ENCYCLOPAEDIA
JUDAICA

ENCYCLOPAEDIA JUDAICA

SECOND EDITION

VOLUME 21
Wel–Zy

Fred Skolnik, *Editor in Chief*
Michael Berenbaum, *Executive Editor*

MACMILLAN REFERENCE USA
An imprint of Thomson Gale, a part of The Thomson Corporation

IN ASSOCIATION WITH
KETER PUBLISHING HOUSE LTD., JERUSALEM

THOMSON
GALE

Detroit • New York • San Francisco • New Haven, Conn. • Waterville, Maine • London

THOMSON
GALE

ENCYCLOPAEDIA JUDAICA, Second Edition

Fred Skolnik, *Editor in Chief*
Michael Berenbaum, *Executive Editor*
Shlomo S. (Yosh) Gafni, *Editorial Project Manager*
Rachel Gilon, *Editorial Project Planning and Control*

Thomson Gale
Gordon Macomber, *President*
Frank Menchaca, *Senior Vice President and Publisher*
Jay Flynn, *Publisher*
Hélène Potter, *Publishing Director*

Keter Publishing House
Yiphtach Dekel, *Chief Executive Officer*
Peter Tomkins, *Executive Project Director*

Complete staff listings appear in Volume 1

For more information, contact
Macmillan Reference USA
An imprint of Thomson Gale
27500 Drake Rd.
Farmington Hills, MI 48331-3535
Or you can visit our internet site at
http://www.gale.com

LIBRARY OF CONGRESS CATALOGING-IN-PUBLICATION DATA

Encyclopaedia Judaica / Fred Skolnik, editor-in-chief ; Michael Berenbaum, executive editor. -- 2nd ed.
v. cm.
Includes bibliographical references and index.
Contents: v.1. Aa-Alp.
ISBN 0-02-865928-7 (set hardcover : alk. paper) -- ISBN 0-02-865929-5 (vol. 1 hardcover : alk. paper) -- ISBN 0-02-865930-9 (vol. 2 hardcover : alk. paper) -- ISBN 0-02-865931-7 (vol. 3 hardcover : alk. paper) -- ISBN 0-02-865932-5 (vol. 4 hardcover : alk. paper) -- ISBN 0-02-865933-3 (vol. 5 hardcover : alk. paper) -- ISBN 0-02-865934-1 (vol. 6 hardcover : alk. paper) -- ISBN 0-02-865935-X (vol. 7 hardcover : alk. paper) -- ISBN 0-02-865936-8 (vol. 8 hardcover : alk. paper) -- ISBN 0-02-865937-6 (vol. 9 hardcover : alk. paper) -- ISBN 0-02-865938-4 (vol. 10 hardcover : alk. paper) -- ISBN 0-02-865939-2 (vol. 11 hardcover : alk. paper) -- ISBN 0-02-865940-6 (vol. 12 hardcover : alk. paper) -- ISBN 0-02-865941-4 (vol. 13 hardcover : alk. paper) -- ISBN 0-02-865942-2 (vol. 14 hardcover : alk. paper) -- ISBN 0-02-865943-0 (vol. 15: alk. paper) -- ISBN 0-02-865944-9 (vol. 16: alk. paper) -- ISBN 0-02-865945-7 (vol. 17: alk. paper) -- ISBN 0-02-865946-5 (vol. 18: alk. paper) -- ISBN 0-02-865947-3 (vol. 19: alk. paper) -- ISBN 0-02-865948-1 (vol. 20: alk. paper) -- ISBN 0-02-865949-X (vol. 21: alk. paper) -- ISBN 0-02-865950-3 (vol. 22: alk. paper)
1. Jews -- Encyclopedias. I. Skolnik, Fred. II. Berenbaum, Michael, 1945-
DS102.8.E496 2007
909'.04924 -- dc22
2006020426

ISBN-13:

978-0-02-865928-2 (set)
978-0-02-865929-9 (vol. 1)
978-0-02-865930-5 (vol. 2)
978-0-02-865931-2 (vol. 3)
978-0-02-865932-9 (vol. 4)
978-0-02-865933-6 (vol. 5)
978-0-02-865934-3 (vol. 6)
978-0-02-865935-0 (vol. 7)
978-0-02-865936-7 (vol. 8)
978-0-02-865937-4 (vol. 9)
978-0-02-865938-1 (vol. 10)
978-0-02-865939-8 (vol. 11)
978-0-02-865940-4 (vol. 12)
978-0-02-865941-1 (vol. 13)
978-0-02-865942-8 (vol. 14)
978-0-02-865943-5 (vol. 15)
978-0-02-865944-2 (vol. 16)
978-0-02-865945-9 (vol. 17)
978-0-02-865946-6 (vol. 18)
978-0-02-865947-3 (vol. 19)
978-0-02-865948-0 (vol. 20)
978-0-02-865949-7 (vol. 21)
978-0-02-865950-3 (vol. 22)

This title is also available as an e-book
ISBN-10: 0-02-866097-8
ISBN-13: 978-0-02-866097-4
Contact your Thomson Gale representative for ordering information.
Printed in the United States of America

10 9 8 7 6 5 4 3 2

TABLE OF CONTENTS

Illuminated "W" used to represent the sound of the initial letter of the Latin word Vere. *The figures represent Ecclesia and Synagoga. Detail from the* Missal of Paris, *France 12th century, Paris, Bibliothèque Nationale, Ms. Lat. 8884, fol. 130.*

WEL-WY

WELENSKY, SIR ROY (Roland; 1907–1991), Rhodesian statesman. Welensky was a leading figure in the political life of Northern Rhodesia (now Zambia) and Southern Rhodesia for nearly 25 years. He was a member of the National Council of the Railway Workers' Union and a founder of the Northern Rhodesia Labor Party. During World War II Welensky was director of manpower and a member of the executive council (1940–53). He campaigned for federation of the two Rhodesias in close association with Sir Godfrey Huggins (Lord Malvern), the first prime minister of the Federation, whom he succeeded in 1956. Welensky advocated a policy of "partnership" between the white and non-white races of the Federation. The partnership failed, either because it was unworkable or because, as many claimed, it was never properly applied owing to white opposition, and the Federation broke up in 1963 despite all Welensky's efforts. He retired from politics, settling as a farmer in Southern Rhodesia, and wrote an account of the Federation in *Welensky's 4,000 Days* (1964). In 1966, Welensky tried to come back to politics but was defeated in the election. One of 13 children of Michael Welensky (from Lithuania), a boardinghouse keeper, and his Afrikaner wife who converted to Judaism on their marriage, Welensky maintained links with Jewry. In his teens he was a railroadman, took up boxing, and in 1926–28 was the heavyweight champion of the Rhodesias. He lived his last year in England.

BIBLIOGRAPHY: D. Taylor, *The Rhodesian* (1955); G. Allingham, *The Welensky Story* (1962). **ADD. BIBLIOGRAPHY:** ODNB online; R. Welensky, *Welensky's 4000 Days: The Life and Death of the Federation of Rhodesia and Nyasaland* (1964).

[Lewis Sowden]

WELLER, MICHAEL (1942–), U.S. playwright. Born in New York, Weller was educated at Brandeis and Manchester University. He entered the New York theater scene in 1972 with his play *Moonchildren*. He followed this great success with a number of finely crafted scripts, including *Fishing* (1973); *The Greatest Little Show on Earth* (1974); *The Bodybuilders* (1975); *Grant's Movie* (1976); *Dwarfman* (1977); *Loose Ends* (1978); and *Spoils of War* (1988). Weller's other plays include *Split* (1979); *Barbarians* (1982); *The Ballad of Soapy Smith* (1985); *Ghost on Fire* (1987); *Lake No Bottom* (1991); *Buying Time* (1995); *What the Night Is For* (2002); and *Approaching Moomtaj* (2004).

Weller wrote the screenplay for the film version of the musical *Hair* (1979) as well as for *Ragtime* (Oscar nomination for Best Screenplay, 1981); *Lost Angels* (1989); the TV version of *Spoils of War* (1994); and was a writer/producer of the TV series *Once and Again* (1999–2002).

Weller was a co-founder of the Mentor Project at the Off-Broadway Cherry Lane Theatre. He also worked as an adviser for several emerging theater companies. In 2005 the Broken Watch Theater Company named its new venue in New York City the Michael Weller Theater.

[Jonathan Licht / Ruth Beloff (2nd ed.)]

WELLESZ, EGON JOSEPH (1885–1974), musicologist and composer of Jewish origin. Wellesz, who was born in Vienna, was a pupil of Arnold *Schoenberg and one of the first to follow his twelve-tone system. He was also his first biographer (1921). He studied musicology with Guido *Adler and in 1913 became a lecturer at the University of Vienna. In 1929 he was appointed professor of the history of music and specialized in research on Baroque opera.

Wellesz's greatest significance, however, lies in his study of Byzantine church music, and the music of the Oriental churches in general, on which he came to be considered the greatest authority of his time. As early as 1915 he discovered the Oriental maqāma *principle in the Serbian liturgy. Soon afterward he found the lost key for deciphering the musical notation of the medieval Byzantine chant. This caused a general reorientation in the study of the early history of music.

Wellesz was forced to leave Austria in 1938. He went to Oxford, where from 1940 he lectured on the history of music. In 1948 he was appointed university reader in Byzantine music. His *History of Byzantine Music and Hymnography* (1949, 1963[3]) has become an undisputed standard work on this subject, on which he also wrote a great number of special studies.

In 1931 Wellesz became general editor of *Monumenta Musicae Byzantinae*, in 1957 coeditor of the monumental *New Oxford History of Music* (of which he himself edited Vol. 1), and in 1966 coeditor of the periodical *Studies in Eastern Chant*.

Wellesz was also very productive as a composer, his compositions including some ten operas and ballets, eight symphonies, and a great number of orchestral and chamber music.

BIBLIOGRAPHY: R. Schollum, *Egon Wellesz: eine Studie* (1963); Redlich, in: *Musical Quarterly*, 26 (1940), 65–75; Reti, *ibid.*, 42 (1956), 1–13, incl. bibl.; Tillyard, in: E. Wellesz and M. Velimirović (eds.), *Studies in Eastern Chant*, 1 (1966), XIII–XV; MGG s.v.; Grove, Dict, and supplement.

[Edith Gerson-Kiwi]

WELLESZ, JULIUS (1872–1915), Hungarian rabbi and scholar. Wellesz, born in Budapest, was ordained at the Budapest Rabbinical Seminary in 1890 and received a Ph.D. at Budapest University (1895) for a thesis on Abraham de Balmes as a philologist, *Abrahám de Balmes mint nyelvész*. An eminent preacher, Wellesz served as rabbi in several Hungarian cities, including Csurgo, Nagybittse, and Obuda. Some of his speeches were published separately, and others in the Hungarian Jewish homiletical review, *Magyar Zsinagóga*. He also devoted himself to philological research and contributed various studies on the Hebrew Bible, Midrashim, and Jewish folklore, but his main interest was in researching Franco-German responsa literature of the 11th–13th centuries.

Among his writings are *Isaak b. Moses Or Zaru'a* (in MGWJ, 48 (1904)); *Ueber R. Isaak b. Moses Or Sarua* (in JJLG, 4 (1906)); *Ḥayyim b. Isaac Or Zaru'a* (in REJ, 53–59 (1907)); and *Meir b. Baruch of Rothenburg* (in REJ (1909–11), 2 parts). His excellent monograph on Rashi, *Rasi Elete és működése* (Hung., 1906) was acclaimed by Jewish scholars and attracted attention abroad.

BIBLIOGRAPHY: M. Weisz, in: *Magyar Zsidó Szemle*, 32 (1915): I. Schmelczer, in: *Studies in Bibliography and Booklore*, 8 (1966), 10–16.

[Imre Schmelczer]

°**WELLHAUSEN, JULIUS** (1844–1918), German Semitist. Born in Hameln, Wellhausen was the son of a Lutheran clergyman, He studied in Goettingen under H. Ewald and was professor of theology in Greifswald from 1872 to 1882. However, he resigned from this position because he did not believe himself equal to the task of "preparing the students for serving the Protestant Church." He was professor of Oriental studies in Halle from 1882 to 1885, in Marburg from 1885 to 1892, and in Goettingen from 1892.

Wellhausen summed up the conclusions of the 19th-century Pentateuch criticism and based upon it a new comprehensive view of the history of Ancient Israel. He also analyzed the Gospels of the New Testament and the pre-Islamic and early Islamic tradition of the Arabs. In his first important book, *Der Text der Buecher Samuelis* (1871), Wellhausen made consistent use of the Septuagint in order to arrive at the original text of Samuel; in his second important book, *Die Pharisaeer und die Sadducaeer* (1874), he followed mainly Josephus and the New Testament in his description of the two parties and their relationship. He then turned to the tradition concerning the beginnings of Ancient Israel. In *Die Composition des Hexateuchs* (1889), he put forward a new and modified hypothesis concerning the four sources: Jahwist (J), Elohist (E), Deuteronomy (D), Priestly Code (P). Taking as his starting point the works of K.H. Graf and A. Kuenen, he reversed the chronological order: he dated the Priestly Code, which had until then been regarded as the oldest source (*Grundschrift*, "primary source"), from the period after the Babylonian Exile. In 1878, he analyzed the remaining historical books (Bleek-Wellhausen, *Einleitung in das Alte Testament*, "Introduction to the Old Testament," 4th–6th editions, 1878–93) and he applied the conclusions of this research in his historiography *Geschichte Israels* (1878; later *Prolegomena zur Geschichte Israels*, 1882; *Prolegomena to the History of Ancient Israel*, 1885) in which he revived the theses of W.M.L. de Wette and W. Vatke. He considered the Priestly Code and Chronicles as sources not for the history of Ancient Israel but only of post-Exilic Judaism. Ancient Israel did not yet know theocracy as a hierocratic institution but only as an idea. The actual law originated only shortly before the Exile (Deuteronomy); after the Exile it became the basis of the canon in the form of the ritual law written down by the priests. In 1894, Wellhausen wrote his *Israelitische und juedische Geschichte* ("The History of Ancient Israel and of the Jews") as a development of the sentence "YHWH the God of Israel, Israel the people of YHWH," which he called the "foundation on which the collective consciousness of Israel has rested at all times." He included in this history, as a matter of course, a chapter on the Gospels, though later he published this only with reservations. He concerned himself with the Arabs first of all for the sake of the history of Ancient Israel, namely in order to "become acquainted with natural man in whom the law of the Lord was implanted by priests and prophets." He believed that the best explanation of the religion of Ancient Israel was to be found in the religion of the pre-Islamic Arabs (*Reste arabischen Heidentums*, 1887). Here also, a critical appraisal of the sources led him to a historiographic synthesis: *Das arabische Reich und sein Sturz* (1902).

Wellhausen was not only a penetrating analyst, but also an excellent writer. He had a great deal of effect even on his adversaries, who attacked him vehemently, for instance with the claim (today definitely disproved) that he was a Hegelian. The driving force behind his historiography was a delight in the free development of human individuality. His view of Ancient Israel has been corrected in many details by the further development of literary criticism (H. Gunkel) and recent research on the Ancient Near East.

BIBLIOGRAPHY: A. Rahlfs, in: K. Marti (ed.), *Studien zur semitischen Philologie and Religionsgeschichte* (1914), 353–68; O. Eissfeldt, in: RGG^3, 6 (1962), 1594–95: L. Perlitt, *Vatke und Wellhausen* (1965); F. Boschwitz, *Julius Wellhausen, Motive und Masstaebe seiner Geschichtsbeschreibung* (1968^2).

[Rudolf Smend]

WELLS (Heb. בְּאֵר, *be'er*, pl. בְּאֵרוֹת, once (Jer. 6:7) בָּיִר, perhaps rather to be read בֵּיר), shafts dug from the surface of the ground to the groundwater. They are of utmost importance in countries with limited rainfall, where springs and perennial streams are few, and particularly vital in nomadic society, since they provide water for the tribe and their livestock (Gen. 29:2). At times rivalry develops among the nomads for the possession of a well. Wells range in size from great shafts many feet deep to shallow pits, depending on the geological formation of the area and its general water level. Biblical wells were located in the wilderness (Gen. 16:14), in valleys (Gen. 26:17), near cities (Gen. 24:11), in fields (Gen. 29:2), and in courtyards (II Sam. 17:18). In order to keep the water supply uncontaminated and to prevent people or animals from falling in, wells were covered (Gen. 29:3; Ex. 21:33). Wells were often designated by specific names in order to commemorate tribal history, such as Esek, Sitnah, and Rehoboth (Gen. 26:20–22). *Be'er* is an element of several place-names, e.g., Beer-Lahai-Roi (Gen. 16:14) and Beer-Sheba (Gen. 21:14), indicating the existence of well-known wells in these places.

Wells are to be distinguished from *cisterns (בּוֹר, pl. בּוֹרוֹת), i.e., subterranean waterproof chambers which store the runoff from roofs, etc. (cf. Lev. R. 18:1, where R. Akiva sees in the word בּוֹרְאֶיךָ (Eccles. 12:1) a combination of בּוֹר, בְּאֵר and בּוֹרֵא).

In the Aggadah

Among the "ten things which were created on the eve of the Sabbath" (cf. Creation, i.e., which are of semi-miraculous character) is enumerated "the mouth of the well." The reference is to the well mentioned in the Song of the Well (Num. 21:16–18). According to the *aggadah* this well, which was created to reward *Miriam for singing the Song of the Sea (Exod. 15:21, Num. R. 1:2), accompanied the children of Israel throughout their wanderings in the wilderness, and disappeared when she died. It was, however, restored through the merit of *Moses and *Aaron, who are the "princes" who "dug it" (v. 17), and it disappeared on Moses' death (Shab. 35a, Ta'an. 9a). According to some, however, the references are to the well of the rock which Moses struck (Num. 20:7–11).

WELLSTONE, PAUL (**David**; 1944–2002), U.S. senator. Wellstone was born in Washington, D.C., and raised in Arlington, Va.; his parents were Russian immigrants. He earned his degrees at the University of North Carolina (B.A. 1965, Ph.D. 1969) and taught political science at Carleton College, Northfield, Minn., from 1969 to 1989. He ran unsuccessfully for Minnesota state auditor in 1982. He was the co-chair of the Minnesota Democratic presidential primary campaign of Jesse Jackson in 1988. In 1990 he was elected to the U.S. Senate, defeating an incumbent Republican, Rudy *Boschwitz, marking the first time in American history that two self-identified Jews had run for the Senate against one another. Boschwitz, itching for a rematch, passed up an open seat in 1994 and ran against Wellstone in 1996, but Wellstone again prevailed, this time handily. While running for reelection again against another Jew, Norman Coleman, Wellstone was killed in a plane crash, along with his wife, daughter, and five other people in October 2002.

Wellstone was an activist in progressive causes from the time he was an undergraduate. He marched for civil rights for African Americans and wrote his doctoral thesis on black militancy. At Carleton, he demonstrated against the Vietnam War and supported other causes, such as ending South African apartheid and providing legal assistance to the poor. In the Senate, Wellstone took active liberal positions on social and political issues, including human rights, health care, social security, worker safety, the environment, abortion, gun control, and campaign finance reform. He sought to strengthen government health, welfare, and education programs and increase their funding.

He opposed the North American Free Trade Agreement (NAFTA) in 1993; he opposed both the Gulf War of 1991 and the Iraq War of 2003, whose authorization he voted against in one of his last Senate votes in October 2002 – the only Democrat in a close race for reelection to do so. He was a loving and critical supporter of Israel, and vigorously opposed Israeli settlements. He enthusiastically supported the peace process. He also was sharply critical of the Palestinian Authority and its failure to conclude peace and accept moves toward a two-state solution. A Wellstone legacy is that he brooked no double standards on human rights and peace and was widely respected for the integrity of his views and for his personal decency. This integrity and decency made him a respected senator, one who could work with the arch right winger Senator Helms on religious freedom and with Conservative Senator Domenici on mental health strengthening government support.

Wellstone had also grown as a Jew, visiting Israel for the first time in 1991, studying Judaism with Rabbi Bernard Raskas of St. Paul, who secured a commitment from Wellstone to study a Jewish text for at least 15 minutes daily. Wellstone felt comfortable in Jewish Progressive circles. He and his wife had not raised their children as Jews, yet their three children felt themselves to be Jews, an example of what Daniel Elazar calls the permeability of identity boundaries in contemporary America.

Former vice president Walter Mondale was coaxed into running for Wellstone's seat in the last days before the election; Norman Coleman defeated him.

[Drew Silver (2nd ed.)]

WELNER, PINCHES (1893–1965), Yiddish and Danish author and journalist. Born in Lodz, Poland, he joined the *Bund in 1904, emigrated first to Argentina, then to Denmark in 1913, and earned his livelihood as a weaver and tailor. Later he made his name as a Yiddish writer and as Denmark's chronicler of East European Jewish life. He also wrote for the general and Jewish press in Scandinavia and other countries and contributed to Yiddish journals in many countries.

Welner's books only appeared after World War II (his early works were generally written originally in Yiddish, but published first in his Danish translation). *In Yene Teg* ("In Those Days," 1958; Danish tr. *I hine Dage*, 1949) deals with the Nazi persecution of the Danish Jews and their famous escape across the Øresund in 1943, a theme that also inspired a later work, *Bay di Bregn fun Oresund* ("On the Shores of the Øresund," 1957; Danish tr. *Ved Øresunds bredder*, 1953). The Polish *shtetl*, with its traditional Jewish types, retained its hold on Welner's imagination and provides the setting for *Den Brogede Gade* ("The Confused Street," 1960); there is also some vivid description and autobiographical material in *Fra Polsk jøde til dansk* ("From Polish to Danish Jew," 1965), which depicts Jewish refugee life in Denmark before and during World War I. Welner published several other books, the last of which, *Fremmed fugl* ("Strange Bird," 1966) is a collection of short stories. A vice president of *YIVO, Welner was an active Zionist, serving as president of the Danish branch of the Iḥud Olami (*Po'alei Zion), which he himself had founded. In 1946 he published *Krigen mod jøderne* ("War against the Jews"), an attack on the British policy in Palestine.

BIBLIOGRAPHY: *Dansk skønlitteraert forfatterleksikon 1900–1950*, 3 (1964), s.v. **ADD. BIBLIOGRAPHY:** LNYL 3, (1960), 483–5.

[Torben Meyer / Jerold C. Frakes (2nd ed.)]

WELSH, ARTHUR L. (**Al**; 1881–1912), pioneer U.S. aviator. Welsh, who was born near Kiev, Russia, was taken to the United States in 1890. In 1905 he joined the U.S. Navy, serving for four years. His interest in flying led him to join Orville Wright's flying class in 1910, and after several months, when he had learned to fly solo, he joined the Wright Brothers Aviation School in Dayton, Ohio, as an instructor. He tutored many important U.S. aviators, including General Henry H. Arnold, U.S. Army Air Force Chief of Staff during World War II. Welsh established many flying records and won a number of trophies, including the George Campbell Cup for altitude at Belmont Park in 1911. His trophies and records are at the National Air Museum of the Smithsonian Institution in Washington, D.C. In 1912 Welsh was assigned by the Wright Brothers to supervise flight training for the War Department at College Park, Maryland. He died in a plane crash during a flight intended to establish a new altitude record.

BIBLIOGRAPHY: S.H. Holland, in: *The Record* (Jewish Historical Society of Greater Washington), 4 (1969), 9–22.

[S.H. Holland]

WELT, DIE ("The World"), the first modern Zionist weekly, founded by Theodor *Herzl, which first appeared in Vienna on June 4, 1897, and, starting with the Fifth *Zionist Congress (Dec. 1901), served as the official organ of the *World Zionist Organization until World War I. From January 1906, after the Zionist Executive had moved to Cologne (1905), the paper was accordingly published there, but, from October 1911 until its last issue of September 25, 1914, in Berlin.

The paper was initiated by Herzl as a privately financed venture to disseminate the Zionist idea, to prepare the first Zionist Congress, and to reply to Jewish critics like W. *Bambus. Herzl was assisted by his brother-in-law, Paul Naschauer (1867–1900), as official publisher, and by S.R. *Landau as first editor-in-chief, who was succeeded by S. *Werner on October 8, 1897. Herzl himself, who had attended to almost every technical detail and initially supplied much of the content, agreed to stay anonymous in order to defuse a severe conflict with his employers at the *Neue Freie Presse*, E. *Bacher and M. *Benedikt, who strongly opposed Zionism. In the first two years Herzl spent a great deal of his own money on *Die Welt*, until he founded a separate joint-stock company together with Heinrich Rosenbaum. Although the paper, after ten months, had only found 280 subscribers in Vienna, its circulation eventually rose to a high of 10,000 a week.

In his first editorial, on June 3, 1897, Herzl defined the guidelines of the new paper: "Our weekly is a 'Jew Paper' [*Judenblatt*]. We take this word, which is supposed to be a term of calumny, and wish to make it a word of honor. … *Die Welt* will be the organ of those men who wish to lead Jewry out of these times into a better era." Herzl deliberately chose a yellow cover, once the *"badge of shame," now to become a "badge of honor," and inserted a *Magen David with a depiction of the Eastern Mediterranean in the title, designed by H. *York-Steiner. Appearing on Fridays, *Die Welt* reported on Jewish and Zionist events, fought antisemitism and assimilation, introduced Hebrew and Yiddish literature in translation, and demanded improvements in the Jewish life of the Diaspora and Ereẓ Israel. As Elon stated in his biography of Herzl (1975), the paper was "a new turn in 'parochial' Jewish journalism in the West; aggressive, polemical, belligerent, witty, it dared to discuss Jewish problems and travails openly, with uncommon candor."

Until April 1899, *Die Welt* was edited by S. *Werner, succeeded by Erwin Rosenberger (until June 1900), Isidor Marmorek (until Dec. 1900), B. *Feiwel (until July 1901), A.H. Reich (until March 1902) and Julius Uprimny (until Dec. 1905). From January 1906, Feiwel, together with A. *Coralnik, continued the paper in Cologne, succeeded by Julius Berger, and finally Moritz Zobel, who remained its editor also in Berlin from October 1911. A Yiddish publication of the same name appeared for about a year (1899–1900). From 1907, the Hebrew *Haolam* ("The World") also served as an international Zionist organ until 1950. *Die Welt* ceased publication in September 1914. The title of Herzl's paper was revived by the Vienna weekly *Die Neue Welt* (1927–38) of R. *Stricker and again, in 1947, by the Vienna monthly *Neue Welt*, which has continued to appear in the early 21st century as *Illustrierte Neue Welt*. Digitized versions of Herzl's *Die Welt* and Stricker's *Die Neue Welt* are available online in Compact Memory's "Internetarchiv juedischer Periodika."

ADD. BIBLIOGRAPHY: A. Boehm, *Die Zionistische Bewegung* (2 vols., 1920–21); A. Bein, *Theodor Herzl* (1934); R. Lichtheim, *Die Geschichte des deutschen Zionismus* (1954); A. Elon, *Herzl* (1975); M. Faerber, in: *The Jewish Press That Was* (1980), 354–9; J. Toury, in: *Zionism*, No. 2 (1980), 159–72; idem, in: *Smanim*, No. 6 (1981), 51–67; idem, *Die Juedische Presse im Oesterreichischen Kaiserreich* (1983), 92–102; Y. Eloni, *Zionismus in Deutschland* (1987); R.S. Wistrich, *The Jews of Vienna in the Age of Franz Joseph* (1990); J.H. Schoeps, *Theodor Herzl 1860–1904* (1995).

[Josef Fraenkel / Johannes Valentin Schwarz (2nd ed.)]

WELTSCH, FELIX (**Baruch**; 1884–1964), philosopher and publicist; cousin of Robert *Weltsch. Born in Prague, from 1910 to 1939 Weltsch served as a librarian at Prague University and from 1940 at the National Library in Jerusalem. From 1919 to 1938 he was editor of the Zionist weekly **Selbstwehr* ("Self-Defense") in Prague. He left Czechoslovakia with a group of 150 emigrants to Palestine on the night preceding the occupation by the Germans (March 14–15, 1939). In his first book, *Anschauung und Begriff* ("Intuition and Concept," 1913), written together with Max Brod, he developed his own theory on the relation of concept to observation. In 1918 he published a juridical-philosophical study called *Organische Demokratie* ("Organic Democracy"), followed by his major philosophical work, *Gnade und Freiheit* ("Mercy and Freedom").

Among his major essays are: "*Nationalismus und Judentum*" ("Nationalism and Judaism," 1920); "*Zionismus als Weltanschauung*" ("Zionism as an Encompassing Philosophy," 1925), written together with Max Brod; "*Judenfrage und Zionismus*" ("The Jewish Problem and Zionism," 1929); *Palaestina – Land der Gegensaetze*, ("Palestine – Land of Contrasts," 1929); *Anti-semitismus als Voelkerhysterie* ("Antisemitism as Hysteria of the Nations", 1931).

In *Das Wagnis der Mitte* ("The Daring of the Center," 1937, 1967²) he developed his philosophy of the creative center. In his pamphlet *Allgemeiner Zionismus* ("General Zionism") he tried to apply this philosophy to Zionist ideology and policy.

Among Weltsch's later works is *Ha-Di'alektikah shel ha-Sevel* ("The Dialectic of Suffering," 1944), in which he revealed his general theory of the dialectics of the "spiral." Thought goes around in a circle, but it rises above it. Thus, from despair, from the destruction of the idea in matter, the flame of the idea bursts forth anew and recharges itself toward its formation in a new reality. In *Teva, Musar u-Mediniyyut* ("Nature, Morals, and Policy," 1950) he considered how the feeble spirit can survive in the body and the material world. The solution was not the subjugation of nature by the spirit, but the "Law of Minimum." Nature does not have to fill all the vacuum of possibilities, but only a part of it that is required by the spirit in order to exist in the world. In political terms this means security, but the minimum of security; armament, but the minimum of armament; and likewise, the minimum standard of living, violence, etc. In 1954 Weltsch edited *Prag vi-Yrushalayim* ("Prague and Jerusalem"), a collection of essays on Jewry and Zionism in Bohemia and Moravia in memory of Leo Herrmann.

Weltsch was a close friend of Franz Kafka. Among his articles about Kafka are "The Rise and Fall of the German-Jewish Symbiosis: The Case of Franz Kafka" (in the *Year Book of the Leo Baeck Institute*, Vol. 1, 1956), "Religion und Humor im Leben und Werk Franz Kafkas" ("Religion and Humor in Franz Kafka's Life and Work", 1957; Heb. 1959), and "Franz Kafka's Geschichtsbewusstsein" ("Franz Kafka's Consciousness of History") in *Deutsches Judentum, Aufstieg und Krise* (1963). He also published a work on the philosophy of Henri Bergson and a study entitled *Das Raetsel des Lachens* ("The Enigma of Laughter," 1935).

BIBLIOGRAPHY: S.H. Bergman, in: *Haaretz* (March 5, 1937; Oct. 20, 1950); MB (Nov. 27, 1964); M. Brod, in: *Zeitschrift fuer die Geschichte der Juden*, 1 (1964), 201–4.

[Samuel Hugo Bergman]

WELTSCH, ROBERT (1891–1982), Zionist editor and journalist. Born in Prague, while a student he joined the Zionist students' society Bar Kochba. During World War I he served as a frontline officer in the Austro-Hungarian army. In 1920 he participated in the Prague Conference at which the Ereẓ Israel *Ha-Po'el ha-Ẓa'ir Party formed a union with *Ẓe'irei Zion organizations in Eastern and Central Europe (Hitaḥadut). In the same year he was appointed editor of *Die *Juedische Rundschau*, the organ of the Zionist Federation of Germany, which was widely read by German-speaking Zionists all over Europe. In 1921 he was elected by the 12th Zionist Congress at Carlsbad as alternate member of the Zionist Executive representing Hitaḥadut. Weltsch retained his post as editor of *Die Juedische Rundschau* until 1938, when he left Berlin and settled in Jerusalem. Until 1945 he edited the German-language weekly *Yedi'ot shel Hitaḥadut Olei Germanyah* (afterward also the organ of the Aliyah Ḥadashah Party) and also contributed articles to *Haaretz*. From 1946 he lived in London as the *Haaretz* correspondent there. He lived his last years in Jerusalem.

In the Zionist movement Weltsch called for an understanding with the Arab national movement, and for many years he was close to the *Berit Shalom movement, which supported the creation of a bi-national state in Ereẓ Israel. A series of articles he wrote in 1933, after Hitler came to power, earned him fame throughout the Jewish world and had a profound effect on the morale of German Jews; one of the articles, published on April 1, 1933, bore the title "Tragt ihn mit Stolz, den gelben Fleck" ("Wear It with Pride, The Yellow Badge"), which became the slogan for German Jews who had found their way back to Jewish values. The entire series was published in a special volume under the title *Ja-Sagen zum Judentum*. In 1963 he edited *Deutsches Judentum, Aufstieg und Krise*. *Festschriften* were published in his honor for his 60th and 70th birthdays (1951, 1961).

[Walter (Shlomoh) Gross]

°**WENCESLAUS IV** (1361–1419), German emperor from 1378 to 1400 and king of Bohemia from 1378 to 1419; son of Charles IV. Wenceslaus, who was in constant pecuniary need, continued his father's policy of relinquishing his legal and economic rights over the Jews (see *servi camerae regis) in return for financial benefits. After protracted negotiations, on June 12, 1385, he concluded a treaty at Ulm with the Swabian *League, whereby, for an indemnity of 40,000 florins, any debts to Jews of less than one year's standing were to carry no interest, while the others were to be computed as capital and interest and the total reduced by one quarter. In order to carry out this project, all the Jews in the kingdom were imprisoned simultaneously, their pledges and records were confiscated, and they were thrown on the mercy of the city councils which were given the right to arbitrate in disputes between them and their debtors. This measure, which barely alleviated Wenceslaus' financial needs, caused economic havoc throughout the country. Five years later Wenceslaus arrived at an agreement with the chief princes of his lands, secular and clerical, whereby they were to be freed from all debts to Jews in return for high indemnities. This measure, a severe blow to the cities in possession of the promissory notes given by Jews, was not fully carried out. In 1398 Wenceslaus had to promise that he would not again cancel debts to Jews.

Though Wenceslaus offered special rights to the Jews of *Eger (Cheb) in return for compensation, he was prompted by economic considerations. He acquiesced in the massacres of the Jews in *Prague and *Goerlitz in 1389, and tried to profit from them.

BIBLIOGRAPHY: A. Sussmann, *Die Judenschuldentilgungen unter Koenig Wenzel* (1907); Baron, Social^2, 9 (1965), 160f., 202, 318; Bondy-Dworský, nos. 154, 190.

WENDLAND, PAUL (1864–1915), German classical scholar. Wendland was professor at the universities of Kiel, Breslau, and Goettingen. His main field of study was the religious beliefs of the classical world and their relations to Judaism and early Christianity (*Die Hellenistisch-roemische Kultur in ihren Beziehungen zu Judentum und Christentum* (1912^2). He also edited the Greek text of the Letter of Aristeas (*Aristeae ad Philocratem epistula* ..., 1900), as well as some writings by Philo (*Neu entdeckte Fragmente Philos* ..., 1891). He wrote the following works on Philo: *Philo's Schrift ueber die Vorsehung* (1892) and *Philo und die kynisch-stoische Diatribe* (1895).

[David Flusser]

WENDROFF, ZALMAN (pseudonym of **Zalman Vendrovsky**; 1877–1971), Yiddish author. Born in Slutsk, Belorussia, Wendroff moved to Lodz at the age of 16, worked in a factory, studied dentistry, and published his first articles about Jewish life in Lodz, in the journal *Der Yud*. Emigrating to England, he was befriended by the anarchist thinker Rudolf Rocker, who helped him publish short stories in anarchist and Zionist journals. The 1905 Revolution found him back in Russia, where he worked as a teacher of English. With the collapse of the revolution, he left for the U.S. In New York, he wrote humorous sketches, articles and short stories for both the anarchist *Fraye Arbeter Shtime* and the Orthodox daily, *Morgn-Zhurnal*. When the latter journal sent him as its correspondent to Russia, he made his home in Warsaw for seven years, also writing for Warsaw's Yiddish daily, *Haynt*. From 1915, he lived in Moscow, working for Jewish organizations during World War I and in the Commissariat for Nationalities after the 1917 Revolution. At the same time he continued to act as correspondent for Yiddish dailies in New York, Warsaw, and Vilna.

Wendroff's stories appeared in various periodicals, in booklets which sold for a few pennies each, and in collections, beginning with *Humoresken un Ertseylungen* ("Humoresques and Stories," 1911, 1921^2). Most popular were two Yiddish volumes which appeared under the Russian title *Pravozhitelstvo* (the legal term for the right to live outside the *Pale of Settlement; 1912). In humorous and tragic tales were described the life of Jews who, though not allowed to dwell outside the Pale, somehow managed to circumvent Czarist restrictions and to carry on a harried existence in forbidden cities as artisans, businessmen, and students. Wendroff had difficulty finding his place in Soviet literary circles, and Moses Litvakov criticized him for taking the line of least resistance and becoming an imitator of Sholem Aleichem. In the 1920s, his articles appeared regularly in the New York *Forverts*.

His book, *Afn Shvel fun Lebn* ("On the Threshold of Life," 1941), appeared just before the German assault upon Moscow. During World War II he worked for the Moscow foreign-language radio service. After the war he was accused of cosmopolitanism and contact with enemy agents and was arrested in 1950 and condemned to ten years' imprisonment. Released in 1956, he returned to Moscow, where he was treated as the doyen of surviving Yiddish writers and contributors to *Sovetish Heymland*. His last Yiddish book, *Undzer Gas* ("Our Street") appeared in Moscow in 1967.

BIBLIOGRAPHY: Rejzen, Leksikon, 1 (1926), 1002–07; LNYL, 3 (1960), 487–90; *Pinkas Slutsk* (1962), 134f., 389f. **ADD. BIBLIOGRAPHY:** Z. Vendrof [Wendroff], *When It Comes to Living* (2004); G. Estraikh, *In Harness: Yiddish Writers' Romance with Communism* (2005).

[Jerucham Tolkes / Gennady Estraikh (2nd ed.)]

WENGEROFF, PAULINE EPSTEIN (1833–1916), author of *Memoiren einer Grossmutter. Bilder aus der Kulturgeschichte der Juden Russlands in 19. Jahrhundert* ("Memoirs of a Grandmother: Scenes from the Cultural History of Russian Jews in the Nineteenth Century"; 2 vols., Berlin, 1908, 1910). Wengeroff was born in Bobruisk into the upper echelons of Russian Jewry. The prosperous Epsteins were pious and strict in their religious practice, but Pauline's father, Judah Epstein, an accomplished Talmud scholar, was also an enthusiast of Haskalah and encouraged his daughters in their study of German. In 1849, Pauline married Chonon Wengeroff, who became a successful banker and served on the city council of Minsk. The couple had seven children. The first volume of *Memoiren einer Grossmutter*, published when Wengeroff was in her seventies, details the observance of the Jewish holy days and festivals in her parental home in the 1840s. Following the success of this work, she wrote a second volume that expanded her childhood recollections into a complex autobiography.

Written after the end of the Russian Haskalah, the memoirs depict traditional Jewish culture and family, their disintegration, and the emergence of Jewish modernity from a female perspective. Wengeroff's two volumes, whose significance for the history of Jewish folklore, haskalah, and assimilation was recognized from the beginning, were republished during her life and posthumously. They are a significant source on women's ritual practices, socialization of girls, and the role of gender in the experience of Jewish modernity. Skillfully crafted and written, they are also the first full-fledged self-referential writing by a woman in the history of Jewish literature to refract an age through the experience of women and to achieve publication through the author's efforts. Wengeroff is not simply an apologist for tradition; she shared many of the core values of the Haskalah and wrote in German. But she excoriates the wanton abandonment of tradition by modernizing Jewish men and their encroachment on women's control of the family, which robbed women of the ability to transmit Judaism, with catastrophic results.

Wengeroff's children included Semyon *Wengeroff, a prominent historian and critic, who converted to Christianity. Her daughter, Zinaida (1867–1941), was a renowned Russian literary critic who emigrated to the United States. Wengeroff considered the conversions of several of her children her greatest tragedy. In her later years, in addition to writing *Memoiren*, she devoted herself to providing vocational and Jewish education to impoverished young women.

BIBLIOGRAPHY: J.R. Baskin, "Piety and Female Aspiration in the Memoirs of Pauline Epstein Wengeroff and Bella Chagall," in: *Nashim*, 7 (2004), 65–96; S. Magnus, "Women and Pauline Wengeroff's Writing of an Age," in: *Nashim*, 7 (2004), 28–64; idem, "Sins of Youth, Guilt of a Grandmother: M.L. Lilienblum, Pauline Wengeroff, and the Telling of Jewish Modernity in Eastern Europe," in: *Polin*, 18 (2005).

[Shulamit S. Magnus (2nd ed.)]

WENGEROFF (Vengerov), SEMYON AFANASYEVICH (1855–1920), Russian literary and intellectual historian. Wengeroff's numerous works include monographs on Turgenev, Goncharov, and Gogol, as well as studies of literary critics such as Belinsky. Wengeroff was also a renowned bibliographer and editor of scholarly reference works, including the unfinished six-volume biobibliographical dictionary of Russian writers and scholars, *Kritiko-biograficheskiy slovar russkikh pisateley i uchenykh* (1889–1904). His other achievements include the establishment in 1917 of the Russian Book Chamber *(Rossiyskaya knizhnaya palata)*, which was still publishing weekly guides to all printed matter published in the U.S.S.R. 50 years after his death. Wengeroff ultimately converted to Russian Orthodoxy, probably because baptism was indispensable to a scholarly career in Czarist Russia. His mother, Pauline *Wengeroff, recalled in her memoirs (in L.S. Dawidowicz (ed.), *The Golden Tradition* (1967), 160–8) that her son was once expelled from school for refusing to kneel before an icon. Of Wengeroff's sisters, one married the writer Nikolai *Minski, another Leonid *Slonimski, a third was Zinaida Wengeroff (see Pauline *Wengeroff), and another was Isabel Wengeroff (Vengerova) 1877–1956), pianist and music teacher at the Curtis Institute in Philadelphia.

BIBLIOGRAPHY: A.G. Kalentyova, *Vlyublyonny v literaturu: ocherk zhizni i deyatelnosti S.A. Vengerova* (1964); A.G. Fomin, *S.A. Vengerov, Kak organizator i pervy direktor Rossiyskoy knizhnoy palaty* (1925).

[Maurice Friedberg]

WERBEL, ELIAHU MORDECAI (1806–1880), Hebrew author. Werbel was born in Ternopol, East Galicia, and educated at the secular Jewish school established by Joseph *Perl. From 1839 he taught at a similar school in Odessa founded by Bezalel Stern, until the school's closure by government order in 1874. He wrote a long literary poem *Edim Ne'emanim o Ḥuldah u-Vor* ("Faithful Witnesses or a Weasel and a Hole," 1852).

The poem's theme is borrowed from an ancient legend, mentioned in the Talmud and elaborated upon in the *Arukh*, of a weasel and a hole who avenge the disloyalty of a man to a young lady whom he had promised to marry. The poem is written in the euphuistic style of the period and was the source for the play *Shulamit* (1886), by Abraham Goldfaden (son-in-law of Werbel) and for poems by many other authors. Werbel contributed regularly to the monthly *Ha-Boker Or*, in which his *Tokhen Alilah*, four literary poems on the blood libel, appeared in 1881. His Hebrew translations of poetry and prose were collected in his book *Siftei Renanot* (1864). He also completed the Hebrew translation of Lessing's *Nathan der Weise* begun by Abraham Ber Gottlober (1874). Unlike many of his contemporaries he neither criticizes nor satirizes the older generation.

BIBLIOGRAPHY: F. Lachower, *Toledot ha-Sifrut ha-Ivrit ha-Haḥadashah*, 2 (1963), 168–70; G. Bader, *Medinah va-Ḥakhameha* (1934), 93–94.

[G.El.]

WERBER, BARUCH (1810–1876), Hebrew author and editor. Born in Brody, Galicia, he began his literary career writing for the Hebrew weekly *Ha-Mevasser*. In 1865, he founded the weekly *Ivri Anokhi* in Brody, editing it until his death. This was devoted primarily to news and popular science, and although it had a conservative and moderate orientation, sharply attacked the ultra-Orthodox Galician followers of the *rebbe* of *Belz. Among his writings are: *Megillat Kohelet*, an introduction and commentary to Ecclesiastes (1862, 1876); *Toledot Adam*, a biography of the French public figure, Albert Cohen (1870).

BIBLIOGRAPHY: Gelber, in: *Arim ve-Immahot be-Yisrael*, 6 (1955), 219–20; Kressel, Leksikon, 1 (1965), 703–4.

[Gedalyah Elkoshi]

WERBLOWSKY, RAPHAEL JUDA ZWI (1924–), scholar in the field of comparative religion. Born in Frankfurt on the Main, Werblowsky lectured at Leeds University, the Institute of Jewish Studies, Manchester University (1951–56), and then at the Hebrew University, Jerusalem, where he was a professor from 1962, and served as dean of the Faculty of Humanities from 1965 to 1969. Among his published works are *Lucifer and Prometheus, a Study of Milton's Satan* (dissertation, with an introduction by C.G. Jung, 1952); *Das Gewissen in juedischer Sicht* (1958); *Joseph Karo – Lawyer and Mystic* (1962; dealing mainly with Karo's mystical experiences as recorded in his *Maggid Meisharim); Anti-semitisme, anti-Zionisme* (with H. van Praage, written in Dutch, 1969); and *Beyond Tradition and Modernity* (1976). Werblowsky translated from Dutch into English J.L. Palache's *Semantic Notes on the Hebrew Lexicon* (1959) and was editor of the *Encyclopedia of Jewish Religion* (with G. Wigoder, 1965, 1990^2) and *The Oxford Dictionary of the Jewish Religion* (1997). He represented Israel at many international conferences on Jewish-Christian relations. For the first edition of the *Encyclopaedia Judaica* he was a consulting editor and the divisional editor of Judaism.

WERFEL, FRANZ (1890–1945), Austrian novelist, playwright, and poet. The son of a prosperous Prague manufacturer, Werfel was a friend of Max *Brod and Franz *Kafka. He rejected the business career his father chose for him, and echoes of their disagreement are apparent in the story, *"Nicht der Moerder, der Ermordete ist schuldig"* (1920). While working as a publisher's reader in Leipzig (1911–14), Werfel attended the university there. His earliest verse collections, *Der Weltfreund* (1911), *Wir sind* (1913) and *Einander* (1915), substituted religious intoxication for the skepticism and sophistry to which his Austrian contemporaries were largely addicted. In his *Euripides: Die Troerinnen* (1915), an expressionist adaptation of the classical tragedy, war is seen through the eyes of the conquered and enslaved. Three years in the Austrian army on the Russian front (1915–17) confirmed Werfel in his pacifism, and the war poems of *Der Gerichtstag* (1919) voiced his longing for the rejuvenation of a blood-drenched world through love and universal brotherhood. After the war Werfel became a freelance writer in Vienna and Berlin. In *Beschwoerungen* (1923) he ecstatically called for a new, Dionysian comradeship with all creation – man, beast, and stone. Werfel's marriage in 1918 to Alma (Schindler) Mahler, the daughter of a famous Austrian painter and widow of the composer Gustav *Mahler, established him in Viennese society. Turning to the theater, he triumphed with the trilogy *Spiegelmensch* (1920) and his drama *Bocksgesang* (1921), but had less success with *Juarez und Maxmilian* (1924), a play about the ill-fated Hapsburg emperor of Mexico, and *Paulus unter den Juden* (1926; *Paul among the Jews*, 1928). In *Der Weg der Verheissung* (1935; *The Eternal Road*, 1937), a biblical play set to synagogal music by Kurt *Weill and staged in New York by Max *Reinhardt, Werfel revealed his spiritual homelessness and the tragic ambiguity of his religious position. When he abandoned expressionism for historical themes, Werfel portrayed not the lords and victors, but rather the lowly and defeated. His epic novel *Die vierzig Tage des Musa Dagh* (1933; *The Forty Days*, 1934) depicted the hopeless struggle of the Armenians against the Turkish hordes. Werfel never actually embraced Christianity, although his essay, *Die christliche Sendung* (1917) was a step in that direction. Toward the end of his life he reassessed his position as a Jew in *Zwischen Oben und Unten* (1946), where he declared that God would one day settle the reckoning in Israel's favor. He also wrote: "Religion is the everlasting dialogue between humanity and God. Art is its soliloquy."

In 1938, Werfel fled to France. When the German army invaded France in 1940, he fled once more and managed to reach the United States. He spent his last years in California, where he completed *Das Lied von Bernadette* (1941), an account of the visionary of Lourdes. This became famous in the English-speaking world as *The Song of Bernadette* (1942) and was later made into a motion picture. *Jacobowsky und der Oberst* (1944; *Jacobowsky and the Colonel*) was a tragicomedy about the flight of a Polish aristocrat and a resourceful little Jew before the German advance into France. During his exile in France, from 1938 to 1940, Werfel wrote a novel depicting the life of the Jews in Burgenland and their sufferings after the annexation of Austria by the Nazis. The manuscript was hidden for years and was first published posthumously in 1954, under the title *Cella und die Ueberwinder* (Frankfurt; republished in East Germany, 1970). The book is one of the most powerful literary expressions of the Holocaust and represents an entirely new aspect of Werfel's creative work. Other novels by Werfel were *Verdi. Roman der Oper* (1924; *Verdi: A Novel of the Opera*, 1925), which promoted a Verdi revival in Germany; *Der veruntreute Himmel* (1939); and *Stern der Ungeborenen* (1946; *Star of the Unborn*, 1946). *Gedichte aus den Jahren 1908–1945*, a collection of Werfel's best poems, was published in 1946.

In the postwar years there was an increasing interest in Werfel both in West and East Germany, and his works continue to appear in English as well. Among the doctoral theses on him, mention should be made of D. Kuhlenkamp's *Werfels spaete Romane* (1971), which contains an extensive bibliography.

BIBLIOGRAPHY: R. Specht, *Franz Werfel* (1926); L. Zahn, *Franz Werfel* (1966), incl. bibl.; W. Braselmann, *Franz Werfel* (1960), incl. bibl.; L.B. Foltin (ed.), *Franz Werfel 1890–1945* (Eng., 1961), incl. bibl.; A. Werfel, *And the Bridge is Love* (1958); R. Kayser, in: G. Krojanker, *Juden in der deutschen Literatur* (1926), 17–26; W. Haas, *Gestalten* (1962), 228–36. **Add. Bibliography:** P.S. Jungk, *Franz Werfel, A Life in Prague, Vienna, and Hollywood* (1991); L. Huber, *Franz Werfel: An Austrian Writer Reassessed* (1992); J.T. Michaels, *Franz Werfel and His Critics* (1994).

[Sol Liptzin / Yehouda Marton]

°WERGELAND, HENRIK ARNOLD (1808–1845), Norwegian poet. Wergeland occupies a unique place in the cultural history of Norway as a leading figure in intellectual and national life in the 1830s and 1840s. In his *Norges Konstitutions Historie* ("History of the Norwegian Constitution," 1841–43), he praised the constitution of 1814 but also voiced his displeasure (in Section II of the work) at the illiberal prohibition of Jewish immigration, a view which he also expressed in a number of newspaper articles. In 1839 Wergeland submitted to the Storting (parliament) a detailed proposal to rescind this prohibition (see *Norway), emphasizing considerations of justice and reconciliation. In his popular work, *Indlaeg i Jødesagen* ("Essays About the Jewish Question"), Wergeland spoke out against anti-Jewish prejudice, writing about Jewish religion, nationality, and patriotism, the occupations of Jews, their philanthropic activities, and moral excellence. Although he did not disregard the economic advantages which the admission of Jews would bring to Norway, moral considerations were of paramount importance to him; Christianity, justice, and charity demanded that the prohibition be rescinded. His collections of poetry, *Jöden* ("The Jew," 1842), and *Jödinden* ("The Jewess," 1844), contributed greatly toward creating a sentiment favorable to the Jews. They were translated into German under the title, *Der Jude und die Juedin* (1935), by the Oslo rabbi, Julius Samuel. Many of these poems, which still appear in anthologies, and which are also used in schools, have Jewish themes. In his essay *Jødesagen i det norske storting* ("The Jewish Cause in the Norwegian Parliament"), Wergeland described the parliamentary debate of 1842. He corresponded with prominent Jews in other countries, particularly in Sweden. After his death Scandinavian (primarily Swedish) Jews erected a memorial to him at his grave. It was unveiled in 1849 at a well-attended public ceremony and in the presence of three Swedish Jews, who had come to Norway with letters of safe-conduct. In 1851 the prohibition against Jewish immigration was rescinded.

Wergeland was instrumental in creating the special way Norwegians celebrate May 17, Norway's Constitution Day. Every May 17 children all over Norway march through the main streets in brass bands followed by children dressed in their best clothing or national costumes, singing, cheering, and waving Norwegian flags. On the morning of this day members of the Jewish community of Oslo (DMT) commemorate Wergeland, as they have since the 1920s, by gathering at his grave before the parades begin. A member of the Jewish Youth Organization (JUF) delivers a speech and lays a garland of flowers on the grave. The Norwegian national anthem is then sung. In latter years the speeches have addressed the importance of following in Wergeland's footsteps with regard to present-day prejudices.

BIBLIOGRAPHY: J.B. Halvorsen, *Norsk Forfatter-Lexikon*, 6 (1908), s.v.; Seip, in: *Edda*, 27 (1927), 113–45; Summit, in: *American Hebrew* (Sept. 8, 1939); F. Bull and F. Paasche, *Norsk Litteraturhistorie*, 3 (1932), 113–319; H. Koht and H. Jaeger, *Henrik Wergeland, V Brev, Retsinlaeg*, 1 (1930); L. Amundsen, *Brev til Henrik Wergeland 1827–1845* (1956); O. Mendelsohn, *Jødenes historiei Norge gjennom 300 år*, 1 (1969). **ADD. BIBLIOGRAPHY:** "Wergeland, Henrik," in: *Aschehaug Leksikon*.

[Oskar Mendelsohn / Lynn C. Feinberg (2nd ed.)]

WERNER, ERIC (**Erich**; 1901–1988), musicologist and composer. Born in Ludenberg (near Vienna), Werner attended the Berlin Hochschule fuer Musik, graduating in 1924. He studied piano, organ, and composition in Vienna and Berlin (with E. Kornauth, F. Schreker, and F. Busoni), and musicology in Vienna, Prague, Berlin, Göttingen, and Strasbourg (with G. *Adler, R. Lach, G. Schünemann, C. *Sachs, J. Wolff, F. Ludwig, and T. Gerold), as well as Judaic studies and comparative religion (with M. *Buber, I. *Heinemann, J. *Horowitz, and E. Mueller). He earned his doctorate at the University of Strasbourg, in 1928, after submitting his dissertation in Latin, under the guidance of Théodore Gérold. His thesis deals with a comparative study of the Western Christian and Jewish forms of cantillation motives. After teaching at Holzminden and at the conservatory and gymnasium in Saarbrücken, Werner became lecturer at the rabbinical seminary in Breslau in 1935–38, and also taught Latin and music at the Jewish high school there. In 1938, seeking refuge from the Nazi regime, he and his wife emigrated to the United States, where, in 1939, he was invited to join the faculty at Hebrew Union College (Cincinnati) as A.Z. *Idelsohn's successor, remaining until 1951. There his full schedule included teaching, directing the choir and worship services, and serving as organist. The college's magnificent Edouard *Birnbaum collection provided material for his early research. His conception of a school of sacred music in New York, linked with Rabbi Stephen Wise's Jewish Institute of Religion (founded in 1922), was ultimately realized in 1950. Resettling in New York, he continued teaching until his retirement in 1967. From 1967 until 1971 he was the head of the department of musicology founded by him at Tel Aviv University.

A Guggenheim Fellowship (awarded in 1957) supported research on his work *The Sacred Bridge; the Interdependence of Liturgy and Music in Synagogue and Church During the First Millennium*, 2 vols. (London, 1959; New York, 1984), the first major synthesis of a basic direction of inquiry in both Jewish and European musicology. Werner's pathfinding studies encompassed such diverse topics as comparative Jewish and Christian chant, synagogue liturgy in medieval times, and the traditional music of Ashkenazi Jewry. Highly critical of the Wagner circle, he also wrote on Mozart, *Mahler, and Bruckner, and contributed a significant biography on *Mendelssohn. His book *Mendelssohn: A New Image of the Composer and His Age* (1963) is another significant reinterpretation. Mathematics, philosophy, and aesthetics are central facets in many of his writings. His liturgical music settings reflect current musical trends while preserving unity in the spirit of tradition.

ADD. BIBLIOGRAPHY: NG[2]; MGG; Baker, Biog, Dict; Riemann-Gurlitt; J. Cohen, *Bibliography of the Publications of Eric Werner* (1968); in: *Yuval*, 1 (1968); I.J. Katz, "Eric Werner (1901–1988): A Bibliography of his Collected Writings," in: *Musica Judaica*, 10 (1987–88), 1–36.

[Bathja Bayer / Israel J. Katz (2nd ed.)]

WERNER, HEINZ (1890–1964), psychologist. Born in Vienna, Werner served as professor of psychology at Hamburg University from 1926 and emigrated to the United States in 1933. After teaching briefly at Michigan, Harvard, and Brooklyn College, Werner assumed the Clark University professorship which he occupied for the rest of his career. His major interests centered on the expressive-symbolic and perceptual processes. He did work on child development, especially with regard to word comprehension. His best-known book is *Comparative Psychology of Mental Development* (1948, 1957), which is essentially a revision of his earlier *Einfuehrung in die Entwicklungspsychologie* (1926, 1933[2], 1953[3]). In it he expressed the conviction that developmental psychology should not serve merely as a subject matter, but as a method of study. In 1957, Werner's department at Clark University was expanded into an Institute of Human Development, and Werner became a major proponent of the developmental viewpoint in the world of psychology. In 1960 there appeared *Perspectives in Psychological Theory: Essays in Honor of Heinz Werner*, edited by B. Kaplan and S. Wapner, which contains, inter alia, a list of some 150 articles and books by Werner. He coauthored *Symbol Formation* (1963), an organismic-developmental approach to language and the expression of thought. Upon his death, Clark University renamed its department the Heinz Werner Institute of Developmental Psychology.

BIBLIOGRAPHY: H.A. Witkin, in: *Child Development*, 36 (1965), 307–28, incl. bibl.

[Aaron Lichtenstein]

WERNER, MICHAEL (1912–1989), sculptor. Werner was born in France but grew up in Austria, where he was educated, as well as at Oxford University, and in Paris. He settled in England in 1938 and held his first one-man exhibition of sculpture in 1949. He subsequently exhibited regularly in London galleries, as well as in mixed international collections. His commissions include portrait busts of George Bernard Shaw, for the Royal Court Theatre, London; a head of W.H. Auden, and a mural of 18 panels for Foxford School, Coventry. Werner was also a distinguished teacher and in 1968 became Senior Tutor at Watford School of Art and other institutions. In the 1960s he became well known for his innovative collages.

[Charles Samuel Spencer]

WERNER, SIEGMUND (1867–1928), one of Herzl's early aides and editor of *Die Welt*. Born in Vienna, Werner completed his studies in medicine in 1896. In his student days he was a member of national-Jewish and Zionist societies, and when Herzl came upon the scene, Werner became one of his devoted assistants. In 1897, he succeeded the first editor of *Die Welt*, Saul *Landau, retaining the appointment until the middle of 1899 and reassuming the editorship for the period 1903–05. His leading articles, as well as the general policy of the paper, conformed to Herzl's views; during the *Uganda Scheme controversy, he accorded both sides equal treatment, a policy which also coincided with Herzl's wishes. He was at Herzl's side when Herzl died and wrote a gripping description of this experience in *Die Welt*. Werner continued as editor until the paper was moved in 1905 to Cologne, which became the seat of Zionist headquarters. Later he moved to Iglau, Moravia, where he took up the practice of dentistry, while continuing his Zionist activities. He was the author of a book of verse (1903). Werner's exchange of letters with Herzl was published by Joseph Fraenkel in *Dr. Siegmund Werner, ein Mitarbeiter Herzls* (1939); his correspondence with Nathan *Birnbaum was published in *Shivat Ẓiyyon*, 2–3, pp. 275–299.

BIBLIOGRAPHY: Y. Lamm, in: H. Gold (ed.), *Die Juden und Judengemeinden Maehrens* (1929), 249–50.

[Getzel Kressel]

WERSES, SAMUEL, (1915–), Hebrew literature scholar and educator. Born in Vilna, Poland, Werses emigrated to Palestine in 1936, where he studied Hebrew literature, completing his doctorate in 1947. From 1953 until his retirement in 1983, he was member of the Hebrew literature department of the Hebrew University. He was awarded the Israel Prize in 1989 for research in Hebrew literature. His research focused on Haskalah and modern Hebrew literature, with an emphasis on studying literary genre as they developed and their links to world literature. Among his works are *Mi-Mendele ad Hazaz* ("From Mendele to Hazaz," 1982) and *Haskalah ve-Shabta'ut* ("Haskalah and Shabbateanism," 1988), a study of trends and forms in the literature of the Haskalah (1990), a book on Agnon (2000), and *Mi-Lashon el Lashon: Yeẓirot ve-Gilgulehen be-Sifruteinu* (1996). Together with Ch. Shmeruk, he edited a book on the cultural life of the Jews in Poland between the two World Wars (*Bein Shetei Milḥemot Olam*, 1997). A bibliography of his works was prepared by R. Schenfeld in 2002.

[Fern Lee Seckbach]

WERTH, ALEXANDER (1901–1969), British journalist and author. Born in St. Petersburg and educated in Glasgow, Werth started his career on Glasgow papers and became Paris correspondent of the *Manchester Guardian* (1932). He went to Moscow as *Sunday Times* and BBC correspondent in 1940, and from 1949 was Paris correspondent of *New Statesman* and New York *Nation*. He wrote mainly on France and Russia, including *The Destiny of France* (1937), *France and Munich* (1939), *Leningrad* (1944), *The De Gaulle Revolution* (1960), *The Khrushchev Phase* (1961), *De Gaulle* (1965), and *Russia at Peace* (1968). His *Russia at War, 1941–1945* (1964), based in part on his experiences as a correspondent there, remains one of best and most vigorous accounts of the Nazi invasion of the USSR.

Werth entered the Majdanek death camp with Soviet forces in July 1944 and was one of the first Western correspondents to report in detail on a Nazi extermination camp, nine or ten months before the more famous accounts of the liberation of German concentration camps like Buchenwald.

WERTHEIM, family of German department store owners, originating from Stralsund. In 1876 ARTHUR WERTHEIM established a small dry goods store in Stralsund. His son, GEORGE WERTHEIM, introduced new practices, such as fixed prices and low markups, which ensured the store's success and led to the opening of a second store at Rostock. Subsequently George and his three brothers ventured into Berlin, where they concentrated on inexpensive mass consumer goods and soon added two additional stores. The 1905 turnover of the main store reportedly totaled the equivalent of $15 million. The building standing on one of Berlin's main thoroughfares, and designed by Alfred *Messel, became a landmark of the German capital. In 1908 WOLFF WERTHEIM separated from his brothers to open another department store in Berlin which, however, failed to equal the former achievement. In 1933 the company owned seven stores. After World War II it became part of the Hermann *Tietz corporation, Hertie, and descendants of the founders retained a considerable interest in the establishment.

BIBLIOGRAPHY: J. Hirsch, *Das Warenhaus in Westdeutschland* (1910), passim.

[Edith Hirsch]

WERTHEIM, ABRAHAM CAREL (1832–1897), Dutch banker, philanthropist, and political leader. Trained in banking, he joined the bank of his uncle, Abraham Wertheim (1803–1889), who later became his father-in-law. The firm, Wertheim and Gompertz, developed into a leading banking institution, and Wertheim achieved recognition as a leader in his field. He played a prominent role in the establishment of many important commercial, industrial, and shipping enterprises. He also shared in promoting the development of the state railroads. In the 1870s he successfully introduced many large-scale United States loans on the Dutch market.

The name A.C. Wertheim is proverbial for his welfare work. Every morning before office hours he would receive the needy with their requests for financial support without making any distinction as to religion or social status. When in 1855 the Society for Public Welfare (Maatschappij tot Nut van 't Algemeen) first accepted Jews, Wertheim became a member and advanced to chairman of the national board. Under his direction a modern hospital in Amsterdam, a society for the blind, and an organization for the improvement of common housing were established.

Being particularly erudite Wertheim also participated in the cultural field. He was involved in the founding of the main national theater company (Het Nederlandsch Tooneel) and the Dutch Dramatic Arts Academy. When the Amsterdam Municipal Theater burned down in 1890 he made a generous contribution to start its immediate reconstruction. He was instrumental in the acquisition of valuable artifacts by museums.

For many years Wertheim served as a member and later as chairman of the board of the Amsterdam Ashkenazi Community. His formula for well-integrated Jewish life in the Netherlands was "to be a Jew in the synagogue and a burgher in the streets."

Politically he was the leader of the Amsterdam Liberals, whom he represented as a member of the North Holland Provincial Council and from 1886 to 1897 of the national Senate. A park in Amsterdam has been named after him.

BIBLIOGRAPHY: A.S. Rijxman, *A.C. Wertheim 1832–1897* (1961).

[Daniel M. Metz (2nd ed.)]

WERTHEIM, MAURICE (1886–1950), U.S. banker. Born in New York, he was vice president and secretary of the United Cigar Manufacturers' Company from 1907 to 1913. In 1915 he joined the investment banking house of Hallgarten and Co., and in 1927 he established his own firm, Wertheim and Co. He served on the War Production Board and the Board of Economic Welfare during World War II. He was a patron of art and education, and his financial contributions enabled the liberal journal *The Nation* to continue publication when it was in financial straits during the Depression. Wertheim was a founder of New York's Theater Guild and a member of the Harvard Fund Council. He was president of the *American Jewish Committee (1941–43) and played a prominent part in bringing together opposing forces in American Jewish communal life. He was the father of Barbara *Tuchman.

[Joachim O. Ronall]

WERTHEIM, ROSALIE (Rosy) MARIE (1888–1949), composer. Wertheim was born in Amsterdam and exhibited musical gifts from an early age. In addition to studying piano and voice, she studied composition with Bernard Zweers and Sem Dresden. She taught piano and solfege at the Amsterdam Muzieklyceum. Her early interest in social work and concern for the working classes grew into a deep commitment. She taught piano to poor children, supported a number of needy families from her own income, conducted a children's chorus in a low-income neighborhood, and conducted the Jewish women's chorus of the Religieus Socialistisch Verbond in Amsterdam.

In 1929 she moved to Paris to study composition with Louis Aubert. Her home became a haven for Dutch artists and composers, and a veritable salon for leading French composers such as *Milhaud, Honegger, Messiaen, Jolivet, Ibert, and Elsa Barraine. Between 1929 and 1935, her works were frequently included on concert programs in Paris. In 1935 she left Paris for a year in Vienna, studying with Karl Weigl. She spent the next two years in the United States, where her music was well received in the New York Composers' Forum. During her time in the States she also worked as foreign correspondent for Dutch newspapers, as she had done in Paris and Vienna. She returned to Amsterdam to find a quickly deteriorating situation. Forced into hiding during the Nazi occupation, she gave secret concerts in the basement of her home, frequently presenting works by Jewish composers, whose music had been outlawed.

Like many of her Dutch contemporaries in the 1910s and 1920s, Wertheim was drawn to French music, particularly the works of Debussy, Ravel, and Stravinsky. Among her most successful works were the *Piano Concerto*, written in 1940 and premiered by the well-known and respected conductor of the Residentie Orchestra, Willem van Otterloo; the *Divertimento for Chamber Orchestra* (1934) and the *String Quartet* (1932), both performed in New York; a piano suite; and a *Trio for flute, clarinet, and bassoon.* Her music is often cheerful, neo-classical in style, and at times quite playful.

BIBLIOGRAPHY: "Rosy Wertheim," in: *Mens en Melodie* 4 (1949), 220; de Ridder, Kate. "Rosy Wertheim," in: *De Vrouw en Haar Huis* 7 (1948), 252–54. H. Metzelaar, "Rosy Wertheim," in: S. Sadie (ed.), *The New Grove Dictionary of Music and Musicians* (2001^2), 302.

[Melissa de Graaf (2nd ed.)]

WERTHEIMER, ASHER (1844–1918), British art dealer. One of the most famous fine art dealers of his time, Wertheimer inherited his Bond Street business from his father, SAMSON (d. 1892), who founded it in the mid-19th century. He developed it into one of the most significant in Britain, a rival to *Duveen Brothers and other dealers who sold art to the very rich. Wertheimer bought many works from the Russian nobility for sale in the West, and in 1898 paid the colossal sum of £122,000 for 83 paintings from the Hope Collection. Wertheimer is best remembered today for the famous portraits of him and his family painted by John Singer Sargent. Wertheimer left over £1.5 million at his death, a vast fortune at the time.

[William D. Rubinstein (2nd ed.)]

WERTHEIMER, CHAIM ERNST (1893–1978), Israeli biochemist. Born in Buehl, Germany, he was appointed professor at the University of Halle in 1927. Emigrating to Ereẓ Israel in 1934, Wertheimer became head of Hadassah's Chemical Laboratory in Jerusalem and later of its Clinical Biochemistry Laboratory. He was a founder and the second dean of the Hadassah-Hebrew University Medical School. Internationally known for his research on diabetes and fat metabolism, he was awarded the Israel Prize for Medical Science in 1956 and the Bunting Prize of the American Association for Diabetes Research in 1964.

[Lucien Harris]

WERTHEIMER, EDUARD VON (1848–1930), Hungarian historian. Wertheimer was born in Pest. He became a lecturer at the University of Kolozsvár in 1877 and later held successive professorships at two law schools, Nagyszeben and Pressburg. In 1900 he was elected a corresponding member of the Hungarian Academy, and in 1903 was knighted and given the surname "de Monor." On his retirement in 1914, he was appointed a privy councilor (Hofrat). He spent the last years of his life in Berlin.

Wertheimer's principal scholarly interests were the foreign policy of the Hapsburg monarchy and the history of Hungary during the early years of the 19th century. His main work in the former field was *Gróf Andrássy Gyula élete és kora* ("Graf Julius Andrássy, his life and his time," 3 vols., 1910–13), a study of dualism and the role of Hungary. His important contributions to 19th-century history were *Ausztria és Magyarország a XIX század első tizedében* ("Austria and Hungary during the First Decade of the 19th century," 2 vols., 1890–92); and *Az 1811–12 magyar orszaggyülés* ("The Hungarian Diet of 1811–12," 1899). Among his other books were: *Bismarck im politischen Kampf* (1929); *Die drei ersten Frauen des Kaisers Franz* (1893), and *Der Herzog von Reichstadt* (1902; *The Duke of Reichstadt, Napoleon II*, 1905).

[Baruch Yaron]

WERTHEIMER, JOSEPH RITTER VON (1800–1887), Austrian pedagogue, philanthropist, and merchant. Born in Vienna of a well-to-do Jewish family, Wertheimer first served as a clerk in his father's commercial activities and soon became his partner. Though involved in the practical world of commerce, Wertheimer used his free time to study pedagogics. In his twenties, he embarked on a trip through Germany, Italy, France, and England in order to broaden his cultural background. His interest in pedagogical matters led him to take particular note of English kindergartens, and he returned home eager to further the building of kindergartens in Austria. As a first step, he translated a work on kindergarten schooling which he called *Ueber fruehzeitige Erziehung und englische Kleinkinderschulen* (1826, 1828). Despite vociferous opposition to the "feather-brained scheme," Wertheimer founded the first kindergarten in Vienna in 1830 with the cooperation of a Catholic priest, Johann Lindner. Subsequently other kindergartens were founded in many Austrian cities. He also established the Allgemeine Rettungsgesellschaft, a society for assistance to released criminals and guidance for juvenile delinquents.

Wertheimer was deeply involved in Jewish activities. In 1840 he organized the Verein zur Foerderung der Handwerke unter den Israeliten, an organization which enabled thousands of Jewish children to learn useful occupations. In 1843 he established a Jewish kindergarten and in 1860 a Society for the Care of Needy Orphans of the Israelite Community, which established an orphan asylum for girls. As trustee, and later as president, of Vienna's central communal body and founder and president of the Israelitische Allianz zu *Wien (1872–87), Wertheimer played a leading role in the struggle to achieve equal social and political status for Jews. In 1842 he advocated the emancipation of Austrian Jews in his *Die Juden in Oesterreich…* (2 vols., 1842), published anonymously, because such works were then prohibited. He also wrote, among other books, *Therese: Ein Handbuch fuer Muetter und Kinder-*

waerterinnen (1835) and *Die Stellung der Juden in Oesterreich* (1852). He was editor of the *Jahrbuch fuer Israeliten* (11 vols., 1855–65).

Wertheimer's services were recognized by the Austrian emperor who, in 1868, conferred upon him the order of the Iron Crown and the accompanying title of nobility.

BIBLIOGRAPHY: G. Wolf, *Joseph Wertheimer* (Ger., 1868); Wininger, Biog. s.v.; K. Wurzbach, *Biographisches Lexikon*, 55 (1887), 124–30; M. Grunwald, *Vienna* (1936), index.

[Morton Mayer Berman]

WERTHEIMER, MAX (1880–1943), founder of Gestalt psychology. Wertheimer was born in Prague, Czechoslovakia. After studying philosophy and psychology, he spent some years in independent investigation until, in 1910, he arrived at the University of Frankfurt, where he began the studies with which his name is connected. There he met Wolfgang Koehler and Kurt *Koffka, with whom he formed a lifelong association and who helped pioneer the Gestalt movement. In 1916 he went to lecture at Berlin University and returned to Frankfurt in 1929 as professor of psychology. With the rise of Hitler in 1933, Wertheimer emigrated with his family to the United States, joining the faculty of the New School for Social Research in New York City.

Gestalt psychology begins with the observation that experiences and actions are not adequately described as a sum of elements, that there are innumerable psychological facts – such as melodies and visual forms – that also refer to qualities in wholes only. Wertheimer proposed that there are wholes with their own properties and tendencies that are not discoverable in their isolated parts, that a whole determines what the properties of its parts will be. This statement of the problem of part-whole relations, central to Gestalt theory, broke decisively with the presuppositions of atomistic psychology.

Wertheimer's perceptual investigations laid the concrete foundations of Gestalt psychology. In 1912 he showed that the experience of movement cannot be split up into a sum of successive sensations, that it is an effect of stimulus events cooperating to produce a new unitary outcome. His account of the principles of perceptual grouping was another major contribution. How does mosaic of discrete stimulations produce a unitary percept? The discovery of this question was one of Wertheimer's great achievements. Investigators had previously taken the formation of units for granted; Wertheimer showed that this was a central problem for the psychology of perception. He identified certain selective principles of grouping, among them those of proximity, similarity, closure, common fate, and good continuation. He held that one principle, that of Praegnanz, was inclusive of the others, the principle that grouping tends toward maximal simplicity and balance, or toward "good form." In this manner he established that perception is a product of organization. Gestalt psychology revolutionized the modern study of perception and affected the outlook in other areas of psychology. Wertheimer related the problems of Gestalt theory to issues of logic, aesthetics, and ethics. Keenly sensitive to the human implications of psychological doctrines, he questioned prevalent assumptions about man as a creature of habit and the relativism of his values.

BIBLIOGRAPHY: W. Koehler, in: *Psychological Review*, 51 (1944), 143–6; E.B. Newman, in: *American Journal of Psychology*, 57 (1944), 428–35; S.E. Asch, in: *Social Research*, 13 (1946), 81–102; R.I. Watson, *The Great Psychologists* (19682), 436–57; A.S. Luchins, in: IESS, 16 (1968), 522–7 (incl. bibl.). **ADD. BIBLIOGRAPHY:** V. Sarris, *Max Wertheimer in Frankfurt*... (Ger., 1995); M. Wertheimer, in: *Der Exodus aus Nazideutschland* 1997) 191–206; D.B. King and M. Wertheimer, *Max Wertheimer and Gestalt Theory* (2005); J.G. Benjafield, in: *A History of Psychology* (2005), 170–6.

[Solomon Asch]

WERTHEIMER, SAMSON (1658–1724), Court *Jew in Vienna; scholar, *shtadlan*, and philanthropist. Born in Worms of a learned father, Wertheimer studied at the yeshivah in Frankfurt. In 1684 he married the widow of Nathan Oppenheimer and through her family came into contact with Samuel *Oppenheimer, who brought him to Vienna, appointing him manager of his affairs and presenting him to Emperor Leopold I. The wealthiest Jew of his day, from 1694 to 1709 Wertheimer was the chief administrator of the financial affairs of the emperors Leopold I, Joseph I, and Charles VI. He placed enormous sums at the disposal of the government, particularly during the Spanish War of Succession and the war against Turkey, and acted as court agent to the emperor and the rulers of Saxony, Mainz, Trier, and the Palatinate. Emperor Leopold I had such confidence in Wertheimer that he also entrusted him with diplomatic missions. On the occasion of the marriage of the emperor's brother, Prince Charles Philip, to the daughter of the king of Poland, Wertheimer succeeded in obtaining from the latter a dowry of 1,000,000 florins; in appreciation of this the emperor awarded him 1,000 ducats and presented him with his portrait. Paintings of the king of Poland and three prince electors were found in his estate. After the death of Oppenheimer in 1703, Wertheimer was appointed chief agent of the court (*Hoffaktor*); he then found new sources of income for the imperial treasury by improving the salt industry of Siebenbuergen, increasing the export of salt by removing several customs stations and by leasing the mines. At the same time he organized the monopoly of the Polish salt trade, arranging for and financing the transfer of the salt from *Wieliczka to Hungary and Silesia. The conference of Utrecht (1714), which brought to an end the Spanish War of Succession, was financed by the Wertheimers, who also paid the expenses of the Austrian ambassador. Ten imperial soldiers guarded his house and he was known by the title of *Judenkaiser* (Jewish Emperor). He invested his fortune in over half a dozen houses and estates in Vienna, Austria, and Germany. Together with other Court Jews, he saved the Jews of Rothenburg from expulsion by the payment of a large sum of money. He also intervened successfully with the authorities on behalf of the communities of Worms and Frankfurt. Speaking for all the Jewish communities in the empire, in 1700 he appealed to the emperor against the incitement of Johann *Eisenmenger; as a result, the emperor forbade the latter's antisemitic book to be circulated. Because of poor health, Wertheimer generally conducted his affairs from his home in Vienna and did not travel extensively, as was the custom of other Court Jews.

Wertheimer was offered the office and title of *Landesrabbiner of Hungarian Jewry for his aid in reestablishing communities and synagogues ravaged by warfare; the title was confirmed by the emperor and was the only one he used, though Moravia, Bohemia, and Worms accorded him similar honors. A scholar and patron of scholars, he financed the printing of the Babylonian Talmud undertaken at Frankfurt (1712–22) by his son-in-law, Moses *Kann. Some of the sermons he delivered in the synagogue in his home have been preserved. He also left behind manuscripts that dealt with various aspects of *halakhah*, Midrash, and Kabbalah. He built a large synagogue in Eisenstadt and one in Nikolsburg. Judah *he-Ḥasid and his group were supported by Wertheimer, who bore the title of *Nesi Ereẓ Israel* and was in charge of the transfer of money collected throughout Europe to the Holy Land (see *Hierosolymitanische Stiftung).

In his old age, Wertheimer retired from court affairs, handing them over to his son WOLF, who was instrumental in organizing the diplomatic effort for the repeal of Maria *Theresa's expulsion of Prague Jewry. Wolf went bankrupt in 1733 after Bavaria had refused to honor its debts to him. These were eventually acknowledged after more than 20 years of litigation; payments, in installments, to his sons commenced after his death (1763). Wolf's grandsons, JOSEPH (1742–1811), HERMANN (1750–1812), and LAZAR (1740–1818), became members of the nobility, with the title Edler von Wertheimstein, in 1791, 1792, and 1796 respectively. Most of their descendants were baptized.

BIBLIOGRAPHY: M. Grunwald, *Samuel Oppenheimer und sein Kreis* (1913); B. Wachstein, *Die Inschriften des alten Judenfriedhofes in Wien* (1912–1917), index; J. Taglicht, *Nachlaesse der Wiener Juden* (1917), no. 279, 272–5 (Heb., no. 9, 22–25); M. Grunwald, *Vienna* (1936), index; S. Stern, *The Court Jew* (1950), index; Y. Rivkind, in: *Reshummot*, 4 (1925), 309–17; M. Lemberger, in: *Gedenkbuch im Auftrage des Kuratoriums*, A. Engel (ed.), (1936), 74–88; L. Bato, *Die Juden im alten Wien* (1928); D. Kaufmann, *Samson Wertheimer* (1888); idem, *Urkundliches aus dem Leben Samson Wertheimers* (1892); M. Braun, in: *A.S. Schwarz Festschrift* (1916), 499–507; MHJ, 3 (1937); 5 (1960); 10 (1967); 11 (1968); 12 (1969), indexes; H. Schnee, *Die Hoffinanz und der moderne Staat*, 3 (1955), index; 4 (1963), index; 5 (1965), index.

[Yomtov Ludwig Bato]

WERTHEIMER, SOLOMON AARON (1866–1935), rabbinical scholar and bibliophile. Wertheimer, born near Pressburg (Bratislava), Slovakia, grew up in Jerusalem. He became interested in the many rare books he found in Sephardi yeshivot and, despite penury, began to collect Hebrew books and manuscripts, particularly Oriental ones, including some unique specimens. Wertheimer was one of the first to publish some of the Cairo *Genizah* treasures.

His Midrash collections, containing some hitherto unknown works, are *Battei Midrashot* (4 parts, 1893–97), *Leket Midrashim* (1903), and *Oẓar Midrashim* (2 parts, 1913–14). A revised and enlarged two-volume edition of these collections appeared during 1948–53, edited by his grandson A.J. Wertheimer. Wertheimer also published geonic and medieval responsa: *Kohelet Shelomo* (1899), *Ginzei Yerushalayim* (3 parts, 1892–97), *Zikkaron la-Rishonim* (1909), and *Ge'on la-Ge'onim* (1925). Among his original works are *Darkah shel Torah* (1891), on the methodology of *halakhah* and *aggadah; She'elot Shelomo* (2 parts, 1932–33), responsa; *Be'ur Shemot Nirdafim sheba-Tanakh* (1924; 1953^2), a work on biblical synonyms. The revised edition of the last by his sons includes a biography and a bibliography of his published books and numerous manuscripts, among them commentaries on Bible and Mishnah, a *siddur*, a Passover *Haggadah*, and a supercommentary on Naḥmanides' Bible commentary. Wertheimer also contributed to learned periodicals and was active as a preacher.

[Zvi Kaplan]

WERTHEIMER, STEF (1926–), Israeli industrialist. Born in Germany, he came to Palestine with his family in 1937. After service during Israel's War of Independence he continued with the development of armaments. In 1951 he founded the ISCAR (Israel Carbides) company, which became a world leader in the production of precision carbide metalworking tools. In 1981, after four years in the Knesset, he devoted his efforts to developing the Galilee, with a residential project, Kefar Veradim, and the Tefen industrial park. He initiated the establishment of several other Galilee industrial parks. These enterprises generated 10,000 jobs in 150 plants and together with ISCAR around $2 billion in annual exports.

Wertheimer was a creative and innovative thinker. The ISCAR complex is enhanced by works of art and even an industrial museum, and to create a bright and cheerful atmosphere, Wertheimer had all the factory floors painted yellow. In 1991 he received the Israel Prize for special contribution to society and the state. In 2006 ISCAR was sold to Oscar Buffett for $4 billion.

[Fern Lee Seckbach]

WESEL, BARUCH BENDET BEN REUBEN (also called **Benedict Reuben Gomperz**; d. c. 1753), German rabbi and author. Baruch Benedict was called Wesel after the town where he was born. He was a member of the distinguished *Gomperz family of Germany and western Europe. His grandfather, Elijah Gomperz, was a Court Jew of Frederick William I of Prussia and through his influence greatly assisted his coreligionists. His father was a wealthy Berlin merchant. In 1724 Wesel was appointed one of the three members of the Breslau *bet din* and wrote a commendation for the *Sha'arei Tefillah* of Solomon Zalman Hanau. In 1728 the *Council of Four Lands appointed him rabbi of the Polish community in Breslau. That same year he wrote a commendation for the printing of the Pentateuch in Dyhernfurth. He inherited a considerable fortune from his father, engaged in business, and did not take a salary from the community. Unsuccessful management of his business affairs, however, led to his financial ruin, and in 1733 the community reinstated his salary. He subsequently applied to be exempted from the high taxes imposed upon wholesale merchants and to be transferred to the category of second-class taxpayers. His application was rejected, however, and he was imprisoned, compelled to pay, and deprived of the title rabbi. He was expelled from Breslau in 1738, but was permitted to take up residence in the neighboring villages. When Frederick II conquered Silesia in 1740, Wesel sent him a laudatory poem in Hebrew and German, written as an acrostic of his name, and Frederick noted this. Subsequently, in 1744, when 12 Polish-Jewish families were granted a permanent permit to live in Breslau, and when a special privilege was granted to Polish merchants, Wesel was elected chief rabbi of Breslau, and the Prussian government recognized him and his community. The same order also permitted the Jews to establish a cemetery in Breslau (previously they had to use the cemetery of Dyhernfurth). Wesel suggested that the funds for the cemetery and for taxes generally be raised from a special tax imposed on meat. However, he did not live long enough to consecrate the cemetery, and he himself was buried in Dyhernfurth. Ten of his responsa were published in 1745 under the title *Mekor Barukh* and republished with additions by his son in 1771.

BIBLIOGRAPHY: D. Weinryb, in: *Tarbiz*, 9 (1938), 65ff., 85; M. Brann, in: *Jubelschrift ... Graetz* (1887), 229, 237ff.; idem, in: *Festschrift ... J. Guttmann* (1915), 237; Halpern, Pinkas, 474.

[Itzhak Alfassi]

WESKER, ARNOLD (1932–), English playwright. Born of immigrant Yiddish-speaking parents (the father was a tailor) in London's East End, Wesker held various jobs after he left school, including kitchen porter and pastry cook. These laid the foundations of his early plays, which have an autobiographical content. *The Kitchen* (1960), for example, is at once a literal representation of life behind the scenes in a restaurant and an allegory of the struggle, competition, and near-slavery of the social world. Wesker is best known for the trilogy of plays entitled *Chicken Soup with Barley, Roots*, and *I'm Talking about Jerusalem* (1959–60). These constitute an ambitious attempt to probe the symptoms of a sick society. *Chicken Soup with Barley* deals with Jewish society in the East End of London during the 1930s and 1940s; it shows the idealistic socialism, which was the main barricade against Sir Oswald Mosley's fascist movement, giving way to an easy, postwar conformity. *Roots* represents these same decadent values subsisting in a country community. In *I'm Talking About Jerusalem*, Wesker shows a young couple endeavoring to establish an ideal community in the country in the immediate postwar period of 1946. These plays are written in realistic prose with a poetic undercurrent. Though partly inspired by the disillusionment of his time, Wesker also exhibits a visionary quality and a desire for reform and renewal.

In *Chips with Everything* (1962), apparently based upon Wesker's own period of national service in the Royal Air Force, the characters are shallow stereotypes, the officers tyrants and decadents, the men simple philistines or easily led slaves. In the 1960s a great deal of Wesker's energy went into forming and administering "Centre 42." This organization, named after a Trade Union Congress resolution supporting the arts, was intended to sponsor festivals and eventually to institute its own cultural program. Its cultural basis at the beginning rested solidly on Wesker's own plays, which took an unashamedly propagandist turn in *Their Very Own and Golden City* (1966). A late play is *Denial* (2000).

Six Sundays in January has some Jewish interest. The title is that of the first story in the volume and was published in the *Jewish Quarterly* in 1958 and in *Modern Jewish Stories* in 1963. Wesker's writings have been translated into 17 languages. With Harold *Pinter, he is probably the best-known contemporary Anglo-Jewish playwright. He has written an autobiography, *As Much As I Dare* (1994).

BIBLIOGRAPHY: G. Leeming and S. Trussler, *The Plays of Arnold Wesker: An Assessment* (1972). **ADD. BIBLIOGRAPHY:** R.W. Dornan, *Arnold Wesker Revisited* (1995); idem. (ed.), *Arnold Wesker: A Casebook* (1998); G. Leeming, *Arnold Wesker – The Playwright* (1982); R. Wilcher, *Understanding Arnold Wesker* (1991).

[Philip D. Hobsbaum]

WESSELY, NAPHTALI HERZ (**Hartwig**; 1725–1805), Haskalah poet, linguist, and exegete. Wessely's ancestors had fled Poland during the Chmielnicki pogroms and settled in Wesel on the Rhine, from where the family took its name. Born in Hamburg, Wessely spent his childhood in Copenhagen, where his father was a purveyor to the king of Denmark. He received his religious education at the yeshivah of Jonathan *Eybeschuetz, who influenced him greatly, and read literature and scientific works in a number of European languages, Associated with the Feitel Bank, Wessely's business affairs took him to Amsterdam and Berlin. In Berlin he met Moses *Mendelssohn and contributed a commentary on Leviticus (Berlin, 1782) to the *Biur*.

Wessely began his literary career with the Hebrew translation of the apocryphal work *Wisdom of Solomon* (from Luther's German translation), to which he appended a brief commentary, later elaborated into a full-length exegesis, *Ru'aḥ Ḥen* (Berlin, 1780; Warsaw, 1885). He pioneered in the revival of biblical Hebrew, and his translation, written in the vivid and lofty style of the Scriptures, prompted later Haskalah writers to translate apocryphal works into biblical Hebrew. The linguistic problems he encountered led to a number of philological works such as *Gan Na'ul* (or *Levanon*; 2 vols., Amsterdam, 1765–66; Lemberg, 1806), a work on Hebrew synonyms and roots, and *Yein Levanon*, a commentary on the mishnaic tractate *Avot* (Berlin, 1775; Warsaw, 1884), which also concentrates on linguistic aspects. While Wessely's focus is often linguistic, his exegesis shows also wide knowledge and learning, and his commentaries were well received by orthodox scholarship. He is, however, mainly known as a poet – *Shirei Tiferet* (1789–1802) is the major literary work of the German Haskalah – and as a pioneer in education and an advocate of the Enlightenment through his *Divrei Shalom ve-Emet* (1782), a call in support of the Edict of Tolerance (*Toleranzpatent, 1782) of Joseph II of Austria.

Poetry

Shirei Tiferet ("Poems of Glory"), Wessely's magnum opus, is a long epic on the life of Moses and the Exodus from Egypt, modeled after similar epical works by Klopstock and Schiller. Embellished with legends from the Talmud and the Midrash, the work is essentially didactic and is suffused with the rationalist spirit of the age. Thus the concept of the mission of the Jewish people is reflected in the description of the revelation at Sinai; the quest for salvation and for an end to the suffering of the Jewish people also clearly echo throughout the poem. Divided into six parts, containing 18 cantos, the narrative of the poem stretches from the persecution of the Jews by Pharaoh and Moses' birth to the giving of the Law. Wessely's great prosodic innovation was the introduction of the alexandrine (the 12-syllable heroic line of contemporary French poetry) into modern Hebrew poetry. The poem, however, is little more than a narrative in verse of the Bible story, its principal aim being didactic rather than aesthetical. Wessely, in the rabbinic tradition, intended his poem to be a commentary on certain obscure passages in the Bible, yet at times he used the narrative only as a pretext to display his poetic virtuosity and his structural prowess.

While the work as a whole may be of little literary merit, there are certain beautiful poems, such as the lyrical introductions to the cantos which are invocations to God. There are also a number of fine poetic passages in the cantos themselves: some describe feelings, while others are didactic in content, such as the depiction of Israel's mission and its destiny in the seventh canto. *Shirei Tiferet* served as a model to later Hebrew poets. The epic was published in full after the poet's death (Prague, 1809), and sections of it were translated into German and French.

Among his other poetic works is *Mehallel Re'a*, an introduction to the translation of Exodus. In his commentary to Exodus, Wessely criticizes the inadequate, faulty educational methods in the contemporary Jewish schools. He also wrote a number of occasional poems.

Wessely was a trailblazer in style. The syllabic meter and the strophic structure he introduced became standard models for Hebrew poets for over 60 years. He also revived the biblical Hebrew style in literature and lent to the language flexibility and vividness.

Linguistic Method

Striving to use a lofty biblical style in order to recreate the flavor and form of biblical writing, Wessely tried to arrive at the original meaning of synonyms in the Bible. His approach was philological rather than exegetical, and he viewed the problem not only from a theoretical and abstract point of view, but primarily practically, i.e., how to use the synonyms for rhetorical purposes. This pragmatic approach also determined Wessely's method in his studies of the Hebrew language. He demanded that biblical Hebrew provide him with the necessary linguistic means and devices for his literary needs. His great sensitivity to the language allowed him to grasp the spirit of the biblical tongue and to penetrate its mysteries. Psychology for him was the key to an understanding of the language in general, and of the individual meaning of synonymic words in particular. The Hebrew language seemed to him as vital in his time as it had been in the ancient past and, though it was not spoken, it remained superior to all other living tongues. Hence his philological assumption that there are no synonyms in Hebrew (an assumption which is in accord with the principle accepted in linguistics that language does not suffer excess and either rejects superfluous words or invests them with new meaning), a characteristic he ascribed only to Hebrew because of his mystical relation to the language. Wessely, however, was extreme in his theory and refused to acknowledge the possibility of synonyms even in poetry; he thus attributed new meaning to an idea repeated in different words. The starting point of his philological research is not the word itself, but the concept that the written words give rise to. He therefore ascribed a separate meaning to each word and disregarded the connotations that have accrued to a word in the course of the historical development of the language.

Wessely's linguistic theory also influenced his style and he showed the way for the writing of pure biblical Hebrew. His prose style, however, is a fusion of Hebrew styles of different historical periods.

Commentary

Imrei Shefer, a commentary on Genesis, is the fruit of lectures given by Wessely to young audiences in Berlin. Portions of the work were published by *Mekiẓe Nirdamim (Lyck, 1868–71). Mendelssohn also asked him to write a commentary to Leviticus (Berlin, 1782) for the *Biur*. Writing in a light and flowing style, Wessely explains every Hebrew word and refers to earlier commentators. He attempted to reconcile the plain meaning of the Scriptures with the commentaries in the Talmud and the Midrashim by means of a detailed analysis of every word, a method which often led to lengthy and sophistic distortions of the simple meaning of the text. Mendelssohn edited the work; he shortened it, interpreted difficult passages that Wessely had failed to explain, and added comments to passages in which the opinions of the two scholars differed. The Gaon of Vilna, *Elijah b. Solomon Zalman, praised the work, but the *maskilim* considered it too scholarly.

Educational and Public Activities

Wessely's epistle *Divrei Shalom ve-Emet* (Berlin, 1782), is a call to the Jewish community of Austria to comply willingly with the order of the Edict of Tolerance of the Austrian emperor Joseph II to open schools for Jewish children in which German would be taught. The work is the first methodical composition in Hebrew on Jewish education written in the spirit of the Haskalah. Wessely distinguishes between two types of studies: what he called *Torat ha-Adam* ("human knowledge"), and instruction in the Law of God. The acquisition of human knowledge demands instruction in subjects which are necessary to man's relationship with man, namely, a training in general subjects and ethics, i.e., secular studies common to the human race. The divine teachings are the heritage of the people of Israel alone and are identical with the Torah of Moses. Jewish education should be founded on both studies, with a schooling in human knowledge preceding divine subjects, since these should serve as a basis for the study of Torah. Without general education it is impossible to understand divine teachings. Wessely came to the conclusion that he who studies the Torah without acquiring common human knowledge, will, when he grows up, become a burden upon society.

His opinions were strongly opposed by the Orthodox, especially by Ezekiel b. Judah *Landau of Prague, *David Tevele b. Nathan of Lissa, and the Gaon Elijah of Vilna. A bitter controversy ensued. Wessely responded to the rabbis in his epistles *Rav Tov le-Veit Yisrael* (Berlin, 1782); *Reḥovot* (Berlin, 1785); and *Mishpat* (Berlin, 1784), all of which were later collected under the title *Divrei Shalom ve-Emet*; sections were translated into French, German, Dutch, and Italian.

Wessely also wrote a number of other works, the most important of which is *Sefer ha-Middot* or *Musar Haskel* (Berlin, 1784), a collection of essays on the essence of the soul and its faculties. The work reflects contemporary philosophical and ethical German thought. *Sefer ha-Middot* became popular among learned Jews in Eastern Europe. Some of Wessely's works are still in manuscript.

BIBLIOGRAPHY: Z. Fishman, in: *Ma'anit* (1926), 17–20; incl. bibl.; J.S. Raisin, *Haskalah Movement in Russia* (1913), index; Zeitlin, Bibliotheca, 413–18; J.L. Landau, *Short Lectures on Modern Hebrew Literature* (19382), 62–74: P. Sandler, *Ha-Be'ur la-Torah shel Moshe Mendelssohn ve-Si'ato* (1940), 136–45; E. Carmoly, *Wessely et ses écrits* (1829); W.A. Meisel, *Leben und Wirken Naphtali Hartwig Wessely's* (1841); Klausner, Sifrut, 1 (19522), 103–50; incl. bibl.; D. Sadan, *Be-Ẓetekha u-ve-Oholekha* (1966), 51–54; M.S. Samet, in: *Meḥkarim… le-Zekher Ẓevi Avneri* (1970), 233–57. **ADD. BIBLIOGRAPHY:** G. Elkoshi, Introduction to *Mivḥar Ketavim* (1952); B. Shahevitch, *Be'ayot be-Signon ha-Perozah ha-Masa'it shel Reshit ha-Sifrut ha-Ivrit ha-Ḥadashah* (1963); N.H. Rosenbloom, *Ha-Epos ha-Mikrai me-Idan ha-Haskalah ve-ha-Parshanut* (1983); E. Breuer, "Naphtali Herz Wessely and the Cultural Dislocations of an 18th Century Maskil," in: S. Feiner and D. Sorokin (eds.), *New Perspectives on the Haskalah* (2001).

[Joshua Barzilay (Folman)]

WESSELY, WOLFGANG (1801–1870), Hebrew scholar and jurist; the first Jew to hold a full professorship in Austria. Born at Trebitsch, Moravia, in 1829, he was the first Jew to receive a doctorate in philosophy from Prague University; four years later he received a doctorate in civil law, and later published legal studies. He also applied for a doctorate in canon law, but as a Jew, was rejected. Wessely first served as a teacher of religion at a Jewish school in Prague and compiled a catechism, *Netib Emuna* (1841), which went through eight editions. In 1844, after the death of the Hebrew censor, Carolus *Fischer, Wessely applied for the post of translator at this office, also presenting the authorities with a proposal for the "establishment of an institute for the science of Judaism [*Wissenschaft des Judentums] and its rabbinical literature at the local university." The conservative leaders of the Prague community, M. *Landau, Samuel Freund, and S. Rapoport, were hostile to Wessely's proposal, and also questioned his qualifications for initiating it. However, Christian academic opinion was on Wessely's side. In 1846 Wessely began to lecture at Prague University on Hebrew and rabbinical literature before a mixed Christian and Jewish audience. In 1851 he was appointed, in addition, extraordinary professor of criminal law. He promoted the introduction of the jury system into Austria. In 1861 he became a full professor at the university.

BIBLIOGRAPHY: O. Muneles (ed.), *Bibliographical Guide to Jewish Prague* (1956), index; G. Kisch, *Die Prager Universitaet und die Juden* (1969), index.

WEST, MAE (1893–1980), U.S. actress, writer, and singer. Born Mary Jane West in Brooklyn, New York, to John P. West and Matilda Delker-Dolger, a German Jewish model and dressmaker, at seven West was winning talent shows. A year later she joined Hal Claredon's stock company in New York. By 1907, she was a vaudeville performer with Frank Wallace, whom she married in 1911 and separated from a few months later. In September 1911, West appeared on Broadway in *A la Broadway* and then in *Hello, Paris*. In 1912, she appeared in *A Winsome Widow* and developed a solo act later that year. In 1918, she starred in the comedy musical *Sometime*, followed by the musical revue *The Mimic World* (1921). In 1926, West wrote and starred in the play *Sex*, which drew the attention of censorship groups. After more than a year on stage, policed arrested West and the cast of *Sex* on obscenity charges; West served ten days in jail and paid a $500 fine, becoming a national celebrity. West became a success with such plays as *Diamond Lil* (1928), which featured the line, "Why don't you come up sometime and see me?"; *Pleasure Man* (1928); and *The Constant Sinner* (1931) (the latter two closed over censorship issues). West went to Hollywood in 1931, appearing in the film *Night After Night* (1932). She went on to write her next eight films, which included *She Done Him Wrong* (1933), based on *Diamond Lil*; *I'm no Angel* (1933), with Cary Grant; *Belle of the Nineties* (1934); *Goin' to Town* (1935); *Klondike Annie* (1936); *Go West Young Man* (1936); *Every Day's a Holiday* (1938); and *My Little Chickadee* (1940), which paired West with W.C. Fields. In 1942, Wallace returned to sue West for divorce and alimony; West made an undisclosed settlement. Her 1943 film *The Heat's On* did not fare well with critics, and West returned to Broadway with *Catherine Was Great* (1944). In 1948, West starred in the short-lived *Ring Twice Tonight*, which was followed with a revival of *Diamond Lil* (1948–51). West toured with the nightclub act Mae West and Her Adonises from 1954 to 1956, and released several albums of her songs, starting with *The Fabulous Mae West* (1955). She made an appearance on the television sitcom *Mister Ed* (1964) and an ill-fated return to the silver screen in the sex-change comedy *Myra Breckinridge* (1970) and *Sextette* (1978), an adaptation of her play *Sex*.

[Adam Wills (2nd ed.)]

WEST, NATHANAEL (pseudonym of **Nathan Wallenstein Weinstein**; 1903–1940), U.S. novelist. Widely regarded as one of the most distinguished American novelists of the 1930s, West was the son of Russian-Jewish immigrants who had settled in New York City, and a brother-in-law of the writer S.J. *Perelman. He began his first novel during his student days at Brown University. Later published as *The Dream Life of Balso Snell* (1931), this was a surrealistic fantasy dwelling on human corruption. It shows the influence of western European symbolists such as James Joyce and other modern experimental writers, particularly those of France. For six years, beginning in 1927, he was a hotel manager in New York. During that time he worked at developing a prose style marked by economy of diction, poetic richness, and psychological depth, and published his second novel, *Miss Lonelyhearts* (1933). Though it was his masterpiece, it was not a popular success. It depicted a once-cynical newspaper columnist dispensing compassion, love, and help to victims of personal or social failure. *A Cool Million* (1934) satirized American fascists veiling themselves in democratic values, myths, and history. From 1935 he worked in Hollywood, remaining there as a scriptwriter until his death in an automobile accident. His fourth novel, *The Day of the Locust* (1938), was a grim satire of American life set in Hollywood. West's achievement rested primarily upon his ability to portray the sordidness, violence, humor, and tragedy of American life. Self-rejection was epitomized in his change of name from Nathan Weinstein and was perhaps the cause of his virtually antisemitic ridicule of Jews and Jewishness in his novels. West was active in movements against Nazism, economic exploitation, and abridgment of democratic rights.

BIBLIOGRAPHY: V. Comerchero, *Nathanael West: The Ironic Prophet* (1964); J.F. Light, *Nathanael West* (1961); S.E. Hyman, *Nathanael West* (1962), University of Minnesota Pamphlets on American Writers, no. 21; J. Martin, *Nathanael West: The Art of His Life* (1970); J. Herbst, in: *Kenyon Review*, 23 (1961), 611–30; R.H. Smith, in: *Saturday Review*, 40 (1957), 13–14.

[Brom Weber]

WESTCHESTER COUNTY, county in New York State. Located immediately north of New York City, and ranked 12th among American counties in per capita personal income, Westchester County is home to the eighth largest Jewish community in the nation, numbering 129,000 in 2002.

Established in 1683, the 500 square mile county was predominantly rural before the introduction of commuter railroads in the mid-19th century. Jews have lived in Westchester since colonial times. In the early 18th century the family of Jechiel Hays migrated from Holland. His sons and grandsons were farmers and shopkeepers in Rye, New Rochelle, Bedford, North Castle, and Pleasantville. The Hays family has preserved Jewish continuity in the county ever since, though some have maintained residences in both New York City and Westchester. Prominent figures were Daniel Peixotto *Hays (d. 1923), Democratic Party figure, Jewish communal activist, and second mayor of Pleasantville; and Arthur Hays *Sulzberger (d. 1968), publisher of the *New York Times*.

The Hays family was not typical; the Jewish population grew only after the eastern European migration of 1880–1924 that formed America's core Jewish population. Most of the immigrants were storekeepers and artisans living and working in cities and villages in the southern, eastern and western fringes of the county. They labored long hours to feed, clothe, and provide simple comforts for local residents and sustain their own large families. Some Jews ventured into the countryside as itinerant peddlers. A few owned and operated farms. Jewish communal life revolved around self-help organizations, kosher grocery and butcher shops, and 17 traditional synagogues. A smaller group of acculturated Jews owned large local businesses or commuted to work in New York City. Along with prospering Russian-born Jews, they established Reform synagogues in the southernmost cities of Yonkers, Mount Vernon, and New Rochelle.

In the 20th century, Westchester Jewry underwent three periods of rapid expansion. The first was the 1920s. A boom in cheap transportation facilitated commutation to Manhattan and the Bronx. When modestly priced automobiles, a new parkway system, and comfortable railroad cars made suburban living attractive, a Jewish middle class found its way to the county. The pattern of settlement was uneven. Jewish commuters and established local businessmen resided comfortably along the tree-lined streets of the southern tier cities and centrally located White Plains. Jewish developers sold Scarsdale lots to other Jews. Jews were not, however, welcome in the other "first class villages" of Bronxville, Rye, Larchmont, and Pelham Manor; nor were they wanted in sections of northern Westchester and some Hudson River villages.

Until the Great Depression Jewish-owned stores and factories brought prosperity to Westchester cities and villages. New wealth facilitated the formation of synagogues as well as the expansion of local communal institutions and chapters of the major Jewish organizations.

Some Jews, however, never made it to the middle class; they remained in low-income, low status occupations, toiling as milkmen, trolley conductors, prison guards, ferry operators, and junkmen, unable to accumulate enough capital to establish stable businesses.

A cohort of radical factory workers and storekeepers from New York City formed summer camps and colonies in northern Westchester. During the summer months they enjoyed fresh air, green grass, wholesome recreation, and endless political debates.

The second period of Westchester Jewry's rapid expansion was the post World War II era (1946–1970), when new social and political factors facilitated increased Jewish settlement. As a result of the increased openness in American society and new laws, heretofore-insurmountable barriers crumbled. After the federal government outlawed restrictive residence clauses in 1948, Jews purchased houses in villages along the Hudson River and Long Island Sound, as well as in developing sections of Mt. Vernon, Yonkers, New Rochelle, and White Plains. The Jewish concentration in Scarsdale swelled incrementally to form about a third of the population.

That antisemitism was not dead, however, is indicated by two phenomena, one far more disconcerting than the other. Country clubs, long the bastion of upper-class snobbery, remained closed to Jews (who formed 11 of their own). Much more serious were the Peekskill Riots. For several years a consortium of the summer camps and colonies invited bass-baritone Paul Robeson, a multi-talented African-American singer, actor, and political radical, to perform. After the Labor Day concert of 1949, local ruffians, screaming anti-black, anti-Communist and anti-Jewish epithets, pelted cars and buses exiting the grounds. Police looked on impassively while the rioters damaged vehicles, inflicting injuries upon the passengers.

Untouched by the Peekskill incident, many Jews welcomed new opportunities to live and work in the county. Teachers found positions heretofore denied them. Some Westchester-born college-educated sons (and later, daughters) returned from war and university to apply new technology and selling techniques to their fathers' businesses. Others preferred to practice law and medicine near home to commuting to New York.

During the immediate postwar period Jewish communal life flourished. People who had seldom attended religious services in the city joined synagogues when they moved to Westchester. They raised money to help Orthodox, Conservative and Reform congregations relocate existing institutions and construct new ones in villages where none had existed before. Premier architects Philip Johnson, Marcel Breuer, and Louis Kahn designed houses of worship in Port Chester, Scarsdale, and Chappaqua.

As the excitement of newness abated, economic and social circumstances again restructured the Westchester Jewish community. In the 1970s and 1980s embattled school systems, high taxes, and societal problems rendered the southernmost cities less desirable. Major synagogues in Yonkers and Mt. Vernon merged, relocated further north, or gave up the ghost. The second wave of feminism and inflated housing prices brought women into the workplace; consequently fewer devoted energy to congregational sisterhoods and Hadassah. As well, predominantly male Jewish organizations, such as the Jewish War Veterans and B'nai B'rith, no longer attracted newcomers. Remaining service, defense, and charitable organizations moved their headquarters to south-central Westchester – i.e., the area centered in White Plains, Scarsdale, and northern New Rochelle.

Change was also apparent in the business and professional profile of Westchester Jewry. While many Jews continued to commute to New York City, an ever-increasing minority worked closer to home. The professional staffs of area hospitals became disproportionately Jewish. Corporate chains slowly ground down the independent pharmacies, privately owned clothing stores, and dry goods emporia. The result was that few shops along the Main Streets of Port Chester and New Rochelle, for example, heavily Jewish in the early 20th century, remained under Jewish ownership. Consequently sons and daughters who returned to Westchester after college took over only those family businesses that were sizeable or cutting-edge. Otherwise, they found opportunity in the corporate parks and professional offices constructed all over the county.

The most recent Jewish influx began in the early 1990s. At a time when the population of American Jewry and New York Jewry remained static, Westchester Jewry experienced a 40% growth, from 91,000 in 1991 to 129,000 in 2002. Housing costs and lack of space in built-up areas moved the population northward. By 2005, northern Westchester matched south-central Westchester in Jewish population and affluence. A case in point is the fact that the Reform congregations of Chappaqua and Bedford nearly match the largest temples in Scarsdale and White Plains in size, beauty and membership.

Judaism in northern Westchester presents an uneven pattern. On the one hand Jewish religious practice is weaker in northern Westchester than in areas closer to New York City. More Jews in this area are married to non-Jews, and for many others, Judaism is a seasonal matter. In 2002 about three-quarters attended a *seder* and fasted on Yom Kippur, but only 16% lit Shabbat candles and 7% kept kosher. On the other hand, recent arrivals to northern Westchester have launched a number of new Jewish institutions. Pleasantville, home to the pioneering Hays family, but with a weak Jewish presence through most of the 20th century, now hosts the Richard J. Rosenthal JCC and the Pleasantville Community Synagogue. Newcomers have initiated Jewish study groups, havurot, and congregations in villages with no previous Jewish address. Most Northern Westchester synagogues identify as Reform, but with a decidedly independent streak. Publicity for The Jewish Family Congregation, South Salem, for example, boasts that it "practices Reform Judaism with a traditional flavor."

In the early 21st century, however, the core of Westchester Jewish life nevertheless remained in south-central Westchester. More Jews there than in other sections of the county observe Jewish rituals and attend synagogue on a regular basis, contribute to Jewish causes, visit Israel with some regularity, enroll their children in Jewish schools, and supply leadership for Jewish organizations in the county and New York City.

For all Westchester Jewry, there was a discernable Jewish profile. In 2002 Westchester Jews constituted 9% of Jewish households in the eight counties of the UJA/Federation of New York service area (New York City, Long Island and Westchester). Half (51%) belonged to synagogues, a considerable advance over the 43% regional total. Among Westchester Jews 42% identifed as Reform, 31% as Conservative and 9% as Orthodox, a deviation from the comprehensive New York profile, where the percentages are more balanced: 29%, 26% and 19% respectively. In a child-centered region, over half of the Jewish children are enrolled in supplementary schools connected to synagogues, while 31% attend four Jewish day schools and two high schools that follow Orthodox or Conservative models. A few adolescents travel to Jewish high schools in New York City.

Virtually all children in Jewish families attend college or university, and many do not return to Westchester. The future of Westchester Jewry depends upon opportunities in business and the professions and the continued appeal of life in New York and its environs.

BIBLIOGRAPHY: B.R. Shargel and H.L. Drimmer, *The Jews of Westchester, a Social History* (1994); B.R. Shargel, "Leftist Summer Colonies of Northern Westchester County, New York," in: *American Jewish History*, 83:3 (September, 1995); New *York Population Studies*, UJA Federation of New York, 1991 and 2002.

[Baila Round Shargel (2nd ed.)]

WESTERBORK, the main transit camp for Dutch Jewry during the German occupation of Holland. The camp, situated in an extremely isolated region in the northeast of the country, had been set up by the Dutch government in 1939 with a financial guarantee from Dutch Jewry, in order to shelter numerous Jewish refugees fleeing from Germany who crossed the Dutch frontiers illegally. The first group came on Oct. 9, 1939. The camp held some 750 refugees when, on July 1, 1942, the Germans took command, after extending it considerably. From that date, more than 100,000 Jews arrested throughout the country remained for several days or weeks in Westerbork, where they had to work before being deported to other camps, primarily Nazi death camps, as part of the "final solution of the Jewish problem" (see *Holocaust: General Survey). During this period the camp was continually overcrowded. On Oct. 2, 1942, 13,000 Jews were imprisoned in Westerbork in one single *Aktion*. Thousands of them had to sleep on the floor without mattresses or blankets. Food and sanitary conditions were deplorable. By September 1944, a total of 93 trains, consisting of 20 trucks and containing 1,000–2,000 Jews, left Westerbork. Jewish officials were in charge of the internal organization and held responsible for maintaining law and order among the internees. Of those deported 54,930 went to Auschwitz in 68 transports, and 34,313 to Sobibor on 19 transports; most of these prisoners were killed upon arrival. In addition, 4,771 went to Theresienstadt, which itself was a transit camp. Nine transports were sent to Bergen-Belsen with 3,762 inmates. A special Jewish police force was created for this purpose. The most important task of these Jewish officials was to determine the order in which Jewish families were to be deported. Most of the Jewish officials, including their president, had been selected from the German-Jewish refugees who constituted the older segment of the Westerbork population. This frequently gave rise to serious conflicts, especially between Dutch and German Jews. Westerbork had its own theater, where famous German artists who had fled to Holland gave performances, as well as an orchestra. An excellent hospital, with a capacity of 1,725 beds, had 120 surgeons, more than 1,000 employees, and a completely equipped operating theater, various clinics, a pharmacy, and laboratories. The camp also maintained various schools and a playground for children, workshops for the repair of clothes and shoe shops, a bathhouse, and a post office. At the end of the war, only 900 Jews remained in Westerbork when the Canadians liberated the camp. The German commander, A.K. Gemmeken, was sentenced by a Dutch court to 10 years' imprisonment. Among those deported from Westerbork on one of the last trains in September 1944 was Anne *Frank and her family.

BIBLIOGRAPHY: J. Presser, *The Destruction of Dutch Jewry* (1969), 406–64, and index; P. Mechanicus, *Waiting for Death* (1968); W. Warmbrunn, *The Dutch under Nazi Occupation 1940–1945* (1963), 61–68, 167–80; A.J. Herzberg, *Kroniek der Jodenvervolging* (1956), passim.

[Abel Jacob Herzberg / Michael Berenbaum (2nd ed.)]

WESTERN WALL (Heb. הַכֹּתֶל הַמַּעֲרָבִי), that section of the western supporting wall of the *Temple Mount which has remained intact since the destruction of the Second Temple (70 C.E.). It became the most hallowed spot in Jewish religious and national consciousness and tradition by virtue of its proximity to the Western Wall of the Holy of Holies in the Temple, from which, according to numerous sources, the Divine Presence never departed. It became a center for mourning over the destruction of the Temple and Israel's exile, on the one hand, and of religious – and in the 20th century also national – communion with the memory of Israel's former glory and the hope for its restoration, on the other. Because of the former association, it became known in European languages as the "Wailing Wall" (or similar appellations). Most of the Western Wall of the Temple Mount, which was about 1,580 ft. (485 m.) long, is hidden by the buildings adjoining it. The accessible portion of the Wall was (until June 1967) no longer than 91 ft. (28 m.) from the Maḥkama building garden on the north to the Prophet's Gate (Barclay's Gate below the Moghrabis' Gate) on the south. In front of it ran a stone-paved alley no wider than 10 ft. (3.3 m.) bordered on its west by a slum area, the Moghrabi Quarter, established in the 14th century. The Wall above ground consisted of 24 courses of stones of different types of dressing and decreasing in size and age, reaching a total height of 58 ft. (18 m.) with 19 ft. (6 m.) above the level of the Temple Mount. In Warren's work in the 19th century 19 more courses were detected buried underground, the lowest founded on the natural rock of the Tyropoeon Valley.

In 1968 the ground in front of the Wall was excavated to reveal two of the buried courses of stone, and the Wall as it exists today consists of eight courses of huge, marginally dressed ("Herodian") stones from the Second Temple period, above which are four layers of smaller, plainly dressed stones from the Moslem (Umayyad) period, eighth century. The upper stones were constructed from the Mamluk period and later. Jewish travelers since the Crusader period used to marvel at the immense dimensions of the lower stones – average height 3¼ ft. (1 m.), and length 10 ft. (3.3 m.), but some as long as 39 ft. (12 m.) and weighing over 100 tons – and believed (incorrectly) that they were part of Solomon's Temple. In order to withstand the pressure of the soil and debris fills situated behind the Wall, the courses of stone were laid with a slight batter, with each row being set back about two inches relative to the one beneath it. The Wall thus slants slightly eastward. This factor, the weight of the stones, and the accuracy of the cutting accounts for the unusual stability of the Wall.

In Jewish Tradition and History

Since 135 C.E. (the failure of the *Bar Kokhba revolt), the prayers of Israel both in Ereẓ Israel and throughout the Diaspora were directed toward the site of the destroyed Temple. The Temple itself as well as all the structures on the Temple Mount were completely effaced, and thus the walls, the only remnants of the Temple Mount, became endeared to the Jews. It cannot be determined with certainty from what point prayers were offered just at this particular section of the Western Wall. The Midrashim already refer to the general sanctity of the Western Wall of the Temple in the fourth century C.E., perhaps referring to the time of Julian the Apostate. They speak of "the Western Wall of the Temple" or of "the Western Gate," from which the Divine Presence never moves, which was not destroyed and never will be destroyed (Ex. R. 2:2; Num. R. 11:2, etc.). It seems probable, however, that the rabbis were referring to the Western Wall of the Holy of Holies and that its indestructibility is symbolic rather than actual, since that wall was in fact destroyed. The notion of the ever-present **Shekhinah* therefore became associated with the Western Wall (of the Temple Mount). An 11th-century source – referred to as the "prayer at the gates" document – is known from the Cairo **Genizah*, and according to it Jews conducted prayers next to the Western Wall not in the present location but farther north immediately opposite the Holy of Holies of the Jewish Temple, i.e., in the area in front of "Warren's Gate." In the 12th century *Benjamin of Tudela mentions Jews coming to the Western Wall for prayers and to the "Mercy Gate," but it is possible that the other walls to the south and east also served a similar purpose. Later visiting rabbis (12th–15th centuries) also refer to the walls of the Temple Mount, but they, too, are not site-specific in terms of a gathering spot for Jewish worship along the Western Wall. The Western Wall is not mentioned at all by *Naḥmanides (13th century) in his detailed account of the Temple site in 1267 nor in the report of *Estori ha-Parḥi (14th century). It does not figure even in descriptions of Jerusalem in Jewish sources of the 15th century (e.g., Meshullam of Volterra, *Obadiah of Bertinoro, etc.). The name Western Wall, used by Obadiah, refers – as can be inferred from the context – to the southwestern corner of the wall, and there is no hint that there was a place of Jewish worship there.

It is only from the 16th century that Jews began praying at the present location and this is clear from the available sources.

Thenceforth all literary sources describe it as a place of assembly and prayer for Jews. According to a tradition transmitted by Moses *Ḥagiz, it was the sultan Selim, the conqueror of Jerusalem, who recovered the Wall from underneath the dungheap which was hiding it and granted permission to the Jews to hold prayers there. No Muslim sources about Jerusalem bear any evidence of Arab interest in the Western Wall. The nearby area became Muslim religious property at least as early as in the 13th century, and from 1320 there is mention of the Moghrabi Quarter established there.

With the expansion of the Jewish population in Ereẓ Israel from the beginning of the 19th century onward, and with the increase in visitors, the popularity of the Western Wall grew among Jews. Its image began to appear in Jewish folkloristic art (upon ritual articles, seals, and title pages) and later also in modern art drawings (B. Shatz, J. Steinhardt, M. Chagall, and others). It also became a subject of literary creation. The 19th century also saw the beginning of the archaeological study of the Western Wall. In 1838 *Robinson discovered the arch since named after him, immediately south of the Western Wall, and in the 1850s J. Barclay investigated the lintel of an ancient gate (now in the corner of the women's section; see *Temple, The Second). In 1865 C.W. *Wilson described the arched structure previously discovered by Tobler in the 1830s. From 1867 Sir Charles *Warren sank shafts around the perimeter walls of the Temple Mount and was able to ascertain its full height on three sides. Excavations were conducted to the south of the Western Wall, beneath Robinson's Arch, to the southwest corner of the Temple Mount, as well as along the southern Temple Mount Wall, by B. Mazar from 1967 to 1978. More recently excavations were made beneath Robinson's Arch by R. Reich and Y. Bilig. To the north of the Western Wall, excavations were made along the Western Wall of the Temple Mount by the Ministry of Religious Affairs, and following that systematically by D. Bahat.

During the 19th century attempts were made on behalf of the Jewish community in connection with the Wall. In the 1850s Ḥakham Abdullah of Bombay failed in his efforts to buy the Wall. Sir Moses Montefiore tried in vain to obtain permission for placing benches or for installing a protection against rain there. Permission to pave the street was, however, granted. Occasionally a table for the reading of the Torah was placed near the Wall, but had to be soon removed at the demands of the Muslim religious authorities. In 1887 Baron Rothschild offered to buy the whole Moghrabi Quarter, and have it demolished. He proposed to the government that for the funds received the Waqf should obtain other lands and resettle there the residents evacuated from the Moghrabi Quarter. Although negotiations reached an advanced stage the plan never materialized for reasons not properly clarified to the present day. It is probable that objections were raised not only on the part of the Waqf, but also on the part of the rabbis and communal leaders of the Sephardi community on whose full cooperation Rothschild made conditional his handling of this delicate matter. It appears that certain rabbis observed that the conditions laid down for the designated Jewish sacred trust (*hekdesh*) would convert the area into a public domain (*reshut ha-rabbim*) with regard to carrying on the Sabbath and thus create halakhic difficulties. In addition interests and counter-interests among the trustees of the various Sephardi sacred trusts foiled the plan.

Shortly before World War I, a further attempt to purchase the surroundings of the Western Wall was made by the Anglo-Palestine Bank. These negotiations were interrupted by the outbreak of the war. In 1912 the Turkish authorities ordered the removal of a partition between men and women, benches, a glass cupboard for candles, a table for reading the Torah, etc., about the introduction of which the Waqf had complained.

After the Balfour Declaration and the British Mandate had given the Jews a recognized national status in Ereẓ Israel, they began to add national significance to the traditional religious significance of the Western Wall. The Arab mufti incited his community against the Zionists (who, he claimed, intended to seize control of the Wall) by proclaiming it a sacred Muslim site which he named after the legendary horse "Al-Burak," upon which Mohammed is supposed to have ridden to Jerusalem and which he allegedly tied to this wall during his visit. Many intercommunal conflicts about the Western Wall occurred in the 1920s. In order to antagonize the Jews the mufti ordered the opening of a gate at the southern end of the street thus converting it into a thoroughfare for passersby and animals. In addition the Muslims deliberately held loud-voiced ceremonies in the vicinity. They also complained again about the placing of accessories of worship near the Wall, and a partition (between men and women) was forcibly removed – by the British police – on the Day of Atonement 1928. In August 1929 an instigated Muslim crowd rioted among the worshipers and destroyed ritual objects and, following the excitement and unrest this created, murderous riots broke out a few days later.

The British set up a committee of inquiry and consequently an international committee (consisting of a Swede, a Swiss, and a Dutchman) was appointed by the League of Nations to resolve "the problem of the Wall." Although this committee ascertained that the place was indeed holy to Jews well before the time of Saladin (i.e., 1187), this was most likely a reference to the holiness of the Temple Mount as a whole, with no clear chronological data as to the origins of the worship at the Western Wall being available to them. The committee met in Jerusalem, in the summer of 1930, and the results of "the trial of the Wall," as it became known, were as follows:

(a) the Muslims had absolute ownership of the Wall;

(b) the Jews had the uncontested right to worship and to place seats in the street;

(c) the Jews were not to blow the *shofar* there.

The Arabs objected. The Jews accepted, except for the prohibition to blow the *shofar*, which was considered a searing humiliation. Indeed, each year nationalist youths would blow the *shofar* near the Wall at the termination of the Day of Atonement, which would always lead to the intervention of the British police.

From December 1947, after bloody incidents with the Arabs, Jews were no longer able to approach the Western Wall, and after the capitulation of the Jewish Quarter (of the Old City) in May 1948, Jews were prevented for 19 years from even looking at the Wall from afar. The paragraph in the cease-fire agreement granting freedom of access to the holy places was not kept by the Jordanians.

The Wall was liberated on the third day of the Six-Day War (June 7, 1967) by Israel's parachutists breaking through the "bloody gate," which the mufti had opened. The Moghrabi Quarter was immediately demolished and on the first day of Shavuot, one-quarter of a million Jews swarmed to the place. Subsequently the buildings placed against the Wall in its continuation southward were removed. The entire cleared area in front of the Western Wall was leveled and converted into a large paved open space. The lower square near the Wall is the prayer area, where one may find people praying or studying, either singly or in groups, day and night throughout the year. Since the liberation of the Wall, it has hosted national events and ceremonies, such as bar mitzvahs, the swearing in of new IDF troops, and memorial and religious services with the attendance of government officials. Under Israeli administration, the excavations made by Warren in 1867, north of the Wall beneath the Muslim structures, were renewed and extended, uncovering the continuation of the Wall northward beyond Wilson's bridge. To the south, too, archaeological excavations progressively revealed the impressive extent of the Wall. One of the main findings of the excavations was the Wall's tunnel, 488 meters in length. The tunnel passes near the foundations of the Western Wall of the Temple Mount and is considered the closest point to the Holy of Holies (*Kodesh ha-Kodashim*). Inside the tunnel is located the Warren Gate, one of the gates to the Temple which were closed by the Muslim Waqf. The tunnel was opened to the public in 1996 by order of Binyamin *Netanyahu, then Israel's prime minister. It led to violent clashes between Palestinians and Israeli police and soldiers which cost the lives of 15 Israelis and numerous Palestinians. Another site in the Wall complex is the archeological garden, located south of the Wall and consisting of remains of Jerusalem from the Second Temple period, mainly *mikva'ot* (see **mikveh*). In addition, there is a Herodian commercial street, with the remains of shops, which led visitors towards the Temple Mount. At the southern edge of the Wall a pile of hewn stones bears witness to the destruction of the Temple. Among the stones, archeologists have found a special one chiseled on five sides. The inscription led them to believe that it was the one used by the priest to announce the beginning of the Sabbath to the people of Jerusalem. Near the archeological garden is the Davidson Center, a glass building with four underground floors where exhibits from the Second Temple and Byzantine periods are on display.

BIBLIOGRAPHY: A.M. Luncz, in: *Yerushalayim*, 10 (1913), 1–58; idem, in: *Lu'aḥ Ereẓ Yisrael*, 20/21 (1914–15–16), 1–8; *The Western or Wailing Wall in Jerusalem*; Memorandum by the Secretary of State for the Colonies, Cmd. 3229 (1928); *Protocol of the 14th Session of the Permanent Mandates Commission of the League of Nations* (1928), 205–7; C. Adler, *Memorandum on the Western Wall* (1930);

Report of the Commission of the Palestine Disturbances of August 1929, Cmd. 3530 (1930); J. Ya'ari-Poleskin, *Baron Edmond Rothschild*, 1 (Heb., 1930), 206–19; J. Triwaks, *Mishpat ha-Kotel* (1931); C.D. Matthews, in: *The Muslim World*, 22 (1932), 331–9; P. Grayewsky, *Sippurei Kotel ha-Ma'aravi* (1936); E.R. Malachi, in: *Lu'aḥ Yerushalayim*, 12 (1951/52), 275–81; Z. Vilnay, *Yerushalayim – Ha-Ir ha-Attikah* (1967³), 97–109; M. Hacohen, *Ha-Kotel ha-Ma'aravi* (1986²); M. Natan, *Ha-Milḥamah al Yerushalayim* (1968⁶), 311–21; M. Har El, *Zot Yerushalayim* (1969), 229–40; M.A. Druck and Z. Steiner (eds.), *Album ha-Kotel ha-Ma'aravi* (1969). **ADD. BIBLIOGRAPHY:** D. Bahat, *The Illustrated Atlas of Jerusalem* (1990); D. Bahat, "The Western Wall Tunnels," in: H. Geva (ed.), *Ancient Jerusalem Revealed* (1994; expanded ed., 2000), 177–90; D. Bahat, "Since When Have Prayers Been Made at the Western Wall?" in: *Eretz-Israel*, Kollek Volume (2006); "The Archeological Garden in Jerusalem," in: *Yedioth Aharonoth* (Aug. 15, 2001).

[Jacob Auerbach / Dan Bahat and Shaked Gilboa (2nd ed.)]

°**WESTERWEEL, JOHAN** ("**Joop**"; 1899–1944), Dutch educator and Righteous Among the Nations. Born in Zutphen, the Netherlands, to parents belonging to the Darbyite Church, also known as the Plymouth Brethren, Johan (better known as Joop) Westerweel attended a denominational teachers college and developed a personal philosophy that combined elements of socialism with his own version of evangelical Christianity. His first teaching job was in the Dutch East Indies (today Indonesia), but he was soon in trouble for protesting the exploitation of the native population by the Dutch masters. When he refused to report for compulsory military training because of his pacifistic beliefs, he was expelled from the colony. Returning home, he joined the teaching faculty of a school, and later became principal of a Montessori school in Rotterdam. It was there, some while later, that he first came into contact with Jewish refugees from Germany and learned about the plight of the Jews under Hitler. Thus came about his contact with the Dutch branch of *He-Ḥalutz, an organization that prepared young people for a life of pioneering and agricultural work in Palestine and which had a training farm in Loosdrecht, near Amsterdam. In August 1942, when the 50-or-so trainees and instructors at the farm learned that they were slated for deportation within a few weeks, the group's leaders, Menachem Pinkhof and Joachim ("Shushu") Simon, turned to Westerweel for help; he had already temporarily hidden several Jews in his home. After listening attentively to their plans to help build a new society in Palestine, though opposed to nationalism in any form, he was impressed by their idealism and concluded that he had at least found a cause worthy of his fundamentalist piety, combined with his faith in socialism and his contempt for the Nazis. Immediately swinging into action, Westerweel set in motion a far-ranging plan to temporarily hide the farm's staff and students with friendly gentile families, assisted by trustworthy persons since then known as the Westerweel group, and then gradually move them to neutral Spain, whence they would proceed to Ereẓ Israel. To get to Spain meant traveling hundreds of miles across German-occupied Belgium and France, armed with forged papers. Westerweel organized and personally directed virtually every aspect of this operation, aided by his wife, Wilhelmina, and about a dozen underground activists, escorting most of the escapees all the way from the Netherlands to the Franco-Spanish border on the peak of the Pyrenées mountains. One of them recalled his parting words one freezing afternoon in 1944 high up in the mountains. "You are on the threshold of freedom. Soon you will arise in the land of freedom and will fulfill your goal of building Ereẓ Israel as a homeland for the world's Jews. I wish each of you happiness and good luck, but do not forget your comrades who fell along the road and by sacrificing their lives paved the way for your journey to freedom.… Remember the world's suffering, and build your land in such a way that it justifies its existence by providing freedom for all its inhabitants and abandoning war." Not long afterward, on March 11, 1944, he was arrested by the Germans at a Dutch-Belgium border-crossing point; Wilhelmina had already previously been arrested and confined to the Vught concentration camp. Brutally tortured, Joop refused to divulge the names of his associates. He was executed on August 11, 1944, just a few days after an attempt to rescue him ended in failure. He had once told his Jewish associates, "You're wrong in thinking I am helping you because you are Jewish. Even if you were blacks or Hottentots, no matter what, I would help you in the name of justice, for you are in need." While awaiting execution, Joop Westerweel penned a farewell message to his Jewish friends. It reads in part: "There they are … all my comrades, standing side by side with me; together we have advanced along this road to confront the enemy.… Whether I die or live is now all the same to me. A great light has dawned within me, enriching me. It is time for silent thoughts. The night is dark and long. But I am fully aglow from the splendor within me." His wife, Wilhelmina, was dispatched to Ravensbrueck concentration camp and luckily survived. The couple's four children were in hiding with friends. In 1963, Yad Vashem awarded Joop and Wilhelmina Westerweel the title of Righteous Among the Nations.

BIBLIOGRAPHY: Yad Vashem Archives M31–32; I. Gutman (ed.), *Encyclopedia of the Righteous Among the Nations: Netherlands*, Vol. 2 (2004), 823–25; M. Paldiel, *The Path of the Righteous* (1993), 138–41.

[Mordecai Paldiel (2nd ed.)]

WESTHEIMER, FRANK HENRY (1912–), U.S. organic chemist. He was born in Baltimore, Maryland, and educated at Dartmouth College and Harvard University, where he received his M.A. and Ph.D. He was National Research Fellow at Columbia University (1935–36) before joining the department of chemistry at the University of Chicago (1936–1954) where he became professor (1948). During this period he supervised the National Development Research Council's Explosives Research Laboratory (1944–45). He was Morris Loeb Professor of Chemistry at Harvard (1954–83) after which he became professor emeritus. Westheimer was among the first chemists to apply physical techniques to analyzing biochemical reactions, and he made outstanding contributions to understanding the molecular mechanics of reactions involving phosphate esters, biphenyls, and beta-keto acids. He was a renowned teacher with a great interest in chemistry education; the Westheimer Report (1965) was the first to assess its relevance to U.S. public affairs. His many honors include the Cope Award (1982), the National Medal of Science (1986), the Priestley Medal (1988), and the Willard Gibbs Medal (2003). He was a foreign member of the Royal Society of London and was a member of the President's Science Advisory Committee (1967–70).

[Michael Denman (2nd ed.)]

WESTHEIMER, RUTH (1928–), sexologist and broadcaster. Born Karola Ruth Siegel to an affluent family in Frankfurt, Germany, she was sent to boarding school in Switzerland while her parents attempted to arrange passage for the rest of the family out of Nazi Germany. She was never to see them again; it is probable that they died in Auschwitz.

A staunch Zionist, she immigrated to Palestine at age 16, where she joined the Haganah and learned Hebrew. She moved to Paris in 1950, where she earned a degree in psychology from the Sorbonne. Moving to the U.S. in 1956, she received her doctorate in education from Columbia University in 1970.

Westheimer became familiar to millions of radio and TV viewers and listeners as Dr. Ruth, dispensing frank, unambiguous, commonsensical advice on sexual matters in a thickly European-accented English to callers. She received her initial break in the media in 1980 when WYNY-FM, a New York City radio station, gave her a late-night slot for her show *Sexually Speaking*. By 1983 it was the top-rated radio show in New York City and cleared the way for her to move into television with the widely syndicated *The Dr. Ruth Show* (1984–91). She also hosted the TV talk show *What's Up, Dr. Ruth?* (1989–90). From 2000 she appeared as Dr. Ruth Wordheimer in the educational/fantasy TV series *Between the Lions* on PBS. She also had a syndicated newspaper column called "Ask Dr. Ruth."

Advocating good sex in the context of loving relationships, Dr. Ruth also used books to spread her message. Her many publications include *Dr. Ruth's Guide to Good Sex* (1983); *Dr. Ruth's Guide to Married Lovers* (1986); an autobiography, *All in a Lifetime* (1987); *Sex and Morality* (1991); *Dr. Ruth's Guide to Safer Sex* (1992); *The Art of Arousal* (1993); *Dr. Ruth's Encyclopedia of Sex* (1994); *Sex for Dummies* (1995); *Heavenly Sex: Sexuality in the Jewish Tradition* (with J. Mark, 1995); *The Value of a Family* (with B. Yagoda, 1996); *Grandparenthood* (1998); *Pregnancy Guide for Couples* (with A. Grunebaum, 1999); *Power: The Ultimate Aphrodisiac* (2001); *Romance for Dummies* (2002); and *Human Sexuality* (with S. Lopater, 2002).

She maintained ties with Israel, visiting frequently and cooperating in joint projects with Israeli academics and publishers. In that sphere, she wrote *Surviving Salvation: The Ethiopian Jewish Family in Transition* (1993).

BIBLIOGRAPHY: B. Multer, *The Dr. Ruth Phenomenon* (1987); M. Scariano, *Dr. Ruth Westheimer* (1992).

[Rohan Saxena and Ruth Beloff (2nd ed.)]

WESTPHALIA, region in Germany. During the Middle Ages Jews lived not only in the duchy of Westphalia but also in many of the bishoprics, cities, and earldoms of the region known as Westphalia. Jews were present in most areas by the beginning of the 13th century; many came from *Cologne, where a flourishing community existed at the end of the 12th century. They generally settled in small numbers; the first organized communities existed in *Muenster, *Minden, and *Dortmund, where Archbishop Conrad of Cologne granted the Jews a charter of privileges in 1250. Until the middle of the 14th century, they were under the jurisdiction of the country nobles. Later, with the strengthening of the towns, the Jews were placed under the municipal jurisdiction, and the number permitted to settle was limited. They earned their livelihood primarily by moneylending. The Jews of Westphalia were victims of the *Black Death persecutions in 1348–49, but during the second half of the 14th century they returned to the towns from which they had fled or had been expelled. Despite local expulsions, Jewish settlement continued in Westphalia. In the latter part of the 17th century, as well as in the 18th century, Jewish autonomy was severely restricted by governmental control and regulation. Nevertheless, the number of Jews increased. They were engaged not only in moneylending but also as merchants in gold, silver, cloth, and livestock.

The establishment of the Kingdom of Westphalia by Napoleon in 1807 brought a dramatic change in the status of the Jews. The Napoleonic kingdom was located to the west of Westphalia and was made up of portions of Hanover, Hesse, and other states. On January 27, 1808, the Jews were granted civic rights and – as the first Jews of Germany – could settle throughout the kingdom, engage in the profession of their choice, and had total freedom of commerce. After a few months, a *consistory was founded using the French institution as a prototype, and existed from 1808 to 1813 in the capital, *Kassel. Its president was Israel Jacobson, financial adviser to King Jerome Bonaparte, assisted by rabbis Loeb Mayer Berlin (1738–1814), Simon Kalkar (1754–1812), and Mendel Sternhardt (1768–1825). Also participating in the work of the consistory were two scholars, David Fraenkel (1779–1865), publisher of *Sulamit*, and Jeremiah *Heinemann (1778–1855). The secretary was S. Markel, the attorney for the municipal council of Kassel. Its task was the supervision of all Jewish activities in Westphalia. Innovations in the religious service were introduced that aroused considerable controversy, and new schools were formed, including a seminary in Kassel for the training of teachers and rabbis in 1810. Of particular interest was the experimental school in Kassel that combined secular and Jewish studies. Westphalia was divided into seven districts, each with its rabbi and his assistant. Jews were compelled to choose family names. Many were attracted by the liberal policies of the kingdom, and by 1810 the number of Jews had risen to 19,039. In 1813, however, the kingdom was abolished, and with it the consistory was dissolved.

Parts of the region known as Westphalia were included in the Prussian province of Westphalia in 1816, and the status of the Jews became similar to that of their coreligionists of Prussia. Together with them, they gradually obtained their *emancipation between 1847 and 1867. In 1881 an organization of Westphalian communities was formed. The notorious antisemite Adolf *Stoecker was active in Westphalia at the end of the 19th century. The Jewish population of Westphalia numbered 21,595 in 1932 (0.45% of the total). The principal communities were *Gelsenkirchen (population 1,440); Muenster (600); *Bielefeld (860); *Bochum (1,152); Dortmund (3,820); and *Hagen (650).

The rise of Nazism led to considerable Jewish emigration from Westphalia, as well as intensive adult education efforts on the part of the Jewish community. Many synagogues were destroyed in November 1938, and mass deportations emptied Westphalia of its Jews by 1941.

The community was renewed after the war, and a number of synagogues rebuilt. In 1946 Westphalia became a part of the modern federal state of North Rhine-Westphalia. There were 924 Jews living there in 1970. In 1989 the nine Jewish communities in Westphalia numbered 745. In 2004 there were ten communities with 7,204 members. The biggest communities are Dortmund (3,409); Bochum (1,147); and Muenster (753). This remarkable increase of membership is explained by the immigration of Jews from the former Soviet Union after 1990. In 1992 the Jewish museum of Westphalia was opened in the small town of Dorsten.

BIBLIOGRAPHY: A. Gierse, *Die Geschichte der Juden in Westfalen waehrend des Mittelalters* (1878); F. Lazarus, in: MGWJ, 58 (1914), 81–96, 178–208, 326–58, 454–79, 542–61; B. Brilling, in: *Westfalische Forschungen*, 12 (1959), 142–61; idem., *Rheinisch Westfalische Zeitschrift fuer Volkskunde*, 5 (1958), 133–62; 6 (1959), 91–99; H.C. Meyer, *Aus Geschichte und Leben der Juden in Westfalen* (1962), bibliography, pp. 242–57; B. Brilling and H. Richtering (eds.), *Westfalia Judaica* (1967), includes bibliography; *Germania Judaica*, 2 (1968), 880–1; 3 (1987), 2055–60; L. Horwitz, *Die Israeliten unter dem Koenigreich Westfalen* (1900); A. Lewinsky, in: MGWJ, 50 (1906); G. Samuel, in: ZGJD, 6 (1935), 47–51; M. Stern, in: *Ost und West*, 17 (1917), 255–68. **ADD BIBLIOGRAPHY:** H. Stratmann and G. Birkmann, *Juedische Friedhoefe in Westfalen und Lippe* (1987); W. Stegemann (ed.), *Juedisches Museum in Westfalen* (1992); C. Gentile (ed.), *Begegnungen mit juedischer Kultur in Nordrhein-Westfalen* (1997); K. Menneken (ed.), *Juedisches Leben in Westfalen* (1998); G. Birkmann, *Bedenke, vor wem du stehst. 300 Synagogen und ihre Geschichte in Westfalen und Lippe* (1998); E. Brocke, *Zeitzeugen. Begegnungen mit juedischem Leben in Nordrhein-Westfalen* (1998); M. Sassenberg, *Zeitenbruch 1933–1945* (1999); M. Brocke, *Feuer an Dein Heiligtum gelegt* (1999); A. Kenkmann (ed.), *Verfolgung und Verwaltung* (2001[2]); S. Gruber and H. Ruessler, *Hochqualifiziert und arbeitslos* (2002). **WEBSITE:** www.jmw-dorsten.de.

[Zvi Avneri / Larissa Daemmig (2nd ed.)]

WEST VIRGINIA, state in the E. Central section of the U.S. Coal mining has been the predominant industry, but with automation the number of coal miners has declined and there has been some migration out of the state. The Jewish population has also declined. From a reported high in 1956 of 6,000, the Jewish population fell to 4,755 in 1967 and, in 2001, 2,300

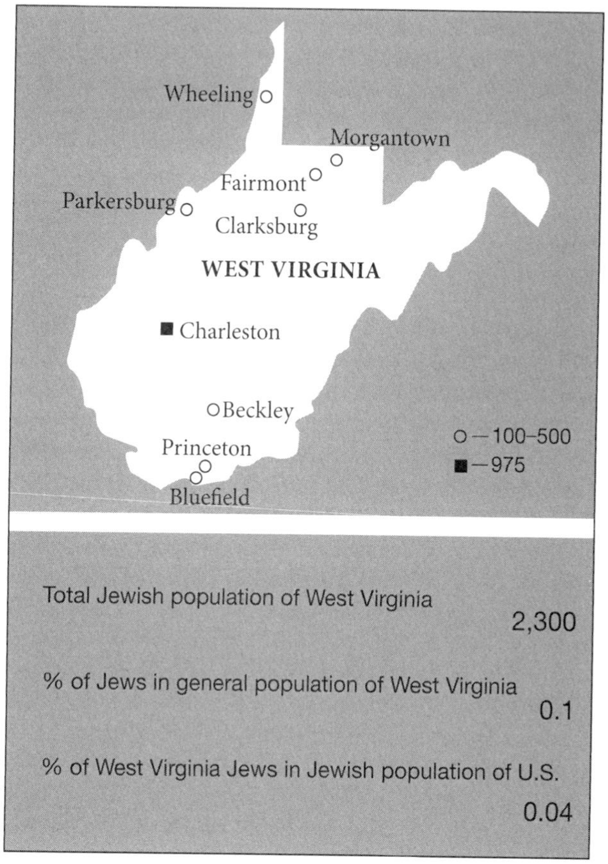

Jewish communities in West Virginia. Population figures for 2001.

out of the total population of 1,808,000. The 2001 figures for the major Jewish communities were Beckley, 120; Bluefield-Princeton, 200; Charleston, 975; Clarksburg, 110; Fairmont, 140; Morgantown 200; Parkersburg, 110; and Wheeling, 290. Jewish life in the state has been largely a coextension of the religious organization. The first congregation, Leshem Shomayim, was formed in Wheeling in 1849; Charleston's B'nai Israel was formed in 1873. West Virginia's congregations, their numbers permitting, have always tried to maintain rabbinical leadership on a regular basis. The smaller congregations, unable to do so, have, especially in the southern part of the state, welcomed Reform student rabbis. Over a period of two or three decades more than 60 such rabbis served the smaller communities.

In addition to the congregations themselves, there are congregational women's organizations in most of the communities and congregational men's organizations in a few. Both the Zionist Organization and Hadassah are represented in five of the communities. The National Council of Jewish Women has a chapter only in Charleston. Fund-raising is conducted by a Federated Jewish Charities organization in Charleston, Huntington, and Bluefield-Princeton; in Wheeling it is conducted under the auspices of a Jewish community council. In the last few years there has been a considerable influx of Jewish students from the northern cities. Morris Harvey College in Charleston has roughly 300 Jewish students; Marshall University in Huntington, 65; and West Virginia University in Morgantown, 300. The state university has a Hillel Foundation which was directed by Rabbi Herbert J. Wilner, who also served as spiritual leader of Morgantown's Congregation Tree of Life. Jews have always taken a vigorous part in public affairs. In 1957–58, Harold L. Frankel served as mayor of Huntington. Serving in the West Virginia House of Delegates (lower division of the state legislature) in the early 1970s were Ivor F. Boiarsky, Simon H. Galperin, Jr., and Leo G. Kopelman. Paul J. Kaufman was a member of the Senate. Fred H. Caplan was a member of the five-man Supreme Court of Appeals. Others serving in the previous decade in the House of Delegates were David A. Abrams, David M. Baker, Stanley E. Deutsch, and Fred H. Caplan. Rabbis, too, have been prominently involved in state affairs. Rabbi Martin Siegel of Wheeling was chairman of the West Virginia Arts and Humanities Council; Rabbi Samuel Cooper, from 1932 rabbi of Charleston's B'nai Jacob Congregation, was chairman of the West Virginia Human Rights Commission. Rabbi Samuel Volkman, rabbi of Charleston's B'nai Israel Congregation from 1952 and regional director of the Union of American Hebrew Congregations from 1957 to 1959, served as a member of the West Virginia Advisory Committee to the U.S. Commission on Civil Rights.

[Samuel Volkman]

There were two synagogues in Charlestown, a traditional congregation with an Orthodox rabbi and a Reform Congregation. There was a Conservative Synagogue in Clarksburg and a joint Conservative/Reform Congregation in Huntington. There were Reform Synagogues in Logan, Martinsburg, Parkersburg, Welsch, Wheeling, and Williamson

BIBLIOGRAPHY: A.I. Shinedling, *West Virginia Jewry: Origins and History, 1850–1958*, 3 vols. (1963).

°WETTE, DE, WILHELM MARTIN LEBERECHT (1780–1849), German biblical scholar and theologian; born at Ulla, near Weimar, and died in Basle. De Wette came from a family of Protestant clerics of Dutch origin. He was appointed privatdocent in theology at the University of Jena in 1805. From 1807 to 1810 he was professor of biblical exegesis at Heidelberg. At *Schleiermacher's suggestion he was invited to join the newly established faculty of theology in Berlin, but his liberal views caused his dismissal in 1819. He returned to Weimar and stayed there until he was offered the post of professor of ethics and theology at Basle in 1822. This marked the beginning of the second phase of his scholarly activity, during which he became more and more conservative in his views, thereby arousing the antagonism of the rationalists, to whom he had himself previously belonged.

In his lifetime, de Wette was one of the most renowned theologians and religious scholars. In Bible criticism, his main contributions are to be found in his early writings – his dissertation on Deuteronomy, written in Latin (*Dissertatio critico-exegetica, qua Deuteronomium a prioribus Pentateuchi libris diversum* ..., 1805) and his book *Beitraege zur Einleitung in das Alte Testament* (2 vols., 1806–07). As against the "fragments" hypothesis prevailing at the time, he maintained the unity of the Book of Deuteronomy and pointed out its unique qualities, both in form and contents. It was he who linked Deuteronomy to the reform introduced by *Josiah (II Kings 22–23), concluding that the book had been composed in that period. He also asserted that the Former Prophets were edited by the Deuteronomistic school, and deprecated the historical reliability of the books of Chronicles. These conclusions eventually became cornerstones of modern biblical scholarship and established de Wette as one of the great biblical scholars of the 19th century. Another noteworthy work of de Wette in the field of biblical criticism was his *Commentar ueber die Psalmen* (1811, 1836[4]) which betrays J.G. Herder's influence, stressing as it does the aesthetic aspect of the text. This was also the first attempt to classify the Psalms on the basis of literary genres, a method subsequently developed by Hermann *Gunkel. De Wette's German translation of the Bible (1809–11), including the Apocrypha, is distinguished by its strict adherence to the original, sometimes to the extent of sacrificing the fluency of the translations.

BIBLIOGRAPHY: E. Staehelin, *Dewettiana, Forschungen und Texte zu W.M.L. de Wettes Leben und Werk* (1956); H.J. Kraus, *Geschichte der historisch-kritischen Erforschung des Alten Testaments* (1956), 160–79; R. Smend, *W.M.L. de Wettes Arbeit am Alten und am Neuen Testament* (1958).

[Menahem Haran]

WETTSTEIN, FEIVEL HIRSCH (1858–1924), Polish historian. Wettstein spent his whole life in his native Cracow, where he owned a bookstore. Through the influence of his teacher, Ḥayyim Nathan *Dembitzer, and while still young, he began to study the history of the Jews in Poland, especially in Cracow, from material available in old responsa and in the minute books and archives of communities and societies. His monographs (published in various periodicals) illuminated obscure periods in the history of the Jews of Poland and served as valuable sources for historians of Polish Jewry such as Meir *Balaban and others. Wettstein's studies are distinguished by careful scholarship and the avoidance of unfounded conjectures.

His works include *Kadmoniyyot mi-Pinkesa'ot Yeshanim le-Korot Yisrael be-Polin bi-Khelal u-vi-Cracow bi-Ferat* (1892); a biography, *Le-Toledot S.J. Rapaport* (1900); *Devarim Attikim mi-Pinkesei ha-Kahal bi-Cracow* (1901); and *Le-Korot ha-Yehudim be-Polin u-ve-Yiḥud bi-Cracow* ... (1918).

BIBLIOGRAPHY: A. Cuch, in: *Haaretz* (July 24, 1924); G. Bader, *Medinah va-Ḥakhameha* (1934), 93.

[Gedalyah Elkoshi]

WETZLAR, city near Koblenz, Germany. Evidence for the presence of Jews in Wetzlar dates from after 1250, but Jews probably settled there as early as 1200. Although in 1265 Archbishop Werner of Mainz promised to protect the Jews of Wetzlar, toward the end of the century they were among those Jews accompanying R. *Meir b. Baruch of Rothenburg in his attempted emigration from Germany. A *Judengasse* (see *Jewish Quarter) in Wetzlar dates from 1292; a synagogue was established by 1318. Both Jews and Christians acted as moneylenders in the city, lending a considerable sum to Emperor Louis IV in 1347. In 1349 the *Black Death persecutions brought an end to the community, but by 1360 Jews were once more residing in the city. In 1382 King *Wenceslaus extended the privilege of admitting Jews to the municipal council of Wetzlar. There were 20 Jews in the city in 1385 and 30 in 1442. In 1524 the municipal authorities sought to regulate *kasher* slaughtering, and in 1544 they unsuccessfully attempted to expel the entire Jewish community. By 1546 there were 50 Jews in Wetzlar. They were all expelled in 1598, but by 1604 some had returned, their number growing to 80 by 1625. A cemetery was consecrated in 1626; until then burial had taken place in Frankfurt. In the second half of the 16th century Isaac Levita, a Jew born in Wetzlar, was appointed to teach at the University of Cologne after he had converted to Protestantism. Also of prominence during the period were R. Joel of Wetzlar (d. 1698) and R. Solomon b. Simeon Wetzlar, author of *Ḥakirot ha-Lev* (Amsterdam, 1731).

The 18th century brought with it a significant rise in Jewish economic activity. Around 1735 Leib Wetzlar was a known business associate of Joseph Suess *Oppenheimer, and Abraham Wetzlar (1715–1799) became a financier of the imperial court. Although the population was legally limited to 12 families of **Schutzjuden* for most of the 18th century, in actuality 18 to 20 families, comprising some 100 persons, lived in Wetzlar during that time. In 1756 a synagogue was dedicated by the Jewish community. Some amelioration of discriminatory practices against Jews was brought about by Napoleonic reforms, beginning in 1803, but a reaction to this followed again after Wetzlar's incorporation into Prussia in 1815. By 1823 there were 101 Jews in the city. In 1880 there were 210; and in 1933 there were 132. Although the community supported a religious school, it considered itself under the jurisdiction of the rabbinate of Marburg. It maintained a synagogue, a cemetery, and a philanthropic organization. During the Holocaust, 41 Jews from the district emigrated and 68 perished.

BIBLIOGRAPHY: *Germania Judaica*, 2 (1968), 882–5; K. Watz, *Geschichte der juedischen Gemeinde in Wetzlar von ihren Anfaengen bis zur Mitte des 19. Jahrhunderts (1200–1850)* (1966); Aronius, Regesten, 291 para. 706; A. Kober, *Cologne* (Eng., 1940), 174–5; FJW, 226; *Statistisches Jahrbuch des deutsch-israelitischen Gemeindebundes* (1903), 78.

[Alexander Shapiro]

WETZLAR VON PLANKENSTERN, aristocratic Austrian family. The first identifiable member of the family was AMSCHEL WETZLAR of Frankfurt (d. 1605?); one of his descendants moved to Offenbach where ABRAHAM WETZLAR (c. 1714–1799) was born. During the Seven Years' War (1756–63) Abraham became an army contractor for Austria and amassed a large fortune. In 1763 he received the title of court agent and six years later obtained permission (together with Isaac *Arnstein) to live among the Christians of Vienna (other distinguished Jews received this privilege only in 1782). On Feb. 17, 1776, he converted to Catholicism and adopted the name Karl from his godfather, Count Pálffy. Shortly thereafter he addressed an obsequious letter to the emperor, enumerating his services to the state, and requesting to be elevated to the nobility with the title of imperial counselor, the one sign of favor from which he had been excluded by his former religion. His request was granted by Joseph *II who remarked: "Since part of his family is already baptized and the rest will soon follow, I agree to the requested ennoblement." During the next three years his ten children were all baptized and received the title von Plankenstern; only LEONORE (1732–1813), his wife, remained true to her religion, unsuccessfully opposing the apostasy of her family. Karl Abraham, determined to become the equal of his fellow noblemen, was accepted into the ranks of the aristocracy and was invested with the estates he had acquired in Lower Austria.

Karl Abraham's daughters married into respected aristocratic families, as did his four sons. The latter did not possess their father's business acumen and the family fortunes gradually declined. All his grandsons entered the army or navy. His son RAYMUND (1752–1810) married Joanna Theresia von Picquigny (1749–1793), herself a daughter of a recently converted French army supplier. Raymund, a music lover, was Mozart's landlord, patron, and godfather to his eldest child. Other distinguished descendants were IGNAZ (1787–1841), who married into the Arnstein family and received Austria's highest military decoration in 1815; HEINRICH ADOLF (1813–60), who joined the Ottoman army and became a Muslim; GUSTAV (1813–1881), who attained the rank of field marshal-lieutenant; and KARL VON BEMBRUNN, who became an actor in 1810 after being captured by the French and forced to swear not to fight against them. He appeared on the stage under the pseudonym Carl Carl, much to the displeasure of his former comrades.

BIBLIOGRAPHY: B. Wachstein, *Archiv fuer juedische Familienforschung* 1 (1913); 2 (1914).

WEXLER, HARRY (1911–1962), U.S. meteorologist. Born in Fall River, Mass., Wexler entered the Federal Weather Bureau in 1934 and was appointed head of the research section of its scientific services in 1946. From 1955 until his death, he was research director of the Weather Bureau and was also chief scientist in the U.S. Antarctic Expedition during the Third International Geophysical Year, of which he was one of the main organizers. One of Wexler's important published contributions dealt with the high concentration of ozone in the Antarctic atmosphere. He advanced a theory which shed light on the mechanism of air circulation at the South Pole and stressed the importance of ozone as a trace element. He studied volcanic dust and its influence on the world's climate and climatic variations and on the expansion of storms in the upper atmosphere.

BIBLIOGRAPHY: *Modern Men of Science* (1966), 520–1; *Nature*, 196 (Oct. 27, 1962), 318–9.

[Dov Ashbel]

WEXLER, ROBERT D. (1951–), U.S. educator. Wexler was born in Los Angeles in 1951 and received his early Jewish education at Wilshire Boulevard Temple, a Reform congregation. He was introduced to traditional Judaism when he attended a local Orthodox summer camp, where he met his future wife, Hannah Goldhaar, and became profoundly influenced by her family, who were Holocaust survivors and deeply committed to Zionism.

While attending UCLA as an undergraduate, Wexler began taking classes at the Los Angeles branch of the Hebrew Union College (HUC), with the intention of becoming a Reform rabbi. But he was increasingly drawn to a more observant life style and a more traditional theology, and in 1969 he left HUC and enrolled part-time at the University of Judaism (UJ).

After receiving his B.A. in sociology in 1971, he enrolled full-time at the UJ's new pre-rabbinic program, and later spent three years in the rabbinical school of the Jewish Theological Seminary in New York, where he was ordained in 1977. In order to prepare himself for possible future immigration to Israel, Wexler spent those same three years in New York earning an M.B.A. degree from Baruch College of the City University of New York. Wexler also taught at JTS's Prozdor High School. Before returning to Los Angeles in 1978, he spent a year on the faculty of Princeton University in the Department of Near Eastern Languages.

At the invitation of then-president David Lieber, Wexler was invited to join the faculty of the University of Judaism in 1978. Wexler also enrolled in a doctoral program at UCLA, where he received both an M.A. and Ph.D. from the Department of Near Eastern Languages. At the University of Judaism, Wexler filled a variety of administrative positions before succeeding David Lieber as president in 1992.

Wexler became an adherent of the social philosophy of Mordecai Kaplan and the concept of Judaism as a civilization. Recognizing the growing trend away from denominationalism, Wexler quickly steered the UJ toward a nondenominational position within the Jewish mainstream.

During the first decade of his presidency, Wexler launched three major initiatives: the Ziegler School for Rabbinic Studies, the Center for Israel Studies, and the Ziering Institute. In 1995 he founded at the UJ the Ziegler School of Rabbinical Studies, which was the first American rabbinical school in the western United States.

The Center for Israel Studies was created in response to Wexler's growing conviction that American Jews needed to be educated more fully about the history, politics, and culture of the modern state of Israel. In 2001 the UJ inaugurated a lecture series at the Universal Amphitheater, which has been attended by over 5,000 people annually. Serving as moderator of the series, Wexler gained a reputation for his interviews with national political figures, such as former U.S. president Bill Clinton, former Israeli prime ministers Ehud Barak and Shimon Peres, and former U.S. secretaries of state, Henry Kissinger and Madeleine Albright.

In addition to his work at the University of Judaism, Wexler served in a variety of community leadership roles. He chaired the Los Angeles Federation's Commission on Israelis and the Committee on Jewish Education.

[Iris Waskow (2nd ed.)]

WEXLER, WILLIAM ABE (1913–2000), U.S. communal leader. Wexler, born in Toledo, Ohio, was an optometrist practicing in Savannah, Georgia, from 1938. He served a term as alderman in Savannah in 1946–47. He first took on a national leadership position as chairman of the United Jewish Appeal from 1951 to 1956 and led the Israel Bond drive from 1957 to 1963. Wexler was president of B'nai B'rith from 1965 until 1971. Under his aegis B'nai B'rith maintained an action policy that encouraged participation by young people through Hillel Foundations and the Young Adult groups, despite turbulence and disaffection among students; solidified the Jewish community's efforts to support Israel, through B'nai B'rith and through the Conference of Presidents of Major American Jewish Organizations, which Wexler chaired from 1968 to 1972; and aided in the campaign in support of Soviet Jewry. In 1971 he succeeded Nahum *Goldmann as president of the *World Conference of Jewish Organizations.

WEXNER, LESLIE H. (1937–), U.S. entrepreneur, civic leader, and philanthropist. Born in Dayton, Ohio, Wexner moved to Columbus, Ohio, when he was a teenager. After graduating from Ohio State University, he worked briefly in his father's clothing shop. In 1963 his own merchandising career began when he borrowed $5000 from an aunt and opened the first "The Limited" store in Columbus, Ohio. "The Limited" (now "Limited Brands") has grown to encompass thousands of stores throughout the United States, but Wexner's corporate headquarters and home remain in Columbus. In recent assessments by *Forbes* magazine, his wealth has been estimated at $2.6 billion.

The Wexner Foundation and the Wexner Heritage Foundation (now part of The Wexner Foundation) were established by Wexner in 1984. The Wexner Heritage program was designed to provide young American Jewish lay leaders with a two-year intensive Jewish learning program, thus deepening their understanding of Jewish history, values, and texts and enriching their leadership skills. By the end of 2005, approximately 1,500 North American Jewish leaders from 31 cities had participated in the program.

In 1988 The Wexner Foundation introduced a Fellowship Program for outstanding rabbinical students and graduate students in Jewish education and Jewish communal service programs. The same year the foundation established a grants program for academic institutions of all types to build and improve training programs for Jewish community professionals. Eventually, the Fellowship Program was expanded to include top candidates for academic Jewish studies and the cantorate. By the end of 2005, approximately 300 outstanding Jewish professional leaders from a wide array of religious affiliations and professional groupings had participated in the Wexner Graduate Fellowship Program.

Additionally, in 1988, the Wexner Israel Fellowship Program was created. Annually, up to 10 outstanding mid-career Israeli public officials are selected to study for a master's degree in the mid-career program of Harvard's Kennedy School of Government. The goal of the fellowship is to provide Israel's next generation of public leaders with advanced leadership and public management training. As of the end of 2005, 163 Israeli public officials had participated in the Israel Fellowship, including leaders who had gone on to become director generals of government ministries, generals and commanders in the Israeli military, and top advisors to prime ministers.

The Wexner Foundation appeared early on the scene of Jewish private philanthropy and in many ways pioneered a new field that has grown to include dozens of private foundations that devote themselves on a national and international scale to the needs of the Jewish people. The Wexner Foundation has never wavered from its focus upon Jewish leadership, and its professionalism, standards of program excellence, and strong relationships with Jewish communities and organizations have created a model of practice for Jewish private philanthropy that has passed the test of time.

Wexner's leadership among major Jewish philanthropists was evidenced by his role in helping to convene and ultimately lead a group of some two dozen philanthropic peers in an effort that was known technically as the "Study Group" but more widely as the "Mega Group." This group of elite Jewish philanthropists was formed in 1991 and developed as an effort to conduct a high-minded philanthropic discussion about the pressing issues of the Jewish people. The group motivated a number of individual and collaborative philanthropic initiatives that, arguably, would not have otherwise occurred, including the Partnership for Excellence in Jewish Education, Birthright Israel, the upgrading of national Hillel, and more. Wexner co-chaired the group with Charles Bronfman during the final years of its existence. While the group no longer exists in its original form, successor groups have surfaced and many of the original members continue to work closely with each other as a result of the associations they developed within the Study Group.

Leslie Wexner's wife, Abigail Wexner, an accomplished attorney, has emerged as a major civic and philanthropic leader in her own right, and has also worked closely with The Wexner Foundation in shaping its programs and future. Mrs. Wexner has served as Chair of The Columbus Foundation and as Chairman of the Board of Children's Hospital, Columbus. She is nationally recognized as a leader who has spearheaded cutting edge programs and services addressing domestic violence in central Ohio and beyond.

Leslie Wexner's philanthropy revolves around a belief in the centrality of leadership and its potential to shape the future. This passion for developing leaders is at the heart of the programs of the Foundation, but extends far beyond them as well.

In business, his storied rise as the son of working class immigrants who became the innovator of specialty retailing in America is near legendary. Wexner began his company in 1963 with one store in Columbus, Ohio. "The Limited" had sales of $473 on the first day of business and first year sales of $160,000. Today, as Chairman, President and CEO of Limited Brands, he leads a company that operates more than 3700 stores, including Victoria's Secret, Express, The Limited, Henri Bendel, Bath and Body Works, and The White Barn Candle Company. Sales for Limited Brands exceeded $9.4 billion in 2004.

In civic life, Wexner's leadership was the force behind the development of the Wexner Center for the Arts at Ohio State University, behind the creation of the Wexner Institute for Pediatric Research at Children's Hospital, and that elevated Columbus' United Way to successes never before imagined. By example, he has sought to "give back" to the community in many ways. He is also a founding member of the Ohio State University Foundation, Chairman of the Columbus Partnership, and Chairman Emeritus of the Ohio State University Board of Trustees.

Wexner serves as Visiting Instructor of Leadership at Harvard University's Kennedy School of Government, where he also sits as a member of the Visiting Committee. His annual lectures on leadership at Harvard are attended by a wide cross-section of students, faculty, and community leaders. The Wexners also spearheaded the development of the Center for Public Leadership at the Kennedy School. Directed by David Gergen, the Center has already become one of North America's most prestigious academic initiatives for the study, teaching, and development of public leadership.

In Jewish life, his leadership activities have been widely acknowledged, including honorary degrees from Yeshiva University, Hebrew Union College, the Jewish Theological Seminary of America, and Brandeis University. In Central Ohio, Wexner's leadership of the Columbus Jewish Federation and his role in developing Wexner Heritage Village (a campus of services and residences for the elderly), the Wexner Jewish Student Center at Ohio State University, and other model programs underscore a personal philosophy that integrity in philanthropy must begin at home, in one's own community, and expand outward from that basis.

In the final analysis, Wexner's impact upon the Jewish people will be his investment in Jewish leaders – in Israel and in North America. Wexner's leadership programs take seriously the responsibility and capacity of leaders to shape a new future for the Jewish people. His programs are pluralistic and embrace the wide sweep of diversity within Jewish life, while building community and commonality from that diversity. Many imagine that there will be Wexner Israel Fellows who will become prime ministers of the State of Israel, Wexner Graduate Fellows who transform Jewish professional leadership into a new force for change in the coming century, and Wexner Heritage alumni who will rethink and rebuild their Jewish communities into more relevant, responsive and dynamic organizational forms. Meanwhile, Wexner and his wife continue to exercise their own leadership, in business, politics, and civic and Jewish life – forever learning and teaching the meaning and promise of mobilizing others around the enduring values and challenges of human life.

[Larry Moses (2nd ed.)]

WEYL, MEIR BEN SIMḤAH (1744–1826), German rabbi. Weyl was born in *Lissa and studied under Ẓevi Hirsch of Janow. He arrived in Berlin in 1783 and was soon elected head of the *bet midrash* and *dayyan*. After Hirschel Levin's death (1800) the reform-minded community leaders delayed his appointment as rabbi until 1809, when they reluctantly made him *Vize-Ober-Landrabbiner*. His patriotic sermons of 1809–13 won him renown. One such sermon of 1813 was republished after World War I as proof of Jewish patriotism. Weyl battled against the Berlin *Haskalah movement and its chief representative, David *Friedlaender. An acknowledged talmudic authority as well as a vehement opponent of Reform, in 1818 the Orthodox elements in the community of Copenhagen appealed to him in their conflict with a Reform group. He sharply attacked the use of German in prayer, and largely through his efforts a royal order was issued dated Dec. 23, 1823, that Jews were to pray only according to their previous custom. When in 1824 the elders of the Berlin community contemplated establishing a teachers seminary and invited L. *Zunz and L. *Bendavid to plan the syllabus, Weyl retaliated by appealing directly to Altenstein, the minister of religion, with his own plan, which was approved. For lack of community support, however, the plan for a seminary was soon dropped. Weyl held halakhic discussions with Akiva *Eger of Posen and Solomon Zalman *Posner of Warsaw.

BIBLIOGRAPHY: MGWJ, 28 (1879), 568–70; M. Stern, *Aus der Zeit der deutschen Befreiungskriege*, 1 (1918); idem, in: *Jeschurun*, 13 (1926), 187–95, 290–308; G, Weil, in; MGWJ, 76 (1932), 385–9; idem, in; JJS, 8 (1957), 91–101; H. Fischer, *Judentum, Staat und Heer in Preussen* (1968), 107–9.

WHEAT, grain belonging to the genus *Triticum*, of which many species exist. Several species of *Triticum* are grown in Israel, some called *ḥittah* (pl. *ḥittim*) and others *kussemet, kusmin*, and *shippon* (for this identification see *Five Species).

(1) *Ḥittah* is the name applied to two species grown in Israel: hard wheat – *Triticum durum*, and bread wheat – *Triticum vulgare* (*aestivum*). The former is called "dark" and the latter "white" in the Mishnah (BB 5:6). The name *ḥittah*, with slight variations, is common to all the Semitic languages, mostly in the form of *ḥintah*, connected with the verb *ḥanot* ("to project"), because the grains project from the pales of the ear of the wheat when it ripens. In rabbinic literature these are termed *levush* ("garment"). When threshed, these *levushim* disintegrate and the grain emerges. Hence the saying: "In the time to come [at the resurrection] the righteous will rise [dressed] in their own clothes. This can be deduced a fortiori from a grain of wheat. If a grain of wheat that is buried naked sprouts up with many garments …" (Ket. 111b). *Ḥittah* is the most valuable of the five species of cereal. According to one *aggadah*, "the tree of knowledge was *ḥittah*" (Sanh. 70b). It is mentioned first among the seven species with which Israel is blessed (Deut. 8:8). It requires good and well-tilled land, and an abundance of *ḥittim* symbolizes well-being and peace (Ps. 81:17).

Wheat, like *barley, is sown at the beginning of the winter, but it develops more slowly (Ex. 9:31–32) and ripens about two months after barley, from which the *Omer* is brought on Passover. Seven weeks later "the firstfruits of the *ḥittim* harvest" are offered (Ex. 34:22). Ezekiel (27:17) mentions "*ḥittim* of Minnith" which "Judah and Israel" peddled, the reference being to the locality of Minnith in the land of Ammon (Judg. 11:33). Similarly, Arbelite and Midian *ḥittim* are mentioned as excellent varieties (TJ, Sot. 9:13, 24b; Shab. 9:6, 12b). The *aggadah* refers to 500 confections made from *ḥittim* (Lam. R. 3:17 no. 6). The choicest *ḥittim*, used in meal-offerings, came from Michmas and Zoniḥah (Men. 8:1). Wheat was dearer than barley, and according to Josephus (Wars 5:427), it was the food of the rich. During the time of the Mishnah and Talmud, however, when the agricultural situation in Israel improved, wheat became the common food of all. "One who grows wheat is sure of his bread, but one who buys wheat in the market, his future is doubtful" (Men. 103b).

(2) *Kussemet* or *kusmin* has been identified with emmer wheat – *Triticum dicoccum*, a plant which has grown in Israel from earliest times. Remnants have been found in excavations in Israel and in Egyptian tombs. A similar species, *Triticum dioccoides*, grows wild in Israel and apparently is the species from which emmer wheat originated. The discovery of this species by Aaron *Aaronsohn in Rosh Pinah in 1906 caused a sensation in the botanical world. He maintained that it was the "mother" of all species of wheat, an opinion still upheld by some botanists. The general opinion, however, is that it is the "mother" of emmer wheat only. Like the *ḥittah*, the *kussemet* was not smitten by the hail in Egypt because it ripens late and its growth is slow (Ex. 9:32). Isaiah (28:25) enumerates it among the crops sown by the farmer, and it was also included in the mixed bread that Ezekiel ate for 390 days (Ezek. 4:9). In rabbinical literature it is always included among the five species of corn. In taste it is very like *ḥittah* (Ḥal. 4:2; Pes. 35a), but its nutritional value in relation to bulk is less because of the chaff that sticks to the grains (BM 40a). To remove these husks the wheat was moistened and trodden by cattle so as to release the grain (BM 89b and Rashi). In Aramaic *kussemet* is called *gulba* (Men. 70a), a word meaning "cut" or "shorn," a similar connotation to *kussemet*, which comes from *kasam* meaning "clipper of hairs" (cf. Ezek. 44:20). The name derives from the short hairs of the ears which look as though they have been cut. Another species of wheat, spelt wheat or *Triticum spelta*, identified by some commentators with *kussemet*, has similar characteristics, but no remnants of spelt from the biblical period have been found in the region. It seems that it is the *shippon* of rabbinical literature.

(3) *Shippon* is also enumerated among the five species of corn. For the law of *mixing of species it is regarded as belonging to the same species as *kussemet* (*kusmin*; Kil. 1:1), but in taste it is associated with barley (Pes. 35a). These indications are compatible with spelt, which resembles emmer wheat but has a barley flavor. Apparently its growth was not very widespread (at the present day also, its growth is very limited), and it is mentioned only a few times in rabbinical literature. This identification is mentioned by the *Arukh* (s.v. *dashr*). Now, however, it is usual, following Rashi, to identify *shippon* with rye – *Secale cereale*. This identification cannot be accepted, as this plant is not suited to the conditions of Ereẓ Israel and was not grown there. It is also erroneous, as is usually done, to apply the name *kussemet* to buckwheat – *Fagopyrum esculeutum* – since it was never grown in Israel and does not fit any of the descriptions of *kussemet*.

BIBLIOGRAPHY: Loew, Flora, 1 (1926), 767–801; J. Feliks, *Olam ha-Ẓome'aḥ ha-Mikra'i* (1968²), 142–51; idem, *Kilei Zera'im ve-Harkavah* (1967), 27–32. **ADD. BIBLIOGRAPHY:** Feliks, Ha-Ẓome'aḥ, 60, 83, 161.

[Jehuda Feliks]

WHITE, HARRY D. (1892–1948), U.S. economist. Born in Boston, Mass., White spent his early years in his father's hardware business, and for several years taught on Sunday mornings at the Home for Jewish Children in Dorchester. After serving overseas during World War I, White became head of Corner House, a settlement house in New York City, and worked as director of a summer camp for boys. While studying for his doctorate at Harvard, he was an instructor in economics; from 1932 to 1934 he taught at Lawrence College in Wisconsin.

White moved to Washington in 1934 to serve as a financial expert at the U.S. Treasury. He became the chief economic analyst for the U.S. Tariff Commission, but soon returned to the Treasury Department to serve as the principal economic analyst in the division of research and statistics, and in 1936 as assistant director of research. In 1938 White was made director of monetary research. His monetary proposals were accepted as the basis for the Bretton Woods Conference, attended by representatives of 44 nations. The "White Plan," which was accepted over the "Keynes Plan," called for the establishment of international trade based on the gold monetary unit. White became assistant secretary of the Treasury in charge of monetary research and foreign funds control in 1945 and the following year was made U.S. executive director of the International Monetary Fund. While in the Treasury Department, he managed the currency stabilization fund, represented the Treasury at committee meetings of the Economic Defense Board, and was a trustee of the Export-Import Bank. He is considered the author of the "Morgenthau Plan" for dealing with postwar Germany, and of other postwar economic plans. White was accused of giving information to a wartime Soviet spy ring and of pushing certain employees toward positions in government in which they would have access to information. He endured a congressional investigation while suffering from heart trouble, which was greatly aggravated by the strain of the sessions, and he died before the investigations had been concluded. White wrote *The French International Accounts: 1880–1913* (1933) and he updated F.W. Taussig's *Some Aspects of the Tariff Question* (1934³).

BIBLIOGRAPHY: N.I. White, *Harry Dexter White; Loyal American* (1956); *New York Times* (Aug. 18, 1948).

WHITE, MORTON GABRIEL (1917–), U.S. philosopher. Born in New York, White received his Ph.D. from Columbia University in 1942. He taught physics at City College, Columbia, and at the University of Pennsylvania. In 1948 he joined the staff at Harvard as professor of philosophy, where he taught until 1970. From 1954 to 1957 he served as chairman of the philosophy department. From 1970 to 1987 he was a professor at Princeton's Institute for Advanced Study. After retiring from teaching, he was named philosophy and intellectual history professor emeritus at the institute's School of Historical Studies.

White's main philosophical contributions are in the areas of epistemology and social and political philosophy. Such works as *The Origin of Dewey's Instrumentalism* (1943) and *Social Thought in America* (1949) reveal the influence of American pragmatism in his thought. White also wrote on the paradox of analysis, a dilemma which holds that all analysis is either trivial or false, and on the analytic-synthetic distinction. In his paper "The Analytic and the Synthetic: An Untenable Dualism" in *John Dewey: Philosopher of Science and Freedom* (ed. by S. Hook, 1950), White contends that the distinction is one of degree and not one of kind, as traditional philosophers maintain.

Among his other important publications are *Toward Reunion in Philosophy* (1956); *Religion, Politics and the Higher Learning* (1959); *The Intellectual vs. the City* (with L. White, 1962); *Foundations of Historical Knowledge* (1965); *Science and Sentiment in America* (1972); *The Question of Free Will* (1993); his autobiography, *A Philosopher's Story* (1999); *A Philosophy of Culture* (2002); and *From a Philosophical Point of View* (2004).

[Arthur Stroll / Ruth Beloff (2nd ed.)]

WHITE, ROBERT MAYER (1923–), U.S. meteorologist. Born in Boston, Mass., White received a B.A. degree in geology from Harvard University and M.S. and Sc.D. degrees (1950) in meteorology from the Massachusetts Institute of Technology. White was president of the National Academy of Engineering from 1983 to 1995. Prior to that, he was president of the University Corporation for Atmospheric Research (UCAR). He served in scientific leadership positions under five U.S. presidents. He was appointed chief of the U.S. Weather Bureau and the first administrator of the National Oceanic and Atmospheric Administration. His years of government service include positions as U.S. Commissioner to the International Whaling Commission and U.S. Permanent Representative to the World Meteorological Organization. He is credited with bringing about a revolution in the U.S. weather warning system with satellite and computer technology. Before joining the government, he founded one of the first corporations devoted to environmental science and services.

White was the Karl T. Compton Lecturer at the Massachusetts Institute of Technology in 1995–96. He was a senior fellow at UCAR and the H. John Heinz III Center for Science, Economics, and the Environment. His many awards include the Rockefeller Public Service Award for the Protection of Natural Resources and the International Meteorological Organization Prize.

[Bracha Rager (2nd ed.)]

WHITE, THEODORE H. (**"Teddy"**; 1915–1986), U.S. journalist and author. White was born in Boston, Massachusetts. He studied at Harvard University, graduating in 1938. His grandfather was a rabbi from Pinsk who spent his last days in pious devotion at the Western Wall in Jerusalem. In his autobiography *In Search of History* (1978), White refers to his Jewish and Hebrew education. "What I learned, then, from age 10 to age 14, when I went on to evening courses at the Hebrew College of Boston was the Bible …." "We learned it, absorbed it, thought in it, until the ancient Hebrew became a working rhythm in the mind, until it became a second language. Memory was the foundation of learning at the Hebrew school, and the memory cut grooves on young minds that even decades cannot erase. Even now, when a biblical phrase runs through my mind, I am trapped and annoyed unless I convert it into Hebrew – whereupon the memory retrieves it from Boston, Mass., where little Jewish-American boys were forced to learn of nomads and peasants of three thousand years ago, forced to learn of spotted lambs, of the searing summer and of the saving rains (Yoreh and Malkosh)." In later years, he used to make his own Haggadah for Passover written on special cards and assigning the parts to his children. In his youth, Teddy White helped to organize the student Zionist activists on the New England campuses in the Avukah (Torch) Society. He helped organize a boycott of German goods in Boston. White was "lured" however to other interests which he defined as Harvard and history. A year after graduating from Harvard, Teddy White was *Time* magazine's war correspondent in China and, by 1945, at the age of 30, he was Time Bureau Chief. His first book (with Annalee Jacoby) was *Thunder Out of China* (1946). Between 1948 and 1953, White was in Europe and wrote *Fire in the Ashes* (1953). Returning to the U.S., White became a national political correspondent for *The Reporter* magazine, then for *Colliers*, and then for *Life*. He also published two novels (*The Mountain Road* [1958] on the evacuation of Chinese and American armed forces and *The View from the Fortieth Floor* [1960] on his 1950s stint at *Collier's* magazine) and one play and wrote several television documentaries.

White achieved his greatest acclaim as the author of a series of books called *The Making of the President* for 1960, 1964, 1968, and 1972 elections, for which he won the Pulitzer prize, and a wrap-up volume called *America in Search of Itself*, published in 1982. He had planned a 1976 "Making of the President" book, but the Watergate scandal led him to write *Breach of Faith* instead.

[Shimshon Arad (2nd ed.)]

WHITE PAPERS, British government statements of policy presented to parliament; they played an important part in the history of Mandatory Palestine. Six such documents were issued between the years 1922 and 1939:

(1) Statement of Policy June 1922 (Churchill White Paper);

(2) Statement of Policy October 1930 (Passfield White Paper);

(3) Statement of Policy July 1937 (on the Peel Commission's report);

(4) Statement of Policy December 1937 (appointment of the Woodhead Commission);

(5) Statement of Policy November 1938 (on the Woodhead Commission's report);

(6) Statement of Policy May 1939 (MacDonald White Paper).

The Churchill White Paper (1922)

This document, for which Winston *Churchill was responsible as colonial secretary, contained the first important official statement of British government policy after the *Balfour Declaration. While reaffirming the declaration, it stated that there was no question of Palestine becoming "as Jewish as England is English" and that the Arabs need have no fear of "the disappearance or the subordination of the Arabic population, language or culture in Palestine." The Balfour Declaration, the statement continued, did not "contemplate that Palestine as a whole should be converted into a Jewish National Home, but that such a Home should be founded in Palestine." The development of the Jewish National Home meant "not the imposition of a Jewish nationality upon the inhabitants of Palestine as a whole, but the further development of the existing Jewish community [which, in another passage, was said to have "national" characteristics] with the assistance of Jews in other parts of the world, in order that it may become a center in which the Jewish people as a whole may take, on grounds of religion and race, an interest and a pride." To enable this community to develop, however, "it is essential that it should know that it is in Palestine as of right and not on sufferance," the statement declared. That was why international guarantees were necessary.

The statement went on to say that Jewish immigration must continue, but must not exceed "whatever may be the economic capacity of the country at the time to absorb new arrivals"; that the government intended "to foster the establishment of a full measure of self-government"; and that, as the next step, it proposed to set up a Legislative Council consisting of 12 elected and ten appointed members, headed by the high commissioner. The Zionist Executive reluctantly accepted the policy set out in the statement, while the Palestinian Arabs did not.

The Passfield White Paper

This was issued by the colonial secretary, Lord Passfield (Sidney Webb), in the wake of the riots of 1929. The causes of the riots and the situation in Palestine had been investigated by the Shaw Commission (see *Palestine, Inquiry Commissions), and an inquiry into land settlement, immigration, and development had been carried out by Sir John Hope Simpson, who was pessimistic as to the possibilities of further Jewish immigration and settlement without displacing Arabs (see Palestine, Inquiry Commissions). A central theme in the White Paper, which was issued simultaneously with the Hope Simpson report, was the argument that under the terms of the *Mandate and the Balfour Declaration, "A double undertaking is involved, to the Jewish people on the one hand and to the non-Jewish population on the other." It rejected the view that the passages regarding the Jewish National Home were the principal feature of the Mandate.

The statement dealt with practical policy under the heads: security, constitutional development, and economic and social development. It declared that the government "will not be moved from their duty by pressure or threats" and that "any incitements to disorder or disaffection, in whatever quarter they originate, will be severely punished." It proposed the establishment of a Legislative Council, with a composition similar to that proposed in the Churchill White Paper. If any section of the population failed to cooperate, steps would be taken to ensure the appointment of the requisite number of unofficial members. In any case, the statement continued, the high commissioner would continue to have the necessary power to enable the Mandatory to carry out its obligations.

The White Paper accepted Hope Simpson's conclusion that "for the present and with the present methods of Arab cultivation there remains no margin of land available for agricultural settlement by new immigrants," with the exception of reserves held by Jewish agencies. It severely criticized the principle of Jewish labor, which, it implied, was detrimental to the Arab population, and "difficult to reconcile" with Zionist declarations of a desire to live in friendship with the Arab people. Transfers of land would be permitted only insofar as they did not interfere with the land development plans of the Palestine Administration. In determining the "economic capacity" of the country to absorb new immigrants, not only Jewish but Arab unemployment must be taken into account, and Jewish immigration would be suspended if it was held to prevent Arabs from obtaining employment.

The White Paper was severely criticized by some British statesmen as a departure from the obligations of the Mandate. *Weizmann resigned from the presidency of the Jewish Agency in protest, declaring that the White Paper went far toward "denying the rights and sterilizing the hopes of the Jewish people in regard to the National Home" and aimed at "crystallizing the development of the Jewish National Home in its present stage." A special British cabinet committee entered into negotiations with representatives of the Jewish Agency, which resulted in a letter from Prime Minister Ramsay MacDonald to Weizmann on Feb. 13, 1931, which was to be communicated as an official document to the League of Nations and embodied in a dispatch as an instrument to the high commissioner. Ostensibly, the letter was no more than an interpretation of the Passfield White Paper, but in reality it canceled much of its anti-Zionist implications. It reemphasized "that the undertaking of the Mandate is an undertaking to the Jewish people and not only to the Jewish population of Palestine" and reaffirmed the preamble of the Mandate, which includes the Balfour Declaration and the historical connection of the Jewish people with Palestine. The letter also stressed the positive obligations of the Mandate, such as facilitating Jewish immigration and encouraging settlement by Jews on the land.

The White Paper of July 1937

This was a statement of British government policy issued together with the report of the Royal Commission on Palestine (the Peel Commission). It stated that the British government accepted the commission's partition plan in principle and would take the necessary steps to put it into effect. Until the establishment of Jewish and Arab states, the government would not surrender its responsibilities for peace, order, and good government throughout Palestine. In the interim period, two steps would be taken: "to prohibit any land transactions which might prejudice such a scheme" and to limit immigration between August 1937 and March 1938 to 8,000.

The White Paper of December 1937

This consisted of a dispatch from W. Ormsby-Gore, the colonial secretary, to A.G. Wauchope, the high commissioner for Palestine, announcing the appointment of the Woodhead Commission to consider the details and practical possibilities of a partition scheme. If the government regarded the new partition scheme as "equitable and practicable," it would refer it to the League of Nations. After that body's approval "a further period would be required for the establishment of new systems of government," possibly including a system of cantonization or separate Mandates for the new Arab and Jewish areas.

The White Paper of November 1938

After the publication of the Woodhead Commission's findings, which, in effect, canceled out the recommendations of the Peel Commission, the British government came to the conclusion that the political, administrative, and financial difficulties involved in the "proposal to create Arab and Jewish independent states inside Palestine are so great that this solution of the problem is impracticable." Instead, the government would "make a determined effort" to promote "an understanding between the Arabs and the Jews." With this end in view the government would convene a conference (see *Saint James' Conference) with representatives of the Palestinian Arabs and of neighboring states … and of the Jewish Agency to confer about "future policy, including the question of immigration into Palestine." If no agreement was reached "within a reasonable period of time" the British government would take its own decision.

The Malcolm MacDonald White Paper (May 1939)

The failure of the St. James' Conference led to the publication of the White Paper of May 1939. Since the Royal Commission's partition proposal had "been found to be impracticable," the British government had devised "an alternate policy." In order to remove any doubts, the statement continued, "His Majesty's Government now declares unequivocally that it is not part of their policy that Palestine should become a Jewish State." Moreover, they would indeed regard it as "contrary to their obligations to the Arabs under the Mandate ..." The government was charged with the development of self-governing institutions and regarded it as "contrary to the spirit of the Mandate" to keep the Palestinian population for ever under a Mandatory regime. It announced that "The objective of His Majesty's Government is the establishment within ten years of an independent Palestine State" in which the essential interests of both Arabs and Jews should be safeguarded. There would be a transitional period during which the "people of Palestine will be given an increasing part in the government of the country." Both sections would have an opportunity to participate, but "the process will be carried on whether or not they both avail themselves of it." In the first stage, steps would be taken to place Palestinians – Arabs and Jews in proportion to their respective populations – in charge of government departments.

IMMIGRATION. The government decided to curtail Jewish immigration. The principle of economic absorptive capacity, established in the White Paper of 1922 was to be replaced by a new, political, principle. The British government claimed it could not find in the Mandate any support for the view that immigration must be allowed to "continue indefinitely," or that economic absorptive capacity must be the only consideration. Although Jewish immigration had been absorbed economically, the Arabs' fear of indefinite Jewish immigration had also to be taken into account in deciding immigration policy. To expand the Jewish National Home indefinitely, the government believed, would mean "rule by force," and it had therefore decided "to permit further expansion of the Jewish National Home by immigration only if the Arabs are prepared to acquiesce in it." During the next five years Jewish immigration would be limited to 75,000, bringing the Jewish population up to approximately one-third of the total population of Palestine. After the end of the five-year period no further Jewish immigration would be permitted "unless the Arabs of Palestine are prepared to acquiesce in it," and the government "will not be under any obligation to facilitate the further development of the Jewish National Home by immigration regardless of the wishes of the Arab population."

LAND TRANSFER. In certain areas, the statement declared, there was no room for further transfers of Arab land, and in other areas transfers must be restricted. The high commissioner would, therefore, be given general powers to prohibit and regulate transfers of land, and on Feb. 28, 1940, the high commissioner promulgated the Land Transfer Regulations, in fact dividing the country into three zones: Zone A, including the hill country and certain other areas – 64% of Palestine – in which the transfer of land to anyone other than a Palestinian Arab was prohibited, save in exceptional circumstances; Zone B, including the Jezreel Valley, eastern Galilee, most of the Coastal Plain (except for the Tel Aviv district), and the Negev – 31% of the area – in which transfers were permitted only in specified circumstances; and Zone C – 5% of the country's area – which would remain a "free zone."

The White Paper was regarded by the Zionist movement and many outside it as a final betrayal of Britain's obligations to the Jewish people under the Balfour Declaration and the Mandate. The announcement of this policy at the outset of the Jewish mass flight from Europe became the starting point for the active struggle of the *yishuv* against the Mandatory regime in Palestine.

BIBLIOGRAPHY: H.N. Howard, *The King-Crane Commission* (1963); Great Britain, Colonial Office, *Palestine Disturbances in May 1921 Report* (Cmd. 1540, 1921); idem, *Palestine Disturbances of 1929 Report* (Cmd. 3530, 1930); idem, *Palestine Royal Commission Report* (Cmd. 5479, 1937); idem, *Palestine Partition Commission Report* (Cmd. 5854, 1938); idem, *Statement on British Policy in Palestine* (Cmd. 1700, 1922) – The Churchill White Paper; *ibid.* (Cmd. 3692, 1930) – The Passfield White Paper; *ibid.* (Cmd. 5513, 1937) – On the Peel Commission Report; *Dispatch to the High Commissioner of Palestine* (Cmd. 5634, 1937) – Appointment of Woodhead Commission; idem, *British Statement of Policy* (Cmd. 5893, 1938); *ibid.* (Cmd. 6019, 1939) – MacDonald White Paper; *Anglo-American Commission of Inquiry ... Report* (1946); *Proposals for the Future of Palestine* (Cmd. 7044, 1947); United Nations Special Committee on Palestine Report (1947).

[Daniel Efron]

WICKED PRIEST (Heb. כֹּהֵן הָרֶשַׁע, *Kohen ha-Resha*), character mentioned in the *Dead Sea Scrolls as the inveterate enemy of the *Teacher of Righteousness. He was a man of whom better things were once expected: "He was called by the name of truth when first he arose, but when he ruled in Israel his heart was exalted and he forsook God, and dealt treacherously with the ordinances for the sake of wealth. He looted and amassed the wealth of the men of [v]iolence who rebelled against God; and he took the wealth of nations, adding to himself iniquity and guilt, and acted in ab[om]inable ways with every defiling impurity" (1QpHab. 8:8–13). He is described as "the priest who rebelled [and transgressed] the ordinances of [God]" (1QpHab. 8:16ff.), "the priest whose shame was mightier than his glory, for he did not circumcise the foreskin of his heart but walked in the ways of drunkenness to quench his thirst" (1QpHab. 11:12ff.). He "wrought abominable works and defiled the sanctuary of God" and in the cities of Judah he "plundered the wealth of the poor" (1QpHab. 12:8–10).

He is chiefly reprobated for his attack on the Teacher of Righteousness: he laid hands on him in an attempt to kill him. But God, according to the commentary (from Cave 4) on Psalm 37, delivered the Teacher from him and reserved a fearful judgment for the Wicked Priest, "delivering him into the hands of the violent of the gentiles to execute[vengeance]on him" (on Ps. 37:32ff.). There was one special occasion when he manifested his enmity toward the Teacher: that was when he "pursued after the Teacher of Righteousness to swallow him up in his hot fury, even to his place of exile, and on the occasion of the sacred season of rest, the Day of Atonement, he appeared among them to swallow them up and make them stumble on the fast-day, their sabbath of rest" (1QpHab. 11:4–8). This suggests that the Teacher and his company observed a different *calendar from the Wicked Priest, so that what was the Day of Atonement for the former was a secular day for the latter.

But condign judgment awaited the Wicked Priest. "Because of the [evil] done to the Teacher of Righteousness and the men of his council, God gave him into the h[ands of]his[en]emies, to afflict him with a stroke, to make him waste away in bitterness of soul, because he acted wickedly toward His elect" (1QpHab. 9:9–12). Because of his rebellion against the ordinances of God, "they smote him with the judgments of wickedness, and wrought horrors of sore diseases on him and deeds of vengeance on his body of flesh" (1QpHab. 8:17–9:2). Because of his shameful drunkenness, "the cup of[Go]d's fury will overwhelm him, to add to his[shame and]ignominy" (1QpHab. 11:15ff.). Because of his plundering "the poor" (by whom perhaps the members of the Qumran community are specially intended), "God will condemn him to destruction even as he plotted to destroy the poor" (1QpHab. 12:5ff.).

Since the Qumran community apparently maintained the exclusive right of the house of Zadok to the high priesthood, a high priest of any other line would be to them a wicked (i.e., illegitimate) priest *ex hypothesi*. But the references quoted above point to one Wicked Priest par excellence. Many suggestions about his identity have been made, ranging in date from the apostate Menelaus, appointed by Antiochus IV in 171 B.C.E. (so H.H. Rowley) to Eleazar b. Ananias, captain of the Temple at the outbreak of the war against Rome in the autumn of 66 C.E. (so C. Roth, G.R. Driver). He has even been identified with Paul of Tarsus (so J.L. Teicher). But the majority verdict favors one of the Hasmonean priest-rulers, though there is no unanimity as to which of them should be preferred. The principal choices are Jonathan (so G. Vermes, J.T. Milik, E.F. Sutcliffe); Simeon (so F.M. Cross); Alexander Yannai (J.M. Allegro, W.H. Brownlee, J. van der Ploeg) and Hyrcanus II (A. Dupont-Sommer). In some cases these identifications (e.g., those with Menelaus and Eleazar) are closely tied in with identifications of the Teacher of Righteousness, and since the description of the Wicked Priest is generally applicable to so many figures known to the history of the period, only an agreed conclusion (which is not yet in sight) on the time when the teacher arose and his community was organized will carry with it a definitive solution to the problem of identifying the Wicked Priest.

BIBLIOGRAPHY: H.H. Rowley, *Zadokite Fragments and the Dead Sea Scrolls* (1952), 67ff., passim; J.M. Allegro, *Dead Sea Scrolls* (1956), 95ff.; J.T. Milik, *Ten Years of Discovery in the Wilderness of Judaea* (1959), 65ff., 84ff.; E.F. Sutcliffe, *Monks of Qumran* (1960), 42ff.; F.M. Cross, *Ancient Library of Qumran* (1958), 107ff.; A. Dupont-Sommer, *Essene Writings from Qumran* (1961), 351ff.; C. Roth, *Historical Background of the Dead Sea Scrolls* (1958), 10ff., passim; G.R. Driver, *Judaean Scrolls* (1965), 267ff.

[Frederick Fyvie Bruce]

WIDAL, FERNAND (1862–1929), French physician, born in Algeria, where his father served as an army doctor. He studied medicine in Paris and worked there. In 1894 he was appointed associate professor, in 1911 full professor, and in 1912 he was elected member of the Academy of Sciences. He instituted a vaccination against typhoid fever in 1888. The innovation was adopted universally and it was used by all the armies that participated in World War I. In 1896 he discovered a method for the serological diagnosis of typhoid fever, which was named after him and became the prototype for the serodiagnosis of other communicable diseases. He also developed methods for diagnosing different diseases by determining the types of cells in inflammatory exudates, thus establishing the basis of cytodiagnosis. His most important contribution to pathological physiology was his recognition of the significance of chloride (in table salt) in causing edema, and he instituted a low-salt diet in cases of fluid retention in the body, which is used nowadays universally. In his research on kidney diseases, he worked on the significance of renal failure, which manifested itself in the defective ability of the body to excrete blood nitrogen. He described the various forms of jaundice, especially those caused by hemolysis, and demonstrated the fragility of red blood cells in cases of familial jaundice. He also did research work on anaphylaxis, streptococcal infections, cardiovascular diseases, and the nervous system.

BIBLIOGRAPHY: S.R. Kagan, *Jewish Medicine* (1962), 250–1; Achard, in: *Progrès médical*, 44 (1929).

[Joshua O. Leibowitz]

°**WIDMANSTETTER, JOHANN ALBRECHT** (**Widmanstadius**, or **Lucrecius**; 1506–1557), Austrian statesman, humanist, and Orientalist. An outstanding Catholic scholar, Widmanstetter became chancellor of Lower Austria and rector of the University of Vienna. He traveled widely, learning Arabic in Spain and Hebrew among Spanish Jewish exiles in Naples. He was also able to conduct a correspondence in Hebrew and his bookplate was phrased in Latin, Hebrew, and Syriac. Widmanstetter's teachers included Johann Reuchlin, David b. Joseph ibn Yaḥya, Baruch of Benevento, and Benjamin d'Arignano. In 1529, he met the Christian Hebraist Egidio (Aegidius) da *Viterbo in Venice, and three years later attended lectures on the Kabbalah held at the Naples home of Judah Abrabanel's brother Samuel. Widmanstetter collaborated with Guillaume *Postel in the publication of the first edition of the Syriac New Testament (Vienna, 1555) and attributed errors in the Koran to the influence of the Kabbalah. He collected many rare Hebrew and Oriental manuscripts and printed works (some obtained from Elijah Levita), which were later bequeathed to the Munich Royal Library.

BIBLIOGRAPHY: J. Perles, *Beitraege zur Geschichte der hebraeischen und aramaeischen Studien* (1884), 184f.; M. Mueller, *Johann Albrecht von Widmanstetter* (1907); U. Cassuto, *Gli ebrei a Firenze nell' età del Rinascimento* (1918, s.v.; H. Striedl, in: *Franz Babinger Studies* (1952); F. Secret, *Les kabbalistes chrétiens de la Renaissance* (1964), 121–3; Baron, Social², 13 (1969), 180, 397, 405.

[Godfrey Edmond Silverman]

WIDOW (Heb. אַלְמָנָה, *almanah*; pl. אַלְמָנוֹת, *almanot*).

Biblical Period

The Hebrew substantive *almanah*, usually translated "widow," often does not simply denote a woman whose husband is dead, but rather a once-married woman who has no means of financial support, and is therefore in need of special legal protection. Many widows would fall into such a classification because of their husbands' death, but others who could rely on the support of a new husband (by levirate marriage or otherwise), an adult son, or a father-in-law, would not. Thus, the *almanot* as a class in Israelite society in biblical times were often considered as comprising not merely women whose husbands had died but, rather, once-married women who no longer had any means of financial support. Such being the case, many famous biblical widows (e.g., Ruth, Orpah, and Naomi (Ruth 1–4); Abigail (I Sam. 25); Bath-Sheba (II Sam. 11)), will not be discussed in this article. Since they are never referred to as *almanot*, there is doubt as to whether they were regarded as such. All of them must have had some means of financial support. Only women who are specifically called *almanah* will be dealt with here.

IN EARLY LEGAL CODES. The main evidence for the above definition of the Hebrew word *almanot* comes from several sections of the Middle Assyrian Laws, where the Akkadian etymological equivalent of *almanah, almattu*, denotes the woman in question:

> [If], while a woman is still living in her father's house, her husband died and she has sons [she shall live where she chooses in] a house of theirs. [If] she has no [son, her father-in-law shall marry her to the son] of his choice… or if he wishes, he may give her in marriage to her father-in-law. If her husband and her father-in-law are both dead and she has no son [only then] has she the status of a woman without male support (*almattu*); she may go wherever she pleases (par. 33; in: Pritchard, Texts, 182).
>
> When a woman has been given [in marriage] and the enemy has captured her husband, if she has no father-in-law and no son, she shall remain for two years [at her husband's estate]. During those two years, if she has not sufficient to live on, she shall come forward and [so] declare; she shall became a ward of the palace; …She will stay for two years [at her husband's estate] and then she may live with the husband she chooses. They [the judges] will draw up a document for her [stating she is] a woman without male support (*almattu*). If in later days, her missing husband has returned home, he may take back his wife who was married to an outsider… (par. 45; in: Pritchard, Texts, 184; cf. also pars. 28, 34, in: Pritchard, Texts, 182, 183) and Hammurapi Law Code, par. 177 (in: Pritchard, Texts, 174)).

In all the Akkadian codes, women whose husbands have died, but who do have some means of support, are not given any particular title and are never called *almattu* (e.g., Middle Assyrian Laws, par. 46). According to G.R. Driver, "these considerations suggest that a woman became an *almattu* only when there is no one with a duty to support her" (in: Driver and Miles, *The Assyrian Laws*, in bibl., 225). Further evidence for this definition of *almattu* is found in the usage of the Akkadian *almānūtu*, "lack of support by a male householder" (abstract formation of *almattu*): *bēl bīti imâtma bītu šû almānūtam illak*, "The owner of the house will die, and that house will have no male to support it" (A. Boissier, *Documents assyriens relatifs aux presages* (1894–99), 5:2; cf. CAD, vol. 1, pt. 1 (1964), 362). There are only a few cases in the biblical law codes where *almanah* does not agree with the definition of the Akkadian *almattu*. These are the laws concerning the ineligibility of the *almanah* to become the wife of the high priest (Lev. 21:14) or, unless she is the widow of a priest, to become the wife of any priest (Ezek. 44:22; the rabbis, however, by artificial exegesis, make this verse mean the same thing as Lev. 21:14 – ordinary priests are not prohibited from marrying any widow): the right of the priest's daughter to return to her father's house and partake of *terumah* should she become an *almanah* (Lev. 22:13), and the vow of the *almanah* being legally binding on her (Num. 30:10). In these cases, but only in these, *almanah* must be translated as "widow." Note that in each of these cases the term *almanah* is juxtaposed to terms having to do with marital status – *betulah*, "unmarried woman" (Lev. 21:13, Ezek. 44:22) and *gerushah*, "divorced woman" (Lev. 22:13; Num. 30:10; cf. Lev. 22:12; Num. 30:7ff.). Elsewhere, there is a general pronouncement against the mistreatment of the *almanah* (Ex. 22:21) and there are many other cases, where the humanitarian nature of the author of Deuteronomy (cf. Weinfeld, in bibl.) caused him to prescribe many new laws concerning the protection of the *ger*, "stranger," *yatom*, "fatherless," *almanah*, and levite. In these cases, *almanot* must refer to "women once-married who no longer have any means of financial support." One may not keep the garment of the *almanah* as a pledge (Deut. 24:17), nor turn back and pick up dropped sheaves during harvest time (Deut. 24:19), dropped fruit from olive trees (Deut. 24:20), or grapes that have fallen off the vine (Deut. 24:21); for these must go to the *almanah* and the other classes mentioned above. These socially disadvantaged groups must be permitted to partake of the third-year tithes (Deut. 14:29; 26:12, 13), the freewill contributions made on the occasion of Shavu'ot (Deut. 16:11), and to rejoice during Sukkot (Deut. 16:14). There is also a curse against anyone who would subvert the legal rights of these disadvantaged groups (Deut. 27:19), and God is described as the protector of the rights of these classes (Deut. 10:18). It should also be mentioned that some scholars claim that there is evidence in the Ugaritic texts for the giving of a special dispensation to the *almnt* during time of war. However, the passages in question from the Keret Epic (I Krt 96–97, 184–5) are very obscure and have been interpreted by other scholars quite differently. No conclusions should be drawn until some additional evidence of a more concrete nature is found.

AS TITLE OF INDIVIDUALS. The earliest and by far the most famous biblical personage given the title of *almanah* was Tamar, the daughter-in-law of Judah (Gen. 38). When Judah's son Er died, leaving Tamar a childless widow, Judah told Onan, his secondborn, to live with Tamar as husband and wife so as to beget an offspring for his dead brother (see Deut. 25:5–10). Onan, bearing in mind the fact that the offspring, whom he would have to bring up, would not count as his, practiced only *coitus interruptus* with her (Gen. 38:9). For this, God punished him with death, and the responsibility passed on to the third and youngest of the three sons, Shelah. However, Judah, fearing that marriage to Tamar was unlucky, claimed that Shelah was too young to fulfill his duty and sent Tamar away to live in the house of her own father "as an *almanah*" (Gen. 38:11). Given paragraph 33 of the Middle Assyrian Law Code quoted above, it is interesting to note that Tamar was called an *almanah* only when Judah, her father-in-law, sent her out of his house. It might reasonably be asked whether Tamar would have been called an *almanah* at all had she remained in the house of her father-in-law.

When Shelah grew up and Judah still did not give him to her as a husband, she resorted to the following ruse. At a time when Judah was likely to be attracted by a sexual opportunity, she removed "her garments of *almanah*-hood," i.e., "the clothes of her status as *almanah*," and sat down, veiled, in a spot where she knew that Judah was to pass and where a woman sitting alone was likely to be taken for a prostitute. Judah, not recognizing her because of her veil, became her customer. When he later learned that his daughter-in-law was pregnant, Judah at first ordered that she be burned (Gen. 38:24). When Tamar, however, privately proved to him that he was the father of her child, he publicly declared that not she but he was at fault, since her conception through him was justified by his failure to give her to Shelah. The legal background of the episode is not only Deuteronomy 25:5ff. (levirate marriage), but also the Middle Assyrian Laws referred to above, for only the latter provides evidence that the father-in-law has the privilege of deciding to which of his surviving sons the widow is to be given or even of taking her for himself. Elsewhere, the woman hired by Joab to play the part of an *almanah* so as to induce David to take back his son Absalom (II Sam. 14:1ff.) claims (verse 5): "I am an *almanah*. My husband died." Both Hiram (I Kings 7:14) and Jeroboam I (I Kings 11:26) are designated as sons of an *almanah*. With respect to the latter, who was responsible for the splitting of the United Monarchy, there is a very interesting, somewhat parallel, Akkadian omen, which occurs many times: *mār almattim kussi'am isabbat*. "The son of an *almattum* will seize the throne" (A. Goetze, *Old Babylonian Omen Texts*; Yale Oriental Series, 10 (1947), 41:30).

Finally, Elijah is sent by a divine call to the house of an *almanah* whose son he later revives (I Kings 17). This woman is described as having no means of livelihood, living in abject poverty, and being on the verge of starvation (I Kings 17:12). Clearly, she is not merely a widow, but rather "a woman once married who no longer has the means of financial support."

AS A SOCIALLY DEPRIVED CLASS WHICH MUST BE PROTECTED. From the time of Urukagina of Lagash (c. 2400 B.C.E.), there is recorded evidence concerning the special responsibility of the Mesopotamian king to protect socially disadvantaged groups. In law codes, both in the prologue of Ur-Nammu (c. 2100 B.C.E.) and the epilogue of Hammurapi (c. 1800 B.C.E.), the king claims to have fulfilled this obligation. Hammurapi, for example, states that he wrote his laws:

> *dannum ensam ana la habalim*
> *ekutam almattam sutesurim*,
> In order that the mighty shall not wrong the weak,
> In order to provide justice for the homeless girl
> and the once married woman without financial support
> (Epilogue, xxvb:59–62).

Also the two Ugaritic kings mentioned in the epics are spoken of as either having fulfilled or not fulfilled this responsibility. In the Keret epic, King Keret's son twice accuses him of neglecting his duties:

> *ltdn dn almnt*
> *lttpt tpt qsr nps*,
> You do not judge the cause of the *almnt*,
> Nor adjudicate the case of the wretched (II Krt 6:33–34; cf. 45–48)
> *lpnk ltslhm ytm*
> *b'd kslk almnt*,
> You feed not the fatherless before you,
> Nor the *almnt* behind your back (II Krt 6:48–50)

Conversely, in the Aqhat Epic, King Daniel is portrayed as a righteous king:

> *ydn dn almnt*
> *ytpt tpt ytm*
> Judging the cause of the *almnt*,
> Adjudicating the case of the fatherless (II D 5:7–8; cf. I D 23–25 [restored]).

Here it should be observed that the parallelism *ytm//almnt*, used in two of the above Ugaritic quotations, is also present in Hebrew poetry (e.g., Isa. 1:17, 23; Ps. 68:6). Another parallel pair of words which exist in both Hebrew and Ugaritic is Hebrew שְׁכוֹל//אַלְמֹן (Isa. 47:8, 9) = Ugaritic *tkl//ulmn* (SS 8–9), which is probably to be translated "bereavement//status of being an *almnt*."

The Hebrew prophets often spoke out against the upper-class exploitation of the *almanah* and the other disadvantaged social groups. These protests can be found in the words of First Isaiah (e.g., 1:17, 23; 10:2), Jeremiah (e.g., 7:6, 22:3), Ezekiel (e.g., 22:7), Zechariah (7:10), and Malachi (3:5). Perhaps the clearest parallels to the Ugaritic and Mesopotamian evidence quoted above, however, are those biblical passages which speak of God as the protector of these disadvantaged classes:

> Father of the fatherless, and judge of the *almanot* is God in his holy abode (Ps. 68:6; cf. 146:9).

AS A DESCRIPTION OF A CITY. The above definition of *almanah* is indirectly supported by those biblical passages in which cities are called *almanah* (Isa. 47:8, 9; 54:4; Jer. 51:5; Lam. 1:1). In those passages where the city involved is Israel (Isa. 54:4; Jer. 51:5; Lam. 1:1), the traditional interpretation has always been to translate *almanah* as some kind of temporary widow whom God has left for the time being. This image would correspond with the divorce imagery of Hosea concerning God and Israel (Hos. 1–3). However, aside from the problem of understanding what a "temporary widow" is (cf. Rashi, Lam. 1:1), there is also the much more severe problem of understanding how this imagery could apply to Babylon (Isa. 47:8, 9). However, if *almanah* is understood as referring to a city with no means of independent support, i.e., a vassal or tributary nation, all cases of this metaphor then make sense. In the case of Babylon, the nation which was once "mistress of kingdoms" (Isa. 47:5, 7) will now become like an *almanah*. Thus, according to this interpretation, "mistress of kingdoms" and *almanah* are exact opposites and Babylon's punishment becomes much more fitting – she who once subjugated many nations will now become subjugated herself. In the case of Israel becoming an *almanah*, in Lamentations 1:1 this interpretation is further corroborated by the parallelism in that verse: "She has become like an *almanah*//She has become like a tributary nation."

[Chayim Cohen]

In Jewish Law

From the legal point of view, a widow is a woman who was married in a valid marriage and whose husband has died; if any doubt arises as to her widowhood, she will have to prove that she was so married (for the origin of the word "widow," see Levy, J., Neuhebr Tal, s.v. *alman*). The rabbis of the Talmud exegetically explained the name *almanah* ("widow") as being derived from the words *al maneh* ("because of the *maneh*"), i.e., because her statutory **ketubbah* is a *maneh* (= 100 zuz) and not 200 as in the case of a virgin (Ket. 10b).

PERSONAL STATUS. A widow is generally free to marry any man except a high priest (Lev. 21:14); if she marries the latter she becomes a *ḥalalah* (see **Yuhasin*; Lev. 21:15; Kid. 77a; Sh. Ar., EH 7:12). For the prohibitions imposed upon her in consequence of her previous marriage, see Prohibited *Marriages, and for the law prohibiting the widow of a childless brother to marry without prior *levirate marriage or *ḥaliẓah*.

RIGHTS AND OBLIGATIONS. The widow is entitled to the return of all her property of whatever kind, since her ownership of it is not affected by marriage (see *Husband and Wife; for the difference in this respect between the different kinds of her property, see *Dowry). In Jewish law a widow does not inherit her husband (see *Succession), but she is entitled to her *ketubbah* and the rights due to her by virtue of its provisions, which the husband's heirs must satisfy out of the estate; the most important of these provisions relate to her maintenance. She is entitled to the said rights by virtue of her being the widow, and it is therefore unimportant whether and to what extent she possessed property during the marriage. Her said rights arise upon marriage by virtue of law: "a man, upon marrying a woman, becomes bound to her in respect of the statutory *ketubbah*... and her right to be maintained out of his property and to live in his house after his death throughout her widowhood" (Maim. Yad, Ishut 12:1; Sh. Ar., EH 59:1–2); but they become due only upon her husband's death, since the *ketubbah* is "like a debt payable at some future date and will be recoverable only after the husband's death..." (Maim. Yad, Ishut, 16:3; Sh. Ar., EH 93:1). Since the said rights accrue to the widow by virtue of her *ketubbah*, they do not exist if she has lost her right to the *ketubbah* (see *Divorce).

Inasmuch as the rights of the widow arise upon her marriage and not upon the husband's death, he cannot prejudice them by his will, and any testamentary disposition to the effect that the widow shall not be entitled to her *ketubbah* or maintenance out of his estate is void (Ket. 68b; Sh. Ar., EH 69:2; 93:3). No express reference need be made to these rights in the *ketubbah* deed since they arise upon the marriage as a condition laid down by the *bet din* (*tenai bet din*), i.e., by virtue of law, although they are based upon her being entitled to a *ketubbah* (Ket. 52b; Sh. Ar., loc. cit).

SATISFACTION OF THE WIDOW'S RIGHTS OUT OF THE ESTATE. According to talmudic law, a widow can enforce her *ketubbah* and its provisions, including maintenance, only against the immovable property which forms part of the estate (Ket. 81b; Sh. Ar., EH 100:1). However, since the development of trade and the decrease of landholding among Jews led creditors to rely also upon the movables of debtors for repayment of their debts, the *geonim* ordained that the movable property of the estate should also be attachable for the widow's rights (Tos. Ket. 51a; Rosh to Ket. ch. 6:5; Sh. Ar., EH 100:1). Since the time of Maimonides, it has become customary to include in every *ketubbah* deed a provision rendering the husband's movable property so attachable, whether acquired at the date of the marriage or to be acquired by him thereafter (Maim. Yad, Ishut, 16:8; see *Lien).

SATISFACTION OF THE WIDOW'S RIGHTS AGAINST PURCHASERS. The husband's property being subject to the *ketubbah*, the widow may, in the event of the estate being insufficient to cover it, follow the property in the hands of the purchasers, i.e., recover the amount of the *ketubbah* out of immovable property which the husband or his heirs have transferred to others. This remedy, however, is not available with regard to movables so transferred, since, contrary to the case of immovable property, where the purchaser can be required first to find out whether the vendor can indeed transfer it free from all encumbrances, in the case of movables, owing to regulations of furthering commerce (*takkanot ha-shuk*), that cannot be required lest commercial stability would thereby be impaired (Ket. 51a; Sh. Ar., EH 100:1). On the other hand, if the husband has transferred his property by way of *donatio mortis causa* (see *Wills), the widow is entitled to be satisfied for her *ketubbah* out of the movable property also, inasmuch as in such a case the property has passed upon death, subject to her rights which accrued to her already in his lifetime (Sh. Ar., ḤM 252:1, EH 100:1, and *Rema* ad loc.). The rabbis, however, also prescribed that for her maintenance the widow cannot proceed against purchasers (see above) even in respect of immovable property, since the amount to be recovered is not a determinate sum but may vary periodically with her requirements, and a purchaser cannot know the precise debt for which the property is charged (Git. 48b, 50b and *Rashi* ad loc.; Sh. Ar., EH 93:20). On the other hand, as in the case of the *ketubbah*, the widow here may also recover from property transferred by way of *donatio mortis causa* (Sh. Ar., ḤM 252:1, EH loc. cit.). The said limitations upon the right of the widow to receive her *ketubbah* and maintenance from the husband's property which has been transferred to others do not apply if it was transferred fraudulently in order to deprive the widow of it, as "the sages of the Talmud set themselves against anyone who intends to defraud and negate his act" (Resp. Rosh, 78:1 and 3). Accordingly, upon proof that the heirs intend as a means of evasion to dispose of the immovable property of the estate and that her maintenance rights will be prejudiced thereby, she may apply to the court for a prohibitory injunction against them; but she cannot do so in regard to movable property of the estate, since the above-mentioned geonic regulation does not extend to such property (Yad, Ishut, 18:11–13 and *Maggid Mishneh* thereto; Sh. Ar., EH 93:21).

THE WIDOW'S MAINTENANCE. The widow is generally entitled to receive the same maintenance as she was entitled to receive during the husband's lifetime. The same rules therefore apply, e.g., maintenance will include clothing, residence, medical expenses, use of household articles, and the like. Similarly, the principle also applies that "she rises with him but does not descend with him," i.e., that she is entitled to the same standard of maintenance she was entitled to during her late husband's lifetime (Ket. 48a and 103a; Sh. Ar., EH 94:1 and 5). To some extent her said right to maintenance is affected by the very fact of her widowhood, since the personal relationship upon which her rights were based during her husband's lifetime is now absent, and she is now alone, so that her requirements are reduced. For this reason, although entitled to reside in the same apartment in which she lived with her husband, she is no longer entitled to occupy the whole of it if she, being alone, is not in need of it even in order to maintain her social status (Sh. Ar., EH 94:1; *Rema* ad loc. and commentaries PD 19, pt. 2 (1965), 338). Similarly, she is not entitled to transfer ownership of the apartment to others nor to let the whole or part of it, since the right of residence is conferred upon her in order to enable her to maintain her social status but not to make a profit (Sh. Ar., loc. cit.). The right of the widow with regard to the apartment is merely to have the use of it; therefore, upon her death, it returns to the heirs of the husband only, and does not form part of her estate (*Beit Shemu'el* 94, n. 4).

This right of residence is not affected by sale of the apartment by the heirs, and the new owner cannot evict the widow from it (Sh. Ar., EH 94:4). Where the widow is unable to live in the apartment, for instance, if it is destroyed, she is entitled to receive out of the estate an amount necessary for renting another suitable apartment (*Ḥelkat Meḥokek* 94, nos. 6, 7). If the widow survives with small children of the husband, both boys and girls, and the estate is insufficient to maintain all of them, her right prevails; if, however, the young children surviving with her are either all boys or all girls, they all take equally (Ket. 43a and Tos. ad loc.; note the alternative opinion in Sh. Ar., EH 93:4; see also EH 113:6 regarding the priority of the widow's maintenance to the right of the daughters to their dowry out of the estate, and for the reason for the aforesaid distinction, see *Beit Shemu'el* and *Ḥelkat Meḥokek* to EH 93:8–9).

THE WIDOW'S CLAIM FOR PAST MAINTENANCE. A widow is entitled to maintenance, also for the time prior to her claim, since there is no reason to assume that she has waived her right to it. This contrasts with the right to maintenance of a wife who is entitled to it only as from the date of claim onward. If the widow has not claimed for a long period – such as when, being a wealthy woman, she delays for three years or, being poor, she delays for two years – she is presumed to have waived the past maintenance unless the presumption is rebutted by the facts, such as by the fact of her right having been secured by a pledge or mortgage (EH 93:14 and see *Limitation of Actions).

THE WIDOW'S RIGHT TO HER EARNINGS AND THE INCOME FROM HER PROPERTY. Parallel to the rule prevailing during the husband's lifetime concerning his right to the wife's earnings, the heirs are entitled to the widow's earnings in consideration of her maintenance (Sh. Ar., EH 95:1). On the other hand, they are not entitled to the income from her property, as is the husband to the income from the wife's property – since to the husband it is due in consideration of her redemption only, i.e., of his obligation to ransom her if she is taken captive so that she can return and live with him as his wife, a reason not applicable in respect of the heirs. Correspondingly, the heirs are under no obligation to ransom her either when she has fallen into captivity or finds herself in a similar situation, for instance, when she cannot return from abroad except upon payment of a considerable sum which she does not possess (Ket. 52a; Yad, Ishut, 18:5 and 8; Sh. Ar., EH 78:8; 94:7; 94:4).

EXPIRATION OF THE WIDOW'S RIGHT TO MAINTENANCE. Since the widow is entitled to maintenance by virtue of the provisions of the *ketubbah* (see above), i.e., only while entitled to the *ketubbah*, her right to maintenance will expire upon her no longer being entitled to the *ketubbah*, i.e., if she has lost her right to it by virtue of law or if she has actually received payment of it from the heirs. Likewise, since one of the conditions in law connected with her maintenance is that she shall not be "ashamed," i.e., to enable her to preserve the honor of her husband, she will lose such right upon her voluntarily claiming her *ketubbah* in court – for by doing so she implicitly declares herself no longer concerned with the honor of her husband or with his heirs (Ket. 54a; Sh. Ar., EH 93:5; and *Ḥelkat Meḥokek*, n. 13).

The widow's right to maintenance also ceases if she remarries (see *Marriage), because under the *ketubbah*, which is the source of her right, she is entitled to maintenance during widowhood only. According to most of the authorities, she even loses her maintenance upon her engagement for a new marriage – although by it alone she does not create a new personal status – because by it she shows that she no longer wishes to preserve the honor of her first husband and remain his widow (Ket. 52b; 54a; Sh. Ar., EH 93:7 and *Rema* ad loc.).

THE PROBLEM OF DENIAL OF MAINTENANCE BY INVOLUNTARY RECEIPT OF THE KETUBBAH. Since the widow – if she has not lost her right to maintenance otherwise (see above) – is entitled to maintenance only so long as she has not received or claimed her *ketubbah* by legal process, opinion was divided already in the time of the Mishnah as to whether the heirs may compel her to receive it and thereby be released from their obligation to maintain her. It was finally decided that this question depends upon custom, because maintenance of the widow is one of the provisions of the *ketubbah*, and in all matters relating to the *ketubbah*, "local custom," i.e., the custom of the place of marriage, applies, such custom being considered a condition of the marriage and therefore not to be varied but with the consent of both spouses (Sh. Ar., EH 93:3 and *Ḥelkat Meḥokek*, n. 5). According to the custom of the people of Jerusalem and Galilee, the choice lay with the widow alone, and therefore they inserted in the *ketubbah* deed a term, "You shall dwell in my house and be maintained in it out of my estate throughout the duration of your widowhood" (Ket. 52b; 54a and Tos. ad loc.). According to the custom of the people of Judea, however, the choice was left with the heirs, and there the corresponding term in the *ketubbah* deed was therefore, "until the heirs shall wish to pay you your *ketubbah*" (*ibid.*). As regards this difference in custom it was said that, while the people of Jerusalem cared for their honor, the people of Judea cared for their money (TJ, 4:15, 29b). The *halakhah* was decided in accordance with the custom of Jerusalem and Galilee, i.e., whenever there is no other fixed custom or rabbinical *takkanah*, the choice lies solely with the widow, and the heirs cannot deprive her of maintenance against her wishes (Ket. 54a and Tos. ad loc.; Yad, Ishut, 18:1; Sh. Ar., EH 93:3; and see *Conflict of Laws).

Inasmuch as economic conditions during marriage may so change that the estate might be insufficient to provide both for the maintenance of the widow and for inheritance for the heirs – a state of affairs which the husband certainly did not intend – many of the authorities were of the opinion that it is proper to make a *takkanah* permitting the heirs to deprive the widow of her maintenance by payment to her (against her will) of her *ketubbah* (*Rema* EH 93:3 and *Pitḥei Teshuvah* thereto, n. 5). Accordingly, various *takkanot* were made in the matter and the most well known, cited also in the Shulḥan Arukh, are those known as the *Takkanot* of Toledo, Spain, of the 13th century, which in their main provisions laid down that the heirs may discharge their obligation for the widow's maintenance by payment unto her of her *ketubbah*, which, if it amounts to more than half the value of the estate, shall be deemed to be discharged by payment unto her of half such value (Resp. Rosh 55; Sh. Ar, EH 118 and commentaries).

In Ereẓ Israel there is a distinction between the Sephardi and Ashkenazi communities. The former follow the author of the Shulḥan Arukh, i.e., that the choice lies with the widow alone and the heirs cannot rid themselves of the obligation for her maintenance against her wishes (Sh. Ar., EH 93:3). The Ashkenazim permit the heirs to do so by payment unto the widow of the *ketubbah* even if she does not agree to it. That is certainly the situation when the widow was the second wife of the deceased, but it is also customary with a first wife, although the rabbinical courts endeavor to get the parties to agree to a fair arrangement under which the widow will not lose her maintenance. At any rate, the heirs are not entitled to evict the widow from the marital home, and she is to be provided with the household utensils and silverware forming part of the estate, the size of the estate being taken into account (*Pithei Teshuvah*, nos. 5 and 6 to Sh. Ar., EH 93; *Sha'arei Uzzi'el*, 2 (1946), 244, nos. 14, 15; *Beit Me'ir*, EH 93:3; 94:1).

THE STATE OF ISRAEL. As to the personal status of the widow in the State of Israel, the rules of the *halakhah* generally apply, both in the rabbinical courts and in the secular civil courts, in the latter except insofar as private international law imports other rules. With regard to the widow's financial rights, however, the Succession Law of 1965 provides that the *halakhah* shall apply in the rabbinical courts alone, and only if all the interested parties have expressed their consent to it in writing (sec. 155). Failing such consent, jurisdiction is in the civil courts alone, and these apply the provisions of the said law only (secs. 148 and 151). Under these provisions the widow is entitled to a part of the estate as an heir. In addition, if she is in need of it, she is also entitled to maintenance out of the estate; the amount of such maintenance is fixed by the court, taking into account all the circumstances, and particularly to what she is entitled as an heir and the extent of her *ketubbah* (secs. 56–65).

[Ben-Zion (Benno) Schereschewsky]

BIBLIOGRAPHY: G.R. Driver and J.C. Miles, *The Assyrian Laws* (1935); idem, *The Babylonian Laws* (1952); H.L. Ginsberg, *The Legend of King Keret* (1946); M. Held, in: Leshonenu, 18 (1953), 117, 154–5; A. van Selms, *Marriage and Family Life in Ugaritic Literature* (1954); M. Weinfeld, in: *Tarbiz*, 31 (1962), 1–17; F.C. Fensham, in: JNES, 21 (1962), 129–39; A.L. Oppenheim et al. (eds.), *The Assyrian Dictionary of the Oriental Institute* (1963), 362–64; A.F. Rainey, *A Social*

Structure of Ugarit (1967). LEGAL ASPECTS: Gulak, Yesodei, 3 (1922), 38–40, 88–91, 95f., 99; Gulak, Oẓar, 98, 156f.; ET, 2 (1949), 16–20; 4 (1952), 744; B. Schereschewsky, *Dinei Mishpaḥah* (1967²), 236–70; M. Elon, in: ILR, 4 (1969), 130–2; Elon, Mafte'aḥ, 4f. **ADD. BIBLIOGRAPHY:** M. Elon, *Ha-Mishpat ha-Ivri* (1988), 1:191, 253, 325, 373, 428, 458, 461, 470, 531, 640, 649, 651, 653, 671f., 676, 682f., 689, 692; 3:1413; idem, *Jewish Law* (1994) 1:215, 296, 389, 452; 2:522, 559, 562, 573, 646, 792, 803, 805, 808, 829f., 834, 841f., 850, 854; 4:1683; *idem, Ma'mad ha-Ishah, Mishpat ve-Shipput, Masoret u-Temurah, Arakhehah shel Medinah Yehudit ve-Demokratit* (2005) 278–90.

WIEDENFELD, DOV (1881–1965), *rosh yeshivah* and *posek*, popularly known as the "Tshebiner Rav." Belonging to a prominent Galician rabbinic family, he received his education from his father Jacob, the author of the *Kokhav mi-Ya'akov* (1933), and from his own brothers, R. Isaac, the rabbi of Grimailov, and R. Nahum, the rabbi of Dubrovitsa. Although widely recognized as a scholar, R. Dov refused to enter the rabbinate and instead became a businessman in Trzebinia. In 1923, following the death of Trzebinia's rabbi, Wiedenfeld acceded to the requests of the community to become its spiritual leader. He now officially opened a yeshivah in Trzebinia which soon attracted 70 students, and his opinion in halakhic questions was eagerly sought by his colleagues throughout Galicia and Poland. Many of his decisions were later recorded in his *Dover Meisharim* (3 vols., 1937–51). During World War II he escaped from Trzebinia to Lvov and was later exiled to Siberia by the Communists. Here, under the most trying conditions, he still continued his talmudic studies, recording his new interpretations on scraps of paper and pieces of wood. In 1946 Wiedenfeld arrived in Jerusalem following Chief Rabbi Isaac *Herzog's intervention with the British government. There he reestablished his yeshivah, which he named *Kokhav mi-Ya'akov* and continued to respond to the many inquiries on Jewish law which he received. Following the death of R. Isaac Zeev *Soloveichik in 1960, Wiedenfeld was considered the final authority of his generation by many Orthodox Jews.

BIBLIOGRAPHY: B. Landau, *Ha-Ga'on mi-Tshebin* (1967).

[Aaron Rothkoff]

WIELICZKA, town in Cracow province, S. Poland, in the historic region of *Lesser Poland. Rights to exploit the celebrated salt mines in Wieliczka were leased by Jews, including Saul *Wahl, from the 14th to the end of the 18th century. However, an organized Jewish community was established there only in the second half of the 19th century. The Jewish population numbered 614 in 1890, 981 (15.5% of the total) in 1900, and 1,700 in 1921.

[Abraham N. Poliak]

Holocaust Period

On the outbreak of World War II there were about 1,300 Jews in Wieliczka. The Germans occupied the town on Sept. 7, 1939. In summer 1942 the Jews from the whole county were concentrated in Wieliczka. The Jewish community was liquidated on Aug. 27, 1942, when 8,000 Jews from Wieliczka and its vicinity were deported to *Belzec death camp, 500 to Stalowa-Wola forced labor camp, and 200 to Plaszow concentration camp. After the war the Jewish community of Wieliczka was not reconstituted.

WIELUN (Pol. **Wieluń**, Rus. **Velyun**), district town in the province of Lodz, Poland. Jewish merchants settled in Wielun about the middle of the 16th century when the town prospered as a station on the commercial route from Poland and Lithuania to Silesia. A privilege, *de non tolerandis Judaeis*, was granted to Wielun in 1566. A Jewish settlement was reestablished at the close of the 18th century. There were 70 Jews (6% of the population) in Wielun in 1808; 642 (16.5% of the population) in 1857; and 2,732 (38%) in 1897. When the town was rebuilt after the great fire of 1858, the head of the local community, Leib Kon, succeeded in thwarting the plans for erecting a Jewish quarter. The overwhelming majority of Jews earned their livelihoods as craftsmen and a minority engaged in commerce. The first synagogue (1799) was situated in an ancient building acquired from a monastery. A large synagogue was built in its place in 1855. Until 1848 the Jews buried their dead in the cemetery of Dzialoszyn. In the early 1850s, as a result of a cholera epidemic, a local cemetery was acquired. From the 1850s the influence of *Ḥasidism began to be felt in the community. At the close of the century R. Menahem Mendel Grynberg held rabbinical office. During World War I hundreds of Jewish workers from Lodz found refuge in Wielun. In 1921 Jews numbered 4,818 (44% of the population). Between the two world wars Jewish craftsmen (65% of the working population in the community) formed trade unions (as builders, carpenters, tinsmiths, locksmiths, barbers, etc.). The town's transportation was developed by Jewish initiative in providing buses and lorries. The community's educational institutions included a talmud torah, Yesodei ha-Torah, *Yavneh schools, a *Beth Jacob school, and a large yeshivah in which about one-third of the Jewish pupils studied. Both the *Zionist movement and *Agudat Israel were active in the community, and delegates from the Jewish population were an important factor in the municipal council. Before the Holocaust there were outbreaks of antisemitism in the town: a boycott of Jewish trade, attacks on the synagogue and its worshipers, and there was an attempt to provoke a blood libel (1937).

[Arthur Cygielman]

Holocaust Period

About 4,200 Jews lived in Wielun in 1939. During World War II the town underwent heavy bombardment and the Jewish hospital was among the numerous buildings destroyed. The ancient synagogue of Wielun was also destroyed and part of the Jewish population escaped to the nearby city of *Zelow. When that town was occupied by German forces, most of the Jews returned and found shelter in barracks and in damaged buildings. The Germans soon began to kidnap able-bodied Jews in the streets for slave labor in what became daily raids. Jewish slave labor was used for the construction and repair of the roads and buildings, and in demolition work (including that of the synagogue). Another group of Jews was forced to build a swimming pool for the Germans, using tombstones from the Jewish cemetery for paving it. Pillage of Jewish property went on without interruption. Even the liturgical objects and the library of manuscripts in the synagogue were looted by the Nazis. Several hundred Jews from the neighboring villages escaped to Wielun, but the Jewish population constantly decreased as a result of either "voluntary" or forced transfers to other parts of Poland. In February 1942, the Germans publicly executed ten Jews on the pretext that they violated the prohibition against the preparation of kosher meat. In June 1942, the president of the *Judenrat was murdered by the Germans, and during that same summer the ghetto was surrounded by German police and a large number of Jews were deported to an unknown destination. The liquidation of all the Jewish communities in Wielun county began on Aug. 22, 1942, when the entire Jewish population (about 10,000) from the neighboring towns and villages were driven to Wielun and kept in the Augustine Church without food or water for several days. The sick, the weak, and the old were murdered in the church, and the rest, together with the Jews of Wielun, were sent to the death camp at *Chelmno. Only a small number of physically fit were sent to *Lodz Ghetto.

[Danuta Dombrowska]

BIBLIOGRAPHY: R. Mahler, *Yidn in Amolikn Poyln in Likht fun Tsifern* (1958), index: M. Bersohn, *Dyplomataryusz dotyczący Żydów w Polsce* (1910), no. 190; J. Goldberg, *Stosunki agrarne w miastach ziemi wietuńskiej w drugiej połowie xvii w xviii wieku* (1960); W. Wilczyński, in: *Informator Wieluński* (1934); I. Schiper, *Dzieje handlu żydowskiego na ziemiach polskich* (1937), index.

WIENER, family of medalists active in Belgium. JACQUES (1815–1899) was the oldest of three brothers who were to become famous as medalists. Born in the Rhineland of Hungarian immigrants, he was apprenticed at the age of 13 to his uncle L. Baruch, a fine engraver in his own right. The two signed some earlier medals jointly. At the age of 30 Wiener was the first to conceive the idea of engraving in precise detail the exterior and interior of a monument on the obverse and reverse of a medal. He engraved with great delicacy ten medals of famous Belgian churches. This he followed with a series of 41 medals, issued between 1850 and 1865, illustrating the most famous European buildings. He also engraved the first Belgian stamps, and for many years was head of the government plant issuing these stamps. Among the hundreds of medals of this master, there are several of Jewish interest, e.g., the 1841 Opening of the Jewish Home for the Aged in The Hague and the 1861 Opening of the Synagogue at Cologne.

Leopold (1823–1891) studied with his older brother Jacques and then became a pupil of David d'Angers in Paris. In 1847 he returned to Belgium and started engraving a series of large historical medals which commemorated contemporary events and became very popular. In 1864 he was appointed first engraver to the Belgian mint, holding the post until his death. He was responsible for all the currency of Leopold II – some 150 pieces. At the same time he continued striking medals. He also had a considerable reputation as a sculptor; several of his monumental works still adorn public places in Belgium. One medal of special Jewish interest is his 1859 portrait study of Henri Loeb, chief rabbi of Belgium.

Charles (1832–1888) was the third and youngest of the Wiener brothers and, perhaps, had the most brilliant career. He studied at Brussels and Paris where he was a student of Oudiné. In 1865 he settled at The Hague as engraver to the king of Holland, but moved to London, where he was assistant engraver at the Royal Mint. He then went to Lisbon as chief engraver of the Portuguese coins. Returning to Brussels in 1867, Charles devoted himself to medals, which he produced in large number, some in conjunction with his brother Jacques. His English pieces have best withstood the test of time. Of Jewish interest are three portrait medals: E.A. Astruc, chief rabbi of Belgium; Jules Anspach, mayor of Brussels; and a dual portrait of Sir Moses and Lady Judith Montefiore.

[Daniel M. Friedenberg]

WIENER, ALEXANDER S. (1907–1976), U.S. immunohematologist. Born and educated in New York, he was appointed professor of forensic medicine at the New York University School of Medicine in 1938. Together with Karl *Landsteiner, Wiener discovered the Rh human blood factor. He also worked out in detail the serology, genetics, and nomenclature of the entire Rh blood group system. He discovered the Rh blocking antibody and was the first to introduce exchange transfusion for the treatment of erythroblastosis fetalis. Other blood group factors discovered by Wiener include Kell, Ca, U, M^e, and the I-i blood group system. Wiener wrote books and articles in the field of blood groups and acted as a member of the editorial boards of several leading medical publications.

BIBLIOGRAPHY: S.R. Kagan, *Jewish Medicine* (1952), 273–4.

[Fred Rosner]

WIENER, ALFRED (1885–1964), public figure. An Arabist by education, he served as secretary to Paul *Nathan from 1911 to 1914. After serving in World War I Wiener became active in the CV (*Central-Verein deutscher Staatsbuerger juedischen Glaubens) of which he became secretary general. He belonged to the pro-Palestine wing of the CV which, from 1929, collaborated in the non-Zionist part of the enlarged Jewish *Agency and the Keren *Hayesod. At the end of 1933, with the help of Professor David *Cohen, he founded the Jewish Central Information Office in Amsterdam which was brought over to London in 1939 and was later named Wiener *Library. The rest of his life was dedicated to this institute.

BIBLIOGRAPHY: C.C. Aronsfeld, in: WLB, 18, no. 2 (1964), 13–14; idem, in: *Theokratia*, 1 (1967/69), 144–59; R. Weltsch, in: YLBI, 9 (1964), XXVIII–XXX; A. Paucker, *Der juedische Abwehrkampf* (1967).

[Yehuda Reshef]

WIENER, ERNEST EDOUARD (1882–1973), Belgian soldier and engineer. A grandson of Jacques *Wiener, he was born in Brussels to a family which played a prominent role in Belgian arts, finance, and politics. He entered the Military Academy in 1899. While a lieutenant, he studied electrical engineering at the Montefiore Electro-Technical Institute in Liège, from which he graduated in 1909. During World War I, he was appointed to important commands and was wounded while trying to rescue some soldiers under artillery fire. From 1929 to 1936, he was in charge of studies at the Military Academy, first as assistant director and then as director. In 1940, he was a major-general commanding Transmission Troops and Services at Supreme Headquarters. As a prisoner of war for five years in German camps during World War II, he showed great dignity both as a soldier and as a Jew, and when he retired from active service in 1946, he was made a lieutenant-general, the highest rank in the Belgian Army.

During his life, Wiener was active in scientific and technical societies and was president, inter alia, of the Belgian section of the International Electro-Technical Committee. Following the family tradition, he became a member of the Consistoire Central Israélite de Belgique, the official representative body of Belgian Jewry. He was elected president in 1938, but could only act as a delegate until 1950, when he assumed the post with full title, occupying it until 1956. Most of his efforts were devoted to the reconstruction of the religious communities throughout the country and to the reorganization of several communal services. General Wiener was decorated by the British, French, and Belgian governments.

[Willy Bok]

WIENER, HAROLD MARCUS (1875–1929), English Bible scholar. Wiener was born in London. Although a lawyer by profession, he devoted most of his life to biblical research. He settled in Palestine in 1924, believing that a religious renaissance was imminent. His main objective was to minimize the conflict between the various religions in the land, and he devoted the last five years of his life to a rapprochement between Arabs and Jews. He supported an Arab school and provided funds for scholarships for young Arabs. His house was called the House of Humanity. Despite these activities, Wiener was killed by an Arab gang on Aug. 13, 1929. He said to his attackers, who did not recognize him, *ana yahud* ("I am a Jew"), and these words sealed his fate.

In his studies Wiener insisted that the Pentateuch was written by Moses, but developed a critical method of biblical interpretation, by which, using the ancient versions, he attempted to establish a correct text. Wiener was prominent among those who opposed the J. *Wellhausen school of Bible research by scholarly methods. Among his major works are *Essays in Pentateuchal Criticism* (1909); *The Origin of the Pentateuch* (1910); *Prophets of Israel in History and Modern Criticism* (1923); *Early Hebrew History and Other Studies* (1924); and *Posthumous Essays* (1932). In addition, the following essays were reprinted separately: *Notes on Hebrew Religion* (1907); *The Date of the Exodus* (1916); *The Religion of Moses* (1919); *The Main Problem of Deuteronomy* (1920); and *Altars of the Old Testament* (1927).

BIBLIOGRAPHY: JL, s.v. (incl. bibl.); Waxman, Literature, 4 (1960^2), 650–3.

[Yehuda Komlosh]

WIÉNER, JEAN (1896–1982), French pianist and composer. He was born in Paris to a family of Austrian origin. He studied at the Conservatoire de Paris with A. Gédalge. After World War I he was among the first to defend jazz music in France. Between 1920 and 1924 he organized the Concerts Wiéner, which contributed to making known his friends, the French "Group of Six" (Honegger, *Milhaud, Auric, Poulenc, Tailleferre, Durey), as well as the works of M. de Falla, I. Stravinski, A. Schonberg, A. Berg, and A. Webern. It was in that framework that D. Milhaud conducted the first performance of Schoenberg's *Pierrot Lunaire*. Along with Clement Doucet he formed a piano duo, which gave 2,000 concerts between 1925 and 1939. His compositions were strongly influenced by American jazz, which he helped to popularize in France. Among his works are *Franco-American Concerto* (1922–23), piano and violin music, an operetta, and music for the cinema, theater, radio, and television.

[Amnon Shiloah (2nd ed.)]

WIENER, LEO (1862–1939), philologist and historian of Yiddish language, literature, and folklore. Born in Bialystok, Poland, he studied at the University of Warsaw in 1880, and then in Berlin. In 1882 he immigrated to the U.S. He became a lecturer in the department of Germanic and Romance languages at the University of Kansas (1892–95), and taught in the Department of Slavic Studies at Harvard University (1895–1930), becoming assistant professor in 1901 and professor in 1911. Wiener published articles on Yiddish linguistic elements in Polish, German, Ukrainian, and Belorussian (1893–1904). In his work *The Popular Poetry of the Russian Jews* (1899), he not only studied Yiddish folk poems but analyzed the poetry of *badḥanim*. He was the first to introduce the poetry of Morris *Rosenfeld, who had been a sweatshop worker, to the general public by translating his poems into English (*Dos Liderbukh*, "The Songbook," 1897) under the title *Songs from the Ghetto* (1898). In 1898, Wiener traveled to Europe to collect material for his pioneering volume, *The History of Yiddish Literature in the Nineteenth Century* (1899). I.L. *Peretz encouraged him and Abraham Elijah *Harkavy, librarian at the Asiatic Museum of St. Petersburg, presented him with a thousand Yiddish books, which formed the basis of the Yiddish collection of the Harvard University library. After the turn of the century Wiener's interest in Yiddish declined. He compiled a valuable anthology of Russian literature (2 volumes, 1902–03) and translated Tolstoy into English (24 volumes, 1904).

He was the father of Norbert *Wiener.

BIBLIOGRAPHY: Rejsen, Leksikon, 1 (1926), 984–6; LNYL, 3 (1960), 447–9; N. Wiener, *Ex-Prodigy; My Childhood and Youth*

(1953); S. Niger, *Bleter Geshikhte fun der Yidisher Literatur* (1959), 283–93.

[Sol Liptzin]

WIENER, MAX (1882–1950), Reform rabbi, author, and theologian. Born in Oppeln (Germany), he studied at the University of Berlin, where he received his Ph.D. in 1906, and at the Juedisch-theologisches Seminar in Breslau and the Lehranstalt fuer die Wissenschaft des Judentums in Berlin. He was ordained there in 1908.Wiener served the congregations in Duesseldorf, where he was assistant to Rabbi Leo *Baeck (1909–12), and then as rabbi in Stettin. He was a chaplain in France with the German Army during World War I. In 1926 he moved to Berlin where he was a communal rabbi for the liberal congregations. He succeeded Julius *Guttmann at the Lehranstalt fuer die Wissenschaft des Judentums. He was active as a member of the national board of directors of the Juedischer Kulturverband, which was constituted to give work to unemployed Jewish artists and musicians by having them perform in concerts and theatrical performances, as well as lectures for the Jewish community. He was one of the great scholars saved by the Hebrew Union College and its visionary president Julius *Morgenstein, and brought to the United States, literally plucked from the fire. Together with other scholars, including Abraham Joshua *Heschel, he was invited to HUC, where he became a member of the faculty and a congregational rabbi in Fairmont West, Virginia. He later moved to Congregation Habonim in New York, which was a synagogue in Washington Heights composed of German Jewish refugees, in what euphemistically became known as the "Fourth Reich" in Manhattan.

Wiener saw the essence of Judaism in the teaching of the prophets (*Die Anschauungen der Propheten von der Sittlichkeit* ("The Prophetic View of Ethics," 1909)), but he was critical of 19th-century Reform (*Juedische Religion im Zeitalter der Emanzipation*, 1933 – a standard work) and took a position sympathetic to Zionism and the historical character of Judaism and the Jewish people. Wiener also published *Juedische Froemmigkeit und religioeses Dogma* (1924); *Religion in dieser Zeit* (1934); and compiled *Abraham Geiger und liberales Judentum* (posthumous 1962). He was on the board of the *Reconstructionist* and served as editor of the *Jewish Lexicon* (1927; his work was adapted for the *Universal Jewish Encyclopedia*).

His son THEODORE WIENER (1918–) was librarian at the Hebrew Union College–Jewish Institute of Religion, Cincinnati, from 1959, after serving as rabbi in a number of Reform congregations. From 1964 Wiener was supervisor of the Hebrew Language Unit in the Descriptive Cataloging Division at the Library of Congress. He published bibliographies of Leo Baeck (1954), Samuel *Cohon (1956), and Solomon B. Freehof (1964) and was co-translator with E. Spicehandler of B. Felsenthal's letters to J.H. Schorr (1958).

BIBLIOGRAPHY: Liebeschutz, in: YLBI, 5 (1960), 35–57; K.M. Olitzsky, L.M. Sussman, and M.H. Stern (eds.), *Reform Judaism in America: A Biographical Dictionary and Sourcebook* (1993).

[Jakob J. Petuchowski / Michael Berenbaum (2nd ed.)]

WIENER, MEIR (1893–1941), poet, novelist, and literary critic. Born in Cracow, Wiener received a traditional and secular education and was influenced by his tutor, Ben-Zion Rappaport. During World War I he studied at the universities of Basel and Zurich, later living in Vienna, Berlin, and Paris (1918–26). After immigrating to the Soviet Union in 1926, he became a Soviet citizen, living and working in Kharkov, Kiev, and, from 1933, Moscow. During World War II he volunteered for the Soviet army and was killed near the city of Vyazma during the defense of Moscow. Until his departure for the Soviet Union he wrote mostly in German, including *Messias* ("Messiah," 1920), a collection of mystical meditative elegies; *Die Lyrik der Kabbalah* ("The Lyric of the Kabbalah," 1920), a selection of Hebrew religious poetry in free translation with introductory notes; *Von den Symbolen* ("On Symbols," 1924), an aesthetical-philosophical treatise; political articles, philosophical essays and book reviews, mostly on Jewish subjects, published in the periodicals *Jerubbaal*, *Esra*, *Der Jude*, *Menorah*, *Wiener Morgenzeitung* and others. Together with H. *Brody he published *Mivḥar ha-Shirah ha-Ivrit* ("Selection of Hebrew Lyric," 1922) from the Middle Ages, with his own Hebrew introduction. He began writing Yiddish poetry and fiction in the early 1920s, but was unable to find a publisher for his works outside the Soviet Union. His extensive literary activity up to 1926, which also includes the expressionistic Yiddish novel *Ele Faleks Untergang* ("Ele Falek's Downfall"; written in Berlin in 1923, published in Kharkov 1929), reflects his search for a mode of expression adapted to the conceptual and emotional struggle of the young Jewish intelligentsia between the world wars. He attempted to define Jewish identity and destiny while vacillating between spiritual Zionism and Martin *Buber's teaching on the one hand, and social political radicalism and expressionistic trends in art and literature on the other. He probed deeply into traditional Hebrew poetry and Jewish mysticism and their human and religious significance for modern people in general, and the Jews in particular. His personal and ideological disappointments, lack of a sense of mission, and absence of a place in the intellectual life in Western and Central Europe, as well as his contacts with leftist circles in Berlin and Vienna, including Soviet Yiddish authors Leyb *Kvitko and *Der Nister, caused him to immigrate to the Soviet Union, where he concentrated his energy and talents on Yiddish literature. His main work there was devoted to the research and publications of the Jewish scientific institutes in Kharkov, Kiev, and Moscow in the 1920s and 1930s, where he also played an important role as counselor, editor, and teacher. He headed the Department of Yiddish Language and Literature at Moscow State Pedagogical Institute (1934–38) and directed and participated in the editing of Yiddish literature ranging from folk-song collections and the anonymous comedy *Di Genarte Velt*, to the writings of Solomon *Ettinger, Israel *Axenfeld, Sholem Yankev *Abramovitsh, and *Sholem Aleichem. His editions have served as models ever since; his prefaces to these editions were collected along with additional articles and published in his book *Tsu der Ge-*

shikhte fun der Yidisher Literatur in Nayntsentn Yorhundert (2 vols., 1945–6²). Although this book had not been planned as a comprehensive study, it is, together with his later book, *Vegn Sholem Aleichems Humor* (1941), one of the most notable achievements of criticism and investigation of 19th-century Yiddish literature. Wiener's books evince penetrating knowledge of the subject against a broad literary and cultural background, but also show the author's dependence on Marxist conceptions and Soviet ideological trends predominant at the time. He also published works on Marxist literary theory, theoretical problems in folklore, and criticism of such contemporary Yiddish writers in Russia and abroad as H. Leyvick, David *Bergelson, Perez *Markish, Leib Kvitko, and Itzik *Kipnis. Despite his declared allegiance to Marxist criticism, he had to defend himself in 1932 against critics who accused him of "dangerous deviationism." Towards the end of the 1930s, the emphasis of his research shifted from the sociological aspects of literature towards the issues of style and psychology of literary characters. He continued to write fiction, including the story of Cracow Jews in the 17th century, *Kolev Ashkenazi* (1934, 1939²) and the unfinished novel *Baym Mitllendishn Yam* ("At the Mediterranean Sea," 1936) set in Venice of the first half of the 17th century. Some of Wiener's works were published posthumously in *Sovetish Heymland: the story *Los Khudios* ("The Jews"; 10, 1968), and his fascinating memoirs which include vivid descriptions of his family and the Jewish Cracow of his childhood and youth (9, 10, 1969). But his major novel, tentatively titled *Der Groyser Roman* ("The Great Novel"), portraying the Jewish literary and artistic scene of Berlin of the early 1920s in which Wiener actively participated, remains unpublished.

BIBLIOGRAPHY: LNYL, 3 (1960), 449–50; Ch. Shmeruk (ed.), *Pirsumim Yehudiyyim bi-Verit ha-Mo'aẓot* (1961), index; 466; G. Scholem, in: *Der Jude*, 6 (1921), 55–69; N. Mayzel, in: *Yidishe Kultur*, 1 (1965), 17–27; E. Rosenthal, in: *Di Goldene Keyt*, 66 (1969), 63–96. **ADD. BIBLIOGRAPHY:** E. Shulman, in: *Pinkas far Forshung fun der Yidisher Literatur un Prese*, 2 (1972), 77–144; M. Krutikov, in: R. Robertson and J. Sherman (eds.), *The Yiddish Presence in European Literature: Inspiration and Interaction* (2005), 73–86.

[Chone Shmeruk / Mikhail Krutikov (2nd ed.)]

WIENER, NORBERT (1894–1964), U.S. mathematician; inventor of the science of cybernetics. Born in Columbia, Missouri, Wiener was a child prodigy. He was the son of Leo *Wiener, historian of Yiddish language, literature, and folklore and professor of Slavic languages, who made incessant intellectual demands on his son (and who did not reveal their Jewishness – a fact discovered by Norbert Wiener only when he was in his teens). Wiener began to read scientific books at four, and by seven was familiar with the theories of natural scientists, such as Darwin, and with psychiatrists such as Charcot and Janet. He entered Tufts University at 11, and obtained his Ph.D. at Harvard University at 18. At Cambridge, England, he studied under such world-famous personalities as the philosopher Bertrand Russell and the mathematician G.H. Hardy. Wiener's main innovation as a mathematician was to develop a mathematics based upon imprecise terms reflecting the irregularities of the physical world. He sought to reduce these random movements to a minimum in order to bring them into harmony. During World War II, he applied his concepts to work connected with antiaircraft defense, and this led to advances in radar, high-speed electric computation, the automatic factory, and a new science he created called cybernetics, a word he coined from the Greek word for "steersman," meaning the study of control. This followed his attempt as a mathematician to find the basis of the communication of information, and of the control of a system based on such communication. Wiener suggested the use of cybernetics in diagnostic procedures and indicated the similarity between certain types of nervous pathology and servomechanism (goal-directed machines such as guns which correct their own fixing malfunctioning). His book *Cybernetics* (1948) was a scientific bestseller and transformed him into a public figure as the pioneer of computer development. For the last 17 years of his life he refused to take part in any military research. His book *The Human Use of Human Beings* (1950) sought to alert the layman to the dangerous social consequences of his theories. He wrote an autobiography in two parts: *Ex-Prodigy* (1953) and *I Am a Mathematician* (1956).

[Maurice Goldsmith]

WIENER, PHILIP PAUL (1905–1992), U.S. philosopher. Born in New York, Wiener taught at City College from 1933. He was a founder of the *Journal of the History of Ideas* (1940) and was its executive editor. In 1960 he became the vice president of the International Society for the History of Ideas, and in 1958–59 was the president of the Peirce Society. Wiener's interest was in examining the development of ideas in terms of their cultural connections and relationships.

He wrote *Evolution and the Founders of Pragmatism* (1949) and *Readings in Philosophy and Science* (1953); He edited works on the history and philosophy of science, on the history of ideas, and on C.S. Peirce, and translated works from the French. His edited works include *Leibnitz Selections* (1951); *Roots of Scientific Thought* (with A. Noland, 1957); *Ideas in Cultural Perspective* (with A. Noland, 1962); *Charles S. Peirce: Selected Writings* (1966); *Renaissance Essays* (with P. Kristeller, 1968); *Basic Problems of Philosophy* (et al., 1972); *The Dictionary of the History of Ideas* (1973); and *Violence and Aggression in the History of Ideas* (1974).

ADD. BIBLIOGRAPHY: J. Miller, *Evolution and the Founders of Pragmatism* (1950).

[Richard H. Popkin / Ruth Beloff (2nd ed.)]

WIENER, SAMUEL (1860–1929), Hebrew bibliographer. In 1887 Samuel Wiener was called upon by the Royal Academy of Sciences in St. Petersburg to work in its department of Hebrew and Yiddish books at the Asiatic Museum attached to the Academy. He assisted Moses Aryeh Leib *Friedland (1825–1899), the wealthy St. Petersburg communal worker and philanthropist, in acquiring and arranging a large and valuable collection of Hebrew books and manuscripts entrusted to the Asiatic Museum in 1892.

His large bibliographical work *Kohelet Moshe* (Bibliotheca Friedlandiana), which lists all the books in Hebrew characters of the Asian Museum, remained unfinished; the first seven volumes, covering the letters *alef* to *kaf* and a total of 5,507 entries, were published (1893–1918), and the eighth volume, containing the letter *lamed*, was edited by Joseph Bender, and published in 1936. This bibliography is unequaled in Hebrew for its accuracy and itemization. In his work *Reshimat Haggadot Pesaḥ* ("List of Passover *Haggadot*," 1901), Wiener describes about 900 Passover *Haggadot*. He also edited and completed the work of I.T. Eisenstadt, *Da'at Kedoshim* (1897–98).

BIBLIOGRAPHY: A. Marks, in: *Hadoar*, 8 (1929), 387 8; A. Tauber, in: KS, 6 (1930), 108; LNYL, 3 (1960), 451–2; E. Simon, in: *Mitteilungen der Soncino-Gesellschaft*, 6 (1930), 27–28.

[Gedalyah Elkoshi]

WIENER GESERA, persecutions of Jews in *Vienna and its environs in 1421. The early 15th century was a period of rising hatred of the burghers of Vienna against the Jews, kindled in part by Jewish wealth. The *Hussite heresy had widespread reverberations in Austria at the time, and it was generally held that Jews and Hussites maintained close contact. Duke Albert V, inclined to religious fanaticism and disturbed by the Hussite rebellion, was also deeply in debt to Jewish moneylenders and without the means of repayment. At Easter 1420 a rumor was spread among the population of Vienna that a rich Jew named Israel had bought consecrated *Hosts from the wife of a Church sexton in Enns, and distributed them among other Jews who desecrated them. The Jews who were implicated were brought to Vienna, imprisoned, and tortured. On May 23, 1420, the Jews were rounded up in all the cities and towns of Austria and their possessions taken from them. The wealthy were imprisoned in Vienna, while the poor were put into boats without oars on the Danube at the mercy of the stream. Some Jews were held captive in houses, others in the synagogues. Children were separated from parents and husbands from wives, and an attempt was made to convert them to Christianity. The rabbis of Italy appealed to Pope Martin V for his intervention on behalf of the Jews of Austria. He reacted by threatening with excommunication anyone who forced Jews to convert. Nonetheless, many of the children taken from their parents were carried off to monasteries and there forcibly converted. A great many of those imprisoned committed suicide, including those held in the synagogues; the last one alive, R. Jonah, set fire to the corpses and died on the funeral pyre. The Jews who were left, 120 women and 92 men, were burned at the stake on March 12, 1421. All the property of the Jews passed to Duke Albert. The stones of the synagogue were used in building the university. Some Jews escaped to Bohemia; a very few managed to maintain an illegal existence in Austria. The proud Vienna community numbering between 1,400 and 1,600 existed no longer, and the city became known in Jewish tradition as "Ir ha-Damim" ("The City of Blood").

BIBLIOGRAPHY: S. Krauss, *Die Wiener Gesera* (1920); M. Grunwald, *Vienna* (1836), 34–37: A. Zehavi-Goldhammer, in: *Arim ve-Immahot be-Yisrael*, 1 (1946), 191–3; O.H. Stowasser, *Zur Geschichte der Wiener Gesera von* 1421 (1920).

[B. Mordechai Ansbacher]

WIENER LIBRARY, Jewish information institute in London, founded in 1934 in Amsterdam as the Jewish Central Information Office, by David Cohen, its president, and Alfred *Wiener, its director. The aim of the institute was to communicate material on the realities of *national socialism to Jewish organizations and leaders for effective action with the authorities of their respective countries. It collected, inter alia, Nazi news publications (up to the end of World War II). The institute supplied information for the defense of David *Frankfurter and for the trial of the publishers of *The Protocols of the Elders of Zion* in Switzerland. At the end of 1938 a special collection of material on the November *Kristallnacht* was initiated. In the spring of 1939 the seat of the institute was transferred to London. The Amsterdam branch and most of its personnel became victims of the Nazis. During World War II the library collaborated with the British authorities and the BBC. Special stress was laid on the collection of material on war criminals, which was supplied to the International Military Tribunal in Nuremberg. In recognition of these services the library received the bulk of the copies of prosecution documents. In 1946 a bi-monthly, *The Wiener Library Bulletin*, was initiated. With volume XIX, no. 3 (1965), its publication ceased, but it was replaced by a new publication under the same title with a change in interests and contents. The 19 volumes are a treasure of information on Nazism, Fascism (including neo-Nazism and neo-Fascism), Jewish affairs, and the Holocaust in particular. After the death of Alfred Wiener in 1964, Walter Z. *Laqueur became director of the library. He inaugurated the *Journal of Contemporary History* (1966), catalogs of the book collection, and monographs on the library's research subjects. Four catalogs of the library had been previously published.

[Yehuda Reshef]

At the end of 1974 it was announced that the Wiener Library would be transferred to Tel Aviv University; the move was completed in 1980 with a microfilm library, covering periodicals, press archives, and rare books, to be maintained in London. From 1974 to 1980 Tel Aviv University contributed to the maintenance of the library in London. Despite the move of some of its holdings to Israel, it continues as the Institute of Contemporary History and Wiener Library, at Devonshire Street in central London. It contains one of the largest libraries of books and archives relating to the Holocaust period in Europe, over 50,000 items. Its director in 2005, Ben Barkow, was the author of *Alfred Wiener and the Making of the Holocaust Library* (1997). The Library publishes a newsletter and other works and holds lectures and conferences.

BIBLIOGRAPHY: J. Robinson and P. Friedman, *Guide to Jewish History under Nazi Impact* (1960), 108–9; Wiener Library; *The Wiener Library, Its History and Activities*, 1934–1945 (1946); R. Weltsch, in: YLBI, 9 (1964), xxix–xxx.

WIENER NEUSTADT, city in Lower Austria. Jews were living there soon after the city's foundation in 1192. Gravestones in the Jewish cemetery date from 1252 and 1261. In 1277 the rights of the Jews in the city were somewhat curtailed, but the Jewish community developed, flourishing in particular in the 15th century. In proximity to the synagogue were a square, a garden, and a poorhouse. The name of one communal leader, Joseph b. Moses Knoblauch, who "did many good deeds for the congregation," is mentioned in *Leket Yosher* (ed. by J. Freimann, 2 (1903), 40). In 1416, when the Jews of Wiener Neustadt were ordered to pay more than one-fifth of their income in taxes, a "communal regulation was drawn up for collection of the tax by two persons in authority and the other scholars among them" (Israel Isserlein, *Terumat ha-Deshen*). The Jews of Wiener Neustadt took part in its defense, and their rabbi "would permit them to do all manner of work on the Sabbath to protect [the city] from its enemies, in accordance with the instructions of the gentile citizens and noblemen" (*Leket Yosher*, pt. 1, 68).

From the mid-13th century on, many noted rabbis lived in Wiener Neustadt, including *Ḥayyim b. Moses; Moses *Taku; *Ḥayyim b. *Isaac; R. Shalom; Isaac *Tyrnau; and Israel *Isserlein. There was an important yeshivah there during the 15th century. In the second half of that century John *Capistrano visited Wiener Neustadt and preached against the Jews. After several anti-Jewish decrees, the Jews were expelled from the city in 1496. The synagogue was converted into a church. Refugees from Oedenburg (Sopron), Hungary, settled in the city in the early 18th century, totaling 535 persons in 1708. However, clerical agitation and popular pressure forced them to leave soon afterward. Jewish peddlers and merchants, mainly from nearby *Burgenland, continued to visit the city but they were not allowed to stay overnight. In 1848 J.H. Friedenthal settled in Wiener Neustadt, and by 1869 there were 173 Jews living there. Permission to open a cemetery was not granted until 1889. A Moorish-style synagogue was built in 1902; it served 1,059 persons in 1923 when Rabbi H. Weiss officiated.

In the early 1930s there were 1,300 Jews. In May of 1938, there were 347. During *Kristallnacht* (Nov. 9–10, 1938) homes, furniture, and bank accounts of Jews were confiscated by the S.A.; the Jews there who did not emigrate were expelled or transported to Vienna. In January 1968 three Jews lived in Wiener Neustadt.

BIBLIOGRAPHY: *Germania Judaica*; M. Pollak, *Juden in Wiener Neustadt* (1927); S. Eidelberg, *Jewish Life in Austria in the XVth Century* (1962); L. Moses, *Juden in Niederoesterreich* (1935), index; MHJ, 4 (1938), index s.v., *Newnstat*, 6 (1961); 8 (1965); 9 (1966), index s.v. *Bécsujhely*.

[Haim Hillel Ben-Sasson]

WIENIAWSKI, HENRI (1834–1880), Polish violinist and composer. Born in Lublin, Wieniawski entered the Paris Conservatory at the age of eight and three years later won the first prize in violin. After his first concert in St. Petersburg in 1848, he appeared in Finland, the Baltic provinces, and Poland. After further study in Paris (1849), he toured Europe with his brother Joseph, pianist, and in 1850 was appointed solo violinist to the czar. He taught at St. Petersburg for a year and then toured the U.S. with the pianist Anton *Rubinstein from 1872 to 1874. From 1874 to 1877 he taught in Brussels. Wieniawski's perfect technique, combined with warmth and delicacy, gained him wide admiration. After the fashion of other virtuosos, he also composed many works for the violin, including two concertos and his popular *Légende*, which he frequently played with his brother. His music is notable for its Slavic idiom and temperament, often exaggerated.

His brother, JOSEPH (1837–1912), studied in Paris and later in Weimar under Liszt. From 1866 he taught at the Moscow Conservatory and founded his own piano school. After a sojourn in Warsaw, where he directed the Music Society, 1875–76, he settled in Brussels and became professor at the conservatory. His works include a piano concerto, waltzes, mazurkas, and Études.

BIBLIOGRAPHY: J. Reiss, *Henryk Wieniawski* (Pol., 1931); I. Yampolski, *Genrik Venyavskiy* (Rus., 1955); L. Delacroix, *Joseph Wieniawski* (Fr., 1908); MGG, s.v.; Grove, Dict., s.v.

[Meir Katz]

WIERNIK, PETER (1865–1936), U.S. Yiddish journalist. Wiernik was born in Vilna, but emigrated to the U.S. in 1885 and settled in Chicago, where he wrote for the Yiddish Chicago Daily Courier. From 1901 to 1936 he was editor for New York's most important Yiddish daily, the *Jewish Morning Journal*. His editorials, possessed of intelligence, good taste and tolerance, advocated a fusion of modern Orthodoxy and Americanism, and evinced a coolness to political Zionism and hostility to socialism. In addition to Yiddish, he also wrote in Hebrew and English, and was for a time editor of the *Amerikaner*. Besides the editorials, Wiernik's most important work was his *History of the Jews in America* (1912; 1931, reprinted 1972). His Yiddish autobiography, written in 1934, appeared weekly in the *Morning Journal*, Sept. 2–Dec. 23, 1951. He was also active in communal matters and was a member of the executive of the Joint Distribution Committee.

BIBLIOGRAPHY: Reisen, *Lexicon*, 1, 990–93, LNYL, I–II, 456–59.

[Joseph Hirsch (2nd ed.)]

WIERNIKORSKI, JUDAH (1823–1901), Russian rabbi. Born in Slonim, Judah was known as an *illui* ("child prodigy"). At the age of 10, he is said to have been completely conversant with three of the six orders of the Talmud: *Mo'ed*, *Nashim*, and *Nezikin*. At the age of 11, he married a cousin and remained in his father-in-law's house until he was 13. He then went to study with R. Isaac of Volozhin and in 1840 under R. Israel *Lipkin in Vilna. Deciding to devote himself to teaching rather than accept a rabbinical appointment, Judah was given the position of *rosh yeshivah* of Slonim by R. Joshua Isaac in 1861. He remained there until 1900 when he immigrated to Ereẓ Israel to spend his last days. He died in Jerusalem.

His works include *Penei Yehudah*, novellae on the tractates *Shabbat* and *Ketubbot* (1870); *Leket Yehudah*, sermons (1872); and *Penei Yehudah* on *Bava Kamma* and *Keritot* (1890). The manuscript of his *Penei Yehudah* on *Pesaḥim* and a commentary on the *Sefer ha-Bahir* ascribed to *Neḥunya b. ha-Kanah were burnt in a fire in his town.

BIBLIOGRAPHY: *Aḥi' asaf*, 9 (1901), 428–9.

WIERUSZOWSKI, HELENE (1893–1978), German-U.S. historian. Born in Elberfeld, her career in historical research was ended in 1933 by the Nazis. After teaching in Spain and Italy, she emigrated to the United States in 1940. In 1949 she joined the history faculty at City College, New York, becoming the first full-time female member of City College's department of history. Her most important books are *Vom Imperium zum nationalen Koenigtum* (1933), *The Era of Charlemagne* (with S. Easton, 1961), *The Medieval University* (1966), and *Politics and Culture in Medieval Spain and Italy* (1971). She wrote an essay on "Peter von Aragon und die Juden; Eine Politik des gerechten Ausgleichs" (in *Estudis Universitares Catalans*, 22 (1936), 239–62).

ADD. BIBLIOGRAPHY: E. Polak, *A Medievalist's Odyssey: Helene Wieruszowski, Scholar* (2004).

WIESBADEN, city in Germany. Individual Jews lived in Wiesbaden in the 14th and 15th centuries. During the 16th century the local count gave them protection against the opposition of the city. In 1620 a number of Jewish refugees arrived there but had to leave after six years. Other Jews, however, were permitted to reside there from 1638. They numbered five families in 1697, nine in 1724, and 11 in 1747. At that time a synagogue, cemetery, and a bathhouse were established. The countess Charlotte in 1732 prohibited the establishment of further synagogues, the public discussion of religion, and profits on moneylending exceeding 5–6 percent. By 1803 there were 14 Jewish families living in Wiesbaden and 42 in the vicinity. Abraham *Geiger introduced his first reforms while acting as rabbi there (1832–38). Forty Orthodox families established an independent community in 1876. The Jewish population numbered 990 in 1875; 2,744 (2.5 percent of the total) in 1910; 3,088 (3 percent) in 1925; 2,713 (1.7 percent) in 1933; and 1,232 (0.7 percent) in 1939. The teacher and reader of the adjacent community of Biebrich was the celebrated scholar Seligmann *Baer. The community maintained a number of educational and welfare institutions, including a "Lehrhaus" for Jewish adult education.

After the rise of the Nazis to power, the Jews of Wiesbaden suffered persecution like those in the rest of Germany. The synagogues were burned in 1938. In 1942, 1,100 Jews were deported from Wiesbaden; during August 1942, 40 Jews committed suicide.

In 1965 there were 350 Jews living in Wiesbaden (0.1 percent of the total population). A new synagogue was opened in 1966. The Jewish community numbered 319 in 1989; 400 in 1990; and 692 in 2004. The increase is explained by the immigration of Jews from the former Soviet Union. A small museum, financed by the city, has an exhibition of the Jewish history of Wiesbaden.

BIBLIOGRAPHY: P. Lazarus, *Die juedische Gemeinde Wiesbaden 1918–1947*, (1949); H. Thomae (ed.), *Weg und Schicksal. Aus der Geschichte der Wiesbadener Juden* (1966); *Germania Judaica*, 2 (1968), 904; 3 (1987), 1642–43; *Festschrift zur Fuenfzigjahrfeier des Synagogen-Gesangvereins zu Wiesbaden* (1913). **ADD BIBLIOGRAPHY:** B. Post (ed.), *Juden in Wiesbaden. Von der Jahrhundertwende bis zur "Reichskristallnacht"* (1988); D. Lottmann-Kaeseler (ed.), *Osteuropaeisches Judentum in Wiesbaden* (1991) (Begegnungen, vol. 2); L. Bembenek and H. Dickel, "Ich bin kein deutscher Patriot mehr, jetzt bin ich Jude," in: *Die Vertreibung juedischer Buerger aus Wiesbaden (1933 bis 1947)* (1991); H-G. Buschmann and E. Vollmer, *Die sieben juedischen Friedhoefe Wiesbadens* (1997). **WEBSITE:** www.am-spiegelgasse.de.

[Ze'ev Wilhem Falk]

WIESEL, ELIE (Eliezer; 1928–), journalist, novelist, professor, human rights activist, and Nobel Peace Prize recipient. Born in Sighet, Romania, in a town that became part of Hungary in 1940, Wiesel was raised in a fervently Orthodox and ḥasidic milieu. Prior to 1944, life in Sighet seemed normal, at least to a young studious boy. The Germans invaded Hungary in March 1944, Jews were ghettoized in April, and in May 1944, Elie, his parents, and three sisters were deported along with the rest of Sighet's Jews to Auschwitz, where his mother and younger sister were killed and he survived with his father and two older sisters. He remained in Auschwitz until the infamous death marches of January 1945 and then was forcibly evacuated to Buchenwald, where his father died from exhaustion, starvation, and despair. After his liberation at the Buchenwald concentration camp on April 11, 1945, he was among the 400 Jewish war orphans transferred by the Oeuvre de Secours aux Enfants (Children's Aid Society) to France, where he was later reunited with his older sisters, Hilda and Bea. From 1948 to 1951, he studied philosophy, psychology, and literature at the Sorbonne, and continued his Jewish learning with a talmudic scholar named Shushani, a figure who later would appear in a number of his novels and lectures. He supported himself by writing for the French newspaper *L'Arche* and the Israeli daily *Yedioth Aharonoth*. Wiesel was drawn to the writings of the contemporary French existentialists Albert Camus, André Malraux, and Jean-Paul Sartre, and the Catholic writer François Mauriac, who encouraged the young reporter to write about the suffering of the Jews in the Nazi death camps.

Wiesel had in fact taken notes of his experiences and thoughts from the first days of his liberation, even while recovering in the hospital. He felt compelled "to trace the tragedy back to its origins and causes," but fearing that the event was "so profound that it cannot be transmitted at all," he vowed to wait ten years before publishing a book on the subject. In 1956, the same year he left Paris and settled in New York, Wiesel's 250-page abbreviated memoir of life in the camps, *Und di Velt hot Geschvign* ("And the World Was Silent"), appeared in Buenos Aires. An abridged version, translated from Yiddish to French (*La Nuit*) with an introduction by François Mauriac, was issued in 1958, and two years later in English (*Night*). A classic in Holocaust literature that is widely used in high schools and colleges, *Night* paved the way for publication of other first-person accounts by Shoah survivors, whom Wiesel recalls "were afraid or shamed to broach the subject."

Night was followed by two novels, *L'Aube* (1960; *Dawn*, 1961) and *Le jour* (1961; *The Accident*, 1962), both dealing with the postwar experiences of Holocaust survivors. Writing in French, Wiesel established his characteristic themes and storytelling style in three subsequent novels: *La ville de la chance* (1962; *The Town Beyond the Wall*, 1964), *Les portes de la forêt* (1966; *The Gates of the Forest*, 1966), and *Le mendiant de Jérusalem* (1968; *A Beggar in Jerusalem*, 1970), which won the Prix Medicis in Paris. Wiesel also publicized the plight of Soviet Jews in a nonfiction account based on his visit to the Soviet Union, *Les Juifs du silence* (1966; *The Jews of Silence*, 1966).

Wiesel's essays on the importance of memory and the struggle against injustice in a post-Holocaust world are included in several collections: *Le chant des morts* (1966; *Legends of Our Time*, 1968), *Entre deux soleils* (1970; *One Generation After*, 1970), *Un Juif aujourd'hui* (1977; *A Jew Today*, 1978), and the three-volume collection, edited by Irving Abrahamson, *Against Silence: The Voice and Vision of Elie Wiesel* (1985). His later essay collections include *From the Kingdom of Memory* (1990) and *After the Darkness* (2002). His autobiography appeared in two volumes: *Tous les fleuves vont à la mer* (1994; *All Rivers Run to the Sea*, 1995) and *Et la mer n'est pas remplie* (1996; *And the Sea Is Never Full*, 1999).

Drawing on his childhood ḥasidic roots, Wiesel based several books on the stories and folklore of famous *rebbes*, their religious struggles and the battles they waged against despair: *Célébration hassidique* (1972; *Souls on Fire*, 1972), *Four Hasidic Masters* (1978), and *Contre la mélancolie: celebration hassidique II* (1981; *Somewhere a Master*, 1982). From 1967, Wiesel gave an annual lecture series at New York's 92nd Street Y, popularizing Jewish learning and the midrashic style of teaching. These and other lectures, which focus on portraits of biblical, rabbinic, and ḥasidic figures, are collected in *Célébration biblique* (1975; *Messengers of God*, 1976), *Images from the Bible* (1980), *Five Biblical Portraits* (1981), *Silences et mémoire d'hommes* (1989), *Sages and Dreamers* (1991), and *Wise Men and Their Tales* (2003).

Wiesel wrote two plays – *Zalmen, ou la folie de Dieu* (1968; *Zalmen, or the Madness of God*, 1974) and *Le procès de Shamgorod* (1979; *The Trial of God*, 1979), and a cantata, *Ani Maamin* (music by Darius Milhaud, 1973). The idea of *The Trial of God* came from an event he witnessed in Auschwitz – a *bet din* called to put God on trial for failing to act. This play, with its perplexing, unanswered questions, generated considerable dialogue with Christian theologians. As Wiesel wrote in *Night*, "I did not deny God's existence, but I doubted His absolute justice." Many of Wiesel's works question God's silence, but even more, they question human silence in the face of persecution and injustice.

Wiesel wrote several essays emphasizing the importance of historical memory, particularly in reaction to Holocaust deniers and anti-Zionists. "Anyone who does not actively, constantly engage in remembering and making others remember," he wrote, "is an accomplice of the enemy." For Wiesel, the Holocaust is "the ultimate event" that has changed everything that follows and consequently should change our response to human suffering. This theme reverberates through his later novels: *Le serment de Kolvillag* (1973; *The Oath*, 1973), *Le testament d'un poète juif assassiné* (1980; *The Testament*, 1981), *Le cinquième fils* (1983; *The Fifth Son*, 1985), *Le crépuscle, au loin* (1987; *Twilight*, 1988), *L'oublié* (1989, *The Forgotten*, 1992), *Les juges* (1999; *The Judges*, 2002), and *Le temps des déracinés* (2002; *The Time of the Uprooted*, 2005). His books are written in French, and many were translated into English by his wife, Marion (married 1969; they have one son, Elisha).

Wiesel has taught the humanities, religion, philosophy, and literature at several colleges and universities, including City College, City University of New York from 1972 to 1976, Yale University from 1982 to 1983 as a Henry Luce Visiting Scholar, and Boston University in 1976. As a survivor, author, professor, and public figure (he was the chairman of the United States President's Commission on the Holocaust, then founding chairman of the United States Holocaust Memorial Council in Washington, D.C.), Wiesel has leveraged his moral authority in support of the State of Israel, Soviet Jewry, and oppressed peoples everywhere. He brought world attention to the plight of Miskito Indians in Nicaragua, Cambodian refugees, South Africans under apartheid, Muslims in Bosnia, Tutsis in Rwanda, Sudanese in Darfur, and other victimized groups. Wiesel was also a vocal critic of those who would dishonor the memory of the victims by the denial, trivialization, or political exploitation of the Holocaust. His most famous intervention came on April 19, 1985, on the occasion of President Ronald Reagan's presenting him with the United States Congressional Gold Medal. Wiesel publicly implored the president to cancel his planned visit to the cemetery in Bitburg, Germany, where members of the SS are buried. Speaking "truth to power," Wiesel stated, "that place is not your place, Mr. President. Your place is with the victims of the SS."

Wiesel received a number of international honors, including the Nobel Peace Prize (1986); *Grand-Croix de la Légion d'Honneur* (France, 2001); *Grã-Cruz da Ordem Nacional do Cruzeiro do Sul* (Brazil, 2001); Order of Merit of the Republic of Hungary (2004); the King Hussein Award of the Hashemite Kingdom of Jordan (2005); and more than 100 honorary degrees from universities worldwide.

In awarding him the Peace Prize, Nobel Committee Chairman Egil Aarvik characterized Wiesel as "a man who has gone from utter humiliation" to become a "messenger to mankind… to awaken our conscience, because our indifference to evil makes us partners in the crime." In 1987, using his Nobel Prize money, he and his wife, Marion, established the Elie Wiesel Foundation for Humanity, which organizes international conferences in pursuit of strategies to combat hatred and indifference.

Refusing to surrender to despair, Wiesel's literary works and public activism continue to stress "the importance of remaining human in an inhumane world, of affirming hope in man – in spite of man."

[Aron Hirt Manheimer and Bonny V. Fetterman (2nd ed.)]

WIESELTIER, MEIR (1941–), Hebrew poet and translator. Born in Moscow, Wieseltier came to Israel as an eight-year-old child. He grew up in Netanyah and later studied English literature, history, and philosophy at the Hebrew University. In the early 1960s, having spent some time in England and France, he became one of the leading figures of the so-called "Tel Aviv Circle" (with Yona *Wallach and Yair Hurvitz) which sought to break with the ironic, impersonal, and non-political writing of poets such as Nathan *Zach and imbue Hebrew poetry with a refreshing, avantgardist and experimental spirit. Wieseltier was co-founder of the literary magazine *Siman Keriah*. His first collection of poems, *Perek Alef, Perek Beit* ("Chapter 1, Chapter 2"), appeared in 1967, followed two years later by *Meah Shirim* ("100 Poems"). Other collections include *Kaḥ* ("Take It," 1973), *Davar Optimi, Asiyat Shirim* ("Something Optimistic, The Making of Poems," 1976), *Penim va-Ḥuẓ* ("Interior and Exterior," 1977), *Moẓa el ha-Yam* ("Exit into the Sea," 1981), *Kiẓẓur Shenot ha-Shishim* ("The Concise Sixties," 1984), Ii *Yevani* ("Greek Island," 1985), *Mikhtavim ve-Shirim Aḥerim* ("Letters and Other Poems," 1986), and *Maḥsan* ("Storehouse," 1994). Wieseltier's poetry is subjective, often unconventional in diction and tone, and occasionally deliberately full of pathos. Loss, death, and the ambiguities of the human predicament are the major themes of his oeuvre. Underlying some of the poems is a pronounced disdain for bourgeois norms and superficial ideologies and at the same time an ambivalent relationship to Tel Aviv, the city in which he resides. His "poetry of iconoclasm," as it was once defined, shows the influence of French surrealism and of modern Anglo-American poetry. Wieseltier is also known as one of the finest translators of English, French, and Russian poetry into Hebrew. He translated a number of Shakespearean tragedies and novels by Virginia Woolf, E.M. Forster, and Charles Dickens. In 2000 he was awarded the Israel Prize for literature. A collection of selected poems in English translation appeared under the title *The Flower of Anarchy* in 2003; individual poems have been translated into various languages. Further information concerning translation is available at the ITHL website at www.ithl.org.il.

BIBLIOGRAPHY: E. Sharoni, "Poem-Making as Life's Way of Struggle," in: *Modern Hebrew Literature*, 3:3 (1977), 41–47; Y. Hurvitz, "*Ha-Sha'ot ha-Gedolot ve-ha-Temunah ha-Nidaḥat*," in: *Siman Keriah*, 7 (1977), 464–67; O. Bartana, "*Lo Navi be-Doro*," in: *Davar* (September 21, 1984); Y. Besser, "*Ha-Ra'av le-Millim ve-Koved ha-Adamah*," in: *Yedioth Aharonoth* (August 7, 1981); M. Perri, "*Kol ha-Guf Panim*," in: *Siman Keriah*, 18 (1986), 402–12; G. Moked, "*Al 'Mikhtavim' shel M. Wieseltier*," in: *Akhshav*, 51–54 (1986), 548–51; Y. Oppenheimer, "*Dibbur ke-Davar Optimi: Al M. Wieseltier*," in: *Ḥadarim*, 6 (1987), 70–80; Sh. Yaniv, "Wieseltier and the Evolution of the Modern Hebrew Ballad," in: *Prooftexts*, 9:3 (1989), 229–46; A. Hirschfeld, "*Mul ha-Even ha-Kashah ha-Mitkatevet*," in: *Efes Shetayim*, 2 (1993), 34–43; S. Nash, "*Elohim ve-Adam be-Shirat M. Wieseltier*," in: *Hadoar*, 81:10 (2002), 27–29; N. Buchwitz, "*Shittut be-Merḥav Lo Mukar: Safah Poetit Ḥadashah bi-Khtivato shel Wieseltier ha-Ẓa'ir*," in: *Alei Siaḥ*, 48 (2002), 106–21; idem, "*Ha-Postmoderniyyim ha-Rishonim*," in: *Gag*, 10 (2004), 26–43.

[Anat Feinberg (2nd ed.)]

WIESENTHAL, SIMON (1908–2005), the world's most famous "Nazi-hunter," the personification of the efforts to bring Nazi war criminals to justice after World War II. Born in the Galician city of Buczacz, then part of the Austro-Hungarian Empire and after World War I part of independent Poland (today located in Ukraine), Wiesenthal was forced to study architectural engineering at the Technical University in Prague due to restrictive Polish quotas on Jewish students. After completing his studies, he returned to Poland, obtained certification as an architect, and began working in his profession in the (then) Polish city of Lwow (Lvov).

During World War II, Wiesenthal was incarcerated in nine concentration and labor camps, among them Janowska, Plaszow, Auschwitz, Gross-Rosen, and Mauthausen, from which he was liberated, barely alive, on May 5, 1945, by the United States Army. During the course of the war, he narrowly escaped death several times, and twice attempted to commit suicide to avoid being tortured. It was these close encounters with almost certain death, and his conviction that many Jews far more worthy than himself had perished in the war, to which he attributed his strong motivation to lend significance to his own survival. A postwar incident, shortly after liberation, in which Wiesenthal was beaten by a former kapo in Mauthausen, who was summarily punished by the American commander of the camp, who assured the Jewish survivor that the supremacy of the rule of law had been restored, deeply influenced his decision to abandon his profession and devote his life to the efforts to facilitate the prosecution of Holocaust perpetrators.

Wiesenthal began his career with the War Crimes Unit of the U.S. Army in Austria and later, in 1947, established the Jewish Historical Documentation Center in Linz, where he collected the testimonies of hundreds of Holocaust survivors. In 1954, however, Wiesenthal closed the center due to waning interest in the prosecution of Nazi war criminals, which he primarily attributed to the growing tensions of the Cold War. In his opinion, the perpetrators of the Holocaust were the biggest beneficiaries of the hostility between the superpowers, which severely limited the efforts to bring them to justice. He sent his files to Yad Vashem, and went to work for Jewish organizations assisting refugees from Eastern Europe.

In 1961, however, following the *Eichmann trial in Jerusalem, Wiesenthal opened the Documentation Center in Vienna and resumed his efforts to bring Nazi war criminals to justice, a mission which he continued virtually until his death. Although he played no role in the actual capture of Eichmann, who was kidnapped by the Mossad in Argentina in 1960 and brought to Israel to stand trial, Wiesenthal gained international stature due to his connection to the case. In 1947 he had prevented Eichmann's wife, Vera, from having Eichmann declared officially dead by an Austrian court (which would have led to the removal of his name from the lists of wanted criminals) and was the first to point to Argentina as his possible haven. After he closed his office in 1954, Eichmann's file was the only one he kept.

Over the years, Wiesenthal played a crucial role in the exposure and apprehension of numerous Nazi war criminals, many of whom were prosecuted and punished. Among his most famous cases were those of Treblinka and Sobibor commandant Franz Stangl, whom he tracked down to Brazil; notoriously cruel Majdanek guard Hermine Braunsteiner Ryan, whom he found in the United States; Sobibor deputy commander Franz Gustav Wagner (Brazil); and Karl Silberbauer (Austria), the Gestapo operative who arrested Anne *Frank and her family in their hiding place in Amsterdam. In addition, Wiesenthal played a prominent role in the ultimately successful worldwide efforts to convince the West German government not to impose a statute of limitations on the prosecution of Nazi war criminals whose implementation was scheduled to go into effect in 1979.

Throughout his life, Wiesenthal stressed the importance of remembering the crimes of the Holocaust and preserving the accuracy of the historical record. In that respect, he achieved worldwide status as a spokesperson for both the survivors and the victims of the Holocaust, an achievement which perhaps surpasses his role as a "Nazi-hunter." His accomplishments in this role were largely significant during the 1950s and 1960s, when there was little public interest in the subject of the Holocaust.

Wiesenthal's work was guided by three major principles: the primacy of the rule of law, his refusal to categorize people by their religion or ethnic origin, and the importance of noting the fate of the Nazis' non-Jewish victims. Thus he steadfastly opposed revenge attempts, emphasized the fact that the nations that produced killers also had Righteous Gentiles, and consistently stressed the fact that the Jews were not the Nazis' only victims. These points found expression in the numerous books he wrote, especially in his best-known works, *The Murderers among Us* (1970) and *Justice Not Vengeance* (1989). In *The Sunflower* (1970) and the novel *Max and Helen* (1982), he explored the themes of forgiveness and reconciliation.

A stubborn defender of his views, Wiesenthal was involved in two well-publicized controversies, one with Austrian chancellor Bruno *Kreisky, whom he criticized for including former Nazis in his government, and a second with the World Jewish Congress, which questioned his apparent lack of enthusiasm for their campaign to prosecute Austrian president (and former UN secretary-general) Kurt Waldheim for war crimes he ostensibly committed during World War II. Various detractors accused him of claming credit for the achievements of others, particularly in the Eichmann case.

In 1979, the *Simon Wiesenthal Center was established by Rabbi Marvin *Hier in Los Angeles. While a separate organization, its high-profile activities, both in the fight against antisemitism and the continued efforts to bring Nazi war criminals to justice, have added to Wiesenthal's international stature and fame, though his association with the organization that bore his name was limited. The recipient of numerous honors, doctorates, and prizes, his efforts to perpetuate the memory of the victims and hold their killers responsible were most appreciated during his last years, when public interest in the Holocaust reached unprecedented heights.

[Efraim Zuroff (2nd ed.)]

WIESNER, JEROME BERT (1915–1994), U.S. electrical engineer and educator; president of the Massachusetts Institute of Technology (MIT). Wiesner, who was born in Detroit, Michigan, was associate director of the broadcasting station at the University of Michigan from 1937 to 1940 and assisted in developing modern electronic techniques for use in the speech department. In 1940 Wiesner was appointed chief engineer of the Acoustical and Record Laboratory in the Library of Congress. During World War II, he was consecutively: associate leader of the radio frequency development group at MIT's radiation laboratory; project engineer of a key radar development program; group leader of Project Cadillac which was assigned to devise an airborne radar system; and a member of the Los Alamos Laboratory staff (1945). Wiesner returned to MIT as assistant professor (1946), and subsequently held several other university posts before being appointed provost in 1966. In 1971 he was named its president – the first Jew to be appointed to that position, which he held until 1980. He was a member of the President's Science Advisory Committee (1957), served as staff director of the American Delegation to the Geneva Conference for the Prevention of Surprise Attack (1958), and in 1961 was appointed special assistant for science and technology by President Kennedy. From 1962 to 1964 he was director of the Office of Science and Technology. Wiesner played an important role in the development of the concept of scatter transmission and in the application of statistical methods to communications engineering. He was a member of the board of governors of the Weizmann Institute from 1964, and advised on education and science policy in Israel. He wrote *Where Science and Politics Meet* (1964).

WIESNER, JULIUS VON (1838–1916), Austrian botanist. Born in Moravia, Wiesner showed an early bent for botany, publishing his first scientific paper, on the flora of the vicinity of Brno, when he was hardly 16 years old. After receiving his Ph.D. at the age of 22, he taught plant physiology at the Vienna Polytechnic Institute and at Mariabrunn. In 1873, Wiesner was made professor of plant anatomy and physiology at the University of Vienna, where he remained for 36 years, until his retirement in 1909. Wiesner was one of the founders of modern economic botany.

His major work in this area was *Die Rohstoffe des Pflanzenreiches* (1873), a comprehensive treatment of the world's plants as sources of gums, resins, fibers, and other economically valuable products. No less outstanding were Wiesner's contributions to basic botanical science. He did important research on the effect of light on plants, on the process of chlorophyll formation, and on the power of movement in plants. In his *Die Elementarstructur und das Wachstum der lebenden Substanz* (1892), Wiesner put forward a theory (now only of historical interest) that the cell is not the ultimate unit of life but is composed of simpler elementary units, which he called "plasomes."

BIBLIOGRAPHY: K. Linsbauer et al. (eds.), *Wiesner und seine Schule* (1903); Molisch, in: *Berichte der deutschen botanischen Gesellschaft*, 34 (1916), 88–99.

[Mordecai L. Gabriel]

WIEVIORKA, ANNETTE (1948–), historian. She was born in Paris to a Jewish family of Polish origin. Her grandfather Aby was a noted Parisian Yiddish poet and a translator from Yiddish into French. In her youth, Wieviorka was a convinced Maoist who went to China with her husband and her son, and worked as a French teacher in Canton, between 1974 and 1976. She wrote a book about her experience in China (*L'écureuil de Chine*, 1979). A high school teacher in Paris from 1976 to 1990, she started doing research in French history and opened a new field, the history of collective memory of the Holocaust in France. Her important dissertation on the making of the memory of deportation in France just after the liberation, published in 1992, proved to be a pathbreaking work. In her book she thoroughly studied the way French public opinion discovered the atrocities of the Nazi camps, and how the French administrations and the French army helped in liberating the camps. In addition, she focused on the reception of the very first testimonies given in France by Jewish survivors. In her complete scanning of these testimonies, she argued that, far from being shy of testifying, the survivors were immediately active in trying to describe the horror they had witnessed and had gone through, but that nobody was then ready to hear their statements: the handful of survivors wrote numerous books, which were not read. With the passing of time, the French leaders were ready to acknowledge the sufferings of Resistance fighter deportees, more of whom survived their deportation as they were not sent to Auschwitz. The historian concluded that "Buchenwald masked Auschwitz." As a researcher Wieviorka entered the National Center for Scientific Research (CNRS) in 1990, and she continued her work on the memory of the Holocaust in France. Among many other books, she wrote a short work, *The Era of the Witness* (*L'ère du témoin*, 1998; English, 2006), in which she asserted the central role of witnesses in the remembrance of the Shoah in contrast to works of scientific research. Starting in 1961 with the Eichmann trial in Jerusalem, she described this trend up to the early 21st century, when the words of an Auschwitz survivor are almost sanctified. Between 1997 and 2000, she was a member of the official commission, appointed by the prime minister, in charge of searching for looted Jewish assets and properties in France. An advocate for the rights of Jewish families to fully recover what had been taken, she explained the necessity of this research to appease the tensions that arose in France. In France, Wieviorka is a public figure, who regularly appears in the media to explain the Holocaust to a wider audience. Her short book on Auschwitz, targeting a teenage audience, *Auschwitz expliqué à ma fille* (1999), is a worldwide bestseller, translated into a dozen languages. Her publications include *Les livres du souvenir, mémoriaux juifs de Pologne* (1983); *Le procès Eichmann* (1989); *Déportation et génocide, entre la mémoire et l'oubli* (1992); *Mille ans de cultures ashkénazes* (ed. et al., 1994); *Passant, souviens toi…* (1995); *Le Procès de Nuremberg* (1995); *Les Procès de Nuremberg et de Tokyo* (1996); and *Auschwitz, 60 ans après* (2005).

[Jean-Marc Dreyfus (2nd ed.)]

WIGNER, EUGENE PAUL (1902–1995), Nobel laureate in physics. Wigner was born in Budapest and was one of a small number of extraordinarily talented Hungarian-born physicists who contributed to the transformation of Newtonian physics. Wigner obtained his doctorate from the Technische Hochschule (later Universitaet) in Berlin in 1925, where his contacts with physicists of equal standing were established at colloquia of the German Physical Society. He worked at a Kaiser Wilhelm Institute, followed by the University of Goettingen, until his recruitment by Princeton University in 1930, a move precipitated by his early perception of the Nazi menace. In 1936–38 he worked at the University of Wisconsin before returning to Princeton. He moved to the University of Chicago (1942–45) to contribute to the Manhattan Project, before becoming director of research and development at the Clinton Laboratories (later Oak Ridge National Laboratory) (1946–48). However, from preference for teaching and research, he returned to Princeton for the rest of his career. His main interests in theoretical physics concerned quantum mechanics and nuclear reactions but later became more philosophical. He was awarded the Nobel Prize in 1963 (jointly with Maria Goeppert-Mayer and Hans Jensen) for the invariance principle, which concerns the rules governing observable physical events. He was also a practical engineer. His involvement in the Manhattan Project arose from his fear that the Nazis might develop nuclear weapons, and he helped to prepare Einstein's letter to President Roosevelt. He contributed to the design of the first experimental fission reactor in Chicago and the first reactor for plutonium production at Hanford. His honors included the U.S. Medal of Merit (1946), the Fermi Prize (1958), the Atoms for Peace Award (1960), and the U.S. National Medal of Science (1969). In 1970 he was elected a fellow of the Royal Society and other learned societies, including the National

Academy of Sciences and the American Academy of Art and Sciences. He was a member of the General Advisory Committee to the U.S. Atomic Energy Commission from 1952 to 1957, was reappointed to the Committee in 1959, and served on it until 1964.

[Michael Denman (2nd ed.)]

WIGODER, BASIL THOMAS, BARON (1921–2004), British lawyer. Wigoder was born in Manchester, son of Philip I. Wigoder, a prominent local Zionist, and educated at Manchester Grammar School and Oxford. At Oxford he was president of the Union. After his military service in World War II, he joined the Liberal Party and unsuccessfully contested a number of elections. From 1963 to 1965 he was chairman of the Liberal Party executive and in 1965–66 of the Liberal Party Organizing Committee. He ceased much of his political activity in the mid-1960s and concentrated on his legal work, acquiring recognition through his appearances in leading criminal cases. In 1966 he was made a Queen's Counsel and in 1971 a Recorder of the Crown Court. In 1974 he was created a life peer, and served as Liberal Whip in the House of Lords.

WIGODER, GEOFFREY (1922–1999), editor. Born in Leeds, England, Wigoder was educated at Trinity College, Dublin, Oxford, Jews' College, London, and the Jewish Theological Seminary, New York. In 1949 he settled in Jerusalem. He was director of Israeli radio's Overseas Broadcasts, founder-director of the Oral History department and Jewish Film Archives in the Hebrew University's Institute of Contemporary Jewry, historical adviser to the Diaspora Museum (Beth Hatefutsoth) in Tel Aviv, and founder-director of the Steven Spielberg Film Center at the Hebrew University. In 1991 he was visiting professor of Modern Jewish Studies at the University of Manchester. Wigoder succeeded Cecil Roth as editor in chief of the *Encyclopaedia Judaica* in 1970 (having previously been deputy editor in chief) and edited its year books from 1981 and the CD-ROM edition. He is author of *Abraham ben Hayya's Meditation of the Sad Soul, The Story of the Synagogue, Jewish-Christian Relations after World War II*, and *Jewish Culture.* He edited many reference works, including *The Standard Jewish Encyclopedia, Dictionary of Jewish Biography, Encyclopedia of Judaism, The Oxford Dictionary of the Jewish Religion* (with R.J.Z. Werblowsky), *New Encyclopedia of Zionism and Israel, Illustrated Dictionary and Concordance of the Bible, Jewish Art and Civilization*, and the three-volume *Encyclopedia of Jewish Life Before and During the Holocaust.*

Wigoder was one of the pioneers in the field of interfaith relations and Jewish-Christian dialogue. He served as the Israeli representative of the International Jewish Committee for Inter-Religious Consultations for over 20 years, becoming its chairman late in life.

WIHL, LUDWIG (1807–1882), German poet and journalist. Born in Wevelinghofen, near Aachen, Wihl received a good Jewish education and then studied philosophy and Oriental languages. His doctoral thesis on Phoenician inscriptions so impressed his teacher at the Munich University, the philosopher F.W. von Schelling, that he was recommended for a professorship. As he refused to abandon Judaism, the post was denied him, and he had to earn his living as a journalist. Wihl contributed to the periodicals of the Young Germany movement, especially to *Gutzkow's *Phoenix*. After the publication of his first volume of poems in 1836 he visited Paris. There he met *Heine, about whom he wrote in unflattering terms, and Heine's retaliatory attack was so vicious that it destroyed Wihl's reputation as a poet. During the revolution of 1848 Wihl published an article which was so outspoken that he had to flee to France to escape a prison sentence. He taught German literature and philosophy at Grenoble until the outbreak of the Franco-Prussian War in 1870, when he sought a final refuge in Brussels.

Wihl's works include *Geschichte der deutschen Nationalliteratur* (Altona, 1840); *Westoestliche Schwalben* (Mannheim, 1847), a collection of verse; and *Le mendiant pour la Pologne* (Paris, 1864), poems in French and German.

BIBLIOGRAPHY: L. Fraenkel, in: ADB, 42 (1897), 469–72 (incl. bibl.); T. Zlocisti, in: *Ost und West*, 1 (1901), 269–70.

[Sol Liptzin]

WIJNKOOP, DAVID (1876–1941), Dutch Communist. Born in Amsterdam, Wijnkoop was the son of the Amsterdam rabbi Joseph David (1842–1910), who manifested himself as a "*rebbe* of the people," a position, which led to a serious break with the chief rabbi of Amsterdam, J.H. Dünner (1833–1911). This conflict was one of the factors which turned his son, David, into a rebel. David Wijnkoop, future first leader and talented propagandist of Dutch Communism, was attracted to Marxism as a student. At first he joined the Labor Party (SDAP) and in 1905 he became a member of its executive. But as one of the founders of the radical-Marxist newspaper *De Tribune* he was expelled from the party. In 1909 Wijnkoop founded his own social democratic party, initially called the Social Democratic Party, which became the Communist Party of Holland (CPH; later: CPN) in 1918. He was the CPH's chairman and sat in the Second Chamber of parliament from 1918 to 1940 as a Communist representative. He was also a member of the Amsterdam municipal council and the North Holland provincial council. Between 1925 and 1930 Wijnkoop became involved in a heated party struggle and was dropped by Moscow. He then founded an independent Communist Party. In 1930 the two parties fused after Wijnkoop publicly confessed his guilt.

Though David Wijnkoop is said to have expressed his support for the Second Zionist World Congress, in 1898, this sympathy was short-lived. In 1903, in protest against the *Kishinev pogrom, the Dutch Zionist Movement and the Labor Party (SDAP) each organized a protest. It was Wijnkoop who, on behalf of the SDAP, gave a Marxist interpretation of the Russian anti-Jewish violence. According to him the pogrom was both an expression of the conflict between peasant and moneylender, and an instrument of the czarist regime to suppress the revolutionary tide.

After his comeback in 1930 Wijnkoops position within the CPH was fairly weak. He died in May 1941, a few months after the February strike against the Nazis in Amsterdam, and was accompanied to his grave by hundreds of people.

BIBLIOGRAPHY: A.J. Koejemans, *David Wijnkoop. Een mens in de strijd voor het socialisme* (1967); L. Giebels, *De zionistische beweging in Nederland 1899–1941* (1975); S. de Wolff, *Voor het land van belofte. Een terugblik op mijn leven* (1978); A.F. Mellink, in: *Biografisch Woordenboek van het Socialisme en de Arbeidersbeweging in Nederland*, 1(1986) 155–59; H. de Liagre Böhl, *Met al mijn bloed heb ik voor u geleefd. Herman Gorter 1864–1927* (1996); E. Gans, *De kleine verschillen die het leven uitmaken. Een historische studie naar joodse sociaaldemocraten en socialistisch-zionisten in Nederland* (1999); J.W. Stutje, *De man die de weg wees. Leven en werk van Paul de Groot 1899–1986* (2000); Gt Voerman, *De meridiaan van Moskou. De CPN en de Communistische Internationale, 1919–1930* (2001).

[Evelien Gans (2nd ed.)]

WILBUSCHEWITZ, family of pioneers in Ereẓ Israel. The head of the family, ZE'EV WILBUSCHEWITZ, was a landowner who lived near Grodno, Lithuania, and whose children joined the Zionist movement. His eldest son, ISAAC, went to Ereẓ Israel with the *Bilu group in 1882, but contracted yellow fever, returned to Russia, and drowned in the Neimen River. GEDALIAH WILBUSCHEWITZ (1865–1943), a mechanical engineer, went to Ereẓ Israel in 1892 and was a founder of a machine and metal-casting factory in Jaffa. This was the first Jewish enterprise of its kind in the country. During World War I he served as chief engineer of Jamal Pasha's headquarters in Damascus. After the war he worked as an engineer in Haifa. He published "*Mi-Zikhronot Ḥalutz ha-Ta'asiyyah ha-Ivrit*" in *Sefer ha-Aliyah ha-Sheniyyah* (1947). MOSHE WILBUSCHEWITZ (1869–1952), a chemical engineer and inventor, improved the margarine production process and invented a type of whole-meal bread (*leḥem ḥai*). He went to Palestine in 1919 and was one of the founders of the Shemen edible-oil products factory in Haifa. He held novel opinions on meteorology and climatology and established a special laboratory bearing his name at The Hebrew University campus on Mount Scopus in order to engage in research in this field. NAḤUM WILBUSH (WILBUSCHEWITZ; 1879–1971) was a mechanical engineer. He moved to Ereẓ Israel in 1903 and founded Atid, the first edible-oil factory in the country, at first situated in Ben Shemen and later in Haifa. He was a member of the Zionist Organization's delegation to East Africa to survey the possibilities for Jewish settlement in Uganda, and his book *Ha-Massa le-Ugandah* (1963) is a diary of this journey. During World War I, he served as an engineer in the Turkish army and was responsible for supplying water to the forces stationed in the Damascus region. Their sister was Mania Wilbuschewitz *Shochat.

BIBLIOGRAPHY: Tidhar, 2 (1947), 939, 950;4 (1950), 1705: 5 (1952), 2430.

[Yehuda Slutsky]

WILCHEK, MEIR (1935–), biophysicist. Born in Warsaw, Wilchek saw his youth disrupted by World War II, which he spent in Russia, mostly in Siberia. His family came to Israel in 1949 and eventually settled in Reḥovot where he finished high school. He received his doctorate from the Weizmann Institute and joined the department of biophysics, becoming professor in 1974 and later chairman. He was awarded numerous prizes, including the Rothschild prize for chemistry in 1987, the Wolf Prize for medicine in 1987, and the Israel Prize in life sciences (1990) for his discovery and development of the technology of chromotographic linkage. He was a foreign associate of the U.S. Institute of Medicine and National Academy of Science and a member of the Israel Academy of Sciences.

WILD BULL (Heb. רְאֵם, *re'em* or רֵים, *reim*), a powerful animal (Num. 23:22) whose strength is primarily in its horns (Deut. 33:17). It is parallel to the strong ox (*ibid.*; Isa. 34:7) but, unlike the ox, cannot be domesticated (Job 39:10–11). The animal referred to, the *Bos primigenius*, is called in Akkadian *rimu*, and was an extremely powerful animal which is depicted in many Assyrian hunting scenes. It was relentlessly hunted and, as a consequence, was entirely exterminated a few generations ago. In Arabic the name *rim* is given to the *antelope, the *Oryx leucoryx*. The biblical *re'em* apparently applies to this animal also, as in Psalms 92:11, which refers to the yard-long horns of the antelope. Similarly, the *Sifrei Deuteronomy* (323) declares that "the horns of the *re'em* are beautiful but it is not strong." In the *aggadah* the *re'em* is depicted as an animal of fabulous size. Because of its size, Noah could not bring it into the ark and tied it to the outside (Gen. R. 31:13). To David it looked like a mountain (Mid. Ps. to 22:25). In later Midrashim the *shor ha-bar* ("wild ox") is reserved, like the *Leviathan, for the banquet arranged for the righteous in the world to come. In earlier sources, however, the reference is to the *behemoth. In the *halakhah* there is a discussion as to whether the *shor ha-bar* is a *kilayim with the ox (Kil. 8:6; Tosef., *ibid.*, 1:8). R. Yose in the Mishnah (Kil. 8:6) regards it as belonging to the category of beasts (non-domesticated animals), while the sages classify it as a (domesticated) animal. The Jerusalem Talmud explains the difference, in that the latter regard it as an animal that was originally domesticated but escaped and reverted to its wild state, while the former holds that it was always wild (*ibid.*, 8:6, 31c). R. Yose identifies it with the *te'o* of Deuteronomy 14:5, but it is not clear whether he means the bison or the *buffalo.

BIBLIOGRAPHY: Lewysohn, Zool, 127ff.; Tristam, Nat. Hist, 146–50; J. Feliks, *Animal World of the Bible* (1962), 9, 21.

[Jehuda Feliks]

WILDENSTEIN, French family of art collectors, connoisseurs, and dealers. NATHAN (1851–1934) opened a small shop in the Rue Laffitte in Paris in 1890 and by the end of the century was considered one of the five most important art dealers in Paris. He opened a gallery in New York in 1903.

His son GEORGES (1892–1963), born in Paris, followed the family tradition, studied French art and joined his father in the business. In 1902 his catalog for the Fragonard exhibition at the Louvre became the model for all later catalogs. He wrote several biographies of French painters: Aved (1922), Louis Moreau (1923), a book on Lancret (1924), and one on Chardin (1933). He opened two more branches of the gallery in London and one in Buenos Aires. In 1941 he settled in the United States.

Daniel Leopold (1917–2001), Georges' son, an art dealer, was born in France. He went to the United States in 1940 and from 1959 to 1962 was chairman of the board of Wildenstein and Company Inc., New York. He wrote articles on art for many magazines both in the United States and in France.

BIBLIOGRAPHY: *Gazette des Beaux-Arts* (July 1963), supplement.

WILDER, BILLY (1906–2002), U.S. film director and writer. Born in Vienna, Wilder began as a newspaperman, and got his start in the film industry in Berlin by writing scripts. He left Germany in 1933 and reached Hollywood in 1934. At Paramount studios he collaborated with Charles Brackett, a former drama critic for *The New Yorker*, and together they wrote 14 successful films, including *Ninotchka* (1939); *Ball of Fire* (1941); *Double Indemnity* (1944); *The Lost Weekend* (1945); *A Foreign Affair* (1948); *The Emperor Waltz* (1948); and *Sunset Boulevard* (1950). After they had parted in 1950, Wilder wrote successes such as *Stalag 17* (1953); *Sabrina* (1954); *The Seven Year Itch* (1955); *Love in the Afternoon* (1957); and *Witness for the Prosecution* (1958). Wilder, whose films were characterized by novel situations and swift dialogue, teamed with I.A.L. Diamond to make *Some Like it Hot* (1959); *The Apartment* (1960); *Irma la Douce* (1961); *The Fortune Cookie* (1966); and *The Private Life of Sherlock Holmes* (1970). Many of these he also produced and directed.

Other Wilder films include *The Spirit of St. Louis* (1957); *One, Two, Three* (1961); *Kiss Me, Stupid* (1964); *Avanti!* (1972); *The Front Page* (1974); *Fedora* (1978); and *Buddy Buddy* (wrote, 1981).

For more than a quarter of a century, Wilder was one of the most successful filmmakers in Hollywood. His many accomplishments and accolades include six Oscars – two for direction, three for screenwriting, and one for producing. In 1986 he received a Lifetime Achievement Award from the American Film Institute. In 1988 he received the Irving G. Thalberg Memorial Award, given to "a creative producer who has been responsible for a consistently high quality of motion picture production."

ADD. BIBLIOGRAPHY: T. Wood, *The Bright Side of Billy Wilder, Primarily* (1970); M. Zolotow, *Billy Wilder in Hollywood* (1977); C. Crowe, *Conversations with Wilder* (1999); E. Sikov, *On Sunset Boulevard: The Life and Times of Billy Wilder* (1999); R. Horton (ed), *Billy Wilder: Interviews* (2001); C. Chandler, *Nobody's Perfect: Billy Wilder, a Personal Biography* (2002).

[Stewart Kampel / Ruth Beloff (2nd ed.)]

WILDER, GENE (Jerry Silberman; 1933–), U.S. actor. Born in Milwaukee, Wisconsin, Wilder received a B.A. from the University of Iowa. He taught fencing before making his off-Broadway debut in Arnold Wesker's *Roots* in 1961. Moving on to the Broadway stage, Wilder appeared in *The Complaisant Lover* (1961); *Mother Courage and Her Children* (1963); *One Flew over the Cuckoo's Nest* (1963); *The White House* (1964); and *Luv* (1964).

He made his film debut as the undertaker in *Bonnie and Clyde* (1967). Wilder was nominated for an Academy Award for his next film, *The Producers* (1968), and from then has starred in a variety of comedy vehicles (also writing and directing some of them), including *Start the Revolution without Me* (1970); *Willy Wonka & the Chocolate Factory* (1971); *Everything You Always Wanted to Know about Sex but Were Afraid to Ask* (1972); the drama *Rhinoceros* (1974); *Blazing Saddles* (1974); *Young Frankenstein* (written with Mel Brooks; Oscar nomination for Best Adapted Screenplay, 1974); *The Adventures of Sherlock Holmes' Smarter Brother* (wrote, directed, 1975); *Silver Streak* (1976); *The World's Greatest Lover* (1977); *The Frisco Kid* (1979); *Stir Crazy* (1980); *Hanky Panky* (1982); *The Woman in Red* (1984); *Haunted Honeymoon* (1986); *See No Evil, Hear No Evil* (1989); *Funny about Love* (1990); *Sunday Lovers* (1990); and *Another You* (1991).

Wilder also appeared in several TV movies; had guest roles on a number of television shows; starred in the sitcom *Something Wilder* (1994–95); and was the voice of the Letterman on the children's educational program *The Electric Company* (1972–77). In 2003 he was nominated for an Emmy for his appearance on the sitcom *Will and Grace*.

Wilder has been married four times, with his marriage (1984–89) to comedienne and co-star Gilda *Radner the most publicized. After she died of ovarian cancer, Wilder co-founded Gilda's Club, a support group to raise awareness about the disease.

His autobiography, *Kiss Me Like a Stranger: My Search for Love and Art*, was published in 2005. He also wrote *Gilda's Disease* (with Dr. S. Piver, 1996).

BIBLIOGRAPHY: G. Radner, *It's Always Something* (1989).

[Jonathan Licht / Ruth Beloff (2nd ed.)]

WILDER, HERTZ EMANUEL (1888–1948), activist, Yiddish journalist, and newspaper editor. Wilder was born in a Romanian village at the foot of the Carpathian Mountains. He was educated in *ḥeder* and public schools in Craiova, and graduated from a commercial state school in Bucharest, where he became active in Jewish literary and Zionist circles. He immigrated to Canada in 1903 and settled in Winnipeg, where he lived until his death. He was employed in banking, business, and printing.

Wilder was active in Winnipeg Jewish institutional life, and played leadership roles in causes such as education, war relief, and immigrant aid. He also served as first English secretary of the Canadian Jewish Congress, and as vice president of the Zionist Organization of Canada. His Yiddish poems, short stories, and articles on Jewish and non-Jewish issues and historical materials on Jewish settlement in Western Canada appeared in the *Winnipeg Dos Folk* and *Der Kanader Yid* (renamed *Dos Yidishe Vort*, 1915). In 1915 Wilder assumed ownership of the *Israelite Press*, and until 1933 served as president and managing editor of the bilingual Yiddish-English weekly *Dos Yidishe Vort/Israelite Press*, which briefly appeared as a daily in 1928. As editor, Wilder fostered Yiddish literature and encouraged contributions by young Yiddish writers. Wilder was a pioneer of the Anglo-Jewish press in Western Canada, and in 1920 he founded the short-lived weekly *Guardian*, where he published his English translations of Yiddish literature. Wilder left the weekly *Dos Yidishe Vort* for financial reasons, but returned as co-publisher in 1946 and contributed a regular English language column until his death.

BIBLIOGRAPHY: C.L. Fuks, *Hundert Yor Yidishe un Hebreyishe Literatur in Kanade* (1982), 106; H. Gutkin, *Journey into Our Heritage: The Story of the Jewish People in the Canadian West* (1980), 179; L. Levendel, *A Century of the Canadian Jewish Press: 1880s–1980s* (1989), 24.

[Rebecca E. Margolis (2nd ed.)]

WILDERNESS or desert; (Heb. מִדְבָּר, יְשִׁימוֹן, צִיָּה). In most biblical passages *midbar* refers principally to an uninhabited, uncultivated land (e.g., Jer. 2:2; 22:6; Ps. 107:4, 33–36) but sometimes also denotes complete desolation (e.g., Num. 20:4–5; Deut. 8:15). In defining desolation there is, in effect, no difference between *midbar* and the corresponding nouns, *yeshimon* and *ẓiyyah*, which are partially identical with it. However, *midbar* is the more comprehensive concept since it includes also marginal land on the borders of the *yeshimon*, "the pastures of the wilderness," and even settlements on its fringes (cf. Isa. 42:11, "the wilderness and the cities thereof"). At times *midbar* signifies a pasturage for flocks (Ex. 3:1; Ps. 78:52), the word being derived, it is suggested, from the Aramaic *dbr*, which denotes leading sheep to pasture.

In the Bible various tracts of wilderness are called after adjacent territories or settlements, such as the wilderness of Edom (II Kings 3:8), Moab (Deut. 2:8), Damascus (I Kings 19:15), Judah (Judg. 1:16), En-Gedi (I Sam. 24:2), Beer-Sheba (Gen. 21:14), Maon (I Sam. 23:24, 25), Shur (Ex. 15:22), Kadesh (Ps. 29:8), Gibeon (II Sam. 2:24), Jeruel (II Chron. 20:16), and Tekoa (20:20).

Palestine was a frontier country which was sometimes raided by marauders from the wilderness who spread havoc and destruction. During the second millennium B.C.E., a period of decline, which continued for centuries, overtook Transjordan as a result of the incursion of nomads of the wilderness. In the Israelite period (first millennium B.C.E.) too, marauders made inroads into the country and pillaged the permanent settlements, leaving devastation in their wake. The rural culture and urban settlement in Palestine and in countries of the East generally were based on a constant state of vigilance against the tribes of the wilderness.

The Bible mentions perils of the wilderness which endanger man's life – hunger, thirst, wild animals. The wilderness is an "evil place" (Num. 20:4–5), and its wide expanses constitute a threat to human beings (Deut. 1:19; 8:15; Isa. 21:1). It is described as a land of the shadow of death, or of thick darkness (Jer. 2:6, 31).

While not ignoring the hardships of the wilderness, the distress of the Israelites, who had come out of Egypt, in Sinai and in the Negev, their hunger and thirst, their complaints and rebelliousness against the terrors of the *yeshimon*, the Bible sometimes regards the wilderness as the cradle of Israel's sins. The sins in the wilderness – whether the making of the golden calf (Ex. 32–33), the rebellion of Koraḥ and his company (Num. 16–17), or the episode of Baal Peor (Num. 25) – became a symbol for all succeeding generations. Thus several Psalms refer to the Israelites' grave sins in the wilderness which determined their fate (Ps. 78:14–41; 106:14–33). Ezekiel makes particularly strong references to the sins of the generation of the wilderness, both fathers and children, and sees in these sins an original sin, as it were, which persisted from the time the Hebrews lived in Egypt, and the punishment for which is visited upon all generations (Ezek. 20:7–26).

In contrast to the negative view of the wilderness period as an age of sin, several prophets refer to it as a time of the nation's purification at the dawn of its history. Thus Hosea and Jeremiah compare Israel to the youthful wife of God whom he found "in the land of great drought," and who followed and cleaved to Him "in a land that was not sown" (Jer. 2:2–4:6; Hos. 2:16–17; 9:10; 13:5). Engraved in the people's memory was the tradition of God's revelation at Sinai and in the wilderness of Seir and the Negeb (Ex. 19:20; Judg. 5:4–5; Hab. 3:3–7). At Sinai, according to this tradition, the Israelite religion crystallized, the Ten Commandments, the laws, and the statutes were given, and the covenant between Israel and its God was made. There, too, Israel enjoyed the special providence of God and was chosen as His people, a theme emphasized particularly in Deuteronomy.

However, the view of the wilderness as the scene of the purification from sin does not mean that the prophets idealized either the essential character of the wilderness or nomadic existence as a way of life (see *Nomadism). This theory, whose main protagonists have been Budde, Stade, Meyer, Flight, and others, is without foundation. The prophets never set the wilderness in opposition to an agricultural civilization, frequently used by them to symbolize a life of abundance and tranquility. Even the *Rechabites did not advocate a return to the wilderness, and there is no proof that they in fact had their home there (cf. the interpretations of Hos. 2:16–17; 12:10 in the Book of *Hosea, and the articles referred to in connection with those interpretations). What can be said on the positive side is that as early as in biblical times the wilderness served as a refuge for anguished, embittered men, whether rebels against society or recluses in search of seclusion (I Sam. 24:1–2; 26:1–4; Job 30:3–8). It is against this background, and not on the basis of idealization, that Jeremiah's yearning, "Oh for a lodging place for wayfarers in the wilderness, that I might leave my people" (Jer. 9:1) is understood. Seclusion in the wilderness, as a historical phenomenon, is known from Second Temple times.

In the Aggadah

The two ways of evaluating the generation of the wilderness, alluded to in the Bible, persisted in the *aggadah*, though in a new idiom, and formed the subject of conflicting views between R. Eliezer and R. Akiva. Whereas the latter held that the generation of the wilderness has no share in the world to come and will not stand at the last judgment, R. Eliezer applied to them the verse (Ps. 50:5); "Gather My saints together unto Me; those that have made a covenant with Me by sacrifice" (Sanh. 10:3). The entire subsequent midrashic tradition follows his line of approach. The Israelites of the wilderness generation are called Darda (Heb. דרדע = דר, "generation," and דע, "knowledge"; cf. I Kings 5:11), "because they were extremely knowledgeable [בני דעה]" (Mid. Prov. to 1:1). The verse (Song 3:6) "Who is this that cometh up out of the wilderness" is interpreted as "her [Israel's] rise dates from the wilderness" (Song R. 3:6, no. 1), since from it came all Israel's virtues in Torah, prophecy, and kingship. However, the diasporas are also compared to the wilderness.

BIBLIOGRAPHY: J.W. Flight, in: JBL, 42 (1923), 158–226; S. Nystroem, *Beduinentum und Yahwismus* (1946); N. Glueck, *The Other Side of the Jordan* (1940); A. Reifenberg, *Milḥemet ha-Mizra ve-ha Yeshimon* (1950); S. Talmon, in: A. Altmann (ed.), *Biblical Motifs* (1966), 31–63; S. Abramsky, in: *Eretz Israel*, 8 (1967), 31–63.

[Samuel Abramsky]

WILDMANN, ISAAC EISIK (**Haver**; 1789–1853), rabbi in Poland-Lithuania. He served as rabbi in the communities of Rozinoi, Volkovysk, Tikocyn, Siauliai, and Suwalk. In addition to his eminence in *halakhah*, he was a kabbalist in the tradition of the school of *Elijah b. Solomon Zalman, the Gaon of Vilna, and wrote *Magen ve-Ẓinnah* (Koenigsberg, 1855), a defense of Kabbalah against the attacks of Judah Leone *Modena's *Ari Nohem*. Wildmann was a prolific writer in both *halakhah* and Kabbalah.

His works include *Beit Yiẓḥak* (Suwalk, 1836), on the negative and positive commandments; *Binyan Olam*, responsa on *halakhah* (Warsaw, 1851); *Beit Olamim* (1889) on the *Idra Rabba*, a part of the Zohar; *Yad Ḥazakah* (1842), a commentary on the Passover *Haggadah; Pitḥei She'arim* (1888), a detailed exposition of Isaac *Luria's kabbalistic system; *Be'er Yiẓḥak* (1889), a commentary on the rabbinical collectanea *Likkutei ha-Gra* of the Gaon of Vilna.

BIBLIOGRAPHY: Fuenn, Keneset, 95.

[Zvi Meir Rabinowitz]

WILENSKY, MICHAEL (1877–1955), Hebrew philologist. Born in Kremenchug, Ukraine, Wilensky was raised in a hasidic family of the *Chabad movement. He studied at a Chabad *yeshivah* and at the University of Berne, where he received his doctorate in 1912. He went on to specialize in mathematics at the University of Kazan, Russia. After the 1917 Revolution he settled in Odessa. There his interest in Jewish studies was aroused by Ḥ.N. *Bialik, and he worked on the staff of Tarbut until 1920. In 1921 he left for Berlin to join *Dvir Publishing. He edited Abraham ibn Ezra's grammatical works, *Safah Berurah* and *Moznayim* (both not published), contributed articles to historical journals and to the German *Encyclopaedia Judaica*, and worked with the Verein zur Gruendung einer Akademie fuer die Wissenschaft des Judentums. His principal accomplishment in Berlin was his publication of Jonah *ibn Janaḥ's *Sefer ha-Rikmah*, accompanied by his own elaborate annotations (vol. 1, 1929; vol. 2, 1931, 1964[2]). In 1934 Wilensky escaped from Germany to Lithuania, and in 1935 he arrived in the U.S. There, upon the invitation of Julian Morgenstern of Hebrew Union College, Cincinnati, he compiled a catalog of all the manuscripts in the institution's library.

BIBLIOGRAPHY: N.H. Tur-Sinai et al, in: M. Wilensky (ed.), *Sefer ha-Rikmah*, 1 (1964[2]), introd.

WILENSKY, MOSHE (1910–1997) Israeli composer. Born in Warsaw, he studied composition and conducting at the state conservatory of Warsaw. After graduating there he left in 1932 for Israel. He was pianist at the "Matate" satiric theater and composed music for songs, as well as background music for documentary movies made by the Carmel studios. At the Matate Theater Wilensky discovered Yemenite songs through the repertoire of singer Esther Gamlieli. When the Li-la-lo Theater was created in 1944, Wilensky was offered the job of "house composer" and met there singer Shoshana *Damari, who was to become the principal performer of his songs. During the War of Independence, Wilensky and Damari toured army posts and performed for soldiers. In 1949, they left for a series of performances in the United States where they remained almost a year. Wilensky wrote the melodies for many of the songs of the Chizbatron, the first of the army bands created during the War of Independence. From the 1950s onwards Wilensky set to music hundreds of songs for singers and army bands. He also wrote the scores for a number of musical comedies such as *Shulamit* (1957), *Fishka*, and *Same'aḥ ba-Namal*.

Wilensky was among the founders of the Artists and Composer's Union. In 1961 he became director of the light music division of Kol Israel, a position he held for many years.

Many of his songs are considered to be among the best of Hebrew music, and Wilensky was awarded the Israel Prize in 1983. He composed songs to the texts of many famous Israeli poets, and his songs appear in hundreds of booklets and discs. Among the books containing selections of his songs are *Tamid Kalaniyyot Tifraḥna* ("Poppies Will Always Bloom," 1978) *Al ha-Kevish Yare'aḥ* ("On the Road Is a Moon," 1982), *Moshe Wilensky, Zer Kalaniyyot* ("Moshe Wilensky, a Bouquet of Poppies," 1980).

[Nathan Shahar (2nd ed.)]

WILENSKY, YEHUDAH LEIB NISAN (1870–1935), Zionist leader. He was born in Chechersk, Belorussia. In 1891, while a student in Berlin, he joined the Benei Moshe Society and the Russian-Jewish Scientific Society. He was a delegate to the First Zionist Congress and attended all subsequent congresses until his death. Responding to Theodor Herzl's call for the "conquest of the communities," he gave up his profession as chemist and became government-appointed rabbi of the Nikolayev community from 1903 to 1906. He democratized the life of the community, introduced modern Hebrew education, and promoted Jewish *self-defense against pogroms. His activities on behalf of an investigation into the role played by the authorities in the pogrom that took place in Nikolayev in October 1905 led to his arrest and expulsion from Russia. For the next five years, Wilensky lived in Berlin, where he was on the staff of the Hilfsverein der deutschen Juden and utilized his position to further understanding between German and East European Jewries. In 1911 he returned to Russia and, after the 1917 Revolution, was elected chairman of the Kharkov Jewish community. In 1919 he led a Jewish delegation that met with the "White" Army general Anton *Denikin to urge the cessation of pogroms by his troops. When the Red Army took over southern Russia, Wilensky had to flee the country by way of the Caucasian border, reaching Palestine in 1920. During the period 1921–32 he served as a Keren Hayesod emissary in Europe and South America (Chile made him its honorary consul in Jerusalem) and was particularly successful in propagating Zionism in Romania. His memoirs and letters, together with a monograph about him written by his daughter Miriam *Yalan-Stekelis, were published in 1968.

BIBLIOGRAPHY: M. Yalan-Stekelis, in: *He-Avar*, 13 (1966), 134–49.

[Yehuda Slutsky]

WILENTZ, ROBERT N. (1927–1996), U.S. jurist. Born in Perth Amboy, New Jersey, Wilentz attended Princeton University, received his B.A. from Harvard, and his law degree from Columbia. He joined his father's law firm in Perth Amboy and practiced from 1952 to 1979. He was elected to the New Jersey legislature in 1966 and served until 1969. He was in the U.S. Navy in World War II. In 1979 he was appointed chief justice of the New Jersey Supreme Court for a seven-year term, and his appointment was made permanent in 1986. Under his administration, the New Jersey Supreme Court achieved a reputation for not being reluctant to move creatively towards adjudication in areas previously untouched by judicial action.

DAVID WILENTZ (1896–1988), father of the chief justice, was the attorney general of New Jersey who prosecuted Bruno Richard Hauptmann in 1932 for the kidnapping-murder of the twenty-month-old son of Charles A. Lindbergh. In 1919 he founded the law firm Wilentz, Goldman, and Spitzer, which grew to become the largest law firm in Central New Jersey.

[Milton Ridvas Konvitz / Ruth Beloff (2nd ed.)]

WILHELM, KURT (1900–1965), rabbi. Born in Germany, he studied at German universities, at the Jewish Theological Seminary in Breslau, and in New York. Wilhelm officiated as rabbi in Germany from 1925 until 1933 when he immigrated to Palestine. In 1936 he founded the Liberal congregation Emet ve-Emunah in Jerusalem where he served as rabbi until 1948, when he went to Stockholm to officiate as chief rabbi of Sweden. He also lectured at Stockholm University on Jewish subjects. Wilhelm advocated a positive and moderate liberalism, similar to Conservative Judaism. He belonged to the circle which supported Arab-Jewish understanding, and was active in promoting Jewish dialogue with Christianity and other religions. He published a number of scholarly collections: *Juedischer Glaube* (1961) on Judaism and *Wissenschaft des Judentums* (1967) on German Jewish scholarship, among others.

BIBLIOGRAPHY: Weltsch, in: AJR *Information* (July 1965); YLBI, 11 (1966), 356, no. 5186; H. Tramer, in: *Theokratia*, 1 (1967–69), 160–85; H. Bergman, in: K. Wilhelm (ed.), *Wissenschaft des Judentums im deutschen Sprachbereich*, 1 (1967), v–ix.

[Hugo Mauritz Valentin]

WILKES-BARRE AND KINGSTON, cities in N.E. Pennsylvania with a Jewish population of 3,000 (in 2005). The first Jews were Moses Libien from France (1835), Hirsch Koch (1836), and Martin Long (1838) from Bavaria. By the 1840s, 13 Jews lived in Wilkes-Barre and held Orthodox services as Congregation B'nai B'rith which became Reform in 1860. Rabbi Albert Friedlander was their leader. In 1970 they moved to Kingston, had 220 members, and were led by Rabbi Arnold Shevlin. By 2005 they had 200 households, with Rabbi Fred Davidow officiating.

East European Jews arrived in the 1870s, forming five Orthodox congregations. The principal Orthodox congregation is Ohav Zedek, founded by Hungarian Jews in 1902. Rabbi Isadore Mayer Davidson became chief rabbi in 1920.

Conservative Temple Israel was founded in 1922 and is the largest with 450 families, led by Rabbi Larry Kaplan and Cantor Ahron Abraham. Abraham D. Barras was rabbi from 1952 to 1983 and initiated bat mitzvah ceremonies. He took Christian clergy on Temple Israel tours to Israel and Egypt and led a mission to Israel and Rome, where they had an audience with the pope and the chief rabbi of Rome.

The Jewish Community Center was founded as the YMHA in 1863. Louis Smith was the director of the JCC from 1925 until 1976. He was very influential and recognized for his excellence by national UJA. Julia Lieberman created Home Camp, and K'Ton Ton camp was directed by Evelyn Gurbst. In 2005 JCC membership was 901 families, its executive director was Don Cooper. The JCC lists 1,500 men and women who served in the military. A senior kosher meal program and day care were initiated, and the JCC camp was renovated. The Jewish Federation sponsors the United Jewish Campaign. In 1999 there appeared a book on Wilkes-Barre Jewry, *The Jews of Wilkes-Barre: 150 Years 1845–1995 in the Wyoming Valley of Pennsylvania*, edited by S. Spear, P.J. Zbiek, E.C. Levin, and M. Levin.

The first Jew elected to office was Abram Salsburgh who served as district attorney of Luzerne County from 1904 to 1910. Some long-serving communal leaders were Rabbi Marcus Salzman, 35 years; Rabbi Isadore Davidson, 43 years; Rabbi Mayer Pernikoff, 47 years; Rabbi Abraham D. Barras, 31 years; Arnold Shevlin, 22 years; and Louis Smith, 52 years.

Men and women of achievement were Judge Max Rosenn and Jesse Choper, who became dean at the University of California Law School; Dr. David Rutstein, first chair of Harvard Medical School's department of preventive medicine, and Harry Reich, the first surgeon to perform a laparoscopic hysterectomy; Mendy Rudolph, NBCA referee, and Sandy Padwe, dean of Columbia University Graduate School of Journalism. Barbara Weisberger was with the Pennsylvania Ballet; Louis Teicher joined Arthur Ferrante playing duo pianos. Martin Yudkovitz was president of NBC Interactive Media. Sanford J. Ungar, author, editor, and former NPR host, was President of Goucher College. David Horowitz was a United Nations journalist, and his brother Emanuel Winters Horowitz wrote short stories. Their father was Cantor Aaron Horowitz.

The United Hebrew Institute is the local Jewish day school. It provides an academic foundation with modern technology in secular and religious studies. The current director is Rabbi Eli Kugielsky. There are two other denominational Hebrew schools. The Jewish Family Service, directed by Dorothy Schwartz (1952–74) and now by Howard Grossman, offers counseling and assistance.

Wyoming Valley has excellent interfaith relationships. Five churches contributed to the construction of Temple B'nai B'rith's first building. Esther B. Davidowitz was the Jewish editor of *Your Life is Worth Living* by Bishop Fulton J. Sheen.

The five local colleges exemplify this cooperation. Penn State, W.B., had many Jewish advisory board members, faculty, and administrators. Mimi Unger Fredman has been chair of the Penn State Board of Trustees. King's College has Jewish members on its board, faculty and administration. Attorneys Harold Rosenn and Murray Ufberg served on the College Misericordia Board of Trustees as vice chairmen with other Jewish board members. Sister Carol Rittner and Sister Siena Finley taught Holocaust courses. College Misericordia has an outstanding Jewish Elderhostel program. The first president of Wilkes University, Dr. Eugene S. Farley, invited Jewish participation. There were many Jewish faculty, administrators, and trustees. Robert S. Capin was a teacher, dean and president of Wilkes College. Buildings were named by Aaron Weiss, Max Roth, Nathan Schiowitz, Robert Fortinsky, Arnold Rifkin, and Robert S. Capin. Louis Schaffer, Joseph Savitz, and Eugene Roth served as chairmen of the board of Wilkes University. Luzerne County Community College was founded in 1966. William Davidowitz was co-chairman of the building committee. Jewish citizens served on their Board of Trustees and as faculty members. Sheldon Spear taught a Holocaust course. Generous Jewish philanthropy has been consistent for all institutions.

In 1911 Seligman J. Strauss was elected judge on the Luzerne County Court of Common Pleas, followed by Jacob Schiffman from 1962 to 1970. Perry J. Shertz sat on the Superior Court as an associate judge in 1980. Nochem Winnet became judge of the Municipal Court. The Honorable Max Rosenn has a life appointment as judge of the U.S. Court of Appeals on the Third Circuit, with a courthouse named after him. Rosenn, Jenkins and Greenwald was the first law firm with Jewish partners, followed by Winkler, Danoff and Lubin. There were approximately 60 Jewish lawyers (in 2005).

Wilkes-Barre city councilmen included Joseph K. Weitzenkorn, Maurice Ziegler, and Jacob D. Groh. Marvin Rappaport, Sallyanne Rosenn, Mimi Cohen, and Wilbur Troy were elected to Kingston Borough Council. Ethel Price served as County Commissioner. In 1931 Herman J. Goldberg was an assistant district attorney. Richard Goldberg became chief Luzerne County solicitor and retired as a full colonel in the PA National Guard. Arthur Silverblatt was first assistant district attorney. David Schwager became solicitor for the county assessors.

The physicist David Bohn wrote a quantum mechanics text and reformulated Einstein's theories. Architect Samuel Z. Moskovitz designed 600 buildings and was president of the American Institute of Architects. Photographer Mark Cohen exhibited at the New York Museum of Modern Art.

Judge Rosenn said, "The Jews of Wilkes-Barre and Kingston have the support and friendship of the larger community. And we have a history of over one hundred and fifty years to learn from and build upon."

BIBLIOGRAPHY: S. Spear et al. (eds.), *The Jews of Wilkes-Barre: 150 Years 1845–1995 in the Wyoming Valley of Pennsylvania* (1999); M. Greenwald, *Temple B'nai B'rith: A Chronological History, 1845–1987, Wilkes-Barre, Pennsylvania* (1989).

[Esther B. Davidowitz, Alfred S. Groh, and Steven Davidowitz (2nd ed.)]

WILLEN, JOSEPH (1897–1985), U.S. social welfare and fund-raising executive. Born in Kushnitsa, Russia, Willen immigrated to the U.S. in 1905. He served in the U.S. Army in World War I. Subsequently he joined the staff of the Federation of Jewish Philanthropies of New York. After serving in a number of capacities, he was executive vice president of the federation from 1942 to 1967, serving as executive consultant from 1967. During his tenure, the federation raised approximately $360,000,000 in its annual campaigns. Willen pioneered the federation's fund-raising techniques, organizing donors into separate committees for professions, localities, and fraternal and benevolent societies, as well as professionalizing the Women's Division fund-raising efforts. Known as a master of philanthropic fund-raising, Willen initiated and directed the federation's successful $200,000,000 "City of Life" campaign for new buildings and institutions. He also served as director of the Greater New York Community Council, on the New York City Welfare and Health Council, and on many Jewish institutions. He was a member of the board of trustees of Brandeis University (1963–73).

Willen's first wife, PEARL LARNER WILLEN (1904–1968), was a communal leader in human welfare organizations. She served the National Council of Jewish Women as chairman of the committee on public affairs (1951–54), vice president (1951–63), and president (1963–66), and was president of the

International Council of Jewish Women (1954–57). She was also a member of the board of governors of The Hebrew University and was active in civil rights and poverty programs and organizations. In 1965 she was one of the driving forces in the Women in Community Service's coalition to help at-risk young women in the U.S. find employment through the Job Corps.

°**WILLIAM OF AUVERGNE** (c. 1180–1249), French theologian and philosopher. Born in Aurillac, William was professor of theology at the University of Paris and bishop of that city from 1228 until his death. His principal work is *Magisterium divinale*, a collection of treatises which includes *De primo principio*, or *De trinitate* (1228), *De anima* (1230), and *De universo* (between 1231 and 1236). William's writings are contained in *Opera omnia* (2 vols., Paris, 1674; repr. 1963). In his writing William combined two tendencies, which during their development in the 12th century had been kept apart: the systematization of theological doctrines and the philosophic investigation of man's position in the universe. But methodologically he distinguished between philosophy and theology, holding that philosophy is an independent discipline with its own rules. A member of the first generation of Paris masters to utilize Aristotelian, Islamic, and Jewish thought, William followed Aristotle and Maimonides in his psychology and cosmogony and the Platonic-Neoplatonic tradition, which he knew to a large extent through Augustine, in metaphysics, cosmology, and epistemology.

William had high regard for the Jewish Neoplatonist Solomon ibn *Gabirol, whose *Mekor Ḥayyim* he read in a Latin translation. However, William considered Gabirol, whom he knew as Avicebron, an Arab by nationality and perhaps a Christian by religion. Although he admired Gabirol, William disagreed with him in holding that the world was created directly and freely through God's will without any intermediary beings.

William was also familiar with, and drew upon, Maimonides' *Guide of the Perplexed*, which became known in Latin translation in the West in the 1240s. He utilized, especially, Maimonides' description of the sublunar world and his criticism of the Greek doctrine of the eternity of the world. However, although William cites Avicebron by name, he does not mention Maimonides, probably because he knew Maimonides was a Jew. Evidence for this view is William's contention that the Jews betrayed their own religion and were worthy of condemnation. He held that at first the Hebrew people were content with the Torah and Prophets, but later they were seduced into believing incredible stories, referring to the Talmud. He felt there were only a few exceptions – men who had lived among the Arabs and became philosophers (*De universo* 1:3, 31). This view is paralleled in a papal legate report defending the suppression of the Talmud (1239–47) as not conflicting with the Church's consideration of Judaism as a *religio licita*. William had been a member of the legate's court in Paris.

BIBLIOGRAPHY: S. Grayzel, *The Church and the Jews in the XIII Century* (1966²), index; D. Knowles, in: *The Encyclopedia of Philosophy*, 8 (1967), 302–3; J. Guttmann, *Die Scholastik des dreizehnten Jahrhunderts in ihren Beziehungen zum Judenthum und zur juedischen Literatur* (1902), 13–32.

[Hans Liebeschutz]

WILLIAMS, CHARLES (1893–1978), British film and broadcasting music composer. Born Isaac Cozerbreit in east London, the son of a Jewish concert singer, Charles Williams – as he was known from the time of World War I – worked as a freelance musician in silent films in London in the 1920s, becoming one of the most distinguished writers of film music for the British cinema and, later, an equally important composer of theme music for British radio and television. His best-known works include "The Dream of Olwen," often played as a serious short piano concerto, *While I Live* (1947), and "The Jealous Lover," originally composed in 1949 for the film *That Dangerous Age* and revived in 1960 as the theme from Billy Wilder's *The Apartment*, winning an Oscar. Williams also composed the theme music for the Australian Broadcasting Corporation's television programs, played several times a day on Australian television, "Majestic Fanfare" (1952), and such BBC theme music as "The Young Ballerina" (1951) for *The Potter's Wheel*.

BIBLIOGRAPHY: ODNB online.

[William D. Rubinstein (2nd ed.)]

WILLNER, ITAMAR (1947–), Israeli chemist. He was born in Bucharest, Romania. He completed his Ph.D. studies in chemistry in 1978 at the Hebrew University of Jerusalem. After postdoctoral research at the University of California, Berkeley, he joined the Institute of Chemistry at the Hebrew University of Jerusalem in 1982. In 1986 he was appointed as professor at the Hebrew University. His research activities over the years attempted to combine biomolecules with synthetic and chemical assemblies to yield materials and systems of new functions and properties, and to prepare man-made materials that mimic biological functions. The research fields developed by him include light-induced electron-transfer and artificial photosynthesis, molecular electronics and optoelectronics, biomolecular electronics and optoelectronics, nanotechnology and nanobiotechnology, and the control of surface properties by functional monolayers and thin films. Until 2004 he co-authored over 420 papers and scientific chapters in books, and presented the research results at numerous worldwide symposia. His pioneering accomplishments were recognized with many international and national awards and distinctions. Among them are the Kolthoff Award (1993), the Max-Planck Research Award for International Cooperation (1998), the Israel Chemical Society Award (2001), and the Israel Prize in chemistry (2002). He is a fellow of the American Association for the Advancement of Science (AAAS), a member of the Israel Academy of Sciences, and a member of the European Academy of Sciences.

[Bracha Rager (2nd ed.)]

WILLOW (Heb. עֲרָבָה, *aravah*). The Bible describes the willow as a tree that grows rapidly near water (Isa. 44:4) and in whose shade the *Behemoth reclines (Job 40:22). The exiles from Judea hung their harps on willows by the rivers of Babylon, loath "to sing the Lord's song in a foreign land" (Ps. 137:2). The willow is one of the *Four Species and is characterized as possessing "neither taste nor fragrance," thus symbolizing those among Israel "who are neither learned nor possessed of good deeds" (Lev. R. 30:12). Although the identification of the *aravah* with the willow is undoubted, it should be noted that in the time of the Mishnah philological problems had already arisen in connection with this identification. The *amora* Ḥisda states that after the destruction of the Temple the name of the *aravah* (*Salix*) and *ẓafẓafah* (poplar, *Populus*) were interchanged (Shah. 36a), and in fact in Arabic it is the poplar which is called *a'rb* (Heb. *aravah*) and the willow, *ẓafẓaf* (Heb. *ẓafẓafah*). The rabbis pointed out the difference between these two genera with regard to validity for the precept of the Four Species: "The willow has a red stalk, an elongated leaf and a smooth [leaf] edge. The *ẓafẓafah* has a white stalk and a round leaf with a serrated edge" (Suk. 34a). The conclusion finally reached is that the willow with the serrated leaf is also valid (*ibid.*). The willow was also used during the festival of Tabernacles, the altar being decorated with willow branches which were brought from Moẓa near Jerusalem. There is undoubtedly a connection between the willow growing by the waterside and the prayer for water on Hoshana Rabba, as well as the prayer for rain on Shemini Aẓeret (eighth day of solemn assembly), the last day of Tabernacles, when "they are judged in respect of water" (RH 1:2).

The willow is a very useful tree. Its soft branches were used for wicker work (Bik. 3:8). The wood withstands rot and was therefore used for building boats called *arba*, the spelling for *aravah* in Aramaic and Syrian. Its fruit contains soft fibers, which are the *petilat ha-idan* ("wick of bast"), used as wicks for lamps (Shab. 2:1). Though not a fruit tree, according to the agricultural folklore of the period fruit trees could be grafted on to it (see TJ, Or. 1:2, 61a). Two species of willow, the *Salix acmophylla* and *Salix alba*, as well as hybrids of both species, grow wild in Israel on the bank of streams and rivers. Another species, *Salix babylonica*, the weeping willow, originated in China.

BIBLIOGRAPHY: Loew, Flora, 3 (1924), 323–37; J. Feliks, *Olam ha-Ẓome'aḥ ha-Mikra'i* (1968^2), 113–5. **ADD. BIBLIOGRAPHY:** Feliks, Ha-Ẓome'aḥ, 115.

[Jehuda Feliks]

WILLOWSKI, JACOB DAVID BEN ZE'EV (Heb. רידב״ז, **Ridbaz**; 1845–1913), Lithuanian talmudist and *rosh yeshivah* in Ereẓ Israel. Willowski was born in Kobrin, Russia. In his youth his brilliant attainments were already recognized. In 1868 he was appointed rabbi at Izballin; in 1876 of Bobruisk; and in 1881 "*moreh ẓedek* and *Maggid meisharim*" (teacher and preacher) of Vilna, the title accorded to the spiritual leader of that community, since it had no official rabbi. He later successively served as rabbi of Polotsk, Vilkomir, and Slutsk. At Slutsk he founded a yeshivah which soon became famous throughout Russia. In 1903 he moved to the United States where he was appointed chief rabbi of a group of Orthodox congregations in Chicago. He was also designated the *zekan ha-rabbanim* ("elder rabbi") of America by the then newly organized *Union of Orthodox Rabbis. However, due to what he considered to be the neglect of religious life there, he left the United States in 1905 and immigrated to Ereẓ Israel. He settled in Safed where he founded a large yeshivah named Torat Ereẓ Israel, popularly known as "Yeshivat ha-Ridbaz." He took issue with R. Abraham Isaac *Kook, then rabbi of Jaffa, for his lenient ruling permitting farmers to work the land during the Sabbatical Year. When the Sabbatical Year came in 1910, Willowski urged them not to work the land, and established an international charity fund to sustain those who followed his decision. His published talmudic works and responsa gained him a worldwide reputation as a preeminent rabbinical scholar. He was particularly renowned for his two commentaries to the Jerusalem Talmud, one of which followed the method of *Rashi in explaining the meaning of the text, while the other, in the manner of the **tosafot*, was a deeper and more critical exposition. These commentaries, together with the text of the Jerusalem Talmud, were published in 1898–1900.

He also wrote *Migdal David* (1874) and *Ḥanah David* (1876), both containing novellae and comments on the Babylonian and Jerusalem Talmuds; Responsa (1881); *Nimmukei Ridbaz*, a commentary to the Pentateuch (1904); *Responsa Beit Ridbaz* (1908); and annotations on R. Israel of Shklov's *Pe'at ha-Shulḥan* (1912).

BIBLIOGRAPHY: A. Rothkoff, in AJHSQ, 57, 4 (1967/68), 557–72; *Yahadut Lita*, 3 (1967), 46; O.Z. Rand (ed.), *Toledot Anshei Shem* (1950), 44.

[Aaron Rothkoff]

WILLS (Heb. צַוָּאָה). A will is a person's disposition of his property in favor of another in such manner that the testator retains the property or his rights to it until his death. There are three different forms of wills, each governed by different legal rules as regards their time of coming into effect and their scope and manner of execution. These are *mattenat* (or *ẓavva'at*) *bari*, i.e., a (literally) gift by a healthy person; *mattenat* (or *ẓavva'at*) *shekhiv me-ra*, i.e., a gift by a person critically ill; and *meẓavveh meḥamat mitah*, i.e., a gift in contemplation of death. There are detailed biblical provisions regarding the legal order of *succession (Num. 27:8–11; Deut. 21:16–17). However, save for isolated hints (see e.g., Job 42:15), there is no biblical provision regarding the possibility of a person determining the disposition of his property after his death in a manner not according with the rules laid down for the legal order of succession.

Mattenat Bari

A person who wishes to give his property to a person who is not his legal heir must divest himself of it during his lifetime so that the property shall not, on his death, automatically be dealt with in accordance with the laws of succession (*Rashbam*, BB 135b). He may, however, donate the body of the property by way of a gift taking immediate effect, while retaining for himself the usufruct of the property until his death (BB 8:7: "From today and after my death"). This is a *mattenat bari*. In form this disposition by will is identical to donation in the case of regular gift. Since the legator transfers his property to the legatee "from today," he may not afterward retract from the will, although the legatee only becomes entitled to the usufruct of the property after the legator's death (Sh. Ar., ḤM 257:6, 7). A will from which it may be inferred that the transfer (**kinyan*) is "from today and after death," is regarded as one in which these words are expressly stated (BB 136a; Tur and Sh. Ar., ḤM 258). It is not possible for the legator to bequeath by way of *mattenat bari* any property except that which is then in his possession (*Rema*, ḤM 257:7; see also *Contract). If the legator employs the words, "from today if I should not retract until after my death," or "from today if I do not retract during my lifetime," he is free to retract from the bequest (Tos. BM 19b; Sh. Ar., ḤM 257:7).

Mattenat Shekhiv me-Ra

A *shekhiv me-ra* is a person who is "ill and confined to bed." According to Maimonides, a *shekhiv me-ra* is "a sick man whose entire body has been weakened and whose strength has waned because of his sickness, so that he cannot walk outside and is confined to bed" (i.e., critically ill; Yad, Zekhiyyah 8:2). Unlike the *mattenat bari*, the provisions of a *mattenat shekhiv me-ra* come into effect on the death of the legator (*ibid.*), since the scholars enacted that the latter form of testacy should be regarded in law as a form of inheritance which comes into effect on the benefactor's death (BB 149a). The scholars enacted far-reaching alleviations with regard to the formalities of conveyance by *mattenat shekhiv me-ra*, dispensing with the need for a formal *kinyan* since "the instruction of a *shekhiv me-ra* has the same force as a document written and delivered" (Git. 13a) and because this was a *takkanah* of the scholars aimed at easing the mind of the sick person (Yad, Zekhiyyah 8:2). The wishes of the testator may be expressed orally or in writing, or by implication (BB 156b; Git. 15a; Sh. At., ḤM 250:7). The will may be an unwitnessed, handwritten deed, to be delivered to the beneficiary (Git. 71a; see Yad, Naḥalot 4:1).

If this form of will is formulated orally by a *shekhiv me-ra* before witnesses, the latter may reduce its terms to writing for delivery to the beneficiary. The delivery may take place during the testator's lifetime or after his death, since this instrument is written solely as a record of the testator's oral statements which immediately on recital take effect as the will (*Sma*, ḤM 253, n. 77).

The special validity which attaches to a *shekhiv me-ra* will is forfeited if the testator should employ one of the regular forms of *kinyan* for gift (Ket. 55b), since in so doing he manifests his intention to effect no more than a regular *mattenat bari*. This result would follow, for instance, if the benefactor should effect a *kinyen sudar* or *ḥazakah*, a lifting or pulling, or a gift *aggav karka* (incidental to land generally; Tos. BB 152a; Tur, ḤM 250:28; Yad, Zekhiah 8:10, 11; *Sma*, ḤM 250, n. 54), or, similarly, if he should draw up a deed, or declare his will and tell the witnesses to draw up a deed for delivery to the beneficiary (Yad, Zekhiyyah 8:12, 13). If the testator declares, orally or in writing, that his resort to a *kinyan* customary for a gift is meant to add rather than detract from his true purpose (a procedure known as *yippui ko'aḥ*), or if it should be apparent that he erroneously believed a *kinyan* was required to effect a *mattenat shekhiv me-ra*, the fact of the *kinyan* will not detract from the validity of the will as a *mattenat shekhiv me-ra* (*Taz*, ḤM 250:17).

The will of a *shekhiv me-ra* is valid only if the testator "gave all his property and left nothing [for himself]; but if he left a part it is like the *mattenat bari* which is only acquired by a formal *kinyan*." The explanation for this is that a *shekhiv me-ra* who only disposes of part of his property does not do so in the expectation of his death – otherwise he would dispose of all his property; hence it is inferred that he intends to make a regular *mattenat bari*, which leaves no room for application of the rabbinical enactment that his instruction "has the same force as a document written and delivered" (Sh. Ar., ḤM 250:4; BB 151b). At the same time, even if a *shekhiv me-ra* leaves part of his property (for himself), his disposition will require no *kinyan* if it is made *meḥamat mitah* – that is, when it appears from his statements, explicitly or implicitly, that the disposition is made by him in the apprehension of death (Sh. Ar., ḤM 250:7; BB 151b). This is in fact the position in practically every case of a will made by a *shekhiv me-ra*. The will of a *shekhiv me-ra* may be retracted from by the testator (Yad, Zekhiyyah 9:15) by way of his oral or written expression of the wish to revoke the will (*Rashbam*, BB 152b). The revocation need not be express and will be implied if the testator makes another will relating to the same property (TJ, BB 8:7, 16b; BB 135b; Yad, loc. cit.). Revocation of part of a will is regarded as a revocation of the whole (BB 148b), and the same consequence follows if the testator should will his estate to several persons and afterward revoke his bequest to any one of them (*Rema*, ḤM 250:12). The will of a *shekhiv me-ra* is automatically revoked on the latter's recovery from his illness (Git. 72b), notwithstanding any prior express stipulation by him to the contrary. This is explained on the grounds of an enactment by the scholars that the expressed wishes of a *shekhiv me-ra* should be fulfilled out of apprehension for the mental agony which the latter might suffer if left in doubt about the fulfillment of his wishes; hence, on his recovery, the justification for the *takkanah* falls away, since he is once again in a position to make the disposition in any manner he desires (Resp. Rashba, vol. 1, no. 975).

Meẓavveh Meḥamat Mitah

The scholars widened the concept of a *shekhiv me-ra* in recognizing as equally valid the will of a "healthy" person if made *meḥamat mitah*, that is, in contemplation of death – *mortis causa*. A "healthy" person is regarded as having willed his property *meḥamat mitah* in one of the following circumstances: when he is seriously ill (even though he does not fall within the definition of a *shekhiv me-ra* – see above); when he is about to be executed under the law of the land; when he sets out with a caravan on a desert journey; and when he leaves on a sea voyage (Git. 65b, 66a and *Rashi* ad loc.). These four circumstances correspond to those in which it is incumbent to offer thanksgiving to the Almighty (Psalm 107; Ber. 54b). A disposition *meḥamat mitah* requires no formal *kinyan*, whether it relates to all or only a part of the testator's property (Yad, Zekhiyyah 8:24; Sh. Ar., ḤM 250:8). The manner of evolution of the law concerning a *meḥamat mitah* disposition is described in the language of the Mishnah, pertaining mainly to the laws of divorce but extended also to the laws of wills, as follows: "At first they used to say: If a man was led forth in chains and was about to be executed under the law of the land and said, 'Write out a bill of divorce for my wife,' they would write it out and deliver it [because being in a state of bewilderment he said only 'write out' and did not manage to say also 'deliver']… Then they changed this and said, 'Also if a man went on a voyage or set out with a caravan.' R. Simeon Shezuri says, 'Also if a man was at the point of death'" (Git. 6:5). The *halakhah* was decided according to R. Simeon (TJ, Git. 6:7, 48a).

Some scholars held that it was only in the matter of granting a divorce that a valid *meḥamat mitah* disposition was constituted in any one of the four above-mentioned circumstances (*Piskei ha-Rosh*, BB 9:18; *Beit Yosef*, ḤM 250, no. 13), and that any other *meḥamat mitah* disposition was only valid in the case of a person seriously ill or one about to be executed, but not in the other two cases. The scholars made this distinction on the basis that in the latter two cases the testator harbors the intention of returning to his home (Rosh, loc. cit.), or that death is not imminent (Nov. Rashba, BB 146b; *Maggid Mishneh*, Zekhiyyah 8:24). Other scholars (*Beit Yosef*, loc. cit., quoting Alfasi, Maimonides, and Naḥmanides) took the view that there was no reason for distinguishing between a divorce and the disposition of property by will for this purpose.

A "healthy" person whose will is not made within the framework of one of the above-mentioned circumstances is not regarded as a person willing his property *meḥamat mitah*, notwithstanding his express declaration that he is acting as such out of fear that he might die suddenly (Resp. Rashba, vol. 1, no. 975; vol. 3, no. 118; Sh. Ar., ḤM 250:14). Hai Gaon was of the opinion that if a "healthy" person willed his property in the apprehension of sudden death and in fact died shortly thereafter, his will was to be regarded as one *meḥamat mitah* (Judah b. Barzillai, *Sefer ha-Shetarot*, no. 54; *Keneset ha-Gedolah*, ḤM 250, *Beit Yosef*, no. 131).

Undertaking and Acknowledgment or Admission (Odita, Hoda'ah)

One of the telling limitations imposed by Jewish law on the different forms of testamentary disposition is the fact that the disposition is valid only in respect of property in the possession of the testator at the time the will is made (Yad, Mekhirah 22:1, 5). To overcome this limitation there evolved the use of a will formulated as an undertaking, since the law, although it precluded any possibility of a person transferring property not yet in existence or possessed by him (in his *reshut*), presented no obstacle to undertaking an obligation in respect of such property (Resp. Rashba, vol. 3, no. 118). Such an undertaking could be affected in writing or before witnesses, and also by way of an acknowledgment (of indebtedness) called *odita*. According to one view an *odita* may only be affected by a *shekhiv me-ra* (*Ittur*, s.v., *Hoda'ah*; *Or Zaru'a*, no. 477, 4).

If the aforesaid undertaking is made in writing and the instrument is delivered before witnesses, the beneficiary may recover it even from *nekhasim mesh'ubadim* (i.e., encumbered and alienated property; see *Lien; but if not so delivered, the beneficiary may only recover from *nekhasim benei ḥorin* ("free property"; *Maggid Mishneh*, Mekhirah 11:15; Sh. Ar., ḤM 40:1 and *Siftei Kohen* thereto, no. 3). In the case of an undertaking before witnesses, the benefactor declares, "Be witnesses unto me that I obligate myself," and the witnesses acquire from him (Yad and Sh. Ar., loc. cit.). The acknowledgment may also be made by the benefactor acknowledging indebtedness in writing or by declaring before witnesses: "Be witnesses unto me that I am indebted"; in this event the witnesses do not require a formal acquisition (*kinyan*) from the benefactor (*Sma* 40:1; *Netivot ha-Mishpat* 40, *Mishpat ha-Urim* n. 1 and *Mishpat ha-Kohanim*, n. 3).

A testamentary disposition by undertaking or acknowledgment is irrevocable, whether effected by a *bari* or a *shekhiv me-ra*, and in the latter case the disposition is not revoked on the benefactor's death (R. Isaac, in Tos. BB 149a; Sh. Ar., ḤM 250:3). The usual time specified for fulfillment of the undertaking is an hour before the death of the benefactor so that the beneficiary should be unable to demand fulfillment during the benefactor's lifetime, since the due date of fulfillment is ascertainable only after the latter's death. However, it is essential that the due time of fulfillment be fixed at a date within the benefactor's lifetime, since an undertaking falling due for fulfillment after the promisor's death is void (Resp. Maharik, no. 89). Testamentary dispositions of this nature have been customary throughout the Diaspora in various forms and degrees of complexity. It is possible that the use of this form of will was adopted to avoid giving the appearance that the inheritance was being diverted from the legal heir – conduct of which the Mishnah says "The sages do not approve of him" (BB 8:5); it was therefore preferred through the means of such an undertaking to avoid a legal devolution of the estate. Widespread use of such an undertaking was made in the *shetar ḥaẓi zakhar*, a deed by means of which a father gave his daughter a share of the property equal to one-half of a son's portion (under the laws of succession). This deed, given to the daughter upon her marriage, may be regarded as a form of irrevocable will of the father (the deed being irrevocable in order to ensure the father's donation to his daughter and her husband). In this case, too, the time of fulfillment usually specified is one hour before the father's death. In order to overcome the difficulty of donating a specified portion of one's estate upon a daughter's marriage, at a time when the exact extent of the estate is still unknown, the following procedure was laid down: the father acknowledges that he owes his daughter a sum of money exceeding the estimated value of one-half of a son's share, adding a condition that the heir shall have the option either to pay this amount to the daughter of the deceased, or to give her a share of the estate equal to one-half of a son's portion (*Naḥalat Shivah*, no. 21; *Rema*, ḤM 281:7 and EH 108:3).

Mitzvah to Carry out the Wishes of the Deceased

Although a will may be invalid for one reason or another, it may still be recognized in certain circumstances in terms of the rule that "It is a *mitzvah* to carry out the wishes of the deceased" (Ket. 70a, Git. 14b). Thus it is the duty of the legal heirs to carry out the wishes of the testator, and this is a duty which the courts will enforce. However, the above rule is not always to be applied as a strict legal duty, and when the duty is merely a moral one, the court will not compel compliance with the testator's directions (*Shevut Ya'akov*, vol. 1, no. 168). The rule applies to the bequest of both a *bari* and a *shekhiv me-ra* (Yad, Zekhiyyah 4:5; Sh. Ar., ḤM 252:2) whether made orally or in writing (Tos., BB 149a). The rule's scope of operation is a matter of scholarly dispute; there are three different views:

(1) that it applies only in respect of property deposited with a trustee, at the time of the bequest, so that he should carry out the latter (Resp. Ritba, no. 54; *Rema*, ḤM 242:2);

(2) that it applies even when the property is not deposited as mentioned above, provided that the legal heir of the deceased has been directed to carry out the bequest and does not object thereto (Resp. Ritba, loc. cit.; *Sha'arei Uzzi'el*, 1 (1944), no. 21);

(3) that it is applicable in every event, and even if the bequest has not been directed to any of the legal heirs, the latter are obliged to carry it out (*Haggahot Mordekhai*, BB no. 666). According to the aforementioned rule, ownership of the bequested property does not automatically pass to the beneficiary, but the duty is imposed on the legal heirs to transfer the said property to him (*Rashi*, Git. 14b; *Mordekhai*, BB, no. 630), from which derives an important distinction between a will taking effect by virtue of the above-mentioned rule and the wills of a *bari* and a *shekhiv me-ra*, namely: in the former case the beneficiary is not entitled to recover the bequested property from third-party purchasers (*Haggahot Mordekhai*, BB, no. 666), where he does have this right in the latter case (Resp. Rosh 86:5; Sh. Ar., ḤM 111:9 and 257:6).

Capacity to Bequeath

A person's legal capacity to make a bequest is generally coextensive with his capacity to make a regular gift, but there are a number of special rules relating to the former:

(1) Although, according to some of the *posekim*, a minor generally requires his guardian's approval in order to make a gift (Yad, Mekhirah 29:7; Sh. Ar., ḤM 235:2), such approval is unnecessary as regards a *mattenat shekhiv me-ra*. The explanation for this apparently lies in the fact that a *mattenat shekhiv me-ra* falls due after the benefactor's death, whereas guardianship terminates on the minor's death, and also because the primary task of a guardian is to safeguard the minor's interests, a task which falls away on the minor's death (Resp. Maharam Alshekh, 101).

(2) It is doubtful whether the tacit *shekhiv me-ra* bequest of a deaf-mute (*ḥeresh*), is valid, even though his tacit, regular gift is valid. The doubt arises from the fact that both the possibility of alienating by implication and a *mattenat shekhiv me-ra* derive from rabbinical enactment, whereas the rule is that "one does not add one *takkanah* to another" (BM 5b). On the other hand, it is possible that the rule, "the instruction of a *shekhiv me-ra* has the same force as a document written and delivered," applies also to the tacit acts of a deaf-mute – even with regard to his disposition of land and despite the fact that he cannot do so by way of a regular gift (*Kesef ha-Kedoshim*, 250:6).

(3) A proselyte has no capacity to make a *shekhiv me-ra* bequest: "A *mattenat shekhiv me-ra* has been given the same force by the rabbis as an inheritance; therefore where there can be inheritance there can also be gift and where there cannot be inheritance there also cannot be gift" (BB 149a). Hence, in view of the fact that a proselyte who leaves no offspring conceived after his proselytization has no heirs (Tos. BB 149a), he cannot make a *mattenat shekhiv me-ra* (Sh. Ar., ḤM 256:1 and *Rema* thereto). According to some scholars, his capacity to bequeath is only limited as regards offspring conceived before his proselytization and who are not his legal heirs, but his *shekhiv me-ra* bequest made to any other person is valid (Sh. Ar., ḤM 256, *Sma* thereto n. 3). Other scholars hold that the *shekhiv me-ra* bequest of a proselyte is of no effect, regardless of who the beneficiary may be (*Hassagot Rabad* on *Rif*, BB 149a, in the name of Hai Gaon; *Hassagot Rabad* on Yad, Zekhiyyah 9:7). According to another view, the rule that it is a *mitzvah* to carry out the wishes of the deceased does not apply to a proselyte (Tos., BB 149a; Tur, ḤM 256:7–9; *Rema*, ḤM 256:1).

Capacity to Benefit from a Bequest

A person's legal capacity to benefit from a bequest is generally coextensive with his capacity to receive a regular gift, but here, too, there exist a number of special rules:

(1) According to some of the *posekim* a proselyte cannot receive a *mattenat shekhiv me-ra* (Rabad, quoted in *Shitah Mekubbeẓet*, BB 149a and *Tosefot Rid*, ad loc., end of no. 14).

(2) Even the *posekim* who hold that a person cannot give a regular gift to his offspring as long as they are *embryos, agree that it is acceptable for him to make them a *shekhiv me-ra* bequest (*Beit Yosef* and *Derishah*, ḤM 210, no. 3; *Siftei Kohen*, ḤM 210, n. 1).

A person who lacks capacity to benefit from a bequest, may benefit from it if it is executed in the form of assignment to a third party on his behalf. This possibility also applies in the case of a *mattenat shekhiv me-ra*, and it is possible to benefit an embryo in this manner, even according to the *posekim* who reject the possibility of a *mattenat shekhiv me-ra* in favor of an embryo (Tur, ḤM 210:1).

Subject Matter of the Bequest

In general the restrictions placed on the possible subject matter of a regular gift are applicable also as regards the subject matter of a bequest. According to certain *posekim*, a person cannot make a *mattenat shekhiv me-ra* and retain for himself the usufruct of the property in question, even though this may be done in the case of a regular gift (Rabad, quoted in *Beit Yosef*, ḤM 209:10; opinion quoted by *Rema*, ḤM 209:7). The reason for this is that a *mattenat shekhiv me-ra* is acquired after the benefactor's death so that his retention of the usufruct is solely for the benefit of his legal heirs and not for himself. A bequest may be made of property in kind and also in the form of a fixed payment (Ta'an. 21a; Ket. 69b), or by establishing a fund, with the income from it designated for a particular purpose (*Pithei Teshuvah*, ḤM 246, n. 2). It is possible for the testator to nominate an executor (*apotropos*) of his estate (Tur, ḤM 250:1 and 33). There is also an opinion that a *shekhiv me-ra* may entrust the executor with the actual decision as to division of the estate (*Mordekhai*, BB, no. 600).

At times wills have included charitable bequests. When such a bequest is made in a manner whereby the principal is established as a perpetual fund, while the income from it is dedicated to the charitable purpose, the estate – or the portion concerned – is known as a *keren kayyemet* (Resp. Rashba, vol. 3, no. 295; *Keneset ha-Gedolah*, YD 253; see also *Consecration and Endowment).

Form and Wording of Wills

It is desirable that it be indicated in the will whether the testator is a *bari* or a *shekhiv me-ra*, although omission to do so does not affect the will's validity (Yad, Zekhiyyah 9:22; Tur, ḤM 251:3). In the case of a dispute between the legal heirs and the beneficiaries under the will, the burden of proof as to the testator's state of health devolves on the latter, since the legal heirs are deemed entitled (*muhzakim*) to the estate's assets and "the burden of proof rests on the claimant" (Yad and Tur, loc. cit.; Sh. Ar., ḤM 251:2). The following are the customary versions, since talmudic times, to describe the testator's state of health: for a *mattenat bari*, "while he was walking on his feet in the market"; for a *mattenat shekhiv me-ra*, "while he was ill and confined to his bed"; and for a *shekhiv me-ra* will reduced to writing only after the testator's death, "and from his illness he died" (BB 153a, 154a), this version being essential since the disposition will be void if the testator should not die from the illness (BB *ibid.*; Sh. Ar., loc. cit.).

The testator must employ the phraseology which is effective for transfer of title in regular gifts. Thus it is necessary for the testator to use a verb denoting gift (*natan*, "gave," etc.; BB 148b; Sh. Ar., ḤM 253:2). A *shekhiv me-ra* testator who bequeathes in favor of his legal heir may employ a verb denoting inheritance (ḤM 281:3). The phraseology used by the testator must clearly show that the testator is alienating the asset concerned and not that he is promising to transfer title to it (*Rashi*, Git. 40b). Use of the past or present tense confers title but not use of the future tense (Yad, Zekhiyyah 4:11; Sh. Ar., ḤM 245:1). On the other hand, a *shekhiv me-ra* will couched in the future tense, is valid since in this case the testator speaks of a gift to take effect in the future – after his death. However, even a *shekhiv me-ra* will is invalid if phrased as a mere promise (*Beit Yosef*, EH 51–end of s.v. שנים; *Maggid Mishneh*, Yad, Mekhirah 2:8; *Bah*, ḤM 253:2). Language phrased in the form of a request to the testator's legal heirs to give specific assets to the beneficiaries under the will is valid and effective (*Piskei Maharam*, no. 99; *Rema*, ḤM 250:21).

As in all cases of gift, the will of both a healthy person and that of a *shekhiv me-ra* must be executed in public, and the testator must direct the witnesses to sign the will in like manner: "… Sit in the markets and public places and write for him openly and publicly a deed of gift" (Yad, Zekhiyyah 5:1, 4; BB 40b; Tur, ḤM 242:7). A *mehamat mitah* testator is not required to direct that the disposition be made public (Yad, Zekhiyyah 9:2), but if he should expressly direct the witnesses to keep his will secret, it will be invalid (*Perisha*, ḤM 242:4).

Interpretation of Wills

Wills are generally subject to the same principles of interpretation as are all other documents (see *Interpretation). The process of *umedana* ("estimation") is of particular application to the interpretation of wills – that is the process of endeavoring to fathom the mind of the testator in order to understand his true intention – and the will itself is virtually the exclusive means to do this. The legal heirs of the deceased are deemed to be in possession of his property. Hence, a person claiming under the will is subject to the rule that "the holder of a deed is always at a disadvantage," for the reason that "the burden of proof rests with the claimant" (Bik. 2:10; Ket. 83b), and the beneficiary under the will accordingly has the burden of proving that the testator's intention was such that the will should be interpreted in his favor. The aforementioned rule only applies where doubt has arisen with regard to the interpretation of the will, and it does not operate in order to void the will entirely (Resp. Ribash, no. 145; Sh. Ar., ḤM 42:9).

The principle of estimation may serve to entirely invalidate a will. Thus in a case where a *shekhiv me-ra*, in the belief that his son is dead, bequeaths all his property to another, the disposition will be invalid if it should subsequently transpire that the son is alive – and in this event the latter will inherit from his father (BB 146b). Similarly, in certain circumstances a beneficiary under a will may become the mere custodian of the estate assets should it be so determined as an outcome of estimation that it was this that the testator intended (BB 131b; Sh. Ar., EH 107 and ḤM 246:4–12).

Various rules were determined with regard to the interpretation of certain expressions in a will. Thus with reference to a *shekhiv me-ra* will, it was laid down that the term *banim* means "sons" and excludes daughters (TJ, Ket. 13:1, 35d) and that the intention of the testator who bequeaths all his property to his *banim*, when he has one son only and daughters, is to bequeath all to his son (BB 143b and see the biblical texts there cited; Yad, Zekhiyyah 11:1). Disputed in the Talmud is the intention of the testator who bequeaths to his *banim* when he has a single son and a grandson, and it was decided that in such a case it is not intended that the grandson be included (*ibid.*).

If a will contains contradictory directions which cannot possibly be reconciled with each other, the direction recorded last in the will prevails, on the assumption that the testator has repudiated the earlier direction (BB 10:2; Yad, Malveh 27:14; Sh. Ar., ḤM 42:5). However, when the contradiction emerges from the directions contained in one and the same passage of the will, the later reference is of no special import and the rule that "the holder of a deed is always at a disadvantage" applies (*ibid.*).

Authority to interpret documents is in general entrusted to the courts. With regard to a *shekhiv me-ra* will this authority is sometimes entrusted to the persons present at the time of its execution (BB 113b; Sh. Ar., ḤM 253:1). Thus if a *shekhiv me-ra* bequeathed his property in the presence of three persons, the latter may adjudge in the matter of the will and with reference to any doubt arising in connection with its interpretation (*Rema*, ḤM 253:1). However, if these persons were requested to be present as witnesses to the will, they will be disqualified from acting as judges in matters concerning the will (*Beit Yosef*, ḤM 7:6; Sh. Ar., ḤM 7:5). Another opinion that they will be disqualified even if they were not requested to serve as witnesses but intended to act as such (*Rashbam*, BB 113b) was rejected by a majority of the *posekim* (Tos. BB 114a; Sh. Ar., loc. cit.). Three persons present at the time of the testamentary disposition may only act as judges in connection with it when the will is made in the daytime, since the *halakhah* is that the adjudication shall not take place at night (see *Bet Din*; Sh. Ar., ḤM 5:2 and 253:1). If sums of money are bequeathed by a *shekhiv me-ra* to several persons, and it transpires that the latter's estate is lacking in funds, the position will depend on the way in which the bequest is worded. If the wording is, "give two hundred *zuz* to A, three hundred *zuz* to B, and four hundred *zuz* to C," each of the persons mentioned receives only his proportionate share of the available amount; if, however, the wording is, "give two hundred *zuz* to A, thereafter three hundred *zuz* to B and thereafter four hundred *zuz* to C," the parties will take precedence in turn in accordance with the order in which their names are mentioned (Yad, Zekhiyyah, 10:13, 14).

Accrual of Rights under a Will

The beneficiary under a *mattenat bari* becomes entitled to the disposition in accordance with the terms of it, that is to the body of the property immediately and to its fruits upon the donor's death. In this case the beneficiary's right to the body of the donated property is a regular proprietary right, which he may, therefore, sell even during the donor's lifetime, and if the beneficiary should predecease the donor, the former's heirs become entitled to the donation (Sh. Ar., ḤM 257:4). The beneficiary under a *shekhiv me-ra* will becomes entitled to the bequeathed property upon the testator's death since a *shekhiv me-ra* will is subject to the same law as is succession according to law (see above). Therefore, if the beneficiary should predecease the testator, the former's heirs do not become entitled to anything at all (Sh. Ar., ḤM 125:9 and *Siftei Kohen*, thereto, 36).

Renunciation of Rights under a Will

In general, a person's refusal to accept property given to him as a gift will be effective if the refusal is made before the property comes into his possession, and in this event he does not become entitled to it (Ker. 24b). In the case of a gift or bequest made in the beneficiary's presence, the latter must at this very stage express his refusal of it (Sh. Ar., ḤM 245:10); if he should wish to renounce a gift or bequest not made in his presence, he must do so immediately on becoming aware of it (Rif, *Halakhot*, BB 138a; *Piskei ha-Rosh, ibid.*; Yad, Zekhiyyah 9:13). A renunciation made by a beneficiary who remains silent for a period after having become aware that the gift or bequest has been made is ineffective (Yad, Zekhiyyah 9:14; Sh. Ar., ḤM 245:10). The renunciation must be made in an unequivocal manner, and the beneficiary must clearly state that he has no intention at all of becoming entitled to the gift or bequest and that it is a nullity *ab initio* (Yad, Zekhiyyah 9:13; Sh. Ar., ḤM 245:7 and *Sma* thereto, n. 18).

Fideicommissary Bequests

The testator may direct that particular assets shall be given to the beneficiary for a limited period and that after this period these assets shall pass to another. A will is generally made in this form when the testator wishes to ensure that his property shall not, after the beneficiary's death, pass to the latter's heirs but shall go to some other person (Yad, Zekhiyyah 3:9; Sh. Ar., 241:6; *Rema*, ḤM 248:3). In principle there is no restriction on the possible order of successive beneficiaries which the testator may determine, but in practice this right is qualified by the requirement that all the beneficiaries must be alive at the time the gift or bequest is made (Resp. Rosh, no. 84:1 and 2). Each beneficiary under such a will in turn enjoys the usufruct of the bequeathed property and has the right to deal with the latter as with his own property – even to sell it.

A moral prohibition was imposed on the sale of such property by any one of the fideicommissaries – save for the last beneficiary mentioned in the will – since this was held to amount to a frustration of the testator's original intention; a sale effected by one of the fideicommissaries contrary to the above prohibition is nevertheless valid (BB 137a; Yad, Zekhiyyah 12:8, 9). A disposition of the bequeathed property by way of a *shekhiv me-ra* will on the part of a fideicommissary is ineffective, since the property only passes into the new beneficiary's possession after the testator's death and at this time the property is no longer the latter's but that of the fideicommissary next in line in terms of the original will (BB 137a; Yad, Zekhiyyah 12:10).

In the case where property is bequeathed to an unmarried woman, "to you and thereafter to A," and the woman subsequently marries, the property will not pass in turn to A but the woman's husband will become entitled to it (Ket. 95b); however, if a bequest of this nature is made to a married woman, the beneficiary next in line will in turn succeed to the property, since this will be assessed to have been the testator's true intention (Ket. loc. cit.;Yad, Zekhiyyah 12:12; Sh. Ar., EH 91:2 and ḤM 248:8).

Where property is bequeathed by a *shekhiv me-ra* will to a legal heir of the testator "to you and thereafter to A," the property will not upon the beneficiary's death pass to A but to the beneficiary's legal heirs (Yad, Zekhiyyah 12:7; Sh. Ar., ḤM 248:1; BB 129b and *Rashbam*, ad loc.). The explanation for this is as follows: since in a *shekhiv me-ra* will the property only passes to the beneficiary after the testator's death, and since the beneficiary is a legal heir of the testator, the former becomes entitled to the property by virtue of the law of the Torah and the testator may not stipulate that his property shall after the beneficiary's death pass to A and not to the beneficiary's legal heirs, for this is a stipulation contrary to the law of the Torah and therefore void; this rule is referred to in the Talmud as *yerushah ein lah hefsek* ("an inheritance cannot be terminated"; BB 129b, 133a).

Takkanot Concerning the Form and Execution of Wills

In many communities different *takkanot* were enacted with regard to various documents which, in particular, obliged those executing the documents to do so before a scribe or rabbi (Sh. Ar., ḤM 61:1), both as a protection against forgeries and in order to make the documents publicly known (*Baḥ*, ḤM 61:1). At times it was laid down that a document executed contrary to a particular *takkanah* was of no effect and a fine was even imposed on the person who executed it (S. Buber, *Anshei Shem* (1895), 225f.). In some cases it was necessary for certain deeds to be publicly announced in the synagogue (Resp. Ribash, no. 88; Resp. Rashba, vol. 3, no. 431). The manner of execution of wills was specially dealt with in a number of *takkanot*. Thus two years after the expulsion of the Jews from Spain, the *takkanot* of Fez were enacted which included, among others, this *takkanah*: "Whoever shall wish to make a gift or will, whether male or female, shall do so before the *ḥakham* or *dayyan* of the town, otherwise the gift or will shall be of no worth" (*Kerem Ḥamar*, vol. 2, no. 11). This *takkanah* was later extended (*ibid.*, no. 19) and a further *takkanah* prescribed that "any *shekhiv me-ra* will or gift which shall not be made before the *ḥakham* or *dayyan* of the town shall be null and void; that is, everything that a *shekhiv me-ra* shall do is void if not done before a *dayyan*" (*ibid.*, 36a/b, *takkanot* pertaining to ḤM, no. 4). These *takkanot* were apparently enacted for two reasons: to ensure that the testator was of sound mind when making the will, and so that the scholar could stress before the testator the fact that the latter was transferring the inheritance from his legal heirs to someone else, a consequence looked upon with disfavor by the scholars (*Mishpatim Yesharim*, no. 2:161, and see above). Similar *takkanot* were enacted also in Jerusalem (Resp. Mabit, no. 2, pt. 2, no. 1).

Jerusalem Takkanot

It was the custom that the estate of a person who died in Jerusalem without leaving any heirs in Ereẓ Israel passed to the public, a custom apparently aimed at preventing the authorities from taking the estate. The public would administer the estate, and if the heirs of the deceased later came to claim the estate, it would be sought to influence them to leave part of it to the community chest. At a later stage a *takkanah* was enacted to the effect that the estate of a deceased person without any heirs in Ereẓ Israel actually passed to the public (see Rivlin, in bibl.). However, even after the enactment of this *takkanah* a person could still keep his estate from passing to the public by making a will. A deterioration in the position of Jerusalem Jewry led to the enactment of a number of further *takkanot* in this connection. Thus in 1730 there was a reinstatement of an ancient *takkanah* which laid down that a will had to be executed before communal representatives and that it was necessary that there be present a representative of the communal leadership of Constantinople, communal appointees, as well as a **parnas* and scribe of the community and, failing this, the will would have no validity. At the same time it was expressly laid down that a person could bequeath as he wished before the above-mentioned persons (*Sefer ha-Takkanot ve-Haskamot… Yerushalayim…* (1883[2]) 24b, 25b, 26a). In 1737 a far-reaching *takkanah* was enacted which forbade a person without heirs in Ereẓ Israel from making a will (*ibid.*, 18a/b). When this *takkanah* was circumvented by persons who made a *mattenat bari* abroad before coming to settle in Ereẓ Israel, there was enacted a *takkanah* in 1776 which rendered invalid various kinds of wills, including a *mattenat bari* "from today and after my death," whether executed in or outside of Ereẓ Israel (*ibid.*, 29a/b). In 1810 Ashkenazi Jews (*Perushim*) began to settle in Ereẓ Israel, and they objected to the above *takkanot*. For some years a dispute was waged in regard to these *takkanot*, and in the end they were not followed by the Ashkenazi Jews (see Rivlin, in bibl., p. 61).

Takkanot Concerning Disposition of the Property of Spouses

The Toledo *takkanot* enacted in favor of the wife's family were aimed at preventing the entire assets contributed by the wife to her husband from passing to the latter on her death. These *takkanot* provided that the wife's relatives – who would normally inherit from her in the event that she survived her husband – should receive one-half of her estate. It was decided by Asher b. Jehiel that a wife could not dispose of her property by will so as to leave it all to her husband or some other person and thereby frustrate the object of the above *takkanot* (Resp. nos. 55:1 and 40:2). In consequence of the decision, *takkanot* were enacted in the communities of the Spanish exiles which expressly incorporated the import of the decision into the Toledo *takkanot*. The exiles of 1391 who settled in North Africa enacted – under the guidance of R. Simeon b. Ẓemaḥ *Duran – a series of *takkanot*, the third of which, among others, rendered it forbidden for a woman to make any form of will in which she purported to transfer one-half of her estate "to any person in the world save to any offspring she has by her husband who would be her nearest heir; and if she has done so, it shall henceforth be null and void" (*Tashbeẓ*, 2:292).

From the statements of the *posekim* of the Moroccan communities, it appears that despite the existence of various *takkanot* which followed those of Toledo, it still remained possible for a woman to make gifts to her husband or other persons (*Mishpat u-Ẓedakah le-Ya'akov*, pt. 2, no. 83; *Mishpatim Yesharim*, no. 2:211). On the other hand it was decided there that a *shekhiv me-ra* bequest made by a woman in which she gave a large part of her property to her husband was invalid (*Ner Ma'aravi*, no. 1:16). Another *takkanah* enacted in Fez imposed restrictions on the husband's freedom to make a testamentary disposition of his property by prescribing that if the wife objected to the *shekhiv me-ra* will of her husband, her share – or that of her heirs – in the estate would remain unaffected by the will. Another *takkanah* laid down that before distribution of the estate in accordance with the existing *takkanot*, there were to be recovered from it *mattenat bari* but not *shekhiv me-ra* bequests to which the wife of the deceased objected (*Kerem Ḥamar*, vol. 2, 34b, no. 6; the scholars were divided on the interpretation of this *takkanah* – see *Mishpatim Yesharim*, no. 2:268).

In consequence of the migrations of the Spanish exiles similar *takkanot* to those of Toledo were enacted in many communities of the Mediterranean countries. In some places a woman was expressly precluded from bequeathing part of her property to her husband; this was prescribed, for instance, in the *takkanot* of Arta (*Torat Ḥayyim*, EH 24), apparently enacted in 1597 (see Resp. Ranaḥ, no. 25).

In the State of Israel

In the Succession Law of 1965 the Knesset partly adopted and partly rejected different principles pertaining to testamentary dispositions in Jewish law. The *mattenat bari* and *shekhiv mera* forms of will were adopted both in formulation and content (sec. 23; M. Elon, in: ILR, 4 (1969), 133f.). The Law – in reception of Jewish law principles and contrary to English law – empowers the court to give effect to a formally defective will when there is no doubt as to its genuineness (sec. 25).

[Shmuel Shilo]

A Will Formulated as a Request

Rabbi Israel Isserlein (Resp. Terumat Ha-Deshen, *Pesakim u-Ketavim*, (Ashkenaz, 15th century), 99) was asked about a will in which the testator turned to his son, requesting him to waive a particular debt that someone owed him; the question was whether this request was in fact an integral part of the will or merely a request or recommendation. His answer was that he was inclined to view this as a will in every respect, and that the use of the form of request, rather than instruction, was merely in order for the matter to be dealt with amicably. The Rema (Sh. Ar., ḤM, 250:21) ruled, on the basis of this responsum, that where a will is drafted in the form of a request, it is to be considered as a statement of a *shekhiv mera*, of one who is critically ill, and therefore to have the binding force of a will. Other halakhic decisors expressed doubts regarding this matter, in view of the fact that further on in this responsum Rabbi Isserlein himself questioned whether this was in fact the law (*Ḥiddushei Rabbi Akiva Eiger*, ad loc.; *Beit Yosef*, ḤM 253).

Rabbi Isserlein's responsum and Rema's ruling were considered in decisions of the rabbinical courts in the State of Israel when adjudicating a case in which the language of the will was framed as a request. The Regional Rabbinical Court in Petaḥ Tikvah (File 1862/28) ruled that, even according to the opinion of the Rema, an additional reason is needed in order for the request to be considered a will, noting that in his responsum Rabbi Isserlein had explained that the provision was framed as a request in order for the matter to be dealt with amicably. Thus, only where there is an additional rationale to explain the background for using the form of request, such as that brought by Rabbi Isserlein, which explained the background of the request, may a request be viewed as a provision of a will. In the appeal, the Israeli Rabbinical Court of Appeals (5731/4, 8 PDR 240) rejected the reasoning of the Regional Rabbinical Court and stated that Rabbi Isserlein's opinion implies that any request constitutes a will unless there is cause to believe otherwise, in which case an additional rationale is needed, and the decision of the Rema is applicable to any ordinary case of a will written as a request (*ibid.*, pp. 245–47).

A similar question came before the Israeli Supreme Court when the deceased left a letter recommending to the person whom he had designated as his heir not to accept the inheritance (CA 202/85 *Kleine-Beck v. Goldberg*, 41(2) PD 753; *per* Justice Menachem Elon). The family of the deceased argued that this constituted a revocation of the will, whereas the person designated as heir argued that this was only a recommendation. The District Court ruled according to the responsum of Rabbi Isserlein – namely, that a request constitutes a will and thus the earlier will must be viewed as having been revoked. The Supreme Court ruled that a distinction must be made between a request, that must be viewed as a will under Jewish Law, and the case under consideration, in which the document at issue was a letter containing a recommendation, that could not even be considered as a request; hence its language should not be viewed as a will, and the letter did not revoke the earlier will (*ibid*, pp. 768–70).

Enforcing a Defective Will

Wills that are drafted by notaries, in accordance with the laws of the State, often contain elements that would be considered defects according to Jewish Law and that would, prima facie, prevent their execution. Nevertheless, the accepted practice is to uphold such wills and to regard them as valid, pursuant to the principle of custom (see *Custom). The basis for this position is the responsum of the Radbaz (1:67) ruling that the custom is to uphold instruments of the non-Jewish legal authorities. Even though the rule is that custom generally cannot override or invalidate rulings based on Torah, here there is no actual invalidation of Torah law governing inheritance, but simply a ruling that the gift was a valid gift on the basis of custom. A similar ruling was given by Rabbi David Ḥai Hacohen (*Resp. Radakh* 26:3; Italy-Greece, 16th century).

According to the opinion of some of halakhic authorities such wills should be upheld pursuant to the principle of *dina de-malkhuta dina* (see **Dina de-Malkhuta Dina).* Some are of the opinion that this is only possible when an act of acquisition (*kinyan*) was performed at the time the will was written (*Arukh ha-Shulḥan*, ḤM 68:6), while according to others no such act is necessary (Resp. Iggerot Moshe, *Even Ha-Ezer*, nos. 104–105).

There are additional cases in which a will is inconsistent with the requirements of Jewish Law and the rabbinical courts nevertheless make an effort to uphold these wills relying, inter alia, on the following solutions:

1. In cases in which it may be inferred from the language of the document that the testator is only transferring ownership after his death (i.e., where the testator writes that he bequeaths his property "*after* my death"), this wording may be interpreted as "bequeathing in the contemplation of my death" (see *supra*), inasmuch as there is a tendency in the rulings of halakhic decisors of recent generations to broaden the possibilities of viewing the will of a healthy person as "a will in the contemplation of death."

2. The use of the rule "it is a *mitzvah* to carry out the wishes of the deceased," as cited above, while adopting the approach that broadens its application beyond the cases in which the property has been transferred to a trustee. This is especially the case where the will bequeaths the property for a charitable purpose.

3. Where funds deposited in a bank account are bequeathed. In such cases inasmuch as the funds have been deposited with the bank in accordance with the bank's procedures, which require the bank to transfer the money to the heirs pursuant to the will, which is probated according to civil law, it is authorized to and required to act according to its procedures.

In the State of Israel – Later Developments

As stated above, some of the sections of the Succession Law, 5725 – 1965, adopted various provisions of Jewish Law. An example of this is Section 42(b) of the Succession Law, dealing with the case of consecutive heirs, which provides, inter alia, that the first heir "may deal with what he received as his own and the second shall only take what the first has left." This provision is consistent with the provisions of Jewish Law, as discussed at length above. In a case decided by the Supreme Court (CA 749/82 *Moston v. Wiederman*, 43(1) PD 278), the testator provided in his will that his property would be bequeathed to his wife and that upon her death it would pass to his legal heirs. After studying and discussing the sources of Jewish Law on this subject, the Court ruled that the testator's wife was entitled to the property and was entitled to carry out any legal transaction regarding them, including their sale, but that she could not bequeath them in her will to other beneficiaries. This was because immediately upon her death the ownership of the property returns to the legal heirs of the first testator, in accordance with the provision of Jewish Law that the first beneficiary may transfer the estate in any manner except by will, not even by way of a *shekhiv me-ra's* will to other beneficiaries (*ibid*, pp. 289–93; *per* Justice Menachem Elon); for a detailed discussion of the aspects of this subject in Jewish law see *Law and Morality).

The origin of Section 23 of the Succession Law in the Jewish Law regarding *shekhiv me-ra* served as the basis for the interpretation given to this section by the Supreme Court in the *Koenig* decision (FH 40/80 *Koenig v. Cohen*, 36(3) PD 701). That case involved a will that a woman left on a piece of paper, undated and unsigned, a moment before she took her life. The justices' opinions were divided regarding the legal validity of the will. Justice Menachem Elon ruled that the document should be regarded as a will in contemplation of death, given that a *shekhiv me-ra's* will and a will in contemplation of death are valid even without a *kinyan*, and even if there were not two witnesses at the time it was drawn up, there is a presumption, by virtue of the special circumstances involved in its drafting, that it reflected her considered wishes and decision (Rambam, Yad, *Zekhiyah u-Matanah,* 8:2, 4, 24, 26; *Sema*, ḤM 253:1). In view of this, the will in the case under consideration, that had no date and to which there were no witnesses, must be validated, notwithstanding its omissions and defects (*ibid*, pp. 733–38).

In another decision (CA 2555/98 *Abergil v. Ben Yair*, 53(5) PD 673), the Supreme Court ruled that the drafting of a will pursuant to the rules of Jewish Law, in the manner of granting a gift while alive, is to be treated by the civil courts as a will and not as a gift, and the provisions of the Succession Law, 5725 – 1965, will apply rather than those of the Gift Law, 5728 – 1968. The Court (Justice Y. Englard) cited the Jewish Law sources discussed above, dealing with the will of a healthy person by way of a gift while living, ruling that Jewish Law indeed considers it a gift, and not a will. However, this is because this is the only recognized way under Jewish Law to distribute the estate to parties other than the legal heirs; hence, this act must be judged according to its *substance*, and should be regarded as a *will* rather than as a *gift* (p. 686 of the decision). In view of this, the Court ruled that even a will drafted in accordance with Jewish Law must fulfill the requirements of Succession Law 5725 – 1965 regarding wills. It should be noted that, regarding this approach of the civil courts, there were those who commented that the decision represents a degree of restriction of the freedom to enter into contractual agreements, inasmuch as it does not permit a person to give his property as a gift in accordance with the model of a "living gift" under Jewish Law.

[Menachem Elon (2nd ed.)]

BIBLIOGRAPHY: L. Bodenheimer, *Das Testament unter Benennung einer... Erbschaft...* (1847); M. Bloch, *Das mosaisch-talmudische Erbrecht* (1890); M.W. Rapaport, in: *Zeitschrift fuer vergleichende Rechtswissenschaft*, 14 (1900), 1–148; Gulak, Yesodei, 3 (1922), 113–45; idem, Oẓar, 110–31; idem, in: *Tarbiz*, 4 (1933), 121–6; idem, *Das Urkundenwesen im Talmud* (1935), 125–36; Herzog, Instit, 1 (1936), 152–4; 2 (1939), 29f.; S. Assaf, in: *Emet le-Ya'akov... Freimann* (1937), 8–13; E. Rivlin, in: *Azkarah... ha-Rav... Kook*, 3 (1937), 559–619; H. Cohn, in: *Yavneh*, 3 (1949), 80–105; A. Freimann, *ibid.*, 106–10; ET, 1 (1951³), 86–88, 251–3, 255; 7 (1956), 114–34; A. Karlin, *Divrei Mishpat*, 1 (1954), 46–81; R. Yaron, *Gifts in Contemplation of Death in Jewish and Roman Law* (1960); A. Kimmelmann, *Ẓavva'at Bari ve-Ẓavva'at Shekhiv me-Ra be-Dinei Yisrael...* (1963); idem, in: *Sinai*, 55 (1964), 145–55; E.E. Urbach, in: *Divrei ha-Congress ha-Olami ha-Revi'i le-Madda'ei ha-Yahadut*, 1 (1967), 133–41; Elon, Mafte'aḥ, 139f., 168–73, 242–5; idem, in: ILR, 4 (1969), 126–40. **ADD. BIBLIOGRAPHY:** M. Elon, *Ha-Mishpat ha-Ivri* (1988), 1:89f., 133f.,361, 364, 369, 417, 476, 651, 653, 670f., 680, 683, 763; 2:992, 1284, 1290; 3:1332, 1395, 1404f., 1412f., 1575f., 1592; idem, *Jewish Law* (1994), 1:99f., 149f., 436f., 440, 446; 2:509, 580, 805, 808, 828f., 839, 843, 940, 962; 3:1200, 1533, 1540; 4:1591, 1663, 1673f., 1681f., 1875f., 1895; idem, *Ma'amad ha-Ishah* (2005), 255–96; M. Elon and B. Lifshitz, *Mafte'aḥ ha-She'elot ve-ha-Teshuvot shel Ḥakhmei Sefarad u-Ẓefon Afrikah* (legal digest) (1986), 2:260, 266–75; B. Lifshitz and E. Shochetman, *Mafte'aḥ ha-She'elot ve-ha-Teshuvot shel Ḥakhmei Ashkenaz, Ẓarefat ve-Italyah* (legal digest) (1997), 2:187–91; I. Gruenfeld, *The Jewish Law of Inheritance* (1987); M.A. Rabilo, "*Al Matanot ve-Yom ha-Mavet*," in: *Sefer Ha-Zikharon le-Gad Tedeski* (1996), 581–606; Y. Rivlin, *Ha-Yerushah ve-ha-Ẓava'ah be-Mishpat ha-Ivri* (1999); H.S. Shaanan, "*Ẓava'ah ke-Halakhah*," in: *Teḥumin*, 13 (1992–1993), 126–317.

WILLS, ETHICAL. The Bible contains examples of wills given by the great sages, especially that of Jacob (Gen. 49), but they possess no special religious or ethical theme. This holds true for the Testament of the Twelve Patriarchs, one of the major works in the *Apocrypha and Pseudepigrapha written during the Second Temple period and shortly after its destruction. The prototype of the medieval ethical will may be found in the Book of Proverbs, where much of the practical ethical advice is given in the manner of instructions from a father to his son.

Talmudic literature contains many aggadic passages quoting or purporting to quote deathbed instructions by great sages to their pupils. These passages, collected by I. Abrahams in the first chapter of his anthology *Hebrew Ethical Wills* (2 vols., 1926), do not concentrate on ethical themes, though some contain ideas similar to those that appear later in the medieval literature. However, Hebrew ethical wills of the Middle Ages are not a direct development of these sayings.

In the Hebrew poetry of the classical Andalusian period there are some examples of ethical wills, for instance, a poem of Samuel ha-Nagid dedicated to his son Yehosef (*Yehosef Kol Asher*) before one of his battles with Granada's army. Seeing death very close, Samuel collected in the poem the best advice for his son.

Medieval ethical wills are an integral part of medieval Hebrew *Ethical Literature, which, although it undoubtedly has deep roots in the traditional talmudic and midrashic literature, is mainly a product of medieval ideologies – i.e., Jewish philosophy, Ashkenazi Ḥasidism (see *Ḥasidei Ashkenaz), and Kabbalah. The aim of ethical literature was to apply theological, psychological, and anthropological conclusions of the ideologies to the everyday life, social and religious, of the average Jew. Various types of literary works were developed for this purpose: ethical treatises dealing with several moral problems, according to subjects or alphabetical order; monographs and homiletical works that deduced ethical norms from the ancient texts; and the ethical will that began to develop in European Jewish communities during the Middle Ages.

Ethical wills differ from other kinds of ethical literature in several ways. Whereas ethical literature usually gives a lengthy theoretical basis for behavioral requirements, ethical wills ordinarily only point out the right way, disregarding the ideological foundations. Thus they are a more practical, behavioral type of literature, close in some respects to the literature of the *hanhagot* (see *Ethical Literature) whose sole aim is to instruct the reader in right behavior in the manner of halakhic literature (but dealing with some subjects not covered by *halakhah*). The literary form of the will – as teachings given by a dying father to his sons gathered around his bedside – does not leave much space for elaborations on or explanations of the traditional basis for the commandments. Ethical wills, therefore, comprise short ethical treatises, very practical in character.

In many ethical wills, every paragraph opens with the words "my son." Sometimes legends arose describing in detail the circumstances under which the will was given. Some wills are described as letters sent by a father, who was far away (in Palestine, for instance), to his sons, instructing them in the basic moral and ethical teachings. In later generations this became an accepted literary form for any short work dealing with the basic ethical norms. The titles of such works, especially in Eastern Europe in the 18th century, suggest a will, e.g., *Naḥalat Avot* ("Inheritance of the Fathers"). It is doubtful whether any extant work of this sort was actually a will, the term "will" having been used only to imply that here in a short form is the essence of the ethical teachings of a certain writer.

Their literary form made ethical wills popular and respected, with readers looking upon them as the last will and testament of a great scholar that should be accepted and followed. Naturally, some writers created pseudepigraphic works, attributing them to great sages of their time who did not happen to write such a treatise themselves. Medieval and early modern times offer examples of such pseudepigraphical works, from the "will" attributed to Maimonides to that attributed to *Israel b. Eliezer Ba'al Shem Tov. The *Ẓavva'at ha-Rivash* (1793) was attributed to the Ba'al Shem Tov, although the work was mainly a compilation of sayings primarily from the writings of Dov Baer of Mezhirech.

The literary form of the will also influenced writers of major ethical works. Jehiel b. Jekuthiel of Rome, author of the *Ma'alot ha-Middot*, a major ethical book of the 13th century, used the form of the will, with the words "my son" beginning many parts of the work. Even Isaiah b. Jacob ha-Levi *Horowitz, whose family produced several ethical wills (see below), used this form in his monumental ethical work *Shenei Luḥot ha-Berit*.

Probably the earliest extant ethical will in Hebrew, a translation from the Arabic, comprises a short chapter in the **Mivḥar ha-Peninnim*, a collection of ethical epigrams attributed to Solomon ibn *Gabirol and translated into Hebrew by Judah ibn *Tibbon. The chapter entitled "The Gate of the Commandment of the Scholar to his Son" includes various epigrams on almost all aspects of human behavior and is part of the philosophical ethical literature, although the philosophical presuppositions are almost nonexistent within the chapter itself.

Another early example is the treatise **Orḥot Ḥayyim* ("Ways of Life"), first attributed to the talmudic sage *Eliezer b. Hyrcanus, and later to the 11th-century Ashkenazi scholar *Eliezer (ha-Gadol) b. Isaac of Worms. Modern scholars disagree about the date of this work – Zunz considers that it was written early in the Middle Ages, about the eighth century, whereas G. Scholem holds that it forms part of the literature which emanated from the same circle that produced the Zohar in the 13th century. *Orḥot Ḥayyim*, a popular work, is a fine example of the literary genre – it includes, in short paragraphs addressed to the writer's sons, advice and instruction about practical, behavioral problems in ethical, moral, religious, and social life, without any specific ideological basis (which is one of the reasons why it is so difficult to determine its time and place of composition). Judah ibn *Tibbon's ethical will, written about 1190 and addressed to his son Samuel, who translated Maimonides' *Guide of the Perplexed* from Arabic to Hebrew, is one of the classics in this genre. Although the will contains the usual detailed and practical instructions from a father to his son on moral behavior, it also is characterized by features rarely found in ethical wills. For example, the will is introduced and concluded by a poem, and within the body of the will there are a number of poetical passages, some of which were taken from *Samuel ha-Nagid's *Ben Mishlei*. A second unusual feature is Judah's reference to many details of family life, his designation of bridegrooms for his daughters and a bride for his son. Apparently the testament is an actual private ethical will from one person to another, and not just a literary work. Thirdly, in this work, also known as "A Father's Admonition" (*Musar Av*), the author clearly reproves his son for his laziness, his lack of interest in books in general and in Arabic in particular, and many other faults of character which seem incongruous in the man who translated the *Guide of the Perplexed*. Perhaps parts of the will were written when Samuel was quite young, and other parts were added later. In addition, the author dwells at length upon the right way to maintain and preserve a library, for Judah possessed one of the most important libraries of his time.

From the 13th century, ethical wills became not only a popular Hebrew literary genre, but also customary practice within certain families. Apparently the custom was maintained in the family of *Asher b. Jehiel (father of the author of the *Turim*), which moved from Germany to Spain. Extant are the "Rules" which R. Asher gave to his family, and a will addressed to the sons of R. Jacob, the son of R. Asher. It is probable that R. Judah, Jacob's brother, also wrote such a will which had come down as an anonymous work.

This custom seems to have been prevalent in one of the most important families in Eastern Europe during the 16th and 17th centuries, the Horowitz family, whose place of residence was usually Prague. In the 16th century Abraham *Horowitz wrote the important ethical will which became widely known as an independent ethical work, *Yesh Noḥalin*. His son, Jacob, wrote a will in the form of emendations of and additions to his father's ethical book, and the two works were often printed together. The grandson, Shabbetai Sheftel *Horowitz, the author of *Shefa Tal*, carried on the family tradition. Although many of this family were kabbalists who helped to spread Lurianic Kabbalah in Eastern Europe, kabbalistic ideas do not occupy a major place in their ethical wills.

Ethical wills sometimes reflect major controversies and trends within Judaism. The 13th-century will of Joseph ibn Kaspi of Provence, known also as *Sefer ha-Musar* ("The Book of Ethics") or *Yoreh De'ah* ("Teacher of Knowledge"), reflects the fierce controversy between the practitioners of Jewish philosophy, especially the followers of Maimonides, of which Ibn Kaspi was one, and their opponents. Ibn Kaspi tries to reconcile the idea of philosophical knowledge as the supreme religious value with the traditional expressions of devotion. Another glimpse into major problems in the history of Jewish thought is provided by the will of *Elijah b. Solomon Zalman of *Vilna (the Vilna Gaon), who addressed a will to his sons when he set out for Palestine (which he never reached). The will expresses the extreme pietism and devotion of the opponents of Ḥasidism in the 18th century. Elijah advised his sons that in order to avoid interrupting their study of Torah they should never set foot outside their houses unless it was absolutely necessary. He even advocated praying at home because the many people congregated in the synagogue might prove distracting or inspire evil thoughts. From these strictures it is not surprising that he was the leader in the opposition to Ḥasidism. In general, ethical wills reflect in a concise and clear way the main concerns of the writer and the social or ideological group within Judaism to which he belongs.

BIBLIOGRAPHY: I. Abrahams, *Hebrew Ethical Wills*, 2 vols. (1926, 1948[2]); H.H. Ben-Sasson, *Hagut ve-Hanhagah* (1959), passim.

[Joseph Dan]

WILLSTAETTER, RICHARD (1872–1942), German organic chemist and Nobel laureate. Willstaetter, who was born in Karlsruhe, became professor at Munich in 1902, and three years later professor at the Technische Hochschule in Zurich. His research showed that chlorophyll, the essential agent for plants to absorb sunlight and carbon dioxide for synthesis, has two components, contains magnesium, is closely analogous to the red pigment of blood, and contains phytol. He was awarded the 1915 Nobel Prize in chemistry "for his researches on plant pigments, especially chlorophyll." In 1912 he became director of a new Kaiser Wilhelm Gesellschaft zur Foerderung der Wissenschaften in Berlin-Dahlem, and studied other plant pigments, the carotenes, and the anthocyanins. In World War I he was awarded the civilian Iron Cross for work on gas masks. In 1915 he became director of the State Chemical Laboratory. At a time when enzymes were still considered to be mysterious agents specific to life processes, he emphasized the view that they are chemical substances.

When by 1924 suitable Jewish candidates were being rejected for positions in the university, Willstaetter reacted to this manifestation of antisemitism by resigning his chair at the University of Munich. He devoted himself to scientific organizations, publications, special lectures, and industrial consultations. In March 1939 the Gestapo ransacked his house and ordered him to leave Germany. He went to Locarno, Switzerland, where he died. His autobiography, *Aus meinem Leben*, appeared in 1949.

BIBLIOGRAPHY: E. Farber (ed.), *Great Chemists* (1961), 1367–74; Robinson, in: *Journal of the Chemical Society*, pt. 1 (1953), 999–1026; idem, in: *Obituary Notices of Fellows of the Royal Society*, 22 (1953), 609–34; T.N. Levitan, *Laureates: Jewish Winners of the Nobel Prize* (1960), 36–38.

[Samuel Aaron Miller]

WILMINGTON, the largest city in Delaware, midway between New York and Washington, some 27 miles south of Philadelphia and 70 miles north of Baltimore. In 1995, 7,600 Jews, 56% of Delaware's Jews, lived in Wilmington and its suburbs. Since 1879, when Delaware's first Jewish organization, the Moses Montefiore Society, was formed, Wilmington has been the center of Jewish life in the state.

Central European and native-born Jews who came to Wilmington from neighboring American cities established the Moses Montefiore Society. Within a few years, eastern European Jews arrived in large numbers. In addition to working as tailors, shoemakers, milliners, and shopkeepers, many of them worked in Wilmington's expanding shipbuilding, railroad car and morocco plants as carpenters or unskilled laborers. The eastern Europeans quickly outnumbered the founders, but the groups worked together to build Wilmington's synagogues and agencies. (See *Delaware.) Given Wilmington's prosperity, the Jewish population grew quickly from 94 people in 1879 to nearly 4,000 by 1920.

Wilmington's moment of glory was the 1918 War Relief Campaign sponsored by the American Jewish Relief Committee. Recognizing the full extent of the suffering in Europe, the AJRC set a national goal of 30 million dollars, an unattainable goal for Jews alone. The agency chose Wilmington, which was known to have very good relations between the Jewish and general community, for an experimental appeal to non-Jews and assigned it a goal of $75,000. With the generosity of Wilmington's established leaders, Pierre duPont and members of the duPont family, Senator Willard J. Saulsbury, then president pro tem of the U.S. Senate, and Wilmington's industrial leaders, the campaign surpassed its goal and raised $125,000. Wilmington became known nationally as the model city of charity and good will, the place where the campaign became "not only a Jewish movement but a human movement."

During the World War I era, the most affluent members of the Jewish community moved north across the Brandywine River, but most Jews continued to live and work in the downtown area. They ran many of Wilmington's leading stores like J.M. Lazarus' Wilmington Dry Goods, Snellenburg's, Keil's, and Braunstein's. By the 1960s, 35% of Wilmington's Jews had moved to the suburbs; only 53% still lived in the city. To meet the new reality, community leaders closed the old Jewish Community Center and built a new one in northern New Castle County on Garden of Eden Road in 1969. Adas Kodesch Shel Emeth (Orthodox) and Temple Beth Emeth (Reform) also moved out of the downtown area in mid century. Beth Shalom (Conservative) was always north of the Brandywine River.

As Wilmington developed into a corporate capital and then a financial/banking center, many Jews found jobs in those fields as well as in other professions. In 1995, 55% of Wilmington's Jews had a four-year college degree or a graduate degree. The vast majority of Wilmington's Jews lived in the suburbs; few lived in the city. The total population of the city and suburbs had not increased much, from an estimated 7,200 Jews in 1962 to an estimated 7,600 in 1995. A multi-year expansion and renovation of the Garden of Eden Campus began in 2003 following a community wide campaign that raised more than 21 million dollars.

During the World War II era, Jewish education became a community priority. The Jewish Federation of Delaware, which was formed in 1935, led a community effort to establish a United Hebrew School. Although the school closed after about 13 years, the focus on education continued. Wilmington Gratz Hebrew High School, a branch of the successful Philadelphia school, opened in 1965. Albert Einstein Academy, the state's only Jewish day school, began in 1970. The Florence Melton Mini School brought its adult education program to Wilmington in 2001.

At the end of the 20th century, 33.3% of Wilmington's Jews defined themselves as Conservative, 30% as Reform, 7.3% as Orthodox, 0.8% as Reconstructionist and 27.7% as Just Jewish.

BIBLIOGRAPHY: Ukeles Associates, Inc., *1995 Jewish Population Study of Delaware, Summary Report*; H. Bluestone, *The Jewish Population of Northern Delaware – 1962– A Demographic Study*; H. Bluestone, *A Historical Review of a Century of Jewish Education in Delaware, 1876–1976*; Toni Young, *Becoming American, Remaining Jewish: The Story of Wilmington, Delaware's First Jewish Community, 1879–1924* (1999); Toni Young (ed.), *Delaware and the Jews* (1979).

[Toni Young (2nd ed.)]

WILNA, JACOB BEN BENJAMIN WOLF (d. 1732?), rabbi, *posek*, and Shabbatean kabbalist. His name indicates that he was born in Vilna. He was a member of the circle of *Judah Ḥasid (Segal) ha-Levi, but it is not clear if he joined this circle while still in Europe and went with them to Ereẓ Israel in 1700 or whether he went there earlier. In any case, he clearly studied Kabbalah in Vilna. While in Jerusalem, he attempted to join the Sephardi community and was a member of the *bet ha-midrash* of Abraham *Rovigo and a member of the *Yeshivah Bet Ya'akov Ferrera* of the Sephardim. In 1707 Jacob signed the ordination of David *Oppenheim with the leaders of the Ashkenazi community in Jerusalem. In Jerusalem he associated with Nathan Nata *Mannheim, a member of the circle of Judah Ḥasid. The two collaborated in the writing of *Me'orot Natan*, which includes the *Me'orei Or* of Meir *Poppers, with their commentary *Ya'ir Nativ* (Frankfurt, 1709). Between 1702 and 1725, he left Jerusalem three times, twice as an emissary of the Ashkenazi community. Jacob visited Turkey, Germany, Holland, and Italy, propagating Kabbalah wherever he went. In 1726 he returned to Safed and from 1728 served as the rabbi of Safed and as head of the yeshivah. He was a moderate Shabbatean and material on his "belief" is included in Shabbatean manuscripts. Jacob was considered the authoritative kabbalist by his contemporaries in Turkey, Ereẓ Israel, Italy, and Poland. His eminence in Kabbalah is attested by Abraham *Gershon of Kutow (Kuty). He died in Safed at an old age. His glosses on *Tikkunei Zohar* were published with the text (in Orta Koi, near Constantinople, 1709).

His son ḤAYYIM NISSIM YERUḤAM (1704?–1775), kabbalist and rabbi, was born in Jerusalem, and was also a Shabbatean kabbalist. He, too, joined the Sephardi community. Ḥayyim left Jerusalem on several occasions on missions for the Ashkenazi community and later became one of its scholars. Apparently he died in Damascus. There is no evidence for the view that Jacob Wilna was the ancestor of the *Elyashar family.

BIBLIOGRAPHY: Yaari, Sheluḥei, 337–40; M. Benayahu, in: *Yerushalayim*, 4 (1953), 203–14; idem, in: *Sefunot*, 2 (1958), 147; idem, *Rabbi Ya'akov Elyashar* (1960), 11–12.

[Abraham David]

WILPON, FRED (1936–), U.S. sports executive and real estate developer. Wilpon, who was born in Brooklyn, N.Y., graduated from the University of Michigan. He worked for Hanover Equities Corporation in New York from 1959 to 1969, rising to vice president. He joined Peter Sharp & Co. as a vice president and two years later co-founded the realty investment concern Sterling Equities of Manhasset, N.Y., which developed and invested in real estate. From 1972, Sterling Equities and its affiliates purchased or developed over 17 million square feet of commercial property, 45,000 residential units, 8.5 million square feet of retail property, and three major sports complexes. In 1980 Wilpon and Saul Katz, the founders of Sterling Equities, acquired a partnership interest in the New York Mets professional baseball team, one of the major sports franchises in the United States. In 1985 Sterling invested in Pathogenesis Laboratories, a medical research company focused on treatments for cystic fibrosis. Five years later Sterling joined with American Securities Capital Partners to form the first of four investment funds that invested in and managed real estate in 43 states. In 2000, he and Katz co-founded, and Wilpon became chairman of, the Brooklyn Baseball Company, owner of the Brooklyn Cyclones, a minor league team. It marked the return of baseball to Brooklyn, which had been without a professional team since the departure of the Brooklyn Dodgers in 1956. In 2002 Sterling became full owner of the Mets, and Wilpon remained chairman and chief executive through the early years of the 21st century. His son Jeff was senior executive vice president and chief operating officer of the Mets. Other members of the Wilpon family served on the board of directors. Wilpon was a member of the New York City Housing Task Force and served as a trustee of the Jewish Institute for Geriatric Care in New Hyde Park, N.Y.

[Stewart Kampel (2nd ed.)]

°WILSON, SIR CHARLES WILLIAM (1836–1905), English army officer and topographer. Wilson entered the Royal Engineers in 1855. He directed the survey of Jerusalem (1864–66) and the survey of Sinai (1868–69) for the Ordnance Survey. He later served as consul in Turkey, intelligence officer during the wars in Sudan (1884–85), and director-general of the Ordnance Survey from 1886 to 1894, when he retired from military service with the rank of major-general. His publications on Ereẓ Israel include the first exact map of Jerusalem (1864), which still serves as the topographical basis of the Old City; explanatory notes on the map (1865); and a map of the Sinai Peninsula (1869). Wilson also contributed to the volume on Jerusalem (1880) in the series *Picturesque Palestine*. During his work Wilson identified remains of the bridge which connected the Temple Mount with the Upper City in the Second Temple period; this has been named after him. He was one of the leaders of the ill-fated expedition to rescue General Gordon in the Sudan in 1885 and was knighted the same year. Wilson again visited Palestine in 1899 and 1904, trying to discover sites relating to early Christianity.

BIBLIOGRAPHY: Ch. M. Watson, *The Life of Major-General Sir Charles William Wilson* (1909). **ADD. BIBLIOGRAPHY:** ODNB online.

[Michael Avi-Yonah]

°WILSON, HAROLD, BARON WILSON OF RIEVAULX (1916–1995), British prime minister. Wilson was the son of an industrial chemist in Huddersfield, Yorkshire, and was educated at Oxford. He entered Parliament in 1945, serving as the youngest member of Clement *Attlee's cabinet in 1947–51. He became leader of the Labour Party in 1963 and served as prime minister in 1964–70 and 1974–76. Wilson had particularly close relations with members of the Jewish community, especially as his confidential advisors, such as his solicitor and confidante Lord *Goodman and a Yorkshire industrialist, Lord *Kagan, from whom he sought economic advice.

Wilson admired Jews for those qualities he saw in himself: intelligence, social commitment, and an ability to rise above class-imposed obstacles.

No fewer than 40 Jews were elected as Labour members of Parliament at the 1966 general election (out of 363 Labour MPs), and the Wilson years probably marked the zenith of the nexus between British Jewry and the Labour Party, especially among those who were young during the time of fascism. Subsequently, many in the Jewish community moved to the political right. Like most social democrats of his generation, Wilson was a strong supporter of Israel and wrote a book on the subject, *The Chariot of Israel: Britain, America, and the State of Israel* (1981).

BIBLIOGRAPHY: ODNB online.

[William D. Rubinstein (2nd ed.)]

WILSON, "SCOTTIE" (1891–1972), painter. Britain's best known "naive" painter, Wilson was an endearing eccentric. He was born Lewis Freeman to eastern European immigrant parents in the Jewish section of the Gorbals slum district of Glasgow. Some sources state that he was born in London, although "Scottie" refers to his place of birth and the broad accent he retained all his life. His formal education ended at the age of nine, after which he worked with an elder brother as a street-trader in Glasgow. In 1906 he enrolled in the Scottish Rifles and served in India and South Africa. His later work bears some resemblance to Indian bazaar painting, and he regularly incorporated in his works the design of the lotus flower. During World War I he served on the western front, after which he returned to street-trading in London and Scotland. In the early 1930s he immigrated to Canada, working as an itinerant trader between Toronto and Vancouver. It was there that his artistic career started. He often related the tale of finding a beautiful gold pen, with a broad nib, which inspired him to doodle; images and faces seemed to flow from the pen involuntarily and he became obsessed with the results. Dozens of notebooks became filled with elaborate decorative patterns, fantasies based on images of childhood, in which nature was always beautiful and humans were always ugly. He began to use colored inks in delightful images of elaborate gardens, with fountains and resplendent flora and fauna. His favorite artist was Blake, whose mystical innocence is reflected in his work. After World War II he returned to London, and within a short time considerable interest was shown in his work. In Paris he was greatly encouraged by the artist Jean Dubuffet, who showed a particular interest in the work of children and eccentrics. Exhibitions of his drawings brought Wilson considerable fame; he was commissioned to paint murals for the National Bank of Switzerland, Basle, and dinner services by the Royal Worcester Porcelain Company. His work was acquired by the Tate Gallery, London, the Museum of Modern Art, New York, the Musée d'Art Moderne, Paris and many other public collections. Among the numerous works about Scottie Wilson is a monograph by Mervyn Levy (1966). More have appeared since his death.

ADD. BIBLIOGRAPHY: G. Melly, *It's All Writ Out for You: The Life and Work of Scottie Wilson* (1986); A.J. Petullo and Katharine Murrell, *Scottie Wilson: Peddlar Turned Painter* (2004); G.A. Schreiner, *Scottie Wilson* (1979).

[Charles Samuel Spencer]

WILSON, SOL (1896–1974), U.S. painter, printmaker, educator. Born in Vilno, Russia, now Poland, Wilson emigrated to the U.S. in 1911. He studied art at Cooper Union and the National Academy of Design. Like many other American artists of his generation, he worked for the Works Project Administration during the Depression: among his public works were the paintings *The Indian Ladder* (1940) for the town of Delmar in New York and *Outdoor Sports* (1942) for Westhampton Beach, also in New York. His paintings of figures, interiors, and landscapes reveal the influence of his art teachers, George Bellows and Robert Henri. His visits to Massachusetts fishing villages resulted in numerous images of fisherman, boats, and harbors, such as *Torn Sail* and *Provincetown Deck*, rendered in expressive jewel tones of red, green, blue, yellow, or in a palette of earth tones, exemplified in *To the Island*. Wilson taught at the Art Students League and the American Artists School. He lived predominantly in New York, but also spent time in Provincetown and Rockport, Massachusetts. His work has been exhibited at the Art Institute of Chicago, the Carnegie Institute, the Corcoran Gallery, the National Academy of Design, the Library of Congress, and the Whitney Museum, among other places. His work can be found in the collections of the Biro-Bidjan Museum, Russia, the Brooklyn Museum, the Metropolitan Museum of Art, and the Smithsonian, among other museums.

BIBLIOGRAPHY: B. Melosh, *Engendering Culture: Manhood and Womanhood in New Deal Public Art and Theater* (1991).

[Nancy Buchwald (2nd ed.)]

°**WILSON, WOODROW** (1856–1924), 27th president of the United States (1913–21). Wilson tried to remain neutral during World War I but finally led his country into the conflict. After victory, he helped design the Versailles settlement, to which the U.S. Senate refused assent. Although Louis D. *Brandeis, whom Wilson appointed to the Supreme Court, oriented the president to the Zionist program, Wilson's prior approval of the Balfour Declaration derived from Allied grand strategy. Thereafter, Wilson displayed increased interest in the Jewish National Home concept and on several occasions gave it his public blessing, much to the chagrin of State Department personnel. Wilson also helped write into the 1919 treaties guarantees for the minority enclaves (including Jews) in the newly created states of eastern Europe. Wilson's benevolence toward Zionist aspirations reflected his concern for all suppressed nationalities and an idealism toward the future of the Holy Land stemming from a rich Christian background. In Wilson's day, the affinity between the United States and world Jewry was translated into Zionist terms.

BIBLIOGRAPHY: Adler, in: JSOS, 10 (1948), 303–34; Lebow, in: *Journal of Modern History*, 40 (1968), 501–23.

[Selig Adler]

WINAWER, BRUNO (1883–1944), Polish playwright and novelist. A Warsaw physicist, Winawer wrote many successful comedies in the style of G.B. Shaw. His belief that technical progress was the basis for social and political change found expression in his novels and in plays such as *Roztwór profesora Pytla* ("Professor Pytel's Chemical Solution," 1919) and *R.H. Inżynier* ("R.H., the Engineer," 1923).

WINCHELL, WALTER (1897–1972), U.S. newspaper columnist. Winchell, a New Yorker by birth, began contributing theatrical gossip to the house organ of a theater chain when he was a young vaudeville actor. This led the New York *Graphic* to give him his own column, "On Broadway," in 1924, and in 1929 he moved to Hearst's *Daily Mirror*. Over the years he gained a position of unmatched power among newspaper writers. His sources included presidents and kings, industrial tycoons, the leaders of show business, and gangster racketeers. His popularity was due mainly to the sensational disclosures for which he became a byword. In the mid-1950s, at the peak of his career, he had an estimated public of more than 35 million readers as a syndicated columnist in more than 2,000 daily newspapers.

Winchell ruled the airwaves from 1930 to 1957, when he captivated radio audiences with his colorful, fast-paced, delivery of entertainment news, gossip, and innuendo. In 1956 he debuted on television, hosting *The Walter Winchell Show*, a weekly variety program; and from 1957 to 1958 he hosted *The Walter Winchell File*, a series about the crime stories he had covered while working with the New York City Police Department. Most memorable to television viewers at the time was Winchell's rapid-fire narration on the popular crime drama series *The Untouchables* (1959–63), based on the 1930s exploits of real-life FBI special agent Elliot Ness and his team, and mobster Al Capone and his henchmen.

The TV biopic *Winchell* was made in 1998, directed by Paul Mazursky and starring Stanley Tucci in the title role. Winchell was inducted into the Radio Hall of Fame in 2004.

His book *Winchell Exclusive: Things That Happened to Me – and Me to Them* was published in 1975.

As founder of the Damon Runyon Cancer Fund in 1946 in memory of his writer friend, Winchell raised millions of dollars for cancer research and care. By 2005 the foundation had invested more than $170 million in cancer research, supporting some 3,000 scientists in the U.S.

BIBLIOGRAPHY: H. Weiner, *Let's Go to Press: A Biography of Walter Winchell* (1955). **ADD. BIBLIOGRAPHY:** H. Klurfeld, *Winchell: His Life and Times* (1976); M. Machlin, *The Gossip Wars* (1981); J. Mosedale, *The Men Who Invented Broadway* (1981); M. Herr, *Walter Winchell* (1990); N. Gabler, *Winchell: Gossip, Power, and the Culture of Celebrity* (1994); L. Stuart, *The Secret Life of Walter Winchell* (2003).

[Bernard Lewis / Ruth Beloff (2nd ed.)]

WINCHESTER, cathedral city in Hampshire, S. England. Jews are first mentioned there in 1148 when, in the survey of city property, Benedict and Ursulinus are recorded as tenants of the bishop. A community subsequently grew up and was possibly visited by Abraham *Ibn Ezra, who mentions the city in his astronomical writings. It was the only large town in England where there were no anti-Jewish disorders in 1190, but a *blood libel resulted in some disturbance two years later. It ranked fourth in the *Donum*. During the 13th century the community was one of the most important in England and an *archa was situated there. The Jewish quarter was in the heart of the city (the present Jewry Street). The constable of Winchester Castle was also Keeper of the Jews. A tower in the castle was known as the Jews' Tower – either because Jews were permitted to take refuge there or because it was used for their periodical imprisonments. The community experienced a series of child-murder accusations between 1225 and 1235. It may have been in connection with one of these that in 1235 the leading member of the community, Abraham Pinch, was hanged in front of the synagogue which he himself maintained. The most tragic event occurred in 1262, when Simon de Montfort sacked the Jewish quarter in Winchester. Among outstanding local capitalists in the second half of the 13th century was Licoricia, who was murdered in 1277; her son Benedict was among the Winchester Jews hanged in 1278 on a charge of coin clipping. Benedict fil' Abraham of Winchester, on the other hand, was the only known English Jew in the Middle Ages to be admitted to the Merchant Guild (1268). Another son of Licoricia, Asher, scratched an inscription, recorded by John Selden, on the wall of his dungeon in Winchester Castle, where he was imprisoned when the Jews of England were arrested in 1287. About this time, the principal Winchester synagogue was confiscated. Approximately 16 local Jewish householders remained by the time of the expulsion of the Jews from England in 1290, their wealth valued at £44. No organized Jewish community has existed there in recent times.

BIBLIOGRAPHY: JC (Sept. 16, 1892), 14; Abrahams, in: JHSET, 2 (1894–95), 102; Stokes, *ibid.*, 10 (1921–23), 193–4; Adler, *ibid.* (1928 31), 171–2; idem, in: JHSEM, 4 (1942), 1–8; C. Roth, *Jews of Medieval Oxford* (1951), index, s..v. *Winchester, Licoricia, David*, etc.; Roth, England, index; Turner, in: *Hampshire Review*, 21 (1954), 17–21. **ADD. BIBLIOGRAPHY:** H.G. Richardson, *English Jewry Under the Angevin Kings* (1960), index; R.B. Brown and S. McCartney in JHSET 39 (2004), 14–34; S. Bartlet in *Jewish Culture and History* 3(2) (2000), 31–54; P. Allin in JHSET 27 (1982), 32–39; J. Hillaby and R. Sermon in *Trans. Bristol & Gloucs. Archaeol. Soc.* 122 (2004), 142–143.

[Cecil Roth / Joe Hillaby (2nd ed.)]

°**WINCKLER, HUGO** (1863–1913), German Orientalist and Bible scholar. Winckler was born in Graefenhainichen. He became a lecturer at Berlin University in 1891 and professor extraordinary in 1904. During the first years of his scholarly activity, he devoted himself to the study of Assyrian inscriptions; he published the Sargon inscriptions in 1889, as well as various studies on the ancient Near East which included a history of Israel, *Geschichte Israels*... (2 vols., 1895–1900), and a work on the code of Hammurapi, *Die Gesetze Hammurabis*... (1902). In 1903–04 he took part in the excavations of Sidon and from 1906 to 1912 was in charge of the German excavations at Boghazköy (ancient Hattusas, the capital of the Hittite Empire in Asia Minor). There he was successful in discovering the royal Hittite archives, opening the history of the Hittite kingdom to the scholarly world. Winckler did not, however, live to see the deciphering of the Hittite language. He was one of the founders of the pan-Babylonian school in the study of the Bible. These scholars claimed that there was a single common cultural system, overwhelmingly influenced by the Babylonians, which extended over the whole of the ancient Near East. This school assumed that the Bible was also rooted in this culture, and not merely influenced by it. The other prominent exponents of this school were Winckler's disciples, F. *Delitzsch and A. *Jeremias.

Winckler's other publications included a critical edition (written with L. Abel) of the Tell el-Amarna letters, *Der Thontafelfund von El-Amarna* (2 vols., 1889–1900); a German translation of these letters, *Die Thontafeln von Tell-El-Amarna* (2 vols., 1896); *Das Alte Westasien* (1899); and publications in the series *Der Alte Orient*.

BIBLIOGRAPHY: O. Weber, in: *Mitteilungen der Vorderasiatisch-Aegyptischen Gesellschaft*, 20 (1915), 13–24.

[Michael Avi-Yonah and Menahem Haran]

WINDER, LUDWIG (1889–1946), Bohemian journalist and writer. Born in Schaffa in Moravia, Winder grew up in nearby Holleschau, where he was raised in an atmosphere of religious rigor. After moving to Vienna, he worked for the liberal newspaper *Die Zeit* before joining the editorial staff of the nationalist *Deutsche Zeitung Bohemia* in Prague. In 1917, he published his first novel, *Die rasende Rotationsmaschine*, which illustrates the difficulties Jews from religious eastern communities faced in integrating themselves into modern western society. Subsequent novels, such as *Die juedische Orgel* (1922) and *Hugo: Tragoedie eines Knaben* (1924), deal primarily with the desperate struggle of young eastern Jews for a secular existence, and show – as the posthumously published manuscript *Geschichte meines Vaters* suggests conclusively – autobiographical traces. Throughout his writings, Winder perceives modern Jewish existence as a state of alienation and psychic deformation, limited by confining traditions and antisemitism. In later novels, he shifted his focus towards the history and downfall of the Austrian Danube monarchy, vividly envisioned in *Die nachgeholten Freuden* (1927), *Der Kammerdiener* (1945), and especially in *Der Thronfolger* (1938), which, critical of the Austrian Archduke Franz Ferdinand, was immediately banned. A member of the so-called "Prague circle" and a close friend of Max Brod, Felix Weltsch, Johannes Urzidil, and Oskar Baum, Winder fled Prague in 1939 with his wife and older daughter (his younger daughter died in Bergen-Belsen in 1945), settling in England, where he lived until his death. During his last years, he finished two additional novels: *Die Novemberwolke* (1942), a story about emigrants during a bombing night in London, and *Die Pflicht* (1943), which deals with Czech resistance to the German invaders.

BIBLIOGRAPHY: K. Krolop, *Ludwig Winder (1889–1946)* (1967); M. Pazi, in: *German Quarterly*, 63 (1990), 211–21; J. von Sternburg, *Gottes boese Traeume. Die Romane Ludwig Winders* (1994); C. Spirek, in: *Exil* 17 (1997), 45–55; A.A. Gassmann, *Lieber Vater, lieber Gott?...* (2002).

[Philipp Theisohn (2nd ed.)]

WINE, fermented grape juice. (For wine in biblical times, see *Food.) Wine was a popular beverage in talmudic times. Produced in winepresses called *bet ha-gat* (Tosef., Ter. 3:7), and stored in wine cellars called *heftek* or *appotik* (Av. Zar. 2:7), the newly pressed wine, prior to fermentation, was known as *yayin mi-gat* ("wine from the vat"; Sanh. 70a); *yayin yashan* ("old wine") was wine from the previous year, and that from earlier vintages, *yashan noshan* ("old, very old"). The last was usually diluted by one-third with water in order to reduce its potency.

Varieties of Wine

Several varieties of wine are mentioned in the Talmud:

(1) *aluntit* ("old wine mixed with clear water and balsam," Av. Zar, 30a);

(2) *kafrisin* ("caper wine," Ker. 6a; according to Rashi, Cyprus wine);

(3) *ilyaston* ("a sweet wine produced by drying the grapes in the sun for three days, and then treading them in the midday heat"; BB 97b; Men. 8:6);

(4) *me'ushan* ("from the juice of smoked or fumigated sweet grapes"; Men. *ibid.*);

(5) *appiktevizi* ("an aperitif"; Shab. 12a);

(6) *pesinyaton* ("a bitter wine"; TJ, Av. Zar. 2:3, 41a);

(7) *ẓimmukin* ("raisin wine"; BB 97b);

(8) *inomilin* ("wine mixed with honey and pepper"; Shab. 20:2);

(9) *enogeron* ("wine added to oil and garum"); and

(10) *kunditon* ("wine mixed with spices"; TJ, Av. Zar. *ibid.*). Matured sour wine was called *ḥomeẓ* ("vinegar").

Attitude of the Rabbis to the Consumption of Wine

The rabbis considered that wine taken in moderation induces appetite, "sustains and makes glad" (Ber. 35b), and is beneficial to health. "Wine is the greatest of all medicines: where wine is lacking, drugs are necessary" (BB 58b). Old wine, in particular, benefits the intestines, though ordinary wine may do harm (Ber. 51a), an assertion corroborated by the story of the rabbi who was cured of a severe bowel disorder by drinking 70-year-old apple wine (Av. Zar. 40b). R. Eleazar suggested (Meg. 16b) that "old wine" was among "the good things of Egypt" which Joseph sent to his aging father (Gen. 45:23), whereas according to some opinion the "tree of knowledge" of which Adam ate was a vine (Ber 40a; Gen. R. 15:7).

The rabbis deliberately rejected the suggestion that abstention from wine and meat be mandatorily instituted as a sign of mourning for the destruction of the Temple. They maintained that such a decree would impose unbearable hardship on the public (BB 60b). At the end of days wine will form an integral part of the eschatological banquet (Ber. 34b). The rabbis are known to have indulged; some, notably Mar Ukva (Shab. 140a) could drink with ease, while others, like R. Judah (whose capacity was severely tested by the four *seder* cups, Ned. 49b) could not. The rabbis even suggested that wine was an inducement to the advancement of their chosen calling. R. Huna maintained that it "helps to open the heart to reasoning" (BB 12b), and Rabbah advised students whose supplies of wine were limited to drink it in large mouthfuls, in order to secure the maximum benefit (Suk. 49b). Sleep or a long walk (BB 10a; Er. 64b) was prescribed for those who interpreted this advice too literally and became heavy with drink.

Excessive consumption of alcohol was frowned upon and overindulgence was thought to be injurious to health, as was shown by Abba Saul (a gravedigger by profession), who, upon examining the skeletons of various corpses, deduced what the effect of liquor was on the bones (Nid. 24b). A prayer recited in a state of intoxication is "an abomination" (Er. 64a).

Wine in Religious Ceremonies

The ceremonies of *Kiddush and *Havdalah on Sabbaths and Festivals should be performed with wine (Pes. 105b–6a). Only in countries where beer is the national beverage may the latter be substituted for *Havdalah* (Pes. 107a). Four cups of wine must be drunk at the *Passover *seder*, two cups at weddings, and one at circumcisions. Indeed, the goblet of wine and the benediction recited over it symbolize the festivity of the occasion. During the nine days of *Av, wine may only be drunk at *Kiddush* on Sabbath.

In accordance with the biblical injunction to "give strong wine to him that is ready to perish, and wine unto the bitter in soul" (Prov. 31:6), a "cup of consolation" was offered to the bereaved after a funeral at the "meal of comforting." Originally, it was ten glasses of wine to which were added four more (Ket. 8b). In modern times this practice has been discontinued (Tur, YD 378).

Before drinking wine, a special benediction is recited "for the fruit of the vine" (Ber. 6:1; Sh. Ar., OḤ 202:1), in contrast to the *She-ha-Kol* benediction, which is the normal blessing for all juices extracted from fruit or vegetables. Grace, after eating food prepared from the designated produce of Ereẓ Israel (grapes, figs, olives, pomegranates, or dates), is also recited after drinking wine (Sh. Ar., OḤ 10:8, 11; see *Grace after Meals). One who leads a group of three or more males in the recitation of the Grace after Meals may pronounce the blessing over a cup of wine, which is then sipped by those present (Sh. Ar., OḤ 190). When drinking in company, it is customary to wish one another *le-Ḥayyim* ("to life"; Shab. 67b).

Wine of Gentiles

Wine consecrated by gentiles for idol worship is called *yein nesekh* ("libation wine") and, like anything so dedicated, is absolutely forbidden. A person may not drink such wine, derive any benefit from it, nor handle it (Sh. Ar., YD 133:5–6). Any food or drink brought into contact with more than one-quarter of a *log* of *yein nesekh* (or *setam yeinam*, see below) is rendered unclean (Av. Zar. 31a).

Wine processed and/or bottled by gentiles for regular use (and not idol worship) is called *setam yeinam* ("ordinary wine"). It is, however, equally forbidden in order to avoid the suspicion that it may possibly be *yein nesekh*, and to avert intermarriage with non-Jews resulting from social intercourse with them (Deut. 7:7; Sanh. 106a; Av. Zar. 36b, and Rashi, loc cit). The prohibition did not include "boiled wine" (Av. Zar. 29b); wine whose taste was dominated by its content of honey and spices; nor, according to some opinions, an alcoholic beverage consisting of one part of wine to seven parts of water; nor other alcoholic beverages (e.g., whiskey, beer, etc.).

The interdiction against the drinking of non-Jewish wine is so severe, that even if a gentile merely touches wine prepared by a Jew it is still prohibited, unless the bottle was securely corked and sealed. Most later rabbinic authorities ruled, however, that if a gentile touched the wine of a Jew with the intention of causing him damage by "defiling" it, the Jew may drink the wine; this is done in order to discourage other gentiles from following suit. The "gentile" referred to above is one who "serves idols"; "the wine of a non-Jew who does not serve idols is forbidden as far as drinking is concerned (because of the fear of intermarriage), but the Jew may trade in it since there is no fear of idolatry. If a gentile, however, touches the wine "by accident," it is permitted, even for consumption. Many authorities maintain that since non-Jews have ceased to be idolaters, their touch should always be considered "accidental" and the wine thus fit for consumption (Isserles to Sh. Ar., YD 124:24). Some authorities also state that a Jew who drinks wine belonging to a Christian has not committed a sin which would invalidate him as witness before a rabbinic court (Isserles, Responsa, ed. Cracow 1640, no. 124; later editions omitted this responsum).

In the rapidly changing society of modern times, where the Jewish community must inevitably come into closer contact with the non-Jewish world, these laws are mainly honored in the breach except among the Orthodox. The Rabbinical Assembly of the Conservative movement in the United States has ruled that non-Jewish wine may be consumed generally, but only Jewish (*kasher*) wine may be used for religious ceremonies.

See also the various types of alcoholic beverages.

BIBLIOGRAPHY: Eisenstein, Dinim, 168f.

WINE, SHERWIN (1928–), Humanist rabbi. Born in Detroit, Michigan, Wine left his Conservative Jewish upbringing to found the world's first non-deified Jewish movement known as Humanistic Judaism. Self-described as strongly Jewish but with a focus on culture rather than religion, Wine earned degrees from the University of Michigan and Hebrew Union College in an effort to build a career as a counselor to the Jewish people. In 1963, he founded the Birmingham Temple in suburban Detroit, the first Humanistic congregation.

In the Birmingham Temple's library, a Torah stands on a pedestal, one of the "good books" offered there. Humanism focuses on Judaism as a culture and humans as self-reliant.

Wine established the Birmingham Temple with eight families who wanted to belong to a Jewish community without the trappings of formal religion. The Temple membership now numbers about 400 families.

In 1969, he helped establish the Society for Humanistic Judaism as a national outreach vehicle for the movement. In 1986, the International Federation of Secular Humanistic Jews was formed to connect Humanistic Jews around the world. Wine became the dean of the International Institute for Secular Humanistic Judaism in North America. The movement started ordaining rabbis in 1992, two of whom succeeded Wine upon his semi-retirement in 1997.

He was involved in organizing the Leadership Conference of Secular and Humanistic Jews, the Center for New Thinking, the North American Committee for Humanism, the Humanist Institute and the Conference of Liberal Religion. He is the author of "Humanistic Judaism," "Judaism beyond God," "Celebration," and "Staying Sane in a Crazy World." Wine also contributed to *Judaism in a Secular Age: An Anthology of Secular Humanistic Jewish Thought*.

Before founding the Humanistic movement, Wine served two years in Korea as a U.S. Army chaplain and several years as a rabbi at Reform pulpits in Detroit and Windsor. Wine believes the Jewish people survived history by human will. Today, the secular Humanistic movement involves more than 30,000 people across North America, but it has yet to gain acceptance by the rest of the Jewish movements.

[Lynne Schreiber (2nd ed.)]

WINE AND LIQUOR TRADE.

Talmudic Period

The strict prohibition against the use of gentile wine during the talmudic period, originally limited to wine used in idolatrous libations but later extended to include all non-Jewish wine (Av. Zar. 2:3, and 36b), must of necessity have concentrated the Jewish wine trade in the hands of Jews. Apart from this, however, there is no evidence of any specific Jewish aspect to the wine trade during this period. There are references to Jewish keepers of wine taverns (Lev. R. 12:1). A certain difference may be detected between Ereẓ Israel and Babylonia. Whereas in the former, a Mediterranean country, Jews drank wine in preference to other alcoholic beverages, in Babylonia the brewing of beer and other alcoholic beverages was much more common. Some of the Babylonian *amoraim* were brewers, among them R. Papa, who was regarded as an expert and amassed a considerable fortune from it (Pes. 113a; BM 65a). However the vine was cultivated in the neighborhood of Sura and Jews were engaged in the manufacture and sale of wine (Ber. 5b).

Middle Ages (to 16th Century)

As a result of both the historio-economic and the religious factors, during the Middle Ages viticulture was one of the branches of agriculture in which Jews had traditional interest and technical proficiency. The rabbinical responsa and **takkanot* provide ample instances of the endeavors made by Jews to obtain supplies of suitably pure wine and the arrangements made for doing so. This was perhaps one of the main reasons why the Jews continued to engage in viticulture longer than in other types of agriculture in this period, though from the 11th century the sources mention that Jews in Western Europe also drank mead. In several areas, Jewish winegrowers or vintners also sold wine to Christians. In the region of Troyes, the teacher of *Rashi (b. 1050) used to sell "from his barrel to the gentile" (Rashi, Resp., no. 159). The Jews of Speyer and Worms were licensed by the emperor in 1090 "to sell their wine to Christians" (Aronius, Regesten, nos. 170–1).

The antagonisms created by the sale of a product to which Jews and Christians attached divergent sacral usages and regulations are reflected in complaints such as that "on the insolence of the Jews" by archbishop *Agobard of Lyons, who wrote (c. 825): "As to wine which even they themselves consider unclean and use only for sale to Christians – if it should happen that some of it is spilt on the earth, even in a dirty place, they hasten to collect it and return it for keeping in jars." The problem is even more strongly presented by Pope *Innocent III in his letter of January 1208: "At the vintage season the Jew, shod in linen boots, treads the wine; and having extracted the purer wine in accordance with the Jewish rite they retain some for their own pleasure, and the rest, the part which is abominable to them, they leave to the faithful Christians; and with this, now and again, the sacrament of the blood of Christ is performed." The description may apply either to Jewish vintners and vineyard owners or to Jews who made arrangements with Christian owners to permit the Jews to extract pure wine in accordance with Jewish law.

In the Muslim countries the Jewish wine trade assumed considerable proportions, as indicated by examples from 12th-century Egypt. It is reported in 1136 that "four partners [all Jews] joined in the production of wine with the enormous sum of 1,510 dinars"; upon liquidating the partnership and paying their taxes, all expressed their satisfaction (S.D. Goitein, *Mediterranean Society* (1967), 364). In about 1150 a Jewish estate included 1,937 jars of wine, worth about 200–300 dinars (*ibid.*, 264). The amounts cited indicate that such thriving business had Muslim customers besides Jews and Christians. In England, in the 12th and 13th centuries, Jews imported wine, and "were exempt from paying any custom or toll or any due on wine, in just the same way as the king himself, whose chattels they were" (Roth, England, 102–3; cf. also 115, note). In Central Europe, Jewish drinking habits were already gradually changing in the 13th century, as shown by the man who asked R. *Meir b. Baruch of Rothenburg for his opinion "about beer [i.e., whether this might be used for **Kiddush*], for in his locality there is sometimes a lack of wine." R. Meir answered: "There is no wine in Westphalia, but in all [other] principalities there is abundant wine; and there is wine in your city throughout the year. It seems to me that you personally drink mostly wine; and if at the end of the year there is some dearth of wine you will find it in your neighborhood.... Certainly you know that it is proper to recite *Kiddush* over wine" (Meir b. Baruch of Rothenburg, Resp., ed. by Y.Z. Kahana, vol. 1, nos. 72, 80).

While by the 15th century Jews must have practically ceased to own vineyards and practice viticulture, trade in wine and other alcoholic beverages was becoming a major Jewish occupation in the German and west Slavic lands. This was part of the general trend of increasing commerce between town and country in this period in which Jews took an active part, not least because they were expelled from the larger cities (see *Expulsions). The competition of the Jewish vintner was an object of complaints by the guilds, such as that of Regensburg in 1516 (cf. R. Straus, *Urkunden und Aktenstuecke zur Geschichte der Juden in Regensburg* (1960), 291, no. 833). In part, this commerce was combined with credit extension, as explained by Jews in Regensburg in 1518, who lent money to the boatmen carrying wine to the city and were sometimes repaid in kind (*ibid.*, 358, no. 988).

In both Muslim and Christian Spain, the sale and consumption of wine in the Middle Ages were subject to taxation by the autonomous Jewish communal administration. The unbroken records give evidence of the significant scale on which Spanish Jewry engaged in business. Copious wine drinking by the upper Jewish social strata is also frequently mentioned in Jewish poetry in Spain. After 1391 exiles from Spain carried their wine trade to Islamic countries, and occasionally aroused opposition from their hosts. These traditions and trends were in part continued, in part considerably modified, in the course of the 16th and 17th centuries.

[Haim Hillel Ben-Sasson]

16th Century to Modern Times

From the 16th to the 19th centuries the production and sale of alcoholic beverages was a major industry in Poland-Lithuania and Russia. It also occupied an important place in the economy of Bohemia, Silesia, Hungary, and Bessarabia. As essentially connected with agriculture, it was carried out in rural estates and formed one of the main sources of revenue for their proprietors. The Jews entered this industry under the **arenda* ("rental") system in the rural economy in which by the 16th century they played an essential role. The Jewish tavern keeper became part of the regular socioeconomic pattern of life in the town and village. The association of the Jew with this activity contributed another negative feature to the popularly created image of the Jew while also affecting Jewish living habits and standards. The alcoholic beverage industry afforded to the Jews a variety of occupations and a source of livelihood enabling them to raise their living standards.

In almost all the rural estates in Poland, the owners held the monopoly over the production and sale of alcoholic beverages, and the heavy drinking habits of the peasants in these countries made it a highly lucrative prerogative. The participation of Jews took the form of leasing in one of the following ways: The lease of breweries, distilleries, and taverns which was part of the wider *arenda* system in Poland and in Ukrainian and Belorussian territories: often, the lease of breweries and distilleries, together with taverns, formed a separate concession; the basic leasehold concession of the single tavern, which was rented either directly from the noble estate owner or from a larger-scale Jewish leaseholder. All leases were granted for a limited term, often for three years, sometimes for one year only. Jewish communal regulations (*takkanot*) effectively limited competition between Jews in bidding for the leases at least to the end of the 17th century (see *Councils of the Lands). Tavern keepers were the largest group of Jews occupied in the industry. They frequently belonged to the poorer class of Jew who had contact with the peasants.

The industry also accounted for an appreciable number of brewers and distillers who worked for the brewery or distillery leaseholders as employees. They were sometimes also employed by taverners. In the middle of the 17th century, this group represented about 30% of the Jews engaged in the production and sale of alcoholic beverages on Polish territory. On the crown estates, the income from the production and sale of alcoholic beverages amounted to 0.3% of the total revenues in 1564, and to about 40% in 1789, an immense increase directly connected with the participation of the Jews in this industry.

Jews also played a similar role in the towns. The location privileges accorded to townships in Eastern Europe usually granted the municipality the right to lease production and sale of alcoholic beverages in the town to an individual local resident. Jews also often competed with other townsmen for this concession, and were generally more ready to supply credit than their Christian competitors. In 1600 the magistrate of Kazimierz complained: "The Jews are not permitted to keep taverns, and yet they deal openly in the sale of vodka, wine, and mead; they hire musicians to tempt in people" (M. Balaban, *Dzieje Żydów w Krakowie i na Kazimierzu*, 1 (1931), 197). Jewish sources confirm the nature of the competition that took place in the cities. The communal regulations for the district of Volhynia of about 1602 enjoin that:

In order to prevent the entry… [to Jewish houses] of gentiles, who came to buy on Saturdays and Festivals, they [the Jewish taverners] should all of them be compelled to take down the sign that they hang up over the entrance to the house on weekdays to let it be known that there is beer and mead inside for sale. That sign shall they take down before the beginning of Sabbath until its end (see H.H. Ben-Sasson, in: *Zion*, 21 (1956), 199).

In *Belaya Tserkov in about 1648, 17 taverns were owned by Jews, although the Jewish population consisted of only 100 families. In towns in Poland and Lithuania where the monopoly was held by the city, it was also leased to Jews. The municipal prerogative was usurped by the manorial owners of the towns during the 17th century, and the concessions for production and sale of alcoholic beverages were leased to Jews on an increasing scale. In the old crown cities, Jews also often leased the tavern from the city authority.

In the second half of the 16th and the first half of the 17th century, a considerable number of Jewish distillers, brewers, and taverners were thus occupied on the estates of the magnates situated in the Belorussian and Ukrainian territories under Poland. Ruin came in 1648–51, following the *Chmielnicki uprising. After the truce was concluded between Poland and Russia in 1667, Jewish taverners could again settle in the Ukraine in the region on the right bank of the River Dnieper; the lands on the left bank passed to Russia, from which Jews were excluded. Jewish taverners were not therefore found in the latter area until the end of the 18th and beginning of the 19th century. The proportion of Jews gainfully engaged in the production and sale of alcoholic beverages amounted in 1765 to 15% of the Jewish residents in the towns, and at the period of the partitions of *Poland-Lithuania (1772–95) to about 85% of Jewish residents in rural areas. In 1791 it was estimated that if the Jews were to be debarred from leasing taverns, about 50,000 people would have to replace them in this occupation, and this was used as an argument against the Russian authorities when they wished to exclude the Jews, in territories then annexed to Russia, from this source of livelihood.

In the period before 1648, Jewish participation in the liquor trade as taverners gave rise to social tensions, which are reflected in contemporary Jewish works and communal regulations, while furnishing a source for anti-Jewish accusations and conflicts between the peasants and Jewish taverners. Antisemites ascribed the drunkenness prevalent among the peasants, and their permanent state of indebtedness, to the wily Jewish taverner, who also extended credit to them. During the 17th and 18th centuries there were uprisings against Jewish leaseholders on numerous estates in Poland, and the complaints of the peasants on the crown estates were often taken up by the courts. After 1648, as opportunities for employment narrowed with the progressive deterioration in Poland of the economy and culture, the hostility intensified and conditions became more difficult for the Jews, in particular for the keeper of the single tavern. He was at the mercy of the despotic noble who ruled the village. In his autobiography Solomon *Maimon recalls vivid childhood memories of the tribulations of a Jewish leaseholder in the 18th century.

Toward the end of the 18th century, in particular after the *Haidamack massacres of 1768, spokesmen of Polish mercantilist and physiocratic theories represented the presence of Jews in the villages and taverns as highly detrimental to Polish economy and society. With few exceptions, the opinion prevailed that the Jewish leaseholders were responsible for the deterioration of the towns and the misery of the countryside. To gain control of these concessions was of greatest importance to the impoverished Polish towns, as the production and sale of alcoholic beverages was a principal branch of the urban economy and its principal source of revenue. Elimination of Jews from this occupation became, therefore, one of the main slogans of the All-Polish middle-class movement between 1788 and 1892. The Polish Sejm ("diet") had passed a bill in 1776 establishing the prior right of the citizen to the lease of the production and sale of alcoholic beverages in smaller towns. However, few candidates with the necessary capital could be found, and these soon had to give it up. As a result, in these towns also the lease passed to Jews. In 1783 an order was issued in Belorussia debarring Jews from traffic in alcoholic beverages in the towns, and the income from taverns was given to the municipalities; but this was canceled in 1785.

Following the partitions of Poland-Lithuania, the Jews in the taverns and villages became the scapegoats of the Russian and Polish ruling classes for the poverty and wretchedness of the peasants. These classes were closely bound by social interests and class consciousness, although divided by national and religious enmities. In the large tracts now occupied by Russia the peasants were of the Greek Orthodox faith, and although despised socially, were now the concern of the Russian authorities. The allegation against the Jew as "the scourge of the village," intoxicating the ignorant peasant because of the misery of his lot, became a spurious slogan for social reform for both the rulers of Russia and their Polish opponents. Elimination of Jewish taverners had started even before the partitions of Poland, and subsequently proceeded with the approval of the Russian governors.

The other states which had gained Polish territory also took up this policy, although with less concentration. The Patent of Tolerance issued by the Austrian emperor *Joseph II in 1782 ordered all the owners of estates to discharge Jewish leaseholders from their domains within two years. This decision was, however, not carried out. About 1805 the Prussian authorities prepared a ban against leasing taverns to Jews, but owing to the occupation of the country by Napoleon, it was never put into effect. In 1804 Russian legislation prohibited Jews from living in the villages. In the period of Napoleon's ascendancy, the Russian authorities refrained from taking action, and in 1812 the orders were suspended. However, after 1830, the stereotype of Jewish guilt for the drunkenness of the peasants was widely propagated in the Polish press. Steps were taken for supervision of the Jews in the name of benefiting the peasant. In Bessarabia the participation of Jews in the production and sale of alcoholic beverages was limited in 1818. Legislation passed in Russia in 1835 prohibited the Jews from selling alcoholic beverages on credit to the peasants, and canceled all the peasants' debts to Jewish taverners. A law of 1866 permitted Jews to lease breweries and distilleries only in towns and villages inhabited by Jews. These measures had little result. In Belorussia between 1883 and 1888, 31.6% of the distilleries in the province of Vitebsk and 76.3% in that of Grodno were Jewish-owned. Full rights to produce and trade in alcoholic beverages in Russia had been permitted to Jews belonging to the category of "merchants of the first class," but after 1882 restrictions were also applied against them.

The part played by Jews in the liquor industry continued to concern the Russian government well into the 20th century, even though assuming other forms. The emancipation of the peasants, cancellation of the compulsory quota of consumption, and abrogation of the monopoly of the estate owners changed the economic character and social aspects of the problem. In independent Poland between the two world wars, various economic and legal measures were taken to drive the Jews from this branch, including regulations for hygiene and manipulation of the state monopoly on the sale of vodka. The development of capitalist industry and trade in the second half of the 19th century and freer access to Jews to take up crafts, enabled many Jews in Eastern Europe to enter other branches of the economy. Even so, the image of the Jew invoked by antisemites in Eastern Europe still made frequent use of the hated Jewish taverner.

The feelings of loathing with which the Jew regarded his place behind the tavern counter is powerfully expressed by the poet Ḥ.N. *Bialik. The taverner and his family saw themselves placed at the:

> meeting between the gates of purity and defilement.../ There, in a human swine cave, in the sacrilege of a tavern, /in streams of impious libation,... /over a yellow-leaved volume, /my father's head appeared, the skull of a tortured matter... /... in smoke clouds, his face sick with sorrow, eyes shedding blood... /the faces were monstrous... the words a filthy stream... /To a child's ear alone... /serenely quietly flowed, the murmur of Torah... the words of the living God... /He [the taverner] would sit... among stretched-out revelers,/... mounting the scaffold each day, thrown to the lions each day... (trans. by Robert Friend, in S.Y. Penueli and A. Ukhmani (eds.), *Anthology of Modern Hebrew Poetry*, 1 (1966), 47–48.)

[Jacob Goldberg]

IN NORTH AMERICA. In addition to the prohibition against partaking of non-Jewish wine, its ceremonial use for various occasions, such as **Kiddush* and on all festive occasions, as well as the need for all wine and liquors to be *kasher* for Passover, observances both practiced even by those who were not particular with regard to non-Jewish wine for ordinary use, resulted in a specific Jewish trade in wine (and for Passover in other liquors) for specific Jewish consumption in all countries. The needs of the Jewish population were met by local manufacturers especially where wine could not be imported from Ereẓ Israel.

U.S. Jews tended to make their wine personally or in small shops. The 19th amendment to the U.S. Constitution and the Volstead Act, which prohibited the manufacture and sale of intoxicating beverages, made an exception in favor of such beverages when needed for religious purposes. Abuses of this privilege by some Jews to supply the illegal liquor market disturbed U.S. Jewry. They led to the issuance of a controversial responsum by the talmudic scholar Louis Ginzberg, *Teshuvah al Devar Yeinot,* etc., permitting grape juice to be used for religious purposes instead of wine. Following the end of Prohibition in 1933, the business of several Jewish wine manufacturers reached national proportions, supplying the non-Jewish as well as the Jewish market. In the U.S. few Jews were tavern keepers. However, they were prominent among distillers and retailers. Such families as Bernheim, Lilienthal, and Publicker were important distillers, and the general prominence of Jews as retail merchants included the selling of bottled liquor.

Some Jewish firms grew to considerable proportions in Europe as well as the U.S. Many expanded their activity to include general trade in wine and liquors and this may be the origin of the extensive representation of Jews in the English public house trade, for example, the firm of Levy and Franks.

Sedgewick's, owned by the *Bronfman family of Canada, became one of the largest distilleries in the world.

WINE INDUSTRY IN EREẒ ISRAEL. In Ereẓ Israel a few small winepresses were owned by Jews, mainly in the Old City of Jerusalem and in other ancient cities inhabited by Jews, before the beginning of modern Jewish settlement in the second half of the 19th century. These were simple household winepresses, catering chiefly to local consumption. The raw material was supplied by Arab vineyards in the surrounding hill regions. The first vines of European variety were planted at the *Mikveh Israel agricultural school founded in 1870. The school also built the first European-style wine cellar, which is still in use. With the beginning of modern Jewish settlement, the first vineyards were planted at *Rishon le-Zion and later in other moshavot. Baron Edmond de *Rothschild, who sponsored early Jewish pioneer settlement in Ereẓ Israel, had high hopes that viticulture would develop as one of the main economic bases for the Jewish villages. He invited specialists from abroad, who selected high-grade varieties in order to produce quality wines. After the harvest of the first crops, he built large wine cellars at Rishon le-Zion (1889) for Judea, and at *Zikhron Ya'akov (1892) for Samaria. These cellars were equipped with refrigerators to retard fermentation and thereby improve quality.

The Baron paid high prices for the grapes in order to assure the settlers a decent standard of living. Economic prosperity resulted in a rapid development of viticulture, and, at the end of the century, vineyards covered about half of the total Jewish land under cultivation. In the course of time, millions of francs were paid to maintain high wine prices, and many settlers concentrated on making wine as their sole occupation. A large overstock of wine accumulated, and wine surpluses continued to increase until a crisis was reached. It was decided to uproot one-third of the vineyards in order to reduce the size of the crop and maintain prices. The winegrowers were compensated by the Baron, and, instead of vineyards, planted almond trees, olives, and the first citrus groves. In 1890–91, the vineyards in Samaria and Galilee were attacked by phylloxera, which ruined the *Rosh Pinnah plantations. The infected vines had to be uprooted and replaced by pest-resistant plants brought from India.

In 1906 the management of the wine cellars at Rishon le-Zion and Zikhron Ya'akov was handed over to the farmers, who founded the Carmel Wine Growers Cooperative. At the same time, several private wine cellars, such as Ha-Tikvah and Naḥalat Ẓevi were established. Their wine was sold both locally and abroad. During World War I, the local wine found a greatly increased market among the German, British, and Australian troops passing through the country. After the war, however, the Ereẓ Israel wine industry lost its principal markets: Russia, because of the Revolution; the United States, because of Prohibition; and Egypt and the Middle East, because of Arab nationalism. The industry had to undergo a period of adaptation. The acreage under grapes was reduced, chiefly in Judea, where vineyards were replaced by citrus groves. On the other hand, additional areas were planted, mainly in the Zikhron Ya'akov area. During World War II, new plantations were developed on a smaller scale, and with the establishment of the State of Israel (1948), the wine-growing areas covered about 2,500 acres (10,000 dunams). At that time there were 14 wine cellars in Israel.

Large new areas were planted in the Negev, the Jerusalem area, Adullam, and Galilee – some of which had never previously been considered suitable for wine growing. With successive waves of immigrants, drinking habits have changed. During the earlier period 70%–75% of the wine consumed was sweet, but later, two-thirds of the total consumption was dry wine. The Israel Wine Institute, established in cooperation with the industry and the government, undertakes research for the improvement of wine production in Israel. Preference is given to wine plantations in the hilly regions. Varieties of better quality are selected, and new varieties are introduced. Israel wine is exported to many countries of the world. It is widely in demand among Jews for ritual purposes but efforts have been made to broaden the market.

[Nathan Hochberg]

The Israeli wine industry underwent a revolution starting in the 1970s and now numbers hundreds of wineries, ranging from leaders like Golan Heights, Carmel, and Barkan Wine Cellars to boutique wineries like the prize-winning Domaine du Castel in the Judean Hills. Israeli wines are now served in quality restaurants in 40 countries, with exports of $13 million in 2005 and domestic sales of around $150 million. Around 7,500 acres of vineyards produce about 50,000 tons of grapes a year

BIBLIOGRAPHY: S.B. Weinryb, *Neueste Wirtschaftsgeschichte der Juden in Russland und Polen* (1934); J. Hessen, *Istoriya Yevreyskogo naroda v Rossii* (1925); R. Mahler, *Yidn in Amolikn Poyln in Likht fun Tsifern* (1958); I. Rychlikowa, *Studia nad towarową produkcją wielkiej własności w Małopolsce w latach 1764–1805* (1966); J. Burszta, *Społeczeństwo i karczma* (1951); R. Rozdolski, *Stosunki poddańcze w dawnej Galicji*, 2 vols. (1962); Ringelblum, in: *Sprawy narodowościowe*, 8 (1934); I. Schiper, *Dzieje handlu żydowskiego na ziemiach polskich* (1937); Ettinger, in: *Zion*, 20 (1955), 128–52; 21 (1956), 107–42; H.H. Ben-Sasson, *ibid.*, 21 (1956), 83–206; Goldberg, in: BŻIH, 59 (1966); C. Roth, in: JHSET, 17 (1953), 39–43; J. Katz, *Tradition and Crisis* (1961), index; N. Hochberg, *Giddul ha-Gefen*, 2 vols. (1954–55); D. Idelovitch (ed.), *Rishon le-Ẓiyyon 1882–1941* (1941); A. Ever ha-Dani, *Toledot Aguddat ha-Koremim* (1966); Z. Carmi, *Anaf ha-Gefen ve-Ta'asiyyat ha-Yayin be-Yisrael* (1963).

°**WINGATE, ORDE** (**Charles**; 1903–1944), British Army officer who served in Palestine during the 1936–39 riots. Wingate was born in India into a nonconformist family; his grandfather had helped conduct a Church of Scotland mission in Budapest for poor Jews and his parents served as missionaries. He was raised on the Bible and kept it at his side throughout his life. Wingate was commissioned in 1923. From 1928 to 1933 he served with the Sudan Defense Force and also studied Arabic and Semitics. In February 1934 he was sent on a one-man mission to search for the mysterious Zarzura oasis in the Libyan Desert (reported in the *Geographical Journal*, 83 (1934), 281–308). In 1936, after his promotion to captain, he was posted to Palestine and played a leading role in fighting the Arab terror campaign, particularly the attacks on the Iraqi-Haifa pipeline, for which he was awarded the D.S.O. He gained the confidence of the *yishuv* authorities, established contact with the *Haganah, and with its help formed the Special Night Squads (SNS), a unit made up largely of Haganah fighters whom he trained in unorthodox but highly successful tactics in countering and preventing Arab attacks. Wingate became a passionate supporter of the Jewish cause in Palestine; the *yishuv* responded in kind and referred to him as "*Ha-Yedid*" ("The Friend"). His highly individualistic character, disregard for the conventional rules of military behavior, and his propagation of Zionism finally resulted in 1939 in his being transferred from Palestine with an endorsement in his passport stating that "the bearer … should not be allowed to enter Palestine." He had, however, left a lasting impression upon the country, and some of the young Jews whom he had befriended and trained were to become military leaders in the State of Israel.

In the early stage of World War II, Wingate commanded an antiaircraft battery in Britain. In 1941 he was "rediscovered" and assigned to lead a force against the Italians in Ethiopia. He played a decisive role in the liberation of the country (he was joined in the campaign by some of the former SNS fighters, at his own request) and was at Haile Selassie's side when the emperor reentered Addis Ababa. His talents were then employed in Burma, where he trained and led the Chindits, a special jungle unit that operated behind the Japanese lines. Winston Churchill, who regarded Wingate as a man of genius, invited him in 1943 to join him in his meeting with Roosevelt in Quebec. Wingate was killed in an air crash in the Burma jungle in 1944 and buried at Arlington National Cemetery in Virginia, U.S. By then he had become a major-general.

Wingate's personality and military genius made a profound impact on the *Palmaḥ and the Haganah and, through them, on the Israeli Defense Forces. He, in turn, dreamed of leading the army of the future Jewish state. His devotion to the Jewish people and Ereẓ Israel persisted up to his death. In a letter to a friend in Palestine (1943) he wrote, in Hebrew, "If I forget thee, O Jerusalem…." Israel has not forgotten *Ha-Yedid.* A children's village on the slopes of Mt. Carmel is named Yemin Orde, the College of Physical Education near Netanyah and a forest on Mount Gilboa bear his name, and there is a Wingate Square in Jerusalem. His wife, Lorna, although a gentile, was a leader of *Youth Aliyah in Britain.

BIBLIOGRAPHY: C. Sykes, *Orde Wingate* (1959); A.I. Hay, *There Was a Man of Genius* (1963); W.G. Burchett, *Wingate's Phantom*

Army (1946); L. Mosley, *Gideon Goes to War* (1955); C.Y. Rolo, *Wingate's Raiders* (1944). **ADD. BIBLIOGRAPHY:** ODNB online; J. Bierman and C. Smith, *Fire in the Night: Wingate of Burma, Ethiopia, and Zion* (1999); P. Mead. *Orde Wingate and the Historians* (1987).

[Moshe Dayan]

WINGER, DEBRA (1955–), U.S. film actress. Born in Cleveland Heights, Ohio, Winger spent two years of her youth in Israel (where she served for three months in the army and worked on a kibbutz). She returned to the U.S. and first came to serious notice as John Travolta's co-star in *Urban Cowboy* (1980). She was subsequently chosen for the female lead opposite Richard Gere in *An Officer and a Gentleman* (1982), for which she received her first Best Actress Oscar nomination. Winger went on to appear in such films as *Terms of Endearment* (Oscar nomination for Best Actress, 1983); *Legal Eagles* (1986); *Black Widow* (1987); *Betrayed* (1988); Arthur Miller's *Everybody Wins* (1990); *The Sheltering Sky* (1990); *Leap of Faith* (1992); *A Dangerous Woman* (1993), *Wilder Napalm* (1993); *Shadowlands* (Oscar nomination for Best Actress, 1993); *Forget Paris* (1995); *Big Bad Love* (produced, 2001); *Radio* (2003); and *Eulogy* (2004).

On television, she appeared three times in 1976–77 in the role of Wonder Girl on the series *Wonder Woman*.

She was married to actor Timothy Hutton from 1986 to 1990. She married actor Arliss Howard in 1996.

BIBLIOGRAPHY: M. Cahill, *Debra Winger: Hollywood's Wild Child* (1984).

[Jonathan Licht and Ruth Beloff (2nd ed.)]

WINIK, MEIR (1886–1966), agronomist. Born in Odessa, Winik graduated as a technological engineer from the Polytechnic of Warsaw. Immigrating to Ereẓ Israel in 1906, he was employed as a chemical engineer at the wine cellars of Rishon Le-Zion and in 1910 proceeded to Paris to study the fermentation of grapes and soil problems at the Pasteur Institute and the National Agricultural Institute. Returning to Ereẓ Israel, he introduced many modern scientific processes in the manufacture of wine and the improvement of grape strains and soil quality. He enlisted in the Jewish Legion of the British Army during World War I and after the war taught chemistry at the Agricultural School of Mikveh Israel. He was awarded the Israel Prize for Agriculture in 1956.

WINKLER, HENRY (1945–), U.S. actor, writer, director, and producer. Winkler was born in New York City to Harry Irving Winkler, a lumber executive, and Ilse Anna Maria (née Hadra), German Jews who had escaped the Nazis before the beginning of World War II. Winkler attended high school at the Horace Mann School in Riverdale, New York, and graduated from Emerson College with a bachelor's degree in 1967. After receiving a master of fine arts degree in drama from Yale in 1970, the five-foot-six actor appeared in dozens of commercials before making his film debut in the 1950s gang feature *The Lords of Flatbush* (1974) with the then unknown Sylvester Stallone. Winkler joined the cast of the 1950s sitcom *Happy Days* (1974–84), achieving pop stardom as the motorcycle-riding mechanic Arthur "Fonzie" Fonzarelli, a role that earned him two Golden Globe awards. While still on *Happy Days*, Winkler starred in films such as *Heroes* (1977) and *Night Shift* (1982), directed by *Happy Days* co-star Ron Howard. In 1978, Emerson College honored Winkler with a doctorate in Hebrew literature. After *Happy Days,* he concentrated on coproducing the television show *MacGyver* (1985–92) and directing feature films such as *Memories of Me* (1988) and *Cop and a Half* (1993). Winkler served as executive producer for Rob *Reiner's *The Sure Thing* (1985) and the film *Young Sherlock Holmes* (1985). He stepped out from behind the camera again to star in the made-for-television movies *Absolute Strangers* (1991) and *The Only Way Out* (1993), as well as for the shortlived sitcom *Monty* (1994). Winkler also returned to feature films with roles in *Scream* (1996), *The Waterboy* (1998), *Little Nicky* (2000), and *Holes* (2003). In 2003, the dyslexic Winkler and Lin Oliver began releasing titles in the ongoing Hank Zipzer book series for young adults, which focused on the misadventures of a fourth-grader with learning difficulties. In 2005 he starred in the CBS series *Out of Practice.*

[Adam Wills (2nd ed.)]

WINKLER, IRWIN (1931–), U.S. film producer. Born in New York City, Winkler graduated from New York University. He served in the army beginning in 1951. After a brief stint as an agent at the William Morris agency, he went to Hollywood in 1966. His first production, with a partner, Robert Chartoff, was *Double Trouble* (1967), starring Elvis Presley (instead of the star he intended for the role, Julie Christie). From that point, Winkler and Chartoff went on to produce some of the most provocative films of the 1970s and 1980s, including John Boorman's *Point Blank* (1967); Sydney Pollack's *They Shoot Horses, Don't They?* (1969), which garnered nine Academy Award nominations; John Avildsen's *Rocky* (1976) and the four other *Rocky* movies; Martin Scorsese's *New York, New York* (1977), starring Liza Minnelli and Robert De Niro; and *Raging Bull* (1980), with De Niro as the boxer Jake LaMotta; as well as *The Right Stuff* (1983), based on Tom Wolfe's book about the nation's first astronauts. On his own, Winkler produced such films as Costa-Gavras' *Betrayed* (1988) and *Music Box* (1989) as well as Scorsese's *Goodfellas* (1990). Winkler then turned to directing, and made films like *Guilty by Suspicion* (1991), which he also wrote, starring De Niro; *Night and the City* (1992), based on Jules Dassin's film noir; the suspense thriller *The Net* (1995), with Sandra Bullock; and *At First Sight* (1999), with Val Kilmer and Mira Sorvino. His films amassed 12 Academy Awards from 45 nominations, including four best picture nominations. He also directed and produced the critically acclaimed drama *Life as a House,* starring Kevin Kline, Hayden Christensen, and Kristen Scott Thomas, and *The Shipping News* (both 2001), based on the Pulitzer Prize-winning novel by E. Annie Proulx and starring Kevin Spacey, Julianne Moore, and Judi Dench. Winkler teamed with Kline again for *De-Lovely* (2004), a biography of the songwriter Cole Porter.

Three of Winkler's films were listed on the American Film Institute list of the top 100 films of all time.

[Stewart Kampel (2nd ed.)]

WINKLER, LEO (Judah; 17th century), leader of the Vienna Jewish community at the time of the expulsion of the Jews from the city in 1670. By profession a physician, he graduated from the medical school in Padua in 1629. He corresponded with the Christian Hebraist Johann Christoph *Wagenseil, and ably represented the community when it was threatened with expulsion. In conjunction with Herz *Coma and Enoch *Fraenkel he signed a letter to Manuel Texeira requesting the intervention of Queen Christina of Sweden on behalf of the Jews. With Coma he offered 100,000 gulden to *Leopold I to enable 1,000 Jews to remain in Vienna. He was also among the signatories of the request for assistance to the Venice communities. His sons ISAAC and JACOB graduated as physicians in Padua in 1669. Winkler apparently later settled in *Poznan (Posen), where Jacob was a physician.

BIBLIOGRAPHY: D. Kaufmann: *Die letzte Vertreibung der Juden aus Wien* (1889), 69, 129, 132, 138, 146, 222; M. Grunwald, *Vienna* (1936), index.

[Meir Lamed]

WINNIK, HENRY ZVI (1902–1982), Israeli psychiatrist and psychoanalyst. Winnik was born near Chernovtsy (Bukovina) into a family of intellectuals and Zionists. His postgraduate experience included laboratory work with F. Georgi, and in psychiatric hospitals in Chemnitz and Berlin. In Berlin he met Wilhelm *Reich and Otto *Fenichel, through whom he entered psychoanalysis. He was trained at first at the Berlin Psychoanalytic Institute, leaving with the advent of Hitler in 1933. He continued in Vienna with noted supervisors such as Helene *Deutsch, maintaining his contact with clinical psychiatry. He became a training analyst in 1938 and, on Anna *Freud's advice, left for Bucharest to develop analysis there. Political events there, however, and the outbreak of the war did not permit him to work. He left for Palestine in 1942 where he became the director of the Geha mental hospital of Kuppat Ḥolim, developing modern methods of institutional care. In 1950 he became the director of its Talbieh mental hospital in Jerusalem.

From 1944 he was a member of the executive of the Israel Neuropsychiatric Society, and its chairman from 1961 to 1965. Winnik had met Max *Eitingon in Berlin and joined him at the Psychoanalytic Institute in Palestine. In 1955 he became its chairman – a post he held four times. From 1954 he was professor at The Hebrew University-Hadassah Medical School in Jerusalem. He founded the *Israel Annals of Psychiatry* and served as its editor-in-chief. His testimony in Israel's courts contributed to the establishment of the principle of irresistible impulse. Winnik published many papers on a broad range of psychiatric, psychoanalytic, and forensic subjects.

[Louis Miller]

WINNINGER, SOLOMON (1877–1968), biographer. Winninger was born in Gura-Humorului, Bukovina, and worked as a post office official in Czernowitz (Chernovtsy) until 1941. In 1950 he settled in Israel. Winninger's *Grosse juedische Nationalbiographie* (7 vols., 1927–36) contains 14,000 biographies of prominent Jews. A further 17,000 (Ms., Jewish National and University Library) remained unpublished.

BIBLIOGRAPHY: D. Lazar, in: *Ma'ariv* (Dec. 20, 1968).

[Nathan Michael Gelber]

WINNIPEG, capital of Manitoba, Canada, the province's largest city and the center of Jewish life in the province. In 2001 Winnipeg's 14,765 Jews constituted only 2.2 percent of the city's population of 661,730. However, they also constituted fully 97 percent of all Jews in Manitoba. In 1881 there were only 23 Jews in Winnipeg. That number grew to 1,164 in 1901 and reached a high of 19,376 in 1961 before beginning a gradual decennial decline to less than 15,000 in 2001. Winnipeg has also dropped in size from third to eighth place among Canadian cities, while the city's Jewish population dropped from third to fourth place among Canadian Jewish communities behind Toronto, Montreal, and Vancouver.

Jewish congregational life began early in Winnipeg's history. In 1883, after the first influx of Jews from Russia, an attempt was made to establish a single congregation in Winnipeg, but disagreements between the earlier Jewish residents and recently arrived and more Orthodox immigrants prevented agreement. In 1887 a *Manitoba Free Press* church survey found "three congregations of the Hebrew faith" but no synagogue building and suggested that if united, "the Hebrews would form a congregation of respectable numbers, and … soon possess a building creditable to themselves and to the city." In 1889 unity was achieved and Shaarey Zedek, the first synagogue, was founded, but a group favoring a "*sefardishe minhag*" soon started the Rosh Pina synagogue.

In the 1960s Winnipeg had 12 synagogues plus the Chesed Shel Emes funeral home. The two largest congregations, Shaarey Zedek in the city's south end and Rosh Pina in the north end, were Conservative; the others were Orthodox and all but one in the north end, where most Jews then lived. In 1965 the Reform Temple Shalom was opened in the south end, and in 1976 a new conservative synagogue, Beth Israel, opened in the north. By the end of the century the majority of Winnipeg Jews had moved from the north end to the south end. Declining membership forced a merger of the three largest north end congregations: Rosh Pina, B'nai Abraham, and Beth Israel, to form Etz Chayim on the premises of Rosh Pina. In 2005 Winnipeg had nine synagogues, six in the north end, including a Lubavitch Center with north and south end branches.

In 1883, Beth El religious school opened, teaching Bible and Jewish history in English to 50 students; a year later Russian newcomers opened a *ḥeder*, with 12 students instructed in Yiddish. In 1902 a King Edward Talmud Torah, named for the new British monarch, opened next to the synagogue. The

B'nai Zion Congregational Hebrew School opened in 1906. Five years later the two schools united with 250 students, and in 1913 a new Talmud Torah building was opened, doubling as a Jewish community center.

Secular Jewish life also flourished in Winnipeg. In 1914 Labor Zionists and Socialists opened the Yiddish Radical School, renamed after I.L. Peretz in 1915. By 1921 the more radical Arbeiter Ring Yiddish school was established, and at one point Winnipeg had five Yiddish secular schools. In 1919 the Peretz School Muter Farein opened the first kindergarten in the city and a year later started a Jewish day school, possibly the first of its kind in North America. By 1963 the I.L. Peretz Folk School was the only remaining Yiddish secular school and in 1983 it merged with the Talmud Torah, which by then had north and south branches, and also operated the Joseph Wolinsky Collegiate. In 1997 the Talmud Torah north and south branches were closed and Jewish education in Winnipeg became consolidated in the Gray Academy at the Asper Jewish Community Campus, opened that year in the south end on the bank of the Assiniboine River. The Herzliah Congregation operates Ohr Hatorah, an Orthodox elementary day school.

There has also been a longstanding Jewish presence on campus. In 1915, a Menorah Society was formed at Winnipeg's University of Manitoba. It sponsored varied Jewish campus activities, including annual Jewish theater productions such as an English-language version of Shalom Aleichem's *It's Hard to Be a Jew.* In response to accusations that the university maintained quotas on Jewish and other minority enrollment in the Medical School, in 1943 the Avukah Zionist Society undertook to investigate. By the end of 1944 they succeeded in exposing the quota system and forced an end to the system. During World War II, Hillel organized on campus and helped initiate Jewish studies courses in 1950–51. By 1964 the University of Manitoba established the first Judaic Studies Department in Canada, headed by Rabbi Zalman Schachter, founder of the Jewish Renewal Movement. In 1989 the department was disbanded, just as Jewish Studies departments were growing in other Canadian universities.

Winnipeg's Jewish community has been characterized by vibrant organizational life. By 1900 **landsmannshaften* and benevolent societies were growing, and the Winnipeg Zionist Society had 100 members. In 1909 B'nai B'rith was established and United Hebrew Charities was organized. Concern that United Hebrew Charities was controlled by Jews in the city's south end led to formation of the North End Relief Society, but the two groups joined forces in 1914. That year Winnipeg and the farm settlement in Lipton, Saskatchewan, became the first two communities in Canada to collect funds for Jewish war relief. In 1915 the Western Jewish Fund for the Relief of War Sufferers was established, and in 1916 Winnipeg hosted a conference of 18 western centers that called for the establishment of a Canadian Jewish Congress. A year later Winnipeg hosted the 15th national convention of the Canadian Zionist Federation, and in 1919 a delegation of 20 Winnipeg Jews participated in Montreal meetings organizing the Canadian Jewish Congress.

By 1920 Winnipeg had a Jewish Orphanage and Children's Aid Society, an Old Folks Home, a YMHA Center, and a Jewish Immigrant Aid Society and, by the mid-1920s, the Orphanage, the Old Folks Home, and Hebrew Relief became beneficiaries of centralized fundraising by the Federated Budget Board, and in 1938 a Jewish Welfare Fund was established to raise funds for Jewish schools and social agencies. In the 1950s a new YMHA Community Center was built which housed the Welfare Fund, the Canadian Jewish Congress, and Zionist Organization regional offices. In the 1960s, the Winnipeg Congress Council had representatives of every local Jewish organization, and Congress Western Region Council had members in Beausejour, Brandon, Dauphin, and Portage la Prairie. The Welfare Fund, Congress and the Zionist organization jointly ran the Combined Jewish Appeal for local, national, Israeli, and overseas agencies. During the 1967 Six-Day War crisis, Winnipeg played an exemplary role in the national Israeli Emergency Campaign.

In 1973 the Welfare Fund and the CJ Congress office merged to form the Winnipeg Jewish Community Council – later the Jewish Federation/Combined Jewish Appeal. In 1997 the Asper Jewish Community Campus was opened in three remodeled Winnipeg heritage buildings on the south bank of the Assiniboine River. The campus houses the Gray Academy of Jewish Education, the Rady Community Centre, successor to the YMHA; the Jewish Heritage Centre of Western Canada, including the Jewish Historical Society and Archives, the Marion and Ed Vickar Jewish Musem and the Freeman Family Holocaust Education Centre; the Kaufman-Silverberg Library, the Berney Theatre and offices of Federation / CJA, Jewish Foundation of Manitoba (founded 1964), Jewish Child and Family Services, Winnipeg Jewish Theatre, B'nai B'rith, and Winnipeg Zionist Initiative. Winnipeg North has a thriving Gwen Secter Senior Centre sponsored by the National Council of Jewish Women and a Na'amat Hall (Pioneer Women), which is also used by United Jewish Peoples Order for public forums and a Yiddish Mameloshen group. The Sholem Aleichem Community runs a Sunday school and sponsors secular holiday events.

Concerned with the gradual decline in Winnipeg's Jewish population, in the late 1990s the Jewish Federation started "Grow Winnipeg," a program of outreach to Jews, especially in Latin America. By 2005 this program had brought 168 South American Jewish families to Winnipeg, comprising 482 individuals. The total number of new arrivals was 564 families, comprising nearly 1,500 individuals, including people from Argentina, Russia, and Israel. These newcomers receive special community services and their presence is reflected in the publication of columns in Russian and Spanish, as well as Hebrew and Yiddish, in the *Jewish Post and News.* For most of the 20th century Winnipeg was served by three Jewish papers, the Yiddish-language *Israelite Press* (*Yiddishe Vort*) founded in 1917, which became bilingual before it ceased publication in 1981, and the English language *Jewish Post* founded in 1925 and *Western Jewish News* founded a year later. The two English language papers merged in 1987.

Very conscious of its history, the Winnipeg Jewish community has been a leader in archival and museum preservation and in celebrating community history. The local Archives Committee was instrumental in organizing both the Canadian Jewish Congress Archives Committee and the Jewish Historical Society of Western Canada. In 1972 the Jewish Historical Society mounted an exhibit entitled "Journey Into Our Heritage," exploring the history of the Jews of Western Canada. It ran for six months at the Manitoba Museum, toured Canada, and was exhibited at the Museum of the Diaspora in Tel Aviv.

Jews in Winnipeg have also made a prominent contribution to the larger community. Perhaps nowhere is this more true that in the legal system. Samuel *Freedman was the first Jew named to the Manitoba Court of Queen's Bench (QB) and later to the Court of Appeal, serving as Manitoba Chief Justice in 1971–83; Israel Nitikman was appointed a judge to the Court of the QB in 1962. In 1967 Roy Matas was appointed a judge to that court and was elevated six years later to the Court of Appeal. In 2005 the Manitoba Court of Appeal had three Jewish judges, the Court of Queen's Bench had seven Jewish judges out of 40, and there were also seven Jews on the Provincial Court.

BIBLIOGRAPHY: A. Chiel, *The Jews in Manitoba: A Social History* (1961).

[Abraham Arnold (2nd ed.)]

WINOGRAND, GARRY (1928–1984), U.S magazine photojournalist and advertising photographer who developed an unusual style of "street" photography that helped change the nature of the genre. He photographed primarily on the streets of New York, the city in which he was born, portraying passers-by with an immediacy and physicality rarely found in still images. "I photograph to find out what something will look like photographed," he said of his method, which incorporated rapid-fire shooting technique, wide-angle lenses and skewed framing for a satirical and sometimes disturbing vision that became popular in the 1970s. His pictures, which deceptively resembled snapshots, were crammed with activity. By traditional standards, critics said, the pictures represent the opposite of real-world photography. But they have the vitality, incongruity, and inexplicability of daily life. John Szarkowski, director of the Museum of Modern Art's photography division, called Winogrand "the central photographer of his generation." In a show at the Modern in 1988, Winogrand's work was divided chronologically: work from the 1960s on women (many published in the 1975 book *Women Are Beautiful*); on zoos (from *The Animals*, a 1969 book and show), and on public events in which the presence of the news media is significant (from "Public Relations," Winogrand's show at the Modern in 1977). In 1978, Winogrand, who freed himself from convention by tilting the frames of his images in an effort to develop fresh ways to depict the world, moved to Los Angeles. There, where street life took place in cars, Winogrand made many pictures from the front seat of an automobile. The images relegated human beings to a far distance.

To be a great photographer, Winogrand claimed half-seriously in the 1970s, was first, to be Jewish. The best ones, in his opinion, shared this birthright. By his definition, Jewish photographers were nervy, ironic, disruptive of artistic norms, and proud outsiders. Winogrand left behind some 2,500 rolls of exposed but undeveloped film, plus 6,500 developed rolls for which no contact sheets had been made, making a total of 300,000 unedited images. The Modern arranged to have the film developed and contacts prints made.

[Stewart Kampel (2nd ed.)]

WINSTEIN, SAUL (1912–1969), U.S. physical organic chemist. Winstein was born in Montreal, Canada. He did research at the California Institute of Technology, Harvard University, and the Illinois Institute of Technology. From 1947 he was professor of chemistry at the University of California at Los Angeles (1947).

WINSTON, ROBERT, BARON (1940–), British physician, broadcaster, and fertility expert. Winston graduated from London University as a gynecological surgeon and became a noted pioneer of fertility and IVF techniques. He is well-known both for his scientific papers and for his programs on BBC television such as *The Human Body* (1998), *The Secret Life of Twins* (1999), and *Superhuman* (2000), which drew large audiences. Winston was professor of fertility studies at Imperial College School of Medicine, London, and received a life peerage in 1995. He served as chair of the House of Lords Select Committee on Science and Technology and was awarded the Royal Society's Faraday Gold Medal.

[William D. Rubinstein (2nd ed.)]

WINSTON, STAN (1946–), U.S. director and visual effects artist. Winston grew up in Arlington, Virginia. After graduating from the University of Virginia in 1968, Winston moved to Los Angeles to be an actor. Influenced by Lon Chaney, who did his own makeup in *Phantom of the Opera* (1943), Winston became a makeup apprentice with Walt Disney Studios. He worked 6,000 hours for Disney, which culminated in his first Emmy win for the television movie *Gargoyles* (1972). Among his first jobs after leaving the studio in 1972 were cosmetically aging actress Cicely Tyson to 110 in the television movie *The Autobiography of Miss Jane Pittman* (1974), which led to another Emmy win, and makeup work on the set of the miniseries *Roots* (1977). He earned his first feature film makeup credit for *The Wiz* (1978), and received his first Oscar nomination for his work on the robot comedy *Heartbeeps* (1981). In 1978, he founded Stan Winston Studio in Van Nuys, California. Winston provided visual effects and second-unit direction for the groundbreaking science fiction film *The Terminator* (1984). This collaboration with director James Cameron led to his helming the special effects unit and creating alien effects for *Aliens* (1986), which won Winston his first Oscar. In 1987, he earned a third Oscar nomination for his creation of the alien in *Predator* (1987), and in 1988 he directed his first feature film, *Pumpkinhead*. Winston earned a fourth Academy Award nod for makeup work on Tim Burton's *Edward Scissorhands* (1990), but won Oscars for makeup and visual effects when he joined Cameron on the big-budget *Terminator* sequel, *Terminator 2: Judgment Day* (1991). The Penguin makeup he created for Danny DeVito in Burton's *Batman Returns* (1992) led to his seventh Academy Award nomination, and after directing his second feature, the straight-to-video *The Adventures of a Gnome Named Gnorm* (1994), Winston won a fourth Oscar for creating the life-sized dinosaurs in *Jurassic Park* (1993). Winston, Cameron, and Industrial Light and Magic designer Scott Ross joined forces in 1993 to form Digital Domain, a computer animation special effects company whose first project was the much publicized adaptation of Anne Rice's *Interview With the Vampire* (1994). However, he and Cameron eventually resigned from the company in 1998. Winston signed a development deal with DreamWorks in 1996, and one year later he founded Stan Winston Productions, which provided special effects, animatronics and makeup for films such as *The Lost World: Jurassic Park* (1997), which earned him his ninth Oscar nomination; *End of Days* (1999); *Jurassic Park III* (2001); *A.I. Artificial Intelligence* (2001), his 10th Academy Award nod; *Pearl Harbor* (2001); *Terminator 3: Rise of the Machines* (2003); and *Constantine* (2005).

[Adam Wills (2nd ed.)]

WINTER, GUSTAV (1899–1943), Czech journalist and author (brother of Lev Winter, the statesman). He was press officer of the Czechoslovak mission to the League of Nations in Geneva, and Paris correspondent for *Právo Lidu* ("The People's Right"), the organ of the Social Democratic Party. Winter was regarded as the best-informed Czech correspondent in France.

He published *Státníci dnešní Francie* ("French Statesmen of our Days," 1927), and *Kniha o Francii* ("Book on France," 1930) for which he received the highest Czechoslovak literary award. *To není konec Francie* ("This is Not the End of France," 1941) was published in London, where he had fled after the fall of France. Winter was also the author of a book of poetic reportage on Spain, *Don Quijote na rozcestí* ("Don Quixote at the Crossroads," 1935) and translator of Čapek and Masaryk into French.

[Avigdor Dagan]

His brother LEV (Leo) WINTER (1876–1935), Czech politician, was born in Hroby in S. Bohemia. Winter studied law at Prague University and joined the Czech Social Democratic Party at the age of 19. In 1907 he was elected to the Austrian Reichsrat (Parliament) and reelected in 1911. In the Austrian Parliament he was active in committees on social legislation. In 1918 he was a member of the revolutionary Czech National Council and became minister of social welfare in the first Government of the Czechoslovak Republic. In 1923 he presented to Parliament the Social Insurance Law, which had been drafted primarily by him. He served two more terms as minister of social welfare and was member of parliament until his death. He wrote several books on social and legal problems, and also translated the first volume of Marx's *Kapital* into Czech. Winter took no part in any Jewish activities.

[Chaim Yahil]

BIBLIOGRAPHY: GUSTAV WINTER: F. Klatil, *In Memoriam Gustava Wintra* (Czech, 1944); E. Hostovsky, in: *Jews of Czechoslovakia*, 1 (1968), 447–8, 523; Ceskoslovenski, *Biografie*, 3 (1936).

WINTER, JACOB (1857–1941), German rabbi and scholar. Born in Hungary, Winter served from 1886 as rabbi in Dresden and received the honorary title of professor from the king of Saxony for his scholarly work.

His main achievement was the three-volume encyclopedic work, *Die juedische Litteratur seit Abschluss des Kanons* (3 vols., 1894–96), a prose and poetry anthology with biographical and literary-historical introductions, edited in cooperation with the German Orientalist August *Wuensche and leading scholars of the time. The work became a standard reference book on post-biblical Jewish literature. An earlier study by Winter was *Die Stellung der Sklaven bei den Juden...* (1886). Together with Wuensche, he also translated into German (with annotations) the halakhic Midrashim *Mekhilta* (1909) and *Sifra* (1938), and edited the second volume of M. Lazarus, *Die Ethik des Judentums* (1911).

WINTER, PAUL (1904–1969), New Testament scholar. Born in Czechoslovakia, Winter by profession was a lawyer in his native land until the Nazi occupation in 1939. Escaping from Czechoslovakia, he joined the free Czech forces in the Middle East, where he served for several years and participated in the battle of El-Alamein and the Normandy landings. After his release from the armed forces he settled in England, where he lived until his death. In his later years he suffered great poverty. His main contribution to scholarship was *The Trial of Jesus* (1961), which created a great deal of interest in the scholarly world with its thesis that Jesus was not condemned by a Jewish court but by the Romans for political, not religious, crimes. He was regarded as one of the leading New Testament scholars of his time.

[Seymour Siegel]

WINTERNITZ, EMANUEL (1898–1983), musicologist who specialized in organology, musical iconology, and art history. Born in Vienna, he studied piano, musicology (under his uncle, Oscar Kapp), and composition (under Franz Schmidt). After serving three years in the Austrian army during World War I, he studied law at the University of Vienna (earning an LL.D., 1922), and lectured on aesthetics and the philosophy of law at the Volkshochschule and at the University of Hamburg. From 1929 he practiced corporate law, while undertaking private studies in music and musical instruments. Fleeing

Nazi-occupied Austria, he immigrated to the United States in 1938. There, he was lecturer at the Fogg Museum of Harvard University (1938–41), and in 1941 at the Metropolitan Museum of Art (New York). In 1942 he was appointed Keeper of the museum's musical instruments. From 1949, until his retirement in 1973, he served as curator of musical instruments. His most successful concert series "Music Forgotten and Remembered," utilizing the museum's instruments, ran for 18 consecutive years. In 1972, both he and Barry *Brook established the Research Center for Music Iconography. He was a lecturer at Columbia University (1947–48) and taught as visiting professor at Yale, Rutgers, CUNY, and SUNY at Binghamton. His publications include *Musical Autographs from Monteverdi to Hindemith* (1955), *Musical Instruments of the Western World* (1966) *Musical Instruments and their Symbolism in Western Art* (New York, 1967), and *Leonardo da Vinci as a Musician* (1982).

BIBLIOGRAPHY: Grove Music Online; MGG.

[Israel J. Katz (2nd ed.)]

WINTERNITZ, MORITZ (1863–1933), Orientalist. Born in Horn, Austria, Winternitz received the degree of doctor of philosophy in 1886 from the University of Vienna. In 1888 he went to Oxford, where he spent the next ten years acting in various educational capacities, including teacher of German and librarian at the Indian Institute (1895). In 1899 he became instructor of Indology and general ethnology at the German University of Prague, and in 1911 was appointed professor of Sanskrit.

Winternitz's main work was *Geschichte der indischen Literatur* (3 vols., 1908–22; *History of Indian Literature*, 3 vols., 1927–59; 1959–63²). His other works include *A Catalogue of South Indian Sanskrit Manuscripts Belonging to the Royal Asiatic Society of Great Britain and Ireland* (1902), *A Concise Dictionary of Eastern Religion: Being the Index Volume to the Sacred Books of the East* (1910); *Die Frau in den indischen Religionen* (1920), and *Rabindranath Tagore* (Ger., 1936). Winternitz also edited several Sanskrit texts.

BIBLIOGRAPHY: *Festschrift M. Winternitz* (1933).

WINTERS, SHELLEY (**Shirley Schrift**; 1922–2006), U.S. actress. Born in East St. Louis, Ill., Winters appeared in the operetta *Rosalinda* (1942). Her first successful film was *A Double Life* (1948). Later she became famous for her interpretation of two prototypes – a street girl and a mother. In 1959 she won an Oscar for her supporting role in *The Diary of Anne Frank*, and in 1965 she won another Academy Award for *A Patch of Blue*. Her other films, which number more than 120, include *The Great Gatsby* (1949); *Frenchie* (1950); *A Place in the Sun* (Oscar nomination for Best Actress, (1951); *Executive Suite* (1954); *Mambo* (1954); *I Am a Camera* (1955); *The Big Knife* (1955); *The Night of the Hunter* (1955); *The Chapman Report* (1962); *Lolita* (1962); *The Balcony* (1963); *Alfie* (1966); *Harper* (1966); *The Three Sisters* (1966); *Enter Laughing* (1967); *The Poseidon Adventure* (Oscar nomination for Best Supporting Actress, 1972); *Blume in Love* (1973); *Diamonds* (1975); *Next Stop, Greenwich Village* (1976); *King of the Gypsies* (1978); *The Magician of Lublin* (1979); *S.O.B.* (1981); *The Delta Force* (1986), *An Unremarkable Life* (1989); *Stepping Out* (1991); *The Pickle* (1993); *Heavy* (1995); *The Portrait of a Lady* (1996); *Gideon* (1999); and *La Bomba* (1999).

On Broadway, Winters appeared in such plays as *Rosalinda* (1942–44); *Oklahoma!* (1943–48); *A Hatful of Rain* (1956); *The Night of the Iguana* (1962); *Who's Afraid of Virginia Woolf?* (1965); *Under the Weather* (1966); *Minnie's Boys* (1970); and *The Effect of Gamma Rays on Man-in-the-Moon Marigolds* (1978).

She appeared frequently at Jewish benefit rallies.

Winters was married to actors Vittorio Gassman (1952–54) and Anthony Franciosa (1957–60).

She wrote the autobiographies *Shelley: Also Known as Shirley* (1980) and *Shelley II: The Middle of My Century* (1989).

[Jonathan Licht / Ruth Beloff (2nd ed.)]

WINTERSTEIN, ALFRED (1899–1960), Swiss biochemist. Winterstein was born in Zurich where his father, Ernest Heinrich Winterstein (1865–1949), was professor of chemistry. He joined the faculty of Zurich's Polytechnicum (1934). He became a senior director of the Hoffmann-La Roche Company in Basle. His fields of research included hematology, vitamins and carotenoids, and hormones.

WINTROBE, MAXWELL MYER (1901–1986), U.S. hematologist. Wintrobe was born in Halifax, Nova Scotia, and graduated in medicine from the University of Manitoba, Winnipeg. He worked in the departments of medicine at Tulane University, New Orleans (1927–30), and Johns Hopkins University, Baltimore (1930–43), before becoming professor and chairman of the department of medicine at the newly established University of Utah (1943–67), where he was distinguished professor of medicine until his retirement in 1977. Wintrobe's main clinical and research interests were in hematology, and he contributed greatly to the major expansion of clinical practice, teaching, and research in this field. He introduced exact laboratory techniques which form an essential part of modern hematological practice. His textbook on clinical hematology, in 2005 in its 10th edition, became a standard work. His many honors include election to the U.S. National Academy of Sciences (1973). He was also a member and chairman of the Scientific Advisory Committee to the Scripps Research Foundation (1964–74).

[Michael Denman (2nd ed.)]

WIRSZUBSKI, CHAIM (1915–1977), classical scholar. Born in Vilna, Wirszubski settled in Palestine in 1934. He taught classics at the Hebrew University from 1948 (from 1956 as professor).

He published *Libertas as a Political Idea at Rome during the Late Republic and Early Principate* (dissertation, 1950) and edited G.R. Moncada's *Sermo de Passione Domini* (1963). He translated Spinoza's *Theological-Political Tractae* (*Ma'amar Teologi-Medini*, with notes, 1961) into Hebrew and wrote an introduction to the Hebrew translation of Tacitus' *Annals* (*Sifrei ha-Shanim*, 1962). Wirszubski dealt in two lectures with Flavius Mithridates and his Latin translation *Liber Redemptionis* (*Nosaḥ Kadum shel Perush Moreh Nevukhim…*) of Abraham Abulafia's kabbalistic commentary on Maimonides' *Guide* (1964, 1969). He also devoted some articles to the Shabbatean movement.

°**WIRTH, CHRISTIAN** (1885–1944), *SS-Sturmbannfuehrer* instrumental in the mass extermination of Jews in German-occupied Poland. Wirth was born in Oberbalzheim, Wuettemberg, where he was a career criminal police detective. He became a member of the Nazi Party in 1931 and joined the SS in 1939. He was assigned to Operation T-4, the German program to "eliminate life unworthy of living" – to murder the mentally retarded, the physically infirm, and the handicapped – and from October 1939 until August 1941 he was chief of office staff and personnel at the "*euthanasia" killing center at Hartheim. As an inspector of killing facilities at all other "euthanasia" killing centers, Wirth developed gas chambers for killing institutionalized persons with disabilities. In late autumn 1941, he transferred to Lublin District, where he was assigned to develop the Belzec killing center. In 1942 Globocnik appointed him inspector of the SS Special Detachments with overall supervisory responsibility for Belzec, Sobibor, and Treblinka. At these three Aktion Reinhard camps more than 1.5 million Jews were killed. There were less than 200 known survivors. Belzec was open for only ten months as a killing center; the other two camps were open for less than two years each. They were closed when their jobs were done and the Jews of Poland were virtually all murdered. When these camps closed, Wirth and his colleagues Globocnik, Hering, and Oberhauser were transferred to Trieste in December 1943 where he commanded an SS *Einsatzkommando* "R" group. Wirth was reported killed by partisans in Istria in May 1944.

BIBLIOGRAPHY: G. Reitlinger, *The SS: Alibi of a Nation* (1956), 279–83; R. Hilberg, *Destruction of European Jews* (1961, 1985, 2003), index.

[Michael Berenbaum (2nd ed.)]

WIRTH, LOUIS (1897–1952), U.S. sociologist. Born in Gemuenden on the Main, Germany, Wirth emigrated to the United States as a young man and studied medicine and social work and then sociology. He taught at Tulane University and from 1940 to 1952 at the University of Chicago. He was an editor of the *American Journal of Sociology*, regional director of the National Resources Planning Board, director of planning of the Illinois State Postwar Planning Commission, and president of the Social Science Research Council (1932, 1937), the American Sociological Society (1947), and the International Sociological Association (1949). In addition, Wirth was active in the American Council on Race Relations and the American Jewish Committee.

A foremost representative of the Parkian school of sociology, Wirth combined theoretical insight with intensive practical application. His position was that sociology was concerned with unique phenomena only insofar as knowledge of them was required for the purpose of valid generalization and scientific prediction. His intense concern with the maintenance and development of democratic institutions and the furtherance of social justice led to his interest in the elimination of discrimination against racial and cultural minorities, in systematic socioeconomic planning, and in a workable theory of public opinion and mass communication. Methodologically, Wirth was a typologist, combining the "ideal type" construction of the German sociologists Max Weber and Ferdinant Toennies with the formulation of what may be called "real types," which is the hallmark of the Parkian school of sociology. A typology of minorities is contained in "The Problem of Minority Groups," in *The Science of Man in the World Crisis* (ed. Ralph Linton, 1945), and in "Morale and Minority Groups," in *American Journal of Sociology*, 47 (1941/42). His theory of urban sociology is expounded in "Urbanism as a Way of Life," *American Journal of Sociology*, 44 (1938/39). *The Local Community Fact Book* (1938) presents a model for the investigation of urban phenomena. Wirth's interest in the sociology of knowledge is documented in his preface to the English edition of Karl Mannheim's *Ideology and Utopia* (1936).

Wirth was intensely interested in the sociology of the Jews, as part of his general interest in the incorporation of minorities in a democratic state. His dissertation *The Ghetto* (1928, 1956²) analyzes the Jewish settlement on Chicago's west side not merely as a physical abode but as a state of mind; the outward pull of the larger society and discriminatory rejection by that society correspond to flight from the narrow restrictions of the ghetto and longing for its sheltering intimacy. Wirth saw the solution of the dilemma in the abolition of discrimination and complete acceptance of the democratic way of life.

[Werner J. Cahnman]

WISCHNITZER, MARK (1882–1955), historian, sociologist, and communal worker. In his youth Wischnitzer lived in Galicia, Vienna, and Berlin. On returning to his native Russia, he devoted himself to the study of Jewish history. From 1908 to 1913 he edited the section on the history of the Jews in Europe in the Russian-Jewish *Yevreyskaya Entsiklopediya* (from the third volume on). From 1909 to 1912 he lectured at the institute of Baron David Guenzburg in Petrograd on Oriental affairs and Jewish scholarship. From 1914 to 1916 he was the initiator and editor of *Istoriya Yevreyskogo Naroda* ("History of the Jewish People") in Moscow. He was also a member of the society for Jewish history and ethnography in Petrograd and participated in its quarterly *Yevreyskaya Starina* ("The Jewish Past"). From 1919 to 1921 he stayed in London, where he engaged in journalism and continued his research. From 1921 to 1937 he was secretary of the *Hilfsverein der Deutschen Juden, in which he engaged in welfare enterprises for the Jews of eastern Europe, visited the regions of Jewish settlement in Russia, and finally (1933–37) concentrated on organizing the emigration of Jews from Nazi Germany to the countries of the West and overseas. During the period he lived in Berlin, Wischnitzer served with his wife, Rachel Wischnitzer, as director of the Jewish publication *Rimon* in Berlin and London (1922–24) and from 1925 was editor of the history section in the *Encyclopaedia Judaica* in Berlin. He occupied himself with the history of the Jewish guilds in Poland and Lithuania during the 17th and 18th centuries and devoted a study to them in Yiddish (1922). His *History of Jewish Crafts and Guilds*, which includes a list of his previous works on the subject, was published posthumously in 1965. He also published *Die Juden in der Welt* (1935).

After leaving Nazi Germany, Wischnitzer entered the service of the *American Jewish Joint Distribution Committee in Paris (1938); however, World War II compelled him to go to the Dominican Republic (1940) and then to the United States (1941). He continued his communal service in the U.S. with the Council of Jewish Organizations and Welfare Funds and worked on editing the *Universal Jewish Encyclopedia*. He devoted his work *To Dwell in Safety, The Story of Jewish Migration Since 1800* (1948) to general Jewish migration. He published the memoirs of Dov Ber *Birkenthal, in the description of whose life and times both literary and social views are intertwined; this appeared as *Zikhronot R. Dov mi-Boliḥov* (1922, repr. 1969; *The Memoirs of Ber of Bolechow* (1922)).

His wife RACHEL WISCHNITZER (née Bernstein; 1885–1989) was a scholar of Jewish art. Born in Minsk, she studied architecture in Paris. She edited the first periodicals for Jewish art, *Rimon* (in Heb.) and *Milgroym* (in Yid.; 1922–24), while she was in Berlin. These were printed by the Rimon publishing house which her husband had established. During this period she was director of the Jewish museum in Berlin (1934–38) and published *Gestalten und Symbole der juedischen Kunst* (1935), as well as contributing to the German *Encyclopaedia Judaica* and many other periodicals. In 1940 she went to the U.S., where she served as contributing editor for Jewish art of the Universal Jewish Encyclopedia (1948) and also wrote on the synagogue of *Dura-Europos. She wrote *Synagogue Architecture in the United States* (1955) and *The Architecture of the European Synagogue* (1964). Rachel Wischnitzer strove to clarify the development of Jewish iconography, especially the literary background to the development of subjects and symbols in Jewish art, e.g., her book on Dura-Europos is replete with biblical and talmudic passages which enlighten the artistic intent. She was also a firm advocate of using the values of traditional Jewish art in the works of modern Jewish art.

BIBLIOGRAPHY: Winninger, Biog, s.v.; *Wilson Library Bulletin*, 30 (1955/56), 298.

[Abraham N. Poliak]

WISCONSIN, a state in the north-central U.S.; Jewish population of approximately 28,000 in a general population of about 5.5 million (2001), or 0.5%. German, Bohemian, Austro-Hungarian, and a smaller number of English Jewish immigrants were among the earliest settlers in Wisconsin, arriving from the 1840s to the 1860s with French, English, German, and Scandinavian gentiles. Yet the first known Wisconsin Jew was Jacob Franks, a fur trader of English ancestry who settled in Green Bay in 1793. His associate and nephew, John Lawe, served in the first Wisconsin Territory Legislature in 1836 and was a county judge. The first organized Jewish community arose in Milwaukee in 1844. By 1856, the city had three synagogues. In Wisconsin's capital, Madison, Jews organized a benevolent society in 1858 and built a synagogue, Shaarei Shamayim, in 1863. The building, one of the oldest remaining synagogues in the United States, has been moved from downtown to a city park. Another early settler, Alsatian-born Bernard Schleisinger Weil, owned thousands of acres of farmland northwest of Milwaukee. The town of Schleisingerville (later renamed Slinger) was named for him. He was the first Jew to serve in the Wisconsin Legislature – four years after statehood was declared in 1848. English-born John Meyer Levy, another influential newcomer, arrived in the Mississippi River settlement of La Crosse in 1845. He succeeded in business and served as mayor from 1860 to 1861 and 1866 to 1868. Levy held the first known worship services there (interfaith) and co-founded the first synagogue in Wisconsin's third

Total Jewish population of Wisconsin	28,000
% of Jews in general population of Wisconsin	0.5
% of Wisconsin Jews in Jewish population of U.S.	0.45

Jewish communities in Wisconsin. Population figures for 2001.

Jewish community. In addition to Milwaukee and Madison, German Jewish immigrants were prominent in business and politics in Appleton, an industrial and university city whose first rabbi was Mayer Samuel Weiss, father of illusionist Harry Houdini, born Erich Weiss. The 19th-century Wisconsin Jewish population was estimated at 2,600 in an 1880 study. So it was the mass Russian and eastern European Jewish immigration from 1881 to 1924 that gave the state most of its Jews. By 1899, the Jewish population had risen to 10,000, then to 28,000 in 1920, and more than 39,000 in 1937, the peak year. Most of the second wave of immigrants came to Milwaukee, where the established Jewish community formed the Settlement House. The facility offered classes to immigrants that led to publication of the long-running *Settlement Cookbook*. Other Russian and eastern European Jews spread around the state, creating Orthodox Jewish communities in two dozen municipalities in the 1920s and 1930s and accounting for a Jewish presence in some 180 more – primarily as merchants. In 1904, five immigrant families cleared land for a Jewish farming settlement in central Wisconsin. Part of a national Jewish agricultural movement, the Arpin settlement grew to 20 families and in 1915 established the county's only synagogue. Poor crop yields and a lack of marriageable young Jews compelled most families to leave by 1922. Sheboygan Jewry exceeded 1,000 in the 1920s and 1930s. With three Orthodox synagogues and several *shoḥatim*, Sheboygan was known among U.S. Jews as "Little Jerusalem." Other traditional Jewish communities with synagogues developed in: Antigo, Ashland, Hurley, Marinette, Superior, and Wausau in the north; Eau Claire and La Crosse in the west; Beloit, Madison, and Monroe in the south; and Appleton, Fond du Lac, Green Bay, Kenosha, Manitowoc, Milwaukee, Oshkosh, and Racine in the east. After the war, most of the smaller Jewish communities shifted to Conservative or Reform Judaism, building or buying new synagogues in a dozen cities. By the year 2000, Wisconsin's synagogues were centralized to 14 municipalities, but Jews remain a presence in nearly 70 communities. Most of the small-town synagogues serve Jews in outlying areas. Regional havurah groups meet regularly in Waukesha County, west of Milwaukee; Door County, on Wisconsin's Lake Michigan peninsula; and the northernmost three counties – Douglas, Bayfield and Ashland. The University of Wisconsin campuses in Milwaukee and Madison house Centers of Jewish Studies, both founded with the help of the Wisconsin Society for Jewish Learning. B'nai B'rith, once a unifier for Jewish men and their families throughout the state, has faded, though the B'nai B'rith Youth Organization reaches a plurality of Jewish teens. Hadassah, National Council of Jewish Women, and Na'amat USA continue to attract women. The Milwaukee Jewish Federation and Madison Jewish Community Council raise funds and coordinate local Jewish activities. Wisconsin Jews who attained national recognition include Israeli Prime Minister Golda *Meir, of Milwaukee; Sens. Herbert *Kohl of Milwaukee and Russell *Feingold of Madison, both Democrats; Socialist Victor *Berger; playwright and novelist Edna *Ferber of Appleton; Newton Minnow, chairman of the Federal Communications Commission; Martin F. Stein of Milwaukee, national chairman of the United Jewish Appeal and CLAL; Depression-era photographer Esther Bubley of Phillips; Allan H. "Bud" *Selig of Milwaukee, commissioner of major league baseball; jazz pianist and scholar Ben Sidran of Madison; and Yiddish poet Alter Esselin of Milwaukee.

[Andrew Muchin (2nd ed.)]

WISDOM; WISDOM LITERATURE.

Connotation of Wisdom

Wisdom (Heb. *ḥokhmah*) has a wide range of meanings in different contexts, as illustrated in stories about Solomon, the traditional paragon of wisdom: cunning (I Kings 2:6, 9), moral discernment (3:9, 12), understanding of justice (3:28), encyclopedic knowledge (5:9, 14 [4:29, 34]), literary skill (5:12, [4:32]), and ability as ruler (5:21 [5:7]). In Job 39:16–17 and Ecclesiastes 2:3 it means simply intelligence. Its primary meaning is superior mental ability or special skill, without a necessary moral connotation (Ex. 35:31–33; II Sam. 14:1ff.). The *ḥakham* was the knowledgeable man, hence a counselor, teacher (Ex. 35:34; Prov. 12:15). Skills were acquired through training, *musar* (Prov. 1:2–6); life situations called for counsel, *ʿeẓah* (I Kings 12:8; Prov. 1:30). The highest skill was that of living successfully, with divine and human approval. The idea of wisdom as a fundamentally ethical and religious quality of life is developed in Job, Proverbs 1–9, the Wisdom Psalms, and Daniel, and later in Ben Sira, Wisdom of Solomon, and Tobit. Special senses of *ḥokhmah* are understanding of dreams and omens (Gen. 41:15, 39; Dan. 1:17); knowledge properly belonging to God alone (Gen. 3:22; Ezek. 28:2–3); and righteousness, in eschatological times (Dan. 11:33; 12:10; the term here is *maskilim*).

As a historical phenomenon, biblical wisdom designates a distinctive cultural tradition and scholarly activity in the history of ancient Israel, continuing in early Judaism and Christianity. It was a way of thinking and an attitude to life that emphasized experience, reasoning, morality, and general human concerns not restricted to Israelites. Its interest was in individuals and their social relationships rather than in the distinctive national religion and its cult. A generalized religious element was present from the first in wisdom's recognition of the rightness of a certain order of life; only in its later stages – as in Ben Sira – were the wisdom and the national-religious traditions joined together. In keeping with this striving for order and equilibrium, the wisdom teachers sought to provide rules and examples of personal morals and, on a theoretical level, meanings and values through reflection, speculation, and debate.

History of the Wisdom Tradition

The history of the wisdom tradition in Israel can be sketched only in broad strokes because the evidence is slight and often ambiguous. Wisdom was a tradition as old as the society itself, a constant factor in its daily life rather than a self-conscious movement. The folk wisdom rooted in the mores of family and tribe has left traces in popular proverbs (Gen. 10:9; I Sam. 24:14; I Kings 20:11) and in references to local sages (II Sam. 14:2; 20:16). With the advent of the monarchy, royal counselors became influential (II Sam. 16:20ff.; I Kings 12:6ff.), and in effect, some were cabinet ministers (I Kings 4:1ff.; Isa. 36:3). Professional scribes and a literate elite court were probably mainly responsible for the production of wisdom and other literature later attributed by tradition to King *Solomon himself (I Kings 5:9–14 [4:29–34]; cf. Prov. 25:1). Temple scribes would be engaged in the composition of psalmody.

In the eighth century Hezekiah's men engaged in collecting Solomonic proverbs (Prov. 25:1) and probably also in assembling the religious and other writings of Judah and Northern Israel. That Isaiah had been a teacher of youth is implied by his opponents' mockery (Isa. 28:9–10; cf. 19:11–12). Both Isaiah and Jeremiah found themselves in conflict with royal counselors who thought themselves wise, i.e., politically expert (Isa. 29:14ff.; Jer. 9:22 [23]; 38:1ff.). Jeremiah clashed with the temple scribes as well (8:8). In *Baruch we see a professional scribe at work (Jer. 32:9ff.; 36:4). When Jerusalem fell to the Babylonians, the exiled scribes undoubtedly carried with them scrolls around which literary activities were centered in their new community.

After the Return, when Judah became a semi-independent temple state under a Persian governor, religious authority was assumed by priests and scribes as custodians of the national-religious tradition. This tradition had now taken form as the Torah and other sacred books, which implied changes in the status of the learned. Ezra the priest bore the official title "secretary of the Law of the God of heaven" (Ezra 7:12). The Torah was both code and creed; it was also the summation of Israel's distinctive religious wisdom (Deut. 4:6). Temple scribes and wisdom teachers turned their attention to Torah study, with two results: the two streams of wisdom tradition and covenant theology coalesced, and a new kind of wisdom piety developed (cf. Ps. 1, 119). At the same time the folk wisdom of home and marketplace continued, but with a more positive ethical and religious orientation as in Proverbs 1–9 and Ben Sira. Independent thinkers like *Koheleth and the author of the Wisdom of Solomon in the Hellenistic period began to write in more philosophic language, and found a following among their compatriots.

International Background and Setting

The international background and setting of Hebrew wisdom are acknowledged in the Bible itself and have become fully evident with increasing knowledge of the literary remains of ancient Near Eastern peoples. Solomon's wisdom is said to have surpassed that of Egypt and the *Kedemites (I Kings 5:10–11 [4:30–31]). The wise men of Egypt are referred to again in Genesis 41:8 and Isaiah 19:11–12; those of Edom in Jeremiah 49:7 and Obadiah 8; those of Phoenicia in Ezekiel 27:8–9; 28:3–5; and those of Persia in Esther 1:13. Although in Babylonia "'wisdom' refers to skill in cult and magic lore… [there is] a group of texts which correspond in subject matter with the Hebrew Wisdom books" (W.G. Lambert; cf. Dan. 1:20).

In Egyptian thought the cosmic order and the moral order were one, to be realized in thought, speech, and behavior. Characteristic documents are the "Instructions" by a king or high official to his son, such as those of Ptah-hotep, Merika-Re, Ani, and Amen-em-opet (cf. Pritchard, Texts, 412ff.). Amen-em-opet bears remarkable similarities to Proverbs 22:17–24:12. Other Egyptian wisdom works are The Divine Attributes of Pharaoh, The Song of the Harper, The Eloquent Peasant, and The Dispute over Suicide (Pritchard, Texts, 405–10, 431–34). The last two, like Job, touch on an innocent sufferer's cry for justice and the dubious value of a sufferer's life. Another type of Egyptian wisdom is found in the onomastica or "noun lists" with their comprehensive outline of knowledge; these may have influenced Genesis 1; Psalms 148; Job 38–39; etc.

Mesopotamian wisdom writing originated with the Sumerians. They too produced noun lists of phenomena, and introduced evaluations of them in dispute fables, e.g., between summer and winter, cattle and grain (Pritchard, Texts^3, 592–3). Human experiences and character were portrayed in adages, parables, and anecdotes (Pritchard, Texts^3, 593–4). Corresponding to the "Instruction" form are the Counsels of Wisdom, Counsels of a Pessimist, Advice to a Prince, Teachings of *Ahikar (the last of Assyrian origin but preserved in Aram; Pritchard, Texts^3, 595–6). In the "problem" writings, the main issues are death and the suffering of the righteous. In the Gilgamesh Epic, the hero goes in search of the secret of immortality and learns that only gods are deathless. In the Dialogue of Pessimism, death is seen as the great equalizer. In a Sumerian poem "Man and his God" an upright man who suffers has no recourse but to pray for deliverance. Two works from the Kassite period in Babylonia deal with the same theme: in "Let me praise the Lord of Wisdom" a sufferer reflects that trouble comes without apparent reason, because humans cannot know the will of the gods; in "The Babylonian Theodicy" the issue is debated by a sufferer and his friend, their views corresponding broadly to those of Job and his friends (Pritchard, Texts^3, 589–91, 596–604). The Sumerian gods represented forces with which humans must come to terms, whereas the Babylonian gods were more thought of as subject to moral standards, like human beings. To the Egyptians *ma'at* ("truth, right, justice") was a cosmic reality to which even the gods were subject. The Egyptians looked for judgment and compensation in the afterlife. In Babylonia (as in Israel until a late period, cf. Dan. 12:2) appropriate rewards or punishments were expected in the present life, and divine justice was often called in question.

No wisdom writings survive from Edom or Phoenicia. Ugaritic literature includes maxims in the father-to-son form, and presumably a more extensive Canaanite wisdom literature existed.

The Wisdom Books of the Hebrew Bible

These wisdom books are *Proverbs, *Job, and *Ecclesiastes, with which *Psalms and Song of Songs are associated in

Roman Catholic tradition. Significantly, all these are among the Hagiographa (*Ketuvim*), the part of the Hebrew Bible most remote from the interests of the Torah, and the last part to be approved as scripture. Most of the other works in the Hagiographa have some connection with wisdom in form, in content, or historically. In addition, though not accepted as canonical in Jewish tradition, two major wisdom books and some shorter works from pre-Christian Judaism were included in the Greek and Latin Bibles: the Wisdom of *Ben Sira, a latter-day Book of Proverbs; the Wisdom of *Solomon, a treatise on Hebrew wisdom addressed both to Jews and to non-Jews; *Tobit, a morality tale incorporating two short collections of precepts; the poem in Baruch 3:9ff. calling on Israel to return to the ways of wisdom; an account of a wisdom contest inserted in I Esdras at 3:1–4:41; and three highly colored parabolic tales added to the Greek version of Daniel.

The great variety comprised within the category of wisdom literature is evident. These writings have in common the theme and practice of wisdom as a distinct way of life and thought, and employ certain favorite literary forms and a characteristic vocabulary. The theme is developed with different emphases: on the one hand traditionally conservative, didactic, and worldly-wise, on the other hand radically critical and theologically innovative. The first is carried out by various methods of authoritative instruction; the second – on a more sophisticated level – by challenging accepted ideas and stimulating original thought. It will be noticed that the religious component of wisdom teaching becomes more explicit as time goes on.

Wisdom was not seen as a natural endowment, though the capacity to attain it might be considered a natural endowment. Wisdom had to be learned, and could be taught. Even so, it remained a divine gift rewarding those who desired it enough to submit to its discipline (Prov. 2). The two principle methods of teaching were *musar* (instruction, training) and *ʿeẓah* (counsel, persuasion), according to whether the teacher's authority was imposed or freely sought. A parent's instruction was mandatory and entailed correction of the disobedient (Prov. 23:13). To the extent that the teacher in a school assumed the parental role (Prov. 1:8) his words had the same dogmatic tone. In the main, however, the teacher's *musar* was an appeal to reason and conscience, and to the pupil's own desire for knowledge and understanding. This is evident in the variety of literary forms found in the wisdom writings, whose primary objective was to teach: the sentence saying or proverb; the rhetorical question; the admonitory precept or maxim and their expansion into longer discourses; soliloquy and debate; descriptive, metaphorical, and meditative poetry; parable and allegory; the imaginative tale and the illustrative anecdote.

Precepts express the imperatives of social order or religious belief; with the teacher they take the form of exhortation to which is added a statement of motive or result (cf. Prov. 19:20; 25:17). Often the imperative is implied rather than expressed (Prov. 25:27a). In Proverbs 1–9 precepts are expanded into ten longer discourses beginning "My son(s)!" In the two poems in 1:20–33 and chapter 8 wisdom itself is personified as a female; in the former she berates fools for their refusal to listen, and in the latter appeals for a hearing on grounds of her priceless worth and her prime role in the creation of the world. Behind this personification lies the reality that there is regular reference to wise women in the Bible (Judg. 4:29; II Sam. 14:2; 20:16) and that a mother might teach her son (Prov. 6:20). Some scholars view Wisdom as an ancient Hebrew goddess. Precepts predominate in 22:17ff., the section closely resembling the Instructions of Amen-em-opet.

A proverb is a short pregnant sentence or phrase whose meaning is applicable in many situations and which is made memorable by vivid imagery or witty expression, often marked by alliteration or assonance. It draws attention positively or negatively to an order of life, right values, and proportions. The prosaic folk saying is brief and pointed: "From wicked men comes wickedness" (I Sam. 24:14 [13]) or "One donning armor should not boast as if he were taking it off" (I Kings 20:11). The proverbs of two (or more) lines in a parallelism, characteristic of Solomonic proverbs in Proverbs 10:1ff. and 25:1ff., have been expanded probably for teaching purposes as cue and response. Examples of folk sayings supplemented in this way are Proverbs 11:2a; 12:11a; and 26:17a. Sayings in the form of a culminating numerical progression like Proverbs 30:18–19 are a kind of riddle, also suitable as a teaching tool.

The art of composing vivid narratives, similes, and metaphors also serves the purposes of the teacher. The word *mashal* ("likeness") has a wider connotation than "proverb." Its commonest form is the simile: "Like clouds and wind that bring no rain is a man who boasts of giving but does not give" (Prov. 25:14). When a simile is expanded into a short story, it becomes a parable. The best-known parables in the Hebrew Bible come from the prophets Nathan and Isaiah (II Sam. 12:1ff; Isa. 5:1–7); the only developed wisdom parable also is found in Isaiah, in 28:23–29. Ecclesiastes 9:13–16 is sometimes cited as a parable but strictly this is rather an illustration since in a parable the audience is expected to recognize the analogy and draw its own conclusions. Although the wisdom teachers do not use the parable, they do make effective use of teaching illustrations. In Proverbs 1:11–14 the very words of the thugs who are tempting the unwary youth are quoted, and 6:12–13 is a true-to-life description of the conspirator. In Proverbs 7:6ff. there is a graphic sketch of the prostitute's behavior and in 23:29ff. one of the drunkard's.

An allegory relates to a metaphor as a parable relates to a simile. In Ecclesiastes 12 the approach of death is pictured in terms of the onset of darkness in a village street. The metaphor of wisdom, personified as a woman (Prov. 7:4), is developed in the poems of Proverbs 1:20–33, where she speaks like a prophetess, and in chapter 8 (cf. Ecclus.), where she speaks of YHWH's co-worker in the creation of the world. In Proverbs 9 wisdom and folly are personified as rival hostesses inviting men to different kinds of banquets.

The paradigmatic narrative, which evokes admiration for a hero or heroine evincing moral qualities deserving of imitation, was another tool of the wisdom teachers. The story may be quasi-historical, as in the case of the story of Joseph in Genesis. It may be clearly fictional, as with Ruth, Daniel 1–6, Esther, and Judith. The prose folk tale which introduces the poem of Job serves the same purpose. The wisdom characteristics of the Joseph story have been pointed out by G. von Rad: a man of unusual ability, intelligence, and moral integrity is shown as triumphing over all adversities, and becoming the principal counselor at the court of Pharaoh. The story in Genesis 3 of human disobedience and expulsion from Eden also has certain wisdom features. The wondrous tree and the talking snake belong to the world of the fable, but these are only incidental. The story can be read as a parable of human alienation from God through disobedience, and illustrates graphically the subtle process of temptation. More important, it probes profound problems in the sphere of wisdom: the nature and limitations of human knowledge and the relation of knowledge to morality. Humans claim to decide for themselves what is good and what is evil, in response to desire, but in asserting their independence find themselves exiled from life and good to a world of death and evil.

See Books of *Proverbs, *Job, and *Ecclesiastes.

Wisdom Psalms

The Wisdom Psalms are those with resemblances to the characteristic themes, tone, literary forms, and vocabulary of the wisdom tradition. They appear to be the products of a new type of personal piety which developed after the Exile, when the written Torah replaced prophecy as YHWH's living voice to His people. Scribal experts in the handling and interpretation of scripture had assumed a new position of religious authority, and the wisdom, prophetic, and cultic traditions were mingled. "God" in the generalized sense of older wisdom writings was now definitely identified with YHWH, the covenant God of Israel.

Some Psalms, such as 1 and 37, are unified compositions representing this new wisdom piety. In others the sapiential features are apparent only in certain parts (e.g., 94:8–13). In still others a poem of another type has been labeled as a wisdom poem (Ps. 2:12d; 111:10). The Psalms with the best claims to be classed as Wisdom Psalms are 1, 19b, 32, 34, 37, 49, 78, 112, 119, 127, 128, and 133. Their most significant feature is that they are addressed primarily to a human audience rather than to God, and their tone is didactic or hortatory. The presence of wisdom vocabulary and stylistic forms can be observed. Psalm 37 is an alphabetical acrostic comprising a series of precepts and proverbs commending a life of piety. Psalm 49 identifies itself as a *mashal*, or wisdom utterance, concerning a riddle (*ḥidah*). Psalm 127 consists of two expanded proverbs.

The principal themes of the Wisdom Psalms are:

(1) the antithetical ways of life of the righteous and the wicked;

(2) the appropriate rewards and retribution in store for each respectively;

(3) the qualities and behavior of the righteous as evoking admiration;

(4) study of the Torah as the focus of piety and a source of pure delight;

(5) life and vitality as fruits of righteousness, which is true wisdom;

(6) personal trust in YHWH;

(7) the search for light on problems of faith;

(8) encouragement to faith and obedience through reflection on YHWH's mighty acts on behalf of His people (see also *Psalms).

The Concept of Wisdom

The concept of wisdom as developed in the long course of Israel's cultural and religious history is different from and broader than the various meanings and uses of the term *ḥokhmah* (see above). All these denote elements and aspects of one thing – the activity of mind – introducing order in place of confusion, expanding and structuring knowledge, and purposefully directing the actions of men. The continuity of the wisdom tradition lay in the constant enlargement and enrichment of this faculty of applied intelligence.

At first the noun *ḥokhmah* denoted simply the state of being wise. It was no more than a linguistic correlative of the adjective *ḥakham* ("wise") and the verb *ḥakham* ("to be wise"), the adjectival use being basic. The wise were more capable, knowledgeable, skillful, intelligent, imaginative, and resourceful than their fellows, who consequently would look to them for counsel and leadership. The sharing of knowledge made of the wise man a teacher. Confidence in his counsel imbued him with the potentiality for leadership and ultimately for government. The general orderliness observable in the natural world called for an order of values as well as a structure of power in human society, and for meaning to justify both. Stimulated by access, through literacy, to the ideas of other wise men, the counselor became a thinker, concerned with understanding and moral judgments as well as with knowledge. Worshipping a God whose commands were not arbitrary but ethically conditioned, this counsel passed beyond the defensive morality of the tribe and the prudential morality of the individual to an ethic resting on beliefs held to be sacred.

If men could be wise to some degree in this deeper sense, God axiomatically was all-wise, good, and just, despite any appearances to the contrary. The creative and providential ordering of the world were acts of divine wisdom, which is sovereign, creative, and dynamic. Thus wisdom becomes fully conceptualized when personified pictorially in Proverbs 8 as a personal instrument of God in the planning and implementation of the created order.

BIBLIOGRAPHY: W.G. Lambert, *Babylonian Wisdom Literature* (1960); B. Gemser, *Sprüche Salomos* (1963²); O. Eissfeldt, *The Old Testament, an Introduction* (1965); R. Gordis, *The Book of God and Man* (1965); idem, *Koheleth the Man and his World* (1968); W. McKane, *Proverbs* (1970). **ADD. BIBLIOGRAPHY:** R. Harris in: J. Gammie and L. Perdue, *The Sage in Israel and the Ancient Near East* (1990), 3–17. See bibliographies to *Ecclesiastes, *Proverbs, and *Job.

[Robert B.Y. Scott]

WISE, GEORGE SCHNEIWEIS (1906–1987), sociologist; first president of *Tel Aviv University. Born in Pinsk, Poland, he went to the U.S. to study in 1926 and graduated from Columbia University in 1930. He served as associate director of its Bureau of Applied Social Research from 1949 to 1952, and lecturer on the sociology of Latin America from 1950 to 1952. For his assistance in the anti-illiteracy campaign in Mexico in 1944–46 he was decorated with the order Aguila Azteca by the Mexican government in 1946, and was visiting professor at Mexico University from 1956 to 1957. Long a supporter of The Hebrew University, he was chairman of its board of governors from 1953 to 1962. In 1963 he was elected president of the newly established Tel Aviv University, which developed rapidly during his tenure of office. In 1971 he became its chancellor. Apart from wide business interests, he took part in Jewish public activities in the United Jewish Appeal and other bodies. He is author of *The Breakdown of Parental Authority in Polish Immigrant Families in the United States* (1931), *Caudillo* (1951), a study of Latin American dictatorship, and *Mexico de Aleman* (1952).

WISE, ISAAC MAYER (1819–1900) U.S. Reform rabbi, architect of Reform Judaism in America. Wise was born in Steingrub, Bohemia, and studied at yeshivot in Prague and Vienna. In 1843, he became the rabbinical officiant (Religionsweiser) in Radnitz, Bohemia. Disillusioned about career prospects for Jews in central Europe, he emigrated to the United States in 1846. He became rabbi of Congregation Beth El in Albany, N.Y., introducing reforms such as mixed seating, choral singing, and confirmation. In 1847, he joined a **bet din* in New York, presided over by Max *Lilienthal, and conceived the idea of its authorizing a single ritual for the American Jewish community. The attempt proved abortive; but in 1848, he issued a call for a meeting the following year to establish a union of congregations. Again the attempt failed, but Wise persisted in advocating the idea. Meanwhile, he was earning a reputation as a writer, contributing regularly to Isaac *Leeser's *Occident* and the New York Jewish weekly, *Asmonean*. In 1850, as Wise pondered accepting the position of rabbi of Congregation Beth Elohim in Charleston, South Carolina, disagreements among the members of Beth El over Wise's reforms caused a split in the congregation that erupted into an actual melee at Rosh Hashanah services; Wise and his followers left to form a new congregation, Anshe Emeth, the first synagogue in the United States to be established with mixed seating from the outset.

In 1854, Wise became rabbi of Congregation B'nai Jeshurun in Cincinnati, Ohio, where he remained for the rest of his life. Within a few months of his arrival, he began to publish a national weekly, *The Israelite*, later renamed the **American Israelite*, and a German supplement *Die Deborah*. By the end of the year, he had founded Zion College, which combined Hebrew and secular studies. In 1855, he issued a call for a synod that would be the guiding authority of American Judaism, and succeeded in organizing a rabbinical conference, which met that year in Cleveland. The conference agreed to call a synod and adopted a platform that recognized the Bible as divine and declared that it "must be expounded and practiced according to the comments of the Talmud." The Orthodox, as represented by Isaac *Leeser, were at first satisfied, but soon grew suspicious of Wise's intentions. Moreover, the Cleveland Platform was scathingly attacked as treachery to the cause of Reform by David *Einhorn, a radical Reformer from Germany who had just become a rabbi in Baltimore. The plan for a synod collapsed.

Wise nevertheless went ahead with some of the projects discussed at Cleveland. In 1856, he published *Minhag America*, a prayer book that modified traditional Hebrew ritual. Despite repeated setbacks, Wise always returned to his advocacy of a union of congregations, a common prayer book, and a college to train American rabbis. He expounded his ideas not only in his writing but in repeated visits to the scattered Jewish communities of America. The recriminations over the Cleveland Conference, and then the Civil War, deferred practical action. The establishment of the *Board of Delegates of American Israelites (1859) and Maimonides College (1867) by traditionalist forces aroused his sarcastic hostility.

Wise showed no sympathy for the Abolitionist agitation which preceded the Civil War. He venerated the American Union and was prepared to tolerate slavery rather than contemplate its dissolution. During the Civil War, he joined the "Copperhead" Democrats and even accepted their nomination to be a candidate for the Ohio State Senate, until his congregation forced him to withdraw from the race. After the Civil War, Wise renewed his push for a union of congregations. He attended the 1869 rabbinical conference in Philadelphia organized by Einhorn (see *Reform Judaism), but distanced himself from its resolutions, fearing that their radical standpoint would put an end to the dream of a comprehensive union of American synagogues under his leadership.

The next few years were punctuated by fierce exchanges between Wise and the more Germanic and radical Reform eastern rabbis – who refused to attend rabbinic conferences organized by Wise in Cleveland, Cincinnati, and New York. In 1873, lay leaders in Cincinnati closely associated with Wise succeeded in forming the *Union of American Hebrew Congregations, a loose confederation of congregations primarily from the South and West. Wise was particularly focused on one of the UAHC's objectives – the establishment of a rabbinical college. In 1875, he was appointed the first president of *Hebrew Union College. The famous *treife* banquet served on the occasion of the first ordination of HUC rabbis ended all hope for a unified American Judaism. The observant stormed out and, for a time, there was only Reform Judaism and everybody else. (More than 125 years later, at the inauguration of David Ellenson as president of HUC, a kosher meal was served, a mark of significant transition within Reform Judaism.)

For the remainder of his life, Wise labored in the interests of the college. He was devoted to his students, earning their affection in return. He ordained more than 60 rabbis and continued to lead them as the founding president of the *Central Conference of American Rabbis, a position he held from 1889 until his death. During his lifetime, when it came to key developments in the shaping of the Reform movement's ideology, Wise was relegated to a secondary position: the Pittsburgh Platform of 1885 (see *Reform Judaism) was the work of Kaufmann Kohler, and the Union Prayer Book was based on Einhorn's *Tamid* rather than Wise's *Minhag America*. On another front, the influx of a large community of eastern European Jews thwarted his prediction that Orthodoxy would not survive on American soil; with that reality, Wise's vision of a singular American Judaism was doomed, and the basic pattern of denominational Judaism established. But Wise's foresightedness and tenacity in laying its three institutional cornerstones earned him the title "founding father" of the indigenous Reform movement in America – and insured that his legacy, rather than the short-lived victories of his radical Reform rivals, would ultimately prevail. (His strident opposition to political Zionism also influenced the Reform movement for nearly half-a-century; eventually, however, Reform Judaism joined the Zionist fold.)

Although known more as a leader than a scholar, Wise did write a number of books: *History of the Israelitish Nation* (1854), *Minhag America* (1856), *Minhag America* (1866), *The World of My Books* (n.d.), *Selected Writings of Isaac M. Wise, with a Biography* (ed. Philipson and Grossman, 1900, rev. 1969), and *Reminiscences* (ed. David Philipson, 1901, rev. 1945).

BIBLIOGRAPHY: Kerry M. Olitzky, Lance J. Sussman, Malcolm H. Stern, *Reform Judaism in America: A Biographical Dictionary and Sourcebook* (1993).

[Bezalel Gordon (2nd ed.)]

WISE, JONAH BONDI (1881–1959), U.S. Reform rabbi. Son of Isaac Mayer *Wise, he was ordained by Hebrew Union College in 1903. In 1904 he was appointed to Mizpah Temple, Chattanooga, Tennessee, and in 1906 to Temple Israel, Portland, Oregon. While in Portland he established a weekly Jewish newspaper, *The Scribe*. In 1925 Wise moved to New York and there served as rabbi of the Central Synagogue until his death. Within his congregation he did not depart from the classical pattern of Reform Judaism; family connections and an aptitude for social life helped to establish his position. In 1934 he established the weekly radio program "Message of Israel." He was an active worker for the *American Jewish Joint Distribution Committee, serving as national chairman 1931–38. He visited Europe several times on its behalf and represented it at the Evian Conference on Refugees, 1938. In the following year he became national chairman of the United Jewish Appeal, though he rejected Zionism.

BIBLIOGRAPHY: S. Caumann, *Jonah Bondi Wise* (1966).

[Sefton D. Temkin]

WISE, LOUIS ELSBERG (1888–?), U.S. organic chemist. Born in New York, Wise was appointed in 1919 professor of forest chemistry at New York State University (Syracuse). In 1933 he became professor of organic chemistry at Rollins College, and from 1941 was at the Institute of Paper Chemistry at Lawrence College, Wisconsin. His contributions were mostly on the chemistry of wood.

WISE, ROBERT EARL (1914–2005), U.S. film producer and director. Born in Winchester, Indiana, Wise worked at RKO studios from 1933 to 1943, and edited Orson Welles' classic, *Citizen Kane* (Oscar nomination for Best Editing, 1941). He was made a director in 1943 and became one of Hollywood's most successful filmmakers. He won four Academy Awards – as director and producer of *West Side Story* (1961), and co-director and producer of *The Sound of Music* (1965), one of the most profitable films ever made. In all, he directed more than 40 films. Among them are *The Body Snatcher* (1945); *The Set-Up* (1949); *The Day the Earth Stood Still* (1951); *Executive Suite* (1954); *Somebody Up There Likes Me* (1956); *Until They Sail* (1957); *I Want to Live* (Oscar nomination for Best Director, 1958); *Run Silent, Run Deep* (1958); *Two for the Seesaw* (1962); *The Haunting* (produced, 1963); *The Sand Pebbles* (produced, Oscar nomination for Best Picture, 1966); *Star* (1968); *The Andromeda Strain* (produced, 1971); *Two People* (produced, 1973); *The Hindenburg* (produced, 1975); *Audrey Rose* (1977); *Star Trek – The Motion Picture* (1979); *Rooftops* (1989); and the TV movie *A Storm in Summer* (2000).

Among his many honors and awards, Wise received the Irving G. Thalberg Memorial Award in 1967 for his contribution to the industry as a creative producer, and the American Film Institute Life Achievement Award in 1998. Wise served as president of the Directors Guild of America from 1971 to 1975, and as president of the Academy of Motion Picture Arts and Sciences from 1985 to 1988. He was active in the civil rights movement in Hollywood.

BIBLIOGRAPHY: S. Leeman, *Robert Wise on His Films: From Editing Room to Director's Chair* (1995); F. Thompson, *Robert Wise: A Bio-Bibliography* (1995).

[Ruth Beloff (2nd ed.)]

WISE, STEPHEN SAMUEL (1874–1949), U.S. rabbi and Zionist leader. Born in Budapest, Hungary, Wise was taken to the United States at the age of 17 months. From childhood he was determined to become a rabbi like his father, Rabbi Aaron Wise, who, together with Alexander *Kohut and Gustav *Gottheil, rabbi at Temple Emanu-El, helped to prepare him for the rabbinate. He was graduated with honors from Columbia University at the age of 18. Ordained in 1893 by Adolph *Jellinek of Vienna, he became assistant rabbi of New York City's Congregation B'nai Jeshurun, and assumed full responsibility after the death of Rabbi Henry S. Jacobs.

In 1900, shortly before marrying Louise Waterman, Wise became rabbi of Temple Beth Israel in Portland, Oregon, where for the next six years he pioneered in interfaith cooperation, social service, and civic leadership. His sermons are collected in *Beth Israel Pulpit: Sermons* (2 vols., (1905–06). He also served as unpaid commissioner of child labor for Oregon.

In 1902 Wise received his Ph.D. degree from Columbia University for his translation and editing of Solomon ibn Gabirol's *Improvement of the Moral Qualities.* For the Jewish Publication Society he translated the Book of Judges for their English version of the Bible, submitting his work in 1908.

Wise had begun his Zionist career during the late 1890s, helping to articulate the movement's ideology and organize its followers. A founder of the New York Federation of Zionist Societies in 1897, he led in the formation of the nationwide Federation of American Zionists in 1898 and served as honorary secretary until 1904, in close cooperation with Theodor Herzl. He had met Herzl at the Second Zionist Congress in Basle in 1898 and at that time agreed to serve as American secretary of the world Zionist movement. In 1914 he was instrumental in creating the Provisional Executive Committee for General Zionist Affairs and later headed it.

He acted as an important intermediary to President Woodrow *Wilson and Colonel Edward House in 1916–19, when, with Louis D. *Brandeis and Felix *Frankfurter, he helped formulate the text of the Balfour Declaration of 1917. He spoke on behalf of Zionist aspirations in Palestine at the Versailles Peace Conference of 1918–19, where he also pleaded for the cause of the Armenian people. He was vice president of the Zionist Organization of America from 1918 to 1920 and president from 1936 to 1938. On several occasions he served as chairman of the United Palestine Appeal. Though he worked closely with Chaim *Weizmann, David *Ben-Gurion, and Abba Hillel *Silver, he often disagreed with them on specific policies and broke relations with Weizmann in the 1920s and with Silver in the 1940s. His views at times conflicted with those of the Zionist organizations as well. Yet Wise always sought unity for the movement, which did not at that time have the backing of a united Jewry or the sympathy of the non-Jewish community. His *Great Betrayal* (1930), written with Jacob De Haas, reviews the history of British policy toward Palestine up to the Passfield White Paper in 1930.

To direct American Jews into pro-Zionist channels, lead them to more liberal objectives in the United States, and create a more democratic base in American Jewish life, Wise led in the organization of the American Jewish Congress, first on a provisional basis in 1916–19, then more permanently in 1920; he served as vice president in 1921–25 and as president or honorary president until his death. It was regarded as an alternative to the more established and more quiescent American Jewish Committee, which was dominated by the German-Jewish establishment that had been in the United States for a generation or more. The American Jewish Congress was more activist and more public in its protests.

Wise sounded the first warnings of the dangers of Nazism to the Jewish and non-Jewish world and sought to organize opposition to it and protection for the victims of Hitler. He organized a movement to boycott German goods in 1933, seeing it as appropriate public protest, against the advice of some German Jews in Germany who urged caution and that American Jews not to be provocative. In 1936 he organized the World Jewish Congress and headed it until his death in 1949. As a Zionist leader, president of the American and World Jewish Congresses, and co-chairman of the *American Jewish Conference, he presented the Jewish cause to President Franklin D. Roosevelt and the U.S. State Department, as well as to the general public, Jewish and non-Jewish. He was the recipient of the all important telegram from Gerhart Riegner that was sent to him in August 1942 via the State Department but never delivered to him. He received it from a second source, Samuel Silverman, a member of the British Parliament, It said:

> That there has been and is being considered in Hitler's headquarters a plan to exterminate all Jews from Germany and German controlled areas in Europe after they have been concentrated in the east. The number involved is said to be between three and a half and four million and the object to permanently settle the Jewish question in Europe.

The telegram spoke explicitly of Zyklon B. It should be noted that the telegram that Wise received, important as it was, was already long out of date. The Final Solution was already operative policy of Germany in all occupied territories. At Wannsee, the list was of 11 million Jews and the death camps of Belzec, Sobibor, and Treblinka were fully operative, the deportation of the Jews of Warsaw had began more than a month before.

Wise took this information to the State Department, which informed him that they already knew of it but could not confirm it; they requested that he not go public with the information until it could be confirmed. In November they confirmed this information to him and Wise did go public, but the State Department did not confirm it to the press, so Wise's release of this information was unofficial, from a Jewish rather than a governmental source.

Wise led the one meeting that the Jews had with President Roosevelt in 1943, which lasted some half an hour. It began with some banter between the president and Wise, and then a prayer was recited. Wise presented the president with a briefing paper, and the president indicated that he knew what was happening. He asked for concrete suggestions and there were few. The president then spoke for almost all the remaining time and, at the end of the allotted time, the meeting was interrupted by staff and concluded.

History has not been kind to Wise, who tried to lead a divided American Jewish community during the most perilous time in Jewish history. He was known in his day as an activist who had been protesting Nazism at its inception and led Stop Hitler Now rallies in 1943 and onward. Yet he is regarded by the younger generation as a symbol of ineffective and timid Jewish leadership, just when boldness and brilliance were required. He is regarded as too close to President Roosevelt and reluctant to criticize him for fear of wounding him politically. Some, but not all, of the criticism is unfair, as many who write judge him by the power and influence of the Jewish community in the last third of the 20th century and not by the reality of his time.

Beyond his public role lay the commitment to his vocation as a rabbi. Wise first sprang into national prominence in 1906 when, after preaching trial sermons at Congregation Emanu-El in New York City, he rejected overtures to serve as rabbi because his demand for a "free pulpit," not subject to control by a board of trustees, was refused. His famous "Open Letter to the Members of Temple Emanu-El of New York on the Freedom of the Jewish Pulpit" is reprinted in his autobiography, *Challenging Years* (1949, pp. 86–94), with a discussion of Louis Marshall's denial that the congregation had called Wise to its pulpit (cf. *Louis Marshall, Champion of Liberty: Selected Papers and Addresses*, vol. 2, 1957, note pp. 831–7). A year later he returned from Oregon to New York and founded the Free Synagogue, based on freedom of pulpit, free pews to all without fixed dues, outspoken criticism of social ills, the application of religion to their solution, and an extensive program of social welfare. His sermons are collected in *Free Synagogue Pulpit: Sermons and Addresses* (10 vols., 1908–32).

In 1922 he launched the Jewish Institute of Religion (JIR), a new kind of seminary which provided training of rabbis from all branches of Judaism, education of Jewish scholars, and preparation of leaders for community service. He served as president until 1948, when JIR merged with *Hebrew Union College in Cincinnati, Ohio, and Nelson *Glueck assumed the presidency.

A social liberal, Wise was co-founder of the National Association for the Advancement of Colored People in 1909 and the American Civil Liberties Union in 1920. He pleaded for clemency and justice on behalf of Sacco and Vanzetti in 1927. He was also active in organizations such as the Child Labor Committee, the Old Age Pension League, the Religion and Labor Foundation, and the League to Enforce Peace. Also, he battled for the rights of workers to organize, and championed the strike against the U.S. Steel Corporation in 1919 and the Passaic textile union strike in 1926. He actively campaigned for Woodrow Wilson in 1912 and 1916, and later supported the candidacies of Alfred E. Smith, Norman Thomas, and (from 1936 on) Franklin D. Roosevelt. With John Haynes Holmes, he headed the City Affairs Committee which exposed corruption in New York City and finally succeeded in forcing the resignation of Mayor James J. Walker in 1932.

Like his Christian counterparts and friends, Walter Rauschenbusch, Josiah Strong, and Washington Gladde, Wise was a forthright, forceful, and influential preacher of social concerns. His opinions and attitudes are expressed in his *Child Versus Parent* (1922); *As I See It* (1944), a collection of his articles for the journal *Opinion*, which he edited from 1936 to 1949; *Personal Letters of Stephen S. Wise* (1956, ed. by J.W. Polier and J.W. Wise); *Stephen S. Wise: Servant of the People – Selected Letters* (1969, ed. by CH Voss). The complete collection of Wise's papers, donated by his daughter Justine to Brandeis University, have been fully catalogued by the American Jewish Historical Society.

[Carl Hermann Voss]

His wife, LOUISE WATERMAN WISE (d. 1947), was a communal worker, artist, and translator. In her youth she came under the influence of Felix *Adler, founder of the Ethical Culture movement, and was imbued by him with a passion for social justice. During her husband's rabbinate in Portland, Oregon, she founded that city's Visiting Nurse Association. In New York she established, in 1914, the Free Synagogue's Child Adoption Committee. She presided over this first Jewish agency of its kind, and by the time of her death, when it was taken over by New York's Federation of Philanthropies, more than 3,500 Jewish children had been placed in private homes. In 1933 she organized and became the first president of the Women's Division of the American Jewish Congress. As refugees from Germany began to come in greater numbers, she established Congress Houses which provided temporary homes for thousands of refugees. Mrs. Wise's translations of Aimé Pallière's *Unknown Sanctuary* and Edmond Fleg's *Why I Am a Jew, My Palestine*, and *The Land of Promise* helped to popularize these works for English readers. Her paintings of portraits, landscapes, and moving representations of persecuted Jews were widely exhibited. Their son JAMES WATERMAN WISE (1901–1983) held various positions as an organization executive, including director of the Stuyvesant Neighborhood House in New York City, and national secretary of Avukah, the U.S. students' Zionist Federation which he helped to found in 1925. He was editor of *Opinion*, a special correspondent for New York dailies, and a popular radio commentator. His published works include *Liberalizing Liberal Judaism* (1924); *Jews Are Like That* (under the pseudonym Analyticus, 1928); *Legend of Louise*, a brief biography of his mother (1949); and *A Jew Revisits Germany* (1950). In the early 1950s he moved to Geneva where, as an art connoisseur, he engaged in the purchase of paintings for private collectors and museums in the U.S.

[Morton Mayer Berman]

Rabbi Wise's daughter, JUSTINE WISE POLIER (1903–1987), attorney and jurist, was born in Portland, Oregon. Admitted to the New York bar in 1928, she subsequently became the first woman referee in the Workmen's Compensation Division of the New York State Department of Labor (1929–34). She subsequently served as a justice in the Domestic Relations Court of New York City from 1935 to 1962. Justine Polier served as a special adviser to Eleanor Roosevelt in the Office of Civilian Defense in 1941 and 1942. From 1962 on she was a judge in the New York State Family Court.

Her Jewish and civic activities included service as president of Louise Wise Services (from 1941), the Wiltwyck School for Boys (from 1960), and the national women's division of the American Jewish Congress (1948–1956); chairman of the national executive committee of the women's division of the American Jewish Congress (1956–1960); member of the executive of the World Jewish Congress (from 1956); member of the White House Planning Conference on Civil Rights (1965); and as New York delegate to the White House Conference on Children (1960). Among her works on child welfare, psychiatry, and the law are *Everyone's Children, Nobody's Child* (1941); *Back to What Woodshed?* (1956); *View from the Bench: the Juvenile Court* (1964); and *The Rule of Law and the Role of Psychiatry* (1968).

[Carl Hermann Voss]

BIBLIOGRAPHY: CH Voss, *Rabbi and Minister: The Friendship of Stephen S. Wise and John Haynes Holmes* (1964); idem, in: AJA, 21 (1969), 3–19; J.W. Wise, *Legend of Louise: The Life Story of Mrs. Stephen S. Wise* (1949). **ADD. BIBLIOGRAPHY:** D. Wyman, *The Abandonment of the Jews* (1985); H. Feingold, *The Politics of Rescue* (1970); H. Feingold, *Bearing Witness* (1995).

WISEMAN, ADELE (1928–1992), Canadian author. Wiseman was born and raised in Winnipeg, Manitoba. Her parents had emigrated from the Ukraine in 1923 and spent two years in Montreal before settling in Winnipeg's North End, a vibrant enclave of Jewish, German, Ukrainian, and Slavic immigrants. Wiseman earned a B.A. in English and psychology from the University of Manitoba in 1949. Following graduation, she lived in London, Rome, and New York, where she wrote and worked at a number of jobs. From 1964 to 1969 Wiseman lived in Montreal, where she taught English at Sir George Williams (now Concordia) University and Macdonald College of McGill University. She was later writer-in-residence at several Canadian universities and head of the May Studios (Writing Program) at Banff Centre for the Arts. She married the marine biologist Dmitry Stone in 1969 (from whom she was later divorced) and had one daughter.

Wiseman published two novels, *The Sacrifice*, which won the Governor General's Literary Award for Fiction in 1956, and *Crackpot* (1974). Both novels employ biblical metaphors, are set in (the unnamed city of) Winnipeg, and explore the lives of Jewish immigrants who settle on the Canadian Prairies. *The Sacrifice* is the tragic story of a butcher who murders a local temptress. The biblical story of Abraham and Isaac resonates throughout Wiseman's narrative. Her own Abraham – once proud and certain – is transplanted from the Old to the New World, where he loses his third son and his precarious hold on life in a novel that charts the demise of a patriarch. *Crackpot* shifts from the tragic to comic mode and experiments with narrative form and perspective. The work celebrates the resilience of Hoda, an obese Jewish prostitute whose life, like Abraham's, is shattered by moral and spiritual challenges.

Wiseman also wrote two plays (*The Lovebound*, ca. 1960; *Testimonial Dinner*, 1978); two books for children (*Kenji and the Cricket*, 1988; *Puccini and the Prowlers*, 1992); and three works of nonfiction (*Old Markets, New World*, 1964; *Old Woman at Play*, 1978; *Memoirs of a Book Molesting Childhood and Other Essays*, 1987). The short story "Goon of the Moon and the Expendables" appeared in *Malahat Review* (vol. 98 (1992), 5–44). Her correspondence with a fellow writer and friend is available in *Selected Letters of Margaret Laurence and Adele Wiseman* (1997).

[Ruth Panofsky (2nd ed.)]

WISEMAN, FREDERICK (1930–), U.S. producer, director, and writer. Born in Boston, Massachusetts, Wiseman graduated from Williams College in 1951 and from Yale Law School in 1953. After serving as a graduate fellow for one year at Harvard, he was drafted into the army, serving from 1954 to 1956. After working briefly as an assistant to the Massachusetts' attorney general, Wiseman went to Paris, where he studied experimental filmmaking from 1956 to 1958. After he returned to the United States, he taught at Boston University's Institute of Law and Medicine from 1958 to 1961 and served as a research associate at Brandeis University from 1962 to 1966. In 1964, he bought the rights to Warren Miller's 1963 novel *The Cool World* and produced a film version directed by Shirley Clarke. He directed his first film in 1966, *Titicut Follies*, a stark documentary about the conditions at the Massachusetts Correctional Institution at Bridgewater. While his films feature no commentary and no music, Wiseman acknowledges that his fly-on-the-wall films are edited in a way that conveys his point of view. After *Titicut Follies*, Wiseman made *High School* (1968), an examination of the experiences of middle-class students in a Philadelphia high school. In 1968, he contributed to the screenplay for *The Thomas Crown Affair*, but was never credited for his work. Wiseman followed up his documentary films with *Law and Order* (1969) and *Hospital* (1970), an emergency room expose that earned Wiseman a best documentary Emmy. In 1970, he established Zipporah Films, a distribution company named for his wife. From 1971 to 1981, Wiseman had contracts with PBS to shoot one film per year with no limits on time or subject, to be shown first on New York's WNET. His studies included *Basic Training* (1971); *Juvenile Court* (1973); *Welfare* (1975); *Meat* (1976); and *Sinai Field Mission* (1978), which featured American soldiers on a peacekeeping mission in the Sinai Desert; and *Manouevre* (1979). In 1980, Wiseman made the fictional film, *Seraphita's Diary*. He continued his documentary filmmaking with such films as *Racetrack* (1985), *Deaf* (1986), *Blind* (1987), *Zoo* (1993), and *High School II* (1994), a return to topics introduced in 1968. His *La Comédie-Française ou L'amour Joué* (1996) was another departure for Wiseman, focusing positive attention on an institution. Wiseman continued to direct documentaries and dramas, most notably the Holocaust drama *The Last Letter* (2002), but also branched out into theater direction. In 2004, Wiseman wrote and directed *The Last Letter*, an off-Broadway show based on Vasily Grossman's 1960 novel *Life and Fate*.

BIBLIOGRAPHY: "Wiseman, Frederick," in: Contemporary Authors Online (2004); "Wiseman, Frederick," in: *Encyclopedia of World Biography* (1998²); "Wiseman, Frederick," in: *International Dictionary of Films and Filmmakers, Volume 2: Directors* (2000⁴).

[Adam Wills (2nd ed.)]

WISEMAN, SHLOIME (1899–1985), Canadian teacher, Yiddish and Hebrew translator, and critic. Wiseman emigrated to

Montreal from Dinovitz, Podolia, in 1913. He was the son of the teacher Shmuel Wiseman, who was a *maskil*, a Bible specialist, and a Hebraist. Shloime, following in his father's footsteps, earned both a B.A. (1920) and M.A. (1923) in pedagogy from McGill University in Montreal even as he was beginning his career as a teacher in the city's Yidishe Folk Shule, a leftist afternoon school created in 1914. A gifted teacher, in 1920 he was offered the directorship of the institution. He held that position until his retirement in 1969. He also served as lecturer in Hebrew at Sir George Williams University (1953–55) and was the first principal of Montreal's Jewish Teachers' Seminary (1952).

In addition to teaching, Wiseman immersed himself in Montreal's Yiddish-speaking community and its cultural life. As a young teacher he also began writing for the Montreal Yiddish press about pedagogy and the responsibilities of teachers in the maintenance and dissemination of Jewish culture. His first serious text appeared in 1916 and he continued to submit articles in Yiddish, Hebrew, and English to Canadian Jewish newspapers and specialized American periodicals. But Wiseman did not limit himself to articles about pedagogy. He also wrote about literature and philosophy. In 1931, he published a three-volume literary anthology for Yiddish schools entitled *Dos Vort*. In 1955, working in collaboration with Mordecai Husid, he published a collection of poems written by the late J.J. *Segal under the title of *Letste Lider*. Wiseman demonstrated his skill as a Hebrew literary critic and translator in 1956 when he assembled, translated, and published a selected anthology of 28 American short-story writers entitled *Mesapperim Amerikayim*. In 1976 Wiseman also published a Hebrew translation of the work of the ancient Greek philosopher Epictetus.

[Pierre Anctil (2nd ed.)]

WISLICA (Pol. **Wiślica**), village in Kielce province, central Poland; town in Sandomierz province in the kingdom of Poland until 1795. Jews settled in Wislica at the beginning of the 16th century. In 1542, after the townsmen obtained a royal privilege (*de non tolerandis Judaeis*) excluding Jews from Wislica, the Jews settled in the suburbs outside the town wall. During the war with Sweden (1656), 50 Jewish families were massacred by Stefan *Czarniecki's soldiers. At the end of the 17th century, Jews settled again in Wislica. An organized community was established at the beginning of the 18th century. A synagogue was then built in the outskirts of the town and a cemetery opened. In 1765, 184 Jews living in the suburbs and 72 in the surrounding villages paid the poll tax. In 1815 Wislica was included within Congress Poland. Until 1862, as Wislica was situated near the Austrian border, the settlement of Jews there was restricted. In 1827 there were 785 Jews living in Wislica (47.1% of the total population). Their number increased to 1,370 in 1857 (69%). Their main occupations were commerce on a small scale, crafts, and transportation. In 1921 there were 1,341 Jews living in Wislica (63%).

Holocaust Period

On the outbreak of World War II there were about 1,500 Jews in Wislica. The community was liquidated on Oct. 3, 1942, when 3,000 Jews from Wislica and its vicinity were deported to *Jedrzejow and from there to the *Treblinka death camp. The community was not reconstituted after the war.

BIBLIOGRAPHY: Halpern, Pinkas, index; R. Mahler, *Yidn in Amolikn Poyln in Likht fun Tsifern* (1958), index; B. Wasiutyński, *Ludność żydowska w Polsce w wiekach XIX i XX* (1930), 53; L. Lewin, *Die Judenverfolgungen im zweiten schwedisch-polnischen Kriege* (1901), 16; I. Schiper, *Dzieje handlu żydowskiego na ziemiach polskich* (1937), index.

°**WISLICENY, DIETER** (1911–1948), German *SS officer. Originally a journalist, he joined the SS in 1934 and also the SD, where he served in its headquarters in Berlin (see *Gestapo). In 1936 he was appointed head of its Jewish subsection (II 112), but was transferred in 1937 to the SD in Danzig. *Eichmann, who had been one of his subordinates in II 112, got him attached in 1940 to the RSHA's Jewish section (IV D4). Wisliceny was sent to Slovakia as "adviser" for Jewish affairs in the German legation. Slovakia was an ally of Germany and quite responsive to it. He supervised the introduction of the anti-Jewish legislation in Slovakia. In the spring of 1942 he organized the deportation of 55,000 Slovak Jews to Poland. When deportations were stopped, inter alia by the intervention of the Church and some say even the government, Wisliceny started negotiations on the *Europa Plan with the "Working Group" (see Gisi *Fleischmann and Michael *Weissmandel), which believed that it had come upon a formula for saving the Jews by ransom. An initial sum was given Wisliceny, who reported it to his superiors; more was promised but could not be delivered. But the initial acceptance spurred the Working Group into activity to obtain the money and offer it to Nazi officials. In March 1943 Eichmann sent him to *Salonika to deport the Jewish community. Wisliceny carried out his task in two months, utterly destroying the Jewish community and sending it to Auschwitz. He stayed in Greece until the end of 1943, when he returned to Slovakia. From March 19, 1944, he served on the staff of Eichmann's special commando in Hungary. He organized the mass deportations of 437,402 Jews on 147 trains within 56 days. Once again Jewish leaders tried to approach him in an effort to save the Jewish community. He was the liaison in the negotiations with the Relief and Rescue Committee of Budapest in the so-called Blood for Goods exchange. In December 1944 Eichmann had become suspicious of him, and arranged his transfer to the section of the Gestapo dealing with Slovak affairs. At the end of the war Wisliceny surrendered to the Americans and served as an inexhaustible source of evidence. After having been both a prosecution and defense witness at the International Military Tribunal in Nuremberg, he was extradited to Czechoslovakia. After a prolonged trial in Bratislava he was condemned to death and hanged (1948). During his incarceration he wrote important affidavits regarding the Final Solution, his boss Adolf Eichmann, the Mufti of Jerusalem, and the proposed Blood for Goods exchange.

BIBLIOGRAPHY: International Military Tribunal, *Trial of the Major War Criminals*, 24 (1949), index; J. Lévai, *Black Book on the Martyrdom of Hungarian Jewry* (1948), passim; R.L. Braham, *Hungarian Jewish Catastrophe: A Selected and Annotated Bibliography* (1962), index; L. Rothkirchen, *Ḥurban Yahadut Slovakia* (1961: incl. comprehensive Eng. summary), index; M. Molho and J. Nehama, *Sho'at Yehudei Yavan 1941–1944* (1965), 134–40 and index; Reitlinger, *Final Solution* (1953), index; Hilberg, *Destruction of the European Jews* (1961), index. **ADD. BIBLIOGRAPHY:** Y. Bauer, *Jews for Sale: Nazi-Jewish Negotiations 1933–1945* (1994).

[Yehuda Reshef / Michael Berenbaum (2nd ed.)]

°**WIŚNIOWIECKI, JEREMI** (1612–1651), a Polonized Russian prince, one of the most powerful magnates of Poland-Lithuania in the 17th century. Wiśniowiecki owned enormous estates in the Ukraine on the Dnieper River which were exposed to Cossack and Tatar invasions. The Jews who settled there were murdered during the Cossack riots. Wiśniowiecki had a private army of about 3,000 soldiers. He was a gifted military commander and was successful in many battles against the Cossacks and Tatars, especially in the years 1648–51. Wiśniowiecki also defended the Jews living on his estates against the Cossack units under *Chmielnicki. Nathan Nata *Hannover, author of the chronicle *Yeven Meẓulah*, written in the 17th century, glorified Wiśniowiecki. He wrote that the latter was the mainstay in the fight against the Cossacks, the cruel enemy of the Jews.

BIBLIOGRAPHY: W. Tomkiewicz, *J. Wiśniowiecki (1612–1651)*, 1933.

[Jacob Goldberg]

WISSE, RUTH R. (1936–), scholar of Yiddish literature. A naturalized U.S. citizen born in Cernauti, Romania, Wisse received her undergraduate degree from McGill University in 1957 and her doctorate in 1969. She was assistant professor of Jewish literature at McGill from 1968 to 1971 and was a senior lecturer at Tel Aviv University and The Hebrew University of Jerusalem from 1971 to 1973. She returned to McGill as associate professor in 1975 and was appointed professor in 1978 and chairperson of the Department of Jewish Studies in 1986. She joined Harvard University in 1993, serving as director of the Center for Jewish Studies until 1996, when she was named Martin Peretz professor of Yiddish literature.

Wisse is considered a leader in the revival of interest in Yiddish literature and in the study of the Yiddish language. Her critically acclaimed work *The Modern Jewish Canon: A Journey through Literature and Culture* (2000), an overview of what she defines as the notable Jewish literary works of modern times, has been said to define the modern Jewish experience through the Jewish literature of the 20th century. Her literary defense of the State of Israel, *If I Am Not for Myself–: The Liberal Betrayal of the Jews* (1992), generated a divided critique. Here Wisse contends that liberalism, which would seem to offer promise for modern Jews, has instead fostered an environment that has allowed a propaganda campaign against the Israeli cause. Criticized for an oversimplification of the Arab-Israeli conflict and for using revelations about her personal life in what was termed a political diatribe, the book nevertheless was considered a compelling argument by some reviewers.

Wisse's academic reputation rests on her edited collections of Jewish literature and her literary criticism. In addition to *The Modern Jewish Canon*, her works include *The Schlemiel as Modern Hero* (1970), *A Little Love in Big Manhattan* (1988), and *I.L. Peretz and the Making of Modern Jewish Culture* (1991). She served as editor of *A Shtetl and Other Yiddish Novellas* (1972) and *The I.L. Peretz Reader* (1990), and as co-editor, with Irving Howe and Chone Shmeruk, of *The Penguin Book of Modern Yiddish Verse* (1987).

She is also prominent politically, advocating strong support for Israel and combating what she perceives to be a surge in antisemitism at the turn of the 21st century. It was Wisse, among others, whom literary critic Leon Wieseltier had in mind when he described the "ethnic panic" among American Jews. She opposed a chair in Holocaust studies at Harvard. "It's a strange idea," she said, "You don't have a chair in modern Jewish history, but you have one on the destruction of the Jewish people." She was a member of the search committee, which rejected all candidates for the position; the chair remained unfilled and the money was returned to the donor.

A fellow of the American Academy for Jewish Research, Wisse is the recipient of numerous awards and honors, including the J.I. Segal Award for Literature in 1971 and 1989, the Torch of Learning Award from The Hebrew University in 1993, and the Jewish Cultural Achievement Award from the National Foundation for Jewish Culture in 2001.

[Dorothy Bauhoff (2nd ed.)]

WISSENSCHAFT DES JUDENTUMS (Ger.; "Science of Judaism"; in Hebrew *Ḥokhmat Yisrael*).

Origin and Definition

The term "Wissenschaft des Judentums" first made its appearance among young Jewish intellectuals during the 1810s and 1820s. Its principal objective, as it was then defined in the *Zeitschrift fuer die Wissenschaft des Judentums* (1822), was the study of Judaism by subjecting it to criticism and modern methods of research. It was emphasized that research must encompass Judaism in its most comprehensive sense: its cultural heritage, the totality of conditions under which it existed and faced its destiny, "the knowledge of Judaism through its literary and historical documentation, and… a statistical knowledge of Judaism in relation to the Jews of our time in all the countries of the world" (*ibid.* pp. 1, 18). The use of the term "science" sought to exclude an approach devoid of criticism of tradition and presupposed principles and beliefs to be proved *a posteriori* by debate or casuistry.

The desire for a scientific knowledge of Judaism gave rise to research at first in Germany (during the early 1820s) within a limited circle of young Jews, the second generation of the Berlin Haskalah. Later it became the legacy of all the important Jewish communities and one of Judaism's outstanding manifestations in modern times. With the development of the Science of Judaism, its ramification into many spheres and subjects (Bible criticism, Talmud, Jewish literature of all periods, history and archaeology, religious philosophy, and the like), "Science of Judaism" came to signify the totality of studies concerning the Jewish people and of Judaism. In several countries these studies came to be referred to by such terms as "Judaistica," "Judaica," and "Jewish Studies."

Motives, Determining Factors, Generations

The desire for a scientific knowledge of Judaism was not solely theoretical, but was essentially a public trend, a response to the demands which had emerged as a result of the changes in the conceptions, the world outlook, and the Jewish feeling of most of the intellectuals of the younger generation. It was connected with the Jewish awakening among the younger generation and which one of its contemporaries (Lazar *Riesser) described as the return to their people of "unruly sons and carefree daughters" who had previously "trodden upon all that was designated as Jewish." This awakening was also a reaction to the violent anti-Jewish propaganda which was conducted in German literature by the German student movements and to the *Hep! Hep! pogroms which deeply affected the second-generation *maskilim*; this awakening was also connected with the improvement of their intellectual standards and in a deepening of their philosophical views. The best among them were attached to the cultural heritage of Judaism and did not reconcile themselves to its abrogation and disappearance within German society. They were aware of the fact that in Germany modern Hebrew literature was being led "to the grave" (Zunz) because of the voluntary integration of the Jews within German culture and language. The indifference of the younger generation to Judaism and their estrangement from the heritage of generations, accompanied by contempt for Judaism, its values, and its honor, not only endangered Judaism but also struck a severe blow at the image of the modern Jew: one who despised his past and was ashamed of it, was regarded as a wretched and deficient human figure by the intellectual and moral leaders of the time.

All the *maskilim*, and those who had been aroused to work in favor of their people, shared a renewed feeling of Jewish identity and a desire to introduce widespread reforms into the "house," to which they were returning, in which they wished to remain, and within which they intended to work; by nature these reforms were widespread and touched upon beliefs and views, ways of life and the structure of society, education, and culture, and schools and synagogues. The "House of Israel" was to be presented, both internally and externally, in all its cultural values and historical splendor. They believed that civic equality of the Jew, which was not accompanied by the recognition of the cultural value of his Judaism, was of little importance. This feeling of Jewishness had permeated into considerably wide circles of that generation. This called for a spiritual self-determination equivalent to a recognition of Judaism as a subject of scientific investigation. Serious research would also serve as a solid basis in the struggle for the survival of the Jewish community and would lead to the complete adaptation of Jewish life within state and society. That life would thus benefit from a new and more spiritual image of Judaism, of which it stood so much in need.

From the beginning "Science of Judaism" was thus marked by three elements: self-consciousness, propaganda for internal consumption, and the pleading of its cause before the outside world. These three factors were in evidence throughout, though not to an equal extent or in the same form. As the development of Jewish education and culture during the 19th and 20th centuries internally and the struggle for status externally followed the same pattern throughout the Diaspora, so did "Science of Judaism" in all the countries in which it was cultivated.

These views were voiced by L. Zunz in a statement that only "Science of Judaism" of a standard recognized in the world of European scholarship would be able to bestow upon Judaism the status and the respect which was due to it and gradually arouse the best elements of the Jewish people and unite them. It was therefore the task of Jewish science to win for the Jews a recognized and equal status in the world of culture and spiritually unite the Jewish people. Scholarly activities were to be devoted principally to the study of Hebrew literature, in which resided the spiritual uniqueness of Judaism. These basic views of the early days of the movement greatly influenced the choice of research areas and the course of its development.

Five factors determined the development of the movement, established its trends, marked and singled out its spheres of research, and marked the boundaries between successive generations. These were the following:

(1) the extent of Torah erudition and Hebrew Haskalah in the European countries inhabited by Jews;

(2) the level of humanistic studies in these countries and the extent in which Jews could benefit from general education;

(3) the political, legal, and social status of the Jews in these countries and their struggle for equality;

(4) the cultural, religious, and public ferment within the Jewish population of these countries and the internal polemics within the communities; and

(5) the type of Jewish classes to which Jewish Science addressed itself, and the organizations upon which the scientific activity in the research of Judaism was based. In accordance with the permutations and changes in these factors, the history of Jewish Science – from its beginnings until our time – can be divided into four generations:

(A) the generation of its founders – 1822–54, from the appearance of Zunz's *Zeitschrift fuer die Wissenschaft des Judentums* (1822 to that of *Monatsschrift fuer die Geschichte und Wissenschaft des Judentums* in 1851/52 and the establishment of the Juedisch-theologisches Seminar in Breslau (1854);

(B) the generation of consolidation and organization – 1854–96, to the discovery of the *Genizah (1896) and the first attempts to summarize the achievements of the "Science of Judaism" (1894);

(C) the generation of confusion and compilation – 1896–1925, to the opening of the Judaistic Institute of the *Hebrew University in Jerusalem; and

(D) the generation of renewal and growth – from 1925 to the present day which is the generation of transition "from the Science of Judaism to Jewish Sciences."

Leopold Zunz

"Science of Judaism" was born with the publication by Leopold *Zunz of his pamphlet *Etwas ueber die rabbinische Literatur* (1818) and his first articles in *Zeitschrift* (on place names in Spain mentioned in Hebrew-Jewish literature; on *Rashi, and his outline of a future statistics of Judaism).

Scientific interest in the Jewish cultural heritage and its history was, however, born before Zunz. The Hebrew poet Solomon *Levisohn, who during his brief life and under most difficult conditions engaged in research work into the language of the *Mishnah (*Beit ha-Osef*, 1812) and the phraseology on the Bible (*Melizot Yeshurun*, 1816), published many lectures in German on Jewish history (1820) and also wrote the first biblical geography in Hebrew (*Meḥkerei ha-Areẓ* 1819); Zunz's colleague I.M. *Jost also preceded him with his *Geschichte der Israeliten* (9 vols., 1820–29). Though written more in the Haskalah spirit than in that of scientific research, it nevertheless made a considerable impression on the public. Zunz, however, was the man who symbolized the "Science of Judaism"; he was the first to lay down a detailed program for it, and his works were the first which in practice contained the methods of research which it was to adopt. By his idealism and humanistic fervor and by his ambition to introduce the Jewish cultural heritage into general humanism by and through scientific study of Judaism, Zunz became the symbol of the whole of the "Science of Judaism."

The program which Zunz outlined in his *Etwas ueber die rabbinische Literatur* was the study of Hebrew literature and its history; it included the study of Judaism in all its manifestations: theology, religious worship of Israel; Jewish law, Hebrew literature in particular, of every category and form, including that on the natural sciences and technology and the contribution of the Jews to their development. Jewish ethics and education, which in reality are the practical conclusions of the outlook and the views of generations, also figured in Zunz's program. He also had a program for research into the Judaism of his day. In his essay on Jewish statistics he declared that the purpose of these "statistics" (in those days, this term signified "social science," sociology) would be to acquire a complete picture of the contemporary Jewish condition by a systematic study of that entity which was the result not only of "origin and religion" but also of common language and history and which showed itself in specific qualities and outlook, professional structure, and organized arrangements. Zunz also outlined the methods to be adopted for the collection and the study of data; he had demonstrated them in his earlier work, which abounds in instructions on research methods, such as examination of sources to ascertain the periods and the places of authors, their personalities, and the reliability of the evidence which they handed down. He also pointed out sources which had not yet been exploited (commemorative coins, tombstone inscriptions, etc.), as well as the importance of responsa as a historical source particularly for the history of the economic life of the Jews. Zunz also drew the attention of researchers to community registers and their importance as a historical source.

The methodical innovation in Zunz's work on Rashi lay in the collecting and comparative study of manuscripts of Rashi's commentaries. From Rashi's works he drew information on the man and his work, his family, his studies, the languages with which he was familiar, and the extent to which he employed them – even a description of his library. The little book made a great impression, especially on Torah students in Western and Eastern Europe, who had become familiar with general culture to varying degrees. They discovered that the Torah was a world by itself and could be of interest to an enlightened man. Many of Zunz's contemporaries admitted this influence and the important role which it played in their lives. To a large extent, all the scholars of the first generation of Jewish Science were the disciples of Zunz: they learned from his methods and followed his example.

The First Generation of Scholars

During the first generation of the promoters of the "Science of Judaism" the foundations were laid for research into all the spheres of Judaism. Of the eight outstanding scholars, S.J. Rapoport, Zunz, S.D. *Luzzatto, and Krochmal – the elders of that generation – and Z. *Frankel, *Geiger, *Munk, and Steinschneider – its younger members – each devoted himself to a specific sphere, opened new vistas for their study, and paved the way for their successors.

The first member of the "generation of the founding and establishment" of the "Science of Judaism" was S.J.L. *Rapoport, whose field was the research of talmudic and rabbinic literature and the history of those periods. His work encouraged and paved the way for a scientific approach to talmudic and rabbinic literature as a source for the study of Jewish history. Rapoport aimed at the enlightenment of the Jewish nation and the strengthening of its self-consciousness. Zunz, on the other hand, who came to be influenced by Rapoport, devoted himself mainly to the history of Jewish liturgy. His meticulous attention to detail, and the interlacing of these details with historical periods and localities and the development of Jewish religious and intellectual life, raised his works to the rank of classics, retaining their importance to the present day.

The early scholarly activity of Samuel David Luzzatto was connected with Hebrew linguistics and the Targum Onkelos, followed by biblical exegesis. His main importance lies in the discovery of numerous and important Hebrew manuscripts and their publication, among them collections of poems by *Judah Halevi (*"Betulat Bat Yehudah,"* 1840; *"Diwan,"* 1844). The wide influence Luzzatto had on his generation is essentially due to his critical evaluation of the past. He fought against disruptive trends in Judaism, the delusions of the emancipation, and the whole outlook of his generation. He called for the existence of Judaism as a separate religious-national entity living according to its usages and the principles of its ethics. He appraised earlier conflicts with the viewpoint of those of his day (*Meḥkerei ha-Yahadut*, ed. Tevunah, Warsaw, 1913). Thus, he was to a certain extent responsible for extracting the "Science of Judaism" from the domain of individual scholars engaged in research and making it a public concern.

Nahman *Krochmal's *Moreh Nevukhei ha-Zeman* ("Guide of the Perplexed of the Generation") was published in 1851 but was written during the 1830s, after the publication of the biographies of Rapoport, Luzzatto's criticism of A. *Ibn Ezra and *Maimonides, Zunz's work on homiletics, and Jost's history. This "Guide" was an attempt to provide a philosophical-historical answer to the problems of the time: how to prevent the disintegration of Jewry by making it conscious of its unity; by salvaging at least part of the authority of religious tradition and strengthening it through sacrificing some of it; by an attempt to strengthen the belief in the future of Judaism; and by finding methods of adapting it for its future task. Krochmal's work summed up the early achievements of the "Science of Judaism" in fostering Jewish self-consciousness: it included Zunz on the spiritual unity of the nation throughout the generations, the nationalist element in enlightenment (Rapoport), and the faith of Luzzatto in the eternity of the Jewish people and its religious character. Krochmal's historical-critical approach paved the way for further research. Jost had described Jewish history in all its periods but Krochmal was the first to adumbrate a unified conception of Jewish history as a whole. The "Guide," both in content and form, ranks among the most important works of the "Science of Judaism" and Hebrew literature in general.

Frankel, Geiger, Munk, and Steinschneider

Although Zunz had pointed out on the title page of his *Gottesdienstliche Vortraege* (1832) that it was "a contribution to the study of antiquity, Bible criticism, and the history of literature and religion," only the younger members of the founding generation devoted their work to biblical and religious research and laid the foundations for its future development. Zacharias *Frankel did this for Jewish law, the history of *halakhah*, and the study of the Talmud. With scholarly caution and care in phrasing and conclusions Frankel established the historical factor in the evolution of Mishnah, the *Talmud, and the *halakhah*, pointing out its principal stages.

The work of Abraham *Geiger, the leading spokesman of the religious reform movement, extended over many spheres of the "Science of Judaism," such as the study of the Bible versions, the ancient *halakhah*, and Jewish sects, and subjects ranging from the languages of the Mishnah, the Hebrew poetry of Spain, and the biblical exegesis of France to the Jewish scholars of Italy during the 16th and 17th centuries. For Geiger all these had the internal evolution of Judaism in common; the reformer occasionally introduced contemporary polemics, consciously or unconsciously, into the study of the past. His largest work was *Urschrift und Uebersetzungen der Heiligen Schrift in ihrer Abhaengigkeit von der inneren Entwicklung des Judentums* (1857). Though subsequent research refuted most of Geiger's conclusions, his contribution to the development of the "Science of Judaism" should not be ignored. There was a great methodical innovation in Geiger's system: the textual discrepancies in the Bible were used by him as the foundation for a history of Judaism. The "Urschrift" aroused strong polemics and its reformist orientation impaired its influence, though it inspired students in later generations.

Solomon *Munk and Moritz *Steinschneider were the first scholars of Oriental philology, particularly Arabic, among the founders of the "Science of Judaism." They developed new methods of research into medieval Jewish literature, in general, and the contribution of the Jews to the development of the sciences, in particular. Munk was the first to make use of the Arabic sources in the study of the history of Jewish literature and thought. His essays on the medieval Jewish scholars who wrote in Arabic, such as *Saadiah Gaon, Joseph ibn *Aknin, and Jonah *Ibn Janaḥ, were based on Arabic sources and presented these scholars in a new light. His research into the history of Jewish philosophy was of prime importance. In his *Mélanges de Philosophie juive et arabe* (1859) he revealed Solomon ibn Gabirol as the author of *Fons Vitae* and in his edition of the Arabic original of Maimonides' "Guide" (1856–66) he laid the foundation for the study of medieval Jewish philosophy.

Steinschneider opened new vistas of bibliographical Jewish literature which won him the title of "father of Jewish bibliography." Three of his works are of particular value: his survey of "Jewish Literature," his catalogs of Hebrew manuscripts, and his books on the Hebrew translations of the Middle Ages and the Arabic literature of the Jews. His survey of Jewish literature was the first comprehensive review of the literary activity of the Jews in all languages and at all periods, from the conclusion of the Bible until the end of the 18th century. Steinschneider's catalogs of the Hebrew manuscripts of five large European libraries (*Bodleian of Oxford, Leyden, Berlin, Minsk, and Hamburg) disclosed treasures of Jewish literature and culture which had hitherto been hidden. The meticulous accuracy in his description and the astonishing knowledge which underlies them became a wonder; they continue to guide scholars in their research into the numerous problems which these discoveries initiated. His works on the translations and the Arabic literature of the Jews became the basis for research into the Jewish history, literature, and culture of the Middle Ages.

Plans for University Faculties; Periodicals; Influence on a Wider Public

The "Science of Judaism" of the founder generation was concentrated in the hands of individuals. They worked in this field "for its own sake" and in their hours of leisure, as they had to teach in schools (Zunz, Munk, and Steinschneider), hold rabbinical office (Rapoport, Frankel, and Geiger), or were engaged in business (Krochmal). Luzzatto was the only one who, as lecturer at the rabbinical seminary in Padua, was more or less directly connected with his scholarly activity. The ideal of the Jewish scholars of those days was the opening of a faculty for the sciences of Judaism or Jewish theology in one of the universities. Zunz declared this at the outset of his activity, Geiger preached in favor of this, and there was even a public demand for the foundation of a "Jewish theological faculty" and a "Jewish seminary" in Germany. Committees were set up and funds were raised (1838). During the brief spring of the Revolution of 1848, Zunz submitted a memorandum to the University of Berlin on the allocation of a place to the "Science of Judaism," but the university rejected this proposal. In reality, the "Science of Judaism" had little appeal for the public and was restricted to the scholars engaged in the subject.

In about 1838 Geiger attempted to amalgamate all those engaged in the "Science of Judaism" into one group. It was joined by over 20 people, including Jost, Zunz, Rapoport, Munk, J.N. Derenbourg (see *Derenburg family) and others. Even though this society was not properly "organized," it faithfully expressed one of the characteristic traits of the generation: a readiness to assist colleagues, including scientific collaboration. It was no accident that one of the literary forms of the publications of the "Science of Judaism" in that generation was that of the "letter," or "epistle," in which scholars and researchers described their work to each other. There were not periodicals exclusively consecrated to the "Science of Judaism"; even Geiger's *Wissenschaftliche Zeitschrift fuer Juedische Theologie* (1834–48) was mainly devoted to contemporary problems which, in the opinion of Geiger, were bound up with its struggle for Reform by the creation of a "Jewish theology" based on historical criticism.

The research work of the "Science of Judaism" was published in the Hebrew periodicals of the Haskalah movement (**Bikkurei ha-Ittim* (1821–32) of Jeiteles in Prague, **Kerem Ḥemed* (1833–56) of Goldenberg in Galicia; *Ziyyon* (1841–42) of Jost and M. *Creizenach in Frankfurt; *Pirḥei Ẓafor* (1841–44) of Vilna) and in the German-Jewish press, such as L. *Philippson's *Allgemeine Zeitung des Judentums* (1837–1922), J. *Fuerst's *Der Orient* (1841–51) and Jost's Israelitische Annalen (1839–41) of which only one of the latter (*Orient*) contained a special literary supplement of scientific standard. Yet this first generation of the "Science of Judaism" was of great historical importance. A desire to explore the past grew among many of the intellectuals of the younger generation. Dozens of authors and students from every quarter, the old and the young, from Germany, Austria (mainly Bohemia, Moravia, and Galicia), France, Italy, Poland, and Russia – some of whom eventually achieved fame – published studies and reviews, articles and notes on the "Science of Judaism" in Jewish periodicals, in Hebrew and other languages. Among them were also scholars whose principal scientific activity was in other spheres, but who felt the need to engage themselves also in the "Science of Judaism."

Disrespect toward Judaism and contempt for its past was on the decline among Jewish and Christian intellectuals, while self-respect was rising among the Jewish public. From this point of view the influence of the "Science of Judaism" was more powerful among the Jewish masses of Eastern Europe: the inclination toward Hebrew of the Haskalah movement and its nationalist tendencies bore the imprint of the "Science of Judaism" and the new perspective on the Jewish past and culture which it had given to that generation. The polemics on religious reforms which perturbed West European Jewry, particularly German Jewry, were also considerably influenced by the "Science of Judaism" and took place against a scholarly background. As a result of this the public became aware of the necessity to promote the development of the "Science of Judaism," to consolidate it, and to organize it.

Rabbinical Seminaries, Learned Societies, and Periodicals

The establishment of the *Juedisch-theologisches Seminar in Breslau (1854) marked the beginning of the second generation of the "Science of Judaism." This was the first institution which made it possible for scholars to devote themselves entirely to the "Science of Judaism." They also could train new generations of students by associating them in the probing of the problems which held the attention of their teachers. Z. Frankel, who headed the seminary for 20 years, was aware of its scientific mission in addition to its practical objectives – the training of rabbis, and during the first years also of teachers. For the first time a modern curriculum for the dissemination of higher Jewish learning was established. It was based on new methods of research while aiming at appropriate standards of knowledge in Bible, the Talmud, and rabbinic literature. The scientific standard of the first teachers (Frankel, the historian *Graetz, the classical philologist Jacob Bernays (see *Bernays family), and the teacher of Jewish religious philosophy Manuel *Joel), the strict demands on the students' preliminary knowledge, and the relationship between their Jewish education and their university studies, as well as the encouragement given to the students in their research projects, assured the success of the foundation.

Approximately 100 of the 300 students who graduated from the seminary during the first 40 years of its existence engaged in Jewish scholarship and published research work, among them Israel Levy, Saul Horowitz, Adolf *Schwartz, Alexander *Kohut, W. *Bacher, J. *Theodor, M. *Guedemann, D. *Kaufmann, N. Porges and J. Perles, H. *Gross, and J. *Freudenthal and Jacob Gutmann. These scholars published much of their research in the *Monatsschrift fuer Geschichte und Wissenschaft des Judentums*, which was founded by Frankel in 1851 and continued to appear until 1939.

The Breslau Seminary became the model for most rabbinical seminaries founded during this period in several countries, and which became centers of the "Science of Judaism." In Berlin the *Hochschule (Lehranstalt) fuer die Wissenschaft des Judentums was founded by Geiger in 1870, and its Orthodox counterpart, E. *Hildesheimer's Rabbinical Seminary, in 1873. The Bet ha-Midrash Lilmod u-Lelamed of Vienna was founded by A. *Jellinek in 1863; the *Ecole Rabbinique was transferred to Paris in 1859 and Jews' College was established in London in 1856. The Landesrabbinerschule of Budapest was founded in 1877 and the Juedisch-theologische Lehranstalt in 1893. Leading Jewish scholars such as A. Berlin, J. *Barth, D. Hoffmann, I.H. *Weiss, M. *Friedmann, M. *Friedlander, Israel *Abrahams, W. Bacher, D. Kaufmann, L. *Blau, A. *Buechler, and A. Schwarz headed and taught at these seminaries. Higher institutes for the training of rabbis were also founded in the United States, such as the Jewish Theological Seminary in New York and *Hebrew Union College in Cincinnati, although at first they did not influence the development of the "Science of Judaism."

In addition to rabbinical seminaries, several other institutions were founded and a number of societies were organized during this period for the promotion of Jewish scholarship (see *Learned Societies). In 1855 the Institut zur Foerderung der israelitischen Literatur was established by Philipson, Jellinek, and Jost. The Zunzstiftung was established in 1864 (on the occasion of Zunz's 70th birthday); the interest from it was placed at his disposal for the rest of his life, after which it was consecrated to works in the spirit of Zunz. In 1864 the *Mekiẓe Nirdamim society was founded, whose aim it was to publish important Hebrew manuscripts. In 1869 Moses *Montefiore founded the Yeshivat Ohel Moshe vi-Yhudit in Ramsgate; it was to give aged scholars the possibility of pursuing their work in material security. In 1880 the Société des Études Juives was founded in Paris; its organ became the *Revue des Études Juives (1880), which rivaled the "Monatschrift" in importance and is still published. All these institutions and societies helped in the progress of the "Science of Judaism." Important *libraries were attached to them, building up collections of manuscripts and rare books.

About 20 periodicals devoted to the "Science of Judaism" were published during that period. These publications were often somehow connected with the above institutions and published by them with the active collaboration of their teachers and students. Apart from those already mentioned, these were the *Magazin fuer Geschichte, Literatur und Wissenschaft des Judentums*, published in Berlin by A. *Berliner and D. Hoffmann (1874–93), the *Jewish Quarterly Review (London, from 1889), and the *Hebraeische Bibliographie*, published by Steinschneider (1858–82). Important periodicals and literary organs were published in Hebrew, mainly on the initiative of individual scholars, such as Senior Sachs' **Kerem Ḥemed* (1854–56) and *Ha-Yonah, Ha-Teḥiyyah* (1851–57), of Schorr's **He-Ḥalutz* (1852–89); Blumenfeld's *Oẓar Neḥmad* (1856–63); T.H. Weiss' and M. Friedmann's *Beit ha-Midrash* and *Beit ha-Talmud* (Vienna, 1881–89); and Kobrak's *Jeschurun (1856–78).

Almost all Hebrew periodicals published articles as well as manuscripts in the field of the "Science of Judaism," some of them by prominent scholars. Among them were S.J. *Fuenn's weekly, later monthly, **Ha-Karmel* (1860–80), P. *Smolenskin's **Ha-Shaḥar* (1869–85), and among the annuals Sokolow's **Ha-Asif* (1885–89, 1894) and S.P. *Rabbinowitz's *Keneset Yisrael* (1886–88). **Ha-Maggid* (1856–1903), the first weekly Hebrew newspaper, carried a special section, *Ha-Ẓofeh le-ha-Maggid*, most of which was consecrated to the "Science of Judaism" and published contributions of Jewish scholars from Eastern and Western Europe. The large correspondence on subjects of the "Science of Judaism" also shows the wide interest taken in it within the Jewish communities of the East and the West.

During this period the development of the "Science of Judaism" was marked by a strong historical trend. Much attention was given to the history of the Jews in the lands of their dispersion, to the countries and their communities, and to their beliefs and views. In their usages and institutions it was possible to determine the evolution from one period to another and from one country to another. This historical trend was the result of external and internal circumstances. The struggle for emancipation continued during all the years which followed upon the formal granting of equality. Jews were compelled to struggle not only for the practical application of this equality but also for its public recognition.

The *antisemitism which emerged in the course of the 19th century in the form of a popular movement and as a platform for the political organization of the masses intensified this struggle. Jewish communities were obliged to stress the historical foundation of their demands and claims. It was believed that they would then be regarded as an organic part of the state or country, as they had participated in their political and cultural development. This is evident in the activities of the historical societies and commissions, which were then formed in almost every country (the first in Germany in 1885, from Steinschneider's circle) for the collection of historical records on Jewish settlements and their history, and their subsequent publication.

Historiography

The same trend was responsible for such studies as those of Darmesteter on Rashi's *La'azim* and the French exegetic literature (1872); Guedemann's *Geschichte des Erziehungswesens* (1880–88); and studies on Jewish philosophy during the Hellenistic period (Freudenthal) and the Middle Ages (Jacob Guttmann). Internal conflicts within the communities were also responsible for the historical trend in the "Science of Judaism." All the factions in the polemics on religious reforms sought to find support in historical research: either to prove that non-organic and "incidental" strata had been added to the basic structure of Judaism according to time and place, and these should be rejected; or out of a desire to preserve the integrity of historical Judaism and its continuity while accepting the principle of evolution within it and historical change as a fact; or by explaining by means of historical research the changes within the framework of Judaism which was in itself stable and immutable.

In practice, historical research constituted an encounter of all the trends of Judaism with the past. The historical approach within the "Science of Judaism" was due to a large extent to the influence of H. Graetz and his work. Together with the 11 volumes of his Geschichte, Graetz published 150 preliminary studies on all the periods of Jewish history (mostly in the *Monatsschrift*). These studies provided ample material for later historians. Graetz's influence is also reflected in areas in which the "Science of Judaism" made particular progress during this second period: the history of the Oral Law and medieval and modern Jewish history. To the first belongs Karaite studies by Simḥah Pinsker, P. Frankel, and A. *Harkavy; I.H. Weiss' *Dor Dor ve-Doreshav* (1871–91) and the polemical researches of J.H. *Schorr and Abraham Krochmal; and the studies of Leopold *Loew (e.g., *Die Lebensalter in der juedischen Literatur*, 1875). With their many-sided work Bacher and David Kaufmann followed to a considerable extent in the footsteps of their teacher Graetz. They did influential research in the fields of *aggadah* and Hebrew philology (Bacher) and on Jewish and religious philosophy and communal and family history. They also paved the way for a history of Jewish art and archaeology (D. Kaufmann).

Research into the language of the Talmud and the Targums were undertaken by Jacob *Levy in his dictionaries, Kohut's *Arukh ha-Shalem* (1878–92), and Fuenn's *Oẓar Leshon ha-Mikra ve-ha-Mishnah* (1884–1900). A. *Neubauer and A. *Berliner wrote on the geography of the Talmud, and R.N. *Rabbinovitz did pioneer work on the text of the Babylonian Talmud, *Dikdukei Soferim* (1868–86). In the sphere of Jewish history, the most influential writers were M. *Wiener, M. *Kayserling, and Joseph *Jacobs, developing new methods in the use of new sources for the study of history of the Jews in various countries. The growth of large Jewish libraries with their collections of manuscripts and the opening of the great general libraries to Jewish scholars, as well as the publication by them of manuscript catalogs, encouraged scholars to publish the "secrets" of bygone generations. The number of works that were published from manuscripts during this period, whether for the first time or in different versions, amounted to several hundreds of the medieval period alone.

The scholars of the older generation were joined by younger ones who published manuscripts in the fields of their particular interest. These critical editions, with their notes and introductions, succeeded in drawing attention to subjects which had been neglected, perhaps owing to the limited material available. First among the scholars in this field were Solomon *Buber (Midrashim and medieval *halakhah*), Berliner (Rashi's Pentateuch commentary, Targum Onkelos, historical texts), Derenbourg (Saadiah), Harkavy (the period of the *geonim*, texts and records on the history of the Jews in Russia), Senior *Sachs (Gabirol's poetry with commentaries), Jellinek (minor *Midrashim* from Kabbalah literature), A. Neubauer (historical texts), and David Kaufmann (historical and literary texts).

The three elements which fashioned the character of the second generation "Science of Judaism" – the rabbinical seminaries, the concentration on local Jewish history, and the emphasis on the publication of manuscripts – were responsible for a decline in the "Science of Judaism" and the self-criticism with which its past and future prospects were viewed. The framework of the rabbinical seminaries, in which the link between general and Jewish scholarship was tenuous (the student studied general sciences at the universities), kept distinguished scholars away, as they did not wish to confine themselves to a "ghetto" (Steinschneider), or it made them join the universities at a later stage (J. Bernays and I. *Goldziher). This lowered the standard of instruction in these institutions. In addition, the practical objective (the rabbinate) of the seminary course did not assure a continuation of the scholarly work, except for the limited number of those who took up a teaching career. Criticism of the "Science of Judaism" at the close of the 19th century was expressed in a current saying: its protagonists are rabbis who begin with the publication of a medieval text and end with writing the history of their community, or that of one of the neighboring communities.

This was the situation during those years in which the changes in the status of the Jew called for stock-taking by every Jewish intellectual. Antisemitism had succeeded in isolating the Jews socially. The emancipation of the Jews had constantly to be fought for, and this perturbed the Jews in general, as well as every individual Jew to varying extents. As a result of the constant tension, this self-consciousness became a moral necessity for every Jewish intellectual who did not wish to abandon his people in the hour of its plight. The pogroms and persecutions which took place in Russia became a Damoclean sword for all Jews, and the mass emigration from Russia through Central and Western Europe on its way to the transatlantic countries revived universal Jewish ties which had been weakened over the past generations. Collaboration in matters of Jewish concern in various countries was encouraged, and a whole network of world Jewish organizations and institutions of unprecedented dimensions in Jewish history came into being.

These activities, which were marked by high organizing ability and financial generosity, accompanied Jewish misfortunes at the time of the Russian pogroms (1881–1920). They also called for a fundamental assessment and serious scientific study of the Jewish situation. The nationalist movement whose slogan was "Rebellion against the Exile" (see *Ḥibbat Zion and *Zionism) considered as one of its first tasks a renewal of Jewish historic consciousness by imparting to the intelligentsia a knowledge of Judaism and its values, based on the results of scientific research. The nationalist movement did in fact initiate literary activities with the aim of "ingathering" the outstanding works of the past in accordance with contemporary requirements (*Aḥad Ha-Am and the establishment of the publishing house *Achiasaf*). Preliminary plans were drawn up for a "summing up" of the "Science of Judaism" and its achievements in the form of an *encyclopedia (*Oẓar ha-Yahadut* of Aḥad Ha Am) which would pass on to the present-day generation the "Torah" of Judaism clearly and without scientific discussions.

The Socialist and revolutionary agitation gave Jewish historical research a new subject – the working classes. It called for research into the Jewish economy, the way of life of the masses, and the promotion of a popular national culture for which there was a growing demand; it was to be fostered and had to be considered from a scientific angle. As a result, the objectives of the "Science of Judaism" and its methods became problematical and led to a number of experiments in promoting and planning research. These became the outstanding characteristics of the third generation of the "Science of Judaism."

The establishment of institutions and organizations for the promotion of the "Science of Judaism," such as the *Gesellschaft zur Foerderung der Wissenschaft des Judentums (Berlin, 1902) and the Verein zur Gruendung und Erhaltung einer Akademie fuer die Wissenschaft des Judentums (Berlin, 1920), was an innovation in that these were not connected with rabbinical seminaries and had no other objective but the promotion of science. Another innovation was the establishment of societies and institutions for the promotion of research in subjects with which the "Science of Judaism" had not dealt until then, such as Jewish ethnography (in the framework of "the Historical-Ethnographical Society" of St. Petersburg; the "Ethnographical – Historical Expedition" of *An-Ski, 1912); research into Jewish statistics (Verein fuer Juedische Statistik, Berlin, 1902), the publication of a special periodical for Jewish demography and statistics (in German, under the editorship of A. *Ruppin); Jewish art ("*Society for Jewish Folk Music," St. Petersburg, 1908), the exploration of Palestine and its antiquities (the Palestine Exploration Society was founded in Jerusalem, 1919); and similar projects.

There was also an innovation in the surveys which were carried out by Jewish organizations and were of importance to all subsequent research. The collection of material on the economic situation of the Jews in Russia (in 1898–99) by a team of experts for the *Jewish Colonization Association (*Recueil de matériaux sur la situation économique des Israélites en Russie*, 2 vols., Paris, 1906–08; there is also a Russian edition) became the basis of all subsequent research on the Jewish economy in Russia (Jacob *Lestschinsky). The two volumes which contained the material on the pogroms in Russia (*Die Judenpogrome in Russland*, 2 vols., 1910), which were published by the Zionist Relief Fund (under the editorship of L. *Motzkin), were a contribution of great importance in this sphere. A fresh development was the rise of non-commercial publishing companies such as *Achiasaf*, Warsaw, and the *Jewish Publication Society of America (Philadelphia), one of whose aims was the propagation of the "Science of Judaism."

Such ventures often foreshadowed institutions. Thus "YIVO" (Yidisher Visnshaftlikher Institut, established in 1925) was heralded by *Der Pinkas* ("Yearbook on the history of Yiddish literature and its language, folklore, criticism and bibliography"; Vilna, 1912), edited by S. *Niger. This annual published B. Borochov's "Documents on the Philology of Yiddish Language Research." The friends of Yiddish and popular Jewish culture grouped themselves around him. The third generation of the "Science of Judaism" had three achievements to its credit:

(1) The summing up of the "Science of Judaism" in *The Jewish Encyclopaedia* (see *Encyclopedias; 1901–06), which was devoted to the "history of the Jewish people, its religion, its literature, and its customs from antiquity to the present era";

(2) The planning of basic reference books, which required the collaboration of scholars;

(3) The discovery of the *Genizah*.

The *Jewish Encyclopaedia*, which formed the basis of the *Yevreyskaya Entsiklopediya* (1908–13; see *Encyclopedias) and the *Oẓar Yisrael* (1906–13; see *Encyclopedias), was published with the participation of Jewish scholars from many countries, as well as a large number of non-Jewish scholars. This encyclopedia summed up the achievements of the "Science of Judaism" in every sphere.

The Gesellschaft zur Foerderung der Wissenschaft des Judentums, one of whose principal tasks was the publication of reference books of a high standard, was unable to complete its program, though in those works it did publish it raised the standards of the "Science of Judaism" and met the demands of the time. The society turned to several Jewish scholars who had achieved repute for their contributions to the general sciences and encouraged them to carry out work in the field of the "Science of Judaism." The society thus published, among others: Georg *Caro's *Sozial-und Wirtschaftsgeschichte der Juden im Mittelalter und der Neuzeit* (1908–20), Eduard *Mahler's *Handbuch der juedischen Chronologie* (1916), Samuel *Krauss' *Talmudische Archeologie* (3 vols., 1910–12), and I. *Elbogen's *Der Juedische Gottesdienst in seiner geschichtlichen Entwicklung* (1924). The program for an Akademie fuer die Wissenschaft des Judentums, which was submitted by its first director (Eugen *Taeubler), envisaged a *Forschungsinstitut* whose members, mostly younger scholars, took on specific projects in their respective fields of study. These were discussed at the meetings of the institute under the guidance of its director. Some of the scholars who worked in the Akademie later became prominent in the "Science of Judaism."

The investigation of the Cairo *Genizah* by Solomon Schechter (1847–1915) and the publication and study of its contents had a revolutionary impact on the "Science of Judaism." It made research possible on periods and subjects in which lack of source material had made research difficult. Out of the *Genizah* Schechter published about two-thirds of Ben Sira in the Hebrew original (1899); materials on the life of Saadiah and his writings; material on the history of the Jews of Palestine during the 11th century; and material on the history of Jewish sects. *Genizah* research enriched the "Science of Judaism" during the first years after its discovery and added new chapters on Jewish history and literature, particularly in the field of Midrash and the literature of the *geonim* (Louis *Ginzberg, Israel *Davidson, and Jacob *Mann), in that of prayers and hymns (Davidson and Elbogen), and in Jewish history in the Orient, particularly Egypt and Palestine (Mann, R. *Gottheil, and others). The progress of the "Science of Judaism" in the United States is also linked with the personality and work of Schechter. At the Jewish Theological Seminary of America, of which he was the head from his arrival in New York (1902), he gathered a team of scholars (Louis Ginzberg, Israel Friedlander, A. *Marx, and I. Davidson), built up its library, which later became one of the largest Jewish libraries – it is particularly rich in Hebrew manuscripts – and raised the seminary to the rank of one of the leading institutions of the "Science of Judaism."

In Eastern Europe, especially in Russia, where almost half of the world's Jewish population lived, the "Science of Judaism" made little progress in spite of intensified Jewish consciousness and a strong nationalist movement. The government – under the influence of the leaders of Orthodox Jewry – would not authorize the establishment of a seminary for the training of modern rabbis and Jewish scholars. Those engaged in the study of Jewish sciences were either authors and scholars, who as a result of publicistic discussions on contemporary problems had passed on to the study of Jewish history (S. *Dubnow, S. *Ginsburg, P. *Marek, J. *Hessen, S.P. Rabbinowitz, B.Z. *Katz), or rabbis and Torah scholars who had adopted, under the influence of the "Science of Judaism," modern methods (such as B. Ratner in his *Ahavat Ẓiyyon vi-Yrushalayim* (1904–17) on the text of the Jerusalem Talmud and H. *Tchernowitz (Rav Ẓai'ir) in his *Le-Toledot ha-Shulḥan Arukh ve-Hitpashetuto; Ha-Shilo'aḥ*, 1899–1900). Others, speaking out in defense of traditional Judaism by exposing the inner contradictions of the *Haskalah, tried to offer a better understanding of Judaism and its moral values (S.A. Horodezky, W. Jawitz), or to refute the conclusions of the "Science of Judaism" and its historical criticism (Isaac ha-Levi).

Only a few Jewish scholars in Eastern Europe, most of whom had been educated in Western Europe, made a substantial contribution to the "Science of Judaism" writings, at least partly in Hebrew (S.A. *Poznański). Contributing western scholars included Abraham *Kahana in "*Perush Madda'i la-Tanakh*" and *Horodezky in *Ha-Goren*. The influence of the "Science of Judaism" in Eastern Europe extended to Palestine, where particular emphasis was put on Hebrew linguistics and the geography of Ereẓ Israel (E. *Ben-Yehuda's massive *Millon* (dictionary) and his "Memoirs"; the activities of the *Va'ad ha-Lashon* (see: Academy of Hebrew Language) periodical, 10 volumes; and A.M. *Luncz's *Jerusalem* (1882–1917). These studies also found an echo outside Palestine (D. *Yellin, the brothers J.J. and A.S. *Yahuda, E. *Gruenhut, A.M. Toledano). Some of the leading scholars (M. Friedmann and W. Bacher, A. Berliner and A.E. Harkavy, S.A. Poznański and S. Krauss, D. Kaufmann and M. Steinschneider) cooperated with them. There was also a certain increase in Hebrew publications dealing with subjects of the "Science of Judaism." The initiative of Bialik in 1923 (with I. Elbogen, J.N. *Epstein, and N.H. *Tur-Sinai (Torczyner)) to publish *Devir* (periodical for the "Science of Judaism") appeared to herald a new era. Its program included "research on the present condition of living, creative Israel," and research into "popular literature" and "Jewish literature of the last century."

With the establishment of the Hebrew University in Jerusalem, a new era began for the "Science of Judaism." For the first time it found itself in its entirety within a framework of an institution of higher education and learning – with Jewish life in all its manifestations and developments as its object – to which the Jewish social reality in its ancient homeland gave a territorial-historical continuity and national and cultural stability. These factors widened the spheres of research. New, or almost new, subjects came to the fore, such as the archaeology and geography of Ereẓ Israel, talmudic philology, Jewish Hellenism, Hebrew law, Jewish mysticism, modern Hebrew literature, Yiddish and its literature, Jewish sociology, and the study of contemporary Jewry. Judaic studies thus replaced the "Science of Judaism." This development also influenced the "Science of Judaism" in the United States, almost the only country in the Diaspora where it continued to advance as a cultural-spiritual factor in the life of its Jewish community. As for other countries, particularly in Central and Eastern Europe, the "Science of Judaism" was integrally bound up with the struggle of the Jewish communities for their survival in an age in which Jewish diaspora existence was threatened by assimilation, on the one hand, and persecution and extermination, on the other.

BIBLIOGRAPHY: GENERAL: I. Elbogen, *Ḥokhmat Yisrael*, 2 (1923), 1–15; S. Bernfeld, *Dor Ḥakham* (1896); N. Rotenstreich, *Ha-Maḥashavah ha-Yehudit ba-Et ha-Ḥadashah*, 2 (1950), 35–51; G. Scholem, in: *Lu'aḥ ha-Areẓ* (1948), 94–112; L. Zunz and A. Wolf, *Ḥokhmat Yisrael be-Reshitah* (1963); L. Wallach, in: HJ, 8 (1946), 35–60; M. Wiener, in: *YIVO Annual*, 5 (1950), 184–96. FIRST GENERATION: S. Bernfeld, *Toledot Shir* (1949); N. Glazer, in: *Zion*, 26 (1961), 208–14; A.H. Weiss, *Zikhronotai* (1895), 86–173; Klausner, Sifrut, 2 (1937); S.P. Rabbinowitz, *Rabbi Zekharyah Frankel* (Heb., 1898); idem, *Rabbi Yom Tov Lipman Zunz* (Heb., 1897); Graetz, Gesch, 11 (1900), 488–502; S. Schechter, *Studies in Judaism*, 1 (1911), 46–72; 3 (1924), 47–143. SECOND GENERATION: A.M. Luncz, (ed.), *Yerushalayim*, 2 (1847); M. Braun, *Geschichte des juedish-theologischen Seminars in Breslau* (1904); idem, *Heinrich Graetz* (Ger., 1917); G. Kisch, *Das Breslauer Seminar* (1963). THIRD GENERATION: Aḥad Ha-Am, *Al Parashat Derakhim*, 1 (1923), 5–13; I. Elbogen, in: MGWJ, 1928), 1–5; L. Finkelstein, in: C. Adler (ed.), *The Jewish Theological Seminary of America* (1939); J. Guttmann, *Die Akademie fuer die Wissenschaft des Judentums* (1929); Lucas, in MGWJ, 71 (1927); S. Schechter, *Studies in Judaism*, 2 (1908), 1–30. FOURTH GENERATION: J. Klausner, *Ha-Universitah Shellanu* (1932); L. Roth, *Limmud Gavoha ve-Ḥinnukh ha-Dor* (1944); *Ha-Universitah ha-Ivrit bi-Yrushalayim Kaf-He Shanah* (1950); A. Trakower, in: *Koveẓ Madda'i le-Zekher Moshe Schorr* (1945); *Al ha-Ḥinnukh ha-Universita'i* (1962); Z. Scharfstein, *Toledot ha-Ḥinnukh* *be-Yisrael ba-Dorot ha-Aḥaronim*, 2 (1917), 310–41; C. Adler (ed.), *The Jewish Theological Seminary in America* (1939); N. Stif, *Di Organizatsye fun der Yidisher Visnshaft* (1925): S. Niger, in: YIVO *Bleter*, 2 (1931), 1f.; S. Weinreich, *ibid.* 17 (1941), 1–13; G. Scholem, in: *Judaica* (1963), 147–63. **ADD. BIBLIOGRAPHY:** J. Borut, "*Verein fuer Juedische Geschichte und Litreatur* at the End of the Nineteenth Century," in: *Leo Baeck Institute Year Book*, 41 (1996), 89–114; A. Brämer, *Rabbiner Zachraias Frankel: Wissenschaft des Judentums und conservative Reform im 19. Jahrhundert* (2000); M. Brenner, "Juedische Geschichte an deutschen Universitäten. Bilanz und Perspektive," in: *Historische Zeitschrift*, 266 (1998); M. Brenner, A. Kauders, G. Reuveni, and N. Roemer (ed. with commentary), *Juedische Geschichte lesen. Texte der juedischen Geschichtsschreibung im 19. und 20. Jahrhundret* (2003); M. Brenner and S. Rohrbacher (eds.), *Wissenschaft vom Judentum: Annäherungen nach dem Holocaust* (2000); M. Brocke, "Gershom Scholem. Wissenschaft des Judentums zwischen Berlin und Jerusalem," in: *Freiburger Rundbrief*, New Series 5:3:178–86; J. Carlebach (ed.), *Wissenschaft des Judentums. Anfaenge der Judaistik in Europa* (1992); D. Ellenson, *Wissenschaft des Judentums, Historical Consciousness, and Jewish Faith: The Diverse Paths of Frankel, Auerbach, and Halevy*, Leo Baeck Memorial Lecture, 48 (2004); N.N. Glatzer, "The Beginnings of Modern Jewish Studies," in: idem, *Essays in Jewish Thought* (1978); E. Hollender, "'Verachtung kann Unwissenheit nicht entschulding.' – die Verteidigung der Wissenschaft des Judentums gegen die Angriffe Paul de Lagarde. 1884–1887," in: *Frankfurt Judaistische Beitraege*, 30 (2003), 169–205; R. Horwitym, "German Romanticism and its Influence on 'The Science of Judaism," in: *Proceedings of the 8th World Congress of Jewish Studies*, Division B (1982), 107–14 (Heb.); A. Jospe (ed.), *Studies in Jewish Thought. An Anthology of German-Jewish Scholarship* (1981); P. Mendes-Flohr, "Wissenschaft des Judentums at the Fin-de-siécle," in: M. Graetz and A. Mattioli (eds.), *Krisenwahrnehmungen im Fin de siécle: Juedische und katholische Bildungseliten in Deutschland und der Schweiz* (1997), 67–82; M.A. Meyer, "Two Persistent Tensions within *Wissenschaft des Judentums*," in: *Modern Judaism*, 24:2; (May 2004), 105–19; T. Rahe, "Leopold Zunz und die Wissenschaft des Judentums. Zum 100. Todestag von Leopold Zunz," in: *Judaica*, 42:3 (1986), 188–99; P. Schaefer, "Judaistik – juedische Wissenschaft in Deutschland heute. Historische Identitaet und Nationalitaet," in: *Saeculum. Jahrbuch fuer Universalgeschichte* (1991), 199–216; M. Schluelter, "Juedische Geschichtkonyeptionen der Neuyeit. Die Entwuerfe von Nachman Krochmal und Heinrich Graetz," in: *Frankfurter Judaistische Beitraege* (October 1990), 175–205; I. Schorsch, *From Text to Context. The Turn to History in Modern* Judaism (1994); G. Scholem, *Judaica*, 6: Wissenschaft des Judentums (1997); E. Schulin, "Zur Geschichteder Wissenschaft des Judentums," in: *Storia della Storiografia*, 30 (1996), 135–39; P. Simon-Nahum, "Wissenschaft des Judentums in Germany and the Science of Judaism in France in the Nineteenth Century: Tradition and Modernity in Scholarship" (Comment, Nils Römer), in: M. Brenner, V. Caron, and U.R. Kaufmann (eds.), *Jewish Emancipation Reconsidered. The French and German Models* (2003), 39–54; H. Soussan, *The Science of Judaism: From Leopold Zunz to Leopold Lucas*, Brighton: Centre for German-Jewish Studies. University of Sussex (Winter 1999); H. Soussan, "The Gesellschaft zur Foerderung des Wissenschaft des Judentums, 1902–1915," in: *Leo Baeck Institute Year Book*, 46 (2001); 175–94; H. Wassermann, *False Start. Jewish Studies at German Universities during Weimar Republic* (2003); N. Waszek, "Hegel, Mendelssohn, Spinoza. Beitraege der Philosophie zur Wissenschaft des Judentums? Eduard Gans und die philosophischen Quellen des 'Veriens fuer Kultur und Wissenschaft der Juden," in: *Menora* (1999), 187–215; C. Wiese, *Wissenschaft des Judentums und protestantische Theologie im wihelmanischen Deutschland. Ein Schrei in Leere?* (1999); K. Wilhelm (ed.), *Wissenschaft des Judentums im deutschen Sprachbereich. Ein Querschnitt*, Schriftenreihe Wissenschaftlicher Abhaldlungen des Leo Baeck Instituts, 16, 2 vols. (1967).

[Benzion Dinur (Dinaburg)]

WISSOTZKY, KALONYMUS ZE'EV (1824–1904), merchant, philanthropist, and supporter of *Ḥibbat Zion. Born in Zhagare (Kovno province), Wissotzky attended yeshivot and then tried his hand at agriculture. Having failed, he became a businessman and, in 1858, he moved to Moscow, where he established the famous tea firm that bears his name (*Aḥad Ha-Am was at one time manager of its London branch). He became a wealthy man and took an interest in public affairs, especially by subsidizing charitable institutions and causes. Wissotzky was one of the earliest adherents and supporters of the Ḥibbat Zion movement in Russia. In 1885 he visited Ereẓ Israel on behalf of the movement and prepared a survey of the general condition of the *yishuv* and of the new settlements that was to have a profound effect upon the practical work of Ḥovevei Zion in the country. For the rest of his life, he maintained his philanthropic activities, supporting Hebrew literature in particular. (*Ha-Shilo'ah, the Hebrew monthly, was financed by him in the first years of its existence.) Under Aḥad Ha-Am's influence he donated 20,000 rubles for the publication of a Hebrew encyclopedia for Jewish studies (1894). This project being canceled, the money was given instead to the society of *Marbei Haskalah* in Russia. According to his will, his entire share in the Wissotzky tea firm (one million rubles) was given to charity, including national Jewish purposes, among them the establishment of the Haifa Technion. In 1898 he published *Kevuẓat Mikhtavim* ("Collection of Letters"), which contains his impressions of the trip to Ereẓ Israel and various other documents relating to his activities in behalf of Ḥibbat Zion.

BIBLIOGRAPHY: M.M. Dolitzky, *Mofet la-Rabbim* (1892); A. Druyanow, *Ketavim le-Toledot Ḥibbat-Ẓivyon ve-Yishuv Ereẓ-Yisrael*, 3 vols. (1919–32), indices; M. ben Hillel Hacohen, *Olami*, 5 (1929), 63–70.

[Getzel Kressel]

WISTRICH, ROBERT S. (1945–), British-Israeli historian and writer on antisemitism. One of the best-known contemporary historians of antisemitism and related topics, Robert Wistrich was born in the Soviet Union but lived in England. He was educated at Cambridge and London Universities. Wistrich held chairs at London University and the Hebrew University of Jerusalem. From 2002 he was director of the Vidal Sassoon International Center for the Study of Antisemitism in Israel. His many books include *Revolutionary Jews From Marx to Trotsky* (1976), *Socialism and the Jews* (1982), and *Antisemitism: The Longest Hatred* (1991), which was made into a successful television series.

[William D. Rubinstein (2nd ed.)]

WITKON, ALFRED (1910–1984), Israeli jurist. Born in Berlin, Witkon settled in Palestine in 1935 and engaged in private practice and teaching at the Jerusalem Law School until 1948, when he joined the Israel Defense Forces, becoming a captain in the Legal Corps. He was president of the Jerusalem District Court from 1948 to 1954, when he was nominated to the Supreme Court. He lectured on tax legislation at the Hebrew University of Jerusalem and at Tel Aviv University and published numerous contributions to law journals, and in particular in the Israel Law Review. His major publications, all of which are in Hebrew, were *Law and Society* (1954), *Law and Politics* (1965), and *Laws of Taxation* (1969).

BIBLIOGRAPHY: *Jerusalem Post* Archives.

[Alexander Zvielli]

WITNESS (Heb. עֵד), one that has personal knowledge of an event or a fact. The evidence of at least two witnesses was required for convicting the accused (Num. 35:30; Deut. 17:6; 19:15; cf. I Kings 21:10, 13). Commercial transactions of importance took place in the presence of witnesses at the gate of the town (Gen. 23; Ruth 4); when a document was drawn up, it was signed by witnesses (Jer. 32: 12). The witness of a grave offence, such as enticement to idolatry, was bound by law to expose the offender; if the penalty for the crime was stoning, the witness was obliged to throw the first stone (Deut. 13:7ff.; cf. Lev. 24:11; Num. 15:33). False testimony is banned (Ex. 20:14 [16]; 23:1; Deut. 5:17 [20]; cf. Prov. 6:19; 14:25, et al.). The convicted false witness bears the penalty that would have been inflicted upon the accused (Deut. 19:16–21; cf. Sus. 60–62; Jos., Ant. 4:219; Code of Hammurapi, 1–4-Pritchard, Texts, 166).

A curse could be publicly uttered against a witness who withholds testimony (Lev. 5:1; Prov. 29:24; cf. Judg. 17:2). Lasting inanimate objects, such as stones (Gen. 31:48), the moon (Ps. 89:38), or poems can be invoked as witnesses: "Therefore, write down this poem and teach it to the people of Israel; put it in their mouths, in order that this poem may be my witness against the people of Israel" (Deut. 31:19; cf. vs 21, 26). The Lord Himself is sometimes called upon as witness (Gen. 31:50; Mal. 2:14), or as a prosecuting witness (I Sam. 12:5; Jer. 29:23; 49:5; Micah 1:2; Mal. 3:5). By its very existence, Israel is a witness of the fact that God is Redeemer and Lord of history (Isa. 43:9–10; 44:6–9). There is nothing in biblical law concerning the qualification of witnesses, but, according to Josephus, the credibility of the witnesses is established by their past life, while neither women nor slaves were allowed to testify (Jos., Ant. 4:219).

In Jewish Law

DEFINITION. Jewish law distinguishes between attesting and testifying witnesses. The former are required to be present at, and then and there attest, formal legal acts which failing such attestation, are normally invalid; the latter are required to testify in court, either to an act previously attested by them or to any fact they have witnessed. The rules on competency (see below) apply to testifying witnesses only. a document duly attested by at least two attesting witnesses and confirmed by the court (see Sh. Ar., ḤM 46:7–8) is admitted as evidence and equivalent to oral testimony in civil cases, and need not be proved by testifying witnesses (Sh. Ar., ḤM 28:12).

The distinction between testifying and attesting witnesses has practical significance also for purposes of modern Israel law. While the validity of an act governed by Jewish law (e.g., marriage or divorce) may depend on the competency under Jewish law of the attesting witnesses, which will have to be determined according to Jewish law, the competency of testifying witnesses, even concerning acts governed by Jewish law, will always be determined by the law of the court (*lex fori*) in which the evidence is taken.

THE TWO-WITNESSES RULE. As a general rule, no single witness alone is competent to attest or testify: there must always be at least two (Deut. 19:15; Sif. Deut. 188; Sot. 2b; Sanh. 30a; Yad, Edut 5:1). The following are some of several exceptions to the general rule: whenever two testifying witnesses would be sufficient to prove a claim, one is sufficient to require the defendant to take an *oath that the claim is unfounded (Shev. 40a; Ket. 87b; BM 3b–4a; Yad, To'en 1:1); thus, in the case of widow claiming on her *ketubbah* or the holder of a bill claiming on it, where a single witness has testified that the claim had already been settled, the interested party will be required to take the oath before being allowed to recover (Ket. 9:7; Sh. Ar., ḤM 84:5). Conversely, a party who has partly admitted a claim will be excused from taking the oath if he is corroborated by at least a single witness (*Rema* ḤM 87:6; *Beit Yosef* ḤM 75 n. 3); and the testimony of a single depositary who still held the deposit was considered sufficient to prove which of the rival claims to a deposit was valid (Git. 64a; Sh. Ar., ḤM 56:1). A woman is allowed to remarry on the testimony of a single witness that her husband is dead (Yev. 16:7; Eduy. 6:1, 8:5; Ber. 27a; Ket. 22b–23a); and the testimony of a single witness is normally sufficient in matters of ritual (Git. 2b–3a; Yad, Edut 11:7). In criminal cases, both witnesses must have witnessed the whole event together (cf. Mak. 1:9), but in civil cases, testimonies of various witnesses to particular facts, as well as a witness and a document, may be combined to satisfy the two-witnesses rule (Sh. Ar., ḤM 30:6).

COMPETENCY. Maimonides lists ten classes of persons who are not competent to attest or testify, namely: women, slaves, minors, lunatics, the deaf, the blind, the wicked, the contemptible, relatives, and the interested parties (Yad, Edut 9:1).

(1) *Women.* By the method of *gezerah shavah* (see *Interpretation), it is derived from Scripture that only men can be competent witnesses. Maimonides gives as the reason for the disqualification of women the fact that the bible uses the masculine form when speaking of witnesses (Sif. Deut. 190; Shev. 30a; Sh. Ar., ḤM 35:14; Yad, Edut 9:2), but Joseph Caro questioned the validity of this derivation in view of the fact that "the whole Torah always uses the masculine form" (*Kesef Mishneh* to Yad, Edut 9:2). Another reason was suggested in the Talmud: that the place of a woman was in her home and not in court (Shev. 30a; cf. Git. 46a), as the honor of the king's daughter was within the house (Ps. 45:14. It is perhaps

noteworthy that the Tur (ḤM 35) omits women from the list of incompetent witnesses). Women are admitted as competent witnesses in matters within their particular knowledge, for example, on customs or events in places frequented only by women (*Rema* ḤM 35:14; *Darkhei Moshe* ḤM 35, n. 3; *Beit Yosef, ibid.*, n. 15; *Terumat ha-Deshen* Resp. no. 353); in matters of their own and other women's purity (Ket. 72a; Ket 2:6); for purposes of identification, especially of other women (Yev. 39b); or in matters outside the realm of strict law (BK 114b). In post-talmudic times, the evidence of women was often admitted where there were no other witnesses available (cf. e.g., Resp. Maharam of Rothenburg, ed. Prague, no. 920; Resp. Maharik no. 179), or in matters not considered important enough to bother male witnesses (Resp. Maharik no. 190; *Sefer Kol Bo* no. 116). In Israel, the disqualification of women as witnesses was abolished by the Equality of Women's Rights Act, 5711 – 1951.

(2) *Slaves*. Witnesses must be free Jewish citizens (*Benei Ḥorin u-Venei Berit*; BK 1:3), excluding both slaves and non-Jews (BK 15a; Yad, Edut 9:4; Sh. Ar., ḤM 34:19). The evidence of non-Jews is admitted if secular law so requires (*Maggid Mishneh*, Malveh 27:1), as well as to attest or identify documents made in non-Jewish courts, or whenever the court sees no reason to doubt their objectivity (*Tashbeẓ* 1:78; *Beit Yosef* ḤM 34, n. 22; *Baḥ* ḤM 34:32; *Keẓot ha-Ḥoshen* 68, n. 1; Tos. to Git. 9b).

(3) *Minors*. A person is incompetent as a witness until he reaches the age of 13. Between the ages of 13 and 20, he is competent as a witness with regard to movable property, but in respect of immovable property he is competent only if he is found to have the necessary understanding and experience (BB 155b; Yad, Edut. 9:8; Sh. Ar., ḤM 35:3). From the age of 20, all disqualification by reason of age is removed.

(4) *Lunatics*. In this category are included not only insane persons (for definitions see *Penal Law), but also idiots and epileptics (Yad, Edut 9:9–10; Sh. Ar., ḤM 35:8–10).

(5) *The Deaf*. Both the deaf and the dumb are included in this category (see *Deaf-Mute). "Despite the fact that their vision may be excellent and their intelligence perfect, they must testify by word of their mouth, or must hear the warning which the court administers to them" (see *Practice and Procedure), and as they cannot speak or hear, they cannot testify (Yad, Edut 9:11; Sh. Ar., ḤM 35:11).

(6) *The Blind*. "Despite the fact that they may be able to recognize voices and thus identify people, they are by Scripture disqualified as witnesses, for it is written, 'whether he hath seen or known' [Lev. 5:1] – only one who can see can testify" (Yad, Edut 9:12; Sh. Ar., ḤM 35:12).

(7) *The Wicked*. According to the Bible, "the wicked" or "the guilty" are unjust witnesses (Ex. 23:1), therefore they are a priori disqualified. They may be divided into five groups: criminals, swindlers, perjurers, illiterates, and informers. "Wicked" or "guilty" are epithets attributed to persons who have committed capital offenses (Num. 35:31) or who are liable to be flogged (Deut. 25:2), hence these are incompetent witnesses (Yad, Edut 10:2; Sh. Ar., ḤM 34:2). A person who has committed any other offense or who is liable to any other punishment is also deemed incompetent as a witness, although not in the Bible (*Rema* ḤM 34:2). Into the category of swindlers fall thieves and robbers (Sh. Ar., ḤM 34:7); usurers (*ibid.*, 34:10); tricksters, gamblers, and gamesters (Sanh. 3:3; Sh. Ar., ḤM 34:16), as well as idlers and vagabonds who are suspected of spending their leisure in criminal activities (Yad, Edut 10:4; Sh. Ar., ḤM 34:16). Tax collectors who do not work for a fixed salary, but receive as remuneration a portion of the moneys collected, are suspected of appropriating more than is due to them, and therefore are incompetent witnesses (Yad, loc. cit.; Sh. Ar., ḤM 34:14); another reason for their disqualification was said to be that they were suspected of undue preferences and discriminations in assessing tax liabilities (*Rema* ḤM 34:14). Once a witness was found guilty of perjury, he would no longer be a competent witness, even after he had made good any damage caused by his false testimony (Sanh. 27a; Yad, loc. cit. Sh. Ar., ḤM 34:8). A man who has no inkling of Bible and Mishnah, nor of civilized standards of conduct (*derekh erez*), is presumed to be idle and disorderly (Kid. 1:10) and therefore incompetent as a witness (Kid. 40b; Yad, Edut 11:1; Sh. Ar., ḤM 34:17). This presumption is rebuttable by evidence that, notwithstanding the man's illiteracy, his conduct is irreproachable (Yad, Edut 11:2–4; Sh. Ar., loc. cit.). A fortiori, agnostics (*eppikoresim*) and heretics, including those who transgress law or ritual from conviction or malice, are wholly and irrevocably disqualified (Yad, Edut 11:10; Sh. Ar., ḤM 34:22). Though not technically transgressors of the law, *informers are considered worse than criminals and hence incompetent (Yad, loc. cit.; Sh. Ar., loc. cit.).

(8) *The Contemptible*. It is presumed that people who do not conform to the conventions of society, for example, by eating in the streets (Kid. 40b), or walking around naked while working (BK 86b), or accepting alms from non-Jews in public (Sanh. 26b), would not shrink from perjuring themselves, and therefore are incompetent witnesses (Yad, Edut 11:5; Sh. Ar., ḤM 34:18).

(9) *Relatives*. The biblical injunction that parents shall not be put to death "for" their children, nor children "for" their parents (Deut. 24:16), was interpreted as prohibiting the testimony of parents against children and of children against parents (Sif. Deut. 280; Sanh. 27b), and served as the source for the disqualification of relatives in general (Yad, Edut 13:1). The Mishnah lists as disqualified relatives: father, brother, uncle, brother-in-law, stepfather, father-in-law, and their sons and sons-in-law (Sanh. 3:4); the rule was extended to cover nephews and first cousins (Yad, Edut 13:3; Sh. Ar., ḤM 33:2). Where the relationship is to a woman, the disqualification extends to her husband (Yad, Edut 13:6; Sh. Ar., ḤM 33:3). The fact that a disqualified kinsman does not maintain any connection with the party concerned is irrelevant (Yad, Edut 13:15; Sh. Ar., ḤM 33:10). Witnesses who are related to one another are incompetent to attest or testify together (Mak. 6a); similarly witnesses related to any of the judges are incompetent (Sh. Ar.,

ḤM 33:17). As relatives are incompetent to testify for or against the party to whom they are related, a fortiori the party himself is incompetent to testify for or against himself, for "a man is related to himself" (San. 9b–10a; Yev. 25b). But while the incompetency of the relatives results only in their testimony being inadmissible as evidence, there can be no "testimony" of a party at all (*Piskei ha-Rosh* Mak. 13–14; Rosh. Resp. no. 60:1; Nov. Ramban Mak. 6b; Nov. Ran Sanh. 9b; Resp. Ribash nos. 169 and 195), and everything he says in court is properly classified as pleading.

(10) *The Interested Party.* A witness is disqualified where any benefit may accrue to him from his testimony (BB 43a; Yad, Edut 15:1), as where he has some stake in the outcome of the proceedings (Sh. Ar., ḤM 37:1; Yad, Edut 15:4). However, the benefit must be present and immediate and not speculative only (Sh. Ar., ḤM 37:10). The question whether some such direct or indirect benefit may accrue to a witness is often puzzling: "these things depend on the discretion of the judge and the depth of his understanding as to what is the gist of the case at issue" (Yad, Edut 16:4; Sh. Ar., ḤM 37:21). It is a "well-established custom" that where local usages or regulations are in issue townspeople are competent witnesses, even though they may, as local residents, have some interest in the matter (Rosh, Resp. 5:4; Sh. Ar., ḤM 37:22). The same "custom" would appear to apply to attesting witnesses who were appointed as such by authority (cf. Sh. Ar., ḤM 33:18). In criminal cases, there is no disqualifying "interest"; thus, the kinsmen of the murdered man are competent witnesses against the murderer, those of the assaulted against the assailant, and the victim of an offense against the accused (*Rema* ḤM 33:16; *Siftei Kohen* ḤM 33 n. 16).

DISQUALIFICATION. No witness may say that he is (or was) wicked so as to disqualify himself from attesting or testifying (Sanh. 9b; Yad, Edut 12:2; Sh. Ar., ḤM 34:25). A party who wishes to disqualify witnesses of the other party has to prove their incompetency by the evidence of at least two other competent witnesses (Sanh. 3:1; Yad, Edut 12:1; Sh. Ar. ḤM 34:25). Disqualification as a witness is not regarded as a penalty, and hence no previous warning is required; but in cases of improper or contemptible conduct and minor transgressions, it has been suggested that a person should not be disqualified as a witness unless previously warned that this would happen if he persisted in his conduct (Yad, loc. cit.; Sh. Ar., ḤM 34:24).

Where a witness attested an act or a document, he cannot testify that he was incompetent to do so (Ket. 18b & 19b; Yad, Edut 3:7; Sh. Ar., ḤM 46:37). It might be otherwise if his signature could be identified only by his own testimony: if he could be heard to deny his signature, he ought also to be heard to say that his signature was worthless (Ket. 2:3; Sh. Ar., ḤM loc. cit.) – always provided he did not incriminate himself.

Where the court has reason to suspect that a person offered as a witness is incompetent, it may decline to admit his testimony (*Rema* ḤM 34:25; Yad, To'en 2:3), and ought to turn him down as an attesting witness (Sh. Ar., ḤM 92:5 and *Siftei Kohen* ad loc.). Where a witness has given evidence, and it subsequently transpires that he was incompetent, his evidence will be regarded as wrongly admitted and the case be reopened only if the incompetence was derived from Scripture or had been announced by public proclamation (Sanh. 26b; Yad, Edut 11:6; Sh. Ar., ḤM 34:23). A person called to attest or testify together with another person whom he knows to be incompetent as a witness must decline to attest or testify, even though the incompetence of the other is not yet known or proven to the court (Yad, Edut 10:1; Sh. Ar., ḤM 34:1). The rationale of this rule appears to be that since the incompetence of any one witness invalidates the evidence of the whole group of witnesses to which he belongs (Mak. 1:8; Yad, Edut 5:3; Sh. Ar., ḤM 36:1), if the first man attested or testified notwithstanding the other's incompetence, the evidence would be nullified (cf. *Siftei Kohen* ḤM 34, n. 3). In civil cases, parties may stipulate that, notwithstanding any incompetence, the evidence of witnesses named shall be accepted and acted upon by the court (Sanh. 3:2; Yad, Sanhedrin 7:2; Sh. Ar., ḤM 22:1).

Disqualification no longer holds: in the case of criminals, after their punishment is completed (Yad, Edut 12:4; Sh. Ar., ḤM 34:29); in the case of wicked persons not liable to punishment, when it is proved to the satisfaction of the court that they have repented and that their conduct is now irreproachable (*ibid.*) – there are detailed provisions as to what acts constitute sufficient proof of repentance (Yad, Edut 12:5–10; Sh. Ar., ḤM 34:29–35); and in the case of relatives, after the relationship or affinity has come to an end (Yad, Edut 14:1; Sh. Ar., ḤM 33:12).

REMUNERATION. As a financial interest in the testimony disqualifies the witness, the stipulation or acceptance of remuneration for testifying invalidates the evidence (Bek. 4:6). However, where the witness has returned the fee he received before testifying, his evidence is admissible; the acceptance of remuneration in itself is not a cause of incompetence, but is visited with the sanction of invalidating the evidence as a deterrent only (*Rema* ḤM 34:18). The rule prohibiting remuneration is confined to testifying witnesses only; attesting witnesses may always be remunerated (*ibid.*) and there are express provisions for the remuneration of witnesses attesting divorces (Sh. Ar., EH 130:21). A man suspected of accepting money for giving evidence is not a credible witness and should never be believed (Tosef. Bek. 3:8). A man who hires false witnesses to testify for him is answerable to Heaven, though not himself criminally responsible (see *Penal Law; Yad, Edut 17:7; Sh. Ar., ḤM 32:2; *Rema* ad loc.).

DUTY TO TESTIFY. Any person able to testify as one who has seen or learned of the matter who does not come forward to testify is liable to punishment (Lev. 5:1), but the punishment will be meted out to him by God only (see *Divine Punishment; BK 55b–56a). While in criminal cases the witness is under obligation to come forward and testify of his own accord, in civil cases the duty to testify arises only when the man is summoned to do so (Yad, Edut 1:1; Sh. Ar., ḤM 28:1). Kings are exempt from the duty to testify (Sanh. 2:2; Yad, Edut 11:9) and though high priests are generally exempt, they must testify for the king (Yad, Edut 1:3). The duty relates only to matters which the witness has seen himself, or which he has heard from the mouth of the accused or a party to the action; a man may not testify to things of which he has no personal knowledge (*Rema* ḤM 28:1), nor may he testify on what he has heard other people telling him, however true and trustworthy it may appear to him (Yad, Edut 17:1,5), and any such testimony is regarded as false (*ibid.*).

Persons who were 'planted' and hidden on the premises to overlook a certain act or overhear certain words are not admitted as witnesses (Yad, Edut 17:3), except in the case of prosecution against inciters to idolatry (Sanh. 7:10; Sanh. 29a, 67a). A witness whose memory is defective may be allowed to refresh it by looking at what he had written at the time, or even by listening to the evidence of other witnesses (Ket. 20b; Yad, Edut 8:2; Sh. Ar., ḤM 28:14; *Beit Yosef* ḤM 28, n. 13–14), but not by what the party tells him, unless that party is a scholar and not suspected of using undue influence (Yad, Edut 8:3). Yet the fact that the witness recognizes some contemporary handwriting as his own does not render the writing admissible in evidence if he does not remember the facts to which that writing relates (Sh. Ar., ḤM 38:13; cf. Yad, Edut 8:1). There is no presumption that the passage of time adversely affects any witness' memory (Sh. Ar., *ibid.*).

EXAMINATION. The biblical injunction, "thou shalt then inquire and make search and ask diligently" (Deut. 13:15), was literally interpreted to require testifying witnesses to be subjected to three different kinds of examination: enquiry (*ḥakirah*), investigation (*derishah*), and interrogation (*bedikah*; Sanh. 40a). Originally, the rule was held to apply in all cases, both civil and criminal (Sanh. 4:1), but it was later relaxed to apply in criminal cases only, and possibly in cases of tort, so as not to render the recovery of debts too cumbersome and thus "shut the doors before borrowers" (Sanh. 3a, 32a; Yev. 122b; Yad, Edut 3:1; Sh. Ar., ḤM 30:1). It is the duty of the court, Maimonides says: "to interrogate the witnesses and examine them and question them extensively and probe into their accuracy and refer them back to previous questions so as to make them desist from or change their testimony if it was in any way faulty; but the court must be very careful lest, by such examination, 'the witness might learn to lie'" (Yad, Edut 1:4 based on Sanh. 32b). The purpose of the examination is, of course, to find out if the witnesses are truthful and consistent; even though all potentially untruthful witnesses have already been sifted and excluded by disqualification, further precautionary rules were deemed necessary to make sure of the witness' veracity.

Ḥakirah is the examination relating to the time and place at which the event at issue occurred (Sanh. 5:1; Sanh. 40b). Every examination starts with questions of this kind, which are indispensable (Nov. Ran. Sanh. 42a). The particular legal importance of this part of the examination is due to its function as sole cause for allegations of perjury (Yad, Edut 1:5).

Derishah is the examination relating to the substance of the facts at issue: who did it? what did he do? how did he do it? did you warn him beforehand? etc. (Sanh. 5:1, 40b). Or, in civil cases, how do you know the defendant is liable to the plaintiff? (Sanh. 3:6). As this line of examination is likewise indispensable, it is regarded in law as part of the *ḥakirah* (Yad, Edut 1:4).

Bedikah is a sort of cross-examination relating to accompanying and surrounding circumstances and not directly touching upon the facts in issue (Yad, Edut 1:6). The more a judge conducts examinations of this kind the better (Sanh. 5:2), because it leads to the true facts being established (Deut. 13:15; Sif. Deut. 93, 149; Sanh. 41a). On the other hand, questioning of this kind is dispensable, and judgment may be given on the testimony of witnesses who have not been so cross-examined (Nov. Ran Sanh. 40a). The conduct and amount of cross-examinations is at the discretion of the judges; they ought to insist on it whenever there is the least suspicion of an attempt to mislead or deceive the court (*din merummeh*; Shev. 30b–31a; Yad, Sanh. 24:3 and Edut 3:2; Sh. Ar., ḤM 15:3). Such suspicion may arise, for instance, where several witnesses testify in exactly the same words – which would not normally happen unless they had learned their testimony by heart (TJ, Sanh. 3:8; *Piskei ha-Rosh*, Sanh. 3:32; Sh. Ar., ḤM 28:10). In these cases, cross-examination should concentrate on points on which suspicion arose and not be allowed to spread boundlessly (Nov. Ran, Sanh. 32b; Ribash, Resp. no. 266; *Rema* ḤM 15:3). If, notwithstanding all cross-examination, the witnesses are consistent in their evidence but the judge is not satisfied that they are telling the truth, he should disqualify himself and let another judge take his place (Shev. 30b–31a; Sanh. 32b; Yad, Sanh. 24:3; Sh. Ar., ḤM 15:3), or he might even, if satisfied that there had been an attempt to mislead the court, furnish the innocent party with a certificate in writing to the effect that no other judge should entertain the suit against him (Rosh, Resp. no. 68:20).

DISPROOF. Where two sets of witnesses contradict each other on a matter material to the issue, i.e., under either *ḥakirah* or *derishah* as distinguished from *bedikah* (Yad, Edut 2:1), the evidence of either set is insufficient in law to establish the facts at issue. The reason is that there is no knowing which of the two groups of witnesses is testifying to the truth and which is lying (Yad, Edut 18:2, 22:1; Sh. Ar., ḤM 31:1). Where, however, there are inconsistencies or contradictions within the evidence of one set of witnesses and none within the other, the evidence of the consistent group will have to be accepted – the other being dismissed as untruthful because inconsistent. After a fact has been established judicially on the strength of the testimony of two (or more) consistent witnesses, the findings of fact will not necessarily be affected by contradictory witnesses coming forward after judgment (TJ, Yev. 15:5), but the court may always reopen a case where fresh evidence becomes available (see *Practice and Procedure).

Contradictions on matters not material to the issue will not normally affect the admissibility of the testimony (Sanh. 41a; Nov. Ran ad loc.), though the court may reject the testimony as unreliable because of contradictions on immaterial points (Yad, Edut 2:2). It seems that in civil cases, contradictions must always relate to matters material to the issue in order to warrant their rejection as insufficient (Sanh. 30b; Yad, Edut 3:2; Sh. Ar., ḤM 30:2). Where one witness positively testifies to a fact material to the issue, and the other testifies that the fact is unknown to him, the testimony of the former is deemed to be contradicted; where the fact testified to is not material to the issue, the ignorance of the second witness does not amount to contradiction (Yad, Edut 2:1). As there is no knowing whether the contradicting or contradicted evidence is true, neither will be regarded as perjury. While evidence of perjury must be given in the presence of the perjured witnesses, evidence contradicting previously given testimony may be given in the absence of the former witnesses (Ket. 19b–20a; Yad, Edut 18:5).

Where the evidence of witnesses to the effect that a man is "wicked" and hence incompetent to testify is contradicted by other evidence, even though the first evidence is insufficient in law to disqualify him, the man will not be admitted as a witness because of the doubts arising on his credibility (Yad, Edut 12:3); but there is a strong dissent holding that every man is to be presumed competent until proven otherwise by valid and conclusive evidence (Tos. to Ket. 26b s.v. *Anan*; *Shitah Mekubbeẓet* Ket. 26b).

[Haim Hermann Cohn]

Further Aspects

DEFINITION. In contrast to Western legal systems, in which the litigant has the right to testify, Jewish law distinguishes between litigants and witnesses, and the laws governing the plaintiff and the defendant are distinct from the laws of testimony. Research has thus far illuminated the foundation and legal rationale for the distinction between a litigant – who may plead his/her own case but not testify – and a witness, who testifies for another (Hefetz, *Mikkumah shel Edut ba-Mishpat ha-Ivri*). In modern times, jurists have proposed anchoring the principle that "A litigant cannot be a witness" in the Israeli laws of evidence (Draft Bill for Amendment to Testimony in Civil Cases, by Dr. S. Ginnosar and Dr. Y. Kister).

Certain scholars have attempted to characterize testimony as a special means of proving matters and deciding a case. The institution of testimony (the set of witnesses) is a quasi-judicial one for the determination of facts, similar to the jury in Anglo-American law. Qualification for testimony is determined by competency requirements that are fundamentally similar to those for membership in the judiciary (Hefetz, *Mikkumah shel Edut*; Ettinger, *The Role of Witnesses*).

A person's classification as a witness and his belonging to a set of witnesses turns on the question of whether the witnesses' function is to witness a particular act or to testify in court (this distinction is largely similar to that between constitutive witnesses, *eidei kiyyum*, and testifying witnesses, *eidei ra'ayah*). Witnesses appearing in court officially receive that status at the stage at which the court administers the admonishment (Mishnah, Sanh. 3:6; 4:5). However, the criterion differs regarding witnesses who observe an event for the purposes of attesting to it. One scholar (Radzyner, *Hatra'ah be-Edim u-Teḥilat Edut*) suggested that Rabba's statement in the Talmud, "Did you come to observe an event or to testify?" refers to a case in which the witnesses were summoned in advance to witness a certain act (Makk. 6a). According to this understanding, in all cases in which the witnesses are called upon to attest to an event, or to sign a document, when a question of their legal competency arises the purpose of their coming must be ascertained. If a relative or legally incompetent person states that he came to testify, the contract is disqualified. The first stage in defining the summoned witnesses as a set of witnesses begins from the moment they intended to attest to the event, and not just to observe it.

TESTIMONY RECORDED IN LEGAL DOCUMENTS (SHETAR). A central rule regarding the validity of signed documents as admissible evidence is the dictum of Resh Lakish, that "signatures of witnesses to a document are as reliable as if their evidence had been investigated in the *bet din*." The accepted interpretation of this dictum is that this refers to biblical law, which makes a substantive distinction between attesting to a document and other forms of testimony (including the affidavit). In most forms of testimony one cannot waive the requirement that witnesses be interrogated by the court, whereas documents can be accepted as evidence without the court conducting any enquiry pertaining to the witnesses who signed it. On the other hand, one of the scholars (Sinai, *The Geonic and Maimonidean Approach to Testimony Recorded in Legal Documents*) demonstrated that certain 12th-century *rishonim* (e.g., Maim., Edut 3:4; R. Simḥah of Speyer, cited in *Mordekhai* on Kiddushin, pt. 569–570) had another conception, whose sources are found as early as the works of the *geonim* (see Rav Sherira Gaon, cited in *Sefer ha-Terumot*, Pt. 13, sec. 1:3), and which is also consistent with the simple meaning of the talmudic sources. According to this conception, the biblical conditions for the admissibility of testimony do not distinguish between attesting to a document and other forms of testimony. Under biblical law all forms of testimony must be given by witnesses in court, thus enabling their examination and interrogation by the court, in accordance with the talmudic rule. "By biblical law, both monetary and capital cases require inquiry and investigation" (Sanh. 32a); the admissibility of written testimony was the result of a rabbinic enactment, "so as not to close the door to borrowers" (Maim., *ibid*). Nevertheless, even according to the latter view, written testimony is valid even under biblical law in cases of ritual matters (*issur*) and especially regarding a *get*, because these as distinct from capital and monetary cases, do not need to be clarified by the court (Maim., Yad, Gerushin 7:24; cf. Sinai's interpretation, ibid., p. 126). This is likewise the conception evinced by Maimonides' comments on examination and interrogation of the testimony that frees a woman from the bonds of *aginut*, regarding which he writes that the Sages allowed a woman to remarry on the basis of testimony that the husband had died, "even on the basis of a written document, and without examination and interrogation." The reason for this is that "the Torah insists upon testimony by two witnesses and the other rules concerning testimony only in those matters, the truth of which cannot be ascertained except out of the mouths of witnesses and by their testimony, as, for example, when they testify that A has slain B or has made a loan to B. But in matters that can be ascertained through means other than the testimony of the particular witness, where he cannot clear himself if he is exposed as a false witness, as when he has testified that so-and-so is dead, the Torah does not so insist, because in such cases it is uncommon for a witness to testify to a falsehood" (Yad, Gerushin 13:29).

In explaining this ruling, one of the scholars focused on the basic distinction between matters requiring a court ruling, such as capital and civil cases, regarding which the stringent rules of testimony are applied, and ritual matters, including the release of an *agunah*, in which the matters permitted or prohibited are applicable by themselves, irrespective of the court ruling (Sinai, *Investigation of Agunah Witnesses*, 360–364).

THE TWO WITNESS RULE. One of the scholars showed that the rule "by two witnesses shall a matter be established" should not be regarded as an all-inclusive and rigid rule and that, in fact, the courts rely as a matter of course on less than two witnesses, as well as on circumstantial evidence (H.S. Hefetz, "According to Two Witnesses?: Circumstantial Evidence in the Bet Din in Practice" (Hebrew), *Takdim*, 2 (1989), 59–84. See also *Evidence.)

In one of the decisions of the Israeli Supreme Court, Justice Silberg relied on the concept that testimony of one witness is sufficient to compel an oath by the opposing litigant, in support of the view that testimony of one witness is only considered as contested if it was rejected by opposing testimony (CA 88/49 *Rosen v. Biali*, 5 PD 72, 73, 78–80).

COMPETENCY. In any case of hearing testimony, courts operating on the basis of Jewish law are required to determine the competency of the witnesses, and in many cases are unable to accept the testimony of incompetent witnesses. Nonetheless, one of the foremost rabbinical judges, who subsequently served as chief rabbi of Israel, stressed that

> It goes without saying that the *bet din* is authorized to hear the truth from any person, in any form, to form an impression. Even where the witnesses are incompetent under halakhic principles, their testimony may aid them in drawing conclusions based on common sense presumptions (*umdana*) or as proof of an objective reality. In many cases, the court is empowered to use its discretion to rule in reliance on other forms of proof and common sense conclusions, even in the absence of valid testimony. (Rav A. Bakshi-Doron, "*Kabbalat Edim be-Bet ha-Din*," in: *Torah she-be-al Peh*, 22 (1981), 81–88, 84).

A comprehensive study by Hayyim Hefetz dealt with the status of circumstantial evidence (Hefetz, *Ra'ayot Nesibatiot*; on matters of evidence and presumption, see *Evidence). The difference between testimony proffered by competent witnesses as opposed to that of incompetent witnesses has been explained by one scholar (Ettinger, *The Role of Witnesses*) as being based on a fundamental distinction between testimony and credibility. This distinction is manifested in the willingness to accept testimony of incompetent witnesses (such as testimony for an *agunah,* that her husband died), even though they are not considered as "witnesses" in the formal sense, though their testimony is relied upon.

Women. The Scriptural source for the disqualification of women as witnesses is both amorphous and disputed. This substantiates the theory forwarded by one scholar, who stated that the disqualification of women as witnesses was an accepted rule among the talmudic sages, who attempted to establish its biblical source even though it was not of explicit scriptural origin (Ettinger, *Isha Ke-Ed be-Dinei Mamonot*, p. 245).

One scholar suggested that the historical reason for disqualification of women as witnesses was based, not on a supposed lack of intelligence, nor on a lack of understanding of the imperative of telling the truth, but rather because, inasmuch as women are not accustomed to dealings in the marketplace, they are not used to earning a living or dealing with public affairs. Their lack of understanding of the ways of the world and the market place, a skill acquired by virtue of practical encounter and dealings with other people, renders them unequipped to understand the actions of others and hence to testify regarding their actions (S. Albeck, *Ha-Ra'ayot be-Dinei ha-Talmud*, Ramat Gan, 1987, p. 97).

Both of these positions served to explain the legal, as opposed to the historical, reason for a woman's disqualification as a witness: is it owing to her lack of reliability (for she is liable to withdraw her testimony "having been tempted or out of fear"; see Tosefta Ket. 3:3, ed. Lieberman; Maim., Yad, Gerushin 13.29); or is the disqualification a "scriptural edict" (*gezerat ha-katuv*), and not based upon unreliability (Resp. Rashba, attributed to Naḥmanides, no. 128). The practical difference between the two approaches is crucial, as demonstrated by one of the scholars (Ettinger, *ibid.*, 249–50). If the disqualification is substantively based on the woman's lack of reliability, there could at least theoretically be a change in the law. Such a change would be effected by way of interpretation, assuming that the factual-social reality had changed, to the extent of eliminating any presumption of a difference of any nature between men and woman in terms of their reliability for testimony. On the other hand, if the disqualification is a formal one, the tendency would be to limit the scope of the prohibition, and to waive it under certain circumstances, in the same way as when the law is altered directly by force of an enactment.

The more lenient approach to acceptance of a woman's testimony is usually found in the Ashkenazi tradition, whereas the tendency of Spanish medieval scholars is to totally ban women as witnesses. It may be presumed that this dispute reflects differences in the status of women in the two parallel Jewish societies of that time. Scholars of that period have shown that Jewish women enjoyed a better status in Ashkenazi society than in Sephardi society, and that as such the Ashkenazi authorities did not hesitate to limit the scope of the prohibition on women as witnesses (Ettinger, *ibid.* 255).

Two chief rabbis of Israel commented on the issue of accepting women's testimony in our times, as follows: Rav Ouziel argued that a woman was disqualified as a witness because she was liable to lack precision in her testimony due to her lack of experience in commercial-market affairs. Based on this reasoning he infers that in all matters with which they are familiar, we may rely on their testimony, and that the community is therefore empowered to enact regulations to validate a woman's testimony in contemporary times (Resp. Mishpatei Uziel, ḤM no. 20). In this context, a significant step was taken by Rabbi Herzog, as indicated in his decisions given when serving on the Rabbinical Court of Appeals in 1948 (collection of decisions of the Chief Rabbinate, ed. Z. Warhaftig, 1985, p.11). Rav Herzog states that the rabbinical judge has discretion to evaluate the testimonies, and if he deems that the witnesses are telling the truth, he is even entitled to accept a woman's testimony.

The Wicked. The Talmud discusses the question of how to characterize a "wicked" person who is disqualified as a witness (Sanh. 27b). According to Rava, only the "wicked who robs" is disqualified – in other words, a person who transgressed an offense of a monetary nature. According to Abbaye, any "wicked" person is disqualified. The *halakhah* was codified in accordance with the latter view. Their dispute may quite possibly turn on the reason for disqualifying the wicked person for testimony. According to Abbaye, for whom the disqualification also applies to strictly religious offenses, its source lies in a Scriptural edict. Rava, however, who limits the disqualification to the financially wicked, apparently sees its source as being the unreliability of the witness who is a criminal (this interpretation is suggested by *Nimmukei Yosef* on Rif, ad loc. 5b of the Rif, s.v. *itmar*). From Maimonides *Mishnah Commentary*, in Sanhedrin 3:3, one scholar inferred (Sinai, *Be'ur Shitat ha-Rambam be-Inyan Kashrutam shel Resha'im le-Edut*), that a distinction must be made between one who violates prohibitions concerning monetary matters (*ḥamsan*), and one who transgresses non-monetary offences. With respect to the latter the prohibition derives from a Scriptural edict, whereas for the former there is a substantive rational reason – namely, the fear of perjury. A similar approach is taken by *Keẓot ha-Ḥoshen*, 52:1). This is also the approach evidenced in the comments of Justice H. Cohn regarding suspected tax evaders, of whom he writes that "This renders them suspect of perjury, for just as they do not recoil from obfuscations and lies in order to evade tax [or another kind of breach of the law], they will similarly not shy away from obfuscation and lies in order to win their case. This is the obvious rationale of the Torah in its disqualification of wicked persons as witnesses, inter alia 'those who take money that is not theirs' (in the language of Maimonides, *Edut* 10.4)" (CA 41/75 *Nili v Shlomi*, 30 (2) PD 3, 6–7).

It is suggested in the research literature that one view the disqualification of the wicked – even if they had not committed monetary offenses – as part of the overall approach of the Torah, and not just as a specific "Scriptural edict" (Sinai, *ibid.*, 298). There are numerous commandments in the Torah in respect of which the "wicked" are not considered as belonging to the community of Israel (Yad, Gezelah va-Avedah 11:2; Mamrim 5:12; Evel 1:10; Edut 11:1). On this basis, we may reasonably surmise that, with respect to testimony, the biblical innovation was that all wicked persons are disqualified for testimony, and as such they are subsumed within the general system of witnesses who are excluded from the Community of Israel. Conceivably, one could add that proffering testimony is regarded as a religious duty, in which not all can partake.

The reason for disqualifying the wicked for testimony has important legal ramifications in our times, regarding the issue of the competence of witnesses who are not religiously observant. In a 1948 judgment, Chief Rabbi Herzog wrote (*Collection of Decisions of the Chief Rabbinate,* ed. Z. Warhaftig, 1985, p. 137) that the offender's disqualification is rooted in his unreliability only, for which reason "one must have taken into consideration that in a time… and place where… non-observance is widespread… this kind of offense will not necessarily impugn the reliability of the witnesses." Consequently, in his view, "If it is clear to the Court that this person [i.e., who does not live a traditional religious life] is not likely to perjure himself for personal benefit, then he may be accepted as a valid witness."

Another legal ramification of the rationale for disqualifying the wicked for testimony that emerges from Maimonides' *Mishnah Commentary* (ibid.) relates to the possibility of the wicked person regaining the status of competent witnesses. As indicated by one of the scholars (Sinai, *ibid.*, 300–308), Maimonides' view is that, with respect to those who committed monetary offenses, their return to the status of legitimate witnesses is contingent upon their allaying our fears that they may perjure themselves for monetary gain. Accordingly, they must abandon "the path of the sinners," and their repentance must be unequivocal. The criterion for such repentance is that they be placed in a situation that invites the commission of the offense that they were accustomed to committing, yet despite having the opportunity of committing the offense, they desisted. This would constitute irrefutable proof of the sincerity of their repentance, that they had freed themselves of their lust for money, and thus we need no longer fear their return to the path of sin. Nonetheless, the recovery of their status as competent witnesses may still be contingent upon the particular circumstances and nature of the crime (Yad, Edut 12).

Persons guilty of non-monetary transgressions only regain competence as witnesses after receiving the punishment of flagellation (Yad, Edut 12.4). The reason, as indicated in Maimonides' *Mishnah Commentary* (*ibid.*), is that those subject to flagellation return to competence even without repentance, because their initial disqualification is not rooted in the fear that they will lie, but derives rather from the Scriptural edict: "Put not thy hand with the wicked to be an unrighteous witness." Hence, having received lashes, they are once again regarded as "thy brother" and regain their competence, even in the absence of repentance (Sinai, *ibid.*, 309–310).

Incidentally, in one of the judgments of the Israeli Supreme Court, Deputy President Menachem Elon wrote that "based on the overarching principle of 'after receiving lashes – he is like your brother' (Mishnah, Makkot 3:15), Jewish law prescribed a series of rules intended to rehabilitate the criminal who served his sentence, and thus preserve his rights as a human being, as your brother and as your neighbor" (ALA 18/84 *Karmi v. State Prosecutor,* 44 (1) PD 353, 375), and also receives expression in the Crime Register and Rehabilitation of Offenders Law, 1981, which is based on the principles of Jewish law (see judgment, ibid; Elon, *Ha-Mishpat ha-Ivri*, pp. 1434–1435)

In another Supreme Court judgment, Justice Silberg alluded to the concept taken from Jewish law in responsa of the *aḥaronim*: to wit, that a person disqualified as a witness due to the offense committed as a result of and in connection with his testimony, is only disqualified after completing his testimony. (CA 238/53 *Cohen v. Attorney General*, 4 PD 4, 30–31).

The Interested Party. A fascinating question that arose in modern times relates to the status in Jewish law of a witness who turns state's evidence (i.e., one offered immunity from punishment for his own crimes in return for testifying against another criminal). The various problems posed by a conviction resting on the testimony of a person who turned state's evidence is a classic example of the "interested party" and of one who "receives benefit for testifying." All of these issues are dealt with in a comprehensive study (E. Shochetman, *Eduto shel Ed Medinah le-Or ha-Mishpat ha-Ivri*). In terms of being "an interested party," the author argues that such a person should be disqualified as witness, because the consideration given him for his testimony is given by one party (the prosecution – District/State attorney), because he is under pressure for his testimony to be consistent with that given to the police during his preliminary interrogation, and because it must conform with the prosecutor's anticipations. Another problem is the granting of immunity against criminal prosecution in return for giving testimony, which constitutes the granting of benefit to the witness in return for his testimony. This is in direct contravention of the commandment to give evidence gratuitously, and under Mishnaic law, such testimony is invalid (Mishnah, Bekhorot, 4:6). The *halakhah* in this matter is in accordance with the view of Rema (ḤM 34:18). On this basis, the author concludes that even in terms of the law of "he who receives benefit for testifying," the state's witness should be disqualified. On the other hand, Shochetman suggests that the institute of "states evidence" might be validated by the enactment of a regulation allowing the court discretionary power to deviate from regular laws of evidence, in an attempt to provide a halakhic solution for situations in which an offender whose guilt is clear may still escape punishment altogether.

DISQUALIFICATION. A comprehensive study concerning the prohibition against self-incrimination in Jewish law was conducted by A. Kirschenbaum (*The Criminal Confession in Jewish Law*), some of the main aspects of which will be discussed below. The talmudic principle that invalidates a person's confession to a criminal offense is without parallel in any of other legal system, whether in the ancient world, in the medieval period, or in modern times. Jewish law determined that no person could be convicted on the basis of his own confession, both with respect to considering the confessor as "wicked," his disqualification as a witness, and with regard to punishment. The author of the above study distinguished between the theoretical halakhic rule, which totally denies the admissibility of a criminal confession, and practical *halakhah*, which was prepared to accept it, as dictated by the exigencies of the period. However, even when an admission was accepted, the original *halakhah* left its imprint, and whenever the exigencies of the period did not compel deviation from the classical *halakhah* – i.e., the vast majority of cases – the courts would abide by the classical position of Jewish law. It should be noted that the Israeli Supreme Court also gave expression to the classical position of Jewish law (see e.g. Justice Elon, Cr.A. 543/79 *Nagar v. State of Israel*, 35 (1) 113). Over the last few years there has been growing support for deviation from the principle of admitting a confession of an accused. In fact, in one of the judgments, Justice Dalia Dorner expressed a lone opinion that drew inspiration from Jewish Law, as a system in which human experience lead to the creation of a rule that disqualifies the admission of the accused (FH 4342/97 *State of Israel v. Al-Abid,* 51 (1) PD 736, par. 3 of judgment).

DUTY TO TESTIFY. The religious duty to testify exists even when the witness is not called upon to testify by the interested party, for conceivably the litigant may not even be aware of the existence of that witness. In a decision given by the Tel Aviv Rabbinical Court, File 15453/5745, the court ruled that in view of this halakhic duty, "the claim of immunity is not accepted (i.e., in accordance with Section 90 of the Chamber of Advocates Law, 5721 – 1961), because that claim contradicts the biblical command 'If he does not utter it, then he shall bear his iniquity' (Lev 5:1)."

Unlike the accepted rule in many legal systems, under Jewish law there is no automatic swearing of a witness to tell the truth. However, "Should the court perceive a need dictated by the times, to impose an oath on them so that they shall say the truth – it may do so" (Rema, ḤM 28:2). The halakhic position was adopted in Israeli law in the Rules of Evidence Amendment (Warning of Witnesses and Abolition of Oath) Law, 5740 – 1980, which provides that "Notwithstanding anything provided in any other law, a witness about to testify in any judicial or quasi-judicial proceeding shall not be sworn" (Section 1). Nonetheless, the court was conferred discretion to swear in a witness "Where the court has reason to believe that swearing a witness may assist in discovering the truth." However, under those circumstances "the witness may, after stating that he does so for reasons of religion or conscience, make an affirmation rather than taking an oath, unless the court is satisfied that he does not invoke those reasons in good faith." Even where the witness does not make an oath, the court must warn him that he must tell the whole truth, and nothing but the truth, and that he will be liable for the penalties prescribed by law if he fails to do so (Section 2). The procedure for warning witnesses is further expanded in *Practice and Procedure.

A highly instructive innovation pertaining to secret monitoring appears in a judgment of Justice Menachem Elon (FH 9/83 *Military Court of Appeals v. Vaknin*, 43 (2) PD 837, 857–859), where it states that "under special circumstances secret monitoring is a mitzvah, as when needed in order to create evidence in a case of serious criminal activity (incitement and enticement), in which case 'witnesses are hidden behind a partition' (Mishnah, Sanh. 7:10) and it is permitted in order to create evidence with respect to any kind of criminality" (see Rabbi Joseph Babad, *Minḥat Ḥinukh*, §462). Justice Elon's comments were cited approvingly by Rav S. Dikhovsky, "*Ha'azanat Seter,*" in: *Teḥumin*, 11 (1990), 299–332, at 302–3.

In another interesting decision of Justice Türkel, a precedential rule was crystallized in a matter yet to be addressed by Israeli case law. The question concerned a judge giving testimony at the witness stand (LCA 3202/03 *State of Israel v. Yosef*), 58 (3) PD 541, at par.10 of judgment). Justice Türkel relied on the sources of Jewish law regarding the retaining of the dignity of the *dayyan*, in addition to the sources dealing with the possibility of taking testimony from a learned scholar in his home, in deference to his revered status (Maim., Yad, Edut 1:2). Justice Türkel drew an analogy from these sources to the immediate question of the judge as a witness.

EXAMINATION. In a court procedure conducted in accordance with Jewish law, the judge is charged with the examination of witnesses, and in principle the litigants and their attorneys do not have the possibility of examining the witnesses. (Regarding court's intervention in the judicial proceedings, see *Practice and Procedure.) In this context, the Rules of Procedure of the Rabbinical Courts of Israel establish a new and interesting arrangement. Regulation 89 (Section 1) states that: "The witness presents the testimony and is then examined by the *Bet Din*. After that, he can be examined by the party that summoned him, and then by the opposing party." The principal examination is inquisitorial, conducted by the *Bet Din* itself, and followed by examinations conducted by both parties (examination in chief, and cross-examination). Insofar as the examination of witnesses by the litigants is purely for purposes of promoting the *Bet Din*'s examination, the *Bet Din* has broad discretion in the examination of witnesses, and is even empowered to deviate from this format where circumstances necessitate it. Section 3 of the aforementioned regulation states "the *Bet Din* is permitted to ask further questions at all times, and to allow the litigants or any one of them to do so." Regulation 90 provides: "The *Bet Din* is permitted to disallow any question presented to a witness and to terminate the questioning of a witness by the litigants, if the *Bet Din* suspects that the question may mislead or prompt the witness to lie, or if the *Bet Din* deems the question superfluous, insulting or intimidating." A similar arrangement (to that provided in said Regulation 90) was established by the Israeli legislator in the Amendment of Procedure (Examination of Witnesses) Law, 5718 – 1957.

In the Israeli Supreme Court, Justice Menachem Elon relied on the procedures for examining witnesses in Jewish law to indicate the importance of the cross-examination (Cr.A. *Hag' Yichyeh v. State of Israel*, 45 (5) PD 221, 264–265.)

In the vast majority of civil suits and personal status suits, the *Bet Din* is not required to conduct a rigorous, punctilious examination of the witnesses, the like of which is mandatory in criminal cases, and the degree of its intervention (which for the most part did not consist of professional *dayyanim*) in the examination of witnesses was minimal. The following alternative grounds for leniency with regard to procedural strictures relating to competency of the *dayanim* and examination of witnesses were invoked by the Sages: "in order not to lock the door on borrowers" (Sanh. 32b); "in order to lock the door on perpetrators of injustice" (*Piskei Ha-Rosh*, to Sanh. 81.1); and "public policy" or "to distance tortfeasors" (Ha-Meiri, in *Bet Ha-Beḥirah* on Sanh. 3b, at p. 6 (Ralbag ed.)). These reasons are applicable both with respect to matters involving financial loss and, in effect, in most civil matters, as well as in matters concerning personal status. As shown by one of the scholars (Sinai, *The Court's Intervention in Litigation According to Jewish Law*, p. 249), the position adopted by halakhic authorities was that strict compliance with the two aforementioned limitations would severely impair the efficiency of the judicial system, precisely concerning those issues with which the rabbinical courts are frequently engaged on a daily basis. This position relied inter alia on the explicit talmudic testimony that in regular matters involving monetary loss, lenience was permitted and matters were heard even before non-professional judges so that suits could be heard by lay judges who were not experts in the secrets of examination and investigation. This in turn engendered a parallel policy of leniency regarding the extent to which the *dayyanim* were involved in the process of examining witnesses, and the abrogation of the obligation to conduct a punctilious examination and investigation in those fields (i.e., monetary, personal status). The result was the conducting of an efficient hearing in every-day matters. Moreover, even in the realm of personal law, the accepted approach is that the *Bet Din* does not conduct a rigorous, meticulous examination of the witnesses (Yeb. 122b). A number of explanations have been offered to explain this tendency: the purpose and role of the witnesses and of the *Bet Din* in matters of personal status as distinct from capital and civil matters; or the tendency towards lenience that characterizes the laws of the *agunah*; or against the background of "*takkanat ha-lovim*" (so that lenders will not be deterred from loaning) (Sinai, *Ḥakirat Edei Hagannah – Le-Hithavvutan shel Tefisot Mishpatiyyot*).

With regard to reliance on written records, it should be added that in a recent ruling of the District Court in Jerusalem (CF (Jer) 4177/02 *Ashkenazi v. Gandin*, (unpublished) par. 6; delivered in 2005) Judge Yosef Shapira accepted the testimony of the defendant-doctor in a medical negligence suit, to the effect that the plaintiff had never actually visited her clinic. His acceptance of this testimony was based inter alia on the presumption that had the plaintiff actually visited her clinic, she would presumably have examined him at the time and recorded his particulars in his patient card, in view of his being a new patient. This factual determination was based on Jewish law, which permits reliance on records in booklets or the computer, in accordance with the *halakhah* codified in the Shulḥan Arukh (ḤM 91.5).

An interesting example of reliance on the Jewish law regarding examination of witnesses appeared in a recent decision of District Court Judge Pilpel (CF (TA) 2070/00 *Avidan v. Avidan* (Tak-Dis 2005 (2), 5676, 5681). The case concerned a suspicion of fraudulent signature on a deed, in the context of the English legal doctrine of "*non-est factum*." In her decision, Judge Pilpel wrote that, "this subject and the decision thereon were already discussed in ancient times by the Babylonian *geonim*" (see *Oẓar ha-Geonim le-Ketubbot*, 183, pp. 92–93). The *geonim* were asked about the validity of a deed when it was known that the witnesses signed thereon were illiterate. They responded that such a situation is "a total farce" and would sow suspicion in any reasonable person's heart, and accordingly the nature of the signature demands examination (Dr. Y. Sinai, "The Geonic and Maimonidean Approach to Testimony Recorded in Legal Documents (*Shetar*)" in: *Dinei Israel*, 22 (2003), 111).

Regarding fraudulent claims see *Practice and Procedure.

DISPROOF. In one of the first decisions of the Israeli Supreme Court it was ruled (per Justice Simha Assaf) on the basis of the Talmud (Sanh. 41a) that a distinction must be made between a conflict that involves the core of a given matter and one regarding trivial conditions. The distinction is explained as follows: "If one of the witnesses was not precise in the details of his testimony, this does not perjure his entire testimony. It is precisely the perjured witnesses, who have carefully coordinated their testimonies, who are more able to submit perfect testimony, without any contradictions. Truthful witnesses, on the other hand, may contradict one another, and even contradict themselves in unimportant details, especially in those pertaining to peripheral aspects of the event, because they were not in a relaxed state of mind, and they were shocked by the confusion and pandemonium that resulted from the event" (Cr.A. 3/48 *Katz-Cohen v. Attorney General*, 2 PD 681, 686–687). Justice Assaf's contention was that contradictory witnesses should not necessarily be disqualified where the contradiction relates to non-substantive matters. In another Israeli Supreme Court judgment, he found additional support for this contention in the words of Rav (TJ Sanh. 4:1, 22a), who when hearing witnesses whose testimony was substantially similar, to the extent of their using the same words, he suspected them of being false witnesses who had coordinated their testimony, and he would investigate and examine them. However if their testimony was not couched in precisely the same wording, each of them describing the event using different words, then he would only investigate to ensure that their testimony provided a sufficiently accurate description of the event so as to be relied upon.

Justice Assaf offered a further justification for this rule stating that, "Just as no two prophets prophesize in the same style, then *a fortiori* two laymen (Resp. *Zikhron Yehudah*, by R. Judah ben Asher, no. 72)" (Cr.A. *Suleiman v. Attorney General*, 6 PD 824, 826).

In another judgment of the Israel Supreme Court, Justice Silberg invoked the principle whereby "testimony that cannot be refuted is not valid" in an interesting manner, as the basis of the requirement for corroborating evidence in sexual offenses. Justice Silberg justified the need for external corroborative evidence in addition to the testimony of the complainant as follows: "Since the testimony of the complainant is almost always 'testimony that cannot be refuted' given that it concerns intimate matters that occurred behind closed doors, where no-one can see, and hence there are no witnesses for the defense who can help the innocent person who is under suspicion" (Cr.A. *Saadia v. Attorney General*, 16 PD 1860, 1862).

[Yuval Sinai (2nd ed.)]

BIBLIOGRAPHY: Z. Frankel, *Der gerichtliche Beweis nach mosaisch-talmudischem Rechte* (1846); N. Hirsch, in: *Jeschurun*, 12 (1865/66), 80–88, 109–22, 147–65, 249–58, 382–94 (Germ.); I. Tonelis Handl, *Die Zulaessigkeit zur Zeugenaussage und zur Eidesablegung nach mosaisch-rabbinischem Rechte* (1866; Hebr. and Germ.); L. Loew, in: Ben Chananja, 9 (1866), Suppl; repr. in his: *Gesammelte Schriften*, 3 (1893), 335–45; M. Bloch, *Die Civilprocess-Ordnung nach mosaisch-rabbinischem Rechte* (1882), 43–53; I.S. Zuri, *Mishpat ha-Tahmud*, 7 (1921), 43–53; Gulak, Yesodei, 2 (1922), 28, 30, 134ff.; 4 (1922), 150–63; idem, Oẓar, 305–11; S. Kaatz, in: *Jeschurun*, 15 (1928), 89–98, 179–87 (Germ.); Z. Karl, in: *Ha-Mishpat ha-Ivri*, 3 (1928), 89–127; A. Gulak, in: *Tarbiz*, 12 (1940/41), 181–9; Z. Karl, in: *Ha-Peraklit*, 5 (1948), 81–85; ET, 1 (1951^3), 88–90, 117–9, 225f.; 2 (1949), 14f., 60, 65, 137, 247, 252f., 300f.; 3 (1951), 160f., 378f.; 5 (1953), 46–51, 337–43, 381–5, 517–22, 528f.; 6 (1954), 199f.; 7 (1956), 290–5, 383–5, 638–64; 8 (1957), 352f., 429–131; 9 (1959), 64–103, 729–46; 11 (1965), 242; A. Weiss, *Seder ha-Diyyun* (1957), 86–124, 206–54; J. Cohen, in: *Ha-Torah ve-ha-Medinah*, 11–13 (1959/62), 517–40; S. Atlas, in: *Sefer Yovel… Abraham Weiss* (1964), 73–90; H. Jaeger, in: *Recueils de la Société Jean Bodin*, 16 (1965), 415–594; Elon, Mafte'aḥ, 206–18; G. Holzer, in: *Sinai*, 67 (1970), 94–112. **ADD. BIBLIOGRAPHY:** M. Elon, *Ha-Mishpat ha-Ivri*, (1988), 424–34, 497–504, 596–97, 816–18, 1341–42, 1424–34; idem, *Jewish Law: History, Sources, Principles*, 397–99, 607–9, 1697–1707; M. Elon, B. Auerbach, D. Hazin, M Sykes, *Jewish Law ("Batei ha-Din")*, in: *Torah she-be-al Peh*, 22 (1981), 81–88; S. Dikhovsky, "*Ha'azanat Se-*

ter," in: *Teḥumin*, 11 (1990), 299–312; S. Ettinger, *"Ishah ke-Ed be-Dinei Mamonot be-Mishpat ha-Ivri,"* in: *Dinei Yisrael*, 20–21 (2000–2001), 241–67; S. Ettinger, "The Role of Witnesses in Jewish Law," in: *Dinei Yisrael*, 22 (5763), 7–37; H.S. Hefetz, *"Mekoman shel Raa'yot Nesibatiot ba-Mishpat ha-Ivri,"* in: *Mishpatim* 1 (1968), 67ff.; idem, *"Mekomah shel Edut ba-Mishpat ha-Ivri,"* in: *Dinei Yisrael*, 9 (1978–1980), 51–84; idem, *"Al pi Shenei Edim Yakum Davar – Ha-Omnam? Ra'ayot Nesibatiot be-Vet ha-Din – Halakhah Le-Ma'aseh,"* in: *Takdim*, 2 (1989), 59–84; A. Kirschenbaum, *The Criminal Confession in Jewish Law* (Heb., 2005); N. Neriah, *"Edut shel mi she-Eino Mekayyem Torah u-Mizvot,"* in: *Teḥumin*, 13 (1992–1993), 417–21; J.A. Polak, "Some Social and Societal Implications of Law of Witnesses," in: *Jewish Law Association Studies*, 4 (1990), 55–68; A. Radzyner, *"Hatra'ah be-Edim u-Teḥilat Edut,"* in: *Dinei Yisrael*, 20–21 (2000–1), 515–51; E. Shochetman, *"Eduto shel Ed Medinah le-Or ha-Mishpat ha-Ivri,"* in: *Mishpatim*, 11 (1981), 139–73; Y. Sinai, *"Bi'ur Shitat ha-Rambam be-Inyan Kashrutam shel Resha'im le-Edut,"* in: *Ma'agal*, 12 (1998), 289–310; idem, *"Ḥakirat Edei Agunah – Le-Hithavvutan shel Tefisot Mishpatiyyot,"* in: *Shenaton ha-Mishpat ha-Ivri*, 22 (2001–3), 329–68; idem, "The Geonic and Maimonidean Approach to Testimony Recorded in Legal Documents (*Shetar*)," in: *Dinei Yisrael*, 22 (Heb., 2003), 111–49; idem, *The Court's Intervention in Litigation According to Jewish Law* (Heb., 2003), 188–282.

°**WITTE, SERGEY YULYEVICH, COUNT** (1849–1915), Russian statesman. Between 1892 and 1903 he was finance minister and exerted much influence in the economic and foreign policies of Russia. In 1894 he introduced the government monopoly in the alcoholic liquors trade, a measure which removed within a few years tens of thousands of Jewish families from this branch of the economy. Witte was opposed to the aggressive policy of Russia in the Far East and, after the defeat of the Russian army in 1904, led the delegation which signed the Peace Treaty of Portsmouth with Japan (1905). He was among the advocates of the Constitution of October 1905 and headed the Council of Ministers until April 1906. As a result of these activities and his efforts to obtain foreign loans, Witte met with Jews both in Russia and western Europe, as well as in America. He criticized the discriminatory policy and spoke against the persecution of the Jews, which he believed was responsible for the active participation by Jews in the Russian revolutionary movement and the difficulties encountered by the Russian government in its foreign policy and on the international financial market.

When *Herzl visited St. Petersburg, during the summer of 1903, he conferred with Witte on the subject of obtaining authorization for issuance of shares in Russia by the Jewish Colonial Trust. During his last years Witte wrote his memoirs (3 vols., 1922–23), which contain material on the economic and political history of the Jews in Russia.

[Yehuda Slutsky]

WITTENBERG, YIẒHAK (**Itzig**; 1907–1943), first commander of the Jewish fighters' organization in the Vilna ghetto (Fareynegte Partizaner Organizatsye, United Partisan Organization, FPO). He was born into a working class family and worked as a tailor before the war and was a Communist from his youth. During the Soviet occupation of Vilna he was a Communist activist. He became one of the leaders of the Communist underground during the German occupation.

The fighters' organization was established in the ghetto after the Nazis systematically murdered more than 40,000 Vilna Jews, after transporting them to the site of the massacre at *Ponary. After the organization was established, Wittenberg was chosen commander. He headed the training program and was an outstanding officer. On July 15, 1943, one of Wittenberg's contacts was caught by the Nazis outside the ghetto, who were apparently unaware of the existence of the FPO. On the evening of the same day, the leaders of the fighters' organization were ordered to appear before Jacob Gens, the chief of the Jewish police in the ghetto, to provide an explanation. The commanders appeared at the appointed hour, and after a short period *SS men broke into the office by the side door with their guns pointed at the fighters. They were ordered to identify Wittenberg, but refused to answer, until Gens himself pointed him out. Wittenberg was handcuffed and taken out in the direction of the gate of the ghetto, but his captors never succeeded in getting him there. The ghetto fighters attacked the SS men and in an exchange of fire succeeded in freeing Wittenberg. Instead of attacking the ghetto and destroying it with Wittenberg inside, the SS handed Gens an ultimatum that he must turn Wittenberg over to them before 3:00 A.M. or they would destroy the ghetto and all its inhabitants.

Due to the tempestuous situation created in the ghetto after Gens repeated the ultimatum, it was necessary to extend the time to 6:00 A.M. At first, people were unwilling to believe Gens' testimony that the Germans intended to destroy the ghetto. Two camps quickly emerged: representatives of the fighters, who believed that under no circumstances was Wittenberg to be given over to the Nazis; and those who supported Gens and demanded that it was necessary to spare the ghetto and hand Wittenberg over to the Germans at the appointed hour, so as not to endanger the entire ghetto for the sake of one man. They also felt that the time was not ripe for a general uprising. The exchanges between the two sides reached the proportions of a civil war in the eyes of the Nazis, who stood on the side waiting for the time to run out. The fighters opened up negotiations with the chief of police with the intention of offering a volunteer to deceive the Germans or to claim that Wittenberg had escaped. But Gens rejected the suggestion. The fighters were close to despair, seeing all their preparations for the fateful day collapsing because of one incident, and they demanded that Wittenberg give the order to fight. But Wittenberg was not prepared to allow Jew to fight Jew until his fighters reached their real enemy. Full of confidence, he walked out into the deserted street, approached the ghetto gate, and turned himself over to the Germans. He was subsequently tortured and died. Some say that he took his own life in prison.

BIBLIOGRAPHY: J. Robinson, *And the Crooked Shall be Made Straight* (1965), 219, 343 note 235; M. Rolnik, *Ani Ḥayyevet le-Sapper* (1965), 89–92. **ADD. BIBLIOGRAPHY:** Y. Arad, *Ghetto in Flames:*

The Struggle and Destruction of the Jews in Vilna in the Holocaust (1980).

[B. Mordechai Ansbacher / Michael Berenbaum (2nd ed.)]

WITTGENSTEIN, LUDWIG (1889–1951), Austrian-British philosopher who profoundly influenced Anglo-Saxon analytic philosophy through his analysis of language; brother of the musician Paul *Wittgenstein.

Life

Wittgenstein was born in Vienna in 1889, the eighth and youngest child in a well-off and cultured family. He had three Jewish grandparents. As a child he was baptized, but he never was a religious Catholic. After a private education at home, he attended school in Linz, where, coincidentally, Adolf Hitler also was a pupil. He studied engineering in Berlin and then went to Manchester, England, to study aerodynamics. There he read Bertrand Russell's *Principles of Mathematics* and became interested in logic and the logical basis of mathematics. In 1911 he met Gottlob Frege (1848–1925) who demonstrated that one can derive mathematics from logic, and singled out the problem of the inaccuracy of language. Frege referred him to Russell, whom Wittgenstein visited in the same year, and who stimulated him to be active in philosophy.

What vividly interested him was language. In 1913 and 1914, he worked during long periods in Norway in order to clarify logic. With the outbreak of World War I he became a volunteer in the Austrian army. In 1916 the first version of his famous *Tractatus Logico-Philosophicus*, Wittgenstein's essay on language and logic, was ready. In the same year, he left for the front. In 1918, he was taken prisoner of war in Italy. Upon his return to Vienna, he studied to become a teacher and gave away his personal fortune.

At first, Wittgenstein could not find a publisher for his *Tractatus*. It was finally published in 1922 in the series *Annalen der Naturphilosophie*. He worked as a gardener and also as a teacher in several elementary schools. He was successful when teaching superior pupils, but was a failure with other pupils, whom he treated harshly. In 1925 he again visited England where he became an advanced student, and in 1929 received his Ph.D. on the basis of his *Tractatus*. In 1930 he started teaching in Cambridge. The *Tractatus* was the only work he published, although he desired also to publish his later work *Philosophische Untersuchungen*.

Teaching at the university did not prevent Wittgenstein from opposing any form of academic philosophy. He developed a growing resistance toward the mathematical and scientific way of thinking as the only ways of philosophizing. In 1935 he pondered immigrating to Russia. In 1939 he was promoted to the rank of professor.

During the difficult years of the Shoah, the Wittgenstein family in Vienna were considered non-Jewish, thanks to a friend, the Catholic teacher Ludwig Hänsel, who had access to leading political figures of that time. It was probably on instructions of Arthur *Seyss-Inquart, who was responsible for the destruction of Dutch Jewry and who was tried in the Nuremberg trials, that the family was not killed.

For some time, Wittgenstein left his academic position and worked in a London hospital. In 1948 he left for Ireland. In the summer of 1949, he visited America, where he became ill. In 1950 he returned to London, without a job and without money. During the last months of his life he wrote *On Certainty*. He died in 1951.

Work

Customarily, one distinguishes between Wittgenstein's early work, the *Tractatus* (1922), and his later work, e.g., the *Philosophical Investigations* (published posthumously in 1953).

Fortunately, there exists Wittgenstein's voluminous *Nachlaß*, of which various manuscript were published, as *Zettel*, *On Certainty*, *Remarks on the Foundations of Mathematics*, *Culture and Value*, and *Remarks on the Philosophy of Psychology*. There are further the *Notebooks 1914–1916* and, finally, the notes made by his students, e.g., *The Blue and Brown Books*, *Lectures and Conversations on Aesthetics*, and *Psychology and Religious Belief*.

The Vienna Circle interpreted his early work in the direction of logical positivism, on the basis of the picture-language discussed in the *Tractatus*. It is, however, questionable if there is enough supporting evidence for speaking of Wittgenstein I and II. It is the same person who, during his entire life, developed a critique of language, attacking the picture theory of meaning. In all of his philosophical activities, he waged "the battle against the bewitchment of our intelligence by means of our language" (*ein Kampf gegen die Verhexung unsres Verstandes durch die Mittel unserer Sprache*) (*Philosophical Investigations*, 109) and wanted the reader to take upon himself the task of clarifying his language. The theory developed in the early work was written to be rejected, and the *Investigations* clarified the questions that were raised in the *Tractatus*. Wittgenstein wanted the old thoughts and the new ones be published together.

Philosophical problems were for him first of all problems of language. He was convinced that, if one would study the logic of language, one would be able to solve many philosophical problems.

Investigation of the Use of Language

The *Tractatus* describes the limitations of language. Logic is what is "true." There is the simple tautological equation A = A. Further, there is the formula A is not not-A: I cannot eat and not eat at the same time. Finally there is the dilemma: or A or not-A: or it rains or it doesn't.

Wittgenstein doubts if one really says something with this logic that it is true under all circumstances. Mathematics, too, is logic: it is a priori true, not based upon experiments: 5 and 5, for instance, is 10, and one does not have to verify that. Finally, Wittgenstein maintains in his *Tractatus* that only scientific utterances give certainty about reality. But scientific utterances are not necessarily true: reality could also be different.

The last sentence of the *Tractatus* (7) reads: "Whereof one cannot speak, thereof one must be silent." (*Wovon man nicht sprechen kann, darüber muß man schweigen*). Through this sentence, Wittgenstein makes much of human life unspeakable, at least in the logical picture-language. The entire domain of speaking on ethics and God has to remain separated from the purely descriptive language. Ethical utterances are authoritative, but distinguished from utterances on facts. About God you cannot speak as about things in the world. Aesthetic and ethical judgments cannot be expressed within logical language, they are not facts and cannot be pictured in thought. Real questions, questions of life, are not scientific questions. Picture-language is thus problematical. Wittgenstein therefore found it useful to study ordinary language with its different language games. Philosophy can, accordingly, be a remedy against the bewitchment of thought by language.

THE COMPLEXITY OF ORDINARY LANGUAGE. It was Wittgenstein's life task to understand ordinary language. One may say for instance that one "has" a book, that one "has" children, or that one "has" a headache. All these are different forms of "having" which are not reducible to each other. One cannot solve this complex reality by speaking about the "essence" of having (as did Plato), which would transcend all these forms of "having." Neither can one reduce something to something else, as is frequently done in psychology. All this proves that we are "bewitched" by wrong visions on language.

The word "essentially" was for Wittgenstein a word that one has to avoid. He left out the "eternal" truth beyond or above reality and concentrated upon the detail that always deviates from a preexisting "essence." We should stop using the word "essentially," as if in having a child, a book or a headache the same unchangeable "having" would return. This would come to being guilty of a logical way of speaking (A = A), that says nothing.

Wittgenstein and Judaism

Recent research has investigated Wittgenstein's thought in light of his Jewish background. Rush Rhees has written on Wittgenstein's self-understanding. He notes that, in 1936, Wittgenstein confessed to his friends and family that he was more Jewish than was generally known. In his book on Wittgenstein and Judaism, Ranjit Chatterjee writes that, with this confession, Wittgenstein indicated that in his work, one may find many a Jewish element, and that Wittgenstein developed an intellectual Jewishness and expressed his inner Jewish feeling in a disguised way. Wittgenstein also remarked to his friend M.O'C. Drury that his own thinking is not Greek, but "one hundred percent Hebrew thinking." With his "Hebrew thinking" he wanted to unmask the idolatry of picture language. On the other hand, Steven Schwarzschild saw Wittgenstein as being alienated from his Jewishness, and as suffering from self-hatred.

BIBLIOGRAPHY: DETAILED BIOGRAPHIES: B. McGuiness, *Wittgenstein: A Life. Young Ludwig 1889–1921* (1988); R. Monk, *Ludwig Wittgenstein. The Duty of Genius* (1990). ON WITTGENSTEIN: A. Ambrose (ed.), *Wittgenstein's Lectures, Cambridge 1932–1935* (1979); G. Anscombe, *An Introduction to Wittgenstein's Tractatus* (1959); C. Barrett, *Wittgenstein on Ethics and Religious Belief* (1991); O. Bouwsma, in: J.L. Craft and R. Hustwit (eds.), *Wittgenstein: Conversations 1949–1951* (1986); R. Chatterjee, *Wittgenstein and Judaism. A Triumph of Concealment* (Studies in Judaism 1) (2005); T. De Mauro, *Ludwig Wittgenstein: His Place in the Development of Semantics* (1967); P. Engelmann, *Letters from Ludwig Wittgenstein, with a Memoir* (1968); K.T. Fann, *Wittgenstein's Conception of Philosophy* (1971); H.L. Finch, *Wittgenstein: The Later Philosophy* (1977); G. Hallett, *A Companion to Wittgenstein's* Philosophical Investigations (1977); W.F. Hermans, *Wittgenstein* (1992); A. Janik and S. Toulmin, *Wittgenstein's Vienna* (1972); A. Janik, *Essays on Wittgenstein and Weininger* (1985); S. Kripke, *Wittgenstein on Rules and Private Language* (1982); N. Malcolm, *Ludwig Wittgenstein. A Memoir*, with Wittgenstein's letters to Malcolm (1984); B. McGuiness, "Wittgenstein and the Idea of Jewishness," in: J.C. Klagge (ed.), *Wittgenstein: Biography and Philosophy* (2001), 221–36; D. Pears, *Wittgenstein* (1970); M. Perloff, *Wittgenstein's Ladder; Poetic Language and the Strangeness of the Ordinary* (1999); G. Pitcher (ed.), *Wittgenstein: The Philosophical Investigations* (1966); R. Rhees (ed.), *Ludwig Wittgenstein: Personal Recollections* (1981); S. Schwarzschild, "Wittgenstein as Alienated Jew," in: *Telos*, 40 (1979), 160–65; D. Stern, "Was Wittgenstein a Jew?" in: James C. Klagge (ed.), *Wittgenstein: Biography and Philosophy* (2001), 237–72; B. Szabados, "Was Wittgenstein an Anti-Semite? The Significance of Anti-Semitism for Wittgenstein's Philosophy," in: *Canadian Journal of Philosophy*, 29 (1999), 1–28; C. Wright, *Wittgenstein on the Foundations of Mathematics* (1980).

[Ephraim Meir (2nd ed.)]

WITTGENSTEIN, PAUL (1887–1961), pianist. Born in Vienna, Wittgenstein studied and made his debut there in 1913. During World War I he lost his right arm at the Russian front and embarked on an extraordinary career as a one-handed pianist. He left Austria in 1930 and after 1933 settled permanently in the United States. His repertoire consisted of works he had adapted or those especially written for him, such as Ravel's *Concerto for Left Hand*, Richard Strauss' *Parergon zur Symphonia Domestica* and *Panathenaeenzug*, and many other concert and chamber works by Erich Wolfgang *Korngold, Benjamin Britten, and Hans Gál. He published a pedagogical work, *Schule der linken Hand.*

WITTKOWER, RUDOLF J. (1901–1971), historian of art and architecture. Born in Berlin, he studied at the universities of Berlin and Munich. From 1923 to 1928 he worked in Italy, and in 1924 was appointed lecturer at Cologne University. When Hitler came to power, Wittkower emigrated to England and became professor at the University of London (1949–55). In 1954 he moved to the United States, where he was made chairman of the department of art history and archaeology at Columbia University, New York.

Wittkower is known for his studies of Italian Renaissance and Baroque art, such as *Art and Architecture in Italy 1600–1750* (1958) and books on Bernini and the Caracci. His *Architectural Principles in the Age of Humanism* (1949), a study of the principles underlying the architecture of the Italian Renaissance, influenced the thinking of students of architecture.

ADD. BIBLIOGRAPHY: D.M. Reynolds, *Selected Lectures of Rudolf Wittkower: The Impact of Non-European Civilization on the Art of the West* (1989); R. and M. Wittkower, *Kuenstler. Aussenseiter der Gesellschaft*, (1993); R. Wittkower, *Allegorie und der Wandel der Symbole in Antike und Renaissance* (1996).

WITTLIN, JÓZEF (1896–1976), Polish poet, author, and translator. Born in Dmytrów, Galicia, Wittlin was raised in Lvov and served in the Austro-Hungarian army during World War I. From 1919 onward he was connected with the Polish expressionist group centered in the periodicals *Zdrój* and *Skamander* and in 1927 moved from Lvov to Warsaw. An outstanding exponent of Polish expressionism, Wittlin first achieved fame with his verse collection *Hymny* (1920), which resembled German expressionist writing. His two other major works were a modern Polish translation of Homer's *Odyssey* (1924) and the novel *Sól ziemi* (1936; *The Salt of the Earth*, 1939?). A prolific writer, he also published many stories, sketches, and essays, as well as various translations of foreign classics, from the Sumerian *Gilgamesh Epic* (1922) to Hasek's *The Good Soldier Schweik* (1931). Wittlin made his mark as the leading pacifist writer in Poland between the world wars. After fleeing to France and Portugal, he emigrated to the U.S. in 1941 and settled in New York, where he became a coeditor of the Polish émigré weekly *Tygodnik Polski*.

BIBLIOGRAPHY: *Słownik współczesnych pisarzy polskich*, 3 (1964), 512–7; N. Wallis, in: *Pologne littéraire* 6 (1931), 58.

[Stanislaw Wygodzki]

WIZEN, MOSHE AHARON (1878–1953), Hebrew grammarian. Born in Rozwadow, Galicia, Wizen was reared in a traditional ḥasidic atmosphere, and at the same time acquired proficiency in several languages. He started to teach at the age of 18, and in 1904 he went to Switzerland for two years to study at the University of Berne. In 1906 he moved to Lemberg, and worked there until the outbreak of World War I, when he was drafted into the army. After the war he settled in Vienna, where he taught in the Jewish Teachers' Seminary established by Zvi Hirsch Perez *Chajes. In 1938 he immigrated to Ereẓ Israel; he directed Hebrew language courses in Tel Aviv.

As a young man, Wizen published poems and feuilletons in *Ha-Pisgah* and *Ha-Maggid*; but his subsequent labors were devoted primarily to linguistic research. Wizen wrote a comparative grammar of Hebrew and other Semitic languages, *Torat ha-Lashon – Sefer Dikduk Sefat Ever* (1923). However, unlike his predecessors, he did not confine himself to the language of the Bible, but also included in his work linguistic forms found in the rabbinic and post-rabbinic period (indicating by different symbols the time when each word was first used). He dealt systematically with vocalization, inflection, and word-formation. He provided comprehensive paradigms of the conjugations and the declensions, including forms that do not appear in the sources but are nonetheless implied by virtue of the system.

While Wizen's general classification of the parts of speech is based upon that of the medieval grammarians, his internal classifications of words derive from the approach adopted by modern grammarians of the Hebrew language. His division of the noun (greatly influenced by that of Brockelmann into declension groups and groups of derivatives) accords with present-day linguistic theory, as do his description and explanations of the vowels (as for example his treatment of the "intermediate" or "half-sounded" *šewa*). He supported his description of the Hebrew verb-root by comparison with Akkadian and explained the forms of the verb in different conjugations by comparison with proto-Semitic, adding notes to illuminate any apparently irregular form; and following Abraham *Ibn Ezra, he also wrote a section on incompatible consonants in the root – a subject avoided by later grammarians.

[Menahem Zevi Kaddari]

WIZO (Women's International Zionist Organization), women's Zionist movement founded in London on July 11, 1920, at an international conference of women Zionists convened by the Federation of Women Zionists of the United Kingdom.

History and Organization

The leaders of the new movement were Vera *Weizmann, Rebecca *Sieff, Romana Goodman, Edith Eder, and Henrietta Irwell. Rebecca Sieff was the first president of WIZO and held this office until 1963, then becoming honorary life president until her death in 1966. At the time of WIZO's establishment, the British administration in Palestine had just been established and the new Russian regime had given rise to considerable Jewish emigration from Russia that was expected to turn to Palestine. The women Zionist leaders felt that since the women immigrants, even more than the men, would have to adjust to a new way of life, they should be prepared and trained. It was felt that women Zionists throughout the world would be more sensitive to this task than the Zionist movement in general and that therefore a special women's organization was needed. WIZO's original program of activities was divided into three categories: professional and vocational training for women, with special emphasis on preparation for agricultural pioneering; education of women to relate to their society as informed and civic-minded citizens; care and education of children and youth.

During the first 20 years of its existence, WIZO had its headquarters in London and built up a network of federations throughout Europe (with the exception of the U.S.S.R.) and in most other countries of the world (except the U.S., where *Hadassah already existed). The headquarters were then transferred to Tel Aviv. In 1970 Raya *Jaglom was elected president, serving until 1996. During her term of office, WIZO was established in the U.S. in 1981. In 1996, Michal Modai, former chairman of the executive of the Israel Federation and of the World WIZO Executive, was elected president of World WIZO. Helena Glaser, chairperson of the WIZO Israel Federation, was elected chairperson of the World WIZO Executive.

After World War II the number of federations was considerably reduced, since the communist bloc and most of the Muslim countries were excluded, but this was soon counteracted by the gradual reopening of the European federations, some of them actually on the heels of the liberators.

By 1996, with the end of the cold war and the opening up of the communist bloc, WIZO had renewed activities in Hungary and the Czech Republic (then Czechoslovakia), both in 1990, and groups had also been started in Latvia, Lithuania and Estonia. Furthermore, in 1981, after reaching an agreement with Hadassah, it also started working in the United States, where it has a dynamic, constantly growing federation.

WIZO's quarter of a million members are organized in 50 federations throughout the world in the following countries: Argentina, Australia, Austria, Barbados, Belgium and Luxembourg, Bolivia, Brazil, Canada, Chile, Columbia, Costa Rica, Curacao, Czech Republic, Denmark, Dominican Republic, Ecuador, Finland, France, Germany, Gibraltar, Great Britain and Ireland, Greece, Guatemala, Holland, Honduras, Hong Kong, Hungary, Israel, Italy, Jamaica, Japan, Mexico, New Zealand, Norway, Panama, Paraguay, Peru, Portugal, Singapore, South Africa, Spain, Sweden, Switzerland, Trinidad, United States, Uruguay, Venezuela, Zaire, and Zimbabwe.

WIZO is recognized by the UN as a Non-Governmental Organization (NGO) and as such has consultative status with the UN Economic and Social Council (ECOSOC) and UN International Children's Emergency Fund (UNICEF).

WIZO is a member of the *World Zionist Organization and of the *World Jewish Congress and is on the executive of both. It is also on the board of governors of the Jewish Agency.

The highest governing body of the movement is the world WIZO Conference, which meets every four years in Israel, determining overall policy and approving the budget and activity reports. It is composed of representatives from all the federations according to the size of their membership. The conference elects the president of World WIZO and the World WIZO Executive which is composed of 50 members: 25 members resident in Israel (most of them heads of the World WIZO departs that run the various WIZO institutions and services in Israel) together with heads of the 25 largest Diaspora federations. The executive elects the chairman and treasurer. WIZO is a non-partisan organization of volunteers, both at the leadership and grass roots level.

Of all WIZO's federations the Israel federation is by far the largest, with close to 100,000 members organized in 145 branches in all parts of the country. While the Diaspora federations concentrate mainly on Jewish and Zionist education, strengthening the bond with Israel and fundraising to help finance WIZO's work in Israel (and also to some extent social and educational projects in their own countries), the Israel federation works directly with and on behalf of the local population, including those of the minority communities. It defines its aims in these fields as follows: to advance the status of women, defend their rights and achieve gender equality in all fields; to combat domestic violence; to assist in the absorption of new immigrants and to contribute to family and community welfare, with special emphasis on single parent families, women, children, and the elderly.

Status of women has always been a priority of the Israel federation. The Equal Rights for Women Law of 1952 was passed on the initiative of then WIZO Israel chairman Rahel Kagan, who represented the organization in Israel's first Knesset. Today, WIZO remains active in this field.

World WIZO, too, has in recent years become active in promoting women's rights and the federations work in close cooperation with other women's organization's in their own countries and are represented on all national and international bodies dealing with women's affairs. The movement participated actively in the UN's conferences on the status of women in Mexico, Copenhagen, Nairobi, and Beijing.

In addition to advancing the status of women, the main aims of the entire movement are, nevertheless, focused on Israel and remain largely what they have been ever since the organization's beginning: to provide for the welfare of infants, children, youth, and the elderly. While during waves of mass immigration, the stress was placed on immigrant absorption services, today the most urgent need is deemed to be combating violence in the family. All WIZO's services and institutions in Israel are set up after close consultations with government and local authorities and have their full cooperation.

The following description of WIZO's 800 institutions and services in Israel presents a clear picture of the condition and needs of the population of Israel.

Institutions and Services

EARLY AGE CARE AND EDUCATION. WIZO's 234 day institutions serve 15,000 infants and small children and include day care centers, special multi-purpose day care centers for high risk children, toddlers' homes, pedagogical centers, after-school centers, therapeutic child centers, toys and games libraries, and four residential family units (Neve WIZO).

FOR CHILDREN AND YOUTH. Catering to 34,700 older children and youth are 11 schools and youth villages and 78 youth clubs.

The schools, which were among WIZO's earliest projects, were established originally either to train girls and young women for a pioneering agricultural life or to provide a home for child survivors of the Holocaust. Today, these day and boarding schools provide vocational, agricultural, and artistic training at a variety of academic levels, ranging from special education to a post–high school level college of design. The student populations consist of both native Israelis and new immigrants; outstanding students as well as low achievers; children from well-established families and welfare cases.

Also in this category are a shelter for girls in distress (Beth Ruth), facilities for the rehabilitation and advancement of marginal youth, and remedial army preparation courses for drop-out girls.

FOR WOMAN AND FAMILIES. WIZO has two shelters for battered wives and a half-way house project; four centers for the prevention and treatment of domestic violence; hot lines in Hebrew, Russian, and Amharic, for battered women; a rape crisis center and hotlines; and 28 legal advice bureaus on family matters (also dealing with specific problems of new immigrant women and single-parent families. Beit Heuss is a recreation home with supportive workshops for women and couples with a common problem.

Assistance is given in immigrant absorption, including special services on caravan sites.

For the elderly there are 100 clubs and sheltered employment facilities as well as a Parents' Home.

Other WIZO services are vocational training and advancement for women, summer camps for needy mothers of large families, and care for families of war victims and single-parent families.

BIBLIOGRAPHY: Grove and Pollak (eds.), *The Saga of a Movement – WIZO 1920–1970* (1971); Herzog and Greenberg, *A Voluntary Women's Organisation in a Society in the Making – WIZO's Contribution to Israeli Society.* **WEBSITE:** www.wizo.org.

[Rosa Ginossar / Aliza El-Dror (2nd ed.)]

WLOCLAWEK (Rus. **Votslavsk**), city in central Poland. Jews began to settle in Wloclawek at the beginning of the 19th century. The Jewish population numbered 208 in 1803, 4,248 in 1897, 6,831 (21% of the total population) in 1909, and 10,209 (18.3%) in 1931. In the interwar period Zionist and other national groups were active in the community. In the census of 1931, 96% of the Jews declared their mother tongue to be Yiddish or Hebrew. Among the outstanding personalities of Wloclawek were R. Judah Leib *Kowalsky, a leader of the Mizrachi movement in Poland, and Abraham Leib Fuks, a physician and a Zionist leader. There was a Jewish gymnasium in the city and two weeklies in Yiddish – one Zionist, and the other Zionist-Revisionist.

[Yehuda Slutsky]

Holocaust Period

When World War II broke out, the Jewish community of Wloclawek, with approximately 13,500 persons out of a general population of 60,000, increased in size as refugees came in from neighboring communities. The German army occupied Wloclawek (renamed Leslau) on Sept. 14, 1939, and incorporated it in the Warthegau district (see *Poland) of Germany. Liquidation of the Jewish community began almost immediately, with the active help of the local Germans (*Volksdeutsche*) and the support of the Polish population. All the synagogues were destroyed by fire. Hundreds of Jews were taken hostage and ransoms for them were extorted. In December 1939 deportations to eastern Poland began. Many Jews fled to nearby towns and to *Warsaw, while 3,000 remaining Jews who were segregated into a ghetto (October 1940) suffered from the food shortage and disease. The *American Jewish Joint Distribution Committee helped many destitute families, and a soup kitchen was opened. Until the liquidation of the ghetto on April 27, 1942, the Jewish cemetery served as a clandestine meeting place for instructing Jewish children, and even for theatrical performances and a makeshift library for exchanging books. At the end of April 1942 the inmates of the ghetto were all sent to *Chelmno extermination camp, and the ghetto was burned down by the Nazis.

Contemporary Period

When the war was over, the surviving remnants of the Wloclawek Jewish community gradually returned to their home town in search of relatives and friends. In 1946, some Jews who returned from the Soviet Union resettled in Wloclawek. The JDC helped to organize cooperatives of Jewish tailors and dressmakers, and Jewish cultural life was renewed. In the first few years after the war the military commander of Wloclawek was a Jew, Michael Weinstein. In 1946 he successfully averted a pogrom on the Jewish quarter by incited peasants. In the course of the following years most of the Jews of Wloclawek left for Israel, the last ones settling there after the Six-Day War (1967).

[David Dori]

BIBLIOGRAPHY: *Vloẓlavek ve-ha-Sevivah, Sefer Zikkaron* (1967, Heb. and partly Yid.); Y. Trunk, in: *Bleter far Geshikhte*, 2 (1949), 64–166; *Yoyvel-Bukh fun Branch 611 Arbeter Ring* (1951).

WLODAWA (in Jewish sources: **Vlodavi**), city in Lublin province, eastern Poland. Jews first settled there in the second half of the 16th century. A community was organized in the early 17th century under the jurisdiction of the *Brest community. In 1648 *Chmielnicki's armies massacred the local Jews, as well as others who had taken refuge there, and set fire to their houses. However, the community was reconstituted soon afterward. In the second half of the 17th century a stone baroque-style synagogue was built; enlarged 100 years later, it was still standing in 1970. In the 18th century the Jews of Wlodawa engaged in the leasing of estates, the timber trade, tailoring, and tanning. In 1765 there were 630 Jews who paid the poll tax. The community grew rapidly, numbering 2,236 (74% of the total population) in 1827 and 4,304 (72%) in 1857. It decreased to 3,670 (66%) in 1897. In the 19th century Wlodawa Jews engaged in commerce in agricultural products and manufacture of alcoholic liquor, as well as tailoring, furriery, and hat-making. *Ḥasidism gained many followers in this period.

Between the two world wars, in independent Poland, all Jewish parties were active in the city. The Jewish population numbered 4,196 (67% of the total) in 1921. In the 1929 municipal elections, 11 Jews were among those elected for the 24 seats. The last rabbi of the community, Moses Baruch Morgenstern, perished in the Holocaust.

[Shimshon Leib Kirshenboim]

Holocaust Period

In 1939 there were 5,650 Jews living in Wlodawa. The German army entered the town in mid-September 1939 and immediately subjected the Jews to persecution. However, no ghetto was established at the beginning, and until the end of 1941 life for Jews in Wlodawa was somewhat easier than in most of occupied Poland. The situation deteriorated drastically at the beginning of 1942. In April 1942 about 800 Jews from *Mielec, in Cracow province, and about 1,000 Jews from Vienna were deported to Wlodawa. On May 23, 1942, the first deportation to *Sobibor death camp took place (the exact number of deportees is unknown). In June 1942 all the children up to the age of ten were taken to Sobibor and murdered. On Oct. 24, 1942, the entire Jewish population was sent to death in the Sobibor gas chambers. During these deportations hundreds of Jews fled to the forests and organized partisan units, the best known of which was commanded by Yehiel Grynszpan and operated in conjunction with Soviet and left-wing Polish guerrillas. Most of the Jewish partisans fell in the forests, but a few score managed to survive until the liberation of the Wlodawa region, while several others succeeded in crossing the River Bug and joined Soviet partisans in the Polesie forests.

In the late autumn of 1942 the Germans ordered the establishment of a special ghetto in Wlodawa for all Jews who voluntarily left their hiding places in the forests of the northeastern Lublin province. They were promised that no further deportations would take place. Several thousand Jews who had taken refuge in the forests, but who lacked arms and food supplies and could not survive the winter there, trusted the German promise, and settled in the new Wlodawa ghetto. On April 30, 1943, all were deported to Sobibor and murdered. Jews from Wlodawa who managed to survive in the partisan units left Poland immediately after the war. The Jewish community in Wlodawa was not reconstituted.

[Stefan Krakowski]

BIBLIOGRAPHY: Halpern, Pinkas, index; S. Dubnow (ed.), *Pinkas ha-Medinah* (1925), index; B. Wasiutyński, *Ludność żydowska w Polsce w wiekach XIX i XX* (1930), 34, 63, 64, 77, 201, 210; A. Wein (ed.), *Żydzi a powstanie styczniowe* (1963), index; N.N. Hannover, *Yeven Meẓulah* (1966), 57, 58; BŻIH, no. 21 (1957), 21–92.

WODZISLAW (Pol. **Wodzisław Śląwski**), town in Katowice province, southern Poland. Jewish settlement in Wodzislaw dates from the 17th century. The Jews there mainly engaged in commerce, and a number of wealthy merchants used to do business at the great fairs of Leipzig and Breslau. The community numbered 200 Jewish householders in 1655–56, at the time of the Polish war with Sweden. Toward the end of the 17th and during the 18th centuries, the Wodzislaw community attained considerable influence. It ranked as a principal *kehillah* within the communal framework (see *Councils of the Lands), and its leaders also took an active part in the affairs of Polish and Lithuanian Jewry as a whole. Rabbis of Wodzislaw include Menahem b. Zalman Gabais, author of *Neḥamat Ẓiyyon* (Frankfurt, 1677), Joseph Joske b. Herz of Lvov, and Samuel b. Uri Shraga *Phoebus, author of *Beit Shemu'el*. The Jewish population in Wodzislaw numbered 1,002 in 1765, 1,563 (72.5% of the total) in 1857, 2,667 (73.6%) in 1897, and 2,839 (73.2%) in 1921.

[Nathan Michael Gelber]

Holocaust Period

On the outbreak of World War II there were about 2,400 Jews in Wodzislaw. In September 1942, 300 Jews from Wodzislaw and its vicinity were deported to the *Treblinka death camp. The Jewish community was liquidated in November 1942 when the remaining 300 Jews were deported to *Sandomierz and shared the fate of that community. After the war the Jewish community of Wodzislaw was not reconstituted.

BIBLIOGRAPHY: B. Friedberg, *Luḥot Zikkaron* (1904²); I. Schiper, in: *YIVO Historishe Shriftn*, 1 (1929), 85–114; I. Halpern, Pinkas, index.

WOGUE, LAZARE ELIEZER (1817–1897), French rabbi, scholar, and journalist. Wogue, born in Fontainebleau, was ordained in 1843 at the École Centrale Rabbinique in Metz. In 1851 he began to teach German and theology there (in 1859 it became the Séminaire Israélite de France and was transferred to Paris), retaining his two chairs until his retirement in 1894. From 1868 Wogue was also director of the *talmud torah* of the Séminaire Israélite. The most important of his many scholarly works is a translation of the Pentateuch with commentaries (1860–69), which is the one used in the *Bible du Rabbinat* edited by Z. Kahn.

Among his other publications are *Le Rabbinat Français au XIXe siècle* (1843), *Le Guide du Croyant Israélite* (1857, 1898²), *Histoire de la Bible et de l'Exégèse biblique jusqu'à nos jours* (1881), a French translation (1882) of the first two volumes of *Geschichte der Juden* by H. Graetz, *Esquisse d'une théologie juive* (1887), and *La Prédication Israélite en France* (1890). He also translated various Hebrew works. Among the manuscripts he left is a tract on theology. A prolific writer, Wogue wrote many articles which were published in such Jewish periodicals as *La Paix* and *l'Union Israélite*. He was editor in chief of *l'Univers Israélite* during 1879–95.

BIBLIOGRAPHY: M. Reines, in: *Oẓar ha-Sifrut*, 5 (1896), 143–53; *L'Univers Israélite*, 52 (1896/97), 132–8.

[Colette Sirat]

WOHL, HENRYK (1842–1907), Polish revolutionary. Born in Warsaw into a patriotic family supporting Polish independence, Wohl took part in the Polish uprising of 1863, and became head of a department in the insurrectionist government. After the collapse of the revolt, he was condemned to death by the Russians, but the sentence was commuted to life imprisonment with forced labor in a remote part of Russia. After serving 20 years he was allowed to return to Poland. On his grave in the main avenue of the Jewish cemetery in Warsaw, a memorial of three unpolished stones symbolizes Poland under the three partitions. The memorial was the center of many demonstrations during the Czarist domination of Poland.

[Abraham Wein]

WOHLBERG, MOSHE (**Max**; 1907–1996), *ḥazzan*. Wohlberg was born in Humene in Czechoslovakia. When he was four, his family moved to Budapest, where he sang with the choir of the Rombach synagogue. He studied in the *yeshivot* of Nagy Karoly and Szatmar. His family moved to the United States, where he completed his Hebrew studies at the Herzliah Hebrew Teachers' Institute in New York. He studied music with Arnold Zemachson, sang in the choir of the Metropolitan Opera, and held several positions as cantor in the United States. His chief activity was in the field of training cantors, and he had hundreds of students. From 1948 to 1951 he was the second president of the Cantors Assembly. From 1952 he was professor of liturgy at the Cantors' School of the Jewish Theological Seminary in New York. He was considered an authority on prayer rites and published many articles on the history of liturgy. His published compositions can be found in collections such as *Chemdat Shabbat* and *Yaḥad B'kol* (Cantors Assembly). A recording of his singing of 19th-century compositions by *ḥazzan*-composers of the period is available through Musique Internationale Chicago

[Akiva Zimmerman / Raymond Goldstein (2nd ed.)]

WOHLGEMUTH, JOSEPH (1867–1942), rabbi, educator, and theologian. Wohlgemuth, born in Memel, as a child moved with his family to Hamburg, where his grandfather, Isaiah Wohlgemuth, became stipendiary rabbi (Klausrabbiner). Wohlgemuth studied at the Berlin Rabbinical Seminary and at the university, teaching at the same time and for many years afterward at the Adass Yisroel religious school. In 1895 he was appointed tutor and lecturer in religious philosophy, homiletics, and practical *halakhah* at the seminary, where he exercised considerable influence on several generations of students for the Orthodox rabbinate. In 1932 broken health forced him to retire to a sanatorium in Frankfurt.

Wohlgemuth's published works include: *Die Unsterblichkeitslehre in der Bibel* (1899); *Beitraege zu einer juedischen Homiletik* (1904); *Das juedische Religionsgesetz in juedischer Beleuchtung* (2 vols., 1911–19), a study of the problem of *Ta'amei ha-Mitzvot* (the ideology of the practical commandments); *Bildungsprobleme in der Ostjudenfrage* (1916); *Das Tier und seine Wertung im Judentum* (1930); and *Grundgedanken der Religionsphilosophie Max Schelers* (1931). His *Der badische Gebetbuchentwurf...* (1907) and *Gesetzestreues und liberales Judentum* (1913) are a defense of Orthodoxy against Reform. In *Der Weltkrieg im Lichte des Judentums* (1915), he extolled Germany's "civilizing mission." Wohlgemuth also translated (with J. Bleichrode (1899, 1939[7]) M.Ḥ. Luzzatto's ethical guide, *Mesillat Yesharim* (1906) into German. In 1914 he founded the monthly **Jeschurun*, which under his editorship became (to 1930) the leading Orthodox periodical in the spheres of Jewish scholarship and thought, and to which he contributed important articles – both on scholarly subjects and on current affairs. A Festschrift was issued in honor of his 60th birthday (*Juedische Studien*, 1928).

His son, JUDAH ARI WOHLGEMUTH (1903–1957), educator and author, taught at Jewish schools in Telsiai, Lithuania, and Riga, Latvia, before spending eight years with his family in a labor camp in Siberia. Wohlgemuth published *Vom Denken und Glauben unserer Zeit* (1935); *Fragt immer: gut oder boese* (1954), dealing with the religious and philosophical problems raised by the Holocaust; and a trilingual poem, "Pesaḥ be-Novosibersk 1942" (1963), written in exile in Siberia.

BIBLIOGRAPHY: J.A. Wohlgemuth, in: L. Jung (ed.), *Guardians of Our Heritage* (1958), 533–50; Y. Aviad, *Deyokena'ot* (1962), 209–12; I. Gruenfeld, *Three Generations* (1958), index; H. Schwab, *History of Orthodox Jewry in Germany* (1950), index; idem, *Chachme Ashkenaz* (1964), 125–6.

°WOJDA, CAROL FREDERICK (1771–1846), senior official in the senate of the Duchy of Warsaw (see *Poland), and member of the committee for Jewish affairs established in 1808. Wojda presented his proposals for solving the "Jewish problem" to the senate in 1809, recommending changes in the Jewish way of life, abrogation of communal and judicial autonomy, educational reform including the teaching of Polish and German, acceptance of European dress, and prohibition of the sale of liquor by Jews. The changes were to have been effected within ten years, after which emancipation was to be granted to Jews in the "productive" professions and to educated businessmen. To accelerate the process of assimilation, Wojda proposed that Jewish residence in the towns not be restricted to special quarters. He also recommended the establishment of a *consistory on the French model to deal with Jewish affairs. Wojda's program was not even debated. In 1815 he presented to the head of the committee for Jewish affairs a memorandum incorporating this plan.

BIBLIOGRAPHY: R. Mahler, *Divrei Yemei Yisrael, Dorot Aḥaronim*, 3 (1955), 71–79; 4 (1956), 219; Wischnitzer, in: *Perezhitoye*, 7 (1909), 166–72; Goldstein, in: *Yevreyskaya Starina*, 12 (1928), 301–14.

[Nathan Michael Gelber]

WOLBERG, LEWIS ROBERT (1905–1988), U.S. psychiatrist and psychoanalyst. Born in Russia, Wolberg was taken to the United States at the age of nine months. When he completed his training, he was appointed clinical professor of psychiatry at the New York University Medical School and a training analyst at the New York Medical College from its beginning in 1943. He was a founder of the American Academy of Psychoanalysis. Although trained in psychoanalysis in its more classical form, he rapidly became aware of the need for innovations. He was a pioneer in the field of dynamic psychiatry and contemporary psychotherapy. In 1945 he founded the Postgraduate Center for Mental Health, of which he was medical director and dean, and later dean emeritus. Here he created a model community mental health center based upon a multidisciplinary approach to treatment, training, research, and prevention. He was in the forefront of new ways to bring a mental health orientation to the individual, the family, the neighborhood, the nation, and the international community. A leading authority on hypnosis, Wolberg pioneered the use of this technique for more than 50 years. He was an outstanding teacher and a member of many psychiatric associations and published extensively in professional and popular periodicals.

His most important books are *Hypnoanalysis* (1945), *The Technique of Psychotherapy* (2 vols, 1954), *Medical Hypnosis* (2 vols., 1948), *Short-Term Psychotherapy* (1965), *Psychotherapy and the Behavioral Sciences* (1966), *The Dynamics of Personality* (1970), *Hypnosis, Is It for You?* (1972), and *The Practice of Psychotherapy* (1982).

ADD. BIBLIOGRAPHY: P. Buirskl (ed.), *Frontiers of Dynamic Psychotherapy: Essays in Honor of Arlene and Lewis R. Wolberg* (1987).

[Yehudith Shaltiel]

WOLBROM, town in Cracow province, Poland. Jews settled there at the end of the 17th century. An organized Jewish community existed from the 18th century under the jurisdiction of the Cracow community. In 1765 there were 303 Jews in Wolbrom who paid the poll tax. The town was incorporated in Congress Poland in 1815. In 1827 the Jews numbered 724 (27% of the total population). Following the economic development of the town in the 19th century, the number of Jews increased to 1,466 (59%), despite the restrictions on Jewish settlement in force there between 1823 and 1862, because of the town's proximity to the Austrian border. The main occupations of the Jews were petty commerce, weaving, tanning, and locksmithing. In the 19th century Ḥasidism had a strong influence in Wolbrom. Between 1897 and 1921 the number of the Jews increased from 2,901 to 4,276 (59%). Before the outbreak of war in 1939, there were about 5,000 Jews living in Wolbrom.

Holocaust Period

During World War II, under the German occupation, Wolbrom came under the province of Cracow of the General Government. The Germans entered Wolbrom on the first day of the war, Sept. 1, 1939. Scores of people were immediately shot. Afterward all the Jewish inhabitants were driven out of Wolbrom in the direction of Zawiercie. On the three-day march many succumbed to torture by the guards. On September 7 the surviving Jews returned and were set at forced labor, particularly in the forests. In the fall of 1941 a ghetto was established in Wolbrom which the Jews were forbidden to leave, under pain of death. Nearly 8,000 Jews, among them about 3,000 deportees and refugees, were concentrated inside the ghetto. The liquidation of the Jews in Wolbrom ghetto began on Sept. 6 or 7, 1942, when the German police and Ukrainians drove all the Jews to the railway station, where the Germans carried out a *Selektion*. About 2,000 old and weak persons were taken to the forest where mass graves had been made ready. After undressing completely, they were shot. The remaining Jews at the station were loaded on to train cars that evening. At the stopovers the Germans cast away the corpses of those who had suffocated in the cars. The deportees were taken to *Belzec death camp. Some hundreds of men were chosen by selection and transported to labor camps. After the liquidation of the Jewish community in Wolbrom, the Jewish cemetery became the site of executions for Jews found or denounced while hiding. From mid-September 1942 until the end of 1944 nearly 400 Jews were shot in this manner.

Only some 300 Jews from Wolbrom survived the war. They did not resettle in Wolbrom, and most of them emigrated.

BIBLIOGRAPHY: Halpern, Pinkas, index; R. Mahler, *Yidn in Amolikn Poyln in Likht fun Tsifern* (1958), index; B. Wasiutyński, *Ludność żydowksa w Polsce w wiekach XIX i XX* (1930), 53; *Landsmanshaften in Israel* (1961), 78–79; E. Podhovizer-Sandel, in: BŻIH, no. 30 (1959), passim.

[Danuta Dombrowska]

WOLF (Heb. זְאֵב), the *Canis lupis*, is frequently mentioned in the Bible and rabbinical literature as a wicked and cruel beast (Ezek. 22:27) found in desert regions (Jer. 5:6) which seizes its prey at night (Zeph. 3:3; Hab. 1:8). Wolves were a serious danger to flocks of sheep (cf. Isa. 11:6). The Mishnah states that "when there is a visitation of wolves," i.e., when they appear in packs, the shepherd cannot be held liable for the loss of the sheep of which he is in charge (BM 7:9). Wolves are stated on an occasion to have killed 300 sheep (TJ, Beẓah 1:160a), and to have torn to pieces two children in Transjordan (Ta'an. 3:6). The wolf is like a big sheep dog (cf. Ber. 9b). According to the Mishnah, "a wolf and a dog," though similar, constitute *mixed species (Kil. 1:6). Even in recent times wolves have been known to attack flocks of sheep in Ereẓ Israel. It can get into the fold and strangle a number of sheep (on occasions sucking their blood, cf. Ezek. 22:27), but it carries off only one sheep, sometimes carrying it a considerable distance to its lair in the mountains of Transjordan. The Midrash to Psalms 10:14 mentions the legend of Romulus and Remus being suckled by a she-wolf.

BIBLIOGRAPHY: S. Bodenheimer, *Ha-Ḥai be-Arẓot ha-Mikra*, 2 vols. (1949–56), index; J. Feliks, *Animal World of the Bible* (1962), 35. **ADD. BIBLIOGRAPHY:** Feliks, Ha-Ẓome'aḥ, 223.

[Jehuda Feliks]

WOLF, U.S. family of communal leaders with branches in Philadelphia and Washington. The brothers ELIAS WOLF (1820–after 1881) and ABRAHAM and LEVI WOLF (1811–1893) were born in Bavaria and emigrated to the United States. Elias Wolf arrived about 1840, going to Philadelphia. He obtained a good education, particularly in Hebrew. After a few years he went to Wilmington, North Carolina, and in 1850 to Ulrichsville, Ohio. He settled permanently in Philadelphia in 1856, where with his brothers he managed the family manufacturing interests. The family established and kept a close association with Rodeph Shalom Congregation, with Elias Wolf serving as vice president in 1867 and as president in 1871.

All of Elias Wolf's five sons took part in communal life in Philadelphia. EDWIN (1855–1934) was born in Ulrichsville a year before his father returned to Philadelphia for good. He was educated in public schools and then joined his father's business, taking over when the latter retired in 1877. Subsequently he left the firm due to ill health and in the 1880s worked with his brothers in their various enterprises. In later life he held a number of civic and communal positions, serving on the Philadelphia Board of Education, to which he was elected in 1901, as president of the Jewish Publication Society from 1903 to 1913, and as chairman of the Board of Governors of Dropsie College.

Edwin Wolf's son MORRIS (1883–1978) was born in Philadelphia. He graduated from the University of Pennsylvania and was admitted to the Pennsylvania Bar in 1903. For more than 50 years he was a senior partner of the well-known firm of Wolf, Block, Schorr, and Solis-Cohen in Philadelphia, which he had founded in 1903. He served as assistant district attorney for the city of Philadelphia in 1909–10, as state deputy attorney general in 1913–14, and as a member of the Court of Common Pleas after 1930. One of his legal clients was the noted book dealer Abraham Simon Wolf *Rosenbach. Morris became a prominent bibliophile and book collector in his own right as a result of his contacts with Rosenbach.

Morris' son EDWIN WOLF II (1911–1991) was a librarian, historian of U.S. Jews, and bibliographer. At age 18 he began a long association with Abraham Simon Wolf Rosenbach, preparing most of the catalogs for the Rosenbach Company. Toward the end of his years with Rosenbach (to 1952), whose career he describes in *Rosenbach: A Biography* (1960), he managed the Philadelphia office of the firm. During World War II he served in military intelligence as a French and German interpreter and in counterintelligence. After he left the Rosenbach Company in 1952, he became librarian for the Library Company of Philadelphia (from 1953 to 1984), the oldest subscription library in the United States, with extensive Judaica holdings. In addition to his work in preserving the documents of the past, Wolf was also instrumental in presenting new works through the Jewish Publication Society of America. Elected a trustee in 1935 "in place of his grandfather," as he notes in one of his elegantly concise annual reports (see American Jewish Year Book), he served as president (1954–59) and from 1965 as chairman of the publications committee.

Edwin Wolf II wrote *History of the Jews of Philadelphia from Colonial Times to the Age of Jackson* (1957), with Maxwell Whiteman; *Philadelphia: Portrait of an American City* (1975); and many monographs. His catalogs include *Descriptive Catalogue of the John Frederick Lewis Collection of European Manuscripts* (1937); *William Blake 1757–1827* (1939), prepared with Elizabeth Mongan, *William Blake's Illuminated Books: A Census* (1953; repr. 1968), edited jointly with Geoffrey Keynes; *Bibliothesauri: Or Jewels from the Shelves of the Library Company of Philadelphia* (1966); *A Flock of Beautiful Birds* (1977); and *Legacies of Genius: A Celebration of Philadelphia Libraries* (1988).

[Claire Sotnick and Hillel Halkin]

WOLF, ABNER (1902–?), U.S. neuropathologist. Born and educated in New York City, Wolf was appointed professor of neuropathology at the College of Physicians and Surgeons from 1951 and at Columbia Presbyterian Medical Center from 1964. Wolf served as president of the American Association of Neuropathologists (1951–52) and the New York Neurological Society (1956–57). He was a member of numerous professional societies and published extensively. He was editor in chief of the *Journal of Neuropathology and Experimental Neurology* from 1963.

WOLF, ABRAHAM (1876–1948), English philosopher. He was professor of logic and scientific method at University College, London, concurrently lecturing at the London School of Economics and Political Science. From 1931 until his retirement in 1941, he was dean of the faculty of economics and political science at the University of London. He was a member of the editorial board of the *Encyclopaedia Britannica* and was also the editor of the *History of the Sciences Library.* His main works deal with logic and scientific method, Spinoza, Nietzsche, and the history of science. He also wrote on higher education in Nazi Germany and in German-occupied countries.

ADD. BIBLIOGRAPHY: "Abraham Wolf," in: S. Brown (ed.), *Dictionary of Twentieth Century British Philosophers* (2005).

[Samuel Hugo Bergman]

WOLF, ALFRED (1915–2004), rabbi, community leader, and interreligious pioneer. Born in Eberbach, Germany, to Hermann and Regina Levy Wolf, Alfred Wolf was one of five rabbinic students brought to the United States by Hebrew Union College in 1935 to continue their studies away from Nazi persecution.

Wolf earned a B.A. at the University of Cincinnati in 1937, was ordained at HUC in 1940, and completed a Ph.D. in religion at the University of Southern California in 1961. Wolf held pulpits in Toronto, Ontario, and Dothan, Alabama (1940–46), before serving as the Union of American Hebrew Congregation's Southeast Council Regional Director (1945–46) and then moving to Los Angeles to serve as the UAHC's Western Regional Director (1946–49). In 1949, he joined Edgar F. Magnin and Maxwell Dubin to become the third member of Wilshire Boulevard Temple's rabbinic staff, which provided religious leadership for the West's largest congregation. After retiring as Wilshire's Senior Rabbi in 1985, he served as director of the American Jewish Committee's Skirball Institute on American Values and became its director emeritus in 1996.

Wolf's influence on Jewish life in Southern California was immediate and far-reaching. In 1946, there were only six Reform congregations in the greater Los Angeles area. Three years later, thanks in part to his energetic efforts with the UAHC – and the Jewish population explosion – there were 18. Upon his arrival at Wilshire Boulevard Temple, he initially focused his attention on creating programs for Jewish youth. He reinstated the bar mitzvah, built up the religious school to 2,000 students, and, most significantly, started one of the nation's first Jewish summer camp programs, which eventually included Camp Hess Kramer (1952) and Gindling Hilltop Camp (1968) on 200 coastal acres in Malibu. Wolf's concept for Jewish camping had its roots in the hills of Germany, where the life-long hiker led Jewish youngsters on outings even after Hitler's ascent to power. The Malibu camps have been attended by more than 50,000 children and are used throughout the off-season by numerous community groups from across the region.

Wolf was determined to assume a leadership role in promoting community and interreligious relations in America. He served as chairman of the Los Angeles County Commission on Human Relations, offering important guidance in the aftermath of the 1965 Watts Riots, and in 1969 he co-founded the Interreligious Council of Southern California, which became the first such organization in the U.S. to encompass virtually all of the world's major religions. In 1987, Wolf was selected to address Pope John Paul II on behalf of the entire Southern California Jewish community during the pontiff's historic visit to Los Angeles.

Among Wolf's numerous other active affiliations were the Southern California Board of Rabbis, the Pacific Association of Reform Rabbis, the Hebrew Union College-Jewish Institute of Religion Board of Governors, the National Commission on Interfaith Relations, the American Jewish Committee's Los Angeles Executive Board, the Los Angeles Jewish Federation Council, and the American Academy of Religion.

[Robin Kramer (2nd ed.)]

WOLF, ARNOLD JACOB (1924–), U.S. Reform rabbi. Wolf was born in Chicago, Illinois, and received his B.A. from the University of Cincinnati in 1945. He chose to remain at Hebrew Union College rather than to move to New York's Jewish Theological Seminary when Abraham Joshua *Heschel left HUC along with students such as Samuel Dressner and Richard L. Rubenstein. In 1948, he was ordained at *Hebrew Union College, which awarded him an honorary D.D. in 1973. Following ordination, he served as assistant rabbi of Emanuel Congregation in Chicago (1948–51; 1953–57), interrupting civilian life to serve as a chaplain in the U.S. Navy during the Korean War (1951–53). He was also the first director of the Summer Camp Institutes of the National Federation of Temple Youth (1948–51). In 1955, he became rabbi of Chicago's Congregation B'nai Joshua (1955–57), while launching his own television and radio programs broadcast over the Midwest affiliates of the CBS and ABC networks. In 1957, he was founding rabbi of Congregation Solel, an experimental synagogue in the Chicago suburb of Highland Park (1957–72). He also taught at the University of Chicago Divinity School, Loyola Marymount University, and the College of Jewish Studies (now Spertus Institute).

In 1972, he decided to leave the pulpit, and Wolf was appointed Jewish chaplain at Yale University, where he also lectured in the philosophy department and served as a commissioner of the Board of Ethics of the city of New Haven. His years on campus were marked by a particularly Jewish brand of social activism: he was chairman of Breira, a group that aimed for shared responsibility by Israeli and Diaspora Jewry for Middle East peace (1973–75), opposed Israel's settlements policy, and sought to talk with the Palestinians. He was a founding contributing editor (with Eugene *Borowitz with whom he had been a fellow student at HUC) of *Sh'ma, A Journal of Jewish Responsibility*. He was also the first official Jewish representative to attend a World Council of Churches Assembly (1975).

In 1980, Wolf returned to Chicago to become rabbi of Illinois' oldest Jewish congregation, Kehilath Anshei Maarav-Isaiah Israel, where he became emeritus in 2000. He resumed leadership roles in the community, becoming president of the Chicago Association of Reform Rabbis (1995–96). In 2002, he was named resident scholar at the Foundation for Jewish Studies in Washington, D.C.

Wolf, who served as theology editor of *Judaism* magazine from 1998, wrote more than 350 essays as well as four books: *Challenge to Confirmands: An Introduction to Jewish Thinking* (1963), *Rediscovering Judaism: Reflections on a New Theology* (1965), *What Is Man?* (1968), and *Unfinished Rabbi* (1998). He also co-edited (with Lawrence *Hoffman) *Jewish Spiritual Journeys* (1997).

[Bezalel Gordon (2nd ed.)]

WOLF, ERIC ROBERT (1922–1999), anthropologist. Born in Vienna, Austria, in 1922, Eric Robert Wolf was an anthropologist who studied peasant societies. Born in an upper middle class family, his family moved to Sudetenland in 1933. His father was an Austrian textile factory manager; his mother was a member of Russian nobility. Wolf grew up on the Czech-German border at the time the Nazi Party was in its ascendancy and antisemitism was on the increase. His father sent him to England to the Forest School in Walthamstow; his family later escaped Germany and immigrated to England, where they were interred as enemy aliens. They eventually moved to the United States in 1940. When World War II broke out, Wolf was studying biochemistry; he left his studies and served in one of the U.S. Army's mountain troop divisions, earning a Silver Star. He returned to school at the end of the war, changing fields to anthropology. He graduated from Queens College in New York City in 1946 and finished a Ph.D. at Columbia University in 1951. He began his career as an academic, first at the University of Illinois and later at the University of Virginia, then Yale and the University of Chicago. He spent 10 years on the faculty at the University of Michigan, from 1961 to 1971, before moving to the Herbert H. Lehman College and Graduate Center at the City University of New York, as a distinguished professor, until his retirement in 1992.

Immediately after graduate school, Wolf focused his work on Mexican history and civilization, looking at the progression of culture and community from pre-Hispanic to Hispanic Mexico. While at Columbia, Wolf became acquainted with Marxism, which led him to his studies of peasantry and their role in complex societies. In the 1950s, he became part of a group of anthropology scholars known as "neo-evolutionists," who challenged the established culturalist tradition. His first book, *Peasant Wars of the Twentieth Century,* examining six political uprisings, was published in 1969. Later in his career he did ethnographic research on Alpine communities, integrating historical and ethnographic perspectives, introducing the notion of ecological constraints on development. Active in the antiwar movement during the Vietnam War, he continued his peasant studies, publishing several influential studies of peasant revolutions. He wrote the book many regard to be the masterpiece of his career in 1982, *Europe and the People Without History.* In this book, Wolf argued market forces created tribes just as they created civilizations and nations. These forces changed world populations by creating giant labor migrations such as the European expansions into Africa, the Americas and the Orient and that the common people in the world were both agents of this change as well as its victims. His last work in 1999, *Envisioning Power Ideologies of Dominance and Crisis*, compared the violent regimes of the Aztec, the Kwakiutl of the Pacific Northwest, and the Nazis. In addition to being a scholar of great reputation, Wolf was also a dedicated teacher who embraced teaching undergraduates when he might have easily excused himself from such duties. Wolf died in Irvington, New York, of colon cancer.

[David Weinstock (2nd ed)]

WOLF, FRIEDRICH (1888–1953), German playwright, author, and essayist. Wolf, who was born in Neuwied am Rhein, rebelled against his middle-class Jewish upbringing and ran away from home, hoping to become a painter in Munich. After varied experiences working on Rhine steamers and even in the Salvation Army, he qualified as a physician and served as a German medical officer during World War I. Wolf's growing opposition to the war led to his confinement in a mental hospital, where he was allowed to treat other patients. A member of the short-lived Dresden Soviet (1919), he joined the Communist Party in 1928, became active in leftist intellectual circles, and visited the U.S.S.R. in 1931. Two years later he immigrated first to Switzerland, and then to France, where he lived until 1941, except for the time he spent fighting in the republican army during the Spanish Civil War. In 1941 Wolf escaped from a detention camp in occupied France and made his way to the U.S.S.R., where he became a radio propagandist and a co-founder of the Communist-sponsored Committee for a Free Germany (1943). He returned to Germany as a Red Army medical officer in 1945. From 1950 to 1951 he was East Germany's ambassador in Warsaw.

Wolf's early expressionism dominated his plays such as *Mohammed* (written 1917, publ. 1924) and *Der Mann im Dunkel* (1925), but political engagement characterized his many later works. These include the dramas *Der arme Konrad* (1924), *Cyankali* (1929), *Die Matrosen von Cattaro* (1930; *The Sailors of Cattaro*, 1935), *Florisdorf* (1935, Eng. 1935), and *Das trojanische Pferd* (1937). Other works published before World War II (many printed in Moscow) were *Der Sprung durch den Tod* (1925) and *Die Nacht von Béthineville* (1936), stories; and *Zwei an der Grenze* (1938), an autobiographical novel. Wolf's best-known drama, *Professor Mamlock* (1933, first as *Dr. Mamlocks Ausweg*; Eng. 1935), was widely circulated among exiled democrats and underground resistance workers. He published a stream of stories and plays during and after World War II, including the autobiographical *KZ Vernet* (1941), *Zwei Kaempfer vor Moskau* (1942), *Heimkehr der Soehne* (1944), *Menetekel oder die fliegenden Untertassen* (1952), and the drama, *Thomas Muenzer* (1953). Wolf also wrote essays on the theater and published five volumes of collected plays (1946–49). He was twice awarded East Germany's National Prize (1949, 1950). Between 1960 and 1967, a 16-volume edition of his complete works appeared.

BIBLIOGRAPHY: W. Pollatschek, *Das Buehnenwerk Friedrich Wolfs* (1958); idem, *Friedrich Wolf* (1960); A.Soergel and C. Hohoff, *Dichtung und Dichter der Zeit*, 2 (1963), 392–7. **ADD. BIBLIOGRAPHY:** H. Haarmann and K. Siebenhaar, "Lebensform und Tendenzkunst: zum Fruehwerk Friedrich Wolfs," in: *Internationales Archiv fuer Sozialgeschichte der deutschen Literatur*, 10 (1985), 113–34; K. Hammer, "Konzepte der Menschenveränderung. Friedrich Wolfs Weg zum Dramatiker der Arbeiterklasse," in: *Weimarer Beitraege*, 34 (1988), 1941–61; L. Hohmann, *Friedrich Wolf: Bilder einer deutschen Biographie. Eine Dokumentation.* (1988); F. Wolf, *Auf wieviel Pferden ich geritten … Der junge Friedrich Wolf. Eine Dokumentation*, ed. by E. Wolf and B. Struzyk (1988); H. Muller (ed.), *F. Wolf, Weltbürger aus Neuwied. Selbstzeugnisse in Lyrik und Prosa. Dokumente und Dokumentarisches, Bilder und Briefe*, ed. for his 100th birthday by H. Mueller (1988); *Mut, nochmals Mut, immerzu Mut! Protokollband*, Internationales wissenschaftliches Friedrich-Wolf-Symposium der Volkshochschule der Stadt Neuwied vom 2.–4. Dezember 1988 in Neuwied aus Anlaß des 100. Geburtstages von Dr. Friedrich Wolf, 23.12.1888 in Neuwied (1990); A. Grenville, "From Social Fascism to Popular Front: KPD Policy as Reflected in the Works of Friedrich Wolf, Anna Seghers and Willi Bredel, 1928–1938," in: R. Dove and S. Lamb (eds.), *German Writers and Politics 1918–1939* (1992), 89–102; K. Jarmatz, "Zur Rezeption des Werkes von Friedrich Wolf in der frueheren DDR und BRD," in: D. Sevin (ed.), *Die Resonanz des Exils* (1992), 299–312; G. Labroisse, "Rezeption von Exilliteratur im Horizontwandel. Ferdinand Bruckners 'Die Rassen' und Friedrich Wolfs 'Professor Mamlock' in Zürich (1933 bzw. 1934) und Berlin (1948 bzw. 1946)," in: D. Sevin, *Die Resonanz des Exils* (1992), 154–63; H. Mueller, "'Ich warte nicht, bis man mich hier verhaftet.' Das Moskauer Exil der Familie Friedrich Wolf," in: *Tel Aviver Jahrbuch für deutsche Geschichte*, 24 (1995), 193–216; D.K. Heizer, *Jewish-German Identity in the Orientalist Literature of Else Lasker-Schüler, Friedrich Wolf, and Franz Werfel* (1996); A.W. Barker, "Anna Seghers, Friedrich Wolf, and the Civil War of 1934," in: *The Modern Language Review*, 95:1 (2000), 144–53; idem, "Karl Kraus, Friedrich Wolf and the Response to February 1934," in: G.J. Carr and E. Timms (eds.), *Karl Kraus und 'Die Fackel'* (2001), 163–69; C. Jakobi, "Antisemitismuskritik und Judendarstellung im deutschsprachigen Exildrama 1933–1945: Anmerkungen zu drei Stuecken von Wolf, Brecht und Hasenclever," in: C. Balme (ed.), *Das Theater der Anderen* (2001), 205–27; P. Schneck, "Mamlok und Mamlock 1937. Eine Literaturgestalt wurde lebendig. Der Berliner Zahnarzt Hans-Jacques Mamlok und Friedrich Wolfs Drama 'Professor Mamlock'," in: A. Scholz and C.-P. Heidel (eds.), *Das Bild des juedischen Arztes in der Literatur* (2002), 130–39; A. Scholz and W. Kohlert, "Ärzte, Heiler und Patienten im Werk des Arztes und Dichters Friedrich Wolf," in: A. Scholz and C.-P. Heidel (eds.), *Das Bild des juedischen Arztes in der Literatur* (2002), 120–29.

[Godfrey Edmond Silverman]

WOLF, FRUMET (**Francisca** née **Brilin**; 1770–1849), community leader. Born in Pressburg (Bratislava) into a prominent scholarly and wealthy family, she married a widower, Chajjim Joachim Wolf of Eisenstadt. An intelligent, compassionate woman, Frumet was appalled at the domination of the community by a small oligarchy of wealthy men, who were totally insensitive to the community's needs. In 1793 she wrote a pamphlet, *Pasquill Zettelech*, circulated anonymously in the community, sharply critical of the wielders of power in the community and their policies. The pamphlet was confiscated and destroyed, but not before its content caused a great stir among the Jews of the city. A ban of excommunication was pronounced not only against the anonymous author, but also against anyone involved in the distribution of the pamphlet. At that point, Frumet identified herself as the authoress. She was fined and forbidden to attend synagogue for a certain time after a plea for clemency was made on the part of her husband. The issue remained a subject of public debate, involving, among others, representatives of the patron of Eisenstadt, Duke Esterházy, until it was finally resolved in 1804. After the death of her husband, Frumet Wolf continued to manage his business and even succeeded in strengthening and enlarging it. She was also well known in Eisenstadt and Burgenland as a philanthropist, assisting the poor financially and providing them with counseling in their private lives. Her will, written in German, is preserved, and is an important source for information on the cultural and economic life of the Jews of Eisenstadt.

BIBLIOGRAPHY: B. Wachstein, *Die Grabinschriften des alten Judenfriedhofes in Eisenstadt,* (1922), 252–62; idem, *Die Inschriften des alten Judenfriedhofes in Wien*, 2 (1917), 285–9; idem, *Urkunden und Akten zur Geschichte der Juden in Eisenstadt…*, 1 (1926), 212–22, 252–62; 2 (1926), 402–22; E. Wolf, *Die Familie Wolf* (1924), 119–21; O. Abeles, *Zehn Juedinnen* (1931), 83–93.

[Yehouda Marton / Albert Lichtblau (2nd ed.)]

WOLF, GERSON (1823–1892), Austrian historian and educator. Wolf was born in Holleschau (Holesov), Moravia. After a brief preoccupation with talmudic studies in Nikolsburg he moved to Vienna, where he studied pedagogy, philosophy, and languages. In 1849 he published a booklet, *Die Demokratie und der Sozialismus*, and several radical articles. Although he was ordered to leave Vienna in the wake of these publications, he managed to stay with the help of influential friends. In 1852 he was imprisoned for a number of weeks on suspicion of being a revolutionary. In 1854, after having worked in several schools, he was appointed a teacher of religion in the Vienna community and became inspector of its religious studies in 1884. Wolf founded a youth library and, together with others, an aid organization for poor Jewish students in Vienna. In addition to surveys and documents on the history of the Jews in Worms, Bohemia, Moravia, and Austria (particularly of the Jews in Vienna), he published a textbook for Jewish schools and a survey of the Austrian educational system. He also wrote biographies of I.N. *Mannheimer and J. *Wertheimer. His works include *Ferdinand II und die Juden* (1859); *Judentaufen in Oesterreich* (1863); *Die Vertreibung der Juden aus Boehmen 1744* (1869); *Geschichte der Juden in Wien 1156–1876* (1876); *Die alten Statuter der juedischen Gemeinden in Maehren* (1880); and *Die Juden* (1883). Wolf wrote regularly for the *Monatsschrift fuer Geschichte und Wissenschaft des Judentums* (1858–87) and published a series of articles in the periodical *Ha-Mazkir* (1858–61).

BIBLIOGRAPHY: B. Wachstein, in: *Zeitschrift fuer die Geschichte der Juden in der Tschechoslowakei* 1 (1930), 17–36, (incl. bibl.). **ADD. BIBLIOGRAPHY:** [No author], in: *Oesterreichische Wochenschrift.* 9 (1892) 45, 804–805.

[Zvi Avneri / Mirjam Triendl (2nd ed.)]

WOLF, GUSTAV (1887–1947), German artist. Wolf began his artistic training at the private school of Hans Thoma (1839–1924), who wanted to promote Wolf's talent and encouraged him in his own style of art. Wolf's paintings belong to symbolism, including motifs of his own experiences, imagination, and visions, such as mythical creatures, as do his woodcuts *Zehn Holzschnitte I–X* from 1910. Wolf served as professor of graphic arts at Karlsruhe until the Nazis came to power. In 1938, Wolf emigrated to the United States. Living in exile, horrified and frustrated by the Holocaust, Wolf created in 1945 several expressionistic paintings with illustrations of the Jewish victims in the concentration camps. He was primarily a printmaker. His publications include *Die Schoepfungstage* (seven lithographs, with the biblical texts on the creation of the world), color woodcuts for a novel by Jacob Picard, and a portfolio of etchings, *Vision of Manhattan*. His work is characterized by vivid imagination and emotional intensity. Most of his artistic works are exhibited at the Gustav-Wolf-Kunstgalerie in Oestringen, Germany.

ADD. BIBLIOGRAPHY: J.E. von Borries, *Gustav Wolf: Das druckgraphische Werk* (1982); B. Brähler, *Gustav Wolf (1887–1947). Eine Weltanschauung in Bildern.* Registry of artistic heritage in Oestringen (2000; Catalogue raisonné); Gustav-Wolf-Kunstgalerie Oestringen, *Gustav Wolf. Schöpfer visionärer Kunst* (1995).

[Jihan Radjai-Ordoubadi (2nd ed.)]

°**WOLF, JOHANN CHRISTOPH** (1683–1739), German bibliographer, *Hebraist, and Orientalist. Born at Wernigerode (Prussia). Wolf studied Hebrew at Wittenberg University and, during study tours in Holland and England, met such Christian Hebraists as Vitringa, *Surenhuis, *Reland, and *Basnage. He became professor of Oriental languages and literature at the Hamburg gymnasium (1712) and was an ardent collector of Hebrew books and manuscripts. Deciding to devote himself to publishing a full list of all extant Hebrew books, he utilized the noted David *Oppenheim collection at Hanover for this purpose. The result of Wolf's research was his *Bibliotheca Hebraea* in 4 volumes (Hamburg, 1715–33).

Volume 1 (1715) contains an alphabetical list of Jewish authors with biographical notes. Volume 2 (1721) is divided into subject headings such as Bible, Apocrypha, Masorah, Mishnah, Talmud, Kabbalah, Hebrew grammar and antisemitic literature, with a short description of the nature of the books listed. Volumes 3 (1727) and 4 (1733) are supplements to the first two. Although he drew upon the works of bibliographers who preceded him (especially *Bartolocci and *Bass), Wolf offered in his *Bibliotheca* thousands of corrections and additions to the works of his predecessors. In 1829, when the Oppenheimer library was acquired by Oxford University for the *Bodleian collection, M. *Steinschneider used Wolf's *Bibliotheca* as the basis for the compilation of his Bodleian catalogue, referring to Wolf's work on almost every page. Until Steinschneider's catalogue, Wolf's *Bibliotheca* was considered the best Jewish bibliography, and Christian scholars for over a century and a half derived their knowledge on such works as the Mishnah and Talmud from Wolf's book.

Wolf also wrote a history of Hebrew lexicons (his Ph.D. dissertation at Wittenberg, 1705) and a book on the *Karaites, *Notitia Karaeorum* (Hamburg, 1714). He bequeathed his library, containing some 25,000 Hebrew books and manuscripts, to the city library of Hamburg.

BIBLIOGRAPHY: Zunz, Gesch, 14–15; Bertheau, in: ADB, 44 (1898), 545–8; Steinschneider, in: ZHB, 5 (1901), 84, no. 417; Steinschneider, Cat Bod, xxxiv–xxxvi; 2730–32, no. 7394 (here called: Wolfius (Jos. Christoph)). **ADD. BIBLIOGRAPHY:** C.G. Joecher, *Allgemeines Gelehrten Lexicon* (1751) [1961], 2053–2055 (with bibl. of Wolf's works); Sh. Brisman, *A History and Guide to Judaic Bibliography* (1977), 13–15.

[Abraham Meir Habermann / Aya Elyada (2nd ed.)]

WOLF, LEYZER (pseudonym of **Eliezer Mekler**; 1910–1943), Yiddish poet. His bizarre parodies, grotesques, and dramatic sketches bridged popular and elite impulses in the literary group *Yung-Vilne. His first book, *Evigingo* (1936), was an exotic parody of Europe printed in the Roman alphabet. The collections *Shvartse Perl* ("Black Pearls," 1939) and *Lirik un Satire* (1940) gathered poems published previously in the Yiddish press. In 1938–39, he mentored *Yungvald*, a group of younger aspiring writers, including Hirsh *Glick. Wolf died of hunger while a war refugee in Soviet Uzbekistan. A posthumous volume, *Di Broyne Bestye* ("The Brown Beast," 1943), satirized fascism. A selection of his best poems, *Lider* (1955), included a critical introduction and biographic sketch by Leyzer Ran.

BIBLIOGRAPHY: LNYL, 3 (1960) 278–9; S. Belis, in: *Portretn un Problemen* (1964), 115–36; J. Cammy, in: *Polin: Studies in Polish Jewry*, 14 (2001), 170–91; E. Shulman, *Yung-Vilne* (1946), 40–4.

[Justin D. Cammy (2nd ed.)]

WOLF, LUCIEN (1857–1930), Anglo-Jewish publicist and historian. Wolf, who was born in London, was the son of a Bohemian political refugee who worked as a pipe manufacturer. He began writing for newspapers at the age of 17. His first regular employment was with the *Jewish World*, of which he later became editor (1905–08). His fluency in French and German was an asset in this profession, and he gradually became known as a foreign affairs expert. His articles in the *Fortnightly Review* and elsewhere, under the pseudonym "Diplomaticus," commanded wide attention. From 1890 to 1909 he was foreign editor of the then-influential *Daily Graphic*. Aroused by the pogroms of 1881, Wolf became extremely interested in Russian affairs, acquired a reputation as an expert in the field, and edited the bulletin *Darkest Russia* (1912–14). He was supplied clandestinely with information through a network initiated by Isaac Elhanan *Spektor. Wolf's anti-Russian attitude made it difficult for him to continue to work as a foreign correspondent after Great Britain's entry into World War I as Russia's ally. In 1917 he became the secretary of the Joint Foreign Committee (of the *Anglo-Jewish Association and the *Board of Deputies of British Jews). As such, he attended the postwar Paris Peace Conference, where he was regarded as a spokesman of "western" Jewry. Although he strongly opposed Jewish nationalism in any form, he was largely responsible for the *Minorities Treaties to safeguard the civil and religious rights of central and eastern European Jews. Subsequently, he acquired a reputation as an authority on minorities problems at the sessions of the *League of Nations at Geneva. Originally an admirer and, to some extent, supporter of Herzl, Wolf later became the principal English spokesman of anti-Zionism, though after 1905 he collaborated with *Zangwill in the Jewish Territorial Organization (see *Territorialism). His hopes that the Wilsonian settlement in Europe at the close of World War I would lead to the protection of its Jewish populations proved tragically naïve.

He had early begun research in Anglo-Jewish history, which he continued throughout his life. He wrote the centennial life of Sir Moses *Montefiore (1884), was one of the organizers of the Anglo-Jewish Historical Exhibition of 1887, and founded the Jewish Historical Society of *England in 1893 (serving repeatedly as its president). His principal work was on the "middle period" of Anglo-Jewish history (after the expulsion of 1290) and on the resettlement. His contributions, based almost wholly on original sources, were of primary importance and placed the study of the subject on a new basis. These researches attracted Wolf to the history of the Marranos. He edited reports on trials of Jewish interest from the *Canary Islands Inquisition records and in 1925 prepared a report on the contemporary Marranos of *Portugal, a historical contribution of great importance. He contributed a most important article to the 11th edition of the *Encyclopedia Britannica* on antisemitism, on the history of which he was the recognized authority in the English-speaking world. His collected *Essays in Jewish History*, edited by Cecil Roth in 1934, contains an account of his life. In the non-Jewish sphere he wrote a life of the English statesman Lord Ripon (1921). During the last 30 years of his life, he was hampered by almost total blindness (only partly relieved by an operation) but triumphantly overcame it. An account of Wolf's wartime activities is Mark Levene's *War, Jews, and the New Europe: The Diplomacy of Lucien Wolf, 1914–1919* (1992).

BIBLIOGRAPHY: Roth, in: L. Wolf, *Essays in Jewish History* (1934), 2–34, 37–47 (bibl.), 51–69; M. Beloff, *Lucien Wolf and the Anglo-Russian Entente* (1951); Frankel, in: JHSET, 20 (1959–61), 161–88; Szajkowski, in: *YIVO Bleter*, 43 (1966), 283–96; idem, in: JSOS, 29 (1967), 3–26. **ADD. BIBLIOGRAPHY:** ODNB online.

[Cecil Roth]

WOLF, RICHARD RIEGEL (**Subirana Lobo, Ricardo**; 1889–1982), plenipotentiary minister of Cuba in Israel (1961–73), scientist, and founder of the Wolf Foundation in 1975. Born in Hanover, Germany, he was a socialist during the government of the Kaiser, member of the then illegal Social-Democratic Party and the German Zionist movements of the left. He immigrated to Cuba in 1913.

As a student of chemistry, he made an important discovery related to the recovery of residual iron during the founding process, which was successfully applied in steel mills around the world, making him a millionaire. In addition to Cuba, Germany, and Israel, he also lived at times in Barcelona, Italy, and Istanbul. In 1924, he married Francisca Subirana, a Cuban, and, contrary to tradition, adopted her surname.

Although a successful businessman, he actively supported the Cuban Revolution and its leader, Fidel Castro, from the beginning. He became an advisor to the government and promoted support for Land Reform. In 1961, he was named head of the Cuban Diplomatic Mission in Israel, the only Cuban embassy that the Revolutionary Government established at no cost because, as he had promised, Wolf paid for the building, salaries, and costs of representation.

He planted the basis for a fertile relationship between Cuba, his adopted country, and Israel, through the creation of a Friendship Association that substituted for official channels and promoted the collaboration of Israeli agricultural technicians with Cuba. Despite the difficulties imposed by the political alliances of the two countries, he added a profound dimension to the understanding of and empathy with Jewish reality among the Cuban leadership.

When Cuba broke off diplomatic relations with Israel in 1973, Wolf, who was 84 years old, decided to stay in Israel. He and his wife Francesca founded the Wolf Foundation that awards prizes to outstanding scientists and artists, irrespective of their nationality.

BIBLIOGRAPHY: M. Corrales, *The Chosen Island: Jews in Cuba* (2005).

[Maritza Corrales (2nd ed.)]

WOLF, SIMON (1836–1923), U.S. lawyer, communal leader, and lobbyist. Born in Hinzweiler, Germany, Wolf, the son of Levi Wolf and nephew of Elias *Wolf, went to the United States in 1848 and settled in Ulrichsville, Ohio. In 1860 he served as an alternate delegate to the Democratic national convention, but shortly thereafter formed a lifelong allegiance to the Republican Party. Disillusioned with a business career, Wolf studied law in 1862 and went to Washington, where he opened a law practice. After the presidential election of 1868, when he publicly defended General Ulyssses S. *Grant against charges of antisemitism stemming from a Civil War incident, Wolf was rewarded with the post of recorder of deeds for the District of Columbia. He held this post until 1877, when political pressures forced his resignation, and then served as a judge of the municipal court in the district. In 1881 he became the United States consul in Egypt, where he tried to foster trade between the two countries. In 1882 Wolf resumed his law practice in Washington, D.C. At that time Washington was sufficiently provincial to allow easy access to all political leaders and Wolf availed himself of this privilege; he soon viewed himself as a spokesman for the U.S. Jewish community to the federal government and claimed a personal acquaintance with every president from Lincoln through Wilson.

A skillful organizer, Wolf was the representative of *B'nai B'rith in Washington, serving as its president in 1904. Early in his career he acquired the permanent chairmanship of the Committee on Civil and Religious Rights of the *Union of American Hebrew Congregations (see *Board of Delegates of American Israelites). He scored several achievements in social justice and liberal legal interpretations, which included a ruling from the immigration authorities that persons dependent on private charities were not liable to deportation as public charges, and the postponement for four years of the enactment of a restrictive immigrant literacy bill. He was said to have saved some 103,000 aliens from deportation through personal intervention. Wolf publicized the plight of Russian and Romanian Jewry by securing in 1870 the appointment of a Jew, Benjamin F. *Peixotto, as consul to Bucharest; by urging the publication of Secretary of State John Hay's Romanian Note, reiterating basic rights for Jews; by helping to effect the quick release of the Kishinev Petition, aimed at world censure of Russian antisemitism; and by working for the abrogation of a discriminatory Russo-American commercial treaty (1911). As a spokesman for Reform Judaism, Wolf opposed governmental attempts to identify Jews as a group and was vociferous in denying Zionist aspirations, a matter in which he claimed assurances from President Wilson. Jealous of his prerogatives, Wolf engaged in internecine quarrels with the *American Jewish Committee. A member of the Washington Board of Charities and of its Board of Education, he served as president of the Washington Hebrew Congregation. Wolf wrote numerous articles and two large works: *The American Jew as Soldier, Patriot and Citizen* (1895), a study of Jews in the U.S. armed forces (1774–1865), and an autobiography, *The Presidents I Have Known* (1918). A collection of *Selected Addresses and Papers* appeared in 1926. His papers are on deposit at the American Jewish Historical Society.

Wolf's son, ADOLF GRANT (1869–1947), was born in Washington, D.C., admitted to the bar in 1893, and for 11 years conducted a law practice in Washington. In the early 1900s he was appointed associate justice of the Supreme Court of Puerto Rico, serving on the bench until 1941, when he retired. He was also a member of the Commission of Uniform State Laws (Puerto Rico) from 1918 to 1930.

BIBLIOGRAPHY: M.J. Kohler, in: AJHSP, 29 (1925), 198–206; D.H. and E.L. Panitz, *ibid.*, 47 (1957), 76–100; E.L. Panitz, *ibid.*, 53 (1963), 99–130; 55 (1965), 57–97.

[Esther Panitz]

WOLFE, Canadian family. RAY D. WOLFE (1917–1990), entrepreneur and philanthropist, and ROSE SENDEROWITZ WOLFE (1919–), social worker, community leader, fundraiser, and philanthropist, were both born into eastern European immigrant working-class families in Toronto. They married in 1940 after Rose graduated with a degree in social work and Ray with a degree in arts from the University of Toronto.

Ray, who had failed his university courses in finance and commerce, masterminded the growth of a small family produce wholesaler into the Oshawa Group – one of Canada's largest food-drug-department store businesses. After serving in the Royal Canadian Air Force in 1943–46, Ray returned to his floundering family business and as chairman and CEO built it into a major Canadian corporation. He established a personal reputation for business acumen, honesty, and philanthropy. He was appointed to the boards of large Canadian corporations, becoming the first Jew to sit on the boards of Canadian Pacific Limited and the Bank of Nova Scotia. He was very active in the Jewish community, serving on the boards of the Canadian Friends of Haifa University, Canada-Israel Institute for Industrial Research and Development, and the Canadian Council of Christians and Jews. He was chair of the United Jewish Welfare Fund, a governor of Toronto's Mount Sinai Hospital, and founding publisher and chair of the weekly *Canadian Jewish News*. The Ray D. Wolfe Fellowship, which supports advanced research in Jewish studies at the University of Toronto, was established in his memory by the Canadian Jewish News. In 1980 Ray was awarded the Order of Canada.

In 2000, the Rose and Ray Wolfe Chair in Holocaust Studies was established at the University of Toronto. The chair was created by Rose and reflected her long association with the university and her devotion to social welfare and human rights issues. Rose's early social work career with Toronto's Jewish Family and Child Service placed her with Jewish youngsters who had survived the Holocaust and entered Canada as orphans in 1947–48. This professional work led Rose to a career as a volunteer which focused on education, social justice, and community relations. She was active in more than 20 social, cultural, and educational organizations. From 1983 to 1991, while an officer of the Canadian Jewish Congress (Ontario), Rose served as chair of the Joint Community Relations committee devoted to improving Jewish relations with other ethnic groups, the media, and government. She was also a member of the board of the Banting Research Institute, McMichael Canadian Art Collection, and the Pearson College of the Pacific. Among her affiliations, Rose was a director of Mount Sinai Hospital, where the family established the Ray D. Wolfe Department of Family Medicine.

Rose's many positions included the presidency of the Jewish Family and Child Service in Toronto, the Women's Division of the UJA, and the Federation of Jewish Women's Organizations. She became the first female president of the Toronto Jewish Congress (later the UJA Federation of Greater Toronto), responsible for all Jewish social agencies and educational institutions, and in 1991–97 she served as the first Jewish chancellor of the University of Toronto, where she had long been a key fundraiser. She was honored with an honorary doctor of laws degree from the University in 1998, the Human Relations Award from the Canadian Council of Christians and Jews in 1985, and the 1980 Jewish National Fund's Negev Dinner. Rose Wolfe was awarded the Order of Ontario in 1982 and the Order of Canada in 1999.

BIBLIOGRAPHY: D. Francis, *Controlling Interest. Who Owns Canada?* (1986), 152–57.

[Paula Draper (2nd ed.)]

WOLFE, ALAN S. (1942–), U.S. scholar of political science. Born in Philadelphia, Wolfe received his bachelor's degree from Temple University in 1963. He did graduate work in political science at Vanderbilt University and in 1967 received his Ph.D. in political science from the University of Pennsylvania. From 1966 to 1968 he was an assistant professor of political science at Douglass College, and from 1968 to 1970 was assistant professor at the College of Old Westbury of the State University of New York. Wolfe taught as a visiting scholar at several universities, including Harvard and the University of California at Berkeley. In 1979 he joined the faculty of Queens College as an associate professor, later becoming a full professor of sociology.

In 1991 Wolfe was named the dean of the Graduate Faculty of Political and Social Science and the Michael E. Gellert Professor of Sociology and Political Science at the New School for Social Research. In 1993 he joined Boston University as university professor and professor of sociology and political science. He was named the director of the Boisi Center for Religion and American Public Life at Boston College in 1999, also holding an appointment as professor of political science.

A contributing editor of *The New Republic* and *The Wilson Quarterly*, Wolfe also wrote for *Harper's*, *The Atlantic Monthly*, and *Commonweal*. He wrote *America's Impasse: The Rise and Fall of the Politics of Growth* (1981), in which he argues that differences between the Republican and Democratic parties have diminished as the demands of economics have become paramount. His works *One Nation, After All* (1998) and *Moral Freedom: The Search for Virtue in a World of Choice* (2001) were selected as *New York Times* Notable Books of the Year. His many other works include *The Transformation of American Religion: How We Actually Practice Our Faith* (2003), *An Intellectual in Public* (2003), and *Return to Greatness: How America Lost Its Sense of Purpose and What It Needs to Do to Recover It* (2005).

Wolfe received numerous grants and awards, including grants from the Russell Sage Foundation, the Templeton Foundation, and the Lilly Endowment. He was the George Herbert Walker Bush Fellow at the American Academy in Berlin in

2004, and he received the Award for Public Understanding of Sociology from the American Sociological Association in 2001. He served as an advisor to President Bill Clinton for the State of the Union Address in 1995.

[Dorothy Bauhoff (2nd ed.)]

WOLFE, BERTRAM DAVID (1896–1977), U.S. historiographer. Born in New York City, Wolfe became involved in radical politics, first as a socialist and later as a member of the Workers (Communist) Party. He edited the party's organ, *The Communist*, 1927–28. In 1929 he was expelled from the party and became active in the Communist opposition group. He thus became what was called a "Lovestoneite," one of the Right Opposition the party expelled along with Jay Lovestone. Wolfe later broke with the Marxist left.

Wolfe and his wife, Ella, had experience of the Soviet Union in the early years of Stalin's rule and knew the Russian leader personally. Wolfe's scholarly work was chiefly in the field of Marxist history and Soviet affairs. His book *Three Who Made a Revolution* (1948) is a biographical study of Lenin, Trotsky, and Stalin. Among his other works are *Keep America out of War* (with N. Thomas (1939); *Communist Totalitarianism* (1961), first published under the title *Six Keys to the Soviet System* (1956); *Marxism, One Hundred Years in the Life of a Doctrine* (1965); *Strange Communists I Have Known* (1965); *The Bridge and the Abyss* (1967); and *An Ideology in Power* (1969). *A Life in Two Centuries: An Autobiography* was published in 1981. He was also the biographer of Diego Rivera, e.g., *The Fabulous Life of Diego Rivera* (1963).

Wolfe was a fellow of the Russian Institute of Columbia University and the Hoover Library.

ADD. BIBLIOGRAPHY: G. Lennard (ed.), *Lenin and the 20th Century: A Bertram D. Wolfe Retrospective* (1984); R. Hessen (ed.), *Breaking with Communism: The Intellectual Odyssey of Bertram D. Wolfe* (1990).

[Ezra Mendelsohn / Ruth Beloff (2nd ed.)]

WOLFE, HUMBERT (Umberto Wolff; 1885–1940), English poet and critic. He was born in Milan but was taken as a baby to Bradford, England, where his father was a wool merchant. He was naturalized in 1891. Wolfe was educated at Bradford Grammar School and Oxford and went into the civil service, where he rose to be deputy secretary at the Ministry of Labor (1938–40). During World War I, from 1915 to 1918, he held an important position in the Ministry of Munitions. Wolfe's first published poems, a collection entitled *London Sonnets* (1920), were characterized by a certain facetiousness and by an attempt to imitate colloquial speech. Other early works included *Shylock Reasons with Mr. Chesterton* (1920), *Circular Saws* (1923), *Lampoons* (1925), *Humoresque* (1926), and a long verse satire on the popular press, *News of the Devil* (1926). His first real success was a volume of light verse entitled *Cursory Rhymes* (1927). Later volumes, notably *Requiem* (1927), took life more seriously. *The Uncelestial City* (1930) represented an unsuccessful return to his earlier manner, and volumes in his more usual strain which appeared over the next ten years added little to his reputation. He translated Rostand's *Cyrano de Bergerac* (1937) and wrote an English adaptation of Jenő *Heltai's Hungarian verse comedy, *The Silent Knight* (1937). His critical writings include studies of Herrick, Shelley, and Tennyson. Wolfe was only mildly interested in Jewish affairs but translated Edmond *Fleg's *Wall of Weeping* (1929) and some of *Heine's poems. His autobiographical works, *Now a Stranger* (1933) and *The Upward Anguish* (1938), reveal his sense of alienation from Jews and Judaism; in 1908 he had become an Anglican. Rather incongruously, Wolfe also wrote excellent accounts of the Ministry of Munitions during World War I which are highly regarded as administrative history.

BIBLIOGRAPHY: Leftwich, in: *National Jewish Monthly* (Jan. 1941); N. Bentwich, in: *Menorah Journal*, 31 (Jan.–March 1943), 34–45. **ADD. BIBLIOGRAPHY:** ODNB online; P. Bagguley, *Harlequin in Whitehall* (1997).

[Philip D. Hobsbaum]

WOLFENBUETTEL, town in Lower Saxony, Germany. There was a small Jewish community in Wolfenbuettel during the 18th century. In 1781 a synagogue was erected to replace the prayer room that had previously been in use. After a new synagogue was dedicated in 1893, the old one was used as a private dwelling. A cemetery was acquired by the community in 1724 (it was desecrated in 1938). The small community is mainly known for the Jewish school that was established in the town. In 1786 Philip Samson and his brother Herz, **Landrabbiner* and *Court Jew of the duke of Brunswick, founded a *bet midrash* for poor boys, under the directorship of Philip, where four to five hours a week were set aside for secular studies (German, arithmetic, etc.). Ten years later another school was founded, endowed by Herz's widow. In 1806–07, under the influence of Israel *Jacobson, the schools amalgamated and revolutionized their curriculum. Less emphasis was given to talmudic studies, which were eventually replaced by catechism. The innovations were carried out by one of the first pupils, S.M. Ehrenburg, who conducted the earliest confirmation ceremony in 1807. The first to be confirmed was Leopold *Zunz, who taught in the school for five years; his contemporary at school was the historian I.M. *Jost. Attendance at the Samsonsche Freischule grew from about a dozen pupils in the late 18th century to 150–200 a century later, when it had become a recognized *Realgymnasium* (high school). It included a hostel. French and English were taught, and Jewish studies included Bible with Mendelssohn's translation, Jewish laws and customs, and a little Jewish history. The trend was that of liberal Judaism. The school was closed on Sabbaths and open on Sundays. In 1928 it was closed following the post-World War I inflation. There were 125 Jews living in Wolfenbuettel in 1932 and 112 in 1933. They maintained two philanthropic organizations. The community ceased to exist during World War II. There are memorials at the Jewish cemetery (from the 1970s and 1980s). A memorial (inaugurated in 1988) and a commemorative plaque (inaugurated in 2000) are dedicated to the former synagogue. In 2005 a new memorial was built to commemorate the Jewish citizens who lived in Wolfenbuettel during the Nazi era.

BIBLIOGRAPHY: H. Schulze in: *Zeitschrift fuer die Geschichte der Juden*, 3 (1966), 1–11; idem, in: *Braunschweigisches Jahrbuch*, 48/49 (1967–69), 23–61, 62–85; M. Eliav, *Ha-Ḥinnukh ha-Yehudi be-Germanyah* (1960), index. **ADD BIBLIOGRAPHY:** R. Busch, *Samsonschule Wolfenbuettel 1786–1928. Ausstellung aus Anlass der 200. Wiederkehr des Gruendungstages* (Veroeffentlichungen des Braunschweigischen Landesmuseums, vol. 46) (1986); *Sie werden lernen von deinen Worten. Kostbare hebraeische Buecher in der Herzog August Bibliothek* (1988); M. Berg, *Juedische Schulen in Niedersachsen* (Beitraege zur historischen Bildungsforschung, vol. 28) (2003).

[Abraham J. Brawer]

WOLFENSOHN, JAMES DAVID (1933–), international peace envoy, Olympian, philanthropist, investment banker and president of the World Bank. Wolfensohn was born in Sydney, Australia, and enrolled at age 16 at Sydney University, where he discovered a latent talent for fencing. Five years later, Wolfensohn fenced for Australia in the 1956 Olympics. That same year he completed his law degree and the following year, was accepted to do an M.B.A. at Harvard.

After a few years, he returned to Australia where his career as an international investment banker took seed. Over the years he held several executive-level positions in firms in Australia, the U.S., and the United Kingdom. In his late forties, he opened his own boutique investment bank.

Passionate about the performing arts, he was always closely involved in a range of cultural activities. As chairman of the board of Carnegie Hall, he was a driving force behind its restoration.

When he was appointed chairman of the board of trustees of the John F. Kennedy Center for the Performing Arts in Washington, D.C., the center was economically and philosophically troubled. He changed its focus, concentrating on education and increasing performance and outreach initiatives. For his contribution to the arts, Wolfensohn received numerous awards, including a Knight Commander of the Most Excellent Order of the British Empire.

As a committed philanthropist, he was devoted to humanitarian causes. He was president of the International Federation of Multiple Sclerosis Societies and personally financed AIDS initiatives for the disabled. Widely recognized for his voluntary work, he was decorated by the governments of Australia, Brazil, France, Germany, Georgia, Morocco, Norway, Peru, Pakistan, and Russia.

A proud Jew, Wolfensohn chaired the Jerusalem Foundation, was a director of the Jerusalem Music Center and a member of the advisory committee of Yad Hanadiv. He won the American Jewish Committee Herbert H. Lehman, Human Relations Award, and was a trustee of the Fifth Avenue Synagogue.

Wolfensohn received nine honorary doctorates, served as chairman of the board of the Institute for Advanced Study at Princeton University, and was a fellow of the American Academy of Arts and Sciences and of the American Philosophical Society. He was a member of both the Council on Foreign Relations and the Century Association of New York and an honorary trustee of the Brookings Institution.

During his presidency of the World Bank between 1995 and 2005, Wolfensohn made poverty reduction the raison d'etre of the Bank and changed its face by describing the challenge of development in terms of people not numbers.

As his term at the bank was ending, in 2005 the Quartet of powers – the United States, Russia, the United Nations and the European Union, which had joined together to help to attain peace in the longstanding Arab/Israeli conflict – appointed Wolfensohn as their special envoy for peace.

[Jill Margo (2nd ed.)]

WOLFENSTEIN, ALFRED (1888–1945), German poet, playwright, and translator. Born in Halle an der Saale, Wolfenstein qualified as a lawyer but lived as a freelance writer in Berlin and Munich until he emigrated to Prague after the Nazis came to power. In 1938 he fled to Paris and, after the German occupation, wandered through France, eventually returning to the capital under an assumed name. The liberation found him seriously ill, and he committed suicide in a hospital. Wolfenstein was an expressionist poet with no overt political or social outlook. He always emphasized the loneliness of the artist but confessed his Jewishness in the essay *Juedisches Wesen und neue Dichtung* (1922).

His verse collections include *Die gottlosen Jahre* (1914), *Die Freundschaft. Neue Gedichte* (1917), and *Menschlicher Kaempfer* (1919). He also published lyrical dramas and a collection of 30 stories, *Die gefaehrlichen Engel* (1936). His other works include a prizewinning biographical study of the French poet Rimbaud (1930) and various translations from French and English. He edited two volumes of the poetry annual *Die Erhebung* (1919, 1920) and an anthology of world poetry, *Stimmen der Voelker* (1938).

BIBLIOGRAPHY: H. Mumm, *Alfred Wolfenstein. Eine Einfuehrung in sein Werk und eine Auswahl* (1955).

[Rudolf Kayser]

WOLFERT, IRA (1908–1997), author and journalist. Best known for his reporting during World War II and for his Pulitzer Prize-winning book, *Battle for the Solomons* (1943), Wolfert also wrote *American Guerrilla in the Philippines* (1945) and published short stories in various magazines. His novel, *Tucker's People* (1943), was based to a very large extent on material he had gathered as a reporter. It was filmed in 1948 as *Force of Evil.* In 1948 he published *An Act of Love*, with characters burdened by their Jewishness. His career fell into eclipse over the next two decades but interest in his work revived somewhat in the 1970s.

WOLFF, ABRAHAM ALEXANDER (1801–1891), chief rabbi of Copenhagen. Born in Darmstadt, Germany, he graduated from the University of Giessen in 1821, writing for his dissertation *Der Prophet Habakkuk* (Darmstadt, 1822). Some years later he wrote *Torat Yisrael*, a textbook on Judaism which was translated into Dutch, Danish, and Swedish. After serving in the rabbinate of Giessen for two years, in 1828 he was appointed chief rabbi in Copenhagen, continuing in office for over 62 years. During this period, Wolff, who combined the traditional spirit with a modern outlook, had a decisive influence in shaping the character of the Denmark community. He succeeded in reconciling the traditional and liberal parties. In the new synagogue, built on his initiative in 1833, Wolff was able to unify the disintegrated community. He instituted the traditional services with revisions, accompanied by a sermon. Many of his sermons have been published. He provided a Danish translation of the prayer book (1856) and translated the Pentateuch and *haftarot* (1891–94, part published posthumously). In *Talmudfjender* (1878) he replied to attacks by some Danish clergymen on the Jews and Judaism. Wolff also wrote *Bibelhistorie for Skole og Hjem* (1867), a biblical history for Jewish school and home use, and defended his innovations in the ritual in *Ateret Shalom ve-Emet*, or *Stimmen der aeltesten glaubwuerdigsten Rabbinen ueber die Pijutim* (1857). He was awarded the title of professor and created a Knight of the Order of Danebrog.

BIBLIOGRAPHY: T.H. Erslew, *Almindeligt Forfatter-Lexicon*, 3 (1853), and supplement, 3 (1868); Simonsen et al., in: *Jodisk Familienblad* (May 15, 1929); B. Balslev, *Danske Jøders Historie* (1932), 54–57, 74f., 114f.; Edelmann, in: *Dansk biografisk Leksikon*, 26 (1944), 242–7; Wilhelm, in: YLBI, 3 (1958), 319–21; C.D. Lippe, *Bibliographisches Lexicon*, 1 (1881), 542–6.

[Leni Yahil]

WOLFF, ALBERT LOUIS (1884–1970), conductor and composer. Born in Paris, Wolff was associated with the Opéra Comique, becoming chorus master in 1908, conductor in 1911, and principal conductor in 1922. In 1924 he was made musical director of the Théatre des Champs Elysées, and later conducted the Concerts Lamoureux and the Concerts Pasdeloup. Famous as a conductor of French music, he toured widely in Europe and in South America (1940–45) and conducted at the New York Metropolitan Opera (1919–21). His best-known work is the opera *L'Oiseau bleu* (1919).

WOLFF, BERNHARD (1812–1879), also **Bendit Wolff** or **Wolff-Benda**, German journalist and publisher. Born the second son of the Berlin banker Marcus Wolff (1759–1835), Bernhard Wolff was trained in medicine but took up journalism. After the death of his father, who had lost all his assets, Wolff joined the old Berlin book publishing firm Vossische Buchhandlung as part-owner, translating scientific works from French and English. Shortly before the 1848 revolution he acquired the *Berliner Bank-, Börsen- und Handelszeitung* and, in April 1848, was among the founders of the liberal Berlin daily *National-Zeitung*, which he managed till 1850, finally becoming its owner.

In 1849, with the backing of the electrical entrepreneur Werner Siemens (1816–1892), Wolff established the world's first telegraphic news agency in Berlin, the Telegraphisches Korrespondenzbuero Bernhard Wolff, later called Wolff's Telegraphisches Bureau (WTB). WTB was to become the most important German news agency, expanding to other German cities and several European capitals, and even taking over *Reuter's office in Berlin. In 1865, WTB was transformed into a joint-stock company, the Continental Telegraphen Compagnie; the Prussian government also started to subsidize WTB. Wolff remained director of the firm until the 1870s; from the 1870s on, WTB had official standing, being virtually owned by the German government. In 1933, the Nazis changed the name of WTB to Deutsches Nachrichten-Bureau (DNB) which, in 1946, became the Allgemeiner Deutscher Nachrichtendienst (ADN), the official news agency of the German Democratic Republic. In 1994, it merged into the Deutscher Depeschen-Dienst (DDP) agency. Wolff's *National-Zeitung* eventually became part of the *Mosse publishing house. Wolff died in Berlin.

BIBLIOGRAPHY: L. Salomon, *Geschichte des Deutschen Zeitungswesens*, 3 (1906); F.M. Feldhaus, in: ADB, 55 (1910), 661–2; F. Fuchs, *Telegraphische Nachrichtenbueros* (1919); Wininger 6 (1931), 311–2; J. Jacobson, *Die Judenbuergerbücher der Stadt Berlin 1809–1851* (1962), no. 920, 481; J. Wilke (ed.), *Telegraphenbueros und Nachrichtenagenturen in Deutschland* (1991); D. Basse, *Wolff's Telegraphisches Bureau 1849 bis 1933* (1991); H.J. Teuteberg and C. Neutsch (eds.), *Vom Fluegeltelegrafen zum Internet* (1998).

[Johannes Valentin Schwarz (2nd ed.)]

WOLFF, CHARLOTTE (1897–1986), pioneering Jewish lesbian physician, psychotherapist, and sexology researcher in Germany and England. Born in Riesenburg, West Prussia, but raised in Danzig and Dresden, Charlotte Wolff matriculated at the University of Freiburg in 1920 and studied in Königsberg and Tübingen before completing her doctorate in medicine in Berlin in 1926. In 1931, she began working in the Institute for Electrophysical Therapy at the Neukölln clinic and was appointed its director the following year. She also had a small private medical and psychotherapeutic practice. An active member of the Verein Sozialistischer Ärzten (Association of Socialist Physicians), Wolff did volunteer work in a marriage counseling center in Berlin, distributing family planning information and providing poor women with contraception devices.

After the Nazi takeover in 1933, Charlotte Wolff was dismissed from her position in the outpatient clinic and was detained briefly by the Gestapo. Soon thereafter, she managed to escape to France and then England and began researching and writing books on chirology; she initially supported herself by analyzing hands because, as a refugee, she was not permitted to practice medicine. In 1937, Wolff became a permanent resident of England and gained permission to practice as a psychotherapist. In 1941, she was made a Fellow of the British Psychological Society and in 1947, she became a naturalized British citizen, but she was not officially reinstated as a physician until 1952.

In the 1960s, while writing her first autobiography, homosexuality became Charlotte Wolff's new field of research. She published *Love Between Women* (1973), a landmark study based on interviews with more than a hundred lesbians. She later wrote a book on bisexuality and a 1986 biography of Magnus Hirschfeld, the pioneering German-Jewish sexologist. In the 1970s, her books began to be translated into German; she was invited to come to Germany to speak about her experiences and her research on homosexuality and bisexuality in 1978 and again in 1979. As a Jew and a lesbian, Wolff believed that she was a quintessential outsider belonging to two persecuted minorities, but towards the end of her life, she found acceptance in British and German lesbian feminist circles, making important contributions to the study of homosexuality in both her adopted country and her native land. Other books include *Studies in Hand Reading* (1936); *The Human Hand* (1942); *The Hand in Psychological Diagnosis* (1950); *On the Way to Myself: Communications to a Friend* (1969); and *Hindsight* (1980).

BIBLIOGRAPHY: R. Alpart, *Like Bread on the Seder Plate* (1997), 141–49; H. Pass Freidenreich. *Female, Jewish, and Educated* (2002); R. Wall, *Verbrannt, verboten, vergessen* (1988), 211–13.

[Harriet Pass Freidenreich (2nd ed.)]

WOLFF, GUSTAV (1834–1913), British shipbuilder. Wolff was born in Hamburg to a Jewish family which had been baptized as Lutherans. He came to Liverpool in 1849 to join his uncle, a partner in a large firm of shipowners, and served an apprenticeship in engineering. From 1857 he was a partner in the Belfast shipbuilding firm of Harland & Wolff, which became one of the largest in the world and was also a leading manufacturer of shipping equipment such as marine rope. Much of the prosperity of late Victorian Belfast was due to his firm, which employed 15,000 men at the time of his death. Wolff served as a Unionist (Conservative) member of Parliament for a Belfast seat from 1892 until 1910. Although he was an Anglican, he maintained extensive contacts with the Jewish community in Britain and with overseas Jewish entrepreneurs, such as Albert *Ballin in Germany. Wolff died soon after his firm built its most famous ship. Tragically, it was the *S.S. Titanic.*

BIBLIOGRAPHY: ODNB online; DBB, 5, 854–59; M.S. Moss and J.R. Hume, *Shipbuilders to the World: 125 Years of Harland & Wolff, 1861–1986* (1986).

[William D. Rubinstein (2nd ed.)]

WOLFF, HERMANN (1845–1902), concert manager and music critic. Born in Cologne, Wolff served for some time as Anton *Rubinstein's secretary. In 1881 he founded the concert management firm in Berlin bearing his name (later known as H. Wolff and J. Sachs), which became well known throughout Europe and was associated not only with the promotion of individual artists but also with the organization of important concert series in Berlin and Hamburg. Wolff was also editor of the *Neue Berliner Musikzeitung* (1878–79) and coeditor of the *Musikwelt.*

WOLFF, JEANETTE (1888–1976), prominent German Jewish Socialist. Born in Bocholt, Westphalia, she qualified as a nurse, later became an educationist and, after moving to Belgium, joined the Socialist Party and became active in the Labor Youth Movement. She returned to Germany in 1910 where she continued her political activity, and after her marriage took an increasing interest in Jewish activities, joining the German Jewish Women's Organization, which she represented on the Council of the Red Cross during World War I. After the war she became a prominent member of, and public speaker for, the Society of German Citizens of the Jewish Faith. As a result of her fearless denunciation of Nazism, she was placed under protective custody when the Nazis came to power and, although released in 1935, was continually harassed by the Gestapo and was eventually deported to the Riga ghetto and other camps. Returning to Berlin in 1946 she rejoined the Socialist Party, was elected a deputy to the West Berlin House of Representatives, and from 1952 to 1961 was a member of the Bundestag. Wolff continued her Jewish activities. She was cochairman of the Union of German Jewish Women, vice chairman of the Central Council of Jews in Germany, and chairman of the Society for Christian-Jewish Cooperation.

She was awarded the Great Service Cross of the German Order of Merit of the West German Government and the Leo Baeck Prize of the Central Council of Jews in Germany in 1975.

Wolff wrote *Sadism as Lunacy* on her experiences in the concentration camps, in which she attempted to analyze objectively the reasons for Nazi barbarity. Her autobiography *Mit Bibel und Bebel* remained in fragments and was published in 1980.

ADD. BIBLIOGRAPHY: W. Albrecht, "Jeanette Wolff – Jakob Altmaier – Peter Bachstein. Die drei Abgeordneten jüdischer Herkunft des Deutschen Bundestages in den 50er und zu Beginn der 60er Jahre," in: J. Schoeps (et al), *Menora. Jahrbuch fuer deutsch-juedische Geschichte 1995* (1995), 267–99; G. Lange, *Jeanette Wolff. 1888–1876. Eine Biographie* (1988); C. Moss, "Verfolgung und Vernichtung in juedischen Selbstzeugnissen: Jeanette Wolff und Marga Spiegel," in. J.-P. Barbian, M. Brocke, L. Heid (eds.), *Juden im Ruhrgebiet. Vom Zeitalter der Aufklaerung bis in die Gegenwart* (1999); B. Seemann, *Jeanette Wolff. Politikerin und engagierte Demokratin (1888–1976)* (2000).

WOLFF, JOSEPH (1795–1862), world traveler and Christian missionary to the Jews in the Oriental Diaspora. Born in Weilersbach, Bavaria, the son of a rabbi, he converted to Catholicism in 1812. He was admitted to the Collegio Romani in 1816, but after being expelled because of his heretical views, he moved to England and joined the Anglican Church. In 1827 he married the daughter of the Earl of Oxford, and their son was Sir Henry Drummond Wolff, the well-known diplomat and politician. He studied Oriental languages and theology at universities in Vienna and Tuebingen, among others. Thereafter he became a missionary to the Jews, traveling to Palestine, Kurdistan, Mesopotamia, Turkey, Persia, Khurasan, Bukhara, India, Yemen, Abyssinia, and many European countries.

He undertook his first great missionary journey to the Orient in 1821, which he described in *Missionary Journal and Memoirs of Reverend Joseph Wolff* (3 vols. London, 1827–29). After touring the British Isles and Holland in 1827, and Palestine and Cyprus in 1829, in 1831 he undertook his second journey to Asia, which he described in *Researches and Missionary Labours Among the Jews, Mohammedans, and other Sects (1831–1834)* (2 vols., London, 1835). In 1836 he traveled to the U.S., where he delivered a sermon before Congress in Washington, received a degree at Annapolis, Maryland, and was ordained as deacon in New Jersey. In 1838, however, he returned to England, accepting a parish in Somerset and occupying this office until his death. He left in 1843 for a second journey to Bukhara, having offered to search for Charles Stoddart and A. Conolly, two high-ranking English officers imprisoned by the emir of Bukhara. However, they had been executed before his arrival, and Wolff himself narrowly escaped a similar fate. The Bukharan episode is described in *Narrative of a Mission to Bukhara to Ascertain the Fate of Colonel Stoddart and Captain Conolly* (2 vols., London, 1845), which ran into seven editions.

His writings contain interesting and valuable details about the Jews and Jewish communities in the regions he had visited, but because of his missionary zeal and erratic character, Wolff's data lack objectivity and reliability.

BIBLIOGRAPHY: J. Wolff, *Travels and Adventures. An Autobiography*, 2 vols. (1861); H.L. Palmer, *Joseph Wolff; His Romantic Life and Travels* (1935); G. Wint (ed.), *Mission to Bokhara* (1969).

[Walter Joseph Fischel]

WOLFF, THEODOR (1868–1943), German journalist, politician, and editor-in-chief of the *Berliner Tageblatt* (est. 1872). Born in Berlin, the son of a wholesale dealer, Wolff joined the publishing house of his uncle Rudolf *Mosse in 1887. There he trained as a clerk and started writing for the *Berliner Tageblatt*. In 1889, together with Maximilian *Harden, he was among the founders of the Freie Buehne, an independent theater modeled after the Théatre-Libre in Paris. He was appointed chief Paris correspondent in 1894 and reported the *Dreyfus trial, side by side with his colleague Theodor *Herzl from Vienna. In 1906, he was called back to Berlin as editor-in-chief of the *Berliner Tageblatt*, which he made a leading liberal paper in and outside Germany until 1933. In his widely read Monday evening editorials, signed "TW," Wolff followed a policy of Franco-German understanding and Anglo-German rapprochement. At the outbreak of World War I he opposed extreme nationalist tendencies and annexationist demands. Often in difficulties with the censor, he was for some time forbidden to write. In 1918, together with E. *Feder and others, Wolff was among the founders of the German Democratic Party (DDP) but resigned in 1927 largely because of its rather right-wing *Kulturpolitik*. Until 1932, he served as a political advisor to Gustav Stresemann (1878–1929) and Heinrich Bruening (1885–1970).

After the rise of Hitler, Wolff, regarded as a leading representative of the Weimar system, was forced to flee Germany and left Berlin on the night of the *Reichstag* fire (February 27, 1933). Via Munich and Austria, he first went to Zurich and, in 1934, on to Nice. In 1937, he was officially expatriated. He continued his literary and journalistic work, contributing to papers such as the *Pariser Tageblatt* of G. *Bernhard and the *Aufbau* in New York. In autumn 1941, his visa to the U.S. expired before he was able to use it. In May 1943 he was arrested in Nice by the Italian army, handed over to the Gestapo and sent to Germany, where he was detained at several concentration camps, including Sachsenhausen and Oranienburg. In August 1943, he was taken to the Jewish hospital in Berlin-Moabit, where he died the following month.

Besides novels and plays, Wolff published various volumes of political surveys and memoirs, including *Der Heide* (1891), *Der Untergang* (1892), *Die Suender* (1894), *Die stille Insel* (1894), *Niemand weiß es* (1895), *Die Koenigin* (1898), *Pariser Tagebuch* (1908), *Spaziergänge* (1909), *Vollendete Tatsachen, 1914–1917* (1918), *Das Vorspiel* (1924), and *Anatole France* (1924). After 1933 there appeared *Der Krieg des Pontius Pilatus* (1934), *Der Marsch durch zwei Jahrzehnte* (1936; reprinted in 1989 as *Die Wilhelminische Epoche*), and *Die Schwimmerin* (1937); posthumously published was *"Die Juden." Ein Dokument aus dem Exil 1942/43* (1984).

In 1961, the foundation of the Hamburg paper *Die Welt* established the Theodor-Wolff-Preis for outstanding journalistic achievements.

ADD. BIBLIOGRAPHY: Wininger 6 (1931), 316; W.E. Mosse, in: LBIYB, 4 (1959), 237–59; G. Schwarz, *Theodor Wolff und das "Berliner Tageblatt"* (1968); E. Feder, *Heute sprach ich mit...* (1971), index; W. Becker, *Demokratie des sozialen Rechts* (1971); B.B. Frye, in: LBIYB, 21 (1976), 143–72; W. Koehler, *Der Chefredakteur Theodor Wolff* (1978); bhdE, 1 (1980), 834; E. Kraus, *Die Familie Mosse* (1999), index; B. Soesemann, *Theodor Wolff. Ein Leben mit der Zeitung* (2000); C. Goldbach, *Distanzierte Beobachtung. Theodor Wolff und das Judentum* (2002); D. Fabisch, *Der Publizist Theodor Wolff* (2004). Edited works: B. Sösemann (ed.), *Theodor Wolff. Tagebücher. 1914–1919* (2 vols., 1984); idem (ed.), *Theodor Wolff...* (3 vols., 1993–97); M. Broehan (ed.), *Theodor Wolff...* (1992).

[Erich Gottgetreu / Johannes Valentin Schwarz (2nd ed.)]

WOLFF, WERNER (1904–1957), U.S. existential psychologist. Born in Berlin, Wolff was one of the first to introduce existentialist psychology in the U.S. In 1933 he left Germany, spent three years at the University of Barcelona and then settled in the United States. He worked at Columbia (1940–42) and served as professor at Bard College in Annandale-on-Hudson, New York, from 1942 onward. He studied the expression of personality in complex movements, in children's drawings, and in handwriting, and wrote books on his findings.

WOLFFSOHN, DAVID (1856–1914), second president of the World Zionist Organization. Born in Dorbiany, Russian Lithuania, Wolffsohn received a religious education. In 1873 his parents sent him to live with his brother in Memel (now Klaipeda) in order to avoid conscription to the czarist army. He studied at a *talmud torah* under Rabbi Isaac *Ruelf, who later became one of the leading forerunners of the *Ḥibbat Zion movement, and who very much influenced Wolffsohn. At an early age Wolffsohn began to earn his living in Loebau, East Prussia, and in Lyck, where he made the acquaintance of David *Gordon, the editor of the Hebrew newspaper *Ha-Maggid* and one of the first proponents of Ḥibbat Zion. He moved from place to place and worked at various jobs, at one time even as a peddler. He finally settled down in the timber trade, first working for others, and later independently, becoming prosperous.

Wolffsohn's bent for public life was first displayed in his activities in various Jewish communities. This did not appear to satisfy him, however, and he joined various cultural and philanthropic organizations. He finally found his place when he chanced to hear a lecture in Cologne given under the auspices of the Society for Jewish History and Literature. This forum was utilized by Max *Bodenheimer to propagate his Jewish nationalist ideas. After one of Bodenheimer's lectures, which had aroused the opposition of the majority of those present, Wolffsohn rose to defend the speaker and his views. After making Bodenheimer's acquaintance in this way, he began to find an outlet for his public activities in Ḥibbat Zion. Wolffsohn was possessed of an unassuming nature, which prevented him from pushing himself to the fore. In later years he was almost the only one of Theodor *Herzl's associates who lacked a formal secular education, and continuous association with all the "Doctors" in Herzl's circle most probably gave rise to guarded feelings of inferiority.

Wolffsohn was one of many whose latent sympathy for the Zionist idea was fired by the appearance of *Der Judenstaat*. He met Herzl in the autumn of 1896, was immediately captivated, and promised his assistance, especially in matters of finance. From then on he was Herzl's constant companion, and is one of those most frequently mentioned in Herzl's diaries. His imagination was set aflame by Herzl's political vision, which, despite Wolffsohn's habitual reserve and cultivated image as a "businessman," motivated him throughout.

Wolffsohn's debt to Herzl is universally recognized; what is less well known, however, is the fact that Herzl owed much to Wolffsohn as well. Herzl, who knew almost nothing of Jewish life, found in him a teacher and a guide. At the height of the preparations for the First Zionist Congress, in the sphere of protocol so dear to Herzl's heart, Wolffsohn gave the Zionist Movement its first two symbols: the colors blue and white on the model of the *tallit*, for the movement's flag, and the ancient term *shekel, for the Zionist members' due. He was the moving spirit behind the founding of the *Jewish Colonial Trust, which he directed until his last days, as well as of all the other financial and economic institutions of the movement. Despite his enormous admiration for Herzl, Wolffsohn never hesitated to disagree with him on matters with which Herzl was insufficiently acquainted. It was this quality above all that endeared him to Herzl, who portrayed him in glowing terms as "David Litwak" in his novel *Altneuland*. Wolffsohn accompanied Herzl on his journey to Ereẓ Israel to see Emperor William II (1898) and on his journeys to Turkey. Herzl's death was a terrible blow to Wolffsohn, who, in lieu of the eulogy forbidden by Herzl, swore to cherish his memory by repeating the words "If I forget thee, Jerusalem, let my right hand forget its cunning" at his graveside. Herzl nominated him as the guardian of his children, and Wolffsohn, himself childless, was a loving and devoted father to them until he died.

Herzl's death was a critical blow to the Zionist Movement, then split between those in favor of the *Uganda Scheme and those opposed to it, and on more or less parallel lines between the political Zionists and the "practical" ones. Herzl had managed to bridge these differences by his personal authority, but he left no one to take his place. Wolffsohn was a member of the delegation that asked Max *Nordau to take Herzl's place. Nordau refused, but suggested instead that Wolffsohn himself was the most suitable candidate, and, at the conference of the Zionist Federation of Germany (Cologne, April 1905), Adolph *Friedemann offered Wolffsohn the presidency. His consistent rejection of these proposals, which was both honest and modest, was prompted by his conviction that no one person, least of all himself, was worthy to take Herzl's place. In the end, a triple leadership was agreed upon: Wolffsohn, Nordau, and Otto *Warburg. This compromise was accepted by the Seventh Zionist Congress, which elected him chairman of the Executive and the Zionist General Council.

Wolffsohn's leadership of the Zionist Movement was overshadowed by tragedy. The giant figure of Herzl constantly before him and the rest of the movement was the source of a great deal of bitterness in his life and a spur to the opposition that began to appear at the start of his tenure. Wolffsohn built up his self-confidence very slowly, until he came to the point where he was a competent enough speaker to parry the thrusts of the opposition. His roots in eastern European Jewish life added to his confidence and enabled him to introduce elements of humor and traditional associations into his speeches, which the Jewish masses found very appealing.

The Seventh Zionist Congress not only put an end to the Uganda Scheme but also effected a programmatic innovation by achieving a compromise between the "practical" and the political Zionists that called for settlement activity within the framework of the *Basle Program. Practical work in Ereẓ Israel was not made conditional on the attainment of a "charter." Although Wolffsohn tried to reconcile differences in the Zionist camp, full unity was not achieved because each side believed he was putting the other side's program into effect. This moderate position became his guiding policy, but it could not be viable for any length of time because it encountered much opposition, despite the fact that Wolffsohn made executive posts available to his staunchest opponents.

After Wolffsohn moved the central Zionist office to Cologne, the *Jewish National Fund center, under Bodenheimer, was transferred there as well. He invited Nahum *Sokolow to act as general secretary of the Zionist Organization and founded the official Hebrew newspaper of the Zionist Organization *Haolam* (1907), which was initially edited by Sokolow. He took part in the conference of Jewish organizations in Brussels (1906) that met to organize matters concerning emigration. Although the practical results of the conference were insignificant, its value lay in the fact that the Zionist Organization made its appearance side by side with other worldwide Jewish organizations. When his health collapsed, Wolffsohn set out on a holiday to South Africa (1906), a journey which was transformed into a triumph for Zionism and became the foundation stone of the South African Zionist Federation. On his return he visited Ereẓ Israel and published his impressions in *Die Welt*.

The compromise between the political and the "practical" Zionists, which took place at the Eighth Zionist Congress in The Hague (1907) and was theoretically expressed in Chaim *Weizmann's famous speech on "synthetic Zionism," found its mediator in Wolffsohn, who restrained both sides at once. His emphasis on efficiency in practical work earned him the epithet "*kaufmaennisch*," a barb directed against him by both sides. He revealed his ability as a leader capable of deciding between extremely opposed views and methods, while simultaneously insisting that everything was being done in the spirit of Herzl. All the practical programs then being instituted (the opening of branches of the Jewish Colonial Trust in Ereẓ Israel, the beginnings of settlement, the activities of the JNF) were, in Wolffsohn's opinion, a continuation of the plans and the activities of Herzl's period. He was elected president by 135 votes to 59.

Afterward Wolffsohn went to Turkey, but was prevented from seeing the sultan by the outbreak of the revolution of the Young Turks (1908), which disrupted all his arrangements. At this time he also showed himself capable of decisive action by agreeing to grant a JNF loan to the first settlers of Aḥuzat Bayit, the nucleus of Tel Aviv, despite widespread opposition on the grounds that the requested loan was against the regulations of the JNF. Great demonstrative value was attached to Wolffsohn's journey (accompanied by Sokolow) to Russia in 1908 and to the splendid reception he was accorded by Prime Minister Stolypin, Foreign Minister Isvolsky, and other members of the government. Although his attempts to secure legal status for the Zionist Organization in Russia were unsuccessful, the downtrodden Jews of Russia experienced a degree of gratification at the show of cordiality with which he was received by the government. On the outbreak of the revolution of the Young Turks, Wolffsohn was one of the few Zionists to retain his composure and refuse to be drawn into the excited political scheming rife in the movement. Instead, he proceeded to organize a branch of the Jewish Colonial Trust in Constantinople and found and acquired newspapers there for the propagation of the Zionist point of view. In 1908 he also visited Hungary, where the Zionists were under severe attack from the assimilationists with government assistance, and succeeded in seeing the prime minister and lessening the tension to a certain extent.

Wolffsohn, who enjoyed Nordau's support, was again elected president of the Zionist Organization, despite the opposition to him that gained in strength, reaching its climax at the Ninth Congress in Hamburg (1909). He did everything in his power to bring the opposition, the "practical" Zionists, closer to the leadership, but all his efforts were in vain. His health was rapidly failing and, finally, proved insufficient to meet the demands of the struggle with the opposition. At the Tenth Congress (Basle, 1911) he resigned from the leadership of the movement, retaining only the directorship of the financial and economic institutions. The center of the movement moved from Cologne to Berlin, and Wolffsohn, apart from remaining active in the above institutions, also undertook various journeys on behalf of the cause. He intended to settle in Ereẓ Israel and even learned to speak Hebrew with this end in view, but he died before this could be accomplished. He was buried in Cologne, and in 1952 his remains were brought to Israel and interred next to Herzl's grave on Mt. Herzl in Jerusalem. His estate provided the means for the National and University Library building in Jerusalem, which also houses his archives, including diaries and letters, and contains a room named in his honor.

It was only after Wolffsohn's death that his personality and work were fully appreciated. Only then was he recognized, even by his opponents, as a man of the people who had risen from the ranks by virtue of decades of devoted work. He was also a symbol of the synthesis between East and West, combining the best qualities of both European Jewish communities. His good nature, however, made him an easy prey for all those who considered Herzl's successor fair game for any treatment they cared to mete out to him. This was the source of the tragic quality that permeated the period of his leadership of the Zionist Movement.

BIBLIOGRAPHY: E.B. Cohn, *David Wolffsohn* (Ger. 1939, Eng. 1944); A. Robinsohn, *David Wolffsohn* (Ger. 1921); T. Herzl, *Complete Diaries*, 5 vols. (1960).

[Getzel Kressel]

WOLFOWSKI, MENAHEM ZALMAN (1893–1975), Hebrew writer and translator. Born in Russia, Wolfowski served in the Russian army during World War I and immigrated to Ereẓ Israel in 1921. After working for three years in road and building construction, he turned to teaching and editing, working for the Miẓpeh and Ha-Kibbutz ha-Me'uḥad publishing houses. Wolfowski published poems, stories, criticism, and articles in various periodicals and literary anthologies in Ereẓ Israel.

His books of poetry are *Sofei Shevilim* (1928) and *Shirim u-Fo'emot* (1953). He also published the short story collections *Yeled Yullad Lanu* (1950) and *Beit Yisrael* (1963), and a series of books for young people. In 1968, a collection of his essays and memoirs appeared, *Kerovim ba-Nefesh*. After the death of M. *Poznanski, he completed the edition of J.Ḥ *Brenner's writings (vols. 2–3, 1960–67). Wolfowski translated more than 50 books, including works by Turgenev, Dostoevski, and Tolstoy, as well as historical works and children's books.

BIBLIOGRAPHY: Kressel, Leksikon, 1 (1965), 695–7. **ADD. BIBLIOGRAPHY:** G. Shaked, *Ha-Sipporet ha-Ivrit*, 1 (1977), 425–29.

[Getzel Kressel]

WOLFSBERG, small town in Carinthia, S. Austria; under the rule of the Bamberg bishopric in the 13th century. Jews are first mentioned there in 1289, and in 1304 the duke of Carinthia granted them a charter of privileges, which was renewed in 1311. During the Host libel at *Pulkau (1338), the Jews of Wolfsberg were accused of having stolen the consecrated bread of the Eucharist, having made it bleed, and having tried to burn it. More than 70 Jews were burned at the stake on August 19, and the community disappeared. In 1346 one Jew was permitted to resettle in Wolfsberg.

BIBLIOGRAPHY: *Germania Judaica*, 2 pt. 2 (1968), 918–9.

[Meir Lamed]

WOLFSKEHL, KARL (1869–1948), German poet. Born in Darmstadt, Germany, he claimed descent from the patrician *Kalonymus family, which settled in Mainz more than a thousand years before his birth, and insisted on his right to regard himself as a representative of the authentic German spirit. After his university studies he came under the influence of the lyric poet Stefan George (1868–1933) whom he hailed as his master and with whom he collaborated in the publication of the three-volume *Deutsche Dichtung* (1901–03) and the *Blaetter fuer die Kunst* (1892–1919). From 1899 to 1932 Wolfskehl's Munich home was the meeting place of the George Circle and Wolfskehl himself its only Jewish member. His early lyrics, which began to appear in 1897, his *Gesammelte Dichtungen* (1903), and *Der Umkreis* (1927) all follow the standards of George's neoclassicism, and there was also a powerful mystic current in his writing. Three traditions shaped Wolfskehl's poetic personality: the German, the Greco-Roman, and the biblical. The biblical influence appeared in 1905 in the lyrical drama *Saul*, but it was only after he left Germany in 1934 that Jewish themes became dominant in his verse. Wolfskehl lived in Italy and Switzerland until 1938 and thereafter in New Zealand. Because both his German and his Jewish feelings were so deep-rooted, the persecution of Jews by Germans was profoundly shocking to him, and in the autobiographical song *An die Deutschen* (begun in Rome in 1934 and completed in New Zealand in 1944; published 1947) the homesick poet took leave of his native land.

Other poems reflecting his heartbreak are those in *Die Stimme spricht* (1934) and in the volumes published posthumously, *Hiob* (1950), and *Sang aus dem Exil* (1951). The correspondence of Wolfskehl's last decade in Auckland (*Zehn Jahre Exil…*, 1959) gives clear insight into his later, more universalist and cosmopolitan, outlook. In 1960 a hitherto unpublished work appeared in Amsterdam in German under the Hebrew-German title *Kalon Bekawod Namir – "Aus Schmach wird Ehr"* ("We will Exchange Disgrace for Honor"; cf. Hos. 4:7). His *Gesammelte Werke* was published in two volumes in 1960.

BIBLIOGRAPHY: P. Berglar, *Karl Wolfskehl. Symbolgestalt der deutsch-juedischen Tragoedie* (1964).

[Sol Liptzin]

WOLFSOHN, JULIUSZ (1880–1944), pianist, critic, and composer. Born in Warsaw, Wolfsohn studied piano at the conservatories in Warsaw, Paris, and in Vienna, where he wrote music and criticism for the *Montagblatt*. On his return to Poland in 1925, he wrote for *Muzykai Rytm* and lectured on Jewish music and musicians and on the interpretation of Chopin. Wolfsohn settled in the United States in 1933. He composed a number of works on eastern European Jewish themes, including *Jewish Rhapsody, Hebrew Suite*, and *Twelve Paraphrases on Jewish Melodies*.

WOLFSOHN-HALLE, AARON (1754–1835), writer. Born in Germany, Wolfsohn-Halle taught in a Jewish public school in Breslau from 1792 to 1807, serving the last five years as its principal. Among the most radical of the early *maskilim*, he was one of the editors of **Ha-Me'assef* during its Berlin period, and editor in chief in 1797. Among his own various contributions to the periodical was the play *Siḥah be-Ereẓ ha-Ḥayyim* (in *Ha-Me'assef*, vol. 7, 1794–97), in which *Maimonides and Moses *Mendelssohn meet in paradise. The author praises Mendelssohn and combines his own radical views of the Haskalah with acrimonious remarks against the Talmud and the Kabbalah. His school text, *Avtalyon* (Berlin, 1790–1814[3]), the first written for Jewish pupils, was a pioneer attempt to relate Bible stories in simplified Hebrew prose. In addition, Wolfsohn-Halle published the books of Job (1826) and I Kings (1827) in the Mendelssohn translation, with his own commentary; wrote in German, translating some biblical books into German; and published works in Yiddish, including *Reb Ḥanokh ve-Reb Yosefkhi*, a satirical play replete with Haskalah didacticism. An earlier Hebrew version of this play, written in the 1790s, recently discovered, was published in 1955 (PAAJR, vol. 24, with notes). In 1995, a new transcription of *Leichtsinn und Froemmelei. Ein Familiengemaelde in drei Aufzuegen* appeared, edited by G. Och and J. Strauss, and following the Breslau edition of 1796.

BIBLIOGRAPHY: Rejzen, Leksikon, 1 (1928), 904–10; idem. *Fun Mendelssohn biz Mendele* (1923), 25–68; Z. Zylbercweig, *Leksikon fun Yidishn Teater*, 1 (1931), 652–4.

[Getzel Kressel]

WOLFSON, ELLIOT (1956–), U.S. professor of Judaic studies. He received a bachelor of arts and master of arts degree from Queens College (1979) and a master of arts (1983) and doctoral degree (1986) from Brandeis University. He conducted research at The Hebrew University, Jerusalem, in 1984 and 1985 and was a fellow at the International Center for the University Teaching of Jewish Civilization in the Diaspora. In 1986 and 1987 he was an Andrew W. Mellon Teaching Fellow in the Humanities at Cornell University.

Wolfson taught at Queens College in 1988–89, then at the Jewish Theological Seminary of America from 1989 to 1993. He taught at Princeton University in 1992, was a visiting professor at the University of Chicago and the Russian State University for the Humanities, and an adjunct professor of Jewish history at Columbia from 1989 to 2000. Wolfson became an assistant professor of Hebrew and Judaic Studies at New York University in 1987, then an associate professor in 1991, and he was appointed professor in 1995. In 1996 he was named the Abraham Lieberman Professor of Hebrew and Judaic Studies. He served as the director of Religious Studies from 1995 to 2002.

Wolfson's research interests include the history of Jewish mysticism, comparative mysticism, the phenomenology of religion, hermeneutics, literary theory, and gender studies. His works include *The Book of the Pomegranate: Moses de León's Sefer ha-Rimmon* (1988); *Through a Speculum That Shines: Vision and Imagination in Medieval Jewish Mysticism* (1994); *Circle in the Square: Studies in the Use of Gender in Kabbalistic Symbolism* (1995); *Abraham Abulafia – Kabbalist and Prophet: Hermeneutics, Theosophy, and Theurgy* (2000); *Pathwings: Poetic-Philosophic Reflections on the Hermeneutics of Time and Language* (2004); and *Language, Eros, Being: Kabbalistic Hermeneutics and Poetic Imagination* (2005). *Through a Speculum That Shines* received in 1995 an award from the American Academy of Religion.

Wolfson edited *Rending the Veil: Concealment and Secrecy in the History of Religion* (1999) and coedited, with A. Ivry and A. Arkush, *Perspectives on Jewish Thought and Mysticism* (1998). He wrote extensively for academic journals, including the *Association for Jewish Studies Review, Harvard Theological Review, Jewish Quarterly Review*, and others, and contributed to many collections of essays, including *Gender and Judaism* (1995) and *Perspectives on Jewish Thought and Mysticism* (1998).

A fellow of the American Academy for Jewish Research, Wolfson is a member of the American Academy of Religion, the World Union of Jewish Studies, and the Medieval Academy of America.

[Dorothy Bauhoff (2nd ed.)]

WOLFSON, HARRY AUSTRYN (1887–1974), historian of philosophy. Born in Belorussia, Wolfson received his early education at the Slobodka yeshivah. Emigrating to the United States in 1903, he studied at Harvard and, from 1912 to 1914, held a traveling fellowship from Harvard, which enabled him to study and do research in Europe. In 1915 he was appointed to the Harvard faculty, becoming professor of Hebrew literature and philosophy in 1925. From 1923 to 1925 he also served as professor at the Jewish Institute of Religion. Wolfson received many academic honors for his pioneering researches. He was a fellow of the American Academy for Jewish Research, serving as its president from 1935 to 1937, and a fellow of the Mediaeval Academy of America. He was president of the American Oriental Society in 1957–58, and also held membership in the American Academy of Arts and Sciences. In 1958 he was awarded the prize of the American Council of Learned Societies. In 1965 the American Academy for Jewish Research published the *Harry Austryn Wolfson Jubilee Volume* (in English and Hebrew) in his honor.

Wolfson – whose writings are marked by a mastery of the philosophic literature in the several languages in which it was written, penetrating analysis, clarity of exposition, and felicity of style – wrote many books and articles. (A bibliography, appearing in the *Jubilee Volume* (Eng. sec., pp. 39–49), contains 116 items, which were published between 1912 and 1963.) His early articles, several of which dealt with issues in the philosophies of Crescas and Spinoza, were followed by his first book, *Crescas' Critique of Aristotle*, which, though completed in 1918, was not published until 1929. The volume contains a critical edition of part of Crescas' *Or Adonai* (the section dealing with the 25 propositions which appear in the introduction to the second part of Maimonides' *Guide*), an exemplary English translation, and an introduction; but of special importance are the copious notes which take up more than half of the volume. In these notes Wolfson discusses, with great erudition, the origin and development of the terms and arguments discussed by Crescas, and he clarifies Crescas' often enigmatic text. In the introduction (pp. 24–29) Wolfson describes the "hypothetico-deductive method of textual study" which guided him in all his works (see introductions to his other books). Akin to the method used to study the Talmud known as *pilpul*, this method rests on the assumptions that any serious author writes with such care and precision that "every term, expression, generalization or exception is significant not so much for what it states as for what it implies," and that the thought of any serious author is consistent. Hence it becomes the task of the interpreter to clarify what a given author meant, rather than what he said, and he must resolve apparent contradictions by means of harmonistic interpretation. All this requires great sensitivity to the nuances and implications of the text and familiarity with the literature on which a given author drew. Like the scientific method, the "hypothetico-deductive" method proceeds by means of hypotheses which must be proved or disproved, and it must probe the "latent processes" of an author's thought.

The investigation of the background of Crescas' thought involved Wolfson in an intensive study of the commentaries on Aristotle's works written by the Islamic philosopher Averroes. However, most of these commentaries existed only in manuscripts, and so Wolfson proposed the publication of a *Corpus Commentarionum Averrois in Aristotelem* (in: *Speculum*, 6 (1931), 412–27; revised version, *ibid.*, 38 (1963), 88–104). This corpus was to consist of critical editions of the Arabic originals, and of the Hebrew and Latin translations; and it was to contain English translations and explanatory commentaries by the editors. The Mediaeval Academy of America undertook to sponsor this project and Wolfson was appointed its editor in chief. By 1971, nine volumes of the series had appeared.

In 1934 Wolfson's two-volume *The Philosophy of Spinoza* appeared. Applying the "hypothetico-deductive" method, Wolfson undertook to unfold "the latent processes" of Spinoza's reasoning. Following the arrangement of Spinoza's *Ethics*, Wolfson explained the content and structure of Spinoza's thought and discussed extensively the antecedents on which he drew. By the time he had completed his *Spinoza*, Wolfson had conceived the monumental task of investigating "the structure and growth of philosophic systems from Plato to

Spinoza," working, as he put it, "forwards, sideways, and backwards." As work on this project progressed, he continued to publish articles. His next book, *Philo: Foundations of Religious Philosophy in Judaism, Christianity, and Islam*, appeared in two volumes in 1947 (1948[2], 1962[3]). *Philo had until then been considered an eclectic or a philosophic preacher, but Wolfson undertook to show that behind the philosophic utterances scattered throughout Philo's writings there lay a philosophic system. More than that, he held that Philo was the founder of religious philosophy in Judaism, Christianity, and Islam, and that "Philonic" philosophy dominated European thought for 17 centuries until it was destroyed by Spinoza, "the last of the medievals and the first of the moderns."

After publishing more articles, Wolfson in 1954 completed another two-volume work, *The Philosophy of the Church Fathers* (1964[2]). However, he decided to publish only the first volume, which appeared in 1956. Following the pattern established in his *Philo*, but allowing for differences occasioned by Christian teachings, Wolfson devoted this volume to faith, the Trinity, and the incarnation, discussing not only the orthodox but also the heretical views.

In 1961 a collection of Wolfson's articles appeared under the title *Religious Philosophy: A Group of Essays*.

[Arthur Hyman]

WOLFSON, SIR ISAAC (1897–1991), British financier and philanthropist. Wolfson was born and grew up in a poor district of Glasgow, the son of a picture frame maker who had migrated from Bialystok. After leaving school at the age of 14, Wolfson worked for his father as a traveling salesman. He moved to London in 1922 and went into business, joining the Great Universal Stores a decade later and becoming its chairman in 1946. He made the GUS Group one of the world's foremost industrial and commercial empires. He built up a chain of nearly 3,000 retail stores, dealing in furniture and soft goods, developed the largest mail order business in Britain, and controlled a road transport organization in Britain second only to the nationalized British Road Services. His interests in Britain and the U.S. extended to banking, insurance, building, real estate, and shipping.

After World War II Wolfson began to devote himself more intensively to Jewish and general philanthropy. In 1955 he formed the Wolfson Foundation which by 1970 had distributed over £20,000,000 (approximately $56,000,000) in charitable contributions to numerous establishments in Britain and the British Commonwealth for the advancement of health, education, the liberal arts, science and engineering, youth and student welfare, and various other humanitarian and academic purposes. He became associated with business undertakings in Israel and used the profits to further his philanthropic interests there. The Edith and Isaac Wolfson Trust provided funds for building the Supreme Rabbinical Center in Jerusalem (Hechal Shlomo, named for his father), 50 synagogues throughout the country, and the Kiryat Wolfson housing projects for new immigrants in Jerusalem and Acre, which included schools and synagogues. He contributed to the development program of The Hebrew University of Jerusalem, the Technion, and especially the Weizmann Institute of Science. Wolfson was made a baronet in 1962 in recognition of his public services. In 1963 he became the only non-scientist to be elected a Fellow of the Royal Society. He founded Wolfson College at Oxford with a contribution of £2,000,000, which was matched by a similar endowment by the Ford Foundation, and in 1977 also founded Wolfson College, Cambridge. He was appeal chairman of the Joint Palestine Appeal of Great Britain and Ireland from 1950 onward, and president of the *United Synagogue. By the time of his death he had given away £130 million to various philanthropic causes and was probably the greatest British philanthropist of his time. His son BARON LEONARD WOLFSON (1927–) succeeded him as chairman of GUS and was president of the Jewish Welfare Board from 1972 to 1982. Also a great philanthropist, he was given a life peerage in 1985.

BIBLIOGRAPHY: S.J. Goldsmith, *Twenty 20th Century Jews* (1962), 129–35. **ADD. BIBLIOGRAPHY:** ODNB online.

[Julian Louis Meltzer]

WOLFSON, THERESA (1897–1972), U.S. economist. Born and raised in Brooklyn, Wolfson received her B.A. from Adelphi College in 1917, her M.A. from Columbia University in 1923, and her Ph.D. from the Brookings Institution in 1926. A specialist in labor economics and industrial relations, she researched and published studies on discrimination against women in the workplace and within trade unions. A researcher, activist, and educator, Wolfson began her long career investigating wage standards and working conditions in the New York garment industry. She worked as a field agent for the National Child Labor Committee (1918–20), as executive secretary of the New York State Consumers League (1920–22), and then as director of education at the Union Health Center of the International Ladies Garment Workers Union (1925–27). Wolfson married Dr. Iago Galdston in 1920 and the couple had two children. Following a 1935 divorce, Wolfson married Austin Bigelow Wood, a professor of psychology at Brooklyn College, in 1938.

In 1928 Wolfson was appointed instructor of economics at the Brooklyn branch of Hunter College, soon to become Brooklyn College, and was subsequently promoted to the rank of professor of economics and labor relations. She also taught adult education courses for the ILGWU, the Headgear Workers Union, and the Summer School for Office Workers, as well as courses in the continuing education program at Sarah Lawrence College after her retirement from Brooklyn College in 1967. During her lifetime, Wolfson's students dedicated a collection of books on labor-management relations at Brooklyn College Library in her honor; after her death, her colleagues established an annual scholarship for graduate study in labor economics in her memory.

In addition to her book, *The Woman Worker and the Trade Unions* (1926), Wolfson published many scholarly and popular articles and was on the editorial board of *The Woman Today*. She served on the public panel of the War Labor Board (1942–45); the national panel of arbitrators of the American Arbitration Association; the State Board of Mediation (1946–53); the Kings County Council Against Discrimination (1949–53); and as New York chapter president and member of the executive board of the Industrial Relations Research Association. In 1957, she received the John Dewey Award of the League for Industrial Democracy in recognition of her achievements as mediator of industrial disputes. Theresa Wolfson's extensive papers can be found in the Kheel Center for Labor-Management Documentation in the Catherwood Library at Cornell University.

BIBLIOGRAPHY: A.J. Lyke. "Wolfson, Theresa," in: *Jewish Women in America*, 2:1487–88; R. Milkman (ed.), *Women, Work and Protest* (1985).

[Harriet Pass Freidenreich (2nd ed.)]

WOLFSTHAL, CHUNE (1851–1924), composer. Born in Tysmenitsa, Galicia, Wolfsthal was the son of a cantor. Together with his six brothers he organized the well-known Kapelle Wolfsthal ensemble in Tarnopol. It toured widely and entertained both at gentile social functions and at ḥasidic courts. After service as a military bandmaster, Wolfsthal became conductor at the Jewish Theater in Lvov but was forced to flee to Vienna in 1914, and returned to Tarnopol after the war. The operettas which he composed, *Der Teufel als Retter, R. Jehuda Halevi, Der komische Ball, Die Malke Schwo, Die Tochter Jeruschulajims, Die Drei Matunes* (from the story by I.L. Peretz), and *Bostenai* were written in the classical pattern of Johann Strauss and Suppé operettas. They were played in every Jewish theater in the world and made Wolfsthal's reputation second only to that of Abraham *Goldfaden. He also composed waltzes, marches, and dances which attained great popularity. Despite his success, Wolfsthal lived and died in poverty.

WOLKOWISKI, JEHIEL BER (1819–1903), wealthy merchant and leader of the community of Bialystok. A dynamic personality, Wolkowiski was outstanding for his brilliant economic initiative. He amassed a fortune by trading textiles from factories in Germany and succeeded in marketing them in an efficient manner at the fairs of Lithuania and Ukraine. As a result of his connections with the Russian authorities he acted as the leader of the community for 50 years (1850–1900), in spite of its lack of official status. His control over the administration of several banks also enabled him to exert influence on the municipal leaders and the local police, and he developed many charitable institutions in the community. Their officials acted upon his instructions. He did many favors for individuals, and became well known for saving Jewish youths who had been forced into military service. Although he possessed a limited education, Wolkowiski maintained a religious atmosphere in his home and a special *bet midrash*, which continued to exist until World War II. An opponent of Ḥibbat Zion and Zionism, he attacked R. Samuel *Mohilewer. In 1894 the authorities granted him a special status according to which he could vote and be elected to office.

BIBLIOGRAPHY: A.S. Herschberg, *Pinkas Bialystok*, 1 (1949), 249–68.

[Moshe Landau]

WOLLENBORG, LEONE (1859–1930), Italian statesman. He became famous especially as founder of the savings and agricultural cooperative credit banks. He founded the first of them in 1883. Wollenborg was elected as deputy in 1893; he was appointed undersecretary at the Ministry of Finance in 1898, and he became minister of finance in 1901. Wollenborg became senator in 1914.

BIBLIOGRAPHY: C. De Benedetti (ed.), *Il Cammino della Speranza: gli Ebrei e Padova*, vol. 2 (1998), 99.

[Massimo Longo Adorno (2nd ed.)]

WOLLHEIM, GERT H. (1894–1974), German expressionist painter, born in Dresden. From 1911 to 1913 Wollheim studied in Weimar at the school of fine arts. Among his teachers were Gottlieb Forster and Albin Egger-Lienz. As a young artist he exhibited in Herwarth Walden's progressive Der Sturm Gallery in Berlin. During World War I, he fought on the eastern and western fronts and was wounded in the stomach, an experience which became crucial for his later art work. His work is violent and contorted, and stresses the element of the grotesque. Some of his compositions mingle figures in everyday dress with figures of masqueraders. In 1919 he left Berlin for Duesseldorf, where he created many of his woodcuts, etchings, and paintings to express his terrible experiences of war. The monumental triptych *The Wounded* has the figure of a soldier in the position of the crucified Jesus, with lacerated belly, as its centerpiece (1919, private collection). Wollheim shared his studio in Duesseldorf with his friend Otto Dix and joined the association Das Junge Rheinland as well as the Aktivistenbund 1919, a group of young leftist intellectuals and artists.

In 1933 he emigrated to Paris, where he founded the Kollektiv Deutscher Kuenstler in 1936–37. In 1938 the Nazis showed three works of Wollheim in their exhibition "Degenerate Art" in Munich as examples of accomplished madness. From 1939 to 1942 he was detained in the camps at Vierzon, Ruchard, Gurs and Septfonds, France. In 1942 he was able to escape to Nay, where he and his wife were hidden by a peasant woman. In 1947 he emigrated to New York. In 1961, on the occasion of the exhibition at the Museum of Art, Duesseldorf, he visited Germany for the first time since 1933. In 1971 his work was on exhibition in Berlin. Wollheim died in New York.

Today the art of Wollheim is considered to be a synonym for aggressive avant-garde art and the attempt to illustrate the inner feelings of mankind in hyper-expressionist painting. His surreal and fantastic landscapes with monstrous figures and symbols point to the work of Hieronymus Bosch, such as *Paradis terrestre* (1936, private collection) or *The Kingdom of Punctuation Marks* (1953, private collection). Moreover, he went on to represent the abuses of the Nazi regime in expressive forms, as in *Gurs VII: Death Transport* (1940, private collection) and *Six Millions* (1962, Museum Duesseldorf). Most of his paintings, some 450 works according to the estimate of the artist himself, were either destroyed in, or have been missing since, World War II.

BIBLIOGRAPHY: Galerie Remmert und Barth, *Gert H. Wollheim zum 90. Geburtstag: Gemälde, Aquarelle, Zeichnungen, Druckgraphiken* (1984); Verein August Macke Haus e.V. (ed.), *Gert H. Wollheim. Phantast und Rebell* (2000); S. v. Wiese (ed.), *Gert H. Wollheim 1894–1974*, monograph and catalogue (1993; with catalogue raisonné).

[Jihan Radjai-Ordoubadi (2nd ed.)]

WOLMAN, ABEL (1892–1989), U.S. sanitary engineer, pioneer in problems of environmental pollution. Born in Baltimore, Maryland, Wolman became professor of sanitary engineering at his alma mater, Johns Hopkins University, lecturing there from 1937 to 1957. Working in the field of water supply and sewage, Wolman did much toward maintaining proper sanitation throughout the United States. He was an early advocate of a national water policy, and as early as 1946 demanded that industry assume responsibility for alleviating pollution. He was consulted by the U.S. Public Health Service, the U.S. Departments of Defense, Agriculture, and the Interior, the Red Cross, the Tennessee Valley Authority, the American Railroad Association, and many municipalities. An authority on environmental sanitation at the UN, Wolman's expertise was sought in India, Ceylon, Taiwan, Argentina, Brazil, and the Arctic. He was chief consultant for Israel's Jordan River project and, from 1958, consultant for all water development in Israel. Disposal problems took on a new dimension with the worldwide proliferation of atomic activity, and Wolman was appointed by the U.S. Atomic Energy Commission to evaluate the dangers of cumulative radiation. In 1967 he became a consultant on biotechnology in the atmosphere for the National Aeronautics and Space Administration (NASA). Wolman served as president of the American Public Health Association and was editor of the *Journal of Public Health*. A prolific contributor to professional journals, he wrote on such diverse subjects as malaria, ice engineering and the legal aspects of water supply. Many of his articles are reprinted in *Water, Health and Society: Selected Papers by Abel Wolman* (G.F. White, ed., 1969). He was co-author of *The Significance of Waterborne Typhoid Fever Outbreaks* (1931), and was the editor of *The Manual of Water Works Practice* (1925). For a period of 60 years Wolman succeeded in focusing his attention on the total human environment, responding in both technological and human terms to the threats to the environment that result from technological progress.

WOLMARK, ALFRED (1877–1961), British painter. Born in Warsaw, he was taken to the East End of London as a child and studied in the Royal Academy Schools. He made his reputation at the Whitechapel Art Exhibition of 1906, where his work was praised by perceptive art critics. In his early period, he painted Whitechapel scenes and Rembrandtesque studies of Jewish subjects, such as rabbis and talmudic students. Later he developed into a brilliant colorist. His use of color was so bright that in an exhibition of the International Society of Artists no English painter dared hang work next to his. His work was finally placed next to Van Gogh's. Wolmark did portraits of many noted literary figures and, in 1925, provided illustrations for an edition of the works of Israel *Zangwill. A retrospective exhibit of Wolmark's work was held at London's Ben-Uri Gallery in 2004.

ADD. BIBLIOGRAPHY: ODNB online.

WOLOFSKY, HIRSCH (1878–1949), Canadian Yiddish publisher and author. Wolofsky was born in Shidlovtse (Szydlowiec), Poland, into an observant ḥasidic community to which his father was crown rabbi. He received a traditional religious education until orphaned at 15. He moved to Lodz, married, and immigrated to Canada via England in 1900 to join a brother in Montreal. In 1907 Wolofsky founded Canada's first enduring Yiddish daily, the *Keneder Adler* (Canadian Jewish Eagle), and served as managing editor until his death. Wolofsky's newspaper served a wide readership across ideological lines. It promoted Jewish education, establishment of a Canadian Jewish Congress, creation of a Jewish Community Council (Va'ad Ha'ir), and building of a Jewish hospital.

The *Adler* attracted Jewish writers of international renown such as Hebraist Reuben Brainin, who served as editor from 1912 to 1915, and featured many of Canada's Yiddish writers. Wolofsky's *Adler* subsidized the literary and scholarly pursuits of its associates and published many of their books. Among the books published was Canada's first Yiddish book: Moshe Elimelech Levin's *Kinder Ertsiyung bay Yidn* ("Children's Education Among Jews," 1910), and a local edition of the Talmud, the *Adler's Shas Talmud Bavli* or, as it became popularly known, the *Montreoler Shas* ("Montreal Talmud," 1919).

Wolofsky also wrote for the *Adler*. He published three Yiddish books: a travelogue titled *Eyrope un Erets-Yisroel nokh dem Veltkrig* ("Europe and the Land of Israel after the World War," 1922), a volume of contemporary commentary on the weekly Torah portions, *Fun Eybign Kval* ("From the Eternal Source," 1930), and a book of memoirs, *Mayn Lebns Rayze* ("Journey of My Life," 1946; Eng. tr. 1945, Fr. tr. 2000). In addition, Wolofsky served as publisher of the Anglo-Jewish weekly the *Canadian Jewish Chronicle* (founded 1914). He held various leadership positions in the Montreal Jewish community, including the vice presidency of both the American Union of Polish Jews and the Canadian Jewish Congress.

BIBLIOGRAPHY: L. Levendel, *A Century of the Canadian Jewish Press: 1880s–1980s* (1989).

[Rebecca E. Margolis (2nd ed.)]

WOLOMIN (Pol. **Wołomin**), town in Warszawa province, east central Poland. The town developed toward the close of the 19th century, and, situated on the Warsaw-Bialystok railway line, became a commercial and industrial center. Jews numbered 3,079 (49.3% of the total population) in 1921. Although they were active in the town's development, during the 1930s they were ousted from their positions and by 1939 their proportion in the town's population had fallen to 22% (3,000 Jews). In general, Jews earned their livelihood from commerce, from such crafts as dyeing, baking, tailoring, and joinery, and from renting houses to summer guests. Some Jews also owned tanneries and glass factories. Communal and cultural activities revolved around the Peretz Library and the *Maccabi and *Ha-Po'el societies. Jews won five of the municipal council's 24 seats in the 1934 elections. Ze'ev Bergeisen, who was rabbi from the early 1900s until the Holocaust, had a profound influence on the life of the Jewish community.

[Shimshon Leib Kirshenboim]

Holocaust Period

On the outbreak of World War II there were about 3,000 Jews in Wolomin. A large-scale *Aktion* took place on Oct. 4–6, 1942, when over 600 Jews were shot in Wolomin and the rest deported to the *Treblinka death camp. After the war the Jewish community of Wolomin was not reconstituted.

WOLOWSKI (Schor), Christian family in Poland of Jewish origin. In 1755–56, its members joined the *Frankists, after which they converted to Catholicism. Until the 1830s the Wolowski family exclusively married apostate Frankists, but subsequently they also contracted mixed marriages.

ELISHA SCHOR, the first known of the ramified Wolowski family, was a descendant of Zalman Naphtali Schor, rabbi of *Lublin. For many years Elisha Schor held the position of *Maggid* in the community of *Rogatin, and was among the leaders of Shabbateanism in the southeastern sector of the Polish kingdom. In 1755, with his sons and his son-in-law Hirsch Shabbetais, the husband of his daughter Hayyah, he joined the sect of Jacob Frank, whom he regarded as the loyal successor of Shabbateanism. It was at Elisha's initiative and with his participation that the disputation with the rabbis was held at *Kamenets Podolski in June 1757; he also signed the *Patshegen ha-Ta'anot ve-ha-Teshuvot* ("Summary of the Arguments and the Replies"). After the death of Bishop M. Dembowski, the patron of the Frankists, Elisha was compelled in the autumn of 1757 to flee across the Turkish border with his followers. He died there during a popular outbreak against the members of the sect.

The children of Elisha Schor, Solomon, Nathan, Lipman, Hayyah, and their families adhered to the Frankist sect, until their conversion to Christianity in 1759, when they changed their name to Wolowski (Pol. *wol* = Heb. *shor*). They held various positions in the court of Jacob Frank in Poland and in Offenbach.

FRANCISZEK LUKASZ WOLOWSKI, son of Solomon and grandson of Elisha, became secretary of King Stanislaus II Augustus, and was raised to the nobility in 1791. JAN KANTY WOLOWSKI (1803–1864), jurist, great-grandson of Elisha Schor, held the position of secretary of state in Congress Poland and was one of the draftsmen of the civil code of Poland. In 1839 he was raised to the nobility by Nicholas I and in 1861 was appointed dean of the faculty of law at the University of Warsaw. He was the only former Frankist not ashamed of his Jewish origin, of which he was even proud.

FRANCISZEK WOLOWSKI (1776–1844), jurist and statesman, great-grandson of Elisha Schor, was a member of the Polish Sejm (Parliament) in 1818 and between 1825 and 1831. He was raised to the nobility in 1823. In 1830, at the time of the Polish uprising, he opposed emancipation of the Jews. After the suppression of the uprising, he emigrated to France with his family. His son LOUIS FRANCOIS WOLOWSKI (1810–1876), French economist and statesman, born in Warsaw, took part in the Polish uprising of 1830–31, and later emigrated to France. In 1834 he began to publish the periodical *Revue de législation et de jurisprudence*. From 1848 to 1851 he was a delegate in the constituent and legislative assembly of France. In 1852 he founded the Crédit Foncier bank. In 1871 he was elected to the National Assembly. His important works are *Etude d'économie Politique et Statistique* (1864); *La Question des banques* (1864); and *L'Or et l'argent* (1870).

BIBLIOGRAPHY: J. Emden, *Sefer Shimmush* (Amsterdam, 1758), 80, 82; J. Bernstein, in: *Juedisches Literaturblatt*, 27 (1882), 107; A. Kraushar, *Frank i frankiści*, 2 (1895), 11, 20, 33, 53, 91; T. Jeske-Choinski, *Neofici polscy*, (1904), 100–3; M. Balaban, *Le-Toledot ha-Tenu'ah ha-Frankit*, 1 (1934), 114–5, 117, 118, 120–3, 139; I. Schiper, *Dzieje handlu zydowskiego na ziemiach polskich* (1937), index; S.A. Kempner, *Dzieje gospodarcze Polski porozbiorowej*, 1 (1920), 97–105; J. Shatzky, *Geshikhte fun Yidn in Varshe*, 1–2 (1947–48), indexes; M. Roztworowski, *Dyaryusz Sejmu 1830/31*, 4 (1912), 6–8.

[Arthur Cygielman]

WOLPE, DAVID E. (1908–), Yiddish writer. Born in 1908 in Keidan in Kovno province (Lithuania), Wolpe was educated in both the traditional *ḥeder* and in the Tarbut Hebrew high school. Fired early with socialist ideals, he joined the Zionist-socialist youth movement Ha-Shomer ha-Ẓa'ir at 16 and became the founding editor of its Hebrew journal, *Ha-Nesher*. In 1930 he immigrated to Palestine as a pioneer of the organization's kibbutz, today Kibbutz Bet Zera, one of the oldest and most prosperous kibbutzim in the Jordan valley. He also worked in the orange groves and vineyards of the Jewish settlements Binyaminah and Petaḥ Tikvah, before leaving the kibbutz in 1933 to become a building laborer in Tel Aviv. Returning to Europe in 1936, Wolpe joined the Lithuanian army, but from 1941 was interned in the Kovno ghetto, from which, in 1944, he was transported to Dachau. In 1945 he was among the survivors liberated by the U.S. army. Sent to recover in the St. Ottilien Hospital in Bavaria, he met and married there an 18-year-old Jewish refugee and fellow patient. In 1951 Wolpe immigrated to South Africa, where he immediately plunged into the Yiddish literary life of Johannesburg, becoming a prolific contributor to all the local Yiddish and Hebrew journals and serving as editor of South Africa's only Yiddish monthly, *Dorem Afrike* (1954–70). He serialized his memoirs, *A Yid in der Litvisher Armey* ("A Jew in the Lithuanian Army") in

South Africa's only Yiddish newspaper, the *Afrikaner Yidishe Tsaytung* (1959–60).

Wolpe's first love was poetry, and in 1978 he published his collected verse, written over a period of some 30 years, in the substantial volume, *A Volkn un a Veg* ("A Cloud and a Way"). Much praised when it first appeared, this anthology was awarded the prestigious Itsik Manger Prize in Israel in 1983. He also published a volume of literary essays, *A Vort in Zayn Tsayt* ("A Word in Its Time," 1984); a critical study of the work of Abraham *Sutzkever, *Mit Avrom Sutskever iber Zayn Lidervelt* ("The Poetic World of Abraham Sutzkever," 1985); a collection of short stories, *Heymen, Khaloymes, Koshmarn* ("Homes, Dreams, Nightmares," 1987); two further volumes of poems and essays, *Krikveg* ("The Way Back," 1991) and *Iber Mayne Vegn* ("Along My Roads," 2002); and a two-volume autobiography, *Ikh un Mayn Velt* ("I and My World," 1997–99). In his nineties Wolpe continued to write from his home in Johannesburg. His abiding contribution to Yiddish literature was well summed up in the citation for the Manger Prize: "He is full of poetic paradox: his ever-present unrest and doubt are an expression of emotional creative nature."

[Joseph Sherman (2nd ed.)]

WOLPE, DAVID J. (1958–), U.S. congregational rabbi, orator, teacher, and writer. Wolpe was born in Harrisburg, Pennsylvania. His early education was in Jewish day schools in Harrisburg and later at Akiba Academy in Philadelphia. Wolpe's father, Rabbi Gerald Wolpe, served as the spiritual leader of Philadelphia's Har Zion Congregation, one of the flagship congregations of the Conservative Movement.

Wolpe attended the University of Pennsylvania, where he received his B.A. degree in English literature; he also spent a year studying abroad at the University of Edinburgh. Wolpe enrolled in the University of Judaism's (UJ) pre-rabbinical program in 1982 and was immediately identified as one of their most promising students. During his two years at the UJ, Wolpe published his first monograph, "Secret Thought and Normal Mysticism." He also served as a rabbinic intern at Congregation Adat Ariel in North Hollywood. After spending a year studying at the Schechter Institute and The Hebrew University in Jerusalem, Wolpe continued his studies at the Jewish Theological Seminary (JTS) from which he was ordained in 1987.

Wolpe joined the faculty of the University of Judaism in 1987 and taught there for eight years. He also served as director of the library and as special assistant to UJ President Robert Wexler. In 1995 Wolpe took a position at JTS as both an instructor in Jewish Thought and as assistant to Chancellor Ismar Schorsch.

A frequent contributor to a variety of Jewish and general periodicals, Wolpe's first book, *The Healer of Shattered Hearts*, appeared in 1990. This was followed by *In Speech and In Silence* (1992), *Teaching Your Children about God* (1993), *Why be Jewish?* (1995), *Making Loss Matter* (1999), and *Floating Takes Faith* (2004).

Wolpe was persuaded to return to Los Angeles to accept the position of senior rabbi of Sinai Temple in 1997. Since his arrival, the congregation has increased from 1,150 member families to over 1,800. He inaugurated Friday Night Live, an innovative Shabbat evening program that draws over 1,700 single Jewish adults each month. In general, Wolpe attracts in excess of 1,000 attendees for each Shabbat morning service.

After returning to Los Angeles, Wolpe undertook a part-time lecturer position at the University of Judaism, where he teaches homiletics. He also serves as a lecturer in modern Jewish thought at the University of California at Los Angeles.

In 2002, Wolpe generated considerable controversy when, during a Passover sermon, he opined that the Exodus story was most likely not the record of an actual event, citing a lack of archeological evidence. He was, however, insistent that the mythic narrative remains important for the Jewish people.

With the retirement of Ismar Schorsch from the position of chancellor of the Jewish Theological Seminary in 2005, Wolpe was heralded as a likely candidate to succeed him. Nevertheless, Wolpe elected to remain at Sinai Temple. In an article that appeared in the Los Angeles *Jewish Journal* in December 2005, he urged that Conservative Judaism be reconceived in terms of the covenantal relationships that Jews have forged with God, one another, and with the rest of the world. He advocated that the name of Conservative Judaism be officially changed to Covenantal Judaism.

[Robert Wexler (2nd ed.)]

WOLPE, HOWARD ELIOT III (1939–), U.S. congressman and scholar. A native of Los Angeles, Wolpe attended public schools there. He earned his bachelor's degree from Reed College in 1960 and received a Ph.D. in African studies from the Massachusetts Institute of Technology in 1967. His doctoral work included two years of field study in Nigeria.

From 1967 to 1972, Wolpe taught in the political science department of Western Michigan University in Kalamazoo, specializing in African political systems. He also served as a consultant to the Peace Corps. Developing an interest in local politics, Wolpe was elected to the Kalamazoo City Council in 1969. In 1972 he was elected to the Michigan State Legislature, the first Democrat to represent Kalamazoo. He served there until 1976, when he ran unsuccessfully for the U.S. Congress. He was subsequently hired as the regional representative of U.S. Senator Donald Riegle. In 1978 Wolpe was elected to Congress as representative of Michigan's Third Congressional District, traditionally a Republican stronghold.

Following his reelection to Congress in 1980, Wolpe was appointed chair of the Africa Subcommittee of the Foreign Affairs Committee, a position he held from 1981 to 1992. Considered a compassionate proponent of economic aid to emerging African nations, Wolpe was a leading critic of American military aid to Zaire, and he opposed the Reagan administration's requests for increased military aid to Kenya, the Sudan, Morocco, and Tunisia. He was highly critical of South African apartheid. He argued throughout his legislative career for a more informed consideration of African perspective in formulating U.S. policy toward African nations.

In 1992, following reformulation of Michigan's congressional districts, Wolpe retired from Congress. He then served under President Bill Clinton as special envoy to Africa. He was named the director of the Africa Program at the Woodrow Wilson International Center for Scholars in Washington, DC, a program aimed at promoting dialogue among policymakers and academic specialists regarding U.S. policy toward African nations.

Wolpe is the author of several books, including *Urban Politics in Nigeria* (1974), *Nigeria: Modernization and the Politics of Communism* (as editor, with Robert Melson, 1971), and *United States and Africa: A Post-Cold War Perspective* (with David F. Gordon and David Miller, Jr., 1998). He was a visiting fellow in the Foreign Policy Studies program of the Brookings Institution. Wolpe also headed the Burundi Leadership Training Program, funded by the World Bank and the U.S. Agency for International Development, which aims to reduce factionalism in post-conflict Burundi.

[Dorothy Bauhoff (2nd ed.)]

WOLPE, STEFAN (1902–1972), composer. Born in Berlin, Wolpe studied at the Berlin Academy of Music under Paul Juon and Franz Schreker. In 1933 he settled in Jerusalem, where he taught at the Palestine Conservatory of Music until 1938 and greatly influenced the first generation of locally educated composers. He subsequently settled in the United States and from 1951 taught at various New York institutions. His music belongs to the Schoenberg and Webern schools and shows strong Jewish influence. Among his compositions are a ballet, *The Man from Midian* (1940); an oratorio, *Israel and his Land*; a cantata, *Jigdal*; and chamber and choral works.

WOLPER, DAVID LLOYD (1928–), U.S. producer of films and television documentaries. Born in New York, Wolper's first commercial venture was to buy old Hollywood films and to sell them to the infant television industry. In 1958 he formed Wolper Productions. His film *The Race for Space* (1959) established his reputation as an independent documentary producer and earned an Academy Award nomination for Best Documentary. Other notable productions were *The Miracle* (1959); *Biography*, a weekly TV series (1961–64); *The Making of the President, 1960* (1963); the TV series *Hollywood and the Stars* (1963); *The Legend of Marilyn Monroe* (1964); *National Geographic Specials* (1964–75); *Let My People Go* (1965), the story of the creation of the State of Israel; *The Rise and Fall of the Third Reich* (1968); *The Unfinished Journey of Robert Kennedy* (1970); *Victory at Entebbe* (1976); the TV miniseries *Roots* (Peabody Award and an Emmy for Outstanding Series, 1977); *Hollywood: The Gift of Laughter* (Emmy nomination, 1982); the TV miniseries *The Thorn Birds* (1983); *Liberty Weekend* (two Emmy nominations, 1986); *The Betty Ford Story* (1987); *Murder in Mississippi* (Emmy nomination, 1990); *The Plot to Kill Hitler* (1990); *Dillinger* (1991); the miniseries *Queen* (Emmy nomination, 1993); and the TV miniseries *The Mists of Avalon* (2001).

Wolper also ventured into feature film production. His movie credits include *The Devil's Brigade* (1968); *If It's Tuesday It Must Be Belgium* (1969); *Willy Wonka and the Chocolate Factory* (1971); *This Is Elvis* (1981); *Imagine: John Lennon* (1988); *Murder in the First* (1995); *Surviving Picasso* (1996) and *L.A. Confidential* (1997).

In 1985 he received the Jean Hersholt Humanitarian Award. Wolper wrote *Producer: A Memoir* (with D. Fisher, 2003).

[Jonathan Licht / Ruth Beloff (2nd ed.)]

WOLPERT, LUDWIG YEHUDA (1900–1981), German sculptor and designer. Wolpert was born in Hildesheim, Germany, the son of an Orthodox rabbi. In 1916 he went to Frankfurt-on-the-Main, where he studied at the School for Arts and Crafts until 1920. After a few years working as a sculptor, Wolpert registered again at the school and specialized in metalwork. His teachers, among others, were the Bauhaus artist Christian Dell and the silversmith, sculptor, and designer of Judaica Leo Horovitz, son of the Orthodox rabbi Marcus *Horovitz. Under the guidance of Leo Horovitz, Wolpert became involved in creating modern Jewish ceremonial art. His famous Passover set, created in 1930, is made out of silver, ebony, and glass (replica in the Jewish Museum, New York; the original is lost) and reveals the strong influence of the Bauhaus designers of the late 1920s who worked under the slogan "form follows function." The same concept also guided the creation of a modern set of Torah silver commissioned by the family of Reuben Hecht for the Orthodox Frankfurt synagogue at the Friedberger Anlage, which was destroyed in 1938. Before Wolpert emigrated to Palestine in 1933, some of his works were shown in the exhibition *Cult and Form* (1931, Berlin et al.) and in an exhibition of ceremonial art in the Berlin Jewish Museum (1932). From 1935 he taught metalwork at the New Bezalel School for Arts and Crafts in Jerusalem. Wolpert's personal achievement is the introduction of Hebrew letters as the dominant artistic element in the creation of Jewish ceremonial art. This is visible in one of his most outstanding works, a Torah Ark in copper and silver (1948, Harry S. Truman Library, Independence, Missouri), where the Hebrew text represents an integral part of the whole design. In 1956 he was invited to New York to establish the Tobe Pascher Workshop for Jewish ceremonial objects at the Jewish Museum. During his time in the U.S. Wolpert took part in designing several synagogue interiors and exterior furnishings, such as at Temple Emanuel, Great Neck, New York, and the Beth El Synagogue, Minneapolis, Minnesota. Until his death in 1981 he directed the workshop and had a great influence impact on his students, such as his daughter Chava Wolpert-Richard and Moshe Zabari.

BIBLIOGRAPHY: *Ludwig Yehuda Wolpert. A Retrospective* (Catalogue, Jewish Museum, New York, 1976); M. Spertus, "Ludwig Yehuda Wolpert, 1900–1981," in: *Journal of Jewish Art*, 8 (1981), 86.

[Philipp Zschommler (2nd ed.)]

WOLSEY, LOUIS (1877–1953), U.S. Reform rabbi. Wolsey, born in Midland, Michigan, was ordained in 1899 by Hebrew Union College. From 1899 to 1907 he led Congregation B'nai Israel in Little Rock, Arkansas. He then served as rabbi at Congregation Anshe Chesed, Cleveland, leading in the construction of its Euclid Avenue Temple. When he left this congregation in 1925, it had increased from 150 to over 1,300 families. He was rabbi at Philadelphia's Rodeph Shalom Congregation from 1925 to 1947. Wolsey helped lead Reform organizations as president of Hebrew Union College Alumni Association (1914–16), executive board member of the Union of American Hebrew Congregations (1925–29), and president of the Central Conference of American Rabbis (1925–27). He was a founder in 1926 of the World Union for Progressive Judaism, and was chairman of the committee that revised the *Union Hymnal* published in 1936.

Although comparatively favorable to nonpolitical aspects of Zionism during his Cleveland years, Wolsey was one of the group of rabbis who opposed the Central Conference resolution for the establishment of a Palestinian Jewish military unit in 1942, and he led the dissident group through several conferences that formed the *American Council for Judaism. He resigned his council vice presidency in 1946 to protest its stand against unrestricted Jewish immigration to Palestine, and resigned from the council itself in 1948. Wolsey found it irreligious and anti-humanitarian in the face of "a harried European Jewry," and demanded that it dissolve. Likewise, "the Zionist movement… should dissolve into a unity of world Jewry for the creation of a Jewish culture and a Jewish life in Israel."

BIBLIOGRAPHY: S. Halperin, *Political World of American Zionism* (1961), index.

WOMAN. This article is arranged according to the following outline:

THE HISTORICAL PERSPECTIVE

Biblical Period

Recovering the lives of Israelite women in the biblical period is difficult because the major source, the Hebrew Bible, focuses on national concerns rather than on the lives of ordinary individuals and also because its principal interest is in the lives of men rather than those of women. In addition, the biblical text postdates, often by centuries, the periods it purports to record. Another problem is that much of the Bible originates in and reflects the urban setting of Jerusalem, whereas most Israelites lived in agrarian households in small villages or walled agricultural towns that were not true cities. However, a multidisciplinary approach, using biblical data along with information produced by archaeology and also ethnographic data and interpretive models from anthropology, can bring the women of ancient Israel into view.

The Hebrew word *ishah* means both "wife" and "woman," signaling the fact that a woman's identity was virtually inseparable from her status as a married woman. It was inconceivable that a woman might willingly live on her own apart from a family structure. Israelite marriage was not the kind of love-based companionate relationship that is the ideal in the modern world; rather, it was a heterosexual pairing meant to provide offspring to assure generational continuity in a land-based society. The conjugal pair with their children would also constitute a work force sufficient to meet the needs of a family in an agrarian society; and the children would be the ones to care for their parents should they survive into old age. Having children was a non-negotiable necessity.

MARRIAGE AND CHILDREN. The Bible does not have a term for "marriage" as such. The formation of a marital bond is indicated by saying that a man "takes" a woman. The narrative of the courtship of Isaac and Rebecca, for example, culminates in the statement that "he took Rebecca and she became his wife" (Gen. 24:67). That a man "takes" a wife is a reflection of the patrilocality of Israelite households. That is, the bride would move to the household of the bridegroom, who usually resided with his own family. An extended family would thus be formed, although each constituent nuclear family might have its own abode within a family compound. The incest laws in Leviticus may have originated to deter problematic sexual intimacy among members of a complex household group.

Financial arrangements generally accompanied marriage except among the poorest families. Although there are no "marriage laws" as such in the Bible, information in narratives indicates that a bride's family typically provided a dowry, usually consisting of moveable property such as jewelry, clothing, and household utensils. In wealthier families, livestock and servants might also be included (see Gen. 24:59; 29:24, 29). The dowry could be supplemented by the groom and his family (Gen. 24:53). Although her husband would have had some access to the dowry during the duration of the marriage, it theoretically remained the woman's possession.

Another marital payment was made by the groom's family to that of the bride. This betrothal gift, sometimes erroneously called "bride price" (*mohar*; see Gen. 22:17; 34:12; I Sam, 18:25), has often been interpreted as evidence that a man purchased a woman. The fact that a word sometimes used for "husband" is *ba'al*, which can (but does not always) mean "master," has also been adduced to claim that a woman is the property of her husband. Similarly, the use of the verb *kanah*, which can mean "to buy" but more generally "to acquire," to describe Boaz' marriage to Ruth (Ruth 4:10) has also been interpreted as an indication of male ownership of women. However, such assertions are now known to be flawed.

In anthropological perspective, the dowry as well as the betrothal gift functioned in overlapping ways to maintain the viability of a family. The betrothal gift would provide some compensation to a woman's family, who would lose the labor of a daughter upon her marriage. The dowry would constitute a woman's chief means of support in the event of widowhood or divorce, especially if she had no sons or if her father was deceased. And the two payments together served to establish and solidify alliances between a woman's natal family and her marital one. Such connections were important in agrarian communities; they served to increase the likelihood of mutual aid in the event of economic or other difficulties, not unusual in Israelite households living in marginal ecological zones. Betrothal and dowry payments together served important economic, social, and legal functions.

To refute the notion of male ownership of women is not the same as establishing equality in the relationship. Perhaps the greatest imbalance was in the area of sexuality. Once a woman was betrothed, her fiancé, and then her husband, had exclusive rights to her sexuality. The patrilineal nature of Israelite society, with land and property transferred across generations via the male line, is likely the reason for the stringency in biblical legal precepts dealing with a woman's sexuality. The gender asymmetry in the treatment of sexuality is evident in Deuteronomy 22:13–21, in which a bridegroom claims that his wife is not a virgin. The ensuing elaborate procedure for dealing with this accusation reflects the value of virginity as a means to assure a groom of his paternity of children she will bear. Gender disparity is also evident, for similar reasons, in the different treatment of women and men in biblical adultery laws (Lev. 20:10; Deut. 22:22–28), where sex between a married man and an unmarried woman is discouraged but not proscribed. Concern for heirs is also a factor in the institution known as levirate marriage, in which a childless widow would marry her deceased husband's brother, with the first son produced by that liaison considered the dead man's heir (Deut. 25:5–10; cf. the narratives of Tamar, Gen. 38, and Ruth). The case of the daughters of Zelophehad (Num. 26:33; 27:1–11; 36:1–12) would seem to mitigate the absolute nature of Israelite patrilineality; however, the inheritance of land by daughters in that case is accompanied by provisions that the land would remain within the clan.

The powerful male interest in transmitting property to biological heirs is also a factor in the existence of polygamy, or rather polygyny (more than one wife), in ancient Israel, as in the ancient Near East in general. Monarchs may have had multiple wives as a sign of their high status and to solidify political alliances, and wealthy individuals may have had more than one wife as a sign of affluence. But in most instances, taking a second wife or a concubine would have occurred because the first wife did not produce offspring. The Genesis narratives give us the impression that polygyny was common. However, shorter life spans for women than for men (meaning a shortage of women of child-bearing age) and the fact that most people probably lived near the poverty level (meaning the inability of a family to support multiple wives) would have precluded polygyny for all but the wealthy. Indeed, many biblical texts, such as Genesis 2:24, the Song of Songs, several passages in wisdom literature, and even legal rulings such as Exodus 21:4–5, reflect a monogamous norm.

Although dissolution of a marriage was sometimes unavoidable, very little is known about provisions for divorce. Isaiah 50:1 mentions a bill of divorce (cf. Mal. 2:14, which refers to a marriage contract), indicating that formal documents were used for establishing or dissolving a marriage, although probably only for people of means. The sole biblical text with divorce rulings, Deuteronomy 24:1–4, addresses a particular situation, the case of a man seeking to remarry a woman to whom he had once been married. Unfortunately, it gives the impression that only men could initiate divorce in the biblical period. Information from extra-biblical sources (e.g., the Elephantine papyri) and indirect information from other biblical texts, such as the narrative of a Levite's secondary wife leaving him (Judg. 19:2), provide reason to contest that notion.

WOMEN IN HOUSEHOLD LIFE. It would be incorrect to assume that women were subordinate to and dominated by men in all aspects of life. Indeed, with few resources available from outside the household, the relationship between a woman and her husband was one of interdependence and complementarity in the various functions of household life.

As the primary unit of social existence, the family household was the locus of the activities necessary for the maintenance and continuity of life. Family life was task-oriented; without the labor of both women and men, and also children, survival in the marginal habitat of the highlands of Ereẓ Israel would not have been possible. But the responsibilities of all family members were not the same. The division of labor by gender, albeit with some overlap, was the most efficient way to accomplish the myriad of household tasks. In addition to procreation, households served the economic, educational, and religious needs of their members.

Economic Roles. Women's economic roles, which included growing field and horticultural crops and keeping domesticated ruminants (mainly sheep and goats), were manifold and complex. Although they participated to some extent in the male-dominated agricultural tasks of growing grains and also helped tend orchards and vineyards, especially in labor-intensive harvest periods (see Ruth 2: 8–9), their own agricultural activities probably involved growing garden vegetables and herbs. Women's major contributions to the household economy were largely the time-consuming food- and fiber-processing jobs, the former on a daily basis and the latter more likely on a seasonal basis. That is, the agricultural products of the household had to be transformed into edible and wearable form through the expertise and labor of women.

Cereal products were the most important food source in the biblical period, with bread providing an estimated 50% of the daily caloric intake. The transformation of grain into edible form involved parching or soaking, grinding, and heating and/or leavening. With an average family size of six persons, three hours of work per day would have been required to produce enough edible grain. With the assistance of older children, women did the work of bread production and also processed and prepared supplementary foodstuffs, mainly fruits, vegetables, and legumes and also dairy products. Some of these would have been eaten raw; but many, such as milk, olives, capers, grapes, nuts, figs, and dates, were also variously churned, pressed, pickled, roasted, or dried on a seasonal basis. Meat would have been eaten rarely, probably only at festivals.

The onerous nature of these food preparation tasks was offset by certain positive aspects. Unlike the often frustrating male tasks of growing field and horticultural crops, in which yields could be drastically affected by periodic droughts or infestations of insects, food preparation, even of limited amounts, always yielded a finished product. Thus, women experienced constant gratification from their daily work, repetitive as it was. Another positive feature was the mastery of technology involved, for the various food-processing procedures each involved considerable technical skill.

Just as important as the individual benefits were the social and political aspects of food preparation. Grinding implements are often found in clusters in the archaeological recovery of dwellings from the biblical period, indicating that women from neighboring households gathered together, undoubtedly to chat and sing, during the long hours spent preparing grains and other foods. The time spent together helped forge women into informal social networks in a way that the more solitary tasks performed by men did not. These networks also constituted a social safety net for Israelite women, facilitating assistance when illness or emergency threatened a neighboring household. Moreover, as is known from ethnographic studies of agrarian households in pre-modern settings, these networks operated on a political level as well. That is, women gained access to information that influenced community decisions made by male officials. Such indirect female political power is typically unrecognized but nonetheless real.

Women's economic roles extended beyond food processing. They gathered garden or wild herbs and plants to concoct medicinal substances used in folk remedies. Although sophisticated ceramic vessels may have been procured from traveling potters or urban workshops, women, perhaps several in a village, likely produced simple storage jars, cooking pots, and serving bowls for everyday use. However, perhaps the most important household activity, because of its potential for commercial activity beyond the household (see Prov. 31:13 and 24), was textile production.

Spinning, weaving, and sewing were woman's domain in the ancient Near East from time immemorial. The discovery in dwellings of the biblical period of spindle whorls, weights used in vertical, warp-weighted looms, and bone needles and weaving tools testify to the production of fabrics in Israelite households. Like grain processing, the procedures involved in making textiles were often time-consuming and tedious. It takes several hours of spinning, for example, to produce the amount of yarn or thread needed for an hour of weaving. Women in pre-modern cultures typically do textile work together; indeed, some of the procedures, such as weighting and even working a warp-weighted loom, were best done by women working in tandem. The personal, social, and political benefits that accrued to women (and their daughters) as transformers of food products were intensified by the shared experience of working with fibers to produce garments and coverings for their families and perhaps also for barter or sale.

Educational and Managerial Roles. The primary care of young children was the mother's responsibility. The child-care component of a woman's workday was subsumed into her daily obligations, no doubt with the assistance of older children and elderly parents. From a very young age, children assisted in household tasks, with women supervising offspring of both genders until boys were old enough to accompany their fathers into the fields. Given the absence of any formal or institutionalized education in the biblical period, except perhaps for a handful of upper-class urban males, women were the chief educators and socializers of both boys and girls in their early years and into adolescence. Fathers surely educated sons in the tasks and activities performed mainly by males. The educative roles of women are not very visible in the Bible, where the mention of sages and elders gives the impression of a male monopoly in teaching skills and inculcating traditional practices and beliefs. However, an understanding of the dynamics of an agrarian household indicates the prominence of women in this role.

A mother's educative role was hardly trivial. It involved instruction in the technologies of household life, in appropriate behavior (as reflected in many of the precepts in the book of Proverbs), and also in the transmission of culture and values more generally. However androcentric and upper-class Proverbs may be, it is nonetheless clear from the frequent parallelism of "mother" and "father" (1:8; 4:3; 6:20; 15:20; 19:26; 20:20; 23:22, 25; 28:24; 30:11, 17) that both parents had important educative roles. And because women had more contact hours with children, their interactions with offspring were of foundational significance in transmitting many aspects of Israelite culture from one generation to the next. It is hardly an accident that the very notion of "wisdom," which includes technical expertise as well as social sagacity, has important female aspects, arguably rooted in the broad role of women in caring for and socializing their children. Note that the biblical word for wisdom in the Bible, *ḥokmah*, is feminine; wisdom is personified as a woman in Proverbs (1:20–33; 3:13–18; 4: 1–9; 7:1–5; 8:1–36; 9:1–6; 14:1); the "strong woman" (*eshet ḥayil*) of Proverbs 31 is characterized as speaking wisdom and teaching kindness (verse 26); and two narratives feature "wise women" (II Sam. 14:1–20; 20:14–22) with none featuring a "wise man."

A woman's educative role was not limited to the instruction of her own children. In the complex, multi-generational Israelite households, older women served as household managers, instructing their own children as well as daughters-in-law and nieces in the array of tasks performed by women as well as in appropriate behaviors. The fifth commandment (Ex. 20:12 and Deut. 5:6) and the demanding (and probably idealized) family laws of Exodus 21:15, 17 and Leviticus 20:9, which were likely concerned with the behavior of adult children in multi-generational households, underscore the authority of both parents. This is in contrast to some ancient Near Eastern societies that apparently favored men over women in assigning authority over offspring. Another indication of female authority in household life is the fact that mothers predominate in the Bible as the ones who name their children. In light of women's extensive educative and managerial roles, the appearance of the phrase "mother's household (*bet 'em*)" rather than the usual "father's household (*bet av*)" several times in the Bible is noteworthy. "Mother's household" appears in passages dealing with the internal life of the household (Gen. 24:28; Ruth 1:8; Songs 3:4; 8:2) and seems to indicate that women controlled most household activities (as in the case of the Shunammite woman, II Kings 4:8–37; 8:1–6), whereas men controlled supra-household lineage interactions.

Religious Roles. The predominance of women in household education and management may have been replicated in household religious roles. Although the Bible's focus is on temple or tabernacle and on national or communal practices, there are clear indications of family celebrations that punctuated the annual religious calendar. For example, Passover in its origins was likely a home-based spring festival involving specific kinds of food preparation; the other major festivals, similarly grounded in the agricultural calendar, no doubt involved family feasting. Household Sabbath traditions are difficult to trace back to the biblical period, but the manna provisions for the seventh day, as well as post-biblical sources, indicate festal meals were part of the holy day of rest. The domestic celebration of festivals and observance of Sabbath are inconceivable without special meals requiring women's culinary expertise and labor.

In addition, women undoubtedly participated in celebrations at shrines near their homes and even initiated cultic activity. The Hannah narrative is instructive in this regard (I Sam. 1–2). Hannah accompanies her husband and his secondary wife and their children to an annual sacrifice at the cult center of Shiloh. In addition, she comes "before the Lord" to make a vow and a sacrifice in the hopes of ending her barrenness. Although post-biblical textual traditions try to obfuscate her role, the Masoretic text clearly indicates that Hannah, having become pregnant and given birth to Samuel, fulfills her vow by bringing sacrifices to Shiloh. Although Deuteronomy 16:16 does not enjoin women to participate in the pilgrimage festivals in Jerusalem, they were not precluded from doing so. Moreover, other passages in Deuteronomy (e.g., 12:12; 16:11, 14) are gender-inclusive in their instructions for bringing sacrifices and celebrating at the central shrine. And dozens of priestly passages use the gender-inclusive term *nefesh*, indicating that women as well as men were mandated to offer certain sacrifices (see, e.g., Lev.2:1 and Num. 5:6).

The participation of women in extra-household religious life and in family celebrations was only part of their religious roles. Those religious activities carried out *only* by women, known through archaeological and ethnographic evidence, were arguably the most important aspects of women's religious lives. Women in pre-modern cultures typically coped with the many problems related to childbearing, which today would be dealt with by medicine, through behaviors that might be termed "magic" but were clearly religious in nature. Facing the possibility of barrenness, childbirth complications, difficulty in lactation, and high infant mortality rates (as many as one in two infants did not survive to the age of five), women performed a variety of rituals in order to keep away the evil spirits thought to be the cause of problems and to attract benevolent ones to assure reproductive success. Many of these apotropaic practices, such as wearing shiny amulets or eye beads to avert the "evil eye," tying a red thread around the wrist or ankle of newborn (cf. Gen. 38:28, where such a thread is a marker), keeping a light burning in a birthing room or place where an infant sleeps, salting and swaddling a newborn (see Ezek. 16:4), continued into the post-biblical period and are found in Muslim and Christian as well as Jewish families well into the 20th century.

Women's household religious praxis can be understood to have empowered them in respect to their concerns about life-and-death matters. Their religious activities focused on the welfare of their families and themselves. Women were ritual experts, for they possessed the requisite knowledge to perform rituals in a prescribed and efficacious way using specific materials and artifacts. Such knowledge was transmitted across generations by older women to younger ones, just as experienced priests educated younger ones in the intricacies of communal ritual. Moreover, household rituals dealing with childbirth were carried out for women by women, including neighbors, relatives, and sometimes midwives (I Sam. 4:20; cf. Ruth 4:13–17). Women's religious practices were profoundly important components of their adult lives.

WOMEN OUTSIDE THE HOUSEHOLD. The midwives who assisted Israelite women in childbirth were religious specialists as well as health-care practitioners, since prayers and potions are part of the culture of childbirth in traditional societies. Other female religious specialists may have included temple servitors (Ex. 38:8; I Sam.2:22). There were surely diviners, as is apparent from the strong anti-divination passage in Ezekiel 13:17–23 addressed to a group of female prophets. Yet not all female prophets were viewed so negatively. Miriam (Ex. 15:20) and Deborah (Judg. 4:4), two of the most prominent women in the Bible, are called prophets, as are Huldah, the first person to issue a ruling establishing the authenticity of a text as God's word (II Kings 22:14–16), and Noadiah, a leader of the postexilic community (Neh. 6:14). Many other religious specialists are reviled, as in the gender-inclusive denunciations in Leviticus 19:31; 20:6, 27; Deuteronomy 18:11, a sure sign that women's services were being utilized. Women served as necromancers, mediating between dead ancestors and their living relatives, as the story of the medium of Endor (I Sam. 28:7–25) suggests. Women also were sorcerers and are specifically condemned as such (Ex. 22:18; cf. Isa. 57:3).

Other female professionals, less explicitly religious, are also mentioned in the Bible. Deborah is a "judge," a charismatic military leader, as well as a prophet. The wise women of Tekoa and Abel help resolve national crises. Troops of female musicians appear in several instances in which military victory attributed to divine intervention in human affairs is celebrated (Ex. 15:21; I Sam. 18:6–7; II Sam. 1:20; Ps. 68:25; Jer. 31:4,13). These cases reflect a special musical genre, unique to women, involving drums, dancing, and singing. Women as well as men are mentioned as professional singers (II Sam. 19:35; Ezra 2:65; Neh. 7:67; Eccl. 2:8; 12:4) and perhaps even temple singers (I Chron. 25:5–6). As is true in many traditional societies, women were deemed more expert in mourning rituals than men (Jer. 9:17–20; Ezek. 32:16). And some women, perhaps those unable to support themselves in any other way, are depicted as prostitutes, an occupation condemned in priestly texts but viewed matter-of-factly in narratives about the heroines Rahab (Josh. 2,5) and Tamar (Gen. 38), and the two women who brought their dispute to Solomon (I Kings 3:16–28).

These varied professional activities are noteworthy because they negate the image of women as confined to the household. In addition, recognizing their existence has important implications for understanding the lives of the women engaged in these occupations on a part-time or full-time basis. Many of these professional specialists, including musicians and singers, mourning women, wise women, and even midwives and prophets, functioned in groups or were connected to each other in loose, guild-like associations. The "daughters" learning dirges in Jeremiah 9:20 and wailing over Saul in II Samuel 1:24 are analogous to "sons" in the phrase "sons [company; disciples] of the prophets" (e.g., II Kings 5:22; 6:1) in that they constituted a guild of professional mourning women. The biblical silence about other such groups does not mean that they did not exist; informal organizations of women with technical expertise in certain areas, such as birthing or healing, are found widely in ancient cultures, including in neighboring Mesopotamia and Anatolia. These women would gather occasionally or even at regular intervals to share knowledge, train newer members of their group, and, in the case of musical professions, compose songs and rehearse in preparation for performances.

Membership in such groups, which typically are organized hierarchically with senior or more talented members earning the esteem of the others and exercising control of group functions, provided women with opportunities to experience prestige and status. Moreover, whether they functioned in groups or as individuals, female professionals provided necessary services for their communities. In so doing, they had the opportunity to experience the benefits of contributing to the public weal. Moreover, those whose roles were performative, as ethnomusicologists have shown, were likely to have subverted or suspended existing hierarchies during performances by virtue of the rhetorical power of their expressive acts. It is noteworthy that societies in which women have rich opportunities for extra-household association are generally considered the least repressive with respect to gender.

CONTESTING THE IDEA OF PATRIARCHY. The term "patriarchy" has not been used in this discussion of women in the biblical period. To be sure, Israelite society was both patrilocal and patrilineal: the major public offices were held mainly by men; and men controlled women's sexuality. Yet the conventional wisdom about pervasive male, or patriarchal, dominance in hierarchical structures affecting all domains of Israelite life can be disputed. If "patriarchy" means that men dominate or monopolize all the pursuits that a society most values, then it is incumbent to ask whether all members of a society value the same pursuits and also whether women themselves have important or even autonomous roles in relation to those pursuits.

Power in pre-modern communities is hardly unitary. There were multiple loci of power in Israelite society, with women as well as men shaping household and community life. The gendered spheres of life within the household, except for sexuality, can be considered complementary rather than hierarchical; men controlled certain activities and subsistence tasks, women had sole expertise and responsibility in others, and some were shared. Furthermore, the existence of female professionals means that there were women's groups with their own hierarchies and that women functioned in public roles, some of which, including mourning, midwifery, certain types of musical performances, perhaps sorcery, were largely or exclusively female.

Anthropologists studying pre-modern societies who are dissatisfied with the shortcomings of existing models of sociocultural complexity have suggested that *heterarchy* rather than *hierarchy* is a better way to understand complex traditional societies. The term *heterarchy* refers to an organizational pattern in which "each element possesses the potential of being unranked (relative to other elements) or ranked in different ways, depending on systemic requirements." Social systems can be related to each other laterally as well as vertically. In this conceptualization, the activities of Israelite women can be considered subsystems, each with its own rankings and statuses. Especially in professional groups but also in informal networks, women exercised leadership and dominance vis-à-vis other women in the system. Looking at women's systems, along with those of men, as constituents of the heterarchical complexity of Israelite society rescues women from the notion of oppression, as implied by the term patriarchy, and allows a more nuanced reading of their lives.

[Carol Meyers (2nd ed.)]

Post-Biblical and Talmudic Period

The authors who left their imprint on history did not view post-biblical Jewish women as equal to men, just as they were not viewed as equal in the Greco-Roman, Semitic, Egyptian, or Persian societies in which Jews lived. The difference between Jews and their neighbors is to be found in the explanations offered for women's lower status. Jews of late antiquity located the origins of female inequality in the narratives and injunctions of the Hebrew Bible. Women's subordinate position was understood as a consequence of Eve's role in Genesis 2:4–3, both as a secondary creation and as guilty of the original sin. Thus, the second century B.C.E. Jerusalemite sage Ben Sira accuses all women of bringing death to the world, obviously referring to the incident in the Garden of Eden (Ecclus. 25:24), and a Jewish pseudepigraphic composition, usually referred to as the *Book of Adam and Eve*, further elaborates this theme. Later midrashic literature continues in the same vein. Women are said to be punished for bringing death into the world: they suffer while giving birth, are subjected to their husbands (as already suggested in Genesis 3:16), and confined at home as in a prison, and must cover their heads when they go out (*Avot de Rabbi Nathan* B, 42). Their function at funerals (preparing the body, mourning the dead) are understood as consequence of their responsibility for human mortality. Even the special commandments reserved for women – lighting the Sabbath candles, setting aside the *ḥallah* portion, and the laws pertaining to menstruation (*niddah*) – are viewed as retribution for that sin (e.g. Gen. R. 17:8).

Contemporary concerns and Hellenistic influence merged with the biblical justification for women's subordination. In one midrash the rabbis compared the biblical story of the creation of women with the Greek Pandora myth, which also depicted woman as a secondary creation who released all evils, including death into the world, when she opened a forbidden box. In the midrashic version, Eve is compared to a woman whose husband gave her all his property save one barrel, which she was not to open. Yet, she could not contain her curiosity, opened it, and unloosed scorpions and snakes (Gen. R. 19:10). The rabbis compare this anecdote to the story of Adam and Eve, who were told to eat from all trees except the tree of knowledge. However, Eve ate from it and consequently she and Adam and all their descendants experienced suffering.

LEGAL POSITION. Jewish women's secondary legal position also has its origins in the Hebrew Bible, particularly in injunctions in the legal sections of the Pentateuch. However, biblical law was of Semitic origin, and reflected a society that upheld polygyny and bride-price marriages. Internal developments, however, as well as influence from Greek and Roman practice, tended toward monogyny and dowry marriages. Thus, some biblical injunctions associated with women were reevaluated and reformed.

Numbers 27 (1–11) discusses the daughter's right in her father's inheritance. The daughters of Zelophad had no brothers, and demanded of Moses the right to inherit. Moses recognized the justice of their claim and ruled in their favor, but his decision clearly stated that Jewish daughters could inherit from their fathers only where there are no sons and if they married within their own tribe (Num. 36:10). Although this ruling is often upheld as an example of an emendation favoring women in biblical law, it was certainly not egalitarian (since it denied other daughters the right to inherit). It also prevented further egalitarian legislation in this field in late antiquity, since the Bible itself made a clear distinction between sons and daughters. Thus, Second Temple Pharisees, in their legal dispute with their Sadducees opponent (TJ, BB 8:1, 16a), zealously upheld this ruling as the final word on the matter. Their opponents, on the other hand, were probably influenced by the Greco-Roman world, in which women were equal heirs to their fathers. They claimed that this law is unfair, and therefore could not reflect the divine intention. Their reliance on the sages of the gentiles (*ḥakhmei goyim*) is stated explicitly in the source. Yet the Pharisee position won the day.

*Levirate marriage is the obligation of a childless widow to marry her dead husband's brother, discussed in Deuteronomy 25:5–9. The rabbis of late antiquity maintained this institution and an entire tractate in the Mishnah (*Yevamot*) is devoted to its intricacies. The Talmuds greatly praise Rabbi Yose, who took his sister-in-law in levirate marriage (e.g. TJ, Yev. 1:1,2b). However, the Bible also includes, albeit grudgingly, a move to release the levirate bride from her levir. This action is called *ḥaliẓah*, and requires a ritual in which the reluctant levir is denigrated – his rejected intended spits in his face and removes his shoe. Despite praise for levirate marriage, its practice was almost completely abandoned by the end of the second century C.E., as it often clashed with a tendency toward monogyny, at least in the Land of Israel. One talmudic text suspects all levirate matches as emanating from lust of the partners, and likens the offspring of such unions to bastards (*mamzerim* – Yev. 39b). The rabbis ceased to view this release ritual as a negative dereliction of duty and maintained that in their day *ḥaliẓah* was the norm rather than the exception. Thus, we see how in some cases post-biblical Judaism maintained biblical law without maintaining its spirit.

Some biblical laws concerning women were greatly expanded. One such example is the laws of menstruation (*niddah*), which are discussed in Leviticus 15:19–24. It is not clear whether these laws originally applied to the entire female population. Some scholars maintain that they were intended for the separation and special elevation of the priestly caste. During the Second Temple period, however, the laws of *niddah* were strictly upheld by most segments of Jewish society and greatly elaborated upon by the rabbis in the Mishnah. They state specifically that members of the Sadducee sect and of the Samaritan denomination observed these rites differently (Nid. 4:1–2), obviously indicating that control of women and their actions was a site of sectarian struggle. After the destruction of the Temple, most purity regulations were abandoned. *Niddah* regulations, however, were upheld and even expanded. For example, the rabbis demanded that a woman examine her internal parts often, to discover whether she was or was not bleeding. This is because they maintained that everything a woman touches between one examination, when she discovered herself pure, and the next, when she was found to be menstruating, is retroactively defiled (Nid. 1:1). They demanded that women who had ceased to bleed at the end of their menstrual periods further refrain from immersion in the ritual bath (*mikveh*) and sexual intercourse with their husbands for seven additional "clean" (or "white") days, to ensure absolutely that they would not defile (Nid. 33a). This phenomenon suggests a significant rabbinic anxiety over ritual impurity in the marital context and women's unruly biological functions in general.

Another biblical institution was the test of the bitter water (*sotah*), according to which a wife suspected of infidelity could be tested by a magical procedure in the Jerusalem Temple (Num. 5). In this ritual the woman was brought to the priest who revealed her hair, tore her clothes and made her drink water mixed with earth and ink. This test, so it was believed, would reveal the woman's guilt. The ritual was still practiced in Second Temple times, but was strongly criticized and perhaps even abandoned altogether toward the end of the period. Rabban *Johanan ben Zakkai, an important rabbi of the last generation before the destruction of the Temple, is reported to have secured the abandonment of this practice (Mish., Sot. 9:9). Whether the report is correct or is a retroactive projection on earlier times is not clear. In any case, the problematic nature of this institution may be reflected in the fact that the biblical text of the *sotah* was inscribed on a golden tablet and donated to the Temple toward the middle of the first century B.C.E. This donation came from an influential Jewish convert and foreign queen – Helene of Adiabene – probably as a political statement on the *sotah* debate (Mish., Yoma 3:10). This does not mean, necessarily, that women supported the procedure, while men (like Rabban Johanan ben Zakkai) rejected it. It suggests, more likely, that this woman – Helene – and this man – Rabban Johanan ben Zakkai – were to be found on different sides of the debate. In any case, after the destruction of the Temple the institution was often viewed as ineffective. Guilty women, it was maintained, could withstand the test if they had a meritorious past (Sot. 3:4). The water also tested men who were accused of the same transgressions (Sot. 5:1). This literary trend indicates that rabbinic texts represent Rabban Johanan ben Zakkai's side of this debate.

Many issues associated with women's legal and social status simply are not dealt with in biblical legislation and significant innovations occurred in Second Temple and talmudic Judaism. Thus, according to rabbinic sources, the rabbinic leader *Simeon ben Shetaḥ, instituted the Jewish marriage contract, the *ketubbah*, during the Second Temple period (Tosef., Ket. 12:1; TJ, Ket. 8:11, 32b–c; TB, Ket. 82b). The meaning of this innovation was that several of the woman's rights in marriage were made legally binding by a written document, including financial support for the widow and divorcée. Marriage contracts were produced by some of the societies with which the Jews came in contact, such as the Greeks. Furthermore, we know that marriage contracts were a reality and not a rabbinic fiction, because contemporaneous Jewish marriage documents were discovered in the Judean Desert in the mid-20th century. Although all of these documents were written for Jews, they are diverse in nature and are written in Aramaic or in Greek. They also display a plethora of traits that are incompatible with the rabbinic *ketubbah* but can be easily traced to Greek and Roman legal tradition. These documents, most of which predate the Mishnah by several decades, attest to the early legal and historical origins of the rabbinic institution of the *ketubbah*, even as they reveal alternative literary models.

THE CULT AND PUBLIC LIFE. Some scholars speculate that women may have held some sacred offices in the First Temple. However, with the final victory of monotheism in Judaism at the beginning of the Second Temple period (early sixth century B.C.E.), women were completely excluded from officiating in Jewish cultic practices. Their secondary role in the cultus was exemplified by the existence of a women's court in the Jerusalem Temple, beyond which women were not allowed to proceed into the holy precincts unless they were bringing a special sacrifice (Jos., War 5:198–99, Mish., Mid. 2:5–6). Furthermore, women had no official role in the Temple staff. The only mention of women in association with the running of the Temple is that of weavers of the Temple veil (*Syrian Baruch Apocalypse* 10:19; Tosef., Shek. 2:6). Weaving in general was a traditional feminine occupation, and women weavers producing sacred garments were present in many Greek Temples at the time. Nevertheless, in our sources, even this minor appearance of women on the scene of the Temple was played down. Thus, while the Tosefta clearly mentions the women weavers (Tosef., Shek. 2:6), its more authoritative counterpart, the Mishnah, mentions only the male supervisor of these activities in a parallel passage (Mish., Shek. 5:1).

After the destruction of the Second Temple, the exclusion of women from Jewish religious activities continued within rabbinic legislation, which exempted them from virtually all time-bound commandments, including daily prayer, the wearing of phylacteries, residing in the Sukkah, and going on pilgrimages (Mish., Kid. 1:7). These commandments, as opposed to others which are not time-bound, are clearly cultic in nature. Women's exclusion from them meant their expulsion from Jewish cultic life.

However, outside the official Temple cult, women were not legally barred from any office and took part in various public functions. This can be exemplified foremost by the fact that in Second Temple times a female member of the Hasmonean dynasty served as queen (Alexandra *Salome (Shelomẓiyyon); 76–67 B.C.E. – Jos., Ant. 13:407–32). She inherited the throne from her husband (in the same way that contemporaneous Egyptian-Ptolemaic queens gained their thrones). In an earlier episode, *Josephus (the main historical source for the queen's reign) tells us that Shelomẓiyyon's father-in-law had also attempted to appoint his wife as heir some 30 years earlier, although his attempt failed when his son seized power and had the queen executed (Jos., Ant. 13:302). From this we may surmise that there was a struggle within the Hasmonean dynasty between those who maintained that the queen should succeed her husband and others who believed it was a son's right. Queenship was obviously a secular office, but it is significant that a woman held this office because the monarch (in this case Shelomẓiyyon) was hierarchically positioned above the religious establishment. Thus, it was the queen who nominated the high priest, and not *vice versa*. Not surprisingly, Shelomẓiyyon nominated her elder son to the office.

Following the destruction of the Second Temple (and in the Diaspora even during its existence), the synagogue took over the many of the cultic functions of the Temple. Since the synagogue was not included in the biblical cultic system, exclusion of women from communal and religious participation was not yet entrenched. Inscriptional evidence, particularly from the Diaspora, reveals that some women carried titles such as *archisynagogos (head of synagogue), presbyter (elder), or mater synagogos (mother of the synagogue), apparently indicating that women played central synagogue roles alongside men.

Alternative religious outlets were also available to women during Second Temple times. For example, they took an active interest in the programs of Jewish sects and could join some as full-fledged members. Philo describes the Diaspora ascetic sect of the *Therapeutics. This Jewish-Egyptian group chose to withdraw from human society and live a life of contemplation in the desert. It consisted of both male and female members, whose burdens and responsibilities were of equal value. The nature of the interaction between the sexes in that sect can be described as "equal but separate" (Philo, *De Vita Contemplativa*).

The Pharisee sect seems to have encouraged women's involvement and support. They were sponsored not just by the Hasmonean queen Shelomẓiyyon but also by Herodian women and by women of the high-priestly families. Probably too, women were not just sympathetic supporters but active members of the group. Thus, rabbinic texts dealing with the *ḥavurah* (apparently the Pharisee table-fellowship) indicate that equal demands were made of men and women (Tosef., Dem. 2:16–17). The invisibility of women in Pharisaism, reflected in most rabbinic texts, results from an androcentric authorship, as well as a deliberate attempt by later rabbis to erase women's presence and, indeed, all sectarian characteristics from the earlier Pharisees.

Women may also have been involved in the activities of the *Dead Sea Sect. Dead Sea scrolls mention women elders and female scribes. They also discuss in detail laws applying to all the family and one document describes the responsibility of the sectarian wife to give evidence against her husband in cases were his behavior transgresses sectarian law (see below). Female skeletons, discovered in the cemetery of Qumran, were probably those of members of the Dead Sea Sect buried in the communal cemetery.

It is likely that women were active participants in the various sectarian organizations that fomented the revolt against Rome in the years 66–73 C.E., of which the *Zealots were but one. Most of our evidence for women's participation in these groups refers to the company that followed *Simon bar Giora. We hear both that women constituted part of his entourage (Jos., War, 4:505) and that his wife was one of his constant companions (*ibid.*, 4:538). But more circumstantial evidence is also available. Both the Jewish writer Josephus and the Roman historian Tacitus refer to women who joined in the fighting against Rome (Jos., War 3:303; Tacitus, *Histories* 5, 13:3). Women were present on Masada and took part in the famous suicide pact practiced by the defenders of the rock (*ibid.*, 7:393). Furthermore, women served as prime role models in the two main ideological innovations of the Zealot movement of the revolt against Rome. The first was personal zealotry, in which an individual aided his or her community by assassinating a public figure. The best literary example of such an action is the female heroine *Judith, who, by slaying the general Holofernes, delivered her people from foreign conquest. The second ideology typical of the zealot movement was the idea of self-inflicted martyrdom, namely suicide rather than subjugation to the enemy. This was practiced by Jews throughout the war against Rome and is nowhere better exemplified than on Masada. The only literary role model for this action from Second Temple times is the mother of the seven Maccabean martyrs, portrayed in the fourth book of Maccabees. In this later composition, the mother chooses to take her own life rather than subject herself to the will of the Greek ruler (IV Macc. 17:1).

Finally, there is little doubt that Jewish women became important supporters of the Jesus movement prior to the Crucifixion. Jesus' followers included women, and when he was arrested, and all his male supporters deserted him, it was women who cared for his burial, and were thus the first witnesses to his resurrection. These women, it should be remembered, were Jewish and not Christian, and their story belongs to Jewish history.

Women's support for sectarian organizations and nascent religious and ideological movements is a universal social phenomenon. Within Second Temple Judaism, such affiliation was a means of social and vocational expression for marginalized groups, such as women, who were barred from participating in the official power and influence systems. However, once sects like the Pharisees and Christians achieved political success, they not only legislated against women's holding positions of equality and power but also attempted to erase any traces of the central roles women had once played.

Women are frequently portrayed in late antique Jewish sources as exercising magical power; they are accused of being witches and practicing sorcery (e.g. TJ, Sanh. 7:19, 25d; TB, Sanh. 67a). Most stories of witchcraft and magicians in rabbinic literature focus on women: one tradition mentions a female leader of sorceresses (TB, Pes. 110a), while another tells of a woman whose healing powers are a guild secret (TJ, Shab. 14:4, 14d). This association of women with the occult by male writers in androcentric sources may reflect unsympathetic interpretations and misunderstandings of women's religious and even professional activities, of which we now know very little. Women's intensive involvement in the medical profession, as well as their roles as midwives and cooks, gave them knowledge of herbs and chemical processes, adding to their expertise as potential healers. When their healing efforts were unsuccessful, however, these failures could be represented as malicious malpractice, sorcery, and poisoning. At one point in Second Temple history this disparaging attitude toward women's activity seems to have erupted into a full-scale witch-hunt. This event, which probably took place during the reign of Queen Shelomẓiyyon, is recorded laconically in rabbinic literature. The Mishnah states simply that Simeon ben Shetaḥ (apparently Shelomẓiyyon's Pharisee advisor) hanged 80 women in Ashkelon (Mish., Sanh. 6:4). The Jerusalem Talmud, however, specifically identifies the women as witches (Sanh. 6:9,23c). Since witch-hunts are a universal phenomenon, a historical kernel for this story seems certain.

In fact, very few Jewish women frequented public places or filled important offices in late antiquity. Although the sources exerted considerable energy to bring this minority of independent and assertive women under male control, most Jewish women were engaged in home-based activities. For these women the sources are both prescriptive and descriptive.

WOMEN AND THE RABBIS. The most complete literary corpus dealing with women's position in Judaism in antiquity is found in the Order of Women (*Nashim*) in the Mishnah (edited ca. 200 C.E.). This collection is an attempt to organize neatly the messy issue of patriarchal control of women in Jewish law. As a consequence, rabbinic literature, particularly the Mishnah, is more restrictive toward women's participation in public and private life than the picture of actual life that seems to emerge from Second Temple sources. For example, rabbinic literature excludes women altogether as witnesses in a court of law (RH 1:8; Sif. Deut. 190). During the Second Temple period, however, women apparently did serve in such a capacity. In the Dead Sea sect, for example, one text suggests that wives were encouraged to give evidence against their husbands in the sect's tribunal (1QSa 1:10–11). This was not a very feminist piece of legislation, since it was intended to distill in female as well as male members the priority of loyalty for the sect over loyalty for one's spouse. Yet, it indicates that the rejection of women as witnesses, later considered a time honored Jewish tradition, was unknown to the Dead Sea sect. Similarly, in descriptions of Herod's court women are often portrayed as giving evidence in important trials (e.g. Jos., Ant. 17:65).

Divorce constitutes another example. The right to divorce in the Bible, described incidentally as part of the law that forbids a man to remarry his wife after she was married to another (Deut. 24:1–4), does not give the husband the absolute prerogative to dissolve a marriage. Rabbinic literature, however, constructs divorce as a unilateral action, reserved to the husband alone (Mish., Git. 9:3). Nevertheless, one of the documents discovered in the Judaean Desert seems to indicate that outside of rabbinic circles women could and did initiate divorce proceedings. In this document a woman by the name of Shelomẓiyyon, daughter of Joseph of Ein Gedi, sends her husband, Eleazar son of Hananiah, a document terminating their marriage. The words she uses to describe the transaction are "a bill of divorce and release," just as in the mishnaic text (Git. 9:3). This document is one example of how reading rabbinic literature alone as a reflection of Jewish social reality in late antiquity may distort our view.

The codification of rabbinic sources also brought about a tightening of control over women within rabbinic circles themselves. The entire corpus of rulings associated with the House of Shammai was rejected wholesale by the descendents of the House of Hillel who edited the Mishnah. While the Shammaitic corpus may, in general, have displayed a more somber view of life, it likewise represented a more benign view of the position of women in Judaism. Thus, the House of Shammai supported a woman's right to run her business transactions independently (Ket. 8:1) and argued for the reliability of a widow's testimony regarding the death of her husband, demanding a full payment of her wedding settlement into the bargain (Ed. 1:12). And since Bet Shammai accepted the unilateral nature of rabbinic divorce, they protected women by limiting considerably the grounds on which a husband could sue for divorce (Git. 9:10).

Other examples of the curtailment of women's rights within rabbinic literature are found in the early rabbinic composition *Sifrei Deuteronomy*, usually assigned to the influential school of Rabbi Akiva. In its insistence that various nouns in the Hebrew Bible that could be understood collectively should be understood as referring only to males, *Sifrei Deuteronomy* exempted women from a large number of roles and activities. For example, it interpreted the phrase "and you shall teach them to your sons" [rather than the alternate reading "to your children"] (Deut. 11:19) to mean that the Torah viewed only sons but not daughter as entitled to learn Torah (Sif. Deut. 46). Likewise the biblical words, "You shall set up a king over you" (Deut. 17:14) were understood as ruling queenship illegal (Sif. Deut. 157). Interestingly, the same composition mentions with great admiration the queenship of Queen Shelomẓiyyon (Sif. Deut. 42). Such contradictions, however, are hardly surprising within a literature that was in the process of transforming itself in new directions and attempting to conceal earlier practices.

Rabbinic literature, however, is not uniform, and a tightening of control over women may be evident in one of its compositions, while the reverse may be detected in another. Judith Hauptman has shown that while the Mishnah is restrictive, careful reading of its sister collection of legal traditions, the Tosefta, can reveal a less rigid attitude toward women's position. For example, while the Mishnah reserves procreation as a commandment to men alone, the Tosefta can envision a situation where women are equally commanded to fulfill it. Unlike the Mishnah, however, the more benign Tosefta never became canonized and its rulings never became law.

The rabbis who composed rabbinic literature were, in the main, scholars who envisioned a society that valued learning above all. Learning became an important status symbol and a means of achieving social mobility that endowed its initiates with social privileges. Men were encouraged to learn Torah and become literate. For this reason, the rabbis' attitude toward women's literacy and the learning of Torah is of special importance. To begin with, rabbinic literature displays some ambivalence on this question. The Mishnah presents the issue as a dispute between two sages in which one rabbi is specifically quoted as supportive of teaching daughters Torah (Sot. 3:4). The more lenient Tosefta even suggests that women were not altogether absent from rabbinic academies. Thus, a woman by the name of Beruriah is mentioned as formulating a halakhic principle (Tosef., BM 1:6). However, by the time that the Babylonian Talmud came to be composed the idea of a female students was so unusual that the rabbis transformed Beruriah into a superhuman scholar (TB, Pes. 62b). At the same time, their restrictive policy toward the freedom and independence of women in all walks of life eventually won the day in this field as well, and women were exempted and then barred from all participation in Jewish learning (see in particular TB, Kid. 30a). This meant, of course, that throughout Jewish history Jewish women have produced very little written evidence and have, for the most part, remained mute to us.

In most respects, late antique Jewish attitudes towards women, with small nuances, conformed to larger social norms in the cultures in which Jews thrived. While it is difficult to know the extent to which the attitudes and practices codified in rabbinic writings were actually realized in the various environments in which Jews lived, one can confidently state that the idealized society delineated in rabbinic literature is patriarchal and androcentric. Women are constructed as second class dependents whom are generally under the aegis of a male relative. Independent women of means, such as widows and divorcées, were seen as potentially disruptive and social custom strongly encouraged their remarriage and return to male control.

[Tal Ilan (2nd ed.)]

Medieval Islamic World and Spain

THE ISLAMIC EXPERIENCE. The lives of Jewish women in regions under Islamic rule were influenced in many ways by the social mores of Muslim culture. Polygamy and concubines, for example, permitted under Islamic law, were also features of Jewish family life. While Jewish women of prosperous families were not literally isolated in women's quarters as were Muslim women of comparable social status, community norms dictated that the woman's place was in the home. In addition, reports indicate that Jewish women wore black veils outside the home so as not to be distinguished from Muslim women. In some countries, the robes and pants women donned were quite similar to those of the men, but the veil revealed their gender.

Although available information for the early days of Islam is rather limited, sources refer to two unusual Jewish women of this era. A poet from Yemen named Sarah was apparently a contemporary of the prophet Mohammed (570–632); she was said to have been a guerilla fighter who was murdered by a Muslim agent. One of her extant poems in Arabic, recorded in *Kitab l-Aghani*, a 10th-century collection edited by Abu al-Faraj al-Isbahani, immortalizes the infamous massacre of the Jewish tribe, the Banu *Qurayza, by Arab forces.

Dahia Al-*Kahina, a convert to Judaism, led North African Berber tribes who thwarted the Arab military in its first attempt to conquer the Maghreb at the end of the seventh century. The details of her policies are rather muddled as are the dates of her rule, but she apparently destroyed settlements under her own sovereignty in the mistaken hope of dissuading the Arabs from pursuing a second attack from the south. In the long run, the Arabs triumphed and gained access to all of North Africa and eventually to Spain. However, until this defeat, Dahia was a successful ruler of Byzantines, Jews, and Christians in the region for a considerable amount of time. Arab historians record the defeat of this Berber Jewish queen; in his 14th-century accounts, Ibn Khaldun glorified the remarkable victory of Islam over this "cruel" monarch.

With the conquest of Spain in 711, Arab culture strongly shaped the subsequent development of the Spanish Jewish community. Poetry flourished, first in Arabic and later in Hebrew, and a few examples of women who were proficient in this art survive. Qasmunah of Andalusia was adept in writing verses in the genre known as *muwashshaḥ*, a rather difficult style because of the frequent variations that are part of its format, rhyme, and meter. Her writings reflect not only a familiarity with Arabic poetry, but display intelligence, cultivation, and originality. Her father trained her in the art of writing poems in this genre; his technique was to compose a line by himself and then challenge her to complete the verse with her own complementary line. The father is recorded as Ishma'il Ibn Bagdalah and it is possible that this name is a distorted version of Ibn Nagrilla, or *Samuel ha-Nagid (993–1055), who is known to have had a daughter.

Genizah Society. The majority of available source material concerning medieval Jewish women in the Muslim world is found in the documents of the Cairo *Genizah* (950–1250). Painstaking reconstruction of *Genizah* fragments that began in 1947 and ended in 1984 have demonstrated that the wife of *Dunash ben Labrat, the 10th-century poet who initiated the use of Arabic poetic forms in Hebrew, was also a poet in her own right in Spain. Her reconstructed poem begins, "From the wife of Dunash ben Labrat, to him." In a tragic and nobly restrained style, it refers to a forced separation between a husband and his wife and infant son; promises of faithfulness and love abound. In his reply, Ben Labrat refers to his wife as "an erudite woman like you." Ezra Fleisher has recounted the tale of this reconstruction as well as what is known of the authors; he suggests that this nameless woman might well be the first known proficient female Hebrew poet (E. Fleisher, "On Dunash Ben Labrat and His Wife and His Son," *Jerusalem Research in Hebrew Literature*, 5 (1984), 189–202 (Heb.)).

A similarly fascinating reconstruction from *Genizah* fragments was achieved by Joseph Yahalom and Edna Engel concerning the life of another Jewish woman from the upper echelons of society, in this case a convert from a wealthy French Catholic family who married David Narbonne, a respected member of an elite Jewish family from Provence in the second half of the 11th century. Her conversion to Judaism infuriated her Catholic relatives, so the couple crossed the Pyrenees into Spain to avoid their wrath. Narbonne and his wife eventually settled in Manyo, but as fate would have it, this community suffered a pogrom; Narbonne was murdered in the synagogue and two of the couple's children were taken captive. The community provided the widow with a loan to redeem her children and a letter of recommendation to fellow Jews in other communities to come to her aid. A second letter continues her saga. The convert remarried but was still being pursued by her relatives. The latter eventually located her, at which time she was incarcerated and sentenced to death. A daring rescue was carried out, the prison guards were bribed, and this woman was whisked away from her cell in the dead of night. Since these documents were found in the Cairo *Genizah*, one assumes that she eventually sought refuge in Egypt where her Christian family would have no standing. It is admirable to see how the Jewish communities in Spain supported this woman, giving her loans and letters to enable her survival despite the fact that she was essentially an outsider, a non-Spanish convert to Judaism (E. Engel, "The Wanderings of a Convert from Provence" (Heb.) and Y. Yahalom, "The Manyo Epistles: The Handwriting of a Rural Scribe from Northern Spain" (Heb.), *Sefunot*, 7 (1999), 13–21; 23–33).

While most of the information from the Cairo *Genizah* repository concerns the Jews of medieval Fustat (Old Cairo), *Genizah* sources also document a larger Mediterranean society. This was due to the mobility of numerous members of this community and their ongoing contacts with Jews in Yemen, India, North Africa, and Spain. S.D. Goitein translated the letter of a medieval trader from Fustat who traveled between Aden and India after having lost all of his initial investment in a shipwreck. His wife, and especially her father, felt that he had more or less abandoned her, and one of their missives asks that he send her a divorce writ. His long letter of reply, in which he defended his personal conduct and emphasized his own suffering, alluded to letters from his wife which had been characterized by frequent rebukes. Another letter translated by Goitein contains information about a merchant who left a concubine and son behind in his travels, making no provisions for them; presumably these were not unusual occurrences. Some men were absent for lengthy periods of time, and their wives and other members of the family begged them to return and rejoin the family. Rabbis such as Maimonides were quite concerned with husbands who abandoned their wives and families, often because they had wed other women and begun parallel families elsewhere.

While the men, in their role as merchants, did the majority of the traveling, some women had to leave their homes because of marital alliances and visits to family members who resided elsewhere; often the *kebira* or matron of the family was sent on a mission that could only be entrusted to her. *Genizah* documents refer to a woman who had fled from the land of Israel during the Crusades and who appealed to the congregation for aid during services, stopping the prayers at the permitted time as was acceptable for those whose cases were urgent and needed to be brought to immediate attention. In a letter stamped with the caliph's seal, a wealthy matron admonishes emissaries assigned to bring funds to the Holy Land not to delay their journey but to set forth immediately to alleviate the suffering of those in need of support.

Literacy. Women were concerned with education and sometimes they themselves were rather literate. Joel Kraemer has unearthed numerous letters from the *Genizah* written by women. While some of these might have been dictated to scribes, the custom of paying a professional to stylize a letter was common for both men and women and does not necessarily establish literacy or illiteracy on the part of the sender. Many of the discovered letters allow us to hear the voices of women whose language was not necessarily as elegant as that of the men, but whose messages were clear and direct, often reflecting a respectable level of literacy.

Some women had dowries that included writing tables and others left instructions in their wills for their sons as well as their daughters to be given private lessons. A question posed to Maimonides referred to a group of girls receiving lessons from a paid teacher; the girls had apparently been misbehaving and had vexed their blind teacher who swore he would never teach them again.

As traditional as *Genizah* society appeared to be, nonetheless there were women who diverged from the norm. In the 12th century, the daughter of Samuel ben Ali of Baghdad, a Babylonian *gaon*, taught at her father's yeshivah in a modest fashion. She was reported to have had expertise in Scripture and Talmud.

At the same time, a study of two responsa by Maimonides reveals the story of an impoverished woman in 12th-century Cairo who was desperately trying to care for two children while her husband was absent for long periods of time. She found a solution by teaching in a school run by her brother. She continued in her capacity at the school even after her brother also left the city, indicating that she was respected for her abilities.

The community's vote of confidence in her teaching was manifested by the fact that the parents of the pupils continued to bring their children to her school even though they had other alternatives. The uniqueness of this set of responsa lies in the fact that one hears both sides of the story. The husband first asked the court if he could have permission to marry a second wife, although their marriage contract clearly stated that he could not do so without the first wife's permission (which was not forthcoming). Maimonides informed him that this was an ironclad clause, but if he desired to restrain his wife from teaching, he could do so legally and with the support of the court. The wife then presented her case. After describing the years of abandonment and neglect with which she had to contend, this anonymous teacher argued that her husband had been repeatedly undependable in the past, that she had built up her student clientele over time, and that were she to give up her teaching she would not easily be able to resume her school should her husband again disappear. Maimonides's remedy is that the Jewish rabbinical court compel the husband to divorce his independent wife on the grounds that he had not fulfilled his legal obligation to support her. Moreover, he advises the wife to refuse all relations with her husband and to forfeit her marriage portion, probably long ago squandered in any case, since these actions, too, would constitute grounds for divorce. After that, Maimonides says, "She will have disposition over herself, she may teach what she likes, and do what she likes"; however, he rules that "if she stays with her husband, he has the right to forbid her to teach."

Innovations and Aberrations in Jewish Law. In medieval Ashkenazi society, women were influenced by the high level of piety that had permeated Christian society and began to initiate changes such as observance of time-bound commandments. No similar developments have been discovered in the medieval Sephardi or Oriental world. The rabbis did not encourage female observance of men's commandments, and women who taught children Bible appear to be among the most learned Jewish females in their Muslim-influenced environment.

However, some women did rebel against religious authority. Maimonides' responsa offer information on a "*Mikveh* Rebellion." At the end of the 12th century, many Egyptian Jewish women discontinued bathing in the ritual bath, preferring to use public bathhouses or to wash their bodies at home under more pleasant conditions than contemporaneous *mikva'ot* apparently afforded. The Egyptian rabbis were infuriated by this tactic, which, in their eyes, was akin to following Karaite practice. This rebellion seemed to have been organized and successful and lasted several years until it was decisively quelled, proving that the women were easily not deterred by the serious threats made by the rabbis.

In later periods, women also banded together to make similar decisions that were unpopular with the rabbis, also around issues of ritual immersion. When the water at the ritual bath was deemed too cold, women refused to go; in Cairo, Jerusalem, and Hebron, women entered the Turkish bath after *mikveh* immersion. Some used the ancient canal of Cairo which was rejected as an option by rabbis like the Radbaz (*David ibn Zimra) because the water did not flow all year round; nevertheless, the women continued using it. Some women whom did not want to wait until the conclusion of the Sabbath to bathe, moved things up and immersed a day earlier. In sixteenth-century Damascus, there were women who went to bathhouses during the day and when the rabbis discovered this, they had a lock installed; undeterred, some of the women broke down the door in defiance of the rabbis.

Marriage. Polygamy, or more accurately polygyny (the practice of a man having more than one wife) was a feature of Jewish life in the Islamic world where Muslim men were permitted to take up to four wives. Needless to say, a husband's taking a second wife presented a threat to the first wife. As early as 1100, the *nagid* *Mevorakh ben Saadiah, following talmudic precedent, declared that a protective clause could be included in the marriage contract (*ketubbah*) to prevent polygamy. M.A. Friedman has named this "the monogamy clause" and determined that it was included in most contracts in the *Genizah* period. In addition, fathers who were anxious to protect their daughters included clauses regarding their right to work, to retain earned income, etc. While one would assume that only wealthy men could afford second wives, this was not always the case (such as the aforementioned teacher's husband). In some instances, husbands took a second wife when the first wife appeared unable to bear children.

Professions. Women could maintain a certain level of independence if they had monetary sources of their own. On the whole, wealthy working women like the broker *Wuhsha al-Dalala, seem to be the exception to the rule, although there were professional teachers, especially of crafts taught to girls. Many women earned money from needlework, particularly embroidery; entrepreneurial women served as brokers who collected the spun threads, textiles, and embroidery work of other women and sold them to merchants. In addition, there were women in traditional professions such as midwives, keeners, healers, and landladies who rented out property they owned.

WOMEN IN MEDIEVAL SPAIN. Unfortunately, no significant collection of documents about Jewish social life has been found in Spain and thus the reconstruction of women's lives, particularly during Islamic rule (8th–11th/13th century) is not very comprehensive. The influence of Islam on the Jewish community and upon its women was similar to that of *Genizah* society: seclusion of women was considered to be the ideal; polygamy was acceptable; and having sexual relations with concubines appears to have been accepted social custom. The ruling of R. *Gershom mandating monogamy did not apply to the Sephardi or Oriental communities. Although the rabbis in Castile expressed occasional opposition to the practice of polygamy, prominent figures in Spanish Jewry, such as the 14th-century leading Aragonese rabbi *Ḥasdai Crescas, had two wives. In the matter of *yibbum or ḥalizah* for a childless widow, Ashkenazi rabbis preferred *ḥalizah*, releasing the widow from any obligation to marry her brother-in-law. Sephardi rabbis, however, often showed a preference for *yibbum* (marriage of the widow to her husband's brother); the fact that he might already be married was not a matter of concern in this environment.

Rabbinical leaders were in disagreement on whether maintaining a concubine was acceptable; many believed this practice would prevent less desirable forms of sexual immorality such as adultery with married women. *Naḥmanides, for example, felt that it was preferable for men to support concubines rather than to indulge indiscriminately in relations with numerous women. Jews often had Muslim female servants or slaves and the masters frequently had sexual relations with them; at times these women converted and married their former masters. A ban was issued by the community of Toledo in 1281 against taking Muslim concubines but apparently was not very effective.

Jewish men frequented bordellos and did not seem to discriminate concerning the prostitute's religious preference. There was a Jewish brothel in 13th-century Saragossa. Some of the rabbis debated as to whether it was preferable to choose a Jewish versus non-Jewish prostitute. Since frequenting a brothel was something of a luxury, it was generally an option for men with financial means.

Girls were engaged to be married at a very early age both in Jewish and Muslim society. Often the groom was considerably older than the bride. In both societies, the young bride was frequently widowed at a tender age; this was the fate of many orphaned Jewish girls who were married off to much older men. If the widow remarried and her second husband died, she was considered a "murderous wife" (*katlanit*). Based on talmudic legal precedent, such a woman was not permitted to marry a third husband, even if she was still quite young, since she was considered dangerous to men. This trend was exacerbated with the growing popularity of mysticism in Spain. The *Zohar discouraged remarriage for widows as the deceased husband was supposedly waiting for the wife whose spirit was linked with his; a struggle with the new husband might even result in the latter's demise. Maimonides objected to branding these young widows as "untouchables" and ruled in favor of a third marriage for these widows. Avraham Grossman has claimed that Maimonides' principled stance against superstition and his pragmatic response to a real social problem had a great impact on sages who acted after him in Spain and in the Muslim world, as well as in Ashkenazi periphery, and saved "thousands" of women from a bitter fate (A. Grossman, "The Killer Wife," *Tarbiz*, 50 (1998), 531–61 (Heb.)). This issue also arose following the riots and forced conversions of 1391 when many women were also left widowed. Following Maimonides, it was generally accepted that if a husband had died as a martyr or as the result of the plague, the designation of "murderous wife" (*katlanit*) would not be applied to the widow and she would be allowed to re-marry.

Jewish women in Spain engaged in traditional professions as midwives, wet nurses (for Christian families too), healers, and peddlers, as well as merchants and moneylenders. Poorer women would work in the ritual bathhouse or for the burial society. Again, there is sparse material available concerning women in the Muslim period, although they seem to have been more active in the economy under Christian rule. Women were present in the marketplace and many middle class women took over for their husbands in their absence due to travel or after their deaths. In the 14th century, women dealt in foodstuffs, handicrafts, spinning, weaving, leather crafts, and the manufacturing as well as sale of footwear.

Inheritance and Guardianship. The widow stands out as the most active and independent woman in Jewish society, especially if she had financial means. She might have inherited from her father or husband, as a stipulation in the will itself, in the form of a gift, or as a condition in the marriage contract. There seems to have been some positive influence from Christian and Muslim society concerning bequests to widows or daughters who would not normally have inherited anything under Jewish law. In Egypt, for example, daughters were often given a tenth of the deceased father's estate (as compared to an eighth in Islamic law). The option also existed in Muslim countries whereby the father could leave his estate to a Muslim institution such as a children's endowment. The result was that his children, male and female, were granted perpetual use of his estate and Jewish inheritance customs would effectively be bypassed. These unusual methods were accepted, albeit grudgingly, by the Jewish community because claims taken to Muslim courts would have resulted in even more favorable results for the women in the family.

At the beginning of the 13th century, a change occurred regarding the fate of a woman's property if she predeceased her husband. Originating in Toledo, the decision was made that if the couple had children, the surviving husband no longer inherited everything as was customary in talmudic law, but had to share with the next generation. The sons and daughters shared equally with the husband and if there were no children, the woman's mother would receive half the dowry if she had provided it; otherwise, the estate was divided between the husband and heirs from his wife's father's side of the family. This regulation stood out in sharp contrast to the customs in the Levant, such as the Damascus regulation, which favored the traditional method; after the 1492 expulsion from Spain, the regulations co-existed, although some rabbis were unhappy with the situation. In the 16th century a compromise was made whereby two-thirds of the deceased wife's dowry went to her husband and the rest to her relatives, unless there were children; in that case, he was entitled to all of her property. This too was subject to additional changes.

Another difference between local inheritance customs is reflected in the assessment of the marriage contract. The Spanish custom was to record a sum to represent the total value of the dowry whereas the Jews in the Middle East listed the value of each item individually. The latter method proved to be detrimental to the woman as values appreciated and depreciated and items that could still be used were returned in order to deduct their value. According to Lamdan, in dealing with dowries as well as monetary assessments, the Spanish system favored the women; this might have been due to the fact that they were a wealthier community than those of the Middle East and more concerned with protecting their daughters in case they were widowed or divorced.

On the other hand, a husband could sidestep Jewish custom and make his wife an heir, even a universal or main heir, should he predecease her. In Christian Spain, many Jews did so in Latin wills upheld by Christian courts. As a result, the widow gained a large degree of independence. Widows were also named as guardians both of property and of their children, often as part of a committee. This joint guardianship was not due to lack of confidence in the women, but in order to protect them from being burdened with sole liability. Many examples of female guardians as part of a group can be found in Aragon, even though the local law did not advocate the formation of committees. These women often continued their husbands' businesses or engaged in their own. Quite a few of them were engaged in money-lending, particularly in the new community of Perpignan in the 13th century; some were married although most were widows. The tendency in this community, for example, was for widows (both Christian and Jewish) not to re-marry. These women did not want to lose their newly independent status or to complicate the lives of their heirs by collecting their dowries. The communities did not pressure them, most likely because they were contributing to the local economy and were not a drain on local resources.

Post-1492. The expulsion of 1492 resulted in a chain of upheavals for the Spanish Jewish community and affected many other Diaspora communities as well, especially those that received the exiles. Immediate effects included impoverishment and the breakdown of family units, for some members preferred to convert. In addition, many of the exiles were robbed, raped, and killed en route to their chosen destination. Serious problems resulted, including women whose husbands had converted to Christianity and had not given them divorce papers. Dilemmas faced the rabbis in Diaspora communities who needed to decide the fate of these potentially "chained women" (*agunot*). Problems of this sort were particularly acute in Salonika. Many of the rabbis did not want to cut off ties to their *Converso brethren and thus discourage their future possible return to Judaism. In addition, decisions had to be made as to whether an apostate was considered a *levir* in case his brother died childless and left a widowed sister-in-law. If the rabbis ruled that the convert was still part of the community, the decision left the women at a disadvantage as it was nearly impossible either to get a divorce or perform *ḥaliẓah* long distance. As time passed, the rabbis' attitudes changed and became more lenient in terms of the women's situation.

Most of the Jews who left Spain came into contact with other Sephardi and Oriental Jews; the nature of this contact depended upon their destination. Jewish women in the Ottoman Empire at this time were relatively independent, and engaged in moneylending, petty commerce, artisanry, and real estate. Some embroidered and others sold needlework. Some were brokers for products made by Muslim women who did not have the option of entering a public domain like the marketplace. There is even a record of a women welder in 16th-century Cairo. Many of these women had stipulations in their marriage contracts stating that their handiwork belonged to them. Goitein commented that in medieval Cairo, ready-made food could be purchased in the market; it seems that this was still the case in the late 15th century as well (R. Obadiah of Bertinoro). Cairo *Genizah* letters written by female exiles from Spain clearly reflect a new level of independence created by the experience of immigration and the encounter with non-Iberian communities.

[Renée Levine Melammed (2nd ed.)]

Medieval Christian Europe

Between the rise of Islam (seventh century) and the 15th century, most Jews lived outside the Land of Israel, with significant populations in the Muslim worlds of North Africa, the Middle East, Western Asia, and Spain (Sepharad). Far smaller numbers of Jews lived in Christian Europe (Ashkenaz). One of the major intellectual endeavors of medieval Judaism was the continuation of the talmudic enterprise through collections of rabbinic answers to legal questions (responsa literature), the production of legal codes, and biblical and talmudic commentaries. These sources confirm that medieval legal authorities continued rabbinic patterns in ordaining separate gender roles and religious obligations for men and women, and in relegating females to secondary, enabling positions. However, norms and customs of local environments were also factors in how Jewish social life developed, since Jews assumed the language, dress, and many of the social practices of their non-Jewish neighbors, including cultural attitudes regarding appropriate female behavior. In medieval Christian Europe where Christian women had a wide range of public and private social, economic, and religious roles, the position of Jewish women markedly improved, relative both to the talmudic era and to the situation of Jewish women in Muslim countries. The reason, beyond a larger environment that was relatively supportive of female initiative, was the economic success that transformed the relatively small Jewish communities of Ashkenaz into a bourgeois society. As Jews prospered in trade and money lending, Jewish women played increasingly vital and often autonomous part in their family's economic lives, both as merchants and as financial brokers, allowing them to achieve almost unprecedented status and power in Jewish communal life.

The small Jewish communities of medieval Christian Europe lived in an atmosphere of religious suspicion and legal disability. Beginning with the period of the major Crusades (1096–1204), Jews were gradually limited from virtually any source of livelihood but moneylending; following 1215, they were often compelled to wear distinctive clothing and badges. By the end of the Middle Ages, Jews were expelled from areas where they had long lived (including England in 1290, and Spain in 1492); those who remained in Central Europe after the mid-16th century were compelled to live in crowded ghettos. Despite their political insecurity, the Jews of Ashkenaz enjoyed a high standard of living and were significantly acculturated. This is evident in the women's names that appear in extant sources of various kinds: Alemandina, Belassez, Blanche, Brunetta, Chera, Columbina, Duzelina, Fleur de Lys, Floretta, Glorietta, and the like, are far more common in our various sources than biblical appellations. (Jewish women in the Muslim realm similarly tended to have names of Arabic derivation).

WOMEN'S HIGH STATUS. Prior to the mid-12th century, most Jewish men were merchants and many traveled extensively. Like the Christian women of the upper bourgeoisie and lower nobility among whom they lived, Jewish women were often left to manage things at home while husbands were absent. And like Christian women, Jewish women had significantly more freedom of movement and higher social status than women in the Muslim world. This high status is indicated, in part, by the large dowries Jewish women brought into marriage. Since the capital with which a young couple started life had its origin mainly in the bride's portion, parents demanded strong guarantees in the *ketubbah* (marriage contract) that the bride would be treated with respect, that her marriage would have some permanence, and that she would have financial security. While the dowry of a deceased childless wife legally belonged to her husband, a 12th century enactment made all the dowry returnable to the father should his daughter die in the first year of marriage. This was to encourage fathers to endow their daughters generously; if a woman died in the second year of marriage without children, one half was to be returned.

A further recognition of the high status accorded to Jewish women in this milieu, as well as an indication of the influence of the prevailing mores of the Christian environment, is the 11th century *takkanah* (rabbinic ruling) forbidding polygyny for Jews in Christian countries. This change in traditional Jewish law is attributed to Rabbi *Gershom ben Judah (c. 960–1028), the first great rabbinic authority of West European (Ashkenazi) Jewry. A. Grossman suggests that the edict forbidding polygyny was also motivated by the involvement of many German Jewish men in international trade which often involved lengthy sojourns in Muslim countries. Some of these merchants may have married second wives while absent from home for long periods of time; the problem of deserted wives and their children is often referred to in Jewish legal literature from the Muslim environment and R. Gershom's ban (of excommunication) may have been intended to prevent such callous behavior that also strained community welfare resources. The important *takkanah* that no woman could be divorced against her will also originates in this time period. In fact, divorce appears to have been less common among Jews in medieval Christian Europe than in the Muslim milieu, perhaps because it was not a sanctioned act within Christian society. It was also the custom here, as in Muslim lands, for

Jewish husbands to leave their wives with a conditional divorce document when they set out on journeys so that their wives would be free to remarry should they fail to return after a specified length of time.

MARRIAGE. Jewish girls in this society, despite rabbinic prohibitions to the contrary, were betrothed very young, often at the age of eight or nine. A young woman might be married at 11 or 12, while her husband would be almost the same age. The responsa of R. *Meir of Rothenburg (d. 1293) records an instance of a young girl, married before the age of twelve, who went to court against her mother who had interfered in a marital dispute between the young bride and her husband. R. Meir ruled that the young wife is in no way bound by agreements her mother made without her knowledge and he takes for granted that it is the young woman who is in control of the couple's financial resources (*Teshuvot R. Meir*, Cremona edition, no. 217).

Early marriages were motivated by the religious desire to remove young people from the sexual tensions which might lead to sin. Economic factors were also operative since a well-dowered young couple could support themselves immediately, learning the business at the same time. Marriages could form an enduring and profitable partnership between two wealthy families, while settling a young daughter well proved her desirability and increased her family's prestige. Conversely, a broken engagement might give rise to rumors concerning the rejected bride and her relatives that could harm her own future marriage chances and those of other family members. Such anxieties contributed to an 11th-century *takkanah* imposing a ban of excommunication against those who violated a betrothal agreement; in most cases the guilty parties were bridegrooms and their families.

One topic on which the sages of France and Germany spoke out very strongly, and another indication of women's prominent social status, was the impermissibility of spousal abuse for any reason. Wife-beating was recognized as grounds for divorce; methods of enforcing the granting of a divorce in such cases were taken far more seriously than in any other part of the Jewish world. Concerning one such case, R. Meir of Rothenburg wrote, "A Jew must honor his wife more than he honors himself. If one strikes one's wife, one should be punished more severely than for striking another person.... If [the abuser's] wife is willing to accept a divorce, he must divorce her and pay her the *ketubbah*" (*Teshuvot R. Meir*, Prague edition, no. 81; cf. Cremona edition, no. 291).

Jewish medieval literature expresses positive attitudes towards marriage and sexuality that were at odds with medieval Christian teachings, which enjoined celibacy on the representatives of the Church, and taught that the only purpose of marital sexuality should be procreation. It is not surprising that Christian writers criticized Jewish sexual behavior, real and imagined. Influence from the Christian environment may account for the ambivalence towards sexuality characteristic of the German-Jewish pietists of the 12th and 13th centuries, the *Ḥasidei Ashkenaz, whose writings, such as *Sefer *Ḥasidim* (Book of the Pious), express not only an obsessive concern with the ubiquity of extramarital sexual temptations, but also a profound ambivalence about the joys of licensed sexual activities. Although a happy marital relationship lessened the likelihood of involvement in illicit sexual temptation or activity outside marriage and was, therefore, a good thing, they were concerned that it might also distract a man from God, who should be the focus of his greatest and most intense devotion (Baskin, 2006). One unfortunate consequence of the dissonance occasioned by these contradictory mandates was the objectification of all women and their frequent representation as vessels of sexuality and erotic distraction in certain pietistic Jewish writings.

During the Middle Ages, marriages between Jews and members of other religions were generally forbidden by religious and secular law in both Muslim and Christian realms. This is not to say that liaisons between Jews and non-Jews did not exist; they were common and at many different levels of intensity, but for a romance between a Jew and a non-Jew to progress to a recognized marriage, one of the parties to the relationship would have to convert. Generally speaking, it was the woman who did so.

Even without the possibility of marriage, Jews and gentiles were involved in a variety of sexual contacts, ranging from visits to prostitutes, involvement with maidservants, a recognized relationship with a mistress or lover, to common-law marriages. A romantic relationship which led to tragic consequences may have existed between *Pulcelina, a prominent 12th century moneylender, and Count Thibaud of Blois. All such liaisons were decried by both Jewish and non-Jewish authorities, and offenders, particularly those involved in permanent or semi-permanent relationships, were sometimes prosecuted by Church authorities, occasionally receiving the death penalty. There was more tolerance on the Church's part of Christian men having affairs with Jewish women, probably because Jewish mistresses were likely to adopt their lover's faith; indeed, the seduction/conversion of a Jewish girl by a Christian suitor became a popular theme in Christian literature. Not surprisingly, Jewish authorities objected to such relationships far more strenuously than the much more common occurrence of Jewish men keeping a Christian mistress, or maintaining sexual involvements with non-Jewish servants. There is no doubt that concern about all Jewish-Christian sexual liaisons was among the factors leading to efforts by the Church to isolate Jews from Christians; it was most likely because of fear of sexual contacts between Christians and Jews that Church legislation (beginning with the Fourth Lateran Council of 1215) forced Jewish women to wear a distinguishing badge at a younger age than was required for Jewish men, and often insisted that women wear humiliating attire, such as one red slipper and one black.

ECONOMIC ACTIVITIES. Jewish women's economic activities generally supplied a part or even the whole of the family income, sometimes allowing their husbands to devote themselves to study. This economic success empowered Jewish women not only in their domestic lives but in the religious and communal realm, as well. The medieval responsa literature is replete with references to women's business undertakings and to their frequent meetings and travels with Jewish and gentile men for business purposes; no objections are cited anywhere to women's wide ranging freedom of action. That women who traveled could be at risk from violent attacks was an accepted part of their economic lives, as it was of men's. *Sefer Ḥasidim* gives evidence of this: "A woman who was traveling heard that a group of gentiles was approaching her and she feared they might rape her. In such a case, she is permitted to dress in a nun's clothing so that they will think she is a nun and not attack her sexually. And if a woman traveling hears that a group of Jewish ruffians is approaching her, she is permitted to dress in non-Jewish dress and say that she is a gentile. She may warn them that she will cry out and report them, and she may also cry out at once in order that gentiles will come to help her, even if they kill the ruffians" (SḤ Bologna ed., par. 702). A responsum of the 12th-century German sage, R. Eliezer b. Joel Halevi, concerns a woman who set out on trade with two Jewish men, one of whom raped her during the journey. On the question of whether or not the woman was also culpable, in that she had acted immodestly by being alone with men contrary to talmudic law, R. Eliezer replied in the negative, saying "Day after day women go forth with two or three men, and seeing that the sages of Torah offer no protest, are unaware that it is forbidden" (*Or Zarua* I, p. 166, no. 615).

Women engaged in all kinds of commercial operations and occupations, but moneylending was especially preferred; widows would frequently continue their financial activities, occasionally in partnership with another woman (see *Banking and Bankers). Such entrepreneurship undoubtedly required some degree of literacy in the vernacular and training in mathematics and bookkeeping skills. *Licoricia of Winchester was a highly successful Jewish businesswoman in England who had direct business dealings with the king. Her five sons, known as "sons of Licoricia," continued their mother's business after her murder in 1277. Some women were involved in craft activities they learned from their fathers or husbands, as well, and there are references in Jewish and Christian sources to independent Jewish women who practiced medicine or worked as midwives. Several medieval obstetrical treatises in Hebrew, apparently intended for female midwives, indicate that at least some women involved in medical practice were literate in that language (Barkai; Shatzmiller).

RITUAL OBSERVANCE. All Jewish women acquired domestic skills in childhood. These included not only the rudiments of cooking, needlework, and household management, but also the rules of rabbinic Judaism applicable to home and marriage. Basic religious training was considered essential so that a woman would know how to observe dietary laws, domestic regulations pertaining to the Sabbath and festivals, and the other commandments relevant to her family life and her relations with her husband. *Sefer Ḥasidim* ordains that a father is required to teach his daughters those practical commandments and halakhic rules essential for correct observance, but goes on to warn that "an unmarried man should not teach a girl, not even if the father is present, for fear that he will be sexually aroused or she will be overcome by her passions." Rather a father should teach his daughter and a husband should teach his wife (SḤB, par. 313).

Particular anxiety is expressed in several sources that women should not only be assiduous but also expeditious in observing "family purity" regulations. In his 14th-century ethical will, R. *Eleazar of Mainz advised his daughters to "scrupulously obey the rules applying to women," advising that "they should carefully watch for the signs of their periods and keep separate from their husbands at such times .... They shall be very punctilious and careful with their ritual bathing, taking with them women friends of worthy character" (Abrahams, pp. 209–10). *Sefer Ḥasidim* endorses similar sentiments and advises against using *mikveh* immersion as a bargaining pawn in domestic quarrels: "A father should tell his daughter who is about to be married not to postpone the time of her immersion in the *mikveh,* and not to say to her husband, 'I will not immerse in the *mikveh* unless you give me a certain amount of money or such-and-such gift'" (SḤB, par. 506). *Sefer Ḥasidim* also mentions a woman who refused to immerse in the *mikveh* until her miserly husband agreed to purchase books and donate them to charitable purposes. The husband complained to a rabbinic authority who told him, "Blessed is she for having brought pressure on you to perform a good deed. This is her only means of compulsion." To the wife, however, the sage said, "If you can find another way to persuade your husband to act generously, then well and good, but don't pressure him by withholding marital relations, because he will have sinful thoughts, you will keep yourself from becoming pregnant, and you will only increase his anger" (SḤB, par. 873).

Some women used their refusals to immerse in the *mikveh* as a strategem out of an unhappy marriage when their husbands would not agree to a divorce. A wife who refused sexual relations was considered a *moredet*, a rebel, and was subject to a daily monetary fine; when the value of her dowry had been exhausted, the husband was compelled to divorce her. Such an expedient might be acceptable to an unhappy wife who had the financial support of her relatives. In cases where rabbinic authorities determined that a woman had refused sexual relations or fled because her husband was repulsive to her, to escape blatant physical or emotional abuse, or due to a lack of economic support, her husband could be compelled to give her a divorce and return her dowry.

Jewish customary law concerning the menstruating woman (*niddah*) became more exclusionary in the Middle Ages, particularly in the Christian sphere. According to the highly influential **Baraita de-Niddah*, a book apparently of the geonic period, the *niddah* was forbidden to enter a synagogue, to come into contact with sacred books, to pray, or to recite God's name. These customs were followed in many locales during the medieval and early modern eras, although they have no basis in *halakhah*. Generally, they were endorsed by rabbinic authorities who praised compliant women for their piety. Even where menstruating women did attend and enter fully into synagogue services, one late fifteenth century source reported, "They take care only not to look at the Torah scroll when the sexton displays it to the congregation" (Jacob Landau, *Sefer ha-Agur*, sec. 1388).

RELIGIOUS PRACTICE. While most Jewish boys were literate in Hebrew, and some became quite learned, only a few girls from elite families ever learned much Hebrew. However, lack of Hebrew learning was not seen as an impediment to religious practice and prayer for either women or men, since as *Sefer Ḥasidim* advises, "one should learn the prayers in a language one understands, for prayer is first and foremost an entreaty of the heart and if the heart does not understand what issues from the mouth how can the supplicant benefit? It is better to pray in whatever language [the person] praying understands" (SḤB, par. 588).

An indication of women's high status in Ashkenaz is their voluntary assumption of religious practices from which they were exempt in talmudic Judaism. Women, for example, were permitted in 12th-century Germany and northern France to perform and to recite blessings over time-bound positive precepts, such as putting on *tefillin* (phylacteries) even though they were exempted from them by *halakhah*; the 12th-century scholar, R. *Simḥah of Speyer included women among the quorum of ten people required to recite the grace over meals. Another example of women's assumption of ritual roles in the public domain is the insistence of prominent women in serving as godmother (*sandeka'it*) at the circumcision of a son or grandson. R. Meir of Rothenburg, a major rabbinic leader of the 14th century, attempted to abolish this practice, since he believed the presence of perfumed and well-dressed women in the synagogue among men was immodest. His failure to do so (this custom continued until the beginning of the 15th century), indicates Jewish women's high status and financial clout in the communal realm of Ashkenaz. However, as the political and economic situation of European Jewish communities gradually worsened, beginning in the 13th century, and traditional practice and laws were reasserted, most of the gains Jewish women had achieved, in this and other areas of daily life, were firmly curtailed.

Some learned women, usually from rabbinic families, led prayers for the other women of their communities. Among women who are described as women's prayer leaders are the 12th-century *Dulcea, the wife of R. *Eleazar of Worms, discussed below, and Urania of Worms of the 13th century, whose headstone epitaph commemorates her as "the daughter of the chief of the synagogue singers.... she, too, with sweet tunefulness officiated before the women to whom she sang the hymnal portions." The Worms synagogue had a separate room in which women's prayers took place, perhaps with a peephole into the larger sanctuary so that the prayer leader could keep her place in the service.

Jewish women appear to have been less likely than men to choose the always available option of conversion to Christianity, perhaps because the benefits such conversion offered to a woman were far fewer than those available to a man. A number of legal queries to rabbinic leaders deal with the question of a woman's divorce from a converted husband. The rabbinic authorities did everything possible to free a Jewish wife from such a marriage and guarantee the return of her property so that a remarriage might occur.

Women are strikingly prominent in 11th-century Hebrew Crusade chronicles which describe the devotion of numerous Jewish women who actively sought death for themselves and their children rather than apostasy. Some scholars have suggested that many of the horrific events narrated in these Hebrew chronicles are imaginative reconstructions, meant to express the high esteem in which women were held in Ashkenazi society and to provide didactic models for future generations of women who might confront similar circumstances. Some have also wondered if women are praised so highly in order to cast shame on men of their own times who were very far more likely than women to become Christians. S. Einbinder has pointed out a deliberate downplaying of female agency in later Jewish liturgical poems on themes of martyrdom that focus more on women's passivity and vulnerability to male assault. This difference in the portrayal of women may be no more than a reflection of the formulaic conventions of the poetic genre. However, given the steady deterioration of women's legal status in Ashkenaz during this same time period, Einbinder's suggestion that "the rabbi-poets increasingly emphasized the sanctity of family bonds and rabbinic authority" to the detriment of female agency and independence is quite persuasive. By representing women as "defenseless and violated," male authors enhanced their own communal power in an effort to rally other men in opposition to a common enemy against whom all Jews were increasingly powerless.

PERSONAL DOCUMENTS. Many ideals of medieval Jewish family life, including the value placed on education, are evident in the medieval ethical will. Such moral testaments, left by a parent for his or her children, sum up the author's life's experience and values, and advise offspring on the proper conduct of their lives. One example is the will of Eleazar b. Samuel of Mainz, a 14th-century Jew of whom nothing else is known. Eleazar's will urges all his children to attend synagogue in the morning and evening, and to occupy themselves a little afterwards with "Torah, the Psalms, or with works of charity." His daughters are particularly requested to obey the laws applying to women, "modesty, sanctity, and reverence should mark their married lives," and they must "respect their husbands and be invariably amiable to them." Daughters, as well as sons, are admonished to live in communities among other Jews so that their children may learn the ways of Judaism, and, significantly, he insists that "they must not let the young, of either sex, go without instruction in the Torah [Hebrew Bible]." Eleazar specifically requests that his daughters prepare beautiful candles for the Sabbath, and that they refrain from risking money in games of chance, although they may amuse themselves for trifling stakes on New Moons, days customarily celebrated as holidays by Jewish women. Eleazar urges his children to avoid "mixed bathing and mixed dancing and all frivolous conversation." He further suggests that his daughters "ought to be always at home and not be gadding about." Nor should they stand at the door, watching whatever passes: "I ask, I command, that the daughters of my house be never without work to do, for idleness leads first to boredom, then to sin. But let them spin, cook, or sew." Eleazar's obvious concern for his daughters' educations, for their mode of life, and his knowledge of the pitfalls they might encounter is vibrant testimony to a Jewish society in which women played many active roles (Abrahams, 209–10).

The esteem granted a beloved wife, and a description of her activities, is found in the lament of an important spiritual leader, R. Eleazar ben Judah of Worms, known as the Roke'aḥ, for his exemplary wife, Dulcea and his two daughters, killed by intruders in their home in 1197. He relates that Dulcea, who supported her family and her husband's students through her business ventures, was also involved in religious activities, attending synagogue regularly, sewing together 40 Torah scrolls, making wicks for the synagogue candles, and instructing other women and leading their prayers. Of his thirteen-year-old daughter, the father poignantly wrote that she had "learned all the prayers and melodies from her mother. She was pious and wise, a beautiful virgin. She prepared my bed and pulled off my boots every night. Bellette was nimble about the house, and spoke only truth, serving her Maker and spinning and sewing and embroidering." And of his younger daughter, Hannah, Rabbi Eleazar remembers: "Each day she recited *Shema Yisrael* and the prayer that follows it. She was six years old and could spin, sew and embroider, and entertain me by singing" (Baskin, 2001).

MYSTICISM AND FOLKLORE. While celibacy and monastic living allowed some Christian women to be recognized as scholars, saints, and mystics, rabbinic insistence on universal marriage forbade any access to such life alternatives for Jewish women. Formal Judaism offered no adult avenues through which Jewish women could express their spiritual aspirations beyond marital devotion, maternal solicitude, observance of domestic Jewish rituals, and acts of charity to others. Jewish religious leaders criticized women who adopted ascetic practices such as fasting, prayer, and acts of personal deprivation; these traditional male methods of expressing devotion to God were seen as a dereliction of a woman's primary duties to her husband and family, and were suspect even in the unmarried girl and the widow (cf. Sot. 22a).

Given these prohibitions, it is not surprising that medieval Jewish mysticism was an essentially male endeavor. Moreover, in the gender imagery which pervades medieval Jewish mystical writings, the male, created in the divine image, is construed as the dominant, primary sex, while females are seen as passive and secondary. In sexual union female distinctiveness is effaced, and similarly, by analogy, the **Shekhinah*, the feminine aspect of the divine, will ultimately be absorbed by the preeminent male entity, the **Ein- Sof* (the infinite and eternal aspect of God), from which she was originally derived. While the *Shekhinah* as bride is a positive symbol, pointing to divine unity, the *Shekhinah* alone, sometimes represented as a *niddah*, is dangerous, since the unconstrained female and her menstrual blood are linked to the demonic forces responsible for evil in the world.

Many of the negative attitudes towards women entrenched in rabbinic traditions are prevalent in medieval Jewish folklore, as well. One example is traditions about the demon *Lilith. These are synthesized in the 11th-century *Alphabet of Ben Sira*, where rabbinic speculation about the "first Eve," who refused to submit to Adam's mastery and established herself as an independent sexual entity, merges with legends about demons who kill infants and endanger women in childbirth. In later Jewish folklore and mysticism, Lilith is the exemplar of rebellious wives and the fiendish enemy of submissive women and their children. Associations between women and witchcraft, already present in rabbinic literature, also appear in *Sefer Ḥasidim,* which assumes that even the most pious woman has the potential, however unwitting, to tempt a man to sin or sinful thoughts.

[Judith R. Baskin (2nd ed.)]

Early Modern Period

SEPHARDI DIASPORA. As R.L. Melammed comments above, the experience of immigration and the encounter with non-Iberian communities offered some female exiles from Spain, particularly those with significant financial resources, a new level of empowerment and independence. Powerful widows, such as Benvenida *Abravanel, and Doña Gracia *Nasi (1510–1569), both of the 16th century, continued their deceased husbands' business ventures successfully, intervened with rulers on behalf of threatened Jewish communities, and were renowned for their philanthropy and their support of Jewish culture and learning.

Benvenida Abravanel, niece of the statesman-philosopher Isaac *Abravanel, married her first cousin, Samuel. The couple left Spain in 1492 for Italy and Don Samuel became head of the Jewish community in Naples. Benvenida was an educated woman who established a good relationship with the duchess of Tuscany. When the Jews of Southern Italy were threatened with expulsion in 1541, Benvenida used her influence to negotiate a postponement of the decree. Following her husband's death in 1547, she took over his business concerns and attained important trade privileges. Benvenida also gained renown as a pious and charitable woman, much given to fasting, whose home was a center of study and culture.

Gracia Nasi was born a New Christian and was baptized as Beatriz de Luna in Portugal. Her husband Francisco, whom she married in 1528, left her half of his property when he died in 1536. Once the Inquisition was established in that same year, Doña Gracia realized that Portugal was no longer a viable home for a crypto-Jew and with her family resolved to return to an open observance of Judaism elsewhere, taking care to move slowly to preserve the maximum amount of their fortune. Ultimately, the family ended up in Constantinople where Doña Gracia supported numerous scholars and rabbis and aided in the publication of scholarly works.

Because of her connections, wealth, mobility, and foresight, Doña Gracia managed to escape the reach of the Inquisition. However, many other crypto-Jewish women were not so fortunate. As the Spanish and Portuguese Inquisitions became obsessed with discovering unfaithful New Christians (see also *Conversos), women were particularly at risk, since they played a crucial role in perpetuating Judaism in this period. Without communal institutions or leadership, the home became the sole center of Jewish continuity and women were central in preserving Jewish domestic rituals, especially the dietary laws and Sabbath observance. Such practices were always dangerous, since servants often testified to the Inquisition about their employers' judaizing activities. Numerous crypto-Jewish women were arrested and tortured, and many sacrificed their lives as martyrs for their faith in the course of the 15th and 16th centuries.

WOMEN IN THE PUBLIC SPHERE IN ITALY, 1600–1800. Since the 19th century historians have asserted that Renaissance Italy was a period in which women attained a new and more equal status in society, and Jewish writers have accepted this view concerning Italian Jewish women, as well. Close examination of the various sources of Jewish communal history in the early modern period, however, demonstrates that while women did function in some public capacities in Italian Jewish communities, there was not a significant departure from traditional attitudes about appropriate female roles. Nevertheless, the Jewish communities of Italy were highly acculturated and there were opportunities for a few unusual women to shine in literature and the arts.

At least two Jewish women in 17th-century Italy became distinguished published writers in Italian. Devora *Ascarelli translated Hebrew liturgical poetry into rhymed Italian, presumably for use by female worshippers. Her *Abitacolo degli oranti*, completed in 1537 and published in 1601, may be the earliest published work in Jewish literature written by a woman. The most accomplished Jewish woman of this period in terms of education and literary productivity was the writer and poet Sara Coppio *Sullam (1592–1641). Born to a wealthy and prominent Jewish family in Venice, Sullam married Jacob Sullam, a local Jewish leader. She formed a salon of mostly Christian men of letters for whom she provided financial support as well as intellectual friendships that sometimes soured. As a female Jewish writer, Sullam was an ideal target for accusations intended to undermine her accomplishments as a woman and a Jew. However, she was able to respond to her detractors in witty and biting prose and poetry. Another talented woman of this period was the professional singer known as Madama Europa De' *Rossi, a highly accomplished performer in the court of the Gonzaga family in late 16th and early 17th century Mantua and the sister of the composer and musician Salamone De' *Rossi.

As early as the 13th century in Italy, certain rabbis allowed girls to receive a Jewish education. Most young women learned to read and write Italian at school or at home, and some learned Hebrew, as well. Teachers of girls were often women and those who taught Hebrew were known as *rabbit* or *rabbanit*. Other women, often widows, offered instruction in domestic skills. Two women of this period exceptional for their learning were sisters, Fioretta (Bat Sheva) Modena and Diana Rieti. According to the Venetian rabbi Leon *Modena (1571–1648), Fioretta's nephew, the women had mastered Torah, Mishnah, Talmud, Midrash, Jewish law, and Kabbalah (Modena, *Ḥayyei*, fol. 15b). At the age of 75, after the death of her husband, Solomon da Modena, Fioretta set out to live in Safed, a city known for its many mystics.

An interesting feature of the early modern Italian Jewish community is the licensing of specific women to act as ritual slaughterers and to porge (*nikkur* or *treibern*) animals. This contrasts with efforts by rabbis elsewhere in Christian Europe to limit women's rights to be involved in kosher slaughtering and porging. The probable reason for this liberality was so women could provide food for their families in isolated locations, such as summer houses in the mountains, or in distressed circumstances (see **Sheḥitah*: Women and *Sheḥitah*).

CENTRAL EUROPE. The invention of printing in the 15th century, which made the dissemination of popular literature practicable and inexpensive, played an important role in expanding Jewish women's religious lives and piety in Central and Eastern Europe in the early modern period. Female access to reading matter in the vernacular had a transformative effect for many women, deepening their knowledge of Judaism and Jewish traditions and even empowered a few women to become writers, themselves. Rabbinic injunctions against women's learning were believed to apply to Talmud study but not to the Bible or legal rulings necessary for women's everyday activities. While Jewish women were generally ignorant of Hebrew, most were literate in Jewish vernaculars (Judaeo-German (Western Yiddish) in Central Europe and Yiddish in Eastern Europe, written in Hebrew characters), which had long been essential to women's economic activities. Translations of the Hebrew Bible, the first books to be printed in the Jewish vernacular, gave women access to Judaism's holy texts. Particularly popular were the *Taytsh-khumesh*, first published by Sheftl Hurwitz in Prague in 1608 or 1610, and the *Tsenerene*, by Yankev ben Itzkhok Ashkenazy (c.1590–1618), both of which included homilies on the weekly biblical readings from the Torah and Prophets, as well as stories, legends, and parables drawn from rabbinic literature, the Zohar and other mystical texts, and histories and travel accounts. **Musar* literature, ethical treatises which discussed proper conduct, woman's religious obligations, and her relations with her husband, such as the *Brantshpigl* ("Burning Mirror") by Moses ben Henoch *Altschuler (1596), and the *Meneket Rivkah* of Rebecca bas Meir *Tiktiner of Prague (d. 1550; posthumously published in the early 17th century), were also available to female readers. These vernacular books intended for women were also read by Jewish men, many of whom were not possessed of significant Jewish scholarship; they were printed in a special typeface, *vayber taytsh* ("women's vernacular") based on the cursive Hebrew hand women were taught for business contracts, marriage agreements, and correspondence.

Although all the Hebrew and Aramaic prayers of the standard liturgy were translated into Judaeo-German/Yiddish, they were never as central to women as **tkhines*, supplicatory prayers which were intended for female use in Jewish rituals and in worship, both in the synagogue and at home. Collections of such prayers began to appear in the 16th century. C. Weissler has pointed out that while much of this literature was written by men for women, and represents men's conceptions of women's religious lives, *tkhines* do demonstrate what women prayed about and offer insight into how they understood the meanings of their religious acts.

Although some attributions of *tkhines* to female authors or editors seem doubtful, there were women like Rebecca Tiktiner who wrote and published *tkhines* collections. Weissler has written that *tkhines* written by women sometimes articulate both the sanctification of women's traditional roles and a critique of them. Sarah Rebecca Rachel Leah *Horowitz (c. 1720–c. 1800), the highly educated author of the *Tkhine imohes* ("*Tkhine* of the matriarchs"), emphasizes the power and importance of women's prayer. In the *Shloyse she'orim* ("Three Gates"), *Sarah bas Tovim (probably 18th century) made use of rabbinic and mystical texts in Yiddish to construct a new vision of women's religious lives in which women's prayer was as significant as men's.

Collections of prayers and religious texts in Yiddish and in European vernacular languages, intended for female use, were produced into the 20th century. *Stunden der Andacht* ("Hours of Devotion"), a German prayer book for women written by Fanny *Neuda (d. 1894) went through 28 editions by the 1920s and was also translated into English. These prayers for women reflect a personal rather than a communal understanding of Judaism, one in which women often called upon the biblical matriarchs to intercede with God on behalf of the worshiper and her family. Inasmuch as some of these prayers were written by women, they also represent some of the earliest extant expressions of female spirituality in Jewish tradition.

COURT JEWS. One early modern woman who wrote in her own voice was Glikl bas Judah Leib (*Glueckel of Hameln; 1646–1724). Her autobiography, written to drive away the melancholy that followed her husband's death and to let her children know their ancestry, is an engrossing document which interweaves and juxtaposes pious tales and moralizing with Glickl's accounts of events in her own life and those of her loved ones. Born into the prosperous Court Jew milieu of Central Europe, Glikl was well read in Judaeo-German literature, and had some knowledge of Hebrew and German as well; her memorial notice characterizes her as "a learned woman" (*melummedet*), unusual praise in her time and place. Betrothed at 12, married at 14, and the mother of 14 children, Glikl was active in business and pious in religious observance, including regular synagogue attendance. At the threshold of modernity, both as a woman and as a Jew, Glikl's business activities reflect the growing economic participation of Jews in the non-Jewish world, while her religious and secular educations speak to the broader horizons and new educational opportunities available to some 17th century Jews – including women.

Esther Schulhoff Aaron *Liebmann (c. 1645–1714) came from the same milieu as Glikl. Married first to Israel Aaron (d. 1673), supplier to the Brandenburg court and founder of the Berlin Jewish community, Esther subsequently wed Jost Leibmann. Liebmann's first wife, Malka, was Glikl's niece and Liebmann himself learned the jewelry business from Glikl's husband, Ḥayyim Hameln. Esther and her husband were the court jewelers to Frederick I of Prussia and the leading family in the Berlin Jewish community. Esther worked actively alongside her husband and successfully carried on their business after her husband's death. Like many Court Jews, Liebmann's fortunes depended on the favor of the ruler. After the death of Frederick I and the accession of Frederick William I in 1713, Esther Liebmann was put under house arrest and released only after she had paid the king a substantial fine.

WOMEN, MYSTICISM, AND MESSIANIC MOVEMENTS. Women are connected with both mysticism and the messianic movements that are a significant feature of Jewish history in early modern Europe. This phenomenon first appeared among crypto-Jewish women in Spain. As R. Melammed has written, Conversas, observing secretly, in the hope of salvation, were likely candidates for a mystical or messianic penchant. During the post-expulsion period, several women and girls experienced visions and delivered messianic prophecies, particularly in the La Mancha and Extremadura region of Castile. Between 1499 and 1502, Mari Gómez of Chillón and Inés, a 12-year-old from Herrera, inspired a renewal of Jewish observance, with special emphasis on fasting, based on their predictions of the imminent arrival of Elijah, heralding messianic redemption in the Land of Israel. This movement was quickly extinguished by the Inquisition: Inés was burned at the stake in 1500 and Mari Gómez escaped to Portugal.

In 1524–1525, Benvenida Abravanel, a wealthy exile from Spain who had settled in Italy, became an enthusiastic supporter of the messianic pretender David *Reuveni (d. 1538).

She is said to have sent him financial support, a silk banner with the ten commandments written in gold on both sides, and a Turkish gown of gold cloth.

Rachel *Aberlin (second quarter of the 16th century, Salonika (?)–first quarter of 17th century, Damascus (?)), is described as a mystic in *Sefer ha-Ḥezyonot* ("The Book of Visions"), the memoir of her contemporary Ḥayyim *Vital. Vital, the most prominent disciple of the greatest 16th century kabbalist, Isaac *Luria, refers to "Rachel Aberlin" and "Rachel ha-Ashkenaziah" frequently in entries that provide rare insight into the mystical religiosity of early modern Jewish women in the period preceding Shabbateanism. Aberlin is portrayed in *Sefer ha-Ḥezyonot* as a woman who regularly experienced mystical visions, from pillars of fire to Elijah the Prophet. She is said to have been "accustomed to seeing visions, demons, souls, and angels." Aberlin seems to have been an important figure to other women in her community, who regarded her as a spiritual leader.

Sarah, one of the wives of the preeminent messianic figure of the early modern period, *Shabbetai Ẓevi (1626–1676), continues to be an enigma to historians. Apparently a survivor of the 1648 Chmielnicki pogroms in Poland who had been brought up as a Christian, Sarah attracted attention with her beauty and her claims that she was destined to marry the messiah. According to some reports, Sarah was an erstwhile prostitute, who had traveled from Poland to Amsterdam and then to Italy, where she worked as a servant for various Jewish families and institutions. Exactly how she and Shabbetai Ẓevi were brought together is unknown. However, the couple was married in Cairo in March, 1664. At least one source reports that Shabbetai married her because of her ill repute, so as to fulfill the word of the prophet Hosea, "take yourself a wife of whoredom" (1:2). Sarah, who subsequently gave birth to a son and a daughter, converted to Islam shortly after her husband in 1666. In 1671, Shabbetai divorced Sarah, even though she was pregnant, and arranged a marriage with another woman. He then changed his mind and took Sarah back. She died in 1674.

An interesting facet of Shabbetai Ẓevi's messianic claims was his promise to ameliorate the secondary status of women in Judaism. He allowed women in synagogues he visited in Constantinople, Smyrna, and Salonika to be called up to the Torah. According to G. Scholem, Shabbetai is reported to have promised in 1665 that he would lift the "curse of Eve" from women, and added, "Blessed are you, for I have come to make you free and happy like your husbands, for I have come to take away Adam's sin." Scholem has suggested that Shabbetai may have been attracted by "the audacity of Sarah, the reputed harlot, because he cherished the dream of the reparation of Adam's sin and of the consequent restoration of woman to her original freedom" (p. 405). Scholem goes on to say the idea that the messiah would repair Adam's sin was current in Lurianic mystical writings but that Shabbetai seems to have been the first to make the connection in terms of the emancipation of women.

Eva *Frank (1754–1816), daughter of the charismatic Shabbatean leader Jacob *Frank (1726–1791) played a major role in the messianic and antinomian Frankist movement. Originally named Rachel, she is referred to in Frankist writings as the Lady, the Virgin, or *Matronita*, the Aramaic name of the mystical female entity *Shekhinah*. She became known as Eva following the conversion of her family to Christianity in 1760. Jacob Frank saw himself as the eternal messiah and told his followers that Eva-Rachel should be recognized as the mystical royal figure of the *Shekhinah* who would lead them as a messianic redeemer in his temporary absence. Ultimately, Frank claimed, he would be reborn and united with his daughter in "the unity of Messiah and *Shekhinah*." After Jacob Frank's death in 1791, Eva led the Frankist community in its hopes of imminent messianic redemption. Even after she died, many Frankist families continued to keep her portrait and honored her as a saintly woman who was falsely reviled.

ḤASIDISM. The development of the pietistic/mystical movement Ḥasidism in 18th-century Poland had a profound and lasting impact on East European Jewry. Ḥasidism brought no improvements for women's status, however, and in some ways intensified negative views of women already present in Jewish mysticism and traditional rabbinic Judaism. Ḥasidic tradition preserves descriptions of daughters, mothers and sisters of rabbinic leaders who are said to have themselves led ḥasidic communities and to have adopted rigorous standards of personal piety. Among them are Sarah Frankel *Sternberg (1838–1937), daughter of ḥasidic Rabbi Joshua Heschel Teomim-Frankel and wife of the *ẓaddik* Ḥayyim Samuel Sternberg of Chenciny, a disciple of the famed Seer of Lublin. After her husband's death, she is said to have functioned successfully as a *rebbe* in Chenciny and was highly regarded for her piety and asceticism. Her daughter, Hannah Brakhah, the wife of R. *Elimelekh of Grodzinsk, was an active participant in the life of her husband's court. A. Rapoport-Albert has pointed out that there is little written documentation about these women and that their authority was based on their connection to revered male leaders.

The one apparent example of a woman who crossed gender boundaries to achieve religious leadership in a ḥasidic sect with some success was the well-educated, pious, and wealthy Hannah Rochel Werbermacher (1815–1888?), known as the Holy Maid of *Ludomir. Werbermarcher, who acquired a reputation for saintliness and miracle-working, attracted both men and women to her "court," to whom she would lecture from behind a closed door. Reaction from the male ḥasidic leaders of her region was uniformly negative, and pressure was successfully applied on Hannah to resume her rightful female role in marriage. Although her marriages were unsuccessful, they had the intended result of ending her career as a religious leader, at least in Poland. Around 1860, Werbermacher moved to Jerusalem where she re-established herself as a holy woman. Here, too, she attracted a following of ḥasidic women and men, as well as Sephardi and possibly some Muslim Arab women, and led gatherings at the Western Wall, the Tomb of Rachel, and her own study house.

Ḥasidism, in its emphasis on mystical transcendence, and on male attendance on the rabbinic leader, the *zaddik* or *rebbe*, to the exclusion of the family unit, contributed significantly to the breakdown of the Jewish social life in 19th–century Eastern Europe. Similar tensions between family responsibility and devotion to Torah were also present among the non-ḥasidic learned elite of this milieu, where wives tended to assume the responsibility for supporting their families while husbands were studying away from home. D. Biale has noted that the sexual ascetism of the homosocial ḥasidic courts and rabbinic yeshivot of the 18th and 19th centuries offered young men a welcome withdrawal from family tensions and the threats of modernity. However, the negative attitudes toward human sexuality they found in these environments were often openly misogynistic, incorporating many demonic images of women from rabbinic, kabbalistic, and Jewish folklore traditions.

[Judith R. Baskin (2nd ed.)]

Modern Central and Western Europe: 1780 to 1939

The *Haskalah, the Jewish Enlightenment movement which began in late 18th century Germany, brought enormous changes to Jewish religious, political, and social life in Central and Western Europe. Receptive to modernity and European culture, the Haskalah insisted that Jewish acculturation to the mainstream mores and customs of the public sphere was not incompatible with adherence to Jewish tradition and rituals in the private domain of home and synagogue. While the goals of Jewish political emancipation and achievement of full civil rights, with their accompanying economic benefits, were central to this movement, some of its supporters also championed religious change within the Jewish community. Most modern forms of Jewish religious practice, *Reform Judaism, *Conservative Judaism, and Modern *Orthodoxy, were shaped in this milieu. Moses *Mendelssohn, the founder of the Haskalah in Central Europe, and others of his circle, also advocated social change in gender relations, opposing arranged marriages and advocating love matches.

Adoption of the language and values of the non-Jewish world tended to occur first among the wealthiest Jews who had frequent economic dealings with non-Jews. D. Hertz and B. Hahn are among those who have chronicled the lives of women from Berlin's wealthy Jewish elite in the last decades of the 18th century. In a Jewish society in which girls received only minimal religious education, instruction in music and modern languages, together with exposure to a new world of secular novels, poetry, and plays, distanced young women from brothers and husbands whose lives were focused on traditional Jewish learning and commerce and finance. It is not surprising that many of these wealthy and accomplished women, such as Henriette *Herz, Dorothea *Mendelssohn, Rahel Levin *Varnhagen, and Fanny von *Arnstein (a Berlin native who moved to Vienna), found success in a *salon society where gentiles and Jews mixed socially. For some of these women, divorces from Jewish husbands were followed by conversions to Christianity and marriage to gentile suitors, often from the impecunious nobility. The absolute number of women who followed this course was small and their motives for doing so were complex. However, for these Jewish women, abandoning Judaism meant integration into the dominant upper-class culture and society. In making the choices they did these women experienced "at an early date and in a gender-specific way the basic conflict between group loyalty and individual emancipation that would torment so many European Jews in the two centuries to follow" (Hertz, 1991, p. 198).

The experiences of Jewish women of the salon world were not typical for most Western and Central European Jewish women. Scholars like M.A. Kaplan and P.E. Hyman have shown that by the mid-19th century processes of acculturation and assimilation, followed in some cases by dissolution of minority ties through conversion and/or intermarriage, were generally quite different for women and men. Gender tended to limit the assimilation of Jewish women, rendering their progress to integration halting and incomplete in comparison to Jewish men. Confined to the domestic scene, restricted in their educational opportunities, and prevented from participating in the public realms of economic and civic life, Jewish women had far fewer contacts with the non-Jewish world. Rather, women were encouraged to cultivate a home-based Judaism in which spirituality was expressed in domestic activities. As Kaplan has demonstrated through memoirs, diaries, personal correspondence, and cookbooks, at a time when male synagogue attendance and ritual performance was declining, it was most often women who transmitted Jewish values to their families through a form of domestic religion which united traditional Jewish cooking and some form of home observance of the Sabbath and other holidays. Perhaps because they had been excluded from so many public rituals to begin with, women's Judaism was essentially domestic, and in secularized homes they were often the last to preserve elements of Jewish tradition. Sigmund Freud, for example, persuaded his wife to drop all religious practices, but throughout their marriage Martha Freud and her husband argued over her wish to light candles on the Sabbath.

Rachel *Morpurgo (1790–1871), the Italian Hebrew poet, is an exceptional example of the impact of the Haskalah on a Jewish woman. Born in Trieste, she was a relative and close friend of Samuel David *Luzzatto (1800–1865), a major figure in modern Jewish thought and Hebrew literature, with whom she studied Hebrew religious texts and poetry for many years. Morpurgo's extensive education was acquired at home, alongside her brother and cousin, from private tutors and family members. Like Italian Jewish women of previous generations Morpurgo worked in the family business, as a turner on a lathe, a skill she learned from her uncle and father. After her marriage to Jacob Morpurgo in 1819, she was no longer able to give much time to study and writing since her husband disapproved of these activities and insisted that she devote herself to domestic duties. Prior to her marriage Morpurgo had maintained an extensive Hebrew poetic correspondence with Luzzatto; he published her writings 30 years later in *Kokhevei Yiẓḥak* (1847) to enormous acclaim. Morpurgo's poems and letters were collected and were published as an anthology entitled *Ugav Raḥel* (ed. V. Castiglioni [1890], rep. 1943).

In 19th century England, a significant number of Jewish women worked in the public domain to hasten Jewish enlightenment and emancipation and to further religious reform. These include active advocates of liberal Judaism like Lily *Montagu, and writers of both fiction and non-fiction with Jewish themes directed to Jewish and gentile audiences such as Grace *Aguilar (d. 1847), and the sisters, Marion *Moss (1821-1907) and Celia *Moss (1819–1873). In her extremely popular book, *The Women of Israel*, Aguilar defended the exalted position of women in Judaism, highlighting what she described as women's traditional role in hastening redemption as "teachers of children" and through other domestic activities. M. Galchinsky has noted that despite their uplifting messages, Jewish women's success in the world of literature was profoundly threatening to the men of their milieu; while male Jewish reformers were compelled to support at least a degree of female emancipation in principle, they were determined to limit, trivialize, and undermine women's writing and influence in the public sphere.

Nineteenth century domestic Judaism throughout Central and Western Europe not only reflected traditional Judaism's preferred positioning of women in the private realm of husband and family, but was also a form of Jewish conformity to the Christian bourgeois model of female domesticity which put religion in the female sphere. Jewish literature and the Jewish press of the late nineteenth century, both in Europe and the United States, where the Jewish community prior to 1881 was overwhelmingly of Central European origin, described the Jewish woman as the "guardian angel of the house," "mother in Israel," and "priestess of the Jewish ideal," and assigned her primary responsibility for the Jewish identity and education of her children. This was a significant indication of acculturation in an ethnic group in which men had historically fulfilled most religious obligations, including the Jewish education of their sons. Moreover, this shifting of responsibility for inculcating Jewish identity and practices to women led rapidly from praise to denigration, as commentators began to blame mothers for their children's assimilation. Such criticisms not only allowed men to ignore the implications of their own assimilationist behavior, but also revealed central tensions in the project of acculturation itself, including a communal inability to prevent individual defections to the larger society.

Reform Judaism, which sought to offer 19th century Western and Central European Jews a modernized form of Jewish belief and practice emphasizing personal faith and ethical behavior rather than ritual observance, proclaimed that women were entitled to the same religious rights and subject to the same religious duties as men in both home and synagogue. Emphasis on religious education for girls and boys, including the introduction of a confirmation ceremony for young people of both sexes, and an accessible worship service in the vernacular, also made the new movement attractive to many women. Pressure from young women may have prompted the Reform rabbinate to adopt the innovation of double ring wedding ceremonies in which not only men but women made a statement of marital commitment. In fact, however, European Reform Judaism made few substantive changes in women's actual synagogue status, offering no extension to women of ritual participation in worship and maintaining separate synagogue seating for men and women well into the 20th century (see *Synagogue: Women and the Synagogue).

Emulation of Christian models of female philanthropy and religious activism played a significant part in middle-class Jewish women's establishment of service and social welfare organizations in the 19th and early 20th century centuries in Germany and England. Such organizations as the *Juedischer Frauenbund in Germany (founded in 1904 by Bertha *Pappenheim), the Union of Jewish Women in Great Britain (founded in 1902), and the *National Council of Jewish Women in the United States (founded in 1893), cooperated in the international campaign against coercion of poor women into prostitution. They also argued for greater recognition of women within their respective Jewish communities as "sustainers of Jewish communal life and guardians against defection from Judaism." Women's activism in Europe and Great Britain positively affected the Jewish community in such areas as social welfare services, feminist trade unionism, support for women's suffrage, and agitation for religious change. Women who worked for these goals also blurred the boundaries between traditional male and female spheres as they acquired administrative expertise and assumed authoritative and responsible public roles.

While most Jewish women in Central Europe in the first decades of the 20th century conformed to the bourgeois models of early generations and focused their energies on home responsibilities and volunteer organizations, some achieved less conventional lives. Jewish women made up a disproportionately large percentage of the early generations of women who sought university education and professional training in Germany and Austria in the early 20th century. Many of these women made important contributions as academics, educators, social scientists, scientists, and physicians and helped pave the way for far larger numbers of middle-class professional women in the late 20th century. H.P. Freidenreich, has written that in an era when married women had a difficult time advancing their professional lives, many university women chose to devote themselves to their careers, tending not to marry or to marry later in life. While most university-educated non-Jewish women tended to become teachers, Jewish women followed the patterns established earlier by Jewish men, and became physicians, scientists, and social scientists, as well as academics and lawyers. A number applied their professional skills to improving the lives of women and children. Many female Jewish physicians specialized in gynecology or pediatrics and advocated for the widespread availability of contraception and legalized abortion; female psychiatrists and psychoanalysts often focused on childhood disorders and trauma. Unlike most of their Christian counterparts, Jewish university women tended to be on the political left. Mostly from highly acculturated middle class Jewish homes, few of these women were connected with the organized Jewish community prior to 1933.

Most of the discrimination these women faced in the early inter-war period was due to their gender, since educated women, in Europe and elsewhere, were often unpaid and underemployed. Even those who achieved academic positions rarely achieved tenure or the recognition they deserved, whether in Germany or Austria, or elsewhere after emigration. Antisemitism also played a role in limiting job opportunities before 1933. With the advent of the Nazi era, professional women, as all Jews, were forced to flee Europe in order to survive. Those who were able to leave Germany and Austria, often at a relatively advanced age and under adverse circumstances, had mixed success in reconstructing their lives and careers.

M.A. Kaplan has chronicled the everyday tyranny German Jews experienced under the Nazi regime from the perspectives of gender, delineating the ways in which women were more sensitive to the experience of discrimination, how women were usually more anxious to leave and risk uncertainty abroad, how women often were compelled to assume "male" roles within and outside the family, and how being female shaped an individual's destiny. After 1933, drastic changes for Jews in the public domain transformed occupational patterns in Jewish families. As Jewish businessmen and professionals were forced from their occupations, many married women had to enter the job market for the first time, often after training in service occupations. Although economic prospects were poor for all, women showed more adaptability than men. And as the family became a refuge from Nazi-imposed social, economic, and psychological hardships, women felt obligated to run their households smoothly even while functioning as the family's wage earner and advocate in the outside world.

Kaplan has also shown that parental desires to keep daughters at home, and preferential treatment of boys by Jewish welfare organizations providing career training, meant that girls were usually only 25 to 30 percent of participants in these vocational programs, often to their detriment. Still, as the situation of Germany's Jews worsened, community efforts to save all young people grew. By 1939, 82 percent of children 15 and under and 83 percent of young people between 16 and 24 had managed to escape Germany.

Following the pogrom of November 1938, more than 20,000 Jewish men were arrested while women witnessed the vandalizing of their homes. From this point on women rescued men, pulled together immigration papers, and where possible extricated their families from increasingly certain disaster. However, gender also played a role in emigration; by 1939, women, mostly elderly, were 57.5 percent of Germany's Jewish population, and they died disproportionately in Hitler's camps, a trend that has been documented for all European Jewish women.

Kaplan has also examined the situation of Jews who had intermarried, noting that almost all German Jews who survived Nazism without emigrating were partners in mixed marriages. While the Nazis condemned such unions and encouraged their dissolution coercively, gender played a crucial role, since Nazi sexism privileged couples with "Aryan" men over those with Jewish men. Nevertheless, "Aryan" men were more likely than "Aryan" women to divorce or abandon a Jewish spouse, although many mixed unions endured almost unbearable pressures.

[Judith R. Baskin (2nd ed.)]

Eastern Europe in the 19th and 20th Centuries

Jewish women in Eastern Europe were marginalized by both ethnicity and gender. In some respects, their individual and collective stories were cut from the same cloth as the larger Jewish historical narrative; at the same time, gender also had a distinct impact in the arenas of religion, family and work, education, culture, and political life.

Female spirituality was deeply embedded in Ashkenazi Judaism. While women possessed a rudimentary understanding of Jewish theology, commandments, and values, they were excluded from participation in public worship and study. As a result, "female variants" of elite male culture emerged with new styles of prayers and learning. The recitation of **tkhines* or supplicatory prayers formed an integral part of women's piety. Unlike formal liturgy, these Yiddish prayers, which addressed everyday concerns and the three female commandments (**ḥallah*, **niddah*, and *hadlakah* or lighting *candles), were voluntary, personal, and could be recited at any time. In lieu of Hebrew and Aramaic texts, women (and "men who are like women" in their lack of Hebrew knowledge) read popular religious literature in the vernacular such as the *Tsenerene* ("Go Forth and See"), a collection of homilies on the weekly Torah portion. To facilitate greater participation of women in their section of the synagogue, architects in Poland began to include women's annexes (*wibershule*) starting in the 16th century, which later became integral parts of the buildings as "women's sections" (*ezrat nashim*). Moreover, the sacralization of popular customs such as *kneytlakh legn* (candlemaking from wicks used to measure graves) lent greater value to female religious rituals.

Gender ideals also shaped Jewish women's status and roles in the family and in the social world of the *shtetl (see *Shtetl: Women and the Shtetl), the small towns where most East European Jews lived. A patriarchal division of labor allocated domestic chores and child rearing to women. However, in contrast to the cult of middle class domesticity in the West, economic necessity and cultural ideals forced the majority of East European women to contribute to the family economy. As a rule, most couples labored together to earn a livelihood by running a family business or earning separate wages. Sometimes, however, the onus of breadwinning fell disproportionately on the shoulders of Torah scholar's wives so that the husbands could study. I. Etkes suggests that elite society of religious learning was successful in constructing women's tacit acceptance of these roles as a privilege that bestowed cultural prestige. While they formed a small minority, these wives in turn served as a "legitimating symbol" to be emulated by ordinary women. Ḥasidic wives whose husbands spent all their time in the company of fellow Ḥasidim or the *rebbe* assumed a similar burden. Yekhezkel *Kotik (1847–1921) was particularly critical of the extreme poverty in which many of these families lived. With the onset of industrialization in the late nineteenth century, many Jews left the shtetl for the large cities of the Pale of Settlement. Women began to work in workshops and factories where they dominated the needle and garment trades. By 1921, Jewish women who worked in industry comprised 55.9 percent of Jewish wage earners in Poland.

Despite the modicum of power that Jewish women exercised in the family economy and household, they were vulnerable in matters of family law. In czarist Russia, where Jews retained autonomy over their own marriages and divorces, rabbinic authorities adjudicated all cases based on *halakhah*; in Galicia, Jews rejected civil marriage, which had been introduced by the Hapsburg state in 1783, and continued to follow religious procedures. Jewish women became increasingly powerless in divorce suits and not simply because of their husband's unilateral prerogative to dissolve marriages. More important was the breakdown of rabbinic control over these broad rights, which had served to protect women previously. As a result, wives found it difficult to secure a *get* (bill of divorcement) from husbands for wife beating and other reasons or to protest a coerced divorce. In response, some resorted to new strategies by turning to state courts and government institutions to enforce or overthrow a rabbinic decision and to secure their monetary rights. Despite these innovative venues, Jewish women still suffered from specific disabilities under Jewish law, especially as **agunot* ("chained" women who were unable to remarry).

The Jewish Enlightenment movement in Eastern Europe, which began in the last few decades of the nineteenth century, was very different from the Haskalah in the West, lacking both the emphasis on Jewish achievement of political rights and civic equality, and the impetus for religious reform, since neither were likely to be achieved in the conservative Eastern European environment. Nor was the impoverished and predominantly small town Jewish population an appropriate constituency for the middle-class norms and values of the West. Rather, the Haskalah in Eastern Europe was a secularizing process which caused many to discontinue religious observance while fostering a Jewish national/ethnic identity, often linked to socialist and/or Zionist political goals. East European women were frequently in the forefront of this movement of cultural transformation.

Women's political involvement was due, in part, to the fact that Jewish women gained greater exposure to the secular world as a result of a gendered system of education in Eastern Europe. While boys received a formal religious schooling starting at an early age, most girls obtained an informal domestic education. The Orthodox community did not begin to provide vehicles for female religious education until after World War I (see Sarah *Schenirer, founder of the *Beth Jacob school network). At a minimum, a large segment of women gained literacy in Yiddish in order to read devotional literature. Alongside these sacred books, it was not uncommon to find popular tales about knights (*Bove Maaseh*) or the adventures of Sinbad the Sailor (*Centura Ventura*). These reading habits made it easy for women to shift to secular Yiddish popular literature by Isaac Meir *Dik, *Shomer, and others. In middle-class and wealthy families, daughters studied foreign languages, music, and art with private tutors without any censure from the Orthodox establishment. Others attended the newly secular schools for girls throughout the Russian empire. Ita Kalish, who grew up in a ḥasidic family observed that the sons studied at the *shtibl* while the girls learned about the "purity of Polish culture" in foreign schools. While not all women were educated, the "benefit of marginality" granted them access to new, modern ideas and prepared them to serve as agents of acculturation in their homes.

Moreover, girls and women in East European Jewish society, where the strong capable woman shrewdly interacting with the outside world was the dominant cultural ideal, were also secularized by their active participation in public economic life. In many ways late 19th century Eastern European women were far more involved in the process of Jewish assimilation than women in Western Europe or the United States. This is evident in the large numbers of East European Jewish women who sought higher education and professional training in Western Europe, a significantly higher percentage of female conversions to Christianity, and particularly in female involvement in a wide range of political movements, discussed below, which offered women opportunities for activism and leadership unavailable in traditional Jewish society.

The Jewish community of Eastern Europe had many social strata. Jews at the higher economic levels moved beyond shtetl society and had closer contacts with the wider world far earlier than their less prosperous co-religionists. The memoirist Pauline Epstein *Wengeroff (1833–1916), who grew up in a wealthy household in the 1830s and 1840s with a father and brothers-in-law who were extremely receptive to the promises of the Haskalah, was an unusually well-informed and well-read woman for her time and place. She received private tutoring in German and Russian as an adolescent, and she became a great enthusiast of literatures in both these languages. In the early days of her marriage she helped her husband improve his German skills, a necessary accomplishment for success in business. This emphasis on a Jewish culture deeply intertwined with the broader intellectual and artistic interests of the modern world was central to the Wengeroffs' family life and values. C. Balin has studied the literary remains, both published and unpublished, of a number of Russian-speaking daughters of prosperous middle-class urban Jews in the late 19th and 20th centuries. Like Wengeroff's daughters, some of these acculturated young women attended gymnasia, learned European languages, and earned university degrees, following educational, artistic, and professional paths comparable to those of many contemporaneous middle-class Jewish girls in Western Europe.

However, with education and acculturation, many Jews of the higher social echelons lost any sense of allegiance to the Jewish people or heritage. Wengeroff wrote her autobiography, *Memoiren einer Grossmutter: Bilder aus der Kulturgeschichte der Juden Russlands im 19. Jahrhundert* (Berlin, 1913; 19192), towards the end of her life. She presents herself as the casualty of significant social transformations which had undermined the female role for which she had been prepared and called into question many of the values with which she was raised. Nor did she see her tragedy as affecting only herself. As she wrote of the baptisms of her children: "Gradually this sorrow lost the significance of a personal tragedy and turned more and more into a national tragedy. I grieved not just as a mother, but as a Jew, for the entire Jewish people, which was losing so many of its strong members" (p. 226).

Wengeroff, in her own way, was part of a larger cohort of Jewish women in Eastern Europe at the end of the 19th and in the early decades of the 20th century who began to explore the greatly enlarged opportunities for self-expression offered by modern secular culture by writing poetry and prose, in languages that included Yiddish, Hebrew, Polish, Russian, and German. While male supporters of the Haskalah in Eastern Europe lauded the process of modernization, they expressed deep ambivalence about the notion of female equality and the intrusion of women into their cultural domain. Nonetheless, *maskilot* like Miriam *Markel-Mosessohn, Devorah Ephrati, Hannah Bluma Sultz, Sarah Shapira, Sarah-Feiga Foner Meinkin, and others became an integral part of the Haskalah movement as producers of culture. The "anxiety of authorship" led some to write under pseudonyms while others adopted palimpsestic writing to hide the true meanings in hidden layers – a strategy used by *maskilim* in general. However, in the case of the *maskilot*, their hidden layers concealed an authentic feminine voice as well as the opinions of an enlightened individual. Up through the interwar years, Jewish women continued to contribute to the Russian and Polish language press and published their own volumes of literature, poetry, or history. However, estrangement from Jewish life frequently accompanied self-realization: to become a Jewish woman writer was to become a cultural anomaly. Often the price of such achievement was equivocal exile from a male culture profoundly uncomfortable with female intellectual assertiveness.

Disillusionment with the old order and aspirations to create a more egalitarian society drew Jewish women into the public political arena. Inspired by the works of Alexander Herzen, Nikolai Chernyshevskii, and other influential writers, women joined the Russian revolutionary movements in disproportionate numbers starting in the 1870s. From the onset, personal and political liberation were intricately connected as Jewish women rebelled against patriarchal oppression and legal disabilities. The most famous revolutionary, Gesia Gelfman, ran away from her prosperous Orthodox home on the eve of her wedding to join the People's Will and participate in the assassination of Alexander II.

However, by the end of the 19th century, the composition and nature of Jewish involvement with socialism (see *Socialism: Women and Socialism) was transformed by the growth of a massive Jewish artisanal working-class in the cities of Eastern Europe. As Jewish women flocked into light industry, primarily the needle trades, but also tanning, bristle making, and cigar and cigarette production, many began to organize as workers and as Jews to protest their exploitative working conditions. Jewish women joined the socialist-oriented *Bund when it formed in Vilna in 1897, comprising one-third of its membership, and occupied many of its middle rank leadership roles, much to the chagrin of traditional families. In the early 1920s, the Bund established a separate women's division, the Yidishe Arbeter-Froy Organizatsie (YAF) and two sister youth groups (Zukunft and Sotsialistisher Kinder Farband) – a common practice among leftists groups in Poland. The women's auxiliary focused on the critical needs of working women, especially the need for child care. While the Bund articulated egalitarian ideals, female activists complained that gender relations and roles had changed little in the family. Male activists expected their wives to perform all their traditional domestic roles even at the expense of missing meetings and activities. As in most revolutionary parties, broader political goals took precedence over the woman's question. Jewish feminist activists persisted and founded the Jewish Women's Association in 1920.

Other women, like Puah Rakovsky, chose to devote their political energies to *Zionism. Two newspapers, *Di froy* (The Woman) and *Froyen-shtim* (Women's Voice) appeared in the mid-1920s with the goal of combining Zionist and feminist aspirations. Both sought to encourage women in their dual struggle as the female half of an oppressed and persecuted people.

Jewish women's lives changed abruptly with the outbreak of World War II. Studies have shown that gender played a critical role in the different male and female responses to crisis and strategies for survival during the Shoah. Prewar socialization proved critical in the early years. In Poland, Jewish women who had significant familiarity with the Polish language and customs as a result of sex-segregated education comprised the majority of Jews who lived on the Aryan side. A Yad Vashem survey found that women were more successful in their disguise due to greater confidence in their physical appearance (i.e., no circumcision), lack of a Jewish accent, fine Polish mannerisms, and attentiveness to the feelings and reactions of others. Moreover, they were more likely to receive assistance from non-Jewish individuals and organizations. These women participated in resistance and rescue activities as couriers and fighters.

Prewar gender roles also persisted in the ghettos. Women assumed the traditional role of caring for their families; however, basic domestic tasks such as feeding the children now required great ingenuity and courage. All Jews, including former housewives, were forced to work in order to survive. Wage differentials in the ghetto were substantial: women often received two-thirds or three-quarters the pay of male workers; moreover, they had a more difficult time finding scarce jobs due to their lack of skills. Another obvious distinction was women's reproductive capacity, which was the target of infamous Nazi policies. In the ghettos, Germans instituted a policy of compulsory abortion. Women with young children and visibly pregnant women were immediately exterminated in the death and labor camps. Women were also more likely to experience rape and sexual harassment at the hands of foster family members, fellow inmates and guards. Testimonies reveal that German commanders selected the most beautiful girls as personal "housemaids" at their own discretion. Some women had no choice but to enter sexual relationships in order to obtain better rations or conditions. In the ghettos and camps, women devised new strategies to survive emotionally and mentally. In contrast to men, many of whom stopped washing or shaving, the majority of women attempted to take care of their personal hygiene. They also formed surrogate families, especially camp sisters and mothers, to provide mutual aid and sustenance.

At the end of World War II, the majority of East European Jewish women survivors opted to immigrate to Israel or America, leaving behind a rich historical legacy.

[ChaeRan Freeze (2nd ed.)]

North America

FROM THE COLONIAL PERIOD TO 1945. Jewish women in colonial America continued their accustomed domestic roles while simultaneously integrating themselves into the wider culture. Often they did so ingeniously, adjusting, adapting, and reinterpreting American forms to serve their Jewish purposes. The first two Jewish women known by name in North America, Ricke Nunes and Judith Mercado, most likely widowed heads of families, were among the 23 Jews who arrived in New Amsterdam in 1654 from Brazil.

Most colonial Jewish women were respectable matrons; their households, as in the case of Rebecca Machado *Phillips (1746–1831), who bore twenty-one children, could be quite large, but others were much smaller. Certainly, dietary laws were followed in many homes. When, in 1774, Hetty Hays suspected that she had bought meat that was not properly kashered, she was ordered to "do Cassarar [kasher], or properly Clense, all her Spoons, plates and all other utensals, used in her House" (Snyder, 25). The extent of observance of traditional **niddah* regulations in this early community is unclear. The first known communal **mikveh* was built by the Jews of Philadelphia in 1786.

Abigaill *Franks (1696?–1756), whose letters form the largest body of writings by a Jewish woman in North America, honored the Sabbath and holidays and kept kosher. She told her son Naphtali never to eat anything at her brother's home, because she knew his household did not observe the dietary laws. Franks ensured that her daughters as well as her sons learned Hebrew. But, she also displayed an independence of mind typical of other American Jewish women. Yearning for a modernized Judaism, she wrote in 1739, "I Must Own I cant help Condemning the Many Superstions wee are Clog'd with & hartly wish a Calvin or Luther would rise amongst Us[.] I Answer for my Self… I don't think religeon Consist in Idle Cerimonies" (Smith, 17). The costs of the open society and such impulses were high. When Franks's daughter Phila married outside the faith, her spirit was crushed; none of Abigail's two dozen grandchildren seems to have passed on Judaism to the next generation.

On Sabbaths and festivals Jewish women joined their male relatives in worship. The second synagogue built in colonial America, in Newport, Rhode Island in 1763, was constructed with an upper level women's gallery that dispensed with the additional grilles and curtains found in European synagogues. This established a pattern in American synagogue architecture in which woman could see and be seen (see *Synagogue: Women and the Synagogue).

In 1820 the Jewish population in the United States was less than 3,000. Jews lived out their lives among their Christian neighbors and represented Judaism to them, inviting Gentile friends to celebrate with them at their weddings and circumcisions. Early America's Jewish women joined these Christian friends and neighbors to aid others. In 1801, Rebecca Machado Phillips and some 20 other Philadelphia women, Christians and Jews, including Rebecca *Gratz (1781–1869), founded the Female Association for the Relief of Women and Children in Reduced Circumstances. Jewish women also supported the needs of their own community; in 1782, when Philadelphia's Jews built a new synagogue, Rebecca Phillips and Grace Nathan raised funds to purchase its ritual objects.

In the 19th century Rebecca Gratz was the epitome of Jewish American female volunteerism. Also a founder of Philadelphia's Orphan Asylum, she is best remembered for her endeavors on behalf of the Jewish people. Gratz founded the Female Hebrew Benevolent Society in 1819 to aid the Jewish poor and protect them from Christian missionizing. In 1838, when she established the first Hebrew Sunday School in America, she launched the prototype of a new educational setting for America's Jewish children and opened a new avenue for Jewish women's communal activism as teachers.

Between 1820 and 1880, America's Jewish population grew to 250,000, mainly due to immigration from German-speaking lands. In 1846, eleven women from New York's Temple Emanu-El established the Unabhängiger Orden Treuer Schwestern. The only independent female fraternal order then in America, it eventually sparked a web of lodges offering newly American Jewish women mutual aid in times of emergency and sickness and guaranteeing members a decent burial.

Another important public avenue for Jewish women's piety was literature. Penina *Moïse (1797–1880) of Charleston, South Carolina, published poems in the leading papers and periodicals of her day. She was superintendent of Beth Elohim Congregation's Sunday school and was the author of the first American Jewish hymnal; many of her hymns were used in the Reform movement well into the 20th century. Periodicals directed at American Jewish women, such as *Die Deborah*, published in German between 1855 and 1902, and **American Jewess*, the first English-language periodical for American Jewish women, edited by Rosa *Sonneschein in 1895–99, informed and entertained female readers and also provided vehicles for Jewish women's writing.

The best known Jewish female writer was poet Emma *Lazarus (1849–1887). In the early 1880s, deeply disturbed by the Russian pogroms whose refugees she met through her work with the Hebrew Emigrant Aid Society, she called for founding a Jewish state in Palestine ("The Jewish Problem," 1883). Her 1883 magnum opus, "The New Colossus," inscribed on the pedestal of the Statue of Liberty, portrays America as the "Mother of Exiles" welcoming "the huddled masses yearning to breathe free."

Between 1881 and 1924, some two million East European Jews streamed to America. Propelled by grinding poverty, violent pogroms, and the dislocations of revolutionary turmoil and war, theirs was overwhelmingly a migration of families. When the male head of the household journeyed ahead, as Israel Antin, father of author Mary *Antin, did in 1891, he spent the next years scrimping and saving to buy passage for his wife and children. This migration utterly transformed American Jewry. By 1930 the 4.4 million American Jews, 3.6 percent of the U.S. population, comprised nearly a third of world Jewry.

Domestic concerns were central to the East European Jewish immigrant women and their daughters who lived in the crowded tenements of immigrant enclaves such as New York's Lower East Side, Boston's North End, and Chicago's West Side. Many strove to adhere to Judaism despite significant economic need. When the price of kosher meat soared from 12 to 18 cents a pound in New York in 1902, immigrant mothers broke into butcher shops, set meat afire, and shared recipes for meatless meals to compel their neighbors to honor their kosher meat boycott.

Established and prosperous American Jewish women, generally of Central European origin, were anxious to help their struggling and impoverished co-religionists. The *National Council of Jewish Women, founded in 1893 by Hannah Greenebaum *Solomon (1858–1942), protected Jewish immigrant girls traveling without guardians from falling into *prostitution. They and other middle-class American Jewish women established vocational training and classes for immigrants to learn American customs. East European Jewish immigrant women also established their own social welfare agencies. Poor immigrant women who had fallen upon hard times, like the newly widowed, and entrepreneurial women, who wanted to buy cloth to sew or coal to heat the bathhouse, could borrow money from immigrant women's credit networks operated by those just slightly better off than they.

Jewish American women had frequently participated in the economic lives of their family. In the colonial era, married Jewish women managed family businesses while their husbands traveled and widows kept kosher boardinghouses. In the 19th century, many Jewish women "helped out" in family businesses, selling clothing and canned goods, saddles and blankets from behind the counters of the dry goods stores their husbands owned in the small towns dotting the landscape of the South and the West. But 19th-century middle-class propriety in America, as in Western and Central Europe, expected women to busy themselves with their homes and families while leaving economic concerns to their men. Following these bourgeois ideals, many Jewish women, prior to 1880, eschewed the public world of business for the private sphere of their homes.

East European Jewish immigrants, however, came from a world which desperately needed and valued women's contributions to the family economy. In Russia young Jewish women had worked primarily in the needle trades. Their mothers sold goods in the marketplace. Immigrant Jewish women came to America expecting to work, and they, especially the unmarried, found employment in the burgeoning ready-made clothing industry. Married Jewish women contributed to the family economy in other ways, taking in piecework to sew at home or opening their tenement apartments to boarders. They also sold goods from pushcarts on the streets or worked in the family's five-and-dime or soda fountain. Later in the 1920s and 1930s, their daughters, aspiring to white-collar work, became salesclerks and bookkeepers. Those who were able to take advantage of New York's tuition-free Hunter College would go on to teach in the city's ever-expanding public schools.

But it was Jewish women's employment in the garment industry, especially in the dress and waist trade, that shaped their politics. Some immigrant working girls had already participated in political movements, unions, and workers' actions in Europe. Low wages, poor working conditions, and frequent layoffs propelled many others into the *International Ladies' Garment Workers Union (see *Socialism: Women and Socialism). In the 1909 "Uprising of the 20,000" the shirtwaist makers struck, seeking a fifty-two-hour workweek and paid overtime. This labor action helped launch "The Great Revolt," which spread to Philadelphia, Chicago, Cleveland, and Kalamazoo and emboldened the American labor movement. By 1919, half of all garment workers were members of a union. Fannia M. *Cohn,* Rose *Schneiderman,* Pauline *Newman, and Clara Lemlich *Shavelson,* all East European-born, experienced the shirtwaist strike as the formative event of their activist youth, as did Theresa *Malkiel, who later became an important Socialist Party activist and immortalized her experiences in the novel, *Diary of a Shirtwaist Striker* (1910). Many female Jewish trade unionists such as Bessie Abramowitz *Hillman, continued their socialist-inspired activism through progressive and reform politics in the New Deal. Labor unrest also provides a context for the neighborhood politics of kosher meat boycotts and the rent strikes Jewish women would stage into the 1930s. Not surprisingly, these same immigrant women actively campaigned for the New York State suffrage bill in 1917.

As immigrant Jewish women and their American-born daughters ascended to the middle-class, they acculturated to middle-class norms that presented women as wives and mothers who were largely uninvolved in economic endeavors and political crusades. American Jewish women with time for leisure pursuits adopted the Chinese game of mah jongg; vacationed with their children in Jewish bungalow colonies in the Catskills, while their husbands spent the week at work in the city; and became consumers of culture, of the theater, movies, and literature. But, most importantly, middle-class leisure allowed America's Jewish women to invent new spaces for themselves in American Judaism that became essential to sustaining Jewish life in America (see *Synagogue: Women and the Synagogue; *Philanthropy: Women and Philanthropy).

Synagogue sisterhoods encouraged women to be exemplary Jewish wives and mothers, to extend the boundaries of their home to the synagogue, equipping its kitchens, and catering its lunches. By 1923, women affiliated with each of the denominational synagogue movements of American Judaism, Reform, Conservative, and Orthodox, had created national organizations of synagogue sisterhoods (see *National Federation of Temple Sisterhoods, *Women's League for Conservative Judaism; Carrie Obendorfer *Simon; Mathilde Roth *Schechter). Other American Jewish women found places in the ladies' branches of *landsmannschaften or the socialist brotherhood of the Yiddish-speaking *Arbeter Ring*, or *Workmen's Circle.

Zionism, the movement for a Jewish homeland in Israel, also commanded American Jewish women's energies, enthusiasms, and commitments. In 1912, Henrietta *Szold, one of the most remarkable Jews of her era, transformed a small Zionist study circle into *Hadassah, the Women's Zionist Organization of America, which would grow into the largest women's organization in America. Through it and other women's Zionist groups, including *AMIT (Mizrachi Women's Organization of America), founded in 1925 by Bessie Goldstein *Gotsfeld; *ORT (Organization for Rehabilitation through Training); and *Pioneer Women, American Jewish women would help support human needs in the State of Israel into the 21st century.

Jewish women in America continued these commitments at home and abroad, even as the Great Depression strained their household economies and propelled some back into the workforce. In the 1930s, America's Jewish women also struggled against the growing menace of Nazi persecution. In the 1930s, the women of the American Jewish Congress picketed Woolworth's to boycott the sale of German goods and battled antisemitism at home. The shelters they established in the 1930s to house refugees fleeing Nazism would soon house allied soldiers as America entered World War II.

Not all Jewish women were concentrated in the Eastern part of the United States. Nevertheless, even those in the Midwest and West, like Rachel *Calof (1876–1952), who was a homesteader in North Dakota, faced the same challenges: how to raise and sustain a Jewish family in the midst of America. They found similar answers in the synagogue sisterhoods they joined in Omaha, Nebraska, and the Hadassah chapters they founded in Detroit, Michigan. Frances Wisebart *Jacobs (1843–1892), known as Denver's "Mother of Charities," helped organize and led the Hebrew Ladies' Benevolent Society, founded the nonsectarian Denver Ladies' Relief Society, and served as the impetus behind the founding of National Jewish Hospital for Consumptives. Florence Prag *Kahn (1866–1948) of San Francisco, the first Jewish congresswoman, was elected in 1924 to the United States House of Representatives for the first of six two-year terms. And Ray *Frank (1861–1948), a California native who spent some years in the Pacific Northwest, was the first Jewish woman to preach and lead religious services from a North American pulpit.

1945–2005. In the 60 years since the end of World War II, America's Jewish women remained devoted to their homes and families, synagogues and Jewish organizations, although they lived out these commitments in new settings These included the emerging Jewish suburbs and cities with growing Jewish populations, like Miami and Los Angeles. Making these neighborhoods their own, women shopped at the Jewish bakeries and kosher butchers that cropped up. They helped start new synagogues and supported educational and social programs for their children from pre-school through the high school years. They imported Ḥanukkah lamps and candlesticks from Israel and sold them in gift shops run by the sisterhoods in their new temples. With antisemitism waning in American life, these women, increasingly the daughters and the granddaughters of the East European Jewish immigrants, also discovered opportunities to acculturate more fully into the American scene. Hence, for many, Jewish commitments became but a single strand in the design of their lives, perhaps more intensive when their children were young, and less so earlier and later.

Ḥasidic communities took shape in North America in the interwar period and grew substantially after World War II. Ḥasidic women continue to stand out from the rest of America's Jewish women with distinctively modest dress and head coverings (see *Ḥasidim: Women in Ḥasidism). Ḥasidic daughters mostly eschew higher education, marry young, usually meeting their husbands through professional matchmakers, and have large families. While many in the ḥasidic world were born into it, some Jewish women have entered this world from the outside.

A high level of education is characteristic of most American Jewish women: 1990 figures indicated that over 85 percent of Jewish women aged 30–39 had gone to college and 30 percent had gone on to graduate school. Similarly, three-quarters of Jewish women aged 25–44 and two-thirds of those aged 45–64 were part of the labor force. Moreover, an increasing number of Jewish women over the decades have entered and achieved in the professions, the entertainment industry, and the arts. American Jewish women have a long history, as well, of success as business entrepreneurs in a number of industries, including cosmetics, dolls and children's toys, fashion, and the food and hotel industries (see Beatrice *Alexander; Jennie *Grossinger; Ruth Mosko *Handler; Estee *Lauder; Judith *Leiber; Mary Ann Cohen *Magnin; Regina *Margareten; Mollie *Parnis; and Ida Cohen *Rosenthal). The ground-breaking two-volume reference work, *Jewish Women in America: An Historical Encyclopedia*, ed. Paula E. Hyman and Deborah Dash Moore (1997), provides biographies of the hundreds of Jewish women who have made significant contributions in numerous areas of endeavor to American and American Jewish life from the colonial period to the present.

American Jewish women, including Betty *Friedan, Gloria *Steinem, and Letty Cottin *Pogrebin, have been in the forefront of the second wave of American feminism that began in the late 1960s (see *Feminism). At the same time, individual Jewish women have carved out personal places in American judicial and political life. Among them are Congresswomen Bella *Abzug, N.Y. Supreme Court judges Birdie *Amsterdam and Judith *Kaye; Supreme Court Justice Ruth Bader *Ginsberg; and United States Senators Barbara *Boxer and Dianne *Feinstein, both from California.

Feminism has also led to major changes in women's status and roles in American Judaism, including the equality of women in synagogue worship outside of Orthodox Judaism (see *Synagogue: Women and the Synagogue; *Liturgy), a plethora of new opportunities for Jewish learning for girls and women across the denominations, and the flourishing of Jewish feminist scholarship and theology (see *Feminism; *Theology: Feminist Theology). The public honoring of young women's coming of age in the synagogue, the *bat mitzvah, had become widespread by the late 1960s.

Since the 1970s American Jewish women have also been ordained as rabbis and cantors (see **Ḥazzan*; **Semikhah*: Ordination of Women; *Rabbi, Rabbinate; *Synagogue); the first American female rabbi, Sally *Priesand, was ordained in 1972. Occupying a historic place in the annals of Judaism, female rabbis have sought to open worship and practice to women's particular concerns. Their astonishing creativity, part of the emergence of feminist Judaism, has produced new prayers and ceremonies for conception, pregnancy, and childbirth; for those grieving infertility, suffering stillbirth, and turning to adoption; for the onset of menses and the completion of menopause; and for healing after rape, for remaining single, and for acknowledging marital separation (see *Ablution; *Birth; *Marriage; **Mikveh*; **Niddah*; *Feminism; *Theology: Feminist Theology; *Liturgy). Furthermore, feminism has also encouraged the inclusion within the Jewish community of many women formerly marginalized, including single women, divorced women, and lesbians (see *Feminism; *Lesbians; *Synagogue: Women and the Synagogue).

Feminism has brought alterations to all sectors of Jewish communal life. Certainly many women have given up the hours they once devoted to volunteer activities for fulltime employment, Many women who continue to volunteer now divert their energies to causes beyond the Jewish community, especially those that support and further gender equality. This has resulted in a decline in numbers and an aging of volunteers in many of the established Jewish women's organizations and synagogue sisterhoods at century's end. Nevertheless, feminism has also allowed for the creation for new avenues for Jewish women's communal and religious activism. These include adult *b'not mitzvah*, feminist *seders*, *Rosh Ḥodesh* groups (see *Bat Mitzvah; *Passover: Women and Passover; *New Moon), and the new spaces for women's projects which have sprung up in Jewish community centers and federations.

Although an increasing number of qualified women professionals are employed in Jewish agencies, the Jewish communal sphere has been slow to recognize and encourage female leadership potential. This resistance to women in positions of authority is indicative of the sexual politics of contemporary Jewish identity in general. While some men will continue to resist what they perceive as female encroachment on male hegemony in the public domain, others may simply abandon Jewish communal institutions and Judaism to women altogether. As S.B. Fishman has cautioned, the stakes for American Jews are significant since, "The American Jewish community not only shares in all the human consequences of feminism but also carries with it the additional responsibility of preserving three thousand years of Jewish history and culture and confronting the problems of a numerically challenged population as well" (Fishman, 247). However, if the past is any indication, forces from outside the Jewish community will be as influential as any from within in determining the roles of women in American Judaism and American Jewish life in the 21st century.

[Pamela S. Nadell (2nd ed.)]

Modern Muslim Worlds

The position of Jewish women and gender relations in the countries of the modern Muslim world, including Turkey, Iran, Iraq, North Africa, Yemen, and the Middle East, were shaped by Jewish law and traditions, the practices of the surrounding Muslim society, and the gradual penetration of Western ideas, customs, and political influence. Due to the wide geography and heterogeneous social and cultural composition and political life of the Muslim world, the amount of external influence on Jewish life varied. It tended to be strongest in urban centers (where most Jews lived) in those countries with closer ties to the West. Internal communal initiatives also brought about new developments and with the passing of time gender relations among Jews in most regions gradually changed from patterns developed in the medieval era.

A division between the realms of women and men was intrinsic to the Muslim world: women were in charge of maintaining the home, while men provided the material means for the family's existence. These well-defined differences in gender roles were also followed in Jewish communities and they had implications for behavior, division of physical space, work, religious activity, education, spirituality, and recreation. An unquestioned gender hierarchy led to different attitudes towards men and women throughout their lives. The birth of a boy was welcomed and celebrated with traditional Jewish rites and particular local ones, while the birth of a girl was rarely celebrated, and at times even deplored. Upon death, too, formal attitudes were different; ceremonies honoring deceased women were rare. Gender preference also had an impact on marriage since lack of male children was considered the woman's fault. If the first wife did not give birth to a son within a certain period of time (usually ten years), a husband could divorce her or marry a second wife, even if daughters had been born.

Gendered space was characteristic of the Muslim world and of the Jewish communities who lived within it. Women spent most of their time within their household whereas men went outside for work and spiritual activities. Most occupational, social, cultural, and religious activities were gender-based; any mixed gender activities occurred mainly within the family circle. Consequently, the internal structure of the home was gender-based, with kitchens and sleeping quarters perceived as the women's space, with men's temporary admittance there at night, while men occupied the public areas of the house. Women in towns rarely stepped outside the house; when they did, they were usually accompanied and veiled. Clothing restrictions were usually less strict for young girls. Urban women were also restricted regarding the places they could visit, usually limited to the homes of other women, the gender segregated ritual bath, the cemetery, and the synagogue. The latter, however, was considered men's space, and most did not have a special women's section until modern times. Sporadic female synagogue attendees observed the service from windows or gates. Markets were also male space and men usually did the daily shopping. Some urban women carried out trades among women, Jewish and even Muslim, but this was unusual, and rarely brought them in contact with men. Gender segregation and clothing restrictions were somewhat lighter in rural areas where most community members were relatives and women's work required departure from the restricted limits of the house.

These social divisions by gender had implications throughout life. Males were part of the women's world only as toddlers; partial separation started when the boys went to school, and culminated once they went out to work. As they grew older, both genders met mainly in close family circles or among a somewhat larger group during special family or seasonal celebrations. Even on these occasions, men and women were often segregated; in many regions men and women ate apart at home and celebrated separately during larger gatherings. This lengthy separation resulted in shyness between married couples; in some locales they hardly spoke with each other, did not use each other's names, and were ignorant about sexual issues, resulting in late pregnancies.

Many female responsibilities remained the same throughout life, but their degree, intensity, and character were also based on the woman's stage within the overall life cycle. Upon their marriage brides usually moved to the extended family household of their husbands where the mother in-law or oldest matriarch headed the female hierarchy. The position of women was also influenced by socioeconomic and geographical settings. Women on the margins – the poor and those living in small isolated villages – had more freedoms.

Regular female household duties included food preparation and serving, cleaning and heating, and care taking, especially of children. The basic duties of women in urban and rural regions were similar, but concepts of what constituted a household were different, based on socioeconomic and geographic conditions. In the village, demographic conditions enlarged the physical space: since the community was smaller, most members were in various degrees of kinship, thus allowing women to have freer contact with men. This enabled women to carry out regular duties outside the house, not only in the attached garden, but also in far away fields. These duties, in turn, made it possible for women to mingle with women outside their family as well as with men, both Jewish and gentile.

The position of rural women was also shaped by economic factors. Women worked in the vegetable garden attached to the house and drew water and fetched wood. Rural girls drew water daily from a source that either belonged exclusively to Jews or to the whole village. This resulted in the village well becoming a center for social interaction. Men were attracted to these gatherings of young women, but due to the large concentration of members of both genders who were often kin, there was little opportunity for privacy in these meetings. Still, these gatherings could result in the formation of couples, although parental approval for marriage was required. In town, on the contrary, until a late period, male water sellers brought water to homes, and rain water was collected in reservoirs.

In the village, wood for cooking and heating was usually fetched weekly by a group of women who left early in the day. They often had to walk a great distance and returned carrying a heavy load on their heads. This activity was accompanied by songs which strengthened group identity and consolidation and served as a diversion from hard labor. Although fetching wood was carried out in groups, and usually did not bring women in contact with men, some urban rabbis objected to it because it was in contrast to city modes of behavior and modesty.

Traditionally, some women worked outside their home due to economic need or in order to perform unique female assignments. In the first category were maids, petty merchants, peddlers, and even ritual butchers (in Yemen), while in the second category were midwives, cosmeticians (mainly for brides), and mourners. Some women gained income from handicrafts which they produced at home by spinning, knitting, weaving, or embroidery. Most women gave their earnings to their male guardians – be it father, brother, or husband. Nonetheless, throughout the period, women often had independent authority over their dowry, and thus some economic power. Older women, and especially widows, had the most social and economic independence, and could invest in economic enterprises and contribute to various private and communal causes, including the establishment of religious institutions and the writing of Torah scrolls.

Towards the second half of the 19th century changes emerged in urban areas as a result of harsher economic conditions, the growing presence of European enterprises, and the increase of employment opportunities following the introduction of new jobs. Increased availability of formal education, including vocational training, also played a significant role. At first, female wage earners were mainly from among the poor, who worked outside their household as long as they were single; married women still rarely worked outside their homes. Initially most jobs were an extension of traditional women's tasks or related to their handicrafts. Thus, a large number of women worked as maids, mostly, but not exclusively, in Jewish households. Those with skills such as needlework and ironing worked either in gender segregated workshops or at home. Only gradually, in the 20th century, did women start to enter mixed-gender workplaces, as nurses, factory workers, and office employees. Even then, women often worked separately. Nonetheless, opportunities for unsupervised intergender interaction increased among Jews and between Jews and gentiles. The opening of kindergartens and girls' schools called for the employment of female teachers and directors. This led to temporary migrations of single women and married couples, mostly within the *Alliance Israélite Universelle (AIU) educational network, mainly from Turkey and Morocco. With the spread of state schools, especially after independence, Jewish women also began to teach in non-Jewish schools (e.g., in Morocco).

With the passing of time, a growing number of women wanted to join the workforce not only out of economic necessity, but also in order to satisfy their personal ambitions, interests, and desire for public service; some regarded it as a means for self affirmation and independence. This tendency was the strongest in those urban centers which were exposed to Western influences, in countries such as Turkey and Morocco. However, despite the growing numbers of women in the workforce, they rarely reached leadership positions, even in fields where their number was high, like teaching. This resulted from their lesser leisure time due to continued responsibilities at home and from continuing gender bias against women in managerial roles.

The different status of women and men was reflected in their educations. Education for men was intended to enable them to participate in synagogue worship and communal affairs and to prepare them to support their families financially. Girls' education, too, provided them with tools to perform their specific tasks. Since their world was mainly domestic, they learned how to maintain a Jewish home, mostly from older female relatives. All home activities had a specific Jewish character and were performed within a broader Jewish framework. Thus, the preparation of food was ruled by strict religious laws regarding *kashrut*, with further instructions for the Passover festival. In addition, girls learned some Hebrew prayers which related to women's religious obligations, such as lighting the Sabbath lights. In time, girls were instructed in regulations governing ritual purity and received some sex education. Girls, who were mainly illiterate, memorized appropriate religious rules and prayers from their female relatives, most of whom had gained their knowledge in a similar way.

Women were not required or expected to participate in the formal male conducted communal service in the synagogue and thus had no need to be instructed in Hebrew. Some girls did learn to read Hebrew, usually from male relatives. On a few occasions, little girls were sent to mixed-gender schools, but their studies lasted a shorter time than the boys'. Although it was very rare, some women became teachers of little children, while a very few others were renowned for their Jewish learning. While all males had a Hebrew name (sometimes in addition to one in the local dialect), many women had names in the vernacular or in European languages, further distancing them from the more prestigious male culture.

A major component of female spirituality was women's poetry, which was part of their life and in their local dialect. Such poetry expressed the individual and the group at work, recreation, celebration, and worship. It dealt with daily issues and events, including specific feasts and celebrations, matters of belief, and private life. Girls were exposed to it from an early age, hearing older female relatives sing individually or together in private or at work, during leisure time, family celebrations (especially at weddings), seasonal feasts, and while honoring the Torah and local places of worship like synagogues and tombs of saints.

Since women tended to be illiterate, their poetry was oral and given to constant change. While many songs had a basic pattern, individuals often improvised to emphasize specific events, personalities, and places relating to a particular occasion. Women usually sang only for women or in family gatherings. Those who sang to a larger non-kin, mixed-gender audience were often from a lower social status and were despised. Female poetry was also a channel for inter-communal and inter-denominational contact and influence. At times, women mixed with the crowds surrounding singers of another group, even belonging to another religion, to learn new songs and melodies. Thus, female poetry and music eased the burden of heavy labor, strengthened group ties, served as a means of artistic expression and form of worship, and even served as a bridge between communities.

Men's poetry, on the other hand, was more rigid and less understood by the masses. Much of it was religious poetry in Hebrew, unintelligible to the majority who knew only the local Jewish dialect. It was mostly created by known poets and sung by professionals. Even the poetry in the local dialect was generally composed by individuals and much less given to improvisation. Consequently, it was easier to preserve and study men's poetry. But although many men listened to this art form, only relatively few could fully understand and appreciate it or contribute to its development. Women, on the other hand, could enjoy, participate, and contribute to their poetry throughout life, regardless of age, status, or occupation.

Women of several households used to gather in their limited leisure time, talking, singing, and doing their handicrafts, which were often intricate artistic creations, unique to specific regions and the bearer's stage in life. During these meetings, female poetry was sung by any member of the group. Girls were exposed to this rich creative environment from an early age, observing visual art in its development, hearing poetry while it was composed, and becoming aware of intimate issues related to family life. Thus, although most girls were illiterate, they acquired the skills of creativity from a tender age and developed their own forms of spirituality in a supportive environment.

The long established cultural equilibrium in Jewish communities under Islam was shattered when new educational systems were introduced, although in many cases schools were established in response to indigenous requests. Among the major elements active in modern Jewish education, including female education, were the Paris-based Alliance Israélite Universelle, beginning in the 1860s (mainly in Morocco, Turkey, Palestine, Iraq and Iran), and the Zionist movement, through local activists and emissaries from Palestine (mainly in Iraq, Tunisia, Morocco, and Libya) during the 20th century. Other modern schools were mostly foreign or, later, run by the state. Communal educational systems were slow to change, and usually did so in response to outside competition. Jewish leadership often opposed modern education because it was geared towards alien value systems and threatened to dispossess traditional functionaries. The opposition was less fierce towards formal female education, both because the community did not provide one and because a secular or Jewish system could draw girls away from missionary schools. Still, in some places, like Iraq and Palestine, there was rabbinic opposition to any formal female education out of fear that educated girls, as the mothers of the next generation, would champion change. Formal female education not only made women literate, but also facilitated another major departure from tradition, the mass entry of women into teaching.

Early girls' schools emphasized vocational training, complemented with a few academic subjects. The focus on vocational education was an effort to attract poor girls, who would acquire profitable professions which could be performed at home. There was a fear that emphasis on academic studies would come at the expense of mastering household skills and would make girls feel superior to their environment and even equal to men, thereby diminishing their chances to marry. Since Muslim girls rarely received formal vocational training at the time, Jewish girls encountered little competition in the professions they learned in school.

Jewish girls' schools were established later than schools for boys, there were usually fewer female than male students, and even fewer girls passed the level of primary education. This was due to continued communal desire for women to marry young and to the fact that secondary education was usually mixed. Schools were mostly segregated by gender, but mixed schools (with either separate-gender classes or mixed ones) existed too, mainly for economic reasons in small communities. Although the attendance of Jewish girls at missionary or state schools increased their chances of meeting gentiles, some Jewish parents sometimes selected missionary schools, as was the case in Egypt and Aden, because of the European languages they taught and the free tuition they offered. Similarly, parents opted at times for state schools, as was the case in Iraq and Iran, because of their sheer number in comparison to Jewish schools, especially at the high school level. In the republic of Turkey, all foreign, religious, and communal schools were gradually closed beginning in the late 1920s.

Those Jewish girls who did receive modern educations often became agents of change. However, the gap between expectations and reality tended to be wide for educated young women. Even when they managed to enter the "men's world," they generally held lower rank jobs with virtually no likelihood of advancement.

Leisure time activities were traditionally gender-based. Women's meetings often incorporated an element of work, private or communal. In addition to home gatherings, adult women met towards the week's end to clean the synagogue and prepare it for the Sabbath, while neighboring women provided them with refreshments. On these occasions female poetry was sung in praise of the Torah scroll. Women frequented the synagogue for worship much less than men. Most women could not pray from prayer books and usually voiced improvised prayers, blessings, and wishes in the vernacular, sending kisses to the Torah scroll. Women were also active in self-help societies, mainly for the needy, including poor brides and the sick. Men's leisure time activities were more text-oriented, usually in the form of prayers or community sponsored study groups, where men passively listened to readings from religious literature or chanted Psalms. Men also met for recreational purposes in coffee houses and drinking places.

Towards the end of the 19th century, new leisure time activities sprang up side by side with traditional ones. Many of the new patterns resulted from foreign influences and the new educational systems. The AIU was very active in this respect, especially in Morocco and Turkey. In anticipation of the foundation of an AIU school, a local AIU committee was established to advance AIU goals, to promote the establishment of an AIU school, and then to serve as a support group for the school. Most AIU committee members were men, but a few women participated too, usually when supporting girls' and mixed schools. The AIU also triggered the establishment of welfare-oriented organizations, which included many female members. Following a few years of a school's existence, an alumni organization was established, supporting the school, mainly through paid cultural and social activities. These organizations were at first often gender-based, but gradually attracted women and men for mixed-gender activities.

The 20th century witnessed the establishment of specific organizations for youth, focusing at first on recreation (mainly sports, parties, and performances), often as an offshoot of an adult organization (e.g., the Maccabi sport organization establishing Young Maccabi). The earlier organizations of this kind were mainly for men, but women were accepted as guests; only at a later stage (mostly in the 1940s) were women admitted as full members or in a separate branch.

The next step, taken mainly in Palestine, Iraq, Tunisia, Morocco, and Libya, was the establishment of ideologically focused Zionist youth organizations. Established by local Zionists and with the support and at times the guidance of emissaries from Palestine, these youth organizations aimed to change the world view of the youth and thus of the community at large. One of their central goals was to create a "New Jew," a term incorporating both men and women, based on an ideal of gender equality. Consequently, the youth movements were for both genders, although some of their activities were gender-based. Deep-rooted concepts, however, were slow to change: girls were less active in mixed group discussions, there were fewer girls than boys in most movements, and fewer still in leadership positions. And although the movements advocated the equal place of women in the new, productive (i.e., agricultural and industrial) workplace, fewer women joined the agricultural training farms (*hakhsharah*), and both there and in the clubs women carried out traditional female tasks, such as cleaning and cooking. Most often, "New Women" found themselves living in a conceptually old world, regardless of their personal spiritual and professional metamorphosis.

Traditional gender divisions had implications on marriage. Only in the village could young people of both genders meet relatively freely, usually when girls performed their daily task of drawing water. Even in villages, however, the final decision concerning marriage rested with the parents. In some regions, young men could influence the choice of their bride through the intervention of local, even Muslim, dignitaries. In urban settings, where most Jews lived, the opportunities for young people to meet were very limited. Apart from family gatherings, which were often gender segregated, some regions had special events which enabled the youth to meet. A very famous occasion took place in Tripoli, Libya, on the last day of Passover, when girls stood beautifully dressed outside their homes, waiting for young men to indicate to their parents which girl they wanted to marry, leaving the negotiations to the parents. Much of the matchmaking was conducted during the informal meetings of family and neighborhood women, who knew quite well the most intimate details about each other and their families. Although girls were usually allowed to reject a prospective bridegroom, they were not supposed to initiate the choice, and the decision of the couple was based mainly on an occasional glimpse. The older women, on the other hand, knew much of the family background and the character of the younger generation and based their decisions on this information. The economic details of the marriage were settled by the fathers. After a decision was made, the couple was not supposed to meet until the wedding.

Most first time brides were in their early teens with somewhat older grooms. At times, though, girls were forced to marry old men. In many places girls unmarried by their mid-teens were considered old spinsters, almost unmarriageable, except to less sought after men, including the poor, disabled, or old. Marriage of minors, even below the age of ten, took place relatively rarely, and happened mainly in Yemen. In some places, babies were given out in marriage, but these agreements were sometimes broken. As a result of Muslim influence, polygyny was accepted among Jews in the Muslim world, but Jewish law required that both wives be treated equally, sexually and economically. Polygyny was not widespread and happened mainly among Yemeni and Kurdish Jews and in rural areas or when the first wife did not give birth to a son.

Preparations for weddings were elaborate, culminating in a week of festivities. The bride, for whom this was the major public event of her life, was adorned and wore luxurious clothing and jewelry (which at times passed from one bride to another). Before the wedding, the bride and her female relatives went to the *mikveh* (ritual bath), an occasion which could be used by her future female in-laws to watch for any hidden physical imperfection.

The introduction of European educations, the operation of youth movements, and the entrance of women into the workforce gradually changed these practices, mainly in the urban centers. Modern educators tried to keep girls in school, in part to postpone the age of marriage. The AIU was active in this trend from the late 19th century on, trying to influence communal leaders to permit marriage only above a certain age. Many couples met as a result of the activities of youth movements (mainly beginning in the 1940s). The entrance of women into the workforce delayed the age of marriage and facilitated contacts among young people, even of different religions and nationalities. As a result, over time most engaged couples knew each other and even chose each other and the marriage age rose, although parental consent for marriage was usually required. These changes took place mainly in the urban centers and on the Mediterranean and Atlantic coasts. They were much less common in Iran, Yemen, and rural hinterlands.

[Rachel Simon (2nd ed.)]

Israel

THE OLD YISHUV. Throughout the early modern and modern periods, until the end of the 19th century, the Jewish population of Palestine was centered in Jerusalem. This population, primarily made up of spiritual seekers from all parts of the Jewish world, survived on charitable contributions from Diaspora communities. These **ḥalukkah* payments, distributed separately by Ashkenazi and Sephardi religious authorities, were originally intended to enable Jewish men to devote their lives to Torah study and prayer. However, demographic data demonstrates that women, mainly widows who had come to the Holy Land to spend their remaining days visiting sacred sites and preparing themselves for the next world, were the majority of the Jewish population of Jerusalem in the 19th century and they also benefited significantly from *ḥalukkah*. As M. Shilo has shown, in the course of the 19th century the male religious establishment linked *ḥalukkah* to pious and modest behavior by the enforcement of by-laws (*Takannot Yerushalayim*) that applied to men and women alike. A number of these regulations constructed all women as objects of sexual temptation and attempted to limit severely women's presence in the public domain. Any mingling between men and women was looked upon as a sin, and husbands and the fathers were expected to supervise the women of the family to preserve the sanctity of the community and to ensure that the family received its allotted share of *ḥalukkah*. Women and their needs were always subordinated to a traditional male view of how society should be arranged.

From the late 19th century on, with the growth of Zionist movements of various kinds, the population of the Old Yishuv (Jewish settlement) was augmented with increasing numbers of immigrants, from both Eastern Europe and from Middle Eastern Jewish communities, such as Yemen. Zionists from Eastern Europe were particularly intent on building up the land and engaging Jews in economic endeavors. In this era the highly religious nature of the Jewish communities of Jerusalem (of both European and Middle Eastern origins) slowly began to change owing to the influx of largely secular immigrants and infusions of funds from Zionist organizations abroad. The areas of transformation with special impact for women included the introduction and external funding of various educational alternatives for girls, including vocational training, and gradual improvements in health care options.

THE NEW YISHUV. The inequality in the treatment of the sexes exemplified in the Old Yishuv community of Jerusalem continued to be a reality in the modern Jewish settlement of the land. The pioneers of the First Aliyah (1882–1903) and Second Aliyah (1904–18), included both men and women. Most of the women of the First Aliyah accompanied their husbands and settled into domestic roles in agricultural settlements (moshavot) or urban environments. The women of this immigration, many of whom were as deeply committed as their husbands to their new lives in Palestine, faced a difficult struggle to achieve any public recognition and participation. Many of the idealistic young people of the Second Aliyah, inspired by the fervor of Labor Zionism, had been trained to work the land in Zionist training schools in Russia, which stressed the equality of women and men. On arriving in Palestine, most young single women, a significant minority among the second wave of immigrants (17–18%), found their options limited and their choices narrowed, simply as a result of their gender. Feeling betrayed by their male comrades, who did not support their struggle, and limited by male perceptions of their biological inequality, unmarried women were virtually unemployable as agricultural workers, and were forced to survive by providing the men with kitchen and laundry services. As Raḥel *Yanait, wife of Israel's second President, Izhak *Ben-Zvi, and a noted educator and writer recalled of those days. "In the thick of that passionate movement toward the land the women workers suddenly found themselves thrust aside and relegated once more to the ancient tradition of the house and the kitchen. They were amazed and disappointed to see how the cleavage was opening, the men comrades really united themselves with the land, but they, though on it, not becoming part of it. The united front was cracking" (*Plough Woman*, 109). Or as Ziporah Bar-Droma put it, "In Palestine there came a parting of the ways. Over there in the Russian exile, men and women had been equal comrades in the movement. We worked together, suffered together in the prisons and in the remote countries to which we were expelled; the moment the first pioneer certificates reached us, admitting us into Palestine, we were divided into the two classes: men comrades and women comrades…. And when we landed we were actually separated into two groups: In the one group were those who were 'building the country' and in the other were those who would take care, in every day matters, of 'the builders of the country'" (PW, 145).

Denied membership as single women in most collective settlements, and refused employment as agricultural workers, a few women founded successful female agricultural and urban collectives, and women's training farms. Such women's farms excelled particularly as tree nurseries. Raḥel Yanait, as an early settler, wrote: "With our own hands we raised, on our soil, tens and hundreds of thousands of shoots, and a kind of bond was created between our fruitful little corners and the wild bare hills around us. We were participants in the great task of re-afforesting the country" (PW, 112). Here on their own farms, women were able to forge their own connection to the land, and their belief that they were helping to build something new went hand in hand with their own feeling of self-renewal. Yet for every place for a woman in such a settlement, there were dozens who were turned away for lack of resources to provide them support and employment.

In the years following World War I, the majority of single women in the Yishuv were unable to find agricultural employment. In order to survive, many ended up working in cities as cooks or laundresses, seamstresses or clerks, or maids in private homes. Under the immigration regulations imposed by the British mandate on the Third Aliyah (1919–23), women were allowed to enter Palestine as dependents, wives, and elderly mothers, but only to a limited extent as prospective workers who could receive a labor immigration permit. Although men and women immigrated in roughly similar numbers (36 percent were women), two-thirds to 90 percent of all women came as dependents, as compared to 10 to 20 percent of all men. Labor permits were allocated to over 50 percent of all men and to only 10 percent of the immigrant women. Moreover, the vast majority of adult Jewish women who immigrated to Palestine had little relevant occupational experience to enable them to become active, equal partners, let alone self-sufficient members, of their new community. In these years many of the goals of the Second Aliyah were being implemented, including the establishment of the Histadrut, the General Federation of Hebrew Labor (1920) and the Women Workers' Movement (1921).

Some of women's complaints about the inequity of their situations were met by the *kibbutz movement, at least for that small group of women who gained entry into a kibbutz. Many of these kibbutzim were dedicated to bold social restructurings of the family in order to create a society in which each individual would achieve economic independence. In such a social setting wives would not be dependent upon their husbands and would no longer be subservient to them. In the kibbutz the family was to be renewed in such a way that men and women would be equal and independent partners sharing common goals; here, women were to be emancipated from the demands of the home and from childcare so that they might work productively and creatively with men in building the land.

Yet even on the kibbutz, women mainly worked in the kitchens and laundries. And here, in this experimental setting, woman's role in childcare raised issues which remain problematic. Many kibbutzim opted for bringing up children collectively in children's houses under the care of nurses and teachers. Parents would only see their children for an hour or two each day. In this way mothers would be freed to function as independent members of the collective, and children would benefit from a feeling that all the adults of the kibbutz were concerned for their development and care. Yet as one kibbutz theorist, Eva Tabenkin, admitted in the early 1930s, perhaps collective child rearing asked too much, "We are worried constantly by one thought: how can we bring into the life of the child which is being cared for in the home, the bright glance and the loving smile of the mother for which even the tiniest creature instinctively longs?" "But," she went on to say, "we cannot forget what was in our minds when we approached the whole problem at the beginning, what ideals and wishes we had regarding life in Palestine generally and our own lives in particular. For it is only as part of a high cultural life that the group upbringing of children has meaning, and only in the larger setting of a general ideal will we find the strength to continue seeking, through this form, a loftier and finer life for ourselves and our children" (PW, 159).

Most women in the Yishuv were married mothers of children. The pre-Zionist communities of both the Ashkenazi Orthodox and Jews of Middle Eastern origin were strongly committed to the establishment of families. Women of these communities tended to marry at a relatively early age. Many among the more recent Zionist immigrants arrived already married and most others married, as well. Community studies conducted in Jerusalem and Haifa in the 1930s indicate that by 35 to 40, all but five percent of Jewish women in the Yishuv had married, and the majority of women bore children. Despite the varied Zionist utopian visions of the new Jewish society to be built in Palestine, traditional gendered divisions of labor and patterns of authority tended to be preserved in the Jewish families of the Yishuv, with the exception of the kibbutz experiment described above.

Few married women in the Yishuv worked outside their homes. Those who did faced the inevitable conflicts of the working woman who must leave her children in the care of another with few social supports. "What is a mother to do," one woman asked, when, "in spite of the place which the children and the family as a whole take up in her life, her nature and her being demanded something more. This woman cannot divorce herself from the larger social life. She cannot let her children narrow down her horizon. And for such a woman there is no rest" (PW, 164). "Am I at fault," asked the writer, Golda *Meir (then Meyerowitz), "if after giving my family a place in my heart there is something left over which has to be filled by things outside the family and the house?" Society, she acknowledged, can offer no easy answer, for as Meir wrote, "This eternal inner division, this double pull, this alternating feeling of unfulfilled duty today toward her children, the next day toward her work. This is the burden of the working mother" (PW, 165).

As D. Bernstein has written of pre-State Israel, women's unequal and marginal position in the labor market, and their sole responsibility for family care, created a distinctly different life pattern for women as compared to that experienced by men. Since the private sphere, where women were central, was all but invisible and since women were only intermittently visible in the all important public sphere, women were essentially excluded from power and influence as the Yishuv moved towards the immense challenges of statehood in the years following World War II.

ISRAEL SINCE 1948. Modern Israel continues to be far from progressive where the status of women in concerned, and is, at the beginning of the 21st century, more conservative than most other western democracies on women's issues (see *Feminism: Feminism, Zionism, and the State of Israel). Despite significant achievements and continuing progress, as a whole Israeli women continue to earn less that their male counterparts, are less visible and influential in the political arena, do not share equal responsibilities or privileges in the military, have unequal rights and freedoms in family life and law, and are secondary in shaping the nation's self image and cultural orientation.

The unequal status of Israeli women is a result of generations of past discrimination in Jewish tradition in general, as well as the additional impact of highly conservative Middle Eastern cultures on many Israelis from Muslim countries. Women suffer numerous disadvantages in the workplace, mandated by paternalistic legislation and the expectation that women will also assume most household responsibilities. Israeli women continue to fulfill the traditional Jewish role of enablers, supporting their husbands and sons, who hold the primary power and powerful jobs, and whose lives are at risk in defending the state. Only a small number of Israeli women reject women's subsidiary roles; most believe that women will not achieve equality as long as war and conflict is a dominant theme in Israeli society.

Jewish women in Israel are significantly disadvantaged in personal status issues. When the State of Israel was established in May, 1948, the Declaration of Independence stated that "The State of Israel will maintain equal social and political rights for all citizens, irrespective of religion, race, or sex," a sentiment reiterated in 1949, in the basic guidelines of the first government of Israel. Yet 1953 legislation awarded the Orthodox religious establishment monopolistic control over marriage and divorce for all Jewish citizens, thus legalizing women's substantial legal disadvantages in the *halakhah*, particularly in areas of family law. There is no civil marriage or divorce in Israel, nor do Reform, Conservative, or Reconstructionist Judaisms, with their more egalitarian approaches, have any official standing. Particular problems are connected with the dissolution of Jewish marriages since, according to *halakhah*, a Jewish woman cannot obtain a divorce without the permission of her husband. Many men refuse to grant their wives a divorce document, sometimes attempting to extort large sums of money from the estranged wife's family before they will comply with a religious court's ruling and agree to the legal dissolution of the marriage. Many refuse to comply at all, leaving the wife in legal limbo. The issue of the over 5,000 *agunot*, women who cannot obtain a divorce because their husbands refuse to grant one or because the husbands cannot be located, is the best known instance of the inability of the Orthodox rabbinate to deal with real social problems which cause immense pain and suffering to women and their families. Only recently have women begun to fight back, forming an International Coalition for *Agunah* Rights, reflecting an intensive effort to reform what are perceived as unjust and discriminatory divorce proceedings in rabbinical courts worldwide.

Although women are eligible for military service, most women in the army are assigned to education, clerical work, and training. Fewer than half of all eligible women are actually conscripted because they are not really needed, although army technology is beginning to create more equal tasks for the Israeli woman. Moreover, since the beginning of the 21st century rapid changes in women's opportunities in the military have been underway. In early 2000, the Israeli Defense Forces decided to deploy women in the artillery corps, followed by infantry units, armored divisions, and elite combat units. The Navy also decided to place women in its diving repair unit. At the beginning of 2004, about 450 women were in combat units; in late 2005, it was announced that three female pilots, including one combat pilot, would shortly complete training and join the nine other female soldiers in Israel's Air Force.

Given the historical pattern of secondary female military roles, however, women remain poorly represented in the upper echelons of the military, as they are in public and political life and in the civil service and academia. Since an important premium is put on military background as the necessary precondition for public office, women have found it very difficult to break into the political system.

Prolonged military conflict highlights various norms which are antithetical to the promotion of gender equality. These include the glorification of the hero and of macho-like ideals which may be necessary to ensure a continued commitment to defense and security. These values tend to glorify military prowess and to stress loyalty and commitment which are carried over from military to civilian life. One consequence of the emphasis on national security is that what are seen as women's issues, particularly in the areas of health, education, and welfare, are almost always given low priority in terms of policy considerations. More significantly, women have not been able to articulate their position on matters of general concern because the primary questions on the national agenda have come to be defined as male issues requiring an expertise that only men have acquired.

A report on the status of women in Israel in 2004 presented by the Israel Women's Network to the Committee for the Advancement of the Status of Women is Israel's parliament (Knesset) indicates that of 121 countries in which women are included in the legislature, Israel, despite having once been led by a woman prime minister, ranks 66th. Women constitute only 15% of Israel's 120-member Knesset, placing Israel somewhere between the Arab world and developing countries in its attitude to female politicians. The Committee for the Advancement of the Status of Women and individual female Members of Knesset are attempting to advance women's status through legislation. Their initiatives address a variety of gender issues such as equality at work, violence against women, welfare, health, and fertility concerns. The Authority for the Advancement of Women, established by law in 1998, is authorized to encourage, coordinate, promote and monitor the government's and the local authorities' activities regarding women's status, to promote legislation, and to advise the government on the enforcement of laws promoting the status of women. It is also expected to initiate research and to enhance public awareness through the media and education. The growing awareness of the status of women in the early 21st century has led to an increasing presence of women in managerial and decision-making positions. Prime Minister Ariel *Sharon included a record number of women ministers (three) and deputy ministers (two) in his government.

Israeli women are highly educated. Approximately 22% of Israel's women have 13–15 years of formal education compared to 20% of men, although 4.5% of women have no schooling compared to 1.8% of men. However, while 57% of all academic degrees are earned by women, and 46% of the doctoral students are women, only 22% of senior faculty members and 7.8% of full professors are women.

Government figures indicate that in 2000, 45.44% of the labor force were women, of whom only 15.8% worked full time, compared to 34.1% of the men. The average monthly salary for women was 60.18% of men's wages and the average wage-per-hour was 80.5% of that of men. In general, women worked mostly in lower-paying jobs, in services, education, health, welfare and clerical positions, and were significantly less represented in prestigious and lucrative occupations. Government statistics also indicate that violence against women is a serious problem in Israel, ranging from spousal abuse, sexual violence, sexual harassment, incest, and trafficking in women for prostitution. It is estimated that a significant number of women suffer from domestic violence. Facilities for their support and care are woefully inadequate.

The Israel Women's Network, founded by Alice Shalvi in 1984, is an advocacy group for women's rights that concentrates on legislative and political efforts to overcome discrimination against women in the workplace, military, religious courts, and in the healthcare and educational arenas. With particular attention to violence and sexual harassment, the IWN helped secure passage in 1998 of legislation criminalizing sexual harassment and holding both the harasser and employer responsible for civil damages. In recent decades, Israel's nascent feminist movement has begun to bring cases to Israel's Supreme Court (see below: The Judicial Perspective) on issues as diverse as access to abortion, women's right to be elected to and hold seats on municipal religious councils, and the ability of women's prayer groups to hold services at the Western Wall.

Several feminist organizations emerged beginning in the 1980s that called for return of the occupied territories to Palestinian control, and condemned the violence and impoverishment in those territories. Women in Black was founded in 1988 to hold weekly silent vigils of Israeli and Palestinian women calling for an end to the occupation. It now has an international peace network and has been nominated for the Nobel Peace Prize. New Profile is a feminist organization that seeks to change Israel from what it perceives to be a militarized to a peace-seeking culture, and works especially on educating children for peace (see essays in Fuchs). At other end of the political spectrum, Women in Green advocates the annexation of Judea and Samaria and supports continued Jewish settlement there.

This increased feminist activity, influenced by the women's movement throughout the Western world, is indicative of the gender and religious tensions that characterize Israeli society in 2006.

Similar concerns are also evident in the kibbutz movement at the beginning of the 21st century. Recent studies indicate that the ideology of equality with which the movement began has never been realized. At present, the division of labor parallels occupational profiles outside the kibbutz, with women predominating in education, childcare, food preparation, and laundry, while men more commonly choose revenue producing occupations in agriculture and industry. One consequence is that women are seen as providing services while men, who are seen as earning money for the kibbutz, come to be regarded as the experts in management and fiscal policy making. Thus men are far more likely to be elevated to leadership positions in the kibbutz, thereby gaining disproportionate power, status, and respect. Similarly, changes in the organization of family life on the kibbutz have added to women's burdens. Where once virtually all kibbutzim provided separate housing for children, who would spend a few hours of relaxation time with their parents, today children almost never sleep in children's houses. This means that women assume the primary responsibility for child care and the increase in household tasks associated with a family sharing living quarters which were often intended only for two. It is not surprising that there is growing dissatisfaction with kibbutz life among younger women who struggle with the contradiction of being "homemakers without homes" (Palgi; essay in Fuchs).

In microcosm, the status of women in Israel is a result of generations of past gender discrimination from a variety of sources, both religious and cultural, together with the problems of inequality which surface in a society experiencing an ongoing state of military conflict. The legal advocacy and political activities of some women in recent times constitute alternative approaches to combating women's unequal roles, but fundamental transformations in Israel's legal structure are necessary if these are to be realized. Similarly, true change for women will only come when the adjudication of family law issues is removed from the sole control of the Orthodox rabbinate which has been inflexible in easing the discriminations against women inherent in halakhic tradition.

[Judith R. Baskin (2nd ed.)]

THE JUDICIAL PERSPECTIVE: WOMEN AND THE ISRAELI COURTS

The issue of the status of women, by its very nature and its significance for society and the family, exemplifies the importance of finding a synthesis between *halakhah* and the needs of the place and time. This was true over the generations, in the worlds of the *tannaim,* the *amoraim* and the *geonim,* in the world of the medieval authorities (*rishonim*) as well as of the *aḥaronim,* during their various periods and dispersions. Since the beginning of the Emancipation period, new considerations and elements have arisen, and special creativity has been evident since the restoration of Jewish political independence in the State of Israel.

Justice M. Elon opens his discussion of the topic (*Ma'amad ha-Ishah – Mishpat ve-Shipput, Masoret u-Temurah: Arakhehah shel Medinah Yehudit ve-Demokratit* (2005), pp. 17–18 (henceforth Elon, *Ma'amad ha-Ishah*) with the following words:

> The issue of the status of women is one of the striking examples of creativity in the world of *halakhah* in days of old and in our times. The word *halakhah* is derived from the root *halokh* ("go"), as explained by Rabbi Nathan ben Rabbi Yehiel of Rome, author of the *Arukh*, in the 11th century: "that which goes from of old until the end [of time], or [that way] in which Israel goes." I am inclined to add that the word *halakhah* bears the additional aspect of creativity. That is, the halakhic Sages viewed themselves as commanded to *go* forward, to *lead halakhah* in a creative manner and in accordance with the circumstances of their time; that is, *halakhah* goes (*holekhet*) forward. Regarding

> the issue of the status of women, this "going" of the *halakhah*, which includes accommodating its foundations and principles to the needs of the time and the place, is given very prominent and creative expression. Nonetheless there are a number of grave issues relating to the status of women that have been partially resolved, but have not yet found their full resolution, such as the problem of women who have been refused a divorce, abandoned wives, and the like; and we must work hard to find a convenient and satisfactory solution (see **Agunah*). In general, however, the status of women in Judaism has from its very beginning been dynamic, in a state of constant creativity, especially in comparison with parallel systems. Halakhic creativity has always found expression in *theoretical study*, through examination of the halakhic principles and statutes, and in the *practical application* of those principles in changing circumstances. In every realm, but especially in that of the law and all its branches, *halakhah* is forced to deal with the question of how on the one hand, to continue the past, from the starting point of the existing *halakhah* – to continue the chain; while, on the other hand, to study and apply the *halakhah* with creativity and in a manner appropriate to the times. Creativity in this context means resolving the needs of the *present*, its problems and demands, through a deep and fitting analysis of the world of Jewish Law and its principles in the *past*, in order to find the appropriate path toward the *future*.

The issue of the status of women, with the great creativity that has been demonstrated therein, serves as an example of the manner in which Judaism has found a *synthesis*, which today is called a synthesis of the values of the State of Israel as a Jewish and democratic state (see *Values of Jewish and Democratic State).

This article will give a number of concrete examples taken from Israeli law and the rulings of the Israeli Supreme Court, an appreciable portion of which are the rulings of Deputy Chief Justice of the Supreme Court, Justice Menachem Elon, who gave a number of concrete decisions on issues pertaining to the status of the women. These examples provide a wealth of material regarding the reciprocal influence of *halakhah* and society; of pluralism and differences of opinion; of activism and restraint; creativity and the avoidance thereof; and the like. All this material provides an impressive picture of how and in what manner the "Jewish" and "democratic" elements of the State of Israel have been combined, how the "Jewish" element has been influenced by the "democratic" and how it has preceded it. Some topics relating to the status of the women have already been discussed at length in other entries; see, for example, **Agunah*; *Husband and Wife; *Parents and Child; *Wills; *Succession; *Maintenance, **Ketubbah*. These topics will not be discussed here in detail, but references will be made to certain conclusions that may be drawn from them.

Husband and Wife

The relationship between husband and wife is central to the issue of the status of women, and has been discussed extensively and often in the legal system (see, for example, Cr.A. 92/2157, *Padida v. the State of Israel*, 47 (1) PD 81; CA 79/458 *Nir v. Nir*, 35 (1) PD 518; and cf. *Husband and Wife). It has been noted that the fundamental legal principles underlying this relationship are based on the words of the *beraita* (Yev. 62b): "Our Rabbis taught: The man who loves his wife as himself, and honors her more than himself [Rashi, s.v. *yoter*: Because disgrace is more difficult for a woman than for a man] who guides his sons and daughters in the right path and arranges for them to be married near the period of their puberty, of him Scripture says: 'And you shall know that your tent is at peace, and you shall visit your habitation, and shall miss nothing.' (Job 5:24)." This, in brief, is the structure of the family cell, as viewed by the Sages. Maimonides codified this law in similar fashion: "Therefore the Sages laid down that a man shall honor his wife more than his own self and shall love her as he loves himself, and shall constantly seek to benefit her according to his means… and shall speak gently with her; that he shall be neither sad nor irritable" (Yad, *Ishut* 15:19). Similarly, the Talmud states: "Rabbi Helbo said: A man should always be careful about his wife's honor, for blessing is found in a man's house only on account of his wife. As it is stated: 'And he treated Abraham well for her [= Sarah's] sake' (Gen. 12:16)" (BM 59a). In his discussion of this issue, Justice Elon states (*Ma'amad ha-Ishah*, pp. 194–228, at 195):

> These are the fundamental demands. But social reality, throughout the generations and the dispersion, did not always meet them. Thus, a series of judicial rulings discuss cases of violence and abuse on the part of a husband toward his wife, and aggressive and inappropriate behavior on the part of a wife toward her husband. The halakhic authorities responded in resolute fashion, whether by way of judicial decisions or by way of legislation of special enactments. These issues have been discussed in the rulings of the Israeli courts, and the deliberations and rulings follow Jewish Law – its sources, its deliberations, and its rulings.

The substantive difference between Jewish Law over English law with respect to the rape of a woman by her husband has also been discussed in this context (see: CA 80/91, *Moshe Ben Meir Cohen v. the State of Israel*, PD 35(3) 281). Justice Elon summarizes the issue as follows (*Ma'amad ha-Ishah*, p. 228): "Jewish Law rescued the honor of women in the State of Israel from the dread of the 'democratic' norm, taken from English law, by which a husband has the right to rape his wife. The ancient Jewish norm, established thousands of years ago, established that a woman is not 'a captive in the hands of her husband,' and thus protects the rights and dignity of a woman. This is the law that is appropriate for the State of Israel as a Jewish and democratic state, Jewish *before* democratic."

A Woman's Economic Rights

The mutual respect that must be demonstrated between husband and wife in their personal relations has already been noted. A number of examples of creativity regarding the status of women in the area of economic rights should also be noted. They include: the independence of a woman's economic status; her right to compensation at the time of divorce; joint property rights in assets acquired during the marriage (see also Elon, *Ma'amad ha-Ishah*, pp. 229–54). These topics have been discussed at length in the entry *Husband and Wife, *Maintenance, **Ketubbah*, and others.

In terms of halakhic creativity and the protection of the status of women in Judaism, a fundamental principle is that "a woman is not considered her husband's daily laborer in exchange for maintenance." According to *halakhah*, a man is obligated to provide his wife with maintenance (not only food, but also medical expenses, raiment, lodging and all her other necessaries), and in exchange is entitled to the benefit of her handiwork (Yad, Ishut 12:1–4). The woman may, of her own choice, waive her maintenance, keeping for herself the proceeds of her handiwork. The husband does not have the parallel right: he cannot deny his wife maintenance by waiving the benefit of her handiwork.

Creative decisions regarding the woman's status were also given with respect to property relations between husband and wife. This began in the rulings of the rabbinical courts in the 1940s, even before the establishment of the State of Israel. The issue is discussed in CA 2/77 *Azugi v. Azugi*, PD 33(3) 1, 17ff [henceforth: *Azugi*] and in CA 630/79, *Lieberman v. Lieberman*, PD 35(4) 359, 372–73. Justice Elon summarizes the issue as follows (*Ḥakikah Datit* (1968), pp. 165–67):

> One of the great innovations of the rabbinical courts in the area of divorce law is the wife's right to receive a certain financial sum at the time of divorce, in addition to her *kettubah*. This sum varies according to the circumstances of the particular case. The rabbinical courts refer to this additional sum as compensation. According to the accepted law prior to this innovation, except for in certain cases, at the time of divorce a woman was entitled to receive her *kettubbah* and to take back the property that she had brought into the marriage. This property included: (a) *nikhsei ẓon barzel* – that part of the woman's property that the couple agree will be given to the almost total ownership of the husband, to the extent of his accepting responsibility for any damage caused thereto, and which, upon the termination of the marriage, the woman would receive the value of in accordance with the sum stipulated in the *kettubah;* and (b) *nikhsei melog* – that part of the woman's property whose principal remains in the wife's ownership even after the marriage, but whose fruits (the proceeds of the principal) belong to the husband. The husband bears no responsibility for damage to *nikhsei melog*. Upon dissolution of the marriage – whether by death or divorce – the woman receives the value of the *nikhsei melog* at the time of termination of the marriage. Hence, if their value rises, she profits, and if their value decreases, she loses. The *halakhah* did not recognize the wife's right to receive, at the time of divorce, a share of the assets accumulated during the period of the marriage, unless the parties had an agreement to that effect, even though these assets often come into existence through the combined efforts of husband and wife. This problem has troubled every legal system, and the Knesset considered various private bills regarding a married couple's joint property. It was against this background that the institution of monetary compensation awarded to a woman at the time of divorce came into being through the rulings of the rabbinical courts.

Another innovation related to the woman's economic rights was the establishment, through the rulings of the Israel Supreme Court (*Azugi ibid.*), of the principle of partnership in property acquired during marriage according to Jewish Law. The law regarding partnership in property was created and developed by the justices of the Supreme Court on the basis of the presumed intention of the two spouses to join their assets, and does not follow automatically from the marital bond between them. This bond serves as the background for the couple's conduct and for additional factors in the lives of the married couple that serve as the basis for the legal presumption of partnership in their assets. The legal reasoning that gives validity to the partnership in assets lies in the presumption of implied agreement that may be inferred from these facts and circumstances. This presumption draws its legal force from the fundamental principles of Jewish Law regarding freedom of contract and power of custom – in all its various forms – that finds expression in tendencies in Israeli society and in the creative and decisive power of presumptions.

Succession Rights of Daughters and Wives

The issue of succession in Jewish Law was treated in the entry *Succession. The daughter's standing as lawful heir of her father's estate went through many stages of development and creativity: beginning with the story of the daughters of Zelophehad, who claimed that, as their father had died without leaving a son, and that unless they inherited him, his name would disappear from his family, because his estate would not remain within his family (Num. 27:1–11; 36:1–12); continuing in talmudic law, through the periods of the *geonim*, the medieval and early modern authorities; and down to the post-Emancipation period, in the various centers of Jewish life. The influences of the diverse socio-economic realities at the various stages are evident. Prior to the establishment of the State of Israel, the inheritance rights of daughters were discussed by the two chief rabbis, Herzog and Ouziel. The issue found its resolution in Succession Law, 5725 – 1965, which recognizes no distinction between sons and daughters (see *Ma'amad ha-Ishah*, pp. 255–78).

According to the early *halakhah*, the husband is heir to his wife's estate, but the wife is not a legal heir to that of her husband (Yad, Naḥalot 1.8). By rabbinic enactment, a widow is entitled to reside in the same apartment in which she lived with her husband, and to receive the same maintenance from his estate as she was entitled to receive during his lifetime. These provisions apply automatically, even if the husband did not explicitly commit himself to them in his wife's *ketubbah*. This issue underwent many changes over the course of the generations. In the Ordinances of the rabbinical courts of the Land of Israel of 5703 (1943) (Ordinance 174, 182–183), the rabbinical court agreed that the husband's estate be divided in accordance with the Mandatory Succession Order of 1923, which awards a woman a share in the estate (see: *Ma'amad ha-Ishah*, pp. 279–96).

The Right to Vote and the Right to Be Elected to Public Office

THE RULING IN THE SHAKDIEL CASE. The issue of a woman's right to vote and to be elected to public office was discussed in the *Shakdiel* case (HC 87/153 *Leah Shakdiel v. Minister of Religious Affairs et al.*, PD 42(2) 221). This ruling is the subject of a detailed discussion in *Ma'amad ha-Ishah* (pp. 51–101), which opens as follows:

> The ruling in the *Shakdiel* case, which was given in May 1988, prior to the passing of Basic Law: Human Dignity and Liberty in 1992, constitutes a classic example of the need for creative interpretation for the resolution of new problems arising in different times and places, and the method of this interpretation. Through an analysis of this ruling, we learn about differences in opinion among the halakhic authorities regarding the necessity and appropriateness of fitting a particular issue in the world of *halakhah* into the new social reality in which they are living. The great creativity evident in their method may serve as an important source of inspiration as we occupy ourselves with the question of the synthesis of the Jewish heritage with the needs of a modern democratic state.
>
> Mrs. Leah Shakdiel – a resident of the town of Yeroḥam in the Negev, a teacher of Judaic studies, an Orthodox Jewess and a member of the Yeroḥam Municipal Council – turned to the Israeli Supreme Court sitting as the High Court of Justice regarding the decision that had been taken to disqualify her from serving as a member of the religious council of Yeroḥam. The claim of the respondents to the petition – the Municipal Council, the local rabbi, the Minister of Religious Affairs and the Committee of Ministers – was that a tradition exists, according to which women are not to be nominated for membership in a religious council. This was supported by an opinion of the Council of the Chief Rabbinate that women may not be permanent members of religious councils. The concern was likewise raised that Mrs. Shakdiel's membership would disrupt the orderly course of activity of the religious council.
>
> After examining all the factual material before him and the claims and arguments of the parties, and after taking note of the sources of *halakhah* and Jewish Law, and the legal material of the laws of the Knesset and the rulings of the courts, Justice Elon concluded that Mrs. Shakdiel's petition should be allowed. The ruling therefore stated: "We therefore decide that she (i.e., Shakdiel) shall be included in the membership of the Yeroḥam religious council, as a nominee on behalf of the municipal council, as her nomination had been presented to the Minister of Religious Affairs with the formation of the religious council."

The Bible, the Talmud, and later sources mention distinguished women – prophetesses, judges, queens, and wise and scholarly woman. These were isolated incidents; the guiding rule – one of great significance in the edifice of the Jewish family over the generations – was: "All the glory of the king's daughter is within" (Ps. 45:14). This verse was taken to mean that a woman earns merit by educating her children and managing her home, and that it is not womanly to be involved in public affairs. A clear and concise expression of this theme is found in Maimonides' reading of Deuteronomy 17:15: "'You shall set a king over you.' "One does not place a woman on the throne, as it said: 'a king over you' – and not a queen. Likewise, for all offices in Israel, only a man may be appointed" (Yad, *Melakhim* 1.5). Maimonides' opinion that men alone may be appointed to public office, and not women, was the accepted position for many years. This was the customary and accepted norm in the general social and economic realms as well. This position was subjected to question in light of changing time and place at the beginning of the previous century, when the question arose whether women should be granted the right of franchise. The question arose primarily in relation to elections of the institutions of self-government of the Jewish community in the Land of Israel just after the end of World War I. It might be recalled that, until then, women had been denied the right to vote in most countries throughout the world, and that it was only during the latter half of the 1910s that women were given full rights to vote and to stand for election in most states and provinces of the United States and Canada, and in Russia, England, and Germany. In some countries, such as France, this right was only granted as recently as 1944, and in Switzerland as late as 1971.

The views of the rabbinical scholars on this issue fell into three camps. The majority opinion was that women should not be granted election rights, whether active, i.e., the right to vote, or passive, i.e., the right to be elected. Some of the authorities held that women have active election rights but not passive ones. A third camp was of the opinion that there is nothing in the *halakhah* to prevent women from exercising both active and passive election rights – that is, women may both vote for and be elected to public and governmental office.

Rabbi Abraham Isaac ha-Kohen Kook, chief rabbi of the Land of Israel, one of the leading halakhic authorities and thinkers of the Zionist movement, belonged to the camp that denied women both active and passive election rights (see: *Ma'amarei ha-Ra'ayah, Kovez̩ Ma'amarim me-et ha-Ra'ayah Kook zaz̩al*, Jerusalem 1984, pp. 189–94). Rabbi Kook discussed the matter from three perspectives: in terms of the law – whether it is permitted or forbidden; in terms of public welfare – whether or not granting women the right of franchise will bring good to the community; and in terms of the ideal – whether our moral consciousness obligates granting election rights or denies it. From the legal perspective, Rabbi Kook followed the earlier halakhic authorities in maintaining that the duty of public service is imposed on men, and not on women. He was also concerned about problems of modesty stemming from a mingling of the sexes in public life. As to the public welfare, Rabbi Kook advocated maintenance of the connection with the sources of Judaism and the Bible, in the name of which the nations of the world recognized at that time the rights of the people of Israel to the land of Israel. "As regards the ideal status of women" – that is, absolute equality of men and women – Rabbi Kook says that "that was a vision for the future… that is as yet entirely unreflected in contemporary cultural life, which is corrupt from within, even though it sparkles from without." Out of concern about injury to the delicate fabric of life and the balance between family life and public life, Rabbi Kook had reservations about granting election rights to women. In his usual manner, he based his decision not only on abstract halakhic principles, but upon his understanding of the delicate balance in the social reality of his time. This position was also advocated by Rabbi

Hayyim Ozer Grodzinski, of Vilna, Lithuania, and Rabbi Israel Meir ha-Kohen of Radin, near Vilna.

An entirely different approach was taken in a responsum written by Rabbi Ben Zion Ouziel, chief Sephardi rabbi of the Land of Israel (see *Resp. Mishpatei Uziel*, vol. 3, ḤM, no. 6). Regarding active election rights, Rabbi Uziel argued that there is no halakhic rule, implicit or explicit, that denies such rights. As for passive election rights, he was of the opinion that the position of Maimonides, according to which " only a man may be appointed for all offices in Israel" only applies to appointments by the Sanhedrin. Regarding a woman's eligibility for public office, however, there is no question of *appointment*, but only of *acceptance*. For by means of the elections a majority of the community expresses its opinion, consent, and trust as regards the elected persons, empowering them to supervise all public affairs; "even Maimonides admits that there is no hint of prohibition in this respect." As for the considerations of public welfare and modesty, Rabbi Ouziel wrote that:

> Reason would have it that there is no licentiousness in any serious conference or useful discussion; and every day, men meet with women on commercial business and negotiate with each other, yet none of this produces any alarm or outcry. Indeed, even those given to sexual abandon do not contemplate forbidden acts while they are seriously bent on their business affairs. The admonition of our Rabbis, 'Do not converse too much with a woman' (Mishnah, Avot 1:5), refers to unnecessary idle talk, the kind of conversation that leads to sin. It does not apply, however, to a conversation or debate about important public affairs; and sitting together for the purpose of public work, which is Divine service, does not engender sinful habits or lead to levity. The entire Jewish people, men and women, are holy and are not to be suspected of breaching the bounds of modesty and morality… In conclusion: (a) A woman has the full right [to participate in] elections so that she may be obligated to obey the representatives chosen to lead the people. (b) A woman can also be elected if the community consents and so legislates (*supra*, pp. 34–35).

Other views expressed on this issue were based on a different analysis of the social reality of the period, through which women were granted an allowance to vote and to be elected to public office by distinguished Rabbis (Shakdiel case, pp. 251–54). A different line of reasoning appeared in a responsum by Rabbi Yehiel Weinberg, who served as head of the Rabbinical Seminary in Berlin (*Resp. Seridei Esh*, vol. 2, no. 52, vol. 3 no. 105). He writes:

> "With respect to your question of women's election rights, Rabbi D.Z. Hoffman allowed them to vote but not to be elected; but the Rabbis in the Land of Israel, as well as Ḥafeẓ Ḥayyim and Rabbi Ḥayyim Ozer Grodzinski and others, barred even this active election right. On the other hand, Chief Rabbi Ouziel, in his *Resp. Mishpatei Uziel*, permits women to both vote and to stand for election. So why should I thrust myself into the controversy between those who permit and those who prohibit; *let time take its course and render the decision*."

Justice Elon interpreted this position as follows (*Shakdiel* case, pp. 260–61):

> That expression should not be regarded as an evasion of decision-making duty; rather, it embodies one of the methods employed in halakhic decision-making. As is known, custom is one of the sources of *halakhah*. At times custom serves to decide the law where there are different opinions among the halakhic authorities; sometimes it decides the law on a question that has arisen in practice and to which there is no known answer in the existing *halakhah* (a lacuna); and at times custom not only adds to the existing *halakhah* but even alters one of its rules. This latter function of custom is limited to civil or monetary law alone and, with certain exceptions, does not apply to matters of religious law (*issur*)… As for the role of custom in deciding the religious law where there are differences of opinion among the halakhic authorities, it states in the Talmud, in response to the question of how to decide the law when the authorities are divided: "Go out and see what the people are doing" (Ber. 45a; Eruv. 14b; TJ Pe'ah 7:5). "Let time take its course and render the decision," as Rabbi Weinberg put it, is thus an accepted method of decision-making: let the ultimate ruling be in accordance with the custom followed by the public. (See *Custom.)

Rabbi Moses Feinstein also discussed this issue in the course of a responsum (*Resp. Iggerot Moshe*, YD, vol. 2, no. 44) regarding "the widow of a scholar who was a *kashrut* supervisor, who has been left penniless and lacking means of sustenance for her orphan sons. She being a modest woman and truly God-fearing, and also wise, understanding, and responsible, [the question is] whether one may rely upon her to take the place of her husband as a supervisor, in this manner to provide for herself and her sons." Rabbi Feinstein ruled that "there is no reason for apprehension regarding her trustworthiness, for if she is regarded as a worthy woman who knows and understands how and what to supervise, she may be relied on." Further on, Rabbi Feinstein concludes that, while the office of *kashrut* supervisor is a position of authority, a woman may nevertheless be appointed to this office. In Rabbi Feinstein's view, Maimonides' ruling that only men may be appointed to an "office" is not based on any Talmudic source, but represents "his own reasoning," and there were many authorities who disagreed. "Therefore, because of the widow's great need for her sustenance and that of her orphan sons, one may rely on those who disagree with Maimonides and appoint her as a supervisor in her husband's stead" (*Shakdiel,* pp. 261–62).

The ruling on the sensitive matter of the *Shakdiel*, which was based on Jewish Law, concludes as follows:

> We are aware of the sensitivity of the halakhic, social, and public aspects of the matter. We are also aware of the grave reservations entertained by those entrusted by law with the power of decision, who have rightly sought to avoid an ideological or quasi-halakhic confrontation with the halakhic authorities in Israel today… But none of this is sufficient to free us from the decree of the Israeli law which prohibits discrimination against the petitioner that would exclude her from membership in the Yeroḥam religious council… It pains us that the decision [of the Chief Rabbinate of Israel] was not in favor of the petitioner, even though a decision in her favor would have the sanction of the *halakhah*, according to the opinion of prominent authorities" (*Shakdiel* pp. 271–72).

The Halakhah and Women's Study of Torah

THE RULING IN THE NAGAR CASE. Another example of creativity regarding the status of women in our time – which was also the subject of judicial rulings – relates to the study and teaching of Torah by women and to women. In the *halakhah*, this issue also relates to the issue of parent-child relations (see *Parent and Child). The issue of Torah study and the related issue of parent-child relations was subject to the judicial rulings of the Israeli Supreme Court, especially in the *Nagar* case, which was brought before a "Special Tribunal" composed of Chief Justice of the Supreme Court Meir Shamgar, Deputy Chief Justice Menachem Elon, and *dayyan* of the Rabbinical Court of Appeals Rabbi Joseph Kapaḥ (ST 81/1, *Yehiel Nagar v. Orah Nagar*, PD 38(1) 365 (henceforth *Nagar*)). The case began as a question of parent-child relations, but it came to include a comprehensive discussion of the issue of women and Torah study – both learning and teaching. It should be noted that the Nagar ruling relates to the status of women in the *domestic-social setting*, whereas the ruling in the Shakdiel case (which was given after the *Nagar* ruling) relates to the status of women in the *public setting*. The question to be decided in the Nagar case was: who has the right to decide about a child's education, his father or his mother? The case involved a divorced couple who disagreed about the educational system in which to enroll their children. The father, who was newly Orthodox, wished to enroll his children in the religious educational system, whereas the mother who continued her previous life-style, objected. The rabbinical court ruled that since *halakhah* imposes the obligation to educate his children on the father, he is entitled to decide on the type of education. In the framework of this case, the Supreme Court discussed two issues: the one, a parent's right and obligation to decide on a child's school; and the second, Torah study for women.

A PARENT'S RIGHT AND OBLIGATION TO DECIDE ON A CHILD'S EDUCATION. Justice Elon opened his discussion regarding the right and obligation to decide about a child's education as follows:

> With all due respect, it seems to me that the unequivocal assertion of the rabbinical court, that the obligation to educate his children devolves upon the father, and therefore it is he who has the exclusive right to decide on the form of that education, would not have withstood appeal in the Rabbinical Court of Appeals, had such an appeal ever been heard. Not only does this assertion contradict the Women's Equal Rights Law regarding equal rights of guardianship of the father and the mother, which requires that equal consideration be given to the preferences of the father and the mother regarding their children's education; with all due respect, it seems to me that this assertion does not even correspond to the accepted view on this issue in the world of *halakhah* of our time.

The ruling notes that various medieval authorities were of the opinion that Rabbi Johanan and Resh Lakish disagree on the question whether the obligation to educate a child in the performance of *mizvot* falls exclusively upon the father or also upon the mother (Naz. 28b; and Meiri, *Bet ha-Beḥirah*, ad loc.). Modern authorities also disagree on this matter (see: R. Abraham Danzig, *Ḥayyei Adam*, Sect. 66, no. 2: "A father is obligated to educate his son and daughter, and some say that the duty of education applies to the mother as well"; Rabbi Jacob Ettlinger, *Arukh le-Ner*, Suk. 2b). Moreover, the primary burden of education usually falls upon the mothers, "who send their children to school, oversee them to assure that they engage in Torah study, show them compassion when they come home from school, and encourage them with treats to desire Torah study" (Rabbi Jonah Gerondi, *Iggeret ha-Teshuvah*, no. 72). Mothers also bear greater responsibility for rebuking their children than do fathers, "because they are available and found more often at home" (Rabbi Isaiah Horowitz, *Shenei Luḥot ha-Berit, Sha'ar ha-Otiyot, Derekh Erez̧*). A mother's obligation finds explicit mention in Scripture: "My son, hear the instruction of your father, and do not forsake the Torah of your mother" (Prov. 1:8).

The right and duty to educate a child is a central factor with respect to his custody. In the context of custody rights, according to *halakhah*, the term education, includes, in addition to Torah study, vocational training and, most importantly, fashioning the child's personality. It is thus that halakhic scholars account for the assumption that the daughter must always be with her mother and, above the age of six, the son with his father: "For just as a mother will instruct her daughter in the way of girls, so a father will instruct his son what befits him" (Rabbenu Yeroḥam, *Toledot Adam ve-Ḥavah, Sefer Ḥavah*, Sect. 23:3); "And he must teach him the method of study and the ways of men" (*Resp. Rashba, ha-Meyuḥas la-Ramban*, no. 38; see also *Resp. Radbaz*, vol. 1, no.429). This is the basis for the ruling of the Rabbinical Court of Appeals that the distinction between boys and girls with respect to custody of a child over the age of six applies even when the parents are not religiously observant: "Even in a case where the two parties fail to educate their children toward the practice and study of Torah, the obligation of a father to his son and the right of the son vis-à-vis his father, is that the son should be near his father and in close connection with him, so that he may strengthen his masculine identity and character traits" (Rabbinical Appeal 33/39, p. 259, following R. Kapaḥ). Moreover, as for a son's education, "a father can teach his son what he is obligated to teach him, even if he is not with him, e.g., by hiring a teacher or apprenticing him to a craftsman" (responsum of R. Isaac Molina, published from a manuscript by Abraham David, *Kiryat Sefer* 44 (1969), 557). This has special significance in our day, when a child's education, in all its various forms, takes place in a wide variety of educational institutions. Thus, the Rabbinical Court of Appeals issued a ruling relating to the aforementioned distinction and making reference to a disagreement between Maimonides and Rabbi Abraham of Posquières (Yad, Ishut 21.17): "However, regarding a son who studies Torah, surely Maimonides writes… that the teacher must teach them all day long and part of the night, in order to train them to study during the day and at night… Thus, the father is not left with any time to teach his son, but only that he should be under his supervision for eating and sleeping, and regarding this it may be argued that the father has no priority over the mother" (File (Jerusalem) 24/42, p. 17, per R. Abraham Shapira).

This was also the conclusion in the *Nagar* case (p. 403): "While these arguments were put forward regarding the right of custody over the son, they also have considerable implications for the question of the priority given to the father to decide the form of [his son's] education-schooling. Since the child's education is no longer provided personally by the father, and it is not the father who teaches him, but rather the teachers in his school and his rabbis, it stands to reason that these should act as the agents of both the parents and with their consent."

TORAH STUDY FOR WOMEN. According to the *halakhah* in the Mishnah and Talmud, a father must teach his son Torah, but a mother is exempted from this obligation (Kid. 29a, Mishnah and Gemara *ibid.*). This law is summarized by Maimonides (Yad, Talmud Torah 1:1): "Women… are exempt from the study of Torah; but a father is required to teach his minor son Torah; as it is said: 'You shall teach them to your sons and speak of them' (Deut. 11:19). A woman is not required to teach her son, since only those who are obligated to study are also obligated to teach."

As early as in the tannaitic period, differing views were expressed regarding this "triple" exemption of women – the exemption of a mother with respect to teaching her son, of a woman with respect to study, and of a daughter with respect to being taught by her father. According to Ben Azzai, "One is obligated to teach his daughter Torah," while Rabbi Eliezer ben Horcanus took the view, "Whoever teaches his daughter Torah is considered as if he taught her *tiflut*" – licentiousness (M., Sot. 3:4). Although various talmudic and post-talmudic sources have spoken in praise of wise and learned women, the view of Rabbi Eliezer came to be accepted as the law.

With the passage of time, the law on this subject underwent a number of changes; the prohibition against teaching Torah to women was constructed more narrowly, both in terms of the subjects permitted to be taught (the Written Law and various laws with practical relevance) and how deeply the material should be taught. The *halakhah* established that a woman is under no obligation to study Torah, and therefore is not obligated to teach Torah. This was essentially the situation until different rulings and conceptions penetrated the world of *halakhah*, a small number over the course of history, and far more in recent generations.

The social changes that have transpired in recent times have had an evident and far-reaching effect on halakhic decision making regarding Torah study for woman and by women. Rabbi Zalman Sorotzkin, one of the leading authorities in the world of yeshivot, has ruled: "Recent times are not like earlier times: in earlier times, Jewish families lived according to the rules of the Shulḥan Arukh, and it was possible to learn the entire Torah from daily life at home… But today… not only is it *permitted* to teach Torah and reverence towards God to the daughters of our generation, but there is *an absolute duty* to do so, as we have explained; and it is a great *mitzvah* to establish schools for girls to implant in their hearts a pure faith and [to teach them] Torah and the commandments…" (Rabbi Zalman Sorotzkin, *Moznayim la-Mishpat*, 1955, sec. 42).

Halakhic decision-making does not break completely with the existing *halakhah*, but rather limits it, and distinguishes between prior and newly developing *halakhah*. In light of the contemporary social and ideological reality that is undergoing fundamental changes, women today are integrated in all areas of activity, in the academic world, in the business world, and in all social life. This reality is no longer commensurate with the conclusions drawn in a different time and under different circumstances, based upon the principle of "All the glory of the king's daughter is within" (Ps. 45:14). Familiarity with and knowledge of the halakhic sources is necessary for both men and women in order to deal with the challenges of the time. For this reason the prohibition to teach one's daughter Torah has been restricted. Rabbi Moshe Malka, head of the rabbinical court of Petaḥ Tikvah, summarized the matter as follows: "Rabbi Eliezer would certainly admit that it is not at all forbidden to teach a woman even the Oral Law, so that she may be able to exercise care in observing all the laws of the Torah that pertain to her work and activities. Indeed, it is our duty to educate her to the fullest extent possible…" (*Resp. Mikveh ha-Mayyim*, vol. 3, YD, no. 21).

The permission granted to women to study Torah, which has been understood by some as an obligation, was expanded in a ruling of Justice Elon, with the agreement of Dayyan Kapaḥ, to also include an obligation imposed on the woman to teach her children Torah (*Nagar,* pp. 406–7):

> In summary, as we have seen, the law that a father is obligated to teach his son Torah, but the mother is exempt, is based on the law that the father himself is obligated to study Torah, and the woman is exempt from such self-study, following the rule that only one whose duty it is to learn has a duty to teach. In our day, after such an fundamental change has taken place, that not only is there no prohibition, but women are even obligated to study Torah, and women not only study for themselves, but also teach the children of others, the conclusion seems to follow that the obligation to teach a son Torah falls equally upon the father and the mother, following the rule that whoever has the duty to learn has also the duty to teach. All the more so this is true when we are dealing with fulfilling the obligation by way of expressing an opinion regarding the school to which the son should be sent. And were I not hesitant, I would say that the Rabbinical Court of Appeals, had it been asked to deal with obligation of educating children, both sons and daughters, would have concluded that it is a joint right and obligation falling upon both parents, subject of course to the special education that a father must give to his son and a mother to her daughter through understanding of and identification with the children of their own gender.

WOMEN'S PRAYER. Another issue that the Supreme Court was asked to consider in connection with the status of women in the world of *halakhah* was that of public prayer conducted by women (see: HC 257/89 *Anat Hoffman et al v. the Trustee over the Western Wall et al.*; and HC 90/2410, *Susan Alter et al. v. the Minister of Religious Affairs*, 48 (2) PD 265–358 (henceforth Women of the Wall); Elon, *Ma'amad ha-Ishah*, p. 119–193).

The issue of women's prayer, their obligation and their exemption, and other related topics, has been discussed at length in the literature of *halakhah* and Jewish thought. The discussion has greatly expanded in recent times in light of the social changes that have transpired. The halakhic questions that have arisen in this connection relate to the laws of prayer: First, is a woman permitted to wear a *tallit*? And second, is she permitted to carry a Torah scroll and read from it? These two questions relate to another issue, namely, the nature of public prayer conducted by women.

Underlying these issues is the halakhic principle stating that women are exempt from time-bound positive commandments, that is, those whose performance depends upon a fixed date or time (e.g., during the day and not at night, during particular hours of the day, on specific days or festivals, and the like; M., Kid. 1:7; Kid. 32a; Maim. Yad, Avod. Zar. 12:3; Yad, Ẓiẓit 3:9; Sh. Ar., OḤ, 17:2; S.J. Berman, "The Status of Women in Halakhic Judaism," in: *Tradition*, 14 (1973) 11–13). Various rationales have been offered for this exemption (see, for example, R. Elyakim Ellinson, *Bein ha-Ishah le-Yoẓerah: Ha-Ishah ve-ha-Mitzvot* (vol. 1, second ed., Jerusalem, 1982), p. 30ff.) According to the prevalent view, a woman is exempt from these obligations so as to make it easier for her to fulfill her role in the world, and not because of any inferiority in relation to the man. In the world of Judaism, the primary role assigned to a woman is to build the home and family – "All the glory of the king's daughter is within" (Ps. 45:14). Hence, the Sages determined that any *mitzvah*, whose performance depends on a particular time, is not binding upon a woman, so as not to make it more difficult for her to fulfill that role.

This rationale is already found in the halakhic literature of the Middle Ages (see: *Sefer Abudraham ha-Shalem: Seder Tefillot shel Ḥol*, Pt. III, *Birkot ha-Mitzvot*), and was well-summarized by Rabbi Moses Feinstein (*Resp. Iggerot Moshe*, OḤ, pt. 4, no. 49):

> For most women in the world are not wealthy, and the burden of child-rearing, which is the most important work for God, blessed be He, and for the Torah… Women's nature is more amenable to child-rearing, for which reason they were granted the leniency of not being obligated in Torah study and the time-bound positive commandments. Therefore, even if the circumstances of living in the world would change for all women, and for wealthy women at all times, and even were it possible to transfer child-raising to certain men and woman, as in our country – Torah law would not change, nor even rabbinic law. … You must understand that this is not because women are lower in the level of holiness than men, for with respect to holiness they are equal to men regarding obligation in *mitzvot*. For the command of *mitzvot* is due only to the holiness found in Israel, and all the verses regarding holiness were said to the women as well. At the beginning of the conditions for receiving the Torah: "You shall be My own treasure from among all peoples… and you shall be to Me… a holy nation." All this was said to the house of Jacob, namely, the women, and told to the children of Israel, that is, the men. And wherever you find the matter of the holiness of Israel, it also refers to women. Therefore, women also recite blessings over the commandments, using the formula, "Who has sanctified us with His commandments," like men, even over those commandments that the Torah did not obligate her [to fulfill]. It is merely a leniency for some reason that God, blessed be He, wished to be lenient with them, as explained above, but not because of some deficiency, God forbid. As for the obligations between husband and wife, the husband is obligated to honor his wife, and the wife her husband, with no distinction. And many women were prophetesses and they were governed by all the laws of prophecy like men. They are praised for many things, both in Scripture and in the words of the Sages, of blessed memory, even more so than men. There is no belittlement of their dignity or anything else in the fact that they are exempt from Torah study and the time-bound positive commandments. And there is no reason for resentment whatsoever. This, you must explain over and over again."

A unique rationale for the exemption regarding time-bound positive commandments given to women was suggested by Rabbi Samson Raphael Hirsch, pioneer of the school of Torah with *derekh ereẓ* (in his commentary to Lev. 23:43): "Their exemption from time-bound positive commandments is most certainly not on account of their being considered in any way of lesser worth or importance. Rather, it seems to us much more likely that the Torah did not impose these commandments upon women because it did not consider it necessary that they be demanded of women. God's Torah takes it for granted that women have greater love and more devoted enthusiasm for their God-serving calling, and that this calling involves less danger in their case than for men whose devotion to Torah is more exposed to the temptations which occur in the course of business and professional life. Accordingly, it does not find it necessary to give women these spurring reminders to remain true to their calling, or warnings against weaknesses in their business lives.

Justice Elon summarized the issue in his ruling in the Women of the Wall case (pp. 305–6):

> The "exemption" from time-bound positive commandments – such as public prayer, *shofar* blowing (on Rosh ha-Shanah) and taking the *lulav* (on Sukkot) – does not deprive a woman of permission to fulfill these positive commandments if she so desires. According to many halakhic authorities, when a woman fulfills a time-bound positive commandment, she is also permitted to recite the same appropriate blessing as that said by men: "Who has sanctified us with His commandments and commanded us…" (*Tosafot*, Kid. 31a, s.v. *delo mafkidna*; Ramban, ad loc., s.v. *man de-amar li*; Ritva, novellae, ad loc., s.v. *katvu ba-Tosafot*; Ra'avyah, vol. 2, no. 597).

Based on the above, the halakhic authorities ruled that a woman who wishes to participate in congregational prayer is not counted toward a *minyan*, the required quorum of ten. This was based upon the reasonable and logical reason that one who is exempt from the *mitzvah* cannot be counted in the obligatory quorum that constitutes the *minyan*. The same rationale has been applied to a man who is exempt from *mitzvot* under certain circumstances. Thus, for example, a person whose close relative died but has not yet been brought to burial is classified as an *onen* – a person in the initial stage of mourning immediately after the death prior to the burial. During this period, he is exempt from the obligation to fulfill *mitzvot*, due to his emotional state and his preoccupation with the burial. According to many halakhic authorities, during this period of *onenut*, since he is exempt from the obligation to pray, he is not counted toward a *minyan* (*Sheyarei Keneset ha-Gedolah*, OḤ, 55; *Hagahot Bet Yosef*, 4; *Resp.* Paraḥ Mateh Aharon, vol. 1, no. 19; *Resp.* Shevut Ya'akov, vol. 2, no. 25).

For this reason, women are counted toward the required quorum with respect to obligations that for one reason or another bind them (e.g., Megillah reading, public sanctification of God's name, and others). Moreover, according to some halakhic authorities, women are obligated in prayer, but they are not obligated in *congregational prayer* (Ber. 20a–b; Maim. Yad, Tefillah 1:2; Sh. Ar., OḤ, 106:1–2, and *Magen Avraham*, ad loc., no. 2).

There is a difference of opinion as to whether women are obligated in all three daily prayers – the Morning, Afternoon, and Evening services – or only in some of them. According to one of the most noted authorities of the past century, Rabbi Israel Meir of Radin, women are obligated to recite the morning and afternoon services (*Mishneh Berurah* on Sh. Ar., OḤ 106.4). Others are of the opinion that women are not at all obligated in prayer, given that it is a time-bound positive commandment. According to *halakhah*, a *minyan* of ten men is required in order to fulfill the obligation of communal prayer, and only in a *minyan* may "matters of holiness" – that is, prayers and blessings which sanctify God, such as *kaddish*, *barekhu* and *kedushah* – be recited (Meg. 23b), and only in a *minyan* does the prayer leader repeat the *Amidah* prayer. Women are not counted toward a *minyan* of ten, for reasons that we will explain below. There are other matters as well – e.g., the priestly blessing, the special *zimmun* recited in the presence of ten, and others – that require a quorum of ten men. The halakhic authorities disagree about the underlying rationale (see Maim., Yad, Tefilah 8:4–6; Sh. Ar., OḤ, 55:1, 69:1). As stated above, women are not counted toward the required minyan, except in certain special cases, according to certain halakhic authorities (see: A. Frimer, "Women and Minyan," in: *Tradition*, 23:4 (1988), pp. 54ff.; A. Weiss, *Women at Prayer* (1990 (13–56)).

It follows from all the above that *halakhah* does not take a hierarchical or condescending attitude toward women. On the contrary, women have "greater affection and more devoted enthusiasm" than men, and it was unnecessary for time-bound positive commandments to be required of them. The halakhic exemption granted women is rooted in *halakhah*'s great attentiveness to the special circumstances of a woman's life, the fact that the burden of child-rearing falls primarily on her shoulders. It is, therefore, clear that she is permitted to take part in the observance of such *mitzvot*, even if she is not obligated to do so (see: D. Sperber, "*Tefilat Nashim*," in *Minhagei Yisra'el* (vol. 7, Jerusalem, 2003), pp. 68–81).

Halakhah's attitude toward the new phenomenon of-women's "prayer groups" has been discussed in light of the sources cited above. The discussions begin with concrete halakhic questions, e.g., wearing a *tallit* and reading the Torah.

Women are exempt from wearing *ẓiẓit* (ritual fringes) and wrapping themselves in a *tallit*, for this is a *mitzvah* that is considered among the time-bound positive commandments, its obligation being limited to daytime, as opposed to night. However, as stated earlier, while women are *exempt* from the obligation to fulfill time-bound positive commandments, they are *permitted* to do so. This applies to the *mitzvah* of *ẓiẓit* as well. In fact, it is in the context of his discussion of this *mitzvah* that Maimonides records the general principle. He states as follows (Yad, Ẓiẓit 3:9): "Women… are exempted by scriptural law from the obligation of having fringes on their garments… If women… desire to wear garments with fringes, no objection is raised, but they do not recite the blessing. The same is the rule with respect to other positive precepts from the obligation of which women are exempt. If they wish to fulfill them without reciting the blessing, no objection is raised." R. Abraham of Posquières agrees that women may fulfill such precepts (*Hagahot ha-Rabad*, ad loc.), and adds that they may even recite a blessing (see also Rabad's comment to *Sifra*, *Vayikra*, *parshata* 2).

There are divergent views in the world of *halakhah* regarding whether or not women who fulfill time-bound positive commandments of their own volition are permitted to recite a blessing. Rabbi Moses Feinstein, in the previously mentioned responsum (*Resp. Iggerot Moshe*, OḤ, part 4, no. 49) rules that, just as women are permitted in general to fulfill time-bound positive commandments and to recite a blessing over them, so too regarding *ẓiẓit*, "a woman who so desires may don a four-cornered garment that is different than a man's garment, put fringes on it, and fulfill the *mitzvah*." But he adds a reservation that runs throughout the responsum: "Clearly, however, this only applies when her soul yearns to fulfill the precepts, even though she was not commanded. Since, however, this is not her intention, but only an aspect of her protest against the Torah, this is not at all an act of *mitzvah*, but, on the contrary, a forbidden act, involving the heresy of believing that the laws of the Torah can be changed." Justice Elon commented on this reasoning (*Ma'amad ha-Ishah*, pp. 131–32):

> "The requirement is that one must perform a *mitzvah* for the purpose of fulfilling the mitzvah, and not out of disregard for a halakhic rule, motivated by 'the alien consideration' of objecting in principle to the exemption because it is offensive to women. In the world of *halakhah* this requirement serves as a firm foundation for legislating enactments, instituting customs and introducing changes into them. The litigants presented us with a letter written by Rabbi Tendler, Rabbi Feinstein's son-in-law, clarifying his father-in-law's position as to his concern that the women's prayer groups are motivated by alien considerations, as stated above, and that the permission to wear a *tallit* applies only when it is clear that their intention is for the sake of

Heaven, without any questioning of Israel's Torah and customs. This argument is included among the moral understandings of the world of *halakhah*, which serve as a weighty factor in *halakhah*'s policy of decision-making in general, and in especially sensitive issues, like the one before us, in particular.

In both earlier and more recent generations, there were women who were accustomed to wear a *tallit* and recite a blessing, with the approval of the halakhic authorities (see Y.Z. Kahana, *Teshuvot, Pesakim u-Minhagim Maharam mi-Rotenburg*, p. 141, no. 24; *Resp. Ẓemaḥ Ẓedek*, OḤ, no. 3, which goes into a full and detailed discussion of the issue; Y.M. Toledano, *Ner ha-Ma'arav*, p. 155; and see S. Ashkenazi, *Ha-Ishah ba-Aspaklariyat ha-Yahadut*, 1953, vol. 1, p. 137). It was nevertheless not the general custom of women, at least not in recent generations, to wear *ẓiẓit* or enwrap themselves in a *tallit*, unlike the case regarding other time-bound positive commandments, such as blowing the *shofar*, waving the *lulav*, or sitting in the *sukkah*, which they were accustomed to fulfill. The reason lies in the custom, first mentioned by the Maharil, that women should abstain from so doing (*Resp. Maharil ha-Ḥadashot*, Jerusalem, 1977, OḤ, no. 7, pp. 13–14). The custom is cited by the Rema (Sh. Ar., OḤ, 17.2) as follows: "Nevertheless, if [women] wish to wrap themselves [in a *tallit*] and recite the blessing, they are permitted to do so, just as is the case with the other time-bound positive commandments… It appears, however, as haughtiness. Therefore, they should not wear *ẓiẓit*, since it is not an obligation on the person." According to some more recent authorities, the common practice today is in fact that women do not wear *ẓiẓit* (*Kaf ha-Ḥayyim*, OḤ, 17, no. 8; *Arukh ha-Shulḥan*, OḤ, 17:2–3, and see there the explanation offered by the author of the *Arukh ha-Shulḥan* regarding what the Rema says that "it appears as haughtiness," and his conclusion: "Therefore, we do not allow her to practice this *mitzvah*, and thus is the custom, and there must be no deviations"; cf. Rabbi S. Yisraeli, "*Nashim be-Kiyyum Mitzvot*," in *Ha-Ishah ve-Ḥinukhah* (Emunah, 1980, p. 29).

As for the issue of Torah reading by women, most halakhic authorities maintain that a woman is exempt from the obligation of public Torah reading, since it is regarded as a time-bound positive commandment (*Tosafot*, R.H. 33a, s.v. *ha-Rabbi Yehudah, ha-Rabbi Yose*; and see there a detailed discussion of most of the topics discussed here; Ran on Alfasi, Meg. 23a, s.v., *ha-kol olin le-minyan shiv'ah*; *Resp. Maharsham*, vol. 1, no. 158; *Arokh ha-Shulkhan* OḤ, 182:6). The *mitzvah* of public Torah reading is defined as a time-bound positive commandment, since it is limited to specific times. Women, therefore, are not counted toward the quorum of ten required for the Torah reading, just as they are not counted toward the quorum of ten required for congregational prayer. They are, however, permitted to read the Torah in the context of women's prayer groups. A question arises regarding the *barekhu* blessing that accompanies the Torah reading, since that falls into the category of *devarim she-bi-kedushah*. Rabbi Tendler summarized the issue in his aforementioned letter: "They may also read from a Torah scroll, but they must be careful to do so in such a way that it not be mistaken for public Torah reading. For example, they may not recite a blessing in public; either they should rely on a blessing that had been recited earlier, or if such a blessing had not yet been recited, they should recite it quietly to themselves." The letter concludes: "There is no absolute prohibition for a menstruating woman to gaze upon or touch a Torah scroll. While it is proper to be stringent, nevertheless it has become customary to be lenient in the matter." It is on this basis that the question of a women's *minyan* was discussed.

Before the modern period, women generally did not go to synagogue for the purpose of congregational prayer. In modern times, women began to attend synagogue services on the Sabbath and festivals. The prayer service and Torah reading was conducted entirely by the men and in the men's section. The woman sat in the women's section that was set apart from the men's section. They played a solely passive role in the service, that is to say, in the women's section, they recited the entire prayer service that was recited and conducted in the men's section. In the last generation, certain women have expressed the desire to conduct a prayer service that would be composed and conducted entirely by women, but not as was customary in a *minyan* composed of men – that is, with *kaddish*, *barekhu*, and other such elements – but rather without these passages, so as not to violate the laws of *halakhah*. These women referred to such services as "prayer groups" or "*tefillah* groups," in order to distinguish between them and a men's *minyan*. Some Orthodox rabbis have supported these women's prayer groups; others, however, while recognizing and encouraging the social and intellectual achievements of religiously observant women in our day, object to women's "prayer groups," and view them as a serious violation of *halakhah* (Women of the Wall, pp. 306–7).

Today, the number of women's "prayer groups" is not large; they were first established in the United States, and there are only a few of them in the State of Israel. The two approaches of Orthodox Jewry, while agreeing on many points, differ bitterly on this issue, the controversy having found widespread written expression. Rabbi Herschel Schechter ("*Ẓe'i Lakh be-Ikvei ha-Ẓon*," in *Beit Yiẓḥak*, 17 (1985), 118, at p. 127 (henceforth: Schechter)) maintains that: "We have never seen nor heard of such a practice of arranging a separate Torah or *megillah* reading for women, or of arranging separate *hakafot* for women. The obligation falls upon us to continue the tradition of our fathers and their fathers before them regarding the manner of observing the *mitzvot*." Therefore, "since women had never been accustomed to observe the *mitzvot* of prayer and Torah reading in this manner, we must not deviate from the tradition of our fathers, and make up new practices… Not only must we continue the tradition of our fathers, but there is also a prohibition to deviate from customary practices. While it is true that 'we have never seen' is not proof, nevertheless, the *Shakh* (YD 1:1) has already explained… that in any event such conduct establishes a custom… and thus these practices involve [the violation of] the prohibition of changing customs" (*ibid.*, pp. 128–29).

This approach was not accepted by Justice Elon who stated (Women of the Wall, p. 313): "This assertion is not free of uncertainty. The absence of a custom does not necessarily constitute proof of the negation of that arrangement; in certain situations there exists a lacuna which may be filled, when the time and the need arrive – obviously, when this does not involve [the violation of] a halakhic prohibition."

Rabbi Schechter views Orthodox women's prayer groups as a "falsification of the Torah" (p. 119), because "it is their intention to show everyone that women are as important as men." According to Rabbi Schechter, the congregational prayer of these Orthodox women involves a violation of the prohibition against adopting non-Jewish practices (*ibid.*, p. 131). For "it is known that these practices were not introduced in our time in a vacuum, but as a result of the general movement for the liberation of women, whose objective in this area is licentiousness, to equate women with men in every way possible" (*ibid.*). The reference here is not to non-Jewish practices in general, but to "non-Jewish practices regarding the performance of religious duties" (*ibid.*). Justice Elon commented on this (Women of the Wall, pp. 321–25):

> With all due respect to the distinguished author, it is difficult to fully understand what he means. Why should we suspect those who participate in the public prayer groups designed for women and conducted by them of such grave intentions and objectives, when their entire conduct demonstrates their meticulousness about *halakhah*: for example, not to recite *devarim she-bi-kedushah*, such as the prayer leader's repetition of the *Amidah* and the like? Does this not in itself prove that the objective of the organizers of the women's public prayer services – with their observance of the framework of *halakhah* and its laws – is [to fill] a spiritual need that stems from knowledge of the *mitzvot* and *halakhah*, of the Torah and the ways of Torah scholars and thinkers? This seems so, particularly in light of the fact that these young girls, teenagers, and women, are meticulous about the ways of *halakhah*, both trivial and serious, and have studied for many years in educational institutions that promote Torah and *derekh ereẓ*, and it is because of this education that they seek their own expression, within the framework of *halakhah*, by way of prayer groups, the subject of our discussion.

In Rabbi Schechter's sharp objection to women's prayer groups, even when they do not constitute a "*minyan*," he relies on the rulings of two of the generation's leading authorities, Rabbi Moses Feinstein and Rabbi Joseph B. Soloveitchik. Rabbi A. Weiss correctly noted that Rabbi Schechter was imprecise on this point. As for the position of Rabbi Soloveitchik, nothing was ever committed to writing, and the view that is attributed to him was reported by rabbis and disciples who had consulted with him. According to their reports, Rabbi Soloveitchik did not object to the existence of women's prayer groups per se, but to particular elements that were practiced in such groups, such as the recitation of the blessing before and after the Torah reading (see Rabbi Weiss, *ibid.*, pp. 107–8). As for the position of Rabbi Moses Feinstein, this is stated explicitly in a detailed responsum (*Resp. Iggerot Moshe*, OḤ, pt. 4, no. 49), mentioned earlier. This responsum does not give voice to an objection in principle to women's prayer groups, when their intentions are in fact for the sake of Heaven, but only to certain changes adopted in such prayer groups regarding Torah reading (see Rabbi Weiss, *ibid.*, pp. 108–10). As stated in earlier comments, according to Rabbi Schechter, the world of *halakhah*, by its very essence, is not stagnant; it is open to new laws and enactments, according to the needs of the time and place. There are, however, matters and principles regarding which halakhic creativity must demonstrate great caution, and according to him, the matter under discussion is included among them. He is aware of the changes that have occurred in recent generations regarding the social standing of women, their knowledge of *halakhah* and their general education, but he argues that all these do not justify the changes involved in women's prayer groups, that are influenced by alien and non-halakhic considerations, with all that they involve with respect to the centrality of prayer and the synagogue in Jewish tradition (see, *ibid.*, end of p. 125 and p. 127ff. regarding "the pillar of *mitzvah* in the deeds of *mitzvah*, and pp. 130–31 regarding the special stringency concerning "synagogue traditions").

Rabbi Weiss espouses the opposite view. In his comprehensive monograph on the topic, he concludes his discussion of women's prayer groups with the following (pp. 123–24): "Within Halakhic guidelines, woman may participate in women's prayer groups, as long as these groups fall into the halakhic category of *tefillah* and not *minyan*… Participants in such groups are not rebelling against Torah Judaism. Quite the contrary. They are seeking to instill greater religious meaning in their lives. Their purpose is not to diminish the Torah, but to enhance their Jewish commitment and halakhic observance… Their quest to reach nobly to attain this lofty objective should be applauded."

THE WOMEN OF THE WALL CASE. The issue of women's prayer was dealt with by the Israeli Supreme Court on several occasions. The first ruling (Women of the Wall case) involved two petitions presented by women who wished to conduct their prayer service in the Western Wall plaza, while carrying Torah scrolls, wearing *tallitot*, and reading out loud from the Torah. The prayer of these women aroused the fierce objection of the overwhelming majority of those praying at the Wall – both men and women – which was accompanied by disturbances and physical and verbal violence. Justice Elon issued a detailed and comprehensive ruling on the matter, close to a hundred pages in length, based on the above-cited and other sources. While he was of the opinion that a women's *minyan* does not contradict the Jewish character of the state, *he ruled that there must be no deviations from local custom, because changes in custom will result in strife and quarreling.* He concludes his ruling as follows (pp. 350–51):

> It is clear beyond all doubt that granting the petitions before us will give rise to exceedingly difficult, bitter, and sharp controversy, accompanied by violence that will end in bloodshed. It is an uncontested fact that the overwhelming majority of people visiting the Western Wall day and night for the purpose of prayer are counted among those who maintain and believe,

> honestly and innocently, that the changes sought in the two petitions before us involve a desecration of the prayer site adjacent to the Western Wall. Not only would these changes lead to very difficult and violent controversy, but the laws of *halakhah* would prevent people, men and women, from conducting their prayers at the Wall… It is clear and unnecessary to say that the petitioners have the right to pray as they please in their congregations and synagogues, and nobody will prevent them from doing so. The freedom of worship of the petitioners remains firmly in place. However, owing to the uniqueness of the Western Wall, and the great sensitivity in the holiest place to the entire Jewish people, prayer in this unique and special place should be conducted in accordance with the common denominator that allows for the prayer of every Jew; namely, in accordance with the custom that has prevailed there for generations.

It should be noted that the Supreme Court addressed the issue in two additional, later occasions (HC 3358/95 *Anat Hoffman et al v. Administrative Director of the Prime Minister's Office et al*, PD 54(2) 345; HC 4128/00, *Administrative Director of the Prime Minister's Office v. Anat Hoffman et al*, PD 57(3) 289).

BAT MITZVAH CELEBRATIONS. As we have seen, practice and custom (see **Minhag*) have had great impact upon decision-making in matters related to the status of women. In this context it is interesting to examine the attitude of the halakhic authorities to the celebration of bat mitzvah of a young girl who has reached the age of maturity (*Ma'amad ha-Ishah*, pp. 137–42). It should first be noted that Rabbi Yehiel Weinberg discussed the issue (*Resp. Seridei Esh*, vol. 3, nos. 93–96) whether it is permissible to perform circumcision of an infant, or that of an adult who had not been circumcised in infancy, under anesthesia, in order to lessen the pain and suffering caused by the procedure. He answers in the negative, especially with respect to the circumcision of an adult. In another responsum, Rabbi Weinberg was asked about celebrating the bat mitzvah of a girl upon reaching her 12th birthday, just as it has always been customary to celebrate a boy's bar mitzvah upon his reaching the age of 13. On this matter, he answered in the affirmative, namely, that a celebration should be held for a girl as well. What is common to the two responsa is that they both deal with innovative practices, the one regarding circumcision, and the other regarding the celebration of bat mitzvah. In a lengthy and detailed responsum, Rabbi Weinberg explains his negative reply regarding the use of an anesthetic during circumcision, arguing that this possibility had already existed in ancient times, during the Talmudic period, but it had met with the opposition of the halakhic authorities for the halakhic reasons detailed in his responsum. This being the case, we apply the principle that "the custom of Israel is considered Torah," and do not deviate from the customary practice. In contrast, regarding the celebration of a girl's bat mitzvah, Rabbi Weinberg's reply was in the affirmative, and the reasoning expressed in his responsum is very instructive. Indeed, bat mitzvah celebrations had not been customary in previous generations, and thus, "there are those who argue against allowing a bat mitzvah celebration, on the grounds that it contradicts the custom of the earlier generations, who did not practice this custom" (*ibid.*, p. 297, col. 1). However, he refutes this argument:

> In truth, however, this is not a [valid] argument, for in earlier generations it was unnecessary to engage in girls' education, for every Jew was full of Torah and fear of God, and the air of every community in Israel was filled with the spirit of Judaism… Now, however, the generations have drastically changed… [Moreover,] It pains the heart that with regard to general education – the teaching of languages, secular literature, natural sciences, and humanities – people are concerned about girls in the same way that they are concerned about boys, but they totally neglect religious education – the study of Scripture and the ethical literature of the Sages, and training in the practical *mitzvot* that are binding upon women. Fortunately, the leading authorities of the previous generation recognized the problem and established institutions of Torah and religious strengthening for Jewish girls. The establishment of the great and comprehensive network of Bet Ya'akov schools is the noblest demonstration of our generation. Common sense and pedagogical principle almost demand that we celebrate a girl's reaching the obligation of *mitzvot*. The distinction made between boys and girls regarding the celebration of their maturity seriously offends the sensitivities of the girl who comes of age (*ibid.*, p. 297, col. 2).

As for the concern of "alien considerations" underlying the introduction of the new practice of celebrating a bat mitzvah – that is to say, such celebrations involve an imitation of non-Jewish practices – Rabbi Weinberg says as follows:

> Our brothers who have recently introduced the practice of celebrating a bat mitzvah say that they have done so in order to strengthen in the heart of a girl who has reached [the age of] *mitzvot* her love for Judaism and its commandments, and to arouse a feeling of pride in her Judaism and in her being the daughter of a great and holy people. It is of no concern to us that the Gentiles also celebrate confirmation whether for boys or for girls; they conduct their ceremony and we ours; they pray and bow down in their churches and we bow down and prostrate ourselves and give thanks to the King of Kings, the Holy One, blessed be He (*ibid.*, p. 297, col. 1).

Justice Elon summarizes this issue in the aforementioned Women of the Wall case:

> In summation, a custom that deviates from a pre-existing custom, such as using anesthetics during circumcision, should not be accepted; for this is the power of custom, that it becomes law, and there is no halakhic justification to change it, unless it is justified in the light of the social changes and legitimate ideological changes in the world of *halakhah*. On the other hand, introducing a new custom, such as celebrating a girl's bat mitzvah, which does not contradict the existing law, and whose non-existence in the past stems from a specific social-ideological reality that has now entirely changed… It is right and fitting that it be accepted, on its own merits and in order to prevent a situation in our generation, as formulated by Rabbi Yehiel Weinberg, in which "the distinction made between boys and girls regarding the celebration of their maturity seriously offends the sensitivities of the girl who comes of age."

The practice of celebrating a girl's *bat mitzvah* upon her reaching the age of 12 was also discussed by Rabbi Moses Feinstein (*Resp. Iggerot Moshe*, OḤ, no. 104). Rabbi Feinstein raises doubts about the propriety of introducing the custom of a bat mitzvah celebration, and he sees such a celebration, not as a *se'udat mitzvah* [a meal constituting a *mitzvah*], but merely a birthday party." Rabbi Feinstein absolutely forbids the celebration of a bat mitzvah in a synagogue, but permits it at home. He adds that this celebration involves the alien consideration of imitating a practice observed in circles that do not accept *halakhah* whatsoever.

Rabbi Feinstein's responsum implies that he was not in favor at all of introducing the custom of celebrating bat mitzvah. In this connection, there is an interesting ruling of the former chief Sephardi rabbi of Israel, Rabbi Ovadiah Yosef, who views the celebration in a positive light, and even promotes it: "It seems that there is certainly a *mitzvah* to arrange a joyous meal for the bat mitzvah, according to what Maharshal (R. Solomon Luria) says in *Yam shel Shelomo* (*Bava Kamma*, Ch. 7. 37) that there is no *se'udat mitzvah* greater than a bar mitzvah banquet… Since she becomes obligated in the *mitzvot*, and she is like an adult who is commanded to perform the *mitzvot*, regarding all the *mitzvot* that are binding upon a woman, [the celebration] is certainly a *mitzvah*" (*Resp. Yabi'a Omer*, Vol. 6, OḤ, no. 29, sec. 4). Rabbi Yosef discusses the issue again in another responsum (*Resp. Yeḥavveh Da'at*, vol. 2, no. 29), where he writes (p. 111): "In truth, opposing bat mitzvah celebrations allows sinners to accuse the Sages of Israel of depriving the daughters of Israel and discriminating between boys and girls." He also cites and relies upon the words of Rabbi Yehiel Weinberg, in responsum no. 93, that this does not involve emulation of non-Jewish practices, and the non-celebration of a bat mitzvah involves discrimination against girls and a serious offense to a girl's sensitivities. Further on, R. Yosef relies on additional responsa of contemporary Sephardi sages, including Rabbi Ovadiah Hadayah, who allow bat mitzvah celebrations (*Resp. Yaskil Avdi*, vol. 5, OḤ, no. 28). Rabbi Ovadiah Yosef refers to the position of Rabbi Moses Feinstein, who raised doubts about the propriety of celebrating a bat mitzvah, as stated earlier, and expresses his disagreement: "But with all due respect, his words are incorrect, for since she becomes obligated in the *mitzvot*, and she is like an adult who is commanded to perform the *mitzvot*, regarding all the *mitzvot* that are binding upon a woman, [the celebration] is certainly a *mitzvah*" (*Resp. Yabi'a Omer, ibid.*)

Rabbi Ovadiah Yosef summarizes his ruling as follows (*Resp. Yeḥavveh Da'at*, *ibid.*): "The practice of making a celebration and festive meal of thanksgiving in honor of a bat mitzvah girl on the day she reaches 12 years and a day is a good and fitting practice. And it is preferable that they speak there words of Torah, as well as praises of God. One must be meticulously careful to observe the rules of modesty according to our holy Torah… And God will not withhold good from those who walk uprightly." (Regarding bat mitzvah celebrations, see *Ma'amad ha-Ishah*, pp. 137–42, 145, 149–150).

AGUNOT. A major and central topic relating to the status of woman in the world of Judaism is the topic of *agunot* (wives who are unable to receive a *get* due to husband's recalcitrance or disappearance). This discussion of this issue began in the tannaitic period and continues to this very day, and it is a striking example of creativity and decision-making in the world of *halakhah*, in accordance with the time, place and situation, and in accordance with the truth of the law and the truth of the judge. It is an instructive example of the influence of historical reality on the methods of creating and fashioning *halakhah*, and regarding the integration of *halakhah* and society in the world of Judaism – thoughts, doubts and differences of opinion. The issue is multi-faceted – an entire world of *halakhah* and Jewish thought. (For a detailed discussion, see *Agunah).

In this context we will cite the following comments of Justice Elon's (M. Elon, *Ḥakikah Datit be-Ḥukei Medinat Yisra'el u-bi-Shefitah shel Batei ha-Mishpat u-Batei ha-Din ha-Rabbaniyyim* (1968), pp. 182–84):

> *Halakhah* has the capability, the authority, and the duty to resolve, those problems, the results of which contradict the goals of the halakhic system itself, and which from the perspective of *halakhah* itself, must be resolved. The classic example of such problems are cases of *agunah*, whether resulting from the disappearance of the husband or other similar situations. Needless to say, *halakhah* has no interest in causing the woman pain and suffering; *halakhah*'s sole interest is that a married woman not take another husband, and that a *yevamah* (widow whose husband died without offspring) who did not perform *halitzah*, not be permitted to others. There may be ways of not regarding the woman as a married woman, for example, by way of a condition attached to the marriage and by way of a nullification of the betrothal – as a result of which the widow will not be regarded as a *yevamah*. This manner of solution was introduced by Mahari Brin (Sh. Ar., EH, 157:3). In such cases, *halakhah* has both the authority and the duty to resolve these problems, for it is the goal of *halakhah* that the woman – every woman –not remain an *agunah*. This is the background of the extensive discussion found in halakhic literature of ways to release an *agunah*, beginning with Rabban Gamaliel the Elder through countless generations of those who made enactments and proposed solutions in order to save a woman from being and suffering as an *agunah*. It should be stated and emphasized that the way to resolve the matter is not easy, if only for the reason that in recent centuries the tendency has been to make little or no use whatsoever of ordinances in this sensitive and delicate area of marital law. However, the needs of the individual and the community, and most importantly, the essence and goals of *halakhah* itself, necessitate the speedy resolution of these problems in the framework of *halakhah* and by the halakhic authorities.

It should again be noted that a partial resolution of the problem of *agunot* has been reached through the legislation and judicial rulings of the State of Israel, i.e., through the sanctions (*harḥakot*) mentioned in Rabbinical Courts Law (Enforcement of Divorce Judgments) 5755 – 1995 (see: *Ma'amad ha-Ishah*, pp. 351–52). These sanctions follow in the footsteps of the enactments of Rabbenu Tam, one of the greatest Tosafists of the 12th century. The coercive force of such sanctions is limited, when the husband refuses to submit and continues in his perverse and abusive ways, despite the sanctions imposed upon him. Similarly, these sanctions are effective only when the *agunah's* husband lives within the borders of the State of Israel, but not when he lives outside the country, where Israeli law cannot be executed or enforced. It may, however, be assumed that the very passage of the law of sanctions in the State of Israel has had a certain impact on Jewish courts around the world, especially when the sanctions are based and rooted in the world of *halakhah* in the ordinances of Rabbenu Tam.

The fitting and complete resolution of this problem would lie in the enactment of a *takkanah* allowing for the retroactive nullification of the marriage, based on a two-thousand-year-old enactment of Rabban Gamaliel the Elder, *nasi* of the Sanhedrin in the Land of Israel. Today, when the Land of Israel and the State of Israel have once again been reestablished as the center of the Jewish people – out of this new reality there have emerged the need and the possibility of resolving the problem of *agunot* by way of the enactment of a *takkanah* allowing for nullification of the marriage, an enactment initiated in the Land of Israel and in the State of Israel, around which the entire Jewish people throughout the Diaspora will rally.

A change as blessed and as momentous as the change that has transpired in our days with the establishment of the State of Israel can and should bring about the restoration of the enactment, the basis of which is found in the tannaitic period, and which was in effect for many generations– namely, nullification of a marriage based on the principle that a man takes a woman under the conditions laid down by the rabbis, and the rabbis – the halakhic authorities in the Land of Israel and the dispersion – may annul the marriage. This is the way of resolving the *agunah* problem and of redeeming the *agunot* from their plight (see *Ma'amad ha-Ishah*, pp. 297–372).

Conclusion

In one of the major rulings the Israeli Supreme Court dealing with the status of women, the court stated the following: (Shakdiel case, pp. 269–70):

> It need scarcely be said that in the world of the *halakhah* we do not discuss purely legal-halakhic questions, in the sense of juridical rights and duties. Rather, the ideological and normative values of Jewish religious life are inherent in and inseparable from the subject of the discourse. For there is a great principle: "Read not *halikhot* [ways], but *halakhot* [laws]." In the same way we can say by way of paraphrase: "Read not *halakhot*, but *halikhot*. For the laws of justice and the ways of life are intertwined. The scholarly passages here cited are not limited to the exposition of the legal issues, but also contain lengthy and detailed discussions of the conceptual implications of Jewish family life – the roles of the father and the mother, of woman and man, domestic harmony, the concept of modesty, and so on. This is because examination of these concepts is essential to the juridical-halakhic ruling on our subject. However, these important concepts must be addressed according to both their original significance and their contemporary setting, as we have learned from the passages quoted.

At the end of the book, *Ma'amad ha-Ishah – Mishpat ve-Shiput, Masoret u-Temurah: Arakhehah shel Medinah Yehudit ve-Demografit* (pp. 453–56), Justice Elon writes:

> We have chosen a concrete example, a specific topic, which contains a combination of "Jewish" and "democratic," with the objective of analyzing the detailed laws, *halakhot* and principles in it; how the laws, *halakhot* and principles work and how they were applied in the social, economic and practical reality in which they were activated and applied; how "this one came and taught about that one, and that one came and completed this one, and they became as one in our hands." For there is no comparison between a general examination of principles and a detailed discussion of its practical applications in daily life… which is an issue that lives, breathes, acts, is acted upon, is activated and activates, diversified and many-faceted – in every period and in every society.

Rabbi Samuel Harkevalti writes (*Resp. Ma'ayan Ganim*, no. 313): "The women whose hearts made them willing to approach the work, the work of God, out of their choice of good, they will ascend the mountain of God, and rest in His holy place, for they are distinguished women. And it is incumbent upon the Sages of their generation to glory and honor them, and strengthen their hands, 'Go and succeed, may Heaven help you.'" It seems that the issue of the status of women that is dealt with in many entries in this Encyclopedia and in many rulings of the Israeli Supreme Court have created a synthesis between its being a Jewish state and its being democratic.

Justice Elon concludes his book (p.456):

> Out of all this, so we hope, it will be easier for us to understand the importance, the necessity and the possibility of executing and fulfilling the role and mission imposed upon us, as stated in Basic Law: Human Dignity and Liberty and Basic Law: Freedom of Occupation: "to establish in a Basic Law the values of the State of Israel as a Jewish and democratic state" – the strength and creativity of the Jewish together with the democratic. May this be the reward of our toil and study.

[Menachem Elon (2nd ed.)]

BIBLIOGRAPHY: HISTORICAL PERSPECTIVE: BIBLICAL PERIOD: E.W. Barber and E. Wayland, *Women's Work: The First 20,000 Years* (1994); D. Bloch, "Marriage and Family in Ancient Israel," in: K.M. Campbell (ed.), *Marriage and Family in the Biblical World* (2003), 33–102; R.M. Ehrenreich, C.L. Crumley, and J. Levy (eds.), *Heterarchy and the Analysis of Complex Societies* (1995); T. Eskenazi. "Out of the Shadows: Biblical Women in the Postexilic Era," in: *Journal for the Study of the Old Testament*, 54 (1992), 25–43; M. Gruber, "Women in the Cult according to the Priestly Code," in: *The Motherhood of God and Other Studies* (1992), 49–68; C. Meyers, *Discovering Eve: Ancient Israelite Women in Context* (1988); idem, "The Drum-Dance-Song Ensemble: Women's Performance in Biblical Israel," in: K. Marshall (ed.), *Rediscovering the Muses* (1993), 49–67, 234–38; idem, "The Hannah Narrative in Feminist Perspective," in: J. Coleson and V. Matthews (eds.), *Go to the Land that I Will Show You* (1994), 117–26; idem, "Everyday Life: Women in the Period of the Hebrew Bible," in: C.A. Newsome and S.H. Ringe (eds.), *Women's Bible Commentary* (expanded edition) (1998), 251–59; "Everyday Life in Biblical Israel: Women's Social Networks," in: R.E. Averbeck, M.W. Chavalas, and D.B. Weisberg (eds.), *Life and Culture in the Ancient Near East* (2003), 185–204; "Material Remains and Social Relations: Women's Culture in Agrarian Households of the Iron Age," in: W.G. Dever and

S. Gitin (eds.), *Symbiosis, Symbolism, and the Power of the Past: Canaan, Ancient Israel, and Their Neighbors from the Late Bronze Age through Roman Palestine* (2003), 425–44; *Households and Holiness: The Religious Culture of Israelite Women* (2005); C. Meyers, T. Craven, and R.S. Kraemer (eds.), *Women in Scripture: A Dictionary of Named and Unnamed Women in the Hebrew Bible, the Apocryphal/Deuterocanonical Books, and the New Testament* (2000); L.G. Perdue, J. Blenkinsopp, J.J. Collins, and C. Meyers, *Families in Ancient Israel* (1997); L.E. Stager. "The Archaeology of the Family in Ancient Israel," in: BASOR, 260 (1985), 1–35; R. Westbrook, *Property and the Family in Biblical Law* (*Journal for the Study of the Old Testament*, Supplement 113 (1991). POST-BIBLICAL AND TALMUDIC PERIOD: C.M. Baker, *Rebuilding the House of Israel: Architectures of Gender in Jewish Antiquity* (2002); J.R. Baskin, *Midrashic Women: Formations of the Feminine in Rabbinic Literature* (2002); D. Boyarin, *Carnal Israel: Reading Sex in Talmudic Culture* (1993); B. Brooten, *Women Leaders in the Ancient Synagogue* (1982); H.M. Cotton, "Introduction to the Archive of Salome Komaise," in: *Discoveries in the Judaean Desert*, 27 (1997), 158–95; C.E. Fonrobert, *Menstrual Purity: Rabbinic and Christian Reconstructions of Biblical Gender* (2000); B. Halpern-Amaru, *The Empowerment of Women in the Book of Jubilees* (1999); J. Hauptman, *Rereading the Rabbis: A Woman's Voice* (1997); T. Ilan, *Jewish Women in Greco-Roman Palestine* (1995); idem, *Mine and Yours are Hers* (1997); idem, *Integrating Women into Second Temple History* (1999); G. Labovitz, "'These Are the Labors': Constructions of the Woman Nursing her Child in the Mishnah and Tosefta," in: *Nashim: Journal of Jewish Women's Studies and Gender Issues*, 3 (2000), 15–42; A.J. Levine (ed.), *"Women Like This": New Perspectives on Jewish Women in The Greco-Roman World* (1991); J. Neusner, *A History of the Mishnaic Law of Women*, vol. 5 (1988); M. Peskowitz, *Spinning Fantasies: Rabbis, Gender and History* (1997); M.L. Satlow, *Jewish Marriage in Antiquity* (2001); A. Schremer, *Male and Female He Created Them: Jewish Marriage in the Late Second Temple and Mishnah and Talmud Periods* (Heb., 2003); E. Schuller, "Women in the Dead Sea Scrolls," in: M.O. Wise, N. Golb, J.J. Collins, and D.G. Pardee (eds.), *Methods of Investigation of the Dead Sea Scrolls and the Khirbet of Qumran Site: Present Realities and Future Prospects* (*Annals of the New York Academy of Science*), 722 (1993), 115–31; D. Sly, *Philo's Perceptions of Women* (1990); J.E. Taylor, *Jewish Women Philosophers of First Century Alexandria* (2003); C.W. Trenchard, *Ben Sira's View on Women: A Literary Analysis* (1982); V. Shulamit, *Women and Womanhood in the Stories of the Babylonian Talmud* (1999); idem, *Women in Jewish Society in the* Talmudic Period (Heb., 2000); J.R. Wegner, *Chattel or Person: The Status of Women in the Mishnah* (1988). MEDIEVAL ISLAMIC WORLD AND SPAIN: H.Z. Hirschberg, "The Berber 'Kahena'," in: *Tarbiz*, 26:4 (1957), 370–83 (Heb.); N. Roth, "The Kahina: Legendary Material in the Accounts of the 'Jewish Berber Queen,' in: " *The Magreb Review*, 7:5–6 (1982), 122–25; J.M. Nichols, "The Arabic Verses of Qasmuna Bint Isma'il Ibn Bagdalah," in: *International Journal of Middle Eastern Studies*, 13 (1981), 155–58; J.A. Bellamy, "Qasmuna the Poetess: Who Was She?," in: *Journal of the American Oriental Society*, 103:2 (1983), 423–24; S.D. Goitein, *A Mediterranean Society*, 1:127–30; 3 (1978, rev. 1988); idem, *Letters of Medieval Jewish Traders*, tr. from the Arabic, 220–26, 335–38 (1973); J. Kraemer, "Women Speak for Themselves," in: S.C. Reif, *The Cambridge Genizah Collections: Their Contents and Significance*, 178–216 (2002); J. Blau, *Maimonides' Responsa*, 1:51–53; 71–73; 2:525 (1958); R.L. Melammed, "He Said, She Said: The Case of a Woman Teacher in Maimonides' Twelfth Century Cairo," in: *Association for Jewish Studies Review*, 22:1 (1997), 19–36; idem, "Sephardi Women in the Medieval and Early Modern Periods," in: J.R. Baskin (ed.), *Jewish Women in Historical Perspective*, 128–47 (19982); M.A. Friedman, *Jewish Marriage in Palestine: A Cairo Genizah Study*, 2 vols. (1980–81); A. Grossman, *Pious and Rebellious: Jewish Women in Medieval Europe* (2004); R. Lamdan, *A Separate People: Jewish Women in Palestine, Syria and Egypt in the Sixteenth Century* (2000); Y.T. Assis, "Sexual Behavior in Mediaeval Hispano-Jewish Society," in: A. Rapoport-Albert and S.J. Zipperstein (eds.), *Jewish History: Essays in Honor of Chimen Abramsky* (1988), 25–59; R. Winer, *Women Wealth and Community in Perpignan, c. 1250–1300* (2005); E. Klein, "Protecting the Widow and the Orphan," in: *Mosaic*, 14 (1993), 65–81; J.L. Kraemer, "Spanish Ladies from the Cairo Geniza," in: *Mediterranean Historical Review*, 6 (1991), 237–67. MEDIEVAL CHRISTIAN EUROPE: I. Abrahams, *Hebrew Ethical Wills* (1926); R. Barkai, *A History of Jewish Gynaecological Texts in the Middle Ages* (1998); J.R. Baskin, "Jewish Women in the Middle Ages," in: J.R. Baskin (1998), *Jewish Women in Historical Perspective* (1998), 101–27; idem, "Dolce of Worms," in: L. Fine (ed.), *Judaism in Practice* (2001), 429–37; idem, "Women and Ritual Immersion in Medieval Ashkenaz," in: *ibid.*, 131–42; idem, "Medieval Jewish Models of Marriage," in: *The Medieval Marriage* (2005), 1–22; idem, "Women and Sexual Ambivalence in *Sefer Hasidim*," in: JQR, 96 (2006), 1–8; R. Chazan, *European Jewry and the First Crusade* (1987); S. Einbinder, "Jewish Women Martyrs: Changing Representations," in: *Exemplaria*, 12:1 (2000), 105–28; A. Falk, *Jewish Matrimonial Law in the Middle Ages* (1966); A. Grossman, *Pious and Rebellious: Jewish Women in Medieval Europe* (2001; trans. 2004); J. Shatzmiller, "Femmes médecins au Moyen Ages," in: *Histoire et Société* (1992), 1:167–75; K.R. Stow, *Alienated Minority* (1992). EARLY MODERN PERIOD: H. Adelman. "Finding Women's Voices in Italian Jewish Literature," in: J.R. Baskin (ed.), *Women of the Word* (1994), 50–69; idem, "Italian Jewish Women," in: J.R. Baskin (ed.), *Jewish Women in Historical Perspective.* (1998), 150–68; D. Biale, *Eros and the Jews* (1992); N. Deutsch, *The Maiden of Ludmir* (2003); R.L. Melammed, *Heretics or Daughters of Israel?* (1999); idem, "Sephardi Women in the Medieval and Early Modern Periods," in: J.R. Baskin (ed.), *Jewish Women in Historical Perspective* (1998), 128–49; A. Rapoport-Albert, "On Women in Hasidism…," in: A. Rapoport-Albert and S. Zipperstein (eds.), *Jewish History*, (1988), 495–525; M. Keil. "Public Roles of Jewish Women in Fourteenth and Fifteenth-Centuries Ashkenaz: Business, Community, and Ritual," in: C. Cluse (ed.), *The Jews of Europe in the Middle Ages (Tenth to Fifteenth Centuries).* (2004), 317–30; G. Scholem, *Sabbatai Sevi* (1973).; E. Taitz, S. Henry, and C. Tallan, *The JPS Guide to Jewish Women* (2003); C. Weissler, *Voices of the Matriarchs: Listening to the Prayers of Early Modern Jewish Women* (1998). MODERN CENTRAL AND WESTERN EUROPE: 1780 TO 1939: D. Biale, *Eros and the Jews* (1992); H. Freidenreich, *Female, Jewish, and Educated* (2002); M. Galchinsky, *The Origin of the Modern Jewish Woman Writer* (1996); B. Hahn, *The Jewess Pallas Athena. This Too a Theory of Modernity* (2005); D. Hertz. *Jewish High Society in Old Regime Berlin* (1988); P.E. Hyman. *Gender and Assimilation in Modern Jewish History* (1995); M. Kaplan, *Between Dignity and Despair* (1999); idem, *The Making of the Jewish Middle Class* (1991); L.G. Kuzmack. *Women's Cause* (1990). EASTERN EUROPE IN THE 19th AND 20th CENTURIES: C.B. Balin, *To Reveal Our Hearts: Jewish Women Writers in Tsarist Russia* (2000); T. Cohen, *Ha-Aḥat Ahuvah ve-ha-Aḥat Senu'ah: Bein Meẓiut le-Bidyon be-Te'urei ha-Ishah be-Sifrut ha-Haskalah* (2002); C. Freeze, P.E. Hyman, and A. Polonsky (eds.), *Jewish Women in Eastern Europe. Polin* 18 (2005); P.E. Hyman, *Gender and Assimilation in Modern Jewish History* (1995); I. Parush, *Reading Women: Marginality and Modernization in Nineteenth-Century Eastern European Jewish Society* (2004); N. Sokoloff, A. Lerner, and A. Norich, *Gender and Text in Modern Hebrew and Yiddish Literature* (1992); C. Weissler, *Voices of the Matriarchs* (1998); D. Ofer and L.J. Weitzman (eds.), *Women in the Holocaust* (1998). NORTH

AMERICA: J. Antler, "Zion in Our Hearts: Henrietta Szold and the American Jewish Women's Movement," in: P.S. Nadell (ed.), *American Jewish Women's History: A Reader* (2003), 129–49; H.R. Diner, *A Time for Gathering: The Second Migration, 1820–1880* (1992); S.B. Fishman, *A Breath of Life: Feminism in the American Jewish Community* (1993); S.A. Glenn, *Daughters of the Shtetl: Life and Labor in the Immigrant Generation* (1990); S. Goldstein, "Profile of American Jewry," in: *American Jewish Year Book*, 92 (1992): 77–173; P. Hyman. *Gender and Assimilation in Modern Jewish History* (1995); idem, "Immigrant Women and Consumer Protest," in: P.S. Nadell (ed.), *American Jewish Women's History: A Reader* (2003), 116–28; J.W. Joselit, *New York's Jewish Jews: The Orthodox Community in the Interwar Years* (1990); idem, *The Wonders of America: Reinventing Jewish Culture, 1880–1950* (1994), 161–62; A.F. Kahn and M. Dollinger, *California Jews* (2003); E. Lerner, "Jewish Involvement in the New York City Women's Suffrage Movement," in: *American Jewish History*, 71 (June 1981), 442–61; S.W. Levine, *Mystics, Mavericks, and Merrymakers: An Intimate Journey among Hasidic Girls* (2003); J.R. Marcus (ed.), *The American Jewish Woman: A Documentary History* (1981); R.J. Markowitz, *My Daughter, the Teacher: Jewish Teachers in the New York City Schools* (1993); M. McCune, "Creating a Place for Women in a Socialist Brotherhood: Class and Gender Politics in the Workmen's Circle, 1892–1930," in: *Feminist Studies*, 28:3 (2002), 585–612; D.D. Moore, *To the Golden Cities: Pursuing the American Jewish Dream in Miami and L.A.* (1994); P.S. Nadell and R.J. Simon, "Ladies of the Sisterhood: Women in the American Reform Synagogue, 1900–1930," in: M. Sacks (ed.), *Active Voices* (1995), 63–75; Irwin Richman, *Borscht Belt Bungalows* (1998); L.M. Schloff. *"And Prairie Dogs Weren't Kosher": Jewish Women in the Upper Midwest since 1855* (1996); R. Sheramy. "'There Are Times When Silence Is a Sin': The Women's Division of the American Jewish Congress and the Anti-Nazi Boycott Movement," in: *American Jewish History*, 89:1 (2001), 105–21; E. Smith, "Portraits of a Community," in: P.S. Nadell (ed.), *American Jewish Women's History: A Reader* (2003), 13–25; H. Snyder, "Queens of the Household: The Jewish Women of British America, 1700–1800," in: P.S. Nadell and J.D. Sarna (eds.), *Women and American Judaism* (2001), 15–45; S. Tenenbaum, "Borrowers or Lenders Be: Jewish Immigrant Women's Credit Networks," in: P.S. Nadell (ed.), *American Jewish Women's History* (2003), 79–90; B.S. Wenger. "Budgets, Boycotts, and Babies: Jewish Women in the Great Depression," in: P.S. Nadell (ed.), *American Jewish Women's History* (2003); C. Wilhelm. "The Independent Order of True Sisters: Friendship, Fraternity, and a Model of Modernity for Nineteenth-Century American Jewish Womanhood," in: *American Jewish Archives Journal*, 54:1 (2002), 37–63; A. Witznitzer. "The Exodus from Brazil and Arrival in New Amsterdam of the Jewish Pilgrim Fathers, 1654," in: *Publications of the American Jewish Historical Society*, 44 (Dec. 1954), 80–97. MODERN MUSLIM WORLDS: S. Deshen, "Women in the Jewish Family in Pre-Colonial Morocco," in: *Anthropological Quarterly*, 56 (1983), 135–38; D. Bensimon-Donath, *L'Evolution de la femme israelite à Fes* (1962); M. Jacobs, *A Study of Cultural Stability and Change: the Moroccan Jewess* (1956); F. Malino. "The Women Teachers of the Alliance Israélite Universelle," in: J.R. Baskin (ed.), *Jewish Women in Historical Perspective* (1998), 248–69; S. Manasseh, *Daqqaqat: Jewish Women Musicians from Iraq* (1990); M.M. Caspi (trans.), *Daughters of Yemen* (1985); S. Reguer, "The World of Women," in: R.S. Simon, M.M. Laskier, and S. Reguer (eds.), *The Jews of the Middle East and North Africa in Modern Times* (2003), 235–50; D. Rouch, *'Immah, ou, Rites, coutumes et croyances chez la femme israelite juive d'Afrique du nord* (1990); R. Simon. *Change Within Tradition among Jewish Women in Libya* (1992); N.A. Stillman and Y.K. Stillman, "The Art of a Moroccan Folk Poetess," in: *Zeitschrift der Deutschen Morgenlandischen Gesellschaft*, 128 (1978), 65–89. ISRAEL: D. Bernstein (ed.), *Pioneers and Homemakers: Jewish Women in Pre-State Israel* (1992); idem, *The Struggle for Equality: Urban Women Workers in Prestate Israeli Society* (1987); E. Fuchs (ed.), *Israeli Women's Studies: A Reader* (2005); R. Haut, "*The Agunah* and Divorce," in: D. Ornstein (ed.), *Lifecycles* (1994), 188–200; L. Hazleton, "Israeli Women: Three Myths," in: S. Heschel (ed.), *On Being a Jewish Feminist* (1983), 65–87; T. Moore (ed.), *Lesbiyot: Israeli Lesbians…* (1994); H. Naveh (ed.), *Gender and Israeli Society* (2003); M. Palgi, "Women in the Changing World of the Kibbutz," in: *Women in Judaism*, 1 (1997); M. Raider and M.B. Raider-Roth (eds.), *The Plough Woman: Records of the Pioneer Women of Palestine* (1932; 1975; critical edition 2002); S.S. Sered, *What Makes Women Sick? Maternity, Modesty, and Militarism in Israeli Society* (2000); S. Sharoni. *Gender and the Israeli-Palestinian Conflict* (1994); M. Shilo. *Princess or Prisoner? Jewish Women in Jerusalem, 1840–1914* (2005); B. Swirski and M. Safir (eds.), *Calling the Equality Bluff: Women in Israel* (1991). JUDICIAL PERSPECTIVE: WOMEN AND THE ISRAELI COURTS: M. Elon, *Ha-Mishat ha-Ivri* (1988), 1:274, 339, 465, 468, 496, 514, 517, 537, 541, 542, 568, 569, 637, 638, 649, 651, 654–55, 664ff., 684, 886, 723, 757, 763; 2:886, 1389; 3:1474,1511ff.; idem, *Jewish Law* (1994), 152–53, 296–97, 361–64, 1653, 1656, 1660, 1665–68, 1671, 1679–80, 1684, 1757–58, 1760, 1765, 1787–91, 1798, 1802, 1805–7, 1824–1826, 1827; idem, *Ma'amad ha-Ishah – Mishpat ve-Shipput, Masoret u-Temurah; Arakhehah shel Medinah Yehudit ve-Demokratit* (2006); idem, *Jewish Law (Mishpat Ivri) Cases and Materials*, 404–20, 493–522; *Anat Hoffman et al. v. the Trustee over the Western Wall et al.*; HC 90/2410, *Susan Alter et al. v. the Minister of Religious Affairs*, PD 48(2) 265–358; HC 87/153, *Leah Shakdiel v. Minister of Religious Affairs et al.*, PD 42(2) 221; Cr.A. 92/2157, *Padida v. the State of Israel*, PD 47(1) 81; CA 79/458, *Nir v. Nir*, PD 35(1) 518; ST 81/1, *Yehiel Nagar v. Orah Nagar*, PD 38(1) 365; M. Firshtik, "Violence against Women in Judaism," in: *Journal of Psychology and Judaism*, 14 (1990), 131–53; *Ha-Ishah ve-Ḥinukhah, Asufat Ma'amarim be-Halakhah u-be-Maḥashavah* (1980); A. Grossman, *Ḥasidot u-Moredot* (2001); D. Frimer, "Women and Minyan," in: *Tradition*, 23:4 (1988), 54ff.; A. Weiss, *Women at Prayer* (1990), 13–56.

WOMEN'S LEAGUE FOR CONSERVATIVE JUDAISM. Founded in 1918 as the National Women's League of the United Synagogue of America, this new organization responded to the call of Solomon *Schechter to harness women's energies and talents to promote an American Judaism that was rooted in history and tradition. In 1918, his widow Mathilde Roth *Schechter, Women's League founding president, drafted the blueprint for its future work as the coordinating body of Conservative synagogue sisterhoods. She led Women's League to set an agenda that included service to home, synagogue, and community, with special concern for youth and adult education, the blind, and the welfare of students at the Jewish Theological Seminary. By 1925 Women's League had grown from 26 founding sisterhoods to 230, with a membership of 20,000 women. In 2005, its goals remained much the same as at its founding: to strengthen and unite its 700 synagogue women's groups; to help their 120,000 members perpetuate Conservative Judaism in the home, synagogue, and community; and to strengthen their bonds with Israel and with Jews worldwide.

In its first decades Women's League created student houses, the first in New York in 1918, to serve as homes away from home for Jewish students and also Jewish servicemen on leave. Its education department published books to deepen its members' Jewish knowledge, including Deborah Melamed's *The Three Pillars: Thought, Worship and Practice* (1927) and the popular *Jewish Home Beautiful* (1941) by Betty D. Greenberg and Althea O. Silverman. Women's League also began publishing its magazine Outlook in 1930. Educating its members and enhancing their observance of Jewish tradition remained a priority of Women's League over the years. In 1931 it helped establish the Women's Institute of Jewish Studies at the Jewish Theological Seminary. In 1993 it formed *Kolot Bik'dushah* to recognize those of its members who have mastered the skills of leading services and reading from the Torah. Women's League saw as its special task to help raise funds to enhance student life at the Seminary. In addition, Women's League helped the Jewish blind though the Jewish Braille Institute. The organization's commitment to liberal political and social issues emerged in the resolutions its members adopted over the years.

In 1972 the association formally changed its name to the Women's League for Conservative Judaism, signifying that it was no longer a subsidiary of the United Synagogue, but rather an independent body of Jewish women dedicated to Conservative Judaism. At the same time Women's League expressed an increasingly forceful position calling for egalitarianism in the Conservative synagogue.

BIBLIOGRAPHY: *They Dared to Dream: A History of the National Women's League, 1918–1968* (1967); S.R. Schwartz, "Women's League for Conservative Judaism," in: P.E. Hyman and D. Dash Moore (eds.), *Jewish Women in America: An Historical Encyclopedia*, vol. 2 (1997), 1493–97; M. Scult, "The Baale Boste Reconsidered: The Life of Mathilde Roth Schechter (M.R.S.)," in: *Modern Judaism* 7, 1 (February 1987), 1–27.

[Pamela S. Nadell (2nd ed.)]

WOOD. In Hebrew the word ʿeẓ (עֵץ) means both "tree" and "wood" (also "stick"). The Bible speaks of special craftsmen for woodworking, *ḥarashei ʿeẓ*, who worked in the various branches of wood manufacturing (Ex. 31:5; II Sam. 5:11; I Chron. 22:15, et al.). The Bible also mentions several types of wood which were treated for various purposes; gopher wood (Gen. 6:14), cedar wood (Ezra 3:7; et al.), acacia wood (Ex. 38:1, et al.), juniper wood (בְּרוֹשׁ; I Kings 6:34), almug wood (I Kings 10:11), and olive wood (I Kings 6:31). Apparently, cedars and cypress trees were used primarily for the construction of ornate buildings, while the other types were used mainly in the construction of furniture, other articles, and utensils. Cedars and almug wood were imported from abroad, mainly during the period of the monarchy, while acacia and olive trees were common in Palestine.

The Bible mentions wooden handles and axes (Deut. 19:5), spear handles (II Sam. 21:19), etc. Stone implements were attached to the wooden handles by tying them together with sinews or ropes, while metal blades of various shapes and having different uses were attached to wooden handles by tying them with cords, by driving one end into the wood, and by making a metal hole into which the wood was inserted and riveted. The Bible mentions a number of pieces of wooden furniture which were used in the Temple and the Tabernacle: the table of display (Ex. 25:23–30), the ark (Ex. 25:10–14), the altar for burnt offerings (Ex. 38:1), and the incense altar (Ex. 37:25). In connection with the laws of uncleanness and purification, the Bible mentions various wooden articles (Lev. 15:12). These are mainly various household utensils: mortars, dishes, spoons, etc. The number of wooden objects from the biblical period which have been discovered in the archaeological excavations in Israel is very small because of decay. The richest in wooden furniture and vessels are the MB II tombs in Jericho, where many tables, bowls, combs, jugs, and toilet boxes were preserved. When the Bible sharply criticizes idol worshipers, it indicates that they are worshipers of wood and stone, the work of men (Deut. 4:28). The use of wood in the construction of houses in Palestine is most variegated. It began with the building of huts from branches which were cut down and left in their natural state, and continues, until today, with the use of processed wood in the consolidation of frames of building and in the covering of wooden structures, as columns for reinforcing walls, for the roofing of clay, stone, or straw buildings, and for making doors and windows.

[Ze'ev Yeivin]

Wood Offerings

On nine different specified dates during the year, designated families brought wood offerings for the Temple sacrificial service. On the 15th of *Av, the priests, levites, and all those not certain of their tribal descent were permitted to join the family designated for that day in bringing the wood offering (Ta'an. 4:5). One of the reasons given for the joyful celebrations on the 15th of Av is that each year on this day felling trees for the altar was discontinued. The reason given is that after this time the strength of the sun lessens and its rays are no longer sufficiently strong to dry the fresh-cut logs (Ta'an. 31a). The wood most preferred for the altar was boughs of fig trees, nut trees, and oil trees (Tam. 2:3).

The rabbis praised the family of Salami Netofah for their efforts in getting wood to the Temple at a time when the ruling authorities placed guards on the roads to prevent Jews from bringing wood to the altar. This family conceived the stratagem of making the logs into ladders which they carried on their shoulders. When stopped by the guards the family explained that they were going to use the ladders to take down young pigeons from the dovecote. Once past the guards, they dismantled the ladders and brought the logs to Jerusalem (Ta'an. 28a).

BIBLIOGRAPHY: W.M.F. Petrie and H. Mackay, *Heliopolis, Kafr Ammr and Shurafa* (1915), pl. xxv; H. Fechheimer, *Kleinplastik der Aegypter* (1921), p. 148; C. Singer et al., *History of Technology*, 1 (1954), 688, 700.

WOOG, MAYER (1833–1896), Yiddish playwright. Born in Hegenheim, Woog was the most representative writer of 19th-century Alsatian Yiddish theater. His comedies of village manners present a Jewish world in tension between tradition and modernity as well as in its relations with the gentile environment. The plays are characterized by their quadrilingualism (Yiddish-Alsatian, Alsatian, German, and French) and their written form (Gothic script). Their primary themes are marriage (*Der Gaasejopper macht Chasene*, "The Goat-Seller Marries," 1877), medicine (*Bas Jechido*, "The Only Daughter," 1884), and market conversation (*Schmues-Berjendes*, "Gossip," 1880, and *Deforim Beteilim leeri Keilim*, "Chatter," 1888).

BIBLIOGRAPHY: A. Starck, in: *Domaine Yiddish*. YOD 31–32 (1990), 145–57; A. Wackenheim, in: *La littérature dialectale alsacienne*, 1 (1993), 203–55.

[Astrid Starck (2nd ed.)]

WOOLF, BOB (1928–1993), pioneering U.S. sports and entertainment agent who emerged in the mid-1960s as the first of a generation of agents and lawyers who altered the way athletes are paid – from five-figure salaries in the 1960s, before free agency, to $250 million for multiyear contracts today. His sports clients included Larry Bird, Carl Yastrzemski, Joe Montana, Julius Erving, Doug Flutie, and Vinny Testaverde; his entertainment clients included Larry King, Gene Shalit, and New Kids on the Block; he negotiated big deals with Donald Trump, Ted Turner, Roone Arledge, and Red Auerbach. Woolf's family moved from Portland, Maine, to Boston when he was 16, and he graduated from Boston Latin School, and later from Boston College (1949), where he received a four-year basketball scholarship. After obtaining his law degree from Boston University Law School, and enlisting for a two-year stint in the U.S. Army, Woolf opened a successful Boston practice. In 1964, Earl Wilson, a Boston Red Sox pitcher who used Woolf as a tax lawyer, asked him also to handle his endorsement contracts. This led, in 1966, to Woolf's first contract negotiation with a team for Wilson. Since most players had no contract representation, Woolf quickly built a stable of clients, representing nine of the 12 Boston Celtics in their late 1960s championship years, and 14 of the members of 1967 Boston Red Sox. Within five years, Woolf had acquired 300 clients in all sports in all major cities. Woolf was not only an agent, he was a fan. His office in Boston's John Hancock building overlooked Fenway Park, with a telescope aimed at the mound and batter's box. Woolf estimated that he had negotiated more than 20,000 contracts by 1992, but grew increasingly concerned by the spendthrift ways of young clients who did not know the value of a million dollars. "I'm very Jewish-oriented," said Woolf in 1992, "[and] … I'm proud of the basketball tournament that's been held in my name in Israel for the past 15 years." Woolf's widow, Ann, administers the Bob Woolf Foundation. Woolf is the author of *Behind Closed Doors* (1976) and *Friendly Persuasion: My Life as a Negotiator* (1990).

[David Brinn (2nd ed.)]

WOOLF, SIR HARRY, BARON (1933–), British judge. Born in Newcastle-upon-Tyne, the son of a builder and architect who later moved to Scotland, and was educated at Fettes, a leading Scottish public school, and London University, Woolf was a barrister before being appointed a High Court judge in 1979, serving until 1985 when he began an impressive rise up the ranks of the British judiciary. He served as a lord justice in 1985–95, a lord of appeal in ordinary with a seat in the House of Lords in 1992–96, master of the rolls in 1996–2000, and lord chief justice from 2000. He is known for his often controversial decisions, generally in the direction of insisting on the welfare of prisoners. Woolf was president of the International Jewish Lawyers' Association from 1993. He was knighted in 1979 and made a life peer in 1992.

[William D. Rubinstein (2nd ed.)]

WOOLF, LEONARD (**Sidney**; 1880–1969), English publisher and writer. The son of a London barrister who was a member of the Reform synagogue, Woolf had ambivalent feelings about family and religious loyalties and, as a convinced rationalist, saw little virtue in any religion. Woolf's father died when he was 12, leaving his family in some difficulties. He attended St. Paul's School and Cambridge on scholarships. As a classical student at Cambridge, he became friendly with a group of intellectuals who were to form the nucleus of London's famous "Bloomsbury Circle." They included John Maynard Keynes, Lytton Strachey, E.M. Forster, and J.T. Stephen, whose sister, Virginia, Woolf married. At Cambridge, Woolf was the first Jew elected to the "Apostles," the famous secret debating society. From 1904 until 1911 he was a colonial administrator in Ceylon, responsible for governing 100,000 people while still in his twenties. From this experience he acquired a lifelong hostility to British imperialism. In 1917 Leonard and Virginia started the Hogarth Press as a hobby: it became famous through the publication of Virginia's novels, T.S. Eliot's *The Waste Land*, the English translation of *Freud's works, and S.S. Koteliansky's translations from the Russian. Just as his experiences as a civil servant in Ceylon had led Leonard Woolf to disapprove of imperialism, so the sight of poverty in the East End of London converted him from liberalism to socialism. He joined the Fabian Society and became involved in the political, trade union, and economic aspects of the British Labour movement.

His two outstanding political works were *International Government* (1916), an early blueprint for the League of Nations, and *Empire and Commerce in Africa* (1920). Woolf was on the editorial staff of the *Contemporary Review* (1920–21), literary editor of *The Nation* (1923–30), and coeditor of *The Political Quarterly* (1931–59). He was also closely associated with *The New Statesman and Nation*. His books include: *The Village in the Jungle* (1913), inspired by his stay in Ceylon; *Hunting the Highbrow* (1927), essays; *Quack, Quack* (1935), a book about dictatorship; *Barbarians at the Gate* (1939); and *After the Deluge* (2 vols., 1931–39), and its sequel, *Principia Politica* (1953), a study of communal psychology. Woolf wrote an outstanding series of autobiographical works: *Sowing* (1960), *Growing* (1961), *Beginning Again* (1964), *Downhill All the Way* (1967), and *The Journey, Not the Arrival, Matters* (1969). Although a significant figure in his own right, Woolf is best remembered today as the husband of Virginia (1882–1941), who has attained almost cultlike status since her death. The nature of their relationship, and Woolf's own role in formulating her iconic status, have been the subjects of continuing debate, as has been her response to his Jewish origins. Similarly, the "Bloomsbury Group" has generated a veritable industry among biographers and literary historians.

BIBLIOGRAPHY: *Times Literary Supplement*, 66 (May 4, 1967); *The Times*, (August 15, 1969). **ADD. BIBLIOGRAPHY:** ODNB online; P.F. Alexander, *Leonard and Virginia Woolf: A Literary Partnership* (1992); G. Spater and I. Parsons, *A Marriage of True Minds: An Intimate Portrait of Leonard and Virginia Woolf* (1977); D. Wilson, *Leonard Woolf: A Political Biography* (1978).

[Renee Winegarten / William D. Rubinstein (2nd ed.)]

WOOLF (Wulff), MOSHE (1878–1971), Israeli psychiatrist and author. Born in Odessa, Russia, Woolf studied medicine in Berlin. Here he started his psychiatric training under Mendel and Jolly and soon became Ziehen's first assistant in the laboratory of the Charité, the university hospital in Berlin. In 1907, while working at Mendel's psychiatric sanatorium, he made his first acquaintance with Freud's works, which proved crucial to his further scientific development. He joined the sanatorium of Berlin-Lankwitz and in 1908 became Juliusburger's assistant. When Karl Abraham returned from Zurich at that time and joined the same sanatorium, he became Woolf's teacher and introduced him to psychoanalysis proper. In 1911 he returned to Russia as the only trained analyst in that country, where his many widespread and diverse activities eventually resulted in the acknowledgment and development of psychoanalysis. After the revolution he joined a large psychiatric outpatient clinic and taught at the second medical clinic of the University of Moscow. At the same time he did additional work at the psychoanalytically oriented children's home of Zermakow. Although he lived in Russia, he became a member of the Vienna Psychoanalytical Society in 1912. In 1927 he left Russia for political reasons and returned to a psychoanalytic institution, the Tegelsee sanatorium, where he worked under Ernst Simmel until 1930.

In 1933 he emigrated to Palestine. Max Eitingon, who arrived in Palestine in the same year, together with Woolf and I. Schalith founded the Palestine Psychoanalytic Society in 1934. After Eitingon's death, Woolf became president of the Israel Psychoanalytic Society, a position he held for ten years.

Woolf's earliest paper on children was "Beitraege zur infantilen Sexualitaet" (1912), which dealt with some cases of momentary loss of consciousness which Woolf considered caused by hysteria. "Phantasie und Wirklichkeit im Seelenleben des Kleinkindes" (1934) was delivered to an educational board of the Communist Party, in order to influence it not to forbid the reading of fairy tales. His paper, "Prohibitions Against the Simultaneous Consumption of Milk and Flesh in Orthodox Jewish Law" (1945), historically and analytically traces the sources for ritual laws applying to food and to Passover. Some of his publications are considered basic contributions to the psychoanalytic theory, for example, "Fetishism and Object Choice in Early Childhood" (published in *Psychoanalytical Quarterly* 15 (1946), 450–71).

BIBLIOGRAPHY: R. Jaffe, in: F. Alexander et al. (eds.), *Psychoanalytic Pioneers* (1966), 200–9.

[Gad Tadmor]

°WOOLLEY, SIR CHARLES LEONARD (1880–1960), English archaeologist. From 1905 to 1907 he was assistant keeper in the Ashmolean Museum, Oxford. His earliest excavation work was carried out in England (Corbridge, 1906–07), Nubia (1907–11), and at Carchemish, Turkey (1912–14). In 1914 he took part, along with T.E. Lawrence, in the expedition surveying Sinai and the Negev, which was a cover for the British military mapping of the Sinai Peninsula. Their report, *The Wilderness of Zion* (1915), presents the first detailed description of the Byzantine cities of the Negev. During World War I Woolley served as a military intelligence officer and was taken prisoner by the Turks in 1916. He was an officer in the military administration in north Syria in 1919, at which time he resumed excavation at Carchemish. This was followed by work at Tell *el-Amarna in Egypt (1921–22), and at *Ur of the Chaldees (1922–34), where he discovered the royal tombs of the first dynasty with their magnificent treasures, and also uncovered the city dating from the time of Abraham (Ur III). He then directed excavations in southern Turkey (Hatay province), first at el-Mina (ancient Greek port of Poseidium) from 1936 to 1937 and afterward at Tell Atshana (1937–39), where he unearthed the remains of the *Alalakh kingdom. During World War II he was archaeological adviser to the British War Office and after the war again excavated at Tell Atshana (1946–49). In addition to his excavation reports, he wrote *Ur of the Chaldees* (1929); *The Sumerians* (1929); *Middle East Archaeology* (1949); *A Forgotten Kingdom* (1953); several popular works, especially *Digging Up the Past* (1930); and his memoirs, *Spadework in Archaeology* (1953).

[Michael Avi-Yonah]

WORCESTER, town in central England. It was founded around 1159 and had a small Jewish population until the late thirteenth century. After the persecutions under John, the regents for Henry Ill confirmed the right of Jews to live there unmolested. In 1219, however, Bishop William de Blois promulgated restrictive measures against them. The so-called "Parliament of Jews" was held at Worcester in 1241, when 109 representatives of the 21 recognized Jewish communities were summoned to apportion a tax levy among themselves. The Jews suffered greatly in the Barons' Revolt (1264–65). Their expulsion from the city to Hereford was secured by Eleanor, the queen mother, in 1275. There were few Jews in Worcester in the 19th century. A small community was founded during World War II. The Jewish population in 1968 was 56, but no organized community exists today.

BIBLIOGRAPHY: Roth, England³, index; M. Adler, *Jews of Medieval England* (1939), index; H.G. Richardson, *English Jewry under Angevin Kings* (1960), index. **ADD. BIBLIOGRAPHY:** J. Hillaby in *Worcs. Archaeol. Soc. Trans.* 3S 12 (1990), 73–122.

[Vivian David Lipman / Joe Hillaby (2nd ed.)]

WORCESTER, U.S. city in Massachusetts, 40 mi. (64 km.) W. of Boston. Its population was 172,648 (2000 census), with an estimated Jewish population of 10,000 in the city and surrounding area, which includes such communities as Westborough, Northborough, Shrewsbury, Fitchburg, and Leominster.

The earliest settlement of Jews in the Worcester area occurred during the American Revolution when the British occupied *Newport, R.I., and several Jewish families, headed by Aaron *Lopez, a wealthy shipping merchant, left that city to live for the duration of the war in Leicester, five miles from Worcester. After the war the Leicester community dissolved when the Jewish families returned to Newport. Worcester had no permanent Jewish settlement until after the Civil War, when the *Straus and Gross families established stores in the city. In 1870 Jewish immigrants from Eastern Europe began to come to Worcester in larger numbers.

Congregations

The first congregation, Sons of Israel, was established in 1877, and a burial society was formed the same year. As the Jewish population grew, congregations – all located on the East Side – multiplied to total 13. With the shift of the Jewish population to the West Side of the city, most of them closed. Sons of Jacob and Shaarai Torah (1904), which was merged with Sons of Abraham (1887), have survived.

In 1968, three Orthodox congregations remained on the East Side – Sons of Jacob; Sons of Zion, a small congregation; and Shaarai Torah – Sons of Abraham, at the synagogue erected in 1906. A West Side branch of Shaarai Torah – Sons of Abraham was established in 1959. Rabbi Joseph Gold, who came to the congregation in 1954, served both branches. Earlier rabbis included Meyer Greenberg (1947–54) and Gershon Appel (1943–47), who pursued his Ph.D. at Harvard and went on to congregations in Seattle and New York before becoming a professor of philosophy at Stern College. In addition to Shaarai Torah – Sons of Abraham, there were in 1968 five other congregations on the West Side.

Temple Emanuel (Reform), established in 1921, moved to permanent quarters in 1923. In 1949 it erected a large synagogue which was considerably expanded in 1961. The congregation grew rapidly to become the Jewish community's largest, with a membership of over 1,300 families. Maurice M. Mazure, the first rabbi (1923–26), was followed by Julius Gordon (1926–29), Levi A. Olan (1929–48; d. 1984), and afterwards by Joseph Klein and Jordan Milstein. Hugo Chaim *Adler, who achieved fame as a composer of synagogue music, was cantor of Temple Emanuel from 1939 until his death in 1955.

Congregation Beth Israel (Conservative), formed in 1924, built a house of worship in 1939, and in 1959 erected a larger synagogue. Its rabbis included Herbert Ribner (1948–55), Abraham Kazis, who began in 1955, and was followed by Joel Pitkowsky.

Congregation Beth Judah (Orthodox), founded in 1948, was headed in 1968 by Rabbi Reuven Fischer. Congregation Tifereth Israel (Orthodox), established in 1959, was led in 1968 by Rabbi Herschel Fogelman. It was associated with the Chabad *Lubavitch movement. Temple Sinai (Reform) was established in 1957; its rabbi (1970) was John J. Rosenblatt. In 2005 Seth Bernstein was the rabbi.

Congregations in Westborough include Beth Tikvah, whose rabbi was Fred Benjamin, Bnai Shalom, whose rabbi was Laurence Milder, and Chabad, whose rabbi was Micoel Green.

In addition to the congregational school, the Ivriah School, a community *talmud torah* supported by the Worcester Jewish Federation was formed in 1927 by combining the Hebrew Free School (established 1905) with the existing Orthodox congregational schools. It ceased to exist in the 1980s, but in the early 21st century there were two day schools, the New Jewish Academy established in 2005 (the successor to the Solomon Schechter Day School), a community transdenominational school which recognizes and respects all forms of Jewish practice, and the Yeshiva, the Chabad-Lubavitch day school.

Community Organizations and Leadership

In 1920 a number of existing charitable organizations were combined to form the United Jewish Charities, later the Jewish Social Service Agency, and in 1968 called the Jewish Family Service. The Jewish Community Council, formed in 1936, and the Jewish Welfare Fund, established in 1939, were merged in 1947 to form the Worcester Jewish Federation. The Jewish Community Center, established in 1950, used the old Temple Emanuel building until its new structure was built in 1966. The Jewish Home for the Aged, founded in 1915, at first served also as an orphanage but by 1968 was restricted to caring for the aged and infirm.

In the early years of the community Jews were mainly peddlers and small-scale shopkeepers. By the 1960s they were engaged in every branch of industry and commerce and in all professions. Among Jews in public office was Joseph C. Casdin, a member of the City Council from 1956, who served his fourth term as mayor in 1968. Past City Council members include Louis Glixman, Elias Pofcher, and Israel Katz. Other officials include Elton Yasuna, who served on the School Committee, and Edward Landau, elected to the committee in 1967; Archibald M. Hillman (d. 1959), assistant city solicitor and, later, city solicitor; Wilfred B. Feiga, assistant clerk of Superior Court (1922–65) and president of the Free Public Library (1932; 1966); Judge Jacob Asher (d. 1956), special justice of the Central District Court; and Judge Joseph Goldberg, appointed to the Central District Court in 1953. There was an additional Jewish mayor in Worcester, Jordan Levy. First elected to the City Council in 1978, he was mayor for eight years.

The playwright S.N. *Behrman has described some of the colorful personalities in the Jewish community during his youth in his partly fictional and partly autobiographical *Worcester Account* (1954). A weekly newspaper, the *Jewish Civic Leader*, served the community from 1923.

[Joseph Klein]

The Worcester Jewish Federation was re-named the Jewish Federation of Central Massachusetts in 1997 to more accurately reflect the area that the Federation serves: not just the city of Worcester, but all of Worcester county, including the Westborough area (which includes Westborough, Northborough and Shrewsbury). The Westborough area is the home to a JCC, a Conservative congregation, Beth Tikvah, and a Reform Temple, Bnai Shalom. Chabad has a presence there as well.

Clark University is located in Worcester. It has a distinguished Judaic Studies program staffed by, inter alia, Everett Fox, who wrote an important translation of the Torah based on the principles of the Buber-Rosenzweig translation of the early 20th century, and Debórah Dwork, who headed its graduate program in Holocaust Studies, the first of its kind in the United States. Clark boasts that it was the only university to invite Sigmund Freud to lecture during an American visit. Neighboring Holy Cross University has an annual lecture on the Holocaust and programs in Jewish-Catholic relations.

BIBLIOGRAPHY: Mopsik, in: JSOS, 7 (1945), 41–62.

[Howard Borer (2nd ed.)]

WORD, in the Bible, primarily renders the Hebrew *davar*, but also *omer* (pl. *amarim*), *imrah*, and *peh* (lit. "mouth"). "The word of the Lord," an oft-recurring scriptural phrase, signifies a divine communication to man that reveals God's character or His will, as in Isaiah 50:4ff. This revelation can assume many forms, such as oracles (e.g., Judg. 20:18ff.), visions (e.g., Amos 7:1ff.), and dreams (e.g., Gen. 15:12ff.), as well as prophecy and religious teaching in general, including the divinely given laws. In the broadest sense, the Scriptures taken as a whole, and subsequently the totality of Jewish spiritual teaching, fall within the connotation of God's word. In certain biblical passages, the divine word is personified, e.g., "So shall My word be that goeth forth out of My mouth: it shall not return unto Me void, except it accomplish that which I please, and make the thing whereto I sent it prosper" (Isa. 55:11; cf. also Ps. 33:6; 147:15). This biblical feature has antecedents in Sumerian and Babylonian literature, where the "word" is an agent of the gods' beneficence, but more especially of their wrath. In wisdom literature this process of hypostatization becomes even more marked, only *ḥokhmah* ("Wisdom") is substituted for the divine word, to which it is closely related ideologically (e.g., Prov. 8:1ff.; 9:1–6; Job 28:12–28). However, throughout the Hebrew Bible the figurative character of the personification is never in doubt.

A further stage in the evolution of the concept of the divine word is reached in apocryphal and rabbinic literature. Here the Word emerges as a distinct entity (cf. Wis. 18:15; Mekh., Be-Shallaḥ, 10; Avot 5:1). Furthermore, there arose a negative attitude toward the attribution to God of any anthropomorphic characteristics or the use of language that appeared to detract from the divine dignity. To avoid anthropomorphisms, the Targum employs the *memra* ("utterance"). For example, Deuteronomy 1:32 is rendered, "… ye have not believed in the *memra* of the Lord." Thus the *memra* connotes the manifestation of God's power in creating the world and in directing history. It acts as His messenger and is generally analogous to the *Shekhinah* ("Divine Presence") and the Divine Wisdom. New and fateful significance was given to the Word by Philo's doctrine of the Logos (the Greek term means both "word" and "reason"). On the one hand, Philo borrowed some of his ideas from the Stoics (Logos as the active and vivifying principle of the universe), who in turn are indebted to Heraclitus ("the dividing Logos," which creates by the fusion of contrasts); he was also influenced by Plato's "theory of ideas." On the other hand, Philo's Logos is rooted in the biblical idea of the creative word of God, the Targum's *memra*, the mystical concepts of the *merkavah* ("divine chariot"), the *Shekhinah*, the name of God, and the names of the angels. The multi-faceted character of the Logos is reflected in the many metaphorical epithets applied to it by Philo: "divine thought," "the image of God," "the firstborn son," "the archpriest," "the paraclete of humanity." Philo paved the way for later Christian theology. In the prologue to John's Gospel (1:14) this is carried farther, and "the Word made flesh" is identified with Jesus. Philo's Logos is no more than an "archangel of many names," the rational principle in the divine nature, the creative mediator between God – the One who is all-perfect and all-good – and the world of matter, which is inherently evil; but the Johannine Logos is a separate divine entity. At this stage the Word created an impossible gulf between Judaism and its daughter faith.

[Israel Abrahams]

WORKMEN'S CIRCLE (Yid. **Arbeter Ring**), U.S. socialist and culturally oriented Jewish fraternal order; founded in New York in 1892 by Jewish immigrant workers and chartered on a national basis in 1900 for the twofold purpose of providing its members with mutual aid, health, and death benefits, and other fraternal services, and of supporting the labor and socialist movements throughout the world. Dedicated to the promotion of progressive Yiddish culture, the Workmen's Circle developed a broad spectrum of cultural activities, including publication of books and magazines, promotion of adult education, sponsorship of singing and dramatic clubs, etc.

During its early period, the leadership of the Workmen's Circle shared the assimilationist-cosmopolitan attitudes of some of the earliest founders of the Jewish labor movement in North America. Later, with an influx of *Bundist immigrants who had either been active in or supporters of the unsuccessful Russian revolution of 1905, a more explicitly Jewish consciousness – secular, progressive, and Yiddish-language–based – was introduced to the Workmen's Circle. These ideas permeated its governing bodies, while individual branches included within their ranks individuals associated with a range of secular movements on the political left.

In 1916, it entered the field of Jewish education by resolving to establish schools for Jewish children, with the first Workmen's Circle afternoon school opening in 1917. The I.L. Peretz schools subsequently became the largest network of

Jewish secular *shuln* (schools) in the United States and Canada.

For many years, the Workmen's Circle was an important repository of socialist sentiment. Many of its activists were active in the Socialist Party, trade unions, and the larger Jewish labor movement. As a result, it became known as "the Red Cross of the labor movement," and was proud of the appellation. A founder and leader of the People's Relief Committee during World War I years, in 1934 it was a founder, and for many years the backbone, of the *Jewish Labor Committee. It also spearheaded the formation of the *Congress for Jewish Culture in 1948.

While initially sympathetic to the Bolshevik Revolution and the new Soviet regime, the Workmen's Circle was critical of the Soviet government's repression of non-Communist socialists. Internecine battles of the early 1920s within the entire U.S. left, not just the Workmen's Circle, pitted Communists against Socialists, and by 1929, the organization became explicitly anti-Communist in orientation. Communists and their allies either left of their own accord or were expelled at that time. Many of those who left were active in the formation of the International Workers' Order and its Jewish People's Fraternal Order. After that breach, the Workmen's Circle often struggled against Communist ambitions within the Jewish community in general, and the environment of the Jewish labor movement in specific.

Starting with the Roosevelt Administration, many in the organization left the socialist world, joining New Deal Democrats. Some left out of conviction that the Democrats were enacting parts of the socialist program. The anti-war position of the Socialist Party in the pre-Pearl Harbor period affected others. The post-war years brought about a gradual move from socialism and social democracy. Bundist anti-Zionism was never as strong in the U.S. as in Europe, and it has been a staunch, albeit not uncritical, supporter of the State of Israel since its formation. At the turn of the 21st century, the organization was far from its explicitly socialist origins, but in a more general sense part of the liberal/left, having as a general goal the creation of *a shenere un besere velt*, "a more beautiful and better world."

Along with other groups that were initially fraternal organizations which drew their membership primarily from the immigration community, the Workmen's Circle had to confront the challenge of establishing a following among native-born Jews, and those whose first, and often only, language was English, not Yiddish. This challenge was especially severe as the founders and their children died off, although it did make headway among the offspring of the older members. In 1925, the Workmen's Circle had its peak membership of 87,000. This was when the wellspring of Jewish immigrants from Europe was closed by U.S. immigration policy changes, and the organization's membership began to decline. In 1967, it was down to 64,000, in over 420 branches, 98 of which were English speaking. By 1978, the number was 55,000; in 1998, 25,000; and by 2005, 15,000, in some 200 branches, virtually all of which were English speaking. As the organization moved away from a "benefits" orientation to focus on public programs of Yiddish and Jewish culture, education and social action, however, the historic definition of "dues-paying membership" has become less relevant to the organization: in 2005, it was estimated that nearly 50,000 individuals were involved to some degree with the Workmen's Circle via attendance at WC-sponsored events, as contributors, purchasers of goods and services including benefit policies, Jewish Book Center, etc. The same is true when looking at the branch structure, which was formed when communication was primarily face-to-face, and the Jewish community was less mobile. In recent years, WC activities and structure are more district- or region-oriented (e.g., Boston, Los Angeles, Detroit), and often WC work is national in nature. Some branches are simply remnants of the structure of earlier generations.

At the end of 2005, there were 15 WC-sponsored or associated *shuln*, many of which were the core of a local Workmen's Circle group. It maintains two geriatric centers for aged community members, and operates Circle Lodge, a summer resort/vacation center, and Camp Kinder Ring, a children's camp founded in 1927, both in the Catskills, Dutchess County, New York. The WC also sponsors the Folksbiene Theater, a Yiddish theater founded in 1915 as an amateur venue, which today operates under professional direction and supports several choirs. The Yiddish publication, *Der Fraynd*, founded in 1910, and the English-language *Workmen's Circle Call*, founded in 1933, both ceased publication in the 1990s. Ironically, in 2005, negotiations with the English-language *Jewish Currents* – which had roots in the U.S. Jewish Communist camp – led to a cosponsorship by the Workmen's Circle and the Association for Jewish Secularism.

BIBLIOGRAPHY: M. Epstein, *Jewish Labor in U.S.A.; an Industrial, Political and Cultural History of the Jewish Labor Movement* (1950–1953); Y. Sh. Hertz, *50 yor arbeter ring in yidishn lebn* (1950); M. Hurwitz, *The Workmen's Circle: its History, Ideals, Organization and Institutions* (1936); J. Jacobs, *The Workmen's Circle* (2004); S. Niger, *Eyn Kamf far a Nayer Dertsiung* (1940); J.J. Shapiro, *The Friendly Society: A History of the Workmen's Circle* (1970); Y. Yeshurin and Y.Sh. Hertz, *Arbeter ring boyer un tuer. Nyu-york: Arbeter ring boyer un tuer komitet*, [biographical dictionary of Workmen's Circle founders and activists] (1962); A.S. Zaks, *Di geshikhte fun arbeyeter ring, 1892–1925* (1925).

[Charles Bezalel Sherman / Arieh Lebowitz (2nd ed.)]

WORLD CONFERENCE OF JEWISH ORGANIZATIONS (COJO), roof organization established in Rome in 1958 with the participation of the following organizations: *American Jewish Congress, *B'nai B'rith, *Board of Deputies of British Jews, *Canadian Jewish Congress, Conseil Représentatif des Juifs de France (CRIF), Delagación de Asociaciones Israelitas Argentinas (*DAIA), Executive Council of Australian Jewry, Jewish Labor Committee, South African Jewish Board of Deputies, and the *World Jewish Congress. Avraham *Harman of the Zionist Executive participated in convening the first meeting of COJO (together with Nahum *Goldmann of the World

Jewish Congress and Philip *Klutznick of B'nai B'rith), but the World Zionist Organization decided not to affiliate with COJO formally. At the initial meeting, these organizations decided to establish COJO as a consultative group on a two-year trial basis, after which they would decide whether they wished to disband or create a fully functioning world Jewish organization dealing with all matters concerning Jewish life. They also decided to explore the desirability of establishing a world council on Jewish education.

Two years later, at a meeting in Amsterdam, the organizations decided neither to disband nor to transform COJO into a fully functioning international organization but to continue COJO on an ongoing basis as a consultative group, meeting from time to time to keep each other informed on problems of mutual concern. Nahum Goldmann was elected as chairman, Label *Katz (of B'nai B'rith) as co-chairman, and Yehuda Hellman as secretary-general. COJO subsequently met regularly at least once a year and deliberated such problems as Soviet Jewry, the Middle East situation, Jews in Arab countries, the Arab boycott, problems of Jews in South America, and other issues.

In 1962 COJO convened in Israel a world conference on Jewish education. Although elaborate plans were laid down, administrative difficulties, differences of opinion, and a lack of funds prevented these plans from fully materializing. At a meeting in Geneva in 1969, COJO adopted the recommendation of a special subcommittee and abandoned the plans for a world conference on Jewish education in favor of a more modest project under the aegis of a COJO Commission on Jewish Education to be established in Jerusalem. Elected to head this commission were Ḥayyim Finkelstein, chairman of the Jewish Agency's Department on Jewish Education, and Jay Kaufman (d. 1971), executive vice president of B'nai B'rith.

At the meeting in Jerusalem in the winter of 1965, COJO further regularized its work by adding to the list of its officers a vice chairman representing the Board of Deputies of British Jews. One year later a representative of DAIA was also elected as a vice chairman. In 1967 the World Zionist Organization became a full member of COJO, and Louis A. *Pincus and William A. *Wexler became co-chairmen. (In 1971 W.A. Wexler was elected president.) On the eve of the Vatican Council II meeting (Feb. 27, 1962), COJO submitted a memorandum to the Vatican on behalf of its member organizations. At their 1970 meeting, the officers of COJO recommended that a clearinghouse be established for the dissemination of relevant documents and information to serve the needs of member organizations and enhance the airing of views and ideas. Although the growth of COJO was slow and undramatic, the members managed to keep together and met regularly to discuss problems of mutual interest.

[Yehuda Hellman]

WORLD JEWISH ASSOCIATIONS. This article is confined to organizations that encompass Jews and Jewish activities cutting across the borders of various countries. Associations of this nature have existed for more than a century. Among the histories of dispersed communities of ethnic, religious, or any other character, nowhere can one find the same wealth of organizational experience in the political, social, and cultural spheres as among the Jews. Three interrelated features characterize these organizations: (1) all their activities are international, as Jews throughout the world constitute a single entity; (2) through its organizations Jewry relates itself to international bodies and their laws; (3) organization is the quality that all Jewish communities must have in common and is what unites them. A nation without president, government, or distinct framework of services, it nevertheless has representatives – "*negotiorum gestores*" in Herzl's terminology – and leaders of sectional organizations who engage in deliberations on lines of policy, "administrative" activities, and independent political action in both the foreign and social arenas. The community, scattered as it is, has its common needs and services, its financial structure, and its patterns of loyalty.

Nevertheless, all of its services are decentralized, and since they must be geared to practical demands they are in constant flux. They include organs of protection and are based on principles of protection. In these efforts, Jewry has to rely on international law and its institutions, and it can only do so through organization. However, there can be no comprehensive organization – whether for protection, welfare, education, fund-raising, or emigration – unless there is a non-governmental organization (NGO) arrangement for it.

Since World War II, the special status of NGOs has been consolidated, mainly in the form of "consultation" with the main intergovernmental organizations (IGOs), primarily the United Nations. As a social phenomenon, however, the NGO is far older, as are its functions and achievements in the history of Jewry. Jews, on their part, played an important role in developing the awareness, within the organized international community, of the need to recognize the status of NGOs and their public services. Jewish world organizations became a pioneering force in the field of international group activity and group protection. The history of this policy, often pursued under the greatest sacrifices and against the heaviest odds, is a vital part of Jewish history. Organization proved to be the main precondition for self-assertion and protection. The whole organizational preparation of Israel's statehood developed within strict NGO patterns, and the same holds true for minority protection in the interwar period and the negotiation of restitution after the Holocaust.

Early Conditions and Organized Charity (19th Century)

With the possible exception of the struggle for Greek independence (and the political activities of Irish emigrants to the United States) international organization developed within Jewry earlier than within any other dispersed community. It was a response to dire need, preceding any clear definition or practicable anticipation of its future. This transition from the generally amorphous condition of Jewry as late as the 18th century occurred with the French Revolution (the Emancipation Act of 1791) and Napoleon's *Sanhedrin, which, whatever the purposes it was meant to serve, or the objections to it, established an organ representing several branches of the Jewish world community. In addition to the French participation, there were 18 representatives from Piedmont, 16 from Regno, and several rabbis from Germany. Joseph David *Sinzheim, the rabbi of Strasbourg, presided. His summary of the session was issued in a proclamation in French and Hebrew, an indication that it was also addressed to Jews abroad. In one of the early Jewish papers in French, *L'Univers Israélite* (1851), Jules Carvallo proposed the establishment of an international Jewish congress, mainly with a view to protecting Jews in the Middle East.

After the Napoleonic era certain developments took place at the intergovernmental political level, and already at the Congress of Vienna (1815) a number of Jewish problems was discussed. The rise in status of some wealthy Jews on the one hand, and new concepts of law invoked by outstanding Jewish lawyers and politicians on the other, initiated a new kind of activity, as symbolized in the joint journey to Cairo of Moses *Montefiore from London and Adolphe *Crémieux from Paris to appeal against the judgment in the Damascus blood libel. In a sense, the establishment of the *Alliance Israélite Universelle (1860), the first Jewish NGO and one of the first international NGOs in general, was a formal expression of the change in organized Jewish activities. Sister organizations in London (*Anglo-Jewish Association) and Vienna (*Israelitische Allianz zu Wien) followed soon after. At the same time, certain wealthy Jews had been carrying out widespread international charity work, serving in effect as substitutes for entire welfare organizations, with knowledgeable secretaries at headquarters and agile agents abroad. These included such renowned figures as Sir Moses *Montefiore, Baron Maurice de *Hirsch, Baron Edmond de *Rothschild, Baron Horace *Guenzburg, Jacob H. *Schiff, and Julius *Rosenwald. Later, the work initiated by them was carried on either by foundations which they established (*Jewish Colonization Association, *PICA) or formal organizations like *ORT and the American Jewish *Joint Distribution Committee (JDC).

Organization for Welfare and Protection

The foreign interests of the Alliance Israélite Universelle and the Anglo-Jewish Association soon shifted from the Middle East to Russia and Eastern Europe. A series of conferences, missions, and welfare organizations characterized the next half century. "The public demonstration, the conference, the international gathering for Jewish purposes, now a phenomenon of everyday life in Jewry, owe their origin to the [Anglo-Jewish] Association and to the Alliance" (Nahum Sokolow). Matters took a similar course in the United States, though still focusing on local welfare and the settlement of Jewish immigrants, mainly from Russia. A vast network of organizations was created: *B'nai B'rith, founded in 1843, became an international order in 1882; HIAS (see *United Hias Service) developed during the 1880s; the *American Jewish Committee was founded in 1906, and the American Joint Distribution Committee in 1914. The three latter organizations, though American only, developed worldwide services for Jews in many countries – the Jewish response to World War I and the postwar disaster in Russia and the Succession States.

With the rise of Emancipation, European Jewry experienced several severe shocks: in the 1880s pogroms and persecution in Russia and Romania and a ritual murder trial in Austria-Hungary (*Tiszaeszlar), and in 1890s the Dreyfus affair in France. Jewry began to react, both out of great and urgent need and as a result of the consolidation of the economic and professional power of individual Jews. Up to World War I, the main organizational effort was concentrated in areas of distress. It found its expression in a proliferation of welfare organizations (including the *Hilfsverein der deutschen Juden, founded in 1901) and in the emergence of organizations for "self-emancipation" and other activities, such as the *Ḥibbat Zion, the socialist *Bund (established in 1897), and the Zionist Organization (founded in the same year, see *Zionism).

Jewish Political Activity: Zionist "Negotiorum Gestio"

Radical reforms were proposed by Theodor Herzl. He rejected both the affirmation of Diaspora life and belief in assimilation or socialism or a retreat into a secluded religious community as enduring solutions of the Jewish problem. He emphatically denied that welfare and charity should be envisaged as long-term methods. Only the establishment of a Jewish state was comprehensive enough a foundation upon which to build a permanent edifice. Herzl quickly arrived at the conclusion that here was need for a world Jewish organization which would take account of all principal factors involved: exodus, settlement, and protection. Organizations should not only be an instrument for foreign policy, but also a body as democratic as possible under the specific conditions of a dispersed nation, designed to incorporate the political will of Jewry; to represent it, to elect its leaders, and to plan its policy. Before providing the nation with territory on which to settle, Herzl wanted to provide it with those organs necessary for its full identity, political activity and functioning. In Herzl's vision, Jewish national self-determination, as an organizational and political proposition, would have to crystallize according to two legal postulates: first, that the Zionist movement be recognized as the *negotiorum gestor* for Jewry as a whole; and second, that Jewry's return to Ereẓ Israel would give rise to a "national home for the Jewish people secured under public law." Herzl did not succeed in obtaining the charter for the "national home," but he succeeded in organizing the Zionist movement, first of all by convening a Zionist Congress "as our first national institution," with several functional subsidiaries.

The First Test: World War I and Its Aftermath

The great test came under the conditions that brought about the dismemberment of the Ottoman Empire, the victory of the principle of national self-determination, and the establishment of the League of Nations as guarantor of the mandates and minorities regimes. In this context, the Zionist vision became politically relevant. Herzl's yearning for a "charter" now proved to have opened a door toward internationalization of the Jewish problem in regard to both method and settlement. The League of Nations' Mandate for Palestine was based on the idea of a Jewish National Home. Thus, at the end of World War I, Palestine was drawn into the orbit of supra-governmental as well as Jewish non-governmental organization. Article 4 of the League of Nations' Mandate called for the establishment of a Jewish Agency, by implication a Jewish body broader than the Zionist Organization, which was nonetheless recognized as such *per interim*. At the Annual Zionist Conference of 1922, the Zionist Organization formally assumed the rights and duties of the Jewish Agency for Palestine. It also expressed the wish that "the Jewish Agency shall represent the whole Jewish people. "The Zionist General Council also passed a resolution (in February 1923) providing that "the controlling organ of the Jewish Agency shall be responsible to a body representative of the Jewish People." Consent was also given to negotiate with leading non-Zionists and various Jewish associations for their participation in an "Agency" to be active in Palestine. An agreement for the establishment of this Jewish Agency was signed in Zurich on Aug. 14, 1929.

Simultaneously with the establishment of the mandate system, the League of Nations created the Permanent Mandates Commission, a supervisory organ for mandate administration, thus creating the formal prerequisites for the protection of group rights, through which representatives of the group organized as an NGO had *ex lege* access to the leading intergovernmental organizations and the possibility of appeal against the mandatory. The procedure was by way of petition and reviews ("observations") or mandatory reports. The Jewish Agency for Palestine came to be regarded by Jews and many non-Jews as the "Jewish State *in statu nascendi*" (*ha-medinah be-derekh*). It assumed a vital function: to represent effectively the interests of Jewry at large in matters pertaining to its National Home. Great Britain, as the mandatory power, was thus faced by an organization representing not only the Jews of Palestine but world Jewry in its relation to Palestine. This role was revived after World War II, when it prevented Great Britain from disposing of Palestine in a deal with the Arabs. Thus, during the interwar period, when Jewry had just acquired a certain minority consciousness (see below), the Zionist movement pressed it in the direction of a community consciousness, or, properly speaking, a definite nationalist consciousness.

Minority Rights and Organization for Reconstruction and Protection

With the Peace Conference of 1919, a stage was reached whereby an organized Jewish world effort for minority rights and self-protection could have developed, having for the first time a definite organization with which to apply at first to the Peace Conference itself and later to the resulting League of Nations. Nevertheless, this development was uneven and fortuitous. From the end of 1918, several Jewish delegations began to converge toward Paris, mainly from the vast belt of political chaos that spread from the Baltic to the Black Sea. New states were emerging and claiming recognition, and the question was whether the international community should not insist on prior guarantees for the rights of minorities and of those groups (being the most outstanding) which would have no state of their own to protect their rights and interests. Anxious to establish a united Jewish front, these Jewish delegations associated themselves with the initiative of the representatives of the *American Jewish Congress, to set up (on March 25, 1919) a coordinating Comité, des Délégations Juives auprès de la Conférence de Paix, presided over by the president of the American Jewish Congress, Julian *Mack, with Louis *Marshall of the American Jewish Committee and Nahum *Sokolow of the Zionist Organization as vice president and Leo *Motzkin as general secretary. Most regional bodies were represented on the Comité as was the B'nai B'rith. However, the Alliance Israélite and the British Joint Foreign Committee refused to participate, although they too intervened politically. Formally, the Jewish delegations had only the status of petitioners. They spoke in the name of elected "congresses," "councils," or federated Jewish communities, and the Comité des Délégations Juives claimed to be the spokesman for more than 10,000,000 Jews. The main approach in 1919 was based on the idea that a minority had rights that an organized representative organization could invoke before an authoritative diplomatic forum acting in the name of international law. In words more appropriate to current procedural concepts, a situation developed in which the protection of beneficiary rights arising out of minority treaties was confined to non-governmental entities operating in constant "consultation" with the IGO.

Nevertheless, the impetus of 1919 soon slackened. In 1927 the Comité des Délégations Juives was reorganized, and a Council for Jewish Minority Rights was established at Geneva to underscore its permanent role. In truth, the real struggle still lay ahead when the Council reentered the arena. In May 1933 it had to plead before the League Council (and in October 1933 before the General Assembly) for the Bernheim petition, to the effect that certain measures of the newly established Hitler regime in Germany were "null and void for Upper Silesia." The petition was successful and showed that individual complaints, if based on international law, could be processed with the aid of an interceding non-governmental body of international standing.

An additional form of consultative function for non-governmental bodies was created in October 1933, when an autonomous Office of the High Commissioner for Refugees (Jewish and other) coming from Germany was established by the General Assembly of the League of Nations. The Office had a governing body consisting of government representatives and an advisory council made up of representatives of "private organizations."

Organizations for relief operated alongside political ones. About a dozen new Jewish organizations had sprung up or had been reorganized since the end of World War I, most of them of welfare type. The enormous devastation resulting from World War I, the new regime in Soviet Russia and the famine there, and the establishment of other regimes gave rise to activities which generally confirmed the existence of Jewish solidarity throughout the world. An immense organization had emerged in the United States for fund-raising (mainly the JDC) and in Europe and other parts of the world for on-the-spot relief, reconstruction, and emigration.

The World Jewish Congress

Hitler's successes on the domestic front made it apparent that Jewry had to prepare for a fight on an international scale against Nazism, its agents – the German settlements throughout the world – and their local antisemitic allies. Leo Motzkin was one of the first to assert that the Council for Jewish Minority Rights must become a fighting political organization in the name of Jewry as a whole. Stephen *Wise, Louis *Lipsky, and other leaders of the American Jewish Congress associated themselves with his initiative, as had Nahum *Goldmann and others in Europe. A reorganization of such scope proved necessary, since it became clear that the postwar period of protection of minority rights under League of Nations patronage was drawing to an end.

In 1932 the first world Jewish conference was convened in Geneva: 17 countries were represented, but the American Jewish Committee, the B'nai B'rith, the Board of Deputies of British Jews, and the Central-Verein Deutscher Staatsbuerger juedischen Glaubens in Germany still refused to participate. Four years later, in August 1936, the *World Jewish Congress (WJC) was formally Founded by 280 delegates from 33 countries assembled at Geneva. Their aim was to create "a permanent address for the Jewish people." The WJC became a voluntary, cooperative association of federations of local Jewish organizations. It did not interfere with the internal life of any federation or community, but it also maintained that no single community or organization, however important and influential, should be entitled to act unilaterally on behalf of the community or any branch of it without being empowered to do so; nor should any community, however small, be excluded from joint action. The WJC declared that it "does not seek to be regarded as [the] 'Government' of the Jewish people outside Palestine." At the international level, it had to assume the function of the Comité des Délégations Juives. It directed a few diplomatic campaigns against Germany, Poland, Romania, and Nazi-occupied Austria. In 1938, at the International Refugee Conference at Evian, the WJC had to fight for the very right of the Jew to be considered a refugee and thus claim the rights of first asylum and transit migration in the countries bordering on Germany.

World War II

Jewry entered World War II as its first victim rather than an ally; it lacked even the limited status and facilities of the various governments-in-exile. The possibility of non-governmental action was considerably reduced, being limited to a few humanitarian efforts *in extremis*. The paradox was that at a time when community consciousness was at its peak, operational capacity was at its lowest. Nevertheless, two problems kept organized efforts alive: the welfare problem of the remnants of European Jewry and the political problem of Jewry in Palestine. It is a tribute to their organizational capacity that the postwar Jewish organizations succeeded in realizing three major aims:

(1) to ensure favorable developments in regard to Palestine;

(2) to secure reparations from West Germany and thus a modicum of relief for more than a million survivors; and

(3) to maintain consultations and later consultative status with the newly established IGOs, particularly the United Nations, UNESCO, and the Council of Europe.

In San Francisco, where the United Nations was established in 1945, it was again the Jewish Agency for Palestine that acted as the representative of the Jewish people vis-à-vis Palestine as well as the nascent Jewish State, particularly when the "first round" was fought in UNCIO for what became Article 80 of the Charter. After the War, when the Anglo-American Commission arrived in Palestine in 1946, it reported that the Jewish case was "presented at full length and with voluminous written evidence, in three series of public hearings: in Washington by the American Zionists, in London by the British Zionists, and finally, and most massively, by the Jewish Agency in Jerusalem. The basic policy advocated was always the same – the so-called Biltmore Program of 1942." The same can be said about the discussions with *UNSCOP in Palestine as well as at UN headquarters on the basis of the UNSCOP report. In this struggle, the Jewish case, as presented by the Jewish Agency, was supported by all the major Jewish organizations. As earlier, the mere fact of having been organized in a democratically structured world organization – the Zionist Organization – had allowed Jewry to respond to events through organized representations, which had been the case from 1917 on, when the Balfour Declaration had been published, up to July 7, 1948, when for the first time a representative of the State of Israel was invited to attend a meeting, the 330th, of the Security Council of the United Nations.

Another aim during the postwar years was to provide for the preservation of human rights in at least three of the five peace treaties with former Nazi satellites – Romania, Hungary, and Bulgaria. By coincidence, these countries were the only ones still to have Jewish minorities, to have turned communist, and to have been obligated by post-World War I arrangements. However, the effort was unsuccessful: no trace remained of the minority rights established in Eastern Europe after World War I. The situation was different in the West. The experience leading to Jewish world community consciousness, which had become rooted in 1933 with the ascension of Hitler to power, did not cease after the War. The War ended with valuable property remaining without owners but traceable to public or private Jewish ownership. It was pointed out that survivors within a given group had the most valid right to advance the thesis of collective restitution. After the Paris Reparations Conference of December 1945, the Jewish Agency for Palestine and the JDC were appointed as "field organizations" for the implementation of a part of the program established by the Conference, and a new era commenced for Jewish NGOs. A major achievement was the establishment in 1951 of the World *Conference of Jewish Material Claims against Germany, the most representative body established thus far, and of a parallel committee for Austria in 1952. These organizations, as well as the Jewish Restitution Successor Organization (JRSO) and the Jewish Trust Corporation for Germany (JTC), established the principle that NGOs can be partners in international legal negotiations and agreements with sovereign or other entities, the outstanding case being the Wassenaar Protocol of Sept. 10, 1952, between the Claims Conference and the government of the Federal Republic of Germany. Moreover, JRSO, together with the JTC for Germany, Ltd., London, and the Branche Française de la JTC, entered into agreements with Bonn (1956) on the payment of compensation in lieu of restitution. Among all the Western states, only in the case of Austria have these efforts met with frustration during all these years.

Jewry's transition from World War II into a greatly changed Europe must be viewed against the background of the Holocaust. The Claims Conference, powerful enough to guarantee annual allocations of $10,000,000 for public use over 12 years, began to plan reconstruction. Roughly 75% of this sum went for basic programs of relief, economic rehabilitation, emigration and resettlement, and 10–15% was allocated for cultural and educational reconstruction. The balance was divided more or less equally between legal aid and historical research into the Holocaust. In 1960 a Standing Conference on European Jewish Social and Welfare Services was established to make formal the *de facto* cooperation existing among local communities and voluntary agencies, such as JDC, ORT, HIAS, etc. Its greatest achievement was the resettlement of refugees from Algeria in France and Israel. Upon winding up its activities, the Claims Conference used its last allocation of over $10,000,000 to establish the Memorial Foundation for Jewish Culture.

Summary

If within a decade or so after the end of World War II, the most urgent needs for Jewish survival were fulfilled – the establishment of the State of Israel, the resettlement of *Displaced Persons, survivors, and refugees, and the repossession of ownerless Jewish property – the continued existence of Jewish NGOs nevertheless became necessary. There were many reasons for this. The need for protection of Jewish minorities became progressively acute in Communist and Arab countries. The B'nai B'rith Anti-Defamation League (active in the United States, Canada, and Mexico) also found a vital field of activity. The fight against racial and religious prejudice and intolerance and several other issues concerning human rights became one of the central themes within leading IGOs (the United Nations, UNESCO, ILO, the Council of Europe). Finally, there has been a tendency for education to replace welfare as the major Jewish concern.

The American Jewish Conference on Soviet Jewry, which, together with similar bodies in Israel and Europe, sponsored the World Conference of Jewish Communities on Soviet Jewry (Brussels, 1971), became a potent factor in the struggle for the rights of the Jews in the Soviet Union. Despite the looseness of its organization, or perhaps because of it, participation and representation on a very wide scale was made possible. The same also holds true for the Comité International pour la Déliverance des Juifs au Moyen Orient established in Paris (1970) to act on behalf of the remaining Jews in distress in Arab countries.

Since 1945 there has been a tendency to establish new organizations and seek consultative status for them with the United Nations or their agencies. Up to 1961 there were no less than 22 new or regrouped Jewish NGOs. Thus, out of 20 Jewish NGOs in the group of principal organizations (international or national with several areas of operation: see chart), six are postwar creations or adaptations, nine have direct and five indirect consultative status with the UN Economic and Social Council (ECOSOC), and several an analogous status with other IGOs. Moreover, six national organizations indirectly enjoy such consultative status (see also *United Nations, Specialized Agencies and Other Bodies).

The proliferation of organizations added impetus to a phenomenon long observed in Jewish organization: their coalition or federalist nature. Thus, the Zionist Organization and the Jewish Agency have been governed for decades by carefully balanced coalitions, under conditions of continually renewed attempts at broadening partnership. They became the operational vehicle for world Jewry's participation in Israel's activities and development as the National Home of Jewry. (According to the Jerusalem Program of 1968, the main aim of Zionism is the unity of the Jewish people and the centrality of Israel in Jewish life.) In this sense it should be compared to earlier organizations. The Comité des Délélegations Juives was formed in response to external circumstances. Its membership was heterogeneous in many respects, but they united in what they viewed as a common purpose. Later, the World Jewish Congress was established as a federation of "national" Jewish associations. If these were "roof organizations" with functions of coordination, some less formal solutions were adopted wherein coordination required no permanent executive apparatus, such as the *World Conference of Jewish Organizations (COJO, founded 1958) and the U.S. Conference of Major Jewish Organizations (generally known as the Presidents' Conference). The main Jewish organizations are represented in all, or most, of these coordinating bodies: the JDC, the Jewish Agency, B'nai B'rith, and the World Jewish Congress. On the other hand, in some of them the absence of the American Jewish Committee is conspicuous. In many of them there is little contact between the organization and the Jewish population at large, and the situation is still similar to what it was at the time of Baron de Hirsch and his welfare secretariats. Jewry is still to a large degree governed by self-perpetuating oligarchic establishments, and the process of full democratization, as envisaged by Herzl, remains a vision of the future.

Jewish world organizations have until now contributed little that is new toward maintaining the consciousness of a common faith, culture, and destiny in Jewish communities.

It is still the position that while many organizations engage in educational activities on a local and national scale, only the Zionist Organization is at present important, though still an inadequate, educational agency on a world scale. (Attempts to establish a World Council for Jewish Education have failed so far; a well-attended World Conference on this subject had met in Jerusalem in August 1962). The main problem of contemporary Jewish world organization is whether its current political activity is sufficient to create a meaningful pattern of activity on behalf of the dispersed Jewish community as a whole – that is, a pattern in which both the Israel-centered part of Jewish identity and heritage and the contribution of Diaspora Jewry to the world's pluralist societies will be recognized as representing an independent entity. Both are confronted with obstacles – the main ones being old-fashioned antisemitism and the latter-day New Left. Nor has much changed in local intergroup relations, the various guest-nations still finding it easier to accommodate the different shades of local acculturation and compromise of Diaspora Jewry than an Israel-oriented Jewry. On the other hand, considering matters in the light of Jewish experience. it would seem that there is hardly any more support, or room, for a Dubnovian affirmation of a Diaspora Jewish culture, notwithstanding the need of the various Jewish NGOs to derive authority for their fight for the consolidation of human rights in general, and Jewish rights in particular, as representatives of a definite cultural identity and interest within a structuralized open society.

Nota Bene

While it is quite clear that the sole purpose of Jewish associations has been the maintenance of the Jewish community, particularly in its dispersal across the often fortuitous boundaries of non-Jewish nations, there have been malicious allegations that it was the intention of Jewry "to rule the world," even if this involved the destruction, or at least corruption, of the non-Jewish nations (see *Elders of Zion, Protocols of the Learned). While it is difficult to eradicate such aberrations, a study of the activities of the organizations previously described reveals nothing more than a desire to be left in peace to develop freely and autonomously.

BIBLIOGRAPHY: J. Lador-Lederer, *International Non-Governmental Organizations* (1963), 126–57; H.M. Sachar, *The Course of Modern Jewish History* (1958); I. Cohen, *Contemporary Jewry* (1950); I. Elbogen, *A Century of Jewish Life* (1953); M.I. Soloff, *How the Jewish People Lives Today* (1952); A. Tartakower, *Am ve-Olamo* (1963) (for further bibliography see articles on the various organizations mentioned in the article).

[Josef J. Lador-Lederer]

WORLD JEWISH CONGRESS (WJC), a "voluntary association" of "representative Jewish bodies, communities, and organizations" throughout the world, organized to "assure the survival, and to foster the unity of the Jewish people" (arts. 1 and 2 of its constitution). The central Jewish communal bodies and major representative organizations of more than 60 countries belong to it (1969). Its immediate aims are: to coordinate the common interests of its member organizations; to defend the rights, status, and interests of Jews and Jewish communities; to encourage and assist the creative development of Jewish social and cultural life throughout the world; and to act on behalf of its member organizations before governmental, intergovernmental, and other international authorities with respect to matters which concern the Jewish people as a whole (art. 2 of the constitution). The organization does not intervene in the domestic political affairs of any country (art. 3). Only democratic bodies which remain autonomous are entitled to membership, which will be granted, as a general rule, to only one representative national Jewish body of any country (art. 4). A plenary assembly is the supreme authority of the Congress (art. 5), and an executive committee and a governing council conduct the affairs of the organization (art. 8).

History

The origin of the concept of the World Jewish Congress may be found in the early cooperative efforts by Jewish communities around the world in religious, legal, political, and relief matters. The origin of the World Jewish Congress can be traced to ideological developments within the American and European Jewish communities during and after World War I. In 1919 the *Comité des Délégations Juives was established, led by Leo *Motzkin, and, after three preparatory conferences, the first World Jewish Congress convened in Geneva, Switzerland, in 1936. 280 delegates represented the Jews of 32 countries under the leadership of Stephen *Wise and Nahum *Goldmann.

Policy and Action

The history of the World Jewish Congress is involved in the most tragic period of contemporary Jewish life – Nazi barbarism, rescue attempts, and relief and rehabilitation programs. The World Jewish Congress played a central role in the creation of Jewish policies with regard to the peace treaties, the prosecution and trial of Nazi war criminals, the adoption of a scheme of indemnification and reparations for Jewish victims of the Holocaust, and the rehabilitation of Jewish life in the years after the war.

Action on behalf of Jewish communities exposed to particular dangers, like those of Eastern Europe and Arab countries; relations with non-Jewish religious bodies; the fight against neo-Nazism and antisemitism; representation before international organs (the United Nations, UNESCO, regional intergovernmental organizations, and others); and, above all, the preservation of the identity of Jewish communities in view of the increasing trend to assimilation, are on the agenda of the different departments of the WJC. It maintains four branches of its executive – in North America, South America, Europe, and Israel – as well as a research branch, the Institute of Jewish Affairs, formerly in New York and presently in London, to execute its policies and direct its activities.

In 1981, Edgar M. *Bronfman was elected president of the World Jewish Congress. Under his leadership through the early years of the 21st century the WJC was in the forefront of the struggle for Soviet Jewry, the campaign to expose the

Nazi past of Kurt Waldheim and achieve moral and material justice for victims of the Holocaust and their heirs, and the fight against antisemitism and right-wing extremists like Jorge Haider as well as defense of Israel in the international arena.

BIBLIOGRAPHY: Institute of Jewish Affairs, *Unity in Dispersion* (1948); N. Robinson, *The United Nations and the World Jewish Congress* (1955); Institute of Jewish Affairs, *The Institute Anniversary Volume* (1962); World Jewish Congress, *From Stockholm to Brussels* (1966); S.S. Wise, *Challenging Years* (1949), passim.

[Natan Lerner]

WORLD LABOR ZIONIST MOVEMENT, organizational framework encompassing the *Israel Labor Party and groups in the Diaspora actively supporting it. Until 1968, before the merger of *Mapai, *Aḥdut ha-Avodah (B), and *Rafi in Israel, this function was carried out mainly by "Iḥud Olami Po'alei Zion-Z.S. Hitaḥadut," which served as the world union of Mapai and its Diaspora supporters. From the earliest days of organized Zionism, there have been groups that combined a belief in Zionism with an attachment to the doctrines of socialism. The emphasis of these groups would sometimes be placed on one or another of the ideologies. Socialist Zionist circles criticized the Zionist movement in its early days because it concentrated on the political task of securing a National Home, disregarding the need to create a Jewish working class imbued with progressive ideas and a search for social justice. The Zionist socialist groups had their divisions and different trends. They had developed independently in various countries and were directly influenced by the revolutionary and social democratic movements of their respective countries. As far back as the First Zionist Congress (1897), an attempt was made to create an international union of Zionist socialists. In the early part of the 20th century, groups began to be established in the large Jewish centers of Russia, Poland, Austria, Galicia, and England. The publications of Ber *Borochov and Nachman *Syrkin, the former following Marxist reasoning and the latter a more idealistic approach, influenced the groups toward different ideological trends.

After World War I the differences crystallized. On one end was the Left Po'alei Zion, almost completely Marxist, which opposed cooperation with "bourgeois" Zionism; in the center the *Po'alei Zion, which sought to become the labor wing of the organized Zionist movement; and at the other end *Ẓe'irei Zion-Hitaḥadut, a moderate Jewish labor movement centered on the pioneering efforts in Ereẓ Israel. The two parties, Po'alei Zion and Hitaḥadut, were linked ideologically with the labor parties in Ereẓ Israel; Po'alei Zion with Aḥdut ha-Avodah and Ẓe'irei Zion – Hitaḥdut with *Ha-Po'el ha-Ẓa'ir. The contacts with parties in Ereẓ Israel had a decisive influence upon the development and the activities of the Zionist labor groups in the Diaspora. Thus when the two main labor parties in Palestine united and established the Mapai Party (1930) the merger prepared the ground for the union of the two parallel parties in the Diaspora.

In 1931–32 a number of consultations were held in the countries of the Diaspora and the conditions for attaining a complete union of the two parties were discussed. These discussions were successful to the degree that the decisive majority on both sides were won over to the idea, although there were smaller groups that did not accept the merger and broke away. It was not until 1932 that a world organization was established at a conference in Danzig, where organized labor movements from Palestine were also represented for the first time. The Palestine parties had themselves effected union, and the parties in the Diaspora followed their lead. The movements united in most European countries, notably Poland, Eastern Galicia, Germany, Romania, Czechoslovakia, Lithuania and Latvia, Bulgaria, Yugoslavia, Greece, and in the United States and South America. In each case, however, there were groups which did not join the merges, especially the left Po'alei Zion groups, which broke away and later aligned with the internal Mapai opposition group, Si'ah Bet, later called Aḥdut ha-Avodah after it split from Mapai (see *Aḥdut ha-Avodah B). The world organization centered on Mapai became known as the Iḥud Olami and its secretaries were Anselm Reiss and Aryeh *Tartakower.

The Iḥud Olami was not only an ideological movement. Although no obligation was placed upon its members to settle in Palestine, the atmosphere created encouraged *aliyah* and "self-realization." The movement extended the maximum help to the *He-Ḥalutz groups that had sprung up all over Europe. The parties affiliated with the Iḥud Olami organized professionals and artisans within the framework of Ha-Oved. The deteriorating economic position of the Jewish masses in Eastern Europe brought tens of thousands of people into the movement. In the course of time it became a valuable and large source for *aliyah*. The movement also took an active part in the struggle for Jewish rights in postwar Europe but its main emphasis was on building up Ereẓ Israel in accordance with pioneering labor ideology. Material that flowed from the nerve center in Ereẓ Israel was distributed, and emissaries, particularly from collective and cooperative labor settlements in Palestine, were encouraged to work in the Jewish communities in order to intensify their Zionism and promote Hebrew education and *aliyah*, pioneering, and settlement. The Iḥud Olami maintained contact with branches in Europe, the United States, South America, South Africa, and Australia. In North Africa there were well-organized groups in Algeria, Tunisia, and Morocco.

The Iḥud Olami formed a united labor wing of the Zionist movement and played a leading role in the debates at the Zionist Congresses and in the manning of the various positions. For many years, the principal positions on the *Jewish Agency Executive were held by representatives of the Iḥud Olami. In 1936–37 the head office of the Iḥud Olami was transferred to Palestine, and a succession of leading members of Mapai acted as secretary-general: Melech Neustadt (Noy); Haim *Shurer; Yiẓhak Harkavy; and Meir Argov.

In 1968, following the creation of the Israel Labor Party by merging Aḥdutha-Avodah (B), Mapai, and Rafi, in Israel, a world conference was called to amalgamate the two supporting movements in the Diaspora (Rafi had no Diaspora organization). A single organization was created at this conference called the World Labor Zionist Movement. Yiẓhak Korn, who had been serving as secretary-general of the Iḥud Olami, was elected secretary-general of the united movement. In the last years of the 1960s the united labor Zionist movement became an influential factor in the World Zionist movement. It was the initiator of the move to separate the functions of the Jewish Agency from those of the Zionist Organization in order that the latter might concentrate on the tasks of encouraging *aliyah*, Jewish education, and the mobilizing of the Jewish masses for Zionism. The creation of a special *aliyah* movement in the Western countries was largely the fruit of Labor Zionist movement initiative. The movement extended its activity to embrace work among students and the parents of children attending Jewish day schools. Its constituent parties were active among non-Jewish labor movements, notably the Labor Friends of Israel in Britain, which did much to combat anti-Israel propaganda. In the ensuing decades it continued to promote the Labor Zionism philosophy, supporting youth movements and other organizations abroad.

BIBLIOGRAPHY: *Be-Shaḥar ha-Tenu'a h: Shishim Shanah la-Tenu'ah ha-Ẓiyyonit-Sozyalistit* (1965); A. Tartakower, *Tenu'at ha-Ovedim ha-Yehudit*, 3 (1931).

[Moshe Rosetti]

WORLD SEPHARDI FEDERATION. Since the establishment of the Zionist movement, efforts have been made to organize the Sephardi communities throughout the world in support of settlement in the Land of Israel, and were accelerated after World War I and the Balfour Declaration. Various organizations were formed, particularly among the youth, and a Conference of Sephardi Communities was held during the World Zionist Congress in Vienna in 1925. Many Sephardi leaders opposed this on the grounds that it would give rise to separation between Sephardi and Ashkenazi Jewry. Mr. Picciotto, a Syrian Jew who lived in London, was elected chairman. As a result of his efforts, a number of agricultural settlements of Sephardi Jews were established, including Kefar Ḥittim, Zur Moshe, and Beit Ḥanan. However, the organization was dissolved after a short time.

In 1947 an organization of Sephardi Jews in the Land of Israel was set up under the leadership of E. Eliyashar, who visited South America to establish links between the Sephardi communities there and the *yishuv* in the Land of Israel. In 1950 contacts were also made with Sephardi communities in France, England, and the United States. A preparatory meeting was convened in Paris to establish a Sephardi World Congress, and among its members were David Sitton, Ovadiah Kimhi, Mr. Kaxbalko of London, and Simian Nissim of the United States.

The Congress was held in Paris in November 1951, and A. Ben-Roy of London was elected president with E. Eliyashar and Bekhor Shitrit (then Israel's minister of police), Elias Taubal of South America, and the Ḥakham S. Gaon of the English Spanish and Portuguese Congregation, as vice presidents.

Headquarters were established in London, but because of the opposition of the Left Sephardi workers in Israel, an attempt to make it a worldwide organization failed.

During the Second Sephardi Congress held in Jerusalem in May 1954, additional efforts were made to reach an understanding between the two parties, but they failed. As a result of this crisis, Mr. Ben-Roy resigned, and Mr. Sebag-Montefiore of London was elected. The new president, a non-Zionist, opposed joining pro-Zionist organizations in general and the Zionist Federation in particular. Both the Left and the Right in the Israeli branch tried in vain to persuade him to change his attitude. As a result, Sebag-Montefiore resigned and two months later Eli Nachmias, of the Sephardi community of Paris, was elected president. Though he warmly endorsed all cultural activities in Israel, he refused all contact between the Federation and any Zionist organizations. This attitude was strongly criticized by Sephardi Zionists both in the Diaspora and in Israel, and as a result Mr. Nachmias resigned.

After 1967, a new leadership emerged under Eliyahu Eliyashar of Jerusalem and Edgar Abravanel of Paris. The dynamic director-general Gad Ben-Meir in London added much vitality to the World Sephardi Federation. Emphasis was placed on scholarships for disadvantaged Oriental youth in Israel, and strengthening programs that would help them finish high school, pass matriculation exams, and advance to university.

In February 1973, Nessim David Gaon, a leader of the Sephardi community in Switzerland, was elected fourth president of the Federation. His activity on behalf of the economically distressed and his support for educational institutions in Israel were well known and appreciated, and he was highly regarded by the heads of the state and of the Zionist movement. His election gave the Federation considerable power.

Even before his election, during the 28th Zionist Congress held in Jerusalem in February 1972, the Sephardi Federation had been accepted as a member of the Zionist Organization, which gave the Federation new status in the eyes of Sephardi Jewry. In response to a request by the Federation's delegates to the Congress – which numbered 15 members from Israel and abroad – a special department of the Zionist Organization was established to deal with their problems on an international basis. As a result, delegates were sent to Sephardi communities in the United States, Canada, France, and England. For the first time in the history of Zionist activities among Sephardi Jews, youth groups from the United States, Canada, France, S. America, and Iran participated in special seminars organized for them in Israel. This youth, hitherto dissociated from Zionism and the building of the Jewish State, began to absorb the Zionist doctrine, and on their return became enthusiastic supporters of the State of Israel. The activities in Israel were concentrated mainly in the field of education. Thanks to the initiative of the Federation's president, a special fund was established for students and the economically underprivileged.

It was agreed to establish a special course at the University of Haifa for the training of public leaders from among the inhabitants of development towns and distressed areas. The course opened with 90 students who were chairmen of councils and heads of departments in development towns. It was agreed to establish similar courses in the universities of Beersheba, Bar Ilan, Tel Aviv, and Hebrew University of Jerusalem, and by the end of 1977 a total of 800 students participated. At the end of the 1970s funds were made available to establish an institute for Sephardi studies at the Hebrew University of Jerusalem called Misgav Yerushalayim, which now publishes scholarly works on Sephardi and Oriental Jewry in literature, history, and language, and organizes large-scale international conferences every four years.

At a plenary conference held in Geneva in 1979, a new structure was decided upon for the Federation, whereby the presidium was to consist of ten representatives each, from Israel and the Diaspora, the former including four delegates from the Likud, three from the Labor Alignment, two from the religious parties, and one independent, while the latter would have two delegates each from the U.S., Latin America, and France, and one each from Britain, Canada, Spain, and the rest of Europe.

In the 1980s and 1990s, the World Sephardi Federation was dormant. By 1985 the budget of the Department of Sephardi Communities of the Jewish Agency was cut to such an extent that it had no funds for activities and only paid salaries. By and large the World Sephardic Federation failed to deal with issues of Sephardi identity, education, rabbinic training, intermarriage and assimilation in the Diaspora, and Sephardi/Mizraḥi poverty and alienation in Israel. The organization remains closed to the outside world and to the Sephardic public in the Diaspora and Israel, and has failed to cultivate or attract young leadership, admit women, and include and unite the extremely fragmented Sephardi/Mizraḥi public consisting of more than 70 diverse ethnic groups throughout the Diaspora and in Israel.

The World Sephardi Federation has since moved its headquarters to Israel. Since the death of Shelomo Abutbul, who was the head of the Va'ad Edah ha-Sefardit of Tel Aviv-Yaffo, the archives of the World Sephardi Federation have remained in a warehouse in Tel Aviv and off-limits to the public and interested researchers.

[David Sitton / Yitzchak Kerem (2nd ed.)]

WORLDS, THE FOUR. The use of the term "world" in the sense of a separate spiritual unit, a particular realm of being, came to the halakhic kabbalists from the heritage of neoplatonism. At an early stage, from the beginning of the 13th century, many such "worlds" are mentioned, representing a mixture of original Jewish, gnostic, and neoplatonic concepts. In the development of the doctrine of the ten *Sefirot*, each *Sefirah* was considered as a complete world in itself which, in a way, had a mystical topography of its own. The world of *emanation could be seen as such a unit, but so could every single component or some of its configurations. Medieval philosophy knew of three worlds: the higher world comprising the separate intelligences often identified with the angels, the middle world of the spheres of heaven, and the lower, sublunar, world of nature and man. It was a natural step to add the world of the Godhead which could be identified with the world of emanation (*Aẓilut*, or the ten emanations) to this scheme. That way, four worlds would emerge. However, this did not occur in the development of the Spanish Kabbalah, where the doctrine of the four worlds originated. Rather, it had its origin in speculations connected with the interpretation of Isaiah 43:7: "Everything called by my name – for my glory I have created it, have formed it, yea I have made it." The three words used here, creation, formation, and making or achieving (*beri'ah, yeẓirah, asiyyah*), were interpreted by many authors as pointing to the progressive stages of divine activity. These stages could be seen in two perspectives: as declining from the purely spiritual to the material, or as progressing from as yet undetermined forms of being to more and more manifest ones, which in the stage of "making" would achieve a perfect shaping of the original divine purpose. In kabbalist literature these two tendencies complement each other and appear beside one another, first in the writings of the kabbalists of Gerona and later in several parts of the *Zohar. The Hebrew word *asiyyah* combines the two meanings of making and acting, and it was in this latter sense of activity that the term was frequently used by the kabbalists.

In the writings of *Azriel of Gerona, the three potencies of creation, formation, and activity are already defined as being comprised within the highest potency of divine emanation (*Aẓilut*), but they are never spoken of as worlds. This transition occurred first in the writings of *Moses b. Shem Tov de Leon. In one of his Hebrew books, *Maskiyyot Kesef*, written after 1293 (MS Adler, 1577), he quotes from an unknown source called *Yerushalmi* – in fact a lost part of the *Midrash ha-Ne'lam* in the Zohar – a statement according to which the soul of man "is from the world of creation and from the world of formation, and its completion [or perfection] is nowhere but in the world of action which is this our world." When a man leaves the world, his soul is comprised of all the three worlds – if he actually has fulfilled his task. Allusions to such three worlds are indeed found in the Aramaic text of the Zohar without being elaborated (for instance: 1, 62a). Another stage of this development is documented by the *Tikkunei Zohar*, the latest stratum of the Zohar which clearly differentiates between four stages in the development of creation without calling them "worlds." The author knows of "ten *Sefirot* of *Aẓilut* in which the king, his real self and his life, are one," whereas this is not the case in the "ten *Sefirot* of *beri'ah*, or creation": "The highest cause radiates into the ten *Sefirot* of *Aẓilut* and the ten of *beri'ah*, and also shines in the ten orders of the angels and the ten spheres of heaven, and he calls these ten ranks of angels the ten *Sefirot* of *Yeẓirah*, or formation." In other passages of the same stratum four manifestations of the figure of man are already mentioned, clearly pointing to four layers of being: they know of an "Adam of *Aẓilut*, an Adam of *beri'ah*, of *yeẓirah*, and of *asiyyah*" (1, 22b, and end of *Tikkun* 67).

These are the preparatory stages from which a fully fledged theory of four worlds emerged at the beginning of the 14th century, particularly in the writings of *Isaac b. Samuel of Acre and the anonymous "treatise on emanation," Massekhet *Aẓilut. Here, God is said to have created four worlds, corresponding to the four letters of His name:

(1) the world of *Aẓilut*, which is like a garment of light to the source of all being;

(2) the world of *beri'ah*, creation, which is essentially the sphere of the throne of God and the seven palaces surrounding it;

(3) the world of *yeẓirah*, formation, which is the world of the *Merkabah seen by Ezekiel, and of the ten ranks of angels, dominated by *Metatron;

(4) the world of *asiyyah*, filled with the lower ranks of angels, who receive the prayers of man, but also with the hosts of *Samael and his devilish companions. This world is dominated by the angel *Sandalfon. Evidently there was no clear-cut definition of the status of the sublunar terrestial world which sometimes is made a part of the fourth and sometimes remains outside of this hierarchy. The realm of the powers of evil, the *kelippot*, could be identified with the world of *asiyyah*, at least as a part of it, but could be located outside this scheme, as indeed it sometimes was in later writings.

It is equally clear that this order of four worlds expressed a declining order of being, from the divine down to the nearly or completely material. This scheme could be relatively easily combined with the teachings of the Zohar, and became accepted doctrine of the kabbalists from the early 16th century onward. Especially the worlds of *beri'ah* and *yeẓirah* were elaborated in great detail in the writings of Moses *Cordovero and Hayyim *Vital, Isaac *Luria's disciple. Cordovero tended to include the realm of the *kelippot* and the whole visible creation within the fourth world of *asiyyah*, whereas the Lurianic Kabbalah tended to differentiate between them. According to Luria, only the fall of Adam brought about the confusion between the spiritual world of *asiyyah* and the material world of the *kelippot* which, in the messianic period, will again be completely separated from each other. The basic structures of the five *Parẓufim*, the configurations of the ten *Sefirot* described under anthropomorphic symbols, are repeated all over the four worlds. Luria's descriptions of the world of *beri'ah* is much more complicated than in former sources. The seven palaces in this structure are seen as exterior projections of its basic substance, and there is considerable vacillation regarding the place of Metatron and Sandalfon who appear in the worlds of both *beri'ah* and *yeẓirah*, apparently representing different stages of their manifestation. Metatron, the highest of all angelic structures, is even said to have his head in the world of *beri'ah*, his ethereal body in *yeẓirah*, and his feet in *asiyyah*. The teachings regarding the latter three worlds in Luria's Kabbalah are almost completely new and were meant to add to the many stages which the mystical *meditation must traverse in order to fix itself on the realm of divinity.

BIBLIOGRAPHY: M. Cordovero, *Pardes Rimmonim*, ch. 16; H. Vital, *Ez Hayyim*, chs. 42–50; [I. Sarug], *Limmudei Aẓilut* (1897), 23d–34a; N. Bacharach, *Emek ha-Melekh* (1648), 167d–178d; J. Ashlag, *Talmud Eser Sefirot*, 6 (1966?), 1887–2033; G. Scholem, in: *Tarbiz*, 2 (1931), 415–42; 3 (1932), 33–66; E. Gottlieb, in: *Divrei ha-Congress ha-Olami ha-Revi'i le-Madda'ei ha-Yahadut*, 2 (1968), 329f.

[Gershom Scholem]

WORM. The word *tola'at* or *tole'ah* is employed in the Bible and the Talmud both for destructive caterpillars and for the rainworm; sometimes the combination *rimmah ve-tole'ah* (= maggots and worms) occurs. One of the curses in the commination of the Bible is that "the worm" shall eat the vines (Deut. 28:39). The Talmud (Ḥul. 67b) speaks of "the worm in the roots of the vines," referring to the beetle *Schistocerus*. The worm which smote Jonah's *kikayon* (Jonah 4:7) was presumably the caterpillar of a beetle of the genus *Capnodis* or *Cerambyx*. The Midrash states that "this worm makes the tree barren" (Mid. to Ps. 22:7). The worms that caused the manna to rot (Ex. 16:20) were fruit-fly maggots. In the Bible *rimmah ve-tole'ah* symbolizes the decomposition of the body after death (Isa. 14:11; Job 21:26), since these feed upon the decaying corpse. Man is compared to them because of his end and his frailty (Isa. 41:14; Job 25:6). They are the maggots of the carrion flies *Lucilia* and apparently also the rainworm *Lumbricus*, found in large quantities in soil rich in rotting organic material. This last is called *shilshul* in rabbinic literature (RH 24b) and in modern Israel.

BIBLIOGRAPHY: J. Feliks, *Animal World of the Bible* (1962), 129, 139. **ADD. BIBLIOGRAPHY:** Feliks, *Ha-Ẓome'aḥ*, 283.

[Jehuda Feliks]

WORMANN, CURT (1900–1991), librarian. Born in Berlin, he served from 1923 as assistant head and, later, head of the department for Adult Education of the Kreuzberg district of Berlin, as well as teaching at the Berlin Library School. In 1933 he settled in Palestine and became academic librarian at the Tel Aviv Municipal Library (1937–47). He then became director of the Jewish National and University Library in Jerusalem (1947–68). When the library on Mount Scopus became inaccessible (1948), Wormann showed great resourcefulness in providing books for faculty and students. Under his direction, hundreds of thousands of books looted by the Nazis were salvaged after the war and acquired for the University Library. The library collection tripled and the collection of manuscripts grew to 25,000 items. Many valuable collections of printed books and manuscripts were acquired during this period.

In 1956 Wormann founded, with the aid of UNESCO, a graduate library school in Jerusalem, which significantly improved library standards in Israel. He served as president of the Israel Library Association from its establishment in 1952 and represented Israel at UNESCO and International Federation of Libraries conferences.

Wormann's published works include: *Der deutsche Bauernroman* (1923); *Die russische Literatur der Gegenwart* (1931); and *Autoritaet und Familie in der deutschen Belletristik nach dem Weltkrieg* (1936).

BIBLIOGRAPHY: *Davar* (Dec. 2, 1960); *Haaretz* (Oct. 6, 1968); *News from the Hebrew University* (Oct. 1968); MB (Jan. 2, 1970).

[Shlomo Shunami]

WORMS, city in Germany. Documentary evidence points to the settlement of Jews in Worms at the end of the tenth century. The community grew during the 11th century, and a synagogue was inaugurated in 1034. In 1076–77 there was already a Jewish cemetery, which has been preserved and is the oldest in Europe. At the end of the 11th century the role of Jewish merchants in Worms was of such importance that they are mentioned by King Henry IV in a privilege document of 1074 before "the other inhabitants of Worms." Around 1090 the king granted to the Jews of Worms a charter of privileges similar in most respects to the charter granted to the Jews of *Speyer. The Jews of Worms were granted freedom to travel without restriction throughout the kingdom (they visited the fairs of *Cologne) and to engage in commerce without paying customs duties. They were authorized to function as moneychangers, and could hire Christian workmen, wetnurses, and maidservants. The Jews were granted the right to own movable and real property. It was forbidden to convert their children forcibly to Christianity, and a Jew who converted lost his share in his father's property. In lawsuits between Jews and Christians, each litigant was to be judged according to his own legal code; Jewish as well as Christian witnesses were necessary before judgment could be passed against a Jew. Lawsuits between Jews would be judged according to Jewish law. The Jews were subject to the king's jurisdiction only. They were given extensive autonomy and could choose their own leadership, subject only to certification by the king.

A number of distinguished scholars were active in Worms during this period: among the "Sages of Worms" were Judah b. Baruch, a disciple of R. Gershom b. *Judah and a prominent halakhic authority; the hymnologist Meir b. *Isaac; Jacob b. *Yakar and Isaac b. *Eleazar, teachers of *Rashi during his stay in Worms; Kalonymus b. Shabbetai of Rome, who became head of the yeshivah after the death of R. Jacob b. Yakar; and Solomon b. *Samson, a halakhic authority and hymnologist who may well have been the *Episcopus Judaeorum* ("Bishop of the Jews") to whom the charter of Worms was addressed. While the scholars of *Mainz engaged exclusively in the study of Talmud, those of Worms also commented on Bible and Midrash and composed *piyyutim*.

This flourishing period was interrupted by the persecutions of the First *Crusade that took place in May 1096. The crusaders, drawn from the simple townfolk and the peasants of the surrounding villages, attacked the Jews in Worms. Some of them were killed in their homes or took their own lives, while others found refuge in the palace of the bishop, until they were overwhelmed and massacred or chose to kill their children and then themselves. The number of martyrs reached 800. Only a few saved themselves by accepting baptism, but in the following year Henry IV allowed them to return to Judaism.

After a short while a new community was established in Worms, and in 1112 Emperor Henry V renewed the customs exemption which his father had granted to the Jews of the city. In the meantime, Jewish economic activity there had taken a new direction: commerce was replaced by *moneylending. At the time of the Second Crusade in 1146, the Jews of Worms fled to fortresses in the surrounding region until the danger had passed. Subsequently the community grew in numbers. The synagogue was renovated (1174–75) and a women's gallery was added (1213); a new *mikveh* was constructed (1186), and the cemetery was enlarged (c. 1260).

During the 13th century the Christian bishop assumed jurisdiction over the Jews in lawsuits with Christians, as well as in criminal law. He also collected a tax from them, in addition to that imposed by the king. The civic status of the Jews was determined by the municipal council. The Jews received its protection and were obligated in return to defend the town in case of attack. During the siege of Worms, in 1201, the Jews took part in its defense. Their obligation to military service later was exchanged for a payment toward the fortification of the city. A regular tax which the Jews paid to the city is first mentioned in 1265. During the 13th and 14th centuries the kings transferred to the city an ever greater portion of the taxes paid by the Jews, and the municipal authority over the Jews thus became more extensive. Finally, in January 1348, Charles IV waived all the royal rights over the Jews of Worms in favor of the city. The community was led by 12 elected *parnasim*. The bishop of Worms appointed one of them "Bishop of the Jews" for life. The last "Bishop of the Jews" died in 1792.

The scholars of Worms took part in the rabbinical *synods which were convened in the Rhineland, as well as in the drafting of communal regulations for the three communities of Speyer, Worms, and Mainz, which had wide-ranging influence on Ashkenazi Jewry (see *Shum). The most important halakhic authorities of Worms in the period were the *paytan* Menahem b. *Jacob; Eleazar b. *Judah, disciple of Judah he-Ḥasid ("the *Pious"), the author of *Sefer ha-Roke'aḥ*; and Baruch b. Meir and his son Meir of Rothenburg (*av bet din* of Worms; d. 1281). From the beginning of the 14th century there was, however, a spiritual decline in the community, and its influence waned.

On Second Adar 10, 5109 (1349), at the time of the Black *Death, anti-Jewish violence broke out in Worms. Some Jews managed to escape to Sinsheim, *Heidelberg, and other localities in the *Palatinate; all the other members of the community set fire to themselves in their homes or were massacred by rioters. The property of the Jews was confiscated by the town, but the latter was also compelled to pay assignments which the king had granted to several of his creditors on account of the tax which was due to him. The local authorities therefore considered it advantageous to authorize the settlement of the Jews in the city once more (1353–55).

This third community fixed the day of Adar 10 as a perpetual fast day. The new community did not acquire the splendor of the past. Even so Jacob Moses *Moellin (the Maharil) preferred to live there in his old age and died in Worms in 1427. The kings and governors of the Palatinate renewed the "seals" of the community from time to time, but an uprising of craftsmen in 1615 caused the Jews to flee from the town; the synagogue and the cemetery were desecrated. Samuel Bacharach, the rabbi of the community, was among the refugees. In 1616 the uprising was subdued by the governor, and the Jews returned to Worms. The first *parnas* of the renewed community was David Joshua Oppenheim, who in 1624 built the *bet midrash* attributed to Rashi. Another *parnas*, Abraham b. Simeon Wolff Oppenheim, was the father of the noted David *Oppenheim. Samuel *Oppenheimer and Samson *Wertheimer, who achieved fame in Vienna, were also natives of Worms. The rabbinical office was then held by the kabbalist Elijah b. Moses *Loanz. From 1650 to 1670, Moses Samson b. Abraham Samuel *Bacharach acted as rabbi and *av bet din* of Worms. It was in his days that Jephthah Joseph Yozpa, a scribe, recorded the legends then current in Worms on the glorious past of the community (*Sefer Ma'aseh Nissim*, Amsterdam, 1696).

Ten years after Worms had been set on fire by the French, in 1689, the community of Worms was again reconstituted. The first rabbi appears to have been Jair Ḥayyim b. Moses Samson *Bacharach (d. 1702), author of *Ḥavvat Ya'ir*. During the 18th and 19th centuries Worms no longer ranked among the important communities of Germany, even though it was still renowned and remained attached to its ancient customs. During the 19th century there were about 800 Jews living in the city. They were granted civic rights along with the Jews of *Hesse, and in 1848 a Jew was elected mayor of Worms.

Holocaust and Contemporary Periods

On the eve of the rise of the Nazis to power, in 1933, there were 1,016 Jews living in Worms. Many Jews emigrated following the boycott of Jewish goods and other forms of harassment. A concentration camp was set up in the vicinity of the city. Nazi persecution stimulated communal activity in the sphere of Jewish adult education, and, after the expulsion of Jewish children from the public school, a Jewish school was founded in Worms in 1936. The ancient synagogue and the *bet midrash* of Rashi were destroyed on *Kristallnacht*, Nov. 9–10, 1938, but the cemetery was saved from destruction by Dr. Ilert, a benevolent non-Jew. Ninety-seven Jews were taken to concentration camps. By May 1939 only 316 Jews remained in Worms. During World War II, in 1941–42, the remaining Jews in Worms were deported to concentration camps and few survived. After the end of the war some Jews again settled in Worms, but the community was not reorganized. The German authorities rebuilt the synagogue and the *bet midrash* from their ruins (1961) and preserved the ancient cemetery. The archives of the community of Worms of 1522 were sent to the General Archives of Jewish History in Jerusalem.

In 1982 the Jewish museum of the history of the Jewish community in Worms was opened at Rashi House, located on the site of the former *bet midrash*. The cellar and parts of the first floor originate from the second half of the 14th century; the rest of the building was erected in 1982. In 2005, a celebration was held in the city to commemorate the 900th anniversary of Rashi's death. In 2005 there were 133 Jews living in Worms, members of the Jewish community in Mainz. The majority are immigrants from the former Soviet Union who moved to Germany after 1990.

BIBLIOGRAPHY: L. Lewysohn, *Sechzig Epitaphien von Grabsteinen des israelitischen Friedhofs zu Worms* (1855); B. Rosenthal, in: MGWJ, 83 (1939), 313–24; A. Epstein, ibid., 40 (1896), 509–15, 554–9; 45 (1901), 44–75; 46 (1902), 157–70; idem, in: *Gedenkbuch David Kaufmann* (1900), 288–317; E. Carlebach, *Die rechtlichen und sozialen Verhaeltnisse der juedischen Gemeinden Speyer, Worms und Mainz…* (1901); L. Rothschild, *Die Judengemeinden zu Mainz, Speyer und Worms* 1349–1438 (1904); S. Rothschild, *Aus Vergangenheit und Gegenwart der israelitischen Gemeinde Worms* (1929); J. Kifer, in: ZGJD, 1 (1929), 291–6; ibid., 5 (1935), 85–199; S. Schiffmann, *Heinrich IV und die Bischoefe in ihrem Verhalten zu den deutschen Juden zur Ẓeit des ersten Kreuzzuges* (1931); M. Grunwald, in: REJ, 104 (1938), 71–111; A. Kober, in: PAAJR, 14 (1944), 149–220; 15 (1945), 68–71; E.L. Rapp and O. Boecher, *Die aeltesten hebraeischen Inschriften Mitteleuropas in Mainz, Worms und Speyer* (1959); O. Boecher, *Die alte Synagoge zu Worms* (1960), includes detailed bibliography; Germ Jud. 1 (1963), 437–74; 2 (1968), 919–27; Aronius, Regesten, index; A. Habermann, *Gezerot Ashkenaz ve-Ẓarefat* (1946); Finkelstein, Middle Ages; K. Duewell, *Die Rheingebiete in der Judenpolitik des Nationalsozialismus vor 1942* (1968), index; R. Krautheimer, *Mittelalterliche Synagogen* (1927), 151–76; **ADD. BIBLIOGRAPHY:** J. Schammes, *Wormser Minhagbuch* (Heb., 1992); J.L. Kirchheim, *The Customs of Worms Jewry* (Heb., 1987); F. Reuter, *Warmaisa. 1000 Jahre Juden in Worms* (1987^2); *Germania Judaica*, vol. 3, 1350 – 1514 (1987) 1671–97; O. Boecher, *The Old Synagogue in Worms on the Rhine* (DKV-Kunstfuehrer, vol 181) (2001); A. Haverkamp and K. Birk, Karin (eds), *The Jews of Europe in the Middle Ages* (2004), 59–81. CD-ROM: K. Schloesser, *Die Wormser Juden 1933 – 1945*. Dokumentation (2002).

[Zvi Avneri]

WORMS, AARON (1754–1836), rabbi in France, born in Geislautern, Saar, son of R. Abraham (Aberle) Joseph. Aaron attended the yeshivah at Metz directed by R. Aryeh Loeb b. Asher *Guenzburg. In 1777 he became rabbi in Kriechingen (Créhange), Lorraine, and in 1785 was appointed *dayyan* in Metz and principal of its yeshivah. From 1813 he served as deputy rabbi, and from 1831, rabbi of Metz.

Although strictly orthodox, he was sympathetic to those desiring the integration of Jews into gentile society through "improvement of morals." During the French Revolution, he joined the National Guard and served as a member of the *Assembly of Jewish Notables and the Great *Sanhedrin (1806–07), where he expressed the view that the granting of civil rights to the Jews would encourage them to assume added responsibilities toward the state. In the Sanhedrin he gave an address on the relations between Jews and non-Jews according to the Talmud, in which he maintained that the phrase *ovedei kokhavim u-mazzalot* (idolators) does not apply to the non-Jews of the present time. On the contrary, the Talmud enjoins a spirit of brotherhood between Jews and non-Jews. He also expressed the view that it is preferable to pray in the vernacular and to understand what one is saying than in Hebrew if one could not understand it. For this reason he took no part in the "temple controversy" in Hamburg in 1818/19. Worms also opposed the retention of customs which had their basis in superstitious beliefs, as well as the exaggerated use of *piyyutim* in the prayers. R. Aaron encouraged the foundation of an educational institution in Metz where children were also taught secular subjects. He urged Jews to learn and practice crafts.

His work *Me'orei Or* was published anonymously in seven parts, the first three between 1790 and 1793; the last four, published between 1819 and 1831, were entitled *Be'er-Sheva, Or la-Mo'ed, Ben Nun*, and *Ken Tahor.* It examines questions of *halakhah* in the Talmud and Shulḥan Arukh and the origins of *minhagim*, and elucidates *aggadah*. Certain sections of the work include a "*mahadura batra*" ("final rescension") which complements the commentary and notes in the body of the work. He included in his works a considerable number of poetical compositions, *piyyutim* for festivals, Sabbath songs and hymns, and *seliḥot* for the High Holydays. He also published a commentary on the *Maḥzor* and the Passover *Haggadah*.

BIBLIOGRAPHY: A. Cahen, in: REJ, 13 (1886), 114, 119–124; N. Bruell, in: *Beit Oẓar ha-Sifrut*, 1 (1887), 20–31; M. Catane, in: *Aresheth*, 2 (1960), 190–8; N. Netter, *Vingt siècles d'histoire d'une communauté juive* (1938), 291–2.

[Yehoshua Horowitz]

WORMS, ASHER ANSHEL (1695–1759), German physician and Hebrew author. In 1723, Asher was appointed physician at the Jewish hospital at Frankfurt on the Main, a position he occupied until his death. He was interested in a wide range of subjects: mathematics (in his youth he wrote a textbook entitled *Mafte'aḥ ha-Algebrah ha-Ḥadashah* ("Key to Modern Algebra"; Offenbach, 1721), physics, logic, ethics, metaphysics, grammar, and, particularly, Hebrew literature and the masorah. His most important work in this last area was *Seyag la-Torah* ("A Fence around the Torah"), published posthumously by his son, the physician Simeon Wolf Worms (Frankfurt on the Main, 1766). It comprises three essays dealing with the nature of the masorah, the masoretes and their times, their identification with the Tiberias schools or with *Ezra and his group, an explanation of the abbreviations used by them, and a correction of the errors that had crept into the masorah. Asher held that "in every generation diligent scribes arose" who preserved the masorah, until the masoretes of Tiberias "corrected all the errors that had occurred in it from the days of Ezra to their own times," and that the masoretes were not the inventors of vocalization, but its transcribers. In the introduction to the work, Worms accused Joseph Heilbronn of Eschwege, who had seen the manuscript before publication, of plagiarizing whole sections of it in his commentary on the masorah, *Mevin Ḥiddot* (Amsterdam, 1765). Heilbronn attempted to defend himself in a pamphlet, *Merivat Kodesh* (Amsterdam, 1766), to which Simeon Wolf Worms replied in his pamphlet *Prodogma Ḥadashah* (Amsterdam, 1767). The controversy was settled by Wolf *Heidenheim who confirmed, on the basis of the first page of *Mevin Ḥiddot*, which he had in his possession, all the charges of plagiarism leveled against Heilbronn.

BIBLIOGRAPHY: M. Horovitz, *Frankfurter Rabbinen*, 3 (1884), 62–64; idem, *Juedische Aertze in Frankfurt am Main* (1886), 35–39; Berliner, in: MWJ, 13 (1886), 62; Harris, in: JQR, 1 (1889), 256; H. Friedenwald, *Jewish Luminaries in Medical History* (1946; reprinted 1967), 152; M. Hendel, *Temunot min he-Avar* (1955), 36, 47.

[Yehoshua Horowitz]

WORMS, DE, family originating in Frankfurt and prominent in finance and politics in England in the 19th century. They traced their descent back to R. Aaron *Worms whose grandson, BENEDICT DE WORMS (d. 1824), married Jeanette von Rothschild in 1795. The family subsequently settled in London where Benedict, with his sons, MAURICE BENEDICT (1805–1867) and GABRIEL BENEDICT (1802–1881), established the family retailing business. As a result of a visit to Ceylon, his sons built up one of the biggest and best cultivated tea plantations on the island, known as the Rothschild Estate. Their brother, SOLOMON BENEDICT (1801–1882), spent some time there doing pioneering work on the estate. In 1871 he was made a baron of the Austrian Empire for financial services and charity, and three years later was granted a warrant to use this title in Britain in recognition of his work in Ceylon. His eldest son, BARON GEORGE (1829–1912), was vice president of the Royal Society of Literature (1896–1900) and headed the family firm. He wrote *The Currency of India* (1876). Solomon Benedict's third son, HENRY (first Baron Pirbright; 1840–1903), was educated at London University and became a barrister, but, after a short time at the bar, assisted his brother George in conducting their father's retailing business. He entered Parliament in 1880 as a Conservative and in 1885 was made parliamentary secretary to the Board of Trade in Lord Salisbury's first government. He was the first professing Jew to hold ministerial office in a Tory government. In 1888, the year he was made a member of the Privy Council, Henry represented Britain at the international conference for the abolition of sugar bounties and was elected its president. He was undersecretary of state for the colonies from 1888 to 1892. In 1895, in Lord Salisbury's third administration, he was given a peerage. In Parliament he championed the cause of oppressed Romanian Jews. He held a number of communal offices, including those of treasurer and vice president of the United Synagogue. He was also president of the Anglo-Jewish Association (1872–86) until forced to resign after attending the marriage of his daughter at church. He was a Fellow of the Royal Society and a man of considerable erudition. His books included *The Earth and Its Mechanism* (1862); *The Austro-Hungarian Empire* (1870) and *England's Policy in the East* (1877).

BIBLIOGRAPHY: P.H. Emden, *Jews of Britain* (1943), 282–6; J.M. Shaftesley (ed.), *Remember the Days* (1966), index; Roth, Mag Bibl, 155; Lehmann, Nova Bibl, 115; JC (Oct. 27, 1882). **ADD. BIBLIOGRAPHY:** ODNB online; C. Bermant, *The Cousinhood* (1971); G. Alderman, *The Jewish Community in British Politics* (1983).

WORMS, RENÉ (1869–1926), French social scientist. He taught chiefly economic subjects at the University of Caen, the École des Hautes Études Sociales, the Institut Commercial, and the École des Hautes Études Commerciales in Paris. Worms' importance for sociology rests largely with his organizational activities. He was the founder of the *Revue internationale de sociologie* (1892), the Institut International de Sociologie (1893), and the organizer of the annual sociological congresses, as well as the Bibliothèque Sociologique Internationale. Worms and the institutions which he helped to create became the major points of resistance against the prevailing Durkheimian influences in French sociology. As an author, he started by standing for an organicistic approach to society but modified his position later in life.

The best-known work of Worms's organicistic period is *Organisme et société* (1896); others are *Eléments de philosophie scientifique et de philosophic morale* (1891), *Psychologie collective et psychologie individuelle* (1899), *Philosophie des sciences sociales*, 3 vols. (1903–07; 2nd ed. 1913–20), *Les principes biologiques de l'évolution sociale* (1910), *La sociologie; sa nature, son contenu, ses attaches* (1921), as well as numerous articles in the *Revue internationale de sociologie.*

BIBLIOGRAPHY: A. Ouy, in: *Revue internationale de sociologie*, 33 (1925), 577–80; C.M. Case and F. Woerner, in: *Sociology and Social Research*, 13 (1929), 403–25.

[Werner J. Cahnman]

WORMSER, ANDRÉ (Alphonse Toussaint; 1851–1926), composer. Born in Paris, Wormser won the Rome Prize in 1872 for the cantata *Clytemnestre*. He composed successful operas, orchestral and choral works, piano pieces, and songs. His best-known composition is the pantomine "wordless opera," *L'Enfant prodigue* (1890).

WORMSER, OLIVIER BORIS (1913–1985), French diplomat and member of banking family, born in Paris. He began his career in 1933 as a foreign service officer upon his appointment as an attaché to the French embassy in Rome. He taught law briefly at the University of Dijon (1938–39) and in World War II joined the Free French movement in London. After his return to France, he occupied key posts in policy formulation, particularly in the field of economics, and as an administrator in the Ministry of Foreign Affairs. In 1966 he became French ambassador to the Soviet Union and in 1969 governor of the Banque de France.

[Joachim O. Ronall]

WORMSER, SECKEL (Isaac Loeb; 1768–1847), talmudist and kabbalist, born in Michelstadt in Hessen. He received his talmudic education in Frankfurt on the Main, in the yeshivah of Nathan Adler, and followed in his footsteps, accepting a rigorously ascetic "hasidic" way of life and turning to kabbalistic studies. After his first marriage he returned, about 1790, to Michelstadt where he maintained a yeshivah for many years and served, at first unofficially, until 1822 as a recognized district rabbi. About 1810, after the death of his wife, he lived for some time in Mannheim. For years, his "ḥasidic" behavior and extreme vegetarianism created considerable tension between him and the majority of his small community, but his reputation as a master of occult powers spread rapidly and Wormser became known throughout Germany as the "Ba'al Shem of Michelstadt." He denied any such supernatural power but agreed to receive people who sought his advice and guidance, giving them natural remedies, specifics, and sometimes amulets. He became particularly known for his treatment of lunatics. Among the Jews of southern Germany many traditions survived regarding his miraculous cures and other feats. He studied German philosophy and was particularly attracted by Schelling. In 1825 his house and large library were destroyed by fire. Of his talmudic writings, preserved by his descendants, almost nothing was published. A catalogue of his second library is preserved in Ms. Heidenheim 206, in the Central Library in Zurich.

BIBLIOGRAPHY: M. Wormser, *Das Leben und Wirken des zu Michelstadt verstorbenen Rabbiners Zeckel Loeb Wormser* (1853); H. Ehrmann (Judaeus), *Der Baalschem von Michelstadt: kulturgeschichtliche Erzaehlung* (1922; contains also memories about him from a contemporary manuscript).

[Gershom Scholem]

WORMWOOD, according to most commentators to be identified with the scriptural לַעֲנָה (*la'anah*). It indicates evil (Deut. 29:17; Amos 5:7; et al.) as does the drinking of the liquid extracted from it (Lam. 3:15; et al.). In Arabic it is called *shi'ah* and in Syriac *shiha*. Consequently the opinion has been expressed that the *si'aḥ* in the phrase עֲלֵי שִׂיחַ in Job 30:4 means "the leaves of the wormwood." The Peshitta identifies *aḥad ha-siḥim* ("one of the shrubs") of the desert under which Hagar cast Ishmael with wormwood (Gen. 21:15).

Several species of wormwood grow wild in Israel in the sandy and desert regions. The most common is *la'anat ha-midbar* ("desert wormwood"), the *Artemisia herba-alba* whose juice has a very bitter taste. It is possible that wormwood juice was extracted from it, as, despite its bitterness, it was regarded by the ancients as having therapeutic qualities. The Romans used to give it (absinthium) to the victors of the chariot races to drink since "health is an honorable prize" (Pliny, *Historia Naturalis* 27:45–46). In Greek, wormwood is called *apsinthion* (as the Septuagint translates *la'anah*). The Talmud (Av. Zar. 30a) mentions "bitter *apsintin* wine," i.e., wine to which *apsinthion* (wormwood) was added, not unlike modern vermouth, which is wine to which the species *Artemisia absinthium* has been added ("wormwood" is probably a corruption of the word vermouth).

BIBLIOGRAPHY: Loew, Flora, 1 (1928), 386; H.N. and A.L. Moldenke, *Plants of the Bible* (1950), index; J. Feliks, *Olam ha-Ẓome'aḥ ha-Mikra'i* (1968²), 180, 200.

[Jehuda Feliks]

WOROSZYLSKI, WIKTOR (1927–1996), Polish poet, editor, and translator. Born in Grodno, Woroszylski began writing in 1945 and was chief editor of the literary weekly *Nowa Kultura* (1956–57). His works include the verse collections *Ojczyzna*

("Fatherland," 1953) and *Wiersze i poematy wybrane* (1955); *Noc komunarda* ("Night of the Communards," 1949); and a comprehensive study of the Soviet poet Mayakovski (1965; *The Life of Mayakovsky*, 1970). He also published translations from Russian literature.

WORSHIP, service rendered to God and comprehending both the attitude of reverence and love toward the Deity and the activity – in conduct as well as ritual – in which the homage finds expression.

Terminology

The biblical vocabulary of worship is extensive and varied. The following are the principal terms employed:

1. *hishtaḥawah*, "to prostrate oneself," is the most frequently used (86 times);
2. *ʿavad*, "to serve";
3. *yare'*, "to revere";
4. *sheret*, "to minister," especially in a cultic sense;
5. *darash*, "to seek, inquire";
6. *sagad* (Heb.), *seged* (Aram.) (both in Daniel), "to bow."

There are also other terms used to express various liturgical acts and the feelings of joy awakened by worship.

Ideological Basis

The earlier version of this entry hewed closely to the position of Yehezkel *Kaufmann whose work, though ingenious, overstated the contrasts between Israel and its neighbors. In addition, as was true of his contemporaries, Kaufmann equated the religion of ancient Israel with the religion of the Bible. The present revised entry concentrates on the biblical view of worship, namely that Israelites must worship Yahweh alone, without equating that view with the actual patterns of worship in ancient Israel, which require separate investigation. For all its distinctiveness, Israelite religion fit neatly into ancient Near Eastern patterns. Like their neighbors, the Hebrews had no concept of nature or its immutable laws. As such, they believed that it was possible to influence the powers that be in human favor by acts of ritual and worship. God might sometimes be spoken of as beyond human understanding (Isa. 40:28; 55:9; Ps. 145:3; Job 5:9) but is accessible nonetheless. Humans turn to the divine, sometimes out of a sense of wonderment and awe, of reverence and gratitude, of joy and trust, which call forth a desire for adoration and thanksgiving. At other times distress and danger impel people to seek God's help, for He is the ultimate source of salvation (Isa. 43:11; Hos. 13:4). God is perceived as both near (Ps. 145:18) and far (Ps. 22:12). Sin estranges humans from God. In biblical thinking rebellion against the Divine will, revealed in His commandments, and the breaching of His eternal covenant, creates a gulf between divinity and humanity, which only atonement can bridge. Penitents seek expiation for their transgressions through confession and sacrifice (Lev. 4 and 16). There are times when the acts of an inscrutable providence result in human challenge and protest (Gen. 18:24; Jer. 12:1ff.; Job, passim). Biblical worship had room for all these human reactions.

Israel's contemporaries had forms of worship analogous to those of Israel; Hebrews and their neighbors shared the notion that it was possible for humans to have some control over their destinies. Both Yahweh and his divine contemporaries demanded the service of the clean of hand and pure of heart (Ps. 24:4; Egyptian Book of the Dead, chapter 125).

Humans have always been conscious of a certain duality in divine worship. In a Hittite inscription designated *Instructions for Temple Officials* it is stated:

> Are the minds of men and of the gods generally different? No! ...When a servant is to stand before his master, he is bathed and clothed in clean [garments]; he either gives him his food, or he gives him his beverage. And because he, his master, eats [and] drinks, he is relaxed in spirit and feels one with him. But if he [the servant] is ever remiss, [if] he is inattentive, his mind is alien to him. And if a slave causes his master's anger, they will either kill him... (ANET, Pritchard, Texts, p. 207).

The author discerns a twofold approach to the deity:

(a) the avoidance of uncleanness and whatever else may vex the divinity;

(b) the provision of offerings.

The same negative and positive approaches to God are reflected in the positive precepts and prohibitions of the Torah. The two aspects are found, for example, in the ritual laws of purification and the ceremonial observances, respectively. They are likewise discerned on the higher level of ethical conduct: wrongdoing is to be eschewed and righteousness is to be pursued in the service of God (Isa. 1:16–17). For worship is not solely or even primarily a matter of ritual. It is of supreme significance that in Micah's formulation of the fundamentals of religion two of the three requirements ("to do justly and to love loving kindness") concern human relationships, and only the third ("to walk humbly with thy God") refers to the Deity (6:8). The Hittites and the Hebrews depicted their gods in human imagery. Both required just and ethical conduct along with ritual, as did the Egyptian and Mesopotamian gods.

Emphasis is often given to the antithesis between cultic observances and righteous conduct. The former is deemed to belong to the priestly conception of religion, whereas the prophets, it is held, rejected ritual and stressed the spiritual approach to God. To some extent this is true. The fact that prophets often railed against the mechanical potency of ritual proves that the concept had deep roots, encouraged of course by the priesthood (Lev. 16:30, 34), whose income depended on it (Hos. 4:8). Yet, the Bible does not show a hard and fast dichotomy. Priests could also be prophets (Jeremiah, Ezekiel); prophets, when necessary, emphasized the importance of ritual requirements (Ezek. 40–48; Haggai 1:2ff.; Mal. 1:8, 12–14). The Torah ordains cultic regulations in juxtaposition to its formulation of ethical principles (e.g., Ex. 20:8–14; Lev. 19:15–22), or synthesizes them into a single law (e.g., Deut. 16:14). Late prophetic teaching lent support to this view (Mal. 3:4–5). The attempt to interpret liturgical and ethical requirements as diametrical opposites serves to compartmentalize the life of the worshiper; the Bible seeks to make it whole. It points to the ultimate purpose of religion in key passages like these: "And thou shalt love the Lord, thy God..." (Deut. 6:5); "And thou shalt love thy fellow as thyself" (Lev. 19:18); "For I desire loving kindness and not sacrifice..." (Hos. 6:6). Worship unites in itself both outward forms and religious inwardness. At the same time some of Israel's religious teachers realized that there was a tension between the observance of the external rites and the inner content of religion in which lurked the danger of formalism and hypocrisy. The prophets inveighed against these tendencies. They denounced corrupting wealth and callous indifference to the needs of the poor (Amos 3:12, 15; 4:1ff.; 5:11; 6:4–6); sacrifices and celebrations that were rooted in unrighteousness and insincerity (Amos 5:21ff.; Isa. 1:11ff.); and taking advantage of religious festivals to engage in illicit sexual behavior (Amos 2:7; Hos. 4:13ff.); whoring after the Baals (Hos. 2ff.; Jer. 3:1ff.); the intemperance and evildoing of priests and false prophets (Isa. 28:7ff.; Hos. 4:4–10); and the horror of sacrificing children to Moloch/Baal (Jer. 7:31; 32:35; cf. Lev. 18:21; Deut. 18:10). Even the Temple was not spared when it ceased to be a center of holiness (Jer. 7:11ff.; Micah 3:12). The prophets did not hesitate to condemn practices that were inherently good but had become vitiated by dishonorable conduct and iniquitous living (Amos 5:21–24; Isa. 1:11ff.; Jer. 6:20). The prophets did not disapprove of sacrifices if offered in sincerity and truth (Mal. 3:4). It was to falsehood and evil that they were opposed. They demanded loyal obedience to the will of God instead of the sacrilege of a cult that was no more than blasphemous hypocrisy (Hos. 6:6; Jer. 7:21–23; Micah 6:6–8; cf. Ps. 51:16ff.). Righteous living was fundamental to true worship. But in a different constellation of circumstances the later prophets, in particular, urged earnest devotion to the forms of organized religion as vital to the survival of the faith and the nation.

The Elements of Biblical Worship

The fabric of Israel's worship was woven of many strands. These may be summarized as acts of purification; dietary laws; sacrifices, tithes, and other offerings; the observance of the Sabbath, festivals, and fast-days; and prayer understood in its broadest sense.

The laws of defilement and purity – largely in Leviticus (e.g., 14:9; 15:11; 17:15–16), Numbers (ch. 19), and Deuteronomy (e.g., 21:1–9) – and the dietary regulations (Lev. 11; Deut. 12:16; 14:4ff.), irrespective of their conjectured origin, form in the Bible part of the law of holiness (Lev. 11:44). "I shall wash my hands in innocence" (Ps. 26:6; cf. 73:13; 24:4).

In a sense, the sacrifices – both public and private – the firstlings, the first fruits, as well as the tithes and other priestly and levitical dues (Ex. 13:11ff.; Lev. 1–7; 27:30–33; Num. 5:9ff.; 15:18ff.; 18:8ff.; Deut. 12:17ff.; 14:22–29; 15:19ff.; 24:19–21; 26:1–14) are comparable to taxes, rents, and fines (R.H. Pfeiffer). Yet as was true in other ancient religious systems, the sacrificial system was a dramatic approach to the divine, an act of homage and thanksgiving (Ps. 24:1; I Chron. 29:14), or of expiation (in His grace God accepts the oblation instead of the sacrificer's life). Hence when the true significance of the offerings was forgotten it was said that God actually revoked them (Isa. 1:11; Ps. 50:8ff.).

The Sabbath and the other holy days of Israel's calendar have played an immeasurable role in developing and ennobling Israel's worship. The attempt to find the origin of the Sabbath in the Babylonian *šapattu* has proved abortive. Whatever its origin, the idea of the Sabbath in the scriptural context is a unique institution, meant to articulate divine sovereignty over time, just as the sabbatical year articulates divine sovereignty over territory. From one point of view, it was Israel's answer to the Egyptian bondage; any human being, even a slave, needs rest. Not only humans, but also animals require recuperation from toil (Ex. 23:12; Deut. 5:12–15). In the Exodus version of the Decalogue, the Sabbath assumes cosmic significance; it becomes a memorial to the story of Creation (Ex. 20:8–11; cf. Gen. 2:1–4). Nor were the prophets less emphatic in stressing the hallowed character of the day (Isa. 58:13–14; Ezek. 20:20), and Nehemiah took stern measures to enforce its observance. An extension of the Sabbath idea is to be seen in the sabbatical year (Ex. 23:10ff.; Deut. 15) and in the year of jubilee (Lev. 25).

Like the Sabbath, the festivals were designed to bring the worshiper nearer to God. They were occasions of deep religious joy (Deut. 16:15; Neh. 8:10ff.). Biblical religion, while deploring all forms of intemperance and overindulgence, nevertheless looked askance at asceticism. Wine was created to gladden the human heart (Ps. 104:15). The Lord was to be served in gladness (Ps. 100:2; cf. Shab. 30b). Modern research has conjectured that certain biblical festivals are derived from earlier lunar and solar celebrations in antiquity, or are related to Canaanite agricultural feasts, which have been adapted to Israelite thinking. Without entering into the validity of these theories, it must be stressed that the religious significance of these observances is not in their supposed origin, but in their scriptural presentation. The paschal offering and the Feast of Unleavened Bread (Ex. 12; Deut. 16:5–6; Ezek. 45:21), and the Feast of Tabernacles (Booths) or of Ingathering (Ex. 23:16; 34:22; Lev. 23:34ff.; Num. 29:12–39; Deut. 16:13–15; 31:10–13) mark respectively the barley harvest and vintage time. As such they had a thanksgiving character; they gave expression to the Israelite's gratitude to God for the earth's bounty. But to the agricultural aspect a historical element was added: Passover calls to mind the deliverance from Egyptian bondage (Ex. 12–13; 23:15; Deut. 16:1–8) and Tabernacles is a reminder of the Lord's care for Israel during their desert wanderings (Lev. 23:43). Israel found God not only in the phenomena of the world, but also in the providential course of events. This historical insight plays an important role in Israel's worship, both in its ceremonial and in its prayers (e.g. Ps. 136; I Chron. 16:8ff.). The Feast of Weeks (Ex. 34:22; Deut. 16:10 – also called the Feast of the Grain Harvest (Ex. 23:16) and the Day of First Fruits (Num. 28:26) – is in its biblical setting a purely agricultural celebration, but in rabbinic times it evolved into the festival of the giving of the Torah at Sinai. Characteristically, too, when farmers brought their first fruits before the Lord, they expressed gratitude in a succinct historical review (Deut. 26:5–10). Minor celebrations, such as Purim (Est.) and Ḥanukkah (the Festival of Dedication; see I *Macc. and II *Macc.) based on Hellenistic models, obviously have a historical motif. The same is true of the fast days of the fifth and seventh months (Zech. 7:3–5), recalling the fall of Jerusalem. But the Day of Atonement (Lev. 16) is entirely religious in character; and the Day of Blowing the Horn, called New Year – Rosh Ha-Shanah – in rabbinic literature (Lev. 23:24; Num. 29:1), and the New Moon (Num. 28:11ff.; I Sam. 20:5ff.; II Kings 4:23, etc.) and the Feast of the Wood Offering (Neh. 10:35; 13:31) were likewise unrelated to historical events. It should also be noted that the special sacrifices (Num. 28–29) which marked all the major celebrations served to emphasize the religious nature of these occasions; and the inwardness of these observances was illuminated by prophetic teaching (Isa. 1:11ff.; 58:3ff.; Joel 2:13).

Finally it should be observed that biblical worship might be individual and collective. Examples of personal worship abound throughout the Bible: the Patriarchs, Moses, Joshua, Hannah, and Hezekiah, among others. Without doubt David composed a number of prayers (cf. II Sam. 7:18–29) and some of his compositions are certainly in the Book of Psalms. But apart from this, the Book of Psalms contains a variety of prayers and hymns that voice the personal supplications, hope, faith, and joy of the authors. These may have been subsequently adapted to national or congregational use, but their individual significance was not wholly lost. To the same category of worship belong also the private sacrifices brought to the Temple, although the ritual formed part of the general priestly ministrations.

At the same time the Bible ordains and illustrates various forms of public worship. Of this aspect of worship the Bible likewise furnished innumerable examples (the public sacrifices; the Temple choral services; the statutory assembly prescribed in Deut. 31:10ff.; and historic occasions like those described in I Kings 8:1ff.; Neh. 8:1ff., etc.). The synagogue services of a later period continued the tradition of congregational prayer and study, without excluding opportunities for personal religious meditation.

Developments in Israel's Worship

Biblical religious rites clearly underwent a continuous process of development. The biblical account of worship in the patriarchal age reflects practices originating in different times and places. Altars were built and the name of YHWH proclaimed (Gen. 12:7–8; 13:4). Tithes were given (Gen. 14:20) and sacrifices offered (Gen. 22:13; cf. 4:3–4; 8:20). The Lord entered into a covenant with Abraham, the accompanying ritual being reminiscent of *Mari customs (Gen. 15; cf. Jer. 34:18). Prayer (Gen. 24:12ff.) and acts of purification (35:2ff.) are mentioned. The Patriarchs blessed their children (27:27–29, 39–40; 49:3ff.) and Jacob made a vow (28:20ff.). The Lord blessed the Patriarchs, assured them of His salvation, and promised the land of Canaan to their children (12:2ff.; 26:3–5; 24; 28:13–15, etc.). In some cases the patriarchal tales reflect family religion that persisted through time in ancient Israel, without an elaborate priesthood or sanctuary; the theophany granted a family elder could determine the site of worship.

The *Tabernacle and its cult (Ex. 25–31; 35–40) reflect worship in monarchic as well as exilic and post-exilic Israel. Prophets like Amos, Hosea, and Jeremiah held that the wilderness period determined the basic character of Israel's authentic worship (Amos 5:25; Hos. 2:16–17; Jer. 7:21–23).

At times, syncretism was rife; the prohibitions against taking over Canaanite sacred sites and practices (Deut. 12:2–3; 30–31) prove that such was the case. At times YHWH was worshiped under the guise of Baal; or along with him (I Kings 18; II Kings 21:3). Saul, Samuel, and David were zealous advocates of the worship of Yahweh alone to exclusion of all other gods, while other kings like *Solomon (see I Kings 11:4), *Ahab, and *Manasseh worshiped other gods alongside Yahweh. David united the nation and chose a central site for worship at the new capital, Jerusalem. He assembled the material for the future Temple and reorganized the priesthood (II Sam. 8:7–12; 17–18). He is said to have enriched Israel's psalmody and introduced instrumental music into public worship (Amos 6:5; I Chron. 15, 16, and 25). He also organized a processional ceremony in which the Ark of the Covenant was brought to Jerusalem, perhaps on one of the great festivals (II Sam. 6; cf Ps. 24 and 132). Solomon built the central Temple in Zion, where worship was strongly ecclesiastical – mediated by the priests and levites – and markedly national, with universal tones appearing in Second Temple writings (Isa. 56:6–7; 66:23; Zech. 14:16–19).

[Israel Abrahams / S. David Sperling (2nd ed.)]

Second Temple

The Babylonian Exile seemed at first to be the final catastrophe which must quench the last flickering flame of Israel's true faith (Ezek. 20:32; Ps. 137). But it was just at this tragic juncture in its history that the Jewish people rose to the full stature of its national greatness. Under the inspiration and direction of prophets like Ezekiel and the so-called Deutero-Isaiah, the exiled people transmuted disaster into a new vision of life, which they proceeded to implement with unflagging vigor. Prayer, by no means absent from pre-Exilic worship, began to play an ever greater role; many psalms were composed or elaborated at this period. The first tentative steps were also taken towards the collection of Israel's sacred literature. It may well be that the foundations were then laid of the concept of synagogal worship, which differed radically from the Temple service. It was decentralized, the stage replaced the priest; prayer was substituted for the altar-offerings, scriptural reading and interpretation became a vital component of religious life; and the seeds of religious study and preaching began to burgeon. The accent was on spiritual education. In the words of R.T. Herford: "In all their long history, the Jewish people have done scarcely anything more wonderful than to create the synagogue. No human institution … has done more for the uplifting of the human race." Even if there were no synagogues actually established in the Exile (but see Ezek.

11:16; 33:30–32), they were certainly to be found in Judea by the fourth century B.C.E. They did not rival the Temple but complemented and survived it.

Upon the return of the exiles, in several stages, under the benignant Persian rule, Jewish religious life assumed new spiritual dimensions and an unprecedented dynamism. The people turned their back completely on idolatry, and worship became more spiritualized (cf. Ps. 26:6ff.). Under the persistent urging of the prophets Haggai, Zechariah, and Malachi, the Temple was rebuilt and its worship acquired new dignity and earnestness. The daily and festival sacrifices were, in time, accompanied by a unique treasury of psalmody, to which choral and instrumental music lent great beauty. Ezra, like a second Moses, made the nation Torah conscious as never before (cf. Ps. 1 and 119). Nehemiah, by his firm and able administration, gave the people greater unity and inner strength. According to some historians (notably L. Finkelstein), some of the earliest rabbinic traditions are to be traced back to the Exile period. Be that as it may, Judaism became in the early days of the Second Temple era an impregnable religious citadel that served to preserve Jewish identity, without government or country, through long centuries. But in the final analysis Israel's worship was neither primarily prophylactic nor narrowly national. It was perhaps Israel's greatest contribution to spiritual civilization, and its seminal power was such that it provided the framework and much of the content of Christian and Islamic worship to this day.

[Israel Abrahams]

BIBLIOGRAPHY: Y. Kaufmann, Toledot; W.O.E. Oesterly, *The Jewish Background of the Christian Liturgy* (1925); I. Elbogen, *Der juedische Gottesdienst in seiner geschichtlichen Entwicklung* (1931³); N.H. Snaith, in: H.W. Robinson (ed.), *Record and Revelation* (1938); H.J. Kraus, *Gottesdienst in Israel* (1954); D.R. Ap-Thomas, in: VT, 6 (1956), 225–41. **ADD. BIBLIOGRAPHY:** R. Albertz, *A History of Israelite Religion in the Old Testament Period,* 2 vols. (1994); K. van der Toorn, *Family Religion in Babylonia, Syria and Israel* (1995); M. Haran, *Temples and Temple Service in Ancient Israel* (1995); S. Geller, in: A. Berlin and M. Brettler (eds.), *The Jewish Study Bible* (2004), 2021–40.

WORTSMAN, YECHESKIEL CHARLES (1878–1938), Zionist journalist. Born in Zvonets, Podolia, Wortsman completed his studies in chemistry at Basle University. During his student days he was active in the Zionist Movement and, together with Chaim *Weizmann, Nachman *Syrkin, and others established the first Zionist society in Berne. He also participated in the First Zionist Congress in Basle (1897). Wortsman began his journalistic activities at an early age and contributed articles to the Yiddish press on current affairs which were devoted principally to promoting Zionism. He also wrote one of the first Zionist propaganda pamphlets in Yiddish, *Vos Vilen di Tsionistn* (1901), and a booklet on the Jewish National Fund (1903). In 1904 he began to publish a Yiddish journal in London entitled *Di Yidishe Tsukunft.* From 1907 Wortsman lived in the United States, and for the rest of his life played a role in the Yiddish press there and in Canada, both as an editor and a regular contributor.

[Getzel Kressel]

WOSK, family of Canadian businessmen and philanthropists. Brothers BENJAMIN (1913–1995) and MORRIS (1917–2002) came to Vancouver, British Columbia, from Russia in 1929. They were sponsored by their cousin ABRASHA WOSK (1899–1980), one of the founders of the Vancouver Jewish community's Home for the Aged and the Achduth Society, which provided loans to immigrants. Together, Ben and Morris built the Wosk department store chain and acquired considerable real estate holdings, concurrently becoming major philanthropists and community leaders. For Ben's work with such charities as the B.C. Heart Foundation and Lions' Club, and many hundreds of individuals whom he helped without fanfare, he was named to the Order of Canada in 1978. He was also a major donor to the Schara Tzedeck synagogue and new Vancouver Jewish Community Centre, which is home to the Wosk Auditorium. Morris Wosk likewise made many significant contributions to both local and international causes. He was a prominent promoter of Israel Bonds and the Jewish National Fund of Canada, as well as numerous educational and health facilities such as the Vancouver General Hospital. In 1995 he commissioned four Torah scrolls for Vancouver's newest Jewish congregations. His long association with Simon Fraser University (SFU) included capital fund donations for the construction of the Morris J. Wosk Centre for Dialogue, an institute for the promotion of discussion and mutual understanding. In 1999 Morris and his son, Rabbi Dr. YOSEF WOSK, provided an endowment to establish a publishing arm for the Vancouver Holocaust Education Society. As the director of SFU's Interdisciplinary Program in the Department of Continuing Studies, Yosef has continued the Wosk family's close relationship with the university, as well as the tradition of philanthropy and support of Israel. He is the founder of SFU's Philosophers' Café, the world's largest series of café discussion gatherings. Morris's other two sons, Mordechai and Ken, have also been active in Jewish causes and philanthropy in Vancouver. Morris's wife, Dena, was a supporter of the arts, especially music.

[Barbara Schober (2nd ed.)]

WOUK, HERMAN (1915–), U.S. novelist and playwright. The son of Russian immigrants, Wouk was born in New York City. For six years he worked as a radio writer and, when the United States entered World War II, joined the Navy as a line officer, serving in the Pacific for four years. Wouk's wartime experiences gave him the material and background for his best seller *The Caine Mutiny* (1951). It sold 3,000,000 copies, won the Pulitzer Prize for fiction, was turned into a successful Broadway play by the author (*The Caine Mutiny Court Martial,* 1954), and was later made into a motion picture. Wouk's other novels include *Aurora Dawn* (1947), a satire on the advertising business; *The City Boy* (1948); *Marjorie Morningstar* (1955), the story of a stage-struck Jewish girl; *Youngblood Hawke* (1962), about the tribulations of a successful writer; and *Don't Stop the Carnival* (1965). A leading Orthodox layman, Wouk taught English at Yeshiva University. *This Is My God*

(1959) was his best-selling affirmation of faith in traditional Judaism, reached after much self-examination and exposure to the non-religious influences of his college years and public life. Wouk's *Winds of War*, regarded as one of his best novels, was published in 1971. It led the *New York Times* bestseller list for 24 weeks. The sequel, *War and Remembrance* (1978), dealing with the Holocaust in the framework of the major battles of World War II, also topped the *New York Times* bestseller list. His later works include the novel *Inside, Outside* (1985) which deals with Judaism in private life and in politics, and *The Will to Live On: This Is Our Heritage* (2000). He was vice president of the Fifth Avenue Synagogue and endowed several Jewish educational causes in the U.S. and Israel.

BIBLIOGRAPHY: R. Gordis, in: *Midstream*, 6 no. 1 (1960), 82–90; S. Brown, in: *Commentary*, 13 (1952), 595–9; E. Feldman, in: *Tradition*, 2 (1959), 333–6; S.J. Kunitz, *Twentieth Century Authors*, first suppl. (1955), s.v.; *Current Biography Yearbook 1952* (1953), 649–50. **ADD. BIBLIOGRAPHY:** L. Mazzeno, *Herman Wouk* (1994).

[Joseph Mersand]

WOYSLAWSKI, ZEVI (1889–1957), Hebrew writer and critic. Woyslawski studied at the Odessa yeshivah, at the Oriental Studies Academy founded by Baron Guenzburg in St. Petersburg, and at Odessa University. His literary career began in 1918 in *Ha-Shilo'ah. Three years later he left Russia as one of the group of writers headed by *Bialik and settled in Berlin. There he contributed to the periodical *Haolam* and edited the publication *Atidenu* (1923–24). He emigrated to Palestine in 1934 and played a prominent role in literary life: as a member of the Central Committee of the *Writers' Association, editor of its literary journal *Moznayim* (1942–47), chairman of the Israel branch of PEN, and a member of the Hebrew Language Academy. In his philosophical writings, Woyslawski examined the essence of recent Jewish culture against the background of European culture. His main contribution to the study of Hebrew literary criticism was the introduction of the sociocultural method of analysis. He wrote *Yeḥidim bi-Reshut ha-Rabbim* on the Jews in European culture (1956), and translated Shemaryahu *Levin's autobiography into Hebrew, as well as works by Hermann Cohen, Martin Buber, Schopenhauer, Freud, and other philosophers. Woyslawski felt that the test of the Hebrew language was its ability to convey other cultures, a strength that he displayed in his translations.

His books include *Eruvei Rashuyyot* (1944); *Ḥevlei Tarbut* (1946), a sociological study of national and linguistic problems; *Be-Mazzal Ma'adim* (1952); *Al ha-Mizpeh* (1959); *Orot ba-Derekh* (1960); *Ha-Roman ve-ha-Novellah be-Sifrut ha-Me'ah ha-Tesha Esreh* (1961); *Mishnat Zimmel al Ru'aḥ ha-Rekhushanut* (1966).

BIBLIOGRAPHY: S. Halkin, *Modern Hebrew Literature* (1950), 167; G. Elkoshi, *Naḥalat Ẓevi* (1966), bibliography of his works: *Atteret Ẓevi: ha-Ish ve-Haguto* (1962).

[Efraim Shmueli]

WRESCHNER, ARTHUR (1866–1932), psychologist. Born in Breslau, Wreschner began his career in the field of philosophy, writing a doctoral dissertation on Kant's and Platner's theories of knowledge for the University of Berlin. He remained at the university to study medicine, and after receiving his degree in 1900, moved to Zurich. There he became instructor in psychology at the Technische Hochschule and at the university where, in 1910, he was appointed professor. Wreschner wrote a number of scholarly books, his specific interests being reflected in *Methodologische Beitraege zu psychophysischen Messungen* (1898); *Die Reproduktion und Assoziation von Vorstellungen* (1907–09); *Die Sprache des Kindes* (1912); and *Das Gefuehl* (1931). His son WALTER WRESCHNER (1904–), an attorney, became president of the Israelitische Kultusgemeinde in Zurich in 1955, and was president of the Keren Hayesod for Switzerland.

WRITERS' ASSOCIATION IN ISRAEL (Heb. אֲגֻדַּת הַסּוֹפְרִים הָעִבְרִים בְּיִשְׂרָאֵל), organization of Hebrew writers established in 1921 in Tel Aviv by a conference of 70 writers, presided over by Nahum *Sokolow. Attempts to found a Hebrew writers' association in Russia and other East European countries had been made by Mordekhai b. Hillel Hacohen, but they proved unsuccessful, generally due to difficulties in procuring a license from the czarist authorities. When the association was founded in Ereẓ Israel, its objectives were set as "the cultivation and growth of Hebrew literature through the cooperative efforts of Hebrew writers; and the defense of the spiritual and material interests of those in the field of literature." The founding conference of the Writers' Association also accepted a resolution "to demand that the Zionist Organization regard Hebrew literature as an integral part of Zionist work and support it."

In the middle of the 1920s, after Ḥayyim Naḥman *Bialik and a group of Hebrew writers from Russia settled in Palestine, substantial impetus was given to the activities of the association. Bialik actively participated in the literary life of the country and declared that:

> The goal toward which the Writers' Association aspires is not to make writers in a flock, all of whose members dance to the tune of the same pipe and are under the staff of the same shepherd. We desire and aspire to diversify, to the joy of blessing and plenty. Each must travel his own special path, the path with which God has blessed him; each will demand of himself according to the path he has chosen and according to the gift God has given him. We ask only one thing: that we will all be infused with one consciousness-that the writers are the servants of the nation and of its eternal values.

In 1928 Bialik was elected president of the Writers' Association. Its organ, *Moznayim* ("Scales"), began as a weekly and then became a monthly. Over the years, many changes were made in the journal and it went through crises and periods during which publication ceased. Editors changed, and with them so did the trends of the publication, but the journal survived and provided an opportunity for literary men of various schools and points of view to contribute. After Bialik's death in 1934, Saul *Tchernichowsky was elected president of the association, and he continued to serve in this capacity until his death in 1944.

The association published series of books, founded funds to aid writers, and in special instances concerned itself with finding work for writers in need. It maintained ties with publishers to determine fair fees for writing and translation. Under the aegis of the association, literary collections were published, meetings and conventions held, a rest home was established for writers at Zikhron Ya'akov, and a house was purchased in Nehorah, in the heart of the newly developed Lachish region, for writers to use.

From 1948, with the establishment of the State of Israel, the mass immigration and growth of the population, the association received new members and broadened the scope of its activities. Among its projects are: the Makor Library for the encouragement of original works, in whose framework six books of fiction, poetry, criticism, and philosophy appear each year; Nefesh Books, which serve as a memorial to writers by publishing their works for the first time or reissuing them; the regularly published "Popular Selection of Our Literature" – selections of the representative works of various authors in popular editions; and the *Collection of Israel Writers*, a large annual in which works by authors of various ages and literary schools are brought together.

From 1951 the association ran the Asher Barash Institute of Records, which serves as one of the important bio-bibliographical sources for research into modern Hebrew literature, especially for students. The institute operates in the following fields: bibliographical records, keeping of archives, collection of newspaper items on writers, and the collection of photographs of writers from various periods of their lives. Among the publications of the institute are the collection *Genazim*, which appears every two years and includes material from the archives never before published; the quarterly *Yedi'ot Genazim*, which provides material about dead authors when the anniversary of their birth or death falls during the period of publication.

The Writers' Association is represented in a substantial number of literary prizes awarded in Israel, such as the Fund for the Encouragement of Original Creations, established in honor of Yiẓhak Lamdan, which is funded by part of the association's budget. Each year it frees a specific number of writers for a period so that they may complete their literary work. The Prime Minister's Fund for Creative Writing was founded by Levi Eshkol in 1968 on the initiative of the Writers' Association. Each year it awards prizes to five authors in order to free them from their daily work for a year and enable them to devote their time to realizing a literary goal. The association also hosts authors – both Jewish and non-Jewish – from abroad.

More than 300 writers belonged to the association in the beginning of the 1970s, and anyone who has published two books is eligible to submit an application for membership. Efforts were made to bring new immigrant writers into the association, and a decision was taken to accept new immigrant authors who did not write in the Hebrew language. The association initiated a project to translate works by these writers into Hebrew (Shevut) in order to both bring these works to the Hebrew-reading public and aid in the cultural absorption of the writers themselves.

The conference of the Writers' Association serves as a forum to discuss problems in the field of Hebrew literature and often resulted in intellectual clashes between different generations and schools of writers. It meets every two years during Passover, and its deliberations also cover problems of a political nature. The offices of the association, including the editorial offices of *Moznayim*, and the Asher Barash Institute, are housed in Bet ha-Sofer, in Tel Aviv, named in honor of Tchernichowsky. The building also contains the Tchernichowsky Museum. The Writers' Association is represented in the Institute for the Translation of Hebrew Literature. The association maintains branches in Jerusalem and Haifa, which carry out their own literary activities, lectures, symposia, and the publication of the yearbooks *Jerusalem* and *Carmelit*, respectively.

[Dov Chomsky]

WRITING (Scripts, Materials, and Inscriptions).

SCRIPTS AND MATERIALS

General Survey

From the end of the third millennium B.C.E., the art of writing was practiced in the ancient Near East (see *Alphabet). Here, the pictographic, cuneiform, and hieroglyphic scripts were invented and developed. In particular Canaan, situated on the cultural crossroads between Egypt and Mesopotamia and beneficiary of their scribal traditions, produced new indigenous writing systems. Some, like the Byblian pseudo-hieroglyphs, the enigmatic Balua stele, or the inscribed bricks from Deir ʿAllā, ancient Succoth, were limited to specific centers. These short-lived systems indicate a high degree of scribal experimentation and originality. It is no wonder then that the Canaanites invented the alphabet. They discovered that their language contained some 30 phonemes and that each one could be represented by an individual sign. The social effects of this revolutionary discovery were not to be felt for several generations.

Between the 17th and 12th centuries B.C.E., the primitive, pictograph-like alphabet was employed in Shechem, Gezer, Tell al-Ḥāsī, Tell al-ʿAjūl, Beth-Shemesh, Megiddo, Tell Rehov, Tell Beit Mirsim, and Lachish. These inscriptions are generally called Proto-Canaanite. Another, larger group, the so-called Proto-Sinaitic inscriptions (1500 B.C.E.) were probably written by a colony of northwest Semitic slaves who worked the mines in Wadi Ma'ara, near Sarābīṭ al-Khādim. It seems that this script generally served a religious function and may have been developed by a Canaanite priesthood. Certainly, all official government documents were written in cuneiform (e.g., el-Amarna letters) which obscured the alphabetic script.

It was during this period that a novel attempt to employ the alphabet was initiated at *Ugarit (1370–1200 B.C.E.). Perhaps as a result of the desire to express the local literature in its own medium, a cuneiform alphabet, influenced by the dominant Mesopotamian system, was devised. A similar trend may be noted in other Canaanite cities as well (Beth Shemesh, Taanach, Mount Tabor). This script as well as an earlier attempt to adapt the cuneiform signs to surfaces other than clay by giving them linear form (personal name incised on a pottery jar from Hazor, arrowhead from Lebanon) did not survive the disappearance of the Babylonian scribal centers in Canaan and Syria toward the end of the Bronze Age.

The political and cultural break with Mesopotamia, as well as the administrative needs of emerging young societies, accelerated the development of the linear alphabet. The letters were simplified, beginning the process that was to evolve into a cursive form. The first alphabetic system to emerge was the 22-letter Phoenician script, which appeared by about 1100 B.C.E. Most likely it was this script, or a slightly older form, that is found on bronze arrowheads in Beth-Lehem and Lachish. This system retained the general form and order of the earlier alphabetic scripts and probably the mnemonic device for its study – all thanks to a strong local scribal tradition. It was the Phoenician alphabet that was to be adopted by the Israelites, Arameans, and later by the Greeks. The new medium was adopted early in Israel's history and deeply affected its civilization. Monotheism was grasped now in terms of a written covenant between God and Israel. The central cult object was the Decalogue cut in stone, and later became the Torah scroll. Israelite religion elevated writing from a means of recording the mundane to a medium of revelation.

Perhaps it was because of the relative simplicity of the alphabet or the fact that Israel had no conservative scribal class with vested interests, that biblical society as a whole became "book-centered." Any tribesman, even a non-priest, could emerge as a literate leader (Josh. 8:32–35; 24:26).The establishment of the monarchy and the process of urbanization resulted in a greater diffusion of writing (among members of the government service, army personnel, the mercantile class, stonemasons, ivory cutters, potters, and others; see the following section). By the time that Deuteronomy appeared in the late seventh century, it might be taken for granted that a king could read, and that there would be enough people in a town who could write the Decalogue or a portion of it on the gates of a city or a house (Deut. 6:9; 17:18).

By Hezekiah's time, a great deal of literary activity was going on. Older written traditions were collected and edited (Prov. 25:1). The classical prophets, or their disciples, wrote down their messages. Prophesies were illustrated by written texts (Isa. 8:1; Jer. 17:1; Ezek. 37:16; Hab. 2:2), which could only have meaning for a populace with a reasonable number of readers (cf. Isa. 10:19). Furthermore, a paleographic study of Hebrew epigrapha indicates an increased diffusion of this skill toward the end of the monarchy. Similarly, the wide use of inscribed personal seals bearing fewer designs and iconographic motifs again argues for a growing literate social body during the First Temple period.

Writing Surfaces

STONE. Stone is the earliest known writing surface; it continued to be used throughout the ages, especially when permanence was desired. Three main types of stone inscriptions can be noted in the ancient Near East: a) monumental inscriptions for public display; b) seals made of semiprecious stones; and c) flakes or pieces of soft stone (e.g., limestone) which constituted cheap writing material.

Monumental Inscriptions. Both Egypt and Mesopotamia had long traditions of writing on stone. The latter area, poor in natural stone, imported the material for royal inscriptions. During the second millennium B.C.E. several Egyptian kings set up their victory stelae in Canaan: Thutmose III, Seti I, Ramses II, and Ramses III. This custom was followed by Sheshonk I (935–915), the biblical Shishak, at Megiddo. Assyrian kings, as well, left several stone monuments describing their victories in Canaan and indicating the extent of their rule. Tiglath-Pileser I (1114–1076 B.C.E.) set up an inscription at Nahr el Kalb, as is already noted by Shalmaneser III (858–824 B.C.E.) who did the same. The latter erected a second stela on Mt. Baal Rosh, which some scholars identify as Mt. Carmel, while Tiglath-Pileser III (745–727 B.C.E.) erected one in the vicinity of Wadi el-Arish, the biblical Brook of Egypt. Isaiah, in referring to such "boundary stones," said: "In that day there shall be an altar to the Lord in the midst of the land of Egypt and a pillar at the border thereof 'To the Lord'" (19:19).

Fragments of a three-dimensional stone inscription of Sargon II, discovered during excavations at Ashdod and dating to between 712–705 B.C.E., have also been published. Prior to the establishment of the Israelite monarchy, there seem to have been few local stonemasons in Canaan (II Sam. 5:11). The earliest stone monuments were probably not inscribed at all. They were composed of natural, unfinished stone found at hand (Gen. 31:45–48; Josh. 4:3; I Sam. 7:12; 15:12; II Sam. 8:13). The emphasis upon unhewn stones in the cult reflects the presedentary stage of Israelite history (Josh. 8:31). While this was generally the case, it was during this period of Israelite history that stone was first used as a writing surface for documents of religious importance. Foremost was the Decalogue, incised on two stone tablets (Ex. 24:12; 34:1; Deut. 4:13). At Shechem, the covenant was rewritten on large natural stones, smoothed over with plaster (Deut. 27:2–3; Josh. 8:32; cf. 24:25–26).

With the establishment of the Davidic monarchy and the subsequent influence of Phoenician material culture (I Kings 7:13ff.), monumental inscriptions must have been composed though they have yet to be found (cf. II Sam. 18:18; Ps. 2:7). This is suggested by the many monumental inscriptions discovered in neighboring countries (see below). These monumental inscriptions can be classified into four types: (1) Display inscriptions proclaiming the king's achievements in subduing his enemies and bringing prosperity to the local citizens. Among the northwest Semites, these documents are characterized by the introductory formula: "I, N. (son of N.) king of PN." Generally, much credit is given to the patron deity who came to the king's aid in the time of his distress. The document usually concludes with a series of curses against those who might want to damage its text. (2) Votive inscriptions recording donations, the name of the donor, and the name of the recipient deity, and noting the donor's piety. The text concludes with a request for a blessing, usually long life (cf. I Kings 3:11ff.). (3) Funerary inscriptions noting the name of the deceased and his title or profession, and containing a word to potential grave robbers that there are no valuables in the sepulcher, and a curse on anyone who disturbs the dead. These notices were written on the sarcophagus or at the entrance to the tomb. (4) Border markers and treaties, a legal genre defining the relationship between two parties. The former, known as *kudurrus* in Mesopotamia, were most extensively used during the Kassite period. The most impressive known treaty written on stone is the Sefire inscription between Matti'el and Barga'yah (c. 750 B.C.E.) composed in Aramaic.

Seals. Many *seals found in and around Israel are decorated with various scenes or designs that are derived ultimately from Egyptian or Phoenician iconographic motifs. Most often, there was a space or register left empty for the name of the buyer. Besides his own name and that of his fathers, he would note also his title ("scribe," "chamberlain," "servant of king…"). Some seals have a dedicatory formula, as well, and may indicate that the seal was a votive offering, especially when cut in the positive. The seal was used to indicate ownership, and was often impressed on jars before firing. It also served to verify standard measures, or, in official documents and letters, the name and authority of the sender (I Kings 21:8; Esth. 8:8).

Flakes. Flakes or small pieces of stone were used as a cheap writing surface for business notations or school texts. The most famous Hebrew inscription of this type is the *Gezer Calendar written on limestone and shaped to roughly resemble the rectangular form of a writing tablet. It is most probably a school text, an assumption corroborated by the fact, among others, that at least one side is a palimpsest.

PAPYRUS. The papyrus reed, cultivated from earliest times especially in the Delta, was a major natural resource of ancient Egypt. The hieroglyphic sign for Lower Egypt is the papyrus plant. Papyrus was found in the Ḥuleh swamp, though in limited quantities, and near the Naḥal Arnon in Transjordan. During the Arab conquest it was introduced into Sicily where it can still be found.

In Egypt, it was an all-purpose plant used for making, among other things, clothing and boats (cf. Ex. 2:3; Isa. 18:2); primarily, it was employed as a writing surface. The earliest written papyri date from the Fifth Dynasty (2750–2625 B.C.E.), though uninscribed rolls have been found dating to as early as the First Dynasty (c. 3000 B.C.E.). Pliny the Elder, the Roman naturalist (d. 79 C.E.), gives a detailed description of the manufacture of papyrus writing material:

> The raw material taken from the tall plants – some as high as 35 feet – consisted of strips cut lengthwise from the pith of the three-sided stalks. Strips of equal length and quality were then arranged on a flat surface, in the manner of latticework, in a horizontal and vertical layer, the former representing the recto and the latter the verso side of the sheet. Through the application of pressure and water from the Nile – perhaps with the occasional addition of glue – the layers were merged into a fairly homogeneous mass, which was then exposed to the sun. After drying, the sheets were rubbed smooth with shells or ivory and perhaps whitened with chalk. Excess moisture was forced out by additional pounding.

The manufacture and trade in papyrus was probably always a royal or state monopoly. Such was the case in the time of the Ptolemies and Caesars. J. Černy has even suggested that the Greek word "papyrus" is derived from an original, though undocumented, *p3 – pr – ʿ3*, "the [stuff] of Pharaoh," indicating a royal monopoly. The earliest reference to papyrus in Canaan is found in the Egyptian text "The Journey of Wen-Amon to Phoenicia" (c. 1090 B.C.E.). Smendes (Ne-su-Ba-neb-Ded), the founder of the 21st Dynasty and ruler of Lower Egypt, sent 500 rolls of papyrus to Zakar-Baal, king of Byblos, in partial payment for a shipment of cedars. This large quantity of writing material most likely reflects the extensive use of the alphabetic script by this time in Canaan, which is corroborated by the repeated references to written documents in the story (letters, royal records, and stelae). Byblos became an agent for the export of papyrus throughout the Mediterranean lands. So much so that it gave its name to the product: in Greek, *biblos* came to mean "book" or "papyrus," and from this the word "Bible" is derived. By Herodotus' time, papyrus had become the standard writing material for most of the ancient world surrounding the Mediterranean Sea (*Persian Wars*, 5:58). It was to remain in use until replaced by true paper, brought from China between the seventh and tenth centuries C.E. There is no specific reference to papyrus in the Bible (but cf. Isa. 23:3). Some scholars, though, infer from the description in Jeremiah 36:23–25 that the prophet's scroll was made of papyrus, which is more easily cut and less odorous than leather.

The earliest Hebrew papyrus dates from the late eighth or early seventh century B.C.E. and was discovered in 1951 in Wadi Murabbaʿāt in the Judean Desert. This palimpsest contains the remains of a letter and instructions for the delivery of food supplies. Several clay bullae from the sixth century bear the marks of papyrus fibers upon which they were impressed. The most famous is the impression of *Igdlyhw ʾšr ʿl hbyt* (*Le-Gedalyahu ʾasher ʿal ha-bayit*; cf. II Kings 25:22) found at various sites in Judah.

The oldest known Aramaic papyrus is a letter discovered in Saqqāra, Egypt, from a king by the name of Adon to his Egyptian overlord. Most scholars agree that it was sent from the Philistine coast, possibly from Ashdod, just before Nebuchadnezzar's invasion in 604 or 598 B.C.E.

The second half of the first millennium B.C.E. saw the widespread use of papyrus for sundry government, religious, and personal documents. Of particular Jewish interest are the *Elephantine papyri (late fifth century). They include official letters and private papers that shed much light on the internal affairs, religious life, and relations with gentile neighbors in this military colony situated near the First Cataract on the Nile. Among these documents, is a fragment of the oldest known version of the Sayings of Ahikar. A small number of the Dead Sea Scrolls were also written on this material.

ANIMAL HIDES. Sheep, goat, and calf hides, after proper preparation, served as one of the principal types of writing surfaces in the Fertile Crescent. There is no contemporary record of preparation of this material, which probably did not differ from the modern process. The skins were washed, limed, dehaired, scraped, washed a second time, stretched evenly on a frame, scraped a second time, inequalities being pared down, and then dusted with sifted chalk and rubbed with a pumice. In the earlier period, the skin was prepared to receive writing only on the hairy side, though in exceptional cases, such as in a long text, it was inscribed on both sides (Ezek. 2:10; cf. Er. 21a).

During the Hellenistic period the skins were treated so as to receive writing on both sides. The improved method was attributed to Eumenes II (197–158 B.C.E.), whose capital, Pergamum, gave its name to the new product – "parchment." In due time, a distinction was made between the coarser and finer types of this material. The latter was manufactured from more delicate calfskin or kidskin, especially from stillborn calves or lambs, and was called "vellum." By the second century C.E., vellum began to compete with papyrus. In the next two or three centuries, with the introduction of the codex, its popularity was assured and it superseded ordinary parchment for the most valued books.

The earliest mention of a leather writing surface is found in an Egyptian text from the Fourth Dynasty (c. 2550 B.C.E.), while the oldest extant example of such a writing surface dates from the 12th Dynasty (2000–1800 B.C.E.). It continued to be used in Egypt until the Arab conquest, though to a limited extent, because of the ubiquitous papyrus.

The use of skins as a writing surface first appeared in Mesopotamia in eighth-century Assyrian reliefs. No doubt, this surface was introduced by the Aramean scribes who found clay tablets unsuitable for their alphabetic script. The fifth-century Greek historians Herodotus and Ctesias noted that the barbarians continued to use leather for writing, while on the Greek mainland this substance had been replaced by papyrus. Ctesias remarked that the Persians wrote their royal records on *diphtherai*, i.e., skins. This has been corroborated by the discovery of 12 letters belonging to Arsames, the satrap of Egypt (fifth century B.C.E.), where the cache was found.

There is no explicit biblical reference to writing on leather, nor are there extant leather rolls, prior to those discovered at Qumran. In spite of this, there is general agreement that throughout the First and Second Temple periods the ancient Israelites primarily used animal hides on which to write their official documents and religious literature. Leather is a much more durable surface than papyrus. The sheepherding Israelites, like the Arameans and the Transjordanian nations, were more likely to use this local resource than to import Egyptian papyrus. During the Second Temple period the references to writing on animal hides are clearer. They no doubt reflect a continuation of the earlier period, since there was no reason to change suddenly to leather at this time.

The Dead Sea Scrolls are the earliest Hebrew texts written on leather that have been discovered so far. They provide firsthand evidence of the ancient scribal technique of preparing and writing on this surface. This scribal tradition was codified by the rabbis (Tractate *Soferim*) and is still followed in the writing of Torah scrolls, *mezuzot*, and **tefillin*.

POTTERY. By far the largest number of inscriptions from the biblical period were written on *pottery. The material can be classified into two distinct types: (1) whole pots that bear a short notice, inscribed either before or after firing and (2) *ostraca, or broken potsherds, generally bearing longer inscriptions. While there is no biblical reference to this writing surface, this cheap and easily available material was widely used not only in Israel but throughout the ancient world. The inscriptions on pottery usually give the owner's name, the capacity of the jar, i.e., *bt lmlk*, "royal bath," or a dedicatory notice. An example of the latter has been found on a pot bearing the word *qdš*, "holy," at Hazor, and on another container in the excavations at Tell Beer-Sheba, which was probably used for a *minḥah* offering at the local sanctuary (Y. Aharoni).

From the end of the eighth century B.C.E., it became customary to indicate important data on the handles of jars. Generally, this was done by impressing a seal on the soft clay before firing. Some 80 "private" and about 800 *lmlk* seal impressions were counted. The latter indicate a standard capacity assured by the king, as well as noting one of the four Judean cities where the contents were "bottled" (Hebron, Ziph, Socoh, and *mmšt*). Most of the inscribed handles from Gibeon were incised after firing and probably indicate a tax formula: *Gbʿn, Gdr, Amryhw*, i.e., "(To) Gibeon (from the village) Gedor (sent by) Amaryahu."

Ostraca (singular: ostracon) is the technical term for potsherds that were used for writing. Pottery was particularly suitable for those scripts employing pen and ink or brush and paint, though the surface might be incised as well. The earliest literary reference to ostraca is that of the fifth-century Athenian custom of voting powerful and dangerous citizens into exile. In order to do so, 10,000 ostraca had to be inscribed with the unlucky man's name. The term "ostracism" is derived from this custom. In Israel, small pieces of potsherds seem to have been used in local lotteries in biblical Arad and Masada of the Second Temple period. (For a list of the ostraca of ancient Israel known at present see Inscriptions, below.) A survey of the ostraca shows that this surface was used for letters, tax dockets, fiscal notices, name lists, and at least one court petition. The cheapness of the material indicates the secondary importance of most of the inscriptions or possibly the hard-pressed circumstances at the time of writing, when papyrus and leather were reserved for more important documents. Furthermore, the ostraca provide some idea of the caliber and diffusion of writing among the bureaucracy, army personnel, and local scribes in ancient Israel.

CLAY. This substance was the standard writing material in Mesopotamia from the third to the first millennia B.C.E. The alluvial soil of the Tigris-Euphrates valley made clay the most readily available and thus the cheapest form of writing material in this area. This medium spread with the cuneiform script to the Elamites, Hittites, and Canaanites.

The Ugaritic literature and the el Amarna letters, in addition to other smaller archives (Alalakh, Taanach) and single documents from Syria and Canaan, were inscribed on clay. With the decline of Mesopotamian influence toward the end of the second millennium B.C.E., this writing surface became obsolete. Furthermore, suitable clay was not commonly found in this area, nor was it easily adaptable to the emerging linear alphabet. The only biblical reference to an incised clay tablet is one found in a Babylonian context and interestingly not an inscription but rather a "blueprint" of Jerusalem: "Son of man, take thee a tile [*levenah*] and lay it before thee and trace upon it a city, even Jerusalem" (Ezek. 4:1).

METALS. Various inscriptions from the ancient and classical worlds have been found written on gold, silver, copper, bronze, and lead. These artifacts corroborate the many Hebrew and north Semitic literary sources which mention these writing surfaces. A small (6.7 cm. × 2.2 cm.) gold case from the north Syrian kingdom of Sm'al bears the dedicatory inscription: "This *smr* fashioned by Kilamuwa son of Ḥayya, for Rakabel. May Rakabel grant him long life" (c. 825 B.C.E.). Similarly, Yehawmilk, king of Byblos (fourth century B.C.E.), presented a gold votive inscription to his divine patroness. In ancient Israel, this precious metal was employed in Temple ornaments and priestly vestments. The high priest's diadem was made of gold and inscribed: "Consecrated to the Lord" (Ex. 28:36–38).

Examples of ex-voto inscriptions on silver platters were found near Ismailiya in north Egypt. One of them reads: "This Qinu the son of Gashmu, king of Kedar, offered to Hani'ilat." These date from the fifth century B.C.E. The donor may be the son of Nehemiah's enemy Geshem the Arab (Neh. 6:1ff.).

The famous Copper Scroll from Qumran is a unique find. This writing surface was chosen specifically to record a list of fabled treasures. Its weight and inflexibility would make it an impractical writing surface for frequently read scrolls.

Bronze seems to have been a more common writing surface. Beginning in the 1950s and 1960s, inscribed bronze arrowheads and javelin heads as well as a spatula were discovered in Phoenicia and Israel. Some have been explained as cultic or magical texts. These inscriptions date from the 12th century to 950 B.C.E. and, therefore represent paleographically the earliest form of the Phoenician alphabet. Several inscriptions in the so-called pseudo-hieroglyphic script of Byblos were written on bronze as well.

There is a growing collection of bronze weights, many of which were cast in the form of animals or parts of the human body. One turtle-shaped weight found at Ashkelon reads "quarter shekel" (cf. I Sam. 9:8) and weighs 2.63 gm. Another of the same design from Samaria reads "a fifth" and weighs 2.499 gm.

There are many references in Greek and Roman sources to lead as a surface for magical texts and even for such literary works as that of Hesiod. Probably following this tradition, a lead scroll inscribed with Psalm 80 in Greek was found at Rhodes. No such material is known from ancient Israel, though some have understood the term *'oferet*, "lead" (Job 19:24), as referring to such a writing surface. Apart from the bronze weights, inscriptions on metal were generally of a religious nature, many of which bore dedicatory formulas and were ultimately donated to a temple treasury.

IVORY. Excluding several personal seals, most, if not all, inscriptions on ivory can be classified into two types: joiners' markings and dedicatory formulas (cf. below Wax). The former are single letters of the alphabet incised on the back of ivory inlays in order to facilitate the process of assembling them. The ivory inlays found in the palace at Samaria are indicative of contemporary styles of decorative art favored by the Israelite aristocracy (Amos 3:15).

As was the case with precious metals, ivory was donated to the patron deities. Of particular interest is one of the Megiddo ivories dated between 1350–1150 B.C.E. which bears the hieroglyphic inscription:

> The Singer of Ptah, South-of-His Wall
> Lord of the Life of the Two Lands [i.e., Egypt] and Great Prince of Ashkelon. Kerker.

The dedication is to the Egyptian god Ptah, who is here called by three of his titles, the third of which indicates a cult seat in Ashkelon. The votaress Kerker seems to be a singer at that Canaanite temple. W.F. Albright has suggested that she be identified with Calcol, a pre-Israelite singer of renown (I Kings 5:11).

Ivory gifts were presented to the king as well. An example may be found in a recently discovered ivory piece from Tell Nimrūd, ancient Calah, dating to the mid-eighth century B.C.E. The legible part of the inscription is in good Hebrew (probably from Samaria) and reads *mmlk gdl*, "from the Great King." This title is probably a Hebrew translation of the well-known Akkadian royal epithet *šarru rabû* (cf. II Kings 18:19; Isa. 36:13). There is a similar ivory inscription from Arslan Tash, north Syria, which reads *lmrn ḥz'l* "for our lord Hazael" (I Kings 19:15). It was most likely among the spoils taken from Damascus in 796 B.C.E. by Adad-nirâri III, king of Assyria.

WOOD. Wood was employed throughout the ancient world as a writing surface. Egyptian inscriptions have been preserved on wooden statues and sarcophagi, as well as on wooden tablets coated with stucco which were frequently used for school exercises. The Bible seldom explicitly mentions this surface.

The earliest clear reference to writing on wood is found in connection with an attempt to challenge Aaron's priestly authority and is employed in substantiating his legitimacy: "Speak to the Israelite people and take from them – from the chieftains of their ancestral houses – ...12 staffs in all. Inscribe each man's name on his staff... also inscribe Aaron's name on the staff of Levi..." (Num. 17:17–26). The inscription is the simple type indicating ownership and was probably incised *le-Aharon* – the writing surface being almond wood (verse 23).

Ezekiel employed a wood writing surface in his famous prophesy of the restoration of national unity (37:16–23): "And thou, son of man, take thee one stick [*ʿeẓ*] and write upon it: 'For Judah' [*li-Yhudah*] and for the children of Israel his companions; then take another stick, and write upon it: 'For Joseph' [*le-Yosef*], the stick of Ephraim, and all the house of Israel his companions; and join them for thee one to another into one stick, that they may become one in thy hand" (verses 16–17).

P.J. Hyatt has suggested, *en passant*, that the prophet may have used wooden writing tablets and joined them together in the form of a diptych, i.e., a two-leaved "book." This suggestion might be reconsidered in the light of the later discovery of such writing material from Mesopotamia (see following paragraph) as well as the prophet's known use of other local surfaces (Ezek. 4:1) and general familiarity with the scribal art. Wooden writing boards may be implied in the undefined term *luḥot* (Hab. 2:2). Since clay tablets were not used in Israel at this time and stone tablets are usually defined as such (Ex. 24:12; 31:18; Deut. 4:13, et al.), the prophet may have been referring to tablets of wood. Furthermore, the verb *be'er*, as shown by Z. Ben Ḥayyim, means to incise on a hard surface.

WAX. It has long been known that wax writing surfaces were employed in Egypt, Greece, and Italy during the Classical period. In addition to much pictographic evidence, especially from Italy, a school text from Fayyum, Egypt, from 250 B.C.E. was found that had a red wax surface and on the reverse one in black. Properly treated, wax has the quality of being a lightweight substance that can be easily reused.

This surface is mentioned in older literary sources from Mesopotamia. An important discovery at ancient Calah during the 1950s were 16 ivory boards with the same number of wooden boards in a well in Sargon II's palace (717–705 B.C.E.). They were constructed so as to contain an inscription on wax. One of the tablets was still covered with beeswax, compounded with sulphide of arsenic or orpiment, bearing the text of a well-known astrological text *Enuma Anu Enlil*. Since these boards were tied or hinged together forming a diptych, triptych, or polyptych, they may be called the earliest known form of the book.

An Aramean scribe holding an oblong, book-shaped object, with ribbed markings at the edge for hinges, is clearly depicted on the stele of Bar-rākib, king of Sm'al. This picture predates the above Calah material by about a quarter of a century and demonstrates the Western Semites' familiarity with this writing surface.

GRAFFITI. These are rough scratchings of names, short notices, and etchings incised by an unpracticed hand on walls or on natural stone surfaces. Two examples of graffiti from the biblical period were discovered during the 1960s. In 1961 several short notices were found in a burial cave northeast of Lachish dating from the sixth century B.C.E. One or two seem to be prayers and another a series of curses. The longest inscription reads: "The Lord is God of the World, the mountains of Judea are His, the God of Jerusalem." From ninth-century Kuntillet Ajrud in Sinai we have mention of YHWH and his *Asherah. Later, several other graffiti have come to light from Khirbat al-Kawm, in the same general vicinity as the above. From this eighth-century site we have again mention of YHWH and his Asherah. Here again several curse formulas have been scribbled on the walls of a family tomb.

TATTOO MARKS. A more unusual writing surface was the human skin, originally incised with a slave mark indicating ownership, but occasionally with a sign demonstrating fidelity to a deity. It was done by cutting into the skin and filling the incision with ink or a dye. This method is already noted in the Mishnah: "If a man wrote [on his skin] pricked-in writing [he is culpable]... but only if he writes it and pricks it in with ink or eye-paint or aught that leaves a lasting mark" (Mak. 3:6). The Bible categorically forbids this practice: "You shall not make gashes in your flesh for the dead or incise any marks (*ketovet qaʿaqaʿ*) on yourselves; I am the Lord" (Lev. 19:28). While this was generally the rule, there seem to have been cases where devotees of YHWH did incise His name on their arms. Isaiah may be referring to this custom when he says: "One shall say: 'I am the Lord's'; And another shall call himself by the name Jacob; and another shall inscribe his hand 'Belonging to the Lord'..." (44:5; cf. also Job 37:7), and perhaps figuratively: "Surely I have graven upon your palms: Thy sealings (!) are continually before me" (Isa. 49:16). Furthermore in Elephantine, slaves of Jews were marked with the name of their owner (Cowley, Aramaic, 28:2–6), as was the general practice.

Writing Equipment

THE PEN. Several different types of writing implements were employed in accordance with the different types of surfaces. Inscriptions on stone or metal required a chisel, whereas for clay or wax a stylus would suffice. In Mesopotamia, the stylus was made of reeds, hardwood, or even bone and metal. There is no pictographic evidence from ancient Israel nor is there any artifact that can be definitely identified as a stylus. The literary sources do mention at least two kinds of tools for writing on stone: an "iron pen," *ʿeṭ barzel*, and a hard stone stylus, *ẓipporen shamir* (Jer. 17:1; Job 19:24). The *ḥereṭ* may have been a tool for working on metal or wood (Ex. 32:4).

The Egyptians used a rush, cut obliquely and frayed at the end forming a brush, to write with ink on papyrus, hides, ostraca, and wood. A similar type of pen seems to have been used on the Samaria and Lachish ostraca. This instrument was probably called "the scribe's pen," *ʿeṭ sofer*, [*soferim*] (Jer. 8:8;

Ps. 45:2), in order to differentiate it from the stone engraver's "iron pen." Likewise, the *ḥereṭ ʾenosh*, the "common or soft stylus" (Isa. 8:1), is not the same as that mentioned above.

At the end of the third century B.C.E., Greek scribes living in Egypt invented a new type of reed pen pointed and split at the end. The quill, used to this day by Torah scribes (*soferei setam*), was introduced during the Middle Ages in Ashkenazi communities.

From earliest times, the Egyptians wrote in black and red ink. Black ink was made from carbon in the form of soot mixed with a thin solution of gum. This solution was molded and dried into cakes, which were mixed with water before use. In producing red ink, red ocher, or red iron oxide was substituted for carbon.

In Israel, a similar type of black ink was probably used, though the Lachish ostraca show traces of iron. The Hebrew word for ink is *deyo* (Jer. 36:18), a term whose etymology is uncertain. In at least one of its solutions, the ink did not easily penetrate the writing surface and could be erased with water (Num. 5:23). Most of the Dead Sea Scrolls were written with a carbon ink, while the badly damaged *Genesis Apocryphon* was written with the metallic mixture.

The copy of the Septuagint presented to Ptolemy II was written with a gold additive (Aris. 176), a practice followed among some circles in writing the Tetragrammaton but which the rabbis specifically forbade (Sof. 1:9).

PEN CASE AND PALETTE. The ancient Egyptians carried their brushes in a hollow reed case. They added to this a wooden palette containing two depressions for the cakes of black and red ink. This was joined by a cord to a small cup designed to hold water for moistening the ink. A stylized drawing of these three pieces became the hieroglyphic sign S Š, meaning "writing" or "scribe." Later the pen case and palette were combined and easily carried on the belt (cf. Ezek. 9:2–3, 11). An Egyptian ivory pen case dating from the time of Ramses III was found at Megiddo. The biblical term for this item is *qeset*, derived from the Egyptian *gsti*. A razor for cutting leather or papyrus (Jer. 36:23) and probably a straight edge for ruling lines as well as a cloth or sponge for erasures completed the equipment required by the scribe.

[Aaron Demsky]

INSCRIPTIONS

The number of inscriptions found in Palestine is relatively small. The only monumental inscription of the type known from neighboring lands found there (except for a three letter fragment from eighth-century B.C.E. Samaria) is the Tell Dan Inscription (bibliography in Schwiderski, 409). This Aramaic inscription has attracted wide attention because it appears to mention "the House of David." This paucity of material is undoubtedly due to the fact that Palestine often served as a battlefield and many of its principal cities were frequently destroyed.

The earliest inscriptions in a language closely related to Hebrew are (a) those in the Proto-Byblian script, which has not been fully deciphered as yet, from the early second millennium; (b) those in the Proto-Sinaitic pictographic script from the 15th century B.C.E. found at Sarābīṭ al-Khādim; and (c) those in the *Ugaritic cuneiform alphabet from Ras Shamra. The Proto-Canaanite inscriptions on artifacts from Gezer, Lachish, and Shechem ranging from the 17th to the 14th centuries B.C.E. are closely related to the Proto-Sinaitic, while short tablets in a form of the Ugaritic alphabet from Beth-Shemesh, Kawkab al-Hawāʾ, and Taanach are from the 14th–13th centuries B.C.E. and early alphabetic writing comes from a variety of sites of the 13th–12th centuries B.C.E. There is still some degree of disagreement as to the deciphering of these brief inscriptions. Inscribed bronze arrowheads from the end of the 12th century found at Al-Khaḍr, near Beth-Lehem, and similar artifacts from a slightly later period found at other sites provide a link with the later developed Phoenician-Hebrew script.

The earliest Phoenician inscriptions are those from Byblos, beginning with that on the Ahiram sarcophagus from the tenth century and those of the other members of Ahiram's dynasty. The earliest Hebrew inscription is on a limestone plaque from Gezer; it contains an agricultural calendar and was written toward the end of the tenth century (see *Gezer Calendar). The Moabite stone from about 840 B.C.E. (discovered in 1868) recounts, in a dialect close to Hebrew, the rule of Omri over Moab (II Kings 3) and subsequent Moabite victories over Israel. It is of prime linguistic importance, but also gives an insight into Moabite religion and the history of the period (see *Mesha Stele). The fragmentary Amman Citadel Inscription, whose language is very close to Hebrew but whose meaning is far from certain, is also from this period. The Kulamuwa inscription in Phoenician from Zenjirli, in southwestern Turkey, celebrates the victory of Kilamuwa over his enemies and records his role in bringing prosperity to his people. One of the earliest Aramaic inscriptions was found near Aleppo. It is dedicated to Melqart, god of Tyre, and comes from the middle of the ninth century B.C.E. (COS II, 152–53). Of great importance is the bilingual Aramaic and Akkadian royal inscription found at Tel Fekherye in 1979 (Swiderski, 194, with bibliography; COS II, 153–54). Minor Aramaic inscriptions have also been found at En-Gev, Hazor, and Tell Dan in Galilee.

From the late ninth and the eighth centuries there are a number of Hebrew inscriptions: (a) a series of small inscriptions from Hazor which contain primarily names; (b) the *Samaria ostraca: 63 dockets written in ink on potsherds referring to deliveries of oil and wine. Although they are short – listing the regnal year, a place name, a personal name, and a quantity of oil and wine – they allow an insight into the administration of the Northern Kingdom. They shed light on the northern dialect of Hebrew and since they contain many Baʿal names, they are of use in discussion of the religious situation in the Northern Kingdom; (c) the Tell Qasīla ostraca: one refers to a shipment of oil, while another reads: "gold of Ophir for Beth-Horon, 30 shekels"; (d) a series of *seals that can be ascribed to this period, some containing names familiar from the Bible such as Ahaz, Jeroboam, and Isaiah; and e) the inscription *qdš* on vessels from Beer-Sheba and Hazor.

The *Siloam tunnel inscription, discovered in 1880, dates from the end of the eighth century. It commemorates the completion of the tunnel between the "Virgin's Spring" and the pool of Siloam – whose purpose was to bring water to the city (cf. II Kings 20:20; II Chron. 32:30). The six-line inscription is written in straightforward Hebrew. From this period also come tomb inscriptions found in caves in the village of Silwān such as that of the royal steward "...yahu, who is over the house" (cf. Isa. 22:15). The papyrus palimpsest from Murabbʿāt may be dated to the end of this period, while a jar inscription found at Azor, near Jaffa, reading *lšlmy* is in the Phoenician script.

It is from this century that there are important Phoenician and Aramaic inscriptions from Syria and southwest Turkey. The Karatepe inscription, from the Adana area, is the longest Phoenician inscription known to date. It commemorates the victories and deeds of King Azitawadda of the Danunians and was inscribed upon orthostats and statues as part of the city gate along with a version in hieroglyphic Hittite. In phraseology and idiom it is often very close to biblical Hebrew and sheds light on the religious practices of the period. There are also texts in the Ammonite language from this period: a) the inscription of King Yariḥʿazor of Beth ʿAmmon; and b) the Ammonite text in Aramaic script from Deir ʿAllā.

The Aramaic inscriptions include the Zakkur inscription (c. 775) commemorating the victory of Zakkur of Hamath and Luath over the Aramaic league under Bir-Hadad son of Hazael of Damascus. This inscription contains important references to prayer and prophecy. The Sefire treaty inscriptions from north Syria contain the treaty made by the king of Arpad and his overlord, the king of the Kashkeans. This is the longest extant inscription in early Aramaic. It contains details concerning the parties to the treaty, the witnessing gods, imprecations upon the treaty breaker, details of the treaty's provisions, and also geographic information. Besides its philological importance, it has supplied considerable information of a cultural and historical nature and has clarified biblical terms and formulas. Of the Aramaic inscriptions from Zenjirli, two (Hadad, Panamu) are in the local dialect (Samalian; known already from Kulamuwa's time) while the others are in Early General Aramaic. They are important for Aramaic religion and also attest to the growing power of the Assyrians under Tiglath-Pileser III.

Phoenician had spread during these centuries to the Mediterranean isles and inscriptions have been found in Cyprus, Sardinia, and elsewhere. The incantation plaque, in Aramaic script but Phoenician language, from Arslan Tash in upper Mesopotamia attests to the continuity of literary idiom and to the symbiosis of the Canaanite and Mesopotamian cultures among the Arameans in the early seventh century. The spread of Aramaic as the lingua franca of the Near East (cf. II Kings 18:26) is seen in the use of Aramaic on an ostracon containing a letter found at Ashur and also in the use of Aramaic dockets on cuneiform tablets at Ashur and elsewhere. Two inscribed funerary stelae in Aramaic come from Neirab near Aleppo. An interesting ostracon from Nimrūd presents a list of exiles with typical Israelite names. Excavations at Nimrūd have also produced inscribed objects (bronzes, ivories, and ostraca) in Hebrew, Aramaic, and Phoenician.

In Palestine during the seventh century, Hebrew inscriptions are found on seals, weights, measures of capacity, and jar handles. *Weights bearing the inscription *bqʿ* or *pym*, both known from the Bible, and *nṣp* are found in many Judahite sites and the words *hīn* and *bat* (*bt lmlk*) – well known from the Bible as names of units of cubic measure – have been found on pots and jugs. There are, from the mid-seventh century onward, an important series of jar handles engraved with the winged sun disk scarab seal, or *ṭet* symbol, with the royal stamp reading *lmlk*, "of the king," and the name of one of four cities: *šwkw* (Socoh), *hbrn* (Hebron), *z (y)p* (Ziph), and *mmšt* (unidentified). The legend *lmlk* refers to weights and measures standardized by the royal administration. The *lmlk* and *ṭet* symbols are found at a later period on jars from Phoenicia, Elephantine in Egypt, and Carthage. The jars were in all likelihood used for wine. From the reign of Josiah there are a number of ostraca from a site south of *Yavneh-Yam. The longest one consists of 14 lines in which an agricultural worker, protesting his innocence, petitioned a superior asking for the return of a cloak wrongly taken from him (cf. Ex. 22:25). The language reflects the legal terminology of the period (i.e., line 10: "and all my brothers will testify for me," *y ʿnw ly*). The graffiti from the area of El-Qom, near Hebron, are primarily tomb inscriptions recording the name of the owner of the tomb. Inscriptions on a bowl and a decanter were also found there, as well as inscribed weights. The Hebrew ostraca found at *Arad are from the late seventh century. They are concerned mainly with the delivery of wine, flour, bread, and oil to certain persons and also to the Kittim (*ktym*), a term used in the Bible for people from Cyprus or the Aegean isles. Small ostraca bearing the names of the priestly families Pashhur (*pšḥr*) and Meremoth (*mrmwt*), known from the Bible, were also found. One ostracon has a reference to the Korahites (*bny qrh*), and another to the Kerosites (*qrwsy*), known from Ezra 2:44 and Nehemiah 7:47 as a family of temple servants, and also to the Jerusalem temple (called *byt whwh*). There are also references to the city Ramath-Negeb and to the Edomites and to events in the area.

The Ophel ostracon found in Jerusalem and containing a poorly preserved list of names with patronymics and residences in all likelihood belongs to the beginning of the sixth century. The jar handles from al-Jīb reading *gbʿn* (together with personal names) has clinched the identification of that site with Gibeon. Three inscriptions in a cave at Khirbat Beit-Lay, south of Jerusalem, are of religious significance since they ask help of YHWH and refer to Judah and Jerusalem. The 21 ostraca found at Tell al-Duwayr (commonly known as the "*Lachish letters") are of prime importance since they come from the period shortly before the destruction of the Temple in 587 and reflect the circumstances of that period. Only seven are well enough preserved to offer a continuous text. They contain lists of names, simple business documents, and the correspondence of the military governor Yaush and his subordinates. They are written in idiomatic classical Hebrew and contain interesting expressions such as the oath *ḥyhwh*, "as Yahweh lives." There is also a reference to a prophet in these texts. Many of the personal names found in these ostraca are familiar from the literature of the period. Seals of the period contain names such as Gedaliah, Jaazaniah, and that of King Jehoiachin. Seals from Ammon, Moab, and Edom are known from this and earlier periods. An Aramaic letter, written by a ruler of one of the cities of the Philistine coast, was found at Saqqarah in Egypt.

The excavations at Lachish produced for the post-Exilic period an interesting inscribed incense altar (*lbnt*ʾ) which may have been dedicated to the Lord (line 3: *lyh* – if this reading is correct). Recent excavations have greatly increased the number of inscribed objects found in Palestine from the Persian and Hellenistic periods. From Arad alone there are about 100 ostraca in Aramaic from the late fifth century; they deal primarily with matters of local economy. An ostracon from approximately the same period was found at Ashdod referring simply to a plot of land as 'Zebadiah's vineyard' (*krm zbdyh*; in Ashdodite? cf. Neh. 13:24). Ostraca in Aramaic from this period have been found at Tell al-Fārʿa and Beer-Sheba in the south and at Tell Saʿīdiyya in the Jordan Valley. An ostracon from a slightly earlier period was found at Heshbon in Moab.

The earliest stamp seals of the Persian period are those inscribed *msh* (or *mwsh*). There are several types of *yhd, yhwd*, and *yh* stamps from this period with the *yh* stamps presumably the latest. The coins from Judah are also inscribed with the legend *yhd* in archaic Aramaic lapidary script. Some stamps have *yhwd* plus a name; the stamps from Ramat Raḥel contain a name and in all likelihood the word *pḥr*ʾ, "the potter."

The Aramaic papyri found in a cave in the *Wadi Daliya are dated from 375 to 335 or slightly later. The content of all the papyri is legal or administrative and they were executed in Samaria. They deal with possession of slaves and also with loans, sales, and marriages. The name Sanballat appears on both papyri and sealings. The papyri were probably hidden in these caves by refugees from Samaria at the time of Alexander the Great's conquests. Aramaic ostraca from En Gedi and Elath from the early fourth century have been published; and from the latter site ostraca in Phoenician and Edomite are known. The Tobiah inscriptions from ʿAraq el-Emir in Transjordan stem typologically from this period.

A revival of the Paleo-Hebrew script takes place during this period. It is found on seals from Daliya and Makmish and also on several coins. It is frequently found on the jar stamps of the third century from Judah, on stamps inscribed with *yhwd* (Yehud) plus symbol, and on the pentagram stamps bearing the inscription *yršlm* (Jerusalem). This script is then used for some texts found at Qumran and on Hasmonean coins and also on those of the first revolt and the Bar Kokhba revolt. It is from this late Paleo-Hebrew script that the Samaritan script developed. The earliest Samaritan inscription, found in the Ionian capital at Emmaus, stems in all likelihood from the first century C.E.

Many of the important inscriptions from the Phoenician coast such as the Eshmunazor, Bodashtart, and Tabnit funeral inscriptions, etc., as well as those from Umm al-ʿAwāmid, come from the Persian and Hellenistic periods. These inscriptions are replete with phrases reminiscent of biblical idiom (e.g., stock (usually, but erroneously, "root") below, boughs (usually, but erroneously, "fruit") above) and religious phraseology that clarify biblical references (e.g., "a place to lie on with the Rephaim"). Inscribed ostraca, seals, and coins are also found. In the east, Phoenician spread to Greece and Egypt; Cyprus, Malta, Sardinia, Sicily and the isles remain a source of written material. In the west, Carthage, rich in inscriptions, became an important center of Phoenician culture, and from there it radiated to Spain, the Balearic islands, and southern France. The sacrificial tariffs from Marseilles and Carthage list animal offerings with payments due to the priests and the sharing of sacrifices. Scholars have noted marked similarities to the Priestly Code. The bilingual Phoenician-Etruscan Pyrgi inscriptions from fifth-century southern Italy have great linguistic importance, while many Punic and neo-Punic inscriptions from North Africa provide an insight into the continuity of Canaanite culture and language outside the Phoenician mainland. Jars inscribed in Phoenician were found at Bat Yam and Shiqmona; a lead weight was found at Ashdot-Yam.

Aramaic became the official language of the Achaemenid Empire and inscriptions in this language are found for this and later periods in North Arabia, Egypt, Turkey, Georgia, Syria, Iraq, Iran, Afghanistan, and India. The many papyri and ostraca from Elephantine, Hermopolis, and elsewhere in Egypt, and the Arsham letters are of prime importance. The Sheikh Faḍl inscriptions (fifth century) mentioning Tirhaka, Neco, and Psammetich and the silver bowls from Wadi Tumilat, mentioning Gashmu the Kedarite (cf. Neh. 2:19; 6:1, 2, 6) are noteworthy. Aramaic versions (on papyrus) of the Behistun and Naksh-i Rustam inscriptions of Darius I, albeit fragmentary, are known. The Taymāʾ inscription attests to the penetration of Aramaic culture into North Arabia and the many Aramaic dockets on Neo-Babylonian cuneiform tablets (fifth century) attest to the spread of Aramaic there. These tablets often record business transactions of the Judean exiles.

The Aramaic-Lydian bilingual from Sardis and the boundary, funerary, and commemorative inscriptions found elsewhere in Turkey and later in Armenia are of philological and cultural interest. In these countries, Greek often superseded Aramaic during the Hellenistic period. In those areas in which Aramaic remained a language of spoken or written communication, national scripts developed such as the Jewish, Nabatean, Palmyrene, Elymaic, Hatrene, and Syriac. The earliest Nabatean script was found at Ḥaluṣa (c. 170 B.C.E.); other inscriptions were found at ʿAvdat and in the Sinai Peninsula. It is in this script that the inscriptions in Palestine of the late Second Temple period are written. Among the inscriptions from the late period of the Second Temple besides those found at Qumran on jars and ostraca, leather parchment, papyrus, and metal, which cannot be enumerated here, the following may be noted: (1) the Jason Tomb inscriptions in Aramaic from the period of Alexander Yannai; (2) the inscriptions on ossuaries usually listing simply the name of the person reinterred therein. Three are worthy of particular attention: (a) from the Bethpage cave whose lid contained a list of workers; (b) from Givʿat ha-Mivtar in north Jerusalem mentioning "Simon, builder of the sanctuary" (*smwn bnh hklh*); and (c) from Jebel Hallat eṭ-Ṭūri which declared that all the valuables in the ossuary were a *qorban* to God; (3) the Bene Ḥezir inscription on a tomb in the Kidron Valley; (4) the Aramaic inscription now in the Israel Museum in Jerusalem that announced the removal of Uzziah's bones to their new resting place; (5) the inscriptions found during the excavations at the Western and Southern retaining walls of the Temple mount, especially the one reading *lbyt htqyʿh*, "to the place of the (trumpet) blowing," which surely came from the Herodian Temple; (6) the small stone weight found in the "burnt house" in the "Jewish Quarter" of Jerusalem bearing the name of the highly placed priestly family Kathros (*qtrs*); (7) the relatively long Aramaic inscription in Paleo-Hebrew script found in a burial cave in Givʿat ha-Mivtar; (8) inscribed objects from Masada including 14 biblical, apocryphal, and sectarian scrolls. Jugs are inscribed with their owner's name; column drums are marked, and a great number of ostraca contain Hebrew names and a variety of letters. The name Ben Ya'ir (*bn y'yr*) surely refers to Eleazar ben Jair the Zealot leader.

[Jonas C. Greenfield]

IN THE TALMUD AND HALAKHAH

The tremendous importance attached by the talmudic sages to the art of writing is reflected, according to one interpretation, in Mishnah *Avot* 5:6, which includes among the "ten things which were created on the eve of the Sabbath" (of creation, i.e., which partake of the semi-miraculous) *ha-ketav ve-ha-makhtev* ("writing and the instrument of writing"). The usual explanation is that the phrase applies to the writing of the Decalogue, which is mentioned afterward, but another view is that it applies to the art of writing as a whole. On the other hand there was the realization that the committal of doctrine to writing had a possibly deleterious effect in that it introduced an inflexibility and a finality to doctrine which should remain flexible and elastic. According to I.H. Weiss (Dor, 1, 1–93), it was this which lay behind the prohibition on committing the Oral Law to writing. The Written Law was final and decisive; its interpretation had to remain open to adjustment.

Writing, its materials, its regulations, and its instruments play a prominent part in the *halakhah*. They are important in the laws of writing a **Sefer Torah*, which must be written on parchment with a quill and indelible ink (the same applies to **tefillin* and **mezuzot*, with slight variations). An exception is the portion of the **Sotah* (the woman suspected of adultery – Num. 5:11–31), since the Bible explicitly states that the writing had to be erased in the bitter waters. There are different regulations for the writing of a bill of divorce, and lastly there is the prohibition of writing on the Sabbath, and the regulations as to what constitutes writing. It is almost entirely in connection with those laws that the many details concerning writing and writing materials occur (cf. especially Shab. 12:3–5, Git; 2:3–4 and the corresponding Tosefta and the relevant discussion in the Talmuds). Whereas for the writing of the *Sefer Torah* and other sacred writings only parchment made from the hide of permitted animals could be used, after the required treatment, bills of divorce could be written on paper made from papyrus. The prohibition of writing on the Sabbath applied to all permanent writing materials. A differentiation is made between permanent writing materials and non-permanent ones. In the former the Mishnah enumerates olive leaves and a cow's horn, to which the Tosefta (Shab. 11 (12):8) adds carob leaves or cabbage leaves. It is difficult to see how they could be used widely. Non-permanent writing materials are given as leaves of leeks, onions, vegetables, and the sorb apple tree.

Owing to the scarcity and high cost of paper, particularly parchment, it was used more than once, by rubbing out the writing with stone and superimposing new writing. It is this palimpsest which is referred to in the dictum of Elisha b. Avuyah, who compares learning as a child to "ink written on clean paper" and learning in one's old age to "ink written on erased paper" (Avot 4:20; Git. 2:4, where erased paper is equated with *diftera* (Gr., διφθέρα), hide which has been treated with salt and flour, but not with gall nuts).

A similar distinction is made between permanent and non-permanent inks. To the former belong ink proper (*deyo*), caustic, red dye, and gum (Shab. 12:4; Sot. 2:4). The Tosefta (Shab. 11 (12):8) adds congealed blood and curdled milk, as well as nutshells and pomegranate peel, which were widely used for making dyestuffs. Ink was made from a mixture of oil and resin, which hardened and to which water was added. Any oil or resin could be used, but the best quality was that of olive oil and balsam (Shab. 23a; 104b). The most permanent ink, however, was made by adding iron sulphate or vitriol (*kankantum* or *kalkantum*, properly קלקנתים, Gr. χάλκανθον) to the ink, which made it a deep black, and it was therefore also used as boot-blacking (Git. 19a). This admixture made the ink completely indelible and was therefore prohibited for use in writing the passage of the *Sotah* (Er. 13a). Non-permanent inks were made from "taria water" (juice of wine), fruit juices, and juice of gall nuts (Git. 19a). There is an interesting reference to invisible writing: "These people of the East are very cunning. When one of them wishes to write a letter in secret writing to his friend he writes it with melon water and when the recipient receives it he pours ink over it and is able to decipher the writing" (TJ, Shab. 12:4, 13d; Git. 2:3, 44b).

It would appear originally the custom to use gold lettering for the writing of the *Sefer Torah*, since the Midrash (Song. R. 1:11; cf. *ibid.* 5:11) applies the verse "we will make the circlets of gold, with studs of silver" (Songs 1:11) to the writing and the ruled lines respectively. According to the Letter of Aristeas, the *Sefer Torah* presented by Eleazar the high priest to Ptolemy Philadelphus was written in letters of gold (cf. Jos., Ant., 12:89). However, such ostentation was later forbidden and tractate *Soferim* (1:9) states, "it is forbidden to write [a *Sefer Torah*] in gold. It happened that in a *Sefer Torah* of Alexandria all the divine names were written in gold, and when it was brought to the notice of the sages they ordered it to be hidden away." There is also mention of Queen *Helena of Adiabene having the passage of the *Sotah* written on a gold tablet (Yoma 37a; Git. 60a). Simeon b. Lakish, however, said that it referred only to the initials. The professional scribe, the *livlar* (librarius), used a *kalmus* (calamus), a quill made of reeds (Shab. 1:3; cf. Ta'an. 20b). For ordinary writing the *makhtev*, a two pointed pin, or stylus, was used, one end for writing and the other for erasing (Kel. 13:2; Tosef., Kel.; BM 3:4). The inkwell, called a *kalmarin* (καλαμάριον), was provided with an inner rim to prevent spilling (Mik. 10:1). This inkwell was used by ordinary people. The inkwell of the scribe, called the *bet deyo* (ink container), had a cover (Tosef., Kel. BM 4:11) and mention is made of the "inkwell of Joseph the Priest which had a hole in the side" (Mik. 10:1).

Pen, paper, and inkstand are referred to as "things of honor" in a peculiar context. Rabban Simeon b. Gamaliel states that any idol which bears something in its hand is forbidden. The Jerusalem Talmud makes an exception in the case of "something of honor" and specifies "paper, pen, and inkwell" (Av. Zar. 3:1, 42c bottom). The word *kalmarin* is also used for the pen-case (Yalk, Num. 766). Among the other instruments of the scribe were the *olar*, the pen-knife used for cutting the reed to make the quill (Kel. 12:8; Tosef. Kel.; BB 7:12); the *izmel*, a knife for cutting the paper (Targ. Jon. to Jer. 36:23; Heb. *ta'ar*, cf. Targ. Jon. to Ps. 45:2); and the *sargel*, a sharp instrument for drawing the lines on the parchment or paper. For sacred writings the *sargel* had to be made from a reed (TJ, Meg. 1:11, 71d; Sof. 1:1). "Writer's sand" was used to dry the ink (Shab. 12:5).

After the invention of printing, the question was raised whether the laws of writing – e.g., with regard to the *Sefer Torah*, the prohibition of writing on the Sabbath, and the writing of a bill of divorce – apply to the printed word (cf. Resp. Samuel di Medina (Maharashdam) YD 184; B. Slonik, Resp. *Masat Binyamin* 94).

[Louis Isaac Rabinowitz]

BIBLIOGRAPHY: GENERAL LITERATURE: P.J. Hyatt, in: BA, 6 (1943), 71–80; B. Maisler (Mazar), in: *Leshonenu*, 14 (1946), 166–81; D. Diringer, *The Alphabet* (1949^2); J. Gelb, *A Study of Writing* (1952); G.R. Driver, *Semitic Writing: From Pictograph to Alphabet* (1954^2); M.D. Cassuto, in: EM, 1 (1955), 79–89; W.W. Hallo, in: JBL (1958), 324–38; J. Licht and M.D. Cassuto, in: EM, 4 (1962), 372–77; A.L. Oppenheim, *Ancient Mesopotamia* (1964), 228–87; D.R. Hillers, in: BASOR, 173 (1964), 45–50; F.M. Cross, in: *Eretz Israel*, 8 (1967), 8–24 (Eng. sec.); idem, in: BASOR, 190 (1968), 41–46; S. Yeivin, in: B. Mazar (ed.), *Ha-Avot ve-ha-Shofetim* (1967), 17–24; J. Naveh, in: HTR, 61 (1968), 68–74. STONE: A.T. Olmstead, in: JAOS, 41 (1921), 372; D. Simons, *Handbook for the Study of Egyptian Topographical Lists Relating to Western Asia* (1937); W.F. Albright, in: BASOR, 87 (1942), 254; H.L. Ginsberg, in: *Louis Ginzberg Jubilee Volume* (1945), 171; B. Porter and B.L.B. Moss, *Topographical Bibliography of Ancient Egyptian Hieroglyphic Texts, Reliefs and Paintings*, 7 (1951), 369f.; N. Avigad, in: IEJ, 3 (1953), 137–52; idem, in: EM, 3 (1958), 68–86; idem and M.D. Cassuto, *ibid.*, 4 (1962), 380–90; H. Tadmor, in: *Eretz Israel*, 8 (1967), 241–5; L. Della Vida, in: *In Memoriam Paul Kahle* (1968), 162–6. PAPYRUS: B. Landsberger, in: OLZ, 17 (1914), 265; A. Cowley, *Aramaic Papyri of the Fifth Century B.C.* (1923); W.F. Albright, in: JBL, 56 (1937), 145–76; E.G. Kraeling, in: JNES, 7 (1948), 199–201; H.L. Ginsberg, in: BASOR, 111 (1948), 25–26; G.J. Thierry, in: VT, 1 (1951), 130–1; F.G. Kenyon, *Books and Readers in Ancient Greece and Rome* (1951^2); E.G. Kraeling, *The Brooklyn Museum Aramaic Papyri* (1953); J.T. Milik, *Les grottes de Murabbâat* (1961); F.M. Cross, Jr., in: BASOR, 165 (1962), 34–42; idem, in: BA, 26 (1963), 110–21; N. Avigad, in: IEJ, 14 (1964), 193–4; J. Naveh, in: *Leshonenu*, 30 (1966), 68. LEATHER: O. Schroeder, in: OLZ, 20 (1917), 204; R.P. Dougherty, in: JAOS, 48 (1928), 109–35; E. Chiera, *They Wrote on Clay* (1938); H. Tur-Sinai (Torczyner), *Lachish Letters* (1938); B. Maisler (Mazar), in: JPOS, 21 (1948), 117–33; idem, in: *Eretz Israel*, 1 (1951), 66–67; D. Diringer, *Early Hebrew Inscriptions* (1953), 331–9; Y. Yadin, in: IEJ, 9 (1959), 184–7; idem, in: *Scripta Hierosolymitana*, 8 (1961), 9–25; S. Iwry, in: JAOS, 81 (1961), 27–34; R. de Vaux et al., *Discoveries in the Judean Desert of Jordan*, 3 (1962), 201ff.; E. Stern, in: EM, 4 (1962), 846–78; H. Donner and W. Roellig, *Kanaanaeische und aramaeische Inschriften* (1962–64), nos. 183–8, 190, 192–9; J. Naveh, in: *Leshonenu*, 30 (1966), 69ff.; Y. Aharoni, in: BASOR, 184 (1966), 13–19; idem, in: BA, 31 (1968), 2–32; Pritchard, Texts, 501, 502. IVORY, WOOD, WAX, GRAFFITI, TATTOO MARKS: M. San Nicolò, in: *Orientalia*, 17 (1948), 59–70; I. Mendelsohn, *Slavery in the Ancient Near East* (1949), 42ff.; M.E.L. Mallowan, in: *Iraq*, 16 (1954), 59–114; M. Howard, *ibid.*, 17 (1955), 14–20; D.J. Wiseman, *ibid.*, 3–13; A.R. Millard, *ibid.*, 24 (1962), 45–51; J. Naveh, in: IEJ, 13 (1963), 74–92; W.G. Dovers, in: HUCA, 40–41 (1969–70), 139–204. INSCRIPTIONS: G.A. Cooke, *A Text-Book of North Semitic Inscriptions* (1903); Diringer, Iscr; A. Reifenberg, *Ancient Hebrew Seals* (1950); S. Moscati, *L'epigrafia ebraica antica* (1951); H. Donner and W. Roellig, *Kanaanaeische und aramaeische Inschriften* (1962–64); Y. Yadin, *Masadah* (1966), 168–91; N. Avigad, in: IEJ, 17 (1967), 100–11; idem, in: *Near Eastern Archaeology in the Twentieth Century* (1970), 284, 287–95; R.D. Barnett, in: *Eretz Israel*, 8 (1967), 1–6; F.M. Cross, in: *ibid.*, 8–24; 9 (1969), 20–27; idem, in: D.N. Freedman and J.C. Greenfield (eds.), *New Directions in Biblical Archaeology* (1969), 41–62; Y. Aharoni, *ibid.*, 25–39; J. Peckham, *The Development of the Late Phoenician Scripts* (1968); J. Naveh, *The Development of the Aramaic Script* (1970); idem, in: IEJ, 20 (1970), 33–37; idem, in: *Near Eastern Archaeology in the Twentieth Century* (1970), 277–83. IN THE TALMUD AND HALAKHAH: L. Loew, *Graphische Requisiten und Erzeugnisse bei den Juden* (1871); L. Blau, *Studien zum althebraeischen Buchwesen* (1902); Krauss, Tal Arch, 3 (1912), 144–58. **ADD. BIBLIOGRAPHY:** J.C. Gibson, *Textbook of Syrian Semitic Inscriptions* (3 vols.; 1971, 1975, 1982); J. Naveh, *Early History of the Alphabet* (1982); B. Sass, *The Genesis of the Alphabet and its Development in the Second Millennium B.C.* (1988); J. Jamieson-Drake, *Scribes and Schools in Monarchic Judah* (1991); J. Fitzmyer and S. Kaufman, *An Aramaic Bibliography, Part 1: Old, Official, and Biblical Aramaic* (1992); A. Lemaire, ABD, 6:999–1008; J. Tropper, *Die Inschriften von Zincirli* (1993); J. Hoftijzer and K. Jongeling, *Dictionary of the North-West Semitic Inscriptions* (HDO; 2 vols., 1995); M. Haran, *The Biblical Collection…* (1996); M. O'Connor, in: P. Daniels and W. Bright (eds.), *The World's Writing Systems* (1996), 88–107; N. Avigad and B. Sass, *Corpus of West Semitic Stamp Seals* (1997); N. Na'aman, in L. Handy (ed.), *The Age of Solomon* (1997), 57–80; F. Cross, *Leaves* *from an Epigrapher's Notebook* (1993); D. Schwiderski, *The Old and Imperial Aramaic Inscriptions*, vol. 2 (2004); S. Ahituv, *Handbook of Ancient Hebrew Inscriptions* (2005²).

WRONKI (Ger. **Wronke**; in Jewish sources: **Vronik**), town in Poznan province, western Poland. The Jewish community of Wronki was first organized in the early 17th century. In 1607 permission was granted to build a synagogue, and in 1633 a royal privilege confirmed the rights of the Jews in the town. They engaged in wholesale trade and crafts; toward the end of the 17th century they participated in the *Leipzig fair. At that time representatives from Wronki served in important posts on the *Council of the Lands. In 1765 the poll-taxpaying Jews of Wronki and surrounding villages numbered 483. Their occupations included tailoring, goldsmithery, and weaving. The debts of the community then reached the enormous sum of 200,000 zlotys. From 1793 up to 1918 the town was under Prussian rule. In 1808 there were 543 Jews in Wronki (32% of the total population); 791 (35%) in 1840; 604 (24%) in 1871; 528 (12%) in 1895; 380 (8%) in 1905; 314 (6.5%) in 1910 and 187 (4%) in 1921. In the 1860s the local Jews started to move westward to Berlin and other large German cities. When the city was annexed to Poland in 1918 the Jewish population continued to dwindle.

[Shimshon Leib Kirshenboim]

Holocaust Period

On the outbreak of World War II Wronki had 31 Jews. On Nov. 7, 1939, all the Jews were deported to the Generalgouvernement via Buk, in Nowy Tomysl county. In the small town of Buk about 1,300 Jews from many other places in the districts of Poznan (Posen) and Inowroclaw (Hohensalza) were concentrated, and sent a month later to the Mlyniewo camp near Grodzisk Poznanski (Suedhof). From there they were sent on to Sochaczew-Blonie county in the Warsaw District, where they were allowed to disperse among the small towns of the region.

[Danuta Dombrowska]

BIBLIOGRAPHY: Halpern, Pinkas, index; A. Heppner and J. Herzberg, *Aus Vergangenheit und Gegenwart der Juden… in den Posener Landen* (1909), index; I. Schiper, *Dzieje handlu żydowskiego na ziemiach polskich* (1937), index; B. Wasiutyński, *Ludność żydowska w Polsce w wiekach XIX i XX* (1930), 167.

WRONSKY, SIDDY (1883–1947), expert in social welfare and social pedagogy. Born in Berlin, she was an influential figure in bringing about the professionalization of social work in Germany and Palestine. She began her training as a teacher and specialized in *Heilpaedagogik*, working as a volunteer in a school for developmentally disabled children. In 1908 she became the director of the Archiv fuer Wohlfahrtspflege, and she also served as co-editor of the prestigious journal *Deutsche Zeitschrift fuer Wohlfahrtspflege*. She taught at the social work training school that was founded by Alice Salomon, the Soziale Frauenschule, in Berlin, as well as at the Deutsche Akademie fuer soziale und pädagogische Frauenarbeit. Through her writing and teaching, she introduced new and modern methodologies for the treatment of welfare recipients through an emphasis on individualized care.

In addition to her role in German social welfare, she was also a centrally important figure in Jewish social welfare after World War I. She became a member of the board of the newly founded Zentralwohlfahrtsstelle der deutschen Juden (Central Welfare Bureau of German Jews) and served on a variety of its commissions dedicated to reforming Jewish social welfare. Wronsky became a Zionist through her work with East European refugees in Berlin during World War I and helped found a Zionist women's organization. In 1933, she was dismissed from her positions and fled to Palestine shortly thereafter. In Palestine, she worked in the social department of the Va'ad Le'ummi and founded the first social work education school, the Sozialschule Jerusalem of the Va'ad Le'ummi. She died in 1947, shortly before the founding of the State of Israel.

Her major works include *Leitfaden der Wohlfahrtspflege* (with Alice Salomon, 1921); *Methoden der Fuersorge* (1930); and *Sozialtherapie und Psychotherapie in den Methoden der Fürsorge* (1932).

BIBLIOGRAPHY: F.M. Konrad, "Paradigmen sozialpaedagogischer Reform in Deutschland und Palaestina. Zur Erinnerung an Siddy Wronsky (1883–1947)," in: *Soziale Arbeit*, 36 (1987), 459–67.

°**WUENSCHE, AUGUST KARL** (1839–1913), German scholar of the Bible and *aggadah*. Wuensche, who was born in Haimwalde, Germany, was a pupil of Franz *Delitzsch and Julius *Fuerst. He wrote commentaries on Joshua (1868) and Joel (1872), and also general studies such as *Die Schoenheit des Alten Testaments* (1906), and *Die Bildersprache des Alten Testaments* (1897). His main researches, however, were in rabbinic literature. His translations into German of the *aggadot* of the Jerusalem and Babylonian Talmuds, *Der Jerusalemitische Talmud … Haggadischen Bestandteilen* (1880), and *Der Babylonische Talmud…* (1886–89) gave Wuensche a great reputation among scholars. He also translated the *Midrash Rabbah*, the *Pesikta de-R. Kahana*, and the Midrash of the five scrolls, as well as a five-volume collection of Midrashim from the *Beit ha-Midrash* of A. *Jellinek entitled *Aus Israels Lehrhaus* (1907–10). Of great importance is Wuensche's three-volume anthology of Jewish literature after the conclusion of the Bible, *Die juedische Literatur seit Abschluss des Kanon*, (1894–96), which he edited with Jacob *Winter. His other works include: *Neue Beitraege zur Erlaeuterung der Evangelien aus Talmud und Midrasch* (1878); *Die Raetselweisheit bei den Hebraeern* (1883); and *Die Freude im Alten Testament* (1896).

[Jerucham Tolkes]

WUERTTEMBERG, state in Germany. There is evidence that the Jewish community of *Heilbronn in Wuerttemberg was one of the earliest in Germany. An inscription bearing the name of "Nathan the Parnes" on the entrance of the *mikveh* apparently dates from the latter half of the 11th century. Information on Jewish settlement in Wuerttemberg becomes more definite in the early 13th century. Jews are known to have settled in 65 localities there before the *Black Death persecutions. These settlements suffered during the *Rindfleisch massacres of 1298 and again in the *Armleder uprising of 1335–37 but soon recovered. At that time the more important Jewish communities were centered in Heilbronn, *Ulm, *Esslingen, and Schwaebisch Gmuend. At first the Jews paid their taxes directly to the king, the count of Wuerttemberg, or to a nobleman to whom the king had granted taxing privileges; from the middle of the 14th century, however, most cities acquired taxation rights over the Jews living within them. Jews in positions of financial responsibility were helpful to many cities during a period of territorial expansion in the 14th century. During the 15th century, however, many Jews in Wuerttemberg became impoverished due to heavy taxation and the official cancellation of debts that were owed to them. Throughout the 15th century the Jews were alternately enabled to settle or expelled by the nobles, and by the end of the century they had been banished from most of the towns. In 1521 a decree was issued expelling the Jews from the entire duchy. Nevertheless, some of them managed to remain in many of the small villages during the 16th and 17th centuries. Jewish settlement in Wuerttemberg was substantially renewed only in the 18th century when Jews were first allowed to visit fairs and trade in cattle; later they were allowed to settle permanently in the duke's private lands and several other limited areas. With the aid of Joseph Suess *Oppenheimer, several Jews were granted residence in *Stuttgart and Ludwigsburg.

The dukes subsequently enacted more liberal regulations concerning Jewish settlement, such as the Hochberg Regulation of 1780. During the 18th century they retained a number of *Court Jews who aided significantly in the economic development of the duchy. When Napoleon added large areas to Wuerttemberg in 1806, the Jewish population rose from 534 to 4,884; by 1817 there were 3,256 Jews living in 79 localities. Jews were permitted to live in cities such as Ulm, from which they had previously been excluded. The body tax (*Leibzoll) was abrogated and Jews were accepted in the army. The improved attitude toward the Jews did not deteriorate after Napoleon's downfall. In 1828 a law was issued obliging Jewish children to receive a secular education; this, however, applied only to shopkeepers and craftsmen and discriminated against peddlers, cattle traders, brokers, and moneylenders. The law recognized the organization of local communities, and in 1831 a central Jewish executive was created in Stuttgart that functioned under governmental supervision. The constitutions of the local communities were drawn up along similar lines to those applied to the Christian communities. The chief rabbi was a government official; but when the chief rabbi Joseph Meir, who was of Reformist bent, tried to introduce the 60 *Hymns of Israel*, mostly of his own composition, into the traditional liturgy, most congregations refused to adopt the proposal, although it came from an official source. However, the Jews did not gain full civil equality in Wuerttemberg until April 25, 1828, and their religious life still remained subject to governmental supervision. Full autonomy was granted in 1912 and was supplemented by additional legislation approved in 1924. The Jewish population increased from 8,918 in 1828 to 11,916 in 1925, organized in 51 communities. By 1933 the number had decreased to 10,023, in 43 communities.

Holocaust Period

Antisemitism was already a significant political factor in Wuerttemberg at the end of the 19th century. With the growth of Nazism from 1925 to 1933, the party became increasingly active in its propaganda campaign against the Jews. After the rise of the Nazis to power, the boycott of Jewish goods, as well as general harassment, led many Jews to emigrate from Wuerttemberg, and 9,000 left there in 1935. While the Zionist movement had not been generally strong in Wuerttemberg, 200 Jews from the village of Rexingen immigrated to Palestine in 1938 to found the settlement of *Shavei Zion.

In October 1938 Jews of Polish extraction were deported back to Poland. On Nov. 9–16, 1938, 18 synagogues in Wuerttemberg were burned to the ground, and 12 others were severely damaged; 875 Jews were imprisoned. Jewish enterprises were "aryanized" and a systematic plan was put into action to rid Wuerttemberg of its Jewish communities. From 1941 to 1945, there were 12 deportations totaling 2,500 Jews from Stuttgart; 260 committed suicide before deportation. Only 180 survived the war; 200 Jews who had intermarried were spared deportation.

[Zvi Avneri]

Contemporary Period

After the Holocaust a few Jews returned to Wuerttemberg. The community of Stuttgart was reconstituted and a new synagogue built; for the most part, what was left of the Jewish community in Wuerttemberg were unused synagogues and abandoned cemeteries.

The Jewish community of Wuerttemberg numbered 677 in 1989 and 2,881 in 2004. The increase is explained by the immigration of Jews from the former Soviet Union. In 1989 the majority lived in Stuttgart; in 2004 about 45 percent lived outside Stuttgart. There are branch communities in *Ulm (founded 2002), Reutlingen, and Hechingen. New branches were to be established in Heilbronn, Heidenheim, and Schwaebisch-Hall.

[Zvi Avneri / Larissa Daemmig (2nd ed.)]

BIBLIOGRAPHY: P. Sauer, *Die juedischen Gemeinden in Wuerttemberg und Hohenzollern* (1966); *Germania Judaica*, 2 (1968), 928; 3 (1987), 2075–78; L. Adler, in: ylbi (1960), 287–98; *Juedische Gotteshaeuser und Friedhoefe in Wuerttemberg* (1928); A. Taenzer, *Die Geschichte der Juden in Wuerttemberg* (1937). **ADD. BIBLIOGRAPHY:** A. Taenzer, *Die Geschichte der Juden in Wuerttemberg* (1937, reprinted 1983); H. Dicker, *Creativity, Holocaust, Reconstruction: Jewish Life in Wuerttemberg, Past and Present* (1984); U. Jeggle, *Judendoerfer in Wuerttemberg* (Untersuchungen des Ludwig-Uhland-Instituts der Universitaet Tuebingen, vol. 90) (1999^2); R. Gregorius, *Das juedische Schul- und Erziehungswesen in Wuerttemberg* (1806–1933) (2000); *Juedische Gotteshaeuser und Friedhoefe in Wuerttemberg* (1932, reprinted 2002); E. Kraiss and M. Reuter, *Bet Hachajim – Haus des Lebens. Juedische Friedhoefe in Wuerttembergisch-Franken* (2003). **WEBSITE:** www.alemannia.de.

WUERZBURG, city in Bavaria, Germany. The Jewish community of Wuerzburg was founded around 1100. The Jews settled near a swampy area that was, however, in the center of the town. Some lived outside this quarter, and there were Christians living among the Jews. In 1147, at the time of the Second Crusade (see *Crusades), the Crusaders, reinforced by rabble from the surrounding countryside, attacked the community. Three rabbis, a scribe, and three other Jews were publicly martyred. The bishop of the town ordered that the bodies of the martyrs be gathered and buried in his garden; he later sold the site to the community, which converted it into a cemetery. During the 13th century the number of Jews grew considerably, not only as a result of natural increase but also through the addition of newcomers ariving from *Augsburg, *Mainz, *Nuremberg, and *Rothenburg. A *Judengasse* is noted in 1182, a school in 1170, and a synagogue in 1238. In the 12th and 13th centuries Wuerzburg became an influential and important center of Jewish learning. Foremost among the scholars associated with the city during the period were Joel ha-Levi, son-in-law of *Eliezer b. Nathan (Raban) of Mainz; his son, *Eliezer b. Joel ha-Levi (Rabiah); *Isaac b. Moses ("Or Zaru'a") of Vienna, who taught in the yeshivah at Wuerzburg; and his celebrated students *Meir b. Baruch and Mordecai b. Hillel. Of note also were *Eliezer b. Moses ha-Darshan, Samuel b. Menahem, and Jonathan b. Isaac. This large community was destroyed in the *Rindfleisch persecutions of 1298. About 900 Jews lost their lives, including 100 who had fled from the surrounding area to seek refuge in Wuerzburg.

The community was subsequently renewed, this time principally by Jews from *Cologne, *Strasbourg, *Bingen, and *Ulm, as well as from Franconia, Thuringia, and Swabia. The Jews paid taxes to both the bishop and the king. In practice, the Jews were under the protection of the bishop, who governed them through a series of regulations issued on his own initiative. His protection aroused the objection of the townspeople, but after the Jews had aided in the financial expenditure of fortifying the city, the burghers were more sympathetic. However, during the *Black Death persecutions of 1349, the Jews were accused of poisoning the wells in Wuerzburg; in desperation they set fire to their own houses on April 21, 1349, and perished. Among the martyrs was Moses ha-Darshan, head of the yeshivah. The survivors fled, some to *Erfurt, *Frankfurt, and Mainz, and the bishop took possession of their property.

By 1377 Jews were to be found once more in the city; at the beginning of the 15th century a community had been reconstituted and the cemetery returned to Jewish possession. A new synagogue was built in 1446, but the community remained small in the 15th century. In 1567 the Jews were expelled from the town and settled in nearby Heidingsfeld. Bishop Julius expropriated the cemetery in 1576, and he founded a hospital on its site, which still exists. While a few Jews lived in the city during the following centuries, the community was not renewed until the 19th century. In 1813 there were 14 families in the city, and the rabbi of Heidingsfeld then settled in Wuerzburg. The synagogue was inaugurated in 1841. Isaac Dov (Seligman Baer) *Bamberger acted as rabbi from 1839 to 1878. In 1864 he founded a teachers' seminary from which hundreds of teachers graduated and taught in the Jewish schools of Germany. The yeshivah founded during his lifetime was also renowned. Wuerzburg became the spiritual center for the numerous village communities of Franconia. They prayed according to the *minhag* of Wuerzburg and addressed their halakhic questions to the rabbis there. In 1884 a Jewish hospital was founded in Wuerzburg. The Jewish population numbered 2,600 (2.84 percent of the total) in 1925, and 2,145 (2.12 percent) in 1933.

With the rise of Nazism, many Jews emigrated from Wuerzburg. On Nov. 9–10, 1938 (*Kristallnacht*), the synagogue was destroyed. From 1941 to 1945 the 1,500 remaining Jews were deported to concentration camps. After the war, 52 Jews returned to their city. In 1967 there were 150 Jews living in Wuerzburg; they had a community organization and possessed a synagogue and an old-age home.

The synagogue was consecrated in 1970. The Jewish community numbered 179 in 1989 and 1,045 in 2004. The increase is explained by the immigration of Jews from the former Soviet Union. In 2001, construction began on Shalom Europa, a new cultural and community center located next to the synagogue. Slated for completion in 2006, the center was to house offices, classrooms, a club for senior citizens, the Ephraim Gustav Hoenlein Genealogy Project of the Ronald S. Lauder Foundation (founded in 2002), and a documentation center of Jewish history and culture in Lower Franconia. The former old-age home, which is part of the complex, was rebuilt by the Ronald S. Lauder Foundation and houses the Lauder Chorev Center for educational seminars and youth get-togethers.

In 1987, when a house in Wuerzburg-Pleich was demolished, 1,508 Jewish gravestones and gravestone fragments were discovered, dating from 1138 to 1347. This was the largest such find in the world. The stones will be exhibited in the community center.

BIBLIOGRAPHY: *Historische Zeitschrift*, 17 (1867), 177–81; J. Weissbart, *Geschichtliche Mitteilungen uebers Ende der alten, Wiedererstehung und Entwicklung der neuen israelitischen Gemeinde Wuerzburg* (1882); L. Loewenstein (ed.), in: *Blaetter fuer juedische Geschichte und Literatur*, 2 (1901), 59–60; 3 (1902), 105–8; 4 (1903), 38–39, 150–3; H. Bamberger, *Geschichte der Rabbiner der Stadt und des Bezirks Wuerzburg* (1905); M.L. Bamberger, *Ein Blick auf die Geschichte der Juden in Wuerzburg* (1905); idem, *Beitraege zur Geschichte der Juden in Wuerzburg-Heidensfeld* (1905); D. Weger, *Die Juden im Hochstift Wuerzburg waehrend des 17. und 18. Jahrhunderts* (diss., 1920); M. Bohrer, *Die Juden im Hochstift Wuerzburg im 16. und am Beginn des 17. Jahrhunderts* (diss., 1922); M.A. Szulwas, *Die Juden in Wuerzburg waehrend des Mittelalters* (1934); idem, in: *Shmuel Niger-Bukh* (1959), 176–92; idem, in: *Between the Rhine and the Bosporus* (1964), 15–31; J. May, in: ZGJD, 8 (1938), 99; H. Hoffmann, in: *Mainfraenkisches Jahrbuch*, 5 (1953), 91–114; *Germania Judaica*, 1 (1963), 475–96; 2 (1968), 928–36; 3 (1987), 1698–1711; Baron, Social[2], 9 (1965), 181–4. **ADD. BIBLIOGRAPHY:** H. Schultheis, *Juden in der Dioezese Wuerzburg 1933–1945* (1983); U. Gehring-Muenzel, *Vom Schutzjuden zum Staatsbuerger. Die gesellschaftliche Integration der Wuerzburger Juden. 1803–1871* (Veroeffentlichungen des Stadtarchivs Wuerzburg)

(1992); R. Flade, *Die Wuerzburger Juden. Ihre Geschichte vom Mittelalter bis zur Gegenwart* (1996[2]); I. Koenig, *Judenverordnungen im Hochstift Wuerzburg (15.–18. Jahrhundert)* (1999); C. Daxelmueller and R. Flade, *Ruth hat auf einer schwarzen Floete gespielt. Geschichte, Alltag und Kultur der Juden in Wuerzburg* (2005). **WEBSITE:** www.shalomeuropa.de.

[Zvi Avneri / Larissa Daemmig (2nd ed.)]

WUHSHA AL-DALLALA, 11th century *Cairo businesswoman or banker. Born in *Alexandria as Karima, the daughter of a banker named Ammar, she became known as Wuhsha (the desirable one or the one pined for) al-dallala (the broker). After moving to Fustat, she married Aryeh of Sicily and gave birth to a daughter whose name does not appear in her will, but rather in later documents; the couple subsequently divorced. Her name is mentioned in many *Genizah documents, either because of her extensive business transactions, including loans, or because her descendants were identified by their connection to her.

*Goitein first discovered Wuhsha's existence from a document dated 1098 in which she expressed annoyance at receiving a court summons based on a business associate's minor claim. Unlike most of the more secluded women in the Jewish community, no introduction was deemed necessary when she appeared in court. One of the most impressive documents extant is her will, written in Arabic at the turn of the century. In it, she provided for ornate funeral arrangements and left considerable sums of money to her surviving brother and to one of her two sisters; the largest bequest was to her son, as well as funds to provide him with a private tutor. Generous donations were left for all four Cairo synagogues, for the needy, and for the cemetery.

Wuhsha never re-married but rather took a lover from Ashkelon with whom she shared an apartment. When she became pregnant, Wuhsha feared social ostracism of her son (which would prevent a desirable marriage) and arranged a surprise visit to her chambers by male witnesses so as to record a deposition confirming that Hassun was the father of her child. Apparently Wuhsha chose not to marry her companion in order to deny him access to her wealth. In her will Wuhsha canceled a considerable debt Hassun owed her but made clear that he was not to receive a penny from her estate.

Wuhsha's deviation from social norms did not pass unnoticed; on one Yom Kippur the president of the Iraqi synagogue expelled her from the congregation. Her later bequest to this very synagogue could be interpreted as acceptance of her fate or, alternatively, as a way for her to have the last word, knowing that her money would not be refused. Wuhsha was an independent and determined woman whose life decisions were not always popular. She clearly left a distinct impression on her peers and on their descendants.

BIBLIOGRAPHY: S.D. Goitein, "A Jewish Business Woman of the Eleventh Century," in: *Jewish Quarterly Review* (*Seventy-Fifth Anniversary Volume*), (1967), 225–42; idem, *A Mediterranean Society*, 3 (1978; rep. 1988), 346–52.

[Renée Levine Melammed (2nd ed.)]

WUNDERBAR, REUBEN JOSEPH (1812–1868), Latvian-born educator and historian. Wunderbar wrote a book about the Jewish colonists in the Kherson region (1840) and was invited by Max *Lilienthal to become a teacher at the Jewish school in Riga of which he was for a time the director. In 1848 he returned to his native Mitau (Jelgava) and became a teacher of religion and a government interpreter, and on several occasions he served as the community's government-appointed rabbi. He published many articles in German-Jewish periodicals and wrote a study on the Jewish calendar. Wunderbar's importance as a historian rests primarily on two of his books which have retained their value as a source of information and research. The first, *Geschichte der Juden in den Provinzen Liv und Kurland* (1853), is a pioneer work on the history of the Jews in *Courland, based on independent research in archives and the use of rare manuscripts and paintings. The second book, *Biblischtalmudische Medicin* (1850–60), is also a pioneer work in the field, despite several inaccuracies and some errors. Although Wunderbar had no formal training, he had a surprising understanding of medical matters.

BIBLIOGRAPHY: Y. Leibowitz, in: *Tav Shin Vav... Shenaton Davar* (1947), 343f.; M. Bobe, *Perakim be-Toledot Yahadut Latvia* (1965), 196–202.

[Joshua O. Leibowitz]

WUNDERLICH, FRIEDA (1884–1965), economist. Born in Berlin, she became a leading expert in the fields of national economy, labor legislation, sociology, and social politics. She taught at the Vocational Institute (Berufspaedagogisches Institut) in Berlin and from 1924 to 1933 was an editor of the periodical *Soziale Praxis*. She took an active part in political life and was town councilor for Berlin (1926–33), and a member of the Prussian Parliament (1930–33). When Hitler rose to power she left Germany for the U.S., where she became professor of sociology and social politics at the Graduate Faculty of Political and Social Science at the New School for Social Research.

In Germany she published many books and articles, such as *Hugo Muensterbergs Bedeutung fuer die Nationaloekonomie* (1920); *Die Bekaempfung der Arbeitslosigkeit in Deutschland seit Beendigung des Krieges* (1925); *Der Kampf um die Sozialversicherung* (1930); and *Versicherung, Fuersorge und Krisenrisiko* (1932). In the U.S. she wrote *Labor under German Democracy* (1940) and *British Labor and the War* (1941).

BIBLIOGRAPHY: J. Meyer, in: *Social Research*, 33 (1966), 1–3; S. Kaznelson (ed.), *Juden im deutschen Kulturbereich* (1959), 681, 696, 856.

[Shalom Adler-Rudel]

WUPPERTAL, city in North Rhine-Westphalia, Germany; formed by the amalgamation of Elberfeld, Barmen, and other towns in 1929. Elberfeld had a Jewish population by the latter part of the 16th century – in 1593 every Jew had to contribute ten thalers for the defense of the town. An expulsion order of 1598 was carried out only half-heartedly. Sixty Jewish families were admitted in 1671. A new *Judenordnung* ("Jews' Statute") was introduced into the duchy of Juelich in 1749, imposing a heavy tax burden. The yarnmakers of Elberfeld had always strenuously opposed Jewish settlement, and in 1794 all Jews were expelled from the town, returning when it was under French rule (1806–15). Their position then greatly improved. In 1808 there were nine Jewish families in the town, and 21 in 1818. A synagogue was built in 1865. In 1875 the number of Jews in Elberfeld was 813, growing to 1,104 in 1880; 1,705 in 1905; and 3,000 in 1932. The poet Else *Lasker-Schueler was born there.

After the 1794 expulsion, Jews were admitted into Barmen under French rule; however, by 1877 there were no more than ten families in the town. The community numbered 584 in 1905, and 750 (0.33 percent of the total population) in 1926 (unchanged in 1933).

The number of Jews in Wuppertal was approximately 3,500 (0.8 percent) in 1933, but had decreased to just over 1,000 in 1939, plus about 650 so-called *Mischlinge* (mixed Jews). In November 1938 the synagogues were destroyed and many Jewish inhabitants deported to *Dachau. Most of those who remained at the outbreak of war in 1939 perished in the Holocaust. A "branch" of the *Buchenwald concentration camp operated outside Wuppertal in 1942–43. A small Jewish congregation was re-established after 1945, numbering approximately 150 persons in 1967.

The Jewish community numbered 82 in 1989 and 2,293 in 2004. The increase is explained by the immigration of Jews from the former Soviet Union. A new synagogue was consecrated in 2002. In 1994 a new cultural and educational center was opened in memory of the members of the Jewish community who were expelled and killed during the Nazi era. Built on the site of the destroyed synagogue in Elberfeld, it serves as a venue for exhibitions, lectures, and seminars. Wuppertal is the seat of the Else Lasker-Schueler Society, founded in 1990.

BIBLIOGRAPHY: E. Jorde, *Zur Geschichte der Juden in Wuppertal* (1933); *Monumenta Judaica, Handbuch* (1963), index; K. Duewell, *Die Rheingebiete in der Judenpolitik des Nationalsozialismus vor 1942* (1968), index. **ADD. BIBLIOGRAPHY:** K. Schnoering, *Auschwitz begann in Wuppertal. Juedisches Schicksal unter dem Hakenkreuz* (1981); P. Busmann, *Auf den Schatten gebaut. Von der inneren zur aeusseren Entstehung der Begegnungsstaette Alte Synagoge Wuppertal* (1996); U. Schrader and H. Jakobs, *Ma Towu… Alte Gebetbuecher der Juedischen Kultusgemeinde Wuppertal* (2000); L. Goldberg, *Dies soll ein Haus des Gebets sein fuer alle Voelker* (2002); T. Ahland and U. Schrader (eds.), *Haus des Lebens. Der juedische Friedhof in Wuppertal-Barmen* (2004).

[Larissa Daemmig (2nd ed.)]

WURZBURGER, WALTER S. (1920–2002), rabbi, academician, communal leader. Wurzburger was among the most important Modern Orthodox rabbinic leaders and intellectuals in the latter half of the 20th century. Born in Munich, he escaped the Holocaust by immigrating to the United States in 1938, ultimately receiving ordination at the Rabbi Isaac Elchanan Theological Seminary of *Yeshiva University and an M.A. and Ph.D. in philosophy from Harvard University. After serving as rabbi of Chai Odom in Dorchester, Massachusetts (1944–53) while at Harvard, Wurzburger was called to the pulpit of Congregation Shaarei Shomayim in Toronto, Canada's largest Orthodox congregation, and was regarded as a shining light in Canadian Jewry. In 1967, he assumed the pulpit of Congregation Shaarey Tefila in Far Rockaway, New York, which, under the leadership of Rabbi Emanuel *Rackman, had become one of America's preeminent Orthodox synagogues. He taught philosophy at Yeshiva College from 1961 and served both as president of the (Orthodox) Rabbinical Council of America and of the Synagogue Council of America. Wurzburger was one of Rabbi Joseph B. *Soloveitchik's most ardent disciples and he carried his teacher's philosophy and theology into the public arena through his articles and lectures, and as editor-in-chief of *Tradition*, the widely respected journal of the Rabbinical Council of America. He received the National Rabbinic Leadership Award of the Orthodox Union. Wurzburger's most important work was *The Ethics of Responsibility* (JPS, 1994) in which he described the Jewish ethical value system which flowed from the *halakhah*, Judaism's legal parameters. He also wrote *A Treasury of Tradition* (1967, 1994). He was a contributing editor of *Sh'ma* and a representative of a time when Modern Orthodoxy was liberal in its orientation, embracing all denominations of Jews and cooperating with the non-Orthodox rabbinic world.

[Stanley M. Wagner (2nd ed.)]

WURZWEILER, GUSTAV (1896–1954), U.S. banker and philanthropist. Wurzweiler was born in Mannheim, Germany. After serving in the German forces during World War I, he established his own banking firm and accumulated a fortune. When he left Nazi Germany for Belgium in 1936, Wurzweiler managed to take out much of his wealth. He lived in Brussels from 1936 to 1941, and then emigrated to the United States where he again established himself successfully as a financier. In 1950 he became a member of the New York Stock Exchange. An Orthodox Jew, Wurzweiler established the Gustav Wurzweiler Foundation in 1950 to aid Jewish cultural, social, and educational agencies, with emphasis on higher education, research in Jewish history, aid to the handicapped, and support for congregations.

By 1970 about 100 institutions had received grants, with the Leo Baeck *Institute a major beneficiary. Among the foundation's grants was $1,000,000 in 1962 to the Graduate (renamed Wurzweiler) School of Social Work of Yeshiva University, augmented in 1968 by a $500,000 grant to establish a doctoral program.

WYDEN, RONALD STEPHEN (1949–), U.S. senator. Ron Wyden is the son of a German Jewish refugee, Peter Wyden, who was the author of *Stella*, a book about the most beautiful girl in his class in Germany who used her beauty as a weapon in survival. One of his grandfathers edited the works of Schopenhauer. His father worked for the *St. Louis Dispatch* and *Newsweek*, so Ron Wyden grew up in St. Louis and Washington, D.C. Among his classmates was Hubert Humphrey III, son of the senator and vice president. He then moved to Palo Alto where he played basketball in high school and at the University of California Santa Barbara before an injury ended his playing days. Only then did he begin to take his studies seriously, and he graduated from Stanford before moving to the University of Oregon to study law.

In Portland, he worked as a campaign aide to Senator Wayne Morse and then as director of the Gray Panthers organizing the elderly. His first effort in politics was to sponsor a referendum for reducing the price of dentures. He ran for Congress at the age of 31 from Portland and, after Robert Packwood resigned, he ran for the Senate in 1996, defeating Gordon Smith, who later became his Senate colleague, by a small margin in a tight race. It was the first race in the country to use mail ballots alone.

In the Senate he worked with Charles Grassley to insist on disclosures of senatorial holds. He was known for his work on behalf of the elderly. During the Reagan Administration and again in the George W. Bush Administration he was an ardent defender of Social Security. He joined with Republican colleagues of the Senate and the House to ensure that the Internet be tax-free, and restricting spam. He was active concerning the environment, sponsoring with Henry Waxman the Clean Air Act. He was also active in the campaign against tobacco. Although he opposed Oregon's assisted suicide law, he defended it against Congressional efforts to override state law with federal regulation. He was a strong advocate for a woman's right to choose and sought to bring RU 486, the morning after pill, to the United States. He also served on the Senate Intelligence Committee and was a firm voter against the Iraq war.

BIBLIOGRAPHY: K.F. Stone, *The Congressional Minyan: The Jews of Capitol Hill* (2000); L.S. Maisel and I. Forman (eds.), *Jews in American Politics* (2001).

[Michael Berenbaum (2nd ed.)]

WYGODZKI, STANISLŁAW (1907–1992), Polish poet and author. Born in Bedzin, where his father, Isaac Wygodzki, was a leading Polish Zionist, Wygodzki was attracted to Communism in his youth and in 1925 was condemned to two years' imprisonment for his political activities. He began his literary career in 1928 with contributions to the literary weekly *Wiadomości Literackie*, later writing for *Głos Literacki*, *Miesięcznik Literacki*, and other periodicals. Wygodzki's first verse collection appeared in Moscow in 1933. During World War II he was deported from the Bedzin ghetto to Auschwitz, where he managed to survive until the liberation. In 1947 Wygodzki returned to Poland and resumed his literary work. He published many volumes of poetry and prose, including *Pamiętnik miłości* ("Diary of Love," 1948), *W kotlinie* ("In the Dell," 1949), *Widzenie* ("Encounter," 1950), *Pusty plac* ("Empty Square," 1955), and *Koncert życeń* ("Request Concert," 1960). Wygodzki's works reflect his deep concern for the fate of his fellow-men, their moral purity and strength, and his struggle against social evils. His books were translated into many languages. Wygodzki also published translations from Yiddish literature (including Sholem *Asch). *Zatrzymany do wyjaśnienia* ("Detained for Explanation") which, confiscated in Poland in 1957, appeared in Israel (in Hebrew) in 1968. He emigrated to Israel in that year. He was the *Encyclopaedia Judaica* departmental editor (first edition) for Polish literature.

BIBLIOGRAPHY: *Pinkas Bendin* (Heb., 1959), index; W. Sadkowski, *Penetracje i komentarze* (1967), 134–45; *Kultura*, 11 no. 254 (Pol., 1968), 70.

WYLER, WILLIAM (1902–1981), U.S. film director and producer. Born in Mulhouse, Alsace, Wyler emigrated to the United States in 1920 with his uncle, Carl *Laemmle, head of Universal Pictures. In 1925 he directed the first of 50 two-reel Westerns, starting his long series of major works, first with Universal and then in association with other studios. An early success was the film version of Elmer *Rice's play *Counsellor-at-Law* (1933), as well as the adaptation of Sinclair Lewis' *Dodsworth* (Oscar nomination for Best Director, 1936). He broke new ground with *These Three* (1936), the successful adaptation of Lillian Hellman's *The Children's Hour*, a play with a lesbian theme. Four more milestones in his directorial career were *Jezebel* (produced, 1938); *Wuthering Heights* (Oscar nomination for Best Director, 1939); *The Letter* (Oscar nomination for Best Director, 1940); and *The Little Foxes* (Oscar nomination for Best Director, 1941). During World War II he served as an officer with the U.S. Air Force, where he made the documentary *The Memphis Belle* and the Navy film *The Fighting Lady*, which won an Oscar for Best Documentary.

After the war, Wyler directed such distinguished films as *The Heiress* (produced; Oscar nomination for Best Picture and Director, 1949); *Detective Story* (produced; Oscar nomination for Best Director, 1951); *Roman Holiday* (produced; Oscar nomination for Best Picture and Director, 1953); *The Desperate Hours* (produced, 1955); *Friendly Persuasion* (produced; Oscar nomination for Best Picture and Director, 1956); *The Big Country* (produced, 1958); *The Collector* (Oscar nomination for Best Director, 1965); *How to Steal a Million* (1966); *Funny Girl* (1968); and his final film, *The Liberation of L.B. Jones* (1970).

Wyler was among Hollywood's foremost filmmakers and was the recipient of many honors, including three Academy Awards, for directing *Mrs. Miniver* (1942), *The Best Years of Our Lives* (1946), and *Ben-Hur* (1959). In 1966 he received the Irving G. Thalberg Memorial Award, for the consistently high quality of his motion picture production. In 1976 he received the American Film Institute's Lifetime Achievement Award.

ADD. BIBLIOGRAPHY: R. Freiman, *The Story of the Making of Ben-Hur* (1959); A. Madsen, *William Wyler, The Authorized Biography* (1973); M. Andregg, *William Wyler* (1979); B. Bowman, *Master Space: Film Images of Capra, Lubitsch, Sternberg, and Wyler* (1992); J. Herman, *A Talent for Trouble: The Life of Hollywood's Most Acclaimed Director, William Wyler* (1995).

[G. Eric Hauck / Ruth Beloff (2nd ed.)]

WYNN, ED (**Isaiah Edwin Leopold**; 1886–1966), U.S. comedian. Born in Philadelphia of an immigrant family from Prague, Wynn was known for 60 years as "The Perfect Fool." His early appearances on Broadway included *The Deacon and the Lady* (1910); *Ziegfeld Follies of 1914*; *Ziegfeld Follies of 1915*; *The Passing Show of 1916*; and *Sometime* (1918). In 1919, when earning $1,700 weekly, he joined a choristers' strike and was then blacklisted by managements. Using his savings, Wynn wrote, staged, composed the music, and performed in the *Ed Wynn Carnival* (1919–21); *The Perfect Fool* (1921–22); and *The Grab Bag* (1925) on Broadway. He later performed in *Manhattan Mary* (1927), and wrote, staged, produced, and performed in *Simple Simon* (1930–31); *The Laugh Parade* (1932); *Boys and Girls Together* (1941); and *Laugh, Town, Laugh* (1942). During the 1930s he became one of the first radio comedy stars, creating the role of the Texaco Fire Chief.

His films roles include *Follow the Leader* (1930); *The Chief* (1933); the voice of the Mad Hatter in *Alice in Wonderland* (1951); *The Great Man* (1956); *Marjorie Morningstar* (1958); *The Diary of Anne Frank* (Oscar nomination for Best Supporting Actor, 1959); *Cinderfella* (1960); *The Absent-Minded Professor* (1961); *Babes in Toyland* (1961); *Son of Flubber* (1963); *The Patsy* (1964); *Mary Poppins* (1964); *Those Calloways* (1965); *The Greatest Story Ever Told* (1965); *The Daydreamer* (1966); and *The Gnome-Mobile* (1967).

Wynn had many forays into television as well. He hosted the *Camel Comedy Caravan* variety show (1950), starred in *The Ed Wynn Show* sitcom (1958–59), and was a guest on dozens of panel, variety, and drama series. He appeared in the TV drama *Requiem for a Heavyweight* (1956) and the TV movies *Meet Me in St. Louis* (1959), *Miracle on 34th Street* (1959), *The Golden Horseshoe Revue* (1962), and *For the Love of Willadean* (1964). In 1950 he was awarded an Emmy for Most Outstanding Live Personality, and *The Ed Wynn Show* won an Emmy for Best Live Show. He earned Emmy nominations for three of his drama series performances (1957, 1958, and 1961).

He was the father of actor Keenan *Wynn (1916–1986).

BIBLIOGRAPHY: K. Wynn, *Ed Wynn's Son* (1959).

[Ruth Beloff (2nd ed.)]

WYNN, KEENAN (**Francis Xavier Aloysius**; 1916–1986), U.S. actor. Born in New York, the son of Ed *Wynn (1886–1966). Keenan toured in stock companies and appeared on the New York stage and on television before making his debut in films in *See Here, Private Hargrove* (1944). His Broadway performances include *Remember the Day* (1935), *Hitch Your Wagon* (1937), *The Star-Wagon* (1937), *One for the Money* (1939), *Two for the Show* (1940), *The More the Merrier* (1941), and *Strip for Action* (1942).

A long-standing character actor, Wynn made more than 100 television appearances and performed in more than 170 films. He was nominated once for an Emmy for his performance in an episode of the TV series *Police Woman*. Of his career Wynn is said to have commented, "My billing has always been 'and' or 'with' or 'including.' That's all right; let the stars take the blame."

Wynn's feature film roles include *The Hucksters* (1947), *My Dear Secretary* (1949), *Annie Get Your Gun* (1950), *Royal Wedding* (1951), *Kiss Me, Kate* (1953), *The Man in the Gray Flannel Suit* (1956), *Don't Go Near the Water* (1957), *A Hole in the Head* (1959), *The Absent-Minded Professor* (1962), *Dr. Strangelove* (1964), *The Patsy* (1964), *The Americanization of Emily* (1964), *The Great Race* (1965), *Finian's Rainbow* (1968), *MacKenna's Gold* (1969), *Loving* (1970), *The Mechanic* (1972), *Snowball Express* (1972), *Nashville* (1975), *High Velocity* (1976), *Just Tell Me What You Want* (1980), *Best Friends* (1982), and *Black Moon Rising* (1986). Wynn's final role was as Butch in the TV pilot and comedy series *The Last Precinct* (1986).

Wynn's autobiography, *Ed Wynn's Son*, was published in 1959.

BIBLIOGRAPHY: N. Wynn, *We Will Always Live in Beverly Hills* (1990).

[Ruth Beloff (2nd ed.)]

WYNN, SAMUEL (1891–1982), Australian wine merchant and communal leader. Born Shlomo Weintraub near Lodz, Wynn was educated at a local yeshivah and joined the family wine-making business. He came to Melbourne, Australia, in 1913 to escape conscription into the czarist army and opened a vineyard near Stawell, Victoria. Wynn bought his first wine-retailing shop in Melbourne in 1918 and began bottling his own vermouths and wines in the mid-1920s. In 1927 he established Australian Wines Ltd., which, by the mid-1940s, were the largest winemakers and retailers in the country. In the post-war era Wynn Estates Pty. Ltd., as it was then known, became internationally known and probably Australia's most famous brand of wines. Wynn was also closely connected with Jewish causes, twice serving as president of the Zionist Federation of Australia. His wife IDA (née Siegler, c. 1896–1948), a Canadian, was a philosopher who was a friend of Martin *Buber, as well as a leading Australian Zionist and president of Australian WIZO.

BIBLIOGRAPHY: ADB, 12, 590–91; H.L. Rubinstein, Australia I, 193–94, 559–60; A. Wynn, *The Fortunes of Samuel Wynn: Winemaker, Humanist, Zionist* (1948).

[William D. Rubinstein (2nd ed.)]

WYNN, STEVE (**Stephen Alan**; 1942–), U.S. casino developer. Wynn was born in New Haven, Conn., and raised in Utica, N.Y. His father, Michael Weinberg, ran a string of bingo parlors in the eastern United States and died shortly before Wynn graduated from the University of Pennsylvania in 1963. Wynn took over the family's bingo operation in Maryland and did well enough to accumulate the money to buy a small stake in the Frontier Hotel and Casino in Las Vegas. In the early 1970s, Wynn was part of a land deal with two titans of the Las Vegas casino industry, Howard Hughes and Caesars Palace, and they won a controlling interest in the Golden Nugget. Wynn renovated, revamped, and expanded the Golden

Nugget, whose annual profit soared from a little over $1 million to over $12 million. Wynn built another Golden Nugget in Atlantic City, N.J., in 1984. In 1984 Wynn was estimated to be worth $100 million. In 1986 he bought a large piece of land next to Caesar's Palace. He then sold the Atlantic City Nugget for $440 million and used much of the money to build the Mirage, a 3,000-room hotel and casino, in 1989. The Mirage set a new standard for size and lavishness. It featured an indoor forest and an outdoor "volcano," and with high-quality room appointments the Mirage was a great success. The Mirage was financed largely with junk bonds issued by Michael *Milken and it proved to be enormously successful, further enhancing Wynn's image in Las Vegas. Wynn expanded further on his concept of the luxury casino with the Bellagio, which had an artificial lake, an indoor conservatory, and an art gallery in which Wynn displayed museum-quality artworks, and branches of high-end boutiques and restaurants located in Paris, San Francisco, and New York. Mirage Resorts was sold to MGM Grand in 2000 to form MGM Mirage. With the money he made on the deal, Wynn built a new resort, the Wynn Las Vegas, which opened in 2005. According to Forbes magazine, Wynn became a billionaire in 2004, when his net worth was estimated at $1.3 billion. Wynn's art collection, on display to the public at Wynn Las Vegas, includes paintings by Picasso, Vermeer, Van Gogh, Gauguin, Warhol, and Matisse.

[Stewart Kampel (2nd ed.)]

WYOMING, a central Rocky Mountain state in the western United States. Its total population in 2000 was 493,782, ranking it the least populated state in the nation. Its Jewish population was approximately 400. The 140-year history of the Jews of Wyoming is a paradigm for the Jewish experience in the West and in America.

By 1868, the gleaming tracks of the Union Pacific Railroad had reached southeastern Wyoming. The opportunities in Cheyenne and Laramie, both nicknamed "Hell On Wheels," attracted a number of German Reform Jews, who had deserted their homeland after the egalitarian reforms of the Revolution of 1848 failed to materialize. Those who ventured to Wyoming were mostly peddlers or frontier merchants who dealt in clothing, liquor, cigars, and sundry items. Intent on fitting in, they noted with satisfaction that they were readily accepted as fellow pioneers. Ernestine Rose, a close friend of Susan B. Anthony, rode up and down the territory on horseback and in stagecoaches campaigning to grant full equality to women. Her mission was successful. In 1869, Wyoming granted women the right to vote and is nicknamed "The Equality State." "Jew Jake" (Jacob Louis Kaufman) built a roadhouse in La Belle in 1879 to service the cowboys as they rode through during the great Texas cattle drives. And legend has it that, as early as 1890, Max Meyer's dry goods store contracted with the John B. Stetson Company to make 10-gallon hats to sell to both rodeo and range cowboys.

Between 1881 and 1914, a flood of eastern European Jews from the Pale of Settlement crowded into the United States.

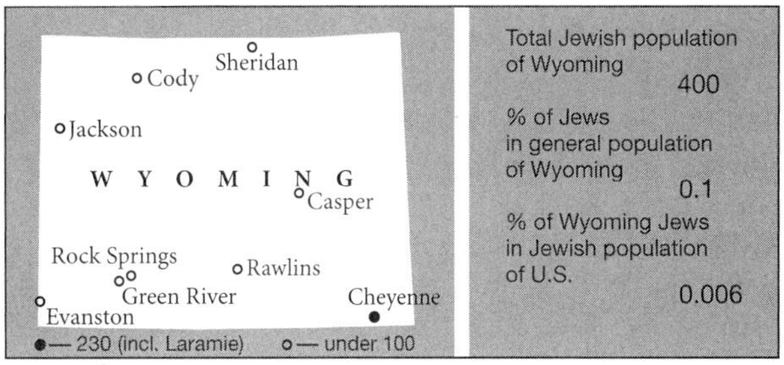

Jewish communities in Wyoming. Population figures for 2001.

Philanthropist Baron de Hirsch funded the Jewish Agricultural Society, an organization whose mission was to spread Jews throughout America. They sent some newly arriving immigrants to Wyoming to fulfill their agricultural dreams. The population of these would-be farmers in towns like Huntley was so high that it was necessary to hire a Yiddish-speaking teacher to instruct their children in public school. Other Jews were lured to Wyoming as a result of two Congressional Homestead Acts, which gave land to settlers in exchange for improving upon it. Primarily Orthodox Jews, this second wave of immigrants brought with them their customs, tools, and rituals; setting up synagogues, sacred burial grounds, and kashering capabilities. By 1919, the Orthodox synagogue in Cheyenne quietly absorbed the remnants of the Reform community into its own. Wyoming was indeed a place to strive for "a sack and a shovel, and shovel in the gold."

Opportunities for Jews in this rugged land were limited only by the extent of their imaginations.

Fred Goodstein, operating American Pipe and Supply, came to Casper in 1923 to take advantage of Wyoming's oil boom. He undoubtedly became the wealthiest man in the state, and more likely, the entire Rocky Mountain region. In 1930, Sol Bernstein opened what would become the largest mail-order western-wear store in the world. From the mid-1930s to the mid-1950s, Wyoming's Jewish communities reached their strides. Anchored by stable marriages and successful businesses, Wyoming's Jews continued to be gratified by the feeling that both America and their adopted state had smiled upon them. New synagogues were built in Casper and Cheyenne. Weddings and bar mitzvahs were frequent enough to make full-time rabbis a necessity. Prayer books, Torahs and worshipers were plentiful throughout the state. The *Wyoming Jewish Press* was published in newspaper form by Abe Goldstein between 1930 and 1940. During WWII, a burgeoning of Jewish military personnel brought more Jews to Wyoming. Those that stayed and married invigorated and further strengthened Wyoming's vibrant and visible Jewish community. Subsequent to the war, a small wave of Holocaust survivors found the people and opportunities of Wyoming to be safe and relatively free of antisemitism.

From the mid-1950s to the mid-1970s, college education of Wyoming's Jewish youth was an expected norm. The comforts and success of Jewish life in Wyoming was now perceived as a possible liability for the immigrants' progeny. The entire baby-boom generation was encouraged by their parents to seek Jewish mates and professional career opportunities in locations other than the high plains. Intermarriage, divorce and a seeming lack of religious observance ran rampant among Wyoming's Jews, just as it did throughout most of America.

The end of the 20th century marked a new pattern of immigration and observance for Wyoming's Jews. No longer concerned with escaping the political and social persecutions of their ancestors, this new immigration is often comprised of people searching for the rewards of material success they have achieved in other places. Jackson Hole in the Grand Tetons is a prosperous second-home destination for those wanting a reprieve from the pressures of frenzied city life, and is the fastest-growing Jewish community in the state. James Wolfensohn, former head of the World Bank, and Alan Hirschfield, former president and CEO of Columbia Pictures, call Wyoming their home. Throughout the state, women no longer are content to silently witness ritual practices previously reserved for men only. And other long-time residents make conscious choices to live meaningful Jewish lives apart from an organized Jewish community.

Questions abound. Are the new Jews of Wyoming or merely in Wyoming? Are they observing real Judaism or inventing a new style that is far afield from the laws of the Torah? Is the strain and excitement of changing religious interpretation inherent to keeping Jewishness alive? Is it simply a divine right to be a Jew, regardless of the details? Answers vary, but it is certain, after more than 140 years on the high plains, that the Jews of Wyoming still find ways to keep themselves and their progeny ever-conscious of their Jewish lives. To those that have wandered in the wilderness for thousands of years, the landscape called Wyoming is familiar territory.

Institutional Data

The highest concentration of Jews in Wyoming is to be found in the areas surrounding Jackson, Casper, Cheyenne, and Laramie. There are synagogues in Casper and Cheyenne and ongoing official community gatherings in Jackson and Laramie. The University of Wyoming supports an active branch of Hillel. There is currently no full-time rabbi in the state, though Jackson brings in a rabbi monthly and on holidays. Cheyenne employs a part-time cantor and Casper and Cheyenne have weekly lay-led services. Laramie's community has monthly and holiday lay-led services. All communities bring in a trained rabbi or cantor for High Holy Day services. Casper, Jackson, and Cheyenne have sacred burial ground, with Cheyenne having an active *ḥevra kaddisha*. All communities have at least one Torah, women are counted in *minyanim*, and each has an education program for youth and adults. Cheyenne, the oldest congregation, has a stream-fed *mikveh* and a fully equipped kosher kitchen.

BIBLIOGRAPHY: P.D. Wolin, *The Jews of Wyoming: Fringe of the Diaspora* (2000)

[Penny Diane Wolin (2nd ed.)]

WYSZKOW (Pol. **Wyszków**), town in Warszawa province, eastern central Poland. The first Jews settled in Wyszkow in the late 18th century. In 1827 the Jewish population numbered 278 (29% of the population). Throughout the 19th century no restrictions were put on Jewish settlement, and in 1857 the Jewish population had reached 1,067 (67%). The wealthier Jews engaged in the timber trade and the brewing of beer; others engaged in tailoring, fishing, carpentry, tanning, haulage, and shopkeeping. In the late 19th century the community was influenced by the ḥasidic groups of *Aleksandrow and Gur (*Gora Kalwaria). In 1897 Wyszkow contained 3,207 Jews (64%). At the beginning of the 20th century a Jewish workers' union was formed, and during the uprisings of 1905 the Jewish youth organized *self-defense. A Jewish library opened in 1909. After the Red Army retreated in 1920, some officers of the Polish army accused the Jews of Wyszkow of treason, almost inciting a pogrom.

Between the two world wars Abraham Cytryn headed the "Bet Yosef" yeshivah, which had 250 students. There was a CYSHO school (see *Education) between 1925 and 1930 and a *Beth Jacob school. Jacob Aryeh Morgensztern, who later led the *Radzyn Ḥasidim, served as rabbi of the community until 1932. He was succeeded by his son, David Shelomo Morgensztern, who was killed in the Holocaust. Economic competition in the 1930s caused an increase in antisemitism. Mordecai *Anielewicz, commander of the Warsaw ghetto uprising, originated from Wyszkow.

[Arthur Cygielman]

Holocaust Period

At the outbreak of World War II there were about 5,000 Jews in the town. The German army entered Wyszkow on Sept. 11, 1939, and organized anti-Jewish riots in which 65 Jews were shot. A few days later, the entire Jewish population was expelled and forced to move eastward into Soviet-occupied territory. After the Warsaw ghetto uprising, the survivors of the Jewish Fighters' Organization formed a partisan unit named after Mordecai Anielewicz that operated in the forests near Wyszkow. After the war, no Jewish community was reconstituted in Wyszkow.

[Stefan Krakowski]

BIBLIOGRAPHY: *Słownik geograficzny Królestwa Polskiego.* 14 (1895), 147–8; Żydowska Rada Narodowa, *Sprawozdanie z działalności tymczasowej żydowskiej Radzie Narodowej…* (1921); B. Wasiutyński, *Ludność zydowska w Polsce w wiekach XIX i XX* (1930), 25; T. Berenstein and A. Rutkowski, in: BŻIH, 38 (1961), 3–38; 39 (1961), 63–87; D. Shtokfish (ed.), *Sefer Vishkov* (1964).

WYSZOGROD (Pol. **Wyszogród**; Yid. **Vishegrod**), town in Warszawa province, eastern central Poland. A Jewish settlement in Wyszogrod is mentioned for the first time in 1422, when Jews received authorization from Prince Ziemowit IV (c. 1352–1426) to engage in commerce and crafts and to establish their own institutions. During the 16th century Jews established workshops for weaving. In the second half of the

18th century a synagogue was erected, built of stone in the late baroque style according to plans by the architect David Friedlander; it was destroyed by the Nazis in 1939. In 1765 the 684 Jews paid the poll tax, and 1,410 Jews paid the poll tax in 208 surrounding villages. The community numbered 2,883 (90% of the total population) in 1808; 2,458 (73%) in 1827; and 2,841 (74%) in 1857. From the mid–19th century many Jews moved from Wyszogrod to Plock and Warsaw; in 1897 there were 2,735 (66%) Jews in the town and in 1921, 2,465 (about 57%). During the 1920s eight of the 12 members of the municipal council were Jews. Because of the town's location on Poland's principal waterway, the Vistula River, Jews there engaged in interurban trade. Their position deteriorated, however, on the eve of World War II as a result of antisemitic pressure and boycott propaganda. N. *Sokolow was born in Wyszogrod. The last rabbis to hold office were David Bornstein (until 1922) and Naphtali Spivak, both of whom died in the Holocaust.

[Shimshon Leib Kirshenboim]

Holocaust Period

At the outbreak of World War II there were about 2,700 Jews in Wyszogrod. On Nov. 19, 1942, the Jewish community was liquidated when the Jews were expelled to Czerwinsk and Nowy Dwor, and from there deported to the *Treblinka death camp. After the war the Jewish community was not reconstituted.

BIBLIOGRAPHY: Halpern, Pinkas, index; R. Mahler, *Yidn in Amolikn Poyln in Likht fun Tsifern* (1958), index; B. Wasiutyński, *Ludność żydowska w Polsce w wiekach XIX i XX* (1930), 22; S. Pazyra, *Geneza i rozwój miast mazowieckich* (1959), passim; I. Schiper, *Dzieje handlu żydowskiego na ziemiach polskich* (1937), index; A. Kubiak, in: BŻIH, 8 (1953), 77, 89–91.

WYZANSKI, CHARLES EDWARD, JR. (1906–1986), U.S. jurist. Born in Boston, Massachusetts, Wyzanski received his A.B. from Harvard College in 1927 and his LL.B. from Harvard Law School in 1930. He served as law clerk to Judge Augustus N. Hand and Judge Learned Hand, practiced law in Boston, and then joined the New Deal Administration of President Franklin D. Roosevelt as solicitor, later serving as acting secretary of labor in the Department of Labor (1933–35). From 1935 to 1937 he was on the staff of the solicitor general, arguing the constitutionality of the Wagner National Labor Relations Act and the Social Security Act. Named U.S. district judge for the district of Massachusetts, he took his seat in 1942, becoming the first Jewish judge of the United States District Court of Massachusetts. In 1966 he was elevated chief judge of the court and served in that capacity until 1971, when he assumed senior status.

Wyzanski served as president of the board of overseers of Harvard University and, from 1952, was a trustee of the Ford Foundation. In the role of teacher, Wyzanski was a lecturer in government at Harvard University (1942–43) and in law at Massachusetts Institute of Technology (1949–50) and Stanford University (1949–51). In 1974 he was a professor of law at Columbia University.

Wyzanski received many public and academic honors. His essays have been collected under the title *Whereas: A Judge's Premises* (1965; paperback repr., *New Meaning of Justice*). He contributed to the *Harvard Law Review* and other professional and popular magazines. Considered one of the ablest judges on the federal bench, Wyzanski's decisions were respected as far-reaching and erudite. He believed that, although it was important to learn the principles of the law, it was even more necessary to accept the challenge of understanding them. In his analysis of the Nuremberg Trials in 1946, he noted that law is not power but restraint on power, a maxim he endeavored to apply in his legal thinking.

Harvard established the Judge Charles Wyzanski Award, a prize given to students who are interested in the law, vigorous conversation, and theoretical and practical issues of justice.

ADD. BIBLIOGRAPHY: D. Lawson (ed.), *Ten Fighters for Peace: An Anthology* (1971); P. Irons, *The New Deal Lawyers* (1982).

[Julius J. Marcke / Ruth Beloff (2nd ed.)]

The letter "X" is set against an illustration of the story of Balaam and his ass (Num. 22), with a rhyme in which the animal asks his master why he is maltreating him. Page from a book of designs for the alphabet, Libro en el quell hay muchas suertas de letras historiada ... *by Juan de Yciar, Saragossa Spain, 1955, London, British Museum, c. 53, c. 24 fol. 15r.*

XA-XI

XANTEN, town in Germany. The first documentary evidence for the presence of Jews in Xanten dates from the period of the First *Crusade when Jews from *Cologne sought refuge there. On June 27, 1096, the crusaders reached Xanten as well, and some 60 Jews were either killed or had committed suicide. Among the martyrs were Moses ha-Kohen, rabbi of Xanten, and an unidentified proselyte. In 1197 the Rhenish communities paid the bishop for permission to bury the six martyrs of Neuss in the Xanten cemetery. Though Jewish moneylenders were found in Xanten in the 13th century, the market day was held on the Sabbath so as to exclude Jews from trade (1236). The community suffered badly during the *Black Death persecutions of 1349. Reports from the 15th and 16th centuries point to Jewish activity as moneylenders. In the 17th and 18th centuries there were apparently only small numbers of Jews in Xanten. From 1690 Xanten was the meeting place for the Rhenish Jewish Diet and in 1787 a special building, which also contained a synagogue, was set aside for the assembly's meetings. In 1860 the community had its own elementary school; in 1890 it counted 85 persons. A butcher and former *shoḥet*, Adolf Wolff Buschoff of Xanten, was the victim of a blood *libel in 1892. Accused by a Catholic of murdering a Christian boy, a charge taken up by the antisemitic press, Buschoff was arrested but then discharged for lack of evidence. A debate in the Prussian Diet, which gave the antisemite A. *Stoecker an opportunity to fulminate against the Jews, resulted in the arrest of Buschoff for a second time; but a jury at Cleves found him innocent (1892). The community did not survive this agitation and gradually decreased to 30 persons (9.6 percent of the population) in 1916 and 14 in 1930. The synagogue was destroyed by the Nazis in November 1938.

BIBLIOGRAPHY: J. Freimann, in: *Festschrift… S. Dubnow* (1930), 163–71; S. Braun, in: *Allgemeine Wochenzeitung der Juden in Deutschland* (March 10, 1961); K. Schilling (ed.), *Monumenta Judaica Handbuch* (1963), index; *Germania Judaica*, 1 (1963), 497–500; 2 (1968), 936–7; Aronius, Regesten, index; A.M. Habermann, *Gezerot Ashkenaz ve-Ẓarefat* (1946); Salfeld, Martyrol.

XANTHI (Ksanthi, Xanthie, Eskedje), city located in northeastern Greece in the region of Greek Thrace between Drama and Cuomotini. This town in the past has had the reputation for producing the best tobacco in the world.

At the beginning of the 20th century, several Jewish families came to the city from Adrianople, Didymoteikhon, and Salonika. In 1913, they established a Jewish community there. The Jews spoke Judeo-Spanish and only in 1926 did they establish a synagogue. In 1924, the Jewish community represented by David Arditis, Abraham Tabach, Abraham Bellos, and Yehuda Cohen purchased a plot of land for a synagogue and community center at the junction of Anatolikis Thrakis Street and Stavrou Hadjistavrou Street. The basilica of the synagogue was influenced by the Reform synagogues of Europe and the Great Synagogue of Edirne. Next to the synagogue was a two-floor community center, where the school was on the ground floor, the first floor was for the office of the headmaster, and the second floor housed the community center. The Sephardi Jewish community of Xanthi was a central cultural community for the Jews of Thrace.

In 1913, after the Balkan wars, Xanthi was annexed to Bulgaria. In 1913, there were 1,290 Jews in the area of Xanthi. Under the Bulgarians, a branch of the organization Hahistadrut leSafa veLeTarbut Ivrit (The Federation for the Hebrew Language and Culture), which was founded in Bulgaria in 1914, was started in Xanthi. In 1918, in Xanthi a branch of Kadima was formed for the dissemination of the Hebrew language and culture and to educate toward Jewish nationalism through Hebrew language, Hebrew literature, Jewish history, and Ereẓ Israel geography classes. The branch also organized literary evenings, hikes, and parties, started a library, and translated material from Bulgarian and Hebrew to Judeo-Spanish. It had 55 members, most of whom were graduates of the Jewish French Alliance Israélite Universelle school system.

Many of the Jews were tobacco workers, artisans, and small merchants. The Jewish community had two philanthropic organizations: Agudat Bikur Holim and Agudat Nashim, a women's organization.

After World War I, in 1919, Greek sovereignty replaced Bulgarian rule. During the Bulgarian retreat, the Bulgarians accused the Jews of having received the Greek army joyfully. One of the Bulgarian newspapers exploited this accusation and attacked all of Bulgarian Jewry. In 1919, there were 70–74 Jewish families (some 300–350 people). During the Asia Minor war of 1922, the community had 700 members. At the beginning of the 1920s, it was estimated that 250 Jewish families lived in relative prosperity. Most Jews lived in the poor neighborhood of Pournali or Pournari, the wealthier Jews lived in Ano Poli (Upper Town).

In 1910, Mois Bassat, an anti-Zionist assistant principal of Alliance Israélite Universelle schools, changed his outlook, became a Zionist, and was chosen as president of the new B'nai Zion Zionist league in Xanthi.

In the early 1920s, the Zionist organization B'nai Zion was active, led by the dentist Isaac de Botton. From time to time, the organization raised money for the Jewish National Fund. In 1922, Isaac de Botton edited the Judeo-Spanish Zionist newspaper *La Fuerza*. In 1924, he published the Judeo-Spanish periodical *El Progresso*. The periodicals wrote on local and regional events, and news from the Jewish world. On the occasion of the inauguration of the Hebrew University of Jerusalem in 1925, he issued *Leumi* (National) in Judeo-Spanish. In 1922 the youth of the community organized into the Zionist HaTikva sport organization. In the mid-1920s, a Jewish scout troop organized in Xanthi, and they eventually allied with the Salonikan Jewish Boy Scout Chapter Maccabee. There was also a Jewish youth theater group, which was highly praised in the local press, and a Music and Sports Association. The community also had the club Cercle Israélite.

In 1923, Yitzhak Daniel was named the honorary president of the Jewish community, and David Arditti was president. Another six men were on the Executive Committee, as well as the chief rabbi Haim ben Avraham and school principal Yitzhak Meshulam. The Executive Committee determined community dues, and appointed members to committees that dealt with Bikur Holim, the synagogue, and education. The community received an annual allotment from the municipality for operating expenses, and the Ministry of Public Education via the governor general of Thrace contributed an annual sum for religious institutions and communal education. The next communal rabbi was Avraham Haviv for most of the 1920s, followed by Rabbi Raphael Nissim Latin.

In the early 1920s, the new Jewish school had 44 boys and 67 girls. The students paid tuition and there were teachers for Greek and French. Yitzhak Meshulam was the principal. In the absence of Hebrew, which was criticized in the Zionist organ *La Fuerza,* it was decided to give the management of the school to the Alliance Israélite Universelle, and Avraham Benveniste of Salonika was hired to be principal and French teacher. In 1924, 150 children were enrolled in the school. In the early 1930s, during the depression, the construction of a school ran into financial problems, and in 1934 the Bank of Athens proposed to sell the school structure in a public auction. The community went into action, found financial help from private businessmen like Karl Shefer, and businesses, and managed to pay the bank. The new principal was Vitali Matalon, who also taught French. The Zionists demanded that Hebrew be taught and that it be taught by members of the Zionist organizations Hatze'irim Hayehudim, which was founded in 1934 and had 80 members, and HaTikva. In 1936, after a court case involving the Jewish community and the widow of the deceased, the community finally received the estate of the tobacco worker Yitzhak Daniel, who died in 1924. A large sum of 1,200,000 drachmas was to be divided as follows: 200,000 for the building of the synagogue, 500,000 for the land for a synagogue, and a scholarship fund of 500,000 for scholarships for two students annually.

In 1937, during the Metaxas dictatorship in Greece, the school received an increased allocation from the government, and solved the school's water shortage problems by putting in a water system. On the other hand, the same nationalist government in the same year ordered that weekly hours for the instruction of Judaism be cut, including the teaching of Hebrew, religion, and history. In 1938, the community was further enraged when, within a few days, the government ordered the school to collect all religious books, i.e., prayer books, weekly Torah portion lessons, holiday *maḥzor* prayer books, psalm books, Midrashim, and commentaries on *Me'am Loez.*

Three major tobacco companies in Xanthi belonged to Jews: Commercial, Herman Spearer, and David Arditis' company, which manufactured cigarettes. Jews also worked in the flour industry, the textile trade, ready-made clothes, haberdashery, leather accessories, and other industries.

In 1934 Leon Amarilio sat on the Municipal Council, and in 1938, David Attas was president of the Jewish community.

In 1934 the community numbered 1,100, but by World War II the community only numbered 120–140 families (600 people).

In April 1941, Xanthi was occupied by the Bulgarians, allies of the Nazis, who already decided in December 1940 to implement anti-Jewish legislation and the Nuremberg laws. The Bulgarian military forces began pillaging and plundering the Jews.

The Jews were compelled to wear the yellow Star of David, and they were forbidden to work in their professions in commerce and industry.

Jews had to mark their homes with a sign stating they were Jews. They could not leave the city and they had a nightly curfew. Gangs robbed Jewish stores and there were random checks in Jewish houses. Communication with the outside world was blocked and the Bulgarian government confiscated Jewish property. On February 22, 1943, the Bulgarian commissar for Jewish affairs, Alexander Belev, came to Xanthi to supervise deportation plans and preparations. At midnight March 4, 1943, the Bulgarians arrested 550 Jews in Xanthi and took them to a tobacco warehouse on 1 Salaminas Street. Only six escaped from the internment. The day of the arrest, the local tobacco merchant Yehuda Perahia was in Cavalla and managed to escape to Salonika. They were transferred to Drama by trucks and from there they were loaded on trains to Dupnitza in Bulgaria and were exposed to horrid conditions. Then on March 19, 1943 they were sent to Lom by train and from there taken by boat to Vienna and then sent by train to Treblinka where they met their deaths. The Bulgarians looted Jewish homes and shops. After the liberation, Yehuda Perahia returned to Xanthi and resumed his job as the head of a commercial tobacco company. He eventually donated his Judeo-Spanish newspaper collection from before World War II Salonika to the Ben-Zvi Institute Library in Israel. He would pray in Cavalla on holidays. In the 1960s the members of the family of Jak Cazes left the city to migrate to Israel.

In 1963, the community center was sold to the Boy Scouts. The dilapidated synagogue building in Xanthi was sold in 1992 and demolished in 1995. The cemetery is still on Xanthis-Diomidias Street beyond the train tracks. It is walled, but abandoned, and contains a few graves dating after 1923.

On March 3, 2001, the Municipality of Xanthi organized a memorial event for the annihilated Jews and the next day a memorial plaque was put in a wall in the tobacco warehouse at 1 Salaminas Street, to remind the local residents of the forced exodus of the Jews from there, their removal from the city, and the end of the Jewish community. Thomas Exarhos' book in Greek on the Jews of Xanthi, published by the Cultural and Development Center of Thrace, was presented within the framework of the special events.

BIBLIOGRAPHY: B. Rivlin, "Xanthi," *Pinkas ha-Kehillot Yavan* (1999) 381–388; E. Messinas, "Preserving Jewish Heritage in Greece," in: *Archeology*, September 23, 1998; "The Jewish Community of Xanthi," at: www.kis.gr/xanthi-en.html; T. Exarchou, *I Evrai stin Xanthi (O kosmos pou chathike alla then ksechastike)* (2001).

[Yitzchak Kerem (2nd ed.)]

XENOPHON OF LAMPSACUS (second century B.C.E.), author of a fanciful travel book in Greek. He has been identified with Xenophon, author of a guide to Syria, quoted anonymously on the subject of Jerusalem's topography in Eusebius, *Praeparatio Evangelica*, 9:36.

XIMENES, SIR DAVID (1776–1848), English army officer. Born in London, into a distinguished Jewish family, Ximenes joined the British army and served in North America. He returned to Britain in 1805 and commanded the 62nd Regiment in Ireland. He later fought in Italy, Spain, and Portugal. Ximenes was knighted in 1832 and retired with the rank of lieutenant general in 1847. He had no direct connection with the Jewish community.

ADD. BIBLIOGRAPHY: J. Picciotto, *Sketches of Anglo-Jewish History* (1875), 303–4.

XIMENES, SIR MORRIS (**Moses**; c. 1762–1837), English magnate. Born in London, Xiemenes was a member of the Stock Exchange and made a fortune. In 1792 he was the leading spirit in an unsuccessful expedition, partly composed of and mainly supported by London Sephardim, for the colonization of the island of Bulama off the west African coast. In 1802 he declined to serve as warden of the Bevis Marks synagogue and was converted to Anglicanism. During the Peninsular War (1812–15) Xiimenes raised and commanded a brigade of Wargrave Rangers. He acquired a country estate and built a mansion at Bear Place in Berkshire. Ximenes became a captain of militia, sheriff of Berkshire, and a knight. He is mentioned by name in Frederick Marryat's novel *Olla Porida* (1841) as the only well-known person in England whose name began with an "x." He was the brother of Sir David *Ximenes.

BIBLIOGRAPHY: A.M. Hyamson, *Sephardim of England* (1951), 201f.; Roth, in: JHSET, 14 (1935–39), 14–16; 15 (1939–45); 16–18; J. Picciotto, *Sketches of Anglo-Jewish History* (1956²), 295–7, 476.

[Cecil Roth / William D. Rubinstein (2nd ed.)]

XIMENES (Ish Yemeni), SOLOMON MORDECAI (d. 1825), Sephardi rabbi. Ximenes' antecedents are unknown, but from

1769 to 1770 he served as the last Hakham of the Sephardi community of Hamburg, succeeding Jacob Bassan. Later he entered the service of the London Sephardi community as a teacher and member of its *bet din* and gave expert evidence of Jewish marriage law in lawsuits in 1793 and 1798. His views embroiled him in disputes with the community; he expressed contrition in December 1804 but was again at loggerheads with it in 1811. In 1800 he published in London Part 1 of his bizarre work *The Expected Good end ... containing the birth of Jacob, his dream of the ladder, various objections on some of the verses of King Solomon. Some observations on the structure of the Tabernacle. Temple of Solomon ..., etc.* He was active in Freemasonry. He hebraized his name to Ish Yemeni.

BIBLIOGRAPHY: J. Picciotto, *Sketches of Anglo-Jewish History* (1956^2), 102, 458; Roth, Mag Bibl 271.

XIMENES (JIMENES) DE CISNEROS, FRANCISCO (originally Gonzales, 1436–1517), ecclesiastical statesman and regent of Castile from 1516 to 1517. After studying at Salamanca and Rome until 1465, Ximenes claimed the archpriesthood of Uceda, despite the archbishop of Toledo's wish that he resign; he was consequently imprisoned for six years. Inflexible resolution and personal austerity characterized his career. He joined the Franciscans, becoming Queen Isabella's confessor in 1492, archbishop of Toledo and chancellor of Castile in 1495, and grand inquisitor and cardinal under Ferdinand in 1507. He died hours after his dismissal by the youthful Charles v.

Ximenes, allegedly with the help of Jews, captured Oran in 1509 while crusading against the Moors of Africa. Although he was an unrelenting inquisitor of lapsed "New Christians" (2,500 were burned during his office), he strove to check inquisitional abuses (extortionism, immorality, etc.), but could not enforce central registration of "familiars" or gangs maintained by the inspectors. Since inquisitional charges without the naming of witnesses were preferred, defense was hampered; when the New Christians offered Charles (as they had earlier with Ferdinand) 800,000 crowns to reform the procedure, the monarch refused, dissuaded by Ximenes' intervention.

Conversos suffered no discrimination at the university founded in 1500 by Ximenes at Alcalá de Henares (Latin, "Complutum") – the site of his early schooling – unlike the situation at other Spanish universities. The "Complutensian Polyglot" Bible (6 vols., 1513–17), produced through Ximenes' personal initiative and patronage, was the first Bible with parallel Hebrew, Greek, Latin, and (for the Pentateuch) Aramaic texts; a Hebrew vocabulary was appended. For this work, significant manuscripts and competent editorship were sought, the latter from among converted Jews (Alfonso de *Zamora, Pablo Coronel, Alfonso de Alcalá). Four of the Hebrew codices utilized survived, but the form of the text presupposes also manuscripts from no later than the ninth century with the simpler Babylonian punctuation. These were apparently sold as waste to a fireworks maker in 1739, but their survival in Spain until the expulsion testifies to the strong Babylonian influence on medieval Spanish Jewry.

BIBLIOGRAPHY: Alvaro Gomez de Castro, *De rebus gestis Francisci Ximenii* (1569); K.J. von Hefele, *Der Cardinal Ximenes* (1853); H.C. Lea, *History of the Inquisition in Spain*, 4 (1906), 618ff.; P.E. Kahle, *The Cairo Genizah* (1959^2), 124–129; M. Bataillon, *Erasme et l'Espagne* (1937), passim; Basil Hall, in: G.J. Cumin (ed.), *Studies in Church History*, 5 (1969), 114–46.

[Raphael Loewe]

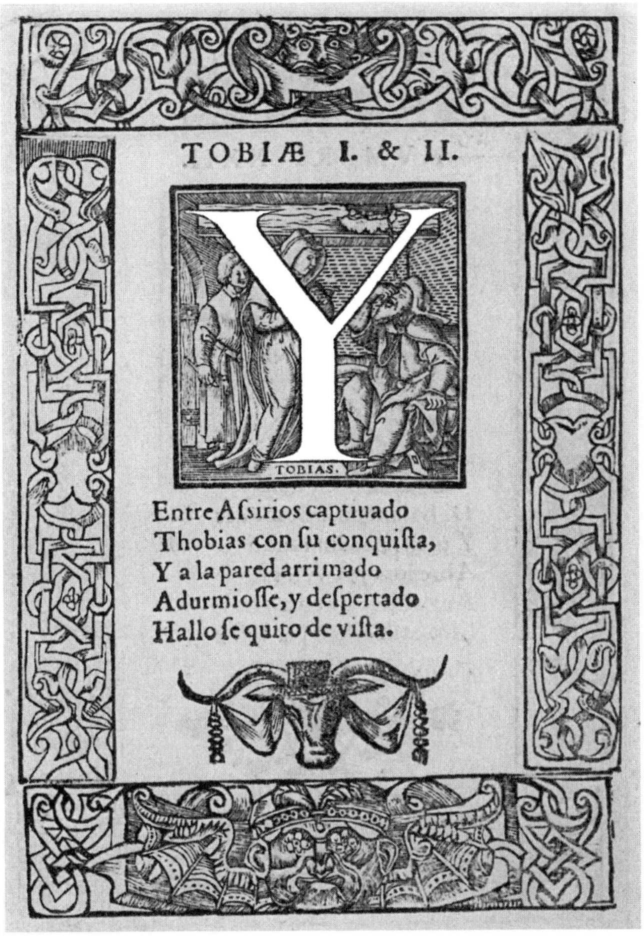

The letter "Y" set against an illustration of Tobit awakening to find himself blind (Tob. 2:9–10), with a rhyme describing the event. Page from a book of designs for the alphabet, Libro en el quell hay muchas suertas de letras historiada ... *by Juan de Yciar, Saragossa Spain, 1955, London, British Museum, c. 53, c. 24 fol. 15v.*

YA-YZ

YA'ACOBI, GAD (1935–), Israeli politician, member of the Seventh to Twelfth Knessets. Ya'acobi was born in Kefar Vitkin where he attended high school. After serving in the IDF in 1953–56, he studied economics and political science at Tel Aviv University and completed an M.A. in economics in 1959. Ya'acobi was assistant to Minister of Agriculture Moshe *Dayan in 1960–61, and headed the Agricultural Planning and Development Center in the Ministry of Agriculture (1961–66). In 1965 he was one of the founders of the *Rafi Party, and in 1966–69 was a member of the Histadrut Central Committee, and of the Ḥevrat ha-Ovedim Executive. In 1967 he participated in the Harvard University International Seminar, headed by Professor Henry *Kissinger. Ya'acobi became a member of the Labor Party Bureau in 1968, when the party was first established. He was first elected to the Seventh Knesset in 1969, and served as deputy minister of transportation under Golda *Meir in 1969–74, and as minister of transportation under Yitzhak *Rabin in 1974–77. In 1977–84, when the Labor Alignment was in opposition, he served as chairman of the Knesset Economics Committee and as chairman of the Socioeconomic Committee of the Labor party. In 1980–82 he taught political science at Haifa University.

In the National Unity Government formed in 1984 Ya'acobi was appointed minister of economics and inter-ministerial coordination. He later changed the name of his ministry to the Ministry of Economic Planning. In this position Ya'acobi stood behind the organization of the Task Force established together with Jewish businessmen from abroad to encourage investments in Israel. After making numerous proposals over the years for electoral reform, soon after the formation of the National Unity Government he was appointed chairman of a joint Labor-Likud Committee on electoral reform that proposed changing the Israeli electoral system to a mixed system in which half the Knesset members would be elected in multi-member constituencies and the other half on the basis of proportional representation. However, while the reform was approved by the Labor Central Committee, it was rejected by that of the Likud, and the idea was buried. In 1987, following the resignation of Amnon *Rubinstein from the Ministry of Communications, Ya'acobi was appointed in his place, and continued to serve in this position from 1988 until March 1990 when the Labor Party left the National Unity Government. After Ya'acobi failed to be elected to the Thirtenth Knesset, he was appointed by Minister for Foreign Affairs Shimon *Peres as Israel's permanent representative to the United Nations, serving in this position in 1992–96. Next he served as chairman of the board of directors of the Israel Electric Corporation until 1998, and in 2000–03 was chairman of the Ports and Railways Authority. Ya'acobi started teaching political science at Tel Aviv University in 1998, and from 2003 taught at the Interdisciplinary Center in Herzliyyah. He was a member of the Ben-Gurion Foundation, the Rabin Center, the Alterman Foundation, and served on the boards of directors of several corporations.

In addition to having written numerous books on politics and reminiscences, Ya'acobi has written three children's books, poetry, and articles in the press. Among his works are *The Government of Israel* (1982) and an autobiography, *Ḥesed ha-Zeman* (2002).

[Susan Hattis Rolef (2nd ed.)]

YA'ALEH VE-YAVO (Heb. יַעֲלֶה וְיָבֹא; "may [our remembrance] arise and come ... before Thee"), the name of the additional prayer recited on the new moon and on festivals, during the evening, morning, and afternoon *Amidah* (with the exception of Rosh Ha-Shanah and the Day of Atonement), and during the *Grace after Meals. First mentioned in the Talmud (Ber. 29b; Sof. 19:7), its style is similar to that of the early *paytanim*. The name is derived from a phrase in its opening line. Specific mention is made of the occasion on which it is said (e.g., "this day of Passover") in the body of the request for "deliverance, happiness, grace, kindness, mercy, life, and peace." According to Rashi, it is also a "supplication for Israel and for Jerusalem, and for the reinstitution of the Temple service and of the sacrifices of the day" (Rashi to Shab. 24a). For this reason the prayer is recited during the 17th benediction in the *Amidah* and the third in the Grace after Meals, which deal with those subjects. The problem as to whether its omission during the recital of either of these benedictions requires that it be repeated is answered differently according to the occasion and the festival (Sh. Ar., OḤ 424: 1). In communal worship, when in the course of this prayer the reader recites the phrases "remember us O Lord our God, thereon for good," "be mindful of us for blessing," and "save us unto life," it is customary for the congregation to respond to each with "Amen."

BIBLIOGRAPHY: E. Munk, *The World of Prayer*, 1 (1961), 150f.; Eisenstein, Dinim, 169.

YA'ALON, MOSHE (1950–), 17th chief of staff of the IDF; known by the nickname Boogie. Ya'alon was born in Israel as Moshe Smolansky. He was a member of the No'ar ha-Oved ve-ha-Lomed youth movement and joined kibbutz Gerofit. During the Yom Kippur War he fought on the southern front as part of the paratroop reserves. After the war he rejoined the army and underwent officer training. From 1974 to 1978 he commanded a platoon and company in the Naḥal brigade. In 1978 he commanded the paratroop reconnaissance unit in the Litani operation in Lebanon. In 1986 he was promoted to colonel and given command of the elite General Headquarters reconnaissance unit, while in 1990 he was given command of the paratroop brigade. Subsequent command positions included Judea and Samaria, Army Intelligence, and the Central Command. In 2000 he became deputy chief of staff and in 2002 chief of staff, serving just three years, without the customary one-year extension, against the background of his opposition to Sharon's Gaza disengagement plan. During his service as chief of staff, the IDF had to contend with the second Intifada and terrorist attacks on Israel's civilian population. During his long service he completed a B.A. in political science at Haifa University.

[Shaked Gilboa (2nd ed.)]

YAARI, ABRAHAM (1899–1966), bibliographer, historian, translator, and librarian. Yaari, brother of Yehudah *Yaari, was born in eastern Galicia and settled in Palestine in 1920. He taught at a Tel Aviv school, and worked in the Hebrew National and University Library from 1925. Beginning his literary career by publishing reviews and articles on education, Yaari later specialized in literary studies, bibliography, and the history of Jewish settlement in Palestine. He rediscovered little-known Hebrew books, especially those printed in the Oriental countries, see e.g., his *Reshimat Sifrei Ladino* (1934) and *Ha-Defus ha-Ivri be-Arẓot ha-Mizraḥ* (1936–40). He published letters, memoirs, travel descriptions from hitherto unknown manuscripts, and many bibliographies which he supplemented by comprehensive introductions.

Among Yaari's works are *Sheluḥei Ereẓ Yisrael* (1951), a comprehensive anthology concerning the emissaries of Ereẓ Israel; *Iggerot Ereẓ Yisrael* (1934, 1950^2), an anthology of letters relating to Ereẓ Israel from the Babylonian Exile to modern times; *Diglei ha-Madpisim ha-Ivriyyim* (1943), about Hebrew printers' marks; *Zikhronot Ereẓ Yisrael* (2 vols., 1947), 120 memoirs from the 17th–20th centuries in Palestine (abridged English version, *The Goodly Heritage*, 1958); *Ha-Maḥazeh ha-Ivri ha-Mekori ve-ha-Meturgam...* (1956^2), a bibliography of plays presented in Hebrew and in Hebrew translation; *Bibliografyah shel Haggadot Pesaḥ* (1960), a major work describing 2,717 different editions of the Passover *Haggadah; Toledot Ḥag Simḥat Torah* (1964), describing customs of the festival in various communities in different eras; and the posthumously published *Ha-Defus ha-Ivri be-Kushta* (1967), a history of Hebrew printing in Constantinople (Istanbul) from 1504. He also translated many writers into Hebrew and was one of the editors of the bibliographical journal *Kiryat Sefer*.

BIBLIOGRAPHY: I. Tishby, *Netivei Emunah u-Minut* (1964), 108–42; KS, 42 (1966/67), 246–51 (obituaries); N. Ben-Menaḥem, *ibid.*, 252–7 (list of Yaari's writings).

YA'ARI (Wald), ME'IR (1897–1987), ideologist and leader of *Ha-Shomer ha-Ẓa'ir and *Mapam; member of the First to Seventh Knessets. Ya'ari was born in Rzeszow, Galicia. He moved to Vienna before the outbreak of World War I, and volunteered for the Austrian army at the age of 17, serving as an officer until the end of the war. In 1919 Ya'ari began agricultural training on the estate of a Jewish landowner near Vienna. He joined one of the first groups that constituted Ha-Shomer ha-Ẓa'ir in Vienna, which at the time combined romanticism with Martin *Buber's philosophy and Gustav *Landauer's socialism. In 1920 Ya'ari settled in Palestine, living at first in Kinneret, where he participated in the construction of the Tiberias-Ẓemaḥ and Tiberias-Tabgha roads. Later he lived in Upper Bitania with a group of friends who engaged in hard physical labor. The nightly conversations there eventually evolved into the collection of essays titled *Kehilliyyatenu* ("Our Community"), describing the conflict between the romantic Zionist dreams and the harsh reality of Ereẓ Israel.

As the leading ideologist of Ha-Shomer ha-Ẓa'ir Ya'ari was largely responsible for changing it from a romantic youth movement into an indigenous political and educational body with a defined Left-wing ideological platform. For close to half a century he played a key role in forging the basic principle of "ideological collectivism," stating that the *kibbutz could not exist unless it was based on collectivism, in the economic, socio-cultural, and ideological-political spheres.

Ya'ari adhered to Ber *Borochov's doctrine of a synthesis between settlement work and class struggle, and attempted to base Mapam, established in 1948, on "an alliance between city workers and agricultural settlements." Although for many years Ya'ari, who was a Marxist, openly and emphatically supported the socialism of the Soviet Union, he denounced its injustices, and voiced his criticism of the Soviet attitude toward Soviet Jewry, and toward Zionism. Ya'ari was the first secretary general of Mapam, serving in this position from 1948 to 1971. He was first elected to the First Knesset as the leader of Mapam. By the mid-1950s, following the doctors' trials in Moscow, and Mordechai Oren's trial in Prague, he became increasingly disenchanted with Soviet socialism. After the 1967 Six-Day War he strongly supported the alignment of Mapam with the *Israel Labor Party, and in his last Knesset – the Seventh Knesset elected in 1969 – ran on the Alignment list. He supported the Alignment until 1984, when the Labor Party decided to join a National Unity Government with the Likud.

Among his writings are *Be-Meri Vikku'aḥ* ("In the Revolt of Debate," 1940); *Be-Derekh Arukah* ("The Long Road," 1947); *Ketavim* ("Writings," 1947); *Kibbutz ha-Galuyot ba-Aspaklaryah shel Yameinu* ("Ingathering of the Exiles in Our Time," 1954); *Mivḥanei Dorenu* ("Trials of Our Generation," 1957); *Be-Siman Aḥdut ve-Aẓma'ut* ("For Unity and Independence," 1968); and *Ba-Ma'avak le-Amal Meshuḥrar* ("In the Struggle for Freed Labor," 1972).

BIBLIOGRAPHY: L. Eshkol, *Mul Kitrugo shel Me'ir Ya'ari* (1960); M. Chizik (ed.), *Haguto u-Manhiguto shel Me'ir Ya'ari* (1988); D. Zayit and Y. Shamir (eds.), *Dyokano shel Manhig ke-Adam Ẓa'ir: Me'ir Ya'ari, Pirkei Ḥayyim 1897–1927* (1992); Y. Hurwitz, *Me'ir Ya'ari: Pe'ulato be-Derekh Arukah* (1994).

[Jacob Amit / Susan Hattis Rolef (2nd ed.)]

YAARI, MENAḤEM (1935–), Israeli economist. Yaari was born in Jerusalem and studied at the Hebrew University and Stanford University in California. A professor of mathematical economics at the Hebrew University, Yaari was director of its Institute for Advanced Studies between 1985 and 1992. From 1991 he was a member of Israel Academy of Sciences and Humanities and served as a vice president in 1994–95. In 1992–97 he was president of the Open University. In 1999 he became chairman of the Jerusalem Music Center Executive Committee. Yaari published papers on subjects such as consumerism under conditions of uncertainty, the allotment of resources over time, and insurance and economic justice. In 1987 he received the Israel Prize for economics. In 1994 he was awarded the Rothschild Prize in social sciences.

YAARI, YEHUDAH (1900–1982), Hebrew writer; brother of Abraham *Yaari. Born in Galicia, Yaari joined the Ha-Shomer ha-Ẓa'ir movement, and in 1920 emigrated to Palestine. He worked in Ruḥamah and Kiryat Anavim, as well as on the building of the Afulah-Nazareth highway. He became one of the founders of the first Ha-Shomer ha-Ẓa'ir kibbutz, eventually settling with the group in Bet Alfa. In 1926 he left the kibbutz and moved to Jerusalem, where he was employed at the National Library. He studied librarianship in New York (1928–30), and afterward took on a teaching post in Canada (1931–33). On his return to Palestine, he was appointed to a position in the head office of the Keren Hayesod, which he held until 1955. From 1955 to 1957 he was cultural attaché at the Israel Legation in Sweden and other Scandinavian countries. He served as director of the Department for Cultural Relations of the Foreign Ministry (1957–61) and as consul general in Amsterdam (1961–62). Yaari is one of the representative writers of the Third Aliyah, depicting the lives and struggles of those Jews who went to Ereẓ Israel after World War I. In his novels and stories he recreates the figures of the devoted young *ḥalutzim* who cleared the swamps of the Ḥuleh in the Galilee (as Yaari himself did). But his ties to Europe are still strong, and he contrasts the destruction of the *shtetl with the rise of the new settlement in Palestine. His publications include the novels *Ka-Or Yahel* (1932; *When the Candle was Burning*, 1947) *Shoresh alei Mayim* (1950), and several collections of short stories.

BIBLIOGRAPHY: A. Kariv, *Iyyunim* (1950), 204–8; S. Kremer, *Ḥillufei Mishmarot be-Sifrutenu* (1959), 206–11; Y. Keshet, *Maskiyyot* (1954), 229–39; *Sefer ha-Aliyah ha-Shelishit*, 2 (1964), 882–92. **ADD. BIBLIOGRAPHY:** D. Sadan, "*Bein ha-Mishpetayim*," in: *Karmelit*, 11–12 (1966), 75–90; Sh. Kadari, in: *Haẓofeh* (Kislev 18, 1970); A. Lifschitz, "*Havayatah shel Tekufah: Al Sippurav shel Y. Yaari*," in: *Yerushalayim*, 7–8 (1973), 223–228; N. Govrin, "*Al Yeẓirato shel Y. Yaari*," in: *Yedioth Aharonoth* (December 25, 1980); D. Laor, "Beginning Anew," in: *Modern Hebrew Literature*, 8: 1–2 (1982/83), 33–40; G. Shaked, *Ha-Sipporet ha-Ivrit*, 2 (1983), 322–35.

[Getzel Kressel]

YAD (Heb. יָד). The word *yad*, in addition to its primary meaning of "hand," has three secondary meanings in Hebrew.

(1) The pointer used by the reader to indicate the place during the reading of the Torah (see *Torah Ornaments). The *yad*, however, of which there are many artistic designs, is more than an ornament. In order to ensure that the scroll would not be touched by the bare hands because of its sanctity, the rabbis enacted that hands which touch the scroll (see *Sefer Torah) become unclean in the second degree (Yad. 3:2 and 4:6, where Rabban Johanan b. Zakkai answers the satirical question of the Sadducees about this apparently paradoxical law that the holiest of articles should render unclean). Although the laws of ritual cleanness no longer apply, the Talmud states "He who holds a *Sefer Torah* naked will be buried naked" (Shab. 14a), and as a result the *yad* was introduced.

(2) A memorial or a monument (cf. Isaiah 56:5). In II Sam. 18:18 it is stated, "Now Absalom in his lifetime had taken and set up for himself a pillar which is in the king's valley... and he called the pillar after his own name and it is called the Yad of *Absalom unto this day." On this basis the word is used in modern Hebrew for memorial. It is, however, largely applied to a memorial institution rather than to a monument. Thus the institution set up in Jerusalem to commemorate the victims of the Nazi Holocaust is called *Yad Vashem, the memorials for fallen soldiers Yad la-Banim, and for individuals, Yad Ben-Zvi, Yad ha-Rav Herzog, and so on.

(3) The *Mishneh Torah* of Maimonides is most commonly referred to as the Yad, the first word of the phrase "*yad ha-ḥazakah*" (the "mighty hand" – cf. Deut. 34:12). Maimonides did not give this name to the work. It refers to the fact that it contains 14 books, the numerical equivalent of *yad* being 14.

[Louis Isaac Rabinowitz]

YADAYIM (Heb. יָדַיִם), tractate in the order *Tohorot – Mishnah and Tosefta – dealing with the laws of washing the hands (see *Ablution) and their ritual impurity. The Mishnah contains four chapters.

The first deals with the quantity of water needed, and the vessels and water suitable for washing the hands. The second chapter discusses invalid washing of hands, the part of the hand to which the law of impurity applies, and doubtful cases of impurity of the hands. Chapters 3 and 4 deal with the *halakhot* of impure hands, in particular with the Holy Scriptures that "render the hands ritually unclean" (see *Ablution). Included in this is the question of whether the Songs of Songs and Ecclesiastes render the hands unclean. As this was one of the problems which occupied the attention of the sages "on that day" (when they appointed Eleazar b. *Azariah (3:5 in place of the *nasi* Rabban *Gamaliel), many other *halakhot* are included which have nothing to do with impurity of hands but were discussed "on that day" (4:1–4), since they were all found together in the source before Judah I *("Rabbi"). For the same reason when at the end of the tractate (4:6) a dispute is cited between the Pharisees and the Sadducees about holy writings rendering the hands impure there are added three other disputes between the Pharisees, Sadducees, and Judeo-Christians (4:7–8). As a result *Yadayim* contains valuable sources for the problem of the establishment of the biblical canon and the history of the *halakhah*.

The Tosefta contains two chapters. Chapter 1 and the beginning of chapter 2 (1–8) are parallel to chapters 1 and 2 of the Mishnah, but they include many *halakhot* not mentioned in the Mishnah and at times their order differs from that of the Mishnah. On the other hand the second part of the Tosefta (2:9–20), corresponding to chapters 3 and 4 of the Mishnah, is poorer. It contains mainly *beraitot* parallel to the Mishnah or adding a few details to it. At the end of the tractate (2:20) there are preserved two more disputes on the Second Temple period that are of great historical importance; one between the Pharisees and the Boethusians, the second between the Pharisees and the *tovelei shaharit* ("the morning bathers"; see *Ablution).

[Moshe David Herr]

YAD ḤANNAH (Heb. יַד חַנָּה), two kibbutzim in central Israel near Tūl Karm, founded as a single settlement in 1950 by Ha-Kibbutz ha-Me'uḥad. The members, immigrants from Hungary and Israel-born youth, split in 1954 into two parts. One, affiliated with the Israel Communist Party, maintains the existing village and constitutes the only communist-affiliated settlement in the country. The group remaining with Ha-Kibbutz ha-Me'uḥad built Yad Ḥannah Bet in the vicinity. Both settlements were exposed border outposts until the Six-Day *War (1967). Both kibbutzim had economies based on irrigated field and fodder crops, citrus groves, flower cultivation, and other branches. In the mid-1990s, the kibbutz affiliated with the Communists had 76 inhabitants, while the kibbutz belonging to Ha-Kibbutz ha-Me'uhad had 140. In 2002 the combined population was 117. Subsequently the kibbutz filed a request to change its status to a moshav in order to absorb new members and ensure the future of the settlement. The name commemorates Hannah *Szenes.

[Efram Orni / Shaked Gilboa (2nd ed.)]

YADIN (Sukenik), YIGAEL (1917–1984), Israeli archaeologist; second chief of staff, and politician, member of the Ninth Knesset. Born in Jerusalem, Yadin was the son of the archaeologist Eliezer Lipa *Sukenik. He went to the Hebrew Gymnasium in Jerusalem, and at the age of 15 joined the Haganah. In 1935 he started studying archaeology, history, and Arabic at the Hebrew University of Jerusalem. Following the outbreak of the Arab disturbances in 1936, Yadin left his studies in favor of active military service. He was first engaged in field units, and later in command and training. In 1939 he was appointed as Yitzhak *Sadeh's adjutant. In 1943 he was appointed head of the Operations Section in the Haganah General Staff. Following disagreements with Sadeh, he returned to his studies, receiving his M.A. in 1945. In 1947, not long before the UN approval of the partition plan of Palestine, he was recalled by David *Ben-Gurion for active military service, filling a variety of positions in the course of the War of Independence. When Ya'akov *Dori fell ill, Yadin served as acting chief of staff. In this period he objected to the plan to capture the Latrun area, and Ben-Gurion's decision to disband the *Palmaḥ. Yadin served as the military advisor to the Israeli delegation to the armistice talks with Egypt in Rhodes, and participated in the talks that followed in Lausanne. In 1949, following Dori's retirement, Yadin received the rank of lieutenant general, and was appointed as Israel's second chief of staff. As chief of staff he reorganized the IDF and established the standing army, compulsory military service, and the reserves system. In December 1952, at the age of 35, he resigned, as a result of differences of opinion with Ben-Gurion over cuts in the IDF budget. He then devoted himself to scientific work at the Hebrew University in the field of archaeology and research into Israeli antiquities. He became a lecturer at the Hebrew University in 1953, and received his Ph.D. in 1955 for a thesis on the "War of the Sons of Light against the Sons of Darkness," one of the *Dead Sea Scrolls. For this study Yadin received the 1956 Israel Prize for Jewish studies. In 1955 he was appointed lecturer in archeology at the Hebrew University and ran the excavations at *Hazor, which continued from 1955 to 1958, and again in 1968. His other famous excavations were in the Qumran caves in the Judean Desert in 1960–61, at *Masada in 1963–65, and at Megiddo in 1966–67. He was appointed professor in 1963. In his excavations Yadin employed thousands of volunteers from Israel and abroad and trained a new generation of young archaeologists in Israel. He also helped bring archaeology to the general public and was a popular lecturer and broadcaster. He gained international acclaim for his historical-philological decoding and interpretations of the Dead Sea and Judean Desert scrolls. Upon his initiative, the Shrine of the Book was built at the Israel Museum in Jerusalem, to house the scrolls. In 1968 Yadin became editor of the archaeological journal *Kadmoniot*. Yadin often cast new light on basic problems of the biblical, Second Temple, mishnaic, and talmudic periods, not only through the excavations themselves, but through an original approach that brought the actual artifacts into a general cultural context, with special reference to contemporary literary evidence. Yadin was critical of Moshe *Dayan's private archaeological exploits and collection of antiques.

On the eve of the Six-Day War, Yadin served as military advisor to Prime Minister and Minister of Defense Levi *Eshkol, until Dayan was appointed minister of defense. Following the Yom Kippur War, Yadin was appointed one of the five members of the Agranat Commission established to inquire into the events and developments leading up to the war. In the late 1950s he headed a movement that called for reform of Israel's electoral system. However until 1976 he rejected all offers to enter the political arena. In that year, against the background of popular dissatisfaction with the ruling Labor Alignment, and growing protest, he established the *Democratic Movement for Change (DMC), together with Prof. Amnon *Rubinstein, Shmuel *Tamir, Me'ir *Amit, and others. The DMC ran in the elections to the Ninth Knesset in 1977, receiving an impressive 15 seats. However, even though the DMC joined the new government established by Menaḥem *Begin, and Yadin was appointed deputy prime minister, Begin had a majority in the Knesset without it, and soon the new party disintegrated. Yadin remained in the government until Begin formed his new government in August 1981 after the elections to the Tenth Knesset, but had little influence, and lost much of his popularity. From September 1978 to March 1981 he belonged to a parliamentary group called the Democratic Movement, and after this group ceased to exist remained a single MK, without any formal status. In August 1981 he retired from politics to return to academic life until his death in 1984.

Among his writings are *Ha-Megillot ha-Genuzot mi-Midbar Yehudah* ("The Hidden Scrolls from the Desert of Judea," 1957); with Chaim Rabin, *Aspects of the Dead Sea Scrolls* (1958); *Military and Archeological Aspects of the Conquest of Canaan in the Book of Joshua* (1960); *The Scroll of the War of the Sons of Light against the Sons of Darkness* (1962); *The Art of Warfare in Biblical Lands in the Light of Archaeological Study* (1963); *Apocrypha Ecclesiasticus: The Ben Sira Scroll from Masada*, with introduction, emendations, and commentary (1965); *Masada: Herod's Fortress and the Zealots' Last Stand* (1966); *Bar Kokhba: The Rediscovery of the Legendary Hero of the Second Jewish Revolt Against Rome* (1971); *Hazor, the Rediscovery of a Great Citadel of the Bible* (1975); *The Temple Scroll; the Hidden Law of the Dead Sea Sect* (1985); and *Investigations of Beth Shean: The Early Iron Age Strata* (1986). Among works he edited are *Jerusalem Revealed: The Archeology in the Holy City 1968–1974* (1975), and *The Documents from the Bar Kokhba Period in the Cave of Letters: Hebrew, Aramaic and Nabatean-Aramaic Papyri* (2002).

Yigael Yadin's brother YOSEF (1920–2001) was one of the founders of the *Cameri Theater in Tel Aviv and participated in numerous plays and films. He was awarded the Israel Prize for screen and theater arts in 1991.

BIBLIOGRAPHY: *Masada: The Yigael Yadin Excavations. Final Reports* (1989–99); N. Asher Silberman, *A Prophet from Amongst You: The Life of Yigael Yadin: Soldier, Scholar, and Myth Maker of Modern Israel* (1993).

YADLIN, AHARON (1926–), Israeli politician. Yadlin was born in Ben Shemen, Israel. He became a member of kibbutz Ḥaẓerim, of which he was general secretary. From 1950 to 1952 he was a member of the Executive Council of the *Histadrut and from 1955 to 1957 served as principal of Bet Berl, the Labor Party's educational center. Yadlin was elected to the Fifth Knesset in 1961 and re-elected through the Ninth Knesset, serving as deputy minister of education from 1966 to 1972. In the latter year he was elected secretary of the Israel Labor Party, and in 1974 was appointed minister of education and culture, retaining the office until the general election of May 1977 when the Alignment was defeated. He was reelected to the Ninth Knesset, but in January 1979 resigned, in accordance with a kibbutz decision on the rotation of Knesset members, and returned to his kibbutz. After his retirement he served as chairman of the Prime Minister's Fund for Hebrew Writers and as chairman of the Postal and Philatelic Museum at the Eretz Israel Museum.

YAD MORDEKHAI (Heb. יַד מָרְדְּכַי), kibbutz in southern Israel, between Ashkelon and Gaza, affiliated with Kibbutz Arẓi, Ha-Shomer ha-Ẓa'ir. Yad Mordekhai was founded by a group from Poland in 1943, during the Nazi Holocaust in Europe, in a drive to enlarge Jewish settlement in Ereẓ Israel toward the south and Negev. In the *War of Independence (1948), the invading Egyptian army, in its advance along the coastal highway, concentrated its tank, artillery, and aircraft forces in an attack on the kibbutz, but was held at bay by the sparse number of settlers for six days. The village was by then reduced to ruins and the survivors, carrying their wounded, succeeded in slipping through the ring of siege and reaching Jewish positions miles away (May 1948). The site was retaken in October 1948. The kibbutz was rebuilt on a far larger scale, but still occupied a border position (close to the Gaza Strip) until the *Six-Day War in 1967. In 2002 the population was 699. The economy was based on farming and the kibbutz also marketed honey and manufactured computerized irrigation systems as well as operating a shopping center. The kibbutz maintains a museum of the *Holocaust and ghetto resistance. A large bronze statue in memory of the ghetto fighters and a reconstruction of the 1948 battle site are located there. The name commemorates Mordecai *Anielewicz.

WEBSITE: www.yadmor.org.il.

[Efraim Orni]

YAD VASHEM (The Holocaust Martyrs' and Heroes' Remembrance Authority), Israel's and the Jewish people's national Holocaust memorial institution. The name is taken from Isaiah 56:5, "And I will give them in my house and within my walls a memorial and a name (a *Yad Vashem*)… that shall not be cut off." Yad Vashem is dedicated to perpetuating the memory of the victims of the *Holocaust, and to research, documentation, publication, and education. Plans for a project for a lasting remembrance began during World War II, initiated by Mordechai Shenhavi, and were approved at the first post-war meeting of the General Zionist Council (London, 1945) whereby an institution was set up, headed by the *Va'ad Le'ummi. After the creation of the State of Israel, the minister of education and culture, Ben-Zion *Dinur, proposed the setting up of a Remembrance Authority in Jerusalem, on Har Hazikaron (the Mount of Remembrance), for the "six million members of the Jewish people who died a martyrs' death at the hands of the Nazis and their collaborators." The task of Yad Vashem is "to gather in material regarding all those Jewish people who laid down their lives, who fought and rebelled against the Nazi enemy and their collaborators, and to perpetuate their memory and that of the communities, organizations, and institutions which were destroyed because they were Jewish…"

The complex that makes up Yad Vashem extends over 50 acres. It includes the Holocaust History Museum and Hall of Names, Holocaust Art Museum, Exhibitions Pavilion, Visual Center, Learning Center, synagogue, unique outdoor monuments, and the most important repository of information on the Holocaust in the world. At its height, the annual number of visitors to Yad Vashem has surpassed two million people.

A decade in the making, the new Holocaust History Museum combines the best of Yad Vashem's expertise, resources, and state-of-the-art exhibits to take Holocaust remembrance well into the 21st century. The new Holocaust History Museum occupies over 4,200 square meters, mainly underground. Both multidisciplinary and interdisciplinary, it presents the story of the Shoah from a unique Jewish perspective, emphasizing the experiences of the individual victims through original artifacts, survivor testimonies, and personal possessions. Its 180-meter–long linear structure in the form of a spike cuts through the mountain with its uppermost edge – a skylight – protruding through the mountain ridge. Galleries portraying the complexity of the Jewish situation during those terrible years branch off this spike-like shaft, and the exit emerges dramatically out of the mountainside, affording a view of the valley below. Unique settings, spaces with varying heights, and different degrees of light accentuate focal points of the unfolding narrative. The museum building was designed by renowned Israeli architect Moshe Safdie. The display was designed by Dorit Harel.

At the end of the Museum's historical narrative is the Hall of Names – a repository for the "Pages of Testimony" commemorating the names and biographic details of Jews who perished during the Holocaust. Pages of Testimony are filled out by family members, friends, or neighbors, many of them survivors of the Holocaust, and serve as symbolic "*maẓevot*" or "tombstones" for their loved ones. On these special acid-free pages the following are inscribed in full: the name of the victim, his or her date and place of birth, the place of residence before the war, the profession, the parents' and spouses' names, and where and when they perished during the Holocaust. A photograph is attached when available. The Pages of Testimony are preserved in special "Yizkor files," classified according to the Hebrew alphabet by the family name and the first name of the victim. The Pages of Testimony have now been digitized and are available online in the Central Database of Shoah Victims' Names, which also includes names from historical documentation and other sources. The number of Jews commemorated in the database to date is close to 3.1 million.

The Hall of Remembrance is a solemn tent-like structure that allows visitors to pay their respects to the memories of the martyred dead. On the floor are the names of some of the Nazi murder sites throughout Europe, and in front of the memorial flame lies a crypt containing ashes of victims. The Hall of Remembrance was designed by architect Aryeh Elhanani.

The Valley of the Communities is a massive outdoor monument to the Jewish communities that were destroyed or damaged in World War II. Seen from the floor of this unique site, the rock walls rise up to a height of some 30 feet or more, and are engraved with the names of more than 5,000 communities, symbolically embedded forever in the very bedrock of Israel. The Valley itself extends over two and a half acres, and is a labyrinth of courtyards and walls, of openings and dead ends arranged to roughly correspond to the geographic arrangement of the map of Europe and North Africa. The Valley of the Communities was designed by Israeli architects Dan Zur and Lippa Yahalom.

The Children's Memorial, hollowed out from an underground cavern, is a tribute to the approximately 1.5 million Jewish children who perished during the Holocaust. Memorial candles, a customary Jewish tradition to remember the dead, are reflected infinitely in a dark and somber space, creating the impression of millions of stars shining in the firmament. The names of murdered children, their ages, and countries of origin can be heard in the background. The Children's Memorial was designed by Moshe Safdie.

The Memorial to the Deportees is an original cattle-car, appropriated by the German Railway authorities and given to Yad Vashem by the Polish authorities. It stands on an iron track which juts out from the slopes of Yad Vashem into the Judean hillside.

Other features are the Avenue and Garden of the Righteous Among the Nations, which honor those non-Jews who risked their lives to help the persecuted Jews in the Holocaust, the Monument to the Jewish Soldiers, the Partisans' Panorama, and the sculpture garden.

The Yad Vashem Archives is the largest and most comprehensive repository of documentary material on the Holocaust in the world. In its ongoing work collecting documentary materials, it has accumulated approximately 68,000,000 documentary pages on the Holocaust to date, close to 300,000 still photographs, as well as thousands of audio and videotaped testimonies of survivors. Yad Vashem's library has the world's most comprehensive collection of books on the Holocaust. It holds more than 112,000 titles in 52 languages, and thousands of periodicals.

The International School for Holocaust Studies is the only school of its kind in the world. With 17 classrooms, a modern multimedia center, resource and pedagogical center, an auditorium, and more than 100 educators on its staff, the school caters annually to more than 100,000 students and youth, 50,000 soldiers, and thousands of educators from Israel and around the world. Courses for teachers are offered in eight languages other than Hebrew, and the school also sends its professional staff around the world for the purpose of Holocaust education. In addition, the school arranges symposia and offers online teaching courses, as well as developing a variety of educational programs and study aids on the Holocaust. The educational rationale of the School places a strong emphasis on Jewish life before the war, daily life of Jews during the Holocaust, and the return to life of Holocaust survivors. Yad Vashem age-appropriate educational materials are multidisciplinary, multidirectional, and multifaceted and are available in many languages both in print and online.

In 1963, Yad Vashem embarked upon a worldwide project to grant the title of Righteous Among the Nations to non-Jews who risked their lives to save Jews during the Holocaust, and did not precondition such aid by any reward or compensation. To this end, Yad Vashem set up a public commission headed by a retired Supreme Court justice, which is responsible for granting the title. The commission is guided by certain criteria, and meticulously studies all pertinent documentation, including primary evidence by survivors and other eyewitnesses before reaching its decision. As of January 2006, 21,310 people had been recognized as Righteous Among the Nations. A person thus recognized is awarded a specially minted medal bearing his/her name, a certificate of honor, and the privilege of his/her name being added on the Righteous Wall of Honor in the Garden of the Righteous Among the Nations. An amendment to the Yad Vashem Law stipulates that any Righteous is entitled, on request, to receive honorary citizenship.

The International Institute for Holocaust Research plans and carries out often groundbreaking research projects, organizes international seminars and conferences, coordinates joint projects with far-flung research institutes, and hosts research fellows from Israel and around the world. Research publications include the annual journal *Yad Vashem Studies*, since 1957, and a series on Jewish communities in Europe under the title *Pinkasei ha-Kehillot* ("Encyclopedia of the Communities"). Through its Publications Department, Yad Vashem publishes approximately 40 books in Hebrew and English annually, including research publications, documents, diaries, and memoirs. Yad Vashem's landmark publications include *Documents on the Holocaust* (1981), *The Encyclopedia of the Holocaust* (a joint publication, 1990), and Yad Vashem's international conference proceedings, the first of which discussed rescue attempts during the Holocaust (1968). Recent important publications include *The Encyclopedia of the Righteous Among the Nations* (six volumes through 2006), *The Auschwitz Album, A Comprehensive History of the Holocaust* (11 volumes to date in Hebrew; the whole series is being published in English in cooperation with the University of Nebraska), the Search and Research series, *Last Letters from the Holocaust*, and *The Wolfsberg Machzor 5705*. Yad Vashem also issues a quarterly magazine in Hebrew and English.

Yad Vashem's website, www.yadvashem.org, contains extensive online resources about the Holocaust, including thousands of photos, documents, testimonies, and artifacts as well as online exhibitions, classroom activities, commemorative ceremonies, and lesson plans. In addition, the Central Database of Shoah Victims' Names provides online access to the names and biographical details of millions of Holocaust victims.

The official State ceremony opening Holocaust Martyrs' and Heroes' Remembrance Day, on 27 Nisan, is held at Yad Vashem, attended by the president and prime minister of Israel, government ministers, Holocaust survivors, and thousands of members of the public.

Yad Vashem is the most visited site in Israel after the Western Wall. Many hundreds of official visitors of the State come to Yad Vashem each year, and it is protocol for all visiting foreign ministers, prime ministers, and heads of state to include Yad Vashem in their itinerary. On March 23, 2000, Pope John Paul II paid a historic visit to Yad Vashem and spoke of the imperative to remember the Holocaust.

Ben-Zion Dinur and Aryeh L. Kubovy were respectively first chairman of the Yad Vashem Directorate and first chairman of the Yad Vashem Council. Subsequently, Katriel Katz, Gideon *Hausner, Yosef *Burg, and Prof. Szewach Weiss have been chairmen of the Council and Yitzhak *Arad (1972–93) and Avner *Shalev (1993–), chairmen of the Directorate.

BIBLIOGRAPHY: Y. Weitz, "Shaping the Memory of the Holocaust in Israeli Society of the 1950s," in: *Major Changes within the Jewish People in the Wake of the Holocaust: Proceedings of the Ninth Yad Vashem International Historical Conference* (1996), 497–516; J.E. Young, "Yad Vashem: Israel's Memorial Authority," in: *The Texture of Memory: Holocaust Memorials and Their Meaning* (1993), 243–61; M. Brog, "'The Memory of a Dream is a Blessing': Mordechai Shenhavi and Initial Holocaust Commemoration Ideas in Palestine, 1942–1945," in: *Yad Vashem Studies*, 30 (2002), 297–336; B. Gutterman and A. Shalev (eds.), "To Bear Witness: Holocaust Remembrance at Yad Vashem" (2005); R. Stauber, *Lesson for This Generation; Holocaust and Heroism in Israeli Public Discourse in the 1950s* (Heb., 2000).

YAGUPSKY, MÁXIMO (1906–1996), Argentinean Jewish intellectual, community leader, and teacher. He was born in La Capilla, one of the Jewish agricultural colonies administrated by ICA, in the province of Entre Ríos, Argentina, to parents who were immigrants from Bessarabia. He started his general and Jewish studies in the local Jewish school in the colony and later studied in public schools. He continued studying Jewish subjects with his father and with a local rabbi. He was a teacher in Buenos Aires in Jewish schools of the Cursos Religiosos network maintained by the Congregación Israelita and ICA and in the 1930s was supervisor of the schools of this network in the provinces. Appearing in the local Jewish press, his articles expressed a Jewish national and Zionist position. Yagupsky was director of the Editorial Israel which published many Jewish books in Spanish in the 1940s and in the 1950s. From 1946 to 1948 he directed the Latin American Department of the American Jewish Committee in New York and in 1948 he opened a branch of this institution in Buenos Aires and acted as its director until 1961. From then and until 1968 he was the director of the American Jewish Committee in Israel. In that year he returned to Buenos Aires.

Yagupsky translated the *siddur* and the Torah into Spanish. He published *Soliloquios de un judío* ("Monologues of a Jew," 1986). In the book *Conversaciones con un judío* ("Conversations with a Jew," 1977) edited by Mario Diament, Yagupsky shared his thoughts and memories. He edited the journals *Comentario* ("Commentary") in Buenos Aires and *Amot* in Tel Aviv. He was also active in Jewish journals in Spanish, Hebrew, Yiddish, and English. In 1988 he received the Prize for Intellectual Merit of the Latin American Jewish Congress.

[Efraim Zadoff (2nd ed.)]

YAGUR (Heb. יָגוּר), kibbutz in northern Israel, in the Zebulun Valley, 7 mi. (11 km.) S.E. of Haifa, affiliated with Ha-Kibbutz ha-Me'uḥad. Yagur was founded in 1922 by the "Aḥavah" group of *Gedud ha-Avodah ("labor legion"), whose members came to the country with the Third *Aliyah. Yagur soon became the largest kibbutz in the country. In addition to developing mixed, intensive farming and industry, it provided a large number of laborers for the Haifa port, and the Haifa industrial zone. In the 1936–39 Arab riots, Yagur suffered from repeated attacks. In June 1946 the kibbutz was subjected to a severe arms search by the British Army. After the *Haganah's central arms cache was discovered there, many members were taken to detention camps. In 1970 Yagur had 1,150 inhabitants. In the mid-1990s the population was approximately 1,390, but by the end of 2002 it had dropped to 1,080. Yagur is considered a wealthy kibbutz. It operated a packaging plant in partnership with American National Can, a kitchen cabinet plant, a large plant nursery, a TV studio, a theme park and activity center for children. Yagur's farming branches were field crops, orchards, dairy cattle, and poultry and included the manufacture of cooking and table oil. Inside the kibbutz is a disco club attracting people from all over the area. Yagur also ran a vocational training school for alternative medicine as well as several cultural institutions. The name Yagur is mentioned in Joshua 15:21, in reference to a different site.

WEBSITE: www.yagur.com.

[Efraim Orni / Shaked Gilboa (2nd ed.)]

YAḤAD (Heb. יַחַד; "union" or "unity"). This term is used in the Bible most often adverbially in the sense of "together." In some of the *Dead Sea Scrolls it appears as a designation of the group usually identified as the *Qumran sect or community. The Qumran *Community Rule is entitled the "Rule [*serekh*] of the *yaḥad*," and the members of its community are called "men of the *yaḥad*" (1QS 6:21, etc.; possibly also CD 20:32). Knowledge of this community must be based principally on those Dead Sea Scrolls which can reasonably be recognized as its own documents, along with such evidence from the excavations at Khirbet Qumran as can be correlated with the contents of these documents. The identification of the word *yaḥad* on an ostracon discovered in 1996 at Qumran, and which would have confirmed its location at Qumran, has been challenged.

Origin and Organization

The origins of the *yaḥad* appear to be described in the *Damascus Document, which suggests a number of stages (1:3–12). First, a remnant of Israel was allowed by God to survive the Babylonian exile; then these were "visited" by God and a "seedling" (*shoresh matta'at*) sprouted "to possess the land." After 20 years of "groping the way," God raised for them a "*Teacher of Righteousness" to "guide them in the way of his heart." It is this last stage, under the leadership of the "Teacher," that in the opinion of most scholars accords with the formation of the *yaḥad*. The earlier stages appear to represent a wider movement that, after the emergence of the *yaḥad*, no doubt continued, since the Damascus Document (1:13–2:1) suggests that the Teacher's appearance generated conflict with a group led by the "Spouter of Lies" – presumably a polemical reference to a rival leader within the existing group. The death of the *moreh ha-yaḥid* (perhaps to be emended to *moreh ha-yaḥad*) is mentioned in CD 20:14. In the Habakkuk **pesher*, no doubt a product of the *yaḥad*, the "Liar" is mentioned also, though the Teacher is opposed mainly by a "Wicked Priest," a figure thought to be a national leader but absent from the Damascus Document. Because of this and other discrepancies between the accounts, it is impossible to decide why the *yaḥad* came into existence. Broadly speaking, two possibilities exist: that it consisted originally of the followers of a "Teacher" who split with the leadership of an existing movement; or that the Teacher was the founder of a new movement that separated from the rest of Judaism and later assumed different forms, including the *yaḥad*. On the former view, inner-sectarian motives may have been instrumental in the formation of the *yaḥad* – such as the Teacher's claim to be an eschatological leader (see CD 6:11), in which case the existing movement arose for reasons (such as differences over calendar and purity laws) that the *yaḥad* inherited in addition to its own distinct ideology. On the latter view, the *yaḥad* is more probably a penitential movement, reacting to the conviction that divine anger was about to befall Israel. Further possible clues might lie in the *Thanksgiving Hymns (*Hodayot*), if they could be read autobiographically as compositions of the Teacher, for they represent the author as the persecuted founder of a community, articulating a profound belief in his existential, and probably eschatological, redemption and fellowship with the heavenly beings. The Community Rule itself does not mention the teacher, but contains passages (cols. 8–9) that in the opinion of many scholars, represent the original aims and organization of the *yaḥad*. On this view, a nucleus of 15 men – three priests and 12 laymen – formed its core. Among the convictions held in these passages is that the land cannot be atoned for by the existing sacrificial cult, which is corrupt; instead a human sanctuary, containing an inner, priestly "holy of holies" must fulfill this function, without sacrifice, by living lives of utter holiness. To this end the members were to segregate from the "sinful" and make a "way in the wilderness" (Isa. 40:3) in order to study the law. This is often interpreted as entailing a physical withdrawal to the Judean Desert, to the west shore of the Dead Sea.

That the *yaḥad* evolved over its history has long been deduced by scholars on the basis of analysis of the Community Rule, and has been confirmed by the recovery from Cave 4 of editions differing from the Cave 1 text. For example, the "men of the *yaḥad*" in 1QS 5:1 are "men of the Torah" in 4QSe 1:1, while the Cave 4 texts refer only to the authority of the "congregation," but in 1QS, the "sons of Zadok" usually (but not always) hold sway. In addition, the "discourse on the two spirits" in 1QS 3–4 is absent from many of the Cave 4 editions. Reconstructing the growth of this document is complicated by the fact that while literary and structural considerations suggest that the Cave 1 version is the latest, it seems palaeographically to be the earliest. However, the disciplinary rules in 1QS 5–7 appear in all editions and are thus part of the earliest organization of the *yaḥad*, and in many respects they agree with a similar code in the Cave 4 versions of the Damascus Document. There were two stages in the novitiate, each lasting one year. Those who completed the first year deposited their private property with the community treasurer, but not until the completion of the second year, if the candidate made the grade, was it merged with the common stock. Anyone who "knowingly deceived with regard to property" was excommunicated for one year from "the purity of the many" and had his rations reduced by one quarter. Longer or shorter terms of this excommunication from sharing in the solemn acts of fellowship, together with reductions of rations for a stated period, were the customary penalties for breaches of discipline. For more heinous offenses complete expulsion was laid down. "The many" (*ha-rabbim*) is the designation of the general membership of the community, while the spiritual leader is called *maskil* (both terms appear in Daniel 11 and 12). The whole membership met in assembly from time to time. Rules of precedence were laid down with regard to the taking of their seats – first the priests, then the elders, then the others, each in his position – and standing orders were strictly enforced. Anyone who wished to speak might stand up and say, "I have a word to say to 'the many,'" and if he received permission he might speak. Speaking out of turn, interrupting, or behaving indecorously during the session received appropriate punishment.

Religious Practice

The *yaḥad* appears to have been a celibate, male group. Communal meals, worship, and consultation were regular features of daily life. Such activities could be carried out by any group of ten, provided one of them was a priest. Among other things, it was the priest's privilege to say grace before he and his companions partook of a communal meal. In each group of ten, there was always one (though not always the same one) engaged in the reading and exposition of the Law. The night was divided into three watches, and during each watch one-third of the membership stayed awake to listen to the reading and exposition and to voice the appointed blessings. The community's abstention from common worship at the Temple was primarily due to their belief that such worship was unacceptable to God under the prevailing establishment; but participation would have in any case been difficult since they observed as a matter of religious duty the *calendar prescribed in the Book of Jubilees and not the lunisolar calendar by which the sacred years in the Temple were reckoned. The *yaḥad* attached great importance to ceremonial washing; the purificatory ablutions which the levitical law prescribes for the priests appear to have been obligatory for all the members. They were not merely initiatory but were performed frequently. Yet it is made clear that ceremonial washing in itself had no cleansing efficacy if a person's heart was not right with God. The washing of the body was acceptable only if it was the outward sign of inward purity.

Eschatological Expectations

Beliefs about the future are not entirely consistent among the writings of the *yaḥad*, though it certainly believed, whether prompted by scripture or calculation or both, in an imminent divine judgment. The members of the community came to regard themselves not merely as the remnant of Israel but as on one side of a dualistic universe, in which light and darkness (or truth and falsehood) were balanced and opposing forces. Each side comprised both angelic and human beings, and was led by its respective heavenly "prince," and light would finally conquer darkness. Such a developed dualistic doctrine is found only in texts associated with the *yaḥad*, though dualistic and predestinarian tendencies are also present in the Damascus Document. Zoroastrian influence on this developed dualism is probable. Yet more traditional, Jewish expectations of the future are represented by belief in the coming of a prophet and the "anointed ones of Aaron and Israel" (1QS 9:11). In that new age the anointed priest would be paramount, the lay Messiah being subordinate to him (as in Ezek. 44:3ff.). The Davidic Messiah may be the "star ... out of Jacob" (Num. 24:17) to whom reference is made in a number of Qumran documents (CD 7:19; 4Q *Testimonia*; 1QM 11:6), in which case he should be the commander of the Children of Light (see *Sons of *Light) in their end-time struggle against the children of Darkness (depicted in the *War Scroll), though strangely he does not appear, only his shield. In this depiction of this final struggle, which can be assigned to the *yaḥad*, dualistic and nationalistic perspectives are combined, with the "children of Light" taking on the identity of Israel, and the "children of Darkness" led by the Kittim, almost certainly the Romans. The war would end in the defeat of the nations and victory for "Israel" but would also represent light vanquishing darkness and evil disappearing forever. That cosmic, national, and sectarian perspectives can be merged into a single coherent expectation is hard to imagine, but the War Scroll (in its various editions) may represent an attempt to do just that.

Suggested Identifications

The members of the *yaḥad* – and those of its parent movement – have been identified at one time or another with Essenes, Zealots, Sicarii, Pharisees, Sadducees, Jewish Christians, and Karaites. The majority verdict favors the Essene identification. Qumran fits the elder Pliny's description of the Essene community, but Josephus and Philo suggest a wider dispersal, which fits better the community of the Damascus Document. There are impressive similarities between the evidence of the Qumran texts and the first-century accounts of the Essenes; yet there are points of difference too. The identification of the community with the Zealots was once supported by several scholars, and Hippolytus says that one branch of the Essenes was known as Zealots (Philosophumena 9:21). Some scrolls possibly originating at Qumran were found at Masada. Qumran itself was apparently attacked by the Romans during the war of 66–70; and the War Scroll envisages a battle that involved Rome. But there are links with Pharisees in the extension of levitical purity beyond the priesthood and in devotion to Torah observance, while connections with Sadducees might be seen in some of the *halakhah* preserved among the Scrolls. It remains possible that the *yaḥad* was none of these, but an otherwise unknown sect among many movements that may have arisen during one of the most turbulent religious and political eras in Jewish history, between the Maccabean revolt and the war with Rome.

ADD. BIBLIOGRAPHY: S. Talmon, "The Sectarian YXD – A Biblical Noun," in: VT, 3 (1953), 133–40; A.R.C. Leaney, *The Rule of Qumran and Its Meaning* (1966); S. Metso, *The Textual Development of the Qumran Community Rule* (1997); J.H. Charlesworth (ed.), *The Rule of the Community and Related Documents* (1994); F.M. Cross and E. Eshel, "Ostraca from Khirbet Qumran," in: IEJ, 47 (1997), 17–28; A. Yardeni, "A Draft of a Deed on an Ostracon from Khirbet Qumran," in: IEJ, 47 (1997), 233–37; P.R. Davies, *Behind the Essenes* (1987), 87–105; idem, *Sects and Scrolls* (1966), 139–50.

[Frederick Fyvie Bruce / Philip R. Davies (2nd ed.)]

YAHIL (Hoffmann), CHAIM (1905–1974), Israeli diplomat and Zionist. Yahil was born in Wallachisch Meseritsch, Austro-Hungary (later Czechoslovakia), and founded there the local branch of the Zionist youth movement, Blau-Weiss, and later became a member of the movement's national council in Czechoslovakia.

He immigrated to Ereẓ Israel in 1929, but later returned to Europe where he received his Ph.D. in political science, in Vienna. He then engaged in social and Zionist activity in Prague, returning to Ereẓ Israel in 1939.

During World War II he was a member of the Haifa and, subsequently, Tel Aviv Labor Councils. In 1945 he was among the first Palestinian emissaries to liberated Europe, as director of the Palestinian Relief Unit under the auspices of UNRRA, sponsored by the Jewish Agency. In this connection he was involved in all activities concerning Jewish Displaced Persons, their organization, education and movements into Germany by *Beriḥah and from Germany by *Aliyah Bet.*

Upon the establishment of the State of Israel he was accredited to the Occupying Power as the first Israeli Consul in Munich. From 1951 he was a member of the Israeli Foreign Service, serving successively as director of information, deputy-director of the Reparations Mission to Germany, ambassador to Scandinavia, and director-general of the Israeli Foreign Ministry (1960–64). Subsequently, he established and headed the Diaspora Center, a joint enterprise of the Israeli Government and Jewish Agency (1965–68) which enabled him to foster Israeli-Diaspora relations. He was appointed the first chairman of the Israel Broadcasting Authority (1965–72). He was the *Encyclopaedia Judaica* divisional editor for contemporary Jewry.

During his term of office relations with Africa were developed and technical cooperation with developing countries institutionalized. Yahil was a firm believer in socialism, but after a life-long association with the Labor Zionist party, he left it in 1972, becoming a founding member and leader of the Land of Israel Movement, which advocated an undivided Israel.

His first work *Trager der Verwirklichung, Die Zionistische Arbeiterschaft im Aufbau* (1938) was published under his original name Chaijim Hoffmann; he also published *Scandinavian Socialism in its Implementations* (Hebrew, 1966). After his death there appeared *Hazon U-Ma'avak* (1977), a selection of articles he wrote between 1965 and 1974, and *Israel's Foreign Relations*, Vols. I and II (1976), jointly with Meron Medzini.

YAH RIBBON OLAM (Aram. יָהּ רִבּוֹן עָלַם; "God, master of the universe"), one of the most popular Sabbath table hymns (*zemirot). The hymn, written in Aramaic, was composed by the 16th-century kabbalist poet, Israel b. Moses *Najara ("Israel" is the acrostic of the five verses), and is based on Daniel 3:32–33. It was first published in a second and enlarged edition of his *Zemirot Yisrael* (Venice, 1600). The hymn, which has been set to innumerable tunes, contains no allusion to the Sabbath. It is a song of praise to the "King of Kings," who rules the world in His endless power and glory. After describing the wonders of God's creation, the poem concludes with a prayer that God may redeem Israel and restore Jerusalem, "the city of beauty."

YAHRZEIT (Yid.; Ger. **Jahrzeit**; lit. "year time," i.e., anniversary), the anniversary of a death. For the determining of the *yahrzeit*, see *Mourning. The commemoration of the *yahrzeit* (on the Hebrew date of the anniversary) is observed both for outstanding individuals and for parents; though some extend it to the other five close relatives for whom mourning is enjoined, brother and sister, son and daughter, and spouse. With regard to the former, *Rashi finds authority for it as early as the amoraic period. He quotes from a geonic responsum on the *riglei* ("festivals"), there mentioned as an amoraic institution: "the anniversary of the death of a great man was established in his honor, and when that day arrives, all the scholars in the region assemble and visit his grave with the ordinary people, and hold a ceremony there" (to Yev. 122a). The only *yahrzeits* which occur in the calendar in one way or another are the 7th of *Adar, the traditional date of the death of Moses (though observed only by minor liturgical changes and as the most common date for the annual banquet of the *ḥevra kaddisha*), *Lag ba-Omer, the traditional date of death of Simeon b. Yoḥai (observed by popular pilgrimages to his grave at Meron); and the 3rd of Tishri, the Fast of Gedaliah (see *Fasts and Fasting), which is stated to be the day "on which Gedaliah b. Ahikam was murdered" (RH 18b; this was not observed as a *yahrzeit* but for its historical implications). The only biblical worthy whose day of death is recorded is Aaron (Num. 33:38), but the day is not commemorated. The Ḥasidim commemorate the *yahrzeit* of their respective dynastic leaders, but the commemoration takes a joyous form as the day on which he was translated on high. In recent times annual commemorations of such national figures as Herzl, Bialik, Rabbi A.I. *Kook, Z. *Jabotinsky, and past presidents of the State of Israel have been instituted.

Detailed regulations have been laid down for the observance of family *yahrzeits*. Where he is able to do so, the *yahrzeit*, as the person observing it is also called, conducts the weekday service, and even if not, recites **Kaddish*. If the Torah is read on that day, he is called to the reading of the Torah; otherwise, he is called on the preceding Sabbath. A 24-hour memorial candle is lit for that day, as a symbol of the verse "the soul of man is the lamp of God" (Prov. 20:27). Fasting is recommended as an act of piety (Isserles, YD 402:12), but is not commonly observed.

The first known authority to employ the word *yahrzeit* was *Isaac of Tyrnau in his *Minhagim* book, and he is followed by Mordecai Jaffe (*Levush Tekhelet*, no. 133). Among the Sephardim the observance is called *naḥalah*, but so widespread is the use of the word *yahrzeit* that despite the fact that it is Yiddish, it is often found in Sephardi religious works. Filial piety has made the *yahrzeit* one of the most widely held observances in Judaism. Even in small communities where there is difficulty in assembling the necessary *minyan* for the congregational service, special arrangements are made for such worship when there is a *yahrzeit*. Its observance is an act of pious commemoration and emphasizes faith in the immortality of the soul.

BIBLIOGRAPHY: Eisenstein, Dinim, 154f.; H. Rabinowicz, *A Guide to Life* (1964), 103–13.

[Louis Isaac Rabinowitz]

YAHŪD, collective noun and appellative for Jews in pre-Islamic Arabian poetry, the *Koran, and Islamic literature, cognate with the less common plural *hūd* and the uniquely Koranic *hāda*, a verb that means "to be Jewish" or "to practice Judaism." For the most part *Yahūd* is used to describe either the Jews of, or slightly preceding, *Muhammad's time or Jews living anywhere between then and the time of the writer employing the term. This is in distinction to the equally widespread *Banū Isrā'īl* which – with some significant exceptions in the Koran and its commentaries, where it refers to Muhammad's Jewish contemporaries – generally indicates ancient Israelites from the period of the patriarchs and the exodus from *Egypt all the way down to Jesus and the destruction of the Second Temple (and thus this designation often includes Christians). A third term, *ahl al-kitāb* (people of the book, scriptuaries), is essentially a timeless epithet for the Jewish people (though it, too, frequently encompasses Christianity). While the latter two labels are sometimes employed in neutral or even positive contexts, the *Yahūd* are almost invariably portrayed as evildoers.

According to Islamic tradition Muhammad first came into consistent contact with Jews after the *hijra* – the emigration of the fledgling Muslim community from Mecca to Yathrib/Madīna (*Medina) in 622 C.E. – where a number of Jewish tribes (chief among them the Banū *Qaynuqā', *Naḍīr, and *Qurayẓa) had once dominated, but now were dominated by, the pagan Aws and Khazraj. Though at the beginning Muhammad wooed the Jews – including them in his "Contract of Madīna," adopting many of their rites, and presenting himself as the successor to the illustrious line of biblical prophets – their unwillingness to accept his new dispensation (and their frequent mocking of the same) soon soured relations between the Muslim and Jewish communities. After the Battle of Badr (624 C.E.) the Banū Qaynuqāʿ were exiled from Madīna and their property confiscated in punishment for alleged fifth-column activity, and the Banū Naḍīr shared their fate the following year in the wake of the Battle of Uḥud. The Banū Qurayẓa were dealt with far more harshly following the Battle of the Trench (627 C.E.), their 800 or so men publicly executed in the center of town and their women and children sold into slavery. In 628 C.E. the northern Jewish fortress of Khaybar, whither many members of the exiled tribes had fled, was reduced by Muslim forces. The survivors were allowed to remain on their land in exchange for a tribute consisting of half the annual produce. (Muhammad married the wife of the "king of Khaybar" – the 17-year-old Ṣafiyyah – after torturing her husband to death for not revealing the whereabouts of his treasure. This was his second wife of Jewish origins.) The Jews of Khaybar were finally expelled after Muhammad's demise by the second caliph, ʿOmar, in fulfillment of Muhammad's dying injunction that "two religions shall not coexist in Arabia."

The portrayal of Jewish norms and historiography in Islamic classical literature ranges from the impressively accurate (including near verbatim recapitulations of biblical and midrashic passages and relatively sophisticated rehearsals of talmudic *sugyot*) to the confused, propagandistic, and fantastic (Jews excise urine-splattered flesh, pluck each other's eyes out in retribution, are enjoined by the Torah to forgo booty in war, and believe Ezra is the son of God as Christians believe Jesus is the son of God; Jewish law forbids the consumption of geese and ducks, prohibits the use of sand for purification if water cannot be found, and commands its adherents to slaughter a yellow heifer if an unidentified corpse is found in a field; the Second Temple was destroyed by Antiochus, the *shekhinah* was the head of a dead cat, the messiah is known in Jewish tradition as *al-dajjāl* ("the deceiver"), King David had one hundred wives and Moses accompanied his people into the promised land). With rare exceptions, the Jews are perceived in Muslim literature as the historical epitome of excess and evil and – having been abandoned by God as a result of such noxious traits – also the model of misery. They may be said to function as the emblem of all that Muslims should not be, a kind of *sunna* (exemplary tradition) in reverse. They will ever be Islam's nemesis (far more so than the Christians), until they are ultimately defeated and destroyed in the Eschaton.

BIBLIOGRAPHY: A. Geiger, *Judaism and Islam* (trans. F.M. Young) (1970); S.D. Goitein, *Jews and Arabs: Their Contacts through the Ages* (1955), esp. chap. 4; C. Adang, *Muslim Writers on Judaism and the Hebrew Bible* (1996); H. Lazarus-Yafeh, *Intertwined Worlds* (1992); B. Wheeler, *Prophets in the Qur'an: An Introduction to the Qur'an and Muslim Exegesis* (2002); U. Rubin, *Between Bible and Qur'an: The Children of Israel and the Islamic Self-Image* (1999); G. Newby, *The Making of the Last Prophet: A Reconstruction of the Earliest Biography of Muhammad* (1989); N. Stillman, *The Jews of Arab Lands: A History and Source Book* (1979); G. Newby, *A History of the Jews of Arabia: From Ancient Times to their Eclipse Under Islam* (1988); M. Cohen and A. Udovitch, *Jews among Arabs: Contacts and Boundaries* (1989); S. Wasserstrom, *Between Muslims and Jews: The Problem of Symbiosis under Early Islam* (1995).

[Z.A. Maghen (2nd ed.)]

YAHUDA, ABRAHAM SHALOM (1877–1951), Orientalist. Born in Jerusalem of a Baghdad family, Yahuda was taught by his brother ISAAC EZEKIEL YAHUDA, who was 13 years his senior and the author of a comprehensive collection of Arabic proverbs (*Mishlei Arav*, 1932). At the age of 15 he published his first book (*Kadmoniyyot ha-Aravim*, "Arabs' Antiquities," 1895^2). He went to Europe to study Semitics at Heidelberg and Strasbourg, where he was the pupil of Th. *Noeldecke. From 1904 to 1914 Yahuda lectured at the Berlin Hochschule (Lehranstalt) fuer die Wissenschaft des Judentums and from then to 1922 was professor at the University of Madrid. During World War I, while in Madrid, he tried to persuade King Alfonso XIII to use his influence with the emperors of Germany and Austria on behalf of the Jews of Ereẓ Israel. These activities were later criticized by Chaim Weizmann in his autobiography *Trial and Error* to which Yahuda replied in his *Dr. Weizmann's Errors on Trial* (1952). After 20 years of travel during which time he acquired a valuable collection of books and manuscripts – part of which he later sold to the British Museum – he became professor at the New School for Social Research, New York in 1942. He died in New Haven, Connecticut.

Yahuda's published works include his critical edition of the Arabic text of Bahya ibn Paquda's *Duties of the Heart* (1912), to which he also wrote *Prolegomena* as his doctoral thesis (1904); a volume of Hebrew poems (*Kol Arvi ba-Midbar*, 1903); *Bagdadische Sprichwoerter* (1906); *Jemenische Sprichwoerter aus Sanaa* (1911); and a collection of papers on Jewish-Arab relations (*Ever ve-Arav*, 1946). The publication of his *Die Sprache des Pentateuch in ihren Beziehungen zum Aegyptischen* (1929; *The Language of the Pentateuch in Its Relation to Egyptian* (1933); popular English edition *The Accuracy of the Bible*, 1934), in which he claimed strong Egyptian influence on the language of the Pentateuch – particularly in the stories of Joseph, the exile in Egypt, and the Exodus – produced worldwide discussion, but his theories were rejected by Bible and Oriental scholars as well as Egyptologists. Yahuda himself did not change his views, which he continued to proclaim in lectures.

A considerable part of Yahuda's library was bequeathed to the Jewish National and University Library. It contains about 1,500 manuscripts, mostly Arabic, but some hundreds are in Hebrew and other languages; some are illuminated and very valuable.

[Martin Meir Plessner]

YAHUDI, YUSUF (1688–1755), Bukharan poet. Yahudi was an exponent of that branch of Persian poetry in Hebrew characters which began with *Shahin and *Imrānī of Shiraz. His poems included an ode devoted to the praise and glory of Moses and hymns in honor of biblical heroes such as Elijah as well as other poems bearing his name in acrostic, some of which are bilingual and trilingual and form even today an integral part of the spiritual heritage of the Persian-speaking Jews of Bukhara. His Tajiki version of *Haft Braderan* ("The Seven Brothers"), based on the Midrash on the martyrdom of *Ḥannah and her seven sons, and his commentary to *Megillat Antiochus* are still popular. Yusuf Yahudi was also noted for his translations of the religious songs of Solomon ibn *Gabirol and Israel *Najara, which were collected in *Judeo-Persian songbooks such as *Yismaḥ Yisrael.*

Under his influence a school of Jewish poets in Bukhara came into existence whose members followed his example in composing Judeo-Persian poetry in their own dialect.

BIBLIOGRAPHY: W. Bacher, in: ZDMG, 53 (1899), 389–427; idem, in: ZHB, 3 (1899), 19–25; W.J. Fischel, in: L. Jung (ed.), *Jewish Leaders* (1953), 535–47.

[Walter Joseph Fischel]

YA'ISH, BARUCH BEN ISAAC IBN (15th century), philosopher and translator. Probably born in Spain, Ibn Ya'ish lived and died in Italy. He had a good knowledge of Hebrew, Latin, and Arabic. Ibn Ya'ish wrote a Hebrew commentary in ten chapters on Avicenna's *De Medicamentibus Cordialibus* ("On Cardiac Remedies") entitled *Be'ur la-Sammim ha-Libbiyyim*, in which he quotes Aristotle and Averroes (Bodl, Ms. Mich., Add. 16).

He translated Aristotle's *Metaphysics* into Hebrew from the Latin at the request of Samuel Ẓarphati, under the title *Mah she-Aḥar ha-Teva* (Bodl. Mich., 421). In the introduction to his translation Ibn Ya'ish explains that he based his translation on the Latin, rather than the Arabic, because the Arabic was confused. It also seems that Ibn Ya'ish had a role in producing a Hebrew translation of an anonymous Latin commentary on Aristotle's *Ethics*. A commentary on the Song of Songs, Ecclesiastes, Proverbs, and Job, which is called *Mekor Barukh* (Constantinople, 1576), and which bears the name Baruch ibn Ya'ish, was written by Ibn Ya'ish's great-grandson and namesake.

BIBLIOGRAPHY: Steinschneider, Cat Bod, 774, no. 4508; Steinschneider, Uebersetzungen, 157–8, 218, 485, 701; Michael, Or, 626.

[Hirsch Jacob Zimmels]

YAKHINI, ABRAHAM BEN ELIJAH (1617–1682), kabbalist and preacher, one of the leaders of the Shabbatean movement. Yakhini was born and lived his entire life in Constantinople. He was a pupil of R. Joseph di Trani and an influential preacher in the community. From adolescence, he was attracted by Lurianic *Kabbalah and wrote books and sermons according to the Lurianic system. He would note his dreams in his books. These dreams are of great interest. Yakhini was also a rhetorician and a poet; in 1655 he published *Hod Malkhut*, an imitation of Psalms. He knew of Shabbetai *Ẓevi while the latter was in Constantinople in 1658. However, there is no indication that Yakhini believed his messianic claims. His detailed notes on Kabbalah from 1658 to 1663 are preserved in a manuscript (*Sefer Razi Li*) and contain no indication of Shabbateanism. Only with the outbreak of the Shabbatean movement in the fall of 1665 did Yakhini join the "believers." He became its leading disciple and major spokesman in Constantinople. He also traveled to Smyrna and was appointed as a "King of Israel" by Shabbetai Ẓevi in December 1665. After Shabbetai Ẓevi's apostasy, Yakhini persisted in his belief and remained the head of the Shabbatean minority in Constantinople. He maintained personal contact and corresponded with Shabbetai Ẓevi and the rest of the movement's leaders. His relations with the rabbis of Constantinople, who now took a negative view of Shabbateanism, were tense. But apparently they did not dare harm him. He circulated books and poetry in honor of Shabbetai Ẓevi and the Shabbatean faith until his death, and in the last year of his life he contacted Abraham Miguel *Cardozo. Even after his death, Yakhini continued to influence Shabbatean circles, especially the sect of converts to Islam, the *Doenmeh of *Salonika. The many tales about him in *Me'ora'ot Ẓevi*, (1813) are not based on historical sources but are the products of the imagination of an anonymous author who wished to write a novel on Shabbetai Ẓevi.

Of Yakhini's numerous works there have been preserved in manuscript *Sefer Razi Li* and *Peli'at Da'at* (Ms. Adler), *Sefer Vavei Ammudim* (Ms. Oxford), sermons on Shabbetai Ẓevi written between 1681 and 1682, a book of various notes which was in the possession of R. Abraham Danon, several pamphlets on the Lurianic Kabbalah, and sermons and poems in honor of Shabbetai Ẓevi. A long letter to the Christian scholar Warner (Ms. Leiden) is preserved.

BIBLIOGRAPHY: Scholem, Shabbetai Ẓevi, index, s.v. *Ha-Yakhini*; Amarillo, in: *Sefunot*, 5 (1961), 245; A. Freimann (ed.), *Inyenei Shabbetai Ẓevi* (1913), 13; A. Epstein, in: REJ, 26 (1893), 209ff.; A. Danon, *ibid.*, 58 (1909), 272ff.

[Gershom Scholem]

YAKIR, YONAH (d. 1937), Soviet general. Born in Kishinev, Yakir commanded the 45th division of the Red Army during the Civil War and was later promoted to general with command of the Kiev district. He was one of the founders of the Red Army armored corps and in 1937 was made military commander of the Ukraine and a member of the Supreme Military Council. Shortly afterward Yakir was arrested on charges of spying and executed. He was posthumously rehabilitated in 1945 and a postage stamp was issued in 1954 in his memory.

YAKNEHAZ (Heb. יַקְנְהַ"ז), abbreviation composed of the initials of the Hebrew words; יַיִן *yayin* ("wine"), קִדּוּשׁ *Kiddush ("sanctification"), נֵר *ner* ("light"), הַבְדָּלָה *Havdalah ("separation"), and זְמַן *zeman* ("time," meaning blessing of the time, i.e., *She-Heḥeyanu*). The word served as a mnemotechnic aid for the correct sequence of the benedictions of the *Kiddush* on the eve of a festival which coincides with the conclusion of a Sabbath. The abbreviation originates in the Talmud (Pes. 102b–103a), and sounds similar to the German phrase "*jag den Has*" ("hunt the hare"). Hence also the hare-hunting scenes in many illustrated Passover *Haggadot* (e.g., *Haggadah of Mantua*, 1561).

YAKNEHAZ (pseudonym of **Isaiah-Nissan Hakohen Goldberg**; 1858–1927), Yiddish and Hebrew writer. Born in a village near Minsk, Yaknehaz began, in 1878, writing Yiddish and Hebrew literary essays which aroused great interest. A decade later, *Sholem Aleichem reprinted the most famous of these, *A Brif fun Lite keyn Amerike* ("Letter from Lithuania to America"), in which, as in hundreds of later tales and sketches, Yaknehaz portrayed the life of the small Jewish town in a simple unsophisticated style. He was popular among the masses for almost half a century. His influence on young Abraham *Reisen was considerable. After the Russian Revolution, he continued to publish in the Soviet Yiddish periodicals. The government of Soviet Belorussia granted him a pension. His collections of stories appeared in Minsk in 1940–41.

BIBLIOGRAPHY: Rejzen, Leksikon, 1 (1926), 1273–75; LNYL, 4 (1961), 271f; Kressel, Leksikon, 1 (1965), 413f.

[Shlomo Bickel and Sol Liptzin / Gennady Estraikh (2nd ed.)]

YAKUM (Heb. יָקוּם; "He Shall Rise"), kibbutz in central Israel, in the southern Sharon, 7 mi. (11 km.) S. of Netanyah, affiliated with Ha-Kibbutz ha-Arẓi ha-Shomer ha-Ẓa'ir. Yakum was founded in 1947, during the struggle of the *yishuv* with the Mandatory government. The founders were Israeli-born graduates of the Ha-Shomer ha-Ẓa'ir movement, joined mainly by immigrant youth from Holland, Bulgaria, and France. In 1970 Yakum had 358 inhabitants, in the mid-1990s the population increased to 470, rising still further to 523 by 2002. Farming was based mainly on plantations and dairy cattle. The kibbutz had a factory for specialized plastics products. In addition, it benefited from its proximity to the Tel Aviv conurbation. It had an interest in a nearby gas station, operated a convention center, and developed a hi-tech industrial park on its land.

WEBSITE: www.yakum.co.il.

[Efraim Orni / Shaked Gilboa (2nd ed.)]

YALAN-STEKELIS (formerly **Wilensky**), **MIRIAM** (1900–1984), Hebrew poet and writer of children's literature. Born in Russia, Miriam Yalan-Stekelis immigrated to Ereẓ Israel in 1920, and lived in Jerusalem, working at Hadassah. From 1926 she was in the Slavonic Department (heading it 1929–56) of the Jewish National and University Library. Her husband was Moshe *Stekelis.

In 1922 she began to publish (two poems in *Ha-Ḥayyim*) and subsequently her works appeared in various newspapers and journals. Her children's poetry which first appeared in 1934 (mainly in *Davar li-Yladim*) was followed by many children's books. She received the Israel Prize for children's literature, 1957, and published three volumes of collected works, *Shir ha-Gedi, Yesh Li Sod, Ba-Ḥalomi* (1958–63). *Sheker*, a collection of three stories, appeared in 1966. A collection of poems and stories (*Shirim ve-Sippurim*) was published in 1987. Miriam Yalan-Stekelis translated to and from Hebrew, including Russian folktales into Hebrew, *Peraḥ ha-Shani* (1952), and the diaries and letters of J. Trumpeldor into German. In 1968 she published the memoirs of her father, Yehudah Leib Nisan *Wilensky, to which she added much biographical material.

ADD. BIBLIOGRAPHY: Y. Zoref, *Shirat ha-Yeladim shel M. Yalan-Shtekelis* (1991). M. Regev, "Bein Zikkaron Otobiografi le-Sippur Yeladim,," in: *Ma'agalei Keriah*, 22 (1994), 21–25; M. Rosenberg, *Iyyunim bi-Shetayim mi-Yẓirot M. Yalan-Shtekelis* (1993).G. Almog, *Tefisot Olam ve-Gishot Ḥinukhiyyot bi-Yẓiratah shel M. Yalan-Shtekelis li-Yeladim* (1995); R. Garon, *Reẓef u-Temurah be-Shirat ha-Yeladim shel M. Yalan-Shtekelis* (1996); R. Gonen, "*Miryam Yalan Shtekelis bi-Re'i ha-Iyyur*," in: *Iyyunim be-Sifrut Yeladim*, 12 (2002), 39–59; G. Almog, "*Bein Sippur le-Shir: M. Yalan-Shtekelis*," in: *Iyyunim be-Sifrut Yeladim*, 13 (2003), 63–73.

[Getzel Kressel]

YALKUT (HA-) MAKHIRI (Heb. יַלְקוּט הַמָּכִירִי), an anthology of aggadic Midrashim by Machir (Makhir) b. Abba Mari, on the lines of the **Yalkut Shimoni* but more limited in scope. The following extant portions have been published: Isaiah (1893) by J.Z. Kahana-Spira; Hosea (in: JQR, 15 (1924/25), 141–212) by A.J. Greenup; the rest of the Minor Prophets (1909–13) also by Greenup; additional fragments of Hosea and Micah in the *Gaster Anniversary Volume* (1936), 385–73) by J. Lauterbach; Psalms (1900) by S. Buber; Proverbs, chapters 2–4 (1927) by J.M. Badhab; Proverbs 18–31 (1902); and fragments of Proverbs 2, 3, 13, and 14 (in: E. Gruenhut, *Sefer ha-Likkutim*, 6 (1903) by E. Gruenhut. In the extant introductions at the beginning of Isaiah and Psalms, Machir mentions a *Yalkut* to the "Prophets, Jeremiah, and Ezekiel." In view of this separate mention of Jeremiah and Ezekiel, Greenup assumes that "Prophets" refers to the Early Prophets and that the author intended to cover all the books of the Bible, excluding those covered by the *Midrash Rabbah*. This, however, is doubtful; the "Prophets" may refer to the later prophets and the Hagiographa. It is certain, however, that only part of the original *Yalkut* has been preserved.

The *Yalkut* includes quotations from many sources: the tannaitic and amoraic literature and many of the homiletical Midrashim. The sources are usually given, though sometimes merely "Midrash" or "Midrash *Aggadah*" is stated; also, the quotations are not always to be found in the existing editions of the sources indicated. Machir is usually exact in giving the actual language of his sources, and as he had many manuscripts (apparently of Sephardi origin) before him, his work is often a basis for restoring the correct reading. There is no information about Machir or the period when the *Yalkut* was compiled. The author traces his ancestry back six generations, but these ancestors cannot be identified. The colophon to the Leiden manuscript states that it was sold in 1415, thus determining the latest possible date the work was compiled. Most scholars attribute it to the 14th century, but Gaster was of the opinion that it was compiled in the 12th century, apparently in Spain, and assumed that the author of part two of the *Yalkut Shimoni*, who according to Gaster lived in the 14th century in Spain, made use of the *Yalkut (ha-) Makhiri*, abridging and summarizing it. This theory has, however, been disproved by Epstein. Both Epstein and Buber claim correctly that neither anthologist knew the other and point out that they differ in their method of citing sources, that each of them cites Midrashim unknown to the other, and that certain Midrashim were known to them under different names. That it was compiled in Provence, the generally accepted opinion, merely because the name Machir was known there, is not supported by internal evidence or by the local dialects. On the contrary, Machir's use of a *Deuteronomy Rabbah* (published by S. Lieberman, 1940, 1965[2]) which was known only in Spain and the statement of Shabbetai Bass in the *Siftei Yeshenim* (Amsterdam, 1680, 29, no. 42) possibly relying upon a tradition that "the *Yalkut (ha-) Makhiri* was compiled before the Spanish expulsion" (*Kunteres Aḥaron*,) at least tends to support the assumption that Machir came from Spain.

BIBLIOGRAPHY: S. Buber, in: *Ha-Ḥoker*, 2 (1894), 88–96; J. Piumer, in: *Me'assef*, 2 (1902), 37–43; M. Gaster, in: REJ, 25 (1892), 44–64 (= *Studies and Texts*, 3 (1925–28), 57–68): idem, *Exempla of the Rabbis* (1924), 35–39; A. Epstein, in: REJ, 26 (1893), 75–82: Zunz-Albeck, Derashot, 415.

[Jacob Elbaum]

YALKUT SHIMONI (usually referred to as **"the Yalkut" of Simeon of Frankfurt**) the best known and most comprehensive midrashic anthology, covering the whole Bible. Some scholars (S.J. Rapoport, etc.) claimed that its author and compiler was Simeon Kara, the father of Joseph Kara and a contemporary of Rashi, but A. Epstein showed that there is no basis for this view. He proved that the Simeon mentioned by Rashi is not the compiler of the *Yalkut* and attributed it to a Simeon ha-Darshan, who lived in the 13th century. Nothing is known of this Simeon, except for a reference by M. Prinz to a "Rabbenu Simeon, chief of the preachers of Frankfurt." The copyist of the Oxford manuscript of 1308, as well as the publishers in Salonika, simply refer to him as *ha-darshan* ("the preacher"), but Prinz's view that he came from Frankfurt is supported by the traditions of the Jews of that town. Zunz dated the Midrash to the 13th century based on the facts that Nathan b. Jehiel of Rome, Rashi, and other 12th-century scholars did not know the *Yalkut*, its use of sources which date at the earliest from the end of the 11th century (according to Zunz – including *Exodus Rabbah, Numbers Rabbah, Midrash Avkir, Divrei ha-Yamim ha-Arokh*, etc.) as well as the fact that Azariah dei *Rossi had a manuscript of it written in 1310. Not all of Zunz's arguments are valid. For example, Rapoport has shown that the *Yalkut* does not utilize *Exodus Rabbah* and *Numbers Rabbah*, but Zunz's view as to its date prevails, despite Gaster's claim that it was compiled in Spain in the 14th century. The attempt of Aptowitzer to predate it to the middle of the 12th century is not convincing. Nevertheless, the *Yalkut* began to circulate widely only at the end of the 15th century, becoming popular and relied on to such an extent that the study of its midrashic sources was neglected. The reason for its late circulation lies in the historical circumstances of those times. The copying of a work of such great volume as the *Yalkut* was difficult and the period was equally barren in creativity in other spheres. The first to mention the *Yalkut* was Isaac Abrabanel, and his son Samuel possessed a copy of part of the *Yalkut* to the prophets.

The aim of the compiler of the *Yalkut* was to assimilate the bulk of rabbinical sayings at his disposal, following the order of the verses of the Bible. It contains more than 10,000 statements in *aggadah* and *halakhah*, covering all the books of the Bible, most of its chapters, and including commentaries on a substantial part of individual verses. He collected material from more than 50 works (in *halakhah* and in *aggadah*) both early and late. The *Yalkut* is the only source for some of them, including *Sifrei Zuta, Yelammedenu, Midrash Esfah, Midrash Avkir, Midrash Tadshe, Devarim Zuta*, etc. The identification of these works was made possible in part by the author's custom of noting the source for his statement (in the manuscripts they are in the margin, in the first printed edition in the text, and in later printed editions again in the margin). These source-notes, however, are incomplete; in hundreds of places no reference is given and even in cases where they are, mistakes and corruptions have crept in, many of them in the late editions.

The *variae lectiones* of the *Yalkut* are of great importance, but great caution must be exercised in relying upon them, especially as regards the later editions, for three reasons: Sometimes the compiler based himself on faulty manuscripts; his method of assembling statements from various sources and combining them caused him at times to abridge and even alter them; and editors and printers used a free hand in altering passages according to their own views. Their tendency, in the words of M. Prinz in the introduction to his edition (Venice, 1566), was to straighten out the words "that were topsy turvy, first things last and last things first, omissions and additions, letters and words distorted and crossed out, partially obliterated and worked over," at times adding to the corrupt state of the text.

Many paragraphs in the *Yalkut* are numbered and are commonly designated *remazim* ("allusions") by the author, though he sometimes employs the term *siman* ("sign") and in a number of places *erekh* ("topic"). The total number of these *remazim* is 966 (963 in the Salonika edition) for the Pentateuch and 1,085 for the other books of the Bible. The method followed in numbering the *remazim* is puzzling: the author does not number each quotation, and although there are numbers covering a few lines dealing with a single dictum (Isaiah 444 has 3 lines) there are also some of exceptional length containing numerous statements extending to several columns (cf. Deut. 938). There are *remazim* which cover the commentary to two successive paragraphs and some even to two successive books. Zunz regarded this numbering as arbitrary, but it seems probable that it served an internal need of the book itself, its purpose being not to divide the work into sections, but to indicate those statements to which he intended to refer in some other part of his work. In fact, in the Oxford manuscript and in the Salonika edition, the number is placed by the side of the particular statement to be referred to elsewhere and not at the beginning of the section (this explanation was put forward by H.Z. Finkel of Jerusalem, and cf. D. Hyman, in: *Hadorom*, 12 (1960), 144–7 and *Mekorot Yalkut Shimoni* (1965), 6–7). In addition to these *remazim*, in various books there is an added division whose nature is not always clear. From the indications in the first edition, it is clear that the author follows the order of books of the Bible given in the Talmud (BB 14b), placing Jeremiah and Ezekiel before Isaiah. In the printed editions the accepted order has been followed, and in consequence the printers, at the beginning of the commentary to Isaiah, quoted the relevant passage from *Bava Batra*, "the sages have taught that the order of the prophets is Joshua, Judges, Samuel, Kings, Jeremiah, Ezekial, Isaiah, the Twelve," and explaining that this accounts for the order in the numbering of the *remazim*. From the Venice edition (1566) onward the numbering is also corrupt.

The numbering of the Psalms in the *Yalkut* differs from the traditional one. The anthologist notes the number at the beginnings of each Psalm and only gives 147. This division was customary in the amoraic period, and the author apparently took it from the Midrash to Psalms which interpreted the verse (Ps. 22:4) "Yet thou art holy, O Thou that art enthroned upon the praises of Israel" (i.e., Jacob) to mean that "the 147 Psalms in the Book of Psalms correspond to the 147 years of Jacob." This division appears only in the Salonika edition and was subsequently blurred. The chief printed editions of the *Yalkut Shimoni* are Salonika editions, Prophets and Hagiographa (1521) and Pentateuch (1526). To this edition a *kunteres aḥaron* (addendum) was added (at the end of part 1) containing 256 *remazim* from the *aggadot* of the Jerusalem Talmud, with deviations from the present order of the tractates and 55 *remazim* from the *Midrash Yelammedenu* on the Pentateuch to all of which cross-references occur in the main work. This addendum was omitted from all subsequent editions. Since then the *Yalkut* has been published frequently but many errors have crept into it. For accurate reading one can rely only on the Salonika edition, which was published from manuscripts, and on the manuscripts available today in the libraries of Oxford, Vienna, Parma, and Hamburg, although they are mostly fragmentary and even in their totality do not cover all the books of the Bible. A. Epstein, in dealing with the differences between the Salonika and Venice editions, proved that the editor of the Venice edition, Meir Prinz, used the printed Salonika edition as the basis of his edition, although he made many changes to it at his discretion, and this impaired it. Hyman, in his *Mekorot Yalkut Shimoni* to the Prophets and Hagiographa, gives the sources of the *Yalkut* in accordance with the manuscripts and first editions and adds his own sources. He also gives the passages, including several long and important ones, which occur in the first edition and in the manuscripts but were excluded from the later editions by the censor.

BIBLIOGRAPHY: Zunz-Albeck, Derashot, 146–9, 443–7; A. Epstein, in: *Ha-Ḥoker*, 1 (1891), 85–93, 129–37; idem, in: *Ha-Eshkol*, 4 (1902) 273–5; 6 (1909), 183–210; idem, *Mi-Kadmoniyyot ha-Yehudim* (1957; = vol. 2 of his *Kitvei*), 278–327, 351–4; idem, in: REJ, 26 (1893) 75–82; M. Gaster, *The Exempla of the Rabbis* (1924), Eng. pt. 21–39; E.Z. Melamed, *Midreshei Halakhah shel ha-Tanna'im be-Talmud Bavli* (1943), 68–70; D. Hyman, in: *Hadorom*, 12 (1960), 144–7; idem, *Mekorot Yalkut Shimoni* (1965), introd; S. Abramson, in: *Sinai*, 52 (1963), 146.

[Jacob Elbaum]

YALON (originally **Distenfeld**), **HANOCH** (**Henoch**; 1886–1970), Hebrew linguist. Born in Trutky, near Lopatin in Galicia, Yalon was influenced by his older brothers who had become *maskilim*, and became well versed in the Hebrew literature of the *Haskalah. At the age of 22 he went to Lemberg (Lvov) where he taught Hebrew. He studied Akkadian at Lemberg University and during World War I moved to Vienna where he studied Semitic languages at the university.

Yalon was invited in 1921 to teach at the Mizrachi Teachers' Seminary in Jerusalem, where he was employed until 1946. He then devoted his life solely to research. In 1962 he received the Israel prize for Jewish scholarship. In 1963 a jubilee volume was published in his honor.

Yalon's published work is comprised only of articles, most of which were collected in three books: *Mavo le-Nikkud ha-Mishnah* ("Introduction to the Vocalization of the Mishnah," 1964); *Pirkei Lashon* ("Studies in the Hebrew Language," 1971; posthumously); and *Megillot Midbar Yehudah* ("Studies in the Dead Sea Scrolls," 1967). He also edited *Kunteresim le-Inyenei ha-Lashon ha-Ivrit* (vol. 1, 1937–38; vol. 2, 1938–39; altogether four issues); and *Inyenei Lashon* (two issues, 1942–43).

Yalon's achievements as an innovator in the field of research on the Hebrew language were considerable. His studies cover all periods of the history of the Hebrew language: the Bible, mishnaic Hebrew, *piyyut*, medieval grammarians, Hebrew poetry in Spain, rabbinical Hebrew, grammarians of more recent centuries, and the Haskalah literature down to the contemporary spoken language. Yalon was the first to recognize the importance of the living traditions of Hebrew, especially that of the Yemenite community. While teaching at the Mizrachi Seminary, whose students came from all ethnic groups in the country, he observed the differences between the living traditions. He found that the Yemenite tradition was close to Hebrew and Aramaic with the Babylonian vocalization. Up to this time it was customary to dismiss the oral traditions of the various communities as "errors." Yalon, however, showed that sometimes their traditions had a Hebrew basis which was different from that transmitted by the masoretes of Tiberias.

His approach established research in mishnaic Hebrew grammar on a new basis. Like J.N. *Epstein, by whom he was greatly influenced, and S. *Lieberman, he realized that the printed versions of mishnaic Hebrew texts were unreliable and therefore one must go to the manuscripts. Consequently he showed that between the grammar of mishnaic Hebrew and biblical Hebrew there were far greater differences than had been thought up to his time.

His achievements were no less in the field of criticism. Yalon wrote about scholars who were fixed in their views which were based on past and dated scientific methods. Outspoken and very sharp in his criticisms, Yalon showed great courage in his attack. His critical activity was admirable for he persisted in it knowing that it would have little effect. Only toward the end of his life he realized that his teachings, and not those of his rivals, had triumphed in the research of Hebrew linguistics in Israel. To the public at large Yalon was known mainly as the scholar who had vocalized the six books of the *Mishnah (with a commentary by Ḥ. *Albeck, 1952–58, 1958–59²). Yalon did not aim at a pure scientific vocalization which would reflect the original form, but at times he even left the faulty vocalization which had become sanctioned through the acceptance of all the communities for many generations.

BIBLIOGRAPHY: *Sefer Ḥanokh Yalon* (1963), 9–50; Y. Kutscher, in: *Haaretz* (April 13, 1962, March 27, 1970, March 30, 1971).

YALOW, ROSALYN SUSSMAN (1921–), U.S. medical physicist and Nobel laureate in physiology or medicine. Yalow was born in New York and received her B.A. from Hunter College (1941) and M.S. and Ph.D. in nuclear physics from the University of Illinois under the direction of Maurice Goldhaber (1945). After teaching at Hunter (1946–50), she started her long association with the Bronx Veterans Administration Hospital. She set up the radioisotope service over the period 1950–70 and became head of the nuclear medicine service (1970–80), senior medical investigator (1972–92) and director of the Solomon A. Berson Research Laboratory (1973–92). She was also appointed research professor (1968–74) and distinguished service professor (1974–79) in the department of medicine of the affiliated Mt. Sinai School of Medicine. Yalow was professor at large at Albert Einstein College of Medicine and Yeshiva University (1979–85) and chairperson of the department of clinical science at Montefiore Hospital in the Bronx (1980–85). She was professor emeritus from 1985 and Solomon A. Berson Distinguished Professor at Large at Mt. Sinai School of Medicine from 1986. Her collaboration with Solomon Berson began in 1950 and lasted until his death in 1972. They developed the technique of radioimmunoassay which became the standard method of measuring small amounts of peptide hormones and other substances in blood and tissues for research and routine clinical purposes, and they established the basic principles of subsequent immunoassays. Throughout her career she made major contributions to studies of hormones and especially insulin in health and disease. Yalow was awarded the Nobel Prize for this work (1977) jointly with Roger Guillemin and Andrew Schally. Her other honors include the Gairdner Award (1971), the inaugural Hagedorn Memorial Lecture (1973), membership in the U.S. National Academy of Sciences (1975), and the Lasker Award for Basic Medical Science (1976). Yalow was an early advocate and role model for women's right to pursue a career in science.

[Michael Denman (2nd ed.)]

YALTA, city and port in the Crimea, Russia. The winter palace of the czar's family, Livadiya, was situated near the town and as a result Jewish residence was restricted. From 1837 to 1860 Jews were forbidden to live there at all. Between 1860 and 1893 the prohibition was lifted, but from 1893 only those Jews who were registered as inhabitants or those with rights to reside anywhere in Russia were authorized to remain there. The others, including sick persons who had been sent there for convalescence, were expelled. In 1897 there were 1,025 Jews (approximately 8% of the total population) in Yalta. By 1926 their numbers had increased to 2,353 (6.2%). With the German occupation of Crimea at the end of 1941, the Jews who had remained in the town were concentrated in a ghetto and on Dec. 16–17, 1941, about 1,500 people were murdered.

By 2005, Yalta had a Jewish community center and a charity center called Hesed Naftul. In 2004, for the first time in 80 years, a Sefer Torah was brought to the town by a group of rabbinical students.

BIBLIOGRAPHY: *Merder fun Felker* (1945).

[Yehuda Slutsky]

YALTA (fourth century C.E.), wife of Naḥman (d. 320) and daughter of the Exilarch (Kid. 70a). When Naḥman entertained prominent scholars he would ask them to send her their greetings. On one occasion he asked Rav Judah, a prominent contemporary, who was visiting him on a legal matter, to send her greetings. Judah objected, however, quoting successive statements in the name of Samuel as to the impropriety of having associations with women. Yalta thereupon sent a message to her husband: "Settle his case before he makes you appear like any ignoramus" (*ibid.*, 70a–b). On another occasion, when her husband was entertaining *Ulla, and the latter stubbornly refused to send her any wine of the cup over which he had recited a blessing, she reportedly broke 400 jars of wine in her anger (Ber. 51b). She also apparently had a sharp tongue, and commented on his refusal, "Gossip comes from peddlers and vermin from rags," i.e., what can you expect from a man like that? (*ibid.*). When dissatisfied with the ruling of one rabbi she appealed to another, apparently concealing from him the fact that she had already consulted one (Nid. 20b). She once said to her husband, "The Torah has permitted something of a similar taste for everything it has forbidden; I would like to eat meat in milk," whereupon he told the butcher to give her roasted udder (Ḥul. 109b).

BIBLIOGRAPHY: Hyman, Toledot, 757f.

[Harry Freedman]

YAMIM NORA'IM (Heb. יָמִים נוֹרָאִים; "Days of Awe"), a term applied to the period from the first day of *Rosh Ha-Shanah until the *Day of Atonement and more particularly to these two festivals. This period is more commonly referred to as the *Ten Days of Penitence. *Yamim Nora'im* is also the title of a compilation on the subject by S.Y. *Agnon.

YAMMIT REGION.

Upbuilding

Of all the new regions whose development was projected after the 1967 Six-Day War, the northeast corner of Sinai initially appeared to be the least promising. This was the Rafiah Salient, which later became known as the Yammit Region, an area whose thick dune cover gave it the aspect of a typical desert. With a scant rainfall of 5–8 inches per year, it was obvious that water for development purposes would have to be taken from Israel's scanty supply. Prospects for future settlement seemed poor. The region was inhabited by several thousand semi-sedentary bedouin, who eked out their livelihood from flocks of sheep and goats, some date-palm groves and rhicinus bush plantations, and small vegetable plots in the depressions between shore dunes. Occasionally they supplemented their income by selling quails, which they caught along the shore during the season of migratory flight.

However, Israel's ruling party at the time, the Alignment Party, felt the necessity of creating a barrier in this region between Egypt and the Gaza Strip, even though in principle they were not opposed to the return of territories for peace. For this reason, it was decided to develop the area.

Once construction was begun, Yammit soon proved its superiority to other regions of settlement, in several respects: The sand dunes were found to be well suited to drip irrigation farming, and the mild climate was beneficial to crops. The water supply was augmented by a shallow coastal aquifer, although it was still necessary to obtain water from Israel's national carrier. It therefore became possible to plan for a larger area of cultivation and a larger population than were originally envisaged. The fine beaches were a tourist attraction. Moshe Dayan, among others, suggested developing Yammit as Israel's third Mediterranean seaport, and industrial firms considered the possibilities for establishing various enterprises. The planning authorities also intended substantial improvements for the local Bedouin as well. Yammit was also blueprinted as a favorable inflow site for the projected Mediterranean–Dead Sea saltwater canal.

By 1977, the year of Sadat's peace initiative, the town of Yammit had over 2,000 inhabitants and was growing fast. By 1981, another 2,000 were living nearby, in the rural center of Avshalom, the kibbutzim Sufah and Ḥolit, and the moshavim Dikla, Ḥaruvit (Tarsag), Ne'ot Sinai, Netiv ha'Asarah, Nir Avraham, Peri'el, Sadot, Talme Yosef and Ugdah. Several more settlements were in the planning stage, and reclamation work by JNF crews was under way. Over 12,000 dunams were under irrigation. Roses, carnations and other flowers were being cultivated in more than 200 greenhouses, as well as under light cover and in open fields. Citrus groves, vineyards and orchards of tropical fruit such as mangoes were flourishing. The settlers tended vegetables, principally out-of-season winter crops, both in greenhouses and in the open. Their fruit and flowers found a ready market in Europe. Scientists contributed their expertise in the areas of water usage, new equipment, construction of greenhouses, seed selection, etc., thus enhancing Israel's reputation for agricultural research. Moshav Sadot, with 70 families and a population of over 350, was one of several settlements which greatly increased their farm production by employing bedouin laborers. They incurred criticism from the Moshav Movement and Labor circles in general for this step, which was seen as a departure from their ideological principles and an inducement to outside Arabs to settle nearby and swell the region's non-Jewish population. A modern, well-equipped regional school was established near Sadot, and Yammit also established educational facilities. In the south of the region, the Etam military airport was considered the most advanced of its kind.

To the Evacuation

Even after Sadat's visit to Jerusalem, it was generally felt that everything possible should be done to retain the Yammit Region. The Likkud government later agreed to suspend the establishment of new Yammit Region settlements while continuing to develop those already in existence. This was done as a gesture to Egypt and the U.S. But Egypt adamantly insisted on a return to the pre-1948 borders, and the 1978 Camp David Accords dashed any hope that Egypt would permit the settlers to remain in Sinai after it was returned to her. In the Knesset discussion on Camp David, both the Likkud coalition and the Alignment opposition defined the evacuation of the area as Israel's most painful concession, but most held it to be an unavoidable step in the peace process. (There were, however, dissenters in both parties, and in the religious and nationalist parties as well.) Among certain circles the hope was expressed that something might occur in the two-and-a-half years remaining before the set evacuation date, which would prevent the evacuation of the Sinai settlements, without, however, interrupting the peace process. Begin decreed that everything should proceed normally in the region until the very last day. In July 1981 the chairman of the Knesset Security and Foreign Committee, Moshe Arens, expressed his reservations concerning the decision to cede northern Sinai, and in August Prime Minister Begin declared that Israel would have to reconsider the evacuation timetable if the Egyptian president continued to stall on renewal of talks on autonomy in Judea and Samaria. Sadat's murder (October 6 1981) raised expectations among the opponents of evacuation that the timetable might be postponed, but this was not the case. One week later the Israel government unanimously agreed to proceed with implementation of the peace treaty as planned. On October 20 President Mubarak announced his intention of continuing the peace process even after Egypt had received all of Sinai. Some Israelis feared that the Sinai evacuation would set a precedent affecting all the administered regions, but others felt that it was a conciliatory step that could win Western and Egyptian acceptance of a continued Israeli presence in Sinai.

These speculations disrupted plans for the orderly liquidation of property in Sinai, with minimal losses to the settlers and the State. They also hampered plans for developing the Pitḥat Shalom (Peace Salient) area in the northwestern Negev, to where most of the Yammit villages were due to be transferred.

It was generally accepted that the settlers should be compensated for the time, money and pioneering efforts that they had invested in the Yammit area. Furthermore, it was hoped that generous remuneration would encourage them to found new settlements elsewhere in Israel. But as a result of the uncertainty surrounding the actual evacuation of Yammit, costs soared and negotiations were protracted. Moreover, opinions differed as to the extent and nature of the compensation, and the amount to be deducted for income tax. The government offered advance payment to the settlers to enable them to prepare in good time for their new lives elsewhere, and after much controversy, the Knesset adapted the Compensation Law on March 30, 1982.

More serious was the struggle with the "League for Preventing the Sinai Retreat" (also known as "Ma'oz"). At its core were *Gush Emunim and the Ha-Teḥiyyah Party (an extreme nationalist political party), but it had many other sympathizers, including some within the government. In May 1979, when Ne'ot Sinai (the settlement closest to El-Arish) was handed over to Egypt six months in advance as a goodwill gesture, volunteers from the League joined local settlers in protesting the move and clashed violently with Israeli soldiers who were sent to remove them.

Ma'oz initiated the founding of new settlements in the westernmost part of the area. Ḥaruvit was established at the time when the Knesset was endorsing the Camp David Agreement, Aẓmonah in 1980, Ḥaẓar Adar in December 1981, and Ma'oz ha-Yam as late as January 1982. Groundbreaking ceremonies were attended by many sympathizers, including some from the Labor Party. These gatherings, although unauthorized, were permitted to take place. The movement also occupied houses left by settlers who had returned to the "Green Line" (the original boundaries of the State of Israel). Ha-Teḥiyyah demanded a plebiscite on evacuation, and the League's nationwide street poll claimed to have collected 700,000 signatures. More volunteer "nuclei" were created in Yammit, Talme Yosef, and Nir Avraham, with the number of "squatters" mounting to 200, and later 350 families. However, not all the veteran settlers welcomed their presence and there were cases of blows and quarrels. Government reaction was divided between those who demanded a forceful reaction and those who advised moderation.

At the end of February 1982 the army set up road blocks to prevent all but genuine inhabitants from entering the area. Defense Minister Ariel Sharon declared March 1 to be the evacuation date, instructing the army to refrain from using violence under any circumstances. The Yammit and Merḥav Shelomo regions were pronounced military zones. Tension rapidly mounted, the inhabitants staged a demonstration of passive resistance to the army, and supporters in Israel declared hunger strikes. Evacuation was postponed until April 1, but permission was obtained for the settlers to remain for the Passover holiday.

On April 19, the army began to remove the resisting settlers and Ma'oz militants. Rabbi Meir Kahane, leader of the Jewish Defense League, rushed from New York to Yammit, where some of his followers were threatening to commit suicide in their bunker rather than comply with the army. He managed persuade them to leave. From April 23, all remaining buildings and installations were systematically reduced to rubble and then flattened, and roadways were torn up. Resistance eventually petered out with no serious clashes. The last Israelis departed on April 25, and by April 26, 1982, all of Sinai was in Egyptian hands.

[Efraim Orni (2nd ed.)]

YAMPOLSKY, BERTA (1934–), choreographer and artistic director of the Israel Ballet. Born in Paris to Russian parents, Yampolsky immigrated at a young age with her family to Israel. She studied with Valentina Archipova Grossman and Mia *Arbatova and continued her studies at London's Royal Ballet. She and her husband, Hillel Markman, were leading soloists in many dance companies all over the world and returned to Israel in 1964. In 1967, the husband-and-wife team established the Israel Ballet. As its choreographer, she produced dramatic ballets, abstract and contemporary in the neoclassical style. In 1977, in Santiago, Chile, she was awarded the prize for the best foreign choreographer for her work entitled *Dvořák Variations*. She created most of the dances for the company, including *The House of Bernarda Alba* (1978), *Carmen* (1980), *Untitled* (1981), *Mendelssohn Concerto* (1982), *Opus 1* (1983), *The Nutcracker* (1985), *Two by Two* (1989), *Harmonium* (1989), a full-length version of *Romeo and Juliet* (1989), *Valse Mephisto* (1992), *Gurre Lieder* (1996), *Ecstasy* (1998), and *Medea* (1999). The repertoire of the company includes a number of works by George Balanchine, as well as works by Roberto Lazzini, Heinz Spoerli, Roberto Trinchero, and the renowned work of John *Cranko, *Onegin*.

In 1998, she received the Minister of Education and Culture Lifework in Dance Award. In 2004 the company numbered 35 dancers, most of them Israeli-born, some immigrants from the former U.S.S.R. and the rest from Western countries. The troupe performed in Israel and at major dance festivals abroad.

BIBLIOGRAPHY: R. Eshel, in: *Israel Dance Quarterly*, 7 (December 1995), 12–20; idem, in: *Dance Today – The Dance Magazine of Israel*, 2 (July 2000), 85–93.

[Ruth Eshel (2nd ed.)]

YANG-CHOU (formerly **Wei-yang**), city in Kiangsu province, China. It had connections with the Jewish community of *Kaifeng. A few scattered references to Jewish and Chinese individuals from Yang-chou are found in the Chinese stele inscriptions of the Kaifeng Jews, dating from 1489 and 1512, and several Chinese officials from Yang-chou helped in the preparation of these inscriptions. A member of the Kaifeng Chin family had his home in Yang-chou, but he donated "a copy of the Scriptures of the Way [*Tao*], and set up the second gateway" in the Kaifeng synagogue. The oral tradition of the existence of a sizeable community and even of a synagogue in Yang-chou cannot be corroborated.

BIBLIOGRAPHY: W.C. White, *Chinese Jews*, pt. 2 (1966²), 27, 42, 46, 47.

[Rudolf Loewenthal]

YANKOWICH, LEON RENE (1888–1975), U.S. jurist. Born in Romania, he went to the U.S. in 1907. In 1927 he was appointed to the Superior Court bench in Los Angeles County, California, and in 1935 he became a judge of the Federal District Court. He sponsored social legislation for women, was an authority on the law of libel, and as judge became famous for liberal decisions in favor of illegitimate children and in favor of the federal government's claim of mineral lands against the claims of Standard Oil Co. of California.

[Milton Ridvas Konvitz (2nd ed.)]

YANNAI, or **Yannai Rabbah (the Great)**, early third century Palestinian *amora*. It seems highly likely that the late "*tanna*" Yannai, who is mentioned in Avot 4:14, and Tosefta Sanhedrin 2:5, is to be identified with the early *amora* Yannai (S. Friedman, Language and Terminology in Talmudic Literature). According to a genealogical scroll found in Jerusalem, Yannai was descended from the high priest, Eli (TJ, Ta'an. 4:2, 68a). Yannai transmitted some halakhic rulings in the name of Judah ha-Nasi (TJ, Ḥag. 3:2, 79b), but his main teacher was Ḥiyya, whom he consulted in difficult cases, and who predicted that Yannai would one day to be a leader in Israel (TJ, Dem. 7:1, 26a). Yannai's daughter married a son of Ḥiyya (Ket. 62b), and he also had a son, Simeon (TJ, MK 2:2, 81a). Though Yannai is recorded in one place as having prayed in Sepphoris (TJ. Ber. 4:6, 8c), Halevi maintains that he always lived in Akbara in Upper Galilee. There he established an academy (TJ, Er. 8:4, 25a), where his pupils lived as a family and tilled the land in addition to their studies (TJ, Shev. 8:6, 38b). The rulings of the academy of Yannai are frequently quoted in the Talmud. His best known pupils were *Oshaiah (Ket. 79a), *Aibu (Kid. 19a), and above all, Johanan and Resh Lakish, who transmitted many of his halakhic decisions (TJ, Kil. 8:1, 31b; BK 52a and 115a; et al.). After his death his pupils turned to Yohanan for guidance (TJ, Shev. 8:6, 38b). Yannai was noted as both a halakhist and an aggadist. An important principle enunciated by Yannai has become part of the general Jewish outlook: danger may not be incurred in the expectation of a miracle (Shab. 32a). He counseled submission to the ruling power (Zev. 102a), and permitted the fields to be sown in the sabbatical years (regarding its force as only rabbinical) to meet the government's heavy taxation (Sanh. 26a). He also ruled leniently with regard to tithing (BM 87bf.).

Yannai was a wealthy man (Kid. 11a), owning an orchard (MK 12b) and vineyards (BB 14a). He was very charitable and at one time, for certain religious reasons, declared the fruit of his orchard free to all for one year (MK 12b). His sensitivity to the feelings of the poor is indicated in his dictum, "Better not to give charity at all, than to shame the recipient by giving it to him in public" (Ḥag. 5a). He compared the man who studies without fear of God to one who makes his door before erecting the building (Shab. 31b). The commandments would retain their validity, he held, even after the *Resurrection of the Dead (Nid. 61b). According to a tradition in the Babylonian Talmud, in his last testament he enjoined his children not to bury him in white, lest his place be among the wicked and he would appear like a bridegroom amid mourners, nor in black, lest his place be amid the righteous, and he would appear like a mourner amid bridegrooms (Shab. 114a).

Apart from Yannai the Great, there were several other *amoraim* of this name. Since the name is often given without patronymic or title, it is not always clear to whom it refers. Yannai b. Ishmael, a Palestinian *amora* of the late third century, is mentioned several times. Laws are quoted in his name concerning liturgy (Ta'an. 14a) and in several aggadic passages, one concerning the tragic victims of Bethar (Git. 58a) and others dealing with biblical themes (BM 86b). A general plea for tolerance may be read into the reply he attributes to Abraham's visitors, who, when he invited them to wash their feet (Gen. 18:4), rebuked him: "Do you take us for Arabs who worship the dust of their feet? Ishmael (who does likewise) has already issued from you" (BM 86b).

BIBLIOGRAPHY: Hyman, Toledot, 758–64ff.; Frankel, Mevo, 103a–104a; Bacher, Pal Amor; Weiss, Dor, 3 (19044), 45f.; Halevy, Dorot, 2 (1923), 273–80; Ḥ. Albeck, *Mavo la-Talmud* (1969), 161f.

[Benjamin Cohen]

YANNAI, liturgical poet, one of the principal representatives of the old Palestinian *piyyut*.

References to Yannai in the Sources

Yannai is first mentioned in *Kirkisani's *Kitāb al-Anwar* (beginning of the tenth century) once, together with Eleazar (i.e., *Kallir) and Phinehas, as a composer of Hebrew hymns, and in two other places as an authority on religious law. Kirkisani mentions that *Hai (b. David), head of the Pumbedita academy, and his father, after having found rabbinical sources for all but two rules in *Anan's Karaite code of law, finally found these in Yanai's *Ḥazzanah*. Around the same time *Saadiah names the following among the "elder poets" whose verses he declares as models: *Yose b. Yose, Eleazar *(Kallir), *Joshua, and *Phinehas. An anonymous manual of poetry from Saadiah's circle cites poems by the "famous Yannai" as the example of rhymed prose. An anonymous poem of similar provenance, and the grammarian *Yehudi b. Sheshat (second half of the tenth century), name Yannai and Kallir in succession. *Gershom b. Judah (*Me'or ha-Golah*) states that Yannai, whom he cites as one of the earliest authors, composed *kerovot* for all weekly Torah portions. Finally, in a Hebrew manuscript (Munich, Ms. 69) and in a liturgical work of Ephraim of Bonn, Yannai is named as Kallir's teacher. Ephraim adds that in "Lombardy" (i.e., Italy), Yannai's hymn "*Onei Pitrei Raḥmatayim*" is not recited because he was considered to be Kallir's murderer: he supposedly put a scorpion in his pupil's sandal, thus causing his death.

Rediscovery of Yannai's Works in the *Genizah*

Yannai is not mentioned in later literature; modern research made his name and works known again. The scholars who first engaged in research on Yannai had only fragments of a *kerovah* ("*Onei Pitrei Raḥamatayim*") and a *piyyut* ("*Az Rov Nissim*") from the Passover *Haggadah* as material (it was later discovered that this *piyyut* was part of the *kerovah*). Yannai's personality was brought into new light only in the 20th century with the discovery and publication of Cairo **Genizah* fragments. In 1901 S.H. Wertheimer published two poems attributed to Yannai (*Ginzei Yerushalayim*, 2 (1901), 18b). In 1903 S. Poznański found a list of books where the *Ḥazzanah* of Yannai is mentioned as a special work (JQR, 15 (1903), 77, no. 12). Davidson's publications opened new horizons for research into Yannai. In 1910 he found a *Genizah* fragment with quotations and beginnings of poems from the "*Maḥzor Yannai*"; this established the existence of a greater poetic work of Yannai's. In 1919 he found in some Greek-Hebrew *genizah*, fragment palimpsests (published by F.C. Burkitt in *Fragments of the Book of Kings* (1897), and by C. Taylor in *Hebrew-Greek Cairo Genizah Palimpsests*, 1900) some of Yannai's *kerovot* which were thought lost, and which he later published with notes by L. Ginzberg (*Maḥzor Yannai* (1919)). In 1928 Davidson found – following a suggestion by Brody – three other poems by Yannai among the *Genizah* fragments in the Bodleian Library: he published them in *Genizah Studies* (vol. 3, 1928). Paul Kahle published, in the *Masoreten des Westens* (1927; 24–27 (Heb. part) with Ger. translation, 59–66), two poems that had already been published as anonymous in 1898–99, with supralinear (Palestinian) vocalization, which he recognized as Yannai's. Apart from that, Kahle found some *Genizah* fragments in Cambridge (Taylor-Schechter Collection) and in Leningrad/St. Petersburg (Collection of the Archimandrite Antonin), which also contained *kerovot* by Yannai and which were in part published by M. Kober (1929). Many more texts by Yannai were identified by J. Schirmann in the large *Genizah* collections especially in Cambridge in 1931 and 1932. They were photographed for the Archives of the Berlin Institute for Research of Hebrew Poetry, together with thousands of other *Genizah* fragments. M. Zulay discovered many more unknown texts by Yannai among the fragments and collected all Yannai's works known to him, in a critical edition (1938). Zulay, more than any other researcher, was interested in Yannai, and apart from important text editions, also conducted intensive research into Yannai's language. J. Mann (1940), S. Widder (1941), I. Sonne (1944), Zulay himself (1947), A. Diez-Macho (1955), and A. Murtonen (1958) published important additions to Zulay's preceding work. Among the most recent publications of Yannai's poetry, it is worth mentioning J. Yahalom's (1978), and above all the edition of Z.M. Rabinowitz (1985–87), with the additions and comments of N.M. Bronznick (2000).

Yannai's *Kerovot*

Davidson established already in his first publication the scheme of the structure of Yannai's *kerovot*, which with some modifications is still valid. (It is doubtful that Yannai invented the special structure of the *kerovah*; its regular and rather complicated features make a slow evolution probable.) This type of *kerovah* served as the model for all his successors, although they differ in many details. Yannai wrote essentially two kinds of *kerovot:*

(1) The *kedushta*, a poem for the Sabbath *Shaḥarit* (morning service) based on the first three benedictions of the *Amidah* and dealing with the biblical portion of each Sabbath. The third *kedushta* contains Yannai's name in an acrostic; it also alludes to the *haftarah* of the relevant biblical portion;

(2) The *shivata*, for the *Musaf* and the eve of Sabbaths and festivals, based on seven benedictions of the *Amidah* (the first three and the last three being always included).

Yannai's Dates

A close relationship between the older Palestinian Midrashim and Yannai's poetry can be established by numerous parallels in content and style. It cannot be determined, however, whether the Midrashim influenced his poetry, or whether both, belonging to approximately the same period, represent the same spirit in somewhat different forms. It is difficult to accept Yannai's compact style with its many allusions to classical sources as his own creation. Between Yannai and *Yose b. Yose – his only predecessor known by name – there is a linguistic disparity which can be explained only by assuming several intermediary stages in language development between them. Furthermore, it is clear that Yannai lived some centuries before Saadiah, who already considers Yannai to belong to the dim past. As historical perspective was undeveloped in Kirkisani's day, his reference (see above) does not prove that Yannai lived before Anan, but only that a later author (Hai b. David) found two points of Karaite law in Yannai's work. The tale of Yannai's relation to Kallir, being legendary, does not help in the determination of Yannai's dates, apart from the fact that Kallir's dates too are uncertain. While modern scholars have accepted the sixth–seventh century as a dating for Yannai, an older one (fourth–fifth century) is also possible.

Yannai's Provenance

For several reasons, it is obvious that Yannai must have lived in Palestine. His *kerovot* are written according to the *triennial Palestinian cycle; only Christians are named as Israel's enemies; and his name is usually spelled יַנַּיי, according to the usage of the Jerusalem Talmud, and not יַנַּאי. Other Diaspora countries were not yet Jewish cultural centers and, therefore, cannot be taken into account. What Gershom b. Judah says of him (see above) has been fully confirmed by modern research. Yannai's *Ḥazzanah* (Arabization of the Hebrew *ḥazzanut*, "liturgy") must have contained *kerovot* to all the portions of the (triennial) Palestinian cycle; used by the Palestinian community in Cairo, it was fragmentarily preserved there in the *Genizah*. The work could have been considered as a source of religious law, as it contained, apart from the *aggadah*, much halakhic material. With the rapid diffusion of Kallir's works, though, it became obsolete and lost its standing in literature.

Yannai was probably the first, or one of the very first, to introduce into the tradition of Jewish liturgical poetry the rhyme and the alphabetic and nominal acrostic.

BIBLIOGRAPHY: A. Harkavy, *Zikkaron la-Rishonim ve-Gam la-Aḥaronim*, 1, pt. 5 (1891), 106–9; P. Kahle, *Masoreten des Westerns*, 1 (1927), 24–27, 59–66, 87 (Heb. pt.); I. Davidson (ed.), *Maḥzor Yannai* (1919), Heb. with Eng. introd.; idem, *Genizah Studies in Memory of Dr. Solomon Schechter*, 3 (1928), 1–47, passim; Elbogen, in: JJLG, 20 (1929), 21-69; J Mann, in: AYSLL, 46 (1929/30), 275–7; M. Zulay (ed.), *Piyyutei Yannai li-Shema Yisrael* (1933) = YMHSI; idem, "*Meḥkerei Yannai*", in: *Studies of the Research Institute for Hebrew Poetry II* (1936), 213–391; idem (ed.), *Piyyutei Yannai* (1938); idem, "*Iyyunei Lashon be-Fiyyutei Yannai*," in: *Studies of the Research Institute for Hebrew Poetry VI* (1946), 161–248; idem, in: *Semitic Studies in Memory of Immanuel Loew* (1947), 147–57 (Heb. pt.); Lieberman, in: *Sinai*, 4 (1939), 221–50; S. Widder, in: *Jubilee Volume… Prof. Bernhard Heller* (1941), 37–60 (Heb. pt.); J. Sonne, in: HUCA, 18 (1944), 199–220; A. Díez-Macho, in: *Sefarad*, 15 (1955), 287–313, 324–40; Spiegel, *ibid.*, 314–23 (Eng.); idem, in: YMHSI, 7 (1958), 137–43; idem, in: MEWJ, 74 (1930), 94–104; Z.M. Rabinowitz, *Halakhah ve-Aggadah be-Fiyyutei Yannai* (1965); idem, in: *Tarbiz*, 38 (1969), 384–94; J. Yahalom, in: *Leshonenu*, 31 (1966/67), 211–6; N. Fried, in: *Sinai*, 61 (1967), 50–66; 62 (1968), 127–62; J. Schirmann, in: *Keshet VI* (1964), no. 4, p. 45–66; A. Mirsky, *Reshit ha-Piyyut* (1965), 74–85; idem, in: *Schirmann Jubilee Volume* (1970), 347–62; H. Yalon, *Pirkei Lashon* (1971), passim; E. Fleischer, in: *Sinai*, 64 (1968/69), 176–84. **ADD. BIBLIOGRAPHY:** E. Fleischer, in: *Hebrew Liturgical Poetry in the Middle Ages* (1975), passim (Heb.); idem, in: *Ha-Yoẓerot* (1984), passim; J. Yahalom, *A Collection of Geniza Fragments of Piyyute Yannai* (1978); B. Chiesa, in: *Henoch*, 2 (1980), 333–48; T. Carmi, *The Penguin Book of Hebrew Verse* (1981), 215ff.; W.J. van Bekkum, in: EOL, 27 (1983), 120–40; Z.M. Rabinowitz (ed.), *The Liturgical Poems of Rabbi Yannai according to the Triennial Cycle of the Pentateuch and the Holidays* (1985–87); idem (ed.), *Maḥzor Piyyutei R. Yannai la-Torah ve-la-Mo'adim* (1985); A. Kor, *Yannai's Piyyutim: Evidence of the Hebrew in Ereẓ Israel during the Byzantine Period* (1988) (diss., Heb.); N.M. Bronznick, *Piyyutei Yannai: Be'urim u-Ferushim im Hazza'ot Menumakot le-Tikkunim ve-Hashlamot* (c. 2000).

[Jefim (Hayyim) Schirmann]

YANNAI (Jannaeus), ALEXANDER (b. c. 126–76 B.C.E.), Hasmonean ruler of Judaea (103–76 B.C.E.), son of John Hyrcanus; was high priest and king. According to Josephus, Yannai was hated by his father and for this reason was forced to spend his childhood in Galilee. When his eldest brother, Aristobulus, inherited the high priesthood from their father, he was imprisoned together with other brothers and his mother for fear they would attempt to seize power. Upon the death of Aristobulus, his widow, Salome Alexandra, designated Yannai as the successor, and the new high priest married his sister-in-law, in accordance with the Jewish rite of levirate.

Since Josephus holds that Aristobulus had already transformed the government into a kingdom, he also assumes that Yannai inherited the kingship from him. However, Strabo's assertion (16:2, 40) and the testimony of Aristobulus' and Yannai's coins may support the opinion that Aristobulus never was a king and that Yannai became a king only at a later stage of his rule.

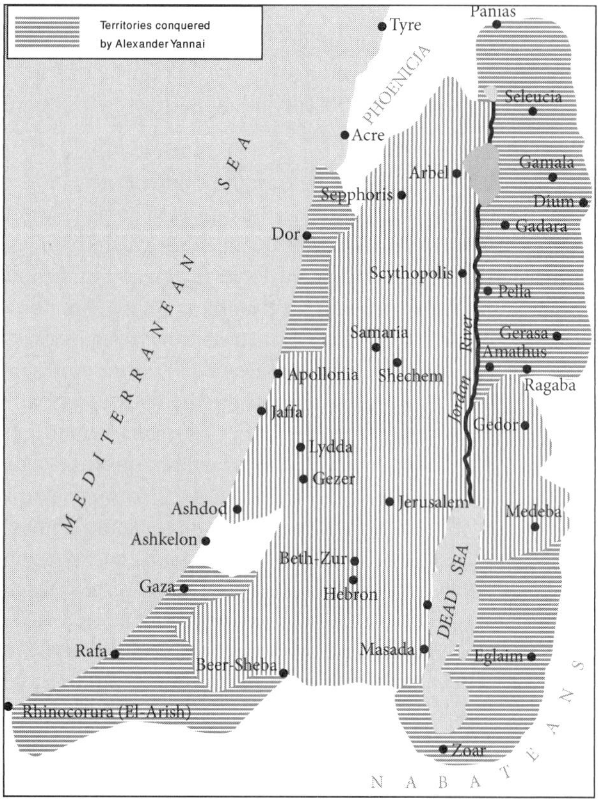

The kingdom of Alexander Yannai, 103–76 B.C.E. Based on Zev Vilnay, New Israel Atlas, *Jerusalem, 1968.*

The political history of Judaea under Yannai may be divided into four periods. The first period extends from 103 until about the year 95. At the start of his rule, Yannai took advantage of the dissensions inside the Ptolemaic kingdom and besieged one of the most impressive Ptolemaic strongholds on the Mediterranean coast: Ptolemais (Acco). Ptolemy Lathyrus, who previously was compelled to retreat to Cyprus by his queen Cleopatra III, his mother, promptly reacted. While leaving part of his army besieging Ptolemais, he invaded Judaea and defeated Yannai. The latter was saved only by Cleopatra's intervention. She launched a military campaign against Lathyrus, took again Gaza and Ptolemais, and forced him to retreat again to Cyprus. Thus freed from Lathyrus' threat, Yannai seems to have turned to Transjordan, perhaps in order to take revenge upon Lathyrus' allies, notably Theodorus, the tyrant of Amathus. Yannai succeeded in conquering Gadara in Transjordan, and Amathus. In the meantime, Cleopatra met her death, while Lathyrus carried on waging war against his brother Ptolemy Alexander. As a result, Yannai turned again to the Mediterranean coast, and this time, he succeeded in subduing Gaza (c. 96). By this time, he had gained control of the entire coastal region from Mount Carmel in the north down to the Egyptian border (with the exception of Ashkelon).

The second period extends roughly from c. 95 to 88. It seems that strengthened by his successes, Yannai assumed the title of king only at this stage of his rule, thus claiming to be free of any other political power. In any case, Yannai's military policies may have overly angered the Jewish population and a civil war broke out, which lasted six years and whose leaders were probably the Pharisees. Since they were unable to defeat the king's army reinforced by mercenaries, they called the Seleucid overlord of Judaea, Demetrius III, to come and fight against Yannai. Demetrius invaded Judaea and defeated Yannai near Shechem (89/88 B.C.E.). Taking advantage of Yannai's weakness, the *Nabateans compelled him to relinquish the territories he previously conquered in Transjordan.

In the aftermath of his defeat, Yannai was compelled to renounce the title of king. He seems to have spent the next three years fighting his Jewish opponents and recovering from his bitter defeat. Having subdued their most powerful stronghold, Bethoma, he made his opponents prisoners, and bringing them back to Jerusalem, he ordered eight hundred of them to be crucified. Both Josephus and Qumranic *Pesher Nahum* echo the horror of such a cruel deed.

The last period of his rule (84–76 B.C.E.) was the culmination of his power and of the territorial expansion of his kingdom. Both Ptolemaic Egypt and Seleucid Syria were on their decline. Although he still endured attacks from Seleucids, Antiochos XII Dionysus attempted to again subdue Judaea on his way against the Nabateans and from Nabateans themselves, when Aretas became the ruler of Damascus. However, with the appearance of the Armenians under Tigranes in 83 B.C.E., and Lathyrus' death in 80 B.C.E., Yannai got rid of his old enemies and felt free to recapture most of the territory east of Jordan, the Decapolis and Golan. New series of coins were struck bearing the title of king once again.

Yannai met his death while besieging Regev, a fortress east of Jordan. According to his will, the throne went to his widow. He left two sons, Hyrcanus and Aristobulus, the former nominated high priest by Alexandra, until the civil war which erupted after the death of their mother (67 B.C.E.).

Yannai and the Pharisees

Josephus on the one hand and rabbinic sources on the other record a number of clashes between Yannai and the Pharisees (e.g., Ant., 13:372–383; Kid. 66a; Sot. 47a; Sanh. 19a). However, according to Josephus (Ant., 13:400–404), on his death bed the king advised his wife to yield a certain amount of power to them, so that she could govern with no problems.

Yannai and Qumran Literature

Yannai appears at least in two Qumranic compositions. *Pesher Nahum* is indignant of the way the "Lion of Wrath" took revenge of "those who seek smooth things" by hanging men alive after Demetrius' unsuccessful attempt to conquer Jerusalem (1Qp Nahum 1:2–8). The historical coincidence points to Yannai's deed against his opponents, mainly Pharisees (here surnamed "those who seek smooth things").

Although the king is named "Alexander Yannai" by Josephus and "Yannai the king" by rabbinic literature, his full name was "Alexander Jonathan" (or "Yehonathan") as attested to by his coins. Therefore most scholars think a previously unknown prayer (4Q448) recalls him when speaking of "Jonathan the king." The editors understood the prayer as "for the welfare of King Jonathan and his kingdom." However the meaning of the biblical phrases quoted by the author suggests another interpretation. It is rather a call to God to arise against Jonathan the king so that God's kingdom may be blessed.

Another group of texts, mainly *Pesher Habakkuk*, recalls the way the "Wicked Priest" persecuted the "Teacher of Righteousness," the head of the Dead Sea sect, and his group. The phrase "Wicked Priest" seems to aim at the High Priest living in Jerusalem, contemporary of the Teacher of Righteousness. Thus some scholars identify this figure with Alexander Yannai, while other scholars seek to identify him with one of his predecessors or successors. An additional hypothesis suggests to understand the phrase "the Wicked Priest" as a generic surname referring to each of the Hasmonean rulers, one after the other. The various opinions seem to result from the supposed times of the Teacher of Righteousness.

BIBLIOGRAPHY: Derenbourg, Hist., 95ff; Schuerer, Hist., 82–90, 95; A. Schalit, in: *Eretz Israel*, 1 (1951), 104–21; C. Rabin, in: JJS, 7 (1956), 3–11; A. Schalit, in *Theokratia*, 1 (1967/59), 3–50 (Ger.); M. Stern, "Thrachides – Surname of Alexander Yannai in Josephus and Syncellus," in: *Tarbiz*, 29 (1959–60), 207–9 (Heb.); E. Schuerer, *History*, rev. and ed. by G. Vermes, F. Millar, and M. Black, vol. 1 (1973), 219–28; A. Negev, "The Early Beginnings of the Nabatean Realm," in: PEQ (1976), 125–33; M. Stern, "Judaea and her Neighbors in the Days of Alexander Jannaeus," in: *The Jerusalem Cathedra*, 1 (1981), 22–46; A. Kasher, in: *Cathedra*, 41 (1986–7), 11–36 (Heb.); D.R. Schwartz, "On Pharisaic Opposition to the Hasmonean Monarchy," in: *Studies in the Jewish Background of Christianity* (1992), 46–56; E. Eshel, H. Eshel, and A. Yardeni, "A Qumran Composition Containing Part of Ps. 154 and a Prayer for the Welfare of King Jonathan and his Kingdom," in: IEJ, 42 (1992), 199–229; E. Main, "For King Jonathan or Against? The Use of the Bible in 4Q448," in: M. Stone and E. Chazon (eds.), *Biblical Perspectives: Early Use and Interpretation of the Bible in Light of the DSS* (1998), 113–35.

[Emmanuelle Main (2nd ed.)]

YARCHO, NOE (Noah; 1862–1912), Argentine physician. Yarcho was one of the first to practice medicine in the settlements of the *Jewish Colonization Association (ICA) in Argentina. Born of a religious family in Slutsk, Russia, he worked for a while in England and in 1893 he left for Argentina, accompanied by his wife, sister of the cooperativist leader Miguel *Sajaroff. They settled in the center of the Jewish settlements of Entre Ríos. In 1894 Yarcho faced an exanthematic typhoid epidemic which exhausted the newly arrived settlers. He later wrote the first medical study on this disease to be published in Argentina. He practiced his profession with fervent idealism, striving to give spiritual as well as physical help to the Jewish and native settlers of the vast region.

[Lazaro Schallman]

YARDENAH (Heb. יַרְדֵּנָה), moshav in northern Israel, 7 mi. (12 km.) N.E. of Beth-Shean, affiliated with Tenu'at ha-Moshavim. Yardenah was founded in the framework of the "town to country movement" in 1952 by laborers originating from Iraqi Kurdistan. The moshav, with 370 inhabitants in 1968, was outstanding among the Jewish settlements for the large size of its families. Ever since its founding Yardenah suffered from enemy attack and, in the period after the *Six-Day War (1967), came under particularly frequent and heavy shelling from Jordanian artillery from beyond the border. Intensive field crops, especially cotton, constituted the prominent farming branch. In 2002 Yardenah's population was 439. The name is derived from the nearby Jordan River.

[Efraim Orni]

YARĪM, town in the central mountains of *Yemen, about 60 miles (100 km.) south of *San'a on the way to Ta'izz, built on a 2,400 m high plateau and dominated by the massif of nearby Mount Sumarrah, which rises to about 3,000 m. Yarīm is rich in historical sites, including Ḥimyari. In antiquity, the Yarīm area was the core of the state of Ḥimyar, which ruled over much of southern *Arabia from about 115 B.C.E. to 575 C.E. The Ḥimyari capital was Ẓafar, about 10 miles (15 km.) south of Yarīm. In the geonic period there existed in Yarīm an important community which contributed to the Babylonian academies. One of the last *geonim* complained to two inhabitants of Yarīm that their townspeople had stopped sending contributions to the academy and demanded that what was legally owing to the academies be sent to him. There is no further record of Jews in Yarīm until the 18th century, when the traveler *Niebuhr makes a parenthetical reference to them. He writes that when, in 1763, the grave of one of his fellow travelers, who had been buried in Yarīm, was desecrated, the Jews were forced to see to his reburial, since they had to perform all lowly tasks. During the last generation before the emigration to Israel, the 100-family Jewish community dwelt in a separate neighborhood, with four synagogues. Their leader was R. Ḥayyim Qāfiḥ, whose father Mussa Qāfiḥ functioned as the regional governor under the Ottoman Turks, entitled to judge Jews as well as Muslims. Some of the Jews were wholesale traders, but most of them were craftsmen: weavers, ironsmiths, cobblers, potters, and carpenters.

BIBLIOGRAPHY: D. Goitein, in: *Tarbiz*, 31 (1961/62), 361; C. Niebuhr, *Travels through Arabia…*, 1 (1799^2), index; Y. Tobi, "The Jewish Community in Yemen," in Y. Tobi, *Moreshet Yehudei Teiman* (1977), 101–2.

[Yosef Tobi (2nd ed.)]

YARIV (Rabinowitz), AHARON (1920–1994), Israeli soldier and politician. Yariv was born in Riga, Latvia, and immigrated to Ereẓ Israel with his parents in 1935. He joined the *Haganah in 1938 and in World War II served in the Palestinian units of the British army and with the Jewish Brigade.

On the outbreak of the War of Independence he was appointed deputy-commander of the Alexandroni Brigade and subsequently commander of the Carmeli Brigade. He was later appointed head of operations of the Israel Defense Forces and from 1954 to 1956 headed the newly formed Staff School of the Army. In January 1964, he was appointed chief of military intelligence, a position he held until his release from the army in 1972 when he was appointed adviser to the prime minister on the war against terrorism abroad, serving in that capacity until 1973. On the outbreak of the Yom Kippur War he was appointed assistant to the chief of staff, and headed the negotiations for the disengagement of forces with Egypt on the Cairo-Suez road. Elected to the Eighth Knesset on behalf of the Israel Labor Party he was appointed minister of communications in the government of Golda Meir in March 1974 and minister of information in the government of Yitzhak Rabin in June of that year, but resigned in January 1975.

YARKON or **ME-YARKON** (**Jarkon**; Heb. מֵי [הַ]יַּרְקוֹן), river on the border of the tribe of Dan, which is described as passing Bene-Berak, Gath-Rimmon, and "Me-Jarkon, and Rakkon, with the border over against Joppa" (Josh. 19:45–46). The majority of scholars, regarding the form Rakkon as a haplography, identify the Yarkon mentioned there with the river known in Arabic as Nahr al-ʿAwjā, the second largest source of water in Israel. The Yarkon rises from the vicinity of Tell Aphek (Ra's al-ʿAyn), approximately 8 mi. (13 km.) from the sea, and after describing a bow to the north, falls into the sea at Tel Aviv, after a course of approximately 16 mi. (26 km.). It receives several tributaries, of which the Naḥal Natuf (Wadi Deir (Dayr) Ballūṭ), from the north, and the Naḥal Aijalon (Wadi al-Muṣrā), from the south, are the largest. At present, the river is barred by a sandy spit, but in ancient times it was navigable for a certain length. This explains the existence of an ancient port and storage center at Tell Qasīle, approximately 2 mi. (3 km.) inland, on the northern bank of the river.

The name Yarkon is derived from the root *yarok* ("green"), which refers to the color of its waters. According to Greek legend, it was in the waters of this river that Perseus washed his sword after killing the dragon and liberating Andromeda on the rocks before Jaffa; therefore, at certain seasons, its waters run red. This fact is explained by the red soil (*ḥamrāʾ*) through which the Yarkon runs. In the Mishnah (Par. 8:10), it is referred to as Me-Puga, the waters of Pegai (the Greek name for Tell Aphek, from where the river rises). It is listed in the Talmud (BB 74b) and elsewhere as one of the four rivers of the Holy Land; due to its swampy origin, its waters were unusable for service in the Temple. As the most prominent of the east-west water courses passing the coastal plain, the Yarkon served as the boundary of the territories of Jaffa, Philistia, and Judea at various times. Passage over it was sufficiently difficult to cause the course of the Via Maris to be diverted so as to pass Tell Aphek, a fact which explains the importance of this site. Alexander Yannai tried to use the line of the river as an obstacle to the advance of the Seleucid army southward by fortifying it. Remains of his fortifications have been found at various places in Tel Aviv.

In early Arab times, the Yarkon was called Nahr Abu Fuṭrus, a corruption of the name *Antipatris, the city founded by Herod at Tell Aphek. On its banks the famous battle of al-Tawwāḥīn between the Tūlūnid Egyptian and the Abbasid troops was fought for the possession of Palestine in 885. In Crusader times, it was known as the "River of Jaffa" (Flum de Japhe), rising at the "tower of the silent springs" (*Toron quod superiacet surdis fontibus*). Even at that time it was called Nahr al-ʿAwjā ("the tortuous river") by the Arabs, a name which the Crusaders corrupted to les Loges. The first accurate mapping of the Yarkon was made by Jacotin in 1799. In the 19th century, its basin became one of the centers of Jewish settlement, beginning with Petaḥ Tikvah and then Bene-Berak, Ramat Gan, and Tel Aviv. Its waters were used for irrigation and other purposes by the settlements along its course; a project to exploit it for generating electricity had to be given up. The crossing of the Yarkon by Allenby's army in 1917 marked the culmination of the first British campaign in Palestine. In recent years, half of its waters have been diverted to irrigate the Negev, thus reducing its level and drying out its bed drastically. The establishment of new settlements and industries along its course introduced pollutants into the water. As a result, only in the eastern part of the river, near its sources, is there running water. Its western part contains seawater. In 1988 the Yarkon Authority was established to clean up the river, and a large park, the Yarkon Park, was created on its western bank. However, the river remained polluted, and the Maccabiah tragedy of 1997, when a bridge collapsed as the Australian contingent crossed it, cost people their lives due to exposure to the polluted waters of the Yarkon.

BIBLIOGRAPHY: S. Avizur, *Ha-Yarkon…* (1957); B. Maisler (Mazar), in: *Eretz-Israel*, 1 (1951), 45ff.; idem, in: IEJ, 1 (1951), 61ff., 125ff., 194ff.; M. Avnimelech, in: BIES, 15 (1950), 2ff.; idem, in: IEJ, 1 (1951), 77ff.; J. Kaplan, in: BIES, 16 (1951), 17ff.

[Michael Avi-Yonah / Shaked Gilboa (2nd ed.)]

YARKONAH (Heb. יַרְקוֹנָה), moshav in central Israel, in the southern Sharon south of Hod ha-Sharon. Yarkonah was founded in 1932 by veteran farm laborers of the "illegal" immigration and *Third Aliyah who, in the initial years, developed their homesteads and farms while continuing to earn their livelihood as hired laborers. After the *War of Independence (1948), two more moshavim, Adanim and Neveh Yarak, were established in the neighborhood. In 1970, Yarkonah had 110 inhabitants, in the mid-1990s the population grew to approximately 150, and in 2002 to 272. Its farming consisted mainly of citrus groves.

[Efraim Orni]

YARKONI, YAFFA (1925–), Israeli popular singer. Born in Givatayim, Yarkoni first became known during the War of Independence in the *Ḥishtron* military troupe, whose repertoire mainly suited the salon, e.g., the tangos "*Sheḥarḥoret*," "*Ḥabibi*," and "*Al Na Tomar Li Shalom*." At the same time, Yarkoni also sang military songs such as "*Bab el-Wad*." Although these were seen as a break with her previous style, in fact many songs, like "*Ha'amini Yom Yavo*," shared features of both. Shortly after the war, Yarkoni also became a leading singer of children's songs like "*Aggalah im Susah*," a song that combines Russian and Oriental influences. Yarkoni also followed folkloristic trends, especially in the masterful recordings with the Emanuel Zamir group. She remained a leading figure in Israeli popular music during the 1950s and 1960s. She performed the winning songs in 1965 and 1966 Israel Song Festival. In the 1970s she participated in several children's song festivals. Around 1970 she had new successes, such as "*Keshehayinu Yeladim*" (1969) and "*Pamela*" (1971). After the early 1970s she recorded few new songs but did produce new versions of her old repertoire, many of them collected in a 5-CD compilation of her songs (1998). In 1998, Yarkoni was awarded Israel Prize for her achievements in the field of Hebrew song.

BIBLIOGRAPHY: Y. Rotem, "Yaffa Yarkoni" (www.mooma.com).

[Yossi Goldenberg (2nd ed.)]

YARMOLINSKY, AVRAHM (**Abraham**; 1890–1975), U.S. literary scholar and biographer. Born in the Ukraine, Yarmolinsky immigrated to the U.S. in 1913. He was head of the Slavonic division of the New York Library (1918–55) and was active in stimulating Slavonic research.

His major works include *Turgenev: The Man, His Art, and His Age* (1926); *Dostoevsky, A Life* (1934; republished in 1957 as *Dostoevsky, His Life and Art*); and *Literature under Communism* (1969), a study of literary policy under Stalin after World War II. He translated (with his wife Babbette *Deutsch) *Modern Russian Poetry* (1921), *Contemporary German Poetry* (1923), and *Russian Poetry* (1927). Yarmolinsky's Jewish interests were reflected in his study, *The Jews and Other Minor Nationalities Under the Soviets* (1928). He also wrote *Road to Revolution* (1957) and edited an *Anthology of Russian Verse, 1812–1960* (1962).

BIBLIOGRAPHY: S.J. Kunitz (ed.), *Twentieth Century Authors*, first supplement (1955); H.M. Lyndenberg, in: *New York Public Library Bulletin*, 59 (March 1955), 107–32, list of works; R. Yachnin, *ibid.*, 72 (June 1968), 414–9, list of works 1955–67.

[Sol Liptzin]

YARMUK (Heb. יַרְמוּךְ), a confluent of the Jordan River on its east side. The Yarmuk is the second largest river in Ereẓ Israel (after the Jordan) in volume, and the third largest in length (after the Jordan and Naḥal Paran); it is the largest river in Jordan. The etymology and meaning of the name are unknown. The Yarmuk is first mentioned in Hebrew in the Mishnah: "The waters of the Jordan and the Yarmuk are invalid because they are mixed waters" (Par. 8:10), i.e., it was forbidden to use them for sprinkling in cases of uncleanness, for which purpose only running water is permitted (Num. 19:17). According to *Estori ha-Parḥi, the mixed waters in the Mishnah refer to the waters of Ḥammat-Gader, which empty into the Yarmuk (*Kaftor va-Feraḥ*, 7, ed. Luncz, p. 125) – thus the Mishnah considered the Yarmuk as the river starting at Ḥammat-Gader and its continuation below. In the Babylonian Talmud (BB 74b) and *Midrash Tehillim* (to 24), on the other hand, the entire course of the river is called the Yarmuk, since it is enumerated as one of the four rivers comprising the border of Ereẓ Israel. The Yarmuk appears in variant spellings in Greek and Latin: Pliny the Elder, in the time of the destruction of the Second Temple, mentions it as Hieromices (not Hieromax) and it appears as such on coins of Gadara; on the Peutinger Map it appears as Heromicas. Byzantine writers of the 8th–11th centuries refer to it as Hiermochthas or Thos. In Arabic the lower course is called Nahr al-Yarmuk and the middle course is called Shariʿat al-Munaḍira.

On maps the upper course coincides with Wadi Zaydī, the longest intermittent stream joining the Yarmuk. Wadi Zaydī rises in the heights of Mt. Bashan and receives water from ephemeral streams descending from Tell al-Jaynāʾ and Tell al-Kulayb, for about 12½ mi. (20 km.). In the mountains it contains water all year long. In the tableland it passes by Bozrah and Edrei, and after this point its continuation, called Wadi al-Madān in Arabic, contains water most of the year and often all year long. About 9 mi. (15 km.) northwest of Edrei the Madān is joined by Wadi al-Dhahab, which also descends from the Bashan, and 2 mi. (3 km.) after this junction a tributary with abundant and perennial water – Wadi al-Bajja – empties into the Dhahab. Wadi al-Bajja issues from a small lake and springs in Muzayīb. From this junction and below, the Yarmuk is a perennial river even in years of drought. After Edrei the bed of the Yarmuk deepens and after passing the mouth of the Bajja it becomes a deep gorge, which is much lower than the plateau on both its sides.

The tributaries to the east and west have not cut courses as deep as the Yarmuk and the smaller they are the higher is the level from which they fall to the bed of the Yarmuk. Waterfalls are thus created – in the small tributaries, right on the slope of the Yarmuk, and in the large tributaries, which have hollowed out channels as deep as the main bed, at some distance away. The waterfalls are especially numerous during heavy rains, when water also rushes down the ephemeral streams. The first large permanent waterfall is situated near Zīzūn north of the Yarmuk. About 3 mi. (6 km.) west of Zīzūn the Yarmuk receives the al-Shallāla River, which flows from the south from northern Gilead near the Jabbok; it is a perennial stream for the last 12½ mi. (20 km.) of its course. Then the al-ʿAlān River flows from the Bashan plateau and joins Wadi al-Iḥrayr (or Ḥarīr) near its mouth. In Arabic the ʿAānl is called "*nahr*," i.e., a perennial stream, but this is true for only about 9 mi. (15 km.) of its length. The Iḥrayr rises in the northern Bashan tableland near the large village of Sanamayn, and the network of its tributaries also extends through the northern part of Mt. Bashan. Because of its large drainage area, huge quantities of water rush down during torrential rains and contribute much to the flooding of the Yarmuk.

The last large tributary of the Yarmuk is Nahr al-Ruqqād, which rises in northern Golan near Tell al-Shaykha and passes through the eastern part of the Golan. From the mouth of Wadi Shallāla to Ḥammat-Gader, the Yarmuk plain forms an arc to the north whose chord is about 12 mi. (19 km.) long, and when the lower part of the Shallāla is added, a semicircle is formed with a diameter of about 13½ mi. (22 km.). Inside the arc several small streams from the Gilead empty into the Yarmuk. From Ḥammat-Gader the Yarmuk flows in an easterly direction, and when it enters the Jordan Valley, it turns southeast to follow the southern slope of the valley. As long as the Yarmuk is in a gorge, its bed is 56 to 63 ft. (17 to 19 m.) wide and only a few small sections are not affected during its flooding. In the Jordan Valley the bed at first is only slightly lower than its banks but after several hundred meters the river bed cuts deeply into the soft marl soil.

A famous battle between the Byzantines and the Arabs was fought on the banks of the Yarmuk on Aug. 20, 636. Outflanked by the Muslims from the northeast and blinded by a desert wind from the sandy south, the Byzantine army perished in the ravines of the river gorge; this battle decided the fate of Syria in favor of the Muslims. In memory of this victory, the "Liberation Army" of Fawzi al-Kaukji in 1947 called itself the "Army of the Yarmuk"; it was defeated and dispersed in 1948 near *Mishmar ha-Emek.

To utilize the Yarmuk's water for irrigation by gravitation, it must be diverted before it leaves the gorge either into a canal extending along the eastern end of the Jordan Valley or into a high aqueduct. The former method was used by the Jordanians in 1960–62 and the latter by Jews in Jordan Valley settlements. In 1908 a railway line was installed through the Yarmuk Valley to connect Haifa with the Hejaz railway (now operating from Damascus to Maʾon in Edom), but in 1948 this linkup with Haifa was cut and the railway's importance ceased. From 1920 the Yarmuk formed the boundary between Syria and Jordan. Its name regularly crops in talks about a regional peace agreement in the Middle East, due to its importance as water source for Israel, Syria, and Jordan.

BIBLIOGRAPHY: Abel, Geog, 1 (1933), 483–4; M.G. Ionides and G.S. Blake, *Report on the Water Resources of Transjordan* (1939): N. Glueck, *The River Jordan* (1946); Avi-Yonah, Geog, 159.

[Michael Avi-Yonah / Abraham J. Brawer / Shaked Gilboa (2nd ed.)]

YARON, REUVEN (1924–), Israeli scholar of Roman and ancient Near Eastern law. Yaron, born in Vienna, settled in Palestine in 1939. He taught jurisprudence at the University of Aberdeen (1956–57) and in 1957 began to teach Roman law at the Hebrew University in Jerusalem, and subsequently taught ancient Near Eastern law as well (from 1962). In 1967 he became dean of the law faculty at the Hebrew University. Yaron was an excellent Romanist and a leading historian of ancient Oriental law in the contemporary period, noted for his mastery of the sources and philology, methodological acumen, imaginative grasp of the legal milieu of antiquity, and selection of fundamental topics. His work testifies to the necessity of a background in non-Jewish legal developments for an understanding of Jewish ones. Yaron was appointed director of the Jewish National and University Library, Jerusalem, in 1973, resigning in 1978 when he was appointed head of the Israel Broadcasting Authority.

Yaron's works in English include *Gifts in Contemplation of Death in Jewish and Roman Law* (1960); *Introduction to the Law of the Aramaic Papyri* (1961); and *The Laws of Eshnunna* (1969, 1988^2). His Hebrew publications include *Ha-Mishpat shel Mismekhei Yeb* ("Laws of the Elephantine Documents," 1961) and *Meḥkarim be-Mishpat Romi* ("Studies in Roman Law," 1968).

YARON (Zinger), ẒEVI (1921–1977), Zionist thinker and educator. Born in Rzeszow, Poland; his family moved to Belgium in 1925. He escaped alone to England in 1940, studied at Yeshivat Etz Ḥayyim in London, and at Manchester University. During his stay in England he became a leading member of the Religious Zionist Youth Movement (Baḥad), serving as *madrikh* of the Thaxted Hachsharah Farm from 1945 to 1947 and director of the Mercaz Limud in Manchester from 1947 to 1950.

In 1950 he immigrated to Israel and was a founder of kibbutz Lavi in the Galilee, director of the cultural department of *Ha-Kibbutz ha-Dati from 1953 to 1957, deputy editor of the religious weekly *Panim el Panim*, and director of the religious section of the Youth and He-Ḥalutz Department of the Jewish Agency. He also taught at the School for Overseas Students of the Hebrew University.

He was a member of the Israel Interfaith Committee, editor of the quarterly *Forum*, and founder and first editor of *Ammudim*, the monthly of Ha-Kibbutz ha-Dati. His major work in addition to numerous articles on religion and state was *Mishnato Shel ha-Rav Kook* (The Teachings of Rabbi Kook, 1974).

YAROSLAVSKY, YEMELYAN (Gubelman; 1878–1943), Russian communist leader, publicist, and historian. Born in Chita, Yaroslavsky joined the Russian Social-Democratic Workers' Party at its founding in 1898 and became a close collaborator of Lenin. He moved to St. Petersburg in 1903 and participated in the revolution of 1905. During the Bolshevik Revolution of 1917, he was a leader of the armed uprising in Moscow and an active figure of the Communist Party. In 1923, he was made a member of the Central Committee of the Party. Yaroslavsky was one of Stalin's principal supporters. In 1921, he became one of the three secretaries of the Party Central Committee and in 1934 was made a member of the strategic Party Control Commission. He served on the Central Executive Committee of the U.S.S.R. and was a deputy to the Supreme Soviet. He was also a member of the editorial board of both the Party newspaper, *Pravda*, and the Party's theoretical organ, *Bolshevik*. Yaroslavsky acquired a notorious reputation as chairman of the League of Militant Godless, the Party organization that campaigned on behalf of atheism against all religions. He was the coauthor of an important history of the Soviet Communist Party, editor of the periodical *Istoricheskiy Zhurnal* ("History Journal"), and served on the editorial board of *Istorik-marksist* ("The Marxist Historian"), a major scholarly journal. During World War II he was head of the Communist Party's propaganda department.

BIBLIOGRAPHY: S. and B. Webb, *Soviet Communism: A New Civilization* (1944^3), index; E.H. Carr, *Socialism in One Country*, 2 vols. (1958–59), indexes.

[William Korey]

YARROW, SIR ALFRED, FIRST BARONET (1842–1932), British shipbuilder. Yarrow was the son of an Anglican merchant; his mother, Esther Lindo, came from an old Sephardi family. Yarrow was educated at University College School, London, and was then apprenticed to a marine engineer. The firm he founded in the 1860s, Alfred Yarrow & Co., became one of the leading naval boat builders in the world, producing 29 destroyers and many gunboats and other vessels for the Royal Navy. Yarrow pioneered the torpedo boat as well as a variety of important innovations in ships' boilers and propellers and introduced aluminum and other lightweight materials into ship design. In 1906–8 he moved his works from London to the River Clyde near Glasgow. He gave very substantial sums to charity and in 1916 was made a baronet (a hereditary knight.) His son SIR HAROLD YARROW, Second Baronet (1884–1962), was chairman of the firm for 40 years.

BIBLIOGRAPHY: ODNB online; B. Baxter, "Alfred Fernandez Yarrow," in: A. Slaven and S. Checkland (eds.), *Dictionary of Scottish Business Biography 1860–1960*, 1 (1986), 245–47; A. Borthwick, *Yarrow & Co. Ltd., 1865–1977* (1977).

[William D. Rubinstein (2nd ed.)]

YARROW, PETER (1938–), U.S. folk singer, producer, composer, songwriter, member of the folk trio Peter, Paul and Mary. Born in New York City, Yarrow began his singing career after graduating from Cornell University. He moved to Greenwich Village, where he met Noel "Paul" Stookey and Mary Travers and formed the group Peter, Paul and Mary, which become the most popular folk group of the 1960s, as well as leaders of the 1960s folk revival. The group made its debut in 1961 at the Bitter End coffeehouse, a bastion of folk music, and recorded its eponymous debut album the following year, which spawned such hits as "Five Hundred Miles" and "Lemon Tree," as well as covers of Pete Seeger's "Where Have All the Flowers Gone" and "If I Had a Hammer." The album remained on the Billboard Top 100 for the next three years. "If I Had a Hammer" won the trio the first of its two Grammy Awards, for Best Performance by a Vocal Group and Best Folk Recording. The group's 1963 album, *In the Wind*, with its cover version of Dylan's "Blowin' in the Wind," sold 300,000 copies in less than two weeks. "Puff, the Magic Dragon," written by Yarrow as a college student in 1958, was first released on 1963's *Moving* and became a No. 1 single, and one of the most popular children's songs of all time. Yarrow's involvement in the U.S. civil rights movement led the group to sing "If I Had a Hammer" at the historic March on Washington in 1963, as well as to participate in the Selma-to-Montgomery march in 1965. Yarrow was an active participant in the anti-Vietnam War movement, and coproduced numerous events for the peace movement. The group supported Senator Eugene McCarthy's presidential campaign for the democratic nomination in 1968, and independently released a single titled "Eugene McCarthy for President." Yarrow married the senator's niece, Mary Beth McCarthy, and the couple had two children, but later divorced. *Album 1700* (1967) initially spawned two hits, "I'm in Love With a Big Blue Frog," and "I Dig Rock and Roll Music," but it was not until two years later when DJs started playing "Leaving on a Jet Plane," a song by the then-unknown John Denver, that the album saw a No. 1 hit. In 1970, Yarrow pleaded guilty to taking "immoral and indecent liberties" with a 14-year-old girl who came to his hotel room for an autograph, and subsequently served three months in jail. He was pardoned by President Jimmy *Carter in 1981. By the time the group broke up in 1970 to pursue solo careers, it had earned eight gold and five platinum albums. Yarrow continued to focus on his songwriting and political activism, and produced three Emmy Award-winning CBS specials based on "Puff the Magic Dragon." In 1978, Peter, Paul and Mary reunited for an antinuclear benefit, which led to sporadic reunion shows throughout the 1980s. The group released a record of new material in 1988, *A Holiday Celebration*, and subsequently released several live albums and a few new albums of original material. Their children's album, and accompanying television special, "Peter, Paul and Mommy, Too," won the group a Grammy and an Emmy. The group was inducted into the Vocal Group Hall of Fame in 1999.

[Harry Rubenstein (2nd ed.)]

YASKI, AVRAHAM (1927–), Israeli architect. Born in Kishinev, Yaski was brought to Palestine in 1935. A prizewinning architect, he designed the social sciences wing of the Givat Ram campus of the Hebrew University, the IBM building in Tel Aviv, the Ben-Gurion University of the Negev campus, and the Gilo neighborhood in Jerusalem. In 1982 he was awarded the Israel Prize for architecture.

YASSER, JOSEPH (1893–1981), organist, musicologist, and theorist. Born in Lodz, Poland, he began his musical studies in Moscow at the age of six under the pianist Jacob Weinberg. In 1917, he graduated from the Moscow Conservatory, where he studied with Alexander Goedicke and Leonid Sabaneyev. There he was appointed director of the Organ Department and concurrently served as organist for the Bolshoi Theater. Following a three-year sojourn in China, where in Shanghai he directed a choral society; he immigrated to the United States in 1923. Settling in New York, he established a reputation as a performing artist, whose organ recitals earned him positions at prestigious Reform synagogues, and ultimately as organist and choirmaster at Temple Rodeph Shalom from 1929 to 1960.

He published an important treatise, *A Theory of Evolving Tonality* (1932), which postulates the evolution from the primitive pentatonic (5-tone) through the diatonic (7-tone) and chromatic (12-tone) scale to the formation of an ultrachromatic scale of 19 microtonal intervals of equal size. His second and controversial treatise on *Medieval Quartal Harmony* (1938) proposed the 4th as a preferred interval over the 5th for accompanying plainchant. Yasser wrote articles on various aspects of Jewish and Russian music, served on the faculty of the Cantors' Institute at the Jewish Theological Seminary (1952–60), and was one of the founders of the American Musicological Society (1935); he was actively involved with the Jewish Music Forum (1945–55) and the National Jewish Music Council (1944–60).

BIBLIOGRAPHY: MGG²; NG²; A. Weisser, *Selected Writings and Lectures of Joseph Yasser: An Annotated Bibliography* (1979); H. Berlinski, "Joseph Yasser (1893–1981): A Personal Recollection," in: *Musica Judaica*, 4 (1981–82), 113–20.

[Israel J. Katz (2nd ed.)]

YASSKY, HAIM (1896–1948), medical administrator in Palestine. Born in Kishinev, Bessarabia, Yassky took part in underground Zionist activities and in Jewish *self-defense in Odessa. He went to Palestine in 1919, just before his final medical examinations. After working as a sanitary inspector, he went to Geneva, completing his medical studies and specializing in ophthalmology. He joined the *Hadassah Medical Organization in 1921. In 1924 he successfully tackled the scourge of trachoma in Judea and earned wide recognition. Appointed director of Hadassah Medical Organization in 1931, he initiated the erection of the Rothschild-Hadassah University Hospital on Mount Scopus (1939), a medical center that established high standards in the Middle East. He developed blueprints for the Jerusalem Medical School and for the immigrant medical service. Yassky was killed by Arabs in the massacre of April 13, 1948, while leading staff and colleagues in a convoy from the city to Mount Scopus. The Hadassah Hospital in Beersheba and the chair of social medicine at the Hebrew University-Hadassah Medical School were named after him.

[Eli Davis]

YATED NEEMAN, Israeli daily newspaper published in Benei Berak. Established in 1985, *Yated Neeman* is the acronym of "*Yoman Da'at Torah*" ("Torah Opinion Journal"). It was founded as a rival newspaper by the Degel ha-Torah Party after Rabbi Eliezer *Shach, the spiritual leader of Lithuanian ("Litvak") Jews, resigned from the Council of Torah Sages – the umbrella group of ḥaredi rabbis – after the Council declined to publish his views in the Agudat Israel party newspaper *Hamodia* in a dispute with the Gur Rebbe over sanctioning the erection of a hotel in Tiberias at the site of Jewish graves. Its founding editor was Moshe Grylick. In 1988 he was succeeded by Natan Grossman.

Yated Neeman and *Ha-Modi'a* remained the only party newspapers in Israel, the former reflecting the views of Degel ha-Torah, as when it refused to take advertisements for housing in the ḥaredi town of Emanuel because it was beyond the "green line"; Shach argued that *piku'aḥ nefesh* (the saving of life) took precedence over the biblical injunction not to relinquish Jewish land in Ereẓ Israel.

In addition to party journalism, it also acted as an educational instrument. The newspaper was controlled by a spiritual committee, whose censors examined the contents of each issue – editorial and advertising – prior to publication to ensure it did not offend ḥaredi sensibilities. Sex-related content and pictures of women were taboo in conformity with ḥaredi views on modesty (*ẓeniyut*). The names of women journalists on the newspaper were abbreviated. Much crime went uncovered. Entertainment and sports were also not covered. In aspiring to build the model Jewish society, the ḥaredi newspaper was also a channel to educate readers in the historical ḥaredi opposition to Zionism as premature vis-à-vis the coming of the Messiah, and to attack Israeli institutions like the Knesset and the Supreme Court for making decisions regarded as running counter to Torah values.

It published eight pages daily, including national political news, news about the Lithuanian ḥaredi sector, and world news. On weekends it had two supplements: a magazine, and a *kadosh* section containing inspiring essays by rabbis on the weekly Bible reading, Jewish law, and Jewish history. On Thursdays there were family supplements geared to women and on Tuesdays a children's supplement.

Shach's death in 2001 left a void. The dispute over whether Rabbi Elyashiv or Rabbi Steineman would become Shach's recognized successor was also played out in *Yated Neeman*. The editors became divided, with the daily edition, edited by Grossman, identifying with Rabbi Elyashiv and the Sabbath edition identifying with Rabbi Steineman.

Nineteen percent of ḥaredim read *Yated Neeman* daily in 2005, and 21% read the Sabbath eve issue. A 1995 survey found that 64% of the newspaper's readers defined themselves as Lithuanian ḥaredim and 22% were undefined ḥaredim (only 7% replied that they were ḥasidim). The newspaper had to contend with a rival ḥaredi commercial press, which grew in the 1980s and 1990s. A weekly English-language newspaper broke away from the Hebrew paper and was published in the United States. In conformity with the ḥaredi rabbinic ban on the Internet, the newspaper had no website.

BIBLIOGRAPHY: M. Mikolson, "Ḥaredi Newspapers in Israel" (Heb.), in: *Kesher*, 8 (1990); Y. Cohen, "Mass Media in the Jewish Tradition," in D. Stout and J. Buddenbaum, *Religion & Popular Culture* (2001); Israel Advertisers Association, *Seker Ḥasifah le-Emẓa'ei Tikshoret: Ḥaredim* (1995).

[Yoel Cohen (2nd ed.)]

YATES, SIDNEY RICHARD (1909–2000), U.S. lawyer and congressman. Born in Chicago, Illinois, Yates received a B.A. from the University of Chicago in 1931 and a Juris Doctor degree in 1933. He was admitted to the Illinois bar in 1933, and practiced law in his own firm. He was assistant attorney to the Illinois Bank Receiver (1935–37) and assistant attorney general attached to the Illinois Commerce Commission (1937–40). He served in the U.S. Navy during World War II (1944–46). First elected to Congress in 1948, Yates was on the Appropriations Committee and the Committee on Small Business of the House of Representatives for ten years. In 1962 he yielded his seat to run successfully for the Senate. The following year President John F. Kennedy appointed him U.S. representative to the Trusteeship Council of the United Nations, with the rank of ambassador. There he served until 1964, when he returned to his former position in the House of Representatives, remaining there until 1999. A friend of Adlai Stevenson, he was always considered a liberal. He opposed the supersonic transport (SST) and the Sentinel antiballistic missile system (ABM), fought for ecology measures, urban housing improvements, and changes in the electoral system. Yates was a member of the American Veterans Committee, the Decalogue Society of Lawyers (editor of its bulletin in 1947), and the Chicago Council of Foreign Relations.

YAVETS, ZVI (1925–), historian. Yavets was born in Czernowitz, Romania, and made his way to Palestine in 1944. He obtained his doctorate from the Hebrew University of Jerusalem in 1956, and after few years as a lecturer at the Hebrew University of Jerusalem, he moved to Tel Aviv University in 1959. In 1962–64 he served as dean of University of Addis-Ababa in Ethiopia. In 1964 he was appointed as dean of Humanities in Tel Aviv University and from 1966 he was chairman of the Department of History at Tel Aviv University. In 1970 he became chairman of the Graduate School of History. Yavets also held the Lessing Chair in Roman History from 1976. His book *Princeps and Plebs* (1969) was of seminal importance to the field of Roman history. His other books – he wrote 23 and edited 9 – and over 50 articles made significant contributions to the study of Greek, Roman, and Jewish history in ancient times. He was awarded the Israel Prize for the humanities in 1990.

[Fern Lee Seckbach / Shaked Gilboa (2nd ed.)]

YAVIN, ḤAYYIM (1932–), Israeli TV news presenter. Yavin began his media career in 1956 on Israel's Kol Israel radio station as a news, entertainment, and music presenter. In 1962 he helped start up a new radio station, Ha-Gal ha-Kal, which later became Reshet Bet, Kol Israel's second station. Subsequently he became a producer, editor, and presenter in the documentary department. When the Israeli government decided to establish a TV channel, he was chosen to present the first news edition. From then on he was the main presenter of the nightly news on Israeli TV. He also produced TV documentaries and taught in academic institutions. Yavin was famous for his announcement of Menaḥem *Begin's 1977 election win with the single word *mahapakh* ("upset"), which marked a dramatic highpoint in Israeli broadcasting and became a Hebrew idiom. In 1977 he was awarded the Israel Prize for media.

YAVNE'ELI (Jawnieli, Warshavsky), SHEMUEL (1884–1961), labor leader in Ereẓ Israel. Born in Kazanka, a village near Kherson, Ukraine, Yavne'eli went to Ereẓ Israel in 1905, worked as an agricultural laborer in Judea, and contributed to the labor periodicals, particularly *Ha-Po'el ha-Ẓa'ir.* In 1911 he was sent to *Yemen at his own request by the Palestine Office of the Zionist Organization to study the Jewish community there and encourage it to migrate to Ereẓ Israel. He undertook two lengthy journeys in Yemen: one from *Aden through Sanʿa to Hodeida, and the other from Aden to *Hadramaut, reaching *Habbān. Yavne'eli rode on mules and donkeys; he was bearded and dressed in Yemenite fashion. The Jews of Yemen and Hadhramaut saw in him a harbinger of the imminent redemption of the people and the land of Israel through *aliyah* and by tilling the ancestral soil. The journey lasted over a year, and subsequently large groups of Yemenite Jews migrated to Ereẓ Israel, reaching it before the outbreak of World War I. The journey is described (with documents) in Yavne'eli's book, *Massa le-Teiman* ("Journey to Yemen," 1952). He was a member of the executive committee of the *Aḥdut ha-Avodah Party and later a member of the *Mapai central committee. He was also active in the *Histadrut in the cultural and educational spheres, and also in the social insurance system.

His other books include: *Bi-Negohot ha-Yamim* (collected articles 1951) and *Aliyat ha-Yesod* (1952). He edited the writings of Berl *Katznelson and published studies in Zionist history: *Tekufat Ḥibbat Ẓiyyon* (2 vols., 1961[2]) and *Be-Vokrah shel Tenu'ah* (1939). Three volumes of his collected works appeared in 1961–62 (bibliography of his writings, vol. 3, 335–56).

BIBLIOGRAPHY: Z. Shazar, *Or Ishim* (1963[2]), 203–9; Tidhar, 8 (1957), 3026–27.

YAVNEH, development town in central Israel, 5 mi. (8 km.). S.W. of Reḥovot. At the end of the 19th century the population of the Arab village Yibn, on the site of historical *Jabneh, increased due to the proximity of such Jewish settlements as *Gederah and *Reḥovot, which supplied opportunities for hired labor and constituted markets for farm products. Arab farmers added garden crops to their grain fields and later planted citrus groves. In 1943 the village had about 3,600 inhabitants and in 1947 about 4,000. During the *War of Independence *Haganah forces occupied Yibnā in May 1948, thereby halting the Egyptian army's advance against Jaffa and Tel Aviv. From the end of 1948 Jewish immigrants were housed in the abandoned village, and in 1949 a number of moshavim – Ben Zakkai, Bet Gamli'el and Benayah – were founded in the vicinity. Yavneh gradually became a semi-urban agglomeration and received municipal council status. In the first phase, small trade, hired labor in farming and industry, and some auxiliary farming formed a narrow economic base. Living standards were low, housing was often primitive, and social cases were numerous. With progressive industrialization, including the transfer of several enterprises from the Tel Aviv area to Yavneh, the town progressed economically, particularly in the 1960s. It contains leather, textiles, metals, and other industries. New housing quarters were built and social and educational standards improved. Its population increased from 1,600 in 1953 to over 10,100 in 1970. By the mid-1990s the population was 25,600, further rising to 31,700 in 2002 and occupying an area of 12 sq. mi. (30 sq. km.). Yavneh received city status in 1986. The main latter-day economic branches were industry, crafts, commerce, and services. A splendid *Mamluk building is traditionally held to house the tomb of R. *Simeon ben Gamaliel II, the Sanhedrin president at Jabneh.

WEBSITE: www.yavne2000.net/yavne/index.html.

[Efraim Orni / Shaked Gilboa (2nd ed.)]

YAVNEH (Heb. יַבְנֶה), kibbutz in the southern Coastal Plain of Israel, about 5 mi. (8 km.) S. of the town of Yavneh, affiliated with Ha-Kibbutz ha-Dati. It was founded in 1941 by pioneers from Germany. They were later joined by members from English-speaking and other countries and by Israeli-born graduates of the *Bnei Akiva movement. Yavneh soon became a center of the religious kibbutz movement and set up a yeshivah, Kerem be-Yavneh, and a *Youth Aliyah village, Givat Washington. In 1970, Yavneh numbered 645 inhabitants; a further 200 lived at the yeshivah. In the mid-1990s the population was approximately 730, rising to 1,030 in 2002. The kibbutz developed intensive, mostly irrigated farming as well as having poultry, turkeys, dairy cattle, and field crops. It also produced cattle feed and had a hatchery turning out 600,000 chicks a week along with a food preserves plant and watch factory. The historical name Yavneh was chosen for the kibbutz for its proximity to the historical site of *Jabneh.

[Efraim Orni / Shaked Gilboa (2nd ed.)]

YAVNEH-YAM, LEGAL DOCUMENT FROM, an inscribed potsherd (maximal measures: 8 × 6 in., or 20 × 16 cm.) containing a Hebrew letter of 14 lines, found in the guardroom of an ancient fortress excavated at Meẓad Ḥashavyahu by J. Naveh (1960), about one mile south of Yavneh-Yam (Minat-Rubin). The examination of the pottery found on the site (partly East Greek sherds of the Middle Wild Goat Style from 630–600 B.C.E.), the historical and geographic considerations, as well as the paleographic evidence indicate that the fortress was built by *Josiah king of Judah (640–609 B.C.E.).

The letter begins with the following phrase: "Let my lord the governor hear the word of his servant." The addressee apparently was Josiah's military governor in the newly conquered coastal area which formerly belonged to the Philistines. In the letter, written by a local scribe, a reaper, who was employed in harvesting at a royal estate named Ḥaẓar-Asam, complains of the confiscation of his coat by a man named Hoshaiahu the son of Shobai, evidently the governor's official. It seems that the charge in question was one of idling. The reaper requests the governor to return his garment, because he has finished his quota and his fellow reapers are prepared to testify his innocence.

This document sheds light on laws concerning negligence in the biblical period, well known from cuneiform sources (see

Driver-Miles in bibl.). Exodus 22:25–26, which admonishes the creditor to give back the debtor's garment "before the sun goes down," reflects a similar situation, and was instituted to protect the debtor.

BIBLIOGRAPHY: G.R. Driver and C. Miles, *Babylonian Laws*, 1 (1952), 461ff.; J. Naveh, in: IEJ, 10 (1960), 129–39; 14 (1964), 158–59; idem, in: *Leshonenu*, 30 (1965), 69–71; S. Yeivin, in: *Bibliotheca Orientalis*, 29 (1962), 3–10; F.M. Gross in: BASOR, 165 (1962), 34–46; I. Sh. Shifman, *Epigrafika Vostoka*, 16 (1963), 21–28; Sh. Talmon, in: BASOR, 176 (1964), 29–38; J.D. Amusin and M.L. Heltzer, in: IEJ, 14 (1964), 148–57; Pritchard, Texts^3, 568; L. Delekat, in: *Biblica*, 51 (1970), 453–70 (includes an extensive bibliography).

[Joseph Naveh]

YAVOROV (Pol. **Jaworów**), city in Lvov oblast, Ukraine, within Poland until World War II. The first information about Jewish settlement in Yavorov dates from 1538. The community increased during the 16th and 17th centuries. In 1627, 56 Jewish families are recorded, 23 of them houseowners; besides merchants and artisans the community included viticulturists. An agreement concluded in 1641 between the Jews and burghers of Yavorov regulated the social and economic status of the Jews of the city. Many Jews in Yavorov perished during the *Chmielnicki massacres in 1648. The community was later reconstituted; in 1658 it received assistance from King John Sobieski, the owner of the city, in building a magnificent wooden synagogue. Within the communal framework, the Yavorov congregation formed part of the borough of *Lvov, and played an important role in community affairs. The Jewish population in Yavorov numbered about 700 in 1765; 1,837 (about 21% of the total population) in 1857; 2,405 in 1921; and 2,950 (about 27.5%) in 1931. Among scholars of Yavorov, the best known are Ḥayyim b. Leib, *parnas* and leader of the Councils of the *Lands from 1673 to 1690; the preacher Berechiah *Berakh the younger, who lived in Yavorov between 1725 and 1730; and Jehiel *Altschuler (about 1753).

[Aryeh-Lieb Kalish]

Holocaust Period

Before the German invasion (June 1941), the Jewish population of Yavorov numbered more than 3,000. Early in July 1941 the Germans ordered the Jews to remove all ritual articles and prayer books from their homes, throw them into the flames of the burning synagogue, and stand by and chant religious melodies. That month 15 persons were shot. In April 1942, 1,000 young Jews and in July, 100 girls were deported to the Janow camp. On Nov. 7–8, 1942, an *Aktion* took place: 1,300 persons were deported to the *Belzec death camp and about 200 were shot on the spot. Some 200 persons found refuge in hideouts but were discovered and shot a few days later. The remaining Jews were concentrated into the ghetto, where Jews from Mosciska, Krakowiec, Sadowa Wisznia, Wielkie Oczy, Szklo, Ozomle, and other nearby towns were also brought. In the spring of 1943 an organized group of youths fled to the forest. They obtained arms and conducted partisan activities in the Lubaczewski area. Artur Henner headed one group and Henry Gleich another. Most of the youths fell in battle. On April 18, 1943 the ghetto was liquidated. Some Jews hid in bunkers in the Janow forest, but most of them were exterminated.

[Aharon Weiss]

BIBLIOGRAPHY: E. Webersfeld, *Jaworów, Monografia Historyczna, Etnograficzna i Statistyczna* (1909).

YEAR (Heb. שָׁנָה, *shanah*), the period during which the earth makes one complete revolution around the sun. This period corresponds roughly to 12 revolutions of the moon around the earth. The determination of the length of a year and its 12 parts for fixing agricultural, cultic, and political cycles led to the development of calendars. Three of these are clearly attested in the Bible. The most common one, which is accepted by the priestly stratum of the Pentateuch (e.g., Lev. 16:29), designates the months of the year numerically as do the pre-Exilic prophets (e.g., Jer. 28:1). Elsewhere in the Pentateuch, as in the pre-Exilic historical books, the months are given names of apparently Canaanite origin. The Book of Deuteronomy employs each system once (Deut. 1:3; 16:1). Post-Exilic writings designate the months by names of Babylonian origin.

The priestly calendar called for a solar year made up of 12 months of 30 days each. Thus the sun and moon were to "serve as signs for the set times – the days and the years" (Gen. 1:14), but not for the months. Consequently, the duration of the Deluge – from the 17th of the second month to the 17th of the seventh month – was exactly 150 days (Gen. 7:11; 8:3–4).

In this calendar the days were counted from sunrise, as noted by Ibn Ezra in his commentary on Genesis 1:5. Leviticus 23:32, however, may point to the reckoning of days from the end of twilight.

The first month of the year in the priestly calendar was that in which Passover fell (Ex. 12:1–2, 18). Thus there were five and a half months intervening between the first day of the Feast of Tabernacles (Lev. 23:39ff.) and the beginning of the new year and exactly six months between the former and the first day of the Feast of Unleavened Bread. A second biblical calendar, that of the Covenant Code (Ex. 21–24) and the Smaller Covenant Code (Ex. 34) designated the Feast of Ingathering as the end of the year (Ex. 23:16) or the turn of the year (Ex. 34:22). In this calendar, therefore, the Feast of Unleavened Bread would presumably come in the seventh month. The latter was designated by the name Abib, "green ear of grain," rather than by number.

The designation of this month by name and the general agreement that the Covenant Code reflects the early monarchical period or the period of the Judges have led to the assumption that the calendar of JE is the same as that referred to in I Kings 6–8. There it is stated that the foundations of Solomon's Temple were laid in the month of Ziv (I Kings 6:1,37), that the Temple was completed seven years later in the month of Bul (I Kings 6:38), and that it was dedicated in the month of Ethanim (I Kings 8:2). The special word for month (Heb. *yeraḥ*) used in these contexts which is attested altogether only 12 times in the entire Hebrew Bible, refers specifically to a lunar month. In each of these passages in I Kings the narrator gives the equivalent date according to the priestly calendar. The lunar month of Ziv is therefore designated also as the second 30-day month (Heb. *ḥodesh*).

Evidently the transition from a year of named lunar months to a year of numerically designated months of 30 days each took place between the time of King Solomon and the redaction of the Book of Kings. The months of the later calendar were designated by the term previously employed for New Moon (Heb. *ḥodesh*, e.g., I Sam. 20:18).

The calendar of the early monarchy corresponds to the *Gezer Calendar in three respects. These are (1) the lunar month (Her. *yeraḥ*); (2) the association of the names of months with agricultural phenomena; and (3) the beginning of the year with the ingathering (Heb. *ʾasif*).

There is no biblical evidence as to how the lunar calendar of the early monarchy was reconciled with the solar year. It is obvious, however, that this agricultural calendar could not ignore it. The 360-day priestly calendar, however, may very well not have been reconciled with the true solar year by intercalation inasmuch as the Egyptians assumed a 360-day year down to 237 B.C.E.

The third biblical calendar, which is first attested in Zechariah 1:7 and 7:1, employs the Babylonian month names, which go back to the calendar of Nippur that antedated Hammurapi. According to rabbinic tradition, these names were imported by those who returned to the land of Israel from the Babylonian Exile (TJ, RH 1:2, 56d). It is most likely that these immigrants also introduced the lunar-solar calendar and the intercalation of a month to reconcile the lunar and solar years, a characteristic of the Babylonian calendar. The adoption of the Babylonian calendar was also responsible for the custom of reckoning the day from the previous evening (e.g., Esth. 4:16; Dan. 8:14). While Zechariah and Esther (Esth. 2:16, et al.) clarify dates in the priestly calendar by reference to the Babylonian system, Nehemiah (Neh. 2:1) employs only the Babylonian names of months.

The Book of Jubilees and the Book of Enoch both reflect sectarian tendencies which regarded the Babylonian lunar-solar calendar as offensive to God as the eating of blood (Jub. 6:38). The sectarians opposed the rabbis' adjustment of the calendar based on the observation of the moon, and they insisted on no deviation from a year of 52 weeks and 364 days (Jub. 6:30–32). The 364 days were attained by counting 12 months of 30 days each and four intercalary days (I En. 82:6). Despite speculations to the contrary, the testimony of the sources admits of no further adjustments.

It has been widely asserted that the priestly calendar's numbering of the months beginning with that in which Passover falls reflects the Babylonian *akītu*-festival or spring New Year. Y. Kaufmann, however, has argued convincingly that both the spring and the autumn New Years are of equally ancient native Israelite origin. Thus the very oldest biblical calendars (Ex. 23:15; 34:18) begin the numbering of the festivals with the Feast of Unleavened Bread while even the priestly calendar figured the beginning of the agricultural year from the seventh month of the liturgical year (Lev. 25:8; cf. Deut. 11:12; 31:10).

Aside from the 50 days which intervene between Passover and Pentecost (Lev. 23:16; Deut. 16:9), there is no evidence for a pentecostal calendar in ancient Israel. The theory which assumes such a calendar is based on a most dubious interpretation of the time-unit *ḫumuštum* mentioned in Old Assyrian economic texts from Cappadocia.

In the Pentateuch years and months are sometimes numbered from the Exodus (Ex. 19:1; Num. 9:1) as in I Kings 6:1. The pre-Exilic prophets and historical books generally number the years in accordance with the years of the reign of the kings of Israel and Judah while post-Exilic writers number the years with reference to the years of the reign of the ruler of Persia (Haggai 1:1; Neh. 2:1).

In Jewish tradition, the religious year begins in the month of Nisan, while the civil year (e.g., in reigns of kings or in contracts) in Tishri.

BIBLIOGRAPHY: M. Muss-Arnolt, in: JBL, 11 (1829), 72–94; B. Meissner, *Babylonien und Assyrien*, 1 (1920), 125ff.; J. Morgenstern, in: HUCA, 1 (1924), 13–77; Kaufmann Y., Toledot, 2 (1960), 491–8; de Vaux, Anc Isr, 178–93; M. Gruber, in: *Journal of the Ancient Near Eastern Society of Columbia University*, 1 (1969), 14–20; R.T. Beckwith, in: *Revue de Qumran*, 27 (1970), 379–96.

[Mayer Irwin Gruber]

YEDIDYAH (Heb. יְדִידְיָה), moshav in central Israel, 3 mi. (5 km.) N.W. of Netanyah, affiliated with Tenu'at ha-Moshavim. Yedidyah was founded in 1935 by settlers from Germany and had 285 inhabitants in 1970. In the mid-1990s the population was around 395, further increasing to 489 in 2002. Its economy was based mainly on citrus groves, olive plantations, flowers, plant nurseries, dairy cattle, and poultry. The moshav was named after the philosopher Philo (Yedidyah).

[Efram Orni / Shaked Gilboa (2nd ed.)]

BIBLIOGRAPHY: www.kyedidya.org.il

YEDINTSY (Rom. **Edineți**), town in N. Moldova in the region of Bessarabia. Yedintsy developed in the first half of the 19th century from a village into an urban settlement as a result of the settlement of Jews who were then coming to Bessarabia. In 1897 the Jews numbered 7,379 (72 percent of the total population) and in 1930 5,341 (90.4 percent). The writer Judah *Steinberg lived there at the end of the 19th century. The institutions of the community included a hospital, established in 1930, and a *Tarbut school.

[Eliyahu Feldman]

Holocaust Period

The town was occupied by Germans and Romanians on July 5, 1941. Within two days 500 to 1,000 Jews were murdered. Women and young girls were raped and some of them committed suicide. The victims were buried in three large ditches and the Jewish gravediggers who had interred the bodies were in turn murdered and buried on the spot. Romanian gendarmes and troops were assisted in the massacre of the Jews by many of the peasants living in the area. In the middle of August a concentration camp was set up at Yedintsy, where all surviving Jews and those from different places in the north of Bessarabia, particularly from *Bukovina, were interned. In September there were about 12,000 Jews in the camp. Many of the inmates succumbed to disease, cold weather, hunger, and thirst; 70 to 100 persons died every day. On Sept. 16, 1941 all the inmates of the camp were deported to *Transnistria and only a few managed to survive. The few dozen families still alive at the end of the war settled either in Chernovtsy or in Israel. Only a handful chose to return to Yedintsy. In the late 1960s the Jewish population was estimated at about 200. There was no synagogue although the Jewish cemetery was still extant.

[Jean Ancel]

BIBLIOGRAPHY: T. Fuks, *A Vanderung Iber Okupirte Gebitn* (1947), index; Eisenberger, in: *Arbeter Vort* (Nov. 29, 1946); M. Carp, *Cartea neagră*, 3 (1947), index; BJCE.

YEDIOTH AHARONOTH, afternoon daily newspaper founded in Tel Aviv in 1939 by Nahum Komerov. The following year the newspaper came into the possession of a printer named Alexander *Mozes. Its editorial operation was administered by Alexander's father, Yehudah, who took on the title of publisher, and brother, Noah. The paper consisted of mostly two pages daily, and had a circulation of only 30,000. Facing heavy financial losses, the family sold half of the newspaper's stock to *Mapai in 1949. But its major crisis had occurred a year earlier in February 1948, when its editor, Dr. Azriel *Carlebach, and most of its journalistic and administrative staff walked out overnight, partly because of excessive intervention by management in editorial matters, and a lack of clear demarcation between editorial content and advertising interests. The group formed their own newspaper, **Maariv*, to be owned and run by journalists. *Maariv* grew to became Israel's largest newspaper with an estimated circulation of 200,000. Rebuilding *Yedioth Aharonoth*, Yehudah Mozes appointed Dr. Herzl *Rosenblum as editor, with responsibility for the op-ed pages and a daily signed editorial which appeared for over 40 years until his retirement in 1986. Dov *Yudkovsky, the managing editor for news, conceived the newspaper to be the "the people's newspaper," with both a tabloid appearance and editorial matter of interest to readers from the professional classes. With the death of Yehudah in 1955, Noah Mozes became publisher. By the end of the 1960s, *Yedioth Aharonoth* drew even with *Maariv* in its circulation war, and in the mid-1970s took over the lead, maintaining its position since. Its publication schedule gradually moved to the early morning. By the end of the century, the newspaper had achieved a very high circulation: a 2005 Teleseker survey reported that 42% of Israelis read it daily, and 54% the Friday weekend issue.

The newspaper's financial structure is centralized, with its company stock comprising 100 basic shares and 1,400 regular shares. The basic share stock was divided between family members. Following Noah Mozes' death in a traffic accident in 1986, his son, Arnon ("Noni"), became publisher and sought to monopolize the running of the newspaper and its associated operations by buying out the stock of other family members. Dov Yudkovsky, who was Yehudah Mozes' cousin, was fired, and he moved to *Maariv* where he became editor. In the 1990s the newspaper became involved in the so-called wiretapping affair with *Maariv*. Editor Moshe Vardi and assignments editor Ruth Ben Ari received suspended sentences. Vardi was reinstated afterward and continued as editor until his retirement in 2004, upon which Rafi Ginat, an Israel Television journalist, was appointed editor.

In 2000 the newspaper created an Internet website, Y-Net, with a separate reporting staff. In 2005 it had 3.3 million users monthly. The newspaper's growth in the 1980s and 1990s extended to a chain of 17 local newspapers, special interest publications including women's magazines, shares in the Channel 2 television network, and book publishing.

[Yoel Cohen (2nd ed.)]

YEFET, SARAH (1934–), Israeli historian specializing in the biblical historiography of the Second Temple period and the Jewish interpretation of the Bible in the Middle Ages. Yefet was born in Petaḥ Tikvah. She received her Ph.D. in Bible studies from the Hebrew University of Jerusalem in 1973, becoming a lecturer (1973) and professor (1987) in the Department of Bible Studies there. From 1984 to 1986 she was the head of the department. From 1990 to 1993 and in 1996 she served as professor in the Beit Midrash for Jewish Studies in Jerusalem. During these years she was a visiting professor in various universities in the United States and Britain, including Berkeley, Oxford, Harvard, and Cambridge. In 1996–97 she was the chairwoman of the academic committee of Magnes Press and in 1997–2001 she was the head of the National and University Library. Yefet published many articles and books, among them *Rabbi Samuel ben Meir's Interpretation of Ecclesiastes* (1985); *Rabbi Samuel ben Meir's Interpretation of Job* (2000); *Studies in Bible* (1986); and *The Bible in the Light of Its Interpreters* (1996). In 2004 she received the Israel Prize for Bible studies.

[Shaked Gilboa (2nd ed.)]

YEFINGAR, Jewish agricultural settlement on the River Ingul (Kherson district, Nikolaev province of Ukraine), which existed from 1809 to 1941. The first settlers attracted by the political support of the Czarist government for agriculture were, evidently, from Lithuania. There were 48 families with 276 people who originally took up viticulture and kitchen-gardening. In 1897, Yefingar had a Jewish population of 2,038 out of a total population of 2,226 and had a Jewish school. Under the Soviets a Jewish collective farm was established in Yefingar which became one of the most prosperous in the province. With the German attack on Russia in June 1941 almost all the male population was called up military service; several days before the arrival of German forces teenagers and all means of transportation were mobilized. The other inhabitants were not evacuated. After Yefingar was occupied by the German troops, all the remaining Jews (521 people) were executed by the Germans and their local accomplices on September 10, 1941. After the war Yefingar was renamed Plyushchevka. The inscription on the monument there, set up with great difficulty by relatives of those massacred, does not indicate that the victims were Jews. No Jews now live in the village and the former Jewish cemetery has been destroyed.

[*Shorter Jewish Encyclopedia in Russian*]

YEFROYKIN, ISRAEL (1884–1954), socialist and communal leader, born in Vieksniai, Lithuania. In 1904 he became active in the Zionist socialist group *Vozrozhdenie. He was among the founders in Russia of the monthly *Yidishe Velt* in 1912 with S. *Dubnow, I. *Zinberg, and others. After the February 1917 Revolution he organized with S. Dubnow, N. *Shtif, and others the Yidishe *Folkspartei. In 1920 he went to Paris with a delegation of the *YEKOPO (Jewish Relief Committee), and directed its central office there until its liquidation in 1925. He was one of the founders of the *World Jewish Congress in 1936. With E. *Tcherikower he published *Oyfn Sheydweg* ("On the crossroads," Paris 1939), a literary anthology. During World War II he took refuge in Montevideo, Uruguay, where he was coeditor of the review *Shriftn* and joined the Po'alei Zion – Hitaḥadut party. He subsequently returned to Paris, where between 1948 and 1952 he edited the review *Kiem*. His writings include *In Kholem un oyf der Vor* ("In Dream and Reality," 1944); *A Kheshbn Hanefesh* ("Introspection," 1948); and *Kedushe un Gevure bay Yidn Amol un Haynt* ("Self-Sacrifice and Heroism by Jews in the Past and Today," 1949).

BIBLIOGRAPHY: Dvoretsky, in: *Di Goldene Keyt*, no. 20 (1954), 199–211; Halpern, in: *Zukunft*, 59 (1954), 269–71; Y. Gruenbaum, *Penei ha-Dor* (1957), 245–9.

YEḤI'AM (Heb. יְחִיעָם), kibbutz in northern Israel, 7 mi. (12 km.) E. of Nahariyyah, affiliated with Kibbutz Arẓi, ha-Shomer ha-Ẓa'ir. Yeḥi'am was founded by pioneers from Hungary and Israel-born youth in 1946, at a time of maximum tension between the *yishuv* and Mandatory authorities. Its establishment in the brush-covered mountain terrain near the crusader castle ruin Jūdīn was valued as a step of political importance. In the *War of Independence, the isolated kibbutz held out against overwhelming odds using the castle as a fort. A convoy of 47 men to reinforce Yeḥi'am was ambushed and wiped out near *Kabri (March 28, 1948). The siege was lifted in May 1948. The front lines finally receded from Yeḥi'am with Operation Ḥiram (October) which cleared all of Galilee. In 1970 Yeḥi'am had 415 inhabitants, dropping to 362 in 2002. Its economy was based on citrus groves, plantations, and poultry. The kibbutz also produced meat products and operated guest rooms. The name commemorates Yeḥi'am Weitz, who fell with 13 comrades on June 17, 1946, in an action to blast the Achzib bridge (*Gesher ha-Ziv).

[Efraim Orni]

YEHOASH (pseudonym of **Yehoash Solomon Bloomgarden**; 1872–1927), Yiddish poet and translator. Yehoash was born in Virbalen, Lithuania, and as a boy he read maskilic literature as well as studying Torah with his father, briefly attending the yeshivah of Volozhin, only to begin a career as a Hebrew poet. At the age of 17 he took his first Hebrew poems to Warsaw, where I.L. *Peretz encouraged him to continue writing Hebrew and Yiddish lyrics. The following year Yehoash immigrated to the U.S. He made no headway either as a Hebrew poet or in various callings – bookkeeping, tailoring, peddling, and Hebrew teaching. For a decade he faced severe privations until he contracted tuberculosis and went to the Denver Sanatorium for Consumptives in 1900 to recuperate. There he remained for almost ten years, maturing as a Yiddish poet, publishing his poems, ballads, fables, and translations in leading dailies, periodicals, and literary almanacs. In his early 30s, he undertook to translate the Bible into a modern Yiddish which would combine scholarly precision with simple idiomatic language, a task to which he devoted the rest of his life. While at work on this translation, he prepared, together with Charles D. Spivak, his physician and the co-founder of the sanatorium, a Yiddish dictionary, first published in 1911, which defined about 4,000 Hebrew and Aramaic words used in Yiddish and which went through many editions as a basic reference work.

Returning to New York in 1909, Yehoash had to struggle to make a living, even though his fame was worldwide and Yiddish periodicals in many lands gladly published his contributions. In January 1914, he left for Ereẓ Israel and settled in Reḥovot. He mastered classical Arabic and translated portions of the Koran and Arabian tales into Yiddish. When the Ottoman Empire entered World War I, he returned to New York and published the story of his experiences in three volumes of travel sketches, *Fun New York biz Rekhovot un Tsurik* ("From New York to Reḥovot and Back," 1917–18; Eng. *The Feet of the Messenger*, 1923). His sojourn in Ereẓ Israel as well as his knowledge of Arabic proved useful to him in his work on the translation of the Bible. Although he had published a Yiddish rendering of several biblical books including Isaiah and Job in 1910, he realized the inadequacy of this initial attempt and began anew. His more adequate rendering, starting with Genesis, appeared in installments in the New York daily *Der Tog* from 1922. At the time of his death only the Pentateuch translation had been published, but the rest of the biblical books were printed from his manuscripts. His version was hailed as a contribution of national significance. The translator drew upon idiomatic treasures of various Yiddish dialects, upon the *Khumesh-Taytsh* (the Old Yiddish, word-for-word translation of Pentateuch), vocabulary used by *melammedim* in Ashkenazi schools for many generations, and expressions of the **Ẓe'enah u-Re'enah* (*Tsene-Rene*), with its archaic patina. Yehoash was thus able to retain the rhythm and flavor of the Hebrew to a larger extent than preceding Bible translators. The two-volume edition, with parallel Hebrew and Yiddish texts, distributed in tens of thousands of copies, became a standard work for Yiddish-speaking homes throughout the world. In 1949, Mordecai Kosover edited Yehoash's notes to the Bible, which afforded an insight into the translator's many years of wrestling with the sacred text.

Yehoash, who also translated Longfellow's *Hiawatha* and the *Rubáiyát* of Omar Khayyam into Yiddish, was far ahead of his time in terms of his own poetry. When the first edition of his *Gezamelte Lider* ("Collected Poems") appeared in 1907, he was widely hailed as a first-rank artist. His lyrics were reprinted in anthologies and school texts, and were translated into many languages. An English translation, *Poems of Yehoash*, by Isidore Goldstick, appeared in 1952, and a Hebrew version (1957) was a cooperative venture by a number of significant Hebrew writers, including Jacob *Fichmann and Dov *Sadan. Yehoash's two later lyric volumes (1919 and 1921) linked him with *Inzikhism, the modernist trend of introspection in post-World War I Yiddish poetry, the leaders of which acclaimed him as their forerunner. Yehoash gave expression in his lyrics to his awareness of a divine force permeating the universe. He re-imagined in verse biblical and post-biblical legends, tales from medieval Jewish chronicles, and ḥasidic lore, versified fables from the Talmud, Aesop, La Fontaine, and Lessing, and created new fables of his own. He wrote romantic, ghostly ballads, but he also felt the spell of Peretz, his lifelong friend, and strove for classical purity and perfection in rhythm and rhyme.

Yehoash also influenced American Jewish poetry in English, notably the modernist work of Louis Zukofsky.

BIBLIOGRAPHY: Rejzen, Leksikon, 1 (1928), 1244–53; LNYL, 4 (1961), 233–44; B.V. Vitkevich, *Yehoash-Bibliografye* (1944); A.A. Roback, *Story of Yiddish Literature* (1940), 201–8; J. Glatstein, *In Tokh Genumen* (1956), 64–9; A. Glanz-Leyeles, *Velt un Vort* (1958), 26–45; S. Liptzin, *Flowering of Yiddish Literature* (1963), 190–7; C. Madison, *Yiddish Literature* (1968), 165–81; Waxman, Literature, 4 (1960^2), 1021–3, 1103–4. **ADD. BIBLIOGRAPHY:** A. Waldinger, in: *Revue Internationale de la Traduction*, 44:4 (1998), 316–35; B. Grin, in: *Yidishe Kultur* (1970), 21–4; S. Noble, in: *Tsukunft* (1970), 299–301; H. Schimmel, in: *Paideuma* (1978), 559–69.

[Melech Ravitch]

YEHOSHUA, AVRAHAM B. (1936–), Israeli novelist, short-story writer, playwright, and essayist, considered both nationally and internationally one of the foremost Israeli writers; recipient of all the literary prizes awarded in Israel including the prestigious Israel Prize (1995). He was also awarded many international prizes, such as the National Jewish Book Award in the U.S., the Jewish Quarterly-Wingate prize in the U.K., and the Boccatio and Lampeduza prizes in Italy. Yehoshua's books have been translated into 26 languages, and many of his stories and novels have been adapted for the theater, cinema, television, and opera.

While Yehoshua's literary works focus on the hidden realms of the individual psyche embedded in its familial, social, and cultural context, his challenging essays address ideological, political, and ethical issues. In these essays Yehoshua questions the very tenets of Israeli society: Judaism, Zionism, religion and nationalism, the Israel-Palestinian conflict, and antisemitism.

A.B. Yehoshua was born in Jerusalem, the fifth generation of a Sephardi family on his father's side, and the first generation on his mother's side. His father, Jacob Yehoshua, an Orientalist by training, wrote a number of books recounting the life of the Sephardi community in Jerusalem from the end of the 19th century to the beginning of the 20th, and two books on the Palestinian press of that time. While his father's occupation with the language, history, and culture of the Palestinians probably opened Yehoshua's eyes to their unique plight and thus indirectly influenced his *Weltanschauung* in general, his father's numerous books served him in the writing of his most acclaimed novel, *Mar Mani* (1990; *Mr. Mani*, 1992). The background of his mother – Malka née Rosolio, born to a rich merchant in Morocco – was a source of inspiration for his novel *Massah el Tom ha-Elef* (1997; *Voyage to the End of the Millennium*, 1999). Although Yehoshua's family was observant, his parents, avid Zionists, sent him to a secular school, the Hebrew Gymnasium in Jerusalem. Yehoshua was also active in the scout movement. His early exposure to the moderate Sephardi version of Jewish tradition along with his secular education and Zionist ideology contributed to a lifelong preoccupation with the complex theme of identity which underlies all his writings.

Upon the completion of his military service (1957), Yehoshua began studying Hebrew literature and philosophy at the Hebrew University of Jerusalem. At that time, he started publishing his first short stories, later collected in his first book *Mot ha-Zaken* (1962). After his graduation, he taught literature in Jerusalem, and then moved to Paris, where he spent the next four years (1963–67). There he served as a school principal and later as the general secretary of the World Union of Jewish Students. During his stay in Paris, he also completed his second book of short stories and novellas, *Mul ha-Ye'arot* (1968; *Three Days and a Child* 1970). In all, Yehoshua published four collections of short stories before he wrote his first novel, a genre to which he has devoted most of his later writings.

Yehoshua's early stories drew immediate attention from literary critics: some were critical of the nightmarish impact of an absurd, alienated reality presented in those stories, others recognized the influence of Agnon and Kafka on his early stories, acknowledged his unique talent, and predicted that he would leave his mark on Israeli literature. Whereas the first volume of stories is surrealistic and grotesque, placed in a no man's land, his later stories, though still grotesque and terrifying, have become more realistic, placed in the familiar settings of Israeli scene. The gripping plots, a hallmark in all of Yehoshua's writing, evolve around single, lonely, and lethargic characters controlled by underlying destructive powers, unconsciously driven to their unavoidable ends.

Returning to Israel shortly after the 1967 war, Yehoshua joined Haifa University as the head of the department for the advancement of immigrant and minority students. Five years later he was appointed professor of comparative and Hebrew literature (1972); a position he held until his retirement in 2002. Following the Six-Day War and its ensuing upheaval, Yehoshua became involved in various left-wing movements and started publishing essays in which he elaborated his ideological and political stance. His active participation coupled with his intellectual and rhetorical skills have made him one of the major spokesmen for the Zionist left wing and the Israeli peace camp, at home and abroad. Many of his thought-provoking and often controversial essays were later published in two volumes: *Bi-Zekhut ha-Normali'ut* (1980; *Between Right and Right* 1981), and *Ha-Kir ve-ha-Har* (1989). Another volume of essays, *Kokha ha-Nora shel Ashmah Ketanah* (1998), focuses on the moral dilemmas underlying all great literary texts.

After the publication of his first novel, *Ha-Me'ahev* (1977; *The Lover*, 1978), Yehoshua wrote eight novels, exploring innovative artistic forms, enlarging the historical scope from which the narrative is told, tackling new terrains, retrieving the writers' lost "authority over sociological, economical, historical, and ideological issues."

In *Ha-Meahev* and in *Gerushim Me'uḥarim* (1982: *A Late Divorce*, 1984), his second novel, the plot is retold by different voices and from different points of view, thus reflecting the essence of the polyphonic Israeli society and giving voice to hitherto muted voices within that society, such as that of a slightly deranged expatriate, or an Arab-Israeli youth (*Ha-Me'ahev*). The scene of events in these, and in most of Yehoshua's novels, is the family, where identity is forged and which also serves as a mirror of society. The first novel encounters the chain of events of a family in a state of deterioration following the father's attempt to revive his long-lost libido by introducing two lovers into the household. The second novel expounds the effects of a bitter and fatally late divorce on the three children of the family, leading to the ultimate destruction of the father.

Hailed by readers and critics, *Mar Mani*, Yehoshua's most ambitious novel, is one of the most interpreted novels of modern Hebrew literature. Like its predecessor *Molcho* (1987; *Five Seasons* 1989), its unique perspective is achieved by juxtaposing the Sephardi angle with the Ashkenazi one: whereas in *Molcho* Yehoshua's narrator follows Molcho, a Sephardi Jerusalemite, throughout the first year of mourning following the death of his "yekke" Ashkenazi wife, in *Mar Mani* Yehoshua employs a polyphonic device in a highly artistic and innovative manner, unfolding the story of more than five generations of a Sephardi family, the Manis, through five one-sided dialogues related by "outsiders," mostly Europeans, about their fatal encounter with one or more of the Manis. In particular, the genealogical novel explores the often disastrous effects of the unconscious, personal and collective, on individuals as well as on nations. The novel encompasses close to 200 years, and explores new terrain (such as Poland and Crete), different cultures (such as the Minoan), and diverse languages (such as Yiddish and Ladino), attempting to understand in depth the complex relationship between Judaism and Zionism, Israel and the Diaspora, religion and nationalism, and above all, the human psyche, where the struggle to make sense of it all takes place.

Wanderlust, restlessness, and a drive to uncover unconscious desires and anxieties send many of Yehoshua's characters on eventful journeys to unknown continents where the confrontation with the irrational is inevitable, such as: Benji's passage to and from India in *Ha-Shivah me-Hodu* (1994; *Open Heart* 1995); Ben Attar's marine voyage to Europe at the end of the first millennium in *Masah el Tom ha-Elef'*; Professor Rivlin's repeated travels to Jerusalem, the West Bank, and an Arab village in the Galil in *Ha-Kalah ha-Meshaḥreret* (2002; *The Liberating Bride*, 2004); and the Via Dolorosa journey of the manager of the human resource division to an unnamed northern country in *Sheliḥuto shel ha-Memuneh al Mashabei Enosh* ("The Mission of the Human Resource Man," 2004). Yehoshua's strength in portraying dramatic situations, often by means of fatal albeit healing confrontations, was also expounded in his plays such as *Layla be-Mai* (1969; "A Night in May," 1974), and *Ḥafaẓim* (1986; "Possessions," 1993), and many of his stories and novels have been adapted for the theater such as *Mar Mani*; for the cinema: *Ha- Me'ahev;* and in 2005 his own libretto based on *Masah el Tom ha-Elef,* for the opera.

BIBLIOGRAPHY: R. Alter (ed.), in: *Modern Hebrew Literature* (1975), 353–56; N. Sadan-Loebenstein, *A.B. Yehoshua: Monografiyah* (1981); G. Morahg, "Reality and Symbol in the Fiction of A.B. Yehoshua," in: *Prooftexts*, 2 (1982), 179–96; H. Bloom, "Domestic Arrangements," in: *New York Times Book Review* (Feb. 19, 1984); G. Ramras-Rauch, *The Arab in Israeli Literature* (1989), 125–47; A. Balaban, *Mr. Molcho* (Heb., 1992); G. Morahg, "A.B. Yehoshua: Fictions of Zion and Diaspora," in: L.I. Yudkin (ed.), *Israelis Writers Consider the Outsider* (1993), 124–37; N. Ben-Dov (ed.), *In the Opposite Direction: Articles on Mr. Mani by A.B. Yehoshua* (Heb., 1995); H. Herziig, *Ha-Kol ha-Omer Ani* (1988), 217–33; B. Horn, *Facing the Fires: Conversations with A.B. Yehoshua* (1997); G. Shaked, *Ha-Sipporet ha-Ivrit* (1998), 158–80; Z. Shamir and A. Doron (eds.), *Massa el Tom ha-Elef: Mivḥar Ma'amarim* (1999).

[Doreet Hopp (2nd ed.)]

YEHUD (Heb. יְהֻד, יהוד), urban settlement in central Israel, 8 mi. (12 km.) E. of Tel Aviv. On the site, mentioned in Joshua 19:45 as one of the towns of the tribe of Dan, ancient tombs, coffins, and remnants of structures were found. An Arab village on the site, named Yahdiyya, expanded in the 20th century, as a result of the development of the region by Jewish settlement. Earlier, several of the founders of *Petaḥ Tikvah, who had to evacuate that settlement temporarily because of the danger of malaria, stayed at Yehud between 1882 and 1893. In Israel's *War of Independence Yahūdiyya was taken, together with the nearby Lydda Airport, by Israel forces in July 1948 and evacuated by its Arab inhabitants. At the end of the same year the first Jewish settlers arrived, and the place soon absorbed numerous newcomers from various countries, subsequently increasing its population from 3,200 in 1950 to 8,600 in 1970. The original plan to base local settlement on full or auxiliary farming was gradually superseded by urbanization and industrialization, as Yehud became part of the outer ring of the Tel Aviv conurbation. In 1951 Yehud received municipal council status and in 1955 it received city status. Its area is 1.6 sq. mi. (4.1 sq. km.). While a number of inhabitants continued to be employed in other centers of the Tel Aviv region, industry, with 32 local enterprises (motor cars, sweets, knitting, textiles, and other branches), became the principal foundation of Yehud's economy. To a certain degree the town also served as a commercial center for settlements of the vicinity (Neveh Efrayim (Monosson), Savyon, Gannei Yehudah, etc.). In the mid-1990s the population was approximately 17,300, increasing to 22,000 in 2002.

[Shlomo Hasson /Shaked Gilboa (2nd ed.)]

YEHUDAI BEN NAḤMAN (**Yehudai Gaon**) head of the academy of Sura c. 757–61. Yehudai was one of the scholars of Pumbedita, but the Exilarch Solomon b. Ḥasdai transferred him to Sura, because "there was no scholar in Sura who was his peer in knowledge" (*Iggeret Sherira Ga'on*, ed. by B.M. Lewin (1921), 107) – despite his advanced age, the fact that he was blind, and as an exception to the tradition of Sura not to appoint as its head anyone who had not been educated there. During his period at Sura, his brother Dudai served as *Gaon* of the Pumbedita academy. Yehudai is referred to as "light of the world, holy and pure" and *Sherira states that "we may not do what Yehudai refrained from doing" (*Teshuvot ha-Ge'onim*, ed. by J. Mussafia (1864), no. 43). His pupils included Ḥaninai b. Huna and Natronai Nasi b. Ḥakhinai; the most distinguished was Ray Abba (Rabbah), the author of a collection of *halakhot*. Yehudai is the first in the geonic period to whom or to whose pupils is attributed the authorship of a book, the *Halakhot Pesukot. In *halakhah* Yehudai based himself entirely upon the Babylonian Talmud and the traditions of the **savora'im* and merely gave the final ruling of the Talmud, omitting the halakhic discussion. He attempted to reestablish talmudic law and averred that he had always replied to halakhic questions with proof from the Talmud as interpreted by his teachers in practice (*Ginzei Schechter*, 2 (1929), 558). He was the first *gaon* to compile responsa, 131 of which are extant; these are distinguished by their brevity, merely giving the ruling without quoting the sources or the reasons for his decision. In consequence of his ambition to make the Babylonian Talmud and the customs of the Babylonian academies authoritative throughout the Diaspora, Yehudai was the first *gaon* to establish contact with the Jewish communities of North Africa. He protested to the Jews of Ereẓ Israel that their customs were "customs due to persecution" which originated in the religious persecutions in that country at the close of the Byzantine era, and demanded that they accept the customs of Babylon. Some scholars assert that these opinions of Yehudai were very much a matter of conjecture and exaggeration. According to *Pirkoi ben Baboi, a pupil of Yehudai's pupil, Rav Abba, who reproduced certain passages of Yehudai's in his own work, the scholars of Ereẓ Israel opposed him and continued to rely upon their ancient custom and traditions. In some cases Yehudai's rulings did not accord with the custom of Sura. Thanks to his activity, however, the influence of the Babylonian academies spread and the Babylonian Talmud became the sole authority for halakhic ruling. Yehudai and his pupils fought fiercely against the spread of *Karaism in Babylonia, and succeeded in defending the Oral Law by stressing the importance of the Talmud and the especial authority of the scholars in these areas (e.g., family law) challenged by the Karaites. According to some, however, Yehudai's aim in his work was not to combat Karaism since *Anan effected the communal schism only during the last years of Yehudai, and the need to consolidate and summarize halakhic material is understandable even without the rise of Karaism. In consequence of his blindness, Yehudai's rulings and directives were written by his pupils and as a result many interpolations by his pupils found their way into his works. Yehudai is described by Pirkoi b. Baboi as "great in sanctity and purity, in piety and in humility, and meticulous in the observance of all the precepts. He dedicated himself to Heaven, and brought people nearer to the Torah and its precepts" (*Ginzei Schechter*, 2 (1929), 556f.).

BIBLIOGRAPHY: Mann, in: REJ, 70 (1920), 113–48; Mann, Egypt, 1 (1920), 280; Mann, Texts, index; L. Ginzberg (Ginzburg), *Ginzei Schechter*, 2 (1929), index; Lewin, in: *Tarbiz* (1930/31), 392f., 398; V. Aptowitzer, in: HUCA, 8–9 (1931–32), 397–400; idem, *Meḥkarim be-Sifrut ha-Ge'onim* (1941), 13–17, 26f., 91–93; M. Margalioth (ed.), *Halakhot Keẓuvot* (1942), 11f. (introd.); idem (ed.), *Hilkhot ha-Nagid* (1962), 3, 17 (introd.); S. Assaf, *Tekufat ha-Ge'onim ve-Sifrutah* (1955), 48f.; Hirschberg, Afrikah, 1 (1965), 136, 226–28; Baron, Social^2, index; Dinur, Golah, 1, pt. 2 (1961^2), index; pt. 3 (1961^2) 52, 113, 249; pt. 4 (1962^2), 474f., 478f.

[Yehoshua Horowitz]

YEHUDI BEN SHESHET (or **Sheshat**; second half of tenth century), Spanish Hebrew grammarian and poet. A student of *Dunash b. Labrat, Yehudi wrote, between 970 and 990, a work against the responsa of the students of *Menaḥem b. Saruk written in reply to Dunash's criticism of their teacher (the only manuscript of the work was published by S.G. Stern in 1870, and again by M.E. Varela in 1981). Yehudi's work is composed like the responsa of Dunash and those of the students of Menaḥem: the first part is in metric form (154 verses in the same meter and rhyme of Dunash's panegyric to Ḥisdai and of the answer of the disciples of Menaḥem, attacking the adversaries directly), and is followed by rhymed prose serving as introduction to the second part, which contains explanations of metalinguistic subjects in the poem. From this work, the names of several of Menaḥem's students are known: Ibn *Kapron, Judah b. David *Ḥayyuj, and Isaac b. *Gikatilla.

Yehudi deals with 42 questions, answering the greater part of the objections which Menaḥem's students had made against Dunash. In 21 responsa, explanations are given for some biblical terms. In ten responsa Yehudi deals with roots of several words and lexical units to which they belong. In one responsum, Yehudi replies to the objection voiced by Menaḥem's students concerning the introduction of Arabic metric patterns into Hebrew poetry. In four responsa he deals with objections against Dunash's usage of several words. Yehudi defends his teacher by citing biblical usage. Three responsa object to some usages of Menahem and his students. Another deals with the position of *dalet* and *tet* in the classification of the letters of the alphabet into "root" letters and "servile" letters (prefixed, infixed, suffixed), defending Dunash's point of view against all the other medieval grammarians. In the last responsum, Yehudi admits that one objection made by Dunash was based on a misunderstanding.

While discussing the meaning of specific terms, Yehudi also comments on general questions of grammar that go beyond the specific problem, e.g., dealing with the meaning of the word *kemaḥ* ("flour," Gen. 18:6). Yehudi deals also with the meaning of the term *ke-mashma'o* ("as its meaning"), which had been used by Menaḥem 161 times in his *Maḥberet*. A matter of principle, such as to what extent Aramaic is to be relied upon when explaining a Hebrew term in the Bible, is dealt with in the discussion on the meaning of the word *piggeru*, interpreted by Menaḥem as "they stayed behind" and by Dunash, basing himself on the Targum, as "they were destroyed; they were weakened" (1 Sam. 30:10). In dealing with the word *lo* (Ex. 21:8), he also explores the general problem of *keri* and *ketiv*. Generally, Yehudi does not bring new opinions but repeats those of Dunash, adding intricate arguments which border sometimes on insult and abuse. Nevertheless, Yehudi does make some original contributions; in the discussion of the term חוֹנָךְ (*ḥonakh*, Ps. 53:6), for example, he remarks that there are grammatical forms impossible in the Bible, but possible in post-biblical (paytanic) usage. On other occasions he maintains that the Hebrew language in his time has reduced to a very sorry state, and there are forms that might have been found in it had we known the language in its fullness. Like Dunash, he defends linguistic comparatism, known at least in the work of Saadiah, against the anti-comparatist attitude of Menaḥem and his disciples.

BIBLIOGRAPHY: N. Allony, *Torat ha-Mishkalim* (1951), 194 (index); W. Bacher, *Die hebraeische Sprachwissenschaft vom x bis zum xvi Jahrhundert* (1892), 34f., 39; H. Hirschfeld, *Literary History of Hebrew Grammarians*… (1926), 31; S. Pinsker, *Likkutei Kadmoniyyot* (1860), 159 (third pag.); S.G. Stern (ed.), *Sefer Teshuvot* (1870), LXXVI, 1–44; D. Yellin, *Toledot Hitpatteḥut ha-Dikduk ha-Ivri* (1945), 107–12. **ADD. BIBLIOGRAPHY:** E. Varela, *Teshuvot Talmid Dunash ha-Levi ben Labrat* (1981); A. Sáenz-Badillos, in: *Sefarad*, 46 (1986), 421–31; C. del Valle, *Historia de la gramática hebrea en España. Vol. 1: Los Orígenes* (2002), 365–70.

[David Tene / Angel Sáenz-Badillos (2nd ed.)]

YEIVIN, ISRAEL (1923–), Hebrew Language scholar, son of Yehoshua Heschel *Yeivin. Israel Yeivin was born in Berlin and in 1925 came with family to Palestine. In addition to supervising the ancient literature section in the Academy of the Hebrew Language's Historical Hebrew Language Dictionary project, he did research on ancient biblical manuscripts as part of the Hebrew University Bible project. He was professor in the Hebrew University Hebrew Language department. In 1989 he received the Israel Prize for research in the Hebrew language. Among his books are *Keter Aram Zova, Nikkudo u-Te'amav* ("Keter Aram Zova. Its Vocalization and Cantillation Signs," 1969) and *Masoret ha-Lashon ha-Ivrit ha-Mishtakefet ba-Nikkud ha-Bavli* ("The Hebrew Language Tradition as Reflected in the Babylonian Vocalization," 1985; Ha-*Masorah la-Mikra'i* ("The Biblical Masorah," 2003).

[Fern Lee Seckbach]

YEIVIN, SHEMUEL (1896–1982), Israeli archaeologist. Born in Odessa, he studied at the Herzlia Gymnasium in Tel Aviv and the universities of London and Berlin, specializing in Egyptology and Semitic philology. He took part in the excavations at Luxor (1924) and Beth-Shean (1924–28) and in the University of Michigan expedition to Seleucia in Iraq (1929–37). He was co-director with J. Krause-Marquet of the excavations at Ai (1933). He was a member of the Hebrew Language Committee (1935–42); chairman of the Jewish Palestine Exploration Society (1944–46); chief Hebrew translator for the British Mandatory government of Palestine (1944–48); director of the Department of Antiquities in Israel (1948–61); secretary and then editor of the *Encyclopaedia Biblica*; professor of biblical history and archaeology at Tel Aviv University; and member of the Hebrew Language Academy. In 1968 he received the Israel Prize for Jewish studies. His publications include *Toledot ha-Ketav ha-Ivri* (1939), *Milḥamot Bar Kokhva* (1946), and *Kadmoniyyot Arẓenu* (1955), an archaeological handbook written jointly with M. Avi-Yonah.

[Michael Avi-Yonah]

YEIVIN, YEHOSHUA HESCHEL (1891–1970), Hebrew writer and editor. Born in Vinnitsa, Ukraine, Yeivin studied medicine, but gradually left his profession in favor of literature. After emigrating to Palestine in 1924, he joined the founders of the Revisionist movement in 1928 and henceforth became an editor of its press and a regular contributor to it.

His first literary articles and essays appeared in *Haolam* of Odessa, and he continued to publish in *Ha-Tekufah* and other periodicals. In the Revisionist press he published articles and novels on historical subjects. In 1959 he won first place in the Israel Bible Contest. His books include: *Sippurim* (1928); *Be-Sod Ḥalalim* (1930); *Uri Ẓevi Greenberg, Meshorer Meḥokek* (1938); *Milḥemet Beit Ḥashmonai* (a story about the Hasmoneans, 1953); *Ha-Ḥayyah ha-Revi'it* (1949); *Mi-Me'onot Arayot* (stories of the underground movement, 1954); *Bi-Shevilei Emunat Yisrael* (essays, 1960); and *Ha-Malkhut Asher Lo Tissof* (1967).

BIBLIOGRAPHY: Kressel, Leksikon, 2 (1967), 73–74.

[Getzel Kressel]

YEKOPO (acronym of **Yevreyskiy komitet pomoschi zhertvam voyny** – "Jewish Relief Committee for War Victims"), organization formed in Russia after the outbreak of World War I to succor Jewish war victims. The need for such relief was most urgent because many Jewish communities were situated in the battle regions and had already suffered heavily during the first days of the war. Many refugees streamed to the rear from the front. The situation deteriorated with the intensification of the anti-Jewish policy adopted by the military authorities, which at first took the form of the detention of Jews as hostages and subsequently of mass expulsions from the battle regions. These persecutions reached their climax in the great expulsion of the Jews from the provinces of *Kovno and *Courland in the spring of 1915. It was also necessary to support the tens of thousands of families of Jewish soldiers. The committee of Petrograd rapidly became the central committee to which all the local branches addressed themselves. Its task was to raise funds and distribute them among the local committees and the various bodies that preoccupied themselves with the different relief activities as well as the organization and supervision of relief activities in various places. The committees of Moscow (YEVOPO) and of Kiev (KOPE) were of particular importance.

The YEKOPO was headed by members of the older intelligentsia and the leading capitalists of St. Petersburg, such as Baron A. *Guenzburg, H. *Sliozberg, D. *Feinberg, M. *Vinawer, L. *Bramson, and J. *Brutzkus. The brunt of the practical work, however, was carried out by "accredited" officials of the committee who came mainly from the ranks of the popular intelligentsia and more particularly from among the members of the Jewish Socialist parties. The committee received much support from the older societies, such as the *Society for the Promotion of Culture among the Jews of Russia, *ORT, *Jewish Colonization Association (ICA) and *OZE. Relief took the form of arrangements for the transportation of the refugees; the provision of escorts for their convoys; provisional arrangement for their nutrition, clothing, and accommodation; the provision of medical care; the organization of "medical-sanitary units"; the care of children and, later, efforts to find them employment and occupations; the establishment of credit funds; the development of vocational schools and courses, etc. In addition, the committee represented the Jewish population before the authorities in its demands for assistance to the Jewish war victims.

For internal and external political reasons, the government recognized the committee and encouraged it by granting authority to its delegates and workers; they received the status of government officials, a factor of prime importance during the period of the hostilities. The committee also maintained relations with the general public institutions, such as the All-Russian Alliance of Towns, and zemstvo workers. By the end of 1916, the committee had provided its services to 240,000 Jews (out of the estimated total of 350,000 Jewish war refugees). The funds received by the central committee in Petrograd until then – 31,000,000 rubles – were derived from the sources as shown in the table below.

The important allocation of the government is also of historical and political significance, as is the considerable contribution of the Jews of the United States. The participation of Russian Jewry in this relief enterprise was larger than is apparent in the table, because many of the funds which were collected in the provinces did not pass through the treasury of the central committee but were directly spent by the local committees. A considerable part of the communities' funds were derived from a system of compulsory contributions.

Source	Total in rubles	%
Russian government	17,179,000	55.8
General Russian Relief Committee	292,000	0.9
American Jewish Joint Distribution Committee (United States)	7,258,000	23.6
British Jewry	1,693,000	5.5
South American Jewry	403,000	1.3
France (through Rothschild)	250,000	0.8
Contributions of the Jews of Petrograd	2,012,000	6.5
Contributions of the Jews in the provinces	1,700,000	5.6
Total	30,787,000	100.0

The activities of YEKOPO also encompassed the Jews of the regions occupied by the Russian army in Galicia and Bukovina. In the execution of their tasks, several divergences of opinion emerged between the workers of the committee, mainly over cultural problems (religious or secular education, schools in the Russian, Hebrew or Yiddish languages), with each side attempting to divert the relief activities in the direction of its own outlook. Much material on the history of this relief work is to be found in the central periodical of YEKOPO, *Pomoshch* (1915–16; later *Delo Pomoshchi*, 1916–17). After the Revolution of February 1917, when the focus of the political activity of Russian Jewry was transferred to the public organizations and the parties, YEKOPO pursued its relief work in a restricted sense. It also continued its activities during the civil war years, when the central role was played by the committee of Kiev (KOPE). In 1920, with the establishment of the Jewish-Soviet relief organization *Idgeskom*, the YEKOPO was in practice absorbed by it. The committee of YEKOPO continued to function in the provinces of *Vilna and *Novogrudok, within the borders of independent Poland, where it concentrated efforts on the rehabilitation of the communities which had been severely affected by World War I and the Polish-Soviet war. The committee was then headed by Dr. Z. *Shabad and was mainly supported by the *American Jewish Joint Distribution Committee (JDC).

BIBLIOGRAPHY: YEKOPO, *Report for Aug. 1914–June 1917* (Rus., 1917); I. Trotki, in: J. Frumkin, et al. (eds.), *Kniga o russkom yevreystve* (1960), 495–7 (= *Russian Jewry 1860–1917*, 1966); M. Shalit (ed.), *Oyf di Khurves fun Milkhomes un Mehumes* (1931).

[Yehuda Slutsky]

YEKUM PURKAN (Aram. יְקוּם פֻּרְקָן; lit. "may deliverance arise"), the name of two prayers recited in the Ashkenazi rite immediately after the reading of the *haftarah* on the Sabbath. Written in Aramaic, the prayers derive their name from their opening words. Both are very similar in form. The first consists of a prayer for the welfare of the students in the academies of Ereẓ Israel and Babylonia, their teachers, the exilarchs, and the judges. Many of the phrases of this prayer resemble those of the *Kaddish de-Rabbanan* ("the scholars' *Kaddish*"). In modern times, some communities have added the phrase *Ve-di be-khol arat galvatana* ("and all that are in the lands of the dispersion") in order to make this prayer more meaningful (Baer's *Siddur*, 229). The second is a more general prayer for the welfare of the congregation, similar in content to the Hebrew prayer *Mi she-Berakh* which follows it. The prayers are not found in the Babylonian *siddurim* of *Amram Gaon and *Saadiah Gaon, although they were probably written in Babylonia. The first is found in the *Maḥzor Vitry, and the second in the *Roke'aḥ* of *Eleazar b. Judah of Worms (1160–1238). Both prayers are absent from the Sephardi rite, although a similar but more lengthy prayer entitled "Prayer for the Congregation" is found in some Yemenite prayer book manuscripts (Duschinsky, in bibl., 194–7).

These prayers are not recited on festivals. A reason given for this is to enable the worshippers to leave the synagogue earlier and enjoy the meals which they are permitted to cook on the holidays (S. Shuck, *Siddur Rashban* (Vienna, 1894), 20b).

BIBLIOGRAPHY: Duschinsky, in: *Livre d'Hommage … S. Poznański* (1927), 182–98.

YELLIN, pioneer family in modern Ereẓ Israel. YEHOSHUA (1843–1924), pioneer in Ereẓ Israel, was born in Jerusalem, the son of the prosperous Yellin-Tavia family from Lomza, Poland, that immigrated to Ereẓ Israel in 1834. He married into the Yehuda family of Baghdad and learned Arabic and Oriental customs in the home of his father-in-law, Shelomo Yeḥezkel Yehuda. In 1860, under the auspices of the British consul, James *Finn, he and his father purchased land in the village of Kalonya (Colonia) on which the settlement of Moẓa was established in 1891. Yehoshua was one of the founders of Naḥalat Shivah, the third Jewish quarter of Jerusalem built outside the Old City by residents of the city (1869).

In 1876 he belonged to the group that tried to buy government lands near Jericho for the establishment of a settlement to be called Petaḥ Tikvah – an attempt that failed because of the opposition of the Turkish government in Constantinople. In 1882 Yellin entered his son David, born in Jerusalem, at the Alliance Israélite Universelle school just opened in Jerusalem and was thus the first member of the Ashkenazi community to ignore the boycott imposed by its rabbis (led by Rabbi Moshe Yehoshua Leib *Diskin) on study in schools. As a punishment he was deprived of his allocation from the *ḥalukkah. In 1897 he was elected a member of the Jerusalem Town Council and served in this capacity until 1901. In his later years he wrote memoirs, *Zikhronot le-Ven Yerushalayim* ("The Memoirs of a Son of Jerusalem," 1924), which are a source for the history of the old Jewish community in Jerusalem at the end of the 19th century.

[Yehuda Slutsky]

His son, DAVID YELLIN (1864–1941), was a distinguished teacher, writer, scholar, and one of the leaders of the *yishuv*.

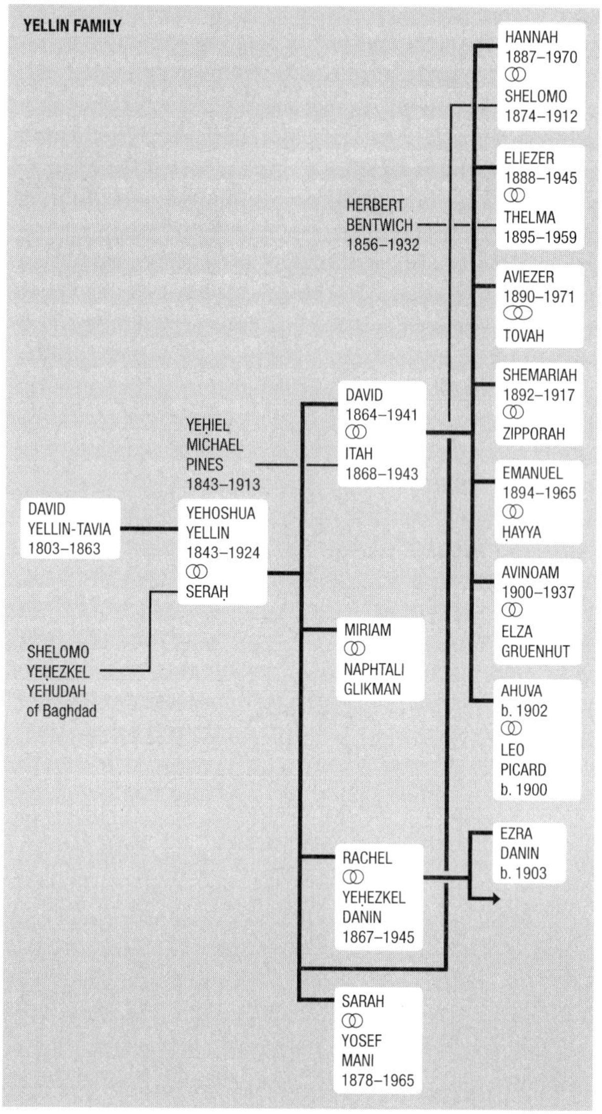

David studied at the Eẓ Ḥayyim yeshivah and also acquired a general education and knowledge of both Eastern and Western languages. In 1882 he became a pupil (later teacher) in Jerusalem at the Alliance Israélite Universelle school and at the Laemel school. In 1903 Yellin was one of the organizers of the founding conference of the *Teachers' Association at Zikhron Ya'akov and was the association's president. In 1912 he became deputy director of the teachers' seminary founded by the *Hilfsverein der Deutschen Juden (Ezra) in Jerusalem. During the language controversy, when the Hilfsverein tried to introduce German as language of instruction, he founded the Hebrew Teachers' Seminary (later at Bet ha-Kerem in Jerusalem) and was its principal until his death. In 1926 he was appointed professor of Hebrew poetry of the Spanish period at the Hebrew University. His knowledge of Arabic language and literature brought him to a deep understanding of Hebrew poetry written in Spain, and he published a number of works by Spanish Hebrew poets. In addition to research works in the field of poetics, he wrote *Torat ha-Shirah ha-Se-faradit* (1941), in which he described the techniques of various poets, types of poems, meters, and the influence of Arabic poetry on that of Hebrew poets in Spain. Yellin was active in the development of Jerusalem and its institutions, participating in the establishment of new quarters and public buildings such as the Zikhron Moshe quarter, the Laemel school, and the Bet ha-Kerem Seminary. Together with his father-in-law, Y.M. *Pines, and E. *Ben-Yehuda, Yellin sat on the Va'ad ha-Lashon (Hebrew Language Committee). He also helped to establish the National Library and organize *B'nai B'rith in the country. He was a member of the Ottoman parliament (1913) and a leader of the Jewish community's aid committee during World War I. He was among the first public figures in the country to join the Zionist movement openly, took part in Zionist Congresses, and in 1917 was exiled by the Turks to Damascus. From 1920 to 1925 he was a member of the Jerusalem Town Council and deputy mayor, introducing the municipality's first Hebrew seal. From 1920 to 1928 David was chairman of the Va'ad Le'ummi (National Council of the Jews of Palestine) and appeared as a Jewish representative on the League of Nations "Wailing Wall Committee" (1931).

Apart from textbooks (the best known is *Mikra le-Fi ha-Taf*, 1900–01), and translations from Arabic (*Shirat Shemu'el Ben Adaya*) and from European languages (e.g., *The Vicar of Wakefield*), David published many studies on Hebrew language and grammar (e.g., *Dikduk ha-Lashon ha-Ivrit*, 1942; *Toledot Dikduk ha-Lashon ha-Ivrit ve-Hitpattehutah*, 1947); and on the Bible (among them commentaries on the books of Job and Isaiah, 1927). The first two volumes of his selected writings, which appeared in 1936 and 1939, contain a selection of his articles in the Hebrew press in Jerusalem and are a valuable source on the history of the *yishuv*. David Yellin was a symbol of the integration of the Ashkenazi and Sephardi communities in Ereẓ Israel, which was also expressed in his scholarship. He was also a leader in education as it developed in the *yishuv*.

David's second son AVIEZER (1890–1971), educator, was born in Jerusalem and attended the Laemel school and the Ezra Teachers' Seminary. He taught in Bulgaria in 1910 and later in the Ezra Seminary. During World War I he founded the first Hebrew girls' school in Damascus. Aviezer was one of the founders and leaders of the *Maccabi and scout movements in Israel. He was a delegate to the first Asefat ha-Nivḥarim (Elected Assembly of Palestine Jews) and a member of the Jewish Communal Council in Jerusalem. In 1925 he became a member of the central committee of the Teachers' Association and served as its secretary until 1956 when he was elected as its honorary president. He wrote many articles on education, sports, and current affairs.

[Benzion Dinur (Dinaburg)]

David's fifth son, AVINOAM (1900–1937), educator and Orientalist, was born in Jerusalem. He translated *The Book of Ahikar the Wise* from the Syriac and Aramaic into Hebrew (*Sefer Aḥikar he-Ḥakham*, 1937) and published modern text-books for the study of Hebrew and classical Arabic (the latter together with Levi *Billig), as well as numerous studies and articles. A member of the Hebrew Language committee (Va'ad ha-Lashon), he became supervisor of Jewish schools in the British Mandatory administration. He was killed in Jerusalem by Arab rioters.

BIBLIOGRAPHY: *Minḥah le-David* (1935), 7–15 (bibliography); B. Dinur, *Benei Dori* (1963), 86–99; Malachi, in: *Hadoar*, nos. 12 and 19 (1941); I. Yellin, *Le-Ẓe'eza'ai*, 2 vols. (1938–41); Orlinsky, in: JQR, 32 (1941/42), 221–5; M. Attias, *Sefer ha-Te'udot shel ha-Va'ad ha-Le'ummi* (1963), index; Tidhar, 1 (1947), 475–6; 2 (1947), 569–70. 705–7.

YELLIN-BENTWICH, THELMA (1895–1959), Israeli cellist and pedagogue, a leading personality in the creation and shaping of musical life in Israel. She was born in England as the ninth child of the aristocratic Bentwich family, all the members of which received professional instrumental training. She studied at the Royal College of Music in London, and was accepted by Pablo Casals as a private pupil. In 1915 she founded in London the all-women trio with Myra *Hess and Jelly d'Arranyi. Yet the tensions of the life of a traveling professional soloist did not suit her nature. In 1919 she joined her brother and two sisters who had already settled in Jerusalem and married Eliezer Yellin, the son of David *Yellin. In 1921 she founded the Jerusalem Music Society which pioneered high quality weekly concerts of chamber music in Jerusalem to a cosmopolitan audience of Jews, Arabs, British, German, and members of other nationalities. The backbone of these concerts was the Jerusalem String Quartet, the first in the country, with her sister, violinist Margery Bentwich. In 1951 she joined the Israeli String Quartet with Lorand and Alice Fenyves (violins) and Oeden *Partos (viola). She also appeared with the Philharmonic and radio orchestras and taught cello and chamber music at the academies of music in Tel Aviv and Jerusalem as one of the most admired cello pedagogues in the country. Her plans for a "music gymnasium" for talented children came to fruition in 1962 in Tel Aviv when the Thelma Yellin Gymnasium was opened.

BIBLIOGRAPHY: M. Bentwich, *Thelma Yellin, Pioneer Musician* (1964); J. Hirshberg, *Music in the Jewish Community of Palestine 1880–1948* (1995).

[Jehoash Hirshberg (2nd ed.)]

YELLIN-MOR (Friedman), NATHAN (1913–1980), one of the leaders of *Loḥamei Ḥerut Israel and Israeli politician, member of the First Knesset. Born in Grodno, Poland, Yellin-Mor completed his studies as an engineer in Warsaw, where he joined the Berit ha-Ẓiyyonim ha-Revizyonistim and *Betar movements and in the late 1930s supported extreme activism, associated, in Palestine, with the *Irgun Ẓeva'i Le'ummi (IZL). In 1938–39 Yellin-Mor edited the short-lived Warsaw Yiddish daily *Di Tat*, which was an IZL organ. After the outbreak of World War II, Yellin-Mor managed to reach Palestine and joined Avraham *Stern, who decided to break away from the IZL and establish a new organization that was called Loḥamei Ḥerut Israel (Leḥi). In 1941 he traveled to Syria on behalf of Stern, with the purpose of reaching neutral Turkey in order to contact representatives of Nazi Germany and offer them cooperation against the British in exchange for a mass evacuation of European Jews to Palestine. However, he was arrested by the British in Syria and imprisoned in Palestine. In 1943 he escaped from a detention camp with a group of his colleagues through a tunnel. After his escape Yellin-Mor became one of a triumvirate of Leḥi leaders, replacing Stern, who was murdered by the British in 1942, concentrating on military operations until 1948.

He was arrested together with other Leḥi members by the Israeli police after the assassination of the UN mediator Count Folke Bernadotte in the fall of 1948. An Israeli military court found him guilty of membership in a terrorist organization but acquitted him of complicity in Bernadotte's assassination. Yellin-Mor was included in the general amnesty granted by the Provisional Government, and ran in the elections to the First Knesset in 1949 on the "Fighters" (*Loḥamim*) ticket that was made up of former Leḥi members. However, he was the only member elected, and soon after his election to the Knesset, he underwent an ideological shift that took him to the extreme Left. Together with Uri *Avneri, he established in 1956 a political group called "Semitic Action" (Ha-Pe'ulah ha-Shemit), which supported the idea of a Jewish-Arab federation in the territory of Mandatory Palestine that would form part of a broader Middle East federation. Yellin-Mor was not elected to the Second Knesset, went into business, and edited a journal called *Etgar* ("Challenge"), in which he professed his views. After Avneri entered the Knesset in 1965, Yellin-Mor left all direct political activity.

His writings include *Loḥamei Ḥerut Yisrael: Anashim, Ra'ayonot, Alilot* ("Loḥamei Ḥerut Yisrael: People, Ideas, Deeds," 1975) and *Shenot be-Terem* ("The Years Before," 1990).

[Susan Hattis Rolef (2nd ed.)]

YEMEN, country in S.W. corner of the Arabian Peninsula; capital, Sanʿa.

The Land and the People

The southern part of the Arabian Peninsula is called al-Yaman (the south), after which the country is named in the West. In pre-Islamic times there were five separate political entities in this area, the history of which is known only in epigraphic sources from the tenth century B.C.E.: Ma'īn (with the capital Qarnāw), Ḥimyar (ʿAfar), Sabā (Mārib), Katabān (Tamnā), and Ḥaḍramawt (Shabwah). The country was politically united under the Ḥimyari kingdom from the fourth century C.E. The Ḥimyari king Abūkarib adopted the Jewish religion in 384, which was retained until 525/530, when *Dhū Nuwās, the last Ḥimyari king was defeated and killed by the invading Christian army from Abyssinia. In 570 the country was conquered by the Sassanid Persians and in 629 was taken over without a fight by the Muslim army. Since then Yemen has been a Muslim country, although its ruling dynasties have changed many times and almost never has Yemen constituted one political entity. After being a remote province of the *Umayyads and the *Abbassids it was actually ruled by different local families, until it fell under the rule of a Zaydī imām, Yaḥyā al-Hādī ilā al-Ḥaqq. His successors became the main political and religious power except for relatively long intervals: 1173–1229 (Egyptian Abbassids), 1229–1454 (Rasūlīs), 1454–1526 (Banū Ẓāhir), 1536–1636 (*Ottoman Turks), 1872–1918 (Ottoman Turks). But even during these intervals the Zaydīs kept their power in the northern part of the country. Since *San'a was the political and religious center, except during the Rasūlī period with the capital Ta'izz, the far southeastern region of Yemen, Ḥaḍramawt was never under the control of the central government but only under that of various local sultans. Part of the country with its important seaport of *Aden was actually under British control between the years 1839 and 1967. In 1962 the Zaydī imamate came to its end in consequence of the republican revolution and since then Yemen has been a Muslim republic. In 1990 Yemen and the State of South Yemen, established after the British had evacuated Aden, were united into one state for the first time in history to include all south Arabia, up the border of Oman in the east. Religiously the country is evenly divided between Zaydīs in the north and the central plateau and Shāfi'īs in the southern lowlands and Ḥaḍramawt.

As an orthodox Muslim state Yemen was always hostile to the Jewish settlement in the Holy Land since the first mass *aliyyot* from Yemen in 1882 and actually tried to prevent them. Later, after the establishment of the State of Israel in 1948, Yemen was one of the seven Arab states who sent their armies against the newborn Jewish state. Yemen never recognized Israel *de jure* or *de facto* and in the early 21st century was one of the radical Arab and Muslim states in terms of its political relation to Israel.

History

There are no documents or other reliable sources about the beginning of Jewish existence in Yemen. The traditions of the Jews of Yemen themselves relate that a large group of Jews left Jerusalem some years before the destruction of the First Temple following the prophecies of Jeremiah. They first came to some localities in Yemen, called Resh Galut, such as San'a, Tan'im, and Dhamār. According to their tradition, the Jews of Yemen rejected the call of Ezra to return to the Holy Land since they anticipated that the Second Temple would be destroyed as well. This tradition may be supported by their pronunciation of Hebrew, which fits that of Judea, like that of the medieval Jews of Babylonia, and differs from the Galilean (Tiberian) pronunciation maintained by all other Jewish communities; and the counting of the years from the ninth of Av since the destruction of the First Temple, a unique custom not existing in any other Jewish community. However, the first certain evidence of Jewish life in Yemen is the tombs of Ḥimyarī Jews in Beth She'arim, dated to the beginning of the third century C.E., which means that at least in the second half of the second century C.E. there already were Jewish settlements in Yemen.

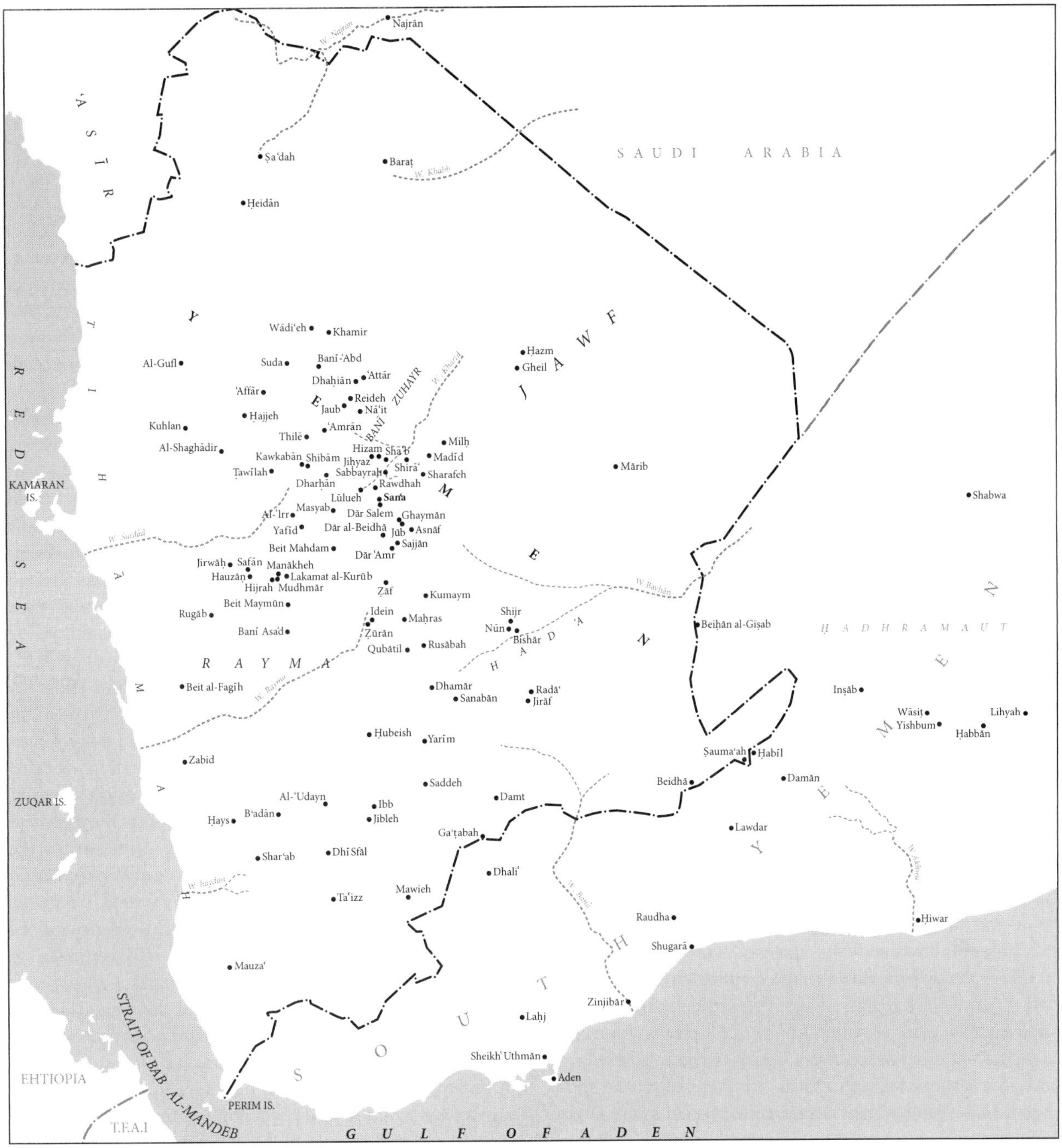

Jewish communities in Yemen before the mass emigration to Israel, 1949–50.

One may conclude, then, that Jews left Judea southward after the destruction of the Second Temple (70 C.E.) and eventually arrived in Yemen to build their new life.

Judaism in pre-Islamic Yemen gained more and more power and influence. The crucial step was in early 380, when the Ḥimyarī king Abūkarib adopted Judaism as the formal religion of the kingdom. Polytheism was completely rejected and for 150 years all inscriptions, the almost ultimate source for pre-Islamic history, were monotheist or Jewish. During that time, a bitter struggle developed between Judaism and Christianity in Yemen, culminating with Yūsuf Dhū Nuwās (522–525/530). But when the foreign army of Aksūm, the Christian power in Ethiopia, intervened and invaded the country, as a response to the punitive expedition of Yūsuf against the rebellious Christians in Najrān, the Jewish regime of Ḥimyar came to its end and the Jews lost their strong standing in the country. From early Muslim sources, however, we learn that Judaism spread out among many Arab tribes, especially in Ḥaḍramawt. The next big step in the degradation of Judaism and Jews in Yemen took place in 629, when the country was taken by the victorious Muslim army of *Muhammad. Suddenly the Jews became *dhimmīs*, namely second-degree subjects protected by the government in return for paying a special tax (only for adult males) – the *jizyah*. It seems that only a few of the Jews of Yemen converted to Islam, although there is not the slightest information in terms of numbers. However, early Muslim sources are quite informative about Yemeni Jews – or about those Jewish scholars who converted to Islam and enriched it with endless Jewish traditions and stories, frequently lost in genuine Jewish sources. To name just a few we may mention *Ka'b al-Aḥbār, 'Abd Allah ibn Sallām, 'Abd Allah ibn Sabā', and Wahb ibn Munabbih.

We know almost nothing about the Jews in Yemen during the Umayyad and first Abbassid periods up to the end of the 9th century, when the Zaydi imamate was established in northern Yemen in 897 by Yaḥyā al-Hādī ilā al-Ḥaqq. From a rare document preserved in his *sīrah* (biography) we know that basically he did not adopt discriminatory and humiliating regulations against the Jews but forbade Jews to build synagogues and hold Muslim slaves. It is notable that he did not prevent Jews from owning lands and even confirmed their right to buy new lands from Muslims.

Again, for more than 250 years, Jewish and Arab sources are almost completely silent regarding Yemeni Jews, but from the scarce information we have it is clear that the Jews of Yemen maintained close relations with the *geonim* in the Babylonian Jewish centers. However, as a result of the growing importance of Yemen and especially of its southern seaport of Aden in international commerce from the Mediterranean basin to *India, the Jewish community of Yemen rises from oblivion, particularly in the documents of the Cairo **Genizah*. During the 11th, 12th, and 13th centuries, Yemen and its Jewish community were like a suburb of *Egypt and its large Jewish Egyptian community. Yemenite Jewry of that time was an integral part of the Jewish world in the vast Muslim area from the shores of the Atlantic to India. In the 12th and 13th centuries, in the course of which Yemen constituted an important part of the Ayyubid dynasty in Egypt, it had special communal and religious relations with *Maimonides and his son Abraham, both of them heads of the Jewish community in Egypt and close to the government. These special relations were first shaped when Maimonides acted on their behalf in the Ayyubid court in Cairo and sent them his famous *Epistle to Yemen* (1172) to lead them away from their belief in the false messiah who appeared at that time in Yemen and to comfort them. Generally the Ayyubid period (1172–1254) was quite happy for the Jews, except for a short time when Mu'izz al-Dīn Ismā'īl (1196–1201) forced them to convert to Islam, a tragic episode ending with his sudden death.

The transition of the government in Yemen from the Ayyubid to the Rasūlī dynasty (1254–1454) did not radically change the political and economic conditions of the Jews. Despite the sparse details in Muslim sources about some Jews who had converted to Islam, there is a good likelihood that in general the Jews lived calmly and securely. They could maintain their close relations with Egyptian Jewry under the rule of the *Mamluks and excel in their literary production, which was the richest and the most diverse in their history. Matters changed with the rise of Banū Ẓāhir in 1454, particularly as a result of another Jewish false messiah who attracted many Jews as well as Muslim followers. Not only was the rebellious messiah killed, but Jews were no longer allowed to dwell in the vast area of Ḥaḍramawt, claimed by the fanatic Muslims to be the land of the pre-Islamic prophet Hūd. This ban was only the first in an unceasing trend to limit the boundaries of Jewish settlement in Yemen. No wonder, then, that the Jews of Yemen looked with hope to Portuguese activities on the seacoast of southern Yemen during the first decade of the 15th century, and some of them even helped them as spies.

Shortly after that, the Zaydī imams, who for several centuries had been pushed to their strongholds in the north, gained power and took control of larger territories in the central plateau where large Jewish communities lived. It should be noted that the Zaydī attitude towards Jews had been greatly altered during the 15th century under the impact of the writings of Ḥanbalī scholars, becoming less tolerant, as attested in legal books of Zaydī scholars. But then came the Ottoman Turks who pushed the Zaydīs back to the north after gaining control of the central plateau, including San'a. In spite of the formal improvement of living conditions of the Jews under the Turks, as the new strict regulations against them were abrogated, they suffered severely from the unceasing war between the Ottoman armies and the Zaydī rebels. This situation came to a head in late 1620, when Faḍlī Pāsha, the Turkish governor in the southern lowlands, arrested the leaders of the Jews, trying to win the sympathies of local Muslims. Nevertheless, the Jews were accused by the Muslim Yemenis of being collaborators of the Turks. When eventually the Yemenis, led by the Qāsimīs, the new dynasty of imāms, succeeded in driving the Turks out of the country in 1636, the Jews were submitted to new anti-Jewish Zaydī regulations.

It was just a question of timing for the fanatically religious Imām al-Mutawakkil Ismā'īl (1644–1676) as to when to act to bring about the total annihilation of Jewish existence in Yemen, a question regularly discussed in Zaydī legal writings since the middle of the 16th century. This occured in 1667, in the wake of the messianic expectations of Shabbateanism throughout Yemen, as well as all over the Jewish world, when a group of San'anī Jews, led by Slaymān Jamāl, one of their scholars, asked the governor of San'a to hand the government over to him. The reaction of Imām Ismā'īl was quick and harsh. He legally abrogated the status of the Jews as a protected minority and applied to scholars of both the Zaydī and Shāfi'ī schools regarding the question of whether Yemen is like the Ḥijāz where non-Muslims are not allowed to dwell. After years of hesitation he adopted the ruling of these scholars, who believed that Yemen was a part of the Ḥijāz, and on his deathbed he instructed his heir, Imām al-Mahdī Aḥmad (1676–1681), to carry out this ruling. The immediate meaning was unequivocal: the Jews could no longer live as Jews in Yemen; they had to choose between Islam and death. The new imām chose a third alternative, to expel the Jews from Yemen. But eventually, for logistic reasons, they were expelled to *Mawzaʿ, a small town in the west of the country, not far from the seaport of Mochā, where living conditions were almost unbearable.

After about a year and a half, the Jews were allowed to return to their towns and villages, although not to same quarters and houses, all of which had been confiscated by the government. They had to build new houses in new neighborhoods, outside the wall in walled cities. For more than two generations the social, economic, and spiritual situation of the Jews was quite bad. It was only in late 1720, under the community leadership of Shalom Iraqi, who served three imāms as collector of taxes and was responsible for the mint house, that the Jews rehabilitated their life, particularly economically as the Jews took part in the new commerce with British India. But that was only for a short time, owing to the jealousy of the Muslims over the growing wealth of the Jews. In 1762 Iraqi was thrown into prison, when he was more than 80 years old, his wealth and property were confiscated, and all synagogues in San'a were closed for 30 years. It was then that the spiritual leadership, headed by R. Yiḥye (d. 1805), held the reins of the Jewish community and rescued it from moral and communal decline. But this could not help the politically and economically deteriorating status of the Jews, a trend which continued and even worsened during the 19th century, up to 1872, when Yemen was conquered by the Turks.

For many years after the British had taken over Aden (1839) and the Turks had invaded Yemen (1849), the Jews of Yemen looked forward to the total occupation of the country by a Western power and tried hard to involve other Jewish communities, especially in England, on their behalf. This could be attained only after the Turks had entered San'a in 1872. In principle, the new rulers canceled the traditional Muslim anti-Jewish regulations, in accordance with Ottoman policy in the entire Empire. Indeed, the situation of the Jews improved during the Turkish occupation and their ties with coreligionists in Europe were strengthened, especially with Jewish settlements in the Holy Land to which the Jews of Yemen started to immigrate in mass beginning in 1882.

These two trends opened a completely new period in the history of the Jews of Yemen during which immigration to the Holy Land was a main political and social factor with a decisive impact upon all aspects of life. Another major factor was the centralist and ultra-orthodox regime of Imām Yaḥyā (1904–48), who led the rebellion against the Turks after his father's death in 1904. He wrested significant authority from the Turks in 1911 regarding internal and religious issues (Jews included), and eventually obtained the entire governing authority in 1918 after the Turks had evacuated the country. Yaḥyā strictly implemented the traditional Zaydī policy regarding the Jews, including two harsh edicts: (a) the orphans' edict, according to which every Jewish orphan was to be taken by the government from his family and raised as a Muslim; (b) the latrine decree, according to which the Jews had to clean the streets and the public baths and lavatories (in order to humiliate them). As an expression of identification and sympathy with Arabs in their conflict with the Jews in the Holy Land, he published a regulation prohibiting Jews from leaving Yemen for that country. But on the other hand he followed a very firm policy of protecting the Jews and severely punished any Muslim, either a regular citizen or a government officer, who harmed them.

However, what had a greater effect on the worsening conditions of life of the Jews during Yaḥyā's reign was his general despotic conduct toward his subjects, Muslims as well as Jews. To gain maximum control over his subjects and to prevent any possibility of revolt against him, Yaḥyā imposed extremely high taxes on the Muslims, particularly the peasants, and set up many factories and companies to deprive Jews of their main source of income, the crafts, which were the primary occupation they were allowed to practice. The Jewish community grew poorer and poorer and instead of the financial help sent by the Jews of Yemen to the new Yemenite communities in the Holy Land during the Ottoman occupation, the Yemenite Jews in the Holy Land collected money and sent it to their brethren in Yemen. Understandably, many Jews tried hard to escape from Yemen and immigrate to the Holy Land, despite the prohibition of the imām. Thus, almost more than a third of the Yemenite Jews had settled in the Holy Land prior to the establishment of the State of Israel in 1948.

Thus, the Jewish community in Yemen experienced much turmoil during the years 1900–1951. In the beginning of the 20th century Yemen was severely afflicted by famine caused by three years of drought (1903–1905), and many Jews died or left in order to find food. The circumstances were particularly terrible in San'a, which was besieged by the rebellious army of Yaḥyā, where more than half (according to one estimate almost 90%) lost their lives. This event, remembered by the Jews of Yemen as *ḥawzat al-nafar* (the siege during which a handful of wheat was sold for one real), triggered the internal immigration of Jews, a phenomenon strengthened in the time of Imām Yaḥyā because of the worsening economic conditions and the immigration to the Holy Land or to British Aden, where the Jews lived in improved conditions. In consequence of this turmoil the traditional social structure of Jewish communities in Yemen was weakened and the negative results could be felt in different aspects of life.

Another factor which shook the communal structure in San'a and in its vicinity was the scandalous controversy over the *Kabbalah. Influenced by the enlightenment movement of Jewish Europe (Haskalah), either by scholars visiting Yemen, such as Joseph Halévy (1869/70) or Eduard *Glaser (1882–1894), or by publications that reached Yemen, some relatively young San'ani Jews, headed by R. Yiḥye, established a kind of reform group, completely negating the Kabbalah or any mystical element in Judaism. This controversy resulted in rich literary productions (see below), but on the social level it was highly destructive, as the community of San'a was splintered in 1910 into two hostile factions, avoiding intermarriage or eating the meat slaughtered by the other side. This controversy was the main social issue in the San'ani community up to its total immigration in 1949–1951. It was transferred to the Holy Land, where it still exists in the 21st century.

Social Position

The basic factor which determined the social status of the Yemenite Jews was the religious-political arrangement imposed on them by the Muslim regime since 629, the **dhimma*, namely, the protection they got from the government in return for the **jizyah*, the tax each male adult had to pay. This arrangement was more effective in the center than in the remote regions of the country, where Jews lived among the tribes and their relations were based on the tribal pre-Islamic social institute of *jār*. The protection bestowed by the sheikh and his men upon the Jew, as upon any other weak person within the tribal community, was based on the issue of honor and had nothing to do with Islam. The general trend in the social status of Jews among Muslims in Yemen was one of deterioration, since even the Zaydī regime eventually adopted all anti-Jewish restrictive and humiliating regulations established by the most extremist Sunnī religious scholars or rulers. Although on the declarative level Jews were not compelled to convert, the entire history of the Jews in Islamic Yemen was an unceasing struggle with the attempts of the government and Muslim society to turn them into Muslims. Indeed, conversion to Islam was a distinct phenomenon among the Jews of Yemen, even though it never stemmed from a real and deep conviction of the truth of Islam.

Basically, the Jew was considered by Yemeni Muslims as an inferior human being, devoid of any rights. Jews were not allowed to build more than two-story houses, carry arms, wear light-colored garments, ride mounts except donkeys (and even then only sidesaddle like a woman), or live among Muslims; also they were ordered to wear sidelocks so as to be recognized as Jews, speak humbly to Muslims, and walk only to the left of a Muslim. The Jew had to be very careful when speaking about Islam or Muslim institutions, as any sign of criticism or disparagement against them might end in capital punishment. In principle Muslim and Jewish communities did not interact; but in contrast to cities and towns, where Jews were completely secluded in neighborhoods, there was a more lenient approach in villages, where the style of life produced more diverse possibilities for social or other kind of encounters between Jews and Muslims. No wonder then that the cultural distance in all aspects, spiritual as well as material, between village Jews and Muslims was much less clear-cut and decisive than that between townfolk Jews and Muslims.

Economic Situation

By and large, Yemeni Jews were very poor. Only rarely do we hear about rich Jews in Yemen, when they could freely deal in international or nationwide trade, as in the 11th, 12th, and 18th centuries or during the second Ottoman occupation (1872–1918). The outcome of the ceaseless social and religious pressure on the Jews was their being the poorest component of the Yemeni population. It is true that almost all the citizens of Yemen were poor because of endless military struggles and the despotism of the rulers, as in the time of Imām Yaḥyā (1918–1948), but the Jews suffered also due to their social inferiority and their exclusion from the main source of livelihood – agriculture. Most Jews were artisans and could make quite a good living in days of peace and calm. However, this situation was rare and in the customary situation of political turmoil and disorder or during frequent years of natural afflictions like drought and locusts, there was no demand for the crafts of the Jews. The best proof of the poverty of the Jews of Yemen is the list of the *jizyah* payers, where most of them are recorded as *adnā* (lowest), and only a small number as *a'lā* (highest). There were only a few families who could boast of their wealth, made via international commerce through Aden or Ḥudaydah, such as the Ḥibshūsh family or Israel Ḥubayri, who made his fortune as the exclusive importer of arms from Germany and Belgium for Imām Yaḥyā's army. Famine was then the main reason for conversion to Islam, particularly because Jews were not helped by the government with food as were Muslims.

Messianic Expectations

The messianic activity of the Jews of Yemen was one of their most characteristic features even in pre-Islamic times, from the fall of Yūsuf Dhū Nuwās in 525/530 in the war against Ethiopian Christians to the rise of *Muhammad. The appearance of Muhammad stimulated messianic expectations among the Jews. Some scholars ascribed to 'Abdallah ibn Sabā, the Jewish convert to Islam at the start of the new religion, and similarly to other proselytes, an important role in conveying messianic notions to Islam, particularly the Shīʿī branch. On the other hand, the Zaydi sect, which was the foremost religious-political force in Yemen from the end of the 9th century, and which belonged to the Shīʿa, elevated the Imām to a meta-human level and did not adopt the idea of the Hidden Imām, existing in abstentia (*ghaybah*), whose advent was awaited by all (*al-mahdī al-muntaẓar*). Yet Muslim Yemen was not free of messianic tension throughout the generations, especially among the Sunni (Shāfiʿi) section of the population, most of it in the south; and often Jewish and Muslim messianic activities nurtured each other. For example, some Muslims followed Jewish messiahs. Moreover, the strong Jewish belief that on a certain day, Messiah, the Son of David, would be revealed, would redeem the Jews of Yemen, and bring them to their land seeped into Muslims in Yemen, and indeed made them fearful lest they be punished for their unfavorable treatment of Jews. By contrast, the authorities, whether Zaydī or Sunnī, were highly suspicious of the Jews' messianic faith, regarding any activity stemming from it as rebellion against the government requiring a swift response. Such reactions to the display of messianism in Yemen since the 12th century contributed to the continuous decline in the political and social status of the Jews of Yemen and the shrinking of the areas of their settlement.

Immigration and Settlement in Ereẓ Israel

Throughout their history, the Jews of Yemen had ties with the Jewish settlement in Ereẓ Israel. From the *Genizah* documents and *Alḥarizi's *Taḥkemoni* we learn about the Yemenite community in Ereẓ Israel. Many years later, R. Obadiah of *Bertinoro reports on Jews of "the Land of Aden," namely Yemen, who immigrated to Ereẓ Israel, probably in the middle of the 15th century. Since then we have little evidence about individuals or solitary families from Yemen making *aliyah*. It was only in 1881 that the flow of Jews left Yemen for Ereẓ Israel, in consequence of three factors: (a) encouraging information about the living conditions there and the rumors about land distributed there to any Jew who came on *aliyah*; (b) improvement in sailing conditions from Yemen to Ereẓ Israel, then both provinces of the *Ottoman Empire; (c) the disappointment with the Turkish government in Yemen.

The first immigrants came to Jerusalem in August 1881 to establish a separate community there; in contrast to previous immigrants from Yemen they blended with the Sephardi community. Many others from Yemen joined this community, most of them from San'a and settled first in the Old City of Jerusalem and from 1885 in new neighborhoods built specially for them outside the walls, like Kefar ha-Shiloaḥ, Mishkenot, and Naḥalat Ẓevi. In 1908, Yemenite Jews in Jerusalem numbered more than 2,500, constituting an independent community after attaining a *firman* from the Ottoman government. Some of the immigrants settled in *Jaffa and there established a smaller community (350 in 1903). In 1908 village Jews of north Yemen started to immigrate and settle in young Hebrew moshavot like Reḥovot. Like them, thousands of immigrants who came from the south of Yemen (Shar'ab), following the mission of Shemu'el Yavne'eli, settled in most of the moshavot in Judea and the Galilee, numbering about half the total population and making their living from agriculture, either as hired laborers or independent farmers. At the end of World War I there were 4,500 Yemenite Jews in the country. The flow of emigrants from all over Yemen was renewed after World War I, this time more to the urban center of Jaffa-Tel Aviv and the new Hebrew towns, as small businessmen, laborers, and retailers. Between the two world wars more then 15,000 left Yemen illegally for Ereẓ Israel through Aden, where they obtained immigration certificates from the British Mandatory government. By the outbreak of World War II there were about 28,000 Yemenite Jews in Ereẓ Israel.

In early 1920 the Zionist movement in Ereẓ Israel started to act in Aden and later in Yemen, in order to encourage and help Jews to emigrate. But owing to the hostile attitude of Imām Yaḥyā to Zionism nothing could be done. It was only in the mid-1940s, that the imām eased his policy, responding to the grave economic situation of his Jewish subjects. Emissaries of the Zionist institutions in Ereẓ Israel acted in Yemen on the eve of the establishment of the State of Israel. Thousands wandered on the routes from all over Yemen to Aden, the only seaport in south Arabia from which Jews could emigrate. With the help of the British authorities in Aden, there was built, next to the city of Aden, Camp Ge'ullah in which the refugees from Yemen were received and well treated by Zionist emissaries and even got a modern Zionist education to facilitate their absorption in the Promised Land. This activity was the basis of the overall emigration of Yemenite Jewry following the establishment of the State of Israel in 1948 and the murder of Imām Yaḥyā, who was considered the ultimate protector of the Jews, in the same year. Aḥmad, the new imām, decided to let the Jews leave his country to Israel, on two conditions: they had to sell all their property to Muslims and to teach the Muslims their crafts. Both conditions were not properly fulfilled, but in any event more than 50,000 Jews left the country in 1949–51, through Aden, except for some several thousands who preferred to stay, clinging to their property or hoping to collect on loans owed by Muslims. A thin trickle of emigration continued until 1954 and even later in 1962, on the eve of the republican revolution. Since then, up to the early 1990s, an iron curtain had fallen on the Jews of Yemen. Some left, however, nominally to the U.S., but most to Israel. No more than 200 Jews still live in Yemen.

Since their first emigration to Jerusalem in 1881, Yemenite Jews dreamed of settling in their old-new homeland as farmers. That was the hope when they settled in Kefar ha-Shiloaḥ and that was what stimulated their leader R. Avraham Naddāf (1891–1920) to purchase land for agricultural settlement and to establish the Shivat Zion society designed for the same goal. Actually Yemenite Jews lived as farmers in Naḥalat Israel Rama not far from Jerusalem for about a year (1895/6). In addition to their agricultural settlements next to the Hebrew moshavot, they established prior to the founding of the State of Israel two independent moshavim – Elyashiv (1933) and Ge'ulim (1945). But the archives of the Hitaḥadut ha-Teimanim, the main Yemenite organization in Ereẓ Israel, inform us that the Zionist organizations did not respond positively to their initiatives to establish agricultural settlements. However, after the mass immigration of Yemenite Jews in 1949–51, the policy was to take them out of the transit camps (*ma'barot*) and settle them in abandoned Arab villages and later in new localities as farmers, in more than 50 places. Soon it became clear, however, that not all Yemenite Jews were fit or wanted to be farmers, and many of them left for the urban settlements, leaving only about 35 Yemenite moshavim. Since then, Yemenite immigrants and their descendants practice all kinds of professions marking their increased social and political acculturation in the State of Israel.

Literary and Scholarly Activities

It is impossible to present a complete picture of Jewish literature in Yemen, as a considerable part is still hidden in unpublished manuscripts. Available sources do not attest that there existed a Jewish literature in Yemen prior to the 10th century.

However, it is probable that the writings of the Sages in Ereẓ Israel and Babylonia, namely the Talmud (Babylonian, not Palestinian) and the Midrashim arrived in Yemen and were preserved there in carefully copied manuscripts. Jewish Yemenite literature constitutes an integral part of Jewish literature in the Muslim-Arabic realm from *Spain to *Persia. In its first steps Jewish literature in Yemen echoes Jewish literature produced in the major Jewish spiritual centers: *Italy, *Iraq, Ereẓ Israel, Spain, North Africa, and Egypt. Thus its first work is probably a Judeo-Arabic translation made by Zechariah ben Sa'īd al-Yamanī of Josippon's *History of the Jews during the Second Temple*, a Hebrew work composed in Italy in 933, or the anonymous *Maḥberet ha-Tījān*, a compendium of the reading rules of the Bible as known from the Eastern tradition and *Saadiah. The third work is a Judeo-Arabic commentary of *Alfasi's compendium to the Talmud tractate *Ḥullin*, by an anonymous author, seemingly of the 11th century. A fourth work of the same time is the enlarged adaptation of the Ereẓ Israeli scholar Rav Nathan ha-Yeshivah's *Commentary on the Mishnah*. The first original work is the ethical-philosophical *Bustān al-ʿUqūl*, written again in Judeo-Arabic by Nethanel berav Fayyūmī around 1150. It is not, then, an accident that all the aforementioned works are in Judeo-Arabic, as since the 10th–15th centuries Yemen Jewry was culturally well immersed in Arab-Muslim culture, just like other Jewish communities in Spain, North Africa, and the East. But there is a highly significant difference, because for all the other communities the proximity to Arab-Muslim culture had been curtailed around 1250.The period from 1150 to 1500 was the most productive for Jewish literature in Yemen in various fields: (a) Poetry – Hebrew poetry in Yemen started in the second half of the 12th century, first by Sa'īd ben Marḥab, who was still influenced by ancient Ereẓ-Israeli *piyyut*, then by his contemporary Daniel berav Fayyūmī, probably Nethanel's brother, who was already influenced by the Spanish school of Hebrew poetry. They both wrote liturgical poems. A later poet who lived before the beginning of the 13th century was Abraham ben Ḥalfon, from whom we have remnants of his *dīwān* of both liturgical and secular poems. The latest poet in that period was David ben Yesha' ha-Levi (around 1500). (b) Biblical Commentary – this is the richest field of literary activity in that period in Yemen, of which we mention here only four works. The earliest is *Nur al-ʿĀlam* by Nethanel ben Yesha (1329) on the Pentateuch, but two other more important commentaries on the Pentateuch are *Midrash ha-Ḥefeẓ* by Zechariah ha-Rofeh (first half of the 15th century) and *al-Wajīz al-Mughnī*, still in manuscript, by David ben Yesha ha-Levi. A commentary on the early Prophets was compiled by Abraham ben Solomon (14th century), only partly published. (c) Midrashic Compilations – the most comprehensive of which is *Midrash ha-Gadol* by David ha-Adani. (d) *Halakhah* – most of the works are commentaries on *Maimonides' *Mishneh Torah*, like that by Zechariah ha-Rofeh. (e) Philosophy – in this category, too, most of the works are commentaries on Maimonides' works, especially *Guide of the Perplexed*. But there were many other works, characterized by their allegoric tendency regarding the *aggadah* of the Sages and even biblical figures and stories. This tendency was influenced on one side by the Maimonidean school in Spain and on the other by Ismā'īlī writings which flourished in Yemen. The most interesting work of this Yemeni school is *Kitāb al-Ḥaqā'iq*, compiled by the rabbis of Ẓā'dah, who were harshly criticized by the rabbis of San'a. Another kind of philosophical compositions, unique to Yemen, is *masā'il*, short discussions providing answers to philosophical questions, like that of Ḥoker bi-Shelomo (first half of the 15th century). (f) Lexicography – most of the compilations in this category were Hebrew-Arabic lexicons, aimed at enabling the understanding of the Mishnah and Maimonides' *Mishneh Torah*, such as *al-Jāmi'* by David ben Yesha ha-Levi. (g) Science – mainly astronomy, needed for establishing the Hebrew calendar, and lists of medicines, like *kitāb al-wajīz* by Zechariah ha-Rofeh. The most prolific writers who acted in almost each of the above-mentioned fields and more are Sa'adiah ben David ha-Adani, David ben Yesha ha-Levi, and Moses al-Balīdah (1475–1525). Most of the works in the period under discussion, except poetry and *Midrash ha-Gadol*, were in Judeo-Arabic.

The 16th century was a transitional period between two major schools of Jewish literature in Yemen: the medieval one focused on Midrash, *halakhah*, and philosophy, mostly in Judeo-Arabic, with a rationalistic orientation, while the other focused on poetry and Kabbalah, mostly in Hebrew and with strong mystical nuances. The most important character in that transitional time was Yiḥye (Zechariah) al-Ẓāhirī, mainly known for his *Sefer ha-Musar*, of the *maqāma* genre, strongly influenced by Al-Ḥarīzī's *Taḥkemoni* and Immanuel's *Maḥbarot*, but also for his poems and *Ẓedah la-Derekh*, the commentary on the Pentateuch, both with rich kabbalistic motifs borrowed from the new school of *Safed which he visited himself. The new school of Jewish Yemeni literature started with the poet *Joseph ben Israel (d. in the 1620s), the founder of classic Jewish poetry in Yemen, characterized by the growing importance of its Arabic element and its openness to the Yemeni Muslim poetry in terms of structure (*muwashshaḥ*) and literary motifs. However, the most prominent figure in Jewish Yemenite poetry, who overshadowed his predecessors as well as his successors, is Shalom Shabazī (1619– after 1680), a younger relative of Joseph ben Israel, both of the Sharabi *Mahsta* family in southern Yemen. Shabazī was a prolific and gifted poet from whom we have about 850 poems. But it should be stressed that Arabic completely disappeared from the new school, except in poetry and a very few folklore-type works or those aimed for less-educated people.

The closer relations between Yemenite Jewry and Jewish spiritual centers and the reinforced encounter with their different traditions and customs resulted first in a comprehensive attempt to adjust Yemenite traditions with these foreign but prestigious traditions. The major scholar who dedicated almost all of his writings to that end was Isaac Wannah (first half of the 17th century), a prolific writer, mainly known for the prayerbook he compiled (*Pa'amon Zahav*) and the commentary he attached to it (*ḥiddushin*), being a dedicated propagandist of the Kabbalah. However, the tendency of neglecting the genuine ancient Yemenite traditions provoked strong resistance among San'ani scholars in the 18th century, who tried to find the golden mean. This was worked out primarily by Yiḥye Ṣaliḥ (d. 1805), the president of the San'ani Jewish court, who was the unchallenged spiritual and communal leader of Yemenite Jewry for more than 40 years. To support his work he searched ancient manuscripts and documented oral and written traditions on all aspects of religious and communal life. He was accepted in Yemen as the ultimate religious authority and his numerous works are so considered until today.

The 19th century presents in general a very pale image of Jewish Yemenite literature, since most of the production by that time was chiefly additions to and commentaries on Ṣāliḥ's works. No wonder, then, that under the alleged impact of Jewish European scholars, some young San'ani scholars, headed by Yiḥye Qāfiḥ (*Kafaḥ) set out to improve the spiritual level of Yemenite Jewry by a complete rejection of kabbalistic literature and customs, including the Zohar, and a return to the medieval school, based on the Talmud and the Judeo-Arabic philosophical literature of Saadiah Gaon and Maimonides. The trend of this new school, very active in the first half of the 20th century and severely criticized by the "orthodox" majority of the Jewish community, yielded a rich literary production, the culmination of which was that of Rabbi Joseph *Kafaḥ, the grandson of Yiḥye Qāfiḥ, already in Israel (he left Yemen in 1943, d. 2000), who was awarded the Israel Prize (1969). In the framework of this production one field should be specifically noted, that of chronological works, which had already been started in the 18th century by Sā'īd Ṣa'dī and Yiḥye Ṣāliḥ. The tendency of searching Yemenite tradition and history continued in Ereẓ Israel, first by Yemen-born scholars like Abraham Naddāf and later by younger scholars, natives of the new land. Close to this kind of cultural activity one may mention the Yemenite poets and prose writers, whose prominent figure is Mordechai *Tabib, who were spokesmen of their communal brethren and described the difficulties of their cultural and economic acculturation.

Culture and Art

Yemenite Jewry had developed a very particular and rich tradition in all aspects of material culture: music, dance, architecture, clothing, embroidery, gold and silver crafts, and so forth. Although we may find not a few common characteristics with the neighboring material culture of the immediate close circle of the Muslims in Yemen or of farther circles like that of India or East Africa, it is convincingly clear that material Jewish culture was different from the Muslim one. This is much more unequivocal regarding what is connected to religious life, such as the music of the synagogue or the shaping of ceremonial objects like Ḥanukkah candles or Torah cases. All that unfamiliar culture, brought to the Holy Land when Yemenite Jews first came en masse in 1881, attracted scholars and artists, like A.Z. Idelsohn and Boris Shatz in Jerusalem. The former established there around 1910 the Shirat Israel (Poetry of Israel) institute, designed to train young Yemenites in their musical traditions, while the latter established in 1906 an association named Bezalel with the goal of promoting Yemenite gold and silver craft, embroidery, and other handicrafts. To that end he set up workshops in Jerusalem and in the moshavah of Ben-Shemen, where Yemenite artists worked and trained for industrial production. In general, Yemenite material culture was sympathetically welcomed in Ereẓ Israel, and the latter's newly shaped culture derived some of its representative elements in music, dance, and artistic works from Yemenite tradition.

The Yemenite community had scores of artists of all kinds, some of them expressing Yemenite tradition, others more rooted in general Israeli culture. The most active field is music. Since the first woman singer, Brachah *Zefirah, a native of Jerusalem, who had a magnificent career in Ereẓ Israel as in Europe, there were, and still are, scores of Yemenite singers, mostly women, who stand in the forefront of light music in Israel. The most famous name is that of Shoshana *Damari (d. 2006), who left Yemen in 1930 when she was a year old and received the Israel Prize in 1988. A much more diversified artist was Sarah *Levi-Tannai, born in Jerusalem in 1911, poetess, composer, and choreographer, and the founder of *Inbal, the most important Yemenite artistic institution in Israel (1949); for many years, this dance theater was the best artistic representative of the young State of Israel in the U.S. and Europe, performing scores of musicals about the folklore of Yemenite Jews. While Yemenite singers in Israel could derive their tradition from the folklore of their families in Yemen, Yemenite painters could not, as painting or any kind of plastic art had not existed in Yemen, excluding a limited engagement with manuscript illumination. This explains why this field of art came relatively later than others to Yemenites in Israel. Two names out of fewer than 20 may be mentioned here: Avshalom Ukkashi and Itamar Siyani, who hold an honored place among Israeli painters. Of all fields of art, only one is still vital and flourishing in its original form after two thousand years: singing. This widely requested cultural product is performed not only by Yemen-born singers like Aharon Amram, but by scores of Israeli-born singers, of the second and even the third generation of people who came from Yemen. Admittedly, this cultural element, along with the traditional Yemenite performance of the prayer in the communal synagogue (and Yemenite dishes as well), symbolizes the intense wish of many of the Yemenites not to be over-acculturated in Israel and completely lose their unique cultural emblems.

[Yosef Tobi (2nd ed.)]

Music Tradition

Today as in the past the Arabs say that the best and the most genuine music comes from Yemen. Unfortunately very few examples of Yemenite Arab music have been studied. The few melodies published in the Western World are not sufficient to draw any conclusions about Yemenite music, and about the possible similarities and dissimilarities between Arab and Jewish music in Yemen. Meanwhile Yemenite Jewish music (studied through the Yemenite Jews in Palestine and Israel, never in Yemen itself) can only be compared with Jewish music in other Middle Eastern countries. Although there are many basic similarities of intent, content, and application, the musical differences are so great that they place Yemenite Jewish music outside the sphere of the musical culture of the Middle East as known today. Some of the differences are the following:

(1) Biblical cantillation does not conform to the cantillation of other Middle Eastern Jews who follow primarily the so-called Babylonian (Baghdadi) tradition.

(2) Prayer song is almost entirely in strict rhythm, and rudimentary harmony and polyphony, in contradistinction to the free rhythm and heterophony found in other Oriental communities.

(3) Folk song is based on the unusually rigid segregation of men and women resulting in different language, content, melodies, form, and style, as if men and women were living in totally different worlds – a phenomenon not observed in any other Jewish community.

(4) There are no musical instruments and therefore no instrumental (art) music, so much beloved elsewhere in the Middle East.

(5) Dance is limited to ceremonial functions such as weddings, men and women being separated to such an extent that they developed different styles.

MASORETIC CANTILLATION. The cantillation is wordbound (logogenic) without any noticeable melisma. The Hebrew text follows the masoretic accents, while the Targum uses a melodic phrase which is shortened or lengthened according to the number of syllables in the sentence. The range of the accents is small, preferably within a third, but fourths and fifths also occur (*sof pasuk*). The movement is stepwise with an occasional third. No pentatonic is discernible. The Targum employs only three successive notes in a *parlando*-melody. The mode resembles the **maqām bayat* in outline (D-/E-F-G-A-/B-C-D), rhythm follows the word-rhythm, the form follows the structure of each individual sentence with clauses and half-clauses, and the voice practice is nasal, sometimes throaty and guttural. The melodic images are so distinctive that once heard they are never forgotten. Cantillation has exerted its powerful influence on the prayer tunes and semireligious songs of Yemenite men. Among the Jews of the world the Yemenites are the only ones to follow the mishnaic precept to read the Targum publicly in the synagogue, a custom long ago abandoned by the others, since Aramaic, once the vernacular of Israel, is no longer in use except by Kurdish Jews (but even they no longer recite the Targum publicly in the synagogue, although they do employ it at home for study).

PRAYER SONG. Communal singing is in fortissimo and in strict rhythmical unison – nobody rushes forward or stays behind. There is, however, no melodic unison but instead chanting in parallel fourths and fifths, often superimposed in *organum*. This type of singing is totally unknown to other Middle Eastern Jews. Whether rhythmical rudimentary harmony and polyphony are indigenous to Yemen, or a remnant of Temple service in Israel, or an African influence is open to investigation. Since there are other isolated regions in the Middle East showing similar features (Turkmen, Anatolian, Samaritan), it is not impossible that the music of the Yemenites represents an old stratum which was later overlaid by the all-pervasive Middle Eastern music in Islamic times. Extended solo singing within the service is not as frequent as in other communities. The Yemenites prefer to sing in rhythmic unison or divided into two choruses responding to each other. There are, however, special occasions when solo becomes important. One of these occasions is a prayer for rain in case of severe drought. A short motive is repeated over and over again, the tense emotion driving the pitch higher and higher with every repetition, until the difference between the initial and final pitch level amounts to a major third. All Yemenite prayer songs can be classified into 15 types of melody, expressing context, mood, and associations with holidays. All 15 melody types can be broken down into motivic materials and modes. Both are used in a totally Oriental way but do not seem identical with any known Arabic musical system. The motives may be used in the improvisational Arab manner, and the modes may be likened to certain Arabic *maqāmāt*, but the intervals are different.

SEMIRELIGIOUS SONG. Semireligious song is performed outside the synagogue and in the home on holidays and festivities. It is the exclusive property of the men. The texts are always religious and in Hebrew and Aramaic. There are a variety of forms with and without meter: *Hallelot, Zafāt, Hidduyot, Neshid, Shirot,* and *Shabbat Shirot*. Except for *Hallelot* all songs require alternating choruses of at least four men. The first verse is sung by the principal singer, who introduces the melody and is followed by two alternating choruses. After having repeated the melody through several verses of the song, the principal singer introduces another melody; the more changes of melody the more prestige to the singer who introduces the melody and is followed by two alternate choruses. Many of the songs are influenced by the synagogue and often do not employ meter. Others are metrical and are used for dancing. The meters can be complicated and alternating (7/8 or 2/4:3/4). The listeners do not join in the singing but accompany the performers with handclapping. Women are excluded from participation except for *Zafāt*, in which they may play a simple percussion instrument (drum or metal platter) and interpolate their high vocal trills or ululations. The men often dance while singing religious texts.

SECULAR SONG. Just as the semireligious song is the exclusive domain of the men, so is secular song the sole domain of the women. Women never attend synagogue and are totally unfamiliar with the men's spiritual world. They do not know Hebrew and all their songs are in Arabic. Barred from the men's spiritual world, the women create their own and express it through narratives, recitation of historical events, songs of love and courtship, marriage, birth, and death, the joys and sorrows of domestic life. They sing while working at home at a trade like embroidery or silversmithing, and while performing such daily chores as grinding flour or baking bread. Women's songs do not bear any melodic similarity to men's songs since even at such an important event as a wedding, celebrations take place in separate quarters. On the whole, women's songs are a great deal simpler than men's songs. The melodies consist of one, two, or three parts and are sung in unison or heterophony. The meter is simple (binary or ternary) and almost all songs can also be danced. The modes employed are *maqāmāt*-like but do not belong to any known system. Augmented seconds are absent and if present are indicative of a foreign intrusion.

MUSICAL INSTRUMENTS. No musical instruments were permitted in Yemen under the fanatical Shiʿa sect, except for the imam's military band. Musical instruments and phonographs were banned and the cinema and foreign broadcasts frowned upon. However, music was played in secret even though if discovered the perpetrators were severely punished. It is no wonder that Yemenite Jews, one of the lowest castes in Yemen, did not play musical instruments except for empty tin cans, copper trays (*ṣaḥn*), and on occasion drums. All instrumental accompaniment in contemporary Yemenite song was acquired in Israel as part of the general acculturation.

DANCE. Men and women never dance together and rarely see each other dance. The men often accompany their semireligious song by dancing, which is graceful, light, and includes leaps in the air and movements reminiscent of Indian dance. The women hardly move at all while dancing; their movements are slow, dignified, and restrained. The excitement, exuberance, and increasing speed of the movements observed in the male dancing style is totally lacking.

COMPATIBILITY WITH WESTERN MUSIC. It is worthy of note that many elements of Yemenite Jewish music were absorbed by Israel folk song and left its imprint on it. One explanation may lie in the greater compatibility of European and Yemenite music, which expresses itself in (rudimentary) harmony and polyphony, the preference for strict rhythm and meter, the almost total absence of melisma, and a somewhat diatonic tendency, in contradistinction to other Middle Eastern musical forms which are often heterophonic, free in rhythm and meter (or so complicated that they sound to the untutored as free meter), highly melismatic, and microtonal. While Middle Eastern song is totally incompatible with European musical structure, Yemenite song is not. This is why it should not be classified as "Middle Eastern" music, but must be considered apart. Whether it belongs to an ancient Middle Eastern stratum which was obliterated with the coming of Islam and only survived in certain isolated areas, or is a special development of Yemen or a remnant of Temple music preserved by the Yemenite Jews must still be determined.

[Johanna L. Spector]

BIBLIOGRAPHY: R. Ahroni, *Yemenite Jewry* (1986); idem, *The Jews of the British Crown Colony of Aden* (1994); idem, *Jewish Emigration from the Yemen 1951–98: Carpet without Magic* (2001); E. Brauer, *Ethnologie der jemenitischen Juden* (1934); B. Eraqi-Klorman, *The Jews of Yemen in the Nineteenth Century* (1993); L. Gilad, *Ginger and salt: Yemeni Jewish Women in an Israeli Town* (1989); S.D. Goitein, *From the Land of Sheba: Tales of the Jews of Yemen* (1947); idem, *Ha-Temanim* (1983); R. Gruber, *Israel Without Tears* (1950); H. Hazaz, *Mori Sa'id* (1956); H.Z. Hirschberg, *Yisrael ba-Arav* (1946); I. Hollander, *Jews and Muslims in Lower Yemen: A Study in Protection and Restraint 1918–1949* (2005); A.Z. Idelsohn, *Melodien*, 1 (1914); E. Isaac and Y. Tobi, *Judaeo-Yemenite Studies* (1999); P.S. van Koningsveld, J. Sadan and Q. al-Samarrai, *Yemenite Authorities and Jewish Messianism* (1990); Y. Tz. Langermann, *Yemenite Midrash: Philosophical Commentaries on the Torah: An Anthology of Writings from the Golden Age of Judaism in the Yemen* (1996); H.S. Lewis, *After the Eagles Landed: The Yemenites of Israel* (1989); Alessandro de Maigret, *Arabia Felix* (2002); R. Meissner, *Die suedjemenitische Juden* (1999); E. Muchawski-Schnapper, *The Jews of Yemen* (1994); idem, *The Yemenites: Two Thousand Years of Jewish Culture* (2000); G.D. Newby, *A History of the Jews of Arabia* (1988); Y. Nini, *The Jews of Yemen 1800–1914* (1991); T. Parfitt, *The Road to Redemption: The Jews of Yemen 1900–1950* (1996); Y. Qāfiḥ, *Halikhot Teiman* (1961); idem, *Ketavim* (1989); A. Qoraḥ, *Sa'arat Teiman* (1954); C. Rathjens, *Jewish Domestic Architecture in Sana, Yemen* (1957); Ch. J. Robin, in: *Arabia* 1 (2003), 97–172; idem, in: JSAI 30 (2005), 1–51; Ḥ. Sa'dun, *Yemen* (2002); H. Tawil, *Operation Esther: Opening the Door for the Last Jews of Yemen* (1998); Y. Tobi, *Yehudei Teiman ba-Me'ah Ha-Yod-Tet* (1976); idem, *Iyyunim bi-Megillat Teiman* (1986); idem, *Tema*, vols. 1–8 (1990–2001); idem, *Avraham ben Ḥalfon – Shirim* (1991); idem, *The Jews of Yemen* (1999); idem, *Yehudi be-Sherut Ha-Imam, Ish ha-Asakim ve-Soḥer ha-Neshek Israel Subayri* (2002); Y. Tobi and Sh. Seri, *Yalkut Teiman* (2003²); M. Weingarten, *Changing Health and Changing Culture: the Yemenite Jews in Israel* (1992); I. Yesha'yahu and Y. Tobi, *Yahadut Teiman: Pirkei Meḥkar ve-Iyyun* (1976); M. Zadoc, *Yehudei Teiman – Toledoteihem ve-Orḥot Ḥayyeihem* (1967); I. Ben-Zvi, *The Exiled and the Redeemed* (1957), index; A. Grohmann, *Suedarabien als Wirtschaftsgebiet*, 1–2 (1922–33); C. Rathjens and H. v. Wissmann, *Landeskundliche Ergebnisse* (1934), 133–6 and fig. 64; B.M. Lewin, in: *Ginzei Kedem*, 3 (1925), 14–23; S.D. Goitein, in: *Sinai*, 33 (1953), 225–37; idem, in: *Tarbiz*, 31 (1961/62), 357–70; idem, *Studies in Islamic History and Institutions* (1966), 329–50; H.Z. Hirschberg, Afrikah, index s.v. *Madman*; D.Z. Baneth, in: *Tarbiz*, 20 (1950), 205–14; Y. Kafaḥ, in: *Sefunot*, 1 (1956), 185–242; 2 (1958), 246–86; 5 (1961), 399–413; Y. Ratzhabi, *ibid.*, 2 (1958), 287–302; 5 (1961), 339–95; idem, in: KS, 28 (1952), 255–78, 394–409; idem, in: *Zion*, 20 (1955), 32–46; idem, in: *Yeda Am*, 5 (1958), 85–89; N. Robinson, in: J. Freid (ed.), *Jews in the Modern World*, 1 (1962), 50–90. MUSICAL TRADITION: Idelsohn, Melodien, 1 (1914); J.L. Spector, in: R. Patai et al. (eds.), *Studies in Biblical and Jewish Folklore* (1960), 255–89; R.B. Serjeant, *Prose and Poetry in Hadramaut* (1951); W. Leslau, *Music of South Arabia* (1951; recordings); N.D. Katz, *Culturally Determined Dichotomy in the Musical Practice of the Yemenite Jews, with Special Reference to Women's Songs* (unpublished Master's Thesis in the Jewish Theological Seminary of America, Dept. of Ethnomusicology, 1969); E. Gerson-

Kiwi, in: *Yuval*, 1 (1968), 177–81; idem, in: G. Reese and R. Brandel (eds.), *The Commonwealth of Music in Honour of Curt Sachs* (1965), 92–103; S. Hofman, in: *Taẓlil*, 9 (1969), 150–1; Y. Ratzhabi, *ibid.*, 8 (1968), 15–22; A. Shiloah, *ibid.*, 9 (1969), 144–9; A. Herzog (ed.), *Renanot*, fasc. 5–6 (1959), no. 1; fasc. 7 (1960), no. 3; fasc. 9 (1961), no. 1; fasc. 10 (1962), no. 1; idem, in: M. Smoira (ed.), *Yesodot Mizraḥiyyim u-Ma'araviyyim ba-Musikah be-Yisrael* (1968), 27–36.

YEROḤAM (Heb. יְרֹחָם), urban settlement in southern Israel, in the northern section of the Negev Hills, 9 mi. (14 km.) S.W. of Dimonah. In 1951, it was founded on a site called in Arabic Tell Rakhma near a junction of roads, one of which was built under the British Mandate with a view to carrying out trial drillings for oil in the vicinity. New immigrants from Romania, Iraq, North Africa, etc., settled there. Initially, it was planned to base the settlement on agriculture (therefore the site was called at first Kefar – village – Yeroham), but when this failed it took on the character of a *ma'barah whose inhabitants worked in road building and other public works and in mining of glass, sand and ceramic clays in the nearby Makhtesh Gadol and Makhtesh Ramon. There was, however, no full employment, and for a long time the inhabitants had to live in transitory wooden huts. In the 1960s, the situation gradually improved with the development of the Oron phosphate field, inhabitants of Yeroḥam finding employment in the *Sedom-Dead Sea Works and the establishment of successful local factories (glass and glass bottles, soft beverages, etc.). Yeroḥam's importance as a road station on the Eilat-Beersheba highway diminished, however, with the construction of the Sedom-Eilat and Revivim-Sedeh Boker highways. The serious water problem was largely solved with the construction of a local storage dam of floodwaters in the gorge of Naḥal Revivim, near a dam of the Roman period. Yeroḥam attained municipal council status in 1959 and grew from 229 inhabitants in 1954 to 5,400 in 1970. With the arrival of new immigrants, the population increased to 6,810 in the mid-1990s and 8,610 in 2002. The municipal area is 13 sq. mi. (34 sq. km.). The main economic branches of Yeroham remained industry and public services, with unemployment high as a result of failing factories and income considerably below the national average.

[Shlomo Hasson / Shaked Gilboa (2nd ed.)]

YERUSHALMI, RINA (1939–), Israeli theater and opera director, founder and artistic director of the Itim Theatre Ensemble and professor of acting and directing at the department of theater arts at Tel Aviv University. Born in Afula, Yerushalmi grew up in Haifa where she started her studies in dance. Her education combined dance, movement, and acting. In England she studied classical dance along with the Laban technique and the Alexander technique. She continued her studies of the Laban technique in Germany with Kurt Joss. In Israel she worked with Moshe Feldenkrais on the Feldenkrais technique. Yerushalmi also studied acting with Nola Chilton, Peter Brook, and Joe Chaikin. She studied Noh and Kyogen in Tokyo, Japan, at Carnegie Mellon University in Pittsburgh, PA, and in New York.

Yerushalmi directed in Israel and in the U.S. Her preferred materials were classical plays of Shakespeare, Pirandello, Lorca, Ibsen, and Beckett.

In 1989 she gathered young unknown actors and founded her own group, the Itim Theatre Ensemble. Their first production, Shakespeare's *Hamlet* (1990), performed in the rehearsal studio of the Cameri Theater of Tel Aviv, was a huge success. Yerushalmi's interpretation of *Hamlet* was based on the physical and spiritual presence of the actors on stage, their collective effort to create on stage a fictional world based on theatrical images and metaphors, and the interaction between their gestures and movements and the audience's imagination. Shakespeare's *Romeo and Juliet* (1991) and Buchner's *Woyzeck* (1992) followed. In each one of these productions Yerushalmi developed her special dramaturgy methods. She adapted the plays and inserted different materials, not always dramatic, thus enlarging their scope and opening them to various readings. The performance was fresh, young, and energetic and the theatrical space was filled with fantastic accessories and stage elements intended to broaden the theatrical framework of the performances.

In 1994 Yerushalmi set off to create her spectacular Bible Project. The project originated in her wish to research the cultural roots of Israeli society. She was intent on finding out whether the Bible was still approachable to Israeli-born, non-religious young people. This research took her and her actors to the desert, where they read the Pentateuch and were overwhelmed by the beauty of the text and the relevance to modern-day Israel. Yerushalmi adapted the Torah (the Pentateuch) without adding or changing the texts, thereby creating two performances: *Va-Yomer va-Yelekh* ("and he said and he went," 1996), and *Va-Yishtaḥu va-Yar* ("and they bowed and he saw," 1998). The result was a dynamic, theatrical performance of beautiful stage images and a unique experience of actors' group work. The Bible Project was performed for more than five years in Israel and in Hamburg, Berlin, London, and New York.

In 2001, Yerushalmi set out on another big project: this time she was led by the wish to analyze vengeance on the personal, the familial, and the national levels. It brought her back to Greek tragedy, to ancient and modern plays dealing with the Trojan War. The result was *Mythos*, a four-hour performance in which the events of the Trojan War were repeated in order to show their influence on the lives of the last generation, that of Electra and Orestes, the victims who become murderers because of the heritage of vengeance they carried along. The relevance to the Israeli-Palestinian conflict was evident, although Yerushalmi did not insert any contemporary indications in the text or in the stage design. The images on stage were constructed of different components – a stage design that deconstructed the stage as the myth unfolded, while huge projections and scientific explanations of the astral system accompanied the scenes. The actors working as a collective body, the chorus facing Electra and Orestes, incarnated the different characters of the plots, but most of all they danced, sang, and lamented, following the tradition of the ancient Greek chorus. *Mythos* was performed in Israel for two years. It was also invited to Zurich and to the Summer Festival of the Lincoln Center in New York.

Yerushalmi worked at the Israeli Opera. In 1997 she directed Humperdinck's *Haensel und Gretel*, and in 2000 she directed Richard Strauss' *Elektra* for a production of the Jerusalem Festival in Caesarea. Yerushalmi received many prizes and awards for her performances: in 1990 she received the Margalit prize for *Hamlet;* in 1992 the Moshe Halevi theater prize for *Woyzeck*, best directing and extraordinary contribution to Israeli theater; in 1998 an award of the Israeli Academy of the Theater for the Bible Project; and again in 1999 the Milo award for the Bible Project; the Rosenbaum award for the founding of the Itim Theatre Ensemble; in 2005 the Landau prize of Mif'al Ha-Payis for excellence in creating an original, powerful, and total theatrical language. In 2001 she received an honorary doctorate from the Hebrew University of Jerusalem. She was the recipient of the Unesco Fellowship for Theater Research and of the Corporation for Public Broadcasting (CPB) fellowship for television, U.S.

BIBLIOGRAPHY: F. Rokem, "Witnessing Woyzeck: Theatricality and the Empowerment of the Spectator," in: *SubStance*, 31:2–3 (2002), 167–83; P.W. Marx, *Theater und kulturelle Erinnerung: Kultursemiotische Untersuchungen zu G. Tabori, T. Kantor u. R. Yerushalmi* (2004).

[Nurit Yaari (2nd ed.)]

YERUSHALMI, YOSEF HAYIM (1932–), U.S. scholar of medieval and modern Jewish history. Yerushalmi was born in New York, graduated with a B.A. from Yeshiva University in 1953, took his doctorate at Columbia in 1966, and was ordained at the Jewish Theological Seminary of America in 1957. He was appointed assistant professor of Hebrew and Jewish history at Harvard University in 1966 and full professor in 1970; in 1972 he was elected a fellow of the American Academy of Jewish Research. In 1976–77 he was a fellow of the National Endowment for the Humanities; in 1978 he was appointed chairman of the Department of Near Eastern Languages and Civilization at Harvard; in 1978, Jacob Safra Professor of Jewish history and Sephardic civilization; and in 1980 director of the Center for Israel and Jewish Studies at Columbia University and Salo Wittmayer Baron Professor of Jewish history, culture, and society, focusing on medieval and modern Jewish history. A specialist in Sephardic and Marrano studies, he is editor of *Studia Sephardica*. Yerushalmi was chairman of the Publications Committee of the Jewish Publication Society of America, and from 1987 to 1991 served as president of the Leo Baeck Institute in New York.

Among his many works are *From Spanish Court to Italian Ghetto; Isaac Cardoso, a Study in 17th Century Marranism and Jewish Apologetics* (1971); "The Inquisition and the Jews of France in the Time of Bernard Gui," in: *Harvard Theological Review*, 63 (1970), 317–376; *Haggadah and History* (1973); *The Jewish People and Palestine* (with C. Berlin, 1973); *The Lisbon Massacre of 1506 and the Royal Image in the Shebet Yehudah* (1976); *Zakhor: Jewish History and Jewish Memory* (1982); *Freud's Moses* (1991); *Ein Feld in Anathoth* (1993), and *Sefardica* (1998). He has also prepared authoritative editions of M. Kayserlings' *Bibliotheca española-portugueza-judaica* (1971); and A. Herculano's *History of the Origin and Establishment of the Inquisition in Portugal.*

YESHAYAHU-SHAR'ABI, ISRAEL (1908–1979), Israeli politician, member of the First to Eighth Knessets. Yeshayahu was born in Sadan, *Yemen, where he received a traditional *ḥeder* education and attended the yeshivah of Rabbi Yihye Kafah. In Yemen he was active in the Dor De'ah Movement. In 1929 he immigrated to Palestine and worked as a farm laborer in the vineyards and on road construction. Soon, however, Yeshayahu entered political life as a member of Mapai, and was active in the Histadrut, serving from 1934 to 1948 as head of the department for immigrants from Yemen and other Muslim countries. In 1948 he was appointed by David Ben-Gurion as deputy government secretary in charge of contacts with the Knesset, and in 1949 was elected to the First Knesset on the Mapai list. From 1948 to 1952 he was active in organizing the immigration of the Jews from Yemen and was sent to Aden to organize Operation "Magic Carpet." He served as a deputy speaker in the Fourth, Fifth, and Sixth Knessets, and served on various Knesset committees. In 1967, he was appointed minister of postal services, holding the position until January 1970, when he was appointed secretary-general of the Israel Labor Party. In the Seventh Knesset he served as chairman of the Knesset House Committee, until, following the death of Re'uven Barkat, he was appointed speaker of the Knesset in 1972. He remained in the position until after the elections to the Ninth Knesset in 1977.

Among his writings are *Mi-Teiman le-Ẓiyyon* (prepared with Shimon Garidi, 1938) and *Ba'al ha-Taltalim ve-Od Sippurim* ("The Curly One and Other Stories," 1979). He was co-editor with Yosef Tobi of *Yahadut Teiman: Pirkei Mehkar ve-Iyyun* ("The Jewry of Yemen: Chapters of Research and Study," 1975).

BIBLIOGRAPHY: Y. Gal-Ron, *Kitvei Yisrael Yeshayahu* (1984).

YESHEVAV THE SCRIBE (end of the first half of the second century C.E.), *tanna*. A pupil of Joshua b. *Hananiah, he was a reliable transmitter of his master's opinions. Even his great colleague, *Akiva, who had opposed him on a halakhic issue, changed his mind and accepted Yeshevav's view which, the latter claimed, had been handed down by his teacher (Ḥul. 2:4; Tosef., Ḥul. 2:9) – this is the only Mishnah which mentions his name. On other occasions Akiva usually opposed him. Once when Yeshevav had gone to the trouble of locating some human bodies in order to declare the area around them a graveyard site, Akiva bluntly told him, "All your trouble was in vain" (Tosef., Oho. 16:3; Naz. 65a). When Akiva declared the offspring of all prohibited unions to be *mamzerim* Yeshevav exclaimed, "Come, let us cry out against Akiva b. Joseph…" (Ket. 29b, et. al.). Yeshevav was extremely generous and he once gave away all his property to the poor. This step was opposed by Rabban Gamaliel *II (TJ, Pe'ah 1:1, 15b, cf. Ket. 50a). Yeshevav is counted among the Ten *Martyrs put to death by the Romans. He is mentioned as being in the company of four other rabbis at Sepphoris in Galilee (Tosef., Kel. BB 2:2), where they were apparently hiding during the Hadrianic persecution. According to a later Midrash (*Midrash Elleh Ezkerah*, in: A. Jellinek (ed.), *Beit ha-Midrash*, 2 (1938^2), 71) he was 90 years old when he was executed, and his parting message to his disciples was "Support one another, and love peace and justice; perhaps there is hope."

BIBLIOGRAPHY: Hyman, Toledot; I. Konovitz, *Ma'arekhot Tanna'im*, pt. 3 (1968), 260 1.

[Moses Aberbach]

YESHIVA CHOVEVEI TORAH, rabbinical school in New York City. Situated near Columbia University on the upper West Side of Manhattan, Chovevei Torah was founded in 1999 by Rabbi Avi Weiss, senior rabbi of the Hebrew Institute of Riverdale and a former instructor at Yeshiva University (YU). It positioned itself as a Modern Orthodox alternative to the Rabbi Isaac Elchanan Theological Seminary, the YU rabbinical school. Weiss and his backers believed that the YU seminary had moved so far toward Orthodox sectarianism that the moderate elements of Orthodoxy – those that endorsed secular education as a positive good, favored ameliorating the status of women under Jewish law, sought cooperation with non-Orthodox forms of Judaism, and advocated religious Zionism – no longer had a yeshiva with which they could identify. Chovevei Torah focuses on producing practicing rabbis, Jewish educators, and Hillel directors who, over time, might change the face of American Orthodoxy, making it, in Weiss's words, "open" and "nonjudgmental" rather than combative and exclusionary. To that end, students in the four-year program are given full scholarships on condition that, after ordination, they serve as rabbis for at least three years. The curriculum gives less attention to Talmud study than other Orthodox seminaries and more to nuts-and-bolts skills required in the rabbinate, such as pastoral counseling and interpersonal relations. In the view of many observers, the fortunes of Chovevei Torah could well play a decisive role in the development of American Orthodox Judaism.

[Lawrence Grossman (2nd ed.)]

YESHIVA UNIVERSITY, institution of higher education in New York City. The Rabbi Isaac Elhanan Theological Seminary (RIETS, named for R. Isaac Elhanan Spektor), the nucleus around which Yeshiva University grew, was founded in 1897 by Rabbis Moses Matlin and Yehuda David Bernstein, and David Abramowitz, as a small institution for the advanced study of Talmud, attracting primarily immigrant youth. RIETS was the first advanced yeshivah in the United States. However, Yeshiva University dates its inception from 1886, when Yeshivat Eṭẓ Chaim, an elementary school which was merged with RIETS in 1915, was formed. Following student turmoil over the question of secular studies in 1906 and 1908 the school's administration was reorganized and some secular studies were permitted. Early presidents of the institution included Rabbi Moses Zebulun (Ramaz) *Margolies, Rabbi Bernard *Levinthal, and David Cohen. In 1915, Bernard *Revel became president and head of the faculty. In 1916 an accredited high school which combined talmudic and secular studies was opened. In 1922 the institution absorbed the Teachers Institute, which had been founded in 1917 by the Mizrachi Organization of America. In 1928 Yeshiva College accepted its first students. The high school, the college, RIETS, and the Teachers Institute were now all subdivisions of one institution, located in the Washington Heights section of New York City, which was to continue to expand its number of divisions as well as students. In 1970, RIETS was reincorporated as an "affiliate" of the university, a distinct legal entity with its own board.

Since its inception RIETS has devoted itself almost entirely to the teaching of Talmud and codes, the basis of the religious tradition, in a manner no different from any traditional yeshivah. The course of study culminates in a four-year program leading to *semikhah* ("rabbinical ordination"). For students of exceptional ability there are several *kollelim* (advanced study programs) that provide training in deciding complex issues of Jewish law. There were over 300 students in the rabbinical program in 2006, whose entrance requirements include a college degree in addition to extensive preparation in Talmud. Some courses in practical rabbinics were given for many years. From 1955 rabbinical students were also required to take courses in such subjects as Bible, Jewish history, philosophy, and Hebrew literature, and in recent years additional requirements have been instituted in the area of practical rabbinics. Yeshiva University has ordained about 2,600 rabbis since its inception. Over 70 percent of its active rabbinical graduates serve the Jewish community today in some formal capacity – as rabbis, teachers and educators, or communal workers – although the number entering the pulpit rabbinate has declined.

At the undergraduate college for men (Yeshiva College) and at the college for women (Stern College), which opened in 1954, students pursue a dual program of studies, taking courses in Jewish subjects as well as a normal load of secular subjects. Both colleges, with their combined enrollment in 2006 of 3,000 students, seek to impart mastery by the students of two intellectual worlds, the religious world and the secular one. There have been periods in the past, especially in the 1960s, when the emphasis was on integration within the curriculum of both worlds so that the content from one area of study may shed light or direction on the other. The talmudic faculty of Yeshiva University has always included some of the outstanding rabbinic scholars of the world. Preeminent among its faculty was Rabbi Joseph B. *Soloveitchik. An increasing number of the talmudic faculty are graduates of the institution. In 1943 Samuel *Belkin, a talmudic authority and Semitic scholar, succeeded to the presidency, left vacant by the death of Bernard Revel in 1940. Under Belkin's leadership the institution greatly expanded. In 1945 it was elevated to university status. It includes such specifically Jewish divisions and programs, in addition to those already mentioned, as the Bernard Revel Graduate School of Jewish Studies, the Azrieli Graduate School of Jewish Education, the Belz School of Jewish Music, and two high schools.

There are four alternative Jewish divisions in which all Yeshiva College students must also be enrolled: the Mechina Program (formerly called the James Striar School, for students with little background in Jewish studies); the Isaac Breuer College (which stresses Hebrew language and literature); and two that concentrate on Talmudic studies – the Irving Stone Beit Midrash Program and the Mazer School.

The secular, nonsectarian divisions of Yeshiva University have undergone the greatest expansion since 1945. These divisions now include the Ferkauf Graduate School of Psychology; the Wurzweiler School of Social Work; the Benjamin N. Cardozo School of Law; and probably best known of all, the Albert Einstein College of Medicine and its affiliated Albert Einstein College Hospital. While these divisions include a diverse student body and a distinguished non-Jewish as well as Jewish faculty, they do, in varying degrees, reflect Yeshiva University's orientation to Orthodox Judaism. All divisions observe the requirements of Jewish law and offer courses that explore the Jewish dimension of the field being studied. The Wurzweiler School requires all students to attend courses in Jewish sociology and in Jewish social work values. On the undergraduate level, the Sy Sims School of Business enables students both at Yeshiva College and Stern College to major in business-related areas.

In addition to its educational and other scholarly activity, the university plays a major role in the Jewish community through its Community Service Division. This division is responsible for rabbinic and teacher placement, conducts adult education and extension courses, provides educational services to many *Talmud Torahs* and youth groups, and sponsors seminars throughout the United States. The approximate enrollment in the various schools and divisions of Yeshiva University in 2006 was 6,000.

[Charles S. Liebman]

Developments since the 1970s

The economic situation of the country and the pressing needs of the state of Israel hurt Yeshiva University's ability to raise funds in the early 1970s. Following the retirement of Dr. Samuel Belkin in 1975, Dr. Norman *Lamm was elected to succeed him as president of the university in 1976. Lamm proved a potent fundraiser, rescuing the institution from the brink of bankruptcy. But another challenge appeared that threatened the university: the growing polarization of American Orthodox Judaism. While Yeshiva had traditionally serviced the educational needs of the so-called "modern Orthodox," for whom the combined religious-secular curriculum was essential, the Orthodox community was now turning rightward, and, partially as a result of the year or more that most Orthodox high-school graduates were spending at Israeli educational institutions, there was a demand for more rigorous religious classes and less emphasis on secular disciplines. In its undergraduate recruitment efforts, Yeshiva University sought to adapt to the new mood, competing for students with the sectarian yeshivot that were skeptical about college rather than with the nation's top universities. Its efforts, however, were complicated by the emergence of *Touro College, which promised a more rigorously Orthodox environment for those seeking higher secular education, and three new institutions that tried to fill the vacuum in the modern Orthodox sector that Yeshiva University had apparently abandoned: *Edah, an educational and consciousness-raising group; the *Jewish Orthodox Feminist Alliance (JOFA); and *Yeshivat Chovevei Torah, which trained rabbis to fill modern Orthodox pulpits. The secular graduate schools of Yeshiva, meanwhile, chafed at what they saw as a growing fundamentalist strain within the university.

Yeshiva University's internal contradictions came to a head with the announcement, in 2001, of Dr. Lamm's impending retirement and elevation to the post of chancellor. Since the classical Orthodox rabbi-scholar model typified by Revel, Belkin, and Lamm had not been cultivated within the institution for a quarter-century, there was no one in that mold to take over the presidency. It was not until 2003 that a new president was inaugurated, Richard Joel, previously the president of Hillel, the organization of Jewish college students. Neither a rabbi nor an academic – the job of Rosh Yeshiva at REITS remained with Lamm and Joel was president of the University – Joel, enjoying the advantage of the financial cushion provided by his predecessor's fund-raising, appeared committed to reorienting the university back toward its modern Orthodox roots, but in such a way as to retain the loyalties of the more tradition-bound rabbis. He energetically set out to increase enrollment, boost morale, upgrade student services, and strengthen the university's bonds with the American Jewish community through the creation of a Center for the Jewish Future.

[Lawrence Grossman (2nd ed.)]

BIBLIOGRAPHY: G. Klaperman, *The Story of Yeshiva University* (1967); idem, in: AJHSP, 54 (1964), 5–50, 198–201; AJYB, 68 (1967), 367, index; C.S. Liebman, *ibid.*, 66 (1965), 62–65; 69 (1968), index. **ADD. BIBLIOGRAPHY:** J. Gurock, *The Men and Women of Yeshiva University* (1988); V. Geller, *Orthodoxy Awakens: The Belkin Era and Yeshiva University* (2003).

YESHIVOT. The name yeshivah was applied to institutes of talmudic learning of three distinct kinds:

(1) the academies in Ereẓ Israel and Babylonia in which the Mishnah was studied by the *amoraim* and which produced the Jerusalem and Babylonian Talmud (see *Talmud, Babylonian and *Talmud, Jerusalem);

(2) the academies of Sura and Pumbedita which in the geonic period were the central authoritative religious bodies for world Jewry;

(3) local institutions for the pursuit of talmudic studies which developed in the post-geonic period. This article deals with the third category only; for the others see *Academies.

The Yeshivot in Islamic Countries and in Western and Central Europe to the 15th Century

The first yeshivot outside Babylon and Ereẓ Israel were already established during the time of the *geonim*. *Pirkoi b. Baboi in the eighth century testifies to their existence in North Africa and in Spain, and in the tenth century yeshivot arose in the Maghreb – in Fez, in Gabès, in Sijilmassa, and in Tlemcen. The Kairouan yeshivah, where *Ḥushi'el b. Elhanan, regarded as its founder, and *Jacob b. Nissim were active, became especially famous. In Egypt there was a renowned yeshivah in Fostat headed by *Elhanan b. Shemariah, and he and other heads of yeshivot in Egypt were termed *reish bei-rabbanan* ("head of scholars") or *rosh ha-seder* ("head of the order"). In Egypt an effort was even made to revive the geonate and during the 12th century the head of yeshivot in Fostat bore the title **gaon*. *Maimonides, who gave public discourses in Fostat, may have headed a yeshivah. There were still important yeshivot in Egypt in the 16th century, headed by *David b. Solomon ibn Abi Zimra, Bezalel *Ashkenazi, and others.

The yeshivot of Ereẓ Israel moved to Damascus after the *Crusades and remained there until the end of the 12th century. There was also an important center of talmudic study in *Aleppo. The largest yeshivah in Oriental countries, headed by the last of the *geonim*, was in Gabhda, where there were also nine small yeshivot.

In Spain yeshivot are mentioned as existing in Lucena and in Barcelona in the middle of the eighth century, but definite evidence of them exists only from the tenth century onward. In the middle of that century *Moses b. Ḥanokh founded a large yeshivah in Córdoba, where he was succeeded by his son, Ḥanokh. The yeshivah of Granada was headed by *Samuel ha-Nagid and after him by his son Joseph. The yeshivah of Lucena attracted many students from outside Spain and continued to exist for some 250 years. Among its pupils were Jonah *Ibn Janāḥ and *Judah Halevi, among its later heads Isaac ibn Ghayyat, Isaac *Alfasi, and Joseph *Ibn Migash. The *Almohad invasion brought about the ruin of the yeshivot in southern Spain and they were replaced by the great yeshivot of Aragon and Castile.

The yeshivot of Barcelona and Toledo flourished in the time of Solomon b. Abraham *Adret, *Asher b. Jehiel, and *Nissim b. Reuben Gerondi, continued to exist until the persecutions of 1391, and exercised great influence upon the yeshivot of France and Germany. Subsequently, and until the expulsion, there were many yeshivot in Spain and by a resolution of the leaders of the communities of Castile in 1432 the duty was even imposed upon every rabbi to establish a yeshivah in his community. At that time the yeshivot of Isaac *Campanton and Isaac de *Leon in Toledo, Isaac *Aboab II, and of Samuel de Valensi became well known. Even Joseph *Jabez, who castigates the scholars of his generation for their secular outlook on life, admits that at the time of the Spanish expulsion the number of yeshivot in Castile was greater than it had ever been.

The first yeshivah in southern France was at *Narbonne, apparently founded in the tenth century. Among its heads (in the 12th century) was *Abraham b. Isaac, author of *Ha-Eshkol*. When *Benjamin of Tudela visited Lunel he found there an important yeshivah, whose pupils, although from other towns, were supported by the local community. The pupils of the yeshivah of Posquières were maintained at the personal expense of its head, *Abraham b. David. The yeshivot at *Béziers, Marseilles, and Montpellier also gained a great reputation. A vivid description of the method of learning in the yeshivot of Provence has been preserved in the work of *Jedaiah b. Abraham ha-Penini, who studied in the yeshivah of Béziers. In northern France the pupils and descendants of *Rashi headed the yeshivot – Jacob b. Meir *Tam at Ramerupt and *Isaac b. Samuel at Dampierre. Students were attracted to them from afar, even from the Slavonic countries. According to one tradition 60 scholars of the Dampierre yeshivah took part in the halakhic discussions which served as the basis for the **Tosafot*. There were also important yeshivot in Orleans, Falaise, Sens, Coucy, and Chinon. The yeshivah of *Jehiel of Paris had 300 students. *Moses b. Jacob of Coucy relates that the students of the French yeshivot were so assiduous in their studies that they even slept in their clothes. The expulsion of the Jews from France in 1306 put an end to the yeshivot there; on their return an effort at revival was made by Mattathias Treves, who founded a yeshivah in Paris after 1360, but it did not succeed.

In Germany the yeshivah of R. *Gershom b. Judah in Mainz, to which pupils came even from Spain, was especially renowned. His pupils continued his activity both in Mainz and in *Worms. In the 11th, and still more in the 12th–13th centuries, there flourished the yeshivot of Speyer, Regensburg, Bonn, and Paris. The students made their way on foot, a custom preserved also in the following generations, and they were welcomed by the Jews of each locality with great honor. After the destruction of the *Rhine communities in the persecutions accompanying the *Black Death (1348–49), Austria became the center for study of the Talmud, and pupils began to stream to the yeshivot of Vienna from the north and the west. As a result of the activity of Isaac Or Zaru'a it became a Torah center as early as the 13th century, as did Wiener-Neustadt, where Israel *Isserlein was active, and Krems. In Prague, Bohemia, there were already yeshivot in the 12th century, headed by pupils of Jacob Tam, but their main flowering was from the end of the 15th century.

In Italy teaching institutions for Talmud existed at a very early period, and some scholars ascribe to Italy a special historical function in the chain of handing down the teaching of Oral Law in Europe. However, both the problem of its relationship to the Torah of Ereẓ Israel as well as of its influence upon the yeshivot of Europe that arose after it have not been sufficiently clarified and are subjects of dispute. In any event there was already a yeshivah in Venosa in the ninth century. Yeshivot, important in their time, existed then and in the tenth century within the Byzantine possessions in the south – at Oria Otranto, and Bari – and also in central Italy at Lucca – from where the *Kalonymus family brought the study of the Talmud to Mainz – and subsequently at Siponto and at Rome. The Jewish centers in the south were destroyed in the later Middle Ages and the northern ones declined in standard. A new impetus to the study of Talmud in Italy was given in the 15th–16th centuries by the arrival of the exiles from Germany and France.

[Simha Assaf]

The Shifting of Yeshivah Centers in the 15th–18th Centuries

Although the political and economic position of the Jews in Germany, Austria, and Spain became increasingly precarious, the yeshivot continued their activities and even increased in number. Yeshivot such as those headed by R. Jacob *Moellin (Mainz), R. Jacob *Weil (Nuremberg, Augsburg), R. Isaac Canpanton (Castile, Spain), and R. Israel Isserlein (Krems, Austria) attracted large numbers of students. However, there was a continuous shifting of the Jewish population to southern and Eastern Europe and study centers moved to Italy, Bohemia, and Poland-Lithuania. R. Moses *Muenz (Minz) opened a yeshivah at Poznan (Poland), and R. Joseph *Colon at Pavia (Italy). R. Jacob *Pollak of Nuremberg moved first to Prague and then to Cracow, students flocking to him wherever he went.

The 16th and 17th centuries witnessed a large concentration of yeshivot and widespread Torah learning in Poland-Lithuania. Among outstanding yeshivah heads were R. *Shalom Shakhna (Lublin), R. Moses *Isserles (Cracow), R. Solomon *Luria (Ostrog, Lublin), R. Judah *Loew (Prague, Poznan, Nikolsburg), R. Mordecai *Jaffe (Prague, Grodno, Lublin), R. Joshua *Falk (Lvov), R. Samuel *Edels (Ostrog), R. Isaiah *Horowitz (Ostrog, Prague), R. Yom Tov Lipmann *Heller (Prague, Vladmir-Volynski (Ludmir), Cracow), and R. Menahem Mendel *Krochmal (Nikolsburg). In Lithuania, important yeshivot were at Brest-Litovsk, Pinsk, and Slutsk. This illustrious stage in the history of the Ashkenazi yeshivah was summed up, if somewhat exaggeratedly, by R. Nathan *Hannover in his *Yeven Meẓulah*: "There were yeshivot in each and every community." During the same period, yeshivah centers sprang up in Italy, Greece, Turkey, and Ereẓ Israel. Important institutions were headed by R. Judah *Minz (Padua; see Elijah *Capsali's vivid account, in: REJ, 79 (1924), 28–60), R. Joseph *Ottolenghi (Cremona), and later by R. Moses *Zacuto (Mantua). Renowned yeshivot were also maintained at Venice and later at Leghorn. The influx of refugees from Spain into the Levant caused a marked upsurge in the study of the Talmud there as is evident by such famous heads of yeshivot as R. Elijah *Mizraḥi (Constantinople), R. Joseph *Taitaẓak and R. Samuel di *Medina (Salonika), R. *Levi b. Ḥabib and later R. Jacob *Ḥagiz (Jerusalem), R. Jacob *Berab and R. Joseph *Caro (Safed), R. *David ibn Abi Zimra (Jerusalem, Cairo). Yeshivot of importance were also supported by the Smyrna community.

After the 1648–49 massacres (see *Chmielnicki) the Polish-Lithuanian yeshivot declined, though they were still attended by students from Western Europe. Scholars from Eastern Europe were increasingly to be found as rabbis and heads of yeshivot in German communities, such as Frankfurt on the Main, Fuerth, Hamburg-Altona, Halberstadt, and Metz. Famous heads of yeshivot in these communities in the 18th century included R. Jacob Joshua *Falk, R. Zevi *Ashkenazi, R. Jonathan *Eybeschutz, R. Raphael *Kohen, and R. Phinehas *Horowitz. The Prague yeshivah continued to flourish under R. Ezekiel *Landau, and yeshivot were established in Hungary (Eisenstadt, Pressburg). The Sephardi yeshivah Etz-Ḥayyim in Amsterdam made a special name for itself, while the yeshivot in the Ottoman Empire were declining steadily. In Italy R. Isaac *Lampronti attracted many students to his yeshivah in Ferrara. By the close of the 18th century the *Haskalah in the West and acute impoverishment in the East had caused many yeshivot to close, and the number of students at the surviving ones was lower than ever.

Organization and Inner Life

Prior to the 16th century, the Ashkenazi yeshivah had only been loosely affiliated with the local community, being mostly the semiprivate undertaking of the scholar who headed it. Almost every talmudic scholar who attained the position of a rabbi would open a yeshivah and he was responsible for meeting its financial requirements. The well-to-do students paid for their studies and upkeep, while the poor ones were supported by communal charity. Many communities paid special taxes to the city for the right to have students from other places at the local yeshivah.

Gradually the yeshivot became more closely connected with the communal administration. By the middle of the 16th century a new type of "community yeshivah" (*yeshivat ha-kahal*) had crystallized, while the former, semiprivate type continued to exist side by side with it, usually supported by wealthy rabbis or by laymen through charitable trusts. The communal yeshivot were subject to the rules (*takkanot*) laid down by the general councils of entire areas, defining their administrative and scholastic functions in the minutest details, such as the universal duty of the communities to maintain and support yeshivot; qualifications of yeshivah heads; admission of students; curriculum; supply of books; graduation of students; distribution of meals for students among members of the communities. In Spain rules regulating the organization of yeshivot had already been promulgated by the Council of Valladolid in 1432. In Italy and Germany numerous little synagogues were endowed by wealthy donors where masters were "enclosed" (hence their name: *Klaus* in German and *Hesger* in Hebrew) with a small number of students. There was also a tightening of social relations between the yeshivah and the community. While students usually conducted separate prayer services with the rabbi, local religious traditions were binding on the yeshivah congregation, and in matters of rabbinical jurisprudence arising in the community the rabbi consulted senior members of his yeshivah (*benei yeshivah*), and local legal cases were brought up for discussion in the plenum of the yeshivah.

Masters and students were in constant personal contact. Many students were "wandering scholars," moving from one yeshivah to another, urged on by necessity or thirst for knowledge. The youngest were aged 13, but the middle-aged, married *baḥur* was not exceptional. At some yeshivot the students organized some form of self-government. Many of them tried to supplement their material resources by teaching young children, copying manuscripts, acting as cantors in outlying communities, and even engaging in some moneylending. While yeshivah students were not known for committing excesses and outrages like university scholars, there were occasional outbursts of merry-making. Their life was devoted to high moral and intellectual ideas, yet it was not somber and other-worldly.

Curriculum

The subject matter of instruction at the Ashkenazi yeshivot was almost exclusively the Oral Law as expounded in the Talmud and its commentaries and supercommentaries of the French-German school. Few traces can be found of formal Bible lectures. This was not universally considered satisfactory, and it came under sharp attack from Sephardi scholars, at whose yeshivot much more time was devoted to Bible and aggadic literature. Nevertheless, the advocates of the Ashkenazi curriculum stressed its greater relevance to religious practice and effectiveness for developing the intellect. However, the private scholarly interests of students were more diversified. In the 15th century a favorite preoccupation was the typically humanistic study of *minhagim*, the local customs and traditions, and students also recorded in great detail the religious practices of their masters. Later this gave rise to a systematic study of codificatory literature (*posekim*), and in Italy, where the pope had banned the Talmud in 1559, this became the central part of the curriculum. At the Etz-Ḥayyim yeshivah in Amsterdam senior students were required to write responsa to set questions on topical matters of *halakhah*. Kabbalistic studies, though increasingly popular, never became part of the formal Ashkenazi studies, as they did in Italy and in the Levant. Secular studies were practically unknown at the Ashkenazi yeshivot, although in Renaissance Italy suggestions were made for combining Torah with the study of science. The academic year was divided into two semesters, with few vacations and holidays. Gradually the vacations were prolonged, especially in the autumn, as masters and their students visited the trade fairs (see *Markets and Fairs) where scholars used to convene to discuss matters of academic and public interest.

For methods of study see *Pilpul*.

Degrees and Graduation

The first grade attained by a young yeshivah student was that of *baḥur*, and upon reaching a certain degree of academic independence he was made a *meshuḥrar*. A student of many years' standing and high scholastic merit was given the title of *ḥaver*. Toward the end of the 14th century the academic and rabbinical title of *morenu* was introduced and the rules of graduation and ordination (*semikhah*) were stabilized. This had become necessary in order to safeguard the academic standard of the rabbinate against the perils of dispersal and migration. However, as soon as *semikhah* was formalized, a process of institutionalization set in, enabling mediocre scholars to attain rabbinical authority and privilege, a fact which was much lamented by leading rabbis. Here and there *semikhah* became a source of income for rabbis, and it was necessary for communities and general councils to issue *takkanot* defining the conditions under which a student could be known as *morenu*. By the end of the 16th century the titles of *morenu* and *ḥaver* lost their purely academic character and were increasingly used as symbols of social status.

Despite persecution, dispersion, and changing social and economic conditions, the ideals of Torah study persisted throughout the Middle Ages. Study was one of the supreme modes of worship, and the central position of scholars and scholarship in the communities made the yeshivah one of the main pillars of Jewish life.

[Mordechai Breuer]

Lithuania and Russia

Documentary evidence exists of yeshivot in Lithuania and Belorussia in the 16th century. By a resolution of its first assembly in 1622 the Council of Lithuanian Jewry obliged every community with a rabbi to maintain a yeshivah with a suitable number of pupils. The large communities were authorized to supervise the implementation of the resolution. An agreement between the rabbi and his community on a limitation of the number of pupils was of no validity. The pupils of the yeshivah were maintained by the members of the community, who made themselves responsible for providing for the material needs of the students not as became customary later on a daily basis ("*essen teg*," literally "eating days") but for a period of two to four weeks. Jews in the neighboring villages were also obliged to help maintain the yeshivah pupils. "Between terms" (from the 15th of Av to the first of Ḥeshvan, and from the 15th of Shevat to the first of Nisan), the pupils lived in the homes of the village Jews. As this caused them to slacken in their study of the Talmud, in 1639 the council limited the students' stay in the villages to the months of Nisan, Elul, and Tishri. Subsequently this practice was abolished completely. The communities also undertook the obligation of supplying the yeshivot with copies of the Talmud and other books. The Lithuanian yeshivot, which were mainly concentrated in the regions of Grodno (Brest-Litvosk), Vilna, and Minsk (Pinsk, Slutsk), never reached the level of the Polish yeshivot and in the 18th century continued to decline. According to the testimony of Joseph Krinki, a pupil of Ḥayyim of Volozhin, the yeshivah in Zamet, which in the past had been a center of Talmud study, ceased to exist.

A new era in the spiritual life of the Jews of Lithuania, however, was inaugurated by *Elijah b. Solomon, the Gaon of Vilna, whose pupils established a network of yeshivot in Lithuania and Belorussia. The most important of these was founded in 1802 in *Volozhin, near Vilna, by Ḥayyim of Volozhin (see Ḥayyim *Volozhiner), the Gaon of Vilna's most distinguished pupil. Only talented students with a good grounding were accepted. Ḥayyim continued the Gaon's method and like him was opposed to the method of *pilpul* prevailing in the yeshivot of Poland. His successor, his son Isaac, made great efforts to make the yeshivah acceptable to the government. From 1854 until its closure by the government in 1892, the yeshivah was headed by Isaac's son-in-law, Naphtali Ẓevi Judah *Berlin (the "Neẓiv"), during whose time its standard rose. The number of students from all parts of Russia and even beyond reached 400. To maintain the yeshivah and needy students, emissaries were dispatched to all the communities of Russia, and even to the United States. From the yeshivah of Volozhin came most of the rabbis and talmudic scholars of Russia in the 19th century. As a factor against the inroads of Haskalah it had a great influence on the spiritual life of the Jews of Russia, as a result of which the representatives of the Haskalah fought against it fiercely. The Russian government, which regarded the Haskalah movement with greater favor, treated the yeshivah with suspicion and several times ordered its closure. The yeshivah was indeed reopened several times after the death of Berlin in 1893, but it never regained its previous eminence. Alongside it there existed other large yeshivot in the towns of Mir (Minsk region), Vilna, Minsk, etc. In the 1870s and 1880s the yeshivot of *Slobodka and *Telz (Telsiai) were founded. The number of their pupils exceeded 300 and they were in some degree intended to make good the deficiency caused by the closure of the Volozhin yeshivah. The Telz yeshivah, headed by Eliezer *Gordon (d. 1910), was distinguished by its rational method of study and the strict arrangement of its studies. The students were obliged to complete five classes of *shi'urim*. In the yeshivah, Keneset Israel (not to be confused with the Keneset Yiẓḥak institute in the same town), founded in Slobodka by disciples of Israel (Salanter) *Lipkin, members of the *Musar movement, particular stress was laid upon the learning of *musar*, prayer with devotion, and the fulfillment of precepts. This approach aroused opposition for fear that the stress on the devotional and ethical teaching of the Talmud was likely to limit its intensive study. However, in the last decades before the Holocaust the system prevailed in most Lithuanian yeshivot. Mention must also be made of the yeshivot of Lomza, Radzyn, Novogrudok, Slutsk, Malch, and Bryansk. The adherents of the Chabad ḥasidic movement maintained a yeshivah in Lubavich with 400 pupils and had branches in other towns. The curriculum of the ḥasidic yeshivot naturally devoted considerable time to ḥasidic doctrine.

The new trends in the spiritual life of the Jews of Russia found an echo among the youth in the yeshivot. In many places the masters endeavored to keep the students from any contact with secular literature, and in Slobodka in particular there was strict supervision. The movement toward acquiring general culture did not touch the ḥasidic yeshivot at all, perhaps since most of them were in small towns far from the cities. Money for their maintenance was collected by emissaries who were at the same time wandering preachers. Apart from the large yeshivot there existed in several localities small yeshivot for the local youth supported by the community and the neighborhood. Since married students were not accepted in the yeshivot and the codes were not studied in them, those married students of the Talmud who wanted to become ordained for the rabbinate would unite in **kolelim*. Such *kolelim* existed in Volozhin (in a branch of the yeshivah), in Eishishok, Minsk, Vilna, and other places. An exceptionally high standard was attained by the Perushim *kolel* in Kovno headed by Isaac Elhanan Spektor (d. 1897), which in the 1890s had more than 200 students. Both the members of these *kolelim*, whose studies lasted from three to four years, and their families, were adequately supported.

In the last decades before the Holocaust the tendency developed to admit other Jewish studies (Bible, Hebrew, etc.) besides Talmud into the curriculum as well as secular studies. One such reformed yeshivah was founded in Lida, in 1905 by Isaac Jacob Reines, with the intention not only of providing general culture for rabbis and teachers but also of furnishing students who intended engaging in business with comprehensive Jewish knowledge. It had about 300 pupils. The yeshivah founded in 1905 by Ḥayyim *Tchernowitz (Rav Ẓa'ir) in Odessa was meant to be an advanced school for Jewish studies and an academy for rabbis, equipped with the apparatus of modern scholarship. The scientific method was practiced in all branches, even in Talmud. In its early period *Bialik and *Klausner were lecturers there, in addition to Tchernowitz. After the Bolshevik Revolution all the yeshivot in the Soviet Union were closed. Until the Holocaust yeshivot remained in Lithuania in Slobodka, Telz, and Ponevezh (Panevezyas); in Poland they remained in Mir, Kletsk, Baranovichi, Radzyn, Warsaw, and elsewhere. In Lublin a large yeshivah was opened under the leadership of Meir *Shapira.

[Simha Assaf]

Yeshivot in the 20th Century

From the beginning of the 20th century it became clear to Orthodox Jewry that only an orderly and organized religious education could serve as a protective barrier against the spread of general cultural trends and the new social movements of the time. As a result, at the very time that the influence of Torah in the life of the individual and the community was being undermined, yeshivah learning and education, which had previously been a matter for the religious intellectual elite only, became an accepted and widespread feature in the life of the young men of Orthodox Jewry as a whole. With the improvement of the economic status of the Jews in Europe and the United States and the improvement in methods of communication and in means of propaganda, the possibilities of establishing a material basis and organizational framework for the subsistence of rabbi and students were created. Consequently the number of yeshivot and their students continued to increase. The improvement in their economic situation and the general recognition of their importance freed them to a great extent from dependence upon the community and its institutions, and in consequence the importance and the personal influence of the heads of the yeshivot rose; through their many students who were dispersed throughout numerous communities, they became the leaders of the whole of Orthodox Jewry, and their influence was greater than that of the rabbis of the communities. In ḥasidic Poland, too, at the beginning of the 20th century there was a large increase in the number of yeshivot affiliated to the courts of the different *ẓaddikim despite the special standpoint of *Ḥasidism on this question. During this era, particularly between the two world wars, the yeshivot of Lithuania attained a position of hegemony in Torah Judaism.

The quantitative growth and the rise in social status which are among the prominent external marks of yeshivot in the 20th century brought with them many changes in the structure and essence of yeshivot in the Jewish world, leading to a change in the very connotation of the whole concept. However, the increase in the number of yeshivot and the growth in the number of students brought in its wake a decline in the average standard of the pre-yeshivah preparation, and in consequence also in the standard of studies at the yeshivah itself. Spiritual movements in Orthodox Jewry, like the different trends of *musar* and Ḥasidism, on the one hand, and the increasing need for the acquisition of general spiritual values under the pressure of modern life on the other, all brought about a strengthening of the educational basis in the yeshivot, and this, to no small degree, at the expense of the instructional basis. Although the basic structure remained the same, the large yeshivot increasingly assumed the character of places of education in Judaism, while higher studies were mainly connected with *kolelim*. One of the conspicuous consequences of this process was the founding of the "minor yeshivot" designed to provide their pupils with a level suitable for regular study in the standard yeshivot. These yeshivot constituted a kind of intermediate stage between elementary and higher education, and the age levels of the students were roughly between 13 and 18. As in the large yeshivot, study was in principle self study but it took place under the continuous and intensive supervision and guidance of teachers and supervisors.

The Holocaust brought the yeshivot of Eastern and Central Europe to an end, but in a number of Western countries which had no yeshivot or where yeshivot had ceased to exist a number of large ones were established. From the mid-20th century the greatest number of yeshivot, and the most important of them, was centered in Israel and in the United States, but they were also found in many other Western countries (e.g., in *Gateshead, England). The *Chabad movement was especially active in this direction, establishing yeshivot in France, Australia, and North Africa.

Yeshivot in Ereẓ Israel

Israel became the greatest center of yeshivot, having the greatest number of yeshivot and students since the talmudic era. In Israel there were also to be found the greatest number of diversified types of yeshivot each of which had a character of its own.

(1) The yeshivot of the old *yishuv*, the oldest in the country, pertained to the very structure of this *yishuv* and were to a great degree connected with the *kolelim* and with the system of the *ḥalukkah*. They provided talmudic education for large numbers. Most of the students were of mature age, some continuing their study during their whole lifetime. Generally speaking about 20 to 30 men, mostly married, were concentrated in such a yeshivah and they received a minimal material support. In most of these yeshivot the system of study was undefined. The larger yeshivot of this type, with hundreds of students (like Eẓ Ḥayyim, or Ḥayyei Olam in Jerusalem), had a character similar to that of the ordinary large yeshivot, and tuition was given in Yiddish. With this type should be connected a number of yeshivot that studied Kabbalah.

(2) The Sephardi yeshivot, the largest and oldest of which was Porat Yosef in Jerusalem, still followed the old Sephardi pattern of study, strong stress being placed on the preparation of religious functions for Oriental communities all over the world.

(3) The central yeshivot, removed from Eastern Europe to Israel (like Slobodka-Hebron), or whose heads reestablished them with the same composition and names, the same applying to the large ḥasidic yeshivot transferred from their center in Poland.

(4) Yeshivot Hesder, yeshivot which combine Israel army service with intensive yeshivah studies. In 1991 there were 3,300 students in the program. In that year the program was awarded the Israel Prize in recognition of its students excelling in the study halls and in the IDF's elite combat units.

An important aspect of yeshivot in Israel were the *kolelim* which developed greatly and in which the young men continued their studies after marriage and at a higher level. These *kolelim* were dependent on the large yeshivot and were an important factor in raising the level of studies in the whole yeshivah. From these *kolelim*, unlike those of the old *yishuv*, the scholars passed after five to ten years to serve as rabbis, *dayyanim*, or teachers at yeshivot. Some of them worked at preparing manuscripts of rabbinic works for publication, in a scientific manner. A number (like Merkaz ha-Rav and Kol Torah in Jerusalem) gave all the tuition in Hebrew but in most the official *shi'ur* was still given in Yiddish, even though most of the learning was conducted in Hebrew.

Another very important change was the attempt to combine secular studies within the framework of the classical yeshivah and at a parallel standard. The idea first arose among German Orthodoxy (see A. *Hildesheimer; S.R. *Hirsch) as an expression of the aims of *Torah im Derekh Ereẓ* ("Jewish with secular learning"), but without any connection with the activity and programs of Orthodox proponents of the Wissenschaft des Judentums or the various types of rabbinical seminary. Chiefly in Ereẓ Israel – and later in the State of Israel – numerous new types of yeshivah were created which combined the classical learning within their compass with various and diversified forms of secular studies organized according to the pattern of the different general schools and subject to the general directions, inspection, and examinations of the state Department of Education. The essence of the attempt and the most successful were the *yeshivot tikhoniyyot* ("high school yeshivot") which finally emerged as the minor yeshivah in which the instruction during the first half of the day was devoted to Talmud with secondary school studies in the afternoon. The talmudic studies in these yeshivot were dominated by the Lithuanian system of study. The success of the attempt brought about its diversification into combinations of "vocational yeshivot" and "agricultural yeshivot," etc. Many minor yeshivot and *yeshivot tikhoniyyot* existed in Israel, and most of the pupils continued in the large yeshivot. The first yeshivah that began to move in this direction was the yeshivah of Ha-Yishuv he-Ḥadash (the "new settlement") in Tel Aviv, established by Rabbi M.A. *Amiel, in which only the evening hours were devoted to secular studies and a fifth year was added to make it possible for the students to take the state matriculation examination. A greater, more direct influence was achieved by the yeshivah of the *Bnei Akiva movement (see *National Religious Party) in Kefar ha-Ro'eh, which became the pattern for about 20 other yeshivot. These yeshivot competed with the religious grammar schools and even encroached upon them. From the teaching standpoint, the two parts, the sacred and the secular, remained uncombined but side by side, but educationally a successful combination was achieved. On the establishment of the State of Israel the heads of the yeshivot came to an agreement with the Ministry of Defense that their students would be exempt from military service, on grounds of recognition of the duty to help in the spiritual rebuilding of Judaism after the Holocaust. This agreement had no legal validity but was an ad hoc arrangement according to which the yeshivah students were regarded as receiving deferment for the duration of their studies. The arrangement was viewed with mixed feelings by the public, even including religious circles, and many yeshivah students interrupted their studies in order to do their military service. In a number of yeshivot there existed various arrangements that combined yeshivah studies with active service, particularly in the framework of *Naḥal.

Most yeshivot in Israel were administratively combined under a loose roof organization, called Va'ad ha-Yeshivot; about ten yeshivot with around 500 students were connected with the Iḥud ha-Yeshivot of the *Neturei Karta. Few yeshivot were definitely associated with a specific religious political party, but most of their heads and students were close to *Agudat Israel and supported it. Those yeshivot closer to the National Religious Party served as a factor inclining their party in a more conservative direction.

The arrangement whereby the State of Israel supported a limited number of yeshivah students (originally 400) designated "professional religious scholars," granting them draft exemptions as well, has mushroomed into a system where the great majority of ultra-Orthodox men (some 80,000 in 2006, half married) study full time. The economic and social consequences of maintaining such a "society of scholars," in the phrase of Menachem Friedman, are a subject of constant debate in Israel.

Yeshivot in the United States

There were large yeshivot of the kind traditional in Eastern Europe, some being actually the original yeshivot transferred there with their students during World War II. Also, many large yeshivot, whose main creation was in the United States, became an important factor in Jewish life there. *Yeshiva University was a valuable contribution of American Jewry to the development of the yeshivah. In this institute the yeshivah studies were no different in quality from the European version and at the same time it contained a large university. This yeshivah brought an important change in the situation of Orthodoxy in the United States, succeeding in raising a new generation of rabbis and spiritual guides who brought about a revival of Orthodox Jewry and had a great influence throughout the whole of the United States. Another great American yeshivah institute is the Beth Midrash Govoha in Lakewood, New Jersey, with 3,000 students in the early 2000s. Founded in 1943 by R. Aaron *Kotler on the rigid Lithuanian model that demanded full-time study, it now offers a Bachelor (and even Master) of Talmudic Law degree which allows students to go on to graduate school. Thus, unlike their Israeli counterparts, the American "Litvaks" are able to ultimately enter the job market in high-paying professions ranging from law and medicine to high-tech industry.

[Adin Steinsaltz]

BIBLIOGRAPHY: Guedemann, Gesch Erz; Assaf, Mekorot; N. Isaacs, *Study as a Mode of Worship* (1925); L. Ginzberg, *Students, Scholars and Saints* (1928). POST-GEONIC PERIOD: Islamic Countries: S. Goitein, *Sidrei Ḥinnukh bi-Ymei ha-Ge'onim u-Veit ha-Rambam* (1962); Provence: Z. Benedikt, in: Tarbiz, 22 (1951), 85–109; I. Twersky, *Rabad of Posquieres* (1962), 19ff.; Italy: A. Marx. in: *Sefer ha-Yovel... L. Ginzberg* (1945), 271–304; M.A. Szulwas, in: *Horeb*, 10 (1948), 105–28; Roth, Dark Ages, ch. 8; France and Germany: M. Guedemann, in: MGWJ, 13 (1964), 68–70, 97–110, 384–95, 421–44; E.M. Lipschulz, in: *Sefer Rashi* (1956), 188–212; Urbach, Tosafot, ch. 1, 13; S. Schwazfuchs, *Etudes sur l'Origine et le Developpement du Rabbinat au Moyen-Age* (1957); J. Katz, *Tradition and Crisis* (1961), ch. 18; I.A. Agus, in: *Studies and Essays in Honor of A.A. Neuman* (1962), 1–16; Roth, Dark Ages, ch. 9–10; M Breuer, in: *Zion*, 33 (1968), 15–46; S. Rozman, *Sefer Zikhron Kedoshim li-Yhudei Carpatoruss-Marmarosh* (1968; Yid.), 149–63. EASTERN EUROPE: I.H. Weiss, *Zikhronotai* (1895); J. Trachtenberg, in: *Jewish Education*, 11 (1939), no. 2; I. Fishman, *The History of Jewish Education in Central Europe from the End of the Sixteenth to the End of the Eighteenth Century* (1944); H.H. Ben-Sasson, *Hagut ve-Hanhagah* (1959), ch. 11. **ADD. BIBLIOGRAPHY:** M. Friedman, *Haredi Society: Origins, Trends, and Processes* (Heb., 1991); W.B. Heimreich, *The World of the Yeshiva: An Intimate Portrait of Orthodox Jewry* (1999).

YESHURUN, AVOT (pseudonym of **Yehiel Perlmutter**; 1904–1992), Israeli poet. Born in Volhynia, he immigrated to Palestine in 1925, and his poems first appeared in *Turim*, in 1934. Among Yeshurun's published volumes of poetry are *Al Ḥokhmat Derakhim* ("The Wisdom of the Road," 1942, under his original name); *Re'em* (1961), and *Sheloshim Ammudim shel*

Avot Yeshurun ("Thirty Pages," 1965); *Ha-Shever ha-Suri-Afrikani* (1974; translated into English as *The Syrian-African Rift*, 1980); *Homograph* (1985); and *Ein Li Akhshav* ("I have no now," 1992). A collection of all his poems (*Kol Shirav*) was edited by his daughter, Helit Yeshurun, with a forward by B. Harshav (1995). He sets personal experience against the background of national problems. At first his poetry found its inspiration in the Bedouin world in a kind of ancient alliance between two peoples nurtured in the same region. Following the Israel War of Independence, he saw the Arab people's exile from Palestine and the Jewish tragedy in Europe as a "common Holocaust." The Eastern European Jew and the Palestinian Arab share a common destiny. This is reflected in his poetic idiom which is studded with Yiddish and Arab elements as well as Hebrew-Arabic puns. Yeshurun's unconventional style, his distortions of syntax and his idiosyncrasies of rhyme and diction reflect his attempt to forge a new idiom. His autobiography appeared in *Massa*, 1 (Jan. 1965). He was awarded the Israel Prize in 1992. For translations into various languages see the ITHL website at www.ithl.org.il.

BIBLIOGRAPHY: S. Burnshaw, et al., *The Modern Hebrew Poem Itself* (1965), 89–91; Kressel, Leksikon, 2 (1967), 107. **ADD. BIBLIOGRAPHY:** Sh. Sandbank, in: *Masa* (May 19, 1978); Y. Besser, in: *Yedioth Aharonoth* (January 23, 1981); B. Ziffer, in: *Haaretz* (January 9, 1981); N. Zach, in: *Yedioth Aharonoth* (October 5, 1984); Y. Oppenheimer, *Shirat Avot Yeshurun* (1992); E. Zoritte, *Shirat ha-Pere ha-Aẓil: Biografyah shel Avot Yeshurun* (1995); G. Moked, *"Dikt ve-Ḥol be-Palestinah,"* in: *Akhsahv* 64 (1996), 134–38; Y. Oppenheimer, *Tenu Li le-Daber Kemo she-Ani, Shirat Avot Yeshurun* (1997); O. Wolkenstein, *Ha-Zikkaron bi-Yẓirotehem shel Avot Yeshurun u-Franz Kafka: Model Psikho-semioti* (2000); A. Kinslter, *Ke-Dag ha-Karev el ha-Ḥakah*," in: *Helikon*, 59 (2004), 26–34.

[Yonah David]

YESODOT (Heb. יְסוֹדוֹת; "Foundations"), moshav shittufi in central Israel, near Ḥuldah, affiliated with Po'alei Agudat Israel. Yesodot was founded in June 1948 in the short interval between the battles during the War of Independence for the opening of the Jerusalem corridor. The site was near a large army camp which British forces had turned over to the invading Iraqi units, but which was stormed and taken by Jewish units. The settlers were immigrants from Germany and Romania. Its farming mainly consisted of intensive field and garden crops (e.g., flowers), cattle, and poultry. In the mid-1990s, the population of Yesodot was about 300, growing to 362 in 2002.

[Efraim Orni]

YESUD HA-MA'ALAH (Heb. יְסֻד הַמַּעֲלָה), moshavah with municipal council status in northern Israel, in the Ḥuleh Valley. Yesud ha-Ma'alah was established in 1883, as one of the earliest settlements in the country, by settlers originating from the Polish town of Mezirech. The first settlers lived in reed huts near Lake Ḥuleh. They endured great hardship due to malaria, the scarcity of food, and lack of medicine. In the initial years, the settlers' agricultural inexperience resulted in negligible harvests. Although Baron Edmond de *Rothschild included Yesud ha-Ma'alah in the settlement network receiving his support, progress continued to be very slow. Attempts to develop specialized branches, e.g., plants for perfume and mulberry groves for silkworm cultivation, failed, and the village subsisted on unirrigated grain crops in spite of the nearness of the sweet water lake. The situation slowly improved in the 1940s, when the Palestine Jewish Colonization Association (PICA) transferred the land to the settlers and a group of youth from the moshavim, Benei Peled, joined the village population. Farming was intensified and the threat of malaria was finally overcome. After the *War of Independence (1948), a small number of immigrants was absorbed. With the draining of the lake in 1958, Yesud ha-Ma'alah received additional farm land. In 1970 the village had 432 inhabitants. By the mid-1990s the population had doubled to 865, increasing further to 1,160 in 2002. Its farming was based on citrus groves, deciduous fruit orchards, and flowers. Other sources of livelihood were tourism (guest rooms) and small enterprises. The 2,960-dunam (740-acre) Ḥuleh Nature Reserve, where a remnant of the former lake and swamps with their unique vegetation and wildlife is preserved, is located nearby. The name Yesud ha-Ma'alah is mentioned in Ezra 7:9.

WEBSITE: www.gal2000.org.il/yesod/ymain.htm.

[Efraim Orni / Shaked Gilboa (2nd ed.)]

YE'USH (Heb. יֵאוּשׁ; lit. "despair"), despair of property. A person's ownership of property ceases when it is apparent that he has made up his mind that the property will be out of his possession forever (see *Ownership). This occurs

(a) where he has indicated that he conveys the property to another in which case it ceases to be his the moment the latter acquires it (see *Sale; *Acquisition, Modes of),

(b) where he abandons it, or

(c) where he despairs of it (*ye'ush*), thus ceasing to be the owner of it and no further act is required of him. *Ye'ush* means that under certain circumstances the owner indicates that he has lost all hope of recovering his property. *Ye'ush* is distinguished from acquisition and abandonment since it is only possible in respect of an object which is out of the "despairing" person's possession. Despair of an object still in the owner's possession is not considered *ye'ush*. Similarly, for property to be despaired of it must be against the owner's wish, for he despairs because the object has been lost or stolen; but if the owner gives up the object of his own free will, it is abandonment, and not *ye'ush*. *Ye'ush* may be apparent either from the owner's speech or behavior, or from the circumstances in which the right went out of his possession. In the first instance, if the owner has said: "What a misfortune that I have suffered a loss of money!" (BM 23a) he has indicated that he has despaired of recovering his money, and the same applies to any other expression having the same meaning. Similarly, if a river carries away logs and their owner does not pursue them, he has indicated his despair (BM 22a). In the second instance, if a lost object has no identification marks, it is presumed that the owner has despaired of it and that it has become ownerless (*hefker*), belonging to whoever finds it. This is also the case with an identifiable object which has been lost in a place frequented by the general public (BM 21b), or where a long time has passed since it was lost (Rashi, BM 23b). According to the Jerusalem Talmud (BM 2:1, 8b) and Maimonides (Yad, Gezelah 11:10), even property which is lost to its owner and to all persons, for instance if carried away by the river, may be kept by its finder, since the owner has given it up for lost. The circumstances in which the object is found create the presumption of *ye'ush* if most people would have despaired of the object in such circumstances; and it is immaterial that the owner protests that he had not given up hope, for it is presumed that surely in his heart he has, in fact, despaired. Even if he has not, the finder may disregard such an exceptional state of mind. If the circumstances are such, however, that most people would not usually despair, then *ye'ush* must be preceded by a specific act or speech by the owner (Maharik, no. 3:2).

Ye'ush does not require an act on the part of the despairer, only an indication of his state of mind, as is the case in all other cases whereby the ownership ceases by an indication of the owner's mind (abandonment and conveyance). Thus *ye'ush* cannot apply to the legally incompetent (BM 22b). The case where the owner cannot know that he has lost the object in circumstances that would usually result in *ye'ush*, is the subject of a dispute between Abbaye and Rava (BM 21b). According to Abbaye constructive *ye'ush* (i.e., if the owner does not know that he has a reason to despair) is not deemed to be *ye'ush* because, since the owner has not yet set his mind to the fact that the property is lost and irretrievable, the ownership thereof has not ceased. The finder will therefore gain ownership of the lost article only if he has found it after most people would have already known of its loss and despaired thereof. According to Rava constructive *ye'ush* is deemed to be *ye'ush* because, when the owner of the lost property learns of its loss, it is to be presumed that he will despair of it, and his reason for not yet despairing thereof is his ignorance of the true state of affairs. This dispute concerning *ye'ush* extends to acquisition as well, as in the case where a person confers property on another which does not belong to him without the knowledge of the owner, and the owner subsequently consents thereto; because acquisition, like *ye'ush*, is only the cessation of ownership by the owner's resolving that the property will never return permanently into his possession.

The concept of *ye'ush* is employed in the laws of lost property and in the laws of theft and robbery. In such cases the property goes out of the owner's possession and, accordingly, when it appears that the property will not be recovered by the owner, there is justification for *ye'ush*. Thereafter the finder or thief or robber acquired ownership of the property. According to Tosafot (BK 66a, s.v. *Hakhi*) a finder who has taken lost property before any *ye'ush*, acquires it after there has been *ye'ush*, but has to pay the owner its value, in accordance with the laws of robbers. According to Naḥmanides (*Milḥamot ha-Shem*, BM 26b) if the finder takes the lost property with the intention of returning it, but subsequently changes his mind, the lost property never becomes his since the owner's *ye'ush* is, in fact, not *ye'ush*; but if the finder takes the lost property in order to keep it, he acquired it after there has been *ye'ush*. As to the laws of theft and robbery, various disputes are recorded in the Talmud, dating back to the day of the *tannaim*, as to when it was usual for a person to despair of converted property. There are some who think that only in the case of theft is there *ye'ush*; others contend that there is *ye'ush* only in the case of robbery; still others maintain that there is *ye'ush* in both cases. It is also disputed whether *ye'ush* is itself indicative of genuine despair in the owner's heart or whether a change of possession is also required (i.e., that the object pass into the hands of a third party), or a change of name (i.e., that the object becomes so transformed that people call it by another name) for the *ye'ush* to be genuine (see *Theft and Robbery). In the law of the State of Israel *ye'ush* is of no consequence, and ownership does not cease as a result of despair.

BIBLIOGRAPHY: J.S. Zuri, *Mishpat ha-Talmud*, 6 (1921), 57; S.S. Zeitlin, in: *Sefer ha-Yovel Levi Ginzberg* (1946), 365–80; B. Cohen, in: *Yisrael* (1950), ed. by A.R. Malachi, 89–101; reprinted Cohen's *Jewish and Roman Law* (1966), 10–22 (Heb. sect.); S. Albeck, in: *Sefer ha-Shanah Bar-Ilan*, 7–8 (1970), 94–116.

[Shalom Albeck]

YEVAMOT (Heb. יְבָמוֹת; "Levirate Marriages"), first tractate in the order *Nashim*, in the Mishnah, Tosefta, and Babylonian and Jerusalem Talmuds. In the Cambridge manuscript it is called *Nashim* ("Women"), a title which is partly justified by the great variety of laws it contains appertaining to women, far beyond those of levirate marriage with which it primarily deals. The Mishnah of *Yevamot* consists of 16 chapters.

Chapter 1 enumerates 15 categories of women who, since they are forbidden to marry the levir, thereby exempt their co-wives from levirate marriage or *ḥaliẓah*. It continues with the enumeration of six other relatives the prohibition of whose marriage with the levir is of more stringent character and the marriage of whose co-wives to the levir is permitted. Chapters 2–6 discuss in detail every other aspect of the obligations and exemptions regarding levirate marriage and *ḥaliẓah*. Mishnah 6:3, which deals inter alia with the prohibition of the marriage of a kohen to a woman who has been released by *ḥaliẓah*, serves as a transition point for the discussion of a large variety of laws applying to women and the forbidden degrees of propinquity. The discussion on the stated subject of the tractate is not resumed until chapter 12, although individual *mishnayot* do deal with this subject. Thus the rest of chapter 6 deals with the women who are permitted to marry priests or a high priest and with the laws of procreation. Chapter 7 deals with the circumstances in which a woman of priestly rank or her slave are deprived of the right to eat *terumah*, while chapter 8 deals with the opposite, priests who are forbidden to eat *terumah* though their wives and slaves may do so, leading to a discussion of all those categories of men or women who as a result of personal physical defects or national origin (e.g., Ammonites and Moabites) are forbidden to many Jews. Chapter 9 lists women who are permitted to their husbands but forbidden to their levirs and vice versa, and those permitted and forbidden to both; it concludes with the circumstances under which a woman may eat *terumah*. Chapter 10 deals with the case of a woman who remarried because of an erroneous report of the death of her husband abroad and with its legal consequences for married life (see Prohibited *Marriage). Chapter 11 deals with the prohibition against marriage with a woman who has been raped or seduced (or her relatives), and the laws appertaining to the marriage of a child of doubtful fatherhood. Chapter 12 lays down the number of judges necessary to constitute the special *bet din* for *ḥaliẓah* and the details of the ceremony and its requirements. Chapter 13 deals with *me'un* (see Child *Marriage) and generally with the laws connected with the marriage of minors. Chapter 14 deals with the laws of the marriage of deaf-mutes and imbeciles with one another and with a normal person. Chapters 15 and 16 deal with the acceptance of evidence of the death of a husband, son, or levir on the part of a woman who returns from abroad; it also deals with other aspects of the evidence needed for presumption of death.

The *halakhot* of Mishnah *Yevamot* belong to an early period and include a relatively large number of the disputes of Bet Shammai and Bet *Hillel, and some of them even precede the time of these two schools (see above 15:1 and 2). A substantial section dates from the period before the halakhic differences between the schools were decided. This is implicit in the tradition which praises the fact that "although Bet Shammai and Bet Hillel are in disagreement about rival wives (1:4), sisters (3:1), a doubtfully married woman, etc., yet Bet Shammai did not abstain from marrying women of the families of Bet Hillel, nor did Bet Hillel abstain from marrying women of the families of Bet Shammai. This teaches you that they showed love and friendship toward one another, putting into practice the text [Zech. 8:19]: 'Love ye truth and peace.' Although these forbade and those permitted, they did not refrain from acts requiring ritual purity in the presence of one another, thus fulfilling the text [Prov. 21:2]: 'Every way of a man is right in his eyes; but the Lord weigheth the hearts'" (Tosef. 1:10 and 11). The Mishnah in its present form stems from Judah ha-Nasi, but it contains many anonymous *mishnayot* belonging to the school of Akiva and his disciples. In particular the formulas of the general statements ("Some are permitted their husbands and forbidden their levirs, permitted their levirs and forbidden their husbands," etc.) in chapter 9 accord with the method and teaching of Akiva (see Epstein, Tannaim, 87).

The Tosefta has 14 chapters. The Mishnah to chapter 9, which, as stated, is from the school of Akiva, has no parallel in the Tosefta, but the contents of Tosefta *Yevamot* parallels and supplements the Mishnah to a great extent, even though the order differs. Of Mishnah 6:6, which discusses the precept to be fruitful and multiply, Ben Azzai says in Tosefta 8:4, "Anyone not engaged in procreation is considered by Scripture as diminishing the image (of the Creator) since it says [Gen. 9:6–7]: 'for in the image of God made He man. And you, be ye fruitful and multiply.' Eleazar said to him: 'Words are beautiful when they come from one who performs them. Some preach well and practice well, Ben Azzai [who was celibate] preaches well but does not practice well." Ben Azzai retorted: 'I cannot help it, my soul is in love with Torah; the world can be carried on by others'" (see also Yev. 63b). The Mishnah also lays down that if a man married and lived with his wife ten years but she has no children, he may not abstain from procreation (*ibid.*); the Tosefta (8:4) adds that the period of residence outside Ereẓ Israel is not counted. A *baraita*, reflecting the state of the *halakhah* before it was decided in accordance with Bet Hillel, is cited in Tosefta 1:13 to the effect that whoever wishes to follow the stricter practices of both Bet Shammai and Bet Hillel, of him the Bible says (Eccles. 2:14): "the fool walketh in darkness,' while he who follows the lenient practices of both Bet Shammai and Bet Hillel is wicked; but one must follow either both the leniencies and stringencies of Bet Shammai or of Bet Hillel."

The themes of tractate *Yevamot* are considered the most difficult of the Talmud. One of the *halakhot* that emerge from this tractate is that the sages were exceptionally lenient in problems of *agunah (88a). They permitted a wife whose husband had disappeared to remarry on the testimony of a single witness, of a woman, and the like; and even on the basis of a mere rumor of her husband's death, the woman is permitted to remarry (16:6 and 7). A great variety of cases are quoted to give examples of the application of these *halakhot* in practice (see Yev. 120ff.). The tractate discusses the problem of proselytization and the indispensability of circumcision and ritual bathing (46a–b) as part of its rite. According to one view "Proselytes are hurtful to Israel as a sore on the skin" (109b). Similarly opinions differ on whether proselytes for the sake of marriage or to "enjoy the royal bounty" should be accepted. The *halakhah* accepts them as proselytes (24b). Praise of family life is implicit in the statement: "A Jew who has no wife lives without joy, without blessing, and without goodness" (62b). On the other hand the lives of a number of sages who suffered severely from their wives are described, and to them is applied the verse (Eccles. 7:26): "And I find more bitter than death the woman" (63a–b). As evidence for these ideas, verses are cited from Ben Sira (26:3f.): "a good wife is a good gift… an evil wife is as leprosy to her husband" (see ed. Segal, p. 156ff.). Among the maxims quoted, the following are worthy of mention: "It is religious duty to obey the sages" (20a); "a judge should always imagine that a sword is lying between his thighs and Gehenna is open beneath him" (109b); and "scholars increase peace in the world" (122b). A parallel to IV Maccabees 2:10 – "For the law ranks above affection to parents" – is the statement: "Since one might have assumed that honoring father and mother should supersede the Sabbath, therefore it is stated (Lev. 19:3) 'Ye shall fear every man his mother and his father, and ye shall keep my Sabbaths,' all of you have the duty to honor Me" (5bff.).

There is not much *aggadah* in the Jerusalem Talmud to *Yevamot*. The statement that R. Ḥiyya b. Ashi was quick to mate his ass soon after it had given birth reveals the knowledge of natural processes on the part of the sages; that such mating is most desirable is also mentioned by Aristotle and Pliny (see S. Lieberman, *Hellenism in Jewish Palestine* (1950), 186f.). A statement of great importance (12:1, 12c) is: "Were the prophet Elijah to come and say [that] *ḥaliẓah can be performed with a shoe, he would be obeyed, that it cannot be performed with a sandal, he would not be obeyed, since the majority is accustomed to perform *ḥaliẓah* with a sandal, and custom takes precedence over the *halakhah*" (cf. TB, Yev. 102a). In a similar vein it states (TJ, 7:2, 8a): "Any *halakhah* about which the *bet din* vacillates and the law is unknown, go and see how people act and act accordingly", *Yevamot* was translated into English by I.W. Slotki in the Soncino edition of the Talmud (1936).

BIBLIOGRAPHY: H. Albeck, *Shishah Sidrei Mishnah, Nashim* (1954), 7–16; A. Weiss, *Al ha-Mishnah* (1969), 44–46; Epstein, Tannaim, 87ff.

[Yitzhak Dov Gilat]

YEVPATORIYA (**Eupatoria**; in Jewish sources the Tatar name of the city Göslöw [Koslov] is also found), city on the western shore of the Crimean peninsula, Ukraine. A large Jewish community existed there under Tatar rule from the 15th to 18th centuries. The Russian conquest at the end of the 18th century caused much suffering to the Yevpatoriya community, many of whom fled to Turkey. At the time of the Russian annexation of Crimea there remained approximately 100 Karaite families and a few Rabbanites (Tatar-speaking *Krimchaks). During the 19th century the Karaite community in Yevpatoriya became the largest in Russia and the spiritual center of the Karaites. The chief Karaite *ḥakham* of Russia had his seat in Yevpatoriya. His status as leader of the community was recognized by the Russian government in 1837. A Hebrew Karaite press (Göslöw press) was established there in the 1830s and functioned until the 1860s. Abraham *Firkovich published the works of the early Karaites there. A school for cantors, headed by the Karaite Hebrew author Elijah *Kazaz, was established in 1894. There was a magnificent Karaite synagogue in Yevpatoriya, and the community had a museum and library containing many rare manuscripts and books. In 1897 the community numbered 1,592 Rabbanites (mainly of Lithuanian or Ukrainian origin) and 1,525 Karaites (together forming 18% of the total population). There were pogroms in Yevpatoriya in 1905. After the 1917 Revolution, the last Karaite *ḥakham* moved to Constantinople. The Jewish population (both Rabbanite and Karaite) numbered 2,409 in 1926 (10.6% of the total). Toward the end of the 1920s several Jewish agricultural settlements were established northeast of Yevpatoriya. After Crimea was occupied by the Germans, at the end of 1941, the Rabbanite Jews in Yevpatoriya were murdered, but the Karaites escaped, not being regarded as Jews.

[Yehuda Slutsky]

YEVREYSKI KOMISSARIAT (Jewish Commissariat). The central commissariat for Jewish national affairs was a government organ of the Soviet regime for carrying out the nationality policies of the Communist Party among Jews. The Jewish Commissariat functioned from January 20, 1918, through April 1924 (alongside commissariats of other national minorities) within the framework of the People's Commissariat for Nationalities Affairs headed by *Stalin. Simon *Dimanstein was appointed commissar of the Jewish Commissariat with the left Socialist-Revolutionary I.G. Dobkovsky serving as his deputy. A number of returning emigrés and anarchists alienated from Russian Jewry who had joined the Bolsheviks worked in the Jewish Commissariat. Until mid-1918 the left *Po'alei Zion, headed by Tzevi Fridlander, also participated in the work of the Jewish Commissariat. Only a few Jewish writers (including Samuel *Niger and Daniel *Charney) cooperated with the Jewish Commissariat in publishing its organ – the first Soviet newspaper in Yiddish *Die Warheit* ("Truth") which appeared from March 8 to August 1, 1918. A group was established within the Jewish Commissariat to work with the impoverished segment of the Jewish population. A department of culture and education headed by N.O. *Buchbinder controlled Jewish schools; it had its own, *Evreyskaya tribuna* ("Jewish Tribune," 1918, nos. 1–4). During 1918, 13 local Jewish commissariats were established (in Vitebsk, Eltse, Mogilev, Perm, Tambov, and elsewhere). Under the influence of proponents of autonomy (mainly from Po'alei Zion), the central Jewish Commissariat, through its newspaper, called for the establishment of local Jewish councils (soviets) or Jewish sections attached to local soviets "to strengthen the Soviet authorities and combat the national bourgeosie" and also able to convene an all-Russian conference to determine the forms of organization of Jewish life in Soviet Russia and for electing a commissar for Jewish affairs. Following the July 1918 congress of Jewish communities which met in Moscow with the participation of representatives of various Jewish political parties, the Jewish Commissariat rejected the idea of democratic Jewish autonomy. The election by the congress of a central bureau to coordinate the work of Jewish institutions led to repression by the Soviet authorities. All non-Bolsheviks were removed from the Jewish Commissariat. There was established the *Yevsektsiya (Jewish Section) of the Communist Party which in close cooperation with the Jewish Commissariat submitted to Party control the resolution of all problems of Soviet Jewish life.

At the first conference of the Jewish Commissariat and the Yevsektsia (in October 1918 in Moscow) there were officially chosen a commissar of the Jewish Commissariat (Dimanstein) and a board of the Commissariat which was charged with liquidating all institutions of the Jewish community. The decree closing down the Center Bureau of Jewish Communities and transferring all communal resources and property to local Jewish commissariats was published in June 1918 but the closure of synagogues and the liquidation of communal institutions, *yeshivot*, *ḥadarim* (traditional primary schools), and schools with instruction in Hebrew began earlier (in Orel, Perm, and other cities).

As early as 1918 the Jewish Commissariat published the anti-Zionist brochure of Z. Grinberg *Die zionistn oif der Idisher Gas* ("The Zionist on the Jewish Street"). In the Jewish Commissariat circular of July 23, 1919, on the closing of communal institutions Dimanstein announced the impending liquidation of *Tarbut, *He-Halutz and other Zionist "bourgeois organizations." Nevertheless, the Jewish Commissariat hardly fought against Zionism, for which it was criticized in the Communist Party press. At the insistence of the Yevsektsiya the Jewish Commissariat declared Hebrew a "reactionary language" and on August 30, 1919, the People's Commissariat of Education banned the teaching of Hebrew in all educational institutions. Books in Hebrew then began to be removed from libraries.

As the Bolshevik doctrine of the transformation of the peoples of the Soviet state into a "single Soviet nation" became more dominant, the functions of the Jewish Commissariat as a government organ became correspondingly more narrow. In late 1918 the handling of issues of Jewish culture and education was transferred to the Yevburu (the Jewish Bureau), a body attached to the People's Commissariat of Education, and other areas of work with Jews were included in the sphere of activity of the appropriate commissariats. In January 1919 local Jewish commissariats were transformed into Jewish departments attached to provincial committees of the Communist Party and in early 1920 the Jewish Commissariat became a department of the People's Commissariat for Nationality Affairs. Both theoretical and practical guidance in regard to measures to "Sovietize" the labor and culture of the Jews of the Soviet Union were concentrated in the hands of the Yevsektsiya.

[*The Shorter Jewish Encyclopaedia in Russian*]

YEVSEKTSIYA (plural *Yevsektsii*), Jewish sections of the propaganda department of the Russian Communist Party from 1918 to 1930. *Lenin, the founder and leader of the Communist Party, denied that the Jews were a living nation and saw assimilation as the progressive solution to the Jewish problem in Russia. This view gained currency in party circles as a result of the debate between the Russian Social-Democrats and the *Bund at the beginning of the 20th century. When the Communist Party took power in November 1917, however, it was faced with the fact that millions of Jews, speaking their own language and maintaining their own social institutions, existed in Russia, and with the necessity of establishing some temporary agency to deal with them until such time as they had assimilated among their neighbors. In January 1918 a "Jewish Commissariat" headed by S. *Dimanstein was created, and Jewish sections (*Yevsektsii*) were organized in local party branches on the model of the national sections which were then being established to direct party work among other non-Russian peoples.

The first conference of the Jewish sections and representatives of the Jewish Commissariat in the provinces took place in Moscow in October 1918; their function was defined as the propagandizing of Yiddish-speaking workers and the establishment of the "dictatorship of the proletariat" among the Jews. It was strongly emphasized that the Jewish sections had no national goals and that Yiddish was to be simply regarded as a necessary means of communication with the Jewish masses, on no account valuable in itself. The conference decided on "systematic destruction of Zionist and bourgeois institutions," with the *kehillot*, *hadarim*, Hebrew schools, and Zionist parties heading the list. A central bureau headed by S. Dimanstein was elected. At the second conference, which was attended by representatives of communist parties and related organizations from the Ukraine and Belorussia, economic activity among the Jews was decided upon. The essential aim of this economic activity was the cooperative organization of "semi-proletarian elements" (i.e., craftsmen and artisans), and the mass settlement on the land of erstwhile Jewish merchants, deprived of their means of livelihood by the revolution.

During the same year a considerable proportion of the Jewish left-wing parties joined the Jewish sections as organized bodies or as individuals. At the third conference (July 1920), which represented 1,743 active members, 34 of the 84 delegates were erstwhile Bundists, 11 were previously United Socialists ("Fareynikte"), and 7 were previously members of *Po'alei Zion. The heads of the Jewish sections kept a close watch on the ex-members of these Jewish parties to see that no hint of their Jewish national allegiance was introduced into their new party work. Fear of being accused of "nationalistic and Zionist deviations" was so pervasive in the Jewish sections that they were wary of endorsing any comprehensive plan for Jewish rehabilitation in Russia, even when put forward by such outstanding Communist leaders as Kalinin, Smidovich, and *Larin. The third conference decided that the Jewish sections were no more than "technical [Communist] Party tools." At this time head offices were established in the Ukraine and Belorussia. Active in the Jewish sections besides Dimanstein were A. Merezhin, M. *Rafes, M. *Frumkin ("Esther"), M. Levitan, M. *Litvakov, A. *Tshemeriski, and M. Kipper.

With the help of government agencies, the police, and the internal security forces, the *Yevsektsiya* initiated and executed the liquidation of Jewish *kehillot*, the confiscation of synagogue buildings, the closing of yeshivot, *ḥadarim*, and Hebrew schools, the closing of libraries, and the banning of books. They fought the remnants of Jewish political and cultural organizations to the bitter end (*He-Ḥalutz, *Habimah, Left Po'alei Zion) or attempted to take them over (Kultur Lige, *ORT). The destruction of the existing Jewish framework was accompanied by attempts to create a Jewish Communist culture; a Jewish press in Yiddish, headed by the dailies *Der Emes* (Moscow), *Der Shtern* (Kharkov), and *Oktyabr* (Minsk), which had a circulation of 27,000 at the end of the 1920s, was founded; publishing houses which printed books in tens of thousands of copies were established; a network of primary and secondary schools was created; and a few departments of Jewish culture were even created in institutions of higher learning. In 1924 the Jewish sections were made responsible for integrating "classless elements" into the Soviet economic system by directing them to industrial and agricultural labor. A public company "OZET" ("Land Cultivation Company") was set up under the direction of the Jewish sections to assist in the Jewish settlement project. Cultural work was intensified, and Yiddish became the official language in trade unions and youth and women's organizations with a predominantly Jewish membership.

Attempts were made to adapt Soviet institutions in towns with large Jewish populations in order to serve the Jewish public in their mother tongue. The Jewish sections were also made responsible for bringing the problems involved in their activities among the Jewish population before the central and local Communist Party committees. Territorial programs for Jewish settlement on the land were put forward; this culminated in the proclamation of *Birobidzhan in the Far East as an area of Jewish settlement (1928). Contrary to their initial "technical" program, the Jewish sections began to serve also as consolidatory factors in Jewish life. At the council of Jewish sections in 1926 a struggle between different trends took place. The council expressed reservations both with regard to the assimilationists in the Communist party, who saw any separate work among the Jewish population as a nationalist deviation, and with regard to those who saw the work of the Jewish sections as "a way of preserving the Jewish people"; it redefined the sole function of the Jewish sections as the introduction of socialism among the Jewish masses.

While the revolution had created the conditions for the agricultural settlement of Jews and the consolidation of some of them as a separate national unit in a separate territory, the great majority of Jews were to find the solution to their social and economic problems in the transition to heavy industry, and were inevitably to assimilate among the masses of non-Jewish workers. When Soviet policy swung leftward at the end of the 1920s, the fate of the Jewish sections was sealed. In January 1930, within the context of the general liquidation of the national sections of Communist Party institutions in the Soviet Union, it was decided to liquidate the Jewish sections. Jewish section activists in practice continued to work among the Jewish population until 1934, but the scope of their work became more and more limited. The imprisonment and liquidation of Jewish section activists, which began in 1934, continued until the late 1930s and was accompanied by the gradual liquidation of educational and cultural institutions and other achievements of Jewish autonomy; their liquidation was completed by the end of the 1940s.

BIBLIOGRAPHY: S. Agurski, *Der Yidisher Arbeter in der Komunistisher Bavegung* (1925); *Alfarbandishe Baratung fundi Yidishe Sektsies fun der AKP (b)* (1926); S. Agurski, *Di Yidishe Komisariatn un di Yidishe Komunistishe Sektsies* (1928); N. Gergel, *Di Lage fun di Yidn in Rusland* (1929); M.G. Rafes, *Orcherki istorii yevreyskogo rabochego dvizheniya* (1929), 217–54; B. Slutski, *Leksikon fun Politishe un Fremd-Verter* (1929), 78–83; S. Agurski, in: *Bolshaya Sovetskaya Entsiklopediya*, 24 (1932), 337–8; J. Lestschinsky, *Ha-Yehudim be-Rusyah ha-Sovyetit* (1943); S.M. Schwarz, *The Jews in the Soviet Union* (1951), 100–1; M. Altshuler, *Reshit ha-Yevsektsiya, 1918–1921* (1966).

[Yehuda Slutsky]

°YEVTUSHENKO, YEVGENI ALEXANDROVICH (1933–), Soviet Russian poet. A prolific author of topical verse, Yevtushenko became one of the standard-bearers of the liberal Soviet intelligentsia during the years following Stalin's death. After the appearance of his first poems in 1949, Yevtushenko chose subjects that were, for the most part, expressions of revolt against the traditions of the Stalin era. Though a non-Jew, Yevtushenko also wrote the most famous single poem of the Holocaust: *Babi Yar* (first published in *Literaturnaya Gazeta*, Sept. 19, 1961, see *Babi Yar). This short but moving description of the site of the Nazi massacre of Kiev's Jews and of the thoughts that the site evoked in the poet unleashed a furious controversy. Neo-Stalinists accused Yevtushenko of a variety of crimes, the most dangerous being the insinuation that antisemitism continued to exist in the U.S.S.R., and that the Jews were martyred by the Nazis not merely as Soviet citizens, but also as Jews – a fact carefully silenced by official Soviet historiography. Russian public opinion was sharply divided. To be for or against Yevtushenko was tantamount to being a foe or an advocate of antisemitism. As if to underline the fact that the choice of *Babi Yar's* theme was no accident, Yevtushenko returned briefly to the subject in his long narrative poem, *Bratskaya GES* (1967; *The Bratsk Station*, 1966), in which one of the protagonists is Izi Kramer, a Jewish survivor of a Nazi camp, now an engineer in Siberia, who continues to be haunted by his tragic past. In 1963, Yevtushenko published *A Precocious Autobiography*, which contains his account of the writing of *Babi Yar*, and the general antisemitic mood of the young Stalinists. In 1970 a new collection of his poems was printed in Russia which omitted *Babi Yar* and some of his most outspoken anti-Stalinist poems.

BIBLIOGRAPHY: G. Reavey (tr. and ed.), *The Poetry of Yevgeny Yevtushenko, 1953–1965* (1965); P. Johnson and L. Labedz, *Khrushchev and the Arts; the Politics of Soviet Culture, 1962–1964* (1965); M. Decter, in: *Commentary*, 36 (1963), 433–7.

[Maurice Friedberg]

YEZD, city in central Iran, probably built by Yazdegerd I (399–420). That Yezd was a center of Jewish scholars in the early Middle Ages is attested by a ninth-century Hebrew manuscript of the Later Prophets with masoretic notes which was found there; it is one of the oldest known biblical manuscripts composed by Persian Jews. The Yezd community's spiritual leader, Mulla Or Sharaga, (d. 1794), who is mentioned in a few Judeo-Persian letters of the early decades of the 19th century, maintained close contacts with the Jews of *Meshed. In 1928 an *Alliance Israélite Universelle school was established in the city. Jews from Yezd were among the earliest immigrants to Palestine and many families settled, mainly in *Safed and

*Jerusalem. In 1948 there were about 1,000 Jews in Yezd and in 1973 fewer than 400; it was reported that after the 1979 Islamic revolution only five families remained.

BIBLIOGRAPHY: E.N. Adler, *Ginzei Paras u-Madai – The Persian Jews, their books and ritual* (1898?), 20; A. Marks, in *Soncino-Blaetter*, 2 (1927), 114; I. Ben-Zvi, *Meḥkarim u-Mekorot* (1966), index. **ADD. BIBLIOGRAPHY:** Y. Sharga, *Mi-Yazd le-Ereẓ ha-Kodesh* (1987); A. Netzer, "Jews of Yezd," in: *Shofar* (Mar.–Apr. 2003), 22ff. (in Persian).

[Walter Joseph Fischel / Amnon Netzer (2nd ed.)]

YEZIERSKA, ANZIA (1885?–1970), U.S. novelist. Anzia Yezierska was reared in an Orthodox home in Russia and was taken to New York at the age of 16. Her life was a mixture of poverty (which she emphasized through her novels) as well as education and literary attainment. Her experience of conditions on the Lower East Side of New York gave authenticity to her first collection of short stories, *Hungry Hearts* (1920), which established her reputation as a realist. Its success raised her for a short time from poverty in New York to riches in Hollywood, but unable to endure that life for long she returned to New York.

Her subsequent books, which also dealt with the adjustment of the Jewish immigrant to American life, were *Salome of the Tenements* (1923); *Children of Loneliness* (1923); *Bread Givers* (1925): *Arrogant Beggar* (1927); and *All I Could Never Be* (1932). In later life she reassessed the traditional values rejected in her youth and found that they gave a heightened meaning to life. Her autobiography, *Red Ribbon on a White Horse*, appeared in 1950.

Remarkably, she had a love affair with John Dewey, whom she met in 1917 at Columbia University. Their affair was brief, and he spurned her. Their relationship occupies Norma Rosen's novel *John and Anzia: An American Romance* (1989).

Fortunately, her works have been rediscovered, especially by feminists. Yezierska's portraits of strong, self-willed women helped a new generation of readers understand both the constraints placed upon Jewish women and the vitality needed to break the bonds of custom.

ADD. BIBLIOGRAPHY: J.A. Boydston (ed.), *The Poems of John Dewey* (1977); L. Henrickson, *Anzi Yezierska: A Writer's Lfe* (1988); D. Konzett, *Ethnic Modernisms: Anzia Yezierska, Zora Neale Hurston, Jean Rhys, and the Aesthetics of Dislocation* (2002); J. Martin, *The Education of John Dewey: A Biography* (2002); C. Schoen, *Anzia Yezierska* (1982).

[Sol Liptzin / Lewis Fried (2nd ed.)]

YEẒIRAH, SEFER (Heb. סֵפֶר יְצִירָה; the "Book of Creation"), the earliest extant Hebrew text of systematic, speculative thought. Its brevity – no more than 1,600 words altogether even in its longer version – allied to its obscure and at the same time laconic and enigmatic style, as well as its terminology, have no parallel in other works on related subjects. The result of all these factors was that for more than 1,000 years the book was expounded in a great many different ways, and not even the scientific investigations conducted during the 19th century succeeded in arriving at unambiguous and final results.

Sefer Yeẓirah is extant in two versions: a shorter one which appears in most editions as the book itself, and a longer version which is sometimes printed as an appendix (for the important differences between the two versions, see A. *Epstein, in: MGWJ, 37 (1893), 266). Both versions were already in existence in the tenth century and left their imprint on the different types of the numerous manuscripts, the earliest of which (from the 11th century?) was found in the Cairo *Genizah* and published by A.M. Habermann (1947). In both versions the book is divided into six chapters of *mishnayot* or *halakhot*, composed of brief statements which present the author's argument dogmatically, without any explanation or substantiation. The first chapter in particular employs a sonorous, solemn vocabulary, close to that of the *Merkabah literature. Few biblical verses are quoted. Even when their wording is identical, the different arrangement of the *mishnayot* in the two versions and their resultant altered relationship one with the other color the theoretical appreciation of the ideas.

Contents and Structure

The central subject of *Sefer Yeẓirah* is a compact discourse on cosmology and cosmogony (a kind of *ma'aseh bereshit*, "act of creation," in a speculative form), outstanding for its clearly mystical character. There is no foundation for the attempts by a number of scholars to present it as a kind of primer for schoolchildren (e.g., S. Karppe, *étude sur la nature et les origines du Zohar* (1901), 16ff.), or as the first Hebrew composition on Hebrew grammar and orthography (according to P. Mordell). The book's strong link with Jewish speculations concerning divine wisdom is evident from the beginning, with the declaration that God created the world by means of "32 secret paths of wisdom." These 32 paths, defined as "ten *Sefirot beli mah*" and the "22 elemental letters" of the Hebrew alphabet, are represented as the foundations of all creation. Chapter 1 deals with the *Sefirot* and the other five chapters with the function of the letters. Apparently the term *Sefirot* is used simply to mean "numbers," though in employing a new term (*sefirot* instead of *misparim*), the author seems to be alluding to metaphysical principles or to stages in the creation of the world.

The use of the term *Sefirot* in *Sefer Yeẓirah* was later explained – particularly in Kabbalah literature – as referring to a theory of emanation, although the book does not mention that the first *Sefirah* itself emanated from God and was not created by Him as an independent action. The author emphasizes, though ambiguously, the mystical character of the *Sefirot*, describing them in detail and discussing the order of their grading. At least the first four *Sefirot* emanate from each other. The first one is the "spirit (*ru'aḥ*) of the Living God" (the book continues to use the word *ru'aḥ* in its dual meaning of abstract spirit and air or ether). From the first *Sefirah* comes forth, by way of condensation, "one Spirit from another"; that is first the primal element of air, and from it, issuing one after the other as the third and fourth *Sefirot*, water and fire. From the primal air God created, or "engraved" upon it, the 22 letters; from the primal waters, the cosmic chaos; and from the primal fire, the Throne of Glory and the hosts of the angels. The nature of this secondary creation is not sufficiently clear because the precise terminological meaning of the verbs employed by the author – e.g., engraved, hewed, created – can be interpreted in various ways. The last six *Sefirot* are of a completely different nature, representing the six dimensions (in the language of the book the *keẓavot*, "extremities") of space, though it is not expressly said that they were created from the earlier elements. Even so it is emphasized that the ten *Sefirot* constitute a closed unit, for "their end is in their beginning and their beginning in their end" and they revolve in each other; i.e., these ten basic principles constitute a unity – although its nature is not sufficiently defined – which is not considered as identical with the divinity except insofar as the first stage of its creation expresses the ways of divine Wisdom.

The author, no doubt intentionally, employs expressions borrowed from the description of the *ḥayyot* ("living creatures") who carry the Throne of Glory in the chariot (*merkavah*; Ezek. 1), and seems to be establishing a certain correlation between the "living beings" and the *Sefirot*, describing the latter as the king's servants who obey his commands and prostrate themselves before his throne. At the same time they are also the dimensions (*amakim*) of all existence, of good and even of evil. The fact that the theory of the significance of the 22 letters as the foundation of all creation in chapter 2 partly conflicts with chapter 1 has caused many scholars to attribute to the author a conception of a double creation: the one ideal and pure brought about by means of the *Sefirot*, which are conceived in a wholly ideal and abstract manner; and the other one real, effected by the interconnection of the elements of speech, which are the letters. According to some views, the obscure word "*belimah*," which always accompanies the word *Sefirot*, is simply a composite, *beli mah* – without anything, without actuality, ideal. However, judging from the literal meaning, it would seem that it should be understood as signifying "closed," i.e., closed within itself. The text offers no more detailed explanation of the relationship between the *Sefirot* and the letters, and the *Sefirot* are not referred to again. Some scholars have believed that two separate cosmogonic doctrines basically differing from one another were fused in the book, and were united by a method resembling neo-Pythagorean theory current in the second and third century B.C.E.

All the real beings in the three strata of the cosmos: in the world, in time, and in man's body (in the language of the book: world, year, soul) came into existence through the interconnection of the 22 letters, and especially by way of the "231 gates"; i.e., the combinations of the letters into groups of two representing the possible roots of the Hebrew verb (it appears that the author held that the Hebrew verb is based on two consonants). The logical number of 231 combinations does not appear in the earliest manuscripts, which fixed 221 gates or combinations, and which are enumerated in a number of manuscripts. Every existing thing somehow contains these linguistic elements and exists by their power, whose foundation is one name; i.e., the *Tetragrammaton, or, perhaps, the alphabetical order which in its entirety is considered one mystical name. In chapters 3–5 the 22 basic letters are divided into three groups, according to the author's special phonetic system. The first contains the three matrices – *immot* or *ummot* (meaning elements, in the language of the Mishnah) – *alef, mem, shin* (אמש), which in turn represent the source of the three elements mentioned in a different context in chapter 1 – air, fire, water – and from these all the rest came into being. These three letters also have their parallel in the three seasons of the year (according to a system found among Greek and Hellenistic writers) and the three parts of the body: the head, torso, and the stomach. The second group consists of seven "double" letters, i.e., those consonants which have a hard and soft sound when written with or without a *dagesh* (*bet, gimmel, dalet,* and *kaf, pe, resh, tav*). The presence of the letter *resh* in this group gave rise to various theories (cf. S. Morag, in: *Sefer Tur-Sinai* (Torczyner; 1960), 207 – 42). Through the medium of the "double" letters were created the seven planets, the seven heavens, the seven days of the week, and the seven orifices of the body (eyes, ears, nostrils, mouth), and they also allude to the basic opposites (*temurot*) in man's life. The 12 remaining "simple" letters (*ha-peshutot*) correspond to what the author considers as man's chief activities; the 12 signs of the zodiac in the heavenly sphere, the 12 months, and the 12 chief limbs of the body (*ha-manhigim*). In addition he gives also a completely different phonetic division of the letters, in accordance with the five places in the mouth where they are articulated (gutturals, labials, velars, dentals, and sibilants). This is the first instance in which this division appears in the history of Hebrew linguistics and it may not have been included in the first version of the book. The combination of these "basic letters" contains the roots of all things and also the contrast between good and evil (עֹנֶג וְנֶגַע, *oneg ve-nega*).

There is an obvious connection between this linguistic-mystical cosmogony, which has close parallels in astrological speculation, and magic which is based on the creative, magical power of the letters and words. In fact it might well be said that *Sefer Yeẓirah* speaks of "the letters in which heaven and earth were created," as according to the Talmud, Bezalel, the architect of the tabernacle, possessed the knowledge of their combinations (Ber. 55a). From this point stem the ideas connected with the creation of the **golem* by an ordered recitation of all the possible creative letter-combinations. Whether *Sefer Yeẓirah* itself initially was aimed at magical ideas of this type is a subject on which opinions differ, but it is not impossible. According to a talmudic legend (Sanh. 65b) R. Ḥanina and R. Hoshaiah (fourth century) used to occupy themselves with *Sefer Yeẓirah*, or – as an ancient variant has it – with *Hilkhot Yeẓirah*; by means of it a "calf three years old" was created for them, which they ate. Whether these *Hilkhot Yeẓirah* are simply the book in question or its early version cannot be decided for the moment, but it must be stressed that accompanying the very earliest texts of *Sefer Yeẓirah* were introductory chapters emphasizing magical practices which are presented as some kind of festive ritual to be performed on the completion of the study of the book (Judah b. Barzillai's commentary, 103–268).

Time of Composition

*Zunz (GV 175), *Graetz in his later works, *Bacher, Bloch, and others were of the opinion that *Sefer Yeẓirah* was composed in the period of the *geonim*, around the eighth century. This dating was in line with the general tendency of those scholars to assign a late date to the composition of the mystical works on the mysteries of the creation and Merkabah, a trend which modern scholarship can no longer uphold. They also talked of hypothetical Arab influence (which was not actually proved). In his early work on Gnosticism and Judaism (1846), Graetz tended to correlate the time of its composition with that of the Mishnah or the beginning of the period of the Talmud, and this view was shared by Abraham Epstein, Louis Ginzberg, and others, who dated its composition between the third and sixth centuries. Leo *Baeck tried to prove that *Sefer Yeẓirah* was written under the Neoplatonic influence of Proclus, possibly in the sixth century. The Hebrew style, however, points to an earlier period. Epstein already proved its proximity to the language of the Mishnah, and additions can be made to his linguistic proofs. The book contains no linguistic form which may not be ascribed to second- or third-century Hebrew. In addition, a number of links with the doctrine of divine wisdom and with various Gnostic and syncretistic views indicate an earlier period; analogies between *Sefer Yeẓirah* and the views of Markos the Gnostic of the school of Valentinus had already been noticed by Graetz.

The doctrine of the *Sefirot* and the language system hint at neo-Pythagorean and Stoic influences. Stoic is the emphasis on the double pronunciation of "*bagad kafat*." Some of the terms employed in the book were apparently translated from Greek, in which the term στοιχεῖα indicates both elements and letters; this duality finds its expression in the Hebrew term *otiyyot yesod* ("elemental letters"), i.e., letters which are also elements. The material which F. Dornseiff (*Das Alphabet in Mystik und Magie*, 1925) collected from the linguistic mysticism of Greek syncretism contains many parallels with *Sefer Yeẓirah*. Illuminating, in this connection, is *Sefer Yeẓirah*'s view of the "sealing" of the six extremities of the world by the six different combinations of the name YHW (יהו) which (unlike in the Bible) occurs here as an independent, fundamental Name of God, playing the part of its corresponding name in Greek transcription ἰάω, which is extremely frequent in the documents of the Gnostics and in religious and magical syncretism. The idea that every act of creation was sealed with the name of God is one of the earliest tenets of Merkabah mysticism and is already found in *Heikhalot Rabbati* (ch. 9); in Gnostic systems and some which are close to Gnosis this name has its function in establishing the cosmos and in defining fixed boundaries for the world. Combinations of this name, which in Greek consists of vowels and not of consonants, appear frequently in Greek magical papyri. The author of *Sefer Yeẓirah* did not yet know the symbols for the Hebrew vowels and in place of the Greek vowels he employed the Hebrew consonants יהו, which are both vowel letters and components of the Tetragrammaton. There is common ground here between the speculations of *Sefer Yeẓirah* and the projections of Gnostic or semi-Gnostic speculations on the fringe of Judaism or outside it during the early centuries of the Common Era. It is difficult to decide whether the ten *Sefirot* or the rules of the 32 paths have to be explained or understood in the spirit of the Gnostic aeon doctrine or in that of the Pythagorean school, both views being possible. The function of the letters of the Hebrew alphabet in the construction of the world is mentioned in an ancient fragment from *Midrash Tanḥuma* dealing with the creation: "The Holy One, Blessed Be He, said: 'I request laborers.' The Torah told Him: 'I put at Your disposal 22 laborers, namely the 22 letters which are in the Torah, and give to each one his own'" (E. Urbach, in: *Koveẓ al Yad*, 6 (1966), 20). This legend is extremely close to the basic idea in *Sefer Yeẓirah*, chapter 2, and it is impossible to know which was the earlier.

To sum up, it may be postulated that the main part of *Sefer Yeẓirah*, though it contains post-talmudic additions, was written between the third and sixth centuries, apparently in Palestine by a devout Jew with leanings toward mysticism, whose aim was speculative and magical rather than ecstatic. The author, who endeavored to "Judaize" non-Jewish speculations which suited his spirit, presents a parallel path to Jewish ecstatic Gnosis of the *Heikhalot* type of literature, which has its roots in the same period. This "Judaizing" is also apparent at the end of the book, which presents Abraham, the first to believe in the oneness of God, as the one who first studied the ideas expressed in the book and actually practiced them – maybe an allusion to the use of magic mentioned above. From this derived the late view claiming Abraham as the author of the book, called in several manuscripts *Otiyyot de-Avraham Avinu*. The attribution of *Sefer Yeẓirah* to R. *Akiva only makes its appearance in the Kabbalah literature from the 13th century onward, no doubt in the wake of the late Midrash *Otiyyot de-Rabbi Akiva*.

Commentaries on *Sefer Yeẓirah*

The earliest reference to *Sefer Yeẓirah* appears in the *Baraita di-Shemu'el* and the poems by Eleazar ha-*Kallir (c. sixth century). Later on the book was of great importance both to the development of Jewish philosophy before *Maimonides and to the Kabbalah, and scores of commentaries were written on it. *Saadiah Gaon explained the book (at the beginning of the tenth century) as an early authoritative text. On the basis of the longer version which was at his disposal he introduced changes and new divisions. The Arabic text with a French translation by M. *Lambert was published in Paris in 1891. Saadiah's commentary was translated into Hebrew several times from the 11th century onward and had a considerable circulation (Mss. in Munich and Paris). In 955/6 the commentary on the short version by Abu Sahl *Dunash ibn Tamim was made in Kairouan. Parts of this Arabic original were discovered in the Cairo *Genizah*, and it was preserved in various editions originating from a later revision and an abbreviated form of the original version, mainly in different Hebrew translations. One of these was published by M. *Grossberg in 1902. The commentary was apparently based on the lectures of Isaac *Israeli, Abu Sahl's teacher. G. *Vajda made a detailed study of this commentary. A third commentary from the tenth century was written in southern Italy by Shabbetai *Donnolo and published by D. *Castelli in 1880, with a comprehensive introduction. The most important of all literal commentaries is the one composed at the beginning of the 12th century by Judah b. Barzillai of *Barcelona, published by S.Z.H. Halberstamm (Berlin, 1885). *Judah Halevi commented on many parts of the *Sefer Yeẓirah* in his *Kuzari* (4:25). Abraham *Ibn Ezra's commentary on the first chapter, which was known to Abraham *Abulafia, was lost, as were some other commentaries from the 11th and 12th centuries, including one by the rabbis of Narbonne. In the 11th century poems were even composed on the doctrines of *Sefer Yeẓirah*, e.g., by Ibn *Gabirol (ed. by Bialik and Rawnitzki pt. 2, no. 58) and by Ẓahallal b. Nethanel Gaon (Davidson, in: HUCA, 3 (1926), 225–55 and additions by E. Baneth, in: MGWJ, 71 (1927), 426–43).

A great many commentaries on *Sefer Yeẓirah* were written within the circles of the *Ḥasidei Ashkenaz, among them that of *Eleazar b. Judah of Worms which was published in its entirety in Przemysl in 1889, and one later attributed to Saadiah Gaon (from the beginning of the 13th century), of which only a part is printed in the usual editions; also noteworthy is the commentary by *Elhanan b. Yakar of London (c. 1240), edited by G. Vajda (in: *Kovez al Yad*, 6 (1966), 145–97). The number of commentaries written in the spirit of the Kabbalah and according to the kabbalists' conception of the doctrine of the *Sefirot* comes close to fifty. The earliest of these, by *Isaac the Blind, is also one of the most difficult and important documents from the beginnings of Kabbalah. It is published at the end of G. Scholem's lectures on *Ha-Kabbalah bi-Provence* (1963). The commentary of Isaac's pupil *Azriel b. Menahem of Gerona appears in the printed editions as the work of *Naḥmanides. The actual commentary by Naḥmanides (only on the first chapter) was published by G. Scholem (in: KS, 6 (1930), 385–410). Almost the entire commentary by Abraham *Abulafia (Munich Ms. 58) is contained in the *Sefer ha-Peli'ah* (Korets, 1784, fols. 50–56). This kabbalist, in one of his works, enumerates 12 commentaries which he studied in Spain (Jellinek, *Beit ha-Midrash*, 3 (1855), 42). From the 14th century come the comprehensive commentary by Joseph b. Shalom *Ashkenazi, written in Spain and erroneously attributed in printed editions to R. *Abraham b. David (G. Scholem, in: KS, 4 (1928), 286ff.); the commentary by Meir b. Solomon ibn *Sahula of 1331 (Rome, Angelica library, Ms. Or. 45); as well as the *Meshovev Netivot* (Ms. Oxford) by Samuel *Ibn Motot. Around 1405 Moses *Botarel wrote a commentary citing a considerable number of false quotations from his predecessors. A number of commentaries were composed in Safed, among them one by Moses b. Jacob *Cordovero (Ms. Jerusalem) and by Solomon Toriel (Ms. Jerusalem). From then on commentaries in the spirit of Isaac *Luria proliferated; for example, by Samuel b. Elisha Portaleone (Ms. Jews' College, London), by David *Ḥabillo (Ms. of the late Warsaw community); from among these the commentary by *Elijah b. Solomon, the Gaon of Vilna (1874), and the book *Otot u-Mo'adim* by Joshua Eisenbach of Prystik (Pol. Przystyk; 1903) were printed.

Printed Editions and Translations

Sefer Yeẓirah was first printed in Mantua in 1562 with the addition of several commentaries, and has since been reprinted a great many times, with and without commentaries. In the Warsaw 1884 edition – the most popular one – the text of some commentaries is given in a considerably distorted form. *Sefer Yeẓirah* was translated into Latin by the Christian mystic G. *Postel and printed even before the Hebrew edition (Paris, 1552). Another Latin edition with commentaries was published by S. Rittangel in 1652. Translations appeared, mostly with commentaries, in English, by I. Kalisch (1873), A. Edersheim (1883), W. Westcott (1911), K. Stenring (1923), Akiva ben Joseph (*The Book of Formation*, 1970); in German by J.F. von Meyer (1830), L. Goldschmidt (1894; which, quite unfoundedly, professes to give a critical Hebrew text), E. Bischoff (1913); in French by Papus (1888), Duchess C. de Cimara (1913); in Italian by S. Savini (1923); in Hungarian by B. Tennen (1931); and in Czech by O. Griese (1921).

BIBLIOGRAPHY: H. Graetz, *Gnosticismus und Judenthum* (1846), 102–32; A. Epstein, *Mi-Kadmoniyyot ha-Yehudim* (1887), 40–9; idem, in: MGWJ, 38 (1893), 75–8, 117–20, 226–9; idem, in: REJ, 28 (1894), 95–108; 29 (1894), 61–78; W Bacher, *Die Anfaenge der hebraeischen Grammatik* (1895); P. Mordell, *The Origin of Letters and Numerals According to the Sefer Yetzirah* (1914); D. Neumark, *Toledot ha-Filosofyah be-Yisrael*, 1 (1921), 100–6; G. Scholem, *Bibliographia Kabbalistica* (1933), s.v. *Jezira*; idem, in: KS, 31 (1956), 379–96; idem, *On the Kabbalah and its Symbolism* (1965), 165–87; L. Baeck, *Aus drei Jahrtausenden* (1938), 382–97; G. Vajda, in: REJ, 106 (1941), 64–85; 107 (1947), 99–156; 110 (1949), 67–92; 112 (1953), 5–33; 113 (1954), 37–61; 122 (1963), 149–66; idem, in: *Annuaire de l'Ecole Pratique des Hautes études* (1959–60), 3–35; idem, in: *Oẓar Yehudei Sefarad*, 5 (1962), 17–20; A.M. Habermann, in: *Sinai*, 20 (1947), 241–65; P. Merlan, in: *Journal of the History of Philosophy*, 3 (1965), 167–81; N. Séd, in: RHR, 170 (1966), 159–84; E. Rosh-Pinnah (Ettisch), in: JQR, 57 (1967), 212–26.

[Gershom Scholem]

YEẒIV PITGAM (Heb. יְצִיב פִּתְגָם; "true and strong is the proverb"), name of a *reshut* in Aramaic for the morning service of the second day of *Shavuot. It is found in the Ashkenazi ritual only, and is recited after the reading of the first verse of the *haftarah*. *Yeẓiv Pitgam* is similar in theme and style to the Aramaic hymn *Akdamut*, which is recited on the first day of Shavuot. It describes the majesty of the Divine revelation at Mount Sinai and concludes with a prayer for Divine grace and protection for the keepers of the Torah. *Yeẓiv Pitgam* consists of 15 verses, the initial letters forming acrostically the author's name: Jacob b. R. Meir Levi. Some authorities identify the author with Jacob b. Meir (of Orleans), the grandson of Rashi.

BIBLIOGRAPHY: Elbogen, Gottesdienst, 193, 335; Davidson, Oẓar, 2 (1929), 420–1, no. 3527.

YIDDISHER KULTUR FARBAND (**YKUF**), a U.S. association for preserving and developing Yiddish culture in Yiddish and in English. Yiddisher Kultur Farband was founded in 1937. Other branches of the international YKUF were established in various countries, among them the English branch, which was still active in 1971. The organizing meeting was an international congress of Yiddish culture, the first to be held; about 100 delegates attended, 11 from the United States. The first chairman of YKUF was the writer A. *Mukdoni; the secretary (to 1957) was Zishe *Weinper, a poet and an efficient fundraiser for YKUF. Financial support also came from the Jewish People's Fraternal Order.

YKUF established the monthly *Yiddishe Kultur* in 1938 and Nachman Meisel, who had edited a Yiddish literary magazine in Poland, became its editor (to 1964). In 1970 the journal appeared seven times a year and its editor was Itche Goldberg. Until 1971 YKUF published over 250 books, including Yiddish fiction and poetry, memoirs, history, and anthologies. With the passing of a generation of secular Yiddish speakers, the activities of the Kultur Farband slowed and the organizational activities atrophied. In 2006 Itche Goldberg, at over 100 years of age, led its limited activities.

BIBLIOGRAPHY: IG, *Yiddishe Kultur.*

YIDDISH LANGUAGE, language used by Ashkenazi Jews for the past 1,000 years. Developed as an intricate fusion of several unpredictably modified stocks, the language was gradually molded to serve a wide range of communicative needs. As the society which used it achieved one of the highest levels of cultural autonomy in Jewish history, the Yiddish language too became an unusually vivid record of Jewish cultural specificities.

The Speech Community

From its beginnings in the tenth century and until the end of the 18th, Yiddish was the virtually uncontested medium of oral communication among Jews from Holland to Ukraine, from Livonia to Romania, as well as in the Ashkenazi communities in Italy, the Balkans, Palestine. Alongside Hebrew, it was also an important medium of literary and other written communication (see *Yiddish Literature). Then, in response to the Emancipation, there arose a strong interest in converting Ashkenazi society from the use of Yiddish to that of other, non-specifically Jewish vernaculars. This striving, successful in most of the German-language sphere and in Holland, had only marginal effects in Eastern Europe. There, on the contrary, the number of Yiddish speakers increased rapidly as the Jewish population burgeoned, and a new flowering of Yiddish literature, contemporary with the rebirth of Hebrew literature, took place. The great migratory movements of the late 19th and early 20th centuries caused the Yiddish community to expand among Ashkenazi immigrants around the world (South America, U.S., Canada, Australia, etc). The development of an active press, a theater, secular educational systems through the secondary-school level, teacher training institutes, and research institutions caused the language to be utilized in a great variety of new functions. Official prohibitions on the public use of Yiddish virtually disappeared in Europe after World War I; in some areas, notably in former U.S.S.R., the language was even granted official status.

NUMBER OF YIDDISH SPEAKERS. The actual number of Yiddish speakers at any time is difficult to calculate because of poor or non-comparable statistics; the best estimates on the eve of World War II reckon with 11 million speakers. This number was drastically reduced by the Holocaust and by a massive shift to other primary languages. In the Americas and in Israel, the shift seems to have been largely voluntary, although encouraged by official organs; in former U.S.S.R., it was coupled with severe, official repressive measures – the closing of schools and other institutions in the 1930s, the liquidation of literature, press, and theater in 1949, with only a limited revival in the post-Stalin period. However, among traditionally multilingual Ashkenazi Jews everywhere, knowledge of Yiddish, at least as a second language, continues to be widespread. In fact, while the use of the language as a primary vernacular has been declining, interest in it, both sentimental, seriously intellectual and in universities, has been rising. Yiddish language is still spoken in the ultra-Orthodox world and among secular Jews in the main communities in the world. This development must be related to the growing ability of Jews in many parts of the world to integrate their European past with the modern European, American, or Israel culture. Thus the measurement of the present knowledge of Yiddish, and its novel place in the Jewish cultural economy, requires tools far subtler than those of ordinary censuses.

MODERN STANDARD YIDDISH. Over the centuries, Yiddish in its vast territorial scattering became regionally differentiated, but for written communication fairly uniform standards were maintained. This was true of the old literary language, which held sway until the early decades of the 19th century, and is true again of Modern Standard Yiddish, which developed as a supraregional formation from the middle of that century. The worldwide relative homogeneity of standard Yiddish is all the more remarkable in view of the fact that it developed without the aid of coercive forces such as are usually provided by a national state (especially through a unified school system); what uniformity there is must be attributed to the sheer centripetal, nation-forming will of the speech community. As in other languages, written usage has been standardized more fully than spoken discourse. However, with the literary language as a basis, standards of orthoepy have also evolved. (In some countries the theater cultivated a pronunciation tradition separate from that which prevailed in public life and in the Yiddish schools.) The structural sketch in the following sections is based mainly on the standard language, with only passing references to regional variations.

Sound System

In the main, the Yiddish sound system has been determined by those German dialects which contributed the bulk of its basic lexical stock. The language thus has a distinctive expiratory stress, which, though its place in a word is not fully predictable, nevertheless functions in several characteristic distributions. Secondary stresses seem to be less prominent than in German – possibly as a result of Slavic influence. The vowel system is of the triangular type, with three degrees of opening and two positions of articulation:

i		u
e		o
	a	

The most frequent diphthongs are made up of *I* following *e, a*, or *o*. Glottal stops generally do not occur. Consonants form a highly symmetrical array:

m	n	n'			
b	d	d'		g	
p	t	t'		k	
v	z	z'	ž	r	
f	s	s'	š	x	h
	l	l'			

Unlike German, the subseries of stops and fricatives are distinguished not by tenseness, but by voicing – probably an influence of the Slavic languages, which also contributed the palatal order. Unlike German, too, is the occurrence of voiced consonants at the ends of words. The influx of vocabulary from Hebrew-Aramaic and Slavic sources has created numerous word-initial clusters unknown in standard or dialectal German (*bd-*, *px-*, for example).

Regional varieties of Yiddish display much richer vocalic distinctions ranging from an opposition between short, open *i* and long, close *i*, to patterns with full parallel sets of short and long vowels. Also to be found in the dialects are front rounded vowels (*ü*) and diphthongs ending in *-w*. In the matter of consonants, on the other hand, it is the standard language which seems to incorporate the richest distinctions. Some regional varieties lack the *h* phoneme, some distinguish fewer palatals, and some, in Western Yiddish, collapse the voice distinction. The articulation of *r* fluctuates regionally between apical and uvular.

An important though still little studied feature of the Yiddish sound system consists of its intonational resources. Numerous syntactic-semantic distinctions are capable of being systematically conveyed by the melodic modulation of sentences.

Writing System

The graphic basis of Yiddish writing is the Hebrew *alphabet, with some standardized diacritics: אַ, אָ, בּ, וּ, יִ, ײַ, כּ, פּ, פֿ, שׂ, and תּ. Most words of Hebrew-Aramaic origin retain the traditional orthography; the rest of the vocabulary is rendered in a system with generally excellent one-to-one correspondence between sounds and letters or letter groups, but retaining, of course, the traditional Jewish conventions, such as those concerning final shapes of letters and initial silent א. (The letters בֿ, ח, כּ, שׂ, תּ, and ת occur only in words of Hebrew-Aramaic origin.) In the course of its evolution, Yiddish has witnessed the increasingly systematic use of א for *a* and latterly also for *o*, although the specialization of אַ and אָ is of mid-19th century origin. The use of ע as a vowel symbol – apparently an Ashkenazi invention, already attested in the 14th century – also became systematized in the course of time. The representation of diphthongs and unstressed vowels, and the conventions on word separation, have varied considerably through the centuries.

The present-day orthographic standards were promulgated in 1936. Although some publishing houses have not yet adhered to them in all details, the actual variations are relatively minor. In the first half of the 20th century, the historical-etymological spelling of words of Hebrew-Aramaic origin was abandoned in various countries, on grounds either of anti-traditionalistic ideology or of linguistic rationalism; here and there the tradition has been reinstituted. In former U.S.S.R. the use of special shapes of final letters was reintroduced in 1961.

Grammar

The basic grammatical plan of Yiddish follows the German model, but a number of important innovations have developed. In syntax, the word order of main and subordinate clauses has been made uniform; the distance between nouns and their determiners, as well as between the subparts of verb phrases, has been decreased. On the other hand, new word order devices for expressing continuity of discourse and for the de-emphasis of epithets have emerged. The nominal system continues to be characterized by four cases and three genders; the genitive, however, has blossomed into a possessive while losing most other functions; after prepositions, the accusative has been eliminated. The German distinction between a weak and strong adjective inflection has been virtually abandoned, while a new distinction between inflected predicate adjectives has evolved. Many nouns have been distributed among the (mostly inherited) patterns of pluralization. The formation of diminutives, among adjectives as well as nouns, has flourished, apparently with a push from the Slavic languages. In the verb, all tenses and moods except the present indicative have come to be formed analytically. A fairly systematic distinction between perfective and imperfective aspect, as well as numerous new aspect-like and voice-like categories, has been developed in a completely un-German direction. The present participle of verbs, too, has been assigned novel functions. The morphological details of the conjugation have in many instances been subject to innovation, and new classes of periphrastic conjugation, especially for verbs of Hebrew origin, have grown up.

Of the regional variations in the grammar of colloquial Yiddish the most significant are related to changes in the case and gender system. In Central as well as in Northeastern Yiddish (see below dialectical differences) the distinction between dative and accusative has collapsed. In the northeast, this has been accompanied by a radical restructuring of the gender system, leading to an abandonment of the historical neuter and the evolution of a new system of four quasi-genders with a high degree of semantic motivation. In general, it appears that the eastern dialects have been the most innovating; it is there that the novel use of inflected adjectives in the predicate and the "sensitivity" of verbs to aspect distinctions have progressed farthest.

VOCABULARY. Yiddish vocabulary is characterized by its multiple origins: German, Hebrew-Aramaic, Romance, Slavic, and "international."

USE AND FUSION OF SEVERAL STOCKS. The mechanical attribution of Yiddish words to ultimate etymological sources, however, yields a highly unrealistic view of the specificities of the language. Thus the word *mentsh* is formally related to German *Mensch*, but some of its important meanings ("employee"; "reliable, mature person") are specific Yiddish innovations which are obscured when the German original of the "outer form" of the word is recalled. Similar reservations apply to vocabulary of other sources. Thus, in *unterzogn* ("breathe into a person's ear"), the prefix and stem remind one of German *unter* and *sagen*, but German *untersagen* has no corresponding meaning; the sense of the Yiddish word can be explained much better as a "loan translation" of a Slavic prefixed verb (cf. Ukrainian *pid-skazaty*). In many common words, such as *oyszogn* ("to disclose") neither German nor Slavic languages provide an explanation of the Yiddish phenomenon. In short, the complex fusion of the several stocks and the rise of purely internal innovation is as important a principle in the formation of Yiddish vocabulary as the multiplicity of its origins.

It is also important to bear in mind that only a restricted portion of the stock languages has been utilized in Yiddish. For example, German has hundreds of stems which are completely unattested in Yiddish (e.g., *schweifen, Laster, fade*). Likewise, Yiddish has adopted from Hebrew *maskem* (*zayn*) and *muskem* (*vern*) "agree," "be agreed upon"; it has taken *madrekh* (*zayn*) "(to) guide," but not the expected *mudrekh* (*vern*) "(to be) guided." The actual vocabulary of Yiddish therefore stands out as a concrete historical formation against the background of its potential sources; the end product could not, as it were, be predicted from knowledge of the ingredients. Yiddish has also preserved elements from the stock languages which have died out in their original habitats; examples related to German are *shver* ("father-in-law"), *eydem* ("son-in-law").

Contrary to a widely held popular view, elements of Yiddish vocabulary have no functions which can be strictly correlated with their respective origins. Thus, material of Hebrew-Aramaic descent is found to have festive, neutral, or even vulgar connotations, depending on the individual word. To be sure, some topical domains have favored vocabulary from a particular source (e.g., rabbinical learning, from Hebrew-Aramaic; agriculture, from Slavic), but individual items have been redistributed in many cases.

The nature of the fusion process makes it difficult to calculate the proportions of vocabulary contributed by various stocks. This task is further complicated by the existence of "blends" such as *mefunitse* ("fastidious woman"), in which one word points in two historical directions simultaneously, *mefunak*, from Hebrew and-*itse*, from Slavic.

German, Romance, and Slavic Contributions. With reference to the German contribution to Yiddish vocabulary, it must be pointed out that no single form of German served as the source, but that Yiddish drew upon a *sui generis* combination of medieval city dialects. For the better part of a century, it was customary among linguists to derive the Germanic vocabulary of Yiddish from Middle High German. A more critical stance has recently led to the unearthing of significant dissimilarities between the German component of Yiddish and the language of German courtly poetry.

The Yiddish words of Romance origin, though nowadays few in number, are of considerable prominence in the language (e.g., *léyenen* "read," *bentshn* "bless"). They are venerable vestiges from the earliest stages of the language, when it was still forming on the lips of immigrants into Germany from the Romance lands (see below, Historical Development).

The Slavic languages have contributed not only thousands of lexical items but also numerous productive patterns for the formation of new words. Within the Slavic component, the most prominent part has been played by Polish, Ukrainian, and Belorussian; the oldest contacts with Czech, and the most recent ones, with Russian, have left far less numerous traces. The impact of non-Slavic languages in Central and Eastern Europe – Hungarian, Romanian, Lithuanian, and Latvian – has on the whole been of a strictly regional nature and has not penetrated the common literary language. In some cases, various Slavic languages contributed competing words (e.g., *pyeshtshen* "pamper," of Polish origin coexisting with *pesten*, of Ukrainian descent); in other cases, a single word has become diffused throughout Yiddish (e.g., *blondzhen* "stray," from Polish), or semantic specializations, a priori unpredictable, have emerged (e.g., *plónte(r)n* "confuse" < Pol., *pla tac, pluten* "act in light-minded manner" < Ukr., *plutaty*).

INTERNATIONAL COMPONENT. The "international" component of Yiddish, no less than the others, must be understood in its specificities. Thus, *fabrík* ("factory"), in a German-like form, has displaced older *fábrike*, of Polish-Russian origin; on the other hand, *relígie* ("religion"), which resembles the Slavic forms (cf. Pol., *religia*), has completely driven out the German-derived *religión*. The presence of *eyrope* ("Europe") side by side with *nevróz* ("neurosis"), in which the same Greek diphthong is represented alternately by *ei* and by *ev*>, illustrates different routes of importation, one via west European, the other Russian. As in so many other languages, "Neo-Latin" terminology has not only been adopted, but has also stimulated the development of parallel coinages out of native resources *shédredik* ("vertebralis"); *iberklangik* = *supersonish* ("supersonic").

Dialectical Differences

The bulk of Yiddish dialectological research, since its beginnings in the 1880s, has been concerned with phonological differences between the dialects. This concern is understandable not only in the light of the predominant interest in sound laws among several generations of linguists, but also in view of the diversity of vowel developments in Yiddish together with the regularity of this diversification.

While the main contours along which the European Yiddish language territory is divided have been known for some decades, no definitive hierarchy of dialect divisions could be obtained on the basis of phonological evidence alone. In recent years, the materials available to dialectology have been greatly enriched, especially in domains other than phonology, and a new impetus has developed toward the re-investigation of the geographic diversification of Yiddish, with increased attention to settlement history and mutual cross-influences among regions.

WESTERN AND EASTERN YIDDISH. The overriding dichotomy of the old Yiddish language territory in Europe is into a western and an eastern wing. The western half, roughly covering Holland, Alsace-Lorraine, Switzerland, and most of Germany, is also associated with peculiarities in synagogal ritual in the pronunciation of the Hebrew liturgy, and with folk customs unknown in the east. Among the lexical boundaries between east and west are *davnen/orn* ("pray") and *sider/tfile* ("prayer book"). Phonologically, Western Yiddish as a whole can be distinguished by the occurrence of /ā/ long in such words as / kāfn flās / *koyfn fleysh* ("buy meat"). Western Yiddish itself is, however, far from homogeneous. Some of its subregional differences can be explained as latter-day adjustments of a once more uniform language to local forms of German; it is apparent, however, that other forces, internal to the Jewish community, have also been at work in the formation of the Western Yiddish dialectal landscape.

Reconstucted Proto Yiddish Vowel[1]	Western Yiddish	Eastern Yiddish			
		South Yiddish		North-East Yiddish	Examples
		Central Yiddish	South-East Yiddish		
A_{11}	a	A	o	a	*gas* ("street") *shabes* ("Sabbath")
A_3	ō/ā	u/ū	u	o	*trogn* ("carry") *brokhe* ("blessing")
E_3	ē	Ai	ei	ei	*sheyn* ("beautiful") *meylekh* ("king")
E_4	ā	Ai	ei	ei	*fleysh* ("meat")
E_5	ē	ē	ei/I	e	*veg* ("road") *teve* ("nature")
I_4	ai/ei	ā	a	ai	*mayz* ("mice")
U_3	ō/au	oi	oi	ei/eu	*hoyzn* ("trousers") *toyre* ("Torah")
U_4	ā	oi	oi	ei/eu	*koyfn* ("buy")
U_1	o/y	I	I	u	*hunt* ("dog") *shutef* ("partner")
U_3	ȳ	ī	i	u	*bruder* ("brother") *shure* ("line")
U_4	au	ō/ou	oi/u	oi/au	*hoyt* ("skin")

1 The conventional labeling of the reconstructed vowels corresponds to the increasingly widespread usage in current linguistic literature (see bibliography). The pairs of forms separated by the diagonal solidus represent subdialectal variants.

Between west and east, the countries south of the Carpathian Mountains occupy a midway position. The western part – Bohemia, Moravia, west Slovakia, west Hungary – are characterized by a Yiddish dialect which was, on the whole, lexically east European but phonologically West European. The Yiddish of the eastern part – the Hungarian lowlands, Transylvania, and Carpathorussia – can be understood as a fusion of the west-Transcarpathian dialect with dialects brought by ḥasidic immigrants from Galicia.

DIVISIONS OF EASTERN YIDDISH. Within the eastern wing of Yiddish territory there is a salient three-way division, in which the southeast (roughly, Ukraine, Romania, and parts of eastern Galicia) occupies a pivotal position between the northeast (Belorussia, Lithuania, Latvia) and the center (Poland proper, western Galicia). Using the phrase *koyfn fleysh* once more as a criterion, we find it in the form / kejfn flejš / in the northeast, / kojfn flajš / in the center, and in the "compromise" version / kojfn flejš / in the southeast.

The split between the Northeast and the rest of East European Yiddish must have begun even before the middle of the 16th century along the dividing line between the Kingdom of Poland and the Grand Duchy of Lithuania. The relatively self-contained nature of these two basins of Jewish colonization, as well as the possibly disparate origins of colonists entering each basin, are likely causes of the early differentiation. A separate issue is the "intermediate" quality of Southeastern Yiddish between that of the Northeast and the Center. It may be related to the mid-16th century re-orientation of the area from Lithuanian to Polish allegiance; on the other hand, we must also reckon with the possibility that the old common non-Lithuanian Yiddish has been more faithfully preserved in the southeast, whereas in Poland it has evolved further under the differential impact of fresh immigration and influence from the west. The separation of historical strata in the formation of such dialectal entities as Belorussian Yiddish and the sorting out of boundary phenomena everywhere into those which were imported and those which were formed in situ, are among the problems with which Yiddish dialectology is preoccupied.

Historical Development

The historical study of Yiddish is hampered by a shortage of texts from the earliest periods and by the highly conventionalized nature of the literary language in which so many of the surviving texts are written. In consequence, many supplementary methods must be used. Reports of contemporaries, both Jewish and non-Jewish, must be sifted; inferences from general historical facts must be coupled with deductions from such knowledge as we have of the history of the stock languages. Above all, reconstructions from attested forms of modern spoken Yiddish must be used as correctives to the interpretation of texts.

PERIODIZATION. It is safe to say that no event was more decisive in the development of Yiddish than its movement into a Slavic environment and its withdrawal from the reach of German norms. It was under Slavic influence, above all, that aspects of the grammatical system were restructured and that "normal" genetic relation of Yiddish to German was weakened. It is only fitting, therefore, that the periodization of the history of Yiddish reflect this realization. The most widely accepted scheme uses the approximate years 1250, 1500, and 1700 as the major turning points.

EARLIEST YIDDISH. The period of Earliest Yiddish, until 1250, is the time before Slavic contact was established. It is in this period that Jews from northern France and northern Italy, speaking a language they called Laaz, established their first bridgeheads in German-language territory in the kingdom of Loter (i.e., Lotharingia). There is reason to believe that they were simultaneously exposed to more than one variety of Christian German, and it is plausible that their speech remained, for many generations, rife with phonetic and lexical imports from the Laaz language, even though the number of surviving vestiges has constantly been reduced. It is in this period, too, that the old Diaspora pattern of reaching into the sacred language for additional vocabulary, along with the custom of writing the vernacular in the Jewish script, must have been transferred from the Laaz areas to Ashkenaz. Although we have no continuous texts from this period, it seems likely that at this early time the basic fusional formula for the subsequent utilization of multiple stocks was already established. Through the use of indirect evidence, it is even possible to discern the effects on Earliest Yiddish of specific historical developments, such as the increasing isolation and mobility of Jews during and after the Crusades, or the changes in the Hebrew tradition associated with the arrival of Babylonian teachers in Ashkenaz.

OLD YIDDISH. It is in the Old Yiddish period (1250–1500) that Yiddish speakers made contact with Slavs and Slavic-speaking Jews – first in southeastern Germany (*Bavaria*) and Bohemia, then in Poland and still further east. Large numbers of new communities were founded in the new environment and existing communities speaking Knaanic (a Slavic-based Jewish language) were converted to Yiddish. In this period, too, even before the development of printing, a relatively uniform literary language developed. Although many more documents have perished than survived, the language is now amply attested in various stylistic ramifications – in poetry, in *taytsh-khumesh* (Bible translation), and the official records of communal scribes.

MIDDLE YIDDISH. The next period, Middle Yiddish (1500–1700), is marked by the vigorous expansion of eastern Ashkenaz and consequently by the withdrawal of an increasing proportion of Yiddish speakers not only from continuous German territory, but also from the vicinity of German-speaking cities in the east. The linguistic monuments of this period, including numerous volumes of narrative and expository prose, make the evidence increasingly richer. Private letters, verbatim testimony of witnesses, and comical verse for the first time offer the modern scholar an insight into spoken usage, while the detailed comparison of variants in repeated editions of stock works enables us to reconstruct some of the diversities and changes of the language in that period. However, the continuing uniformity of the written language and the shortage of texts of East European provenance hides from view the crucial processes of dialectalization and Slavization which must have gone on at the time.

MODERN YIDDISH. The Modern Yiddish period, after 1700, witnessed a slow but almost fatal decline of Yiddish in the West. The old literary standard, increasingly remote from the living speech of the East European majority, finally collapsed, and a new standard, on an Eastern Yiddish base, began to form about 1820. For some decades, there was uncertainty about the dialectal base and the authoritativeness of literary German models; with the development of a press and a self-conscious literature in the 1860s, however, a supradialectal formation with only limited reliance on German patterns gained rapid ascendancy. The use of the language in organized social movements and in quickly accelerating literary activity reached a high point of self-consciousness in the *Czernowitz Yiddish Conference of 1908. The subsequent introduction of Yiddish as a medium of school instruction, of scholarly research, and of regional administration contributed to the lexical expansion and stabilization of the language. Modernistic poetry was particularly imaginative in exploring the Yiddish potential of enrichment from within.

YIDDISH AND HEBREW. The preceding discussion has sketched the important role played by the sacred language in the formation of Yiddish and in the determination of its graphic image. A few more detailed points may now be taken up separately.

The principal strata of the learned tradition from which Yiddish has drawn have been the Pentateuch, the daily prayers, and the technical discourse of the yeshivah. Because the boundary lines between biblical Hebrew, mishnaic Hebrew, and Aramaic were only vaguely observed in rabbinical use of the sacred language, it is more accurate to speak of the "Hebrew-Aramaic" than of the "Hebrew" stock in the formation of Yiddish. In most recent times, of course, Palestinian and Israel Hebrew have exerted an influence on Yiddish, both within the country and abroad; Yiddish now has such doublets as (traditional) *alíe* ("call to read a lesson from the Torah in the synagogue"), and (modern) *aliá* ("immigration to Palestine/Israel").

HISTORY OF HEBREW-ARAMAIC-YIDDISH CONTACT. Although more or less the same stock has at all times been available in its entirety to all Ashkenazim, the entry of a particular form from Hebrew-Aramaic into Yiddish must be regarded as a concrete historical event in place and time. Thus, there are words of Hebrew-Aramaic origin which have become current in some regions but are unknown in others (*rak*>, "continuously," in Northeast Yiddish, *ives*, "biting words," in Alsace). There are also marked regional differences in the forms or Hebrew-Aramaic words merged into Yiddish which are unrelated to the systematic dialectal differentiation of Yiddish (e.g., *nadn* "dowry" in Central and Southeast Yiddish, *nadán* in Northeast and Transcarpathian Yiddish, *nedunye* in most of Western Yiddish). A further argument for the concrete historicity of Hebrew-Aramaic-Yiddish contact is the fact that early Yiddish texts contain forms of Hebrew-Aramaic origin which have since become extinct in the language (e.g., *mekabets zayn*, "go begging").

WHOLE AND MERGED HEBREW. Hebrew-Aramaic elements which entered Yiddish have, of course, been subjected to the phonological and grammatical norms of the recipient language; this has differentiated many of them from their equivalents within Ashkenazi Hebrew proper. The result of this distinction is described by the pair of technical terms, Whole Hebrew and Merged Hebrew.

Some of the peculiarities of Merged as opposed to Whole Hebrew, such as the shift of the stress or the neutralization of unstressed vowels, are accounted for by the exigencies of Yiddish phonological and grammatical structure. But there are other peculiarities, not explainable in such a way, which are of particular value in elucidating the outlines of rabbinical Hebrew as a distinct historical branch of the sacred language. Quite a few forms suggest caution against oversimplified conceptions of Hebrew historical grammar. Significant, too, are discrepant treatments of individual Merged Hebrew words and the re-systematization of such discrepancies into new patterns.

The existence of synonym pairs, of which one member is of Hebrew-Aramaic origin and the other stems from elsewhere, has endowed some domains of Yiddish vocabulary with a double register characteristic of Jewish Diaspora languages. To be sure, the semantic or stylistic difference between the members of the pairs is not always the same: in *seyfer*, *shulkhn* (as against *bukh*, *tish*) the reference is to a book of traditional Jewish content and to the ritual synagogue table for unrolling the scroll of the Torah (sacred vs. profane); in *akhlen*, *eynaim* (as against *esn*, *oygn*), the Hebrew-origin term connotes crassness and vulgarity; in *mashtin zayn*, "urinate," *aver*, "bad odor," the Hebrew-origin terms function as euphemisms for their synonyms of other origins.

YIDDISH INFLUENCE ON HEBREW. For many centuries Yiddish has been exercising a reverse influence on Hebrew. Rabbinical writings of the 13th century already contain turns of phrase which would be unintelligible except as loan translations from Yiddish, and, as time went on, the recourse to Yiddish as a source both of direct borrowing and of calquing, increased. This pattern led to easily parodied excesses in ḥasidic literature, but was utilized moderately and creatively in the shaping of modern literary Hebrew by Sholem Yankev *Abramovitsh (Mendele Mokher Seforim) and his contemporaries. In the revived spoken language of Palestine and Israel, Yiddish has had a profound impact not only on the phonetic structure of the language, but also on the developing distinction between perfective and non-perfective verbal constructions, in the fashioning of new idioms, and in the vocabulary of slang. The patterned difference between what may be called Merged Yiddish and Whole Hebrew has made possible previously unavailable stylistic distinctions.

History of Yiddish Studies

Yiddish studies go back to the 16th century, when German humanists saw in the script and in certain aspects of the vocabulary and grammar of this language a convenient bridge to the learning of Hebrew. In the subsequent period Yiddish also attracted the attention of theologians concerned with missionizing among the Jews, and of police officials and others interested in cryptic Jewish speech and Yiddish as a source of German thieves' cant (see *Avé-lallemant). The science of Judaism in the 19th century paid only scant attention to Yiddish, and the developing Germanic philology was slow in coming to appreciate the historical significance of this language. The foundations of a modern scholarly approach to Yiddish were laid by scattered individuals – L. *Saineanu in Bucharest, who furnished the first dialect monograph, and A. *Landau in Vienna, who set an example in matters of text editing, scholarly commentary, etymology, and the study of the subtle but pervasive impact of Slavic. In the first two decades of the 20th century Yiddish studies remained the domain of private persons with varying levels of university preparation. A new beginning was made in the 1920s with the founding of institutions devoted, partly or completely, to the study of Yiddish: chief among them were the institutes affiliated with the Ukrainian and Belorussian academies (Kiev and Minsk) and the *YIVO (Yiddish Scientific Institute) in Vilna. These institutions became the centers of large-scale, systematic collecting of material and of the preparation of capital works such as dialect atlases and dictionaries. The serial publications established by these institutes provided a forum for the printing of text editions, collections of folk language, and analytic studies. Systematic training of aspirants in Yiddish studies became available for the first time. The several institutes also played the role of normative authorities, first with respect to orthography, and eventually also in some areas of terminology.

The suppression of Jewish scholarship by the Soviet regime and the Holocaust brought about the almost complete annihilation of scholarly personnel and collections. The American branch of YIVO, however, became the focus for its postwar reorganization and that of Yiddish studies. A new phenomenon, almost without precedent before World War II, was the introduction of Yiddish into the curricula of universities. The development of advanced Yiddish studies at the Hebrew University in Jerusalem created a fresh opportunity for coordinating Yiddish studies with training in other Judaica, while the activities centering around Columbia University in New York helped to integrate Yiddish linguistics with general linguistics on a broader scale than before. A renewed interest in Yiddish studies has also been in evidence in Western Europe, especially in western Germany, France, Netherlands, in Eastern Europe and in America.

See also *Yiddish Literature.

BIBLIOGRAPHY: The main works up to 1958 are inventoried in Uriel and Beatrice Weinreich, *Yiddish Language and Folklore: a Selective Bibliography for Research*, (1959). The most important current literature is covered in the annual bibliography issue of the *Publications of the Modern Language Association* (of America). Significant recent collections of studies are *For Max Weinreich on His 70th birthday* (1964); U. Weinreich, et al. (eds.), *The Field of Yiddish* (1965–68), fifth collection, 1993. Periodicals and miscellaneous volumes devoted completely or in part, to the study of Yiddish are: *YIVO Bleter* (since 1931; first in Vilna, after World War II in New York); *Yidishe Shprakh* (since 1941, New York). DICTIONARIES: Y. Mark and J.A. Joffe (eds.), *Groyser Verterbukh fun der Yidisher Shprakh*, 4 vols. (1961–80); N. Stutshkov, *Oytser fun der Yidisher Shprakh* (1950); U. Weinreich, *Modern English-Yiddish, Yiddish-English Dictionary* (1968). LINGUISTIC GEOGRAPHY: M.I. Herzog, *The Yiddish Language in Northern Poland* (1965), with extensive bibliography; M. Kosover, *Arabic Elements in Palestinian Yiddish* (1966). HISTORY: M. Weinreich, *Geshikhte fun der Yidisher Shprakh*, 2 vols. (1968); J.A. Fishman, *Yiddish in America* (1965); Birnbaum, in: JJS, 72 (1961), 19–31. YIDDISH AND HEBREW: U. Weinreich, *Ha-Ivrit ha-Askhenazit ve-ha-Ivrit she-be-Yidish, Beḥinatan ha-Ge'ografit* (1965; first published in *Leshonenu*, vols. 24 and 25); H. Blanc, in: U. Weinreich et al. (eds.), *The Field of Yiddish*, 2 (1965), 18–20. **ADD. BIBLIOGRAPHY:** A. Harkavy, *Yiddish-English-Hebrew Dictionary* (1928, reprinted, 1988); M. Aptroot and H. Nath, *Araynfir in der yidisher shprakh un kultur* (2002); J.G. Bratkowsky, *Yiddish Linguistics, a Multilingual Bibliography* (1988); A. Fishman (ed.), *Sociology of Yiddish* (1980); idem, *Never Say Die! A Thousand Years of Yiddish in Jewish Life and Letters* (1981); J.C. Frakes, *Early Yiddish Texts* (2005); M.I. Goldwasser, *"Azhoras Noshim": a Linguistic Study of a Sixteenth Century Yiddish Work* (1982); D.-B. Kerler, *The Origins of Modern Literary Yiddish* (1999); Y. Lifshitz and M. Altschuler (eds.), *Briv fun Yidishe Sovetishe Shreibers* (1980); Y. Niborski and B. Vaisbrot, *Yidish-frantseyzish verterbukh* (2002); Y. Niborski and S. Neuberg, *Verterbukh fun loshn-koydesh shtamike verter in yidish* (1997); D.G. Roskies, *Against the Apocalypse – Responses to Catastrophe in Modern Jewish Culture* (1984); D. Sadan, *A Wort ba-Shteit: Shpaziren tsvishen Shprakh un Literatur*, 2 vols. (1979); C. Shmeruk, *Sifrut yidish, perakim letoldotehah* (1978); idem, "Can the Cambridge Manuscript Support the Spielman Theory in Yiddish Literature?," in: *Studies in Yiddish and Folklore* (1986), 1–36; idem, "Hebrew-Yiddish-Polish: A Trilingual Jewish Culture," in: Y. Gutman, E. Mendelsohn, and Ch. Shmeruk (eds.), *The Jews of Poland between Two World Wars* (1989), 285–311; E. Timm, *Graphische une phonische Struktur des Westjiddischen* (1987); idem, E. Timm, *Yiddish Literature in a Franconian Genizah* (1988); S. Tsaftman, *Bein Ashkenaz le-Sefarad – Le-Toledot ha-Sippur ha-Yehudi bi-Ymei ha-Beinayyim* (1993); Ch. Turniansky, "*Le-Toledot ha-'Taytsh-Ḥumesh' – 'Ḥumesh mit Ḥibur'*," in: *Iyyunim be-Sifrut – Devarim she-Ne'emru ba-Erev Likhvod Dov Sadan Bimlot lo Shemonim ve-Ḥamesh Shanah* (1988); M. Weinreich, *The History of the Yiddish Language* (1980); U. Weinreich and M. Herzog (eds.), *The Language and Culture Atlas of Ashkenazic Jewry*, (1992). S. Kumove, *Words Like Arrows – A Collection of Yiddish Folk Sayings* (1984); Kahn, *Portraits of Yiddish Writers* (1979); D. Sadan, *Teuren un Tiren* (1979); Ch. Shmeruk, *The Esterke Story in Yiddish and Polish Literature* (1985).

[Uriel Weinreich]

YIDDISH LITERATURE.

This articles is arranged according to the following outline:

INTRODUCTION

Yiddish is one of a number of languages that Jews have assimilated into their culture from their foreign environment during their long exile (see *Jewish Languages). These languages were "Judaized" and, at least initially, served primarily as a means of everyday communication. They were regarded as of lower status than the ancient and holy language, Hebrew, which enjoyed almost exclusive dominance in the realms of religious ritual and scholarship. Yiddish, developing and flourishing side by side with the Hebrew-Aramaic which continued to be the unifying medium of communication among Jews of all lands of the dispersion, is unique. While Judezmo (popularly known as *Ladino), *Judeo-Arabic, *Judeo-Persian, and other Jewish languages also developed a linguistic identity, a rich folklore, and a variety of literary genres, none can claim as copious and diversified a literature as that which flourished in Yiddish, nor did any of them reach the geographical spread of Yiddish, nor equal it in number of speakers. During the second half of the 19th century at the latest, all the literary genres found in modern European literature had also become vehicles of expression in Yiddish.

A parallel may be drawn between the relationship of Latin literature to the vernaculars of medieval Christendom in European literature and that of Hebrew to Yiddish in Jewish culture. The transition of Yiddish from a medium of daily communication and a popular literature to a comprehensive and highly developed literary and intellectual vehicle of creativity was complex. Hebrew, it was formerly thought, was the sole medium of reading and writing of the intellectual strata of Jewish society until the 19th century. Yiddish, it was said, catered only to the masses, answering mainly the spiritual needs of the less educated, especially women. Hebrew writings expressed the highest aesthetic, intellectual, social, and religious ideals of the society; Yiddish literature, it was assumed, answered the needs of the untutored and of women. Yiddish literature until the end of the 18th century, it was formerly thought, consisted either of educational material written by intellectuals or popular works by writers from the readers' own social class. This schema ignores the best of both early Yiddish (i.e., Old and Middle Yiddish) literature and the flowering of a sophisticated Yiddish literature in northern Italy in the late 15th and 16th centuries. As regards women, there is clear evidence that they made up a sizable portion of the reading audience of early Yiddish texts; some were also active participants in the printing industry, whether as typesetters, printers, or authors.

With the rise of the *haskole* [*Haskalah] movement at the end of the 18th century, modern Yiddish literature gradually developed into an independent medium in all modes of intellectual and artistic expression. By the end of the 18th century, the conventional and standardized Yiddish literary language which had attained its most definite form in the 16th, or at the latest in the early 17th century, had become stereotyped. Spoken and literary Yiddish differed widely, the latter having been maintained almost solely to answer the need for a uniform written medium understood by Yiddish speakers of Western and Eastern Europe. Literary Yiddish had become an artificial language. The end of the 18th and beginning of the 19th centuries saw the birth of a literary language based on the Yiddish dialects of Eastern Europe. At the same time, Yiddish almost ceased to be a creative medium in Western Europe, the Haskalah movement and emancipation having encouraged linguistic assimilation. West European Jewish writers adopted European languages as media of expression, a process that affected East European Jewry much later.

Extant pre-18th century manuscripts, printed books, and small pamphlets are sadly lacking in many spheres, a natural outcome of the persecutions, expulsions and wanderings forced upon European Jewry. This dearth is also due to an attitude to Yiddish, a legacy of previous generations that saw only Hebrew as holy and of value. Modern research into early Yiddish literature started shortly before World War I. The results published in the 1920s and 1930s need to be revised because of the ideological concepts and methodology then current, because of important texts discovered since, and because of more recent studies. This state of affairs is no less true regarding modern Yiddish literature, a field in which relatively little scholarly research has been done. The following survey could well be reshaped by future findings.

UNTIL THE END OF THE 18TH CENTURY

The Bible in Yiddish Literature

From its beginning Yiddish literature was largely based on the Bible and its interpretations, talmudic legends, and midrashim. For centuries, efforts were made to impart Bible knowledge in Yiddish, as evidenced by glosses in margins of Hebrew manuscripts (at least from the 12th century), manuscript glossaries for individual books of the Bible, and works such as *Mirkeves haMishne / Seyfer R' Anshl* [*Mirkevet ha-Mishna – Sefer R' Anshl*, Cracow, 1534], a dictionary and concordance for the entire Bible, which is the first known Yiddish printed book. In some manuscripts traces have been found of interlinear translations that simulated the syntax, grammar and semantics of the Hebrew original. Complete translations of the Pentateuch were published in Constance (1544), Augsburg (1544), and Cremona (1560). Translations were made of single books of the Bible, e.g. Psalms (Venice, 1545), and of the entire Bible (Amsterdam, 1676–9, 1679).

This literary creativity in Yiddish continued earlier oral efforts by the Jewish settlers of southern Germany who had adopted the local vernacular. The traditional oral study of the Scriptures in Yiddish among descendants of these German Jews in Israel and in the U.S. is a living assertion of the earlier creative process. In modern times, the threads of this literary expression were taken up by Sholem Yankev *Abramovitsh (Mendele Moykher-Sforim/Mokher Seforim], Y.L. Perets (*Peretz), Khayim Shoys (Ḥayyim Schauss], and others, in their translations of individual books of the Bible, and by *Yehoash [Yehoyesh / Solomon Bloomgarten) in his translation of the entire Scriptures. Yehoash's work is standard among secular Jews in the Yiddish-speaking world (latest revised edition 1941; online "YIVO" edition at *Di Velt fun Yidish* website). (To grasp the status accorded to this poet until recently in the Yiddish world, see the special Yehoash issue of *Di Goldene Keyt* 72 (1971)). The poetic translation of Yitskhok Katsenelson (Itzhak *Katzenelson) in the early 1940s in the Warsaw ghetto placed the Bible in the forefront again as a source for Yiddish literary inspiration.

Yiddish scriptural translations closely adhered to the text, usually rendering it literally. By drawing on the traditional Hebrew biblical commentaries, the Yiddish translations gained authority. The process of translation was to render into Yiddish each Hebrew word of the original by a parallel Germanic component, despite the fact that many of the Hebrew words in the text were understood by all Jews and in use in Yiddish. For a long time, translators of the Bible followed a definite structure and linguistic pattern in consequence of which idioms, stylistic and linguistic forms no longer used in the spoken language were preserved in the oral and written study of the Bible. The sanctity of the Hebrew original imputed to these early translations explains why these archaisms were preserved, becoming a main source for stylization in modern Yiddish literature.

EPIC. The 14th century marked the beginning of Yiddish rhymed biblical tales. (Christian rhymed versions of the Bible are almost all psalters). In the Cambridge University Library manuscript T.-S. 10K22, from the Cairo *Genizah, the stories of Abraham, Joseph, and Moses (written *ca.* 1382) are in verse. The epic poem about the binding of Isaac (*Akeyde* [*Akedah]) seems to have been very popular for centuries and has been preserved in various manuscripts and printed texts up to the 18th century. The Book of Esther and the midrashim based on it, also in great demand, are known to have been rendered into Yiddish in poetical form from the 15th century onward. This literary activity reached its zenith in the **Shmuel Bukh* ("Book of Samuel," Augsburg, 1544) and **Melokhim Bukh* ("Book of Kings," Augsburg, 1543), biblical epics believed by some to have been written in the 15th century. Later works structurally imitated these earlier compositions, e.g., *Joshua* (Mantua, 1562/64), *Judges* (Mantua, 1564), *Isaiah* (Cracow, 1586), and *Daniel* (Basel, 1557). The metrical structure common in popular German epic poetry (four lines of six stresses with a prominent caesura in each line and an *aabb* rhyme scheme) was adopted, sometimes with the acrostic and strophe of the Hebrew *piyyut* (e.g., the rhyme scheme *aaaa* in the poem on the sacrifice of Isaac). The style and structure of these poems reflect cotemporal German poetic conventions.

In these mainly anonymous poetic adaptations, the original Bible story was embellished with talmudic legends and midrashim to augment the narrative element of the tale. The poets, possessing as they did profound knowledge of the Hebrew sources, were faithful to the content and spirit of these additions. We can assume that this literary creativity was, *inter alia*, born of the need to produce an offset and possible substitute for the alien "fictitious" adventure stories which had spread to the Jewish public. Except for some isolated works and poetic adaptations, written as late as the 17th century, e.g., *Kehiles Yankev* [*Kehilas Ya'akov*, Fuerth, 1692], this type of literary activity ceased. From the end of the 16th century it made way for homiletic prose, whose subjects and themes were culled from the same sources.

HOMILETIC PROSE. The *Tsenerene* (**Ẓe'enah u-Re'enah*) by R. Jacob b. Isaac Ashkenazi of Janow was a very popular work in the genre of homiletic prose. A miscellany of tales, homilies, midrashim, and exegetical comments woven around a Yiddish rendering and paraphrasing of the Pentateuch, the *haftoyres* [*haftarot*] and the *megiles* [*megilot*], the work is written in a lively, simple, and flowing style. The commentaries and midrashim supplementing and expounding the selected biblical passages were well known. The work is assumed to have appeared first in the 1590s. (The first preserved unicum was apparently published at Hanau, 1622, but was preceded by at least three editions which have been lost.) Reprinted up to the present, it has gone through over 210 editions. Another work ascribed to Rabbi Jacob b. Isaac Ashkenazi, *Seyfer haMagid* [*Sefer haMagid*], popular for generations, is a translation of *Neviim* [Prophets] and *Ksuvim* [Hagiographa] printed alongside the Hebrew text with a paraphrase of Rashi's commentary. Published at the beginning of the 18th century under the title *Magishey Minkhe* [*Magishey Minkha*] with an edition of the *Khumesh* [Pentateuch] written in the same style, the book became increasingly popular. It may be assumed that the widely-read works of R. Jacob b. Isaac Ashkenazi helped perpetuate the archaic style dominating Yiddish literature until the end of the 18th century, a style which ignored the developments in the spoken tongue, especially the changes that occurred in Yiddish in Eastern Europe. The 1786 Lemberg re-edition of the *Tsenerene* systematically repatterned the language to conform to modern Eastern Yiddish [Kerler 1999, p. 100]. Though lacking exegetical and homiletical originality, this prose is faithful to the Hebrew-Aramaic sources that the contemporary Jewish community at large knew well. Its novelty lies mainly in the popular style and the new literary forms into which the ancient cultural treasures were cast.

DRAMA. Yiddish biblical drama, adapting Scripture stories more freely than any of the other genres, appeared on the Yiddish literary scene at the latest by the 17th century. This late date (in comparison to European literatures) may be due to the ban imposed by the rabbis on the theater, in force particularly in medieval Europe where the Christian Church controlled drama. The establishment of professional theatrical companies and troupes in Germany in the 17th century led to the secularization of the theater and to the relaxation of the ban, thus making way for the Yiddish drama. The latter confined itself, however, to biblical subjects: *Akheshveresh Shpil* ("Ahasuerus Play," earliest ms. 1697, printed text Frankfurt am Main, 1708); *Mekhires Yoysef* ("Selling of Joseph," Frankfurt am Main, before 1711); *Dovid un Golyes* ("David and Goliath," Hanau, 1717); and *Moyshe Rabeynu Bashraybung* ("Moses Our Teacher Description," mid-18th century).

Yiddish biblical drama shows clear influences of the non-Jewish theaters of the time, mainly in the setting and in the introduction of comic characters. Although non-Jewish plays on the same themes may have served as models and sources for Yiddish drama, all elements or motifs that were incompatible with the Jewish outlook were replaced by material culled from midrashim which added rich dialogue to the original biblical story. The midrash thus was a vital literary source whose wealth of subjects, themes, and actual language lent a note of originality to the development of the biblical themes in the dramas. Generally presented at Purim when prohibitions and bans were relaxed, these plays fit the festive mood of the holiday. The oral tradition of the *Purim shpiln* ("Purim plays"), also including dramatic works on other biblical themes, bears clear traces of these early 17th and 18th century Yiddish dramas. The tradition was alive in Eastern Europe up to World War II, and in the isolated instance of the Bobover ḥasidim is still alive today.

Liturgy

The canon of Jewish liturgy had become fixed before Yiddish literature developed, and this may be the reason there was little original prayer and religious lyrical writing in Yiddish. The earliest Yiddish verse (preserved in the Worms *makhzer* [*Makhzor*, high-holiday prayer book, 1272] reads: "gut tak im betag shevayr dis makhzor in bes hakneses trag" ("May the person who carries this holiday prayer book to the synagogue be blessed"). This benediction, found only in this source, was merely an embellishment and did not form part of the standard liturgy. Most of the liturgical activity was in translation. From the 15th century onward, Yiddish translations of individual prayers and of entire prayer books were well known and current in the Jewish community; the first printed Yiddish prayer book (Ichenhausen, 1544) contains prayers for the entire year. However, the main function of translations of prayers into Yiddish was to aid understanding of the Hebrew-Aramaic texts; according to tradition, they alone were acceptable for devotional service.

In Yiddish, however, there were spheres in which to express religious feelings and devotion. The *tkhine*, a non-standard prayer of individual and private supplication adapted for various purposes, is outside the body of the liturgical canon. Mainly considered prayers for women, *tkhines* are often attributed to women authors. Written mainly in prose, these supplications are characterized by simplicity and emotionality. They are found as early as the 16th century in printed Yiddish texts, sometimes in prayer books with Yiddish translations. They were widely published in small books and in special collections that are still printed today.

Yiddish religious poetry also found an outlet in those ceremonies which did not yet have a set of fixed rules and customs governing them, mostly ceremonies conducted specifically in the home (Sabbath and festival meals, the Passover *seder*, weddings and circumcisions). By the 15th century, not only were popular Hebrew *piyyutim* and hymns translated into Yiddish, but Yiddish poems were specifically composed for such celebrations and festivities. Bilingualism characterized this poetry: some of the poems were written both in Hebrew and in Yiddish so that the entire company might fully participate. Contrary to the Hebrew text, which in accordance with the tradition of the Hebrew *piyyut*, was studded with learned quotations, the Yiddish text was characterized by poetic simplicity and vivid descriptions directly reflecting the times and mores. Structurally, this Yiddish poetry is marked by a symbiosis of two strophic forms drawn from two separate literary sources: the strophe of the Hebrew *piyyut*, adapted to the linguistic peculiarities of Yiddish, and the German strophe, particularly that of the folk song. The Yiddish poems were often written and adapted to German folk melodies popular among Jews (e.g., a Hebrew and Yiddish song in honor of the Sabbath sung to the melody of the German *Herzog Ernst*, as early as the middle of the 15th century). This poetry was also a vehicle for various types of parodies that were especially popular at Purim.

Ethical Literature

This wealth of Yiddish literary activity developed directly and naturally out of an established and organized Jewish society whose way of life was in no small measure influenced by a didactic literature consisting of books of customs (*mineg* (*minhog*)), and ethical conduct (*muser* (*musor*)). The Yiddish literature on traditional conduct mainly instructed the Jewish community in how to behave during synagogal worship and at domestic festivities and religious ceremonies. Custom books in Yiddish are found in early manuscripts which, with the dissemination of the art of printing, were frequently reprinted, with only minor changes, up to the end of the 18th century. In his *Early Yiddish Texts* (*text no. 31*), J.C. Frakes edits an excerpt from a north Italian manuscript of a book of customs (Paris, Bibliothèque Nationale, ms. hébr. 586, fos. 117r–118r; dated 1503). The first printed Yiddish comprehensive guide to customs appeared at Mantua in 1590.

Ethical writings were one of the most important genres in early Yiddish insofar as numbers of exemplars actually read. In a simple and clear style easily understood by the average person, they taught ideal religious and social behavior for the individual and society as a whole. This literature denounced (often excessively) any conduct which deviated from the standards of the authors. The ethical writings, also based on accepted Hebrew sources, were to a large extent translations of Hebrew ethical literature, e.g., *Seyfer Mides* ("Book of Qualities" [Sefer Midot], Isny, 1542), the first comprehensive printed Yiddish ethical work translated and published before the Hebrew text *Orkhes Tsadikim* ("Way of the Just," Prague 1581). [See L. Prager & B.S. Hill, "Yiddish Mss. in the British Library," in: *The British Library Journal*, 21/1 (Spring 1995), 86–8 and footnote 39; see also EJ 12: 1458–60]. *Lev Tov* ("Good Heart," Prague, 1620) and *Simkhes HaNefesh* ("Joy of the Soul" [Simkhas HaNefesh], first part Frankfurt, 1707; second part, containing a collection of poems and hymns including the music, Fuerth, 1727) were two original Yiddish ethical works, well known in Jewish society and often reprinted.

The many parables and exemplary tales included in ethical writings established a close link between this literature and the *exemplum and *hagiography. Traces of the first written Yiddish exempla and hagiographies, the origin of which was undoubtedly in homily and oral literary traditions, e.g., folklore, are contained in a number of tales found in scattered manuscripts and small books (most of which are lost) appearing in Venice in the middle of the 16th century. The story titles point to the decisive influence that the Hebrew legend had on this literature. The **Mayse Bukh* ("Story Book" [*Ma'aseh Book*]), which was first published in Basel in 1602, is a comprehensive compilation of 257 stories based largely on talmudic and midrashic tales, though some are culled from other sources. Direct influences of the novella and the folktale, genres current in contemporaneous non-Jewish European literature, can be detected in many of the narratives; others are hagiographical accounts about *Khsidey Ashkenaz* [Khasidey Ashkenaz] with the obvious time gap between contemporaneous life and historical and legendary memories. These hagiographical tales are also comprised in the *Mayse Nisim* ("Miracle Tales" [*Ma'aseh Nissim*], Amsterdam, 1696) and are found in a number of small works in which local legends, whose protagonists are prominent historical figures, are developed. The principal purpose of exemplum and hagiographical literature was didactic and it formed the mainstream of Yiddish narrative prose up to the end of the 18th century.

The *Mayse Bukh* also testifies to Yiddish fable literature, although the first extant works in that genre are found in the much earlier Cambridge *Genizah* manuscript of 1382. The fables are free translations into Yiddish from fables of the time known originally in Hebrew, often with a modified moral. The **Ki Bukh* ("Book of Cows") is the first Yiddish collection of fables (the first edition apparently at Verona, 1595; a slightly revised reprint appeared at Frankfurt, 1697, under the name Moses Wallich). Eli Katz in his splendid critical edition indicates that "What distinguishes the tone" of the latter from its sources or possible influences "is its hominess": the stork in the first fable prepares *kreplekh*; the crow in the second fable blesses the new moon. A translation of the Hebrew *Mishlei Shu'alim* ("Fox Tales") appeared at Freiburg in 1583.

Although virtually all Yiddish authors prior to the second decade of the 20th century commanded both Hebrew and Yiddish to some degree, and though there are numerous Hebrew works printed with their translations in Yiddish, the intimate relationship between the two languages is best seen in the too little understood organically dual Hebrew and Yiddish poem such as the early 17th debate poem, a distinct kind of *muser* writing, *Seyfer Mase u-Merive* [Sefer Masso u-Merivo] ("Essays and Disputations," 1627) by R. Aleksander ben Isaac Pfaffenhofen. This rhymed bilingual poem contains an intricately developed disputation between poverty and richness in rhymed Hebrew and Yiddish parallel texts. Evidence points to the author's intention to publish, but it was not until 1985 that the rare Bodleian manuscript was "redeemed" in a scrupulously edited edition by Chava Turniansky. Bilingual Hebrew/Yiddish poems date from the 14th to the 18th centuries in genres such as wedding song, Sabbath hymn, debate poem, and ethics poem.

"Historical" Songs and Writings

Up to the end of the 18th century, current historical events and contemporary Jewish life found expression mainly in long narrative poems called *lider*, which were put to music. This type of poem resembles the popular German *historische Lieder* (long poetic narratives on current events). *Megiles Vints* ("Vinz Scroll," a bilingual poetic work in Hebrew and in Yiddish) by Elkhonen Heln is one of the earliest extant poems of this type. It describes the sufferings of the Jews of Frankfurt am Main during the Fettmilch riots (1612), how Fettmilch and his rabble forced them to leave the city, and their eventual return. The 40 or so extant historical *lider* (from the beginning of the 17th to the end of the 18th century) – some of them bilingual with parallel Hebrew texts – are remnants of a poetry very popular in its time. The variety of topical subjects that found expression in this verse published in small cheap pamphlets close to the time of the events they describe point to its functional merit both as public commentary and news. The poems describe expulsions, blood libels, massacres, and natural calamities in the life of Ashkenazi Jewry from Vilna in the north to Ofen in the south, from the Ukraine in the east to Holland in the west.

The authors often showed a highly developed historical sense. A vehicle of communication on current historical events, these *lider* were at the same time emotionally charged, a reaction to contemporary non-Jewish literature of the same kind which described the same events in the form of anti-Jewish accusations. Elements of the ancient *kina* ("lamentation") and the Hebrew *piyyut* ("liturgical hymn") can be clearly discerned, as well as stylistic and structural forms adopted from German poetry of the genre. The poetry also contains balladic elements and is occasionally interspersed with lyrical digressions. As far as can be ascertained from the extant poetry, the writers seem to come from the lower echelons of Jewish leadership, and the events related were thus seen and expressed in the light of norms found in popular ethical literature. Most of this poetry has little literary merit, but measured against the background of Yiddish literature of the 17th and 18th centuries, its value is to be found in its originality and its ability to depict vividly the historical present – at that time hardly expressed in any other literary genre. The art, though slightly modified, was alive in Eastern Europe up to World War II. Its final remnants, preserved by survivors of the Nazi concentration camps and the ghettos, were gleaned from the last transmitters of this oral tradition of the "historical" *lid*.

Also very popular in Yiddish were historical writings, a literature almost entirely translated from Hebrew. *She'eris Yisroel* (Amsterdam, 1743), an original work by Menakhem Man *Amelander, was one of the few exceptions. It was written as a sequel to the Yiddish translation of *Josippon (first printed in Yiddish in Zurich in 1546, and thereafter in numerous editions). Included in this literature somewhat arbitrarily since it fits neatly into no one genre is an untitled and quite extraordinary work that is conventionally (although inaccurately) referred to as the *Zikhroynes* ("Memoirs") of Glikl bas Leyb (since 1898 conventionally known as Glikl Hamil or *Glueckel of Hameln, 1645–1719). A widow with many children, Glikl by force of character and sagacity overcomes the many difficulties that she encounters in her long life. Hers is a timeless work of ethics and moral edification which – almost incidentally – also vividly describes the writer's life and illuminates the Jewish and general society in which she lived.

Transcriptions of German Works

Jewish authors and readers were familiar with certain types of German literature as evidenced by linguistic and stylistic conventions and structural patterns and forms found in poetical adaptations of biblical tales and other types of Yiddish poetry taken from German verse. Thus German popular literary works were well known and understood among Jews in German-speaking countries, despite the fact that their language was not exactly identical with that of their environment. Until the beginning of the Haskalah (middle of the 18th century) this literature was transmitted mainly orally or by transcription of the works into the Hebrew alphabet. While the majority of Jews were able to read and write Hebrew, they were not able to read the Roman alphabet (*galkhes*), especially those circles that were most attracted to secular German literature.

The art of transcription into the Hebrew alphabet thus became prominent in Yiddish literature. Traces of the many German works transcribed can be found in manuscripts from the 14th century onward (*Dukus Horant* / "Duke Horant" in the Cambridge *Genizah* manuscript of 1382) and in printed works until the 18th century. German works that reached the Jewish reader were generally restricted to those popular with the German lower classes. Among these there was a popular folk literature, especially the folk song, which is extant in modified form and preserved even in collections of East European Jewry (compiled and written down from the oral tradition from the end of the 19th century). The early transcribed literature includes fantastic adventure tales which in many cases may be seen as folk literature and, from the end of the 16th century, a popular genre known in German literature as the *Volksbuch* ("chapbook"). Some of the transcriptions come from a written source while others were drawn from oral tradition. Slanders against Jews were excised from most of these works, the Jewish transcriber usually trying to expunge anything that was liable to offend the Jewish reader. Occasionally, however, accusations against Jews and other derogatory remarks are left in the transcribed version.

Transcriptions into the Hebrew alphabet adhered to certain methods that can be roughly reduced to the following: (1) excision of Christian religious references; (2) use of opprobrious expressions common among Jews for Christian terms and objects (such as *tifle* [contemptuous term for "church"] instead of *kirche* ["church"] in *Dukas Horant*); (3) use of neutral expressions for religious terms (e.g., "glaykh bay den tor" instead of "in di kirkhn" in *Sheyne Magelone* ("Beautiful Magelone," Fuerth, 1714); (4) the Judaization of Christian terms (*shul* ["synagogue"] instead of *kirkhe* in *Zibn Vayzn Maynster Bikhl* ("Book of the Seven Wise Masters," Basel, 1602). One method was not necessarily used consistently in any one transcription, nor was one method prevalent at a given period. In most works, the transcriber applied all the possibilities mentioned, while in others, not even the Christian terms were deleted.

A number of these works transcribed from writings whose roots were in the German environment presented literary problems beyond that of transcription and the changes made to Christian references. Such a work is the Yiddish *Kinig Artis Houf* ("King Arthur's Court," earliest manuscript from the 15th–16th century), whose sources are not known and which was later (17th century) adapted in *ottava rima*, imitating Elye Bokher's [Elijah Baḥur *Levita's] poetic adaptations from Italian (see below).

"Secular" Yiddish Literature in Italy

The growth rate of an original "secular" literature in Yiddish may possibly have been slowed by the great ease with which Jews were conversant in German literature. Thus the end of the 15th century and the 16th century were a flourishing period in Yiddish literature among the Jews of northern Italy. These Ashkenazi immigrants cut off from the German environment retained Yiddish as a living tongue at least until the late 16th century. The outstanding creative mark of the period is the original "secular" Yiddish literature to which it gave birth. Many Yiddish works in manuscript were produced and a variety of Yiddish books was published in such cities as Venice, Cremona, Mantua, and Verona. Though rooted in non-Jewish sources, the Yiddish writings were not transcriptions but original works whose vitality survives to the present day.

One of the major Jewish writers of the time in Italy was Elye Bokher [Elijah Baḥur Levita] who, until the end of the 18th century, was the central figure in Yiddish literature. A Hebrew scholar in the fields of grammar, linguistics, and Bible, and a friend and teacher of Christian humanists, he was a man of comprehensive and deep knowledge in a number of intellectual and cultural spheres. He was a versatile poet, sensitive to poetic form with which he experimented freely. Undoubtedly, not all of his Yiddish works have survived. Among his extant writings is his translation of the Book of Psalms (first printed in Venice in 1545), two poetic pasquinades, and the romance *Bovo d'Antona* ("Bovo of Antona," written in 1507, first printed at Isny, 1541, and known as the **Bove Bukh* in later editions). Either Elye Bokher or a disciple of his composed *Pariz un Viene* ("Pariz and Viene," Sabbioneta, 1555/6; first extant ed. Verona, 1594). Only recently has a complete copy of the text been discovered (Verona, Biblioteca del Seminario Vescovile, Fonds Venturi, no. 192) which has clarified much concerning both the period and the genre (see the exemplary edition by Ch. Shmeruk in collaboration with E. Timm [1996]). Adaptations from popular Italian stories, these romances point to the authors' complete freedom in the treatment of their material, made possible by the rendition into a language alien to the sources and by adaptation of the content for the Jewish reader. This literary freedom was, however, limited for the transcriber of German writings and for the translator (including Elye Bokher) of the sacred or semi-sacred Hebrew sources.

Elye Bokher reduced the *Bovo d'Antona* narrative from the 1,400 stanzas of the Italian source to 650 stanzas in the Yiddish, eliminating some of the erotic elements and including his own original additions – sometimes in a lyrical, sometimes in a delicately humorous vein. He also Judaized his characters at times, as transcribers from Roman into Hebrew script had occasionally done before him. While in the works of the latter, the Judaized material – whether situation or character – was sporadic, random, and out of context, Elye Bokher exploited the technique to create comic effects that formed a natural and integral part of the whole. His readers did not find it strange that medieval knights and kings good-humoredly observed Jewish customs and manners.

While the two works, which imitate the style and form of the sources, were written in *ottava rima*, the author felt that Yiddish was not easily adaptable to the Italian models. In the process of adapting the *Bovo d'Antona*, he developed an original stanza whose rhyme scheme was that of the *ottava rima* (*abababcc*) and which had alternate masculine and feminine rhymes. In this stanza, by skillfully integrating the natural accentuation of the Yiddish language and the syllabic principle governing the Italian language, he invented an exact iambic meter (in which the *Pariz un Viene* was also later composed), anticipating similar developments in other European literatures. Elye Bokher's poetic language is vivid and rich, and his rhymes are varied, partly because he included rhyme schemes from German, Hebrew, and Italian. Yiddish rhyme, usually based on a single component of the language, thus broke with the traditional conventions.

Despite the popularity of the *Bove Bukh* (known in corrupted texts in Eastern Europe up to the 19th century), Elye Bokher's Yiddish literary efforts did not substantially influence the development of Yiddish literature. This has been attributed to the decline of Yiddish in Italy at the beginning of the 17th century and to the cultural environment of the other European Ashkenazi communities which, until the beginning of the 19th century, was not receptive to a poet of Elye Bokher's caliber.

MODERN LITERATURE

Until World War I

Two Haskalah comedies written in the 1790s by Isaac Euchel and Aaron Wolfsohn mark the end of Yiddish literature in Western Europe. While in the 19th and 20th centuries parodies of German literature were written in Western Yiddish (generally transcribed into the Roman alphabet), they are marginal phenomena among Jews who, as readers and writers, had become integrated into German culture. The groups of Yiddish writers in Berlin and Vienna after World War I are branches of the Yiddish literature that developed in Eastern Europe.

The desire to eliminate the popular Yiddish *Purim shpil*, stemming from an open disdain for the "corrupt" language, Yiddish, was one of the reasons that prompted the writing of the two aforementioned comedies. In the plays only the undesirable characters speak Yiddish, while the laudable characters speak, or at least try to speak, a "proper" language, i.e., "pure" German. It is doubtful whether the educational aims of Euchel or Wolfsohn achieved anything with regard to the language problem. These comedies were, in fact, a manifestation of the assimilative tendencies which were crystallizing at the time – irrespective of the desires of these authors – and which ultimately brought about the extinction of Yiddish literature in Western Europe. The society denied the very right of the language to exist and used it only for jokes – and even then only so long as there were Jews who could understand the puns and were still familiar with the environment from which they were becoming progressively estranged.

There was a symbolic and highly significant difference in principle between the comedies written in Germany and those of the East European Haskalah, written in Yiddish, even though the latter may have been written under the influence of the former, and both had similar aims. This type of comedy became one of the accepted genres in modern Yiddish literature in the 19th century. From the anonymous comedy *Die Genarte Velt* ("The Deluded World," 1816?), the comedies of Shloyme Etinger [S. *Ettinger] and Yisroel Aksnfeld [I. *Axenfeld], to the plays of Sholem Yankev *Abramovitsh [Mendele Moykher-Sforim/Mokher Seforim] and Avrom Goldfadn [A. *Goldfaden], this type of drama not only fulfilled the authors' aims of disseminating the ideas of the Haskalah and modernizing Jewish society in Eastern Europe, but also facilitated (though not always deliberately or consciously) the transition of Yiddish literature from a folk literature to a modern one.

HASKOLE (HASKALAH). Although the *maskilim* ("enlighteners") in Eastern Europe disapproved of Yiddish in principle and used it only as a medium for the dissemination of their ideas among the masses who understood no other language, their use of the language came to serve as the basis for the development of a modern literature. An important, perhaps decisive, factor was the realization that the character and expressive power of the language were compatible with the environment. Yiddish was an effective tool for Haskalah writers who were unable to express themselves with the same ease and effectiveness in Hebrew, although in principle that language remained the ideal.

This response, often unconscious, to the possibilities of Yiddish may clearly be seen in the writings of Mendl Lefin [Mendel *Levin (Lefin)], Yoysef *Perl (beginning of the 19th century), and in later authors (up to the beginning of the 20th century) who wrote in Hebrew and Yiddish. Until the second half of the 19th century, no Jewish writers used the non-Jewish languages current in Eastern Europe, and until World War I, only a fairly narrow stratum of the Jewish intelligentsia had a thorough command of these languages.

The literature written in East European Yiddish – from the period of the Haskalah comedies to that of the wide geographical expansion of Yiddish literature in the late-19th and the 20th centuries, both in the countries where it took shape and in those lands to which the emigrants brought it – has been an arena fraught with tensions and metamorphoses. The turbulence endemic to Yiddish literature stems from a variety of sources: consciousness of the social and national purpose of Yiddish literature in describing the fundamental internal changes in Jewish society since the beginning of the 19th century; resistance to hostile external forces; the attitude to the Yiddish language itself, and to Jewish culture as a whole, especially to Hebrew and Hebrew literature; and its relationship to modern trends in Western literatures. All these elements constituted the background and motivating force for the rapid development of Yiddish literature.

From its inception, Yiddish literature in Eastern Europe saw the clash between Ḥasidism and Haskalah, one that assumed various forms in the course of time and continues to this day. Ḥasidism represents a mystical, romantic approach to life, while the Haskalah in all its variations is fundamentally rationalist and in its literary expression "realistic."

ḤASIDISM. Ḥasidism from the 18th century tried to renew Jewish religious and social life on a mystical and emotional basis and created a literature of its own in Yiddish. In comparison with Hebrew ḥasidic literature, Yiddish ḥasidic literature is limited in scope and in its forms of expression. However, it is of immense importance as a direct source for all genres of modern Yiddish literature. The latter was nourished by its spirit, its outlook, and its characteristic narrative themes.

Ḥasidism produced two basic types of stories: (1) Hagiographies that glorified the founders and leaders of Ḥasidism by describing their marvelous deeds. The first important collection of this type, *Shivkhey haBesht* ("The Praises of the Baal Shem Tov," 1815), is derived from oral traditions in Yiddish which were first collected and committed to writing in Hebrew. Immediately translated into Yiddish in three independent versions, the work started a chain of hagiographical oral and written literature which influenced Yiddish prose and poetry until the period of the Holocaust. (Yitskhok Katsenelson's poem on the rabbi of Radzyn, written in the Warsaw Ghetto in 1942/43, was based on authentic stories of this kind current at the time in the ghettos of Poland.) (2) Religious, mystic stories of which the tales of R. *Naḥman of Bratslav are among the most remarkable in all of Yiddish literature. Composed between 1806 and 1809, these tales appeared in a bilingual version (Yiddish with a Hebrew translation) in 1815. They are an original manifestation of religious mysticism in the garb of symbolist fiction and are the only works of their kind in Yiddish literature. Some of the themes are drawn from folk literature and anticipate important motifs of modernism which later appeared in Yiddish literature: the dichotomy in the soul of modern man between simple and unquestioning faith on the one hand, and rationalism and rationalization of life on the other. Within the ḥasidic movement itself, the narrative genre of the school of R. Naḥman had no successor. However, with the advent of modern symbolist trends in Yiddish literature in the late 1890s, his tales were a source for the works of Y.L. Perets, D. *Ignatoff, Der *Nister, and others.

STRUGGLE BETWEEN HASKALAH AND ḤASIDISM. The struggle against Ḥasidism and its literature – and, in a large measure, against its Yiddish narrative literature – was one of the main objects of Yiddish Haskalah writings in Eastern Europe. The anti-ḥasidic motif is a characteristic feature of satirical Haskalah literature (Yisroel Aksnfeld, Y.Y. Linetski [I.J. *Linetzky], and others) which included both parodies and deliberately confusing versions founded on ḥasidic literature itself (Y. Perl). For a fairly long period, the aggressive bias and open didacticism of the mainstream of Haskalah Yiddish literature limited its artistic possibilities for satire on the one hand and artificial pathos on the other. These works included, it is true, the poetical and dramatic writings of Sh. Etinger, in which the tendentious aims of the Haskalah were not particularly virulent, as well as the numerous stories of Ayzik-Meyer Dik [Isaac Meyer *Dick], which are a connecting link between the traditional didactic and ethical tales and the trends of the Haskalah. The real turning point, however, in the one-sided outlook of the Haskalah came in the works of Sh.Y. Abramovitsh.

SHOLEM YANKEV ABRAMOVITSH (MENDELE MOYKER-SFORIM). Abramovitsh's great talent and artistic power enabled him to rise above his original declared motives as an adherent of the Haskalah. Despite the pungent satirical elements which are especially apparent in his early works, he drew a complex and unbiased picture of a way of life and a gallery of characters of which he had previously disapproved. He was perhaps the first Yiddish Haskalah writer who ceased to attack Ḥasidism, and to describe the movement and its problems in his work. The Haskalah, in its beginnings and its later simplistic forms, concentrated on the internal struggle within Jewish society. The struggle was rooted in the naive expectation that the authorities in each country would support its aim of breaking down the barriers between the Jew and his environment in return for their readiness to give up specific Jewish characteristics. Abramovitsh marks a change in this attitude.

The allegorical *Di Klyatshe* ("The Nag," 1870) forms a turning point in Abramovitsh's writings. He was disappointed in his expectations of external support, as well as profoundly conscious of the uniqueness of the Jews, which he believed should be sustained. His view found expression in an active and comprehensive criticism of failings in Jewish society, which he already at that stage regarded as the outcome of conditions forced upon the Jews because of their status within a hostile Christian society. This attitude is one of the most characteristic elements of his later work and the reason why he rewrote earlier stories after the 1870s. He wanted to balance the grotesque, which was derived from the earlier satirical themes, with pathos and emotionalism. Despite the satire and the grotesque, his work is an unrivaled realistic reflection of a stable Jewish way of life which disintegrated with bewildering rapidity and whose very existence became problematic for his successors. His language and style were forged out of varied literary traditions and based on a combination of two basic dialects of the spoken language, northern and southern. They thus form a uniform literary language and are a turning point in Yiddish literature, one that led ultimately to modernization and integration with general literary trends. That change occurred in Abramovitsh's later years, and he neither participated in nor encouraged it.

The same factors that led to the change in his outlook and manner of writing also brought new trends of thought to the fore in East European Jewry, and, at the same time, new trends and elements in its literature. These can be seen in the poetry of Sh.*Frug, who moved from Russian to Yiddish. He introduced into Yiddish poetry both modern lyricism in nature poetry and an individual character. A poet of strong national feelings, he gave expression to modern national trends, Zionism, and the beginning of the labor movement. Toward the end of the 19th century, these became the main foci of activity among the intelligentsia within Jewish society and sparked its modern literature in Hebrew and Yiddish.

THE LABOR MOVEMENT. While modern Hebrew literature developed in the wake of Zionism, which was its principal spiritual mainstay, the ideological affinities of Yiddish literature were more complex. The founders and leaders of the Jewish labor movement, most of whom came from the intelligentsia, had adopted the co-territorial language. They soon realized the need to conduct their propaganda in Yiddish in order to disseminate their views more effectively. Before long, however, Yiddish became for the labor movement not merely an instrument but a cultural asset of national and intrinsic value, especially in its non-Zionist sections. Yiddish and its literature thus received from the labor movement an ideological background giving wide and dynamic public support which it had previously lacked, despite its development in Abramovitsh's time and sporadic declarations in its favor from the beginning of the 19th century (Y.Sh. Bik and Y.M. *Lifshits) which had been of scant practical value.

The adherence of the Jewish masses to the labor movement and its propaganda methods at the time, created a new trend in Yiddish literature which closely bound education with revolutionary propaganda. The writers of this trend expressed and emphasized the sufferings of the Jewish worker, both as worker and Jew, and summoned him to struggle against his exploiters within and without and to sacrifice himself for social, political, and national liberation. The Yiddish poetry of previous periods, which rarely succeeded in rising above the level of popular entertaining verse (e.g., Binyomin-Ze'ev Eyrenkrants [Benjamin (Wolf) *Ehrenkranz], M. *Gordon, Elyokum Tsunzer [E. *Tsunser] and to some extent, Avrom Goldfadn and Y. *Gordin) was now supplemented by a new poetry. Though still primitive in expression and limited in its imagery and symbolism – which were borrowed and adapted to the phraseology of the labor movement – it was inspired by a powerful faith and inner fervor. The most successful of this poetry was written in the U.S. as early as the 1890s by Moris Vintshevski [M. *Vinchevsky], Moris Roznfeld [M. *Rosenfeld], D. Edelshtat, and Y. *Bovshover; it also reached the labor movement in Eastern Europe and served it well.

While in the U.S. Yiddish poetry was largely dominated by social considerations and what remained of popular entertaining verse, the main feature of Yiddish prose was the straightforward description of the life of the immigrants, mingled with sentimental nostalgia for the lands of their origin (e.g., Z. *Libin). In theater, the struggle continued between the music hall and the beginnings of artistic drama (e.g., Y. *Gordin and L. *Kobrin). In Eastern Europe, on the other hand, the position was already more complex during the 1890s, which, up to World War I, was dominated by the ramified and highly influential work of Sholem-Aleykhem (*Sholem-Aleichem) and Y.L. Perets, who are rightly regarded, with Abramovitsh, as the classic authors of Yiddish literature.

Both Sholem-Aleykhem and Perets went through the growing pains of the Haskalah, but for both it was a passing phase at the beginning of their literary careers. Both of them – particularly Perets – sympathized with the rise of the Jewish labor movement while responding to the problems raised by other Jewish national movements. The distinctive feature of both authors, however, was their success in resisting the restraint of ideological trends that might have fettered their artistic freedom. Although both were involved with the sufferings and problems of their generation, each in his own way refused to surrender to the conventions, or to the demands and criticisms of politicians and critics who wanted to restrict the function of Yiddish literature to that of an instrument for education and the realization of social and political ends.

SHOLEM-ALEYKHEM. Although Sholem-Aleykhem (*Shalom Aleichem) was successful both in the novel and in drama, his great and unique talent was manifested mainly in the direct narratives of his various heroes: the monologues of Tevye der Milkhiker ("Tevye the Dairyman"), the letters of Menakhem-Mendl, the stories in the first person of Motl

Peysi dem Khazns ("Motl Peysi the Cantor's Son") and the short stories in which the narrator himself "disappears," and the flow of his heroes' voice is given free rein. His attitude toward the gallery of characters he created, personae that seem to have been taken directly from life, with all their sublime, crooked, and comic features, is one of tolerance, devoid of overt preaching or censure. Even in the tragic situations in which he often placed his characters, he did not lose the capacity to laugh and amuse, although he might have to do so in pain and sorrow. Sholem-Aleykhem's humor and the gripping situations depicted in his stories often obscure the more complex elements in his works, which led to criticism of him for flippancy and shallowness. The journalistic topicality, to which he sometimes gave way because of his newspaper work, became outdated. Sholem-Aleykhem himself realized this, and toward the end of his life he revised his works published over several decades, abridged them, and succeeded in raising his characters to the level of universal figures independent of their origins in time and place.

Menakhem-Mendl, as revised in 1910, is a condensed treatment of material, mainly topical, which had been written around this character since 1892. Sholem-Aleykhem's capacity for self-control, which is outstandingly displayed in this book, shows him as a great artist with a sober and highly developed critical sense. From the beginning of his literary career he did much to develop the literary taste of the Yiddish reading public in his struggle against vulgar popular books which were widespread at the time (though modern critics are far more appreciative of Shomer than Sholem-Aleykhem was in his vituperative *Shoymers Mishpet* ("Shomer's Trial," 1888), and in his editing and publication of the first literary collections in Yiddish (*Di Yidishe Folksbibliotek* / "The Jewish Popular Library, 1888/89). Sholem-Aleykhem's most important contribution, however, was his original literary work. It educated readers from all sectors of Jewish society and attracted them to Yiddish literature. He is still the most popular Jewish author, both in the original and in translation, though it is impossible fully to convey his rich, idiomatic, colorful, and variegated style in any language but Yiddish.

Y.L. PERETS. The work and significance of Sholem-Aleykhem's contemporary Y.L. Perets (I.L. *Peretz) are of a very different kind. Perets's literary heritage comprises poetry, drama, stories, and essays in both Hebrew and Yiddish. His most important contribution as an author consists of his short stories in both languages and his poetical plays in Yiddish. Drawing on folktales and ḥasidic stories, Perets created for himself and many of his successors new patterns in the Yiddish short story. He presented in a modern and artistic form the wealth of tales which had been current in the written and in the oral tradition in a primitive form without damaging their spirit and character. In his ḥasidic tales, Perets started the neo-ḥasidic trend in Yiddish and Hebrew literature, a trend which, in its various developments, has not yet ceased. None of his successors, however, has matched his capacity not only to present the plot element in the stories faithfully, but also to give them a form appropriate to their source. Much in his stories expresses his own ideas and they contain significant layers of ambiguity, ambivalence, and paradox.

Perets's main work in the last ten years of his life was in the field of drama. The final versions of his last two plays, *Di Goldene Keyt* ("The Golden Chain," 1911/12) and *Bay Nakht Oyfn Altn Mark* ("At Night in the Old Market Place," 1914/15), which are among his most important works, reveal despair and disappointment at the solutions presented to the modern Jew by the ideologies of his day. In this mainly pessimistic view of life, the only spark of hope Perets sees is in the return to the traditional ways of Judaism, but even this possibility is presented together with a clear and penetrating perception of the destructive forces working against it. Perets was the only Yiddish author before World War I who dared to undertake such a trenchant self-examination. Although they were based on a neo-Romantic style and symbolism, his plays, especially *Bay Nakht Oyfn Altn Mark*, came close to expressionism, which found its way into Yiddish poetry after his death.

Unlike Abramovitsh and Sholem-Aleykhem, Perets had an affinity for modern trends in general world literature, especially Polish neo-Romanticism. He always succeeded, however, in preserving the Jewish character in his work, and drew his themes from Jewish cultural and traditional sources. He was admired by many of his contemporaries, who began to write under his inspiration and his guidance and in the course of time continued, each in his own way, to expand and deepen the modern elements in Yiddish literature, while constantly wrestling with the problems of their own society (e.g., D. *Pinski, Sh. *Asch, Y.M. *Vaysnberg, A. Reyzn (*Reisen), H.-D. *Nomberg, M. Boreyshe, Y.Y. *Trunk, and many others). Despite differences of opinion in the evaluation of Perets as writer and teacher, he is still a point of departure and a model for Yiddish writers of various camps. Authors like Kh.N. Byalik [*Bialik], Y. Shteynberg [*Steinberg], and S.Y. *Agnon, whose main work was in Hebrew, also wrote in Yiddish, parallel with and in continuation of the tradition of Abramovitsh and Perets.

Several processes vital for the future development of Yiddish literature reached their peak in 1908. A conference in support of Yiddish took place in Czernowitz; a literary journal called *Literarishe Monatshriftn* ("Literary Monthly") appeared in Vilna; and *Di Yugend* ("Youth"), the first organ of a group called Di Yunge ("The Young Ones"), appeared in New York. The aim of the two periodicals was to renew Yiddish literature along the lines of European symbolism.

The *Czernowitz conference had the important effect of increasing confidence, self-respect, and a consciousness of the status of Yiddish literature as a modern literature among authors and readers. At the same time, however, following the attempt of several extremists to have Yiddish (as opposed to Hebrew) proclaimed as *the* national language of the Jews, the conference intensified the rift between the two literatures of the one people, which, until then, had been used together by most Ashkenazi authors. Furthermore, in certain situations – among Yiddish authors adherent to the non-Zionist labor movement and in the Soviet Union after the revolution – these extremist views led to a deliberate denial of Jewry's vital sources and subsequently to a simplified evaluation of the traditional cultural heritage. This linguistic strife has left its marks, though its extremism has abated since World War II.

A number of young writers centered around the two above-mentioned periodicals with the declared purpose of severing Yiddish literature from its commonly accepted mission of raising the cultural level of the masses and providing them with material for edification and entertainment. Under the influence of contemporary trends in world literature, as well as disappointment with social and national ideologies, they demanded the recognition of the rights of Yiddish literature as an independent artistic domain. Some of the younger writers in the U.S., who were themselves recent immigrants from Eastern Europe, also demanded the integration of Yiddish literature and authors in their new home, with all that this implied in adaptation to the new landscape and the speedier rhythms of life in prose and verse. Individualism, aestheticism, pessimism, eroticism, the development of new verse forms, and a new sensibility to life are among the distinguishing characteristics of the young writers associated with these periodicals and of the broad literary periphery that came under their influence without actually joining their groups.

Until the end of World War I, this trend produced many poets in various countries who reinvigorated Jewish poetry with new images and new meters, expanded the range of its subject matter, and wrote lyric poems on a standard not below that of other contemporary literatures. D. Aynhorn (*Einhorn), L. *Naidus, Sh.-Y. *Imber, *Mani-Leyb, I.J. *Shvarts, M.L. *Halpern, H. Leyvik (*Leivick), A. *Margolin, D. Hofshteyn (*Hofstein), Z. Landoy (*Landau), R. Ayzland (*Iceland) – each having an individual poetical style – are a few of the poets in the flood of modern Yiddish poetry which reached its full strength only after World War I. At the same time, Yiddish prose underwent a significant change. The impressionistic style of D. *Bergelson and L.*Shapiro, the symbolist tales (based on the Jewish narrative tradition) of Der *Nister and D. *Ignatoff, the deep-rooted vitality of J. *Opatoshu, the new American scene in the stories of A. *Raboy, all contribute to the modernization process. The plays of Sholem *Ash and Perets Hirshbeyn [*Hirschbein], which laid the foundations for an artistic repertoire in the Yiddish theater, also belonged to the new developments of this period.

Most of the authors who started on symbolist lines in deliberate opposition to the subordination of literature to social ideologies did not generally remain faithful to the literary doctrines which they adopted. In the course of time they found their way to themselves and their environment and helped develop the special character of modern Yiddish literature. They remained alive to the problems of the generation which was struggling under the burden of internal conflicts affecting them as Jews and as inhabitants of the modern world. Perets had expressed doubts in his first Yiddish work (Monish, 1888) as to whether the Yiddish language had the capacity to express sublimity and subtlety, the abstract and the spiritual, or whether it was limited to describing in concrete terms the Jewish way of life and the idiomatic pungency of popular speech. These apprehensions disappeared entirely at the time of World War I and were replaced among Yiddish authors by a confidence in the capacity of the language to prove itself in any field of artistic and literary expression.

After World War I

The three decades following the outbreak of World War I were highly dramatic for the history of modern Yiddish literature. These years saw World War I, the revolutions and pogroms in Russia, migrations and changes of regime, World War II, and, above all, the Nazi Holocaust, which brought East European Jewry, almost the only source for Yiddish authors, to the brink of extinction. These events were the background for transformations in the development of Yiddish literature, which itself directly expressed all facets of the tumultuous period. The continual spread of Yiddish literature and the increased importance of its centers overseas extended its horizons.

At the same time, especially after the Holocaust, emigrant authors were torn between their emotional attachment to the ruined lands of their origin and their aspiration to be integrated in their new homes and establish a new generation of authors there. Before World War I, Yiddish literature was basically bilingual; many authors wrote in both Yiddish and Hebrew and many readers understood both languages. After the death of Perets (1915), Sholem-Aleykhem (1916), and Abramovitsh (1917), this close bond was severed, and no successor arose with the influence and prestige able to bridge the gap. Despite the great tension throughout the period in all centers of Yiddish literature and the constant and drastic decline in the number of readers, the stock of authors and literary output increased. There were important artistic achievements, new depths were plumbed and new literary territory was conquered.

POETRY. While prose dominated Yiddish literature before World War I, in the postwar period it met with competition from poetry. Expressionistic and other verse tendencies showed themselves immediately after World War I along parallel lines in the three main centers of Yiddish literature: the Soviet Union, Poland, and the U.S. Despite differences in temperament and direct reference to the places where it was written, the poetry possessed a common linguistic medium and cultural background. The poets whose works filled *Eygns* (1918, 1920) in Kiev, *Shtrom* (1922–24) in Moscow, *Yung-Yidish* (1919) in Lodz, *Khalyastre* in Warsaw (1922) and Paris (1924), *Albatros* in Warsaw (1922) and Berlin (1923), *In Zikh* (1920–39) in New York, and similar periodicals elsewhere, sought new forms of poetical expression to convey new experiences. The younger generation of poets had endured the ravages of World War I and the revolutions and pogroms in Eastern Europe. Urbanization for them had become inevitable. Their basic attitudes and religious beliefs, which had previously begun to crumble, now seemed to be completely shattered. The strong feeling that these traumas could not be given adequate poetic expression with the means previously regarded as acceptable in Yiddish poetry gave rise to the new poetry, with its free rhythms, which broke the bonds of the conventional, constricting metrical forms and challenged all the conventions of society, Jewish tradition, and the entire self-destructive human race.

At the same time, this verse was saturated with contradictions. Despair and anger, oaths and imprecations, unbelief and deliberate obscurity, eroticism bordering on pornography and exhibitionism, and reverence for vitality and all-conquering technology, which are outstanding features in the work of most of these poets, patterned one side of the coin; the obverse revealed lyrical sensitivity, a readiness – even a yearning – for new solutions, and a nostalgia for the "antiquated" ways of life. This poetry gave voice to the fear of loneliness in the oppressive and overwhelming big city which crushes personality and offers no security. It differed from contemporary non-Jewish work, which is similar in its main tendencies, by close attention to specifically Jewish images and associations drawn from the resources of a Jewish tradition which was visibly breaking up.

One outstanding expression of this poetry of contradictions and inner conflicts was the work of Perets *Markish. In one and the same period, Markish wrote *Volin* ("Volyn," 1939), an idyllic poem of nostalgia for the region of his birth and its Jews, *Di Kupe* ("The Heap," 1921), a poem full of anger, profanity, and unbelief, written as a reaction to the pogroms in the Ukraine, as well as urbanistic poetry packed with new and bold imagery, with a new poetic rhythm, as in the Warsaw collection *Radio* (1922) and in his Paris poems (1922–23). Dating from the same period are his sonnet cycle *Fun der Heym* ("From Home," 1922–24) and *Zkeynes* ("Old Women," 1926), restrained works revealing great epic skill in the closed metrical structure of which this representative of Jewish expressionism was particularly fond.

Among those who belonged to these trends were the introspective poets who founded the *In Zikh* group: A. *Glants-Leyeles, Yankev Glatshteyn [Jacob *Glatstein], and N.-B. *Minkoff in New York; the expressionists U.-Tsvi *Grinberg, M. *Ravitsh, M. *Broderzon, and M. *Kulbak in Poland; and L. *Kvitko, D. *Hofshtein, A. *Kushnirov, and E. *Fininberg in the Soviet Union. They were joined by poets who identified themselves wholly or partially with the new poetic current. As the first impulse died down in the 1920s, the expressionistic tenor grew less extreme, but it left traces on the whole of Yiddish poetry.

THE SOVIET UNION. The desire for solutions, for identification, and for belonging led many of the poets of this generation to the belief that the Soviet Revolution could solve both the social and the national problems of humanity. Most of the Jewish writers in the Soviet Union – including those who left it after the Revolution and returned a few years later – as well as many in Poland, Romania, the U.S., and other centers of Jewish literature, attached great hopes to the Soviet regime. They believed in the continued development of a secular Jewish culture in Yiddish, which took the form in the U.S.S.R. of a school network with Yiddish as the language of instruction, research institutes, theaters, and ramified publishing activity, established with governmental and public finance during the 1920s. As early as the 1930s, however, these expectations were disappointed with the decline and contraction of this cultural activity which, it had been hoped, was to serve as a firm basis for the development of Yiddish literature. Even worse was the constant ideological pressure which was exerted on Yiddish literature, as on other national literatures in that country, because of the Communist Party's desire to transform literature into a propaganda medium and its demand for loyalty to the constantly changing political line, including the struggle against "deviations" which mostly were regarded as "nationalist" and "chauvinist." Yiddish writing and cultural institutions were also impoverished by their forced severance from Hebrew language and literature, from the Jewish past, and even from contemporary Yiddish culture and literature in other countries (unless their content was completely identified with the Soviet regime).

Ideological pressures and incarceration behind the frontiers of the Soviet Union not only limited the opportunities of Yiddish literature but, in practice, annulled some of its great achievements for the sake of a programmatic, declarative, unambiguous, shallow poetry and a prose obedient to the "principles" of socialist realism. Yiddish literature was also affected by the arrest and liquidation of some of its most important writers who had lived and worked in most of the geographical areas from which modern Yiddish literature had emerged. Among those who disappeared or were silenced even as early as the 1930s was the lyricist Izi *Kharik, although he was faithful to the revolution. Moyshe *Kulbak was distinguished not only for his poetry but also for his modernistic prose and drama while he still lived in Poland (until 1928). Kulbak completed and published in the Soviet Union his novel *Zelmenyaner* (1: 1931, 2: 1935) – one of the most original works in Soviet Yiddish prose and the only one with topical, satirical, and grotesque elements.

After a brief lull at the end of the 1930s and the comparative freedom of expression which reigned during World War II, in the course of which Yiddish authors were permitted to express their emotions at the catastrophe which was destroying millions of their people, all remnants of Yiddish cultural activity were suppressed in the Soviet Union by the end of 1948. Most of the Yiddish authors were imprisoned and accused of anti-Soviet and Jewish "nationalist" activity. On August 12, 1952, the most important Yiddish authors were executed. Among the victims during those years were: Perets Markish, whose extensive literary heritage included poems giving powerful expression to sincere and sublime social and national feelings, side by side with expressive lyrical verse, and who managed before his arrest to embody his lament for the Holocaust of World War II in wide-ranging epic verse in his book *Milkhome* ("War," 1948); D. Hofshteyn (*Hofstein), one of the most important lyric poets; L. *Kvitko, a poet who expressed himself in a most original manner in the 1920s and was later distinguished for his children's verse; I. *Fefer, one of the leading representatives of the ideological tendencies of Soviet Yiddish poetry; D. *Bergelson, the former impressionist, a talented novelist and short story writer. Another victim of the first rank was Pinkhes Kahanovitsh, known by his curious pseudonym Der *Nister ("Hidden One"), outstanding until 1929 for his original symbolist stories, who, after seeking new paths that would placate Soviet criticism, started writing his novel *Di Mishpokhe Mashber* ("The Mashber Family," vol. 1 (Moscow, 1939; New York. 1943); vol. 2 (New York, 1948)); he managed to publish two volumes of this extensive, quasi-realistic epic, in which he diagnosed the disintegration of late 19th-century East European Jewish society. Among the victims of the last liquidation was the lyric poet and talented dramatist, Shmuel *Halkin, who came out of prison a sick man and died a few years after his release.

POLAND. Poland, with its periphery in Romania in the south and Lithuania in the north, was the main center of Yiddish literature in this period. Independent and vital, it was the main source from which Yiddish literature overseas could draw after World War I. Most characteristic of the literary center in Poland is the natural growth of Yiddish literature in its Jewish community that, with its long history and tradition, still largely preserved its Jewish character. Even among those social circles in Polish Jewry which abandoned the tradition of their fathers in its religious manifestations, there were sincere efforts to find ways of ensuring the continued survival of the new Jew. For a considerable part of the community and its authors, the very existence of a modern Yiddish literature expressed an attachment to tradition which had assumed a new form in their time. In Poland, Yiddish folklore lived in all its forms. The popular literature of previous generations, both religious and secular, was alive, and new works of the same type were born. Under the aegis of this cultural continuity, the new literature in Yiddish became a vital community asset and was regarded as worthy of admiration and subject for lively discussion. Despite the natural antagonisms between generations, differences in taste and attitude, parents and children in Poland still sat together to read Yiddish literature.

Yiddish literature in Poland was characterized by a rich variety of ideological, political and literary trends, temperaments and forms of expression during the brief period that preceded the destruction of Polish Jewry. The novelists and short-story writers whose careers started before World War I – H.D. *Nomberg, Z. *Segalovitsh, I.J. Trunk, Y.M. Vaysnberg, and others – continued to write, and they were joined by a younger generation – M. Burshteyn, Y. Grin, Sh. *Horontchik, E. *Kaganowski, I.J. *Singer and his brother Y. *Bashevis-Singer, A. Katsizne [*Kacyzne], L. Olitsky, Y. *Perle, L. *Rashkin, Y. *Rabon, Y. *Warshavsky, M. Altman in Romania, Y. Kaplan in Lithuania, and others. Their prose was realistic, with strong tendencies to naturalism. Their trials and tribulations as Jews were almost their principal subject.

Yiddish poets appeared in all parts of Poland: Z. Bagish, Y. *Emiot (Goldwasser), B. *Heller, M. Knapheys, L. Kenigsberg (*Koenigsberg), Y. Kirman, K. Lis, K. *Molodowsky, L. Morgentay, B.L. and M. *Olitsky; Y. *Rubinshtein, S. *Shayevitsh, Kh. Semyatitski [*Siemiatycki], M. Shulsteyn, Y. *Shtern, M. Ulyanover [*Ulianover], S. Zaromb, A. Tseytlin [*Zeitlin], and others. Distinctive tones were added by poets from Galicia, Romania, and Bessarabia: Y. Ashndorf [*Ashendorf], L. Bartish, N. *Bomze, Ade [Ada] Cohen, M. Gebirtig, Y. Groper, B. Horovits [*Horowitz], R. Zhikhlinski [*Zychlinska], M. Karats, Y.Y. Lerner, D. Fogel, Y. Gotlib [J. *Gottlieb], R.*Korn, M. Saktsier, Y. Shudrick, Y. Shternberg [J. *Sternberg], M. Shiml, B. Shnaper [*Schnapper], and from Lithuania, N. Dimantshteyn. The *Yung Vilna* group, which was formed in the 1930s included H. Glik [*Glick], Ch. *Grade, S. *Kaczerginsky, A Sutskever [*Sutzkever], E. Vogler, L. Volf [*Wolf], and others. These (and other) poets represent a broad spectrum of poetical work on a high standard, from the simple, lively poem to intellectual poetry in search of meaning, trenchant in its images and personal symbols, and characterized by great skill in composition and linguistic innovation.

It is difficult to evaluate the achievements of this flood of creative activity, especially as many of the writers fell victim to the Holocaust in their youth before reaching the age at which they would likely have published their best work and before collecting in book form work scattered in periodicals. Others perished before they had developed their talents to the full. Nevertheless, mention should be made of several points specific to Yiddish literature in Poland and the neighboring countries between the two world wars, particularly of new departures created against the background of the cultural continuity from which they sprang.

The great Yiddish lyric poet Itsik *Manger came to Poland from Romania and during his Polish period wrote his major works, *Medresh Itsik: Khumesh-Lider* ("Itsik's Midrash: Pentateuch Poems," Warsaw, 1935) and *Megile-Lider* ("Scroll Songs," Warsaw, 1936), which constitute a continuation of the tradition of poetical adaptations from the Scriptures. The main novelty of these poems is the transference of the biblical characters, together with their actions, to the neighborhood, milieu, conceptions, and idiomatic – often regional – language of the East European Jews. Manger's *Medresh*, in a simple meter close to that of the folk song, is full of humor and rich in imagination, charming with its graceful and melancholy strains. M. Ulyanover, who perished in the Lodz ghetto, wrote modern poems in the tradition of the *Tkhine* and of traditional religious poetry: *Mayn Bobes Oytser* ("My Grandmother's Treasure," Warsaw, 1922).

E. Shtaynbarg [*Steinbarg] in Romania cultivated the fable in Yiddish and achieved a high level of virtuosity in this traditional literary genre that he based on the Jewish milieu

In the spring of 1909 members of the Ahuzat Bayit association met on a sandy area northeast of Jaffa for a drawing of the lottery that would distribute plots of land to build a Jewish neighborhood. *Photo by A. Soskin, Courtesy Eretz Israel Museum, Tel Aviv.*

THE TERM ZIONISM FIRST APPEARED AT THE END OF THE 19TH CENTURY TO DENOTE THE MOVEMENT TO REESTABLISH THE JEWISH HOMELAND IN EREẒ ISRAEL. OVER THE PAST CENTURY, THE NATION OF ISRAEL HAS EXPERIENCED ONE OF THE MOST MIRACULOUS TRANSFORMATIONS IN HUMAN HISTORY. NOWHERE IS THIS MORE CLEARLY REVEALED THAN IN THE VAST DEVELOPMENTS IN ISRAEL'S ARCHITECTURE AND URBAN LANDSCAPE. OFFERED HERE ARE SOME STUNNING BEFORE-AND-AFTER VIEWS OF THE GROWTH OF ISRAEL AS WELL AS SOME OF THE FACES OF ISRAEL'S CITIZENS, WHO HAIL FROM MORE THAN ONE HUNDRED COUNTRIES.

ZIONISM

Nine decades after the lottery of 1909, the large city of Tel Aviv-Jaffa stands on former sandy areas along the Mediterranean coast. The site of the historic lottery gathering is located at the intersection of Rothschild Boulevard and Nahalat Binyamin Street. *Photo: Albatross Aerial Photography.*

TOP: A view of the town of Eilat in its early years (early 1950s). The photograph was taken from the mountains west of the town. The Gulf of Eilat is to the right; in the far background are the Jordanian town of Aqaba and the mountains above it. To the left (north) is the Aravah valley extending all the way to the Dead Sea.

BOTTOM: Eilat in the early 21st century is mostly a tourist-economy town. It boasts a vast hotel area surrounding a man-made lagoon at the head of the Gulf of Eilat. Large numbers of tourists come to the resort town to enjoy its warm sea. Eilat has developed tremendously from the frontier town it was in the early 1950s. *Photo: Albatross Aerial Photography.*

Israelis originally from Kurdistan celebrating the Mimouna festival in Jerusalem. *Photo: David Harris.*

(opposite page) TOP: Mikveh Israel postcard from the Third Zionist Congress celebrating the creation of an innovative agriculture school where different species of fruits and trees were grown. *Photo: The Central Zionist Archive, Jerusalem.*

(this page) LEFT: A very early Jewish National Fund (J.N.F.) certificate given to a donor at the Fifth Zionist Congress in Basel, 1901, for planting olive trees in Ereẓ Israel. *Photo: The Central Zionist Archive, Jerusalem.*

(this page) RIGHT: Herzl's vision at the First Zionist congress at Basel, 1897: declaring "If you wish it, it is no legend." *Photo: The Central Zionist Archive, Jerusalem.*

Breaking the ground for the new site of the Dead Sea Works at the southern end of the Dead Sea in 1949. In 1948 the plant at the northern end of the sea was evacuated due to Israel's War of Independence. The Dead Sea is to the right, Mount Sodom to the left.
Photo: The Central Zionist Archive, Jerusalem.

The Dead Sea tourist area with its very special landscape. *Photo: Albatross Aerial Photography.*

TOP: On August 1, 1939, Jewish laborers in Bat Yam load gravel onto pack camels for use in building sites. *Photo by Zoltan Kluger/GPO via Getty Images.*

BOTTOM: Bat Yam on May 29, 2006. With its high rise hotels and apartment buildings built on the beaches of the Mediterranean Sea, Bat Yam has become a popular tourist destination. It is also a thriving suburban city with a population of more than 130,000 residents. *Photo by Joe Raedle/Getty Images.*

and its deeply rooted cultural traditions. A. Tseytlin, who fought against the expressionists, though he too shared similar tendencies, found in Jewish mysticism sources of inspiration for his poetry and plays. The poetry of Y. Shtern [I.*Shtern], who was associated with the expressionists, is imbued with a pantheistic sensitivity and a longing for religious faith based on an emotional attachment to the teachings of R. *Naḥman of Bratslav. Kh. Grade, in his poem "Musernikes" ("Moralists," 1939), brought to Yiddish literature the world of the seminary students and the traditional scholarship of the *Misnagdim*, who until then had received only marginal attention in Yiddish. Y. Bashevis-Singer found in *Der Sotn fun Goray* ("Satan in Goray," 1932) new solutions in the consolidation and stylization of popular narrative literature. Tseytlin, Manger, and Sutskever also ventured at stylized adaptations of the language and forms of pre-18th century Yiddish poetry. This introversion and deliberate return to earlier literary traditions was a new trend in Yiddish literature, one not fully realized before the Holocaust, which destroyed the communities that gave birth to the Yiddish works in which the tendency was so clearly marked.

There was a wide range of writing in the ghettos of World War II where many authors were incarcerated. Only a small part of the work of the writers killed by the Nazis has survived, having been saved with great devotion and almost by miracle. Among those are the prose fragments by Y. Perle (Warsaw ghetto), stories by Y. *Shpigl (Lodz ghetto), the poems of S. Shayevitsh (Lodz ghetto), a few poems by M. Gebirtig (Cracow ghetto), Hershele Danilevits (Warsaw ghetto), and H. Glik (Vilna ghetto). Above all, the songs and poems, biblical plays, and diary of Yitskhok Katsenelson, who continued the tradition of writing in Hebrew and Yiddish both in the Warsaw ghetto at the brink of death and in the Vittel camp, are an authentic testimony from the valley of death, standing beyond any mere literary evaluation. Ghetto literature found its most agonizing expression in Katzenelson's great lament "Dos Lid fun Oysgehargetn Yidishn Folk" ("The Song of the Murdered Jewish People") which was completed in the concentration camp at the beginning of 1944, in full and appalling knowledge of the destruction of Polish Jewry.

A few writers, like A. Sutskever, R. Briks, and Y. Shpigl – who personally witnessed the destruction of their people, but survived – embody in their work from the ghetto period and the years following the liberation (which is also overshadowed by the Holocaust) the continuity and endurance of Yiddish literature in the face of the extinction which overcame its most vital center, Polish Jewry.

THE UNITED STATES. The most important branch of Yiddish literature outside Eastern Europe between the two world wars was in the United States, especially in New York, where the leading Yiddish writers outside Eastern Europe were concentrated. The literary traditions of the 1890s were represented by older dramatists and novelists like D. *Pinski, O. *Dimov, and A. *Reisen, the poet and short-story writer; the members of the *Di Yunge* group, most of whom had abandoned the symbolist outlook after World War I, continued to write; for many years the founders of the *In Zikh* group and their associates maintained their contacts and in 1929 the *Prolet-pen* organization, which for a short time united the authors of the communist camp, was established. From time to time other sporadic groupings of writers with similar literary, social, and political outlooks arose, but they did not persevere even in maintaining joint periodicals. These external manifestations, however, which are sometimes regarded as a sign of the vitality of Yiddish literature in the U.S., are of secondary importance in comparison with the great achievements of the writers themselves.

In American Yiddish poetry of this period we find the rich lyricism and longings for redemption in the poetic and visionary dramas of H. Leyvik [*Leivick]; the imaginative poetry of M.-L. *Halpern, A. *Glanz-Leyeles, and Y. Glatshteyn [*Glatstein], with its variety of conflicts; the profound enquiry into personal and national problems in the poetry of M. Boreyshe [*Boraisha], with its broad epic scope; the identification with the landscapes of the U.S. in the narrative and idyllic poetry of Y.Y. Shvarts [I.J.*Schwartz]. We must take into account the poetry of E. Oyerbakh [*Auerbach], B. Alkvit, B.Y. Byalostotski [B.J. *Bialostotzky], A. Berger, A.-M. Dilon [*Dillon], Ts. Drapkin [C. *Dropkin], R. Ayzland [*Iceland], L. Faynberg [*Feinberg], Al. Guria (G. Grafshteyn), H. Gold, E. Grinberg [*Greenberg], Y. Heshels, M. Yofe, A. *Katz, Y. Kisin, B. Kopshteyn, H. Kuperman, Z. Landoy [*Landau], B. *Lapin, R. Ludvig [*Ludwig], A. Lutski [*Lutzki], A. Lyesin [*Liessin], *Mani-Leib, A. *Margolin, L. Miler [*Miller], N.B. Minkof [*Minkoff], M. *Nadir, A. Nisenson [*Nissenson], G. Prayl [*Preil], H. Rosenblat [*Rosenblatt], Y.[J.] *Rolnik, S. *Shvarts, Y.Y. Segal, E. Shumyatsher [*Shumiatcher], A. Stoltsnberg, F. Shtock, A.B. Tabatshnik [*Tabachnik], A. Tverski, Y. Teler [I. *Teller], M.Z. Tkatsh [*Tkatch], R. Veprinski, Z. Vayner [Weiner], B. Vaynshteyn [*Weinstein], Y.A. Vaysman, Yehoyesh (*Yehoash), N. *Yud, and many others, the clear personal imprint of whose work distinguishes most of them and places Yiddish poetry in the U.S., especially its great lyrical works, above and beyond the limitations of any literary or ideological school with which they may have identified at any particular time. Yiddish writing in the U.S. also excelled in the novel and the short story: the historical novels and tales of Y.[J.] *Opatoshu; the wide-ranging fiction of the immensely popular and much translated Sh. Ash [*Asch]; the great descriptive powers of Z. Shneyer [Shneur] and Y.Y. Zinger [I.J. *Singer]; the stylized prose of L. *Shapiro; and the works of D. *Ignatoff, M.D. Aplboym [Appelbaum], F. Bimko, B. Glazman, B.*Demblin, N. Brusilov, S. Miler [*Miller] and Y. Roznfeld [J. *Rosenfeld]. Notable, too, is the prose of the distinguished poet Y. Glatshteyn [J. *Glatstein].

While the main external influences on Yiddish literature in other centers had been European – especially that of modern literature in the Slavic countries – in the U.S. these were supplemented by "Anglo-Saxon" influences. The U.S. scene, the great city as an intensive poetic experience, and, in prose, the Americanization of the immigrants – both mainly against the background of New York – are also distinctive features of this period in U.S. Yiddish literature. At the same time, all these local elements were strongly affected by traditional influences and by the problems and tendencies of Yiddish literature in Eastern Europe. The same applied to other centers of immigration nurtured by further waves of immigrant writers and readers. The writers who came from Eastern Europe, who established and still maintain Yiddish literature in its dispersions, did not have the satisfaction – with few isolated and insignificant exceptions – of witnessing the growth of a new generation of Yiddish authors and readers among the native-born children of the immigrants. As a result of the movement of the immigrants and the inability to establish a new generation of readers and writers, Yiddish literature in the U.S. and other overseas countries has continued to be dependent on the countries of its origins. A fervent desire to strike deeper roots in the new centers and important literary achievements which testify to the partial attainment of this aim have not altered this fact.

This problem has been even more obvious since World War II and the destruction of East European Jewry. The authors feel a growing bond with the vanished communities in which they were born – a need to grasp the full meaning of all that was involved in the old Jewry of Europe and erect a monument to its memory, or a desire to find a direct expression for the events themselves. Hence there has again been an increase in the proportion of prose, in the form of numerous books dealing with memories of the past, as well as novels and stories with an obvious autobiographical element. With all the differences in style and narrative skill in this memoiristic literature, there is a palpable effort to remain simple, eschewing novelty or surprise in structure or in narrative point of view beyond the unconcealed "I" of the author or the anonymous narrator whose identity is clear. Parallel with this tendency in prose is a similar tendency in poetry to forego experimentation or innovation and to return to closed metrical forms. This verse also deepens and fully exploits the linguistic and stylistic resources and the mainly traditional imagery which had been mastered by modernistic Yiddish poetry from the beginning of the 20th century.

The works of the authors who reached the U.S. from Poland immediately before, during, or after the war period and who followed these tendencies, mark the most important achievements of this literary center. Paramount among them are the autobiographical epic *Poyln* (7 vols., 1944–57) by Y.Y. [I.J.] Trunk, which sums up, with reverence and nostalgia, the life of the last generations in Polish Jewry. The narrative is also a stylized retelling of the folk literature in which the memory of the Holocaust is a dominant theme. The prose and narrative poetry of Kh.[Ch.] Grade perpetuates the memory of his home city, Vilna, with its many strata and internal conflicts, its spiritual greatness and material poverty. The novels and stories of Y. Bashevis (Isaac *Bashevis Singer) have revealed a new Polish Jewry, one in the grip of lusts and superstitions, together with its inner light and messianic yearnings.

Branches of Yiddish literature multiplied in all the countries to which Jews emigrated from Eastern Europe. Centers such as Berlin and Vienna in the 1920s, or Germany, Austria, and Italy after World War II were clearly transitory from the beginning and disappeared after a few years. Other branches in Europe, in Canada, Latin America (Argentina in particular), South Africa, and Australia, though much shrunken, still exist. The above-mentioned problems of Yiddish literature apply to countries of immigration as well, perhaps even more markedly than to the U.S.; their achievements, especially after World War II, are largely the work of refugee authors from Central or Eastern Europe.

PALESTINE / ISRAEL. Even though Hebrew was the sole recognized language in the resettlement of Palestine, a branch of Yiddish literature was established there quite early. Yiddish writing in the Ashkenazi community in Palestine dates back at least to the 16th century in the form of letters preserved in the Cairo *Geniza*. There were special works in Yiddish in the 17th and 18th centuries describing Erets-Yisroel (*Geliles Erets-Yisroel* [Galilot Erets-Yisrael], "Districts of the Land of Israel," 1635; *Yedey Moyshe* [Yedey Moshe], "The Hands of Moses," 1769), which were followed, at the beginning of the 20th century, by travelogues of Erets-Yisroel by Sh. Ash [Asch] and Yehoyesh [Yehoash] The first signs of writing in Yiddish for its inhabitants in modern times, however, may be seen in the appearance of the periodical *Di Roze* (1877). This and other periodicals that succeeded it, as well as the few books and brochures of various ideological leanings that were published in the country up to World War I do not form links in a continuing chain. It is only after World War I that there emerged in Palestine a group of authors who devoted themselves to Yiddish. They adhered generally to the labor movement and tried, despite the vigorous antagonism to Yiddish among the majority of the new Jewish community, to maintain a distinctive literary movement through a series of literary periodicals and the publication of books by local Yiddish authors. While this activity was long marginal in relation to the major centers of Yiddish literature in Eastern Europe and the U.S., Yiddish creative activity steadily grew after World War II and the establishment of the State of Israel and *changes in the status and importance of this new center became visible.*

It is natural that Yiddish literature in Israel should be more closely attached to the recent past in Eastern Europe than contemporary Hebrew writing, which has already produced several generations of authors who, born and bred in the country, have lost contact with their parents' milieu and traditions. At the same time, Yiddish literature in Israel has developed a new and immediate tie with the new homeland, nourished by and based on former traditions in Jewish culture. The landscape and rebuilding of the country served as the central element in the work of Y.[J.] *Papiernikov]. The most veteran of these poets, he had been writing in the country since the 1920s. The efforts of the *khalutsim* ("pioneers") and life in the *kibbutz* ("collective settlement") have found original expression in the poems of A. *Shamri and A *Lev. New dimensions in the attachment to the Land of Israel as the momentous realization of the resurrection of the generation which directly experienced the Holocaust appear in the post-1947 poems of A. Sutskever. This feeling is characteristic not only of Yiddish literature written within the State of Israel, but is also a prominent theme in the works of many Yiddish writers who, having visited the country, write about it from abroad.

From the 1940s, a varied group of authors lived in cities and kibbutzim in Israel. Among them were: R. *Basman, Y. Birshteyn, H. *Binyomin, S. Berlinski, T. Ayznman, M. Gorin, Y. *Hofer, B. Heler [*Heller], M. *Yungman, L. Olitski [*Olitzky], R. Potash, R. Fishman, A.-M. Fuks [*Fuchs], Ka-Tsetnik [*Ka-Zetnik] (Dinur), Y. Kaplan, A. *Karpinovitsh, M. Mali, M. Man [Mann], Y. Mastboym [J. *Mastbaum], L. Rokhman [*Rochman], Hadase [Hadassah] *Rubin, A. Ribes, Y. Stol, S. Shenhud, A. *Shpiglblat [Spiegelblatt], S. Vorzoger. In 1971 they were joined by poets who came from the U.S.S.R. – R. Boymvol, Y. *Kerler, and Z. Telesin. Though younger on the average than in other centers, at the turn of the century most of the above-named were no longer among the living and the youngest were well into their seventies.

The 1970s and After

For more than a decade after the "liquidations," no original Yiddish works were published in the Soviet Union, but between 1959 and 1970 a few dozen books were issued; from 1961, the literary periodical *Sovetish *Heymland* appeared in Moscow. Despite the obvious talent of some of the contributors to this periodical who survived the "liquidations," there does not seem to be a single writer among them of the stature of their masters and colleagues who met their death during Stalin's last years. *Sovetish Heymland* ceased to appear in 1991 but was soon followed by *Di Yidishe Gas*, also edited by Aaron *Vergelis (1993–97). Morally discredited by many in the Yiddish world, Vergelis continues to have his defenders who see him as an outstanding if difficult and complex personality who made extreme compromises to keep Yiddish writing alive in the Soviet Union.

A small group of writers held their ground in Poland after the Holocaust and continued to bring out a few publications. There too, however, with its small Jewish community, Yiddish literature was a rootless remnant of the pre-Holocaust period and was, to all intents and purposes, completely destroyed in the wave of antisemitism inspired by the Polish government after the Six-Day War. Dozens of authors from Poland and Romania succeeded in leaving these lands during the late 1960s. They reinforced the overseas branches as a continuation of the postwar stream of emigration. However, the Holocaust and the liquidation of Jewish culture in the Soviet Union at the end of 1948, following upon the closing of Russia's gates from the 1920s to the 1970s, blocked the potential human and cultural resources from Eastern Europe which have been almost solely responsible for maintaining the new branches. While in the beginning of the 19th century Yiddish literature was transferred from Western to Eastern Europe, its main centers today remain the U.S. and Israel, reinvigorated as in past decades by East European emigrants who had preserved their connections to Yiddish language and literature. Yiddish letters in the early 21st century are still being fed by the influx to Israel during the 1970s of Yiddish writers from Eastern Europe.

[Chone Smeruk / Leonard Prager (2nd ed.)]

While much of the world tended to forget about or simply ignore the Holocaust for many decades following World War II, the subject continued to be (or became) a primary focus for Yiddish writers everywhere, who have in the ensuing decades produced documentary evidence, memoirs, reports, diaries, fiction, poetry, and other writings directly or indirectly related to the Holocaust. As a result, no serious and comprehensive research on the Holocaust may avoid a profound engagement with this massive corpus of Yiddish-language material now available in published form or in archives.

The dedication of the Leyvik House in Tel Aviv in 1971 by the Israeli prime minister, Golda *Meir (a Yiddish-speaking immigrant from the U.S.), held out the hope of a united Yiddish international community transcending old ideological blinkers. But these blinkers were still in place when Israel's leading Yiddish poet Avrom Sutskever in greeting the World Conference for Yiddish in Jerusalem in 1976 expressed the hope on the opening page of *Di Goldene Keyt* (vol. 90 (1976)) "az tsuzamen mitn tkhies-hameysim funem folk un zayn tate-loshn, vet oykh oyfgeyn in fuler prakht, vi a regn-boygn nokh a regn fun trern-zayn mame-loshn" ("that together with the rebirth of our people and its father-tongue, will also rise in its full splendor, like a rainbow after a rain of tears – its mother-tongue"). Expressions such as these brought tears to the eyes of many, but momentous changes were not to follow.

Nonetheless, all three Yiddish publishers in Tel Aviv – Perets, Hamenora, Yidish Bukh – were active; Yiddish writers from the Diaspora continued to settle in Israel; and Yiddish found a warm home at the Hebrew University where Dov *Sadan and Chone *Shmeruk and their students were changing the face of Yiddish studies, in league with the Columbia University disciples of father-and-son, Max and Uriel *Weinreich and their students at leading universities the world over. This academization has continued and has prospered, but in August 2005 at the 14th World Congress of Jewish Studies in Jerusalem, Israeli Yiddish scholars were barely a quorum among the 1,200 participants. On the other hand, while aware of their small numbers, they knew, too, that they represented a recognized and valued discipline in the larger Judaica Studies universe.

With the influx of established Yiddish writers from Eastern Europe throughout the 1970s, Israel replaced the U.S. as the center of Yiddish literary creativity. The integration of these writers into the new environment is reflected in their increasing use of Israeli themes. The earlier writers preferred to settle in the Tel Aviv area, where the three major Yiddish publishing firms were situated, and where the most prestigious Yiddish literary organ, the quarterly *Di* **Goldene Keyt* ("The Golden Chain"), was published (1949–95). But in the 1970s writers from Eastern Europe began settling in Jerusalem, making it an ever-growing focal point of Yiddish literary activity.

Yerushalaimer Almanakh ("Jerusalem Almanac"), founded in 1973 as the organ of the Jerusalem Yiddish Writers' Association by Yoysef *Kerler (ed.-in-chief, 1973–98), with co-editors David *Sfard (1974–82) and Efroyim Shidletski (1982–92), continued to expand from year to year. The founding editor's son, Yiddish poet and scholar Dov-Ber Kerler (co-editor, 1993–98, and current editor), edited vol. 27 (2003). Twenty-seven substantial volumes in 30 years under conditions of uncertain funding is no small achievement. The 27th volume was issued in partnership with Vilna University's Vilnius Yiddish Institute and the Yung-Yidish ("Young-Yiddish") Center in Jerusalem, both financially vulnerable institutions. However, perusal of the list of contributors to the last issue yields enough names of younger writers to assure that at least for another decade or two there will be no shortage of Yiddish-writing authors. The older readership, of course, continues to decline and the recruitment of a generation of young readers is slow and uncertain.

In 1977 the Yiddish Cultural Association in Jerusalem established the Hurvits Prize for the publication of Yiddish manuscripts by new immigrants. The first work chosen was Meyer Yelin's *Blut un Vofn* ("Blood and Weapons," 1978), sketches and short stories based on the author's experiences and observations in the Kovno ghetto, continuing in the spirit of his earlier volume of short stories, *Der Prays fun Yenem Broyt* ("The Price of That Bread," 1977). His was a fairly typical case of a Soviet writer who emigrated to Israel, became acclimated after the usual immigrant's absorption difficulties, and both published books in Yiddish and saw some of his work translated into Hebrew.

The 1970s could also boast of a thriving literary journal in Tel Aviv, the quarterly *Bay Zikh* ("At Home") that was founded in 1972 as the organ of new-immigrant writers, the work of 13 of whom filled the first issue; subsequent issues included contributions by long-time residents in Israel. The Prime Minister's Prize for Yiddish Literature, established by Golda Meir during her premiership, was awarded in 1976 to the much-honored Avrom Sutskever, and in the following year to the editor of *Bay Zikh*, Yitskhok Yanasovitsh, for his three volumes of essays, *Penimer un Nemen* ("Faces and Names," 1971–5). The journal expired in 1989; its publisher was the Komitet far yidishe kultur in Yisroel ("Committee for Yiddish Culture in Israel").

The Israel Yiddish Writers Association gave recognition and awards in 1976 to Hadase *Rubin, Yosl Lerner, and A. *Shpiglblat, and in 1977 to Ovadye Fels, Nakhmen Rap, Sh. Roytman, and Y. Kaplan. Rap's short stories and sketches, *In Veg tsum Altn Man* ("To the Old Man," 1976), and Roytman's sonnets and lyric poems on Israel, *Mayn Yisroeldik Shoyferl* ("My Israeli Shofar," 1976) deal with contemporary themes, whereas Kaplan's short stories, *Tsaytnshnit* ("Harvest of an Era," 1976), reflect nostalgia for a destroyed Jewish world that barely survives in Jerusalem's Mea She'arim quarter.

Among the most prestigious Israeli Prizes for Yiddish literary and other arts is that named after the great lyric poet Itsik Manger. Its recipients are among the finest Yiddish talents of the period: in 1976 poets Arye *Shamri and Leyzer Aykhenrand; in 1977 poets Hirsh Osherovitsh and Yankev-Tsvi Shargel and the Montreal novelist Yehude Elberg; in 1978 poets Uri Zevi *Greenberg (who wrote in Hebrew and Yiddish), Meyer Shtiker, U.S.-born Rokhl Fishman, novelist Eli *Shekhtman, essayist and editor Mortkhe Shtrigler (Mordecai *Strigler), and famed singer Nehamah *Lifshitz; in 1979 Shloyme Rotman, Shimshen Meltser, Shloyme Shenhod, Avrom Zak and novelist Khave Roznfarb [*Rosenfarb]. In 1980 Tsvi Ayznman, Yitskhok Yanasovitsh, Nakhmen Rap and Shimen-Yisroel Dunski won the prize.

Within a few years after arriving in Israel from the Soviet Union, Hirsh Osherovitsh published several volumes of verse, including *Gezang in Labirint* ("Songs in the Labyrinth," 1977) which consisted almost entirely of poems about Israel which he was unable to publish in the Soviet Union, even though he had served on the editorial staff of *Sovyetish Heymland*; in Paris in 1977 he garnered the Ganopolski Prize. Yehude Elberg, a survivor of the Warsaw ghetto and best known for his novel on the subject *Oyfn Shpits Fun a Mast* ("On the Tip of a Mast," 1974), published in 1976 a collection of his stories *Tsevorfene Zangen* ("Scattered Stalks") that were indeed scattered among periodicals. Eli *Shekhtman, recognized as the foremost novelist among the Soviet immigrants (recipient of the Zhitlovski Prize in 1976, the Eliezer Pines Prize in 1977 and the Itsik Manger Prize in 1978) published Erev ("On the Eve"), his prose epic of Russian-Jewish life from 1905 through the 1970s (first published in a censored version, Moscow 1965), then later in a complete version, Tel Aviv, vols. 1–4, 1974; vols. 5–6, 1979; vol. 7, 1983), followed by *Ringen oyf der Neshome* ("Links on the Soul," 4 vols. 1981–8), and *Tristia* ("Sadness," 1996).

Mordekhay Tsanin, founding editor of Israel's Yiddish newspaper (a weekly now) *Letste Nayes* ("Last News"), a heroic figure in the struggle for Yiddish in Israel, was also a novelist and essayist of distinction. From 1966 to 1985 he published his *Artopanus Kumt Tsurik Aheym* ("Artopanus Returns Home"), a series of six historical novels centering about Artopanus, the wandering Jew, and covering 2,000 years of Jewish experience. The fourth of these books, *Di Meride in Mezhibozh* ("The Revolt of Mezhibozh," 1976), deals with the rise of the Ḥasidic movement in the 18th century. (Tsanin also compiled useful Hebrew–Yiddish (1960) and Yiddish–Hebrew dictionaries (1982)).

The Mendele Moykher-Sforim Prizes for Yiddish Literature established in 1976 by the Tel Aviv Municipality were awarded to the poet Bunem Heler [*Heller] and the prose writer Avrom *Karpinovitsh. In the same year the Yankev Glatshteyn Prize of the World Jewish Culture Congress was awarded to the novelist of the Holocaust Yeshayohu *Shpigl and the poet and literary critic Yitskhok Goldkorn. Within a few years after arrival in Israel, Meyer Kharats published four volumes of verse, including *Shtern oyfn Himl* ("Stars in the Sky," 1977). In 1976 he had been encouraged by receipt of the Yankev Fikhman Prize for Literature; the essayist and authority on the folklore of the Hebrew alphabet Eliezer Lipiner won this prize in 1977. The Czernowitz poet and painter Khayim Zeltser published *Fun Heymishn Brunem* ("From My Fountain," 1976), his second volume of poetry since his arrival in Israel. These include satiric ballads, poems of his suffering under the Soviets and of his new life in Israel.

Moyshe Yungman's lyrics *In Land fun Eliyohu Hanovi* ("In Elijah's Land," 1977); Kalman Segal's narratives, *Aleynkeyt* ("Loneliness," 1977); Efroim Roytman's poems, *Di Erd Zingt* ("The Earth Sings," 1977); Motl Saktsier's lyrics, *Mit Farbotenem Blayer* ("Forbidden Writings," 1977); Rokhl Boymvol's songs of nostalgia and reborn hope, *Fun Lid tsu Lid* ("From Song to Song"); and Rokhl Oyerbakh's [*Auerbakh] reminiscences of the Warsaw Ghetto, *Baym Letstn Veg* ("The Last Road," 1977) are among the rich crop of Yiddish books issued in Israel in 1977, a fairly typical year in the 1970s and 1980s.

Prizes, both for their material and their morale value have always been important in Yiddish literary life, but no award aroused as much interest as did the 1978 Nobel Prize for literature. The entire Yiddish world was cheered when Yitskhok Bashevis (known in America as Isaac Bashevis Singer) won this prize, the first and only time a Yiddish author had been so honored. Yet among a coterie of sophisticates, it was murmured that the prize was not for the Yiddish Bashevis, but for the translated, reworked, Americanized Singer, a perspective argued in *The Hidden Isaac Bashevis Singer* (2002), edited by Seth Wolitz. This line of research had been initiated by Chone Shmeruk who, to cite a single instance, pointed to the censored Jesus reference in Saul *Bellow's generally outstanding translation of "Gimpl Tam," a classic tale misleadingly titled in English "Gimpel the Fool." However, no one who knows Yiddish well, literary gossip aside, can deny the rapid-fire, word-and tone-accurate storytelling genius of Bashevis aka Singer, who was by no means a simple creature.

Yiddish literature continued to age in the 1980s. Almost all its writers were born before the destruction of the Yiddish heartland in Eastern Europe; readers also became fewer. The Yiddish press diminished. The most prestigious daily, the New York **Forverts* (Jewish Daily Forward) was converted in 1982 to a weekly after 85 years of existence. The repertoire of ever fewer theatrical performances consisted of older plays and nostalgic musicals. Novelists, except in Israel, preferred as subject matter the longed-for, destroyed world of yesteryear. Aging survivors of ghettos, Nazi concentration camps, and Soviet gulags published memoirs and narratives of their experiences or participated in Yisker (Yizkor, Memorial) books about perished Jewish communities.

Heroic efforts were made to slow down the decline of Yiddish creativity. Grants, prizes, and awards for Yiddish books multiplied. The World Council for Yiddish and Jewish Culture looked back in 1986 on a decade of support for Yiddish writers, publishers, and journals. Its bilingual annual, *Gesher-Brikn* ("Bridges") featured since 1983 translations of Hebrew works into Yiddish and of Yiddish works into Hebrew. Its monthly organ, *Yidish Velt* ("Yiddish World"), coordinated worldwide Yiddish activities since 1985. In New York the *Biographical Lexicon of Modern Yiddish Literature*, initiated in 1954 by the Central Yiddish Culture Organization (CYCO) was completed in 1981. By then, none of the early editors and administrators (Shmuel *Niger, Yankev Shatski, Moyshe Shtarkman, Yankev Pat, and Khayim Bas) was alive. However, the editors of the final volume, Berl Kagan, Yisroel Noks, and Elye Shulman, succeeded in enlisting 32 writers from all continents for the project, whose eight volumes gave bio-bibliographic entries of more than 7,000 Yiddish writers of the 19th and 20th centuries. In Buenos Aires, Shmuel Rozhanski [Rozhansky] completed in 1984 the editing of the 100 volumes of Masterpieces of Yiddish Literature. The first volume, in 1957, dealt with the pioneer of Yiddish poetry and drama Sh. Etinger (Solomon *Ettinger). The 100th volume bore the symbolic title *Tsu Nayem Lebn* ("Toward A New Life") and consisted of poems, tales, and essays which could serve to counteract the prophets of doom as regards the future of Yiddish.

The 1980s and 1990s may have seen the continued shrinking of the secular Yiddishist community, but significant writing continued to be published, and not only in New York and Tel Aviv. Seven volumes of *Bukarester Shriftn* were completed between 1978 and 1984. Of this annual's editors, Y. Karo, Spanish civil-war veteran Khayim Goldnshteyn and, especially, Volf Tambur, attracted attention with their stories and novels. Leyzer Aykhnrand maintained a lonely Yiddish vigil in Switzerland, where his last poems appeared in 1984, shortly before his death. Yiddish creativity in France was impoverished by the death in 1981 of M. Shulsteyn and B. Shlevin, but the Paris newspaper *Unzer Vort* continued to appear until 1996. In 1980, M. *Waldman published his poems of four decades, *Fun Ale Vaytn* ("From All Distances") and was awarded the Manger Prize in 1983. M. Ram published her short stories *Shteyner* ("Stones") in 1981, was translated into Hebrew and won the Manger Prize in 1984. In 1983 the novelist Y. Finer (pen name of Yitskhok Burshteyn) completed his fictional trilogy *Tsvey Mishpokhes* ("Two Families"). A veteran of the French underground during World War II, much of Finer's fiction deals with the encounter between Polish Jew and native Frenchman. In England, the death in 1983 of Joseph Leftwich and A.N. *Stencl, and in 1984 of Jacob Meitlis removed three strong pillars of Yiddish literature and scholarship and led to the discontinuance of *Loshn un Lebn*, which Stencl had founded and edited since 1946.

In South Africa, the *Yidishe Tsaytung*, edited by Levi Shalit, ceased publication in 1985 but *Dorem Afrike*, edited by Zalmen Levi, continued as the literary organ of the Yiddish writers until 1991. Two of the leading South African Yiddish writers, David *Fram and David Volpe [*Wolpe] continued to publish: Fram's book of poems *A Shvalb Oyfn Dakh* ("A Swallow On the Roof") appeared in 1983 and Volpe published his collected essays in 1984. In Australia, *Melburner Bleter* served as the sole literary organ for its few Yiddish writers, but Yitskhok Kahn won wider recognition with his essays and Sheve Glas-Viner with her ghetto tales. In Canada, Kh.- L. Fuks [*Fox] edited in 1980 a literary lexicon encompassing 422 Canadian writers in Yiddish and Hebrew.

The closing down of *Di *Goldene Keyt* in 1995 created a vacuum not only in Israel where it was published, but in the entire sparse but far-flung Yiddish world. The brave continuance of such serious journals as *Tsukunft* and *Yidishe Kultur* in New York and *Yerusholaimer Almanakh* in Jerusalem only partially filled the void. In 2000 an Israeli government-subsidized *Natsyonal Instants far Yidisher Kultur* ("National Instance for Yiddish Culture") supported the Tel Aviv literary quarterly – which does not actually appear four times a year – *Toplpunkt* ("Colon"), where the last crop of Soviet-born authors to reach Israel met individual young Yiddish authors from around the world. Nos. 1–5 were edited by Hebrew poet and translator Ya'akov Beser and co-edited by Yisroel Rudnitski, the latter becoming editor with No. 6 (Winter 2003).

Aleksander *Shpiglblat wrote his fine account of his family's incarceration in Transnistria during World War II, *Durkhn Shpaktiv fun a Zeyger-Makher* ("Through the Eye Piece of a Watch Maker," 2000). Two years later this former member of Sutskever's *Di Goldene Keyt* editorial staff published *Bloe Vinklen–Itsik Manger, Lebn, Lid un Balade* ("Blue Corners–Itsik Manger, Life, Song and Ballad"), an informal critical biography of fellow Romanian Itsik Manger and one of the most readable Yiddish books of the year. Shpiglblat is now devoting himself to fiction, having published the three-story collection *Shotns Klapn in Shoyb* ("Shadows Knock on the Window," 2003) and *Krimeve; An Altfrenkishe Mayse* ("Krimeve; An Old-fashioned Story," 2005).

Not all Yiddishists are pessimistic as to the fate of Yiddish. It is increasingly recognized that in the urban enclaves of some ḥasidic sects in London, New York, Jerusalem, Bene-Berak, Antwerp – and rural Kiryas Yoyl [Kiryat Yoel] and New Square – and elsewhere, there is an actual increase in the population of native-speakers of Yiddish. The reading interests (beyond religious texts) of these communities are increasingly being served by a small but growing ḥasidic publication industry that now annually produces scores of novels (including historical novels, adventures tales, even spy thrillers), story collections, children's books, and textbooks, in addition to numerous orthodox newspapers and periodicals that include serial narratives (see "Ḥasidic Lierature" under *Ḥasidism). While the literary quality of these texts has indeed improved over the course of recent years, it is nonetheless currently quite impossible to imagine that anything like the development of post-Enlightenment secular Yiddish literature out of traditional Ashkenazi society might recur in this 21st century Orthodox environment. It is in any case still too early to know what kind of literature can develop in such parochial confines and whether it might be valued beyond the borders of those communities (i.e. among secular Jews, where there is, after all, an ever diminishing audience capable even of reading the texts).

Yiddish creative writing of high quality was not rare in the first decade of the 21st century – against a background of more or less habitual prognostications of the death of the language. In Israel the nonagenarian Avrom Sutskever continued to write. A collection of his poems in Hebrew translation *Kinus Dumiot* ("A Gathering of Silences," 2005) received national attention and reviews in the media. Leading Hebrew-language authors and critics participated in this warm reception, a sign of an altered attitude to Yiddish generally as well as reaffirmed recognition of a poet who had lived in Israel for over half a century and was by virtue of *oeuvre* as well as of residence a pillar of Israeli literary culture.

In mid-2005 the veteran Yiddish weekly *Forverts*, edited in New York by a small, relatively young, and highly motivated staff, is electronically reproduced in Israel and distributed so as to arrive, for instance, at a Haifa subscriber's mailbox on Friday morning, with enlarged font to accommodate the elderly, and containing – in addition to news about Yiddish culture the world over – a novel in parts that is well written and worth reading. A number of literary journals continue to appear. There is a strong interest in translating Yiddish books and many high-quality translations have appeared. While there are few Departments of Yiddish in the world, lone Yiddish scholars grace departments of Jewish Studies or of German in leading universities. Conferences of specialists meet to explore central themes such as the shtetl in Yiddish life and letters, Yiddish literature and the Left, or a single important figure like Bashevis or Bergelson. Such symposia and seminars define the Yiddish scene at the beginning of the 21st century.

One needs to consider not only journals in Yiddish, but those in other languages that are devoted in whole or in part to the study of Yiddish literature. Since 1981, *Prooftexts: A Journal of Jewish Literary History*, edited by Alan Mintz and David Roskies, has brought a hitherto rarely encountered sophistication and seriousness to the understanding of Yiddish and Yiddish-related texts. The journals *Polin, Shofar,* and *Jewish Social Studies* have published significant research on Yiddish literature. *Jiddistik Mitteilungen; Jiddistik in Deutschsprachigen Laendern* is an unfailingly informative German-language bulletin for the field of Yiddish studies. Since 1993, the University of Haifa, with the cooperation of Tel Aviv and Bar-Ilan Universities, has issued a Hebrew-language journal which attempts in many ways to be a revived Hebrew version of the old *Yivo-Bleter – Khulyot: Dapim le-Mekhkar be-Sifrut Yidish ve-Zikoteha le-Sifrut Ivrit* ("Links: Pages for the Study of Yiddish Literature and its Connections to Hebrew Literature") (also spelled *Chulyot*) issued its ninth volume in 2005. The journal has been well received in the Israeli academy, but it must be admitted that the pool of contributors is somewhat narrow and will probably remain so unless Israeli universities prove more welcoming to Yiddish studies than they have been up until now.

The opening years of the 21st century proved receptive to new and revisionist perspectives. Conferences, as mentioned above, have convened to air large themes. In this atmosphere, Yael Chaver could write, "The mainstream culture created a historiography that suppressed the Yiddish culture imported into Palestine with the pioneers who were nurtured in it. However, not only did this culture continue to survive but it also produced significant original work" (See "Outcasts Within: Zionist Yiddish Literature in Pre-State Palestine," *Jewish Social Studies*, 7/2 (2001) 39–66). Dan Miron pitted himself against widespread clichés regarding the greatest of Yiddish comic writers, Sholem-Aleykhem, urging us to look more deeply at the writings of a comic master (*Ha-Ẓad ha-Afel be-Ẓeḥoko shel Shalom-Aleykhem* ("The Dark Side of Shalom-Aleykhem's Laughter")). Almost four decades earlier Miron in his still central study, *A Traveler Disguised* (1968) had altered the way we see Abramovitsh. Among Yiddish linguists there is much debate still as to the origins of Yiddish; Hebrew linguists continue to assess the precise role and weight of Yiddish in the formation of modern Israeli Hebrew. We can expect a new generation of Yiddish scholars to ask new questions and formulate innovative replies.

Much of the life of Yiddish today is "lived" on the internet, where Yiddish has colonized very effectively. The "surfer" interested in Yiddish needs simply to type the word "Yiddish" to be ushered into a cybernetic universe where in addition to a few quality way stations there are also shoddy stops, established by presumably well-intentioned persons who believe they are serving a positive cause but merely misrepresent a language which has its rules and a culture which is immensely rich and not to be summed up in clichés or slogans. It is now possible to communicate in Standard Yiddish (Yiddish with all the correct vocalization) on the internet, to publish listservs and electronic journals, to access rare digitized books in the comfort of one's study. The single most important listserv in the field of Yiddish is Mendele, whose existence began in 1991, followed in 1997 by its literary supplement *The Mendele Review*, now in its ninth year. The website *Di Velt Fun Yidish* ("The World of Yiddish") provides both text and audio of classic Yiddish texts, as well as the entire *Tanakh* ("Hebrew Bible") in the outstanding translation of the famed Yiddish poet Yehoyesh (Yehoash, born Solomon Bloomgarten). This site will trace the development of Yiddish Bible translation from its beginnings in the Old Yiddish period until today. It also boasts a compendious index to all the works of the classic author Sholem-Aleykhem (Shalom Aleichem) and an index (in Hebrew) to Droyanov's classic 3-volume anthology of Jewish humor.

The riches of Yiddish literature are available to all. Will they be claimed?

[Sol Liptzin / Leonard Prager (2nd ed.)]

CONTEMPORARY ḤASIDIC YIDDISH LITERATURE

Ḥasidic Yiddish print culture remains rooted in tradition with religious books at its core, but as ḥasidim adapt to contemporary needs and technologies, the range of commercial publications in Yiddish has expanded to include in-house products that accommodate urban and suburban demands for information and entertainment and thus deter temptation from outside sources. Some ḥasidic sects, such as Satmar, Bobov, Belz, Ungvar, Tash, Skver, and others, have made a conscious decision to use Yiddish as a means of maintaining cultural continuity (in contrast to the Chabad (Lubavitch) and the non-ḥasidic Litvish community). The audience for Yiddish publications is thus a relatively small subset of the overall Orthodox population, most of whom use English and Hebrew as vernaculars. While spanning many countries, the niche market for Yiddish publications is highly localized in a few subculture enclaves, mainly in the New York area and in Israel. Writers and illustrators are from within the community, and publications both capitalize on a *heymish* ("homey") quality and are carefully controlled by rabbinic authorities.

Publishers and distribution systems are small in scale, located mainly in Williamsburg and Boro Park, Brooklyn, and in outlying suburbs of New York City (e.g. Monsey, Kiryas Joel, and New Square). Besides marketing to local readers, they also distribute to Israel, Europe (Antwerp and London), and even Australia and Argentina, either by direct shipment or through a network of local and chain bookshops that cater strictly to ḥasidim. Distribution is also becoming available via the Web, although Yiddish-speaking ḥasidim generally have less Web access than other Orthodox populations. While bookstores stock primarily Hebrew *sforim* for men, small sections for women include Yiddish publications, consisting especially of reprints of Yiddish classic women's texts that have been available for centuries: the *Tsene Urene, musar* (moral) works, and assorted prayer books, in addition to inspirational literature, guides to behavior, and more practical books, as women readers crave reading material of a lighter nature. Some Yiddish publications are translations from Hebrew, while others are Yiddish originals. Despite the fact that entertainment and fiction has traditionally been discouraged, scores of lively novels have appeared in recent decades. The ḥasidic taste for the dramatic has encouraged historical fiction, exotic travel literature, and indeed spy novels. Thus, in *Geknipt un Gebindn* ("Knotted and Bound," Brooklyn: Mekor Chaim Press, 1995), Hayim Rozenberg embellishes a true story of an adopted girl in secular Israel who, with the help of a Christian clerk in the U.S., finds her birth mother and her true religious identity. Soon after the destruction of the Twin Towers, a collection of tales of escape and divine intervention appeared: *Himl Signaln in Teror Geviter; Nitsulim un Martirer in der Shoyderlekher Tragedye in Amerike; der September 11*

("Signals from the Sky in Terror; Victories and Martyrs in the Terrifying Tragedy in America on September 11"). Of course the Holocaust is also an important subject: *Antlofn Di Letste Minit: 1944-1945* ("Escaped at the Last Minute: 1944-1945") by the very popular and prolific writer Yair Weinstock, who produces lengthy thrillers at a rapid pace.

The significance of periodicals in Yiddish literature has not been limited to the secular community, and thus serialized fiction has long thrived in ḥasidic weeklies such as *Der Yid* (Brooklyn; primarily Satmar readership), where the factual history of a kidnapped ḥasidic boy in embellished form appeared as a series, *Vu iz Yosele?* ("Where is Yosele?"). Such series function to promote sales as well as prevent temptation by outside sources of entertainment. Other ḥasidic periodicals published in Brooklyn include *Der Blatt* (for the Satmar faction in Kiryas Joel), the Lubavich-sponsored *Algemeyner Zhurnal*, the weekly *Di Tsaytung* (in English on the masthead: "News Report: The Yiddish Newspaper of Record. Brooklyn"), *Der Blick*, *Dos Yiddishe Vort* from Agudat Israel, and *Di Wokh*, all with local news, weather, and traffic for the New York area, but also including international politics and ḥasidic affairs. The magazines, *Der Yidisher Shtral* ("The Jewish Ray") and *Di Yidishe Likht* ("The Jewish Light") are long-established Israeli publications with items of interest to a range of readers. In the U.S., the most widely read magazine is *Mallos*, a professionally produced, wide-ranging cultural quarterly that features articles of religious history and doctrine, a children's section (*Shtayg Hekher* / "Climb Higher"), a section for housewives, and a column called *Mame Loshn* ("Mother Tongue"/"Yiddish"), on Yiddish etymology and usage, a new phenomenon in a community that does not produce Yiddish dictionaries or grammars (although one commonly finds D.M. Harduf's Yiddish-English dictionary (1993) and occasionally even Uriel Weinreich's dictionary (1968) in ḥasidic households). A new Hebrew translation of Yiddish sayings ("Yiddish the Holy Language") also indicates this shift in attitude to Yiddish among Hebrew-reading ḥasidim.

Yiddish literature for school-age children includes inspirational biographies, simplified religious books, and school books. The Satmar girl's school *Beys Rokhl* has published a series of readers in Yiddish, used in Israel as well as Brooklyn, e.g. *Der Inhalt fun Megiles Ester* ("The Content of the Esther Scroll," Beys Rokhl, Brooklyn, 1983). There is also a multi-volume *Entsiklopedye far Yugnt* ("Encyclopedia for Young People," Israel, 1999), as well as Yiddish math books for girls, and board games in Yiddish, like *Handl Erlikh* ("Deal Honestly"), a spinoff of "Monopoly" that emphasizes charity. The market for preschool children is vast, and includes colorful, glossy picture books and coloring books. Among the many popular items is the series *Mitsve Kinder* ("Good Deed Kids"), one volume of which elucidates *Greytn zikh Tsum Shabes* ("Preparations for the Sabbath"), with cassette tapes (Hamatic Press, Brooklyn). A series of colorful books for girls that reinforce their roles in domestic life (by an author who signs herself "Leyele's mother") is produced in Modi'in, Israel. A series for boys (produced in Israel and widely marketed) focuses on miracle-working holy men: *Dertseylungen fun Tzadikim* ("Tales of Saints"), such as *Der Prinz is Gevorn a Yid* ("The Prince Became a Jew," Sifrut Machanayim, Israel). *Nitz Dayn Moyekh* ("Use your Brain," Roebling Distributors, Brooklyn) is a series of Yiddish activity books. Both boys and girls learn their highly differentiated daily routines through stories and adventures, as in *Broynem Ber un Teg fun di Vokh* ("Brown Bear and the Days of the Week," Midos Publishers, Brooklyn). For younger children there is series of coloring books by Nachem Brandwein in Yiddish and English that teaches holidays, blessings, and events.

While some secular Yiddishists deny that contemporary Yiddish-language stories, songs, novels, and periodicals produced by the ḥasidim constitute *belles lettres*, one detects over the course of the last 15 years a growing, albeit unacknowledged, attention to "literary" concerns such as structure, form, and style in ḥasidic fiction. A century and a half ago, modern Yiddish literature developed gradually, haltingly, but directly out of the core of traditional Ashkenazi culture. Whether the similar traditional community of 21st-century ḥasidim will eventually produce literature that appeals to a readership beyond its own cultural borders (if such a readership even exists by that time) remains to be seen. If there is to be Yiddish literature in the future, however, it currently seems unlikely that it can come from any other source.

[Miriam Isaacs (2nd ed.)]

YIDDISH RESEARCH AFTER THE HOLOCAUST

Coming to Terms with the Loss

In the late 1950s, with the first indications in the United States that Yiddish would be given academic status, the poet H. Leivick gave a speech in which he warned of the fate of the language as follows: "I said to myself: look, Yiddish and its literature are soon to reach the upper echelons. But isn't there some fear stirring in your heart, since at the same time Yiddish is departing from the lower echelons of the people?" (H. Leivick, Eseyen un Redes (1963), 105). Leivick's words at the time were echoed widely since they gave precise expression to what seems even now to be the paradoxical fate of Yiddish: the language whose exponents were so proud of its being a language of the masses and of its wide usage, characteristics which made it a bridge between different Jewish communities, is fast disappearing from the marketplace and byways of life, and only small, specialized groups work towards maintaining it. As expected, Leivick concluded his speech with a plea not to accept this situation, and to try to preserve Yiddish as a spoken language for the Jewish people in the Diaspora. But this call, and many others like it, fell on deaf ears. The decline of Yiddish as an everyday language is an ongoing process that seems irreversible. Only among groups of the ultra-Orthodox does Yiddish preserve its status as a spoken language, as another component conferring a unique quality on this way of life that is impermeable to changing times. The Yiddish which until a generation ago was heard in the streets of New York and Buenos Aires, Kiev and Paris, Tel Aviv and Melbourne has retreated to much more limited pockets: it has become the possession of aging groups of speakers, and in the best of cases is the object of yearning of a few of their children or grandchildren, whose ears still catch a Yiddish song and enjoy it, even though in most instances they no longer speak the language fluently. How can one maintain the treasures of the spoken language and pass on its flavor, nuances, and subtleties to a generation that no longer speaks it? This almost Sisyphean aim was and remains one of the main goals of research on Yiddish, which has exercised more than two generations of scholars.

Those who took up this burden, propelled by a deep sense of urgency, were that very generation for whom Yiddish occupied a central place in its cultural world and served as its prime channel of cultural expression: those Jewish intellectuals who were educated in Eastern Europe, although a large part of their research work was carried out elsewhere. The first to sense that time was running out and to gear up for the task of collecting and preserving Yiddish intensively, even at the beginning of the 20th century, were the folklorists (see also below). In other disciplines one must note the linguists Solomon Birnbaum, Judah A. Joffe, Yudel Mark, Max and Uriel Weinreich, the historian Jacob Shatzky, and the literary critics Nahum Baruch Minkoff and Samuel Niger. Some of them did not have formal academic training, and their ongoing work was not carried out in the framework of any academic institution at all; there is no doubt that this deficiency has left its traces in their work, but they did nevertheless have one decisive advantage – intimate acquaintance with the deepest levels of the language and all of its complex byways as well as rootedness in the world from which the new cultural identity of Yiddish had developed and grown. Both the capabilities and limitations of this generation can be seen in an important post-Holocaust project intended to perpetuate Yiddish literary activity: in 1956 the first volume of the *Leksikon fun der Nayer Yidisher Literatur* ("Biographical Dictionary of Modern Yiddish Literature") was published in New York and only a full generation later, in 1981, was the undertaking completed. A supplementary volume was published in 1986 by Berl Kagan. These books are brimming with rich, varied material that makes them a primary resource for anyone dealing with this field. However, the bibliographical underpinning is often lacking, and many biographies were written without proper critical perspective. The deaths of the original editors, Niger and Shatzky, prior to the appearance of the first volume left a decided gap that could not be filled as the work progressed. Thus, the reader can easily see through the course of the volumes just how pressing the hour was with regard to comprehensive projects such as these in the field of Yiddish.

That same generation that grew up against a natural backdrop of Yiddish can claim to its credit after the Holocaust two first-rate lexicographical projects. In 1950 the YIVO Institute for Jewish Research in New York, the leading center for Yiddish scholarship, sponsored the publication of *Der Oytser fun der Yidisher Shprakh* ("The Thesaurus of the Yiddish Language") by Nahum (Nokhem) Stutchkoff (ed. Max Weinreich; reprinted 1991). This was the first collection of the lexical treasurehouse of the language, including words, idioms, and sayings, listed according to themes, as a thesaurus. Then, once the rich corpus of the Yiddish language had been gathered in a much more valuable manner than any previous dictionary of the language, the need was felt even more urgently for additional works. The material that Stutchkoff had collected did indeed serve as the cornerstone for a multifaceted lexicographical undertaking, *Groyser Verterbukh fun der Yidisher Shprakh* ("Great Dictionary of the Yiddish Language"), the first volume of which appeared in 1961 under the editorship of Judah A. Joffe and Yudel Mark. After the death of Joffe, Mark became the sole editor. Towards the end of his life he transferred the project from New York to Jerusalem, and after his death a fourth volume (1980) appeared, after which no more have as yet been published. The four current volumes have some 80,000 lexical entries, words, expressions, and sayings, completing the entries for the letter *alef.* On the surface one might think that this project is still near the beginning, but because the *alef* is employed for a number of the most common functional, grammatical particles in Yiddish, particularly as the prefix of many verb roots, it is reasonable to assume that the volumes now available contain about one-third of the entire vocabulary of Yiddish. These volumes are impressive testimony to the ability of a generation of researchers who grew up within the world of Yiddish to interpret and explain its finest nuances to the point of unlocking the hidden treasures of the spoken language. Even when it might at first glance seem that the editors have sometimes listed a meaning for a word that adds nothing to the previous definition, it turns out that they have discerned an additional shade of meaning that otherwise would have escaped the user and become irretrievable. If one compares the method of definition of entries in the *Groyser Verterbukh* to that employed in similar dictionaries in other languages, it is immediately noticeable that the editors did not limit the definitions, which generally turned out better than expected, for the overly lengthy definitions contain invaluable linguistic and cultural information and turn these volumes into a first-rate document of the widely variegated world of Yiddish speakers throughout its history and in its different centers.

Yet, in certain areas faults resulted from the lack of a research base broad enough for such a comprehensive project. Since Yudel Mark was Lithuanian, in many instances there is a noticeable lack of attention to other dialects of Yiddish, particularly the documentation of Polish Yiddish. There are also gaps in citations from literary material, which are, additionally, inconsistent. Moreover, the editors faced an almost insurmountable difficulty inherent in the language and the conditions under which it developed. Yiddish developed everywhere by contact with the surrounding languages, absorbing from them various influences and many words – some that took root in the language and others that soon fell into disuse. In the distribution of Yiddish outside Eastern Europe, the speakers borrowed from English, Spanish, French, and Modern Hebrew, from where some of the words also entered the written language, especially in newspapers not attentive to a literary standard. The editors of the dictionary faced a serious problem in deciding what standard to apply to such words – to include a great many or to exercise caution in listing words taken from the surrounding languages, whose place in normative, literary Yiddish is doubtful. In most instances the editors dealt with these words quite generously, frequently "hosting" them, although in many cases, such decisions are debatable. Following the death of Yudel Mark the dictionary project was continued jointly by a number of academic institutions: Columbia University, the City University of New York, and Hebrew University in Jerusalem, in association with YIVO. Such cooperation was intended to insure the completion of this enormous undertaking and offer future generations a rich lexical panorama of the language at its different historical periods and stylistic registers, thus rescuing them from extinction. Although no new volumes have appeared in a quarter-century, it is to be hoped that this essential reference tool will yet be completed, since this is a task whose importance and urgency are almost impossible to overstate.

Yet, even the completion of this huge project would not comprehensively account for spoken language usage. The variety of dialects in Yiddish is basic to the language at every level: phonologically, semantically (in different areas different words were used to name the same object), and grammatically. The documentation of this great linguistic richness was the primary goal of *The Language and Culture Atlas of Ashkenazic Jewry*. The aims, scope, and methodology of this project were determined by Uriel Weinreich in 1959, and work was continued after his untimely death in 1967 under the direction of Marvin I. Herzog at Columbia University. Dozens of informants were carefully chosen in order to give balanced representation to the geographical distribution of Yiddish. They were given a detailed questionnaire to complete, the answers to which document a broad range of the aspects of language use and the varied ways in which it expresses the lives of its speakers. It is obvious that the *Atlas* drew most of its material from Eastern European speakers, but it also documented the remnant of the spoken language from the Western Europe (Holland, Alsace and Switzerland), and the data gathered now indicate links, which have not as yet been sufficiently studied, between different centers of Yiddish over a broad territorial range. As time passes and surviving native speakers become both fewer and ever more distanced from the language as it was spoken in its natural setting, the value of the oral documentation increases. The first volumes of the *Atlas* began appearing in 1992, published jointly by YIVO in New York and Max Niemeyer Verlag in Tuebingen, Germany. Three volumes had appeared as of 2005.

By the end of the 20th century most assumed that it was no longer possible to document the Yiddish language from East European speakers *in situ*. Yet the U.S.-born linguist Dovid *Katz, who had been the central figure in Yiddish studies in Oxford, England, for over a decade, relocated to Vilnius (Lithuania; formerly Vilna) in 1999 and began conducting interviews with elderly Jews throughout Lite (the Yiddish designation for the Jewish conception of Lithuania, which includes the Baltics, Belarus, northeastern Poland, and a portion of the extreme northern Ukraine). The information thus gathered by Katz and his students will no doubt prove important to future researchers.

Another area of research that is nearing the zero hour for collection efforts is the study of every aspect of Yiddish folklore – folksongs, sayings, jokes, folktales, folkplays (the *Purim shpil* / "Purim play"). The situation certainly became more urgent after the Holocaust and its consequent linguistic assimilation; although early researchers in Yiddish studies already noted that urgency. Even prior to World War I Y.L. Cahan wrote, in the introduction to a large collection of Yiddish folksongs that he had gathered and published, of the slow decline of the genre, particularly in the large cities, to the point that "it seems to me that it will not be long before the original folksong will become a thing of the past" (Y.L. Cahan, *Shtudyes vegn Yidisher Folksshafung* (1952), 10). If this were true at a time when the sounds of Yiddish were heard everywhere in Jewish Eastern Europe, it is quite obvious how much more pressing the preservation of Yiddish folklore has become in recent decades. New methodologies and technologies now make possible more accurate documentation. Thanks to the efforts of Ruth Rubin, Eleanor Gordon Mlotek, Barbara Kirshenblatt-Gimblett, and others, we now have hundreds of recordings and texts of Yiddish folksongs which are housed in numerous collections in Canada, the U.S., and Israel. The Jewish Folksong Archives, founded by Meir Noy, which is located at Bar-Ilan University, contain cardfiles with detailed information on thousands of songs in Hebrew and Yiddish, on the lyricists, melodies, and place of publication. In the subfield of the study of folktales, the leading institute is the Israel Folktale Archives at Haifa University which sets down the stories of the various Jewish ethnic communities. Unfortunately a large part of the material from East European informants was documented not in the Yiddish original but in Hebrew translation. The publication of Beatrice Silverman Weinreich's *Yiddish Folktales* (1988) made available in English a selection of material collected by YIVO's Ethnographic Commission in the 1920s and 1930s.

The study of East European Jewish music was given an important boost in the 1980s with the founding of YIVO's Max and Frieda Weinstein Archive of Recorded Sound, which assiduously preserves all genres of East European Jewish music, re-recording them using modern technologies (*Klezmer Music 1910–1942*, compiled and annotated by Henry Sapoznik (Folkways Records FSS 34021)). Its work went beyond the area of pure collecting: as young musicians in the United States and eventually around the world rediscovered *klezmer* (East European Jewish instrumental folk) music, they turned to the archives with requests for texts and melodies in order to build their repertoire. By the late 1990s this surge of interest led to a wave of new scholarly work on Yiddish music, as well as the reissue of historic recordings collected as early as 1912–14 on the famous ethnographic expeditions led by Sh. Ansky (*Treasures of Jewish Culture in Ukraine* (Vernadsky National Library of Ukraine, 1997)). The "people of the book," which already for the most part cannot read what was written in the language it spoke until two or three generations ago, now maintains its link to Yiddish through the sounds of its music. As knowledge of the language continually declines among the children and grandchildren of its speakers, the Yiddish song at times becomes the only link to that memory.

One response to declining Yiddish literacy has been to produce works about Yiddish in more widely known languages. In 2002 the YIVO Institute began work on a multi-volume encyclopedia of Jewish life in Eastern Europe. Once completed this work will likely stand as a definitive reference tool on the history and culture of Yiddish-speaking Jewry, while its English-language format reflects the shift away from Yiddish as a Jewish *lingua franca* predicted by Leivick nearly a half-century before. The YIVO Encyclopedia is the most ambitious of recent works built on the underlying assumption that the golden age of Jewish creativity in Yiddish is at an end and that the time has come to take stock of its achievements. Since the pioneers of the field saw Yiddish as the living tongue of the Jewish masses, they placed much emphasis on disciplines such as demography, pedagogy, and sociology that focus on contemporary issues, as well as on the study of the spoken language. By the end of the 20th century there was a shift towards Yiddish research in a retrospective mode, with more work done from a historical perspective and less in the social sciences. The study of Yiddish language use among the *ḥasidim*, the only group to continue to speak Yiddish in large numbers, remains an exception to this rule and a promising area for future research.

The Organizational Framework

NEW CENTERS OF YIDDISH STUDIES. In the period between the two World Wars, when Yiddish cultural activity in all of its manifestations reached its zenith, the Soviet Union was the only country in which Yiddish was granted a recognized status by research institutes and university-level academic institutions. This situation drew scholars from other countries, such as Max *Erik and Meier *Wiener, who hoped to pursue their research uninhibitedly in Russia. But reality upset their dreams and ideological pressure, persecution, and arrests limited the development of their talents, although much of their work in the fields of linguistics, literature, and folklore have even up to the present constituted a touchstone for generations of scholars. Conversely, in Poland and in the U.S., where millions spoke Yiddish, recognition of the language in an academic forum remained a distant, unrealistic dream.

Thus, intensive research on Yiddish outside the borders of Russia was concentrated between the two World Wars in an institution established at the initiative of Yiddishist circles. The YIVO Institute for Jewish Research originated with the memorandum "Vegn a Yidishn Akademishn Institut" ("On a Yiddish Academic Institute") circulated by the linguist Nahum (Nokhem) *Shtif in 1925 in Berlin, which was then the center for the Jewish intellectuals who had left Russia in the early years of the Revolution. But it eventually became clear that the institution could not exist in a western cosmopolitan city that lacked a significant pool of enthusiasts and willing hands to do the work, a pool that might be found – or so they hoped – among Yiddish speakers. The institution established its headquarters in Vilna, "Jerusalem of Lithuania," a city with a glorious historical tradition and only weak signs of linguistic or cultural assimilation. Branches of YIVO were active in other countries and cities, particularly in New York. After the outbreak of World War II and the destruction of the Vilna headquarters, the New York branch became the new headquarters of this institution, due in large part to the intensive work of Max *Weinreich, a central figure in YIVO from its establishment, who had managed to escape Europe at the beginning of the war and to reach the U.S. After the war both patience and faith were necessary even to hope for the continuation of research on Yiddish. Of the Jewish communities of Eastern Europe, particularly Poland, there remained but a few glowing embers. The institutes for Yiddish research in Russia had suffered greatly during the purges at the end of the 1930s and the Nazi occupation; what little remained after the Holocaust was destroyed along with the other familiar manifestations of Jewish culture by the end of 1948. Yet, a number of scholars who had managed to flee in time from the Holocaust and reach safety, such as Max Weinreich and Yudel Mark, dedicated their lives to serving as a real link between the two periods and the two totally differing cultural milieux, prewar Eastern Europe and postwar America. They strove to continue their research activities in places that seemed somehow inappropriate. At the end of the 1940s, the first significant attempts were made at blazing a trail for the study of Yiddish at universities in the U.S. A few years later saw the founding of two university frameworks for Yiddish instruction and research that were of signal importance, in Israel on the one hand, and in the U.S. on the other. In 1951 the Yiddish Department was established at Hebrew University in Jerusalem under Dov *Sadan, and in 1953 Uriel Weinreich, the son of Max *Weinreich, was appointed to the Atran Chair of Yiddish Language, Literature, and Culture at Columbia University in New York. Many of their students and their students' students today teach Yiddish in leading academic institutions in the U.S. and Israel.

After the deaths of Max and Uriel Weinreich two projects were undertaken that symbolize the desire for continuity and renewed growth in a research field that had suffered so much from the vicissitudes of Jewish history in the preceding decades. In 1968 the YIVO Institute for Jewish Research established the Max Weinreich Center for Advanced Jewish Studies, which provided a framework for graduate and post-doctoral training in the fields of Yiddish and East European Jewish studies. The same year Columbia University in cooperation with YIVO established the Uriel Weinreich Program in Yiddish Language, Literature and Culture, an intensive, comprehensive program that annually enables students of every level to make their first acquaintance with Yiddish and its literature and to continue on to more advanced studies. The success of this program prompted other institutions to follow in its footsteps. In the 1990s Oxford was the site of an intensive summer language course, which was essentially transplanted to Vilna with Dovid Katz's relocation there; another such program rotates triennially among Paris, Strasbourg, and Brussels.

In 2005 the Weinreich Program shifted its affiliation to New York University, mirroring YIVO's relocation in 1999 to the Center for Jewish History, a new facility housing several Jewish institutions near NYU's Greenwich Village campus. By this time the Weinreich Center had ceased to offer graduate classes, a gap partly filled since 1999 by the International Research Seminar in Yiddish Culture, led by Avrom Novershtern and David Roskies and held every other summer in New York and Israel alternately. This program conducted entirely in Yiddish provides students with an introduction to the various fields of Yiddish studies, yet as a two-week course it cannot replace the curriculum once offered by the Weinreich Center. The fate of the Weinreich Center reflects a general trend at YIVO, which by the 1990s largely abandoned its advocacy of Yiddish as a vehicle of academic discourse and its sponsorship of original research. Instead it came to function primarily as a facilitator and disseminator of scholarship, emphasizing its unparalleled library and archival collections as well as publications in English often based on material from those collections. The growth of Jewish Studies programs across the United States has partially addressed this lacuna, as the teaching of Yiddish language and culture – in English – became increasingly common on American campuses.

In the U.S. at the start of the 21st century, institutions with faculty positions dedicated to Yiddish include Columbia University, Harvard University, Indiana University, the Jewish Theological Seminary, New York University, and Ohio State University; at Columbia and Ohio State it is possible to receive a degree in Yiddish Studies. Moreover, with the growing acceptance of Yiddish as a subject of study, the language is also taught in Jewish Studies programs at the University of California at Berkeley, the University of Michigan, the University of Texas at Austin, and many others. The emphasis in the U.S. is on the research and teaching of modern Yiddish literature and of historical aspects of Yiddish culture, the latter often carried out within departments of history.

The study of Yiddish in all its aspects – earlier and modern literature, language, and folklore – developed at Hebrew University in Jerusalem under Dov *Sadan, his successor Chone *Shmeruk, and their students Chava Turniansky and Avrom Novershtern. With Shmeruk's death and Turniansky's retirement, the Yiddish Department continues to train graduate students but is much diminished in its scope. Programs for the teaching of Yiddish and its literature now exist at other Israeli universities, however, such as the Rena Costa Centre for Yiddish Studies at Bar-Ilan University. In Germany interest in the field, primarily the study of Old Yiddish literature, flourished with the establishment of chairs of Yiddish at the universities in Trier (1990) and Dusseldorf (1996). The Medem Library in Paris, led by Yitskhok Niborski, continues to function on a high level with an active program of classes and publications in both Yiddish and French.

In the late 1980s and 1990s Oxford, England, became a prominent center of Yiddish studies under the leadership of Dovid Katz and his students, training a generation of young scholars, producing a series of books and journals in Yiddish and English, and sponsoring an intensive summer language course and academic conference. By the end of the century this had all come to an end, with the Yiddish faculty dispersing to take up positions elsewhere, and the program was rebuilt on only a modest scale.

The collapse of the Soviet Union opened new possibilities for Yiddish studies, as formerly unknown materials came to light and as new contacts were made with the surviving Jewish communities of Eastern Europe. Project Judaica, founded in 1991 by the Jewish Theological Seminary, YIVO, and the Russian State University of the Humanities in Moscow, first introduced the study of Yiddish to post-Soviet Russia. After departing Oxford, Dovid Katz settled in Vilna, where he founded the Vilnius Yiddish Institute in 2001 and began a new course of research, teaching, and publishing. These programs have given students in the region the opportunity to study the language and its culture, although the most promising have pursued their training in Israel or the U.S.

THE NEW IDEOLOGICAL CONTEXT. Before the Holocaust, studies of Yiddish and its literature were marked by ideological clashes that were at times quite severe, particularly between those working in the Soviet Union on the one hand and YIVO affiliates in Poland and the United States on the other. In the wake of World War II and the establishment of the State of Israel, longstanding tensions between Yiddishists and Hebraists became increasingly irrelevant, while the rift between Communists and their opponents faded with the end of the Soviet Union. These developments paved the way for a fresh look at topics formerly considered ideologically suspect or at best unimportant, including the comparative study of Yiddish and Hebrew literature and Yiddish culture among Orthodox Jewish communities. The work of both Soviet Yiddish activists and their Communist sympathizers abroad has also been subject to new research, enhanced by material made available in former Soviet archives. These trends can be seen as the fulfillment of the inclusive vision of Jewish culture formulated by such pioneering scholars as Max Weinreich and Dov Sadan, whose work is discussed below.

This is not to imply that the field has been without conflict in recent years. Benjamin Harshav's *The Meaning of Yiddish* (1990) stirred controversy with its stance that Yiddish should be treated as a dead language, demonstrating that the question of its status as a spoken vernacular can still arouse strong emotions. Linguists such as Paul Wexler and Dovid Katz have put forth new controversial theories on the origins of the Yiddish language and its Ashkenazi Jewish speakers, and Katz rejected the unified Yiddish orthography developed by YIVO to devise his own. Some of Katz's ideas are incorporated in *Words on Fire: The Unfinished Story of Yiddish* (2004), which despite its idiosyncrasies is to be welcomed as the first overall history of Yiddish culture in English. Nevertheless, as ideological orthodoxies have broken down, Yiddish scholars now work in a variety of conceptual contexts, ensuring cross-fertilization and the introduction of new methodologies such as the perspective of gender studies which has proven a useful tool of analysis. But any advantages inherent in the situation are dependent upon the ability of those in the field to maintain a common framework of reference, while recognizing the achievements of the past and the value of innovation.

Yiddish Research in the Previous Generation: Concepts and Achievements

THE NEW CULTURAL CONTEXT. Throughout its history Yiddish was the language of a minority group that maintained within itself a very high degree of internal unity. It is therefore not surprising that the history of both the language and its literature serves as an illustrative example of the complex, tense relations between internal traditions and external influences; parallel phenomena can also be discerned in the development of Yiddish research. Until the beginning of the 20th century, few scholars of Yiddish spoke or published in Yiddish. This is true certainly for the non-Jews such as J. Johann Christoph Wagenseil and J. Schudt as well as for those who turned to Yiddish for pragmatic reasons (including missionaries). Even the outstanding scholars of the *Wissenschaft des Judentums*, Leopold Zunz and Moritz Steinschneider, fell into this category. Only at the beginning of the 20th century, with the growing awareness of the cultural value of Yiddish, did there begin to develop in Eastern Europe the study of Yiddish in Yiddish; this process reached its high point with the work carried out between the two World Wars, in Russia on the one hand, and at YIVO on the other. The scholars for whom Yiddish was both a native language and the language in which they published their academic studies considered themselves participants in a wide-ranging cultural creativity that included schools, newspapers and journals, publishing, and theater. It is difficult to name many individuals from this period whose sole occupation was scholarship: they were also active in Jewish political parties, journalism, literary criticism, and the teaching of Yiddish in secondary or higher education. They particularly liked to emphasize the fact that whereas their predecessors had approached Yiddish from the outside, simply as a "dry" object of research, they saw it as a living possession of the people which they nurtured within the framework of an entire range of cultural activity. It is no wonder then that parts of their work seem overly "forced" to contemporary readers, as writing that integrated research with journalism and attempted to promote a clearly defined ideological position. This is true mainly for work carried out in Russia, particularly in the 1930s, where writers were forced to add references to Lenin and Stalin, interpolations that were obligatory in almost any scholarly article. But even to the scholars whose goal was scholarly objectivity, it was clear that their work fit into a wider cultural context.

This cultural context was utterly destroyed by the Holocaust, by the annihilation of Jewish cultural institutions in Russia, and by linguistic assimilation in both East and West, particularly in the U.S. and in Israel. A Yiddish-speaking folk, functioning both as the potential addressees of, and the ideological frame of reference for, scholarly work on Yiddish and in Yiddish, no longer existed. Also gone was the network of schools that had needed terminology in Yiddish for every subject, from physics to psychology. With the teaching of the language gradually diminishing, the issues of normative standards, which in their time had led to great controversies, were no longer pressing: for example, the question whether or not it was necessary to strive for a universally accepted pronunciation. The abandonment of Yiddish as a spoken language necessarily led to a great decline in the field of study and interest on the part of researchers. But the new cultural situation, in which other forces were created for the maintenance of Yiddish in a bilingual or multilingual framework, led scholars to emphasize other aspects and to raise new questions. As in any field of research in the humanities, in this instance, too, the present was leaving its mark on the approaches used to study the past.

THE ACHIEVEMENT OF MAX WEINREICH. The career of Max Weinreich well illustrates this process. Upon his arrival in the U.S. in 1940 he immediately understood how different the new cultural context was in which he had to work; in his lectures and letters he repeatedly compared and contrasted Jewish New York and Vilna, the city that he had left before the war. But such a comparison could only reinforce his own ever-growing awareness that the few elements still shared by the two communities upon his arrival in New York were eroding right before his eyes. Thus Weinreich faced a difficult challenge: the drastic and painful change in cultural context from prewar Vilna to postwar New York necessitated a conceptual and even ideological reorganization. In this regard there is in Yiddish scholarship no more fascinating document than Weinreich's magnum opus, *Geshikhte fun der Yidisher Shprakh* (4 vols., 1973; partial Eng. tr., *History of the Yiddish Language*, 1980; a complete English translation forthcoming from YIVO and Yale University Press will finally make the full scope of this study accessible to a wider audience). This great synthetic work depicts the history of Yiddish in a wide cultural framework. The book itself is noteworthy first and foremost for its advances in research, but some of its more subtle dimensions are just as valuable: on the one hand, its ideological premises and the conclusions drawn from them, and on the other – a feature that seems superfluous – the style and method of approaching the material. On every page of the book the reader can palpably feel that in this case the method of exposition has its own latent significance; Weinreich's style attempted most earnestly to combine the rich vitality of the spoken language with characteristics of scholarly usage, which demands precision and nuance. In his search for a method to formulate his statements, Weinreich did not employ ready-made models from English or German, because he believed that such an academic work as this in Yiddish had to be read differently. Thus his work became a wonderful revelation of the combination of the folk and academy, of Yiddish scholarly and of the hidden richness of the spoken language. The backbone of the book is the discussion which provides abundant examples of the mutual relations between language and culture. Weinreich expresses and summarizes the ideas of scholars who preceded him, defining Yiddish as the language of "the Way of the Shas [Talmud]," i.e., of the traditional Ashkenazi way of life. In light of this definition, readers can only wonder (and become ever more convinced as they read further) whether Weinreich is implicitly questioning the possibility of maintaining Yiddish in the Diaspora among secular Jews outside of its natural cultural framework. But it is striking that Weinreich, the scholar who once subscribed to secular Yiddish ideologies, does not raise this problem explicitly. His detailed discussion of the link between Yiddish and Yidishkayt raises many problematic questions that cannot be avoided by the sensitive reader, but they remain outside of the scope of this comprehensive work. In the section preceding the discussion of more specific aspects of research, Weinreich for the first time set up a broad, conceptual framework of great significance for dealing with all of the languages of the Jews, thereby laying the foundations for a new area of research: the interlinguistics of Jewish languages, which in recent years has become of greater interest. Weinreich showed, with a great many examples, how Yiddish had become a fertile field for the melding of the languages of the surrounding environment – Romance languages, German, and Slavic languages – along with *loshn koydesh* ("the holy tongue"), which was given special status in traditional Jewish society. The nature of Yiddish as a fusion language of various linguistic elements is not, therefore, simply a linguistic fact, but a multidimensional intersection of language and culture. A large part of Weinreich's book is devoted to the description and analysis of the phenomenon of bilingualism and multilingualism among Ashkenazi Jewry, as well as members of other Jewish groups – between Hebrew and the spoken language of the Jews or between those languages and the co-territorial non-Jewish language. Thus Weinreich's work is outstanding in its decidedly interdisciplinary nature. His discussions and analysis of purely linguistic data touch on and illuminate other areas as well, such as the history of the Jews, folklore, literary history, and sociolinguistics.

BILINGUAL DICTIONARIES. An illustrative albeit paradoxical example of the possibilities and limitations simultaneously at hand in the new cultural situation in Yiddish scholarship is the work that by its very nature aimed at bridging cultures – bilingual dictionaries. Such dictionaries were always the high road for Yiddish lexicography, because they were intended initially to answer practical needs, namely to teach European languages to Yiddish-speakers. By contrast Uriel Weinreich's *Modern English-Yiddish Yiddish-English Dictionary* (1968), which is clearly one of the most important Yiddish lexicographical undertakings of its period, addressed first and foremost the needs of the user desiring to acquire Yiddish as an active language. Towards this end Weinreich gives a detailed and normative grammatical description of each Yiddish lexical item, a description that has no parallel in any earlier dictionary of the language. However, the bilingual format of the dictionary limited the scope of the entries. Thus students in need of a reference tool to help them understand Yiddish literary texts must turn to Alexander Harkavy's older *Yiddish-English-Hebrew Dictionary* (1928; reprinted with a new introduction in 1988). Weinreich intended his dictionary to be used both by active Yiddish speakers and by passive readers of the language, and each audience is equally well served by this excellent work, although the latter audience in fact outnumbers the former; additionally, its needs are not adequately met in a work of limited scope that tries to cater to two audiences. Weinreich's dictionary has been supplemented by several specialized lexicographical studies by Mordkhe Schaechter (*English-Yiddish Dictionary of Academic Terminology* (1988), *Pregnancy, Childbirth, and Early Childhood: An English-Yiddish Dictionary* (1991), and *Plant Names in Yiddish* (2005)) and two important reference works published by the Medem Library: Yitskhok Niborski's *Verterbukh fun Loshn-Koydesh-Shtamike Verter in Yidish* ("Dictionary of Words of Hebrew and Aramaic Origin in Yiddish," 1997; 1999[2]) and the bilingual Yiddish-French Dictionary of Niborski and Bernard Vaisbrot (2002). All these include entries for terms lacking in Weinreich and Harkavy, and all are the products of meticulous research. At least for Francophone Yiddish readers, the Niborski/Vaisbrot dictionary has effectively replaced Weinreich for most purposes.

RESEARCH ON OLD AND MIDDLE YIDDISH LITERATURE. The study of early Yiddish literature – the corpus of works written up to the end of the 18th century – is one of the oldest branches of Yiddish scholarship, extending back to the period of the *Wissenschaft des Judentums*, and in some sense even back to the Humanist period. In this field contemporary scholars can draw on the achievements of the past, creating a certain continuity in the research tradition, yet the difference in cultural context has led to new emphases in research and to a different general perspective.

When the *Cambridge Codex of *ca.* 1382 (the earliest extensive codex in Yiddish) was published, it aroused controversy between the Germanist, J.W. Marchand, and Max Weinreich [J.W. Marchand, review of *The Oldest Known Literary Documents of Yiddish Literature*, L. Fuks (ed.), *Word*, 15 (1959), 383–94; M. Weinreich, "Old Yiddish Poetry in Linguistic-Literary Research," in: *Word*, 16 (1960), 100–118. This controversy has been analyzed extensively by Jerold C. Frakes in his *The Politics of Interpretation: Alterity and Ideology in Old Yiddish Studies* (1988)]. At issue was whether to identify the texts in the manuscript as German literature written in the Hebrew alphabet or as Yiddish literature, despite the fact that the language displays few features distinct from co-temporal German. The dispute was based less on the linguistic facts than on the interpretive context in which the researcher tried to explain them. In this regard their disagreement was the forerunner of two contemporary trends in the study of early Yiddish, for there are indeed discernible two different cultural contexts for this discipline: the Germanist scholars at the University of Trier (pioneered by Hans Peter Althaus, Walter Roll, Erika Timm, and now continued by Simon Neuberg) is particularly noteworthy for careful editing and philological analysis of texts (despite the severe limitations imposed by their publishing the texts in an overtly Germanizing Roman transcription); they naturally contribute to the understanding of phenomena of early Yiddish literature by virtue of their approach and training as Germanists. By contrast, among the scholars in Jerusalem (formerly led by Ch. Shmeruk and his student Ch. Turniansky, and now continued by S. Zfatman) a different methodological perspective has been developed, which mainly stresses the internal Jewish context of the works in Old Yiddish literature and the close relations with Hebrew works of the same period, a contact whose most noticeable manifestation is the bilingual text – a work written simultaneously in Hebrew and in Yiddish. Interestingly, the current chair of Yiddish studies in Dusseldorf, Marion Aptroot, trained in Oxford, combines the philological thoroughness of the Trier Germanists with the attention to the Jewish cultural context characteristic of the Jerusalem scholars of early Yiddish (cf. J. Michman and M. Aptroot (eds. and tr.), *Storm in the Community: Yiddish Political Pamphlets of Amsterdam Jewry, 1797–1798* (2002)).

In the first comprehensive works on the history of early Yiddish literature, written in the 1920s and 1930s by Max Erik, Max Weinreich, and Israel Zinberg, the ideological tendency of the writers was clearly discernible in their special appreciation of the "secular" aspects in Old Yiddish works [M. Erik, *Di Geshikhte fun der Yidisher Literatur: Fun di Eltste Tsaytn biz der Haskole-Tkufe* (1928; rpt. 1979); M. Weinreich, *Bilder fun der Yidisher Literaturgeshikhte* (1928); I. Zinberg, *Di Geshikhte fun der Literatur bay Yidn*, 6 (1935), (rpt. 1943; Engl. trans. 1975)]. Ch. Shmeruk thoroughly revised this approach in his book *Sifrut Yiddish: Perakim le-Toledoteha* ("Yiddish Literature: Chapters of its History," 1978; rev. Yid. tr. 1988), which is based on a much wider corpus, including texts discovered in the decades before its publication (the most significant being the Cambridge manuscript mentioned above). He analyzed Old Yiddish literature with regard to its status and role in traditional Ashkenazi society, where the sharp division made between the "secular" and the "religious" by his predecessors proves quite artificial. The new conceptual system stresses the centrality of the Bible as a source and inspiration for early Yiddish literature, and understanding its importance reveals the mutual link between genres previously considered distinct – direct translations of the Bible, paraphrases of the Bible, homiletical works (which gave early Yiddish literature its most popular book, the *Tsenerene* (**Ẓe'enah u-Re'enah*)), biblical epic poetry, and plays based on biblical themes which were presented as *Purim-shpiln*. In his studies of early Yiddish literature Shmeruk cited phenomena parallel to those that Weinreich noted in the history of the language itself: traditional Jewish society, from which Yiddish language and literature developed, did not absorb cultural artifacts from environments that were external to its autonomous way of life. Instead, such cultural elements first passed through a process of "Judaization," which neutralized of their Christian components. This multifaceted process is an outstanding example of the productive meeting of internal traditions and external influences that characterize every aspect of the Yiddish language and its literature. In addition to the discovery and publication of hitherto unknown texts and the enrichment of our bibliographical knowledge, this period of scholarship built up a new conceptual system that aims at properly describing the cultural complexity of Old Yiddish literature.

At the start of the 21st century, the linguistic focus of early Yiddish studies in Europe has broadened to include aspects of communal history, for example in the work of Marion Aptroot and Shlomo Berger on Amsterdam Yiddish publications of the early modern period. In Jerusalem, following Shmeruk's death and Turniansky's retirement, only Zfatman continued her teacher's legacy. Meanwhile, two important publications marked a major advance for the field: the first comprehensive survey of the period in seventy years appeared in Jean Baumgarten's *Introduction to Old Yiddish Literature* (orig. French ed. 1993; ed. and tr. Jerold C. Frakes, 2005). Perhaps more significant is the publication of Frakes' nearly 900-page anthology, *Early Yiddish Texts, 1100–1750* (2004), whose scope, comprehensive notes, and carefully edited texts in the original alphabet make this a landmark work in early Yiddish studies.

MODERN YIDDISH LITERATURE – REAPPRAISING CLASSICAL TEXTS. Dov Sadan, the founder of the Yiddish Department at Hebrew University in Jerusalem, presented an all-encompassing concept of Jewish literature in his comprehensive essay, "*Al Sifruteinu*" ("On Our Literature," 1950), which conceives Jewish literature as a single, broad, many-branched corpus, which includes texts in Hebrew and Yiddish, as well as the works of Jewish authors who wrote in other languages for Jewish readers. One discerns Sadan's striving for totality not only with regard to the languages of modern Jewish literature, but also the mutual relations between its various spiritual trends; while most of his predecessors considered modern literature in Hebrew and in Yiddish as the product of the Haskalah movement and a clear manifestation of the penetration of Jewish society by modernization, Sadan broadens the canvas and attempts to encompass all of modern Jewish intellectual creativity in all of its interwoven manifestations and roots, as they develop from the Haskalah, Ḥasidism, and the rabbinical works of the *misnagdim*. Thus Sadan's broad comprehensive conception deliberately raises doubts as to the legitimacy of privileging secular *belles lettres* above all the rest of the Ashkenazi cultural heritage.

This thesis of an underlying unity in Jewish literature was one of the bases of the comprehensive work by Israel Zinberg, *Geshikhte fun der Literatur bay Yidn* (8 vols. in 10, 1929–37; Eng. tr., *History of Jewish Literature*, 12 vols., 1973–78). Despite the difficult conditions under which Zinberg wrote his work in Leningrad, cut off from other scholars and from the literature of the West, he conceived of a most comprehensive plan for his endeavor, which was to describe Jewish literary creativity in the medieval and modern periods in all languages and genres. Due to his imprisonment and exile, however, he did not manage to complete this wide-ranging work, and its final volume (which was discovered and published in 1965) only reaches the period of the flourishing of the Haskalah in Russia (the 1860s). It was thus Dov Sadan and his students who took upon themselves the task of applying the integrative approach to modern Yiddish literature.

In this context it is natural that the main author to benefit from new exploration of his work would be the bilingual writer S.Y. *Abramovitsh, better known by the persona fabricated in his writings, Mendele Moykher Sforim. To be sure this "split" between the biographical writer and his literary persona was the focal point of the study by Dan Miron, *A Traveler Disguised: A Study in the Rise of Modern Yiddish Fiction in the Nineteenth Century* (1973; reissued 1996), which was based on research directed by Max and Uriel Weinreich. In the first part of his book Miron summarizes the ambivalent position demonstrated by the Haskalah towards Yiddish: despite the fact that most *maskilim* had a contemptuous attitude towards the language, some of them nonetheless laid the foundations of modern Yiddish literature. On this basis Miron articulates the literary and cultural circumstances and conditions in which the young *maskil* Abramovitsh turned to writing Yiddish, to which end he created his most central, vital character – Mendele, who appears in his works in a wide range of incarnations and roles – as the publisher of works given to him, as a Yiddish translator, as a good listener to stories told in his presence, and even as a protagonist in his own right. Miron's study deals with the point where the influence of ideological positions on the act of literary creation becomes discernible, and he proves how the problematic status of Yiddish and the difficulties with which its authors struggled led directly to refined, complex artistic solutions. In 2000 a volume of Miron's studies appeared under the title *The Image of the Shtetl and Other Studies of Modern Jewish Literary Imagination*, further acquainting the English reader with his wide-ranging achievement.

Ch. Shmeruk's *Peretses Yiesh-Vizye* ("Peretz's Vision of Despair," 1971), treats another aspect of the tension between literature and ideology as manifested in I.L. Peretz's symbolist drama, *Baynakht oyfn Altn Mark* ("At Night in the Old Market Place"), where many characters from both the world of the living and the dead express their existential thoughts and doubts while appearing one night against the background of a typical market square familiar from the Jewish milieu of Eastern Europe. Critical reviews in Yiddish perceived the play as a pivotal expression of Peretz's attitude toward a wide range of Jewish ideologies – from the Haskalah to the workers' movements. They felt that his position was exhausted in the final sentence of the play, "in shul arayn!" ("To the synagogue!"), which was taken as a call to return to a traditional Jewish way of life. Shmeruk concurs in essence that the play should be read in a contemporary ideological context, but his tracing of the sources of the various interwoven motifs and allusions reveal many shades of meaning that had gone unnoticed before.

PUBLISHING IN YIDDISH STUDIES. Scholars devoted serious and continuous efforts to publishing selected Yiddish literary texts. Among the most outstanding achievements of this kind, one must mention the anthology *A Shpigl oyf a Shteyn* ("A Mirror on a Stone," ed. Ch. Shmeruk, 1964; 1988²), which includes poetry and prose by 12 Yiddish authors who perished in the Soviet Union. The Yiddish Department of Hebrew University in Jerusalem publishes a series of books, one of whose goals is to collect the Yiddish works of bilingual authors who are known today mainly through their works in Hebrew; in this framework have appeared writings of S.Y. *Agnon, M.Y. *Berdyczewski, Uri Zevi *Greenberg, and Jacob *Steinberg. Likewise, selected works by Isaac Bashevis *Singer, Abraham *Sutzkever, Itzik *Manger, and Israel *Rabon have been published.

For most of the post-Holocaust period, the premier journals for Yiddish studies were the YIVO-*Bleter* ("YIVO Pages"), founded in 1931, and *Di *Goldene Keyt* ("The Golden Chain"), founded in Israel in 1949 by the poet Avrom Sutzkever. Yiddish academic publishing enjoyed a modest upswing in the early 1990s with the revival of the sporadic YIVO-*Bleter* and the founding of several Yiddish journals in Oxford. However, *Di Goldene Keyt* ceased publication in 1995, followed three years later by the Oxford imprints. In addition, journals such as the YIVO *Annual*, which was revived from 1990 to 1996, and *Khulyot* ("Links," 1993–present) created a forum for Yiddish scholarship in English and Hebrew respectively.

In another sign of this linguistic shift, interest among a wide audience in modern Yiddish literature has given rise to an ongoing trend of translations, mainly into English and Hebrew, but also into French, German, Spanish, and other languages. The bibliography by Dina Abramowicz in 1968 listed 247 titles of books translated from Yiddish into English, beginning in 1945 (*Yiddish Literature in English Translation* (1968); idem, *Yiddish Literature in English Translation: List of Books in Print* (1976)), and today that list could be significantly expanded. The awarding of the Nobel Prize to Isaac Bashevis Singer in 1978 increased interest in his works in particular, and in Yiddish literature in general. The New Yiddish Library, sponsored by Yale University Press and edited by David Roskies, has published fresh translations of the modern Yiddish classics and promises to acquaint the English reader with previously inaccessible Yiddish works. In the realm of historical study, YIVO has published translations of important material from its collections, such as the autobiographies of Jewish youth collected in the 1930s and Herman Kruk's diary of the Vilna ghetto (cf. J. Shandler (ed.), *Awakening Lives: Autobiographies of Jewish Youth in Poland Before the Holocaust* (2002) and H. Kruk, *Last Days of the Jerusalem of Lithuania: Chronicles from the Vilna Ghetto and the Camps, 1939–1944*, ed. Benjamin Harshav and trans. Barbara Harshav (2002)).

One of the main demonstrations of this trend is the appearance of two bilingual anthologies which strove to offer the best of Yiddish poetry to a new generation of readers: *American Yiddish Poetry: A Bilingual Anthology*, edited by Benjamin and Barbara Harshav (1986), and *The Penguin Book of Yiddish Verse*, edited by Irving Howe, Ruth R. Wisse and Khone Shmeruk (1987). The bilingual format of the two anthologies makes them the first collections of this type, and it demonstrates that the editors aimed for a varied audience: both the student and the reader of Yiddish literature in the original, as well as the English reader who did not know Yiddish. A comparison of the two volumes is interesting because of the differing approaches of the editors: the Harshavs emphasize the literary achievements, multifaceted quality, and uneasy path of modernism in Yiddish poetry in its most important center, the U.S., and thus their anthology can serve as an excellent introduction for the reader interested in this important branch of modern Yiddish literature; the editors of the *Penguin Book of Yiddish Verse*, which offers a selection of Yiddish poetry of the last one hundred years from the entire Yiddish world, aimed at a wider audience, and their selections were guided more by thematic concerns. They assumed that contemporary interest in Yiddish poetry is based primarily on its Jewish content and its ability to express and describe a world that no longer exists. The selections offered by these two books, therefore, reflect two different, complementary approaches towards the question of how to understand and appreciate the great heritage of Yiddish literature today, while demonstrating the multiplicity of approaches and contexts in which research and teaching in this field are conducted.

Scholars and students of Yiddish studies, who are relatively few in number and widely dispersed across the globe, are perennially frustrated by the difficulties of gaining access to books long out of print, while the costs of printing new works can be prohibitive. The National Yiddish Book Center, which began by accepting donations of Yiddish books collected *en masse* worldwide and selling them to interested libraries and individuals, has revolutionized access to Yiddish materials with its Steven Spielberg Digital Yiddish Library, which produces on-demand reprints of available Yiddish texts. Modern technology has proven a boon in other ways as well. The *Index to Yiddish Periodicals*, a database developed at Hebrew University in Jerusalem, allows researchers to search the content of many important journals, while the on-line forum *Mendele* connects Yiddish specialists around the globe. Such innovative tools, as well as a pluralism of views and methodologies, promise new achievements as scholars continue to develop the various fields of Yiddish research in the 21st century.

[Abraham Novershtern / Cecile Esther Kuznitz (2nd ed.)]

BIBLIOGRAPHICAL SURVEY

Interest in the study of Yiddish language and literature was first displayed by Christian scholars of the 16th–18th centuries (Buxtorf, Wagenseil, Schudt, and others) few of whom, however, had any functional knowledge of either the language or its literature. Their relevant texts concerning Yiddish are edited, translated into English, and analyzed by (1) J.C. Frakes, *Christian Humanists and the Study of Yiddish in Early Modern Europe* (2006). Modern research into Yiddish literature had its proper beginnings in the German *Wissenschaft des Judentums* school of the 19th century. It was primarily M. *Steinschneider who laid the foundations of Yiddish bibliography and, incidentally, also set the end of the 18th century as the limit for the study of Yiddish literature by future exponents of the *Wissenschaft des Judentums*, completely disregarding the new literature that was then being created in Eastern Europe. It was not until the beginning of the 20th century that scholars of East European extraction extended the scope of research to include modern Yiddish literary works.

The methods employed in research on, and criticism of, Yiddish literature do not differ in their essentials from any other modern criticism and literary research. To a certain degree, however, the study of Yiddish literature has until the 1990s lagged behind in adopting more advanced methods. Until World War II such study was characterized by its unwarranted dependence upon the traditional methods of German literary studies and concepts, especially with regard to early Yiddish literature. Furthermore, as a result of its close connections with certain ideologies and preconceived views, the study and criticism of Yiddish literature has retained some undeniable traces of tendentiousness. Those scholars who had inherited the mantle of the German *Wissenschaft des Judentums* tended to overemphasize the relationship between German and Yiddish literature in order to provide evidence of Jewish participation in German culture, or even of a German-Jewish symbiosis. This tendency was revived by modern German scholars. Their interest also centered upon early Yiddish literature, in view of the importance for German studies of pre-modern German texts preserved in the Hebrew alphabet. On the other hand, scholars and critics of Yiddish literature who belonged to the Yiddishist camp and as such had close connections with Jewish labor ideology tended to exaggerate the "secular" basis of early Yiddish literature. With regard to modern literature, Yiddishist scholars sometimes preferred ideological evaluation to aesthetic criticism and study of form. The establishment of a chair of Yiddish literature at Hebrew University in Jerusalem in 1951 paved the way for a renewal of

Yiddish literary studies consciously liberated from the limitations imposed upon them by the tendentiousness of the past and, to some degree, the present also. In recent decades, the study of Yiddish literature and culture is found in a variety of academic disciplines in the Humanities and Social Sciences.

Students of all periods and facets of Yiddish literature should have recourse to a few valuable reference works which, while not specifically devoted to literature, soon prove themselves indispensable. These include the pioneering pamphlet of (2) Uriel and Beatrice Weinreich, *Yiddish Language and Folklore* (1959) and its sequel (3) *Yiddish Linguistics; A Multilingual Bibliography* (1988), edited by Joan G. Bratkowsky. To this may be added (4) *Yiddish Linguistics; A Classified Bilingual Index to Yiddish Serials and Collections 1913–1958* by D.M. Bunis and A. Sunshine (1994). Yiddish studies have so proliferated in recent years that it is useful to have a general guide as well. (5) C.E. Kuznitz's "Yiddish Studies," in Martin Goodman (ed.), *The Oxford Handbook of Jewish Studies* (2002), 541–71 is remarkably comprehensive and insightful.

Up to the End of the 18th Century

The scholar and lay reader interested in Yiddish literature up to the end of the 18th century has to accept the fact that the material available (manuscripts, books, printed pamphlets) is marked by wide gaps in many fields. The erstwhile existence of many Yiddish works is known only from evidence found in secondary sources. See (6) Ch. Shmeruk, "Reyshuta shel ha-Proza ha-Sipurit be-Yidish u-Merkaza be-Italya," *Sefer Zikaron leArye Leona Carpi* (1967). Yiddish books and pamphlets dating back to the 16th, 17th, and 18th centuries are largely unica, existing in single copies only. The most comprehensive collection of manuscripts and books from this period is found in the David Oppenheimer collection, now a part of the Bodleian Library at Oxford University. The Bodleian Hebrew-alphabet (i.e., including but not restricted to Yiddish) manuscript collection is catalogued by (7) Adolf Neubauer, *Catalogue of the Hebrew Manuscripts in the Bodleian Library* (1886; 1994; supplement M. Beit-Arié and R.A. May, 1994), while the Hebrew-alphabet printed books are catalogued by (8) M. Steinschneider, *Catalogus librorum hebraeorum in bibliotheca bodleiana*, 2 vols. (1852–60; 1998), and (9) A.E. Cowley, *A Concise Catalogue of the Hebrew Printed Books in the Bodleian Library* (1929; 1971). Smaller collections, as well as important single manuscripts and books, are to be found in libraries throughout Europe, Israel, and the U.S. An older introduction to the more significant collections of specifically Yiddish books, as well as a bibliography of publications on Yiddish literature up to 1912, is included in (10) Ber Borokhov, "Di Bibliotek fun Yidishn Filolog," *Pinkes* (1913).

A useful bibliography of printed Yiddish works is still (11) M. Steinschneider, "Jüdisch-Deutsche Literatur," in: *Serapeum* (1848–49; 1961), although it is in many respects quite unreliable. Concerning Yiddish manuscripts, their publication and the references to them in various studies, (12) C. Habersaat, "Repertorium der jiddischen Handschriften," *Rivista degli studi orientali*, 29 (1954), 53–70; 30 (1955), 235–249; 31 (1956), 41–49, represents a useful, though difficult, source. Vast collections of early Yiddish texts have been made accessible in facsimile editions via several microfilm publications: (13) Ch. Shmeruk (ed.), "Research Collections on Microfiche: Jewish Studies, Yiddish Books" (1976 ff.); (14) H. Bobzin and H. Suess (eds.), *Sammlung Wagenseil* (1996); (15) H. Suess and H. Troeger (eds.), *Die Hebraica und Judaica der Sammlung Tychsen der Universitaetsbibliothek Rostock* (2002). Digitalized facsimiles of the extensive Hebrew-alphabet collection of the Universitaetsbibliothek, Frankfurt am Main, are available online: http://stub.semantics.de/jd/templates/template.xml?Sprache=eng&js=yes&Skript=Home

Recent decades have seen the discovery of numerous unknown or up to that point incomplete early Yiddish texts; further such discoveries may well still come to light. An outstanding example is the Yiddish rhymed couplet of 1272 found in the Worms *makhzor*, published and analyzed in (16) D. Sadan, "*Ketovet Rishona be-Yidish Kedumah be-Maḥzor Vermeyza*," in: *Kiryat Sefer* 38 (1963), 575–76; (17) M. Vaynraykh, "A Yidisher Zats fun far Zibn Hundert Yor," in: *Yidishe Shprakh* 23 (1963), 87–93 (correction in vol. 24 (1964)), 61–62. The most significant find was the Cambridge University Library manuscript from the Cairo *Genizah*, dated ca. 1382, known already before World War II, but not published until (18) L. Fuks, *The Oldest Known Literary Documents of Yiddish Literature* (c. 1382), 1–2 (1957); (19) *Dukus Horant*, ed. P.F. Ganz, F. Norman, W. Schwarz. (with excursus by S.A. Birnbaum) (1964); (20) H.J. Hakkarainen, *Studien zum Cambridger Codex T-S. 10. K. 22*, 3 vols. (1967–73). The definitive scholarly edition of the codex is (21) E. Katz (ed.), "Six Germano-Judaic Poems from the Cairo Genizah" (Diss. UCLA, 1963). The scholarly controversies surrounding the texts of the Cambridge manuscript (e.g. linguistic and cultural identity of the texts) are comprehensively treated by (22) J.C. Frakes, *The Politics of Interpretation: Alterity and Ideology in Old Yiddish Studies* (1989).

Other discoveries include: the recognition of several dozen glosses in the commentaries of Rashi (11th century) as examples of early Yiddish (see (23) E. Timm, "Zur Frage der Echtheit von Raschis jiddischen Glossen," in: *Beitraege zur Geschichte der deutschen Sprache und Literatur*, 107 (1985), 45–81); a complete text of the renaissance epic, *Pariz un Viene* (Verona, 1594), and the magnificent fable collection of the *Ki-bukh* (Verona, 1595). Such discoveries of early Yiddish texts have transformed the study of early Yiddish by extending the beginnings of Yiddish literature back to a much earlier date and by appreciably broadening its scope far beyond the narrow confines imagined by older scholarship. A radical change is thus called for in the hitherto available and accepted descriptions of early Yiddish works in the standard histories of early Yiddish literature: (24) Elazar Shulman, *Sefat Yehudit-Ashkenazit veSifruta* (1903; 1913); (25) M. Erik, *Vegn Altyidishn Roman un Novele* (1926); (26) M. Erik, *Di Geshikhte fun der Yidisher Literatur fun di Eltste Tsaytn biz der Haskole Tkufe* (1928); (27) M. Vaynraykh [Weinreich], *Bilder fun der Yidisher Literatur*

Geshikhte (1928); (28) Y. Tsinberg [Zinberg], *Di Geshikhe fun der Literatur bay Yidn*, 9 vols. (1929–37; Heb. tr. (1956–60); Eng. tr., 1972–78, esp. vol.. 6 of the Yid. ed.

These works have shortcomings which must be taken into account: the paucity of specific preliminary studies upon which they are based; the lack of a detailed and comprehensive investigation of the relationship between Yiddish and Hebrew literature on the one hand, and German literature on the other; failure to examine the role of Yiddish and Yiddish literature in the broad scope of Jewish culture of the period; and absence of detailed analysis of the nature of the literary genres. Considerable doubt must also be expressed about the "Spielmann" theory of the historical outlines of Yiddish literature, a theory borrowed by Erik and Weinreich from antiquated German literary research and grafted onto Yiddish literature without proper foundation; see: (29 Kh. Shmeruk, "Di Naye Editsye funem Altyidishn Mlokhim-Bukh," *Di Goldene Keyt* 59 (1967) and (30) Ch. Shmeruk, "Can the Cambridge Manuscript Support the Spielman Theory in Yiddish Literature?" in: *Studies in Yiddish and Folklore* (1986), 1–36. Detailed studies of specific works can teach us much, as in (31) M.I. Goldwasser, "Azhoras Noshim": a Linguistic Study of a Sixteenth-Century Yiddish Work (1982).

The lack of up-to-date scholarly surveys of the period has been satisfied by (32) Ch. Shmeruk, *Sifrut Yidish: Perakim leToldoteha* (1978; rev. Yid. tr.), (33) *Prokim fun der Yidisher Literatur-Geshikhte* (1988), and especially (34) J. Baumgarten, *Introduction à la littérature yiddish ancienne* (1993; rev. ed. and tr. by J.C. Frakes, (35) *Introduction to Old Yiddish Literature*, 2005). The recent anthology edited by (36) J.C. Frakes, *Early Yiddish Texts 1100–1750* (2004) provides critical editions of more than a hundred texts representing the broad scope of extant genres from this period (including many of the early texts discussed in the present entry), along with extensive bibliography of scholarly studies; it thus appreciably lessens the scholarly dependence on earlier, methodologically often problematic anthologies, such as: (37) J.C. Wagenseil, *Belehrung Der Jüdisch-Teutschen Red-und Schreibart* (1699); (38) J.J. Schudt, *Jüdische Merckwürdigkeiten*, III. *Theil* (1714); and (39) M. Grünbaum, *Jüdisch-deutsche Chrestomatie* (1882), as well as the first sections of: (40) *Antologye Finf Hundert Yohr Idishe Poezye*, ed. M. Basin, 1–2 (1917); (41) E. Korman *Yidishe Dikhterins, Antologye* (1928). The complex socio-linguistic development of the modern Yiddish literary language is comprehensively analyzed by (42) Dov-Ber Kerler, *The Origins of Modern Literary Yiddish* (1999).

Studies of Bible translations, Bible exegesis, and poems based on the Bible and midrashim, including texts, are included in: (43) W. Staerk and A. Leitzmann, *Die Jüdisch-Deutschen Bibelübersetzungen von den Anfängen bis zum Ausgang des 18. Jahrhunderts* (1923); (44) N. Leibowitz, *Die Übersetzungstechnik der Jüdisch-Deutschen Bibelübersetzungen des 15. und 16. Jahrhunderts* (1931); (45) Sh. Noble, *Khumesh-Taytsh* (1943); (46) Sh. Birnboym, "Zeks Hundert Yor Tilim Oyf Yidish," in: *For Max Weinreich…* (1964); (47) M. Aptroot, "Bible Translation as Cultural Reform: The Amsterdam Yiddish Bibles 1678–1679" (Diss., Oxford, 1989); (48) L. Landau, "A Hebrew-German Paraphrase of the Book of Esther," *Journal of English and Germanic Philology*, 18 (1919); (49) M. Stern (ed.), *Lieder des Venezianischen Lehrers Gumprecht von Szczebrzeszyn (um 1555)* (1922); (50) L. Landoy, "Der Yidisher Medrash Vayosha," *Filologishe Shriftn* 3 (1929); (51) F. Falk (ed.), *Das Schemuelbuch des Mosche Esrim Wearba*, I–II (1961); (52) L. Fuks, *Das Altjiddische Epos Melokhim-Bukh*, I–II (65); (53) P. Matenko and S. Sloan, "The Akeydes Yitskhok," in: *Two Studies in Yiddish Culture* (1968); see also the studies of the Cambridge Genizah manuscript (18–22). The identity of the genre of epic on biblical themes as specifically *midrashic* (and not *biblical* as such) was worked out by (54) D. Sadan, "The Midrashic Background of 'The Paradise' and its Implications for the Evaluation of the Cambridge Yiddish Codex (1382)," in: *The Field of Yiddish*, 2 (1965), 253–62, and (55) W.O. Dreessen, "Midraschepik und Bibelepik," *Zeitschrift fuer deutsche Philologie*, 100 (1981), 78–97.

Texts of the early Yiddish plays are included in the magisterial collective volume: (56) Ch. Shmeruk (ed.), *Maḥazot Mikra'iyyim be-Yiddish (1697–1750)* (1979), that also provides a broad survey of the history and function of drama in Ashkenaz; see also (57) E. Butzer, *Die Anfaenge der jiddischen purim shpiln in ihrem literarischen und kulturgeschichtlichen Kontext* (2003). Earlier discussions include: (58) Y. Shiper, *Geshikhte fun Yidisher Teater-Kunst un Drama*, 1–3 (1923–28); and in the first chapters of (59) B. Gorin, *Di Geshikhte fun Idishn Teater* (1929); on contemporary ḥasidic Purim plays, see (60) Ch. Shmeruk, "Ha-Shem ha-Mashma'uti Mordekhai-Markus: Gilgulo ha-Sifruti shel Idiyal Ḥevrati," in: *Tarbiz*, 29 (1959) and (61) Shifre Epshteyn (Shifra Epstein), *Donyel-Shpil beKhsides Bubov* (Eng. title: *The Daniel-shpil in the Bobover Hasidic Community*) (1998).

On Elye Bokher, see (62) G.E. Weil, Élie Lévita, humaniste et massorète (1963); (63) J. Joffe (ed.), *Elye Bokher: Poetishe Shafungen in Yidish, I* (1949); (33) Ch. Shmeruk, *Prokim* (1988), 97–120, 141–56; (35) J. Baumgarten, *Introduction* (2005), 163–206. (64) *Pariz un' Viene* is edited by Ch. Shmeruk (1996), and he is the subject of an innovative literary analysis by (65) A. Schulz, *Die Zeichen des Körpers und der Liebe: "Paris und Vienna" in der jiddischen Fassung des Elia Levita* (2000).

Texts of songs and hymns can be found in: (66) F. Rosenberg, "Über eine Sammlung Deutscher Volks-und Gesellschaftsliedern in Hebräischen Lettern," *Zeitschrift für die Geschichte der Juden in Deutschland*, 2 (1888), 3 (1889); (67) L. Löwenstein, "Jüdische und Jüdisch-Deutsche Lieder," in *Jubelschrift… I. Hildesheimer* (Berlin, 1890); (68) Y. Shatski (ed.), *Simkhes HaNefesh fun Elkhonen Kirkhon* (1926); (69) Ch. Shmeruk, "The Earliest Aramaic and Yiddish Version of the 'Song of the Kid' *(Khad Gadye)*," *The Field of Yiddish*, 1 (1954); (70) Kh. Shmeruk, "Velkher Yontef Iz Der Bester?," *Di Goldene Keyt* 47 (1963); (71) A. Yaari, "Gilgulo Shel Shir beYidish al Aseret haDibrot," *Kiryat Sefer* 41 (1966).

The *Ma'ase-bukh* has been translated into English by (72) M. Gaster, *Ma'aseh Book,* 1–2 (1934); into German by (73) Ulf Diedrich (2003), both based on the Amsterdam edition of 1732; and into French (with facing page facsimile of the *editio princeps* of 1602) by (74) Astrid Starck, *Un beau livre d'histoires / Eyn shön Mayse bukh*, 2 vols. (2003). See also (75) J. Meitlis, *Das Ma'assebuch, Seine Entstehung und Quellengeschichte* (1933) and (76) I.Z. Sand, "A Linguistic Comparison of Five Versions of the Mayse-Bukh," *The Field of Yiddish*, 2 (1965).

Fictional prose is discussed in (77) Y. Rivkind, "Di Historishe Alegorye fun R' Meyer Sh"ts," *Filologishe Shriftn* 3 (1929); (78) Kh. Shmeruk, "Ha-Sipurim al R' Adam Ba'al Shem ve-Gilguleihem be-Nuskho'ot Shivkhei ha-Besht," *Tsion* 28 (1963). The *Ki-bukh / Seyfer Mesholim* has been translated (with facsimile) by (79) A. Freimann, *Die Fabeln des Kuhbuches*, 2 vols. (1926) and (80) E. Katz, *Book of Fables; The Yiddish Fable Collection of Reb Moshe Wallich* (1994). See also (81) S. Tsfatman, *Bein Ashkenaz le-Sefarad – Le-Toledot ha-Sippur ha-Yehudi bi-Ymei ha-Beinayim* (1993) and (82) E. Timm, "'Beria und Simra': Eine jiddische Erzaehlung des 16. Jahrhunderts," in: *Literaturwissenschaftliches Jahrbuch*, n.s. 14 (1973), 1–94.

Most of the early Yiddish historical songs were listed in chronological order by (83) M. Steinschneider, *Die Geschichtsliteratur der Juden* (1905). The function of such songs is analyzed by (84) Kh. Turniansky, "Yiddish 'Historical' Songs as Sources for the History of the Jews in Pre-partition Poland," in: *Polin*, 4 (1989), 42–52. Editions of representative texts are (85) R. Ulmer (ed.), *Turmoil, Trauma and Triumph: the Fettmilch Uprising in Frankfurt-am-Main (1612–1616)* (2001) [= *Megiles Vints*]; (86) S. Neuberg (ed.), *Das Schwedesch lid* (2000). The relationship of Yiddish drama to German drama is analyzed in (56), of poetry in (66), of prose, in: (87) A. Paucker, "Yiddish Versions of Early German Prose Novels," in: *Journal of Jewish Studies*, 10 (1959).

The Arthurian legends in Yiddish are the subject of (88) L. Landau, *Arthurian Legends or the Hebrew-German Rhymed Version of the Legend of King Arthur* (1912) [with ed.], (89); R.G. Warnock, "The Arthurian Tradition in Hebrew and Yiddish," in: *King Arthur Through the Ages* (1990), 1:189–208 and (90) A. Jaeger, *Ein juedischer Artusritter* (2000). The problems posed by this type of adapted literature were also discussed in connection with the Cambridge manuscript.

The prosody of Yiddish poetry comes in for incidental treatment in general summaries and in connection with the publication of texts; it is dealt with specifically in (91) B. Korman, *Die Reimtechnik der Estherparaphrase Cod. Hamburg 144* (1930), and (92). Hrushovski, "The Creation of Accentual Iambs in European Poetry and their First Employment in a Yiddish Romance in Italy (1508–09)," in: *For Max Weinreich*… (1964).

Modern Literature

Until recently modern Yiddish literature lacked proper treatment in works based on modern methods of research and criticism. Much of the published material is confined to bibliography, biography, impressionistic criticism influenced by current events, eulogies, personal memoirs, introductions to the collected works of individual authors, and anthologies. There is an urgent need for critical editions of the literary works of this period; even the works of such authors as S.Y. Abramovitsh, Y.L. Perets, and Sholem-Aleykhem have not been published in complete and authoritative editions.

(93) The biographical encyclopedia by Z. *Rejzen, *Leksikon fun der Yidisher Literatur, Prese un Filologye*, 1–4, Vilna, 1928–29, which contains basic bibliographical data, and (94) *Leksikon fun der Nayer Yidisher Literatur,* 1–8 (1956–81) are useful guides for initial information about modern Yiddish writers. These works are supplemented by (95) Berl Kagan's *Leksikon fun Yidish-Shraybers* (1986). For bibliography, recourse may be had to the chapters on Judeo-German, Yiddish biography, and bio-bibliography in: (96) Sh. Shunami, *Mafteakh haMaftekhot* (1965). The following work (97) Y. Gar and F. Fridman, *Bibliografye fun Yidishe Bikher Vegn Khurbm un Gvure* (1962) is an important source for the literature of the Holocaust and postwar period.

The principal summaries of modern Yiddish literature are: (98) L. Wiener, *The History of Yiddish Literature in the Nineteenth Century* (1899); (99) M. Erik, *Etyudn tsu der Geshikhte fun Der Haskole, 1789–1881* (1934); (100) M. Viner, *Tsu Der Geshikhte fun der Yidisher Literatur in 19tn Yorhundert*, 2 vols. (1940; 1945–6. These may be complemented by (101) A.A. Roback, *Contemporary Yiddish Literature* (1957), and (102) S. Liptzin, *The Flowering of Yiddish Literature* (1964), and (103) *The Maturing of Yiddish Literature* (1970), as well as the sections on Yiddish literature in volumes 7–8 of (28) and in the additional volume 9 of that work: (104) Y. Tsinberg, *Di Bli-Tkufe fun der Haskole*, vol. 10 (1966). (105) *A Bridge of Longing; the Lost Art of Yiddish Storytelling* (1995) by David G. Roskies is an acute study of Yiddish narration focused on the central figures Nakhmen *Bratslaver, Ayzik-Meyer *Dik, Perets, Sholem-Aleykhem, Der Nister, Itsik Manger and Yitskhok Bashevis [Singer]. (106) The same scholar's earlier *Against the Apocalypse: Responses to Catastrophe in Modern Jewish Culture* (1984) is a seminal work in Yiddish as well as Holocaust studies. (107) Dovid Katz's *Words on Fire: the Unfinished Story of Yiddish* (2004) is a highly individual, footnote-free popular though learned survey.

Among the collections of critical articles and studies, mention should be made of (108) Sh. Bikl, *Shrayber fun Mayn Dor*, 1–2 (1958; 1965); (109) Y. Glatshteyn, *In Tokh Genumen*, 1–5 (1947, 1956; 1960; 1963); (110) A. Tabatshnik, *Dikhter un Dikhtung* (1965); (111) N. Mayzil, *Noente un Vayte*, 1–2 (1929–30); (112) N. Mayzil, *Forgeyer un Mittsaytler* (1946); (113) N. Mayzil, *Noente un Eygene* (1957); (114) N.-B. Minkov, *Zeks Yidishe Kritiker* (1954); (115) Sh. Niger, *Geklibene* Shriftn, 1–3 (1928); (116) Sh. Niger, *Dertseylers un Romanistn*, 1 (1946); (117) Sh. Niger, *Bleter Geshikhte fun der Yidisher Literatur* (1959); (118) D. Sadan, *Avney Bedek* (1962); (119) D. Sadan, *Avney Miftan*, vol. 1 (1962); (120) Sh.- L. Tsitron, *Dray Literarishe Doyres*, 1–4 (1931; 1922); (121) B. Rivkin, *Undzere Prozaiker* (1951).

Comprehensive anthologies include (122) Z. Rejzen, *Fun Mendelson biz Mendele* (1923); (123) N. Shtif, *Di Eltere Yidishe Literatur, Literarishe Khrestomatye* (1929); (124) A. Goldberg, *Undzer Dramaturgye, Leyenbukh in der Yidisher Drame* (1961). The following are anthologies in Hebrew translation: (125) *Akhisefer, Maasef leDivrey Sifrut... veTargumim min haShira haIdit*, ed. Sh. Niger and M. Ribilov (1944); (126) *Al Naharot Tisha Makhzorey Shira miSifrut Yidish*, ed. and tr. Sh. Meltser (1956); (127) M. Basuk, *Mivkhar Shirat Yidish, leman Y.-L. Perets ad Yameinu* (1963). In English translation there are a number of anthologies of prose. (128) I. Howe and E. Greenberg (eds.), *A Treasury of Yiddish Stories* (1953; paperback, 1958) has achieved classic status and may be credited more than any other single volume with bringing Yiddish fiction to the admiring attention of several generations of non-Yiddish-speaking readers. (Noyekh Miller and Leonard Prager have collected and published the Yiddish originals of the entire anthology on the Mendele website under the rubric "Onkelos"). The formidable editorial team composed of the brilliant essayist and critic of literature Howe and the Yiddish intellectual and poet Greenberg compiled a parallel volume (129), *A Treasury of Yiddish Poetry* (1969); an important bilingual anthology of Yiddish poetry (130) is *The Penguin Book of Modern Yiddish Verse*, ed. I. Howe, R.R. Wisse, and Ch. Shmeruk (1987). The 39 poets included in this volume were by the editors' collective judgment admitted to membership in an as yet undeclared poetic canon. Yiddish literature in the U.S. is treated in the following works: (131) K. Marmor, *Der Onheyb fun der Yidisher Literatur in Amerike, 1870–1890* (1944); (132) N.-B. Minkov, *Pionern fun Yidisher Poezye in Amerike*, 1–3 (1956); (133) A. Shulman, *Geshikhte fun der Yidisher Literatur in Amerike, 1870–1900* (1943); (134) N. Shteynberg, *Yung Amerike* (1917; 19302); (135) B. Grobard, *A Fertl Yorhundert* (1935); (136) B. Rivkin, *Yidishe Dikhter in Amerike* (1947); (137) B. Rivkin, *Grunt-Tendentsn fun der Yidisher Literatur in Amerike* (1948); (138) A. Pomerants, *Proletpen* (1935). (139) The entire Yiddish *oeuvre* of Menke Katz translated by Benjamin and Barbara Harshav is presented in *Menke* (2005), introduced by Dovid Katz with a monographic survey of 20th-century Yiddish literary politics in New York.

Anthologies of American Yiddish literature are: (140) *Antologye, di Idishe Dikhtung in Amerike biz Yohr 1919*, ed. D. Landoy (1919); (141) *In Zikh, Antologye* (1920); (142) N. Shteynberg's miscellany *Idish America* (1929) gives a good sense of the literary scene at the time; (143) *Hemshekh-Antologye, fun Amerikaner Yidisher Dikhtung, 1918–1943*, ed. M. Shtarkman (1945); (144) *Amerikaner Yidishe Poezye*, ed. M. Basin (1940); (145) N. Mayzil, ed. *Amerike in Yidishn Vort – Antologye* (1955) is a thematic anthology of America in Yiddish literature in translation; and (146) H. Goodman (ed.), *The New Country, Stories from the Yiddish about Life in America* (1961). (147) Benjamin and Barbara Harshav's *American Yiddish Poetry / A Bilingual Anthology* (1986) is an outstandingly designed book and its translations with the participation of K. Hellerstein, B. McHale, and A. Norich set new standards in the demanding art of poetry translation. (148) The sumptuous two-volume folio *Yiddish Literature in America 1870–2000, Anthology*, ed. E.S. Goldsmith (1999), with its generous allotment of space for all its authors, is a retrospective exhibition.

A bibliography of Yiddish literature in the Soviet Union is included in (149) *Pirsumim Yehudiim beVrit haMoatsot 1917–1960, Reshimot Bibliografiyot*, compiled Y.Y. Kohen, ed. Ch. Shmeruk (1961); (150) A. Abtshuk, *Etyudn un Materyaln tsu der Geshikhte fun der Yidisher Literatur-Bavegung in FSSR 1917–1927* (1934) is of great documentary value for the first ten years of the Soviet regime. The Soviet approach to Yiddish literature in the U.S.S.R. is given in the following collations of criticism: (151) M. Litvikov, *In Umru* 1 (1919), 2 (1926); (152) Y. Bronshteyn, *Atake* (1931), while the non-Soviet approach is to be found in (153) Sh. Niger, *Yidishe Shrayber in Sovyet-Rusland* (1958) and (154) Ch. Shmeruk, "Twenty-Five Years of *Sovetish Heymland* – Impressions and Criticism," in: Y. Ro'i and I. Beker (eds.), *Jewish Culture and Identity in the Soviet Union* (1991), 191–207; a short summary in English is (155) Ch. Shmeruk, "Yiddish Literature in the U.S.S.R.," in: *The Jews in Soviet Russia since 1917*, ed. L. Kochan (Oxford, 1970). See also (156) S. Wolitz, "The Kiev-Group (1918–1920) Debate: The Function of Literature," in: *Yiddish*, 3 (1978), 97–106.

The main anthologies of this literature are (157) *Oyf Naye Vegn, Almanakh, Draysik Yor Sovetish-Yidish Shafn* (1949), and (158) *Dertseylungen fun Yidishe Sovetishe Shrayber* (1969), both edited in the Soviet Union; (159) *A Shpigl oyf a Shteyn, Antologye Poezye un Proze fun Tsvelf Farshnitene Yidishe Shraybers in Ratn-Farband*, ed. Ch. Shmeruk; selected by B. Hrushovski, A. Sutskever and Ch. Shmeruk (1964; rev.ed.1988); (160) *Lo Amut Ki Ekhye, 24 Sippurim mi-Sifrut Yidish be-Vrit ha-Mo'aẓot* (1957), an anthology of Hebrew translations. See also (161) I. Howe and E. Greenberg (eds.), *Ashes Out of Hope – Fiction by Soviet Yiddish Writers* (1977).

Yiddish literature in Poland after World War I is treated in (162) Y.Y. Trunk, *Di Yidishe Proze in Poyln in Der Tkufe tsvishn Beyde Velt-Milkhomes* (1949); (163) B. Mark, *Umgekumene Shrayber fun Getos un Lagern* (1954). Anthologies of this literature from Poland are: (164) *Antologye fun der Yidisher Proze in Poyln Tsvishn Beyde Velt-Milkhomes (1914–1939)*, ed. Y.Y. Trunk and A. Tseytlin (1946); (165) B. Heler, *Dos Lid Iz Geblibn, Antologye, Lider fun Yidishe Dikhter in Poyln, Umgekumene Beys der Hitleristisher Okupatsye* (1951).

Other East European centers of Yiddish literature are the subject of (166) M. Naygreshl, "Di Moderne Yidishe Literatur in Galitsye," *Fun Noentn Over* (1955); (167) Sh. Bikl, "Vegn dem Onhoyb fun der Moderner Yidisher Literatur in Rumenye," *Shmuel Niger-Bukh* (1958); (168) *Oyfshtayg, Zamlbukh: Hundert Yor Yidishe Literatur in Rumenye*, ed. Meyer Rispler.

Anthologies in Israel of Yiddish literature include: (169) *Vortslen, Antologye fun Yidish Shafn in Yisroel / Poezye un Proze* ed. A. Shamri (1966); and (170) M. Khalmish, *Mi-Kan u-mi-Karov, Antologyah shel Sipurei Yidish be-Erez-Yisrael mi-Reishit ha-Me'ah ve-ad Yameinu* (1966); (171) *Yidish-Literatur in Medines-Yisroel / Antologye*, 2 vols. (1991) [edited by H. Osherovitsh, Sh. Vorzoger, M. Yelin, E. Podriatshik, M. Tsanin] [single selections of 204 writers who lived in Israel with brief bio-bibliographical introductions and photographs].

The lack of adequate attention to Yiddish women authors has been belatedly and partially addressed in the anthology of short story translations: (172) *Found Treasures / Stories by Yiddish Women Writers*, ed. F. Forman, E. Raicus, S. Silberstein Swartz, and M. Wolfe (1994). (173) Kathryn Hellerstein has translated and commented upon a wide selection of Kadya Molodowsky's poems in her *Papirene Brikn* (1999), with Yiddish original facing English translation. Dafna Clifford has written perceptively about Esther Kreitman, the relatively little-known sister of the famous Singer brothers: (174) "From Diamond Cutters to Dog Races: Antwerp and London in the Work of Esther Kreitman," in: *Prooftexts*, 23 (2003), 320–37.

Specific problems in poetics and prosody are studied in the following works: (175) D. Hofshteyn and P. Shames, *Teorye fun Literatur, Poetik* (Kharkov 1930); (176) N. Stutshkov, *Yidisher Gramen-Leksikon* (1931); (177) A. Vaynraykh, "Vegn Filtrafikn Gram," *Yidishe Shprakh* 15 (1955); (178) U. Weinreich, "On Cultural History of Yiddish Rhyme," *Essays on Jewish Life and Thought* (1959); and (179) B. Hrushovski, "On Free Rhythms in Yiddish Poetry," *The Field of Yiddish*, 1 (1954).

The quality of translations of Yiddish literature into English has improved in the past decade and with it the quality of anthologies of Yiddish literature in English translation. (180) Hugh Denman lists 90 anthologies of Yiddish literature in English (in *The Mendele Review*, 8.08, July 29, 2004), including one of short fiction edited by the veteran anthologist of Yiddish Joachim Neugroschel. No earlier short story collection approaches the breadth of (181) *No Star Too Beautiful* (2002), which gives recognition to older Yiddish literature. Neugroschel includes extracts from the *Mayse-bukh* and *Tsenerene*, and stories by Anski, Asch, Bashevis, Bergelson, Bimko, Dik, Dinezon, Elye Bokher, Ettinger, Avrom Karpinovitsh, Glikl, Kipnis, Kobrin, Rokhl Korn, Kulbak, H. Leyvik, Linetski, Abramovitsh, Nakhmen of Bratslav, Perets, Der Nister, Nomberg, Yoysef Perl, Yeshue Perle, Pinski, Avrom Reyzn, Khave Roznfarb, Yoyne Roznfeld, Lamed Shapiro, Sholem-Aleykhem, Spektor, Y.-Y. Trunk, and others.

Translation continues to be a challenge to students of Yiddish, who inevitably encounter the half-truth that Yiddish is untranslatable. In a recent effort at rendering Abramovitsh (whose Yiddish, it is claimed, was already somewhat archaic a century ago) freshly and engagingly, the late Ted Gorelik in translating *Fishke the Lame* "conveys the intricacies of Abramovitsh's Yiddish diction by echoing the dialects found in English novels of the 18th and 19th centuries by such authors as Laurence Sterne and Charles Dickens, whose work influenced Abramovitsh." On the other hand, Hillel Halkin, a veteran translator of Hebrew in particular, "strikes a balance between archaic and modern elements of style." (182) S.Y. Abramovitsh, *Tales of Mendele the Book Seller*, ed. D. Miron and K. Frieden (1996), lxii.

For material on research in Yiddish literature see the following: L. Prager, in: J.A. Fishman (ed.), *Never Say Die! A Thousand Years of Yiddish in Jewish Life and Letters* (1981), 529–45; D. Roskies, in: *Prooftexts*, 1 (1981), 28–42; Ch. Shmeruk, in: *Di Goldene Keyt*, 91 (1976), 39–48.

[Chone Shmeruk / Leonard Prager (2nd ed.)]

ADD. BIBLIOGRAPHY: M. Aptroot, in: G. Estraikh and M. Krutikov (eds.), *Yiddish in the Contemporary World* (1999), 43–55; A. Novershtern, in: *ibid.*, 1–19; M. Krutikov, in: *Shofar*, 20:3 (2002), 1–13; C. Kuznitz, in: M. Goodman (ed.), *The Oxford Handbook of Jewish Studies* (2002), 541–71; L. Prager, in: *La Rassegna Mensile di Israel*, 62:1–2 (1996), 451–64; J. Shandler, in: *Conservative Judaism*, 54:4 (Summer 2002), 69–77; M. Isaacs, in: L.J. Greenspoon (ed.), *Yiddish Language and Culture Then and Now* (1998), 165-88; idem, in: D.-B. Kerler (ed.), *Politics of Yiddish* (1998), 85-96; idem, in: J. Sherman (ed.), *Yiddish After the Holocaust* (2004), 131-48; idem, in: *International Journal of the Sociology of Language*, 138 (1999), 9-30; idem, in: *La culture yiddish aujourd'hui* (2004), 14-21; A.F. Roller, *The Literary Imagination of Ultra-Orthodox Jewish Women* (1999); J. Shandler, in: *Pakntreger* (2002), 21-7.

YIDDISH THEATER, FOLKSBIENE. New York City's Folksbiene Yiddish Theater, which the *New York Post* called "one of the city's most remarkable cultural institutions," is America's sole surviving professional Yiddish theater and the longest continuously producing Yiddish theater company in the world. When Folksbiene was founded in 1915 on the Lower East Side, New York City boasted 14 other Yiddish theater companies. True to its name (the People's Stage) the Folksbiene Yiddish Theater is dedicated to producing shows and events that are socially relevant and that foster understanding and cohesion within the broader Jewish community.

From 1915 to 1998 the Folksbiene existed under the auspices of the *Workmen's Circle/Arbeter Ring as a semi-professional company, serving an immigrant community and presenting literary Yiddish plays as well as plays from the world repertoire in Yiddish translation. In 1998 Folksbiene's board of directors ushered in a new era by replacing the company's management and instituting a new mandate to modernize the company and expand the audience beyond its strictly Yiddish-speaking core constituency. Its mission is twofold: to be the custodian of a rich cultural legacy, while developing new works that will add to this legacy. Zalmen Mlotek, noted conductor and Yiddish music specialist, took over the leadership and brought in new and innovative programming.

The Folksbiene became independently incorporated, employed a fully professional staff and performers, and provided English and Russian translations for non-Yiddish speakers. By the fall of 2004, the Folksbiene had ushered in a dramatic expansion of its programming, producing a year-round schedule of mainstage productions and a wide array of other music, literary, and theatrical events. More and more theatergoers with no previous exposure to Yiddish culture flock to the theater to sample all the excitement. In an effort to continue this growth, the Folksbiene instituted an Outreach Program to bring Yiddish performance to communities outside of New York City. Looking forward, the Folksbiene is in the process of establishing itself as a national membership organization and has raised $1.9 million toward building a permanent home.

See also *Theater: Yiddish Theater.

[Zalman Mlotek (2nd ed.)]

YIDISHER KEMFER ("Jewish Fighter"), U.S. Yiddish Labor Zionist publication. Founded in Philadelphia in 1906 as an organ of Po'alei Zion in America, the *Kemfer* appeared as an irregular weekly in New York from 1907 to 1923, as a biweekly from 1924 to 1931 (during which period it was called *Yidisher Arbeter*), for many years thereafter a weekly, then in 1990 a biweekly and, since the mid-1990s, as a bimonthly magazine. Initially sponsored by the Labor Zionist Organization-Poale Zion, later under the auspices of the Jewish National Workers Alliance (renamed the Farband Labor Zionist Order in 1950), and since the mid-1960s by the Labor Zionist Alliance's "Labor Zionist Letters." During its long history, it was edited by such distinguished figures as Kalman *Marmor, David *Pinski, Ber *Borochov, Joel *Entin, Chaim *Greenberg, and Mordechai Strigler. It was for many years an international center for Labor Zionist thought and one of the most eminent Yiddish political and social journals in the United States and indeed in the world. From 1963 through 1995, under Strigler's tenure, the *Kemfer* published such renowned authors as Jacob Glatstein, Chaim Grade, H. Leivik, Abraham Reizen, and Isaac Bashevis Singer. From the summer of 1998, it was edited by Jacob Weitzner.

BIBLIOGRAPHY: D. Smith, "Mordechai Strigler, 76, Editor of Yiddish Forward," in: *The New York Times* (May 12, 1998).

[Hillel Halkin / Arieh Lebowitz (2nd ed.)]

YIDISHE SHTIME, a daily paper published in Kovno (Lithuania). Founded in 1919, it was published by the General Zionist Organization of Lithuania, but became the acknowledged organ of the whole of Lithuanian Jewry. At first the paper consisted only of two small sheets, but from the end of 1920 it ran to eight pages on weekdays and 12 or more at weekends and on holidays. The first editor was L. Garfunkel, who was succeeded in 1921 by A. Elyashiv. R. Rubinstein was chief editor from 1923 and was largely responsible for developing the newspaper and giving it high standing. From time to time *Yidishe Shtime* had regular supplements, such as *Hed Lita* ("Echo of Lithuania") which appeared weekly in Hebrew; *Die Welt*, an illustrated weekly printed in Berlin; and *Musu garsas* ("Our Voice") in Lithuanian. In June 1940, with the invasion of Lithuania by the Russians, the paper and its printing press were nationalized and turned into an organ of the local Jewish Communists. Rubinstein, the editor, was dismissed, imprisoned soon after for the "crime of Zionism," and sent to a concentration camp in northern Russia. The paper survived only a short time until the appearance of the official Communist Yiddish journal, *Kovner Emes* ("Kovno Truth").

[Leib Garfunkel]

YIDISHES TAGEBLAT, New York Yiddish daily newspaper. Founded by K.H. *Sarasohn in 1885, it was regarded as the first Yiddish daily in the world, although it did not publish daily (excluding Saturday) until 1894. The *Tageblat* continued publication until 1928, when it was amalgamated with the *Morning Journal* [*Morgen zshurnal*]. Its first editor was M. Jalomstein, who was succeeded in 1892 by Johann (John) Paley, under whom the newspaper became extremely influential, circulation figures ranging from 30,000 at the end of the century to 70,000 in 1913. The paper had an anti-socialist policy, later taking a more progressive trend but without departing from its position as spokesman for Orthodoxy and the maintenance of Jewish customs, literature, and language.

BIBLIOGRAPHY: Anon, "A Yiddish Daily Paper," in: *Salvation – A New Evangelical Monthly*, vol. 1 (Jan. 1899); Y. Chaiken, *Yidishe bleter in Amerike* (1946); H. Hapgood, *The Spirit of the Ghetto* (1966); Z. Rejzen, *Leksikon fun der Yidisher Literatur, Prese un Filologye*, 4 (1929)

YIGDAL (Heb. יִגְדַּל; "May He be magnified"), opening word of a liturgical hymn based upon the Thirteen Articles of Faith enumerated by Maimonides. Its authorship is attributed to Daniel b. Judah, a *dayyan* in Rome in the first half of the 14th century. It is also ascribed to Immanuel (b. Solomon) of *Rome, the author of the *Maḥbarot* (see: *Maḥbarot Immanu'el ha-Romi*, ed. by D. Yarden, 1 (1957) 90–93; esp. 90 no. 422). *Yigdal* is metrically constructed and has a single rhyme throughout. Although other poetical renditions of these principles of faith were composed during this period, only *Yigdal* became incorporated into the daily liturgy. In the Ashkenazi ritual, it is usually printed at the start of the daily *Shaḥarit* service, but recited as in the Sephardi, Italian, and Yemenite rituals only at the conclusion of the Friday and festival evening services. Ḥasidim do not recite this hymn at all. The Ashkenazi hymn consists of 13 lines, one for each creed. The Sephardi version, on the other hand, contains 14 lines; the final line of this version is: "These are the 13 bases of the Jewish faith and the tenets of God's law."

English translations of *Yigdal*, retaining the rhyme, have been composed, such as that of Alice Lucas (1852–1935). Her rendition begins:

> The living God we praise, exalt, adore!
> He was, He is, He will be evermore!
> No unity like unto His can be:
> Eternal, inconceivable is He.

It concludes:

> He at the last will His anointed send,
> Those to redeem, who hope, and wait the end.
> God will the dead to life again restore.
> Praised be his glorious Name for evermore! (Hertz, Prayer, 7).

[Aaron Rothkoff]

Musical Rendition

The many melodies for *Yigdal* seem to have been composed, evolved, or adapted more or less independently in each local community. Where the Ashkenazi custom prevails, and also in Yemen, the melodies of *Yigdal* are generally based on the prayer mode and, in this sense, tend toward standardization and a lack of individuality. In the Sephardi Diaspora, however, *Yigdal* has a great number of distinct tunes; none of them seems to be particularly old and all of them draw strongly upon the reservoir of free paraliturgical and secular tunes available within the community and from the surrounding population (such as folk song and military marches). The only element common to most of these is the character of the melodies, which, together with the way in which they are sung by the congregation, combines the moods of pride and cheerfulness.

One *Yigdal* melody has achieved particular fame – the so-called "Leoni *Yigdal*". It is attributed to Meyer Leon, called Leoni, who was *ḥazzan* at the Duke's Place synagogue in London (Ashkenazi). Thomas Olivers, a Wesleyan minister, heard Leoni sing this *Yigdal* there; he decided to render the hymn into English and to introduce it into Christian worship together with its melody. (In another version of the story Olivers first translated the text and then went to Leoni to ask for "a synagogue melody to suit it.") Olivers' version, *The God of Abraham Praise*, first published in 1770, became popular immediately, and is sung to this day in the Anglican service as a processional or general-purpose hymn (*Hymns Ancient and Modern Revised*, no. 637, pp. 868–70). It has also been taken into the hymnals of several other English-speaking Protestant denominations. A.Z. *Idelsohn attempted to relate the Leoni *Yigdal* in a large comparative table to a number of Spanish, Basque and Polish folk songs, to a Sephardi melody for the *piyyut Lekh le-Shalom Geshem u-Vo le-Shalom Tal*, and also to the melodies of the Zionist hymns *Dort wo die Zeder* and *Ha-Tikvah*, together with the well-known motive from Smetana's *Moldau*. Not all of the comparisons in the scheme are musicologically valid. In any case, Idelsohn's main objective here, which was to prove the "Jewish roots" of *Ha-Tikvah*, has been invalidated by the discovery of its true antecedents (see *Ha-Tikvah).

[Bathja Bayer]

BIBLIOGRAPHY: Idelsohn, Liturgy, 74: Elbogen, Gottesdienst, 87f.; Davidson, Ozar, 2 (1929), 266f. MUSICAL RENDITION: Idelsohn, Melodien, indices: A. Baer, *Baal T'fillah* (1883^3), no. 432 (4 versions); Levy, Antologia, 1 (1965), nos. 43–62: Idelsohn, Music, 220–5; J. Picciotto, *Sketches of Anglo-Jewish History* (Rev. ed. 1956), 139–40; J. Julian, *Dictionary of Hymnology* (1892), 1149–52; A. Haeussler, *Story of Our Hymns* (1952), index; M. Frost (ed.), *Historical Companion to Hymns Ancient and Modern* (1962), 475–6.

YIḤUS (Heb. יחוס, biblical Heb. יַחַשׂ; "genealogy"), common term for family records, derived from the root יחס ("relationship"). The term is first found in the later books of the Bible, where it means genealogical lists (e.g., I Chron. 9:1, "So all Israel were reckoned by genealogies"). After the return from the Babylonian exile, genealogies were evidently important because those who could not bring evidence of their ancestry, for example, were excluded from the priesthood (Ezra 2:62; Neh. 7:64). The word retained this meaning in the talmudic period where mention is made of a *Megillat Yuḥasin* ("Book of Genealogies"), a commentary on Chronicles whose loss was considered "to have impaired the strength of the sages, and to have dimmed the light of their eyes" (Pes. 62b), where it is related that Simeon b. Azzai said, "I found a book of genealogical records in Jerusalem" (Yev. 49b). The importance of *yiḥus* is revealed in the statement of R. Ḥama b. R. Ḥanina that "When the Holy One, blessed be He, causes His Divine Presence to rest, it is only upon families of pure birth (*mishpaḥot meyuḥasot*) in Israel" (Kid. 70b). There seems, however, to have been some attempt to counter the importance attached to *yiḥus*, as is revealed by such statements as "the learned *mamzer* takes precedence over the ignorant high priest" (Hor. 3:8). In later Jewish tradition considerable importance was attached to *yiḥus* in the matter of arranging marriages (see Sh. Ar., EH chaps. 2–6). Lists of genealogical records were even printed with the express purpose of tracing the *yiḥus* of particular families. Examples of these are to be found in Ḥ.N. and D. Magid's *Mishpaḥat Ginsburg* (1899); S.Z. Kahana's *Anaf Eẓ Avot* (Cracow, 1903); and A. Epstein's *Mishpaḥat Luria* (Vienna, 1901). It was considered particularly valuable to be able to trace one's lineage back to King David. In the introduction to *Migdanot Eli'ezer* (1895), Rabbi E. Ḥarlap of Poland published a family tree showing his descent from King David.

See *Genealogy, *Zekhut Avot, *Family.

YIḤYE, ISAAC HA-LEVI (1867–1932), selected as last chief rabbi of Yemenite Jewry, pupil and grandson of R. Shalom Manẓurah. Yiḥye was known for his Torah learning as well as for his understanding of worldly affairs. Appointed *av bet din* of *San'a in 1901, he became chief rabbi of *Yemen in 1905, holding this position until his death. His rabbinical appointment corresponded with one of Yemenite Jewry's most difficult periods – following upon the war and the severe famine which struck the country in 1903–04. After this the community numbered only a third of its previous size. He reorganized the survivors and restored its religious and communal institutions, both internally and externally with regard to its relations with the central government.

Yiḥye's activities spread throughout Yemen, and by means of emissaries and rabbis he was vigilant in Torah and religious matters throughout the exile; in the fields of education, the rabbinate, matrimony and *takkanot* affecting society. Together with the heads of the San'a community, he strove to found a modern school in the capital. For this purpose they entered into lengthy negotiations with the *Alliance Israélite Universelle, but for various reasons the plan did not materialize. As *av bet din*, his responsa were sent to all parts of Yemen. His numerous activities include the rescue of orphans from conversion and the smuggling of them into Palestine, and his purchase of the land of the Jewish district in San'a from the hands of the Muslim waqf. Yiḥye also maintained contact with the Zionist organization in Palestine and assisted the immigration of Yemenite Jews. As official representative of the Jews, he was treated with honor and respect in the court of the imam and in government circles. He succeeded in using his influence for the benefit of his community.

[Yehuda Ratzaby]

Yiḥye's son, R. SHALOM ISAAC HA-LEVI (1891–?), was *av bet din* and chief rabbi of the Yemenite Jews in Israel (1925–1961) and took part in the educational activities of his community. He was also helpful in editing the responsa of R. Yiḥye *Sāliḥ (parts 1–2, 1946; part 3, 1965) to which he wrote the introduction. In 1955 he edited the Mishnah *Berakhot*, with the commentary of R. Obadiah of *Bertinoro, in Yemenite vocalization.

YINNON (Indelman), MOSHE (1895–1977), Hebrew and Yiddish journalist. Born in Poland, Yinnon was active in the Zionist movement, contributed to the Hebrew press, taught Hebrew, and served as a member of the editorial staff of the Yiddish paper *Haynt*. For a number of years he also edited the Hebrew weekly *Hadoar* in New York City. In 1940 he emigrated to Palestine where from 1943 to 1956 he was editor of the publishing house Mosad Bialik.

BIBLIOGRAPHY: Kressel, Leksikon, 2 (1967), 86.

[Eisig Silberschlag]

YISHTABBAḤ (Heb. יִשְׁתַּבַּח; lit. "Praised"), first word and the name of the blessing which concludes the *Pesukei de-Zimra section of the morning service. *Yishtabbaḥ* is referred to in the Talmud as "the benediction of song," where it is designated as a conclusion of the *Hallel* recited during the Passover *seder* (Pes. 118a; Rashbam ad loc.). The blessing is one of praise for God, declaring that unto Him "song and praise are becoming, hymn and psalm, strength and dominion, victory, greatness and might, renown and glory, holiness and sovereignty, blessings and thanksgivings from henceforth even for ever" (Hertz, Prayer, 107).

Its author is unknown, although some attribute it to a certain Solomon, interpreting שִׁמְךָ לָעַד מַלְכֵּנוּ הָאֵל (*Shimkha la'ad Malkenu ha-El*) as an acronym of his name. Others explain this *notarikon* as being in honor of King Solomon (*Abudarham ha-Shalom* (ed.) Jerusalem (1959), 64). The Zohar places great stress on the proper recitation of this prayer since its 13 individual praises of God activate the 13 attributes of God (Zohar, Ex., 132a). *Yishtabbaḥ* should be recited while standing (Sh. Ar., OḤ 53:1 and *Taz* ad loc.), and it is forbidden to interrupt or converse during this portion of the service (*ibid.*, 51:4; cf. 54:3). Following *Yishtabbaḥ*, half-*Kaddish* is recited to separate the *Pesukei de-Zimra* from the *Shema* and its benedictions which follow.

BIBLIOGRAPHY: Elbogen, Gottesdienst, 85f.; Idelsohn, Liturgy, 84; E. Levy, *Yesodot ha-Tefillah* (1952[2]), 134f.

YIVO (acronym for **Yidisher Visnshaftlekher Institut**) **INSTITUTE FOR JEWISH RESEARCH**, the principal world organization conducting research in *Yiddish and about the history and culture of Yiddish-speaking Jewry. Until 1955, its English designation was the Yiddish Scientific Institute. YIVO sought from its inception to collect and preserve material mirroring Jewish life and to study various Jewish problems objectively and empirically. In this endeavor, YIVO was guided by three basic principles: (1) the peoplehood of Jews, especially as united by the Yiddish language; (2) the enrichment of the life of that people by means of Jewish scholarship; and (3) the application of the most modern methods of research in the quest for a better understanding of Jewish identity and Jewish group phenomena.

The original proposal for a Yiddish academic institute was initiated by Nahum (Nokhem) *Shtif and published in the pamphlet *Di Organizatsye fun der Yidisher Visnshaft* ("The Organization of Yiddish Scholarship," 1925). Shtif argued that Jews should participate in scholarly research in their own language, and that the results of world scholarship be made available to those Jews unfamiliar with languages other than Yiddish. Noting the achievements of various scholars during the preceding decade in new areas of Jewish research, he proposed an institution that would coordinate, conduct, and disseminate such research, as well as standardize the Yiddish language, collect relevant library and archival materials, and train young scholars. Shtif's plan was approved at a meeting organized by Max *Weinreich and Zalman *Rejzen in Vilna on March 24, 1925. The decision to begin work was made later that year at a conference in Berlin held August 7–12, 1925. Although the official seat of the institute was in that German city, Vilna was the most active center of YIVO's work and eventually the location of its headquarters. An American branch was founded in October 1925 and subsidiary branches or support groups were also active in locales around the world including Argentina, Austria, Brazil, Chile, England, Estonia, France, Latvia, Romania, and Palestine. After the outbreak of World War II the American branch, earlier known as the Amopteyl (Amerikaner Opteylung) took over the central direction of the institute (1940).

In the period before World War II YIVO's research was conducted through four sections: (1) History, directed by Elias *Tcherikower and including Simeon *Dubnow, Raphael Mahler, Emanuel *Ringelblum, Ignacy Schipper, and Jacob *Shatzky; (2) Philology, directed by Max *Weinreich and including Y.L. *Cahan, Zelig *Kalmanovitch, Samuel (Shmuel) *Niger, Noah *Prylucki, and Zalman *Rejzen; (3) Economics and Statistics, directed by Jacob *Lestschinsky and including *Ben-Adir, Boris Brutzkus, Julius Brutzkus, Liebman *Hersch, and Mark Wischnitzer; and (4) Psychology and Education, directed by Leibush *Lehrer and including Abraham *Golomb, H.S. Kasdan, Lyuba Konel, Herts Kovarski, and Roza Simkhovitsh. Publications were in Yiddish with summaries in English, German, or Polish. These included each section's series of *Shriftn fun Yidishn Visnshaftlekhn Institut* ("Writings of the Yiddish Scientific Institute," 1925–40), the journal *Yivo-Bleter* ("YIVO Pages," 1931–), and the newsletter *Yedies fun Yivo* ("YIVO News," 1925–). A Bibliographic Center, Library, and Archives collected historic and contemporary research material. Correspondents in Yiddish-speaking communities throughout the world, but most especially in Eastern Europe, were encouraged to study local folkways and to assemble material of historical and cultural significance to send to the institute. YIVO's Vilna period reached its peak with two international conferences organized in 1929 and 1935, which were attended by leading scholars from around the world. In the 1930s Max Weinreich, YIVO's dominant figure, increasingly emphasized the study of Jewish sociology and economic life. In 1934 the institute initiated the Division of Youth Research and the Aspirantur, a training program for young scholars. An Art Section was created the following year and YIVO's efforts to standardize Yiddish spelling finally reached fruition in 1936. By 1939 YIVO had amassed one of the world's largest Judaica collections, including books, press, theatrical memorabilia, photographs, manuscripts and letters of famous personalities, and sundry items connected with Yiddish culture.

After the German invasion of Vilna during the Holocaust, the Nazis established a sorting center for looted Jewish property in the YIVO building in March 1942. They forced YIVO staff members to select the most valuable items to be sent to Germany and attempted to destroy the rest, but many Jews smuggled or hid important items. At the war's end the YIVO headquarters in Vilna was completely destroyed and the New York branch was declared the institute's new center. The materials sent to Germany and some hidden in Vilna were recovered and sent to New York in 1947.

In 1955 YIVO moved to a building at 86th Street and Fifth Avenue and changed its English name to the YIVO Institute for Jewish Research. In this period YIVO pioneered the academic study of the Holocaust and gave increasing attention to the lands to which East European Jews had immigrated, especially to the problems of Jewish acculturation in the U.S. Yiddish writers, scholars, and Jewish communal bodies added to YIVO's collections, while the acquisition of records from the American Jewish Committee and the Hebrew Immigrant Aid Society (HIAS) made YIVO a major center for the study of American Jewish history. The institute also sponsored annual conferences, exhibits, classes, and seminars, which served as a forum for the exchange of ideas and enriched the Jewish cultural scene. Participants in YIVO's Research Planning Commission, organized by Max Weinreich in 1962, included Michael Astour, Gerson D. *Cohen, Alexander Ehrlich, Marvin I. Herzog, and Uriel *Weinreich, with Joshua A. *Fishman as chairman. Major research projects inaugurated by the Commission included: the Interplay of Social and Political Factors in the Struggle of a Minority for its Survival and Creative Development; the Jews of Poland, 1919–1939; and the History of the American Jewish Labor Movement. YIVO sponsored research conferences on the German-Imposed Jewish Councils during World War II; Multilingualism and Social Change: Perspectives on Yiddish; and Economic Aspects of Jewish Life in Poland between the two World Wars. In 1970 the Commission was expanded into a Commission of Research and Training under the chairmanship of Nathan Reich.

Despite the continued leadership of Max Weinreich until his death in 1969, there was a dwindling number of scholars fluent in Yiddish, and the compromise with English became increasingly more pronounced. In 1968 YIVO founded the Uriel Weinreich Program in Yiddish Language, Literature, and Culture, an intensive summer language course; and a graduate component, the Max Weinreich Center for Advanced Jewish Studies. These programs played a crucial role in transmitting knowledge of the Yiddish language and of East European Jewish culture to young American-born scholars, many of whom became leaders in Jewish Studies programs then developing on campuses across the U.S.

YIVO's post-war publications include such standard reference works as Uriel Weinreich's *College Yiddish* (1949) and *Modern English-Yiddish Yiddish-English Dictionary* (1968) and Max Weinreich's *Geshikhte fun der Yidisher Shprakh*, 4 vols. (1973; partial Eng. tr. *History of the Yiddish Language*, 1980). YIVO created the journal *Yidishe Shprakh* ("Yiddish Language," 1941–86), edited by Yudel *Mark and later Mordkhe Schaechter, to treat problems of standard Yiddish. *The YIVO Annual of Jewish Social Science* (later the *YIVO Annual*, 1946–96), whose founding editor was Shlomo Noble, originally included mainly translations from YIVO's Yiddish publications; later volumes contained an increasing proportion of original contributions, especially on Jewish life in America. Under YIVO's auspices, the Yiddish Dictionary Committee was established in 1953 to gather, define, and publish Yiddish lexicographical treasures. Four folio volumes of the *Groyser Verterbukh fun der Yidisher Shprakh* ("Great Dictionary of the Yiddish Language") appeared between 1961 and 1980 (comprising *only* the letter alef), although the project was no longer affiliated with YIVO by the latter date. Bibliographies listing books, journals, articles, and reviews published by YIVO appeared in 1943 and 1955.

In the 1980s YIVO created the Max and Frieda Weinstein Archive of Recorded Sound and the Yiddish Folk Arts Program (popularly known as KlezKamp, later run independently), which played a central role in the revival of *klezmer* (East European Jewish folk) music. With the advent of Perestroika YIVO learned that part of its pre-war collection had survived in Soviet Lithuania, and the archival materials were brought to New York and duplicated in 1995–96. Together with the Jewish Theological Seminary of America and the Russian State University of the Humanities in Moscow, YIVO created the first Jewish Studies program in the former Soviet Union, Project Judaica. In 1992 the first volumes of *The Language and Culture Atlas of Ashkenazic Jewry* appeared, a massive project begun by Uriel Weinreich in 1959 to record Yiddish dialects. YIVO's library and archives continued to expand, in particular with the acquisition of the Bund Archives of the Jewish Labor Movement (1992), while the publication of *The Yiddish Catalog and Authority File of the YIVO Library* (1990) and *The Guide to the YIVO Archives* (1998) greatly improved access to the collections. The 1994 bombing of the AMIA Jewish community center in Buenos Aires severely damaged YIVO's branch there, which had been run independently since World War II. Members of the institute's New York staff traveled to Argentina to assess the damage and offer assistance. In 1999 YIVO relocated to the Center for Jewish History, a facility at 15 West 16th Street in New York housing several Jewish research institutions. At the start of the 21st century YIVO's Library and Archives contained more than 350,000 volumes and 10,000 linear feet of archival material, the world's largest collections documenting Yiddish culture and the experience of East European Jews and their descendants.

ADD. BIBLIOGRAPHY: L.S. Dawidowicz, *From That Place and Time: A Memoir, 1938–1947* (1989); L. Dobroszycki, in: Y. Gutman (ed.), *The Jews of Poland Between Two World Wars* (1989), 495–518; D.E. Fishman, *Embers Plucked from the Fire: The Rescue of Jewish Cultural Treasures in Vilna* (1996); B. Kirshenblatt-Gimblett, in: *YIVO Annual*, 23 (1996), 1–103; C.E. Kuznitz, "The Origins of Yiddish Scholarship and the YIVO Institute for Jewish Research" (diss., 2000); D. Miron, in: *YIVO Annual*, 19 (1990), 1–15; J. Shandler (ed.), *Awakening Lives: Autobiographies of Jewish Youth in Poland Before the Holocaust* (2002); D. Soyer, in: *Jewish Social Studies*, 5:3 (Spring/Summer 1999), 218–43; *Yivo-Bleter*, 46 (1980) (special 50th anniversary issue).

[Sol Liptizin / Cecile Esther Kuznitz (2nd ed.)]

YIẒḤAKI, ABRAHAM BEN DAVID (1661–1729), rabbi, halakhic authority, and kabbalist. Born in Jerusalem, Yiẓḥaki was the grandson of the kabbalist, Abraham b. Mordecai *Azulai, and son-in-law of Abraham Israel Zeevi, a scholar of Hebron. He studied Talmud under Moses b. Jonathan *Galante, and Kabbalah together with Joseph Bialer, grandfather of Ḥ.J.D. *Azulai. He was chief rabbi of Jerusalem, *Rishon le-Zion*, by 1708, and held the position until his death. He also headed a yeshivah. Among his disciples were Moses *Ḥagiz, Isaac ha-Kohen *Rapoport, and Isaac Zerahiah Azulai.

At the beginning of his rabbinate, the inhabitants of Jerusalem suffered from the heavy burden of taxation placed upon them by the government. To ameliorate the situation, Yiẓḥaki went to various European countries and to Turkey as an emissary of the community (1709–16). In 1708, as head of the Jerusalem rabbis, he signed a declaration against the Shabbatean Nehemiah *Ḥayon, and during his journey he vigorously opposed the propaganda conducted by Ḥayon and Miguel Abraham *Cardozo. On reaching Amsterdam in 1712, he encouraged Moses Ḥagiz and Ẓevi *Ashkenazi (Ḥakham Ẓevi) to oppose Ḥayon, who came to Amsterdam in 1713. His father, David Yiẓḥaki, on the other hand, was a foremost supporter of Shabbetai *Ẓevi. On returning to Jerusalem, Yiẓḥaki devoted himself to teaching and writing. Some time later, when the situation of Jerusalem deteriorated and his safety was endangered, he was compelled to flee to Hebron, but later returned to Jerusalem, where he died. He was the author of the responsa *Zera Avraham* (2 pts.; Smyrna and Constantinople, 1732–33).

BIBLIOGRAPHY: Frumkin-Rivlin, 2 (1928), 153–6: Yaari, Sheluḥei, 353 8; Benayahu, in: KS, 28 (1952/53), 33; Toledano, in: *Yerushalayim*, 4 (1953), 215–6; Scholem, Shabbetai Ẓevi, 1 (1957), 199–200; M. Benayahu, *Rabbi Ḥayyim Yosef David Azulai* (Heb. 1959), index; Friedman, in: *Sefunot*, 10 (1966), 490–1.

[Avraham Yaari]

YIẒḤAKI, DAVID (c. 1615–1694), rabbi and halakhic authority of Ereẓ Israel. Yiẓḥaki was born in Salonika, where he studied under Elijah Gevartil, and later immigrated to Ereẓ Israel. He married the daughter of the kabbalist Abraham b. Mordecai *Azulai of Hebron, but appears to have lived in Jerusalem from 1661 to 1665. During the stay of *Shabbetai Ẓevi in Jerusalem (1662–65), Yiẓḥaki was attracted to him and became one of his most devoted followers. He was in Egypt in 1665 and, though at first shaken by Shabbetai Ẓevi's acceptance of Islam in 1666, he remained loyal to him. He presumably returned to Ereẓ Israel but left again in 1666 or 1667 and stayed for some time in Adrianople, where he studied under Shabbetai Ẓevi. After the widespread adoption of Islam in Salonika by the followers of the false messiah in 1683, however, Yiẓḥaki appears to have forsaken the movement completely. He returned to Jerusalem and in 1672 was appointed a *dayyan* in the *bet din* of Moses *Galante (Ha-Magen), after whose death in 1689 he acted as the leading rabbi of Jerusalem, where he died. His sons were Abraham *Yiẓḥaki, one of the leading persecutors of the Shabbateans, and Isaac Yiẓḥaki, a Jerusalem scholar.

BIBLIOGRAPHY: Frumkin-Rivlin, 2 (1928), 73f.; M.D. Gaon, *Yehudei ha-Mizraḥ be-Ereẓ Yisrael*, 2 (1938), 288f.; G. Scholem, in: *Zion*, 6 (1941), 87–89; 13–14 (1948–49), 59–62; Scholem, Shabbetai Ẓevi, 1 (1957), 155, 199;2 (1957), 401, 726; I. Sonne, in: *Sefunot*, 3–4 (1960), 47f.

[Abraham David]

YIZHAR, S. (originally **Yizhar Smilansky**; 1916–2006), Hebrew author who belongs to the first generation of native Israel writers. Born in Reḥovot into a family of writers (see *Smilansky), Yizhar taught at the Ben Shemen youth village and at a Reḥovot secondary school, fought in the 1948 War of Independence, and was a member of the Knesset (Mapai-Rafi) from its inauguration until 1967, when he gave up his seat because of an extended sojourn abroad. Holding a Ph.D. from the Hebrew University, he taught literature and education and was professor at Tel Aviv University.

Yizhar was the first prose writer born in Ereẓ Israel to render into aesthetic experience his profound awareness of the local landscape and scene, and his stories evolve entirely against a Palestinian background. These qualities can already be detected in his first story, *Efrayim Ḥozer la-Aspeset* (published in *Gilyonot* 6, 1938). His characters, imbued with his own deep attachment to the land, are steeped in their immediate surroundings.

His early writings were influenced by the internalized reflective prose rhythms of Uri Nissan *Gnessin and his later works by Joseph Ḥayyim *Brenner's quest for moral truth beyond the pretense of daily convention. Yizhar's distinctive prose style won him his place in Israel literature and is primarily responsible for his influence on the younger Hebrew writers. His lyrical sentences, characteristic of the internal monologue, dominate his early stories, while in later works, particularly in the novel *Yemei Ẓiklag* (1958), he displays a flexibility of language which blends the internal monologue with dialogue, and long descriptions of nature with short rapid passages of action. Yizhar's thorough command of literary Hebrew, his proclivity for linguistic precision, and his ability to draw on contemporary Hebrew without being ensnared by the slang of the moment won him general acclaim. He has, however, been criticized for sacrificing the narrative and plot development to a display of linguistic dexterity and versatility.

Yizhar's characters, mainly youths born in Ereẓ Israel, are involved in a dynamic situation in which they are torn between conflicting moral values. They are faced with the dilemma of whether to follow the dictates of their immediate society (the kibbutz, a group of fighters) or those of their conscience and at the same time strive to preserve their individuality. The tension between these two polar values is sharply delineated in *Sippur Ḥirbet Ḥizah* (1949) and *Ha-Shavui* (1949), two short stories written after the War of Independence, in which Yizhar describes the moral dilemma of the protagonist, a young Israel soldier, who does not dare to revolt against the military authority whose amoralism he rejects. Spurred on by his sensitivity to the suffering of others and his own strong sense of justice, he wants to protest but is paralyzed because he does not wish to lose the esteem of his companions. The inner revolt of the hero (or anti-hero) of *Sippur Ḥirbet Ḥizah* against the expulsion of Arab farmers from their home village is particularly poignant because he sees an injustice perpetrated by Jews, sons of a people that has long suffered from exile and persecution. In *Ha-Shavui*, the anti-hero realizes only too well that he and his friends are sinning against the simple village shepherd whom they hold prisoner for no particular military reason, but merely to relieve their boredom and the humdrum life in a dugout. The protagonists of both stories are unable to adduce enough counterarguments against the collective action, and neither dares to disobey an order or to depart from the accepted framework.

These stories aroused a storm of protest when they appeared. Yizhar was the first writer sharply to reveal the other face of the War of Independence which, though just in itself, inevitably led to moral corruption of victor and vanquished alike. The author, however, was not so much concerned with presenting the clash of two opposing moral systems as with the portrayal of the tragic dilemma reflected in the struggle within the soul of the hero, a character who recurs in all his stories. While fully aware of the moral problems he was posing, Yizhar seemed to be incapable of investing his protagonists with decisive and permanent force of action.

Yemei Ẓiklag, a panoramic war novel, presents a wider scope of the problems and moral contradictions with which the heroes contend. The narrative is a description of the combat experiences of a group of soldiers stationed in a dugout in the south, near the Negev, during a seven-day period of the War of Independence. The theme, the spontaneous reaction of the young fighters to war and its inherent fear of death, also nurtures a strong protest against the ideological and moral values bequeathed to them (the first generation of native-born sons) by the "pioneer generation." The heroes, and apparently the writer himself, see the secular socialist credo as empty of meaning and incapable of forming a moral bulwark on which to lean during their grave internal conflict, born out of war and the simple fear of death. This protest, however, even when expressed most sharply and daringly, is not a philosophy out of which they can formulate their true attitude to war or can understand why they continue to fight and do not flee. Yizhar explains their protest against war and the fear of death and their compulsion to continue fighting as the results of immediate reflexes, and not actions rooted in moral truth or ideal. The narrator fully realizes the weakness of his answer to the moral dilemma and hints at some possible solution lying beyond the scope of knowledge of the protagonists. In the final analysis, however, he admits that there is no answer and that the only way out lies in the renewal of man's rapport with the universe that surrounds him.

The rhythms of his rich prose infuse his minutely detailed recording of natural, technical, or psychological data with a rare lyricism. Yet his love of descriptive writing slows up his narrative flow and weakens the structure of his plot. B. Kurzweil has pointed out this inherent weakness in *Yemei Ẓiklag*, which essentially remains a short story extended into a novel by long and repetitious passages of lyrical prose. He has also suggested that Yizhar's catalog of characters is drawn from the rather narrow world of his contemporaries whose experience – at least as Yizhar has described it – is too limited to afford a background for a full-scale novel.

After 30 years of self-enforced silence, Yizhar published several prose works in the 1990s, many of them autobiographical stories of recollection, reflecting on pre-state Israel. *Mikdamot* (*Foretellings*, 2005), depicts a boy growing up in a Jewish farming community in Palestine and in the growing city of Tel Aviv. The boy's sensual experiences coalesce with the adult's conscious reflection on past experiences. *Ẓalhavim* (1993), a novel, describes an afternoon spent by three teenagers, the author being one of them, in a tangerine grove during the 1930s and focuses on adolescence, the erotic appeal of the earth and the complex relations between fathers and sons. Followed by a collection of stories, *Ẓedadi'im (Asides*, 1996), Yizhar published in 1996 the collection *Eẓel ha-Yam*, three novellas in which the sea becomes a metaphor for the ambigious relationship between man and the universe. The novel *Malkomiyyah Yefeifiyyah* ("Lovely Malcomiah," 1998) is yet another story of adolescence amidst the sights and smells of nature. A shy Ereẓ Israeli youth falls in love with the beautiful, much admired Shula. It is not the plot, but the precise, fine observation of nature, the sensual and lyrical description and the many-layered poetic idiom which typify Yizhar's later prose. Among his other works are *Be-Fa'atei Negev* (1945); *Ha-Ḥorshah Asher ba-Givah* (1947); *Shishah Sippurei Kayiẓ* (1950), two volumes of stories for youth; *Be-Raglayim Yeḥefot* (1959), and *Gilui Eli-*

yahu (1999). Yizhar also wrote articles and essays on political and public affairs. The Collected Works appeared in 1996. Yizhar was awarded the Brenner Prize, the Agnon Prize, as well as the prestigious Israel Prize for literature (1959). *Midnight Convoy and Other Stories* appeared in 1969. Stories were translated into various languages and are included in anthologies, as for example "Habakuk" in: G. Abramson (ed.), *The Oxford Book of Hebrew Short Stories* (1996). For information concerning translations, see the ITHL website at www.ithl.org.il.

BIBLIOGRAPHY: A. Ukhmani, *Le-Ever ha-Adam* (1953), 327–72; Y. Halpern, *Ha-Mahpekhah ha-Yehudit*, 2 (1961), 633–93; D. Kena'ani, *Beinam le-Vein Zemannam* (1955), 94–136; D. Meron, *Arba Panim ba-Sifrut ha-Ivrit Bat Yameinu* (1962), 175–340, incl. bibl.; S. Zemach, *Massah u-Vikkoret* (1954), 241–52; B. Kurzweil, *Bein Ḥazon le-Vein ha-Absurdi* (1966), 376–403; A. Kariv, *Iyyunim* (1950), 190–7; Y. Keshet, *Maskiyyot* (1953), 240–60; E. Schweid, *Shalosh Ashmorot* (1964), 185–201; R. Wallenrod, *The Literature of Modern Israel* (1956), index. **ADD. BIBLIOGRAPHY:** G. Shaked, in: *Ha-Sipporet ha-Ivrit*, 4 (1993), 189–229; N. Shani, *Yiẓẓug ha-Toda'ah ha-Mesapperet bi-Yẓirat Yizhar* (2000); N. Essing, *Lashon Figurativit be-Sipporet shel S. Yizhar* (2001); A. Negev, *Close Encounters with Twenty Israeli Writers* (2003); R. Feldhai-Brenner, "Yizhar's *Ḥirbet Ḥizah*," in: *Inextricably Bonded: Israeli Arab and Jewish Writers Re-Visioning Culture* (2004). G. Nevo: *Shive'a Yamim ba-Negev: Al Yemey Ziklag* (2005).

[Matti Megged / Anat Feinberg (2nd ed.)]

YIZKOR (Heb. יִזְכּוֹר; "He shall remember"), opening word of the memorial prayer, said for departed close relatives on the last day of Passover, Shavuot (the second day in the Diaspora), Shemini Aẓeret, and the Day of Atonement. The word is popularly applied to the whole **Hazkarat Neshamot* service.

YIZRE'EL (Heb. יִזְרְעֶאל), kibbutz in northern Israel at the foot of Mt. Gilboa affiliated to Iḥud ha-Kevuẓot ve-ha-Kibbutzim. In the War of Independence the strategically situated Arab village of Zaʿrīn served as a vantage point from which Arab units harassed Jewish settlements in the Harod Valley and tried to block communications with nearby Afulah. A *Palmaḥ group took the village in an attack on May 30, 1948. A few weeks later a group of Israel-born youth established the kibbutz on the abandoned site. Immigrants from Australia and other English-speaking countries later joined the kibbutz. Farming was highly intensive, based on field crops, almonds orchards, fishery, poultry, and dairy cattle. The kibbutz owned Maytronics for the manufacture of advanced pool-cleaning equipment and Yizrael Tamuz for cables, wires, electronic enclosures, and packaging. In the mid-1990s the population was approximately 515, dropping to 464 in 2002.

WEBSITE: www.yizrael.org.il.

[Efraim Orni / Shaked Gilboa (2nd ed,)]

YOD (Heb. י; יוֹד, יוּד), the tenth letter of the Hebrew alphabet; its numerical value is therefore 10. The Proto-Canaanite form of this letter was a stylized pictograph of a hand (= yad) with forearm , . In the 11th and 10th centuries B.C.E., the yod developed into which basically did not change in the Hebrew (, ,), Samaritan (), and Phoenician (,) scripts. However, the Aramaic cursive reduced it as follows: → → → and in the fourth and third centuries B.C.E. two variants evolved. One resembles the numeral "2" and the other has an inverted-v form . While the Nabatean developed the 2-shaped yod (which turned into the Arabic ya), the Jewish script adopted the inverted-v shape and preserved the small size of the letter (→), so it could be distinguished from the longer waw. From the old Phoenician yod, the Greek iota and the Latin "I" developed. See *Alphabet, Hebrew.

[Joseph Naveh]

YOFFE, ALTER (fl. early 20th century), Zionist Socialist living in Dvinsk. An early member of the Zionist Socialist movement before its division into political parties, he was cofounder of the *Vozrozhdeniye group. He published a pamphlet *Di Ikorim fun Tsionism far Yidishe Arbeter* ("The Principles of Zionism for Jewish Workers"), justifying the class struggle in the Jewish economy and recommending Jewish participation in the general struggle only to the extent that it benefited the Jewish proletariat. Yoffe decided to become a laborer and worked in a furniture factory. He established the first group of worker Zionists in Dvinsk. At the beginning of 1905, he was a co-founder of the territorialist *Zionist Socialist Workers' Party and a member of its first central committee. After the 1905 Revolution, he immigrated to the United States, where he became a lawyer and a member of the Socialist Party.

BIBLIOGRAPHY: *Royter Pinkas*, 1 (1921), 153–73; *Yedi'ot ha-Arkhiyyon ve-ha-Muze'on shel Tenu'at ha-Avodah*, 3–4 (1938), 52–55.

[Mendel Bobe]

YOFFE, MORDECAI (1899–1961), Yiddish poet, translator and literary critic. Born in Dusetos (Dusiat, near Kovno, Lithuania), the son of a village rabbi, Yoffe had both a traditional and a secular education. He began his literary career in Odessa before returning to Kovno; in 1927 he immigrated to Canada, and in 1937 to New York. Between 1953 and 1961 he moved to Israel and back to New York twice. He strove to be a literary intermediary between Hebrew and Yiddish.

His essays on Hebrew writers were collected in *Ringen in der Keyt* ("Links in the Chain," 1939). His translations of Hebrew poetry, to which he devoted most of his creative years, appeared in four volumes (1935, 1939, 1948, and 1958). While accurate in form, they suffer from uniformity. Yoffe's last publication was the anthology *Erets Yisroel in der Yidisher Literatur* ("Palestine in Yiddish Literature," 1961), which includes selections from 94 Yiddish poets.

BIBLIOGRAPHY: Rejzen, Leksikon, 1 (1926), 1287–8.; LNYL, 4 (1961), 292–5; M. Ravitch, *Mayn Leksikon*, 3 (1958), 198–9; A. Lis, *Heym un Doyer* (1960), 159–63.

[Melech Ravitch / Jerold C. Frakes (2nd ed.)]

YOFFEY, family of rabbis and scholars in Russia, England, and Israel. JOSEPH BEN MOSES YOFFEY (Joffe, or Jaffe;

1845–1897), born in Ukmerge (Vilkomir), Lithuania, was rabbi of Pokroy (1874), Salant (1883), and Gorzhd (1886). An ardent supporter of Ḥibbat Zion, he opposed the use on Sukkot of citrons grown outside Ereẓ Israel. In 1881 Yoffey published *Yosef Be'ur*, a commentary on Song of Songs, and in 1890 he wrote *Ahavat Ẓiyyon vi-Yrushalayim*, a three-part work opposing Orthodox anti-Zionism (abridged edition, 1891; full version, 1946). He immigrated to England in 1893 and was appointed rabbi of the Central Synagogue in Manchester. He published *Alim li-Terufah*, a versified ethical work (1895); many responsa (e.g., *Divrei Yosef*) and sermons remain in manuscript form. His son-in-law, ISRAEL JACOB BEN ABRAHAM HA-KOHEN YOFFEY (1874–1934), also born in Ukmerge, succeeded him as rabbi of the Central Synagogue at the age of 23. He founded the Manchester yeshivah and revitalized the *talmud torah*. Together with Rabbi H. Hurwitz of Leeds he organized in 1911 the first conference in England of Eastern European rabbis, with the aim of uniting them. He also convened the first conference of religious Zionists in England (1918), becoming one of the leaders of the Mizrachi movement. He died in Alexandria, Egypt, on the way to Ereẓ Israel. His works are mainly in the field of homiletics, with some *halakhah*. They are *Keneset Yisrael* (1910), *Teḥiyyat Yisrael* (1927), and *Shofar Yisrael* (1931).

His son, JOSEPH MENDEL YOFFEY (1902–1994), born in Manchester, achieved distinction in medicine, and was active in Jewish communal life. Three-times Hunterian professor in the Royal College of Surgeons (London), he was professor of anatomy at Bristol University (1942–67) and dean of the medical faculty. His publications include *Quantitative Cellular Haematology* (1960), *Bone Marrow Reactions* (1966), *Lymphatics, Lymph, and the Lymphomyeloid* (1970; in collaboration). Yoffey settled in Israel in 1967 and became visiting professor of anatomy at the Hadassah Hospital in Jerusalem.

BIBLIOGRAPHY: *Ha-Tor*, 14 no. 20 (1934), 4; JC (May 11 and 18, 1934); *The Times* (May 9, 1934); Yerushalmi (Katzburg), in: *Ha-Miẓpeh* (1953), 491–6.

YOFFIE, ERIC H. (1947–), U.S. rabbi and leader of the Reform movement. From 1996 Yoffie served as president of the Union of American Hebrew Congregations (UAHC), the congregational arm of the Reform Jewish movement in North America. He was the first president of the organization who was completely a home-grown product of the movement. Raised in Worcester, Massachusetts, where his family was active at Temple Emanuel, Yoffie became a national vice president of the North American Federation of Temple Youth (NFTY). He graduated from Brandeis University – Phi Beta Kappa, magna cum laude – in 1969 and was ordained at the Hebrew Union College-Jewish Institute of Religion in 1974. As a young rabbi he served congregations in Durham, North Carolina, and Lynbrook, New York. In 1980 Yoffie joined the UAHC staff as regional director of the Midwest Council, in 1983 he became executive director of the Association of Reform Zionists of America, and in 1992 he was named vice president and director of the Social Action Commission. He was elected UAHC president in 1996 after the retirement of Rabbi Alexander M. Schindler in a seamless transition. In 1999, the *Forward* newspaper ranked Yoffie first in the list of top Jewish leaders, referring to him as a "tribune to the next generation."

The signature to Yoffie's presidency was a fusion of the Reform movement's commitment to social justice and Israel and, at the same time, to such internal issues as promoting adult Jewish literacy and spirituality among Reform leaders and throughout the movement as a whole. Calling for "Torah at the center," Yoffie has used his "bully pulpit" at the union's biennial conventions to launch a series of initiatives to strengthen congregational life in areas of communal worship, adult and religious school education, and Jewish camping. Under his leadership, the union added three camps in the U.S. and Canada. Continuing Schindler's support for outreach programs to intermarried couples, Yoffie urged Reform Jews to invite the non-Jewish spouses in interfaith families to convert to Judaism.

During his presidency, the union moved its longtime New York City headquarters from Fifth Avenue and 65th Street (across the street from Congregation Emanu-El) to more modern and spacious offices at 633 Third Avenue. Proceeds from the sale of the former building were used to fund programs for strengthening the religious foundations of Reform Jewish identity. He also threw his leadership behind a controversial campaign to change the name of the 120-year -old organization from the Union of American Hebrew Congregations to the Union for Reform Judaism (URJ). This effort, which had failed repeatedly over the years, succeeded at the organization's 2003 Biennial in Minneapolis.

An outspoken champion of liberal values, Yoffie sharply criticized the administration of President George W. Bush and the U.S. Congress for awarding tax cuts to the rich at the expense of the poor, and for government efforts to break down the wall separating church and state. In opposition to the religious right, he has defended reproductive rights for women and equal justice for gays and lesbians. He was the only national religious leader to address the Million Mom March in May 2000, urging sensible gun control. In 2004 after the Presbyterian USA voted to divest from certain companies doing business with Israel, Yoffie strongly protested the move but organized high-level meetings with mainstream Protestant leaders and intensified the union's efforts in the area of interfaith relations on both the national and local level. An ardent Zionist who reads the Hebrew press daily, Yoffie has expanded the union's work to strengthen Progressive Judaism in Israel, and has been a strong advocate of Jewish religious pluralism in the Jewish state. Reflecting on the work of the URJ, Yoffie has stated: "We are a union of Jews committed to a particular vision of Jewish life: to spirituality, Torah, and social justice – the highest ideals of Reform Judaism."

[Aron Hirt Manheimer (2nd ed.)]

YOKE (Heb. עוֹל).

In the Bible

The yoke was usually made from a circular wooden halter which was placed on the animal's neck, and harnessed to a plow, cart, or other vehicle. Pegs, two on each side, with the neck of the animal between them, were tacked to the halter from underneath. A harness which encircled the neck of the animal from underneath was attached to these pegs. The remaining parts of the harness which were connected to the cart, plow, or other vehicle were connected to the halter of the yoke itself. The ordinary yoke was designed for two animals, but yokes for only one animal were also common.

The yoke was a symbol of servitude in the Bible. In order to emphasize the weight of oppression, the yoke is sometimes described as of iron (Deut. 28:48). It was also a symbol of the burden of slavery or taxes upon the people (I Kings 12:11), while freedom from oppression was described in poetic and prophetic literature as the breaking of the yoke (Jer. 5:5).

Jeremiah was commanded to go about Jerusalem wearing a yoke on his neck, as well as to send yokes to the kings of the neighboring countries, to indicate that they, together with Judah, should submit themselves to Babylonian rule. At the dramatic public disputation in the Temple with *Hananiah, the son of Azzur, the prophet of Gibeon, the latter broke the yoke which Jeremiah was wearing as a sign that "I will break the yoke of the King of Babylon," while Jeremiah prophesied that in place of the yoke of wood there would come a yoke of iron (Jer. 28).

[Ze'ev Yeivin]

In Rabbinic Literature

In rabbinic theology the yoke is a metaphor of great importance. It is the symbol of service and servitude, and in accordance with the principle that the Jew should be free from servitude to man in order to devote himself to the service of God, the "yoke of the kingdom of man" is contrasted with "the yoke of the kingdom of heaven." The doctrine is fully enacted in the statement of *Neḥunya b. ha-Kanah: "Whoever takes upon himself the yoke of the Torah, they remove from him the yoke of government and the yoke of worldly concerns, and whoever breaks off the yoke of the Torah, they place on him the yoke of government and the yoke of worldly concerns" (*Avot* 3:5). The "yoke of the Torah" here presumably refers to the duty of devoting oneself to study but "yoke" is used in a more specific and restricted sense. The proclamation of the unity of God by reading the *Shema is called "accepting upon oneself the yoke of the kingdom of heaven," while the acceptance of the fulfillment of the Commandments as a whole, referred to in the second paragraph of the *Shema*. is called "accepting the yoke of the Commandments," and it is this which determines the order of the paragraphs. In *Avot* 6:6 the phrase "bearing the yoke with one's fellow" means "sharing his burdens."

[Louis Isaac Rabinowitz]

YOKOHAMA, city in Japan. Opened to foreign trade by Japan in 1859, Yokohama soon blossomed into the country's major port. Among the Westerners who settled here were Jewish merchants and professional people, some of whose graves may still be seen in the city's old cemetery, dated 1869 and 1870. The first organized community was established in 1917, mainly for the purpose of helping the approximately 5,000 Russian Jewish migrants, mainly women and children, who, on their way to join their menfolk in the U.S., were held up in Japan by a change in the American visa regulations. This community continued to exist until 1923, but after the earthquake in that year the majority of Yokohama Jews moved to Kobe. Although some returned, no community was reestablished. During the years of the American military occupation of Japan (1945–52), Yokohama became a center of Jewish life because of the presence of numerous American Jewish soldiers and sailors in the area. Since then the small number of American and European Jews have continued to reside as individuals in the city. Its Jewish cemetery is still used by the Tokyo Jewish community.

YOMA (Aram. יוֹמָא), fifth tractate in the order *Mo'ed*, in the Mishnah, Tosefta, and Jerusalem and Babylonian Talmuds. In the Jerusalem Talmud, in manuscripts of the Mishnah and the Tosefta, and in the geonic literature, the tractate is given its Hebrew name, *Yom ha-Kippurim* ("Day of Atonement"), or briefly, *Kippurim* ("Atonement"). In the Babylonian Talmud, however, it was called *Yoma* ("the Day"), or *Seder Yoma* ("the Order of the Day"; cf. Yoma 1:3), and it may be that its early name was *Seder Yom ha-Kippurim* ("Order of the Day of Atonement"). Of the eight chapters contained in the Mishnah, only the last one deals with the laws of the fast. The first seven describe in a dramatic yet simple style the service of the high priest in the Temple in the order of its performance. This part of the Mishnah does not contain many differences of opinion, and it is distinguished by its uniformity and the continuity in its exposition of the high priest's service, with only a few interruptions regarding incidental details.

There are considerable parallels in the contents of tractates *Yoma* and *Tamid – some even verbatim – although each tractate gives details not found in the other. The statement of Johanan, "Who taught *Yoma*? Simeon of *Mizpah" (Yoma 14b), is not to be regarded as tradition, since its purpose was merely to resolve a contradiction between the two tractates. All that Johanan wishes to convey is that those *halakhot* of the daily sacrifice which appear in *Yoma* and differ from those in *Tamid* were taught by Simeon of Mizpah, who lived in the generation before the destruction of the Temple. At any rate, it is evident that the Mishnah has preserved *halakhot* which belong to an early period, and it follows that the tractate was composed early. Apparently they had already begun to teach and arrange the *halakhot* of the service of the Day of Atonement close to the destruction, but the editor of the Mishnah had before him a source (apparently from the generation before his) in which the early material was intermingled with later additions. The second part of the Mishnah – chapter 8 – is a composite of various sources. The Mishnah concludes with the declaration of R. Akiva, "Happy are you, Israel! Who is it before whom you are cleansed, and who is it that cleanses you? Your Father who is in Heaven." The glowing terms in which this is expressed is possibly a polemic against the Christian belief in cleansing through Jesus.

The Tosefta of *Yoma* consists of four chapters (though one manuscript has five, the second chapter being divided into two), of which the Tosefta chapter 4 is parallel to chapter 8 of the Mishnah, and Tosefta chapters 1–3 correspond with 1–7 of the Mishnah. However, the nature of the first part of the Tosefta differs completely from that of the Mishnah. Not only does the Tosefta not contain a continuous description of the order of the service, but it is quite impossible to understand the Tosefta without the Mishnah. The editor of the Tosefta made use of various sources, many of which contained only short *beraitot* that revolve around and are dependent on the Mishnah, such as those opening with the interrogatives "why" (1:1, 4, 8), "how" (1:5), or "which" (1:9). This portion also contains *halakhot* that are parallel to, or add to, the Mishnah, but has only a few sources that contain material not found, in whole or in part, in the Mishnah (e.g., 1:17–19; 2:5–8). On the other hand it contains many *aggadot* and examples which preserve important historical traditions about personalities and events of the Temple period (1:4; 6, 12, 14, 21, 22, et al.). The end of Tosefta *Shekalim (3:25–27) is apparently the beginning of Tosefta *Yoma*, omitted from it by copyists in error and appended to *Shekalim*. In contrast to the dependence of the first part of the Tosefta upon the Mishnah, the independence of its last chapter is conspicuous. It contains many sources which are almost entirely independent of the Mishnah, and the order of its *halakhot* differs from that of the last chapter of the Mishnah.

Yoma includes a number of beautiful aggadic passages. In the first chapter there is the well-known one: "Why was the first Temple destroyed? Because of the prevalence of three evils: idolatry, immorality, and bloodshed… But why was the Second Temple destroyed, seeing that the people occupied themselves with the Torah and its precepts and practiced benevolence? Because of the prevalence of hatred without cause. Thus you may learn that groundless hatred is of equal gravity to the three sins of idolatry, immorality and bloodshed" (9b). In chapter 7, on the verse (Ex. 25:11) "Within and without shalt thou overlay" (the ark with gold), Rava scholar" (72b), R. Meir used to say, "Great is repentance, for on account of an individual who repents, the sins of all the world are forgiven" (86b).

It was translated into English by I. Epstein in the Soncino edition of the Talmud (1938).

BIBLIOGRAPHY: N. Krochmal, *Moreh Nevukhei ha-Zeman*, ed. by S. Dawidowicz (1961^2), 224f.; H. Albeck, *Shishah Sidrei Mishnah, Mo'ed* (1952), 215–21; idem, *Mavo la-Mishnah* (1959), 71f., 85f.; Epstein, Tanna'im, 36f.; D. Hoffmann, *Die erste Mischna und die Controversen der Tannaïm*, 18 (in: *Jahresbericht des Rabbiner-Seminars zu Berlin pro 5642* (1881–82).

[Moshe David Herr]

YOM HA-ZIKKARON (Heb. יוֹם הַזִּכָּרוֹן; "Remembrance Day"), memorial day observed for those who fell on active service in the Israel War of Independence and subsequently. It is observed on Iyyar 4th (the day before *Independence Day) in solemn civil, military, and religious ceremonies throughout Israel. It begins at sunset and concludes with a siren blast as the stars appear the next day to usher in Independence Day. Memorial candles are lit in army camps, schools, synagogues, and public places, and flags are flown at half-mast. Throughout the day ex-servicemen and soldiers serve as guards of honor at war memorials in all towns and villages, and the families of the fallen participate in memorial ceremonies at military cemeteries. By law, all places of entertainment are closed on the eve of *Yom ha-Zikarron*, and broadcasting and educational bodies are required to stress the solemnity of the day. During the morning a siren marks a two-minute silence, which brings all activity to a standstill. The Israel rabbinate has prescribed special prayers for the previous Sabbath and for *Yom ha-Zikkaron*. They include the recital of Psalms 9: "For the leader, on the death of the son," and 144: "Blessed be the Lord, My Rock, who traineth my hands for war and my fingers for battle."

BIBLIOGRAPHY: *Laws of the State of Israel*, 17 (1962–63), 85; see also bibl. for Independence Day.

[Aryeh Newman]

YOM KIPPUR KATAN (Heb. יוֹם כִּפּוּר קָטָן; lit. "minor day of atonement"), the eve of the new month which became for the pious a day of fast and repentance. The custom of keeping Yom Kippur Katan is a late one, and is not mentioned in the Shulḥan Arukh. It began among the kabbalists of *Safed in the second half of the 16th century and is first spoken of by Moses *Cordovero. The waning of the moon was conceived by the kabbalists as a symbol of the exile of the *Shekhinah* ("Divine Presence") and the diminution of the power of holiness during the Exile, and its renewal as a symbol of the return to perfection in the age of Redemption. They based this conception on the talmudic legend according to which God had said to Israel: "Bring atonement upon me for making the moon smaller" (Ḥul. 60b). In addition to the reading of the Torah and other prayers and *seliḥot*, customary for a fast day, special *seliḥot* were written for the afternoon prayer (*Minḥah*) of Yom Kippur Katan. They are based on the themes of Exile and Redemption. The special service *Tikkun Yom Kippur Katan* was first printed in *Sha'arei Ẓiyyon* (Prague, 1662) by Nathan Nata *Hannover. Later it appeared in different versions and in special books which were very popular until the 19th century. The *tikkun* (special prayer) in *Ḥemdat Yamin* is particularly well known. The first halakhic reference to Yom Kippur Katan appears in *Bayit Ḥadash* by Joel *Sirkes. The celebration of Yom Kippur Katan became widespread because of the many commendations by Isaiah b. Abraham *Horowitz in *Shenei Luḥot ha-Berit*. Later the custom became popular among the pious who observed this day as though it were sanctioned by *halakhah* without any connection with *Kabbalah.

BIBLIOGRAPHY: G. Scholem, *On the Kabbalah and Its Symbolism* (1965), 151–3; idem, in: *Beḥinot be-Vikkoret ha-Sifrut*, 8 (1955), 93–94; A. Yaari, in: KS, 38 (1962/63), 99, 249–50; A. Abeles, *Der kleine Versoehnungstag* (1911).

[Gershom Scholem]

YOM KIPPUR WAR.

Introduction

In September 1973, indications were already noted by Israel Intelligence of a buildup both on the Egyptian and Syrian fronts. These were passed off as routine major exercises which had been taking place at frequent intervals along the borders, and particularly along the Suez Canal front. This appraisal tallied with the assessment of Israel Intelligence that the Arab armies were not yet ready for a major all-out war, and that their leadership was not capable of launching it. This estimate was aided by a highly effective deception plan which was mounted by the Egyptians and the Syrians parallel to the actual military preparations which were set afoot. Nevertheless, the indications on the front gave concern to the Israel High Command, with the result that during the ten days preceding Yom Kippur, the armored forces of Israel, both on the northern and on the southern fronts, were doubled as a precautionary measure.

The week preceding Yom Kippur was one of preoccupation with the decision of Chancellor *Kreisky to close the Schoenau Castle transit camp for emigrants from the U.S.S.R. en route to Israel (see under *Austria). Golda *Meir, prime minister of Israel, who was at a meeting of the Council of Europe in Strasbourg, proceeded to Vienna in an endeavor to persuade Chancellor Kreisky to change his policy, but to no avail. On the evening of her return to Israel on Wednesday, October 3, the Cabinet met, the sole subject of discussion being the crisis with Austria.

On Thursday, October 4, intelligence was received about the departure of Soviet families from Egypt and Syria. This, coupled with the very heavy concentrations of troops along the borders of Syria and Egypt, indicated that a very serious situation had developed. A Cabinet meeting was called for midday on Friday, October 5, in Tel Aviv, at which part of the Cabinet participated. Apart from minor unit mobilization and preparations in the standing army, particularly the Air Force, and cancellation of leave in the army generally, no major mobilization took place.

On Saturday, October 6, Yom Kippur Day, at 4.00 A.M., intelligence was received which confirmed finally that war was about to break out on Yom Kippur Day. Consultations thereupon took place between the Minister of Defense, the Prime Minister, the Chief of Staff, and other staff officers. At approximately 10.00 A.M. total mobilization of the armed forces of Israel was authorized.

The information received that morning from reliable intelligence sources had indicated that the Arab attack would take place at 6.00 in the evening. At 2.00 in the afternoon, however, the Syrian and Egyptian armies attacked simultaneously with their total forces. Thus began the Yom Kippur War.

Throughout the holy day of Yom Kippur, Israel mobilized her forces. One of the miscalculations made by the Arabs was to launch the war on this day when all the manpower of the country was available either at home or in synagogue, and Israel thus saved many valuable hours of mobilization which were to prove vital at a later stage.

On the Northern Front

On the northern front the battle began with air attacks and a heavy artillery bombardment by the Syrians of the Israel front line and Israel headquarters. Three Syrian infantry divisions moved across the line and hundreds of Syrian tanks deployed to attack the Israel positions. Behind these three Syrian divisions were deployed two armored divisions ready to follow up. The Israel line was held by a series of fortifications acting as outposts and observation points and supported in each case by a small force of tanks. This line held: apart from a position on Mount Hermon, not one fortification was captured, though three were evacuated under orders. Tales of incredible bravery were to emerge from the heroic stand of the forces in the fortifications along the Israel line. (See Map: Syrian Attack and Map: Israeli Counter Offensive).

Shortly after the opening of the battle, the GOC Northern Command, Major General Yiẓḥak Ḥofi, divided the Golan Heights front into two sectors, the northern sector from the town of Kuneitra (al-Qunaytira) northward, and the southern sector from Kuneitra southward. By Sunday morning, October 7, Major General Raful Eitan was in command of the division controlling the northern sector and Major General Dan Laner of the southern sector. On the eve of Yom Kippur the General Staff had moved the Seventh Armored Brigade up to the Golan Heights. Thus the battle opened with an Israel force of approximately 180 tanks holding the line against a major Syrian armored assault which was later to develop into an attack of some 1,400 tanks. Israel's Seventh Brigade was deployed in the northern sector with another in the southern sector. The major Syrian thrust came unexpectedly against the southern sector, where this Brigade with a small number of tanks withstood the assault of some 600 Syrian tanks. In the northern sector the first wave consisted of some 250 tanks, the Third Syrian Armored Division being held in reserve. With the opening of the assault, Syrian helicopters landed on Mount Hermon and infantry forces transported by them attacked the position. Within a matter of hours the position, which consisted of barely a section of fighting troops was overrun and taken.

Heavy fighting developed in the southern sector with platoons of the Israel army battling against entire Syrian battalions. Again and again the battle was decided by the sheer force of numbers, with hundreds of Syrian tanks pouring into the sector. Part of the Israel forces withdrew to the area of Naffāḥ. In the northern sector, the Seventh Brigade blocked the enemy advance throughout the fighting. By the night of 6th/7th October, there were Syrian forces on the routes leading to the Sea of Galilee, and their advance elements had reached

Syrian Attack, 6 October 1973

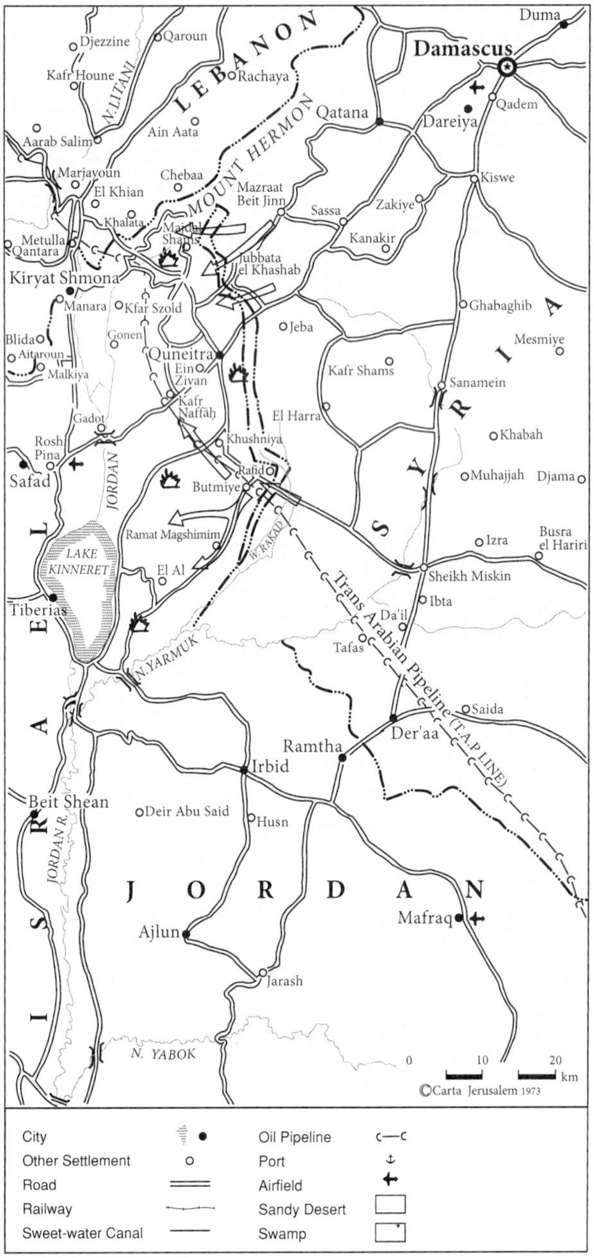

Israeli Counter Offensive

City		●	Oil Pipeline	c—c
Other Settlement		○	Port	↓
Road			Airfield	↓
Railway			Sandy Desert	▢
Sweet-water Canal			Swamp	▢

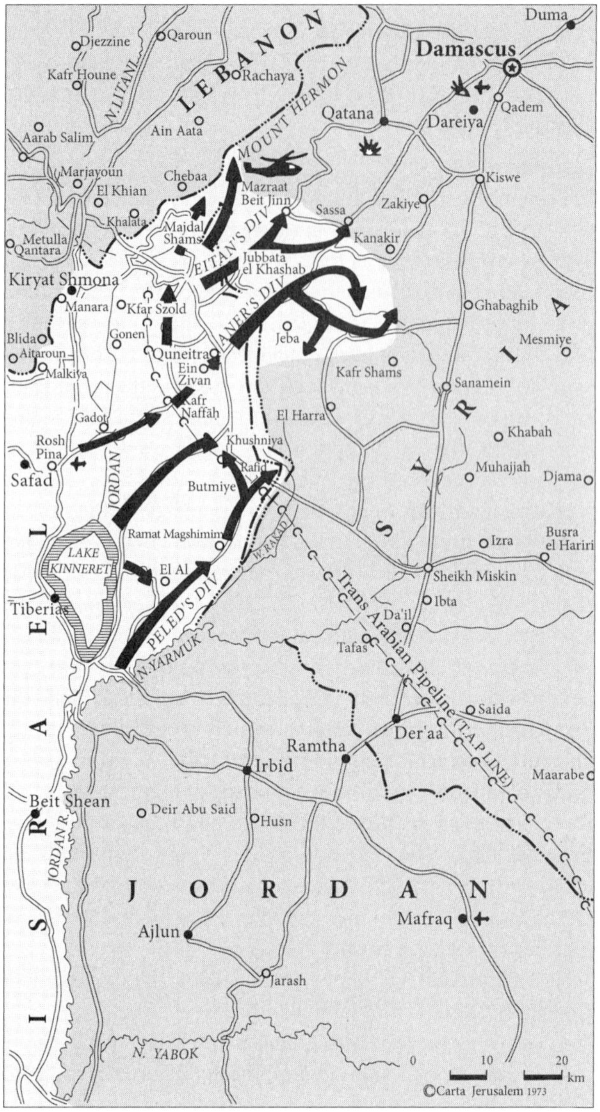

to within 800 meters of the moshav of El Al overlooking the Sea of Galilee.

However, the main battle was joined in the area of Naffāḥ, where the Syrians developed a major thrust. On the Yahūdiyya road, they reached to within 10 kms. of the point where the Jordan enters the Sea of Galilee. On the central route the Syrian forces reached the area of the Naffāḥ camp. On Sunday, October 7, heavy fighting continued all along the line with serious losses being sustained by both sides. At this stage, Northern Command was reinforced by a division commanded by General Moshe ("Musa") Peled. It was resolved that with this new force, Northern Command would move over to a coun-

terattack on Monday, October 8. Peled's division took over responsibility for all the forces on the El Al route and the route parallel to it, both leading to the Rafid crossroads.

By this time, the Brigade in the southern sector had ceased to exist. Both the brigade commander and his deputy were killed, and both battalion commanders had been wounded.

On Monday, October 8, General Peled's division launched the counterattack on the Al Al road against two Syrian tank brigades which had reached to within seven miles of the Sea of Galilee. A heavy battle raged along this route between El Al and Rafid on Monday, October 8, and Tuesday, October 9. By Wednesday, October 10, at 10.00 A.M., the Israel forces had driven the Syrians back to the cease-fire line, inflicting very heavy casualties on them.

On the Seventh Brigade front in General Eitan's divisional area, both sides had fought to a standstill and were wavering, when one of the Israel positions behind enemy lines, which had held out throughout the fighting and was surrounded by the Syrians, reported that the Syrian supply trains were withdrawing. The Syrian attack had been broken. In the area facing the Seventh Brigade, known as the Valley of Tears, north of Kuneitra, some 300 Syrian tanks and armored personnel carriers, abandoned and burnt out, were mute testimony to the incredible bravery which had given this victory to Israel arms.

General Laner's division maintained the pressure around the area of Naffāḥ and along the Tapline route by which the major Syrian effort had advanced. This division gradually cleared the area around Naffāḥ and the area between it and the village of Khushniya which had already been established as a major Syrian supply base and headquarters. General Laner's forces, pushing in a south-easterly direction, gradually drove the Syrian forces back from the area of Naffāḥ towards Khushniya. At this point – on Tuesday, October 9, and Wednesday, October 10 – a two-divisional effort, that of General Laner from the north and General Peled from the south, boxed in the Syrian forces in the general area of Khushniya and destroyed a considerable number of tanks in very heavy fighting. By Wednesday, October 10, General Laner's forces too had reached the "purple line" which was the 1967 cease-fire line on the Golan Heights, and the Syrian forces had either been destroyed or driven out of his divisional area.

On Monday, October 8, units of the Golani Brigade attempted to recapture the Mount Hermon position which had been lost on the 6th, but the attack failed, with considerable losses. Thus by Wednesday, October 10, the Syrian forces had been driven entirely from the Golan Heights, and Israel forces had closed in on the cease-fire line along its entire length.

On the following day, Thursday, October 11, the Israel counterattack into Syria was launched. The operation began at 11.00 A.M. when General Eitan's division, including the Seventh Brigade, broke into the Syrian position in the area of Jubāta, while General Laner's division attacked along the heavily fortified main route to Damascus. General Eitan's division broke through according to plan. General Laner's division also broke in along the main route as planned, but his first brigade ran into a very heavy antitank screen which had remained behind on the ground, undetected. When this brigade was held up the support brigade followed through and took the village of Khan Arnaba. The third brigade followed through along the main Damascus route.

On Friday, October 12, the forces of General Eitan operating in the northern sector reached the village of Mazraat Beit Jinn and established defense positions there. The Seventh Brigade was repulsed in its attempt to take the hill of Tel Shams. To the south, General Laner's division widened its area of penetration as it advanced toward Kanakir. As the division moved towards Kanakir the Iraqi forces which had entered Syria reached the area of battle, the first of its two armored divisions moving forward towards the flank of General Laner's advancing division. General Laner, standing on a hill and directing the battle, saw the Iraqis advancing in clouds of dust across the plain from the southeast. He withdrew his division from the attack and prepared to meet them. Receiving an additional brigade from General Peled's division just in time, he created an armored box into which the Iraqi forces moved unsuspectingly. The battle commenced at 3.00 in the morning. The attack was smashed and the Iraqi forces withdrew, leaving some 80 destroyed tanks on the field of battle. The Israel forces exploited their success and reached the area near Kafr Shams.

On Saturday, October 13, parachute forces captured the vital hill of Tel Shams suffering only four wounded in the battle.

The Syrians developed a counterattack in the area of Beit Jinn on the main route linking Sassa and Tel Shams. In the meantime, the 40th Jordanian armored brigade had entered Syria, and basing itself on Tel Harra, supported the Iraqi forces on their left flank in the counterattacks which were mounted.

General Laner's division counterattacked and captured two very important dominating hills, Tel Aleika and Tel Antar. Counterattacks were mounted in turn by the combined Arab forces – Syrians, Iraqis, and Jordanians – but the Israelis now held a very strong line which the Arab forces failed to penetrate. In the battle which raged in the Iraqi sector, approximately 100 Iraqi tanks were hit with some 80 destroyed, and approximately 40 Jordanian tanks were hit of which 30 were destroyed.

On October 21/22 the Israel forces again mounted an operation to recapture the Mount Hermon position.

Units of a parachute brigade were helicoptered to a point above the Syrian Hermon position while units of the Golani brigade moved up from below. The paratroopers took all their targets. Golani forces moved along three routes, but when they entered battle, the nature of the terrain and the comparatively large enemy force scattered over the hillside endangered their operation. The brigade commander and the battalion commander were wounded and the situation was critical. Additional forces were transported by helicopter to the Golani attackers and the paratroopers began to move down from the captured Syrian position. At the critical moment the operations officer of the brigade took command and organized the assault, and finally broke the enemy in a very costly counterattack.

On October 22, at 10.00 A.M., Mount Hermon was recaptured.

In the battle for the Golan Heights and the attack into Syria the Syrian army lost approximately 1,100 tanks. Some 867 tanks were identified in the Golan area inside the cease-fire line, including a large number of the latest model T62 Russian tanks. Approximately 3,500 Syrians had been killed, and some 370 prisoners taken.

The battle for the Golan Heights was replete with incidents of great bravery and human tenacity. The Israel forces, pitched against a Syrian army whose soldiers fought well, revealed a genius for improvisation. But for this, the Golan

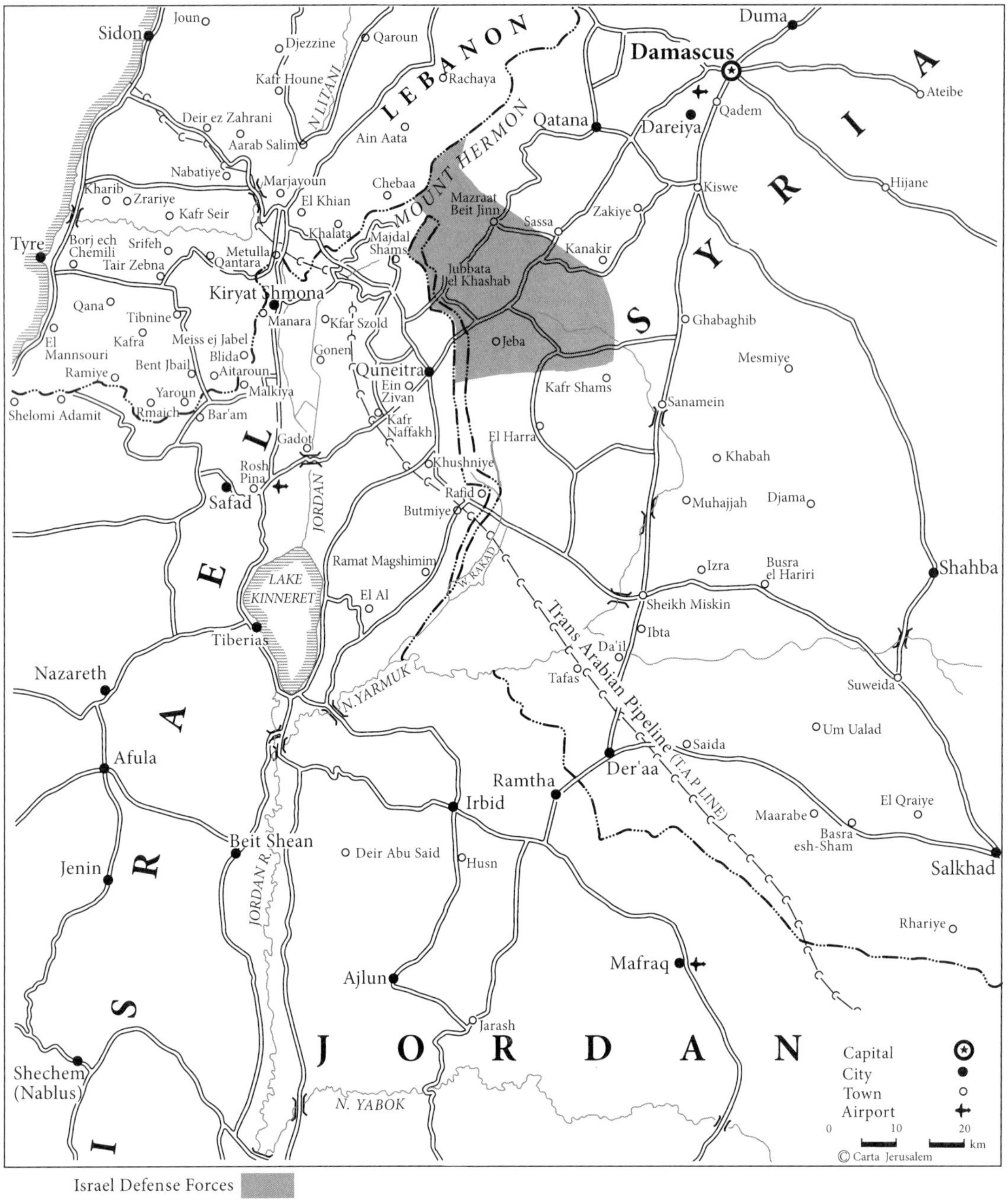

Syrian Front. Situation at the time of cease-fire, October 1973

Heights would have been overrun. At all stages the Israel Air Force fought to support the ground forces and at a later stage began to engage strategic targets within Syria. By the end of the first week most of the Syrian Air Force had been destroyed and ceased to be an element on the field of battle. Furthermore, the Syrian missile system was to a great degree destroyed. Thus Israel's Air Force was free to deal with strategic targets deep in Syria, particularly in the ports on the Mediterranean and in Damascus and other cities.

The Israel forces concluded the battle holding the strategic heights of Mount Hermon which dominate the entire area between the battlefield and the capital, Damascus, and positions as far eastward as Tel Shams, in an area which placed the outskirts of Damascus within range of Israel artillery. This was the situation when the Syrian command finally agreed to a cease-fire as requested by the Security Council on October 22.

In the battle for the Golan Heights, the situation had been saved by the self sacrifice and bravery of the two brigades on the two sectors, coupled with the standing army units in the fortifications which held along the cease-fire line. Their heroic stand enabled Northern Command to mobilize the reserve forces and, despite the overwhelming odds and the initial success of the vast forces of the Syrian army, to mount a counterattack already on the third day of the battle and to drive out the Syrian forces from the Golan Heights two days later. The battle of the Golan Heights will become a classic both as a major armored battle and as a battle of improvization and tenacity leading to the success which placed Israel's forces well on the road to Damascus.

The Egyptian Front

The Egyptian assault on the Bar-Lev line in the area of the Suez Canal came as a complete surprise to the Israel forces, which comprised less than 500 troops manning a line some 100 miles long. At 2.00 P.M. on Yom Kippur, October 6, five Egyptian infantry divisions moved simultaneously across the Suez Canal – some 70,000 troops against less than 500. A clever plan of deception had been prepared which led the Israel command to believe that all the preparations which were readily visible were in fact part of a major exercise. The Israel line was subjected to intense shelling and at the same time Egyptian planes went into action. The forces under General Mandler rushed to occupy the positions which they were due to reach at 4.00 P.M., but by this time Egyptian infantry had crossed the Canal, bypassing the widely dispersed Israel fortifications in the Bar-Lev line, and had deployed in the positions prepared for the Israel tanks on the east bank of the Suez Canal. As the Israel armored forces approached their previously prepared positions in order to engage the enemy crossing the Suez Canal, they were met by a hail of anti-tank Sagger-type missiles fired by the Egyptian troops already in position on the east side of the Canal. These missiles caused heavy casualties to the Israel tanks making the initial assault.(See Map: Egyptian Attack and Map: Israel: Counter Offensive).

In the course of the night of October 6/7, the Egyptians ferried five divisions of infantry across the Canal together with their armor and by means of highly effective and very flexible Russian bridging equipment were able to establish adequate bridges across the Canal to keep their forces supplied. They set up three major bridgeheads across the Canal; one in the north basing itself on the area of Qantara, one in the center basing itself on the area of Ismailia, and the third in the south in the area of the Great Bitter Lake and Suez. The northern effort was under the command of the Egyptian Second Army, the southern under the command of the Egyptian Third Army.

The Israel forces continued to battle in order to contain the initial attack of the Egyptians, and the fortifications along the line continued to hold out on the morning of October 7. The main efforts of the Israel forces were directed towards holding a line along the second line of fortifications some 10 kms. from the Suez Canal, and preventing the Egyptians from enlarging their bridgeheads. An Egyptian effort was mounted on a number of occasions southwards along the Gulf of Suez in the direction of the oilfields of Abu Rudeis, but as in each case this effort required the Egyptian armor to leave the cover of their antiaircraft missile system, the Israel Air Force drove the Egyptian armored forces back, inflicting on them heavy casualties.

The entire Egyptian operation, against which the Israel Air Force mounted attack after attack in an endeavour to destroy the bridges and upset the crossings, was carried out under cover of a dense antiaircraft missile system which caused heavy casualties to the Israel Air Force, particularly because it forced the Israel planes to fly low to avoid the missiles and brought them within range of the conventional antiaircraft guns. The Israel forces that attempted to reach the units besieged in the fortifications of the Bar-Lev line in order to relieve them suffered very heavy casualties. Most of the line had either been captured or abandoned by the third day of battle. The most northerly position in the area of Baluza succeeded in holding out during the whole war and was never taken by the Egyptians. The most southerly position, at Port Tewfik, held out for most of the week, the defenders fighting a very brave battle and surrendering only when they had run out of ammunition, food and medical supplies.

On Monday, October 8, the area was divided by General Gonen, GOC Southern Command, into three divisional areas: the northern division commanded by Major General Adan, the central sector by Major General Sharon and the southern sector by Major General Mandler. On that day, Major General Adan's forces mounted an attack towards the area of the Firdan bridge opposite Ismailia. This attack was held by the Egyptians and General Adan's forces were unable to advance. Pitched battles continued, with the Egyptians throwing heavy infantry concentrations against the Israel armor with a view to inflicting casualties on them by use of antitank missiles. The Israel forces quickly adapted themselves to this new type of warfare, and tactics which they developed limited the losses sustained by this weapon.

Forces under General Sharon managed to reach the water's edge at the northern end of the Great Bitter Lake but the Israel General Command elected to remain in a holding position in preparation for the major armored assault which they expected would develop as soon as the two armored divisions held back in Egypt, the Fourth Division in the south and the Twenty-First Division in the north, moved across the Canal.

On Sunday, October 14, the Egyptian army mounted a major tank offensive and a heavy tank battle raged all day long, with the Egyptian army endeavoring to break out at four different points. The major battle was mounted against General Sharon's forces, in the central sector, where some 110 Egyptian tanks were destroyed in the course of the day. The northern division commanded by General Adan and the southern division commanded by General Mandler were likewise engaged in battle, with a determined attempt being made by the Egyptian Third Army to break out southward along the Gulf of Suez toward the oil fields. This attempt was foiled by the Israel Air Force which destroyed the greater part of an Egyptian brigade. In all, during October 14, the Egyptians lost over 200 tanks in the assault, which failed to achieve any advance.

Egyptian Attack, 6 October 1973

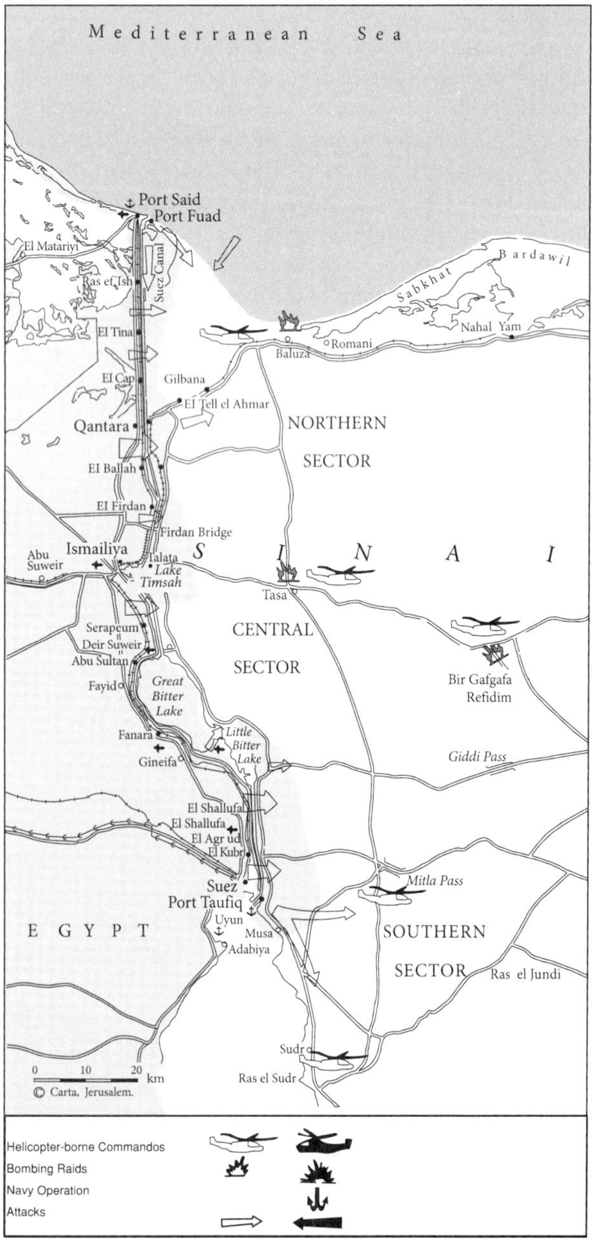

Israeli Counter Offensive

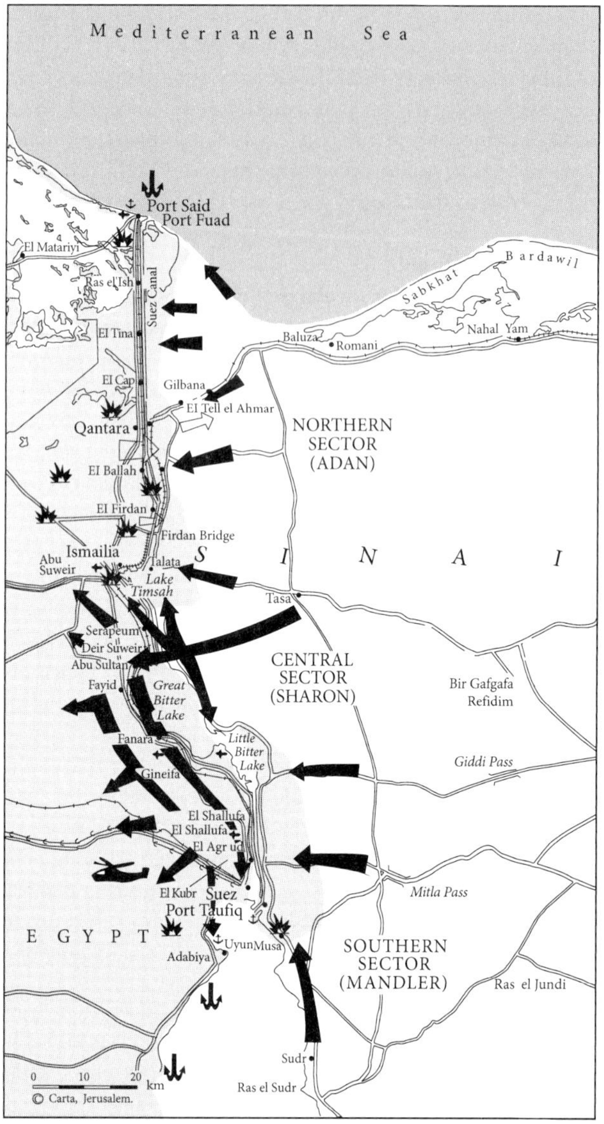

A debate had been in progress in the Israel Command as to the advisability of launching the planned attack across the Suez Canal in order to counter the Egyptian forces which were on the east bank. The chief deterrent factor had been the fact that the two main Egyptian armored divisions, the Fourth and the Twenty-First, were on the west bank. But as soon as they crossed to the east bank and were committed in the battle of October 14, it became apparent to the Israel Command that the time had come to mount the counterattack. Accordingly preparations were made to break through to the Canal at a point already planned in advance at the northern end of the Great Bitter Lake.

This task was assigned to General Sharon's division. On the night of October 15/16, parachute forces led his division across the Canal and established themselves in Egypt on the west bank. On the following day they were joined by elements of an armored brigade which began to widen the perimeter. Taken by surprise, the Egyptian forces on the west bank of the Canal did not offer much determined opposition. There were considerable delays, however, in clearing the area of the corridor to the Canal. Although in preparation for the crossing General Sharon's forces had reached the water's edge, the area through which they maneuvered had not been cleared of Egyptian forces and when the problem arose of resupply and moving down the bridges to the Canal it was found that the Egyptians were in a position to hinder any advance toward the Canal. General Adan's division, which had been designated to follow through after the bridges had been laid across the Canal, was therefore obliged to postpone its operation and engage the enemy in the area of the breakthrough to the Canal so as to create a corridor, widen it and mop up enemy units. At the same time an Egyptian armored brigade moved up from the area occupied by the Third Army along the Great Bitter Lake. General Adan's forces lay in wait and destroyed it. General Sharon's forces by this time were being reinforced on the west bank of the Canal, and with General Sharon in command of the forces both on the east bank and the west bank, they began to push northwards. One of the fiercest battles of the war was fought at the northern part of the corridor leading to the Canal, in a region known as the Chinese Farm.

In the meantime, despite very intense Egyptian bombardment, artillery barrages and air attacks, bridging equipment was brought up and two bridges were thrown across the Canal.

On October 16 and until midday on the 17th, General Adan's forces engaged in heavy battle and cleared the main routes to the bridging areas as well as the corridor leading to the bridges. His forces crossed the bridges which had been thrown across the Canal on the night of October 17/18, their first mission being to destroy as many antiaircraft missile sites as possible and to advance in the general direction of the Geneifa Hills. His forces broke out and began to fan out southward. On the same night Egyptian commando battalions counterattacked from Ismailia southward against the parachute brigade which had crossed the Canal initially, but they were driven back. Large-scale air battles developed in the meantime with the Israel Air Force achieving complete superiority.

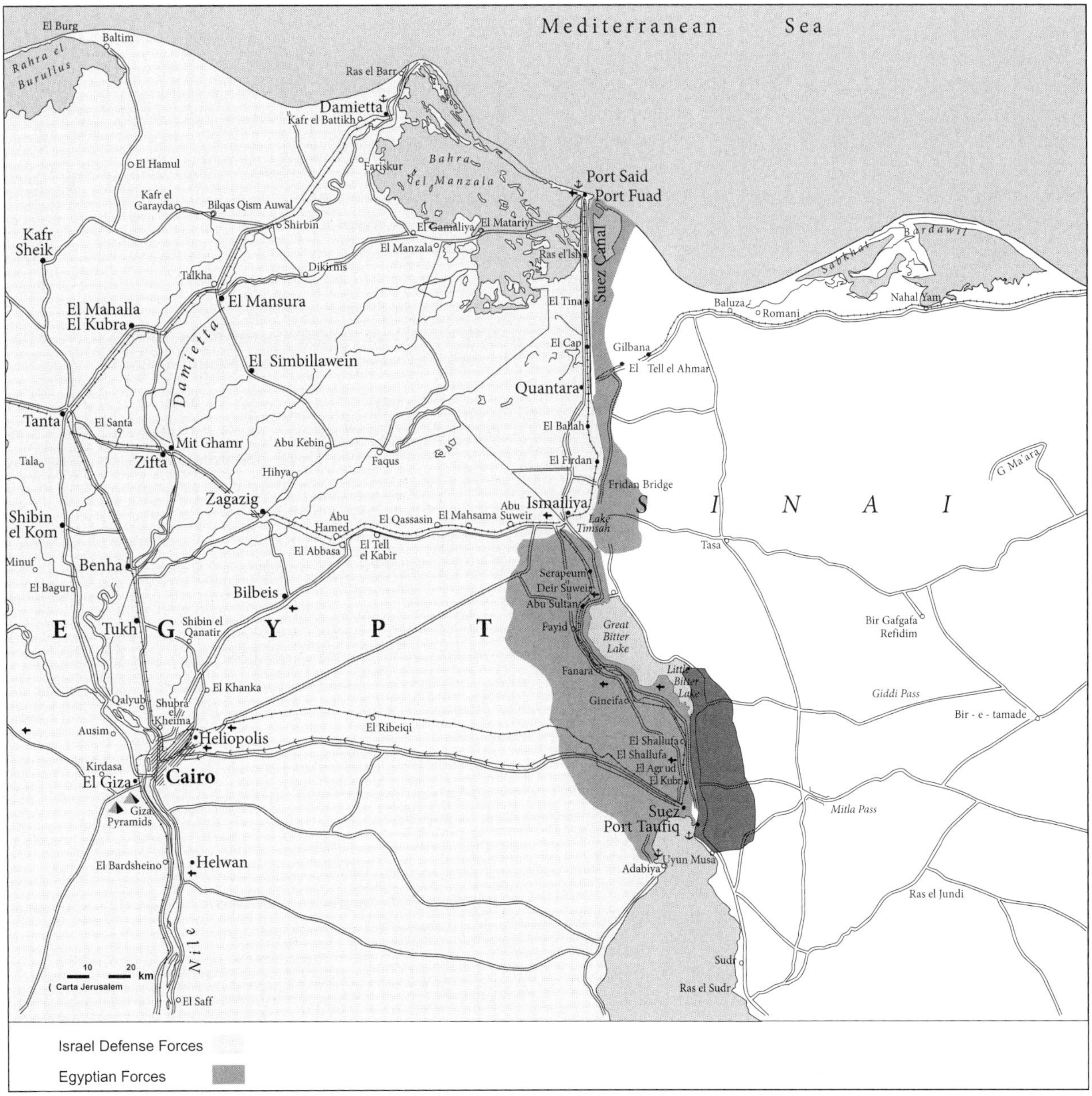

Egyptian Front. Situation at the Time of Cease Fire, October 1973

In the course of the fighting at the end of the first week, Major General Mandler was killed and his brigade was taken over by Major General Kalman Magen.

On October 19 in the evening, General Magen's division crossed the bridges.

Thus the attack on the Israel bridgehead developed, while for two days, until October 18, the Egyptians believed the Israel report that this was a task force designed solely for the purpose of attacking the Egyptian missile sites. There was lack of coordination between the Egyptian Third Army and Second Army, of which the Israel forces took advantage. By October 19 there were already three Israel divisions on the west bank of the Suez Canal. General Sharon's force was obliged to fight through the cultivated area created by the sweet-water canal in the general direction of Ismailia while at the same time endeavoring to remain parallel to the Israel forces on the east bank of the Canal which encountered very heavy opposition from the Egyptian Second Army units. General Adan's forces were ordered to advance in the direction of Geneifa-Suez, while clearing the area of the west bank of the Bitter Lake and the west bank of the Canal itself. General Magen's forces swept inward in a broad arc to the west of Jebel Geneifa directed towards the port of Adabiyah on the Gulf of Suez. General Sharon, who by this stage had advanced some six kilometers northwards from the bridges, began to widen his bridgehead and to push towards Ismailia. By October 22, he had pushed northward to the water purification plant of the town of Ismailia. His forces also attacked northward on the east bank of the Suez Canal in an endeavor to clear the area between the Great Bitter Lake and Lake Timsah. They managed to advance only part of the distance, however, and were not successful in clearing the remainder of that area.

General Adan continued southward along the Suez Canal between the Bitter Lakes and the town of Suez. His forces were in constant contact with the Egyptian forces along the Canal and also with the Egyptian forces operating from the east bank. General Magen reached the Cairo-Suez road and cut it early on October 22.

The Security Council, which had been hastily convened by the Soviet Union, met on October 21 and called for an immediate cease-fire, to come into effect at 5.58 P.M. on October 22. The cease-fire was accepted both by Egypt and Israel, but by the time it came into effect, the Egyptian Third Army found itself cut off and surrounded. Fighting continued after the beginning of the cease-fire primarily because units of the trapped Egyptian Third Army fought desperately to break their way out of the Israel vice, which was tightening. Israel forces counterattacked, and were engaged along the front by Egyptian artillery from all the sectors. General Magen's forces consolidated their gains, closing the ring by taking the Red Sea fishing port of Adabiyah in the Gulf of Suez. General Adan cleared the entire water edge and reached the outskirts of the town of Suez.

The fighting continued in the Suez area. Israel forces, assuming that the fighting was over, moved into the town of Suez, but came up against strong Egyptian points of defense which inflicted heavy casualties on them.

The fighting finally ended on October 24 with the Egyptian forces holding two major bridgeheads on the eastern bank of the Suez Canal to an average depth of about 10 kms., and with the Israel forces occupying some 1,600 sq. kms. of territory inside Egypt from the outskirts of Ismailia in the north to Mount Ataqa and the port of Adabiyah in the south and reaching, at the most westerly point, within some 70 kms. of Cairo. Moreover, Israel had cut off the Egyptian Third Army (comprising some 20,000 troops and approximately 300 tanks) on the east bank of the Canal opposite the town of Suez, and indeed, but for the Security Council resolution calling for a cease-fire, the Egyptian Third Army was doomed and could have been wiped out by the Israel forces within a matter of days.

Thus the war concluded on the Egyptian front, with the Egyptians celebrating the fact that they had achieved an initial success in crossing the Canal and in maintaining bridgeheads on the east bank of the Canal. On the other hand, the Israel forces had effected a counterattack which had given Israel a military situation constituting a good bargaining position with a view to future negotiations.

In the battle with Egypt over 1,000 Egyptian tanks were destroyed and vast quantities of equipment were taken in addition to 8,000 prisoners. Some 240 Israel prisoners were taken and these were exchanged for the 8,000 Egyptian prisoners following the cease-fire agreement signed with Egypt.

Naval Operations

At the outset of the war, the Egyptian navy had blockaded the Straits of Bab el-Mandeb, preventing commercial shipping from entering the Red Sea and reaching Israel's ports. The Israel presence at Sharm el-Sheikh enabled the Israel navy to effect a counter blockade in the Gulf of Suez which obstructed all Egyptian activity in the Gulf and which prevented the supply of oil to Egypt from her own oil wells in the Gulf of Suez.

A naval battle developed between the Egyptian and Syrian navies and a modern Israel navy equipped with missile ships, some of which had been built in Israel, and all equipped with Israel-built missiles. In a number of battles, the first missile battles in naval history, in which both the Syrian and Egyptian navies were engaged, the Israel navy destroyed most of the Syrian navy and part of the Egyptian navy and gained complete control of the seas, both in the Mediterranean and in the Red Sea. The Israeli naval operations were characterized by daring and initiative.

The Cease-Fire

On October 22 the United Nations Security Council passed Resolution 338 calling upon all parties to cease all firing and immediately thereafter to begin the implementation of Security Council Resolution 242 of 1967 in all its parts. It also decided that immediately and concurrently with the cease-fire, negotiations should start between the parties concerned under appropriate auspices, with the aim of establishing a just and durable peace in the Middle East.

On November 11 the cease-fire agreement was signed between Egypt and Israel at Kilometer 101 on the Suez-Cairo Road. This agreement made arrangements for the supply of food, water and medical equipment to the beleaguered town of Suez and for the provision of non-military supplies to the Third Army on the east bank of the Suez Canal. It also made initial provisions for the exchange of all prisoners of war. These arrangements were honored, as was an unwritten undertaking that the blockade of the Straits of Bab el-Mandeb would be lifted.

The Geneva Peace Conference opened on December 21 with the participation of Egypt, Jordan and Israel, under the auspices of the United States and the Soviet Union.

Strategic Considerations

The Yom Kippur War has changed many concepts about modern warfare. It was the first time in history in which a naval missile battle took place. The effect of the antitank missile in the field of battle was much discussed, but as the fighting developed, the Israelis found a solution to this problem. It would appear that the conclusions drawn on this subject were very greatly exaggerated.

On the other hand, the efficacy of the sophisticated antiaircraft missiles, such as the SAM6 Russian missile supplied to the Egyptians and Syrians, proved to be very considerable, and had an important bearing on the course of the air war.

From a purely military point of view, the war which began under the worst possible circumstances that Israel could have envisaged and under the most promising circumstances that the Arab forces could have hoped for and for which they had prepared, resulted in a victory for Israel's forces. As the war developed, the degree of Russian connivance which was evidenced by the major Russian air and sea lifts mounted immediately after the commencement of hostilities in order to resupply the Egyptian and Syrian armies, became increasingly apparent.

To counter this massive Russian air lift and in order to preserve the balance of forces, the United States mounted an air lift to resupply the Israel forces, which had expended a considerable quantity of ammunition and had sustained comparatively heavy losses in the fighting.

The losses in lives in the Yom Kippur War on both sides were heavy: 2,522 Israelis and an estimated 15,000 Egyptians and 3,500 Syrians were killed.

For the political and other aspects of the war, see *Israel, State of: Historical Survey.

ADD. BIBLIOGRAPHY: C. Herzog, *The Arab-Israel Wars* (1982); A. Rabinovich, *The Yom Kippur War: Epic Encounter That Transformed the Middle East* (2004); U. Bar-Joseph, *Watchmen Fell Asleep: The Surprise of Yom Kippur and Its Sources* (2005).

[Chaim Herzog]

YOM TOV BEN ABRAHAM ISHBILI (**Asbili**; i.e., of Seville; known as Ritba – from the initial letters of his Hebrew name **R**abbi **Y**om **T**ov **B**en **A**braham; c. 1250–1330), Spanish talmudist. Famous already in his youth as a scholar, he studied in Barcelona under *Aaron ha-Levi of Barcelona and Solomon b. Abraham *Adret, and was mentioned in an official document of 1280 of the kingdom of Aragon as a *ḥakham* and *dayyan* of the community of Saragossa. Even during the lifetime of his teachers, questions were addressed to him for he was regarded as among the leading Spanish rabbis. When the king's bailiff in Saragossa asked his opinion about the protests of the local Jews against the excessive privileges of the wealthy families Alconstantini and Eleazar, he, despite his youth, condemned their domineering behavior and abuses, whereupon they attacked and seriously injured him.

After the death of his teachers, he was regarded by Spanish Jewry as its spiritual leader. When the community of Daroca introduced certain decrees, it was stated that this was done "in the name of R. Asher [b. Jehiel] and in that of R. Yom Tov b. al-Ishbili" (Resp. Ritba, no. 159). His *bet din* was referred to by contemporary rabbis as "the great and excellent *bet din*" (*ibid.*, no. 43). In his humility, he would apologize if he thought he had used somewhat harsh language in writing to anyone who disagreed with his views (*ibid.*, no. 208). He devoted himself also to the study of philosophy, in particular Maimonides' *Guide of the Perplexed*, acquiring a thorough knowledge of it and comparing its translation with the Arabic original. He also studied the works on logic of the Provencal scholars Samuel ibn Tibbon, Jacob Anatoli, and Gershom b. Solomon.

Yom Tov regarded Nahmanides as "a faithful shepherd" and declared it to be "the glory of the scholars of our land" that they received their Torah from him (*ibid.*, no. 208). Nevertheless he published a work (*Sefer ha-Zikkaron*) in defense of the *Guide of the Perplexed* against Naḥmanides' criticism of it in his commentary on the Pentateuch. In this work Yom Tov did not hesitate to declare that Naḥmanides "went much too far in saying of a great man brimful of the wisdom of the Torah and fully versed in all knowledge that his are empty words." He added that most of Naḥmanides' criticisms originated from his deficient knowledge of philosophical works, and that, not having adequately studied the *Guide*, he was unable to grasp its inner meaning and purpose (*Sefer ha-Zikkaron*). In this defense, Yom Tov did not attempt to blur the dividing line between "the path of truth" followed by Nahmanides and that "of logic" followed by Maimonides, but expressed the view that the latter's course "is very correct according to his outlook," while the former's "is more correct according to his." Generally Yom Tov reaffirms: "there are 70 ways in which the Torah can be interpreted, all of them the words of the living God." Even where he disagrees with Maimonides and accepts the view of Nahmanides, he declares that "all his [Maimonides'] statements are for the sake of Heaven and characterized by great wisdom" (*ibid.*).

Yom Tov's reputation rests upon his novellae to the Talmud, *Ḥiddushei ha-Ritba*. He apparently began writing them from the direct dictation of his teacher Aaron ha-Levi (*Ḥiddushim* to BB 63b, ed. by M.Y. Blau, vol. 1 (1952), 250). When, however, he realized that the work would be inordinately long, he decided to make an abbreviated version. There is even a possibility that he wrote a third "version" to some tractates. These facts give rise to a difficult and complicated literary problem, his novellae to the different tractates being of different "types," and therefore not always of the same quality. It is sometimes very hard to identify them with certainty. His novellae are, in general, very rich in early source material: tosafistic, Spanish, Provençal, and geonic, and display a considerable originality, though he is very much under the influence of his two great teachers.

His novellae have been published many times, and in different editions. Their first editions are: *Berakhot* (1968); *Shabbat* (1967); earlier works on this tractate which purported to be *Ḥiddushei Ritba* were ascribed to him erroneously; *Eruvin, Ta'anit, Mo'ed Katan, Ketubbot* (Amsterdam, 1729; *Pesaḥim* (1864) is not his); *Sukkah* (in *Sheva Shitot le-ha-Rashba*, Constantinople, 1720; wrongly ascribed to Solomon b. Adret); *Rosh Ha-Shanah* (1858); *Yoma* (Constantinople, 1754); *Megillah* (in David Hayyim Samuel Hassan, *Kodshei David*, Leghorn, 1792); *Yevamot* (Leghorn, 1787); *Gittin* (Salonika, 1758); *Kiddushin*, in the very rare edition of the tractate of Sabionetta, 1553, and afterward Berlin, 1715; *Bava Batra* (1952–54); *Bava Meẓia* (1962; the earlier editions are not his); *Makkot* (in *Ḥamishah Shitot*, Sulzbach, 1769); *Ḥullin* (Prague, 1735); *Niddah* (1868 - chapter *Tevul Yom*; in *Ha-Segullah*, 4, Jerusalem, 1937). His other works include: a commentary on *Hilkhot Nedarim* by Naḥmanides (in *Ishei ha-Shem*, Leghorn, 1795); *Hilkhot Berakhot* (at the end of Ḥayyim Isaac Musafia's responsa *Hayyim va-Hesed*, 1844); Responsa (ed. by Y. Kafaḥ, 1959); *Sefer ha-Zikkaron* (by S.H. Halberstamm, in *Ḥiddushei ha-Ritba al Niddah*, 1868; critical edition by K. Kahana, 1956); a commentary on the Passover *Haggadah* in *Peh Yesharim* (1838); *Perush al Hilkhot ha-Rif*, in manuscript: *Sefer ha-Derashot*, his homilies, now lost.

[Ephraim Kupfer]

A complete edition of Ishbili's responsa, edited by Y. Kafaḥ, was first published in 1959. The Institute for Research in Jewish Law of the Hebrew University has now published the first volume of a comprehensive historical index to those responsa (together with that of the responsa *Zikhron Yehudah* of *Judah ben Asher, the son of *Asher b. Jehiel) under the editorship of M. Elon. The volume is the second in the series of the indexes to the responsa literature. The first volume, that of the responsa of Asher b. Jehiel, consisted for the most part of indexes to the legal matters in these responsa and their sources in biblical, talmudic, and post-talmudic literature. The present volume consists of an exhaustive historical introduction, and the subject matter is arranged under different headings, such as the political, juridical, and social status of the Jews as revealed in the responsa, communal organization, family and social life, economic life, realia, etc.

BIBLIOGRAPHY: Graetz, Gesch, 7 (c. 1900), 305; Weiss, Dor, 5 (19044), 57–60; Baer, Spain, 1 (1961), 224, 428; 2 (1966), 452; idem, in: *Zion*, 3 (1938), 45; M.Y. Blau (ed.), *Ḥiddushei ha-Ritba al Massekhet Bava Batra*, 1 (1952), introd.; Yom Tov b. Abraham Ishbili, *Sefer ha-Zikkaron*, ed. by K. Kahana (1956), introd.; J.M. Toledano, *Oẓar Genazim* (1960), 208–10; Yom Tov b. Abraham Ishbili, *She'elot u-Teshuvot*, ed. by Y. Kafaḥ (1959), introd.; Eidelberg, in: *Sinai*, 40 (1957) 41–46.

YOM TOV OF JOIGNY (d. 1190), talmudist, exegete, and synagogal poet. He was a disciple of Rabbenu *Tam of Troyes, the grandson of Rashi. Toward 1180 he settled in *York, probably under the aegis of *Josce, the leader of the community. His halakhic decisions are reported in the *Mordekhai* of *Mordecai b. Hillel (Ket., no. 198) and elsewhere; he was also known as a commentator on the Bible, and he engaged in anti-Christian polemics. Several of his religious poems are preserved, including a ballad-like strophic elegy on the Blois martyrs of 1171, *Yah Tishpokh Ḥamatkha*, written in Andalusian style; each of the four strophes has an allusion to some aspect of the death of the martyrs, asking God to intervene in favor of His people and avenge these deaths. He mentions in particular the names of two of the martyrs, Yehiel and Yekutiel, who had been, like himself, students of Rabbenu Tam. He is also the author of the hymn *Omnam Ken*, for the eve of the Day of Atonement, one manuscript version of which embodies the name Yom Tov in the last verse. He is said to have inspired the heroic mass-suicide of the Jews of York when they were beleaguered in the castle on the Sabbath before Passover in 1190. He and Josce were the last to die.

BIBLIOGRAPHY: C. Roth, *Intellectual Activities of Medieval English Jewry* (1948), 21–22; idem, in: JHSET, 16 (1945–51), 214–5; Kahn, in: REJ, 1 (1880), 233; 3 (1881), 4–5; Gross, *ibid.*, 7 (1883), 43; Jacobs, *ibid.*, 18 (1889), 261; Gross, Gal Jud, 123, 252, 353; Davidson, Oẓar, index; Urbach, Tosafot, index. **ADD. BIBLIOGRAPHY:** S. Einbinder, *Beautiful Death: Jewish Poetry and Martyrdom in Medieval France* (2002), 29f., 51f., 57ff., 62ff.

[Cecil Roth / Angel Sáenz-Badillos (2nd ed.)]

YONATH, ADA (1939–), Israeli chemist. Born in Jerusalem, Yonath received her B.Sc. in chemistry in 1962 and M.Sc. in biochemistry in 1964 from the Hebrew University of Jerusalem. After completing her Ph.D. studies at the Weizmann Institute of Science, Reḥovot, Israel, in 1968 she conducted postdoctoral studies at the Pittsburgh Carnegie-Mellon University and at the Massachusetts Institute of Technology.

In 1970, Yonath joined the Chemistry Department of the Weizmann Institute and established what was for almost a decade the only protein-crystallography laboratory in Israel. In 1984 she was promoted to associate professor and in 1988 she became a full professor. She was the head of the Structural Chemistry Department (1989–90) and the Structural Biology Department (1992–94). From 1988 she was director of the Helen & Milton A. Kimmelman Center for Biomolecular Structure and Assembly and of the Joseph & Ceil Mazer Center for Structural Biology at the Weizmann Institute, where she became the Martin S. Kimmel Professor of Structural Biology. Between 1986 and 2004, in addition to being a faculty member of the Weizmann Institute, she headed the

Max Planck Research Units for Ribosomal Structure in Hamburg, Germany.

Prof. Yonath spent most of her scientific career working to unravel the structure of the ribosome, the cell's "protein factory" which synthesizes proteins according to genetic code instructions. Her 20-year research efforts included pioneering technical advances such as cryo-bio-crystallography, which revolutionized structural biology worldwide. Her studies culminated in 2000 when she determined the structures of the two ribosomal subunits, an accomplishment ranked by the prestigious *Science* magazine as among the most important scientific developments of the year. She then revealed the modes of action of over a dozen antibiotic families, thus paving the way for structure base drug design.

Yonath was a member of the Israeli Academy of Science and Humanities, the U.S. National Academy of Sciences, the European Academy for Science and Art, the EMBO, and of the International Academy of Astronautics. She was the winner of the 2002 Israel Prize in chemistry. She was also the recipient of the First European Crystallography Prize, the Kolthof Award for Outstanding Research in Chemistry, the Kilby International Award, and the Harvey Prize.

[Bracha Rager (2nd ed.)]

YONATHAN, NATHAN (1923–2004), Hebrew poet. Yonathan was born in Kiev, in the Ukraine, came to Israel as a child, and grew up in kibbutz Givat ha-Sheloshah and later in Petaḥ Tikvah. For nearly 40 years he lived in kibbutz Sarid and later in Tel Aviv. He studied Hebrew and general literature, taught in high schools and at university, and was for many years chief editor of Sifriat Po'alim Publishing House and a member of the board of directors of the Israel Broadcasting Authority. Yonathan began publishing poetry in 1940 and his first collection *Shevilei Afar* ("Paths of Dust") appeared in 1951. This was followed by some 20 collections, including *El ha-Nirim ha-Aforim* ("Unto the Furrows Grey," 1954), *Shirim be-Arov ha-Yam* ("Poems at Sea Dusk," 1972), *Ḥofim* ("Shores," 1983), and *Shirim be-Ahavah* ("Poems with Love," 1990). Yonathan was one of the most popular Hebrew poets, not least because so many of his poems were set to music (For instance, *Ḥofim, Yesh Peraḥim, Ne'esaf Tishrei, Shenei Alonim*). His lyrical verse, describing the nature and landscape of Ereẓ Israel, the sea, the rivers, the fauna and flora, is associated with the best of "Israeliness." The private self is nonetheless present in many of Yonathan's poems. Particularly moving are the poems of loss and bereavement he wrote after the death of his son Lior on the first day of the Yom Kippur War ("Poems to Lior," 1974). Yonathan also wrote prose and four books for children, including *Bein Aviv le-Anan* ("Between Spring and Cloud," 1959) and *Lilakh mi-Kevuẓat Ilanot* ("Lilach of the Ilanot Group," 1963). He received many prizes, including the Bialik Prize and the Brenner Prize. An English collection titled *Stones in the Darkness* appeared in 1975. Individual poems have been translated into diverse languages and information concerning translation is available at the ITHL website, www.ithl.org.il.

BIBLIOGRAPHY: A. Feinberg, in: *Al ha-Mishmar* (November 1, 1974); Sh. Levo, "*Bein Melaḥ le-Or*," in: *Davar* (December 18, 1980); E. Sharoni, "Meditative Minstrel of Water Music: Of 'Poems This Far' by N. Yonathan," in: *Modern Hebrew Literature*, 5:4 (1980), 33–36; A. Hermoni, "*Havanat ha-Shir be-Millim u-vi-Temunot*," in: *Alei Siaḥ*, 21–22 (1984), 72–78; Z. Luz, *Shirat N. Yonathan, Monografiyah* (1986); H. Barzel, "*N. Yonathan: Tugah ve-Ahavah*," in: *Moznayim*, 64:9–10 (1990), 24–32; Sh. Yaniv, *Ha-Baladot shel N. Yonathan*, in: *Tura* 2 (1992), 152–159; Sh. Bakshi, in: *Bi-Sedeh Ḥemed* 47 (2004), 95–98.

[Anat Feinberg (2nd ed.)]

YORK, English cathedral city and the principal city in the north of England during the Middle Ages. Jewish capitalists settled there in the middle of the 12th century and attained considerable prosperity. The leaders of the community were Benedict, *Josce, noted for his patronage of scholars, and the tosafist *Yom Tov of Joigny. Benedict and Josce represented the York Jews in the deputation which waited on Richard I at his coronation in September 1189. In the ensuing riots Benedict was seriously wounded and died of his injuries on his homeward journey. In the following March anti-Jewish rioting broke out in York and the Jews, headed by Josce, were allowed by the sheriff to take refuge in the royal castle known as Clifford's Tower. Suspecting the latter's intentions, they later excluded him, were besieged by the mob, and committed mass-suicide rather than submit (*Shabbat ha-Gadol*, March 16/17, 1190). The victims included Josce, R. Yom Tov, and the tosafist Elijah of York. A poignant elegy on the massacre was composed by *Joseph b. Asher of Chartres. A community was reestablished early in the 13th century though it never regained its former importance. The most important Anglo-Jewish magnate of the reign of Henry III, *Aaron of York, archpresbyter of the Jews of England (1236–43), was the son of the Josce mentioned above. The community's cemetery, originally shared with those of *Lincoln and *Northampton, was at a place still known as Jewbury.

York was one of the cities in England which had an *archa and it remained a Jewish center until the expulsion of 1290, when the financial magnate Bonamie of York was given a safe-conduct and was permitted to settle in Paris. A few Eastern European Jews settled in York at the end of the 19th century, and a small congregation has existed since 1892. In 1968 it numbered 45 out of a total population of 106,010, while the 2001 British census found 191 declared Jews by religion. There is an Orthodox congregation. A plan in 2002 by the local council to build a shopping mall adjacent to Clifford's Tower was opposed by the *Board of Deputies of British Jews and the local community.

BIBLIOGRAPHY: Davies, in: *Yorkshire Archaeological and Topographical Journal*, 3 (1875), 147–97; J. Jacobs, *Jews of Angevin England* (1893); A.M. Habermann, *Gezerot Ashkenaz ve-Zarefat* (1945), 127, 152–54; Roth, in: JHSET, 16 (1952), 213–20; Birnbaum, *ibid.* 19 (1960), 199–205; M. Adler, *ibid.*, 13 (1936), 113–55 (= *Jews of Medieval England* (1937), 127–73); E. Brunskill, *ibid.*, 20 (1959–61), 239–46. **ADD. BIBLIOGRAPHY:** R.B. Dobson, *Clifford's Tower and the Jews of Medieval York* (1995); idem, *The Jews of Medieval York and the Massacre of March 1190* (1974).

[Cecil Roth]

YORK-STEINER, HEINRICH ELCHANAN (1859–1934), Zionist publicist and author. Born in Senica (Hungary; now Slovakia), York-Steiner entered business in Vienna in his early youth. Self-educated in literature and art, he went to the U.S., returned to Vienna in 1884, and became director of a publishing house and an editor. After the appearance of *Der Judenstaat*, he joined Theodor *Herzl and became an ardent Zionist. He participated in the March 1897 conference that decided to convoke the First Zionist Congress and was responsible for the technical preparation of the central Zionist organ, *Die *Welt*. At the First Zionist Congress (1897) he submitted, on behalf of the organization commission, the proposals for adapting the constitution of the World Zionist Movement to the legislative requirements of various countries. These proposals became the basis of the Statute of the Zionist Organization. At the Sixth Zionist Congress in Basle (August 1903) he was an outspoken opponent of the *Uganda Scheme. While in Rome, York-Steiner heard about the disappointing results of Herzl's visit there. He called on the papal secretary of state in February 1904 and was finally authorized to state that the Apostolic See would not object to Jewish settlement in Palestine on humanitarian grounds. He published a report on the interview in *Die Welt* (no. 14, 1904).

After Herzl's death York-Steiner fought for strict adherence to Herzl's political Zionism and strongly opposed the gradual expansion of Zionist activities to other spheres in the Diaspora according to the *Helsingfors Program (1906), as well as premature, unorganized settlement in Ereẓ Israel. When the practical Zionists attained the leadership of the movement, he left it (1911). During World War I he visited the U.S. on behalf of the Austrian Freemasons to seek the immediate cessation of hostilities. In the late 1920s he joined the *Revisionist movement, but was no longer active. He settled in Palestine in 1933, having visited the country repeatedly since 1898.

Among his publications are *Kuenstlerfahrten vom Atlantischen bis zum Stillen Ozean* (New York, 1883); *Anti; Croccolos Synagoge; Der barmherzige Bruder* (three stories, 1895); *Mutter Eva* (1897); *Der Talmudbauer* (1904); *Der hohe Kurs* (1908); *Bedeutet der Krieg einen Ausnahmszustand?* (1915); *Vom sterbenden Geld* (1921); *Die Kunst als Jude zu leben* (1928), containing many biographical notes and reminiscences; and "Aus Herzl's letzter Zeit" (in Tulo Nussenblatt, *Zeitgenossen ueber Herzl*, 1929, 213–17). He also published many articles in various Jewish and Zionist magazines.

BIBLIOGRAPHY: L. Jaffe, *Sefer ha-Congress* (1950^2), index; *Tidhar*, 3 (1949), 1413–14. **ADD. BIBLIOGRAPHY:** *Menorah*, 7 (1929), 542; *Davar* (Feb. 18, 1934); P. Arnold (Kellner), *Zikhronot be-Ahavah* (1968), 81–83; Th. Herzl, *Briefe und Tagebuecher* (1982–1997), indices; A. Schnitzler, *Briefe 1913–1931* (1984), 192–93.

[Oskar K. Rabinowicz / Archiv Bibliographia Judaica (2nd ed.)]

YOSE (first half of the fourth century), Ereẓ Israel *amora*. Although always mentioned in the Jerusalem Talmud without patronymic, he is to be identified with R. Yose b. Zevida (Men. 70b: cf. TJ, Ḥal. 1:1, 57c). He transmitted the teachings of Ilai, Ze'ira, and Jeremiah. Yose became a close associate of R. *Jonah, and their joint teachings and discussions fill the pages of the Jerusalem Talmud just as those of Abbaye and Rava characterize the Babylonian Talmud. Yose and Jonah together attended weddings (TJ, Ber. 6:5, 10c), visited the sick (TJ, Shab. 6:9, 8c), and comforted mourners (TJ, Sanh. 6:12, 23d). They also were lifelong business partners in the production of wine (TJ, Ma'as. Sh. 4:9, 55b). When informed of the death of Yose's son, Jonah fasted the rest of the day (TJ, Ned. 8:1, 40d). Yose and Jonah permitted the baking of bread on the Sabbath when compelled to do so at the time of Ursicinus' campaign in Israel in 351 (TJ, Shev. 4:2, 35a). Later they were respectfully greeted by Ursicinus when they went to meet him in Antioch (TJ, Ber. 5:1, 9a). After R. *Ammi moved his academy to Caesarea, Yose and Jonah succeeded to the rectorate of the academy at Tiberias. They had many disciples, some of whom became the leaders of the next generation. Among Yose's prominent students were his own son, Eleazar, and Mani, the son of Jonah. Following Jonah's death (TJ, Ma'as. Sh. 4: 9, 55b) Yose was acknowledged as the leader of Palestinian Jewry, and he received inquiries from as far away as Alexandria, Egypt (TJ, Kid. 3:14, 64d). He sent a detailed calendar to Diaspora Jewry, cautioning them to continue to observe the second day of the festivals (TJ, Er. 3:9, 21c: cf. Beẓah 4b). He was so esteemed by his generation that upon his death his students who were kohanim defiled themselves by carrying his bier (TJ, Ber. 3:1, 6a).

BIBLIOGRAPHY: Hyman, Toledot, 713–7; Ḥ. Albeck, *Mavo la-Talmudim* (1969), 334f.

YOSE BAR ḤANINA (second half of the third century), Palestinian *amora*. Yose was an important member of the academy of Tiberias and was called a "great man" by R. Assi (BK 42b). He was a pupil-colleague of Johanan with whom he sometimes disagreed both in *halakhah* and *aggadah*. His intimacy with Johanan is emphasized in the story told by Ze'ira that Yose b. Ḥanina appeared to him in a dream and told him that he was seated next to Johanan in the Garden of Eden (BM 85b). This intimacy is the cause of some confusion in the sources and in some sayings it is not clear which of them was the author. However, the view that Yose b. Ḥanina was ordained by Johanan on the recommendation of Simeon b. Eliakim is based on an error in the text of the Babylonian Talmud (Sanh. 30b). The correct text in the Jerusalem Talmud makes it clear that Yose b. Ḥanina recommended Simeon b. Eliakim for this purpose to Johanan. Yose b. Ḥanina was a *dayyan* and Rava said of him that "he penetrated to the inner spirit of the law" (BK 39a). As a *dayyan* he was renowned for his leanings toward compromise rather than the application of the strict letter of the law and his plea to the contending parties was that they should not stand upon their legal rights but go "beyond the line of justice" (TJ, BM 6:8, 11a). The Babylonian Talmud has a rule that wherever it says "they ridiculed it in the west" (Ereẓ Israel) the reference is to Yose b. Ḥanina (Sanh. 17b). He was also a great aggadist and apparently an outstanding preacher; he said "whosoever discourses on the Torah in public and his words are not as sweet as honey to his audience… it were better that he had not spoken" (Song R. 4, no. 1). There is probably a personal element in his statements, "Love unaccompanied by reproof is not love" and "reproof leads to love" (Gen. R. 54:3).

Very little is known of the events of his life. He was apparently wealthy (BB 90b), and his children died during his lifetime (Ta'an. 13b). The suggestion that he was the brother of Ḥama b. Ḥanina is a mere conjecture. Among his important pupils was Abbahu; however, his sayings are transmitted by many others. He taught *beraitot*, and as a result, although he was not a *tanna*, his name was attached to halakhic Midrashim, though a *tanna* called Yose b. Ḥanina is also mentioned (Epstein, Tanna'im, 630).

BIBLIOGRAPHY: Bacher, Pal Amor, 1, 2, 3; J.S. Zuri, *Yose bar Ḥanina me-Keisarin* (1926); Z.W. Rabinowitz, *Sha'arei Torat Bavel* (1961), 443–4; Hyman, Toledot, s.v.; Ḥ. Albeck, *Mavo la-Talmudim* (1969), 185–6; Epstein, Mishnah, 307–10.

YOSE (Issi) BEN AKAVYAH (second century C.E.), *tanna*. According to a tradition in the Babylonian Talmud (Pes. 113b), he is identical with Joseph of Huẓal (in Babylonia), Joseph the Babylonian, Issi b. Gur Aryeh, *Issi b. Judah, Issi b. Gamaliel, and Issi b. Mahalalel. The Jerusalem Talmud (BK 3:7, 3d) also identifies him with Yose Kittunta, of whom the Mishnah states that with his death the pious men (*ḥasidim*) came to an end (Sot. 9:15). Bacher disputes these identifications, and regards Issi b. Judah in particular as distinct from Yose b. Akavyah but identical with R. Yose b. Judah "of the Babylonian village" who deprecated study from young teachers, preferring instead "old, experienced masters" (Avot 4:20).

Yose's preference for older teachers is paralleled by the respect in which he held old people in general. In contrast to those rabbis who interpreted Leviticus 19:32, "You shall rise up before the hoary head" as referring to scholars, Yose explained it according to its literal sense (Kid. 32b). He also maintained that honoring one's father takes precedence over the performance of a precept which could be carried out by others (Kid. 32a). He stated that anyone superior in even a single accomplishment should be honored (Pes. 13b) and regarded the premature death of scholars as a divine punishment for lack of self-respect (ARN 29, p. 88). In line with R. Eliezer's opposition to the education of women (Sot. 3:4), Yose excluded daughters from the commandment that a man should teach the Torah to his children (Sif. Deut. 46). In accordance with the ancient practice, he interpreted Deuteronomy 23:26 as applying to anyone, while other rabbis, aware of economic realities, restricted the right of picking ears of grain to laborers employed by the owner of the field (BM 29a). Likewise he insisted on the literal meaning of Exodus 21:14 to include non-Israelites under the provisions of the law of murder (Mekh. Nezikin 4). Yose summed up in brief, pointed phrases, the accomplishments of the leading contemporary scholars (Git. 67a). He took extreme care to check his traditions, and was highly praised by R. Eleazar b. Shammua (Men. 18a). To aid his memory, Yose wrote important traditions in private "secret scrolls" (Shab. 6b) which were not meant for dissemination. He failed to attend *Yose b. Ḥalafta's college for three days because Yose had failed to explain the reasons for his statements (Ned. 81a). Yose was also an expert in biblical exegesis, and his statement that "there are five verses in the Torah, the syntactical construction of which is undecided" (it being uncertain whether a word be read with the first or second section of the verse; Mekh. Amalek 1, Yoma 52a–b, et al.) was incorporated in the masorah.

BIBLIOGRAPHY: Bacher, Tann: Hyman, Toledot, 151ff.

[Moses Aberbach]

YOSE BEN AVIN (fourth century), Palestinian *amora*. Yose b. Avin is frequently mentioned in the Jerusalem Talmud and is one of the last scholars referred to there by name. He was a pupil of Yose of Yokrat and later of Assi (according to the reading of Dik. Sof., Ta'an. 23b). Although he frequently transmitted the words of his predecessors, no one, apart from the anonymous "rabbis of Caesarea" (TJ, Shab. 8:1, 11a; et al.), transmitted sayings in his name. According to one tradition (Yev. 45b) he was also in Babylonia, and statements of his are cited in the Babylonian Talmud, though his name is often interchanged with that of his contemporary, Yose b. Zevida. Similarly, in the Palestinian Talmud he is cited as transmitting Babylonian teachings (TJ, 1:2, 60b) and customs (TJ, Pes. 10:2, 37c). There is great confusion in the sources about his exact dates, and some scholars are of the opinion that there was more than one *amora* *Avin (or Ravin). His son Samuel is also mentioned (TJ, Dem. 4:3, 24a) as well as his son-in-law, Hillel (TJ, Ber. 2:5.5a).

BIBLIOGRAPHY: Frankel, Mevo, 102a; Hyman, Toledot, s.v.; Z.W. Rabinowitz, *Sha'arei Torat Bavel* (1961), 444–47: H. Albeck, *Mavo la-Talmudim* (1969), 336–37.

YOSE BEN DORMASKOS (second–third century C.E.), *tanna*. "Dormaskos" refers to his birthplace, Damascus, as he himself stated (Sif. Deut. 1). The Aramaic form Darmesek occurs also in the Bible (I Chron. 18: 5–6; in Kid. 39a the reading is "ben Durmaskah"). Yose is mentioned once only in the Mishnah (Yad, 4: 3; cf. Tosef., Yad. 2:16), not as the author of a halakhic statement, but as transmitting information from the academy of Jabneh to Eliezer b. *Hyrcanus in Lydda. Yose b. Dormaskos tended to follow the plain meaning of the Bible and explicitly dissociated himself from farfetched interpretations. He used to say with regard to these interpretations "Why do you distort the verses?" (Sif. Deut. 1). Most of his sayings are in *aggadah* (Mekh. Shirah 2, et al.). One *baraita* (Ḥul. 67b) which states in his name that the leviathan is a clean fish is also based upon a biblical verse. Another *halakhah*, that "the law of *orlah does not apply outside Ereẓ Israel", he transmitted in the name of Yose *ha-Gelili (Tosef., Or. end).

BIBLIOGRAPHY: Hyman, Toledot, s.v.

[Jacob Eliahu Ephrathi]

YOSE BEN ḤALAFTA (mid-second century C.E.), *tanna*; the R. Yose mentioned in the Talmud without patronymic. Yose was one of the leaders of the generation after the persecutions which followed the Bar Kokhba War. He was born in *Sepphoris, where his father was one of those who instituted *takkanot* there after the destruction of the Temple (Tosef., Ta'an. 1:14). Yose studied under his father and transmitted some of his teachings (Kelim 26:6; et al.). He also studied under *Johanan b. Nuri in Galilee (Tosef., Kelim, BK 6:4; et al.), and under *Tarfon in Judea (*ibid.*, Shev. 4:4). His main teacher, however, was *Akiva in whose name he frequently transmits *halakhot*, and it was said generally: "R. Akiva his teacher" (Pes. 18a). The Babylonian Talmud numbers him among his last pupils who "reestablished the Torah" (Yev. 62b) and according to one tradition he was ordained by *Judah b. Bava (Sanh. 14a). Other traditions report that he participated in all the conventions of scholars "at the close of the period of persecution," in the valley of Bet Rimmon, in Usha, and in Jabneh (TJ, Ḥag. 3:1; Ber. 63b). During the persecutions he endangered his life to fulfill the precept of circumcision and fled to Asia or to Laodicea (BM 84a: TJ, Av. Zar. 3:1). He followed in the footsteps of his father in Sepphoris in introducing *takkanot* (Sanh. 19a), in giving practical instruction (see Er. 86b), and in preaching in public (Sanh. 109a).

Yose's *bet din* in Sepphoris was reckoned among the most outstanding in Ereẓ Israel (Sanh. 32b). Yose and Judah are frequently found together with the *nasi*, Simeon b. Gamaliel both at Usha and during his various travels (Tosef., Ber. 5:2; *ibid.*, Suk. 2: 2; et al.), and Simeon b. Gamaliel quotes him (Meg. 6b). His influence was still felt in the council chamber during the time of Judah ha-Nasi, the son of Simeon, who withdrew his own view in favor of that of Yose (Shab. 51a), and spoke of him with exceptional respect (Git. 67a). The Talmud states that the *halakhah* was established in accordance with the view of Yose wherever his associates disagreed with him (Er. 46b). Yose is mentioned several times in all the tractates of the Talmud with the exception of *Bikkurim*, *Hagigah*, *Horayot*, and *Me'ilah*, and in the *beraitot* his *halakhot* are frequently given.

His sayings in the *aggadah* are not numerous. Some 16 conversations with gentiles have been ascribed to him, especially those with "a certain matron." Many aggadic sayings quoted in his name deal with theological and cosmological problems, and noteworthy in this connection is his explanation of the name *Makom* ("place") for God: "The Holy One is the place of the world, but the world is not His place" (Gen. R. 68:9). Among others are his sayings: "The Divine Presence never descended to earth, nor did Moses and Elijah ever ascend on high" (Suk. 5a); "On what does the world rest? On the pillars… the pillars upon the waters… the waters upon the mountains… the mountains on the wind… the wind upon the tempest… the tempest is suspended on the arm of the Holy One" (Ḥag. 12b). In opposition to the view of others, Yose held that "man is judged each day" (Tosef., RH 1:13). Yose transmitted many reminiscences and historical traditions of the generations close to him and of the time of the Temple. In his *aggadah* too an important place is given to determining the chronology of the events in Scripture and to the interpretation of the historical material of the scriptural books. The *baraita*, **Seder Olam*, dealing with chronology, apparently had its origin in his school, as testified by Johanan (Yev. 82b). Many traditions record his unpretentious ways and his relations with his fellow men, as well as his piety (Shab. 118b; TJ, Ber. 3:4). Yose is the earliest scholar of whom it is related that he was worthy of having the prophet Elijah reveal himself to him regularly in order to teach him (Ber. 31; et al.). Of his private life, it is reported that he obtained his livelihood by tanning (Shab. 49a–b). He left five sons, all scholars, the best known of them being *Ishmael and *Eleazar.

BIBLIOGRAPHY: Frankel, Mishnah (1923), 174ff.; M. Yoel, in: MGWJ, 6 (1857), 83ff.; B. Ratner, *Mavo le-Seder Olam Rabha* (1896); Bacher, Tann, 2; Epstein, Tanna'im, 126ff.

[Shmuel Safrai]

YOSE BEN JOEZER OF ZEREDAH (first half of the second century B.C.E.), together with his colleague, *Yose b. Johanan of Jerusalem, the first of the **zugot*. Both were disciples of *Antigonus of Sokho. Zeredah, his place of origin, is in the south of Samaria. He was the *nasi* of the Sanhedrin and his colleague was the *av bet din*. They are recorded as having "decreed uncleanness upon gentile countries and upon glassware" (Shab. 14b–15b, TJ, Shab. 1:7, 3c; Pes. 1:6, 27d; Ket. 8:11, 32c). Apparently the main reason for the first decree was to prevent or discourage emigration from Ereẓ Israel. The suggestion that the second decree was for economic reasons is very doubtful. It is probable that it was merely one of the stringencies introduced into the laws of ritual uncleanness and cleanness during the time of the Second Temple. They were the first to differ in the well-known dispute about **semikhah* (the laying on of hands upon sacrifices during the festival), Yose b. Joezer holding that it should not be performed and Yose b. Johanan permitting it (Ḥag. 2:2). Because of their profound erudition and piety both Yoses were called "the grape clusters," and it was said that when they died "the grape clusters ceased" (Sot. 9:9; cf. Tosef., BK 8:13; Tem. 15b).

It is related of Yose b. Joezer "that he was the most pious in the priesthood, yet his apron was [considered] *midras* (uncleanness) for [those eating] hallowed things" (Ḥag. 2:7). The Mishnah (Eduy. 8:4) relates of him: "Yose b. Joezer of Zeredah testified concerning the *ayil kamẓah* locust that it is clean … and that one who has definitely touched a corpse is unclean. And they called him Yose the permitter." It is noteworthy that this testimony – the first mentioned in the sources (see *Eduyyot*) – is in Aramaic, typical of authentic Second Temple traditions. His statement in *Avot* (1:4), however, is in Hebrew: "Let thy house be a meeting place for scholars; sit amid the dust of their feet; and drink in their words with thirst." The Midrash (Gen. R. 65:22) relates that Yose was sentenced to death by crucifixion. On the way to his execution his nephew, Yakum of Zerorot, who is usually identified with the wicked priest *Alcimus, encountered him and taunted him. Alcimus repented and committed suicide. This story, however, does not agree with the description of the death of Alcimus in I Maccabees 9:55–56. The Talmud (BB 133b) relates that Yose gave all his property to the sanctuary and bequeathed nothing to his son because of his unworthy conduct.

BIBLIOGRAPHY: Hyman, Toledot, 729–31; N. Krochmal, *Moreh Nevukhei ha-Zeman (Kitvei Rabbi N. Krochmal*, ed. by S. Rawidowicz (1924), 69); Frankel, Mishnah, 31–4; Weiss, Dor, 1 (1904[4]), 98–102; Halevy, Dorot, 1 pt. 3 (1923), 200–2, 348–50; S. Klein, *Ereẓ Yehudah* (1939), 45; E.E. Urbach, in: *Tarbiz*, 27 (1958), 170; Alon, Meḥkarim, 2 (1958), 185f.; L. Ginzberg (Ginẓburg), *Al Halakhah ve-Haggadah* (1960), 141, 21–27.

[Moshe David Herr]

YOSE BEN JOHANAN HA-TANNA OF JERUSALEM, colleague of Yose b. Joezer of *Zeredah, and one of the *zugot. He is almost invariably mentioned together with his colleague. Yose b. Johanan's maxim in *Avot* (1:5) is: "Let thy house be wide open; let the poor be members of thy household; and engage not in much gossip with women."

[Moshe David Herr]

YOSE BEN JUDAH (second century C.E.), *tanna*. Yose was the elder colleague of Judah ha-Nasi (see Pes. 112b) with whom he held halakhic discussions (Shab. 18a) and whom he accompanied on his tours of the country (Ned. 62a; Gen. R. 76:8). Yose's statements are cited a number of times in four of the six orders of the Mishnah but not in *Zera'im* and *Tohorot*. Many of them are cited anonymously, whence his designation in the Babylonian Talmud, "*stimata*" (Er. 38 b; et al.). Yose is very frequently mentioned in all six orders of the Tosefta. Most of his statements belong to *halakhah* and only a few are in *aggadah*, the best known being that which tells about the two ministering angels who accompany a man when he returns home from the synagogue on the eve of the Sabbath (Shab. 119b). Well known too is his apothegm: "Let your 'yes' be righteous and your 'no' be righteous" (BM 49a). It is possible that Simeon b. Judah was his brother.

BIBLIOGRAPHY: Epstein, Tanna'im, 172–4; Hyman, Toledot, s.v.

[Israel Moses Ta-Shma]

YOSE BEN KIPPAR (end of the second century C.E.), *tanna*. Yose's name does not occur in the Mishnah, but only in the Tosefta and in *beraitot*. He transmits many sayings in the name of Eleazar b. *Shammua (TJ, Shev. 2:4, 33d. Beẓah 4:2, 62c; et al.) and some scholars are of the opinion that whenever he transmits in the name of R. Eleazar without a patronymic the reference is to Eleazar b. Shammua. Yose is the first known emissary sent from Ereẓ Israel to Babylon in order to collect money and offerings for the benefit of the scholars of Ereẓ Israel. He was accompanied by his colleague Dostai b. Yannai, and on account of this mission became involved in a dispute with the local people (Nehardea, in the TB) who demanded the return of their money and even took it back from him by force and under torture (TJ, Git. 1:6, 43d; Git. 14b). According to a passage in the Talmud (Ber. 63a), Yose b. Kippar was sent with "the grandson of Zechariah b. Kebutal" to Babylon in order to dissuade Hananiah, the nephew of Joshua b. Hananiah, from intercalating the year outside Ereẓ Israel. This incident occurred shortly after the Bar Kokhba revolt in 135 C.E. and therefore the chronology makes it difficult to ascribe the incident to him. Consequently some scholars are of the opinion that the reading is a mistake for Yose b. ha-Kappar (see Dik. Sof. 1c.). The Jerusalem Talmud also (ed. 6:13, 40a) specifies the names of other emissaries regarding this incident, and his name does not occur there.

BIBLIOGRAPHY: Hyman, Toledot, 732–3.

[Israel Moses Ta-Shma]

YOSE BEN KISMA (first half of the second century C.E.), *tanna*. Yose lived apparently in Tiberias (Tanḥ. B. Gen. 166; Yev. 96b). An autobiographical story is told of his preferring to live in a place of Torah rather than have all the silver, gold, and precious stones in the world (Avot 6:9). The Palestinian Talmud transmits a tradition in which Yose ben Kisma appears in the company of the fourth generation *tannaim* Eleazar and Yose (TJ Shek. 2:5, 47a). No halakhic statements are transmitted in his name. In the *aggadah* of the Babylonian Talmud, Yose is described as having held that one should submit to Roman rule, and according to this tradition he did not give up this view even during the time of the Hadrianic persecutions. It is related that when he was ill, *Ḥanina b. Teradyon went to visit him. Yose said to him: "Ḥanina, my brother, do you not know that it is Heaven that has ordained this nation to reign? For though she has laid waste His house, burnt His Temple, slain His pious ones, and caused His choice ones to perish, still is she firmly established! Yet, I have heard that you sit and occupy yourself with the Torah, address public assemblies, and keep a scroll of the law in your bosom." Ḥanina replied: "Heaven will have mercy." "I," remonstrated Yose, "am telling you plain facts and you say, 'Heaven will show mercy!' It will surprise me if they do not burn you together with the scroll of the Law." Nevertheless, Yose looked forward to the redemption and believed that Israel would fall into the hands of the Parthians (Sanh. 98a–b). It was said that within a few days Yose b. Kisma died, and all the great men of Rome went to his funeral and made great lamentation for him (Av. Zar. 18a).

BIBLIOGRAPHY: Hyman, Toledot, 735f.; Bacher; Tanna'im; J. Guttmann, in: *Sefer Assaf* (1953), 173f.

[Moshe David Herr]

YOSE BEN MESHULLAM (end of the second century C.E.), *tanna*. Yose was the colleague of Abba Yose b. Dosai and Simeon b. *Eleazar. He transmitted *halakhot* in the name of his brother Nathan (Tosef., Dem. 3: 1). Yose, who belonged to the intimate circle of Judah ha-Nasi, is referred to by name only three times in the Mishnah (Ter. 4:7; Bek. 3:3 and 6:1). It can be proved, however, that several of the anonymous statements in the Mishnah are according to him. He and Simeon b. *Menasya headed the "holy *congregation" of Jerusalem (TJ,

Ma'as. Sh. 2:10, 53d) who ate ordinary food in ritual purity and divided their day into three: one-third for study, one-third for prayer, and one-third for work (Eccles. R. 9:9).

BIBLIOGRAPHY: Epstein, Tanna'im, 182–4; S. Safrai, in: *Zion*, 23 (1957), 189 ff.

[Israel Moses Ta-Shma]

YOSE BEN YOSE (fourth or fifth century C.E.?), the earliest liturgical poet known by name. *Saadiah mentions him as foremost among the famous poets of antiquity (Arabic introduction to the *Iggaron*, and Hebrew translation, ed. A. Harkavy, in *Zikkaron la-Rishonim ve-Gam la-Aḥaronim*, 5 (1891), 50 f.). Of the many theories about him, the only one that appears tenable is that his native country was Palestine, as it has been established beyond doubt that the oldest *piyyut* was developed in that country. Even in the early Middle Ages, nothing was known of the period and the circumstances of his life. He is sometimes called *ha-yatom* ("the orphan") apparently because he bore the name of his father. Others called him "high priest" from which it would seem that he was believed to have lived in the times of the Temple, while others identify him with the *amora* Yose b. Yose. He probably flourished as early as the fifth or even the fourth century. Since these dates cannot be definitely determined, it is not certain whether he is to be regarded as the originator of the artistic *piyyut* or as reliant upon older models no longer extant. Despite his dependence on the picturesque style of the Midrash and occasional neologisms, Yose's language is distinguished by its purity and its lofty poetic diction. He is the only non-Spaniard whose verses Ibn *Janaḥ quotes in his dictionary as ideal models (*Sefer ha-Shorashim* (Berlin, 1893), 305, 419).

Large parts of his compositions have been preserved in the *genizah*, and have been published by M. Zulay and E. Fleischer. A. Mirsky has edited and annotated all his preserved liturgical poems (1977²). Among the unpublished texts of the *genizah* are some which were apparently composed by Yose.

The following poetical compositions are attributed to Yose:

(1) The so-called *Teki'ata* of the German ritual, consisting of three sections appended to the prayers **malkhuyyot*, **zikhronot*, and **shofarot*.

(2) At least three versions of the **Avodah*, namely:

(a) *Azkir Gevurot*, for the *Shaḥarit* of the Day of Atonement (Rosenberg), M. Sachs, *Kovez Ma'asei Yedei Ge'onim Kadmonim* (Berlin, 1856), 1–9, 85–87; H. Brody-M. Wiener, *Mivḥar ha-Shirah ha-Ivrit* (1934), 26–36; A. Mirsky, *Piyyutei Yose ben Yose*, 127 ff.; with English translation: T. Carmi, *The Penguin Book of Hebrew Verse* (1981), 209 ff.; M.D. Swartz and J. Yahalom (eds.), *Avodah: An Anthology of Ancient Poetry for Yom Kippur*, 295 ff.

(b) *Attah Konanta 'Olam be-rov Ḥesed* used in the old French ritual in the Middle Ages, later preserved in the ritual of *Apam, the text of which was published in Rosenberg's *Kovez* II, 111–5 as well as in S.D. Luzzatto's Italian *maḥzor* (Leghorn, 1856); A. Mirsky, *Piyyutei Yose ben Yose*, 178 ff.; M.D. Swartz and J. Yahalom (eds.), *Avodah: An Anthology of Ancient Poetry for Yom Kippur*, 291 ff.

(c) *Asapper Gedulot*, for the *Minḥah* prayer, extant only in a small Cairo *Genizah* fragment (published in I. Elbogen, *Studien zur Geschichte des juedischen Gottesdienstes* (1907), n. 8); A. Mirsky, *Piyyutei Yose ben Yose*, 203 ff.

(3) *Omnam Ashamenu*, a confessional prayer included in the German ritual, translated into German by L. Zunz (Zunz, Poesie, 163); A. Mirsky, *Piyyutei Yose ben Yose*, 118 ff.

(4) *Yozer* (perhaps), of which only the first line *Or Olam Ozar Ḥayyim* remains; see A. Mirsky, *Piyyutei Yose ben Yose*, 217 ff.

(5) Two rhymed verses quoted by Ibn Janaḥ in Yose's name which belong, as M. Zulay has proved, to the rhymed *rehitim* for the Day of Atonement.

(6) Several compositions for the New Year: *Ahalelah Elohai*, ed. A. Mirsky, in: *Piyyutei Yose ben Yose*, 93 ff.

(7) *Efḥad be-Ma'asai*, ed. A. Mirsky, in: *Piyutei Yose ben Yose*, 101 ff.

(8) *Anusah le-Ezrah*, ed. A. Mirsky, in: *Piyutei Yose ben Yose*, 109 ff.

(9) *Etten Tehillah*, for Yom Kippur, ed. A. Mirsky, in: *Piyyutei Yose ben Yose*, 173 ff.

(10) The lamentation *En Lanu Kohen Gadol* traditionally attributed to him, ed. A. Mirsky, in: *Piyyutei Yose ben Yose*, 210 ff.

(11) The *piyyut* on the members of the body *Eftaḥ Sefatai*, ed. A. Mirsky, in: *Piyyutei Yose ben Yose*, 218 ff.

(12) *Az le-Rosh Tattanu*, ed. A. Mirsky, in: *Piyyutei Yose ben Yose*, 219 ff.

And a few more doubtful *piyyutim*.

BIBLIOGRAPHY: Zunz, in: WZJT, 2 (1836), 305–7; Zunz, Poesie, 81, 96, 122, 124, 130, 137; Zunz, Lit Poesie, 26–28, 643–5; Landshuth, Ammudei, 85–88; A. Harkavy, *Zikkaron la-Rishonim ve-Gam la-Aḥaronim*, 1:5 (1891), 105 f.; I. Elbogen, *Studien zur Geschichte des juedischen Gottesdienstes* (1907), 74, 78–81, 118 f.; Elbogen, Gottesdienst, 306–8, 550, 560; Bacher, in: JQR, 14 (1902), 742 f.; W. Jawitz, in: *Festschrift zum siebzigsten Geburtstag David Hoffmanns* (1914), 74–82; Simchoni, in: *Ha-Tekufah*, 12 (1924), 179 f.; Davidson, Ozar, 4 (1933), 398; J. Kenaani, *Millon Konkordanzyoni li-Leshon ha-Piyyutim* (1931), includes a list of Yose b. Yose's *piyyutim* on p. xii; Zulay, in: YMḤSI, 6 (1945), 235 f.; Roth, in: JBL (1952), 171–8; Schirmann, in: JQR, 44 (1953/54), 142–4; A. Mirsky, *Yalkut ha-Piyyutim* (1958), 1–11; Ligier, in: *Nouvelle Revue Théologique*, 72 (1960), 40–45; A. Mirsky, *Reshit ha-Piyyut* (1965); E. Fleischer, in: *Kovez al Yad*, 7 (1968), 1–79. **ADD. BIBLIOGRAPHY:** *Hebrew Liturgical Poetry in the Middle Ages* (1975), 93 ff., passim; idem, in: *Ha-Yozerot* (1984), 19 ff.; W. Horbury, in: *Suffering and Martyrdom in the New Testament* (1981), 143–82; A. Mirsky (ed.), *Piyyutei Yose ben Yose* (1991²); J. Yahalom, *Poetry and Society in Jewish Galilee of Late Antiquity* (Heb., 1999); M.D. Swartz and J. Yahalom (eds.), *Avodah: An Anthology of Ancient Poetry for Yom Kippur* (2004).

[Jefim (Hayyim) Schirmann / Angel Sáenz-Badillos (2nd ed.)]

YOSE BEN ZIMRA (second century C.E.), Erez Israel scholar belonging to the last generation of *tannaim* and the first generation of *amoraim*. According to one tradition, Yose was a priest (Yoma 78a). His daughter married the son of R. Judah ha-Nasi (Ket. 62b). His halakhic sayings are few, most of his dicta belonging to the sphere of *aggadah*, and they occur in the Talmuds and the Midrashim (and once even in the *Mekhilta). His sayings are usually transmitted in his name by Johanan and, particularly, by Eleazar b. Pedat. His statement "If all the inhabitants of the world were to assemble, they could not create a single gnat and put life into it" (TJ. Sanh. 7:19, 25d), directed against sorcerers and magicians, was used against the alleged miracles of sectarians, apparently Christians, who were very common in Ereẓ Israel in his day. He particularly censured talebearers and scandalmongers, whom he compared to those who deny the very foundations of religion (Ar. 15b).

He interprets the word *va-yiven* in Genesis 2:22 to indicate that "woman is endowed with more understanding (*binah*) than man" (Gen. R. 18:1).

BIBLIOGRAPHY: Hyman, Toledot, 722f.; Bacher, Pal Amor; Allon, Meḥkarim, 2 (1958), 36f.; Ḥ. Albeck, *Mavo la-Talmudim* (1969), 161.

[Moshe David Herr]

YOSEF, OVADIAH (1920–), Israeli rabbi. Yosef was born in Baghdad, but when he was four years old he was taken to Jerusalem. At the age of 20, he was ordained rabbi by Ben-Zion Meir *Ouziel. In 1945 he was appointed a *dayyan* in the *bet din* of the Sephardim in Jerusalem. In 1947 he was elected head of the *bet din* of Cairo and deputy chief rabbi of Egypt. During the period of his rabbinate in Egypt he displayed great courage and national pride; he refused to issue proclamations against the State of Israel, forbade contributions for military equipment for the Egyptian army, and also insisted on his right to preach in Hebrew. In 1950, he returned to the young state of Israel and was appointed a member of the rabbinical court of Petaḥ Tikvah and of Jerusalem (1958–65). In 1965 he was appointed a member of the Supreme Rabbinical Court of Appeals in Jerusalem, and in 1968, Sephardi chief rabbi of Tel Aviv-Jaffa. On October 16, 1972, Rabbi Yosef was elected Sephardi chief rabbi of Israel (*rishon le-Zion*), a position he held until 1983.

In 1984, with the encouragement of Lithuanian leader R. Eleazar Menahem *Shach, who had in effect become his mentor, Yosef founded *Shas as an ultra-Orthodox political party aiming to redress the wrong of Eastern underrepresentation in Israeli public life. Shas became a major force in Israeli politics, with a peak of 17 seats after the 1999 Knesset elections and its own school system, El ha-Ma'ayan. With the rise of Shas and as its spiritual leader, Yosef became one of the most prominent and influential figures in the country, given to scathing and often crude pronouncements about the secular world, and in particular Israel's Supreme Court. However, Yosef was also a pragmatist, and though he had fallen under the sway of R. Shach and made his followers part of the closed Lithuanian yeshivah world where secular studies and secular employment were anathema, his own background in the more open society of Eastern Jews, where assimilation was not feared and vocational training was the norm, had made him relatively liberal in his outlook. Thus, in 1979, Yosef consented to serve as president of a rabbinical seminary attached to Bar-Ilan University which would be combined with a B.A. program in the Humanities and Jewish Studies – a kind of Israeli Yeshiva University. However, the outcry in the ḥaredi world of R. Shach and a campaign of pressure and threats caused R. Yosef to back down and repudiate the project. The break with R. Shach came when R. Yosef supported the peace process and permitted Shas to join the Rabin government in 1992. Shas subsequently joined the Netanyahu government in 1996 and then the Barak government in 1999 after reaching its high-water mark of 17 Knesset seats. Since that time, Shas has slipped at the polls and more often than not found itself bypassed in government coalitions, which together with the general recession has had an effect on the funds channeled into its pet projects and led to the near bankruptcy of its school system. Politically it has moved to the right, opposing the 2005 disengagement from the Gaza Strip.

A prolific writer of halakhic works, Yosef published his first work, *Yabbi'a Omer*, at the age of 18 on themes in tractate *Horayot*, and he used the same title for many subsequent collections of responsa (which appeared in Jerusalem in 1954, 1956, 1960, 1964, and 1969). A second set of responsa was published under the title *Yeḥavei Da'at*, and his rulings were codified in *Yalkut Yosef*. In 1970 he was awarded the Israel Prize for Torah literature. He also wrote *Ḥazon Ovadyah* (1952), on the Passover *Haggadah*, in two sections: one halakhic and the other homiletical. The second part was published in an enlarged second edition (1967). Yosef's works are distinguished by their erudition. He is at home both with the Sephardi and Ashkenazi authorities to whom he gives equal weight. His rulings are clear and direct. In general he inclined to leniency in his rulings. Yosef also headed the yeshivah Torah ve-Hora'ah – the Tel Aviv branch of the yeshivah Porat Yosef – as well as the institute for *dayyanim* established by him in Tel Aviv. Among his best-known rulings were those collectively recognizing the *Beta Israel as Jews and affirming the permissibility of giving up land in Ereẓ Israel in exchange for peace.

ADD. BIBLIOGRAPHY: N. Chen and A. Pfeffer, *Maran Ovadyah Yosef: Ha-Biografiyah* (2004); B. Lau, *Mi-Maran ad Maran – ha-Rav Ovadyah Yosef* (2005); J. Lupu, *A Shift in Haredi Society: Vocational Training and Academic Studies* (2004).

[Itzhak Alfassi / Fred Skolnik (2nd ed.)]

YOSE HA-GELILI (beginning of the second century C.E.), *tanna*, one of the scholars of *Jabneh. As his name indicates, Yose came from Galilee (Er. 53b). His teachers there are unknown, but at an early age he went to Jabneh, where he made a great impression in his discussions with Tarfon and Akiva – who also later were his chief disputants (Zev. 57a; et al.). His relations with Akiva were at first those of pupil and teacher, but in the course of time he became his colleague, even saying to him: "Akiva, even if you carry on all day I shall not heed you" (Sifra 6:23; Men. 89a). Akiva held him in high regard, and said: "Not for everyone [would I withdraw] but for you, who are Yose ha-Gelili." His name is not mentioned in the tractate *Eduyyot* because he was still young when the *halakhot* detailed there were established. His *halakhot* are scattered throughout the Talmud, but mainly in the order *Kodashim*. Generally he does not interpret the scriptural verses according to their literal meaning, and in the *aggadah* he inquires as to the intent of the verse. His permanent place of residence is not known. In Tiberias he studied together with Simeon b. Ḥanina (Sif. Zut. to Num. 19:4) and he was also in the south – when he accompanied Tarfon, Eleazar b. Azariah, and Akiva to comfort Ishmael – in Jabneh, and in Lydda, where Tarfon lived.

According to a talmudic tradition, his wife was a shrew and he was persuaded by his colleagues to divorce her, but after the divorce he acted generously toward her and supported her and her second husband, who became blind (TJ, Ket. 11:3). He had three sons: Eliezer, Ḥanina, and one who died during his lifetime. He was also regarded as a wonder-worker whose prayers for rain were effective. Because of the similarity of names some of his statements are confused with those of *Yose b. Ḥalafta and vice versa. Nothing is known of his disciples, and those who transmitted statements in his name are few: Judah b. Ilai, Eleazar b. Shammua, Nathan, Simeon b. Eleazar, anti *Yose b. Dormaskos. Yose ha-Gelili apparently died before the Bar Kokhba War (132–135 C.E.), and according to a medieval tradition his tomb was located near Safed in Galilee.

BIBLIOGRAPHY: Frankel, Mishnah, 132–4; Hyman, Toledot, 738–40; Bacher, Tann index; Z. Vilna, *Mazzevot Kodesh be-Erez Yisrael* (1963^2), 360–1.

[Israel Moses Ta-Shma]

YOSE HA-KOHEN (end of the first century C.E.), *tanna*. Yose, a pupil of *Johanan b. Zakkai, was known for his piety and his teacher designated him a "*ḥasid*" (one of exceptional piety; Avot 2:8). It is related of him that he never sent a letter through a gentile lest he forward it on the Sabbath (Shab. 19a). His piety is also discernible in his apothegm: "Fit yourself to study Torah for it will not come to you as a heritage; and let all your actions be for the sake of heaven" (Avot 2:12). In answer to the question as to "the good way to which a man should cleave" Yose ha-Kohen answered that a man should maintain good neighborly relations (Avot. 2:9). Like most of the *ḥasidim* of the Talmud Yose was not conspicuous in his teaching and very little is known about it (Eduy. 8:2). Yose plays a significant role in the later amoraic versions of the stories concerning early tannaitic involvement in the study of *Merkabah mysticism, along with Simeon ben Nethanel (TJ, Ḥag. 2:1, 77a), or according to another tradition with *Joshua b. Hananiah (TB, Ḥag. 14b). These traditions, however, probably do not preserve authentic historical information about Yose himself or his historical period. Some identify Yose ha-Kohen with Yose Kittunta, of whom it is said that when he died, piety ceased (Sot. 9:15). On the other hand it is certain that he is not to be identified with the Joseph ha-Kohen mentioned in several places (Mik. 10:1; et al.) without the title "Rabbi."

BIBLIOGRAPHY: Hyman, Toledot, 740–1. **ADD. BIBLIOGRAPHY:** S. Wald, "The Mystical Discourse of Eleazar ben Arakh," in: JSIJ (2006).

[Israel Moses Ta-Shma / Stephen G. Wald (2nd ed.)]

YOTVATAH (Heb. יָטְבָתָה), kibbutz in southern Israel, in the Arabah Valley 26 mi. (40 km.) N. of Eilat, affiliated with Iḥud ha-Kevuẓot ve-ha-Kibbutzim. Yotvatah was founded in 1951 as a *Naḥal outpost by Israel-born graduates of youth movements and later joined by pioneers from various countries. Nearby is the Yotvatah playa and one of the largest springs of the southern Arabah, from which the principal water supply was first drawn to Eilat. Situated at an isolated spot near the Jordanian frontier, Yotvatah suffered from frequent enemy attacks. In 2002 its population was 576. It developed methods for progressive oasis farming, producing mainly out-of-season vegetables and flowers, dates and other tropical fruit, etc. Yotvatah ran a dairy for pasteurized milk products, but also sold other products, such as fruit juices. In 1998 part of the dairy was sold to the Straus company, a large family-owned food enterprise. The kibbutz experimented with hydroponics and was active in regional nature research. It set up a small wildlife reserve. The name Yotvatah is biblical (Jotbath; Num. 33:33; Deut. 10:7).

See also: *Jotbath, Jothbatah.

[Efraim Orni]

YOUNG, ALEC DAVID (1913–2005), British aeronautical engineer. Young was born in London and educated at the Central Foundation School before graduating in mathematics from Cambridge University (1935). After postgraduate research in aeronautics he joined the scientific staff of the Royal Aircraft Establishment, Farnborough (1936–46) followed by the College of Aeronautics, Cranfield (1946–54) where he was professor and head of the department of aerodynamics. Between 1954 and 1978 he was professor, head of the department of aeronautical engineering and vice principal (1966–78) of Queen Mary College, University of London, dean of the university faculty of engineering (1962–66), and from 1978 emeritus professor. His research interests included aircraft design, boundary layer problems, and innovative work on the design of ejector seats, parachutes, and jet engines. He made major contributions to elucidating the cause of the Comet crash (1954) and the Munich air disaster involving the Manchester United football team (1958). His many honors include the Order of the British Empire (1964), the Royal Aeronautical Society Gold Medal (1972), election to the Royal Society of London (1973), and the Roy Medal from the International Council for the Aeronautical Sciences (1994). He served as consultant to the Haifa Technion, with which he had strong ties.

[Michael Denman (2nd ed.)]

YOUNG, DAVID IVOR, BARON YOUNG OF GRAFFHAM (1932–), British businessman and politician. Lord

Young of Graffham was born in London, the son of a flour merchant, and the brother of Stuart *Young, who became the chairman of the BBC. Lord Young was educated at a London public school, Christ's College, Finchley, and London University. He became a solicitor and then entered business life, serving as an executive at Great Universal Stores from 1956 to 1961 and as chairman of Eldonwall Ltd. Margaret *Thatcher appointed him to head the Manpower Services Commission from 1982 to 1984, which was concerned with reducing Britain's high unemployment rate. In 1984 she made Young minister without portfolio in her government, with a life peerage. Lord Young was then appointed to Thatcher's cabinet, serving as employment minister in 1985–87 and trade minister in 1987–89. Later he held a variety of senior business appointments and was chairman of Cable & Wireless Ltd. in 1990–95. He was also active in Jewish affairs, serving as president of Jewish Care from 1990. Young is the author of an account of his time in government, *The Enterprise Years: A Businessman in Politics* (1990).

[William D. Rubinstein (2nd ed.)]

YOUNG, JAMES E. (1951–), U.S. Holocaust scholar. Born in California, educated at the University of California, Santa Cruz (B.A. 1973, Ph.D. 1983) and the University of California, Berkeley (M.A. 1976), Young taught at Bryn Mawr College (1983–84), New York University (1984–88), and from 1988 at the University of Massachusetts, Amherst, where he was named professor of English and Judaic Studies and chair of the Department of Judaic and Near Eastern Studies. He was a visiting professor at the universities of Washington, Harvard, and Princeton, and a lecturer at other universities and public forums. He was a fellow of the YIVO Institute for Jewish Research and the Institute of Contemporary Jewry at the Hebrew University, and received fellowships or grants from the Guggenheim and Littauer foundations, the National Endowment for the Humanities, and other scholarly support organizations. Young served on the boards or advisory committees of the New England Holocaust Memorial Committee, the State Museum at Terezin, the International Auschwitz Council of the Polish Ministry of Culture, and the commission for the Holocaust memorial in Berlin, as well as consulting with other national and municipal memorial authorities. He was the curator of "The Art of Memory" exhibition at the Jewish Museum in New York in 1994 and is the editor-in-chief of the *Posen Library of Jewish Culture and Civilization*, a multivolume collection of primary sources, documents, texts, and images sponsored by the Posen Foundation.

Young's scholarly work focused on historical memory and memorialization, and in particular the aesthetics and politics of Holocaust memorials, on which he is a recognized authority. Young's insight that "the motives of memory are never pure" informs his examination of the ways in which contemporary political commitments and exigencies shape what is remembered and how it is memorialized, and how a memorial may become part of a reductive political mythology. He proposes that the "countermonument" – a work of art that interrogates and undermines intended, official meaning – is the best guarantor that viewers will experience a more genuine sense of historical memory not entirely mediated by a heroic or redemptive national narrative. Young examined the process of representing the Holocaust both in personal literary and artistic works and in official public memorials in Poland, Germany, Israel, and elsewhere. His principal publications are *Writing and Rewriting the Holocaust: Narrative and the Consequences of Interpretation* (1988), *The Texture of Memory: Holocaust Memorials and Meaning* (1993), *Holocaust Memorials in History: The Art of Memory* (edited, 1994), *At Memory's Edge: After-Images of the Holocaust in Contemporary Art and Architecture* (essays, 2000). He contributed essays to a number of collected volumes and published numerous articles and reviews in academic as well as less scholarly journals and newspapers.

[Drew Silver (2nd ed.)]

YOUNG, STUART (1934–1986), British public servant. The son of a North London flour merchant, Young entered accountancy at 17, and at 23 was senior partner of his own firm, specializing in corporate finance. He entered British public life as appeals chairman of European Architectural Heritage Year 1975, subsequently becoming a member of the Historic Buildings Council, a trustee of the National Gallery, and a leader of the Architectural Heritage Fund. In 1983 he became the youngest chairman of the governors of the British Broadcasting Corporation. Appointed with a view to the use of his accountancy skills for the internal reorganization of the BBC, he became a champion of its independence from government. An active Zionist from 1950, Young volunteered his services in the 1967 Six-Day War, took a leading part in the raising of funds for Israel, and became president of the Joint Israel Appeal in Britain. Among many other communal appointments, he planned the reorganization of Anglo-Jewish welfare services as chairman of the Central Council for Jewish Social Service. He died of lung cancer at the age of 52.

BIBLIOGRAPHY: *The Times* (Aug. 30, 1986); *Jewish Chronicle* (Sept. 5, 1986). **ADD. BIBLIOGRAPHY:** ODNB online.

[Vivian David Lipman]

YOUNG ISRAEL, NATIONAL COUNCIL OF, an umbrella organization for 146 Orthodox congregations with approximately 25,000 member families in North America. Its sister organization, Yisrael Hatzair – the Young Israel Movement in Israel – has more than 50 synagogues under its aegis. It is headquartered in New York City with regional offices in Florida, California, New Jersey, and Jerusalem. At the beginning of 2006, Shlomo Z. Mostofsky was national president and Rabbi Pesach Lerner was executive vice president.

The National Council's stated mission is to "broaden the appeal of the traditional community synagogue as the central address for Jewish communal life by providing educational, religious, social, spiritual, and communal programming," and also offers synagogues interest-free loans to use for organization and expansion.

The National Council perceives itself as a grass roots association directed by input from lay leadership, including the national board, delegates from each branch synagogue, branch rabbis and presidents and professional staff. The organization holds an annual national banquet, rabbinic and lay leadership conferences, political missions to Washington, D.C., and various rallies and other events to keep members involved and inspired. Among the programs are synagogue support services; the Council of Rabbis; youth programs; rabbinic training and placement; *kashrut* education and services; the American Coalition for Missing Israeli Soldiers; the Eretz Yisrael Commission; the Samuel Zucker Synagogue Revolving Loan Fund; the Women's Division; Lay Leadership Development; Senior League; and various publications (*Viewpoint Magazine*, weekly *Divrei Torah Bulletins*).

The organization was founded about 20 years after the massive flood of Jewish immigrants arrived in New York in the late 19th century to provide a bridge between the old Jewish world and America by creating a positive Orthodox synagogue experience for the immigrants' growing group of Americanized children. Among its founders was Mordecai Kaplan, then an Orthodox rabbi, who saw in the Young Israel a vehicle for strengthening the Jewish identity of the American-born and/or English-speaking young Jews. Sermons were in English, not Yiddish, and there was no charge for honors in the synagogue. The immigrants began to establish their American lives, but it was difficult for observant Jews to get jobs if they refused to work on Shabbat. By then, these Jewish parents, who struggled to lift themselves from poverty, wanted desperately for their children to become economic successes accepted into American society while maintaining traditional practice. It was an almost impossible demand. Yiddish was the lingua franca in most Orthodox synagogues, and the atmosphere was very Eastern European, so that these English-speaking first-generation American Jews began to avoid going to traditional synagogues, because they simply could not connect, and became classic "High Holy Day Jews."

To combat this growing problem, in 1912 15 young men and women decided to form Young Israel on the Lower East Side of Manhattan. Their first activities offered a series of Friday night lectures, presented in English, on Jewish topics. By 1915, they had established a prototypical congregation that would attract young American Jews, did not demand payment for any synagogue honors, and structured itself as a Jewish community center to service a diverse group of Jews within the realm of traditional Jewish observance.

The organization today sets minimum halakhic requirements for *meḥizah*, a practice that put it at odds with the OU, which in the 1950s was less stringent regarding the separation of men and women, a practice that has changed as Orthodoxy moved rightward. Young Israel does not allow synagogue parking on the Sabbath and Jewish holidays and requires that all synagogue officers in member congregations be Orthodox Jewish Sabbath observers. The National Council of Young Israel's mission further states:

> The aims and purposes of the organization shall be to foster and maintain a program of spiritual, cultural, social and communal activity towards the advancement and perpetuation of traditional Torah-true Judaism; and to instill into American Jewish youth an understanding and appreciation of the high ethical and spiritual values of Judaism and demonstrate the compatibility of the ancient faith of Israel with good Americanism.
>
> The organization shall promote cooperation among the constituent branches now existing and which may hereafter be formed, establish a close bond of kinship to the end that their individual and common problems may more easily be solved, and act as the federated and central body for the Young Israel Movement so that its influence as a force in Jewry may be felt and recognized in America and the world over.

WEBSITE: www.youngisrael.org.

[Jeanette Friedman (2nd ed.)]

YOUNG JUDAEA, U.S. Zionist youth organization. Founded in 1909 Young Judaea drew its members from Jewish students. The original group was led by Emanuel *Neumann. It formulated as its goals the advancement of the cause of Zionism; furthering the mental, moral, and physical development of Jewish youth; and the promotion of Jewish cultural ideas in accordance with Jewish tradition. It was affiliated with the *Zionist Organization of America and published a journal, the *Young Judaean*, originally edited by Henrietta *Szold. In 1940 it came under the jurisdiction of the American Zionist Youth Commission, a joint effort of *Hadassah and the ZOA and in 1967 became the sole responsibility of Hadassah. The first settlers in Israel from the Young Judaea movement arrived during World War I, among them members of the *Jewish Legion. At its peak of membership (1948) Young Judaea had over 30,000 members, but along with other Zionist groups in the U.S. it suffered a decline in membership following the establishment of the State of Israel. Each year thousands of young people age 8–18 attend its clubs, conventions, activities, and six summer camps including Tel Yehudah, the movement's senior leadership camp in Barryville, New York. Its Year Course program, founded in 1956, brings more than 400 young people annually to Israel during a "gap year" between high school and college, for a 10-month program of study, community volunteering, and intense engagement with Israeli society. A variety of other programs involve visits to Israel for high school and college students. The Hamagshimim program is for college students up to age 30. In 1973 a group of its members founded kibbutz Keturah in the Aravah.

[Ramie Arian (2nd ed.)]

YOUNGMAN, HENNY (1906–1998), U.S. comedian. Youngman was born in England to Russian-Jewish parents Jacob Youngman (né Yonkel Jungman) and Olga Chetkin. His parents were naturalized American citizens when they met on New York's Lower East Side. They married in 1904 and went to England on their honeymoon, returning to the United

States when Youngman was six months old. The family lived in Brooklyn, and Youngman attended school at PS2, where he was a notoriously difficult student. His first taste of comedy came during high school, when he was hired to fill in for Jewish comedians who refused to work on Yom Kippur. However, Youngman was dragged off stage halfway through his routine at the request of his father, who wanted him back in synagogue. Later expelled from Manual Trades High School, Youngman finished his studies at Brooklyn Vocational Trade School. Youngman started out as a bandleader for the Swanee Syncopators and worked the Borscht Belt hotels; between sets he walked the hotels as a *tummler.* One night at the Nut Club in Pinedale, New Jersey, the club manager asked Youngman to fill in for a headliner who had not shown up. Youngman's comedy act was a hit and he was hired on as the club's comic for two weeks. He continued performing stand-up in New York at bar mitzvahs and nightclubs, and spent his after-hours hobnobbing with celebrities and journalists, including Walter *Winchell, who gave Youngman the moniker "King of the One-Liners." Youngman's delivery was rapid-fire as he often dished out a dozen one-liners in less than a minute. By the 1940s, he was performing six-minute routines on the radio for *The Kate Smith Show.* One evening Youngman was desperately trying to learn his lines shortly before a live broadcast when his wife and her friends came backstage. He took his wife by the elbow, led her to an usher and uttered for the first time his most famous line, "Take my wife … please." In 1973, Youngman published his first autobiography, *Take My Wife … Please! My Life and Laughs*, followed by *Take My Life, Please!* (1991). He also penned a variety of joke books, including *Henny Youngman's Greatest One-Liners* (1970), *Insults for Everyone* (1979), *Take My Jokes, Please!* (1983) and *Take my Wife, Please!: Henny Youngman's Giant Book of Jokes* (1998). Although he made numerous television appearances as a regular guest on such shows as Johnny Carson's *Tonight Show* and *Hollywood Squares*, he spent most of his career touring the world, even performing for Britain's Queen Elizabeth. Youngman was working a twice-nightly show in late 1997, when he contracted a flu which eventually developed into pneumonia, from which he succumbed several months later.

[Adam Wills (2nd ed.)]

YOUNGSTOWN, iron and steel producing center in N.E. Ohio; the general population in 2004 was 77,713; Jewish population estimated at 3,200, a significant reduction from the Jewish population of the 1970s, but one that is proportionate to the general decline of Youngstown's population. An early historical account indicates that some Jews settled in Youngstown in 1826, but the first name of a Jewish settler on record is that of Jacob Spiegel in 1837. The first Jewish immigrants came from Alsace, Bavaria, and central Germany; a second wave was from Hungary and Romania; while early in the 20th century there was yet another heavy influx from Poland and Russia. After World War II several hundred refugee families from Europe were absorbed by the local Jewish community.

The earliest Jewish settlers in Youngstown were mostly merchants, though some were also involved in the founding of the local steel industry. Over the course of the 20th century, however, Jews tended to move upward from small retail businesses – whereas there were once over 100 Jewish grocers in Youngstown, in 1970 there were only a few – into the professions and such fields as steel, aluminum, and plastics fabricating plants, wholesale distributorships, and insurance agencies. In 1970 most heads of families were owners of, or employees in, business and industry. In recent decades the percentage of Jewish professionals declined slightly, as young people graduating college tended to settle elsewhere, in larger urban areas.

The oldest existing congregation in Youngstown in 1970 was Rodef Sholom (Reform), founded in 1867. Three other congregations existed as well: Children of Israel (traditional Orthodox), founded in 1892; Temple Emanu-El (modern Orthodox), founded by Russian and Polish immigrants in 1906; and Temple Anshe Emeth (Conservative), founded in 1924. Several congregations organized early in the 20th century disappeared when their congregants moved from the neighborhoods in which they were established.

From the mid-1960s, most of the Jewish population of Youngstown has moved to the northern and southern suburbs of the city. The community was organized around the Jewish Federation, created in 1935, and the Jewish Community Center, built in 1953. Federation agencies included the Jewish Community Center, a Family and Children's Service, a Community Relations Council, and Heritage Manor, a home for the aged. The 1960s witnessed growing coordination between the congregations and the Jewish Community Center in cultural and youth activities. The community was served by a local paper, the *Youngstown Jewish Times.*

Jews held a wide variety of cultural, civic, and philanthropic positions in Youngstown life, yet for the most part they continued to be excluded from active participation in the local "power structure." No Jews held (1970) executive posts with any of the big national steel companies operating in Youngstown, few ran for public office, and fewer still were elected. From the 1970s the steel companies switched much of their operations overseas, and there are fewer barriers to Jewish participation in the life of the community.

There are four congregations in Youngstown: a Chabad congregation, Children of Israel; a Reform congregation, Rodef Sholom; a Conservative congregation, Ohev Tzedek Shaarei Torah; and a congregation that lists itself as Conservative and Reform, Temple El Emeth. Among the newer activities of the community is an annual Jewish film festival.

BIBLIOGRAPHY: *Youngstown Jewish Times* (1935–); Jewish Federation of Youngstown, Ohio, *Annual Report* (1937); J.G. Butler, *History of Youngstown and the Mahoning Valley, Ohio* (1921), passim.

[Harry Alter / Michael Berenbaum (2nd ed.)]

YOUTH ALIYAH (Heb. עֲלִיַּת יְלָדִים וָנֹעַר, Aliyyat Yeladim va-No'ar; "Children and Youth Aliyah"), a branch of the Zionist movement founded for the purpose of rescuing Jewish children and young people from hardship, persecution, or deprivation and giving them care and education in Ereẓ Israel. It is administered as a department of the *Jewish Agency and supported by voluntary contributions. Youth Aliyah started its activities in Germany on the eve of the Nazis' rise to power and saved many children who had to leave their families or were orphaned by the Holocaust. It extended its work to other countries when the need arose and, particularly after the establishment of the State of Israel, looked after many young people entrusted to its care by new immigrant parents already in the country. It developed its own methods for bringing up young people in youth communities in kibbutzim or in its own centers and children's villages. Between the start of the movement in 1933 and the end of 1970, Youth Aliyah cared for about 140,000 young people, of whom 125,000 received residential care: 44% from Europe and the Americas, 41% from Asia and North Africa, and 15% from families already in Israel.

In 1932 Recha *Freier, a rabbi's wife in Berlin, conceived the idea of taking Jewish young people doomed to idleness in Germany and bringing them up in Palestine. She contacted the *Histadrut, which proposed absorbing them in kibbutzim. The first group of 12 young people was sent out in October 1932 to the *Ben Shemen youth village, and on January 30, 1933, the day Hitler became chancellor, the Juedische Jugendhilfe organization was founded, with the cooperation of Jewish youth movements in Germany, to carry on the work.

In the same year the 18th Zionist Congress in Prague decided on the establishment of a department for the settlement of German Jews and the leadership of the department's Youth Aliyah office was entrusted to Henrietta *Szold, with the assistance, in matters of finance, of Georg *Landauer. In February 1934 the first large group of young people, numbering 60, arrived at the kibbutz En-Harod. A few months later the first religious group was sent to Kevuẓat Rodges, near Petaḥ Tikvah. By the middle of 1935, 600 had been accommodated in 11 kibbutzim, four agricultural schools, and two vocational training centers. In 1935 Hans *Beyth, a youth movement leader, became Henrietta Szold's chief assistant and at the end of the year Hadassah undertook the responsibility for financial support of Youth Aliyah. After the Nazi conquest of Austria and Czechoslovakia its work was extended to cover these countries. The need for the rescue of Jewish children from Europe became even more obvious and urgent after the burning of the synagogues and the drastic anti-Jewish measures in Germany in November 1938. By the outbreak of World War II more than 5,000 had been brought to Palestine – two-thirds from Germany, one-fifth from Austria, and the rest from other countries. For lack of immigration certificates, another 15,000 were sent to Western European countries, especially Britain.

In the early years of World War II (1940–42) it was almost impossible to bring children from Europe and in 1941 Youth Aliyah began to undertake the care of young people already in Palestine. In the same year the first children arrived from Oriental countries (mainly Syria), about 1,000 of them crossing the Palestine frontier illegally. In 1943, 800 children from Poland, who had reached Persia via the Soviet Union and were accommodated in a refugee camp in Teheran, were taken to Palestine. There was a heated controversy in the *yishuv* over the education of these children, most of whom were orphans, religious circles demanding that they be given a specifically religious upbringing. The Jewish Agency finally ruled that those over 14 should choose for themselves and younger children should be brought up according to the way of life of their parents.

After the war, soldiers of the *Jewish Brigade and emissaries from Ereẓ Israel sought out children in Europe and collected them in transit centers set up by Youth Aliyah, the American Jewish *Joint Distribution Committee, *OSE, and local organizations. Between 1945 and 1948, Youth Aliyah brought over to Palestine about 15,000 children from Europe, mostly survivors of the Holocaust. Many of them arrived illegally and were deported by the British authorities to camps in Cyprus, where a youth village, an imaginative institution that prepared thousands of young people for life in Israel, was established at the beginning of 1947.

With the establishment of the State (1948), Youth Aliyah opened wide its doors to child immigration and care. Its leadership passed to Moshe *Kol, who held the post until 1966, when he joined the Israel government and was succeeded by Yiẓḥak Artzi. In 1968 the post was entrusted to Yosef Klarman. Between 1948 and the end of 1970, 93,500 young people passed through its hands – about 52% of them coming from Asian and North African countries, 31% from Europe and the Americas, and 17% from Israel (mostly of African and Asian origin).

Religious youth are brought up in youth villages and institutions, including yeshivot, and in religious kibbutzim, belonging to all trends in religious Jewry. Forty percent of Youth Aliyah wards are accommodated in religious centers. In 1958 Youth Aliyah was awarded the Israel Prize for education for its humanitarian, social, and educational achievements.

Educational Methods

Successive waves of immigration brought in very varied types of children, differing widely in origin, previous education, and social, economic, and cultural background, many of whom had undergone traumatic experiences before their arrival. Youth Aliyah's aim, moreover, was not merely instruction and physical welfare, but education in the widest sense of the term in order to enable the child to find his place and play his part in a new and dynamic society. It was necessary, therefore, to develop new educational methods and forms of youth care, a task that demanded acute pedagogical insight and much initiative and innovation. To integrate the children into the social fabric of the new environment and at the same time give them individual attention, Youth Aliyah utilized two distinctive instruments: the *ḥevrat no'ar* (youth community) and the *madrikh* ("guide," counselor, or youth leader).

The *ḥevrat no'ar* became the characteristic educational unit of Youth Aliyah. It comprised about 40 young people who stayed together for two to four years until the age of 17–18 and constituted a self-contained social group with a large measure of internal autonomy. It might be attached to a kibbutz, which thus became an "educational settlement," or be part of a youth village or other educational institution directly managed by Youth Aliyah. The young people generally devoted four hours to work on the farm or in the workshop and four to study, in addition to communal and group activities.

Each *ḥevrat no'ar* had a *madrikh* and a *metappelet* (house mother) who helped the young people to tackle their personal, emotional, educational, and social problems as individuals and as a coherent and self-disciplined group. In the early years most of the *madrikhim* were temporary, coming from the kibbutzim for a spell of duty, but considerable efforts were made to enhance the status and standards of their vocation as a branch of the teaching profession. Seminaries for Youth Aliyah *madrikhim* and teachers were conducted in coordination with the Ministry of Education and Culture, especially its agricultural education division. Many graduates of Youth Aliyah have become *madrikhim*.

From 1949 onward, the proportion of children from African and Asian countries – mostly from underprivileged homes – rose until in 1953 they constituted 80% of the total. After a study of the problems involved in the care and education of these children, Youth Aliyah educators were able to confirm that there were no "ethnic" causes for their apparent backwardness, which was the result of generations of poverty and neglect. Specially graded curricula were devised for these children, textbooks and teaching materials were designed for the purpose, and teachers were given special guidance in this type of work.

At the beginning of the 1970s, Youth Aliyah was an educational, rather than a rescue organization, bringing up young newcomers from developed countries, as well as from areas of distress. Many were accommodated in youth villages, receiving education on the secondary level – vocational, agricultural, or academic – enabling some of them to prepare for matriculation and – if fit – go on to one of the universities. There was a scholarship fund for gifted children. Youth Aliyah's educational system was recognized by the Ministry of Education and Culture and controlled by its own inspectors. At the Ne'urim-Hadassah center, a joint venture of Youth Aliyah and Hadassah, a large variety of special vocational training courses were held. At Ramat Hadassah and Kiryat Ye'arim there were special courses for educationally backward and emotionally disturbed children. There were also medical and child guidance services.

For children in development areas living with their parents (mostly new immigrants), Youth Aliyah has established day centers in new towns and villages, which it runs jointly with the Jewish Agency and the ministries of Labor and Education. In 1970 there were 15 of these centers, giving a full day's vocational training and general education to more than 1,000 children aged 14–16 who had failed to gain admission to local post-primary schools or had dropped out before completing the course. There were also advanced one-year courses for graduates of the centers (some of them at Ne'urim). Youth Aliyah *ulpanim* were established for young immigrants aged 16–17½. A late innovation was the establishment of foreign-language courses at which young people from abroad can complete their secondary education in their native language up to matriculation standard and at the same time learn Hebrew and Jewish subjects.

Of the 125,000 children and young people taken in by Youth Aliyah up to the end of 1970 (in addition to some 15,000 in day centers), 9% came from Western Europe, 33% from Eastern Europe, 2% from the Americas, 21% from Africa, 20% from Asia, and 15% from Israel. During the year 1970, 1,351 new wards were received: 29% from Israel, 19% from African countries, 19% from Mediterranean countries, 11% from the Americas, 9% from Eastern Europe, 8% from Western Europe, and 5% from other Asian countries. On Jan. 1, 1971, Youth Aliyah had 7,551 wards under its care: about 70% in its 80 residential institutions, 19% in 150 kibbutz centers, 6% at special courses, and 5% at *ulpanim*. In addition, 1,631 young people attended day centers for youth, making a total of 9,182 under Youth Aliyah's care. Youth Aliyah graduates made up over 10% of Israel's Jewish population between the ages of 15 and 50 (50 being more or less the age of the earliest wards in 1971). They are about 20% of the membership of the kibbutzim and 30% in religious kibbutzim.

Youth Aliyah also found many non-Jewish supporters who were impressed by its work, including personalities like Eleanor Roosevelt, who was its World Patron. It is affiliated to various international organizations and is an active member of the International Federation of Children's Communities (FICE) and the International Union for Child Welfare.

Later Developments

From the early 1970s Youth Aliyah accepted large numbers of Israeli-born children. By 1978, nine out of every ten Youth Aliyah students were Israeli-born, from families in distress. During the 1970s Youth Aliyah absorbed many immigrants from the Soviet Union and from Iran. With Operation Moses in 1984, approximately 3,000 Ethiopian children entered Youth Aliyah institutions. During the 1990s Youth Aliyah absorbed many children from the Soviet Union, due to Operation Exodus and subsequent waves of immigration from the CIS, from Ethiopia, through Operation Solomon, and from war-torn Yugoslavia and Eastern Europe.

After 60 years of existence, Youth Aliyah had approximately 300,000 graduates. In 1993–94, out of a total number of 14,000 students, 7,000 were Israeli, 5,200 were Ethiopian immigrants, and 1,800 were immigrants from other countries; 73% of the students were in 70 residential and youth villages, 19% were part of 70 youth groups in kibbutzim, and 8% were in 15 youth day centers. In 2005 it operated five big youth villages for 1,000 native-born Israelis and new immigrants and provided short-term programs to another 12,000.

BIBLIOGRAPHY: R. Freier, *Let the Children Come* (1961); C. Pincus, *Come from the Four Winds – The Story of Youth Aliyah*

(1970); M. Kol, *Youth Aliyah – Past, Present and Future* (1957); idem, *Massekhet Aliyyat ha-No'ar* (1961); N. Bentwich, *Jewish Youth Comes Home* (1944); Ch. Rinott, *No'ar Boneh Beito* (1953); idem, *Kavvim le-Aliyyat ha-No'ar ki-Tenu'ah Ḥinnukhit* (1951); idem, in: K. Frankenstein (ed.), *Between Past and Future* (1953).

[Chanoch Rinott]

YOUTIE, HERBERT CHAYYIM (1904–1980), U.S. papyrologist. Youtie, who was born in Atlantic City, joined the faculty of the University of Michigan in 1929 and was appointed research professor of Greek papyrology in 1946. He was generally considered to be the world's leading authority in nonliterary papyrological matters. From the late twenties he devoted himself to the editing of Greek papyri, primarily those that were found at the Michigan excavations in Karanis, Lower Egypt. In addition to publications of particular groups of papyri – *Papyri and Ostraca from Karanis* (1944), *Archive of Aurelius Isidorus* (1960) – Youtie concerned himself with elucidating the theoretical principles necessary to the modern editor of a papyrus text in order to ensure accuracy and reliability, in his *Textual Criticism of Documentary Papyri*, edited by E.G. Turner (1958). He also wrote *The Papyrologist: Artificer of Fact* (1962); *Scriptiunculae* (1973); and *Scriptiunculae Posteriores* (1981).

His wife, LOUISE CANBERG YOUTIE (1909–2004), was a well-respected decipherer of papyri at the University of Michigan and worked closely with Herbert.

YOVEL, YIRMIYAHU (1935–), Israeli philosophy scholar. Yovel was born in Haifa. He received his B.A. degree in 1959 and his M.A. in 1964 in philosophy from the Hebrew University of Jerusalem. In 1965 he studied philosophy at the Sorbonne and in 1966 moved to Princeton University. In 1968 he received his Ph.D. in philosophy with a dissertation on Kant's metaphysics. In 1966 he joined the department of philosophy at the Hebrew University. In 1972 he became the head of the department. In 1976–78 and 1982–92 he was director of the Bergman Center for Philosophical Studies and in 1992–98 he was chairman of the center. In 1984 he became a professor, and in 1998 he retired. During the 1970s Yovel was a visiting professor at Princeton and the Sorbonne and during the 1980s and 1990s he visited several other universities. In 1986 he founded the Spinoza Institute in Jerusalem, where he led several international symposiums on Spinoza's thought and additional conferences in various fields such as state and religion, identity and tolerance, and religion and secular culture. In the mid-1980s he was appointed chairman of the editorial board of *Iyyun*, the Hebrew journal of philosophy. Yovel was active as a journalist. In 1960–64 he edited the daily news broadcasts of Israeli Radio. During the 1967 Six-Day War he was a military correspondent on the Sinai front. In 1967 he was one of the founders of the Israel Broadcasting Authority and for two terms served on its council. In 1968 he edited the first political documentary for Israeli TV and during the 1973 Yom Kippur War he was a military correspondent on the Egyptian front. From 1975 to 1978 he hosted a TV show called *The Third Hour* on social issues. From 1967 he also wrote columns for *Haaretz* and *Yedioth Aharonoth*. Yovel was also a political activist. In 1977 he established the 77 Group inside the Labor Party, which he left in 1978. In 1982 he opposed the Lebanon War and spoke out on behalf of peace with the Palestinians. Yovel published many books, among them *Kant and the Renewal of Metaphysics, Kant and the Philosophy of History, Spinoza and Other Heretics,* and *Dark Riddle: Hegel, Nietzsche, and the Jews*. In 2000 he received the Israel Prize for philosophy.

[Shaked Gilboa (2nd ed.)]

YOẒEROT (Heb. pl. יוֹצְרוֹת, sing. יוֹצֵר, *yoẓer*), a series of *piyyutim* inserted in the benedictions which precede and follow the *Shema of the morning prayers. *Yoẓer,* the designation of the first *piyyut* (also called *guf ha-yoẓer*), came to refer to the series as a whole. The name is taken from the opening line of the first benediction before the *Shema: Yoẓer or u-vore ḥoshekh* etc.... ("Who createst light and formest darkness"). The *yoẓer* is considered one of the earliest forms of *piyyut*, though it is later than the *kerovah*. The first *paytanim* who composed *yoẓerot* were Eleazar b. Eleazar *Kallir and Joseph b. Nissan of Shaver Kiriathaim. Fragments of *yoẓerot*, however, were found in the Cairo *Genizah* and their literary structure testifies to their having been composed during "the period of the anonymous *piyyut*." This form of *piyyut* was widely known in Middle Eastern countries from the 9th to the 11th centuries. During this period 15 *paytanim* composed full series of *yoẓerot* for each of the weekly Torah portions. In Europe the *yoẓer* was also considered to be the acceptable form of *piyyut*. The *yoẓerot* series was initially intended to replace the established versions of the *Shema* blessings. With time, however, passages of the *yoẓerot* were integrated into the *Shema*. The series thus came to adorn the benedictions and all the other essential passages of the prayer, specifically: *Ha-Kedushah de-Yoẓer* and two verses from *Shirat ha-Yam* ("The Song of the Sea," Ex. 15:11 and 18) which were to be recited before *Birkat ha-Ge'ullah*.

The classical series of the *yoẓerot* consists of seven component parts: (1) The *yoẓer* or *guf ha-yoẓer* which concludes with the reciting of the first verse of the *Kedushah. (2) The *ofan*, the name being derived from the opening lines of the permanent prayer after which it was inserted. The *ofan* served as a bridge between the first and the second verse of the *Kedushah*. (3) *Ha-me'orah*, occasionally referred to in the *Genizah* as *me'orot*. It is named after the text of the concluding benediction, *yoẓer ha-me'orot*, and ends with the first benediction before the *Shema*. (4) The *ahavah*, taken from the second benediction before the *Shema* which immediately follows it (*ha-boher be-ammo Yisrael be-ahavah*) and with which it concludes. (5) The *zulat*, occasionally referred to as *zulatkha* in the *Genizah* (named after the conclusion of the standard verse of the prayer and inserted after it at a later period). In the *Genizah*, it also appears as *emet*, a title derived from the opening lines of the aforementioned text. It concludes with the first of the verses of *Shirat ha-Yam; Mi kamokha*. (6) *Mi* *kamokha* which concludes with the second of the verses of the *Shirat ha-Yam Adonai Yimlokh.* (7) *Adonai malkenu*, named after the permanent text which, according to the Eastern ritual, is recited at this point. It ends with the benediction that concludes the *Shema: Ga'al Yisrael.* The last section was divided into two by the Eastern *paytanim* (9th to 11th centuries): *Adonai malkenu and ve-ad matai.* In Europe, the section is named after the concluding benediction: *Ge'ullah.* In the Eastern series, the *yoẓerot* for the regular Sabbath, and occasionally also those for the festivals, incorporate the opening section of the weekly reading or holiday portion into the body of the *yoẓer*; in the *zulat*, the *haftarah*. Around the tenth century, the Oriental *paytanim* introduced their *yoẓerot* with short opening *piyyutim* called *mazdar* (introduction). In the ancient Ereẓ Israel ritual the *yoẓerot* for the morning prayers in which the *Kedushah de-Yoẓer* is not recited (on weekdays, including special weekdays such as Ḥanukkah, Purim, Rosh Ḥodesh, and *ḥol ha-mo'ed*, and on fast days) consisted only of five parts (without *guf ha-yoẓer* and the *ofan*). Among the components of the Oriental *yoẓerot*, only *guf ha-yoẓer, ofan*, and *zulat* are of any structural length; the other parts of the *yoẓerot* are short. In the European *yoẓerot*, all the component parts developed into separate and comprehensive *piyyutim*. In Spain the *Mi kamokha* was developed monumentally. The Italian and Ashkenazi (German) *paytanim* often omitted the *me'orah*, the *ahavah*, and the passages that follow the *zulat* from their series of *yoẓerot*. Several European *paytanim* composed segments of the *yoẓerot* for various occasions, without carefully integrating them into complete series.

BIBLIOGRAPHY: Zunz, Poesie, 60–65: Elbogen, Gottesdienst, 210f.: M. Wallenstein, *Some Unpublished Piyyutim from the Cairo Genizah* (1956), 22–25.

[Ezra Fleischer]

°YSANDER, TORSTEN (1893–1960), Swedish theologian and scholar of *Ḥasidism. Ysander, a bishop in the Church of Sweden (1936–59), was appointed chaplain to the king in 1939. In 1922 he traveled to the Ukraine and Poland to meet sectarians and Ḥasidim; under the guidance of Jewish friends, he visited the ḥasidic communities in Warsaw and Cracow. The trip strengthened his theory on the dependence of early Ḥasidism on the Russian sectarians, especially the Khlysty, Skoptsy, Molokane, and Dukhabors. His views on the Ḥasidism of *Israel ben Eliezer Ba'al Shem Tov are summarized in his *Studien zum b'eštschen Ḥasidismus in seiner religionsgeschichtlichen Sonderart* (1933). According to Ysander, such Ḥasidism, its customs, dances, songs, mannerisms during prayer, and the institution of the *ẓaddik*, were very similar to Russian sectarian practices. As Ḥasidism became established, it ceased to be a revolutionary sect, and its similarity to the sectarians diminished but never disappeared. Contemporary Ḥasidism only slightly resembles its origins.

BIBLIOGRAPHY: *Bonniers Lexikon*, 15 (1966), 783; Y. Eliach, in: PAAJR, 36 (1968), 57–83 (an independent study corroborating Ysander).

[Yaffa Eliach]

YUD, NAHUM (pseudonym of **Nahum Yerusalimchik**; 1888–1966), Yiddish poet and fabulist. Born in Mogilev province (Belorussia), he received both a traditional and secular education. Although he wrote first in Russian, he subsequently turned to Yiddish while in Warsaw. His first Yiddish poems appeared in 1913 in the anthology *Nisn*, and he wrote for the periodical *Haynt*. When he immigrated to the U.S. in 1916, he was already known in many Yiddish journals, including *Tsukunft, Tog*, and *Kinder Tsaytung*, was a regular contributor to *Forverts*, and published in *Fraynd* and *Der Groyser Kundes*. Yud is especially known for his fables, anthologized in children's textbooks and other collections. His books include *Fablen* ("Fables," 1918), *Lider* ("Poems," 1924), and *In Likhtike Minutn* ("In Bright Moments," 1932).

BIBLIOGRAPHY: LNYL, 4 (1961), 246–7. **ADD. BIBLIOGRAPHY:** B. Kohen, *Leksikon fun Yidish-Shraybers* (1986), 299.

[Israel Ch. Biletzky / Lily O. Kahn (2nd ed.)]

YUDAN (fourth century C.E.) Palestinian *amora*. Yudan was a pupil of Abba (TJ, Ket. 2:4, 26c). He had halakhic discussions with Yose, head of the academy of Tiberias, and transmits many of the dicta of his predecessors, both *tannaim* and *amoraim*. Among those who turned to him with questions was also Mani, the son of Jonah, head of the Tiberias academy who figures prominently in the Jerusalem Talmud (TJ, Kid. 2:6, 62d). Mention is made of Yudan fleeing to Noy (Naveh, Nineveh) in Transjordan, which may have been in 351, during the Roman persecutions of Ursicinus, the commander of the army of Gallus (TJ, Ket. 11:1, 34b). He is not mentioned at all in the Babylonian Talmud but many of his statements, both in *halakhah* and *aggadah*, are found in the Jerusalem Talmud and the Midrashim.

In his homilies Yudan strove to encourage his contemporaries who were persecuted by the Christian kings of Rome, using parables with which he described God's profound participation in Israel's troubles and comforting them with a promise of the impending redemption (Mid. Ps. 20:1). His statement, "The redemption will not come to this nation at one time, but little by little… now they are in great distress and if the redemption were to come all together they would not be able to bear great salvation… therefore it will come little by little and grow gradually greater" (*ibid.* 18:36), may possibly be connected with the temporary respite during the reign of Julian the *Apostate. He comforted his contemporaries by assuring them that their distress in this world would assure their deliverance in the world to come, putting forward an *a fortiori* argument. "Scripture states (Ex. 21:27) 'And if he smite out his bondman's tooth or his bondwoman's tooth, he shall let him go free for his tooth's sake.' If a slave gains his freedom for the loss of his tooth, or a single limb, how much more will this be the case with one assailed by suffering in his whole body" (Gen. R. 92:1). Noteworthy is his statement: "Whosoever supplies the righteous with bread is as though he fulfilled the whole Torah" (*ibid.* 58:8).

BIBLIOGRAPHY: Hyman, Toledot, 616f.; Frankel, Mevo, 95a; Bacher, Pal Amor index; S. Klein, *Ever ha-Yarden ha-Yehudi* (1925) 51–53; Ḥ. Albeck, *Mavo la-Talmudim* (1969), 322.

[Yitzhak Dov Gilat]

YUDELOVITZ, ABRAHAM AARON (1850–1930), rabbi. Born in Navardonik, Byelorussia, he studied with his uncle Rabbi Meir and then at the *Volozhin yeshivah. He was ordained by Rabbi Yom Tov Lippman of Bialystok. He published his first book, *Alim le-Mivḥan*, at the age of 21. He held a number of rabbinical positions in succession and served as rabbi of Salov, Kosnitza, Constantin, Turov, and Kapulia before becoming chief rabbi of Manchester, England, in 1898.

He published seven volumes of responsa, *Beit Av*, from 1896 onward and attended the Sixth World Zionist Congress where he opposed the Uganda proposal. After a half dozen years in Manchester, he immigrated to the United States, first for a congregation in Boston and shortly thereafter to teach at Rabbi Isaac Elchanan Theological Seminary and then in 1906 as rabbi of Bayonne, New Jersey. He then returned to New York to be rabbi of the Eldridge Street Beit Midrash Hagadol. He never affiliated with Agudath Harabonim but instead belonged to Agudath Ha-Rabbonim ha-Ma'atifim, of which he became president. He continued to publish, including five volumes of *Derash Av*. He also inaugurated a short-lived Torah journal, *Ha-Mizpeh*, of which six volumes appeared. His most controversial rabbinical decision in 1927 permitted a woman to appoint an agent on her behalf for *ḥaliẓah* to cancel the levirate marriage. He was roundly criticized by the authorities of his time and his reputation was severely damaged. He died three years later and many of the luminaries would not attend his funeral.

BIBLIOGRAPHY: M.D. Sherman, *Orthodox Judaism in America: A Biographical Dictionary and Sourcebook* (1996).

[Michael Berenbaum (2nd ed.)]

YUDGHAN (**Yehuda**; 8th century), sectarian of *Hamadan (Iran). A pupil of *Abu ʿĪsā al-Isfahānī, Yudghan claimed to be a prophet of his followers, the Yudghanites, who believed that he was the Messiah. The* Karaite historian Jacob al-*Kirkisānī writes in his *Book of Gardens and Parks* (938) that the Yudghanites "prohibit meat and intoxicating drinks, observe many prayers and fasts, and assert that the Sabbath and holidays are at present no longer obligatory." The Muslim historian Al-Shahrastani relates in his *Book of Religions and Sects* (1128) that Yudghan believed the Torah to have an external and internal meaning, a literal and an allegorical interpretation, but different from that held by the *Rabbanite Jews. The Karaite exegete Japheth b. Ali (last third of the tenth century) states that the Yudghanites considered the holidays as mere symbols and asserted that after the destruction of the Temple many laws were no longer obligatory. It is a matter of controversy whether the Yudghanites are referred to by *Saadiah b. Joseph Gaon in his book *Beliefs and Opinions* in which he mentions "certain people who call themselves Jews and maintain that the promises and consolations of the prophets refer to the time of the Second Temple." It is also a matter of controversy whether the scholar *Judah ha-Parsi (Judah the Persian), against whom Abraham *Ibn Ezra (12th century) argues in his works, is identical with Yudghan. A small number of Yudghanites still lived in *Isfahan in the year 938. In addition to the Yudghanites, Japheth b. Ali mentions another sect, the Shadganites, about whom nothing is known. Al-Shahrastani mentions a pupil of Yudghan, Mushkha, who fell in battle against his adversaries. Some Mushkhanites believed that Muhammad was a prophet sent by God to the Arabs and others but not to the Jews because they already have their Holy Scriptures.

BIBLIOGRAPHY: L. Nemoy, in: HUCA, 7 (1930), 328, 383; idem. *Karaite Anthology* (1952), 10, 51, 334, 336, 391; B. Dinur, *Yisrael ba-Golah*, 1, pt. 2 (1961), 232, 233, 234, 236, 274; J. Rosenthal, in: *YIVO-Bleter*, 21 (1943), 77–78; Baron, Social2, 5 (1957), 182, 185, 191f., 219.

[Judah M. Rosenthal]

YUDIKA (**Yudis** (**Judith**) **Tsik**; 1898–1988), poet. She was born in Gorzhd (Gargzdai), Lithuania. Poverty forced her family to send Tsik to live with an aunt in Eastern Prussia, then annexed to Germany. At the outbreak of World War I, at the age of 16, she was imprisoned in a German labor camp as an enemy alien. Released a year later, she took refuge in Sweden, then lived in various cities throughout Lithuania, Russia, and the Ukraine, supporting herself as a teacher in girls' schools and workers' dormitories. In 1917, while living in Yekaterinoslav (Dniepropetrovsk), Ukraine, she became acquainted with the poet Moishe *Teitsh, and under his influence began writing in Yiddish using the pen name Yudika. She attained considerable success, publishing in periodicals and anthologies; these early poems were collected in *Naye Yugnt* ("New Youth," 1923) and *Mentsh un Tsayt* ("Person and Time," 1926). She married and in 1926 had a son. In 1929 she immigrated to Toronto, Canada, with her son but without her husband, and there became an important member of the proletarian school of Yiddish writers, a purely Canadian movement of the 1930s and 1940s. While working in factories to support herself and her son, her poetry was published in journals in Canada and the U.S. Her books of this era are *Vandervegn* ("Migrant Roads," 1934), *Shpliters* ("Splinters," 1943), and *Tsar un Freyd* ("Trouble and Joy," 1949). Her political radicalism is evident in her poetry, much of which, however, is less polemic than might be expected. Her work includes lyric and narrative forms and is concerned with the upheavals facing Jewish life in the old world as well as the new.

BIBLIOGRAPHY: S.A. Fuerstenberg, "Yudica: Poet of Spadina's Sweatshops," in: *Canadian Woman Studies/Les Cahiers de la Femme* 16/4 (Fall 1996), 107f; C.L. Fuks, *100 Yor Yidishe un Hebreyishe Literatur in Kanade*, 141f; LNYL 4, 255f.

[Faith Jones (2nd ed.)]

YUDKIN, JOHN (1910–1995), British physician and nutritionist. The son of Russian Jewish parents who fled from pogroms to London, Yudkin was born in London and educated at Cambridge University. He was professor of physiology at Queen Elizabeth College, London, from 1945 to 1954 and then professor of nutrition – the first such appointment in Britain – at the same institution from 1954 to 1971. Yudkin became internationally known for his attacks on sugar as a leading cause of obesity and disease and for his pioneering emphasis on a proper diet and lifestyle as an antidote to disease. He is the author of such well-known works as *Pure, White and Deadly: The Problem of Sugar* (1972) and *This Nutrition Business* (1977). His works drew concerted attacks from the sugar lobby but were significant in the contemporary emphasis on a healthy lifestyle. Yudkin was a member of the board of governors of the Hebrew University of Jerusalem.

[William D. Rubinstein (2nd ed.)]

YUDKOVSKY, DOV (1923–), Israeli journalist. Born in Poland, Yudkovsky spent 33 months in Auschwitz from where he escaped twice, in each case being recaptured. He reached Palestine, where his cousin, Yehudah *Mozes, publisher of **Yedioth Aharonoth*, made him head of the newspaper's Jerusalem office. After the so-called putsch in which Dr. Azriel *Carlebach, the editor, and most of the newspaper's staff left to found the new newspaper **Maariv*, Mozes appointed Yudkovsky the paper's news editor, and in 1953 managing editor for news. Yudkovsky conceived the newspaper as "the people's newspaper," and notwithstanding its tabloid appearance, filled it with editorial content of interest also to readers from the professional classes. By the mid-1970s *Yedioth Aharonoth* had taken the lead in the circulation war with *Maariv*, credit for which went partly to Yudkovsky's news editorship. In 1984 Yudkovsky was appointed by publisher Noah Mozes one of the newspaper's two directors. But after Arnon ("Noni") Mozes became the publisher following the death of his father, Noah, and sought to centralize his control, Yudkovsky was dismissed in 1989. He then represented the Israeli interests of British media mogul Robert *Maxwell, who appointed him editor-in-chief of *Maariv*. Regarding *Maariv* as a somewhat dull, middle-class newspaper, Yudkovsky sought to liven it up by installing an ultra-modern color press. In 1992 he left the paper and became one of the founders of Koteret, a private college situated in Tel Aviv for journalism training. In 2000 he won the Sokolow prize for journalism and in 2003 the Israel Prize in media.

[Yoel Cohen (2nd ed.)]

YUGOSLAVIA ("Land of the Southern Slavs"), until 1991 a Socialist Federated Republic in S.E. Europe, in the Balkan Peninsula. The various elements of which Yugoslav Jewry was composed after 1918 (i.e., those of Serbia and the Austro-Hungarian countries) were distinct from one another in their language, culture, social structure, and character according to the six separate historical, political, and cultural regions of their origin. These regions were Serbia; Slovenia; Croatia, Slavonia, and Dalmatia; Bosnia-Herzegovina; Macedonia; and Vojvodina. Croatia, Slovenia, Bosnia-Herzegovina, and Macedonia declared their independence in 1991. Serbia and Montenegro became the Federal Republic of Yugoslavia in 1992.

Until 1918

SERBIA. There were some Jews in Pannonia in Roman times. Jews seem to have reached *Belgrade and there were also traces of a Jewish population along the banks of the Danube during the tenth century. Some Jews penetrated into Serbia from Macedonia. During the ninth and tenth centuries many of the Serbians converted to Christianity. The faith of the new Christians at that time was an amalgamation of Christianity, Judaism, and paganism. Benjamin of Tudela, the 12th-century traveler, also mentions the influence of the Jews on the inhabitants of the Balkans. At the time of the conquest of Serbia by Sultan Murad in 1389, the Jews engaged in the sale of salt. Under Turkish rule the Jews of Belgrade played an important part in the trade between northern and southern Turkish provinces which passed through Belgrade. During the period of the Austrian rule over northern Serbia from 1718 to 1739, the government's attitude toward the Jews was generally good. During the Serbian wars of independence (1804–30), some of the Jews fled from Belgrade and in 1807 founded a community, which numbered 280 persons in *Zemun. The Jews supplied arms to the revolutionary army. However, the independence movement, which fomented rebellions against the Turks from time to time, frequently attacked the Jews. In 1831 the Serbian government decreed certain limitations on the crafts in which the Jews were engaged. In 1845 they were excluded from tailoring and shoemaking. During the reign of Milosh Obrenovich, the prince of Serbia, there was a favorable change in the condition of the Jews. However, with the ascent of the Karageorgevich dynasty in 1842, which supported the interests of the Serbian merchants who envied their Jewish rivals, the condition of the Jews took a turn for the worse. A decree of 1856 forbade the Jews to reside in the provincial towns. There were then 2,000 Jews in Serbia. About 1,000 of them settled in Belgrade, while the rest were dispersed in other towns. When Prince Milosh returned to power in 1858, the condition of the Jews temporarily improved. However, during the reign of his son, Prince Michael (1860–68), who was also influenced by the Serbian merchants, the persecutions were renewed. An expulsion decree of 1861 against 60 Jewish families of Šabac was changed during the same year into another decree which authorized the Jews – and this only in their places of residence – to practice the same professions as they had engaged in before February 28, 1861. The Jewish merchants, also in their places of residence, were authorized to trade in raw materials and foodstuffs. These rights, however, could not be transferred to their successors. Concerning real estate, the new decree confirmed a former one which prohibited the purchase of property in the provincial towns.

After the assassination of Michael and the enthronement of Milan Obrenovich, the Serbian parliament voted the emancipation of all citizens, but at the same time confirmed the restrictive decrees of 1856 and 1861. In 1873 the Jews were expelled from the towns of Šabac, Smederevo, and Požarevac. The treaty of Berlin of 1878 accorded civil and political equality to the Jews of Serbia, but it was only in 1889 that the Serbian parliament proclaimed the complete equality of all Serbians without distinction of origin and religion and abolished the restrictive decrees of the previous years. In 1895 there were 5,102 Jews in Serbia, 5,729 in 1900, and 5,000 in 1912. The number of Jews who participated in the Balkan Wars (1912–13) was 500. During the Serbian-Bulgarian war of 1913 and World War I many Jews were decorated.

SLOVENIA. Jews lived in Slovenia from the 13th century until they were expelled in 1496 by Emperor Maximilian I of Austria. The biggest rabbinical center was at Maribor (Marburg) in the Styria district. Maribor had a "Jewish Street" as early as 1277 near the river Drava (Drau) and a synagogue inside the walled city. Rabbi Israel *Isserlein taught there. His official title was "Landesrabbiner fuer Steiermark, Krain, und Korushka." He was succeeded by his pupil R. Joseph b. Moses. Other Jewish communities existed at Ptuj (Poetovia), Celje, Radgona, and Ljubljana. Jews were engaged in viticulture, and traded in horses and cattle.

CROATIA, SLAVONIA, AND DALMATIA. The Croats, who penetrated into the N.W. Balkans in the seventh century and established a kingdom in the tenth, found there several Jewish communities. In the letter of Ḥisdai ibn Shaprut (5:10) to Joseph the king of the Khazars, there is a mention of the "king of the Gebalim" who sent a deputation, which included Mar Saul and Mar Joseph, to Caliph Abdurrahman III of Cordoba. The "king of the Gebalim, the Slavs," whose country bordered that of the Hungarians, was Krešimir, king of Croatia. The messengers informed Ḥisdai that Mar Amram of the court of the Khazar king had come to the land of the "Gebalim." There is little information on the Jews of Croatia from the 10th to 15th centuries. Some Jews lived in the Croatian capital *Zagreb in the 13th and 14th centuries, when they had a chief entitled "magistratus Judaeorum," and a synagogue. Others settled between the Sava and Drava (Drau) and Danube rivers during the 15th century. As long as the economy of the country required the presence of the Jews, they lived there without hindrance. As soon as they were superfluous, they were persecuted and driven out. The Jews were expelled from Croatia and Slavonia in 1456. Croatia together with Hungary passed to the Hapsburgs in 1526, and no Jews lived there for the next 200 years.

Toward the end of the 18th century, Jews from Hungary, Bohemia, Moravia, and especially Burgenland (east Austria) resettled there. In 1776 Jews came to *Osijek and in 1777 to Varaždin and a limited number to Zagreb. At that time there was also a Jewish community in Zemun. R. Judah b. Solomon Ḥai *Alkalai (1798–1878), who lived there from 1825 to 1874, also propagated the ideals of the movement for the settlement of Ereẓ Israel in Šabac and Belgrade. A census of the Jews in 1773, during the reign of Maria Theresa, revealed only 25 families. It was only after the publication of the **Toleranzpatent* in 1782 by Emperor Joseph II that the situation improved and more Jews arrived from the north and the south. The right of residence was granted in 1791. Further rights were granted in 1840, but the "tolerance tax" remained in force. The Jews of Croatia and Dalmatia only received their full emancipation in 1873. Until 1890 the community of Osijek was the most prominent, but from that year the community of Zagreb, founded in 1806, became the leading one. In 1841 an Orthodox congregation was founded in Zagreb. The Jews of Croatia were mostly merchants and some were artisans.

Jews arrived in Dalmatia with the Roman armies. In Solin (Salona), in the vicinity of *Split (Spalato), there are remains of a Jewish cemetery of the third century. There was a Jewish community in Solin until 641, when Solin was destroyed by the Avars. During the Middle Ages, the Jews of Split and Ragusa (*Dubrovnik) engaged in commerce and especially in the brokerage of the trade between Dalmatia and Italy and the Danubian countries. Under the autonomous republic which was established in Dubrovnik during the 15th century, the Jews lived in relative tranquility. The Christian clergy, however, attempted to oppress them and succeeded in spreading *blood libels in Dubrovnik in 1502, 1622, and 1662. During the 16th century, refugees from Spain and Portugal settled in Dalmatia. When Pope Paul IV expelled the Jews from Ancona in 1556, a considerable number of them requested asylum in Dubrovnik. These included the physician *Amatus Lusitanus and his friend the poet Didacus *Pyrrhus, both Marranos. In 1738 the condition of the Jews in Dalmatia deteriorated. The Jews of Split lived in a ghetto until the arrival of the French in 1806. In 1906 the Austro-Hungarian government passed a law which defined the status of the Jewish communities of Croatia, Slavonia, and Dalmatia. In 1870 there were already 10,000 Jews in Croatia, Slavonia, and Dalmatia; 13,488 in 1880; and 17,261 in 1890. After World War I there were 20,000 Jews in Croatia, Slavonia, and Dalmatia.

BOSNIA-HERZEGOVINA. One of the republics in central Yugoslavia with the largest Muslim population (750,000). There is no evidence of the existence of a Jewish community in Bosnia before the expulsion of the Jews from Spain. Tombstone inscriptions prove the existence of Jews in *Sarajevo in 1551. A special quarter was allocated to them later in the 16th century and they lived there until the conquest of the town by the Austrians in 1878. During the rule of Daudji Pasha, who was appointed in 1635, the relations between Turkey and Venice became strained. This had an adverse effect on the commerce of the local Jews. During the siege of Ofen in 1686 many Jews fled to Sarajevo, including Ẓevi Hirsch *Ashkenazi (Ḥakham Ẓevi), who was appointed *ḥakham* there. A change for the worse in the situation of the Jews of Sarajevo occurred in 1833. It was only after payment of a heavy ransom that the Jews were saved from the danger of riots and blood libel. The laws of 1839, 1856, and 1876, which granted the Jews of Turkey equality of rights with the other citizens, also applied to the

Jews of Bosnia. From then onward, some Jews were elected to the Ottoman parliament in Constantinople and the municipal councils. In 1876 Yaver Effendi Barukh was sent to the parliament as the representative of Bosnia. Isaac Effendi Shalom was a member of the *Majlis Idareh* ("Advisory Council to the Vali"). Upon his death, his place was filled by his son Solomon Effendi Shalom, who was also a representative in the parliament. Two Jewish delegates were sent to the Landstag which was opened in 1910. Besides Sarajevo, there were also Jewish communities in the towns of *Travnik, *Banja Luka, Bijeljina, and others. The following data are available on the number of Jews in Bosnia from the end of the 18th century. There were 1,500 Jews in 1780; 8,213 in 1895; 10,000 (Sephardim) in 1923; 13,701 in 1926; 14,000 in 1941 (together with Herzegovina); and 1,298 in 1958. In addition to the Nazis and the Ustaše who were active in Bosnia in World War II, the former mufti of Jerusalem, Ḥājj Amīn al-*Husseini, succeeded in enlisting the support of local authorities in the expulsion of the Jews from the province and their extermination.

MACEDONIA. The earliest Jewish presence was really in Macedonia and Dalmatia. Philo mentions the Jews of Macedonia in *Embassy to Gaius* (*Legatio ad Gaium*), translated into English by F.H. Colson (1962), par. 281, while the apostle Paul delivered sermons in its communities (Acts 20:1–2). A Greek inscription on a pillar of the church – a former synagogue – in Stobi (in the vicinity of the town of Bitolj (*Monastir)) and now preserved in the national museum of Belgrade, serves as evidence of the Jewish settlement during the second and third centuries. In it, Claudius Tiberius Polycharmos relates his Jewish way of life. During the Middle Ages, Jews lived in Bitolj (Monastir), Skoplje, *Ochrida, and Struga. During the reign of the Serbian emperor Stefen Dushan there is a mention of Jewish farmers in Macedonia (conquered by Dushan in 1353). During the 14th century, the renowned grammarian Judah (Leon) Moskoni, whose version of Josephus was published in Constantinople in 1510, lived in Ochrida. During the 16th century there were Jewish communities in *Skoplje, Bitolj, *Niš, Smederevo, and Požarevac. At the time, Skoplje was a commercial center. The Jews traded in wool clothes, "kachkaval" cheese, and also engaged in commerce between Salonika and Constantinople on the one hand and Western Europe on the other. In 1680 *Nathan of Gaza died in Skoplje. His admirers made an annual pilgrimage to his tomb. When the armies of Leopold I approached Skoplje in 1689, the Jews hurriedly abandoned the city. Their synagogues were burnt down and the wall surrounding their quarter also was destroyed by the flames. The Jewish population of Štip was of Salonikan origin. During the 17th and 18th centuries, R. Abraham Motal ha-Paytan ("the hymnologist") and R. Reuben b. Abraham, who wrote the work *Derekh Yesharah* (Leghorn, 1788) and in Ladino *Tikkunei ha-Nefesh* (Salonika, 1765–75), lived in this town. At the time of the upheavals in Turkey which preceded the Balkan Wars, more Jews settled in Macedonia.

VOJVODINA. This was an Austrian frontier region and the residence of Jews was prohibited there. Jews first settled in Vojvodina during the 18th century, but they were exceptions. Most Jewish communities were founded in the 1840s. The Jews of Vojvodina engaged in commerce and in import-export trade. Before World War II there were 19,200 Jews in Vojvodina (Bačka, 14,800; Banat, 4,400). In 1952 there were Jewish communities in *Novi Sad, 275; *Subotica, 403; *Sombor, 46; Senta, 28; and Pančevo, 34, following immigration to Israel by most of the survivors of the Holocaust.

After 1918

With the establishment of the Yugoslav kingdom, about 100 Jewish communities (with 70,000 Jews) were included in the new state. The Jews generally belonged to the middle class, but there were also impoverished communities, such as that of Bitolj. The Jews were well represented in industry, commerce, and artisan activity. They also held an important place in the banking business. There were some professions, such as the army officers, cadres, the upper government services, and journalism, from which the Jews were almost totally absent. The Jews of Croatia and Slavonia were under the cultural influence of Germany and Hungary and surpassed their coreligionists of the other Yugoslav provinces in the economic and cultural spheres. The Jews of Macedonia maintained their Oriental character and their economic and cultural standards were somewhat backward in comparison to the remainder of Yugoslav Jewry. There was a marked Hungarian influence among the Jews of Vojvodina. The Jews did not hold a prominent place in political life, although there were some influential members in the parties. De Majo, an advocate of Belgrade, was elected in 1927 for one term to the parliament (Skupshtina).

Antisemitism as an organized movement was nonexistent. After World War I, some signs of it appeared, but the situation improved again. The Karageorgevich dynasty and the Orthodox Church evinced a favorable attitude toward the Jews. The antisemitic sentiments really originated in Croatia and Slavonia. In Vojvodina, there was some hostility toward the Jews who had been Austro-Hungarians before the war and thus were considered to be the representatives of the alien Hungarian culture.

THE ORGANIZATION OF THE JEWS. The unification of the variegated Yugoslav Jewish population was not easy. Yugoslav Jewry did not form a single unit. In the southern districts, from the Sava and Danube rivers and further, there were essentially Sephardim, while the other provinces were mainly inhabited by Ashkenazim. The Sephardim generally adhered to their Oriental manner of life and the Ladino language, while some others were influenced by the speech and culture of the southern Slavs. In 1939 there were about 43,000 Ashkenazim and 29,000 Sephardim in Yugoslavia. They lived in 121 communities. At a meeting of the communities which was convened in Osijek in 1919, the "Federation of Jewish (Religious)

Communities" was founded. It received government recognition and its activities extended to the fields of religion, culture, and education. In 1923 the chief rabbinate was founded and an association of rabbis was formed. The final status of the communities was confirmed in 1929. The separate union of Orthodox communities, which had refused to join the federation of the communities, also received legal recognition at that time. The Orthodox union consisted of 12 communities and numbered 3,426 in 1935. The spiritual head of the Jewish population was the chief rabbi, Dr. Isaac Alkalay (he held office from 1924 to 1941), who was appointed by the king and resided in Belgrade. The chief rabbi was equal in status to the Orthodox patriarch, the Catholic archbishop, and the Muslim *reis ul-Ulema*. He was also a member of the Yugoslav senate.

EDUCATION AND CULTURE. There were Jewish elementary schools, which had existed before the Yugoslav kingdom, in the towns of *Zrenjanin, Osijek, *Sarajevo, Senta, *Zagreb, and *Zemun. The government prohibited the opening of new elementary schools. In Vojvodina there were yeshivot in Senta, Subotica, Kanjiža, and Ilok. Jewish children attended the general schools, in which two hours weekly were allocated for Jewish religious studies. From 1928 to 1941 there was a seminary in Sarajevo for the training of *ḥakhamim* and teachers on a secondary school level. Among the scholars and authors mention should be made of Lavoslav Šik, a historian of Yugoslav Jewry, the poet Hinko *Gottlieb, and Siegfried Kapper. An important place in Yugoslav literature was held by Isak *Samokovlija, a Bosnian novelist who died in 1955. The headquarters of the Zionist Organization were in Zagreb, where newspapers and periodicals were published.

STATISTICS. In 1926 there was a Jewish population of 73,267 and in 1935, 70,000. According to the census of 1939, there were 71,000 Jews. The decrease in the number of Jews in Yugoslavia can be explained by the increase of *antisemitism in Europe.

[Simon Marcus]

Holocaust Period

In April 1941, Yugoslavia was occupied by German, Hungarian, Italian, and Bulgarian troops. It was divided into several parts: Serbia and the Banat came under direct German military administration; Hungary reoccupied some of the areas it had ceded to newly formed Yugoslavia after World War I; Bulgaria took over Macedonia; and Italy extended its rule over Dalmatia and Montenegro. Most of the remaining territory – Croatia, Bosnia, and Herzegovina – was formed into a new "Independent State of Croatia."

SERBIA AND THE BANAT. On the day after the occupation of Belgrade (April 13, 1941), German troops, assisted by "*Volksdeutsche*" (local Germans), ransacked the Jewish shops. Within a week, the Jews were ordered to register with the police, and eventually 9,145 Jews, out of a total prewar population of about 12,000, were registered. The Jews were removed from public service. The yellow *badge was introduced, and Jews were drafted into forced labor. About 3,500 to 4,000 males from the age of 14 to 60 were forced to clear the buildings that had been razed by the bombardment, while women aged 16 to 40 were given menial tasks in the German military installations. A special police detachment was formed to deal with the Jewish population. A "Jewish Organization" (Jevrejska Zajednica) was created to attend to the needs of the Jewish population. The Nazis forced the organization to collect contributions from the Jews and provide hostages to ensure Jewish compliance with their orders. After the German invasion of the U.S.S.R., the occupation regime became even harsher. In one incident alone, at the end of July, 120 Jewish hostages were shot to death (in the village of Jajinci, near Belgrade). In the Banat, which had a large German minority, after robbing the Jews of all their property and belongings the Nazis placed them in camps and a few weeks later (in September 1941) deported them to Belgrade, adding another 2,500 people to its destitute Jewish population. By the end of September, all Jewish men aged 16 and above were put into a concentration camp, situated in Topovske Šupe, a Belgrade suburb.

Felix Benzler, German consul in Belgrade, and Edmund Veesenmayer, from the German Foreign Office, demanded the concentration of "at least" 8,000 men on an island in the Danube delta and their liquidation there and asked for appropriate pressure on the German military authorities. Adolf *Eichmann was consulted on the matter and proposed the immediate execution of the Jews. He dispatched Franz Rademacher to Belgrade who discovered that of the 8,000 Jewish men, 2,000 had already been shot and there were only about 4,000–5,000 left. He arranged for their execution "by the end of the week" (October 1941). Between Aug. 25 and Oct. 18, 1941, all Jewish men in Nazi hands – those who had been put on forced labor (about 3,000), the deportees from the Banat, and any others that the Nazis had succeeded in apprehending – were concentrated in the Topovske Šupe camp and in the nearby Banjica camp. The massacre began in the early part of September. Day by day, groups of Jews, ranging from 100 to 300, were taken out of the two camps, ostensibly for work in the fields. In fact a total of 4,500 were shot to death, the scene of the crime being either Jajinci or some other site on the opposite bank of the Danube. A group of Jewish refugees from Germany, Austria, and Czechoslovakia who had been on their way to Palestine in September 1940 had been stranded on the Danube for lack of a seaworthy boat to continue their voyage. They had found temporary refuge in the Yugoslav town of Šabac, but when the Nazis occupied the country they were all interned (together with 63 local Jews). Originally their number was 1,300, but 200 refugees, mostly children, had received immigration certificates to Palestine and had departed. In October 1941, all the men were taken to the Danube village of Zasavica and shot; the women and children were deported to the Sajmište camp in Zemun near Belgrade. In February 1942 they were loaded into closed trucks and were gassed while en route to Jajinci. Not a single person escaped from this

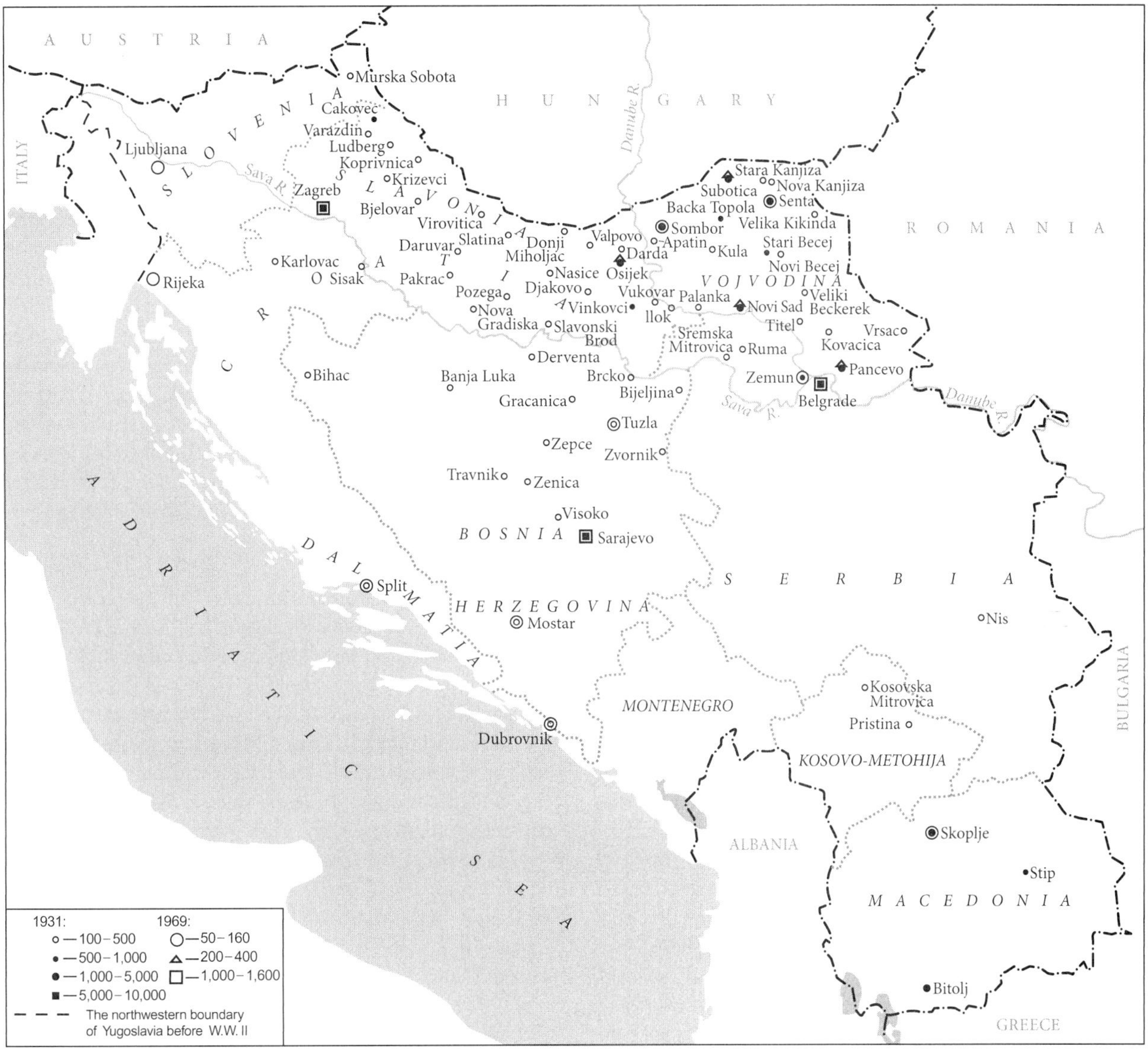

Jewish communities in Yugoslavia in 1931 and 1969. Courtesy Federation of Jewish Communities in Yugoslavia, Belgrade.

camp, and the fate of its inmates was reported by a few Jewish women, wives of gentiles, whom the Nazis had released. In August 1942 a German report stated that the "problem of Jews and gypsies had been solved; Serbia is the only country where this problem no longer exists."

THE INDEPENDENT STATE OF CROATIA. The new Independent State of Croatia (NDH) was headed by Ante *Pavelić, leader of the Ustaše movement, who had been in exile in Italy and Germany and had developed relations with the Nazis. For the Jews, the four years of his rule in Croatia were marked by savage cruelty and terror. Within a few days of the occupation of Zagreb, the Germans, the local Nazis, and the Ustaše combined to deprive the Jews of their property and their status. Nuremberg-style laws were enacted as early as April 30, 1941, followed by the removal of Jews from all public posts and the introduction of the yellow badge. On August 27, a decree was issued expropriating all Jewish-owned real estate, and two months later the Jews were ordered to hand over all other valuables in their possession. In Osijek, a levy of 20,000,000 dinars was imposed upon the Jews within three days of the occupation of the city; in Zagreb, the Ustaše arrested the wealthy Jews in May and kept them hostage until a ransom equivalent to 100 kilograms of gold was provided for their release. Synagogues, cultural institutions, and even Jewish cemeteries were razed by the Ustaše as soon as it came to power.

Early in May 1941, the first concentration camp was established in the Danica factory, in the village of Drinja, near Koprivnica. Mass arrests of Jews were stepped up after the outbreak of the German-Soviet war (June 1941), and a number of additional concentration camps were established in Jasenovac, Stara Gradiška, Loborgrad, and Djakovo. A temporary camp, at Jadovno near Gospić, served as one of the early extermination camps. By July 1941 all the inmates of the Danica camp had been murdered, and by August the inmates at the Jadovno camp had suffered the same fate. The main, and most notorious, of the Croatian concentration camps was situated near Jasenovac, a town on the Zagreb-Belgrade railroad. This camp remained in existence throughout the period of Croatian "independence," and tens of thousands of people were murdered there, among them about 20,000 Jews. It was to these camps that the Jews of Croatia proper were deported. Exact figures are not available, but it is estimated that by the end of 1942, 5,000 Jews had been deported. Further deportations took place as late as 1944. The Jewish communities continued to exist, although they were now largely made up of persons with only one Jewish parent, who were protected by law; Jewish partners of mixed marriages were also saved from deportation due to the efforts of the Catholic Church, and especially the papal nuncio. (About 1,000 such persons survived in Croatia.)

Bosnia and Herzegovina, which were incorporated into "independent" Croatia, had a prewar Jewish population of about 14,000. When the Germans occupied Sarajevo (April 17, 1941), one of their first acts was to set fire to the Sephardi synagogue in the city, the finest structure of its kind in the Balkan countries. They were assisted in this act of vandalism by local Muslims, who, under the influence of their spiritual leaders, were generally hostile to the Jews and willingly collaborated with the Nazis. Hājj Amīn al-Husseini, the ex-mufti of Jerusalem, went especially from Berlin to Sarajevo in order to give his blessing to the Bosnian Muslim division named "Handjar" (Sword), which was among the Croatian puppet state's contributions to the German war machine. This division effectively fought on the eastern front against the Soviet Union, incorporated in the ranks of the Wehrmacht. In the wake of an act of sabotage that occurred at the end of July, nine of the leading Jews of Sarajevo and 12 prominent Serbs were arrested, and within a few days the police announced their execution by a firing squad. Mass deportations began on September 3, when 500 Jews were dispatched to a camp at Kruščica near Travnik; a second transport to the same location took place a few days later. On Oct. 19, 1941, in celebration of "Germany Day," 1,400 Jews were arrested in Sarajevo. Although the community commissars (a Serb and a Muslim) succeeded in getting a few of the Jews released, the community as a whole was panic-stricken and made strenuous efforts to escape. About 1,600 made their way to Italian-occupied Mostar. The largest roundup of Jews was organized by the Germans on Nov. 15–16, 1941, when 3,000 Jews were deported to Jasenovac. Women and children from Bosnia and Herzegovina were taken to the Loborgrad and Djakovo camps. By the end of August 1942, some 9,000 Jews had been deported, and only 120 were left. In the fall of 1941 the Kruiščica camp was liquidated, the men being sent to Jasenovac and the women to Loborgrad. A year later, the Loborgrad camp suffered a similar fate, and those who had survived the first year were now dispatched to the Auschwitz death camp.

The Jewish community of Osijek had been tricked by the Ustaše into building its own ghetto in a factory near the village of Tenje. When the job was completed, the Jews of Osijek and the surrounding area were crowded into the factory, where they lived for a period of two months. In August 1942, the surviving inmates were transported to Jasenovac and Auschwitz. By April 1945, only a little more than 1,000 Serbs and Jews were still alive in the Jasenovac camp. On April 22 they were all crowded into a single factory building to await their death. In a final desperate effort, some 600 of the prisoners broke the gates and attacked the Ustaše guard; for most of them, the effort was in vain, and only 80 saved their lives, among them 20 Jews. The Stara Gradiška camp, a "branch" of Jasenovac, "specialized" in women and children, and no less than 6,000–7,000 children, according to one report, were put to death there. The German consul in Zagreb, Siegfried Kasche, and police attaché Hans Helm reported to Berlin on April 18, 1944 that "Croatia is one of the countries in which the Jewish problem has been solved."

VOJVODINA (BAČKA AND BARANJA). In Vojvodina, occupied by Hungarian troops, the fate of the Jews (and, to a certain degree, the local Serbs) was no different. In Subotica, the main city in Bačka, 250 persons were killed in the first days of the occupation. In Novi Sad, the first slaughter took place on the third day of the occupation, when 500 people, both Jews and Serbs, were murdered. The Jewish community was threatened with deportation to Croatia unless it made an immediate payment of 50,000,000 dinars; after great efforts, 34,000,000 were raised. Altogether, about 3,500 people were killed in Vojvodina in the initial stage, among them 150–200 Jews. Concentration camps were established in various places (Subotica, Stari Bečej, Ada, Odžaci, Bažka Topola), and some 2,000 Jews passed through these camps in the first two months of the occupation. In January 1942, a clash between resistance fighters and a Hungarian troop detachment caused the death of four Hungarian soldiers, and in reprisal 1,000 men, women, and children were rounded up and shot to death. Among the victims of this slaughter were 100 Jews. A few weeks later, a similar action took place at Novi Sad, where 870 Jews – almost a fifth of the total Jewish population of the city – in addition to 430 Serbs were murdered. Thousands more were brought to the banks of the Danube to suffer the same fate when a dispatch from the Hungarian military authorities arrived to put an end to the mass killing.

In 1942 the Hungarians ordered the formation of forced labor battalions into which all Jews and Serbs between the ages of 21 and 48 were drafted. Some 4,000 Jews from Bačka and Baranja were conscripted into the battalions; 1,500 were sent to the Ukraine, near the front, where they succumbed to disease and starvation or were murdered. Only 20 of the entire group survived the ordeal. The others were sent to Hungary and Serbia, where they were put to work in copper mines and on the railroads, together with about 6,000 Hungarian Jews. In spite of the harsh conditions to which they were exposed, they managed to survive for a while. The end came in March 1944, when Hungary was taken over by German forces. On September 17, a transport of 3,600 Jews from the Bor mines (where the labor battalions were concentrated) was dispatched in the direction of Belgrade; about 1,300 prisoners were murdered or died en route and the rest were deported to Germany. A short while later a second transport of 2,500 Jews, which included a large contingent of Vojvodina Jews, was organized. Some of these managed to escape, and several hundred were liberated by Tito's partisans, finding refuge with the population in Serbia and the Banat. The rest of the Jews from Bačka and Baranja were deported on April 25–26, 1944. About 4,000 Jews from the area of Novi Sad were interned at Subotica, while the Jews from the eastern part of Bačka were dispatched to a camp in Baja (Hungary); in May 1944, the group from Subotica was also sent to Baja. Eventually all the inmates of the Baja camp (as well as those of the Bačka Topola camp) were deported to Auschwitz.

MACEDONIA. The majority of Macedonian Jews were concentrated in three cities: in Skoplje (3,795 Jews, including 300 refugees from Belgrade); Bitolj (Monastir; 3,350); and Štip (550). Direct control of the area was in Bulgarian hands, and for the first 18 months persecution of the Jews did not go beyond confiscation of property, forced contributions, and personal insults. In August 1942, a group of 50 refugees from Belgrade was handed over to the Gestapo, which deported them to the Banjica camp; on Dec. 3, 1942, they were put to death in Jajinci. At the beginning of January 1943, further restrictions were imposed on the Jews, and two months later all of the Jewish population of Macedonia was placed in a temporary concentration camp in the "Monopol" tobacco factory near Skoplje. On March 22 a transport of 2,338 Jews was dispatched to the death camps in Poland, followed a week later by two more transports, numbering 2,402 and 2,404 people. Only about 100 Jews returned to Macedonia from these transports. About 150–200 Sephardi Jews were recognized by the Spanish government as Spanish nationals and were not deported; about 120 Jews fled to Albania, and some joined the partisans.

ITALIAN-OCCUPIED AREAS. Compared to the other parts of occupied Yugoslavia, the area under Italian control was a haven for the Jews. In spite of constant pressure by German diplomats – including Kasche, the German consul at Zagreb – the Italians refused to accede to demands to deport Jews and, for a while at least, regarded any measure discriminating against the Jews as incompatible with the honor of the Italian army. Originally there were a small number of Jews in this area, but soon it became a refuge for Jews from Bosnia and Croatia. In August 1941, according to a German estimate, there were between 4,000 and 5,000 Jews in Dubrovnik and Mostar. By November 1941, the Italians went as far as establishing camps for the Jewish refugees, interning refugees from Bosnia and Herzegovina in Kupari (near Dubrovnik) and Jews from Croatia in Kraljevica. In Split there were 2,000 refugees, in addition to 415 local Jews; 500 were sent to the island of Korčula and 1,100 to Italy (mostly to the Ferramonti internees' camp). In June 1943, 2,650 Jewish inmates of camps in Dalmatia were deported to the island of Rab. In all the camps, the Italians extended humane treatment to the Jews.

In September 1943, after the Italian capitulation, Tito's partisan army evacuated 2,000 refugees from Rab; able-bodied men joined the partisans, while the old men, women, and children found refuge in northern Dalmatia. About 300 people – the old and sick, women and their small children – remained on the island, and when the Germans invaded it, in March 1944, they were deported to Auschwitz. A similar fate overtook the Jews in Split. On Sept. 28, 1943, all adult men were interned, and after a while they were deported to Sajmište, where they were all murdered. In March 1944, 300 women and children were deported from Split to Jasenovac where they died.

JEWISH PARTISANS. Yugoslav Jews took an active part in the fight against the Nazis and played a leading role among the organizers of Tito's revolt. Ten Jews were named as national heroes of the resistance. No exact figures are available for the number of Jews who fought with the partisans, because they did not enlist as Jews, and in the early stage no family names were recorded. With one exception, there were no Jewish units. After the war, however, the Federation of Yugoslav Jewish Communities was able to identify 2,000 Jewish names among the members of Tito's formations.

Shortly after the occupation of Belgrade, *Ha-Shomer ha-Ẓa'ir put itself at the disposal of the Communist Party and helped organize the resistance. The first secret radio in Zagreb was operated by two Jewish brothers and the first act of sabotage in Vojvodina was carried out by youngsters of the Jewish youth movement. Individual Jews committed acts of sabotage, and in August 1942 the first group joined the partisans. A Jewish partisan unit was formed in the fall of 1943 from among the Jews evacuated from the Italian camp on the island of Rab. Composed of 250 men, the unit suffered heavy losses in the fighting against the Germans: its ranks were decimated, and the survivors were incorporated into other units. The most prominent Jewish resistance fighter was Moša *Pijade, who became one of Tito's four vice presidents after the liberation.

Contemporary Period

From the end of 1944, when Yugoslavia was liberated, about 14,000 Jews returned to the cities from their places of hiding, the partisan areas, and prison camps. The Federation of Jewish Communities officially reestablished its activities on Oct. 22, 1944, a few days after the liberation of Belgrade, when its surviving chairman, Friedrich Pops, reopened its office. Fifty-six Jewish communities were reconstructed, and the federation, with the aid of the American Jewish *Joint Distribution Committee (JDC), engaged in a variety of welfare projects, including the reopening of the home for the aged in Zagreb, extending material aid to the needy who began to return to their daily lives, etc. It also reestablished its ties with the *World Jewish Congress and other Jewish organizations.

Upon the establishment of the State of Israel (1948), the Federation sought and received permission from the Yugoslav authorities to send material help and organize Jewish emigration to Israel. From the end of 1948 until 1952 about 8,000 Jews, who were allowed to take their property with them, left for Israel. After 1952 the number of Jews remained almost unchanged at 6,500–7,000, of whom 6,200–6,500 were registered in 38 communities. In 1968 there were 1,552 Jews in Belgrade, 1,359 in Zagreb, 1,095 in Sarajevo, 1,320 in six communities (each of which had more than 100 members), 911 in 28 local and district communities (some of which had less than ten members), and another 220 scattered throughout the country. The structure of Yugoslav Jewry is revealed by censuses taken in 1952 and 1957. The first census covered 6,250 Jews who were registered in communities. Of these, 43% were male and 57% female; about 50% were Sephardim (especially in Serbia and Bosnia) and the rest were Ashkenazim (mostly in Croatia and Slovenia). Of the children, 591 were under the age of seven, 818 were in elementary school, 325 were in high school, and 247 were in institutes of higher learning. Among the adults, there were 12 apprentices in various fields, 221 doctors (military and civilian), 41 pharmacists, 21 veterinarians, 82 engineers, 46 technicians, 54 teachers in schools of higher learning, 48 teachers and educators, 27 lawyers, 12 judges (and 33 others held law degrees), 31 journalists, 875 in different branches of administration, 247 economists and administrators in economic enterprises, 4 agronomists, 231 artisans, 33 writers and artists, 73 army officers (not counting medical personnel), 5 noncommissioned officers, 233 on pension, 136 with no profession, 277 in various other professions, 1,435 housewives, 314 elderly people without pensions, 106 chronically ill, 45 seriously crippled, and 257 did not supply details on their professional status. The census of 1957 covered 6,691 Jews including 137 women per every 100 men (contrasted with an average of 106 women per 100 men in the general population). The number of children (up to age 18) was 25.1% of the Jewish, and 38.7% of the total population.

The activities of the Federation of Jewish Communities were founded upon the 1953 law that regulated the activities of religions and churches in Socialist Yugoslavia. But religious life was only part, and not necessarily the outstanding part, of Jewish community life. In 1952 the Federation deleted the word "religious" from its title and the title of the communities associated with it. The communities thus viewed themselves as national Jewish entities, preserving their ties with worldwide Jewish organizations and various bodies in Israel. This attitude was made possible by the liberal Yugoslav policy on the question of nationalities and the support of widespread circles in Yugoslavia for Judaism and for Israel. The Federation devoted much of its efforts to Jewish education. Kindergartens were established in a number of cities (and still functioned in 1969, in Belgrade and Zagreb); youth centers and sections for women, whose activities were directed by appropriate national boards, were set up in some communities; the larger communities reestablished their libraries; and an historical museum was established in Belgrade, including an institute for research on the history of Yugoslav Jewry, in which non-Jewish scholars also participated. Jewish youths were sent to Jewish seminars and studies abroad, and every year summer camps involved between 350 and 400 youth on various levels. Choirs in Belgrade and in Zagreb cultivated Israel and Hebrew music, both religious and secular.

There is special concern regarding the preservation of cemeteries of historic significance and the orderly liquidation of cemeteries and other property of communities which could not be preserved or were displaced by urban-renewal projects. Some synagogues were handed over to local cultural institutions and serve as cultural houses and museums. About 30 monuments have been erected to the victims of World War II in cemeteries and public places.

The Federation of Jewish Communities publishes a monthly organ and an annual *Jevrejski Almanah*. The first almanac appeared in 1954, the seventh, for 1965–67, in 1968. The almanacs cover historical and current-affairs material as well as literary works about the Holocaust. The Jewish youth publish an organ titled *Kadimah*. For a number of years a calendar printed in Serbo-Croatian was put out (containing prayers printed in Latin characters) by the only rabbi (*ḥakham*) to have survived the Holocaust, Menahem b. Abraham Romano (1882–1968) of Sarajevo. In 1952 the Federation published a book titled *Crimes of the Fascist Conquerors and their Collaborators Against the Jews in Yugoslavia*, whose second edition includes a summary in English. The Federation also published a number of basic Jewish books including a translation of a short history of the Jewish people by S. *Dubnow with an epilogue that carries on his concept of the Jewish nation with a Marxist interpretation.

The position of religion in community life weakened. In the community organizations committees for religious affairs have tried to satisfy the needs of the community as much as possible. On holidays the communities often celebrated with communal prayers and meals. No one was left to replace Rabbi Romano upon his death. Religious life was supplemented by observance of days of remembrance, especially for the victims of the Holocaust. Representatives of Yugoslav Jewry participate in many Jewish world conferences. Their ties with Israel were demonstrated – with the agreement of Yugoslav authorities – by fund raising for the Martyrs Forest and the forest in memory of Albert *Vajs (Weiss; 1905–1964), successor to Pops as chairman of the Federation, and mutual visits by delegations of youth and others. After 1966 the Federation expanded its ties with Jewish communities in Eastern European countries. Mutual visits were frequent, not only on occasions of celebration, such as the 400th anniversary of the establishment of the community in Sarajevo (October 1966), but also for discussions on practical matters. Even the Israel-Arab *Six-Day War (1967), which brought about Yugoslavia's one-sided position and the severance of diplomatic relations with Israel, did not change this situation. The Federation's activities were not restricted from above, although it took upon itself specific restrictions in its relations with the State of Israel.

[Cvi Rotem]

In the early 1980s the Jewish population of Yugoslavia was estimated at approximately 5,500, the majority of whom resided in Belgrade, Zagreb, and Sarajevo. Although the regime in Yugoslavia was authoritarian, its internal structure was the most liberal of all Eastern European countries, and the Jewish community enjoyed freedom both with regard to the organization of communal life and the conduct of religious and cultural activities, and most notably with regard to the community's ties with international Jewish organizations. Thus delegates from Yugoslavia regularly participated in the conventions of the World Jewish Congress, the World Conference of Synagogues and Kehillot, etc. From all parts of Yugoslavia, 28 community heads participated in a seminar and study tour in Israel (Oct. 19, 1976–Nov. 2, 1976), organized by the Jewish Agency.

Though not a member of the Warsaw Pact, and with a foreign policy independent of Moscow, since 1967 Yugoslavia adopted an extreme anti-Israel policy with regard to the Middle East conflict. It was the foremost defender and militant champion of sanctions against Israel in all international forums, including the UN and its agencies.

[Eliezer Palmor]

The violent breakup of Yugoslavia which began in 1991 and the bloody civil war that accompanied it had far-reaching and traumatic effects on the 5,000 to 6,000 Jews who lived in the country. Until the division of the country, Yugoslav Jews had belonged to communities joined in autonomous republic-wide organizations which in turn were members of a nationwide Federation based in Belgrade.

Most Jews were concentrated in the capital cities of three of the republics: Zagreb, capital of Croatia, with about 1,200 Jews; Sarajevo, capital of Bosnia-Herzegovina, with about 1,000; and Belgrade, capital of Serbia and also the federal capital, with about 1,500 Jews. The remaining Jews lived in much smaller scattered communities, mostly in Croatia and Serbia's Vojvodina province. Fewer than 100 Jews lived in Slovenia, and only 100 in Macedonia.

There was little overt antisemitism, and the rate of intermarriage was high. Through the 1980s participation grew in wide-ranging programs and activities run by the Federation and the individual communities (with the help of international Jewish philanthropic organizations). These included a summer camp on the Adriatic Sea, annual Maccabi sports competitions, old-age care facilities, women's and youth groups, and educational programs including religion classes, Hebrew classes, and the first Jewish kindergarten in Yugoslavia in more than a decade, which opened in Zagreb, the most active community, in 1989. Yugoslavia had only one rabbi – Belgrade-based Cadik Danon – but by the late 1980s one young man was in Israel studying to become a rabbi, and several others were training as cantors or lay leaders for religious services.

Yugoslavia's Jews also maintained close ties with various international Jewish organizations, and by the late 1980s Yugoslav government officials also met with Jewish and Israeli representatives. At a meeting in New York in July 1987, Yugoslav leader Lazar Mojsov told World Jewish Congress president Edgar Bronfman that he would "work toward better relations with the Jewish world as a whole and with the State of Israel."

A landmark cultural event was a major exhibition on the Jews of Yugoslavia that opened in Zagreb in April 1988 and then was shown elsewhere in the country, attracting tens of thousands of visitors, before going on to the United States and Israel. Belgrade's first Holocaust memorial (aside from memorials in the Jewish cemetery) was dedicated in 1990; it was by the Jewish sculptor Nandor Glid.

The mounting separatism and ethnic tensions that came to the fore in the late 1980s had their effect on the Jewish communities. Some Jews felt that Serbian overtures to Israel including the formation in 1989 of a Serbian-Jewish friendship society and the twinning of various Serbian-Israeli cities were mainly aimed at courting world Jewry to give support to Serbia in its opposition to any decentralization of the state. A leader of the tiny Jewish community in Slovenia warned of possible antisemitism after a youth magazine published *Protocols of the Elders of Zion* in 1990. In Zagreb, Jewish leaders at the end of 1990 expressed concern that Croatian nationalism might prompt a resurgence of antisemitism, but later threw support behind the Croatian government when it seceded from Yugoslavia and became embroiled in civil war.

When the civil war broke out following Slovenian and Croatian secession in the summer of 1991, the status of Jewish communities again became a political issue. Serbs and Croats attempted to discredit each other with accusations of antisemitism. In early 1992 Klara Mandic, a founder of the Serbian-Jewish Friendship Society, visited the United States and in a series of lectures and articles charged the Croatian government of Franjo Tudjman with reviving fascism and antisemitism and planning "genocide" against Serbs in Croatia. Nenad Porges, president of the Zagreb Jewish community, countered by accusing Serbs of antisemitism and expressing support for the Tudjman government.

The civil war led to great suffering and destruction, particularly after fighting spread from Croatia to Bosnia-Herzegovina. Jews had to flee their homes along with hundreds of thousands of other citizens, and Jewish monuments and property were damaged or destroyed along with countless other buildings. Among them, the medieval synagogue in Dubrovnik was damaged by bombs; the Jewish community center in Osijek was hit by shelling; and Serbian fighters used the ancient Jewish cemetery overlooking Sarajevo as a position from which to fire onto the city. In Zagreb, terrorist bombs in August 1991 wrecked the Jewish community offices and prayer hall and also damaged the Jewish cemetery.

Starting in April 1992, the American Jewish Joint Distribution Committee carried out daring air and overland evacuations of almost the entire Jewish population of Sarajevo.

Almost from the beginning of the civil strife, communications between Zagreb, Sarajevo, and Belgrade were difficult or cut altogether. Local Jewish communities became fully autonomous and ultimately independent as the former Yugoslav republics became independent. In Zagreb, gala celebrations in September 1992 marked the reopening of the Jewish community center and prayer hall after a full-scale restoration, partially funded by local authorities, following a terrorist bombing of the year before.

[Ruth E. Gruber]

In the years that followed the breakup of Yugoslavia the Federation of Jewish Communities in Belgrade, although diminished, continued to function, arranging cultural events and publishing Jewish material. In Zagreb, capital of Croatia, a Coordinating Committee headed by Dr. Ognjen Krauss was formed. The Kehillah is now called Zidovska opcina and is similarly active in all fields of Jewish life, especially in publishing cultural reviews and books on historical subjects. In Ljubljana, capital of Slovenia, there exists a Judovska skupina, a small congregation. In Sarajevo, the community, now called Jevrejska zajednica and headed by Jacob Finci, operates from the Ashkenazi synagogue. In Skopje, capital of Macedonia, Jews are organized under the name of Evreiska zajednica. Representatives of these organizations occasionally meet in European Jewish forums abroad and once a year in Dalmatian (Croatian) summer resorts.

Estimated population figure in the early 2000s were as follows: Bosnia-Herzegovina 500, Croatia 1,700, Macedonia 100, Serbia and Montenegro 1,500, Slovenia 100.

[Zvi Loker (2nd ed.)]

Relations with Israel

Between the end of World War II, which saw the creation of Yugoslavia as a Communist federal republic, and the establishment of the State of Israel in 1948, the Yugoslav attitude to Palestine Jewry was friendly and found expression in allowing passage to thousands of "illegal" immigrants to Palestine. From the Yugoslav point of view, this formed part of the anti-imperialist struggle. In 1947 Yugoslavia was elected a member of the 11-nation Special Commission on Palestine (UNSCOP). Its representatives declared their understanding for Jewish aspirations to independence, but eventually took a stand for a binational state, and in the UN Assembly, in November 1947, Yugoslavia did not vote for the partition resolution. However, following the proclamation of the establishment of the State of Israel, Yugoslavia recognized the new state on May 19, 1948; full diplomatic relations and the first trade agreement were quick to follow. The majority of Yugoslav Jews, survivors of the Holocaust, were permitted to go to Israel in 1948–49. In the years 1949 to 1954 relations were cordial. Political, social, and cultural ties were developed through exchange of delegations, as, e.g., between the Socialist Union and Mapai, the Yugoslav trade unions and the Histadrut, and through manifold activities of the respective legations at Belgrade and Tel Aviv.

Although Yugoslav diplomacy was not, even before 1956, generally favorable to Israel's stand in the Arab-Israel conflict, it did preserve a fairly balanced attitude until then. On Sept. 1, 1951, its representative voted, in the Security Council, for free navigation for all nations in the Suez Canal, a resolution hailed at the time as a victory for Israel. Marked deterioration on the Yugoslav side came after the Bandung Conference in 1955 and Yugoslav premier Tito's policy of assembling, and possibly leading, a group of "nonaligned" nations, together with Egypt's president Gamal Abdel Nasser, and Jawaharlal Nehru, prime minister of India. As Tito's collaboration with Nasser went ahead, relations with Israel became cooler. Another important factor in the changed Yugoslav attitude was the improvement of relations between Yugoslavia and the Soviet Union from May 1955. During the Sinai crisis (1956), Yugoslavia adopted an extremely hostile attitude to Israel. It thereafter slowed down and finally stopped most of the positive aspects of bilateral cooperation. Apart from trade, only personal contacts between Jews were permitted to continue. Yugoslavia supported the Arab stand against Israel in all spheres, save for economic boycott.

Yugoslav policy in the Middle East gradually evolved into a completely one-sided, pro-Arab position, culminating in its branding Israel as the "aggressor" in the Six-Day War (June 1967), severing diplomatic relations concurrently with other Communist countries (Romania excluded), and open advocacy of Egyptian-Arab extremist viewpoints. However, the sympathies of the Yugoslav people still seemed to incline toward Israel.

By 1971, the only aspect of Yugoslav-Israel relations which continued unaffected was in the sphere of trade, although Yugoslavia unilaterally suspended, in April 1970, the payments' agreement. Commercial ties started modestly in 1949, with a few hundred thousand dollars' worth of exchange both ways, and grew steadily; at the time of the signature of the third trade agreement in 1966 they had reached six million dollars. Trade was still growing in 1971, being fairly balanced. Yugoslav firms were represented in Israel, and there seemed to be a common understanding to continue with mutually useful trade exchanges.

The main items imported by Israel from Yugoslavia were meat, wood, furniture, boxes for packing citrus, metal products, and sugar. Its exports were cement, citrus fruits and concentrates, phosphates, tires, textile rayons, and plastic products.

[Zvi Loker]

A slightly more favorable tone toward Israel's rights was, however, expressed by the late President Tito during his visit to Romania (Dec. 3–4, 1977), when he said: "Israel exists for many years as a genuine fact, is recognized by the UN and is a member of it; any other view would be unrealistic. Thus, all the Arab states must recognize Israel as a state." Although Yugoslavia had not restored diplomatic relations with Israel broken after the Six-Day War in 1967, commercial and cultural ties as well as cooperation in the areas of sports and tourism burgeoned during the 1980s. Slovenia's Adria Airlines established direct flights to and from Israel in 1989.

During the 1990s Israel established diplomatic relations with the independent states of former Yugoslavia.

[Eliezer Palmor]

Musical Life

The many pictures of shofars discovered on ceramics at the archaeological site in Celarevo on the Danube river (seventh–ninth century C.E.; Khazars?) may indicate the presence of Jewish settlements and were the first pictures of the noted Jewish instrument in this part of Europe. This necropolis is unique for the Balkans and Panonia.

Ancient Jewish communities also existed on the shores of the Adriatic Sea (Split). There is no information about the music of these communities. There is also no information about the Jews of Dubrovnik who settled there from the 12th century C.E.

In the 16th century, a large community of Sephardim immigrated to the Balkans' parts of the Ottoman Empire up to Sarajevo. They learned synagogue music at a school founded by Rabbi David Jakov Pardo in the second half of the 18th century. Basic research on this musical tradition was done between the two world wars by Isak Hendel, Erik Elisha Samlaich, Zhiga Hirschler, and others. Unfortunately, most of the researchers lost their lives during the Holocaust, and the texts and musical transcriptions were lost as well.

From the studies of the contemporary musicologists Cvjetko Richtman (1902–1990), who was the founder of the Institute for the Study of Folklore in Sarajevo, his daughter Dunja Richtman (1970–), and particularly the basic studies of Ankica Petrovic (1978–) on the musical tradition of the Sephardim in Bosnia-Herzegovina, one can infer that there is a great difference between the sacred and the secular music of the Bosnian Sephardim. In this tradition, the melodies of their secular "romances" (*romantigas*) were influenced by medieval Spanish music, while their sacred music preserved more ancient roots from the pre-Ottoman and pre-Arab era. (see also *Greece and *Ladino (Romancero)). A great number of Jewish music documents are archived in the Jewish Museum of Belgrade.

At the time of the national resurgence, the pioneers of "classical music" were of a Jewish origin, both among the Croats (Vatroslav Lisinski, born Fux, 1819–1854) and the Serbs (Josif Schlezinger, 1794–1870). However, there are no Jewish elements in their music.

In the first half of the 20th century, the most prominent Jewish composers in Yugoslavia were Rikard Schwarz, Zhiga Hirscher, Pavao Markovac, Oskar Jozefovich, Robert Herzl, Erih Elisha Samlaich, and Lavoslav Grinski. All of them were killed during World War II.

Among the survivors who immigrated to the United States were the baritone and composer Aaron Marko *Rothmueler (1908–1993), who also wrote *The Music of The Jews* (1958), and the eminent musicologist Dragan Plamenac (1895–1983), known for his studies on music of the 14th and 16th centuries. Among the composers and performers who immigrated to Israel were Paul Raphael Sterk (1904–1979), who composed the symphony *City of David*; Uri Givon (1912–1974), who produced numerous arrangements of Jewish and Israeli songs and compositions; Reuven Yaron, who was brought to Palestine as a child in 1943, studied with M. *Seter, and was killed at the age of 23 in the Sinai Campaign of 1956. His compositions were highly esteemed.

Among the notable performers between the two world wars were pianist Ernest Krauth, conductor Milan Sachs, and violinist Mary Dragutinovic. In the field of light music Abraham Kupferberg and Raphael Blam distinguished themselves.

After World War II Bruno Bjelinski, Miroslav Spieler, Ruben Radica, Dubravko Detoni, and Enriko Josif were active as composers, and performers included singer Breda Kalef, conductor Oskar Danon, violinist David Kamhi, and pianist Andreja Preger.

[Dushan Mihalek (2nd ed.)]

BIBLIOGRAPHY: Rosanes, Togarmah; Grossmann, in: *Am va-Sefer*, 2 (1939), 26–28; Gelber, in: *Zion*, 8 (1943), 35–50; Levi, in: *Shenaton Davar*, 2 (1944), 182–7; Matkovski, in: *Yad Vashem*, 3 (1959), 187–236; Shapira, in: *Bi-Tefuẓot ha-Golah*, 3 (1961), 85–88; Alkalai, in: *Algemeyne Entsiklopedye*, Yidn, 4 (1950), 748–62; Rotem, in: *Gesher*, 10 (1965), 45–49; Ch. Molbech, F.R. Chesney, and E. Michelsen, *Das tuerkische Reich in historisch-statistischen Schilderungen* (1854); I. Loeb, *La situation des Israélites en Turquie, en Serbie et en Roumanie* (1877); N. Leven, *Cinquante ans d'Histoire*, 1 (1911), 93–111; J. Diamant, *Geschichte der Juden in Kroatien bis zur Gleichberechtigung* (1912–13); Hollaender, in: *Jevrejski Almanah*, 4 (1928), 53–58; Glesinger, *ibid.*, N.S. 1 (1954), 60–62, 197–204; Vinaver, *ibid.*, 2 (1955–56), 28–34; Kovačević, *ibid.*, 4 (1959–60), 105–12; *La Yougoslavie d'aujourd'hui* (publié par la section de la presse du Ministère des Affaires Etrangères, 1935); *Jevrejski Narodni Kalendar* (1935–36); *Jevrejski Kalendar za godinu 5713* (Izdanje Saveza Jevrejskih veroispovednich opština FNRJ); Hengel, in: ZNW, 57 (1966), 145–83; *Spomenica 400 Godina od dolaska Jevreja u Bosnu i Hercegovinu* (1966). HOLOCAUST PERIOD: Matkovski, in: *Yad Vashem Studies*, 3 (1959), 203–58, incl. bibl.; Z. Loewenthal (ed.), *Zločini fašističhih okupatora i njihovih pomagača protiv Jevreja u Jogoslaviji* (1957), incl. introd. and comprehensive Eng. summary; R. Hilberg, *Destruction of the European Jews* (1961), index; G. Reitlinger, *Final Solution* (1968²), 385–98; L. Poliakov and J. Sabille, *Jews under the Italian Occupation* (1955), 129–50; B. Arditi, *Yehudei Bulgaryah be-Shenot ha-Mishtar ha-Naẓi 1940–1944* (1962); L. Hory and M. Broszat, *Der kroatische Ustascha-Staat 1941–1945* (1964); M. Novich, in: Z. Shner (ed.), *Extermination and Resistance*, 1 (1958), 180–2; S. Baruch, *ibid.*, 183–5. CONTEMPORARY PERIOD: D.J. Elazaar… [et al.] (ed.), *Balkan Jewish Communities: Yugoslavia, Bulgaria, Greece, and Turkey* (1984); H.P. Freidenreich, *The Jews of Yugoslavia: A Quest for Community* (1977); Rotem, in: *Zion*, 3:2 (Eng., 1952), 30–36; J. Gordon, in: AJYB, 53 (1952), 347–50; L. Shapiro, *ibid.*, 68 (1967), 407–10; A. Vajs, in: *Jevrejski Almanah* N.S., 1 (1954), 5–47; *ibid.* 3 (1957–58), 162; American Jewish Congress, *Jewish Communities of Eastern Europe* (1967), 57–65. **ADD. BIBLIOGRAPHY:** Y. Eventov, "*Toledot Yehudei Yugoslavia*," vol. 1 (with English summary; 1971); J. Rado and J. Major, *Istorija Novosadskih Jevreja* (with English summary; 1972); D. Kečkemet, *Židovi v povijesti Splita* (with English summary; 1971); *Zbornik*, 1 (with English summary; 1971); Z. Loker (ed.), *Pinkas ha-*

Kehillot – Yugoslavia (1988); M. Shelah (ed.), "History of the Holocaust – Yugoslavia" (Heb., 1990); P.B. Gordiejew, *Voices of Yugoslav Jewry* (1999); A. Kerkaennen, *Yugoslav Jewry – Aspects of Post-World War II and Post-Yugoslav developments* (2001).

YUGOSLAV LITERATURE. The Serbs, Croats, Slovenes, Macedonians, Hungarians, and other ethnic groups that constitute the population of former Yugoslavia all have their own distinct cultural traditions, and it is therefore merely for the sake of convenience that they are associated under the heading Yugoslav Literature. The earliest literary activity in the "land of the southern Slavs" (dating back to the ninth century) was the result of the educational and missionary work of Cyril of Salonika and his brother Methodius, Cyril having devised the Slavic (Cyrillic) alphabet still used, within Yugoslavia, by the Serbs and Macedonians (see *Bulgarian Literature).

Biblical and Hebraic Influences

The Bible has been translated and referred to by the southern Slavs since the beginning of their cultural history. The first translation of the Old Testament, by Cyril and Methodius, was intended for the Slavs of Macedonia and according to tradition was based on the original Hebrew. The earliest complete translation, however, was that of Primož Trubar, a Slovenian Protestant, in the late 16th century. Two versions of the Reformation period were a Croatian Lutheran Bible (1562–63) and Juri Dalmatin's Protestant Bible and Psalter (1584), which marked the beginnings of Slovenian literature. Among the translations of the 19th century, a period of national and cultural revival, were those of Matija Petar Katanić in Croatia (1813) and Djura Daničžć in Serbia (1865), both Orthodox. Two 20th-century versions are the (Orthodox) Bible of 1932–33 and Petar Vlasić's Serbo-Croatian Bible (1923–25). In Serbia, biblical tales (such as the "Book of Adam") and religious plays were written during the Middle Ages and until the period of the Turkish invasion in the mid-15th century. Biblical themes were also current in 15th-century Croatian literature. The Hebraic and Greek biblical traditions persisted in Old Slavonic literature and flourished under Byzantine influence among the southern Slavs. Biblical subjects were later popular during the Serbian literary revival in the 19th century. At the beginning of the 18th century, Gavril Stefanović Venclović of Srem translated some 20,000 pages of this old literature into vernacular Serbian.

However, original works on Old Testament themes have been traced to the Renaissance era, when the Croatian poet and humanist Marko Marulić wrote the allegorical Neo-Latin epic *Davidiadis libri XIV* and the first Croatian epic on a religious subject, *Judita* (1501), which was intended to arouse national feelings against the Turkish overlord. Another writer of the 16th century, the Montenegrin poet Mavro-Nikolo Vetranović of Ragusa (Dubrovnik), wrote an outstanding verse play about Abraham, *Posvetilište Abraamovo*, and the apocryphal drama, *Suzana ćista*. After a lapse of almost three centuries, the epic tradition was revived by the Serbian writer Milovan Vidaković, who published his *Istorija o prekrasnom Josifje* (1805) and the apocryphal *Mladi Tovija* (1825). Vidaković, who also wrote the epic *Putešestvije u Jerusalim* (1834), was followed by several other writers: Laza Kostić, a Serbian poet; Petar Petrović Njegoš, vladika (prince-bishop) of Montenegro, the greatest Montenegrin poet; and Silvije Strahimir Kranjčerić, a Croatian poet of Sarajevo. Biblical elements are prominent in the works of all three, Njegoš having composed the epic *Luča mikrokozma* (1845; *The Rays of the Microcosm*, 1953), which betrays the influence of Dante, Milton, and Byron, and Kranjčerić having written *Mojsije*, a poem about the Lawgiver. This interest in biblical subjects was maintained in the 20th century. Miroslav Krleža, the outstanding contemporary writer in Croatia, published dramas on Adam and Eve and Salome, while his colleague and fellow radical, August Cesarec, wrote "Israel's Exodus and Other Legends" on the eve of World War II. Old Testament themes have also inspired two studies of Moses (1932, 1938) by Aron Alkalaj; "King David," a drama by the Belgrade writer, artist, and stage director Raša Plaović; and *Vreme čuda* ("Time of Wonders," 1965), by the Serbian Borislav Pekić which was inspired by biblical legends.

There have been no Yugoslav translations of talmudic and later Jewish religious literature and these have therefore exerted no influence on the local culture. In the 16th century, however, Croatian humanism produced an outstanding scholar in Matthias Flacius Illyricus (Vlachich), a Protestant theologian and philologist who became professor of Hebrew at the University of Wittenberg in 1544. A violent controversialist and fanatical anti-Catholic, he published many scholarly works including a linguistic dictionary of the Bible, *Clavis Scripturae Sacrae seu de sermone sacrarum literarum* (Antwerp, 1567; Basle, 1623). The *Wandering Jew theme also appeared in Yugoslavia with the epic *Ahasver* (1946) by the left-wing Croatian poet and politician Vladimir Nazor. As to classics of modern Jewish literature, works by writers such as Shalom Aleichem and Sholem Asch have been translated from the Yiddish, as have other works by Jewish writers in other languages, notably Isaac Babel, Saul Bellow, Heinrich Heine, and André Schwarz-Bart, all popular among Yugoslav readers and critics.

[Ana Shomlo-Ninic]

The Image of the Jew

In the areas constituting former Yugoslavia, Jews have not, in general, provided writers with a major literary theme. There were two basic reasons for this: the Jewish population was always limited, inconspicuous, and largely cut off from gentile society; and, in the ethnic, religious, and cultural mosaic formed by this Balkan region, a crossroads and battlefield of many nations, native writers in search of the exotic or colorful had no need to seek out the Jew. Until the Holocaust Jews were central characters only in works by Jewish authors. Subsequently they also became an accepted subject for non-Jews.

In the rich folk literature which survived well into the 19th century, the Jews who appear have no individuality and, under the influence of Christian polemical writings, they are often presented as "cursed" and cruel, objects of hatred and derision. Exceptionally, one folk song contains cautious praise for the young Jewess who wishes to marry the exalted hero, Kraljević Marko. During the Renaissance period, Dalmatian poets (e.g., Marulić) adapted biblical and apocryphal subjects and New Testament material, but did not associate the Hebrews of the past with the Jews of their time. Instead, they tended to regard the people of Israel as a symbol of their own nation in its fight against the Turks and as exemplifying the general struggle of humanity. Jewish figures appeared in very few comedies, one being the anonymous *Jerko Škripalo* presented in Dubrovnik during the 18th century, and then from a positive point of view. Serbian and Croatian authors of the 19th-century Romantic school scarcely mentioned contemporary Jews, but when they did, they used them to describe their own situation, as in August Šenoa's *Vječni Žid* ("The Eternal Jew"), or else to express general ideas (as in S. Kranjčević's *Mojsije*, and Vladimir Vidrić's *Dva levita*). Before the First Zionist Congress the Slovenian ex-priest Anton Aškerc published a mordant poem ("Natanova prikazen") about an old rabbi who bewails the homelessness of his people; in answer, the patriarch Abraham assures him that, since the whole world owes money to the Jews, the world is their homeland. In Slovenia, France Pršeren wrote a poem ("Judovsko dekle") about a young Jewess who falls in love with a Christian, but abandons him because of the religious barrier.

With the advent of the realistic novel at the end of the 19th century, the Jew began to figure in the role of the shopkeeper or publican who precipitates the collapse of rural society, as in Josip Kosor's *Rasap* ("Disintegration," 1906), or as a moneylender; always a secondary figure, bereft of individuality, the Jew was invariably presented in an unfavorable light, often with pronounced antisemitic overtones. The Croatian Miroslav Krleža, a militant leftist author and playwright, scattered antisemitic remarks throughout his works, although he placed such comments in the mouths of degenerate, negative types. Otherwise Krleža merely produced the image of a revolutionary, cosmopolitan Jew, oblivious to patriotism or any sense of national identity. Between the world wars the figure of the Jew was mainly the concern of Jewish writers, some of whom restricted themselves to a Jewish readership (e.g., Hinko *Gottlieb). The humorist Zak *Konfino introduced the little Sephardi communities of the Serbian countryside, and Isak *Samokovlija wrote about the ordinary Sephardi Jew of Bosnia. Both writers familiarized the general public with Jewish types whom they presented in an attractive literary style. During and after World War II, dozens of Jewish and non-Jewish authors became preoccupied with the fate of Yugoslav Jewry in verse, drama, and fiction. Since in most cases these works were inspired by actual events, the characters appearing in them acquired a seal of authenticity. The Jew now appeared not only as the innocent victim of Nazi-Fascist bestiality, but also as a courageous fighter who lays down his life to avenge his people or to free his country. This tide, which is still in full spate, carried with it many Jewish and non-Jewish authors of the older generation impelled to supply testimony about the Jewish tragedy, as well as innumerable younger writers for whom the subject served as a powerful literary incentive.

The image of the Jew acquires a classic dimension in the works of the Serbian Nobel Prize winner Ivo Andrić, especially in the two novels which he wrote in German-occupied Belgrade. Within the general racial and cultural panorama of *Travnička hronika* ("The Chronicle of Travnik," 1945) he described the *Athias family's way of life and tribulations, typical of the Sephardi refugees in Western Bosnia at the beginning of the 19th century. These exiles from the West are thrown into the Orient, which corrupts and degenerates them without destroying their self-respect. In *Na Drini ćuprija* ("The Bridge over the Drina," 1945) Andrić affectionately described a beautiful and energetic Ashkenazi Jewess of Tarnow who runs a tavern in an East Bosnian townlet at the close of the 19th century. There the clash of the old and the new provides an anvil for her own achievements and failures. In his short stories, *Pripovetke* (3 vols., 1924–36; *The Pasha's Concubine and Other Tales*, 1969), Andrić described other Jewish figures in a realistic but sympathetic manner. Always deeply involved in their surroundings, they nevertheless keep their distance, either of their own free will or from compulsion.

[Cvi Rotem]

The Jewish Contribution

Although there have been Jewish communities in Macedonia and Dalmatia for 2,000 years or more, the earliest record of Jewish literary activity in the territory of former Yugoslavia dates only from the mid-16th century. The Neo-Latin poet Didacus *Pyrrhus, a Portuguese refugee known also as Flavius Eborensis, Pyrrhus Lusitanus, and Diego Pires (originally Isaiah Cohen), settled in Dubrovnik (Ragusa), where he continued to write verse. After 1492 many Spanish exiles fled to Bosnia (then part of the Ottoman Empire) and settled in Sarajevo, where they were made welcome. However, their new cultural milieu, by contrast with Western Europe, was so low that they virtually ceased to foster scientific and scholarly pursuits. The first Bosnian Sephardi of literary note was the 17th–18th-century Sarajevo kabbalist Nehemiah Hiyya *Ḥayon. With the appointment of David Samuel b. Jacob *Pardo as rabbi of Sarajevo (1765), Jewish studies were revived, flourishing under his son, Isaac Pardo, and under Meir Danon, Eliezar Jichac Papo, and Eliezer Shem-Tov Papo (all 19th century), of whom the last two published works in Ladino as well as Hebrew.

In 1526 Jews were banned from Croatia for more than two centuries; their resettlement dates from the 18th century. Among the newcomers were many intellectuals, notably Siegfried (Vítezslav) *Kapper, an eminent Czech poet who at one time lived in Karlovac and promoted international interest in Croatian and Serbian poetry. From the beginning of the 20th century, Jewish newspapers and magazines such as *Židovska smotra, Gideon* (later titled *Ha-Noar*), *Ha-Aviv* (for youngsters), and *Ommanut* began regular publication. There were two important publishers: Lavoslav Hartman (1813–1881), who issued the first Croatian translations and editions of world classics, and Geca Kon (1873–1941) of Belgrade, who headed the largest Yugoslav publishing house in the period between the world wars. In Belgrade, as in Sarajevo, the first Jewish writers were rabbinic scholars, and secular literature, reflecting the prevalent Sephardi culture, was mainly written in Ladino until World War I. In the late 1830s, during the reign of Prince Miloš, who was sympathetic to the Jews, Hebrew printing began to develop in Serbia; Hajim Davićo was the pioneer Jewish writer in the Serbian language in the late 19th century. During the 1880s many new Jewish literary associations, newspapers, and periodicals in Ladino, Yiddish, German, Hungarian, and Serbo-Croatian were established, including *Jevrejski Glasnik, Zajednica, El amigo del pueblo, Pasatiempo* (Belgrade), and *Alborada* (Sarajevo). Jovan Mandil (1873–1915), a lawyer and journalist of Šabac, Serbia, was the correspondent of the Belgrade dailies *Pravda* and *Beogradske novine*, as well as the founder and chief editor of *Bitoljske novine*. The founder of Sarajevo's first Ladino newspaper, *La Alborada* (1900–01), a scientific and literary weekly, was Abraham Kapon (1853–1930), an author and editor whose works included two dramas, *El Augustiador* (1914) and *Shivat Sion* (1921), a volume of *Poesias* (1922), and translations. Many of his unpublished manuscripts were lost during World War II.

Later Trends

Early in the 20th century numerous Jewish writers and translators introduced Serbian, Croatian, and Bosnian readers to the classics of world literature. Prominent among them were Benko Davičo (brother of Hajim Davičo), who translated Heine; Lav Grin (Ilko Gorenčevi), the art critic; Paulina Loebl Albala; David Pijade, who published original fiction and a translation of Oscar Wilde's *Picture of Dorian Grey*; Bukić Pijade; and Haim Alkalaj.

An entire tradition of *Ladino romances, proverbs, and folklore had been transmitted orally from the late 15th century onward, and, during the 1930s, some Sephardi writers in Yugoslavia tried to revive this culture and to set it down in writing. In this regard the work of Laura Papo Bohoreta, a poet, playwright, and novelist, was especially significant. She published *Ojes mios, La pasiensia vale muche, Tiempos pasados,* and *Avia de ser*, and also wrote a study of the Sephardi woman which was translated into Spanish (1931). Bohoreta died in the Holocaust. Active in the same field was the Hispanicist Kalmi Baruh (1896–1945), born in Sarajevo, whose research in Spain during the late 1920s was later recalled by his friend and compatriot, Ivo Andrić (in: *Jevrejski almanah* (1959/60), 213–5). Baruh devoted much of his time and energy to the study of the Ladino language and the Ladino "romances" of Bosnia (*Jevrejsko-španski idiomi*); and his many essays and studies relating to Ladino culture and Spanish writers were partly republished in *Eseji i članci o španskoj književnosti* ("Essays and Articles on Spanish Literature," 1952). Baruh died shortly after his liberation from the Bergen-Belsen concentration camp.

Jewish Themes

In Serbo-Croatian literature proper, Jews achieved prominence only after World War I. So far as specifically Jewish themes and interests are concerned, the two most important Yugoslav authors were Isak Samokovlija, who wrote only of Sephardi life in Bosnia, and the Zionist poet and author Hinko Gottlieb, who wrote fiction on World War II themes and died in Israel. Other Jewish writers active in the period between the world wars included the poet and editor Samuel *Romano, who translated modern Hebrew verse and prose works, and Stanislav Vinaver. Among the promising young authors who died in the Holocaust were two cousins from Novi Sad: Vitomir Jovanović (pen name of Viktor Rozencvajg), who issued a verse collection, *Naš život* ("Our Life"); and Nenad Mirov (pen name of Alfred Rozencvajg), whose collected poems appeared in *Dve duše* ("Two Souls"), *Kroz jadilovce klance* ("Through the Gorges of Pain"), and *Tri prema jedan za poeziju* ("Three to One for Poetry").

Apart from the versatile author and humorist Žak Konfino, some of whose works deal with Sephardi life in Serbia, most contemporary Jewish writers in Yugoslavia (among whom several have achieved considerable importance) are remote from Jewish tradition and show little interest in either Sephardi or Ashkenazi themes. Outstanding among these was the Communist poet and novelist Oscar *Davičo, whose anti-Zionist and anti-Israel bias was shared by the eminent art historian and essayist Oto Bihalji *Merin. The latter's brother, Pavle Bihalji, a leading publisher, fell victim to the Nazis in 1941. Two authors whose literary career began well before World War II were the poet and playwright Miroslav Feldman and the novelist and literary scholar Ervin *Šinko. The older generation of modern writers was also represented by the Zagreb poet and translator Ina *Jun-Broda, who settled in Vienna and published Serbo-Croatian works in German translation; Julija Najman, who translated from the French and wrote fiction on Jewish themes; and Jožef *Debrecenji, a native of Budapest, who wrote in Hungarian as well as Serbo-Croatian. One of the most translated Yugoslav writers was Erih Koš (1913–), who published novels and short stories, and satires such as *čudnovata povest o kitu velikom takođe zvanom veliki Mak* (1960; *The Strange Story of the Great Whale, also known as Big Mac*, 1962). Other works by Koš include the novel *Il tifo* (1958), an allegory on the tragic aspects of war. Among the leftist social writers who were first active between the world wars were Šinko, Bihalji Merin, and the psychiatrist Hugo Klajn (1894–1981), who taught at the Belgrade Academy of Dramatic Arts and wrote *Šekspir i čovječanstvo* ("Shakespeare and Mankind," 1964).

In the course of the German occupation of Yugoslavia during World War II, the vast majority of the Jews perished and the traumatic effect of this disaster had profound literary repercussions. Personal experiences as a survivor of Auschwitz dominate the works of Djordje *Lebović, who dealt with the concentration camp theme in dramas such as *Nebeski odred* ("Commando Heaven," 1959), *Do viđenja druže Gale* ("Goodbye, Comrade Gal," 1961), and *Haleluja* (1965). Other authors who tackled the same subject included Frida

Filipović (1913–), who published fiction and translations from the French; the poet, novelist, and children's writer Ivan Ivanji; the novelist Danilo Nahmijas; Julija Najman; and Jožef Debrecenji, whose novel *Hideg krematórium: Auschwitz regénye* ("The Cold Crematorium," 1950) first appeared in Hungarian (in Yugoslavia) and was later translated into other languages. Two other works about the Holocaust period by postwar writers were the novels *Testament* by Stevan Kvazimodo, and *Pod žutom trakom* ("Under the Yellow Badge") by Andrija Deak. Two authors of the younger generation who displayed a nostalgic interest in the Jewish tradition were Filip David and Danilo Kiš (1935–1989), whose novels include *Psalm 44* and *Bašta, pepeo* ("Garden, Ashes," 1965).

After 1945 and throughout the 1950s and 1960s, Jewish writers continued to play an important part in Yugoslavia's cultural life as editors and contributors of leading newspapers and periodicals, theater managers, and writers for radio, television, and the motion picture industry. Many of them gained the highest literary awards. *Jevrejski almanah*, the annual publication of the Federation of Jewish Communities in Yugoslavia, promotes the work of aspiring young writers and also contains essays and other contributions by eminent Jewish and non-Jewish authors.

[Ana Shomlo-Ninic]

BIBLIOGRAPHY: N. Strunjaš, in: *Gesher*, 15:1 (1969), 74–84 (= *Jevrejski almanah*, 1965–67). **ADD. BIBLIOGRAPHY:** P. Palavestra, *Jevrejski pisci u srpskoj knjizevnosti* (1988); D. Katan Ben-Zion, *Presence and Disappearance – Jews and Judaism in Former Yugoslavia in the Mirror of Literatures* (Heb., 2002).

YUḤASIN (Heb. יֻחֲסִין), laws dealing with the determination of an individual's personal status and its legal consequences insofar as such a status derives from a person's particular parentage. From the beginning of Jewish history, the ascertainment of an Israelite's *yiḥus, i.e., genealogy or pedigree, was considered of utmost importance, as is evidenced in Scripture (Num. 1:2, 18 and *Rashi* ad loc.; Ezra 2:59–63; 8:1). According to the Talmud, a person's *yiḥus* was also of importance with regard to the amount of the "main" (or statutory) *ketubbah, as for a certain period of time it was ruled that it should be increased beyond the regular minimum in the case of the daughters of priests and of other distinguished families (Ket. 12a–b and Tos. ad loc., s.v. *bet din shel kohanim*).

Determination of Paternity

A person's *yiḥus* obviously cannot be established unless the identity of his parents is known. Identifying the mother generally presents no difficulties but to identify the father it is necessary to distinguish between the offspring of a married and an unmarried woman.

The offspring of a married woman is presumed to have been fathered by her husband, according to the rule that the majority of cases is to be followed, since for the most part a woman cohabits with her husband (Ḥul. 11b; Sh. Ar., EH 4:15). Therefore if the husband denies paternity the onus is on him to rebut this presumption; he will succeed in his claim if he can prove that factually the child cannot be his, for example, if he was away from his wife and never saw her for an unbroken period of at least 12 months prior to the birth of the child (Sh. Ar., EH 14). When a child is born less than 12 but more than 10 months after the husband's separation from the child's mother, the matter will depend on the facts in each case (although the matter is not undisputed in the codes; see Sh. Ar., EH 14 and *Ḥelkat Meḥokek* to 10 and 11): if on the evidence of the mother's conduct there is reason to suspect that she has committed adultery, the court will not be bound by the usual presumption and may decide that the husband is not the father of the child (*Rema*, EH 14); if, however, there is no basis for any such suspicion, it may possibly be held – unless there is some evidence to the contrary – that the fetus tarried in its mother's womb beyond the normal pregnancy period (270 days) and the court may rule that the husband is the father of the child.

The presumption of paternity does not apply where the husband expressly denies it and there is no evidence that he has cohabited with his wife during the relevant period. It must be clear, however, that his denial is based on his own conviction and not on mere speculation, and is in no way contradicted by his own conduct, e.g., if hitherto he has admitted his paternity – expressly or by implication. This *halakhah*, known as *yakir* ("acknowledge"), is based on Deuteronomy 21:17, from which it is deduced that the husband may acknowledge and designate a particular son as his firstborn, in preference to other sons born to his wife after their marriage, even if such a son is younger than the others – the husband thus implicitly declaring that the other ones are not his, but are *mamzerim born to his wife through *adultery (Kid. 74a; Sh. Ar., EH 4:29; PDR 3:97–108). The husband's declaration of a son's bastardy, however, is not believed if the son already has sons of his own, since because of the rule that the son of a *mamzer* is also a *mamzer* this would taint them with bastardy as well, and the Torah has not conferred so wide a power upon the husband (Sh. Ar., EH 4:29). On the other hand, as long as the husband himself does not deny paternity, the wife's declaration that he is not the father of her child will not be accepted as sufficient to exclude the husband's paternity, and this is so even if a third party admits to being the father of the child (Sot. 27a; Sh. Ar., EH 4:15; *Rema*, EH 26:29; see also PDR 7:281, 289). Various questions arise in the case of a child born as a result of *artificial insemination.

In the case of the offspring of an unmarried woman the onus is on the child to prove (through his mother) that the defendant is his father. This is so not only because here the presumption of paternity as in the case of a married woman is inapplicable, but also because the mere fact that the defendant and the child's mother had sexual relations does not necessarily warrant the inference that the defendant is its father (Yev. 69b; Resp. Ribash, nos. 40 and 41). Differing opinions are expressed in the codes on how paternity is to be proved. In the Shulḥan Arukh it is laid down as *halakhah* that the defendant's paternity may only be proved by his own admission (EH 4:26

and *Rema* thereto; Resp. Ribash, *ibid.*). Such an admission need not necessarily be expressed and it is sufficient if facts can be established concerning the defendant's conduct from which an admission of his being the father may be inferred: e.g., his taking the mother to a hospital for her confinement, or paying the hospital bill for the mother or the child, etc. (Resp. Rosh 82:1; *Oẓar ha-Posekim* EH 4, no. 108, 4).

Rules of *Yuḥasin*

The following four categories of offspring are to be distinguished: offspring of parents married to each other; offspring of parents not married to each other; offspring of parents of whom only one is Jewish; and offspring of unknown parents.

OFFSPRING OF PARENTS MARRIED TO EACH OTHER. A child born to a marriage which is valid and not originally prohibited between the parties (see *Marriage, Prohibited), is *kasher* (of unimpaired status), i.e., his (or her) marriage is permitted to any *kasher* Jewess (or Jew; Kid. 69a; Sh. Ar., EH 8:1). Such a child takes the father's status, not that of the mother, in accordance with Numbers 1:2, 18 (and *Rashi* ad loc.; Sh. Ar., EH 8:1). Thus, the son of a priest and an Israelite woman will be a priest and one born of an ordinary Israelite and the daughter of a priest will be an ordinary Israelite. If the marriage of the parents is valid but originally prohibited, the child's status follows that of the tainted parent (Kid. 66b; Sh. Ar., EH 8:4). Hence the offspring of a marriage of which one party is a *mamzer(et)*, will also be a *mamzer* (Kid. 66b; Sh. Ar., EH 4:18); similarly, the son of a priest and a divorcée is called a *ḥalal* (חלל), i.e., profaned, and is unfit for the priesthood, while the daughter of such a marriage is called a *ḥalalah* (חללה) and can not marry a priest (Lev. 21:7; Kid. 77a; Sh. Ar., EH 7:12 and 8:4). Since the laws of the priesthood apply only to priests of unimpaired status (*kesherim*) there is no prohibition against a *ḥalal* marrying a divorcee (Sh. Ar., EH 7:20). Except in matters of priesthood, the *ḥalal* suffers no defect in status and he or she is allowed to marry an Israelite woman or man of unimpaired status (Sh. Ar., EH 8:2). A marriage between such parties not being prohibited, their offspring follows the father's status; i.e., the daughter of an Israelite and a *ḥalalah* is not profane and is permitted to be married to a priest, but the daughter of a *ḥalal* and an Israelite woman is also a *ḥalalah* and so must not marry a priest (Kid. 77a; Sh. Ar., EH 7:16).

OFFSPRING OF PARENTS NOT MARRIED TO EACH OTHER. The mere fact that a child is born out of wedlock does not taint his personal status, nor is he thereby rendered unfit for the priesthood (Yev. 59b–60a; Sh. Ar., EH 6:8). Even though it prohibits fornication, which is punishable with *flogging (Yad, Ishut 1:4), Jewish law, unlike other legal systems, does not render a child illegitimate, with its rights affected, merely because it is the issue of an extramarital union. The sole legal difference – in the present context – between such a child and one born of parents married to each other concerns the question of proving paternity (see above). Upon proof of paternity, the status of a child born out of wedlock is determined in the same manner as if it were born to parents married to each other. This applies only if (at the time of conception) there existed no legal impediment to a marriage between the parents of the child. However, if the parents were not in a position to contract a valid marriage with each other even if they had wished to do so, because their cohabitation would have amounted to incest (including adultery) according to the Torah (i.e., a union between parties prohibited to each other according to biblical law and for whom the punishment is *karet or death), the child will be a *mamzer* and his status thus impaired (Kid. 66b; see *Marriage, Prohibited).

OFFSPRING OF PARENTS OF WHOM ONLY ONE IS JEWISH. Here the rule is that the child takes his mother's status (Kid. 66b; Sh. Ar., EH 4:19). Accordingly, the offspring of a non-Jew and a Jewess is a Jew and is legitimate, subject to the limitation that a priest should not marry such a daughter, or unless the mother is herself a *mamzeret*; in this case the child is a *mamzer*, and this is so even if the Jewess is a married woman whose adulterous relations with a Jew would have made the child a *mamzer* (Sh. Ar., EH 4:19 and 4:5 with commentaries). On the other hand, the offspring of a Jew and a non-Jewish mother is not a Jew, regardless of the will of the parents, since the matter is determined by the objective facts alone. The child therefore can become Jewish only by first being a *proselyte, in the same way as any other non-Jew. Here the status of the father is totally irrelevant and the child, after proselytizing according to Jewish law, will assume the status of a legitimate Israelite like all other proselytes; even if his father is a *mamzer* this will not affect the status of the proselyte child (Kid. 66b, *Rashi* ad loc.; Sh. Ar., EH 4:20). For the case of a child when either one or both of its parents is unknown see **Mamzer*.

The State of Israel

Questions of *yuḥasin* and paternity are apparently regarded as matters of personal status within the meaning of Act 51 of the Palestine Order in Council (1922), and therefore are governed by the personal law of the parties concerned – Jewish law in the case of Jews. The Supreme Court of Israel, however, has so far refrained from adopting a clear stand on the matter and has left it as a *quaere* (PD 5 (1951), 1341ff.; 17 (1963), 2751, 2755). On the question of under what circumstances the offspring of a Jew and a non-Jewish mother can be registered as a Jew for the purposes of the population registration law – registration which in itself does not serve as proof that the person registered is a Jew – the Supreme Court has held, by a majority of five judges to four, that the subjective declaration of the parents should suffice unless it is obviously incorrect (PD 23, pt. 2 (1969), 477–608). With regard to the modes of proof of paternity of a child born of an unmarried mother, the Supreme Court has decided that the general rules of evidence and not the rules of Jewish law shall apply (PD 5 (1951), 134ff.).

[Ben-Zion (Benno) Schereschewsky]

Those Not Allowed to "Enter the Lord's Congregation" According to Biblical Law and the Rabbinical Solutions

The Torah (Deut. 23:4–9) lists certain nations from which no individual may be accepted as an Israelite: Ammonites, Moabites, Egyptians, and Edomites. With regard to the first two, the biblical prohibition applies across the board, with no limitation in time or number of generations, and is justified by observing that "they did not receive you [the Israelites] with food and water along the way when you left Egypt [...] and they hired Balaam son of Beor, from Pethor of Aram Naharaim, to curse you." Regarding the latter two nations, the prohibition is limited to just two generations, so that a third-generation descendant of an Egyptian or of an Edomite could be accepted as a Jew.

Moreover, the prohibition against the Ammonites and Moabites was restricted by tannaitic authorities to males alone (Mish., Yev. 8:3). According to the Talmud (Yev. 76b–77a), this law originated in the court of Samuel the Prophet, who announced this decree before he went to anoint David, a descendant of Ruth the Moabite, as king. Another *mishnah* (Yadayim 4:4) describes a dispute among the late first-century *tannaim* as to whether the ban was still in effect in their day. The controversy is settled with Rabbi Joshua's view prevailing: "Sennacherib came and mixed up [the identity of] all the nations"; hence, the Ammonites of their time were not those Ammonites whose acceptance into the Jewish community is prohibited by the Torah. The established *halakhah* holds, with respect to all four of the aforementioned nations, "Once they... have become commingled with the other permitted nations, they all became permitted" (Maim., Yad, Bi'ot Asurot 12:25), and therefore are "immediately permitted to enter into the Lord's congregation."

Efforts by the Rabbis to Avoid Determining *Mamzer* Status

To the above laws should be added the general principle that a person is presumed to be of fit and proper lineage, even if the factual truth is that he does suffer from some taint. The Mishnah cites a tradition stating that "Elijah will not come [in the future] to declare the pure, impure – nor to declare the impure, pure; nor to distance those who are near or to draw near those who were distanced, but only to distance those drawn near by force and to draw near those distanced by force" (Eduyot 8:7). R. Obadiah of Bertinoro interprets the citation as meaning that Elijah will only distance those who are publicly known to be tainted but were forcibly intermingled among the Jewish people, "but where there is a tainted individual in a particular family, but this is not publicly known, due to the family having intermingled [into the Jewish community], Elijah will let it remain so and let the family retain its presumption of legitimacy." On the basis of these statements, Rabbi Moses Isserles rules (Sh. Ar., EH 2:5) that, in a case in which it becomes clear to someone that one of the ancestors of a given family was a *mamzer*, he is not at liberty to reveal this: "but rather he should let the family continue to be assumed to be as fit and proper, since all families that have assimilated into the Jewish people will be fit and proper in the future." For an extensive discussion of this issue, see *Mamzer.

Tissue Typing and the Establishment of Paternity in the State of Israel

The Talmud (BB 58a) records a case where a man learned that nine of his children were *mamzerim* and only one of them was his real child. Before his death, he bequeathed his property to his real child, but he did not know which one was the real child. When the case was brought before R. Bana'ah, he ordered a test to determine which son, according to his characteristics, was the legitimate heir. *Sefer Ḥasidim* (§232) describes a method, considered scientific by the standards of the time, for determining paternity. Rabbi Samuel Strashun (*Hagahot ha-Rashash*) comments on the above talmudic source that Rabbi Bana'ah nevertheless refrained from employing the "scientific" test mentioned in *Sefer Ḥasidim*, because by doing so he would have revealed that the other sons were *mamzerim*.

With the development of scientific means for identifying family relations by genetic testing of tissues, these principles have become more significant. Rabbinical courts have considered the validity of a scientific test that produces results that contradict juridical presumptions of Jewish law, such as the one mentioned above, that "most acts of intercourse are attributed to the husband." Rabbi Shlomo Dikhovsky (File 866/41 13 PDR, 51) rules that one must accept tissue typing intended to establish paternity for purposes of ruling on child support payments (see *Maintenance), but for establishing *mamzerut* one may disqualify reliance on tissue typing because it is not infallible (p. 60). In a number of cases, the Rabbinical Court of Appeals has ruled that, even for determining maintenance payments, tissue typing to establish paternity may not be used as an absolute criterion, but there is need for supporting evidence as well.

This question was brought before the Israeli Supreme Court (CA 548/78, *Sharon v. Levi*, 35 (1) PD 736 per Justice Menahem Elon), that ruled that in Israeli courts tissue typing for establishing paternity should be admitted as evidence. The court emphasized, however, that:

> Tissue-typing would not, in every case, establish paternity. Moreover, in certain instances the court may decide not to make use of this test, when the test is liable to label a minor as "tainted," e.g., when a married woman claims that while she was married she became pregnant by someone other than her husband, and that the person by whom she became pregnant is the father of her child. If true, this statement would result in the minor being stigmatized as a *mamzer*. In this or in similar cases involving the establishment of status, proof provided by tissue-typing is insufficient to establish paternity (p. 748 of decision).

Thus, in such cases, paternity is to be established based on the juridical presumption that "most acts of intercourse are ascribed to the husband." This ruling is based on Jewish law's sensitivity to a person being stigmatized and branded with *mamzer* status, coupled with the halakhic principles of making various legal presumptions in order to avoid such stigmatization. Further on its ruling, the court cites some of the above-cited Jewish law sources on which it based its ruling.

In another ruling (CA 1354/92, *Attorney General v. Anon.*, PD 48(1) 711, Justice Menahem Elon) based on these considerations, the court ruled that, even when both parents give their consent to tissue typing for establishing the parenthood of a minor, such a test should not be conducted if it may endanger the minor's best interests, inter alia raising doubts about his legitimacy, and that these interests supersede the interest in investigating the truth.

The court added (pp. 739–40) that, although the rabbinical courts have no reason to suspect that such testing would fix an individual's status as a *mamzer*, since only rabbinical courts have the authority to do so, there are two reasons for discouraging such testing: first, acceptance of such findings in a civil court might socially brand the minor – itself a sufficient reason for prohibiting the testing. Second, there is no certainty that the rabbinical court might not change its stance and decide to recognize such results as sufficient to supersede the juridical presumptions cited above:

> Since no one can assure us that if the test is in fact performed and it indicates that the mother's husband is not the father of the minor, a rabbinic court might not accept these results and rule accordingly. As we have seen, the *halakhah* relies on various presumptions and fictions to preclude the tainting of a child as a *mamzer* by reason of his married mother having been impregnated by someone other than her husband. But as we noted, according to the *halakhah* as well, when it is clear that the child cannot be the offspring of the mother's husband, as in a case in which it has been proved that for 12 months there were no relations between the husband and wife, even the *halakhah*, for lack of alternative, declares the offspring a *mamzer*. Thus, several rabbinical courts have ruled against relying on tissue typing for proving paternity (p. 740). (See **Mamzer*.)

Establishing Maternity

With the development in the 1970s and 1980s of techniques for in vitro fertilization, discussion began as to how to decide who is to be considered the mother of a person conceived though such artificial fertilization, in the case where the fertilized egg has been implanted in the uterus of a different woman. Because no direct response to this question can possibly be found in the classic sources of Jewish law, halakhic authorities sought guidance from indirect sources, and even from non-legal sources, as to whether maternity is to be considered a function of pregnancy and birth or of the genetic source of the egg.

There is no uniformity of halakhic opinion on this point. Some have ruled that the genetic mother is the mother, but a majority of the authorities who have addressed the question hold the opinion that the surrogate mother – the mother in whose uterus the fertilized egg was implanted and where it developed until the child's birth – is the mother with regard to all legal entailments (Rav Z.N. Goldberg, *Teḥumin* (1984), 248–59; Rav A.Y. Halevi Kilav, *ibid.*, 260–67; Rav Z.N. Goldberg, *ibid.*, 268–74; Rav. E. Waldenberg, Resp. *Ẓiẓ Eli'ezer*, vol. 20 no. 49). Evidence for this is adduced from the law cited in the Talmud (Yev. 97b) whereby twin males born to a woman who converted to Judaism during her pregnancy are ineligible to marry each other's wives (see *Incest), in accordance with law pertaining to Jewish brothers. This proves that the act of birth creates maternity, for were it not so then the twin children would have been considered their mother's sons from the moment of conception, prior to her conversion, the conversion would have nullified that relationship, and they would not have been considered brothers.

In the State of Israel, the Agreements Relating to the Carrying of Embryos (Approval of the Agreements and Status of Offspring) Law – 1996 establishes a presumption that the birth mother is the mother, and only after the child is delivered to the intended parents do they, by means of a court-issued parenthood decree, become the child's parents for all intents and purposes, even when the fertilized egg originated with the intended mother. Notwithstanding, the law in question (§12 (b)) states that the parenthood decree does not effect any change in the laws of what is permitted or forbidden regarding marriage and divorce.

[Menachem Elon (2nd ed.)]

BIBLIOGRAPHY: A. Buechler, in: *Festchrift Adolf Schwarz* (1917), 133–62, 572; L. Freund, *ibid.*, 163–92; Gulak, Yesodei, 3 (1922), 10; A. Buechler, in: MGWJ, 78 (1934), 126–64; ET, 1 (1951[3]), 3–5, 276f.; 2 (1949), 21f.; 3 (1951), 346; 4 (1952), 741f.; *No'am*, 1 (1958), 111–66; M. Silberg, *Ha-Ma'amad ha-Ishi be-Yisrael* (1965[4]). **ADD. BIBLIOGRAPHY:** M. Elon, *Ha-Mishpat ha-Ivri* (1988), 1:302f., 670, 720, 814; 3:1327; idem, *Jewish Law* (1994), 1:361f.; 2:828, 888, 997; 4:1585; M. Elon and B. Lifshitz, *Mafte'aḥ ha-She'elot ve-ha-Teshuvot shel Ḥakhmei Sefarad u-Ẓefon Afrikah* (legal digest) (1986), 1:166–67; B. Lifshitz and E. Shochetman, *Mafte'aḥ ha-She'elot ve-ha-Teshuvot shel Ḥakhmei Ashkenaz, Ẓarefat ve-Italyah* (legal digest) (1997), 107–9; M. Corinaldi, *Dinei Ishim, Mishpaḥa vi-Yerushah – Bein Dat le-Medinah* (2004), 102–17; Z.N. Goldberg, "Fetal Implant," in: *Teḥumin*, 5 (1983/4), 248–59; A. Kilav, "Test-Tube Babies," in: *Teḥumin*, 5 (1983/4), 260–67; I. Warhaftig and Z.N. Goldberg, "Test-Tube Babies – addendum," in: *Teḥumin*, 5 (1983/4), 268–74; B. Schereschewsky, *Dinei Mishpaḥah* (1993[4]), 352–66; A. Steinberg, *Enẓiklopedyah Hilkhatit Refu'it*, 2 (1990/1), 128–38.

YULEE, DAVID LEVY (1810–1866), U.S. senator. Yulee, who was born David Levy in St. Thomas, West Indies, was taken to the U.S. by his father in 1818. After being educated at Norfolk, Virginia (1819–27), he managed one of his father's Florida plantations. He then moved to St. Augustine, Florida, where he studied law. After admission to the Florida bar (1832), Levy was appointed clerk to the territorial legislature. During the Seminole wars, he became known as a vigorous defender of white settler rights. He was subsequently elected to the legislative council (1836) and to the legislature (1837), and served as a delegate to the Florida constitutional convention (1838). From 1841 to 1845 Levy was the Florida territory's delegate to Congress, where he vigorously campaigned for Florida's admission to the Union. Upon its admission in 1845 he was elected its first senator, the first Jew in the U.S. Senate. In 1846 Levy legally assumed the name of Yulee soon after his marriage to the daughter of ex-governor Wickliffe of Kentucky, and his children were subsequently brought up as Christians. Yulee served as chairman of the Senate Naval Committee in 1846 where he advocated the acquisition of ironclad vessels and opposed the abolition of flogging as a naval punishment. He was defeated for election in 1851, was reelected in 1855, and served until 1861 when he resigned his seat. Although Yulee was a vigorous supporter of slavery and secession, his participation in the Civil War was limited to service in the Confederate Congress. In 1865 he was appointed by the governor of Florida to a commission charged with seeking Florida's readmission to the Union. Before the commission reached Washington, Yulee was arrested and interned in Ft. Pulaski. After his release a year later, he retired from politics and dedicated himself to the highly lucrative business of rebuilding Florida's ruined railway system.

BIBLIOGRAPHY: DAB, 20 (1936), 638; L. Huehner, in: AJHSP, 25 (1917), 1–30; B.W. Korn, *American Jewry and the Civil War* (1951), index.

YULY (**Aben-Yuly**, **Yulee**, **Levy-Yuly**), Moroccan family whose first known member was R. SAMUEL LEVY ABEN-YULY (d. after 1740), scholar, financier, and statesman. He was one of the Jewish favorites of the sultan Moulay Ismāʿil (1672–1727) and the counselor and then all-powerful secretary of the sultan Moulay Abd-Allah (1729–1757), who appointed him **nagid* of Moroccan Jewry. He added the name Yuly, the initial letters of "they shall come and bow down before Thee," Ps. 86:9, to his original name Levy. He died in *Meknès. His son, JUDAH ABEN-YULY, was one of the founders of the Jewish community of *Mogador, where he was appointed "merchant of the sultan" about 1767. Samuel Aben-Yuly's brother, JUDAH LEVY-YULY (d. after 737), was a powerful international merchant in *Salé and *Rabat, where he also managed the financial interests of various sultans and as head of these communities was known as *sheikh*. His serious conflicts with the rival *Ben-Kiki family disturbed the communities of northern *Morocco for a long time.

His son, ELIJAH LEVY-YULY (d. c. 1799), also held the position of "merchant of the sultan" in Mogador and *Tangier; at the end of Muhammad b. Abd-Allah's reign (1757–1790) he became a vizier, in which function he wielded extensive political influence. Samuel *Romanelli, who was acquainted with him and refers to him simply as Elijah Levy, criticizes him at length in *Massa ba-Arav* and asserts that, in order to escape the death penalty which was decreed against him by the sultan Moulay Yazīd (1790–1792), he converted to *Islam, only to die a few months later. Elijah, in fact, took refuge in England, where he died a Jew. His son, MOSES LEVY-YULY (b. c. 1782), who was born in Mogador, left England for the island of St. Thomas in the Caribbean in 1800. He amassed a considerable fortune in the wood trade and in 1816 established himself in Havana (Cuba), where he became an army purveyor. In 1819 he settled in Florida, becoming an influential pioneer when he set up immense plantations. His son David *Yulee was the first U.S. senator from Florida and the first U.S. senator of Jewish origin.

R. SAMUEL BEN BARUCH LEVY ABEN-YULY (d. after 1840) was *dayyan* in Meknès, Tangier, and then Gibraltar. He wrote two works on various religious subjects, *Hadar Zekenim* ("Splendor of the Elders") and *Kol Kallah* ("Sound of the Rabbinical Assembly," 1835), and traveled to Leghorn, where he published R. Pethahiah *Berdugo's *Rosh Mashbir* (1840). R. SOLOMON LEVY ABEN-YULY and R. JOSEPH LEVY ABEN-YULY of Meknès were among the most influential religious leaders of Moroccan Jewry before 1850. SAMUEL LEVY-YULY (1798–1872), born in Mogador, was sent to London as ambassador of Morocco and held this position until 1825. He was a business partner of Judah Guedalla of London and died in Portsea, England. JUDAH LEVY-YULY (1805–1878), born in Portsea, was an influential and wealthy merchant and one of the defenders of the rights of the Jews in Morocco. When Mogador was bombarded by the French in 1844, he was one of the most active organizers of the committee which was formed in London under the presidency of Sir Moses *Montefiore and Baron Anthony Rothschild to bring relief to the town and reestablish its Jewish community. He died in Mogador.

BIBLIOGRAPHY: E. de Avila, *Be'er Mayim Ḥayyim* (1806), 56b–70b; S. Romanelli, *Ketavim Nivḥarim: Massa be-Arav*, ed. by J.H. Schirmann (1968), index; *Voice of Jacob*, no. 93 (March 1, 1845); L. Huehner, in: AJHSP, 25 (1917), 1–29; J.M. Toledano, *Ner ha-Ma'arav* (1911), 132, 199, 229; Miège, Maroc, 2 (1961), passim.

[David Corcos]

YUNGE, DI ("The Young Ones"), American-Yiddish literary movement. Di Yunge was formed (1907) of young immigrant writers who professed themselves literary orphans and sought to create a new path in Yiddish literature. Eschewing the efforts of *Sweatshop Poetry, which preceded them on the literary scene, Di Yunge advocated literature as the communication of impressions rather than concepts and called for the creation of art for its own sake, the highlighting of the voice of the individual, the maintenance of stillness and silence in literature, and a stress on *shtimung* ("mood"), while aiming to emancipate Yiddish literature from didactic moralizing, sentimentality, and propagandizing. Di Yunge published their works in the existing Yiddish press, but also founded many of their own literary journals, including *Yugnt* ("Youth," 1907–8), *Troymen un Virklekhkayt* ("Dreams and Reality," 1909), *Literatur* (1910), *Fun Mentsh tsu Mentsh* ("From Person to Person," 1915), *Ist Brodvey* ("East Broadway," 1916), and, their most successful and sustained periodical, *Shriftn* ("Writings," 1912–26). In addition to publishing original fiction, poetry, and literary and social criticism, Di Yunge sought to enrich the canon of Yiddish literature through translations of masterpieces of foreign literature. Their most ambitious project was their eight volume *Di Verk fun Haynrikh Hayne* ("The Works of Heinrich Heine," 1918). Poets associated with this movement included Moshe Leib *Halpern, *Mani-Leib, Zishe *Landau, Reuben *Iceland, Moses *Nadir, Berl *Lapin, J.J. *Schwartz,

Joel Slonim, M. *Bassin, and A.M. *Dillon. Novelists and short story writers included David *Ignatoff, Isaac *Raboy, Joseph *Opatoshu, and M.J. *Haimowitz. Writers who contributed to later phases of the movement included Menahem *Boraisha, Ephraim *Auerbach, B.J. *Bialostosky, A. *Nissenson, Naphtali *Gross, and Z. *Weinper, and H. *Leivick. The dominance of Di Yunge was not effectively challenged until the rise of *Inzikhizm after World War I.

BIBLIOGRAPHY: A.A. Roback, *Story of Yiddish Literature* (1940), 258–73; R. Iceland, *Fun Undzer Friling* (1954); D. Ignatoff, *Opgerisene Bleter* (1957); B. Rivkin, *Yidishe Dikhter in Amerike*, 2 vols. (1947–59); S. Liptzin, *Flowering of Yiddish Literature* (1963), 206–35; A. Tabachnik, *Dikhter un Dikhtung* (1965); S. Liptzin, *Maturing of Yiddish Literature* (1970), 1–18. **ADD. BIBLIOGRAPHY:** R.R. Wisse, in: *Jewish Social Studies* 38 (1976), 265–76; idem, in: *Prooftexts* 1 (1981), 43–61; idem, *A Little Love in Big Manhattan* (1988).

[Sol Liptzin / Marc Miller (2nd ed.)]

YUNGMAN (Youngman, Jungman), MOSHE (1922–1982), Yiddish poet. Born in Khodorov, Galicia (Ukraine), Yungman worked in Soviet peat camps during World War II. Thereafter he led Zionist youth groups in Italy and immigrated with them to Palestine in 1947. Yungman's first poems appeared in post-liberation Yiddish refugee periodicals in Rome and Munich. Later he often contributed to literary journals in Israel, Paris, New York, and Buenos Aires and was among the founding editors of *Yung-Yisroel* (Haifa, 1954–7). His first book of poems, *In Hinerplet* ("In a Daze," 1947), includes the allegorical pageant "Rosh Ha-Shanah," which was performed in refugee camps. His poetry, celebrating both a world lost and a new world being built, was collected in several volumes, among them: *In Shotn fun Moyled* ("In the Shadow of the New Moon," 1954), *Vayse Toyern* ("White Gates," 1964), *Mayn Tatns Parnoses* ("My Father's Jobs," 1981). He translated some of his poems and several works of contemporary Yiddish writers into Hebrew, and a volume of poems of A. *Shlonsky, *Lider* (1971), from Hebrew into Yiddish.

BIBLIOGRAPHY: LNYL, 4 (1961), 264–5; J. Glatstein, *In Tokh Genumen* (1956), 378–86. **ADD. BIBLIOGRAPHY:** H. Osherovitsh, in: *Di Goldene Keyt*, 110/111 (1983), 228–34.

[Leonard Prager]

YUNG-VILNE ("Young Vilna"), Yiddish literary group, introduced in the daily *Vilner Tog* in 1929 with the headline: "Young Vilna Marches into Yiddish Literature." It aroused excitement through its miscellanies (*Yung-Vilne*, 1934–36), its contributions to local and international Yiddish journals, and individual books of verse and fiction. Principal members included poets Chaim *Grade, Shimshon Kahan, Peretz Miransky, Abraham *Sutzkever, Elkhanan Wogler, and Leyzer *Wolf, prose writers Shmerke *Kaczerginski and Moyshe Levin, and artists Bentsie Mikhtom and Rokhl Sutzkever. Dozens more were associated with the group, whose members were united by generation, place, a shared humanistic orientation, and the encouragement of local intellectuals like Zalman *Rejzen and Max *Weinreich. A Yung-Vilne evening in the Vilna ghetto, the participation of several members in the partisan underground, and the accomplishments of Grade and Sutzkever as leading postwar Yiddish writers assure that Yung-Vilne will be remembered as one of the great incubators of Jewish creativity in interwar Poland.

BIBLIOGRAPHY: L. Ran, 25 Yor Yung-Vilne (1955); E. Shulman, Yung-Vilne (1946). **ADD. BIBLIOGRAPHY:** J. Cammy, in: *Polin: Studies in Polish Jewry*, 14 (2001), 170–91; idem, in: *Judische Kultur(en) im Neuen Europa: Wilna 1918–1939* (2004), 117–33; *Di Goldene Keyt*, 101 (1980) (Yung-Vilne issue); A. Novershtern, in: *The Jews of Poland Between Two World Wars* (1989), 383–98.

[Sol Liptzin / Justin D. Cammy (2nd ed.)]

YUSHKEVICH, SEMYON SOLOMONOVICH (1868–1927), Russian playwright and novelist. An Odessa physician, Yushkevich published his earliest work in 1897 and was encouraged by Maxim *Gorki to write about Jewish life in Russia. In his plays and narrative works he often contrasted poor, but virtuous, Jews with their wealthy, but vulgar, coreligionists.

Yushkevich's plays include *Golod* ("Hunger," 1905), *Dina Glank* (1906), and *Komedia o svadbe* ("The Comedy of Marriage," 1911); and his other works include *Yevrei* ("Jews," 1903), stories; *Khaimka i Yoska* (19052); and *David Levin* (1918). A 14-volume edition of his works appeared in 1914–18. Yushkevich also wrote plays in Yiddish, some of which – such as the highly successful *Miserere* (1910) were also published in Russian (1923). After immigrating to the U.S. in 1920, Yushkevich contributed to the New York Yiddish press and published the novels *Epizody* (1923), which dealt with the Russian civil war, and *Leon Drey* (3 vols., 1928). He died in Paris, and a collection of his works appeared posthumously in 1927.

BIBLIOGRAPHY: S.S. Yushkevich, *Posmertnya Proizvedenya* (1927), 5–117 (introds.).

YŪSUF AS'AR YATH'AR DHŪ NUWĀS (MASRŪQ), the last (13th) and most famous king of the Ḥimyarī kingdom of *Yemen (522–525/530 C.E.–637–640/645 Ḥimyarī Era), who adopted Judaism in 380 C.E. Nothing is known about this important historical figure from any Jewish source, and nothing has been preserved in the historical memory or in the oral and written tradition of the Jews of Yemen themselves. All that was known about him originated in contemporary biased – clearly anti-Jewish – Christian literature in various languages and religious trends. These traditions also found their way into Arabic historical literature by means of South Arabian sources. But the updated epigraphic research since the end of the 19th and the middle of the 20th century, enabled scholars to better understand the story of the Jewish king. The first trustworthy depiction was given by H.Z. Hirschberg (1946), and later by Christian Robin (2003, 2005, and 2006). In the Ḥimyarī inscriptions the Jewish king is mentioned as Yūsuf As'ar Yath'ar *malik kull al-shu'ūb* (king of all nations), but in the Arabic historical sources he is known as Dhū Nuwās. Scholars differ about the meaning of the nicknames *Dhū Nuwās* and

Masrūq. Regarding the first, the common explanation refers to his alleged braids or ponytail, while other say that he was first the *qayl* (king) prince of a small locality named *Nuwās*. As to the second nickname, *Masrūq*, some say that it has the same meaning (the common one) of *Dhū Nuwās*, used by the Najrānīs, while other claim it is a disgraceful nickname used by his opponents: the wicked, the abominable or the killer.

Yūsuf was a descendant of the *tuba'* (royal) family of a Ḥimyarī dynasty, but he was not the son of his predecessor Ma'dīkarib Yu'fūr (519–522). He took control of the kingdom about June 522, after the death of the king who was placed on the throne by the Christian kingdom of Aksūm in Abyssinia. Some sources state that he was the successor of Rabī'ah, a member of the same dynasty; but some scholars believe he was a usurper. Judaism had already been adopted in the Ḥimyarī kingdom by the reformer king Abūkarib at the end of the fourth century, as proved by the total disappearance from that time of polytheistic divinities from the Ḥimyarī inscriptions and the multiplicity of Ḥimyarī Jewish inscriptions along with a complete absence of Christian inscriptions until 530. But Yūsuf himself had converted to Judaism, already prior to his accession to the throne, although there is a tendency in modern Arabic research to deny his Jewish conviction and to allege that he was Nestorian, namely Unitarian Christian (al-Faraḥ, 750), against all unequivocal evidence of epigraphy. However, Yūsuf's policy was to unite all the princely factions in his territory into one Jewish kingdom. After seizing power, Yūsuf revolted against Abyssinia, seeking to throw the foreign Ethiopian invaders out of Yemen. According to Christian sources (Syriac and Greek), as well as early Arabic sources, he conducted a fanatical policy of forced conversion to Judaism; he captured the Ethiopian garrison in the capital of Ẓafār (125 km south of *San'a) and burned the church there as well as other Christian churches in the country, such as that of Makhāwān (modern Mochā). Then he annihilated the Christian population connected with Aksūm and Byzantium, particularly in the coastal areas and in Najrān. But later Yemeni-Muslim scholars of the 10th–12th centuries offer a different story. They write about two Dhū Nuwās, one who indeed destroyed the Christians, and the other, who lived 400 years earlier and was a great king.

Two Christian contemporary sources, the Syrian 'Book of the Himyarites' (*Ketava de-Ḥimyarayya*) and the epistle of Simon of Beit Arsham, relate that Yūsuf maintained political relations with the *ḥakhamim* of *Tiberias, two of whom negotiated with the Christians who were besieged in Ẓafār. Basing himself on this information, Hirschberg put forward the theory about a Jewish international coalition of Mar Zutra, a scion of King David and direct successor to the position of exilarch in Babylonia who had immigrated to Tiberias and was backed by the Persian kingdom, and the Jewish king of Ḥimyar against Christian Byzantium and its allies in the kingdom of Aksūm and in Yemen.

The greatest event of his reign is the capture of Najrān, the large Monophysite Christian stronghold in northern Yemen. Christian sources quote John of Ephesus that Dhū Nuwās decided to persecute the Christians living in his kingdom as a response to the persecution of his co-religionists in their kingdoms, especially in the Byzantine Empire, and that after taking control of the town he burned its Christian residents. The first quoted number of dead in those sources was relatively small – 200 – but in the course of time it was gradually inflated and under their influence (also in Arabic sources, which were separated from the events by hundreds of years), rose to 70,000. Some scholars believe that there is also an allusion to the burning of the Christians in Najran in the *Koran (Sura 85:4–5).

The fall of Najrān and the alleged massacre of its Christians caused an enormous shock in the Christian world, which issued a call for a war of vengeance. Patriarch Timothy of *Alexandria wrote a letter to the Ethiopian emperor Ella Aṣbaḥa III Caleb urging an aggressive action against the Jewish Ḥimyarī king, and the Byzantine emperor Justin I offered the use of 60 ships. The Ethiopian forces, led by Caleb himself, started a crusade and were eventually victorious in a great battle on the shore of Zabīd in 525. Yūsuf, who despite his endeavors could not secure any allies from among the enemies of the Byzantine Empire or from among the local chiefs, was defeated and fell on the battlefield. A South Arabian legend, later infiltrated into modern Jewish literature (Friedberg 1893/9), relates that Yūsuf sprang into the sea astride his horse and was drowned. But in 1931 the German archaeologists Rathjens and Wissmann unearthed his tomb in Ghaymān, southeast of *San'a. Yemen, however, remained a restless province, and Caleb soon granted it independence under the Christian prince Abraha (535–565). Ḥimyar remained under the control of Aksūm until the conquest of the country by the Persian Sassanids c. 570/5.

During the 1950s five inscriptions were discovered within the proximity of Najrān, referring to Yūsuf with clear Jewish elements, all of them from June–July 523 (Ry 508, Ja 1028, Ry 507, Ry 513, Ry 515). These inscriptions enriched the information about the Jewish king. Three of them were written by Sharaḥbīl Yaqbul, the commander of the royal army and a member of the Dhū Yazan family. The two other were written by other officers of the same army. From Ry 507 and Ja 1028 we know the Arabic names of Yūsuf: *As'ar* and *Yath'ar*. The inscriptions Ry 507 and Ja 1028 provide interesting details, like the submission of military units from Najrān. It is hinted that the king suspected the Monophysite Christian community in Najrān of treason. Indeed, the agitation against the king in Najrān was effective and an open revolt broke out. A number of Jews in the town were killed, and its inhabitants openly refused to obey the king's orders. On this occasion Yūsuf would not forgive the inhabitants of the town and he set out to conquer it. The Christian sources concede that the king proposed peace in exchange for the submission of the town and that it was only after he realized that his offer went unheeded that he started to fight.

The Jewish elements are: *"lhn* for *Elohim* (Ry 508, Ja 1028), *Yosef* the name of the king (Ry 508, Ja 1028, Ry 507), *Rb-hd* or *Rb-hwd* – the God of the Jews (Ja 1028, Ry 515), and *Amen* (Ry 513). According to Ch. Robin (2006), however, the depiction of the victories of Yūsuf on his Christian opponents and the destruction of the churches in Ẓafār and Makhāwān (Ry 507, Ry 508, Ja 1028) was the main goal of the inscriptions, intimidating the rebellious Christian Najrānīs. This interpretation of the inscriptions that the conflict between Yūsuf and the residents of Najrān was basically political contradicts the strong impression received from Christian and Arabic sources that it was religious. Robin conjectures that Yūsuf was much less radical than Abūkarib in his religious politics. He just wanted a Jewish government without requesting to establish the organization maintained by Abūkarib. For him his opponents were first of all those foreign powers – Byzantium and Aksūm – who wanted to dominate Yemen, using the Christian Ḥimyarīs, and not Christians as a whole. Yūsuf's ambitions were more political and military than religious.

BIBLIOGRAPHY: H.Z. Hirschberg, *Yisrael ba-Arav* (1946), 76–111; idem, in: *Tarbiz*, 15 (1943/44), 129–43; idem, *Ereẓ Kinnerot* (1950), 80–89; idem, *Kol Ereẓ Naftali* (1968), 139–46; idem, *Yahadut Teiman – Pirkei Meḥkar ve-Iyyun* (1977), J. Ryckmans, *La persécution des Chrétiens Himyarites au sixième siècle* (1956); G.D. Newby, *A History of the Jews of Arabia*, (1988); A. de Maigret, *Arabia Felix* (2002); M. Al-Farḥ, *Tabābiʿat al-Yaman al-Sabʿin* (2002), 749–59; Ch. J. Robin, in: *Arabia*, 1 (2003), 97–172; idem, in: JSAI, 30 (2005), 1–51; A.Sh. Friedberg, *Zikhronot Le-vet David* (1893/9).

[Yosef Tobi (2nd ed.)]

YZRAELY, YOSSI (1938–), theater director and poet, professor in the theater department of Tel Aviv University. Yzraely was born in Jerusalem. After obtaining his diploma from the London Academy of Dramatic Art, Yzraely continued his B.A. studies at Bristol University, and completed his Ph.D. at Carnegie Mellon University in Pittsburgh. He wrote his doctoral thesis on Vakhtangov's staging of *The Dybbuk*. Yzraely taught and directed from 1969. Yzraely served twice as artistic director: at the Habimah National Theater, from 1975 to 1977, and at the Khan Theater in Jerusalem, from 1984 to 1987. In both cases his artistic direction was impressive, albeit controversial. He was a full professor in the Department of Theater Arts at Tel Aviv University, and between 1982 and 1989 he was visiting professor at Carnegie Mellon University in Pittsburgh. Between 2001 and 2005 he published five books of poetry.

Yzraely's first professional directing in Israel was Shlonski's *Uẓ-Li Guẓ-Li* at the Cameri Theater in 1965, which was a great success; the critics hailed the birth of a new theater director. This success was repeated in the productions that followed: Strindberg's *The Creditors* (Zavit Theater, 1966), Mrozek's *Striptease* (Zavit Theater, 1967), Beckett's *Waiting for Godot* (Habimah Theater, 1969), A.B. Yehoshua's *Night in May* (Bimot Theater, 1969), and Seneca's *Medea*. In all of these performances Yzraeli's directing method was based on a personal reading of the text and on the creation on stage of a powerful visual metaphor that brought to life his interpretation of the text with the aid of the actors' movements and gestures, the stage design, the music, and the lighting.

In 1972 Yzraely directed Dan Almagor's adaptation of ḥasidic tales *Ish Ḥasid Hayah* (*Only Fools Are Sad*, Bimot Theater, 1972). The performance enjoyed great success and led to a series of very personal interpretations of Jewish material on the stage. Thus, Yzraely adapted Agnon's novels for the theater while keeping the epic components of the narrative and using theatrical images to enhance the dramatic situations; *Hakhnasat Kallah* (*Bridal Canopy*, Habimah National Theater, 1972), *Sippur Pashut* (*A Simple Tale*, Habimah National Theater, 1979), *Temol Shilshom* (*Yesterdays*, Habimah National Theater, 1982), and *Tehillah* (Khan Theater, 1984) were very powerful performances in which Yzraely established an idiosyncratic theatrical language. He also adapted for the stage Rabbi Nachman of Bratzlav's tales *The Seven Beggars* (Khan Theater, 1979), and a theatrical collage, *Nothing Is More Whole than a Broken Heart*, based on Rabbi Nachman of Bratzlav's dreams, prayers, and tales (State Theater, Heidelberg, Germany, 1981, and Berlin Festival, 1982).

Yzraely is also internationally known for his *mise en scene* of classical drama: Sophocles' *Antigone* (Kresge Theater, Pittsburgh, 1990), *Oedipus* (Haifa Municipal Theater, 1992), Shakespeare's *King Lear* (Shakespeare in the Park Festival, Delaware Park, Buffalo, New York, 1983), *Measure for Measure* (Three Rivers Shakespeare Festival, Pittsburgh, 1985), *Anthony and Cleopatra* (Three Rivers Shakespeare Festival, Pittsburgh, 1989), *Romeo and Juliet* (Shakespeare in the Park Festival, Delaware Park, Buffalo, New York, 1993), and Corneille's *The Illusion* (an adaptation of *L'Illusion Comique*, Khan Theater, Jerusalem, 2002). Yzraely is a specialist in Ibsen's drama. His performances of *Peer Gynt* (Habimah National Theater, 1971), *The Enemy of the People* (Habimah National Theater, 1976), *Little Eyolf* (Khan Theater, Jerusalem, 1987), and *The Wild Duck* (Beer Sheva Municipal Theater, 1987) sought the points of connection between realism and symbolism. In 1987, Yzraely was given the Ibsen Medal by the mayor of Skien, Norway, for his distinguished presentations of Ibsen's plays.

Yzraely's international directing career started at the same time as his Israeli career. From 1966 he directed in Manchester, London, Heidelberg, Berlin, Pittsburgh, Buffalo, and New York. He received important awards and prizes for his performances: the award (twice) for best original production of the year from the Israel Ministry of Education and Culture (for *Utz-Li Gutz-Li* and *Ish Ḥasid Hayah*) and the David's Harp Award (for *Ish Ḥasid Hayah* and for *A Simple Tale*). In 1982 he was chosen by the Pittsburgh press as best director of the year for his staging of *Ghost Sonata*, and in 1986 he was chosen as best director of the year by the Pittsburgh *Post-Gazette* for his staging of *Measure for Measure*.

BIBLIOGRAPHY: G. Kaynar, *Interview with Y.Y.*, in: *Teatron 02* (June 2002), 64–73; idem, "Translation as Realization of Scripted Actions and Staging Metaphor: Y. Yzraely's Reading of Ibsen's *The Lady from the Sea*," in: *Assaph*, 16 (2000), 44–64.

[Nurit Yaari (2nd ed.)]

The letter "Z" used as an "S" at the beginning of the phrase Stetit Salomon ante altare. *The illumination shows King Solomon holding his scepter. Detail from a book of homilies, France, 1170. Cambrai, France, Bibliothèque Municipale, Ms. 528, fol. 249v.*

ZA-ZY

ZABARA, NATAN (1908–1975), Russian Yiddish novelist and playwright. Zabara was born in Rogachev, Belorussia. In the late 1920s he studied at the Institute of Jewish Culture associated with the Ukrainian Academy of Sciences. He began publishing in 1930 and wrote *Radioroman* ("Radio Novel," 1932) about the development of new military technology: novels about the happy life of Soviet Jews, such as *Nilovka* ("Nilovka," 1938), books of essays such as *Mensh un zeitn* ("Peoples and Times," 1938), a novel, *Hein vert geboyrn a velt* ("Today a World is Born," 1965: Russian trans. 1968), reflecting his front-line experience during World War II and his experience as a correspondent for the Soviet press in post-war Germany, and his novel-chronicle *A Poshete Mame* ("An Ordinary Mama," 1967) about G. Chudnovskiy, the first Soviet commander of the Winter Palace and red commissar of the city of Kiev.

Between 1950 and 1956, like the majority of the surviving Jewish cultural figures in the Soviet Union, Zabara was in jail and in prison camp (in Kolyma). He arranged Passover eve services (*sedarim*) for Jewish youth and introduced them to their national traditions and culture. On regaining his freedom, he became one of the first underground teachers of Hebrew in Kiev.

His uncompleted three-part historical novel *Galgal Ḥozer* ("All Repeats Itself," Moscow, 1979) aroused the interest of Jewish readers far beyond the borders of the Soviet Union. The work presents a broad panorama of Jewish life of the Middle Ages – depicting Jewish writers, poets, scholars, philosophers, and patrons of the 13th–14th centuries. Zabara often introduced into his novel sayings and legends taken from ancient sources, often citing them in Hebrew or Aramaic, then translating them into Yiddish. The publication of this was an exceptional event in official, i.e. published, Soviet Jewish literature, which generally avoids works reflecting Hebrew cultural creativity.

[*The Shorter Jewish Encyclopedia in Russian*]

ZABLUDOW (Pol. **Zabludów**), town S.E. of *Bialystok, in N.E. Poland. Jewish settlement in Zabludow began to develop toward the end of the 15th century. The wooden synagogue, built in 1646 and restored in 1765, is one of the best examples of the type in Poland. An important commercial center, Zabludow was the venue of the meetings of the Council of Lithuania (see *Councils of Lands) in 1664 and 1667. The Russian conquest in 1660 caused terrible suffering to the community. The minute book *(pinkas)* of the community, containing its records from 1650 to 1800, and of the burial society (1701–1819) are extant. The Jewish population increased from 831 in 1764 to 2,621 by 1897 (68.6% of the total population). During the 19th century weaving and tanning industries developed in Zabludow. Owing to deteriorating economic conditions, however, many Jews immigrated to the United States between 1905 and 1925. Zabludow reverted to Poland after World War I. In 1939 the community numbered about 2,000. During World War II, the Jews of Zabludow were mobilized by the Germans for work in the tanneries. On November 2, 1942, they were deported to the death camp at *Treblinka.

BIBLIOGRAPHY: Assaf, in: KS, 4 (1925), 307–17; YIVO, *Historishe Shriftn*, 2 (1937), 579–81; Bachrach, in: YIVO *Bletter*, 28 (1946), 317–28; *Mitteilungen zur juedischen Volkskunde*, no. 8 (1901), 162–68; M. and K. Piechotka, *Boznice drewniane* (1957).

[Yehuda Slutsky]

ZABOLOTOV (Pol. **Zablotów**), town in Ivano-Frankovsk (Stanislav) district, Ukraine. The Jewish settlement in Zabolotov developed in the 18th century, and by 1764 there were 986 Jews in the town. From 1772 till 1918 the region was part of the Austrian empire. In the early 19th century there was a strong ḥasidic trend in the community, due mainly to David Hager (d. 1848; see *Kosov), who founded a rabbinic dynasty centered in the town. The *Baron de Hirsch Foundation established a school and a bank. The Jewish population numbered 1,730 (49% of the total) in 1880; 2,009 (50%) in 1890; 2,092 (49%) in 1900; and 2,171 (46%) in 1910. Toward the end of World War I many Jews left Zabolotov because of antisemitic attacks. In 1921 there were only 1,454 Jews (41%) left. Between the world wars the town was under Polish administration.

[Shimshon Leib Kirshenboim]

Holocaust Period

Under Soviet rule (1939–41) the town's Jewish institutions were disbanded. Early in July 1941 Hungarian forces took Zabolotov. The Ukrainians organized pogroms against the Jewish inhabitants. The town passed to direct German rule in September 1941. The Germans imposed a *Judenrat, headed by Neta Feliks, but he was removed shortly after for refusing to fulfill German orders. On Dec. 22, 1941, the authorities carried out an *Aktion* against the Jews, killing and burying 900 Jews in trenches on the road to Trojce. About 100 Jews were shot in the town itself. This was followed by the deportation of 250 Jews on April 11, 1942, to an unknown destination. On April 24 orders were given for the general evacuation of the remaining Jews to the ghetto in *Kolomyya within a three-day time limit. The mass exodus of inhabitants was averted for a few days by the payment of a sum of money, but afterward everyone moved, except for 20 persons designated as "indispensable," who were allowed to stay. In the Kolomyya ghetto the refugees underwent starvation and suffered from disease. About 250 Jews working in the vicinity of Zabolotov were again allowed to live in the town, and were exempt for the meantime from deportation. On Sept. 7, 1942, the remainder of the Jewish community of Zabolotov, along with all the Jews in that district, were sent to Snyatyn. They were all deported to the *Belzec extermination camp. The Zabolotov Jews in Kolomyya were liquidated along with the other inmates of the Kolomyya ghetto in an *Aktion* in January 1943.

Societies of former residents of Zabolotov function in Israel and the U.S.

[Aharon Weiss]

BIBLIOGRAPHY: B. Wasiutyński, *Ludność żydowska w Polsce w wiekach XIX i XX* (1930), 124; R. Mahler, *Yidn in Amolikn Poyln in Likht fun Tsifern* (1958), index; *Ir u-Metim: Zabolotov ha-Meleʾah ve-ha-Ḥarevah* (Heb. and Yid., 1949), a memorial book.

ZABRZE (from 1915 to 1945, **Hindenberg**), industrial city in Katowice province, Poland. The Jews who first settled in Zabrze at the beginning of the 19th century belonged to the congregation of neighboring *Beuthen. An independent community was established in 1872. A synagogue was erected in 1865 and a cemetery opened in 1871. In 1931 there were 1,200 Jews living in Zabrze out of a total population of 70,000. The community was annihilated by the Nazis. The new community formed after World War II consisted mainly of Jewish repatriates from Russia.

ZACH, NATHAN (1930–), Hebrew poet. Born in Berlin, Zach was taken to Palestine by his parents in 1935 and grew up in Haifa. He studied at the Hebrew University and began publishing poetry in the early 1950s in the new journal *Likrat* ("Towards"), which he edited together with Benjamin Hrushovski. A leading member of a group which sought to free Hebrew poetry from pathos, ideological encumbrance, and an over-symbolical texture, he was also active in founding the journal *Akhshav.* In the early 1960s he edited (together with Ori Bernstein) another new journal, *Yokhani*. From 1968 to 1979 he lived in England and completed his Ph.D. thesis on English Literature at the University of Essex. After his return to Israel, he lectured at Tel Aviv University and was appointed professor at Haifa University. His first collection, *Shirim Rishonim* (1955), was followed by *Shirim Shonim* (1961), *Bi-Mekom Ḥalom* (1966), *Kol he-Ḥalav ve-ha-Devash* (1966), and *Nathan Zach* (1962), a selection of his poetry together with critical notes by the editor, Dan Tsalka. Later collections include, among others, *Ẓefonit Mizraḥit* ("North by Northeast," 1979), *Anti-Meḥikon* ("Hard to Remember," 1984), *Keivan she-Ani ba-Sevivah* ("Because I Am Around," 1996) and *Ha-Zamir Kevar Lo Gar Po* ("The Nightingale No Longer Lives Here," 2004). No doubt one of the seminal voices in contemporary Hebrew poetry, a writer who had a decisive influence on other, also younger poets, Zach's nonsymbolic, nonallusive diction marks a conscious break from the literary tradition, particularly from the poetic expression of A. *Shlonsky and N. *Alterman. Zach's oeuvre displays a variety of themes and genres and an astounding virtuosity of language, avoiding sentimentality and highlighting simple imagery. Full of humor, irony, and sophistication, and characterized by dramatic immediacy, his poems contemplate the transience of relationships, the folly of humans, love and death. Repetitions, wordplay, and a distinct rhythmic quality typify many of his poems. Together with Rashed Ḥussein he translated Arabic folk songs, *Dekalim u-Temarim* (1967). Zach also published *Zeman ve-Ritmus eẓel Bergson ve-ha-Shirah ha-Modernit* (1966) and a collection of essays, *Kavei Avir* ("Airlines," 1983); he edited the selected works of Ya'akov *Steinberg (1963). His book *Mot Imi* ("The Death of My Mother," 1997) is an impressive, moving homage to his mother, combining prose and poetry, the descriptive and the meditative. Bodily decrepitude and mental frailty are central themes in the book, as well as the portrayal of the mother, of Italian origin, as a stranger in a country which was to be her home. Zach also published a number of books for children, including *Ha-Nesher ha-Gadol* (2001) and *Devorah, Devorah* ("Devorah, the Bee," 2001). Together with poet Moshe Dor, Zach edited the anthology *The Burning Bush: Poems from Modern Israel* (1977). He also translated several plays for the Hebrew stage, by Max Frisch and Bertolt Brecht. He was awarded the Bialik Prize (1982), the Israel Prize (1995), and the Acum Prize for his life work (2003). Several collections appeared in translation: *Against Parting* (1967), *The Static Element* (1982), *Lost Continent* (French: 1989), *Selected Poems* (Italian: 1996; 1998), *Collected Poems for Children* (Italian: 2003). In 2004, Zach received an honorary doctorate from the University of Geneva for "his contribution to the renovation of the poetry of the second half of the twentieth century." A list of his poems translated into English appears in Goell, Bibliography, 1790–93, and further information is available at the ITHL website at www.ithl.org.il.

BIBLIOGRAPHY: G. Levin, "A Different Matter Altogether: N. Zach," in: *Modern Hebrew Literature*, 5:3 (1979), 43–47; G. Steindler Moscati, "Poesia israeliana: L'ironia ronantica di Natan Zach," in: *Oriente Moderno*, 3:1–6 (1984), 83–94; Y. Mazor, "Israeli Poetry – Between Bridled Sentiment and Exiled Sentimentality: The Case of N. Zach," in: *Modern Judaism*, 8:2 (1988), 157–65; H. Bar-Yosef, "Neo-Decadence in Israeli Poetry 1955–1965: The Case of N. Zach," in: *Prooftexts*, 10:1 (1990), 109–28; Y. Milman, *Romantikah ve-Nikkur be-Shirat Zach* (1995); idem, "The Poetics of Alienation in Nathan Zach's Poetry," in: *Orbis Literarum*, 50:1 (1995), 26–42; M. Haouari, "Intertextualidad en la poesia de N. Zach," in: *Miscelánea de Estudios Árabes y Hebraicos*, 48 (1999), 77–93.

[Anat Feinberg (2nd ed.)]

ZACHARIAS, JERROLD REINACH (1905–1986), U.S. physicist and educator. Born in Jacksonville, Florida, Zacharias joined the staff of the Massachusetts Institute of Technology Radiation Laboratory in 1940. He spent 1945 at Los Alamos working on the atomic bomb project, and in 1946 was appointed professor of physics and director of the nuclear science laboratory at M.I.T., where he pursued research on the radio frequency spectra of atoms. This led to the development of an atomic clock, the first practical atomic frequency standard.

In 1956 Zacharias founded the now internationally known Physical Science Study Committee to devise more effective methods for the teaching of physics. He was named institute professor and director of the Education Research Center at MIT in 1968. He was coauthor of *Medical Education Reconsidered* (1966).

ZACHARIAS, JOHN (1917–), Swedish stage director. At the Boulevard Theater, Stockholm, 1947–50, Zacharias directed *Thieves' Carnival* by Jean Anouilh and *Crimes and Crimes* by August Strindberg. In 1950 he became head of the City Theater of Helsingborg, and in 1953 head of the City Theaters of Norrköping and Linköping, a position he retained for 25 years. Among his most successful presentations were *Drei Groschen Oper*, *The Diary of Anne Frank*, *The Oppenheimer Case*, and *Fiddler on the Roof*.

ZACUTO, ABRAHAM BEN SAMUEL (1452–c. 1515), astronomer and historian. His ancestors were French Jewish exiles who had come to Castile in 1306. In his biblical and talmudic studies he was instructed by his father and R. Isaac *Aboab II, and he attended the University of Salamanca, where he specialized in astronomy and astrology, subsequently becoming a teacher in these fields. At the behest of the bishop of Salamanca, Gonzalo de Vivero, who was his patron and admirer, Zacuto wrote his major astronomical work, *Ha-Ḥibbur ha-Gadol* (1473–78). At this court, Zacuto engaged in astronomical research and writing until the prelate's death in 1480. The bishop, in his will, requested that all of Zacuto's Spanish writings be compiled and bound in one volume and placed in the cathedral library. Zacuto continued his astronomical researches in the service of Don Juan de Zuñiga, grand master of the Order of Knights of Alcántara, and settled in Gata in the province of Cáceres. Under his aegis, he wrote his book on the influence of the stars, *Tratado breve en las influencias del cielo*, to which he appended a treatise on solar and lunar eclipses, *De las eclipses del sol y de la luna*. The work was apparently written in Hebrew, but is extant only in its Castilian translation (published by J. de Carválho in 1928; see bibl.). In 1492, when the Jews were expelled from Spain, Zacuto emigrated to Portugal, where he was appointed court astronomer by King John II. The king's successor, Manuel I, confirmed the appointment. Before sending Vasco da Gama on his sea voyage to India (1496), the king sought the advice of Zacuto, who then lived in the city of Beja, on a calculation of the position of the stars. He foretold the success of the expedition and that the Portuguese would conquer a large part of India. He also instructed the sailors in the use of his newly perfected *astrolabe, his tables, and maritime charts, with which Da Gama's ships were equipped. Da Gama himself also consulted Zacuto in Lisbon before he set sail. In 1497, when King Manuel forced all Jews in his country to convert, Zacuto left Portugal and went to North Africa. Twice he and his son Samuel were taken prisoner, but they finally reached Tunis. In 1504, during his sojourn in Tunis, he completed the *Sefer ha-Yuḥasin* (last edition 1963), a book of genealogies, on which he had worked for many years.

Zacuto's achievements in astronomy were many: his astrolabe of copper, the first of its kind (previously they had been made of wood), enabled sailors to determine the position of the sun with greater precision; his astronomical tables, based on the Alphonsine tables, were an improvement on the latter. They permitted sailors to ascertain latitudes without recourse to the meridian of the sun, and to calculate solar and lunar eclipses with greater accuracy. While frequently quoting his predecessors, Zacuto also draws attention to their deficiencies. Proudly he asserts: "I, Abraham Zacuto, the author, have corrected all the books (containing the Alphonsine tables) in accordance with the tables that I have prepared, and my tables circulate throughout all Christian and even Muslim lands" (*Yuḥasin*, 222a). Zacuto's astronomical findings played an important role in the Spanish and Portuguese discoveries. Columbus used his tables on his voyages, and on one occasion they were instrumental in saving him and his crew from certain death. Knowing from the Zacuto tables that a lunar eclipse was imminent, Columbus threatened the natives that he would deprive them of the light of the moon as well as of the sun. (A copy of the tables, with Columbus' notes, is preserved in Seville). Zacuto's astronomical work *HaḤibbur ha-Gadol* (the Hebrew original is extant in several manuscripts) enjoyed a wide reputation during his lifetime.

In 1481, it was translated into Spanish by Juan de Salaya, who had been professor of astrology and of logic at the University of Salamanca. (In 1931, F. Cantera Burgos published Salaya's translation together with his own, which is based on the original.) His pupil Joseph (Vizinus) Vicinho translated an abridged version of *Ha-Ḥibbur ha-Gadol* into Latin, under the title *Almanach perpetuum celestium motuum*, and then rendered the Latin into Spanish (both were published in Leiria in 1496). Vicinho's version is the only Spanish incunabulum published in Portugal. The two translations were republished by the Portuguese government in 1915 and 1922. In 1496, a revised Latin version of the *Almanach*, edited by Alfonso de Córdova, appeared in Venice. Vicinho's Spanish translation, transliterated into Hebrew characters and entitled *Be'ur Luḥot Kevod Rav Avraham Zakkut* by *Daniel b. Peraḥyah ha-Kohen, was published in the latter's *She'erit Yosef* (Salonika, 1568). The publication was mainly for the Spanish exiles. An Arabic translation of the *Almanach* is extant in Milan (Ms. Ambrosiana 338). *Ha-Ḥibbur ha-Gadol* or sections of it are referred to in Hebrew literature under various titles: *Ha-Ḥibbur ha-Gadol*, *Be'ur Luḥot*, *Luḥot Temidim*, *Tekufot u-Mazzalot*, *Tekhunot Zakkut*, *Almanak*, and *Almagest*.

Sefer ha-Yuḥasin, a work composed in the spirit of the writings of his predecessors (e.g., R. *Sherira b. Ḥanina Gaon, R. Abraham *ibn Daud, author of *Sefer ha-Kabbalah*, Maimonides and others who had written introductions to the Talmud), intended to outline the historical development of the Oral Law and to establish the chronology of the Jewish sages who had transmitted it. Meant for scholarly study by students of Jewish lore, and to stimulate debate, this work at times elucidates a particular law for the specific purpose of fostering greater faith. The originality of the research is mainly contained in the first two treatises of his book, which cover the period of the Second Temple, the Mishnah, and the Talmud. From the standpoint of completeness, these treatises are superior to anything written by Zacuto's predecessors and they laid the foundations for scholarly research by succeeding generations. In numerous passages, he takes issue with Maimonides and R. Abraham ibn Daud, to whose writings he refers as *Kabbalat he-Ḥasid*. Chapters three and four of *Sefer ha-Yuḥasin* discuss the succession of the **savoraim*, the **geonim*, and the rabbis. (In his treatment of the material Zacuto, by and large, follows the line of thought of Abraham ibn Daud.) Chapter five expounds the epoch from the beginning of the rabbinic period in Europe until the author's time (the period of the expulsions from Spain and Portugal). In the latter treatise, Zacuto bases himself on a Hebrew chronicle which was also the groundwork of similar writings by *Joseph b. Ẓaddik of Arévalo and *Abraham b. Solomon of Torrutiel (there is no reason to assume that the latter's work was known to Zacuto). A large part of the treatise, however, is original research and analysis, based on later rabbinic literature. Zacuto incorporated in the chapter the well-known story about the appearance of the *Zohar in Spain, by Isaac b. Samuel of Acre. The author disregarded the critical conclusions that might be drawn from the story and confirmed the belief that the disciples of *Simeon b. Yoḥai had compiled the Zohar. Consequently he relied on the Zohar in matters of *halakhah* and history. The sixth chapter is a chronological outline of the history of various nations and the scientific research and inventions carried out by their scholars. This treatise is based on Latin and Spanish works. While Zacuto's approach to astronomy is scientific in these analyses, his views are restricted by Jewish tradition and *aggadah*. He also seems careless and disparaging in his examination of gentile lore. The advantage in its study he saw mainly in that "it greatly assists the Jews dwelling among Christians to argue with them about their religion." *Sefer ha-Yuḥasin* was first published by Samuel Shalom (Constantinople, 1566) together with an introduction and notes by the editor, as well as a Hebrew translation of Josephus' *Contra Apionem*. It was next published in Cracow (1580–81) with the notes of Moses b. Israel *Isserles, and several times thereafter. In modern times, the work was published by Z.H. *Filipowski (1857) from an Oxford manuscript. It was reprinted (1925, 1963^2) by A.H. *Freimann, together with a biographical and critical introduction, and with corrections and notes that had appeared after Filipowski's publication. The complete sixth chapter, as previously published by A. *Neubauer, is also included.

Little is known of the last years of Zacuto's life. In 1513 he was in Jerusalem and stayed at the yeshivah of R. Isaac Sholal, where he compiled an almanac "in the holy tongue." Various passages in *Sefer ha-Yuḥasin* testify to his interest in the burial sites of the pious in Ereẓ Israel. In 1515 Zacuto was in Damascus. An eschatological passage prophesying the coming of the redemption in 1524 is found in a manuscript ascribed to Zacuto. There is, however, no substantiating evidence that Zacuto was still alive close to that date.

BIBLIOGRAPHY: Steinschneider, Cat Bod, 706–8; M. Steinschneider, *Die Geschichtsliteratur der Juden* (1905), 88–93; idem, in: HB, 19 (1879), 100f.; Graetz, Hist, 4 (1949), 366; Baer, Toledot, 2 (1959), 406, 540; J. Bensaude, *L'Astronomie antique au Portugal á l'époque des grandes découvertes* (1912), 6, 18–29, passim; Griffini, in: *Rivista Degli Studi Orientali*, 7 (1916), 88–92; B. Cohn, *Der Almanach Perpetuum des Abraham Zacuto* (1918); J. de Carvalho, in: *Revista de estudos hebraicos*, 1 (1928), 9–56; Marx, in: *Studies in Jewish Bibliography and Related Subjects in Memory of Abraham Solomon Freidus* (1929), 247f.; idem, in: I. Davidson (ed.), *Essays and Studies in Memory of Linda R. Miller* (1938), 167–70; F. Cantera Burgos, *El judío Salmantino Abraham Zacut* (1931); idem, *Abraham Zacut* (1935); idem, in: *Revista de la Academia de Ciencias de Madrid*, 27 (1931), 63–398; R. Levy, in: JQR, 26 (1935/36), 385–8; C. Roth, in: *Sefarad*, 9 (1949), 1–9; 14 (1954), 122–5; H. Friedenwald, *Jews and Medicine*, 1 (1944), 295–321; *Sefarad*, index volume to vols. 1–15 (1955), 375.

[*Encyclopaedia Hebraica*]

ZACUTO, MOSES BEN MORDECAI (c. 1620–1697), kabbalist and poet. Zacuto, who was born into a Portuguese Marrano family in Amsterdam, studied Jewish subjects under Saul Levi *Morteira (an elegy on the latter's death by Zacuto was published by D. Kaufmann in REJ, 37 (1898), 115). He also studied secular subjects. According to tradition, he later fasted 40 days "in order to forget the Latin language." He was a student in the *bet midrash* of Amsterdam and in his youth traveled to Poland to study in the yeshivot there. Zacuto was attracted by Kabbalah and refers in his letters to his teacher Elhanan, perhaps "Elhanan the kabbalist," who died in Vienna in 1651. He moved to Italy, remaining for some time in Verona. From 1645 he lived in Venice and served for a time as a preacher under Azariah *Figo. Afterward, he became one of the rabbis of the city and a member of the Venetian yeshivah. Between 1649 and 1670 he was proofreader of many books printed in Venice, especially works on Kabbalah. He edited the *Zohar Ḥadash* in 1658, and also wrote many poems for celebrations and special occasions. Zacuto tried to acquire the manuscripts of the Safed kabbalists, especially those of Moses *Cordovero and the different versions of the works of Ḥayyim *Vital. He befriended the kabbalist Nathan Shapiro of Jerusalem and the old kabbalist Benjamin ha-Levi, who served as an emissary from Safed in Venice for two years (1658–59).

At the outset of the Shabbatean movement, Zacuto tended to give credence to the messianic tidings, but he was opposed to innovations such as the abolition of *tikkun ḥaẓot* ("midnight prayers") and other customs. In the spring of 1666, in a letter to Samson Bachi, he took a positive but cautious stand in favor of the movement, mainly supporting its advocacy of repentance. After the apostasy of *Shabbetai Ẓevi he turned his back on the movement and joined the other Venetian rabbis in their action against *Nathan of Gaza when he came to Venice in the spring of 1668. At the same time he openly opposed the Shabbateans in a letter to Meir Isserles in Vienna, and in subsequent years rejected Shabbatean propaganda, despite the fact that his favorite students *Benjamin b. Eliezer ha-Kohen of Reggio and Abraham *Rovigo were among the "believers" (*ma'aminim*). Relations between Zacuto and these two disciples became strained because of their differences, when, for example, the Shabbatean scholar Baer Perlhefter came to Modena and Rovigo supported him. The Shabbateans on several occasions criticized Zacuto, whose conservative temperament displeased them. In 1671 he was invited to serve as rabbi in Mantua, but he did not go until 1673, remaining there until his death. He enjoyed great authority as the chief of the contemporary Italian kabbalists and corresponded with kabbalists in many places. He never realized his desire to settle in Ereẓ Israel.

Zacuto's published exoteric works include his commentary on the Mishnah, *Kol ha-Re-Me-Z*; he was known throughout his life as Re-Me-Z, from his initials (Rabbi Moses Zacuto). Part of the work was published in Amsterdam in 1719. Ḥ.J.D. *Azulai, in his *Shem ha-Gedolim*, noted that the manuscript was twice as long as the printed edition. A collection of halakhic responsa was published in Venice in 1760. A commentary on the Palestinian Talmud is lost. His major activity, however, was in Kabbalah. Zacuto opposed the mingling of the kabbalistic system of Cordovero with that of Isaac *Luria which was then current in some circles (Tishby, in: *Zion*, 22 (1957), 30) and for this reason he criticized Solomon Rocca's *Sefer Kavvanat Shelomo* (Venice, 1670) even though he composed a poem honoring the author (see Zacuto's *Iggerot*, letters nos. 7, 8). He went over the entire corpus of Luria's and Vital's writings and added many annotations under the name *Kol ha-Re-Me-Z* or the abbreviation *Ma-Za-La-N* (*Moshe Zakkut Li Nireh* – "It seems to me, Moses Zacuto"). Many of them are collected in the books *Mekom Binah* and *Sha'arei Binah* of Isaac Ṣabba (Salonika, 1812–13) and they have partly also appeared in different editions of the works of Vital and Jacob *Ẓemaḥ. Zacuto wrote at least two commentaries on the *Zohar. In the first, he continued *Yode'ei Binah* begun by his contemporary Joseph *Ḥamiẓ (up to Zohar 1, 39). Here, Zacuto used many commentaries from the school of Cordovero, the commentary *Ketem Paz* by Simeon *Labi and the first commentary of Ḥayyim *Vital. The printed part contains the commentary up to Zohar 1, 147b (Venice, 1663). For unknown reasons it was never circulated. One copy is extant in the library of the *bet din* in London, but there exist complete manuscripts (e.g., British Museum, Ms. Add. 27.054–27.057). *Mikdash ha-Shem*, his second commentary on the Zohar, was written for the most part according to the Lurianic Kabbalah, and was published in abridged form in the *Mikdash Melekh* of Shalom *Buzaglo. The complete commentary is found in the

Oxford manuscripts Opp. 511, 512, 513, 515, 516, 517. *Mezakkeh ha-Rabbim* (Oxford, Bodleian Library, Ms. Opp. 120), though ascribed to him, was not written by him. A long kabbalistic responsum to the rabbis of Cracow on the copying of Torah scrolls, *tefillin*, and *mezuzot* was published several times, in *Mekom Binah*, in *Kiray Sefer* by Menahem Meiri (pt. 2, 1881, 100–8; separately, Berdichev, 1890). Zacuto arranged *tikkunim* ("special prayers") for several religious ceremonies according to Kabbalah. These were often reprinted and had great influence, especially on the religious life in Italy. They include *Sefer ha-Tikkunim* (a *tikkun* for the eve of Shavuot and Hoshana Rabba; Venice, 1659), *Mishmeret ha-Ḥodesh* (*ibid.*, 1660), *Tikkun Shovavim* (the initials of the first six sections of Exodus), i.e., a *tikkun* for fasts undertaken in expiation for nocturnal ejaculations (*ibid.*, 1673), and *Tikkun Ḥaẓot* (*ibid.*, 1704). All these were arranged under the influence of Benjamin ha-Levi and Nathan Shapiro.

A major part of Zacuto's poetry is devoted to kabbalistic subjects, such as his poems in the book *Ḥen Kol Ḥadash* (Amsterdam, 1712), and in *Tofteh Arukh* (a description of hell; Venice, 1715; see below). Besides this he arranged voluminous *collectanea* on kabbalistic subjects. The first was *Shibbolet shel Leket*, on all the books of the Bible (Scholem, *Kitvei Yad be-Kabbalah*, 1930, p. 153, para. 107). This was followed by *Remez ha-Romez* on numbers, **gematria*, and explanations of Holy Names according to numerology (Ms. British Museum, Margoliouth 853); *Erkhei Kinnuyim*, selections from the Lurianic Kabbalah in alphabetical order (complete in Ms. Jerusalem 110). Parts of this work were published at the end of *Golel Or* by Meir *Bikayam (1737) and at the end of Bikayam's *Me'ir Bat Ayin* (1755). Another anthology, in alphabetical order, was published as *Em la-Binah*, part of his *Sha'arei Binah* (1813). *Shorshei ha-Shemot*, also called *Mekor ha-Shemot*, is a collection of practical Kabbalah according to the order of the magical "names." This work was widely circulated in manuscript and went through several versions by North African kabbalists. A complete manuscript is in Jerusalem (8° 2454). Essays on kabbalistic subjects have remained in several manuscripts; also a number of important collections of Zacuto's letters are preserved, e.g., Budapest 459 (in his own handwriting); Jerusalem 8° 1466; British Museum Ms. Or. 9165 (in his handwriting); Jewish Theological Seminary, N.Y. Mss. 9906 and 11478; and in the Eẓ Ḥayyim Library in Amsterdam, C15. Only a few were published in *Iggerot ha-Re-Me-Z* (Leghorn, 1780).

[Gershom Scholem]

Yesod Olam

Zacuto was the author of the first biblical *drama in Hebrew literature, *Yesod Olam* (ed. D.J. Maroni, 1874; ed. A. Berliner, 1874). The play was not published during the author's lifetime, apparently because it comprised only part (estimated at one-third) of a projected lengthy work portraying Abraham in the major stages of his life as a righteous man on whom the entire world rests. Only the first part (and perhaps not all of it) was finished; this deals with the midrashic legend of the shattering of the household idols in Terah's home, the trial before King Nimrod, Abraham's deliverance from the fiery furnace, and the death of Haran. The play was written according to the classical rules of dramatic theory as they had developed in the 16th and early 17th centuries, but no particular model can be discerned. The author maintained the three unities – of plot, time, and place – even to extremes. No stage effects were introduced and therefore leading characters speak lengthy monologues. The plot is simple and concentrates on the best-known details of the legend while omitting all the minor ones. The hero, Abraham, is portrayed as an exalted and philosophic personality against whom the idol worshipers and the hedonists rebel. The philosophy of the play is rationalist-humanist and Abraham's views are remarkably similar to those of Maimonides; there is no trace of kabbalistic influence.

The style too is classical and the play is composed almost entirely in sonnets. Sentences are generally short and comprehensible, but the language is flowery. Though the vocabulary is largely drawn from the Bible, Zacuto does not hesitate to use talmudic idioms. No details exist from which the exact date of composition can be determined. However, it is clear that Zacuto wrote the play before he became a kabbalist of the Lurianic school. The play treats at length the theory of the immortality of the soul, which is rejected by Nimrod and his sages while Abraham defends it. This is clearly an echo of the dispute over the views of Uriel da *Costa, who angered Sephardi Jewry by his denial of the immortality of the soul. This fact supports the view that the play was written before 1640.

Tofteh Arukh

When he lived in Italy, Zacuto wrote his great dramatic poem, *Tofteh Arukh*. It appears that this work was inspired by Dante's *Divine Comedy*, as the subject matter is the afflictions of the soul in hell. In the opening verses, the dead man recounts his last illness and the arrangements for his burial. Afterward follows the episode of *ḥibbut ha-kever* ("tribulations in the grave"). The angel Duna commences the judgment and trial and with the aid of his angels drags the dead man through the seven sections of hell, showing the terrible punishments suffered by sinners. The conclusion is a description of the difference between the fate of sinners and that of the righteous, and toward the end the angel and the dead man praise God as the true judge. The poem consists of 185 rhymed stanzas of five verses each. The author employs many homonyms, assonances, and word plays, to an extent that becomes tedious. The work attained great popularity, especially among groups of kabbalists, such as *Ḥadashim la-Bekarim*. After its publication (Venice, 1715), a sequel titled *Eden Arukh* was written by Jacob Daniel Olmo. Since the second edition (1743) the two poems have been published together.

[Jozeph Michman (Melkman)]

BIBLIOGRAPHY: A. Apfelbaum, *Moshe Zacut* (Heb., 1926); Ghirondi-Nepi, 225; Landshuth, Ammudei, 2 (1862), 214–21; G. Scholem, *Kitvei Yad be-Kabbalah* (1930), 150–5; idem, in: *Zion*, 13–14 (1949), 49–59; idem, in: *Beḥinot*, 8 (1955), 89; 9 (1956), 83; Scholem,

Shabbetai Ẓevi, 653–4; A. Yaari, *Ta'alumat Sefer* (1954), 54–56, 67–75; idem, in: *Beḥinot*, 9 (1956), 77; M. Benayahu, in: *Sinai*, 34 (1954), 156; idem, in: *Yerushalayim*, 5 (1955), 136–86; idem, in: *Sefunot*, 5 (1961), 323–6, 335; I. Tishby, *Netivei Emunah u-Minut* (1964), index; Steinschneider, Cat Bod, 1989–92. YESOD OLAM: J. Melkman, in: *Sefunot*, 10 (1966), 301–33; idem, in: *Studia Rosenthaliana*, 1, pt. 2 (1967), 1–26; 3 (1969), 145–55. TOFTEH ARUKH: *Tofteh Arukh*, ed. by D.A. Friedman (1922); H. Hamiel, in: *Sinai*, 25 (1949), 304–19; 26 (1950), 101–12; M. Zacuto, *L'inferno preparato (transportato in versi Italiani da S.I. Luzzati*; 1819); C. Foa, *Tofte gnaruch ossia il castigo dei reprobi poema ebraico del secolo XVII di Mose Zacut, versione italiana in., prosa* (1901).

ZACUTUS LUSITANUS (**Abraham Zacuth**; 1575–1642), physician. Born in Lisbon into an illustrious Marrano family and a descendant of Abraham ben Samuel *Zacuto, Zacutus became an important figure among Jewish physicians and had a large practice. His non-Jewish name was Manuel Alvares de Tavara. In 1625 he moved to Amsterdam, where he openly returned to Judaism, was circumcised, adopted the name Abraham, and began to use the name Zacuth in his writings. He engaged in fruitful scientific activity, and published many medical books. His main strength is revealed in his accurate clinical descriptions of plague, diphtheria, exanthematous diseases, and malignant tumors; he was one of the first to describe blackwater fever.

His works were collected in two folio volumes, published posthumously in Lyons (1642). They include *De Medicorum Principum Historia* – a systematic description of all diseases, as investigated by physicians of preceding generations; *Introitus Medici ad Praxin* – 80 principles for the physician in his behavior at work; *Zacuti Pharmacopéa* – a compendium of pharmacy, listing also the new drugs imported from Latin America; *Praxis Historarium* – a survey of diseases in internal medicine; *Praxis Medica Admiranda* – a collection of selected rare cases. He anticipated discoveries that appeared in later medical literature, such as Jacksonian epilepsy as well as stomach disease accompanied by dark vomits (apparently peptic ulcer), which he treated with aluminum silicate. Although his writings were intended for a general readership, they included some autobiographical details which emphasized his Jewish origin.

BIBLIOGRAPHY: E. Carmoly, *Histoire des médecins juifs* (1844), 178–80; H. Friedenwald, *Jews and Medicine*, 2 (1944), 770; S.R. Kagan, *Jewish Medicine* (1952), 126–7; N. Koren, *Jewish Physicians in Eighteen Centuries* (1961); C.G. Joecher, *Allgemeines Gelehrten-Lexicon*, 4 (1751) 2136; J.O. Leibowitz, in: *Harofé Haivri*, 24 (1951), 113–22 (Heb.), 170ff.; S. Kottek, in: 22nd *Congress for the History of Medicine* (1970), 61.

[Joshua O. Leibowitz]

ẒADDIK (Heb. צַדִּיק; lit. "righteous man"), the title applied to an individual who is considered righteous in his relations with God and man. Noah is described as "righteous and wholehearted" (Gen. 6:9), and the Bible is replete with praises of the *ẓaddik*. Acting justly is the *ẓaddik*'s greatest joy (Prov. 21:15), and the righteous man is considered an abomination to the wicked (Prov. 29:27). The righteous live by their faith (Hab. 2:4), and when their number increases the people rejoice (Prov. 29:2). There are whole generations that are righteous (Ps. 14:5), and in the future the entire Jewish people will be righteous and thereby merit inheriting the land forever (Isa. 60:21). The *ẓaddik* will be rewarded with material prosperity, and his merit will endure forever (Ps. 112:3; Prov. 11:31). Even if he stumbles seven times, he will still rise up again (Prov. 24:16), and God will not suffer the righteous to famish (Prov. 10:3) or be forsaken (Ps. 37:25).

Nevertheless, the Bible also recognizes that there are *ẓaddikim* who undergo tribulations. Abraham pleaded against the possibility that the righteous would perish along with the wicked (Gen. 18:23), and Habakkuk described the wicked swallowing up the righteous (Hab. 1:13). Ecclesiastes also probed this dilemma, remarking that "there is a righteous man that perisheth in his righteousness, and there is a wicked man that prolongeth his life in his evil-doing" (Eccles. 7:15).

The rabbis described the righteous as individuals whose behavior went beyond merely fulfilling the letter of the law (BM 83a and Rashi ad. loc.), and as being scrupulous in monetary matters (Sot. 12a). One passage, however, suggests that the *ẓaddik* is on a lower level than he "that serveth God" (Mal. 3:18, and see Ḥag. 9b). According to one interpretation, Noah is only considered a *ẓaddik* because his moral standards were higher than those of his depraved generation (Gen. 6:9; Sanh. 108a; i.e., it was a relative and not an absolute standard). The rabbis praised the righteousness of the *ẓaddikim* as being greater than that of the ministering angels (Sanh. 93a), and held that if the *ẓaddikim* desired, they were capable of creative acts similar to those of God (Sanh. 65b). It was believed that the *ẓaddik* could annul the decrees of God (MK 16b), and that he is constantly remembered for a blessing by virtue of his good deeds (Prov. 10:7; Yoma 38b). The rabbis attributed the barrenness of the matriarchs to God's desire to hear the prayers of the righteous before he would bless them with children (Yev. 64a). It is because of the merit of the *ẓaddikim* that the world exists (Yoma 38b), and God will never destroy the world as long as there are 50 righteous people alive (PdRE, 25; cf. Gen. 18:26). People are divided into three classes: the completely righteous, the completely wicked, and the intermediate class (RH 16b; cf. Ber. 61b); although the verse "For there is not a righteous man upon the earth, that doeth good, and sinneth not" (Eccles. 7:20) implies that the concept of the completely righteous is purely theoretical. The completely righteous are immediately inscribed in the Book of Life on Rosh Ha-Shanah and they are similarly forthwith inscribed for everlasting life on the Day of Judgment (RH 16b).

For the concept of the *ẓaddik* in Ḥasidism, see *Ḥasidism. For the concept of the thirty-six *ẓaddikim* who inhabit the world in every generation, see *Lamed Vav Ẓaddikim.

[Aaron Rothkoff]

ẒADDIK, JOSEPH BEN JACOB IBN (d. 1149), philosopher and poet. Little is known of his life. From 1138 ibn Ẓaddik held the position of *dayyan* in Cordoba. He exchanged verses with

*Judah Halevi and was in contact with Moses *Ibn Ezra, his contemporaries, and wrote liturgical poetry which won praise from Judah *Al-Ḥarizi. His treatise on logic has been lost. His main philosophical work is preserved in a rather clumsy Hebrew translation replete with arabisms, under the title *Sefer ha-Olam ha-Katan* ("Book of the Microcosm") whose translation M. Steinschneider attributes to Nahum ha-Ma'aravi. The Hebrew text has been edited by A. Jellinek (1854) and by S. Horovitz (1903). Maimonides speaks highly of the author, whom he remembers from his early days in Cordoba, and describes his book as one of great significance, although he acknowledges that he had not seen it. Other medieval writers who quote it include David *Kimḥi, *Jedaiah ha-Penini, and Meir *Aldabi.

The *Microcosm* is purported to have been written in answer to a disciple's question as to what constitutes the "everlasting good and the state of perfection" to be pursued by man according to the teachings of the philosophers. The author is motivated to reply to this question by his desire to offer guidance to his generation, which he sees sunk in "the deep sleep of lethargy" and "drunk with the passions of this world," and which "retains of Judaism but the name and of humanity but the corporeal form." Like the Islamic "*Sincere Brethren" and ibn *Gabirol, he declares the "knowing of God and the doing of His will" to be the twin roads leading to man's ultimate felicity. As for a knowledge of God, it is best obtained by way of self-knowledge, seeing that man is but a microcosmic replica of both the corporeal and spiritual worlds. Thus, by self-inspection "man may climb the ascending stages of knowledge until he reaches the divine knowledge… for by arriving at a knowledge of his intelligent soul, he will achieve the knowledge of its Creator." The title of the book thus indicates its central theme. In treating it, the author shows himself to be steeped in the neoplatonic tradition.

The work is divided into four "discourses." The first deals with epistemology, ontology, and the nature of the corporeal world as well as of the human body. The second elaborates the microcosm theme and describes the nature of the vegetative and animal souls, life and death, sleep and the waking state, the rational soul, the intellect, and the spiritual world. In these two discourses the neoplatonic outlook is predominant. The remaining two discourses follow the pattern of *Kalām theology in that the third deals with the principles of theology, especially the unity and attributes of God; the fourth deals with "serving and disobeying God" and "reward and punishment." The work as a whole thus reflects the two then prevailing trends, *neoplatonism and Kalām.

In his theory of knowledge ibn Ẓaddik says of the senses that they perceive only the accidental qualities (the "shells") of things, whereas the intellect knows the genera and species, i.e., true nature of things which lies in their "spiritual being." There are two kinds of knowledge: self-evident and demonstrative. Like *Saadiah Gaon, he admits that tradition is also a source of true knowledge. Following Plotinus, he speaks of the rational soul as a "stranger in this corporeal world… wherefore men can make themselves understood to one another only through the medium of speech," whereas the souls in the celestial spheres do not require such a medium. In his ontology he follows Isaac *Israeli and ibn Gabirol in assuming that (spiritual) matter and form are constituent elements of the spiritual world. Consequently, the duality of matter and form applies to both corporeal and spiritual beings. All beings, furthermore, are composed of substance and accidents. Matter is potential substance which becomes actual substance only when clothed with form. All natural bodies are composed of the elements, and are therefore subject to generation and corruption. The human body participates in the nature of minerals, plants, and animals. Hence in men are found the courage of the lion, the timidity of the hare, the meekness of the lamb, and the cunning of the fox. His description of man's superiority over the animals (the "balance" of the four elements, upright stature, etc.) closely resembles Israeli's treatment of the subject in his *Treatise on the Elements*. Man is a "celestial plant," hence his head, which is his "root," is directed heavenward.

While the analogy between the human body and the corporeal world is manifest to everybody, the analogy between the soul and the spiritual world can be discerned only when the "veil of (spiritual) blindness" is removed. The rational soul is not corporeal. Ibn Ẓaddik's four proofs in support of this argument are derived, for the most part, from Plotinus. The rational soul is a spiritual substance. The body is not its place, but it is the "place" of the body. God created it from nothing in order that "it may proclaim His works and indicate His existence." He interprets Aristotle's definition of the soul in a neoplatonic sense (as did Isaac Israeli before him): The soul is a substance (not an accident) giving perfection to a natural body which is an instrument (of the function of the soul) possessing life potentially; this substance is the cause of perfection in man by virtue of the fact that it is the cause of life in the hereafter. The rational soul, which is "like a king" and which is destined to lead man to his eternal bliss, receives its "light" from the Intellect, the "matter" of which is the "perfect light and clear splendor" which "emanates from the power of the Creator, without an intermediary." This is a literal quotation from Israeli's metaphysical doctrine, which is itself derived from a pseudo-Aristotelian neoplatonic treatise describing the coming-into-being of the Intellect. His dependence on Israeli is pronounced in this as well as in other matters.

In his Divine attributes he takes issue with the Kalām version, and following largely *Baḥya ibn Paquda's view of the unity of God and the exclusively negative sense of all qualities predicated of the Divine essence, he admits only "attributes of action," and holds that God's essence is "incomparable and unknowable." "The eternal will of God" created the world, and the notion of time is inapplicable to this act. Creation is to be attributed "to God's abundant goodness and mercy and to nothing else." Non-recognition of God's goodness is tantamount to the denial of God. Gratitude is the first duty which religion prescribes. From Saadiah, ibn Ẓaddik adopts the distinction between the commandments of reason and those of revelation. But even the latter contain some profound, secret, and subtle meaning, as e.g., the commandment of the Sabbath, which teaches "that the world came into being by an act of Creation"; moreover, the Sabbath symbolizes the future world: for example, just as man will have nothing to eat on the Sabbath unless he has prepared the Sabbath meal during the week days, so he will have no share in the future world unless he prepares himself in this world with good deeds.

BIBLIOGRAPHY: Vajda, in: *Archives d'histoire doctrinale et littéraire du moyen âge*, 24 (1949), 93–181; A. Altmann and S.M. Stern, *Isaac Israeli* (Eng., 1958), index; Guttmann, Philosophies, 144–8; Husik, Philosophy, 125–49; Schirmann, Sefarad, 1 (1954), 544f.; 2 (1956), 686; Wolfson, in: JQR, 55 (1964/65), 277–98. For some older literature see bibliography in: JE, 7 (1904), 265, and JL, 3 (1929), 336.

[Alexander Altmann]

ZADIKOW, ARNOLD (1884–1943), German sculptor and medalist, killed by the Nazis. He was born in Kolberg, Germany, and lived mainly in Munich and Rome, settling in Paris in 1932. His work as a sculptor was smooth, serene, and highly finished. One of Zadikow's sculptures, the figure of the young David, was exhibited in the middle of the entrance hall of the Jewish Museum in Berlin in 1933. He continued his artistic work even when imprisoned in Theresienstadt, where he died.

See also *Art: In the concentration camps and ghettoes.

BIBLIOGRAPHY: M. Brenner et al., *The Renaissance of Jewish Culture in Weimar Germany* (1996).

[Jihan Radjai-Ordoubadi (2nd ed.)]

ZADKINE, OSSIP (1890–1967), sculptor. Born in Smolensk, Russia, Zadkine studied in London. After serving as a stretcher-bearer in the French army in World War I, he resumed his career in Paris. When the Nazis invaded France in 1940, Zadkine took refuge in the United States and taught at the Art Students League in New York. During this time his work was symbolic of the war period, and included "The Prisoner," "The Phoenix," and "The Warrior." After the war he returned to Paris. In his early years, Zadkine was a cubist, but in the early 1920s he felt restricted by the cubist indifference to human beauty. He then developed a freer and more baroque style. His work is more closely linked to tradition than that of most other members of the cubist generation. Features derived from African primitive art blend with those inspired by classical sculpture. His themes are frequently based on Greek mythology or stimulated by figures from literature and from the Jewish and Christian religions ("Job and His Friends," "David," "The Good Samaritan," "Christ"). He achieved world fame with his sculpture, "The Destroyed City," unveiled at Rotterdam in 1953. This monument, which rises 20 feet, is in the form of a mutilated giant, arms upheld in agony, and symbolizes the ruthless bombardment of the Dutch port city by German planes in 1940. Zadkine, whose preferred media were wood and bronze, produced numerous drawings and lithographs, as well as designs for tapestries. His autobiography, *Le Maillet et le ciseau; souvenirs de ma vie*, was published in 1968.

BIBLIOGRAPHY: I. Jianou, *Zadkine* (Fr., 1964); Staedtische Kunstgalerie Bochum, *Ossip Zadkine: Plastiken 1910–1959* (1960).

[Alfred Werner]

ZADOK (Heb. צָדוֹק, "righteous"), priest in the time of king *David. Zadok established a high priestly dynasty which continued until approximately 171 B.C.E., both in the First and Second Temple periods. He first appears, together with *Abiathar, as the priest in charge of the Ark at the time of Absalom's revolt (II Sam. 15:24–37). He and Abiathar joined David in his flight from Jerusalem, carrying the Ark with them, but the king ordered them to return to the capital to inform him of events in Absalom's court. There they had freedom of movement and were able to deliver messages to David about the rebels' intrigues (*ibid.* 17:15ff.). After Absalom's death, Zadok and Abiathar acted according to a message sent to them by David requesting them to suggest to the people that the king should be called back (*ibid.* 19:12–13). They are mentioned next to each other in both lists of David's chief officials (*ibid.* 8:17; 20:25), where Zadok is always mentioned before Abiathar. They are heard of again in the story of the dynastic struggle in David's last days (I Kings 1–2). When *Adonijah plotted to usurp the throne, Zadok remained faithful to David, while Abiathar joined the usurper (*ibid* 1:7,8). When David became aware of the plot, he instructed Zadok and *Nathan the prophet to anoint *Solomon king (*ibid.* 32ff.). For his loyal service in anointing Solomon, Zadok was made chief priest (*ibid.* 2:35), while Abiathar was deposed from the priesthood and banished to Anathoth (*ibid.* 2:26–27). Zadok must have died shortly afterwards, for he is never again mentioned and in the list of the main officials, which was compiled in the middle of the reign, it is his son Azariah who holds the title of priest (I Kings 4:2; the mention of Zadok and Abiathar in verse 4 is probably an interpolation).

Origin

The question of Zadok's origin is extremely obscure, for there is no clear and accurate picture of his background in the Bible. In the narrative he appears, as it were, from nowhere. In II Samuel 8:17 he is called the "son of Ahitub" and seems to be connected with the House of *Eli, but this verse is clearly the result of a textual corruption. Indeed, the prophecy of I Samuel 2:27–36 (cf. I Kings 2:27) makes it clear that the House of Zadok was considered to have supplanted the House of Eli. Nor are the genealogies in Chronicles and Ezra (I Chron. 5:27–34; 6:35–38; 24:3; Ezra 7:2), which treat Zadok as a descendant of the Aaronide house of Eleazar, any more reliable, for they repeat the error of II Samuel 8:17. Zadok thus remains without a genealogy in the ancient texts.

It seems likely, however, that the reason David made Zadok an equal to Abiathar, who had served him loyally from the time of his break with Saul, is connected with the position occupied by Zadok before he entered the service of David. Several hypotheses have been consequently advanced about his origin:

a) Zadok was the priest of *Gibeon, where the Tabernacle stood (cf. II Chron. 1:3), while Abiathar served before the Ark at Jerusalem (Auerbach; Grintz). This hypothesis is based on I Chronicles 16:37ff., where the two are mentioned as the principal sanctuaries in David's time. In support of this theory it is pointed out that after the exile of Abiathar not only was Zadok made the sole chief priest, but Solomon went to Gibeon to sacrifice (I Kings 3:4).

b) Zadok was appointed priest already by Saul, replacing Abijah (= *Ahimelech; cf. Jos., Ant., 5:350; Wellhausen).

c) The proper name Ahio in II Samuel 6:3–4 should be read as *'aḥiw*, "his [Uzzah's] brother," this nameless brother being Zadok (Sellin, Budde). According to this theory Zadok served the Ark at Kiriath-Jearim and afterwards remained at Jerusalem, as one of the two men who carried the Ark (*Uzzah would have been replaced by Abiathar; II Sam. 15:29).

d) Since Zadok does not appear until after the capture of Jerusalem and since his genealogy is not given, he may have been a priest of Jebusite Jerusalem before the conquest by David (Rowley). According to this theory, David permitted him to retain his priestly function in order to help reconcile the old inhabitants to their new master.

It is safer to admit that Zadok's origin is unknown; it can be assumed that he was indeed of levitical origin, though not from the same branch as the house of Eli.

The House of Zadok

I Chronicles 5:34–40 gives a list of the successors of Zadok as head of the priesthood in Jerusalem. It contains eleven names from *Ahimaaz (Zadok's son) to Jehozadak. This gives exactly 12 generations of priests from the building of the Temple under Solomon to its reconstruction after the Exile. The list of Zadok's ancestors given immediately before, in I Chronicles 5:29–34, also contains exactly 12 generations from the erection of the Sanctuary in the desert to the building of the Temple; and 12 generations of 40 years corresponds exactly to the 480 years in I Kings 6:1 as the period from the Exodus to the erection of the Temple. This symmetry is deliberate, and other parts underline the artificial nature of the list. Ahimaaz was undoubtedly Zadok's son (II Sam. 15:36), but Azariah was another son of Zadok, not his grandson (as I Chron. 5:35 states). Moreover, the list is incomplete; though it contains some names which are found elsewhere in the Bible (Azariah, II Kings 4:2; *Hilkiah, II Kings 22:4; *Seraiah, II Kings 25:18; Jehozadak, Hag. 1:1), it omits *Jehoiada (II Kings 12:8), Urijah (or *Uriah; II Kings 16:10; Isa. 8:2), and at least two others who are mentioned in the narrative part of Chronicles itself (II Chron. 26:20; 31:10). Another difficulty is that the series Amariah-Ahitub-Zadok recurs in identical form among the immediate ancestors of Zadok (I Chron. 5:33–34) and among his descendants (verses 37–38). The list, however, seems to express a real fact, namely the continuity of Zadok's line, but it cannot be used as the basis of a detailed history of his house.

J.M. Grintz attempted to reconstruct a list of the high priests by comparing those mentioned in Josephus (Ant., 10:152) with those retained in *Seder Olam Zuta* 5–6. He claims that the list he obtained by this process is authentic and that those names which appear in the list, but not in I Chronicles, represent a lineage other than that of the House of Zadok. This new, otherwise not attested, dynasty (probably of the House of Abiathar) began to serve, according to Grintz, in the Temple after Solomon's death, but was deposed during the reforms of King *Josiah, being, as it seems, suspected of idolatrous inclinations.

J.R. Bartlett, on the other hand, doubts that the high priests of Jerusalem were directly descended from Zadok. He claims that they were rather appointed in each case by the kings, on the basis of merit. According to this view, the term "House of Zadok" was fixed only in Josiah's time, in order to distinguish between the Jerusalemite priests and the priests of the high places.

The fortunes of the House of Zadok after the Exile are reflected in the position given to them in the books of Ezekiel and Chronicles. In Ezekiel 40–48, the exiled Zadokites expect as reward for their faithfulness that they alone shall perform the priestly functions in the new temple; the rest of the levites are to be reduced to the status of servants. The Book of Chronicles shows that after the return this program was not put into practice.

In the Second Temple period, the House of Zadok retained the high priesthood continuously until the Hasmonean revolt. In the Book of Nehemiah (12:10ff.) there is a list of high priests from *Jeshua to *Jaddua, i.e., down to the time of Darius II (cf. Neh. 12:22), or until about 400 B.C.E. This list may be incomplete, and it presumes that the succession always passed from father to son; yet it does collect the information given in Nehemiah, and the name before the last (*Johanan, 12:22) is found in the Elephantine papyri as the name of the high priest in 411 and again in 408 B.C.E. (Cowley, Aramaic, 30:18; 31:17).

There is no information about the following century and a half. After this, Josephus and the Book of Maccabees make it possible to trace the line from Onias *I in the middle of the third century B.C.E. to Simeon the *Just and to Onias *III, who held the office of high priest when Antiochus Epiphanes succeeded to the throne c. 175 B.C.E. His son, Onias *IV, was too young to succeed to his father's office, to which *Jason (II Macc. 4:7,20) and *Menelaus (II Macc. 4:23–26; though not a priest) were successively appointed by bribing the Seleucid ruler to appoint them. After the death of *Alcimus in 159 B.C.E., the office remained vacant for seven years (Jos., Ant., 12:413, I Macc. 9:54–57), until the Maccabean *Jonathan was nominated high priest by Alexander Balas. But only in the early years of *Simeon, Jonathan's successor, was the high priesthood irrevocably transferred from the Zadokites to the Hasmoneans. This seems to have given the appropriate occasion for the crystallization of the *Dead Sea Sect (see, e.g., Cross). The sect probably originated with a group of priests deeply disturbed by prevalent trends, especially in the high priesthood. The Hasmoneans were considered usurpers and the sect maintained the exclusive right of the Zadokites to fill the high priestly office.

Meanwhile, Onias IV had been conveyed by, or had gone with, a number of those who remained loyal to his father's memory to Egypt, where he obtained permission (c. 154 B.C.E.) from the Egyptian king to rebuild a disused temple at *Leontopolis (On) and to appoint "priests of his own race" to serve it (e.g., Jos., Ant., 12:388; 13:62, 79, 185). This last statement can refer only to priests of his own Zadokite family as distinct from the contemporary Hasmonean line in Jerusalem. This Zadokite priesthood presided over the temple at Leontopolis until it was closed by Vespasian in 73 C.E. (Jos., War, 7:433–646).

BIBLIOGRAPHY: A. Cody, *A History of Old Testament Priesthood* (1969), 88–93, 139–40 and passim; W.R. Arnold, *Ephod and Ark* (1917), 61–62; R.H. Kenne Tt, *Old Testament Essays* (1928), 82–90; E. Auerbach, in: ZAW, 49 (1931), 327–28; H.H. Rowley, in: JBL, 58 (1939), 113–41; idem, in: *Festschrift Alfred Bertholet* (1950), 461–72; Wellhausen, Proleg., 115–28; A. Bentzen, in: ZAW, 51 (1933), 173–76; K. Budde, in: ZAW, 52 (1934), 42–50; C.E. Hauer, in: JBL, 82 (1963), 89–94; M.A. Cohen, in: HUCA, 36 (1965), 88–90; R.A. Rosenberg, *ibid.*, 167–70; J.R. Bartlett, in: JTS, 19 (1968), 1–18; J.M. Grintz, in: *Zion*, 23–24 (1958–59), 124–40 (Eng. Sum. I–II); de Vaux, Anc. Isr., index, s.v. Sadoq; E. Sellin, *Geschichte des israelitisch-juedischen Volkes*, 1 (1924), 167; F.M. Cross, *The Ancient Library of Qumran* (1958), 128ff.

[Yuval Kamrat]

ZADOK (late first century B.C.E. and early first century C.E.), Palestinian *tanna*. Zadok was of priestly descent, and is known to have officiated in the Temple. On one occasion, when two priests disputed the right of precedence in offering a sacrifice and one stabbed the other, Zadok quietened the excited congregation by delivering an address, taking as his text Deuteronomy 31:1 (Tosef. Yoma 1:12). In the later talmudic *aggadot* about the destruction of Jerusalem, Zadok is described as having foreseen the destruction of the Temple, and fasted for 40 years in an attempt to prevent it. According to these traditions, his exertions so weakened him that *Johanan b. Zakkai found it necessary to ask Vespasianus, the Roman commander, to supply a physician for him (Git. 56b; Lam. R. 1:5). After the fall of Jerusalem, Zadok joined with other scholars at *Jabneh, where he issued the few halakhic decisions which are recorded in his name (Eduy. 7:1–5). He seems to have been on terms of personal friendship with *Gamaliel, and held an honored place in his Sanhedrin, where he sat on the patriarch's right (TJ Sanh. 1:7, 19c). The Talmud relates that he once spent a Passover in Gamaliel's house (Pes. 76a) and, together with Eliezer b. Hyrcanus and Joshua b. Ḥananiah, was invited to a banquet which the patriarch gave in Jabneh. On that occasion, he expressed his disapproval of the elaborate manner in which their host was praised by his colleagues, who compared the manner in which he served his guests to that of Abraham as described in Genesis 18:8. Zadok exhorted them to praise God instead (Kid. 32a).

Talmudic tradition reports that although Zadok was a pupil of the school of Shammai, he always made halakhic decisions in accordance with the teachings of the school of Hillel (Yev. 15b). He also taught *aggadah*, and the *Pirkei de-Rabbi Eliyahu* ascribes to him sayings concerning the fallen giants, the sacrifices of Cain and Abel, and the Flood. In private life, Zadok was renowned for his piety. Johanan b. Zakkai states that had there been but one other like him the Temple would not have been destroyed (Lam. R. 1:5). His most famous maxim was, "Do not make learning a crown with which to make yourself great, nor a spade with which to dig" (Avot 4:5).

Zadok II

Zadok II was the son of Eliezer and grandson of the above. According to one account, he was taken captive to Rome, where he was sold to an aristocratic household. He was granted his freedom when he refused to marry one of his mistress' beautiful slaves, pleading that he was a member of both a priestly and an influential Jewish family (Kid. 40a).

BIBLIOGRAPHY: Bacher, Tann; Hyman, Toledot, 34–36.

ẒADOK (Wilkenfeld), ḤAIM JOSEPH (1913–2002), Israeli attorney and politician, member of the Third to Ninth Knessets. Ẓadok was born in Rava-Roska in Poland. He attended a Polish gymnasium in Rava-Roska, and later studied philosophy and Jewish Studies at Warsaw University. He was a member of the Gordonia Movement in Poland, and of the Hitaḥadut-Po'alei Zion party. Ẓadok immigrated to Palestine in 1935 and received a law degree from the Government Law School in Jerusalem. He served with the *Haganah and Jewish supernumerary police until 1945, and as an officer in the Israel Defense Forces during the War of Independence. In the first Israeli government formed in 1949 he was appointed deputy attorney general, and in 1952 opened a private law practice, in which he remained until 1974, with an intermission in 1965–6.

Ẓadok was first elected to the Third Knesset in 1955 on the Mapai list. In the Fourth and Fifth Knessets he served as chairman of the Knesset House Committee, and in the Seventh and Eighth Knessets as chairman of the Knesset Foreign Affairs and Security Committee. He served as minister of commerce and industry in the course of the Sixth Knesset, from 1965 to 1966, resigning in November due to differences of opinion with Minister of Finance Pinhas *Sapir. He was appointed minister of justice in the government formed by Yitzhak Rabin in June 1974, serving for a period also as minister for religious affairs. Ẓadok was elected to the Ninth Knesset in 1977, but resigned in January 1978, returning to his private law practice but continuing to be active in the Israel Labor Party and in various public activities.

From 1964 to 1974 Ẓadok served as chairman of the Executive Committee of the Hebrew University, and from 1978 to 1980 he lectured there.

In 1971 he wrote, with Avraham Ben-Naftali, *Sidrei Shilton u-Mishpat* ("Government and Justice Procedures," 1971), and in 1978 he published *Sugyot ba-Mimshal be-Yisrael* ("Government Issues in Israel").

[Susan Hattis Rolef (2nd ed.)]

ZADOK (Isaac) BAR MAR YISHI (Ashi) (also known as **Mar Zadok**), *gaon* of Sura 816–818. Only a few of Zadok's responsa have been preserved, but most of his decisions, halakhic judgments, and ordinances, for example, the imposition of an oath upon a defendant who denies a claim on land (*takkanot shevu'ah al kefirat karka'ot*), were handed down by his successors in the gaonate. The *geonim* speak of Zadok with much reverence, *Amram, for instance, calling him "our master, who enlightens us." *Naḥshon Gaon was his son.

BIBLIOGRAPHY: H. Tykocinski, *Takkanot ha-Ge'onim* (1959), 58–59; Abramson, Merkazim, 2.

[Meir Havazelet]

ZADOK HA-KOHEN RABINOWITZ OF LUBLIN (1823–1900), ḥasidic *ẓaddik*, talmudic scholar, halakist, philosopher, kabbalist, and prolific author. He was born in Kreuzburg (Krustpils), Courland. His father, R. Jacob ha-Kohen, a Lithuanian rabbi, had a positive attitude toward Ḥasidism. R. Zadok was orphaned as a young child and raised by his uncle, R. Joseph ben Asher, a student of R Ḥayyim ben Isaac *Volozhiner. He was recognized as a prodigy from a young age, and known as the "*illui* of Krinik." After traveling throughout Poland and meeting various rabbis (seeking their endorsement on the *me'ah rabbanim* permit) he became a ḥasid and disciple of R. Mordecai Joseph Leiner of *Izbica Lubelska. After R. Leiner's death (1854) R. Zadok approved his close friend, R. Judah Leib *Eger, as the new *rebbe,* while he studied and wrote in piety and seclusion for more than 30 years. Following Eger's death (1888) R. Zadok was persuaded by the ḥasidim to become a *rebbe*. Although he refused to have his writings published during his life, he indicated before his death that he wanted them published posthumously. Most of those that were not in print before the Holocaust were destroyed in the Lublin ghetto. Extant from his writings are such early works as *Sikhat Malakhei ha-Sharet* (1929); halakhic responsa, including responsa to famous rabbis, collected in *Tiferet Ẓevi* (1909) and elsewhere; other halakhic writings; and books of ḥasidic teachings, from his first and best-known ḥasidic book, *Ẓidkat ha-Ẓaddik* (1902), through *Resisei Layla* (1913), *Maḥashavot Ḥaruẓ* (1912) and more, to later works such as *Dover Ẓedek* (1911), *Likkutei Ma'amarim* (1913), *Takkanat ha-Shavin* (1926), *Yisrael Kedoshim* (1928), and *Pokad Akarim* (1922). His late ḥasidic sermons were collected in the five volumes of *Peri Ẓaddik* (1901–24). His writings are deep and flowing, combining sharp intellectual analysis with ḥasidic psychological and mystical sensitivities, and a scholarly interweaving of a wide range of talmudic, halakhic, mystical, kabbalistic, ḥasidic, and philosophical sources. Among his main topics are the unity of God, psycho-spiritual growth, determinism, and sin (expanding on the teachings of R. Leiner), the Oral Law, the significance of the Jewish calendar and holidays, and topics in historiosophy, psychology, hermeneutics, and linguistics. His writings influenced many thinkers, including R. Elijah Dessler, author of *Mikhtav me-Eliyahu*; R. Isaac Hutner, author of *Paḥad Yiẓḥak*; and R. Gedalya Shorr, author of *Or Gedalyahu*.

BIBLIOGRAPHY: S. Unger, *Toldot ha-Kohen* (1924); A.T. Brombreg, *Mi-Gedolei ha-Ḥasidut*, 7 (1954); J. Hadari, in: *Reshit* (1962); *Sinai*, 46 (1960), 353–69; 53 (1963), 75–91; 56 (1956), 84–99; Y. Elman, in: *Jewish Law Association Studies: The Touro Conference Volume* (1985), 1–16; *Tradition*, 21:4 (1985), 1–26; *Journal of Jewish Thought and Philosophy*, 3:1 (1993), 153–87; A. Liwer, "Paradoxical Principals in the Writings of R. Zadok ha-Kohen of Lublin" (Heb., M.A. thesis, 1993); G. Kitsis (ed.), *Me'at la-Ẓadik* (2000); A. Brill, *Thinking God* (2002); S. Friedland, "Written Torah and Oral Torah and Aspects of Revelation and Concealment in the Writings of R. Zadok ha-Kohen of Lubin" (Heb., M.A. thesis, 2003).

[Amira Liwer (2nd ed.)]

ZADOKITES (Heb. *benei Zadok*; "sons of Zadok"), the *Qumran community's description of its members, especially its priestly members. The community conceived part of its duty to be the continuation of the functions assigned in the Torah to the Zadokite priesthood. The passage in Ezekiel 44:15ff., where the privilege of approaching God is reserved for "the priests, the levites, the sons of Zadok" because they remained faithful when the other priests went astray, is interpreted in the Zadokite Admonition as a reference not to one class but to three, indicated by the repetition of the conjunction "and"; "the priests and the levites and the sons of Zadok" (CD 3:21ff.). "The priests are those who turned from impiety in Israel and went out of the land of Judah; the [levites are those who] joined (*nilvim*) with them; the sons of Zadok are the elect of Israel, called by name, who arise in the latter days" (CD 4:2–4). Within the community the framework of priests and levites was maintained, (a) to teach Torah (Mal. 2:7); (b) to undertake what service was possible while the pollution of the Temple by the illegitimate, non-Zadokite, high-priesthood (from 171 B.C.E. onward) prevented them from ministering in it; (c) to make preparation for the day when they would resume the full service of God in a purified temple. In the *Manual of Discipline initiates into the community place themselves "under the authority of the sons of Zadok, the priests, who keep the covenant" and follow the interpretation of the law of Moses revealed to "the sons of Zadok, the priests" (1QS 5:2, 9); here the designation is more expressly confined to the priesthood within the community. "The sons of Zadok, the priests" have a similar authoritative role in the Rule of the Congregation (1QSa 1: 2, 24; 2: 3). The idea that the *Teacher of Righteousness himself was called Zadok (so H.J. Schoeps) is speculative, as is a suggested connection with *Zadok the Pharisee who was Judah the Galilean's comrade-in-arms in 6 C.E. (Jos., Ant., 18:4,9–10).

BIBLIOGRAPHY: S. Schechter, *Documents of Jewish Sectaries* (1970), introd. by J.A. Fitzmyer; A.R.C. Leaney, *Rule of Qumran and*

Its Meaning (1966), 91ff., 165ff.; H.J. Schoeps, *Urgemeinde, Judenchristentum, Gnosis* (1956), 71ff.; G.R. Driver, *Judaean Scrolls* (1965), 226ff.; North, in: *Catholic Biblical Quarterly* (1955), 164ff. (in spite of the similarity of name, to call these Zadokites "Sadducees" is misleading).

[Frederick Fyvie Bruce]

ZADOK THE PHARISEE (early first century C.E.), founder, together with *Judah the Galilean, of the "fourth philosophy" among the Jews of the late Second Temple period (see *Sicarii). This "philosophy" was, in effect, the theoretical basis and justification of the Jewish rebellion against the Romans, and according to Josephus was first introduced by Zadok and Judah during the assessment of Jewish property by the Syrian governor Quirinius (6 C.E.). This assessment, claimed the two rebels, amounted to no less than the enslavement of the Jewish people, and inasmuch as "God alone is their leader and master," there was no alternative but to make a bid for independence. Josephus stresses the zeal which Judah and Zadok inspired in the young, and attributes to them the subsequent strife leading up to the rebellion.

[Isaiah Gafni]

ZAFRANI, HAIM (1922–2004), Jewish scholar, writer, educator, and historian. Haim Zafrani was born in Mogador, *Morocco, where from 1939 to 1962 he taught school and became general supervisor of Arabic in the schools of Morocco. He was also the representative of the *Alliance Israélite Universelle in the country. In 1962 he moved to France where he held the chair in Hebrew at the Ecole Nationale des Langues Orientales Vivantes in Paris from 1962 to 1966 and worked at the Centre National de la Recherche Scientifique (CNRS), also in Paris, from 1966 to 1969. From 1975 he held the chair in Hebrew at the University of Paris VIII, where he was chairman of the department of Hebrew language and Jewish civilization from its establishment in October 1969. Zafrani's studies include the preparation of a critical edition and French translation of the Bible. This is part of a group project involving researchers from Paris, Jerusalem, Tel Aviv, Morocco, and *Egypt. Zafrani also studied and conducted research into the kabbalistic texts and mystical traditions of the Jews of the Maghreb. He published numerous books and many articles on Hebrew, Judeo-Arabic, and Judeo-Berber linguistics, and on Jewish thought in the Muslim West and in Islamic countries. Among his works are *Mille ans de vie juive au Maroc* (1982; Hebrew 1986) and *Kabbale. Vie mystique et magie* (1986), *Poésie juive en Terre d'Islam* (1977; translated into Hebrew), *Littératures dialectales et populaire juives en Occident Musulman* (1980); *Juifs d'Andalousie et du Maghreb* (1996; Spanish 1994); *Two Thousand Years of Jewish Life in Morocco* (2005; French 1998; Spanish 2001); *Ethique et mystique, Judaïsme en terre d'Islam. Le commentaire kabbalistique du "Traité des Pères" de J. Bu-Ifergan* (1991–2002); *Le monde de la légende: littérature de prédication juive en Occident musulman* (2003).

ADD. BIBLIOGRAPHY: N.S. Serfaty and J. Tedghi (eds.), *Présence juive au Maghreb: hommage à Haim Zafrani* (2004).

[Gideon Kouts / Sylvie Anne Goldberg (2nd ed.)]

ZAGARE (or **Zhagare**; Pol. **Zagory**; Yid. **Zager**), town in N. Lithuania on the border between Lithuania and Latvia. It had two separate Jewish communities: Old Zager and New Zager. New Zager was founded at the beginning of the 18th century by Jews who settled on the lands of the nobleman Umjastowski, after oppression by the townspeople. According to the census of 1766, there were 840 Jews in Old Zager and 313 in New Zager. As a result of its proximity to *Courland, Zagare became one of the first centers of the Haskalah movement in Russia and gained renown as "a town full of scholars and scribes." The *maskilim* circle of Zagare, which at the beginning of the 19th century was concentrated around the person of Ḥayyim Zak, became known as "the scholar of Zagare." On the other hand, Zagare was influenced by the centers of traditional Jewish learning of Lithuania; the majority of the Jews remained faithful to tradition and two yeshivot existed in the two parts of the town. Noted personalities born in Zagare include R. Israel *Salanter, Senior *Sachs, Raphael Nathan *Rabbinovicz, the *Mandelstamm family, K.Z. *Wissotzky, J. *Dineson, and the bibliographer A.S. *Freidus. The Jewish quarter in Zagare was among those damaged in 1881 in the outbreak of conflagrations which swept the Lithuanian communities as an accompaniment to the pogroms in southern Russia. After World War I, during the existence of independent Lithuania, this community declined. The Jewish population of the two communities numbered 5,443 in 1897 (c. 68% of the total) and 1,928 in 1923 (41%). After the German occupation of Lithuania in 1941, a ghetto was set up in the town, in which Jews from the neighboring localities were also interned. At the beginning of October 1941, the inhabitants of the Zagare ghetto were murdered.

BIBLIOGRAPHY: H. Frank, in: *Lite*, 1 (1951), 775–84; A. Zagerer, *ibid.*, 1605–07; E. Oshry, *Khurbn Lite* (1951), 234–9; A.S. Sachs, *Worlds that Passed* (1928), 41–44.

[Yehuda Slutsky]

ZAGREB (Ger. **Agram**), capital of the Croatian Republic, formerly Yugoslavia. The first Jews known to have lived in Croatia, and probably in Zagreb, were Mar Saul and Mar Joseph, King Krešimir's emissaries to ʿAbd al-Raḥman III, the caliph of Cordoba in the tenth century. *Ḥisdai ibn Shaprut asked them to convey a message to Joseph, king of the Khazars, on the shores of the Caspian Sea. During the 13th century Jews went to Zagreb from France, Malta, and Albania. Some Jews lived there by the end of the 14th century. The city chronicles of Zagreb for 1444 mention a *domus judaeorum* (community house or synagogue). Little, however, is known about Jewish life and activities, except that they were merchants and moneylenders and that they came from Hungary, Burgenland, or Moravia. In 1526 an expulsion order by Ferdinand I, which was linked to the conversion of most of Croatia into a "military zone," put an end to medieval Jewry's existence in Zagreb, and for more than two centuries no Jews lived there or frequented the city.

New Jewish settlers arrived in Croatia in the mid-18th century from Bohemia, Moravia, and Hungary and about 50 families lived in Zagreb in the 1840s. The community was officially founded only in 1806. In 1841 a smaller Orthodox community came into being. The *ḥevra kaddisha* was established in 1859. The first rabbi of the Zagreb community was Aaron Palota (1809–1849). In 1867 the new synagogue was inaugurated (it was completely demolished in 1941 by the pro-Nazi Ustashe). The building was constructed by Franjo (Francis) Klein, one of the important builders of Zagreb. The spiritual leadership of the community was in the hands of Rabbi Hosea Jacoby for 50 years, and under his guidance a school and a *talmud torah* were opened and religious life was organized. A new cemetery was built in 1878. The philanthropist Ljudevit Schwarz was the prime mover in establishing a Jewish home for the aged; it still functioned in 1970 as the Central Jewish Home for the Aged in Yugoslavia, and was assisted financially by the American Jewish Joint Distribution Committee. Jacques Epstein founded the first public assistance body in Croatia, the Association for Humanism. In 1898 a union of Jewish high school students was created, and became a training ground for future communal and Zionist leaders.

Antisemitism and Croat Nationalism

Croatian representatives were opposed to the official recognition of Jewish civil rights, which were not established until 1873. In 1858 there was a blood libel in Zagreb, and merchant and artisan guilds at times incited the population against the Jews, creating dangerous situations. Jews had to apply to Ofen (Buda), the Hungarian capital, or to the imperial chancery at Vienna, to seek safeguards and protection; later, they also had to apply to the Croat nationalist leader (of the so-called Illyric movement), Ljudevit Gaj.

It is noteworthy that individual Jews already sympathized with the Croatian revival in its early stages (Eduard Breier, Dr. Siegfried Kapper), while others were among the ideological or political leaders of modern Croat nationalism (Isaiah (Joszua) Frank, an apostate, and the lawyer Dr. Hinko Hinković). Frank's name was adopted by the separatist party, whose members were known as "frankovci" (followers of Frank); the same party later became violently fascist and antisemitic under Pavelić and his Ustashe.

Communal Life

The main body of Zagreb Jewry remained aloof from local politics, dedicating themselves to the internal affairs of the community, which became the largest in Yugoslavia. Between the two world wars Zionism drew a strong following in Croatia, and Zagreb was chosen as the headquarters of the Zionist Federation, which was led by Alexander *Licht. The Zagreb community also maintained a number of associations: a Maccabi sports club, a choir, women's and youth organizations, and a union of Jewish employees. The leading Jewish periodicals in Yugoslavia, such as the Zionist weekly *Židov* ("Jew"), were published in the city. Jewish contribution to the development of Zagreb was manifold. Jews were among the pioneers in export (wine and lumber) and local industry (furniture, beer, streetcars, etc.). Lavoslav (Leopold) Hartmann, the first librarian in Croatia, organized lending libraries, and also founded a printing press.

Jews also made a major contribution to science: the first chairman of the community, Dr. Mavro (Maurice) Sachs, was among the founders of forensic medicine in Croatia, and David *Schwarz, who lived most of his life in Zagreb, invented there the first rigid airship. Jews who were prominent in the arts included the painter Oscar Hermann; the sculptor Slavko Bril; the pianist Julius Epstein; and the bandmaster Anton Schwarz. A Jewish art monthly, *Ommanut*, was published there for five years (to 1941), ceasing with the Nazi invasion. Zagreb occupied a central position in the Yugoslav Jewish community. About 12,000 Jews lived there in 1941 after an influx of refugees from Germany, Austria, Czechoslovakia, and later Hungary. Following the German occupation of Zagreb in April 1941, Jews were persecuted, seized for forced labor, and murdered, with survivors sent to Jasenovac and Auschwitz at the end of 1942 and the beginning of 1943. The remnant reestablished the community after the war.

Rabbis Gavro Schwarz and Miroslav (Shalom) Freiberger, both victims of the Holocaust, were initiators of Jewish historical studies. In 1970 the Jewish population of the city was 1,200. After the secession of Croatia from the Yugoslav federation in 1991, a "Coordinating Committee" was formed consisting of a dozen congegations, with an Orthodox rabbi, Kotel Dadon, heading the Zagreb branch. The community, now calling itself Zidovka Opcina published a journal and literary magazine. A Documentation Center headed by Dr. Melita Svob deals with the claims of Holocaust survivors and the collection and publication of statistical and historical evidence. Around 1,000 Jews remained in the early 2000s.

BIBLIOGRAPHY: D.Z., *Zagreb* (1941); G. Szabo, *Stari Zagreb* (1941); L. Glesinger, in: *Jevrejski almanah*, 1 (1954); 2 (1955–56); 8 (1965–67); M. Despot, *ibid.*, 2 (1955–56); L. Šik, in: Židov, 15, no. 37 (1931). **ADD. BIBLIOGRAPHY:** Y. Eventov and Z. Rotem, *Toledot Yehudei Yugoslavia*, 2 vols. (1971, 1991); *Dva stoljeca povijesti I culture Zidova u Zagrebu I Hrvatskoj* (1988); I. Goldstein, *Holocaust u Zagrebu* (2001); M. Svob, *Zidovi u Hrvatskoj*, 2 vols. (2002).

[Zvi Loker]

ẒAHALON, Sephardi family, which after the expulsion from Spain settled in Italy and in Near Eastern countries. Many of them were scholars, rabbis, and physicians. ABRAHAM BEN ISAAC ẒAHALON (16th century) was a talmudic scholar and kabbalist. He wrote *Yad Ḥaruẓim* (Venice, 1595), a work on the calendar, and *Yesha Elohim* (*ibid.*, 1595), a commentary on the Book of Esther. In the introduction to his *Marpe la-Nefesh* (*ibid.*, 1595), a moralistic work based on kabbalistic principles, he complained that he had to travel much, wandering from place to place to find his livelihood. He completed this work in Baghdad in 1593.

JACOB BEN ISAAC ZAHALON (1630–1693) was born in Rome, where he also received a medical education and the degree of *artium ac medicinae doctor* at the university. In 1682 he became rabbi of Ferrara. His best-known work is *Oẓar ha-*

Ḥayyim (Venice, 1683), a manual of medicine, which was the third part of a greater work, *Oẓar ha-Ḥokhmot*. It was divided into 13 parts, the last part, on mental diseases, remaining unpublished because of lack of funds. With the medical information, he also stresses the ethical side of medical practice, gives practical advice to physicians, and urges them to recite weekly the physician's prayer he had composed. In addition he wrote *Margaliyyot Tovot* (*ibid.*, 1665), an abridgment of the *Hovot ha-Levavot* of Baḥya ibn Paquda in 30 parts so that one may read a part a day and complete it monthly. Each part ends with a prayer. In the introduction he mentions eight of his works that were in manuscript. He also wrote a number of responsa which are found in *Teshuvot ha-Remez* of Moses *Zacuto, in the *Paḥad Yiẓhak* of Isaac *Lampronti, and in *Afar Ya'akov* of Nathaniel Segre. He also translated into Hebrew a work of Thomas Aquinas. Jacob was the first in Italy to stress the value of preaching in the synagogue. On November 18, 1656, during the plague in Rome, when the synagogue was closed, he preached from a window to an assemblage on the street. Many of his sermons are extant in manuscript. The *Margaliyyot Tovot* contains a prayer for preachers.

MORDECAI BEN JACOB ZAHALON (d. 1748), his son, succeeded him as rabbi in Ferrara. He was also a physician. He wrote responsa, which were published under the title *Meẓiẓ u-Meliẓ* (Venice, 1715); some of them also appear in the *Paḥad Yiẓhak* and the *Shemesh Ẓedakah* of Samson Morpurgo. He composed a number of *piyyutim*, some of which were included in the service of the Ferrara synagogues. He also wrote *Megillat Naharot* (n.p. 1707), the story of the deliverance of the Jews during a great flood in Ferrara.

YOM TOV BEN MOSES ZAHALON (1559–1619/20) was one of the distinguished rabbis of Safed. He was ordained by R. Jacob Berab II (the grandson of Jacob *Berab I). He served as an emissary of that town between 1590 and 1600, visiting Italy and Holland. After returning to Safed, he was sent to Egypt and Constantinople, where he wrote some 600 responsa, many of which were published by his grandson Yom Tov b. Akiva, a rabbi in Constantinople in the second half of the 17th century, who appended to the volume his own novellae to chapters five and six of *Bava Meẓia* (Venice, 1694). Of interest are Yom Tov b. Moses' responsa to some of the communities of the Orient who sought his advice. Though himself a Sephardi, in a controversy between Sephardim and Ashkenazim he took the part of the Ashkenazim. Though a student of Joseph Caro, when the Shulḥan Arukh appeared, he disapproved of it, attacking it as a work for children and laymen.

Of his books the following should be especially noted: 1. *Magen Avot*: Commentary on *Avot de-Rabbi Natan* (in the Oxford Bodleian Ms.). 2. *Lekaḥ Tov*: Commentary on the Scroll of Esther (Safed, 1577). This was the first book published in Safed; it was published for a second time in a photocopied edition (Jerusalem, 1976). This work contains a long commentary on the sages' sermons on the Scroll of Esther, constituting both a literal and homiletic interpretation. 3. Novellae on tractate *Bava Kamma*. Chapters 5–6 were printed at the end of his responsa (Venice, 1964). 4. A total of 296 of his responsa were printed by Rabbi Yom Tov ben Akiva Ẓahalon in the Venice edition; another 240 responsa can be found in the Oxford Ms. and were published by the Jerusalem Institute (Jerusalem, 1980–81) in two volumes. The responsa deal mostly with subjects pertaining to *Hilkhot Even ha-Ezer and Ḥoshen Mishpat* in the Shulḥan Arukh. Yom Tov Ẓahalon's responsa were accepted as law. They contain historical information and details of customs and reforms in Safed and the Ashkenazi and Sephardi communities in Jerusalem, particularly the inferior position of the latter in comparison with the Ashkenzi community when it came to the distribution of charitable donations.

Ẓahalon reveals himself as forceful, uncompromising and sometimes sharp-tongued, though he tends to accept the opinions of earlier sages. He often disagrees with the rulings of Joseph Caro in the Shulḥan Arukh but also explains at times the language and reasoning of the Shulḥan Arukh.

BIBLIOGRAPHY: Vogelstein-Rieger, 2 (1895), 268–70; Savitz, in: *New England Journal of Medicine*, 213 (1935), 167–76; H. Friedenwald, *The Jews and Medicine*, 1 (1944), 268–79 (on Jacob); L.M. Herbert, in: *Harofe Haivri*, 1 (1954), 98–106. ON YOM TOV B. MOSES: Yaari, Sheluḥei, 238–40; Benayahu, in: *Kobez al Jad*, 15 (1951), 139–93; Nissim, in: *Sefunot*, 9 (1964), 9–20. **ADD. BIBLIOGRAPHY:** D. Tamar, Introduction to *Lekaḥ Tov* (1976), 22–26; Y. Sh. Spiegel, Introduction to Ẓahalon's *Responsa* (1980), 13–31.

[Isaac Klein / Yehoshua Horowitz (2nd ed.)]

ZAIẒOV, RINA (1932–2005), Israeli pediatrician who specialized in blood disorders and malignancy in childhood. She received her M.D. from the Hadassah Medical School of the Hebrew University of Jerusalem (1959) and trained in pediatrics in the U.S., where she developed her lifelong interests. She returned to the Beilinson Medical Center in Petaḥ Tikvah (1966) and became director of the national center for pediatric hematology and oncology (1973–97), professor of pediatrics in the Sackler faculty of medicine of Tel Aviv University (1988), and Josefina Maus and Gabriela Cesarman-Maus professor of pediatric hematology and oncology (1992). She established the department that became Israel's national center for treatment and research in blood disorders and malignant diseases in childhood. The center provided the most advanced methods of diagnosis and treatment, and support for patients and their families. She made major internationally recognized contributions to many clinical and laboratory and epidemiological research programs concerning genetic disorders of blood production, leukemia, lymphomas, bone tumors, tumors of the nervous system, and the genetic disorder Gaucher's disease. Her enthusiasm and humanity were also reflected in the comprehensive program for treatment and support that she established in the community. She had formidable teaching and organizational skills, recognized in her contributions to many national and international committees concerned with organizing clinical care, research, and education. From 1998 she was chairman of Kuppat Ḥolim's program for services in pediatric hematology and oncology. Her many honors included the Geifman Prize for developing pediatric oncology in Israel (1978), the First Prize for Research of the Childhood Leukemia and Lymphoma Conference (2000), the Kadezky Award for oncology research of Tel Aviv University (2001), and the Israel Prize for medical research (2005).

[Michael Denman (2nd ed.)]

ZAK, ABRAM (d. 1893), Russian financier. Zak was born in Bobruisk. An autodidact, he achieved great proficiency in mathematics and foreign languages. He occupied high posts in various financial institutions, and as chairman of the board of the Discount and Loan Bank of Petersburg, he made it the most powerful financial institution of the Russian capital. Zak was often consulted by the State Council and other official bodies on questions of finance, economics and railroad exploitation. He was offered the post of assistant minister of finance with the promise of promotion if he would convert to Christianity, but he refused. He was a member of the Jewish delegation to Czar Alexander III after the pogroms of 1881. He was active in the Jewish community and a member of the *Society for the Promotion of Culture among Jews, distinguishing himself by the great support he gave to Jewish students. Like many of the wealthy Jews of Russia he was opposed to Jewish emigration from Russia and to the establishment of a Jewish National Home.

BIBLIOGRAPHY: Weisenberg, in: YE 7, 659–60; E. Tcherikower, in: *Yidishe Shriften* 3 (1939), 109, 120; L. Greenberg, *The Jews in Russia*, 1 (1944), 173; *ibid.*, 2, (1951), 173.

ZAK, EUGEN (1884–1926), French painter. Born in Poland, he went to Paris in 1901. He was not influenced by the various new trends in painting, but rather harked back to Poussin and the Florentine masters. He endowed his subjects with an unobtrusive stylization and a subtle idealization.

ZAKEN MAMRE (Heb. זָקֵן מַמְרֵא; lit., "rebellious elder"), a scholar who disobeys a decision of the supreme *bet din* in Jerusalem. Its basis is to be found in the Bible: "If a case is too baffling for you to decide… you shall promptly repair to the place which the Lord… will have chosen and appear before the levitical priests, or the magistrate… and present your problem. When they have announced to you the verdict… you shall act in accordance with the instructions given you… And should a man act presumptuously and disregard [them]… that man shall die" (Deut. 17:8–12). There were three courts in Jerusalem; one used to sit at the entrance of the Temple Mount, another at the door of the Temple court, and the third in the Chamber of Hewn Stone (in the *Temple). Each of the first two courts consisted of 32 members, and the third was the supreme *bet din* – the Great *Sanhedrin of 71. If a scholar gave a decision and his colleagues in his town disagreed with him, he and his colleagues were obliged to go to Jerusalem for direction. At first they went to the court at the entrance to the Temple Mount, and each one expressed his opinion. If possible, they reached a decision, but if not, they turned to the second court. If this could not give a decision either, they and the members of the court which had not reached a decision appeared before the Great Sanhedrin in the Chamber of Hewn Stone. If the scholar then returned to his town and ruled or acted in opposition to the view of the supreme *bet din*, he was considered a *zaken mamre* and liable to the death penalty; however, if he merely taught as heretofore but without giving a practical decision, he was exempt (based on the text, "And should a man act presumptuously" (Deut. 17:12; Sanh. 11:2)).

A *zaken mamre* was not liable to the death penalty unless he was an ordained scholar, who was fit to pass judgment and whose decision had validity. His defiance of the supreme *bet din* had to be in a matter which if done willfully carried with it the penalty of **karet*, and if done inadvertently a sin-offering, or in a matter that if done deliberately would lead to a transgression carrying with it the same penalties, for instance, a disagreement on the intercalation of the year that would lead to leaven being eaten during Passover (Sanh. 87a; Maim., Yad, Mamrim, 3:5, 4:2). A *zaken mamre* is liable to the death penalty when he disagrees about a matter whose basis is in the written Torah and whose explanation is from the **soferim* ("scribes"), or about a *halakhah* given to Moses at Sinai, or about something derived from the 13 hermeneutical principles (see *Hermeneutics) whereby the Torah is interpreted, but not when he disagrees on a law of rabbinic provenance which has no basis in the Torah (Maim., *ibid.*, 1:2).

BIBLIOGRAPHY: ET, 12 (1967), 346–64.

[Abraham Arzi]

ZAKHO (**Zakhu**), town in the province of *Mosul in Iraqi *Kurdistan; location of an ancient Jewish community. During the 18th century Zakho was led by the *nasi* Sheikh Eliah the goldsmith. In 1827 there were 600 Jewish families, some of whom were wealthy. They earned their livelihood from raising cattle, as weavers and goldsmiths, and in other crafts as well. They had an old synagogue, followed ancient customs, and spoke Jabal (mountain) Aramaic. In 1848 *Benjamin II found 200 Jewish families in Zakho, some of whom were engaged in commerce and others in weaving. Most of them were wealthy. In 1880 there were 400–500 houses, half of which were owned by Jews. During the same year the town was ravaged by famine and a large section of the population, including many Jews, died. In 1881, 300 Jewish families lived in a special quarter; their political situation and security were in a very precarious state. In 1884 there were 510 Jews, among them merchants, spice dealers, and sheep breeders. In 1888 there were 1,500 Jews. In 1891 the Muslims attacked the Jewish community, looting the houses of the Jews, and set fire to one of the synagogues which was burned down together with its Scrolls of the Law. In 1892 the persecutions intensified. Jews were murdered; heavy taxes were imposed on members of the community; they were required to pay ransom, and many were arrested and tortured. The Tigris overflowed its banks and destroyed 150 Jewish houses; many Jews drowned and synagogues were destroyed.

In spite of all this, there were 300 Jewish families in the town in 1893 and 2,400 Jews in 1906. After World War I their situation improved. They had two large old synagogues; on one of them was an inscription dating from 1780. According to the official census of 1930, there were 26,835 inhabitants, including 1,471 Aramaic-speaking Jews. The decline of the economic standing of northern Iraq following the opening of the Suez Canal in 1869, which shifted the commercial pathway from the overland route (from Europe to India via Aleppo in Syria and northern Iraq) seems to have caused emigration to Baghdad and Palestine. The Jews of Zakho started to emigrate to the Holy Land in the middle of the 19th century, with *aliyah* intensifying after World War I. In the census of 1947 their number had decreased to 1394. They lived in a special quarter and most of them engaged in commerce. When the Iraqis opposed Zionism their situation deteriorated. Jews from Zakho were the first to emigrate to Palestine after 1920. Many settled in *Jerusalem, where they engaged in manual labor as porters, donkey drivers, stonecutters, builders, stone hewers, etc. Six thousand settled there before the establishment of the State of Israel. They built special quarters for themselves, such as Zikhron Yosef, Zikhron Ya'akov, Sha'arei Raḥamim, and others. With the establishment of the state, all the remaining Jewish inhabitants of Zakho emigrated to Israel.

The poetry of the Zakho Jews was published by J.J. Rivlin in *Shirat Yehudei ha-Targum* (1959).

BIBLIOGRAPHY: A. Ben-Jacob, *Kehillot Yehudei Kurdistan* (1961), 58–62; J.J. Rivlin, in: *Sefer Zikkaron le-A. Gulak u-le-S. Klein* (1942), 171–86. **ADD. BIBLIOGRAPHY:** *Enẓiklopedya shel Yehudei Kurdistan* (1993).

[Abraham Ben-Yaacob / Nissim Kazzaz (2nd ed.)]

ZAKHOR (Heb. "Remember"), black Judaizing movement in Mali comprising around 1,000 people. It was founded in Timbuktu in 1993 by the Malian historian Ismael Daidé Haïdara, whose followers claim to be the offspring of Saharan Jews. In a manifesto published in 1996, the members of Zakhor recognize themselves as Jews and declare themselves to be descendants of the Jews of Touat. The Touat, the region at the limit of the Sahara in western Algeria, was, up to 1492, inhabited by Jews involved in trans-Saharan trade. At that time, Sheikh Abd el Krim el Meghili, a scholar and a mystic, exterminated them and ordered the destruction of their synagogues at Siljimassa and Tamentit.

According to Zakhor, some of the Jewish survivors from Touat, following the routes of caravans, took refuge with other Jews settled along the Niger, but their safety was only temporary. Soon afterwards, in 1493, under the influence of the same el Meghili, Askyia Muhammad the Great, the ruler of this region, introduced an edict for the eviction of the Jews of the Songhai. They apparently found themselves in the position of choosing either to renounce their faith or to die. Haïdara, the leader of Zakhor, noted that "the Jews could not go further, in front of the great Nile of the Arabs [that is, the river Niger]. They stopped facing the Koran and the sword. They converted." This was how, he concluded, the black Jews became Muslims. Today, the members of Zakhor portray themselves as a small, early Jewish population which is said to have been superseded by the subsequent Islamic community, with only tiny remnants of Judaism surviving. The heads of the families who founded Zakhor relate that the three families constituting their community from the 16th century, the Levite Kehaths, now named Kati, the Cohens and the Abanas, were not in fact the first Jewish inhabitants of these regions.

In the 11th century, el Bakri and el Idrissi, the great Arab historians and geographers, referred to the presence of populations "who read the Tawrat" in what would become Mali. Abraham *Cresques, the famous Majorcan Jewish geographer, upon establishing the Catalan Atlas, in 1375, presumably located Mali and its emperor, on the basis of information from his Malian co-religionists. Leo Africanus who visited this region in the first part of the 15th century, the Tarikh el-Sudan of the 15th century, and the Tarikh el-Fetash of the 17th century, the essential corpus of sources of information about medieval western Africa, mentioned the presence of Jews in the region of Gao and Tendirma.

Under the aegis of UNESCO, the gradual discovery at Timbuktu of old manuscripts, some of which date back to the 13th century, constitutes an unpublished scientific treasure trove likely to bring much information about the possible settlement of Jews in this area.

BIBLIOGRAPHY: I.D. Haïdara, *Les Juifs à Tombouctou, Recueil de Sources écrites relatives au commerce juif à Tombouctou au XIXe siècle* (1999); J. Oliel, *Les Juifs au Sahara* (1994); M. Abitbol, *Juifs Maghrébins et commerce transsaharien du VIII au XVe siècle,* in Bibliothèque d'Histoire d'Outre-mer, Etudes 5–6, *200 ans d'histoire africaine, le sol, la parole et l'écrit* (1981); T. Lewicki, "L'Afrique noire," in: *Kitab al Masalik wa l-Mamedik d'al Bakri, (XIe siècle), Africana Bulletin,* 2 (1965), 9–14; V. Monteil, "Al Bakri, un routier de l'Afrique," in: IFAN, 30 (1968), 39–116; J. Cuoq, *Bilad Al Sudan, Recueil des Sources Arabes concernant l'Afrique occidentale du VIIIe au XVIe siècle* (1975); O. Houdas and M. Delafosse, *Tarikh el Fattash* (1964); Ch. de La Roncière, *Découverte de l'Afrique au Moyen Age* (1924).

[Tudor Parfitt (2nd ed.)]

ZALCSTEIN, GECL (1773–1841), dealer in books and ancient Polish manuscripts. A follower of the ḥasidic leader *Jacob Isaac ha-Ḥozeh of Lublin, Zalcstein opened a book and antique shop in Warsaw around 1800. On his many visits to the Polish aristocracy he obtained ancient manuscripts and books, thus acquiring an extensive knowledge of Polish works. He aided the historian J. *Lelewel and the bibliographer K. Świdziński in their research, and through his devoted assistance the libraries of the University of Warsaw and other academic institutions were enlarged. His shop became a meeting place for Polish intellectuals. In 1831 Zalcstein founded a mirror factory and transferred the management of his bookshop to his son, LEIB, a Kotsk ḥasid. After a few years of meager success Zalcstein closed the factory and returned to managing his bookshop. In the 1830s, because of his connections with Polish intellectuals, he was suspected of subversive activities by the Russian authorities. His wife took over the shop after his death, and his son Leib engaged independently in book-selling and publishing from 1820 until his death in 1860. His annual *Kalendarz Astronomiczny i Gospodarski* ("Astronomic and Economic Calendar") appeared for 40 years and was a pioneering work of agronomical information in Poland. Zalcstein's younger son, JONAH BAER, also opened a bookshop, and descendants of the Zalcsteins were prominent booksellers, publishers, and antique dealers in Warsaw in the 1920s.

BIBLIOGRAPHY: J. Shatzky, *Geshikhte fun Yidn in Varshe,* 2 (1947–49), indexes; K.W. Wójcicki, *Pamiętniki dziecka Warszawy* (1909), 58–59; S. Kastik, *Zdziejów Oswiecenia zydowskiego* (1961), 192–97.

[Arthur Cygielman]

ZALESHCHIKI (Pol. **Zaleszczyki**), town in Tarnopol district, Ukraine. In 1765 there were 344 Jews who paid the poll tax. The local Jews engaged in small trade and crafts, and later they participated in the resort business. The Jewish population numbered 4,424 (71% of the total) in 1880, and 3,382 (62%) in 1910. There was a strong ḥasidic influence in the community.

[Shimshon Leib Kirsheboim]

Holocaust Period

During the period of Soviet rule (1939–41) all communal activity was prohibited. In the first days after the outbreak of war between Germany and the U.S.S.R. (June 22, 1941), Jews were attacked by the local German population. On Nov. 14, 1941, the first *Aktion* took place and about 800 Jews were killed. Jewish youth were sent to a forced-labor camp in Kamionka. On Sept. 20, 1942, the order was given for all the Jews to move to the Tluste (Tolstoye) ghetto within 24 hours. From there part of the Jews were sent to the *Belzec death camp; others were sent to work camps in the area, while a few tried to find refuge in the surrounding forests. The community was not reconstituted in Zaleshchiki after the war.

[Aharon Weiss]

BIBLIOGRAPHY: B. Wasiutyński, *Ludność żydowska w Polsce w wiekach XIX i XX* (1930), 121; I. Schiper, *Dzieje handlu żydowskiego na ziemiach polskich* (1937), index.

ZALUDKOWSKI, ELIJAH (1888–1943), **ḥazzan* and writer. He was a son of the well-known *ḥazzan* of Kalisz, Noah Zaludkowski (1859–1931), known as "Reb Noaḥ Lieder." Elijah studied with his father and other *ḥazzanim*, and also at conservatories in Milan and Berlin. He held posts as *ḥazzan* in Warsaw, Vilna, and Liverpool, England, and in 1926 went to the U.S. where he officiated in New York and Detroit. Zaludkowski wrote *Di Kultur-Treger fun der Yidisher Liturgie* (1930), containing useful biographies of famous *ḥazzanim*, and published his father's and his own liturgical compositions in *Tefillat No'aḥ va-Avodat Eliyahu.*

ZAM, ZVI HERZ (1835–1915), Russian soldier; the only Jewish officer in the czarist army in the 19th century. Born in Gorengrod, Zam was taken from his home when he was 12 and trained at the *Cantonist military institute at Tomsk. He was posted to an infantry regiment, and, following the introduction of national conscription in 1874, was permitted to enter the cadets' school. He rose to become vice captain (*shtabskapitan*) but was placed in command of the worst company in his regiment at the orders of the war minister, who expressed surprise that a Jew who had remained faithful to his religion should serve as an officer. Within a year Zam had made his company the best in the regiment, but not until 1893, just before his retirement after 41 years in the czarist army, was he promoted to full captain. Zam took an active part in Jewish affairs and was instrumental in providing synagogue facilities for Jewish soldiers.

BIBLIOGRAPHY: Zam, in: *Voskhod* (Nov. 21, 1903).

[Mordechai Kaplan]

ZAMARIS (**Zimri**; late first century B.C.E.–early first century C.E.), Babylonian Jew. Zamaris fled from Parthian Babylonia with a retinue of 500 horsemen and mounted archers, as well as his family. He had taken refuge in Syria, when *Herod heard of his presence. Desirous of strengthening Jewish settlement in *Trachonitis and of creating a buffer zone, Herod offered land to Zamaris, who was not to be taxed. The Babylonians settled and built a village, *Bathyra, which served as a shield both for the Jewish settlements and for the pilgrims from Babylonia traveling to Jerusalem for the pilgrim festivals. Zamaris' son Jacimus organized a bodyguard for the Herodian family. His son Philip remained a close associate of Agrippa. Some are of the opinion that the *Benei Bathyra, who held high office in the administration of the Temple, came from these Babylonian settlers of Bathyra. In any event, it is clear that the Babylonian Zamaris had mastered Parthian military tactics and that his followers (who included mounted archers) were excellent soldiers. Zamaris must have held a substantial place in the Parthian feudal structure. His flight has nothing to do with Parthian "antisemitism," for in this same period other Jewish grandees held considerable power in the empire. Zamaris may have fallen victim to the complex intrigues surrounding the disputed Arsacid throne.

BIBLIOGRAPHY: Jos., Ant., 17:23–31; N.C. Debevoise, *Political History of Parthia* (1938), 145–6; G. Rawlinson, *The Sixth Great Oriental Monarchy* (1873), 240ff.; Neusner, Babylonia, 1 (1965), 38–41.

[Jacob Neusner]

ZAMBIA (formerly **Northern Rhodesia**), Central African republic. The two earliest Jewish settlements in Northern Rhodesia were in Livingstone and Broken Hill. When the railway reached Victoria Falls in 1905, there were enough Jews in Livingstone to start a congregation. By 1910, when the first Jewish wedding in Northern Rhodesia was celebrated, the congregation had 38 members. Jewish pioneers did much to open up the country, developing the cattle trade and ranching. Maurice

Rabb, Harry Wulfsohn, Len Pinshow, Hanan Elkaim, and the Susman brothers, Elie and Harry, were just some of these Jewish immigrants whose enterprise and initiative laid the foundations of the modern-day Zambian economy. The Susman Brothers, who arrived in 1900, were the first to develop large-scale wagon and river transport to Barotseland. Just before 1914, they pegged the Nkana copper mine but could not float a company to open it because the mine was in tsetse fly country. They sold their claim for £250 to what is now the largest copper mine in Zambia. Sir Edmund *Davis, Solly *Joel, and Sir Ernest *Oppenheimer were prominent in developing copper mining. Abe Galaun (1914–2003) arrived in Zambia just before the outbreak of World War II and became a dominant force in the country's meat and dairy business to the extent that Zambian President Kenneth Kaunda dubbed him "the man who feeds the nation." Galaun was involved in a wide range of charitable enterprises and his extensive contribution to Jewish communal life included founding the Council for Zambia Jewry. In 1921, out of a total Jewish population of 110, 48 lived in Livingstone, 11 in Broken Hill, and 25 in Lusaka. In succeeding years the Jewish population grew slowly, increased mainly by refugees from Nazi Germany in the late 1930s. As happened in neighboring Southern Rhodesia and the Belgian Congo, there was a substantial influx of Sephardi immigrants, largely from the Greek island of Rhodes. With the development of the copper mines in the north and the general growth in population and commerce, the Jewish population reached a peak of about 1,200 in the middle 1950s; most lived in Lusaka and the copperbelt centers of Kitwe, Ndola, Mufulira, Chingola, and Luanshya, in each of which there was a small but organized Jewish congregation. After 1960 numbers declined. In 1968, the estimated figure was 500, excluding some 200 on short-term contracts with Solel Boneh (the construction company of the Israel labor federation) and other overseas enterprises. Younger people tended to leave, and most of the older school-age groups were sent to Rhodesia or South Africa for their education. In communal and Zionist affairs Zambian Jewry remained linked until the late 1960s with the Central African Jewish Board of Deputies and Zionist Organization. Thereafter, the Council for Zambia Jewry, after 1993 through its affiliation to the *African Jewish Congress, oversaw the community's affairs. Before Zambia's independence in 1964 Jews played an active role in local government. Jewish mayors served in Livingstone, Broken Hill, Kitwe, and Luanshya. In the political field Sir Roy *Welensky was the leading figure in Northern Rhodesian politics from the 1930s until the Federation was set up in 1953, when he moved to *Salisbury (today Harare) as deputy prime minister; M.G. Rabb was a member of the legislative assembly from 1959 to 1962, and S.W. *Magnus was a member of parliament from 1962 to 1968, when he resigned to become a judge of the high court. As happened in South Africa, some Zambian Jews were active in resistance politics on behalf of the disempowered black majority in the pre-independence era. Most noteworthy of these was Lithuanian-born Simon Zukas, who played an important part in Zambia's independence struggle in the postwar era and in 1952 was in fact exiled on this account by the colonial government. Zukas returned to Lusaka after 1962 and later served as agriculture minister in President Frederick Chiluba's first cabinet (1991). A number of South African Jews who were prominently involved in the struggle against apartheid in their home country, amongst them Joe *Slovo, Ronnie *Kasrils, and Ray Alexander, were based in Lusaka for the greater part of their years in exile before returning to South Africa after 1990. The Zambian Jewish community steadily dwindled in the post-independence era. About 50 Jews remained in 2004, most of them living in Lusaka. Zambian Jewry in the early 2000s comprised a small core of long-term "settlers" and more transient residents engaged in trade, commerce, agriculture, and the professions. The community comes together for religious services on the High Holidays and Passover, as well as for Israel's Independence Day and other Israel-related events. There are eight Jewish cemeteries scattered around the country, and they are maintained by the remaining members of the community, in consultation with the African Jewish Congress.

BIBLIOGRAPHY: H. MacMillian and F. Shapiro, *Zion in Africa – The Jews of Zambia* (1999).

[Maurice Wagner / David Saks (2nd ed.)]

ZAMBROW (Rus. **Zambrov**), town in Bialystok province, N.E. Poland. The few Jews who lived in Zambrow in the early 18th century were not organized into a community being under the jurisdiction of that of *Tykocin (Tiktin). A *ḥevra kaddisha* was established in Zambrow in 1741, but the Jews buried their dead in the cemetery of the neighboring community of Yablonka. In 1765, 12 Jews living in Zambrow and another 462 in the surrounding villages paid the poll tax. In 1808 the Jews of Zambrow numbered 80 (13% of the total population), and in 1837, 320 (31%). A Jewish cemetery was consecrated in the town in 1828, and in 1830 an organized community with a synagogue, *mikveh*, and permanent religious officials were established. At first the members of the Jewish community engaged in the timber and grain trade, and kept inns. From the middle of the 19th century Jewish occupations included raising horses, cultivation of orchards, crafts, and petty trade. In 1857 the community numbered 1,022 (63% of the population). In 1890 the local cemetery was enlarged. A *kasher* kitchen was opened for the hundreds of Jewish soldiers attached to the battalions stationed there. About 400 Jewish houses were destroyed in a great fire in 1895. In 1905–06 Jewish youths and workers, organized within the *Bund, the *Zionist Socialist Workers' Party ("SS") and the *Po'alei Zion, staged a number of strikes in the textile factory and the sawmills. R. Lipa Ḥayyim held rabbinical office in the town from the 1850s until his death in 1882. He was succeeded by his son-in-law, R. Dov Menahem Regensberg, who held the position for several decades.

In 1921 there were 3,216 Jews (52%) living in Zambrow. Between the two world wars, branches of all the Jewish parties were active in the town. An elementary Yiddish school named after Ber Borochov was established in 1919. It was followed by a Hebrew school and a Zionist kindergarten in 1921. R. Shlomo *Goren, Israeli rabbi, was born in this town.

[Arthur Cygielman]

Holocaust Period

Under Soviet administration (1939–41) great changes were introduced affecting Jewish life. All activities of a political or Zionist nature were suppressed, and private enterprise was terminated. Jewish refugees arrived from Ostrow Mazowieck and were offered assistance by the Jewish community. A great number of these refugees were exiled to the Soviet interior. In the spring of 1941 the young Jews were drafted into the Soviet army. After the war between Germany and the U.S.S.R. broke out (June 22, 1941), the town fell to the Germans. A Judenrat was set up on German orders, headed by Gerszom Srebrowicz. It tried to alleviate the suffering of the community, but when it did not comply with all the German demands it was disbanded and a new Judenrat was set up, headed by a man who did not belong to the local community. The first *Aktion* was carried out on Aug. 19, 1941, in which about 1,500 persons were murdered in the region of Szumowo. During a second *Aktion* on Sept. 4, 1941, 1,000 persons were put to death in the locality of Rutki-Kosaki. At the end of December 1941 about 2,000 Jews were forced into a ghetto and subjected to starvation. Typhus epidemics broke out, and the hospital set up to aid the population worked ceaselessly. People began fleeing to the forests in an attempt to join the partisans. The severe conditions of the forest, as well as the antisemitic attitude of the partisans, forced many Jews to return to the ghetto. Nevertheless, some Jews were able to join partisan units which operated in the area of the Pniewa forest. Many of them were killed by members of the Polish underground Armia Krajowa. In November 1942 about 20,000 Jews from Zambrow and the vicinity were rounded up and interned in a former army camp. On Jan. 12, 1943, their transport to Auschwitz began in batches of 2,000 a night. Two hundred elderly and sick were poisoned and disposed of locally. After the war, only a few survivors from Zambrow and the vicinity remained. Others returned from the Soviet Union. Most of the survivors left again for Bialystok and Lodz, and later left Poland. Societies of emigrants from Zambrow were established in the U.S., Argentina, and Israel. A memorial book, *Sefer Zambrov*, in Hebrew and Yiddish with English summary, was published in 1963.

[Aharon Weiss]

BIBLIOGRAPHY: W.A.P. Bialystok, ZOB, 12:1–38 (= CAHJP, ḤM 7546–53); R. Mahler, *Yidn in Amolikn Poyln in Likht fun Tsifern* (1958), index; B. Wasiutyński, *Ludność żdowska w Polsce w wiekach XIX i XX* (1930), 36; *Ha-Meliẓ*, 123 (June 4, 1887); *Ha-Ẓefirah*, 167 (1895); 36 (1897).

ZAMBROWSKI, ROMAN (1909–1977), Polish Communist politician. Zambrowski joined the Communist youth movement as a young man, becoming its first secretary and its representative on the central committee of the Polish Communist Party. He also represented the Polish Communists on the executive committee of the Youth International in Moscow. He was arrested several times by the Polish authorities and imprisoned, among other places, in the notorious Bereza Kartuska concentration camp. During World War II Zambrowski lived in the Soviet Union and became one of the chief organizers of the Union of Polish Patriots sponsored by the Soviet authorities. He took an active part in the formation of Polish army units which fought alongside the Soviet army. His special responsibility was the appointment of political staff attached to these units, and he was a member of the Communist central bureau at Polish army headquarters. After World War II Zambrowski became head of the Polish United Workers' Party. He was a member of the Political Bureau of the Polish government and between 1956 and 1963 was secretary of the party's central committee. For a short time he occupied the post of minister for state control. In 1964, after a quarrel with the group in power led by Wladyslaw Gomulka, he was removed from leading positions in the party and government. During the antisemitic campaign launched by the Polish authorities after the *Six-Day War (1967) he was publicly accused of revisionism and sympathy for Zionism and retired from public life.

[Abraham Wein]

ZAMENHOF, LUDWIK LAZAR (1859–1917), Polish philologist and creator of Esperanto. Born in Bialystok, Zamenhof studied medicine and specialized in ophthalmology. He acquired his interest in philology from his father, who was a language teacher. For several years Zamenhof engaged in research work in the Yiddish language and began to write a Yiddish grammar, which was not completed. From his youth he had contemplated the idea of creating a simple international language which would facilitate and advance relations and mutual understanding between nations. In 1878, he completed the writing of the first pamphlet which contained the fundamentals of the new language. It contained only 900 root words and a grammar with 16 rules. It was published in 1887 under the title *Lingvo Internacia* ("International Language"). Zamenhof signed it with the pseudonym "Doktoro Esperanto" ("Dr. Hopeful"), hence the name of the language. At first Zamenhof encountered opposition and mockery, but he succeeded in gaining numerous enthusiastic supporters in every country, including renowned thinkers and scientists. Zamenhof published translations from German, English, and Russian literature, as well as from the Bible, in order to prove that Esperanto, in spite of its simplicity, could become a literary language. In 1905, in France, he convened the first international congress of Esperantists. In 1910, when the sixth congress was held in Washington, Zamenhof visited the United States and delivered a series of lectures in Esperanto. Two statues were erected in Zamenhof's honor in Poland – one in Warsaw (1928) and the other in Bialystok (1934), his native town. Zamenhof remained close to Jewish problems. He was one of the first members of Ḥovevei Zion, and in 1901 published a pamphlet, *Der Hilelismus*, where he presented Judaism as the philosophy of humanism. He published an Esperanto textbook in Hebrew.

BIBLIOGRAPHY: M. Boulton, *Zamenhof, Creator of Esperanto* (1960); E. Privat, *Life of Zamenhof* (1931); H. Arnhold, *Ein Fuerst ohne Krone* (1920); G. Waringhien, *Lazare Louis Zamenhof, à l'occasion du centenaire de sa naissance* (1959) (= Association Universelle pour l'Espéranto, Document CRD/6–1); I. Lapenna, *Dr. L.L. Zamenhof's Greatness* (1959) (=Universal Esperanto Association, Document RDC/6–2).

[Max Wurmbrand]

ZAMENHOF, STEPHEN (1911–1998), U.S. biochemist. Born in Warsaw, the nephew of Ludwik *Zamenhof, he went to the U.S. in 1939. He worked at Columbia until 1964, when he became professor of microbial genetics and biological chemistry at the School of Medicine of the University of California at Los Angeles. His 250 scientific papers were concerned with nucleic acids, enzymes, growth hormones, immunology, and genetics. He wrote *The Chemistry of Heredity* (1959).

ZAMIR, ITZHAK (1931–), Israeli jurist. Born in Warsaw, Poland, Zamir came to Palestine in 1934. He studied law at the Hebrew University of Jerusalem (M.Jur.) and the London School of Economics (Ph.D.). He was a law professor and director of the Institute for Legal Research and later dean of the Law Faculty at the Hebrew University. From 1978 to 1986 he was attorney general of the State of Israel, and from 1994 to 2001 a justice of the Supreme Court of Israel. He was also founding dean of Haifa University School of Law, president of the Israel Press Council, chairperson of the Israel Council on Tribunals, president of the Israel Association of Public Law, and chairperson of various other public committees.

Zamir wrote several books and many articles in Hebrew and English on various legal subjects as well as articles in the daily press. Among his books are *The Declaratory Judgment* (1962, with Lord Woolf) and *Administrative Power* (Heb., 1996). In 1997 he received the Israel Prize for legal scholarship. Throughout his career Zamir has been a staunch advocate of pluralism, tolerance, and egalitarianism.

[Leon Fine (2nd ed.)]

ZAMORA, city in León, N.W. Spain. Its ancient Jewish community was founded in the same period as those of *Nájera and *Salamanca. The date when the Jewish quarter was erected is not known. It was situated outside the city walls on the site known as Vega, where there was a separate group of houses, as well as the synagogue of the quarter and the Jewish cemetery. Throughout the period of the community's existence, there were three synagogues, one of which was registered in the office of Sancho IV, in 1283.

In 1313 a *Church Council held in Zamora adopted a series of decisions relating to the Jews: Jews were excluded from state functions; the edicts enforcing the wearing of a distinctive *badge were to be maintained, as also those concerning payment of the tithe to the church, the interest rate, and the transfer of newly built synagogues to the possession of the state, among other measures. These decisions of the council influenced the decisions of the Cortes which was convened in that year.

There is no information available on how the persecutions of the Jews in Spain of 1391 affected those in Zamora, but they undoubtedly resulted in conversions and apostasy. The amount of tax which the community paid declined.

During the 1470s and 1480s R. Isaac b. Moses *Arama preached in Zamora. In 1485 an order issued by John II was confirmed; it exempted the Jews of Zamora from providing accommodation for public personalities, with the exception of the king, the queen, and the members of the royal council. In that year Saul Saba – a brother of Abraham *Saba, and a renowned kabbalist and preacher – was condemned to death in Zamora, but details of the accusation and the trial are not known. In 1490 a unique lawsuit concerning a Jewess of Zamora was brought before the crown; she accused Jacob ibn Meir, the son of Isaac of Valladolid, an inhabitant of Zamora, of having ravished her and promising to marry her, and of not keeping his promise. In 1490 the community of Zamora, with that of Seville, contributed toward the redemption of the Jewish captives who had been taken in *Málaga. In 1491 the community paid a sum of 100,650 maravedis toward the war with Granada, in conjunction with a number of communities in the area.

In 1492, following the edict of expulsion from Spain, the Jews of Zamora went to Portugal, and the property of the community and the exiles was handed over to the prosecutor of Saragossa.

At the end of 1492 Zamora became a transit center for Jews who returned from Portugal to Spain in order to convert to Christianity. Several exiles from Zamora achieved fame during the 16th century for their activities in Jewish centers in the Ottoman Empire, of whom the most renowned were Jacob ibn *Ḥabib and Levi b. *Ḥabib.

BIBLIOGRAPHY: Baer, Spain, index; Baer, Urkunden, index; F. Cantera, *Sinagogas españolas* (1955), 349–53; Suárez Fernández, Documentos.

[Haim Beinart]

ZAMOSC (Pol. **Zamość**), city in Lublin province, E. Poland. The first Jews to settle in Zamosc were Sephardim who had been encouraged by the founder of the city, Jan Zamojski, to make it their home in 1588. The synagogue they built was notable for its richly ornamented interior. However, after a single generation the community ceased to exist. Ashkenazi Jews began to settle in Zamosc at the beginning of the 17th century, and during the *Chmielnicki massacres of 1648–49, Zamosc became a refuge for thousands of Jews in the vicinity; many died of hunger and disease while the city was under siege. In 1765, 1,905 Jews were recorded in Zamosc and in the communities within its jurisdiction. During the period that the city was under Austrian rule (1794–1809), the Enlightenment movement (see *Haskalah) found adherents in Zamosc. At the beginning of the 19th century, Joseph Zederbaum (father of Alexander *Zederbaum, editor of the Hebrew newspaper

Ha-Meliẓ), and the scholar and educator Jacob *Eichenbaum were leaders in the city's Haskalah circles. The poet and physician Solomon *Ettinger lived in Zamosc, and the author I.L. *Peretz was born and raised there. A center of rabbinical learning as well as of Haskalah, Zamosc was noted for its many public and private libraries. *Ḥasidism spread to the city during a later period.

Under Russian rule the number of Jewish inhabitants in Zamosc grew from 2,490 in 1856 to 7,034 in 1897 (50% of total), and to 9,000 in 1909 (about 63% of the total population). At the beginning of World War I many inhabitants left the city, since it was located on the Austro-Russian front line. After the war the community was reorganized. It numbered 9,383 in 1921, 10,265 in 1931, and 12,000 in 1939. Between the two world wars a Hebrew school existed in Zamosc as well as a Jewish-Polish secondary school. A local Jewish newspaper *Zamoscer Shtime* was published in the city.

[Yehuda Slutsky]

Holocaust Period

After a few days of heavy bombardment, which especially damaged the Jewish quarter, the German army entered Zamosc on Sept. 14, 1939. Immediately after capturing the city, the Germans organized a series of pogroms, motivated in part by the desire to loot Jewish property. On Sept. 26, 1939, the Germans left Zamosc and the Soviet army entered, but handed the city back to the Germans two weeks later, in accordance with the new Soviet-German demarcation line. About 5,000 Jews left the city at the time that the Soviet army withdrew. The remaining Jewish population suffered Nazi brutality and persecutions, like the rest of the Jews throughout Lublin province.

In October 1939 the Germans selected a *Judenrat and forced it to pay a "contribution" of 100,000 zlotys ($20,000) and the daily delivery of 250 Jews for hard labor. In December 1939 several hundred Jews expelled from *Lodz, Kalo, and *Wloclawek in western Poland were settled in Zamosc. Early in the spring of 1941 an open ghetto was established around Hrubieszowska Street, and the first deportation from Zamosc took place on April 11, 1942 (on the eve of Passover). The entire Jewish population was ordered to gather in the city's market, whereupon gunfire was directed at the crowd killing hundreds on the spot. About 3,000 Jews were forced to board waiting trains which took them to *Belzec death camp. From May 1 to 3, 1942, about 2,100 Jews from *Dortmund, Germany, and from Czechoslovakia were taken to Zamosc. Almost all of them were deported to Belzec on May 27 and murdered. The third mass deportation started on Oct. 16, 1942. All Jews were again ordered to gather in the city's market, and afterward were driven to *Izbica, some 15½ mi. (25 km.) from Zamosc. Many were shot on the way, and the rest, after a short stay in Izbica, were deported to Belzec and murdered. In this deportation the Jews offered passive resistance and hundreds went into hiding in prepared shelters. The Germans brought in Polish firemen to open the shelters by destroying the walls and removing other obstacles. Several hundred Jews were discovered in hiding and imprisoned for eight days in the city's cinema hall without food or water; then all those who were still alive were brought to the Jewish cemetery and executed.

A few hundred Jews fled to the forests. Most of them crossed the Bug River, made contact with Soviet guerrillas in the Polesie forest, and joined various local partisan groups. After the war some 300 Jews settled in Zamosc (270 from the Soviet Union, and 30 survivors of the Holocaust in Zamosc), but after a short stay they all left Poland.

In 1950 a memorial to the Jewish martyrs of the Holocaust from Zamosc was erected in the Jewish cemetery of the city.

[Stefan Krakowski]

BIBLIOGRAPHY: *Zamosc bi-Ge'onah u-ve-Shivrah* (1953), memorial book; M.W. Bernstein (ed.), *Pinkes Zamosc, Yisker-Bukh…* (Yid. 1957); Klausner, in: *He-Avar*, 13 (1966), 98–117; BŻIH, 21 (1957), 21–92.

ZAMOSC, DAVID (1789–1864), Hebrew writer and teacher. Educated in his native Kampen, Poznan, until the age of 13, he then moved to Breslau, where he studied under his uncle, acquired a secular education, and taught for ten years. In 1820, having won a large sum in a lottery, he went into business, but returned to literary and teaching activities after he lost his capital. His poems, stories, plays, translations, and compilations were written mainly for children and schools. His play, *He-Haruz ve-he-Azel, O Yad Haruzim Ta'ashir* ("The Diligent Man and the Lazy Man, or the Hand of the Diligent Will Enrich," Breslau, 1817), is the first modern Hebrew play written for children. Through its allegorical characters – the diligent man, the rich man, the lazy man, and Satan – Zamosc tried to instill moral values into the young.

His other works include: *Pillegesh ha-Givah* (Breslau, 1818), a historical play; *Tokhahat Musar* (Breslau, 1819, 1946^2), a translation of J.H. Campe's moral catechism, *Theophoron*, written in a didactic narrative style, with the Hebrew appearing opposite the original German; *Resisei Meliẓah* (Dyhernfurth, 1820–22; 2 vols.: one consisting of poems and letters, both original texts and German and Hebrew translations; the other of poems by other writers); *To'ar ha-Zeman* (Dyhernfurth, 1821), a play on problems of his time; *Mafte'ah Beit David* (Breslau, 1823), 100 epistles with a German glossary; *Meẓi'at Amerikah* (Breslau, 1824) and *Rabinsonder Yingere* (Breslau, 1825), adaptations of works by J.H. Campe; *Aguddat Shoshannim* (1827), poems and various aphorisms; *Halikhot Olam* (1829), a play; *Esh Dat* (1834), a textbook divided into three parts:

(1) reading exercises in German and Hebrew and a translation of the play *Eldad ve-Tirẓah*;

(2) entitled Ohel David, dealing with Hebrew grammar based on the works of Ben-Ze'ev, Gesenius, and others; and

(3) entitled Shirei David, consisting of miscellaneous poems; *Nahur me-Eden* (1837), a Jewish history for children "with questions and moral thoughts, including a short poem at the end of each chaplet"; a translation of *Ro'ot Midyan O Yaldut*

Moshe by S.F. de Genlis (1843); and various poems dedicated to friends, princes, and kings. He also contributed to *Bikkurei ha-Ittim*, the Hebrew annual (Vienna, 1821–31).

[Getzel Kressel]

ZAMOSC, ISRAEL BEN MOSES HA-LEVI (also **Segal**; c. 1700–1772), talmudist, mathematician, and one of the early Haskalah writers. Zamosc was born in Bóbrka (near Lvov) to an undistinguished family and studied in Zamosc, where he also taught at a yeshivah. His first published work is *Neẓaḥ Yisra'el* ("The Eternity of Israel"; written c. 1737): while essentially devoted to traditional *sugyot*, it is innovative in that it interprets numerous Talmudic passages from a mathematical and astronomical viewpoint. Zamosc proclaims his fidelity to Maimonides and gives reason priority in interpreting tradition. He thus argued that the rabbis of the Talmud held true scientific views, so that, if interpreted correctly, even seemingly "odd" statements in the Talmud turn out to be consistent with science; by contrast, he boldly took to task venerated Talmud commentators who held, for example, that the earth was flat. Conservatives rightly identified this work as subversive and dubbed it *Reẓaḥ Yisra'el* ("The Assassination of Israel"). The scientific knowledge displayed in *Neẓaḥ Yisra'el* is astonishingly broad but outdated (his authorities are Aristotle and Ptolemy): it is drawn exclusively from Hebrew books, almost all medieval. (The only exception is Joseph Delmedigo's *Sefer Elim* (1629), on which Zamosc wrote a commentary, now lost.) The exceptional availability of books in Zamosc, many in manuscript, is perhaps a consequence of the earlier presence there of Sephardi Jews, brought in by its founder, Jan Zamoyski (1541–1605). Israel Zamosc had followers and allies, among them Joel b. Uri Ba'al Shem (the younger). The town of Zamosc became a center of early Haskalah a generation later. In Zamosc, Israel composed a number of further works, of which the (geocentric) astronomical treatise, *Arubbot ha-Shamayim* ("The Windows of the Heaven"), is the only one to survive (in manuscript). His predilection for science notwithstanding, Israel Zamosc was conventional in his respect for the Kabbalah.

In 1741 Zamosc went to Frankfurt an der Oder, where he had *Neẓaḥ Yisra'el* published. He then settled in Berlin, where he taught Hebrew, science, and Jewish philosophy to Aharon Zalman Gumpertz (1723–1769) and Moses Mendelssohn (1729–1786), thus exerting a formative influence on two important figures of the early Berlin Haskalah. He studied (with Mendelssohn's help) German elementary books of science.

In 1744 Zamosc published in Jessnitz his (commissioned) commentary on *Ruaḥ Ḥen* ("A Spirit of Grace"), a 13th-century anonymous popular introduction to philosophy and science. In addition to simple textual interpretations, Zamosc "comments" on the Aristotelian principles in the medieval text by exposing totally incompatible findings of recent – namely, Wolffian – science. The "small animals" observable through a microscope in a droplet of semen elicit his exclamation, "How awe-inspiring is this statement, which our forefathers did not fathom." The new knowledge grounded in experience opened new unexpected horizons, refuting at the same time entrenched (Aristotelian) beliefs and thus undermining traditional authority, including that of Maimonides. Zamosc's is a subversive commentary: a venerated, authoritative text was used to legitimate the introduction of new ideas into a conservative community. This new literary genre was to be employed by later *maskilim*. Yet Zamosc's reception of the new science was limited to its descriptive aspects, and he failed to grasp mathematical physics or to accommodate contemporary philosophy.

The breakdown of all received verities weakened Zamosc's commitment to Maimonides' philosophy and hence to reason and science. Zamosc's views became more conservative and fideist: the commentary on *Ruaḥ Ḥen* paradoxically both exposes recent science and signals its author's turn toward the authority of traditional, including kabbalistic, texts. During the third, conservative, period of his life, spent between Berlin and Brody, Zamosc wrote two further (posthumously published) commentaries on medieval classics, which now accompany the traditional editions of these two works: *Oẓar Neḥmad* ("A Lovely Treasure"), on the *Kuzari*, and *Tuv ha-Levanon* ("Lebanon's Best"), on *Ḥovot ha-Levavot* ("The Duties of the Heart"). Although in these commentaries Zamosc replaced certain outdated medieval scientific ideas with facts from modern science, he held that belief and revelation are superior to reason and science. In 1764 Zamosc contacted Jacob Emden (1697–1776) on matters of *halakhah*.

In an unknown period, Israel Zamosc also wrote *Nezed ha-Dema'* ("A Pottage of Tears"; published posthumously: Dyhernfurth, 1773), a bitter, pessimistic social criticism written in rhymed prose. Its obscure style and intertextual allusions have led to a dispute over the target of its critique. Some scholars have interpreted it as a fierce attack on the ḥasidic movement, which was then becoming prominent: it contains most of the claims against the Ḥasidim used by later opponents – e.g., the allegations that Ḥasidim fostered ignorance, were prone to drunkenness, made unjustified innovations in religious practice, and misled simple people. Other scholars see in *Nezed ha-Dema'* a critique of contemporary Jewish society generally. Perhaps the truth is in between: the work may have been written over a long period of time, so that some passages have a particular target, whereas others are unspecific social criticism, of the kind Zamosc had expressed already in his youth.

Zamosc, who often oscillated between a tone of melancholic discouragement and elation, saw himself as a reformer of the spiritual cum social state of contemporary Jews: he was not only enlightened, but also sought to enlighten his audience. In his last years, he was venerated as an erudite *maskil* in Brody, where he died on April 20, 1772. Later *maskilim* and secular historians rightly gave him a place of pride in the history of the Haskalah. At the same time, Orthodox circles have hailed him as the author of two classic commentaries on standard works of Jewish thought.

BIBLIOGRAPHY: A. Shohat, *Im Ḥilufei Tekufot. Reshit ha-Haskalah be-Yahadut Germanyah* (1960), index, s.v.; G. Freudenthal, "Hebrew Medieval Science in Zamość ca. 1730: The Early Years of Rabbi Israel ben Moses Halevy of Zamość," in: R. Fontaine, A. Schatz, and I. Zwiep (eds.), *Sepharad in Ashkenaz. Medieval Learning and Eighteenth-Century Enlightened Jewish Discourse* (2006); idem, "R. Israel Zamość's Encounter with Early Modern Science (Berlin, 1744); The Subversive Commentary on *Ruaḥ Ḥen* and the Birth of a New Conservative," in: *Thinking Impossibilities: The Legacy of Amos Funkenstein* (2006); R.S. Westman, D. Biale, and D.B. Ruderman (eds.), *Jewish Thought and Scientific Discovery in Early Modern Europe* (1995), 332 ff.; Y. Friedlander, *Be-Misterei ha-Satirah. Hebrew Satire in Europe in the Eighteenth and Nineteenth Centuries*, vol. 2 (Heb., 1989), 9–110.

[Gad Freudenthal (2nd ed.)]

ZAMZUMMIM (Heb. זַמְזֻמִּים), the name given by the Ammonites to the inhabitants of the Transjordanian territory whom they dispossessed (Deut. 2:20). They were part of the nation of giants known as *Rephaim, who formed the ancient population of Transjordan (Deut. 2:10–12, 20–23). The Zamzummim are often identified with the people called Zuzim, mentioned as one of the nations defeated by Chedorlaomer and his allies in Transjordan (Gen. 14:5; Rashi, Gen. 14:5), since the same peoples listed in Deuteronomy 2 are listed in Genesis, with Zuzim substituted for Zamzummim. Some modern scholars explain the name Zamzummim as "to talk gibberish" (cf. Ar. *zamzama*). In the midrashic literature, Zamzummim (interpreted as meaning "great masters in war") is one of the seven names given to the offspring of the alliances between the Canaanite women and the angels (Gen. R. 26: 7; see Gen. 6:1–4).

BIBLIOGRAPHY: S.R. Driver, *Deuteronomy* (ICC, 1895), 40; EM, 2 (1954), 909–10; G.M. Landes, in: IDB, 4 (1962), 934; E.A. Speiser, *Genesis* (1964), 102; L. Koehler and W. Baumgartner, *Hebraeisches und aramaeisches Lexikon zum Alten Testament*, 1 (1967³), 255, 262; Ginzberg, Legends, 1 (1909), 151.

[Gershon Bacon]

ZAND, MICHAEL (1927–), philologist of Persian. Zand was born in Kamenets-Podolski, but was taken to Moscow in 1930. In 1937 his father was killed during the Stalin purges. Zand studied at the University of Moscow and then, when he could not find employment because of his "background," he moved to Stalinabad (now Dushanbe), where he did research at the Tajik Academy of Sciences from 1951 to 1957. In that year, following the posthumous "rehabilitation" of his father, he returned to Moscow, where he became head of the philological department and member of the editorial board of *Narody Azii i Afriki*, the leading Soviet journal of Oriental studies. In 1962 he became a research worker at the Institute of Oriental Studies, U.S.S.R. Academy of Sciences, and in 1964 consulting editor of the *Soviet Literary Encyclopedia*. Having made more than one attempt to leave for Israel, he became involved in the late 1960s in the dissent movement of Soviet intellectuals and in those circles which, despite official disapproval, spread knowledge of Judaism and Israel among Jewish youth.

In 1971 Zand was detained for having led a public demonstration in Moscow of Jews desiring to leave for Israel. His detention became the object of a protest movement addressed by scholars and learned institutions in many countries to the Soviet authorities. He was allowed to leave for Israel that year and was appointed professor of Persian and Tajik literature at the Hebrew University and in 1975 was appointed head of its department of Iranian and Armenian Studies at the Institute of Oriental and African Studies.

Among Zand's publications are *Six Centuries of Glory* (Moscow, 1967) on the history of Persian literature (Persian translation, 1972) in English and in Hebrew; *Jewish Culture in the Soviet Union* (with Ch. Schmeruk, 1973); and *Bukharan and Mountain Jews* (with M. Altshuler and Y. Pinkash, 1973). He was editor (with A. Tartakower and M. Zahave) of *Hagut Ivrit bi-Brit ha-Moaẓot,* studies on Jewish themes and contributions to Hebrew literature by contemporary Russian Jewish scholars (1976). Some of his Hebrew poems, under the pseudonym Menaḥem de-Razin, were sent clandestinely from the U.S.S.R. to Israel and published there.

[Shaul Shaked]

ZANGWILL, ISRAEL (1864–1926), English author. Born in London of a poor Russian immigrant family, Zangwill was first raised in Bristol and then educated at the Jews' Free School in the East End of London and at London University, where he graduated with honors in 1884, and became a teacher. He began his literary career with humorous short stories, but his early life had given him material for work of a far more serious kind. Sensing that he would one day wish to record the world of East London Jewry in novel form, he carefully noted down his early observations and any chance incidents or anecdotes that came his way. These notebooks formed the basis of his "ghetto" novels. Underlying Zangwill's work was also a serious intellectual and spiritual concern with Jewish existence in the Diaspora. This was reflected in the essay on Anglo-Jewry which he contributed to the first volume of the *Jewish Quarterly Review* in 1889. In this article he laid powerful emphasis on the permanent significance of Judaism as a revealed religion; but he also confessed that, in the light of modern skepticism and as a result of the emancipation of the Jews and the breakdown of the ghetto system, Judaism was no longer a viable faith. The Jew, he wrote, was "like a mother who clasps her dead child to her breast and will not let it go." There is a paradox here which indeed runs through Zangwill's life and work. He was passionately devoted to the values of the Jewish past as enshrined in the ghetto, but at the same time he sought to escape from what he felt to be the ghetto's restrictiveness. Like all his major characters, Zangwill was a child of two worlds. The *Jewish Quarterly Review* article attracted the attention of Judge Mayer *Sulzberger of Philadelphia and, as a result, Zangwill was invited to write a novel for the Jewish Publication Society of America. This was the genesis of his internationally successful *Children of the Ghetto* (1892), which records the history of the Ansell family – clearly a reflection of the history of his own family, with Zangwill himself projected as Esther Ansell, the heroine. *Children of the Ghetto* is a mixture of comedy, pathos, trivial episodes, and serious questioning of the nature of Judaism. From a formal and tonal point of view, it is an incompletely unified novel, but it has an epic range and depth and clearly penetrates to the tragedy – as well as the comedy – of Jewish life. All the characters, including the heroine, seek to escape from the ghetto and its religious and social forms, but they nearly all wander back in the end, returning to its spiritual comforts. Among the comic characters is the ghetto poet Melchizedek Pinchas – actually an unflattering pen portrait of Naphtali Herz *Imber, author of *Ha-Tikvah*. *Dreamers of the Ghetto* (1898) consists of a series of sketches based on the lives of historical figures, including the author's father, Moses Zangwill (who ended his days in Jerusalem), Benjamin *Disraeli, Heinrich *Heine, Ferdinand *Lassalle, *Shabbetai Zevi, and Baruch *Spinoza. Most of these men were also affected by the tragic duality of Jewish existence and sought to find some way of mediating between the living inheritance of Judaism and the powerful attractions of the world outside; but, in contrast to the main figures in *Children of the Ghetto*, they nearly all chose the road of apostasy. Other ghetto studies are *The King of Schnorrers* (1894), a hilarious, if imaginary, account of London Jewry in the 18th century; *Ghetto Tragedies* (1893); and *Ghetto Comedies* (1907). Many of these shorter pieces are of only ephemeral significance, but some generate the full power of Zangwill's major work, as for instance "The Diary of a Meshumad" in *Ghetto Tragedies*. This tells the story of the inner conflicts of a Russian Jew, married to a non-Jewess and living his Judaism secretly within himself. Zangwill also wrote many novels without any Jewish content at all. They include *The Master* (1895), the story of an immigrant child from Canada who finally succeeds in becoming a famous artist; *The Mantle of Elijah* (1900), about the events of the Boer War; and *Jinny, the Carrier* (1919), a novel set in mid-19th-century rural England. These now have only historical interest. He also wrote several plays, including *The War God* (1911); *The Cockpit* (1921); and *The Forcing House* (1922). *The Melting Pot* (1909), a drama about Jewish settlement in America, had a long run on Broadway, but its theme ("America is God's crucible, the great melting-pot where all the races of Europe are melting and reforming") was, perhaps, exaggerated. In this work he coined the phrase "the melting pot" to describe America and its immigrants, a phrase which has become proverbial. Zangwill abandoned the idea within a few years. Except for this latter attempt, his plays were not greatly successful on the stage, and his last years were embittered by frustrating struggles with unsympathetic producers. Zangwill also wrote one of the great classics of the "locked room" detective story, *The Big Bow Mystery* (1891).

Zangwill's interests were by no means confined to literature. He took an active part in public questions, including women's suffrage and, during World War I, pacifism. It was to him that *Herzl came in 1895, introducing himself with the words: "I am Theodor Herzl. Help me to rebuild the Jewish state." A year later Zangwill enabled Herzl to address his first London audience, and to that rally of the Maccabeans in 1896 the beginnings of British Zionism may be traced. Zangwill immediately saw the significance of Zionism and became a follower of Herzl and also became a friend of Max *Nordau, whose *Degeneration*, when the English version appeared in 1895, had made a deep impression on him. He joined the Maccabeans' pilgrimage to Ereẓ Israel in 1897 and attended the First Zionist Congress as a visitor. More interested in Jewish nationhood than in the Jewish land, he abandoned official Zionism when the Seventh Zionist Congress (1905) rejected the *Uganda offer. He then founded the Jewish Territorial Organization (see *Territorialism), dedicated to the creation of a Jewish territory in some country that need not necessarily be Palestine. He threw himself into this project with characteristic zeal and energy, recruiting for it the support of the first Lord *Rothschild and of the U.S. philanthropist Jacob *Schiff. The movement's only substantial achievement was the settlement of several thousand Jews in *Galveston, Texas, in the years before World War I. With the issue of the *Balfour Declaration in 1917, Zangwill temporarily returned to his Zionist faith. He became disillusioned, however, as a result of the difficulties encountered by the settlers in Palestine and the opposition of the Arabs and, in his final years, returned to his belief in a territorial solution for the Jewish problem outside Palestine. It is possible to discern a connection between Zangwill's Jewish novels and his political efforts for I.T.O. (see Territorialism). In both, the reality of a Jewish organic existence in the Diaspora is central. A self-governing Jewish territory would be a kind of super-ghetto, perpetuating what was presumably best in the ghetto system without the necessity for a radical spiritual readjustment such as a Jewish renaissance in the Holy Land seemed to demand. Yiddish was, for Zangwill, the true repository of Jewish culture. It is interesting that "ITO land" was not Zangwill's only solution for the Jewish problem. Along with it he paradoxically entertained another idea almost its antithesis: the melting away of Jewish separatism and the absorption of Judaism into a new religion of the future, which would embody the best of Hebraism, Hellenism, and Christianity. Such ideas are set out in his plays *The Melting Pot* and *The Next Religion* and in a number of occasional essays printed at different times.

Zangwill was a brilliant and witty speaker and could always draw a capacity audience of London's Jews. Some of his best-known aphorisms were: "A chosen people is really a choosing people," "Every dogma has its day, but ideas are eternal," and "The history of the ghetto is from more than one aspect the story of the longest and bravest experiment that has ever been made in practical Christianity." His major essays on the Jewish question are collected in *The Voice of Jerusalem* (1920), which contained such biting remarks as: "If there were no Jews, they would have to be invented, for the use of politicians – they are indispensable, the antithesis of a panacea; guaranteed to cause all evils." A further collection of *Speeches, Articles and Letters* was issued in 1937. Zangwill also contributed several verse translations of portions of the liturgy, which ingeniously preserved the original's acrostic and rhyming schemes, to an edition of the *Festival Prayer Book* (1904, and several editions); and he translated a selection of the poems of Ibn *Gabirol in 1903. But his genius did not lie in poetry: his true bent was for comedy and for eloquent narrative and expository prose. His major works were translated into about 20 languages. In 1903 Zangwill married Edith Ayrton (1875–1945), the daughter of a distinguished physicist and the stepdaughter of a Jewish woman, Phoebe Marks Ayrton, herself a distinguished physicist. Edith Zangwill was a noted novelist in her own right.

His younger brother, LOUIS ZANGWILL (1869–1938), wrote under the pseudonym "Z.Z." and achieved some success with his first novel, *A Drama in Dutch* (1894). His other works include *The Beautiful Miss Brooke* (1897), *Cleo the Magnificent* (1898), and a study of the dramatist Richard *Cumberland (1911). Louis Zangwill was, in his earlier years, a chess champion and a gifted mathematician. Israel Zangwill's son, OLIVER LOUIS ZANGWILL (1913–1987), was professor of experimental psychology at the University of Cambridge from 1952 until 1991. He wrote several books on psychology, amnesia, and animal behavior.

BIBLIOGRAPHY: M. Wohlgelernter, *Israel Zangwill: A Study* (1964), incl. bibl.; A. Spire, *Israël Zangwill* (Fr., 1909); J. Leftwich, *Israel Zangwill* (Eng., 1957); M. Freund, *Israel Zangwills Stellung zum Judentum* (1927); N. Glazer and D.P. Moynihan, *Beyond the Melting Pot* (1963), 288f.; H. Fisch, in: *Judaism*, 13 (1964), 107–21; L. Wolf, in: JHSET, 11 (1928), 252–60. **ADD. BIBLIOGRAPHY:** ODNB online; E.B. Adams, *Israel Zangwill* (1971); J.H. Udelson, *Dreamer of the Ghetto: The Life and Works of Israel Zangwill* (1990).

[Harold Harel Fisch]

ZANOAH (Heb. זָנוֹחַ), name of two biblical cities in Judah.

(1) A town "in the Lowland" near Zorah, Jarmuth, and Adullam (Josh. 15:34). It is mentioned in the list of Judean cities with Adullam and Lachish (Neh. 11:30). The inhabitants of Zanoah and their leader Hanun were among those who rebuilt the walls of Jerusalem in Nehemiah's time (Neh. 3:13), and it may be conjectured, therefore, that Zanoah was a center of secondary rank in its district, probably that of Keilah. In the time of Eusebius (Onom. 92:13), Zanoah was a village within the boundaries of Eleutheropolis (Bet Guvrin) on the way to Ailia (Jerusalem). The site is identified with Khirbat Zanūʿ between Beth-Shemesh and the valley of Elah, where pottery of the Late Bronze and Iron II ages, as well as remains from later periods, was found. According to the Mishnah, the quality of the fine flour of Zanua was unsurpassed (Men. 8:1; corrected Mss.).

(2) A Judean city in the mountain region, in the same district as Maon, Carmel, Ziph, and Juttah (Josh. 15:56). Therefore, it was probably to the S.E. of Hebron, but the exact site is unknown.

An agricultural moshav with the name Zanoah, originally of Yemenite Jews, mostly new immigrants, was established south of Beth-Shemesh in 1950. Later the Yemenites were replaced by North African Jews, mostly from Morocco. Its population in 1969 was 318. In the mid-1990s the population was approximately 340

BIBLIOGRAPHY: S. Yevin, in: *Zion*, 9 (1943), 59; Y. Aharoni, in: IEJ, 8 (1958), 30; W.F. Albright, in: BASOR, 18 (1925), 11; M. Noth, *Das Buch Josua* (1938), 65–66; A. Alt, in: PJB, 30 (1934), 13.

[Michael Avi-Yonah]

ZANTE (Gr. **Zakynthos** or **Zakinthos**), city on the island of Zante, the main southernmost island of the Ionian Islands of Greece. Moses *Basola, who passed through Zante in 1522, found about 30 Jewish families and a synagogue. *Elijah of Pesaro mentions in 1563, 20 heads of families of Sicilian and Portuguese origin, mostly wealthy merchants engaged in maritime trade between Venice and Constantinople. The Jews lived in a ghetto which was closed at night. From 1518 they had to wear the Jewish *badge.

The first known rabbi of the community was Joseph Formon, born at Serrai (Seres), in Macedonia, who headed a rabbinical school before being appointed to Zante. During the 17th century R. Jacob b. Israel ha-Levi was the rabbi of Zante. In 1686 the Jewish community numbered about 1,000 people. There was a *blood libel in Zante in 1712. There were two synagogues in the town, one named the Zante Synagogue and the other Candia. The latter was built in 1699 by natives of Candia at a slight distance from the ghetto, destroyed in 1712, and rebuilt in 1716. The Jews engaged in crafts and commerce. As a result of the blood libels and the decline in commerce, they abandoned the town. After some time Jews from Corfu, Crete, Constantinople, Izmir, and other places settled in Zante. They lived under the English from 1815–64. It was forbidden for them to belong to artisan guilds and trade associations and to take part in the political life of the island. In 1891 the Jewish population numbered between 200 and 300. During the Corfu blood libel and ensuing riots of that year, violence erupted in Zante. Although the troops defended the Jews, the mob attacked four Jewish families outside of the Jewish ghetto. Four people were killed, and 11 were injured. One soldier was killed defending the Jews and three Christians were killed when the troops shot at the crowd to defend the Jews.

At the outbreak of World War II the Jewish population numbered 270. With the German occupation many of them sought refuge in the mountains, some 70 to 80 remaining in the town. When on September 9, 1943, the Germans demanded that the Jews of Zakynthos be drafted for forced road work, they were quickly represented by the Righteous Gentiles Metropolit Chrystostemos and mayor Lukas Karrer (the Jewish community president being incapable of doing so), and relieved of the arduous task. The German commander Lut demanded Jewish communal lists, but the two dignitaries claimed that they were the only Jews on the island. The

Jews dispersed throughout the island and until the liberation, some 30 of them died of starvation. A deportation boat arrived from Corfu, but there was no room to add local Jews; the Jews were still dispersed, however, in the countryside villages. The Jews were never deported and though there are numerous theories, none have ever been proven or documented. They include Lut's having a Greek girlfriend who influenced him not to harm the Jews, EDES leader Katevatis threatening Lut continuously with revenge if the Jews were deported, and Metropolit, claiming to have known Hitler from their student days in Munich, reportedly sending a telegram to Hitler requesting him not to deport the Jews. Even at the end of the German occupation in August 1944, Jews were still being pursued in the most remote corners, and not arresting and deporting the Jews of Zakynthos is a highly unusual phenomenon in Nazi-occupied Greece and Europe.

The convoy of Jews that was sent from Corfu to death camps in Poland in June 1944 was too large to permit a halt in Zante and so the Jews there were saved. Those who had fled subsequently returned in September of that year, but shortly afterward a large number of them immigrated to Ereẓ Israel on the illegal immigration boat *Henrietta Szold* in August 1946. They were stopped by the British in the Bay of Haifa and deported to Cyprus, but allowed to come to Ereẓ Israel in December 1946. In 1948 there were 70 Jews in the town, but after the 1953 earthquake most of the Jews left for Athens or Israel. In the 1980s the last Jew died, and the Greek Board of Jewish Communities in Athens oversaw the synagogues and cemetery.

BIBLIOGRAPHY: C. Roth, *History of the Jews in Venice* (1930), passim; I.S. Emmanuel, *Histoire des Israélites de Salonique* (1936); A. Milano, *Storia degli ebrei italiani nel Levante* (1949), passim. **ADD. BIBLIOGRAPHY:** D.H. Stravolemou, *A Heroism – a Vindication, The Survival of the Jews of Zakynthos in the Occupation* (Greek; 1988), 31–35; B. Rivlin, "Zakynthos," in: *Pinkas ha-Kehillot Yavan* (1999), 117–23; Y. Kerem, "The Survival of the Jews of Zakynthos in the Holocaust," in: *Proceedings of the Tenth World Congress of Jewish Studies*, Division B, vol. 2 (1990), 387–94; idem, *The History of the Jews in Greece, 1821–1940*, pt. 1 (1985), 473.

[Simon Marcus / Yitzchak Kerem (2nd ed.)]

ZAPHON (Heb. צָפוֹן), city of the tribe of Gad, listed with Succoth and, as the enumeration of cities in Joshua 13:27 goes from south to north, apparently situated to the north of the latter. The name also appears as that of a family in the genealogy of Gad (Gen. 46:16, as Ziphion; Num. 26:15, as Zephon). The city may have been occupied earlier than the Israelite period, as is indicated by its name, which recalls the Canaanite deity Baal-Zephon; it is possibly mentioned in one of the el-Amarna letters (no. 274) as well. Some scholars assume that Jephthah resided there, for the Ephraimites, in their quarrel with him, gathered at Zaphon. Where the Hebrew text relates that Jephthah was buried "in one of the cities of Gilead" (Judg. 12:7), the Septuagint reads "in his city, Zaphon." In the Jerusalem Talmud (Shev. 9:2, 38d), it is identified with Amtan (Amathus), present-day Tell ʿAmmātā in the Wadi Rājib, but possibly this is due to confusion between a distinguishing epithet and the city name: this particular Zaphon was known as "Zaphon near Amathus." Josephus calls it Asophon; it was there that Alexander Yannai suffered defeat at the hands of Ptolemy, king of Cyprus (Ant., 13:338). Basing his position on the talmudic equation, Glueck identifies it with Tell al-Qaws, a prominent and strategically strong position, about three mi. (5 km.) north of Tell Deir (Dayr) ʿAllā, the assumed site of *Succoth. Pottery on the surface of the tell ranges from late Chalcolithic through Early Bronze Age I–II, Middle Bronze I, Late Bronze II, and Iron Age I–II. The later Zaphon may have been located at Khirbat Buwayb, about 1.4 mi. (2.25 km.) west-northwest of Tell al-Qaws. Albright, however, identifies the ancient site with Tell al-Saʿīdiyya, farther to the northwest on the Wadi Kafranjī, near the Jordan (on the excavations of this mound, see *Zarethan).

BIBLIOGRAPHY: L. Haefeli, *Samaria und Peraea* (1913), 94; C. Steuernagel, *Der Adschlun* (1927), 343; N. Glueck, in: AASOR, 25–28 (1951), 351ff.; W.F. Albright, in: BASOR, 89 (1943), 7ff.; Aharoni, Land, index.

[Michael Avi-Yonah]

ZAPOROZHE (before 1921 Alexandrovsk), city in Zaporozhe district, Ukraine. The Jewish community increased with the rapid development of the town in the late 19th century and in 1897 numbered 5,290 (28 percent of the total population). In 1881 there was an outbreak of *pogroms in the town, whence they spread to the surrounding towns and villages. In 1905 there were again severe pogroms. The Jewish population in 1926 numbered 11,319 (20.3 percent of the total). The growth of the city attracted many thousands of Jews from the impoverished townlets of western Ukraine and Belorussia. In 1932 there were 20,000 Jews in Zaporozhe, of whom about half were industrial workers. It is estimated that this number at least doubled in the period before World War II, which was a time of rapid development for the city of Zaporozhe (whose total population rose from 56,000 in 1926 to 289,000 in 1939). During the German occupation in World War II the Jews who did not succeed in escaping were murdered. In 1959 the Jews numbered 17,400 (4 percent of the total population). There was no synagogue, but *kasher* poultry was available. There was a Jewish section in the general cemetery, and on the outskirts of the city a Jewish mass grave dating from the German massacres.

District of Zaporozhe

Between 1846 and 1855 ten Jewish settlements were founded in the district of Zaporozhe. In 1908 they cultivated 309,000 acres. These settlements were incorporated in 1928 within the Jewish autonomous region named Nei-Zlatopol after the largest settlement. The Jewish population of the district numbered 7,500 (50 percent). The Jewish settlements were destroyed during the German occupation.

BIBLIOGRAPHY: *Die Judenpogrome in Russland*, 2 (1909), 196–203.

[Yehuda Slutsky]

ZARASAI (under the czarist regime **Novoaleksandrovsk**), city in N.E. Lithuania. In independent Lithuania the city was first called Ežerenai and was a district center. In 1838 there were 146 Jews there, among them five merchants; by 1847 the number of Jews had risen to 453. The town's geographic position, near Dvinsk (*Daugavpils), on the main Petersburg (Leningrad)–Warsaw–Berlin highway, had a favorable influence both on its general development and on the growth of its Jewish population; by 1897 there were 3,348 Jews in the town (53% of the total population). During World War I most of the Jews there fled to other parts of Russia, and not all returned to the town after the war. When Lithuania became independent, Zarasai was cut off from its hinterland, with disastrous consequences both for its economy and size of its population; by 1923, the Jewish population had decreased to 1,329 (35% of the total population). The community was composed largely of shopkeepers and artisans, but there were also some professionals. A number of Jewish secular and religious institutions of learning were supported by the community. In World War II, shortly after the Germans attacked the U.S.S.R., Zarasai was occupied by the German army. On Aug. 26, 1941, 8,000 Jews from Zarasai and surrounding communities were taken to a forest near Dusetai and murdered there.

BIBLIOGRAPHY: *Lite*, 1 (1951); *Yahadut Lita*, 3 (1967); *Yisker-Bukh fun Rakishok un Umgegnt* (1952).

[Joseph Gar]

ZARCHI, ASHER (1864–1932), Orthodox rabbi. Born in Kovno, Lithuania, Zarchi later attended the well-known yeshivah of Volozhin. He married in 1883, continued his Talmud studies, and received rabbinic ordination from Rabbi Isaac Elhanan Spektor, the communal rabbi of Kovno, along with Rabbi Isaac Meir of Slobodka and Rabbi Chaim Segal of Yanova.

Zarchi immigrated to the United States in 1891 and served as pulpit rabbi in the Brownsville section of Brooklyn for a year, after which he moved to Des Moines, Iowa, where he was the only Orthodox rabbi. Zarchi played a central role in establishing America's first Orthodox rabbinic union, the Agudat ha-Rabbonim. He helped prepare its initial mission statement. Zarchi stayed in Des Moines until 1903, when he was invited to move to Louisville, Kentucky, by that city's *Vaad Ha-Ir*, to become its community rabbi. Zarchi did not serve any particular pulpit in Louisville but rather served the needs of the entire community.

In Louisville, Zarchi was responsible for *kashrut* supervision and communal charities. He was also the main Hebrew teacher in a small school at the Beth Hamidrash Hagadol. Zarchi was instrumental in forming the Louisville Hebrew School and as chief rabbi of the city, he often traveled to inspect Midwestern mills that prepared flour for *matzah* baking as well as manufacturing plants in Cincinnati, where he gave kosher supervision for Crisco.

Zarchi's life work included articles of Talmud commentary and Jewish law that appeared in such journals as *Ha-Ivri, Ha-Pisgah,* and *Ha-Measef.* He also contributed essays to the encyclopedic work, *Ozar Yisroel*, which was edited by Rabbi Judah David Eisenstein. Zarchi died on June 24, 1932. He had no children. In 1946, the Jewish National Fund of Louisville helped establish an Israeli settlement in his memory and named it Naḥalat Zarchi.

[Lynne Schreiber (2nd ed.)]

ZARCHI, ISRAEL (1909–1947), Hebrew novelist and editor. Born in Jedrzejow, Poland, Zarchi immigrated to Ereẓ Israel in 1929, worked as a laborer, and studied at the Hebrew University (1932–37). He wrote mainly about life in Ereẓ Israel. The pain and anguish that accompanied the efforts of the *ḥalutzim* to acclimatize themselves and take root in Ereẓ Israel are major themes in his works.

His novels include *Olamim* (1933); *Yamim Yeḥefim* (1935); *Ha-Neft Zorem la-Yam ha-Tikhon* (1937); *Har ha-Ẓofim* (1940); *Beit Savta she-Ḥarav* (1941); *Ereẓ Lo Zeru'ah* (1946); *Kefar ha-Shillo'aḥ* (1948); a short story collection, *Ha-Ḥof ha-Nikhsaf*, was published posthumously (1950). He translated works by S. Maugham, J. Conrad, and H. von Kleist, and was one of the editors of *Yalkut Yerushalmi le-Divrei Sifrut* (1942). A. Barshai edited a collection of Zarchi's stories, *Yalkut Sippurim* (with an introduction and a bibliography, 1983). For a list of English translations of his stories, see Goell, Bibliography, 82.

BIBLIOGRAPHY: Toren, in: *Itturim* (1949), 129–36. **ADD. BIBLIOGRAPHY:** G. Shaked, *Ha-Sipporet ha-Ivrit*, 2 (1983), 308–13.

[Getzel Kressel]

ZARCHIN, ALEXANDER (1897–1988), Israeli engineer and inventor. Zarchin was born in Zolotonosha in the Ukraine. After graduating from the Leningrad Technical Institute, he was a member of its staff until 1934. He was imprisoned for a time in a labor camp. He took out patents for evaporative drying, distillation, separation of oxygen from air, and, more importantly, for a freezing process for desalination of water. Zarchin went to Palestine in 1947. His desalination process was developed in Israel and used experimentally to supply water to the town of Eilat.

BIBLIOGRAPHY: Desalination Plants Ltd., *Desalination Plants Ltd: Developers of Zarchin Process* (1962); Tidhar, 14 (1965), 4518–20.

[Samuel Aaron Miller]

ZARCO, JUDAH (16th century), rhetorician and poet. Born on the island of Rhodes, Zarco subsequently lived for some time in Salonika. There he became a member of the Ḥakhmei ha-Shir ("Masters of Poetry"), who held competitions in the art of poetry and who also composed epigrams, poems, and works of rhetoric for various occasions. While still in Rhodes, Zarco had already written love poems and rhetorical works; and when he came to Salonika, he was received with great respect and was extolled by the local poets for his inventiveness.

Zarco composed a *maqāma* entitled *Leḥem Yehudah* (Constantinople, 1560), which he dedicated to the "Maecenas"

Abraham ibn Ḥen. It was published only once and is today a rarity. Its contents run as follows: A certain king had an exceedingly beautiful daughter. He shut her up and took great care that no lover should have access to her. Five princes came and attempted with the help of a certain wise man to enter the locked palace. They disguised themselves and entered, each one in a different manner, and one of them was successful in his stratagem. Zarco took great pains to compose a complicated acrostic that runs the entire length of the *maqāma*, and which has no parallel; but his work was not of the same quality as that of the famous writers of *maqāma*.

BIBLIOGRAPHY: A.M. Habermann, *Toledot ha-Piyyut ve-ha-Shirah* (1970), 232f.; idem, in: J. Zarco, *Leḥem Yehudah* (1970), introduction; Davidson, Oẓar, 4 (1933), 392f.

[Abraham Meir Habermann]

ZAREPHATH (Heb. צָרְפַת), Phoenician city situated between Tyre and Sidon and dependent on the latter. According to the papyrus Anastasi I, which dates to the time of Ramses II (13th century B.C.E.), it was located between Sidon, Ush (Palaetyrus), and Tyre. The prophet Elijah was commanded to go to Zarephath during the great drought in the reign of Ahab (I Kings 17:9–24). There he was met by a widow whom he nourished, miraculously, throughout the barren period; he later revived her dying son. This miracle made a great impression on later generations: it was mentioned in Jesus' discourse at Nazareth (Luke 4:26) and was represented in the wall paintings in the synagogue at *Dura-Europos. Zarephath is mentioned as the farthest limit of Canaan in Obadiah 1:20. In 701 B.C.E. Sennacherib took the city in his campaign against the rebellious cities of Phoenicia and the land of Israel. Josephus locates it between Sidon and Tyre (Ant., 8:320; as Sarept). According to Pliny, purple dye was produced there (5:70). Eusebius refers to it as a "most famous village" (Onom. 162:1). In Byzantine times it was called "large village," and the Aramaic name for it was "the long village" (*Qrita arikta*), probably because it extended for some distance along the seashore. It is so named on a detached fragment of the Madaba Map, in an account of the miracles of the saints Cyrus and John (*Patrologia graeca* 87:3636), and in the *Life of Petrus Iberus* (ed. Raabe, 111, 114). In crusader times, it was a walled village, a fief of Sayette (Sidon) and the seat of a bishop, known as Sarepta. It is now called Ṣarafand, a village on the shore, about 9 mi. (15 km.) south of Sidon, with a tomb of al-Khaḍr (Elijah), which probably replaced the church dedicated to the prophet which was mentioned by Theodosius (*Itinera Hierosolymitana* …, ed. Geyer, 147) and Antonius (*ibid.*, 160). The name is also used in Hebrew for France (which in medieval times excluded Provence).

BIBLIOGRAPHY: R. Dussaud, *Topographie historique de la Syrie…* (1927), 42; Abel, Geog, 2 (1938), 449; M. Avi-Yonah, *Madaba Mosaic Map* (1954), 77.

[Michael Avi-Yonah]

ZARETHAN (Heb. צָרְתָן), site near Adam, mentioned in the account of the damming of the Jordan (Josh. 3:16) and in that of the flight of the Midianites (Judg. 7:22; as Zererah). Beth-Shean, in Solomon's fifth district, is described as being "beside Zarethan, beneath Jezreel" (I Kings 4:12), but most scholars emend this passage by transposing Zarethan to the end of the verse, thus placing it at the farthest limit of the district near Jokneam (Tell al-Mazār?). Solomon had the vessels of the Temple cast between Succoth and Zarethan (I Kings 7:46; II Chron. 4:17, as Zeredah). The identification of the place is in dispute, some scholars placing it west of the Jordan, others placing it to the east of the river. Of the latter, Mazar identifies it with Tell Umm Ḥamād, a large settlement between Adam and Succoth, while Glueck has suggested Tell al-Saʿīdiyya farther to the north, which, however, Albright identifies with *Zaphon. Excavations directed by Pritchard at Tell al-Saʿīdiyya revealed the remains of a Canaanite occupation, as well as an Israelite city (tenth-eighth centuries B.C.E.) with a casemate wall 17 ft. thick, remains of houses with pillared courts, a weaving room with 72 loom weights, and an Iron Age I staircase, roofed over and arranged in two passageways led by 84 steps from the city to the spring. Other finds include early Bronze Age, late Bronze Age and early Iron Age tombs, one of a woman with jewelry, including 575 beads.

BIBLIOGRAPHY: N. Glueck, in: AASOR, 25/28 (1951), 340ff.; B. Mazar, in: *Eretz Israel*, 3 (1954), 26; Y. Aharoni, in: *Bi-Ymei Bayit Rishon*, ed. by A. Malamat (1962), 111; Albright, in: JPOS, 5 (1925), 32ff.; Pritchard, in: ADAJ, 8/9 (1964), 95ff.

[Michael Avi-Yonah]

ZARETZKI, ISAAC (1891–1956), Yiddish linguist and author. Born in Pinsk, he studied mathematics at Derpt University (now Tartu, Estonia) in 1913–17 and published studies on geometric terminology in Yiddish (1923) as well as Yiddish translations of mathematics (1921) and algebra (1924) textbooks. Zaretzki's major contribution, however, was in the field of Yiddish linguistics. After the 1917 Revolution he joined the Jewish Labor *Bund and then the Communist Party (1918), which he left in 1921. He was briefly head of the Jewish Department of the People's Commissariat for Education in Moscow (1920). As the central figure in the movement for a reformed Yiddish orthography, Zaretzki wrote a number of books and articles on the subject, which later received government sanction, becoming the official Yiddish orthography of the Soviet Union, one of whose striking characteristics is the abandonment of the traditional spelling of Yiddish words of Hebrew-Aramaic origin. In the early 1930s he advocated introducing the Latin alphabet for Yiddish, but did not find many supporters among his fellow language-planners.

A leading methodologist in Yiddish language teaching, Zaretzki wrote a number of books in this field while pursuing extensive and intensive research into Yiddish grammar, especially syntax, and was noted for his penetrating observations and generalizations. Foremost among his numerous publications in this field is *Praktishe Yidishe Gramatik* ("Practical Yiddish Grammar," 1926, 1927[2], rev. ed. 1929 under the title *Yidishe Gramatik* ("Yiddish Grammar")). From 1928 he taught Yiddish linguistics at the Second Moscow State University, later transformed into the Moscow Teachers' Training Institute. When the Yiddish department was closed (1938), he became a university lecturer of general and Russian linguistics. He died in Kursk, Russia.

BIBLIOGRAPHY: Reyzen, Leksikon, 1 (1926), 1057–61; LNYL, 3 (1960), 476–8. **ADD. BIBLIOGRAPHY:** G. Estraikh, *Soviet Yiddish: Language Planning and Linguistic Development* (1999).

[Mordkhe Schaechter / Gennady Estraikh (2nd ed.)]

ZARISKI, OSCAR (1899–1986), U.S. mathematician. Zariski was born in Kobrin, Russia, His father was a talmudic scholar who died when Zariski was two, leaving his mother Hannah to support seven children. She did this by running a store, and in fact the family became one of the richest in Kobrin. In 1927 Zariski won a scholarship to Johns Hopkins University in the U.S., where he was professor of mathematics from 1937 to 1945. He was then professor at the University of Illinois and finally at Harvard. Zariski's contribution to mathematics was mainly in the fields of algebraic geometry, modern algebra, and topology, and he is known particularly for his work on algebraic surfaces. Zariski received a Guggenheim fellowship in 1939–40. He was president of the American Mathematical Society in 1969–70 and was editor of the *American Journal of Mathematics*. Among his books are *Commutative Algebra* (2 vols., 1958–60) with P. Samuel; and *Algebraic Surfaces* (1935); he edited the work of R. Dedekind, *Essenza e significato dei numeri* (1926).

[Maurice Goldsmith]

ZARITSKY, MAX (1885–1959), U.S. labor leader. Zaritsky was born in Petrikov, Russia, and was taken to the U.S. in 1905. He became active in the cap and millinery workers' union, rising to president by 1919. Thereafter, he fought to establish union standards throughout the chaotic trades, succeeding with the aid of the New Deal. He was responsible for stabilization and union-management cooperation in his industry. Active in pressuring labor support for national unemployment insurance and for AFL-CIO unity, his socialist heritage was tempered as head of the United Hat, Cap, and Millinery Workers. While ousting Communist influence from his union, he never abandoned the hope for independent labor political action. In 1936 he helped establish the American Labor Party and was a presidential elector for Franklin D. Roosevelt. After 1944 he joined the Liberal Party. A labor Zionist, Zaritsky believed in a Jewish state. As chairman of the American Jewish Trade Union Committee for Palestine, Zaritsky worked, after World War II, on behalf of unrestricted immigration to Palestine and for an independent Jewish Commonwealth. His papers are in Tamiment Library, New York University.

BIBLIOGRAPHY: D.B. Robinson, *Spotlight on a Union* (1948); *New York Times* (May 11, 1959), 27 (obituary).

[Kenneth Waltzer]

ZARITSKY, YOSSEF (1891–1985), Israeli painter. He was born in Borispol, near Kiev, and studied until 1914 at the Academy of Art in Kiev. He then lived in Moscow. In 1923, he went to Palestine, settling in Jerusalem, where he was one of the initiators of the first exhibition of Palestinian artists. In 1927, Zaritsky moved to Tel Aviv, where in 1947–48 he was one of the founders of the "New Horizons" group. Zaritsky was the first Israel artist to hold a one-man show in an important art center, the Stedelijk Museum, Amsterdam, in 1955 – the year he was awarded the Israel Prize. His temperament and his feeling for color led him to concentrate on landscapes. Between 1923 and 1945 he painted mostly in watercolor. Zaritsky's work underwent "periods," each of which has its special characteristic. There are the watercolors of Haifa, Jerusalem, and Safed (1923–26), which contain carefully blended color harmonies as well as sketches in which patches of violent color are applied to the drawing; the "Views over Ramat Gan" (1936–38) show great feeling for composition. His series of "Zikhron Ya'akov" (1939–40) and still lifes (1945) are stages in an evolution toward abstraction. Lastly, his large oils in the "Yehiam" and "Amsterdam" series (1954–55) synthesize all the elements of the evolution, in both brushwork and balance of color. Zaritsky's indirect influence through his pupils Avigdor Stematsky and Yehezkel Streichman contributed to the birth of an abstract-lyricist movement after 1948. This dominated young Israel painters for many years.

[Yona Fischer]

ZARKO (Zarka), JOSEPH BEN JUDAH (14th–15th centuries), Hebrew grammarian and poet in *Spain and *Italy. Zarko was one of the pupils of Profiat *Duran. Apparently in consequence of the 1391 persecutions in Spain he wandered to various towns of Italy, and in 1413 he lived in Pisa and subsequently in the towns of Modena, Ferrara, Cento, Ancona, and Mantua. He apparently died in Mantua. In Italy he engaged in writing and was supported by wealthy patrons, such as Jehiel b. Mattathias of *Pisa and the brothers Isaac and Mordecai *Finzi of Mantua. In practice he was one of the disseminators among the Jews of Italy of the Hebrew poetry and grammatical studies that had developed in Spain.

He was the author of *Rav Pe'alim*, written in 1429, a grammar of the Hebrew language which was frequently copied; and *Ba'al ha-Lashon*, a Hebrew dictionary after the manner of the *Sefer ha-Shorashim* of David *Kimḥi. Poems and letters of his are also extant. Some scholars have erroneously identified him with Joseph b. Isaac Zarko, the teacher of Abraham Portaleone.

BIBLIOGRAPHY: Davidson, Oẓar, 4 (1933), 404; D. Kaufmann, in: REJ, 37 (1898), 306f.; idem, in: MGWJ, 43 (1899), 136–44; S. Poznański, *ibid.*, 50 (1906), 624; S. Simonsohn, *Toledot ha-Yehudim be-Dukkasut Mantovah*, 2 (1964), 516.

[Abraham David]

ZARZA, SAMUEL IBN SENEH (14th century), Spanish philosopher. Although there is little information on Zarza's life, it is known that he lived in Palencia, in Castille, in the second half of the 14th century. Samuel Shalom, the first printer of *Sefer ha-Yuḥasin* (1566), maintains in his notes to that work that Zarza was burned at the stake by the tribunal of Valencia, having been accused by Isaac *Campanton of denying creation. However, historians have proved that this is only a legend.

Zarza wrote a philosophical commentary on the Pentateuch titled *Mekor Ḥayyim* ("Fountain of Life," Mantua, 1559), containing an epilogue in which he described the sufferings of the Jews of Castile during the period of the civil wars between King Pedro and his brother Henry (see Baer, Urkunden, 2, pt. 1 (1936), no. 209). In 1369 he wrote a philosophical commentary on various *aggadot* called *Mikhlal Yofi* ("The Perfection of Beauty," Bodleian Library, Seld. Arch. A. 65). In an introduction to this latter work Zarza wrote that in Toledo alone 10,000 Jews were killed during the period of these civil wars. In *Mekor Ḥayyim*, Zarza mentioned four other works that he wrote that are no longer extant: *Tohorat ha-Kodesh, Eẓe ha-Dat, Ẓeror ha-Mor*, and *Magen Avraham*. Poems in Zarza's honor were written by Solomon Reubeni of Barcelona and Isaac ibn *Al-Ḥadib.

Zarza's philosophical thought is typical, in many respects, of a group of thinkers in his immediate and more distant areas, including Solomon Al-Constantini, Solomon Franco, Shem Tov ibn Shaprut, and Shem Tov ibn Major. Like some of the Torah commentaries of this circle of colleagues, Zarza's *Mekkor Ḥayyim* is both a commentary on the Torah and a supercommentary on Abraham Ibn Ezra. The commentary, interesting in its own right, is also important on account of the variety of sources cited, including fragments of the lost Bible and *aggadah* commentaries of Shem Tov ibn *Falaquera. Zarza's philosophy combines the views of Ibn Ezra and Maimonides. For example, he adopted the Maimonidean negative divine attributes and Aristotelian conception of God as thought itself, while at the same time he adopted Ibn Ezra's Neoplatonic cosmology, combining such terms as "universal soul" and Active Intellect. Zarza also displayed a broad view of astral magic, according to which the Torah's commandments are vessels for attracting astral "spiritual influence" (*ruḥaniyut*). This combination of diverse elements from Maimonidean Aristotelianism, Neoplatonism, and astral magic was characteristic of the 14th-century Neoplatonic school in his area of which Zarza was a major figure.

BIBLIOGRAPHY: Baer, Spain, 373, 449; Steinschneider, Cat Bod, 2496–98; R. Jospe, *Torah and Sophia: The Life and Thought of Shem Tov ibn Falaquera* (1988), Appendix E, "Falaquera's Bible Commentary," 459–84; R. Jospe and D. Schwartz, "Shem Tov ibn Falaquera's Lost Bible Commentary," in: HUCA, 64 (1993), 167–200; D. Schwartz, *The Philosophy of a Fourteenth-Century Jewish Neoplatonic Circle* (Heb., 1996), index; idem, *Studies on Astral Magic in Medieval Jewish Thought* (2005).

[Dov Schwartz (2nd ed.)]

ZARZAL (ZARZAB), ABRAHAM IBN (14th century), Spanish physician and astrologer. Zarzal was favored by Sultan Muhammad IV of Granada. The previous court physician Pharez b. Abraham ibn Zarzal was possibly his father. When the sultan's minister, Reduan, was assassinated, Zarzal, fearing he might be implicated, fled to Castile. Here his reputation as a physician and astrologer, together with the recommendation of the sultan, with whom King Pedro of Castile was on friendly terms, led to Zarzal's appointment to the court of Castile as physician and astrologer. There he worked from 1350 to after 1369.

BIBLIOGRAPHY: H. Friedenwald, *Jews and Medicine*, 2 (1967²), 644–6.

[Nathan Koren]

ZASLAVSKY, DAVID (1880–1965), Russian journalist and publicist. An early opponent of the Bolsheviks, he became one of their most zealous defenders and propagandists. He studied law at the University of Kiev, and in 1903 joined the *Bund, writing manifestos which led to his imprisonment for short periods by the czarist police. He took up journalism in 1904 and was a correspondent for liberal dailies in Yiddish and Russian. In 1917 he was a Bund delegate to the Workers' Councils and opposed the Bolsheviks. When the Bolsheviks seized power in October, he left for Kiev, but acknowledged his error when the Bolsheviks occupied Kiev. In 1920 he published an open letter in which he "confessed" his anti-Bolshevism. In 1925 he published another letter in which he tried to "atone" and asked to be accepted into the Communist Party, but he was allowed membership only in 1934. From 1926 he was a political writer for *Izvestiya*, and from 1928 until the end of his career, for *Pravda*. During the period of the Ribbentrop-Molotov pact he included attacks on the Jews in his articles on international affairs. During World War II he was a member of the Jewish *Anti-Fascist Committee; he was not arrested in 1948/49 with most of the other members of the committee. Zaslavsky was unsparing in his attacks on "deviationists," among them Boris *Pasternak for his novel *Dr. Zhivago*. After the establishment of the State of Israel he was one of its most violent critics in his editorial and feuilleton writing. He studied the treatment of Jews in Russian literature and concluded that it was antisemitic.

Zaslavsky wrote biographies of Plekhanov and Lassalle (1925) and an account of the U.S. Civil War (1926). A collection of his articles was published in 1960 under the title *Day by Day*. Zaslavsky admitted that the Communists had only partially solved the Jewish problem in the U.S.S.R.

BIBLIOGRAPHY: D. Shub, in: *Forward* (June 8, 1965); LNYL, 3 (1960), 554–6.

[Yitzhak Maor]

ZASLOFSKY, MAX ("**Slats**"; 1925–1985), U.S. basketball player and coach, member of the NBA's Silver Anniversary Top 25 Team. A native of Brooklyn, New York, Zaslofsky was an all-scholastic player at Thomas Jefferson High School. He graduated during World War II, and served for two years in the U.S. Navy. After his discharge, Zaslofsky attended St. John's University for a year, where he helped the Redmen to the NIT with his effective two-hand set shot and solid overall court presence. Already 21 years old and married, Zaslofsky chose to turn professional in 1946, playing for the Chicago Stags of the newly formed BAA, which three years later became the NBA. Chicago, led by Zaslofsky's offense, topped the Western Division, and in the playoffs upset Coach Red *Auerbach's heavily favored Washington Capitols before bowing out to the Philadelphia Warriors in the championship. At the end of his rookie season, Zaslofsky was named First Team All-NBA, the youngest player ever to receive that honor (21 years 4 months). In the 1947–48 campaign, Zaslofsky was first in the league in total points (1,007), second in points per game (21.0), and led Chicago to a quarterfinal victory over Boston in the playoffs before losing to Baltimore in the semifinals. In his third season with Chicago, Zaslofsky was again among the top five in most offensive categories. In his last year with Chicago, Zaslofsky led the NBA in free-throw percentage, shooting 84.3 percent. Zaslofsky was named First Team All-NBA each of his four years with Chicago. When the Stags folded in 1950, the now coveted Zaslofsky was won in a mini-lottery by the New York Knicks, whom he immediately helped to two consecutive NBA finals in 1951 and 1952, and was named a starter on the 1952 NBA All-Star East team. Zaslofsky was traded in 1953 to the Fort Wayne Pistons, and the following year he went to the Baltimore Bullets and Milwaukee Hawks before returning to Fort Wayne. During that 1954 season, Zaslofsky became the first of only five NBA players to score 20 or more points in a game for three different teams in the same season. Zaslofsky led the 1954–55 Pistons team to the NBA finals, and contributed to their repeat trip to the finals the following year. When he retired in 1956, Zaslofsky was the third highest scorer in the NBA, with nearly 8,000 points. He came out of retirement in 1967 to coach the New Jersey Americans of the American Basketball Association. The team narrowly missed the playoffs after having to forfeit a tiebreaker game. Zaslofsky retired from coaching the following season. In 2002, the staff of ESPN voted Zaslofsky one of the top ten players in NBA history not to be included in the Hall of Fame.

[Robert B. Klein (2nd ed.)]

ZASTAVNA, town in Chernovtsy district, Ukraine, in N. *Bukovina; until World War I in Austria and between the two world wars in Romania. Jews probably settled in Zastavna toward the end of Moldavian rule in the area; at the beginning of the Austrian conquest there were already Jews in the town. According to the Austrian census, they numbered 17 in 1774 and 33 in 1776. An organized community was established in the early 19th century, though tombstones in the cemetery attest to a regular community life before that period. A Jewish elementary school was established in 1919, and a synagogue built in 1926. In Zastavna, as in other communities of Bukovina. *Ḥasidism had a considerable influence. A Zionist organization was established in Zastavna in 1905. Jews took part in the municipal elections and for some time a Jew was mayor. The Jews in Zastavna were mainly engaged in commerce and crafts, but toward the end of Austrian rule also included wealthy landowners and industrialists (in sugar and alcohol manufacture). The community of Zastavna had jurisdiction over 29 nearby villages, where Jewish landowners were also living. At the beginning of World War I, in 1914, many of the Jews living in Zastavna escaped to Vienna, and most did not return.

Holocaust and Contemporary Periods

In World War II, during the Holocaust period (1941–44) the 635 Jews in Zastavna, like other Jews in Bukovina, were deported to *Transnistria. After the war about 120 survivors returned, but their number gradually diminished through emigration to Israel and elsewhere. By 1971 no Jews remained in Zastavna.

[Yehouda Marton]

ZATEC (Czech **Žatec**; Ger. **Saaz**), town in N.W. Bohemia, Czech Republic. Jews settled in Zatec before 1350. The burghers of Zatec sought to expel them in the early 16th century, but the king did not consent. However, after the publication of the Bohemian expulsion decree of 1541, the burghers attacked the Jews and drove them out of town. Jews did not return until the second half of the 19th century; two Jewish families lived in Zatec in 1852. A cemetery was opened in 1869 and a synagogue built in 1872. The Jews were mainly engaged in the trade and export of hops, an economic activity of national importance. In 1921 the Jewish population numbered 1,082, but by 1930 their number had declined to 760 (4.2% of the total population). The community was destroyed during the Holocaust. In the 1960s the cemetery was still in existence.

BIBLIOGRAPHY: Ger Jud, 2 (1968), 728; E. Maendl and H. Schwenger, in: H. Gold (ed.), *Juden und Judengemeinden Boehmens* (1934), 579–84.

[Jan Herman]

ẒAVA'AT RIBASH, ḥasidic work; full title, *Ẓava'at Ribash ve-Hanhagot Yesharot* ("The Testimony of Ribash [Rabbi Israel Ba'al Shem] and Upright Rules of Conduct"), published in Zolkiew in 1793. (Another Zolkiew edition, which may be earlier, is undated.) The title page ambiguously states that the manuscript was in the possession of the editor, Isaiah of Yanov. Although, on the basis of the title, it was widely believed that the work is the ethical will of Israel Ba'al Shem Tov, Shneur Zalman of Lyady writes: "The truth is that this is not his ethical will and that he made no such will before he departed this life. It is rather a collection of his sayings compiled by others. Although these were insufficiently skilled in translation, the authentic meaning is conveyed" (*Tanya, Iggeret ha-Kodesh*, No. 25). The title of the work is derived from the opening sentences: "It is a command (*ẓava'ah*) of the Ba'al Shem that one must be wholehearted in the service of God." The editor remarks that he has included in the anthology some teachings of Dov *Baer, the Maggid of Mezhirech. In fact, the majority of the teachings recorded are from the school of the Maggid. The work bears a strong resemblance to other collections of ḥasidic material, such as *Likkutei Yekarim* and *Maggid Devarav le-Yaakov*, the same sayings appearing in all these works, though not in the same order or with exactly the same wording.

The work contains the basic ideas of Hasidism, stressing in particular the idea of *devekut*, attachment to God in the mind at all times. Man should cultivate an attitude of equanimity, being indifferent to both the praise and blame of others, and be so devoid of any desire for physical pleasure that it makes no difference to him whether he eats delicacies or coarse, unpalatable food (Nos. 2 and 10). God wishes to be served in many different ways. Even when a man converses with others, his mind can be on God and perform "unifications" (*yiḥudim*) (No. 3). Weeping is an evil. God must always be served in joy. To weep is only advantageous when it is the result of joy in man's attachment to God (No. 45). The fear of God without the love of God is tantamount to melancholy. It is wrong to be overscrupulous in considering how best to serve God. One should be so full of joy at the very opportunity of serving Him that one has neither time nor inclination to ponder over the "how" and "what" of worship (No. 110).

The accusation by the *Mitnaggedim* that *Ẓava'at Ribash* discourages the study of the Talmud is unfounded. However, it is true that *devekut* is the book's ultimate ideal, to which even Torah study is subordinate. The work not only demands of the student of the Torah that he pause frequently during his studies to engage in *devekut*, but states explicitly that the study of the Torah is not an aim in itself but is for the purpose of attaining *devekut* (No. 29). Moreover, prayer is held to be superior to Torah study, a reversal of the traditional scale of values: "The soul declared to the Rabbi [the Ba'al Shem Tov] that the reason the things on high were revealed to him was not because he had studied much Talmud and the Codes, but because of his prayers, which he recited with powerful concentration. That is why he attained such a high rank" (No. 41).

As one of the earliest printed ḥasidic works, *Ẓava'at Ribash* especially aroused the ire of the *Mitnaggedim*. The book was publicly burnt in Vilna at the instigation of Elijah ben Solomon *Zalman, the Vilna Gaon and, according to a ḥasidic tradition, in Prague, by order of Ezekiel *Landau. A ban on the book was declared in Cracow, together with other ḥasidic *bikhlekh* ("booklets"). The work is one of the most popular of ḥasidic writings. The anthology *Sefer Ba'al Shem Tov* (Lodz, 1938), which quotes ḥasidic teachings in the form of a running commentary to the Pentateuch, manages in the course of the book to quote the whole of *Ẓava'at Ribash*. Schochet lists 34 separate editions prior to his own.

BIBLIOGRAPHY: J.I. Schochet (ed.), *Ẓava'at ha-Ribash* (1975), with an Introduction (numbers in the text refer to this edition); S. Dubnow, *Toledot ha-Ḥasidut* (1967), 53–58; 116; 387–88, 455–56; A.M. Habermann, in: *Sefer ha-Besht* (1960); M. Wilensky, *Ḥasidim u-Mitnaggedim* (1970), 1, 42–43; 11, 92–93.

[Louis Jacobs]

ZAVIM (Heb. זָבִים; "Sufferers from Flux"), ninth tractate in the order *Tohorot* in the Mishnah; there is no *Gemara* either in the Babylonian or in the Jerusalem Talmud. The scriptural basis of this tractate is Leviticus 15:1–15, which speaks of the ritual impurity of the *zav*, i.e., a man who has a running issue (probably gonorrhea), and describes in great detail how anybody and anything coming into contact in any manner (directly or indirectly) with the *zav* contracts impurity. Mishnah *Zavim* consists of five chapters.

Chapter 1 discusses the significance of the frequency, intensity, and continuity of the discharge in determining whether the person concerned is considered definitely a *zav* in terms of Leviticus 15:1–15, or whether he is afflicted with a lesser degree of impurity (e.g., a *ba'al keri*, one who suffered an accidental discharge of semen, in terms of Lev. 15:16). Chapter 2 first lists the categories of men to whom the law of running issue applies (including, for example, slaves, minors, and even eunuchs) and then discusses the seven ways of examining a suspected person to ascertain whether or not he is really a *zav*. The last paragraph touches on the difficult problem of *midras* (lit. "treading"), denoting the very high degree of impurity ("father of uncleanness") imparted by a *zav* to a thing on which he stands, sits, lies, etc. (without touching it) and which this thing in turn imparts to a person (including his garments) who stands, sits, lies, etc., on it. The "thing" in question here is called *mishkav* ("couch"), but the law of *midras* would apply to anything used for standing, lying, or sitting on, or for any other relevant activity (e.g., leaning, riding, etc.).

Chapters 3–4 discuss various cases of *midras* in contrast to cases of *hesseṭ* (lit. "shaking"), i.e., the lesser degree of impurity imparted by the *zav*'s moving a person or object without touching him or it, or by the *zav*'s being moved in the same manner. For example, if a *zav* rides with another person on a beast, even if their garments did not touch, an uncleanness of the *midras* category is imparted to the other person. Instances of *hesseṭ* mentioned are, for example, the sitting of the clean and unclean on a beam not firmly fixed, or if they pull a rope in opposite directions. Chapter 5 at first continues the subject of *hesseṭ*, but then discusses different aspects of the impurity of a *zav*, partly in comparison with other kinds of impurity. The last paragraph deals with rabbinical stringencies regarding the imparting of uncleanness to *terumah*. A point to which particular attention may be drawn is that holy books which touch *terumah* make the latter unclean. The apparently strange practice of the priests of storing their holy food next to scrolls of Holy Scripture should be set against the background of this remarkable regulation. It was out of concern not for the holy food, but for the Holy Scriptures, lest they become damaged by proximity to food, that the regulation was made, thus preventing the placing of holy food near books (Shab. 14a).

Mishnah *Zavim* is mainly of ancient origin (Epstein, Tannaim, 96). *Mishnah* 3:1 is its only *Mishnah* discussed in the Babylonian Talmud (BM 105b). Several sources can be detected in *Zavim*. Epstein (Tannaim, 64) attributed chapter 5 (except for *mishnayot* 4–5) to R. Joshua b. Hananiah, and *Mishnah* 1:1 to Akiva's earlier view, which he later changed (cf. Tosefta 1:4–6). *Mishnah* 1:2 is according to the view of R. Meir, while the corresponding passage in the Tosefta 1:8 stems from R. Judah, who refers to Meir in his work as "a certain disciple." The Tosefta contains several topics not mentioned in the Mishnah, such as the discussion on the *zav, zava*, and the leper in chapter 3, on the defiling caused by idol worship in 5:6–8, and the topic of *yayin nesekh* ("wine used in idol worship"). One passage of this Tosefta (1:5) discloses the origin of the *mishnayot* of Akiva: "As R. Akiva stood before his disciples classifying the *halakhot*, he said: Let anyone who knows a reason or law [pertaining to the topic at hand], arise and speak… R. Simeon then spoke in his presence… whereupon [Akiva] said: Not everyone who jumps up [to state a *halakhah*] is to be praised, unless he gives the reason thereof." An English translation is in Danby's *Mishnah* (1933).

BIBLIOGRAPHY: Epstein, Mishnah, index; Ḥ. Albeck, *Shishah Sidrei Mishnah*, Tohorot (1959), 437f.

[Arnost Zvi Ehrman]

ZAWIERCIE (Rus. **Zavertse**), city in Katowice province, S. Poland. Jews settled in Zawiercie in the latter half of the 19th century when the city underwent rapid industrial development. Zawiercie was then in Congress Poland. Jews came to the city from the communities of *Radom, *Belchatow, *Wielun, and Wloszczowa, and became mechanics, smiths, tailors, weavers, clerks, bookkeepers, and tradesmen. In the last third of the century wealthy Jews established a glassworks, an iron foundry, machine, and textile factories. The Gincberg brothers invested 3.5 million rubles in a cloth factory which employed over 200 Jewish workers. There were 1,134 Jews in Zawiercie in 1887 (27% of the total population), and 3,158 (18.5%) in 1897.

At first there was no organized community life in the city and the Jews relied on the services of the neighboring community of Kromolow. The first local synagogue was built in the 1880s. The ḥasidic movement exerted a strong influence on the community. In 1915 Zawiercie was declared a municipality and there followed a period of intense communal development. The Zawiercie community numbered 6,095 (21%) in 1921, and 5,677 in 1931. Between the world wars there were two Jewish schools.

[Shimshon Leib Kirshenboim]

Holocaust Period

On the outbreak of World War II there were about 7,000 Jews in Zawiercie. On Sept. 2, 1939, about 2,000 Jews fled the city just before the entry of the German army. After entering the city, the Germans ordered all Jewish males from ages 17 to 50 to assemble in the city's market. They were all arrested and tortured for 9 days. On May 10, 1940, about 600 Jews from the Zaolzie region of Czechoslovakia were forced to settle in Zawiercie. A ghetto was established there in the summer of 1940. In November 1940 about 500 young Jews were deported to forced labor camps in Germany, where almost all of them perished. In May 1942 about 2,000 Jews were deported to Auschwitz and murdered there. On Aug. 26, 1943, the ghetto was liquidated, and almost all remaining Jews were deported to Auschwitz and murdered. During this deportation over 100 Jews were shot on the spot for offering passive resistance. About 500 Jews were left in the newly established local forced-labor camp, which was in turn liquidated on Oct. 17, 1943. The Jewish community was not reconstituted in Zawiercie after the war.

[Stefan Krakowski]

BIBLIOGRAPHY: B. Wasiutyński, *Ludność żydowska w Polsce w wiekach XIX i XX* (1930), 29; *Carat i klasy posiadające w walce rewolucią 1905–07 w Królestwie Polskim* (1956), index; I. Schiper, *Dzieje handlu żydowskiego na ziemiach polskich* (1937), index; *Zawiercie ve-ha-Sevivah – Sefer Zikkaron* (1958; Heb. and Yid.).

ZAY, JEAN (1904–1944), French socialist politician. Born in Orleans, Zay joined the Radical Socialist Party in his youth and was elected a deputy in 1932. He became undersecretary of state in 1936 and was appointed minister of national education in Léon *Blum's Popular Front government in the same year. He held this position in successive governments until 1940, despite bitter criticism of his support for the republican cause in Spain. Following the fall of France, Zay was arrested and held in prison, and was summarily executed on June 20, 1944.

ZAYIN (Heb. זַיִן ;ז), the seventh letter of the Hebrew alphabet: its numeral value is therefore 7. The earliest form of the *zayin*, in the c. 1500 B.C.E. Proto-Sinaitic inscriptions, consisted of two parallel strokes =, which were later joined by a third stroke I, H. In the tenth century B.C.E. the letter was relatively high I (thus also in the Archaic Greek script), but later became squat. In the Hebrew script it was written I → I, which developed into Samaritan ᘔ, while in the Phoenician script it turned into z (cf. Greek and Latin "Z") and Z. In the Aramaic script it was written as a wavy line ~ which later dropped its extremities \ and then it turned into a vertical stroke I. The vertical *zayin* was preserved in both the Nabatean and Jewish scripts. In Arabic – in order to distinguish it from the *ra* – a diacritic point was added to the *za* ز; in the Jewish script, as the vertical stroke was interchangeable with the *waw*, a rightward hook was added to the letter top. From this form the ז developed. See *Alphabet, Hebrew.

[Joseph Naveh]

ẒAYYAḤ (Ẓiyyaḥ), JOSEPH BEN ABRAHAM IBN (16th century), rabbi and kabbalist. Ẓayyaḥ was apparently born in *Jerusalem. There he completed his *Even ha-Shoham* in 1538. From Jerusalem he went to *Damascus to serve as rabbi of the Mostarabian (the native Jewish) community but paid frequent visits to Jerusalem. He was regarded in his time as an important *posek*. A number of his responsa have been published in some of his contemporaries' collected responsa, such as those of Joseph *Caro, Moses di *Trani, *Levi b. Ḥabib, and others who were on friendly terms with him. A number of his works have remained in manuscript, including a large collection of responsa, two of which were published by S. *Assaf (see bibliography). From one of them it can be inferred that he took an active part in the dispute in *Safed on whether scholars should be exempted from taxation, and he was among those who upheld the exemption.

Three of his kabbalistic works are known: *Even ha-Shoham* (Jerusalem National Library, Ms. 416), in which the author with great profundity combines the kabbalistic doctrine of combination of letters of the alphabet (*ḥokhmat ha-ẓeruf*) with that of emanation (*aẓilut*), a work which was popular among Yemenite Jews; *Ẓeror ha-Ḥayyim* (London, Jews College, Ms. 318), a curious commentary to the *Oẓar ha-Kavod* of Todros *Abulafia. He dedicated both these works to Abraham de *Castro, who was leader of the Jews in Egypt. The third work, *She'erit Yosef* (Vienna, Ms. 260), was compiled in Jerusalem in 1549 and is a kind of supplement to and commentary on his *Even ha-Shoham*. This work is apparently mentioned in the *Torat ha-Kena'ot* of Jacob *Emden (Lemberg, 1870, p. 69), where he states that Nehemiah *Hayon took a number of ideas from the *She'erit Yosef* and made wrong use of them.

BIBLIOGRAPHY: C. Hirschensohn, in: *Hamisderonah*, 1 (1885), 192–201, 255–9; Frumkin-Rivlin, 1 (1929), 67–69; G. Scholem, *Kitvei Yad be-Kabbalah* (1930), 89–91; A.Z. Schwarz, *Die hebraeischen Handschriften in Oesterreich* (1931), 203, no. 260; S. Assaf, in: KS, 11 (1934/35), 492–6; M. Benayahu, in: *Sefunot*, 7 (1963), 103–17.

[Abraham David]

ZBARAZH (Pol. **Zbaraż**), town in W. Ukraine (formerly in E. Galicia). Jews were living there at the end of the 15th century. The cemetery dates from 1510. According to a document of 1593 the city and its entire revenues were leased to Jews and Christians jointly. The Jewish community expanded in the 17th century and a synagogue was erected. The siege on Zbarazh by *Chmielnicki in 1649, its capture by the Turks in 1676, and the *Haidamak raids of 1708 caused terrible suffering to the community. There were 910 Jewish inhabitants in 1765. The number increased under Austrian rule after 1772, reaching 2,896 (35% of the total population) in 1900. The 1931 census records 3,000 Jewish residents. Two followers of Judah *he-Ḥasid originating from here were Isaiah of Zbarazh and his son. Zbarazh was also the birthplace of the folk poet B.Z. *Ehrenkranz.

[Max Wurmbrand]

Holocaust Period

During World War II the Jewish population reached 5,000 with the arrival of refugees from western Poland. After the German occupation, the Jewish survivors from Skalat, Grzymalow, and Podwoloczyska were brought into Zbarazh. On July 4, 1941, a pogrom was carried out and the first Jews were killed. On Sept. 6, 1941, the Jewish intellectuals were ordered to present themselves before the Nazis; 70 persons were murdered in the Lubieniecki forest. In the spring of 1942 some 600 sick and aged persons were marched off toward Tarnopol and murdered on the way. Other Jews were deported to the labor camps of *Kamenka-Bugskaya and Zborow. On Aug. 31–Sept. 1, 1942, an *Aktion* took place and hundreds of persons were deported to the *Belzec extermination camp. Hermann Mueller, head of the Gestapo at Tarnopol, directed the murder of the Jews of Zbarazh. On Oct. 20–22, 1942, 1,000 Jews were deported to Belzec and Lvov Janowska camp. On Nov. 8–9, 1942, a group of more than 1,000 Jews was deported to Belzec. On April 7, 1943, hundreds of Jews were put to death near the city. The ghetto established in the autumn of 1942 was demolished on June 8, 1943. Some Jews hid in the Polish village of Kretowce. Some 60 Jews from the city survived the Holocaust.

[Aharon Weiss]

ZBITKOWER, (Joseph) SAMUEL (1730s–1801), Warsaw merchant, banker, and army purveyor. He settled in Warsaw in 1757 and displayed great ability and initiative in the development of varied types of trade and industry, including timber haulage, working the salt mines, preparation of leather, operating a slaughterhouse, exercise of the monopoly on *kasher* meat, and the operation of brick kilns and a brewery. Because of his great wealth, evidenced by his ownership of houses in Warsaw and estates in the surroundings, as well as through banking operations, he established good connections with ruling circles – Poles, Russians, and Prussians. In 1773 he received through the minister Poniński the title "Elder of the Jews," which gave him the authority to farm taxes and was exploited by him to extort money from the rich men of the community.

In 1788 Zbitkower was appointed *parnas* of the Warsaw suburb of Praga, and in 1796 submitted a petition for the suburb to be granted the status of a separate community. He also received the right to establish a cemetery in Praga, which still has the tombstone describing his achievements. The quarter in which he lived was called Szmulowizna after him. Zbitkower's ability to adapt himself to political change enabled him to obtain the position of official contractor to the Russian army of occupation, and also helped him in supplying the Polish fighters during the *Kosciuszko revolt, Tales were related about his generous actions and his readiness to save Jews from the danger of war and capture. His third wife, JUDITH LEVY of Frankfurt, was well known for her learning and proficiency in German and French, and this enabled her to aid her husband in his connections with members of the government. Despite his poor education, *Zbitkower managed to serve as *shtadlan* for the Jewish community, thanks to his official connections. After his death his widow and his son BEREK amassed great riches. He was the ancestor of the Berkson (or Bergson) family; his great-grandson was the philosopher Henri *Bergson.

BIBLIOGRAPHY: J. Shatzky, *Di Geshikhte fun Yidn in Varshe*, 1 (1947), index; A. Levinson, *Toledot Yehudei Varshah* (1953), 56–60; I. Ringelblum, in: Zion, 3 (1938), 246–66, 337–55; N. Sokolow, in: *Haynt* Jubilee Volume (1928); idem, *Ishim* (1958), 101ff.; J. Flinker, in: *Varshah (= Arim ve-Immahot be-Yisrael)*, 3 (1948), 50–54.

[Moshe Landau]

ZBOROV (Pol. **Zborów**), city in Tarnopol district, Ukraine. The Jewish community had considerable influence in Zborov in the 17th century. The peace treaty signed in Zborov in

1649 between John II Casimir and the Cossack rebel *Chmielnicki forbade Jews to live or work at *arenda* (leaseholding) in the same towns in which Cossack troops were encamped. In 1689 King John III Sobieski gave the Jews rights equal to those of other citizens of the town, with the provision that all legal cases between Jews and gentiles be tried in government courts. Four market days were arranged each year to stimulate economic growth, and Jews were allowed to operate taverns if gentiles did not claim this privilege for themselves. There were 655 Jews in Zborov in 1765; 2,109 (54% of the total population) in 1880; 1,873 (46%) in 1890; 2,080 (40%) in 1910; and 1,184 (32%) in 1921. In the early 19th century Ẓevi Hirsh of Zborov (d. 1841) influenced the community toward Ḥasidism. In 1930 the Jewish quarter was damaged extensively by fire.

[Shimshon Leib Kirshenboim]

Holocaust Period

On the outbreak of World War II, there were about 1,800 Jews in Zborov. In July 1941 an *Aktion* took place and 850 Jews were killed. In September or October 1942 some of the Jews were deported to the *Belzec death camp. The ghetto was liquidated in April–June 1943. A number of Jews were imprisoned in a forced-labor camp in Zborov established at the end of 1941. This camp was liquidated in July 1943 when all its inmates were killed. After the war the Jewish community of Zborov was not reconstituted.

BIBLIOGRAPHY: N.N. Hannover, *Yeven Mezulah* (1966; map); B. Wasiutyński, *Ludność żydowska w Polsce w wiekach XIX i XX* (1930), 121, 130, 147.

ZDUNSKA WOLA (Pol. **Zduńska Wola**), district capital in the province of Lodz, Poland. In 1788 the owners of the town erected at their own expens e a wooden structure to serve as a synagogue to encourage Jewish settlement. Of the 32 families who lived there in 1778, 11 were Jewish, eight of whom earned their livelihood as craftsmen and three in commerce. In addition to the taxes owed to the crown, every Jewish family had to pay 16 to 50 zlotys annually to the owners of the estate. The Jewish community body also had to pay an annual rent of 130 zlotys for the synagogue. In 1825 the settlement was granted municipal status and at the same time the residence rights of the Jews were limited to two streets. In 1827 there were 468 Jews (17% of the total population) in the town. In the 1830s, when Jewish financiers took the initiative of opening a woolcloth industry (with manufacture on a contractual basis), some of them were authorized to erect stone houses beyond the Jewish streets. During the second half of the 19th century Jewish merchants became pioneers in the manufacture of cotton cloth. The rapid industrialization of Zdunska Wola attracted Jews from the surrounding towns as well as from Lithuania. In 1857 the number of Jews had risen to 1,676 (26% of the population), and in 1897 to 7,252 (46% of the total). The majority were engaged as craftsmen, particularly as weavers. At the beginning of the 20th century a class of Jewish industrial workers had already developed.

Until 1828 the community of Zdunska Wola was subject to the jurisdiction of the *Lask community. In 1825 a cemetery was established which was enlarged in 1850. During the 1840s a *bet midrash* was founded, and in 1852 the old wooden synagogue was replaced by a large one with funds contributed by Feibush Opatowski. The community's first rabbi, Levi Cybis, was appointed in 1825. During the tenure of office of Levi Isaac Fleischer (from 1873), Gur and *Aleksandrow Ḥasidism gained ground, while among the Jews of Lithuanian origin *Haskalah was the prevailing influence. Eliezer *Kaplan taught in the secular Jewish schools founded at the beginning of the 20th century.

In 1921 there were 7,885 Jews (42% of the total population) living in the town. Between the two world wars, the community maintained a Hebrew *Tarbut school, an elementary school of the CYSHO (see *Education), a *Beth Jacob school for girls, and a *talmud torah*. The Jewish population numbered 8,819 in 1931. From 1931 antisemitism began to spread in the town, particularly among the German population. In 1936 there was even an attempt to stage a blood libel.

[Arthur Cygielman]

Holocaust Period

There were close to 10,000 Jews, comprising nearly 50% of the total population, in Zdunska Wola at the outbreak of World War II. The German armies entered on Sept. 6, 1939, and immediately destroyed the synagogue and burned all the liturgical objects. In October, in retaliation for the alleged killing of a German policeman, over 3,000 Jews were arrested and kept in prisons in Sieradz for several days. During this *Aktion* many Jews were maltreated and some killed. The extortion of large sums of money and the eviction of Jewish families from predominantly non-Jewish districts followed. In the spring of 1940 a ghetto was formed on the outskirts of the city and over 8,000 Jews were crowded inside. In the meantime the number of Jews in Zdunska Wola increased as a result of the transfer of various groups from other towns and villages in western Poland annexed by Germany. A series of workshops was organized in the ghetto for furriers, tailors, shoemakers, and knitters. Their products were bought by the German army at a low price. On the outskirts of the ghetto Zionist youths received agricultural training on a farm. They helped supply the ghetto with vegetables and milk. In the summer of 1941 the Germans raided the ghetto to collect able-bodied men for labor camps in the Poznan district. Over 1,000 men were seized, with the cooperation of the Jewish police. In 1942 two public executions took place in which ten Jews accused of smuggling were hanged. The Germans picked the festivals of Purim and Shavuot for that purpose. The ghetto was finally liquidated on Aug. 23–24, 1942. The first *Selektion* was carried out in the ghetto and the second in the Jewish cemetery. Over 1,000 able-bodied Jews were sent to *Lodz ghetto, 550 Jews were murdered on the spot, and between 6,000 and 8,000 were transported to the death camp at *Chelmno. Throughout the existence of the Judenrat, its chairman Jakub Lemberg was held in great esteem for his courageous and selfless leadership in which he often risked his life. He also was murdered during the liquidation of the ghetto.

[Danuta Dombrowska]

BIBLIOGRAPHY: J. Smiałowski, in: *Rocznik łódzki*, 2 (1959); D. Dąbrowska, in: BŻIH, 13–14 (1955), passim; I. Tabaksblat, *Khurbn Lodz* (1946), passim; *Zdunska Wola* (Heb., Yid. (same) Eng., 1968); B. Wasiutyński, *Ludnóśść żydowska w polsce w wiekach XIX I XX* (1930), 27.

ZEALOTS AND SICARII.

Introduction

This article deals not only with the group of fighters for the freedom of Israel known from *Josephus as the "Zealots," but includes in its survey other groups with similar aims, particularly the Sicarii.

Judea differed from the other provinces in the east of the Roman Empire in that it never resigned itself to Roman rule and did not willingly become integrated into the Imperial system. From the beginning of the Roman conquest its history was one of bitter struggle accompanied by revolts against the Imperial power. Although there were revolts in the Western parts of the Empire too (in Britain and Gaul and by the Batavi), these were not as frequent and they generally occurred in the early stages of Roman occupation and on the frontiers of the Empire. In Judea, however, a province that lay in the heart of a vital area, between Syria and Egypt, relations with the Roman authorities were in a state of almost continuous tension from the period of *Pompey and *Gabinius until after the *Bar Kokhba War.

The causes of this tension are to be found first and foremost in the religious-ideological conflict between the belief of the Jews in the doctrine that they were the Chosen People and therefore unique and the bitter fact that they were forcibly subjected to the rule of an idolatrous empire which accorded divine honors to its emperors. This empire was the complete antithesis of the spiritual conception and way of life of the Jews, and the tension found its resolution in the strengthening of a messianic-eschatological faith at the center of which stood the hope of the revival of the glory of Israel and the downfall of "the kingdom of arrogance." The intensity of this feeling and these yearnings increased with the passage of time and was nurtured by the deterioration in relations between the Roman administration of the province, which gave its support to non-Jewish elements and based itself on them, and the Jews, as well as by the spiritual and social developments within the Jewish community itself. In the year 66 C.E. the great majority of the people supported the revolt against the procurator Florus, some enthusiastically and some with reservations; only a minority, such as *Agrippa II, were prepared to employ force to suppress the uprising while it was still in its initial stages. The ferment, however, was provided by certain groups among the Jews which developed a specific and definite ideology of objection in principle to Roman suzerainty. Other elements attached themselves to these groups, and their activism was no less positive despite the fact that the principles upon which they based themselves were less clearly defined.

The essential lines of the ideological currents, activities, and main divisions of the Jewish freedom fighters at the close of the Second Temple period can only be drawn in a general way. Fate has willed it that the main source of knowledge of this remarkable phenomenon – the ideology of Jewish liberty in this period – was their inveterate and uncompromising opponent, Josephus. Josephus not only wrote his most important work on this subject, *The Jewish War*, as the official historian of the Flavian dynasty and with personal reasons for denigrating the image of the rebels against Rome; he also developed a theory according to which the extremist elements among them, who constituted only a minority of the people, dragged in their wake the whole Jewish population in the direction of an insane rebellion. Josephus almost completely ignored the messianic-eschatological aspects of the struggle. Nevertheless, even from his prejudiced and one-sided account, something of the ideals which animated the Jewish warriors in their struggle against Rome emerges.

The "Fourth Philosophy" and the Sicarii

In Book 7 of *The Jewish War* (253–74) Josephus distinguishes in a general way between the various parties which took part in the resolute stand against Rome. In respective order, he mentions the Sicarii, the followers of *John of Giscala, the soldiers of *Simeon bar Giora, and finally the Zealots. The main distinctions are exemplified also in incidents which he describes in his detailed description of these sects in the earlier books of *The Jewish War*. Both references help towards an understanding of events. As stated, the Sicarii are mentioned first in the general summary in Book 7. Elsewhere Josephus describes the emergence of this extreme freedom group against the background of the establishment of the Province of Judea, which was connected with the census instituted by *Quirinius, the legate of Syria, in the year 6 C.E. (Ant. 18:4–10). The census was a profound shock to the Jewish people as a whole and it was only after considerable effort that the high priest at the time, Joezer ben Boethus, succeeded in quietening the emotions aroused among the majority of the people. Nevertheless, *Judah the Galilean of Gamala in Gaulanitis joined forces with *Zadok the Pharisee to issue a call for armed revolt, since in their eyes the census represented outright slavery. In their speeches they went so far as to declare that God would come to the aid of those who did not spare themselves in the struggle. According to Josephus, Judah and Zadok were the founders of the "Fourth Philosophy," the other three being the *Pharisees, the *Sadducees, and the *Essenes. After they acquired a great number of followers they involved the Jewish body politic in uprisings and sowed the seeds of the future catastrophes which were to overwhelm the Jewish people. Later on, after he gives a description of the "three philosophies," Josephus returns to Judah, whom he refers to simply as "the Galilean," and gives a succinct account of his "philosophy." According to him the adherents of this philosophy agree in general with the Pharisees, and are distinguished from them only by their unbounded love for freedom and by the fact that they accept God as their only master and leader. They are freely and readily prepared to submit to even the most horrible of deaths and to see their relations and friends tortured rather than accept human domination. Josephus even emphasizes that this resolute determination of theirs is widely known and therefore there is no fear that the truth of what he says will be challenged; on the contrary, he is afraid that he may not have sufficiently emphasized their indifference to torture (Ant. 18:23–5).

In *The Jewish War* (2:117–8) only a precis is given of this. The census of Quirinius is not even mentioned in this connection – only that *Coponius was sent as governor to Judea. During his years of rule a Galilean called Judah incited the people to revolt against the Romans and accused them of cowardice for consenting to pay taxes to the Romans and tolerating the rule of man when their only ruler was God. This man Judah was a "sage" (σοφιστής) and the founded a sect which was entirely different from all the other sects. Zadok the Pharisee is not mentioned at all in the *War*; nor does Josephus mention in this work that, apart from their principle of freedom, the philosophy of the Zealots was identical with that of the Pharisees. Nowhere does he mention the end of Judah the Gaulanite, or Galilean; only in the New Testament (Acts 5:37) is it stated that he was put to death by the Romans.

It seems reasonable to accept the theory of those scholars who identify Judah the Gaulanite with Judah ben Hezekiah, who headed the revolt in Galilee against Varus after the death of *Herod in 4 B.C.E. (Ant. 17:271–2; War 2:56). Thus Judah assembled a large number of followers and attacked the royal palace in *Sepphoris, the capital of *Galilee. According to Josephus he had aspirations to the throne of Judea. And whereas he gives the details of the fate which befell the other leaders of rebellion at that time, such as Simeon of Transjordan and *Athronges and his brothers, and the manner in which the rebellions were suppressed, he is completely silent about the fate of Judah. It would appear that he escaped and reemerged ten years later, by which time his ideology had already been worked out and disseminated among the whole people. The father of this Judah was that *Hezekiah who rose to fame as a fighter and leader in the forties of the first pre-Christian century, during the rule of Julius Caesar, and was executed by Herod at the beginning of his political career when he was appointed governor of Galilee. His execution produced a wave of bitterness in Judea and even resulted in Herod's being summoned before the Sanhedrin in Jerusalem.

Of Hezekiah we are told that he was active in the area bordering on Syria and that his execution by Herod was greeted enthusiastically by the Syrians (War 1:204–5; Ant. 14:159–60). This is easily explained on the assumption that Hezekiah was a native of Gamala in the Gaulanitis, as is mentioned explicitly with regard to Judah, the father of the Fourth Philosophy.

Hezekiah and his son were the founders of a dynasty of leaders of an extremist freedom movement, a dynasty which it is possible to trace until the fall of *Masada and the final crushing of Jewish opposition to Rome. They, the proponents of the Fourth Philosophy, were the first to raise the standard of revolt against the Roman Empire and were the last of those who waged the battle in Ereẓ Israel itself and preached rebellion throughout the length and breadth of the Diaspora. Among the descendants of Judah was *Eleazar b. Jair, the commander of Masada. Eleazar and his men are usually called Sicarii (Σικαριοι) by Josephus, and the same historian also explicitly identifies the Sicarii with the fomenters of unrest after the census of Quirinius (War 7:252–5): "This fortress was called Masada; and the Sicarii who had occupied it had at their head a man of influence named Eleazar. He was a descendant of the Judas who, as we previously stated, induced multitudes of Jews to refuse to enroll themselves when Quirinius was sent as censor to Judea. For in those days the Sicarii banded together against those who consented to submit to Rome and in every way treated them as enemies, plundering their property, rounding up their cattle, and setting fire to their habitations, protesting that such persons were nothing but aliens who so ignobly sacrificed the hard-won liberty of the Jews and admitted their preference for the Roman yoke."

In consequence of this, it should in general be assumed that when Josephus refers to the Sicarii, the reference is to the successors of Judah the Gaulanite, the upholders of the extremist ideology. Apart from the quotation given above in which he identifies the fomenters of unrest in the time of Quirinius with the Sicarii, the first time he feels the need to employ the term Sicarii is against the background of the events during the procuratorships of *Felix (52–60 C.E.) and *Festus (60–62). The word itself is a Latin one, and Josephus points out that it was given to them because of the dagger (*sica*) which they carried concealed in their garments and with which they were accustomed to dispose of their enemies (War 2:255, Ant. 20:186). It is clear that such a pejorative name was first given to them by their Roman opponents.

The name Sicarii appears for the period of the procuratorship of Felix only in *The Jewish War* (2:254–7). They are mentioned there as a new phenomenon and in this context Josephus does not give the connection between them and the Fourth Philosophy. It would appear that the novelty consisted in the technique which they employed to dispose of political opponents. According to Josephus they used to choose particularly the festivals: they would mingle with the crowds and put their opponents to death without any possibility of being identified. Their first victim was *Jonathan (b. Anan), who had previously been high priest. His murder is also described in the parallel passage of the *Antiquities* (20:162–66), where it is stated that it was carried out under the influence of the procurator Felix, who was interested in getting rid of Jonathan by means of the "bandits" (λησταί). Hence no one was punished for the murder of Jonathan. "The 'bandits' adopted the custom of coming to Jerusalem during the festivals and concealing their weapons in the same way and carrying out their crimes." Thus, in the *Antiquities* Josephus describes the same system and methods as he does in the *War* against the background of the procuratorship of Felix, but without mentioning the same Sicarii. In both works Josephus refrains from presenting any ideological explanation of the stimulus behind these acts. The first time Josephus explicitly mentions the Sicarii in the *Antiquities* is during the procuratorship of Festus (Ant. 20:186–7), and he goes on to describe their activities against the background of the procuratorship of *Albinus (62–64 C.E.). During that procuratorship the Sicarii adopted a new tactic of seizing hostages in order to obtain the release of their comrades who had fallen into the hands of the Romans. It was thus that they seized the secretary of *Eleazar, the son of the previous high priest, *Ananias, who served as "captain of the Temple" (στρατηγός τοῦ ἱεροῦ) and sent a message to Ananias that he would be released only in exchange for ten of their men who were being held by Albinus. When they succeeded in this, others were captured and held as hostages and similarly released in exchange for other Sicarii (Ant. 20:208–10).

The New Testament also mentions the Sicarii during the procuratorship of Felix (Acts 21:38). According to this reference the Roman officer Claudius Lysias was of the opinion that *Paul was identical with an Egyptian visionary who had led 4,000 Sicarii into the wilderness. It is, however, highly doubtful if there is any justification for assuming any connection between the Egyptian prophet and the adherents of the Fourth Philosophy.

The few references to the Sicarii in the Talmud already belong to the period of the war itself. First there is the Mishnah (Makhshirim 1:6): "It once happened that the men of Jerusalem hid their fig-cakes in the water because of the Sicarii, and the sages declared them not susceptible [to ritual uncleanness]." Similarly in *Avot de-Rabbi Nathan* (7 p. 20, version (B), ed. Schechter, 1945[2]): "When Vespasian came and surrounded Jerusalem… the Sicarii took the initiative and set fire to all the granaries." In Eccles. R. to 7:12 there is mention of Ben Batiaḥ, "the head of the Sicarii in Jerusalem," and to the same category of information belongs the story of *Abba Sikra, the leader of the *biryonim*, the son of the sister of Rabban *Johanan b. Zakkai (Git. 56a).

As is evident from the interchange of Sicarii and Zealots (*Kanna'im*) in the text of *Avot de-Rabbi Nathan*, and as one can also infer from the use of the name Sicarii in Acts, it is by no means certain that in the talmudic passages the word necessarily refers to the Fourth Philosophy and to the adherents of the Galilean dynasty. It is possible that the word is sometimes used more flexibly than in Josephus.

The suggestion has also been put forward that the "Galileans" mentioned by Epictetus (Arrian, Discourses 4:7, 6) are in fact the disciples of Judah the Galilean, but the accepted view which identifies them with the Christians seems more reasonable.

In the period between the census and the outbreak of the Great Revolt the descendants of Judah are mentioned only once. Two of his sons are referred to – Jacob and Simeon, who were crucified by the procurator Tiberius Julius *Alexander between 46 and 48 C.E. (Ant. 20:102). There is no information as to the activities for which they received this punishment, or whether their area of operation was Galilee or Judea. It is clear, however, even in the absence of such information, that they stood at the center of the rebel activities, and when the opportunity presented itself with the outbreak of the Revolt, *Menahem, one of the descendants of Judah, took a leading part in the events.

After the offering of the daily sacrifice for the welfare of the Emperor was discontinued on the initiative of Eleazar the son of Ananias, and fighting was raging in the streets of Jerusalem between the rebels and those who strove for peace with the Romans, the peace party being aided by the soldiers sent by Agrippa II, there was created a situation whereby the royal troops held control of the Upper City while the rebels were in control of the Temple and the Lower City. The outcome was decided when many of the Sicarii joined forces with the rebels. The army of Agrippa was routed and his opponents broke through into the Upper City and set not only the royal palace on fire, but "eager to destroy the moneylenders' bonds, and to prevent the recovery of debts, in order to win over a host of grateful debtors and to cause a rising of the poor against the rich, sure of impunity," they also burned the archives. This passage seems to point to the extremist social ideology of the Sicarii under the leadership of Menahem.

The fortress of *Antonia also fell to the rebels and a siege was laid to the palace of Herod. At this stage, however, a schism took place. Menahem, who had already gained control of Masada, acquired a rich booty of weapons with which he armed his adherents. He then began to act as the sole leader of the revolt. "He returned like a veritable king to Jerusalem, became the leader of the revolution, and directed the siege of the palace."

Menahem captured the palace of Herod with the exception of the three towers (Hippicus, Phasael, and Mariamne) in which the Roman soldiers took refuge. It was at this time that the former high priest Ananias and his brother were captured and put to death by Menahem's men. His ambition, which apparently had a messianic-eschatological character, aroused the opposition of the other rebels commanded by Eleazar the son of Ananias. They attacked him when he was dressed in royal robes and accompanied by his admirers. In the fight Menahem was placed at a disadvantage. He himself escaped to the Ophel, but was captured and put to death. A similar fate overtook his associates, of whom the most prominent was *Absalom. Many of the Sicarii were killed and a siege was laid to those who hid themselves. Some of them, under the leadership of Eleazar b. Jair, a member of the family of Judah the Galilean, found refuge in Masada, which, as stated, had earlier been captured by Menahem (War 2:422–48).

From this time on the Sicarii ceased to be the guiding factor in the events in Jerusalem. Nevertheless, they continued to exist and it was they who were destined to be the last to hold aloft the standard of rebellion. Although they were no longer in control of Jerusalem and it is not possible to ascribe predominance to them in any part of Jewish Ereẓ Israel apart from Masada, it can be stated with near certainty that many of them continued their activities in other parts of the country and were a factor in the incitement of the people. It is possible to see evidence of this in the explicit and detailed information given of the activities of the Sicarii when, after the destruction of the Temple, they fled to Egypt and Cyrenaica. It is certain that these refugees did not come from Masada nor belong to the soldiers of Eleazar b. Jair, since those all met their end at Masada. These men were completely consistent in their outlook, following the principles of Judah the Galilean, just as before their flight to Egypt and Cyrenaica they had clung to them in Jerusalem and elsewhere in Ereẓ Israel. In addition, the considerable number of the warriors who fought under Simeon bar Giora at the time of the siege is easily explained on the assumption that many Sicarii were included in his army, since they felt themselves more in sympathy with him than with the other leaders in besieged Jerusalem. Their extreme social views bridged the gap between them and Simeon. It might be added that the impression that the Sicarii were an influential factor in besieged Jerusalem is gained to some extent from the above-mentioned talmudic sources. The group of Sicarii who formed a unit under the leadership of Eleazar b. Jair – that group to which Josephus consistently gives the name Sicarii – entrenched itself in Masada and the sphere of its operations was confined to the adjacent area, and there is mention of their attack on En-Gedi (War 4:398–405). When Simeon bar Giora was forced to leave the vicinity of Jerusalem owing to the pressure of Anan ben Anan, he found a temporary refuge with the Sicarii in the wilderness of Judea. They refused, however, to join him in major exploits which would take them far away from their secure base in Masada (War 4:503–7) and there is no further mention of them by Josephus until after the destruction of the Temple. The recent excavations at Masada revealed many potsherds on which the names of the Masada fighters appear. From these sherds one learns of their conscientious observance of the commandments of the Torah, finding expression in such things as their meticulous adherence to the laws of the tithe. Masada is also the only place apart from *Qumran where fragments have been found of the *Dead Sea sect (a scroll of the Sabbath Sacrifice). It seems that its source was the people of Qumran who joined the warriors of Judea at some stage of the war, although one is not entitled to identify the members of the sect, on this account, with the Sicarii or the Zealots. It is a fact that the Essenes participated in the Great Revolt. It was the second senatorial governor of the province of Judea, *Silva, who decided finally to stamp out the last vestiges of Jewish resistance and to capture the last stronghold of the Jews. After all hopes of maintaining this position had failed, and the Romans were poised to storm it, the defenders took the decision to immolate themselves rather than fall into the hands of the Romans. This decision to commit mass suicide was in keeping with the tradition of the Fourth Philosophy. For many of them the choice was in fact between death through torture by the Romans or taking their own lives. Others without doubt had to choose between the difficult alternative of accepting Roman domination, which in their eyes amounted to "Desecration of the Divine Name" (see *Kiddush ha-Shem*) and death. But even those who might have been prepared to accept Roman rule and make a public declaration to that effect could only look forward to cruel slavery, while a life of shame faced the women. It is true that Jewish soldiers had been placed in a similar situation in other localities in Ereẓ Israel, and yet only in isolated instances does one hear of suicide in preference to captivity. Thus there is reference to the suicide of the last defenders of *Jotapata, as well as of many of the defenders of Gamala (War 4:79), the city of origin of Judah, the spiritual father of the movement. Josephus also tells of the two priests Meir the son of Bilga and Joseph the son of Dalaeus who threw themselves into the flames of the Temple, and that the survivors of the Zealots sought their death in the field of battle after the capture of the city. Dio Cassius also reports the suicide of many of the defenders of the Temple.

In this mass suicide the essential principle of the Fourth Philosophy undoubtedly played an important role. They faced the danger of transgressing their religious faith, since in their eyes recognition of Roman rule was tantamount to idolatry. The choice before them therefore was not different in essence from that which faced the Jewish communities of the Rhineland in the First Crusade of 1096 or the martyrs of York in 1190.

The two speeches of Eleazar b. Jair in which he urged his followers to put an end to their lives bear the genuine stamp of the Greek rhetoric of the period of the Roman Empire, and it is not difficult to detect in it characteristic ideas taken from Greek philosophy and literature; at least the Stoic tradition recognized the legitimacy of suicide. But in addition to this it contains also the specific ideas of the Fourth Philosophy as indeed Eleazar b. Jair could give expression to it at that fateful moment. There is also in it something of the historical philosophy of Josephus himself as it finds expression in the *War* generally. Already at the beginning of his speech Eleazar emphasizes the essential idea which inspired him and his men not to become subservient to the Romans or to any man but only to God himself (War 7:323–5): "Long ago, my brave men, we determined neither to serve the Romans nor any other save God, for He alone is man's true and righteous Lord; and now the time is come which bids us put that resolution to the test by our actions. In this crisis let us not disgrace ourselves. We who in the past refused to submit even to a slavery involving no peril, let us not now, along with slavery, deliberately accept the irreparable penalties awaiting us if we are to fall alive into Roman hands. For as we were the first to revolt, so are we the last in arms against them. Moreover, I believe that it is God who has granted us this favor, that we have it in our power to die nobly and in freedom – a privilege denied to others who have met with unexpected defeat" (War 7:407–19).

The influence of the Sicarii refugees was not confined to Egypt. It also embraced the city of *Cyrene and other cities of the Libyan Pentapolis. A certain Jonathan, a weaver by trade, was active in these cities, influencing many of the Jews belonging to the lower classes in Cyrene to follow him to the wilderness where he promised to show signs and wonders, and here also the local Jewish authorities intervened and brought about his arrest by the Roman governor Catullus (War 7:437–40).

As to the extent to which these Sicarii refugees and those who were influenced by their views were a long-range factor in the developments which took place in the lands of the Hellenistic Diaspora, particularly in Egypt and Cyrenaica in the years prior to the revolt during the reign of Trajan and which was its cause, it is difficult to give an answer in the complete absence of sources.

To sum up: it was the outlook of Judah of Gaulanitis and his successors which constituted the most extreme expression of opposition to Roman rule and of Jewish independence. The yearning for the redemption of Israel was the heritage of virtually all sections and classes of the people, but among the adherents of the Fourth Philosophy it led them to immediate action and an activism which knew no compromise, as well as to the recognition that divine aid would come to the energetic and the bold. Acknowledgment of Roman rule was tantamount in their eyes to an affront to divine rule and constituted *Ḥillul ha-Shem*. Consequently they maintained adamantly that it was essential to come out openly in war against Roman rule and also to compel those who disagreed with them to join the struggle. The Hasmoneans in their time had taken up arms when the situation became impossible and the danger of extermination threatened the Jewish faith, but only when the opportune moment came did they act to realize the ancient aspirations of the people for political freedom. The freedom fighters of the school of Judah of Gaulanitis, on the other hand, raised the banner of freedom and opposition to mortal rule without taking account of the realities of the situation. Their ideas fell on fertile ground as a result of the developments which had taken place in the province of Judea and in Jewish society during the last years of the Second Temple period. The eschatological tension which was characteristic of that generation fitted in exactly with the Fourth Philosophy. Nevertheless, only a small number of the fighters for the freedom of Judea during the Great Revolt accepted the specific ideology of the Sicarii of the school of Judah or of the Zealot priests of Jerusalem, between whom and the Sicarii one can posit only a hypothetical connection, as will be seen below. It can also be assumed that, among other groups, the question of leadership and the realization of the eschatological hopes of Menahem constituted from the outset an obstacle to complete identification with the ideology of the Sicarii.

The Zealots of Jerusalem

Among many scholars and in general works one frequently finds that the extreme wing of the freedom fighters which crystallized in the period immediately prior to the destruction of the Temple is identified with the Zealots (Ζηλωταί, *Kanna'im*). Judah of Gaulanitis is regarded as the founder of the Zealots, who are identified as the proponents of the Fourth Philosophy. In the original sources, however, no such identification is anywhere clearly made, and the question is hardly raised of the relationship between the Sicarii, the upholders of the Fourth Philosophy, and the Zealots. Josephus himself in his general survey of the various groups of freedom fighters (War 7:268–70) enumerates the Sicarii first, whereas he mentions the Zealots last. "In this lawlessness the so-called Zealots excelled, a class which justified their name by their actions; for they copied every evil deed, nor was there any villainy recorded in history that they failed to emulate zealously. And yet they took their name from their professed zeal for virtue, either in mockery of those they wronged, so brutal was their nature, or reckoning the greatest of evils good." In presenting the events themselves Josephus first mentions the Zealots in connection with the composition of the temporary government in Jerusalem under the leadership of Joseph ben Gorion after the victory over *Cestius Gallus in the year 66 C.E. Josephus explains why *Eleazar b. Simeon, who distinguished himself in the fighting against the Romans, undoubtedly playing a decisive role, and took possession of most of the booty and the treasury of Cestius Gallus, was not appointed to the government. He explains that he was passed over "because they observed his despotic nature and that the Zealots under him conducted themselves like his bodyguard" (War 2:564). One gains the impression that Josephus is referring here to the Zealots who placed themselves under Eleazar's command as a phenomenon which had existed for some time and does not therefore realize that the reader has not heard of their appearance before.

Despite the fact that Eleazar b. Simeon was temporarily overlooked and not included either in the government of Jerusalem or in the list of the area commanders of the country who were appointed after the victory over the governor of Syria, he nevertheless maintained his decisive influence. In the words of Josephus, "Gradually, however, financial needs and the intrigues of Eleazar had such influence with the people that they ended by yielding the supreme command to him" (War 2:565). Josephus returns to the Zealots in his description of the subsequent events at the end of Book 2 (651) against the background of the preparation for the war against the Romans in 66–67 and underlines the antagonism which existed between Anan b. Anan and those called the Zealots. This latter name becomes more frequent in the context of the fratricidal war which broke out in Jerusalem after the war in Galilee. The war approached Jerusalem towards the end of 67 C.E.; the Roman army was already in control of *Jabneh and *Ashdod and large numbers of refugees and fighters streamed from the different places to the capital and joined the extreme elements there (War 4:138). These reinforced units began to take action against the moderate elements who until then had been in control of the city, particularly against individuals who were suspected of wishing to come to terms with the Romans. The first victim was a certain Antipas, who belonged to the house of Herod and tried to stop the rebels at the outbreak of the revolt. Together with two other members of the royal family he was imprisoned, and shortly afterwards they were put to death. The extremists took a revolutionary step in abolishing the system which had been established since the time of Herod and reserved the *high priesthood to a number of families which in effect constituted the priestly oligarchy. This privilege had not been abolished even in the time of *Agrippa I. The high priesthood had continued to alternate between these oligarchic houses; from time to time the transfer was accompanied by reprehensible dealings, such as the bribery of the appointing authorities. In the years immediately preceding the Revolt the right of appointment was entrusted to Agrippa II, and the last high priest appointed by him was *Mattathias, the son of Theophilus II. It was now decided to introduce a complete democracy in the high priesthood and to choose by *lot. The lot fell upon Pinḥas (*Phinehas) b. Samuel of Kefar Havta. With the aim of portraying this change in the blackest of colors Josephus states that Pinḥas was "a man who not only was not descended from high priests, but was such a clown that he scarcely knew what the high priesthood meant. At any rate they dragged their reluctant victim out of the country, and dressing him up for his assumed part, as on a stage, put the sacred vestments upon him and instructed him as to how to act in keeping with the occasion. To them this monstrous impiety was a subject for jesting and sport, but the other priests, beholding from a distance this mockery of their law, could not restrain their tears and bemoaned the degradation of the sacred honors" (War 4:139–57). This Pinḥas is also mentioned in the talmudic sources, according to which he was a stonemason by trade, but they add that he had married into the House of Hillel. The view expressed by some scholars that this appointment constituted the restoration of the ancient glory of the high priesthood, since he belonged to the House of Zadok, in whose hands the high priesthood had been until the appointment of the Hasmoneans, is highly doubtful and there is nothing to support such a suggestion in the extant sources.

In his actual description of these events, the arrest and execution of the three members of the Herodian house and the revolutionary change in the selection of the high priest, Josephus does not mention the Zealots as such. The subsequent account, however, establishes it as a certainty that it was they who acted as the instigators. At the assembly called at the insistence of the most important of the previous high priests, under the influence of these events, *Joshua b. Gamla and Anan b. Anan castigated those present for their indifference and explicitly incited them against the Zealots. In other words, they attributed to them those actions which they were denouncing. It is in this context that Josephus for the first time explains the name Zealot, which henceforth he uses frequently, "for so they called themselves, as though they were zealous in the cause of virtue and not for vice in its basest and most extravagant form" (War 4:161).

The existing leadership in Jerusalem decided to embark upon an open struggle against the attempts of the Zealots to seize the reins of power. Numbered among these chief opponents, in addition to Joshua b. Gamla and Anan, were Goryon b. Joseph and *Simeon b. Gamaliel (War 4:159). In a rousing address Anan incited the citizens of Jerusalem against the Zealots who had fortified themselves in the Temple, and the Temple Mount was besieged. The struggle was decided in favor of the Zealots only with the entry of thousands of Idumeans into Jerusalem who ranged themselves on the side of the Zealots (War 4:162–304).

The Zealots were now in control of Jerusalem (winter of 67–8 C.E.) and their chief opponents were put to death, among them Anan b. Anan, Joshua b. Gamla, Goryon b. Joseph, and the commander *Niger from Transjordan. Meanwhile, however, a split took place between the Zealots and the Idumeans (War 4:305–65).

At this stage of events John of Giscala was in alliance with the Zealots, although Josephus does not mention his activities either with regard to the fight which took place in Jerusalem or the execution of the leading opponents of the Zealots. It is possible that John contented himself with giving aid to them without involving himself personally in the fight against those with whom he had previously cooperated. The Zealots and John of Giscala were now the two main powers in Jerusalem, but this situation changed fundamentally when Simeon bar Giora wrested control of the Upper City and portions of the Lower City. As a result the capital was divided into three parts. Eleazar b. Simeon continued as the commander of the Zealots, fortifying himself and his men particularly in the Temple. They maintained their hold there as a result of a topographical advantage which made up for their numerical inferiority compared with the men of John (War 5:5–10). After the appearance of *Titus before the walls of Jerusalem in the spring of 70, however, John took the bold step of adding the Zealots to his command; using the excuse of the Festival of Passover, according to Josephus, he infiltrated his armed men into the Temple area and thus established his domination over them (War 5:98–105). From this time onwards the Zealots were under the overall command of John in the same way as the Idumeans accepted the command of Simeon bar Giora. Both of these groups, however, continued to maintain their separate identity (War 5:250) and in the battles which raged between the Romans and the Jews during the siege the Zealots, distinguishing themselves by their courage, achieved a prominence comparable to those who belonged to the other camps (War 6:92, 148).

The sources are silent as to the fate of Eleazar b. Simeon and *Zechariah b. Avkilus, the principal leaders of the Zealots. It would appear that they were killed, or died, before the final fall of the Temple. Of at least one of the outstanding Zealot fighters during the siege, Judah b. Ari, it is known that he escaped from Jerusalem and that many of the fighters rallied around him. In the forest of Jardes they were encircled by a unit of Roman cavalry, while the infantry were cutting down the trees to blaze a trail through the forest. All the Jewish fighters, among whom there must have been many of the Zealots from Jerusalem, fell in the battle, including their Zealot commander Judah (War 7:210–15). Their end was more similar to that of the Sicarii – despite the fact that it was not actually a case of mass suicide but the fall of heroes in the field of battle – than to the fate of Simeon bar Giora or John of Giscala, who fell alive into the hands of the Romans.

There seems little reason to doubt that the priests of Jerusalem were the fomenting element among the Zealots. Their essential base was always the Temple Mount and at least two of their principal leaders, Eleazar b. Simeon and Zechariah b. Avkilus, were priests (War 4:225). To them one may add, as will become clear below, *Eleazar b. Hananiah. Josephus also testifies that three more of their leaders were notables in Jewish society, "Judas the son of Chelcias, and Simon son of Esron, persons of might, along with a man of some distinction, Ezechias of Chobari" (War 5:6).

It would even appear that the very name *Kanna'im* has a priestly connection, in that they consciously regarded themselves as the spiritual descendants of the "Kanna'i" par excellence of Jewish tradition, Pinḥas (*Phinehas) the son of Eleazar (Num. 25:11).

As has been seen, at least immediately after the Roman victory in *Beth-Horon, the *Kanna'im* emerge as a recognized and definite factor, but it is possible to go further back and see as an act of the Zealots the decisive step which from the formal point of view marked the outbreak of the Revolt – the cessation of the daily sacrifice in honor of the Roman Emperor at the instigation of Eleazar b. Hananiah (War 2:409). It appears that despite the fact that he belonged to high priestly circles, his sympathies were all with the *Kanna'im*. It is not out of place to note that according to the talmudic tradition (Git. 56a) this symbolic and decisive act is connected with an individual who is known from Josephus as the second most prominent leader of the Zealots after Eleazar b. Simeon, namely Zechariah b. Avkilus: "Through the scrupulousness of R. Zechariah b. Avkilus our sanctuary was destroyed, our Temple burnt, and we ourselves were exiled from our land." The suggestion that the Zealots received considerable support from Bet Shammai has been put forward in the past and there is undoubtedly some basis for it.31 A consideration of the activity of Bet Shammai at the beginning of the Revolt as described in the halakhic sources fits in perfectly with what has been assumed as the ideology of the *Kanna'im*. Is it, however, possible to see the activities of the *Kanna'im* as the expression of a defined current and a consolidated group in the period prior to the Revolt?

It is certain that Josephus, the primary and most important source, and the only one to describe the ideologies of the Jews at the close of the Second Temple, does not employ the word Zealots at all in respect to the previous events. One cannot, however, infer far-reaching conclusions from this silence, since even at the beginning of the Revolt he does not mention the formation of the sect, and it is only casually that he notes the connection between Eleazar b. Simeon and the *Kanna'im*, referring to them consistently only from Book IV of the *War* onwards. However, even the other sources shed little light on the subject. The reference of *Avot de-Rabbi Nathan* to them (ARN[1], ed. Shechter, 6, p. 32) is already to the days of the war and the siege of Jerusalem, while the statement of the Mishnah (Sanh. 9:6), "If a man stole a sacred vessel or cursed by *kosem*, or made an Aramean woman his paramour, the Zealots may fall upon him," is directed more to a way of life than to a group with a definite ideology. On the other hand, more weight can be given to the name Zealot given to Simeon, one of the disciples of Jesus, in Luke and Acts (Luke 6:15, Acts 1:13).

Nevertheless, without coming to any definite conclusion with regard to the first appearance of this name, the question can be raised of the initial emergence of an ideology firmly maintained by a specific group and active in the life of the Jews during the Second Temple period.

The historians of the 19th century took it as a fact that the Zealots were identical with the adherents of the Fourth Philosophy, and therefore constituted a division of the same movement to which the Sicarii belonged. This opinion was widely accepted by various scholars. On the other hand, in the 20th century certain scholars flatly denied any connection between the adherents of the Fourth Philosophy and the Zealot ideology, and even the emergence of a specific Zealot faction in the period preceding the Revolt. It must, in fact, be conceded that there is no clear evidence in the sources of any connection between the Fourth Philosophy and the Zealots during the Revolt, especially as the interpretation given to the sole reference to the followers of Menahem as "Zealots" (War 2:444) is open to doubt.

Despite this, however, there appears to be a certain connection between the two and the assumption, though far from decisive, is a reasonable one. As mentioned above, Josephus (Ant. 18:4; cf. 18:9) mentions as the two founders of the Fourth Philosophy Judah of Gamala in Gaulanitis and Zadok the Pharisee. Both the name Zadok and his appellation as a Pharisee suggest, on the one hand, that he belonged to the priestly circles and, on the other, that he was a well-known sage. In a hypothetical manner one can posit this Zadok as the formulator of that ideology which later characterized the Zealots of Jerusalem during the Revolt, whose leaders were the priests of the Temple and who were close to the Bet Shammai.

This assumption of a certain connection between the Zealots and the Fourth Philosophy also serves better to explain the decisive importance which Josephus ascribes to the Fourth Philosophy, on which he places the chief blame for the chain of disasters which befell the Jewish people, culminating in the destruction of the Temple. The limitation of the members of the Fourth Philosophy to the Sicarii, whose activity was impressive, in fact, only at the beginning of the Revolt, and even then it was not they who were responsible for the cessation of the daily sacrifice for the welfare of the Emperor, raises the question as to why Josephus found it necessary to underscore with so much emphasis the fateful guilt of the men of the Fourth Philosophy, to make it appear that they were responsible for all the disasters. It is perhaps possible here to add the two different versions of *Avot de-Rabbi Nathan*, in which Zealots are mentioned in one and the Sicarii in the other, and their mention in juxtaposition in the statement of the Church Father Hippolytus, although the passage is far from clear. And lastly, it should be mentioned that neither Zealots nor the Sicarii were prepared to be captured alive by the Romans.

In the light of these considerations it appears that one can posit, albeit with some caution, the hypothesis that there was indeed a certain connection and cooperation between the founders of the Zealots and of the Sicarii during the census of Quirinius, and that from the outset the difference between these two movements was a tangible one. This difference found its expression in the decisive schism which took place during the Revolt after a brief period of cooperation at its beginning.

What then was it that differentiated the Zealots from the Sicarii and the other groups who fought against the Romans for the freedom of Judea? The differences can be enumerated as follows:

1. Whereas the Sicarii obtained their initial inspiration from Gaulanitis and Galilee in the north, the Zealots were directed by a group of priests in Jerusalem, and it was the Temple which was their main stronghold.

2. The Sicarii continued to be loyal to the dynasty of Judah the Galilean, their last leaders being Menahem and Eleazar b. Jair, who were scions of that house; in contrast the Zealots showed no particular loyalty to any house or dynasty.

3. The Zealots were not of the opinion that the eschatological hopes of the Jews found their expression in the person of any of their leaders. Although Eleazar b. Simeon emerges as their outstanding leader, other leaders worked together with him, and the impression gained is that of collective leadership. Side by side with him stood personalities like Zechariah b. Avkilus and the brothers Simeon and Judah, the sons of Ari.

Simeon bar Giora

The program of the Zealots included the reform of the institution of the high priesthood. As soon as they were able to do so they went to the extreme in the direction of democratizing this office by completely abolishing the high priestly oligarchy which had stamped its impression on Jewish society from the time of Herod and, as mentioned above, chose the incumbent by lot. In the siege of Jerusalem during the spring and summer of 70 C.E., however, the leaders of the Sicarii are conspicuously missing, and the leaders of the Zealots were relatively unimportant; although prominent in the affairs of the capital, they did not hold the most important posts. The two commanders in besieged Jerusalem until its fall at the hands of Titus were *Simeon bar Giora of Gerasa and *John of Giscala. It is possible to a certain extent to trace the connections of Simeon with the Sicarii in Masada, as well as to detect the bond that was established during a certain period between John and the Zealots of Jerusalem. Nevertheless it is completely out of the question to maintain that Simeon definitely belonged to the Sicarii or that John became a member of the Zealots. All that it is possible to establish is that there was a certain identification between Simeon bar Giora and the Sicarii as regards their social outlook and that at a certain stage during the struggle John came to recognize clearly that the Zealots were his true allies in a consistent and effective stand against the Romans. Both Simeon and John are mentioned side by side with Eleazar b. Simeon as the commanders in Jerusalem, not only by Josephus but by the Roman historian Tacitus, who enumerates Simeon first and Eleazar last. Titus also regarded Simeon bar Giora as the leading commander and it was he who was chosen by the Romans to exemplify an enemy commander and lead the triumphal procession in Rome. The elevation of Simeon to the position of commander-in-chief was surprising when one takes into consideration his lowly origin and the existence of other individuals more firmly rooted in the tradition of an anti-Roman ideology. Internal developments in Jewish Ereẓ Israel and the abolition of the influential institutions which existed at the beginning of the Revolt, coupled with the charismatic personality of Simeon, go a long way towards explaining his advancement. It would also appear that from the outset Simeon exemplified the strength of certain rebel elements in Jewish Transjordan, an area which had already shown its love for freedom after the death of Herod, when uprisings which broke out in Ereẓ Israel were crushed out by Varus, governor of Syria. From Jewish Transjordan also came one of the important commanders at the outbreak of the Great Revolt, Niger (War 2:520, 566), a man with an outlook and social connections completely different from those of Simeon. The source of Simeon's strength, however, was by no means confined to Transjordan and gradually he became the spokesman of great masses throughout Jewish Ereẓ Israel. Despite the fact that there is no proof that Galileans joined his forces to any extent, it appears that his influence was decisive in the villages of Judea and Idumea. The suggestion has already been put forward that many of the Sicarii joined him – namely, those who did not fortify themselves in Masada. With the murder of Menahem and the departure of Eleazar b. Jair to this isolated stronghold they had lost their traditional leadership. It is a fact that no less than 10,000 out of the 23,400 fighters who defended besieged Jerusalem were directly under the command of Simeon, and to them are to be added 5,000 Idumean soldiers who were associated with them, as against only 6,000 men under the direct command of John of Giscala and 2,400 Zealots who accepted the leadership of Eleazar b. Simeon (War 5:248–50). It thus emerges that under Simeon there were about two-thirds of the total of the defenders of Jerusalem, and the Romans were naturally justified in regarding him as the commander of the enemy forces. As his name indicates, he was descended from proselytes, and he came from *Gerasa, an important Hellenistic city in Transjordan. The ruins of Gerasa and the inscriptions discovered there distinguish it from all the cities in the country and reveal the quality of its life as a Hellenistic city influenced by its Oriental background. Simeon was a young man when the Revolt broke out and was distinguished by his physical strength and courage (ʾαλκῇ δὲ σώματος καὶ τόλμῃ διαφέρων War 4:504). Simeon first acquired fame by his actions against the Roman army which had advanced against Jerusalem under the command of Cestius Gallus. He attacked them from the rear as they were making their way to the ascent of Beth Horon and carried away many of their pack animals as spoil to Jerusalem (War 2:521). When local commanders were appointed to the various districts of Ereẓ Israel by the temporary government, neither Simeon nor the chief hero of the fray, Eleazar b. Simeon, was among them. Already then Simeon had gathered around him many of the rebels in the most northerly toparchy of Judea, that of Acrabatene. In his activities in that area the extreme social policy of Simeon and his followers already became evident. According to Josephus he did not content himself with attacking people of wealth; he even subjected them to physical torture. When Anan b. Anan, who was at that time the central figure in the temporary government in Jerusalem, sent an army against him Simeon apparently could not maintain his position against the authorities in Jerusalem and escaped south to Masada, and henceforth Idumea became his field of action (War 2:652–54), whereas in Jerusalem itself and in the northern part of Judea access was barred to him as long as the temporary government, which had been set up immediately after the victory over Cestius Gallus, was in control.

At first Simeon was regarded with suspicion by the Sicarii in Masada, a fact which proves that under no circumstances can he be regarded as having been one of them. According to Josephus he was permitted access only to the lower part of the fortress. They nevertheless cooperated with him in the raids which he made in the vicinity, since they saw in him "a man of congenial disposition, and apparently to be trusted." New opportunities opened for him, however, when Anan b. Anan fell into the hands of the Zealots. In addition, he increased the number of his followers by proclaiming the emancipation of all slaves (War 4:503–6). His influence spread over all parts of Judea, in the north as well as Idumea, and the masses flocked to his banner, with the result that "his was no longer an army of mere serfs or brigands, but one including numerous citizen recruits, subservient to his command as to a king" (War 4:510). Simeon's growing influence throughout Judea and Idumea brought him into conflict with the Zealots in Jerusalem and with John of Giscala, to whom it became evident that he was depriving them of any hold in Judea beyond the capital. The opponents of the Zealots who escaped from Jerusalem, whatever their ideological outlook might be, found refuge with Simeon (War 4:353). An attempt of the Zealots to restrain Simeon was unsuccessful, but Simeon did not consider his army sufficiently strong to wrest control of Jerusalem, and instead he first tried to bring Idumea under his influence. His attempt to gain control of Herodion ended in failure, but he did succeed in conquering Hebron (War 4:510–37).

Meanwhile the tension between Simeon and the Zealots increased. The latter took Simeon's wife captive in the hope of exerting pressure against him, but, confounded by Simeon's furious reaction, they released her (War 4:538–44) and the conflict in Jerusalem paved the way for Simeon. It would appear that the impetus to invite him to Jerusalem as a counterweight against John and the Zealots came from the Idumeans, and in Nisan (Xanthicus) of 69 C.E. Simeon arrived at the gates of Jerusalem and gained control of a large section of the capital, though his attempt to force the Zealots out of their stronghold in the Temple Mount ended in failure (War 4:566–584). He continued, however, to hold sway over the whole of the Upper City and part of the Lower City, establishing his headquarters in the Tower of Phasael (War 5:169). During the period of the siege Simeon took the initiative in arranging a truce with John of Giscala with the aim of cooperation against their common enemy (War 5:278) and henceforth fought shoulder to shoulder with him. On the other hand he dealt harshly with the upper classes, whom he suspected of collaboration with the Romans. Among those put to death by him were Mattathias b. Boethus and three of his sons (War 5:527–33, 6:114), and he took part together with John in the defense of the Temple before it was destroyed by fire (6:72).

Simeon bar Giora, in contrast to the Sicarii in Masada and the Zealot leaders in Jerusalem, who either committed suicide or fell in the field of battle, did not die during the war. He was taken alive by the Romans and Titus even issued an order to save him for the triumph which he was going to organize in Rome (War 7:25–36). He was sent to his death in that triumph amidst the applause of the Romans, in accordance with Roman custom.

Simeon was beyond doubt the most charismatic figure among the leaders of the Revolt. According to Josephus, his soldiers were prepared to go through fire and water for him (War 5:309) "and his was no longer an army of mere serfs or brigands, but one including numerous citizen recruits, subservient to his command as to a king" (War 4:510). Simeon was first and foremost the leader of the lower classes in Transjordan, Judea, and Idumea. It would be difficult to accord Simeon the epithet of "sage" as Judah and Menahem, the leaders of the Sicarii, are referred to (σοφισταί), nor did his influence and prestige obtain any support from the tradition of a family which for generations had been held in esteem by the people.

The sources are almost completely silent with regard to individual figures who belonged to the camp of Simeon. There is mention of his nephew Eleazar, who distinguished himself in battle (War 6:227), and one of his outstanding aides was Hanan of Emmaus. Nothing, however, is known of the origin or social affiliations of the others, such as Ardala (6:360), Castor (5:322), Judah b. Judah (5:534), Judah b. Mareotes (6:148), Simeon b. Hosaiah (6:148), or Malachi (6:92). One can point to a number of the prominent lines of Simeon's social policy: his vigorous activity against the propertied classes already in the first stage of the war and his emancipation of the slaves. Side by side with these one must underscore the special relationship which he had with his followers.

In accordance with his policy in *The Jewish War*, Josephus tends to ignore the messianic-eschatological element in the Great Revolt. Nevertheless, messianic hopes were associated with Simeon and, as has been stated, in one place (War 4:510) Josephus points out that he was obeyed like a king. There is also a basis for the suggestion that there is a connection between the coins bearing the inscription "*Li-Ge'ullat Ẓiyyon*" ('To the redemption of Zion') and the eschatological hopes which were reposed in the personality of Simeon bar Giora. If, therefore, with regard to social outlook Simeon was close to the general spirit of the Sicarii, there was nevertheless room for disagreement between them in the question of the leadership, since many of the Sicarii found it difficult to recognize the leadership of someone who did not belong to the family of Judah the Galilean. Nevertheless the differences were straightened out to some extent as a result of the absence of a recognized Sicarii leader in Jerusalem after the death of Menahem. Nor should one overlook the fact that whereas the Sicarii leaders, Judah and Menahem, were "sages," the impression gained of Simeon is that of a man who could under no circumstances be regarded as such according to the ideas prevailing in the Second Temple period. The personality of Simeon bar Giora fits in well with the picture one has of many of the popular leaders in the preceding period, during the disturbances which took place after the death of Herod. As is known, at that time there appeared, in addition to Judah b. Hezekiah, who was active in Galilee and conquered Sepphoris, a number of other leaders whose field of action was Jewish Transjordan and Judea itself. One of them was Simeon, the slave of Herod, who was distinguished by his handsomeness, his physical stature and bodily prowess. He assumed the crown and gathered around him a number of followers who proclaimed him king. He also set on fire and looted the royal palace in Jericho. Simeon himself met his death in battle together with his supporters, most of them from Perea (Ant. 17:273–77, War 2:57–59).

Similar to Simeon's conduct and activities were those of another rebel against Herod's son, Athronges, a shepherd by calling and of lowly origin, who also distinguished himself in stature and courage. He also aspired to the throne and, aided by his four brothers, crowned himself. According to Josephus he took a determined line against the Romans as well as against the members of the Herodian house. He made Jews as well as non-Jews suffer if it was to his advantage. Of his activities his attack upon a Roman troop in *Emmaus is mentioned and thus his field of action was in the west of Judea. His activities came to an end as a result of the efforts of Archelaus after he had consolidated his position as ethnarch of Judea (And. 17:278–84; War 2:60–64).

There is a parallel between such figures as Simeon the slave of Herod, Athronges, and Simeon bar Giora. All of them were of lowly origin and all three aspired to the throne, and it is almost certain that this aspiration was connected with the messianic expectations which had become widespread among the people at the time and in the case of all of them these expectations had a social character.

John of Giscala

To an entirely different social milieu belonged *John of Giscala (Gush Ḥalav in Galilee). Josephus, who is practically the sole source for him, displays a special animosity towards the personality of John. Whereas with regard to the individuals and the principles which animated the other freedom fighters he reveals an ideological opposition and blames them for the catastrophes which followed, and, as the near-official historian of the Flavian house he was obliged to denounce them with every kind of denunciation, with regard to John his criticism reveals a profound personal animosity. The roots of this animosity, which runs like a scarlet thread throughout the *War*, and even more so in his autobiography, the *Life*, are to be found mainly in his experiences while serving as commander of Galilee, where John was the most determined and unwavering of his opponents and did everything to have him deposed. This is undoubtedly the source of that hostility and the difference between his description of John and that of the other rebel leaders. The characteristics of John as presented by Josephus (War 2:585–88) reveal such unmistakable signs of contemporary rhetoric as to remind Thackeray, one of the most brilliant students of Josephus, of the description of Catilina by the Roman historian Sallust. "Poor at the beginning of his career, his penury had for a long time thwarted his malicious designs; a ready liar and clever in obtaining credit for his lies, he made a merit of deceit and practiced it upon his most intimate friends; while affecting humanity, the prospect of lucre made him the most sanguinary of men; always full of high ambitions, his hopes were fed on the basest of knaveries. For he was a brigand, who at the outset practiced his trade alone, but afterwards found for his daring deeds accomplices, whose numbers, small at first, grew with his success. He was, moreover, careful never to take into partnership anyone likely to fall an easy prey to an assailant, but selected good, strapping fellows, with stout hearts and military experience." Nevertheless, even Josephus does not attempt to implicate John as one of the inciters of the rebellion against Rome, as a person whose destructive ideology, on the lines of the Fourth Philosophy, was a factor in bringing about the conflagration. John is not mentioned at all as one of those who raised the standard of revolt against the Romans at its outset. On the contrary, when he saw that some of the inhabitants of Gush Ḥalav (*Giscala) were influenced by the ferment, he essayed to restrain them and demanded that they remain loyal to Roman rule (Life, 43). The developments which took place in Galilee, however, as in other regions, in the relations between the Jews and their non-Jewish neighbors caused him to change his attitude. Gush Ḥalav itself was attacked by those non-Jews, who wrought havoc in it. John, who was already then a central figure in the town, armed his followers and made a counterattack against those who had caused the destruction in his town. He gained ascendancy over them and erected a wall around Gush Ḥalav to protect it against similar assaults in the future (Life 44–45). It is also stated that John amassed a fortune through his successful business dealings, which were connected with the sale of the abundant olive oil from Galilee to the Jews of adjacent Syria who refused to use non-Jewish oil.

Josephus testifies that John maintained close contacts with influential circles in the important cities of Galilee such as Gabara, where one of his friends, Simeon, was active (Life 124) and *Tiberias. An important accretion of strength came to him from Jewish refugees from *Tyre (Life 372). Among his friends in Jerusalem was numbered Simeon b. Gamaliel (Life 192). In two parallel narratives in the *War* and in his *Life* Josephus gives the details of John's activity in Galilee prior to the appearance of the Roman army there under Vespasian in 67 C.E. Naturally his description revolves around the personal relations between himself and John. The latter even attempted to influence the leaders of the revolt in Jerusalem to depose Josephus from his post as commander of Galilee. The *Life* in particular gives details of this; of special importance in this episode is the revelation of the close relations and complete mutual understanding which existed between John and Rabban Simeon b. Gamaliel. According to Josephus, Simeon on his part exercised his influence on the former high priests Anan b. Anan and Joshua b. Gamla to come out against Josephus and four emissaries were sent to Galilee for the purpose of deposing him. Their mission ended in complete failure, however, and Josephus continued to serve as commander of Galilee (Life 189–335).

A close examination of Josephus' accounts in his two works gives rise to serious doubts about their credibility, both with regard to the events in Galilee in general and his relationship with John in particular. Two things, however, are clear. One is that John played a leading role in the opposition to Josephus in Galilee and the other is that he cannot under any circumstances be regarded as the mouthpiece of the radical elements. It is known that he maintained excellent relations with Simeon b. Gamaliel, and his opposition to Josephus received the approval of Anan b. Anan.

It fell to John's lot to be the last of the fighters of Galilee. Whereas Josephus surrendered in Jotapata and the last Jewish strongholds in Galilee were captured by the army of *Vespasian and their defenders put to the sword or taken prisoner en masse, John succeeded in escaping from Gush Ḥalav at the head of his men and making his way to Jerusalem (War 4:84–111).

In Jerusalem John at first enjoyed prestige as the outstanding fighter against the Romans and the open opponent of Josephus, who had failed in the defense of Jotapata and whose surrender to the Romans cast suspicion on all his previous conduct of the war. As against this, the success of John in extricating himself with all his men, and bringing them to aid in the defense of Jerusalem, stood out prominently. The fact that he was at the head of an armed force wholeheartedly devoted to him, and subject to his personal command, gave him an advantage over all the other leaders in Jerusalem. The possibility that other refugees from Galilee joined him, since it is a fact that many Jews from Galilee fought in the defense of Jerusalem, including no less than 2,000 from Tiberias alone (Life 354), should be taken into consideration. After his arrival in Jerusalem, John maintained his old ties with the existing Jewish leadership. On the other hand, however, he benefited from the influence of Zealot circles who opposed that leadership, since they saw in him a man of energy and an uncompromising fighter against the Romans. According to Josephus he infused a spirit of courage and hope in the inhabitants of Jerusalem, "extolling their own power, and ridiculing the ignorance of the inexperienced; even had they wings, he remarked, the Romans would never surmount the walls of Jerusalem, after having had such difficulty with the villages of Galilee and having worn out their engines against the walls" (War 4:126–7). When the conflict broke out in Jerusalem between the Zealots and the traditional leadership under Anan b. Anan, John still belonged to the party of Anan but, in consequence of the prestige he enjoyed also among the Zealots, he was chosen by Anan as the intermediary between him and them. According to Josephus he betrayed Anan and it was he who encouraged the Zealots to call upon the Idumeans for aid against the existing leadership (War 4:208–23). Reference has already been made above to the development of the relations between John and the Zealots of Jerusalem which brought about close military cooperation between his men and the less numerous Zealots. In point of fact it was only the appearance of Simeon bar Giora which prevented the concentration of the high command in besieged Jerusalem in the hands of John. After his entry into the capital Simeon remained his sole rival and both served as commanders in the city.

Josephus consistently attempts to place the blame for the desecration of the Temple squarely on the shoulders of John. According to him John requisitioned the wood which had been stored for Temple purposes in order to erect towers for military purposes (War 5:36). When he and his men seized control of the Temple from Eleazar and the Zealots, not only did they exploit the Passover for their own purposes, but the majority of his men were not even ritually clean when they penetrated the Temple precincts (War 5:100), and he concludes, "For he had unlawful food served at the table and abandoned the established rules of purity of our forefathers" (War 7:264). The main purpose of these accusations was to put John in as bad a light as possible. John fulfilled a task of primary importance in the defense of the fortress of Antonia. After its fall he sought refuge in the tunnels, but finally met a fate similar to that of Simeon bar Giora and fell into the hands of the Romans, unlike the Sicarii and the Zealots. But whereas Simeon was put to death by the Romans, John was sentenced to life imprisonment (War 6:434).

John of Giscala represents an outstanding example of the spread of the ideal of liberty into the widest sections of the people. A moderate and peace-loving man from Galilee, an intimate of Rabban Simeon b. Gamaliel and not unacceptable to the ruling oligarchy of the high priesthood (Anan b. Anan), he joined the revolt out of the necessity of the situation at the same time as even the recognized leaders of Jewish society (the heads of Bet Hillel and the high priestly circles) were swept into it by the general enthusiasm. In the course of events, when he came to Jerusalem after the collapse in Galilee, he felt a spiritual affinity to the Zealots there and joined them in their war against the existing leadership, but there is no need to assume that there was any decided ideological identification on his part with the Zealots.

Despite all of Josephus' attempts to besmirch him more than all the other individuals who were active at that period in Jerusalem, he hardly ascribes to him any special acts of cruelty, as he does to Simeon bar Giora. Nor is there any evidence of a socialistic revolutionary outlook or messianic-eschatological ideology in his personality. Nevertheless he was filled with the conviction that God would defend His city (War 6:98–99).

Although it cannot be denied that the picture given here of the various currents in the Jewish freedom movement is to a considerable extent hypothetical, one thing is nevertheless indisputably clear, namely, that the unifying factors among them outnumbered the divisive ones. From this point of view there is perhaps some justification for the view of those historians who are accustomed to speak generally of a Zealot movement which fearlessly raised the standard of revolt against the Roman Empire when it was at the height of its power.

[Menahem Stern]

Later Scholarship

The above classic article by Menahem Stern is reprinted unchanged because it remains the best ordering and interpretation of evidence in Josephus and in Christian, rabbinic, and pagan sources on the rise and spread of the Jewish revolutionary movements from the first century B.C.E. to the aftermath of the destruction of Jerusalem in the 70s C.E. This brief supplement is intended only to clarify, expand, and update certain aspects.

The only point in Stern's article which has to be corrected in light of subsequent scholarship is the final, concluding statement that "the unifying factors among [the Jewish revolutionary groups] outnumbered the divisive ones." Scholars today tend rather to see myriad partisan rivalries and societal fissures in Judea as contributing factors to the outbreak of the rebellion and the massive extent of the destruction it brought. Josephus has succeeded in obscuring the number and variety of revolutionary movements and leaders, and the ancient authors of the other sources had no interest in providing better information. But it seems clear now that the incidental mention of different rebels in Josephus and the New Testament, and the proliferation of small militia-type groups during Josephus' term as general in the Galilee, provide a glimpse into a much wider phenomenon. Moreover, these groups tended to compete with each other more often than they combined to oppose Roman rule in Judea. The chief victims of the Sicarii were all Jews, the recorded activity of other militants seems to have claimed mostly Jewish victims, and the in-fighting in the Galilee and Jerusalem not only resulted in high numbers of casualties but seriously hobbled the Jewish defensive strategy against the Roman attack. Josephus records in disgust and horror that the Sicarii primarily terrorized Jewish opponents, "saying that they were no different from non-Jews" (*allophyloi*): this redefinition of one's kinsmen as foreign is a psychological and rhetorical tactic typical of intense internal conflict.

Connected with this theme, recent work has also favored the picture of wide and enthusiastic participation by the Jewish upper classes in the rebellion. The Jewish ruling class was a heterogeneous group, whose members were in constant tension with each other and with the less privileged groups in Jewish society; this has been especially emphasized in recent studies of patronage in the countryside of Judaea and Galilee. Aristocrats formed their own factions or joined existing ones in order to gain control of the revolt and maintain their status and position overall. Their failure to unify as a class contributed to the widening fractures in Jewish society, and encouraged Rome to view the revolt as a grave threat. Just before the war, "a kind of enmity and factionalism broke out among the high priests and leaders of the Jerusalem populace" who joined hands with "the boldest revolutionaries" to carry out their high-level power feuds (Ant. 20:180, cf. Pes. 57a). Many aristocrats were to be found in the ranks of Simeon bar Giora's organization, and some of John of Gischala's closest associates, before he betrayed them, were also of the ruling class. Eleazar, son of the high priest Hananiah and *sagan* of the Temple, was apparently a member of or very close to the priestly party of the Zealots. And significantly, the first revolutionary government formed in Jerusalem in 66 C.E. and lasting about six months was composed of high priests, noble priests, and lay nobility: the roster of noble rebels is long. These rebellious aristocrats joined the struggle for a variety of motives, including desire to protect their local power and influence, a feeling of genuine outrage at abuses by the Roman procurators, and infection by the messianic fervor and eschatological hopes pervading Judea before the war (which was not, despite conventional belief, limited to the less educated masses).

At the same time, recent work has tried to illuminate, from very uncooperative sources uninterested in the topic, the social and economic hardships and struggles which contributed to the formation and continuing activity of revolutionary groups and the outbreak of rebellion. The aristocrats' inability and the Romans' conspicuous unwillingness to help control what was apparently a festering economic crisis, punctuated by periodic famine and agricultural failure (only dimly perceived in the literary and archaeological evidence), obviously drove some to join anti-establishment movements large and small. But this factor can be overstated, for economic destitution did not always lead to political rebellion; there is no reason to think that the economic situation in Judea was worse than in other peaceable areas of the empire, and the echoes of the slogans and platforms espoused by the Jewish rebel groups have nothing to do with economic injustice. Despite the fact that economic grievance indisputably contributed to the appeal of revolution, especially to the destitute and dispossessed, there is no sound basis for the model of the Jewish rebellion as two rebellions in one, an economic uprising by the peasant against the propertied classes and a national uprising against a foreign empire. Motives were complex, varied, combinatory, changing, and often indistinguishably tangled.

When social hierarchies weaken and the state power proves inefficient, banditry often arises (especially when socio-political instability is exacerbated by economic hardship). Brigandage and piracy were a problem which accompanied the Roman Empire throughout its entire history, particularly in peripheral, less fully Romanized, and less stable areas. The rebels in first-century Judea are routinely labeled *leistai*, "brigands," by Josephus, and there is little doubt that this quasi-legal label, applied indiscriminately to both prominent named and smaller unnamed bands, reflects the official Roman perspective, which viewed political upstarts as no more than criminals and troublemakers to be exterminated, and treated them accordingly. Josephus, when he became a historian, found that this attitude conveniently reflected his personal animus against the militant groups, especially when they attacked wealthy local magnates (but he also absurdly calls his personal enemy John of Gischala a *leistes*, even though John was well-to-do and well-connected, War 2:587). But the term may conceal a much more complex reality than can be teased out of the sources, and much recent work has been devoted to distinguishing between common criminals and "social bandits" on Hobsbawm's model. The problem is one of perception. Josephus' *leistai* did not of course present themselves as common robbers, nor were they perceived as such in the popular imagination, even less so by the other individuals whom they recruited to their ranks. Moreover, whatever "social bandits" existed in Judea seemed to have been infected by, and in turn to have exploited, the growing popular outrage against the Roman Empire and concomitant spreading messianic ideology. Social banditry is (according to the model) a rural phenomenon, yet some of the main revolutionaries – especially the Zealots – seem to have been active in an urban setting. Careful distinctions have to made, and the concept of social banditry as a political act will be found to apply only to the partially visible groups who make brief and enigmatic appearances in the sources. The concept contributes very little to understanding the Zealots and Sicarii, who were selective groups founded and led by literate ideologues who engaged in overtly political terror; the Zealots, as Stern has made clear, were a highly specialized group of mostly priests.

No writings by the Zealots or Sicarii have survived to round out and deepen the picture, no genuine voice of a revolutionary ideologue can be heard directly; belief and actual rhetoric must be filtered out of the considerable distortions and omissions of the existing sources. It remains true that "… there is no direct expression outside Josephus of the ideology of revolt" (Rajak 2002, 177). Yet much recent scholarship has attempted to appreciate the full force of the messianic character and apocalyptic beliefs and professions of many of the revolutionaries, and their impact on the prewar Jewish population at large. The scant indications in Josephus of the messianic nature and eschatological message of many of the rebels – the Sicarii if not the Zealots, and the many "prophets" and unnamed militants mentioned by Stern – combined with the relatively substantial but enigmatic corpus of apocalyptic and messianic texts from the period (e.g., *Psalms of Solomon*, *Assumption of Moses*, *Sibylline Oracles* III and IV, et al.), have been marshaled to create a picture of pervasive messianism throughout Palestinian Jewish society in the first century. But, except for the messianic texts from Qumran (of which the sectarians played no known role in the war), it is not possible to associate any known apocalyptic text with a revolutionary group. Nor should one expect to do so. There is no reason to believe that known groups such as the Zealots or even the Sicarii with their "fourth philosophy," or unnamed groups, wrote their own manifestos or inspirational texts. Messianists who repeated the widely known prophecy of the next world ruler arising from Judea (recorded by Josephus, War 6:312) needed to cite no more than Numbers 24:17, or the eschatological visions in the book of Daniel. It can be said from the available evidence that messianic hopes affected all societal sectors, definitely motivated many of the revolutionary groups agitating for war with Rome, and drove the diehards in Jerusalem to expect salvation until the very end. On the other hand, Josephus tried to demonstrate in his life and writings that it was possible to be a strongly believing Jew and accept accommodation with the Roman Empire, postponing eschatological hopes for an undetermined, distant future.

[Jonathan Price (2nd ed.)]

BIBLIOGRAPHY: W.R. Farmer, *Maccabees, Zealots and Josephus* (1956); H.H. Rowley, in: ZAWB 77 (1958), 184–92; C. Roth, *The Historical Background of the Dead Sea Scrolls* (1958); idem, in: *Judaism*, 8 (1959), 33–40; idem, in: JSS 4 (1959), 332–55; M. Hengel, *Die Zeloten* (1961); S. Zeitlin, in: JBL 81 (1962), 395–8; M. Stern, in: *The Great Man and his Age*, The Historical Society of Israel (1963), 70–78 (in Hebrew); G. Baumbach, in: *Theologische Literaturzeitung* 90 (1965), 727–40; idem, in *Festschrift Leonhard Rost* (1967), 11–18; B. Salomonsen, in: *New Testament Studies* 12 (1965–6), 164–76; S.G.F. Brandon, *Jesus and the Zealots* (1967); idem, *The Trial of Jesus of Nazareth* (1968); K. Wegenast, in: Pauly-Wissowa 2-e Reihe 9 (1967), 2474–99; H.P. Kingdon, in: *New Testament Studies* 17 (1970/1), 68–72; M. Smith, in: HTR 64 (1971), 1–19; S. Applebaum, in: *Journal of Roman Studies* 61 (1971), 155–70; M. Borg, in: JTS 22 (1971), 504–12; G.R. Driver, *The Judaean Scrolls* (1965); Y. Yadin, *The Excavation of Masada 1963/4* (1965); idem, *Masada: Herod's Fortress and the Zealots' Last Stand* (1966); idem, in: JSS, 4 (1959), 332–55; C. Daniel, in: *Numen*, 13 (1966), 88–115 (Fr.); K. Kohler, *Festschrift zu Ehren des Dr. A. Harkavy* (1908), 6–18; F.J. Foakes Jackson and K. Lake, *The Beginnings of Christianity* 1 (1920), 421–5; J.W. Lightley, *Jewish Sects and Parties in the Time of Jesus* (1925), 324–95. **ADD. BIBLIOGRAPHY:** Of the mass of work on Zealots, Sicarii, and other Jewish revolutionaries that has come out since Stern's article, most important is the English translation of M. Hengel's fundamental book: *The Zealots. Investigations into the Jewish Freedom Movement in the Period from Herod I until 70 A.D.*, trans. D. Smith (1989), which, however, uses "Zealots" to mean all revolutionaries and sees messianism as perhaps too much of a determining ideology. M. Stern's other article, "Sicarii and Zealots," in: M. Avi-Yonah and Z. Baras (eds.), *World History of the Jewish People*, 8 (1977), 263–301, should also be consulted. Also of fundamental importance is the English translation of Schuerer: E. Schuerer, *The History of the*

Jewish People in the Age of Jesus Christ, 1–3, rev. and ed. G. Vermes, F. Millar et al. (1973–87), esp. 2:598–606. GENERAL: M. Black, in: O. Betz, K. Hacker and M. Hengel (eds.), *Josephus-Studien. Untersuchungen zu Josephus, dem antiken Judentum und dem Neuen Testament Otto Michel zum 70. Geburtstag gewidmet* (1974), 45–54; L.I. Levine, in: *Cathedra*, 6 (1976), 39–60 (Heb.); D.M. Rhoads, *Israel in Revolution: 6–74* C.E. (1976); S.J.D. Cohen, *Josephus in Galilee and Rome. His Vita and Development as a Historian* (1979); P. Vidal-Naquet, in: *Yale French Studies*, 59 (1980), 86–105; E.M. Smallwood, *The Jews under Roman Rule* (1981); U. Rappaport (ed.), *Judea and Rome – The Jewish Revolts* (1983); U. Rappaport, in: JJS, 33 (1982), 479–93; idem, in: I.L. Levine, *The Jerusalem Cathedra*, 3 (1983), 46–55; G. Jossa, in: *Vichiana (Studi in memoria di Franceso Arnaldi II)*, n.s. 12 (1983), 224–34; V. Nikiprowetzky, in: L.H. Feldman and G. Hata (eds.), *Josephus, the Bible and History* (1989), 216–36; J.J. Price, *Jerusalem Under Siege: The Collapse of the Jewish State, 66–70* C.E. (1992); I. Ben-Shalom, *The School of Shammai and the Zealots' Struggle against Rome* (Heb., 1993); M. Smith, in: W. Horbury, W.D. Davies and J. Sturdy (eds.), *Cambridge History of Judaism*, 3 (1999), 501–68. ON "BANDITS" AND REVOLUTIONARIES, WITH SPECIFIC REFERENCE TO THE JEWISH REVOLT: R.A. Horsley, in: JSJ, 10 (1979), 37–63; idem, in: *Journal of Religion*, 59 (1979), 435–58; idem, in: CBQ, 43 (1981), 409–32; B.D. Shaw, in: *Past & Present*, 105, 3–52 and in: JJS, 44 (1993), 173–203; B. Isaac, in: HSCP, 88 (1984), 171–203; S. Freyne, in: J. Neusner et al., *The Social World of Formative Christianity and Judaism. Essays in Tribute to Howard Clark Kee* (1988), 50–68; T.L. Donaldson, in: JSJ, 21 (1990), 19–40. The classic founding discussion of bandits in modern historiography is E. Hobsbawm, *Bandits* (1969). ON THE SOCIAL AND ECONOMIC FACTORS LEADING TO THE REVOLT: P.A. Brunt: in: *Klio*, 59 (1977), 149–53; M. Goodman, in: JJS, 33 (1982), 417–27; idem, in: JJS, 36 (1985), 195–99; idem, in: A. Kasher, U. Rappaport, and G. Fuks (eds.), *Greece and Rome in Eretz Israel* (1990), 39–55; E. Bammel, in: E. Bammel and C.F.D. Moule (eds.), *Jesus and the Politics of His Day* (1984), 109–28; U. Rappaport, in: A. Kasher et al., *Man and Land in Eretz-Israel in Antiquity* (Heb., 1986), 80–86; M. Goodman, *The Ruling Class of Judaea. The Origins of the Jewish Revolt against Rome* A.D. *66–70* (1987); H. Kreissig, in: L.H. Feldman and G. Hata (eds.), *Josephus, the Bible and History* (1989), 265–77; S. Schwartz, in: F. Parente and J. Sievers (eds.), *Josephus and the History of Graeco-Roman Period* (1994), 289–307; E. Gabba, in: W. Horbury, W.D. Davies, and J. Sturdy (eds.), *Cambridge History of Judaism*, 3 (1999), 84–167. ON MESSIANISM AND APOCALYPTICISM AS THE BACKGROUND TO THE REVOLT AND IDEOLOGY OF THE VARIOUS REVOLUTIONARY MOVEMENTS. I. Gruenwald, in: ANRW, II.19.1 (1979), 89–118; L.I. Levine, in: Z. Baras (ed.), *Messianism and Eschatology* (Heb., 1983), 135–52; G.W.E. Nickelsburg, in: D. Hellholm (ed.), *Apocalyptism in the Mediterranean World and the Near East* (1983), 641–54; R.A. Horsley, in: *Nov. Test.*, 27 (1985), 334–48; R.A. Horsley and J.S. Hanson, *Bandits, Prophets and Messiahs: Popular Movements at the Time of Jesus* (1985); J. Barton, *Oracles of God: Perceptions of Ancient Prophecy in Israel after the Exile* (1986); R. Gray, *Prophetic Figures in Late Second Temple Jewish Palestine: The Evidence from Josephus* (1993); J.J. Collins, in: L.H. Schiffman (ed.), *Archaeology and History in the Dead Sea Scrolls* (1990), 25–51; idem, *The Scepter and the Star: the Messiahs of the Dead Sea Scrolls and other Ancient Literature* (1995); idem, *Apocalypticism in the Dead Sea Scrolls* (1997); A.I. Baumgarten, in: G. Stanton and G. Stroumsa (eds.), *Tolerance and Intolerance in Early Judaism and Christianity* (1998), 38–60; W. Horbury, *Jewish Messianism and the Cult of Christ* (1998); J. Zimmerman, *Messianische Texte aus Qumran* (1998); T. Rajak, in: A.M. Berlin and J.A. Overman (eds.), *The First Jewish Revolt: Archaeology, History and Ideology* (2002), 164–88, with considerable further bibliography.

ZEBAH AND ZALMUNNA (Heb. צַלְמֻנָּע, זֶבַח), two Midianite kings. The Israelites under the leadership of Gideon won a decisive victory over the Midianites. Oreb and *Zeeb, two princes of Midian, were captured and slain (Judg. 7:15–25). With the complete destruction of the Midianite forces, the Israelites were free of the terrors of yearly raids and crop stealing by the peoples from the east (Judg. 6:2–6). Gideon, however, was not satisfied. He was determined to find and kill Zebah and Zalmunna, two other Midianite kings who had managed to survive the great defeat and had fled eastward into the desert. This was a personal quest by Gideon, however, in order to exact revenge for the murder of his brothers, and he did not have the support of the tribes in this expedition. With his 300 men, he managed to rout the surviving Midianite forces and capture Zebah and Zalmunna. Gideon offered the privilege of executing blood revenge to his young son Jether, but the scared youth could not bring himself to draw his sword (Rashi, Judg. 8:20). Zebah and Zalmunna asked Gideon to execute them, so that they would die at the hands of a kingly person like themselves (Judg. 8:4–21; Ps. 83:12).

Y. Kaufmann maintains that Gideon thought his brothers were still alive, otherwise the question "Where are the men…?" (Judg. 8:18) would make no sense. In the same verse he emends הרגתם ("you killed") to נהגתם ("you captured"; cf. Gen. 31:26; Deut. 28:37), as better fitting the meaning of the text. Gideon had heard only of his brothers' capture by the Midianites, and it was from the answer of Zebah and Zalmunna that he learned of their deaths.

BIBLIOGRAPHY: G.F. Moore, *Judges* (1949, ICC), 221ff.; Y. Kaufmann, *Shofetim* (1962), 185–8.

[Gershon Bacon]

ZEBIDAH, family of *paytanim* that appears in several places in the **Genizah* (Judah, Yose his brother, Abraham b. Judah, Isaac and Jacob b. Isaac). The head of the family and its most important *paytan* seems to have been Judah, author of a *kerovah* for the Intermediate Sabbath of Passover, published by I. Davidson (JQR, 21 (1930/31), 255, 266–75). A second signature to this *kerovah*, "*Yehudah mi-Berutah me-Ḥaleb Asah*," would indicate that the family came originally from Syria, some living in Beirut and some in Aleppo. The founder of the family must have lived, at the latest, in the 11th century.

BIBLIOGRAPHY: H. Schirmann, *Shirim Ḥadashim min ha-Genizah* (1965), 87–96. **ADD. BIBLIOGRAPHY:** E. Fleischer, *Ha-Yoẓerot* (1984), 455, 609, 701.

[Menaḥem Zulay]

ZEBULUN (Heb. זְבוּלוּן, זְבוּלֻן, זְבֻלוּן), tenth son of Jacob and the sixth born to him by Leah (Gen. 30:19f.). The tribe of Zebulun is named after him. It was divided into three clans: Seredites, Elonites, and Jahleelites (Num. 26:27) after the three sons of Zebulun (Gen. 46:14). At the census taken in the Plains of Moab the number of men in the tribe over 20 years of age and fit for military service was 60,500 (Num. 26:27). Zebulun held a major position among the tribes of Galilee; it was settled more securely than the others. Unlike the case of the tribes of Asher

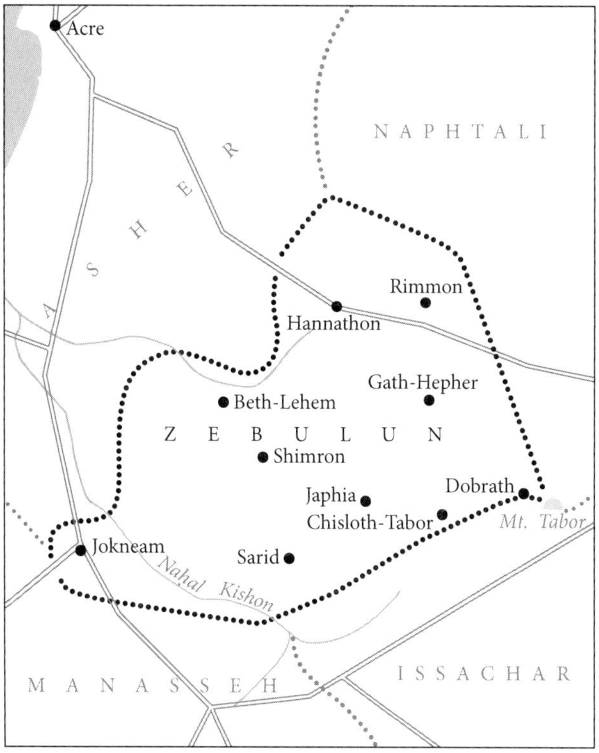

Territory of the tribe of Zebulun. After Y. Aharoni, Lexicon Biblicum, *Tel Aviv, 1965.*

and Naphtali who continued to "dwell among the Canaanites" (Judg. 1:32f.), among Zebulun the Canaanites constituted a minority: "the Canaanites continued to dwell among them" (Judg. 1:30). The tribe was very active in the campaigns of the period of the Judges. The victorious army in the battle by the wadi Kishon was formed of men of Zebulun and Naphtali (Judg. 4:6, 10). Deborah praised them as "a people that put its life in jeopardy to the point of death…" (Judg. 5:18). The men of Zebulun also took part in the Midianite war (Judg. 6:35). The judge Elon was a Zebulunite (Judg. 12:11), as was probably Ibzan of Beth-Lehem (in Galilee in the territory of Zebulun, Josh. 19:15), whom the text juxtaposes with Elon (Judg. 12:8–10).

The importance and strength of the tribe of Zebulun in the period of the united kingdom is also indicated by the mention of Zebulun's army as the largest of the western tribal armies that fought under King David (I Chron. 12:34 [33]). Isaiah mentions the land of Zebulun after the collapse of the kingdom of Israel (8:23 [9:1]). Apparently, it suffered less than other regions during the destruction of the kingdom of Israel. The Zebulunites were not uprooted and were probably the core of the remnant that survived the Assyrian campaigns in Galilee (II Chron. 30:6). Consequently, the last Davidic kings were careful to maintain their ties with the people of Zebulun who were among those who made the pilgrimage to celebrate Hezekiah's Passover in Jerusalem (II Chron. 30:10–11). Manasseh, king of Judah, married Meshullemeth of Jotbah (II Kings 21:19), which, according to S. Klein, was Yotbat-Yodpat (referred to by Josephus as Jotapata), in the land of Zebulun, and her son Amon succeeded Manasseh as king in Jerusalem. Amon's son, King Josiah, also married into the tribe of Zebulun; his wife Zebudah, the mother of King Jehoiakim, was a native of Rumah in the Valley of Beth-Netophah (II Kings 23:36). This is the regnant view, though S. *Mowinckel, in the Norwegian Bible translation, and H.L. Ginsberg, *Marx Jubilee Volume* (1950), 350f. n. 12 prefer to restore the Judean town names Juttah (יוּטָה, יֻטָּה; Josh. 15:55; 21:16) and Dumah (דּוּמָה, var. רוּמָה; Josh. 15:52) respectively.

It has been shown that the populous Jewish community in Galilee in the period of the Second Temple centered around Sepphoris, Jotapata, and the Valley of Beth-Netophah. In all likelihood it was the remnant of Zebulun together with what was left of other tribes, Babylonian returnees, and some Judeans who, together, formed the nucleus of Jewish Galilee which lasted over 1,000 years. The sages were particularly sympathetic toward the tribe of Zebulun, mainly because many of the centers of learning after the destruction of the Temple, such as Bet She'arim and Sepphoris, were in the land of that tribe. The generosity of the wealthy Galileans in supporting the colleges and sages is reflected in rabbinic legends about Issachar and Zebulun (see *Issachar, in the *Aggadah*).

BIBLIOGRAPHY: A. Alt, in: ZAW, 45 (1927), 59–81; M. Noth, in: ZDPV, 58 (1935), 215–30; B. Maisler (Mazar), *Toledot Ereẓ Yisrael*, 1 (1938), 232–7; Abel, Geog, 2 (1938), 62–63; Y. Elitzur and Y.A. Seidman, *Sefer Yehoshu'a* (1953), 84–86; M. Naor, *Ha-Mikra ve-ha-Areẓ*, 2 (1954), 77–81; EM, 2 (1954), 895–901; Y. Aharoni, *Hitnaḥalut Shivtei Yisrael ba-Galil ha-Elyon* (1957); Y. Kaufmann, *Sefer Yehoshu'a* (1959), 217–23; S. Klein, *Ereẓ ha-Galil* (1967[2]), 1–9.

[Yehuda Elitzur]

ZEC, PHILIP (1909–1983), British illustrator and cartoonist. Zec was born in London, the son of an immigrant rabbi and tailor from Russia. He was educated at the St. Martin's School of Art, London. In the 1930s he became one of the most famous poster artists in England, producing the famous poster for the *Flying Scotsman* train and other well-known advertising designs. From 1937 until 1961 he was the chief political cartoonist for the pro-Labour *Daily Herald*, depicting Hitler and the Nazis as strutting buffoons. Zec's most controversial cartoon appeared in 1942. It depicted a torpedoed sailor on a raft and stated below, "The price of petrol has been increased by one penny – Official." The implication, that war profiteering was the official policy of the British government, infuriated many in Parliament. Zec's original caption had been entirely different; the offending words were added by the newspaper. Zec is regarded as among the handful of great British political cartoonists of his time. He served as a director of the *Jewish Chronicle*.

BIBLIOGRAPHY: ODNB online.

[William D. Rubinstein (2nd ed.)]

ZECHARIAH (Heb. זְכַרְיָה; "YHWH has remembered"; end of ninth century B.C.E.), the priest, son of Jehoiada. According to II Chronicles 24:20–22, Zechariah admonished the people in the courtyard of the Temple. They plotted against him and stoned him at the command of *Joash, king of Judah. The latter had forgotten that Jehoiada, Zechariah's father, had once saved his life and made him king (II Chron. 22:11 ff.). As Zechariah died he said: "May the Lord see it, and avenge it." (The historicity of the incident is questioned by H.L. Ginsberg.) The tombstone over the alleged grave of Zechariah son of Jehoiada stands in the Valley of Kidron opposite the Temple Mount in Jerusalem.

[Yehoshua M. Grintz]

In the Aggadah

The *aggadah* about the murder of Zechariah in the Temple concerns Zechariah the son of Jehoiada (II Chron. 24:20 ff.); but in some of the sources he is confused with Zechariah the prophet (Zech. 1:1; Ezra 5:1) and also with the Zechariah mentioned in Isaiah 8:1. The *aggadah* magnifies the crime which was committed by the king and the people: "Seven transgressions were committed by Israel on that day" (Lam. R., Proem 23), among them that he was slain on the Day of Atonement which happened to fall on the Sabbath. Not content with the punishment which King Joash suffered according to the biblical story (II Chron. 24:23 ff.), the *aggadah* tells that after the slaughter in Jerusalem and its environs, Nebuzaradan found the "blood of Zechariah bubbling up." When he inquired as to the nature of this blood, he was first told that it was the blood of sacrifices; but when he investigated and found it not to be so, they admitted whose blood it was. Nebuzaradan said "I will appease him" and he stood and killed in cold blood the members of the Sanhedrin, the priestly class, and the rest of the people – a total of 94,000; but the blood still seethed until Nebuzaradan angrily rebuked Zechariah saying "Do you want me to destroy them all?" Then the blood stopped seething (Git. 57b; Sanh. 96b; Lam. R. *ibid.*; also on Lam. R. 4:13, TJ, Ta'an. 69a–b; Sanh. 96b; cf. also Matt. 23:35 f.). According to some of the versions, Nebuzaradan was so impressed by this example of divine justice that he repented his own misdeeds and was converted to Judaism. Thus the murder of Zechariah was the direct cause of the destruction of the Temple and all the suffering connected with it. Although the story refers explicitly to the First Temple, it seems meant to explain the destruction of the second one, for which no obvious reason was apparent. Hence it is quite plausible that the *aggadah* has in mind similar incidents which happened prior to the destruction of the Second Temple, such as the murder by John Hyrcanus of his brother during the sacrificial service (Jos., Ant., 11:300) or the slaying by Zealots of an innocent citizen, called Zechariah(!), in the Temple (Jos., Wars, 4:335).

[Joseph Heinemann]

BIBLIOGRAPHY: Ginsberg, in: JBL, 80 (1961), 347; de Vaux, Anc Isr., 346, 377, 385. IN THE AGGADAH: S. Baeck, in: MGWJ, 76 (1932), 313–9; H.S. Blank, in: HUCA, 12–13 (1937–38), 327–46; Ginzberg, Legends, 4 (1947[5]), 304; (1946[3]), 396–7.

ZECHARIAH, king of Israel, son of Jeroboam II. Zechariah succeeded to the throne after his father's death in 743 B.C.E. He was assassinated six months later by *Shallum of Jabesh, who seized the throne for about one month (II Kings 15:8–13). It is not possible to determine the reason for his assassination, but presumably it was prompted by external political circumstances.

BIBLIOGRAPHY: Bright, Hist, 253.

[Yehoshua M. Grintz]

ZECHARIAH, son of Jeberechiah, one of the two "faithful witnesses" to *Isaiah's prophecy when he wrote on a sheet "to *maher-shalal-ḥash-baz*" and named his newborn son Maher-Shalal-Hash-Baz ("Plunder hastens, booty speeds"), as a sign that "before the boy knows how to call 'Father' and 'Mother' the wealth of Damascus and the spoils of Samaria shall be carried off before the king of Assyria" (Isa. 8:2–4). There is no other unequivocal reference to Zechariah but, since the father of the prophet *Zechariah had the same name (Berechiah) as the father of this Zechariah, and since several scholars attribute the last six chapters of the Book of Zechariah to an earlier, First Temple prophet, there is a theory that the Isaiah witness is that mysterious prophet. It has also been suggested (by Z. Jawitz) that this is the same Zechariah who instructed Uzziah king of Judah "in the fear of God" (II Chron. 26:5). It is more likely that he is to be identified with Zechariah the father-in-law of King Ahaz (II Kings 18:2; II Chron. 29:1).

BIBLIOGRAPHY: Z. Jawitz, *Toledot Yisrael*, 2 (1897), 28.

[Yehoshua M. Grintz]

ZECHARIAH, the eleventh book of the Twelve Minor Prophets. While the book is attributed to one prophet, in style and content it is clearly separated into two parts:

(1) Chapters 1–8 are written with the return from Babylonian Exile as background, and the name of the prophet and the dates of his prophecy are clear;

(2) Chapters 9–14 are of an eschatological nature and are written in an obscure style with allusions to unclear backgrounds. Contemporary commentaries tend to treat *Haggai-Zechariah 1–8 together, and separately from Zechariah 9–14.

Zechariah 1–8

The introduction to the book attributes the work to Zechariah son of Berechiah son of Iddo the prophet (Zech. 1:1, and 1:7). The prophet's name is mentioned elsewhere in the Book (7:1, 8). He is mentioned as well, along with *Haggai, in Ezra 5:1; 6:14, where he is referred to as the son of Iddo, rather than grandson. In Nehemiah 12:4 and 16, mention is made of a priest named Zechariah of the family of Iddo, who may be Zechariah the prophet. Three of Zechariah's prophecies are dated between the second and fourth years of Darius' reign (520–18 B.C.E.; 1:1, 7; 7:1). This makes Zechariah a contemporary of Haggai. The Talmud (TJ, RH 1:1, 66b) considers the beginning of Zechariah's prophecy to predate Haggai, although in at least one of his prophecies (8:9–13), he appears to refer to concerns of Haggai as matters which preceded him (Haggai

1:2–11; 2:15–19). In all probability, therefore, he was a younger contemporary of Haggai (cf. Zech. 2:8, where he is called *naʿar,* "lad"). The chronological headings of Haggai-Zechariah 1–8 are more detailed than earlier books of the Bible, so much so that we can see that they cover a period of less than two and a half years in the reign of Darius I the Great (522–486). Haggai and chapters 1–8 of Zechariah seem to be part of the same redactional effort. Zechariah sees himself in the line of the pre-exilic prophets (*ha-nevi'im ha-rishonim*; Zech. 1:4; 7:4, 12), whose words of warning were fulfilled over the doubts of the people to whom they were addressed. From the fact that Yahweh's words of doom and destruction of Judah and Jerusalem conveyed by the prophets were fulfilled, Zechariah concludes that Yahweh's promises to do good for Judah and Jerusalem will likewise be fulfilled (Zech. 8:14–15). Indeed, in response to the question of whether the fasts commemorating the disasters of the earlier sixth century should continue to be observed (Zech. 7:3), the prophet responds that these days will be turned into festivals (Zech. 8: 18–19). In contrast to some of the pre-exilic prophets, he is an enthusiastic supporter of the temple (Zech. 2:16), to which he refers as "Yahweh's palace" (*hekal YHWH*; contrast Jer. 7:4 in which that characterization is termed *sheker,* "a lie"), to Mount Zion as the holy mountain and Jerusalem as the city of truth in which YHWH dwells; a holy land (Zech. 2:16; 7:3). Like the pre-exilic prophets he calls for social justice, honesty, and equity and regard for the poor and defenseless (Zech. 7:8–10; 8:16–17). Zechariah makes much use of symbolic visions, seeing in them a connection between the visionary and real objects, by blurring the time and location. Unlike the visions of the pre-exilic prophets, the visions of Zechariah are accompanied by direct or indirect explanations made by the angel who speaks to him, and who serves as an intermediary between the prophet and God. The angel also serves to transmit prophecies from God to the prophet (see below).

Chapters 1–6 contain eight visions (among which some other fragments are inserted; see below). In the first of these (1:8–17), Zechariah one night sees a man astride a red horse standing among myrtle trees "in the depths," or, perhaps, "in the shadow." Behind him are red, sorrel, and white horses. Replying to the prophet's question, the angel explains that the horses symbolize messengers sent throughout the world by God to see what is transpiring (cf. Job 1:7). The image is probably based on the Persian surveillance system. They return with the information that all is tranquil. The angel, apparently disappointed, perhaps because the disturbances following the death of the Persian emperor Cambyses (530–522) had raised hopes of independence among the subject peoples of the empire, prays for the rebuilding of Jerusalem and the cities of Judah which have aroused God's anger for "these seventy years"; the Lord replies that He is jealous for Jerusalem and Zion, and will return to them. In the second vision (2:1–4), which continues along the lines of the first, the prophet sees four horns (like those of a siege ram butting against a wall), which represent the nations that destroyed Jerusalem. Zechariah then observes four craftsmen who go to cut the horns down, i.e., who restore the city. In the third vision (2:5–9), a man sent to measure Jerusalem with a measuring rod is sent away by an angel who states that Jerusalem does not need a man-made wall: it will be inhabited without walls, God being the wall about "the multitude of men and cattle therein." The fourth vision (Zech. 3), the only vision in the Hebrew Bible in which a historical character appears, takes place in heaven, where a court is in session. The accused is the high priest Joshua and the prosecutor is the Satan (Heb. *ha-satan* as in Job 1; a title, not yet a proper name). God rebukes the Satan: "Joshua is a brand saved out of fire" and is not to be harmed. An angel orders that Joshua's filthy garments, symbolic of his human impurity, be replaced with robes and a clean turban. He promises Joshua that if he will walk in the ways of God, keeping His charge, he will have "free access among these that stand by," i.e., among the angels (cf. the symbolic purging by which *Isaiah is qualified to participate in the deliberation of the heavenly council; Isa. 6:1–8). In vague language, the angel prophesies that God will bring "My servant the Branch" (see Zech. 6:12; Cf. Jer. 23:5–6; 33:15–16), a reference to Zerubabel, grandson of the Davidic King Jeconiah deposed in 597. He shows Joshua a stone with seven eyes. The vision is interrupted by an inserted oracle to Zerubabel, promising that it is he who will complete the temple and triumph in his mission through the agency of the divine spirit rather than through military force as might have been hoped during the period of the empire's unrest (cf. Hag. 2:20–23). Following the insertion, the eyes in the stone are symbolically explained (Zech. 4:10b) as the seven eyes of YHWH, which range through all the earth. The prophet then observes a golden lampstand with a bowl above it and seven lamps upon it, and "each of the seven with seven spouts, for the lamps which are on top of it" (see illustrations in IDB 3:66; Meyers and Meyers, pl. 12–14). Two olive trees, one on each side, have branches, which serve as conduits to empty the golden olive oil through two golden *ṣantərot* (?). The two olive trees represent "the two sons of oil who stand by the Lord (*adon*) of the whole earth," i.e., Joshua and Zerubbabel, who will rule jointly and by their close association with Yahweh represent fertility and prosperity (Meyers and Meyers 1988, 276). The prophet sees two more visions (Zech. 5), which are also related to each other. A large scroll, perhaps inscribed with a curse, perhaps the Torah, flies through the air, symbolizing the curse which will fall upon a thief or one who swears falsely. He then sees a tub/container (?) (Heb. *efah*) containing a seated woman, who is being carried "between earth and heaven" to the land of Shinar, i.e., Babylon, by two winged women. A lead disc is thrown over the mouth of the tub and seals it. The angel explains that the woman symbolizes wickedness, which is being expelled to a distant place. The final vision (6:1–8) resembles the first one: four chariots, harnessed to horses of various colors appear between "mountains of brass." They represent the four winds of heaven, which leave after presenting themselves to the Lord, in order to fulfill their task on earth.

The visions are accompanied by a fragment relating a dramatic act of Zechariah (6:9–15). The prophet is ordered to take silver and gold from Heldai, Tobijah, and Jedaiah, who recently returned from the Exile, and to bring it to Josiah son of Zephaniah (the craftsman?) who will make crowns from it. One crown is to be placed on Joshua's head and the other, apparently, is to be reserved for "the Branch" (Zerubbabel), who he prophesies, will build the Temple and "shall bear glory, and shall sit and rule upon his throne." The high priest will stand by his side "and the counsel of peace shall be between both." The crowns are said to have been placed in the Temple as a memorial and to have remained there throughout the period of the Second Temple (Mid. 3:8). The prophet closes with words regarding proselytes who will be brought to the Lord in the end of days.

In chapters 7 and 8, Zechariah turns from matters directly concerning the returning exiles to eternal prophetic concerns. The returning exiles had asked the priests and prophets in Jerusalem if they were still obligated to observe the four fast days connected with the destruction of Jerusalem. Zechariah raises the question of the fundamental purpose of divine worship (cf. Isa. 58). The basic point is not fasting, but ethical conduct – "honest justice… judgment… mercy, and compassion" (7:9), "the honest and equitable justice" (see 8: 16; see *Peace). Transgressing these precepts had brought "wrath," while keeping them would lead to redemption and to the conversion of fasts into occasions of joy and gladness. The point then is to "love honesty and equity" (8:19). Again, he ends with a vision of "many peoples and mighty nations" recognizing the Lord, and turning to Israel to accompany her in the "search for the Lord of hosts in Jerusalem" (cf. Isa. 2).

Zechariah's central themes in chapters 1–8 do not differ significantly from those of the prophets who preceded him. In a sense, their words, to which he regularly alludes, are already Scripture for him. He esteems the Temple service, and at the same time considers the observance of the precepts of righteousness, truth, and peace most important. Jerusalem is God's chosen city and He is jealous for its honor. The future of the non-Jewish nations is also concerned with the city, for they will eventually seek Yahweh and pray to him. They will acknowledge that God (*elohim*) is with the Jews (Zech. 8:20–23). One innovative aspect of Zechariah's prophecy is the special importance he accords to the high priest. This is a result of the changed circumstances of the Persian period, in which it appeared that the Davidic monarchy would not be restored. The prophetic compromise was a dyarchy, in which Zerubabel and Joshua would each sit on a throne (Zech. 6:13) and that "'a counsel of peace' would exist between them," an outcome which failed to materialize. Zechariah, like later *apocalyptic, makes use of an angel, who instructs the prophet, explaining the strange and wondrous visions which the latter does not comprehend. Much in the fashion of the apocalyptists, Zechariah sees angels standing in God's presence, though he does not see God Himself, as previous prophets had dared (1 Kings 22:19; Isa. 6:1–2). Zechariah's language in describing the visions is prosaic and dry, and occasionally even confused; however, some prophetic passages, such as 2:10–17, do rise to lyricism.

Zechariah 9–14

The entire second section of the book (chapters 9–14) lacks any mention of the prophet's name and period. Chapter 9 begins with the word *massa*ʾ ("an oracle"), as does chapter 12. The first half of the chapter (vs. 1–8) contains prophecies of divine punishment of Israel's neighbors: Hadrach, Damascus, and Hamath, all in Syria; Tyre and Sidon; and the Philistine cities of Ashkelon, Ekron, and Ashdod. All are to be destroyed or annexed to Israel. The second half (vs. 9–17) is a prophecy of redemption for Israel: a savior-king will come to Zion to save all "the poor as well as the one who rides an ass, yea a colt, foal of a donkey" (Tur-Sinai; Held). He will put an end to war in Ephraim and Jerusalem, "and he shall speak peace unto the nations, and his dominion shall be from sea to sea." He speaks of the return from captivity, the war of the sons of Zion against the sons of Javan, and God's appearance in battle to save His people.

In chapter 10 the prophet belittles teraphim and diviners as sources of aid. Only the Lord can produce "showers of rain." He mentions God's wrath at "the shepherds," and goes on to describe the victorious battle of the houses of Judah and Joseph against their enemies. He describes the ingathering of exiles from Egypt and Assyria "into the land of Gilead and Lebanon," and the humbling of Egypt and Assyria. In chapter 11 he returns to his prophecy of divine punishment of the evil "shepherds" (cf. Ezek. 34). He himself is called upon to feed some flocks, using two staves, which he names "Pleasant" and "Binders." He (or God?) cuts off three shepherds in one month. It can be understood from what follows that the nation loathes him, paying him 30 pieces of silver, an ancient idiom for a trifling amount, going back to Sumerian (Reiner). He takes this silver and at God's command throws it into the temple for use by the potter. (These verses inspired Matt. 26:15; 27:3–5.) He then announces the breaking of "the brotherhood between Judah and Israel." He prophesies the rise of a "foolish shepherd" who will neglect the flock, and he curses him strongly.

Chapter 12, like chapter 9, opens with the word *massa*ʾ ("an oracle"). Jerusalem will be besieged by many nations, but Yahweh having made Jerusalem into a cup of reeling, these attackers together with their horses will be struck with confusion and madness. In another image, Yahweh makes Jerusalem into a burdensome stone, which cuts anyone who carries it off. In yet a third image of Judah harming all who attack her, Yahweh will make the clans of Judah into a wood-burning brazier or a torch set to a sheaf and they will consume their attackers "on the right and on the left." The next several verses are highly problematic. They seem to indicate some tension between Jerusalem and the Davidides on the one hand and the "tents of Judah" on the other (12:7–8). Verses 10–12 refer to widespread mourning over one who was stabbed, comparable to the loss of a firstborn son or to the mourning over/at

Haddad Rimmon in the Valley of Megiddo. Chapter 13 tells of a fountain of purification, which will be opened for the house of David and the inhabitants of Jerusalem. The names of the idols will be cut off from the land, and the "unclean" spirit will be swept out of the land. Reflecting the new phenomenon that the divine word should be sought in a limited corpus of Scripture, the writer predicts that Yahweh will also remove prophecy from the land. A prophet will be stabbed by his parents for prophesying. Prophets will deny their vocation by attributing to horsing around any wounds that might be taken as a sign of ecstatic behavior. Once again a flock and a shepherd who will be punished are mentioned. Two parts of the nation "shall be cut off and die," and the remaining third will be purified like silver and gold: "They will call my name and I will answer them; I will say 'That is my people,' and they will say, 'Yahweh is my God,'" an exchange drawn directly from Hos. 2:25.

Chapter 14 begins with a siege of Jerusalem. First, Yahweh brings the gentiles to Jerusalem to make war against it. The city is conquered and plundered, half of the people going into exile. The gentile victory though is short-lived because Yahweh himself will go forth to battle the nations; He will first set his feet on the Mount of Olives and it will be split across from east to west. Then one part will shift north and the other south, creating a huge gorge. The Valley in the Hills (Wadi Kidron?) will be stopped up the way it was in the earthquake of the eighth century in King Uzziah's reign. On a day known only to Yahweh, there will be one continuous day, neither day nor night. On that day fresh water will flow from Jerusalem, part of it to the Dead Sea and part of it to the Mediterranean all year round. Yahweh will be King over all the land (*kol ha-areẓ*) of Israel; others "all the earth"), there will be one Yahweh with one name (i.e., no more Yahweh of Samaria, Teiman, etc.) Then all the land (*kol ha-areẓ*) will become (depressed) like the Arabah, so that Jerusalem (in fulfillment of Isa. 2:2) will be raised, after which it will be secure (Zech. 14:11). Having rearranged the topography, Yahweh is now ready to smite all the peoples who attacked Jerusalem at his invitation, as well as their mounts, with a plague that rots their skin, eyes, and tongues (vss. 12, 15). A panic from Yahweh will fall upon all. Judah will join in the fighting and the wealth of all the nations will be gathered to Jerusalem (vs. 14). Finally, every survivor among the nations struck by Yahweh will make an annual pilgrimage to Jerusalem to bow down to Yahweh and to celebrate the Feast of Booths; if not, they shall have no rain. Egypt, which depends on the Nile rather than rainfall, will be punished in some other way if they fail to make the pilgrimage. All of Jerusalem will be pure. "Holy unto Yahweh" will be inscribed on everything from bells on horses to metal pots.

Chapters 9–14 are unclear, and the historical allusions they contain remain contested. There is no apparent temporal connection between them and the contents of the earlier chapters of the book. The two sections differ both in form and style. Much of earlier scholarship concentrated on analyzing the text into sources without attempting to account for why the sources were combined. Contemporary scholarship attempts both. First, 9–14 is now generally subdivided into 9–11 and 12–14, each headed "Oracle, word of Yahweh." But whereas the first heading indicates that the word is directed against various foreign nations, the second is directed against Israel. Though the material is diverse there are several themes in common: military conflict, criticism of leadership, and Jerusalem's future prosperity (see Petersen). There are various reasons why chapters 9–14 were combined with 1–8. For one, both sections contain strange visions. More important, both sections promise the future glory of Jerusalem. Chapter 8:20–23 speaks of all the peoples coming to Jerusalem to seek Yahweh, while chapter 14 concludes with all the nations coming annually to Jerusalem to bow down to Yahweh and to celebrate the Feast of Booths. Jerusalem. As is true of the other late biblical books, both sections of Zechariah constantly quote earlier Scripture, reinterpret it, or allude to it, a process commonly but inaccurately called "intertextuality." (For Zech. 1–8 see Boda; for Zech. 9–14, see charts in Meyers and Meyers 1993, 40–43).

Zechariah in Later Sources

In the Aramaic section of the Book of Ezra (5:1), Zechariah is cited together with Haggai as one of those supporting the building of the Second Temple in the early days of Darius. One passage in Zechariah (1:3) appears to have been quoted in Malachi (3:7). At a later period, some translations of the Bible credited Zechariah with the authorship of several psalms at the end of the Book of Psalms. The Greek translation credits him with Psalms 137 and 138, and in collaboration with Haggai, with 145 through 148; the early Latin version with 112; the Vulgate with 112 and 146, done jointly with Haggai; and the Syriac version in the Polyglot Bible with 126, and 145 to 148. The "addendum" to the Syriac also dates these psalms and describes their use in the Temple. Christianity made much use of Zechariah 9–14, which is the most quoted of the Hebrew prophets in the Gospels, and is second only to Ezekiel in its influence on the Christian apocalypse Revelation. The author of Matt. 23:25 confused our prophet with Zechariah b. Jehoiada of II Chr. 24:20–22, while Matt. 27:9 quotes Zech. 11:12–13, but mistakenly attributes it to Jeremiah.

[Yehoshua M. Grintz / S. David Sperling (2nd ed.)]

In the Aggadah

Zechariah was one of the three prophets to accompany the Exiles who returned from Babylon to Jerusalem; his contribution to the subsequent rebuilding of the Temple consisted of his testimony regarding the site of the altar (Zev. 62a, and Rashi, loc. cit). He prophesied together with Haggai and Malachi, in the second year of the reign of King Darius (Meg. 15a). He could interpret difficult scriptural texts (Er. 21a–b), and he helped Jonathan b. Uzziel to compose the Targum to the prophets (Meg. 3a). Like Haggai and Malachi, he received his learning direct from the early prophets (ARN 1:1). He is identified with Zechariah Meshullam (Neh. 8:4), and was so called because his conduct was blameless (*mushlam*; Meg. 23a). It was only after the death of these three prophets that the Holy Spirit departed from Israel (Yoma 9b).

BIBLIOGRAPHY: G.H. Kraeling, in: AJSLL, 41 (1924/25), 24–33; S. Feigin, in: JBL, 44 (1925), 203–13; B. Heller, in: ZAW, 45 (1927), 151–5; W.W. Cannon, in: AFO, 4 (1927), 139–46; E. Sellin, in: JBL, 50 (1931), 242–9; H. Schmidt, in: ZAW, 54 (1936), 48–60; R. Press, *ibid.*, 45–48; H.G. May, in: JBL, 57 (1938), 173–84; Klausner, Bayit Sheni, 1 (1951[2]), 208–14; K. Galling, in: VT, 2 (1952), 18–36 (Ger.); M. Tsevat, in: *Tarbiz*, 25 (1955/56), 111–7; M. Zer Kavod, *Ḥaggai, Zekharyah, Malakhi* (1957); Y. Kaufmann, Toledot, 3 (1960), 322–33; 4 (1960), 226–74; F.F. Bruce, in: BJRL, 43 (1960/61), 336–53; B. Uffenheimer, *Ḥazonot Zekharyah* (1961); D.R. Jones, in: VT, 12 (1962), 241–59; M. Treves, *ibid.*, 13 (1963), 196–207; for further bibl., see: EM, 2 (1954), 928–9. IN THE AGGADAH: Ginzberg, Legends, index; I. Ḥasida, *Ishei ha-Tanakh* (1964), 143–4. **ADD. BIBLIOGRAPHY:** N. Tur-Sinai, *The Language and the Book* (1954), 390; E. Reiner, in: JAOS, 88 (1968), 186–90; M. Held, in: BASOR, 200 (1970), 32–40; P. Hanson, *IDBSup*, 982–83; R. Smith, *Micah-Malachi* (Word; 1984), 166–293; C. Meyers and E. Meyers, *Haggai, Zechariah 1–8* (AB: 1987); idem, *Zechariah 9–14* (AB; 1998); idem, ABD, 6:1061–65; D. Petersen, ibid, 1065–68; idem, *Haggai and Zechariah 1–8* (1984); idem, *Zechariah 9–14 and Malachi* (1995); M. Saebø, DBI, 2:666–68; A. Kuhrt, *The Ancient Near East c. 3000–330 B.C.* (1995), 647–701; H. Tadmor, in: R. Chazan et al. *Ki Baruch Hu… Studies B. Levine* (1999), 401–12; P. Briant, *From Cyrus to Alexander A History of the Persian Empire* (2002); M. Boda and M. Floyd (eds.); *Bringing Out the Treasure: Inner Biblical Allusion in Zechariah 9–14* (2003); Y. Hoffmann, in: O. Lipschits and J. Blenkinsopp (eds.). *Judah and the Judeans in the Neo-Babylonian Period* (2003), 169–218; R. Albertz, in: idem and B. Becking (eds.), *Yahwism after the Exile* (2003), 49–17; M. Boda, ibid., 49–69.

ZECHARIAH AL-ḌĀHIRI (1519?–1589?), author in *Yemen. A well-known scholar and *dayyan*, Zechariah was well versed in Hebrew and Arabic literature and in philosophy. He traveled widely, journeying to Ereẓ Israel in 1567 and becoming acquainted with scholars there. During the Turco-Yemenite war (1568–73), he was imprisoned, together with the rest of the Jewish community, in *Sanʿa. In prison he wrote his best-known work, *Sefer ha-Musar,* consisting of 45 sections (*maḥbarot*), influenced in subject matter by the *maqāmāt* of Al-Ḥariri and the *maḥbarot* of *Al-Ḥarizi and *Immanuel of Rome. The book includes amusing folklore, animal fables, and riddles, as well as moral and admonitory tales, and contains poems praising particular books and their authors. However, the most important part of the work is the author's description of his travels in Ereẓ Israel, Egypt, Syria, Iraq, Turkey, Persia, and India, and of contemporary events in Yemen. Zechariah described the scholars and systems of learning of the yeshivot of Ereẓ Israel, including that of *Tiberias, which was supported by Gracia *Nasi, and that of Joseph *Caro in *Safed. Among the notables of Safed whom he mentions are Moses of *Trani and Moses *Cordovero. In Ereẓ Israel Zechariah widened his knowledge of *Kabbalah, and later was instrumental in diffusing the Zohar and other kabbalistic works in Yemen. *Sefer ha-Musar* is an important source of information on the Jewish communities of the period, throwing special light on the political, spiritual, and cultural situation of Yemenite Jewry. Zechariah also wrote *Ẓeidah la-Derekh*, a commentary to the Pentateuch (published with the text, 1964), and several works on *halakhah* and *aggadah*.

BIBLIOGRAPHY: Zechariah al-Dahiri, *Sefer ha-Musar,* ed. by Y. Ratzaby (1965), introd.

[Yehuda Ratzaby]

ZECHARIAH BEN AVKILUS (first century C.E.), scholar in the generation of the destruction of the Second Temple. Zechariah was known for his piety and humility, and his conduct was even relied upon to determine the *halakhah* (Tosef., Shab. 16:7). The famous statement ascribed to R. Johanan in TB Git. 56a (cf. Lam. R. 4:23), "The humility of R. Zekharia b. Avkulas destroyed our Temple, burned our Holy of Holies, and exiled us from our land," is in fact a slightly expanded version of the statement of the *tanna* R. Jose found in Tosefta Shab. 16:7 (see: *Five Sugyot*, 106–11), and provided the starting point for the later talmudic tradition which described in great detail the way in which Zechariah's behavior served as an immediate cause of the outbreak of the Roman War. When the rabbis were inclined to overlook the blemish in the animal offered as a sacrifice by the Roman government, in order not to offend Rome, Zechariah objected; and when they proposed that *Bar Kamẓa be put to death to prevent his informing against them to the government, he again objected. The Romans regarded the refusal to offer up the sacrifice as a sign of rebellion on the part of the Jews against the empire and the Roman War broke out, which resulted in the destruction of the Temple.

BIBLIOGRAPHY: Hyman, Toledot, 402; Y. Furstenberg, in: S. Friedman (ed.), *Five Sugyot from the Babylonian Talmud.* (Heb., 2002).

[Zvi Kaplan]

ZECHARIAH BEN BARACHEL (12th century), head of the *Baghdad academy. R. Zechariah was born in *Aleppo, where his father was the leader of the community. While still in Syria, R. Zechariah was renowned for his erudition and "he taught them most of the Talmud by heart." When he went to Baghdad, the head of the academy R. *Samuel b. Eli gave him his learned daughter in marriage, appointed him *av bet din* of the yeshivah, and empowered him to "designate scribes, *ḥazzanim*, community emissaries, and heads of communities." During the same year (1190), R. Zechariah traveled to the communities of Babylonia and Syria in order to raise funds for the academy. After the death of his father-in-law in 1193, he succeeded him. During his visit to Baghdad, R. Judah *al-Ḥarizi described him as "powerful in Talmud, respected, God-fearing, and pious" (*Taḥkemoni*, ed. by A. Kaminka (1899), 190).

BIBLIOGRAPHY: Mann, Texts, index; idem, in: HḤY, 6 (1922), 109 f.; Assaf, in: *Tarbiz*, 1:1 (1930), 106–10; D.Z. Baneth (ed.), *Iggerot ha-Rambam* (1946), 31:2.

[Zvi Meir Rabinowitz]

ZECHARIAH BEN SOLOMON-ROFE (RaZaH; known in Arabic as **Yahya ibn Suleiman al-Tabib**, first half of 15th century), Yemenite scholar and physician. Zechariah lived in *Sanʿa, *Yemen. His midrashic anthology of the Torah and *haftarot, Midrash ha-Ḥefeẓ*, compiled in 1428, is considered one of the most important Yemenite Midrashim. The **Midrash ha-Gadol* is the main source of his work. He was also influenced by *Maimonides' philosophical opinions. All the sources are in Hebrew and Aramaic; he enlarges upon the ideas and comments on them in Arabic.

Zechariah also wrote a commentary, *al-Durrah al-Muntakhabah* ("The Choicest Pearl"), on the *Midrash ha-Gadol*. His admiration for Maimonides is also expressed in several works which he wrote on Maimonides' books: (1) *Sharḥ al-Ḥigbur,* comments in Arabic on the unknown sources of *Yad ha-Ḥazakah* and *Sefer ha-Mitzvot*; (2) an explanation for Maimonides' commentary on the Mishnah, set out in the form of questions and answers; (3) a commentary in Arabic on *Moreh Nevukhim*. His own medical work, *al-Wājiz* ("the Compendium"), consists of three parts and includes the anatomy of the human body, a detailed list of various diseases, and a description of their cures by the use of herbs and other remedies. Two of his works, which were written at the request of his pupils, indicate that he taught in public. Of his works, only the commentary on the *haftarot* (1950) and the Midrash on Song of Songs (1962) have been published.

BIBLIOGRAPHY: Steinschneider, Arab Lit, 249–50, no. 198; idem, in: JQR, 9 (1896/97), 626.

[Yehuda Ratzaby]

ZECHARIAH MENDEL BEN ARYEH LEIB (d. after 1707), rabbi and author. He was born in Cracow, where his father was rabbi of the community. On his father's death in 1671 Samuel *Koidonover was appointed to succeed him, while Zechariah Mendel was appointed rabbi of the main synagogue. Some time after 1674 he was appointed rabbi of Tvrobin and from 1691 to 1700, he was rabbi of Belz. Zechariah was an active member of the *Council of Four Lands; his signature appears on *takkanot* of the council issued during the years 1688–1700.

He was the author of *Ba'er Heitev* on the Shulḥan Arukh, *Yoreh De'ah* (in Sh. Ar., Amsterdam, 1754) and *Ḥoshen Mishpat* (in Sh. Ar., *ibid.*, 1762), a digest of the halakhic comments on the Shulhan Arukh, similar to the commentaries of the same name by Judah b. Simeon *Ashkenazi or Tiktin on *Oraḥ Ḥayyim, Yoreh De'ah*, and *Even ha-Ezer*, by Isaiah b. Abraham on *Oraḥ Ḥayyim*, and by Moses b. Simeon *Frankfurter on *Ḥoshen Mishpat*. Later editions of the Shulḥan Arukh generally contain Zechariah Mendel's *Ba'er Heitev to Yoreh De'ah* and *Ḥoshen Mishpat* and that of Ashkenazi to *Oraḥ Ḥayyim* and *Even ha-Ezer*. Zechariah's son JOSEPH was *av bet din in* Bychawa, Jaslo, and Lublin.

BIBLIOGRAPHY: Ḥ.N. Dembitzer, *Kelilat Yofi*, 1 (1888), 79b; S. Horowitz, *Kitvei ha-Ge'onim* (1928), 58f.; Ch. Tchernowitz, *Toledot ha-Posekim*, 3 (1947), 306ff.; Halpern, Pinkas, 210, 213f., 220, 251, 254.

[Abraham David]

ẒEDAKAH (Heb. צְדָקָה; "righteous act," or "charity"), word derived from the root צדק ("to be correct"). In the Bible, it is variantly used: as righteousness, in the sense of "piety" (Gen. 15:6); as justice (Amos 5:7; 6:12); as right in one's claims (II Sam. 19:29); and, in the plural, as righteous acts (Judg. 5:11; I Sam. 12:7; Jer. 51:10). In later Hebrew literature, it more generally came to mean "charity," implying "acts of justice" but was distinguished from **gemilut ḥasadim* ("acts of kindness"). In the liturgy of Rosh Ha-Shanah and the Day of Atonement, *ẓedakah*, along with "repentance" and "prayer," is said to "avert the evil decree."

ZEDEKIAH (Heb. צִדְקִיָּה, צִדְקִיָּהוּ; "YHWH is my righteousness"), the third son of Josiah (I Chron. 3:15) and the last king of Judah (597/6–587/6 B.C.E.). Zedekiah was 21 years old when he ascended the throne. His mother was Hamutal the daughter of Jeremiah of Libnah (II Kings 24:18; Jer. 52:1). His original name, Mattaniah, was changed to Zedekiah by *Nebuchadnezzar king of Babylonia when the latter appointed him king in place of his brother's son (II Kings 24:17). The change of name is a symbolic expression of Zedekiah's political status as a vassal of the king of Babylonia. Echoes of the vassal pact made between Babylonia and Judah are found in Ezekiel 17:12–14.

From *Jehoiachin, Zedekiah inherited "a humble kingdom" (Ezek. 17:14), a country that was small and weak, subject to a foreign yoke, and divided within. Nebuchadnezzar's campaign against Jehoiakim and Jehoiachin his son brought in its wake the destruction of many cities in Judah, which Zedekiah was prevented from refortifying properly. With Jehoiachin there went into exile some of the honored ones of the country, an important part of the veteran leadership, and many of the craftsmen and experts. Israel's neighbors, especially the Edomites, taking advantage of the difficult position of the kingdom of Judah, made attempts to invade its territory. Ostraca from Arad reveal echoes of the danger that threatened the settlements in the south of Judah from the Edomites. Furthermore, after the exile of Jehoiachin, the kingdom of Judah was under the leadership of inexperienced soldiers and civilians, some of whom were disposed to adventures. Zedekiah himself was not the right leader at the right time. He did not possess those qualities with which he could have prevented the situation from deteriorating to its bitter end – the destruction of the state, of Jerusalem, and of the Temple. The Bible describes him as lacking self-confidence, irresolute, vacillating, Zedekiah was a weak ruler, unsuited for the difficult conditions of the time. Disposed to listen to the advice of *Jeremiah the prophet and not rebel against Babylonia, nevertheless, fearing the princes, he followed their wishes and renounced his allegiance (Jer. 38:5). Zedekiah's position was not an easy one. He ruled only by grace of the king of Babylonia, and Jehoiachin, the preceding king, lived in exile and continued to bear the title of king of Judah even while in Babylonia. There were circles in Judah who hoped for Jehoiachin's return to Jerusalem and for his reappointment as king of Judah (Jer. 28).

During his first years, Zedekiah bore the yoke of Babylonia loyally. It was only in the fourth year of his reign (594/3 B.C.E.) that he showed a tendency to throw off that yoke. In Jeremiah 27 (in verse 1, the reading should be Zedekiah instead of Jehoiakim; cf. 28:1) it is reported that representatives of Edom, Moab, the Ammonites, Tyre, and Sidon assembled in Jerusalem to confer and revolt against Babylonia. The arrival in Jerusalem of the emissaries of the different countries may indicate that Zedekiah took a notable part in initiating the revolt. To the kings subject to Babylonia, that year may have seemed a suitable one for an attempt to throw off the Babylonian yoke; either because of the internal unrest prevailing in Babylonia in 595/4 B.C.E., which is evident from the Babylonian Chronicle, or because of the accession of Psammetichus II to the throne of Egypt (595–589). For reasons that are not clear, the rebellion did not take place. Nebuchadnezzar apparently became acquainted in time with the plot that was being hatched against him and nipped the revolt in the bud by undertaking a campaign to Syria (in 594 B.C.E., according to the Babylonian Chronicle). To this, apparently, belongs the information about the delegation sent by Zedekiah to Nebuchadnezzar to express loyalty (Jer. 29:3), and it is not impossible that he himself journeyed to the king of Babylonia to humble himself before him and express loyalty to him (Jer. 51:59).

The final rebellion of Judah against Babylonia broke out in 589/8 (II Kings 24:20). What prompted Zedekiah to rebel in that year is not clearly known. It is, however, reasonable to assume that he acted not only from a desire to satisfy the wishes of his army commanders, who favored the throwing off of the yoke of Babylonia, but also in coordination with and support of Hophra (589–570), king of Egypt (cf. Jer. 44:30). Echoes of the conspiracy of Judah with Egypt occur in Ezekiel 17 and in Ezekiel's prophecy against Egypt (Ezek. 29). The *Lachish Letters also clearly show that Judah had close ties with Egypt, for important princes of Judah went to Egypt. Letter no. 4 (Rainey, 266–67; COS III, 80) states: "The commander of the host, C[on]iah son of Elnathan, has come down in order to go into Egypt." This army commander undertook a mission to the pharaoh of Egypt on behalf of Zedekiah. Tyre may also have been involved in the revolt, if the statement quoted by Josephus (Apion 1:15ff.) on the siege of Tyre by Nebuchadnezzar king of Babylonia which lasted 13 years can be assigned to this period. It is not impossible that Ammon may also have been a party to the revolt, in view of what is said in Ezekiel 21:24–25 and the subsequent murder of *Gedaliah the son of Ahikam by *Baalis the king of Ammon. At the height of the rebellion, Zedekiah made a covenant with the people "that everyone should set free his Hebrew slaves, male and female, so that no one should enslave a Judite his brother" (Jer. 34:9–11). This act may attest the enthusiasm that came upon various circles among the people during the rebellion. It was, however, not long before all those who had previously been freed were once more enslaved (Jer. 34:11).

The failure of the rebellion was foreseen. Nebuchadnezzar was at the pinnacle of his power, and a treaty of two or three states was unable to oust Babylonia from Syria and Palestine. The internal position in Judah was very grave. The nation was divided about its relations with Babylonia. There were circles that were disposed to rely on Egypt and throw off the yoke of Babylonia. Those who incited the people to rebellion and instilled confidence in them, a confidence that was false, were the army commanders and the prophets, referred to by Jeremiah as prophesying lies. These prophets promised the people that neither sword nor famine would come to Jerusalem and that God would help them in their distress (Jer. 14:13; 21:2). Jeremiah refuted the words of the prophets, prophesied sufferings for the people, and uttered a grievous prophecy on Jerusalem and its Temple (7:14–15; 34:21–22). According to Jeremiah, the fate of the nation had already been determined for destruction, in consequence of its moral and religious sin (6:13; 7:17–19, et al.). Because of his warnings and rebukes, Jeremiah, as well as all those who had similar ideas, were persecuted by the princes and the false prophets (Jer. 26).

The Babylonian answer was not long in coming. Nebuchadnezzar went to Syria and established his camp at Riblah in the land of Hamath (II Kings 25:6, 20; Jer. 39:5), while troops of Chaldeans made their way southward, and laid siege to Jerusalem. The siege lasted for about two and a half years, from Zedekiah's ninth year, in the tenth month, on the tenth of the month, until the city was breached in his 11th year (587 to 586 B.C.E.), in the fourth month, on the ninth of the month (II Kings 25:1–4; Jer. 39:1–2; 52:4–7).

There is no explicit information on the help extended to Judah by the neighboring countries except Egypt. Hophra, king of Egypt, sent a force to help Judah. The Chaldeans besieging Jerusalem withdrew before the Egyptian auxiliary force and lifted their siege of the city (Jer. 37:5; Ezek. 17:29–32; cf. Lam. 4:17). When the Egyptian force returned to Egypt, the Babylonian forces renewed the siege of Jerusalem. At the same time, the Chaldeans, attacking the hill country and the Shefelah, captured the fortified cities of Judah one by one (Jer. 44:2). In Jeremiah 34:7 it is stated that "the army of the king of Babylon fought against Jerusalem and against all the cities of Judah that were left, Lachish and Azekah; for these were the only fortified cities of Judah that remained" (see also Jer. 44:2). In Lachish Letter no. 4 the commander of one of the strongholds writes to the commander of Lachish: "And let [my lord] know that we are watching for the signals of Lachish, according to all the indications which my lord hath given, for we cannot see Azekah." It has been argued that this letter reflects the moment when Azekah, too, fell and the signals from it ceased, but this is unlikely (Begin). Archaeological excavations of the tells to the south of Jerusalem show that many cities, such as Lachish, Beth-Zur, Ramat Raḥel, and Tell Bet Mirsim, were destroyed at this period. The Lachish ostraca reflect the tension and straits of Judah during the last days. Letter no. 6 (Ahituv, 48) indicates that some of the people "were weakening hands," i.e., spreading discouragement about the rebellion. This tallies to a great extent with Jeremiah 38:4, according to which the princes blamed Jeremiah for "weakening the hands" of the soldiers. Jeremiah himself was suspected of treachery when he tried to go over to the land of Benjamin (Jer. 37). He urged the people to give up the fight and surrender to the Babylonians (21:8–10); and indeed some of the people deserted to the Chaldeans (38:19). Zedekiah was not only unable to inspire and encourage the people at this fateful hour, but was afraid of them and in the power of the princes. He himself was not wholeheartedly in favor of the rebellion against Babylonia. If Zedekiah did not abandon Jerusalem during the siege itself, it was because he feared the Judites who were already in the camp of the Babylonians (Jer. 38:19). At the same time, many refugees from the provincial cities had come to Jerusalem, where the situation became intolerable because of the severe famine (Jer. 37:21; 52:6; II Kings 25:3).

When the city was breached on Tammuz 9 (587 or 586 B.C.E.), Zedekiah fled, together with the aristocrats of Jerusalem, toward eastern Transjordan, but was captured in the neighborhood of Jericho and brought to Riblah. There his sons were killed before his eyes, after which he was blinded and sent in chains to Babylonia, where he died (II Kings 25:4–7; Jer. 39:4–7; cf. Ezek. 12:1–14). In the month of Av, on the seventh of the month, Nebuzaradan (Akkadian: Nabû-zēr-iddina), "the captain of the guard" (the Hebrew, a translation of the Akkadian title, literally means "chief cook") came to Jerusalem, demolished the city, burnt the Temple, and took many of the people captive (II Kings 25:11; cf. Jer. 52:29–30). The nobility of Jerusalem were brought to Riblah, where they were executed (II Kings 25:8–21).

[Bustanay Oded]

In the Aggadah

Despite the fact that Nebuchadnezzar demanded that Zedekiah swear fealty to him on a Torah scroll, he did not keep faith and soon rebelled against him (PR 26:129). Nor was this his only treachery toward his overlord. Once he surprised Nebuchadnezzar in the act of eating flesh cut from a living hare. The king adjured him not to relate what he had seen, but Zedekiah reported it to the neighboring kings (Ned. 65a; Tanh. B., Ex. 33). Zedekiah was duly punished for his unfaithfulness. When Jerusalem fell, he tried to escape through a cave extending from his house to Jericho, which tradition identifies with the "Cave of Zedekiah" in Jerusalem. God sent a deer into the Babylonian camp, and in pursuit of the animal the soldiers reached the opening of the cave at the very moment when Zedekiah was leaving it (Rashi, II Kings 25:4). Nebuchadnezzar justified the cruel punishment he meted out to Zedekiah and his sons (II Kings 25:7) because the Jewish king had sinned both according to the laws of God and the laws of the state (PR 26:131a). Nevertheless, Zedekiah did possess virtues. He is particularly praised for having Jeremiah rescued from the mire (MK 28b). God wanted to reduce the world to chaos because of the misdeeds of his generation, but when he considered Zedekiah his anger subsided (Ar. 17a). Jeremiah's prophecy that Zedekiah would "die in peace" (34:5) was fulfilled in that he outlived Nebuchadnezzar, although he died shortly after (MK 28b). He was mourned as the king who represented "the residue of all the previous generations" (Seder Olam R 28). Royalty in Israel is compared to the moon. The bright light of Solomon's reign, which was like the moon at its zenith, gradually waned until it was extinguished with the blinding of Zedekiah (Ex. R. 15:26).

[Aaron Rothkoff]

BIBLIOGRAPHY: Ginzberg, Legends, 7 (1938), 512f. (index); M. Greenberg, in: JBL, 76 (1957), 304–9; Bright, Hist, 306–10; A. Malamat, in: IEJ, 18 (1968), 144–56; Freedy and Redford, in: JAOS, 90 (1970), 462–85. **ADD. BIBLIOGRAPHY:** M. Cogan and H. Tadmor, *II Kings* (AB; 1988), 315–24; S. Ahituv, *Handbook of Ancient Hebrew Inscriptions* (1992); R. Althann, ABD, 6:1069–70; Z. Begin, in: VT, 52 (2002), 166–74; A. Rainey and R. Notley, *The Sacred Bridge* (2006), 264–67.

ZEDEKIAH, the name of several biblical figures.

(1) The son of Chenaanah, one of the prophets of Samaria in the time of *Ahab king of Israel and *Jehoshaphat king of Judah (I Kings 22; II Chron. 18). Zedekiah appears to have been one of the court prophets dependent upon the king and in consequence strove to win Ahab's approval by prophesying what he wished to hear – that he would be successful in the battle of Ramoth-Gilead. For this purpose he even made horns of iron and said: "Thus says the Lord, 'With these you shall push the Arameans until they are destroyed'" (I Kings 22:11). According to the Bible, his words were contrary to those of *Micaiah son of Imlah, a prophet of the Lord, who prophesied defeat for the armies of Israel and Judah. Thereupon Zedekiah obsequiously smote Micaiah on the cheek and presented him as a false prophet, saying: "How did the Spirit of the Lord go from me, to speak to you" (I Kings 22:24; cf. II Chron. 18:23). In reply, Micaiah prophesied to Zedekiah: "Behold, you shall see on that day when you go into an inner chamber to hide yourself" (I Kings 22:25; cf. II Chron. 18:24).

(2) The son of Maaseiah, mentioned together with Ahab son of Kolaiah in Jeremiah (29:21–23). Both were accused by Jeremiah of performing folly in Israel, committing adultery with their neighbors' wives, and speaking in the name of God lying words which He did not command them. Jeremiah prophesied that Zedekiah and Ahab would be punished at the hands of the king of Babylon, and that their fate would serve as a symbol among the exiles of Judah who would say: "The Lord make you like Zedekiah and Ahab, whom the king of Babylon roasted in the fire" (29:22). The background of Jeremiah's prophecy appears to be the support given by Zedekiah and Ahab to opposition to Babylon, in contrast to Jeremiah's view on this matter.

(3) *Zedekiah, king of Judah.

[Hanoch Reviv]

ZEDERBAUM, ALEXANDER (pseudonym **Erez**, "cedar" = Zederbaum; 1816–1893), a pioneer of Jewish journalism in Russia. Born in Zamosc, Poland, he moved to Odessa in 1840, taking an active part in Jewish affairs there and becoming a favorite of the local authorities. He received a permit to publish **Ha-Meliẓ*, the first Hebrew weekly in Russia, and began publication in 1860. Two years later he published *Kol Mev-*

asser, a Yiddish supplement to *Ha-Meliẓ*. Leading Hebrew writers of the day contributed to the papers, which supported the Haskalah movement, opposed Ḥasidism, and kept their readers informed of current events in the Jewish and non-Jewish world. In 1871 Zederbaum transferred *Ha-Meliẓ* to St. Petersburg and began publication of a Russian-language weekly entitled *Vestnik Russkikh Yevreyev* ("Russian Jewish Herald"). Financial difficulties led to the closing of both papers in 1873. Zederbaum renewed publication of *Ha-Meliẓ* in July 1878, during the Russo-Turkish War. He transferred his permit for a Russian-language newspaper to a group of Russian-Jewish intellectuals, who then produced **Razsvet*. In 1881 he began to publish the Yiddish newspaper, *Yidishes Folksblat*. He was an enthusiastic supporter of the Ḥibbat Zion movement from its inception, and its members were among his contributors. The actual editing of *Ha-Meliẓ* in this late period was done by Hebrew writers such as J.L. *Gordon (1880–83 and 1885–88), and A.S. *Friedberg (1883–86). From 1886 *Ha-Meliẓ* appeared as a daily. Zederbaum edited and wrote the leading articles for his newspaper. Though his articles were pompous and verbose, their content greatly appealed to his readers. He was a liberal editor, permitting contributors to express views he opposed, but adding his dissent in a footnote.

Zederbaum published several books in Hebrew and Yiddish, including *Bein ha-Meẓarim* (Odessa, 1864); *Keter Kehunnah* (Odessa, 1868), essays consisting mainly of anti-ḥasidic polemics; and *Di Geheymenise fun Berditshov* (Odessa, 1870). His many detractors accused Zederbaum of dilettantism and a negative attitude toward his collaborators, but in perspective Zederbaum may be viewed as a pioneer of Hebrew journalism who, despite the prevailing political and cultural conditions of Jews in 19th-century Russia, succeeded in creating Hebrew and Yiddish literary platforms where most of the contemporary writers in these languages were able to express themselves.

BIBLIOGRAPHY: Friedberg, in: *Sefer ha-Shanah*, ed. by N. Sokolow (1900), 238–53; Waxman, Literature, 3 (1960), 338ff.; 4 (1960), 433; N. Slouschz, *Renascence of Hebrew Literature* (1909), 162–3; J. Raisin, *The Haskalah Movement in Russia* (1913), 288; Rejzen, Leksikon, 3 (1928), 325–50; *Ha-Asif*, 6 (1893), 169–71; *Aḥi'asaf*, 2 (1894), 452–4; Kressel, Leksikon, 2 (1967), 701–4.

[Yehuda Slutsky]

ZEDNER, JOSEPH (1804–1871), German bibliographer. Zedner, born in Glogau, taught at a Jewish school in Strelitz, Mecklenburg, and was a tutor in the home of the book dealer and publisher Adolph Asher (1800–1853) of Berlin before becoming a bookseller himself. In 1846 he was appointed translator and later assistant librarian in the Hebrew division of the British Museum, London, a post he held until 1869 when he retired to Berlin. He supplied Leopold *Zunz and Moritz *Steinschneider with a great deal of bibliographical information. His main work was the *Catalogue of the Hebrew Books in the Library of the British Museum* (1867). He also edited Abraham Ibn Ezra's commentary on the Book of Esther (1850).

BIBLIOGRAPHY: M. Steinschneider, in: *Magazin fuer die Literatur des Auslandes* (1871), 628–30 (= *Gesammelte Schriften* (1925), 628–34. **ADD. BIBLIOGRAPHY:** AZJ (February 6, 1872), 116–18; G. Deutsch, in: JE, 12 (1906), 650–51; JL, 5 (1930), 1542; D. Kaufmann, in: ADB, 44 (1898), 749–53; F.D. Lucas and M. Heitmann, *Stadt des Glaubens. Geschichte und Kultur der Juden in Glogau* (1991), 475–78, G. Pelger, in: *Festschrift fuer Prof. Dr. M. Brocke* (2005); Wininger, in: JNB, 6 (1979), 352.

[Alexander Tobias / Gregor Pelger (2nd ed.)]

ZE'EIRA (in TB Zeira; c. 300 C.E.), *amora*. Ze'eira was a Babylonian *amora* but later immigrated to Ereẓ Israel. His name is one of the most frequently mentioned in both the Babylonian and Jerusalem Talmuds. Hundreds of dicta in his name are transmitted by many different scholars. He studied in the academy of Sura under Huna and in Pumbedita under Judah b. Ezekiel (Ber. 39a). He transmitted many of the teachings of these rabbis, as well as those of their teachers Rav and Samuel and other great Babylonian *amoraim*. While still in Babylon he evinced a special interest in the teaching of the Palestinian *amoraim* and would request persons going on a visit there to clarify *Johanan's views on certain halakhic matters (Er. 80a; BM 43b). When he was preparing to go to Ereẓ Israel he avoided his teacher, R. Judah, who was opposed to this step (Shab. 41a; Ket. 110a–111a), and left without informing him. It is stated that in his great love for Ereẓ Israel and eagerness to be there, he crossed the Jordan fully clothed (TJ, Shev. 4:9, 35c); another version is that he crossed on a narrow bridge holding onto a rope stretched across the river, maintaining: "How can I be sure that I am worthy to enter a place that Moses and Aaron were not vouchsafed to enter?" (Ket. 112a). In Ereẓ Israel he attended the school of Johanan in Tiberias (Kid. 52a; Nid. 25b). It is related that he underwent 100 (some say 40) fasts in order to forget the Babylonian method of study so that it should not interfere with his absorbing the system prevalent in Ereẓ Israel (BM 85a). He studied under the greatest *amoraim* of Ereẓ Israel in that generation, including Eleazar, Ammi, and Assi. He praised Ereẓ Israel and its teaching, saying: "The very atmosphere of the Land of Israel makes one wise" (BB 158b); "Even the ordinary conversation of the people of the Land of Israel requires study" (Lev. R. 34:7). In Ereẓ Israel Ze'eira obtained *semikhah* and received the title "rabbi." He was meticulous in the care he took both to receive and transmit halakhic traditions (Ber. 28a; Er. 46a; et al.). His chief pupil was *Jeremiah b. Abba.

Ze'eira was reckoned among "the pious ones of Babylon" (Ḥul. 122a) and there are several stories told testifying to his piety when in Ereẓ Israel. Thus it is related that he showed friendship to lawless men who lived in his neighborhood in order to lead them to repentance (Sanh. 37a). To the question of his pupils: "By what virtue have you reached a good old age?", he replied: "Never in my life have I been harsh with my household; nor have I stepped in front of one greater than myself; nor have I meditated on the Torah in filthy alleys; nor have I walked four cubits without *tefillin*; nor have I ever slept, or even dozed in the *bet ha-midrash*; nor have I ever rejoiced at the downfall of my fellow or called him by his derogatory nickname" (Meg. 28a). Another of his dicta was: "A man should not promise something to a child and not keep the promise because he will thereby teach him to lie" (Suk. 46b). Apparently Ze'eira returned to Babylon for some time (Shab. 14a–b), but returned to Ereẓ Israel where he died. The Talmud gives one of the eulogies delivered at his funeral: "The Land of Shinar [Babylon] was his home of birth; the Land of Glory [Israel] reared her darling to fame; woe is me, says Rakkat [Tiberias] for she has lost her choice ornament" (MK 25b). The Babylonian Talmud sometimes mentions in addition to R. Ze'eira an *amora* Rav Zeira. Some assert that he was another *amora* (living at the beginning of the fourth century C.E.). Others maintain that both refer to the same *amora*, who, like all Babylonian *amoraim*, had the title "Rav" before he went to Ereẓ Israel, whereas after he immigrated to Ereẓ Israel and was ordained there, he was referred to as Rabbi Ze'ira (Ket. 43b; Men. 40b; see Rashi Tos. *ibid.*).

BIBLIOGRAPHY: Bacher, Pal Amor; Hyman, Toledot, s.v.; Ḥ. Albeck, *Mavo la-Talmudim* (1969), 233–6.

[Zvi Kaplan]

ẒE'ENAH U-RE'ENAH (Heb. צְאֶנָה וּרְאֶנָה; lit. "Come and See"; Yid. pronunciation *Tsenerene*; title taken from the Song of Songs, 3:11), an exegetical rendering in Yiddish of the Pentateuch, the *haftarot*, and the Five Scrolls. Composed at the end of the 16th century by Jacob b. Isaac *Ashkenazi, it gained universal acceptance among Ashkenazi Jewry. Used primarily by women as reading matter on the Sabbath, it has retained its great popularity up to the present day. The work consists of discourses on selected topics or passages from the weekly portion of the Pentateuch, the *haftarot*, and the Scrolls, the method used being a combination of *peshat* ("literal exegesis") and *derash* ("free interpretation"), interwoven with legends from the Midrash and other sources, stories, and topical comments on moral behavior. The author used numerous sources of which some are cited by name, including *Rashi, Baḥya b. *Asher, and *Naḥmanides. It seems, however, that the major source was the commentary on the Torah by Baḥya; a considerable part of the interpretative material was taken directly from that commentary, rather than from the original sources, and the construction of the interpretative passages in *Ẓe'enah u-Re'enah* also bears a striking resemblance to that employed by Baḥya. No definitive study has yet been made of the sources employed by the author and the manner in which he made use of them; it is clear, however, that he edited and adapted them at will. Generally he avoids the kabbalistic or philosophical passages that are found in his sources; he uses Yiddish throughout (rather than quoting the Hebrew original) and his aim is to provide an easily comprehensible interpretation, interspersed with story elements.

Ẓe'enah u-Re'enah became a book for women, but this, notwithstanding the feminine form of its name, was not the original intention: the frontispiece on the oldest extant edition states that "this work is designed to enable men and women… to understand the word of God in simple language." Like *Meliẓ Yosher*, the other homiletic work by the author, it aimed at both men and women. The date and place of publication of the first edition of *Ẓe'enah u-Re'enah* are not known; the oldest existing edition – of 1622 – is from Basle (although it was actually printed in Hanau); the frontispiece of this edition reveals that it was preceded by at least three other editions, one printed in Lublin and the other two in Cracow, and that by 1622 these earlier editions were already out of print. Over 210 editions have since appeared, first in Central Europe, then in Eastern Europe, and finally also in the U.S. and Israel.

The various early editions show few linguistic differences, but in the 18th-century editions these became so numerous that *Ẓe'enah u-Re'enah* became a kind of laboratory for the Yiddish language. The 19th-century editions also contain textual variations, which sometimes bear the imprint of a particular ideological trend in Judaism (mainly of Haskalah and Ḥasidism). Various parts of *Ẓe'enah u-Re'enah* were translated into other languages. The first was a translation into Latin of the weekly portion, *Bereshit*, by Johannes Saubertus (Helmstadt, 1660, cited in Wolf, Bibl. Hebr. III, 474). The Book of Genesis was translated into English by Paul Isaac Hershon (London, 1855), as was the Book of Exodus, by Norman C. Gore (N.Y., 1965). There are two German translations of Genesis, one by Sol Goldsmidt, published in *Mitteilungen zur Juedischen Volkskunde* (Vienna, 1911–14) and the other by Bertha Pappenheim (Frankfurt, 1930); the chapter "Destruction of the Temple" (which in *Ẓe'enah u-Re'enah* follows the Scroll of Lamentations) was also translated into German by Alexander Eliasberg (Berlin, 1921). There are also many adaptations of *Ẓe'enah u-Re'enah*, varying in the degree of their faithfulness to the original, such as *Tsenerena in Nayer Bearbaytung*, by Judah ha-Kohen Kraus (Pecs (?), 1891); *Tsenerena, Kommet und Shaut!*, by David Schweitzer (Fuerth, 1861); and *Ẓe'enah u-Re'enah* by Herz Homburg, which did not see print and parts of which were recently discovered in manuscript. The title "*Ẓe'enah u-Re'enah*" was also used for various works, one of these a sort of anthology on subjects from the Pentateuch, by Emmanuel Hecht (St. Wendell, 1862?); another is a collection of sermons by Liebman Adler (Chicago, 1887). These two works were written in German; there is also a French-language "*Ẓe'enah u-Re'enah*," a textbook on the weekly portion and the *haftarot*, by Alexander Créhange (Paris, 1846).

Sefer ha-Maggid, a Yiddish work on the Prophets and Hagiographa similar in nature to the *Ẓe'enah u-Re'enah*, was also attributed to Ashkenazi; however it has now been conclusively proven that he was not the author (see Lieberman, bibl.).

BIBLIOGRAPHY: M. Erik, *Geshikhte fun der Yidisher Literatur* (1928), 223–30; Ch. Shmeruk, in: *For Max Weinreich on his Seventieth Birthday* (1964); J. Prijs, *Die Basler hebraeischen Drucke* (1964); Ch. Lieberman, in: *Yidishe Shprakh*, 26 (1966), 33–38; 29 (1969), 73–76. **ADD. BIBLIOGRAPHY:** M. Heyd, in: JJA, 10 (1984), 64–86; J. Baumgarten, in: REJ 144,1–3 (1985), 305–10; J.P. Schultz, in: *Judaism*, 36, 1 (1987), 84–96; J. Carlebach, in: *L'Eylah*, 23 (1987), 42–47; D.S. Bilik, in: *Jewish Book Annual*, 51 (1993), 96–111; J. Ferrer, in: *Jewish Studies at the Turn of the Twentieth Century I* (1999), 43–50.

[Chava Turniansky]

ZE'EV WOLF OF ZHITOMIR (d. 1800), ḥasidic preacher, disciple of *Dov Baer, the Maggid of Mezhirech. His book, *Or ha-Me'ir* (Korets, 1787), is important for its wealth of material on the history of Ḥasidism and teachings of its founders. R. Ze'ev criticized the behavior of the *ẓaddikim* of his day who had abandoned simple living for luxury. An opponent of noisy prayer, he contended that one should pray with *kavvanah*, with the object of elevating one's thoughts and realizing one's insignificance: "One ought to pray with fear and reverence and stand upright and not be heard, and only move the lips" (*Or ha-Me'ir, Terumah*).

BIBLIOGRAPHY: A. Walden, *Shem ha-Gedolim he-Ḥadash* (1870); Dubnow, Ḥasidut (1960^2), 203–4; R. Schatz-Uffenheimer, *Ha-Ḥasidut ke-Mistikah* (1968), index; I. Tishby, in: *Zion*, 31–32 (1966/67), 41–45.

[Zvi Meir Rabinowitz.]

ZE'EVI, ISRAEL BEN AZARIAH (17th century), rabbi and emissary. Born in Salonika, Ze'evi settled in *Jerusalem, where he suffered under the harsh regime of the Turkish governor Ibn Faruk. In a halakhic correspondence with Joseph b. Moses *Trani (later of *Safed and then Constantinople), he described the sufferings of the Jerusalem community, in particular their financial plight (*Responsa Maharit* 2, *Ḥoshen Mishpat*, no. 60). Ze'evi was one of the signatories of a 1646 *takkanah* (regulation) exempting scholars from taxes. He also wrote a number of approbations (**haskamot*) and twice undertook missions on behalf of the Jerusalem community, visiting *Turkey and the Balkan countries. His great-grandson, ISRAEL B. BENJAMIN ZE'EVI (d. 1731), was rabbi of *Hebron for about 30 years and head of a yeshivah founded by the wealthy Abraham Pereira of Amsterdam, and visited Constantinople in 1685 as an emissary of *Hebron. He was the author of *Orim Gedolim* (Smyrna, 1758), consisting of talmudic novellae, sermons, and responsa.

BIBLIOGRAPHY: Frumkin-Rivlin, 2 (1928), 14f.; E. Rivlin (ed.), *Ḥorvot Yerushalayim* (1928), 41, 45f.; Yaari, Sheluḥei, 266–7.

[Abraham David]

ZE'EVI, REḤAVAM (**"Gandhi"**; 1926–2001), Israeli military commander and politician, member of the Twelfth to Fifteenth Knessets. Born in Jerusalem, Ze'evi went to the regional school at Givat ha-Sheloshah. From 1936 to 1944 he was active in the Ha-Maḥanot ha-Olim youth movement, and in 1944 joined the *Palmaḥ, where he got the nickname "Gandhi," for his emaciated appearance. In the War of Independence he was the intelligence officer of the Yiftaḥ brigade. In later years he served as operations officer on the Northern Front, intelligence officer in the Southern Command, and commander of the Golani regiment. In the early 1960s he attended the Command and Staff College of the U.S. Army. In 1964 Ze'evi received the rank of major general, and served as commander of the Central Command, and in 1968 was appointed head of the Operations Branch. A week before the Yom Kippur War he retired from the IDF, but returned to active service during the war in the Operations Branch. During his military career he gained a reputation for his flamboyancy and directness.

In 1974 Ze'evi was appointed adviser to Prime Minister Yitzhak *Rabin and in 1975–77 as the prime minister's advisor on intelligence matters. In 1981 he was appointed director of the Land of Israel Museum in Tel Aviv, serving in this capacity for 10 years, during which he developed the museum but was also criticized for his management of it.

In 1985 Ze'evi started to speak publicly of the need to encourage a voluntary transfer of the Palestinian population from the West Bank and Gaza Strip. Prior to the elections to the Twelfth Knesset in 1988 he established a political party called Moledet. Moledet gained two seats in the Twelfth Knesset, three in the Thirteenth, two in the Fourteenth. In the elections to the Fifteenth Knesset Moledet ran as part of the National Union list.

After the breakup of the National Unity Government in 1990, Ze'evi joined the government as minister without portfolio and member of the Security Cabinet in February 1991, causing an uproar within the Likud, since some of its leading members felt that his views were too extreme. However, less than a year later he left the government, against the background of Prime Minister Yitzhak *Shamir's decision to participate in the Madrid Conference on Peace in the Middle East.

In the course of the Thirteenth Knesset he was one of the strongest opponents of the Oslo Accords in the Knesset, but he strongly condemned Rabin's assassination. He was also one of the mourners of former Major General and MK Mattityahu Peled, despite Peled's left-wing views and his membership in a mixed Jewish-Arab party. In general Ze'evi remained attached to all his former colleagues – including Rabin and Peled – with whom he had served in the Palmaḥ. However, in the Thirteenth Knesset he hit the headlines primarily due to his quarrels with the other two members of his party, one of whom he called "a clown," and the other a "UFO," and bitter verbal exchanges with some of the Arab Knesset Members. Ze'evi did not join the government formed by Binyamin *Netanyahu in 1996, supporting the government from the outside. As a member of the National Union he joined the government formed by Ariel *Sharon in March 2001 and was given the Tourism portfolio. In the periods when he was not a member of the government, he served on the Knesset Foreign Affairs and Defense Committee and on the House Committee. He was murdered by Palestinian terrorists in the Hyatt Hotel in Jerusalem on October 17, 2001. Though Ze'evi's political positions were condemned by many, he was held even by his opponents in high esteem for his integrity and decency. After his murder, his son Palmaḥ contended for the leadership of Moledet, but Rabbi Binyamin (Benny) *Elon was elected.

Ze'evi edited and brought to print a translated series of historical travel books published between 1982 and 1995 by the Ministry of Defense. He also edited, by himself and with others, numerous books relating to geographical locations in Ereẓ Israel, and military issues.

BIBLIOGRAPHY: M. Sheshar, *Siḥot im Reḥavam Ze'evi* (2001); I. Katz, *Aluf Rehav'am Ze'evi 1926–2001: Devarim le-Zikhro* (2001).

[Susan Hattis Rolef (2nd ed.)]

ZEFIRA, BRACHAH (c. 1911–1990), Israeli singer. Born in Jerusalem of Yemenite parentage, but orphaned early, Brachah Zefira spent her childhood in various foster families and became familiar with the different musical heritages of the Jewish and Arab communities. Educated at the *Me'ir Shefeyah Youth Aliyah Village, she went to Europe at the beginning of the 1930s to study singing and acting. In Berlin she met Nahum *Nardi (to whom she was married for a time) who helped shape her style, and was in turn influenced by her. Returning to Palestine, she met the new immigrant composers such as Paul *Ben-Haim, Oedoen *Partos, Alexander Uriyah *Boscovitch, Marc *Lavry, and Menahem *Avidom, to whom she introduced the musical style of the Orient on which they sought to base their work. They arranged many of her songs, composed songs especially for her, and even used some of her songs in their own compositions. She also influenced some of the younger composers. Through her personal appearances and broadcasts, Brachah Zefira, an alto, became the first national folk singer of the *yishuv*. The personal style which she created was compounded of Yemenite, Palestinian-Sephardi, and Arabic elements. In the 1950s, Brachah Zefirah took up abstract expressionist painting.

[Avner Bahat]

ZEHAVI, DAVID (1910–1977), Israeli composer born in Jaffa to parents who had arrived from Romania in 1899. At age 14 Zehavi joined a group of Ha-No'ar ha-Oved, which set up a new agricultural community, kibbutz Na'an (1930). There, in addition to farming, he conducted sing-along sessions. He was the first composer born in Ereẓ Israel, and as such he ranks among the founding fathers of the Israeli folk song together with *Admon, *Ze'ira, *Nardi, and others. In 1927 he composed his first published song, "*Orḥah ba-Midbar*" ("Caravan in the Desert"), whose opening line "*Yamin u-Semol*" ("From right to left …") is often quoted as the title. He composed some 400 songs altogether; 250 of them appeared in print. Many of his songs are considered to be among the best in Hebrew song, such as "*Halikhah le-Kesaria*" (or "*Eli Eli Shelo Yiggamer le-Olam*" ("On the Road to Caesarea," or "My God, My God, Let It Never End"), "*He-Ḥalil*" ("The Flute"), the Palmaḥ song "*Hen Efshar*" ("How Can It Be Possible"), "*Yesusum Midbar*" ("Let the Desert Rejoice"), "*Niggunum*," "*Male'u Asamenu Bar*" ("Our Silos Are Filled with Grain"), and dozens more. In fact, songs make up most of his musical output. He wrote most of them for sing-along performances. Kibbutz members often wrote the lyrics for these songs.

His songs have been published in hundreds of booklets, usually for sing-along evenings, with or without the musical score. They have been recorded by hundreds of singers and ensembles. The publishing house of the cultural wing of the Histadrut has published four collections of his songs: *Song Collection* (1954), *Second Song Collection* (1962), *A Song for David* (1978), and *David Zehavi – Let It Never End* (1981).

David Zehavi also wrote five cantatas for chorale, for soloists, and for a small ensemble. These cantatas, born of scenes of kibbutz life, were composed and performed on the kibbutz.

[Nathan Shahar (2nd ed.)]

ZEICHNER, OSCAR (1916–), U.S. historian. Born in New York City, Zeichner taught at City College, New York, where he became professor of history in 1960, and dean of graduate studies in 1968. After he retired from teaching, he was named professor emeritus of history. His principal interest was the colonial period of American history, and his best-known work is *Connecticut's Years of Controversy, 1750–1776* (1949). He served as president of the Association for the Study of Connecticut History (1975–76); was a member of the American Historical Association for more than 50 years; and was a member of the executive committee of American Professors for Peace in the Middle East.

[Ruth Beloff (2nd ed.)]

ZEID, ALEXANDER (1886–1938), pioneer of the Second Aliyah and one of the founders of the *Ha-Shomer defense organization. Born in Balagansk, Siberia, at the age of 13 Zeid settled in Vilna, where he joined the Zionist labor movement. In 1904 he was one of the first pioneers of the Second Aliyah to reach Ereẓ Israel, where he worked as an agricultural laborer and wagoner in Rishon le-Zion and Petaḥ Tikvah. In Zikhron Ya'akov he was wounded by Arab marauders, and he then worked for some 18 months as a stonemason in Jerusalem. In 1907 he was one of the seven founders of the secret defense organization *Bar Giora, which served as the nucleus of the Ha-Shomer organization, established at Mesḥa (Kefar Tavor) in 1909. Zeid devoted himself to the organization until his death. In 1916 he joined a group of Ha-Shomer veterans who settled in Upper Galilee on the Ḥamara lands near Metullah (now Kefar Giladi). Ten years later he left Kefar Giladi and moved to Tel Ḥai and thence to Sheikh Abrek in the Jezreel Valley to take charge of the guard duty of all the neighboring settlements on behalf of the *Jewish National Fund. Time and again, Zeid was involved in dangerous situations but never abandoned his post, even when wounded by Arab rioters in 1932. He was one of the first to discover the caves near Sheikh Abrek and one of the organizers of the archaeological excavations that revealed the *Bet She'arim necropolis of the mishnaic period. He was killed by Arabs while on guard in 1938. At the site of his death a statue of Zeid on horseback was erected, and the nearby settlement of Givat Zeid, founded in 1943, was named after him. His diaries were edited by E. Smoli under the title *Ḥayyei Rishonim* (1942).

BIBLIOGRAPHY: B. Habas, *Alexander Zeid* (Heb., 1938); M. Smilansky, *Mishpaḥat ha-Adamah*, 4 (1953), 239–49.

[Gedalyah Elkoshi]

ZEIRA, MORDECHAI (1905–1968), composer. Zeira was born in Kiev, Ukraine, and went to Ereẓ Israel after having been arrested in 1924 as a member of a Zionist youth organization. He joined the *Ha-Shomer Ha-Ẓa'ir pioneers' group in Jabneel and worked in road building, fishing, and construction work. Drawn to the theater and impressed by the songs of J. *Engel, he went to Tel Aviv in 1927 and joined the studio of the Ohel Theater. About 1928 Zeira went to Jerusalem for regular music studies with S. *Rosowsky, making his living as a laborer at the Dead Sea Works. In 1933 he settled permanently in Tel Aviv, where he was an employee of the Palestine Electric Corporation, steadily refusing to have his livelihood depend on his compositions. With the outbreak of World War II, Zeira joined an army troupe which entertained Jewish soldiers in the allied forces.

Zeira wrote several hundred songs, of which more than 50 achieved a permanent and beloved place in the cultural heritage of modern Israel. The main influences evident in his work are those of the East European cantorial and Ḥasidic idioms as well as the Russian Romances and revolutionary songs, with the Near Eastern environment as a more covert but nevertheless subtly integrated element. Most important was his own extraordinary gift for melody, lyricism, and emotional intensity, and he may be called the greatest among the creators of the Israel song.

BIBLIOGRAPHY: M. Ravina, in: M. Zeira, 111 *Shirim* (1960), pref.

[Bathja Bayer]

ẒE'IREI ZION (Heb. צְעִירֵי צִיּוֹן, "Young Men of Zion"), Zionist and moderate socialist labor movement, active mainly in Russia. The movement dates from approximately 1903, although its ideological roots go back to previous theories, as e.g., those of Nachman *Syrkin and even Moses *Hess. The year 1903 was one of traumatic experiences and reevaluations in Jewish and Zionist history. The hopes of achieving charter rights to settle Ereẓ Israel were dashed; the *Uganda Scheme controversy led to the secession of the *Territorialists from the Zionist movement and the consolidation of the opposition to *Herzl (the Ẓiyyonei Zion); the outbreak of the *Kishinev pogrom (1903) had a shock effect on the Jewish people and brought many to realize the urgency of the Zionist solution.

Against this background and the existence of an expanding revolutionary movement, Ẓe'irei Zion groups began to emerge almost simultaneously throughout Russia. In the beginning they had neither a formal program nor a socialist "scientific basis," but an unwritten platform was common to all these groups: practical, constructive Zionism based on personal fulfillment through *aliyah*, pioneering, the use of Hebrew, support for the interests of the working masses, participation in the struggle to liberate Russia from czarist autocracy, participation in the struggle for equal rights and national autonomy for the Jews of Russia, the organization of self-defense, and socialist aspirations. The movement's approach to socialism and Zionism is best explained by the statements of Yosef *Sprinzak and Syrkin. The former stated: "We are socialists for the future. With the creation of an independent… new reality in Ereẓ Israel, it will be possible for us to be socialists." In the words of Syrkin: "The ways and means of realizing Zionism are different from those of any other movement of national liberation, which depends on the political power of the oppressed classes, for the Zionist movement must first create the economic power which will then be transformed into political power."

Ẓe'irei Zion devoted itself from the start to practical activities – from collecting funds in *Jewish National Fund boxes to personal fulfillment through *aliyah*. Members of the movement filled the ranks of the Second Aliyah, bringing with them the values of self-labor, collective and cooperative settlement, equality, mutual aid, defense, etc. The settlement in Ereẓ Israel of a Ẓe'irei Zion group from Homel in 1904 is generally regarded as the beginning of the Second Aliyah. Their arrival coincided with the first signs indicating that the Uganda Scheme crisis – emigration from Ereẓ Israel and suspension of settlement work – was wearing off, and they played a vital role in improving the mood in the *yishuv*. Together with workers who arrived before them, they organized the Histadrut ha-Po'alim ha-Ẓe'irim be-Ereẓ Israel, which became the *Ha-Po'el ha-Ẓa'ir Party in October 1905.

Ẓe'irei Zion continued its activities in the Diaspora, mainly in Russia (including Poland and Lithuania). *He-Ḥalutz was founded in Odessa in 1905, and in 1906 a conference of the Bilu'im Ḥadashim (an organization founded by Ẓe'irei Zion in response to Josef *Vitkin's historic call for *aliyah*) was held. The program of the Bilu'im Ḥadashim was very similar to that of the U.S. He-Ḥalutz founded during World War I by David *Ben-Gurion and Izhak *Ben-Zvi and that of the all-Russian He-Ḥalutz established on Joseph *Trumpeldor's initiative after World War I. The alliance between Ẓe'irei Zion and He-Ḥalutz reached its high point during the time of the Third Aliyah.

The Ẓe'irei Zion movement continued to grow without a formal program, but a center was established in 1905 in Kishinev, where a large and powerful local society existed. In the same year, a countrywide conference was held with the aim of consolidating the movement organizationally and ideologically. The latter goal was not realized, however, until the second conference in Kishinev (1906) adopted the Kishinev Program in the following terms: Zionism strives for the renaissance of the Jewish people in Ereẓ Israel; Zionism is borne by working masses; the main motivating forces in Zionism are economic, cultural, and national-political; the concentration of the masses of the Jewish people in their homeland until they constitute a majority there and normal conditions for their free and independent development are created is the solution to the Jewish problem.

In 1910 a Russian-Polish conference of Ẓe'irei Zion took place in Lodz. Like all its predecessors, this meeting was illegal, but unlike them it was discovered by the czarist police and most of the delegates were arrested. Despite the arrests, or perhaps because of them, the conference strengthened the movement by ideological clarification (in the spirit of Ha-Po'el ha-Ẓa'ir) and organizational consolidation. In 1912 an all-Russian conference was held in Minsk. On its agenda were organizational questions, *aliyah*, He-Ḥalutz, and *hakhsharah*, and the convening of a world conference, which was to be held in Vienna in August 1913 to coincide with the 11th Zionist Congress. This meeting of 56 participants in the Zionist Congress (30 from Ẓe'irei Zion organizations in the Diaspora and 26 of Ha-Po'el ha-Ẓa'ir from Ereẓ Israel) laid the foundations for a world federation of Ẓe'irei Zion with permanent connections with Ha-Po'el ha-Ẓa'ir. A prolonged discussion and resolutions on the movement's attitude toward socialism led to disappointment and secessions on both the left and right. The delegates elected a central board to be located in Bialystok and decided to adopt the fortnightly Hebrew paper *Shaḥarit* in Odessa as the movement's organ and to transfer it to Warsaw.

In April 1914 an all-Russian council was held in Vilna, the last before the outbreak of World War I. The main subjects for discussion at this meeting were the condition of the labor movement in Ereẓ Israel, pioneering *aliyah*, and cultural activities. The liberation from the czarist regime by the February Revolution of 1917 caused great ferment among Russian Jews, who then prepared themselves to build their national autonomy in democratic Russia and at the same time to expand their Zionist activities. Ẓe'irei Zion became a mass movement as tens of thousands from all parts of the country swelled its ranks.

The second all-Russian conference of Ẓe'irei Zion, which took place in Petrograd on May 18–24, 1917, was a great event in Jewish life. Three main trends struggled to dominate the conference: socialist, moderate labor, and popular democratic. The presentation of the socialist case was very impressive, but the movement was not prepared to adopt a full-fledged socialist program and declared itself to be the Ẓe'irei Zion Popular Faction in the Zionist Organization in Russia. After the conference Ẓe'irei Zion acted as an independent party and grew rapidly. The party's center in Petrograd was later transferred to Kharkov after the October Revolution and from there to Kiev, which was not yet under Soviet rule. From then on the movement's activities were mainly concentrated in the Ukraine during a period filled with hope of Jewish national autonomy, but mainly dominated by the threatening storm of pogroms. Ẓe'irei Zion then played an important role as organizer of the Jewish *self-defense units and of extensive cooperative enterprises. Its main activities, however, were concentrated on the pioneering *aliyah* movement, promoted through the He-Ḥalutz conference in Kharkov (1918).

At the third conference of Ze'irei Zion, which took place in Kharkov in May 1920, the Popular Faction decided to become the *Zionist Socialist Party – ZS, whereas the "right-wing" faction seceded and joined Ha-Po'el ha-Ẓa'ir, establishing with it the *Hitaḥadut in Prague (1920).

BIBLIOGRAPHY: B. West, *Naftulei Dor* (1945); A. Levinsohn, *Be-Reshit ha-Tenuah* (1947); A. Munchik, *Le-Toledot ẒẒ–ẒS, Ha-Po'el ha-Ẓa'ir, ve-He-Ḥalutz* (1943); I. Ritov, *Perakim be-Toledot ẒẒ–ẒS* (1964).

[Israel Ritov]

ZE'IRI (third century), Babylonian *amora*, also known as Ze'iri b. Hinena (Hinna) in the Jerusalem Talmud. He was born in Babylon but went to Ereẓ Israel in his youth, where he studied under *Hanina b. Ḥama. He later taught in Ḥanina's name that the Messiah would not appear until all the "arrogant ones" had disappeared (Sanh. 98a). His main teacher, however, was *Johanan, whose teachings he later transmitted (e.g., Av. Zar. 53a). Johanan even offered Ze'iri his daughter's hand in marriage. When he declined on the ground that he preferred to marry a woman of Babylonian birth rather than of Palestinian, Johanan retorted, "Our learning is suitable, but our daughters are not?" (Kid. 71b). While in Palestine, Ze'iri was captured by highwaymen and R. Ammi and R. Samuel attempted to attain his release. While they were negotiating with the leader of the brigands, news arrived of neighboring bloody gang warfare, and in the confusion Ze'iri escaped (TJ, Ter. 8:10, 46b; *Penei Moshe* (ad. loc.)). Ze'iri was highly regarded as an expounder of the *beraitot*, and Rava remarked that "every *baraita* not explained by Ze'iri was not truly explained" (Zev. 43b). He eventually returned to Babylon where he taught the Palestinian traditions in the academy of Nehardea (Ḥul. 56a; Ber. 22a). His closest pupil was Ḥiyya b. Ashi (Shab. 109a; Yoma 77b). Others who transmitted his teachings were R. Ḥisda (Ber. 43a), Rabbah (Ned. 46a), R. Joseph (Ned. 46b), Rav Judah (Av. Zar. 61b), R. Naḥman (Av. Zar. 61b), and R. Giddal (Men. 21a).

BIBLIOGRAPHY: Hyman, Toledot, s.v.; Ḥ. Albeck, *Mavo la-Talmudim* (1969), 175–6.

ZEIT, DIE ("The Times"), Yiddish daily newspaper published in London. It was founded in 1913 by Morris *Myer, an immigrant from Romania who had been a prominent Jewish socialist, journalist, and orator. In the first few years the paper served mainly the working class Jewish movements, but Myer changed his views and actively supported the Zionist movement and especially Po'alei Zion. Between the wars the paper gradually took on a more general character and began to publish religious articles. In the early 1920s, there was another rival newspaper (*Di Express*) which however only lasted a few years; thus the *Zeit* was the only Yiddish daily in the whole of Great Britain, although it later became a weekly. With the death of Myer in 1944 the paper was carried on by his son, Harry Myer (1903–1974), but the decline in the number of Yiddish-speaking readers made it difficult for the paper to continue, and it finally closed in 1950. It was the last Yiddish daily in Great Britain.

[Moshe Rosetti]

ZEITLIN, AARON (1898–1973), Hebrew and Yiddish writer. The son of Hillel *Zeitlin, he grew up in Gomel, Vilna, and Warsaw. His early poetic works were lyrical; later, philosophic concepts appeared in his verses, and then followed an attempt to express mystical religious insights within formal rhythmic structures. A philosophic aesthete deeply rooted in Jewish tradition and mysticism, Zeitlin's lyrics are often contemplative liturgic hymns. Well versed in world literature, Zeitlin wrote with equal facility in Hebrew and Yiddish. His early Hebrew poems and essays appeared in the periodicals *Ha-Tekufah* and *Ha-Shilo'aḥ*. His first volume of Yiddish lyrics *Shotns Oyfn Shney* and his longer poems *Metatron* were published in 1922. Four years later he became literary editor of the Warsaw Yiddish daily *Unzer Ekspres*. Zeitlin's poems are filled with visions of true and false messiahs. His drama *Yakob Frank* (1929), written in Yiddish, dealt with two conflicting approaches to God, the one espoused by the God-seeker Jacob *Frank, a disciple of the false messiah *Shabbetai Ẓevi, and the other by the God-finder *Israel Ba'al Shem Tov, founder of Ḥasidism. Another drama was *Brenner* (1929), whose protagonist was J.H. *Brenner, the Hebrew poet who in his younger years had come under the influence of Hillel Zeitlin and was later murdered in the Jaffa pogrom of 1921. Zeitlin's play, *In Keynems Land* ("In No Man's Land"), appeared in Warsaw in 1938. He prophetically described the sadism of the German militarists and warned of the horrors to follow. When the catastrophe came, he was saved; in the spring of 1939, Maurice *Schwartz invited him to New York for the Yiddish Art Theater's premiere of his play. The war prevented Zeitlin's return to his family, all of whom were killed by the Nazis. As contributor to the New York Yiddish daily *Jewish Morning Journal* and professor of Hebrew literature at the Jewish Theological Seminary of America, Zeitlin profoundly influenced the American Jewish scene after World War II. His Hebrew essays, poems, and lectures during his frequent visits to Israel similarly influenced Hebrew literature. A novel set in Palestine, *Brenendige Erd* ("Burning Earth," 1937), dealt with *Nili, the World War I Jewish espionage group. His dramatic poem *Bein ha-Esh ve-ha-Yesha* ("Between Fire and Deliverance," 1957) focused on the destruction of European Jewry. Zeitlin's collected poems, *Gezamelte Lider* (vols. 1 and 2, 1947, vol. 3, 1957), contained the revised versions of the verse he wished to see preserved.

BIBLIOGRAPHY: Rejzen, Leksikon, 3 (1929), 297–9; M. Ravitch, *Mayn Leksikon* (1945), 203–5; S. Bickel, *Shrayber fun Mayn Dor* (1958), 121–32; Z. Zylbercweig, *Leksikon fun Yidishn Teater*, 4 (1965), 3647–51; S. Liptzin, *Maturing of Yiddish Literature* (1970), 172–5; Waxman, Literature, 4 (1960), 1249–50.

ZEITLIN, HILLEL (1871–1942), author, thinker, and journalist. Born in Korma, Belorussia, Zeitlin received the education of a *Ḥabad Ḥasid; self-taught in secular studies, he became troubled by matters of religion and faith. His first work, *Ha-Tov ve-ha-Ra* (in *Ha-Shilo'aḥ*, 5, 1899), was pessimistic in tone and was followed by monographs on Spinoza (1900) and Nietzsche (in *Ha-Zeman*, 1905). Zeitlin was disappointed by secular culture and longed for celestial beauty, a longing expressed in *Maḥashavah ve-Shirah* (2 vols., 1911–12). Shocked by the pogroms in *Kishinev in 1903, he reveals his unceasing anxiety for the survival of the Jew in *Al ha-Zevaḥ* (*Ha-Zeman*, 1905). Out of profound reflection on the fate of the Jew, he returned to religion and came close to Orthodox Judaism, to whose literature he gave a new character. From 1906 he worked for *Haynt* and *Der Moment*, writing for 36 years on both minor topics and serious ones. From 1914 he immersed himself in mysticism and published "visions" in *Ha-Tekufah*. In "*Al Gevul Shenei Olamot*" (*Ha-Tekufah*, 4 (1919), 501–45) he discusses "the origins of mysticism in Israel" on the hypothesis that Judaism is mystical and not rational, concluding, against most scholarly opinions, that Moses de Leon was merely the final editor of the *Zohar, who set forth the teaching of the Zohar in its four subjects – the human body, the soul, the spheres, the Divine – and not the original author. Zeitlin translated the Zohar into Hebrew and wrote a commentary on it, of which only the introduction was published. He became active in the cause of propagating Judaism, publishing *Der Alef-Beys funem Yudentum* ("The Alphabet of Judaism," 1922), in which he establishes a Jewish outlook on the world against a scientific background, as well as books on Ḥasidism, on R. *Naḥman of Bratslav, and on Ḥabad. During his last years, when he foresaw the Holocaust, he called for repentance with enormous fervor – in pamphlets, in speeches, and in organizing special groups of *mekhuvvanim* ("purposeful ones"). Once more despairing, he gave expression to his loneliness in the book containing his last confession, *Demamah ve-Kol* (1936). Zeitlin died a martyr's death, garbed in *tallit* and *tefillin*, on the way to Treblinka on the eve of Rosh Ha-Shanah.

BIBLIOGRAPHY: I. Rabinowich, *Major Trends in Modern Hebrew Fiction* (1968), 100–1; *Ha-Tekufah*, 32–33 (1948), 848–76; 34–35 (1950), 843–8, bibl. by E.R. Malachi; I. Wolfsberg and Z. Harkavy (eds.), *Sefer Zeitlin* (1945); S.B. Urbach, *Toledot Neshamah Aḥat* (1953); idem, *Hillel Zeitlin* (1969); A. Holtz, in: JBA, 28 (1970/71).

[Symcha Bunim Urbach]

ZEITLIN (Zeitlis), JOSHUA (1742–1822), scholar and *shtadlan*. Born in Shklov, Russia, Zeitlin was the disciple of R. Aryeh Leib *Gunzberg, author of *Sha'agat Aryeh*. When the region of Belorussia was annexed by Russia (1772), he became one of the wealthiest merchants in the area and his affairs extended beyond its borders. Under the patronage of Prince Potemkin he was a purveyor and contractor for the government in the regions of "New Russia" which were then transferred from Turkish rule. After the death of Potemkin (1791) Zeitlin retired from business affairs and acquired estates with over 900 serfs. He built himself a palace on the estate of Ustye, to the east of Shklov, where he housed a vast library. Many scholars and researchers, including Menahem Mendel *Levin and Baruch *Schick, frequented his estate. He supported *Elijah b. Solomon the Gaon of Vilna in his dispute against the Ḥasidim and he wrote *Haggahot Ḥadashot* ("New Notes"), on the *Sefer*

Mitzvot Katan, published in the Kopys (Kapust) edition of this work (1820).

BIBLIOGRAPHY: S.J. Fuenn, *Kiryah Ne'emanah* (1915), 271–3; S.J. Horowitz, in: *Ha-Shilo'ah*, 40 (1923), 3–6.

[Yehuda Slutsky]

ZEITLIN, SOLOMON (1892–1976), U.S. scholar of post-biblical literature. Zeitlin, born in Russia, studied in Dvinsk and was influenced by the Ragoshover Illui (R. Joseph Rozin) and R. Meir Simḥah Ha-Kohen. In 1908 he attended the Institute of Baron David *Guenzberg in St. Petersburg, where his roommate was Zalman (Rubashov) *Shazar. Enrolling at the Ecole Rabbinique, Paris, in 1912, Zeitlin received ordination and a doctorate in theology there. His article on "Les 'dix-huit mesures'" was published in REJ, 68 (1914), 22–36. Immigrating to the U.S. during World War I, Zeitlin received a Ph.D. at Dropsie College, Philadelphia, in 1917; his dissertation was on *Megillat Ta'anit as a Source for Jewish Chronology and History in the Hellenistic and Roman Periods* (1922). Zeitlin taught first at Yeshiva College, New York, then became professor of rabbinics at Dropsie College in 1921. As an outstanding authority on the Second Commonwealth period, he wrote over 400 articles and books in the fields of rabbinics, Josephus, the Apocrypha, and Christianity.

Zeitlin's assertions that the so-called Christ passage in Josephus was not authentic but only an interpolation by Eusebius, contrary to the opinion of most scholars, gained him early scholarly fame (JQR 18 (1927/28), 231–55).

His main concern was the analysis of tannaitic sources and the recognition of a clear distinction in historic eras before and after the Temple destruction; differentiating institutions, laws, and concepts.

Zeitlin was the main protagonist against dating the Dead Sea Scrolls in the intertestamental period. His understanding of the continuity of history is reflected in studies on the sources and nature of the teachings of Saadiah Gaon, Maimonides, Rashi, and other sages to ascertain the halakhic process in Judaism. He was the author of many basic writings on Josephus, on Jewish historiography and law, on the crucifixion of Jesus (*Who Crucified Jesus?...*, 1964^4) and on halakhic traditions. He was editor of the **Jewish Quarterly Review* and editor in chief of the Jewish Apocryphal Literature Series. He was also instrumental in organizing the American Academy of Jewish Research in the U.S. Zeitlin's two volumes on the *Rise and Fall of the Judean State* (1968^2) present a definitive view of the Second Temple era, and include comprehensive rabbinic, non-rabbinic, and classical sources. An original and fearless scholar, he stressed that the scholar must not allow theological bias, which often influences writings on the Second Temple era and the Dead Sea Scrolls.

BIBLIOGRAPHY: S.B. Hoenig, *Solomon Zeitlin: Scholar Laureate; an Annotated Bibliography 1915–1970 With Appreciations of His Writings* (1971); *ibid.*, in: JBA, 29 (1971/72), 94–100.

[Sidney B. Hoenig]

ZEITLIN, WILLIAM (**Ze'ev**; c. 1850–1921), bibliographer. Born in Gomel, a member of the Zeitlin family of Shklov, he began at an early age to write poems and to translate from Russian. In the early 1870s he went to Germany to study. After several efforts at creative writing, he turned to bibliography, becoming an outstanding expert, especially in those fields which he pioneered, such as contemporary Jewish literature, the Haskalah, and Zionism. His major work, *Bibliotheca Hebraica Post-Mendelssohniana* (1891–95), in which he lists the Hebrew Haskalah literature from its beginnings to the end of the 1880s, still remains an invaluable aid for the study of that literature. In this book, published in German, only the titles of the works are listed in Hebrew. He also published lists of pseudonyms, the death dates of scholars and writers, and similar material. In *Ha-Maggid* (1873), 5–6, he published, in Hebrew, the first bibliographical article on the Hebrew press.

BIBLIOGRAPHY: A.M. Habermann, in: *Yad la-Koré*, 2 (1951), 146–50; Kressel, Leksikon, 2 (1967), 716.

[Getzel Kressel]

ZEKHUT AVOT (Heb. "Merit of the Fathers"), the doctrine that progeny benefit from the righteousness of their forebears. The exact nature of this concept is a question of great complexity. Some of the references to it would indicate that it is a form of reward granted to the ancestors or an expression of divine love for them; others seem to regard it as a benefit emanating from the superabundance of the ancestors' merit, with little regard for the deserts of the offspring; and yet other sources tend to view it as a spiritual gift to the progeny, who, in turn, must be spiritually qualified to receive it.

The Patriarchs

The idea of merit of the fathers is often mentioned in the Bible and rabbinic literature in relation to the Patriarchs Abraham, Isaac, and Jacob, and in some sources, to the Matriarchs and other biblical heroes as well. There are many instances in the Bible of Israel's being favored, not because of its own merits, but because of those of the Patriarchs, e.g., "And because He loved your fathers, He chose their offspring after them; He Himself... led you out of Egypt" (Deut. 4:37). Similarly, the memory or deeds of the righteous forefathers are often invoked in prayers for the forgiveness or welfare of their descendants, for instance, Moses' supplication after the sin of the golden calf, "Remember your servants, Abraham, Isaac, and Jacob..." (Ex. 32:13), and Solomon's plea, "Remember the good deeds of David Thy servant" (II Chron. 6:42). This practice has been a part of Jewish prayer throughout the ages. The daily and holiday prayer books contain numerous appeals based on the righteousness of the Patriarchs. Prominent among them is the evocation of the heroic sacrifice of Isaac, especially in the liturgy of Rosh Ha-Shanah.

Rabbinic literature contains many statements to the effect that the merit of ancestors affects the welfare of their descendants. Thus it is held that because Judah saved Tamar from burning, his descendants Hananiah, Mishael, and Azariah were saved from the fiery furnace (Sot. 10b). Similarly,

Aaron had descendants who deserved to die, but were spared because of his merit (Yoma 87a). Even within the period of the Patriarchs, it is maintained, the principle of merit of the fathers was operative. The prayer of Isaac to be blessed with children was considered more efficacious than that of his wife Rebekah, because he was not only a righteous man himself but also the son of a righteous man, while his wife Rebekah, although saintly herself, was the daughter of a wicked man (Yev. 64a).

Other Righteous Ancestors

In the rabbinic view, the doctrine of the merit of the fathers relates not only to the Patriarchs and other biblical heroes but also to each man's righteous ancestors. Thus, in the view of R. Akiva, "The father transfers to his son beauty, strength, wealth, wisdom, and length of years" (Eduy. 2:9). Others limit R. Akiva's view, holding that these bounties accrue to the son only as long as he is a minor; thereafter, he attains them only as a result of his own goodness (Tosef. Eduy. 1:14). In another application of the principle the rabbis interpret 1 Chronicles 7:40, "all these were the children of Asher, heads of the fathers' houses, choice and mighty men of valour, chief of the princes…," as indicating that only those who were descendants of an unblemished ancestry were permitted to serve in David's army, so that "their merit and the merit of their ancestors would sustain them" (Kid. 76b). Still another example is the declaration of R. Gamaliel, "Let all men who labor [as leaders] with a community, labor for the sake of Heaven, for the merit of their fathers sustains them" (Avot 2:2). It is related that R. Eleazar b. Azariah was selected as head of the academy over other candidates of equal qualifications, because as a descendant of Ezra, he enjoyed the merit of the fathers.

Qualifications of Efficacy

Despite these and other examples which emphasize the power of ancestral merit, according to many rabbinical sources, merit of the fathers is not effective in all instances. Thus, the wicked king Manasseh is excluded from the world to come, even though his father was the pious Hezekiah, for "a son imputes merit to a father, whereas a father does not impute merit to a son, as it is written 'None can deliver from my hand' [Deut. 32:39]" (Sanh. 104a). Similarly, "R. Kahana taught, let not a man say for the sake of my righteous brother or father I shall be saved, for Abraham could not save his son Ishmael, nor Jacob save his brother Esau… as it is written, 'no man can by any means redeem his brother'[Ps. 49:8]" (Yal. Ps. 46). Thus ancestral merit alone, unaccompanied by the good deeds of the descendants, cannot be relied on, at least not for salvation of the soul, this being primarily a matter of personal attainment (cf. commentary of *Torah Temimah* to Deut. 32:39). This accords with the well-known statement of Hillel, "If I am not for myself, who is for me" (Avot 1:14), which in another source goes on to read, "If I have not gained merit for myself in my own lifetime, who will gain it for me?" (ARN[1] 1:27). Elsewhere (Sot. 10b) the Talmud relates that David interceded on behalf of Absalom and that through this prayer Absalom was raised from Gehenna to Paradise. Some medieval commentators explained this story as implying that it is not the good deeds of the father that save the son but the prayer that accompanies them (Sot. *ibid.*); in the case of David it was not so much his merit as his prayer that succeeded.

Termination of Patriarchal Merit

There is a statement in the Talmud (Shab. 55a; Lev. R. 36:6) to the effect that the merit of the Patriarchs has come to an end, though the exact date of its cessation is a matter of dispute. This being so, the rabbis conclude, Israel can rely exclusively on God's unending mercies (*ibid.*). Some commentators of this talmudic passage pointed out the difference between the covenant and the merits of the patriarchs: even though the merit of the fathers may have come to an end, the covenant with the fathers has not, for it is eternally binding; and the liturgical evocations of the fathers refer essentially to the everlasting covenant with them.

Guilt of Ancestors

Related to the notion of imputed merit is the concept of inherited guilt. The source for this is the verse in the Ten Commandments… "Visiting the guilt of the fathers upon the children upon the third and fourth generation of those who reject Me; and showing mercy to the thousandth generation of those who love Me and keep My commandments" (Ex. 20:5, 6). Elsewhere in the Bible the opposite doctrine is expressed: that guilt is individual and does not pass from one generation to another. "Parents shall not be put to death for children, nor children be put to death for parents; a person shall be put to death for his own crime" (Deut. 24:16). The contradiction between these two verses is resolved by the talmudic sages who suggest (Ber. 7a; Sanh. 27b) that descendants suffer for the sins of their forebears only when they themselves perpetuate the same evil deeds (see Targum Onkelos and commentary of Rashi, Ex. 20:5). This view is even more sharply stated by other rabbis who reject the view of inherited guilt, declaring (Mak. 24a) that Moses' decree "visiting the guilt of the father upon the children" was abrogated by Ezekiel's statement "the soul that sinneth, it shall die" (Ezek. 18:4); according to one 18th-century commentator (Maharsha, Mak. *ibid.*), this implies that even when the sons perpetuate the parental sins, they suffer only their own guilt, not that of their parents.

BIBLIOGRAPHY: R.T. Herford, *Pharisaism* (1912), 213–4, 276–81; S. Levy, *Original Virtue* (1907), 1–42; A. Marmorstein, *The Doctrine of Merits in Old Rabbinic Literature* (1968^2); S. Schechter, *Some Aspects of Rabbinic Theology* (1909), ch. 12; A.I. Kook, *Iggerot ha-Re'ayah*, 1 (1962), 319–22.

[Joshua H. Shmidman]

ZELDA (MISHKOVSKY) (née **Schneurson**; 1914–1984), Israeli poet. Born in Chernigov, Ukraine, where her father was a rabbi, Zelda was brought to Ereẓ Israel in 1925 and settled in Jerusalem, where she received a religious education. In 1950 she married Ḥayyim Mishkovsky, who died in 1970.

Zelda Mishkovsky published poems in various periodicals over the years, but her first collection in book form appeared in 1967 (*Pena'i*). Her second volume (*Ha-Karmel ha-i-Nir'eh*, 1971) consists of poems written in a relatively short period and are mostly connected with her husband's death. Her *Al Tirḥak* (1974) contains 25 poems, followed by *She-Nivdelu mi-Kol Merḥak (*1984). The collected poems (*Shirei Zelda*) were published in 1985.

Zelda's poems aroused considerable interest and surprise on account of her integration of religious verse rooted in the traditional Jewish world with a completely modern sensitivity. Many of the poems describe her relationship with God and details of religious life. In her poems, which are in no way dogmatic, themes dealing with details of religious observance, appear side by side with more universal themes, such as death, immortality, and man's place in the universe. Some of them reveal occasional clashes between the traditional Jewish world and the secular environment, manifested in the juxtaposition of religious symbols and modern objects. In their tone the poems combine naiveté and sophistication.

Some of the characteristics of her poetry establish an interesting connection between her and the Hebrew poetry of the 1960s and 1970s. Thus, like the modern Hebrew poets, she emphasizes the importance of sense perception in the structuring of her inner world: colors, smells, and tastes are factors determining her emotions and moods. These colors and tastes generally pertain to the natural world (smell of flowers, taste of fruit), and in this, too, she is part of the modern school, with its inclination toward nature and the primal in the midst of busy modern life. This is related to a longing for a magic, visionary world which is sometimes identified with the world of childhood. Another common characteristic is the unusual tendency toward the wild and the asocial.

Her books have been hailed by critics and have achieved great popularity. She was the recipient of a number of literary prizes, including the Bialik Prize for literature in 1978. Individual poems have been translated into diverse languages. For information see the ITHL website at www.ithl.org.il.

BIBLIOGRAPHY: H. Barzel, in: *Moznayim*, 2 (July, 1972) 121–32. **ADD. BIBLIOGRAPHY:** Y. Kamer, notes, in: *Leket mi-Shirei Zeldah* (1983); A. Wineman, "Zelda's Poem on Shabbat," in: *Conservative Judaism*, 37:3 (1984), 32–37; idem, "Death, Redeeming Moments, and God in Zelda's Later Poems," *ibid.*, 56:2 (2004), 60–69; A. Zwi, "The Poetry of Zelda," in: *Ariel*, 65 (1986), 58–70; H. Bar-Yosef, *Al Shirat Zeldah* (1988); N. Kobler, "Zelda's Poetry," in: *Journal of Semitics*, 3:2 (1991), 202–9; N. Kobler, "A Touch of Imagination." Zelda's Poetry of Love," in: *Jewish Affairs*, 48:2 (1993), 116–19.

[Abraham Balaban]

ZELDIN, ISAIAH (1920–), founding rabbi of Stephen S. Wise Temple in Los Angeles, creator of the largest Jewish day school within an American Reform congregation, founding dean of the Los Angeles campus of the Hebrew Union College–Jewish Institute of Religion. A visionary, he is the example par excellence of the rabbi as institution builder and leader.

Born in Brooklyn to Russian immigrant parents, his earliest influences rooted him deeply in the life of the Jewish people. His father was a Zionist, a Yiddishist, and a Hebraist, who wrote for both the Yiddish and Hebrew press. Zeldin's parents decided that they would raise their children speaking only Hebrew in the home. In high school he lobbied for the addition of Modern Hebrew to the curriculum. Later, he convinced Brooklyn College, where he earned his bachelor's degree, to accept Modern Hebrew as a legitimate, officially recognized foreign language.

In 1933, at the age of 13, his father took him to a rally protesting the rise of Hitler. It was when he heard Rabbi Stephen S. *Wise address the rally that he decided to devote his life to the well-being and defense of the Jewish people. He was ordained rabbi (1946) by the Hebrew Union College in Cincinnati.

After serving as an assistant rabbi in Newark for two years, he was named assistant dean of HUC-JIR in New York, supervising the faculties of the Schools of Education and Sacred Music.

In 1953, he moved to Los Angeles to become the dean of the College of Jewish Studies, assembling an exceptional faculty, creating a School of Sacred Music and a large School of Education. Within one year, under his leadership, the college became the West Coast campus of HUC-JIR. Within five years he had created a Rabbinical School. Concurrently, he was regional director of the Union of American Hebrew Congregations, overseeing the creation of many new Reform congregations in the area. From 1958 to 1963 he served as rabbi of Temple Emanuel in Beverly Hills.

His greatest contributions to Jewish life were yet to unfold. In 1964 he founded Stephen S. Wise Temple, named for his teacher and mentor. Inspired by Wise's passionate Zionism, as well as his commitment to a rabbi's freedom to speak even the most unpopular of truths from the pulpit, Zeldin built his congregation from a small group of 35 members who met in a living room to a community of 3,500 member families. Respected and admired for his depth and breadth of knowledge, for the lively intellect he brought to the pulpit, as well as for his genuine warmth and engaging manner, his leadership was always marked by an innovative spirit and an uncanny understanding of the zeitgeist and the needs of his community. He set forth a bold vision that his congregants made their own.

When the temple acquired land, the first buildings he erected were classrooms. Jewish education was at the center of his vision. He created the largest synagogue pre-school in Los Angeles and went on to establish an elementary day school of nearly 700 students – all during years that the Reform Movement had not yet committed to the idea of day school education.

At age 70 – with all of his rabbinic colleagues long retired – he took on a challenge which would become the pinnacle of his achievements: the creation of a Jewish high school in which nearly 900 students study every day, the only such school to be operated by a Reform synagogue in North America. The synagogue and its education network – from Parenting Center to pre-school, elementary and high school, as well as its adult learning Center for Jewish Life – are now located on three separate campuses spanning 30 acres.

Over the course of a rabbinic career spanning more than 60 years, his passion for Jewish life, the Jewish people, and Israel never waned. He never stopped building his congregation and its schools which serve as a model nation-wide. He continued to teach and write as he led and inspired.

[Eli Herscher (2nd ed.)]

ZELDOVICH, YAKOV BORISOVICH (1914–1987), Soviet astrophysicist; originally a specialist in nuclear physics. Zeldovich was born in Minsk and studied in Leningrad. From 1931 he worked at the Institute of Chemical Physics of the Academy of Science of the U.S.S.R. During World War II he contributed research to the war effort. He later worked at the Institute of Cosmic Research at the Space Research Institute of the Soviet Academy of Sciences in Moscow (ASUSSR), and from 1964 at the Academy's Institute of Applied Mathematics. In 1958 he was made a member of the Academy of Sciences. Professor at the University of Moscow from 1966, he was one of the founders of contemporary theories of combustion, detonation, and shock waves and the author of a number of works on the theory of the last stages of the evolution of stars and galaxies which involved the theory of general relativity and the theory of gravitational collapse. He has also proposed a number of experiments and methods for verifying cosmological theories. Zeldovich was awarded a Lenin Prize, four Stalin Prizes, and three times hailed as a Hero of Socialist Labor.

[*The Shorter Jewish Encyclopaedia in Russian*]

ZELECHOW (Pol. **Zelechów**), town in Warsaw province, Poland. Jewish settlement in the town dates from the 17th century. Zelechow was celebrated for the high-quality footwear produced there. The ḥasidic rabbi, *Levi Isaac of Berdichev, officiated there from 1772 to 1784. The character of the little town is graphically conveyed in the works of two Yiddish authors who were born there, I.M. *Weissenberg and the poet Y. *Lerer (see bibliography). After the establishment of the Polish republic in 1918, the economic position of Zelechow deteriorated with the loss of the Russian markets. The Jewish inhabitants of Zelechow and district numbered 1,464 in 1765, 2,317 in 1856, 4,930 in 1897 (70% of the total population), and 5,500 on the eve of World War II.

[Yehuda Slutsky]

Holocaust Period

The German army entered Zelechow on Sept. 14, 1939, and on the next day the Nazis burned the synagogue. During 1940–41 over 2,000 Jews, mostly from the surrounding smaller places, were forced to settle in Zelechow. In the fall of 1940 an open ghetto was established there. On Sept. 30, 1942 (during Sukkot), the ghetto was liquidated and all its inmates were transferred to the *Treblinka death camp and exterminated there. Only a few hundred Jews managed to flee. Many of them organized small Jewish partisan units or joined mixed Polish-Jewish-Russian units that were active in the vicinity until the liberation in July 1944. No Jewish community was reconstituted in Zelechow after the war. Organizations of former Jewish residents are active in Israel, the United States, Brazil, and Argentina.

[Stefan Krakowski]

BIBLIOGRAPHY: I.M. Weissenberg, *A Shtetl* (1910); Y. Lerer, *Mayn Heym* (1938); A.W. Yasny (ed.), *Yizkor-Bukh fun der Zelechower Kehile* (1953); *Sefer ha-Partizanim ha-Yehudim*, 2 (1958), 199–205.

ZELENKA, FRANTIŠEK (1904–1944), Czech architect and stage designer. Zelenka was responsible for the design and decor of a great number of original productions in the Czechoslovak National Theater and the Municipal Theater of Prague. His wit found highly successful expression in modern versions of comedies by Molière and Shakespeare and brought him ultimately to the most popular satirical theater of Czechoslavakia, the Osvobozené Divadlo (Liberated Theater). Here he became permanent stage designer for the famous comedies of Voskovec and Werich. After the German occupation of Prague, Zelenka was deported to Theresienstadt, from where he was sent to Poland in 1944 but died on the way. While in Theresienstadt, he showed great resourcefulness in designing theatrical performances for the camp inmates, among them a Czech baroque folklore play about Queen Esther. Zelenka also helped to organize the Jewish Museum in Prague.

BIBLIOGRAPHY: N. Frýd, *Culture in the Anteroom to Hell* (1965).

[Avigdor Dagan]

ZELIZER, NATHAN (1907–2001) U.S. Conservative rabbi. Zelizer was born in Poland and immigrated to the United States in 1921. He earned a B.S. from New York University in 1929 and an M.A. from Columbia University in 1930; in 1931, he was ordained at the *Jewish Theological Seminary. He became rabbi of Congregation Tifereth Israel in Columbus, Ohio, where he was to spend his entire career (1932–73, emeritus until his death) – or so it seemed at the time of his retirement. Arriving at a synagogue whose membership had been decimated by the Depression, he breathed new life into the congregation: under his leadership, it eventually grew from under 50 to 1,100 families. He took a sabbatical from his congregation in order to volunteer as a military chaplain, serving in the Pacific with the U.S. Navy.

Returning to Tifereth Israel after the war, Zelizer developed Jewish educational programs and became involved in civic affairs. Starting in 1947, Zelizer served as a chaplain for the Jewish mental and penal wards of the state of Ohio as well as for the Veterans Administration Hospital in Chillicothe, Ohio. He developed a close relationship with Governor Frank Lauche, asking him to reduce prison sentences for those he believed could be rehabilitated; inmates freed with his help continued to write him over the next 40 years in appreciation for what he had done. During the 1950s, Zelizer served on the Columbus Rent Advisory Board and founded the first Senior

Citizens Center in Ohio, where the elderly were able to spend time engaged in constructive activities. He also hosted a local radio and television show where he interacted with leaders of different religious groups about common challenges and projects; he was invited to speak at African-American and Catholic churches, earning the respect of non-Jewish clergy.

Perhaps Zelizer's greatest contribution to American Jewry came in the 1960s, when he persuaded one of the most prominent Jewish citizens in Ohio, Samuel M. *Melton, a director of Bethlehem Steel, to fund the Melton Research Center (later, Melton School of Education) at the Jewish Theological Seminary in New York City. A pilot program of the innovative new school was established at Tifereth Israel, which became a model educational center for Conservative synagogues. Some 35 individuals credited Zelizer with their career decisions to enter the rabbinate – including his own son, Gerald, who rose to become president of the *Rabbinical Assembly. As a result of his accomplishments, the city of Columbus selected Zelizer as one of its 10 leading citizens, and the Ohio Chamber of Commerce paid him to travel across the state and engage audiences in discussions of important civic issues.

Upon his retirement from Tifereth Israel, Zelizer moved to Boca Raton, Florida, where he was asked to serve as the part-time rabbi of Congregation B'nai Torah. Once again, he built up a sizable institution from practically nothing. When the congregation became too large for a part-time rabbi, he moved on to help found Temple Beth Zion in Royal Palm, Florida. When he left this congregation, he would spend weekends driving to Melbourne, Florida, where he served as the rabbi for Jewish participants in the NASA Space Shuttle project. Because of these activities, one rabbi called Zelizer the "Johnny Appleseed" of the American Jewish community.

In 1985, Zelizer joined forces with another small congregation that formed in Boca Raton to start a Conservative synagogue called Beth Ami. He played an instrumental role in building the Jewish community of Boca Raton, starting a community day school and founding the South County Rabbinical Association. In 1992, he finally decided to retire a "second time," at 87 years of age. On that occasion, the mayor proclaimed Nathan Zelizer Day in the city of Boca Raton.

[Bezalel Gordon (2nd ed.)]

ZELK, ZOLTAN (1906–1981), Hungarian poet. Zelk was one of the *Nyugat* literary generation, but only achieved a position of prominence in the 1950s. His collections of verse, of which several were published, include *Mint égő lelkiismeret* ("Burning Conscience," 1954) and *Zúzmara a rozsafán* ("Hoarfrost on the Rosebush," 1964). He also wrote some outstanding poetry for children. Though an orthodox Marxist, Zelk joined the 1956 revolution and subsequently served two years in prison.

ZELLERBACH, U.S. merchant family. Its founder, ANTHONY ZELLERBACH (1832–1911), was born in Bavaria and went to the United States, settling in Philadelphia, in 1846. In 1856 he traveled to California and went to work for his elder brother MARKS (d. 1891), who was operating a bank at Moore's Flat in Nevada County. In 1868 he settled in San Francisco, and in 1870 established a small paper supply business, primarily dealing with printers. In 1882, with his son JACOB C. (b. 1864), he founded the firm of A. Zellerbach & Son. Another son, ISADORE (1867–1942), known as I.Z., came into the firm in 1887, and the youngest, HENRY (1868–1944), joined somewhat later. In 1907 the company was renamed Zellerbach Paper Company; I.Z. was president. After World War I the company expanded into paper towel milling and newsprint production, and the holding company Zellerbach Corporation was formed in 1928 for financing and administration, becoming through merger Crown Zellerbach Corporation. In 1937–38 the corporation became an operating company. With its international operations and the expansion of manufacturing and marketing into containers, flexible packaging, and other innovations, it became one of the largest paper manufacturers in the world, with sales in the billion-dollar range. The family remains active in its operations.

Members of the family have been active in civic, cultural, commercial, and community activities in the San Francisco area. They have been directors of Congregation Emanu-El of San Francisco, Mount Zion Hospital, the Concordia-Argonaut Club, the San Francisco Art Commission, and the San Francisco Symphony Orchestra. I.Z.'s son HAROLD LIONEL ZELLERBACH (1894–1978), a sales executive and executive committee member of the corporation, and board chairman 1956–1963, served as president of Congregation Emanu-El and was active in many other phases of Jewish community life in San Francisco. JAMES DAVID ZELLERBACH (1892–1963), I.Z.'s eldest son, president of the corporation from 1934 and chief executive officer from 1950, was appointed U.S. ambassador to Italy in 1956 after serving in 1945–48 on the International Labor Organization and in 1948–50 as chief of the Marshall Plan special mission to Italy. Harold's son WILLIAM J. served as president of Zellerbach Paper Company.

[Norton B. Stern]

ZELLICK, GRAHAM (1948–), British academic and university head. Educated at Cambridge and Stanford Universities, Zellick became a barrister and then a professor of law at London University (1982–98). From 1997 to 2003 he was vice chancellor (president) of the University of London. From 2003 he was chairman of the Criminal Cases Review Commission, which investigates alleged miscarriages of justice. For many years he was editor of *Public Law*. Zellick has been associated with a variety of Jewish and pro-Israel organizations.

[William D. Rubinstein 2nd ed.]

ZELOPHEHAD (Heb. צְלָפְחָד), son of Hepher, descendant of Manasseh. He died in the wilderness without male issue (Num. 26:33; 27:1). His five daughters, Mahlah, Noah, Hoglah, Milcha, and Tirzah, requested of Moses that they be recognized as female heirs and granted their father's inheritance of land. They pleaded that although their father had suffered the punishment of dying in the course of the desert wanderings, he had committed no exceptional sin, such as participation in the revolt of Koraḥ, that might merit the destruction of his "name." The case was decided by divine decree in favor of the daughters, and it led to the promulgation of legislation providing for the disposal of the property of a man who died without a male heir (*ibid.* 27:1–11). This ruling occasioned an inter-tribal problem in that, should Zelophehad's daughters marry outside their tribe, the estate would consequently pass into the possession of their husbands and the latter's tribes. By divine decision Zelophehad's daughters were required to marry within the tribe of Manasseh and, in fact, they were given to their cousins. To protect the total tribal inheritances, it was laid down that all heiresses must marry within their own tribe (*ibid.* 36:1–12).

It is of interest that although Zelophehad was descended from Gilead, his daughters received their patrimony from Joshua west of the Jordan (Josh. 17:3–6). In the Samaria Ostraca two of their names, Noah and Hoglah, appear as the names of districts within the territory of Manasseh.

In the *Aggadah*

Both Zelophehad and his father, Hepher, were among those whom Moses had led out of Egypt. Zelophehad himself was therefore entitled to three portions in Ereẓ Israel (two as the firstborn of his father, and one in his own right), and his daughters claimed all three portions when their father died (BB 122b). Moses had to refer this claim to God because, although aware of the general right of a daughter to inherit, he was unsure of their right to claim in addition the dual portion of their father's birthright (*ibid.*, 119a). Another opinion, however, is that Moses did not know whether God had forgiven Zelophehad for the sin on account of which he had died in the desert (Num. 27:3). It was only when God mentioned Zelophehad by name (*ibid.*, 27:7), that Moses knew that he had been forgiven (Zohar 3:157a). Zelophehad was neither one of those who murmured against God (Num. 11:1), nor one who joined the ten spies in their condemnation of Ereẓ Israel (*ibid.*, 14:1), since the participants in both these movements were automatically denied all rights of inheritance in Ereẓ Israel. This was also the punishment of the followers of Koraḥ (which is why Zelophehad's daughters specifically stated that their father did not participate in this sin; Num 27:3; Sif. Num. 133; BB 18b). Judah ben Bathyra maintained that Zelophehad was one of those who "presumed to go up to the top of the mountain" (Num. 14:44); while R. Akiva was of the opinion that it was he who gathered wood on the Sabbath (Num. 15:32; Shab. 96b), the two incidents being juxtaposed (BB 119a).

The daughters of Zelophehad are highly praised for their sagacity in presenting their problem at an appropriate moment, when Moses was expounding the laws of levirate marriage. They showed outstanding exegetic ability in arguing their own case. They are also praised for their virtue, and for the care with which they chose their husbands (BB 119b). Although permitted to marry men from any tribe, they were so careful in their choice that even the youngest waited until she was 40 years old before finding a worthy husband (*ibid.*, 120a).

BIBLIOGRAPHY: G.B. Gray, *Numbers* (ICC, 1903), index. IN THE AGGADAH: Ginzberg, Legends, index; I. Hasida, *Ishei ha-Tanakh* (1964), 373–4.

ZELOW, town in Lodz province, near *Lask, central Poland. Jews settled there in the second half of the 19th century and earned their livelihood mainly in the local textile factories. They numbered 922 (30% of the total) in 1897 and 1,816 (34%) in 1921. In 1939 there were approximately 3,500 Jews in Zelow comprising about 60% of the total population. The Germans entered Zelow on Sept. 6, 1939, and forced the Jewish community into a restricted zone in town. The number of Jews swelled to 6,000 with the influx of refugees from nearby towns. No formal ghetto was established, and the Jews could maintain a certain amount of illegal trade across the border of the General Government. Although the Judenrat supplied able-bodied workers to the German authorities, raids were carried out against people in the streets for forced labor. Prior to the final liquidation of the Jewish community of Zelow the Germans publicly executed ten Jewish prisoners and deported 245 able-bodied men to the *Lodz ghetto. In September 1942 the ghetto was liquidated. Some of the Jews were killed on the spot, others were transported to the extermination camp at *Chelmno, and a few hundred young people were sent to forced labor camps.

BIBLIOGRAPHY: I. Trunk, in: *Bleter far Geshikhte*, 2:1–4 (1949), 64–166 (passim); D. Dabrowska (ed.), *Kronika getta lodzkiego*, vols. 1–2 (1965–1966), passim; idem, in: BŻIH, 13–14 (1955); B. Wasiutyński, *Ludność żydowska w Polsce w wiekach XIX i XX* (1930), 75.

[Danuta Dombrowska]

ZELVA (Pol. **Zelwa**), town in Grodno oblast, Belarus. Jews were accustomed to visit the Zelva fairs from the end of the 15th century. A Jewish community, under the jurisdiction of the Grodno *kahal*, was established in the late 16th century. During the 18th century Jews traded at the local fairs, dealing in horses and in furs imported from Moscow. The lay and rabbinical leaders of Lithuania met at these fairs, and after 1766, when the Council of the Four Lands (see *Councils of the Lands) was disbanded, Zelva became the customary meeting place for rabbis of the region. Excommunications against the Ḥasidim were publicized here in 1781 and 1796, and a plan of action was drawn up to suppress the movement. In 1766 there were 522 Jews who paid the poll tax. In 1793 Zelva was annexed by Russia. There were 864 Jews in 1847, and 1,844 (66% of the total population) in 1897. Between the world wars Zelva was part of independent Poland and possessed *Tarbut and Yavneh schools. In 1921 the Jewish community numbered 1,319 (64%). The community was annihilated in World War II when Jews were executed by the Germans or sent to death camps, but dozens of young people managed to escape into the forest.

BIBLIOGRAPHY: S. Dubnow (ed.), *Pinkas ha-Medinah* (1925), index; E. Ringelblum, in: *Miesięcnik żydowski*, 6 (1932), 516; I. Schiper, *Dzieje handlu żydowskiego na ziemiach polskich* (1937), index.

[Shimshon Leib Kirshenboim / Ruth Beloff (2nd ed.)]

ZEMACH, BENJAMIN (1903–1987), dancer, actor, choreographer, stage director and drama teacher. Born in Russia as the young brother of Nachum Zemach, the founder and leader of the Habimah theater in Moscow with whom he went to the U.S. in 1926. Zemach was active during the 1930s as dancer and choreographer in many progressive left-wing productions organized by such companies as the New Dance Group and other trade-unions-based artistic initiatives in New York during the Great Depression. He opened an independent modern dance school in Los Angeles. His choreographic work was based on Jewish as well as socially conscious themes. He choreographed several large-scale productions at the Hollywood Bowl and created the choreography for Max Reinhardt's film *The Eternal Road* (1936).

In 1971 he came to live in Israel, teaching and producing at the Kibbutz Seminar in Tel Aviv, choreographing for Inbal Dance Theater, finally settling in Jerusalem, where he died in 1987.

[Giora Manor (2nd ed.)]

ZEMACH, NAHUM (1887–1939), theatrical director, founder of *Habimah. Born in Volkovysk, he grew up in Poland and was a successful businessman in Moscow before devoting himself to literature and the theater. In 1912 in Bialystok (with Menahem *Gnessin), he assembled a group of Hebrew-speaking actors who performed *Dymov's *The Eternal Wanderer*, and in the following year he presented the play in Vienna to the members of the 11th Zionist Congress. The company was short-lived; but it was the forerunner of the company called "Habimah" which Zemach founded in Moscow in 1917 and which drew some of its actors from the Bialystok group. Zemach stayed with Habimah until 1926 when he took the company to the U.S. and decided to remain there. His pioneering work with Hebrew theater drew attention to Hebrew as a living language, and when Habimah performed *The Dybbuk* it also demonstrated the vitality of the modern Jewish literary movement. Zemach went to Palestine after Habimah had become established there and for a time directed the Beth-Am Theater. But he returned to the U.S. and in 1937 became manager of the Jewish Theater unit of the Federal Theater Project.

BIBLIOGRAPHY: M. Kohansky, *Hebrew Theater* (1969), index.

ZEMACH, SHLOMO (1886–1974), Hebrew writer. Born in Plonsk (Russian Poland), Zemach spent his youth on his father's estate in the village of Volka. In his youth he was attracted to Zionism, and together with some friends founded the Zionist society Ezra. At the age of 18 he immigrated to Ereẓ Israel, where he became an agricultural worker. He was one of the founders of *Ha-Po'el ha-Ẓa'ir in 1905. In 1909 he went to France. After studying literature and philosophy at the Sorbonne for three years, he attended the Higher Institute of Agriculture in Nancy and graduated as an agricultural engineer in 1914. On the outbreak of World War I he went to Poland and was obliged to remain there, within German-occupied territory, until 1918. He then left for Odessa, where he edited the periodical *Ereẓ*, and engaged in other literary activities. In 1921 he returned to Ereẓ Israel and taught agriculture at the Mikveh Israel school. From 1924 to 1933 he directed the training department of the agricultural experimental station run by the Zionist executive. In 1933 he founded the *Kadoorie Agricultural school and was its principal until 1937. It was only after his retirement that he began to devote himself exclusively to literary work.

Short Stories

Zemach began his literary career as a writer of short stories – one of the first to write about Ereẓ Israel. He described the life of the villager. Averse by nature to idealizations and illusions, Zemach never wrote in a symbolic or allegorical fashion, nor did he make any attempt to depict abstract characters. There is a strong biographical element in his stories and his characters and events are presented within a limited, well defined range of time and place.

Zemach's uniqueness as a writer lies not so much in his narrative gifts as in an outlook which sublimates existence. A sober and discerning observer, lacking in illusions, he treats his heroes' foibles with gentle amusement. The Ereẓ Israel stories that Zemach wrote at the beginning of the century are very different from the idyllic, folkloristic, superficial, and tendentious Zionist stories of other writers. He was able to rise above the eroding stream of life and to free himself in considerable measure from the "bonds of custom," a phrase which became the title of his article on the subject.

Novel

Zemach wrote one novel, *Eliyah Margalit* (1921), which describes the life of young Jewish intellectuals living in Paris during the pre-World War I period. The young men establish a national Hebrew circle, and they discuss the future of their people and the image of the Jew as he will be when he is privileged to live a normal life in Ereẓ Israel. The hero, Eliyah Margalit, a painter, has not yet succeeded in freeing himself of the "burden of inheritance," the oppressiveness of his rigorous education, and the stifling influence of his hometown. He is thus impelled to preach extreme and self-contradictory revolutionary ideas, to rebel against traditional Judaism and demand that epicurean joy in life rule as the supreme value. He believes in the theory that the entire history of the Jewish people after the destruction of the Temple must be blotted out of memory; a new way of life must be created for the contemporary Jew, so that his heart and soul may be rejuvenated and he can live a normal healthy life. He wishes to pass over the hundreds of years spent in the Diaspora, so as to return to the ancient epoch and to the primary source of Judaism.

From the structural point of view, *Eliyah Margalit* is one of those romantic novels which end in inevitable disaster. The spirit of the age and the French background of the novel find expression in the temporary corruption of the hero who emerges from his experience utterly purged and purified. In this respect also Zemach was a pioneer, inasmuch as he was the first Hebrew writer to study the problem of decadence and its effect upon life.

Drama

Zemach's play *Tanḥum mi-Kefar Yano'aḥ* is on the face of it a historical drama. The events take place in the plain of Jericho and in the village of Janoah at the time of the establishment of the Essene sect. The ideas, however, apply to the present. Tanḥum is a young farmer who decides to join the Essene sect, and is followed by Miriam, a girl from his village. But he soon discovers that the strict laws of purification are neither in accord with his temperament nor with his opinions. He is a rebel by nature and dislikes those who are excessively righteous; he much prefers ordinary people, with all their weaknesses. He transgresses the custom of the sect when he shakes hands with a Jewish peddler, thus becoming "defiled by touch." He is unable to forgo reality for the sake of shutting himself away in an ideal world of abstinence and devotion to God. The Essenes accuse him of corrupting the brotherhood and causing defilement among them, and finally they expel him from the sect. Tanḥum and Miriam return to their village, where they are married. He proves himself when the time comes to defend his country and he fights the enemy at the head of the village youth. Zemach thus attempted to refute the view that morality and patriotism necessarily call for abstinence and asceticism, and he championed the individual who loves life but at the same time is ready to sacrifice it in the defense of his country.

Memoirs

Shanah Rishonah ("First Year"; 1952), a volume of memoirs about Zemach's first stay in Ereẓ Israel in 1904, lies on the borderline between fiction and documentary literature. Written in the 1950s, considerably removed in time from the actual events, the author with a critical and discerning eye selected the essential events and utterances that seemed to him the most characteristic, arranging them in such a way as to create a planned, well-designed, and meaningful picture. All the problems and crucial events of the Second Aliyah period are described and illuminated here with critical discernment. A. Zemach wrote down Shlomo Zemach's life story (*Sippur Ḥayai*, 1983).

Literary Criticism

Throughout his literary career Zemach wrote not only belletristic works but also literary criticism. From 1910 onward he systematically and seriously engaged in criticism, publishing scores of essays, articles, and reviews in different periodicals. These have been collected in part in *Be-Arẓot Nod* (1922), *Adam im Aḥerim* (1953), *Massah u-Vikkoret* (1954), *Sheti va-Erev* (1959), *Eruvin* (1964), *Shettei ha-Mezuzot* (1965), and *Massot u-Reshimot* (1968). Ten essays on Bialik (*Al Bialik*) were published in 1978. Zemach regards criticism as "free evaluation, based on a literary truth (not the truth, just a truth), free from all mixture of secondary interests and having two points of departure whose influence is reciprocal, evolved and kept alive through the relationship between the author as agent who creates the work of art and the work of art as agent in that it reveals the author." True criticism derives from the critic's devotion to literature, his principal tools being the power of analysis and of expression. Zemach is totally opposed to the view that criticism is an inferior or parasitic genre of literature; he regards it as a form of literary creativity even though it does not come entirely from the world of feelings but applies logic as well as emotions.

A basic principle of Zemach's critical doctrine is the demand that contemporary Hebrew literature cultivate an attachment to the nation's traditions. He opposes literary phenomena that manifest imitation or detachment. It is the duty of contemporary Hebrew literature to return to its sources, to abandon imitation and foreign patterns and to seek genuine independence.

Throughout his career in criticism Zemach was a fighter. Already in his youth he attacked the "Mendele style" in Hebrew literature; he warned against the danger of "petty realism" involved in this school, demanding that prose should liberate itself from its ties with cultural patterns and soar to the heights of human thought and feeling. In "*Ha-Sifrut va-Ḥalifoteha*" (1926) Zemach maintained that the literature of Ereẓ Israel should broaden its themes, abandon Diaspora motifs, and have the courage to come to grips with the new reality in Ereẓ Israel. He regarded writing on the subject of Ereẓ Israel as a temporary measure. At the same time he rejected modernistic trends in Hebrew literature and remained faithful to traditionalism.

Zemach is perhaps the only contemporary Hebrew critic who attempted to formulate a theoretical basis for his work. He defined his view on the essence of the beautiful in art in the final chapter of *Al ha-Yafeh*. "I do not regard aesthetics as contemplation nor as an escape from the concrete world and an evasion of life; aesthetics is for me a continuation of human activity that transports the actual in nature to the actual in visions; and in the process of shifting, the actual is divorced from its dependence on nature and its laws. Certainly feeling pain, love – is as real as feeling stone, water, dust. Thus an abstract description does not exist. It is not figural, but consists of color splashes and geometric forms and these are real. We are not discussing the 'abstract' and the 'real' but the distinguishing force which gives them significance." *Ha-Seḥok* (1947) also deals with the theory of aesthetics.

For many years Zemach contributed to newspapers and periodicals. His main work as editor was in the periodical *Beḥinot* (1953–57), a platform both for the theory of criticism and for its practice. For a listing of Zemach's works in English translation see Goell, Bibliography, index.

BIBLIOGRAPHY: Biography in: *Ketavim Nivḥarim* (1956); A. Epstein, *Mi-Karov u-me-Raḥok* (1944), 145–52; G. Yardeni, *Tet Zayin Siḥot im Soferim* (1961), 27–38; B.J. Michali, *Le-Yad ha-Ovnayim* (1959), 200–27; Kressel, Leksikon, 2 (1967), 720–2. **ADD. BIBLIOGRAPHY:** D. Sadan, "*Ahavat Shelomo: Devarim al S. Zemach*," in: *Molad*, 1 (1975), 388–91; A. Shapira, "*Bein Sh. Zemach ve-A.D. Gordon*," in: *Shedemot*, 69 (1979), 31–37; H. Shaham, *Mishnato ha-Sifrutit vi-Yzirato ha- Ereẓ Yisra'elit shel Shelomo Zemaḥ* (1981); G. Shaked, *Ha-Sipporet ha-Ivrit*, 2 (1983), 61–65.

[Abraham B. Yoffe]

ẒEMAḤ, JACOB BEN ḤAYYIM (d. after 1665), kabbalist and physician. A member of a Converso family in northern Portugal, he first served as a physician. He decided to go to Ereẓ Israel and passed through Salonika where he studied Torah. Some time between 1610 and 1620, he settled in Safed and learned Talmud and Kabbalah. In approximately 1628 he left for Damascus, and studied the Lurianic Kabbalah under Samuel b. Ḥayyim *Vital. Around 1640 he settled in Jerusalem where he became one of the leading kabbalists. He was among the Jerusalem opponents of *Shabbetai Ẓevi who excommunicated him when he first claimed to be the messiah in 1665.

His many works, which are anthologic in character, lack originality and rely on *Ḥayyim Vital's Kabbalah. Nevertheless, his contribution to the literary consolidation of Lurianic Kabbalah is important, as are his citations of contemporary kabbalists, e.g., *Joseph ibn Tabul. In his introduction to *Kol ba-Ramah*, he complains that Lurianic Kabbalah is not much studied. Ẓemaḥ left many works, partly in manuscript. In the aforesaid introduction he gives details of his literary activities.

His works include: (1) introductions to and glosses on various works; (2) *Zohar ha-Raki'a* (Korzec, 1785), a commentary on sayings of *Sifra di-Ẓeni'uta*, and the *Idra* of the Zohar; (3) *Zer Zahav*, an explanation of every item in the *Oraḥ Ḥayyim* section of the Shulḥan Arukh according to the *Zohar and the Lurianic Kabbalah; (4) *Leḥem min ha-Shamayim* (Munkacs, 1905), a compilation of Lurianic customs of which the printed version differs from the manuscripts; (5) *Nagid u-Meẓavveh* (Amsterdam, 1712), an important anthology of Lurianic customs which served as the basis for *Shulḥan Arukh shel ha-Ari*. Due to frequent republication, many customs of Luria became widely familiar (the manuscript version is much longer than the printed); (6) *Ẓemaḥ Ẓaddik* (Korzec, 1785), kabbalistic homilies; (7) *Kol ba-Ramah* (*ibid.*, 1785), a commentary on the *Idras*; here too the manuscript is longer than the printed version and is preceded by a very important introduction.

BIBLIOGRAPHY: G. Scholem, in: KS, 26 (1950), 185–94; 27 (1951), 107–10: I. Sonne, *ibid.*, 97–106; N. Ben-Menahem, in: *Aresheth*, 2 (1960), 379–83.

[Moshe Hallamish]

ẒEMAḤ BEN ḤAYYIM, *gaon* of Sura (c. 889 to c. 895). Apart from the fact that he was the stepbrother and successor of Nahshon b. Zadok, there is virtually no biographical information concerning him. He is remembered principally for his reply to the question of the perturbed scholars of Kairouan, following the appearance of *Eldad ha-Dani in North Africa. In his responsum, he reassures them that although the customs reported by Eldad often appear at variance with accepted laws, they are not neccessarily heretical, some of the divergences being attributed to variations in local traditions or simply to the forgetfulness produced by a long and perilous journey.

BIBLIOGRAPHY: S. Poznański, in: *Festschrift … A. Harkavy* (1908), 176, 186 (Heb. part); J. Mueller, *Mafte'aḥ li-Teshuvot ha-Ge'onim* (1891), 141; Baron, Social, 6 (1958^2), 221, 241.

[Meir Havazelet]

ẒEMAḤ BEN PALTOI, *gaon* of Pumbedita (872–890), great-grandfather of *Sherira Gaon. Comparatively few of Ẓemaḥ's responsa are signed with his full name. Many more responsa were only signed Rav Ẓemaḥ, but several of these belong to him. Tradition has it that he was the first to compile a systematic dictionary of the Talmud. Not a single fragment of this work has been preserved, and even possible quotations from it are so equivocal that some modern scholars have denied its existence. The lexicon was evidently compiled in order to facilitate the study of the Talmud in lands distant from Babylonia. The lexicon was popular until the end of the Middle Ages.

BIBLIOGRAPHY: S.D. Luzzatto, *Beit ha-Oẓar* (Lvov, 1847), 46b; L. Ginzberg, *Geonica*, 1 (1909), 159–61; S. Poznański, in: JQR, 3 (1912/13), 409f.; J. Mann, *ibid.*, 11 (1920/21), 447f.; B.M. Lewin, in: *Ginzei Kedem*, 5 (1934), 46–48; H.F. Taubes, in: *Scritti in memoria di Sally Mayer* (1956), 126–41 (Heb. section); Abramson, Merkazim, 10, 56.

[Meir Havazelet]

ẒEMAḤ ẒEDEK BEN ISAAC (second half of tenth century), *gaon* of the Sura Academy in Baghdad from about 988 to about 997; descendant of R. *Ẓemaḥ b. Paltoi Gaon. R. Ẓemaḥ Ẓedek reopened the Sura Academy after it had been closed for some 45 years (after the death of R. Saadiah Gaon). In a letter of 953, attributed to Ẓemaḥ Ẓedek, which was probably sent to *Ḥisdai ibn Shaprut in Spain, the writer asked for contributions to the academies of Babylonia and appended a list of halakhic questions which had been addressed to Babylonian *geonim*. R. Ẓemaḥ Ẓedek maintained friendly relations with R. *Elhanan b. Shemariah of Egypt, with whom he had become acquainted when the latter had studied at Pumbedita under R. *Sherira Gaon and his son R. Hai Gaon. R. Ẓemaḥ Ẓedek gave his advice to R. Elhanan in questions concerning the nature and the unity of God.

BIBLIOGRAPHY: E.D. Shapira, in: *Ginzei Kedem*, 3 (1925), 3–13; Mann, in: *Hebrew Union College Jubilee Volume* (1925), 227ff.; idem, in: HUCA, 3 (1926), 309–10; Mann, Texts, 1 (1931), 145–7, 478–9; Abramson, Merkazim, 113, 136.

[Abraham David]

ZEMARAIM (Heb. צְמָרַיִם), city belonging to the tribe of Benjamin and listed among the northern group of its cities next to Beth-El (Josh. 18:22). It probably gave its name to the Mount Zemaraim of II Chronicles 13:4, which was mentioned in connection with a battle between Abijah of Judah and Jeroboam I on the border between Judah and Israel; the text presumes that the place was south of Beth-El. In Shishak's list of conquered towns, it comes after Gibeon and was probably the first Israelite city conquered after his assault on Judah. Zemaraim, therefore, was apparently a city and a mountain in the vicinity of Ramallah. Clermont-Ganneau has suggested that Ra's al-Zemara between al-Ṭayyiba and Rammūn is Mt. Zemaraim; for the city itself, Ra's al-Tāḥūna in al-Bīra has been suggested. The tell occupies one of the highest points in the area and has remains of fortifications and Iron Age pottery.

BIBLIOGRAPHY: G. Dalman, in: PJB, 21 (1925), 58; Clermont-Ganneau, Arch, 2 (1899), 289; B. Mazar, in: *VT Supplement*, 4 (1957), 57ff.; Aharoni, Land, index.

[Michael Avi-Yonah]

ZEMBA, MENAHEM (1883–1943), Polish rabbinical scholar. Zemba came from a poor ḥasidic family. While still a young man, he distinguished himself by his erudition in his approach to the study of the *mishnayot* and a freedom from *pilpul* for its own sake, which was prevalent in his time in Poland. He studied for 20 years, during which time he was supported by his wealthy father-in-law. On the death of his father-in-law (about 1917) Zemba was forced to take over the running of his business, but he was not successful and after years of hardship he agreed in 1935 to become a member of the Warsaw rabbinical council. Until then he had been active in the *Agudat Israel movement, was secretary of the Mo'eẓet Gedolei ha-Torah, and a member of the council of the Warsaw Jewish community. Zemba was one of the last Warsaw rabbis to remain in the ghetto after the first wave of extermination. At a meeting of its surviving leaders on January 14, 1943, he gave rabbinic approval for the uprising. In an inspiring address, he stated: "Of necessity, we must resist the enemy on all fronts.... We shall no longer heed his instructions.... Sanctification of the Divine Name manifests itself in varied ways. During the First Crusade, at the end of the 11th century, the Halakhah ... determined one way of reacting to the distress of the Franco-German Jews, whereas in the middle of the 20th century, during the liquidation of the Jews in Poland, it prompts us to react in an entirely different manner. In the past, during religious persecution, we were required by the law 'to give up our lives even for the least essential practice.' In the present, however, when we are faced by an arch foe, whose unparalleled ruthlessness and program of total annihilation know no bounds, the Halakhah demands that we fight and resist to the very end with unequaled determination and valor for the sake of Sanctification of the Divine Name." On the eve of the revolt, Catholic circles offered their assistance to save the three remaining rabbis of Warsaw, but Zemba gave a ruling against it and died a martyr's death in the ghetto.

Zemba's works acquired great renown among students since they were an unusual amalgam of the dialectical approach common in Poland and the logical and penetrating method of the Lithuanian yeshivot. He published *Zera Avraham* (1920), responsa dialogue with R. Abraham Luftbehr (son-in-law of R. *Meir Simḥah ha-Kohen of Dvinsk); *Toze'ot Ḥayyim* (1921) on the Law of carrying on the Sabbath; *Oẓar ha-Sifri* (1929), *Oẓar ha-Sifra* (1960), and a number of articles which appear in various collections. The manuscripts of many other important works were lost in the Holocaust. Among these were *Menaḥem Yerushalayim*, on the Jerusalem Talmud; *Maḥazeh la-Melekh*, on Maimonides; four volumes of responsa; and a volume of sermons and dialectics which he had prepared for press. Zemba's remains were reinterred in Jerusalem in 1958.

BIBLIOGRAPHY: S. Rothstein, *Rabbi Menaḥem Zemba* (1948); O. Feuchtwanger, *Righteous Lives* (1965), 23–27; *Elleh Ezkerah*, 2 (1957), 38–51; A. Shurin, *Keshet Gibborim* (1969), 98–100; H. Seidman, *Diary of the Warsaw Ghetto* (1957), 281–5; I. Elfenbein, in: L. Jung (ed.), *Guardians of Our Heritage* (1958), 605–16; A. Rothkoff, in: *Jewish Life* (Nov.–Dec. 1969), 41–46.

[Aryeh-Leib Kalish]

ZEMER, HANNAH (1925–2003), Israeli journalist. Born in Bratislava, Slovakia, Zemer was imprisoned in the Ravensbrueck and Malchow concentration camps. She began her journalistic career in Europe, and after immigrating to Israel in 1950 she joined the *Omer* newspaper and subsequently *Davar*, the Histadrut trade union federation newspaper, serving as its Knesset correspondent, political correspondent, news editor, foreign correspondent in the U.S., chief editorial writer, and deputy editor. In 1970 she was appointed the newspaper's editor, thereby becoming the first woman to hold such a position in Israel. Post-Holocaust European Jewry and social welfare in Israel respectively were frequent subjects of her reporting and editing. Although not a feminist, she ensured that women journalists rose in the newspaper's ranks. Reporters enjoyed relatively wide freedom in their writing. Despite the paper's institutional ties to both the Histadrut and the Labor Party, and her own membership in the Labor Party executive, she withstood external pressures on the paper and its editorial staff, producing at times tensions between the Histadrut and the newspaper. Yet despite her stature as an editor, the 20 years she was at the helm was a period of decline for *Davar*, as for the party press as a whole. Circulation declined from 40,000 in 1970 to an estimated 16,000 in 1990, with much of its readership limited to Histadrut members from the secular Ashkenazi sector of the population. There was inadequate financial management, including a decline in advertising, and massive debts which reached NIS 20 million by 1990.

A popular lecturer, Zemer won a number of awards, including Woman of the Year (1978) for her work in communications, the Sokolow prize for journalism, the Herzl Prize, the Nordau Prize, and the Ted Lurie Prize. She sat on the boards of a number of national and Tel Aviv cultural and artistic institutions. She wrote *God Does Not Live There* (Heb.), a personal travelogue paying tribute to lost Jewish communities in Europe.

[Yoel Cohen (2nd ed.)]

ZEMIROT (Heb. זְמִירוֹת "songs").

(1) Term applied by Sephardi, Italian, and eastern communities to the biblical verses, psalms, and doxologies recited before the main part (*yoẓer, *Shema, and *Amidah) of the morning service. The terms *zemirot* and *Pesukei de-Zimra ("Passages of Song"), its Ashkenazi equivalent, are used interchangeably by the authorities as early as *Abudarham (14th century; cf. Sh. Ar., OḤ, 51:1, 8).

(2) In Ashkenazi usage, the table hymns sung during or directly after Sabbath meals. Their recitation was considered meritorious (מצוה) by the early authorities (cf. *Sefer ha-Ḥasidim*, ed. Wistinetzki, 722; *Or Zaru'a*, 2:95). Three groupings achieved prominence and were printed in most prayer books:

(a) eight *zemirot* for the Friday evening meal (*Kol Mekaddesh Shevi'i, Menuḥah ve-Simḥah, Mah Yedidut, Mah Yafit, Yom Shabbat Kodesh, *Yah Ribbon Olam, Ẓur mi-Shello Akhalnu, Yom Zeh le-Yisrael*); the first five apparently date from the early Middle Ages, the last two from the 16th century;

(b) eight for the Sabbath noon meal (*Barukh Adonai Yom Yom, Barukh El Elyon, Yom Zeh Mekhubbad, Yom Shabbaton, Ki Eshmerah Shabbat, Shimru Shabbetotai, Deror Yikra, Shabbat ha-Yom la-Adonai*); 10th to 15th centuries;

(c) nine for the end of Sabbath (*Ha-Mavdil, Eliyahu ha-Navi, *Be-Moẓa'ei (Yom) Menuḥah, Ḥaddesh Sesoni, Agil ve-Esmaḥ, Elohim Yisadenu, Eli Ḥish Go'ali, Addir Ayom ve-Nora, Ish Ḥasid Hayah*); early to late Middle Ages. A number of these are to be found in *Maḥzor Vitry* (11th century) and some were also accepted by Sephardi communities who had their own traditional table hymns. The kabbalists, especially Isaac Luria, added new *zemirot*. Among Sephardi and Oriental Jewry the writing of this type of hymn has continued.

Designated for either home or synagogue, the *zemirot* are not a special literary category. Rather, they belong to the group of songs and liturgical poems called *zemer* or *pizmon* or *shevaḥot* by Sephardi communities; these are not recognized as obligatory prayer. Examples of these *zemirot* are the *bakkashot* ("requests") said each morning before prayer by Sephardi Jews (some of which are recited at meals by other communities) and the many songs dedicated to special occasions such as the Sabbath, festivals, marriage, circumcision, redemption of the firstborn son, *Zeved ha-Bat* (a Sabbath celebration for a newborn daughter), Simḥat Torah, the 15th of Shevat, Ḥanukkah, Purim, etc. Many have been printed in standard and holiday prayer books, while others have been published in collections such as *Shirim u-Zemirot* (Istanbul, 1539). Among collections with *zemirot* not found elsewhere are *Sefer Shir u-Shevaḥah* (1921, ed. by Rafael Ḥayyim Ha-Cohen, 561 songs), *Sefer Pizmonim* (1929, ed. by Mordekhai Ḥayyim Eliyahu Levi, 408 songs), *Sefer Shirim, Tehillat Yesharim ha-Shalem* (1954, ed. by Ẓalah Manẓur, 373 songs).

BIBLIOGRAPHY: N. Ben-Menahem, *Zemirot shet Shabbat* (1949); Idelsohn, Liturgy, 80–83, 151–7; M. Zobel, *Der Schabbat* (1935), 182ff.; Elbogen, Gottesdienst, 81–87.

[Ernst Daniel Goldschmidt]

ZEMLYACHKA (Zalkind), ROZALIYA SAMOYLOVNA (other Party pseudonyms – **Samoylova, Demon, and Osipov**; 1876–1947), Soviet government and Party official. Born in Kiev, daughter of a merchant, she became a member of the Social-Democratic Party in 1896. In 1901 she was a representative of the newspaper *Iskra* in Odessa and Yekaterinoslav. After the Party split of 1903, Zemlyachka became a member of the Bolshevik Central Committee and in 1905 secretary of the Moscow committee of the Russian Social Democratic Workers Party, working in the Party's military organization.

She was arrested on a number of occasions. In 1909 she was secretary of the Baku Party organization and then spent some time abroad. In 1915–16 Zemlyachka was a member of the Moscow bureau of the Central Committee of the Bolshevik Party. During the February Revolution of 1917 she was secretary of the Moscow Committee of the Bolsheviks and participated in the armed seizure of power. From 1918 to 1920 she headed the political departments of the 8th and 13th armies and was the first woman in Soviet Russia to be awarded a medal (that of the Combat Red Banner). From 1920 to 1926 she occupied various Party posts, including, from Nov. 1920, that of secretary of the provincial Party committee in the Crimea where, together with B. *Kun, she carried out a policy of mass terror. From 1926 she was a member, deputy chairman, and then chairman of state and Party control organs. She was notorious for her merciless attitude in regard to Party purges and sanctioned repressions. From 1939 to 1943, in addition to serving in other capacities, she was deputy chairman of the Council of Peoples' Commissars of the U.S.S.R.

[Mark Kipnis and *The Shorter Jewish Encylopaedia in Russian* (2nd ed.)]

ZEMUN (Ger. **Semlin**), town on the Sava river, opposite Belgrade; part of Yugoslavia from 1918. Under Austrian rule Zemun was part of the so-called military area and subject to special regulations. It was therefore difficult for Jews to gain a foothold there, but once they succeeded in settling, they enjoyed relative safety in this "protected doorway to the Balkans."

After the Austrian conquest of *Belgrade in 1717, some Jews from Austria and Germany settled there, but when Belgrade fell to the Ottoman Turks again in 1739, a group of 20 Jewish families fled to Zemun. A small but lively community was thus created inside Croatia, which was exclusively administered by Austrians in view of frequent wars and bargaining with the Turks. In 1746 the *Judengemeinde* was officially recognized, but Maria Theresa granted the first known written privilege to a Jew (Raphael Salomon) to live permanently in Zemun only in 1753. A few years later there was a *Judengasse* (Jewish street, quarter), synagogue, and Jewish school. Jews paid a contribution of 150 florins to the authorities and were goldsmiths, barrel makers, glassworkers, ironmongers, etc. They also traded with Austria; as merchants, they were in an unfavorable position compared with the Austro-Germans, Serbs, and Wallachians (they were forbidden to sell hides or spirits, and the Serbian merchants' guild submitted a petition to the authorities to limit Jewish trade to scrap iron only). In view of their protected situation and due to the commercial importance of Zemun – despite restrictions – the community enjoyed a rare opportunity in being within "military areas," which were generally inaccessible to Jews. In 1772 a decree was issued permitting unlimited Jewish settlement –a striking proof of their usefulness. By 1773, however, the decree was revoked and residence was restricted for a long time to the descendants of the original Jewish settlers. Although checked in its growth, this first Croatian-based community – with its semiautonomous status – played an important role among Yugoslav Jewry.

After the Austrian occupation of Belgrade (1789), some Jews fled first to Zemun, where they found temporary asylum, and later went to Hungary. During an earlier siege of nearby Belgrade, many Jews were robbed and left homeless. On this occasion an aid committee was organized in Zemun and help was received from Hungary (Szeged, Budapest, Sombor, Baja), Croatia (Osijek, Varaždin), Transylvania (Temesvar), Austria (Vienna), and Germany (Leipzig). At the end of the 18th century there were 157 Jews in Zemun. In 1804 Jews manufactured ammunition for Serbian rebels ("first uprising" under Karageorge), and in 1806 Jewish craftsmen also did the same for the Turks, though under duress and surveillance. Almoslino, a Jew, was the Austrian diplomatic agent to the victorious *knyaz* (prince) Karageorge. During the first half of the 19th century 30 new families were granted rights to settle in Zemun, but others migrated to Bosnia. In 1862 the Zemun magistrate asked the military authorities to permit more Jews to settle within the city walls in order to promote trade and replace the war-torn city of Belgrade as a main trading center. Jews were still subjected to a special tax until the abolition of "military zone status" in 1871; in 1881 the "free city of Zemun" abolished all restrictions on Jewish settlers and was attached to the kingdom of Croatia-Slavonia. In 1918 Zemun became part of Yugoslavia

From 1825 to 1843 Judah Ḥai *Alkalai, the famous rabbi and precursor of Zionism, was community leader (*ḥakham*) of Zemun. Among the first group of "privileged Jews" were the ancestors of Theodor *Herzl; his grandfather, Simon Loew Herzl, was a follower of Rabbi Alkalai. He was imprisoned in 1849 for alleged Hungarian sympathies, but (according to the Belgrade City Archives, document no. 552) was released at the community's request in order to celebrate the Jewish holidays. Herzl's grandfather and grandmother (Rebecca, née Billitz) were buried at the Zemun cemetery, while his father Jacob, who was also born in Zemun, moved to Budapest.

In 1941 the community's 500 Jews and its institutions were quickly annihilated. Most of them perished in the barracks of the *saymishte* (fairground), which were prepared for an international exhibition. This was also used as a detention camp for Croatian Jews and others (see *Yugoslavia). Among those who were murdered was the writer and composer Erich (Elisha) Samlaić.

BIBLIOGRAPHY: AZDJ, 23 (1859), 276–7; 26 (1862), 585–6; H. Urbah, in: *Jevrejski Glas*, 13:30 (1940), 4–59; G. Schwarz, in: *Ommanut*, 4:10 (1940); G. Diamant, *A zsidók története Horvátországban* (1942); L. Ćelap, in: *Jevrejski almanah* (1957/58), 59–71.

[Zvi Loker]

ZEMURRAY, SAMUEL (1878–1961), U.S. business executive. Zemurray, who was born in Kishinev, Russia, went to the U.S. at the age of 14. After working at several jobs, he became a banana peddler in Alabama at the age of 20 and quickly rose to wealth. He became co-owner of two tramp steamers, bought 5,000 acres of Honduras land, and formed the Cuyamel Fruit Company. In 1930 Zemurray sold Cuyamel to the competing United Fruit Company for 300,000 shares of the latter's stock, making him its largest stockholder. He retired from business in Louisiana, where he became a vigorous opponent of Huey Long. By 1932 the drastically depreciated value of United Fruit stock caused him to bid for company control. He subsequently became chief of operations, reorganized the company, and was elected president in 1938. In 1951 Zemurray, by then known as the "Banana King," retired to become executive committee chairman. During the early New Deal period, Zemurray was active in the formulation of Agricultural Adjustment Act (AAA) industry codes. He served as an adviser to the Board of Economic Welfare during World War II. During his career, Zemurray was probably the most enlightened of the big U.S. businessmen operating in Latin America. He endowed clinics, housing projects, recreation facilities, and schools for the workers on his Central American plantations at a time when such a course of action was considered visionary, if not lunatic. Zemurray, who was a friend of Chaim Weizmann, was a director of the Palestine Economic Corporation, a generous contributor to Zionist causes, and a supporter of the Weizmann Institute of Science.

BIBLIOGRAPHY: Ch. Weizmann, *Trial and Error* (1949), 312–3.

ZENICA, town in central Bosnia on the Bosna River in a mining belt – where coal was extracted and iron and steel were produced – with corresponding industrial and commercial undertakings. Jews arrived during the 18th century. The oldest tombstone, dated 1747, attests to the Jewish presence at that time. A community was established in 1880 and a handsome synagogue in Moorish style was erected in 1903. In 1910 about 300 Jews lived there. Judah Montiiljo headed the community. Cantors were Moritz Altarac and Moritz Salom. The Zionist group was headed by Otto Loewy and Albert Ozmo.

During the Holocaust all the Jews perished. A memorial was consecrated in 1967. The synagogue was desecrated and plundered but survived; the building serves as a museum.

BIBLIOGRAPHY: PK – *Yugoslavia* (1988).

[Zvi Loker (2nd ed.)]

ZENKEVICH, LEV ALEKSANDROVICH (1889–1970); Soviet researcher in the fields of hydrobiology and invertebrate zoology. Zenkevich was born in what became known as Leninsk, Velograd Province. From 1927 he worked at the Institute of Oceanography of the Academy of Sciences of the U.S.S.R.; from 1930 he was a professor at Moscow University and a member of the Academy of Sciences. He studied the northern and eastern seas of the U.S.S.R., the Caspian Sea, and the Pacific Ocean from 1949 to 1952, heading scientific expeditions. From 1956 he was a member of the UNESCO committee on oceanic sciences and vice president of the special committee on oceanographic research of the International Council of Learned Societies. From 1961 to 1970 Zenkevich headed the oceanographic committee of the Academy of Sciences. He elaborated quantitative methods for studying ocean fauna and devised a theory of the biological structure of the ocean and the evolution of ocean fauna.

[*The Shorter Jewish Encyclopedia in Russian,* Jerusalem]

ZENO, PAPYRI OF, archives of Zeno. Zeno (third century B.C.E.), the son of Agreophontos, was a Greek from Caunus in southern Asia Minor, who settled in Egypt in the reign of Ptolemy Philadelphus (285–246 B.C.E.). There he entered the service of the finance minister, Apollonius, and as his right-hand man fulfilled various functions. He went on an economic mission to Ereẓ Israel and in 259 accompanied his master on his journeys in Egypt itself. From 256 he managed Apollonius' estate in Faiyum and assisted in the development of Philadelphia in that nome. After the death of Ptolemy Philadelphus and the consequent decline of Apollonius' influence, he continued to live in Faiyum and to engage in economic enterprises there.

In 1915 Zeno's archives were discovered at the site of Hellenistic Philadelphia, east of Faiyum. Many hundreds of documents and private letters, as well as accounts, receipts, and contracts were brought to light and have found their way to museums and various universities (Cairo, Michigan, Columbia, the British Museum); the bulk of them have been published. Written for the most part in a better Greek and a more legible hand than in most papyri, these documents shed direct light on the life and activities of Zeno and his associates, and also give a general picture of the economy, administration, law, and mode of life in Ptolemaic Egypt in the middle of the third century B.C.E. They are especially clear on events in the nome of Faiyum, where at that time the land was being reclaimed for cultivation and was the scene of vigorous economic and administrative enterprises. The study of the Zeno documents has enriched the knowledge of the status of the Greek settlers who flocked from various places in the Greek world to seek a future for themselves amid the economic prosperity of Ptolemy Philadelphus' Egypt.

Among these documents are some that throw light on the life of the Jews in Faiyum in the third century B.C.E. In one account reference is made to the Jew Antigonus, in another to the Jewess Johanna, who was apparently in Apollonius' domestic service. An account dealing with bricks mentions the Sabbath, when, it seems, the foreman did not come to work. Among the papyri a memorandum addressed to Zeno by two Jewish tenant farmers (Alexander and Ishmael) mentions a Jewish guard, and has many other references to Jews.

Knowledge of Ereẓ Israel under Ptolemaic rule has been greatly augmented from the account of Zeno's visit, when he traveled through much of the country, while his master Apollonius maintained many and varied contacts with Ereẓ Israel, either in the discharge of his official duties or in the pursuit of his business interests. The Zeno papyri also reveal the existence in the country of Ammon of a military colony comprising men of different origin and headed by *Tobias the father of Joseph who is known from Josephus' *Antiquities*, Book 12. Tobias' influence is evident from his correspondence with Ptolemy and Apollonius found in the archives (257 B.C.E.). The papyri also give new information on the administration and economy of Ereẓ Israel, the slave trade conducted there in which Zeno himself participated, the export of oil to Egypt, Apollonius' extensive estate in Bet Anat in Galilee, and Gaza as the harbor for the export of spices. One of the most interesting facts revealed by the papyri is the independent attitude adopted by village leaders in Ereẓ Israel toward the royal administration; one of them, Yadus (Jaddua?) actually expelled from his village (in Judea or in Edom) the representative of the administration.

Most of the Zeno papyri have appeared in the following publications: C.C. Edgar, *Catalogue Général des Antiquités Egyptiennes du Musée du Caire: Zenon Papyri*, 5 vols. (1925–40); idem (ed.), *Zenon Papyri in the University of Michigan Collection* (1931); W.L. Westermann (ed.), *Zenon Papyri*, 2 vols. (1939–40) (Columbia papyri); "Società italiana per la Ricerca dei Papiri greci e latini," in *Egitto: Papiri greci e latini*, 4–6 (1917–20); The Papyri about Jews have been published in: Tcherikover, Corpus, 1 (1957).

BIBLIOGRAPHY: Tcherikover, in: *Tarbiz*, 4 (1933), 226–47, 354–65; 5 (1934), 37–44; M.I. Rostovtsev, *A Large Estate in Egypt in the Third Century* (1922); C. Préaux, *Les Grecs en Egypte d'après les Archives de Zénon* (1947).

[Menahem Stern]

ZENODORUS (first century B.C.E.), tetrarch of *Trachonitis. Zenodorus leased the domain of Lysanias, who ruled over the land of the Itureans northeast of Galilee and who was put to death by Mark Antony. According to the inscription on his coins, Zenodorus was both tetrarch and priest. The area of his rule included Trachonitis, Auranitis, Bashan, Chalcis, and Paneas. As a punishment for his association with the robbers of Trachonitis, this territory, together with Auranitis and Bashan, was taken from him and transferred to Herod, who was charged with restoring security and order there. This aroused Zenodorus' hatred of Herod and he unsuccessfully attempted to damage Herod's relations with Rome. After the death of Zenodorus his other estates also passed to Herod.

See Jos., Ant., 15:344ff.; Wars, 1:398–400.

[Uriel Rappaport]

ZENTRALE STELLE DER LANDESJUSTIZVERWALTUNGEN, organization dealing with Nazi crimes. The Zentrale Stelle der Landesjustizverwaltungen (Central Office of the Ministries of Justice of the Laender) at Ludwigsburg (Baden-Wuerttemberg) was established in 1958 by an agreement between the ministers of justice of the German Laender. It resulted from the realization that numerous Nazi crimes still remained unsolved and that the work of the various public prosecutors required coordination. Initially, the Zentrale Stelle was competent to deal only with Nazi crimes committed outside the borders of the German Federal Republic against the civilian population, especially the crimes of the *Einsatzkommandos* (special unit commandos) and crimes in concentration and death camps. Subsequently the Zentrale Stelle's sphere of activities was extended to include crimes against prisoners of war and crimes committed inside the territory of what is now the German Federal Republic, particularly by the leading organs of the Reich and Nazi Party. It was not authorized to deal with war crimes – crimes committed in the conduct of war that were unrelated to Nazi ideology. The Zentrale Stelle was not organized as an additional public prosecutor's office. Its task was to make the initial inquiries and submit its findings on particular crimes to the appropriate prosecutor's office, in accordance with existing German legal procedure. It was the duty of the specific public prosecutor to continue the investigation and to decide whether prosecution was warranted. Thus, the Zentrale Stelle was in the nature of a police bureau. It developed into an agency collecting Nazi documents with a bearing on possible criminal prosecution, and also supplied the names of the accused and the witnesses. Some 50 criminal lawyers and 15 crime experts were eventually seconded to the Zentrale Stelle by the Laender. In Israel a bureau for the investigation of Nazi crimes was set up at police headquarters in cooperation with the Zentrale Stelle. By 1985 the Zentrale Stelle had initiated more than 12,000 cases.

ADD. BIBLIOGRAPHY: F. Hellendall, "Nazi Crimes Before German Courts: The Immediate Post-War Era," in: *Wiener Library Bulletin*, 24:2 (Summer 1970); A. Ruckerl, *An Investigation of Nazi War Crime 1945–1978: A Documentation* (1980); idem, "Ludwigsburger Zenstrallstelle," in: Y. Gutman (ed.), *Macmillan Encyclopedia of the Holocaust* (1990).

[Fritz Bauer / Michael Berenbaum (2nd ed.)]

ZENTRALRAT DER JUDEN IN DEUTSCHLAND (Central Council of Jews in Germany), political umbrella organization of Jewish communities in Germany founded in July 1950 in Frankfurt-am-Main. It includes the Jewish state federations (*Landesverbaende*) and communities of the major cities, and was generally accepted as the representative of Jews in West Germany and, since 1990, in reunified Germany. The name signifies a break with the pre-Nazi self-designation of "German citizens of the Jewish faith." Reflecting both the experience of exclusion and the fact that most Jews in postwar Germany were not of German origin, it has remained unchanged throughout its existence. During its early decades its main tasks were the reconstruction of Jewish life and negotiations with German authorities concerning restitution. Since the 1990s, it has been occupied to a large extent with the integration of immigrants from the former Soviet Union.

Its seats have been Frankfurt, Duesseldorf, Bonn, and since 1999, Berlin. The governing body consists of the president, two vice presidents, and six additional members of the executive. Presidents of the Zentralrat were Heinz *Galinski (1954–63, 1988–92), Herbert Lewin (1963–69), Werner *Nachmann (1969–1988), Ignatz *Bubis (1992–1999), and Paul *Spiegel (2000–). In 2005, 87 Jewish communities belonged to the Zentralrat, consisting of about 110,000 members. For the first time, three Liberal Jewish state federations joined the Zentralrat in 2005. The Zentralrat oversees the Jewish Studies College in Heidelberg, the Central Archives for the Research of German Jewry in Heidelberg, and the Zentralwohlfahrtsstelle, responsible for social work. It also serves as the publisher for Germany's only weekly Jewish newspaper, the *Allgemeine Juedische Wochenzeitung*. In addition, it also initiated the annual Leo Baeck Award, whose recipients have shown special merits with regard to Jewish issues in Germany.

BIBLIOGRAPHY: Y.M. Bodemann, *Gedaechtnistheater* (1996); M. Brenner, *After the Holocaust* (1997); J. Geller, *Jews in Post-Holocaust Germany* (2005).

[Michael Brenner (2nd ed.)]

ZENTRALSTELLE DER FUERSORGE FUER KRIEGSFLUECHTLINGE (Central Agency for the Care of War Refugees), set up in Vienna in World War I by the Austrian government to assist Jewish refugees fleeing before the Russian invasion of Galicia and Bukovina. Some of them had fled out of fear of Russian atrocities, and others had been evacuated by the army, often having been forced to relinquish their possessions. About half of the refugees had been left without means. In 1915 there were 137,000 refugees in Vienna, of whom 77,000 were Jews; the rest were Poles, Ukrainians, and some Italians. Large numbers were located also in Bohemia, Moravia, and Hungary, some in camps. The Zentralstelle was financed by the Austrian government, administered by the city of Vienna and directed by the Jewish member of the Vienna council, Rudolf Schwarz-Hiller, and supported by a staff of voluntary Jewish helpers. It provided the refugees with weekly allowances (according to the size of their families), shelter, clothing, nurseries, schools, medical and legal services, and a library and reading rooms. Its work was supplemented by various Jewish organizations. Initially conceived as a temporary measure, the Zentralstelle functioned until the end of World War I, when the situation deteriorated due to the food and housing shortage and to antagonism on the part of some of the local population.

BIBLIOGRAPHY: J. Kreppel, *Juden und Judentum von heute* (1925), 61–70; R. Till, *Geschichte der Stadtverwaltung Wien* (1957), 112.

[Hugo Knoepfmacher]

ZENTRALWOHLFAHRTSTELLE DER DEUTSCHEN JUDEN (Central Welfare Organization of German Jews), founded in 1917 and composed of representatives of welfare bodies, communities, the larger German-Jewish organizations, and professional social workers. It gradually attained a leading position in Jewish welfare work and was recognized and supported by the German government, the *American Jewish Joint Distribution Committee, and the major German welfare bodies. In its first years the Zentralwohlfahrtstelle dealt with the havoc wrought by World War I and the ensuing inflation. It gradually extended its activities to new fields: tubercular cases, nervous and mental diseases, and juvenile delinquency. It initiated, advised, and helped organize regional and territorial organizations. In 1932, 212 institutions (including homes for the aged, asylums, hospitals, and schools) were under its supervision. One of its main duties was the care of Jews from Eastern Europe. It published a number of high-caliber periodicals on social, welfare, and communal work. The Nazi seizure of power in 1933 created a new situation in which the organization's activities consisted of emigration and retraining for occupations open to Jews, the awakening of Jewish consciousness, education, and Zionism. These challenges were met by the establishment of the Reichsvertretung, within which the Zentralwohlfahrtstelle continued to play an important role in the distribution of welfare funds, medical care, and aid. In 1951 the Zentralwohlfahrtstelle was reorganized with its seat in Frankfurt, and after 1990 became increasingly involved with Russian immigrants.

BIBLIOGRAPHY: G. Lotan, in: YLBI, 4 (1959), 185–207. **ADD. BIBLIOGRAPHY:** B. Scheller, *Die Zentralwohlfahrtstellen* (1987); G. Heuberger, *Zedaka* (1992).

ZEPHANIAH (Heb. צְפַנְיָה), Judean prophet whose activity is dated to the reign of King Josiah (639–609). In addition to the usual mention of his father's name (Cushi), his ancestry is traced back four generations to *Hezekiah, possibly the king of that name. If so, Zephaniah was a distant relative of King *Josiah (cf. Zeph. 1:4). He lived in Jerusalem and prophesied there. It has been suggested plausibly that "Cushi" refers to the prophet's ultimate African origin in the area conventionally rendered "Ethiopia," but actually corresponding to contemporary Sudan (Rice). Note also the positive reference to *Cush in Zephaniah 3:10 (cf. Ps. 68:32).

Book of Zephaniah

DATE AND HISTORICAL BACKGROUND. The Book of Zephaniah is the ninth book of the Latter Prophets. The Qumran sectaries wrote a *pesher* (a commentary making use of fulfillment exegesis) on the book, relating it to their own times. The name צְפַנְיָה means "YHWH has hidden," or "YHWH has treasured." The genealogy given in Zephaniah 1:1 traces Zephaniah's ancestry back four generations to a certain Hezekiah, who some have identified with Hezekiah, king of Judah (715–687 B.C.E.), although this identification is sometimes doubted because Hezekiah is not referred to as king (Zephaniah's genealogy was already debated by medieval Jewish commentators). According to the superscription, Zephaniah prophesied during the reign of King Josiah (640–609 B.C.E.). Some scholars would date the work during the reign of Jehoiakim (609–598 B.C.E.); others prefer postexilic dates or at least significant postexilic additions. Ben Zvi opts for an exilic or postexilic dating but despairs of recovering an original seventh-century Zephaniah, or his sayings. The present author is of the opinion that the basic material in Zephaniah corresponds well enough to the period of Josiah's rule, so that with the exception of some later interpolations, the traditional dating offers the best solution

An apparent 50 years' silence of prophetic inactivity is shattered by the forceful and articulate voice of Zephaniah. The long reign of Manasseh (687–642 B.C.E.) witnessed the promotion of cults of other divinities alongside Yahweh, a situation which the Hebrew prophets, with their zeal for the worship of Yahweh alone, opposed. The abuses attacked by Zephaniah in chapter 1, such as astral worship (1:4–5) and aping foreign customs (1:8–9), are largely those decried in Kings (II Kings 21:2–9; 23:4–7), which Josiah's reform (621 B.C.E.) sought to eliminate. The external situation was even more ominous. The breakup of the mighty Assyrian empire with the attendant cataclysmic upheaval was already causing a premonition of doom to pervade the international atmosphere. Such a time was propitious for a sensitive person, steeped in the cultic and literary traditions of his people, to arrive at a deepened meaning of the swiftly approaching Day of YHWH.

COMPOSITION AND STYLE. Despite recent attempts to fragment and/or rewrite the Book of Zephaniah, the overall structure of large units of the book as well as its rhetorical features argue strongly for the basic integrity of the work. The assumption that all passages of hope and eschatological statements must be postexilic is no longer tenable. In fact, there is little in the book that does not fit the historical period in question, nor is there serious internal inconsistency. The style exhibits the magnificent artistry of the author, who utilizes many poetic devices (see Avishur) and reaches sublime heights in the famous hymn concerning the "Day of YHWH" (1:15ff.), "a day of wrath is that day." The Vulgate's translation of *yom evrah ha-yom ha-hu'* by *"dies irae dies illa"* inspired the medieval hymn "Dies Irae," which remains part of the Catholic Requiem Mass. The book also contains the beautiful "Zion Hymn" (3:14–17).

CONTENTS AND MESSAGE. Chapter 1 begins with a prophecy of total destruction (*asof, asef,* cf. Jer. 8:13) of all life and of the inhabitants of Judah and Jerusalem in particular. There is not one word of hope. No one is to be spared. The sin of the people, especially that of the leaders, is pictured in stark and graphic detail: they worship Baal and the host of heaven, they swear by their king (*malkam*; though a god rather than a human king may be referred to here), and turn away from following YHWH. This judgment speech is set within the framework of an ominous portrayal of "The Day of YHWH" in which Zephaniah carries further the concepts of Amos (5:18–20) and

Isaiah (2:6–22). This day, portrayed as the day of YHWH's sacrifice, will be a day of utter darkness and gloom, whose sound of howling and wailing stands in sharp contrast to the silence with which the people are called into YHWH's presence: "Hush before the Lord YHWH" (1:7).

Chapter 2 begins as an oracle of woe against Jerusalem and Judah (2:1–3), which continues the motif of a judgment by fire and calls upon the faithful to actively strive for justice, righteousness, and humility. Perhaps a remnant might be saved (cf. Amos 5:14–15). The warning and promise are supported by an oracle against the Philistines and other coastal people (2:4–7), whose destruction would mean salvation and pasturing for the remnant of Judah. This oracle begins and ends with a double use of roots (הִתְקוֹשְׁשׁוּ וָקוֹשׁוּ – whose meaning is unclear – verse 1, and וְשָׁב שְׁבוּתָם, verse 7; cf. 1:2; 3:20). It may be closely related to the material in chapter 1, providing at least a ray of hope for the faithful remnant. The oracle against Moab and Ammon (2:8–11) is generally regarded as reflecting a later period. However, Moab had long been known for its pride (cf. Mesha Stele and Jer. 48:26–30), an evil which was of special concern to Zephaniah (cf. 2:3; 3:11–12). The chapter concludes with a short statement against Cushites, perhaps referring to the Cushites in Egyptian military service, and a detailed and vivid description of judgment against Assyria and Nineveh, an oracle which appears to have been uttered around the time of the destruction of Nineveh in 612 B.C.E.

Chapter 3 begins as an oracle of woe against Jerusalem and its leaders. This prophecy might very well have been written after the Deuteronomic reformation (621 B.C.E.) and before Josiah's death (609 B.C.E.), reflecting doubts concerning the depth of the reform, a view also expressed by Jeremiah. Following the accusation (3:1–7), the announcement (3:8–13) repeats the threat of total destruction (cf. 1:18), but is transformed by the rhetorical use of כִּי־אָז ("but instead") in verses 9, 11 into a salvation oracle. Zephaniah 3:9 makes use of the ancient Near Eastern motif that distant peoples spoke "twisted tongues" (CAD L, 213), and prophesies that all peoples will have clear speech so that all will call upon the name of YHWH and worship together at His holy mountain. The prophet then breaks into a joyous and exultant Zion hymn (3:14–17), rejoicing that YHWH, the King, in their midst, has taken away their sentence and given victory. His use of the Zion tradition emphasizes his belief that the future is in the hands of YHWH, who alone can change the nature of the people so that they can be humble and righteous (cf. Hos. 2:21–22). The chapter and the book conclude (3:18–20) with an ingathering of exiles, presumably a late addition, so that the people of YHWH might be restored and given fame and praise.

BIBLIOGRAPHY: A.B. Davidson, *The Books of Nahum, Habakkuk and Zephaniah* (1896); S.R. Driver, *The Minor Prophets* (1906); J.M.P. Smith, *Micah, Zephaniah and Nahum* (ICC, 1911); G.A. Smith, *The Book of the Twelve Prophets*, 2 (1929); O. Procksch. *Die kleinen prophetischen Schriften nach dem Exil* (1929); G. Gerleman, *Zephanja: Textkritisch und literarisch untersucht* (1942); S.M. Lehrman, *Zephaniah* (1948, 1961); J.P. Hyatt, in: JNES, 7 (1948), 25–29; C.L. Taylor, *The Book of Zephaniah* (1956); A. George, *Michée, Sophonie, Nahum* (1958); D.L. Williams, in: JBL 82 (1963), 77–88; A. Deissler, *Sophonie* (1964); F. Horst, *Die zwölf kleinen Propheten: Nahum bis Maleachi* (1964); K. Elliger, *Das Buch der zwölf kleinen Propheten*, 2 (1967); M. Bič, *Trois-prophètes dans un temps de ténèbres: Sophonie-Nahum-Habaquaq* (1968). **ADD. BIBLIOGRAPHY:** G. Rice, in: *Journal of Religious Thought*, 36 (1979), 21–31; J. Roberts, *Nahum, Habakkuk, and Zephaniah* (1991); E. Ben Zvi, *A Historical-Critical Study of the Book of Zephaniah* (1991); idem, DBI, 2:669–73; Y. Avishur, in: Z. Weisman (ed.), *Tre Asar Bet* (Olam ha-Tanakh; 1993), 118–35; A. Berlin, *Zephaniah* (AB; 1994); J. Keselman, in: ABD, 6:1077–80; M. Sweeney, *Zephaniah* (Hermeneia; 2003).

[Ivan Jay Ball, Jr. / S. David Sperling (2nd ed.)]

ZEPHANIAH BEN MORDECAI (16th century.), one of the first Karaite scholars from Lithuania. Zephaniah was a spiritual leader and served as a *ḥazzan* of the Troki community in the middle of the 16th century. He was a great-grandson of the scholar Samuel Politi from Adrianople (Turkey). Zephaniah was an authority on *halakhah* and established new regulations about calendation, which were accepted by part of the Karaites in Polish-Lithuanian communities. He was also a teacher of Torah and had many disciples, one of whom was the young Isaac ben Abraham *Troki. Zephaniah was the author of the following works: *She'elot u-Teshuvot be-Hilkhot Sheḥitah* (IOS B 563 (JNUL, mic. 53737)) about ritual slaughter; *Kiddush ha-Ḥodesh ve-Seder ha-Ibbur be-Kiẓẓur*, about calendation. He also composed several liturgical poems. According to A. *Firkovich, in 1528 Zephaniah asked King Sigismund I "to return him his fields and his lands, which had been granted to him by previous kings. The king satisfied his request, confirming his charter, and ordered his servants to return to Zephaniah all the fields which had belonged to him in the past (*Avnei Zikkaron*, (1872), 254), but we have no evidence from other sources confirming this information.

BIBLIOGRAPHY: G. Akhiezer and I. Dvorkin, in: *Pe'amim*, 98–99 (2004), 238–99; G. Akhiezer and D. Shapira, in: *Pe'amim*, 89 (2001), 38–39; B. Gottlober, *Bikkoret le-Toledot ha-Kara'im* (1865), 209; A. Neubauer, *Aus der Petersburger Bibliothek* (1866), 75.

[Golda Akhiezer (2nd ed.)]

ZERAH (Heb. זֶרַח), name of five biblical figures. The etymology of the name is uncertain. It may mean "rising sun" or "brightness" or, possibly, "crimson" (see below).

1) One of the twins of *Tamar (Gen. 38:30; 46:12; I Chron. 2:4). The narrative relates that when the twins were being delivered, Zerah put out his hand and the midwife tied a crimson thread to it to signify his priority of birth. However, he withdrew his hand and his brother unexpectedly emerged. Because of this his brother was named *Perez (Gen. 38:27–30). The Bible seems to ascribe the name to the crimson thread attached to his hand. It has been suggested that Zerah is derived from *zeḥorita*, the Aramaic for *shani* ("scarlet thread").

This story closely resembles that of the twin birth of Jacob and Esau (Gen. 25:24–26), and probably is a variation of the same theme. Zerah became the eponymous ancestor of a Judahite clan, and the narrative of his birth may reflect the prior ascendancy of this clan over that of Perez, and its subsequent decline and supersession by Perez.

2) An Edomite chief descended from both Esau and Ishmael. His father Reuel was born of the marriage of Esau to Basemath, daughter of Ishmael. Zerah was the father of Jobab, an early Edomite king (Gen. 36:13, 17, 33; I Chron. 1:37, 44).

3) Son of Simeon and eponymous ancestor of a Simeonite tribe called the Zerahites (Num. 26:13; I Chron. 4:24). He is referred to as Zohar (Heb. צֹחַר) in Genesis 46:10 and Exodus 6:15.

4) A levite, grandson of Levi, of the family of Gershom (I Chron. 6:6, 26).

5) Zerah the *Cushite (II Chron. 14: 8ff.).

ZERAH BEN NATHAN OF TROKI (1578–1657/8), Karaite scholar. Zerah was born in Birzhe, Lithuania. At the age of five his parents sent him to study in Troki. His first teacher was his relative, Isaac ben Abraham *Troki, in whose house Zerah stayed. After his teacher's demise he studied with Troki's disciple – Joseph ben Mordecai *Malinovski. In 1618 he visited Constantinople for the purpose of study. He was interested in Kabbalah, practical mysticism, astronomy, astrology, mathematics, etc. He is mainly known through his correspondence (from 1620) with the famous Jewish scholar and kabbalist, Joseph Solomon *Delmedigo from Candia, who spent five years in Lithuania as a physician of Prince Krzysztof Radziwiłł. In his letters, Zerah complained that "he had neither friend nor teacher among the Jews," adding that he had important books from many countries in his library. His first letter to Delmedigo included questions on Kabbalah. Later he put to Delmedigo 12 major and 70 minor problems mainly relating to mathematics, astronomy, physics, and medicine. He also discussed "demons, amulets, divination, dreams, and secret remedies and the antithetical temperamental balance called in Greek 'sympathy' and 'antipathy'…" as well as theological problems such as the existence of God, Providence, Heaven and Hell, and Resurrection. These questions were published by Delmedigo in *Sefer Elim* (Amsterdam, 1629). His answer, entitled *Iggeret Aḥuz,* was published by Abraham Geiger in *Melo Chofnajim* with a German translation and notes (Berlin, 1840). Delmedigo's reply expressed his views on Kabbalah, drew Zerah's attention to a series of works on mathematics, philosophy, exegesis, and other subjects, and provided him with a list of his works. Zerah evinced an interest in Philo's writings and asked Delmedigo to translate for him a table of contents and some extracts from Philo from Latin into Hebrew.

Zerah corresponded with Karaite scholars and community leaders from different lands, such as the scholar Joseph ben Moses Maruli of Istanbul and David b. Joshua, a head of the Jerusalem Karaite community. He wrote a letter to *Manasseh Ben Israel after his acquaintance with a Latin work by Manasseh, from which a clergyman from Vilna translated some sections for him into Polish. Zerah offered Manasseh for publication at the latter's printing house in Amsterdam the book *Ḥizzuk Emunah* by Isaac ben Abraham Troki and the liturgical poem by Joseph ben Mordecai Malinovski *Ha-Elef Lekha*. Manasseh did not print the former, presumably because of the fear of censorship, and published the second in 1643.

Zerah wrote a kabbalistic commentary on Song of Songs (W. Nathansohn, Devir, second edition, Warsaw 1883, I, 222); a commentary on *Moreh Nevukhim* by Maimonides (IOS SPb B 383); a number of elegies and a large number of liturgical poems in Hebrew and the Karaite language, of which some were included in the Karaite prayer books.

BIBLIOGRAPHY: Mann, *Texts*, 2 (1935), index, p. 1595; I. Cohen, *Vilna* (1943), 205, 457–8. **ADD. BIBLIOGRAPHY:** A.B. Gottlober, *Bikkoret le-Toledot ha-Kara'im* (1865), 165–66; M. Polliack (ed.), *Karaite Judaism: A Guide to its History and Literary Sources* (2003), index; S. Schreiner, *Studia Judaica*, 2:4 (1999), 165–83; *Sefer Elim*, Odessa (1864).

[Yehuda Komlosh / Golda Akhiezer (2nd ed.)]

ZERAH THE CUSHITE (Heb. זֶרַח הַכּוּשִׁי), military commander who invaded Judah in the time of *Asa. According to a story, preserved only in II Chronicles 14:8–14, Zerah commanded a large army and 300 chariots against Judah and reached the environs of *Mareshah. The Judean army defeated and pursued him to Gerar, conquering the cities in the area and looting many sheep and camels. It has generally been contended by scholars that Zerah was Osorkon I, king of Egypt (c. 914–874 B.C.E.); but Osorkon, like his father *Shishak, was not a Cushite (Nubian) but a Libyan. Furthermore, there is no etymological connection between Zerah and Osorkon, and the characters of their armies were different. According to Albright, Zerah was the governor of a Cushite colony, which was established by Shishak after his campaign in Ereẓ Israel. The settlement of Hamite elements near *Gerar in Philistia during the monarchy is also treated in I Chronicles 4:39–41 (according to the Septuagint; not Gedor as in Masoretic text). Nonetheless, it is more probable that Zerah was a Cushite chieftain from the vicinity of Gerar, who raided and plundered the surrounding areas. Thus, Habakkuk (3:7) mentions Cushite tribes with *Midian (cf. also Num. 12:1).

[Yehoshua M. Grintz]

In the *Aggadah*

Zerah was, for a short period, the owner of all the wealth in the world, which he acquired by capturing from Shishak (king of Egypt), those treasures which the king had taken from Rehoboam (I Kings 14:25ff.). These were the treasures which the Children of Israel had taken from the Egyptians at the time of the Exodus (Ex. 12:36). Ultimately, however, these treasures reverted to Asa, when he defeated Zerah the Cushite in battle (Pes. 119a).

BIBLIOGRAPHY: R.H. Hall, *The Ancient History of the Near East* (1937[7]), 439; Olmstead, Hist, index; Albright, in: JQR, 24 (1934), 370; idem, in: JPOS, 4 (1924), 146–8; Bright, Hist, 214–5. IN THE AGGADAH: Ginzberg, Legends, index; I. Ḥasida, *Ishei ha-Tanakh* (1964), 145.

ZERAHIAH BEN ISAAC BEN SHEALTIEL (Gracian (Ḥen)), philosopher, Bible commentator, and translator. Zerahiah was born in Barcelona to a prominent Jewish family, which for several generations produced rabbis and sages. In the last quarter of the 13th century he was active in Rome. The dates of his birth and death are not known; however, in 1290 he regarded himself as an old man, whose time had come to return to his birthplace and to be buried with his ancestors. Nothing is known about him after 1291.

Zerahiah arrived in Rome in the 1270s, where all his writings known to historians were composed in a 15-year period ending in 1291. In Rome he became a recognized authority in philosophy and in philosophical Bible exegesis, and for some years taught Jewish youth courses in Maimonides' *Guide of the Perplexed*. In contrast with the rabbinic leadership of the Barcelona community, which at that time was decisively influenced by the teachings of *Naḥmanides, the Jewish communal leadership in Rome was supportive of Zerahiah's rationalist-naturalist approach. His authority was recognized by such prominent communal leaders as Rabbi Shabbetai ben Solomon and Isaac ben Mordecai, the pope's physician; they also supported Zerahiah in his bitter controversy with Hillel ben Samuel of Verona over Hillel's conservative interpretation of Maimonides' philosophy. He seems to have been supported by Immanuel of Rome, who wrote a rhymed letter on his behalf to Hillel. Zerahiah thus found the cultural atmosphere of Roman Jewry congenial, but mocked the Ashkenazi Jews ("who never saw light in the sky").

Zerahiah's thought is largely based on the Jewish and Islamic philosophy he studied in Spain, and his writings only slightly echo scholastic concepts. The only Jewish thinker besides Maimonides whose thought Zerahiah knowingly uses was Samuel ibn *Tibbon. Zerahiah believed in the full harmony of Torah and science, or more precisely, between the esoteric meaning of the Torah and the exoteric doctrines of philosophy, a belief at the foundation of his exegetical approach to the Bible. His philosophical outlook was essentially Aristotelian, frequently in accordance with Ibn Rushd's commentaries. Nevertheless, on central ontological questions he took an independent stance. He strongly emphasized the transcendence of God, negating any relation between God and his creatures, but at the same time believed in the pre-existence of supreme "wisdom," a sort of logos originating in God, by means of which, and in cooperation with, the world was created. This "wisdom" is what established the cosmic order, the eternity of the species, and the fixed revolutions of the heavenly spheres. In this context, Zerahiah needed to employ the overtly Neoplatonic imagery of infinite emanation, by which "wisdom" overflowed and filled the whole cosmos. He also adopted a Neoplatonic stance regarding the concept of time, understanding it as a hypostasis independent of bodies (apparently reflecting the influence of the *Liber de Causis* which he translated from Arabic into Hebrew). Zerahiah's concept of prophecy was influenced by the lost Arabic version of Aristotle's *Parva Naturalia*, a version which enabled him to adapt the belief in prophetic revelation in dreams to a philosophic conceptual framework.

Zerahiah sharply criticized the "popular religion" and the cultural world of the early kabbalists, and attacked the belief in magic, **gematria*, reincarnation, and the real existence of Satan. His commentary to Job includes a naturalistic critique of Naḥmanides' thought, but he also frequently differed with more rationalist commentators like Abraham *Ibn Ezra and David *Kimḥi.

Zerahiah was the author of the following:

Original Works

1) Commentary on Proverbs (1288–89), published by I. Schwartz in *Ha-Shaḥar*, under the title *Imrei Da'at* (also known as *Imrei Shefer*) and republished as a separate edition in Vienna, 1871.
2) Commentary on Job (1290–91), published by Schwartz in *Tikvat Enosh* (1862; reprinted, Jerusalem, 1969).
3) Commentary on the Pentateuch, or on certain portions of it, which, however, is no longer extant.
4) Commentary (extant only in manuscript) on parts of Maimonides' *Guide of the Perplexed* (1:1–71 and other passages, especially the 25 propositions appearing at the beginning of Book 2).
5) Letters of Hillel ben Samuel of Verona and to Judah ben Solomon, printed in *Oẓar Neḥmad* (1857).

Translations of Philosophical Works from Arabic into Hebrew

1) Aristotle's *De Anima* (ed. G. Bos, Leiden, 1994).
2) Themistius' paraphrase of Aristotle's *De Caelo* (ed. S. Landauer, Berlin, 1903).
3) Averroes' Middle Commentary on Aristotle's *Physics*, *De Generatione et Corruptione*, and *Metaphysics* (all extant only in manuscript).
4) Al-Farabi's treatise on the nature of the soul (ed. Z.H. Edelman, *Ḥemdah Genuzah*, Koenigsburg, 1856, and by S. Rosenthal, Warsaw, 1857).
5) Pseudo-Aristotle, *Liber de Causis*.

Translations of Medical Works from Arabic to Hebrew

1) Galen's *De Causis et Symptonatibus* (extant only in manuscript).
2) Galen's *Katagene*, ch. 1–3 (extant only in manuscript).
3) Avicenna's *Canon* (unfinished; extant only in manuscript).
4) Maimonides' *Aphorisms* (extant only in manuscript).
5) Maimonides' *Treatise on Poisonous Drugs* (extant only in manuscript).

6) Maimonides' *Shorter Treatise on Sexual Intercourse* (ed. H. Kroner, Bopfingen, 1906).

BIBLIOGRAPHY: Steinschneider, in: *Oẓar Neḥmad*, 2 (1857), 229–45; Steinschneider, Uebersetzungen, 111–24, 125, 146, 160, 262, 295, 652, 681, 764, 765; Steinschneider, Arab Lit, 213–19; Dukes, in: HB, 3 (1860), 99–100; Kirchheim, *ibid.*, 4 (1861), 125–6; Carmoly, in: *Oẓar Neḥmad*, 3 (1860), 109–10; G. Boss, Aristotle's *De Anima*, translated into Hebrew by Zerahiah ben Isaac ben Shealtiel Hen (1994), 1–4; J. Friedman, "R. Zerahiah ben Shealtiel Hen's Commentary on the *Guide of the Perplexed*," in: *Jacob Friedman Memorial Volume* (1974), 3–14 (Heb.); A. Ravitzky, "The Thought of R. Zerahiah ben Shealtiel Hen and the Maimonidean-Tobbonite Philosophy in the 13th Century" (Heb., Ph.D. diss., Jerusalem, 1977); idem, *Al Da'at ha-Makom* (1991), 133–35, 236–43; idem, "Possible and Contingent Existence in Exegesis of Maimonides in the 13th Century," in: *Daat*, 2–3 (1978–79), 89–97 (Heb.).

[Aviezer Ravitzky (2nd ed.)]

ZERAHIAH BEN ISAAC HA-LEVI (known as **Ferrarius Saladi**; late 14th–early 15th century), rabbi of Saragossa and of all the communities of Aragon. A disciple of Ḥasdai *Crescas, he distinguished himself as a talmudist, preacher, physician, and translator, and was one of the leading Jewish participants in the disputation of *Tortosa. During his teacher's lifetime Zerahiah had already begun in his sermons to attack the rationalists who disagreed with R. Ḥasdai. While in Tortosa, he preached to the Jewish disputants in the synagogue. There is an account of this by Solomon ibn Verga: "The opening of his sermon was: 'the similar into the similar is healthy as is the opposite into the opposite' [a saying of Aristotelian origin], on which he delivered an excellent commentary [probably strongly anti-Christian] which can only be understood if heard directly. He completed his sermon with a prayer and supplication" (*Shevet Yehudah*, ed. by A. Shoḥat (1947), 97). During the disputation Zerahiah proved one of the most systematic, incisive, and trenchant of the debators. His comprehensive disquisitions there have been preserved in the Latin protocol of the disputation. This records that on March 16, 1414, Zerahiah presented the conclusions of the Jews on the dogmatic validity of the *aggadot* in which he concluded that the principles of the religion (*articuli legis*) come to the believer by way of faith and tradition alone and do not require any proof, whereas Scripture, as well as the teachings of the Talmud, have to be explained according to these principles; the Christians had also adopted this method. For the Jew, anticipation of the Messiah remains one of the fundamentals of his faith so long as the Jews continue in exile and without a king, and so long as many other conditions have not been fulfilled. Through this methodical and dogmatic approach, structured according to the system of Thomas Aquinas on the subject of the principles of faith, Zerahiah tried to remove the christological interpretation of talmudic *aggadot* from the Christian armory and to exclude the messianic principle of faith from the discussion.

BIBLIOGRAPHY: Baer, Spain, index; A. Pacios Lopez, *La disputa de Tortosa*, 2 (1957), index; *He-Ḥalutz*, 7 (1865), 96–101, 118–9.

[Haim Hillel Ben-Sasson]

ZERA'IM (Heb. זְרָעִים), the first of the six orders of the Mishnah, according to the traditional order as stated by R. Simeon b. *Lakish (Shab. 31a), who states that the order is called "Faith"; although from the words of R. Tanḥuma (Num. R. 13:15–16), it is possible to infer that according to another tradition, *Zera'im* is the second order. With the exception of the first tractate, *Berakhot*, all the tractates in *Zera'im* deal with the agricultural laws which obtain in the Land of Israel, and various suggestions have been put forward for the inclusion of *Berakhot*.

Zera'im contains 11 tractates in the following order: *Berakhot*, 9 chapters; **Pe'ah*, which treats of the gifts to the poor from the produce of the land, namely, gleanings, forgotten produce, and the corner of the field, 8; **Demai*, doubtfully tithed produce, 7; **Kilayim*, mixed species, 9; **Shevi'it*, the Sabbatical Year and the remission of debts, 10; **Terumot*, 11; **Ma'aserot*, 5; **Ma'aser Sheni*, 5; **Ḥallah*, 4; **Orlah*, 3; and **Bikkurim*, 3, making 74 chapters in all. This order departs from the accepted rule that the tractates are given in descending order of the number of chapters and, in fact, according to an early tradition *Shevi'it* and *Kilayim* come between *Terumot* and *Ma'aserot*. There is also evidence that *Demai* was placed between *Kilayim* and *Ma'aserot*. In the Tosefta to *Zera'im*, *Berakhot* has 6 (or 7) chapters; *Pe'ah* has 4; *Demai*, 8; *Terumot*, 10; *Shevi'it*, 8; *Kilayim*, 5; *Ma'aserot*, 3; *Ma'aser Sheni*, 5; *Hallah*, 2; *Orlah*, 1; and *Bikkurim*, 2. There is Jerusalem Talmud for the whole of the order *Zera'im*, but Babylonian Talmud only for *Berakhot*.

BIBLIOGRAPHY: Epstein, Mishnah, 980ff., esp. 987f.; Ḥ. Albeck (ed.), *Shishah Sidrei Mishnah,...Seder Zera'im* (1957), 1–3.

[Zvi Kaplan]

ZERBST, city in Saxony-Anhalt, Germany. A *Judenwinkel* (Jewish lane), which contained houses owned by both Jews and Christians, was mentioned in 1324. Shortly afterward, the Jews seemed to have been forced to move to the east side of the street, where they rented their homes from Christian landlords. A street once named Keverstrasse (*kever* = Heb. "grave"), situated outside the original city walls, may have received its name from a Jewish cemetery. After the establishment of the duchy of Zerbst-Anhalt in 1603, the dukes granted letters of protection to Jewish merchants. The modern community, founded in the mid-19th century, numbered 81 in 1880; 120 in 1932; 95 in 1933; but only 36 on September 1, 1939. It maintained a synagogue, cemetery, and school. During World War II, two forced labor camps were erected in the vicinity. In 1942, 34 of the 36 remaining Jews were deported to the east.

A plaque commemorates the destroyed synagogue and the former Jewish community. Another plaque, in the Jewish cemetery, honors the victims of *Kristallnacht*.

BIBLIOGRAPHY: FJW, 419; *Germania Judaica*, 2 (1968), 939–40; 3 (1987), 1718–19; PK Germanyah. **ADD. BIBLIOGRAPHY:** B. Bugaiski, I. Leubauer, and G. Waesche, *Geschichte der juedischen*

Gemeinden in Sachsen-Anhalt. Versuch einer Erinnerung (1997), 286–91; W. Binger (ed.), *Gedenkorte fuer die Opfer des Nationalsozialismus in Sachsen-Anhalt* (1998), 62.

ZERED, brook or valley of (Heb. נַחַל זֶרֶד, Naḥal Zered), a river valley described as a camping place of the Israelites before the flanking movement which brought them to Jahaz (Num. 21:12). The crossing of the deep rift in the mountains made a deep impression on the Israelites, and this event served as a terminal point for the account of the wanderings in the desert after Kadesh-Barnea (Deut. 2:13, 14). In later Jewish literature, the Zered appears as the border of the area held by the returning exiles from Babylonia (Sif. Deut. 51, et al.). Eusebius mentions it but does not localize it (Onom. 92:10); the Madaba map, however, shows it clearly south of Kerak (Charachmoba). Most scholars identify it with the Wadi al-Ḥasā, which flows in a deep rift for approximately 28 mi. (45 km.) from east to west up to the Dead Sea. The shallow stream has a width of 8.7 yards (8 m.) and a capacity of 300–400 cu. m. per minute.

BIBLIOGRAPHY: Abel, Geog, 1 (1933), 279, 310, 489; 2 (1938), 216; EM, 3 (1952), 630.

[Michael Avi-Yonah]

ZEREDAH (Heb. צְרֵדָה), home town of the Ephraimite Jeroboam the son of Nebat (I Kings 11:26). The reference to Zeredah in II Chronicles 4:17 is a corruption of Zarethan, according to the parallel verse in I Kings 7:46. In talmudic sources it is mentioned as the home town of Yose b. Joezer, an early *tanna* (c. 150 B.C.E.), who, with his colleague Yose b. Johanan, formed one of the **zugot* ("pairs") of Jerusalem (Avot 1:4; Eduy. 8:4; Sot. 9:9; Pes. 17b; Ned. 7:1, 40a; Tosef., BK 8:13). The accepted identification of Zeredah is with Deir Ghassāna in the district of Thamna, 16 mi. (c. 25½ km.) northeast of Lydda. The ancient name is preserved by the village spring, ʿAyn Ṣarīda, This area was originally part of Ephraim but was transferred to Judea, together with the rest of the district, in the time of Jonathan the Hasmonean. As such, it could well be the home town of the *tanna* Yose.

BIBLIOGRAPHY: Press, Ereẓ, s.v.; Albright, in: BASOR, 49 (1933), 26–28; Yeivin, in: BJPES, 14 (1949), 88; Abel, Geog, 2 (1938), 457.

[Michael Avi-Yonah]

ZERUBAVEL (Vitkin), JACOB (1886–1967), leader of *Po'alei Zion; author and journalist. Born in Poltava, Ukraine, Zerubavel at an early age joined Po'alei Zion, which was established at that time by high school students. Together with Izhak *Ben-Zvi, he participated in organizing the self-defense that succeeded in preventing a pogrom in Poltava. In 1906, at the founding convention of Po'alei Zion, he was elected to the central board. He helped Ber *Borochov publish an illegal newspaper and afterward moved to Vilna, with the other members of the central boards. There he was imprisoned for a year and a half, and after he was released Zerubavel left Russia and moved to Austrian Galicia. In Lemberg he was active on the editorial board of the newspaper *Der Yidisher Arbeter* and also helped Borochov, who was in Vilna, to edit *Dos Fraye Vort*, which was printed in Galicia, smuggled into Russia, and distributed clandestinely. In 1910 Zerubavel settled in Ereẓ Israel and was a member of the editorial board of *Ha-Aḥdut*, the Hebrew newspaper of Po'alei Zion (together with Ben-Zvi, David *Ben-Gurion, and Raḥel Yannait *Ben-Zvi). He served as secretary of the central board of Po'alei Zion. Upon the outbreak of World War I, he took on Ottoman citizenship, but because of his sharp criticism in *Ha-Aḥdut* of the persecution of the *yishuv* by the Turkish authorities, he was sentenced to prison; he succeeded in escaping, however, and was sentenced in absentia to 15 years of hard labor.

Zerubavel managed to arrive in the United States in 1915 and served on the editorial board of the organ of Po'alei Zion there, *Der Yidisher Kemfer*. On the outbreak of the Russian Revolution (1917), he returned to Russia and was active in the National Jewish Council of the Ukraine. From 1918 to 1935 he was among the leaders of Po'alei Zion in Poland (from the time of the split in the movement in 1920, he was the head of the central office of Left Po'alei Zion).

He also edited the newspaper *Arbeter Tsaytung*, and was a member of the Warsaw community council. Zerubavel visited Palestine, but the British authorities would not allow him to remain there permanently. Only in 1935 did he receive an official immigration visa.

In Palestine Zerubavel was active in publishing Yiddish books and journals (such as the newspaper *Nayvelt*). He served on the Executive of the *Histadrut. During World War II he was a member of the Rescue Board (Va'ad ha-Hazẓalah). In 1948 Zerubavel was chosen a member of the Zionist Executive and headed the Department of Mediterranean Jewry. He played a role in the unification of Left Po'alei Zion with *Aḥdut ha-Avodah and their integration with *Ha-Shomer ha-Ẓa'ir to form *Mapam. He was also among the founders of the Israel-U.S.S.R. Friendship League and edited its literary organ (in Russian). Zerubavel was active in the Yiddish Writers' Union in Israel and demanded an official status for Yiddish in the State of Israel. In 1951 he returned to work in the Histadrut as director of the Labor Archive.

Zerubavel's activities as a publicist and literary critic in Hebrew and Yiddish continued for 60 years. He published a book on Borochov (in Yiddish, 1926). During his final years he published two volumes of memoirs, *Alei Ḥayyim* ("Leaves of Life," 1960) and *Bi-Ymei ha-Milḥamah* ("During the War," 1966), impressions of his travels in Poland after the Holocaust, and impressions of his travels in the Soviet Union. In 1961 *Sefer Zerubavel* was published in honor of his 75th birthday, including appreciations of the author and a bibliography (covering more than 1,600 items).

BIBLIOGRAPHY: LNYL, 3 (1960), 673–6; Tidhar, 5 (1952), 2298–301.

[Getzel Kressel]

ZERUBBABEL (Heb. זְרֻבָּבֶל; Akk. Zēr Bābili, "scion of Babylon"). Usually recorded as the son of Shealtiel (Ezra 3:2, 8; 5:2;

Neh. 12:1; Haggai 1:1, 12, 14; 2:2, 23), he is mentioned once in a genealogical list as the first son of Pedaiah and the nephew of Shealtiel, the son of exiled King Jehoiachin (I Chron. 3:17–19). This may be the result of a lacuna in the text. Like some of the other Jewish leaders of the period – Sheshbazzar (Ezra 1:8), Mordecai, and Bilshan (Ezra 2:2 = Neh. 7:7) – he bore a Babylonian name, perhaps because of his contact with the Babylonian court (cf. I Esd. 3–5; Dan. 1:3ff.). He worked in close collaboration with Joshua (Jeshua) son of Jehozadak the high priest as leader of the original caravan of repatriates (Ezra 2:2 = Neh. 7:7; Neh. 12:1) and as builder of the Temple, which frequently bears his name (see *Temple). Just as there is confusion about his genealogy, so is there uncertainty about the chronology of events and personalities involved in the reconstruction of the Temple. When in 520 B.C.E., Tattenai, governor of the Trans-Euphrates, inquired concerning who was responsible for building the Temple, the Jews responded that Cyrus had appointed Sheshbazzar as governor to carry out the task (Ezra 5:14–16). According to another account, however, the work was carried out by Zerubbabel, also entitled "governor" (Haggai 1:1, 14; 2:2, 21), and Joshua. The year date of the arrival of the caravan is not given, but it is said to have been in the seventh month (Tishri). The two leaders, in the face of opposition from the neighboring peoples, set up the altar, reinstituted the sacrificial cult, and offered the special sacrifices for Tabernacles. In the second month (Iyyar) of the second year of their arrival, they began the construction of the Temple proper and dedicated the laying of the foundation stone (Ezra 3). The offer on the part of the neighbors to participate in the task was rejected by the two leaders. The former thereupon put forth every effort to bring a halt to the building of the Temple, and work, in fact, did not resume in earnest until 520 (Ezra 4:1–5).

The divine encouragement necessary to bring about resumption of the work was provided by the prophet *Haggai, and a new foundation ceremony was held on Kislev 24 (December 17). On that day the prophet told Zerubbabel that the Lord was about to shake heaven and earth, overturn kingdoms, and make him like a "signet ring" (Haggai 2:18ff.), thereby reversing the prophecy of Jeremiah against Jehoiachin (Jer. 22:24ff.).

Following the lead of Haggai, Zechariah also encouraged the people to rebuild the Temple (Zech. 1:16). He too addressed both leaders, albeit individually, and there is some uncertainty as to the full import of his message. Zerubbabel is mentioned explicitly in only one passage (Zech. 4:6–10), but alluded to in two others (Zech. 3:8; 6:12). In the last two passages mentioned, Joshua is addressed. He is told that the Lord "will raise up for David a righteous Branch," again fulfilling a prophecy of Jeremiah (Jer. 23:5f.; 33:14ff.), who shall build the Temple, bear royal honor, and rule upon this throne. The (high) priest shall likewise rule and a peaceful relationship shall exist between the two. The first passage (Zech. 4:6–10) elaborates: Zerubbabel shall finish the work on the Temple and topple mountains, "not by might nor by power, but by My spirit, says the Lord of Hosts."

These messianic hopes came to naught. Neither Zerubbabel nor Joshua are mentioned by name at the dedication ceremonies of the Temple (Ezra 6:14ff.), nor does Zerubbabel appear further in any official capacity. However, the name of Zerubbabel did not fade from the people's memory. It was early embellished in the apocryphal tale which placed the beginning of his activity in the reign of Darius as one of the king's bodyguards who outdid his companions in a battle of wits and thereby won the right to rebuild the Temple (I Esd. 3:1–5:6; Jos., Ant. 11:31–74). Although even Ezra is absent from Ben-Sira's list of worthies, Zerubbabel is fully praised along with Joshua and Nehemiah (Ecclus. 49:11ff). In the medieval Ḥanukkah hymn *Ma'oz Ẓur* celebrating Israel's past redeemers, the "end of Babel (Babylon)," is associated with Zerubbabel.

[Bezalel Porten]

In the *Aggadah*

Zerubbabel was the grandson of Jehoiachin (PdRK 163). He is identified with *Nehemiah, the name Zerubbabel indicating his Babylonian birth (בבל זרוע; Sanh. 38a). He was born circumcised (ARN[1], 12) and was designated as one of the select servants of God (ARN[2], 43, 121). He later served as one of the members of the Great Synagogue (Introd. to Maim. Yad, 2a). He succeeded Daniel in the service of King Darius and occupied a higher position than all the other servants and officials. He was captain of the three who constituted the royal bodyguard. Once when the monarch slumbered, his guards resolved to write down what each considered the mightiest thing in the world. The first wrote down "wine," the second, "the king," while Zerubbabel wrote, "women are the mightiest in the world, but truth prevails over all." After he awakened, the king, preferring the answer of Zerubbabel, offered to grant any request he would make. Zerubbabel asked for nothing for himself, but asked permission of the king to restore Jerusalem, rebuild the sanctuary, and return the holy vessels. Not only did Darius grant these request, but also gave him letters of safe-conduct and conferred numerous privileges upon the Jews who accompanied him to Palestine (Josippon, Hominer ed. 3:16–20).

Like Daniel, Zerubbabel was also vouchsafed a knowledge of the secrets of the future. The archangel Metatron was especially friendly to him. Besides revealing the time at which the Messiah would appear, he also brought about an interview between the Messiah and Zerubbabel (Zerubbabel, ed. Jellinek, *Beit ha-Midrash*, 2 (1938), 54–57). Together with Elijah, Zerubbabel will also explain obscure Torah passages and reveal its mysteries in the time to come (Midrash in *Halakhot Gedolot*, ed. Hildesheimer, p. 223).

[Aaron Rothkoff]

BIBLIOGRAPHY: Ginzberg, Legends, 4 (1947[5]), 287, 351–2; 6 (1946[3]), 381, 437–9.

ZERUBBABEL, BOOK OF, a work describing the vision of Zerubbabel, last ruler of the House of David. In accordance with the dates given in the text for various stages of the redemption, this work was probably written at the beginning of the seventh century, at the time of the last victories of the Byzantine Empire over Persia (629). To one living in Ereẓ Israel at that time, it might have seemed that the last stage of victory over the Roman Empire and the Christian Church had arrived, and that the coming of the Messiah was imminent. Since no mention is made of the Arabs and Islam, whose invasion shortly thereafter (637) eclipsed these victories, it can be assumed that this is a pre-Islamic work.

Written in biblical style, especially as found in the visions of Ezekiel and Daniel, the book describes the revelation to Zerubbabel of the events of the End of Days by the angel Michael, or Metatron. Besides the figures of the Messiah son of Joseph and the Messiah son of David, which are standard in such apocalyptic writings, two new figures are introduced: Ḥephzi-Bah, the mother of Messiah son of David, who plays a prominent role in the messianic wars; and Armilus (probably Romulus), the enemy, who is depicted as a monster, son of Satan and of a stone monument of a woman. Both a Caesar and a pope, Armilus unites the powers of Augustus and Jesus, thus symbolizing material and religious evil combined. The victory of the Messiah and his mother over Armilus represents that of Judaism over the Roman Empire and the Christian Church. Since the story – a dramatic one of many wars and apocalyptic disasters – has no theological overtones, it was acceptable to every ideological movement of Judaism (except the followers of Maimonides).

Found in countless medieval manuscripts and printed in many different collections, the *Book of Zerubbabel* became the standard source for descriptions of the End of Days and of the coming of the Messiah. In addition, many Jewish thinkers were influenced by it, from Saadiah Gaon, who based a chapter of his *Emunot ve-De'ot* on it, to Nathan of Gaza, Shabbetai Ẓevi's prophet, who used it to prove that Shabbetai was the Messiah. The lasting hatred that Jews felt toward the Roman and Christians throughout the Middle Ages made this work popular for more than a thousand years after its composition.

BIBLIOGRAPHY: A. Jellinek, *Beit ha-Midrash*, 2 (1938), 54–57; I. Levi, in: REJ, 68 (1915), 129–60; Y. Even-Shmuel, *Midreshei Ge'ullah* (1954), 56–88.

[Joseph Dan]

ZEVAḤIM (Heb. זְבָחִים; "Animal Sacrifices"), first tractate in the order *Kodashim*, in the Mishnah, Tosefta, and Babylonian Talmud (there is no Jerusalem Talmud to *Kodashim*). Just as tractate **Ḥullin* is also called *Sheḥitat Ḥullin* ("The Slaughter of Profane Animals", i.e., for human consumption), so *Zevaḥim* has the alternate name *Sheḥitat Kodashim* ("The Slaughter of Sacrificial Animals") in the Talmud (BM 109b, etc.) and deals almost exclusively with the regulations for the slaughter of animals and birds for the Temple worship. The tractate consists of 14 chapters in the Mishnah and 13 in the Tosefta.

Chapter 1 deals with the validity of sacrifices offered up under incorrect designations. Chapters 2–4 deal with irregularities due either to unfitness on the part of those carrying out the rites, in the deed itself, or in the intention with which it was performed. Chapters 5 and 6 detail locations where the various sacrifices of the animals, birds, and meal offerings took place; the sprinkling of the blood of the animals and birds; and the manner of their consumption. Chapter 5 constitutes the basis of the whole tractate, giving a complete enumeration of all sacrifices, and for this reason it was included, from as early as the Seder of Amram *Gaon, in the introductory portion of the daily prayers. Chapter 7 deals with irregularities in the sacrifice of birds. Chapter 8 discusses the mixing up of sacrificial animals and of their blood and limbs after slaughter. Chapter 9 discusses the sanctity which articles incur by being placed on the altar or in the sacrificial vessels. Chapter 10 gives the order of precedence of the sacrifices. Chapter 11 deals with the washing of garments stained by the blood of sacrifices and the laws concerning meat boiled in the sanctified vessels. Chapter 12 is concerned with the rights of the priests to share in the sacrifices. The subject of the last two chapters is sacrifices offered elsewhere than in the Temple, including the Temple of *Onias and the *bamot* ("high places").

Most of the *tannaim* mentioned in the Mishnah belong to the post-Temple period, when the sacrificial system no longer obtained. They nevertheless studied it and even established the *halakhah*. Thus R. Simeon b. Azzai states "I have heard a tradition… that any animal offerings which must be consumed remain valid though slaughtered under a different name…" but the sages did not agree with him (1:3). Nevertheless, the Mishnah contains passages which belong to the Temple period. Although Mishnah 10:8 is given in the name of R. Simeon and the whole of chapter 10 is derived from his Mishnah, Epstein (Tannain 157) maintains that it belongs to the Second Temple period and was only reported by him. Similarly, 3:6 is given in the name of Judah b. Ilai, but it is actually from his teacher Eliezer b. Hyrcanus, who lived during Temple times, as can be seen by a comparison with Tosefta 3:6 (*ibid.*, 189ff.). Mishnah 9:1 cites a law anonymously, and Joshua b. Hananiah and Rabban Gamaliel disagree as to its interpretation. *Tosafot* maintains that the law must therefore have been in existence prior to the recorded dispute, while Rashi is of the opinion that the law was no older than the dispute itself (cf. Halevy, Dorot 1. 5 p. 256 and Albeck, Mishnah (Ger.) p. 105).

The Tosefta includes several passages of aggadic material. Chapter 13 tells the history and laws of the *bamot* and sanctuaries which preceded Solomon's Temple. In 11:16 it tells about the *gedolei kehunnah* ("the leading priests"), who took the hides of the sacrifices for themselves. Despite measures taken to prevent this expropriation, the priests continued this practice until the people adopted the custom of specifically devoting the hides "to heaven." Tosefta 2:17 has an interesting description of the persistent questioning of Eleazar b. Shamua by one of his disciples until a law which had been overlooked was traced to its origin. Realizing that through this persistence on the part of the student his teaching had been restored to the college, Eleazar exclaimed: "Happy are you, the righteous who love the Torah, as it is written, Oh how I love thy Torah! I meditate on it all day."

The *Gemara* contains comparatively little aggadic material. Worthy of mention is the statement "sacrificing without repentance is an abomination" (7b). Another saying speaks of the atoning powers attaching to the high priests' garments (88b). One passage lists the centers of worship before the building of Solomon's Temple (118b). The rabbis stated that the returning exiles built their bronze altar on the very site of the original altar destroyed by the Babylonians. They located it on seeing the angel Michael at worship near an altar which was still standing. According to Isaac Nappaḥa, however, they were assured of the spot when they saw the ashes of Isaac upon the ground as they walked (62a). *Zevaḥim* was translated into English by H. Freedman in the Soncino edition of the Talmud (1948).

[*Encyclopedia Hebraica*]

ZEVI, BRUNO (1918–2000), Italian architect, writer on architecture. He was born in Rome, studied at Harvard University, and on his return to Italy after World War II became a champion of Frank Lloyd Wright. He advocated Wright's organic approach to architecture rather than the rational approach then favored in Italy. Zevi was an active member of the Jewish community and president of the Rome Jewish maternity home from 1950. He was consultant on building problems in Israel. He wrote studies on Frank Lloyd Wright (1945), Erik Gunnar Asplund (1948), and Richard Neutra (1954). He edited and published *L'Architectura*, a monthly magazine. Zevi was appointed professor of modern architecture at Rome University in 1948.

ẒEVI HIRSCH FRIEDMAN OF LESKO (Pol. **Lisko**; d. 1874), Ḥasid, active in Lesko, S.E. Poland; son of Aaron of Ujhely (Satoraljaujhely; d. 1816). He made many journeys to visit the *ẓaddikim* of his time, studying mainly under Ḥayyim *Halberstamm of Zanz, who wrote an approbation to Ẓevi Hirsch's work *Akh Peri Tevu'ah* (Pt. I, 1875; Pt. II, 1876), consisting of homilies on the Pentateuch in which he quotes sayings of the Talmud, numerous teachings of the Tanya and of *Shneur Zalman of Lyady, and the Ḥasidim who preceded him, as well as works written on the Lurianic Kabbalah – the system of Isaac *Luria. Like other Ḥasidim, he considers Creation to be the result of *ẓimẓum* (contraction of the Divine Emanation; see *Kabbalah). The resultant paradox is that this contraction must tolerate the dialectic duality of Good and Evil because though the world was created with justice (*din*) the actual creation shows mercy (*ḥesed*) to its creatures. Similarly, the evil inclination was created for the benefit of man "because the principal purpose of man's creation in the world is to have free choice and overcome his inclination" (ibid.). His work, *Sefer ha-Yashar ve-ha-Tov* (1880), contains homilies for the Sabbath and the festivals. Of his two sons-in-law, ḤAYYIM FRIEDLANDER OF LESKO (d. 1904) wrote *Tal Ḥayyim Berakhah* (1898), novella on talmudic subjects, and *Tal Ḥayyim* (1909), homilies on the Pentateuch, and YOZEFA GOLDBERGER (d. 1908) was a *ẓaddik* and merchant.

BIBLIOGRAPHY: S. Friedlander, *Ahavat Shelomo* (1961); Z.W. Goldberger, *Darkhei ha-Yashar ve-ha-Tov* (1910).

[Esther (Zweig) Liebes]

ẒEVI HIRSCH OF NADWORNA (second half of the 18th century), ethical writer. Ẓevi Hirsch, who was *av bet din* of the community of Nadworna (Nadvornaya), Galicia, wrote a short ethical treatise, *Otiyyot Maḥkimot* ("Instructive Letters"), which consists of ethical advice arranged according to the letters of the alphabet.

The work was first published in Breznitz in 1796, but in an incomplete form; a second edition appeared in Nowy Dwor in 1799. In his preface to the corrected edition Ẓevi Hirsch's son explained that the first edition did not represent an accurate version of the original work, and that he was therefore republishing it from the actual manuscript of his father; he also added an appendix, *Millei de-Avot*, an ethical commentary on *Avot*.

BIBLIOGRAPHY: Benjacob, Oẓar, 32.

[Joseph Dan]

ZEVIN, SOLOMON JOSEPH (1885–1978), rabbi and scholar. Born in Kazimirov near Bobruisk, Belorussia, Zevin studied at the Mir yeshivah under R. Elijah Baruch Kamai, and later at Bobruisk under R. Shemariah Noah Schneerson. At the age of 18, he began to correspond on halakhic subjects with some of the greatest contemporary scholars, such as Joseph *Rozin and Jehiel Michael *Epstein. Zevin was rabbi of several Russian communities, including Kazimirov, where he succeeded his father. On the eve of the establishment of the Soviet regime in Russia (1917–18), he participated in conferences and conventions in Vilna, Moscow, and Kiev, and was elected as a Jewish representative to the Ukraine National Assembly. The Soviet regime granted him, together with R. Yeḥezkel *Abramsky, special permission to edit and publish a monthly journal *Yagdil Torah*, devoted to religious and halakhic subjects. This appeared in Slutsk in 1928, but was discontinued by government order. In 1934 he succeeded in obtaining permission to immigrate to Palestine. Creator of a new halakhic Hebrew style, he was an original critic of contemporary halakhic literature. From 1936 to 1945 he published a weekly review of this literature and an appraisal of religious personalities, and also wrote on current halakhic problems and on halakhic aspects of the festivals. His published works (frequently reprinted) were *Ha-Mo'adim ba-Halakhah* (1944); *Le-Or ha-Halakhah* (1946); *Ishim ve-Shitot* (1952); *Soferim u-Sefarim* (3 vol., 1959), containing reviews of 200 books that appeared from 1938 to 1945; *Sippurei Ḥasidim* (2 vols., 1955–57); *La-Torah ve-la-Moadim* (1961). Zevin was editor of the *Enẓiklopedyah Talmudit* (Talmudic Encyclopedia), founded in 1942. The importance of his work lies in his effective and lucid mastery of the entire complex of talmudic literature. By its concise and informed treatment of the vast material, the *Enẓiklopedyah* has influenced the curriculum in yeshivot and given the public an insight into the theory of the *halakhah*. Zevin received many literary prizes, including the Israel Prize for Religious Literature in 1959. He also served as president of Yad ha-Rav Herzog (Rabbi Herzog World Academy for Torah Research) in Jerusalem (1960–1978), and as a member of the supreme rabbinical council of Israel (1965–1978).

BIBLIOGRAPHY: S. Assaf, in: KS, 24 (1947/48), 10–12.

[Jehoshua Hutner]

ZEYER, JULIUS (1841–1901), Czech poet and author. Zeyer was born in Prague. Although his Jewish mother became an ardent Catholic, Zeyer always remained conscious of his Jewish origin, dreamed of visiting Palestine, and even learned Hebrew. Abandoning the traditional nationalist school of Czech 19th-century literature for a cosmopolitan outlook, in the epic verse, which was his major contribution to Czech literature, he characteristically used subjects from many countries. Jewish themes appear in much of his writing, beginning with the novel *Duhový pták* ("Rainbow Bird," 1874). His short story *Smrt Evy* ("Eve's Death") is based on the biblical account of Cain, and the collection of which it forms part, *Báje Šošany* ("Shoshanna's Tales," 1880), is set in the Frankfurt ghetto. He chose biblical subjects for two dramas: *Sulamit* (1883) and *Z dob růžového jitra* ("From the Times of the Rosy Dawn," 1888), the latter about Isaac's stay in Gerar (Gen. 26:1–12). Other short stories with Jewish themes are *El Cristo de la Luz* (1892), which deals with medieval Toledo, and *Asenat* (1895), a tale of Joseph in Egypt. Zeyer also wrote a number of poems on Jewish subjects.

Outstanding among his works of epic poetry are *Ossianův návrat* ("Ossian's Return," 1885); *Z letopisů lásky* ("From the Annals of Love," 4 volumes, 1889–92); and *Karolinská epopej* ("Carolingian Epic," 1896). His two most important prose works are the novels *Román o věrném přátelství Amise a Amila* ("The True Friendship of Amis and Amil," 1880) and *Jan Maria Plojhar* (1888).

BIBLIOGRAPHY: F.V. Krejči, *Julius Zeyer* (1901); P. Váša and A. Gregor, *Katechismus dějin české literatury* (1925); O. Donath, *Židé a židovství v české literatuře 19, stoleti* (1923); F. Gottlieb, *Jan Maria Zeyer* (1932); idem, in: *Židovská ročenka* (1970/71), 109–19; J.S. Kvapil, *Gotický Zeyer* (1942). **ADD. BIBLIOGRAPHY:** J. Hrabák, *Dějiny České literatury* III (1961); E. Jurčinová, *Julius Zeyer, život českého básníka* (1941); A. Mikulášek et al., *Literatura s hvězdou Davidovou*, vol. 1 (1998); *Slovník českých spisovatelů* (2000).

[Avigdor Dagan / Milos Pojar (2nd ed.)]

ZGIERZ (Rus. **Zgerzh**), city in Lodz province, central Poland. Jews first settled there in the mid-18th century. There were nine Jews living in the city according to a census of 1765, and 12 in 1793. Their main sources of livelihood were the leasing of inns and the sale of alcoholic liquor. Their number had grown to 27 (5% of the total population) in 1808. The situation of the small Jewish settlement deteriorated following the restrictions imposed on the industrial cities by the government of Congress Poland. In 1824, by order of the Warsaw authorities, the Jews of Zgierz, with few exceptions, were compelled to move to a separate small quarter. There they numbered at first 30 families, increasing in the following 25 years to 400 families, although only 24 one-story houses were built in the quarter during that time. In 1851–55 a few streets were added to the Jewish quarter, and in 1862 the restrictions on residence were abolished completely. Jews were also discriminated against in an agreement signed on March 30, 1821, between the Polish administration and German immigrants, in which (paras. 38 and 39) Jews were prohibited from acquiring real estate in the new quarters and from manufacturing or selling alcoholic beverages in the whole city. This became the prototype for similar agreements with other towns.

Despite these restrictions the Jewish population grew, numbering 356 in 1827 (8% of the total) and 1,637 (20%) in 1857. According to data of 1848, 92 Jews engaged in crafts (46 tailors, 10 hatmakers, 11 in the foodstuff branch), and 43 in trading, while 46 were hired workers. In this period cotton and wool mills were founded by Jewish industrialists. An organized community functioned from 1824. A wooden synagogue was built in the 1840s, a *mikveh* and poorhouse were erected in the 1850s, and a large stone synagogue in 1860, followed by a large *bet midrash* in the 1880s. The first rabbi of the community, Shalom Ẓevi ha-Kohen (officiated 1827–77), founded a yeshivah. His son, Solomon Judah, author of *Neveh Shalom*, was rabbi from 1898 to 1940.

The first Jewish school with Russian as the language of instruction was founded in Zgierz in 1885. Toward the end of the 19th century several modern *ḥadarim* of the *Haskalah movement were organized, one by Jacob Benjamin Katzenelson, father of the poet Itzhak *Katzenelson. The Hebrew poet David *Frischmann was born in Zgierz. In 1912 the Yagdil Torah organization was founded, which supported many religious educational institutions. There were cultural associations for literature, art, drama and sport, and in 1911 a branch of *Ẓe'irei Zion was founded, which was active in the cultural sphere, stimulating interest particularly in the Hebrew language and press.

During World War I the Zgierz community instituted a special tax to provide for Jews in Zgierz suffering from hunger or disease. Conditions for Jewish workers in Zgierz were particularly poor, and the community administration sent an appeal (Sept. 28, 1920) to local Jewish industrialists to employ Jewish workers. Polish workers used antisemitic arguments to oppose Jewish industrialists who favored the employment of Jewish workers. The Jewish population numbered 3,543 in 1897, 3,828 in 1921, and 4,547 in 1931.

[Arthur Cygielman]

Holocaust Period

In 1939 there were 4,800 Jews in Zgierz (about 20% of the total population). Immediately after the German occupation persecution of the Jewish population began. On Dec. 27, 1939, about half the total Jewish population – some 2,500 persons – were expelled to the town of Glowno. The rest either managed to escape or were deported across the border to central Poland. A few Jewish tailors and shoemakers, who worked for the Germans, were allowed to remain in the city. In January 1942 they were sent to *Lodz ghetto.

[Danuta Dombrowska]

BIBLIOGRAPHY: Lodz, WAP, *Anterioria Piotrkowskiego Rządu Gubernskiego*, no. 2581; Dyr. Sz. no. 1710–18 (= CAHJP, ḤM 3450, 5686, 5708); B. Wasiutyński, *Ludność żydowska w Polsce w wiekach XIX i XX* (1930), 28; R. Mahler, *Yidn in Amolikn Poyln in Likht fun Tsifern* (1958), index; E. Sonnenberg, *Zgierz ze stanowiska sanitarnego* (1869); B. Wachlik, *Zgierz, szkic historyczny* (1933); J. Goldberg, "Zgierz" (Ms. at Yad Vashem, for inclusion in PK Polin); *Davar* (Jan. 14, 1940), 3; D. Dombrowska (ed.), *Kronika getta łódzkiego*, vols. 1–2 (1965–66), passim; idem, in: BŻIH, no. 13–14 (1955).

ZGURITSA (Rom. **Zgurita**), Jewish agricultural village in N. Moldova, in the region of Bessarabia. Zguritsa was founded in 1853 on an area of over 1,000 acres rented by settlers from Bessarabia. In 1878 the new owner, a Jew, canceled the lease of the estate and Zguritsa lost its status as a Jewish agricultural colony. Its residents were then registered as burghers. From 1890 to 1903 further Jewish settlement in Zguritsa was prohibited by virtue of the *May Laws issued on May 3, 1882. In 1897 Zguritsa's Jewish population was 1,802 (85% of the total population). In 1899, 36 families rented 370 acres in the area, mainly for growing vegetables. Agrarian reform in Romania in 1922 granted plots of land to 150 Jews of Zguritsa. In 1925 the 193 members of the local loan fund included 40 farmers, 25 artisans, and 113 tradesmen. In 1930 there were 2,541 Jews in Zguritsa (83.9% of the total population), supporting a kindergarten and an elementary school both of the *Tarbut organization.

[Eliyahu Feldman]

Holocaust Period

On July 3, 1941 after the outbreak of war, the village was shelled and houses were set on fire. Jews fled to the fields, where they were rounded up after two days by Romanian troops and kept under guard in the open. They suffered general maltreatment (especially the women), and in addition the soldiers practiced shooting, using Jews as their targets. A few days later the Jews were dispatched to *Transnistria and then sent back to Bessarabia, the sick, elderly, and the children dying on the way. Near Cosăuți all the young men were separated from the group, ordered to dig graves, and shot. Jews died every day from disease, hunger, and thirst. In the fall of 1941 they were sent back to Transnistria, and before crossing the Dniester 200 men were removed, ostensibly for work, and shot. The remaining Jews were taken to Tiraspol and Balta. Only a few survived the war.

[Jean Ancel]

BIBLIOGRAPHY: HOLOCAUST PERIOD: Yakir, in: *Eynikeyt* (Feb. 16, 1946); M. Mircu, *Pogromurile din Basarabia*... (1947), 30–37.

ZHDANOV (until 1948 **Mariupol**), city in S. Stalino district, Ukraine. The Jewish community of Zhdanov was founded at the beginning of the 19th century and numbered 111 in 1847. Owing to continuous Jewish emigration from the Lithuanian and Belorussian provinces to southern Russia, the Zhdanov community had increased by 1897 to 5,013 (16.1% of the total population). Seven Jewish settlements were founded in the surroundings of Zhdanov toward the end of the reign of Nicholas I, and by the end of the 19th century their population was estimated at over 3,000. Riots, which lasted three days, broke out in the city in October 1905. In 1926, 7,332 Jews lived in Zhdanov (18% of the city's total population). Jewish life was suppressed at that time. Immediately after the city's occupation by the Germans in October 1941, all the Jews were imprisoned in an ancient military camp outside the city and were shot on Oct. 18, 1941. In 1959 there were about 2,800 Jews (1% of the total population) in Zhdanov. A small synagogue was still functioning there in 1962. Most Jews left in the 1990s.

BIBLIOGRAPHY: *Die Judenpogrome in Russland*, 2 (1909) 227–40.

[Yehuda Slutsky]

ZHERNENSKY, MOSHE ELIYAHU (pseudonym **M.E. Jacques**; 1887–1948), Hebrew writer. Born in Kamenets, Lithuania, he served (from 1929–32) on the editorial board of the Hebrew encyclopedia *Eshkol* in Berlin. He went to Palestine in 1933. His articles on language, problems of translation, modes of poetic expression, and other topics appeared in various journals.

He wrote penetratingly on the Hebrew poetry of the Middle Ages, the poetry of *Bialik, and the writings of *Agnon. Three volumes of his works appeared: *Mi-Saviv* (1929), *Bein ha-Shelabbim* (1940), and *Arugot* (1949). His translations from Russian, French, and German include: *The Brothers Karamazov*, 3 vols. (1921–29), stories by Balzac (1943), and *Gottesdienstliche Vortraege der Juden* by L. Zunz (1947).

BIBLIOGRAPHY: N. Goren, *Demuyyot be-Sifrutenu* (1953), 237–43; Rabbi Binyamin, *Mishpeḥot Soferim* (1960), 342–4.

[Gedalyah Elkoshi]

ZHIDACHOV (Pol. **Żydaczów**) city in Drogobych district, Ukraine (formerly in eastern Galicia). Jewish settlement in Zhidachov began in a comparatively early period, as the existence of an ancient cemetery and wooden synagogue indicates, although no definite date is known. Records show 199 Jews living in Zhidachov in 1765, some 900 in 1910 (about a quarter of the total population), and 823 in 1931. Zhidachov was known for its dynasty of ḥasidic rabbis (*admorim*), descendants of Ẓevi Hirsch Eichenstein of Zhidachov.

Holocaust Period

At the outbreak of World War II there were about 1,000 Jews in Zhidachov, On Sept. 5, 1942, some of the Jews were deported to the *Belzec death camp. On Sept. 30, 1942, a number of them were expelled to *Stry and shared the fate of that community. The remaining Jews were imprisoned in a forced-labor camp in Zhidachov until its liquidation in August 1943. After the war, the Jewish community of Zhidachov was not reconstituted.

ZHIDACHOV, ḥasidic dynasty. The dynasty's founder and most outstanding personality, ẒEVI HIRSCH EICHENSTEIN (1785–1831), was born in the village of Safrin, Hungary. In his youth he was known as a brilliant Torah scholar, and while still a young man, he devoted himself mainly to the study of the *Kabbalah. Under the influence of his brother, Moses of Sambor (d. 1840), he became a Ḥasid and the outstanding disciple of *Jacob Isaac ha-Ḥozeh ("the Seer") of Lublin. In addition, Ẓevi Hirsch studied with *Moses Leib of Sasov, whom he also considered to be his mentor, and with *Baruch of Medzhibezh, among others. Only after the death of Jacob Isaac of Lublin did he become the leader of a large ḥasidic community.

His unique approach to Ḥasidism, which aroused the opposition of other ḥasidic leaders, consisted in strengthening the kabbalistic-philosophical foundation of the movement. He wrote a number of important works on mysticism, and his disciples and followers were distinguished from other streams of Ḥasidism by their open and dedicated study of the system of Isaac *Luria, whose thought they considered to be a direct forerunner of Ḥasidism. Ẓevi Hirsch saw Ḥasidism as the means by which the ideals of the important later kabbalists could be put into practice, and, in addition, he maintained that no understanding of Ḥasidism was possible without a deep knowledge of Kabbalah.

Among his numerous disciples were his brother, Judah Ẓevi of Rozdol, and his nephew, Isaac Eizik of Komarno. The well-known *Malbim (Meir Leib b. Jehiel of Michael) studied Kabbalah under Ẓevi Hirsch. The 11th of Tammuz, the date of Ẓevi Hirsch's death, became a day of celebration, when his disciples, admirers, and the adherents of closely related ḥasidic sects made a pilgrimage to his grave. He was followed as leader of the Zhidachov dynasty by his brothers ISSACHAR LEIB (d. 1832) and MOSES OF SAMBOR, and then by his nephew, ISAAC EIZIK (1804–1872). Isaac Eizik, although a follower of a number of the great ḥasidic leaders of his generation, was primarily a devoted disciple of his uncle Ẓevi Hirsch. In addition, Isaac Eizik wrote ḥasidic works which are firmly based on a kabbalistic foundation and serve as a kind of bridge between Ḥasidism and Kabbalah. Isaac Eizik's sons and grandsons, who were rabbis and communal leaders in several places, continued the tradition of the dynasty, and were **admorim* in several centers.

Among the works of Ẓevi Hirsch are *Sur me-Ra va-Aseh Tov* (1835), preface to *Peri Eẓ Ḥayyim; Peri Kodesh Hillulim* (1836), on *Peri Eẓ Ḥayyim; Ateret Ẓevi* (1836), on the Zohar; *Beit Yisrael* (1834), on the Pentateuch. A book about his life and work is M. Braver's *Ẓevi la-Ẓaddik* (1931).

The works of Isaac Eizik include: *Likkutei Maharia* (1890), on *Yalkut Shimoni; Likkutei Torah ve-ha-Shas* (1886). M. Braver's *Pe'er Yizḥak* (1928) treats of his life and work. The entire Zhidachov dynasty is covered in I. Craker's *Eser Kedushot* (1906), and R. Mahler's *Ha-Ḥasidut ve-ha-Haskalah* (1961), which contains an index.

[Adin Steinsaltz]

ZHIRMUNSKY, VIKTOR MAKSIMOVICH (1891–1970), Russian philologist. Zhirmunsky was born in St. Petersburg, the son of a Jewish physician. He finished Tenishev School (1908) and St. Petersburg University (1912), where he studied German and Romance philology. After graduate study in Munich, Berlin, and Leipzig, he was appointed *privat-docent* at St. Petersburg (1915) and professor at Saratov University (1917). In 1919 he was appointed to the Chair of Germanic Philology in St. Petersburg (later Leningrad) University. Zhirmunsky's earliest scholarly publications were devoted to German Romanticism and modern mysticism (*Nemetskiy romantizm i sovremennaya mistika*, 1914). His dissertation, *Religioznoye otrecheniye v istorii romantizma* ("Religious Renunciation in the History of Romanticism"), was published in 1919. A regular contributor to *Russkaya mysl, Severnye zapiski, Vestnik literatury*, and other periodicals, he published several penetrating and erudite essays on contemporary Russian and European literature. In 1919–21, Zhirmunsky was closely associated with the Society for the Study of Poetic Language (O POYAZ). His later dispute with some of its members (notably B. Eichenbaum) became an important landmark in the history of the Russian Formal School.

A remarkably versatile literary scholar and linguist, Zhirmunsky worked in such diverse fields as theoretical poetics, Russian and comparative literature, Germanic philology, dialectology, Turkic and Slavic folklore, etc. During the 1920s, he published monographs on the composition of lyrical poetry (*Kompozitsiya liricheskikh stikhotvoreniy*, 1921; reprinted 1970), history and theory of rythme (*Rifma*, 1923; reprinted 1970), metrics (*Vvedenie v metriku*, 1925, reprinted 1971), the Romantic tradition in Russia (*Bryron i Pushkin*, 1929, reprinted 1970), and Russian Symbolism (*Poeziya Aleksandra Bloka*, 1922; *V. Bryusov i naslediye Pushkina*, 1922). His collected essays appeared in 1928 as *Voprosy teorii literatury* ("Problems of the Theory of Literature," reprinted 1962). In spite of the political persecution to which Zhirmunsky was subjected for his book *Natsionalny yazyk i sotsialnye dialekty* ("National Language and Social Dialects," 1936), his definitive study of Goethe's influence on Russian literature and a historical grammar of the German language were brought out in 1937–38. During World War II, Zhirmunsky lived in Central Asia. His post-war publications include *Uzbekskiy narodny geroicheskiy epos* ("Uzbek Heroic Epos," 1947), *Kirgizskiy geroicheskiy epos Manas* ("Manas, the Kirghiz Heroic Epos," 1948, 1961), *Nemetskaya dialektologiya* ("German Dialectology," 1956); *Epicheskoye tvorchestvo slavyanskikh narodov i problemy sravnitelnogo izucheniya eposa* ("The Epic Art of Slavic Peoples and the Problems of Comparative Epic Studies," 1958), *Drama A.. Bloka "Roza i Krest"* (1964), etc. Zhirmunky's study of Anna Akhmatova's poetry was published posthumously in 1972.

His *Vredenie v metriku* has appeared in English under the title *Introduction to Metrics* (1965); also in English is his "On Rhythmic Prose," in *To Honor Roman Jakobson*, 3 (1967), 2376–88.

[Omri Ronen]

BIBLIOGRAPHY: *V.M. Zhirmunsky* (1963); *Problemy sravnitel'noy filologii, Sb. st. k 70-letyu chl.-korr.* AN *S.S.S.R. V.M. Zhirmunskogo* (1964); V. Erlich, *Russian Formalism* (1965).

ZHITLOWSKY, CHAIM (1865–1943), Yiddish philosopher and writer. Zhitlowsky was the chief theoretician of *galut* ("Diaspora") nationalism and Yiddishism. Born in a small town near Vitebsk, Russia, he gave up his studies at 15 when he became a Socialist, and moved to Tula in Central Russia, where he joined the Narodniki, the anti-czarist populist movement. Engaged in propaganda among non-Jews, he was completely estranged from Jewish interests, but the pogroms of the 1880s brought him back to Vitebsk and to his Jewish roots. The Ḥibbat Zion movement, and particularly M.L. *Lilienblum, influenced him profoundly without converting him to Zionism. He believed that a full Jewish national life could be lived in the Diaspora. In 1886 he began research in Jewish history at St. Petersburg and in 1887 published his study in Russian on Judaism's historic destiny. A basic idea of this study was that the Jewish people in its difficult struggle for survival had become estranged from the historic ideals which had justified its existence. This study was violently attacked by S. *Dubnow in the Russian press, while the Hebrew press dubbed Zhitlowsky a Jewish antisemite and heretic. In 1888 Zhitlowsky left for Berlin and then moved to Zurich. He tried to convince the Russian Social Democratic leaders in exile of the desirability of issuing propaganda literature in Yiddish for the Jewish masses. He failed because these leaders, including the Jews among them, felt that publications in Yiddish might impede the complete assimilation of Jews to Russian ways. In his Zurich period, he also expressed his doubts as to the necessary connection between socialism and economic materialism. In 1892 he called upon Jewish intellectuals to return to their people, stating that not only equal civil rights but also equal national rights were needed for a Jewish resurgence, because Jews formed a distinct national group and must therefore strive for national emancipation. In 1893 he helped to found the Russian party of Socialist-Revolutionaries in exile and coedited its journal *Russky Rabochy.* He also founded a Jewish Socialist Union, which published socialist literature in Yiddish. He participated as a correspondent in the First Zionist Congress at Basle, 1897, but rejected Zionism as a reactionary movement dangerous for Eastern European Jewry. Only under socialism would Jews be redeemed as Jews and as workers. Jews need not emigrate to Zion. They could engage in productive labor and develop Jewish schools, universities, national and cultural institutions in their present countries. An article entitled "*Farvos Davke Yidish?*" ("Why Yiddish?"), written in 1897 and published in 1900, initiated his intensive activity as the theoretician of Yiddishism. He joined the *Bund in 1898, a year after its foundation, and published in its ideological organ *Der Yidisher Arbeter* his essay, "*Tsionizmus oder Sotsyalizmus*" (1899), in which he argued that socialism was not necessarily linked with faceless cosmopolitanism and nondescript humanity but afforded each nation an opportunity to develop its national uniqueness in multi-national states. The Kishinev pogroms in 1903 brought about a change of ideas and inclined him toward *Territorialism.

In 1904 Zhitlowsky arrived in the United States for a lecture tour on behalf of his Socialist-Revolutionary Party and stirred Jewish immigrant masses with his oratory. His lectures on "Jew and Man" and on "The Future of Peoples in America" opposed the melting-pot philosophy and advanced a United States of harmoniously functioning nationalities. These lectures converted many Yiddish-speaking cosmopolitan socialists into Jewish socialists. While in the United States, he became coeditor of the weekly *Dos Folk*, a territorialist socialist publication, in which he advocated a fusion of socialism and Jewish nationalism, of autonomy in the Diaspora and a Jewish territorial center. Returning to Europe, he was elected to the Second Russian Duma, and participated as chairman in the *Czernowitz Yiddish Conference of 1908. After 1908 he made his permanent home in New York, where he edited the monthly *Dos Naye Lebn* (1908–13), which was revived in 1922 with S. *Niger as coeditor. His two-volume work, *Di Filosofye, Vos Zi Iz un Vi Zi Hot Zikh Antvikelt* ("The Development of Philosophy," 1910), an outgrowth of lectures to American and Canadian audiences, was the first serious history of philosophy written in Yiddish. His *Gezamlte Shriftn* appeared in three editions (10 vols., 1912–19, 1929–32, and 1945–51). A Hebrew edition, *Ketavim*, with an introduction by R. Mahler, appeared in 1961. In 1914 Zhitlowsky visited Ereẓ Israel, became interested in Labor Zionism, and wrote pamphlets in the spirit of *Po'alei Zion. Returning to New York, he joined the staff of the Yiddish daily *The Day* and helped to found the *American Jewish Congress. He was an enthusiastic supporter of the establishment of the *Jewish Legion. Zhitlowsky translated Nietzsche's *Thus Spake Zarathustra* (1919) into Yiddish and wrote scholarly essays on Kant, Einstein, Job, and Faust.

In 1936 Zhitlowsky, who had been a lifelong, bitter foe of dogmatic Marxism and Bolshevism, was shocked into a more friendly attitude toward Soviet Russia by the ever increasing danger of Hitlerism. He endorsed Birobidzhan as the realization of his idea of a Jewish territory for productive Jewish masses. He justified Soviet actions, including the Moscow Trials of 1936. He considered the German persecution of the Jews as a punishment for the negative socioeconomic role played by the Jewish middle classes. As a result he became estranged from all except a pro-Soviet sector of his Jewish admirers during the last years of his life.

As the outstanding ideologist of Diaspora nationalism and Yiddishism, Zhitlowsky influenced the programs of all Jewish national parties, but only in his struggle against assimilationism was his influence profound and enduring, both in the former Russian Pale and among the American Jewish immigrants. More important than his theoretical justification for the existence of Yiddish was his practical application of Yiddish in his journalistic and scholarly style which delineated ideas and philosophical systems.

BIBLIOGRAPHY: Rejzen, Leksikon 1 (1928), 1118–36; LNYL, 3 (1960), 685–705; *Zhitlowsky Zamlbukh* (1929), incl. his bibl. 459–79; N. Mayzel, *Forgeyer un Mittsaytler* (1946), 147–81; S. Bickel, *Shrayber fun Mayn Dor*, 1 (1958), 195–203; 2 (1965), 288–94; S. Liptzin, *The Flowering of Yiddish Literature* (1963), 165–77.

[Jerucham Tolkes]

ZHITNITSKI, MARK (1903–?), Russian artist. Zhitnitski was born in Mogilev, Belorussia, and studied at the Moscow Art Institute from 1925 to 1932. From then until 1936 he worked as a book illustrator in Minsk, but in that year he was sentenced to ten years' hard labor in Siberia. Upon his release he resumed his artistic activity in Minsk for another three years, but was again exiled to Siberia. In 1956 he was "rehabilitated" and accepted as a member of the U.S.S.R. Artists Union. Many of his works have been acquired by Russian museums. Zhitnitski immigrated to Israel in 1971, and there completed a series of paintings entitled *Ha-Kotel ha-Ma'aravi* ("The Western Wall").

ZHITOMIR, city in Zhitomir district, Ukraine. Under Polish rule (until 1792) Jews were not authorized to live in Zhitomir, but some had settled there under the protection of government officials. In 1753 a *blood libel case was brought to court there; two Jews from the surrounding villages were executed and others were compelled to convert. In 1789 the Jewish community numbered 882, about a third of the total population. They comprised innkeepers, merchants, and craftsmen. When the city was annexed by Russia (1792), there were 1,300 Jews, and by 1847 their number had risen to 9,500. During this period, Ḥasidism spread to Zhitomir and *Ze'ev Wolf of Zhitomir was one of the disciples of the *Maggid of Mezhirech. With the establishment of the government-authorized rabbinical seminary there (1847), teachers and pupils of *maskilim* circles gathered in the city; they included H.S. *Slonimski, A.B. *Gottlober, and E. *Zweifel. In 1873 the rabbinical seminary was converted into a seminary for training teachers for the Jewish government schools. This seminary was closed in 1885. The first Jewish vocational school in Zhitomir was established in 1862 and enjoyed a good reputation, but it was closed in 1884 because the authorities believed that its instruction gave the Jews economic superiority over the Christians. *Mendele Mokher Seforim, A. *Paperna, and A. *Goldfaden also lived and studied in Zhitomir, and H.N. *Bialik (who was born in the village of Radi, near Zhitomir) spent his childhood there.

From the 1870s, the community shared in the general decline of the city following dispossession of the region's Polish landowners and the construction of the railroads, which initially bypassed Zhitomir. In 1897 there were 30,748 Jews who formed 46.6% of Zhitomir's total population; their number rose in 1910 to 38,427. Ninety per cent of those engaged in commerce were Jews, as were 60% of the city's craftsmen. In April 1905 pogroms broke out in the city at the government's instigation. The Jewish youth, Zionists and socialists, organized a *self-defense unit and fought with the rioters. About 15 Jews were killed, including the Russian student N. Blinov, who joined the Jewish self-defense action. Ten Jewish youths from the townlet of *Chudnov who were called in to assist the Jews of Zhitomir were murdered on their way there. In January 1919 pogroms were perpetrated by the Ukrainian army and a mob from the neighboring villages; 80 Jews lost their lives and much property was looted. In March 1919, after the soldiers of *Petlyura had captured Zhitomir from the Red Army, riots broke out and 317 Jews were murdered. At the time of the Polish conquest (1920), the Jews suffered from the brutality of the Polish soldiers. As soon as the Soviets gained control of the city, the organized community was liquidated and Jewish life disintegrated. In 1926 there were 30,000 Jews in the city (38% of the total population).

Many Jews fled from the city during the German occupation (1941). Those who remained, as well as many Jews from the neighboring townlets, were imprisoned in a ghetto and executed on Sept. 19, 1941. After the liberation of the city, thousands of Jews, former inhabitants as well as others, returned. According to the census in 1959, there were about 14,800 Jews (c. 14% of the total population) in Zhitomir, but the real number was probably closer to 25,000. There was a well-kept cemetery and a synagogue with a rabbi. During High Holidays thousands congregated in and around the synagogue. Yiddish was often heard in the streets. The synagogue building was ordered to be destroyed in 1962 to make way for a large apartment house, and the Jewish community rented a new apartment for its needs.

Until 1990, the city had approximately 12,000 Jews. After the Iron Curtain was lifted, thousands immigrated to Israel, the U.S., and Germany. Those that remained established congregations throughout the northern and western Ukraine. Zhitomir serves as the headquarters for 167 official congregations, 29 of which have their own synagogue and 28 that have their own daily Torah study groups. The Jewish community in Zhitomir itself has a synagogue, a community center, a *mikveh*, yeshivas, kindergartens, a day school, a university for men, a library, a soup kitchen, a women's club, a boarding house for boys and for girls, and a cemetery.

[Yehuda Slutsky / Ruth Beloff (2nd ed.)]

Hebrew Printing

The first Hebrew printing press in Zhitomir was established in 1804 by the wandering printer Ẓevi Hirsch b. Simeon ha-Kohen, who came from *Zolkiew (Zholkva), where he had worked as a typesetter. He had worked in the printing press in the town of *Nowy Dwor, and had subsequently possessed his own press in 1796 in Kopel, and in 1803–04 in Brezitz (Beresty). Ẓevi Hirsch had his printing press in Zhitomir until 1806, and during the three years of its existence at least nine books were published, five of which were ḥasidic and kabbalistic works. In 1847 a second printing press was established there by the three brothers Ḥanina Lipa, Aryeh Leib, and Joshua Heschel Shapira, sons of Samuel Abraham Abba

Shapira, the printer in *Slavuta. Until 1862 this was one of the only two Hebrew presses the Russian government permitted to operate in the whole of Russia, the other being in Vilna. This press had 18 hand presses and four additional large presses. In 1851 Aryeh Leib broke away and established his own printing press in Zhitomir. In these two establishments only sacred books of every kind were printed. During the years 1858–64 the press of the two brothers printed a beautiful edition of the Babylonian Talmud together with the *Halakhot* of Isaac *Alfasi, while between 1860 and 1867 Aryeh Leib printed an edition of the Jerusalem Talmud.

In 1865 a Hebrew printing press was established by Abraham Shalom Shadov, and in 1870 another one by Isaac Moses Bakst. In 1888 the Hebrew press of Brodovitz was founded, and in 1891 this passed into the possession of his successors. In c. 1890 a printing press was founded by Joseph Kesselman and in c. 1902 it passed into the possession of his widow Rachel, who entered into partnership with Elijah Feinberg. In these three presses all kinds of Hebrew and Yiddish books were printed.

[Avraham Yaari]

BIBLIOGRAPHY: M. Osherowitch, *Shtet un Shtetlekh in Ukraine* (1948), 269–78; Y. Hochfeld, in: *Yalkut Vohlin* (1950), 7:9–12; 10:7–8; A. Yaari, in: KS, 23 (1947), 243–8; H.D. Friedberg, *Toledot ha-Defus ha-Ivri be-Polanyah* (1950[2]), 134–5; S. Ginsberg, in: *Zukunft* (1932), 589–94.

ZHITOMIRSKI, ALEXANDER MATVEYEVICH (1881–1937), composer. Born in Kherson, Crimea, Zhitomirski studied violin with Mlynarsky in Odessa (1892–97) and with Prill in Vienna (1898–1900), where he also studied composition and piano. He graduated from the St. Petersburg Conservatory in 1910, and from 1915 to 1937 he taught there the theory of composition (from 1919 as professor). Among his students were such outstanding musicians as Andrey Balanchivadze, Mikhail Chulaki, Alexander Gauk, Khristofor Kushnarev, Alexander Melik-Pashaev, and Mikhail Yudin. His works include *Symphonic Poem* (1915); *Heroic Poem* for orchestra (1933); a violin concerto (1937); a string quartet (1927); *Elegy* for cello and piano; and songs to Russian, Yiddish, and French words. He was a member of the Society for Jewish Folk Music and collaborated with S. Kiselgov and P. Lvov in the publication of the Society's *Lider Zamlbukh* (1911, 1914[2]).

[M. Rizarev (2nd ed.)]

ZHMERINKA, city in Vinnitsa district, Ukraine. Before the 1917 Revolution it was a rural settlement in the province of Podolia. As it was an important railway junction (Kiev-Mogilev and Odessa-Lvov routes), a Jewish community developed there at the end of the 19th century. In 1897 there were 2,396 Jews (16.6% of the total population) in Zhmerinka. In 1903 it was excluded from the list of rural settlements where Jews were forbidden to reside. There were 5,186 Jews in the city (one-third of the total population) in 1926. During World War II Zhmerinka was incorporated into the Romanian occupation zone (*Transnistria). The Jews who had remained there and refugees from the surrounding district organized themselves into a community, and were joined by several hundreds of Jews who had been expelled from Romania. In June 1942 the Jews were concentrated within a ghetto, where they numbered 3,274. In March 1943 they were employed in forced labor at the railway station and in its vicinity. The Jews participated in the local partisan movement and in the battles for the liberation of the city in March 1944. In 1959 there were about 1,000 Jews (4% of the population) in Zhmerinka. Under the Soviet regime, the Jews gained notoriety for writing a letter to the newspaper *Pravda* in which they requested that the Russian authorities grant them permission to immigrate to Israel.

BIBLIOGRAPHY: PK Romanyah, 1 (1970), 440–1.

[Yehuda Slutsky]

ZHOLKVA (Pol. **Żółkiew**), city in Ukraine (formerly Galicia), renamed Nesterov in 1951. Jewish settlement in Zholkva began in the 16th century and the community became important; entries in its minute book *(pinkas)* commence from 1613. Thousands of Jewish fugitives took refuge in Zholkva during the *Chmielnicki massacres of 1648–49 and helped to defend it from the Cossacks, who agreed to lift their siege on the city on payment of 20,000 gulden. In the second half of the 17th century the community benefited from the general prosperity which Zholkva enjoyed as the patrimony of King John III Sobieski. A number of wealthy Jews with influence at court made their home in Zholkva. The magnificent fortified synagogue built in 1687 with the king's assistance, known as the "Sobieski Shul," was preserved until 1941. The favorable economic and cultural conditions which had made Zholkva one of the leading communities in the province of "Russia" (see *Councils of the Lands) came to an end in the second half of the 18th century; 2,100 Jewish inhabitants are recorded at this period, but in 1770 the city was devastated by a plague in which some 800 Jews died.

Leading members of the Zholkva community included John Sobieski's physician, Simḥah Menahem of Jona; the royal tax farmer Bezalel b. Nathan; the *parnas* Israel Isser b. Mordecai; and the *av bet din* Alexander *Schor. Between 1680 and 1730 Zholkva served as a center of the late Shabbatean movement in Poland (see *Shabbetai Ẓevi). Among the sectarians in Zholkva were Ḥayyim *Malakh, Fischel Zlochover, Isaac Keidaner, and Moses Meir Kaminski. At the end of the 18th century Zholkva became an important center of the Haskalah movement, particularly as Nachman *Krochmal lived there. Among scholars and writers of Zholkva in this period were Baruch Ẓevi Noy, principal of the Jewish-German school; Eliezer Favir, the Yiddish folklorist and author of the *Sippurei ha-Pela'ot* (1800); and Samson ha-Levi *Bloch, author of the popular geographical work *Shevilei Olam*. Ẓevi Hirsch *Chajes acted as *av bet din* between 1828 and 1852. Many of the Zholkva community were occupied in the fur industry, which began to develop in the 19th century and employed hundreds of workers. Emigré furriers from Zholkva, who acquired an international reputation, found their way to the great workshops of Paris, London, and Brussels. Educational and welfare institutions in Zholkva before World War II included a *talmud torah*, schools established by the *Tarbut and *Beth Jacob organizations, and orphanages which also provided vocational training. The annual budget of the community totaled 42,000 zlotys in 1937. The Jews in Zholkva numbered 4,100 (about half the total population) at the end of the 19th century; in 1931 there were 4,500.

[Aryeh-Leib Kalish]

Hebrew Printing

The first Hebrew press in the city was set up by the Amsterdam printer *Uri b. Aaron Phoebus ha-Levi in 1692 under license to John Sobieski. The first production appears to have been novellae by Samuel *Edels. For eight decades Uri Phoebus, his sons, grandsons, and other members of the family (Madpis, Grossmann, Rosanes) printed a great variety of books, covering all branches of Hebrew literature. Productions were generally of a high quality, with handsomely decorated title pages. The Letteris family, who were related to the Uri Phoebus clan, printed in the city from 1794 to 1828, moving their presses from *Lvov. In 1793 A.J.L. Mayerhofer obtained a printing license from the Austrian government, and he and his sons were active till 1830. Originally he was in partnership with M. Rubinstein, but they separated in 1797 and Rubinstein and his son continued on their own until well into the 19th century. Other Hebrew printers of importance in the 19th century were S.P. Stiller, who began work in 1859 and produced a Zohar (1862–64), and J.Z. Balaban, who established a press in 1862.

Holocaust Period

The Jewish population numbered over 5,000 in June 1941. After the outbreak of war between Germany and the U.S.S.R., the quick collapse of the Soviet front prevented Jews fleeing eastward from reaching safety. The Germans entered the city on June 28, 1941, and within a few days burned down its synagogues. Shortly thereafter, a *Judenrat was imposed by the Germans, headed by Febus Rubinfeld. The Germans imposed a "contribution" (fine) of 250,000 rubles, 5 kg. of gold, and 100 kg. of silver to be paid within three days. In early 1942 the Jewish population underwent registration which classified them into three categories: A – able-bodied for hard labor; B – capable of lighter work; C – "non-productive."

In an *Aktion* on March 15, 1942, the Germans rounded up 700 persons in the "C" category and dispatched them to the *Belzec death camp. The Judenrat meanwhile organized varied welfare activities to alleviate the suffering of the community. The Jews who escaped from the death train transports to Belzec were helped in particular. The train station in Zholkva served as a transit point for the death trains from the East. Although education of their children was prohibited, the Jews managed to set up a clandestine education program for groups of six to eight pupils under 30 teachers. In a second *Aktion* on Nov. 22–23, 1942, 2,500 persons were shipped to Belzec. Numerous victims attempted escape from the trains; the rails were strewn with their corpses. Very few made their way back to the city. That month a ghetto was set up for the Jews of Zholkva and the vicinity – mostly from Mosty Wielkie, Dobroszyce, Kulikow, Glinsk, and Wola Wysoka. An epidemic broke out, with a mortality rate rising to 20 a day. On March 15, 1943, over 600 men were taken to the Janowska Street labor camp in Lvov. The Germans and their Ukrainian helpers broke into the ghetto on March 25, 1943, and the inmates were rounded up in Dominikanski Square and taken to Borek forest, about 2 mi. from the city, near the road to Kamenka Bugskaya; there they were murdered and buried in mass graves. One hundred men and 70 women were spared and sent off to the Janowska Street camp. Only 70 others, skilled craftsmen, were still left in Zholkva, interned in a building on Sobieski Street. Some of them were killed later. Zholkva was taken by Soviet forces on July 23, 1944. About 70 Jews survived the Holocaust.

[Aharon Weiss]

BIBLIOGRAPHY: M. Baracz, *Pamiąãi miasta Zółkiew* (1877^2); S. Buber, *Kiryah Nisgavah* (1903); M. Balaban, in: *Jednošć*, no. 40 (1908); *Almanach gmin żydowskich* (1939), index. HEBREW PRINTING: Chajes, in: *Literaturblatt des Orients*, 2 (1841), 665ff.; B…, *ibid.*, 3 (1842), 473f.; M. Balaban, in: *Soncino Blaetter*, 3 (1929/30), 14ff.; Ḥ.D. Friedberg, *Toledot ha-Defus ha-Ivri be-Polanyah* (1950^2), 62ff.

ZHURAVNO (Pol. **Zurawno**), town in E. Drogobych district, Ukraine. In the early 18th century a Jewish community was organized in Zhuravno under the jurisdiction of the Lvov community. The Jews traded in wood and grain, and manufactured spirits. In 1765, 566 Jews paid the poll tax. The Jewish population numbered 2,197 (69% of the total) in 1880; 1,665 (61%) in 1890; 1,546 (53%) in 1900; and 1,338 (48%) in 1910. The hasidic movement of the nearby city of *Zhidachov greatly influenced the community. Between the world wars the town was included in Poland. In that period the Jewish population decreased, numbering only 867 (45%) in 1921.

[Shimshon Leib Kirshenboim]

Holocaust Period

On the outbreak of World War II there were about 1,300 Jews in Zhuravno. On Sept. 5, 1942, 500 Jews were deported to *Belzec death camp. On Sept. 29, 1942, the Jews were expelled to *Stry and shared the fate of that community. The remaining Jews were killed in Zhuravno in June 1943. After the war the Jewish community was not reconstituted.

BIBLIOGRAPHY: B. Wasiutyński, *Ludność żydowska w Polsce w wiekach XIX i XX* (1930), 124.

ZIBA (Heb. צִיבָא), servant of the house of *Saul, probably the official keeper of the household. Ziba informed *David about the whereabouts of *Mephibosheth, the lame son of *Jonathan, when David sought to locate the surviving members of the house of Saul in order to show them kindness or to put them under surveillance (II Sam. 9:1–4). Ziba was appointed the land administrator of Saul's private property which David restored to Mephibosheth. Consequently Ziba's household of 15 sons and 20 servants became servants of Mephibosheth (II Sam. 9:9ff.).

When David was forced to flee Jerusalem during *Absalom's rebellion, he was greeted by Ziba with essential food supplies (II Sam. 16:1ff.). Ziba made David believe that his master Mephibosheth willingly remained in the city in the hope that the throne would be restored to him (II Sam. 16:3). Consequently David transferred all of Mephibosheth's possessions to Ziba on the spot, as it was customary for kings to do with a rebel's property. After Absalom's rebellion was suppressed, Ziba recrossed the Jordan ahead of the king, and may have been of help in persuading the Benjamites to come to welcome David at the Jordan (II Sam. 19:18–19). Mephibosheth was also among those who came to greet the king, and he exposed his servant's duplicity to David, by explaining that he had intended to join David in his flight and that Ziba, taking advantage of his lameness, had made off with the already saddled asses. David, prompted by a feeling of gratitude to Ziba on one hand and a belief in the integrity of Mephibosheth's account on the other, ruled that Saul's property should be divided equally between the two (II Sam. 19:25ff.).

ẒIDDUK HA-DIN (Heb. צִדּוּק הַדִּין; lit. "acknowledgment of [Divine] justice"), the term for the Jewish burial service. The service commences with the recitation of Deuteronomy 32:4, "The Rock! – His deeds are perfect, yea, all His ways are just…" and includes a reading of Jeremiah 32:19; Psalms 92:16; Job 1:21; and other verses. It concludes with Psalms 78:38; Isaiah 25:8; the benediction "Who formed you in judgment…" and the *Kaddish le-Ḥadata*. On the days when *Taḥanun* is not said, Psalm 16 replaces the opening verses in some rites. Various parts of the prayer are mentioned in the Talmud. Ḥanina b. Teradyon quoted the first half of Deuteronomy 32:4 before being executed by the Romans, his wife completed the verse, and his daughter recited Jeremiah 32:19 (Av. Zar. 18a). The special *Kaddish*, which includes references to Erez Israel and expresses a hope that the Temple may be rebuilt, is mentioned in *Soferim* 19:12. The benediction is cited in the Tosefta (Ber. 7:6 in a different version; cf. the *baraita* in Ber. 58b). The present form dates from the geonic period (Zunz, Lit Poesie, 21).

BIBLIOGRAPHY: Abrahams, Companion, ccxxvi–ccxxx; Idelsohn, Liturgy, 171f.

ŽÍDEK, PAVEL (1413–1471), Czech scholar and the first individual of Jewish origin to contribute to Czech culture. Žídek was baptized in his youth and raised as a Hussite but, while studying at Vienna, embraced Catholicism and became a priest. An outstanding scholar, he received doctorates at three universities, earning renown as well as enmity through his learned disputations at Prague, Breslau, and Cracow. Žídek's quarrelsome disposition drove him from place to place until he found refuge at the court of the progressive Czech king George of Podebrad. Žídek's one surviving work is his *Správovna* ("Administration," 1908), a book of suggestions to the king, which prescribes everything from the monarch's attire to the principles of good state administration. Žídek piously concludes that the king should join the Catholic Church, thus uniting all the Christians of his kingdom.

BIBLIOGRAPHY: P. Váša and A. Gregor, *Katechismus dějin české literatury* (1925); J. Staněk, *Dějiny literatury české* (1925). **ADD. BIBLIOGRAPHY:** J. Hrabák, *Dějiny české literatury III* (1961)

[Avigdor Dagan]

ŽIDOVSKÁ STRANA (Czech "Jewish Party"), national Jewish party in Czechoslovakia. It was founded at the first conference of nationalist Jewry held in the Czechoslovak Republic, convened in Prague on the initiative of the Jewish National Council at the beginning of January 1919. The party aimed to secure representation of the Jewish national minority in the institutions of the new state and the local authorities. The party was joined by Zionists of every trend, with the exception of *Po'alei Zion, which advocated independent political activity of Labor, and of Jews of nationalist outlook not within the Zionist Organization. The principal objective, to assure parliamentary representation for the Jewish minority, was not achieved from the beginning, although the Jewish Party gained about 80,000 votes in the first elections (1920) and almost 100,000 votes in the second (1925). This was because the election law stipulated that only a list that obtained 20,000 votes in at least one electoral district, or a sufficient number of votes for the election of a deputy in a district on the first ballot, could be represented. Since the Jews were dispersed throughout the state, they could, even theoretically, obtain this number only in one electoral district – and they failed to do so.

In the third elections (1929), the Jewish Party joined forces with the Polish minority party and thus succeeded in sending its first two deputies to parliament. These were Ludvik *Singer (after his death in 1931 replaced by Angelo *Goldstein) and Julius Reisz. At the fourth elections (1935), it was no longer possible to form a political Polish-Jewish alliance because the Poles had begun to adopt a hostile policy toward the Czechoslovak Republic. The Jewish Party concluded an elections agreement with the Czech Social Democratic Party, which included two representatives of the Jewish Party within its list. Although this decision won the acclaim of Po'alei Zion, it was criticized by conservative circles of the Jewish Party. In these elections Angelo Goldstein and Ḥayyim *Kugel were elected. The Jewish Party was also represented in the provincial diets of Moravia-Silesia and Slovakia, and in many municipal councils. Its outstanding leaders included, in addition to the parliamentary deputies, František Friedmann, Emil *Margulies, and Arnošt Frischer.

Although the party is regularly discussed as a single body, it actually represented three different sectors of Jewry, which in the political sphere also expressed local attitudes and interests. In the Czech-speaking lands (Bohemia, Moravia, and Czech Silesia), the Jews had experienced a long uphill struggle, but by now it had reached a mature stage. In the Czechoslovak Republic, the Jewish Party embodied the desire of the middle class and the secular elements, who expected it to take care of the general needs of the Jewish population, as any Western European party does.

In Slovakia, the party upheld the local interests of the population regarding its religious and social needs. On a national level, it promoted ethnic-Jewish demands and fostered Zionist policies. In this endeavor it clashed with the leaders of the Czech countries; while devout Zionists, they misunderstood the desires of Slovak Jewry. The strength of Slovak Orthodoxy, hostile to Zionism and cherishing its own material and political interests, inhibited the abilities of the party in Slovakia. In Carpatho-Rus the party expressed the desire for modernization within a part of the Jewish masses. Zionism, especially among the youth, also expressed the desire to escape the squalid conditions of Carpatho-Rus. Here the party encountered stubborn opposition on the part of the Orthodox, headed by the ḥasidic rabbi of Mukachevo, Chaim Eleazar Shapira. In elections the Jewish Party, especially in the eastern parts of the Republic, was exposed to machinations and intrigue on the part of the Agrarian Party in cooperation with the Orthodox. There was also competition from Czech, German, and Magyar assimilationists. Another problem expressed itself in the conflict between the need for domestic policies ("Landespolitik") of the electorate and the Zionist desires of the ideological political elites of the party.

During World War II, Frischer represented the Jewish minority in the Czechoslovak National Council in Exile in London. When Czechoslovak independence was renewed after the Holocaust, there was no longer room for political activity by national minorities, and the Jewish Party was not reorganized.

BIBLIOGRAPHY: A.M.K. Rabinowica, "The Jewish Party," in: *The Jews of Czechoslovakia,* vol. 2 (1971), 235–345; M. Crhova, "Jewish Politics in Central Europe: the Case of the Jewish Party in Interwar Czechoslovakia."

[Chaim Yahil / Yeshayahu Jelinek (2nd ed.)]

ZIEGFELD, FLORENZ (1869–1932), U.S. showman. Ziegfeld, born in Chicago, started his career at the Chicago World Fair, 1893, and staged his first production in 1896 in New York. His star was Anna Held, whom he had brought from Europe and later married, and he publicized the show with front-page advertising, a device which subsequently became his hallmark. In 1907, after a visit to Paris, he launched the *Ziegfeld Follies* and presented new editions periodically until 1931. These extravaganzas included lavish arrays of beautiful showgirls and set the standard for Broadway musical revues. Ziegfeld became known as "the glorifier of the American girl" and "the apostle of the beauty show." His many other productions included *Showboat* (1927 and 1932) and *Rio Rita* (1927), which opened at the Ziegfeld Theater built for him by William Randolph Hearst. Ziegfeld's productions brought fame to many stars, including Eddie *Cantor and Will Rogers. The film *The Great Ziegfeld* told the story of his career.

BIBLIOGRAPHY: DAB, 20 (1936), 653–4; L. Morris, *Curtain Time* (1953), 295–6, 308–9, 313–4; *Oxford Companion to the Theater* (1957^2), 854.

[Lee Healey]

ZIEGLER, ARCHIBALD (1903–1971), painter and sculptor. Ziegler was born in London and belonged to the group of "second-generation" Anglo-Jewish artists. Following his first one-man exhibition at the Whitechapel Art Gallery in 1932, he was commissioned to execute a series of large murals at Toynbee Hall, the famous East London community and educational center. His only Jewish commission was for stained-glass windows at the Walthamstow and Leyton Synagogue, London. From 1938 he was a visiting lecturer at the St. Martin's School of Art. Ziegler was closely connected with the Ben Uri Art Gallery and Society, a unique center in London for Jewish art activities. He was principally a painter of landscape, a favorite subject being Hampstead Heath in London, where he lived. In his later years he took up sculpture and had considerable success as a portraitist; his bust of Norman Bentwich was presented to the Hebrew University, Jerusalem.

[Charles Samuel Spencer]

ZIEGLER, IGNAZ (1861–1948), scholar. Ziegler, who was born in Dolny Kubin, Slovakia, studied at the rabbinical seminary and the University of Budapest. During the period of his studies, he was influenced by the Reform movement and from 1888 served as liberal rabbi of Carlsbad, where he accomplished a great deal for the Jewish community. Ziegler sympathized with Zionism.

His research dealt with the Bible, Talmud and Midrash, Jewish religious philosophy, and Jewish history. In his most important work, *Die Koenigsgleichnisse des Midrasch* (1903), he dealt with the "parables of kings in the Midrash" in the light of the historical and factual reality of the Roman Empire. His other important works are: *Religioese Disputationen im Mittelalter* (1894); *Die Geschichte des Judenthums* (1900); *Die Geistesreligion und das juedische Religionsgesetz* (1912); *Dokumente zur Geschichte der Juden in Karlsbad (1791–1869)* (1913); *Das magische Judentum* (1923); and the two-volume *Die sittliche Welt des Judentums*, 2 vols. (1924–28).

BIBLIOGRAPHY: BLBI, 2 (1958–59), 211–22 (autobiography).

[Moshe David Herr]

ZIFF, MORRIS (1913–2005), U.S. rheumatologist. Ziff was born in Brooklyn, New York, and earned his B.S. (1934) and Ph.D. (1937) in chemistry from New York University (NYU) where he was a postdoctoral research chemist with Erwin Chargaff (1939–41). The difficulties of pursuing a career in basic science persuaded him to obtain his M.D. (1948) from NYU Medical College where he worked as a clinical and research rheumatologist (1950–58) and was head of clinical research from 1952. In 1958 he moved to the University of Texas Southwestern Medical School in Dallas as professor of medicine and founding director of the Rheumatic Diseases Division. He became an Ashbel Smith Professor (1981), the highest professorial rank in the university, and he remained chief of rheumatology until 1984. He was founding director of the Harold C. Simmons Arthritis Research Center (1983–84), and he continued his research and clinical activities as professor emeritus until 1999. Ziff pursued a career-long interest in the immunological and inflammatory mechanisms that affect joints in rheumatoid arthritis and are widespread in the body in other rheumatic diseases. He used his laboratory discoveries to develop tests of clinical value for diagnosis and assessing disease activity. His ideas inspired similar research in most major rheumatology centers in the world. His program of integrated laboratory and clinical studies also became an accepted model for organizing research in this field. His identification of cytokines as the factors that stimulate joint inflammation was an important contribution to the current development of monoclonal antibodies for controlling rheumatic diseases. In addition to his research skills, Ziff was an outstanding clinician and teacher. His extraordinary blend of scientific rigor, intellectual curiosity, and human sympathy inspired the 131 research fellows he trained to pursue similar, often outstanding careers throughout the world. His many honors included the Heberden Medal of the British Society for Rheumatology (1964), the Carol Nachman Prize (1974), the Bunim Medal of the Pan-American Congress of Rheumatology (1982), and the first Gold Medal of the American College of Rheumatology (1988).

[Michael Denman (2nd ed.)]

ZIFRONI, ISRAEL BEN DANIEL (16th century), Hebrew printer. Zifroni was a native of Guastalla, near Padua, Italy, and lived in Gazzuolo. In 1567 he worked as corrector in *Sabbioneta for Vicenzo Conti, who produced three works, among them Menahem b. Zeraḥ's halakhic compendium *Ẓeidah la-Derekh*. The period of his finest achievements was 1578–83, when among other works he printed a fine edition of the Talmud (1578–80) for Ambrosius Froben in *Basle, and a Pentateuch with *haftarot*, the Five Scrolls, etc. (1583) for Th. Guarin. Because of difficulties with the Basle city fathers, Froben and Zifroni printed some of their works in *Freiburg-im-Breisgau, such as Aaron of Pesaro's *Toledot Aharon*, Benjamin of Tudela's *Masot*, and a Judeo-German paraphrase of Berechiah ha-Nakdan's *Mishlei Shu'alim* (1584). Zifroni eventually returned to Italy, where he worked for Di Gara of Venice as corrector (from 1588). Zifroni's son MOSES ELISHAMA also became a Hebrew printer and was active in *Mantua for T. Ruffinelli and the brothers I. and S. Norzi (1593–97), after which he joined his father in Venice.

BIBLIOGRAPHY: D.W. Amram, *Makers of Hebrew Books in Italy* (1909), index; M. Steinschneider, *Juedische Typographie* (1938²), 2 ff.; J. Prijs, *Baseler hebraeische Drucke* (1964), index.

ZIKHRONOT (Heb. זִכְרוֹנוֹת; "remembrance" verses), name of one of the benedictions in the *Musaf* prayer of *Rosh Ha-Shanah. This section begins with *Attah zokher* ("Thou rememberest") and contains ten biblical verses (four from the Pentateuch, three from Psalms, and three from the Prophets) praising God who remembered, among other things, *Noah during the flood, the Israelites in Egyptian slavery, and His covenant with Abraham, Isaac, and Jacob. The prayer closes with a plea that God remember the binding of Isaac (see *Akedah), and, through Abraham's merit, bestow mercy upon his descendants. These *Zikhronot* verses express the most characteristic significance of Rosh Ha-Shanah, the Jewish New Year, as a "Day of Remembrance" (*Yom ha-Zikkaron*). At the end of their recital (as with the **Malkhuyyot* and **Shofarot* verses) the *shofar* is sounded. The reciting of the *Zikhronot* on Rosh Ha-Shanah is mentioned already in the Mishnah (RH 4:5–6) and is believed to have been part of the Rosh Ha-Shanah liturgy in the Temple.

BIBLIOGRAPHY: Elbogen, Gottesdienst, 141–4; E. Munk, *The World of Prayer*, 2 (1963), 202–4; Abrahams, Companion, cxcviii f.; Eisenstein, Dinim, 232f.

ZIKHRON YA'AKOV (Heb. זִכְרוֹן יַעֲקֹב), village with municipal council status in N. Israel, on the southern spur of Mount Carmel. Founded in 1882 by Jews from Romania, it was one of the earliest settlements of the Ḥovevei Zion movement. Zikhron Ya'akov was initially called by the Arabic name of the site, Zammrin, which was erroneously supposed to be derived from "Shomron." The following year, Baron Edmond de *Rothschild took a personal and financial interest in the village and named it Zikhron Ya'akov ("Memory of Jacob") after his father, James de Rothschild. On his initiative wine grapes were introduced as a principal agricultural branch, and one of the two large wine cellars established in the country (the other is at *Rishon le-Zion) was built. After a short time, however, the vineyards were seriously hit by the *Phylloxera* pest, and the vines had to be replaced by strains introduced from America. In 1903 a convention of the Jewish settlers of Ereẓ Israel was held at Zikhron Ya'akov to create a kind of Jewish umbrella organization. M.M. *Ussishkin addressed the meeting, at which the *Teachers Association (*Histadrut ha-Morim*) was founded. The physician Hillel *Joffe, known for his fight against malaria, lived in Zikhron Ya'akov, as did the botanist and agronomist Aaron *Aaronsohn and his sister *Sarah, who founded the secret *Nili intelligence group in World War I; their home was later turned into a museum. Zikhron Ya'akov started becoming a holiday resort in the late 1930s and 1940s. One of the first and important centers was the artists' rest home, Bet Dani'el (on the Bentwich-Lange-Friedlaender estate), which was named after the young pianist Daniel Friedlaender. In the first years of Israel's statehood the village expanded considerably when it absorbed many new immigrants. In 1950 Zikhron Ya'akov received council municipal status. In the 1960s, however, its population remained static, with 4,470 inhabitants in 1968. Farming, in which vineyards and other fruit orchards continue to be prominent, was important along with industry (the wine cellar, a hosiery plant producing for export, and smaller enterprises), tourism, and recreation. In

1963 a group of Christians from Germany established a closed community in the northern part of the town, run like a kibbutz and operating factories for air purification systems, blankets, and processed foods. In the mid-1990s the population of Zikhron Ya'akov expanded to approximately 8,090, rising further to 14,300 in 2002 with new neighborhoods coming into existence. The municipality developed the original first street of the moshavah into a tourist attraction.

In 1954 Baron de Rothschild's remains were transferred to a mausoleum, surrounded by beautiful gardens, at Zikhron Ya'akov. Also buried in the village is the labor leader David *Remez, who spent many years there as a pioneer and labor organizer, and in whose honor a large rest house of Kuppat Ḥolim, Bet Remez, is named.

[Shaked Gilboa (2nd ed.)]

ZIKLAG (Heb. צִקְלַג), town apportioned to the tribe of Simeon along with Hormah and Beth-Marcaboth (Josh. 19:5). It was later included in Judah where it was part of the first district, again with Hormah (Josh. 15:31). According to I Samuel 27:6, it was given to David, then a refugee from the persecution of Saul, by Achish, the Philistine ruler of Gath; therefore, at that time, it must have been within the orbit of Philistine power. It was David's base till the time of the battle of Gilboa; after he was sent away from Aphek by the Philistines, he found the city burned by the Amalekites, whom he pursued and destroyed (I Sam. 30). From Ziklag David sent the spoils from this battle to various cities in Judah and there he heard, on the third day after his return, the grievous news of the fall of Saul and Jonathan; after slaying the messenger, he made his famous lament there (II Sam. 1:17ff.). David was joined in Ziklag by his "mighty men" (I Chron. 12:1ff.) and from the city he went to claim the kingship of Judah. It was one of the places inhabited by Jews after the return from the Babylonian exile (Neh. 11:28). Eusebius locates the place in the Daromas (Onom. 156: 11). Most scholars, following A. Alt, have identified Ziklag with Tell al-Ḥuwaylifa, a prominent tell 20 mi. (32 km.) southwest of Hebron, in a pass on the fringe of the Judean mountains; as this site does not seem to fall within the area of Philistine domination, however, *Press and *Aharoni have suggested Tell al-Shariʿa further to the west, which others have identified with Gerar.

BIBLIOGRAPHY: Alt, in: JPOS, 15 (1935), 317ff.; Press, Ereẓ, 4 (1955), 806f.; Aharoni, Land, index.

[Michael Avi-Yonah]

ZILBER, LEV ALEKSANDROVICH (1894–1966). Russian microbiologist, virologist, and immunologist. He was the brother of B.A. *Kaverin. Zilber graduated from St. Petersburg University in 1915 and Moscow University in 1919. He began to work at the Institute of Microbiology of the People's Kommisariat of Health in 1921.

Due to the fact that he was an honest and principled researcher, Zilber more than once suffered repression: between 1937 and 1939 and from 1940 to 1944, he was incarcerated in Soviet "corrective labor" camps. From 1939 to 1940 he headed the department of virology, and in 1945 the department of immunology and malignant growths at the Institute of Epidemiology and Microbiology of the Academy of Medical Sciences of the U.S.S.R. From 1945 he was a member of this academy. His scientific fields of interest encompassed the variability of microorganisms and immunology. In 1937 he described a previously unknown viral disease: Far Eastern tick elephantiasis. In 1945 he began elaborating a viral theory of the origin of cancer. He was awarded a Stalin Prize in 1946 and a joint State Prize posthumously in 1967, for the discovery of the pathogenesis of the Raus chicken sarcoma in other kinds of animals.

[*The Shorter Jewish Encyclopedia in Russian*, Jerusalem]

ZILBERTS, ZAVEL (1881–1949), composer, conductor, and *ḥazzan*. Born in Karlin, near Pinsk, Russia, Zilberts became his father's successor as *ḥazzan* upon the latter's death in 1895, and by the age of 18 he was singing his own compositions. After studying music at the conservatory in Warsaw, he became conductor of the famous Hazomir choral society in Lodz. Between 1907 and 1914 he was choir master in the Central Synagogue, Moscow. He returned to Lodz for another six years before emigrating to the U.S. in 1920. Striving for the establishment of a pure, unaccompanied choral style, he founded the Zilberts Choral Society in 1930 and became musical director of the Jewish Ministers-Cantors Association of America, composing a large number of liturgical pieces and choral arrangements for concert appearances organized by the Association.

His liturgical compositions were often based on motifs from biblical cantillations. His setting of **Havdalah* is widely known and has been sung and recorded by many *ḥazzanim*. Zilberts wrote the biblical cantatas *Jacob's Dream* and *Am Yisrael Ḥai*, and published *Neginot Yisrael* (1932) and *Music for the Synagogue* (1943).

BIBLIOGRAPHY: A. Fishman, in: *Jewish Review* (Feb. 10, 1949); H. Lefkowitch, in: *Proceedings of the Ninth Annual Conference-Convention of the Cantors Assembly of America* (1956), 25–30; I. Rabinovitch, *Of Jewish Music* (1952), 230–2, 240–1.

[David M.L. Olivestone]

ZILBOORG, GREGORY (1890–1959), psychiatrist. Zilboorg was born in Kiev, Russia. He served as a physician in the Russian army, participated in the first revolution in Petrograd in 1917, and was secretary to the Ministry of Labor in the cabinets of Prince Lvov and Kerensky. He edited a daily paper in Kiev until the German occupation. Zilboorg was forced to leave Russia in 1919, when he settled in the U.S. He graduated from the Columbia College of Physicians and Surgeons, New York City, in 1926, and was at the Berlin Psychoanalytic Institute from 1929 to 1930. After 1931 he entered private practice in psychiatry and psychoanalysis. He was a member of the Committee for the Study of Suicide, assistant clinical professor of psychiatry in the New York Medical College, and on the Consulting Delegation on Criminology to the United Nations.

Zilboorg's research and writings extend over several particular fields. His two major works were *The Medical Man and the Witch During the Renaissance* (1935) and *A History of Medical Psychology* (in collaboration with George W. Henry; 1941). His historical work was followed by *Mind, Medicine and Man* (1943), *Sigmund Freud* (1951), *The Psychology of the Criminal Act and Punishment* (1954), and *Freud and Religion* (1958). Among Zilboorg's shorter works three deal with suicide: *Suicide among Civilized and Primitive* (1936), *Differential Diagnostic Types of Suicide* (1936), and *Considerations on Suicide…* (1937). His paper "On Social Responsibility" in *Searchlights on Delinquency* (ed. K.R. *Eissler, 1948) provides an insight into Zilboorg's view of the role of psychoanalysis vis-à-vis the problems of society.

BIBLIOGRAPHY: A. Grinstein, *Index of Psychoanalytic Writings*, 4 (1958); 8 (1965), incl. bibl.

[Louis Miller]

ZILINA (Slovak. **Žlina**; Hung. **Zsolna**; Ger. **Sillein**), town in N.W. Slovakia. After the repulsion of the Tatar invasion in the 13th century, King Béla IV of Hungary elevated Zilina to the status of a royal city and invited Jews and Germans to the abandoned and depopulated town, granting them certain important privileges. The town later suffered severely from various vicissitudes and was repeatedly burned down; the town archives therefore retain no documents concerning Jewish life there in this period.

Many of the inhabitants were German settlers, and the authorities prevented Jews from settling in Zilina. Even the *Toleranzpatent* of Josef II did not alter the situation. In 1840 the Hungarian parliament permitted Jews to settle in most places, but Zilina authorities still tried to prohibit Jewish settlement. Jews settled in nearby villages, such as Rajec and Varin. After the prohibition was lifted in 1840, Jews moved to Zilina. A commercial crossroads, it attracted Jewish businessmen. In 1834 there were 13 Jews in Zilina; in 1840, there were 22; in 1880 there were 619; in 1910 there were 1,467; and in 1940 there were 2,919. Most were deported in 1942 to extermination camps in Poland. In 1947, there were 497 Jews living in Zilina. Some 700 local Jews survived the Holocaust.

In 1852 Jewish communal life began in the town. There was a small synagogue, a *ḥeder*, a *ḥevra kaddisha*, and a cemetery. In 1861 the synagogue was enlarged, and there was a school, a *mikveh*, and a kosher slaughterhouse. After Zilina became an important railway center, more Jews moved in. They established saw mills and textile factories. Through Jewish initiative, Zilina became the center of the Slovakian timber trade.

After the Jewish Congress of 1868, the congregation chose the Reform path until 1921, when several hundred formed an Orthodox congregation. In 1938 a small group of Ḥasidim established a place of prayer following *nusaḥ sefarad*.

The Jewish community became a center of political and cultural activity. With the foundation of the Czechoslovak state, a group of Jews asked to be recognized as Slovaks of the Mosaic creed. They were followed by intensive Zionist activity. The city became a leading center of the Jewish Party, and its candidate served a long stint as deputy mayor. The Zionist movement had a major branch in Zilina, which included several youth movements. The Maccabi sports organization was well established and boasted several national champions.

After the Munich treaty of September 1938, Slovak nationalists, mainly in the Hlinka Slovak People's Party, proclaimed autonomy for Slovakia within the Czechoslovak Republic. The proclamation took place in Zilina. On March 14, 1939, Slovakia proclaimed independence under the aegis of Berlin. The new state immediately embarked on persecuting Jews. All Jewish children were expelled from non-Jewish schools and autonomous Jewish institutions were outlawed. In 1940 many Jews were expelled from Bratislava, and some settled in Zilina. Thus the Jewish population rose to 3,500.

In March 1942 the deportation of Jews from Slovakia to extermination centers in Poland began. Being close to the Polish border and a central transportation hub, Zilina was the final preparation point for Poland-bound transports. The living conditions were so squalid and the Hlinka Guard so brutal that the state had to intervene. While waiting for their transport, the inmates were forced to work on building a soccer stadium, which is still in use.

In 1943–44 the remaining Jewish community helped Jewish refugees from Poland, who had crossed the Slovak border illegally, to cross the Hungarian border to safety. In August 1944 the Slovak Uprising began, and Zilina became a hiding place. Jews caught by the Germans were sent to Poland.

Zilina was liberated in spring 1945, and the small community attempted to rebuild its Jewish life. A synagogue was renovated, and the cemetery was cleaned up. A public kitchen distributed food to the homeless returnees and the Displaced Persons on their way home. Zilina also became a center of *"illegal" immigration (Aliyah B) on the way to Palestine.

The Zionist youth movements flourished, preparing their members for Palestine. In the cemetery a memorial to victims of the Holocaust was erected. In the 1950s the Jews suffered badly under the Communist regime. In 1967 there were 254 Jews in Zilina.

During the Prague Spring of 1968 whoever could leave the country did so; mainly the elderly remained. After the Velvet Revolution (1989), the community organized public life again. The Reform synagogue was sold and became a concert hall. June 17 is the memorial day of the Zilina congregation; in 2004 a memorial to the Jews who perished at the transportation center was erected, made of twisted railway tracks.

BIBLIOGRAPHY: M. Lányi and H. Propper, *A szlovenszkói zsidó hitközségek története* (1933); Z. Lippa and I. Halpert, in: *Die aussaeen unter Traenen mit Jubel werden sie ernten*, ed. by R. Iltis (1959), 206–11. **ADD. BIBLIOGRAPHY:** E. Bàrkàny and L. Dojč, *Židovské náboženské obce na Slovensku* (1991).

[Elieser Beck / Yeshayahu Jelinek (2nd ed.)]

ZILKHA, family of bankers originating in *Baghdad. KHEDOURY ZILKHA (1884–1956), a descendant of textile traders, founded the family banking house in Baghdad in 1899 with a capital of $250. Baghdad's rising importance as a communications and trading center contributed to his success as a banker. Under the threat of extortionists he left Baghdad in 1926 and as a result, interest rates rose considerably in the Baghdad bazaar. In 1927 Zilkha opened a bank in *Beirut, followed by branches in *Damascus (1935) and *Cairo (1937). In 1941 Zilkha settled in the United States where he and his four sons, MAURICE (1917–1964), ABDULLA (1913–), Ezra (1925–), and SELIM (1927–), began to operate a successful worldwide network of financing and foreign exchange operations. In 1950, however, the original Baghdad house was seized by the Iraqi government, and in 1956 the Cairo firm was expropriated by the Egyptian government.

[Joachim O.Ronall]

ZILKHA, NAʿIM (1879–1929), Iraqi lawyer. Zilkha started to practice law in his native *Baghdad in 1904. In 1908 he became a member of the Beirut Court of Appeals, retaining his post for over ten years and rising to deputy president of the court. Returning to *Iraq in 1921, he became deputy president of the *Basra civil courts, and in 1922 president of the Diyala Province civil courts. He was elected to the Iraqi House of Representatives in 1925 and remained a member until his death. He was one of the few young Jews in the Iraqi House of Representatives who had the courage to express opposition to the government. In 1925 he was also appointed lecturer at the Baghdad law school, and became active in the Jewish community council; he was elected chairman of the "Jeshmi Committee," in charge of the secular affairs of the Jewish community, and held this position until his death. He made attempts to introduce reforms in the life of the Jewish community and to restrict the influence of religious dignitaries and the rich; he succeeded in forcing Rabbi *Dangoor to resign from his post as head of the community. Zilkha's sudden death put an end to the reforms that he had initiated.

[Hayyim J.Cohen]

ZILPAH (Heb. זִלְפָּה), handmaid of *Leah and concubine of *Jacob. *Laban gave Zilpah to his daughter Leah as a handmaid on the occasion of Leah's marriage to Jacob (Gen. 29:24; 46:18). A parallel custom is attested in the *Nuzi Documents. When Leah ceased bearing children she presented Zilpah to her husband as a concubine (30:9; 37:2), just as her sister *Rachel had previously done with her own maid *Bilhah (30:3). Two sons, *Gad and *Asher, were born of the union between Jacob and Zilpah (30:10–13; 35:26). Sixteen descendants of Zilpah are listed in the Genesis genealogies (46:18). There is no further mention of Zilpah in the Bible.

ZIM, Israel Navigation Company Ltd., founded in June 1945 by the Jewish Agency, the Histadrut, and the Palestine Maritime League in order to build a merchant fleet that would make the prospective Jewish state independent of foreign shipping, as well as to exploit the sea as a source of income. The word *ẓim* means ships and appears in the Bible (Num. 24:24). The Jewish Agency held 45% of the shares, the Histadrut 45%, and the Palestine Maritime League 10%. Supreme control by the future state was ensured in the articles of the company by a governor's share that gave its owners public-political control. In 1959 the government became a one-third partner in the company; in 1965 its share rose to 80%. Zim's first ship, purchased in January 1947 in partnership with a British company, was the 3,500-ton *Kedmah*, which opened a passenger and cargo service between Haifa and Marseilles. After the establishment of the State of Israel, it became vital to transport immediately the mass of refugees from Europe. Zim then merged with Oniyyot u-Sefinot, a branch of the Mosad, the organization for "illegal" immigration, which at the time owned many boats that had been confiscated by the British authorities. Some of the vessels were found suitable for the transport of immigrants; others were used to form the Israel navy.

In 1951 Zim, for the first time, ordered two new cargo boats. After the reparations agreement was signed between Israel and West Germany, Zim received purchase credits and, between 1953 and 1955, ordered 18 new ships from German shipyards, including two passenger ships for its European lines, two passenger-cargo ships for the transatlantic line, and one tanker. Subsequently Zim had ships built in shipyards in Japan, France, Italy, Yugoslavia, Sweden, and Israel, and by the beginning of 1970 the company owned or operated 60 ships with a deadweight of 1,012,605 tons. In 1964 the 25,000-ton passenger ship SS *Shalom* began service on the Haifa-New York line. The management's decision to provide two kitchens on board – one for kosher and the other for non-kosher food – aroused a violent controversy, and eventually Zim had to operate the ship with only a kosher kitchen. The ship did not make a sufficient profit and was sold in 1967. The passenger service reached its peak in 1960 when four passenger ships were serving Zim. In 1967 Zim employed 3,400 sailors and shore employees. The expansion of maritime training facilities accompanied the development of the fleet. However, passenger service declined in the 1960s as elsewhere in the world and by 1970 Zim owned no passenger ships.

Zim then expanded its cargo lines and began operating specialized ships such as bulk carriers, refrigerated ships, and tankers. Another important field of activity was the operation of tankers carrying oil from Iran to Israel, and petroleum products from Israel to Europe. In the early 1970s Zim established ZCS – ZIM Container Service. The company ordered and built six ships, the first generation of large specialized container ships, as well as shore equipment and containers. During the early 1980s Zim faced another financial crisis, but eventually achieved a turnaround. The year 1985 marked the start of a new era for a leaner, more flexible, and more profitable Zim. In the early 2000s the company constituted an integrated international transportation system, combining a variety of transport-related activities and providing a wide range of services. Zim operates over 80 vessels of all types. Of these, 27 vessels are fully or partly owned and the rest chartered. In 2004 the Israeli government sold its shares (49%) in Zim to Israel Corporation, owned by the Ofer family, transforming Zim into a private company. Zim's ships maintain regular communications with most European countries, the U.S. and Canada, South America, West and East Africa, and countries in Asia, including Hong Kong, Japan, and Australia. The company's rapid and successful development attracted the attention of new countries in Africa and Asia, which invited the company to organize and run their shipping. The national shipping of Ghana and Burma were organized by Zim.

BIBLIOGRAPHY: S. Tolkowsky, *They Took to the Sea* (1964); *Ha-Toren* (monthly of the Zim Co.; 1953–65); *Ha-Yammai ha-Ivri* (1947–62; especially the articles by Captain Ze'ev Ha-Yam). **WEBSITE:** www.zim.co.il.

[Zvi Herman / Shaked Gilboa (2nd ed.)]

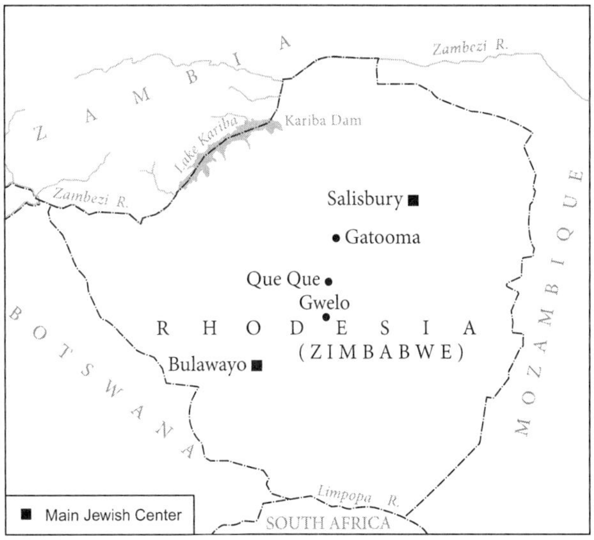

Jewish communities in Zimbabwe (then Rhodesia), 1971.

ZIMBABWE, formerly the British colony of Southern Rhodesia and, briefly, the Republic of Rhodesia. Organized Jewish life in Zimbabwe goes back to 1894 when about 20 Jews were among the purchasers of land in Bulawayo. They established a congregation there in that year, followed by another in *Salisbury (later renamed Harare) in 1895. A third congregation, which remained small, was established in Gwelo in 1901. Individual Jewish traders had penetrated north of the Limpopo 35 years earlier, and a number of Jews were in the occupation column that Cecil Rhodes sent to Salisbury in 1890 as well as in the fighting columns of 1893 and 1896. An important role in the development of Rhodesia was played by Alfred *Beit. The majority of the Jewish settlers were of Russian and Lithuanian origin, although later on an appreciable number of Sephardim came from the Aegean island of Rhodes. The earliest settlers came up from the south, some by way of the east coast through Portuguese Beira. Joe van Praag, who later became mayor of Salisbury, is known to have walked from Beira. There was a small influx of German refugees in the late 1930s, and during the period of prosperity after World War II a considerable number of South African and English Jews settled in Rhodesia. The Jewish settlers founded newspapers and were largely responsible for pioneering efforts in transportation systems, mining, the tobacco industry, cattle and produce marketing, furniture and clothing industries, and the hotel business. As the population began to grow and disperse, a number of synagogues were established. According to census figures, there were 400 Jews in 1900, 1,289 in 1921, 2,219 in 1936, 4,760 in 1951, and 7,060 in 1961. The two main Jewish centers were Bulawayo and Salisbury, with smaller congregations in Gatooma, Gwelo, and Que Que. After 1965, when the ruling white supremacist Rhodesian Front unilaterally declared Rhodesian independence in a bid to perpetuate white minority rule, the Jewish population declined precipitously. UDI resulted in Rhodesia's being increasingly isolated by the international community, and it inevitably led in due course to a long, ruinous civil war between the white minority regime and the various black liberation movements (1976–79). The Jewish population was approximately 5,500 in 1968 and barely a quarter that number 12 years later, when political power finally passed to the black majority. Rhodesia was renamed Zimbabwe and the country's inaugural elections were won by Robert Mugabe's ZANU-PF party. Emigrating Jews largely settled in neighboring South Africa, although a fairly substantial number went to Israel or the U.K. The Jewish population, together with that of the white minority, continued to shrink under Mugabe's increasingly authoritarian rule. In December 1987, only 1,200 Jews remained in Zimbabwe, two-thirds of whom were over the age of 65. Nearly all were living in Harare and Bulawayo, the former midlands communities of Gweru, Kwe Kwe, and Kadoma having by then ceased to function. During the mid-1990s, Zimbabwe entered a sustained period of economic and political turmoil, as Mugabe's ruling ZANU-PF party resorted to ever more totalitarian methods to remain in power amidst crumbling social services, food and other shortages, and hyper-inflation. In 2004, fewer than 400 Jews remained in the country. Despite the attrition, the Jewish communal infrastructure remained intact, with organizations like the Zimbabwe Jewish Board of Deputies, Central African Zionist Organization, women's Zionist groups, and the Union of Jewish Women still functioning. There were three synagogues, all Orthodox, of which two were in Harare and the other in Bulawayo. Sharon School in Harare, whose student body is now 90% non-Jewish, nevertheless provides some Jewish-related instruction for the community's few remaining Jewish children. Savyon Lodge, the Jewish Aged Home in Bulawayo, had

31 Jewish residents in 2004. With an average age of over 70 and no sign of any reversal in the near future of the country's ongoing implosion, Zimbabwe Jewry is today a community coming to terms with its own imminent demise.

BIBLIOGRAPHY: M.I. Cohen, in: *South African Jewish Year Book* (1929). **ADD. BIBLIOGRAPHY:** B.A. Kosmin, *Majuta: A History of the Jewish Community of Zimbabwe* (1980).

[Maurice Wagner / David Saks (2nd ed.)]

ZIMBALIST, EFREM (1889–1985), violinist and composer. Zimbalist was born at Rostov on Don, Russia, and received his earliest musical training from his father, a conductor, before studying at the St. Petersburg Conservatory with Leopold *Auer. He made his European debut with the Berlin Philharmonic Orchestra in 1907. In 1911 he went to the U.S., making his American debut with the Boston Symphony Orchestra, and became one of the most prominent violinists on the U.S. concert scene. In 1914 he married the singer, Alma *Gluck, who died in 1938. In the same year he married Mary Louise Curtis, the founder of the Curtis Institute of Music, Philadelphia, of which he became director in 1941. Zimbalist specialized in the history of early violin music. He composed the opera *Landara* (1956), orchestral and chamber works, songs, and *One Hour's Daily Exercises for Violin* (1918). He left the Jewish faith.

EFREM ZIMBALIST JR. (1923–), U.S. actor, musician, and producer, was the son of Efrem Zimbalist by Alma Gluck but was not of the Jewish faith. He was born in New York where, in 1947 and 1950, he produced three operas by Gian-Carlo Menotti. The last, *The Consul*, won a Pulitzer Prize and the New York Drama Critics' Award. Early minor roles with the American Repertory Theater led to his Broadway debut in *Hedda Gabler* (1948). After the death of his wife in 1950, Zimbalist went into semi-retirement, working with his father. In 1954 he returned to acting, and as the lead in the television series "77 Sunset Strip," won popular acclaim.

BIBLIOGRAPHY: G. Saleski, *Famous Musicians of Jewish Origin* (1949), 12–5; MGG, incl. bibl.

ZIMMELS, HIRSCH JACOB (1900–1975), rabbi and scholar. Zimmels, born in Yavorov, Poland, lectured from 1929 to 1933 at the Juedisch-Theologisches Seminar, Breslau, and from 1934 to 1939 was rabbi of the Israelitische Kultusgemeinde, Vienna. Zimmels left Austria for England after the Nazi *Anschluss* in 1938, and in 1944 was appointed lecturer in Bible, Talmud, and Jewish history at Jews' College London. He became director of studies in 1961 and was principal in 1964–69.

Zimmels' published works, based mainly on his important research into responsa literature, include: *Beitraege zur Geschichte der Juden in Deutschland* (1926); *R. David ibn Abi Simra's (R.D.b.S) Leben und Lebenswerk* (1932); *Die Marranen in der rabbinischen Literatur* (1932); *Magicians, Theologians and Doctors* (1952); and *Ashkenazim and Sephardim* (1958).

[Alexander Tobias]

°**ZIMMERLI, WALTHER** (1907–1983), Swiss Bible scholar. Born in Schiers (Graubuenden), Zimmerli was professor in Zurich (from 1938) and Goettingen (from 1951). The subject of his research is expressed in the title of the collection of his articles *Das Alte Testament als Anrede* ("The Old Testament as a Harangue," 1956) and *Gottes Offenbarung* (1963). In his commentary on Ezekiel (2 vols., 1955–69), he explains in detail the message of the prophet in its historical-traditional context; the present Book of Ezekiel is the result of a later development of the prophetic word within an "Ezekielian school." In his commentary, Zimmerli applies the form-critical method, especially to the theologically significant formulas (e.g., "formula of self-introduction," "statements of realization," "word of proof").

One of his main interests is the marginal position of the Wisdom writings in relation to the theology of the Old Testament (*Zur Struktur der alttestamentlichen Weisheit*, in ZAW, 51 (1933), 177–204); his commentary on Ecclesiastes belongs in this context (*Das Buch des Prediger Salomo*, 1962). In various works Zimmerli deals with aspects of the theology of the Old Testament (*Das Gesetz und die Propheten*, 1963; *Der Mensch und seine Hoffnung im Alten Testament*, 1968; *Die Weltlichkeit des Alten Testaments*, 1971).

[Rudolf Smend]

ZIMMERMAN, CHARLES SASCHA (1897–1983), U.S. labor leader. Zimmerman, who was born in the Ukraine, came to the United States in 1913 and went to work in a New York City knee-pants shop. In 1916 he joined the International Ladies Garment Workers Union (ILGWU) and thereafter the Socialist Party. With the emergence of the American Communist movement after World War I he became a member of the Communist Party, whose faction in the ILGWU he led throughout the early 1920s. In 1926, a year after becoming union manager of the Communist-controlled New York Joint Board, Local 22, ILGWU, Zimmerman organized a general strike. Though he considered the management's eventual settlement offer to represent a substantial victory for the workers, the Communist Party forced a continuation of the walkout, which ended in defeat. The experience had a sobering effect. Zimmerman, although he remained in the Party for a few more years as leader of its Needle Trades Industrial Union, resigned in 1929 and in 1931 he led Local 22 back into the ILGWU. After his return to the ILGWU Zimmerman played an active role in the struggle against Communist influence in the labor movement. He was made vice president of the ILGWU in 1943, a post he long held. He was also active in the American Labor Party in New York State, until his resignation in 1946, after it veered to the left. After World War II, through his activities in the Jewish Labor Committee, Zimmerman was active in the cause of civil rights. In 1949 he became a leader of Amum-Israeli Housing Corporation, an enterprise in low-cost housing in Israel undertaken by the ILGWU and several other American unions.

BIBLIOGRAPHY: M. Epstein, *Jewish Labor in U.S.A.*, 2 vols. (1950–53), index; idem, *The Jew and Communism, 1919–1941* (1959), index.

ZIMMERMAN, HARRY M. (1901–1995), U.S. neuropathologist. From 1930 to 1943 he was professor of pathology at Yale. After World War II he became chief of laboratories of New York's Montefiore Hospital and clinical professor of pathology at Columbia's College of Physicians and Surgeons. From 1963 he was professor of pathology at Yeshiva University's Albert Einstein College of Medicine.

For many years Zimmerman was consultant in pathology and neuropathology to hospitals and institutes, including the Armed Forces Institute of Pathology in Washington, D.C. He was associate editor of the *American Journal of Pathology* (1943–53). He wrote many scientific papers, and coauthored the three-volume work *Neuroradiology Workshop* (1961–68).

[Fred Rosner]

ZIMMERMAN, SHELDON (1942–), U.S. Reform rabbi, administrator. Zimmerman was born in Toronto, Canada, and received his B.A. (1964) and M.A. (1965) from the University of Toronto. In 1970, he was ordained at *Hebrew Union College-Jewish Institute of Religion, which awarded him an honorary D.D. in 1995. Following ordination, he was appointed assistant rabbi of New York City's Central Synagogue, where he was elevated to the position of senior rabbi in 1972 (1972–85). He was also a member of the faculties of Hunter College (1966–69), Fordham University (1971–74) and the New York campus of HUC-JIR, where he taught liturgy and rabbinics (1980–85). Reaching out to those in need, he organized an interfaith coalition of churches with his synagogue and founded the first feeding program for the homeless in the mid-Manhattan area; he also welcomed the first Alcoholics Anonymous group ever to meet in a synagogue. In addition, he served on the national rabbinic cabinets of the United Jewish Appeal, the Jewish National Fund, and State of Israel Bonds, as well as on the boards of the World Center for Jewish Unity and the Synagogue Council of America. He was religious news commentator for the radio station WOR and moderator of the Message of Israel radio broadcasts started by Rabbi Jonah *Wise.

In 1985, Zimmerman became senior rabbi of Temple Emanu-El in Dallas, Texas (1985–96), where was also adjunct professor at Southern Methodist University and Perkins Theological Seminary (1986–89). His civic involvement included serving as chairman of the Interfaith Commission of the Jewish Community Relations Council and on the Committee on Institutional Ethics at Baylor University Medical Center as well as on the boards of Children's Medical Foundation, Jewish Federation of Dallas, and the Chaplains Advisory Board of SMU. He also served as alumnus in residence at HUC-JIR's Los Angeles (1985) and Cincinnati campus (1989).

In the Reform movement, Zimmerman served as president of two of the three cornerstones of Reform Judaism: the *Central Conference of American Rabbis and HUC-JIR. After serving as a member of the executive committee and board of trustees of the Union of American Hebrew Congregations, president of HUC-JIR's Rabbinical Alumni Association and co-chairman of the UAHC-CCAR Joint National Commission on Outreach, he was elected vice president (1991–93) and then president (1993–95) of the CCAR. During his term of office, he was selected by President Clinton to be part of a delegation accompanying Vice President Gore to Warsaw to commemorate the 50th anniversary of the Warsaw Ghetto uprising and was invited to Jerusalem by President Ezer Weizman to participate in a conference of leaders of world Jewry.

In 1996, Zimmerman was named the seventh president of Hebrew Union College-Jewish Institute of Religion. He was credited with restoring prominence to HUC-JIR's faculty; also during his tenure, the Los Angeles school began ordaining rabbis – prior to that students could begin their studies on the West Coast – and would have to complete them in New York and Cincinnati. He resigned in 2000 after an investigation into his conduct as a rabbi several years earlier led to his suspension by the Central Conference of American Rabbis, which never made public the accusation but merely the verdict. Soon thereafter, he was appointed executive vice president of *Birthright Israel in 2001. In 2003, he became vice president of *United Jewish Communities' Jewish Renaissance and Renewal. He returned to the world of academia in 2006, teaching rabbinics at HUC-JIR.

Zimmerman is the author of three family prayer books for Sabbath and the festivals and co-editor of *The Threat of a Mixed Marriage – A Response*. He has contributed to a number of books, including *Alcoholism and the Jewish Community, Twelve Jewish Steps for Recovery* and *Healing of Soul, Healing of Body* – which were informed by his pioneering efforts as a founder of the Federation Task Force on Jewish Alcoholism and the support group JACS – and for which he received the first Marshall Hochhauser Memorial Award. He was also a member of the advisory board of Jewish Lights Publishing and of the publication committee of the Jewish Publication Society of America.

[Bezalel Gordon (2nd ed.)]

ZIMMERN, SIR ALFRED (1879–1957), English political scientist and an authority on international relations. Born in London, the son of a Jewish merchant (his mother was of Huguenot descent), Zimmern was educated at Winchester and Oxford, where he was fellow and tutor from 1904 to 1909. From 1919 to 1921 he held the chair of international relations at the University of Wales-Aberystwyth. In 1930 he returned to Oxford as professor of international relations. Zimmern held several important posts in the British government and was an adviser to the Ministry of Education and the Foreign Office. He was also deputy director of the League of Nations Institute of Intellectual Cooperation from 1926 to 1930 and was special adviser to UNESCO.

Zimmern's writings include *The Greek Commonwealth* (1931^5); *The Third British Empire* (1934^3); *The League of Nations and the Rule of Law, 1918–1935* (1939^2); and *Spiritual Values and World Affairs* (1939). They reflected his understanding of the historic factor in the development of international relations and, as a result, his advice on foreign affairs was sought by various governments. Though Zimmern was not connected with the Jewish community, *Weizmann consulted him on political questions. Zimmern was a lifelong advocate of the outlawing of war, enforced by international agreement, and was, in 1917, one of the first to suggest that war be outlawed by international treaty. He also believed in the inevitable progress of the human race, a proposition for which there was tragically little evidence during his lifetime. After 1947 he lived and taught in New England, dying in Connecticut.

BIBLIOGRAPHY: *New York Times* (Nov. 25, 1957), 31; *Illustrated London News* (Nov. 30, 1957), 941. **ADD. BIBLIOGRAPHY:** ODNB online.

ZIMRI (Heb. זִמְרִי; "my strength or protection [is the Deity]"), son of Salu, chieftain of a Simeonite ancestral house (Num. 25:14). The Israelites profaned themselves at Shittim by whoring with the Moabite women and by joining them in sacrifices to their god Baal-peor (Num. 25:1–2). Incensed, the Lord let loose a plague upon Israel (see Rashi, Num. 25:3) and ordered Moses to execute the ringleaders publicly (Num. 25:4). The earlier offense was further aggravated by Zimri, who brought a Midianite woman into his household (cf. Ibn Ezra, Num. 25:6) in full view of Moses and the assembled community who were bemoaning the plague. In an act of zeal for the Lord which became legendary (see I Macc. 2:26; IV Macc. 18:12), Phinehas son of Eleazar son of Aaron the priest killed both Zimri and the Midianite woman, Cozbi daughter of Zur, of a noble Midianite family. It was his action that turned away the wrath of God from the children of Israel. The plague ceased, but its victims numbered 24,000.

In the Aggadah

In midrashic literature the biblical events are further dramatized in that Zimri openly challenged Moses' leadership and the validity of the Torah. Zimri shamed Moses into silence by reminding him of the non-Israelite origin of his own wife Zipporah (although this was not really a sin since he had married her before the acceptance of the Torah at Sinai). It was Phinehas who prevented complete disaster. He remembered a law which Moses had forgotten in his confusion – that at that time an Israelite caught in the act of openly consorting with a foreign woman was liable to immediate execution by zealots. Advised by Moses to carry out this law, Phinehas executed Zimri and Cozbi, and the threat was ended (Sanh. 82a). In Josephus' amplified version of the story, Moses feared an open confrontation with the rebels and merely exhorted the people to remain faithful to God. Encouraged by his weak reaction, Zimri denounced the law as a tyrannical limitation of man's ability to act according to his own will. The quick action of Phinehas put an end to the rebellion (Jos., Ant., 4:141–56). Phinehas became a symbol for zealous action for the Lord, while Zimri became a symbol for the worst rebellion against God and his Torah: "Fear neither the Pharisees nor those who are not Pharisees, but those hypocrites who resemble Pharisees whose deeds are like the deeds of Zimri, yet they demand the reward of Phinehas" (Sot. 22b).

BIBLIOGRAPHY: G. B. Gray, *Numbers* (ICC, 1912), 386–7; EM, 2 (1954), 931; Ginzberg, Legends, index; I. Ḥasida, *Ishei ha-Tanakh* (1964), 144.

[Gershon Bacon]

ZIMRI (d. 885/4 B.C.E.), king of Israel. When Baasha's son *Elah had reigned only a few months, he was slain by Zimri, commander of half of the chariots. Upon taking power, Zimri executed all the males among the relatives and admirers of Baasha (I Kings 16:11), thus fulfilling the words of the prophet Jehu (I Kings 16:11–14). However, Zimri reigned only seven days, for *Omri, who was in command of the force that was laying siege to the Philistine town of Gibbethon, was proclaimed king by his men. He marched with them to *Tirzah, the royal residence of those days, which he captured without much difficulty. Before Omri reached the citadel in which the royal palace was situated, Zimri set fire to the palace over himself (I Kings 16:8–18). Though his reign was short, Zimri became a symbol of the slave who turns against his master. A generation later, when *Jehu assassinated *Jehoram, the last king of the House of Omri, the dowager queen *Jezebel mockingly addressed him as "Zimri, slayer of his master" (II Kings 9:30–31).

BIBLIOGRAPHY: EM, 2 (1954), 932–3, incl. bibl.

[Gershon Bacon]

ZINBERG, ISRAEL (**Sergei**; 1873–1939), historian of Hebrew and Yiddish literature. Born near Kremenets, Volhynia, into a maskilic family, Zinberg, a chemical engineer by profession and scholar by avocation, published his first work in the field of literary history in 1900 – a monograph, in Russian, on Isaac Baer *Levinsohn. Editor of, and chief contributor to, the Hebrew and Yiddish literature divisions of the Russian-Jewish encyclopedia (*Evreiskaia Entsiklopediia*, 16 vols., 1906–13), Zinberg served on its editorial board. Among the many Russo-Jewish periodicals and Yiddish publications to which he contributed were *Voskhod*, *Der Fraynd*, and *Di Yidishe Velt*, which he also helped to establish in St. Petersburg in 1912 (with S.*Dubnow and S. *Ginsburg). His monograph on old Yiddish literature appeared in *Istoriia evreiskogo naroda* (1914). In 1917, together with S. *Niger, Zinberg edited a Sholem Aleichem memorial volume. During these years he was active in the cultural life of St. Petersburg, wrote for newspapers, and gave lectures which prepared for his monumental *Geshikhte fun der Literatur bay Yidn* ("History of Jewish Literature," 9 vols. in 11, 1929–66), which chronicles Jewish literary creativity from the Spanish period to the end of the Russian Haskalah. In this monumental work, Zinberg displayed much scholarship, erudition, and originality both as critic and historian. Basing the study on primary sources, he combined the study of historical documents, social context, the primary centers of Jewish literature, and the languages used by the writers, and thus succeeded in giving a sense of the unity and diversity of Jewish cultural creativity and writing a readable history, which has become a standard work in its field (Hebrew transl., 1955–60; English transl., 1972–78).

Arrested in 1938 and deported to Vladivostok, where he died the following year, Zinberg was "rehabilitated" by the Soviet government in 1956. At the time of his arrest his papers were confiscated. Discovered later among these papers at the Academy of Sciences in Leningrad was the manuscript of the first part of the final volume of his history. Entitled "The Flowering of Haskalah Literature in Russia," the manuscript, dealing with the early works of S.J *Abramovitsh (Mendele Moykher Seforim), Abraham Uri *Kovner, M.L. *Lilienblum, Isaac Meir *Dik, and I.J. *Linetzki, was published by YIVO and Brandeis University in 1966.

Among Zinberg's other works are *Proiskhozhdenie Sheiloka* ("The Origin of Shylock," 1902), *Zhargonnaia literatura i yego chitateli* ("Yiddish Literature and Its Readers," 1903), *Dva techeniia v evreiskoi zhizni* ("Two Trends in Jewish Life," 1905), and *Istoriia evreiskoi pechati v Rossii* ("History of the Jewish Press in Russia," 1915), a study covering the Hebrew, Yiddish, and Russian Jewish press. A selection of Zinberg's essays, *Kultur-Historishe Shtudien* ("Studies in Cultural History," 1949, ed. by Jacob Shatzky), which appeared in New York, contains original Yiddish essays as well as translations from Russian.

BIBLIOGRAPHY: Waxman, Literature, 4 (1960²), 825ff.; LNYL, 7 (1968), 585–96; Kressel, Leksikon, 2 (1967), 718–9; D. Sadan, *Avnei Miftan* (1962), 251–5.

[Elias Schulman / Jean Baumgarten (2nd ed.)]

ZINNEMANN, FRED (1907–1997), U.S. film director and producer. Born in Vienna, Zinnemann went to Hollywood in 1929, worked as a script clerk, and in 1934 directed a full-length documentary, *The Wave*. Later he applied documentary techniques to feature films, and worked for M.G.M. until 1950, when he started on his own.

Among his most important films are *The Seventh Cross* (1944); *Act of Violence* (1949); *The Search* (Oscar nomination for Best Director, 1949); *The Men* (1950); *Benjy* (produced; Oscar for Best Short Documentary, 1951); *The Member of the Wedding* (1952); *High Noon* (Oscar nomination for Best Director, 1952); *From Here to Eternity* (Oscar for Best Director, 1953); *Oklahoma!* (1955); *A Hatful of Rain* (1957); *The Nun's Story* (Oscar nomination for Best Director, 1959); *The Sundowners* (produced; Oscar nomination for Best Picture and Best Director, 1960); *Behold a Pale Horse* (produced, 1964); *A Man for All Seasons* (produced; Oscar for Best Picture and Best Director, 1966);*The Day of the Jackal* (1973), *Julia* (Oscar nomination for Best Director, 1977); and *Five Days One Summer* (produced, 1982).

Among his many awards, Zinnemann received a Lifetime Achievement Award from the Directors Guild of America in 1970. His autobiography, *Fred Zinnemann: A Life in the Movies*, was published in 1992.

BIBLIOGRAPHY: A. Nolletti (ed.), *The Films of Fred Zinnemann: Critical Perspectives* (1999); N. Sinyard, *Fred Zinnemann: Films of Character and Conscience* (2003).

[Ruth Beloff (2nd ed.)]

ZINOVIEV, GRIGORI YEVSEYEVICH (1883–1936), principal architect of the Communist International and its first chairman. He was Bolshevism's leading advocate of world revolution. He was born Grigori Yevseyevich Radomyslski in Yelizavetgrad (now Kirovograd), Ukraine. His bourgeois parents were Jewish, but Zinoviev, early in his youth, became completely assimilated to Russian life, particularly to the radical Marxist socialism then sweeping broad segments of the intelligentsia. He joined the Russian Social Democratic Workers Party in 1901, and its Bolshevik wing in 1903.

Having played an active role in the 1905 Revolution in St. Petersburg, he was chosen as a delegate to the Stockholm (Unity) Congress of the Social Democratic Party in 1906, where his powerful and inspiring oratory attracted immediate attention and assured him a prominent position in the Bolshevik hierarchy.

During the post-revolutionary period, Zinoviev shared *Lenin's exile and came to be the latter's closest collaborator, writing "everything that Lenin thought was required," whether it be "newspaper articles, circulars to party friends, resolutions, or brochures." He served as an editor of *Proletariy* and *Sotsial-Demokrat*, Bolshevik newspapers, and of *Kommunist*, a Bolshevik journal. In 1912 at the Prague Conference of the Bolsheviks, he was elected to their Central Committee

In the course of World War I, Zinoviev's close relationship with Lenin deepened. Jointly they published a landmark work, *Against the Tide*, attacking both the war and Social Democratic leaders who had supported the war; jointly, they organized the Zimmerwald (1915) and Kienthal (1916) Conferences of dissident Socialist groups; jointly, they rode the "sealed train" that took them back to Russia in April 1917, following the collapse of the czarist regime; and jointly, they went into hiding after the July uprising against the Provisional Government.

Zinoviev, panicking at a moment of crisis, split with Lenin in October on the question of the seizure of power. He feared that a Bolshevik coup at the time would lead to foreign intervention and a counterrevolutionary peasant uprising. Yet Zinoviev remained in the Central Committee of the party and continued to be one of its key figures until the middle of 1926. Early in 1922 he became a member of the all-powerful Politburo. In Petrograd he was the unchallenged "boss" both of the soviet and the party.

If Zinoviev had his hands on the levers of power within Russia, it was in Comintern activity that his influence was most strongly felt. Indeed, he was relieved of national administrative posts so that he might devote the maximum attention to the international revolutionary movement. Until November 1926 he was the chairman of the Comintern's executive committee and the driving force of its presidium. His ideological pronouncements constituted the major premises for the strategy and tactics of Communists everywhere. During 1919–20 his role was especially prominent, with the Comintern character and structure molded largely by him.

However, the retreat of the international revolutionary wave, beginning in 1921, dimmed his luster. The collapse of the "March Action" in Germany (1921), for which he was largely responsible, and the defeat of the revolution in Germany in October 1923, contributed to the decline of his international image. Yet his power within Soviet Russia was unquestioned. Following Lenin's death in January 1924, he joined with *Stalin and Lev *Kamenev to constitute the "Troika" of preeminent party leaders. Together, they drove Leon *Trotsky into political isolation.

The "Troika" foundered on Stalin's doctrine of "socialism in one country" and his aspiration for sole party leadership. Considering Stalin's doctrine a threat to world revolution, a capitulation to the peasants, and the beginning of "Thermidor," Zinoviev joined Trotsky in the "Joint Opposition" formed in July 1926. An intense struggle for power culminated in his complete defeat and ouster from the party in December 1927 at the 15th Party Congress. Zinoviev was a master of the art of intrigue, but found himself completely outmaneuvered by the general secretary of the party.

Seven years later, following the assassination of Sergey Kirov, Zinoviev was arrested. Stalin was now preparing to deliver the final blow to his political opponents and, in August 1936, the first of the "Great Purge" trials was held. Zinoviev, along with 15 colleagues, was formally arraigned on charges of having organized the "terrorist centers" that allegedly had plotted Kirov's murder. Public admissions of guilt by the accused were followed by death sentences, immediately carried out. Zinoviev's name disappeared down the "memory hole" to be resurrected only on occasion as a symbol of treachery.

Even after N. Krushchev's disclosures at the 20th Party Congress in 1956 which hinted that the Kirov murder may have been a frame-up, Zinoviev was not rehabilitated. Current official histories of the party mention his name but rarely, and then only to castigate him, although the 1936 charge of treason is no longer mentioned.

BIBLIOGRAPHY: E.H. Carr, The Interregnum, 1923–1924 (1954), index; idem, *Socialism in One Country, 1924–1926*, 2 vols. (1958–59), index; S. and B. Webb, *Soviet Communism: A New Civilization* (1944[3]), index; L. Schapiro, *The Communist Party of the Soviet Union.* (1962[2]), index.

[William Korey]

ZION (Mount Zion; also *Sion, Mountain of Zion*; (Heb. צִיּוֹן, הַר צִיּוֹן), hill and fortress in Jerusalem. The origin of the name is uncertain. Suggestions have included a rock, stronghold (צִיּוֹן), a dry place (צִיּוֹן), or running water (Hurrian: *ṣeya*). The name Zion was first used for the Jebusite fortress ("the stronghold of Zion"), on the southeast of Jerusalem, below the Ophel and the Temple Mount. On its capture by David it was renamed "City of David" (II Sam. 5:7; I Kings 8:1), and the name later included also the Ophel (Micah 4:8; Isa. 32:14). In poetry Zion was used by way of synecdoche for the whole of Jerusalem (Isa. 2:3; 33:14; Joel 3:5), and "daughter (or virgin) of Zion" referred to the city and its inhabitants (Isa. 1:8; 30:16; Songs 1:5). Zion often referred by way of metonymy to Judea (Isa. 10:24; 51:11) or the people of Judea (*ibid.* 51:16; 59:20). Sometimes Zion referred simply to the Temple Mount (Joel 4:17, 21; Ps. 20:3) and it was this use that became the regular one by the Maccabean period, when the Temple Mount was called "Mountain of Zion" (ὄρος Σιων; I Macc. 7:32–33), as opposed to the lower city, the upper city, and Acra (on the southwestern hill of ancient Jerusalem). By Josephus' time "the stronghold" (of Zion; τὸ φρούριον) was identified with the upper city and the upper agora (Wars, 5:137; cf. Ant., 7:62), which included the sites identified at present with Mt. Zion, as well as David's Tower. By the first century C.E. the whole of that elevation, called Mt. Zion, was surrounded by a wall, part of which (in the southwest section) lay under the present city wall and part (its northern line) ran along the present King David Street, while the eastern wall ran through the present Jewish quarter. The fact that the Acra was situated at the northeast corner, and the royal palaces were there, probably encouraged the belief that Zion was to be identified with this area.

In the first century C.E. a small church was built on the southern end of the hill, and it was identified with the Coenaculum ("Room of the Last Supper"). In 1342 the Franciscans rebuilt it and this is substantially the building surviving to this day. The Franciscans were expelled by the Muslims in 1551 and were permitted to return and build a monastery near there only in 1936. This is the Church of the Dormition of Mary.

The Traveler from Bordeaux (333) cites that a single synagogue, one of the seven synagogues of ancient times, was left on Mr. Zion. This is confirmed by archaeological excavations performed at the northern wall of David's Tomb, where evidence for the existence of a late Roman synagogue was found, which seems to have been repaired during the reign of Julian the Apostate (361–3). The synagogue was associated with David as early as the fourth century, and by the tenth century his grave was located there, probably because of the biblical dictum that he was buried "in the city of David" (I Kings 2:10). It is believed by some that Saladin fortified the Coenaculum and David's Tomb by a wall in the 12th century, but the present city wall runs behind them. In 1524 the site was turned into a mosque of "the Prophet David." After 1948, when Mount Zion was the only section of east Jerusalem to remain in Jewish hands, David's Tomb was once again turned into a synagogue and became the most important pilgrimage center for Jews in Israel (see *Pilgrimage; *Holy Places). The archaeological remains of the Hellenistic Fullers' Quarter just south of the grave have been uncovered. Next to the tomb is "the Holocaust Chamber" dedicated to those who died under the Nazis. The name Zion also lent itself in modern times to organizations connected with Judaism or Jews, e.g., Zionism, Zion Mule Corps, etc.

BIBLIOGRAPHY: Z. Vilnay, *Jerusalem* (1969), index; M. Benvenisti, *The Crusaders in the Holy Land* (1970), 51, 52, 54, 73; B. Mazar, in: *Kadmoniot*, 1–2 (1968), 8–10; M. Avi-Yonah, *ibid.*, 19–20; H.Z. Hirschberg, *ibid.*, 57–59.

ZIONISM.

This article is arranged according to the following outline:

THE WORD AND ITS MEANING

The root of the term "Zionism" is the word "Zion," which very early in Jewish history became a synonym for Jerusalem. It had a special meaning as far back as after the destruction of the First Temple in expressing the yearning of the Jewish people for its homeland. Thus "Zion" is found in the Psalms, "By the rivers of Babylon,/There we sat down, yea, we wept,/ When we remembered Zion" (Ps. 137:1); in the prayer, "And let our eyes behold Thy return in mercy to Zion"; in the poem, "Zion! Wilt thou not ask if peace be with thy captives/That seek thy peace – that are the remnant of thy flocks" (Judah Halevi); and frequently elsewhere in religious and secular literature.

The modern term Zionism first appeared at the end of the 19th century, denoting the movement whose goal was the return of the Jewish people to Ereẓ Israel. It was coined by Nathan *Birnbaum in his journal *Selbstemanzipation* (April 1, 1890). Birnbaum himself explained the term (in a letter of Nov. 6, 1891) as the "establishment of an organization of the national-political Zionist party in juxtaposition to the practically oriented party that existed until now." The term was thus intended to express a political orientation toward Ereẓ Israel in place of the prevailing philanthropic approach. The extent to which the new word filled a need in the young movement can be gauged from the plethora of subtitles of *Selbstemanzipation* from its first appearance until the May 18, 1893 issue, when the definition "Organ der Zionisten" ("Organ of the Zionists") was adopted. However, despite the precise meaning which Birnbaum intended to convey by it, the terms "Zionism" and "Ḥibbat Zion" (see below) were still used interchangeably, and it was only gradually that the meaning of political Zionism, as distinguished from its "practical," almost wholly philanthropic aspect, gained acceptance. This happened finally and unequivocally with the appearance of *Herzl.

Herzl, who knew nothing of the semantic developments of the word Zionism, first used it to denote philanthropic-supported small-scale settlement. It was only when preparations for the First Zionist Congress had commenced and when, at the last moment, two of the speakers at the Congress – R. Hirsch *Hildesheimer and Willy *Bambus, leading members of the *Esra Society – withdrew their participation, due to Herzl's explicit political orientation, that Herzl began to stress the importance of the "Zionist" Congress, to be distinguished from the Ḥibbat Zion movement. The Basle program adopted at the First Zionist Congress explicitly endorsed Herzl's political conception of Zionism. From then on, Zionist history was viewed as being divided into two epochs; Ḥibbat Zion up to the First Congress, and from then on "Zionism," i.e., political Zionism. This did not, however, put an end to the prolonged struggle between the two concepts inside the Zionist movement, between the "political" and the "practical" Zionists, each of whom regarded their approach to the realization of the Zionist aim as the genuine meaning of the term "Zionism." It was at the Eighth Zionist Congress (1907) that Chaim *Weizmann coined a new term, "synthetic" Zionism, which stipulated that the two approaches supplement each other and are in reality two sides of the same coin: political activity is meaningless unless it is based upon practical settlement in Ereẓ Israel, and settlement alone could not develop into desirable proportions without the support of political efforts.

[Gideon Kouts]

FORERUNNERS

On the threshold of modern times, as far as ethnic and historical consciousness is concerned, the Jews were better prepared for a national movement than any other ethnic group in Europe. Before this consciousness could become an ingredient of modern nationalism, it first had to undergo certain transformations. By the same token, however, all peoples had to undergo important changes in their attitudes before they could be caught up by a national movement; they had to elevate the attributes of their ethnic group to ultimate values. Jewish society achieved its nationalist transformation with the appearance of a modern idea, later called Zionism, which purged, so to speak, Jewish messianic belief of its miraculous eschatological elements and retained only its political, social, and some of its spiritual objectives. Even in this phase of development, however, Zionism leaned heavily on the old messianism and derived from it much of its ideological and even more of its emotional appeal (see *Messianic Movements). Yet all this was accomplished only at the end of the 19th and the beginning of the 20th century. Thus, in spite of the fact that the Jews preceded other nations in possessing the potentialities of nationalism, the development of the Jewish national movement in its Zionist form lagged behind that of most of the European nations.

The shattering of the traditional existence of European Jewry, as separate religious-ethnic entities somehow connected with the surrounding estate-structured, prenationalistic society, was followed by a transitional period that partly preceded and partly coincided with that of the forerunners of Zionism. This period was basically rationalistic, aiming principally at the integration of the Jews in the new, rapidly changing European society, but it simultaneously evolved certain features (particularly pronounced in the *Haskalah period), which were later absorbed into the stream of Zionist ideology. One of them was the revitalization and modernization of the Hebrew language, which eventually culminated in the historical achievement of Eliezer *Ben-Yehuda; another, the striving for economic "productivization." An additional trait of this period was the emergence of the politically minded Jewish leader who appraised the world around him realistically, in the light of a defined political activity.

One cannot, however, properly speak of "forerunners" of Zionism such as Rabbi Judah *Alkalai, Rabbi Ẓevi Hirsch *Kalischer, Chaim *Lorje, Rabbi Elijah *Guttmacher, Moses *Hess, and others, before the end of the 1850s or the beginning of the 1860s. Only then could they succeed in uniting the widely scattered adherents of their idea through mutual contact. The factor common to all, their faith that the future existence of the Jewish nation is conditioned by its return to the historical homeland, became a basis of social unity. The difference between the earlier period and the 1860s is not difficult to explain. The 1860s saw the completion of emancipation in most West European countries, and where it was not yet wholly accomplished, it was thought to be just round the corner. As long as the struggle for political equality of the Jews was going on, the idea of Jewish nationalism could not be tolerated, for the argument that the Jews are a separate national entity was one of the main weapons of the gentile enemies of emancipation. From the 1860s on, when the emancipation seemed all but completed, the idea of Jewish nationalism could be propagated as the next phase. Kalischer even suggested that Jewish nationalism was the natural continuation of the emancipation itself.

The old messianic idea, however, did not disappear completely under the impact of rationalism; it remained alive in the Jewish masses. As late as 1840, there was a widespread rumor in the Balkans and in Eastern Europe that the messianic year, which was destined to bring about the great turning point in Jewish history, had arrived. Many held this belief genuinely and were waiting in a state of mental agitation. For one of these believers, Rabbi Judah Alkalai (1798–1878), his messianic expectation became a point of departure for the transition from the traditional, miraculous messianism to a realistic one. This change of conception was caused by the coincidence of the messianic expectation with the rescue of the Jewish community in Damascus, which had been charged with ritual murder, by the two leading figures of French and English Jewry, Adolphe *Crémieux and Sir Moses *Montefiore. As the miraculous events of the redemption failed to appear, Alkalai inferred that the rescue of this one community was a model for the messianic procedure. The future stages of redemption were to be achieved through similar activities of outstanding Jews. Alkalai was an undistinguished preacher of a little Sephardi community in Semlin, near Belgrade. Until the year of his newly found conviction, he was hardly known outside his limited circle, nor did he wish to be known. However, after he became convinced that the era of the Messiah had arrived and that the redemption would have to be achieved by human action, he felt compelled to convey this message to his fellow Jews. In the remaining 37 years of his life, not only did Alkalai publish numerous pamphlets and articles to spread his ideas, but he traveled on two occasions to Western Europe and later settled in Ereẓ Israel in order to convince Jews and non-Jews of the truth of his mission. He tried to induce people to join an organized resettlement of Jewry, or some part thereof, in their homeland and to equip themselves with the attributes of a modern nation. Although Alkalai began as a preacher imbued with the traditional, and especially kabbalistic, sources, he gradually acquired the elements of a modern national conception. He propagated the idea of Jewish national unity through an overall organization of world Jewry, with modernized Hebrew as its common language. Religion would also play its part in the new national life, but as the controversy between Orthodoxy and Reform grew, Alkalai sought a remedy to this in the idea of national unity.

Ẓevi Hirsch Kalischer (1795–1874) developed his ideas on similar lines. A German rabbinic scholar of Polish origin, he refused to accept any position in communal life. The great experience of his youth was the emancipation of the Jews in France and in the German countries at the time of Napoleon. He explained these events in terms derived from Jewish tradition. The emancipation, and even more the ascendance of Jewish individuals (e.g., the *Rothschilds) to unheard-of economic and political influence, appeared to him to be the fulfillment of the old prophecy of liberation which, according to Jewish tradition, was to terminate the exile. It is true that the prophecy was not yet realized, for it entailed the ingathering of the Jews to their homeland. Therefore, as early as 1836, Kalischer appealed to Meyer Anschel Rothschild to buy from Muhammad Ali the whole of Ereẓ Israel, or at least Jerusalem or the Temple area, so as to initiate the miraculous redemption "from below," and later he addressed the same request to Moses Montefiore. By interpreting the events of emancipation in terms of messianism, Kalischer simultaneously transformed these very terms. From the first stage of deliverance, which was brought about by human activity, he inferred the nature of the next stages, which were also to be achieved by human agency. Thus his interpretation of the emancipation led to the demand for the ingathering of at least some part of Jewry in Ereẓ Israel.

In order to place these theories in the correct perspective, one must bear in mind the underlying motives of their promoters. These theories of redemption were derived from a reinterpretation of the messianic tradition in the light of recent historic experiences. In view of later developments, it is important to note that modern antisemitism was not among these experiences. The activities of Alkalai and Kalischer took place during the flourishing period of Middle European liberalism, e.g., between 1840 and 1875, when optimism about the possible integration of Jews into the life of European nations was almost universal. Certain obstacles to achieving full civil rights, as well as some signs of reservation in social rapprochement, were interpreted as residues of waning prejudices. Alkalai and Kalischer were among the optimists. Until the 1870s they never advanced the argument that Jews needed a country to secure their physical existence, which was later to become one of the main planks of Zionism.

The same can be stated about the motives of the socialist Moses Hess. Hess was not an Orthodox Jew but a social revolutionary and philosopher with a Hegelian tinge. His conversion to Jewish nationalism in the 1860s can be understood as the result of the unmaterialized social revolution. Hess based his Zionist ideas on the concept of a national spirit which permeated the life of the Jewish people. Since the dispersion, the "spirit" was embodied in the Jewish religious institutions, but as these institutions were rapidly disintegrating, the gradual disappearance of the Jewish spirit was the most probable – and the most lamentable – prospect. In order to rescue this spirit, the only solution was the reconstruction of national life in the ancient homeland. Hess's argument is phrased in terms of social philosophy, while the emotional climate was provided by resentment against the non-Jewish society which had frustrated the Jews' expectation of being treated as equals. In any event, any diagnosis excluding emancipation as a possible solution to the "Jewish problem" is absent from the theory of Hess, as it is absent from those of Alkalai and Kalischer. More obvious than in the theories of Alkalai and Kalischer is Hess's dependence on the general trend of nationalism in Europe. The use of such terms as "nationality," "national renaissance," and "creative genius of the nation" indicate the source of influence, i.e., romanticism, which provided all the national movements with their respective ideological tools. Hess's *Rome and Jerusalem*, as its title indicates, was written under the impact of events which had led to the unification of Italy in 1859. Hess expressly refers to this fact, calling the Jewish cause "the last national problem," after Italy had solved its own. However, impulses from non-Jewish sources can also be traced in the cases of Alkalai and Kalischer, as both use one characteristic argument in their appeal: Jews, who are the descendants of a holy and ancient nation, should not lag behind the newly created nations of the Balkans.

The real difference between Alkalai and Kalischer on the one hand and Hess on the other, is the spiritual background from which their respective drives stemmed. While the first two were originally steeped in the sources of Jewish tradition, including the Bible, Talmud, and Kabbalah, the last had only a faint idea of these sources from his childhood. He was influenced in his knowledge of Jewish history and its evaluation by the contemporary historian Heinrich *Graetz. However, the fabric of Hess's outlook was woven out of strands which were of modern European, primarily Hegelian, origin. He was far from being a religious Jew, in any traditional sense, and, judging by his earlier activities and writings, he must be counted as one of those Jews who were absorbed by European movements and systems of thought.

Hess was the first figure in Zionist history who did not grow out of Jewish tradition. His Jewishness returned to him after a period of estrangement. Thus, Hess and his two contemporaries, Alkalai and Kalischer, prefigure the two main types of Zionism: one had to overcome the miraculous elements of traditional messianism; and the other, after having forsaken the tradition altogether, had to recover its cultural and political implications.

Attributing the emergence of the Zionist idea to the revitalization and modernization of the messianic utopia does not mean that the mere suggestion of regathering the Jews in their homeland was sufficient for initiating the movement. The historical connection between the Jews and their ancient homeland was indeed a conspicuous feature in Jewish, as well as Christian, tradition. The idea of the restoration of the Jews gained currency, especially in England, where the awakened interest in the Old Testament in the wake of the Puritan revolution strongly stimulated interest in the history of the Jewish nation (see Christian Zionism, below). Imaginative Jewish writers and social projectors also readvanced the idea of establishing a Jewish commonwealth, either in Palestine or elsewhere, with a view to solving the "Jewish problem." A case in point was the efforts of Mordecai M. *Noah, one-time consul of the United States in Tunis, who in 1825 issued an appeal to European Jewry to establish a Jewish state named "Ararat" on the Grand Island of the Niagara River. Noah later fostered the idea of the restoration of Palestine.

At first the general Jewish public either took almost no cognizance of these ideas and their promoters or reacted to them with mockery and derision. Alkalai, who had begun his activities 20 years earlier, succeeded in finding any substantial and lasting support only in the 1860s. From this time on, a connection can be perceived in the activities of the various early Zionists. The three great figures described here not only knew of each other, but also supported each other. They succeeded in founding a more-or-less interconnected society among themselves, together with other, less conspicuous personalities who were influenced by them or who had reached the same conclusions independently. Moreover, from the 1860s onward there is an uninterrupted development, and one may speak of historical causation as the ideas and activities of these early Zionists led the way to the full-fledged Ḥibbat Zion movement, founded in the 1880s under the impact of the Russian pogroms and the rise of modern antisemitism in Germany.

By and large, it cannot be said that the forerunners had succeeded in realizing something of their aim, i.e., the ingathering of Jews in their homeland. Until the 1870s, when anti-Jewish troubles began in Romania, there had been no Jewish exodus from any country in Europe. Instead of producing an idea in order to satisfy a need, the early Zionists were searching for a need which would correspond to their ideas. Kalischer seized any rumor of Jews wishing to emigrate as a God-sent opportunity to prove that people who were ready to go to Ereẓ Israel could be found. Thus he tried to refute the argument that his theory had no hold on reality, but he never tried to prove the social necessity or inevitability of his idea. The first real objectives of Zionism were realized only in the 1880s, when persecutions and defamation in Romania and bloody pogroms and civil disqualifications in Russia set many European Jews into motion.

[Jacob Katz]

ḤIBBAT ZION

*Ḥibbat Zion (Heb. "Love of Zion") was the ideology and movement whose aim was the national renascence of the Jews and their return to Ereẓ Israel. The movement in the 19th century flourished mainly in the large Jewish communities of Eastern Europe (Russia-Poland, Romania). The Ḥibbat Zion societies merged with the Zionist Organization upon its establishment by Theodor Herzl, although some of them continued their formal existence until World War I.

ROOTS OF ḤIBBAT ZION. The Ḥibbat Zion movement derived most of its ideas from the basic values of Jewish tradition: the sense of exile, the longing for redemption, and the religious and spiritual attachment to Ereẓ Israel. Most of the Jews of Eastern Europe, however, were distant from organized political and social activity, and their religious leaders – with a few exceptions – were even opposed to it on the grounds that the coming of the Messiah should not be urged by human endeavor (*dehikat ha-keẓ*) and that it constituted human interference in the ways of providence. The problems of the Jewish national renascence and the settlement of Ereẓ Israel were mainly discussed by individuals who were motivated to action by messianic visions or by the influence of the national awakening of European peoples. Ẓevi Kalischer and Judah Alkalai (see above) had propagated the idea of settling Ereẓ Israel as early as the 1840s and 1850s, and the former had initiated a consultation of several rabbis and representatives of the communities of Germany in 1860 in order to found a company for this purpose. Shortly after this conference Chaim Lorje of Frankfurt on the Oder founded the Jewish Company for the Settlement of the Holy Land. Neither propaganda nor these activities had any substantial effect on the public, however, just as scant attention was paid to Moses Hess's *Rome and Jerusalem* and David *Gordon's articles in *Ha-Maggid*, which supported the settlement of Ereẓ Israel. When the Ḥibbat Zion movement was founded, however, its religious sector was influenced by the ideas and the example of these first rabbis.

The public debate on the question of Jewish nationalism began at the end of the 1860s with the renewed strength of the movement for religious reform in Germany and Hungary. This movement called for the national and cultural assimilation of the Jews and for a break with the national tradition by removing references to Zion and Jerusalem from the prayer book and basing the Jewish religion on its "eternal truths" alone. Peretz *Smolenskin was among those bitterly opposed to these trends, denouncing them in the monthly *Ha-Shaḥar* which he began publishing in 1868. He placed the Jews firmly among the peoples aspiring to national liberation. Eliezer *Ben-Yehuda's important articles "*She'elah Nikhbadah*" ("An Important Question") and "*Od Musar lo Lakaḥnu*" ("We Have Not Learned Our Lesson") in *Ha-Shahar* (1879), relating the national renascence in Ereẓ Israel to the revival of the Hebrew language as a spoken tongue, were an essential contribution to the crystallization of Ḥibbat Zion as an ideological trend.

BACKGROUND TO THE EMERGENCE OF THE MOVEMENT. The Ḥibbat Zion movement arose at a time when developments in Eastern European states were pressing large numbers of Jews to emigrate or engage in intensified social and political activity. At the same time leading advocates of the Enlightenment (*Haskalah) became disillusioned with their faith in the possibility of Jewish assimilation among the nations and were disappointed in their hopes to attain equal rights for Jews. A decisive force in this direction was the series of pogroms in *Russia after the assassination of Czar Alexander II (1881). The fact that the sincere aspiration of the *maskilim* and the Jewish youth to grow closer to the Russian people had been met with a wave of hatred and that the government had been quick to declare the pogroms as the "reaction of the people" to "Jewish exploitation" and had begun to impose severe restrictions on the sources of income, government posts, and admission to institutes of learning available to the Jews caused a severe ideological crisis among the *maskilim*. Many of those who had grown distant from their people began to return to it (visiting the synagogue, participating in fasts, etc.). Others who had previously pinned their hopes on the struggle to change the social system began to realize that this would not automatically answer the "Jewish question." Among those who advocated a national renascence, the realization became apparent that a spiritual and linguistic revival was not sufficient, and that they must set their sights on a real homeland, in which the Jews would not be regarded as aliens. The example of Germany, where a widespread antisemitic movement arose at the end of the 1870s, served as a warning and proof that neither Enlightenment nor emancipation was sufficient to guarantee the status of Jews in their countries of residence. Jewish writers and *maskilim* embarked on a penetrating discussion of antisemitism and its causes. The times, however, were unsuited to ideological discussions alone. The panic-stricken flight of thousands across the borders and the suffering of the refugees in the places where they were concentrated emphasized the need for a speedy and urgent "national solution."

THE BEGINNINGS OF THE MOVEMENT. The majority of the active Jewish public felt that the only solution was to leave Russia; only a small minority, mainly the wealthy and their relatives, opposed emigration. Many societies, especially among the youth, were formed for this purpose, and there were many arguments between those who supported Ereẓ Israel as a "place of refuge" and those who favored the United States. Foremost among the Ḥovevei Zion – those in favor of going to "the land of our fathers," "to which we have historical rights" – was Moses Leib *Lilienblum, who was soon joined by Smolenskin, Leo *Levanda, and others. The journals *Ha-Shaḥar, Ha-Maggid, Ha-Meliẓ*, and *Razsvet* (in Russian) became the disseminators of the ideas of Ḥibbat Zion. Most of the Ḥovevei Zion societies, especially those of the young *maskilim*, advocated radical national programs. The students' society Ahavat Zion, founded in 1881 in St. Petersburg, declared that "every son of Israel who admits that there is no salvation for Israel unless they establish a government of their own in the Land of Israel can be considered a member of the society." The charter of the *Bilu society stated: "The goal of the society is the politico-economic and national-spiritual revival of the Jewish people in Syria and Ereẓ Israel." Some of the societies regarded their aim as imminent *aliyah* to Ereẓ Israel, while others emphasized preparation and the propagation of the concept of the settlement of Ereẓ Israel among the people. All of them, however, agreed upon the means toward settlement as the acquisition of land (either granted by the Turkish government or purchased) and the creation of a class of Jewish farmers and artisans in the country.

Romanian Jewry was aroused by the idea of settling Ereẓ Israel. The Romanian government's devious disavowal of its explicit obligation – according to the decisions of the Congress of Berlin, 1878 – to grant equal rights to all its citizens and the dispossession of growing numbers of Jews from their sources of income had made the true value of those legal guarantees clear to many Romanian Jews and brought them face to face with emigration as the sole solution. At the end of 1881 there were over 30 societies for the settlement of Ereẓ Israel in Romania, and on Jan. 11–12, 1882, a conference of Ḥovevei Zion took place in Focsani and elected a central committee, with its headquarters in Galati. (See also below, Zionist Organization in Romania.)

PINSKER'S "AUTOEMANCIPATION." The new movement was provided with a systematic ideological basis by Leon *Pinsker in his *Autoemancipation*, which appeared in September 1882. Although initially he did not contemplate Ereẓ Israel as the most suitable territory for the Jewish state, he eventually joined the Ḥibbat Zion movement. He came into contact with societies in different localities, and after consultation with Lilienblum, Hermann *Schapira, Max *Mandelstamm, and others (in September 1883) a memorandum was sent out calling for the establishment of a central executive committee to be elected by a congress of delegates from all the Societies for the Settlement of Ereẓ Israel. Shortly afterward the Zerubavel society (with Pinsker as chairman and Lilienblum as secretary) was founded in Odessa and immediately became the central society of the movement; it was followed by the Warsaw society, which was headed by Saul Pinḥas *Rabbinowitz and Isidor *Jasinowski.

SETTLEMENT ACTIVITIES. Many of the Ḥovevei Zion pinned their hopes on the support of the *Alliance Israélite Universelle and on other Jewish organizations. However, when these organizations searched for a haven for the refugees from Russia who were concentrated in Brody, they did not direct their migration to Ereẓ Israel at all: some were sent to the United States and some were returned to Russia. At the conference of delegates from various Jewish groups that met in Berlin in April 1882 to discuss the question of emigration, only Azriel *Hildesheimer came out in favor of settling the refugees in Ereẓ Israel, and his proposal was not met with sympathy. Representatives of the societies nonetheless went ahead, and in the spring of 1882 a considerable number of settlers began to reach Ereẓ Israel, prompting the Turkish authorities immediately to publish orders to forbid further entry. The Ḥovevei Zion turned for aid to their British sympathizer Laurence *Oliphant, and asked him to intervene with the Turkish government, but he had no influence in Constantinople. Among those who succeeded in reaching Ereẓ Israel in July 1882 were 14 members of the Bilu Society who had gone, without any property, to work as agricultural laborers.

Despite the Turkish ban on immigration, the foundations of Jewish agricultural settlement in Ereẓ Israel were laid in that year. In July 1882 Zalman *Levontin and his companions established Rishon le-Zion, and shortly afterward members of the Moinesti society from Romania settled in Rosh Pinnah (which had previously been settled and then abandoned by Jews from Safed). At the same time, the settlement in Petaḥ Tikvah, which had been founded by Jerusalem Jews in 1878 but had later been abandoned, was revived. At the end of 1882, a group of Romanian Jews settled in Zammārīn (later Zikhron Ya'akov). However, the meager resources of the new settlers, their lack of preparation, and the difficulty of local conditions worked against them, and soon after the establishment of the new settlements they were in need of help. It soon became apparent that the various societies in Russia and Romania were in no position to provide the required assistance, and Baron Edmond de *Rothschild was persuaded by Samuel *Mohilever and Joseph Feinberg (of Rishon le-Zion) to assist a group of Jewish farmers from Russia to settle in Ereẓ Israel (they later founded Ekron) and to take the settlement of Rishon le-Zion under his protection. In the course of time most of the settlements became sponsored by Baron de Rothschild; the exception was Gederah, which was founded by the Bilu'im in 1884. The regime of strict supervision of the settlers through the agency of Rothschild's officials was a constant source of friction and rebelliousness. Meanwhile, settlements continued to be founded until the end of the 1880s.

THE ORGANIZATION. Although it was clear to all the active members of Ḥibbat Zion that the movement had to be unified and organized, opinions differed on the form of organization. Younger and more radical elements demanded emphasis on the ultimate national aspirations and open opposition to the philanthropic organizations, while more bourgeois elements advocated moderation and supportive activities. The 100th birthday of Moses Montefiore provided the movement with a suitable occasion for convening all its active members, and the first conference of Ḥibbat Zion took place on Nov. 6, 1884, at Kattowitz (see *Kattowitz Conference). Thirty-five delegates participated in the conference; most of them were from Russian societies, and the rest were from Romania, Germany, England, and France. An account of the movement's achievements proved rather unimpressive. The great tide of Jewish emigration had been stemmed, and even the large Jewish organizations had abandoned hope of guiding and directing it; the Turkish government had closed the gates of Ereẓ Israel, and those few who had succeeded in reaching the country were considered infiltrators. It is therefore not surprising that the main value of the conference was its demonstration of the unity of Ḥibbat Zion and of the Jewish people as a whole. Pinsker hoped to attract Jewish personalities and organizations from the West into the movement. It was decided to call the organization Mazkeret Moshe be-Ereẓ ha-Kodesh and to establish a central committee with headquarters in Berlin, since conditions in Russia made legal activities on behalf of the movement impossible there; until the establishment of this committee, it was decided to set up a temporary committee in Odessa and a subcommittee in Warsaw. The resolutions accepted at the conference concerned mainly practical matters – organizational methods and ways of supporting the settlements. There was no mention, either in the debates or in the resolutions, of the major questions of national revival or the great national goal.

These concessions, however, were in vain. In Germany, not a single Jewish personality of any stature was found to head the proposed committee, and the resolution to establish a Berlin center was cancelled. Neither did other societies of Ḥibbat Zion that were founded in German and English towns succeed in achieving importance. Even the society in Kattowitz, which in 1883 had published the German-language movement organ, *Der Kolonist*, lost its importance. Only the student organization *Kadimah in Vienna, which published *Selbstemanzipation* from 1885 on, survived. The movement in Romania stagnated until the beginning of the 1890s, and the Russian societies were involved with minor affairs. The organization consolidated itself, however; there were almost 100 societies with a membership of approximately 14,000, which collected about 30,000 rubles a year from donations and another 20,000 rubles from various enterprises. Propaganda among the masses was emphasized; preachers (e.g., Ẓevi Hirsch *Masliansky and Judah Leib Yevzerow) and entertainers (e.g., Eliakum *Zunser) did much to spread the ideas of Ḥibbat Zion. Nonetheless, there was friction between the different societies, and opposition to the existing leadership emerged.

In June 1887 the Second Conference, this time of Ḥovevei Zion in Russia, met in Druskininki and resolved to call the movement Ḥovevei Zion. Mohilever attempted to impose an

Orthodox authority over the movement, but was foiled by younger representatives, such as Menaḥem *Ussishkin from Moscow, Ze'ev Berman from St. Petersburg, and Meir *Dizengoff from Kishinev. Pinsker was finally reelected to lead the movement, with six advisers, three of whom were famous rabbis: Mohilever, Naphtali Ẓevi Yehudah *Berlin, and Mordecai *Eliasberg. It was also decided to renew efforts to gain permission from the Russian government to organize the movement. In 1890 Alexander *Zederbaum, editor of *Ha-Meliẓ*, succeeded in obtaining government sanction for the Society for the Support of Jewish Farmers and Artisans in Syria and Palestine, which became known as the *Odessa Committee. The founding conference, which took place legally – for the first time – that year in Odessa, was attended by numerous delegates from all over Russia. Increased contributions enabled the establishment of the settlements of Reḥovot and Haderah (1890–91), the consolidation of Mishmar ha-Yarden, and provided support for the veteran settlements. An executive committee was set up in Jaffa under Vladimir *Tiomkin to supervise the distribution of support and the acquisition of land. The Esra Society in Berlin and other societies in Frankfurt, Paris, and London intensified their activities. The second "Russian Exodus," which took place after the expulsion of Jews from Moscow in 1891, led to increased *aliyah* and to speculation in land, and the Turkish authorities renewed their ban on immigration and settlement.

THE SPIRITUAL CENTER. The "practical" activities of Ḥibbat Zion gave rise to harsh criticism, especially on the part of *Aḥad Ha-Am. This criticism was partially inspired by Aḥad Ha-Am's view that Ereẓ Israel could not provide a solution for the masses of emigrants, but should rather serve as a "spiritual center" to unite all parts of the disintegrating nation. It was in this spirit that the *Benei Moshe society was founded. The crisis in settlement activities after the short-lived increase in *aliyah* at the beginning of the 1890s sowed fresh disillusionment in the ranks of Ḥibbat Zion and strengthened the influence of Aḥad Ha-Am, who had several supporters among the members of the Odessa Committee. Emphasis on the need for spiritual preparation brought about an intensification of the ideological and cultural activities of Ḥibbat Zion, especially after the founding of the Aḥi'asaf publishing house. Despite the importance of Aḥad Ha-Am's criticism, however, his approach could not serve as a basis for the activities of the movement. It is not surprising, therefore, that upon the appearance of Herzl and political Zionism, the vast majority of the Ḥovevei Zion societies joined the new Zionist Organization.

[Shmuel Ettinger]

IDEOLOGICAL EVOLUTION

THE SHOCK OF THE 1880S; POLITICAL ZIONISM. Modern Zionism began with need and in disillusion. The new thinking was a reaction to dramatic and tragic events in Russia. Czar Alexander II was assassinated early in 1881 by revolutionaries, among whom there was one young Jewess in a minor role. Immediately thereafter a wave of pogroms spread all over the country. The physical results of the murder and pillage were dire, but the moral impact of these outrages was even more devastating. It was commonly believed that the perpetrators of these attacks were encouraged and even organized by governmental circles; it was certainly beyond doubt that the authorities did little to defend the Jews against the pillagers and murderers. What was perhaps even more upsetting, at least to elements of the advanced Jewish intelligentsia, was that many liberal and revolutionary circles did not defend the Jews but preferred to see in these outbreaks the first stirrings of social change, in which the Jews were being attacked for their supposed exploitation of the Russian peasants and laborers. The whole system of anti-Jewish restrictions had locked the Jews of Russia into a few miserable middleman occupations, in which they could not help but be "unproductive"; the Jews were as much victims as those whom they were supposedly victimizing. Yet all this was ignored by so advanced a group as the leaders of the populist (Narodnik) movement, even though there were some Jews among them, as they hailed the pogroms as the first necessary revolutionary convulsion.

The conclusion drawn on all sides from this shock was that there was no future for Jews in Russia in the existing regime. A segment of the Jewish intelligentsia turned to revolution and lost all hope in the possibilities of reform in the land. Great masses followed in the path of the substantial trickle of emigration that had begun in the 1870s, and, despairing of any economic future in Russia, they moved westward, chiefly to the United States. In the years between 1881 and 1914 some 2,600,000 Jews from Russia and its immediate neighbors immigrated to the "new land." Some contemporary figures, chiefly Leon Pinsker and Moshe Leib Lilienblum, drew other conclusions. They did not believe that hatred of Jews was limited to Russia alone, or that the problem was ultimately to be solved by emigration to friendlier countries or even by the achievement of emancipation in legal theory. The young Lilienblum was in Odessa in 1881 as an "enlightener," a *maskil*, completing his own secular education, in the certainty that the road to freedom for Jews required their westernization, which would then make them acceptable to "benevolent Russia." He was then also mildly socialist in his political outlook. But cowering before the pogrom mob, it became clear to him, as he was soon to write, that the revolution might take place and yet not bring freedom to the Jews; that they might still be excluded and hated even in a new order; and that the future of Jews lay in the restoration of Jewish nationhood. The more important, and more famous, immediate reaction to the pogroms and to the failure of hope which attended them, was that of an even more committed "enlightener," Leon Pinsker. He left Russia for Central Europe in those months to search for allies for his new views, which he published in German in a pamphlet called *Autoemancipation*. The simple assertion of this essay was that antisemitism, which he called Judophobia, was a permanent psychopathological phenomenon, not only a social one, so long as the Jews were a "ghost nation" – everywhere a minority and nowhere a normal national majority, everywhere "guests" and nowhere "hosts." Antisemitism was "xenophobia," the hatred of the stranger, but it differed from all the usual varieties of such tensions, if not in kind then in degree, as it was the longest lasting and most pervasive form of this malaise. In the light of pogroms Pinsker finally rejected the notion that any amount of change by Jews to make themselves over into the image of their gentile neighbors could finally gain them acceptance in the majority society. He thus agreed with the antisemites that by their ill-will they had proved their case, that the Jews were irretrievably and forever alien, and that the dream of assimilation was not possible, not because the Jews could not assimilate but because the majority would not let them. It followed rationally from these premises that the way to solve the Jewish problem was to remove the Jews from the places of their dwelling, from the situation of abnormality surrounded by hatred, to a territory of their own where they would become a normal nation. Such a place was not necessarily the land of the ancestors in Ereẓ Israel, though Pinsker was aware that there were historic and emotional ties to the land, but rather the most readily available land that was suitable for settlement, preferably on the American continent, where Jews could develop their own autonomy. For all of his disbelief in the promise of the era of the emancipation that Jews would be personally accepted as equals in Europe, Pinsker's outlook was still emancipatory, still rooted in the desire to engineer the acceptance of the Jews as equals in the modern world. What was new was that Pinsker saw this world as consisting of nations which disliked foreigners, so Jews had to cease being foreign by becoming a proper nation. He was in the first stage of awareness that such national equality was not granted as a gift from on high, because the peoples were not generous, but rather as a result of the national effort of those who desired their national dignity.

Those to whom Pinsker turned in Western Europe showed sympathy for him, but thought that he had been totally unnerved by the sight of the pogroms in his country. In Russia itself the few who organized the Ḥibbat Zion movement in 1882 were motivated also by other impulses than the national theorizing of Pinsker. Their concerns were, like those of Alkalai and Kalischer of the previous generation, a blend of the older, religious longing for the messianic restoration of Zion and the new language of modern nationalism, allied to the notion that gradual settlement in Ereẓ Israel was at least a step in the direction of the ultimate consummation. Pinsker reluctantly found in these groups the only possible adherents and he consented to become their leader. Aḥad Ha-Am, his younger contemporary who was to become the major ideologist of this strand of Zionism, insisted after Pinsker's death, and in contrast with Theodor Herzl, that Pinsker's major concerns had been "the revival of the spirit," i.e., the renaissance of the Hebraic culture in a modern key, and that he had never wavered from his commitment to Zion as the only possible land for the endeavor of a Jewish renaissance – and, for that matter, that Pinsker had never dreamt of more than an elite, representative Jewish community in the Land. All this was fairly adequate as a statement of Aḥad Ha'am's own premises, but Theodor Herzl was thoroughly right in his assertion that, had he known of the existence of Pinsker's *Autoemancipation*, he would not have written *Der Judenstaat*. Herzl's views were indeed almost exactly those of his Russian predecessor.

It is now no longer believed that Herzl wrote *Der Judenstaat* in immediate reaction to the beginnings of the Dreyfus Affair, which he witnessed and on which he reported as the correspondent in Paris of the leading daily paper of Vienna. Herzl's shift from a fashionable journalist who believed in the assimilation of Jews into the majority culture had begun earlier, in reaction to renewed antisemitic agitation of the German-speaking world in the 1880s culminating in Karl *Lueger's appointment as mayor of Vienna on an antisemitic platform. Kaiser Franz Joseph had vetoed his election three times, but that such a party could prevail in cosmopolitan Vienna was a major shock. The beginnings of anti-Jewish agitation in the very home of the emancipation, Paris, where the French Revolution had first given equality to some European Jews in 1791, could only confirm that the trouble was real, and pervasive. Herzl was, if anything, even less involved in Jewish cultural concerns than Pinsker, who had been a leader of the "enlighteners" before his conversion to Jewish nationalism and had even so labored among his people in that period. What gave particular bite to Herzl's views was that he made no distinction, explicit or implicit, between "Eastern" and "Western" Jews. This (and not some intellectual belief in the indivisibility of the Jewish spirit) was the meaning, in the context of his thinking and writing in 1896, of his oft-quoted sentence, "We are a people – one people." What he saw was one Jewish situation all over the world, that of a national group which was an anomaly. His first thought had been that of total assimilation and at first he even fantasized about the possibility of leading all Jews to the great cathedral of St. Stephan in Vienna, where their baptism would make an end of antisemitism. He turned away from this "solution" (in which he had been preceded by such figures as David Friedlaender and Napoleon a century earlier, at the dawn of the era of emancipation) because he knew that it would not work, that antisemites hated Jews even after they were totally assimilated. Herzl therefore proceeded to argue in *Der Judenstaat*, exactly like Pinsker, that the essence of the Jewish problem was not individual but national and that the Jews could gain acceptance in the world only if they ceased being a national anomaly. He too spoke of the creation of a commission which would survey the possible territories on which the Jewish State would be founded, and he left open the question as to whether it would be better to opt for Palestine with its historic associations or for some vacant land in Argentina. Intellectually, what was original in Herzl's analysis was his dialectic use of the conception of antisemitism as a "reasonable" form of hatred of the unlike. Herzl argued, on the basis of his bold assertion that he alone understood this phenomenon correctly, that even antisemites

Commission d. Zionisten-Congresses
Wien,
II., Rembrandtstr. 11.

אדון נכבד!

ביום א׳ ב׳ וג׳ אלול ש״ז יתאספו חו״צ בכל הארצות לקונגרס־הציוני בבאזל (בשווייץ). והיום ההוא, שבו יתאחדו אחינו המפוזרים בדעה אחת, יהיה יום נצחון לתחית לאומנו. האספה בבאזל תהיה התחלת תקופה חדשה בהתפתחות תנועתנו.

שם יספרו לנו אחינו מכל פנות הארץ ע״ד מצבם ומגמותיהם, שם יתברר מה התנועה הציונית דורשת ממעריציה. שם תתרכז ותתאחד פעולתנו, שהיתה קרועה לכמה גזרים, ע״י הנהגה כוללת לכל סניפי העבודה. שם תראינה עינינו קבוץ־גליות, שיאחד כל הכחות לפעולה אחת, גדולה וכבירה.

הקונגרס שואף למטרות קרובות ואפשריות. כל הידיעות האחרות על אדתיו קלוטות מן האויר. כל מעשי הקונגרס יהיו בפרסום גמור. בוכוחיו והחלטותיו לא תהיה שום התנגדות לחוקי איזו ארץ ולחובותינו האזרחיים. ביחוד אנחנו ערבים בזה, שכל מעשי האספה יהיו באופן מקובל ומרוצה לחו״צ ברוסיא ולממשלתם הרוממה.

בזה נבקש או׳ך, אדון נכבד, ואת חבריך שבחוגך, שתואילו לבא לבזל ולהשתתף באספתנו. הקונגרס הראשון שלנו הוא התל שהכל פונים אליו. אוהבים ואויבים מחכים לו בעינים כלות. ולכן עליו להראות לכל, כי חפצנו ברור ויכלתנו גדולה. אם לא ימלא הקונגרס את תפקידו, אז תבא ע״כ נסיגה לאחור בתנועתנו לזמן רב. והכל תלוי רק בהשתתפות מרובה של אחינו ברוסיא, ששם רוב מנייננו.

אנו מקוים, שתדעו את חובתכם ותבאו לאספתנו. באספה אפשר יהיה לדבר עברית. בבאזל יש אכסניא כשרה.

דבר בואך מהר נא להודיענו עפ״י הכתבת הנ״ל.

בשם „הועד להכנת הקונגרס הציוני״:

Dr. Theodor Herzl
ראש־הועד

Dr. Marcus Ehrenpreis
המזכיר

Buchdruckerei Max Bruck, Diakovar. 2349.—97.

Invitation to the First Zionist Congress at Basle, 1897. It is signed by Herzl as head of the preparatory committee and Marcus Ehrenpreis as secretary. Jerusalem, Central Zionist Archives.

could and would be enlisted in laboring for a Jewish State, for it would help them solve problems that they had with Jews, who were "unnecessary" in the host societies and whose very existence disturbed social peace. Since he accepted without question that men were reasonable and not demonic (Herzl went so far as to say that the emancipation was basically irreversible), he could only presume that history would inevitably move forward and produce the only possible solution to the tension between the Jews and the majority society, a Jewish State.

The very nobility of his person, the appearance of a man who suggested the ancient prophet and seemed the equal of great statesmen of his own day, lent resonance to Herzl's words, and he was particularly moving to masses of Jews in Eastern Europe precisely because he was a "Westerner" come back to his people. His tactics were perhaps even more important as an original contribution to the formation of the Zionist movement. Into the teeth of the antisemites who had made the word "Jew" into an insult, and of the assimilationists who used such circumlocution as "Hebrew" and "Israelite," he spoke boldly of the *Judenstaat*, which means not "The Jewish State" but, literally, "The Jew State." He saw the Jewish question as an international political question to be attacked in the forum of international politics. He therefore organized the Zionist movement at the First Zionist Congress in 1897 in such fashion that the gathering had about it the aura of a Jewish parliament in session, and he made of his presidency of the movement something reminiscent of the role of a head of state or a prime minister. All of the new instruments that were created – the Zionist Congress as a political forum, the buying of the shekel as an act of allegiance to the national movement, a bank (The *Jewish Colonial Trust) to be financed by the buying of shares, and an official press in several languages to inform the adherents of the political activities of the central body and its principal leader – these did indeed constitute the adumbration of Herzl's bold assertion in his diary at the First Zionist Congress in 1897, "Here I have created the Jewish State."

In the few years that were given him at the head of Zionism, he held consistently, until near the very end of his days, to the line that only the attainment of a charter, of a political document granting Jews near-sovereign rights in the territory that they were to settle, was the first objective of Zionism. He therefore fought against turning the Zionist movement into an instrument of piecemeal settlement, and the aid that was given the early settlements in his lifetime, little though it was, was a concession that he made to his opponents in the movement, the "practical" Zionists.

Herzl bitterly opposed the turning of Zionism toward cultural endeavors either by linking it with the secular Hebrew revival or by coupling Zionism with the national religious orthodoxy of the Mizrachi faction which was arising near the end of his days. For that matter, even though he was himself a certain kind of aristocratic social reformer (he dreamt of a seven-hour day in the Jewish State and even wanted its flag to contain seven stars to mark this social advance), Herzl opposed the setting up of the Socialist faction within Zionism. For him the movement that he had created existed for one purpose: the translation of "a people without a land" to some "land without a people." He did indeed turn his first and major ongoing efforts toward negotiating with the sultan of Turkey for a charter for Jews in Palestine or in its immediate vicinity, but those who opposed him in 1903, when he wanted to accept the proposal of the British Government for a Jewish settlement in East Africa (see *Uganda Scheme), were not entirely wrong in remembering that Herzl's commitment to Zion was unlike theirs, and that on theoretical grounds he had always remained a Zionist created by the "plight of the Jews" (*Judennot*), and not by cultural commitment.

Nonetheless, the bulk of Herzl's followers, even though all assented to his political vision of a national movement treated as an equal among the powers of the world, came to his Zionism with less clear-cut, more complicated motivations. It was not only that individual parties and factions arose, each of which wanted the future Jewish State to take a certain shape and to be constructed consciously in such a direction. More fundamentally, the needs that Zionism served among the mass of its East European believers were not always identical with those which had moved Pinsker and Herzl.

CULTURAL AND "SYNTHETIC" ZIONISM. The basic distinction in contemporary polemics was made around the turn of the century by Aḥad Ha-Am: he refused to believe that it was humanly possible, even under the most favorable conditions, in the light of the Jewish birthrate, for the majority or even any substantial fraction of the Jews of the world to emigrate to their national homeland and thus significantly reduce the population in the Jewish Diaspora. He thus saw the "Jewish plight" as intrinsically insoluble by purely Zionist means, and the Jews could only do what they had already done in the Exile in bad times: either emigrate to more favorable countries, such as America, or temporize with the conditions in Russia. Aḥad Ha-Am himself did a bit of both, eventually emigrating to London, where he practically stopped writing but served in an important way as spiritual guide to the young Chaim Weizmann and a coterie of others. The fundamental problem of the modern age, and the one to which Zionism could indeed address itself, was the crisis not of the Jews but of Judaism, i.e., the rapid and radical disintegration of Jewish faith and identity that was going on everywhere. A secularist and positivist himself, Aḥad Ha-Am did not believe that the process of loss of religious faith was reversible. The function that revealed religion had performed in talmudic and medieval Judaism, that of guaranteeing the survival of the Jews as a separate entity because of their belief in the divinely ordained importance of the Jewish religion and people, it was no longer performing and could not be expected to perform. The crucial task facing Jews in the modern era was to devise new structures to contain the separate individuality of the Jews and to keep them loyal to their own tradition. This analysis of the situation implied, in its very first assertions, a view of Jewish history which Aḥad Ha-Am produced as undoubted and which has since become the common coin of secular Zionist and Israeli historiography: that the Jews in all ages were essentially a nation, and that all other factors profoundly important to the life of this people, even religion, were mainly instrumental values.

A thousand years earlier Saadiah Gaon (d. 942 C.E.) gave expression to the *raison d'être* of the Jew in the pre-modern era when he pronounced that "the Jewish people is a people only for the sake of its Torah," i.e., that Jews exist as the instrument of Judaism. To accept this definition in the modern age of disbelief would mean that contemporary Jews have broken radically with their past, that continuity no longer existed in Jewish history, and that whatever solution could be found for the present situation would address itself to masses of individuals who still bore the name "Jew," in varieties of suffering or quiet desperation and on various levels of pride or self-hatred, to help them make the best of their situation. Such an understanding of Jewish modernity could lead to an assimilationist conclusion, as it had throughout the 19th century. It could also support the basic thesis of Herzl that the Jews existed as a community in his day only because they shared a negative situation, antisemitism, and that this was the one problem which they could, in the here and now, solve together. Those who chose to deal with that problem only by national and

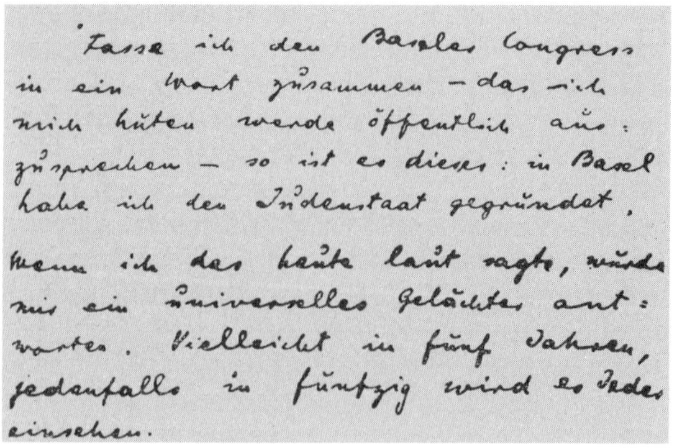
Fasse ich den Basler Congress
in ein Wort zusammen – das ich
mich hüten werde öffentlich aus-
zusprechen – so ist es dieses: in Basel
habe ich den Judenstaat gegründet.
Wenn ich das heute laut sagte, würde
mir ein universelles Gelächter antworten. Vielleicht in fünf Jahren,
jedenfalls in fünfzig wird es Jeder
einsehen.

Extract from Herzl's diary for Sept. 3, 1897, after the First Zionist Congress: "In Basle I founded the Jewish State. ... Maybe in five years, certainly in fifty, everyone will realize it." Jerusalem, Central Zionist Archives.

political means would then be free to evolve whatever culture might suit them. This view of modern Jewish culture was maintained by Hebrew writers and ideologists, such as M.J. Berdyczewski, J.Ḥ. Brenner, and Jacob Klatzkin. They could accept neither Aḥad Ha-Am's notion of ongoing continuity in Jewish history nor, more fundamentally, his description of the "national spirit" as an authoritative guide and standard to which he attributed a majesty comparable to that which the religious had once ascribed to the God of revelation. Brenner regarded the national past and most of the Jewish heritage as weak, desiccated, cringing, and unworthy. There was thus created at the beginning of the 20th century, in part under the influence of Friedrich Nietzsche, a school of thought which wanted to create a Jewish state not only because there had already been a radical break with the Jewish past but in order to realize such a change. These writers wanted to establish a bold and earthy people, whose hands would not be tied by the rules of the rabbis or even by the self-doubts of the prophets. (This trend toward a total break was never attractive to more than a small minority among the Zionists, but it eventually evolved into a heresy to be represented by those few Israel writers and intellectuals who opposed the very notion and term of Jewish peoplehood and Zionism – and were called *"Canaanites."

Of all the schools of thought that were arising within the Zionist movement in its very first few years, Socialist Zionism was, at least in practice, the most important. In the work of its founding father, Nachman Syrkin, and a few years later, of the younger, Marxist, Ber Borochov, a socialist explanation of the "plight of the Jews" was constructed. In this view, the Jews were everywhere rejected aliens because their economic pursuits were "unproductive" or peripheral. For their masses were locked in the Pale of Settlement without any outlet into the modern development of the general society and its economy. They were middlemen, small craftsmen or *luftmenschen* who were not integrally bound to the roots and basic aspects of production and especially not to farming, modern industry, and other forms of primary economic activity. Socialist Zionists did not, of course, blame the Jews for this unhealthy economic situation, for they knew that it was not only a result of many centuries of persecution and discrimination but also of the "judophobia" of the gentile peasants and workers who regarded the Jews as alien "exploiters" and unwanted competitors; the antisemitism which attacked Jews because of their marginal economic role was the source of the very phenomenon that it attacked. This vicious circle produced the "inverted pyramid" of the Jewish economy in the Diaspora, the phenomenon that Jews were fewest in production and became more numerous the further away one went from farms and factories. That was the cause of an inevitable process of mass flight from Russia, Romania, and other countries, which would, in the view of Borochov, eventually propel Jews toward the land within which a proper kind of national economy, a "normal" pyramid, would be created. However, the non-Marxist Labor Zionists, particularly those in Ereẓ Israel, such as A.D. Gordon, who was influenced by Tolstoy, affirmed neither such a historical inevitability of a mass emigration to Ereẓ Israel nor its socialist future, nor did they theorize about the need to create a Jewish national community as a necessary precondition for "healthy class straggle," which could not take place in the Diaspora where both Jewish workers and their employers were trapped by unhealthy circumstances. For Gordon and his pioneering disciples Zionism was an act of will, an affirmation about the dignity of physical labor and the rootedness of man in his own soil, of the desperate necessity to create a new Jewish man in the Land of Israel to replace the disfigured human being who had been shaped by his misery and alienation from nature in the Diaspora. The men of the Second Aliyah, the young pioneers who went to Ereẓ Israel in the first decade of the 20th century, adhered in their majority to some version of the socialist Zionist faith and especially to the notion that the "new man" whom they were creating and exemplifying through themselves was the essential positive feature of Jewish history in the modern era. This group was eventually to become the dominant element among the founders of the State of Israel. It had no doubt from the beginning of its career that it was the creative center of the Jewish world and that, most immediately, the Zionist movement was important insofar as it made their image of the Jewish settlement in Ereẓ Israel possible.

The major thrust of Zionism in the era immediately after Herzl was neither toward his purely political activity for the achievement of the "charter," nor toward small-scale settlement combined with cultural evolution; it was toward "synthetic Zionism." This term was coined by Chaim Weizmann, who had been a young opponent of Herzl in his lifetime and who succeeded to the acknowledged leadership of the movement by 1917, when the Balfour Declaration was obtained from the British Government as the result of prolonged negotiations during which he had been the central figure. Weizmann was, however, not alone in this shifting of the Zionist outlook and policy. Even Herzl's immediate heir in the presidency of the movement, David Wolffsohn, and most of those with whom he surrounded himself, especially Nahum Sokolow, were committed or at least inclined to the cultural, Hebraic renaissance and to the gradual upbuilding of Jewish settlement efforts in Palestine as the ongoing immediate tasks of the movement, while continuing diplomatic efforts and hoping that the time would come when major political arrangements would be possible. Moreover, the very struggle for these achievements, the labor of securing, step after step, "one cow, one dunam" in the Land of Israel, or the laying of the foundations for an educational system in Hebrew culminating in the creation of the Hebrew University in Jerusalem, were the routine ongoing life of Zionism, while those who engaged in these daily endeavors continued to dream of the eventual Jewish commonwealth, to be achieved at some political turning point in history. The handful who were taking the lead in the early years of the century by going to Palestine were moved by visionary considerations, and they regarded themselves, and were regarded within the Zionist hinterland, as a kind of secular priesthood preparing the way for those who would follow. Even in the United States, where the Zionist movement consisted almost entirely of recent immigrants of the same origins as the pioneers in Palestine (so that these American Zionists were then not themselves candidates for joining the pioneer vanguard), the labor for Zion became a quasi-religious experience. Even those "Western" Jews in America who had become Zionists, because they said they wanted to extend philanthropic help to Jewish refugees who chose to go to Palestine, belonged to a generation in American life which was dominated, among both Jews and gentiles, by the "social gospel," the teaching that the meaning of religion is not in metaphysical faith or theology but in the work of social reform in this world. "Synthetic" Zionism thus provided those who adhered to it, everywhere, with such daily commandments as the collecting of money to help the Jewish National Fund purchase dunams for new settlers; with tales of courage and suffering by the pioneers in Palestine; with spiritual uplift at the sight of a cultural renaissance; and with the ultimate hope, sustained even in the decade between 1904 and 1914, that some great political event would come to pass.

The cultural and "synthetic" Zionists emphasized more than the purely "political" Zionists the activity called in Zionist debates *Gegenwartsarbeit*, i.e., "work in the present," in the Diaspora. They included in it not only the task to "conquer" the Jewish community councils, proclaimed by Herzl himself, but also the need for modernized Hebrew education, in new-type *ḥadarim* (called "*ḥeder metukkan*") and in secular-type schools; the establishment of Jewish athletic and sports clubs for the young (Bar Kokhba, later Maccabi, etc.); and, most important of all, the active participation, on separate Jewish tickets, in parliamentary and local elections, particularly in the Austrian Empire, in order to emphasize the existence of specific Jewish national interests in multinational states, crystallize the Jewish public around them and thus erect a barrier against political assimilationism.

Zionism was transformed into a mass movement and into a major political force by World War I. At the outbreak of hostilities the seat of the Zionist executive was in the capital of one of the major warring powers – Berlin; and even though an office was soon established in neutral Copenhagen, there was no possibility of effective central direction in a situation in which major Jewish communities were on both sides of the line. The situation was all the more complicated by two facts: that Palestine was under the control of Turkey, which joined the Central Powers in 1915; and that the largest Jewish community in the world, and the one most disaffected from its own oppressive government, was in Czarist Russia, which was allied to the Western powers. The situation created complex interplays of political forces which resulted in such events as the partial expulsion and total harassment by the Turks in 1917 of the Jewish population of Palestine; the protection of Jews in Palestine by German influence in Turkey in order not to lose support of Jewish opinion in the world as a whole and especially in then neutral America; and, above all, the long deliberations which resulted in the publication by the British government on November 2, 1917, of the Balfour Declaration, in which it declared itself to be in favor of the establishment in Palestine of a Jewish national home, provided that the civil and religious rights of the non-Jews were not impaired. This act resulted from the desire of the British to appeal to U.S. Jewish opinion, whose support for the Allies was questionable until the U.S. entered the war at a very late stage in the British deliberations on Zionist aspirations, and to keep Russia in the war despite its revolutionary upheavals in 1917. Beyond these immediate purposes there was, however, a new atmosphere compounded out of markedly increased Jewish fervor for Zionism. This was a corollary to the rising nationalism among all peoples in Europe, including the Austro-Hungarian Empire, which the Allies were exploiting by promising such subject nations as the Czechs and the Poles their national freedom after the war. The self-determination of subject peoples was made into a central war aim by President Wilson when he announced his Fourteen Points.

LEGION AND SELF-DEFENSE. It was clear early in the war that this convulsion involving all the major European powers would inevitably lead to new political arrangements and thus give room for Jewish aspirations. Some of the Zionists, especially Joseph Trumpeldor, the Russian Zionist leader Vladimir Jabotinsky, and later also such young labor pioneers from Ereẓ Israel as David Ben-Gurion and Izhak Ben-Zvi, believed that one way of making sure that Jews would be taken seriously at the peace table was to organize Jewish military units to fight on the side of the Allies. As a practical matter this was the way to enlist Russian Jews in the West, particularly in England, for while they would not return to their native land to fight for Russia, even if that had been possible, many were eager to enlist as Jews in the Allied cause. The British government was at first not overly enthusiastic or cooperative, but these efforts did result in the establishment of the Jewish Legion – the Zion Mule Corps, which fought at Gallipoli in 1915 and in the Jewish battalions which took the field in 1917. As military formations they were of some importance, but their main significance was in the creation of the modern Jewish military tradition as a conscious national act. In the preparation of the claim for normal Jewish nationhood at the end of the war, something more than a symbolic army had fought beside the ultimate victors. Even earlier, with the very beginnings of Zionist settlement, Jewish armed guards (see *Ha-Shomer) had increasingly protected settlements against thieves and armed robbers. Both of these military traditions coalesced after World War I, when difficulties soon developed in Palestine between Jews and Arabs, into the creation of a semisecret Jewish self-defense organization, the Haganah. There was never sufficiently prolonged quiet in Palestine between the two world wars for Jews ever to be able to imagine that they would be safe without their own self-defense. By the late 1930s there was continuing open warfare between the Jewish and Arab communities, in which the British played an ambiguous role, at best, and in which the Jews could largely depend for their safety only on themselves. By this time *"illegal" immigration in the teeth of British restrictions had become a life-and-death matter for those Jews who could escape Europe. The Zionist movement as a whole, in all its factions, and not only the Revisionists, who had left the Zionist Organization because of its lack of militancy, was in a military struggle with both the Arabs and the British. There had thus evolved a new element which had been im-

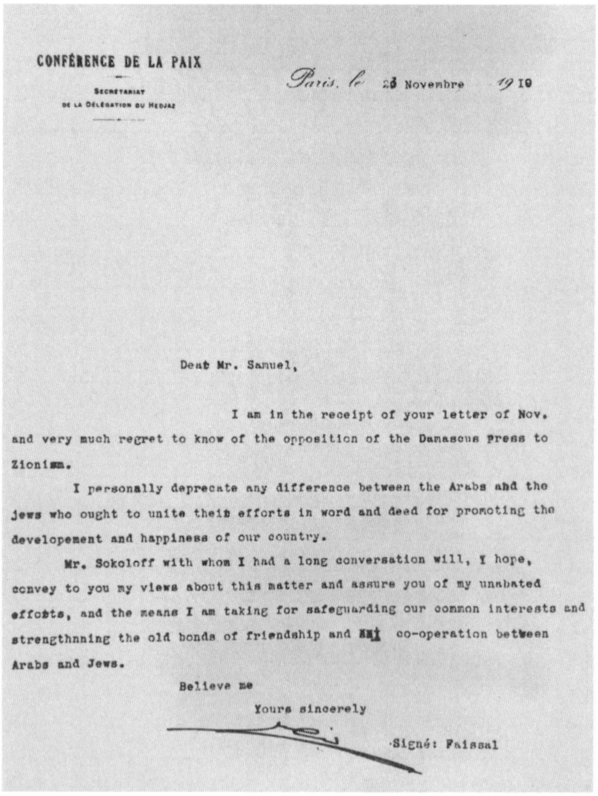
CONFÉRENCE DE LA PAIX

SECRÉTARIAT DE LA DÉLÉGATION DU HEDJAZ

Paris, le 23 Novembre 1919

Dear Mr. Samuel,

I am in the receipt of your letter of Nov. and very much regret to know of the opposition of the Damascus Press to Zionism.

I personally deprecate any difference between the Arabs and the Jews who ought to unite their efforts in word and deed for promoting the developement and happiness of our country.

Mr. Sokoloff with whom I had a long conversation will, I hope, convey to you my views about this matter and assure you of my unabated efforts, and the means I am taking for safeguarding our common interests and strengthnning the old bonds of friendship and co-operation between Arabs and Jews.

Believe me

Yours sincerely

Signé: Faissal

Letter from Emir Feisal, head of the Arab delegation at the Paris Peace Conference, to Herbert Samuel, Nov. 23, 1919, expressing his positive attitude toward Zionism. Jerusalem, Central Zionist Archives.

plicit in the Zionist ideological vision of a normal nation: an increasingly independent military force, which, however small by international standards, was almost from its beginning a substantial power in the immediate region. The existence of armed strength added further "sovereign" dimensions of Jewish self-liberation to the vision of Zionism.

POST-WAR CONSENSUS AND DIFFERENTIATION. As World War I ended, the major arena of Zionist activity was, however, not in Ereẓ Israel but in Paris, where the victors were meeting in 1919 to define the terms of peace. A variety of Jewish groups were officially in the lobbies of this conference. The most assimilated elements from France, England, and the United States would, for the most part, have preferred that the Jewish position at the Peace Conference be simply the demand for full individual liberty in all the states that were then being created in Central and Eastern Europe. The "Western" Jews were projecting the image of what they hoped was and would remain their own status, that of Frenchmen, Englishmen, or Americans who differed from others only in their private adherence to a differing religious faith. The Zionists, headed by Weizmann and Sokolow, came to Versailles to make sure that the intent of the Balfour Declaration (as they hopefully understood it to mean: an act pointing to the creation in measurable time of Jewish political independence in Palestine) would be incorporated in the peace arrangements. The delegates from Eastern Europe were mostly interested in insisting that such new states as Poland and Lithuania, and all the rest, be made to pledge the most solemn guarantees for the rights of national minorities within their borders. For Jews this meant self-definition as a national minority, parallel, for example, to the Ukrainians in Poland, with the right to conduct educational institutions with public money in their own national language, be it Yiddish or Hebrew; the right to self-governing community councils with status before the law; and, most sensitively, the right to appeal to the international community, which was seen to be represented by the League of Nations, over the head of the national government, if minority rights were violated.

There was internal struggle among these various parties in Paris. Out of their interaction there, and largely through the leadership of Louis Marshall, a kind of consensus was achieved which became the actual premise for all Jewish political life in the next decades, the interwar years. It was agreed that all would stand together for the minority rights of Jews in those countries in which the local Jewish population desired such a formulation of its identity. In practice this meant that the Jews of Eastern and Central Europe were publicly defined in new international arrangements as a separate people; for the Zionists this definition meant the possibility of struggling effectively within these Jewish national institutions to orient educational endeavors toward the new Hebraic culture and to prepare the hearts of the people to realize that only in complete national concentration in Ereẓ Israel could there be a Jewish future. Throughout the 1920s and 1930s various other factions were in combat with the Zionists within these new structures of the Jewish community. There was ongoing friction with assimilationist opinion, but this trend never achieved importance in the inner life of the East European Jewish communities outside the Soviet Union. The more serious battles were with the religiously orthodox, who were by then organized to a great degree around *Agudat Israel; this party found Zionism to be too secular. As a counterforce to these views the Orthodox wing of the Zionist movement itself, the Mizrachi, achieved particular importance during these years; it represented the possibility of a synthesis between the new national ideal of self-realization in Ereẓ Israel, through cooperation even with nonbelievers who were laboring in the Zionist cause, and preserving and even refreshing traditional Judaism. The enemies of Zionism on the left were even more serious, because both the Jewish Socialist Bund and the Jewish elements within the mostly illegal Communist Party, in Poland and in several other adjacent countries, had substantial followings. The Zionists countered these visions of a new, revolutionary era by insisting, especially through their own socialist wing, that the new socialist society would have to be formed by the remaking of individual national societies and that, at least in the case of the Jews, rampant antisemitism, which had culminated in the mass slaughter of the Ukrainian pogroms in the post-revolutionary period and became a bitter reality in independent Poland, required that, whatever be the nature of the internal life of a Jewish independent society, the solution to the Jewish problem had to take a Zionist form. Several varieties of Zionist Socialism had been defined in the 1920s, ranging from moderate social democracy to the ultimately Marxist pro-communism of Ha-Shomer ha-Ẓa'ir.

Almost every one of these versions of Zionism, except for the most radical communist option, had existed as a school of thought and even as an organization, in some form, before World War I. However, these parties came to serious maturity in their encounter with the postwar realities: the internal struggles of East European Jewry and, of growing and soon of predominant importance, the battle for the definition of the life and character of the *yishuv*, the Zionist settlement in Palestine, as it increased tenfold, from roughly 60,000 in 1919 to 600,000, in the 1940s. In the interwar period a fully developed form of Jewish communal autonomy and self-government existed there, legally, in the *Keneset Yisrael with its executive body, the Va'ad Le'ummi, which was confirmed by the British Mandate Government and, extra-legally, in the internal discipline and cohesiveness of the Jews in the country. An even more important political process involved these very forces, both in the *yishuv* and among the Jewish masses of Eastern Europe, in their interaction in the World Zionist Organization. The League of Nations' Mandate for Palestine stipulated that an appropriate "*Jewish Agency" cooperate by right with the British authorities in the upbuilding of the Jewish national home, and the Zionist Organization, though obliged to seek the cooperation of non-Zionist Jews as well, was recognized as such an "agency." The most poignant problem during most of those years was the question of Jewish immigration, which was always strictly limited by the British in reaction to Arab opposition and violent outbursts. The World Zionist Organization exercised effective control over the distribution of "certificates," that is, entry permits for new immigrants, up to the number permitted in any one year by the British. How these permits were divided in the Diaspora became a cause for impassioned struggle, both among the various Zionist factions which accepted the discipline of the world body and especially with the Revisionists, who regarded themselves as discriminated against. (This militant group eventually broke away, mainly for political reasons, and declared its Zionist independence in 1935.) The basic solution was an agreement to operate by the "party key," which meant that "certificates" were distributed on the basis of the respective strengths of the various parties in the world Zionist movement and especially in the nascent *yishuv*. The result was that the political composition of the Jewish community in Palestine remained remarkably stable despite the growth of its proportions. This party influence on immigration was part of a picture in which many of those who came, especially after 1933 in flight from Hitler – even though they were admitted as individuals and not as the holders of certificates – had also to find their way within a community which was dominated by parties. Kibbutzim, banks, educational facilities from university down to elementary school, jobs in the administration, and many other things besides were controlled or influenced by parties, which tended to be complete Jewish societies living side by side, each one involving most of the elements of human life, almost from the cradle to the grave. There were parties even before 1914, but in the 1920s the internal life of the Jewish community in Ereẓ Israel had crystallized into the political parties, which largely exist to the present day. The forces which were contending over the nature of the new society were divided into three broad groups. The most powerful were the several kinds of Socialist Zionists, with their roots in the Second Aliyah, in the kibbutz movement, and in the labor unions, which had together formed the overarching organization of all the Jewish workers in Israel (later including Arabs also), known as the Histadrut. These forces strove for a socialist, economically egalitarian, secularist Jewish society. The central sector of the developing Jewish community consisted of middle-class elements. In part, and especially in the case of the first refugees to come from Germany after 1933, these forces consisted of people who arrived with some property. Not all those who came from Eastern Europe wanted to be pioneers in kibbutzim. Some had been accustomed to a middle-class, urban way of life and they wanted to live that way in the new environment. This middle-class group contained many General Zionists allied to the anti-Socialist Revisionists. On doctrinaire grounds they insisted with vehemence that the very future of the Jewish settlement depended on the releasing of the energies of free enterprise. There was one wing of General Zionists who refused to identify, both in Ereẓ Israel and outside it, with any specific middle-class program in the country and who followed the lead of Chaim Weizmann, in particular, in accepting economic and cultural support for the labor sector as well as for private enterprise. But another wing of the General Zionists clung to a more partisan view, so that a continuing battle was fought between Socialist Zionism and the middle-class groups. The tension was often sufficiently great for bitter accusations to be hurled. Such leaders as David Ben-Gurion, in his role as secretary general of the Histadrut, spoke for the Socialists in accusing the Revisionists of being "Fascists"; the partisans of Jabotinsky replied by charging that the Socialist Zionists were using their power not for the good of all but to increase their own political and organizational dominance.

Parallel with this quarrel there was continuing tension over the issue of religion. There had been Orthodox Jews of the old *yishuv* in some numbers in Ereẓ Israel before the new Zionist immigration began, but the earliest arrivals after 1900 were in their overwhelming majority Socialist and secularist, and many of them were anti-religious in a doctrinaire way. The religious Zionist movement, Mizrachi, had indeed been founded in the early years of the century and it had existed as a trend even before, but its direct presence and influence on the life of the new Jewish community in Ereẓ Israel began to be felt only after World War I. By then a labor wing of the religious party, the Ha-Po'el ha-Mizrachi, had arisen, and it proceeded to create its own kibbutz movement. Many of the middle-class immigrants who were arriving in the 1920s and 1930s were personally Orthodox, and they could not imagine a Jewish presence in the land which did not exemplify the values and practices of the religious tradition. Religious Jewry was led by the Ashkenazi Chief Rabbi, Abraham Isaac *Kook, until his death in 1935, who, though he was himself beyond party, was regarded as the spiritual voice and teacher of all religious Jews who accepted a Zionist vision. For Kook the new settlement in the Land of Israel was the "beginning of the redemption." Both his temperament and outlook were broad enough to embrace even the most partisan secularist as an instrument of the divine purpose. Those who followed him could accept such a notion in theory. In practice they were dedicated to the building of an institutional power base for religious Jews, so that they could compete as equals with the other groups and provide equal opportunity in the new country for those who shared the Orthodox religious faith. This body of opinion was deeply concerned that the total temper of the Jewish community should not be secularized. They did not want to become a religious ghetto in a non-religious Jewish society, and they believed that it was their duty to bring religion even to those who opposed it. Orthodox Jews in Palestine joined the battle, immediately after the beginning of the British Mandate government, for the ever wider influence of traditional Jewish practice on the life and the law of the *yishuv*. The struggle between the Socialist and the middle-class elements in Israel's society has been muted in the generation of statehood, for a mixed economy now prevails. The conflict over religion and its relationship to public life has, if anything, become sharper within the sovereign parliamentary life of the Jewish state.

BETWEEN POGROMS AND HOLOCAUST. Ideological stamps were thus deeply impressed on the Jewish community in Palestine. Great numbers of those who came in the 1920s and even in the 1930s chose their paths because they believed in some version of the Zionist vision and found in it their path toward national and personal realization. Nonetheless, the dominant element in creating many more candidates for immigration to Palestine than were ever permitted to arrive was not Zionist ideology, at least not in its cultural, "synthetic" form, but the growing horror of antisemitism, at a time when other doors to safety were closing or were entirely closed to Jews. The sense of disaster was already deeply embedded in the consciousness of European Jews by the events which followed right after the end of World War I. The far greater horrors of the Nazi Holocaust have by now half obscured the murder of about one hundred thousand Jews, including women and children, in the Russian-Polish borderland, where Ukrainian and counter-revolutionary Russian army units systematically engaged in killing Jews in the years 1919–21. These pogroms had a profound effect on the Jewish delegation in Paris, which agreed to plead unanimously for national minority rights because the hatred of Jews as Jews was so rabid in Eastern Europe. Moreover, major figures among Western Jewry increasingly became less doctrinaire. Men such as Louis Marshall could not accept the Zionist notion that all Jews everywhere belonged to a national entity other than that of the majority of the people in the political state into which they were born, and they could not therefore agree that Jews ought to be working for their ingathering in Zion. Nonetheless, such figures responded to the dire need of East European Jews both by trying to alleviate the immediate situation and by accepting that, on purely humanitarian grounds, those who wished to go to Palestine should be helped to do so. Even after the pogroms ended and a certain amount of surface stability was created in Eastern Europe, the largest community outside the United States, that of Poland, was increasingly harassed by a regime of economic exclusion and of *numerus clausus* at the universities and in the professions. Year by year the life of these Jews was becoming more unbearable, and there were occasional pogroms in Poland in the 1930s to underline their misery. The situation was only relatively better in some of the other countries in the area. The "non-Zionists," who were persuaded by Chaim Weizmann in 1929 to join with the Zionists on the basis of parity in creating the "enlarged" Jewish Agency, were moved by a sense of the direst Jewish needs and a growing undercurrent of fear of worse things to come. This, rather than Zionist ideology of any variety, was the dominant note in the development of Zionism itself even before Hitler appeared on the scene, and certainly after 1933.

The sense of need and foreboding had come to formal expression in Zionist thought immediately after World War I. Louis Brandeis, by then a justice on the Supreme Court of the United States, who had served as the leader of American Zionism during the war years, believed that, with the achievement of the Balfour Declaration, the political struggle of Zionism was over and that, henceforth, the Jewish settlement in Palestine should be fostered through the orderly processes of investment, on the highest principles of business accountability. This soon led to a shattering struggle with Weizmann, who continued to believe in the need for a movement of Zionist national consciousness. He wanted the Zionist movement to work toward a *yishuv* which would be a left-wing liberal, in part moderately Socialist, Hebrew-speaking society and he saw its embodiment mainly in the collective and cooperative enterprise of the labor pioneers who needed non-profitable funds, such as the *Keren Hayesod, to create their network of settlements and institutions. In short, Weizmann intended to realize the "synthetic" Zionism which he had defined in the days of his youthful opposition to Herzl. Both Brandeis and Weizmann, despite their differences, wanted to create the Jewish community in Palestine step by step, according to plan, with the presumption that there was time aplenty to do it. Right after World War I Max Nordau, the still-living colleague of Herzl, and later also Vladimir Jabotinsky, arose against such views. Nordau and Jabotinsky did not believe that the Jews of Eastern Europe would find safety in any years of seeming quiet that might follow after the Russian-Polish upheavals, and they were equally convinced that the British government, the holder of the Mandate, would find reasons of its own for making the large-scale immigration of Jews into Palestine an ever more difficult enterprise. Nordau proposed, melodramatically, that without any meticulous planning or preparation, or even arrangement for solid housing, Jews, mainly from the pogrom-afflicted areas, should be led in their hundreds of thousands simply to appear in Palestine. He agreed that many might suffer extreme hardship, but that it was better for that to happen than to wait for the slower horrors in Europe and the hardening of the anti-Zionist policy of the British. At least, this mass movement would immediately achieve majority status for Jews in Palestine and would assure possibilities for the future. This then wild idea of "catastrophic" Zionism was rejected but it remained dormant, and even in the quieter years of the 1920s it was the countertheme to the then dominant notion of "building step by step," according to plan. By the 1930s Jabotinsky and the Revisionists called for the implementation of the "Nordau plan" and for an orderly mass "evacuation" of East European Jewry. Though this call evoked bitter internal controversies among Zionists, Jewish need, and the growing foreboding of worse horrors to come, were ever more the driving force attracting support to Zionism as a solution all over the Jewish world, and beyond its confines.

RELATION TO THE ARABS. Until the immediate aftermath of the Balfour Declaration the Zionist movement had given little serious thought to the question of the Arabs residents in Palestine. Moses Hess in 1861, a generation before Herzl, had imagined that a highly Westernized element such as the Jews would be welcomed by the Arabs because of the leadership that Jews would provide in creating in the entire region an advanced economy and an advancing society. Chaim Weizmann took a comparable tack in 1919 in his encounters with the Arab leader of the time, the Emir Feisal, with whom he signed an agreement in this spirit. The theme was that Jews and Arabs proposed to be good neighbors. However, such figures as Feisal, who was from the *Hejaz, were alien to the immediate Palestinian Arab scene. The politically active elements in the local population were much more hostile and resentful. Despite large Jewish efforts toward conciliation, and the positive effect that such attempts did have on certain Arab circles, the dominant motif in Arab policy was to declare the Balfour Declaration to be an infringement on Arab rights and to insist that, at best, a limited Jewish minority could in the future live on Arab sufferance in the land. At every point in the interwar years at which Jewish immigration became of some consequence, there were Arab riots which invariably caused the British to issue further restrictions against the Jews. This became particularly marked in the decade after 1929, when there were major riots by Arabs. Zionism had thus, perforce, to define itself in much more complicated terms than those of a "people without a land on the way to a land without a people." The very example of its own energies and national purpose was helping to evoke some comparable national emotion among the Arabs in Palestine. In theory, throughout this period the bulk of the Zionist movement never surrendered the ultimate vision of a Jewish state, but the only wing of the movement which made of this the essence of its public position was the Revisionists. All the others concentrated on two immediate objectives: immigration, while trying not to displace Arabs in the process and to compensate generously the few displaced ones, feasible by constantly increasing the "absorptive capacity" of the land through new endeavors; and the devising of formulas for ongoing life together with the Arabs in which no absolute minority ceiling would be placed on the Jews. Among one group on the extreme left, the Marxist Ha-Shomer ha-Ẓa'ir, a bi-national state of absolute parity between Jews and Arabs was defined as its version of the political purpose of Zionism as a whole. A handful of Jewish pacifists of high station, led by such figures as Judah L. Magnes and Martin Buber, formed the *Berit Shalom program in the 1930s; they were willing to go even further than Ha-Shomer ha-Ẓa'ir in placating Arab fears for the sake of peace, but even they, like all the other Jewish groups or leaders (including Ben-Gurion), could find no Arab representatives of rank and power with whom to come to terms. Jewish misery was growing constantly in Europe and the need for mass immigration was ever greater. No Zionist group (and, for that matter, after the appearance of Hitler, no responsible non-Zionist body) could accept the halting of the growth of the *yishuv* even if it meant open hostility with the Arabs, and that is what it indeed meant by the mid-1930s and for the rest of the decade. Jews required freedom of immigration; Arabs demanded its absolute end. The British floundered in the middle, issuing "white papers" and setting draconian quotas on future Jewish arrivals. The situation could not last for all the positions were irreconcilable.

Throughout the years of the British Mandate of Palestine the government in London appointed a whole series of commissions, whenever conflict between Jews and Arabs broke out into open violence, in the vain quest of finding some acceptable compromise. Such efforts became more frequent in the 1930s, when the basic Jewish demand was, as it had to be, mass immigration which could not ever be restricted by Arab veto.

The logic of events, compounded out of the first years of Hitler and the increasing clashes in Palestine between Jews and Arabs, evoked the single most serious study of the Palestine question which was ever undertaken, that by the Royal Commission of 1936, chaired by Lord Peel. In its many hearings, some of them in no less impressive a place than the House of Lords in London, and others in Palestine itself, the major spokesmen of all varieties of Arab and Jewish opinion were heard. There was little essential difference among the views of the Zionist representatives, for even such old antagonists as Weizmann and Jabotinsky spoke in the same terms. Both emphasized the spiritual and cultural elements in Zionism, the vision of the movement of a "new Jew" who would be born in freedom to achieve his own proper dignity. However, the main theme, in the testimony of both, was the misery of Jewish life at that moment. Before the Peel Commission and later, at the Zionist Congress of 1937, when Weizmann proposed that the movement accept, in principle, the Commission's proposal to partition Palestine, he looked especially closely at the life of the Jews in Poland. He said openly that this community was doomed. A third of it, the old people, would no doubt die in Poland; for another third he had no hope; but it was the responsibility of all who could help to make it possible for the last third, the young people, to come to Palestine and start a new and decent life.

In this atmosphere the Peel Commission proposed the division of Palestine into three geographical entities: an Arab state, a Jewish one, and a large enclave, including Jerusalem, to be governed by the British. The proposed map was very nearly impossible, though, for it presumed the kind of goodwill between Jews and Arabs which, had it existed, would have made partition unnecessary. What the proposal did achieve, from the perspective of the Zionist movement, was the first formal suggestion by the ruling power that a Jewish state in at least part of Palestine was a realistic necessity; secondly, the proposal was based on the premise that Jews had a right, because of their need, to large new immigration into the land and that they could achieve this only if they were in political control of their own national destiny. The Zionist movement, after heated debate, which reflected the objections that the proposed state was unviable and that to accept it meant to give up the claim on the whole of the land, reluctantly accepted the partition proposal as a basis for discussion. The negotiations soon died, however, because the Arabs rejected the idea and the British, in the era of appeasement of Hitler, had no stomach for forcing any radical solution. On the eve of World War II, Zionism had, however, defined itself as charged with the responsibility of creating or exercising, whether legally or illegally, as much independence as was necessary to do everything that was possible for the saving of Jews. This had become the dominant motif, and it had a directness and moral urgency which ever wider circles of Jewish and world opinion could not help but accept. The contrast between Jewish farmers in Palestine and their native-born sons, farming their fields and shooting back if necessary at Arab raiders, and the Jews being spat upon in Warsaw or sent to concentration camps, or worse, in Germany was, even before 1939, clear and unmistakable.

AFTER THE HOLOCAUST: "CATASTROPHIC" ZIONISM REVIVED. On the very eve of World War II the British government issued a White Paper in which, in effect, Jewish immigration was limited to a final 75,000. This meant that the Jews of Europe were being left to their destiny; the clear intent was to condemn the Jews in Palestine to be a permanent minority. The whole of the Jewish world was well nigh unanimous in its opposition, in declaring this act to be not only wrong but utterly devoid of moral or legal validity. Soon the war broke out and the Zionist movement, indeed the entire Jewish community everywhere, was inevitably on the side of the Allies. The Jews in Palestine soon tried to organize a volunteer force to fight with the British in the critical Middle Eastern arena, but, on the grounds of "parity," because no such volunteers were forthcoming from the Arabs, the offers were initially rebuffed. The Jewish Brigade eventually came into being. It played a military role especially in the campaign in Italy, but its most important achievement was that here, directly, much of the immediate foundation of the future army of Israel was laid. "Illegal" immigration had been going on straight through the war, for the Zionist movement as a whole had accepted the slogan of David Ben-Gurion: "To fight Hitler as if there were no White Paper and to fight the White Paper as if there were no Hitler." Some of the brutalities that the Nazis had perpetrated were to be seen in Italy, as the Jewish Brigade advanced within the Allied army; and as the war was ending, the men of the Brigade began the work of finding friendly out-of-the-way ports and cooperative officials elsewhere to make it possible to transport to Palestine those Jews who had survived. The armies on the eastern and the western fronts, and especially the Jews among them, were concurrently discovering the unspeakable crimes of Buchenwald and Auschwitz. Perhaps a million Jewish refugees were alive in camps in Europe in May 1945. All those who saw them were overwhelmed by one conviction – that they must be given the kind of new life where they could never again be the object of the horrors that had been done to them. The survivors themselves were most vocal everywhere that they had to be allowed to go to Ereẓ Israel, to take their place in an independent Jewish state.

During the war years the Zionist movement itself had almost completely stripped away all tentativeness or vagueness from its ultimate aims and it had abandoned, at least for the moment, any public concern with the nature of the new Jewish society. That did not mean that within Palestine itself, and within the world Zionist movement, the various parties did not continue to jockey for control of whatever they could regarding resources and position, but from the mid-1930s onward these issues became ever more internal to the immediate scene in the *yishuv*. As a world movement Zionism spoke of "a home for the homeless," and the more bitter and obvious the homelessness was, the greater was the support for all the actions that this slogan required. By 1942 a Zionist conference, the most representative possible under the circumstances, met in New York at the Biltmore Hotel. It announced in the "Biltmore Program" that the "establishment of Palestine as a Jewish Commonwealth" was the war aim of the Jewish people. This program was tacitly adopted by non-Zionists as well. The many years when such words were not spoken even by most Zionists, for fear of complicating the immediate situation among Jews, Arabs and the British, had thus been ended. Within the next year or so, after a bitter battle within the ranks of American Zionism between those who were willing to wait for the end of the war and trust President Roosevelt, and those who believed that American public opinion needed to be enlisted on the widest possible basis, Abba Hillel *Silver emerged the victor over Stephen S. *Wise and, in 1943, Zionism in America entered a militant phase which continued until the State of Israel was achieved. Here, too, it was the growing knowledge and then the absolute certainty of what Hitler had been doing to Jews that made the Zionist demand for freedom, dignity, and independence a great force in American public life.

At the end of the war the Jews were indeed, as the anti-Zionist British foreign minister Ernest *Bevin said, "pushing to the head of the queue." No doors, not even those of the United States, were wide open to the refugees of the greatest single disaster that had ever befallen a people, and it was therefore inevitable that Palestine would have to provide the major part of the immediate solution. The British, weakened greatly by the war, were even less affected and less resolute than they had been in the 1930s; the Arabs were at least as intransigent; the Jews, both in Palestine and elsewhere, were at the highest point of outrage and self-assertion in their entire history. Many intricate maneuvers in Europe, Palestine, and the diplomatic centers of the world resulted finally in the great debate before the United Nations in November 1947 on the future of Palestine. The Jewish Agency, even though it was not a government, was admitted to the debate as the representative of the Jewish people; it stood solidly for the legal and moral right of those to whom promises had been made in the Balfour Declaration and who had suffered so greatly in the recent past to a state of their own in the land which had belonged to their ancestors and in which they had already created much in the 20th century. The end result was a decision reminiscent of the proposals of the Peel Commission a decade before – partition of the land in an unworkable map. This time, however, nothing prevented the formal declaration by the Jews of their own state on the appointed day, May

14, 1948 – neither the ambiguous attitude of the United States in the decisive stage nor the war against this new state which was begun by the Arabs both in Palestine and on its borders even before the formal declaration.

ZIONISM AND THE STATE OF ISRAEL. After the costly battles ended and the state was secure, and even as the war was still going on, refugees by the tens of thousands were brought into Israel. There was little surface difficulty in the immediate years after the achievement of statehood in defining the purpose of Zionism. The state was young, weak, and threatened; the refugees were many and in direst need. The purpose of Zionism, and of the Jewish world which it was by then leading, was to help root the state in secure ground, defend and explain it before world opinion, and either raise funds directly or provide inspiration for such endeavors. Almost immediately, however, the question of Zionist purpose and definition began to be a critical issue, first in isolated instances and then in prolonged debate which raged through the 1950s and into the 1960s. As early as 1949 there was a public break between David Ben-Gurion, the first prime minister of Israel, and Abba Hillel Silver, then the major Zionist figure in the Diaspora. The essence of the quarrel was the unwillingness of the government of the new state to accept any presumption of tutelage from the Zionist movement. Now that a state existed, Zionism could clearly no longer engage in the kind of international politics to which it had been accustomed. The fund-raising had increasingly been engaging Jews of all shades of opinion, and many of the richest and most generous were not Zionists, at least in the formal sense. The bodies which raised funds for Israel were not everywhere, and especially not in the United States, really under Zionist leadership. There were a number of attempts made by post-state Zionism in the Diaspora to define the ongoing purpose of the movement as the cultivation of Jewish national consciousness, the fostering of Hebraic education and the creation of a Jewish life which had as its emotional and spiritual center the life in Israel. Against this there stood, implacably, the figure of David Ben-Gurion, and the majority opinion in Israel which he led. He held that fund-raising and other forms of aid extended by Jews to Israel were an endeavor which was, and quite properly, common to the entire Jewish people. This entitled those involved to be considered "friends of Israel." A Zionist, in the proper sense of the term, could be only one who was preparing himself and his family, no matter how comfortable the society in which he was living, to come in measurable time as an immigrant to the new Jewish state. This outlook finally prevailed in international Zionist councils in the 1960s, and the seal was set on it with a proclamation in 1968 of the Jerusalem Program by the Zionist Congress (see below). In this document the acceptance of *aliyah*, of personal migration as the ultimate ideal, became a sine qua non of belonging to any recognized Zionist group.

It took two decades, however, for Zionists in the Western countries to be willing to reach such a conclusion. In the early years after the establishment of the State of Israel American Zionists in particular had argued that "America is different," that there is a distinction between a Diaspora where Jews were persecuted and the Diaspora of the free countries, where antisemitism was not a major factor and was not likely to increase, because of the rooted democratic tradition of a country such as America, which had no medieval past of hatred of Jews. The unwillingness to accept *aliyah* even as an ideal was ended in part by ongoing pressure from Israel opinion and in part by changing loyalties within American society as a whole, which was becoming less nationalist in the 1960s. The most important cause was, however, internal. During most of this era the president of the World Zionist Organization was Nahum Goldmann, and he became aware, soon after the heady days of the creation of the State of Israel, that intermarriage and spiritual and cultural evaporation were becoming a major threat to the survival of Jewish life in the free world. He argued that the task of the time was to prevent in the very age of Zionist achievement the rapid assimilation of world Jewry. Ever wider circles in the Jewish communities in the Western countries began looking to Israel, to various educational and work programs in the country, especially for young people from all communities of the Jewish world, to provide the occasion and the source for Jewish commitment. In such an atmosphere of growing concern for the Jewish continuity of hundreds of thousands of Jewish families all over the world, the notion that those who chose to live in Israel would certainly remain Jewish in a creative way conquered many previous reservations about *aliyah* as the ultimate personal ideal of a Zionist.

In the 1970s the world Zionist movement retained substantial functions in the upbuilding of Israel's society, both in the bringing of new immigrants, especially from lands where Jews are being persecuted, and in all other areas in which public funds from the Diaspora are properly spent. It continued to conduct and even to expand its endeavors in the strengthening of ties between Jews all over the world and those in Israel. Its governing body, still called the Jewish Agency, formally expanded again, in 1971, under the leadership of its chairman Louis Pincus, after the pattern of an earlier, practically abortive expansion in 1929, to include on the basis of parity representatives of the major Jewish pro-Israel fund-raising organizations everywhere in the world. In these new arrangements the World Zionist Organization and its Executive divested themselves, in favor of the new body, of direct responsibility for the financing and directing of *aliyah* from places of need and of the tasks which flow from this responsibility. Regardless of the formal changes, and even the increase in activities, the question of Zionist definition remains, however.

A major turning point was the Six-Day War in 1967. The days that led up to that event were filled with fear that a small state surrounded by enemies might become the object of a new holocaust. The swift and total victory evoked joy that Jews were now masters of their own destiny and recognized as such throughout the world. The Jewish Diaspora in all countries did not know how deeply it identified both with the fears and the triumphs of Israel until it was in the midst of the actual events. There then came an outpouring of money, political support of the most public kind, and volunteers, the equal of which had not been seen except briefly during the months of Israel's War of Independence. The years between 1948 and 1967, of continued integration of Jews into U.S. society, and into several West European countries, had not affected the strong emotions of self-identification and of identification with Israel which had clearly existed two decades before. Nowhere, during those days, did Jews hesitate to exert pressure on the governments of their countries of residence to support Israel. In France, where de Gaulle had reversed his previous policy and stood against Israel when war came, Jewish demonstrations in Paris evoked from him a remark about the Jews as an "elite people, sure of itself, and domineering." After the initial outrage over the negative rhetoric in which de Gaulle's opinion was couched, the Jews of the world were by 1967 willing to accept the proposition that Jews were indeed a community with opinions, ties, and characteristics which were distinct, and that the major contemporary affirmation of this Jewish distinctiveness was the whole set of relationships which involved all Jews in Israel. Zionism had thus finally succeeded in having the Jewish world accept the idea – and, what is more, feel deeply – that in the 20th century the Jews were a people and not only an international religious community, and that this people found its central expression in the renascent life in Israel.

TENSIONS IN THE U.S. AND THE U.S.S.R. In the last years of the 1960s two other events deeply affected the contemporary understanding of Zionism. In the United States this was the era of major social tension and Jews were not far from the center of all the problems. Race relations deteriorated by the latter years of the decade to physical confrontation and even armed clashes between blacks and whites. In all of the largest cities of the United States Jews had, for historical reasons (they were usually the last occupants of the neighborhoods into which blacks then moved), a substantial stake in the economy of the black ghetto, as storekeepers and landlords. They were often the most visible white men in the life of blacks in the north. In another dimension, younger, politically radical Jewish elements had been among the founders of the most activist movements of black protest, but, as black consciousness became ever more exclusivist, Jews and all other whites were systematically excluded from these movements. Certain administrations, such as that of the public school teachers in New York City, were dominated by Jews, and blacks began to fight hard to occupy their places. On a variety of levels the dream of peaceful integration was thus replaced by confrontation in the name of group identity and group interests. Within such an atmosphere many Jews were pushed toward identification with the specific interests of the Jewish community and its own peculiar destiny. The alternative for some of the young who had cut their teeth politically in the black movement, was to come to Israel.

There was no such direct correlation between the rising tempers over the war in Vietnam and Jewish consciousness. Young Jews were very prominent among the makers of the political protests which rocked the American campus in the late 1960s; but only a very few of those who chose not to fight in the war in Vietnam came to Israel. What was more fundamental was the growing disillusionment in all circles, not only Jewish ones, with the "American dream." For a person to emigrate from America to some less problematic, more satisfying place was now thinkable, and indeed some were even doing so. At such a moment the problem of "dual loyalty" which had troubled the past generation of Jews in America, their need to prove that it was not anti-American to care about Israel, or even to want to go and live there, was no longer of consequence. Fear for their future as Jews was not major, but some element of reaction to antisemitism was widespread. *Aliyah* from America, which neared 10,000 for the first time in the year 1970, was mostly, however, propelled not by the "push" of disappointment in American life, but by the "pull" of the attraction of Israel to Jews who wanted to live its kind of life, as the realization of their own Jewish identity.

In the late 1960s the Jews of the Soviet Union, who had remained inert on the surface under Stalinist persecution, began to assert their Jewishness and their identification with Israel in the most overt ways. The underlying factors here were the classic ones of bitter resentment that Russian Jews felt at the antisemitism which still existed in Soviet society and its administration after half a century of Bolshevik rule, coupled with a surprising amount of deep Jewish feelings, and especially of proud identification with Israel, which still persisted despite the absence for at least a generation of any Jewish schools or communal organizations – for even the communist schools and press in Yiddish had been destroyed under Stalin. In the Soviet Union, too, the Six-Day War had been a turning point. The government was on the Arab side and remained the chief protector and supplier of Egypt and of the most anti-Israel of the other Arab states. Official propaganda was violently anti-Israel, anti-Zionist with strong antisemitic overtones. The Jews of the U.S.S.R., through their most vocal elements, had, however, lost their fear of repression and proceeded to demand the right to leave and to go to Israel. A trickle of such immigration had been permitted by the Soviet authorities earlier and, spasmodically, it was renewed in 1968, even during the years of the most bitter vituperation of Israel by Soviet diplomacy and propaganda. The numbers of those who were permitted to leave reached relatively considerable proportions and the requests that were submitted by Jews were in the tens of thousands. Hebrew was being studied in semi-underground conditions and in many ways connection was maintained, amidst difficulty and some danger, with the Jews beyond the "iron curtain." The right of Soviet Jews to emigrate had become by the end of the decade an international issue of considerable magnitude. The activity on their behalf was widespread throughout the Jewish world, and it acted to recall many Jews who were themselves otherwise alienated, to a sense of their own Jewish identity. In the Soviet Union itself this reassertion of Jewishness was clearly the harbinger of a new era of rebellious national consciousness after the two generations when cultural and linguistic de-Judaization was forced upon the Jews while the doors of gentile society to complete equality and assimilation were not opened to them. For Zionism the Jews coming out of the U.S.S.R. represented an element that had been aggrieved and had so strongly asserted itself as to be a classic fundamental assertion of Zionist theory: the assertion that in any social system the Jew would ultimately find himself in a situation different from that of the majority and discriminated against and that he would have to make his life in terms of that reality.

IDEOLOGICAL PROBLEMS IN ISRAEL. In Israel itself, the first generation of statehood produced essentially two sets of internal cultural problems. Both were not new; both were deeply embedded in tensions inherent in Zionism almost from the beginning. Religious and secular forces fought each other over the role that Jewish religion was to play in the life of the total community. For the religious such questions as whom one married, or whether public transport and all public services were to function on the Sabbath, were not matters of private conscience. They went to the very roots of the issue of why a Jewish state had to be created in Zion in the first place. It was to be something more than a refugee camp, or a large-scale attempt to create a "Jewish Albania." The purpose of this effort was to make it possible for a characteristic Jewish life in line with tradition to be lived in contemporary settings of one's own. Amid the secular forces the imposition by the State of the Orthodox religious rules on personal status, so that, for example, one was not free to marry out of the faith if one chose, or the legal definition of "who is a Jew" only by the norms of rabbinic law (so that children of gentile mothers born and raised in Israel as Jews were not so registered by secular law until 1970), raised great anger. In the view of the secular thinkers a modern state and society required an absolute separation between religion and public order. Another continuing battle was that between those who preferred to regard themselves as Israelis, with little concern or identification either with the Jewish past in the Exile or with the present-day Jewish majority in the Diaspora, and those who kept insisting that Jews in the new state were still primarily Jews and not Israelis. The events of 1967 and the rise of Jewish passion in Soviet Jewry effectively made an end to this latter debate. It became clear to almost everyone that Israel and the Jews of the world stood together in crisis; that even the Jews of the U.S., the richest of Diasporas, did not feel themselves as living on a different plane from the Jews in Israel; and that everywhere the rescue of the Soviet Jews was regarded as a prime purpose. The seal was thus set on a development which had begun with the very foundation of the State in one of its earliest constitutional acts, "the Law of Return," under which any Jew anywhere has the right to claim Israel citizenship upon arrival in the country and his right to immigrate into Israel is inalienable. The government of Israel had made it its duty to intervene diplomatically on behalf of Jewish communities in trouble, from the very beginning of its existence. Israel had never allowed any doubts to persist that the defense of Jewish interests all over the world was an integral element of its foreign policy. It had certainly presumed that world Jewry would stand with Israel and that its policies on all matters of major concern would parallel those of the State. In June 1967 these presumptions of world-wide Jewish support for Israel were fully realized. Soon thereafter there was another demonstration of the principle that defense of Jews all over the world was central to Israel's policy. It took the leading role in the battle which soon broke into the open for the rights of Soviet Jews.

Perhaps the most difficult, in the long run, of the problems of Jewish self-definition in Israel was its relationship to the Arabs. On the one hand there was lasting tension; on the other there was increased contact after 1967 and an ever greater straining to recognize and encounter Arabs as equal human beings. Here, too, the new generation was heir to a moral concern as old as the very beginnings of Zionism. At the beginning of the 20th century Aḥad Ha-Am had expressed the fear that the new Jewish settlement in Ereẓ Israel might be so constructed as to harm the Arabs and he had pleaded for sensitivity to this possibility. In actual day-to-day life throughout the years of Zionist immigration there were not only riots and battles but also friendships and accommodations between the two communities. Eventually every Zionist theory had had to face the question of the Arabs. The newest note after the Six-Day War was sounded by those intellectuals and politicians in Israel who saw the main road to peace in active consent and even cooperation by Israel in the establishment of Palestinian Arab independence in a part of the previous area of Palestine (including Transjordan).

Looking toward the last third of the 20th century, Zionism as an organized movement was weaker than it had been a generation before, but the result of its labors, the State of Israel, was strongly established. As an organization the world Zionist movement inevitably no longer occupied the central place in the Jewish world, for it had been replaced by the government of Israel, but Zionist sentiment now pervaded the whole of Jewish organized endeavor. The possibilities of substantial new immigration were again in view and the Zionist movement continued to assert that the encouragement of such processes was its most characteristic task. But the basic question that Zionism had posed when it first appeared, even before Theodor Herzl, still remained open – and embattled: What would be the nature of the new Jews and of the new Jewish society? To what degree would it be conventionally modern and Western and to what degree would it be connected with the classic Jewish past – or, for that matter, to what degree would the Jews in Israel "de-Westernize" in order, hopefully, to come to terms with the Middle Eastern world within which they were living? If, at the very least, there would be major Jewish communities in the Diaspora for a long time to come, and perhaps permanently, what was to be the continuing relationship between the

Jewish national community in Israel and that Diaspora? How, for that matter, was the continuity of Jewish loyalty in the far-off communities to be fostered and preserved? What, in short, was the new Jew, the Zionist and Israel successor to his ghetto ancestors, to be? In 1971 there were as yet no answers – but it was equally clear that these questions would continue to be wrestled with and lived through for many years to come.

NON-ZIONIST AND ANTI-ZIONIST TRENDS

Zionism, though initially a minority movement, became so central in Jewish thought that eventually the other Jewish ideological trends had to define themselves largely in terms of their attitude to the Zionist idea or to certain essential elements of it, as, e.g., the revival of Hebrew language and culture, the "fixation" on Ereẓ Israel as the only territory for ingathering the Jewish mass migration, the national unity of Orthodox and secular Jews, etc.

AUTONOMISTS AND YIDDISHISTS. Before World War I the bulk of the Jews of the world were living in two multi-national empires, Russia and Austria-Hungary. In both of these regimes minority peoples were conducting struggles for their respective national autonomies. The situation of the Jews was different from that of all other minorities, for they were nowhere a majority in any particular piece of territory that was historically associated with their national identity. Nonetheless, Jews in these regions continued to speak a language of their own, Yiddish, and they were bound together by ties of history and culture and by a network of communal institutions. Zionism was not the only possible national movement among Jews. A variety of other ideologies and movements arose, which refused to accept the idea that Jews were in any sense alien to the places of their dwelling in Europe, or to believe that antisemitism could be ended only by mass emigration. These movements argued that Jews were one of the historic tribes of Eastern Europe, with as much right in the region as the Poles or the Ukrainians. The discrimination against Jews could, and should, be ended by a more vigorous battle for a just social order and by the achievement of national equality for all the national communities in the region. "To do battle at one's positions" was the slogan directed against the Zionists by such schools of thought. Most such non-Zionist nationalists regarded the Hebrew revival as a piece of romanticism and as disguised clericalism. In their view the spoken language of the people, Yiddish, was its natural contemporary speech. A healthy national life could be built only by strengthening that language and its literature and raising it in public esteem from the level of a dialect to that of a respected language.

The most important theoretician of Diaspora nationalism was the historian S. *Dubnow. He himself did not deny the importance of Hebrew, or of Russian, for he wrote all his life in both these languages as well as, of course, in Yiddish; nor did Dubnow deny that there was significance in the developing Jewish community in Palestine. In his historiography Jewish life had always found its leadership in some new emerging center of energies as an older community was declining. In his own day he saw Eastern Europe as the lead community, then erecting tributary centers in Palestine and the United States. He envisaged that Jews everywhere would labor to achieve nationally cultural autonomous institutions, including especially an educational system of their own in their own language. His spiritual disciples organized a party which labored for a system of "Sejms," Jewish "parliaments" or "diets," which should direct the affairs of the various Jewish communities and of the Jewish people as a whole. This principle of "autonomism" was adopted also by the Russian Zionists at their conference in Helsingfors (1906), when czarist Russia seemed to be on the threshold of genuine parliamentary democracy. They, however, regarded it not as an end in itself, but as an element of Zionist *Gegenwartsarbeit*: an instrument for Jewish social and educational activity with the clearly defined aim of ultimate migration and settlement in Ereẓ Israel. Dubnow faced squarely the question that the national situation of the Jews in the Diaspora, in the minority everywhere, was an anomaly, but he did not arrive at the conclusion that this situation should be rectified by the creation of a Jewish commonwealth in Ereẓ Israel. At the core of his outlook was the vision of a future for all humanity in which all of the historic nations would rise to a higher stage of existence in which they would be freed of their dependence on any particular land and would exist as communities on the basis of historic and cultural ties. The paradigm for such communities was what the Jews had become in the Diaspora after the beginning of the Exile; they had persisted in this new and higher form; and so Dubnow saw his vision of Diaspora Jewish national autonomism, or a formulation of the modalities of human association, to be the newest and most profound teaching by Jews for mankind.

There were other, more mundane versions of Diaspora nationalism. Several schools of thought, chiefly under the influence of Chaim *Zhitlowsky, were in favor of the centrality of Yiddish in the national Jewish experience and labored toward the recognition of that language, and of those who lived out their lives in it, as one of the several cultural linguistic communities of Eastern Europe, and of the Western world as a whole. This ideology was crystallized formally at a conference of Yiddishists in 1908 in *Czernowitz. Right after World War I this ideology was expressed by the foundation in Vilna, with branches in other parts of the Jewish world, of the Yidisher Visenshaftlekher Institut (*YIVO-Institute for Jewish Research), which survived World War II and now continues its scholarly and educational endeavors in New York.

The most important single movement to arise in Eastern Europe in the 1890s, in the very months when Herzl was appearing on the Jewish scene, was the Jewish Socialist Bund. This organization was created not primarily in reaction to Zionist stirrings but through tensions within the Russian revolutionary movement. Most of the young Jewish revolutionaries of the day were joining and taking prominent part in the various underground factions, but some began to feel that the Jewish workers could not be approached and made active in the Jewish revolutionary cause except through Yiddish. The announced purpose of the founders of the Bund was thus not a Jewish national one, for initially they proposed only the temporary use of Yiddish as a means to the end of bringing the Jewish workers into the mainstream of the Russian revolution. Yet the gibe by no less a figure than Plekhanov, the father of Russian Marxism, that Bundists are "Zionists who are afraid of seasickness," soon acquired a measure of truth. A Yiddish-speaking party representing the revolutionary will of Jewish workers could not help but become aware that these workers had problems not only with their employers but also with gentile workers. Under the pressure of Zionists, and especially of socialist Zionists, the Bund moved in the direction of accepting the separate culture of Jews as a lasting value worth preserving through "personal cultural autonomy," i.e., the right of every individual to enjoy national, educational, and linguistic life in the framework of a legal minority organization. It clashed on this issue with its fellow social democrats, Jewish and non-Jewish, Menshevik and Bolshevik.

RELIGIOUS AND SECULAR ANTI-NATIONALISM. There were also anti-nationalist reactions to Zionism, and these were much more clearly occasioned by the fact that an organized Zionist movement had arisen. The First Zionist Congress had been intended for Munich and it did not take place there because most of the rabbinate of Germany made a public declaration against the movement, for it would, in their view, call into question the absolute loyalty and integration of Jews as a purely religious community in the European nations. Some 20 years later, in the debates within the British war cabinet which preceded the announcements of the Balfour Declaration, the only Jewish member of the cabinet, Edwin Montagu, argued along the same line, that the recognition of the Jews as a nationality with its homeland in Palestine would call into question his political identity as a British subject who was a Jew only by religion. In 1929 when a group of distinguished non-Zionists joined a reorganized and "enlarged" Jewish Agency for Palestine, on a plane of parity with the representatives of the World Zionist Organization, the non-Zionists maintained that their interest in the Jewish settlement in Palestine was philanthropic and not political, and they indeed remained opposed to any talks of an eventual Jewish state. In the 1940s in the United States anti-Zionist sentiment was represented at its most extreme by the *American Council for Judaism, which maintained not only that its members were Jews by religion alone but that their religion made it incumbent upon them to take only a universalist position, which meant in practice a pro-Arab and anti-Jewish nationalist view of their responsibilities. "Dual loyalty" worried wide circles of Jews, especially in the Western countries, in varying degrees into the 1950s. By then it had become generally accepted, as Nahum Goldmann maintained, that all men have many "loyalties" which live in some tension with each other. The purpose of at least the most extreme of these anti-Zionists was the rapid assimilation of Jews into the total population, and they opposed Zionism because they saw it as a stumbling block to this end.

Zionism was attacked from another side by schools of thought which found it too secular, too modern, and thus too destructive, in their view, of the traditional Jewish values. The religious forces which joined Ḥibbat Zion in the 1880s and which later formed the religious Zionist organization, the Mizrachi, during the first few years of the modern Zionist movement, were a small minority among the Orthodox. The overwhelming majority, especially in ḥasidic circles, saw in such human efforts for the restoration of Jewish nationhood an affront to the command to wait patiently for the Messiah. More seriously, they understood that the definition of Jewry as a modern nation, which meant in immediate Zionist practice that religious believers were to accept equality within Jewry with nonbelievers, portended the eventual end of the supremacy of the Orthodox faith within Jewry. On this point older believers in Eastern Europe found allies in some circles of Westernized Jewry, especially in Germany. Together these groups formed in 1912 the *Agudat Israel, which maintained a consistent involvement in the Jewish community in Ereẓ Israel but was opposed to Zionism as too secular. Its main emphasis was on the defense of the Orthodox Jewish faith everywhere in the world.

TERRITORIALISM AND AGRICULTURAL SETTLEMENT. The movement that was closest to Zionism, *Territorialism, arose out of a split within the Zionist movement itself. In 1903 Herzl brought before the Zionist Congress the proposal of the British that the Jews be given land in East Africa for the development of their own autonomous community. The occasion for this proposal was the dire need of Russian Jewry, in the light of renewed pogroms, and the despair of quickly achieving from the Turks rights for settling Palestine. Thus it seemed that Herzl himself had "moved away from Zion" toward immediate, practical mass settlement to alleviate Jewish need. The proposal to examine the feasibility of the British offer won a bare majority at the last Zionist Congress presided over by Herzl, but it was overwhelmingly defeated after his death. Israel Zangwill, the writer who had been one of Herzl's first followers in England, left the Zionist Organization and founded the Jewish Territorialist Organization (ITO) in 1905. This and similar territorialist bodies continued into the 1930s and 1940s to search for a territory in some part of the world sufficiently empty and available to give the Jews room for the creation of their own national polity. These efforts never succeeded, but something very like what they intended was indeed realized by a non-ideological body, the *Jewish Colonization Association (ICA) which was founded in 1891 by Baron de Hirsch, one of the Jewish magnates to whom Herzl had turned and who had refused to join the Zionist endeavor. Agricultural colonies were created by this trust in several places in the United States and, especially, in Argentina. Though on the local level a kind of autonomous "all-Jewish" life did develop in some places on the American continent for one generation, they never coalesced into full-fledged "territorial" communities. Nowhere did these settlements survive the attraction for their young of higher education in the dominant language and the economic and professional opportunities of the cities.

SOVIET JEWISH CULTURE. In the first two decades after 1917, a kind of Jewish Communist nationalism arose and flourished in the Soviet Union and it was attractive to many Jews outside the borders of the U.S.S.R. But it was short-lived and took a tragic end. In reaction to the Jewish Socialist Bund and to the Zionists the young Stalin had declared in 1913 that there was no such thing as a united Jewish nation, for it lacked a land of its own. Only separate ethnic Jewish groups did exist and were doomed to disappear by assimilation. Nonetheless, during his early years in power he continued the policy of Lenin, to permit the Jews to organize a system of cultural life in Yiddish, provided the Jewish nationality, like all the others in the Soviet Union, made Communism the central political purpose of its cultural activity. Schools on all levels and even college courses in Yiddish were created in the 1920s. Hundreds of books were published and a press and theaters were encouraged. Additionally, with the help of such Western Jews as the Chicago millionaire, Lessing Rosenwald, who was opposed to Zionism, there was some settlement of Jews on the land in southern Russia and the Crimea. An even more grandiose attempt was made to create an autonomous Jewish region on a stretch of land in Siberia, *Birobidzhan. In the later 1930s and particularly after 1948 all of this, including Jewish cultural life in Birobidzhan, was brutally ended. But into the 1930s the reality of Jewish autonomy and the vision of state-sponsored Yiddish creativity in the Soviet Union, allied with its official outlawing of antisemitism, seemed to some Jews in the west, not only of the extreme political Left, an option to be preferred to Zionism. There is no longer any such ideology because repression in the Soviet Union has ended every genuine expression of Jewish life in that country. What existed there in the early 1970s was conducted as an act of semi-clandestine resistance to an unfriendly repressive regime.

[Arthur Hertzberg]

ZIONIST POLICY

Throughout the 19th century, and with increasing potency during the 20th century, nationalism emerged as probably the most powerful political force in Europe, the Americas, and later in Asia and Africa as well. It led to the dismemberment of established empires and to the unification of nations (Italy and Germany); it released creative forces hitherto often suppressed by foreign rule; but it also had other consequences: the identification of state and nation left little room for free and equal development of "minorities." Unlike the Greeks or Romanians, who lived on their own land, the Jews could not attain national self-determination by merely throwing off a foreign yoke. That these developments could not but affect Jewish thought was only natural.

Nineteenth-century Jewry carried very little political weight. Its strivings and efforts could only be of a religious, spiritual, or philanthropic nature. There was no lack of literary expression: countless pamphlets, memoranda, petitions, and sermons were bequeathed by men of renown and by anonymous writers in that century, as well as in earlier times. The general upheaval kindled new hopes. Not only Jewish names, such as Montefiore the magnate, Hess the socialist, and *Disraeli the statesman, are connected with that period, but also many gentile names, such as Lord Palmerston, Lord Shaftesbury, Ernest Laharanne, J.H. Dunant (father of the International Red Cross), and George Eliot. Gentile support for the idea of the Return to Zion reflected the realization that emancipation of the Jews was not enough, and that in addition to recognition of their civil rights, Jews were also entitled to the recognition of their rights as a nation. The sympathy of the few, however, was far outweighed by the hostility of the many. The old antisemitism had been reinforced by "scientific" racial teachings. The last two decades of the century saw the outburst of violent persecutions and pogroms in Eastern Europe, particularly in Russia. These were followed by a mass flight westward, especially to the U.S. The little that Ḥibbat Zion could do in the circumstances was totally inadequate. While hundreds of thousands surged through the gates of the New World, only hundreds succeeded in infiltrating through the more than half-closed doors of the ancient homeland. That these few would in time lay the cornerstone of the Jewish state could only be foreseen by dreamers and visionaries.

THE HERZL PERIOD. If Ḥovevei Zion had sought to reach their goal by quiet and modest labor, Herzl's aim was to achieve a dramatic *coup*, to secure vast funds in order to obtain a guaranteed political basis ("Charter") for a large-scale settlement of Jews. Securing the cooperation of Baron Hirsch or Baron de Rothschild and the consent of the sultan and the German kaiser looked like a shortcut to the goal. He believed that with "millions" it would be possible to obtain a charter or, with a charter, to obtain the millions. Hirsch and Rothschild had already been involved in assistance to Jews in the East in cooperation with the Alliance Israélite Universelle, which had established, inter alia, the first Jewish agricultural school near Jaffa in 1870. Rothschild extended a helping hand to the early settlements in Ereẓ Israel, and Hirsch had set up the Jewish Colonization Association (ICA) with an endowment hitherto unheard of in Jewish affairs. Herzl was received by Hirsch in June 1895 and the result was nil. It was after that interview that Herzl wrote *Der Judenstaat*.

The publication of this clarion call had several consequences. The Jewish national idea, hitherto discussed in small and uninfluential groups, became the subject of heated debate in wider circles. The excited support that came from various quarters – as well as criticism and derision – confirmed Herzl's instinctive feeling that the idea was viable. The territorial aspect also became clearer in his mind: it was to be the ancient homeland and not Argentina or some other place. The keys to Palestine were to be found in Berlin and Constantinople. A man of action, Herzl took his first political steps. He began by seeking a way to approach William II, and the initial results were not discouraging. Anxious to make rapid progress, however, he went to Constantinople (June 1896) in an attempt to see Abdul Hamid II. This proved to be impossible, but Herzl spoke to a number of high officials and a minor order was conferred upon him in the sultan's name.

After further visits to London and Paris in search of political and financial backing, Herzl saw no alternative to organizing a mass movement. Support of a growing number of Zionist groups, especially of students and youth, and encouragement from some Jewish notables enabled him to brush aside the opposition of the assimilated and of rabbinical circles (even Ḥibbat Zion remained cool, fearing Baron de Rothschild's displeasure). The First Zionist Congress met in Basle, Switzerland, in August 1897 and, amid scenes of great enthusiasm, adopted the following formulation of its aim: "Zionism seeks to establish a home for the Jewish people in Palestine secured under public law." The Congress also created the instrument for the implementation of its plan: the World Zionist Organization. Herzl wrote in his diary the prophetic words: "In Basle I founded the Jewish State." And he added a forecast as to the date when the state will become a reality: "…maybe in another five years, at the utmost fifty years." It was 50 years later – almost to the day – that the highest international body, the United Nations, gave its stamp of approval.

One of Herzl's immediate aims – turning the Jewish problems into a "world political problem" – had been achieved in part by the discussions that took place at the Congress itself, in the press, and in the public. Herzl could not have known, for instance, that the German embassy in Berne sent to Berlin a not unsympathetic account of the proceedings, or that this account reached the kaiser's desk and evoked William's remarking that he is all for the Jews moving to Palestine, "the sooner the better." On the other hand, the German consul in Jerusalem made light of the Congress and characterized Zionist aims as utopian. There was to be a change in the kaiser's approach, however. Urged by the grand duke of Baden, one of the more liberal and influential princes in Germany, he reconsidered his previous attitude. On the eve of his visit to Constantinople and Jerusalem in 1898, the kaiser wrote to the grand duke that "the basic idea has interested me, indeed, moved me," and he had come to the conclusion that they were dealing with a "problem of far-reaching significance." Great importance was attached to Jews turning to Germany with gratitude, and he was ready to receive Herzl during his visit to Turkey.

Anxious to have the kaiser put in a good word for Zionism in his talks with Abdul Hamid, Herzl obtained a preliminary audience with William in Constantinople (Oct. 18, 1898) and it seemed that the kaiser had received in a positive spirit both his views and his plea. Von Buelow, the German foreign minister, showed little enthusiasm. It was decided that a Zionist delegation would be officially received by the monarch later, during his visit to Jerusalem. The second audience took place as planned (Nov. 2, 1898), but the spirit was almost totally different. It seemed that the kaiser mentioned the matter in his talks with the sultan, and the latter did not react. The final outcome of Herzl's tremendous effort had been deeply disappointing even though, on the credit side, the whole chapter added somewhat to Zionism's political weight in the eyes of the world, Jewish and non-Jewish.

In search of new approaches, Herzl sought contacts with England and even with Russia; nor was Constantinople written off as yet. Indeed, a new mediator – the Orientalist Armin *Vambery – succeeded in obtaining the decisive audience with Abdul Hamid himself (May 17, 1901); but it proved fruitless. Coupled with the disheartening difficulties on the way to establishing the financial instruments of the movement, which were intended to help in obtaining the charter (the Jewish Colonial Trust), it brought Herzl to the realization that the old road led nowhere and the search would have to turn to other areas, closer to Ereẓ Israel or further away.

England was the first to be approached, and the territory in question was around *El Arish, on the southern border of Ereẓ Israel. London was interested, as it sought to secure the eastern approaches to the Suez Canal. A commission of experts went out to explore the area, which, not unexpectedly, proved to be poor in agricultural land and water resources and could at best absorb a limited number of settlers. Herzl himself visited Cairo (in the spring of 1903) to negotiate with the British representative there, Lord Cromer, and with the Egyptian authorities, but he could not secure the main precondition for any attempt in El Arish – supplies of water from the Nile.

This episode did not sever the first links with London. The second, and more serious suggestion, to come from there related to Uganda. The name Uganda stood then for a number of tribal areas in East Africa where British penetration – first missionary, then commercial and military – went on through the 1870s and 1880s and originally did not prosper. In 1892 the British government decided to abandon the territory, but reversed itself under pressure of missionary and trade interests. Sleeping sickness killed about 250,000 people among the local tribes between 1901 and 1909. Herzl did not know those details when British Colonial Secretary Joseph Chamberlain first spoke to him about the place. Before the matter came up officially, he made another attempt to tackle the Palestine issue by trying to obtain Russian support. In August 1903, several months after the *Kishinev pogrom, he traveled to St. Petersburg and interviewed the notorious minister of interior Plehve (who was assassinated within less than a year) and the minister of finance Count Witte. Once again, the Russian government would not or could not help. On his return journey, he received official news of the new British proposal.

Uganda was not Zion, Herzl knew that and said so at the Sixth Zionist Congress, which met immediately after his visit to Russia. As long as Ereẓ Israel was not obtainable, however, the persecuted people needed a temporary asylum.

Opposition from the old, "pre-Herzlian" Zionists was to be expected, but it was sharper and more widespread than foreseen. In fact, it revealed an accumulation of old dissatisfactions in considerable sections of the movement, especially among the young. The affairs of Zionism were conducted in a way that was far from democratic. Had it produced results, the rank and file would have acquiesced; but all those comings and goings in spheres of "high diplomacy" led away from the main goal, which was Zion. The basic difference between the approach of the leadership and that of the critics became increasingly apparent. The "political Zionists" believed that immigration and settlement could only follow the grant of a "Charter," which would secure the rights of the Jewish people to the land; anything else would be "infiltration" doomed to fail. The "practical Zionists" believed that Jewish rights to Ereẓ Israel were self-evident; immigration and settlement there could not be called "infiltration" and had to proceed under all circumstances. Both sides, however, were conscious of the political significance of the British proposal: at last a mighty world power had recognized the national aspirations of the Jews and was willing to extend a helping hand.

The Uganda Scheme became the Uganda crisis. The Sixth Zionist Congress did not reject the idea outright; with 295 delegates voting for, 178 against, and 132 abstentions, the movement formally accepted the leadership's proposal that a commission be elected to act in an advisory capacity when the Executive sent a mission to the area proposed by England. But the storm that broke loose came as a shock, and it was realized that it would be virtually impossible to proceed with the plan. There were also reports of strong opposition on the part of the British settlers in East Africa and criticism in England itself. Thus, the first debate on Zionism took place in the House of Commons in June 1904, with the participation of the prime minister, A.J. *Balfour and one of the opposition leaders, David Lloyd *George.

In the closing stages of the Zionist Congress, Herzl sought to conciliate the opposition and stressed his continued devotion to what he called "the only country where our people can find rest." But he felt that the breach could hardly be healed. After eight years of superhuman effort and tremendous personal sacrifices, he saw the end approaching. In a final spurt of energy he turned to Rome, where he was received at the beginning of 1904 by King Victor Emmanuel III and by Pope Pius X. The king displayed a warm interest, but there was not much that Italy could do. The pope was ice cold: "If you come to Palestine and settle your people there, we shall prepare churches and priests to convert them." Within a few months after these interviews, Herzl died.

THE TRANSITION PERIOD. That the political activities of the movement could, after the leader's death, no longer be conducted in the same centralized, personal way had been clear to all concerned. After the "natural" successor, Max Nordau, refused to take over, the task fell to another close friend, David Wolffsohn. But he was hardly a political leader, and if the inevitable change came but gradually, it was because the desire to remain faithful to "Herzlian Zionism" dominated the heirs to the leadership and because the main problem inherited by them, Uganda, called for immediate decisions. By then, neither side, the Zionists nor the British, were interested in proceeding with the project. A group of experts went to East Africa in December 1904 and reported in April 1905: the proposed area was not suitable for mass settlement. Meanwhile, practical work in Ereẓ Israel gained priority even before any official change took place in the policy of the movement. One of the first visits paid by Wolffsohn was to Edmond de Rothschild, who promised to aid in practical undertakings in the country. Wolffsohn also visited Vambery, who was not optimistic. In his view, the best way for Zionists was to settle Palestine through quiet work within the existing laws. It was in this direction that the Zionist movement gradually veered after Herzl's death, though it never gave up the political element of its philosophy. The turning point came at the Seventh Zionist Congress (1905) which witnessed the first split in the movement when supporters of Uganda refused to concede defeat. They saw themselves as "territorialists," and with the gates of Ereẓ Israel virtually closed, the "Ugandists" refused to reject a proposal made by a great power at a time when the need to find a refuge for the victims of persecution was at its highest.

The departure of the Ugandists, who established the Jewish Territorial Organization under the leadership of Israel Zangwill, was bound to weaken the movement. But it strengthened the "practical" wing in Zionism (led by M.M. *Ussishkin), which, for the first time, obtained representation on the Zionist Executive. The latter was now composed of three "political" Zionists, three "practical," and Wolffsohn as the balancing force. The controversy did not end at that, and difficulties arose when the territorialists sought to negotiate with governments. Tensions relaxed somewhat when the two organizations found themselves cooperating at a conference called by the Zionists (Brussels, January 1906) in order to discuss assistance to Russian Jews. This also produced meager results.

Wolffsohn and his advisers looked for new political initiatives, though this time – in accordance with an explicit ruling of the Seventh Zionist Congress – not beyond Erez Israel and "adjacent areas." El Arish and Sinai drew renewed attention; Syria and Mesopotamia were considered. Sinai was then causing difficulties between Constantinople and London, which wanted the Turkish-Egyptian border to be fixed as far away from the Suez Canal as possible. A suggestion that the establishment of a Jewish settlement in Sinai may serve as a "compromise" found no support. France displayed no interest at all; when Nordau sought its help on behalf of persecuted Jews in Russia, he was told that France cannot add to the many difficulties of an allied government.

There were other attempts, among them discussions with the foreign minister of the Netherlands about raising the problem of Jewish migration during the second Peace Conference at The Hague. Another proposal spoke of calling a special international conference to deal with the subject. The Dutch thought that it would be appropriate for the initiative to come from England; London felt that a Dutch initiative would be better. A German official promised to take it up with his foreign minister, but no more was heard of it. In the meantime, a fleeting hope arose that it might be possible to renew some of the contacts with Turkey. The sultan's financial troubles were greater than ever, and his officials were looking for help. Twice during the year 1907 Wolffsohn visited Constantinople, and there were moments when he felt that "substantial" progress had been achieved. He no longer spoke of a "Charter" and concentrated on immigration and land acquisition. But the Turks needed vast sums of money, which were, as before, far above the financial ability of the Zionists. The results were therefore the same as during Herzl's desperate journeys. On the credit side, a start had been made for the opening of a bank in Constantinople (The Anglo-Levantine Banking Co.) in which the controlling interest was to be in the hands of the Jewish Colonial Trust (enabling it to appoint the bank's deputy director, who would represent Zionist interests, both financial and political).

THE YOUNG TURKS. When Wolffsohn next visited Constantinople, it was after the situation there had undergone a dramatic change. The revolution of the Young Turks (July 1908) brought to the fore new rulers and widespread hopes. It also restored a relatively liberal constitution; abolished the rule of corrupt palace cliques, of spying, and censorship; and established a parliament. Abdul Harold survived for another eight months and – after a briefly successful counter coup – was replaced by Muhammed v. The years that followed were turbulent and saw almost constant warfare, beginning with the Italian campaign in Tripolitania (1911–12) and through two Balkan wars (1912–13) to World War I and beyond. It was hardly a time for gaining sympathy for Zionism. Whatever progressive ideas the Young Turks may have had initially, chauvinistic tendencies soon prevailed among them. They rejected suggestions for a less centralized regime and for a degree of freedom for the minorities. As far as Palestine was concerned, they proved as inflexible as the rulers they displaced. Nevertheless, conditions of political work in Constantinople itself underwent a slight change.

The Zionist leadership sought to avail itself of the few opportunities that were now to be found on the Bosphorus, mostly for the purpose of explaining the aims and purposes of Jewish settlement in Ereẓ Israel. With the opening of the Anglo-Levantine Banking Co., the post of deputy director was entrusted to Victor *Jacobson, a Russian Zionist with some experience in the Near East. Since the main task had been the proliferation of authoritative information, he was joined by another Russian Zionist, the journalist Vladimir Jabotinsky. A small Turkish publication in French was turned into a well-edited daily, *Le Jeune Turc*. Apart from propaganda, however, there was little that could be done in the political sphere. A visit by Nordau, who had friendly ties with some of the Turkish leaders, produced no change. He was told that the Jews would be allowed to take part in the development of Turkey but would not be allowed to concentrate in any particular area, such as Palestine. Wolffsohn revisited Constantinople (June 1909) to review the situation. This was to be his last visit there. In 1911 he retired from the Executive and was replaced by Otto *Warburg, a "practical" Zionist, as chairman. This time Wolffsohn paid special attention to the attitude of Turkish Jews, of whom only a few showed interest in Zionism; others were indifferent or unfriendly. The community saw much infighting: between Sephardi and Ashkenazi leaders, between those influenced by the French-oriented Alliance Israélite Universelle and the adherents of the German-Jewish *Hilfsverein der Deutschen Juden. Prominent among the opponents were Chief Rabbi Haim *Nahoum (later chief rabbi of Egypt) and a Jewish member of parliament from Baghdad.

THE ARAB PROBLEM. The Arabs themselves had become a significant political factor. As one of the subject peoples, they had little direct say in the past. In Palestine difficulties arose, from time to time, between Jewish settlers and the local population in connection with land purchases, commercial competition, labor disputes, or robberies. Labor troubles multiplied after the Second Aliyah brought young pioneers who sought to "conquer" labor opportunities in all Jewish settlements. But there, as elsewhere in the empire, Arabs were dominated and roughly treated by Turkish officials. The Arab national movement was in its infancy. One of the few who thought of it was Ahad Ha-Am, who wrote as far back as 1891, in a famous article "Truth from Ereẓ Israel":

"We abroad are accustomed to believe that Ereẓ Israel is almost totally desolate at present… but in reality it is not so… Arabs, especially those in towns, see and understand our activities and aims in the country but keep quiet and pretend as if they did not know, and that because they don't see any danger to their future in our activities at present, and they try to exploit us, too, and profit from the new guests while laughing at us in their hearts. But if the time comes and our people make such progress as to displace the people of the country… they will not lightly surrender the place."

The situation began to change after the revolution of the Young Turks. There were some 60 Arabs and a couple of Jews in the parliament, which counted less than 300 members. The Arabs influenced policy (mostly through personal contacts), introduced interpellations, and, in 1911, initiated two full-fledged debates on the dangers involved in Jewish immigration and land acquisition. In one of these debates, the only speaker to refute their accusations was a Bulgarian Socialist member. Government spokesmen more than once made hostile statements stressing Zionist separatist aims. Zionist representatives sought to counteract the assaults by denying separatist intentions. Jacobson also sought to establish contact with Arab members of parliament. The latter feared that government leaders belonging to the Committee of Union and Progress might be unduly influenced by Jews who were among the earliest supporters of the Committee. The Turkish authorities, on their part, chose to make promises to all and fulfilled very few of them.

Not many realized at the time that the struggles in which Turkey had been involved, in the Balkans and elsewhere, were but the opening skirmishes in an approaching world war. Though talk of "partition" of the Ottoman Empire was heard long before and early Zionism itself had been influenced by it, the Zionist movement had to base its day-to-day work on repeated assurances that it did not seek to harm the unity of that empire. When Turkey found itself at war with Italy in *Tripoli, Nordau supported a proposal that a unit of Jewish volunteers be organized to fight side by side with the Ottoman forces. Another Zionist suggestion later spoke of organizing a medical unit to help the Turks in the Balkans. When the veteran Zionist leader Jacobus *Kann of The Hague published a book about a visit to Ereẓ Israel in which he openly stated that the ultimate aim of Zionism is the establishment of a Jewish state there, Jabotinsky, then in charge of Zionist press activities in Constantinople, vigorously protested to Wolffsohn and demanded the suppression of Kann's book.

This attitude did not seem too convincing to the Young Turks, while it made Zionism further suspect in the eyes of Arab nationalists. On the other hand, Zionist tactics were almost inevitably the outcome of the contradiction between the movement's immediate needs and its long-range goals. The immediate necessity was to preserve the existing *yishuv* and to increase, however slowly, the number of new immigrants and settlements. The hopes engendered by the changes in Turkey were soon reflected in growing Jewish activity: the number of settlements established in the years 1908–14 reached almost a dozen and a half. The same period also saw the opening in Jaffa of the Palestine Office of the Zionist Organization under Arthur *Ruppin, the foundation of Tel Aviv, and the formation of organized public bodies of the new *yishuv*. All these naturally strengthened Arab opposition and coincided with the formation of local Arab nationalist groups and the appearance of their first newspapers in the country. Though the stirrings among the Arabs found little reflection in the Jewish press, some Zionist leaders soon realized their importance, and as far back as 1908 Wolffsohn used an expression which was later to be repeated by others: Governments change, but the people remain.

During the last year before the outbreak of World War I the first Arab-Jewish contacts that could be seen as politically significant, were introduced. When the Young Turks started taking stringent measures for the "Ottomanization" of their empire, some of the active Arab nationalists were in search of allies. A few turned to the Jews, who, they hoped, could help them with the press and public opinion in Europe. A director of *Le Jeune Turc*, S. Hochberg, received an invitation to visit Beirut and Cairo in order to meet Arab nationalists. He went there, with Jacobson's consent and with the knowledge of the Young Turks, and, according to reports to his superiors, established a measure of accord. The support of *Le Jeune Turc* had been promised for Arab aspirations, without prejudice to the unity of the empire, as well as help in the European press, while the Arabs undertook to drop their opposition to Jewish immigration and to support Arab-Jewish understanding. Some of this spirit was also reportedly felt at a conference called by the same Arab activists in Paris in July 1913. This time, Jacobson joined Hochberg in the talks but these were inconclusive, though only muted opposition to Jewish immigration was voiced at the conference.

Another attempt at Arab-Jewish understanding was made in 1914. Arab politicians were again in need of propaganda assistance and, in conversations with Zionists in Constantinople, concentrated on Jewish financial aid for the expansion of Arab education, large-scale public works in Arab regions, and preventing the dispossession of Arab *fellahin*. The latter point was met by suggestions that agriculture be intensified, thus making room for new settlers as well as for the existing farmers. Parallel with these conversations, other talks were conducted by Nahum Sokolow, member of the Zionist Executive, who visited Beirut and Damascus in May 1914. Arab participants in these talks suggested a joint conference to be convened later in the summer and attended by members of the Zionist Executive like Sokolow himself, and not by representatives unauthorized to take decisions. Some of the Arabs called for the assimilation of the Jewish settlers among the local majority through the establishment of mixed villages and mixed schools. In the meantime, heavy clouds covered the international horizon. The joint conference which was to meet at the beginning of July was postponed for a few weeks. But on July 28 the first shots of World War I rang out in the Balkans, and on November 5 Turkey became involved in the war on the side of Germany and Austria.

THE STRUGGLE FOR THE FUTURE. That the vast conflict was bound tragically to affect a people whose masses lived on both sides of the frontiers in regions which turned into battlefields soon became all too obvious. The Zionist movement, national in spirit but international in structure, was also bound to find itself in a precarious position. Its headquarters were in Berlin, but the majority of its followers lived in countries at war with Germany or neutral. There were suggestions that the central office should move to Scandinavia. British and U.S. Zionists wanted it transferred to the United States and placed under the leadership of Louis D. Brandeis. Russian Zionists feared that such a step would cause affront to Germany and further antagonize Turkey; they wanted a coordinating bureau in neutral Copenhagen. Thus the old central office remained in Berlin and its representatives stayed in Constantinople, their task more vital than ever: to see to it that the young *yishuv* weathers the storm. Two members of the Executive (Sokolow and *Tschlenow) were sent to London to take charge of political activities there, while another member, Shemaryahu *Levin, went to the United States. Nonetheless, one of the results of the fact that the Zionist headquarters never left Central Europe was the widespread and persistent impression that the movement was under German influence.

Whether Germany itself took it for granted was far less certain. Berlin never took Zionism seriously. Its international character had always been suspect. The recent struggle of the *yishuv* (1913) against German as the language of instruction in the German-Jewish Hilfsverein schools, including the newly founded Haifa Technological Institute, caused considerable irritation. Having achieved the huge political success of involving Turkey in the war as an ally, Berlin would do nothing to place any strain on the friendship. Repeated Zionist initiatives directed at obtaining Turkish – or at least German – expressions of sympathy for Jewish aims in Ereẓ Israel were repeatedly rebuffed. Even where the proposals concerned the rights of Jews in Russian Poland, which was occupied by German troops (Count Bernstorff, German ambassador in Washington, urged his government to promise them equality of rights in the future), Berlin responded negatively, ostensibly because such a step could make it more difficult to achieve a separate peace with Russia at some later date.

Nonetheless, in the military and political vacillations that were to follow, the Germans sought to preserve the precarious status quo in and around Palestine, but even that proved difficult. Soon after the outbreak of hostilities, one of the most ruthless members of the Turkish ruling group, Jamal Pasha, assumed command in Syria and Palestine and began a series of expulsions, some of them explained as military measures, others as the result of the fact that many of the Jews in the country were foreign (mostly Russian), citizens. The grave danger to the very existence of the *yishuv* (which numbered about 85,000) alarmed not only the Zionists but Jewry as a whole. The largest Jewish community (Russia) could do little; its political influence was nil and it had been overwhelmed by its own huge refugee problem, created by the mass expulsion of Jews from the war zones by the Russian army command. There remained only one large section of the Jewish people not directly involved in the war. U.S. Jewry immediately offered a helping hand both to the Jewish victims of the fighting in Eastern Europe and to the *yishuv*. Furthermore, U.S. Jewry had political weight, and the United States was at the time represented in Constantinople by Henry *Morgenthau, who was willing to help. Coming on top of the Turkish atrocities, of which the Armenians were the main victims, reports of harassment in Ereẓ Israel created an atmosphere that was harmful not only to Turkey but to its allies as well. One of the main aims of the Central Powers had been to keep the U.S. neutral. The unpopularity of czarist Russia in wide circles of the United States public played into their hands. There were also great economic interests involved in the struggle for U.S. sympathies. This helped to make the rulers of Turkey realize that turning Jewish Palestine into another Armenia by large-scale massacres may be too costly, and, although Jamal Pasha often acted on his own, the worst fears that were felt in the first months of the war only partly materialized. Before the end of 1915 the German ambassador in Constantinople, Count Metternich, sent a confidential circular letter to his consulates in Turkey explaining their government's "friendly attitude" toward Jewry's aspirations concerning the raising of the spiritual and economic standards of the Jews living in the Ottoman Empire and furthering Jewish immigration and settlement there (Palestine was not mentioned); all this, of course, provided no harm was done to Turkish or German interests.

In the meantime, a Zionist political campaign was slowly gaining ground in Britain. It centered around a younger leader who had become prominent as one of the critics of Herzl's policies – Chaim Weizmann. One of his closest advisers was a much better known critic of Herzl – Aḥad Ha-Am. The political climate in England was unlike that of Germany. For a long time Britain guarded the integrity of the Ottoman Empire until the latter's misgovernment; the steady penetration of German interests into Turkey and the expansion of Britain' own interests in the Near East made that policy no longer tenable. The future partition of the vast Ottoman domains raised great problems and offered great opportunities, including some for the non-Turkish elements in the empire and for the Jews in Palestine. Weizmann was one of those who soon grasped the suddenly unfolding prospects. The history of his efforts is the history of the Balfour Declaration. It was a dramatic struggle in which the chief participants were outstanding leaders of the British government, foremost among them Balfour and Lloyd George, leaders of the Jewish community, split in their attitude to the very idea of a Jewish center in Palestine, and numerous other personalities. An early advocate of the idea was a member of the government, Herbert *Samuel. The search for an acceptable policy formulation proved to be a most complicated task, mainly because other Entente partners, above all France, were also involved.

When the first tentative approaches were made, the Zionists knew nothing of the secret negotiations between Britain and France, which resulted in the *Sykes-Picot Agreement of February 1916, that had already settled the future of Palestine. With the exception of a small enclave including Haifa, in which Britain had a long-standing interest, the country was to be placed under an international administration. Later, Russia was also promised large areas of Turkish territory. These undertakings tied Britain's hands when the discussions on Zionist proposals began making headway. But they also spurred interest. The creators of British policy in the Near East had always viewed France as an undesirable neighbor in the vicinity of Suez. An opportunity to reopen the question, especially as far as Palestine was concerned, increased that interest. The potential propaganda value in America and even in Russia, with their millions of Jews, was not overlooked. The Jews, on their part, were becoming more active in giving expression to their wishes and expectations. The British government consulted the government of the U.S., and obtained the support of Wilson and his administration for the pro-Zionist attitude of the British government. L. Brandeis and S. Wise played an important role in securing the U.S. support. As early as the first days of the war, before Turkey joined the Central Powers, proposals were made that Jewish battalions be raised to fight for the liberation of Ereẓ Israel. In August 1914 London was visited by a well-known figure in the Russian revolutionary movement, Pinḥas *Rutenberg, who sought to obtain the support of Weizmann and others for this idea. In the meantime, young Jews expelled from Ereẓ Israel to Egypt began volunteering for service with the British forces, and the Zion Mule Corps was established in 1915 under British command with a former officer of the Russian army, Joseph Trumpeldor, playing a central role when the unit went to Gallipoli later in the year. This was but the beginning of the prolonged campaigning for the establishment of the Jewish Legion that was stubbornly pursued by Jabotinsky in London and took another two years to obtain its goal. Rutenberg, who went to the United States in 1915 for the same purpose, had been persuaded to postpone it because of the threat of Turkish retaliations in Palestine, and those who influenced him most were two labor leaders from Ereẓ Israel, David Ben-Gurion and Izhak Ben-Zvi, who later, however, in 1917, themselves promoted the idea of the Jewish Legion and joined its "American" battalion. Much of this activity, including Weizmann's political initiative, had not been authorized by the official supreme organs of the Zionist movement; a meeting of its General Council held in Copenhagen in 1916 resolved that the Executive may not negotiate with any country at war with Turkey.

The turning point on almost all the fronts came in 1917. The beginning of March brought the Russian Revolution which overthrew the czar and led, eight months later, to the overthrow of the revolutionary government itself and the establishment of the Soviet regime. April brought the American declaration of war on the Central Powers (but not against Turkey). Soon afterward permission was granted in London for enlistment in Jewish battalions. At the beginning of the same year, the British government, now led by Lloyd George, started "unofficial discussions" with the Zionists. One of the first obstacles that had to be removed was the previous commitment under the Anglo-French Sykes-Picot Agreement. Indeed, it was Sir Mark Sykes himself who conducted the discussions with representative Jews, and with his assistance important moves were made in Paris and Rome. On behalf of the Zionists, Sokolow conducted the negotiations there. This time, even the Vatican was less unbending. Benedict XV told Sokolow: "We shall be good neighbors." A short time later, Sokolow received from the French government assurances of "sympathy for your cause, the triumph of which is bound up with that of the Allies." It may have been a reluctant concession, but it opened the way for a decision by the British cabinet. Significantly, the most persistent opposition there came from Edwin Montagu, the Jewish secretary of state for India, but it could not overcome the equally great persistence of the prime minister and of the secretary of state for foreign affairs. Montagu succeeded, however, in delaying the approval of his government's pronouncement and in watering it down. On Nov. 2, 1917, the Balfour Declaration was issued.

WORDS AND DEEDS. The impact of the Balfour Declaration on Jewish public opinion was immediate, and enthusiasm spontaneous. In many lands there were huge demonstrations and processions displaying the Union Jack side by side with the Zionist flag. But the Jews in Germany and Austria could only celebrate between four walls, and in Russia there were by then large areas under Bolshevik rule or in a state of flux where open identification with an "imperialist power" became imprudent. If one of the purposes of the declaration had been to influence developments in Russia, it came too late, even assuming that Jewish opinion could have had any significant influence amid the political storms that were raging there. On the other side of the trenches, in Germany and Turkey, the semi-official reactions were unexpectedly mild. The German Foreign Ministry was unmoved; Zionist efforts in Berlin to obtain a similar declaration were rebuffed. But in December 1917, Talaat Pasha, one of the Turkish ruling triumvirate, told a Zionist correspondent of a prominent German newspaper that Turkey was favorably disposed to Jewish settlement in Palestine, that existing restrictions would be removed, and immigration would be free within the "limits of the country's absorptive capacity," and that Jews will have the right to free economic and cultural development and to local self-government in the framework of Turkish laws. After the publication of the interview, Jewish and Zionist representatives were called to the Foreign Office in Berlin and an undersecretary told them that his government welcomed Talaat's statement.

The general military situation at the time had not yet been viewed by the Central Powers as hopeless. Even Turkey was far from giving up the struggle, in spite of the British advance in Palestine, which caused, inter alia, the removal of Jamal Pasha (September 1917), but not before he hanged a number of Arab nationalists in Damascus. Turkey was pinning its hopes on a Russian withdrawal from the war, chances of a separate peace, or, at least, a relatively lenient treatment at a future peace conference. But 1918 brought the series of events that left no more illusions. Bulgaria collapsed at the end of September. A few days later came the disintegration of the Austro-Hungarian Empire. Turkey capitulated on October 20, and Germany herself, her power broken on the western front and her people rebelling, deposed the kaiser and signed an armistice on November 11.

Months before this denouement, the new Zionist leadership headed by Weizmann took the first steps toward the implementation of the Balfour Declaration. A *Zionist Commission for Palestine had been formed, including representatives from Britain, America, France, and Italy, and started out for Ereẓ Israel. Two representatives from Russia were elected, but their departure had been postponed. Before leaving, Weizmann was received by King George V. There were high hopes but few illusions. It had been difficult to obtain the international promise; turning it into a reality was bound to be much more difficult. The Turks were out; the Arabs felt immeasurably stronger; the British military administration was totally indifferent and often openly hostile. The Jewish people as a whole had been greatly weakened by the war. Russian Jews were among the chief victims of the internal chaos that followed the October Revolution and of the civil war that was beginning to engulf most of Russia. Polish Jewry was in dire need of help. American Jews saw their most urgent task in rushing aid to Eastern Europe.

The arrival of the Zionist Commission in Ereẓ Israel in April 1918 opened three decades of incessant struggle. The commission's immediate task was to help in restoring the impoverished *yishuv* and preparing the conditions for future immigration. The almost totally negative attitude of the military authorities was a major obstacle, and it also impeded understanding with the Arabs. Contacts were established with Emir Feisal, about to become king of Syria. Weizmann's talks with him, first in Akaba and later in London and Paris, led to the signing of an agreement in January 1919 with Colonel T.E. *Lawrence acting as intermediary. But Feisal's hopes to remain in Syria had been frustrated. The French forced him to flee Damascus in 1920, and though he was compensated by the British, who secured his election as king of Iraq, his understanding with the Zionists remained a dead letter. The stormy events in the Arab world were bound to involve Palestine, to where they were soon directed – partly made to be directed – against the Jews. For the first time attacks were organized on a large scale. In the spring of 1920, Trumpeldor and seven others fell while defending Tel Ḥai in Upper Galilee. Within a few weeks Arab rioting in Jerusalem claimed further victims. Some of the organizers were sentenced to years of hard labor. For the sake of evenhandedness, Jabotinsky and members of the Jewish self-defense received similar treatment. Moreover, official explanations published by the British authorities made the Balfour Declaration look like a scrap of paper. The political pattern then established was to last until the end of British rule in the country.

Elsewhere on the political front things looked somewhat less dismal. Zionist leaders had been given an opportunity personally to present their case at the Paris Peace Conference. They also had a say in the lengthy process of drafting the League of Nations' Mandate for Palestine, even if many of their proposals had not been accepted. The Mandate itself had been entrusted to Britain at San Remo in 1920, although some British leaders wanted it to be taken on by a more than reluctant America. On June 30, 1920, Sir Herbert Samuel arrived in Palestine as its first high commissioner, with every goodwill to serve the people of Palestine as a whole, the Jewish National Home, and British interests. While he was taking the initial steps in establishing a civilian administration, Zionist leaders met in London for their first postwar conference, and the internal difficulties which dogged the movement from its early days again came to the surface. Instead of "political" and "practical" Zionists, it was "east" and "west" this time, symbolized to a great extent by two names: Weizmann and Brandeis. The former wanted a comprehensive program of action embracing political, economic, and cultural matters. His opponents viewed the political chapter as closed with the attainment of international recognition and approval of the Mandate; henceforth efforts were to be concentrated on economics, and particularly on fostering private enterprise. Those in Weizmann's camp proposed the establishment of a large foundation fund – Keren Hayesod – for the upbuilding of the National Home and for the encouragement of private initiative. The "Brandeisists" opposed it. There was a widespread feeling that unless Jewry put to good use the opportunities created by the wartime achievements, they might be irretrievably lost. But the general situation did not work in Zionism's favor, regardless of trend. The strongest appeals addressed to world Jewry evoked only a faint echo. The funds raised were miserably inadequate. Even the limited number of immigrants could not find immediate employment, and crisis chased crisis.

These difficulties opened new opportunities before the opposing side. Samuel's efforts to placate the Arabs were rebuffed. Winston *Churchill's efforts as head of the Colonial Office to do the same by making Feisal king of Iraq and Abdullah emir of eastern Palestine (called Transjordan) where the "Jewish clauses" of the Mandate were not to be applied, fared no better. Less than a year after Samuel's arrival, the country was shaken by the worst outbreak of Arab rioting yet seen there. Its political repercussions led to the publication (in June 1922) of the first of the series of *White Papers which undermined the foundations of what was intended to be the Jewish National Home. No concession, however, satisfied the Arab political leadership, which sought to stop all Jewish immigration and take over the government of the country through institutions with an Arab majority or by other means. This general erosion gave rise to great discontent within the Zionist movement. Weizmann was accused of not being strong enough in his dealings with the Mandatory government since he constantly insisted on Jewish-British relations based on mutual trust. Others accused him of extending too much support to the Zionist labor movement and to unsound economic policies. One of the opposition groups was led by Jabotinsky, who had been brought into the Executive in 1921 but resigned in 1923. Moreover, Brandeis laid down his post as honorary president of the Zionist Organization (June 1921), thus bringing U.S. Zionists into disarray for a number of years. For different reasons, Ussishkin was also soon to leave the chairmanship of the Zionist Executive in Jerusalem (which replaced the Zionist Commission). Even before that, there were changes in its Political Department whose first chief, Commander *Levi-Bianchini (Italian Jewry's representative on the commission) had been killed by Bedouin in an attack on a train near the Syrian border. His successor, M.D. *Eder (a former territorialist) returned to London in 1922, and Weizmann sent to Jerusalem a career officer with diplomatic experience, Lt. Col. F.H. *Kisch, who was to remain at his post for nine difficult years.

Seeking to break the vicious circle of economic predicaments and political setbacks, Weizmann and his colleagues decided to open a new page by bringing into the national effort important non-Zionist elements in Jewry. The idea encountered strong opposition, mainly among those already opposed to Weizmann. However, after lengthy preparatory work, the first conference of the "enlarged" Jewish Agency met in Zurich in 1929 in the presence of a number of outstanding Jews of the generation, among them Albert Einstein, Leon Blum, Ḥ.N. Bialik, Shalom Asch, Louis Marshall, and others. The impression produced by this remarkable gathering had been powerful, and the hopes it reawakened were great. But the reaction in Palestine came almost immediately. After months of Arab incitement motivated by the most potent of weapons – Muslim religious hatred aimed at depriving the Jews of their traditional rights at the Western Wall – there came a wave of murderous attacks. The outbreak was followed by two inquiries. An international commission studied and reported on rights of access to the Western Wall, and a British commission reviewed the political aspects of the situation. The resultant White Paper (1930) issued by the colonial secretary, Lord Passfield (the Labour leader Sidney Webb), led to Weizmann's resignation as president of the Jewish Agency as a protest and a sign that the government can no longer expect his cooperation. A storm followed in the press and in the British Parliament. Official explanations were published by Prime Minister Ramsay MacDonald, but they could but slightly reduce the damage done. Weizmann's own position became untenable, and at the 1931 Zionist Congress Sokolow was elected president in his place. No essential change in the policy of the movement, however, followed. Indeed, Chaim *Arlosoroff, who took over the Jewish Agency's Political Department in Jerusalem from Kisch (who resigned before the Congress), had been Weizmann's devoted disciple. It was also the first time that a representative of Zionist Labour had been entrusted with the political portfolio, which was to remain in Labour hands. Furthermore, with Weizmann away from his old office in London, the center of Zionist policy-making gradually moved to Jerusalem, and this shift was virtually completed after Ben-Gurion joined the Executive in 1933.

Kisch was the model civil servant; Arlosoroff was the statesman-philosopher. Realizing that no change in the situation could be expected unless there was some progress toward a modus vivendi with the Arabs, Arlosoroff was determined to concentrate much of his work in this field. Consequently, he appointed Moshe Shertok (*Sharett) as secretary of the department for his knowledge of Arabic and his strong ties with the country. Arlosoroff's brief term, less than two years (he was murdered on the Tel Aviv seashore in June 1933), coincided with the first years of service of the British high commissioner, Sir Arthur Wauchope. The two established a sincere mutual understanding, and this played a part in government actions when, at the beginning of the Hitler regime, it became imperative that Palestine be opened to a large number of immigrants from Germany. Nonetheless, Arlosoroff also came to the conclusion that although there was no immediate alternative to the former political course of the movement, future alternatives had to be explored. He considered Revisionist demands for a complete change of the system of government in Palestine as unrealistic. But the road hitherto followed, without greater political assistance from Britain and vast sums from the Jewish people, would clearly not bring Zionism nearer to its goal. The world situation also militated against it. In 1932 Arlosoroff foresaw a new international conflagration "in five to ten years." It was imperative to elaborate alternative, even "revolutionary," plans, while continuing to "muddle through." The ideas discussed in those days included plans for the division of the country into "cantons" on Swiss lines. This was an old suggestion made by Jacobson, then head of the Zionist Office at the seat of the League of Nations in Geneva. More radical proposals spoke of establishing a Jewish state in a part of the country where Jews formed a large section of the population (by then the *yishuv* counted about 180,000).

In spite of their vital importance, long-range issues had to give way to urgent current problems, and even these could not be adequately handled when the budget of the Political Department in Jerusalem amounted to $20,000 a year. The latest White Paper (1931) brought in its wake additional inquiries into the problems of land and absorptive capacity – or lack of it, according to British experts. The Jewish Agency tried to reopen the question of settlement in Transjordan; a group of influential sheikhs entered into negotiations with the Jewish Agency on the subject, presumably not without Emir Abdullah's knowledge. The British were adamant: Transjordan was to remain closed to Jewish settlement. Such policies could only weaken the position of the few Arab leaders who were inclined to some sort of understanding with the Jews. Desultory attempts to open discussions with them were made during those years by prominent *yishuv* personalities (J.L. Magnes, Rutenberg, Moshe *Smilansky) and, less important, by a small group called Berit Shalom, which was seeking a binational solution. They found, however, no one in the Arab camp able to enter into binding agreements. The mufti of Jerusalem, Ḥājj Amin al-*Husseini, intended to turn the Palestine problem into a general Muslim problem by calling a Muslim Conference in Jerusalem. Tension and agitation were also fostered by inciting broadcasts from Fascist Italy. In Egypt the beginning of the 1930s witnessed violent disturbances and a general strike in 1933. In the year 1937 independent Egypt was admitted to the League of Nations. The year 1936 saw a general strike in Syria, too, but French consent to grant Syria independence was later repudiated by Paris. Iraq, which joined the League of Nations in 1932, experienced a military coup in 1936. The examples proved infectious. In order to force the British to stop Jewish immigration and place Palestine under an Arab government, and also in order to subdue the moderates within the Arab camp itself, al-Husseini and his followers proclaimed an Arab national strike in 1936. It did not take long for what was supposed to be passive resistance to turn into open rebellion. An Arab Higher Committee was formed to conduct the struggle.

The inquiry instituted by the British this time was the most authoritative ever. A Royal Commission headed by Lord

Peel had been appointed, and before it left for its destination, unusually stringent measures were taken in Ereẓ Israel to restore a semblance of order, with the aid of almost 20,000 British troops. Formally, the Arab leaders only stopped the strike when called upon to do so by the rulers of Iraq, Saudi Arabia, Yemen and Transjordan (Egypt was not among them), but later decided to boycott the commission because the government approved new immigration permits. The commission stayed in the country from November 1936 until the end of January 1937, and toward the conclusion of its hearings Arab representatives testified before it in compliance with another call from the same rulers. The Jewish Agency appeared before the commission in full force, headed by Weizmann who was again its president (reelected in 1935). Sittings were held abroad as well, and statements were heard from Jabotinsky and Samuel, among others. Politically, the results were more dramatic than after any previous inquiry. The commission concluded that the Mandate proved to be unworkable because it was impossible to secure even the minimum of mutual understanding between the two sections of the population necessary for its implementation. After analyzing the various proposals for finding a way out of the impasse, the commission chose partition: dividing the country into a Jewish state, an Arab state, and a mandated zone which was to include Jerusalem. The establishment of a Jewish state had thus become for the first time a proposal from a formal British body. What could not have been foreseen was that at least three other commissions would have to go into the matter and a second world war and the holocaust of European Jewry would be witnessed before the plan – largely modified – would be implemented.

The approaching war was casting ominous shadows. Britain could not face increased complications in a vital strategic region. Parliamentary reactions to the partition plan were unfavorable. Emir Abdullah stood to gain a great deal, for he could do in 1938 what he did in 1948 – take over the area allocated to the proposed Arab state. Abdullah's supporters were secretly with him, but for public consumption their attitude was negative. The Husseini camp was totally uncompromising and ready to renew the fight. Soon the government was compelled to take drastic steps, including the suppression of the Arab Higher Committee and the deportation of extremist leaders; some of them, including al-Husseini, had fled the country earlier. The riots continued, however, and to a large degree became an internecine Arab struggle, claiming numerous victims, mostly among the moderates. The fact that the Jews were also split in their attitude to the partition plan made Britain's retreat from the plan much easier. In spite of Weizmann and Ben-Gurion's pleading in its favor, only a vague compromise resolution could be forced through the Zionist Congress in 1937. By 299 votes to 160 it was agreed that the Executive should "ascertain" in discussions with the British "the precise terms for the proposed establishment of a Jewish State." The non-Zionist partners in the Jewish Agency were far more negative. They did not want a Jewish state; their decisions, including a request to the government to convene a conference of Jews and Arabs, made progress even more difficult.

In 1938 another commission visited Palestine. Though it was called the Partition Commission, there had been a widespread feeling even before it reached Jerusalem that its real purpose was to bury the plan. In the autumn it presented its report, which was negative. It was welcomed not only by Arabs, but also by anti-partition Zionists. But even before that happened, Hitler made his first decisive steps toward war: the annexation of Austria in April and the beginning of the destruction of Czechoslovakia in November. The same month also brought the **Kristallnacht* in Germany. By then the propaganda offensive of the Axis in the Near East had heightened. Anxiety among Jews abroad mounted and led, inter alia, to the presentation of a memorandum on the subject to President Roosevelt by 245 members of both Houses of Congress and 30 governors. In Poland a Jewish Emigration Committee was established under government pressure to seek new "territories"; a study mission went to Madagascar and returned with empty hands. Other territories were mentioned with little hope. By then, an air of inevitability began enveloping Europe and the world. No conditions could be less propitious for an attempt to achieve in 1939 what proved to be elusive before: a fair settlement.

Britain nonetheless considered that the urgent needs of the hour precluded further postponement. Taking up the suggestion that an Arab-Jewish conference be called, the British broadened the scope and invited, in addition to the parties to the conflict, representatives of Egypt, Iraq, Saudi Arabia, Transjordan, and Yemen. Inevitably, the inclusion of the Arab states almost led to a boycott of the conference by the Jews, but the situation was far too grave for that. The Jewish delegation was large and weighty; it included Zionists, non-Zionists, and Agudat Israel. With regard to the leadership of the Palestine Arab delegation, London began by declaring Amin al-Husseini persona non grata and ended by accepting his representative and kinsman, Jamāl al-Husseini, over the opposition of moderate Palestine Arabs. The augury was plain: no agreed proposal could come from such a gathering. The Arabs insisted on their full program: abolishment of the Jewish National Home, an end to Jewish immigration, and Arab self-government. There was no room for give and take. The government of Neville Chamberlain saw itself facing one overriding task: to prepare for the coming war with Hitler. The Arabs could be a menace; the Jews had no choice. Thus, a new White Paper was issued in May 1939. A Palestine state was to be established and the population was to be prepared for self-government over a ten-year period. The future constitution was to include safeguards for the holy places, for the special position of the Jewish National Home, and for British interests. Full independence was made conditional on the creation of good relations between Arabs and Jews. As to immigration, 75,000 Jews were to be admitted in the next five years, after which the continuation of immigration would depend on Arab consent. The regulation of land sales, or their banning in certain areas, was left in the hands of the government.

The White Paper was rejected outright by Jews and Arabs alike. There was sharp criticism in the British Parliament, and only the grave international situation gave the government the needed majority; Labour and some 20 Conservatives (including Churchill) voted against it. The strongest words came from the Mandates Commission of the League of Nations, which stated unanimously that the policy "was not in accordance with the interpretation which… the Commission had placed upon the Palestine Mandate." The matter was to come up before the Council of the League of Nations, due to meet in September, since a change in the terms of the Mandate called for the council's consent. The war started before it met, and the British government considered itself free to act. In the meantime, the extremist Arabs found themselves leaderless as al-Husseini and some of his associates were not allowed to return. This was used by the Arab moderates who saw a chance to gain both the leadership and a compromise that would give the Arabs most of what they wanted. The Jewish leaders in Palestine and abroad refused to cooperate with the British administration, and some extremist elements, mainly the underground *Irgun Ẓeva'i Le'ummi (IẒL), soon turned to the use of force. The Zionist Congress which met in Geneva on the very eve of World War II avoided taking dramatic decisions. With armies massing all over Europe and with the signature of the Molotov-Ribbentrop Pact, it was realized that both valor and wisdom would be needed in the coming struggle.

WAR AND HOLOCAUST. Even before the initial Axis successes brought a direct military threat to Palestine in 1940, tragedy befell European Jewry (see *Holocaust). Its unbelievable dimensions did not become known until later, but there were already large numbers of Jews fleeing from death and trying to reach Palestine. The immediate task was to help in their escape. Next to it was the need to mobilize the *yishuv* for the war. As had been the case a quarter of a century earlier, the British were reluctant to accept Jewish volunteers. Only the early defeats in North Africa weakened this reluctance, and by 1940 many thousands of Palestinian Jews enlisted. The *yishuv*'s economic potential also gradually became a factor of considerable value. The British did not forget their White Paper, however, and in February 1940 introduced crippling regulations concerning land transactions, which caused another bitter outburst on the part of the Jews. The immigration problem had taken on a different character. The British aim was to spread out the use of the 75,000 "certificates" over five years and – if possible – until the end of the war (although nobody could know when that would be). In any case, regular immigration was unlikely to continue under war conditions. Indeed, less than 20,000 immigrants – authorized and unauthorized – entered during the years 1940–42. Furthermore, the fact that the Chamberlain government fell in May 1940 and another administration took over, headed by Churchill and including a number of other friendly ministers, was bound to influence the general political climate.

As to the Arabs, the initial military successes of the Axis made them stake their future on its victory, and many were ready merely to wait for it. Hence the failure of Al-Husseini's call for an open rebellion. The fall of France in 1940 turned Syria and Lebanon into bases of subversion and February 1941 brought about a pro-German putsch in Iraq. Allied countermeasures prevented further deterioration. Al-Husseini turned up in Rome and Berlin in the autumn of 1941, and some Egyptian sympathizers of the Axis (including the future president of the UAR, Anwar Sadat) plotted with Axis men in North Africa. A slight change took place after Rommel's defeat in 1942. British efforts were largely directed at exploiting the improved situation, and in due course a policy of unifying the Arabs evolved, which led to the organization of the Arab League in 1945. Palestine Arabs were granted a voice in the league itself when it was organized, their cause having been included in its charter.

Among the Jews there was a feeling that somewhat friendlier winds were imperceptibly blowing in London. The immediate peril to the *yishuv* had receded, but the dimensions of the tragedy that befell European Jewry were gradually emerging. The need for immigration, and immigration itself, were again coming to the fore. Internal pressures were building up; the wartime "truce" between the British authorities and extremist elements was coming to an end; and violence erupted again in Palestine, this time initiated by the IẒL. The Zionist leadership found it necessary to clarify its own position and seek clarification of the position likely to be taken up by the Churchill government. Much of the thinking harked back to the Royal Commission's proposals, but the formulation adopted at a conference called by American Zionists at the Biltmore Hotel in New York in May 1942 claimed "that Palestine be established as a Jewish Commonwealth." This was later approved by the appropriate Zionist bodies in Jerusalem over the opposition of some of the former anti-partitionists. Outbursts of terror from Jewish extreme underground organizations, including the murder in Cairo of the British minister for the Near East, Lord Moyne, by members of *Loḥamei Ḥerut Israel (Leḥi), again increased the feeling of impending crisis.

YEARS OF DECISION. The end of the war in Europe in May 1945 was followed by the fall of Churchill. Labour, which replaced him, had in the past displayed great sympathy for Zionism, and its party conference had just confirmed its promise to help the development of the National Home by making room for it through "extending the present Palestinian boundaries, by agreement with Egypt, Syria, or Transjordan." The urgent need for action soon became clear with the disclosure that it was necessary to aid in the rehabilitation of hundreds of thousands of survivors of Nazi camps. This could only be done through Anglo-American cooperation. The United States had already become a factor in Middle Eastern affairs, militarily and economically. Now, because of its friendly ties with both Jews and Arabs, it was beginning to become involved politically as well.

In the days immediately following World War II, the voice of the American Jewish community on its own government carried much weight in Washington. This was the culminating point of a generation of sporadic political endeavor by the Zionist movement in America, which had resulted in 1924 in the U.S. government's formally approving the League of Nations Mandate for Palestine and its guarantee of Jewish national rights. Every president of the United States after Woodrow Wilson had made declarations favorable to Zionist aspirations, and the majority of Congress was moved several times to declare its pro-Zionist views, both officially in joint resolutions and informally. With the rise of Nazism, Zionist membership in the United States grew rapidly and the Zionist organizations became a prevailing influence in the community while also widening the circle of friends and supporters in the general community. During World War II there was lively and even bitter disagreement between those Zionists who followed Stephen S. Wise in being ready to rely on the goodwill of President Roosevelt and were therefore willing to remain relatively quiescent, and those led by Abba Hillel Silver, whose orientation was toward the opposition Republican Party and who believed public opinion had to be organized against the government in order to both save Jewish lives in Europe and realize Zionist aims after the war. These forces paved the road to the adoption of the Biltmore platform in 1942, which postulated Jewish independence as the Zionist war aim. Distrust in the goodwill of others and the desire for independence deepened while the news of the Holocaust continued to seep out of Europe. By the winter of 1943 Abba Hillel Silver replaced Stephen Wise as the head of Zionist political affairs and public relations in the United States. With the help of Emanuel *Neumann and a number of others, the American Zionist Emergency Committee, which Silver led, mounted a political offensive throughout the United States and prepared the ground both in the public mind and in political circles for U.S. support of Zionism against the continuing White Paper policy of the British government and for the establishment of a Jewish state. The Zionist forces had a substantial impact on the White House and on Congress, which were responsive to public protest and pressure mounted within the democratic process, and they thus managed (1947–48) to influence the policy of the U.S. government, despite the continuing opposition of the State Department.

The United States also had to shoulder most of the burden of aid to the vast numbers of *Displaced Persons in Europe. The Jewish Agency asked for an immediate grant of 100,000 immigration permits, but Britain, embroiled in a fierce election campaign, was incapable of acting. Two months earlier, a change of leadership had also taken place in the U.S. Roosevelt's successor, President Truman, was anxious to help, and one of his first steps was the dispatch of an envoy to DP camps. The latter recommended resettlement of 100,000 stateless Jews found in the western zone of occupied Germany, and pointed out that "Palestine is definitely… the first choice." This recommendation, with Truman's backing, was sent to London, but the new prime minister, Attlee, could not see his way to accepting it, proposing instead a joint Anglo-American investigation of the entire problem. This was agreed upon in October 1945.

Uncertainty and conflicting pressures had their most damaging effect in the Middle East itself. The Arabs saw new danger to their hopes, raised high by the 1939 White Paper. A reorganized Arab Higher Committee was soon established. The Arab states' position as founding members of the new United Nations gave them a feeling of being able to sway political developments. Now they were incensed by America, even more than by Britain. There were violent demonstrations and attacks on Jews and foreigners. On the other hand, the *yishuv* also found new strength in its very despair. Some 20,000 Jewish troops were beginning to return, well trained, many with war experience, having seen with their own eyes what happened to their brethren in Europe. They, and others in the *yishuv*, vowed "never again!" Acts of violence were becoming widespread. The Haganah, which in the past had concentrated on defense and on preparations for the day of decision, undertook action of its own. Soon the government, with all the forces at its disposal, found itself at war with the *yishuv*. The only respite came during the work of the Anglo-American Committee of Inquiry, whose prospects, however, were prejudiced in advance by the new British foreign secretary Ernest Bevin, who from the outset left little doubt of his hostility. The Labour government inherited a crushing burden of problems of which the Middle East was only one. Britain became unable to continue its imperial role. It was necessary to cut losses and safeguard only the most vital interests. Soon India was to be independent, after being split into two states, and other parts of the empire were to follow. So was Palestine, but at the end of 1945 and beginning of 1946 a way was still being sought to keep Britain in control. Under pressure of immigration needs, a provisional monthly "schedule" of 1,500 permits had been decided upon for the duration of the discussions and it was stated, for the first time, that any proposed settlement would be brought before the United Nations.

The work of the Anglo-American Committee, which started in Washington in January 1946, continued in London and in other places in Europe, then in Jerusalem, Cairo, and a number of other Arab capitals, and ended in Lausanne in March. It was conducted in a highly charged atmosphere. Large numbers of Jewish survivors of the Holocaust were being intercepted on the high seas by the British navy as "illegal" immigrants. Acts of violence in Palestine became a daily occurrence. So did Arab threats, especially after Husseini escaped from Germany on the eve of its surrender and appeared in Cairo. The Palestine Arabs mainly relied on the influence of the Arab states, whose willingness to assist them was proclaimed daily. It was inevitable that the inquiry should seek a compromise, and the final report turned not to partition but to its alternative: a bi-national Palestine state based on parity and under a United Nations trusteeship. To help in meeting pressing needs, 100,000 immigration permits were to be issued, if possible in 1946, and future immigration was to be based on compromise.

With the exception of Washington, no interested party approved the recommendations. Britain's equivocations found expression in official statements and, even more, in Bevin's speeches. The Arabs saw their hopes for Arab rule in Palestine dashed. The Jews, though pleased by the opportunity of rapidly bringing in a large number of Displaced Persons, feared the prospect of unending strife with the Arabs and with the "Trustee," which they expected would be Britain. The breaking point was reached in June 1946, when, in a retaliatory action *Palmaḥ units destroyed a number of rail and road bridges in sensitive points, and the British government hit back by imposing a virtual siege on the *yishuv*: mass searches for arms and incriminating documents were carried out in hundreds of buildings, including the offices of the Jewish Agency; over 2,000 people, among them the members of the Jewish Agency and Va'ad Le'ummi executives, were arrested. The life of the *yishuv* had been dislocated. In time, some of the detainees were freed, but over 700, including Agency and Va'ad Le'ummi leaders, were interned. A short time later, IẒL blew up a wing of the King David Hotel in Jerusalem, housing offices of the government secretariat. The casualties, belonging to all communities, were heavy. The *yishuv* was shocked, and the Jewish Agency condemned the deed. Meanwhile attempts were made in Washington and London to proceed with discussions about the results of their joint inquiry. Another committee, headed by Henry F. Grady (U.S.) and Herbert Morrison (Britain) found it more advisable to go back to the principles of territorial division. It suggested the establishment of a Jewish sector, an Arab sector, and a British sector, including Jerusalem and the Negev, as an intermediary stage that could eventually lead either to a unitary state, to a bi-national one, or outright partition. Administration of common interests such as defense, foreign relations, communications, etc., was to remain in the hands of a British high commissioner. During the initial five years, he was also to appoint presidents of the legislatures of the Jewish and Arab sectors, and his approval would be needed for new legislation. Immigration would also remain under his control after the agreed 100,000 were brought in with American help. The implementation of the scheme as a whole was made conditional on American participation and Arab-Jewish consent.

There was little to recommend this latest compromise, which contained most of the drawbacks of earlier suggestions. Washington withdrew from it almost immediately, and there was much criticism in London. The Arabs insisted on all their original demands, and the Jews refused to accept the plan. Again, London proposed a conference. The Jewish Agency was ready for it but not on the basis of the Morrison-Grady plan. The Arab Executive refused because its conditions (including the participation of Amin al-Husseini) were rejected. Thus, when the conference convened in September 1946, the main parties to the dispute were absent and only the British and Arab governments were represented. No progress could be made, and Britain suggested that the discussions be temporarily suspended for a further attempt to bring in the parties concerned. This was to take place at the beginning of 1947 in order to enable the Jewish Agency to bring the matter before the forthcoming Zionist Congress. To make things easier, the interned Zionist and *yishuv* leaders and a number of other internees were released. By then the Jewish Agency had again disassociated itself from the acts of violence, which were continued, however, by IẒL and Leḥi. Simultaneously, a number of Husseini's men were allowed to return to the country.

When the Zionist Congress met in December 1946 in Basle, it revealed a significant change in the internal situation. The Labour wing of the movement lost some ground, and within its ranks the activist elements had the upper hand. The American Zionists were led by Abba Hillel Silver, a supporter of a more determined policy. Furthermore, the Revisionists rejoined the Zionist Organization. As a result, the Congress refused to participate in the London talks, albeit leaving the door slightly ajar for later reconsideration. The idea of partition had enough support, but no initiative was to come from the Jewish Agency. Finally, the post of president had been left vacant, thus demonstrating the rejection of the Weizmann line. It was the absence of the Zionists that helped the Arab League persuade the Palestine Arab leaders to take their seats at the second round of the London talks in January 1947. An amended version of the Morrison-Grady scheme was put forward by Bevin, designed to meet some of the earlier criticism: cantonal self-government, for instance, in place of provincial authority; a shortened period of trusteeship; 100,000 immigrants in two years instead of one; and no partition. The Arab reply, however, was nevertheless a resounding no. This left things in a worse state than ever because it became obvious that the 1939 White Paper was also dead, a victim of the Holocaust, determined Jewish opposition, Arab conduct during the war and, finally, United States intervention. Left without an official policy, London turned to the United Nations on April 2, 1947. The purpose of this step was made clear in a statement before the House of Commons: "We are not going to the United Nations to surrender the Mandate. We are going to the United Nations setting out the problem and asking their advice as to how the Mandate can be administered. If the Mandate cannot be administered in its present form, we are asking how it can be amended."

THE UNITED NATIONS INVESTIGATES. Though this was the first time that the United Nations was to deal with the Palestine problem, the latter was not unknown to it. Preliminary skirmishes on the subject took place at the San Francisco Conference in 1945 and at the first session of the General Assembly in 1946, when Arab representatives attempted in vain to obtain decisions prejudicial to the Jewish position. The first special session of the General Assembly met between April 28 and May 15, 1947, with the purpose of "constituting and instructing a Special Committee to prepare for the consideration of the Question of Palestine at the second Regular Session" (scheduled to open September 16). The five Arab delegations tried to alter the very purpose of the deliberations on the eve of the session by requesting to amend the subject of discussions by adding to the agenda an item entitled: "Termination of the Mandate over Palestine and declaration of its independence." As before, the Assembly rejected their request; it also refused to exclude from its discussions the problems of displaced Jews in Europe.

For the first time, representatives of the Jews and of Palestine Arabs were heard by the United Nations. When the question arose whether their spokesmen should be heard at a plenary meeting or at a meeting of the Assembly's political committee, Czechoslovakia and Poland, backed by the U.S.S.R., urged for a hearing in the plenary, while Britain and America viewed the committee as the appropriate place for statements by delegations that did not represent member states. The latter view prevailed. The Jewish Agency spokesmen were Ben-Gurion, Silver, and Shertok (Sharett). The Arab Higher Committee was represented by E. Ghouri and H. Kattan.

The burden of the Jewish case was summarized by Ben-Gurion, who told the committee: "... in Palestine you are faced not merely with a large and growing number of Jews, but with a distinct Jewish nation. There are Jews and Jewish communities in many countries, but in Palestine there is a new and unique phenomenon – a Jewish nation, with all the attributes and aspirations of nationhood." The Arab case was presented not only by the spokesmen of the Higher Committee but also by the five Arab member-states, and it was summarized by Ghouri: "We only request the application to us of the principles of the democracies. We are only asking for our national rights. It is... the determined and unequivocal will of the Arabs to refuse to consider any solution which entails or even implies the loss of the sovereignty to the whole or to any part of the country, or the diminution of such sovereignty in any form whatever."

Much of the discussion was procedural, and the great majority of the delegates avoided anything that could be seen as clear commitment to one side or the other. The representative of India (a Muslim) was one of those who did not conceal his leaning to the Arab side, nor did the representative of Turkey. The delegate of China spoke with feeling of "the tragedy of the Jewish people" which contributed so much to the world and which "deserves a national home of some sort, deserves a place it can call its own, in which it can live in happiness, free from social and political discrimination and free from the eternal fear of persecution." Sympathy for Jewish aspirations were expressed by Czechoslovakia and Poland, but the chief surprise came when the Soviet delegate explained the stand of his government. The Soviet regime had long been known for its extreme hostility to Zionism, but the opportunity to hasten the removal of Britain from an area of special interest to the U.S.S.R. was far too important to let that stand in the way. While supporting the Jewish Agency's request for a hearing, Andrei Gromyko spoke of the sufferings of the Jewish people in Europe and said that it was "beyond description." "The fact that not a single Western European state" came to the help of the Jews "explains the aspirations of the Jews for the creation of a state of their own... It is impossible to justify a denial of this right of the Jewish people." The Mandate failed, and both Jews and Arabs call for its liquidation. The best solution would be "the establishment of an independent, dual, democratic, homogeneous Arab-Jewish state," but if that proved impossible "in view of the deterioration in the relations between the Jews and the Arabs," it would be necessary to consider "the partition of Palestine into two independent autonomous states, one Jewish and one Arab."

The divergent views led to dissensions concerning the composition of the proposed UN mission and its terms of reference. Talk of "neutrality" and "impartiality" was found to be of little help, But it was agreed that the UN Special Committee on Palestine (UNSCOP) was to have "the widest powers to ascertain and record facts, and to investigate all questions and issues relevant to the problem of Palestine" and it was to conduct "investigations in Palestine and wherever it may deem useful." It was asked to "give most careful considerations to the religious interests in Palestine of Islam, Judaism, and Christianity" and present its report by Sept. 1, 1947. The only votes against the decision were those of the Muslim states. As to the composition of UNSCOP, it was agreed to make it fully representative of all regions of the world, and to exclude the permanent members of the Security Council and the Arab countries. Two Muslims (from India and Iran) were included, as well as delegates from Australia, Canada, Czechoslovakia, Guatemala, the Netherlands, Peru, Sweden, Uruguay, and Yugoslavia.

Arab dissatisfaction with these decisions found its immediate expression in a boycott by the Arab Higher Committee. The Arab League left the question of its cooperation open in the hope of persuading the mission not to visit refugee camps in Europe. The investigators did, indeed, postpone their decision on the subject until after the hearings in the Middle East. The latter started in the middle of June in an unusually tense atmosphere caused by numerous acts of violence, hangings, and retaliations. It also coincided with the dramatic developments concerning the fate of the refugee ship *Exodus 1947* with over 4,500 men, women, and children who sailed in it to Palestine only to be returned to Germany after a bloody encounter with British forces in Haifa harbor. Nevertheless UNSCOP (presided over by Swedish Chief Justice Emile Sandström) heard Jewish and British representatives, official and unofficial, and visited Arab areas of the country, as well as Jewish ones, spending over five weeks in Palestine. The Arabs who met the UN envoys privately repeated the demands already heard in New York. The Jewish Agency efforts were now clearly directed at achieving partition on fair terms. On its way back, UNSCOP members visited Lebanon, Syria, and Transjordan and heard representatives of the Arab states, who warned against any solution but the one proposed by them. Upon arriving in Geneva, UNSCOP decided to have a subcommittee visit Jewish refugee camps in Germany and Austria, and by the end of August it completed its work.

The UNSCOP report contained 12 general recommendations (11 of them adopted unanimously), a majority plan, and a minority plan. The majority plan, presented by Canada, Czechoslovakia, Guatemala, the Netherlands, Peru, Sweden and Uruguay, called for the partition of Palestine into an Arab state, a Jewish state, and an internationalized Jerusalem, the three to be linked in an economic union. The Jewish state was to include eastern Galilee, the Coastal Plain from a point south of Acre to north of Ashdod, and the Negev. The Arab state was to include western Galilee, central Palestine, and the Coastal Plain from Ashdod to the Egyptian border. The Jerusalem-Bethlehem area was to be administered by the United Nations under a permanent trusteeship. The Mandate was to come to an end, and from Sept. 1, 1947, Palestine was to be administered by Britain for another two years, alone or with the participation of one or more UN members, under UN auspices. The political regimes in the new states were to be "basically democratic." The holy places and access to them were to be safeguarded according to existing rights. Furthermore, the UN was to make speedy arrangements to solve the problem of a quarter of a million Jewish refugees in Europe. With two dissenting votes, UNSCOP also expressed its view that "any solution for Palestine cannot be considered as a solution of the Jewish problem as a whole." The argument of the minority report, concurred in by India, Iran, and Yugoslavia, with Australia abstaining in the vote on both plans, was based on the assumption that "the well-being of the country and its peoples as a whole" outweighed "the aspirations of the Jews." It suggested a federal regime comprising an Arab state and a Jewish state with Jerusalem as capital of a central government in charge of defense, foreign relations, and immigration. There was to be a bicameral legislature based on parity in one house and on proportional representation in the other, and all legislation would require majority support of both. Jewish immigration into the Jewish state was to be allowed for three years within its absorptive capacity. Arbitration was to help in overcoming any deadlock between the states. These proposals were made by less than one-third of UNSCOP and the division of views between the majority and the minority reflected the division within the UN itself, as was to be confirmed three months later.

THE UN DECISION. The UNSCOP report occupied the center of the stage when the regular General Assembly met in New York on Sept. 16, 1947, although there were other important items on the agenda as well. The preliminary discussion on the report took place at an Ad Hoc Committee representing all member states, whose number had increased in the meantime: Yemen and Pakistan had been admitted to the United Nations, thus strengthening the Arab and Muslim front. Apart from that, no new alignments of forces were to be seen during the opening stages of the debate that lasted for over three weeks and was characterized by confusion. The main shift that soon became noticeable was in the tactics of the British delegation, which openly and actively canvassed for the rejection of partition. Arab delegations also increased their pressure. They were outspoken in their threats to Western, and particularly American, interests in their lands, and there were powerful economic and military factors in the United States, Britain, and France which could be – and were – activated in order to defeat the UNSCOP proposals. Indeed, initial American remarks on the subject were reserved and hesitant. On the other hand, threats voiced by the Arab Higher Committee to the effect that what will happen to the Jews in Palestine if the UNSCOP proposals were adopted would "exceed the horrors of Genghis Khan" had the opposite effect. It became clear to a growing number of UN members, and to great sectors of the general public opinion, that decisions must be taken which would prevent these threats being carried out. The Jewish Agency announced acceptance of the majority plan early in the debate. Weizmann's speech before the committee left a profound impression. His role in realizing the ultimate decision of the United Nations in favor of partition and the creation of a Jewish state was of prime importance. Though out of office, for the Zionist Congress in 1946 did not reelect him as president, thus symbolizing its commitment to a more activist policy, Weizmann continued to work both in London and in New York for the creation of a Jewish state. He was particularly successful in moving and impressing President Harry Truman, from whom he secured the binding promise to support the partition proposal, including an outlet on the Red Sea for the proposed Jewish state.

As the discussions progressed, attitudes began to crystallize. The United States and the Soviet Union came out openly for partition. After that, the prospects of the majority plan gaining the necessary two-thirds of the votes grew. More attempts were made to find a compromise, in subcommittees and in the corridors, but the persistent Arab demands for the establishment of what could only be an Arab state with a Jewish minority at the mercy of its adversaries led to the failure of all such efforts. An ominous warning also came from Britain: while accepting UNSCOP's unanimous opinion that the Mandate be terminated, it would take no implementation of a decision that was not acceptable to the parties. This meant noncooperation. The question of implementation became of utmost importance, especially after the British refused to extend their stay in Palestine even for a few weeks beyond May 15, 1948, or to help in the transfer of power to the authorities that were to be established in the Jewish and Arab states. The readiness of the Mandatory power to act in a way that was tantamount to sabotaging an international design for relieving it of a responsibility that had become too great to bear also had an opposite effect. It stiffened resistance to those who refused to accept the majority view. A vote in the Ad Hoc Committee on November 24 rejected an Arab proposal for a unitary state by 29 to 12. On November 25 a vote was taken on the partition plan, somewhat amended by a subcommittee, and it was approved by 25 to 13. This was not yet the two-thirds majority needed in the plenary. Both sides were by now making exerted efforts to gain their objectives. After one or two postponements, which further increased the tension, the decisive vote came on November 29, and it was 33 for, 13 against, and 10 abstentions.

The wave of emotion which followed gave abundant evidence that not only the Jewish people saw the UN verdict as truly historic, but many other nations found in it an expression of the wish to right some of the wrongs of which Jews were victims, particularly the Nazi Holocaust. There were also grave warning signs. Arabs of Palestine reacted by widespread attacks on Jews; large numbers of armed men were coming in from across the borders to participate in those attacks; and Arab governments made no secret of their preparations for large-scale military action on the day of Britain's withdrawal. The UN appointed a small Palestine Commission to help in an organized transfer of power to provisional councils of government in the two proposed states, but the British refused to cooperate with it or even allow it to enter Palestine before the month of May. The commission also reported that while Arab and Jewish police supernumeraries were being organized in towns and villages, only the Arabs were getting arms from the British. Furthermore, while the British continued to supply arms to Arab governments, the United States imposed an embargo on all such supplies to the area, thus forcing the Jews to seek other sources, mainly in Eastern Europe.

A sense of frustration and helplessness was gradually enveloping the UN, which saw the danger that its first major decision might end in failure. While the UN machinery was going through the motions (the Trusteeship Council, for instance, prepared a draft statute for an international administration of Jerusalem), reports from Palestine spoke of mounting disorder, of fighting and casualties, and of British preparations to leave in an atmosphere of what was then called "planned chaos." The implementation commission made partial progress in one sector only: in cooperation with the Jewish Agency for the establishment of the necessary authorities in the future Jewish State. The situation was repeatedly discussed in the Security Council, which had been told by the commission (February 1948) that it would not be able to fulfill its task without armed assistance. A debate started within the Council concerning its own authority: while it was agreed that it may use force for the preservation of peace, there was less agreement about the same right in respect to the enforcement of UN decisions. U.S. views were negative, and they were strongly criticized by the Soviet Union. On March 19 the United States proposed that the work of the Palestine Commission be suspended and a temporary UN trusteeship over the country be established. The proposal had been made by the State Department in Washington without the knowledge of President Truman, as he later explained. The State Department had also been strongly urging Zionist leaders to postpone action on the establishment of the Jewish state for at least a few months, a suggestion that was turned down by the majority of the Jewish Agency members. Furthermore, the U.S. proposed to call another special session of the Assembly to discuss the trusteeship idea.

The new session met on April 16, 1948, and was immediately bogged down in a procedural debate. The United States presented a working paper outlining details of a temporary trusteeship, providing for a government and essential public services in Palestine pending further negotiations. At the same time, the Trusteeship Council was asked by the General Assembly to study measures for the protection of Jerusalem, where fighting was then going on almost without interruption. On April 28 the Council came to an understanding with the parties concerned about a truce in the city, but reports from Jerusalem spoke of continued firing. On May 5 the Council recommended that before the Mandate expired on May 15, a special municipal commissioner for Jerusalem should be appointed by the Mandatory power with Jewish and Arab consent. The candidate for the post never went to Jerusalem, as the Arabs refused to cooperate with him and there was no truce. On May 14, the last day of the Mandate, a Franco-American proposal to establish a temporary international regime in Jerusalem failed to get the necessary support. It had also become clear that the idea of a trusteeship over the whole of Palestine stood no chance. The only outcome of the discussions on that day had been the disbanding of the Palestine Commission and the decision to appoint a mediator, for which task Count Folke Bernadotte of Sweden was later chosen. With the hands of the clock moving toward 6 P.M. in New York (midnight in Palestine and the end of the Mandate), the struggle was still on. But even before the hour came, the United Nations was informed that the establishment of the State of Israel had already been proclaimed in Tel Aviv. A few minutes after 6 P.M. it was announced by the White House that President Truman recognized its provisional government as the de facto government of the new state. Soviet de jure recognition followed a few days later. On May 15, regular forces of Egypt, Syria, Lebanon, and Iraq, including Saudi Arabian contingents, and the Arab Legion of Transjordan with its British officers, invaded Israel, and its newborn defense forces took the field against them.

[Moshe Medzini]

ZIONIST ORGANIZATION

HISTORY. The Zionist Organization was founded at the First Zionist Congress (convened by Theodor Herzl in Basle, 1897) as the structural framework of the organized Zionist movement, "comprising all Jews who accept the Zionist program and pay the shekel." The biblical name *shekel was given to the membership fee of the Zionist Organization.

Though a rudimentary framework of a popular movement had been established by the Ḥibbat Zion, it was only through the foundation of the Zionist Organization that Zionism became a modern, democratic, mass movement, based on a worldwide interterritorial organization and equipped with instruments for political, settlement, and educational activities on a large scale. The most important of these instruments were created during Herzl's presidency (1897–1904): the Jewish

Colonial Trust, to serve as the Zionist bank (1899); the Jewish National Fund (1901), for the acquisition of land as the inalienable property of the Jewish people; and *Die Welt* (1897), as the official organ of the organization.

Herzl died in 1904 before attaining his primary political aim, the Charter, i.e., the grant by the Ottoman authorities of political autonomy in, and the right of settlement of, Ereẓ Israel. The conflict over the Uganda Scheme at the Sixth Zionist Congress (1903) led to a split in the Zionist Organization. When the Seventh Congress (1905) rejected any settlement activities outside the Land of Israel, the Territorialists seceded from the Zionist Organization and founded the Jewish Territorial Organization, which, however, failed to play a significant part in Jewish life and, after the Balfour Declaration, disappeared from the public scene.

The growth of the Zionist Organization is best illustrated by the increase in the total number of shekels distributed: in the two-year period ending with the Eighth Zionist Congress (1907; for the former period, only the sums of the shekel revenues are available) there were 164,333; at the 11th Congress (1913) the number of shekels was 217,231; it steeply rose to 855,590 at the next Congress in 1921, the first to be held after World War I and the Balfour Declaration (although at that time most of Russian Jewry, the mainstay of Zionism, had already been cut off from the main body of the movement); at the 21st Congress, on the eve of World War II (1939), the number of shekel holders exceeded 1,000,000; and at the first postwar and last pre-state gathering, the 22nd Congress in 1946, the shekel figures indicated that 2,159,840 Jews were organized in the Zionist Organization. After Herzl's death, the seat of the organization was transferred from Vienna to Cologne, the residence of Herzl's successor, David Wolffsohn (1905–11). When Otto Warburg headed the organization (1911–20), Berlin became the Zionist capital, but World War I isolated it from the Zionists in the Allied countries, whose activities were centered in London. The purpose of the Zionist Liaison Office set up in 1915 in neutral Copenhagen was to facilitate the contact across the war fronts between the two sections of the organization. London was the capital of the Zionist world during the presidencies of Chaim Weizmann (1920–31 and 1935–46) and of Nahum Sokolow (1931–35), but in 1936 the center was transferred to Jerusalem, although London remained the seat of its president and of some members of the Executive.

When the 18th Congress (1933) had resolved that "in all Zionist matters the duty of discipline in regard of the Zionist Organization must take precedence over the discipline to any other body," the majority of the Zionist Revisionists, led by Vladimir Jabotinsky, seceded from the Zionist Organization and set up the New Zionist Organization, while a minority of Revisionists, under Meir *Grossman, remained in the ranks as the *Jewish State Party. The split lasted until 1946, when the Revisionists returned to the parent body and renewed their participation in the Zionist Congresses.

The First Congress laid down only a rough outline of a few organizational rules. It was the Third Congress (1899) that adopted the first complete constitution (Organisations-Statut) which, substituted by a more elaborated text adopted by the Fifth (1907) and the Tenth Congresses (1911), remained in force until 1921, when a thorough revision of the text and its adaptation to the changed conditions was effected by the 12th Congress. Minor amendments were adopted by each of the subsequent Congresses. In 1960 an entirely new Constitution came into force and thoroughly changed its structure (see below). The 25th and 26th Congresses (1960, 1964) made efforts to broaden the basis of the Zionist Organization by the admission of associate members, i.e., Jewish bodies which endorse the Zionist program without obliging their members to be organized Zionists. These efforts were initiated and supported by the fifth president of the Zionist Organization, Nahum Goldmann (1956–68), who assumed the presidency after the office had been vacant for ten years.

The 27th Congress (1968) adopted the greater part of the recommendations submitted by the Commission on Reorganization, which had been set up by the preceding Congress, and resolved to amend the Constitution accordingly. These amendments, however, affected details like Congress elections or the participation of youth in Zionist territorial organizations, rather than the general pattern and basic provisions of the Constitution.

STRUCTURE. Before the Zionist Organization was divided into parties, it had been organized on a purely territorial basis. According to its early Constitution, the members were organized in local societies that were grouped into regional units, which were in turn subordinated to territorial committees in charge of Zionist affairs in the country concerned. With the emergence of ideological trends and groupings, a type of dualism became characteristic of the structure of the Zionist Organization. According to the Constitution of 1921, the Zionist Organization was structured both horizontally and vertically: on the one hand, there were countrywide organizations comprising all Zionists without regard to their views on special issues – Zionist territorial unions with local branches; on the other, Zionists subscribing to a certain ideology, or, as the Constitution put it, "representing a special point of view," were, under certain conditions, given the privilege of forming a separate union (Sonderverband) which set up territorial branches. The first separate union was the Mizrachi (1902); the *Po'alei Zion followed in 1907; Ha-Shomer ha-Ẓa'ir and the Jewish State Party were founded as separate unions after World War I. The *Ancient Order of Maccabeans, established in Britain at an early stage of the movement, soon became defunct.

During the first decades of activity, the separate unions represented only a small minority of the membership. At the 12th Congress (1921) the delegates affiliated with the territorial unions numbered 376, while those of all separate unions totaled only 136. The membership and strength of the separate unions steadily grew, however, and at the last Congress before World War II (1939) the proportion was reversed: the delegates of the territorial unions numbered 171 and those of the separate unions 386. Furthermore, at the beginning the members of the Zionist territorial unions were called *General Zionists, simply denoting all those who did not belong to any separate union; but a tendency rose and finally prevailed within the General Zionists to adopt an ideology of their own and to transform themselves into a party like the others. Furthermore, this group often split into two wings, at first called Groups A and B, and since the 24th Congress (1956) known as the Union and the Confederation of General Zionists, respectively. On the other hand, the difference between the separate unions and parties not registered as such became blurred and, apart from a few purely formal privileges of the former, ceased to exist for all practical purposes. Because of this differentiation between territorial and separate unions, the Zionist movement in some countries almost disintegrated into several independent parties without common framework, apart from joint committees established for special purposes like the shekel and election boards. As a reaction to this "atomization," several Congresses declared that a United Zionist Federation, based on individual membership and comprising all parties and groups, be compulsory in every country. These and later resolutions, which again made the establishment of a joint territorial framework obligatory, but were content with the collective membership of parties in so-called Zionist Federations, largely remained unimplemented.

The structure of the Zionist Organization underwent a profound change with the promulgation of a new Constitution in 1960. It introduced a new official name, the World Zionist Organization (although the traditional one, Zionist Organization, is still more frequently used); the shekel remained in existence as a token of Zionist allegiance and voting card, but members of the Zionist Organization were no longer individual shekel-payers but collective bodies only, namely Zionist territorial organizations and Zionist territorial and interterritorial associations. The former are either Zionist unions based on the membership of individual Zionists (like that of the Netherlands), or Zionist federations based on the collective membership of Zionist bodies (like that of Belgium), or mixed Zionist federations based on the membership both of bodies and individuals (like that of France). Examples of Zionist territorial and interterritorial associations are *Hadassah and *WIZO (incidentally, the two largest Zionist bodies in the world).

The Constitution of 1960 introduced a far-reaching reform of decentralization. According to the legal construction underlying the Constitution, the Zionist Organization is the "body authorized by its members to act for and on behalf of the movement and all the members for the implementation of the Zionist program." Emphasis is placed on the autonomy of the members: "Every member shall determine the conduct of his affairs, the form of his organization and procedure." Bodies that were affiliated with the Zionist Organization when the new Constitution came into force were considered members under its provisions. New members may be admitted by the Congress or General Council, provided they comply with a number of conditions laid down in the Constitution. One of these provisions is that the body "has regard to the protection of the requirements of all its members and to the fundamental principles of justice." (On the membership of national and international Jewish bodies, see above.)

GOVERNING BODIES. The pattern of internal organization very much resembles that of a sovereign state: the shekel payers are comparable to citizens, the Congress elected by them – and to a certain degree also the General Council – is similar to a parliament, the Executive resembles the government or administration of a country, and the Congress Tribunal and the attorney of the Zionist Organization are its "judicial branch." On the other hand, the Zionist Organization differs from a state in two important respects: it is an interterritorial body and not limited by national frontiers; and it is built on a purely voluntary basis, with no means of enforcing its decisions. The ultimate and gravest sanction it may impose is expulsion from its ranks.

THE ZIONIST CONGRESS. The Congress is the supreme organ of the Zionist Organization. It legislates, receives and considers reports from other organs, determines the financial policy, and elects the president, Executive, General Council, Congress Tribunal, attorney, and comptroller. Until the 26th Congress (1964) the shekel payers chose the Congress either by direct elections or by "unopposed elections," by means of a "united slate" arrived at through interparty agreements. The 27th Congress (1968) was not based on elections but, in accordance with special regulations enacted after the Six-Day War (1967), had the same composition as its predecessor. It decided that future Congresses should not be elected according to a uniform election system, but that each country should itself determine the method of elections of its Congress delegates, provided it does not conflict with generally accepted democratic principles. Until the 24th Congress (1956) the number of delegates allotted to an election area (country) was in direct proportion to the number of shekels sold there. Under the Constitution of 1960, however, the size of the representation is fixed by a special commission "having regard to the size of the Jewish population and the totality of the conditions and activities of the Zionist movement in the country concerned."

In Herzl's time the Congress met every year (apart from 1902); until 1939 it convened once every two years (with the exception of World War I). The Constitution of 1960 legalized the practice of a four-year inter-Congress period.

THE GENERAL COUNCIL. The longer the intervals between Congresses, the greater the importance attaching to the Zionist General Council, also known by its original name of Herzl's times as the Actions Committee. During the inter-Congress period, it has not only legislative functions, but "shall consider and decide upon all matters relating to the Zionist Organization and its institutions." The number of Council members with voting rights in 1968 was 129, compared with 25 in 1921.

The Council meets at least once a year no later than March, since the budgetary year of the Zionist Organization terminates on March 31 and one of the Council's prerogatives is to decide on the budget in years when no Congress is held. It discharges this function either itself or through its Permanent Budget and Finance Committee. It has become general practice that the Congress or the Council fixes the framework of the budget, while the details are determined by the committee acting upon the proposals of the Executive. Over the course of years the importance of the Council has grown because "delegated legislation" has become increasingly frequent, i.e., the Congress has authorized the Council to make decisions or take steps within the jurisdiction of the Congress. Thus, even the Constitution of 1960 was adopted by the Council and not by the Congress. The Council's membership exactly reflects the composition of the Congress, each grouping being represented by a number of members equal to one-fifth of its Congress delegation. Apart from these members with full rights, the Constitution provides for members in an advisory capacity who are entitled to speak but not to vote in the Council's sessions, such as the members of the Executive or Zionist personalities who have been granted seats as "virilists" (i.e., veteran Zionists who are given a seat for their personal merits).

During World War II and up to the 22nd Congress (1946), an Inner General Council in Jerusalem composed of 31 members exercised all functions of the full Council, which could not meet. The presidium of the General Council, consisting of its chairman and 18 members, conducts the meetings of the Council, represents it in external and internal matters, and discharges various duties "imposed by law or referred to by Congress or Council."

THE EXECUTIVE. According to the Constitution of 1960, the Executive, elected by the Congress, is "its executive organ charged with the implementation of the decisions of Congress and Council and responsible to these bodies." Its seat and head office is in Jerusalem, but the Executive may "establish one or more divisions abroad." The branch in London was abolished shortly after the proclamation of the State of Israel (1948), but there is a New York section whose members join their Jerusalem colleagues several times a year for plenary sessions at which general policy is formulated. Day-to-day matters are handled in the almost weekly meetings of the Jerusalem Executive. The Executive acts through its departments, generally headed by one or more of its members. In 1970 the following main departments were in existence: Immigration and Absorption, Youth Aliyah, Youth and He-Ḥalutz, Settlement, Organization, Information, External Relations, Education and Culture – and Torah Education and Culture – in the Diaspora, Treasury, and Administration. Over the years no other governing body of the Zionist Organization has grown in size as much as the Executive, which, originally called the Small Actions Committee, initially numbered five and after Herzl's death seven members. The Executive elected at the first post-World War I Congress (1921) had only 15 members, but that appointed by the 23rd Congress (1951) numbered 19 members and two deputies, while that elected in 1966 included 26 regular members (one without voting rights – WIZO) and one deputy. The 27th Congress (1968) reversed this trend, reducing the number of the Executive members to 14 (among them one representative each of the WIZO and the Sephardim) and empowering the General Council to co-opt up to 5 nonparty Zionist personalities.

THE PRESIDENT. The president elected by the Congress is "the head and chief representative" of the Zionist Organization. He has the full rights of an Executive member. The actual standing of the president is determined less by his constitutional status than by his personality and activities. No president was elected at the 22nd Congress (1946), and until 1956 Nahum Goldmann and Berl *Locker co-chaired the Executive. In 1956 Goldmann was elected president of the Zionist Organization until 1968, when, at the 27th Congress, no president was elected, but Louis Aryeh *Pincus was chairman of the Executive from 1965.

THE JUDICIAL ORGANS. The judicial organs of the Zionist Organization are the Congress Tribunal and the attorney. According to the Constitution of 1960, the Congress Tribunal combines the functions of the former Congress Court and Court of Honor. It consists of a maximum of 25 members including the chairman and up to five deputy chairmen. The Congress Tribunal had jurisdiction to interpret the Constitution; to examine the legality of decisions of central Zionist bodies; to determine disputes between one central Zionist body and another or an individual – except in financial matters; to deal with objections to a postponement of the Congress or a Council session; to verify Congress elections; to deal with appeals from territorial judicial bodies and against decisions of the committees determining the number of Congress delegates and the system of Congress elections; to deal with complaints that the Constitution was infringed or that the interest and prestige of the Zionist Organization damaged. The attorney of the Zionist Organization (formerly Congress Attorney) is charged with representing the interests of the organization before the Congress Tribunal and advising central Zionist bodies in legal matters.

THE COMPTROLLER. The comptroller and his office are a counterpart to the state comptroller of Israel or the comptroller and auditor general of Great Britain. The comptroller's task is to "inspect the financial and economic activities of the Zionist Organization and its institutions and officers of every kind."

ZIONIST ORGANIZATION AND THE JEWISH AGENCY. The term Jewish Agency for Palestine was coined by the Mandate for Palestine promulgated by the League of Nations in 1922, whose article 4 made provision for "the recognition of an appropriate Jewish Agency as a public body for the purpose of advising and cooperating with the Administration of Palestine in such economic, social, and other matters as may affect the establishment of the Jewish National Home and the interests of the Jewish population of Palestine." The Mandate designated the Zionist Organization as the Jewish Agency it envisioned, and until 1929 it functioned in that capacity, i.e., the Zionist Organization and the Jewish Agency were one and the same body. The position changed when at Weizmann's initiative the enlarged Jewish Agency was established at the 26th Zionist Congress (1929) "for discharging the functions of the Jewish Agency as set forth in the Mandate," on the principle of parity between Zionists and "non-Zionists," i.e., Jewish persons and bodies supporting the building of the National Home, without identifying themselves with the political aspirations of Zionism. Thereafter the Zionist Organization and the Jewish Agency were two different bodies, though headed by the same president. When the last "non-Zionist" member of the Jewish Agency Executive, Werner *Senator, resigned in 1947, the complete identity between the Executives of the two institutions was reestablished. This identity existed until 1971. It was confirmed and stressed in the Israel Law on the Status (see below). In that period the difference between the two bodies was one of terminology rather than substance. In practice the name Zionist Organization indicated the activities and functions in respect to the Diaspora, while the designation Jewish Agency was mostly used in connection with work in and for Israel.

After the Six-Day War, when formerly uncommitted sections of the Jewish people identified themselves with the State of Israel to an unprecedented extent, the proposition to enlarge the Jewish Agency and reinstate its separation from the Zionist Organization was again put forward. The 27th Zionist Congress in 1968 authorized the Executive to initiate negotiations with "fund-raising instruments for Israel" with a view to "establishing a direct relationship between the Jewish Agency and such bodies." A year later the General Council approved the principles of the enlargement; in August 1970 the "agreement on the reconstitution of the Jewish Agency" was initialed, and on June 21, 1971, it was signed. Since then the World Zionist Organization and the Jewish Agency have again been two independent and separate bodies, although – similar to the pattern of 1929 – 50% of the members of the governing bodies of the Jewish Agency are designated by the World Zionist Organization. The chairman of the Zionist Executive is chairman of the Assembly and of the Executive of the Jewish Agency, and they have in common a treasurer and comptroller. The agreement included a division of functions between the Jewish Agency and the Zionist Organization, according to which the latter will "continue as the organ of the Zionist movement for the fulfillment of Zionist programs and ideals." Its main field of activity is the Diaspora, and it deals with Zionist organization, information, youth and He-Ḥalutz (pioneering movements), education and culture, external relations, and the activities of the Jewish National Fund, and also encourages and promotes aliyah from free countries.

ZIONIST ORGANIZATION AND THE STATE OF ISRAEL. In April 1948, one month before the proclamation of the State of Israel, the Zionist General Council resolved that after the establishment of the Provisional Government of Israel, "the jurisdiction of the Zionist Executive should comprise settlement, immigration, and all related matters including Youth Aliyah, Zionist information, organization, propaganda and culture, education in the Diaspora, youth and He-Ḥalutz, the development of Jerusalem and the National Funds." This principle of separation of functions was confirmed in a somewhat modified form by the resolution of the subsequent session of the General Council in August/September 1948 and of the 23rd Congress in 1951. Accordingly, while some functions previously exercised by the Zionist Organization have naturally devolved on the government, other functions remained the sole responsibility of the Zionist Organization-Jewish Agency. In Israeli law the mutual relations between the State of Israel and the Zionist Organization-Jewish Agency were put on a firm legal basis by the Law on the Status of the World Zionist Organization – The Jewish Agency – 5713 (1952), article 4 of which declares: "The State of Israel recognizes the World Zionist Organization as the authorized agency which will continue to operate in the State of Israel for the development and settlement of the country, the absorption of immigrants from the Diaspora and the coordination of activities in Israel of Jewish institutions and organizations active in those fields." The details of this status and the forms of collaboration between the Zionist Organization-Jewish Agency Executive and the government of Israel were, as foreseen in article 7 of the law, determined by a "covenant" entered into by them in 1954. A special committee consisting of an equal number of government ministers and Zionist Executive members was set up to coordinate activities, but in practice the delineation of the functions of the Zionist Organization-Jewish Agency has remained in a state of flux. After the Six-Day War proposals were made to increase the government's responsibility for the integration of the immigrants and were widely discussed in Israel and the Diaspora. In June 1968 the government decided to create a special Ministry for Absorption, with the understanding that even after its establishment, certain aspects of absorption of immigrants would remain in the domain of the Executive of the Zionist Organization-Jewish Agency.

[Aharon Zwergbaum]

LOCAL DEVELOPMENT THROUGH THE SIX-DAY WAR

In Australia and New Zealand

Zionism developed more slowly in Australia than in other British dominions. An attempt by Leon Jona to establish a Zionist society in Adelaide after the First Zionist Congress (1897) failed. The first Zionist bodies in the Commonwealth of Australia were the Victorian Zionist League in Melbourne (founded 1907) and the Sydney Zionist Society (1908); from 1913 a West Australian Zionist Society (Perth) was also in existence. In Australia's sister dominion, New Zealand, there were Zionist associations at the time in Auckland and Wellington; the former had developed from a Ḥovevei Zion society founded as early as 1903. Nonetheless, as the Sydney

Zionist Society, the most active of these bodies, wrote in a report to Zionist headquarters at Cologne in 1911, "there were comparatively few enthusiastic Zionists in Australia" and the attitude of the great majority of the Jewish community toward the movement was "apathy, though not hostility." In 1911 the first delegate from Australia, Salomon Pechter of Sydney, made his appearance at the Tenth Zionist Congress in Basle. During the so-called language conflict in Ereẓ Israel in 1914, the Zionist societies in Australia came out strongly in favor of Hebrew and against German as the language of instruction at the newly founded Technion of Haifa.

Efforts to bring all Zionist bodies in the various cities into the common framework of an Australian Federation had begun in 1908. Some bodies, like the Victorian Zionist Association, were directly affiliated with the Zionist Federation of Great Britain. It was only after World War I and the Balfour Declaration that the first all-Australian Zionist Conference took place in Melbourne (1927) and that the Zionist Federation of Australia and New Zealand was established, on the initiative of Alexander *Goldstein. Although its name continued to include New Zealand, the Zionist Council of New Zealand has virtually become an independent organization (close cooperation with the Australian Federation notwithstanding) and has been represented by its own delegates at the Zionist Congresses.

Sir John *Monash, who had been commander in chief of the Australian army in World War I, was elected honorary president of the Zionist Federation. However, the other most distinguished personality of Australian Jewry, Sir Isaac *Isaacs, who had been chief justice and governor general of the Commonwealth, was an anti-Zionist, and during World War II he conducted a press campaign against the Zionists, charging them with disloyalty to Britain and denying the existence of a Jewish people. Rabbi Israel *Brodie, later chief rabbi of the British Empire, served as president of the federation from its foundation until he left Australia in 1937.

During the economic depression at the beginning of the 1930s, the federation declined and its very existence was called in question, but it recovered again toward the end of that decade. During World War II its importance and prestige considerably rose as a result of its political and public relations work. The atmosphere for such activities was favorable because general public opinion in Australia was rather friendly to Zionism. Some strongly pro-Zionist Christian sects, like the Christadelphians, were active there. They even raised funds for Zionist causes. The pro-Zionist sentiment in the Commonwealth was also partly due to the excellent relations between the *yishuv* in Palestine and the Australian troops stationed there during both world wars. Australian statesmen Robert Menzies, Ben Chifley, and John Curtin (prime minister during World War II) were supporters of the Zionist cause. Particularly important was the role of Herbert Evatt, a personal friend of some Zionist leaders and an advocate of the idea of a Jewish state, who as foreign minister was elected chairman of the UN Palestine Ad Hoc Committee (1947). In this capacity he thwarted delaying maneuvers, and firmly directed the proceedings of the committee which culminated in the positive vote for the partition of Palestine in the General Assembly on Nov. 29, 1947.

Characteristic of Zionist life in Australia has been a certain competition, even to the point of rivalry, between the main Jewish centers: Sydney in New South Wales and Melbourne in Victoria. It has become traditional for the federation to transfer its seat periodically from one city to the other. Thus the 24th Australian Zionist Conference held in Melbourne in 1970 decided that the headquarters of the federation should be in Sydney for the next four years. Like the Commonwealth of Australia, the Australian Zionist Federation is organized on federative lines in state Zionist councils (New South Wales, Victoria, Queensland, West Australia, and South Australia) to which all Zionist societies, bodies, and groups of the state are affiliated. There was a total of 60 such bodies in 1970. A distinctive feature of the Australian Zionist Federation is that it embraces all organizations and institutions which are in any way connected with the work for, and support of, Israel. The Jewish National Fund had remained very strong and popular, and Zionist influence is predominant in the Australian Jewish communal institutions.

While the beginnings of Zionism in Australia were slow and precarious, from the late 1960s this community was one of the most Zionist-oriented in the Diaspora. During the Six-Day War between Israel and the Arab states (1967), several hundred young Australian Jews registered as volunteers for Israel, but only a few managed to arrive there in time to aid the war effort. The Zionist Membership Drive 1970/71 resulted in about 13,000 members, i.e., almost 20% of the total Jewish population in the Commonwealth of Australia.

[Aharon Zwergbaum]

In Austria

Austria, as referred to in this article, is understood as the territory of the Austrian Federal Republic as it existed from 1918 to 1938 and again from 1945. The history of Austrian Zionism, in this territorial sense, is almost identical with that of Vienna, where more than 90% of Austrian Jews were concentrated.

Vienna, then the capital of the Hapsburg monarchy with a Jewish population of about two million, had been one of the centers of the nascent Jewish national movement even before Herzl's appearance on the stage of history. Several Jewish national student associations existed, the most notable being Kadimah (founded in 1883). Even the name Zionism was coined in Vienna by Nathan Birnbaum, the most prominent ideologist of these early Zionists. When Herzl published *Der Judenstaat*, he found enthusiastic followers among these forerunners of political Zionism and many other young Jews, particularly students, but met stiff opposition in the Jewish liberal bourgeoisie and the Jewish community establishment. Since Herzl was a resident of Vienna, that city was during his lifetime the capital of Zionism, i.e., the seat of the Zionist Executive (the Inner Actions Committee), the central Zionist organ *Die Welt*, and the Jewish National Fund. Viennese Zionists like Johann *Kremenetzky, M. Schnirer, Alexander *Marmorek, and Oser Kokesch occupied key positions in the Inner Actions Committee. It was also in Vienna that the first Zionist-Socialist movement, Aḥva, emerged in 1898, upon the initiative of Saul Raphael *Landau.

After Herzl's death, Vienna lost its central position in the Zionist world movement, the central institutions having been transferred to Cologne, but Zionism remained a vibrant movement in Austria, albeit with a change of emphasis and leadership. The trend was now on practical Zionism, both in respect to settlement work in Ereẓ Israel and in Jewish national politics in the Diaspora ("Work in the present"), greatly invigorated after the introduction of universal suffrage in 1907. The leaders of the movement in the period prior to World War I were Adolf *Boehm, Robert *Stricker, and Jacob Ehrlich. In 1909, 25 Zionist societies existed in Austria, mostly in Vienna, organized in the Zionistischer Landesverband. The 11th Zionist Congress (1913) was held in Vienna. The great influx of refugees from Galicia during World War I and the obvious victory of the principle of national self-determination at the end of the war further strengthened the Zionist movement.

After the dismemberment of the multi-national Hapsburg monarchy and the establishment of the Austrian Republic, a Jewish National Council was established on Zionist initiative. In the first elections Robert Stricker was elected on a Zionist ticket to parliament and three Zionists to the city council of Vienna. But after some time there was a sharp decline in the Zionist following, mainly due to the attraction of the Social-Democratic Party, which had many Jewish leaders, almost all of them assimilationists and opponents of Zionism. Even in that period of decline there was, however, a bustling and very diversified Zionist activity going on. There were scores of Zionist associations, parties, youth movements, cultural clubs, sports associations, etc. Vienna was the most important transit place for immigrants to Palestine and, therefore, an important meeting place. Upon the initiative of Rabbi Ẓevi Pereẓ *Chajes, who had been appointed chief rabbi of Vienna in 1918, a Hebrew teachers' seminary was established, as well as a secondary school, bearing (after Chajes' death) his name.

From 1918 until 1927 a Zionist daily, the *Wiener Morgenzeitung*, appeared, as well as several weeklies. In 1925 the 14th Zionist Congress assembled in Vienna. In 1932 the Zionists succeeded in realizing Herzl's slogan of the "conquest of the communities," gaining 20 out of 36 seats in the Jewish community council. Desider *Friedmann was elected president of the community. Zionists stood, therefore, at the helm of Austrian Jewry when the catastrophe befell them in 1938. From the Nazi conquest in March 1938 until the outbreak of World War II in September 1939, about one-half of Austrian Jewry succeeded in leaving the country, many of them for Palestine, mostly by "illegal" routes. Almost all of the remaining Jews fell victim of the Holocaust; among them were prominent leaders of Austrian Zionists, like Desider Friedmann, Robert Stricker, and many others.

After World War II Austria was the scene of great Zionist activity, being located on the main route of the *Beriḥah and harboring in its confines many camps of Jewish DPs. In the small reconstituted Jewish community of Vienna a diversified Zionist activity started, all Zionist parties reemerged, but for most of the postwar period the Zionists constituted a minority of the community, while the majority supported the non-Zionist, albeit not anti-Israel, Social-Democratic *Bund werktaetiger Juden*.

[Aharon Zwergbaum / Chaim Yahil]

In Bulgaria

A large part of the predominantly Sephardi and Ladino-speaking Jewish community of Bulgaria was always strongly attached to Zionism, although enjoying full civic rights since the establishment of independent Bulgaria (1878). They were not under pressure to emigrate and suffered little from anti-semitism. Even before Herzl's appearance, there were Zionist societies like Ezrat Aḥim in Sofia, Carmel in Plovdiv (Philippopolis), and Dorshei Zion in Khaskovo. Bulgarian Jews founded the settlement Hartuv in Ereẓ Israel as early as 1896, the same year in which Herzl was surprised and moved by the enthusiastic welcome accorded to him by masses of Jews when his train stopped at the Sofia railway station en route to Constantinople.

Bulgaria was represented at the First Zionist Congress (1897) by Ẓevi Belkovsky, Yehoshua Caleb, and Carl Herbst. Marcus *Ehrenpreis, who became chief rabbi of Bulgaria, had taken a very active part in preparing the Congress and also attended it. The first Bulgarian Zionist Conference took place in 1898 in Plovdiv, which was the Zionist center before Sofia. The leader of political Zionism in Bulgaria during its first stage was, until his tragic death (1899), Josef Marcou *Baruch.

The rapid spread of Zionist societies encountered some opposition on the part of the assimilationists influenced by the French education in the Alliance Israélite Universelle schools, but they were less strong than in other countries. However, the Zionists quickly "conquered the communities," in accordance with Herzl's demand. In 1900 they initiated the convocation of the First National Congress of Bulgarian Jewry, which adopted statutes transforming synagogue groups into veritable communities. The second Congress in 1920 already had a Zionist majority and proclaimed the religious and national solidarity of all Jewish inhabitants of the country, regardless of origin, language, or citizenship. Another Congress took place in 1932. The publication of the central Zionist organ *Ha-Shofar* was started in 1901. Due to Zionist influence, in the 1920s Hebrew became the language of instruction (apart from subjects like Bulgarian history and literature) at all schools maintained by the Consistory, the central Jewish community organization, which were attended by the great majority of Jewish children.

Between the two world wars Alberto Romano, for many years chairman of the Zionist Federation of Bulgaria, and

Masthead of Ha-Shofar, *the Zionist weekly in Hebrew and Bulgarian, published in Plovdiv, November 1935. Jerusalem, Yad Vashem Archives.*

Ḥayyim Aaron Farḥi, chairman of the Consistory and member of the Bulgarian parliament, were among the most important figures in Zionist life. The movement became diversified, and parties and youth movements were set up. The Bulgarian WIZO was founded in 1923; in 1930 Maccabi had more than 3,300 members in 24 clubs; the number of shekel holders reached 8,000, a much higher percentage of the population than in most countries; He-Ḥalutz was training its members for *aliyah* in training farms, such as that near Pazardzhik. After the Revisionist secession from the World Zionist Organization (1935), the New Zionist Organizations set up branches of the Betar movement. They issued their own weekly *Razsvet*. One of their leaders, Benjamin Arditti, was afterward a member of the Israel Knesset from the Ḥerut list.

Hundreds of Bulgarian Jews settled in Palestine during the Mandate period. Some of them established their own settlements, like the moshavim Kefar Ḥittin near Tiberias and Bet Ḥanan south of Tel Aviv. Members of Ha-Shomer ha-Ẓa'ir who settled in Palestine before 1935 founded five kibbutzim.

The Zionists of Bulgaria were active in organizing "illegal" immigration to Palestine before and immediately after World War II. They also assisted Jews from other countries, who fled the Nazis or pro-Nazi regimes, to embark on "illegal" transports from Bulgarian ports to Palestine. All Zionist activities had to cease under the Fascist regime during World War II, but immediately after the country's liberation a Zionist Conference was convened (1944) and a Zionist organ *Zionisticheska Tribuna* was published. In 1946 a United Zionist Organization was set up. In the same year more than 14,000 shekels were distributed and almost 9,000 voters took part in the elections to the 22nd Zionist Congress, at which Bulgaria was represented by four delegates.

The Communist regime, under Georgi Dimitrov, at first displayed sympathy for the newborn State of Israel and permitted all Bulgarian Jews who wished to go to Israel to do so without placing any obstacles in their way. Thus, in the years 1944–49, a real exodus of Bulgarian Jews took place, when 40,000 of them settled in Israel. However, in accordance with the policy of the Soviet bloc, this attitude changed, and in 1949 all Zionist bodies had to disband "voluntarily" and all Zionist activities ceased.

[Aharon Zwergbaum]

In Canada

In 1898, one year after the First Zionist Congress, a Zionist society, Agudat Zion, was formed in Montreal. One year later, five more societies came into existence in Quebec and Ontario and formed the Federation of Zionist Societies, electing Clarence I. De Sola as its first president. The number of Zionist societies increased gradually and conventions were held annually. With the outbreak of World War I, all Zionist work practically came to a standstill, as contact with the *yishuv* was severed; however, the Balfour Declaration revitalized the Zionist activities.

The year 1919 was a turning point in the affairs of the Zionist Federation; De Sola stepped down from the presidency and was succeeded by A.J. *Freiman of Ottawa, and Lilian *Freiman organized the Canadian Hadassah Organization. One year later, Keren Hayesod began its activities. Within the next four years the Labor Zionist Organization was formed. It sponsored a program for Palestine based on a synthesis of socialism and Jewish nationalism. During the same period the Mizrachi Organization was organized by religious Zionists. All these groups participated actively in the Keren Hayesod-United Palestine (Israel) Appeal and the Jewish National Fund (JNF). In 1924 the Labor Zionists added their own annual campaign, which was called the Geverkshaften (later Histadrut) Campaign; M. Dickstein played an important role in this activity. Each of the organizations also organized national women's branches – Hadassah (affiliated with WIZO), Mizrachi Women, Pioneer Women – each conducting active programs and substantial campaigns for institutions in Palestine and later also for Youth Aliyah. The parent bodies also organized youth movements: Young Judea was begun in 1916 by Bernard Joseph (who later, as Dov *Joseph, was military governor of Jerusalem during the siege of 1948 and occupied important cabinet positions in subsequent Israel governments); the *Habonim Labor Zionist organization and Junior Hadassah were formed later.

Organization. In 1966 the Federated Zionist Organization of Canada (FZOC) was established to unify all the existing Zionist organizations into a single framework. It includes the following bodies:

(1) The Zionist Organization of Canada, the oldest and largest of the Zionist organizations, which has branches in most of the sizable communities, as well as fraternal orders in the larger cities. It holds regional conferences regularly, and together with the women's organization, Hadassah (WIZO), and the other Zionist movements, influences the Canadian Jewish community in a large measure.

(2) The Labor Zionist Movement, a federative structure of autonomous Labor Zionist bodies which embraces the United Labor Zionist Party (Po'alei Zion), now united with Aḥdut ha-Avodah; the Farband Labor Zionist Order; and the

Pioneer Women of Canada; as well as Habonim Labor Zionist Youth; and the Israel Histadrut Campaign.

(3) The Mizrachi-Ha-Po'el ha-Mizrachi Organization of Canada, which has three offices (in Montreal, Toronto, and Winnipeg) and a Mishmeret Ẓe'irah of young couples in these centers, as well as its youth movement and a women's division.

(4) The Zionist Revisionist Movement of Canada, with its youth movement, Betar, and women's organization.

(5) The Friends of Pioneering Israel, which is closely affiliated with Mapam in Israel.

The Federated Zionist Organization publishes a monthly entitled *The Canadian Zionist*. The United Labor Zionist Party (Labor Zionist Party and Aḥdut ha-Avodah-Po'alei Zion, affiliated in 1970) publishes *Dos Vort* in Yiddish and English, and a quarterly, *Viewpoints*. Hadassah publishes *Orah, Campaigns and Projects*. The United Israel Campaigns, which have been carried on annually, averaged $3,000,000–3,500,000 (Canadian) a year between 1960 and 1967. In the latter year a special Emergency Campaign brought in an additional $30,000,000. In addition, since 1953 there has been an annual sale of State of Israel bonds, initiated under the leadership of Samuel *Bronfman and E.E. *Gelber. In the first year there were over 10,000 subscribers, with a net sale of $4,500,000. Subsequently there was an annual sale of $3,000,000–3,500,000 up to 1967, and between 1967 and 1970 $4,000,000–5,000,000 annually. The Jewish National Fund has been functioning since the beginning of Zionist activities in Canada. It has concentrated on "Traditional Funds," which link the fund with special occasions in Jewish family life, such as barmitzvahs and weddings. In addition, it has initiated and sponsored special projects, such as the "Negev Dinners," for acquiring funds to plant forests and develop new land projects in Israel. These projects have brought in considerable sums of money over the years.

In 1927 Canadian Zionists bought a tract of 30,000 dunams on the shores of the Mediterranean for $1,000,000, and it was developed as Emek Hefer. In 1952 a convention of Canadian Zionists undertook to redeem an area of 50,000 dunams in the western Negev. In 1955 the JNF of Canada began a project to plant 500,000 trees at Ein Kerem in the Judean Hills, to be known as the Canadian Forest. Canadian Hadassah has sponsored such projects as the Agricultural School for Girls at Nahalal, the Hadassim Children's Village; a hydrotherapy pool for crippled children at Sarafand; a child guidance clinic in Jerusalem; baby crèches; and "Canada Hall" at Hebrew University. Over the years the Histadrut Campaign has sponsored a number of special Canadian projects in Israel, particularly the Amal vocational schools. The Pioneer Women have established Omna, a children's home in Haifa, and a community center at Migdal ha-Emek and have helped maintain the many institutions of the Mo'eẓet ha-Po'alot (Working Women's Council in Israel). In 1955, the Mizrachi Organization began to raise funds for the new Bar Ilan University, and the Mizrachi Women have sponsored a number of their own projects. The Zionist Revisionist group and their women's organization, Jordania, also have special projects. In addition, the Friends of the Hebrew University was organized in 1944 under the national chairmanship of Allan Bronfman. There is also a Canadian Technion Society, under the leadership of D. Lou Harris, as well as a group interested in the Weizmann Institute at Rehovot, in which Samuel J. Zacks, a past president of the Zionist Organization of Canada, was very active during his lifetime.

The various Zionist organizations have summer camps for young people. In 1970 the Zionist Organization of Canada operated eight youth camps between Halifax and Vancouver, with an enrollment of 1,700 youngsters. The Mizrachi-Ha-Po'el ha-Mizrachi ran a Hebrew camp for over 500 youngsters. The Labor Zionist Movement operated a youth camp near Montreal and Camp Miriam at Vancouver. The Keren ha-Tarbut, Hebrew department of the Zionist Organization of Canada, is active in the larger cities (Montreal, Toronto, Winnipeg, and Vancouver). It carries on special programs, such as Hebrew courses, "Hebrew-on-the-air," and *ulpanim*, particularly for those planning to settle in Israel. The Labor Zionist Movement was influential in helping to establish the Canadian Jewish Congress and has been active in that organization throughout the years. The Zionist organizations also assist indirectly in Jewish education. The Labor Zionist Movement is directly affiliated with the Folk Shule and Peretz schools in Montreal and the Bialik Hebrew Day School in Toronto. The public relations department of the Zionist Organization of Canada operates an ongoing program, supplies speakers for the Jewish and non-Jewish service clubs, and assists in the work of the Canadian Israel Association, a non-Jewish organization which has been in existence and active since 1947. Together with the Canadian Jewish Congress and B'nai B'rith, the Zionist Organization of Canada operates a Canadian-Israel Public Affairs Committee.

Aliyah and Settlement in Israel. The first Canadian *ḥalutz*, Ya'akov Pruzhansky, who later changed his name to Aḥvah, arrived and settled in Ereẓ Israel in 1913. During World War I more than 200 Canadians volunteered as members of the Jewish Legion and fought under General Allenby; a fairly large number remained in Palestine. In 1948, during Israel's War of Independence, about 250 young men volunteered their services in *Maḥal, and a certain number remained after the state came into being. The Six-Day War of 1967 evoked an unparalleled response of identification with Israel. Financial contributions were made freely and spontaneously; demonstrations for Israel took place throughout the country; delegations of prominent Canadian Jews visited the prime minister and urged that the Canadian government take a positive stand in favor of Israel's position; blood and plasma were volunteered for shipment to Israel. Over 10,000 volunteers offered themselves and, in spite of traveling difficulties at the time, about 400 left Canada and by devious means reached Israel. Of these, 228 went with the direct aid of the Zionist Organization of Canada and many of them remained and settled permanently.

Even before 1967, but particularly from then on, there has been a steady flow of tourists, students, temporary settlers and many who have made their permanent home in Israel, among them prominent Zionist leaders. It was estimated that in 1971 there were about 3,500 former Canadians residing in Israel.

[Samuel B. Hurwich]

In Czechoslovakia

BEFORE THE ESTABLISHMENT OF THE CZECHOSLOVAK REPUBLIC (1918). The growing tension between Czechs and Germans in Bohemia and Moravia aroused the sensitivity of the Jews to the nationality problem and a positive disposition toward the Zionist idea. Several Jewish nationalist societies were established even before the appearance of Theodor Herzl, especially in Czech provincial cities. The first Zionist society was established in 1893 in the town of Horaždovice in Bohemia. The appearance of Herzl aroused a strong response, especially in the communities of Moravia, due partly to the fact that many of the youth of these communities had come into contact with Herzl and Zionism while studying in Vienna. In 1900 the first Zionist weekly, the *Juedische Volksstimme*, was founded in Brno (Bruenn). Berthold Feiwel and Robert Stricker, among the first Zionist students from Moravia, rose later to leading positions in the world movement. Zionist societies were also established in Prague and the cities of the Sudeten. In the final decade before World War I, the Zionist student association *Bar Kochba, led by Shemuel Hugo Bergman, was outstanding for its high intellectual level. This group adopted not only the political program of Zionism but aimed also at a return to the sources of Jewish spiritual creativity and found contacts with the Jewish cultural and social way of life in Eastern Europe. Their goals blended into the great educational task designed to "renew the image of Jewish man." On the whole this group supported the outlook of the Democratic Faction within the Zionist Organization and cultural Zionism; later on it leaned toward the ideas of A.D. *Gordon. Its initiative led to the publication of the Zionist weekly **Selbstwehr* (1907) and the anthology *Vom Judentum* (1913). From Bar Kochba emerged many Zionist leaders in Czechoslovakia and beyond, S.H. Bergman, Hugo Hermann, and Robert Weltsch. With the expansion of the movement among Czech-speaking students, another, parallel group was founded under the name Theodor Herzl (1909). The student Zionist society Barissia, founded in 1903, supported militant political Zionism. In the last two years before the outbreak of World War I, the first youth movement, *Blau-Weiss, was established. Maccabi and other sports organizations were also established in many communities, as were women's organizations.

In Slovakia, then part of Hungary, Zionism penetrated only into communities in the western areas, which maintained closer contact with Jewry in Vienna and Moravia. The founding world convention of Mizrachi was held in Pressburg (Bratislava) in 1904. Although World War I interrupted the organizational work of the Zionist Organization, it also widened and deepened the national feelings by bringing Jewish soldiers from the West to centers of Jewish life in Eastern Europe, on the one hand, and many thousands of Jewish refugees from Galicia to communities in Moravia and Bohemia, on the other.

In the Republic of Czechoslovakia (1918–39). The establishment of the Czechoslovak Republic signified a victory for the principle of national self-determination, which was also supported by the Zionist movement. The establishment of the new, democratic republic also appeared to be the great hour of the Zionist movement, as the leader of the new state, the philosopher and humanist T.G. Masaryk, had fought against anti-Jewish blood libels, was a great admirer of Aḥad Ha-Am, and was supported in his struggle for national independence by Zionist leaders in the United States and Great Britain. The Jewish National Council was founded on the initiative of Zionists and was headed by the leader of the Prague Zionists, L. Singer, aided by Max Brod, Emil Margulies, chief rabbi Chaim Brody, and others. The council's program aimed toward achieving national, political, and cultural autonomy, built upon the communities as autonomous cells. The movement achieved recognition for the Jewish nationality in the constitution of the republic and protection for the rights of a national minority and also succeeded in building a network of Hebrew and Jewish schools – especially in the eastern areas of the republic, but it never achieved the full realization of Jewish cultural autonomy.

The stress on Diaspora work met with opposition in the Zionist movement, and at the second national conference, held in Brno in 1921, a new leadership was chosen for the Zionist movement. It was headed by Joseph *Rufeisen, who advanced practical activities toward the upbuilding of Ereẓ Israel as the central platform of the Zionist program. The center of the Zionist movement was set up in Ostrava and remained there until 1938. The Zionist Organization in Czechoslovakia, headed by Rufeisen, was outstanding in its efforts for settlement work in Ereẓ Israel, Hebrew and Jewish education, and training of *ḥalutzim*, while the Jewish National Council and the Jewish Party (*Židovská Strana) handled local political matters. On Zionist policy, the majority supported Weizmann's line and based itself on the close cooperation between the General Zionists, headed by Rufeisen, and the Labor Zionists; the Revisionists and Mizrachi also developed substantially.

The Zionists had decisive influence in the communities in Slovakia and Sub-Carpathian Ruthenia. Their opponents were the Czech assimilationist movement, and most fiercely the Communists on one end of the spectrum and the ultra-Orthodox on the other. A pioneering He-Ḥalutz movement had existed since the establishment of the republic and succeeded in founding a number of collective settlements and moshavim in Palestine. Various youth movements were active in the spirit of pioneering and *aliyah*. Zionist influence was also decisive in the sphere of education and in the 1930s in the area of social welfare, especially for the Jews of Sub-Carpathian Ruthenia and the refugees of Nazi persecution. Three Zionist Congresses were held on Czechoslovak territory: the 12th Zionist Congress (1921) and 13th Zionist Congress (1923) in Carlsbad and the 18th Zionist Congress (1933) in Prague.

The Holocaust and After. The destruction of the Czechoslovak Republic, after the annexation of Austria, came in several quick stages: the annexation of the Sudetenland to Germany (October 1938), giving over certain areas to Hungary and Poland (November 1938), the establishment of "independent" Slovakia (March 14, 1939), the conquest of Bohemia and Moravia by the German army turning them into the "Protectorate" (March 15, 1939), and the annexation of the remainder of Sub-Carpathian Ruthenia by Hungary (March 16, 1939). These were also the stages of the destruction of Czechoslovak Jewry, while the Zionists played central roles in attempts to save it. They increased their efforts toward facilitating *aliyah* and emigration. About 15,000 Jews from Czechoslovakia succeeded in reaching Palestine between the autumn of 1938 and the end of 1939, the overwhelming majority by means of "illegal" immigration. Zionists remained in most positions of community leadership both in the "Protectorate" and Slovakia. Under the leadership of the Zionists Jacob Edelstein, Franz Kahn, Otto Zucker and Hannah Steiner, together with the leaders of the pioneering movement, the Zionists preserved their sense of cooperation, national loyalty, and Jewish values in the Theresienstadt concentration camp and even in Auschwitz. They organized means of escape from Slovakia, where the head of WIZO, Gisi *Fleischmann, initiated the *Europa Plan to save European Jewry, and many Zionist youths took part in the partisan uprising in Slovakia in the summer of 1944.

The few who survived the Holocaust tried to reestablish the Zionist movement after the war and save the survivors through *aliyah* and settlement in Ereẓ Israel. Zionist activity was renewed in all parts of the republic. Czechoslovakia was a major transit country for the flow of the *Beriḥah* from Poland. During the Israeli War of Independence (1948), Czechoslovakia was a major source of arms' supply to the new state. Emigration to Israel was permitted, and more than 20,000 Jews, about 40% of the Jewish community, settled there. After a short while, however, the sympathy of the new Communist government in Czechoslovakia for Israel evaporated. Zionist activity was forbidden, and after a time emigration was also halted. In 1952 the Communist government staged a show trial against "Zionism" (see *Slánsky Trial). During the short period of the "Prague Spring" in 1968, under the leadership of Alexander Dubček, expression of sympathy for the State of Israel was again permitted and even *aliyah* was renewed, but organized Zionist activity did not resume and the invasion of the Warsaw Pact armies in August 1968 ended this period of relative improvement.

[Chaim Yahil]

In France

Early History. The Jewish community of France occupies an important place in the early history of Jewish settlement in Ereẓ Israel, due to the initiative of the Alliance Israelite Universelle and of Baron Edmond de Rothschild. The Alliance set up a network of elementary and vocational schools there, the first of which was the Mikveh Israel agricultural school, founded in 1870. Although these activities were similar to Alliance projects in other parts of the Ottoman Empire, this interest in Ereẓ Israel was undoubtedly influenced by the discussions of Joseph *Natonek and Moses Hess with Alliance directors in Paris in 1866. Rabbi Samuel Mohilewer, accompanied by young settlers from Rishon le-Zion, paid a visit to Edmond de Rothschild that served to move him to increase financial, technical, and administrative assistance to new Jewish agricultural enterprises in Ereẓ Israel. Rothschild's intervention was crucial in saving the struggling villages from ruin and in facilitating the development of budding Jewish agriculture. Despite the philanthropic character of Rothschild's undertakings, his paternal attitude, and outbursts of indignation against political Zionism, his contribution was substantial and at a certain stage decisive for the continuation of settlement work.

Paris can also be considered the cradle of political Zionism. It was while in Paris as a correspondent for the *Neue Freie Presse* that Theodor Herzl conceived his Zionist idea and wrote *Der Judenstaat*, and it was in Paris that Max Nordau lived from 1880 to the outbreak of World War I. Among the early Zionists in France were Alexander Marmorek and his brothers Oscar and Isidore, the writer Bernard *Lazare, Miriam Schach, and the sculptor S.F. *Beer. Zadoc *Kahn, France's chief rabbi, supported Zionism and Herzl, but abstained from publicly expressing his support. The Fédération Sioniste de France was established in 1901 and its president until his death in 1923 was Alexander Marmorek. In 1899 he founded the journal *L'Echo Sioniste* which appeared from 1899 to 1905 and again from 1912 to 1914. In 1916 it reappeared under the title *Le Peuple Juif* and remained in existence to 1921. In 1914 the federation had five groups in Paris, one in Nice, and two in Tunis. The great majority of native-born Jews and the official communal bodies, however, were indifferent, if not hostile, to the Zionist program, fearing that their status acquired in the great Emancipation would be placed in jeopardy. This hostility to Zionism did not subside with the Balfour Declaration, although the French minister for foreign affairs, Stephen Pichon, afforded French assent to the declaration. During the Peace Conference at Versailles (1919), two French representatives, the poet André *Spire and Professor Sylvain *Lévi, were members of the committee established by Chaim Weizmann together with N. Sokolow and M. Ussishkin, to present the Zionist views to the conference delegations. Lévi however, who was president of the Alliance, clashed with the committee, since, in his view, the Zionist objectives conflicted with French interests in the Middle East.

Zionism in France appealed mainly to Jewish immigrants from Central and Eastern Europe who arrived there beginning in the 1880s. Thus, the successive leaders of French Zionism were Israel *Yefroykin, Marc *Jarblum, and Joseph Fischer

(Ariel). Fischer founded a bimonthly journal, originally as the organ of the Jewish National Fund, *La Terre Retrouvée* (published from 1928). Jarblum, a leader of Labor Zionism, was its spokesman in the Socialist movement of France and Belgium. He had influence with such men as Léon Blum, Emil Vandervelde, and Camille Huysmans. However, a small number of leading French-born Jews also supported Zionism, among them the poets Edmond Fleg and André Spire. The latter's Zionist writings caused him to split with Charles Péguy and his circle of *Cahiers de la Quinzaine*. In 1915 a group of Jewish and non-Jewish intellectuals established the Ligue Franco-Sioniste, and in 1917 André Spire published *Les Juifs et la guerre*, which dealt with the problem how to present the idea of the Jewish state to the future peace conference. In the same year he established the Ligue des Amis du Sionisme, of which he was the secretary general, and its organ *La Palestine Nouvelle*.

1917–1939. In 1917 a Zionist youth movement was established in Strasbourg, from which the bulk of French immigrants went to Palestine prior to World War II. In 1920 a Zionist students' club was founded in Paris, and in 1921 a Mizrachi group was established with its center in Strasbourg. In 1925 the Union Régionale des Sionistes de L'Est de la France was founded by Léon Metzger and Robert Lévy-Dreyfus. This union was the strongest Zionist organization in France before World War II, and up to the conquest of France by the Nazis in 1941 it retained a separate identity. In 1923 a women's group was founded by Mrs. Richard Gottheil; it later merged with the Women's International Zionist Organization (WIZO). In 1929 French Jews accepted Weizmann's invitation to join the "enlarged" Jewish Agency, and Léon Blum, Leo Zadoc-Kahn, and Henri Lévi represented French non-Zionists in the founding meeting in Zurich in August 1929. In the 1930s the following Zionist organizations existed: Po'alei Zion (Left), founded in 1922; the Union of Zionist Revisionists, founded in Paris in 1925 and becoming the center of its world movement; Po'alei Zion-Hitaḥadut, which included a League for Labor Palestine and the Jewish People's League; Organisation Sioniste de France, founded in 1933, an organization of General Zionists; and the Jewish State Party, founded in 1936. Mizrachi also had a certain following in France, including a group called Yavne and a Yiddish-language journal. In the same period branches of many Zionist youth movements were formed: Bleu-Blanc (General Zionists), Betar (Revisionists), Berit ha-Kannaim (Jewish State Party), Deror (Po'alei Zion-Hitaḥadut), Ha-Shomer ha-Ẓa'ir, Ẓe'irei ha-Mizrachi, Ha-Po'el ha-Mizrachi, and Ha-No'ar ha-Ẓiyyoni. In 1937 the Fédération de la Jeunesse Sioniste et Pro-Palestinienne was founded as a result of the merger between the Jewish scouting movement and a few Zionist youth groups, with a total membership of 5,000.

World War II. From the German occupation in 1940, Zionist activities were centered in the southern area known as Vichy France. In 1941, at a secret conference in Lyons, initiated by J. Fischer (Ariel), a new Zionist leadership embracing all groups was established under the chairmanship of Leonce Bernheim, former chairman of the Zionist coordination committee. At another meeting in Vichy in the same year, the Mouvement de la Jeunesse Sioniste, embracing all youth organizations, was created under the direction of Simon Lévitte and Jules Jefroykin. Both frameworks engaged in educational work, such as the teaching of Hebrew, Jewish history, etc., but devoted their energies mainly to smuggling Jewish refugees into Switzerland and Spain. Young Zionists also played a leading part in organizing Jewish armed resistance to the Nazis (see *France, Holocaust Period).

After World War II. Immediately after World War II, leading French Jews, such as André Blumel, were active in aiding the "illegal" immigration and the *Beriḥah* movement to Palestine though French ports. With the establishment of the State of Israel, Jewish community officials in France adopted an attitude of sympathy, putting an end to their previous hostility. In 1947 the Union Sioniste Française was founded, uniting all Zionists in France and North Africa, led for some time by André Blumel. The transformation of French Jewry by the influx of North African, particularly Algerian Jews, also influenced the Zionist movement there. Migration to Israel increased steadily. French Jewry demonstrated its solidarity with Israel before and after the Six-Day War (1967), and Chief Rabbi Jacob *Kaplan voiced Jewish disapproval of De Gaulle's anti-Israel policies. All traditional Jewish bodies began openly to support Israel, and a Comité de Coordination des Organisations Juives en France, headed by Guy de *Rothschild, was specially created in 1967 for financial aid and information services for Israel. Groups for *aliyah* to Israel were formed, among them Oded, comprising young intellectuals from North Africa. All Zionist parties and most world organizations collecting funds and selling bonds for Israel have branches in France, many of them publishing their own journals, such as the French *Amitiés France-Israel* (since 1953) and the Yiddish daily *Unzer Vort* (since 1945) and *Tsionistishe Shtime*.

[Lucien Lazare]

In Germany

The First Zionist Congress (1897) was attended by more than 40 delegates from Germany, not all of them natives of that country. (The delegation included four representatives from Ereẓ Israel, one of whom, Heinrich *Loewe, was a founder of a Zionist group in Germany even before the appearance of Theodor Herzl.) There were, however, a few bodies in Germany that could be regarded as forerunners of modern Zionism; the Esra society in Berlin (founded 1883) tended to the Ḥibbat Zion; the Russian Jewish Scientific Society in Berlin (1889) which was composed almost exclusively of "Eastern Jews"; the Association for the Promotion of Agriculture and Crafts in Palestine, founded in Cologne in 1892 by Max *Bodenheimer and David Wolffsohn, was in 1897 transformed into the Nationaljuedische Vereinigung and demanded, before the Basle Program, nothing less than a Jewish state. As early as October 1897 the Zionistische Vereinigung in Deutschland (ZVD), a roof organization of all Zionist societies, was set up. The Zionist movement in Germany was distinguished by quality – especially excellent organization and harmonious internal relations – rather than by quantity, since, to quote Richard *Lichtheim: "nowhere was the opposition of Jews to the new movement so widespread, principled, and fierce as in Germany." Herzl's original plan to convoke the First Congress in Munich failed because of the hostility of the German rabbis; the board of the Union of German Rabbis issued a proclamation against the Congress and Zionism (hence *Protestrabbiner).

The slow but steady growth of the ZVD is reflected by the following figures: in 1912 it had 8,400 members and in 1927 some 20,000, 2,000 of whom were members (or "old boys") of the Zionist students' associations organized in the Kartell juedischer Verbindungen; in the same years the number of local branches doubled from 100 to 200. The year 1902 saw the establishment of two Zionist institutions whose influence reached far beyond the borders of Germany: the Zionist weekly **Juedische Rundschau* and the publishing house *Juedischer Verlag. Special importance is attached to the Zionist territorial conference of 1912 because it adopted a resolution obliging every Zionist "to include *aliyah* in the program of his life" or at least to connect his personal fate with that of the national home by means of economic interests.

The influence of the Zionist Federation of Germany was particularly strong during the 15 years in which the headquarters of the World Zionist Organization were in Germany: in Cologne during the presidency of David Wolffsohn (1905–11) and in Berlin during that of Otto Warburg (1911–20), all the more so as one of the chairmen of the ZVD, Arthur *Hantke, was a leading member of the Zionist Executive. It was largely due to the fact that the Zionist headquarters remained in Berlin during World War I, although some Executive members went abroad, and that German Zionists continued to hold key positions in the world movement, that German representatives in Turkey exerted their influence in favor of the *yishuv* and helped to mitigate its persecution. Leaders of German Zionism like Felix Rosenblueth (later Pinhas *Rosen, Israel's first minister of justice), Richard Lichtheim, and Kurt *Blumenfeld held highest office in the world movement even after its seat had been transferred to London.

During the Weimar Republic (1918–1933) the Zionists in Germany continued to be an elite rather than a mass movement. Shekel figures moved round 20,000, and it was only after the Nazis had seized power that the Zionistische Vereinigung in Deutschland reached its maximum membership of 35,000. It always embraced all Zionist parties – with the exception of the Revisionists, who seceded in 1932. When the ascent of the Nazis had conclusively proved the bankruptcy of assimilation, Zionism became the dominant force in German Jewry. The courageous and dignified article of the *Juedische Rundschau*, "Wear the Yellow Badge with Pride," by its editor Robert Weltsch, which was the Zionist reply to the anti-Jewish boycott of April 1, 1933, made Jewish history. The main efforts of the ZVD were now directed at the preparation and promotion of *aliyah* and *hakhsharah* (youth training). Through the *Haavarah, the transfer of Jewish assets to Palestine, some £6,000,000 were saved and infused into the economy of Ereẓ Israel to its great benefit. After the Nuremberg Laws in 1935 the ZVD was subjected to increasing restrictions and in 1938 was dissolved by the authorities.

Immediately after World War II a United Zionist Federation was established by the Displaced Persons. It was very active, but after most of the DPs had left, mainly for Israel, it was dissolved. In 1954 the Zionist Organization in Germany was established, against considerable opposition in the world movement, but when two delegates from Germany were admitted to the 24th Congress (1956), this federation, with its seat in Frankfurt, gained official recognition. Due to the small number of Jews in Germany and to other factors, the scope and quality of its activities fall necessarily short of those of the former ZVD, but it is doing useful work in particular in the fields of fundraising and public relations.

[Aharon Zwergbaum]

In Great Britain

There were many Jewish and non-Jewish forerunners of the Zionist idea and supporters of Jewish settlement in Palestine, as well as an active group of Ḥovevei Zion (see *Ḥibbat Zion), in Great Britain. Thus, political Zionism appeared on the British scene very early. It was in London that Theodor Herzl made his first Zionist speech (at the Maccabean Club in November 1895) and outlined his program in an article in the *Jewish Chronicle*, in January 1896, before the publication of *Der Judenstaat*. He was received with great reservations not only by the Jewish establishment, but even by some of the Ḥovevei Zion. On his next visit, in July 1896, he addressed a mass meeting in the East End and received an enthusiastic response. Among his first supporters and followers were the Sephardi Haham Moses *Gaster, the Hebrew teacher Ephraim Ish-Kishor, the already famous writer Israel Zangwill, and Jacob de *Haas, followed soon after by Joseph *Cowen, Leopold *Greenberg, and Leopold *Kessler. In March 1898 Ḥovevei Zion in Britain joined the Zionist movement mainly under the influence of Herbert *Bentwich and Albert *Goldsmid. As a consequence, the Second Zionist Congress (1898) was attended by 15 delegates from Britain, compared to eight at the First Congress. In January 1899 the English Zionist Federation was founded, with Sir Francis Abraham Montefiore, a grand-nephew of Sir Moses Montefiore, elected the first president of the Federation. Herzl, who from the beginning believed in British support for Zionism, registered the Jewish Colonial Trust as a British corporation (1899), and in 1900 convoked the Fourth Zionist Congress in London, the only Congress during his lifetime not held in Basle. "From here the Zionist idea will soon soar higher and higher," Herzl declared in his opening speech. Most British Zionists supported Herzl in the controversy over the Uganda Scheme, while Jacob K.

*Goldbloom, one of Herzl's first followers, led the opposition. The Zionist movement in Britain suffered a severe blow when Zangwill seceded, in 1905, and founded the Jewish Territorial Organization.

In 1904 Chaim Weizmann settled in England, having received a position at the University of Manchester, and soon gathered around him a group of devoted Zionists who later distinguished themselves in the British and world movement, notably Simon *Marks, Israel *Sieff, Harry *Sacher, and Leon *Simon. In 1914 Weizmann became vice president of the Zionist Federation (under Joseph Cowen as president). World War I opened new political perspectives. An advisory committee on Zionist political activity was formed, composed of Nahum Sokolow and Yeḥiel Tschlenow (members of the world Executive who had moved to London), Cowen, Weizmann, Gaster, and Bentwich. The Zionist Federation became an important factor in these activities. In 1915 it organized a petition demanding "the establishment of a publicly recognized and legally secured Home for the Jewish people in Palestine, as formulated by the Zionist Congress in Basle in 1897." The petition was signed by 77,000 adults out of a total Jewish population of about 300,000. In January 1917 Cowen resigned from the presidency of the Zionist Federation to make way for Weizmann.

In their struggle for British support for the Zionist goals, the leaders of the movement were enthusiastically supported by the federation and advised and supported by Zionists from abroad who spent the war years in London, like Aḥad Ha-Am and Vladimir Jabotinsky, as well as by some British Jews of high social standing, most notably Herbert Samuel and Lord Rothschild. Chief Rabbi Joseph Herman *Hertz came out as a supporter of Zionism, in remarkable contrast to his predecessor Herman Adler, who had denounced Zionism as a fantasy. Still, anti-Zionist sentiments were so strong in the Jewish establishment that the presidents of the Board of Deputies and of the Anglo-Jewish Association, D.L. Alexander and Claude Montefiore, respectively, publicly repudiated Zionist aims in the name of their organizations. The sharp protest by the followers and sympathizers of Zionism forced Alexander to resign. Lord Rothschild accepted the honorary presidency of the Zionist Federation and so became the addressee of the Balfour Declaration. At the first Zionist World Conference after the war, held in London in 1920, Weizmann was elected president of the World Zionist Organization and the seat of the Executive and of the main instruments of the movement were formally established in London, which thus became the capital of world Zionism.

During the 30 years of British administration in Palestine, the activities of the Zionist movement in Great Britain were of utmost importance for the work and struggle of the Zionist Executive, by providing mass support in the political, financial, and cultural fields. Zionist influence within British Jewry increased. In 1929 the Board of Deputies joined the enlarged Jewish Agency for Palestine as a constituent body. In 1939 Selig *Brodetsky, a member of the Zionist Federation, was elected president of the Board of Deputies, and since then only Zionists or staunch supporters of Israel have served in that capacity. Zionist youth movements developed, and there was a significant *aliyah* from Britain. At the 21st Congress (in 1939) Great Britain was represented by 15 delegates, eight representing the Federation (General Zionists), three Po'alei Zion, three Mizrachi, and one the Jewish State Party. The Revisionists, who at that time had already seceded from the World Zionist Organization, also moved their headquarters to London, which was the seat of the Zionist-led European Executive of the World Jewish Congress, as well. In 1944 the Board of Deputies embraced the Biltmore Program by adopting a resolution calling for the establishment of a Jewish state in undivided Palestine, hopefully within the framework of the British Commonwealth. During the years of the struggle and resistance of the *yishuv* after World War II, preceding the independence of Israel, British Zionists took a courageous stand against their government.

After the establishment of the State of Israel, Great Britain naturally lost its central position in the Zionist world, but British Zionists – under the direction of Lavy Bakstansky – continued to distinguish themselves by their generous support of Israel and their increasing influence within the Jewish community of Great Britain. The achievement of raising £11,000,000 in the Emergency Campaign of 1967 (as compared with £2,600,000 raised the year before), as well as the fact that within a few days about 10,000 volunteers for Israel enlisted, about 2,000 of whom actually arrived in Israel, is worthy of note. The most impressive achievement within the framework of the community is the establishment of a network of Zionist day schools since 1953. In 1969 ten schools were operating with an enrollment of over 5,000 pupils.

[Aharon Zwergbaum]

In Holland

The Zionist Federation was established in Holland in 1899 under the name of Nederlandse Zionistenbond. Among its founders was the young banker Jacobus H. Kann, who was a close collaborator of Theodor Herzl. The members of the organization were mainly middle-class intellectuals, and for about 30 years the Zionist movement of Holland was unsuccessful in attracting a wider following among the Jewish proletariat. The movement also encountered violent opposition from Orthodox circles. The chief rabbi of Amsterdam, J.Z. *Duenner, supported the Zionist movement from the start, and some of his close friends founded the Mizrachi movement, led by S. Ph. de Vries. But his colleagues and almost all of his disciples rejected Zionism, and in 1904 the Council of Chief Rabbis (which Duenner refused to join) forbade the Jews to join the Zionist movement. The Eighth Zionist Congress, which was held in The Hague, led to an awakening of the movement. An attempt to establish a Zionist youth movement during that period ended in failure, but the official Zionist organ. *De Joodse Wachter*, founded in 1905, which in time became a weekly, stood its ground.

In 1912 Nehemiah de *Lieme was elected president of the Nederlandse Zionistenbond, and S.A. van Vriesland (who was later to become treasurer of the World Zionist Organization) was elected its secretary. De Lieme consolidated the organization's special character by establishing several principles: the negation of any Zionist work for Diaspora Jewry ("*Gegenwartsarbeit*"); sound economic management in the upbuilding of Ereẓ Israel; the exemplary organization of the Zionist movement in the Diaspora. In Holland, the organization made the following demands: prohibition of the sale of the shekel for obtaining the right to vote at elections to the Zionist Congresses (therefore Holland's representation at all the Congresses fell below the organization's actual strength); membership to be registered personally (not through Zionist parties); insistence on Zionist principles in propaganda as well as fundraising for Ereẓ Israel. De Lieme exerted tremendous influence on his friends and followers, among them S. *Hoofien, later director of the Anglo-Palestine Bank in Palestine, Abel Herzberg, author and politician, and others. In 1914 the world headquarters of the Jewish National Fund were transferred to The Hague, and de Lieme headed the fund for seven years and formulated its principles. In 1920 he was elected to the Executive of the World Zionist Organization, but resigned when his principles were not accepted. After de Lieme's resignation, he returned to the leadership of the Nederlandse Zionistenbond and developed a stance of opposition to the Executive of the World Zionist Organization. Pereẓ (Fritz) *Bernstein also extended this opposition to the political line of Chaim Weizmann, and in his capacity of editor of *De Joodse Wachter* and later as president of the organization, he left his imprint on the movement. Only a small group of Dutch Zionists countered the de Lieme-Bernstein line, among them David Cohen and the Po'alei Zion, founded in 1933 by S. de Wolff. There was also a small Revisionist group, which would not gain much influence because of the anti-Weizmann stance of the whole Zionist Federation.

During World War I the arrival of refugees from Belgium (all of whom were Jews of East European origin) added an important element to the movement. The study of modern Hebrew developed and several newspapers included a Hebrew supplement. In 1917 an organization of Zionist youth groups, Joodse Jeugdfederatie, was established with the moral support of the Zionist leadership and under its aegis. The Jeugdfederatie encompassed many groups throughout the country and held independent activities (publications, lectures, conventions). After about ten years, it was headed by young people, mostly students, who had emerged from its own ranks.

The rise of antisemitism in Germany was a cause for much agitation in Holland, and the 30,000 German Jewish refugees who arrived in the country highlighted the problem. The influence of the Zionist movement increased, and although it had no more than 4,000 registered members, many beyond its ranks accepted the Zionist ideology. Anti-Jewish trends then began to grow in Holland and the local Zionist leadership was inclined to conceal the Jewish national character of Zionism. In opposition to this tendency, a trend calling itself "Radical Zionism," greatly influenced by Lion Nordheim, developed within the youth movements and among the students. It clashed sharply with the Zionist leadership, especially over the following points: the Joodse Jeugdfederatie demanded of its members complete identification with the Jewish people and public detachment from the Dutch nation; it stood for the safeguarding of Jewish national values and traditions and for Jewish education, thus opposing the prohibition of "*Gegenwartsarbeit*"; it propagated the ideal of *halutziyyut* (pioneering) among its members. The rift between the youth movement (which also encompassed religious and labor groups and commanded a membership of 2,000 in 40 branches) reached its climax in 1940. With the German invasion, however, it was decided to establish a joint leadership of all the Zionist organizations in Holland, and this body administered the affairs of the Nederlandse Zionistenbond until its dissolution.

Immediately after World War I, many *ḥalutzim* from Eastern Europe had arrived in Holland to complete their agricultural training with Dutch farmers. During the 1930s *ḥalutzim* also emerged from the ranks of the Joodse Jeugdfederatie. They established three organizations: Ḥevrat Olim (the adherents of Bernstein), Berit Ḥalutzim Datiyyim (religious) and He-Ḥalutz (composed mainly of *ḥalutzim* from other countries, including German refugees). As Holland was not considered to be a danger zone, not even by the World Zionist Organization, over 800 *ḥalutzim* were trapped there for many years. Many of them perished during the war, but 444 were saved, mainly due to the activity of the *Westerweel group. After World War II the Dutch Zionist movement was dominated mainly by the radical trend. Its slogan, which called for massive *aliyah*, led to considerable success. Out of the 25,000 Jews who survived in Holland, some 4,000 settled in Israel between 1948 and 1969, a higher percentage than from any other Western country. During this period most of the Zionist leadership itself migrated to Israel, and the Nederlandse Zionistenbond lost its central position within the remnant of Dutch Jewry. Zionist periodicals in Holland included, apart from *De Joodse Wachter, Tikvath Jisrael* (from 1917), monthly of the youth movement; *Mizrachie* (from 1932), monthly of the Mizrachi movement; and *Jaarboek van de Nederlandse Zionistische Studentenorganisatie* (since 1909).

[Jozeph Michman (Melkman)]

In Hungary

Two strong and opposing forces were influential among Hungarian Jewry from the 1840s: on the one hand a desire to assimilate linguistically and culturally into the Magyar nation, and on the other extreme religious conservatism. In addition, Ḥasidism exerted a substantial influence, particularly in the northern part of the country. These three phenomena were an obstacle to the proliferation of the Zionist idea at the end of the 19th century. Nonetheless, the difficult and extended struggle of the Zionists succeeded in spreading the Zionist idea among relatively small groups throughout the country.

During the period of the Ḥovevei Zion a number of enthusiastic supporters of this movement in Hungary maintained ties with other Ḥovevei Zion beyond the borders. However, even the fact that Theodor Herzl was a native of Budapest and was bound to Hungarian Jewry through familial ties did not facilitate the development of the Zionist movement in Hungary. On a number of occasions Herzl himself declared that Zionism would reach Hungary, but only later on.

In spite of strong opposition to Zionism in religious circles, some Orthodox Jews from Hungary participated in the founding of the world religious Zionist movement. Some Hungarian Jews also settled in Ereẓ Israel during the 19th century and became an important element in the old *yishuv*, but as a rule they bore no ties to Zionism. Representatives from Hungary participated in the First Zionist Congress (1897). One of them, János *Rónai, delivered a speech at the Congress and pointed to the normal condition of life of Hungarian Jewry, but he expressed the fear that this situation would deteriorate and predicted that Hungarian Jewry would then join the Zionist movement. Immediately after the Congress, Rónai, an attorney from Transylvania, began to engage in varied organizational activities, establishing branches of the Zionist movement, heading the national efforts at organizations, and being elected first chairman of the Hungarian Zionist Organization. In preparation for his appearance at the Congress, he wrote an ideological pamphlet in German entitled *Zionismus in Ungarn* (1897), in which he engaged the arguments of both the assimilationist and religious opposition. Another central figure was Samu Bettelheim, who was active in Bratislava. Bettelheim was a religious Zionist, and upon his initiative the first world conference of Mizrachi was convened in his city in 1904. The number of local Zionist groups began to increase, and at the Second Zionist Congress (1898) 32 branches of the Hungarian Zionist Federation were in existence.

In 1908 the Hungarian authorities became aware of the movement and prohibited collecting money for the Zionist funds. Local Zionists alerted the president of the World Zionist Organization, David Wolffsohn. He visited Budapest and was received by the minister of interior, Count Gyula Andrássy, who displayed understanding and even friendship toward the Zionist movement but explained to Wolffsohn that the problem of minorities was very disturbing in Hungary and he could not afford to allow the creation of yet another national minority, the Jewish nation. This approach continued to characterize the position of the Hungarian authorities vis-à-vis Zionism.

At the beginning of the 20th century, some of the students at the University of Budapest became Zionists. In 1903 they founded a society called Makkabea, which played a central role in the propagation of the Zionist idea in the capital and the provinces until World War II. The Zionist press was also established by the initiative of this society. The first Zionist organ was *Zsidó Néplap*, which was published from 1905 to 1907. In 1911 another organ, *Zsidó Szemle*, began to appear under the editorship of József Schőnfeld. These papers, however, did not succeed in penetrating into wider Jewish circles. A Jewish quarterly called *Múlt és Jövő* began appearing in 1911 under the editorship of Joseph *Patai. Although this literary and artistic periodical was not an official organ of Zionism, it clearly identified with the Jewish nationalist and Zionist trend and achieved great popularity (publication ceased during the Holocaust). Zionists were also active in the establishment of Jewish sports organizations that maintained ties with similar groups in Austria.

Feeble attempts were made at the beginning of the century to establish Po'alei Zion in Hungary, but the Jews among Hungarian Social Democrats opposed this idea. The Jewish Territorial Organization (ITO) also set up a branch in Hungary in 1912. Local Zionists became involved in a difficult struggle with the ITO, which was also supported by the non-Zionist Jewish press. In spite of all these difficulties, however, on the eve of World War I there were branches of the Hungarian Zionist Organization in many cities throughout Hungary, and 20 delegates from Hungary participated in the 11th Zionist Congress (1913).

During World War I many active Zionists were mobilized into the army, and some who were captured came into contact with Russian Jews and Zionists. These contacts proved to be very fruitful. During the last months of World War I and the period of the Russian Revolution, Zionists, and especially demobilized officers, organized into self-defense units and in a number of places overcame mob attacks on the Jews. The first short-lived Communist regime in Hungary (1919) displayed open hostility to Zionism, prohibited organizational activities, and forced the Zionist organ to close down for a period.

In the peace treaty that ended World War I, Hungary was divided up, and the Zionist activity in areas annexed to Romania, Czechoslovakia, Austria, and Yugoslavia began to develop independently of the Hungarian Zionist Organization, whose headquarters were in Budapest. Zionist activities continued in the limited area of Hungary, where one of the central problems was the extended struggle to acquire government authorization for the Zionist Organization. The leaders of the Neolog Jewish community also opposed the granting of such authorization, since they regarded Zionism as a breach of Hungarian patriotism. Legalization was finally achieved in 1927, with the Hungarian Zionists receiving strong political support from the Zionist Executive in London. The Pro-Palestine Association exerted influence among those Jews who did not formally join the Zionist Organization.

By the 16th Zionist Congress (1929) many youth movements had already been formed in Hungary, including He-Ḥalutz. A great step forward was the enlargement of the Jewish Agency and the seating of the Hungarian Zionist Joseph Patai, and the chief rabbi of Szeged, Immanuel Löw, who was considered a non-Zionist, on its General Council. In 1937, 17 local branches of the Zionist Organization and 3,600 members existed in Hungary. The number of youth movement members was also substantial. The year 1937 was the last before the cancellation of equal rights for Hungarian Jews (the Hungarian parliament had already begun deliberating the law to reduce their rights, which was passed in 1938). The first anti-Jewish law, the restrictions on Jewish economic activities, and the proximity of German Nazism – after Germany had annexed Austria – increased the interest of Hungarian Jewry in the Zionist movement. Zionist cultural activities expanded, especially those of the youth movements. The number of Jews who wished to go to Palestine, as well as the number of those who realized their desire, was on the rise.

Jewish refugees from Austria, Poland, and other places began arriving in Hungary, and aid was extended to them principally through the framework of the Zionist movement. Efforts to move refugees to Palestine through "illegal" channels were made under Zionist auspices, particularly through the youth movements. With the annexation of northern Transylvania to Hungary in 1940, a group of Transylvanian Zionist leaders experienced in public and political life arrived in Budapest. Among them were Rezsnő Rudolf *Kasztner and the newspaper editor Ernő *Marton. The Zionist Socialist movement was further strengthened during this period, and Béla Dános, its leader, also took upon himself varied activities. Youth leaders arrived from Slovakia and other parts of former Czechoslovakia, bringing with them strong Zionist views. The movement in Hungary was then headed by Ottó *Komoly. Those who came from the annexed provinces, as well as active Zionists who had fled from other countries, were aided by, and extended aid to, the rescue activities of the Zionist movement and to some degree the Aid and Rescue Committee set up for that purpose. The Aid and Rescue Committee established contact with Adolf *Eichmann to discuss rescue plans and sent Joel *Brand, one of the active Zionist Socialists, on his tragic mission. During World War II Hungarian Zionists were active mainly in rescue activities.

After World War II, in 1945, the Zionist Organization in Hungary was reconstituted. Zionist youth movements directed many young people to Ereẓ Israel. The new government displayed hostility toward the Zionist activities from the very start and tried gradually to liquidate the movement. In 1949 the Zionist Organization and all Zionist activities were formally prohibited. A number of trials, directed specifically against Zionists, were later held by the government, and in other trials, including that of László Rajk, some of the defendants were accused of "conspiring with Zionists." The 50-year history of the Zionist movement in Hungary thus came to an end.

In Italy

Because of the small number of Jews in Italy and the fact that they were largely assimilated, Zionism could penetrate only slowly and with difficulty and for years retained an exclusive character. Among the Jewish periodicals, the first to express Zionist ideas at the end of the 19th century was *Il Corriere Israelitico*, which was published in Italian but appeared in Trieste (then under Austrian rule). No Italian delegates were present at the First Zionist Congress in 1897. The Second Congress (1898) was attended by the rabbi of Naples, Joseph Sonnino, who was chosen as delegate without formal elections. He represented the first Zionist groups that had been formed in Italy in Ancona, Rome, Leghorn, Florence, and Naples. Also present at the Second Congress was Felice Ravenna, who was to become the head of Italian Zionism and was to remain its leader for many years, representing it at the Third Congress in 1899, together with two other delegates. It was only in 1901 that the Italian Zionist Federation was formed. Its conventions originally took place every two years in various towns. In 1901 the first Zionist periodical, *L'Idea Sionista*, was founded and survived for ten years; in 1908 the more penetrating *L'Eco Sionista d'Italia* appeared.

At that time Italian Zionism had no important political scope and was troubled by various controversies; its nature was mainly philanthropic. Due to the intervention of some of its exponents, however, Theodor Herzl was received in January 1904 by King Victor Emmanuel III and by Pope Pius X. On that occasion, Herzl had an interview with the Italian minister for foreign affairs and later sent him a written statement. From the beginning, the most active and penetrating Zionist writer and journalist was Dante *Lattes. After Herzl's death the movement experienced a period of decline, and the center of its activities was transferred to Florence, under the leadership of Alfonso *Pacifici. In 1916 the weekly *Israel* was founded there and remained the center of Zionist activity, although it carried no Zionist label.

Immediately after World War I an Italian Jew, naval captain Angelo Levi-Bianchini, was sent by the government as Italian military attaché to General Allenby's General Staff. Under the influence of Chaim Weizmann, he became an ardent Zionist. He was killed in a Bedouin ambush in Syria in 1920. In 1922 Weizmann went to Italy and made his first close contact with Italian Jewry, defining it in his autobiography as follows: "The Italian Jewish community seemed to be a community of *sujets d'élite*. And the *élite* of that community were turning their eyes to Palestine." During the early years of Fascist rule, the relations between the Italian government and the Zionist Organization were so good that in 1928 the Comitato Italia-Palestina was formed to facilitate the contact between Italy and Palestine. Personalities of high standing in politics and literature were among the members of this committee. There had even been talk in 1931 of holding the 19th Zionist Congress at Abbazia (now Opatija, Croatia). The Zionist Revisionist movement was also in touch with the Italian government. Its leader, Leone *Carpi in Milan, published the periodical *L'Idea Sionistica*. The Revisionists founded a naval school at Civitavecchia for the world Betar movement that was several times visited by Vladimir Jabotinsky.

Although the attitude of Mussolini's government became increasingly pro-Arab, Zionism remained active for some years. It maintained agricultural training centers (*hakhsharot*); encouraged contributions to the Zionist funds, which showed increases; replied firmly to controversies in newspapers; and regularly sent delegates to the Zionist Congresses. Following the introduction of the racial laws in 1938, the position of Italian Jewry rapidly deteriorated. The existing Jewish periodicals were ordered to stop publication, the Zionist organizations were dissolved, and Jewish life, with the exception of religious and charitable functions, had to be carried on in secret. This period marked the beginning of a considerable *aliyah* from Italy, whose first pioneers and standard-bearers had been Enzo and Ada *Sereni.

After the interval of World War II, marked by deportations and ruin, particularly during the German occupation, Jewish and Zionist life slowly revived in Italy. Immediately after World War II Italy became a center of widespread and feverish underground activities in the organization of "illegal" immigration of Jewish survivors from Central and Eastern Europe to Palestine (directed by Ada Sereni) and also of secret arms transports for the Haganah. Italian Zionist and communal leaders, among them Raffaele *Cantoni, played a major role in these operations. These facts, as well as the presence of the soldiers of the Jewish Brigade Group from Palestine, created a climate of deep identification of Italian Jewry with the struggle for Jewish independence in Palestine.

Numerous Zionist conventions took place in Italy from 1947 onward and *aliyah* increased considerably. Jewish education, e.g., the great Jewish school in Milan, became Hebrew and Israel-oriented. Italian Zionism, which is numerically still very small because of the limited size of the Jewish community, is now more politically conscious and has more cultural and personal ties with Israel than ever before.

[Giorgio Romano]

In Latin America

The Zionist movement in Latin America grew with the development of the continent's Jewish communities. In most countries Jewish communal and Zionist institutions collaborated from the start, and from the time of the struggle for independence and the establishment of the State of Israel the activities of the Zionist movement have expanded to continental proportions. The movement has sponsored such major continental gatherings as the first Zionist congress in Montevideo (1945); the second Zionist congress in Buenos Aires (1950); the first Jewish Latin American youth convention (Montevideo 1961); a conference convened after the Six-Day War that brought together 527 delegates from Argentina, Uruguay, Chile, Paraguay, and Peru (Nov. 1967); and a South American encounter for the new Zionist generations (Buenos Aires, April 1970).

Argentina. Zionist groups arose in Buenos Aires and in the interior simultaneously with the organization of the First Zionist Congress in Basle. The oldest group (established 1897) was Sion. The Dr. Theodor Herzl League was also influential for several years. As the movement grew, its activities were coordinated by a Federación (established 1904), a central institution which was an extension of the Herzl League. In 1908 it was replaced by Tifereth Zion. The movement's leadership developed within the framework of the Federación Sionista Argentina (established 1913), whose first leaders were Jacobo Joselevich, Nathan Gezang, and Solomon Liebeshutz.

During the early stages of its development, the movement did not tend toward internal political polarization. There were, however, lesser organizations which espoused particular ideological trends: Ḥerut, Socialist Territorialists (established 1905); SS, Socialist Zionists (established 1906); and a Borochovist group, Po'alei Zion (est. 1909), and Ẓe'irei Zion (1918). The two last groups united in 1932 to form Po'alei Zion Ẓe'irei Zion and its periodical *Di Naye Tzait*, established 1918, still exists. The other major local party is the General Zionists, whose official publication is *El Estado Judío*. Ha-Shomer ha-Ẓa'ir, particularly active after World War II, publishes the *Nueva Sion* (established 1947). The Revisionist party (established 1930), which increased its organizational cadres during the struggle of the *yishuv* against the British administration in Palestine, puts out *La idea Sionista*. Mizrachi was established in 1940 on the foundations of previously organized smaller groups.

These parties have sponsored the creation of youth movements which have made significant contributions in the areas of Jewish education and *aliyah*. Women's organizations of each party, as well as WIZO, are also active. The Consejo Central Sionista (established 1948), in which all local Zionist institutions are represented, arose from the reorganization of the Zionist parties and the creation of a Comisión Coordinadora (established 1940). As of 1951 it has undertaken functions previously carried out by the Jewish Agency (established 1937, for Argentina and Latin America). Delegates from Argentina have attended Zionist Congresses since 1925; their presence in previous years had been sporadic. The Zionist Organization of Argentina became one of the central organizations of Argentine Jewry.

Brazil. The first Zionist organizations, Tifereth Zion and Ahavath Zion (1916–17) sprang up in São Paolo and Rio de Janeiro. Smaller centers were also established in the northern provinces. With the founding of the Zionist Organization (1921), a degree of coordination was attained, including collaboration between Ashkenazim and Sephardim. During World War II, when Brazil imposed legislation restricting the internal development of national minorities, the Zionist movement was officially closed down (1938), but it nevertheless continued its activities on a limited scale until 1945, when its legal status was renewed. The reorganized Zionist political parties coordinated into the United Zionist Organization (established 1945). The most influential of these parties were Mapai (organized in the 1920s), General Zionists (since 1947), and the Revisionists. The Keren Hayesod was reorganized in 1946.

The movement encountered difficulties which derived from the complex internal organization of the Jewish community; local autonomous trends and a division according to countries of origin interfered with its collaboration with a centralized communal organization. Nevertheless, communal institutions in the state of São Paolo consolidated their activities with the Zionist Organization in support of the Jewish state and to aid European Jewry. The assimilation of Jewish sectors into Brazilian society, a growing manifestation during and subsequent to World War II, was a contributing factor to the limited influence of the movement during those years. There has been an upswing in the local Zionist movement since the 1950s, particularly after the Six-Day War (1967).

Colombia. The communal life of this small Jewish community, composed of Sephardim who emigrated from Palestine during the crisis years of the 1920s, German-speaking Ashkenazi immigrants arriving since World War I, and refugees from Nazi persecution, was organized with difficulty. The Zionist movement also had a slow beginning due to the restrictive measures adopted by the authorities to prevent the formation of "ethnic islands." The Federación Sionista, together with the Comité Central (established 1936), adopted measures against antisemitism and racial discrimination.

Ecuador and Paraguay. The respective organizations of Ecuador and Paraguay enjoy a limited membership, and they work together with communal institutions. Paraguay, whose minute Jewish population is preponderantly pro-Zionist, has seen an increase in activities in the wake of the Six-Day War.

Chile. Chile's flourishing Jewish community has attained a strong internal organization in which the Zionist movement wields authority and influence. The earliest Zionist initiatives were sporadic. The first stable group was formed in 1911 by members maintaining contact with the Argentinean Zionist movement. An influential figure during this early period was Mauricio Baltiansky. From the first Zionist convention in 1919, the movement became more firmly established. The major blocs were Po'alei Zion (established 1916) and the General Zionist Party (1947). Since the 1930s all Zionist parties and factions have increasingly polarized within the local movement. These include the Pro-Palestine Labor League (1931), the Revisionists (1932), and Mizrachi. Smaller groups such as the Folksfarband and the Grupo Hebraista formed the opposition. Active pioneer organizations are Ivriah (1930), Betar (1933), Bnei Akiva (1940), Kadimah (1944) – from which Ha-Shomer ha-Ẓa'ir grew – Deror-He-Ḥalutz, and Iḥud ha-No'ar ha-Ḥalutzi (1950) of the Po'alei Zion Hitaḥadut. Zionist women's organizations are WIZO (1926) and Pioneer Women (1949).

The firmly organized Zionist Federation of Chile (established 1919) incorporates all political and Zionist organizations, the United Jewish Appeal, and every institution which, if not specifically Zionist, nonetheless identifies with the movement's objectives. Together with the Jewish representative body, the Comité Representativo, it engages in nationwide Jewish education, is involved with cultural activities, and participates in the Central Committee for Jewish Education (established 1946). It sponsors the Instituto Chileno-Israelita de Cultura (established 1950), which is associated with the Comisión de Cooperación Intelectual of the University of Chile. It has also carried out an intensive campaign of political explanation within non-Jewish circles, particularly since World War II and the creation of the State of Israel.

Peru. The Zionist movement in Peru, established at the end of World War I, encountered initial resistance on the part of the Bund and other left-wing groups in the communal institutions and in the Jewish press. After its establishment (1925), the Zionist Federation collaborated closely with the Unión Israelita del Peru, an Ashkenazi community functioning since 1924, and with the Sociedad de Sociedades (1942), representative of the community. Together with the latter, the Zionist Federation sponsors the León Pinelo school (inaugurated 1946). Jewish public opinion in Peru today is preponderantly pro-Zionist. Jewish university students are organized in the Centro Universitario Peruano-Israelita (established 1960–61), which was reorganized in 1969 as the Movimiento Universitario Peruano Israelita. An independent youth group, Kinneret (est. 1962), sponsors immigration to Israel and local communal activities. The Zionist Federation has collaborated with the Comité Pro-Palestina (1945) and works with the Instituto Cultural Peru-Israel.

Mexico. Despite the divergences between Zionists and sectors identified with the non-Zionist left, the Zionist movement exerted increasing influence from the 1920s onward. Both blocs collaborated in certain communal activities, particularly those pertaining to education. Prior to institutional Zionist organization, activities were sporadic (i.e., on behalf of the Balfour Declaration (1917), a Keren Hayesod campaign (1923), etc.). The first organized group was the Po'alei Zion (1923), which published the first Yiddish publication, *Unzer Vort.* Groups with divergent leanings and bereft of specific partisan character collaborated in the Federación Sionista (1925), which later became affiliated with General Zionism. Fragmentation into specific parties and Zionist institutions – according to countries of origin or youth and women's sectors – began during the years immediately preceding World War II: Liga Pro-Palestina Obrera (1934), Pioneras (1935), Revisionists (end of the decade), Organización Sionista Sefardí (1936, functioning jointly with the Sephardi community), WIZO (1938), Ha-Shomer ha-Ẓa'ir – the first pioneer organization (1940) – Mizrachi (1942), Betar (1946), Bnei Akiva (1946), Ha-No'ar ha-Ẓioni (1948), Habonim (1948), Mapam (1948). The youth organizations centralized their activities in the Federación Juvenil Sionista (1943). Each of the trends had its own publication: *Dos Wort* (1947, Po'alei Zion), *Ha-Shomer ha-Ẓa'ir* (1942), *La Voz Sionista* (1948, General Zionists), *Unidad Juvenil* (Po'alei Zion youth), *Avangard* (1948, Mapam), *Unzer Tribune* and *El Heraldo* (Revisionists), *Mizrachi Leben* (religious). The overall organized movement formed the Federación Sionista de Méjico (established 1950), which has since undertaken central leadership tasks, including those of a local communal nature. An index of the movement's scope are the following figures: approximately 400 organized institutions cooperated in the Emergency Palestine Committee of

1946; in 1954 90% of the Jewish population considered itself Zionist, 8% non-Zionist, and 2% anti-Zionist. The Federación collaborates with the Comité Central Israelita, a representative communal institution, and with the Instituto de Relaciones Culturales Méjico-Israel.

Uruguay. This community of strong Zionist leanings had evolved from groups which have collaborated since the earliest stages of their development. In the first group, Agudath Zion, Israel Tschlenow (1914) brought together Zionists of no particular political leanings. The Sephardim founded the "Dr. Herzl" group in 1918; Po'alei Zion was established in 1917. Various trends took shape during the 1930s, and the movement expanded. All the Zionist parties and their pioneer movements and women's institutions are locally represented. The Organización Sionista Territorial, which encompasses the Federación Juvenil Sionista, cooperates closely with the Comité Central Israelita, a representative communal institution. It also collaborated with the Comité Uruguayo Pro-Palestina (1940) and later with the Comité Cultural Uruguay-Israel.

Venezuela. The Zionist Organization has been the most active and influential institution of this small community since its reorganization in 1949. It works together with the Ashkenazi and Sephardi sectors, as well as with B'nai B'rith and the Jewish National Fund. Despite their limited number, the following youth movements also operate: Ha-Shomer ha-Ẓa'ir, Bnei Akiva, Unión de Jovenes Hebreos (est. 1955), which form the Federación Universitaria Sionista Sudamericana. WIZO maintains branches in the capital and in the interior of the country. Affiliation with the Federación can also be individual. It collaborates with the Instituto Cultural Venezuela-Israel.

Central America. Despite their small size, the Jewish communities of Guatemala, Honduras, Nicaragua, Costa Rica, El Salvador, and Panama have organized Zionist institutions. In El Salvador they have functioned since 1946 and enjoy the cooperation of non-Jewish intellectuals and government figures. In Panama and Costa Rica, Zionist activities have found support among the political non-Jewish personalities who have also sponsored relations with the State of Israel. The Zionist movement in the region has increased its activities since 1965 in the wake of the formation of the Federación de Comunidades de America Central, in which the Zionist Organization is also represented.

[Rosa Perla Raicher]

In North African and Asian Countries

The attachment of Oriental Jewry to Ereẓ Israel was a messianic-religious one, expressed in prayers and aspirations and at times in going to Ereẓ Israel to die and be buried there. Until the 1880s migration to Ereẓ Israel was an individual matter and was not undertaken by organized groups.

Organizations. In the late 19th century the European Zionist movement attracted followers and sympathizers in all the Oriental countries, with the exception of remote *Yemen. The first African and Asian countries in which Zionist movements were founded were *Algeria, *Tunisia, and *Egypt. As early as 1898 communities from these three countries sent two delegates to the Second Zionist Congress, convened at Basle. Later on, Zionist organizations were established in *Iraq, China (Shanghai), Turkey, and *Morocco and afterward in *Libya, *Syria, *India, and Singapore. At first groups were set up to read Zionist journals and literature from Europe. Later on, organizations were founded, sometimes several in the same city. Most of these groups were not registered officially, either because registration was not required by law or because Zionist organizations were not permitted, such as in the Ottoman Empire. From the late 19th century to the 1930s these organizations had a limited membership. The few active members devoted most of their time to Zionist fundraising, and not enough attention was given to strengthening Hebrew and Zionist education.

After World War I, though in some places only after the 1930s, an important change took place in the development of Zionist organizations in Oriental countries. Zionist youth movements were established and directed by *sheliḥim* (emissaries) from Ereẓ Israel, for the most part independent of the adult Zionist organizations. The youth movements were generally more successful than the adult organizations for several reasons; they were organized and run by young people who were sent especially for this task and devoted all their time to it; the emissaries were not interested in collecting funds, but engaged in Hebrew and Zionist education; and they even dared to establish underground organizations when Zionist activities were prohibited. When necessary (in Iraq, Egypt, and Libya), the emissaries also established paramilitary underground self-defense organizations in which hundreds of young Jews were trained in the use of weapons in case of anti-Jewish outbursts.

In 1970 when most of the African and Asian Jewish communities had ceased to exist, Zionist organizations survived only in *Iran and in Turkey, where young people are active in Hebrew and Zionist education.

Financial Contributions. Large sums were contributed to the Jewish National Fund by Iraqi and Shanghai Jewry only in the early 1920s. However, most of the money contributed to the JNF between 1920 and 1923 (£36,500 out of a total of £38,470) was given by a Jew who wished to commemorate his brother, and his contribution enabled the establishment of the moshav Kefar Yeḥezkel in the Jezreel Valley. The rest of Iraqi Jewry contributed only £1,970 during that time. Shanghai Jewry contributed over £21,000 from 1911 to 1926, a rather large sum for a Jewish community in that area.

The contributions to the Keren Hayesod were not large, and the number of shekels (i.e., the dues paid for membership in the World Zionist Organization) acquired by the members of these communities was small. During the 1940s a relatively large number of shekels were acquired in the North African

Table 1: Shekels in Muslim and Asiatic Countries, 1922–50

	1922–33	1946	1949–50
Tunisia	7,857	13,296	32,202
Morocco	5,602	11,982	58,339
Algeria		8,100	26,652
Syria, Turkey, Iran	4,302	4,536	20,613
Iraq	4,557		
Egypt	6,724	7,541	–
Libya	?	1,963	7,000
Other Asiatic countries	?	4,325	2,574
Total	30,000	51,743	147,380

and non-Arabic countries in Asia, as shown in Table 1: Shekels in Muslim and Asiatic Countries, 1922–50.

From 1951 fewer shekels were acquired by Jews in the Eastern countries in the wake of the mass *aliyah*. The weakness of Zionist activity in these countries may be explained by the lack of strong communal organizations. The wealthy and the notables in the community were not attracted to Zionism. As the authorities in several Arab countries prohibited Zionist activity, there was no choice but to establish underground organizations. Indeed, it was impossible to conduct either oral or written Zionist education and propaganda. Therefore, the fundraising campaigns also suffered.

Aliyah. Jewish migration to Israel was always large. There are no data, however, as to the number of immigrants prior to World War I. They may be estimated according to those who remained in Palestine and were counted in the census conducted in the State of Israel in November 1948. In that census 462,567 Jews were registered as born abroad. They are divided according to periods of immigration in Table 2: Jews in Israel Born Abroad.

The number of immigrants is actually larger, as Table: Jews in Israel Born Abroad does not include those who died or left prior to 1948. One may assume that the First and Second Aliyah from Asia and North Africa numbered about 6,000; from 1919 to 1938, about 38,000; from 1939 to May 1948, about 25,000. About 33% of Yemenite Jewry, 27% of Turkish Jewry, and 6–8% of Egyptian, Iraqi, and Persian Jewry migrated to Palestine in 1919–48.

By 1971 only several thousand Jews remained in North Africa, out of a community of 500,000. The immigration to Israel from Libya was minimal until the anti-Jewish riots in Tripoli between 1945 and 1948. Immediately after the State of Israel was established, most of Libyan Jewry migrated there, anticipating more disturbances and fearing life in independent Libya. The rich and the educated, who at first remained in Libya, left the country gradually, so that by June 1967 there were virtually no Jews left in Libya.

In 1971 there were only several thousand Jews in Syria. After 1950, however, only half of the Turkish Jews who emigrated went to Israel, the rest settling in other countries. Some of the Jews in Iran, mostly the poor, left for Israel. Persian Jews enjoyed full political and religious freedom until early 1979. In March 1950 the Iraqi authorities permitted Jews who wished to leave to do so, and 124,000 Jews migrated to Israel within two years. In late 1951 there remained only about 6,000 Jews, some of whom migrated later on.

After the establishment of the State of Israel, there was a relatively large emigration of Egyptian Jews (it seems that a substantial part of these Jews were born in Ereẓ Israel and were expelled by the Turks to Egypt during World War I). In 1956–57 the Egyptian authorities expelled thousands of Jews. Some came to Israel, but the majority, particularly the wealthy, emigrated to Europe and America.

Aliyah from Yemen was proportionately larger than that

Table 2: Jews in Israel Born Abroad According to Native Countries and Periods of Immigration

Countries	Until 1918	1918–38	1939–47	1948 and unknown date	Total no. of Immigrants
Yemen and Aden	1,800	8,510	5,676	316	16,302
Syria and Lebanon	459	4,243	5,850	237	10,789
Turkey	399	4,897	4,042	1,214	10,552
Iraq	470	5,272	2,983	277	9,002
Iran	563	2,833	423	97	3,916
The rest of Asia	38	1,451	645	717	2,851
Egypt	152	2,061	2,165	251	4,629
Morocco, Tunisia, and Algeria	468	506	534	3,823	5,331
Libya	7	297	439	507	1,250
Asia and North Africa	4,356	30,070	22,757	7,439	64,622
Rest of Africa excluding South Africa	10	170	164	67	411
Soviet Asia	428	3,025	378	261	4,092
Europe, America, South Africa, and Oceania	7,478	211,424	96,334	76,347	391,583
Unknown	56	576	362	665	1,659
Total	12,328	245,265	119,995	84,779	462,367

of other Oriental communities. In the 70 years from 1881 to 1951, Yemenite Jewry exploited every opportunity to settle in Ereẓ Israel.

[Haim J. Cohen]

In Poland

1897–1918. Prior to the restoration of Polish statehood, Poland's territory remained divided into three sections: one under the administration of Germany, the second of czarist Russia, and the third of the Austrian monarchy. In the German part of former Poland, the very limited Jewish population (no more than around 50,000 at the beginning of the century) was thoroughly assimilated into German culture and displayed little interest in Jewish affairs in general and in Zionism in particular. However, two prominent forerunners of Zionism, Ẓevi Hirsch Kalischer and Elijah Gutmacher, both lived in that part of Poland and published their pamphlets calling for redemption of Zion, but their appeal had no influence upon the community; neither did the first conference of the Ḥovevei Zion movement, which took place in 1884 in the German part of Poland.

The development of Zionism was also slow among the great masses of the Jewish population in the Polish territories of czarist Russia, around 2,000,000 people at that time. A distinction should be drawn between the province of Congress Poland and other parts of the territory. In Congress Poland, which was one of the richest and economically most developed parts of the Russian Empire, the local Jewish population was somewhat influenced by the Polish assimilationist ideology and, on the other hand, the anti-Zionist Orthodoxy. It therefore had to be won over to Zionism with considerable effort. The standard-bearers of Zionism in that part of the country were the so-called "Litvaks," i.e., immigrants who came from Lithuania and the neighboring provinces, who were strongly imbued with Jewish nationalism and ideology and influenced other groups of the Jewish population. Quite different was the situation in other provinces, whose Jewish population was deeply rooted in Judaism, which was much nearer to the idea of Jewish nationalism and adopted the Zionist program with enthusiasm.

These initial differences disappeared in the course of time, however, as the movement conquered growing parts of the Jewish population. It was not particularly disturbed by the authorities, who were inclined to see in Zionism a means of reducing the danger of revolutionary propaganda among the Jews, or by the Polish population, which initially favored the idea of a movement likely to enlarge the scope of Jewish emigration. This situation changed considerably, however, when the Zionist movement proclaimed as a part of its immediate aims the struggle for civic and national rights for the Jewish population, as formulated in the *Helsingfors Program of 1906. The reaction of the authorities was a marked reduction in tolerance toward Zionist activities and antisemitism spread among the Polish population, leading even to an economic boycott of the Jews, which continued until the outbreak of World War I.

The number of adherents of the Zionist movement and the scope of its influence nevertheless grew from year to year. At the beginning the membership was limited mainly to people from the middle class, but the movement subsequently won many adherents among the workers. Although a few groups broke away and joined the territorialist *Zionist Socialist Workers' Party (SS) or the party supporting Jewish autonomism (the "Sejmists," see *Jewish Socialist Workers' Party), the others remained concentrated around the Po'alei Zion Party and tried to combine their socialist ideology with the Zionist program. On the other hand, many groups of Orthodox Jewry had already supported the Ḥovevei Zion, joined the Zionist movement, and decided to establish a special faction of religious Zionists, the Mizrachi. The various groups cooperated closely, although the Po'alei Zion, influenced by the Russian branch with its strong proletarian class character, soon tended to proclaim its organizational independence, stressing the special interests of the Jewish workers.

The situation differed in many respects in Galicia, the Polish part of the Austrian monarchy. The roots of Jewish nationalism and Zionism were much deeper there than in Congress Poland. Not only did the movement of Enlightenment, which considered Jewish nationalism self-evident and whose most prominent representatives lived in Galicia, leave its deep impression on the area, but the organized Zionist movement appeared there years before the First Zionist Congress (1897). The Zionist movement drew its supporters mainly from among the university students and the large groups of the Jewish intelligentsia. It is not surprising, therefore, that Herzl's call was responded to by the masses of the Jewish population, despite the opposition of rather small, if vociferous, groups of assimilationists, the extreme adherents of Ḥasidism, and the unfriendly attitude of the authorities, who were opposed to Jewish nationalism. This opposition grew much stronger when the Galician Zionists conducted a vigorous and relatively successful struggle for civic and national rights for the Jews, whose platform was formulated at the Cracow Conference (1906). In the first election to the Austrian parliament, after universal suffrage had been granted (1907), the Zionists acquired three seats in Galicia. One after another, various groups of the population joined the movement: members of the middle class, considerable groups of wage earners (especially the commercial employees), university and high school students, etc. It was an authentic popular movement, trying simultaneously to satisfy both the cultural needs of the population, through a network of Hebrew schools, and the economic needs, especially by establishment of credit unions in the poor and neglected province of the Hapsburg monarchy. Adolf *Stand and Osias *Thon were the prominent leaders of Galician Zionism in that period.

In Independent Poland. The Zionist movement suffered strongly during World War I, especially in the province of Galicia, which was occupied for almost a year by the Russian army. After the war it was faced with a new situation and new tasks in the reconstituted Polish republic. It emerged as the strongest force in Jewish public life, challenged only by the anti-Zionist Orthodoxy, the Socialist Bund, and for a certain period also the movement of "Folkists" (see *Folkspartei). At the same time, it was faced with the task of merging into one the movement throughout the various parts of the country now united within the borders of the reconstituted Polish state. This task, however, could be accomplished only to a very limited degree. The religious and socialist factions within the Zionist movement developed into full-fledged parties, independent of the parent body, which thus became one party among several others. The religious Mizrachi party consolidated quickly and established its countrywide organization irrespective of the former territorial division. The labor movement, on the other hand, suffered for years from extreme differentiation and many splits, until at the beginning of the 1930s the main groups united in the Po'alei Zion Hitaḥadut. The Left Po'alei Zion remained aloof and outside the World Zionist Organization, which it joined only shortly before World War II. At the other extreme, the Revisionist Party developed, from the second half of the 1920s, to considerable strength. When the Revisionists broke away from the World Zionist Organization in 1935, a minority group split away from them, constituting the Jewish State Party, which remained within the ranks of the World Zionist Organization. Some of these parties were organized on a national basis, comprising the whole of Poland, whereas others, although ideologically united, stuck to the previous territorial division. Only the center party of General Zionists was divided both on territorial and ideological grounds. In Congress Poland they split into the progressive, pro-labor Al ha-Mishmar faction, left by Yiẓḥak *Gruenbaum, and the outspokenly middle-class Et Livnot faction, led by Leon Levite; in Galicia they were divided in the West Galician Federation, under the leadership of Osias Thon and later of Ignacy *Schwarzbart, and the East Galician Federation led by Leon *Reich, Fischel *Rotenstreich, and Emil Schmorak.

The process of internal disintegration and dissent frequently weakened the influence of the Zionist movement. This was especially felt in the field of national and local politics, the main bone of contention between the rival factions. Activities in this field were very pronounced, frequently taking first place in the program of various parties. The Zionist representation in the Polish Sejm grew considerably, especially in the first three parliaments, reaching its climax in the second Sejm with 32 Zionist deputies out of a total of 47 Jewish deputies. It fell considerably, however, in the following parliaments, with the progressing degeneration of democracy in the life of the country, but it still continued to lead the struggle against the ever-growing wave of antisemitism. In the municipalities and the administration of the Jewish communities, however, Zionist influence was overshadowed by that of other political groups, especially the Bund and various Orthodox groups on the right.

In spite of external difficulties and internal frictions, Zionist activities continued with increasing intensity throughout the entire period, securing for Polish Zionism the first place within the world movement, especially in the field of *aliyah* to Ereẓ Israel, and strongly influenced all facets of Jewish life in the country. Polish Jewry was strongly represented in the waves of migration to Palestine between the two world wars, both by worker pioneers and the middle class. The membership of the various pioneering youth movements exceeded 100,000 in the 1930s, with 20,000 in active training (*hakhsharah*) for future life in Ereẓ Israel. Not all of them succeeded in emigrating, as the number of immigration certificates was severely limited by the Mandatory government of Palestine. As a consequence, Polish Jewish youth was also strongly represented in the "illegal" immigration, especially in the later 1930s. Jewish life in Poland during that period can hardly be imagined without *aliyah* as its focal point.

No less felt was the influence of Zionism on cultural life in all its forms. Jewish literature, press, and artistic life all remained under the strongest influence of Zionist ideology. One of the most outstanding fields of activity was education. Of the 250,000 students in Jewish educational institutions in Poland in the 1930s, those in institutions under predominant Zionist influence took first place. This was especially true for the network of the *Tarbut schools (around 40,000 students), with Hebrew as language of instruction, but other networks, such as those under the influence of the Mizrachi and of the Po'alei Zion, as well as the officially nonpartisan organization of Jewish secondary schools in Poland, also actually remained under the overwhelming influence of Zionism, despite assimilationist pressures from the Polish authorities. Zionist influence was also dominant in the press. In the period before World War I special importance may be attributed to the Hebrew daily *Ha-Ẓefirah*, the Yiddish periodicals *Dos Yidishe Vort* and *Tagblat*, and the Polish periodical *Wschód*. In the period between the two world wars virtually all Jewish dailies and periodicals, with the exception of those published by Bund or by Agudat Israel, were either openly Zionist or influenced by Zionist ideology, including the leading Yiddish dailies *Haynt* and *Moment*, the dailies in Polish *Nasz Przegląd*, *Nowy Dziennik*, and *Chwila*, and many weeklies and other periodicals, issued by various Zionist parties and youth movements.

There was hardly any other Jewish community in the world before World War II, with the possible exception of the relatively small communities of the Baltic countries and Bessarabia, in which the influence of Zionism was so strongly felt. All this broke down with the destruction of Jewish life in Poland during World War II. Various Zionist groups, especially groups of Zionist youth, tried for a period to continue their activities underground. They took the lead in the clandestine struggle against the Nazi occupation and in the ghetto uprisings. Zionists who succeeded in escaping from Poland established centers for rescue beyond the border, the most important of them in Vilna until its annexation to the Soviet

Union and later the German invasion of the U.S.S.R. in 1941. Zionist refugees participated actively in the political and rescue activities of various Jewish bodies, notably the World Jewish Congress. Ignacy Schwarzbart in his capacity as member of the Polish parliament in exile represented the Jewish minority before the Polish government in London. The second representative was a non-Zionist, member of the Socialist "Bund" party. Emil Sommerstein in his capacity as chairman of the Jewish Central Committee represented the Jews before the Polish authorities established in the Soviet Union. But all these efforts could not arrest the course of events: the extermination of the great Jewish community of Poland. After the war, surviving Zionists, and especially Zionist youth movements, established escape routes to and from Poland (see *Beriḥah), assembled children who had been hidden in monasteries and in gentiles' homes, and reorganized Jewish education. But after a short period of transition all Zionist activity within Poland was finally liquidated by the Communist regime.

[Aryeh Tartakower]

In Romania

The Jews from the principalities of Moldavia and Walachia had rooted religious ties with Ereẓ Israel. In Jerusalem, Tiberias, Safed, and Hebron there were groups of Jews who had emigrated from these two Romanian principalities, whence they received aid. In the middle of the 19th century the first modern pre-Zionist ideas arose in Romania. Israel Benjamin, known as Benjamin the Second, a native of Fălticeni (Moldavia), advocated Jewish agricultural settlement in Ereẓ Israel in his travel memoirs, which were published in 1856.

The first pre-Zionist groups were established starting in 1873, with the trend for the participants to emigrate to Ereẓ Israel and dedicate themselves to agriculture. The initiative began that year from Nicoresti with a group of 100 families, joined by other families from Tecuci, Ivesti, Galati, Piatra Neamt, Bacau, and Jassy. In 1875 a group from Moinesti sent a delegate, David Schub, to Ereẓ Israel to study the possibilities of settlement. The war between Russia and Turkey in 1877 hindered the continuation of that movement.

The Yishuv Erez Israel Movement. In 1880 Eleazar Rokeaḥ arrived in Romania from Ereẓ Israel to collect funds for an agricultural settlement, Gei Oni, near Safed. He also unexpectedly found candidates for *aliyah* partly because of the difficult living conditions of the Jewish population after the Congress of Berlin (1878). One year after Rokeaḥ's mission, groups that called themselves Ḥevrat Yishuv Ereẓ Israel al yedei Avodat Adamah (Society to Settle Ereẓ Israel by Working the Land) existed in 30 Romanian towns. The members of these groups decided to emigrate with their families. The publisher and editor in chief of *Ha-Maggid*, David Gordon, suggested the creation of a central committee, and on Jan. 11–12, 1882, the first meeting of 32 branches from throughout the country took place in Focsani. The president of the meeting was Samuel *Pineles. It was decided that the first group of 100 families was to leave for Ereẓ Israel before Passover, and resolutions were adopted in order to subsidize the settlement. Among the leaders of the movement were R. Avner Kasvan, Karpel Lippe, the Hebrew writer Israel Teller, and others. The central committee was in Galati, and Pineles was secretary.

In February 1882 the Romanian parliament discussed the "creation of the Palestinian Kingdom," and Prime Minister I.C. Bratianu declared that the Romanian government would give its wholehearted support to this plan. In May 1882 the second meeting with delegates from 28 localities took place in Jassy, with the visit of Laurence Oliphant. The English gentile spoke at the meeting and promised financial aid from non-Jews. Meanwhile Pineles negotiated with the Turkish consul in Galati and, with the approval of the Turkish ambassador in Bucharest, obtained the assurance that Romanian Jews would be able to settle in Ereẓ Israel, except for the Jerusalem region, in groups of 50 to 100 families. At the same time a delegation sent from Bucharest to Constantinople was received by the sultan, the vizier, and the minister of the interior. As a result of these audiences, a decision favorable to the settlement of Romanian Jews was adopted at the meeting of the Turkish cabinet. The sultan, however, refrained from giving his own approval because of the events in Egypt.

The Beginnings of Settlement. While negotiations were taking place, from the spring of 1882, delegates left Romania for Ereẓ Israel in order to buy land there, and, from towns such as Moineşti, Bărlad, Bacău, Bucharest, Tulcea, dozens of families had already emigrated. The group from Moineşti had sent their own delegate, David Schub, who in the summer of that year had bought the lands at Gei Oni, where a previous settlement of Jews from Safed had failed. In August 1882 the first organized 39 families (228 persons), emigrated; the nucleus of this group was formed by those from Moineşti who founded the village of Rosh Pinnah. The central committee also purchased another 6,000 dunams, and Zikhron Ya'akov was founded with 386 settlers. The creation of these two colonies gave an impetus to the *aliyah*, and until the end of 1882 a total of 1,322 settlers had left Romania. In the summer of the same year a movement for agricultural training was started on estates leased by Jews. At the same time, a number of youth organizations held a joint meeting at Galaţi in December 1882 with delegates from 12 towns and founded Aẓilei Benei Israel. In April 1883 a second meeting of the youth organizations took place at which the integration with the Yishuv Ereẓ Israel movement was decided upon. On Sept. 17, 1883, the third meeting of the Yishuv Ereẓ Israel movement took place in Galaţi, and it was decided that the administration of Zikhron Ya'akov would be handed over to Baron Edmond de Rothschild, since the central committee in Romania could not provide sufficiently for the economic needs of the village. In November 1883 Rosh Pinnah, which was in the same situation, also passed to Rothschild's administration. The 60 branches of the movement were dissolved one by one. The central committee ceased its activity in 1884. The pre-Zionist movement was resurrected again in Romania under the influence of the movement in Russia. Between 1890 and 1892, branches of Ḥovevei Zion were formed in some towns. By 1895 such branches existed in 31 towns and two conferences had been held. A central committee was elected under the management of Pineles, and once again groups of potential settlers organized. A plot of 11,000 dunams was acquired in Brustras and a group of 80 families from Jassy, together with another 16 families from Bulgaria, acquired another 18,000 dunams on the east side of the Jordan. Herzl's *Der Judenstaat* was published in 1896, and by the end of that year the first Romanian translation appeared in Botoşani. Pineles started to collect the signatures of those who wished to settle in Ereẓ Israel. Some 50,000 Romanian Jews signed the petition. Shortly before the First Zionist Congress in Basle (1897), the third meeting of Ḥovevei Zion took place in Galaţi, expressing support for Herzl's political Zionism. The First Zionist Congress was opened by a speech of the oldest delegate Karpel Lippe. Pineles was elected vice president of the Congress. During the fourth conference of Ḥovevei Zion in 1898, the Basle Program was unanimously accepted. The number of Zionist groups increased from 26 in 1897 to 136 in 1899.

The deadlock in which the World Zionist Movement found itself caused the number of active Romanian Zionist groups to decrease from 136 in 1899 to 56 in 1911. An additional reason for the decline was the creation of the Union of Native Jews (UEP) in 1910. The Union, which dedicated itself to the fight for local Jewish emancipation, attracted the active participation of many Zionist leaders. But the younger generation of Zionists wanted a Jewish national emphasis within the movement for political emancipation. A group of young scholars, directed by Jacob Nacht, fought against the trend toward assimilation in the UEP by encouraging Jewish cultural activities, e.g., Romanian translations of Hebrew and Yiddish literature and the introduction of Hebrew as a living language in schools. In this spirit the weekly paper *Ha-Tikvah*, edited by Leon Gold, was published in Galaţi in 1914. It had a great influence on Jewish life in Romania and included among its contributors A.L. *Zissu, Mattathias Friedman, and J. Nacht, as well as almost all the more important Jewish writers of Romania.

Between the Two World Wars. In March 1919 the Zionist leadership of Galati published a program of Jewish demands to be presented at the Versailles peace negotiations. It demanded complete political, cultural, and religious autonomy for Jews as a national minority. Under the influence of the young Zionist leaders, the UEP rejected the attempts of the Romanian government to evade again the problem of Jewish citizenship by involved juridical proceedings, as was the case after the Congress of Berlin in 1878. The Jewish population followed the instructions of the UEP leaders and boycotted the government's equivocal laws on Jewish citizenship. Romanian Zionists, together with delegates from the UEP, were included in the Comité des Délégations Juives at the Versailles Peace Conference. After the Jews finally obtained collective naturalization in 1920 as a result of the Versailles peace treaty, there remained the problem of Jewish participation in elections and in the political life of the country. The UEP supported the idea of Jewish candidates. Therefore, in the next year, the UEP joined the Zionists in presenting a separate Jewish list. Because of fraudulent election procedures, not one Jewish deputy was elected. It was only in 1926 that the first Jewish national deputies entered parliament, but they were representatives of territories annexed by Romania after the war: Bessarabia, Bukovina, and Transylvania.

The Zionist Organization in the rest of Romania went on with its policy of neutrality in internal politics. In 1919, at a Zionist conference in Bucharest, it was decided to transfer the central headquarters from Galaţi to Bucharest and to draw the leadership more and more from the younger generation. In the new era after the Balfour Declaration, Zionism became a mass movement whose principal activity was the collection of funds. In 1924 the Zionist group Renaşterea Noastră ("Our Revival") was created, many of whose members had belonged to the student association Hasmonaea. Later, Renaşterea became affiliated with the radical Zionist faction. In 1930, as a result of Renaşterea's initiative, the Jewish Party was created in Muntenia and Moldavia; it included Zionists, especially from the intellectual younger generation. Along with the Jewish-national deputies elected from the annexed territories, such as Michael Landau from Bessarabia, S. Singer and Mişu Weissman were elected to parliament from Muntenia and Moldavia in 1931 and 1932, respectively. At the same time such Zionist groups as Ẓe'irei Zion, Po'alei Zion, Mizrachi, and the Revisionists were formed. Zionist leadership had been drawn from the ranks of the General Zionists until 1930, when the first coalition of radicals and Ẓe'irei Zion was elected to the leadership. The Zionist youth movements remained organized along the traditional lines existing in the World Zionist Organization.

In 1920 Romania's Zionist Organization tried to create a school for teachers of Hebrew at Jassy, but it only functioned one year because the Romanian authorities refused to authorize it. In 1925 a *hakhsharah* farm to train *ḥalutzim* (pioneers for Palestine) was created in Jassy. Between the two world wars Zionist organizations functioned in 71 Romanian towns, and a central Zionist Council was established in Bucharest. WIZO, which had 5,000 members in its branches in 33 towns, set up 17 kindergartens in which the language of instruction was Hebrew. It also established the agricultural and housekeeping school Ayanot at Nes Ẓiyyonah in Palestine. On Mt. Carmel between 1922 and 1925, 3,500 dunams (875 acres) of land were acquired by a Romanian group and given the name Aḥuzah (actually Aḥuzat Herbert Samuel), on which some of its 1,000 members settled. Another Romanian society bought land in the Haifa Bay area.

The Zionist Press. During the interwar period, many Zionist magazines were issued in Romanian. Among the more important publications were: *Ştiri din lumea Evreiască* ("News from the Jewish World"), the official organ of the Zionist Organization; *Renaşterea Noastră* ("Our Revival"), the organ of the radical group, which also expressed the point of view of the Jewish Party; *Drumuri Noi* ("New Roads"), first the Revisionist organ, then the organ of the Jewish State party; and *Tribuna Evreiască* ("The Jewish Platform"; Jassy). In addition, the monthly magazine *Hasmonaea*, organ of the Zionist students, was published regularly.

World War II Period. After the invasion of Poland in 1939, Romania became a transit route for *aliyah* from Eastern Europe. Britain, however, pressured the Romanian government to stop the flow of *aliyah* from and through the country. At the beginning of 1940 the collection of Zionist funds was forbidden, but it was authorized again on Feb. 26, 1940, under the condition that the Zionist leadership would not encourage emigration. In September 1940, however, the government of Ion *Antonescu, which approved of Jewish emigration, came to power and negotiations were held between Zionists and the government on emigration plans. The Zionist Organization continued to work even after December 1941, when all other Jewish organizations were dissolved. The Zionist Organization was dissolved only in August 1942, by the order of Gustav Richter, Eichmann's agent in Romania. However, the Zionist leadership and youth movements clandestinely continued their activities, while the semi-official organ of the German legation, *Bukarester Tageblatt*, carried on a defamatory campaign against the Zionists. The Romanian government continued to negotiate with the Zionists about emigration, and at the same time a Jewish underground, in which Zionist leaders also participated, was formed. From the beginning of 1939 until the very capitulation of Romania in August 1944, 31 ships with more than 13,000 emigrants, some of whom were refugees from Poland, Hungary, and Czechoslovakia, left from Romanian harbors. The Palestine Office of the Zionist Organization in Bucharest succeeded in continuing its activity in the guise of a travel agency. Detecting these underground activities, the Germans initiated the imprisonment of the leaders of the Zionist Organization and the youth movements in January and February of 1944. Diplomatic intervention, especially by the International Red Cross, obtained their release, however. Imminent German defeat and the approach of the Allies allowed A.L. Zissu, a Zionist leader, to obtain from Romanian ministers in June 1944 the authorization to create an emigration office which was to serve as a cover for the underground Zionist Executive. In order to report on the situation of Jews in Romania, the Zionist leaders maintained contact secretly with the Jewish Agency in Jerusalem during the whole period of underground activity.

Post-World War II Period. Soon after the cessation of hostilities in Romania in August 1944, the Zionist Organization resumed its legal activity and attracted many members because of the desire of most Jews to emigrate. The Zionist parties and youth organizations were reestablished, and Zionist weekly magazines began to appear. From 1944 to 1948 a Zionist publishing house, Bicurim, published about 80 volumes of translations from Hebrew literature and works of Zionist history and ideology. Although Britain continued to restrict Jewish migration to Palestine according to the White Paper of 1939, 30,000 Romanian Jews entered Palestine "illegally" before 1948. After World War II the Jewish Communists founded the Jewish Democratic Committee, in which at first the Zionist Socialists also participated. But the latter were eliminated after the creation of the State of Israel as the Jewish Democratic Committee started an anti-Zionist campaign. As a result of the pressure exerted by the Jewish Democratic Committee, the Zionist Organization and its constituent parties were forced to dissolve at the end of 1948. During the summer of 1950 the leaders of the Zionists and the Zionist youth movements were arrested, tried, and condemned to prison. Some were accused of spying and others of inciting against the Communist regime. Finally, in 1955, under a general political amnesty, the leaders were liberated. (Three of them died in prison and some others soon after their arrival in Israel.) From the end of 1949 until the end of 1952 112,652 Romanian Jews left for Israel. Then, for a period of ten years, emigration was effectively stopped, only to start again at various times since 1962. The Jewish Democratic Committee was dissolved in 1953. All in all, about three-quarters of the Romanian Jews who survived the Nazi terror went to Israel.

[Theodor Lavi]

In Russia

Theodor Herzl's activities engendered a revival among the Ḥovevei Zion movement in Russia, and large new groups joined the movement, which soon encompassed masses of people. The number of Zionist societies in Russia increased from 23 to 373 in 1897, the year of the First Zionist Congress. There were 877 societies by May 1899; 1,034 in 1900; and 1,572 in 1903–04. At the First Zionist Congress the Russian delegation accounted for one-third of all the delegates (66 out of 197), among them L. Motzkin, H. Schapira, M. Mandelstamm, V. Tiomkin, and M.M. Ussishkin, and four delegates from Russia were elected there to the Zionist General Council, each of them with a specific function. Y. *Bernstein-Cohen of Kishinev headed the Zionist center of correspondence in Russia (the so-called "Post Bureau"), Mandelstamm was responsible for financial matters. Rabbi S. Mohilever of Bialystok headed the center for cultural activities, and I. Jasinowski of Warsaw headed the center for Zionist literature. For all practical purposes the "Post Bureau" became the organizational center of the Zionist movement in Russia until before the Fifth Zionist Congress (Basle, 1901), when it was replaced by the office of information headed by V. Jacobson. The delegates divided the country into districts and held district conferences. In 1898, prior to the Second Zionist Congress (Basle, 1898), the majority of the first Russian Zionists convened in Warsaw consisting of 160 delegates from 93 cities and towns, among them 14 Orthodox rabbis, supported the demand that the practical settlement activity in Ereẓ Israel continue, as against the position of the "political" Zionists, who supported Herzl's concept that small-scale "infiltration" into the country might harm the prospects of achieving the Charter. Eventually a compromise decision was formulated. The demand of the rabbis at the Zionist Congress to create a rabbinic committee to supervise Zionist cultural work was rejected. Rabbi E.A. Rabinowich of Poltava and other rabbis left the movement, became its opponents, and later organized in Kovno, together with other ultra-Orthodox rabbis, Ha-Lishkah ha-Sheḥorah ("The Black Bureau"), which published books and pamphlets against the Zionist movement.

Among the Russian delegates at the Second Zionist Congress were Chaim Weizmann, Nahum Sokolow, and Shemaryahu Levin, who played increasingly dominant roles in the Zionist movement. At the Fourth Zionist Congress (London, 1900) Russian Zionists were represented by more than 200 delegates, and at the Fifth Congress (Basle, 1901) the *Democratic Faction, headed by Weizmann, M. Buber, Motzkin, and B. Feiwel, was established. It demanded a much greater emphasis on Jewish education and culture on the part of the Zionist Organization. They were opposed by J.J. *Reines and the Orthodox wing forming the Mizrachi movement, which opposed the anticipated secular character of Zionist cultural activity.

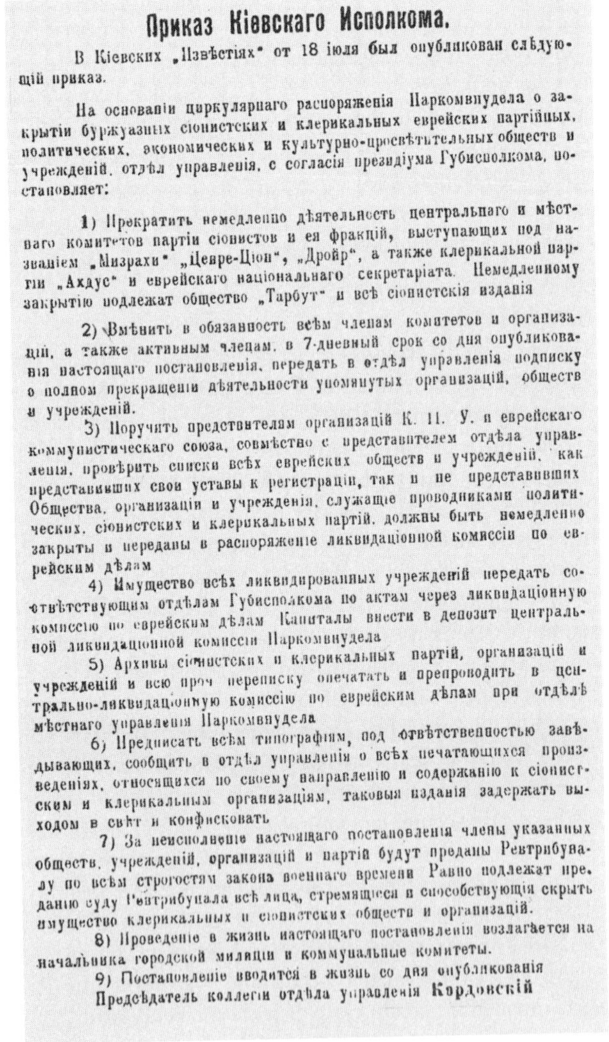
Приказ Кіевскаго Исполкома.

В Кіевских „Извѣстіях" от 18 іюля был опубликован слѣдующій приказ.

На основаніи циркулярнаго распоряженія Наркомвнудела о закрытіи буржуазных сіонистских и клерикальных еврейских партійных, политических, экономических и культурно-просвѣтительных обществ и учрежденій, отдѣл управленія, с согласія президіума Губисполкома, постановляет:

1) Прекратить немедленно дѣятельность центральнаго и мѣстнаго комитетов партіи сіонистов и ея фракцій, выступающих под названіем „Мизрахи" „Цеире-Ціон", „Дройр", а также клерикальной партіи „Ахдус" и еврейскаго національнаго секретаріата. Немедленному закрытію подлежат общество „Тарбут" и всѣ сіонистскія изданія

2) Вмѣнить в обязанность всѣм членам комитетов и организацій, а также активным членам, в 7-дневный срок со дня опубликованія настоящаго постановленія, передать в отдѣл управленія подписку о полном прекращеніи дѣятельности упомянутых организацій, обществ и учрежденій.

3) Поручить представителям организацій К. П. У. и еврейскаго коммунистическаго союза, совмѣстно с представителем отдѣла управленія, провѣрить списки всѣх еврейских обществ и учрежденій, как представивших свои уставы к регистраціи, так и не представивших Общества, организаціи и учрежденія, служащіе проводниками политических, сіонистских и клерикальных партій, должны быть немедленно закрыты и переданы в распоряженіе ликвидаціонной комиссіи по еврейским дѣлам

4) Имущество всѣх ликвидированных учрежденій передать соотвѣтствующим отдѣлам Губисполкома по актам через ликвидаціонную комиссію по еврейским дѣлам Капиталы внести в депозит центральной ликвидаціонной комиссіи Наркомвнудела

5) Архивы сіонистских и клерикальных партій, организацій и учрежденій и всю проч переписку опечатать и препроводить в центрально-ликвидаціонную комиссію по еврейским дѣлам при отдѣлѣ мѣстнаго управленія Наркомвнудела

6) Предписать всѣм типографіям, под отвѣтственностью завѣдывающих, сообщить в отдѣл управленія о всѣх печатающихся произведеніях, относящихся по своему направленію и содержанію к сіонистским и клерикальным организаціям, таковыя изданія задержать выходом в свѣт и конфисковать

7) За неисполненіе настоящаго постановленія члены указанных обществ, учрежденій, организацій и партій будут преданы Ревтрибуналу по всѣм строгостям закона военнаго времени Равно подлежат преданію суду Ревтрибунала всѣ лица, стремящіеся и способствующія скрыть имущество клерикальных и сіонистских обществ и организацій.

8) Проведеніе в жизнь настоящаго постановленія возлагается на начальника городской милиціи и коммунальные комитеты.

9) Постановленіе вводится в жизнь со дня опубликованія

Председатель коллегіи отдѣла управленія Кордовскій

Order of the Kiev local authority closing all Zionist organizations and institutions, July 18, 1919. Courtesy A. Rafaeli-Zenziper, Archive for Russian Zionism, Tel Aviv.

The second All-Russian Zionist Conference was held in 1902 in Minsk (see *Minsk Conference) with the participation of 500 delegates, representing some 75,000 shekel holders. It was the only legal Zionist conference in czarist Russia and aroused much public interest. About 160 delegates represented Mizrachi and about 60 represented the Democratic Faction. After a long and stormy debate on education, a compromise was reached recognizing both educational trends, the secular and the religious.

In 1903 the Russian delegation to the Sixth Zionist Congress (Basle) were the prime movers of the opposition to the Uganda Scheme, which was finally rejected (after Herzl's death) at the Seventh Congress (Basle, 1905), where a minority group seceded and created the Jewish Territorial Organization (see *Territorialism). While territorialism did not gain much ground among most Zionists in Russia, its influence grew in the budding Zionist labor movement. The Zionist Socialists (called SS according to their Russian name Sionisty Sotsialisty) repudiated the solution of the Jewish problem in Ereẓ Israel, devoting their main attention to Jewish migration, which they believed would eventually lead to settlement on a specific territory and thus solve the Jewish problem. Another group in Russian Jewry, known as the "Sejmists," rejected both Zionist and territorialist solutions and advocated instead the struggle for officially recognized Jewish national autonomy in the Diaspora countries. The Zionist Socialist movement Po'alei Zion, under the leadership of B. *Borochov, emerged in 1905–06. Another movement of Socialist-oriented moderate Zionists was Ẓe'irei Zion, which eventually became linked to Ha-Po'el ha-Ẓa'ir in Ereẓ Israel. These movements, which represented Labor Zionism in Russia, soon became popular among the younger generation and the intelligentsia. The main force opposing Zionism in Russian Jewry was also a social democratic party, the Bund, which regarded Yiddish as the sole national language of the Jews and fought against the Zionists and against the cultivation of modern Hebrew.

Prior to the 1905 Revolution, the Zionist movement in Russia abstained from any participation in Russian politics. This abstention was based on the original Zionist concept of "negation of the Diaspora" and rejection of the possibility of Jewish national existence in Russia. The 1905 Revolution brought a radical change in this position. An All-Russian Zionist Conference, known as the Helsingfors Conference (1906) formulated a new Zionist program, that of "synthetic Zionism," which combined the basic negation of Jewish future in exile with the struggle not only for equal rights in the existing Diaspora, but also for the right of self-determination as a national minority group (see *Helsingfors Program). Consequently the Zionists nominated their own candidates in the election to the First Duma, and five out of 12 elected Jewish deputies were Zionists. In the Second Duma one of six Jewish delegates elected was a Zionist. When the czarist government renewed its political repression in 1907, the Zionist movement, like other political trends in Russia, became practically paralyzed.

The Legal Status. Russian Zionists did not request official permission to organize because they did not expect to receive such legitimation for a movement whose world center was located abroad. At first, although the authorities knew of the Zionist activities, on the whole they did not interfere. Later a change for the worse took place in the official attitude toward the Zionist movement and to Jews in general, which culminated in the spring of 1903 in the Kishinev pogrom. In June 1903 the czarist minister of the interior, Plehve, issued a directive prohibiting any Zionist activity in Russia. Herzl then traveled to Russia in order to influence the Russian government in favor of Zionism and to abolish the anti-Zionist decree. Plehve promised Herzl that the government would not interfere, provided that the Zionists did not engage in the organization of Russian Jewry on a national scale, but rather encouraged emigration.

The attitude of the authorities, however, did not improve substantially. The holding of public meetings was prohibited. The Zionists were able, however, to continue their educational and cultural activities, the collection of shekels, and the sale of shares of the Jewish Colonial Trust. Though in November 1904 a Zionist delegation learned from the liberal minister of the interior, Sviatopolsk-Mirsky, that the movement would not be persecuted, a turn for the worse took place again. The resolutions of the Helsingfors Conference increased the government's suspicions. The Zionist Organization was declared illegal. Licenses for local groups named "Palestine" were revoked, and activities on behalf of the Jewish National Fund (JNF) were prohibited (1907). Then David Wolffsohn, president of the World Zionist Organization, went to St. Petersburg (1908) and was promised that activity for the JNF and the Jewish Colonial Trust would be facilitated but the Zionist Organization would not be legalized. In 1910 the persecutions increased, and when the Zionist central committee of Russia met in Moscow with the Russian members of the Zionist General Council, some of them, including the editor of *Haolam*, A. *Druyanow, were brought to trial. The central committee was then transferred to St. Petersburg and the editorial board of *Haolam* to Odessa (1912). The police did not harm the editorial board of the Zionist weekly *Razsvet* and Zionist leaders in St. Petersburg.

The Second and Third Aliyah. The pogroms in Kishinev and Gomel and other forms of oppression, together with the deep disappointment caused by the failure of the 1905 Revolution, stimulated a renewed movement of migration and settlement in Ereẓ Israel. Israel *Belkind went from Ereẓ Israel to Russia seeking support to establish an agricultural school there for the orphans of the Kishinev pogrom. M. Ussishkin, in his pamphlet *Our Program*, and Josef *Vitkin's call from Ereẓ Israel to Jewish youth in the Diaspora for *aliyah* and settlement, contributed to a new wave of pioneering migration. Thus the Second Aliyah started, and it included members of different trends, such as Ẓe'irei Zion, Po'alei Zion, Bilu he-Ḥadash, etc. Among the pioneers were men like Berl *Katznelson, David Ben-Gurion, Izhak Ben-Zvi, Joseph *Sprinzak, and others who later became leaders of the *yishuv* and the Zionist movement during the Mandatory period and during Israel's independence. Middle-class settlers from Russia participated in founding a residential neighborhood near Jaffa, Aḥuzat Bayit, which became Tel Aviv. Settlement societies were founded in various cities in Russia. After World War I the Third Aliyah started as a movement of survivors of the pogroms in the Ukraine and of pioneers who followed Joseph *Trumpeldor.

The Russian Revolution of February 1917 removed all the official obstacles from the Zionist movement, which immediately grew tremendously. An All-Russian Zionist Conference met in Petrograd on May 24, 1917, and its 552 delegates represented 140,000 shekel holders (in 1913 there were only 26,000 shekel holders). The conference reaffirmed the Helsingfors Program and succeeded in drafting a unified program of all Zionist groups for the forthcoming elections to the Russian Constituent Assembly. The newly elected central committee was instructed to take the initiative in convening an All-Russian Jewish Congress. This conference, the first after 1902, was attended by Trumpeldor, who spread his idea about creating a Jewish army to march through the Caucasus to Ereẓ Israel. About 20 delegates supported Jabotinsky's pro-British activity in establishing the Jewish Legion, but the overwhelming majority adhered to the official Zionist neutralism in the World War. The Balfour Declaration of Nov. 2, 1917, which put an end to this neutralist position, made Zionism the dominant trend in Russian Jewry, and in the elections to the All-Russian Jewish Congress the Zionists received the majority of votes. Wartime conditions made the meeting of the Congress impossible, but a Jewish National Council was established in which the various Jewish parties were represented in proportion to the number of seats they had won in the elections to the congress. The Zionists also maintained the Tarbut organization with a network of more than 250 Hebrew-language schools and other educational institutions.

The October (Bolshevik) Revolution of 1917 did not, at first, affect Zionist activities. A Palestine Week, proclaimed in spring 1918, was successfully conducted in hundreds of Jewish communities. Palestine Offices were established in various cities, among them Petrograd and Minsk. Efforts were made to mobilize private capital for investment in Palestine, and various companies were established for the construction of residential and business premises, an oil refinery in Haifa, etc. Trumpeldor founded the *He-Ḥalutz movement. A conference of 149 delegates from 40 Jewish communities in central Russia, which took place in Moscow in July 1918, had a Zionist majority. In the Ukraine, where the Soviet regime was finally established in February 1919, the Zionist movement was in 1918 the dominant force in Ukrainian Jewry. In the elections to Jewish community councils (*kehillot*) there, the Zionists received 54.5% of the vote, and in the elections to the provisional Jewish National Council of the Ukraine in November 1918, about 54% voted for Zionist candidates.

Liquidation and Resurrection in the U.S.S.R. Under Soviet rule Zionism soon became the object of repression and persecution. Zionist parties and organizations were outlawed, their clandestine meetings and regional conferences dispersed by force, and their participants and delegates arrested. The Hebrew language itself was gradually proscribed. Some underground Zionist activity continued, however, in the first decade of the Soviet regime, including the emergence of the pioneering youth movement Ha-Shomer ha-Ẓa'ir as an important factor among young Zionists striving to reach Palestine. In the forefront of the anti-Zionist campaign stood the "Jewish section" (*Yevsektsiya) of the ruling Bolshevik party, whose task it was to eradicate "clericalism" and "bourgeois nationalism" from Jewish life. Various attempts made in the 1920s to achieve a permissive, or at least tolerant, attitude to some aspects of Zionist activity, mainly in the cultural field and emigration to Palestine (such as the semi-official negotiations of the member of the Zionist Executive, M.D. Eder, during his visit to Moscow in 1921 or the exchanges of a Moscow Zionist, Isaac Rabinovich, with high-ranking Soviet personalities in 1926) proved futile. However, until the late 1920s a number of Jews convicted for Zionist activities were allowed to leave for Palestine.

From 1949, and particularly in 1952–53, "Zionism" became an odious catchword in Stalin's anti-Jewish campaigns (see *Slánsky Trials, *Doctors' Plot). After Stalin's death this trend was dormant for several years, until it emerged again under Khrushchev in the 1960s and with particular virulence after the Six-Day War of 1967, when the almost daily attacks against "World Zionism" in the Soviet mass media and "political-education" system achieved an intensity similar to the antisemitic propaganda of czarist times. Meanwhile, from 1948 Soviet Jews showed more and more signs of interest in, and attachment to, the State of Israel, demonstrating their sympathy for it and often their desire to migrate and settle there. These demonstrations took various forms, from many thousands of Jews attending synagogues when members of the Israeli diplomatic mission came to pray or many young Jews who came to greet Israeli delegations to international youth festivals, Israeli sports teams, or folk singers visiting the U.S.S.R., to the famous mass gatherings of Jewish youth singing Hebrew songs and openly declaring their attachment to the Jewish nation and to Israel on Simḥat Torah in and around synagogues of Moscow, Leningrad, and other cities.

This movement became more and more pronounced and daring from 1969, when an increasing number of Jews from various Soviet regions addressed fully signed petitions and protests to the Soviet authorities, the government of Israel, the United Nations, and even to Communist parties in the West, demanding their right – under the Universal Declaration of Human Rights signed by the U.S.S.R., and a convention including a clause that every person has the right to leave any country, including his own, recently ratified by the Supreme Soviet – to leave the Soviet Union for "repatriation to the Jewish ancestral homeland in Israel." There is evidence that this spontaneous movement – which can be defined as "neo-Zionist" – also encompassed private groups of young Jews studying Hebrew, Jewish history, about the State of Israel, etc. The Soviet authorities, particularly the security services, attempted to deter them by arrests, show trials, and other measures of intimidation, but the Jews maintained their campaign for the right to settle in Israel. For further details see *Russia.

[Israel Klausner]

In South Africa

The Zionist Organization found enthusiastic support in South Africa among the new immigrants, mostly from Lithuania, rather than among the Anglicized minority of the "old-timers." The first Zionist associations were established in Cape Town (1897) and Johannesburg (1898). By the end of 1898, a dozen Zionist societies with some 5,000 members were already in existence. A year later the first women's Zionist association was set up in Pretoria. As early as December 1898, 12 years before the Union of South Africa came into being as a political entity, the South African Zionist Federation, including Zionist bodies on the whole South African subcontinent, was established. It was represented at the Third Zionist Congress in Basle (1899) by two delegates. After the Boer War, which impeded the growth of the movement, the Zionist Federation was recognized by the authorities as representative of South African Jewry and entrusted with official tasks, such as the repatriation of Jewish war refugees. Later, this official recognition was transferred to the general communal organization, the South African Jewish Board of Deputies, which, in the course of years, sometimes experienced competition and friction with the federation, but mostly worked in friendly cooperation with it.

In 1908 the *Zionist Record* was founded in Johannesburg as the official organ of the federation; it became the most important South African Jewish newspaper. The sympathies of the leaders of the Afrikaans community, like the generals Louis Botha and J.B.M. Hertzog, were conducive to the progress of Zionism and to its high standing in the country. Field Marshall Jan Christiaan *Smuts was an avowed friend of Zionism and one of the architects of the Balfour Declaration. In later years the Zionist Federation secured his powerful support whenever a major crisis threatened the Zionist cause.

The financial contributions of South African Jewry to the Zionist funds have been outstanding. From 1926 South

Africa occupied the second place in the world (after the U.S.) in fundraising for the Keren Hayesod; its per capita contribution – £1.16 in the 1920s – was by far the largest. The federation's growth is also reflected by the following figures: in 1921 there were 177 bodies affiliated with it, in 1930 about 200, and in 1949 no fewer than 350. Also the Rhodesias, Kenya, and even Belgian Congo then belonged to its jurisdiction. In 1932 the South African Women's Zionist Council was established to coordinate women's work for all Zionist purposes. It became affiliated with WIZO and in 1967 numbered some 16,000 members. The South African Zionist Federation also has a notably strong following among youth. A census taken shortly before the 30th South African Zionist Conference in 1967 showed that four youth movements affiliated with the federation numbered 6,800 active members, divided into 297 units throughout the country, and led by 556 youth group workers.

South African Zionists distinguished themselves as a highly efficient movement that succeeded in assuming and retaining leadership of the Jewish community at large. They have attained outstanding achievements in the fields of organization, financial support of Israel, the building up of an impressive network of schools, and in *aliyah*. About 6,000 Jews from South Africa settled in Israel, including members of collective settlements, men of private initiative, scientists, and public servants.

The South African Zionist Federation has been headed by able leaders, from S. Goldreich (first chairman) to H. Morris and N. Kirschner to B. Gering and I.A. Maisels. Under the successive direction of Jack Alexander, Zvi Infeld, and Sidney Berg, it gained a reputation for its organizational structure and efficiency. Divided geographically into provincial councils and functionally into some 20 departments, it covers a variety of Zionist activities, including fundraising, and embraces all the Zionists of the country, both party members and independents. Up to the early 1930s parties played no significant role in the federation; later the Zionist Revisionists and the Zionist Socialists became especially prominent. It was not until 1946 that the Executive of the federation was elected on a party basis, but it continued to include nonparty members. The number of shekel holders was exceptionally high; it sometimes approached and even exceeded 50% of the adult Jewish population (43,605 shekels in 1946 and 42,949 in 1960).

During World War II the federation also aided refugees passing through South Africa and accorded valuable material and moral support to the "illegal immigrants" who had been deported from Palestine and detained in Mauritius. In 1943 the federation arranged a "plebiscite," and its three points – to open the gates of Palestine to Jewish immigration, to set up a Jewish army, and to establish Palestine as a Jewish Commonwealth – were endorsed by 37,000 Jews. No fewer than 3,000 volunteers offered their services in the War of Independence (1948), and 700 were accepted and fought in Israel. During the period of the Six-Day War, 782 volunteers arrived in Israel from South Africa, but several times this number had registered.

[Aharon Zwergbaum]

In the United States

Jewish immigrants who came to the United States from Eastern Europe in the early 1880s brought the ideas of the Ḥibbat Zion movement with them, and by 1890. Ḥovevei Zion organizations existed in the large Jewish communities of New York, Chicago, Baltimore, Milwaukee, Boston, Philadelphia, and Cleveland. At the same time, newspapers propagating Ḥibbat Zion ideas appeared, two of which were *Shulamit*, edited by J.I. *Bluestone in Yiddish, and *Ha-Pisgah* ("The Summit," 1888–89), a Hebrew paper edited by W. Schur. Following a mass meeting in New York on May 4, 1898, supporters of Zionism established an organization which *Die Welt* called the Zentralverein der amerikanischen Zionisten. Other Zionist organizations appeared in the months before the First Zionist Congress at Basle (1897). Opposition was expressed by upper-class Jews and Reform rabbis. The *Central Conference of American Rabbis passed a resolution in July 1897 denouncing Zionism in sharp terms:

> Resolved that we totally disapprove of any attempt for the establishment of a Jewish state. Such attempts show a misunderstanding of Israel's mission which, from the narrow political and national field, has been expanded to the promotion among the whole human race of the broad and universalistic religion first proclaimed by the Jewish prophets.

By 1898 two major Zionist organizations developed in New York City: the Federation of Zionist Societies of Greater New York, under the leadership of Richard *Gottheil, and the League of Zionist Societies of the United States of North America, under Rabbi Philip *Klein and Michael Singer. They united in February 1898 into the Federation of Zionists of Greater New York and Vicinity. Consolidation at the national level in July 1898 resulted in the establishment of the Federation of American Zionists (FAZ), under the presidency of Gottheil, with Stephen S. Wise as first secretary.

Despite initial progress, the FAZ encountered great organizational difficulties. Many Zionist organizations did not recognize its authority. The most recalcitrant were the scores of independent Zionist organizations in New York based on *landsmannschaften and in Chicago on the Knights of Zion, who organized in October 1898 under the leadership of Leon Zolotkoff. Only in 1913 did the Knights accept the authority of the FAZ. Another obstacle to the growth of the FAZ was the opposition to Zionism from the left, i.e., from East European immigrants who adhered to Socialist organizations and regarded socialism and trade unionism as the solution to Jewish problems as well. Difficulties were increased by the reluctance of the membership, which was primarily from Eastern Europe, to accept the leadership of "Germans," who differed from them in their way of life as well as social class.

In 1902 Jacob de *Haas moved to the U.S. as editor of the FAZ's official paper, *The Maccabean*, and secretary of the organization. He tried to cope with the various organizational and administrative difficulties and to include more organizations under Richard Gottheil's leadership. De Haas instituted the "Shekel Day" and developed elaborate Zionist propaganda. Nevertheless, the FAZ was plagued by financial difficulties. In 1904 Gottheil resigned and Harry *Friedenwald became president. In early 1905 de Haas also resigned and was replaced by Judah Magnes as secretary. With the two new leaders, the Zionist orientation of the FAZ changed. Gottheil and de Haas were "political Zionists" who supported Herzl on the Uganda issue, whereas Friedenwald and Magnes were "cultural Zionists" who tried to adapt Zionism to the American scene. Other important cultural Zionists were Solomon Schechter, president of the Jewish Theological Seminary, and Israel *Friedlaender, also of the Seminary, a Bible scholar and communal leader. These "cultural Zionists" saw Zionism as a renaissance of traditional Jewish values and check on assimilation. Although Ereẓ Israel was for them a cultural center, they did not negate the Diaspora, which they viewed as equal in importance.

The first Labor Zionist (Po'alei Zion) organization was founded in New York City in March 1903. Its ancillary Jewish National Workers Alliance (Farband) was established as a benevolent organization in 1910, in part to attract members who might join the Socialist, anti-Zionist Workmen's Circle. In its initial stages, Po'alei Zion was rejected by the Socialists and regarded with suspicion by the Zionists. Labor Zionism combined Jewish national aspirations with a social philosophy dedicated to the establishment of a new political and economic order both in Ereẓ Israel and the Diaspora. During its first decade, the platform included as priorities: the furthering of Jewish settlement in Palestine, the struggle against assimilation, aid to Jewish workers, and the building of Yiddish folk schools. Its organs, *Der Yidisher Kemfer* (1905, with interruptions) and *The Jewish Frontier* (1934), exerted wide influence, especially in liberal and progressive circles outside Zionist ranks (the latter under the editorship of Ḥayyim *Greenberg).

In 1911 a new FAZ administration whose members were mostly East European was elected. Friedenwald remained honorary president, but the affairs of the organization were handed to the chairman of the executive, Louis *Lipsky. He shared the burden with his associates Abraham Goldberg, Bernard *Rosenblatt, and Senior Abel, who founded the Yiddish organ of the movement, *Dos Yidishe Folk* (1909). Until World War I attempts were made to improve administration, notably by Henrietta *Szold, who functioned as secretary between 1910 and 1911. Newly founded organizations gradually established ties with the FAZ: Po'alei Zion, Hadassah Women's Organization, founded by Henrietta Szold (1912), and the Mizrachi Organization of America (1914). The latter was established in 1911 by Meir Berlin (*Bar-Ilan). In time it became the backbone of the World Mizrachi Organization by virtue of its numbers and resources.

World War I and After. Early in 1914 the Federation of American Zionists, and American Zionism, was small and weak; its membership was static and it was suffering from financial stress. It did enjoy the support of the *Day* and *Morning Journal*, two leading Yiddish dailies. The *Forward*, however, was sharply anti-Zionist out of socialist conviction until it became more sympathetic during the 1920s. With the outbreak of World War I, international Zionist activity became largely centered in the U.S., where the Provisional Committee for General Zionist Affairs (PZC) was established. Louis D. Brandeis, who had his first contact with Zionism through Jacob de Haas, Nahum Sokolow, and Bernard *Richards, accepted its chairmanship. He took up his role with great energy and drew to the Zionist movement Felix *Frankfurter, Louis Kirstein, and Bernard *Flexner, all of whom were also attracted by its democratic and progressive ideas. Under Brandeis' able leadership, the financial situation of the FAZ improved, and membership and political influence increased. Brandeis and his associates were influenced through Horace *Kallen and others by the idea of cultural pluralism, the essence of which is that America is a nation of nations in which different cultures are blended. This theory served to reconcile "Americanism" with Zionism.

After Brandeis' elevation to the Supreme Court in June 1916, he resigned as active chairman but continued to lead the FAZ through his associates, notably de Haas. In 1916 the Po'alei Zion and Mizrachi organizations withdrew from the Provisional Zionist Committee, and in 1917 the federation reorganized all its branches into the *Zionist Organization of America (ZOA), which was based on territorial districts. Brandeis became honorary president, Judge Julian W. *Mack president, Stephen S. Wise and Harry Friedenwald vice presidents.

After the war Brandeis visited Palestine and formed plans to build its future on the basis of large-scale investment and centrally controlled public corporations. He wanted the ZOA to collect funds for specific economic projects. At the London Conference of 1920 his views clashed with those of Weizmann, who wanted to found the Keren Hayesod as a general fund to improve the economy and settlement methods of Palestine, as well as to establish educational institutions. The Brandeis group refused to accept the decisions of the World Zionist Organization, represented by Weizmann. At the Cleveland convention of the ZOA in 1921, in which the issues were debated, a majority rejected Brandeis' views, and as a result he and his close associates seceded from the mainstream of Zionist activity in the U.S. and concentrated their efforts on fostering the economic development of Palestine, as, e.g., through the Palestine Economic Corporation. Louis Lipsky, who led the opposition to Brandeis, became president, with Abraham Goldberg, Emanuel Neumann, Morris *Rothenberg, and others as his collaborators. The Lipsky administration remained in office until 1930. During this period the ZOA concentrated on fundraising but was not very successful. It established the Keren Hayesod in the United States.

Article 4 of the League of Nations Mandate had made specific provision for the recognition of a "Jewish agency" to advise and cooperate with the administration of Palestine as representative of the Jewish people U.S. Jewry, by reason of its tremendous numbers and resources, was a decisive factor in "enlarging" the Jewish Agency. Louis Marshall, the leading American "non-Zionist," convened two nonpartisan conferences to consider Palestine problems in 1924 and 1925. These meetings resulted in proposals to include non-Zionist representation in an enlarged Jewish Agency. The proposal to enlarge the Agency by the co-option of non-Zionists was also approved in principle by the Zionist Congress in 1927, and in that year, following publication of a preliminary agreement between Weizmann and Marshall, a Joint Palestine Survey Commission was appointed. It made recommendations for practical work in Palestine upon which both Zionists and non-Zionists could agree. In August 1929 the constitution of the enlarged Agency was approved and the Americans received the largest number of the 112 seats allotted to non-Zionists (44). However, due to the death of Marshall, the onset of the economic depression, the subsequent political events, and the disorganization of the American section of the Jewish Agency, the Zionists continued to control all activities and policies of the Agency.

The riots in Palestine in 1929, coupled with the U.S. economic crisis, further lowered the morale of the ZOA, whose membership declined to 8,000. There was a general clamor for Brandeis' return. At the convention in 1930, an executive committee of 18, composed mainly of Brandeis' circle, was elected with Robert *Szold its chairman from 1930 to 1932. From 1932 to 1936 Morris Rothenberg functioned as president; Stephen S. Wise succeeded him from 1936 to 1938, followed by Solomon *Goldman in 1938, Edmund Kaufmann in 1940 and Judge Louis E. *Levinthal in 1941.

World War II. With the outbreak of World War II, the ZOA formed the American Emergency Committee for Zionist Affairs, which later became the American Zionist Emergency Council, presided over by Stephen Wise and Abba Hillel Silver. On May 9–11, 1942, at New York's Biltmore Hotel, a Zionist Convention consisting of delegates of the ZOA, Hadassah, Mizrachi, and Po'alei Zion enacted the Biltmore Program which defined the postwar Zionist aim as the establishment of Palestine as a Jewish Commonwealth. From 1945 the Zionist Emergency Council directed the energies and propaganda of the movement to influence the entire Jewish community, the U.S. government, and public opinion to support its demands in Palestine. Through these efforts American Zionists contributed decisively to the political prerequisites for the establishment of the State of Israel on May 14, 1948.

During and after the war, a dissident group, called at first Committee for a Jewish Army and later the Hebrew Committee for National Liberation, agitated in the U.S., mainly through newspaper advertisements, by expounding and supporting the ideas and acts of the Irgun Ẓeva'i Le'ummi (IẒL) in Palestine. The group was headed by an IẒL leader, Hillel Kook (who appeared in America under the name of Peter Bergson), and enlisted the support of several prominent Jews and non-Jews. The style and tactics of the "Bergson group" were the subject of sharp controversies in Zionist circles, particularly among Revisionists and their sympathizers.

In addition to their efforts in the political field, American Zionists were among the most active participants in practical aid to the *yishuv* in its struggle after 1945; they helped with "illegal" immigration, the *Beriḥah*, secret shipment of arms to the Haganah, and great sums of money. The greatest number of volunteers to the *yishuv*'s fighting forces, which were called *Mitnaddevei Ḥuẓ la-Areẓ* (*Maḥal), came from the United States. However, only after World War II, under the impact of the Nazi Holocaust in Europe and, later, the establishment of the State of Israel, did Zionism become accepted by the bulk of the Jewish community in America.

Opposition to Zionism. From the beginning Zionism had encountered great opposition, especially from Reform Judaism. Among the staunchest, most influential opponents were rabbis Emil G. *Hirsch and Kaufmann *Kohler. Other prominent Reform rabbis, however, such as Gustav *Gottheil, Jacob *Raisin, Bernard *Felsenthal, and Maximilian *Heller supported the movement. In 1907 professors Max *Margolis, Henry *Malter, and Max Schloessinger, all strong sympathizers with Zionism, resigned from the *Hebrew Union College faculty, while the Zionists charged that they were forced to resign by the College's anti-Zionist president Kohler. Among the younger generation, Stephen S. Wise, Judah L. Magnes, and Abba Hillel Silver were notable exceptions to the anti-Zionism of the Reform rabbinate. The main body of the Central Conference of American Rabbis was anti-Zionist and delivered pronouncements against Zionism until 1920. After the Balfour Declaration (1917) and the San Remo decision on Palestine (1920), the Reform movement adopted, although unofficially, a position of non-Zionism which allowed cooperation with Zionists in philanthropic enterprises. In 1935 they revised their collective negative stand on Zionism in favor of individual choice, and further conciliation occurred after the "Columbus Platform" of 1937. A small minority group, however, continued with its opposition to Zionism.

In November 1942 the *American Council for Judaism was formed, composed of Reform rabbis and influential lay leaders, such as Lessing *Rosenwald, with Rabbi Elmer Berger as its head. The Central Conference of American Rabbis tried to halt this split within its ranks, but to no avail. Whereas the Reform movement as a whole tended to pro-Zionism, the Council continued its anti-Zionist activities and upon the establishment of the State of Israel it stated:

> The State of Israel is not the state or homeland of the Jewish people: to Americans of Jewish faith it is a foreign state. Our single exclusive national identity is to the United States.

Jewish Orthodox circles were divided nearly from the beginning on the Zionist issue. While the Zionist Mizrachi and the Ha-Po'el ha-Mizrachi found many adherents among the East European Jews, Agudat Israel, a smaller but articulate group, was anti-Zionist out of conviction that Zionism was secularist and incompatible with Orthodox Judaism.

Only during World War II did these groups abate their anti-Zionism, and in 1945, with some internal opposition, Agudat Israel declared its willingness to cooperate with the Zionists. On the fringe of Orthodoxy, extremist opposition to Zionism was continued by the Satmar Rebbe Joel *Teitelbaum, who condemned the Zionists for trying to hasten the redemption by establishing a "heretical" state.

Within the lay leadership of American Jewry, Zionism at first found its strongest opponent in the *American Jewish Committee, whose leadership included at various times, among others, Mayer *Sulzberger, Cyrus *Adler, Irving *Lehman, Louis Marshall, Jacob *Schiff, Felix *Warburg, Oscar *Straus, Cyrus *Sulzberger, and Julius *Rosenwald, all wealthy, of German background, and non- or anti-Zionists. After the Balfour Declaration, however, the Committee tacitly recognized the ZOA as the representative of those Jews directly concerned with the welfare of Palestine, although within the American context the AJC, which was an unelected elite, opposed the "Congress Movement" during World War I, which was advanced by Zionists and based on mass support. During the 1920s the leaders of the AJC were approached by Weizmann in order to establish the enlarged Jewish Agency. Zionist "Diaspora nationalism," however, which the AJC saw as a threat to their position and patriotism, remained an issue of contention between them. Thus, opposition to the Zionists continued in various forms until January 1948, when Judge *Proskauer, under the pressure of the pro-Zionist Jewish consensus in the U.S., declared the committee's acceptance of the Jewish state recommended by the United Nations Special Committee on Palestine (UNSCOP). However, the AJC remained apprehensive about the status of American Jews in the light of a Jewish state. It was willing to support Israel while remaining independent of direct Israel interference in its affairs. In 1950 David Ben-Gurion, as prime minister, exchanged letters on the subject with Jacob *Blaustein, president of the AJC. Ben-Gurion stated that Israel represented only its own citizens and had no claim to speak in the name of the Jews in the Diaspora. The Jews of the United States, as a community and as individuals, owed political loyalty only to the United States, and the Jews in Israel had no intention of interfering in the affairs of Jewish communities abroad. The effect of these letters was the cooperation of the AJC with Israel within defined areas of agreement.

Mass Support and Fundraising. Dedicated supporters of the Zionist movement came from the ranks of Conservative Judaism. Solomon Schechter and his faculty at the Jewish Theological Seminary supported Zionism despite the objection of the Reform-oriented board of directors of the Seminary. The meetings of the Rabbinical Assembly of America were consistently characterized by expressions of sympathy for Zionism. The Reconstructionist movement, under the leadership of Rabbi Mordecai M. *Kaplan, also was always pro-Zionist. It viewed its endeavor in Palestine as a means to achieve a renaissance in Jewish life in America as well. Guided by Rabbi Kaplan's concept of "Jewish Peoplehood," Reconstructionist rabbis worked within the Zionist movement in order to achieve their twofold aim.

From the 1930s on, the ZOA devoted more and more attention to fundraising, mainly in the United Palestine Appeal. There was considerable rivalry with non-Zionist overseas agencies, especially the *American Jewish Joint Distribution Committee (JDC), for the allocation of funds raised in local communities. In 1939–40 the UPA and JDC combined into the *United Jewish Appeal (UJA). The frequent consequence of such cooperation was a lack of emphasis on Zionist ideology in Zionist circles. The situation changed from the 1940s when fund raising and political ideology became indistinguishable. Zionist fundraising became the almost universal expression of Jewish identification and communal participation. In April 1960, following criticism from a U.S. Senate committee and other sources of the practice of returning a small proportion of funds raised for Israel for educational activities in the U.S., an agreement was reached between the Jewish Agency and the leadership of the UJA to establish an entirely American body, the Jewish Agency for Israel, Inc., to budget and allocate funds raised in the United States for immigrant needs in Israel. This body was charged with authorizing the expenditure in Israel of funds contributed in America, thus giving American Jewry a direct say and responsibility in administering its funds in Israel. Aid to Israel by Jews in the U.S. was channeled through the UJA and other overseas agencies, and through the Israel Bond Organization. From 1948 through 1968, the UJA provided over $1,100,000,000. In times of crisis for Israel, the sums collected reached unprecedented proportions, as evidenced at the time of the Six-Day War: in 1966 the sale of Israel Bonds totaled $11,000,000; in 1967, $175,000,000. In 1970–71, in the face of threats to Israel's security, the goal was the largest ever, $1,000,000,000. In addition to fundraising, private investment was fostered by bodies such as the Palestine Economic Corporation (PEC). American contributors and investors were not only declared Zionists, but Jews who felt a sense of identification with the Jewish people. As a consequence, American Jewish philanthropy shifted its main priority from support of American Jewish causes to the support of Israel, and the distinction between philanthropic humanitarianism and political Zionism lost its practical significance.

Aliyah and Youth Movements. Aside from the increase in funds, there was also evidence of greater American immigration to Israel, the ultimate expression of commitment to Zionism. In the first three and a half years of the state's existence (May 1948–December 1951), out of a total of 684,201 immigrants to Israel, only 1,909 were Americans. Until 1961 immigration from the United States was less than 1.1% of the total number of immigrants. Between 1960 and 1967 immigration to Israel from the U.S. was 2,000 per year; immediately after the Six-Day War this figure rose to 5,000 per year. After 1967 a "grass roots" immigration movement started independent of the Jewish Agency, which in 1968 formed the Association of Americans and Canadians for Aliyah. The resolutions of the 27th Zionist Congress (Jerusalem, 1968) stated that all necessary help be extended to this and all other organizations seriously contemplating immigration. Immigration in 1970 and 1971 was approximately 7,000 annually. The Zionist movement in America financially assisted established educational institutions and youth movements (Iḥud Habonim, Young Judea, Bnei Akiva, etc.), summer camps, and also organized tours to Israel. In the 1950s and 1960s membership in these movements declined mostly as a result of the growing Jewish affiliation to the various religious movements and their youth groups.

Organizational and Cultural Impact. After World War II, as a continuation of the framework created by the American Zionist Emergency Council, an American section of the Jewish Agency Executive was established in New York, consisting of leading members of the ZOA, Hadassah, the Labor Zionists, and Mizrachi. They participated regularly in plenary sessions of the Executive, whose main center remained in Jerusalem.

In 1957 Mizrachi and Ha-Po'el ha-Mizrachi (founded in 1925) united into the Religious Zionists of America. The women's organizations of both groups, as well as their respective youth groups, Mizrachi ha-Ẓa'ir and Bnei Akiva, remained separate organizations. In 1923 Labor Zionism formed the Histadrut Campaign, which raised funds for the various institutions of the Histadrut in Israel. *Pioneer Women, founded in 1926, made its main function raising funds for the women's division of the Histadrut (Mo'eẓet ha-Po'alot). The youth affiliated to Labor Zionism, Habonim, administer summer camps and year-round social and cultural programs in North America.

In the late 1960s Zionists became concerned with increasing their propaganda activities through new tactics and approaches, especially on the American campuses where the New Left and black nationalists developed an explicit anti-Zionist ideology which denied Israel's right to exist and supported Arab aims to destroy Israel – an ideology which even attracted a number of Jewish students. Independent radical campus groups (e.g., the Radical Zionist Alliance; see below) emerged throughout the U.S. to counter this ideology from a Jewish point of view.

Partly under the impact of this Zionist revival in the new generation, an important reform took place in the structure of American Zionism. Instead of the relatively weak coordinating body called the American Zionist Council, in which the main parties and organizations were represented, the Zionist Federation of America was established in 1970. Zionist affiliation of individuals became henceforth possible without the intermediary of a particular party or organization.

The voluminous literature and extensive ideological debates on the relationship between American Jewry and Israel indicated the impact made on the Diaspora by the State of Israel. American Jews showed themselves more willing and ready to be identified as Jews, to affiliate with Jewish organizations and institutions, and to send their children to Jewish schools as a result of their ties to Israel. Israel occupies an important place in synagogue activities, sermons, and various religious celebrations, and Israel's Independence Day assumes an important place in the American Jewish calendar. The Israel flag is frequently displayed in synagogues and community centers. In many synagogues prayers for the welfare of the State of Israel and world Jewry are recited on Sabbaths and holidays following that for the welfare of the United States. Both the Conservative and Reform branches attempt to establish themselves in Israel through rabbinical schools and various educational programs.

Another impact of Israel has been the use of the Hebrew language in contrast to the decline of Yiddish. Hebrew songs and Israeli folk dances have become American Jewish popular culture: at weddings, bar mitzvot, and on many college campuses. Jewish art, which traditionally concentrated on East European themes, expanded to include Israeli symbols; Israeli crafts find a wide market among American Jews. Fiction on Israeli life increases rapidly and an extensive periodical literature is directed from Israeli institutions toward American Jewry.

Israel had a profound impact on the ideologies of American Jews. The anti-Zionist American Council for Judaism was the only American Jewish organization which claimed that any suggestions of an ethnic bond among Jews, especially the ideas of Zionism and the creation of the State of Israel, harmed the position of the Jews in America because it placed in question their loyalty to the United States. With the progress of the State of Israel and particularly after the Six-Day War, many of its members and supporters shifted to a more pro-Israel stance, and the Council's influence dwindled considerably. Agudat Israel, on the other hand, which before the establishment of the state held that any state not governed by *halakhah* would be illegitimate, accepted the State of Israel, as did almost all other Orthodox Jewish groups in America.

Jewish religious and welfare institutions in America, such as the National Council of Jewish Women, B'nai B'rith, and the Jewish War Veterans, as well as civic organizations such as the Anti-Defamation League and the National Communal Relations Advisory Council, all adopted an official stand of "non-Zionism." In practice, however, they supported the State of Israel and demands for an American policy of friendship toward Israel. As a consequence, they rejected the suggestion that Jewish ethnic traditions about Zionism and the existence of the State of Israel created conflicts of dual loyalty.

Religious and Ideological Issues. There were, however, issues of concern to some of these organizations. Orthodox Jewry in America felt itself intimately involved in the course of religious affairs in Israel and pressed the state to pursue official religious policies in accord with its own religious beliefs. Similarly, Israeli rabbis commanded influence and respect among similar circles in the United States. The Conservative and Reform movements, on the other hand, were concerned that the legal establishment of religious Orthodoxy in Israel involved discrimination against non-Orthodox Jews there. Some demanded the separation of state and religion or the adoption of forms of religious practice closer to their own points of view. The concern of the American religious groups implies that the religious forms practiced in Israel are of direct relevance to American Jews.

After the establishment of the State of Israel, controversies also arose between Israelis and American Zionists over their relationships in the future. The Americans demanded a separation of the activities of the state from those of the Jewish Agency and the World Zionist Organization, whereas the Israelis wanted Jerusalem to be the center of all the Zionist activities. In addition, there was a great controversy about the meaning of the Diaspora and the obligation to immigrate to Israel. The Americans claimed that America was not *galut* because Jews were secure and not oppressed there (Rose *Halprin) and that the Zionist Organization should not submit to the authority of Israel (Abba Hillel Silver). American Zionists wanted to be recognized as the liaison for all activities between American Jews and Israel. They demanded that, through legislation, Israel recognize their leading position in fundraising and practical work, a demand practically achieved in 1952 through the passage of the Zionist Organization and Jewish Agency Law in the Knesset and the covenant signed subsequently between the Israel government and the Jewish Agency.

American Zionists maintained that the most important issue for the Jews was their survival as a people. Since Jews will continue to live in the Diaspora, only a Zionism that recognized the essential ethnic elements of the Jewish people could keep them from cultural disintegration. For this reason a strong emphasis on cultural continuity, Hebrew, and a strong bond with Israel are the tasks of American Zionism (Ben *Halpern), although since 1967 the furtherance of *aliyah* from the U.S. also became a legitimate part of Zionist activity in America. In essence this is a neo-Aḥad Ha-Am position which sees Israel as the cultural center of the Jewish people but simultaneously dependent on the moral, political, and financial assistance of the Diaspora.

[Jehuda Reinharz]

JEWISH RADICAL ZIONISTS IN THE U.S. *The First Generation of the American Jewish Student Movement, 1968–72.*

> We see ourselves as your children, the children of Jews who with great dedication concern themselves with the needs of the community, the children of Jews who bring comfort to the afflicted, give aid to the poor, who have built mammoth philanthropic organizations, who have aided the remnants of the Holocaust, who have given unfalteringly to the building of Israel, who give more per capita to charity than any other group in America. We are your children and affirm this, but, to paraphrase the Rabbinic aphorism, we want to be not only children – *banim* – but also builders – *bonim*. We want to participate with you in the building of a vision of a great Jewish community. It is when we think of this that we become dismayed with the reality of American Jewish life which we cannot reconcile with what you have taught us to cherish.
>
> It took us several years to realize our confusion of form and essence and to recognize that there was more to Judaism than its poor expressions in the American Jewish community. For some it was a trip to Israel, for others it was the reading of Buber's *I and Thou*, for others an encounter with Ḥasidim, for others it was a traditional Jewish education redirected to confront existential problems, for others the exploration of self could not overlook the Jewish component. The Six Day War forced us to reassess our attachment in deciding to risk our lives if necessary on Israel's behalf. The black awakening reminded us that the melting pot dream was a fool's fantasy and that differences were legitimate. We woke up from the American dream and tried to discover who we really were. For many of us this now means turning our concerns inward into the Jewish community because we are disenchanted with the crass materialism of the larger society. Yet where can we find inspiration in the multi-million-dollar Jewish presences of suburbia? (from a speech by Hillel Levine, Nov. 1969)

Greening and Ethnicity. The Jewish Student Movement, born in the late 1960s, developed out of the American radical tradition and a groping for an authentic Jewish ethnicity that would permit both a highly visible Jewish commitment and an active concern for the social-political milieu.

The tolerant, permissive environment in which the American post-World War II babies were brought up, in a world which knew both the threat of atom bombs and the ease of wealthy America, made for what has been called the "greening of America." "Greening" is the turning inward in search of roots, of community, and toward a celebration of self; it is a rejection of much of what super-industrialized, technologized America, with its overwhelming belief in progress, had brought, without shunning the blessings of that culture, the cheap transportation and mass communication that make possible the ferreting out of like minds.

By the mid-1960s, emerging black self-confidence, which was to become a paradigm of ethnicity and the engulfing anti-Vietnam war spirit were voiced by young voices – at a time when more and more students were shedding the powerless, lethargic modes of the 1950s for an aggressive, assertive mode of demanding. They demanded the right of self-expression, rather than the duties of an apprenticeship to adulthood. In the early 1960s a high proportion of the activists were Jewish, but what can be termed "low-profile Jewish." Their "high profile" applied to their activism. Some, however, influenced by spreading ethnicity ("work within your own community"), sought to identify themselves more consciously as Jews, i.e., to raise their Jewish profile – in greatly varying measures, of course, but clearly to raise it.

American youth, by then a subculture, asserted the right to play the socio-political games of life according to rules of their own. These rules, no doubt, had an ancestry in the collective memories to which these youths were the heirs; but they wished to choose, order, and stack the rules themselves. A tolerant America seemed to allow for this; the "greening of

America" appeared to allow for the "greening of Judaism." It is in this "greening of Judaism," a radicalism precipitated in an ethnic mode, in which Jewish students after 1967, searching for their spiritual and/or primeval, and/or national, and/or cultural roots, began to make bids for power – the power necessary for the assertion of their will. To gain some perspective on their bids, we turn to some seasoned high-profile activists.

Low-Profile Jews, High-Profile Activists. Of the high-profile activists, low-profile Jews who exerted a shaping influence on the Left of the 1960s, Saul Alinsky and Paul Jacobs (both of them influential in the 1930s), Noam Chomsky and Herbert Marcuse (both of them leaving their mark on the 1960s) are of note.

Saul Alinsky, already in the 1930s, stressed the similarities between "democrat" and "radical." He saw his attitude as rooted in the Jeffersonian tradition, and urged would-be radicals to know the "rules of the game" so as to be able to manipulate them to their own ends.

In his essay "Repressive Tolerance," Herbert Marcuse, of similar profile as regards Activism/Judaism, diagnosed the very acquiescence to the primary rules governing a game (situation) as serving to maintain the system, and as not permitting a really radical change. Marcuse's influence on the emerging "New Left" was particularly widespread, especially as regards his notion of repressive tolerance and his objections to the "one-dimensional" man. His notion of tolerance further discredited an already declining regard for the liberal tradition (a decline that Alinsky had presaged in his writings).

The breakdown of the liberal tradition was also a time of emerging influence of the "beyond-the-nation-state" proponents, of whom Noam Chomsky is of particular note. By 1968, speaking from what he termed an Aḥad Ha-Am perspective, he put forth a theory of the desirability of "kibbutzinization" of the Middle East. He proposed that Israel be in the vanguard of those states which would abandon the apparatus of statehood. The ensuing dialectic, in which he had an important role, picked up momentum and lasted for several years thereafter. It was vital to the articulation of the radical Zionist position on the one hand, and the renewed advocacy of the bi-nationalist state, on the other.

Marcuse and Chomsky had a profound influence on the theoretical superstructure of the planning of radical social action in the 1960s.

Paul Jacobs, active as early as Alinsky, and like Alinsky involved at least as much in doing as in theorizing, represents the low-profile Jew, high-profile activist which the new ethnically conscious Jews of the late 1960s rejected. Writing of himself in *Is Curly Jewish?*, Jacobs portrays his "back-drop" Jewishness as it was worked out in the 1930s. By the 1930s assimilation (passing) and denominational Judaism had been added to the paths opened to Jews in the late 19th century: Torah (religious Judaism, self-consciously ideological, given its exposed, defensive posture); Zionism; Socialism (both in its Diaspora-centered and its internationalist varieties). Jacobs chose "socialism" and worked from within a class-consciousness perspective.

He explains his pull to radicalism as a push from Judaism:

> I have a hunch, too, that for me one of the unconscious pressures toward radicalism was that the movement provided an atmosphere in which I could reject being Jewish without any feeling of guilt. One of the first rituals in the radical movement was the adoption of a party name by which one was to be known in the organization.... Even granting the legitimate need we felt to change our names in order to escape possible consequences, why was it that so many of the Jewish radicals took as their cover names ones that were conspicuously non-Jewish? No Comrade Cohen ever adopted Ginsburg as a party name; instead he became Green or Smith or Martin, or something equally bland.

Speaking of encounters between members of the Young People's Socialist League (YPSL) and the Zionist Ha-Shomer ha-Ẓair, Jacobs observes:

> ... the YPSLers (and Hashomer) were very close... politically. They hated the Communists almost as much as we did, primarily because the Soviet Union had set up the remote province of Birobidzhan as its own Jewish state, touting its virtues over Palestine.... They (Hashomer) were convinced that the only salvation for the Jews was in their own land, and because they were socialists, they were committed to making Palestine into a socialist country.... I sat with them for hours... arguing heatedly that Zionism was only another form of petty bourgeois nationalism. But those arguments had none of the rancor and bitterness that were so characteristic of the fight all of us had with the Stalinists.

In 1947 Jacobs joined the staff of the American Jewish Committee:

> ... the emphasis... was not heavily Jewish in those of its operations which related to the non-Jewish world.... My own department, for example, was officially named the "National Labor Service of the American Jewish Committee," but only the name "National Labor Service" appeared on its publications, on the theory that an organization without an open Jewish identification could operate more effectively with non-Jewish groups than one, say, like our rival, the Jewish Labor Committee.

He clearly states that, for himself and many other members of the AJC staff, this arrangement was ideal: "it provided us with a base from which we could fight prejudice and discrimination without any need to be Jewish."

Moving Toward High-Profile Jewishness. The Jewish revolutionary who strives for the liberation of mankind and views Jewish nationalism as merely tribalistic and a retreat from internationalist ideals is of course not a new phenomenon. It was just this perspective of the "steady patriot of the world alone, the friend of every country but his own" that was unanimously rejected by the high-profile Jewish activists of the Jewish Student Movement (JSM). They wished to combine a high-profile activism with a self-consciously assertive high-profile Judaism.

The base of JSM is ethnic, and if concerned with "passing" (being assimilated into, accommodated by) the American culture, it is a minimal passing – that of not being rejected by the host society because of displayed ethnic characteristics.

For JSM, as it grew in the black-is-beautiful hothouse of the American 1960s, the do-it-yourself metaphor, so much a part of American culture, involved a return to classic Jewish texts, a return to *lehrhaus*. Its approach was of the de-schooling sort, which emphasized the student and his personal and intellectual growth, rather than some formal school curriculum. This reflected the general anti-establishment attitude of the times. In this regard, the cultural heroes included men such as Herbert Marcuse and Noam Chomsky, who goaded American youth to that radical perspective known as "New Left."

By 1968 the New Left had moved from a tacit to an explicit anti-Israel stance, and consequently Jews who were moving to a higher ethnic profile were experiencing greater difficulties staying within the fold. At a 1969 meeting, for instance, Students for a Democratic Society (SDS), participating in a teach-in in Washington, D.C., were arguing vehemently against the validity of a separate Jewish group operating in radical politics. Others argued back and by dawn one of the SDS members started quoting verbatim from Mao's little red book. His opponents responded by chanting the morning prayers, the *Shaḥarit*, in Hebrew. This polarization between the mainstream SDS and the more Jewishly conscious activists illustrates the tightrope along which Jews drawn towards the evolving Jewish Student Movement chose to walk.

The earlier American ethic of rugged individualism was being replaced by that of group activity; instead of "pull yourself up by your own bootstraps," there was "work in your community" and "we shall overcome." A dominant mode of behavior had been radicalized in its idiom, and a young Jew faced with existential quandaries and problems of group identities could easily come to think of his search for roots as radical.

Toward Crystallized Stands. Alinsky and Jacobs suggest the tone of the (Jewish) American radical tradition, and Chomsky and Marcuse its intellectual goadings to radical social action. The Students for a Democratic Society served as the paradigm of a radical group and symbol of the New Left of the 1960s.

The aims of the SDS were described by Straughton Lynd in "The New Radicals and Participatory Democracy" (*Dissent*, Summer 1965): "… that the individual share in those social decisions determining the quality and direction of his life; that society be organized to encourage independence in man and provide the media for their common participation."

This was to become characteristic of the Student Non-Violent Coordinating Committee and the "greening of America." The participatory democracy of SDS, with its parallelistic approach – working within the community, i.e., grass-roots as the locus of power; community schools; local papers; a diversity of mini-institutions; free universities – served structurally as the model for much of the behavior of the Jewish Student Movement. By the early 1970s there would be Jewish "free universities" and Jewish studies departments. Even Jewish Community Centers would have "Jewish culture personnel."

M.J. Rosenberg's "To Uncle Tom and Other Such Jews" (*Village Voice*, February 13, 1969) has become a document of its age. It spread among Jews across American campuses like wildfire. It gave voice to the feelings of many young Jews who would "work within your community"; "stand up and be counted as a Jew"; "work on the grass roots level" and who would reconcile, perhaps even subordinate, their politics to their ethnic affiliation. M.J. Rosenberg suggests the spirit of the Jewish Student Movement – both in what allowed it to pass into the American scene and in its insistence on the right to assertion of Jewish power. These are, of course, at least incompatible, and the JSM was ill put to contain both trends for long.

Rosenberg speaks for those of his generation of post-Holocaust, Third Jewish Commonwealth Jews who had begun to opt for grappling with their Jewish heritage and the incorporation of the realities of Jewish existence (perhaps, especially the death trauma of Auschwitz and the birth trauma of Israel) into their daily living.

> The self-hating Jew should have died with the creation of Israel. If the drama enacted in Cyprus, Europe, and Palestine between 1945 and 1948 did not convince him of the blood and guts of his own people then I am not sure anything would.
>
> The Young American Jew… craves assimilation; the very idea of "Jewishness" embarrasses him. If you tell him that he doesn't "look Jewish," he will invariably take it as a compliment. The concept of Jewish nationalism, Israel notwithstanding, he finds laughable. The leftist Jewish student… is today's "Uncle Tom." He scrapes along ashamed of his identity and yet is obsessed with it. He goes so far as to join black nationalist organizations, not as a Jew, but as a white…. His destiny is that of the Jews but he denies what is apparent to the rest of us; he wants to be an "American," a leftist American talking liberation and an aspiring WASP.
>
> The miracle of 1948 was that the Jew did it alone, with the guns he could smuggle and the iron will that is the legacy of Auschwitz…. This makes it so imperative that we ensure that which was won by Jewish heroes on the fields of Palestine will not be lost with the aid and connivance of Jewish moral cowards…. "
>
> The issue is one of Jewish pride. The Jewish professor who makes a point of teaching on Yom Kippur with subtle mockery of those students who stay home,… the Jewish radicals who are prepared to fight for the Czechs, the Greeks, and the Biafrans and yet reject Israel; these are our Uncle Toms and our shame. The Jew must accept his identity … the burden of proof is on you. You who mockingly reject every lesson of your people's history…. In the aftermath of the crematoriums, you are flippant. In the wake of Auschwitz, you are embarrassed. Thirty years after the Holocaust you have learned nothing and forgotten everything. Ghetto Jew, you'd better do some fast thinking.

Rosenberg criticized what he called the "bagels-and-lox society" Hillel Houses. He rejected both their insularity and their programs. The first "generation" of the movement (1968–72) shared this evaluation and engaged the Hillel people in a dialectic which led to a move away from a somewhat hollow home-away-from-home in which one could be quietly, safely Jewish on campus, and toward a Hillel which promoted active Jewish involvement and study.

There was a shift in the reality tests of Judaism – from the edifice temple to the community prayer room, from the classroom to the open *lehrhaus*, from the bagels-and-lox brunch to the communal *sukkah*. The call was to a more public Jewish witnessing and the slogan was: Israel is real; Diaspora is real. A de facto Judaism as labeled by others would not suffice, nor would old patterns of expression be adequate. The goal became to rejuvenate and reauthenticate a living Judaism.

This call and others were heeded by Jews who formed the various groups which make up the JSM. From the Jewish Defense League on the right, to the Radical Zionist Alliance on the left (which so significantly shifted its emphasis from "Jewish radicals" to "Radical Jews") and the communitarian *ḥavurot* located at some apolitical point in between, young Jews stood up to be counted. They demanded some of the access, the means, the space of the American Jewish community. In the ethnic mode of the late 1960s, the relatively Protestant frame of the Reform movement with its over-arching "grand issue" concerns could not satisfy the young Jew seeking expression of his Jewishness; nor did he feel comfortable in other of the traditional denominational Jewish sub-groups. He wanted a nondenominational Jewishness, an ethnically binding frame. He wanted to be part of a group, of a movement. Indeed, by being ethnically bound, by achieving a subculture particularism, he would be able to pass in the new America, to demand power for his group. The new "greened" Jew could be at home as a Jew in the new "greened" America, or so it seemed in 1968–69.

Aliveness of Israel and Diaspora. The greened Jews' move was away from the "Jewishness of survival" which they perceived as the over-mortgaged heritage of their parents. Israel as a safety deposit box for their Jewish identity would not suffice. They wanted a growing, developing Diaspora Jewishness, and adopted the more *au courant* ecological metaphor of "greening," of "return to roots."

A major confrontation developed between the emerging demands of Jewish students and their fathers, i.e., within the Jewish community. Hillel Levine, on behalf of a loosely knit ad hoc group, Concerned Jewish Students (CJS) of Boston, presented a set of demands to the Council of Jewish Federations and Welfare Funds in November, 1969. This confrontation was the first of numerous head-on encounters between "radical" (root-searching) young Jews and the established Jewish communities on a local, regional, and national level. It marked the insistence that they, the young Jews, have a say in determining what was happening in the Jewish community. It was a bid for power. The CJS asserted:

> In affirmation of our Jewishness and our concern for Jewish Survival we feel we can no longer be silent. Distortions in the budget priorities of Jewish Federations have long been decried.... We demand that, while maintaining the generous level of support for Israel, all local federations undertake a drastic and immediate reordering of domestic priorities in their local communities, in order to improve the quality of Jewish cultural life on campus and in the community.

Bill Novak, then of *Response*, a magazine founded by Jewish undergraduates at Columbia, which has operated as "the unofficial intellectual and artistic voice of the new Jewish counter-culture" sounded the call:

> You have a culture, so dig it
> You have a people, work with it
> You have a history and a body of literature,
> Study it!

Meanwhile, Jewish students elsewhere were also responding to the times. 1968 was a year of student demands and new ethnicities. The World Union of Jewish Students (WUJS) is an international federation of Jewish student unions from over 30 countries. In the late 1960s the importance of strengthening WUJS on the North American continent, given the higher-profile Jewish activism, the new ethnicity and the sense of the growing importance of North American Student Jewry, became apparent to both WUJS and its Jewish Agency sponsors.

Certain of the leaders of the Youth and He-Ḥalutz Department of the Jewish Agency, alert to the need for new forms of pat Zionist yea-saying, given changes in fashions and the times, were, in the mid and late 1960s, eager to encourage the formation of Jewish groups, journals, etc., which could serve as vehicles for propagating a concerned Jewish involvement. They accurately sensed the potential usefulness of the campus as medium.

In 1969, at Brewster, N.Y., the assembled representatives of the older national student organizations and the new independent "Jewish Student Movement" decided to create "Network" in order to keep one another informed and to ferment activities.

"Network" stated that its aspirations were grounded in "belief in the unity of the Jewish people. Like most Jews we agree on very little else. Even in our common commitment to the Soviet Jewish struggle and to the flourishing of Israel we differ in our visions and tactics.... We want to share with each other in the rejuvenation of the Jewish people, each of us in his own way...."

Network's aim to "provide Jewish youth organizations with the opportunity to relate to each other without the intervention of the establishment organizations" was a Jewish counter-culture move, toward the grass-roots expression of needs and away from mediating, remote "representation."

WUJS. Particularly dramatic is the history of WUJS's relationship to the World Zionist Organization, to which it was accepted in 1968 (26th Zionist Congress) and within which it was so bitterly attacked over its Arad Program, 1972 (27th Zionist Congress).

In Arad (XV WUJS Triennial Congress) the new "ethnic" Jews who, although committed to Israel and its survival, were critical of the policies of the State of Israel and of Zionist ideology, found that their analyses were not well received by the very authorities who had recently sent them out to struggle with the New Left.

The Zionist establishment had been disturbed at the snowballing anti-Zionism of the "New Left" and correctly realized that a left Zionist force could be an effective response. Thus, at the Brewster conference, where the WUJS appeared on the American scene, and at others which would follow, the Youth and He-Ḥalutz Department under the leadership of Mordekhai Bar-On, lent its weight, experience, and financial backing.

The financial backing did not bring a line-towing to any of the standard acceptable versions of secular Zionism. It is interesting that, given the asserted Jewishness of these new young Zionists, the Department itself underwent a renewed concern with non-secular Zionism. The very polarity, so unfortunately entrenched in Israel life, between the secular and the religious, was challenged. Unlike the Zionist left of an earlier generation, the "Radical Jews" are not programmatically secularist. The "Judaizing" they brought about was part of the dialectic between the Jews of the "movement" and the controllers of the Jewish community. This dialectic took place with the Agency, and within local Jewish communities, and among the supporters of the Jerusalem program of the WZO and the Arad program of WUJS, *et al.*

It did not always entail a neat adherence to the "rules of the game." WUJS barely survived the 1972 WZO backlash response to its Arad program. The Jerusalem Program/Arad Program entanglement is a high point in Jewish Student Movement/Establishment Jewry relations.

Arad Program.

> 1. Zionism is the national and also, by virtue of its territorialistic aspect, the social liberation and emancipation movement of the Jewish people; it is to be realized in Israel. The universalistic task of the Jewish people, as expressed in its prophetic tradition, must arise out of the necessary concentration of the Jewish people in Israel, so that out of this framework, it can devote its energies to the social emancipation of Mankind.
>
> 2. A condition for this realization is: The recognition of the national rights of the Palestinian Arabs, not only as a political step, but as a consequence of Zionist ideology.
>
> 3. The aims of Zionism are (a) the preservation of the existence of the Jewish people, united by their common identity, through the fostering of the Jewish values and strengthening the identity that will bring to a fulfillment in Israel. (b) the abolition of the abnormal situation of the Jewish people living in the Diaspora, by its territorial concentration in the State of Israel. (c) the realization in the State of Israel of a democratic society, just, equalitarian, and peace loving that recognizes the right of self-determination of all peoples. (d) the encouragement of the Jews to become conscious of, and identify with, the liberation struggle of other peoples. (e) the protection of the rights of Jews everywhere.

Contrast this with the resolution of the 27th Zionist Congress, a resolution known as the 1968 Jerusalem Program:

> The aims of Zionism are: The unity of the Jewish People and the centrality of Israel in Jewish life; The ingathering of the Jewish People in its historical homeland, Eretz Israel, through Aliya from all countries; The strengthening of the State of Israel which is based on the prophetic vision of justice and peace; The preservation of the identity of the Jewish People through the fostering of Jewish and Hebrew education and of Jewish spiritual and cultural values; The protection of Jewish rights everywhere.

The contrast between the Arad and the Jerusalem Programs is obvious. In light of the backstage treatment dealt with the WUJS people in overreaction to their program, it is difficult to concede that the disillusionment that followed the ugly rejection could call forth anything but angry tantrums, "children" to "parents." The would-be "*bonim*" received naughty "*banim*" treatment.

Radical Zionist Alliance. In 1969, in Palmer, Mass., the North American Radical Zionist Alliance (RZA) came to life. Child of radical enthusiasms, dreams of Zion, and calculated analyses of power-options, it was to serve as an umbrella organization for Jews working in small groups, united by their concerted search for their Jewish selves, a shared concern for effecting social change, and their differing concerns for the Jewish polity.

"Radical Zionist Alliance" was a name, a category, fashioned to drape around a coalition of voices expressing consonant concerns at a time when to group in America was to group ad hoc – For Women; For Peace; Veterans against Vietnam; American Committee for Peace and Justice; *et al.* Such was the social metaphor.

The RZA groups were largely campus-based. They had begun to establish newspapers, push for Jewish studies on campus (not unlike their co-students who were demanding Black Studies), and to challenge the American Jewish establishment on its priorities in funding and on the quality of their Jewish education.

The newspaper established by RZA, *Nitzotz*, was short-lived. RZA, like its member group, the Jewish Liberation Project in New York, had a complicated relationship to *Mapam*, marked by ambivalence and problems of controlling the "young people." Involvement with Israeli political parties is a characteristic shared with the Jewish Defense League.

The formalizing of RZA seems to have been more a watershed in the institutionalizing of the new radical mode than a commitment to joint programs of action. The numerous conventions (Brewster, Madison, Philadelphia, etc.) and retreats and scrambled get-togethers among different participants in, and adherents to, the idea of the Jewish Student Movement from 1968 to 1972 suggest a pattern of ritualistic confirmation of the invisible community they formed and an occasion for recharging the commitments of the members.

In the general mood of political impotence that followed the May 1970 invasion of Cambodia, many activist Jews began to lose interest in politics or to transform their activism into a super-particularistic Jewish nationalist identity – Jewish Defense League or Soviet Jewry work or a turning to Jewish nondenominational religious movements. The Student Struggle for Soviet Jewry, founded in 1964 by people who later became leaders of various of the other groups, was a rallying point of Jewish involvement for activist Jews of all political persuasions. Those who stressed their RZA commitments toyed with the idea of city-kibbutzim (Urbutz); while on campus they did pro-Israel information work, protested awards to reactionary politicians by Zionist organizations, and confronted the Jewish Defense League.

The demise of RZA by 1972 reflects their disposability to the Jewish establishments (especially to the Zionist establishment for whom they had worked on the campuses); a conformity to the general shift on campuses from political and outer-oriented to spiritual and inner-oriented concerns; and their members' inability to cope with the realities of contemporary Israel life.

In late 1972, the Washington Jewish Student Organization (Seattle) could advertise in "Network" its sponsorship of a conference "of all those interested in detailed discussion of the *theoretical* and *strategic* questions now facing the broadly defined socialist-Zionist movement in North America.... This conference will be *political* and will *not* include seminars on Jewish identity, creative *Shabbatot*, Jewish media, innovative *Halakhah*, Krishna-Mishna or Neo-Hassidism...."

The "spiritual" interests struck from the RZA agenda became the critical interests of the Jewish Student Movement. The "spiritual revolution" which had taken root in the American campuses at the turn of the decade now flourished among the second generation of the Jewish Student Movement.

[Chava Alkon Katz]

In Yugoslavia

Zionism in the countries that united on Dec. 1, 1918, to form the kingdom of the Serbs, Croatians, and Slovenes sprang from three main sources: the traditional national-religious aspirations of Sephardi Jewry, which was permeated with messianic yearnings; the youth of these countries who had studied in Vienna; and the influence of the Ḥovevei Zion movement, which penetrated into these regions from Galicia, especially after the conquest of Bosnia by the Austrian army in 1878. Among the forerunners of Zionism were two rabbis in Croatia, although their activities had no reverberations in their immediate surroundings. Jekuthiel Hirschenstein, the rabbi of Varaždin, gave advice to Moshe Zaks, a Jerusalemite, who tried to engage in a kind of Zionist diplomacy in Vienna and Germany, as shown through their correspondence during the years 1835–38. Judah Hai *Alkalai actively engaged in the revival of Jewish nationhood, both philosophically and in practice, and tried in vain to bring the Jews of the Serbian city of Šabac to Ereẓ Israel after the pogroms of 1865. Viennese Zionism influenced the southern Slavic countries even before the advent of Herzl. David M. Alkalai, a relative of Judah Alkalai, was a member of the Viennese Zionist student group Kadimah, founded by Nathan Birnbaum. He and his wife, Rachel, Alkalai's granddaughter, were among the few representatives from the southern Slavic countries at the First Zionist Congress (1897). The others were Marcus (Mordecai) *Ehrenpreis from Djakovo and Armand *Kaminka from Osijek. Immediately after the Congress, Alkalai founded an association named Zion in Belgrade and, in 1937, he became the second chairman of the Zionist Organization of Yugoslavia. At the turn of the century, Sephardi students from the southern Slavic countries, including Bulgaria, established the Zionist Esperanza Society in Vienna. A student Zionist association, Bar Giora, uniting Ashkenazi and Sephardi Jewish students from the southern Slavic countries, was organized. In 1904 the two societies held meetings together and thus laid the foundation for cooperation between the southern Slavic Zionists. Judeja, a Zionist student organization from Zagreb, joined them in 1908.

Through the initiative of the Osijek Zionists (pioneers of Herzl's political Zionism in Croatia), led by Hugo Spitzer, the Yugoslav Zionist Federation was founded in 1909 within the borders of the Hapsburg monarchy. It united the Zionist groups that had been established in the cities and towns. The first Zionist local group of this kind was founded in 1897 by Nathan Landau, a teacher in the town of Brčko in Bosnia. Other active Zionists of the early period were Gustav Seidemann, Yoḥanan Thau, Raphael Poljokan, and A.D. Levi. Under the influence of the youth who had studied in Vienna, in 1898 a group of high school students in Zagreb formed an organization that produced a generation of leaders. Led by Alexander Licht, they transformed Zagreb from a center of assimilationism into the center of Yugoslav Zionism and the seat of most of its institutions. Licht's brother Herman organized the Jewish working youth. In Belgrade, David Albala, a member of Bar Giora, founded the youth organization Gideon, which also raised a group of active Zionists. Between the Balkan War and World War I there was a discernible emigration of Jews from Bitolj (Monastir), Macedonia, some of whom reached Jerusalem. Active, organized Zionism actually began in Macedonia between the two world wars in close contact with the center in Zagreb. Leon Kamhi was the leader in Bitolj and Josef Behar in Skoplje. In Vojvodina, which belonged to Hungary, assimilationist trends prevailed until the end of World War I.

World War I brought a temporary halt to all Zionist activities in the region, due to the government's prohibition, as well as the drafting of active Zionists into the army. Before the end of the war, however, the movement came to life in Croatia, Bosnia, and also in Vojvodina, partly because of the presence of a few Russian Jewish prisoners of war and Galician Jewish soldiers in the Austrian army garrisoned there. The leader of the Zagreb Zionists then was Lav Stern. The first conference of the Yugoslav Zionist Organization assembled in Zagreb in January 1919, immediately after the establishment of the independent kingdom of Yugoslavia, with representatives from every part of the new monarchy. It served to renew the tradition of undefined unity and cooperation in the

Zionist movement that had been prevalent before World War I and carried on in this role during the years between the two world wars. In 1919 a union of Jewish youth associations was established, uniting most of the students and working youth who had ties with various world Zionist youth movements. The union organized youth assemblies and summer camps. In 1920 the first *hakhshara* and Palestine Office were founded under the chairmanship of Abraham Werber (Avishur), as a result of the influence of pioneers of the Third Aliyah who passed through Zagreb in 1919–20 and the conference of Ha-Po'el ha-Ẓa'ir in Prague (1920). *Hakhsharot* existed until the Nazi occupation, training *ḥalutzim* from Central Europe. The first pioneers from Yugoslavia went to Palestine in 1921, and their *aliyah* continued until the Holocaust, with the numbers depending upon the Mandatory entry permits ("certificates") allocated to Yugoslavia.

Under the leadership of Julius Dohany, in 1929 the Revisionists broke away from the Yugoslav Zionist Organization and set up Betar; the Zionist Organization, however, preserved its encompassing influence under the leadership of Licht, covering the General Zionists and adherents of Labor Zionism, and youth movements from the left Ha-Shomer ha-Ẓa'ir and Tekhelet-Lavan (Neẓaḥ) to General Zionists. The number of religious Zionists was small and their influence minimal.

Although there was full cooperation between the Ashkenazi and Sephardi elements of the community from the end of the 19th century onward, part of the Sephardi community tended to oppose the Zionist Organization because of complaints voiced by the World Sephardi Organization about discrimination against Sephardim in Palestine. Already with the founding of independent Yugoslavia, the frictions between the majority in the movement and the Sephardi separatists deepened because of Yugoslav political issues. The Zionist movement produced women's WIZO groups, the Maccabi movement, and Jewish choirs, orchestras, and amateur theaters. It reinvigorated the existing elementary schools, founded Hebrew kindergartens (the first in Zagreb under the direction of Miriam Weiller), and invited teachers from Palestine. Jewish poets, writers, and researchers consciously devoted their efforts to Jewish topics and thus developed a rich Jewish literature in the Serbo-Croatian language. A monthly Zionist publication *Židovska Smotra* ("Jewish Review") appeared from 1906 to 1914. In September 1917, before the publication of the Balfour Declaration, copies of the Zionist central weekly *Židov* ("The Jew") began to appear, and it was printed up to the Nazi invasion. *Židovska Svijest* ("Jewish Consciousness") and *Jevrejski Život* ("Jewish Life"), a separatist Sephardi publication, were initiated in Sarajevo in 1918 and united in 1928 as *Jevrejski Glas* ("Jewish Voice"). *Gideon* and other youth publications appeared from 1919. A monthly children's publication, *Ha-Aviv*, was published from 1922 until 1941. The monthly publication *Ommanut*, under the editorship of H. Gottlieb, appeared from 1937 until March 1941. In Novi Sad, Vojvodina, various Zionist publications appeared in German, among them *Juedisches Volksblatt*. Books and pamphlets were also published by the periodicals *Židov* and *Jevrejski Narodni Kalendar*.

The Zionists of Yugoslavia worked to win control over the Jewish community councils. Almost all the Jewish communities (with the exception of the small, separate Orthodox communities) came into the hands of a stable Zionist majority until the mid-1930s. This majority was instrumental in the founding of the Federation of Jewish Communities in 1919, led by Spitzer and afterward by Fridrich Pops. The Federation of Jewish Communities was an active force behind national Jewish education, the results of which were evident even after the Holocaust: most of the survivors settled in Israel during 1944–52, and those who remained in Socialist Yugoslavia tried to retain their Judaism by keeping in close contact with the Jewish people and the State of Israel.

[Yakir Eventov / Cvi Rotem]

For later developments, see entries on the individual countries.

RETROSPECT AND PROSPECT

The Twenty-Seventh Zionist Congress which met in Jerusalem on June 19, 1968, outlined the aims of the Zionist Movement thus:

1) To promote the unity of the Jewish people and the centrality of the State of Israel in Jewish Life.

2) To assist the ingathering of the Jewish people in the historical homeland, which is based on the vision of justice and peace of the Hebrew prophets.

3) To preserve the identity of the Jewish people through fostering Jewish, Hebrew, and Zionist education with emphasis on spiritual and cultural values.

The document is known as the Jerusalem Program 1968. It reiterated the resolution which had been adopted by the Twenty-Third Zionist Congress (Jerusalem, August 30, 1951). It proposed that the Zionist organization undertake the following tasks:

1) To encourage immigration and assist in the absorption and integration of the immigrants in Israel.

2) To assist in agricultural settlement in the land and in economic development; to stimulate the pioneering spirit (*ḥalutziyyut*) among the settlers; and to acquire new tracts of land as the property of the Jewish people.

3) To raise funds and encourage investment of private capital.

4) To foster Jewish consciousness by propagating the Zionist idea by means of education and enlightenment.

5) To engage in a political campaign in defense of Israel and of Jewish rights.

IMMIGRATION (ALIYAH). Since the inception of the movement, *aliyah* had been a sacred precept of Zionist ideology and constituted the highest expression of Zionist fulfillment. As Ben-Gurion affirmed, the one and only hope for creative Jewish survival lay in immigration to the Jewish state. It contributes to the national strength and serves as an antidote to the demographic problem. It fortifies the physical bond between Israel and the Diaspora.

Jews have been immigrating to Ereẓ Israel for generations. They were motivated by sentimental and religious reasons. It was only from 1882 that the driving force was nationalism and the aspiration to lay the foundations of a national home, and eventually a state. Each wave of immigration was called *aliyah,* meaning ascent. Between 1882 and 1948 some 550,000 Jews made *aliyah.*

Jews immigrated in spite of the restrictions instituted first by the Ottoman government and subsequently by the British authorities imposed. In the eyes of the Turks and the British this kind of immigration was illegal, but the Zionist Organization considered the prohibition itself as illegal. It is estimated that the total number of *"illegal" immigrants (*aliyah bet*) was 120,000, which constituted about 15 to 20 percent of the Jewish population in Palestine in May 1948 (around 640,000). The figure of 120,000 does not include the Cyprus internees. Even during the hazardous years of World War II (1939–45) immigration did not stop and reached the total figure of both legal and "illegal" immigrants of 62,530. During the period between the end of World War II and May 15, 1948, the total number of immigrants, both legal and "illegal," amounted to 56,480, the infamous 1939 restrictions notwithstanding.

With the establishment of the State of Israel the gates of immigration opened wide. However, as the centers of Jewish communities in Eastern and Central Europe were tragically decimated, the State of Israel and the Jewish Agency turned to other centers. Between May 1948 and the late 1950s entire Jewish communities were transplanted to Israel. Among these communities were, in round numbers: Yemen (42,000), Iraq (125,000), Iran (30,000), Bulgaria (40,000), Yugoslavia (68,000), Czechoslovakia (20,000), Poland (120,000), Romania (125,000), Morocco, Tunisia, Algeria (60,000), Libya (32,000), China (2,250), and Aden (3,500). In addition to the sea route, the Jewish Agency organized accelerated immigration from Yemen, Iraq, and elsewhere (Operation Ezra and Nehemia, Operation Magic Carpet). Immigrants arrived in Israel from 70 countries speaking different languages and reared in different cultures and traditions. The newborn State and the Jewish Agency were confronted with the Herculean task of absorbing them and molding them into one nation.

During the first three years of Israel's existence its population more than doubled. During the 1950s and 1960s, Middle Eastern countries constituted a major source of immigration, while the 1970s saw a renewed wave from the West and the U.S.S.R. In the early 1990s there was a new wave of immigration from the former Soviet Union, as well as from other countries, notably Ethiopia and Argentina. In sum, from 1882 to 2005 more than 3,000,000 Jews immigrated to Israel, an unprecedented figure by world standards. By the end of the 20th century there were almost 100 times as many Jews in Ereẓ Israel as at the beginning of the century (50,000).

A word must be said about the two extraordinary Aliyot from the former Soviet Union as well as from Ethiopia. Isolated from the rest of world Jewry and living under a despotic government, Soviet Jewry was almost written off. However, the ecstatic reception accorded to Golda Meir at Moscow's Great Synagogue demonstrated that Soviet Jewry remained far from moribund in their ethnic loyalties. The emergence of a vibrant human rights movement among Soviet intellectuals was a powerful catalyst that contributed to the emergence of newfound nationalism and self-assertion. The remarkable military victory of the Israel Defense Forces in the Six-Day War was an inspiring source of pride. In consequence, the desire to immigrate to Israel became more powerful. The Soviet government was intransigent and hostile but the Jews did not give in. Their struggle could justly be termed heroic. Some were prepared to face imprisonment, to sacrifice their livelihoods and even life itself. The phenomenon of the "refusnik" fired the imagination of many far beyond the borders of Russia. Demonstrations were held in most of the Western capitals under the banner of "Let My People Go." Jews and gentiles took part in the campaign. It was a remarkable demonstration of solidarity in a cause.

American pressure too made its mark. On January 3, 1975, following resolutions overwhelmingly adopted by the House of Representatives and the Senate, President Gerald Ford signed the Trade Reform Act which incorporated the Jackson-Vanik-Hills Amendment. It made trade with the Soviet Union conditional on relaxation of emigration quotas for Jews wishing to go to Israel. It brought a reluctant Soviet Union to terms. For the Jewish lobby it was a remarkable victory.

During the 1970s, 160,000 Soviet Jews made *aliyah* to Israel, constituting approximately half the number of *olim* who arrived in the country. In February 1985 the best-known Prisoner of Zion, Nathan (Antoly) *Sharansky, was freed from a Soviet prison after a long international campaign for his release. On his arrival in Israel he was accorded a national welcome.

After Mikhail Gorbachev came to power a liberal and open policy was initiated, so that during the first part of 1990 *aliyah* reached a high point – 100,000 *olim* were registered – a number that would have been considered completely improbable a few years earlier.

The Israelis observed all this with amazement and admiration. It was nothing short of miraculous. It presented the government of Israel as well as the Jewish Agency with an unprecedented challenge. The absorption of hundreds of thousands of new immigrants within a short period of time in terms of housing, employment, and integration into Israeli society was a task that seemed beyond the ability of the young state. There were indeed a great many problems. But then a second miracle occurred. Not only did the Russian immigrants adjust to the new conditions with relative ease but within a short period they began to contribute to Israeli life, in economics, culture, science, and medical services. For this was an *aliyah* rich in talent, enterprising and determined. No previous *aliyah* had included so many academics, engineers, technicians, musicians, and scientists. Coming from a country which had been anything but democratic, they showed acute political awareness and their representation in the Knesset (eight seats) in a party called Yisrael be-Aliyah was a testimony to their civic maturity. In short, this was one of the greatest gifts that Israel and the Zionist enterprise had received since its foundation.

The Israelis were spellbound also by immigration of Jews from Ethiopia. They were of an entirely different background. Black-skinned, they lived in the highlands of Gondar province. Considered by their neighbors as falashas (strangers), they identified themselves as *Beta Israel. Their origin was uncertain but it seems that they were Africans who in the early Middle Ages had been converted to Judaism. Although cut off from world Jewry they had preserved Jewish customs and traditions with remarkable tenacity in the face of merciless persecutions at the hands of Christian governments. Nor did their yearning to return to Zion abate at any time. By the 19th century their numbers had dwindled to less than 30,000. In 1948, when the news of the foundation of the Jewish State reached them, they became possessed of a feverish desire to depart to the Land of Promise.

In March 1979, with President Carter's assistance, the government of Israel discreetly transferred funds to Sudan's President Ja'afar Numeiri, who for his part agreed to grant Ethiopian Jews temporary asylum in Sudan. Yet their initial migration of over 9,000 people was a trying ordeal. They went on foot, encountering incredible difficulties – disease, starvation, robbery, rape – until they reached a prearranged base, from which 2,000 were transported to the Red Sea coast and then taken to Israel by the Israeli navy. Five years later, in 1984, Operation Moses was carried out, during which another 7,000 Ethiopian Jews were taken out of Sudan. This time they were flown to Europe and from there to Israel. The Israeli government, jointly with the Jewish Agency, the World Zionist Organization, and other bodies, had done a magnificent job. Operation Moses was followed by Operation Solomon, during which, in May 1991, 15,000 Ethiopian Jews were air-lifted to Israel in 36 planes. About 4,000 remained behind in the Gondar highlands; these too, in due course, were quietly, though less dramatically, transported in small groups to Israel.

The absorption of the Ethiopian Jews and their integration into the Israeli society has proven to be far more difficult than that of *olim* from the former Soviet Union. But at least their physical existence is assured. Their *aliyah* could be truly termed as a heroic implementation of the Zionist ideal without prior education in Zionism.

SETTLEMENT ON THE LAND. Like *aliyah*, settlement on the land constitutes a principal tenet of Zionism. The back to the land movement symbolized the transformation of the Jew's image from that of a "luftmentsh" in the Diaspora to that of a healthy and productive individual rooted in the land. This was palpable evidence of normalization. It showed the world that the Zionist experiment was not a passing phenomenon but a durable entity.

In addition to the social, economic, and political importance of settlement on the land, it had also a strategic value. It defined the borders of the Yishuv and subsequently of the State. Thus Kefar Giladi, Metulla and Tel Ḥai ensured that the Galilee panhandle would become part of the Jewish National Home. The pioneers of the 11 settlements that were established in the Negev on the eve of the proclamation of the State ensured that the Negev would not be cut off from the rest of the country.

Since the beginning in 1882, 1,221 rural settlements have been founded in all parts of the country (944 since statehood), changing its superstructure and landscape beyond recognition. It was the World Zionist Organization that played the major role in implementing this huge enterprise. The Jewish National Fund (the Keren Kayemet le-Israel) was also engaged in agricultural development, acquisition of land, building new roads, and afforestation. The land purchased by the KKL became the property of the Jewish people. It could not be sold and was therefore formally leased by the settlers.

EDUCATION. Education has traditionally been the Jewish forte. It is the asset that Jews throughout the generations have valued the most. A learned man was esteemed as a model to be emulated. Education fortified the Jewish ability to survive in hostile environments. Although emancipation brought its obvious blessings, it was sometimes at the expense of Jewish identity and culture. Acculturation and the consequent assimilation, not to mention intermarriage, have become the greatest threats to Jewish survival. In the United States the number of mixed marriages has already passed the 50% mark. In France, in England, and in Western Europe in general the situation is not much better. This is the price the Jewish people are paying for the enjoyment of life in open societies.

The World Zionist Organization could not remain indifferent to this dangerous trend. The answer lies in education. It should be borne in mind that in the Diaspora 50 percent of Jewish youth do not receive any Jewish education at all, and that only 25 per cent attend Jewish schools. First it should be emphasized that education begins at home. The home and family life play an important part in designing the educational process. It is the parents who provide the initial framework and lifestyle that will prepare the child for Jewish life in a gentile environment. But if the parents themselves are subject to the identity crisis so characteristic of life in the Diaspora, the future of their offspring as Jews does not seem bright.

The school system is meant to ameliorate the situation, and it is here that the Zionist Organization plays its part by inspiring and assisting the local Jewish communities to cultivate Jewish education. In concrete terms teacher-*sheliḥim* from Israel are sent to reinforce the existing staffs of local schools and give them particular direction. They focus on teaching Hebrew, Jewish history, and Zionism and on inculcating greater familiarity with the State of Israel. Their overriding purpose is to strengthen Jewish identity, to induce pride in the Jewish heritage, and to equip the students with the tools to counter anti-Zionist and antisemitic propaganda.

There are two kinds of schools: Jewish day schools and complementary systems of education. Most day schools are on the elementary level. After completion, studies are continued in general schools. The complementary educational system is meant for those parents who for a variety of reasons do not have the option of a full day school. In most cases it is housed on the synagogue premises or in the community cultural center. It has classes on Sundays and thus the system became known as "Sunday School." The program of study at complementary schools focuses on fundamental Jewish concepts, Hebrew, the teaching of prayer, preparation for Jewish festivals, and reinforcing the bond with the State of Israel. The educational effect of this system is limited but still the seeds are being sown. In the United States about 24 percent of young Jews participate in this framework.

In addition to the formal educational system, youth and children enjoy an informal educational experience. In most Jewish communities in the Diaspora there are frameworks which facilitate encounters aimed at the consolidation of Jewish national identity and ideas. These are provided by the Zionist youth movements, which operate practically on parallel lines with the youth movements in Israel. In North America about seven percent of children and youth participate in informal youth movement activities, in the former Soviet Union about 20 percent, and in Latin America 30 percent. Most of the youth organizations maintain strong connections with Israel and Zionism though with different ideological orientations. Moreover, an integral part of their programs are visits to Israel.

Visits to Israel have proved highly effective in the educational process. They have existed since the 1950s and expanded significantly after the Six-Day War. They last for several weeks during the summer vacation and include tours of historical sites of national significance and an introduction to contemporary Israeli society and culture. Since the 1990s these trips have been called named the "Israel Experience." Jewish leaders throughout the world recognized the importance of this particular experiment in stemming assimilation by forging Jewish identity and in educating future leaders. In 2000 a new venture was launched: "The Birthright Israel Project." It is sponsored by Jewish philanthropists, the government of Israel, the Jewish Agency, and Jewish communities throughout the world. The project also enables university students to take courses at institutions of higher learning in Israel free of charge through scholarships. Nearly 40,000 young Jews have visited Israel so far within the framework of the Birthright Israel Project.

Also of importance are summer camps for children and youth financed by communities In the Diaspora. They are popular particularly in North America, where there are over 200 such camps. In some cases camps are active all year round. The participants range from age 8 to 16. The Zionist Organization plays a major role in all the above-mentioned activities. Early in 1981 the World Zionist Organization launched the Jerusalem Fellows program, which aims to recruit young men and women and train them in Israel for leadership positions in the field of education and organization.

In the area of adult education in 2000 the Jewish Agency initiated a program of "People to People" which aims to stimulate intercourse between professional groups and individuals in Israel and the Diaspora. Partnerships between cities in Israel and Jewish communities in the Diaspora in various parts of the world ("Partnership 2000") is yet another example of cooperation and the demonstration of mutual responsibility. Thus, the city of Netanyah is linked to the Jewish community in Cincinnati; Ramleh and the Gezer regional council to Kansas City; Ashkelon to Mexico; Nahariyyah to Belgium, etc. Public lectures, conferences, and seminars add another dimension to adult education. A powerful factor in galvanizing Jewry and enhancing solidarity with Israel are extraordinary events like the Yom Kippur War and the struggle for the rights of Soviet Jews ("Let My People Go") and against all manifestations of antisemitism and the vilification of Israel.

ORGANIZATION. At the outset of the 21st century the supreme body of the World Zionist Organization remained the Zionist Congress – an elected parliament of sorts. It constitutes the organizational arm of the Zionist movement. Its main roles are: to stimulate *aliyah*; to strengthen the State of Israel; to promote Jewish and Hebrew education and cultivate Jewish values; to counter the trends of assimilation and defend Jewish rights. The Congress meets every four or five years and the seats (more than 500) are allocated geographically in the following proportions; 38% for Israel, 29% for the United States; and 33% for all other countries. In Israel delegates are allocated to the Zionist political parties proportionately to their representation in the Knesset.

The Congress elects the Zionist executive, on which major ideological movements and international bodies are represented, as well as the Zionist General Council. The latter body meets once a year between congresses. The chairman of the Zionist executive serves also as chairman of the Jewish Agency and the Executive. Similarly, the treasurer of the World Zionist Organization serves as the treasurer of the Jewish Agency. In 1952 an agreement was reached between the government of Israel on the one hand, and the World Zionist Organization and the Jewish Agency on the other, on a functional distribution. Accordingly, the Zionist institutions took upon themselves all matters relating to *aliyah*, absorption of immigrants, and settlement on the land, while security, finances, trade, employment, etc. are the prerogatives of the government. The agreement was confirmed in a covenant two years later. In 1980 a coordinating commission of these two constituent bodies approved the establishment of a national authority for *aliyah* and absorption.

Between the years 1973 and 2000 the following leaders served as chairmen of the Zionist Executive: Aryeh Dulzin, Pinḥas Sapir, Joseph Almogi, Simcha Dinitz, Yehiel Leket,

Avraham Burg, and Salai Meridor. Since the Twenty-Seventh Zionist Congress, no president had been elected.

There is a body of opinion that maintains that with the establishment of the State of Israel the Zionist Movement had fulfilled its historical task and outlived its usefulness. This is a misconception. The state, as Herzl proclaimed, is not an end in itself but only a means to implement high ideals such as the ingathering of exiles; redemption of land; building of a model society, and serving as a beacon to Jewry and the world at large. So long as these objectives have not been fulfilled, Zionism still has a role to play in Jewish history. Zionism is the embodiment of Jewish nationalism and as long as the Jewish people exist, Zionism will endure as well.

[Isaiah Friedman (2nd ed.)]

ZIONIST UTOPIAS

In the initial stages of the Zionist movement, the borderline between programmatic and utopian writing was blurred. Moreover, Zionist authors and publicists often consciously made use of the utopian form in order to visualize the end product and thereby prove the feasibility of Zionism. Herzl's *Der Judenstaat* is a classic example of a book in which Zionist ideology and utopian visions are present. In a letter to Moritz *Guedemann (August 22, 1895), Herzl writes of the book: "I can now say why it is no Utopia… There have been plenty of Utopias before and after Thomas More, but no rational person ever thought of putting them into practice. They are entertaining, but not stirring" (Complete Diaries 1, 235–6). Herzl's novel *Altneuland*, which was the most famous Zionist utopia, had a great deal in common with the program presented in *Der Judenstaat. Altneuland* sought to indicate the way in which Herzl visualized the realization of Zionism – a Jewish state in which technology would be developed to the highest degree and in which the Jewish intelligentsia would find unlimited opportunities. The new culture, however, would be essentially a European culture, based on a medley of languages and devoid of distinctive Jewish character. It is thus not surprising that Aḥad Ha-Am, to whom the continuity of Jewish culture was the essence of Zionism, was outraged by the book. Herzl envisaged that the Jewish state would become a reality by 1923, 20 years after the publication of *Altneuland*.

Another Zionist utopia, *Massa le-Ereẓ Yisrael bi-Shenat Tat* ("A Journey to Ereẓ Israel in the Year 5800 (2040)," 1893), by the Hebrew writer Elhanan Leib *Lewinsky, which preceded *Altneuland* by ten years, reflects the Zionist dream of East European Jewry, rooted as it was in Hebrew culture. The Hebrew language and the fostering of Hebrew culture occupy a central place in the book, and Aḥad Ha-Am's vision of Ereẓ Israel becoming the spiritual center of the Jewish people reaches fulfillment. In *Ein Zukunftsblick* by Edmund *Eisler (written in 1882 and published anonymously in 1885) both the political and cultural visions of the Jewish state are found. The novel describes the Jewish exodus from Europe and the creation of the state of "Judah" in Ereẓ Israel, which has Hebrew as its official language; the fledgling state is attacked by its neighbors, but vanquishes them all. Eisler even had a nightmare vision of Germany. He exchanged correspondence with Herzl on the subject of his book. In the main, the book reflected the background of European antisemitism and the pogroms in Russia.

Edward Bellamy's book *Looking Backward, 1887–2000* had a profound influence on Zionist utopias. One example was a utopia of political Zionism by Max Austerberg-Verakoff, *Das Reich Judaea im Jahre 6000* (2241), published in 1893. The author, a non-Jew (although possibly of Jewish origin), envisaged a mass exodus of Jews from Europe, their settlement in Ereẓ Israel, and the founding there of a Jewish state with Hebrew as its official language. He discusses the attitude of the Jewish state toward the European power that had been guilty of persecuting the Jews (Russia) and the relations between the citizens of the Jewish state and the Jews who stayed behind in the Diaspora. Austerberg-Verakoff also established contact with Herzl. Another Zionist utopia inspired by Bellamy was *Looking Ahead* (1899) by Henry Pereira *Mendes. A native of England, Mendes settled in the United States and for several decades played an important role in the cultural life of American Jewry. He was one of the first American Jews to respond to Herzl's call, and his book expresses the essence of the Zionist vision: the Jewish state and Jerusalem, its capital, would be the center of world peace, and by the creation of the state, the nations of the world would redress the wrongs they had perpetrated against the Jews throughout the ages. There is also a description of the mass exodus of Jews to Ereẓ Israel; those who stay behind are enjoined to be loyal citizens of their countries, without losing awareness of the temporary nature of their residence outside of Ereẓ Israel.

At the height of the *Dreyfus trial (1898), a utopian extravaganza, "Anti-Goyism in Zion," was published in *Siècle*, a Parisian journal, in March 1898; it later appeared in *Die Welt* in German translation (April 1898) and was also published in Hebrew (1954). Its author was Jacques Bahar, who represented Algerian Jewry at the First Zionist Congress. His work, written under the impact of manifestations of French antisemitism (which also had its repercussions in Algeria), describes a "Dreyfus trial" taking place in the Jewish state, with "Anti-Goyism" playing the role of European antisemitism. He makes the point that in the Jewish state tolerance would prevail and a phenomenon such as the antisemitism that dominated the Paris scene of 1898 would be unthinkable.

Two utopias describe a Jewish state bearing the name "Israel." One, written by the Hebrew author Isaac *Fernhof, describes the ascent of the poor and downtrodden Jews to Ereẓ Israel, where they create an independent state to which they give the name the State of Israel. The book is called *Shenei Dimyonot* ("Two Ideas") – one being the reality as experienced by the author, the other his vision of the Jewish state. The second utopia that refers to the Jewish state as the State of Israel was the work of the Hebrew-Yiddish writer Hillel *Zeitlin. Written in 1919 under the name *In der Medinas Yisrael in Yor 2000* ("In the State of Israel in the year 2000"), it reflects the tremendous impact of the Balfour Declaration upon the Jewish masses. The author foresees the establishment of the state and its growth and development. The work appeared in serial form in *Der Moment*, the Warsaw Yiddish daily, but was never completed. The Balfour Declaration also inspired *Komemiyyut* ("Upright"), a comprehensive work written in Russia in 1920–21 by the Hebrew author Shalom Ben-Avram and published shortly thereafter in the quarterly *Ha-Tekufah*. This utopia contains an astounding accurate vision of mass *aliyah*, the founding of the Jewish state, and the Jew at last straightening his back in the young and vibrant state.

During the British Mandatory period (1918–48), a number of utopias were published in Hebrew (as *Yerushalayim ha-Benuyah* by Boris *Schatz, 1924). They often reflect the contemporary situation – the struggle for Jewish labor and the opposition to the Mandatory regime. When the Jewish state is founded, the problems are foreseen as solved and all unjust decrees abolished.

[Getzel Kressel]

CHRISTIAN ZIONISM

As Zionism is understood to mean a modern Jewish movement aiming at resettlement in the Land of Israel and the revival of an independent Jewish nation, "Christian Zionism," i.e., the active support of Christians for such a movement, could not have preceded the Jewish forerunners of Zionism in the second half of the 19th century. However, Christian Zionism had a long prehistory, deeply rooted in theological thought and messianic expectations. Only gradually, with the emergence of Jewish political and settlement activities in Palestine, did Christian Zionism become more and more secular, pragmatic, and political, though it often still bore the imprint of its religious tradition and motivations. Thus, even in the historic breakthrough of the Balfour Declaration, issued by the British government in 1917, when political expediency was apparently the main factor, religious motives were certainly not absent from the thoughts of men like Lloyd George and Balfour. The importance of the Christian and biblical traditions also became apparent in the attitude toward the State of Israel in the 1950s and 1960s. The Afro-Asian world (including Muslim countries), insofar as it had no biblical traditions – particularly in Central and Eastern Asia – could only gradually "discover" and evaluate the ancient roots of the Jewish renaissance in the Land of Israel, and this realization developed mostly after these states had developed formal relations with Israel on a purely utilitarian basis. The attitude of the Christian world, however, remained clearly influenced by an undercurrent of intimacy derived from the biblical tradition.

The Theological Background. From the time of the Reformation, the belief that Jews should return to the Holy Land, in accordance with the biblical prophecies, became popular mainly among pietistic Protestants and certain groups of English Puritans. It was based on the millenarian concept which held, on the basis of a literal interpretation of apocalyptic prophecies, that the second coming of Jesus was at hand and that he would rule from Jerusalem for 1,000 years (the millennium). The millenarians anticipated not only the return of the Jews to their land but also their conversion to Christianity as important conditions and "signs of the time" prior to the second coming (Advent).

The Restoration movement spread from 16th-century England to other European countries and became particularly strong in the United States from the 18th century. It flooded the Protestant world with publications. Sometimes the Restorationists requested heads of state to take political measures in order to obtain rights for the Jews to settle in the Holy Land. Their activity remained without any practical results, however, until the 19th century, when essential changes took place in the character of the movement and in the motivations of Christians who supported the return of the Jews to the Land of Israel.

Some of the new sects which arose placed this belief at the center of their theology as the fulfillment of the eschatological prophecies which would bring on the end of days and the millennium. In 1830 the Plymouth Brethren were founded in England by John N. Darby (1800–82), whose doctrine of dispensationalist premillennialism asserted that all the biblical prophecies relate to the return of the Jewish people to its homeland prior to the Advent. Before the second coming, however, the Jews and all the other nations will be judged during a period of tribulation, after which Jesus and the Jewish remnant will rule over all the nations from Jerusalem. Many Protestant Fundamentalist churches adopted this outlook and continue to promote it to this day.

In 1844 the Christadelphians were established in England by John Thomas, author of *Elpis Israel*. From the outset, this sect supported the return of Jews to the Land of Israel. Later it offered practical assistance to Jews, such as the support of the Ḥibbat Zion movement, and even the attempt to rescue Jews during the Nazi Holocaust. The Mormons, founded by Joseph Smith in the United States in 1830, held that Jews would return to their land as "a sign of the time" of the second coming. In 1841 the Mormon missionary Orson Hyde was sent to Jerusalem, where he recited a "Zionist" prayer and dedicated the land to the Jews from the top of the Mount of Olives in Jerusalem. The Adventist movement, which emerged in the United States in 1830, split into many sects. A few of these sects view the return of the Jews to the Land of Israel as a fulfillment of their eschatological beliefs, and some of them have moved their center to Israel.

In the 19th century millenarian sects, mostly American, engaged in experiments in settlement in the Holy Land in order to await the approaching Advent of Jesus. All these attempts failed, including the 1851 agricultural settlement at Monthope, near Jaffa, of the American Clorinda S. Minor and the settlement near Jaffa of Reverend G. Adams and a group of Americans from the Church of the Messiah in 1866.

The Emergence of Political Motives. During the 19th century, Christian politicians in various countries attempted to act on behalf of the return of the Jews to the Land of Israel, adding to their religious beliefs the political interests of their countries in the Near East. An outstanding example was Lord Anthony Ashley Cooper, Earl of Shaftesbury (1801–85), who drew up detailed projects for the settlement of Jews in Palestine under British auspices, which he presented to the government and circulated among Protestant heads of state in Europe and in the United States. The beginning of practical Jewish settlement on the land in Ereẓ Israel, and especially the establishment of the Ḥibbat Zion movement and later Theodor Herzl's political Zionism, contributed to an increase in millenarian assistance to the realization of Zionist aspirations. The Canadian theologian Henry Wentworth Monk visited Palestine and assisted in the foundation of the first Jewish settlements. The English mystic Laurence Oliphant, who eventually settled in Palestine, lent aid to the first Jewish pioneers from Russia, tried to intercede on their behalf in Constantinople, and founded an influential Christian group in London to assist the Ḥibbat Zion movement. The Zionist activities of Herzl's friend William H. *Hechler also derived from a deeply religious outlook.

The most famous of the Zionist millenarians in the United States was William Blackstone (1841–1933) of Chicago, the author of *Jesus is Coming*, in which he expounded his belief in the future of the Jews in the Land of Israel according to the dispensationalist conception. He attempted a political realization of his ideas through memoranda to the president of the United States, in 1891 and in 1916, which demanded American intervention for the return of the Jews to the Land of Israel as a solution to the czarist anti-Jewish persecutions. Hundreds of eminent Americans signed these petitions, which stimulated various reactions in the general and the Jewish press. Blackstone participated in several Zionist conventions in the United States and remained a supporter of the Zionist movement until his death.

Archaeologists, Scholars, and Politicians. In the second half of the 19th century some Christians supported the return of the Jews to their homeland out of exclusively humanitarian or political motivations, distinct from theological views. In 1852 Colonel George Gawler (1796–1869) established the Association for Promoting Jewish Settlement in Palestine, which assisted the British consul in Jerusalem in the training of local Jews for agricultural work. He also published practical suggestions for Jewish settlement in Ereẓ Israel as a guarantee for establishing British influence in Syria. The Palestine Exploration Fund, established in England in 1865, was a center for energetic supporters of Jewish settlement in the Land of Israel. Among its members were the archaeologist Charles Warren, who conducted excavations in Jerusalem and foretold Jewish rule in the country, and Claude Reignier Conder (1849–1910), a cartographer and scholar of Palestinian studies who preached and wrote on the realization of the Zionist idea. The Italian philosopher and politician Benedetto Musolino (1809–85) preached Jewish settlement in the Land of Israel as a means of bringing European culture into the Middle East in *La Gerusalemme e il Popolo Ebreo* (1851). Jean Henri Dunant (1820–1910), founder of the International Red Cross, displayed a great interest in a humane solution to the Jewish problem. From 1863 to 1876 he attempted (in vain) to rouse the Jewish organizations in Western Europe to act on behalf of Jewish settlement of Palestine, and he founded the Palestine Colonization Society in London in 1875.

In 1887 the question of Jewish settlement in Ereẓ Israel reached the British parliament. Edward *Cazalet, a well-known industrialist and economist, demanded the return of the Jews to Palestine under British auspices both in his book and in his campaign speeches for parliament. He was the first Christian who regarded Ereẓ Israel as the spiritual and scientific center for Jewry, and he foresaw the idea of a Hebrew university in Jerusalem.

After the Balfour Declaration. In the 20th century, mainly after the Balfour Declaration (1917), another change occurred in Christian activity on behalf of Zionism and the establishment of a Jewish state. The British Palestine Society was established and was active from 1916 to 1924 and from 1930 to 1946 in advancing common interests of British policy and Zionism. Similar Christian organizations were founded in other countries. However, the most vigorous assistance and open support of Zionist aspirations were given by several Christian groups in the United States. In 1930 the Rev. Edward Russell founded the Pro-Palestine Federation, which was joined mostly by clergy. In 1932 the American Palestine Committee was founded. Its members included prominent public figures, statesmen, and officials. The Christian Council of Palestine was founded in 1942 and had a membership of 3,000 clergymen in 1946, mostly from liberal churches. The latter two organizations merged in 1946 as the American Christian Palestine Committee, which had a very influential membership of 15,000. This organization published books and pamphlets on the justice of Zionist aspirations and later to strengthen sympathy toward the State of Israel. After the establishment of the state, gentile friends of Israel founded organizational frameworks for their activities in the form of friendship leagues.

[Yona Malachy]

INTRODUCTION TO ZIONIST BIBLIOGRAPHY

Zionist literature developed in many languages: German (*Rome and Jerusalem* by Moses Hess), Hebrew (*Derishat Ẓiyyon* by Ẓevi Hirsch Kalischer and the articles of D. *Gordon), and gradually in many other languages, not only in countries with large Jewish populations. It also appeared in many forms, from thick volumes to leaflets and periodicals issued at various intervals (dailies, weeklies, monthlies, yearbooks, collections commemorating special occasions, etc.). The variety of form is reflected in the variety of genre: feature writing, essays, chronicles, belles lettres in all its forms (fiction, plays, poetry, etc.), historical research and documentation, and so forth. Zionist literature covers the period from the 1860s to the present and, including all the books, leaflets, articles, and so on, encompasses millions of items.

A difficulty in cataloging this wealth of material is that in the early days of Ḥibbat Zion, the border between "Zionist" material and works on Ereẓ Israel in general was very vague, and this lack of a clear distinction between the two categories was not overcome in later years. Even after the establishment of the State of Israel it was difficult to draw a distinct line between literature on the state and writings on the Zionist movement. Throughout the existence of Zionist literature, therefore, the terms, "Ḥibbat Zion," "Zionist movement," "Ereẓ Israel," and the "State of Israel," have been viewed as loosely synonymous, although the special scope of each concept was clear. Thus it is difficult to differentiate bibliographically between the history of the *yishuv* from the beginning of the 1880s and the history of the movement and political Zionism.

This overlapping in concepts is inevitably reflected in the majority of the works cited below. Characteristic is the subtitle of a recent platform for research, which is entitled *Ha-Ẓiyyonut: Me'assef le-Toledot ha-Tenu'ah ha-Ẓiyyonit ve-ha-Yishuv ha-Yehudi be-Ereẓ Yisrael* ("Zionism: Journal of the History of the Zionist Movement and the *Yishuv* in Ereẓ Israel," vol. 1, 1970). The same problem of exact definition exists in the bibliography *Esrim Shenot Medinat Yisrael* ("Twenty Years of the State of Israel," 1970) by A. Neuberg, in which much Zionist material is found, and the index volumes titled *Palestine and Zionism* (all these items are discussed below).

Bibliographies. As a rule, the bibliographies dealing with Zionism are listed in Shunami's *Bibliography of Jewish Bibliographies* (1965[2]), but not all the material on this subject is found under the headings "Zionism" or "Zionist" in the index (p. 990), and a considerable amount of relevant material is found in other divisions. Bibliographical attention was first paid to the subject of Zionism at the end of the 19th century, even before the advent of Theodor Herzl. Practical efforts intensified with the advent of political Zionism, especially when newspapers throughout the world began to display an interest in Zionism. At a meeting of Russian members of the "Actions Committee" in Minsk, following the Minsk Conference (1902), it was decided to charge G. Belkowsky with the task of publishing a comprehensive bibliography on Zionism. The book came out in Russia under the title *Ukazatel literatury o sionizme* (St. Petersberg, 1903). It did not cite the names of the editors of the bibliography, which Belkowsky revealed after many years in a detailed article on this project (*Haolam*, Sept. 10, 1942, p. 425). The work listed over 4,000 entries in a variety of languages, in three categories: (1) Jewish nationalism; (2) Zionism: Theory and Practice; and (3) Ereẓ Israel.

The second of the three parts, which was to appear later and include literature in Hebrew and Yiddish, was not published because of the conditions in czarist Russia at the time. Hebrew works on Zionism were recorded afterward by William *Zeitlin in his bibliography *Bibliotheca Sionistica* (Frankfurt, 1909; reprint from ZHB, vols. 12–13, 1908–09; includes works from 1852 to 1905).

At the same time a bibliographical project of vast dimensions on Palestine, entitled *Die Palaestina Literatur*, began to be carried out under the editorship of Peter Thomsen. Up to 1971, six volumes had been published, covering the literature from 1895 to 1939 (although the title page of the sixth volume states that it goes down to 1944). This series was published in Germany from 1908 to 1956 (the beginning of the sixth volume includes a biography of Thomsen). Material on Zionism is found only in the first four volumes and in the section on contemporary Palestine; a vast amount of material is listed in several languages (inter alia, bibliographies other than those recorded by S. Shunami).

Since 1944 many bibliographies have appeared, some of a general nature and some devoted to various bodies and institutions of the Zionist movement and Zionist Organization. Among the latest general and detailed bibliographies that include Zionist literature in various languages is *Bibliografiah Ẓiyyonit* (1943), by Abraham Levinson (with the cooperation of N.M. Gelber), which lists 2,400 entries in 17 languages. Bibliographical notations have been added to each section of Yiẓḥak Gruenbaum's work *Ha-Tenu'ah ha-Ẓiyyonit* (vols. 1–4, 1942–54) by G. Kressel (1–2) and Israel Klausner (3–4). With the establishment of the State of Israel, Sophie A. Udin published an important bibliographical listing in English entitled "A List of References Leading to the Establishment of the State of Israel" (in *The Journal of Educational Sociology*, 22:3 (Nov. 1948), 239–47). Finally, *The State of Israel* (1948–68), by Assia Neuberg, contains much material on Zionism in a variety of languages (1970).

Any bibliography, no matter how complete, is by its nature unable to be entirely up-to-date in recording the continuous publication of works each year. Therefore annual bibliographical listings are included in various yearbooks: the *American Jewish Yearbook*, the *Palestine Yearbook*, the *Zionist Yearbook*, the *Jewish Book Annual*, etc. The most complete and correct ongoing bibliographical listing, however, is that published in each edition of the bibliographical quarterly of the Jewish National and University Library in Jerusalem, *Kirjath Sepher*, in the section on "Zionism, Ereẓ Israel, the State of Israel," which covers material published in Israel and abroad. The Zionist Archives in Jerusalem have published a bibliographical bulletin in various forms and at irregular intervals since 1936 (mimeographed). A vast amount of material on Zionism can also be found in the many bibliographies on personalities active in the field; these are listed in the section "Personal Bibliographies" in Shunami. The same is true of bibliographies on institutions and organizations within the Zionist movement, e.g., *Madrikh Bibliografi le-Sifrut Ẓiyyonit-Datit* ("A Bibliographical Guide to Literature on Religious Zionism," 1960[2]), by Yiẓḥak Raphael, which goes beyond the field defined in its title and also includes articles in periodicals and the press, and *Ha-Po'el ha-Mizrachi be-Ereẓ Yisrael* (1968), by Yosef Salmon, which also includes articles.

Press and Periodicals. The press and periodicals, Jewish and non-Jewish, in all languages, contain much important material on the history of the Ḥibbat Zion movement, political Zionism, and everything pertaining to Ereẓ Israel over the past generations, from first-hand documentation (statements, press releases) to news items, commentary, reaction, essays, and research. Periodicals of all sorts, issued at varying intervals, whether published by official institutions of the Zionist Organization or its sympathizers or by those opposed or openly hostile to Zionism, reach into the thousands; and recent research has led to the conclusion that periodical literature attacking Zionism – whether published by Jews or non-Jews – is no less important for the study of Zionism than the publications of official Zionist organs or Zionist sympathizers.

In the beginning the scope of the Zionist press was limited, in direct relation to the size of the movement itself. In the 1860s and 1870s, the Jewish press, in all languages, was generally hostile, or at least apathetic, to the Jewish nationalist movement, with the exception of the *Jewish Chronicle* in England, *Der Israelit* and *Die Juedische Presse* in Germany, *The Occident* in the United States, and the Hebrew *Ha-Maggid* (Prussia). A pioneer of Zionist journalism in Germany was *Selbstemanzipation*, edited by N. Birnbaum, and its successor *Zion*, edited by H. Loewe and Willy Bambus (until Bambus came into conflict with Herzl before the First Zionist Congress). Then Herzl began to publish the weekly *Die Welt* (in German), which later became the first official organ of the Zionist Organization. Afterward organs of the Zionist organizations in various countries began to appear in a number of languages. Over the years Zionist newspapers have been established wherever a Zionist organization functioned, and some non-Zionist newspapers became pro-Zionist or tempered their opposition. At the same time, however (and until World War I), the Jewish press that was not particularly sympathetic toward Zionism – from the Orthodox and Reform movements to the leftist parties in Eastern Europe – was also a substantial force. The change in their attitude came about gradually, as the achievements of the Zionist movement and the *yishuv* became more noticeable and, by the outbreak of World War II, the future of the Jews in Europe grew darker and darker. Finally, a radical change in attitude came about during and after the Holocaust, which practically reversed the situation that had existed during the 1860s and 1870s: a very small minority of the press remained opposed to the Zionist movement and the State of Israel and the majority were devoted to them to one degree or another. Because of this change in attitude, it was practically unnecessary for the Zionist movement to maintain its own organs, although such a press does continue to exist in many countries.

The Hebrew press holds a unique position. Even when it was employed to preach the doctrines of the Haskalah and indifference toward Jewish nationalism and Zionism, the Hebrew language was, by its very nature, a kind of living bridge to Ereẓ Israel. After the illusions of the Haskalah in Eastern Europe had been destroyed, therefore, the Hebrew press was the most loyal instrument of the Ḥibbat Zion movement and afterward of political Zionism, each paper expressing a difference in orientation. Sharp opposition to Jewish nationalism and Zionism in the Hebrew press was inconsequential compared to the overwhelming majority of pro-Zionist publications. The opposition began with *Ha-Emet*, a socialist-oriented paper edited by A.S. Liebermann, and after a number of years it was also expressed in extreme Orthodox circles, thus appearing at opposite poles of the spectrum. Over the years this opposition has taken various forms (today as the pro-Arab Israel Communists, Rakaḥ, and the *Neturei Karta, respectively). An impressive symbol of the developments discussed above was the development of the Zionist leadership and its expression in the press and Hebrew literature through such personalities as Lilienblum, Aḥad-Ha-Am, Sokolow, and many others.

Lists of Newspapers and Indexes to their Contents. These two instruments of aid never kept up with the developments in the field of Jewish and Zionist journalism. For decades lists of Jewish newspapers have appeared, both in various lexicons and separately. Comprehensive listings are the *Tentative List of Jewish Periodicals in Axis-Occupied Countries* (1947), covering the period between the two world wars, and Joseph Fraenkel's *The Jewish Press of the World* (1967[6]), which reflects the situation after World War II. In this period, the distinction between Zionist and non-Zionist publications has become blurred, and any comprehensive list of Jewish publications reflects principally Zionist or pro-Zionist publications (see also Hebrew *Press; for other lists of publications, including those prepared by Fraenkel, see Shunami, Bibliography, second edition, index).

More problematic is the task of getting to the vast amount of material in the press. Indexes of the press, long accepted as standard in the world at large, are still rather innovations in the realm of the Jewish and Hebrew press. Only lately have really useful indexes come into being, but this venture is still in its infancy. One thing must be stressed in regard to material on Zionism: it is not to be found under subject headings such as "Zionism" and the like. Over the last generation Zionism encompassed the entire Jewish world and is thus to be found under thousands of other subject headings. Among the indexes included by Shunami and others that have been issued recently, the following deserve special attention:

(1) S.A. Udin and S. Landress (eds.), *Palestine and Zionism* (vols. 1–11, 1949–58) is organized according to a dictionary catalog (as are the two following works), so that "Zionism" is scattered among an abundance of sources; at the end of each volume of this important index to periodicals is a separate index to books and pamphlets, and it also covers material published in languages other than English from 1946 to 1956.

(2) *Index to Jewish Periodicals*, edited by Miriam Leikind, has been published in Cleveland, Ohio, since 1964 (seven volumes through 1970) and covers material from 1963 onward.

(3) Index to *Ha-Po'el ha-Ẓa'ir*, edited by Isa and G. Kressel (1968). The index to this weekly during the 50 years of its existence is essentially an index to all the events in the Zionist

movement, the *yishuv*, and the labor movement during this period and is the largest index of this kind (in its dimensions and number of entries – more than 100,000) that has yet been published in Hebrew. It is also worth noting that an event located in the index to one newspaper can easily be found, according to the dates, in the rest of the press.

(4) The quarterly of the Jewish National and University Library, *Kirjath Sepher*, lists (beginning with no. 21) with exactness the contents of periodicals on Jewish studies and important articles in the daily press. Anyone wishing to keep up with what is going on in all fields of Jewish studies or any one or set of fields therein must go over each and every issue; for the sake of expediency, however, Issachar Yoel has compiled the *Index of Articles on Jewish Studies* (for 1966ff.), which reviews the yearly output according to special categories, including Ereẓ Israel, Zionism, and State of Israel. It includes an index to the largest number of newspapers and periodicals in this ramified field.

Encyclopedias and Lexicons of Zionism. Every Jewish lexicon obviously contains much material on Zionism, whether on personalities or Zionist affairs. Nonetheless, throughout the decades the need was felt for a special lexicon of Zionism, which would cover all aspects of this subject. The first attempt at this task, which still holds a position of major importance, was the lexicon published by the Zionist Federation in Germany in 1909, *Zionistisches A-B-C Buch*. The entries therein on personalities and Zionist affairs are written with exactitude and provide a comprehensive picture of the Zionist Organization, through the end of the first decade of its existence. The participants in putting the volume together were the heads of the Zionist movement in Germany and Austria. The second venture into this field was the *Leksikon Ẓiyyoni* (1924) of the Hebrew writer S.L. Zitron; however, it is restricted to personalities only. A Zionist lexicon (in Yiddish) of greater dimensions, whose intention was to cover personalities, Zionist affairs, the names of settlements in Ereẓ Israel, etc., began to come out in Warsaw under the title *Tsiyionistisher Leksikon*, under the editorship of B. Zweibaum; however, only one volume was published (1935; up to the middle of the letter "*bet*"). Another Yiddish lexicon published in Warsaw, *Yidisher Gezelshaftlekher Leksikon*, edited by Reuven Ben-Shem (Feldschuh), met a similar fate. Its first volume, which also included personalities, institutions, affairs, etc., came out close to the outbreak of World War II and is preserved in only a few copies throughout the world. It goes up to the middle of the letter "*vav*" and covers primarily Polish Jewry, but it is considered a Zionist lexicon because of the wealth of Zionist material covered therein.

In Palestine, Moshe Kleinman aspired to publish the *Enẓiklopedyah le-Ẓiyyonut* (1947), but was prevented from issuing more than one volume (which goes up to the end of the letter "*gimmel*") by the conditions in the country and finally by his death. Since 1957 *Enẓiklopedyah shel ha-Ẓiyyonut ha-Datit*, edited by Y. Raphael (assistant editor G. Bat-Yehudah), has been published in Jerusalem; it covers personalities only. A large encyclopedic venture covering personalities is David Tidhar's *Enẓiklopedyah le-Ḥalutzei ha-Yishuv u-Vonav*, published from 1947 (19 volumes) which list biographies of personalities in Ereẓ alphabetically, but the indexes to each volume and to the work as a whole facilitate locating an entry. This work contains a wealth of Zionist material, especially in the latter volumes, which contain biographies of personalities in Ereẓ Israel mostly from Eastern Europe, the United States, England, etc. The *Leksikon la-Sifrut ha-Ivrit ba-Dorot ha-Aḥaronim*, by G. Kressel, also contains entries on many Zionist personalities. A two-volume work in English, *Encyclopedia of Zionism*, covering both personalities and Zionist events and affairs, was published in New York under the editorship of Raphael Patai (1971). Note should also be made of the various Jewish *Who's Who* volumes in English, Hebrew, and other languages that have come out in Israel and abroad.

Journals, Research Institutes, and Archives. Material on research into the history of Zionism is found in abundance in Jewish periodicals throughout the world. Especially rich in material are the official organs of the Zionist movement (*Selbstemanzipation, Die Welt, Juedische Rundschau, Haolam*, etc.). Since the beginning of the Zionist movement, however, the need for a special forum for Zionist research has made itself felt. In 1905 a forum of this type appeared for the first time in Germany, known as *Die Stimme der Wahrheit* and subtitled *Jahrbuch fuer wissenschlaftlichen Zionismus* (edited by L. Schoen). The notation "the volume of the first year" expressed the intention to perpetuate this publication, which was not realized. Since then collections honoring the memory of Herzl, for example, have turned into platforms for Zionist research: *Theodor Herzl, A Memorial*, edited by Meyer Weisgal (New York, 1929), and the *Herzl-Jahrbuch*, an annual for research on Herzl and Zionism, only one issue of which (by T. Nussenblatt) was published (1933). In Israel three collections were put out (one of which was in two volumes; 1950–56) under the title *Shivat Ẓiyyon*; they were intended to become an annual (edited by a staff of editors), but publication ceased. In the United States, Raphael Patai published the *Herzl Year Book* (6 vols. 1958–65). In 1970 the first collection on the history of the Zionist movement and the *yishuv* in Ereẓ Israel, *Ha-Ẓiyyonut*, was published under the editorship of Daniel Carpi. All these collections contain mostly research papers and documentary material.

Research institutes have been established at Tel Aviv University (named in honor of Chaim Weizmann) and the Hebrew University, Jerusalem (named in honor of Israel Goldstein). The former has already put out a number of books that investigate various aspects of the history of the *yishuv* and Zionism. The largest and most important archive for the history of Zionism throughout the world is the Central Zionist Archive in Jerusalem, but other archives are found in New York, in Bet ha-Tefuẓot of the University of Tel Aviv, etc. See *Archives.

[Getzel Kressel]

BIBLIOGRAPHY: GENERAL: N. Sokolow, *History of Zionism*, 2 vols. (1919); A. Boehm, *Die zionistische Bewegung*, 2 vols. (1935–37); I. Cohen, *The Zionist Movement* (1946); B. Halpern, *The Idea of the Jewish State* (1961); A. Hertzberg (ed.), *The Zionist Idea* (1960, 1997); R. Learsi, *Fulfillment: Epic Story of Zionism* (1951); Ch. Weizmann, *Trial and Error* (1948); Y. Gruenbaum, *Ha-Tenu'ah ha-Ẓiyyonit*, 4 vols. (1942–54), partial translation into Eng. *History of Zionism*, 2 vols. (1943–46); J. Heller, *The Zionist Idea* (1947); L. Stein, *The Balfour Declaration* (1961); C. Sykes, *Crossroads to Israel* (1965); A. Bein, in: *Herzl Year Book* (1959), 1–27, includes bibliography. ḤIBBAT ZION: N. Sokolow, *Hibbath Zion* (1935); idem, *History of Zionism*, 1 (1919); Y. Gruenbaum, *History of Zionism*, 1 (1943); A. Boehm, *Die zionistische Bewegung*, 1 (1935), 96–150; A. Levinson, *Bibliografiah Ẓiyyonut* (1943), 51–69; A. Druyanow, *Ketavim le-Toledot Ḥibbat Ẓiyyon*, 3 vols. (1919, 1925, 1932); idem, *Pinsker u-Zemanno* (1953); Ḥ. Ḥissin, *Mi-Yoman Aḥad ha-Bilu'im* (1928); B. Dinaburg, *Tekufat Ḥibbat Ẓiyyon* (1932, 1934); S. Jawnieli, *Sefer ha-Ẓiyyonut: Tekufat Ḥibbat Ẓiyyon*, 2 vols. (1942, 1961²); S. Breiman, in: *Shivat Ẓiyyon*, 1 (1950), 138–68; 2–3 (1953), 83–227; I. Klausner, *Ḥibbat Ẓiyyon be-Rumanyah* (1958); idem, *Be-Hitorer Am* (1962); idem, *Mi-Katoviẓ ad Basel* (1965); N.M. Gelber, *Toledot ha-Tenu'ah ha-Ẓiyyonit be-Galiẓyah*, 1 (1958), passim; M.L. Lilienblum, *Derekh La'avor Ge'ullim* (1899); T. Lavi et al. (eds.), PK Romanyah, 1 (1970), 47–60, 213–4 (bibl.). ZIONIST POLICY: C. Sykes, *Crossroads to Israel* (1965); H.M. Sachar, *The Emergence of the Middle East 1914–1924* (1969); Ch. Weizmann, *Trial and Error* (1948); O.K. Rabinowicz, in: *Herzl Year Book*, 1 (1958), 1–106; M. Medzini, *Ha-Mediniyyut ha-Ẓiyyonit me-Reshitah ve-ad Moto shel Herzl* (1934); R.G. Weisbord, *African Zion…*(1966); N. Friedman, J. De Haas, H.M. Kallen et al., *A Memorandum on the Relations between the Ottoman Government and the Zionist Administration* (1913); I. Friedman, in: JSOS, 27 (1965), 147–67, 236–49; idem, in; *Journal of Contemporary History*, 5:2 (1970); P.A. Alsberg, in: *Shivat Ẓiyyon*, 4 (1956), 161–209; Y. Rabi, in: *Middle Eastern Studies*, 4 (Apr. 1968), 198–242; L. Stein, *The Balfour Declaration* (1961); M. Vereté, in: *Zion*, 32 (1967), 76–114; idem, in: *Middle Eastern Studies*, 6:1 (Jan. 1970); J. Kimche, *The Unromantics – the Great Powers and the Balfour Declaration* (1968); M. Medzini, *Eser Shanim shel Mediniyyut Arẓiyisre'elit* (1928); F.E. Manuel, *The Realities of American-Palestine Relations* (1949); idem, in: *Shivat Ẓiyyon*, 4 (1956), 210–39; Zionist Organization, *Political Report* (1921); H.L. Samuel, *Memoirs* (1955); F.H. Kisch, *Palestine Diary* (1938); Ch. Arlosoroff, *Yoman Yerushalayim* (1950); M. Sharett, *Yoman Medini*, 2 vols. (1968–70); R. Meinertzhagen, *Middle East Diary, 1917–1956* (1959); ESCO Foundation for Palestine: *Palestine, A Study of Jewish, Arab, and British Policies*, 2 vols. (1947); V. Jabotinsky, *The Story of the Jewish Legion* (1945); H. Parzen, in: *Herzl Year Book*, 4 (1962), 345–94; S.L. Hattis, *The Bi-National Idea in Palestine during Mandatory Times* (1970); Y. Bauer, *From Diplomacy to Resistance* (1970); D. Joseph, *British Rule in Palestine* (1948); Dinur, Haganah; D. Ben-Gurion, *Medinat Yisrael ha-Meḥuddeshet*, 1 (1969). ZIONIST ORGANIZATION: Zionist Organization, *Protocols of the Zionist Congresses*, in particular of the 1st (1897) and 23rd (1951); idem, *The New Constitution of the World Zionist Organization* (1960); Jewish Agency, *Constitution of the Jewish Agency for Palestine* (1950); Zionist Organization, *Reports of the Executive of the ZO submitted to the Congresses*, in particular to the 22nd (1946); idem, *The Jubilee of the 1st Zionist Congress* (1947). ZIONISM IN AUSTRIA: J. Fraenkel, *The Jews of Austria* (1967), passim; H. Gold (ed.), *Geschichte der Juden in Wien* (1966). IN AUSTRALIA AND NEW ZEALAND: M. Freilich, *Zion in Our Time – Memoirs of an Australian Zionist* (1967); A. Wynn, *Fortunes of Samuel Wynn* (1968). IN BULGARIA: A. Romano, J. Ben, and N. Levy (eds.), *Yahadut Bulgaryah* (1967), 87–606; Ch. Keshales, *Korot Yehudei Bulgaryah* (1969); N.M. Gelber, in: JSOS, 8 (1946), 103–26. IN CZECHOSLOVAKIA: F. Weltsch (ed.), *Prag vi-Yrushalayim* (1953); Ch. Yahil, *Devarim al ha-Ẓiyyonut ha-Tchekhoslovakit* (1967); idem, in: *Gesher*, no. 59–60 (1969); *The Jews of Czechoslovakia*, 2 vols. (1967–71). IN FRANCE: André Spire, *Le Mouvement sioniste 1894–1918* (1919); idem, *Poèmes Juifs* (1919, 1959); A. Bein, *Introduction au sionisme* (1939²); A. Blumel, *Léon Blum, juif et sioniste* (1951). IN GERMANY: M. Bodenheimer, *Prelude to Israel* (1963); R. Lichtheim, *Die Geschichte des deutschen Zionismus* (1954); idem, *Rueckkehr* (1970); K. Blumenfeld, *Erlebte Judenfrage* (1962, Heb. 1963); E. Auerbach, *Pionier der Verwirklichung* (1970). IN GREAT BRITAIN: P. Goodman, *Zionism in England, 1899–1949* (1949); J. Fraenkel, in: *Zionist Year Book* (1959–60), 283–312; idem, in: YIVO *Bleter*, 43 (1966), 72–147; Ch. Weizmann, *Trial and Error* (1948), passim; Zionist Federation of the United Kingdom, *Annual Report* (1968). IN HOLLAND: *Jaarverslagen van het Bondsbestuur van de Nederlandse Zionistenbond; Bishviley Jachid* (1950). IN HUNGARY: Z. Zehavi, *Toledot ha-Ẓiyyonut be-Hungaryah*, 1 (1966). IN ITALY: D. Lattes, in: D. Carpi et al. (eds.), *Scritti in Memoria di Leone Carpi* (1967), 208–18; A.J.M. Pacifici, *ibid.*, 219–29; S. Minervi, *Angelo Levi-Bianchini e la sua opera nel Levante 1918–20* (1967); E. Castelbolognese (ed.), H.E. Sereni, *Ha-Aviv ha-Kadosh* (1947), an anthology of diaries, letters, and essays. IN LATIN AMERICA: P. Schwartzman, *Judiós en América…* (1963), index; I. Austri-Dann (ed.), *Yorbukh fun Meksikaner Yidentum* (1950–52), 331–51; M. Senderey, *Di Geshikhte fun dem Yidishn Yishuv in Chile* (1956), 231–56; J. Shatzky, *Communidades Judías en Latino América* (1952); *Communidades Judías de Latino América* (1968); *Primero Congreso Sionista Latino Americano* (1946); *Primera Convención Juveníl Judia Latino Americana* (1962). IN NORTH AFRICA AND ASIA: H.J. Cohen, *Ha-Pe'ilut ha-Ẓiyyonit be-Iraq* (1969), incl. bibl.; J.M. Landau, *Ha-Yehudim be-Miẓrayim ba-Me'ah ha-Tesha-Esreh* (1967), 126–35. IN POLAND: N.M. Gelber, *Toledot ha-Tenu'ah ha-Ẓiyyonit be-Galiẓyah*, 2 vols. (1958); Y. Gruenbaum (ed.), *Warsaw*, 1 (1953), 357–466; 2 (1959); I. Schwarzbart, *Tsvishn Beyde Velt-Milkhomes* (1958); L. Spizman (ed.), *Antologye fun der Khalutsisher Bavegung*, 3 vols. (1959–62); H.M. Rabinowicz, *The Legacy of Polish Jewry: 1919–1939* (1965); A Tartakower, in: *Algemeyne Entsiklopedye Yidn*, 6 (1963), 147–63. IN ROMANIA: T. Lavi et al. (eds.), PK Romanyah, 1 (1970), 47–61, 101–6, 177–89, 209–24 (incl. comprehensive bibl.); M. Landau, in: *Gesher*, 3:1 (1957), 77–94; 3:2 (1957), 78–91; 3:3 (1957), 101–13. IN RUSSIA: L. Greenberg, *The Jews in Russia*, 2 (1951), 160–202; J.B. Schechtman, *Zionism and the Zionists in the Soviet Union* (1966); idem, in L. Kochan (ed.), *The Jews in Soviet Russia* (1970), 99–124; G.G. Goldman, *Zionism under Soviet Rule 1917–1928* (1960); G. Aronson, in: J. Frumkin, G. Aronson and A. Gildenweiser (eds.), *Russian Jewry 1860–1917* (1966), 144–71; I. Ben-Zvi, *ibid.*, 209–18; S. Baron, *Russian Jews under Tsars and Soviets* (1964), index; A. Rafaeli (Zenziper), *Pa'amei ha-Ge'ullah* (1951); idem, *Ha-Ma'avak la-Ge'ullah* (1956); M. Nurock, *Ve'idat Ẓiyyonei Rusyah* (1963); Y. Gruenbaum, *Ha-Tenu'ah ha-Ẓiyyonit be-Hitpatteḥutah*, 3, 4 (1949, 1954); I. Klausner, *Oppoziẓyah le-Herzl* (1960); A. Levinsohn, *Be-Reshit ha-Tenu'ah* (1947); Y. Erez (ed.) *Sefer Z.S.* (1963); B. West, *Struggle of a Generation: The Jews Under Soviet Rule* (1959); Y. Eliash, *Zikhronot Ẓiyyoni me-Rusyah* (1955); B.Z. Dinur, *Be-Olam she-Shaka 1884–1914* (1958); idem, *Bi-Ymei Milḥamah u-Mahpekhah 1914–1921* (1960); J. Rabinovich, *Mi-Moskva ad Yerushalayim* (1957); *He-Avar le-Divrei Yemei ha-Yehudim ve-ha-Yahadut be-Rusyah* (1952). IN SOUTH AFRICA: M. Gitlin, *The Vision Amazing* (1950). IN THE UNITED STATES: I.S. Meyer (ed.), *Early History of Zionism in America* (1958), includes a series of articles and comprehensive bibliographies; M. Feinstein, *American Zionism 1884–1908* (1965); A. Friesel, *Ha-Tenu'ah ha-Ẓiyyonit be-Arẓot ha-Berit ba-Shanim 1897–1914* (1970), includes a comprehensive bibliography; idem, in: D. Carpi (ed.), *Ha-Ẓiyyonut*, 1 (1970), 121–49; N.W. Cohen, in: AJHSP, 40 (1950/51), 361–94; S. Udin (ed.), *Fifty Years of American Zionism 1897–1947: A Documentary Record* (1947); R.J.H. Gottheil, *The Aims of Zionism* (1899); idem, *Zionism* (1914); M. Rischin, in: AJHSP, 49 (1959/60), 188–201; Y. Shapiro, *Leadership of the American Zionist Organization 1897–1930* (Ph.D. thesis, Columbia, 1964); S.S. Wise, *Challenging Years* (1949); S. Halperin, *The Political World of American Zionism* (1961); C. Reznikoff (ed.), *Louis Marshall, Champion of Liberty*, 2 vols. (1957), index and passim; B. Halpern, *The American Jew, Zionist Analysis* (1956); R. Patai (ed.), *Herzl Year Book*, 5 (1963), contains a series of studies in the history of Zionism in America 1894–1919; H. Parzen, *ibid.*, 4 (1962), 345; 6 (1965), 311–68; idem, in: JSOS, 23 (1961), 235–64; Saul D. Alinsky, *Reveille for Radicals*, N.Y., 1946, 1969; Robert Wolff, Barrington Moore, Jr., and Herbert Marcuse, *A Critique of Pure Tolerance*, N.Y., 1965; Paul Jacobs, *Is Curly Jewish?*, N.Y., 1965, 1973; David Mandel, *On RZA*, in press; Jack N. Porter, ed. and introd., *Jewish Radicalism*, N.Y., 1973; Charles A. Reich, *The Greening of America*, N.Y., 1970; Richard Siegel, Michael Strassfeld, and Sharon Strassfeld, *Jewish Catalog*, N.Y., 1973; James Sleeper and Alan L. Mintz, *New Jews*, N.Y., 1971; *Ellul*, Ellul 5733; *Commentary*, "Revolution and the Jews," 51:2, Feb. 1971; *Response*, "Jewish Radicalism – Then and Now," No. 15, 73–81; No. 19, 105–20; *Net Outlook*, Aron Manheimer, "Radical Zionism Reconsidered," 16:5, June 1973. ZIONIST UTOPIAS: G. Kressel (ed.), *Ḥezyonei Medinah* (1954); idem, in: I. Cohn and D. Sadan (eds.), *Me'assef le-Divrei Sifrut, Bikkoret ve-Hagut*, 8–9 (1968), 456–69. CHRISTIAN ZIONISM: M. Vereté, in: *Zion*, 33 (1968), 145–79: N.M. Gelber, *Vorgeschichte des Zionismus 1695–1845* (1927); F. Kobler, *The Vision Was There* (1956); A.M. Hyamson, in: AJHSP, 26 (1918) 127–64; N. Sokolow, *History of Zionism*, 2 vols. (1919–68), passim, index; Y. Malachy, in: *Herzl Year Book*, 5 (1963), 175–208; 6 (1964/65), 265–302; B. Tuchman, *Bible and Sword* (1956). **ADD. BIBLIOGRAPHY:** W. Laqueur, *A History of Zionism* (1972); S. Avineri, *The Making of Modern Zionism: Intellectual Origins of the Jewish State* (1981); R. Furstenberg, *Post Zionism: The Challenge to Israel* (1997); J. Reinharz and A. Shapira (eds.), *Essential Papers on Zionism* (1995); H.M. Sachar, *A History of Israel from the Rise of Zionism to Our Time* (1996[2]); G. Shimoni, *The Zionist Ideology* (1995); D. Vital, *The Origins of Zionism* (1975).

ZIONIST COMMISSION (Heb. **Va'ad ha-Ẓirim**), a commission headed by Chaim *Weizmann and consisting of Jewish representatives from Great Britain (Leon *Simon, Montagu David *Eder, Joseph *Cowen, and I.M. *Sieff as secretary), France (Sylvain Lévy) and Italy (Angelo *Levi-Bianchini), which proceeded in 1918 after the issue of the Balfour Declaration, with the approval and authorization of the Allied governments, to British-occupied Palestine. The commission arrived in Palestine on April 4, when the northern districts of the country were still in Turkish hands. It was accompanied by Major W. Ormsby-Gore (later Lord Harlech, colonial secretary in 1936–38) as political officer on behalf of the British government, assisted by Major James de Rothschild and Edwin Samuel to serve as liaison with the British military authorities. The commission was to act as "an advisory body to the British authorities in Palestine in all matters relating to Jews, or which may affect the establishment of a National Home for the Jewish people." It was concerned specifically with coordinating relief work, assisting the repatriation of Jews exiled by the Turks, helping to organize the Jewish population and establishing friendly relations with the Arabs, as well as investigating the possibility of the early establishment of a Jewish university. Thus Weizmann then made his first contacts with Emir Feisal and laid the cornerstone of the *Hebrew University on Mount Scopus in Jerusalem. On the other hand, the commission encountered an uncooperative and even hostile attitude from the British military authorities, which studiously refrained from officially publishing the policy embodied in the Balfour Declaration (until May 1, 1920) and practically prevented any Jewish settlement work. The commission had to send strong representations to London against this attitude but achieved little in changing it until the military' administration was replaced in 1920 by the civilian regime under the first high commissioner, Sir Herbert *Samuel.

The idea of dispatching such a commission to Palestine was broached by Weizmann as early as November 1917 in his correspondence with the leading Zionist in the United States, L.D. *Brandeis. At first, no American Jew was attached to the commission, because of American neutrality in the war with Turkey, and no Russian Jew could take part in it because of the revolutionary upheaval in Russia. However, two Palestinian Jews, Aaron *Aaronsohn and Zalman David *Levontin, worked with it. In the autumn of 1919 Menahem *Ussishkin became the head of the commission (following a brief tenure by M.D. Eder), which was the sole representative of the Zionist Organization in Palestine until September 1921, when it was replaced by the Zionist Executive established in Jerusalem after the 12th Zionist Congress. Thus the Zionist Commission was the predecessor of the *Jewish Agency.

BIBLIOGRAPHY: Ch. Weizmann, *Trial and Error* (1949), 265–99; I. Cohen, *The Zionist Movement* (1945), 116–7; Zionist Organization, *Reports to the XII Zionist Congress, Political Report* (1921); A. Friesel, *Reshit Darko shel Weizmann be-Hanhagat ha-Tenu'ah ha-Ẓiyyonit 1917–1921* (Ph.D. thesis, Jerusalem, 1970), 15–35, includes a comprehensive bibliography.

[Daniel Efron]

ZIONIST CONGRESSES, the highest authority in the Zionist Organization; created by Theodor *Herzl. None of the previous attempts to convene general assemblies of the Jewish national movement, some of which were successful and some abortive, succeeded in creating an instrument similar in scope or nature to the Zionist Congresses. Herzl's aim in convening the Congress was "to close the Zionist ranks, bring about an understanding between all Zionists and to unify their endeavors… the Congress will show what Zionism is and wants." His other aim – to establish "the national assembly of the Jewish people" – was realized by many of the Congresses that took place both before and after his death. The problem of the location of the Congress was not confined to the First Zionist Congress alone. Several of the Congresses encountered problems in this sphere until the 23rd Congress, which met in Jerusalem (all subsequent Congresses have been held in Jerusalem). Previous venues were Basle, London, The Hague, Hamburg, Vienna, Carlsbad, Zurich, Prague, Lucerne, and Geneva. During the periods of the Ottoman regime and the British Mandate over Palestine, it proved impossible to hold the Congress in Ereẓ Israel.

The First Congress

The location of the First Zionist Congress was to have been Munich, Germany, but due to the opposition of the community and the *Protestrabbiner, it was transferred to Basle and held on Aug. 29–31, 1897. The historical importance of the Congress lies in the formulation of the *Basle Program and the foundation of the Zionist Organization, which united West and East European Zionists in both an organizational and programmatic sense. Up until that time the East European Ḥovevei Zion (see *Ḥibbat Zion) engaged in settlement activities in Ereẓ Israel, and they now accepted political Zionism as well. The approach termed political Zionism, an essential problem debated at the Congress, was raised and defined by Herzl himself. The settlements founded to date had indeed proved the ability of the Jews to farm the land. The Jewish problem, however, could only be solved by large-scale migration and settlement of the country, which could be effected only with international assistance and recognition. By the Third Congress this was expressed in the term "charter." The means and goals of political Zionism were formulated in a key sentence, possessing four subclauses, the Basle Program.

The First Congress also devised a schedule that was followed by all subsequent Congresses: reports on the situation of Jewish communities in the Diaspora (at the first Congresses, the famous speeches of Max *Nordau), lectures on Ereẓ Israel and settlement activities, and debates on cultural questions, which were extremely stormy at the first few Congresses. Herzl acted as the chairman of the Congress (as he did at all Congresses until his death) and was also elected president of the Zionist Organization.

The Congress made a tremendous impression on both Jews and non-Jews throughout the world. Herzl himself summarized the importance of the First Congress thus: "I no longer need to write the history of yesterday [the day on which the Congress opened]; it is already written by others.... Were I to sum up the Basle Congress in a word – which I shall guard against pronouncing publicly – it would be this: At Basle I founded the Jewish State" (Herzl's diary, Aug. 30, Sept. 3, 1897, *Complete Diaries*, ed. by R. Patai, 2, 580–1). Ḥayyim Naḥman *Bialik even published a poem titled "*Mikra'ei Ẓiyyon*" in honor of the First Congress (for English translations see Goell, Bibliography, 489–90, no. 237). A full list of the participants in the First Congress with biographical and bibliographical details was compiled by H. Orlan in *Herzl Year Book*, 6 (1964–65), 133–52. There is a vast literature on the First Congress including *Warum gingen wir zum ersten Zionistenkongress?* (1922), in which 32 participants recount the motives which prompted their participation in the First Congress, and *Sefer ha-Congress* (1923, 1950^2), an anthology edited by Leib Yaffe. The official language of the first Congresses was German (the minutes were published in this language until the beginning of the 1930s and after that in English). The language spoken from the rostrum was, for many years, also mostly German, but since many delegates spoke a kind of Yiddishized German it was nicknamed "Kongressdeutsch."

The Second Congress

The second meeting of the Zionist Congress was held in Basle on Aug. 28–31, 1898. In his opening address, Herzl called on the Zionists to "conquer the communities," a slogan which later led to the program of "work in the present," i.e., in the Diaspora, in order to deprive various assimilationists of their self-appointed role as spokesmen of the Jewish people. At this Congress the foundations were laid for the *Jewish Colonial Trust and David *Wolffsohn was placed in charge of implementing the project. Leo *Motzkin, who had just returned from Ereẓ Israel, presented a detailed report on the situation of both the new and the old *yishuv*. A group of Zionist Socialists demanding representation for the Jewish proletariat in the leadership of the Zionist Organization made their first appearance at this Congress. Herzl was opposed to splitting the precariously united Zionist camp. The struggle between the "political" and "practical" Zionists had been set aside at the First Congress, and the resolution to establish the Jewish Colonial Trust further narrowed the gap between the two camps.

The Third Congress

Held in Basle on Aug. 15–18, 1899, the Third Congress opened with a report by Herzl of his meetings with Kaiser William II in Constantinople (Oct. 18, 1898) and Jerusalem (Nov. 2), in addition to a casual meeting at Mikveh Israel. While these meetings produced no practical results, their demonstrative value, in the presentation of the Zionist case before the head of a great power, was immense. There was a great deal of debate about the exact meaning of the "charter," first mentioned by Herzl, and the significance of the term "public law" in the Basle Program, i.e., whether the intent was a license from all the powers or only from Turkey. Herzl was persuaded to accept the latter interpretation. It was also resolved that the Jewish Colonial Trust would confine its settlement activities to Ereẓ Israel and Syria. The "practical" Zionists failed in their attempts to gain the Congress' approval for initiating settlement activities before obtaining the "charter," and the theoretical debates on cultural matters, which occupied several Congresses from the Second on, continued. Herzl was preoccupied with political activities, and everything outside this sphere was thrust aside.

The Fourth Congress

On Aug. 13–16, 1900, the Fourth Congress was held in London. The reason for choosing London as the location of this Congress was given by Herzl in his opening speech as follows: "England, great England, free England, England looking over all the seas, will understand our aspirations. From here the Zionist idea will take its flight further and higher, of that we are sure." The Congress bore the imprint of the severe crisis in Romanian Jewry, with many thousands forced to leave the country and those remaining behind subject to pressure and harassment. Herzl viewed the persecution of Romanian Jewry as further proof of the urgent necessity for a Zionist solution. Since the "charter" was still a distant prospect, matters demanding immediate attention came to the fore. The position of the Jewish workers in Ereẓ Israel was also brought up at this Congress.

The Fifth Congress

Herzl presented this Congress, held in Basle on Dec. 26–30, 1901, with the greatest of his achievements – an interview with the sultan. He also presented a report on the initial activities of the Jewish Colonial Trust. These achievements, however, did not satisfy many of the delegates, especially a group of young men who organized the *Democratic Fraction. They advanced the concept of Zionism as an internal Jewish renaissance and demanded serious attention to the problems of Jewish culture, instead of concentrating solely on political activities, which they regarded as sterile. The main achievement of this Congress was the establishment of the *Jewish National Fund (JNF) on the lines proposed by Hermann *Schapira at the First Congress.

The Sixth Congress

In accordance with a resolution taken at the Fifth Congress, the Sixth took place two years after its predecessor (on Aug. 23–28, 1903, in Basle) instead of one, as had been the practice. This was the last Congress in which Herzl participated and was also the stormiest and most tragic. While the "charter" was as far as ever from Herzl's grasp, the pressure for a solution to the Jewish problem was mounting, particularly after the shock of the Kishinev pogrom in the spring of the same year. This situation gave rise to "temporary solutions," such as the *El-Arish project, to which Herzl devoted much of his energies and with whose results he was bitterly disillusioned. In spite of the Kishinev pogrom, Herzl had visited Russia, where he met Minister of Interior Plehve. He also received an official offer from the British government, which was willing to allocate a territory for Jewish settlement in Uganda, East Africa. At the Congress, Herzl advanced this proposal for serious examination, while simultaneously emphasizing that "our views on Ereẓ Israel cannot and will not be subject to change. Uganda is not Zion and will never be Zion. This proposal is nothing more than a relief measure, a temporary means of allaying distress." The vote on the *Uganda Scheme was as follows: 295 in favor, 178 against, and 98 abstentions. At first those opposed to the scheme left the hall, headed by Jehiel *Tschlenow, but were persuaded to return by Herzl personally, who appealed to them not to destroy the Zionist Organization. The Uganda Scheme overshadowed all other matters at the Congress, such as Franz *Oppenheimer's lecture on cooperative settlement, a program that was implemented some years later in the settlement Merḥavyah. Approximately one year after this Congress, Herzl died.

The Seventh Congress

The Congress, held on July 27–Aug. 2, 1905, in Basle, was opened by its new president, Nordau, who delivered a eulogy on Herzl. Immediately afterward, a stormy debate on the Uganda proposal broke out. Opposition to the scheme had grown with the return of the commission of inquiry and its negative report on conditions in Uganda, which it found unsuitable for Jewish mass settlement. Despite the opposition of the Territorialists, who were supported by *Po'alei Zion, the Congress resolved to reject finally the Uganda Scheme and the notion of settlement anywhere except in Ereẓ Israel and its immediate vicinity. The Territorialists, headed by Israel *Zangwill, withdrew from the Congress and the Zionist Organization and founded the Jewish Territorial Association (see *Territorialism). A resolution to the effect that practical settlement activities would not be delayed until public rights had been obtained, but would begin at once, was then passed. Otto *Warburg, who was to become the moving spirit of practical Zionism, made his first impressive appearance at this Congress. He emphasized the political value of limited settlement and the need for introducing it in a systematic way. In place of Nordau, who refused to accept the position, Wolffsohn was elected chairman of the Executive which was equivalent to the head of the Zionist Organization. The center of the Zionist movement moved from Vienna to Cologne, where Wolffsohn lived.

The Eighth Congress

In accordance with Herzl's tradition of keeping the Zionist movement in the public eye, this Congress met at The Hague on Aug. 14–21, 1907, while the Second International Peace Conference was taking place there. The struggle between political and practical Zionists was resolved by the decision that settlement activity in Ereẓ Israel should not be delayed until after the receipt of the "charter." On the contrary, planned small-scale settlement, not exceeding the limits of the Basle Program, was to precede the charter, which would thus be obtained on the strength of these "small" achievements. Wolffsohn was the mediator between the two camps. As Herzl's close friend and loyal disciple, on the one hand, and a sober man of affairs, on the other, he was eminently suited to this function. Weizmann's famous speech on "synthetic Zionism" merged political and practical Zionism into an organic whole and laid a common foundation for both camps. He stated: "We must aspire to a charter, but our aspiration will be realized only as a result of our practical work in Ereẓ Israel." As a result of this approach, the *Palestine Office was founded in Jaffa in 1908 to direct the work of agricultural settlement on behalf of the World Zionist Organization. The office was headed by Arthur *Ruppin.

The Ninth Congress

Held in Hamburg on Dec. 26–30, 1909, this was the first Congress to meet in Germany. The hope that the attitude of the Turkish government toward Zionism would change after the revolution of the Young Turks, which had taken place in the previous year, was expressed by both Wolffsohn and Nordau. A very strong opposition to Wolffsohn's leadership emerged at this Congress and was led by Menahem *Ussishkin, Weizmann, and Nahum *Sokolow and joined by representatives of the workers in Ereẓ Israel, appearing for the first time at a Zionist Congress. They were united in their opposition to the "commercial" approach to the settlement activities, which evaluated every project by its economic efficiency. The decision to begin cooperative settlement according to the Oppenheimer plan was a great concession to the "practical" Zionists, representatives of Po'alei Zion, and the workers of Ereẓ Israel. Wolffsohn was finally reelected president of the Zionist Organization and chairman of the Executive, which also included Warburg and Jacobus *Kann. Friction over Woffsohn's methods, which were also criticized by the political Zionists as not close enough to those of Herzl, did not come to an end with the closing session of this Congress.

The Tenth Congress

This Congress, held in Basle on Aug. 9–15, 1911, earned the name of "The Peace Congress" for ending the quarrels and friction of the "Cologne period" and bringing total victory to the realistic "synthetic" trend in Zionism. In his opening address, which contained the announcement of his resignation, Wolffsohn gave his blessings to the period of Zionist history about to commence after the "Vienna period" and his own "Cologne period." Detailed discussion of practical activity in Ereẓ Israel and Hebrew culture took place. For the first time in the history of the Congresses, a whole session, led by Ussishkin, was conducted entirely in Hebrew. The relations with the Arabs were also discussed in a speech by Shelomo *Kaplansky. The Zionist headquarters were transferred from Cologne to Berlin, and the new leadership consisted of the president Otto Warburg and Arthur *Hantke, Shemaryahu *Levin, Victor *Jacobson, and Sokolow.

The Eleventh Congress

The demonstrative absence of Nordau at this Congress, held in Vienna on Sept. 2–9, 1913, was a silent protest against the abandonment of Herzl's line. Arguments about the body in charge of the Jewish Colonial Trust took place with the Executive and with Wolffsohn and his associates. Ruppin presented a detailed report on the first settlement activities on behalf of the Palestine Office. This report, together with Levin's survey of 30 years of settlement in Ereẓ Israel, were an indirect tribute to "small-scale" deeds. On the suggestion of Weizmann and Ussishkin, it was resolved to establish a Hebrew University in Jerusalem. Bialik made an impressive appearance at the closing session. Wolffsohn, who was the president of the Eleventh Congress, died a year afterward.

The Twelfth Congress

No previous Congress had met in a period so sharply distinguished from the preceding one. This was the first Congress after World War I. It was held in Carlsbad on Sept. 1–14, 1921, after the following crucial events had taken place: the *Balfour Declaration, the British conquest of Palestine, the Bolshevik Revolution in Russia, mass pogroms against Ukrainian Jews, and the London Zionist Conference (1920), at which the *Keren Hayesod was founded. During this period the Zionist movement in America had begun to come to the fore, and the *Brandeis group had clashed with Weizmann's leadership at the London Conference. The Zionist leadership had also been transformed. The "Berlin period" had come to an end with the defeat of Germany in World War I, and the group that had obtained the Balfour Declaration, led by Weizmann and Sokolow, had transferred the Zionist world center to England. At the London Conference, Weizmann was elected president of the Zionist Organization and Sokolow president of the Executive. In addition, the first years after the Balfour Declaration had been marked by anti-Jewish riots in Jerusalem (1920) and Jaffa (1921). Weizmann delivered a report on the political activities of the Zionist Organization during the war and called on the Jewish people to assist in building Ereẓ Israel. Ruppin brought the acquisition of large tracts of land in the Jezreel Valley before the Congress for approval and was opposed by the directorate of the JNF, led by Nehemiah *de Lieme. Bialik, among others, came out in defense of the Jewish workers in Palestine who were the subject of attacks by the "efficiency"-minded group, opposing Weizmann's leadership. For the first time in the history of Zionism, a representative of the workers in Ereẓ Israel, Josef *Sprinzak, was elected to the Executive, which thereafter was situated in London and Jerusalem.

The Thirteenth Congress

On Aug. 6–18, 1923, the 13th Congress was held in Carlsbad. Before it took place, the British Mandate over Palestine had been endorsed by the *League of Nations and the Zionist Organization became officially the *Jewish Agency for Palestine, mentioned in Article 4 of the Mandate and charged with taking steps "to secure the cooperation of all Jews who are willing to assist in the establishment of the Jewish National Home." At this Congress, the proposal to include non-Zionists in the Jewish Agency was debated and aroused bitter opposition from those who considered this a threat to the broad democratic basis of the Zionist Organization. Weizmann defended the proposal against its opponents until it was finally implemented six years later (1929). The possibilities of obtaining financial resources for building up Palestine were debated at length, and Chaim *Arlosoroff delivered a lecture containing a proposal for a planned economic program. The Congress also resolved to open the Hebrew University in Jerusalem.

The Fourteenth Congress

This Congress, held in Vienna on Aug. 18–31, 1925, was much affected by the "prosperity" in Palestine caused by the Fourth Aliyah (mostly from Poland) and the feverish construction of houses and land speculation. It encouraged the view that private enterprise would solve the problems of building Palestine, and criticism of labor settlement methods reached its height. David *Ben-Gurion participated in the debate, delivering a speech on the workers in Palestine and their activities. Ruppin resigned as head of the Jewish Agency Settlement Department, which he had directed for approximately 18 years, and Colonel F.H. *Kisch was appointed to direct the Agency's Political Department in Jerusalem.

The Fifteenth Congress

The prosperity in Palestine was followed by a severe economic crisis and unemployment, which affected nearly 8,000 workers. Hunger and poverty drove many from the country and *aliyah* dwindled. Preoccupation with "breaking the crisis" at the 15th Congress, held in Basle on Aug. 30–Sept. 11, 1927, spoiled the celebrations in honor of the 30th anniversary of the First Congress. Weizmann outlined a proposal for overcoming the crisis, and Ruppin delivered one of his brilliant Congress speeches on pioneering and its meaning for Zionism. The Executive elected did not include a labor representative and its most forceful personality was Harry *Sacher. Eulogies on Aḥad Ha-Am were delivered by Martin *Buber and Nahum Sokolow.

The Sixteenth Congress

Held in Zurich on July 28–Aug. 10, 1929, this Congress, like its predecessor, met in an anniversary year and was opened with a speech by Sokolow on Herzl upon the 25th anniversary of his death. Unlike its predecessor, however, this Congress met during a period of economic recovery in Palestine, improved employment conditions, and the revival of *aliyah*. Weizmann again reported on the enlargement of the Jewish Agency by non-Zionists, which was to be established after the Congress was over. Despite strong opposition to the project (mainly from the *Revisionists), the debate that had lasted for seven years ended with the official establishment of the enlarged body in an impressive meeting with the participation of Weizmann, Sokolow, Herbert *Samuel, Louis *Marshall, A. *Einstein, Lord *Melchett, Leon *Blum, Sholem *Asch, F. *Warburg, and others. The Executive (the "Sacher regime") was severely criticized for its attitude toward Labor Zionism. The Congress ended with the election of a new Zionist Executive, joined by two *Mizrachi representatives (Rabbi M. Berlin and A. Barth), two labor representatives (S. Kaplansky and Y. Sprinzak), and Ruppin.

The Seventeenth Congress

A few days after the establishment of the enlarged Jewish Agency in Zurich, bloody riots broke out in Palestine (August 1929) and were followed in quick succession by the report of the British commission of inquiry into the 1929 disturbances; the *White Paper by the colonial secretary, Lord Passfield; restriction on Jewish immigration; the negative report on the possibility of Jewish settlement by Sir John Hope-Simpson; etc. The commission report and Sir John Hope-Simpson's conclusions were openly hostile to the Zionist movement, the JNF, Jewish labor, and practically all other Jewish activities in Palestine. Weizmann immediately resigned as president of the Zionist Organization in protest to the new British policy. His move, in turn, resulted in the "MacDonald Letter," which retracted much of the negative elements in the new trend.

At the 17th Congress, held in Basle on June 30–July 15, 1931, a number of delegates voiced their protest to Weizmann's policy, which was based upon the fundamental need for maximum cooperation with the British government. The opposition, consisting not only of the Revisionists, but also of many other delegates, claimed that this policy was not justified. The Revisionists demanded that the creation of a Jewish majority and a Jewish state be defined officially as the final aim of Zionism, and when this demand was rejected by the majority, Vladimir *Jabotinsky tore up his delegate's card with the cry: "This is no Zionist Congress," leading ultimately (in 1935) to the secession of the Revisionists from the Zionist Organization. In view of the situation, Weizmann, despite support from the labor wing, refused to withdraw his resignation, and Sokolow was chosen president of the Zionist Organization. In spite of Weizmann's official resignation, however, the Executive of the Zionist Organization, in which the strength of the labor parties had grown with the election of Chaim Arlosoroff as head of the Political Department, actually continued to act along the lines of Weizmann's policy.

The Eighteenth Congress

This Congress, held in Prague on Aug. 21–Sept. 4, 1933, bore the imprint of three events: the advent of the Nazis to power in Germany and growing persecution of German Jewry, economic inflation in Palestine, and the assassination of Arlosoroff. The conflict between the Revisionists and labor reached its height, since the labor representatives believed that the constant incitement by the Revisionists had created the setting for Arlosoroff's assassination. It was finally decided to establish a committee of inquiry into the tragedy. A special session was devoted to the celebration of Ussishkin's 70th birthday. Sokolow was reelected president of the Zionist Organization. The representation of labor on the Executive increased and included Ben-Gurion and Moshe Shertok (*Sharett), who succeeded Arlosoroff as head of the Political Department.

The Nineteenth Congress

Held in Lucerne on Aug. 20–Sept. 4, 1935, this Congress was distinguished by the comprehensive and practical lectures delivered on Diaspora Jewry (Sokolow), the building of Palestine (Ben-Gurion), the JNF (Ussishkin), rescuing Jewish children from Germany – Youth Aliyah (Henrietta *Szold), and the problems of Hebrew culture (Berl *Katznelson). The labor faction, the largest at the Congress, worked out a program for a broad coalition and made it possible for Weizmann to resume the presidency, and Sokolow was chosen as honorary president of the Organization and the enlarged Jewish Agency. Ben-Gurion, who was reelected to the Executive, became more and more its central figure. Sokolow died within a year.

The Twentieth Congress

This Congress was held in Zurich on Aug. 3–16, 1937, and was faced with the responsibility of resolving one of the most difficult problems that had faced the Zionist movement since the controversy over the Uganda Scheme. The report of the Royal Commission on Palestine (Peel Commission) appointed in the wake of the 1936 Arab riots proposed the establishment of a Jewish state in part of the country. There were divisions of opinion between and within the Zionist parties on the issue (with Ben-Gurion of *Mapai, for example, in favor of the proposal and Katznelson against it). In the end it was decided to take note of the finding of the Royal Commission "that the field in which the Jewish National Home was to be established was understood, at the time of the Balfour Declaration, to be the whole of Palestine, including Transjordan," but at the same time, the decision of the Congress empowered the Executive to negotiate with the British government the possibility of securing a more favorable partition of western Palestine than that proposed by the Peel Commission's plan and bring the results to the Congress before a final decision was made. In addition a special session took place in Basle to mark the 40th anniversary of the First Congress. During the session, presided over by Ussishkin, delegates to the First Congress recalled the great event in their lives and in Zionist history.

The Twenty-first Congress

Held in Geneva on Aug. 16–26, 1939, the 21st Congress met on the eve of World War II. The British government had withdrawn its partition plan, conferred with representatives of Jews and Arabs (including Arab governments) at the St. James Conference in London, and published its anti-Zionist White Paper imposing tremendous restrictions on Jewish immigration and purchase of land. The delegates unanimously expressed their strong opposition to the White Paper and declared the readiness of the *yishuv* to fight against the restrictions. Katznelson extolled the "illegal" *immigration program and called for all the energies of the Zionist movement to be channeled into extending its scope, in view of the threatening political situation in Europe. In the atmosphere of impending war the Executive was reelected for another term. Weizmann closed the Congress with the emotion-filled statement: "I have no prayer but this; that we will all meet again alive." Ussishkin, the president of the Congress, expressed his grave concern for the fate of Polish Jewry.

The Twenty-second Congress

The Congress met in Basle on Dec. 9–24, 1946, after World War II and the Nazi Holocaust, which had exterminated most of European Jewry. The *yishuv* had participated in the British war effort and had waged an armed struggle against White Paper restrictions. The Revisionists had returned to the Zionist Organization and were represented at the Congress. The *Biltmore Program (1942) on the establishment of Palestine as a Jewish commonwealth had been approved as the program of the Zionist movement at the first international Zionist conference after the war (New York, 1945). The Anglo-American commission of inquiry (1946) had recommended, inter alia, the abolition of a number of existing restrictions and the settlement of 100,000 Jews in Palestine. The British government had refused to accept these recommendations, and the armed resistance of the *yishuv* had increased. Leaders of the *yishuv* and the Jewish Agency had been arrested (1946). The Morrison-Grady plan for the cantonization of Palestine and its division into four districts (Jewish, Arab, Jerusalem, and Negev) had been announced. The British had proposed a Jewish-Arab conference in London to reach an agreed solution, and the release of the imprisoned Jewish leaders as a preliminary to this conference. The Congress was therefore faced with the necessity of taking a stand on both the Morrison-Grady proposal and the London Conference. Weizmann stressed the importance of the decision on the establishment of a Jewish state in Palestine and the sympathy with which Zionism and the aspirations of the *yishuv* were regarded by President Truman and American opinion. The Congress approved the political program of the Zionist Organization "to establish a Jewish commonwealth integrated into the world democratic structure," turned down the plan for the cantonization of Palestine, and also resolved that "in existing circumstances, the Zionist movement is unable to participate in the London Conference." Weizmann, who was opposed to this last resolution and favored participation in the London Conference, resigned from the presidency, and for the first time in the history of the Zionist Organization the Congress failed to elect a new president.

The Twenty-third Congress

The Congress met in Jerusalem on Aug. 14–30, 1951. Weizmann, now president of the State of Israel, was unable to attend, but in a message to the delegates defined the new situation: "There is a deep symbolism in the fact that the Zionist Congress has not met in our ancient land until it has become ours again… It is only now, since we have attained independence and statehood, that we can fully appraise the paramount place held by Zionist Congresses in the evolution of our movement." The opening ceremony of the Congress took place, symbolically, by Herzl's grave in Jerusalem. The chairman of the Executive, Berl *Locker, summed up the history of the Zionist movement and described the road it had taken from Basle to Jerusalem. The central issue debated at the Congress was the status of the Zionist movement after the establishment of a Jewish state. The Basle Program no longer met the requirements of the new reality and was replaced by the "Jerusalem Program" (see *Basle Program), whose essential clause was: "The task of Zionism is the consolidation of the State of Israel, the ingathering of the exiles in Ereẓ Israel and the fostering of the unity of the Jewish people." The coalition formed after the Congress included all the factions except for the Zionist Revisionists – *Ḥerut. Two chairmen were elected to the Executive: Naḥum *Goldmann in New York and Berl Locker in Jerusalem. One of the resolutions, demanding official recognition of the status of the Zionist Organization by the state, was implemented after the Congress in the World Zionist Organization-Jewish Agency for Palestine Status Law passed by the Knesset on Nov. 24, 1952.

The Twenty-fourth Congress

The Congress, held on April 24–May 7, 1956, was overshadowed by the security situation of the State of Israel, which was threatened by the arms streaming especially into Egypt from the Soviet bloc. Internal affairs in the spheres of *aliyah*, settlement, and organization of fund raising were also discussed.

It was decided to concentrate all funds in the hands of the *Keren Hayesod and United Israel Appeal. Naḥum Goldmann was elected president of the Zionist Organization, an office which had been unfilled since 1946.

The Twenty-fifth Congress

The central issues debated at this Congress, held on Dec. 27, 1960–Jan. 11, 1961, were the relationship of the government of Israel to the Zionist Organization and its official status, in light of the sharp criticism leveled against the Organization by Ben-Gurion; *aliyah*; absorption; Jewish culture and education in the Diaspora. Goldmann was reelected president and chairman of the Executive. After the Congress, Moshe Sharett was elected chairman of the Jerusalem Executive in place of B. Locker, who resigned.

The Twenty-sixth Congress

The slogan "Facing the Diaspora," coined in Goldmann's opening address, was the center of debate at this Congress, held on Dec. 30, 1964–Jan. 10, 1965. After the establishment of the state, Goldmann felt it was necessary to regard the aims of Zionism as the survival of the Jewish nation in the Diaspora and the assistance of the state to the Jewish people. The debate, as usual at Congresses held after the establishment of the state, spread to the sphere of relations between the state and the Zionist Organization, *aliyah* obligations, etc. The Congress resolved on the following as the first of the tasks and functions of the Zionist movement: "The deepening of Zionist awareness and its dissemination as a way of life, based on the recognition of the uniqueness of the Jewish people and the continuity of its history, the unity of the nation despite its dispersion, the mutual commitment of all its parts and their common responsibility for its historic fate, and the recognition of the decisive mission of the State of Israel in assuring its future." Goldmann was reelected president of the Zionist Organization. Sharett, chairman of the Jerusalem Executive, sent his greetings in writing due to the illness from which he died a few months later.

The Twenty-seventh Congress

The Congress was held on June 9–19, 1968, the first in reunited Jerusalem after the Six-Day War. An innovation at this Congress was the participation of youth delegations, students, and members of the *aliyah* movement. The question of *aliyah* was the focal point of the debates, and the decision of the Israel government to establish a Ministry of Immigrant Absorption was approved. Additional paragraphs on the goals of Zionism were added to the Jerusalem Program: "The unity of the Jewish people and the centrality of Israel in its life; the ingathering of the Jewish people in its historic homeland Ereẓ Israel through *aliyah* from all lands; the strengthening of the State of Israel founded on the prophetic ideals of justice and peace; the preservation of the identity of the Jewish people through the fostering of Jewish education, Hebrew, and of Jewish spiritual and cultural values; the protection of Jewish rights everywhere." Goldmann resigned as president of the Zionist Organization and no one was chosen to take his place. Louis *Pincus, who had been elected chairman of the Executive after the death of Sharett, was reelected to this post.

[Getzel Kressel]

The Twenty-eighth Congress

The Congress was held in Jerusalem on January 18–28, 1972, with 559 delegates voting. For the first time in many years, instead of the interparty agreements whereby the number of delegates for each party was determined, elections were held in most countries. The membership drive which preceded the elections revealed a membership of the World Zionist Organization approaching 900,000. In Israel, however, most of the delegates were nominated by the political parties, in proportion to their relative strength in the Knesset. The Sephardi and Oriental communities were represented by some 90 delegates and observers. Another notable feature was the large representation of youth, through the World Union of Jewish Students and the Zionist youth movements. Louis *Pincus was re-elected chairman of the Zionist Executive. The Congress concentrated on the specific tasks of the Zionist Movement in the Diaspora, such as Jewish education, youth work, and the promotion of *aliyah* from the free countries. Considerable attention was devoted to social problems such as the cultural and economic gaps between sections of the population in Israel and the acute housing shortage. A prominent theme of the Congress was the struggle of Soviet Jewry for the right to *aliyah*. A resolution to the effect that Zionist leaders who failed to settle in Israel after two terms of office should forfeit their right to reelection was declared unconstitutional.

The Twenty-ninth Congress

The Congress was held in Jerusalem from February 20 to March 1, 1978. It had been postponed from January 1977, when the Congress Court ruled as unconstitutional a proposal to allow 90% of the election committee in any country to agree on a slate of delegates without elections. Over a million Diaspora Jews registered in preparation for the Congress.

The composition of the Congress faithfully reflected the political change that had taken place in Israel in 1977. The Zionist Labor Movement lost ground to the Likud and the Confederation of United Zionists in the Diaspora, and to the Likud and Democratic Movement for Change in the Israeli delegation. The Likud, with 174 out of the 550 seats with full voting rights, was the largest party, followed by the Confederation, with 113; Labor with 93; Mizrachi, 77; Mapam, 27; DMC, 26; others, 40. There were also 75 representatives of international Jewish organizations.

The Congress resolved that all WZO departments and programs in Israel should be administered in accordance with the principle of equal treatment for all trends in Judaism, Orthodox, Conservative, and Reform.

Arye Leon *Dulzin (Likud) was unanimously elected chairman of the Executive; Likud representatives took over the *aliyah*, youth and He-Ḥalutz, and education departments, and the chairmanship of the Zionist General Council from

Labor, and the settlement department was shared between Labor and the Likud. A Labor representative, however, succeeded Dulzin as treasurer.

[Misha Louvish]

The Thirtieth to Thirty-second Congresses

The 30th–32nd World Zionist Congresses, all convened within the decade 1982–92, exhibit several noteworthy trends. The meetings became progressively less ideological, of shorter duration, attended by more delegates who represented more world Jewish organizations – and were increasingly democratic. Yet the World Zionist Organization has less status in the Jewish world than in previous periods and has lost substantial power to its offspring, the Jewish Agency.

In 1982, the 30th Congress had 656 accredited representatives; two Congresses later, 721 delegates were accredited to the Congress. The 32nd Congress was also the first at which an incumbent chairman of the World Zionist Executive, running for a second term, was challenged by another candidate.

The 30th Zionist Congress met December 7–17, 1982. Even before it opened there were numerous appeals to the Zionist High Court protesting alleged infringements of democratic practices during elections. The High Court felt it had no recourse but to disqualify all representatives of Zionist parties and groupings in the U.S. Meeting in extraordinary session three days before the Congress opened, the Zionist General Council decided to make an unprecedented exception and passed a resolution which empowered the High Court itself to apportion mandates on a one-time basis. The court reluctantly complied. In a judgment against a previous attempt by the Zionist General Council to bypass holding elections for the Congress, Dr. Moshe Landau wrote, "This is not petty legalistic quibbling… when Zionism is attacked and slandered on all sides by the enemies of the Jewish people, it is doubly important that Zionism zealously guard its image as a movement which maintains its own democratic principles."

Worldwide, five election districts held direct elections, indirect elections were conducted in four, but 16 districts opted for a system of mutually agreed lists instead of elections.

The 31st Congress, December 6–11, 1987, was on the whole a democratically elected Congress, boasting a considerable number of first-time delegates. The American Zionist Federation conducted a nationwide election by mail, supervised by the independent American Arbitration Association, in which 183,000 valid votes were cast. However in electoral districts outside the U.S., only 40,000 people actually voted in elections.

The major groups represented at the Congress, by size of representation, were Likud, Labor Zionist Movement, Confederation of United Zionists, Mizrachi, Artzenu (Reform), Mapam, Mercaz (Conservative), Tzomet, and Teḥiyyah. The results showed major gains for the relatively new Zionist organizations of the Reform and Conservative movements, which ate into the traditional base of support held by Hadassah and the Zionist Organization of America. For the first time since 1948, the balance of power in negotiations to form a coalition was held by a bloc representing the Diaspora, composed of the Confederation, Artzenu, and Mercaz. These groups joined with Labor and Mapam to form a majority.

Simcha Dinitz, of Labor, was elected chairman of the World Zionist Organization Executive; Meir Shitreet, of Ḥerut, was elected treasurer.

The issue of religious pluralism in Israel was a major focus of concern at the 31st Congress due to the increased presence of the Reform and Conservative movements. The Congress passed a resolution that called for the "complete equality of rights to all streams of the Jewish religion and [for] granting their rabbis the legal right to perform all life cycle events and other rabbinic functions." This decision was the cause of much agitation in the ranks of the Mizrachi delegation as well as among Orthodox delegates in other groups.

The 32nd Zionist Congress, July 26–30, 1992, was the tenth to be held in Jerusalem since the establishment of the State. There were ten plenary sessions, four of which were of a cultural and festive nature. Consequently the work of the Congress, traditionally marked by earnest debate, was mainly conducted in the committees which submitted their resolutions for ratification at the closing plenary.

The resolutions fell into two categories, declarative and practical. Since the Resolutions Committee that processes the decisions of the various committees before they can be put to a vote at the plenary does not permit any operational resolution which has a budgetary component attached to it, most of the resolutions tend to be declarative.

Simcha Dinitz was re-elected Chairman by a majority of almost 80 percent. A precedent of sorts was established when the losing candidate's faction (Artzenu) was excluded from the Executive that customarily is a wall-to-wall coalition rather than a majority cabinet.

On the whole changes that have occurred in the WZO since the 31st Congress both reflect and are caused by a younger, Israeli-born leadership that tends to be less ideological and more pragmatic.

Simcha Dinitz and Meir Shitreet overlooked the legacy to revitalize contemporary Zionist ideology by reformulating some of its tenets mandated to them by Arye Dulzin in his last years in office. Dinitz chose to operate primarily in the Jewish Agency field abandoning the ideological thrust of the Herẓliyyah Process of 1983. At a meeting held at the home of the president of Israel in 1990, called to discuss "The WZO: Changes in Ideology and Status," Dinitz said, "In essence the crisis confronting the Zionist movement is not ideological but functional. Whereas the WZO is somewhat shabby, dusty, oversensitive, and not terribly efficient, the Jewish Agency is business-like, healthful, robust, and efficient. It is also more ruthless."

Four matters of vital Zionist importance failed to be substantively addressed by the 32nd Congress. These were the diminished standing of Zionist Federations throughout the world; the options regarding partnership with the fundraisers in the Jewish Agency: unification or dissolution; the change in the thrust of the Settlement Department – once the flag bearer of Zionist pioneering – to a Jewish Agency department of urban and rural welfare; and finally, the transfer of increasingly large segments of *aliyah* and absorption work to government care.

Looming in the background of the 32nd Congress was the notion that, in reality, the World Zionist Organization had outlived its mandate. There were some who felt that since the WZO had failed to come to terms with essential aspects central to itself, a courageous discussion was called for and that the 33rd Zionist Congress, which was to be also be the centenary conclave since the first World Zionist Congress was convened in Basle, could be an appropriate occasion.

[Amnon Hadary]

The Thirty-third and Thirty-fourth Congresses

The 33rd Zionist Congress convened in Jerusalem in 1997. With Diaspora Jewish organizations within the Zionist movement now exercising 50% of the vote in the Jewish Agency and similarly in the WZO (through the Joint Authority for Jewish Zionist Education), Israel found itself less central to the overall agenda. The Zionist leadership and intellectuals attempted to define the nature and role of Zionism at the change of the millennium. The principle of religious pluralism figured high on the agenda of the religious streams; however, it took a concerted effort and much adroit negotiation by Chairman Avraham *Burg, to arrive at an acceptable resolution. At this congress a resolution was passed requiring at least 25% of Zionist Congress delegates to be between the ages of 18–30.

The 34th Zionist Congress convened in Jerusalem in 2003. As resolved in the previous Congress, 25% of the delegation was under the age of 30. Under the banner of "Solidarity and Mutual Responsibility: The Jewish People and the State of Israel" it brought together Zionist groups from across the Zionist spectrum to discuss the issue of Israel as a Jewish and democratic state and to look toward a new vision of Zionism.

The Zionist Congress concluded with a series of resolutions reaffirming the centrality of Israel, the importance of immigration, promotion of Jewish Zionist education, increased funding for youth movements, coordinating the fight against antisemitism and anti-Zionism, and settling the Negev and the Galilee. It also issued the following proclamation:

> We, who are assembled at the XXXIV Zionist Congress, held in Jerusalem during the fifty-fourth year since the establishment of the State of Israel and one hundred and five years since the convening of the First Zionist Congress where the right of the Jewish People to national revival in Eretz Israel was declared, hereby do call upon the legislators of the Knesset of Israel to secure in Basic Law the fundamental values of the State of Israel that determine it to be the State of the Jewish People and a Jewish and democratic state;
>
> Whereas the State of Israel was established by the Zionist Movement to be the National Home of the Jewish People and to achieve our two thousand year long aspiration to bring about the Ingathering of the Exiles, national independence, spiritual renaissance and the creation of a society in accordance with the vision of the Prophets of Israel;
>
> Whereas there are those who refute the right of the Jewish People to self-determination in Eretz Israel;
>
> And whereas the character of the State of Israel is determined and expressed, among others, through the Basic Laws that serve as the foundation for the future Constitution of Israel;
>
> Therefore,
>
> We who have assembled at the XXXIV Zionist Congress, convened in Jerusalem in the month of Tamuz in the year 5762, do proclaim that the time has come to provide for the legal status of the Jewish, Zionist and democratic values of the State of Israel in keeping with Israel's Declaration of Independence and the ethos of the State since its inception, and to declare the following principles as the basis for determining the uniqueness, character and raison d'être of the existence of the State of Israel as a Jewish and democratic state.
>
> 1. **The State of Israel is the State of the Jewish People and its capital is Jerusalem.** It is the fulfillment of the aspirations of the Zionist Movement and the aspirations of generations for the independence and sovereignty of the Jewish People in the spirit of the principles of the Declaration of Independence.
> 2. **The State of Israel will be open to the aliyah of Jews and will aspire to bring the Jewish People home.**
> 3. **The State of Israel is a democracy** that respects basic human rights and the heritage of the minorities living in its boundaries, through the safeguarding of equal rights for all of its citizens, regardless of religion, race, sex or nationality. The values of freedom, freedom of religion and conscience, justice and peace are the Jewish heritage of Israel.
> 4. **The State of Israel safeguards** the sites that are holy to all religions from any desecration or other offense that would interfere with freedom of access to members of all religions to their holy places or their sentiments to those sites.
> 5. "**Hatikvah**" is the national anthem of the State. The State flag and the State emblem are those determined by the Law of the Flag and Emblem.
> 6. **The State of Israel is a state whose history is intertwined with the history of the Jewish people.** The Shabbat is the day of rest of the State, the national festivals are its holidays and Hebrew is its language.
> 7. **The State of Israel perceives the encouragement of Jewish settlement in Israel** to a basic value of Zionism and a responsibility of the State and its authorities.
> 8. **The State of Israel, through the fulfillment of its mission, seeks the involvement of the Jewish People** in the building of the Land and in the Ingathering of the Exiles in accordance with the statutes of the State.
> 9. **The State of Israel, as the State of the Jewish People, will act to guarantee** the future existence of the Jewish People; will promote ties between Israel and the Diaspora; and will come to the aid of Jews throughout the world in time of need.
> 10. **The partnership between the State of Israel and the Jewish People** shall find expression through the National Institutions as determined by Law.
>
> On this momentous occasion, here in Jerusalem, we the representatives of the Zionist Movement, call upon the Knesset to adopt these principles among the Basic Laws of the State of Israel as the keystone for ensuring the future of the State of Israel as the Jewish and democratic State of the Jewish People.

Congress Minutes

Minutes of the 1st to the 27th Congresses were published in special volumes from 1898 until 1969. The minutes of the 1st to the 19th Congresses came out in German. Minutes of the First Congress came out in a second edition (Prague, 1911), with introductions by Nordau and Wolffsohn, and were also translated into Hebrew with supplements by H. Orlan (1947) and with the addition of forewords by surviving participants in the First Congress. From the 16th Congress (1929) minutes also include discussions of the Jewish Agency Council, which took place immediately after the closing session of the Congress. Hebrew became the language of Congress minutes with the 19th Congress, whose minutes are also in German; from the 20th Congress, the official records are only in Hebrew. Hugo *Schachtel published the following reference works for the minutes of the first Congresses: an index of the first six Congresses (1905), an index of the Seventh Congress (1906), and the resolutions of the first seven Congresses (all in German, 1906). An index of the minutes of the first four Congresses was compiled at Tel Aviv University (1966–69).

A vast and multilingual literature on the Congresses is to be found in newspapers, journals, and special books, especially during the periods in which Congresses were held. Various catalogues of journals and newspapers are extremely rich in this material, especially the index of *Ḥamishim Shenot Ha-Po'el ha-Ẓa'ir*, and *Zionism and Palestine* (11 vols., 1946–56).

On the role of the Congress within the general structure of the Zionist Organization, See *Zionism, Zionist Organization, Organizational Structure.

BIBLIOGRAPHY: N.M. Gelber, *Ha-Kongresim ha-Ẓiyyoniyyim* (1956). **WEBSITE:** www.jafi.org.il/education.

ZIONIST ORGANIZATION OF AMERICA (ZOA), U.S. organization of General Zionists. In 1898 Richard *Gottheil, who attended the Zionist Congress in Europe, called a New York conference which formed the Federation of American Zionists. To attract support, the Federation began to publish a monthly, *The Maccabean*, in 1901, and *Dos Yidishe Folk* in 1909. The newly formed *Young Judaea (1907) and *Hadassah (1912) joined the Federation, and at a convention in 1918 the various Zionist branches merged into the ZOA. Louis D. *Brandeis was elected honorary president and Julian W. *Mack president. The Mack administration (1918–21) participated in the work of the *Zionist Commission in Palestine. At the Cleveland convention of 1921, Brandeis and his adherents, who differed from Chaim *Weizmann and the world leadership in favoring a policy of private economic investment in Palestine, withdrew from the ZOA. Louis *Lipsky, who supported the *Keren Hayesod, became president, and the ZOA grew numerically, politically, and financially. In 1924 a merger of the annual Zionist major fund-raising efforts created the United Palestine Appeal. After the outbreak of World War II in September 1939, the American Emergency Committee (Council after 1943) for Zionist Affairs (ECZA) began to function. ZOA representatives on the ECZA occupied the front rank in the political struggles and achievements of that period. During 1946–48, U.S. support for the Jewish state was achieved by the exertions of the mobilized Zionist forces, including the ZOA leaders, especially Abba Hillel *Silver and Emanuel *Neumann.

With the founding of the State of Israel on May 14, 1948, the ZOA's role diminished and shifted to fund raising and public relations on behalf of Israel. In 1957 a group of prominent Zionists seceded from the ZOA and organized the American Jewish League for Israel. The ZOA struggled to maintain its position by fostering projects in Israel such as Kefar Silver and the ZOA house in Tel Aviv, and stressing Zionist education and Hebrew culture in the U.S. ZOA supported the Young Judaea youth movement and several Zionist-oriented summer camps. It published a periodical *The New Palestine* which later was called *The American Zionist*. ZOA membership was 147,551 in 1918; 44,280 in 1939; and 165,000 in 1950. Since 1950 there has been a decline in membership.

[Herbert Parzen]

ZOA's influence continued to diminish in the 1980s and early 1990s as the focus of pro-Israel activism shifted to major lobby groups like the American Israel Public Affairs Committee (AIPAC) and as Jewish defense agencies increasingly took on pro-Israel functions.

But the group became more prominent after the 1993 election of Philadelphia activist Morton Klein as ZOA president in a controversy-ridden contest.

While most pro-Israel groups supported the 1993 Oslo agreement, under Klein the ZOA expressed strong reservations, citing ongoing terrorism and continuing statements by Palestine Liberation Organization leader Yasser Arafat rejecting Israel's right to exist. Klein also used his position as a member of the Conference of Presidents of Major Jewish Organization to attack fellow presidents and to criticize individuals including *New York Times* columnist Thomas Friedman, and to lead a campaign against John K. Roth for director of the Research Institute of the U.S. Holocaust Memorial Museum. He tried to prevent the Presidents Conference from endorsing the Peace Process even when this was the policy of the elected government of Israel.

As ZOA became more critical of Israel's participation in the peace process, the group was wracked by internal dissension over the question of whether it was appropriate for American Jews to criticize the policies of an elected government in Jerusalem. That led to several local chapters, led by a prominent group in Baltimore, to disaffiliate from ZOA.

But the shift to the right helped ZOA reestablish a strong fundraising base. The group, and Klein in particular, also became close allies of Christian Zionist groups that became increasingly critical of the Oslo process and U.S. involvement in ongoing negotiations.

ZOA was most effective in raising the issue of American victims of Palestinian terrorism. In the 1990s, it established a Washington lobbying operation that frequently clashed with AIPAC, the leading pro-Israel lobby group, and began working closely and virtually exclusively with right-of-center lawmakers. In 2005 ZOA became a leading U.S. voice against Israel's unilateral withdrawal from Gaza, conducting a vigorous but ultimately unsuccessful advertising campaign in Israel against the withdrawal.

[James Besser (2nd ed.)]

BIBLIOGRAPHY: Zionist Organization of America, *Annual Reports*, 1 (1898–to date); idem, *ZOA in Review*, 1 (1964–to date); M. Feinstein, *American Zionism: 1884–1904* (1965); R. Learsi, *Fulfillment: The Epic Story of Zionism* (1951); H. Parzen, *A Short History of Zionism* (1962); S.H. Sankowsky, *A Short History of Zionism* (1947), 98–107.

ZIONIST SOCIALIST WORKERS' PARTY (or SS, the initials of "Zionists-Socialists" in Russian), territorialist group in Russia founded at a conference held (interrupted as a result of the arrests of its participants) in Odessa, in January–February 1905. The party was the outcome of the rift between two conflicting tendencies in *Po'alei Zion in 1903–04, and though efforts were made to unite the separate groups into a united Zionist Socialist party, the ideological differentiation led to three distinct trends: territorialist, autonomist, and Ereẓ-Israel-centered. There were also differences on the participation of Jewish socialists in the revolutionary struggle in Russia. Among the leaders and activists of the party were: N. *Syrkin, J.W. *Latzky-Bertholdi, the brothers Jacob and Joseph *Lestschinsky, G. *Abramowitz (Avrahami), J. Chernikhov (Danieli), M. Rashkes, M. *Litvakov, A. *Yoffe, M. Shatz-Anin, S. *Niger, the brothers David and Moses Gepstein, J. *Pat, D. *Lvovich, B. Zelikovich (M. Gutman), Samuel *Weizmann, and A. Sokolovski. B. *Dinur (Dinaburg), B. *Katznelson, A. *Harzfeld, M.D. *Remez (Drabkin), as well as S. *Mikhoels, A. Leyeles *Glanz, and Elisha *Rodin, who belonged to it during various periods. In its foundation statement the party adhered to *territorialism, arguing that the essence of Zionism was its "social economic content," and not "the revival of the Jewish land, Jewish culture, and Jewish tradition." Therefore, "there is no organic link between Zionism and Palestine." Because the SS had rejected the purely autonomist principle of "Sejmism," the supporters of the *Vozrozhdeniye group rapidly seceded from it. The party participated in the Seventh Zionist Congress (summer 1905), after which it left the Zionist Organization, supporting the Jewish territorialist organization founded by I. *Zangwill. The first proper convention of the party was held in Leipzig (March 1906) and decided to change its name, but it postponed it until the establishment of a Jewish world socialist organization. A minority within the party did not support its extreme anti-Ereẓ Israel stance.

The SS viewed the future of the Jews in the Diaspora with extreme pessimism and saw an urgent need for a radical solution for fear of catastrophe. The party did not believe in "national cultural autonomy" of the Bundist type, nor in the national-political autonomism of the Sejmists. The absence of a "national economy" and "acute, social-economic and national-political pressures" were leading to the constant impoverishment of the Jewish masses and their "cultural sterility." The formula "non-proletarization" evolving into "non-industrialization," explained the abnormal conditions of the Jewish proletariat and its restriction to small industry and craftsmanship. Thus it could not be "the real bearer of the socialist ideal." The "historical necessity" for realizing the concept of territorialism was linked to the actual flow of Jewish mass emigration, which occupied a central place in the party's ideology. The Jewish emigration, flowing to developed countries and towns, would reach a saturation point. It would be compelled to chance its direction toward agriculture, toward a compact settlement, which would foster "the concentration of the Jewish masses in a free territory." Once political rights would be won this evolution would lead to the formation of a "Jewish national economic organism." This concept lacked, however, any indication as to the role to be played by the party in the realization of Jewish territorialism. The party regarded itself as a social-democratic Marxist party, supported active participation in the revolutionary struggle of Russia, but did not see any organic link between it and the aims of territorialism. In the revolution of 1905–06 its influence reached a peak and it became a factor second in importance only to the *Bund, which regarded it as a serious rival. The party also struck roots in Poland, especially in *Czestochowa (J. Kruk and A. *Syngalowski). It claimed to have 27,000 members and played an active role in Jewish *self-defense and in the trade-union movement. In 1907 it was joined by the Jewish territorialist workers' party, the successor of the "Minsk trend" of Po'alei Zion.

There was also a "SS League Abroad." The party maintained relations with sister organizations in the United States (the "Zionist territorialists," led by N. Syrkin, B. *Zuckerman, and A. Goldberg), England, and Argentina. The SS participated in the Congress of the Second Socialist International at Stuttgart (1907) on a consultative basis, but it was not accepted as a member of the International. In the reaction years, after the abortive revolution of 1905–06, the SS declined greatly in importance and was abandoned by a number of its leaders. Its slogan became "regulation of emigration" (Vilna Convention, 1908), hence its initiative for the calling of a World Emigration Congress, the project of an emigration bank, and its participation in the congresses of the Jewish Territorial Organization. The SS stood for Yiddishism. At its fourth conference (1911) it decided to participate in the life of the Jewish communities, while at the fifth conference (March 31–April 1, 1915), it adopted, for the first time, a positive position on autonomism. The SS participated in the activities of the *ORT, the *Society for the Promotion of Culture among the Jews of Russia, and the *OZE. During World War I the SS adopted an anti-war attitude (fifth conference, 1915) and was opposed to participation in the patriotic war-industrial committees in Russia. After the February 1917 Revolution it substituted in its name the word "territorialist" instead of "Zionist," and adopted – at its sixth conference (April 1917) – the program of national autonomy. Thus the road was open for a union with the Sejmists and the establishment of the *United Jewish Socialist Workers' Party (Fareynigte; June 1917). Several former members of the SS were prominent for their role in Jewish settlement in the Soviet Union (e.g., I. Golde and Y. Liberberg). The organs of the SS included: *Khronik fun der Tsionistish-Sotsialistisher Arbeter Partey* (1905), *Forverts* (Warsaw, 1905–06); *Der Nayer Veg, Unzer Veg* (Vilna, 1906–07), *Der Shtral*, 2 vols. (1907–08), and *Tsukunft* (1913).

BIBLIOGRAPHY: A. Kirzshanski, *Der Yidisher Arbeter*, 2–4 (1925–28), index; B. Borochov, *Ketavim*, 1–3 (1955–66); *Sotsialistisher Teritorializm* (1934), 43–51, 79–115, 140–8; A.L. Patkin, *The Origins of the Russian-Jewish Labor Movement* (1947), 222–8; M. Gutman, *Royter Pinkas*, 1 (1921), 152–73; B. Katznelson, *Ketavim*, 5 (1947), 382–5; B. Dinur, *Be-Olam she-Shaka* (1958), 303–60; M. Katz, *A Dor Vos Hot Farloyrn di Moyre* (1956), 54–57, 156–67, 195–216; I. Gordin, *Yorn Fargangene, Yorn Umfargeslekhe* (1960), 54–116; I. Rubin, *Fundanen Ahin* (1952), 143–91; O. Janowsky, *The Jews and Minority Rights* (1933), index; J. Kruk, *Taḥat Diglan shel Shalosh Mahpekhot* (1968).

[Moshe Mishkinsky]

ZIPH (Heb. זִיף; Wilderness of Ziph, מִדְבַּר זִיף), city of Judah mentioned in the seventh district of the hill country of Judah together with Maon, Carmel, and Juttah (Josh. 15:55); it was also associated with the Calebites (I Chron. 2:42; 4:16). The Ziphites were noted for their loyalty to Saul, to whom they twice revealed the site of David's hiding places in the desert which extended east of the city (I Sam. 23:19ff.; 26:1ff.; cf. Ps. 54:2). Ziph was fortified by Rehoboam and it apparently served as the terminus of his line of defense guarding the southern part of Judah (II Chron. 11:8). The wilderness of Ziph, the desert east of the city, was almost impassable for an enemy army. The importance of Ziph during the Judean kingdom is attested by its appearance (along with Hebron, Socoh, and *mmšt*) on royal seal impressions from Judah. The settlement in Ziph continued to exist in the fourth century C.E.: a village with this name is mentioned by Eusebius in Daromas in the territory belonging to Eleutheropolis (Bet Guvrin; Onom. 92:15ff.). It is last mentioned in connection with the life of St. Euthemios (fifth century). Ziph is identified with Tell Zif, 4½ mi. (7 km.) southeast of Hebron.

BIBLIOGRAPHY: S. Klein, *Meḥkarim Ereẓ Yisre'eliyyim* (1923), 9, 28; A. Alt, in: PJB, 22 (1926), 77; B. Maisler, *Toledot ha-Meḥkar ha-Arkhe'ologi…* (1936), 42, 160; Abel, Géog, 2 (1938), 490; Avi-Yonah, Geog, 105; EM, 2 (1965), 911–3.

[Michael Avi-Yonah]

ZIPPER, GERSHON (1868–1921), leader of the Zionist Movement in Galicia. Born in Monasterzyska, East Galicia, Zipper became one of the outstanding lawyers in Galicia. His special concern was the oppressed and the poor. From his early youth he was an active Zionist. He was a member of the group that published the first Polish-language Zionist periodical, *Przyszloszcz* ("Future") in 1892, and, together with A. Korkis, was the author of a Zionist booklet in Polish, "The Task of Jewish Youth." Zipper was one of the founders of a Galician Zionist organization that preceded by several years the appearance of Theodor *Herzl's *Der Judenstaat*, and became one of the leading protagonists of political Zionism in Galicia. He also became active on the local political scene and played a leading role in the 1911 elections to the Austrian parliament on behalf of a Zionist list. The list, however, suffered a severe defeat as a result of the intimidation practiced by the Austrian administration, in cooperation with the Jewish assimilationists. The following year he visited Ereẓ Israel, where he met Solomon *Schiller, his former associate in Zionist work in Poland, who had become director of the Hebrew high school in Jerusalem. On his return, Zipper organized a campaign for the creation of a building fund for the high school and succeeded in raising the money for the erection of the school building. He was also active on behalf of the *Jewish National Fund. During World War I he served in the Austrian army. On his return to Lvov after the war, he resumed his activities in the Zionist Organization of Galicia and when the Zionist leaders of Lvov were arrested, after the pogrom, Zipper alone was left to lead the struggle with the Polish authorities for Jewish rights. At the beginning of 1919 he founded *Chwila* ("The Moment"), a Polish-language Zionist newspaper.

BIBLIOGRAPHY: B. Ginsberg, *Gershon Zipper* (Yid. 1937); N.M. Gelber, *Toledot ha-Tenu'ah ha-Ẓiyyonit be-Galiẓyah*, 2 vols. (1958), index.

[Getzel Kressel]

ZIPPER, YA'AKOV (1900–1983), Canadian educator and Yiddish author. Zipper was born in Tyszowce, Poland, the son of Rabbi Abraham David *Shtern. After receiving an intensive ḥasidic education from his father and at the traditional *ḥeder*, Zipper became deeply interested in Yiddish culture and education and trained as a teacher in the secularist schools of Poland. Despite his strongly secular views and associations, Zipper always maintained a positive interest in the traditional and religious values of Jewish culture and a love for Hebrew as well as for Yiddish, Jewish folklore, the established Jewish community, and the Land of Israel.

While in Poland, Zipper helped to organize secular schools in Vladimir Volynski and Ustilug. In 1925, he emigrated to Canada, where he became the leader of the Labor Zionist-oriented Yiddish-Hebrew Peretz schools of Winnipeg and, from 1934 until his retirement in 1971, in Montreal. He was an important figure in Canadian Jewish literary circles, being active in the Jewish Public Library, the Poalei Zion, the Jewish Nation Workers' Alliance, the Jewish Writers' Association, and in the educational work of the Canadian Jewish Congress. Under his direction and the leadership of Leiser Zuker (1886–1965), the Peretz School paid special attention to the education of the children of the poor, despite the institution's constantly straitened finances.

Zipper also played a leading part in extending the activities of the Jewish schools of the community to the realm of adult education, so that the Peretz schools became a vital spiritual center for the secular and Zionist community – as did the Jewish People's schools with which they merged in 1971. In this context Zipper's oratorical and literary talents supported his pedagogical training.

A major thrust of Zipper's thinking and teaching was the centrality of East-European folk Jewry in the recent centuries of Jewish history, which is reflected in his considerable literary output, both in Hebrew and in Yiddish. Together with Y.Y. *Segal, Rachel *Korn, Melech *Ravitch, Mordecai Chossid, N.J. Gotlib, and Peretz Miransky, he helped to establish the Canadian – and especially the Montreal – community as one of the important secondary centers of Jewish literature in the mid-20th century. His short stories, book reviews, poems, travel reports, and other writings appeared in scores of periodicals in the United States, Europe, Israel, and South America. His Hebrew style was as original a contribution to Jewish literature as were his Yiddish works. Much of his writing reinterprets biblical and historic themes. His first major work, based upon the biography of the Ba'al Shem Tov, appeared in serial form in *Haolam* (1937–38) and later in book form, both in Hebrew (*Ish Hayah ba-Areẓ*, 1955) and in Yiddish (*Geven iz a Mentsh*, Montreal, 1940). His semi-autobiographical novel, *Oyf Yener Zeyt Bug* (Montreal, 1946), set in Poland after World War I, appeared in a Hebrew version, *Me-Ever Li-Nehar Bug*, in 1957. His *Tsvishen Teykhen un Vassern* (Montreal, 1960), a major fictional work on Jewish life and moods in Polish villages, also appeared in Hebrew, *Bein Naharot u-Neḥalim*, in 1967. He wrote a long elegy on the ruins of the Holocaust, "*Ikh bin Vider in Khurever Heym Gekumen*" (Montreal, 1965). Zipper also edited the *Leizer Zuker Gedenkbukh* in memory of the prominent Poalei Zion educational worker and Canadian Jewish Congress leader.

[David Rome]

ZIPPORAH (Heb. צִפּוֹרָה), wife of Moses. The name of Zipporah's father is variously given as Reuel (Ex. 2:18, 21) and *Jethro (18:2; cf. 3:1), priest of Midian. She was one of seven daughters (2:16). Zipporah bore Moses two sons, Gershom and Eliezer (2:22; 18:3–4). She appears to have accompanied her husband on his return to Egypt when, at a night encampment on the way, she averted his imminent death by circumcising her son with a flint (4:24–26). Zipporah seems to have returned with her children to her father's home in Midian, rejoining Moses at Mt. Sinai after the Exodus from Egypt (18:1–6). Nothing further is recorded of her.

[Nahum M. Sarna]

In the *Aggadah*

Zipporah is praised in the Midrash both for her piety and virtue (MK 16b; Ex. R. 1:32) and for her beauty (Mid. Ps. 7:18). Various explanations are given of her name ("bird"): When questioned by her father about Moses, she ran after him like a bird and returned with him (Ex. R. 1:32); she cleansed her father's house from every vestige of idolatry as a bird collects the smallest crumbs from the ground (*ibid.*); she is compared to the bird used in the purification rites of the leper (Tanḥ. B., Ex. 6). As soon as Jethro realized that Moses was the Hebrew who had fled from Egypt he had him thrown into a pit. During the ten years he spent in the pit, however, Zipporah provided him with food until he was set free (Targ. Jon., Ex. 2:21). The "sending away" of Zipporah after the Exodus is interpreted as meaning that Moses gave her a bill of divorce (Mekh., Amalek, 3). Identifying the "Cushite woman" (Ethiopian) in Numbers 12:1 with Zipporah whom he remarried, the rabbis explain that as a Cushite woman is distinguished by her skin, so was she distinguished by her virtuous deeds (MK 16b).

BIBLIOGRAPHY: S. Talmon, in: *Eretz Israel*, 3 (1954), 93–96 (Heb.), 4 (Eng. summ.); J. Blau, in: *Tarbiz*, 26 (1956/57), 1–3 (Heb.), 1 (Eng. summ.); S. Ben-Shabbat, *ibid.*, 213 (Heb.), 7 (Eng. summ.); H. Kosmala, in: VT, 12 (1962), 14–28 (incl. bibl.); J. Morgenstern, in: HUCA, 34 (1963), 35–70; Ginzberg, Legends, index.

ZIPSER, MAJER (1815–1869), rabbi and leader of the *Neologist movement in Hungary. Born in Balassagyarmat, Hungary, Zipser studied at the renowned yeshivot of *Eisenstadt and *Mikulov, under R. Meir *Eisenstadt and N. *Trebitsch, respectively. The latter granted him his rabbinical diploma (*semikhah*), as did Moses *Sofer though he was not one of his disciples (1837). While still engaged in his talmudic studies, he acquired a broad general education, and graduated from the University of Pest in 1851. In 1844 Zipser was appointed rabbi of *Szekesfehervar. As soon as he assumed his position, he called for reforms in the order of prayer: the exclusion of the *piyyutim* from the obligatory prayers and their recital in silence. Controversies immediately broke out within the community which increased after he consented to give a *get* (divorce bill) in the community, something which had never been done before. Zipser published *Mei ha-Shillo'aḥ* ("Waters of Siloaḥ," 1853) in defense of his attitude. In 1850 he went to England, where he published his apologetic work *The Talmud and the Gospels* (1851). It was republished by the community of London in 1852 as "*The Sermon on the Mount Reviewed*…, in reply to statements made by two members of parliament, Inglis and Newgate." As a result of the disputes in his community, he thought of emigrating, but accepted a call from the community of Rechnitz (Rohonc), where he remained until his death. His other works include *Zur Biographie R. Meir Eisenstadt* (1846–47); *Die juedischen Zustaende unter der 150 jaehrigen Tuerkenherrschaft* (1846–47); *Raphael Meldola* (1846–47); and *Kritische Untersuchung ueber die Originalitaet der im Talmud und Midraschim vorkommenden Parabeln und Sentenzen* (1848). His German translation of Josephus' *Contra Apionem*, entitled *Ueber das hohe Alter des juedischen Volkes gegen Apion*, was edited by A. *Jellinek and published posthumously in 1870.

BIBLIOGRAPHY: Reich, in: *Beth El*, 2 (1868), 265–97.

[Baruch Yaron]

ZIRELSON, JUDAH LEIB (1860–1941), chief rabbi of Bessarabia, communal leader, and author. Born in Kozelets, Ukraine, at the age of 18 he became rabbi of Priluki and in 1908 of Kishinev. When he received a call to Radom, his community opposed his leaving; the leaders of the Radom community submitted the issue to a *bet din* but lost the case. Widely learned and proficient in many languages, Zirelson became a leading Zionist and a regular contributor to Hebrew periodicals in Russia, such as *Ha-Meliẓ, Ha-Ẓefirah, Ha-Zeman, Ha-Peles*, and *Ha-Modi'a*. He dissociated himself from Zionism, however, as a result of a dispute in 1898 about the election of the Va'ad Rabbanim ("Committee of Rabbis"). In 1908 he presided over the Conference of Russian Rabbis which met in St. Petersburg to discuss the Jewish position in Russia. In 1911 he issued an appeal for signatories to the protest against the *blood libel raised during the Beilis case at Kiev. In 1912 he was one of the founders of Agudat Israel and was chairman of the two congresses held by that organization in Vienna (1923 and 1929). A communal leader of the loftiest stature, he was one of the personalities most active on behalf of Russian Jewry. When Bessarabia was incorporated in Romania (1920), he learned Romanian, became the leader of the extreme Orthodox Jewry of that country, and was elected a deputy to the Romanian parliament in 1922 and a senator in 1926. Besides being the chief rabbi, he was for certain periods also the head of the community and even mayor of Kishinev, in recognition of which many honors were conferred on him. In Kishinev he founded numerous institutions, among these its first Orthodox high school. He was shot and killed by the Germans in Kishinev (during World War II).

He was the author of several important works: *Aẓei Levanon* (1922), responsa; *Gevul Yehudah* (1906, 1912^2), responsa; *Hegyon Lev* (1929), homilies and eulogies; *Ma'arekhei Lev* (1932), responsa and homilies; *Derekh Selulah* (1902), essays and poems; and *Lev Yehudah*, 1 (1935), 2 (1961), responsa and addresses. In his works he included many quotations in various languages, being in this respect almost unique in responsa literature.

BIBLIOGRAPHY: M. Slipoi, *Ha-Ga'on Rabbi Yehudah Leib Zirelson* (1948); *Elleh Ezkerah*, 1 (1956), 164–76; LNYL, 7 (1968), 600–1.

[Itzhak Alfassi]

ZIRIDS (Ar. **Banu Ziri**), *Berber dynasty which ruled Ifriqiya (Northeastern Africa, mainly *Tunisia of today) from the late tenth century until approximately 1167. A branch of this family extended Berber rule into *Spain in the 11th century and established its capital at Granada. Under Zirid domination in Northeastern Africa there emerged a vital center of Jewish intellectual life. This became feasible owing to the dynasty's tolerant disposition toward the Jews who generally populated the city of *Kairouan and the commercial ports of Mahdiya and Gabès (today part of southern Tunisia). Kairouan was the residence of the central Jewish leadership and its president, the **nagid*. Perhaps the most illustrious *nagid* in the Zirid era was Ibrahim b. 'Ata, who was court physician to the governors Badis and Mu'izz. He had the title of *negid ha-Golah* bestowed upon him in recognition of his outstanding services both to his local community and to the *Pumbedita Academy.

After the Zirids extended their authority to Spain, the Jews of Granada were able to promote cultural and political activity with no particular curbs on communal freedom exercised by the Zirids. This was especially true once the latter appointed *Samuel ha-Nagid and his son, Joseph, as governmental ministers (viziers). One of the reasons the Jews were properly treated may be attributed to their contribution to the dynasty's financial stability. Following the murder of Joseph ha-Nagid in 1066, Jewish influence declined. The *Almoravids replaced the Zirids as a dominant ruling Berber dynasty in North Africa. Though the Almoravids proved tolerant vis-à-vis their Jewish subjects, this attitude hardly measured up to the golden age enjoyed by the Jews until the mid-12th century.

BIBLIOGRAPHY: S.D. Goitein, *A Mediterranean Society: The Jewish Communities of the Arab World as Portrayed in the Documents of the Cairo Geniza*, vol. 2: *The Community* (1967–71); H.Z. Hirschberg, *A History of the Jews in North Africa*, vol. 1 (1974); N.A. Stillman, *The Jews of Arab Lands: A History and Source Book* (1979).

[Michael M. Laskier (2nd ed.)]

ZISLING, AHARON (1901–1964), labor leader in Ereẓ Israel. Born in the Minsk district, Belorussia, Zisling received both a religious and a secular education. In 1914 he was taken to Tel Aviv by his family. In 1917, when the Turkish authorities ordered the evacuation of Tel Aviv, Zisling studied with a group of deported teachers in Ḥaderah and, under the influence of Joseph Ḥayyim *Brenner, he grew closer to the labor movement. He worked as a laborer in kevuẓat Tirah near Haifa and on the Afulah-Nazareth road and participated in the founding of the workers' collective Ḥavurat ha-Emek, which merged with kibbutz En-Harod. Zisling, who was a delegate to the founding conference of the *Histadrut (1920) and served as secretary of the Jerusalem workers' council (1925–26), was a member of kibbutz En-Harod from its start and a leader of the *Ha-Kibbutz ha-Me'uḥad movement. Among the founders of *Youth Aliyah, he served on its executive board. As a member of the *Haganah command, he participated in the founding of the *Palmaḥ. During World War II, Zisling was a founder of the Friendship League with the U.S.S.R. A leader of the original *Aḥdut ha-Avodah which merged with Ha-Po'el ha-Ẓa'ir to form *Mapai (1930), he led the Si'ah Bet ("faction B") when Mapai split and became a founder of the new Aḥdut ha-Avodah Party (1944) and of *Mapam (1948). He was a delegate to the Asefat ha-Nivḥarim, beginning with the second one, a member of the Va'ad Le'ummi executive, co-founder of Kofer ha-Yishuv (the *yishuv* defense fund), and an active member of central institutions of the Histadrut. In 1947 he was a member of the Jewish Agency delegation to the United Nations. He served in Minhelet ha-Am (People's Administration, see *Israel, State of, Central Governance) and in the provisional Israel government of 1948–49 as minister of agriculture. He was a member of the First Knesset. From 1961 to 1963 Zisling was a member of the Zionist Executive and headed its absorption department.

BIBLIOGRAPHY: Tidhar, 4 (1950), 1571–72.

[Abraham Aharoni]

ZISSU, ABRAHAM LEIB (1888–1956), Romanian Zionist leader and author. Born in Piatra-Neamţ, Zissu was descended from prominent Ḥabad Ḥasidim and was raised in a religious environment. Although he became an important manufacturer, Zissu devoted most of his time to literary and political work of a Jewish or Zionist nature. He joined Leon *Algazi and the philo-Semitic Romanian writer Gala Galaction (1879–1961) in publishing the periodical *Spicul*; was coeditor (from 1908) with M.M. *Braunstein (Mi-Bashan) of the Hebrew monthly *Ha-Mekiẓ;* and in 1919 founded the Romanian Zionist daily *Mântuirea*.

As an active Zionist, Zissu often came into conflict with Jewish assimilationists who headed many Jewish institutions, and in his writing developed a violently polemical style. He wrote several novels and other works on Jewish themes, including *Spovedania unui Candelabru* ("Confession of a Candelabrum", 1926); *Ereticul dela Mănastirea Neamțului* ("The Heretic of the Neamț Monastery", 1930); *Calea Calvarului* ("The Road of Calvary", 1935); and *Samson și Noul Dagon* ("Samson and the New Dagon", 1939). The publication of his study *Logos, Israel, Biserica* ("The Logos, Israel, and the Church", 1937) brought him threats of violence from outraged antisemitic students. From 1944 he headed the Zionist Federation and the World Jewish Congress (Romanian section), and organized the mass emigration to Ereẓ Israel of Romanian Jews. Zissu nevertheless continued his efforts under the Communist regime until he was arrested, tried, and sentenced to life imprisonment in 1954 for Zionist activities. Following his release, he arrived in Israel in 1956, but died a few weeks later.

Abraham Zissu's son. THEODORE ZISSU (1916–1942), who had an English university education, was a practical Zionist. He foresaw the immense importance of the then barren Negev region of Palestine and, after the 1937 Peel Commission, formed the Negev Group to fight for the area's inclusion in any future Jewish state. Zissu conducted a vigorous publicity campaign to this end. During World War II he rose from the ranks to become a British tank officer and was fatally wounded at the battle of El Alamein. His book, *The Negev, Southern District of Palestine*, was published in 1946.

BIBLIOGRAPHY: T. Arghezi, in: *Adam* (July 31, 1929); A. Saraga, *He-Asui li-Veli Ḥet* (1964).

[Abraham Feller]

ZITNITSKY, PINCAS (Pedro) LÁZARO (1894–1967), Argentine journalist, editor, and author. Born in Kiev, Zitnitsky studied law at Kiev, Koenigsberg, and Bonn. He emigrated to Argentina in 1928 and was active in the non-Zionist and Yiddishist left-wing sector of the Jewish community in Buenos Aires and presided over the Tzentral Veltlech Yiddishe Shul Organizatzie (TZVISHO; Central Organization of Jewish Secular Schools) upon its foundation in 1934. He was also one of the directors and a member of the editorial board of the leftist Yiddish daily newspaper *Di Presse* of Buenos Aires. He became a professor of Slavic civilization at the Universidad Internacional de Latino-America, Buenos Aires, in 1959, and vice rector the following year. Zitnitsky was a prolific journalist and essayist. His books include *Forerunners of Scientific Socialism* (1928), *The Meaning of History* (1930), *Peretz: Philosophy and Socialism* (1951), and *A Half-Century of Yiddish Literature* (1952).

ZITRON, SAMUEL LEIB (1860–1930), Hebrew and Yiddish writer and journalist. The son of a distinguished merchant family in Minsk, Zitron was educated at Lithuanian yeshivot. While studying at the Volozhin yeshivah, he became attracted to the Haskalah and in 1876 moved to Vienna, where he became friendly with P. *Smolenskin. After studying for several years in Germany, he began his journalistic career, and for more than 50 years contributed to the Yiddish press and to nearly all the Hebrew periodicals in the Diaspora. In the 1880s to 1890s, he wrote short stories, one of which, "*Yonah Potah*" (1887), aroused popular attention. He joined the Ḥibbat Zion movement in its early days and translated L. *Pinsker's *Autoemanzipation* into Hebrew (it appeared in a censored version, under the title *Im Ein Ani Li Mi Li*). From 1904 Zitron lived in Vilna and edited various newspapers and anthologies. Of special interest are a series of articles on the Hebrew press published in *Haolam*, 4 (1911–14, 1927–30). Based mainly on Zitron's personal experiences and recollections, the articles contain material of historic value, particularly on *Ha-Maggid, Ha-Meliẓ, Ha-Ẓefirah, Ha-Karmel, Ha-Levanon, Ha-Emet*, and *Ha-Kol*. He also wrote about the history of the Yiddish press in the 19th century (*Geshikhte fun der Yidisher Prese*, 1923). With the decline of the Hebrew press in Eastern Europe, Zitron wrote extensively for the Yiddish press, and published many monographs written in a popular style, some of which were later published in book form. Zitron also translated many books into Hebrew (including the works of *An-Ski and the stories of L. *Levanda).

His works include: on the Zionist movement and its precursors, *Toledot Ḥibbat Ẓiyyon* (1913); *Herzl* (1921; Heb.); *Leksikon Ẓiyyoni* (1924); on Hebrew literature and its writers, *Yoẓerei ha-Sifrut ha-Ivrit ha-Ḥadashah* (1922); *Anashim ve-Soferim* (1921); articles in Yiddish, *Meshumodim* (4 vols., 1923–23), *Literarishe Doyres* (4 vols., 1921–23), *Shtadlanim* (1926), *Barimte Yidishe Froyen* (1944).

BIBLIOGRAPHY: Waxman, Literature, index; J. Fichmann, in: *Moznayim*, 29 (1930); Schoenhaus, in: *Haolam* (1930), 28, 490; M. Shalit, in *Davar Musaf* (Nov. 21, 1930); Rejzen, Leksikon, 3 (1929), 286–97; N. Goren, in: *Gilyonot*, 26 (1952), 398–400. **ADD. BIBLIOGRAPHY:** G. Shaked. *Ha-Sipporet ha-Ivrit*, 1 (1977), 223–25.

[Yehuda Slutsky]

ZIV, JACOB (1931–), electrical engineer. Born in Tiberias, Israel, Ziv received his B.Sc., Dip. Eng. (1954), and M.Sc. (1957), both in electrical engineering, from the Technion, Israel Institute of Technology, Haifa. From 1955 to 1959, he was a senior research engineer in the Scientific Department of the Israeli Ministry of Defense and was assigned to the research and development of communications systems. He was sent by the Israeli Ministry of Defense to Massachusetts Institute of Technology and received his D.Sc. degree in 1962. From 1961 to 1962, while studying for his doctorate at MIT, he joined the Applied Science Division of Melpar, Inc., Watertown, Mass., where he was a senior research engineer working in communications theory. In 1962 he returned to the Scientific Department of the Israeli Ministry of Defense as head of the Communications Division and was also an adjunct of the Faculty of Electrical Engineering at the Technion. From 1968 to 1970 he was a member of the technical staff of Bell Laboratories, Inc., Murray Hill, N.J., where he also spent several sabbaticals in later years. He joined the Technion in 1970 and was appointed professor of electrical engineering. From 1974 to 1976, he was dean of the Faculty of Electrical Engineering and vice president for academic affairs from 1978 to 1982. Upon his return full time to the Technion in 1970, he worked on a variety of problems in information theory, including the characterization of the complexity of an information source and the related problem of universal data compression. With Abraham Lempel he wrote a series of papers on the Lempel-Ziv algorithm. His research interests include data-compression, information theory, and statistical communication. In 1982 he was elected a member of the Israel Academy of Sciences and appointed a Technion distinguished professor. In 1993 he was awarded the Israel Prize in exact sciences (engineering and technology). Among his many awards, he has twice been the recipient of the IEEE-Information Theory Best Paper Award (for 1977 and 1979). He is the recipient of the 1995 International Marconi Award, the 1995 IEEE Richard W. Hamming Medal, in 1997 the Shanon Award from the Information Theory Society, and in 2002 the Rothschild Prize for technological sciences. He was chairman of the Israel Universities Planning and Grants Committee from 1985 to 1991 and served as the president of the Israel National Academy of Sciences and the Humanities.

[Bracha Rager (2nd ed.)]

ẒIVION (pseudonym of **Benzion Hoffman**; 1874–1954), Yiddish journalist and essayist. Born in a Latvian village, he joined the *Bund soon after its founding in 1897 and remained a faithful interpreter of its ideology. From 1895 he wrote Hebrew articles and in 1909, the year after his emigration to New York, he edited the U.S. Hebrew journal *Ha-Yom*. However, his main literary medium was Yiddish, in which he is said to have written about 6,000 articles, mostly in the New York Yiddish paper *Jewish Daily Forward*, and in the monthly, *Zukunft*. Although he received a doctorate in science and engineering, he preferred to write about rather than practice in these fields. A correspondent to many national and international conferences, he proved to be a skillful interpreter of complex political problems. His readers valued his independent judgment, his simple style, and his mild humor. He popularized scientific subjects in several books and participated in the English-Yiddish Encyclopedic Dictionary (1915). On the semicentennial of his literary activities, a volume of his, *Far Fuftsik Yor* ("Selected Works," 1948) appeared under the editorship of H.S. Kazdan.

BIBLIOGRAPHY: Rejzen, Leksikon, 3 (1929), 246–51; H.S. Kazdan, Introduction to Ẓivion, *Far Fuftsik Yor* (1948).

[Melech Ravitch]

ZIYANIDS (**Banu Ziyan**), Berber dynasty which ruled intermittently in western *Algeria from 1235 to 1557. This dynasty had its capital in *Tlemcen. It welcomed numerous Jewish refugees victimized by pogroms in Christian *Spain in the 1390s – one hundred years before the mass expulsion of Spanish Jewry. Some Jews enjoyed influence in the Ziyanid court as officials, interpreters, and financial advisers. When Spain and *Portugal conquered parts of Algeria in the 16th century, they sowed panic among the Jews, who fled to *Morocco and other parts of the Maghreb. Some came back after the withdrawal of the occupiers. To maintain their hold over Algeria, the Ziyanids enlisted the aid of the Ottoman Turks. The latter gradually consolidated their hold over the country in the 1550s and remained in relative control until the French conquest of 1830.

BIBLIOGRAPHY: H.Z. Hirschberg, *A History of the Jews in North Africa*, 1 (1974); C.-A. Julien, *History of North Africa: From the Early Arab Conquest to 1830*, ed. and rev. by R. Le Tourneau (1970).

[Michael M. Laskier (2nd ed.)]

ẒIẒIT (Heb. צִיצִית pl. צִיצִיּוֹת, *ẓiẓiyyot*; "fringes"), name of the tassels attached to the four corners of special (four-cornered) garments worn by men in fulfillment of the biblical commandment in Numbers 15:37–41 and Deuteronomy 22:12. It has been suggested that the *ẓiẓit* served as a talisman (*amulet) or that it was instituted in order to distinguish between male and female garments which were very similar in biblical times. In the latter case it served as a protection against immoral conduct (an interpretation derived from Numbers 15:39). Talmudic literature invests the commandment of *ẓiẓit* with exalted symbolism. The rabbis regarded the *ẓiẓit* as a reminder to the Jew to observe the religious duties, giving it a function similar to that of the **mezuzah* on the doorposts and to the **tefillin* on the head and arm. The Talmud brings the parable how a person was saved from sensual sin because he wore fringes (Men. 44a).

The biblical commandment prescribing the entwining of a blue cord in the fringes is regarded as essential because blue, the color of the sky, was also supposed to be the color of the "throne of glory" (Men. 43b). Difficulties in obtaining the dyeing material for this purpose caused rabbinic authorities in the second century C.E. to waive this requirement.

In modern times, each *ẓiẓit* consists of one long and three short white threads which are passed through the holes in the four corners of the garment and folded so as to make eight threads. They are then fastened with a double knot. The long thread (called *shammash*) is wound around the other threads seven, eight, 11, and 13 times and the four joints are separated from one another by a double knot. The *ẓiẓit* thus consists of five double knots and eight threads (a total of 13). This number, together with the Hebrew numerical value of *ẓiẓit* (600), amounts to 613, the number of the biblical commandments of which the *ẓiẓit* are to remind the wearer (Num. 15:39). *Ẓiẓiyyot* of wool or linen are ritually fit for a **tallit* of whatever material. A silk or cotton *tallit*, however, should have *ẓiẓiyyot* of only the same fabric. The minimum length of the *ẓiẓit* threads should be four thumb lengths. If one of the *ẓiẓit* threads is torn, it is customary to replace the whole fringe. A person not wearing a four-cornered garment is exempt from the *mitzvah* of *ẓiẓit* since the religious duty of wearing *ẓiẓit* is not a personal one (*ḥovat gavra*). In order to fulfill this biblical commandment, however, pious Jews always wear a (*tallit katan*) "small four-cornered garment."

Women are exempt from the duty of *ẓiẓit* as the fulfillment of this commandment relates to a specific time and women are exempt from such obligations: *ẓiẓiyyot* have to be worn only during the day, based on the Bible verse "ye may look upon it" (Num. 15:39) which excludes the night.

It is customary to kiss the *ẓiẓiyyot* while reciting the last section of the **Shema* (Num. 15:37–41) in the morning service. The *ẓiẓyyot* of the *tallit* in which males are buried are torn to make them ritually unfit.

BIBLIOGRAPHY: Maim. Yad, Ẓiẓit, 1, 2, 3; Sh. Ar., OḤ 8:24; Eisenstein, Dinim, 349–50; S.R. Hirsch, *Ḥorev*, tr. by I. Grunfeld, 1 (1962), 180–6; IDB, 2 (1962), 325–6.

ZLATOPOL, town in N.W. Kirovograd district, Ukraine. In 1847 the Jewish community of Zlatopol numbered 2,668 and increased in 1897 to 6,373. Zlatopol was the first residence of the *Brodski family who founded there an almshouse, a hospital, and a high school. In May 1919 Ukrainian revolutionaries conducted pogroms in Zlatopol. Approximately 70 Jews were killed and most homes and stores in the town were robbed and burned. In 1926 the Jewish community amounted to 3,863 (61.7% of the population). The community perished under the Nazi occupation. In all, some 1,200 Jewish residents of the city were killed in 1941–42.

BIBLIOGRAPHY: *Reshummot*, 3 (1923), 385–91; Benari, in: *Gazit*, 6 (1944), 10–13.

[Ruth Beloff (2nd ed.)]

ZLATOPOLSKY, HILLEL (1868–1932), Zionist leader, industrialist, and philanthropist. Zlatopolsky was born in Yekaterinoslav. As secretary to Max *Mandelstamm, the Zionist Organization representative for the Kiev district (1897–1905), Zlatopolsky was in charge of the Zionist activities there, as well as of the financial center of Russian Zionists. He played a leading role in organizing the opposition to the *Uganda Scheme. He was one of the founders of the Ḥovevei Sefat Ever Society (Friends of the Hebrew Language, 1907) and was also active in the Histradrut le-Safah u-le-Tarbut Ivrit (Association of Hebrew Language and Culture). He made substantial financial contributions to facilitate the establishment of a network of Hebrew schools, ranging from kindergarten to teachers' seminaries. He also subsidized the Hebrew daily *Ha-Am*, and the *Habimah theater in Moscow and was one of the founders of Omanut, a publishing house for Hebrew textbooks and readers (the latter in cooperation with his daughter Shoshannah and son-in-law Joseph *Persitz). During World War I, he lived in Moscow, but he left Russia in 1919. Together with Isaac *Naiditsch, he was one of the founders of the *Keren Hayesod, and as a member of its first board of directors he conceived the idea of a national tithe. Zlatopolsky wrote articles on Zionism and Hebrew culture, as well as feuilletons, the latter containing a wealth of general Jewish and ḥasidic folklore. Some of his writings were published in two collections, *Bi-Tekufat ha-Teḥiyyah* (1917) and *Sefer ha-Feuilletonim* (1944). He died in Paris, the victim of a murder.

BIBLIOGRAPHY: M. Glickson, *Ishim*, 1 (1940), 231–7; D. Smilansky, *Im Benei Dori* (1942), 175–8.

[Yehuda Slutsky]

ZLOCISTI, THEODOR (1874–1943), physician and one of the first German Zionists. Born in Borchestowa, East Prussia, Zlocisti studied medicine at the University of Berlin and graduated in 1900. He practiced his profession throughout his life, first in Berlin and from 1921 in Ereẓ Israel – initially in Tel Aviv and later in Haifa. During World War I he was the chief medical officer of the Red Cross Mission in Constantinople and director of the Red Cross hospital in that city. In Tel Aviv he served as a member of the city council and its executive committee. Zlocisti played a leading role in the Zionist movement in Germany. In 1893 he was the secretary of the Young Israel Society in Berlin and had an exchange of correspondence with *Herzl. In 1895 he became one of the founders of the first Zionist students' society in Germany; together with his wife he attended the First Zionist Congress and kept up his Zionist activities in Germany until settling in Ereẓ Israel. He took a profound interest in East European Jewry and in Yiddish literature, and in *Aus einer stillen Welt, Erzaehlungen aus der modernen juedischen Literatur* (1910), he published German translations of works by leading Yiddish authors. He also published two collections of verse, *Vom Heimweg* (1903) and *Am Tor des Abends* (1912). He was the author of professional articles and treatises and of a comprehensive work on the climate of Ereẓ Israel, *Klimatologie und Pathologie Palaestinas* (1937).

Zlocisti also revived the writings of Moses *Hess and devoted efforts throughout his life to uncovering documentary material on Hess. He began with the publication of Hess's Jewish writings (*Juedische Schriften*, 1905), to which he added a comprehensive introduction. This introduction was later expanded into a special book (Heb. trans. Y.A. Heller, 2 vols., 1945–46). He also published a selection of his socialist writings, *Moses Hess, der Vorkaempfer des Sozialismus und Zionismus* (1921), a complete edition of *Rome and Jerusalem* (1935), and a shortened edition (1939), including an introduction and comments. He left a collection of Moses Hess's correspondence that was published in Hebrew translation after his death with an introduction by the translator, G. Kressel (1947).

BIBLIOGRAPHY: A. Biram in: *Haaretz* (Dec. 10, 1953); G. Kressel and N. Rotenstreich, in: *Davar* (Jan. 25, 1944).

[Getzel Kressel]

ZLOTOWITZ, BERNARD M. (1925–), U.S. Reform rabbi. Raised in an Orthodox immigrant family on the Lower East Side of Manhattan, Zlotowitz served as a leading voice of the Reform movement of the United States, holding several positions in the Union of American Hebrew Congregations (later the Union for Reform Judaism). His father, Rabbi Aron Zlotowitz, was spiritual leader of a congregation in Brooklyn for 60 years. Accepted into medical school while studying at Brooklyn College (B.A., History, 1948), Bernard Zlotowitz decided on a career in the Reform rabbinate. "I decided I didn't want to be a doctor. My real interest was in trying to serve God and the Jewish people," he says. In college, he re-examined his faith. "Reform answered my religious needs. Reform challenges the origins of the Bible … the nature of God."

After ordination in 1955 from the Hebrew Union College-Jewish Institute of Religion, where he earned a B.H.L, M.H.L. and subsequently a D.H.L. degree, Rabbi Zlotowitz served as a pulpit rabbi at temples in Elmont, N.Y., Nyack, N.Y., Freeport, N.Y., and Charlotte, N.C. He returned to New York City in 1975 to serve as the UAHC's New Jersey regional director. "I wanted to serve more Jews than I was serving in Charlotte," he said. In 1980 he was promoted to director of the New York Federation of Reform Synagogues; he also lectured on Bible at HUC and wrote a "Jewish Q & A" column for *Reform Judaism* magazine.

Zlotowitz worked at the federation until retirement in 1990. From his retirement, he taught at the interdenominational Academy for Jewish Religion in the Bronx, and continued to teach and lecture as the URJ's senior scholar, serving as a resource for the Reform movement's rabbis and lay members on a variety of religious and historical topics, such as the construction of a *mikveh,* and the source of the tradition of sitting *shivah* for an intermarried child.

"My major interest is Bible," he said, "because it's a living book. It's a guide for life."

As a leader of summer trips to Israel sponsored by the National Federation of Temple Youth in 1968–72, he took part in archaeological digs in the Old City of Jerusalem. "I chose to do it. It gave me a tremendous insight into archaeology. It gave me an insight into the history of Jerusalem."

Rabbi Zlotowitz was a life member of NFTY and a board member of the New York Board of Rabbis. He received an Honorary Doctor of Divinity degree from HUC in 1980.

With his wife Shirley he traveled around the world, including most of Europe, as well as parts of Africa, Asia, South America and Africa. During a visit to Germany in 1994, Rabbi Zlotowitz became fascinated by the story of Martin Riesenburger, a preacher and cantor who openly officiated at funerals and led worship services in the chapel of Berlin's major Jewish cemetery during the Nazi era and came to be known as "the last rabbi of Berlin."

Rabbi Zlotowitz researched Riesenburger's life and wrote his biography, still unpublished. "He was a hero. He gave the people hope," Rabbi Zlotowitz said. "He always told them the war would end."

Among his writings are *Abraham's Great Discovery* (1991) and *How Tzipi the Bird Got Her Wings* (1995), both as co-author with Dina Maiben; *Folkways and Minhagim, Art in Judaism; The Septuagint Translation of Hebrew Terms in Relation to God in the Book of Jeremiah* (1981), *The Book of Psalms: A New Translation and Commentary* (co-author with Mark Rozenberg, 1999); he was editor of *One People* (1982).

[Steven Lipman (2nd ed.)]

ZLOTOWITZ, MEIR (1938–), U.S. publisher. Born in New York, son of Rabbi Aron Zlotowitz, a European-born rabbinic scholar, vice president of the Agudat Harabonim in the 1940s and one of the leaders of the Rabbis March on Washington, on the eve of Yom Kippur 5703 – 1943.

Zlotowitz attended Yeshiva Rabbi Jacob Joseph on the Lower East Side of Manhattan, then spent eight years at Mesivtah Tifereth Jerusalem studying under Rabbi Moses Feinstein, from whom he received his ordination.

As a graphic artist, he established *ArtScroll Studios, specializing in illuminated scrolls, brochures, journals, and invitations. In 1976, he produced a translation of and commentary on *Megillat Esther* as a tribute to a recently deceased friend. The book so impressed those who saw it, that he was encouraged to leave his job and to found Mesorah Publications, publishers of the ArtScroll Series, which has over 1,000 titles in print. He founded the organization with Rabbi Nosson *Scherman and Sheah Brander.

When he first began, in quick succession he similarly translated four other *Megillot* and wrote an exhaustive six-volume translation and phrase-by-phrase commentary on the Book of Genesis. During the first decade of the ArtScroll Series, he authored numerous other books, but then reluctantly withdrew from his personal writing and devoted himself to shepherding Mesorah Publications into its period of explosive growth.

Zlotowitz is also president of the Mesorah Heritage Foundation, a not-for-profit organization which funds more than 80 scholars in Israel, America, and Europe who write and edit such scholarly works as the Schottenstein Talmud. Asked what accomplishments mean the most to him, Zlotowitz speaks of the strangers who approach him to say that ArtScroll has transformed their lives.

The success of the ArtScroll/Mesorah series is undeniable. ArtScroll is a fascinating combination of fervently Orthodox Judaism and an American aesthetic that wraps traditional Judaism in a visual idiom acceptable to the American sensibility. Zlotowitz's sense of the visual impact of a book is an indispensable ingredient in its success. Despite what outsiders may think, even the rejectionist Orthodox community that does not embrace modern culture has, perhaps inadvertently, acculturated itself to the offerings and packaging of the American marketplace.

ArtScroll publishes in English and in Hebrew and has brought its own unique styling to the Israeli and American marketplace. In the United States, it represents an important transition between Yiddish and English as the spoken language and the language of Jewish learning for fervently Orthodox Jews in America.

Modern Orthodox scholars have not been uncritical of ArtScroll's success. Its historical studies are wrapped, not in western scholarship, but in hagiography; it seems as if every fervently Orthodox leader or rabbi is without blemish. Others on the right criticize it for enabling and empowering English rather than Yiddish or Hebrew to be the language of contemporary learning.

The Schottenstein Talmud has allowed many who would have otherwise lacked the skill and talmudic virtuosity to participate in *daf yomi* (learning a page of Talmud a day) programs. It has offered those learning in yeshivah the "English" experience of the *bet midrash* and has far outpaced the more sophisticated and erudite commentary of Adin *Steinsaltz in popularity and use.

[Michael Berenbaum (2nd ed.)]

ZMIGROD NOWY, village near Jaslo in Rzeszow province, S. Poland, passed to Austria in 1772, and reverted to Poland after World War I. Jews first settled there in the early 16th century. By the middle of the century they had established an organized community under the jurisdiction of the *Szydlowiec *kahal* in *Sandomierz-Krakow province. In 1692 Menahem Mendel b. Ẓevi Hirsh of Poznan became *av bet din* in Zmigrod Nowy. He was succeeded by Benjamin Wolf who later became rabbi of Dessau and *Metz. In 1765 there were 683 Jews who paid the poll tax living in Zmigrod Nowy, and 1,025 living in 143 surrounding villages; there were 68 Jewish houses in Zmigrod Nowy; a synagogue had been built in the early 17th century. Until Zmigrod Nowy passed to Austria in 1772, Jews there mainly engaged in the import of wines and horses from Hungary, tailoring, and hat making. In the 19th century Jews in Zmigrod Nowy were mainly occupied in trade in timber and grain, the leasing of flour mills and engraving. The Jewish population numbered 1,330 in 1880 (53% of the total), 1,240 (54%) in 1900, and 940 (48%) in 1921.

[Shimshon Leib Kirshenboim]

Holocaust Period

During 1940–41 the Jews suffered from administrative and economic restrictions and forced labor. The Jews of the entire area were concentrated in the city, and in the summer of 1942 hundreds of Jews were killed. Later about 500 people were sent to the Plaszow labor camp, where many of them met their death. The remnants of the community were sent to the *Belzec death camp in the autumn of 1942.

[Aharon Weiss]

BIBLIOGRAPHY: R. Mahler, *Yidn in Amolikn Poyln in Likht fun Tsifern* (1958), index; B. Wasiutyński, *Ludność żydowska w Polsce w wiekach XIX i XX* (1930), 133; M. Balaban, *Historja Żydów w Krakowie i na Kazimierzu*, 2 vols. (1931–36), index; I. Schiper, *Dzieje handlu żydowskiego na ziemiach polskich* (1937), index.

ZMORA, YISRAEL (1899–1983), Hebrew literary critic. Born in the Belz district of Bessarabia, he immigrated to Palestine in 1925. He was one of a group of modernistic Hebrew writers who, from 1927 to 1939, contributed to Tel Aviv's avant-garde literary periodicals *Ketuvim* and *Turim*, and he regularly published critical notices of new Hebrew books and writers in the Palestinian Hebrew press. Zmora founded and edited (1940–54) the literary magazine *Maḥbarot le-Sifrut*. In 1940 he also founded the publishing house with the same name, which published the works of young Hebrew poets, new editions of Hebrew works from the Middle Ages and the Haskalah period, and translations. He was also active as a translator, particularly from French and Russian.

His books include *Anshei Shem Mitloẓeẓim*, under the pen name of Y. Zeh (1933); *Rainer Maria Rilke*, a monograph (1933); *Avraham Shlonsky*, a monograph (1937); *Shenei Mesapperim*, essays on Ḥ. *Hazaz and Jacob *Horovitz (1940); *Sifrut al Parashat Dorot*, essays on literature and writers (3 vols., 1949–50); *Ha-Mesapper Kav le-Kav*, literary analysis of the works of U.N. *Gnessin (1951); and *Nevi'im Aḥaronim*, essays (1953); a collection of poems (1965), *Shloshim Sonetot* (1971) and essays entitled *Ḥamesh Megilot* (1973).

BIBLIOGRAPHY: A. Ben-Or, *Toledot ha-Sifrut ha-Ivrit be-Dorenu*, 2 (1955), 282–4; Tidhar, 3 (1949), 1362f.

[Gedalyah Elkoshi]

ZNAIMER, MOSES (1942–), Canadian television and theater producer, media executive. Canadian broadcasting was revolutionized in 1972 when Moses Znaimer created *Citytv*, an independent Toronto station that redefined community-based television as culturally diverse, spontaneous, and attuned to the growing wired environment. Znaimer's dynamic and complex personal history grew out of the struggle for survival that defined his early years. His parents had fled the German invasion of Poland and were in Kulab, Tajikistan, when Znaimer was born. The family made their way to Shanghai, then settled in Montreal in 1948. A scrappy dynamo, Znaimer later boasted of the police record he accumulated as a youth in Montreal. But he also immersed himself in Bible and Talmud study, identifying with the Jewish prophets as ideologues who fought alone against the Establishment. He graduated in philosophy and politics from McGill University before earning an M.A. in government at Harvard at the age of 20. Drawn by the world of media communications, he went to work for the Canadian Broadcasting Corporation, where he proved a youthful force, working as producer, presenter, and director of historical and current affairs programming.

He eventually left the CBC to pursue his creative dreams. With the help of financial backers, he built *Citytv* into a major Canadian media conglomerate with stations serving niche markets across Canada. In 1984 he created *MuchMusic*, a 24-hour music-video channel that opened the walls between its multicultural presenters and its young viewers. It relied on hand-held cameras and brought the "backstage" of studio television into the foreground. During the 1980s and 1990s Znaimer presided over the expansion of a media empire that came to include 24-hour local news, creative arts, and educational channels. By 2002 he had built 17 specialty channels and eight local outlets spread across Canada, and licensed similar stations from Argentina to Finland. Znaimer also appeared as an actor in motion pictures and produced the ground-breaking play, *Tamara*, a thriller where the audience pursues the assorted plot lines unfolding in different rooms of a single house. He opened a TV museum in Toronto, tracing the history and impact of television around the world. In 2000 Znaimer began *IdeaCity*, a yearly "meeting of minds" which provides a "forum for the high ground of ideas and idealism."

By the time of his retirement from full-time production in 2003, Znaimer had defined a uniquely Canadian media voice. He has been recognized with a number of honorary doctoral degrees and awards for his work in media innovation and his efforts on behalf of race relations in Canada, including the Canadian Council of Christians and Jews Human Relations Award.

[Paula Draper (2nd ed.)]

ZNOJMO (Ger. **Znaim**), town in S. Moravia, Czech Republic. Although Jews are mentioned in a document dated 1052, the document itself is considered a 13th-century forgery. A Jewish tombstone in Znojmo, dated 1256, is the oldest to be found in Moravia; another tombstone there is inscribed 1306. A Jewish quarter was established when the town obtained independent status and is described in a document dated 1330. A synagogue is mentioned in 1341. The community were victims of the massacres following the Desecration of the Host libel of *Pulkau and during the Black *Death (1348). An assessment of an impost on Moravian communities in 1421 indicates that the Znojmo community was then the largest in Moravia. The Jews were expelled from Znojmo in 1454 and subsequently were permitted to enter the town only on payment of a body tax (**Leibzoll*); there was a special inn for visiting Jews.

There was a "Jewish street" in Znojmo, now called "Vesela street" ("the cheerful street"). The first Jews to receive permission to reside in Znojmo settled there in 1851. A congregation (*Kultusverein*) was founded in 1865 and became autonomous in 1876. In 1888 a synagogue was constructed in the Moorish style. In 1848 there were 19 Jews living in the town. In 1857 there were 36; 357 in 1869; 749 in 1921; 786 in 1928; and 675 in 1930.

The Jews contributed significantly to the town's economic development. They pioneered the canning industry, in particular pickles, for which Znojmo became famous.

Znojmo's population, as well as the vicinity, was known for the Judeophobia entrenched there. During the Sudeten crisis (1938), most Jews left Znojmo. The synagogue was set afire during *Kristallnacht* and was later torn down. Some 665 members of the community perished in concentration camps. A congregation was reestablished after World War II. It no longer exists.

BIBLIOGRAPHY: H. Einhorn and B. Wachstein, in: H. Gold (ed.), *Juden und Judengemeinden Maehrens…* (1929), 579–85; A. Engel, in: JJGJC, 2 (1930), 59; I. Reich, *Slavnostni spis… Chevra kadisa ve Znojme* (1929); idem, *Nahrobky… Grabsteine* (Czech and Ger., 1932); Kahan, in: MGWJ, 73 (1929), 382–4; 74 (1930), 134–5, 226–7; E. Baneth, *ibid.*, 133–4; *Jews in Czechoslovakia*, 1 (1968), 390; B. Bretholz, *Quellen zur Geschichte der Juden in Maehren* (1935) index; idem, *Geschichte der Stadt Bruenn* (1934), index; *Germania Judaica*, 2 (1968), index; MHJ, 1 (1903), 411. **ADD. BIBLIOGRAPHY:** J. Fiedler, *Jewish Sites of Bohemia and Moravia* (1991).

[Meir Lamed / Yeshayahu Jelinek (2nd ed.)]

ZOAN (Heb. צֹעַן), ancient city in Lower Egypt; the ancient Egyptian Djanet, Greek Tanis, and modern Ṣan el-Ḥagar in the eastern Delta of Egypt. Zoan is mentioned several times in the Bible. Attempts have been made to identify it with the Hyksos capital of Avaris. According to Numbers 13:22 the city was founded seven years after Hebron. An Egyptian text of around 1330 B.C.E. commemorates the 400th year of the god Set in Avaris; since Set was the Egyptian form of the Asiatic storm god whom the Hyksos worshipped, his establishment in Avaris 400 years earlier would follow closely on the appearance of the Hyksos in the Delta. The Egyptian New Kingdom, particularly the period of Ramses II, is well represented at Tanis, but it was not until after the New Kingdom, in the Twenty-First Dynasty, that Tanis rose to preeminence as the chief city of Egypt. It was a Tanite king who campaigned against Gezer, conquered it, and gave the city as dowry to his daughter, Solomon's wife. The mention of Tanis and its rulers by the prophets (Isa. 19:11, 13; 30:4; and Ezek. 30:14) refers, however, to a different dynasty, the Twenty-Second (Libyan) Dynasty, some of whose rulers continued to reside in Tanis and were buried there. The "field of Zoan" (Ps. 78:12, 43), which is attested on several late statues and stelae (Sekhet Djanet) may have been an alternative name for the city, but more probably it was the name of the surrounding region.

BIBLIOGRAPHY: A.H. Gardiner, *Ancient Egyptian Onomastica*, 2 (1947), 199–201.

[Alan Richard Schulman]

ZODIAC, in astrology, an imaginary zone in the heavens within which lie the paths of the *sun, the *moon, and the planets. The zodiac is divided into 12 signs which are mostly symbolically represented by animals (Gr. Ζώδιον, "a little animal"). The twelve-fold division of the zodiac was first developed by the Chaldean astronomers and was almost certainly suggested by the occurrence of the 12 full moons in successive parts of the heaven in the course of one year. It spread to the West about the beginning of the Christian Era. There is no mention of the zodiac in the Talmud, probably as a result of R. Johanan's statement, based on the verse "Thus saith the Lord, learn not the way of the nations and be not dismayed at the signs of heaven, for the [gentile] nations are dismayed at them" (Jer. 10:2), to the effect that "Israel is immune from planetary influence" (Shab. 156a). It is first mentioned in the *Sefer *Yeẓirah*; and the names given to the 12 signs are direct translations of the Latin names. Thus Aries is called *Taleh*; Taurus, *Shor*; Gemini, *Te'omim*; Cancer, *Sartan*; Leo, *Aryeh*; Virgo, *Betulah*; Libra, *Moznayim*; Scorpio, *Akrav*; Sagittarius, *Keshet*; Capricorn, *Gedi*; Aquarius, *Deli* ("a bucket"), and Pisces, *Dagim*.

According to the *Yalkut Shimoni* (Lev. 418), however, the standards of the 12 tribes correspond to the signs of the zodiac. Thus in the east were stationed Judah, Issachar, and Zebulun, corresponding to Aries, Taurus, and Gemini; Reuben, Simeon, and Gad in the south correspond to Cancer, Leo, and Virgo; Ephraim, Manasseh, and Benjamin in the west with Libra, Scorpio, and Sagittarius; and Dan, Asher, and Naphtali in the north with Capricorn, Aquarius, and Pisces. A long *piyyut* based on the 12 signs of the zodiac, *Yittaḥ Ereẓ le-Yesha*, is included in old *maḥzorim* accompanying the prayer for rain on Shemini Aẓeret, and the signs of the zodiac usually accompany the printed text. This *piyyut* has, however, been excluded from all modern *maḥzorim*, and the only place where the signs appear today are in some calendars. In the *Pesikta Rabbati* (27–28 ed. Freedman p. 133b) a passage occurs which explains the names of the signs homiletically in accordance with Jewish history. The Temple could not be destroyed in Nisan, since the ram which it represents in the zodiac is a reminder of the **Akedah*; Taurus is connected with the calf which Abraham slaughtered for his angelic guests (Gen. 18:7); the Gemini represent Jacob and Esau; while the Temple was destroyed in the month of Av, since its zodiacal sign *Aryeh*, the lion, corresponds to Ariel, a name given to the Temple (Isa. 29:1).

The signs of the zodiac figured prominently in early Jewish art, for example on the mosaic floors of ancient Palestinian synagogues (e.g., *Bet Alfa, *Hammath) as well as in prayer books, on *ketubbot*, etc.

ẒOFIM (Heb. צוֹפִים), place in the vicinity of Jerusalem, which indicated the limits of the city (Pes. 3:8). From this spot, pilgrims approaching Jerusalem first saw the Temple. According to later sources, Jews arriving at Ẓofim and seeing the Temple in ruins were apt to tear their clothes in mourning (TJ, MK 3:7, 83b; Lam. R. 5:18, no. 1). Josephus describes Saphein (the Greek transcription of Ẓofim) as the place where the high priest Jaddua met Alexander the Great (Ant., 11:329). During his march on Jerusalem, Cestius Gallus camped at a spot called Scopus (the Greek translation of Ẓofim = "place of beholding"), 7 furlongs (c. 1 mi.; c. 1½ km.) from the city (Jos., Wars, 2:528; 542). It was also the last camp of Titus in his march on Jerusalem in 70 C.E. (Jos., Wars, 5:67, 106). Ẓofim is usually identified with Ras el-Mesharref to the north of Jerusalem, on the road along the watershed which enters the city from the north and served as the main road on the west. By extension, the name Ẓofim has been applied in modern times to the campus occupied by the Hebrew University until 1948, when it became a demilitarized Israel enclave in Jordanian territory, until reunited with the city during the Six-Day War in 1967.

BIBLIOGRAPHY: Abel, Geog, 1 (1933), 375; Y. Epstein, in: *Tarbiz*, 5 (1934), 386; G. Dalman, *Jerusalem und sein Gelaende* (1930), 28ff.

[Michael Avi-Yonah]

ẒOFIT (Heb. צוֹפִית; "Lookout Point"), moshav in central Israel, in the southern Sharon N. of Kefar Sava, affiliated with Tenu'at ha-Moshavim. Ẓofit was founded in 1933 by farm laborers from Eastern Europe within the framework of the Thousand Families Project (see *Israel, State of: Settlement). Before 1948 the settlers earned their livelihood mainly by working as hired laborers on farms in the vicinity, but gradually developed their auxiliary farms into full-fledged holdings based mainly on citrus groves, dairy cattle, and poultry. Newcomers from Poland enlarged the moshav after 1948. In 1970, Ẓofit had 330 inhabitants. By the mid-1990s the population had grown to 405 approximately, rising further to 720 in 2002. In 1998 the moshav initiated an expansion program aimed at children of moshav members and newcomers. Barely 15% of Zofit residents earned their livings in farming: field crops, beehives, poultry, and plantations. The rest were employed in various occupations.

WEBSITE: www.tsofit.org.il.

[Efraim Orni / Shaked Gilboa (2nd ed.)]

ZOHAR (Heb. זֹהַר; "[The Book of] Splendor"), the central work in the literature of the *Kabbalah.

Introduction

In some parts of the book the name "Zohar" is mentioned as the title of the work. It is also cited by the Spanish kabbalists under other names, such as the *Mekhilta de-R. Simeon b. Yoḥai*, in imitation of the title of one of the halakhic Midrashim, in *Sefer ha-Gevul* of David b. Judah he-Ḥasid; the *Midrash de-R. Simeon b. Yoḥai*, in several books dating from the period of the pupils of Solomon b. Abraham *Adret, in the *Livnat ha-Sappir* of Joseph Angelino, the homilies of Joshua *Ibn Shu'ayb, and the books of Meir ibn *Gabbai; *Midrash ha-Zohar*, according to Isaac b. Joseph ibn Munir (see *He-Ḥalutz*, 4 (1859), 85); *Midrash Yehi Or* in the *Menorat ha-Ma'or* of Israel *al-Nakawa, apparently because he had a manuscript of the Zohar which began with a commentary on the verse "Let there be light" (Gen. 1:3). Several statements from the Zohar were quoted in the first generation after its appearance, under the general title of *Yerushalmi*, in the writings of, for example, Isaac b. *Sahula, *Moses de Leon, and David b. Judah he-Ḥasid, and in the (fictitious) responsa of Rav Hai in the collection *Sha'arei Teshuvah*.

This article is arranged according to the following outline:

The Literary Form of the Zohar
The Unity of the Work
STYLE
SOURCES
LANGUAGE
ORDER OF COMPOSITION
DATE OF COMPOSITION
The Author
Manuscripts and Editions
Commentaries
Translations
Scholarship
Later Research

The Literary Form of the Zohar

In its literary form the Zohar is a collection of several books or sections which include short midrashic statements, longer homilies, and discussions on many topics. The greater part of them purport to be the utterances of the *tanna* *Simeon b. Yoḥai and his close companions (*ḥavrayya*), but there are also long anonymous sections. It is not one book in the accepted sense of the term, but a complete body of literature which has been united under an inclusive title. In the printed editions the Zohar is composed of five volumes. According to the division in most editions, three of them appear under the name *Sefer ha-Zohar al ha-Torah*; one volume bears the title *Tikkunei ha-Zohar*; the fifth, titled *Zohar Ḥadash*, is a collection of sayings and texts found in the manuscripts of the Safed kabbalists after the printing of the Zohar and assembled by *Abraham b. Eliezer ha-Levi Berukhim. Page references in the most common editions of the Zohar and the editions of the *Tikkunim* are generally uniform.

References here to the *Zohar Ḥadash* (ZḤ) are to the Jerusalem edition of 1953. Some of the sections of the book exist separately in manuscript. The sections which make up the Zohar in its wider sense are essentially the following:

(1) The main part of the Zohar, arranged according to the weekly portions of the Torah, up to and including the portion *Pinḥas*. From Deuteronomy there are only *Va-Etḥannan*, a little on *Va-Yelekh*, and *Ha'azinu*. Basically it is a kabbalistic Midrash on the Torah, mixed with short statements, long expositions, and narratives concerning Simeon b. Yoḥai and his companions. Some of it consists also of common legends. The number of verses interpreted in each portion is relatively small. Often the exposition digresses to other subjects quite divorced from the actual text of the portion, and some of the interpretations are quite skillfully constructed. The expositions are preceded by *petiḥot* ("introductions") which are usually based on verses from the Prophets and the Hagiographa, especially Psalms, and which end with a transition to the subject matter of the portion. Many stories act as a framework for the homilies of the companions, e.g., conversations while they are on a journey or when they rest for the night. The language is Aramaic, as it is for most of the other sections of the work (unless otherwise stated). Before the portion *Bereshit* there is a *hakdamah* ("preface"), which would appear to be a typical collection of writings and not a preface as such, unless perhaps it was intended to introduce the reader to the spiritual climate of the book. Many expositions are found in various manuscripts in different places and sometimes there is some doubt as to which particular portion they really belong. There are also discourses which recur in different contexts in two or three places. *Aaron Zelig b. Moses in *Ammudei Sheva* (Cracow, 1635) listed about 40 such passages which are found in parallel editions of the Zohar. A few expositions in the printed editions break off in the middle, and their continuation is printed solely in the *Zohar Ḥadash*. In the later editions, beginning with that of Amsterdam, 1715, these completions are printed as *hashmatot* ("omissions") at the end of each volume.

(2) Zohar to the Song of Songs (printed in ZḤ, fols. 1d–75b); it extends only to the greater part of the first chapter and, like (1), consists of kabbalistic expositions.

(3) *Sifra di-Ẓeni'uta* ("Book of Concealment"), a kind of fragmented commentary on the portion *Bereshit*, in short obscure sentences, like an anonymous Mishnah, in five chapters, printed at the end of portion *Terumah* (2:176b–179a). In several manuscripts and in the Cremona edition (1558–60) it is found in the portion *Bereshit*.

(4) *Idra Rabba* ("The Greater Assembly"), a description of the gathering of Simeon b. Yoḥai and his companions, in which the most profound mysteries are expounded concerning the revelation of the Divine in the form of *Adam Kadmon* ("Primordial Man"). It is of a superior literary construction and the most systematic discourse found in the Zohar. Each of the companions says his piece and Simeon b. Yoḥai completes their pronouncements. At the end of this solemn assembly three of the ten participants meet with an ecstatic death. Among the early kabbalists it was called *Idra de-Naso* and it is printed in the portion *Naso* (3:127b–145a). It is, in a way, a kind of Talmud to the Mishnah of the *Sifra di-Ẓeni'uta*.

(5) *Idra Zuta* ("The Lesser Assembly"), a description of the death of Simeon b. Yoḥai and his closing words to his followers before his death, a kind of kabbalistic parallel to the death of Moses. It contains a companion discourse to that in the *Idra Rabba*, with many additions. Among the early kabbalists it was called *Idra de-Ha'azinu*. This portion concludes the Zohar (3:287b–96b).

(6) *Idra de-Vei Mashkena*, a study session conducted by Simeon b. Yoḥai with some of his students concerning the exposition of certain verses in the section dealing with the tabernacle. Most of it deals with the mysteries of the prayers. It is found at the beginning of *Terumah* (2:127a–146b). The note in later editions that the section 2:122b–3b is the *Idra de-Vei Mashkena* is a mistake. This part is mentioned at the beginning of the *Idra Rabba*.

(7) *Heikhalot*, two descriptions of the seven palaces in the celestial garden of Eden in which the souls take their delight when prayer ascends and also after their departure from the world. One version is short and is inserted in the portion *Bereshit* (1:38a–48b). The other version is extremely long, because it expands on the mysteries of prayer and angelology. It is found at the end of the portion *Pekudei* (2:244b–62b). At the end of the longer version there is an additional section on the "seven palaces of uncleanness," which is a description of the abodes of hell (2:262b–8b). In kabbalistic literature it is called the *Heikhalot de-R. Simeon b. Yoḥai*.

(8) *Raza de-Razin* ("The Secret of Secrets"), an anonymous piece on physiognomy and chiromancy, based on Exodus 18:21, in the portion *Yitro* (2:70a–75a). Its continuation is to be found in the *hashmatot* and in *Zohar Ḥadash* (56c–60a). A second section on the same subject, cast in a different form, was inserted in a parallel column in the back of the Zohar (2:70a–78a).

(9) *Sava de-Mishpatim* ("Discourse of the Old Man"), an account of the companions' encounter with R. Yeiva, an old man and a great kabbalist, who disguises himself in the beggarly appearance of a donkey driver, and who delivers himself of an extensive and beautifully constructed discourse on the theory of the soul, based on a mystical interpretation of the laws of slavery in the Torah. It is inserted as part of the body of the Zohar on the portion *Mishpatim* (2:94b–114a).

(10) *Yanuka* ("The Child"), the story of a wonder child, the son of the old man, Rav Hamnuna, who teaches the companions profound interpretations of the Grace after Meals and other matters, when they happen to be lodging in his mother's house. Stories concerning other children like this are found in other parts of the Zohar. In some manuscripts this story constitutes the section of the Zohar on the portion *Devarim*. In the printed edition it is found in the portion *Balak* (3:186a–92a).

(11) *Rav Metivta* ("Head of the Academy"), an account of a visionary journey undertaken by Simeon b. Yoḥai and his pupils to the garden of Eden, and a long exposition by one of the heads of the celestial academy on the world to come and the mysteries of the soul. It is printed as part of the portion *Shelaḥ Lekha* (3:161b–174a). The beginning is missing, as are certain parts from the middle and the end.

(12) *Kav ha-Middah* ("The Standard of Measure"), an explanation of the details of the mysteries of emanation in an interpretation of the *Shema*, in the form of a discourse by Simeon b. Yoḥai to his son, printed in *Zohar Ḥadash* (56d–58d).

(13) *Sitrei Otiyyot* ("Secrets of the Letters"), a discourse by Simeon b. Yoḥai on the letters of the Divine Names and the mysteries of emanation, printed in *Zohar Ḥadash* (1b–10d).

(14) An interpretation of the vision of the chariot in Ezekiel, chapter 1, printed without a title in *Zohar Ḥadash* (37c–41b).

(15) *Matnitin* and *Tosefta*, numerous short pieces, written in a high-flown and obscure style, serving as a kind of Mishnah to the Talmud of the Zohar itself. The connection between these pieces and the expositions in the portions of the Zohar is clear at times trod and at others tenuous. Most of the pieces appear as utterances of a heavenly voice which is heard by the companions, and which urges them to open their hearts to an understanding of the mysteries. Many of them contain a summary of the idea of emanation and other major principles of Zohar teaching, couched in an enigmatic style. These pieces are scattered all over the Zohar. According to Abraham *Galante in his *Zohorei Ḥammah* (Venice, 1650), 33b, "when the editor of the Zohar saw an exposition which belonged to an argument in a particular exposition from the *mishnayot* and *tosafot* he put it between those pieces in order to give the exposition added force from the Tosefta and the Mishnah."

(16) *Sitrei Torah* ("Secrets of the Torah"), certain pieces on verses from the Book of Genesis, which were printed in separate columns, parallel to the main text of the Zohar, in the portions *No'aḥ, Lekh Lekha, Va-Yera*, and *Va-Yeẓe*, and in *Zohar Ḥadash* in the portions *Toledot* and *Va-Yeshev*. There are several pieces titled *Sitrei Torah* in the printed editions – e.g., *Sitrei Torah* to the portion *Aḥarei Mot* in *Zohar Ḥadash* – but it is doubtful whether they really do belong to the *Sitrei Torah*. Similarly, there are manuscripts which designate the systematic interpretation of creation in 1:15a–22a as the *Sitrei Torah* to this section. However, its character is different from the other examples of *Sitrei Torah*, which contain mainly allegorical explanations of verses on the mysteries of the soul, whereas this piece explains the theory of emanation (in an anonymous discourse) in the style of the main part of the Zohar and the *Matnitin*.

(17) *Midrash ha-Ne'lam* ("Concealed Midrash") on the Torah. This exists for the sections *Bereshit, No'aḥ, Lekh Lekha* in *Zohar Ḥadash*; for *Va-Yera, Ḥayyei Sarah*, and *Toledot* in the main body of the Zohar, in parallel columns; and for *Va-Yeẓe* in *Zohar Ḥadash*. The beginning of the section *Va-Yeḥi* in the printed editions, 1:211–6, is marked in some sources as the *Midrash ha-Ne'lam* to this portion, but there is some reason to believe, with several kabbalists, that these pages are a later addition. From their literary character and the evidence of several manuscripts, the pages 2:4a–5b, and particularly 14a–22a, belong to the *Midrash ha-Ne'lam* to the portion *Shemot*, and 2:35b–40b to the *Midrash ha-Ne'lam* to the portion *Bo*. From this point onward only a few separate short pieces occur in *Zohar Ḥadash*, on the portions *Be-Shallah* and *Ki Teẓe*. Several pieces, very close in spirit to the *Midrash ha-Ne'lam*, are found here and there in the main part of the Zohar, e.g., in the exposition of Rav Huna before the rabbis, in the portion *Terumah*, 2:174b–175a. It is also possible that the pages in the portion *Bo* are of this kind. The language of this part is a mixture of Hebrew and Aramaic. Many rabbis are mentioned in it, and in contrast to the long expositions of the earlier parts we find here mostly short pieces similar to the original aggadic Midrashim. Here and there we can recognize the transition to a more lengthy expository method, but there are no artistically constructed and extensive expositions. As to content, the material is centered mainly around discussions on creation, the soul, and the world to come, with a few discussions on the nature of God and emanation. Most of the sections, after the portion *Bereshit*, expound biblical narratives, notably the deeds of the patriarchs, as allegories of the fate of the soul.

(18) *Midrash ha-Ne'lam* to the Book of Ruth, similar in style and content to the preceding. It is printed in *Zohar Ḥadash*, and was originally printed as a separate work called *Tappuḥei Zahav* or *Yesod Shirim* in Thiengen in 1559. It exists in many manuscripts as an independent book.

(19) The beginning of the *Midrash ha-Ne'lam* to the Song of Songs. It is printed in *Zohar Ḥadash* and is merely a prefatory exposition to the book, without any continuation.

(20) *Ta Ḥazei* ("Come and See"), another interpretation of the portion *Bereshit* in short anonymous comments, most of them beginning with the words *ta ḥazel*, and written in an obviously kabbalistic vein. The first part is found in *Zohar Ḥadash*, 7a, after the *Sitrei Otiyyot*, and the rest was

first printed in the Cremona edition, 55–75, continuing in the *hashmatot* of the Zohar, at the end of volume 1. In some manuscripts (like Vatican 206, fols. 274–86), the two sections are found together, but in most they are missing altogether.

(21) *Ra'aya Meheimna* ("The Faithful Shepherd") – the reference is to Moses – a separate book on the kabbalistic significance of the commandments. It is found in some manuscripts as an independent work, and in the printed editions it is scattered piecemeal among the sections in which the particular commandments are mentioned and printed in separate columns. The greater part occurs in portions from Numbers and Deuteronomy, and particularly in *Pinḥas, Ekev*, and *Ki Teẓe*. The setting of the book is different from that of the main part of the Zohar. In it Simeon b. Yoḥai and his companions, apparently through a visionary revelation, meet Moses, "the faithful shepherd," along with *tannaim* and *amoraim* and other figures from the celestial world, who appear to them and talk with them about the mysteries of the commandments, as if the academy on high had descended to the earth below. This work is quite clearly dependent on the Zohar itself, since it is quoted several times under the name of "the former [or first] book," particularly in the portion *Pinḥas*. The enumeration of the commandments, which is extant in several places and which points to an original order, has become confused (see also below, The Unity of the Work, Order of Composition).

(22) *Tikkunei Zohar*, also an independent book whose setting is similar to that of the *Ra'aya Meheimna*. It comprises a commentary to the portion *Bereshit*, each section (*tikkun*) beginning with a new interpretation of the word *bereshit* ("in the beginning"). The book was designed to contain 70 *tikkunim*, confirming to "the 70 aspects of the Torah," but in actual fact there are more, and some of them are printed as additions at the end of the book. Two completely different arrangements are found in the manuscripts, and these are reflected in the different editions of Mantua (1558), and of Orta Koj (1719). The later editions follow Orta Koj. The expositions in the book digress widely from the subject matter of the portion and deal with quite different topics which are not discussed in the main body of the Zohar, like the mysteries of the vowel points and accents, mysteries concerning halakhic matters, prayer, and so on. The pages in the Zohar, 1:22a–29a, belong to this book and occur in manuscripts as *tikkun* no. 70. Here and there, there is a change in the narrative framework, when it imitates that of the main body of the Zohar and, sometimes apparently continuing the discussion, appears as if it were being held in the celestial academy. The book also has a preface (*hakdamah*) on the model of the preface in the Zohar. Long additional expositions, parallel with the book's opening sections and mixed with other interpretations on the same pattern, are printed at the end of *Zohar Ḥadash* (93–123), and they are usually introduced as *tikkunim* of *Zohar Ḥadash*.

(23) An untitled work on the portion *Yitro*, a redaction, in the spirit of the *tikkunim*, of the physiognomy found in the *Raza de-Razin*, printed in *Zohar Ḥadash* (31a–35b).

(24) A few works printed in *Zohar Ḥadash*, like the "Zohar to the portion *Tissa*" (43d–46b), and the anonymous piece printed as the portion *Ḥukkat* in *Zohar Ḥadash* (50a–53b). These pieces must be regarded as imitations of the Zohar, but they were written without doubt very soon after the appearance of the book, and the first is already quoted in the *Livnat ha-Sappir*, which was written in 1328 (Jerusalem, 1914, 86d).

In addition to these sections there were others known to various kabbalists which were not included in the printed editions, and some of them are completely lost. A continuation of the *Sefer ha-Tikkunim* on other portions known to the author of *Livnat ha-Sappir* (95b–100a) was a long piece on the calculation of the time of redemption. The pieces, which were printed in the *Tikkunei Zohar Ḥadash* (117b–121b), and interpret various verses concerning Abraham and Jacob, seem to belong to this continuation. The "sayings of *Ze'ira*" ("the little one"), which are mentioned in *Shem ha-Gedolim* as being "quasi-midrashic homilies," are extant in Paris Ms. 782 and were included by Ḥayyim *Vital in an anthology which he compiled of pieces from the early kabbalah, and which still exists. The Zohar to the portion *Ve-Zot ha-Berakhah* is preserved in the same Paris manuscript (fols. 239–42), and is a mixture of fragments from the Midrash on Ruth in unknown pieces. It would appear that Moses *Cordovero saw a *Midrash Megillat Esther* from the Zohar, according to *Or Ne'erav* (Venice, 1587, 21b). His pupil Abraham Galante, in his commentary to *Sava de-Mishpatim*, quotes a text called *Pesikta*, from a manuscript Zohar, but its content is not known. There is no direct connection between the literature of the Zohar and the later literary imitations of it that are not included in the manuscripts, such as the Zohar on Ruth, which was printed under the title *Har Adonai* (Amsterdam, 1712).

The opinion of the kabbalists themselves concerning the composition and editing of the Zohar was formed after the circulation of the book. At first the view was widely held that this was the book written by Simeon b. Yoḥai while he was in hiding in the cave, or at least during his lifetime, or at the latest in the generation that followed. Among the kabbalists of Safed, who generally believed in the antiquity of the whole of the Zohar, Abraham Galante, in his commentary to the portion *Va-Yishlaḥ* in the Zohar, thought that the whole work was put together in geonic times from the writings of R. Abba, who was Simeon b. Yoḥai's scribe, and that the book did not receive its present form until that time. This view, which tries to explain a number of obvious difficulties in the chronology of the rabbis who are mentioned in the Zohar, also occurs in *Netiv Mitzvotekha* by Isaac Eisik Safrin of *Komarno. In the 16th century the legend grew up that the present Zohar, which contains about 2,000 closely printed pages, was only a tiny remnant of the original work, which was some 40 camel loads in weight (in *Ketem Paz*, 102a). These ideas are not substantiated by a critical examination of the Zohar.

The Unity of the Work

The literature contained in the Zohar can be divided basically into three strata, which must be distinguished from one another:

(a) the main body of the Zohar, comprising items (1)–(15) in the list above;

(b) the stratum of the *Midrash ha-Ne'lam and Sitrei Torah*, i.e., items (16)–(19); and

(c) the stratum of the *Ra'aya Meheimna* and the *Tikkunim*, i.e., (21)–(23).

Items (20) and (24) are doubtful as regards their literary relationship, and perhaps they belong to material that was added after the appearance of the Zohar. There are, to be sure, definite links between the different strata which establish a chronological order, but a detailed investigation shows quite clearly that each stratum has a definite unity of its own. The question of the unity of the main body of the Zohar is particularly important. The apparent differences are merely external and literary, e.g., the choice of a laconic and enigmatic style at times, and at others, the use of a more expansive and occasionally verbose style.

STYLE. This unity is evident in three areas; those of literary style, language, and ideas. Ever since the historical critique of the Zohar first began, there have been views that regard the Zohar as a combination of ancient and later texts, which were put together only at the time of the Zohar's appearance. At the very least it contains a homiletic prototype, a creation by many generations which cannot be attributed essentially to one single author. This view has been held, for example, by Eliakim Milsahagi (see *Mehlsack), Hillel *Zeitlin, Ernst *Mueller, and Paul Vulliaud, but they have contented themselves with a general conclusion, or with a claim that the *Sifra di-Ẓeni'uta*, the *Matnitin*, or the *Idrot*, are ancient sources of this type. The only scholar who attempted to investigate the early strata in the expositions of the other parts of the Zohar was I. Stern. A detailed examination of his arguments, and also of the general arguments, shows that they are extremely weak. In particular there is no evidence that the *Sifra di-Ẓeni'uta* differs from the other parts of the body of the Zohar except in the allusive style in which it was intentionally written. In actual fact, the literary connections between the different parts of the Zohar are extremely close. Many of the sections are constructed with great literary skill and the different parts are related to one another. There is no real distinction, either in language or thought, between the short pieces in the true midrashic style and the longer expositions which follow the methods of the medieval preachers, who used to weave together different ideas into a single fabric, which begins with a particular verse, ranges far and wide, and then finally returns to its starting point. Practically all the sections are built on an identical method of composition, stemming from variations of different literary forms. From the point of view of construction there is no difference also between the various narrative frameworks, such as the transmission of expositions which originated during the companions' journeys between one city and another in Palestine, especially in Galilee, or the type of dramatic composition that is to be found in the *Idrot*, the *Sava*, and the *Yanuka*. The breaking-up of the material into a conversation among the companions, or into an expository monologue, does not basically alter the subject matter of the exposition itself. Even in the monologues several opinions concerning a particular verse are mentioned side by side while in other parts the different opinions are divided up and assigned to different speakers. Quotations of, or references to, expositions in other parts of the Zohar occur throughout the main body of the book. Some matters, which are discussed extremely briefly in one place, are treated more fully in another exposition. The Zohar, unlike the Midrash, loves to allude either to a previous discussion or to a subject which is to be dealt with later, and this is typical of medieval homilists. An examination of these cross-references, whether of exact verbal citations or of subject matter without precise quotation, shows that the main part of the Zohar is a literary construction all of one piece, despite superficial variations. Statements or ideas which are not reflected in more than one place do exist but they are very few and far between. Even those sections which have a particularly characteristic subject matter, like that dealing with physiognomy in the portion *Yitro*, are connected in many ways with other sections of the Zohar, which deal more fully with topics only briefly mentioned in the former. On the relationship of the *Midrash ha-Ne'lam* to the main body of the Zohar, see below.

One element in the constructional unity of the Zohar is that of the scene and the dramatis personae. The Zohar presupposes the existence of an organized group of "companions" (*ḥavrayya*), who, without doubt, were originally meant to be ten in number, but most of them are no more than shadowy figures. These companions are Simeon b. Yoḥai, his son Eleazar, Abba, Judah, Yose, Isaac, Hezekiah, Ḥiyya, Yeiva, and Aḥa. Several of them are *amoraim* who have been transferred by the author to the age of the *tannaim*, like Abba, Hezekiah, Ḥiyya, and Aḥa. What is narrated of them here and there shows that the author utilized stories in talmudic sources which concerned *amoraim* with these names, and these are not therefore unknown historical figures. These basic characters are joined by certain other rabbis, who usually appear indirectly, or as figures from the generation that preceded Simeon b. Yoḥai. In this connection, one particular error of the Zohar is very important. In several stories it consistently turns Phinehas b. Jair, Simeon b. Yoḥai's son-in-law (according to Shab. 33b), into his father-in-law. Similarly, the father-in-law of Eleazar, Simeon's son, is called Yose b. Simeon b. Lekonya, instead of Simeon b. Yose b. Lekonya. In addition to the regular companions there occasionally appear other characters whom the designation *sava* ("old man") places in the preceding generation, e.g., Nehorai Sava, Yeiva Sava, Hamnuna Sava, and Judah Sava. There is a recognizable tendency to create a fictional framework in which the problems of anachronism and chronological confusion do not arise. On the other hand, neither Akiva nor Ishmael b. Elisha is mentioned as a master of mystical tradition, whereas both appear in the *heikhalot* and the *Merkabah literature. Akiva is introduced only in stories and quotations which come from the Talmud.

The Palestinian setting of the book is also fictional, and, in the main, has no basis in fact. The Zohar relies on geographical and topographical ideas about Palestine taken from older literature. Sometimes the author did not understand his sources, and created places which never existed, e.g., Kapotkeya, as the name of a village near Sepphoris, on the basis of a statement in the Jerusalem Talmud (Shev. 9:5), which he combined with another statement in the Tosefta, *Yevamot* 4. He produces a village in Galilee by the name of Kefar Tarshi, which he identifies with Mata Meḥasya, and tells in this connection of the rite of circumcision which is based on material quoted in geonic literature with regard to Mata Meḥasya in Babylonia. Occasionally a place-name is based on a corrupt text in a medieval manuscript of the Talmud, e.g., Migdal Ẓor at the beginning of *Sava de-Mishpatim*. In the matter of scene and characters there are very close links between the main body of the Zohar and the stratum of the *Midrash ha-Ne'lam*, which follows the same path of mentioning places which do not actually exist. In this section Simeon b. Yoḥai and his companions already constitute a most important community of mystics, but other groups are mentioned as well, and particularly later *amoraim* or scholars with fictitious names who do not reappear in the Zohar. In recent times, several attempts have been made to explain the geographical difficulties, and to give a non-literal interpretation of statements in the Talmud and the Midrashim in order to make them fit the Zohar, but they have not been convincing. Several times the Zohar uses the expression *selik le-hatam* ("he went up thither"), a Babylonian idiom for those who went up from Babylonia to Palestine, thereby changing the scene from Palestine to the Diaspora – "thither" is an impossible expression if the book was actually written in Palestine.

SOURCES. As to the question of the sources of the Zohar, we must distinguish between those that are mentioned explicitly and the true sources that are alluded to in only a general way ("they have established it," "the companions have discussed it"), or are not mentioned at all. The sources of the first type are fictitious works which are mentioned throughout the Zohar and the *Midrash ha-Ne'lam*, e.g., the *Sifra de-Adam*, the *Sifra de-Ḥanokh*, the *Sifra di-Shelomo Malka*, the *Sifra de-Rav Hamnuna Sava*, the *Sifra de-Rav Yeiva Sava*, and in a more enigmatic form, *Sifrei Kadma'ei* ("ancient books"), the *Sifra de-Aggadeta*, the *Raza de-Razin, Matnita di-Lan* (i.e., the mystical Mishnah in contradistinction to the usual Mishnah). With regard to the mystery of the letters of the alphabet, the *Atvan Gelifin* ("Engraved Letters") is quoted, or the "Engraved Letters of R. Eleazar." Works of magic are also quoted, e.g., the *Sifra de-Ashmedi*, the *Zeinei Ḥarshin de-Kasdi'el Kadma'ah* ("Various Kinds of Sorcery of the Ancient Kasdiel"), the *Sifra de-Ḥokhmeta di-Venei Kedem* ("Book of Wisdom of the Sons of Kedem"). Some names are based on earlier sources, like the *Sifra de-Adam*, and the *Sifra de-Ḥanokh*, but matters are referred to by these names which really belong entirely to the Zohar and to its world of ideas. In contrast to this fictitious library, which is clearly emphasized, the real literary sources of the Zohar are concealed. These sources comprise a great many books, from the Talmud and Midrashim to the kabbalistic works which were composed in the 13th century. A single approach in the use of these sources can be detected, both in the sections of the Zohar itself and in the *Midrash ha-Ne'lam*. The writer had expert knowledge of the early material and he often used it as a foundation for his expositions, putting into it variations of his own. His main sources were the Babylonian Talmud, the complete **Midrash Rabbah*, the *Midrash *Tanḥuma*, and the two *Pesiktot* (**Pesikta De-Rav Kahana* or **Pesikta Rabbati*), the Midrash on Psalms, the **Pirkei de-Rabbi Eliezer*, and the Targum *Onkelos. Generally speaking they are not quoted exactly, but translated into the peculiar style of the Zohar and summarized. If a particular subject exists in a number of parallel versions in the earlier literature, it is not often possible to establish the precise source. But, on the other hand, there are many statements which are quoted in a form which exists in only one of the different sources. Less use is made of the halakhic Midrashim, the Jerusalem Talmud, and the other Targums, nor of the Midrashim like the *Aggadat Shir ha-Shirim*, the Midrash on Proverbs, and the *Alfabet de-R. Akiva*. It is not clear whether the author used the *Yalkut Shimoni*, or whether he knew the sources of its *aggadah* separately. Of the smaller Midrashim he used the *Heikhalot Rabbati*, the *Alfabet de-Ben Sira*, the *Sefer Zerubabel*, the *Baraita de-Ma'aseh Bereshit*, the chapter *Shirah* in the *Aggadot Gan Eden*, and the tractate *Ḥibbut ha-Kever*, and also, occasionally, the *Sefer ha-Yashar*. Sometimes the author makes use of *aggadot* which no longer remain, or which are extant only in the *Midrash ha-Gadol*; this is not to be wondered at because aggadic Midrashim like this were known to many medieval writers, e.g., in the homilies of Joshua ibn Shu'ayb, who wrote in the generation following the appearance of the Zohar. The Zohar continues the thought patterns of the *aggadah* and transfers them to the world of the Kabbalah. The references to parallels in rabbinic literature which Reuben Margulies quotes in his *Niẓoẓei Zohar* in the Jerusalem edition of the Zohar (1940–48) often reveal the sources of the expositions.

From medieval literature the author makes use, as W. *Bacher has shown, of Bible commentators like *Rashi, Abraham *Ibn Ezra, David *Kimḥi, and the *Lekaḥ Tov* of Tobiah b. Eliezer. Apparently he also knew the commentaries of the tosafists. He was noticeably influenced by the allegorical commentators of the *Maimonides' school, particularly in the *Midrash ha-Ne'lam*, but also in some of the expositions in the main body of the Zohar. The last commentator whom he used as a source was *Naḥmanides in his commentaries both to the Torah and to Job. Certain verbal usages in the Zohar can be explained only by reference to the definitions in the *Sefer he-Arukh*, and in the *Sefer ha-Shorashim* of David Kimḥi. An important exposition in the section *Balak* is based on a combination of three pieces from the *Kuzari* of *Judah Halevi. In connection with certain customs he bases himself on the *Sefer ha-Manhig* of *Abraham b. Nathan ha-Yarḥi. Rashi's commentary to the Talmud serves as the foundation of several statements in the Zohar, and not only in connection with the Talmud. Of the works of Maimonides, he makes slight use of the commentary to the Mishnah and the *Guide of the Perplexed*, and uses the *Mishneh Torah* more extensively. Several attempts to prove that Maimonides knew the Zohar and made use of it in several of his *halakhot* (more recently that of R. Margulies, *Ha-Rambam ve-ha-Zohar*, 1954) only serve to show the dependence of the Zohar on Maimonides.

The sources of the Zohar among the kabbalistic works which preceded it are also unclear. The *Sefer* *Yeẓirah is clearly mentioned only in the later stratum. The *Sefer *ha-Bahir*, *Ma'yan ha-Ḥokhmah* attributed to Moses, the writings of the Ḥasidei *Ashkenaz and particularly of *Eleazar of Worms, R. *Ezra's commentary to the Song of Songs, and the commentary to the liturgy by *Azriel of Gerona, were all known to the author of the Zohar, and he develops tendencies which appeared first in the writings of the circle of the Gnostics in Castile in the middle of the 13th century (see *Kabbalah). Similarly, the kabbalistic terminology of the Zohar reflects the development of the Kabbalah from the *Sefer ha-Bahir* up to Joseph *Gikatilla, and the term *nekuddah ḥada* ("one point") in the sense of "center" is taken from Gikatilla's *Ginnat Egoz*, which was written in 1274. Terms scattered in several places, like **Ein-Sof*, *avir kadmon*, *ayin* (in the mystical sense), *mekora de-ḥayyei*, *re'uta de-maḥshavah*, *alma de-peiruda*, have their source in the development of the Kabbalah after 1200. The term *ḥaluk* or *ḥaluka de-rabbanan*, for the soul's garment in Eden, and ideas relating to the formation of this garment, are taken from the *Ḥibbur Yafeh min ha-Yeshu'ah* of Jacob b. Nissim (1050). Often the author of the Zohar draws on the Midrashim indirectly by means of the commentaries on them written by the kabbalists who preceded him.

The medieval environment can be recognized in many details of the Zohar apart from those already mentioned. Historical references to the Crusades and to Arab rule in Palestine after the wars are put together with material based on the laws and customs found in the Spanish environment of the author. In the same way his ethical diatribe directed against certain particular immoralities in the life of the community belongs to a specific period of time, as Yiẓhak *Baer has shown. The common customs are characteristic of Christian lands in medieval times. The author's ideas on medicine fit this particular period, which was dominated by the views of Galen. The Zohar does not have any clear ideas concerning the nature of idolatry, and it is dependent on the views of Maimonides which, for their part, were based on the fictitious "literature" of the sect of the Sabeans in Haran. The cultural and religious background to which most of the book, including its polemical parts, is related, is Christian and monogamous. But occasionally we come across allusions to Islam and to contacts with Muslims, and this fits the identification of Castile as the place where the book was written.

Where the ideas of the Zohar concerning *Satan and the ranks of the powers of uncleanness, devils, and evil spirits, and also necromancy and sorcerers, are not taken from talmudic sources, they bear the clear impress of the Middle Ages, e.g., the compact between the sorcerer and Satan, and the worship of Satan by the sorcerers. References to these matters are scattered throughout the Zohar, but they are of one and the same type. The liturgy, which is expounded at length in the sections *Terumah* and *Va-Yakhel*, is not the original liturgy of Palestine, but the Spanish and French version in use in the Middle Ages. The literary form of words supposed to have been used in the tannaitic period is only superficial. The author of the third stratum, in the *Ra'aya Meheimna* and the *Tikkunim*, reveals his environment through some additional material, and it is almost as if he did not wish to conceal it at all. This is particularly noticeable in his lengthy treatment of the social and religious situation of the Jewish communities of his time, a favorite subject which receives a different treatment from that of the main body of the Zohar. The social conditions described here are in no way those of the earlier communities of Babylonia and Palestine but fit, in every detail, what we know of the conditions in Spain in the 13th century. His writing has a distinctly harsh polemical note directed against various groups in Jewish society, a note which is absent from other parts of the Zohar. Typical of this part is the use of the phrase *erev rav* ("mixed multitude") to designate that social stratum in the Jewish communities in which were combined all the blemishes which he noted in his own contemporaries. The author was also aware of the lively controversy between the kabbalists, described in these parts only as *marei kabbalah* ("masters of kabbalah"), and their opponents, who denied both their claim that mysteries existed in the Torah and their knowledge of them.

LANGUAGE. If all hopes of discovering primitive layers in the Zohar through an historical and literary analysis of its various parts are vain, they will be equally frustrated when we turn to a linguistic critique. The language of the Zohar may be divided into three types:

(1) the Hebrew of the *Midrash ha-Ne'lam*;

(2) the Aramaic there and in the main body of the Zohar;

(3) the imitation of (2) in the *Ra'aya Meheimna* and the *Tikkunim*.

The Hebrew is, in fact, an imitation of the aggadic style, but whenever it diverges from its literary sources it is seen to be a medieval Hebrew belonging to a time when philosophical terminology was widely used. The writer uses later philosophical terms quite openly, particularly in the earlier sections and in the Midrash on Ruth. At the same time the transition from this Hebrew to the Aramaic of the *Midrash ha-Ne'lam* itself and of the main part of the Zohar, which linguistically speaking are one and the same, can be clearly distinguished. The natural Hebrew of the author is here translated into an artificial Aramaic. While his Hebrew has counterparts in medieval literature, the Aramaic of the Zohar has no linguistic parallel, since it is compounded of all the Aramaic idioms that the author knew and which he used as the foundation for his artificial construction. The very use of the word *targum* (I, 89a) for the Aramaic language, instead of *leshon Arami*, which was used in the Talmud and Midrash, was a medieval practice. The Aramaic idioms are in the main the language of the Babylonian Talmud and the Targum Onkelos, together with the Galilean Aramaic of the other Targums, but they include only very little from the Jerusalem Talmud. Types of different idioms are used side by side indiscriminately, even in the same passage. Similar differences may be seen in the pronouns, both subjective and possessive, demonstrative and interrogative, and also in the conjugation of the verb. The Zohar uses these interchangeably, quite freely. Sometimes the Zohar adopts the Babylonian usage of a particular form, e.g., those forms of the perfect tense preceded by *ka* (*ka amar*) or the form of conjugation of the third person imperfect (*leima*). At other times the corresponding targumic forms are preferred. With the noun there is no longer any distinction between those forms which have the definitive *alef* suffix, and those which do not have it, and there is complete confusion. Even a form like *tikla ḥada* ("a wheel") is possible here. The constructive case is almost nonexistent and is mostly replaced by the use of *di*. In addition to the usual vocabulary new words are coined by analogy with formations that already exist in other words. So words like *nehiru, neẓiẓu, ketatu* come into being (for new words in the vocabulary, see below). As for adverbs, it uses indiscriminately words from both biblical and Babylonian Aramaic, and translations of medieval terms, like *lefum sha'ata* or *kedein*, in imitation of the use of *az* to join different parts of a sentence as in medieval Hebrew. With all the confusion of these forms there is, nevertheless, some sort of system and consistency. A kind of unified language is created which is common throughout all the parts mentioned above. In addition to the basic forms drawn from the Aramaic idiom there are many characteristics which are peculiar to the language of the Zohar. The Zohar mixes up the conjunctions of the verb, using the *pe'al* instead of the *pa'el* and the *af'el* (*lemizkei* for *lezakka'ah, lemei'al* for *le'aala'ah, lemeḥdei* for *leḥadda'ah*) and also the *af'el* instead of the *pe'al*, e.g., *olifana* for *yalfinan* (among the most common words in the Zohar). It uses incorrect forms of the *itpa'al* or *etpe'el* (the two forms of the verb are indistinguishable), e.g., *itsaddar* or *itsedar, itẓayyar* or *itẓeyar, itzakkei* or *itzekei, itẓerif*, etc. In several instances, although only with certain verbs, it uses the *itpa'al* (or the *etpe'el*) as a transitive verb, e.g., *it'arna milei, le-istammara* or *le-istemara orḥoi, le-itdabbaka* or *le-itdebaka* in the sense of "to attain." It gives new meanings to words, following their medieval usage: e.g., *istallak* with regard to the death of the righteous; *itar*, through the influence of *hitorer*, which in the Middle Ages was used in the sense of "to discuss a certain matter"; *adbakuta* in the sense of "intellectual perception"; *ashgaḥuta* in the sense of "providence"; *shorsha* in the sense of "basic principle." The conjunctive phrase *im kol da* used throughout in the sense of "nevertheless" (*be-khol zot*) is influenced by the translators from Arabic, as is the use of the word *remez* as a term for allegory.

A large number of errors and of borrowed translations constantly recur in the Zohar. The word *pelatarin* is considered a plural form, and *galgallei yamma* a plural form from *gallei ha-yam* ("waves of the sea"). The author writes *bar-anan* instead of *bar-minan* and gives the artificial translation "limb" for *shaifa* through a mistaken guess in the interpretation of a passage in *Makkot* 11b. From the verb *gamar*, meaning "to learn," he coins the same meaning for the verb *ḥatam* (*le-meḥtam oraita*), and there are many examples of this kind. There are several words, whose meaning in the original sources the author of the Zohar did not know, and they are given new and incorrect meanings: e.g., the verb *ta'an* is given the meaning of "to guide a donkey from behind" (an Arabism taken from the *Sefer ha-Shorashim* of David Kimḥi) or *taya'a*, "the Jew who guides the donkey." *Tukfa* in the sense of "lap" is based on a misunderstanding of a passage in Targum Onkelos (Num. 11:12); *boẓina de-kardinuta* as "a very powerful light" is based on a misunderstanding of a passage in *Pesaḥim* 7a. There are a number of words, especially nouns, which have no known source and whose meaning is often unclear. It is possible that they derive from corrupt readings in manuscripts of rabbinic literature, or the author's new coinage in imitation of foreign words which occur in that literature. Most of them begin with the letter *kof* (ק), and the letters *zayin* (ז), *samekh* (ס), *pe* (פ), and *resh* (ר) are predominant: e.g., *sosfita, kaftira, kosfita, kirta, kozpira*. Arabic influence appears in only a very few words, but Spanish influence is noticeable in the vocabulary, idioms, and use of particular prepositions. The word *gardinim* in the sense of "guardians," derived from the Spanish *guardianes*, occurs in every part of the Zohar; the verb *besam* in the sense of "to soften" is a literal translation of the Spanish verb *endulzar*; hence also the common expression *hamtakat ha-din*, which comes from the Zohar. The borrowed translations of *ḥakal* in the sense of "battlefield," and of *kos* in the sense of the "cup of a flower," show the influence of Romance usage. Idioms like *likeḥin derekh aḥeret, kayyama bi-she'elta, istekem al yedoi* (instead of *askem*) *osim simḥah, yateva be-reikanya* (in the sense of "being empty") are all translations borrowed from Spanish. In the *Tikkunei Zohar* there is, in addition, the use of *esh nogah* for "synagogue" (Sp. *Esnoga* = *sinagoga*). The phrase *egoz ha-keshet* as a military term has its source in the medieval Romance languages (*nuez de ballesta*). There are many examples of the use of the preposition *min* ("from") instead of *shel* ("of"); *be* ("in") for *im* ("with); *legabbei* ("in reference to") for *el* ("to") – all resulting from the influence of Spanish constructions.

The linguistic unity of the Zohar is apparent also in particular stylistic peculiarities which are not found at all in rabbinic literature, or which have a completely different meaning there. They occur in all parts of the Zohar, particularly in the *Midrash ha-Ne'lam*, and in the main body of the Zohar. Examples of this are the use of forms on the pattern of "active and not active" – not in the rabbinic sense of "half-active," but with the significance of spiritual activity whose profundity cannot be fathomed; the combination of words with the termination *de-kholla*, e.g., *amika de-kholla, nishmeta de-kholla, mafteḥa de-kholla*; hyperbolic forms of the type *raza de-razin, temira de-temirin, ḥedvah de-khol ḥedvan, tushbaḥta de-khol tushbeḥin*; the description of an action, whose details are not to be revealed, through the use of the form "he did what he did"; the division of a particular matter into certain categories by the use of it… *ve-it*, e.g., *it yayin ve-it yayin, it kayiẓ ve-it kayiẓ*; the use of hendiadys (two terms for the same object), e.g., *ḥotama de-gushpanka* ("seal of a seal"), *boẓina di-sheraga* ("light of a light"). As for syntax, we notice the use of the infinitive at the beginning of a clause, even when the subject of the clause is different from that of the main sentence, e.g., *ẓaddikim re'uyyim le-hityashev ha-olam mehem, ihu heikhala di-reḥimu le-iddebaka dakhora be-nukba*. This is particularly so in the case of relative and final clauses. Another syntactical characteristic is the use of *az* or *kedein* at the beginning of subclauses. All these characteristics are typical of medieval usage, and particularly of the Hebrew of Spanish Jewry, under the influence of the philosophical style, and the author of the Zohar uses them without any concern about their being a late development. The dialectical language in the arguments of the rabbis is taken almost exclusively from the Babylonian Talmud, with the addition of a few terms from the medieval homiletical style, e.g., *it le-istakkala, it le-hitara*. Within the context of this linguistic unity, the Zohar uses different stylistic media with great freedom. Sometimes it deals with an exposition or follows an argument at great length; and at others it is laconic and enigmatic, or adopts a solemn, almost rhythmical, style.

In contrast to the language used in other parts of the Zohar, the language of the *Ra'aya Meheimna* and the *Tikkunim* is poor from the point of view of both vocabulary and syntax. The writer is already imitating the Zohar itself, but he does not have the literary skill of its author. The number of Hebrew words transmuted into Aramaic is much greater here than in the Zohar. The literary goal of the author of the main part of the Zohar is quite different from that of this author, who writes an almost undisguised medieval Hebrew: it is quite clear that he never intended his work to be thought of as a tannaitic creation. The terms Kabbalah and *Sefirot*, which are not used at all in the main body of the Zohar or in the *Midrash ha-Ne'lam*, and which indeed are circumvented by the use of all kinds of paraphrastic idioms, are here mentioned unrestrainedly.

ORDER OF COMPOSITION. An examination of the Zohar following the criteria above shows the order of composition of the main strata. The oldest parts, relatively speaking, are sections of the *Midrash ha-Ne'lam*, from *Bereshit* to *Lekh Lekha*, and the *Midrash ha-Ne'lam* to Ruth. They had already been written according to a different literary pattern, which did not yet assign everything to the circle of Simeon b. Yoḥai alone but which established *Eliezer b. Hyrcanus also, following the *heikhalot* and the *Pirkei de-Rabbi Eliezer*, as one of the main heroes of mystical thought. This section contains the basis of many passages in the main body of the Zohar, which quotes statements to be found only there, and develops its themes, stories, and ideas more expansively. The reverse cannot be maintained. In these early sections, there are no matters whose comprehension depends on a reference to the Zohar itself, whereas every part of the body of the Zohar, including the *Idra Rabba* and the *Idra Zuta*, is full of quotations from, and allusions to, matters found only in the *Midrash ha-Ne'lam*. The contradictions that occur here and there between the two strata on certain points, particularly on matters concerning the soul, may be explained, in the light of the unity that exists between them, as indications of a development in the ideas of the author whose written work emerged from a deep spiritual stirring. Some gleanings into the creative imagination of the author and its development are made possible by the discovery of a new section on the verse "Let there be lights in the firmament of heaven," which parallels the one in the printed editions and in most of the manuscripts, but which differs from it in the extraordinary imaginative conception of the author, and appears to be the first draft of the printed version. This new section is extant only in the oldest manuscript of the Zohar so far known (see G. Scholem, in: *Jubilee Volume… L. Ginsberg* (1946), 425–46), but it provides the first quotation from Zoharic writings to be found in Hebrew literature. In the last two sections of the *Midrash ha-Ne'lam* there are two references to matters which are to be found only in the main body of the Zohar, the writing of which seems therefore to have been started at that time. In the composition of the main body of the Zohar changes occur in literary technique, and in the transition to the exclusive use of Aramaic, and particularly in the decision to treat more expansively the writer's kabbalistic ideas, and those of his circle. The order of composition of the various sections which make up the second basic stratum cannot be precisely determined. There are so many cross-references, and we do not know whether these references were inserted in the final redaction or whether they were there from the very beginning, either referring to something already written or to what the author intended to write later on. In any event, most of the material was written as the result of a profound creative enthusiasm and over a relatively short period of time, so that the question of the order of composition of this section is not vitally important. Even after the author had stopped working on the *Midrash ha-Ne'lam*, which was never completed, he occasionally continued to write passages in the same vein and fitted them into the structure of the main part of the Zohar. This interlocking of one layer with another, despite the obvious differences between them, occurs also between the main body of the Zohar and the later stratum, whose composition begins with the *Ra'aya Meheimna*. The differences here are so great that it is impossible to suppose that the same author wrote both the two earlier strata and the later one. But there is a link between them. The author of the main part of the Zohar began, apparently, to compose a literary work which was anonymous and not associated with any particular literary or narrative framework and which was meant to be a personal interpretation of the reasons for the commandments. He did not finish this work, and the remnants of it are not extant in any one particular manuscript copy. However, the author of the *Ra'aya Meheimna*, who was probably a pupil of the former writer, knew it and used it as the starting point of his comments on several of the commandments, adding his own individual insights, and the new scenery. The differences in outlook and style between these fragments – which, when they do occur, are always at the beginning of the discussion on the commandments – and the main parts of the *Ra'aya Meheimna* are very great. It is almost always possible to determine precisely the point of transition between the fragments of the original text, which may be assigned to the Zohar itself, and the *Ra'aya Meheimna*, which was added to it.

The kabbalists themselves seem to have recognized this distinction. For example, the printers of the Cremona edition of the Zohar made a division on the title page between two sections, called *Pekuda* and *Ra'aya Meheimna*. The pages of the *Pekuda* belong from every point of view to the main body of the Zohar. The author of the later stratum had very different ideas from those of the author of the first. He does not express his ideas at length like the homilists, but links things together by association, without explaining his basic principle. He progresses by means of associations, especially in the *Sefer ha-Tikkunim*.

The author of the *Midrash ha-Ne'lam* and the main body of the Zohar intended from the very beginning to create a varied literature in the guise of early rabbinic material. He did not content himself with putting together the various sections which now form part of the Zohar, but he extended his canvas. He edited a version of a collection of geonic responsa, particularly those of Hai Gaon, and he added kabbalistic material in the style of the Zohar, using particular idioms of zoharic Aramaic, and also in the style of the *Midrash ha-Ne'lam*, all of which he titled *Yerushalmi* or the "*Yerushalmi* version." This edited version appeared at about the same time as the Zohar itself, in order to serve as a kind of indication that the new work was in fact known to the earlier rabbis. It was subsequently printed with the title of the *Sha'arei Teshuvah* responsa, and it misled not only kabbalists of the 15th and 16th centuries, but also scholars of the 19th century, who used it as a proof of the antiquity of the Zohar. One of the first of these was David *Luria in his *Ma'amar Kadmut Sefer ha-Zohar*.

Similarly, the author of the *Midrash ha-Ne'lam* wrote a small book titled *Orḥot Ḥayyim* or *Ẓavva'at R. Eliezer ha-Gadol*, which is connected throughout very closely to the Zohar. It is written in Hebrew but it has all the linguistic ingredients and stylistic peculiarities of the Zohar. In this work Eliezer b. Hyrcanus before his death, which is described at length following the late Midrash *Pirkei de-R. Eliezer*, reveals the paths of virtue and good conduct in an epigrammatic style, and in the second part, adds a description of the delights of the soul in the garden of Eden after death. These descriptions are very close indeed to particular parts of the Midrash on Ruth, and of the portions *Va-Yakhel, Shelaḥ Lekha, Balak*, and other parts of the Zohar. The book was known at first only in kabbalistic circles. It was printed in Constantinople in 1521, and usually each of the two parts was printed separately – the description of the death and the ethical prescriptions in one part, and the description of the garden of Eden in the other. The second part is included in A. *Jellinek's *Beit ha-Midrash* (3 (1938), 131–40). The first part was interpreted at length in the editions of *Orḥot Ḥayyim* by two Polish rabbis, Abraham Mordecai Vernikovsky (*Perush Dammesek Eliezer*, Warsaw, 1888), and Gershon Enoch Leiner (see *Izbica-Radzyn; Lublin, 1903), who tried to prove the antiquity of the book because it was based entirely on the Zohar, and in fact they did prove that the two works were composed by the same author. There are also some grounds for thinking that the author of the Zohar intended to write a *Sefer Ḥanokh* on the garden of Eden and other kabbalistic topics, and a long description from it is quoted in the *Mishkan ha-Edut* of Moses de Leon.

DATE OF COMPOSITION. Calculations of the time of *redemption, which are to be found in several sections of the Zohar, confirm the conclusions concerning the time of its composition. These calculations give an assurance, in various forms, and by means of different interpretations and conjectures, that the redemption will commence in the year 1300, and they expound the different stages of redemption leading to the resurrection. There are variations in the details of the precise dates, depending on the type of theme expounded. According to the Zohar 1,200 years had passed since the destruction of the Temple – a century for each of the tribes of Israel. Israel now stood at the period of transition which preceded the beginning of redemption. According to these dates (1:116–9, 139b; 2:9b; see A.H. Silver, *A History of Messianic Speculation in Israel* (1927), 90–92) it must be assumed that the main part of the Zohar and the *Midrash ha-Ne'lam* were written between 1270 and 1300. Similar calculations are to be found in the *Ra'aya Meheimna* and the *Tikkunim*. The basic date is always 1268. After this the "pangs of the Messiah" will begin, and Moses will appear and will reveal the Zohar as the end of time approaches. This period of transition will come to a halt in the year 1312, and then the various stages of the redemption itself will begin. Moses, in his final appearance, is not the Messiah but the harbinger of the Messiahs – the son of Joseph, and the son of David. He will be a poor man, but rich in kabbalistic Torah. The period of transition is a period of trouble and torment for the sacred group of the people of Israel, represented by the kabbalists, who will join in fierce conflict with their opponents and their detractors. The Zohar itself is a symbol of Noah's ark, through which they were saved from the destruction of the flood. God revealed Himself to the original Moses through the fire of prophecy; but to the later Moses of the final generation He will be revealed in the flames of the Torah, that is to say, through the revelation of the mysteries of Kabbalah. Something of Moses shines upon every sage or righteous man who occupies himself in whatever generation with the Torah, but at the end of time he will appear in concrete form as the revealer of the Zohar. Allusions of this type exist in every section of the latest stratum.

The Author

According to the clear testimony of *Isaac b. Samuel of Acre, who assembled the contradictory information concerning the appearance and nature of the Zohar in the early years of the 14th century, the book was published, part by part, not all at once, by the Spanish kabbalist *Moses b. Shem Tov de Leon, who died in 1305, after he had met Isaac of Acre. This kabbalist wrote many books in Hebrew bearing his name, from 1286 till after 1293. He was connected with several kabbalists of his time, including Todros *Abulafia and his son Joseph in Toledo, one of the leaders of Castilian Jewry, who supported Moses de Leon. From all that has already been said, the Zohar with its various strata was without doubt composed in the years that immediately preceded its publication, since it is impossible to uncover any section that was written before 1270. In actual fact, Moses de Leon was considered by some of Isaac of Acre's colleagues to have been the actual author of the Zohar. When he made some investigations in Avila, the last city in which Moses de Leon lived, Isaac was told that a wealthy man had proposed to marry his son to the daughter of Moses' widow provided that she would give him the original ancient manuscript from which, according to him, her deceased husband had copied the texts which he had published. However, both mother and daughter maintained that there was no such ancient manuscript, and that Moses de Leon had written the whole work on his own initiative. Opinions have been divided ever since as to the worth of this important evidence, and even the attitude of Isaac of Acre himself, whose story, preserved in Abraham *Zacuto's *Sefer ha-Yuḥasin*, which is interrupted in the midst of it, is not altogether clear, for he quotes from the Zohar in a few places in his books without relying on it at length or in main points. An analysis of the Zohar gives no support to the view that Moses de Leon edited texts and fragments of ancient works that came to him from the East. The question, therefore, is whether Moses de Leon himself was editor, author, and publisher, or whether a Spanish kabbalist, associated with him, wrote the book and gave it to him to edit. A decision can be made only on the basis of a comparison of the parts of the Zohar with the Hebrew writings of Moses de Leon, and on the basis of such information as the earliest extant quotations from the Zohar. Research into these questions leads to definite conclusions. In the extant works of Moses de Leon, and also in the earliest citations from the Zohar by Spanish kabbalists between 1280 and 1310, there are no quotations from the *Ra'aya Meheimna* and the *Tikkunim*. It may be supposed therefore that these latter were neither composed nor published by Moses de Leon. Of particular weight in this connection is the fact that Moses de Leon wrote a long work on the reasons for the commandments, but there is no similarity whatsoever between his *Sefer ha-Rimmon* and the *Ra'aya Meheimna*. In complete contrast to this, all his writings are extraordinarily replete with expositions, ideas, linguistic usages, and other matters to be found in the Zohar, from the stratum of the *Midrash ha-Ne'lam* and the main body of the Zohar, including those particular fragments designated above, which constitute the *Pekuda* at the beginning of the sections of the *Ra'aya Meheimna*. Often long sections like these, written here in Hebrew, contain no mention of the fact that they are derived from one source, and the author often prides himself on being the originator of things, which all exist nevertheless in the Zohar. Short pieces in the middle of a longer section are introduced in various ways which show that his real reference is to the Zohar: "it is expounded in the inner Midrashim"; "they say in the secrets of the Torah"; "the pillars of the world have discussed the secrets of their words"; "I have seen a profound matter in the writings of the ancients"; "I saw in the *Yerushalmi*"; "I have seen in the secrets of the depth of wisdom"; and so on. Quotations like these abound in his writings, and some of them are already present in the Aramaic version of the Zohar. There are also a few passages which do not occur in the existing Zohar, either because these particular texts did not survive or because they were not finally published. I. Tishby's opinion is that several of them were introduced only as pointers to what the author intended to write, but he did not in fact manage to write out these matters at length. But it is more likely that the greater part of the Zohar was available to him when he wrote his Hebrew books.

Moses de Leon's Hebrew style reveals in many particulars those idiosyncrasies of the Aramaic of the Zohar indicated above, and we find especially those mistakes and errors of usage which are characteristic of the Zohar and are not found in the works of any other writer. He writes in this style even when his writing does not reflect the actual expositions of the Zohar, but expresses his own personal ideas or adds a new dimension to ideas in the Zohar. He has a completely unfettered control of the material in the Zohar and uses it like a man using his own property. He ties together expositions from different parts of the Zohar, adding to them combinations of themes and new expositions, which are in perfect accord with the zoharic spirit and show that his thinking is identical with that of the Zohar. In many cases his writings constitute an interpretation of difficult passages of the Zohar which later kabbalists did not interpret literally. Whenever in his writings he diverges freely from the subjects treated in the Zohar, his variations do not constitute any proof that he did not understand his "source." Sometimes he openly mentions the true literary sources which are concealed in the Zohar. The long passage from the Book of Enoch which is quoted in his *Mishkan ha-Edut* is written entirely in his own particular Hebrew style. Features which are peculiar to the Zohar, and which distinguish it from other contemporary kabbalistic works, recur in the works of Moses de Leon. These are in particular the exaggerated use of mythical imagery, the sexual symbolism developed with regard to the relationships between the *Sefirot*, and the striking interest shown in demonology and sorcery. Consequently, there is no reason to assume that an unknown author wrote the Zohar in the lifetime of Moses de Leon, and then passed it on to him. The authorship of Moses de Leon solves the problems raised by an analysis of the Zohar together with his Hebrew works. These books were largely written in order to prepare the ground for the publication of the texts of the Zohar which went hand in hand with this work. In particular, the *Mishkan ha-Edut* (1293) is full of recommendations and praise for the secret sources upon which it is based.

The solution of the fundamental question of the identity of the Zohar's author leaves questions which are still open on several counts; e.g., the order of composition of the sections of the main stratum of the Zohar; and the final editing of the Zohar before its texts were publicly disseminated, if indeed there was an editing at all, for there is evidence here for both possibilities. The main question still needing clarification is the relationship between Moses de Leon and Joseph Gikatilla, which apparently was very close and reciprocal. Similarly we still have to solve the problem of the author of the *Ra'aya Meheimna*, who, unlike Moses de Leon, left no other books which can identify him. Whether other kabbalists knew of Moses de Leon's plan and helped him in some way to achieve his aim is not clear. What is clear is that many kabbalists, after the appearance of the book, considered themselves free to write works in the style of the Zohar and to imitate it – a liberty which they would not have taken with Midrashim whose genuineness and antiquity were beyond question. This fact shows that they did not take seriously the claim of the Zohar to be accepted as an ancient source, even though they saw in it a fine expression of their own spiritual world. For books of this type see *Kabbalah.

Manuscripts and Editions

The circumstances surrounding the appearance of the Zohar are not known in detail. The first texts which circulated among a few kabbalists were of the *Midrash ha-Ne'lam*, and the earliest quotations are to be found in two books by Isaac b. Solomon Abi Sahula, the *Meshal ha-Kadmoni* (Venice, c. 1546–50) and his commentary to Song of Songs, which were written in 1281 and 1283 in Guadalajara, where Moses de Leon lived at that time. He is the only author who knew and quoted the *Midrash ha-Ne'lam* before Moses de Leon himself began to write his Hebrew works. Todros Abulafia also possessed such texts and quoted from them in his books. Parts of the main body of the Zohar circulated from the late 1280s. An examination of the quotations from the Zohar found in contemporary writing shows that

(1) they possessed only isolated parts, depending on what each of them could obtain;

(2) they knew a few expositions or parts which do not appear in the Zohar we have;

(3) they made use of it without regarding it as a supreme authority in Kabbalah.

In about 1290 some portions of the Zohar on the Torah were known to *Baḥya b. Asher, who translated several passages word for word in his commentary to the Torah without mentioning his source, and generally used the Zohar widely. Twice, however, he refers to very short passages in the name of the *Midrash R. Simeon b. Yoḥai*. Other sections, including the *Idrot*, were in the possession of Gikatilla when he wrote *Sha'arei Orah*, before 1293. From the anonymous *Ta'amei ha-Mitzvot*, which was probably written in the 1290s, it appears that some passages were known to the author. From 1300 onward there is an increase in the number of quotations actually cited under the specific name Zohar or *Midrash ha-Ne'lam*, which sometimes served as the title for the whole Zohar. Solomon b. Abraham Adret's pupils, who wrote many kabbalistic works, quoted the Zohar only rarely, and they clearly exercised some restraint in the use of it. Menahem *Recanati of Italy also possessed some isolated parts in this time, and he used them widely, mentioning his source in his commentary to the Torah and in his *Ta'amei ha-Mitzvot*. In the latter book he makes a distinction between the *Zohar Gadol*, which consisted mainly of the *Idra Rabba*, and the *Zohar Mufla*. The origin of this distinction is not clear. Recanati possessed only about one-tenth of the Zohar now extant, but he had access to an exposition of the mystery of sacrifices which no longer remains. Among the authors at this time (1310–30) who used the Zohar extensively were Joseph Angelino, the author of *Livnat ha-Sappir*, and David b. Judah he-Ḥasid, who wrote *Marot ha-Ẓove'ot*, *Sefer ha-Gevul*, and *Or Zaru'a*.

The position with regard to the earliest quotations is matched by our knowledge of the earliest Zohar manuscripts. Complete, well-ordered manuscripts did not circulate, and it is doubtful whether they ever existed. Mystics who took an interest in the Zohar made up anthologies for themselves from the texts they were able to procure; hence the great differences in the contents of the early manuscripts. An example of an anthology like this is the Cambridge Ms. Add. 1023, the oldest anthology yet known. It contains material which serves to complete another anthology which is now lost, and includes those parts of the Zohar which the compiler was able to obtain. This manuscript is from the last third of the 14th century, and contains a complete portion, otherwise unknown, of the *Midrash ha-Ne'lam*, which Isaac ibn Sahulah also knew. The Vatican Ms. 202, which is a little earlier, contains only isolated fragments from the Zohar. In the 15th century, manuscripts containing most of the portions of the Zohar were already compiled, but sometimes they still omit whole sections, e.g., the *Idrot*, the *Sava*, etc. (On these manuscripts see I. Tishby, *Mishnat ha-Zohar*, 1 (1957[2]), 110–2.)

The differences between manuscripts of the Zohar and the printed editions are mainly in the field of spelling (words are mostly written *plene* in the manuscripts and in early quotations), and in the relatively large number of romanisms, which were later confused; in the wider use of the preposition *bedil* for *begin*; and in the alteration of the grammatical forms of the Targum and the Babylonian Talmud. There are many differences in the basic text but they are relatively unimportant, and usually different readings of this kind are given in brackets in the later printed editions. There are manuscripts from the 15th century of the *Sefer Tikkunim* as well, such as Paris Ms. 778. The *Ra'aya Meheimna* also exists in separate manuscripts. From 1400 onward the sanctity of the Zohar became more widely acknowledged in kabbalistic circles, and the criticisms of it which were heard here and there in the 14th century (e.g., in Joseph *Ibn Waqar who wrote: "the Zohar contains many errors of which one must be wary, to avoid being misled by them") died down. At this time the spread and influence of the Zohar were confined mainly to Spain and Italy, and it was very slow to reach the Ashkenazi lands and the East. The great elevation of the Zohar to a position of sanctity and supreme authority came during and after the period of the expulsion from Spain, and it reached its peak in the 16th and 17th centuries.

The Zohar was printed amid a fierce controversy between those who opposed its publication, among whom were some important kabbalists, and its supporters (see S. Assaf, *Mekorot u-Meḥkarim be-Toledot Yisrael* (1946), 246–328). The first two editions of the Zohar were published by competing printers in the neighboring cities of Mantua (1558–60) and Cremona (1559–60). The *Tikkunei ha-Zohar* was also published separately in Mantua (1558). The editors of these two editions used different manuscripts – hence the differences in the order and in detailed readings. Immanuel of Benevento who established the Mantua text used ten manuscripts, from which he arranged his edition, and chose the text which he considered to be the best. Among the correctors at Cremona was the apostate grandson of the grammarian Elijah *Levita (Baḥur), Vittorio Eliano. They used six manuscripts. The Mantua Zohar was printed in three volumes in Rashi script, while the Cremona Zohar was in one large volume in square script. Both of them contain a large number of printing errors. Both include the *Ra'aya Meheimna*, but they differ as to the placing of the different *mitzvot*. According to size, the kabbalists called these two editions *Zohar Gadol* ("Large Zohar") and *Zohar Katan* ("Small Zohar"). The *Zohar Gadol* was printed on two more occasions in this form, in Lublin in 1623, and in Sulzbach in 1684. The Polish and German kabbalists up to about 1715 generally used the *Zohar Gadol*. All other editions follow the Mantua format. Altogether the Zohar has been printed more than 65 times and the *Tikkunei Zohar* nearly 80 times. Most of the editions come from Poland and Russia, but there are also printings from Constantinople, Salonika, Smyrna, Leghorn, Jerusalem, and Djerba. In later editions they added the variant readings of the Cremona text and corrected many printing errors. They also added variants and readings from the manuscript of the Safed kabbalists, indications of biblical sources, and introductions. The Zohar was printed twice in Leghorn with an (incorrectly) vocalized text. Those sections in the Safed manuscripts which were not found in the Mantua edition were, except from the *Midrash ha-Ne'lam* to Ruth, printed together in a separate volume in Salonika in 1597, which was called *Zohar Ḥadash* in the later editions. The best of these are Venice, 1658, and Munkacs, 1911. All the sections of the Zohar were included in the complete edition of Yehudah *Ashlag, Jerusalem, 1945–58, in 22 volumes, with a Hebrew translation and textual variants from the earlier editions. The *Tikkunei ha-Zohar* began to appear in 1960, and by 1970 was not completed. A critical edition based on early manuscripts does not yet exist.

Commentaries

The crucial importance of the Zohar in the development of Kabbalah and in the life of the Jewish community can be seen in the vast exegetical literature and the large number of manuals that were composed for it. Most of these commentaries have not been printed, notably the commentary of Moses Cordovero *Or ha-Yakar*, of which five volumes have appeared (Jerusalem, 1962–70) – a complete version of this exists in the library at Modena in 19 large volumes; and the commentary of Elijah *Loans of Worms, *Adderet Eliyahu*, and *Ẓafenat Pa'ne'aḥ*, which exists at Oxford in four large volumes in the author's own hand. The early commentaries to the Zohar have not survived. Although Menahem Recanati mentions his own commentary in his *Ta'amei ha-Mitzvot*, most commentaries are based on Lurianic Kabbalah and do not add much to our understanding of the Zohar itself, e.g., *Zohar Ḥai* of Isaac Eizik Safrin of *Komarno, which was printed in 1875–81 in five volumes, and *Dammesek Eliezer* by his son Jacob Moses Safrin, which was printed in seven volumes in 1902–28. The most important commentary for a literal understanding of the Zohar is *Ketem Paz* by Simeon *Labi of Tripoli (written about 1570), of which only the Genesis section has been printed (Leghorn, 1795), but this also diverges quite often from the literal meaning and offers fanciful interpretations. Second in importance is the *Or ha-Ḥammah*, a compilation by Abraham b. Mordecai Azulai, which includes an abridgment of Cordovero's commentary, the commentary of Ḥayyim Vital which was written in the main before he studied with Luria, and the *Yare'aḥ Yakar*, a commentary by Abraham Galante, one of Cordovero's pupils. Azulai arranged these commentaries together corresponding to each page of the text of the original Zohar. The whole work was printed with the title *Or ha-Ḥammah* in four volumes in Przemysl in 1896–98. It reflects the Cordovero school of Zohar exposition. A very widely known commentary, half literal and half Lurianic, is the *Mikdash Melekh* of Shalom *Buzaglo, a Moroccan rabbi of the 18th century, which was printed in Amsterdam in five volumes in 1750, and several times subsequently. It was printed together with the Zohar itself in Leghorn in 1858. The commentary, *Ha-Sullam*, in Yehudah Ashlag's edition of the Zohar, is part translation and part exposition. These commentaries do not consider the comparison of the Zohar with earlier material in rabbinic literature or in other kabbalistic works. The commentaries of the Gaon *Elijah of Vilna are important, namely *Yahel Or*, and his commentary to the *Sifra di-Ẓeni'uta*, which is characterized by his comparative approach. Both of them were printed together in Vilna in 1882. Among the many commentaries to the *Tikkunei Zohar*, the *Kisse Melekh* of Shalom

Buzaglo must be singled out, and also the *Be'er la-Ḥai Ro'i* of Ẓevi Shapira (printed in Munkacs, 1903–21), three of whose volumes cover only about half the book.

Of the aids to the study of the Zohar the most useful are *Yesh Sakhar*, a collection of the laws in the Zohar, by Issachar Baer of Kremnitz (Prague, 1609); *Sha'arei Zohar*, a clarification of zoharic statements through their relationship to Talmud and Midrash, set out in the order of tractates and Midrashim, by Reuben Margulies (Jerusalem, 1956); a collection of zoharic statements on the Psalms by Moses Gelernter (Warsaw, 1926); and *Midreshei ha-Zohar Leket Shemu'el* by S. Kipnis, three volumes (Jerusalem, 1957–60), a collection of zoharic statements on the Bible with explanation. Keys to the subject matter of the Zohar are to be found in *Mafteḥot ha-Zohar*, arranged by Israel Berekhiah Fontanella (Venice, 1744), and in *Yalkut ha-Zohar* by Isaiah Menahem Mendel (Piotrikov, 1912).

Translations

The question of translating the Zohar into Hebrew had already arisen among the kabbalists of the 14th century. David b. Judah he-Ḥasid translated into Hebrew most of the quotations from the Zohar which he cited in his books. According to Abraham Azulai, Isaac *Luria had "a book of the Zohar translated into the holy tongue by Israel *al-Nakawa," the author of *Menorat ha-Ma'or* in which all the quotations from the Zohar, under the name of *Midrash Yehi Or*, are in Hebrew. In the Vatican manuscripts of the Zohar (nos. 62 and 186), several sections have been translated into Hebrew in the 14th or 15th century. According to Joseph *Sambari, Judah Mas'ud translated the Zohar into Hebrew in the 16th century. A translation of the Zohar from the Cremona edition, dating from the year 1602, is extant in Oxford Ms. 1561, but the more esoteric passages are omitted; the translator was Barkiel Cafman Ashkenazi. The Genesis part of this work was printed by Obadiah Hadaya (Jerusalem, 1946). In the 17th century Samuel Romner of Lublin translated a large part of the Zohar under the title *Devarim Attikim* (Dembitzer, *Kelilat Yofi*, 2 (1960), 25a); this is extant in Oxford Ms. 1563, with rabbinic authorizations dated 1747, showing that they had intended to have it printed. According to Eliakim Milsahagi of Brody, about 1830, in his *Zohorei Ravyah* (Jerusalem Ms.), he translated the whole of the Zohar into Hebrew, and to judge from his excellent style this must have been the finest translation made, but it is now lost together with most of his separate studies on the Zohar. In the 20th century large sections were translated by Judah Rosenberg in *Zohar Torah* in five volumes; and similarly, commentaries on the Zohar to Psalms and the *Megillot* in two volumes (New York, 1924–25; Bilgoraj, 1929–30). This translation is devoid of any literary qualities. The Hebrew writer Hillel Zeitlin began to translate the Zohar, but he did not continue. The preface to the Zohar in his translation was printed in *Metsudah* (London, 1 (1943), 36–82). A complete and extremely literal translation (but not without many textual misunderstandings) is contained in the edition of the Zohar by Yehudah Ashlag. Many selected pieces were translated in a meticulous and fine style by F. Lachower and I. Tishby, *Mishnat ha-Zohar* (2 vols., 1957–61²).

Even before the Zohar was printed, the French mystic G. *Postel had prepared a Latin translation of Genesis and of the Midrash on Ruth, which is extant in manuscript in the British Museum and in Munich. The preface to it was published by F. Secret. The Christian mystic Chr. *Knorr von Rosenroth also made a Latin translation of important parts, particularly the *Idrot* and the *Sifra de-Ẓeniuta*, in his large work *Kabbala Denudate* (Sulzbach, 1677; Frankfurt, 1684), and most of the quotations from the Zohar or translations of those pieces which appeared in other European languages were taken from here, together with all the mistakes of the original translator, e.g., the works of S.L. Mathers, *The Kabbalah Unveiled* (1887); Paul Vulliaud, *Traduction intégrale du Siphra de-Tzeniutha* (1930). A French translation of the three volumes of the standard editions of the Zohar was prepared by Jean de Pauly (the later name of a baptized Jew from Galicia) but it is full of distortions and adulterations and accompanied by a great many false textual references, often to books which do not contain them at all or to books which have never existed. The translation was corrected by a Jewish scholar who knew Talmud and Midrash but did not correct the mistakes in the field of Kabbalah, which he did not understand. This translation, *Sepher ha-Zohar (Le Livre de la Splendeur) Doctrine ésotérique des Israélites traduit… par Jean de Pauly*, was magnificently printed in six volumes in Paris (1906–11). An English translation of the main part of the Zohar, with the omission of those sections which seemed to the translators to be separate works or additions, was *The Zohar* by Harry Sperling and Maurice Simon, published in five volumes in London (1931–34). The translation is in good style but suffers from incomplete or erroneous understanding of many parts of the kabbalistic exposition. A German anthology of many characteristic quotations from the Zohar was made by Ernst Mueller, who was obviously influenced by the teaching of Rudolf Steiner (*Der Sohar, das heilige Buch der Kabbala*, 1932).

Scholarship

Scholarly research into the Zohar did not begin with the kabbalists, however deeply interested they were in its teaching: they accepted uncritically the literary romantic background of the book as historical fact. The Jewish opponents of the Kabbalah expressed doubts about the veracity of this background from the end of the 15th century onward, but they did not delve deeply into a scholarly investigation of the Zohar. Christian interest in the Zohar was not at first scholarly but theological. Many thought they would find support for Christian ideas and developed a "Christian Kabbalah," and most of the writings up to the middle of the 18th century reflect this spirit. No scholarly value can be attached to these efforts. The first critical work was the *Ari Nohem* of Leone *Modena (1639) who questioned the authenticity and antiquity of the Zohar, from the point of view of language and other matters, but he did not undertake a detailed study. The book was printed as late as 1840 (Leipzig), but its circulation in manuscript aroused the wrath of the kabbalists who saw every attempt at critique as an assault upon the sacred, and they replied to it, and to later books which were written in the same vein, with a considerable number of works defending the Zohar, but these are of little historical worth. Leone Modena's critique was also stimulated by a polemic against certain claims of Christian Kabbalah, while that of Jacob *Emden was connected with the struggle against the Shabbateans, who went to extreme lengths of heresy in their interpretations of the Zohar. In *Mitpaḥat Sefarim* (Altona, 1768), Emden concluded on the basis of a large number of specific errors in the Zohar that many sections, and particularly the *Midrash ha-Ne'lam*, were late, although he still assumed that there was an ancient foundation for the main body of the book. The *maskilim* followed him, especially Samuel David *Luzzatto in his *Vikku'aḥ al Ḥokhmat ha-Kabbalah ve-al Kadmut Sefer ha-Zohar* ("An Argument Concerning the Wisdom of the Kabbalah and the Antiquity of the Zohar" (1827), printed in Gorizia, 1852). These two books, Emden's and Luzzatto's, elicited several replies seeking to answer the questions they raised, particularly *Ben Yoḥai* by Moses Kunitz (Vienna, 1815), and *Ta'am le-Shad* by Elia Benamozegh (Leghorn, 1863). The profound inquiries by Eliakim Milsahagi in several books devoted to the Zohar would have much furthered historical inquiry had they been printed and not simply remained in manuscript. He towered head and shoulders above many of the writers who succeeded him. There remain only a few pages of his in the *Sefer Ravyah* (Ofen, 1837) and his introduction *Zohorei Ravyah* (Ms. in National Library, Jerusalem). The great 19th-century scholars of Judaism, *Zunz, *Steinschneider, and *Graetz, went further than Jacob Emden and saw the Zohar as a product of the 13th century. M.H. *Landauer tried to prove that the Zohar was produced by Abraham *Abulafia, and A. Jellinek directed attention once more to Moses de Leon. A. *Frank and D.H. *Joel argued as to whether the teaching of the Zohar was of Jewish or foreign origin, and an echo of this kind of controversy reverberated throughout most of the literature of the *maskilim*, whose very general conclusions were not based on a close attention to detail and are marred by many weak arguments. Because of the lack of precise critical inquiry, scholars chose to solve the problem of the Zohar in accordance with their own subjective views, and the very widespread belief was that the Zohar was the creation of many generations and was only edited in the 13th century. There were also those who admitted that Moses de Leon had a greater or lesser share in the editing. The results of the many studies by G. Scholem and I. Tishby, which were based on detailed research, do not support these theories and lead to the view summarized above. There is no doubt that scholarly research into the Zohar has only just begun and will develop in detail in connection with research into the history of 13th-century Kabbalah in general. In the bibliography works are listed which reflect various points of view.

[Gershom Scholem]

Later Research

Gershom Scholem, the founder of the modern academic study of Jewish mysticism, was particularly interested in the authorship, historical context, and the mythical doctrines of the Zohar. He devoted two chapters in *Major Trends in Jewish Mysticism* to the author of the Zohar and the worldview expressed in its theosophic orientation. Scholem understood the Zohar as a pseudoepigraphic composition – a work deliberately attributed by its authors to someone else – namely a medieval work attributed to Rabbi Shimon bar Yoḥai. He argued that its composition should be dated to the period between the mid-1270s and late 1280s, and concluded that the Zohar was the fruit of a single spiritual-literary genius, Rabbi Moses de León. Scholem suggested that the different literary units within the Book of the Zohar ought to be understood as compositions arising from different periods of the intellectual development of Moses de León. Scholem saw in the Zohar a mythical, innovative composition, created in the heart of medieval rabbinic Judaism, and emphasized its originality and daring more than its relationship to earlier literary traditions. Since Scholem's work, the Zohar has become an integral part of Kabbalah research and found its place in the canon of literary and spiritual works of the Middle Ages.

Isaiah Tishby's research into the Zohar relied on the key assumptions of Scholem's research. His monumental work, *The Wisdom of the Zohar*, now available in English, is the product of academic research which further seeks to bring the treasures of the Zohar to the modern reader who may not be well versed in the text or its language. Tishby's great contribution lies in his classification of the central topics discussed in the Zohar and in his scholarly, detailed, and systematic introductions to these topics. Alongside these studies he translated into Hebrew (together with Fischel Lachower) many select texts from the Zohar.

Yehuda Liebes contributed many ground breaking studies to Zohar scholarship. In his seminal article, "The Messiah of the Zohar," Liebes explored the messianic character of the hero of the Zohar, Rabbi Shimon bar Yoḥai, and the messianism of the entire composition. In this article, he explored many other aspects of the Zohar including zoharic myth and composition, the place of eros and sexuality in the Zohar's unique language, the world of the companions, analysis of the *Idra Rabba* and *Idra Zuta*, different conceptions of *tikkun* (rectification), and the influence of the Zohar on later Jewish mystics. Liebes argues that the zoharic narratives and homilies are necessarily intertwined and must therefore be analyzed with the zoharic story as an essential component of the text, constituting a key to the text's uniqueness and not merely as the insignificant frame for the homilies expounded therein.

In his article, "How the Zohar was Written," Liebes reopened the question of the authorship and composition of the Zohar. He points to a range of content, conceptual, and stylistic factors, which challenged Scholem's view of a single author creating the Zohar. Liebes refocused attention from the question of *who wrote the Zohar* to *how the Zohar was written*. This study concludes that the Zohar is the product of a circle of mystics and not the work of a single author. In his article *Zohar and Eros*, Liebes focused on the place of eros and sexuality as the vital force in the Zohar and that which bestows upon the composition its unique place in the annals of Jewish literature.

Elliot Wolfson has written many important studies on the Zohar and emphasizes the centrality of mystical and ecstatic experience in kabbalistic and zoharic creativity while presenting a critical analysis of earlier approaches to the relationship between theosophy and experiential mysticism in the Zohar. His major claim is that an understanding of the world of the Zohar necessitates an appreciation of the fact that the Zohar is not merely a speculative or theoretical work, but rather presents practical means for attaining ecstatic states of union with or participation in the divine. Wolfson has written extensively on issues of gender and sexuality in the Kabbalah as a whole and especially in the Zohar. He argued for the centrality of male sexuality in both mystical experience and exegetical process in the Zohar as opposed to the secondary and dependant status of the feminine.

In *Kabbalah: New Perspectives*, Moshe Idel explored the spiritual and intellectual characteristics of the kabbalistic climate in which the Zohar was produced. He claimed that the circle of mystics responsible for the Zohar came into being out of the creative processes of a secondary elite of spiritual leadership. Idel distinguishes between a primary elite, comprising those scholars and rabbis who assumed central leadership roles in the community, and a secondary elite, the members of which constituted a second order of leadership characterized by the freedom to choose a creative and innovative path without seeking the approval of the legal and spiritual authorities of the time. In his book *Absorbing Perfections* he focused and extended his detailed and extensive research in the field of kabbalistic hermeneutics in which he explored the nature of the kabbalistic and zoharic symbol and the uniqueness of the symbolic-dynamic interpretation of the Zohar.

In the early 21st century Daniel Matt was working on the monumental enterprise of producing an annotated English translation of the Zohar, based on a critical Aramaic text that he is reconstructing from numerous Zohar manuscripts. As of 2006, three volumes had appeared, covering the Zohar's commentary on Genesis. The complete translation, titled *The Zohar: Pritzker Edition*, is projected to comprise 11–12 volumes.

In his research he has also highlighted the tension between innovation and traditionalism in the zoharic consciousness and has explored the way in which the Zohar as a whole understands itself as representing an alternative Jewish culture to that of classical rabbinic culture.

Arthur Green recently published a popular introductory volume for the Pritzker edition of the Zohar, translated by Daniel Matt.

Charles Mopsik translated into French select parts of the zoharic corpus as well as the writings of Rabbi Moses de León, introduced with detailed commentary which explored the ideological and literary context of this corpus. Mopsik further took issue with Liebes' claim about the circle of the Zohar, arguing again for the solitary literary production of the work by R. Moses de León.

Ronit Meroz heads a project which seeks to publish a critical edition of the Zohar. Her research of the Zohar suggests that through the use of philological-historical tools accompanied with literary ones it is possible to identify different chronological layers in the zoharic text. Meroz seeks to delineate discrete literary units in the composition and to test the hypothesis that different units were composed by different authors who were part of a literary movement. Meroz seeks to locate the beginning of what would later become the Zohar in texts composed as early as the 11th century somewhere in the Middle East. The earliest zoharic literary strata that she has defined is written in Hebrew, while the most refined, rich, and complex one, which Meroz calls the "Epic unit," was composed at the end of the 13th century and has at its center the spiritual biography of R. Simeon b. Yoḥai.

Israel Ta-Shma researched the halakhic world of the Zohar. He showed that the composition of the Zohar portrays Spanish *halakhah* even as it shows its dependence and intimate knowledge of French Jewish customs and liturgical rites.

Melila Hellner-Eshed's book "A River Issues from Eden" provides a detailed phenomenological analysis of mystical experience in the Zohar. The book provides the reader with a lexicon for zoharic mystical experience, reviews the paths and practices through which the Companions of the Zohar attain their mystical experiences as well as the special language and modes of expression which are used in order to describe the mystical experience itself, and its unique characteristics. Hellner-Eshed sees the zoharic literature as having the performative aim of awakening the mystical consciousness of its readers. In her book there is also an exploration of dimensions of self consciousness and reflexivity in the Zohar.

Boaz Huss has explored the question of the appearance, acceptance, canonization, and sanctification of the Zohar. Huss has explored the zoharic comparison between the figures of Moses and R. Simeon Bar Yoḥai, the hero of the Zohar, and the Zohar's preference for Bar Yoḥai over Moses. He claimed that the zoharic portrayal of Rabbi Simeon Bar Yoḥai reflects the self understanding of the Zohar's authors, while the figure of Moses points to the authoritative and kabbalistically conservative character of Naḥmanides. The zoharic portrayal of Rabbi Simeon as superior to Moses, Huss argues, expresses the attempt of the Zohar's authors to circumvent the authority of Naḥmanides and his school and to create a sanctified and canonized kabbalistic literature.

Daniel Abrams in various studies has stressed the necessity of distinguishing between the literary production of zoharic texts and the later historical reception of the disparate texts as a book. His central claim is that kabbalists and scholars alike have projected their expectations and assumptions of the "Book of the Zohar" back on to the earlier history of its composition in late 13th-century Spain. He claimed that there is no evidence as yet to show that the Zohar was written as a book, but rather the book was invented many centuries later as a separate editing effort. Abrams claims as well that the Zohar does not have an "author," as understood in modern conceptions of literature and of the individual.

In her book, *Vision and Speech: Models of Revelatory Experience in Jewish Mysticism*, Haviva Pedaya has written extensively on the religious experience of the Zohar and on strategies for identifying those parts of the Zoharic corpus written in revelatory states.

Oded Israeli wrote a book on the zoharic literary unit known as "*Saba de-Mishpatim*." In his research, he explored the key issues associated with this unit: the date of its composition, its place in the zoharic corpus, and its conceptual and literary characteristics.

The late strata of the Zohar, *Ra'aya Meheimna* and *Tikkunei ha-Zohar*, composed by an anonymous kabbalist in the beginning of the 14th century, have also enjoyed new investigation and scholarly studies. Pinchas Giller dedicated his book, *The Enlightened Will Shine,* to a study of these two later compositions. His later book, *Reading the Zohar*, detailed the various interpretative strategies among later commentators of the Zohar.

Amos Goldreich wrote on the self-image of the author of *Ra'aya Meheimna* and *Tikkunei ha-Zohar*. His edition of an unknown commentary to Ezekiel by this author is due shortly.

From this cursory overview of Zohar research, the great wealth of complex and complicated questions and issues explored by the Zohar's many researchers and interpreters begins to emerge.

[Melila Hellner-Eshed (2nd ed.)]

BIBLIOGRAPHY: G. Scholem, *Bibliographia Kabbalistica* (1933), 66–210; M. Kunitz, *Ben Yoḥai* (1815); S.J. Rapoport, *Naḥalat Yehudah* (1873); S.Z. Anushinski, *Maẓẓav ha-Yashar* (1881–87); D. Luria, *Kadmut Sefer ha-Zohar* (1887); H. Zeitlin, *Be-Fardes ha-Ḥasidut ve-ha-Kabbalah* (1960), 55–279; D. Neumark, *Toledot ha-Filosofyah be-Yisrael*, 1 (1921), 204–45, 326–54; H.S. Neuhausen, *Zohorei Zohar* (1929); idem, in: *Oẓar ha-Ḥayyim*, 13 (1937), 51–59; J.A.Z. Margaliot, *Middot Rashbi* (1937); idem, *Kokho de-Rashbi* (1948); J.L. Zlotnik, *Midrash ha Meliẓah ha-Ivrit* (1938); Y. Baer, in: *Zion*, 5 (1940), 1–44; I. Tishby, *Mishnat ha-Zohar* (1957–61); idem, in: *Perakim* (1967–68), 131–82; Scholem, Mysticism, 156–243, 385–407; idem, in: *Zion (Me'assef)*, 1 (1926), 40–56; idem, in: MGWJ, 75 (1931), 347–62, 444–48; idem, in: *Tarbiz*, 19 (1948), 160–75; 24 (1955), 290–306; idem, in: *Sefer Assaf* (1953), 459–95; idem, in: *Le-Agnon Shai* (1959), 289–305; idem, *On the Kabbalah and its Symbolism* (1965), 32–86; E. Gottlieb, *Ha-Kabbalah be-Khitvei Rabbenu Baḥya ben Asher* (1970), 167–93; R. Margulies, *Malakhei Elyon* (1964²); idem, *Sha'arei Zohar* (1956); S.A. Horodezky, *Ha-Mistorin be-Yisrael*, 2 (1952), 266–339; P. Sandler, in: *Sefer Urbach* (1955), 222–35; M.Z. Kadari, *Dikduk ha-Lashon ha-Aramit shel ha-Zohar* (1970); idem, in: *Tarbiz*, 27 (1958), 265–77; M. Kasher, in: *Sinai Jubilee Volume* (1958), 40–56; S. Belkin, in: *Sura*, 3 (1958), 25–92; A. Franck, *The Kabbalah: The Religious Philosophy of the Hebrews* (1967²); E. Waite, *The Secret Doctrine in Israel* (1913); A. Bension, *The Zohar in Moslem and Christian Spain* (1932); R.J.Z. Werblowsky, in: JJS, 10 (1959), 25–44, 113–35; D.H. Joel, *Midrash ha-Zohar: Die Religionsphilosophie des Sohar und ihr Verhaeltnis zur allgemeinen juedischen Theologie* (1923³); A. Jellinek, *Moses b. Schem-Tob de Leon und sein Verhaeltnis zum Sohar* (1851); Graetz, Gesch, 7, 430–48; I. Stern, in: *Ben Chananja*, 1–4 (1858–62); W. Bacher, in: REJ, 22 (1891), 33–46, 219–9; S. Karppe, *Etude sur les origines et la nature du Zohar* (1901); E. Mueller, *Der Sohar und seine Lehre* (1959³); M. Preis, in: MGWJ, 72 (1928), 167–84; *Etudes et Correspondance de Jean de Pauly relatives au Sepher ha-Zohar* (1933); H. Sérouya, *La Kabbale* (1957²), 198–395; F. Secret, in: *Etudes Juives*, 10 (1964); M. Benayahu, *Ha-Defus ha-Ivri be-Cremona* (1971), 206–9. **ADD. BIBLIOGRAPHY:** *The Zohar: Pritzker Edition*, tr. and commentary by D.C. Matt, vols. 1–3 (2004–6); D. Abrams, "When the 'Introduction' to the *Zohar* was Written, and Changes Within Differing Copies of the Mantua Printing," in: *Asufot*, 8 (1994), 211–26 (Heb.); idem, "The Zohar as a Book: On the Assumptions and Expectations of the Kabbalists and Modern Scholarship," in: *Kabbalah: Journal for the Study of Jewish Mystical Texts*, 12 (2004), 201–32; M. Hellner-Eshed, "*Ve-Nahar Yoẓe me-Eden*": *Al Sefat ha-Havayah ha-Mistit ba-Zohar* (Heb., 2005); B. Huss, "Sefer ha-Zohar as a Canonical, Sacred and Holy Text," in: *Journal of Jewish Studies*, 7 (1998), 275–307; idem, "The Anthological Interpretation: The Emergence of Anthologies of Zohar Commentaries in the Seventeenth Century," in: *Prooftexts*, 19 (1999); idem, "*Ḥakham adif mi-Navi: Rabbi Shim'on Bar Yohai u-Moshe Rabbeinu ba-Zohar*," in: *Kabbalah: Journal for the Study of Jewish Mystical Texts*, 4 (1998), 103–39; idem, "*Hofaato shel Sefer ha-Zohar*," in: *Tarbiz*, 70 (2001), 507–42 (Heb.); P. Giller, *The Enlightened Will Shine, Symbolization and Theurgy in the Later Strata of the Zohar* (1993); idem, *Reading the Zohar: The Sacred Text of the Kabbalah* (2000); A. Goldreich, "*Beirurim bi-Re'iato ha-Aẓmit shel Ba'al Tikkunei Zohar*," in: M. Oron and A. Goldreich, *Masuot* (1994), 459–96; A. Green, *A Guide to the Zohar* (2004); M. Idel, *Kabbalah: New Perspectives* (1998); idem, *Absorbing Perfections* (2002); Y. Liebes, *Studies in the Zohar*, tr. by A. Schwartz, S. Nakache, and P. Peli (1993); idem, *Perakim be-Millon Sefer ha-Zohar* (Heb., 1983); idem, "*Zohar ve-Eros*," in: *Alpayim*, 9 (1994), 67–119 (Heb.); idem, "*Ha-Zohar ke-Renesans*," in: *Da'at*, 46 (2001), 5–11 (Heb.); idem, *Torat ha-Yeẓirah shel Sefer Yeẓirah* (2000); D.C. Matt, "'New-Ancient Words': The Aura of Secrecy in the Zohar," in: P. Schäfer and J. Dan (eds.), *Gershom Scholem's "Major Trends in Jewish Mysticism": 50 Years After* (1994), 181–207; R. Meroz, "Zoharic Narratives and Their Adaptations," in: *Hispania Judaica*, 3 (2001), 3–63; idem, *Yuvalei Zohar: Li-She'elat Mekorotav shel ha-Zohar ve-Ofen Ḥibburo* (Heb., 2006); idem, "*Va-Ani lo Hayiti Sham?*" in: *Tarbiz*, 71 (2002), 163–94 (Heb.); I.M. Ta-Shma, *Ha-Nigleh she-ba-Nistar* (Heb., 2001²); I. Tishby (Heb. trans. and ed.), *The Wisdom of the Zohar: An Anthology of Texts*, tr. David Goldstein (1989); C. Mopsik, *Le Zohar*, vol. 1 (1981); vol. 2 (1984); vol. 3 (1991); vol. 4 (1996); *Le Zohar: Le Livre de Ruth* (1987); *Lamentations, traduction annotation et introduction* (2000); idem, "*The Body of Engenderment in the Hebrew Bible, the Rabbinic tradition and the Kabbalah*," in: *Fragments for a History of the Human Body* (1989), 48–73; H. Pedaya, *Ha-Mareh ve-ha-Dibbur, Sources and Studies in the Literature of Jewish Mysticism*, 8 (Heb., 2002); E. Wolfson, *Through a Speculum That Shines – Vision and Imagination in Medieval Jewish Mysticism* (1994); idem, *The Book of the Pomegranate, Moses De Leon's Sefer ha-Rimmon* (1988); idem, "Beautiful Maiden Without Eyes – Peshat and Sod in Zoharic Hermeneutics," in: M. Fishbane (ed.), *The Midrashic Imagination: Jewish Exegesis, Thought and History* (1993), 155–203; idem, "Hai Gaon's Letter and Commentary on Aleynu: Further Evidence of Moses de Leon's Pseudepigraphic Activity," in: JQR, 81 (1991), 365–410; idem, "Left Contained in Right: A Study in Zoharic Hermeneutics," in: AJS Review, 11 (1986), 27–52; idem, "Letter Symbolism and Merkavah Imagery in the Zohar," in: M. Hallamish (ed.), *Alei Shefer: Studies in the Literature of Jewish Thought Presented to Rabbi Dr. Alexandre Safran* (1990), 195–236 (English section); idem, "Forms of Visionary

Ascent as Ecstatic Experience in the Zoharic Literature," in: P. Schäfer and J. Dan (eds.), *Gershom Scholem's "Major Trends in Jewish Mysticism", 50 Years After* (1993), 209–35; O. Israeli, *Parshanut ha-Sod ve-Sod ha-Parshanut: Megamot Midrashiyyot ve-Hermanoitiyot be-'Saba de-Mishpatim' she-ba-Zohar, Sources and Studies in the Literature of Jewish Mysticism*, 17 (Heb., 2005).

ZOHAR, MIRIAM, Israeli actress. Born in Czernowitz, Romania, Miriam Zohar was in a concentration camp in the Ukraine during World War II. In 1948 she was among the "illegal" immigrants sent to Palestine on the *Pan York*, all of whose passengers were sent to Cyprus. There she began to perform in amateur theater. After arriving in Israel she worked in a Yiddish theater. From 1951, she appeared in *Habimah. In 1986 she co-starred with Lea *Konig in an acclaimed production of Jacob *Gordin's *Mirele Efros*. In 1987 she received the Israel Prize for theater, cinema, and television arts. In 2004 she starred in the film *The Schwartz Dynasty*.

ZOHAR, URI (1935–), Israeli actor, director, singer, comedian; one of the most colorful characters in the history of the Israeli entertainment industry. Until 1977, when he became an observant Jew, he was considered one of the doyens of Israel's entertainment family. Just one year earlier he had been the recipient of the country's most prestigious award, the Israel Prize, in recognition of his cinematic work. However, Zohar's career, which began in the mid-1950s, spanned broad artistic terrain.

Like many of his generation he started out as a member of an army entertainment troupe, teaming up with Chaim *Topol (later to become famous as Tevye in *Fiddler on the Roof*) in the Naḥal band. After completing their national service the two helped found the Baẓal Yarok ("Green Onion") musical-comedy team, which achieved considerable success in the late 1950s, releasing a string of hit songs such as *Adoni ha-Shofet* ("Your Honor") and *Venezuela*.

After Baẓal Yarok disbanded in 1960, Zohar's comedy career blossomed as he worked with top artists such as actor-comedian Shaike *Ofir and writer Ḥayyim *Hefer. He also began to break into radio, cinema, and later television. While at this stage Zohar was chiefly known as a comedian he also contributed to some serious ventures, such as Nathan Axelrod's 1962 film *Tree or Palestine*, which depicted life in pre-state Palestine from the 1930s up to the establishment of the State of Israel in 1948.

When Israeli television started in the late 1960s the charismatic Zohar was a natural choice as frontman for the *What's My Line* TV show, and he was a popular perennial presenter of the Miss Israel beauty contest. Today, Zohar is probably best known for his film directing, which began in 1965 with *Ḥor ba-Levanah* ("Hole in the Moon"), and took a big leap with a string of satirical-farcical efforts such as *Peeping Tom* (1972), *Big Eyes* (1974), and *Save the Lifesaver* (1977). In the early 1970s Zohar was a leading member of the group that put together the highly successful comic-musical *Lul* television series which has now achieved classic status. Iconic singer Arik *Einstein was among his co-stars in the series.

In 1977 Zohar quit the entertainment industry and moved to an ultra-Orthodox neighborhood in Jerusalem. At the time the Israeli public was shocked, considering the *enfant terrible* persona Zohar had cultivated over the years. His ties to Einstein, however, continued as his two eldest sons married two of Einstein's daughters.

[Barry Davis (2nd ed.)]

ZOHARY, MICHAEL (1898–1983), Israeli botanist. Zohary was born in Bobrka, E. Galicia, and went to Ereẓ Israel in 1920. He joined a team of research workers at the Hebrew University under Alexander *Eig. Zohary wrote *Olam ha-Ẓemaḥim* (1954), *Géobotanikah* (1955), and *Flora Palaestina* (2 vols., 1966). Together with Naomi Feinbrun, Zohary published the *Flora of the Land of Israel* (Heb. and Eng., 3 folios, 1945–55). His research covered a wide section of the Middle East and led to his publishing more than 100 papers and books on the flora of the area. In 1952 he was appointed professor of botany at the Hebrew University and in 1954 he was awarded the Israel Prize in Science.

°**ZOLA, ÉMILE** (1840–1902), French novelist and champion of Alfred *Dreyfus. In Zola's 20-volume *Rougon-Macquart* novel cycle (1871–93), a naturalistic portrayal of French social decay under the Second Empire of Napoleon III, there are Jewish characters who often appear in an unfavorable light. However, as with Gundermann in *L'argent* (1891), the Jewish financier invariably has equally unattractive gentile counterparts. Zola's humanitarian socialism, allied to a deep suspicion of clerical politics, determined his stand in the Dreyfus Affair. One of the earliest opponents of Édouard *Drumont, Zola wrote a series of essays defending the Jews, which were published in the daily *Le Figaro* (1896–97) and which stung antisemites to insinuate that his pen had been hired. "The Jews such as they are today are our work," Zola wrote, "the work of our 1,800 years of idiotic persecution" (*Nouvelle campagne*, 1897). He also contrasted the advanced Hebrew concept of the unity of mankind with the racist's primitive insistence on interracial conflict and hatred. Zola's involvement in the Dreyfus Affair reached a climax when he published an open letter to President Félix Faure on the front page of George Clemenceau's radical daily *L'Aurore*, headlined "*J'accuse…!*" (Jan. 13, 1898). He charged the French government and army with conspiring to suppress the true facts and with committing "high treason against humanity" by diverting popular anger from their own reactionary intrigues to the fabricated crime of a hapless, insignificant Jew. Zola's widely publicized accusation gave new heart to the supporters of Dreyfus and led to a prison sentence which the writer avoided by taking refuge in England. It also led many more to suspect that there had been a miscarriage of justice, and resulted in Dreyfus' retrial and eventual vindication.

Zola returned to the case in *L'affaire Dreyfus* (*Lettre à la jeunesse*, 1897; *La vérité en marche*, 1901), where he reiterated his belief in a conspiracy of army officers and clericalists aimed at overthrowing the Republic, and declared: "Truth is on the march; nothing can stop it now." His somewhat oversimplified approach to the problem of antisemitism – which would, he believed, vanish forever with the overthrow of ignorance and superstition – reappears in *Vérité*, the third part of his unfinished novel cycle, *Les Quatre Evangiles* (1899–1903). Here the anti-Dreyfusard thesis propounded by Maurice *Barrès is mercilessly lampooned. Anticipating the final outcome of the affair, which he was not destined to witness, Zola brings his fictionalized account of the case to a successful and morally satisfying conclusion with the vindication of his Jewish hero, Simon, a victim of the *blood libel, and the downfall of the reactionary intriguers.

Zola apparently intended to visit Palestine to gather material for a novel about Zionism, but his plan was never realized. His sudden death, resulting from carbon monoxide poisoning due to a blocked chimney, was allegedly contrived by a reactionary fanatic who gained access to the writer's apartment in the guise of a workman.

BIBLIOGRAPHY: *Le procès Zola*, 2 vols. (1898); M. Josephson, *Zola and his Time* (1928, 1929); J. Romains, *Zola et son exemple* (1935); J. Kaplan, *Témoignages sur Israël* (1949^2), index; H. Guillemin, *Zola, légende ou vérité* (1960); C. Lehrmann, *L'élément juif dans la littérature française*, 2 (1961), 86–89; R. Ternois, *Zola et son temps* (1961); A. Wilson, *Emile Zola, an Introductory Study* (1964^2); B. Dinur, *Ha-"Ani Ma'ashim" u-Mashma'uto ha-Historit* (1949).

ZOLA, GARY PHILLIP (1952–) U.S. Reform rabbi, historian, archivist. Zola was born in Chicago, Illinois, and received his B.A. from the University of Michigan (1973) and his M.A. from Northwestern University (1976). In 1982, he was ordained at *Hebrew Union College-Jewish Institute of Religion, where he earned his Ph.D. in 1991. Following ordination, he was appointed National Dean of Admissions, Student Affairs and Alumni Relations for HUC-JIR. In 1996, he was named executive director of The Jacob Rader *Marcus Center of the American Jewish Archives (AJA), the world's largest archival resource documenting the history of North American Jewry. He was also associate professor of the American Jewish Experience at HUC-JIR in Cincinnati and editor of *The American Jewish Archives Journal*. Under Zola's leadership, the physical home of the AJA tripled in size, making it the world's largest free-standing research institution dedicated solely to the study of the American Jewish experience. Dedicated in 2005, the AJA's Malloy Education Building, which houses electronic classrooms, distance learning centers, and public exhibition galleries, introduced new digital technologies to the field of historical research and archival science.

Zola is credited with initiating the 2004 national commemoration marking the 350th anniversary of the establishment of New Amsterdam's first Jewish community in 1654: he was the organizer of the congressionally recognized Commission for Commemorating 350 Years of American Jewish History, a consortium of research institutions representing a historic collaboration of the Library of Congress, the National Archives and Records Administration, the American Jewish Historical Society and the AJA. As commission chairman, Zola served as guest chaplain at the U.S. House of Representatives and the U.S. Senate. In September 2004, he participated in opening ceremonies for the Commission's historical exhibitions held at the Library of Congress and delivered the invocation at the commission's gala dinner in Washington, DC, where President George W. Bush delivered the keynote address.

Active in both national and local Jewish communal affairs, Zola served as president of the Greater Cincinnati Board of Rabbis (1993–94) and rabbinic consultant to the Ethics Committee of Cincinnati's Jewish Hospital (1993–), as well as on the boards of the Jewish Federation of Cincinnati and the Hillel Jewish Student Center. He was selected twice (1988, 1992) by the American Center for International Leadership to be one of two rabbinic delegates on the Religion Commission of the U.S.A./U.S.S.R. Emerging Leaders Summit. He was president of the Martin Luther King Coalition, and a member of the Boards of Trustees of the Cincinnati chapters of the American Jewish Committee and the Jewish Community Relations Council. He was the winner of the Cincinnati Jewish Federation's Rabbinic Leadership Award (2004) and the Rabbi Roland B. Gittelsohn Prize for most effective congregational project in social action.

A contributor to numerous academic journals, and a former member of the editorial board of the *Journal of Reform Judaism* (1985–1990), Zola wrote *Women Rabbis: Exploration and Celebration* (2004) and *Isaac Harby of Charleston* (1994). He also edited *The Dynamics of American Jewish History: Jacob Rader Marcus's Essays on American Jewry* (1996) and co-edited *A Place of Our Own: The Rise of Reform Jewish Camping in America* (2006).

[Bezalel Gordon (2nd ed.)]

ZÖLD, MÁRTON (1865–?), Austro-Hungarian general. Born in Hungary, Zöld passed out of the military academy in Budapest and was seconded to the infantry. In 1914 he commanded a battalion against Serbia and Montenegro, and was awarded a Hungarian knighthood for valor on the Russian front. In the same year he commanded a regiment on the Italian front. After the establishment of an independent Hungarian state, Zöld was made a full general. He was active in Jewish affairs.

ZOLF, Canadian family. FALEK ZOLF (1898–1961), teacher, author, and essayist, was born in Poland. From 1909 to the outbreak of war in 1914, he attended yeshivah in Poland. In 1916, to avoid compulsory military service, he became an "essential worker" at a Jewish-owned leather factory in Yaroslavl, Russia. With the Kerensky revolution he volunteered for the Russian Army, was sent to the Galician front, was captured by the Germans, and, in 1918, became a prisoner of war in East Prussia. Returning home after his release, he found his mother dead and his village of Zastavia caught up in the civil war that followed the Bolshevik Revolution. A dedicated Labor Zionist, in 1920 Zolf worked in the Jewish reconstruction in postwar Poland, assisted by the American Joint Distribution Committee, and became a teacher at a rebuilt school.

As life became more and more difficult under the antisemitic Polish regime, in 1926 Zolf decided to emigrate. He arrived in Canada in 1926 as a "farm worker" but soon became an itinerant *melammed* (teacher). After more than a year in Canada, he brought his family to Winnipeg, where he became a teacher and later principal of Winnipeg's I.L. Peretz Folk School. His part-fictional autobiography *Af Fremder Erd* (*On Foreign Soil*, 1945) was republished in English translation in 2003 with some Yiddish transliteration by Martin Green. Zolf also published *Undzer Kultur Hemshekh* (*Our Eternal Culture*, 1956), and contributed essays to the Yiddish press.

Falek Zolf's fourth child, LARRY (1934–), a reporter and producer, was born and brought up in Winnipeg's immigrant North End. Larry Zolf earned a B.A. at the University of Winnipeg, won scholarships, and completed an M.A. in history at the University of Toronto. He was with the Canadian Broadcasting Corporation's News and Current Affairs Department in Toronto from 1962. From 1964 to 1966 he worked on the innovative Canadian public affairs program, *This Hour Has Seven Days*, and teamed with Pierre Elliot Trudeau (before Trudeau entered parliament) to interview René Lévèsque, Quebec "Separatist" leader and founder of the Parti Québécois who led his party to power in Quebec in 1976. Zolf later wrote speeches for Prime Minister Trudeau. Zolf also produced an award-winning documentary on computers and published several books including *Dance of the Dialectic* (1973); *Just Watch Me: Remembering Pierre Trudeau* (1984); and *Scorpions for Sale* (1989), a fictional biography. He continued to write an on-line column for the CBC that mixed political commentary with personal reminiscences, often including references to his Jewish roots in the Winnipeg Jewish community, personalities in the community, community politics, and encounters with the non-Jewish world.

Larry Zolf's daughter, RACHEL ZOLF, is a poet whose works include *Her Absence, This Wanderer* (1999) and *Masque* (2004).

[Abraham Arnold (2nd ed.)]

ZOLLER (Zolli), ISRAEL (1881–1956), rabbi and apostate. Born in Brody, Galicia, Zoller spent a great part of his life in Italy. He was chief rabbi of Trieste after World War I, professor of Hebrew at the University of Padua from 1927 to 1938, and, from 1939, chief rabbi of Rome. At the beginning of September 1943, when the Germans entered Rome, he abandoned the community and took refuge in the Vatican. At the end of the hostilities he reappeared to assume his position as rabbi, but was rejected by the community because of his unworthy behavior at the time of the greatest danger. On Feb. 14, 1945, he converted to Catholicism, taking the name of Eugenio Maria (in homage to Pope Pius XII), and returned to the Vatican. In 1949 he was professor of Semitic epigraphy and Hebrew at the University of Rome. He was the author of a large number of works, especially of biblical interpretation, Jewish history, liturgy, and talmudic literature. Among his works are *Israele* ("Israel," 1935), *L'ebraismo* ("Judaism," 1953), and autobiographical reflections entitled *Before the Dawn* (1954). His translation of the tractate *Berakhot* was published by a Catholic publishing house (1968).

BIBLIOGRAPHY: L.I. Newman, *A "Chief Rabbi" of Rome Becomes a Catholic* (1945).

[Sergio DellaPergola]

ZOLLSCHAN, IGNAZ (1877–1948), Austrian anthropologist and physician. Zollschan, who was born in Erlach, Lower Austria, graduated as a doctor and while working in private practice in Carlsbad turned his interests to anthropology. To combat the antisemitic racist theories of Houston S. *Chamberlain, he published his *Das Rassenproblem unter besonderer Beruecksichtigung der theoretischen Grundlagen der juedischen Rassenfrage* (1910, 1925^5). As a Zionist he opposed Jewish Diaspora nationalism. In *Revision des juedischen Nationalismus* (1919) he attacked the Jewish demand for minority rights, and a revised edition of this work with a supplement, "*Der Weg zum Maximalismus*," appeared in the following year. In 1921 he analyzed the condition of Zionism in his *Krise und Sezessionsgefahr im Zionismus und deren Ursachen*. His interpretation of the Zionist problem stimulated the formulation of a current within German Zionism called Binyan ha-Areẓ.

Zollschan recognized the danger to world peace of Nazi racist theories as a tool of rabid nationalism and undertook a struggle to combat them. In 1933 he presented a plan to Thomas *Masaryk for the examination of the theoretical foundations of racialism which was taken up by the Prague Academy of Sciences. The academy submitted a proposal for an international conference on the subject to the leading international and national scientific bodies of the world, including those of the Vatican and the Ecumenical Council of the Protestant Churches. Dr. Beneš, then foreign minister of Czechoslovakia, submitted the plan to the Institute for Intellectual Cooperation of the League of Nations, but the appeasement policy of Great Britain obstructed the involvement of the institute. Zollschan continued his efforts, set up a Society for the Scientific Investigations of the Racial Question in 1937, and in the following year traveled widely throughout Europe to obtain support for his work. One instance of success was the preparation in May 1938 of a papal syllabus calling on all academies to pursue joint scientific research into racial ideologies. The collapse of the Czechoslovak Republic nullified the entire enterprise. Zollschan settled in London, where he published his *Racialism against Civilization* (1942).

[Ephraim Fischoff]

ZOLOCHEV (Pol. **Złow**), town in Lvov district, Ukraine; formerly in Galicia, Poland; between 1772 and 1919 under Austrian rule; ceded to Soviet Russia in 1945. At the end of the 16th century the key leasing enterprises there were in the hands of a Jewish contractor, Israel b. Joseph Eideles (see *Poland; *Arenda). A Jewish community was formed during the 17th century, and in 1716 was required to pay a poll tax of 350 zlotys, while the tax levied on the *Lvov community for the same year was raised to only 140 zlotys. The *Council of the Four Lands would sometimes convene there. The old synagogue of Zolochev was built in the second half of the 17th century. The *Maggid* Jehiel Michael of *Zloczow, an early leader of the Ḥasidim, preached there from 1770. Under Austrian rule the Jews of Zolochev engaged in considerable political activity; between 1891 and 1907. Zolochev, together with *Brody, returned Jewish deputies to the Austrian parliament: E. *Byk, and after his death Joseph Gold, a physician who officiated also as vice mayor of Zolochev. Both acted in conjunction with the other Polish deputies. From 1892 to 1907 there existed a Jewish school supported by the funds of Baron Maurice de *Hirsch. In 1907, 128 Jewish students attended the local secondary school (out of 500).

The Zolochev community numbered 1,150 in 1765; 5,401 (51.9% of the total population) in 1900; 5,744 in 1921; and 5,700 in 1931.

[*Encyclopaedia Hebraica*]

Holocaust Period

When World War II broke out, on Sept. 1, 1939, Jewish refugees from western Poland arrived, and the Jewish population of the town increased to 14,000. Under Soviet rule (1939–41) the Jewish communal bodies were disbanded and the activities of the Jewish political parties were forbidden. A number of the Jewish refugees were exiled to the Soviet interior in the summer of 1940. When the war broke out between Germany and the U.S.S.R. on June 22, 1941, groups of Jews attempted to cross over to the Soviet interior, but were turned back by Soviet patrols. German forces reached Zolochev on July 1. Two days later, in a pogrom perpetrated by Ukrainians, with the sanction of the German authorities, 3,500 Jews were killed in the city's fortress. A Judenrat was set up, headed by Dr. Maiblum, a former deputy mayor of Zolochev. In November 1941, 200 Jews were taken to the forced labor camp in Lackie Wielkie. In early 1942 Jews were sent to labor camps in Kozaki, Jaktorow, Plew, Zawarnice, and Sasov. Many inmates died in these camps from disease or injuries. After a *Selektion*, on Aug. 28, 1942, at the railroad station, 2,700 victims were sent to *Belzec extermination camp. On Nov. 2–3, 1942, in a second *Aktion*, 2,500 Jews were sent to Belzec; among the victims were Samuel Jacob *Imber, the poet. On December 1 a ghetto was set up to include Jews from towns in the vicinity of Zolochev – Olesk, Sasov, and Bialy Kamien. Hunger and disease decimated the inhabitants. Jewish doctors, notably Shelomo Jolek, battled against epidemics. On April 2, 1943, the ghetto was liquidated; the inmates were shot in Jelechowice. A small group of craftsmen, who were spared, organized two resistance units under Hillel Safran and F. Nachimowicz. The latter's group escaped to the forest but were betrayed by a Ukrainian peasant and wiped out after offering resistance. The leaders of the other unit were arrested in the ghetto and the members disbanded. Safran was shot when he attacked his German guard while being led to execution. On Aug. 23, 1943, the labor camps in the vicinity were liquidated. The inmates in Lackie Wielkie offered armed resistance. Soviet forces reentered Zolochev on July 13, 1944. The community was not reconstituted after the war.

[Aharon Weiss]

BIBLIOGRAPHY: S. Mayer, *Der Untergang fun Zloczow* (1947).

ZOLOTONOSHA, city in S.W. Poltava district, Ukraine. Jews began to settle in Zolotonosha at the beginning of the 19th century. In 1847 there were 1,001 Jews, and in 1897 there were 2,769 (about 32% of the population). In October 1905 pogroms broke out in the city, characterized by general looting and the destruction of all Jewish property. In 1926 there were 5,180 Jews in the city (32.5% of the total population). In 1939 they numbered 2,087. When the Germans invaded in September of 1941, they murdered 300 Jews from the surrounding area. Those who were unsuccessful in escaping the city were exterminated: Some 3,500 Jews from the city were executed in November.

[Yehuda Slutsky / Ruth Beloff (2nd ed.)]

ZOLTY, YAACOV BEZALEL (1920–1982), chief rabbi (Ashkenazi) of Jerusalem. Zolty was born in Stavitsk, district Lomza, Poland, and at the age of seven immigrated with his family to Ereẓ Israel where he studied at the Eẓ Ḥayyim and the Hebron yeshivot. In 1951 he was appointed a member of the District *bet din* of Tel Aviv, and the following year to the Jerusalem *bet din*. In 1956 he was appointed a member of the Supreme *bet din* of Israel.

An outstanding rabbinical scholar, Zolty served as head of the Bet ha-Talmud of Yad ha-Rav Maimon from 1966 to 1974 and later as the head of the Yad Aharon Yeshivah, and gave courses in the important yeshivot in Israel. His first published work, *Ginzei ha-Sifrei on* the *Sifrei, was published in 1948 and his responsa, *Mishneh Ya'avitz* on *Ḥoshen Mishpat* (1963) which gained him the Rabbi Kook Prize of the Municipality of Tel Aviv, was followed by a volume of the same name on the Laws appertaining to the Festivals in the *Oraḥ Ḥayyim* (1976).

In 1977 he was appointed chief rabbi (Ashkenazi) of Jerusalem, serving until his death.

ZOMBER, DOV BAER (**Bernhard**; 1821–1884), rabbinic scholar. Zomber was born in Lask, Poland, and studied under the rabbis Joske Spiro of Inowroclaw and Jacob Ettlinger, as well as at the university in Wuerzburg. After settling in Berlin, he taught Talmud there and maintained a boarding house for pupils. In 1871 he was appointed lecturer in Talmud at the *bet ha-midrash* in Berlin, where he served until his death.

He edited the *Shitah Mekubbeẓet* on tractate *Nedarim* (1860), and *Hilkhot Pesaḥim* of Isaac *Ibn Ghayyat with

Zomber's own commentary (1864). He wrote *Ma'amar al Perush Rashi le-ha-Massekhtot Nedarim u-Mo'ed Katan* (1867), a study on Rashi's commentaries on the treatises of *Nedarim* and *Mo'ed Katan*, and *Moreh Derekh* (1870), on Rabbenu Gershom's and Rashi's commentaries on tractate *Mo'ed Katan*. Against the latter Raphael Nathan Nata *Rabbinovicz wrote his *Kunteres Moreh ha-Moreh* (1871). Contributions of his were published in *Ha-Maggid* and in the *Magazin fuer die Wissenschaft des Judenthums*. His study on Judah ben Yakar, an early commentator on the Jerusalem Talmud, which appeared first in the *Monatsschrift fuer Geschichte und Wissenschaft des Judenthums* (1860), was subsequently printed in a Hebrew version with additions by the author in *Ha-Karmel* (1863).

BIBLIOGRAPHY: *Die juedische Presse*, 15 (1884), 236f.; Fuenn, Keneset, 187; P.Z. Gliksman, *Ir Lask va-Ḥakhameha* (1926), 76.

[Tovia Preschel]

ZONANA, wealthy and influential Jewish family in 18th-century *Istanbul. The family held the position of Ocak Bazergânı, the commercial and financial agent of the Janissary corps. It was involved in the administration of the Jewish community of Istanbul, and took part in the committees of deputies entrusted with the affairs of the Jewish communities of Ereẓ Israel. As prominent businessmen and financiers they supported a variety of religious and charitable causes, maintaining yeshivah studies in Istanbul and Ereẓ Israel and financing the printing of rabbinic treatises. The first member of the family to hold the position of Bazergân was DAVID ZONANA, who in 1722 was already portrayed as a prominent figure of Jewish Istanbul (in *Megilat Yuḥasin* by Meyuhas Behor Shemuel of Jerusalem, a guest in David's spacious seashore residence). By the time of the war of 1736–39 David was well established in his position, with considerable influence over promotions and the corps' diverse financial affairs. Later incidents suggest an even greater sphere of influence. When Seyyid Hasan Paşa, agha of the Janissaries since 1738, was appointed grand vizier in 1743, David continued to serve as his personal agent, thus attaining one of the highest ranks possible for Jews in the Ottoman state. When his patron was replaced in August 1746 by a member of a rival faction who also held a personal grudge against him, David was arrested and summarily executed. David's eldest son JACOB (d. 1764) succeeded to his position in the Janissary corps, and continued his activities in the Jewish sphere as a deputy for the Jewish community of Jerusalem. He used his influence in official Ottoman circles to protect, as well as control, the Jerusalem community, involving himself in its internal conflicts. Jacob secured the building (1754–5) of a hostel for Jewish pilgrims and travelers in *Jaffa, the main port of entry en route to Jerusalem, and used his business network to guarantee the transfer of funds designated for the Jerusalem community. SAMUEL HALEVI, son of David's sister, founded a yeshivah in *Hebron and hosted rabbi H.Y.D. *Azulai, the emissary of the Hebron community, during his stay in Istanbul (1757–58). He may have been the unidentified "Levi" who held the position of Bazergân together with Jakob. After 1768 (and until the demise of the Janissary corps in 1826) the position of Ocak Bazergânı was held by several generations of the *Adjiman family, which appears to have been closely related to the Zonanas.

BIBLIOGRAPHY: H. Uzunçarşili, *Kapukulu Ocakları* (1943), 1:407–8; A. Yaari, *Sheluḥei Ereẓ Yisrael* (1951), index; idem, *Ha-Defus ha-Ivri be-Kushta* (1967), index; J. Barnai, "*Ha-Yishuv ha-Yehudi be-Ereẓ Yisrael bein ha-Shanim 1740–1777 u-Kesharav im ha-Tefuẓot*" (Ph. D. diss., Jerusalem, 1975); R.W. Olson, in: JESHO, 20:2 (1977), 185–207; idem, in: JSS, 41:1 (1979), 75–88; J. Barnai, *The Jews in Palestine in the Eighteenth Century* (1992), index; E. Eldem, *French Trade in Istanbul in the Eighteenth Century* (1999), 48–56; Sh. Ecker, "The Paymaster of the Janissary Corps (Ocak Bâzergânı)" (M.A. diss., Tel Aviv, 2002); Y. Ben-Naeh, in: *Etmol*, 29:6 (2004), 28–29.

[Shuki (Yehoshua) Ecker (2nd ed.)]

ZONDEK, family of physicians. MAX ZONDEK (1868–1933), physician born in Wronke in the province of Posen who specialized in surgery and the study of renal diseases. In 1913 he was appointed titular professor of surgery in Berlin. He was the author of numerous publications on surgical subjects, among them *Die Topographie der Niere und ihre Bedeutung fuer die Nieren-Chirurgie* (1903); *Zur Chirurgie der Ureteren* (1905); and *Die chirurgischen Erkrankungen der Nieren und Harnleiter* (1924). His nephew, HERMANN ZONDEK (1887–1979), endocrinologist, was also born in Wronke. He served as assistant at the Charité Hospital in Berlin and later became associate professor at the Friedrich Wilhelm University of Berlin and director of the municipal hospital. He left Germany in 1933, spent a year in England, and then settled in Jerusalem, where he took charge of the internal medical division of Bikkur Ḥolim hospital and subsequently became professor of endocrinology at the Hebrew University.

Hermann was a pioneer in the study of the thyroid gland and disturbances arising from its dysfunction. He was the first to record the cardiac symptoms occurring as the result of thyroid insufficiency. He showed that administration of iodine normalizes the raised metabolism in hyperthyroidism and demonstrated that both thyroid hyper – and hypofunction may be of primary pituitary origin. He made studies on hormonal activity in general and evolved the theory that an endocrine disease may be a result of an abnormal reactivity of the peripheral tissues as well as of a primary endocrine malfunction (peripheral theory). He was the first to point out the inverse relationship between urinary nitrogen and sodium chloride excretion in certain renal disturbances. Zondek made several studies of the pituitary diencephalic system and its relation to certain ocular disturbances. He wrote books and articles on various aspects of endocrinology. His memoirs, *Auf festern Fusse*, appeared in 1982.

His brother, BERNHARD ZONDEK (1891–1966), endocrinologist and gynecologist, was also born in Wronke. He was an assistant in the Charité Hospital in the department of obstetrics and gynecology. He became associate professor at Berlin University and later head of the obstetrical and gynecological department of the municipal hospital in Berlin. When

Hitler rose to power, he left Germany for Palestine where he became professor of gynecology and obstetrics and head of the hormone research laboratory at the Hebrew University of Jerusalem. Bernhard is best known for the pregnancy test which he developed together with Selmar Aschheim in 1927. They demonstrated that the excretion of gonadotropin in the urine is a constant early symptom of pregnancy. His later investigations dealt with methods of preparing estrogenic and gonadotropic hormones, the effect of estrogen in castrates, the induction of uterine bleeding with progesterone, estrogenic substances in the Dead Sea, and hormonal treatments of various diseases. Zondek's contributions significantly advanced the knowledge of hormonal therapy. He was the author of many scientific publications and recipient of many honors. He was awarded the Israel Prize in 1958.

A third brother, SAMUEL GEORG ZONDEK (1894–1970), physician, was best known for his studies on electrolytes and therapy of heart diseases. He developed a theory concerning the relationship between the autonomous nervous system and the electrolytes. He called attention to the importance of potassium for the growth of cells and studied the causes of extra-renal uremia. Samuel Georg was born in Wronke, and in 1926 became associate professor at Berlin University. He left Germany with the rise of Hitler and became chief of the division of internal medicine at Hadassah Hospital, Tel Aviv. He was the author of numerous medical publications.

BIBLIOGRAPHY: S.R. Kagan, *Jews in Medicine* (1952), 279–80, 282–4, 341, 450.

[Suessmann Muntner]

°**ZOPYRION**, an author, otherwise unknown, appearing in a list of Greeks who wrote specifically about the Jews and attested to their antiquity. Josephus (Apion, 1:216) criticizes him for inaccuracy.

ZORACH, WILLIAM (1887–1966), U.S. sculptor and painter. Lithuanian-born William Zorach immigrated with his parents to the United States in 1891, settling in Ohio. Zorach only completed school up to the eighth grade, forced into working because of the family's impoverishment. He studied lithography in the evenings at the Cleveland School of Art in 1903 and soon thereafter he began earning a wage as a commercial lithographer. After he had saved some money, Zorach moved to New York City in 1907 where he received two years of additional training at the National Academy of Design. Again funded by money earned from his work as a lithographer, Zorach went to Paris to study art at La Palette in 1910. In Paris, Zorach met Marguerite Thompson, an American also studying at La Palette. Marguerite's influence, as well as the avant-garde atmosphere in France, effected Zorach's painting style, which became Fauvist in conception. His colorful paintings were first exhibited publicly at the Salon-d'Automne (1911). Financial circumstances forced Zorach back to Cleveland in late 1911, but by December 1912, he had earned enough money as a lithographer to return to New York, where he and Marguerite married. Zorach's paintings remained Fauvist-inspired until around 1916, at which time he adopted a Cubist idiom.

Zorach carved his first sculpture in 1917. He gave up painting entirely to focus on sculpture in 1922. Early sculptures were stylized and angular in conception, akin to the Cubist style of his canvases. Soon Zorach adopted the more rounded, simplified, classicized forms for which he is best known in directly carved works such as the 36-inch-tall mahogany *Mother and Child* (1922, Metropolitan Museum of Art, New York). His first solo exhibition of sculpture was held at the Kraushaar Galleries in New York (1924). Many of Zorach's sculptures, mostly carved out of wood and stone, focus on themes of family.

He executed several public commissions, including a monumental marble figure of Benjamin Franklin (1936–37) for the Benjamin Franklin Post Office in Washington, D.C., and a 16-foot-tall group sculpture, *Builders of the Future*, for the 1939 World's Fair. Upon request, Zorach submitted a design for a proposed memorial for the Jews who perished in the Holocaust. Although the memorial never materialized, a plaster model titled *Monument to Six Million Jews* (1949, Zorach family collection) survives. Designed to be viewed in the round, on one side of the tombstone shaped pedestal topped by a *menorah* stands a woman protecting her child and on the other side a man looking upward to heaven beseechingly.

In addition to his artistic production, Zorach wrote articles on art and two books: a primer on sculpture and his autobiography. He also taught at several institutions, including the Art Students League for 30 years beginning in 1929 and Columbia University (1932–35).

BIBLIOGRAPHY: P.S. Wingert, *The Sculpture of William Zorach* (1938); W. Zorach, *Zorach Explains Sculpture* (1947); J.I.H. Baur, *William Zorach* (1959); W. Zorach, *Art Is My Life* (1967).

[Samantha Baskind (2nd ed.)]

ẒORAH (Heb. צָרְעָה), Canaanite city mentioned in Tell-el-Amarna letter no. 273; later a Danite city mentioned with Eshtaol and Ir (Beth)-Shemesh in one of the city lists (Josh. 19:41). According to the later enumeration of the districts of Judah, Zorah passed to that region, where it was located in the northern district of the Shephelah (Josh. 15:33). The fame of Zorah derives from the story of *Samson. The Danite camp in which his father Manoah lived is defined as situated between Zorah and Eshtaol (Judg. 13:25); Manoah himself is described as a Zorite (Judg. 13:2). Samson was buried between Zorah and Eshtaol (Judg. 16:31). The 600 Danite warriors went forth from the same camp to search for living space for their tribe, hard pressed by the Amorites (Judg. 8:11). According to I Chronicles 2:53, 54, and 4:2, it was settled by families of Judah. It is listed with Aijalon among the fortifications of Rehoboam (II Chron. 11:20). It appears with Jarmuth in the list of places resettled by Jews returning from Babylonian exile (Neh. 11:29). In the Byzantine period, it belonged to Eleutheropolis (Onom. 156:15ff.). It is identified with the former Arab village of Ṣarʿa, situated on a dominating hill north of Beth-

Shemesh near the Jerusalem–Tel Aviv highway, about 15 mi. (25 km.) from Jerusalem.

[Michael Avi-Yonah]

Kibbutz Ẓorah in the Jerusalem Corridor west of Beth-Shemesh is affiliated with Iḥud ha-Kevuẓot ve-ha-Kibbutzim. It was founded in December 1948 by Israeli youth, who were later joined by settlers from South Africa. In 1970 Ẓorah had 431 inhabitants, more than doubling to 945 in the mid-1990s but then dropping to 701 in 2002. In addition to farming (field crops, plantations, turkey, and dairy cattle), the kibbutz manufactured mobility and rehabilitation aids for the handicapped and operated a furniture factory, winery, silk-screen printing studio, and guest house and youth hostel.

[Efraim Orni / Shaked Gilboa (2nd ed.)]

BIBLIOGRAPHY: Aharoni, Land, index; Avi-Yonah, Geog, index. **WEBSITE:** www.tzora.co.il.

ẒORAN (Heb. צוֹרָן), urban settlement in the Sharon region of central Israel. It received municipal council status in 1997. In 2002 its population was 5,660. In 2003 the municipality of Ẓoran was united with that of *Kadimah. Their combined population was 15,709 in 2004.

ZOREF, ABRAHAM SOLOMON ZALMAN (1785–1851), leading figure in the Ashkenazi community of Jerusalem. Born in Kaidan, Lithuania, Zoref set out for Ereẓ Israel with his wife and three sons in 1811. Traveling by way of Odessa and Constantinople, they arrived in Acre after a journey lasting more than five months. They settled in Safed where Zoref worked as a gold- and silversmith (whence his surname, which is Hebrew for silversmith). The outbreak of the plague in 1813 drove him to Jerusalem. There he became associated with *Menahem Mendel of Shklov in the leadership of the small Lithuanian community (*Kolel ha-Perushim*). From 1819 to 1823 and from 1829 to 1833 Zoref traveled in Europe as emissary for this *kolel*; on his second journey he acted on behalf of the Sephardim as well. When Ereẓ Israel came under Egyptian domination in 1831, he went to Cairo to obtain permission with the help of the Austrian and Russian consuls, to rebuild the Judah he-Ḥasid dwellings. The success of his mission, which contributed to the development of the Ashkenazi settlement in Jerusalem, earned Zoref the enmity of the Arabs, who made two attempts on his life, from the second of which he did not recover.

His sons MORDECAI, MOSES, and ISAAC, who adopted the surname Salomon, and his grandson Joel Moses ben Mordecai *Salomon, continued to work for the growth and consolidation of Jewish Jerusalem and Ereẓ Israel.

BIBLIOGRAPHY: Frumkin-Rivlin, 3 (1929), 147, 152, 156, 180, 259; I. Triwaks and E. Steinman, *Me'ah Shanah* (1938), 126–8; M. Solomon, *Sheloshah Dorot ba-Yishuv* (1939), 17–90; Yaari, Sheluḥei, 761–3, 774–7,781f.

[Avraham Yaari]

ZOREF, JOSHUA HESHEL BEN JOSEPH (1633–1700), Shabbatean prophet; the most important figure of the Shabbatean movement in Lithuania. Born in Vilna, he was a silversmith with a modest Jewish education who early inclined to an ascetic way of life. During the persecutions in the wake of the Polish-Swedish War he took refuge, around 1656, in Amsterdam, but returned later to Vilna where he started the study of moral and mystical writings, but remained without talmudic learning. During the messianic upheaval of 1666 he had visions which many compared with those of Ezekiel. He became the outstanding spokesman of the believers in *Shabbetai Ẓevi and persisted in his belief throughout his life. He continued his strictly ascetic behavior, and during several years was said to have never left his home except for the synagogue or the ritual bath. Shortly after 1666 he started to put down the revelations he received in five books, intended to correspond to the books of the Pentateuch. He assembled around him a circle of fervent followers who considered him an oracle, and played in this group a role very similar to that of the later ḥasidic *ẓaddikim*. Stories told about him already have a noticeably "ḥasidic" flavor. He used to make pronouncements not only about the messianic developments and the related mysteries but also concerning political events of his time, such as are recorded by Ẓevi Hirsch *Koidonover in *Kav ha-Yashar* (ch. 12: 1705). People flocked to Ẓoref from all over Poland to ask his advice or to strengthen their Shabbatean faith, He considered himself the Messiah ben Joseph, and Shabbetai Ẓevi the true Messiah, and saw his own role as revealer of the secrets of redemption between the first and the second coming of the Messiah. His written revelations center around the esoteric meanings of the *Shema Yisrael* and by the time of his death were said to have covered about 5,000 pages. Those parts which have survived show clearly that the book was completely built upon elaborate numerological speculations following the *Megalleh Amukkot* of Nathan Nata b. Solomon Spiro (*Spira). These speculations are essentially founded on the *gematriot* of Shabbetai Ẓevi and his own name Joshua (Yehoshua) Heshel (814 and 906), frequently alluding to the year 1666 (in *gematria* 426) as the beginning of redemption. Although the Shabbatean character of Ẓoref's revelations is clear, he did not divulge his faith except to the members of his intimate circle who had to take a formal vow to show discretion and dissimulation before unbelievers. He maintained, directly or through his confidants, a lively correspondence with Shabbateans in Italy and Turkey. A letter written by the Shabbatean leader Ḥayyim *Malakh in 1696, after some visits to Heshel Ẓoref, acknowledges his extreme ingenuity with numbers but expresses great reservations as to his kabbalistic initiation and his psychic powers. During the last years of his life, Ẓoref transferred to Cracow where he married (a second marriage?) the daughter of Jacob Eleazar Fischhof, one of the protectors of the ḥasidic group of *Judah Ḥasid and Ḥayyim Malakh. When this group prepared to journey to Jerusalem, Ẓoref participated in a meeting of its Shabbatean leaders in Nikolsburg toward the end of 1699. Ẓoref died in Cracow. His manuscripts were scattered. Some parts of the collection of his revelations, *Sefer ha-Ẓoref*, came into the hands of the kabbalist Nathan b. Levi, a member of the *Klaus* of *Brody who hid them; however, another part, including his writings from his last years, found its way to *Israel b. Eliezer Ba'al Shem Tov, the founder of Ḥasidism, who held these writings in high veneration without seemingly having been aware of their Shabbatean character. He frequently spoke in their praise, and the tradition of his pupils identified them with those of the mythical rabbi *Adam Ba'al Shem which his son was said to have given to the Ba'al Shem. Adam Ba'al Shem, a legendary figure of the 16th century, and Heshel Ẓoref in the generation preceding that of the Ba'al Shem, coalesced into one figure. Toward the end of his life the Ba'al Shem ordered a copy of the *Sefer ha-Ẓoref* to be made, but this order was executed only more than 20 years after his death. Copies of these copies have been preserved among the descendants of the ḥasidic rabbis Naḥum of *Chernobyl and *Levi Isaac of Berdichev. An attempt by the latter to have the book printed in Zholkva was foiled by Ephraim Zalman Margulies of Brody who recognized its Shabbatean character.

BIBLIOGRAPHY: G. Scholem, in: RHR, 143 (1953), 67–80; idem, *Kitvei Yad be-Kabbalah* (1930), 157f., 161f., 239f.; idem, in: *Zion*, 6 (1941), 89–93; 11 (1946), 170–2; W.Z. Rabinowitsch, *ibid.*, 5 (1940), 126–32;6 (1941), 80–84; Ch. Shmeruk, *ibid.*, 28 (1963), 86–105; A. Freimann, *Inyenei Shabbetai Ẓevi* (1912), 99–103.

[Gershom Scholem]

ZORN, JOHN (1953–), U.S. saxophonist, bandleader, composer, festival organizer, record label founder and owner. If any single figure can be credited with the revival and reinvention of Jewish-American musical culture in the last decades of the 20th century and first decade of the 21st, it would be the mercurial John Zorn. It may not have been Zorn who coined the term "Radical Jewish Culture" to describe the scintillating musical and theatrical hybrids that emerged in that period, but it was Zorn who shaped the constituent elements that became that reality. Zorn, who was born and raised in New York City, began as an avant-garde composer and alto sax player, influenced by such disparate figures as Karlheinz Stockhausen, Ornette Coleman, Ennio Morricone, and Warner Brothers cartoon composer Carl Stallings. His early work is a frequently abstract, almost antiseptic exploration of blocks of sound, focusing on the seams and unlikely swerves and turns between them. He was also fascinated with game theory and frequently applied it to group improvisation with uneven but fascinating results. He worked with a film-noir-influenced band, Naked City; wrote numerous soundtracks for independent films; issued numerous solo albums; and founded the Tzadik record label.

At some point in the late 1980s, Zorn became interested in exploring his Jewish identity, as his label name suggests. Starting with his 1990 album *Kristallnacht*, he began developing a new band, Masada, whose focus was on a specific set of the prolific composer's original compositions, most of them a flavorful blend of Blue Note hard-bop and Middle Eastern themes. The band's book became the basis not only for countless Masada recordings featuring Zorn's powerful alto but also for numerous spin-offs including a string quartet, an electric band, and a rock-inflected group. What Zorn had been attempting was nothing less than the creation of an entire body of new Jewish music for the new millennium.

To that end, he also encouraged many unlikely musicians from the worlds of avant-garde jazz, post-rock, and performance art to explore their own Jewishness on his record label, involving such luminaries as Steve Lacy, Borah Bergman, and Marty Ehrlich, and his own core of superb musical collaborators, including drummer Joey Baron, cellist Erik Friedlander, and pianists Anthony Coleman and Uri Caine among others. Zorn also promoted this new Jewish culture with a series of festivals, concerts and clubs (Tonic and his own The Stone chiefly) that moved the "downtown" scene gradually into the mainstream. Despite much acclaim and the growing success of his vision of Jewish music, Zorn remained a prickly figure, unwilling to speak to the press and intensely private.

BIBLIOGRAPHY: S. Hopkins, "John Zorn Primer," in: *The Wire* (Feb. 1997), at: www.thewire.co.uk; "John Zorn," in: Music-Web Encyclopaedia of Popular Music, at: www.musicweb.uk.net; S. Maykrantz, "John Zorn, a Biography and Discography," at: www.omnology.com/zorn.

[George Robinson (2nd ed.)]

ZRENJANIN (Hung. **Nagybecskerek**), city in the Banat, Vojvodina province, Serbia; formerly called Veliki Bečkerek and Petrovgrad. Zrenjanin was a regional agricultural and trading center. In the first part of the 18th century it was within the Austrian "military area" and thus inaccessible to Jews. The first mention of a Jewish presence there dates to 1760. A *ḥevra kaddisha* was created in 1764, and the community was officially founded in 1790. A Jewish school was built in 1816 and the following year a Jews' judge (*Judenrichter*), Adam Guttmann, was nominated. The first prayerhouse was erected in 1809, and another was built in 1895. The first rabbi was Rabbi Fein, who was followed by David Oppenheim and Maurice Klein. The last held office from 1880 to 1915 and became well known in all Hungarian-speaking communities for his translation of Maimonides' *Guide of the Perplexed* into Hungarian as *A tévelygök utmutatója* (4 vols., 1879–90). Jews traded mainly in hides, cattle, wine, and cereals.

During the Hungarian Revolution of 1848 about 25 Jews participated in the uprising, and the victorious Austrians imposed a collective fine on the community for alleged disloyalty: they had to provide 25,000 boots for the army. In the second half of the 19th century the community played an important role in the Danube basin, smaller communities gathering around it. Zrenjanin Jews gave aid to Belgrade Jews, who had suffered through shelling from the Turkish citadel in 1862 – 100 florins, which was half the sum donated by Budapest. By the turn of the century the community was well established and fairly prosperous. A new Hungarian-style synagogue was inaugurated in 1901 (it was completely demolished in 1941). The Zrenjanin Jewish community suffered during

World War I, but subsequently recovered, and by 1929 it numbered 400 families. Until the Holocaust it was active under rabbis Maurice Niedermann and David Finci, and President Leopold Fleischberger. There was a small Orthodox group. In November 1936 a German antisemitic paper, *Erwache* (a sort of imitation of *Der Stuermer*), was published. Its editor was brought to trial, but the court acquitted him. The community, numbering about 1,300, was almost annihilated by the Hungarians in 1941; the few survivors were deported to Auschwitz. The community was reestablished after the war and in the early 21st century hosted small-scale *Maccabiah Games for Vojvodina's Jews.

BIBLIOGRAPHY: AZDJ, 26:34 (1862); *Ben Chananja*, 5:29ff. (1862); D. Kaufmann, in: REJ, 4 (1882), 208–25; Fischer, in: *Jevrejski almanah* (1925/26), 285–302: Savez jevrejskih opština Jugaslavije, *Zločini fašistskih okupatora … u Jugoslaviji* (1952), 9–13; *Satellite Croatia 1941–1945* (1960), incl. bibl. **ADD. BIBLIOGRAPHY:** D. Colic, "Jevreji u razvoju privrede Banata," in: *Spomenica*, 4 (1979), 11–21; Z. Loker (ed.), *Yehudei Vojvodina be-Et he-Ḥadashah* (1994).

[Zvi Loker]

ZS (Zionist Socialists), Zionist-socialist party, mainly in Russia and Eastern Europe. At its third conference (Kharkov, May 15–20, 1920), the *Ẓe'irei Zion movement in Russia decided to become the Zionist Socialist Party – ZS (The letter "Z" in the shortened name of the party, which stands for the Hebrew or Yiddish word "Zionist," was particularly emphasized in order to distinguish it from the SS, a party called Sionistsko-Sotsialisticheskaya Rabochaya Partiya ("*Zionist-Socialist Workers' Party"), founded in 1904 as a Zionist party but transformed, without changing its name, to a *Territorialist, anti-Zionist party during the conflict over the *Uganda Scheme.) The rising wave of socialist ideas in Russia, as well as the creation of the socialist *Aḥdut ha-Avodah (A) party, in Ereẓ Israel in 1919, induced a decisive majority of this Ẓe'irei Zion conference to adopt the socialist creed and the new name; a "right-wing" minority split off and announced (August 1920) the continuation of the original Ẓe'irei Zion Popular Faction, which later formed the world union Hitaḥadut together with *Ha-Po'el ha-Ẓa'ir.

The ZS joined forces with Aḥdut ha-Avodah in Ereẓ Israel. Soon after the *Kharkov conference a convention of Ẓe'irei Zion in independent Poland decided to adopt a socialist program, and in 1921 Ẓe'irei Zion in independent Lithuania also accepted a socialist program and became ZS parties. The ZS Party in Russia emerged and lived under unique circumstances of revolutionary upheavals, repressions, and persecutions by the anti-Zionist Soviet regime, which was also extremely hostile to any non-Communist socialism. During the decline and disintegration of Jewish public life, especially of the Jewish socialist movements (which were gradually swallowed up in the ruling Communist Party), the burden of the fight for socialist Zionism, and to a great degree also for Zionism as such, was shouldered by the members of the young ZS Party.

ZS had to face not only the Bolshevik regime, the Communist Party, and the ruthless political police ("Cheka"), but also the most implacable of all enemies of Zionism and Jewish socialism, the *Yevsektsia (Jewish section of the Communist Party). In a life-and-death struggle, the ZS operated feverishly on many fronts: in the organization of the party itself, in Zionist activity, in *He-Ḥalutz, in the organization of self-defense against pogroms of counterrevolutionaries, in the youth movement Berit ha-No'ar ha-Ẓiyyoni ha-Soẓyalisti, in the trade unions, in producers', consumers', and credit cooperatives, in rendering productive Jews lacking occupational training and especially in agricultural training and in cultural activities directed toward *aliyah* to Ereẓ Israel. All this was undertaken in a spirit of devotion in the full knowledge that the fight was a losing battle. Arrests and deportations increased, but the ranks closed and activities expanded. ZS members leaped onto every available platform loudly declaring their party's demands – for the democratization of Soviet rule, for cultural-national autonomy, for the rehabilitation of Jewish economic life ruined in the civil war, for the right of *aliyah* to Ereẓ Israel – knowing that they would be arrested on the spot.

The Fourth Congress held in Leningrad in February 1924 decided to intensify activity and publish an illegal Russian-language newspaper (*Hagut ZS*). A climax was reached in August of the same year (on the eve of the Congress of National Minorities in the Ukraine), when the ZS distributed tens of thousands of leaflets denouncing the dictatorial and centralist regime, presenting the economic and cultural demands of the masses of the Jewish people in Russia, and calling for a Zionist-socialist solution to the Jewish problem in general. Both the contents of the leaflet and the manner in which it was distributed under the Cheka terror regime made a tremendous impression on Jews and non-Jews alike, but the party paid a heavy price for it; within a few days 3,000 ZS members and ZS youth had been arrested and sent to join the hundreds of their comrades who had already been jailed and deported to the far north of Russia. Lost leaders were replaced again and again in this emergency situation, but their activities were soon curtailed in turn. The rebellious party was increasingly besieged, and determined efforts were made to break and destroy it completely. Intervention from various quarters, especially from the wife of Maxim *Gorki, Yekaterina Peshkova, brought about the liberation of a certain number of prisoners and their *aliyah* to Ereẓ Israel. With the final establishment of a totalitarian dictatorship under *Stalin, ZS suffocated and disappeared. Only a few of its members survived the years of terror. Thousands died in the deportation camps, after enduring mental and physical torture. In other countries, notably Poland, the Baltic countries (Lithuania, Latvia, and Estonia), and Romania, ZS developed into a legitimate Zionist-socialist movement closely linked with the labor movement in Ereẓ Israel and with He-Ḥalutz, sponsoring pioneering *aliyah* and often taking part in local politics as a link between Zionists and the socialist parties of the respective countries.

BIBLIOGRAPHY: Y. Ereẓ (ed.), *Sefer ẓs* (1963); I. Ritov, *Perakim be-Toledot ẓẓ-ẓs* (1964); A. Rafaeli (Zenziper), *Pa'amei ha-Ge'ullah* (1951), index.

[Israel Ritov]

ZSIGMOND, EDE (1916–1944), Hungarian poet. He came from a Jewish proletarian family. In his poems he expressed his socialist outlook and mourned his deported parents. He perished in labor service at the battle front. A collection of his poems was published posthumously under the title *Elszàntan es szeliden* ("With Decision and with Softness," 1961).

ZSOLDOS (formerly **Stern**), **JENÖ** (1896–1972), Hungarian literary scholar and philologist. Born in Budapest, Zsoldos fought as an officer in the Austro-Hungarian army during World War I. In 1919 he became a teacher and, from 1940 until his retirement in 1965, was headmaster of the Jewish community's girls' high school in Budapest. For a time, he edited the Jewish newspaper *Zsidó Szemle* and, between 1936 and 1943, was editor of the eminent Jewish literary periodical *Libanon*. In his research into Hungarian literature and cultural history Zsoldos devoted himself to a painstaking analysis of the relationship between Hungarian and Jewish literature, laying particular stress on its social significance. In an original and varied style, Zsoldos discussed the relationship between Jews and Hungarians and the manner in which these are reflected in literature. His contribution to philology was also important, and for 30 years he contributed to the periodical *Magyar Nyelvőr*, also publishing Hungarian grammars.

Zsoldos' writings include *A felvilágosodás német zsidó irói és a magyar irodalom* ("German-Jewish Authors of the Haskalah Period and Hungarian Literature," 1934), *Magyar irodalom és zsidóság* ("Hungarian Literature and Judaism," 1943), *A héber mese jelentkezése a magyar irodalomban* ("The Appearance of the Jewish Folktale in Hungarian Literature," 1946), and *1848–49 a magyar zsidóság életében* ("1848–49, in the Life of Hungarian Jewry," 1948).

BIBLIOGRAPHY: *Magyar Zsidó Lexikon* (1929), 1024; *Magyar Irodalmi Lexikon*, 3 (1965), 611.

[Baruch Yaron]

ZSOLT, BÉLA (1895–1949), Hungarian novelist, poet, and journalist. Zsolt, who was born at Komárom, joined the editorial board of the radical Budapest newspaper *Világ* in 1921 and later worked for *Magyar Hírlap* and, from 1933, for *Újság*. In addition, he was editor in chief of the radical weekly *A Toll*. In his editorials, Zsolt subjected his press rivals to merciless attack, especially for their ignorance and corruption, their hatred of European culture and, above all, their virulent antisemitism. During the Nazi era he was sent to a labor camp in the Ukraine and when the Hungarian army chief ordered his release, the command was not obeyed. Finally, as a member of the *Kasztner Group, he was dispatched to Switzerland from Bergen-Belsen. After the war, Zsolt returned to Hungary, where he founded the radical weekly called *Haladás*. In the free elections of 1947, he was elected to parliament on the radical party list.

Zsolt made his name as a novelist and poet. His prose writing, though carelessly constructed, shows great talent for artistic and accurate description, and his bourgeois and petit bourgeois Jews are characters out of real life. Zsolt's attitude toward the Jewish bourgeoisie in his fiction contrasts with his defense of the Jews as a journalist. In his stories, he exposed their corruption and degeneration no less devotedly than he fought for their political and economic rights. Zsolt's verse includes the collection *Zsolt Béla verseskönyve* ("The Book of Poems by Béla Zsolt," 1915). Outstanding among his novels were *Házassággal végződik* (1926; *It Ends in Marriage*, 1931); *Gerson és neje* ("Gerson and his Wife," 1930), on the theme of mixed marriage; *Bellegarde* (1932); *Villámcsapás* ("Thunderbolt" 1937); and *Kakasviadal* ("Cockfight," 1939). He also wrote plays, including *Oktogon* (1932). *Kilenc Koffer* ("Nine Cases." 1947) was a book of memoirs and *Kőért kenyér* ("Bred for Stones," 1939), a collection of articles. Zsolt was continually preoccupied with the problem of the relationship between Jews and non-Jews. This reached a head in the novel *Kínos ügy* ("Distressing Affair," 1935), which showed his descriptive powers at their best. His ambivalence would seem to stem from his own unstable attitude to Judaism: he converted to Christianity, but later reverted to Judaism. Zsolt was the last chronicler of the Hungarian-Jewish assimilated bourgeoisie, and his precise descriptions perpetuated their memory.

BIBLIOGRAPHY: *Magyar Irodalmi Lexikon*, 3 (1965), 611–3.

[Baruch Yaron]

ZUCKER, DAVID (1947–), U.S. film producer. Born in Milwaukee, Wisc., Zucker studied film making at the University of Wisconsin. With a few borrowed video tape decks and an old film camera, Zucker and his brother, Jerry, and a friend, Jim Abrahams, formed Kentucky Fried Theater, a theatrical sketch group, in the back of a bookstore in Madison, Wisc. Moving to Los Angeles in 1972, they presented a satirical blend of videotaped, filmed and live sketches that in five years became the most successful small theater group there. In 1977 the team collaborated on their first feature film, *Kentucky Fried Movie*, essentially an extension of their sketches, and it became a financial success. Their next project created a new film genre. Conceived by David Zucker as a comedy without comedians, the film *Airplane!* featured dramatic actors performing zany dialogue with straight-laced sincerity. The spoof became a surprise hit of 1980, positioning the trio as kingpins of Hollywood comedy. They broke into television in 1982 with the series *Police Squad!*, which did for the detective drama what *Airplane!* did for its genre. Their streak of successful movies continued with the secret agent spoof *Top Secret!* (1984) and the biting farce *Ruthless People* (1986), which became one of the top-grossing films of the year. In 1988 David, on his own, directed *The Naked Gun*, based on *Police Squad!*, and it was a runaway hit. The 1991 follow-up, *Naked Gun 2½: The Smell of Fear*, surpassed the original at the box office. The final installment, *Naked Gun 33⅓*, which David produced, was also another box-office hit. David also co-produced several serious films, including *Phone Booth* (2001).

[Stewart Kampel (2nd ed.)]

ZUCKER, HENRY L. (1910–1998), U.S. community leader in welfare services. Born in Cleveland, Ohio, Zucker graduated from Western Reserve University. He began his career in social services as supervisor of public relations for the Cuyahoga County [Ohio] Relief Administration. He was a consultant for the American Jewish Joint Distribution Committee, helping to restore Jewish communal life in Europe after World War II. From 1936 to 1946, he served the Welfare Federation of Cleveland in several capacities. He was associate director of the Jewish Community Federation of Cleveland (1946–48) and later became its executive vice president, serving in that capacity until 1976. Zucker served as chairman of the advisory committee of the Hebrew Union College's School of Jewish Communal Services in Los Angeles, and was on the Board of Trustees of the United Appeal of Greater Cleveland and on several committees of the Welfare Federation of Cleveland. He held key positions in numerous Jewish and civic institutions. Under Zucker's professional leadership the Jewish Community Federation became one of the most comprehensively organized in the U.S., with the highest per capita donations to its Jewish Welfare Fund. He also established the Cleveland Welfare Endowment Fund, considered one of the largest of such funds in existence.

In 1991 Zucker received the Rosichan Retiree of the Year Award from the Association of Jewish Community Organization Professionals. The award is bestowed on a retired Jewish community organization professional who has had a distinguished career, has served as a role model and who, during retirement, continues to make a contribution to the field.

ZUCKER, JACQUES (né **Jakub Cuker**; 1900–1981), U.S. painter, illustrator, writer. Born in Radom, Poland, Zucker studied art in New York, but received most of his education at the Bezalel School of Art, Jerusalem, and the Académie de la Grande Chaumière and the Académie Colarossi in Paris. During WWI, Zucker fought for Palestine's liberation by enlisting in that country's Royal Fusillier's Jewish Brigade. By the 1920s Zucker had attained a reputation as an artist of landscapes, portraits, and figures. Some of his imagery possessed Jewish themes, such as *Synagogue of the Cabala*. The artist immigrated to the U.S. in 1922 to rejoin his family. Zucker traveled extensively: many of his images depict scenes or objects in Spain, Portugal, Egypt, Israel, and Poland. He divided his time between France and the U.S., and exhibited in both countries. In the U.S., Zucker's work was shown at the Art Institute of Chicago, the Brooklyn Museum of Art, the Metropolitan Museum of Art, New York, the Museum of Modern Art, New York, and the Whitney Museum. Zucker's style demonstrates myriad influences: the German and Austrian Expressionists, such as Oskar Kokoschka and Ludwig Kirchner; the landscapes of Chaim Soutine; and French painters such as Vuillard and Bonnard. Zucker's work is owned by many major museums, including the Jewish Museum, New York and the Israel Museum, Jerusalem. In 1969, the French art critic Claude Roger-Marx wrote a book titled *Jacques Zucker* devoted to the work of the eponymous artist.

BIBLIOGRAPHY: B.P. Solomon, "Portrait of a Lost Master: Film Brings Jacques Zucker to America," in: *The Forward* (Jan. 14, 1994).

[Nancy Buchwald (2nd ed.)]

ZUCKER, JEFF (1965–), U.S. television executive. Zucker, who was born in Miami, Fla., received a bachelor's degree from Harvard University in 1986 after serving as president of the school newspaper, the *Harvard Crimson*. At the *Crimson*, Zucker encouraged a decades-old rivalry with the *Harvard Lampoon*, led by Conan O'Brien, a future colleague. When Zucker failed to gain admission to Harvard Law, he was hired by the National Broadcasting Company to research material for its coverage of the 1988 Olympics in Seoul, South Korea. The following year Zucker became a producer for the highly rated *Today Show* and in 1992 became its executive producer. He introduced rock concerts on the shows and incorporated a mass live audience through a window on Rockefeller Plaza, from which the NBC Studios broadcast. In 2000, at the age of 35, he was named NBC's entertainment president and in 2003 was put in charge of the network's news and cable operations as well. Following a merger with Vivendi Universal, Zucker was promoted to president of its television group in 2004. The following year, Zucker was again promoted by NBC, to chief executive behind the chairman, Robert C. Wright.

[Stewart Kampel (2nd ed.)]

ZUCKER, MOSHE (1904–1987), rabbinic and Arabic scholar. Born in Kopeczowka (near Lutsk), Volhynia, Zucker studied at the Jewish Theological Seminary of *Vienna and the University of Vienna. In 1925 he was ordained as a rabbi, serving as a spiritual leader of a congregation in Vienna and also as a lecturer in the *Beit ha-Midrash* of Jellinek, as well as at the Rambam School. In 1938, with the *Anschluss*, Zucker immigrated to the United States. He served congregations in Brooklyn, New York and Bangor, Maine. In 1947 he began teaching at the Jewish Theological Seminary's Teachers Institute and in 1959 was appointed to the faculty of the rabbinical school of the seminary, where he became professor of Bible commentaries.

Zucker's main works include *Hassagot Rav Mevasser* (1955), an edition of a text by a contemporary of *Saadiah Gaon, based on a unique manuscript in the Firkovich collection in Leningrad, and *Al Targum Rav Sa'adyah la-Torah* (1959). In the latter work Zucker examines Saadiah's Arabic translation and studies on other matters, which are important for the geonic period. He discusses the problem of the *Baraita of the Thirty-two Rules*, ascribed to R. Eliezer b. Yose ha-Gelili, and showed that it is actually part of *Samuel b. Hophni's introduction to his Pentateuch commentary. Zucker also proved that the *Mishnat Rabbi Eliezer* (ed. by H. Enelow) is a late work, probably by a pupil of Saadiah Gaon. Another of his works is "*Keta'im Ḥadashim mi-Sefer ha-Mitzvot shel Ḥefeẓ b. Yaẓli'aḥ*" (PAAJR, 29 (1961), Heb. pt., 1–68). Zucker blended knowledge of the entire *genizah* material and of rabbinic literature. Familiar with the Arabic literature of the geonic period, he reproduced the details emerging from *genizah* studies and also interpreted them in the light of the Jewish and Arabic backgrounds of the period. He proved how deeply the *geonim* were rooted in the general trends of their time.

[David Weiss Halivni]

ZUCKERKANDL, EMIL (1849–1910), Austrian anatomist and physical anthropologist. Born in Raab (Györ), Hungary, Zuckerkandl was appointed assistant demonstrator at the Viennese anatomical institute of Karl von Langer in 1874. Langer charged him with the study of skulls brought back by the expedition around the world of the frigate *Novara* in 1857–59. The results, published in 1875, were a precise anatomical description and an assessment of the influence of various abnormalities in the form of the particular skulls, and their influence upon the racial character. His monograph *Zur Morphologie des Gesichtsschaedels* (1877) contained studies of the ratio between cranial and facial form, prognathism and opistognathism, and provided a summary of these problems among diverse races and comparable primates. After fulfilling appointments at the universities of Vienna and Utrecht, he became professor of anatomy at Graz in 1882. In that year he published "Ueber asymmetrische Kranien, welche ohne Nahtobliteration enstehen," demonstrating the frequency of this phenomenon and explaining its causes by the disproportion between the cranium of the foetus and the diameter of the mother's uterus. This paper was followed by several others, all appearing in *Mitteilungen der Anthropologischen Gesellchaft in Wien* (vols. 4 and 5). His epoch-making book *Normale und Pathologische Anatomie der Nasenhoehle und ihrer pneumatischen Anhaenge* (2 vols., 1882–92) entitles him to be regarded as the founder of modern rhinology.

In 1883 Zuckerkandl participated in the study of the ancient charnel houses in the Austrian Alps at Styria, Carinthia, and Carmola. The results, published in the journal of the Austrian Anthropological Society (1883–88), contributed much valuable information regarding cephalic forms in the area. In 1888 Zuckerkandl returned to Vienna to succeed Langer as professor of descriptive and topographic anatomy and occupied this post until his death. Known as an excellent teacher, he at various periods served as dean of the medical faculty at Vienna. Several anatomical entities discovered and described by him bear his name. His bust, placed in the assembly hall of the University of Vienna, was removed by the Nazis.

His younger brother, OTTO ZUCKERKANDL (1861–1921), was an eminent urologist and surgeon.

BIBLIOGRAPHY: J. Pagel, *Biographisches Lexikon der hervorragenden Aerzte des neunzehnten Jahrhunderts* (1901), 1907–08; C. Toldt, in: *Mitteilungen der Anthropologischen Gesellschaft in Wien*, 41 (1911), 154–6: J. Tandler, in: *Anatomischer Anzeiger*, 37 (1910), 86–96; *Wiener Klinische Wochenschrift*, 23 (1910), 798–800; S.R. Kagan, *Jewish Medicine* (1952), 151, 446.

[Ellen Friedman]

ZUCKERMAN, BARUCH (1887–1970), Labor Zionist leader. Zuckerman was born in Kurenetz, Russia. Steeped in Jewish tradition, he was early drawn to Zionism. Upon his arrival in the United States in 1903 he quickly involved himself in the development of the Labor Zionist movement in that country, becoming one of the founders of the U.S. Po'alei Zion party. When the movement split into territorialist and Palestine-centered factions after the Uganda offer, he went over to the Socialist-Territorialists in 1905, rejoining the Po'alei Zion in 1910. Zuckerman's role in the Labor Zionist movement in the United States was both that of major exponent and of formulator of policy. By virtue of his varied activities as editor, journalist, speaker, and holder of high office in the movement, he became one of the chief spokesmen of the U.S. Po'alei Zion throughout the world. He was a trusted representative of the people in the large Yiddish-speaking sector of the Jewish community. Zuckerman's influence was not confined to his party activities. He played a significant part in the foundation of the People's Relief Committee, serving as its executive director from 1915 to 1924. He was also among the founders and promoters of Farband, the Labor Zionist fraternal order; the Jewish Legion of World War I; the American Jewish Congress; and the Histadrut Campaign.

Zuckerman served as one of the chief representatives of the Labor Zionist movement in the World Organization. A member of the Actions Committee, he was elected to the executive of the Jewish Agency, and was head of its Latin American and Organization Departments from 1948 to 1956. He settled in Israel in 1956 and continued his activities, mainly literary, until his death. In addition to a prolific output of articles and pamphlets, he wrote several volumes of personal memoirs which provide a rich source of historic material for the development of Jewish life and Zionism during the period they cover, among them *Oyfen Veg* (1956) and *Zikhroynes* (1962). Many of his shorter pieces were collected in *Essayen un Profilen* (1967).

[Marie Syrkin]

ZUCKERMAN, BEN (1890–1979), U.S. apparel manufacturer. Zuckerman, who became known as "the dean of the American ready-to-wear coat and suit industry," was a master tailor who never learned how to sew. "You can teach a bear how to dance," he once said. "I can teach a tailor how to work." Zuckerman was born in Romania, one of 13 children. He was a child when his parents brought the family to the U.S. and settled in New Jersey. His formal education ended when he was 15. His first job was sweeping floors in a dress factory for $3 a week. Subsequently, he learned to be an apparel cutter and in 1911 went into business with Joseph Hoffman. Zuckerman & Hoffman made expensive coats and suits. In the late 1920s, the business was dissolved and Zuckerman launched another firm with Morris Kraus. That company liquidated in 1949 and Zuckerman spent the next year traveling through Europe and the U.S. He returned to New York and in 1950, opened Ben Zuckerman, Inc., and presented his first collection. It was designed by Harry Schacter, who would remain with Zuckerman for decades and who eventually added dresses and ensembles to the line. In 1951, Zuckerman won a Neiman Marcus Award for Distinguished Service in the Field of Fashion. In 1952 and 1956 he was presented with Coty American Fashion Critics Awards and in 1961 was inducted into the Coty Hall of Fame. He retired in 1968, but remained connected to the industry, becoming a charter member of the Council of Fashion Designers of America in 1973.

A prominent figure in New York City's garment business for almost 60 years, Zuckerman was known for making clothes in the U.S. that were said to have the look, the feel, and the fit of Paris originals. His coats and suits became popular with numerous prominent women, including Jacqueline Kennedy when she was still First Lady, and his skills at cutting and draping fabric became legendary.

BIBLIOGRAPHY: *New York Times* (June 10, 1961), 11.

[Mort Sheinman (2nd ed.)]

ZUCKERMAN (Cukierman), ITZHAK (Antek; 1915–1981), Warsaw ghetto fighter. Born in Vilna to a traditional Jewish family, he became one of the four commanders of the Jewish Fighting Organization (ZOB) that organized armed resistance to the Nazis in the Warsaw Ghetto. He was educated at Hebrew High School in Vilna and joined *He-Ḥalutz and moved to Warsaw as part of the youth movement. When He-Ḥalutz combined with Dror he became one of two general secretaries organizing the movement throughout Poland. When the war began he escaped eastward to Soviet-occupied Poland and organized underground branches of Dror. In 1940 he returned to German-occupied Poland and became a leader in Warsaw and from there traveled clandestinely to other ghettos, organizing the movement for agricultural training and Zionist education. He met and fell in love with Ẓivia *Lubetkin, a fellow Zionist underground leader. They later married. After word of the Einsatzgurppen activities reached Warsaw, he foresaw that all educational and cultural activities would have to be linked to armed resistance. During the great deportation that commenced on July 23, 1942, and sent 265,000 Jews to the Treblinka death camp in less than 60 days, Zuckerman pressed for active resistance, but his position was rejected at that time. When the ZOB was formed on July 28, 1942, he became part of staff headquarters. He was sent on a secret mission to Cracow to discuss resistance activities and was wounded there in December 1942. Returning to Warsaw with great difficulty, he participated in the preparations for armed resistance and was part of the group that fought the Germans during the January 18, 1943, deportations. He then became commander of one of the three fighting sectors. Because he looked like a Pole and spoke the language without an accent, he was sent out of the ghetto to obtain arms for the ghetto underground from Polish army organizations; he met with rebuttals. When the Uprising broke out on April 19, 1943, Zuckerman was on the Aryan side of the wall. He wanted to return but he received a formal note from ZOB commander Mordecai *Anielewicz and a "very aggressive one" from his wife: "You haven't done a thing so far. Nothing." They were desperate for arms. He returned anyway and helped assist fighters escaping the burning ghetto move through the sewers of Warsaw, which he knew well from his smuggling activities. After the Ghetto Uprising, he also helped organize a Jewish underground among Jews in hiding on the "Aryan" side, the Jewish National Council (Żydowski Komitet Narodowy). The committee distributed information and pamphlets dealing with the situation of the Jewish-led struggle against the Nazis, e.g., known as *Kol mi-Ma'amakim*, which appeared on Aug. 22, 1944. He wrote reports on the activities of the ZOB that were transmitted to the Polish government-in-exile. During the Warsaw Polish Uprising, the fighting of non-Jews in August 1944, Zuckerman commanded a group of fighters, the remnants of the ZOB. Liberated by the Russians in January 1945, he devoted himself to the restoration of the He-Ḥalutz movement and *Beriḥah, the mass movement of East European Jews into Western and Southern Europe on their way to Palestine. He arrived in Palestine in 1947 and was one of the founders of kibbutz Loḥamei ha-Getta'ot. In 1961 served as a prosecution witness at the *Eichmann trial in Jerusalem, where he read from the final correspondence he received from Mordecai Anielewicz. Zuckerman was also one of the founding directorate of the *Ghetto Fighters' House and was editor of its publications. During the 1950s and 1960s as the status of the Warsaw Ghetto Resistance fighters provided the first generation of Israelis with a proud history of the Shoah, Zuckerman's moral voice was often heard. He was interviewed by Claude *Lanzmann in the film *Shoah*, in which he described the aftermath in rather non-heroic terms. "I began drinking after the war. It was very difficult… If you could lick my heart it would poison you." His autobiography, published first in Hebrew and expertly translated into English, ranks together with Czerniakow's Diary and the Ringelblum documents as an indispensable means for understanding the situation of Warsaw's Jews. Aptly titled *A Surplus of Memory*, it is indeed a full, unexpurgated recitation of his memories from that period.

BIBLIOGRAPHY: N. Blumental and J. Kermish, *Ha-Meri ve-ha-Mered be-Geto Varsha* (1965), index; Z. Popkin, in: *Commentary*, 13 (1952), 34–37.

[B. Mordechai Ansbacher / Michael Berenbaum (2nd ed.)]

ZUCKERMAN, MORTIMER (1937–), U.S. developer, publisher. Born in Quebec, Canada, Mortimer Benjamin Zuckerman earned law degrees from McGill University in Montreal and Harvard University and a master of business administration degree from the Wharton School of Business at the University of Pennsylvania. He worked at the Department of Housing and Urban Development before joining the old-line Boston firm of Cabot, Cabot & Forbes, where he revamped the firm's ailing California properties and assembled prime downtown Boston real estate, rising to a senior financial position at the firm. But Zuckerman found the atmosphere too stuffy and left, along with an associate, Edward H. Linde. The California properties became part of their severance package, and they gave Boston Properties, their new venture in 1970, the starting cash flow. Zuckerman also received $4 million from Cabot after a court suit. Boston Properties became active in real estate and developed more than 50 buildings. Zuckerman became a United States citizen in 1977. Three years later he bought *The Atlantic Monthly* magazine, called the spine of Boston's literary community, paying a reported $3.2 million for a faltering magazine with a splendid piece of real estate near the Public Garden. In 1981 Boston Properties shifted its focus to Washington, DC, and built more than 15 buildings, including the Democracy Project, an office complex in nearby Montgomery County, Md., in which Zuckerman's friend, Martin Peretz, publisher of *The New Republic*, and members of the Bronfman family had an interest. Boston Properties also constructed new headquarters for the magazine *U.S. News and World Report*, and in 1984 acquired the nationally distributed newsweekly, the third largest in the country, and half of its real estate. Although he had an editor, Zuckerman, as publisher, decided to write a weekly column for the magazine, showing a strong pro-Israel stance. In 1992, Zuckerman bought *The New York Daily News*, once the newspaper with the largest circulation in the country but a periodical that had seen a fall in advertising and circulation as the city's economy and demographics changed. Zuckerman cut costs at the newspaper, laying off staff members and frequently changing editors. At the same time Boston Properties won the sweepstakes to build one of the most coveted pieces of real estate in Manhattan, the Coliseum site at Columbus Circle, which eventually became headquarters for Time Warner. Zuckerman used his position as publisher of *The Atlantic Monthly, U.S. News*, and *The Daily News* to promote his views on the Middle East. After buying *The Atlantic*, he issued a ban on articles, that, in his estimation, "challenged Israel's right to exist." In *U.S. News*, he chastised the press for bias against Israel in the 2000 Al Aqsa/Temple Mount incident that triggered the second intifada, although his version of the events were later found to be incorrect. Zuckerman was friendly with many governmental officials and key journalists, including A.M. *Rosenthal, who published a profile of Zuckerman when he was executive editor of *The New York Times* but then printed an Editor's Note apologizing for aspersions made in the article about Zuckerman's character and ambitions. Later, after Rosenthal left *The Times*, he wrote his frequently pro-Israel column for *The Daily News*. Zuckerman was active in many Jewish organizations and served as honorary president of the American-Israel Friendship League. He was honored by the American Jewish Committee and the Jewish National Fund, among other organizations. In 2001 Zuckerman became chairman of the Conference of Presidents of Major American Jewish Organizations, an amalgam of 54 groups, becoming one of the foremost spokesmen for Jewish causes.

[Stewart Kampel (2nd ed.)]

ZUCKERMAN, PAUL (1912–1986), U.S. communal worker. Zuckerman was born in Istanbul, Turkey, and was brought to the United States at the age of two. He lived in Detroit where he was chairman and president of a corporation which manufactured and imported food products. President Johnson named him head of the U.S. Food for Peace Committee in Michigan. He gave outstanding service to the Jewish community, both in Detroit and nationally, serving as a director of Sinai Hospital, National American ORT, and the Jewish Community Center in Detroit. He gave the Paul and Helen Zuckerman Auditorium and Conference Center to Detroit's Sinai Hospital and provided the West Bloomfield Township Library with its site.

He was president of the United Jewish Appeal of the United States from 1974 to 1977 and was a member of the Executive of the Jewish Agency and of the Board of Governors of Ben-Gurion University from 1976.

[Frederick R. Lachman (2nd ed.)]

ZUCKERMAN, SOLLY, LORD (1904–1993), British anatomist. Born in Cape Town, South Africa, Zuckerman settled in England, where he first taught at London University (1928–32). As research anatomist to the Zoological Society of London, he studied the behavior of primates, this interest having been stimulated by earlier observations on wild baboons in South Africa. He described his researches in *The Social Life of Monkeys and Apes* (1932). As a research associate at Yale University (1933–34), he extended his primate studies and in *Functional Affinities of Man, Monkeys, and Apes* (1933) dealt with the behavior, comparative physiology, and reproductive patterns of the primates. Zuckerman taught anatomy at Oxford (1934–45) and became Hunterian professor at the Royal College of Surgeons in 1937, also lecturing on anatomy at the University of Birmingham from 1939. During World War II he was scientific adviser to the British armed forces. After the war Zuckerman became increasingly involved in problems of British government policy related to science. He was chairman of the Defense Research Policy Committee (1960–64) and chairman of the Committee on Scientific Manpower (1950–64). From 1966 to 1971 he was chief scientific adviser to the British government. His book *Scientists and War* (1966) dealt with the relation of science to military affairs and social policy. He also wrote *A New System of Anatomy* (1961) and *The Image of Technology* (1968). He was elected a Fellow of the Royal Society in 1943. Zuckerman was knighted in 1956, was awarded the Order of Merit (in 1968), the French Legion of Honor, and the U.S. Medal of Freedom, and received a life peerage in 1971. He married the daughter of the second marquess of *Reading and was a governor of the Weizmann Institute, Rehovot.

[Mordecai L. Gabriel]

ZUCKERMANDEL, MOSES SAMUEL (1836–1917), rabbi and researcher in tannaitic literature. Born in Ungarisch-Brod (Uhersky Brod), Moravia, Zuckermandel studied under Samson Raphael *Hirsch at Nikolsburg (Mikulov) and later at the rabbinical seminary (see *Juedisch-Theologisches Seminar) and the University of Breslau. From 1864 to 1897 he was a rabbi of various congregations, and from 1898 he served as rabbi at the Mora-Leipziger Foundation in Breslau. His life work was the scientific edition of the *Tosefta (according to the Mss. of Erfurt and Vienna (third part), and printed texts, 881–82, second ed. with supplement by S. Lieberman (1937), reprinted with additions (1970)) which, despite its deficiencies, represented a great advance in its time. Zuckermandel was of the opinion that the Tosefta was in fact only a remnant of a great Palestinian *Mishnah (to which the Palestinian *amoraim* resorted) that had remained after the Babylonian **amoraim* had removed part of it, adapted it, and called it the Mishnah. This was rightly rejected by A. *Schwarz and others.

His writings include *Die Erfurter Handschrift de-Tossefta* (1876); *Spruchbuch* (vols. 1–2, 1889–90); *Tosefta, Mischna, und Boraitha* (vols. 1–2, and supplement, 1908–10); *Gesammelte Aufsaetze* (vols. 1–2, 1911–13); and *Festpredigten* (vols. 1–2, 1915). In 1915 his autobiography *Mein Lebenslauf* appeared.

BIBLIOGRAPHY: M. Brann, *Geschichte des juedisch-theologischen Seminars (Fraenckelsche Stiftung) in Breslau* (1904), 204.

[Moshe David Herr]

ZUCKERMANN, BENEDICT (1818–1891), mathematician, librarian, and historian. Born in Breslau, Zuckermann received an education that embraced mathematics and related subjects. After being awarded a doctoral degree at the University of Kiel, Zuckermann returned to Breslau, where he was appointed to the faculty of the newly established Jewish Theological Seminary, headed by Zacharias Frankel, as instructor in mathematics and the natural sciences. In 1857 he was also entrusted with the administration of the Seminary library. Throughout his life he was strictly observant in his religious practice. An authority on the science of the calendar, about which he taught and wrote, Zuckermann was interested in the mathematics of the Talmud and clarified difficult passages.

His article on the complicated law in *Kilayim* 5:5, which appeared with accompanying diagrams in MGWJ (4 (1855), 146–56), shows his erudition in this field. He also specialized in the history of weights and measures of the Talmud; an article on this theme appeared in MGWJ (13 (1864), 295–306, 334–49, 373–84). Several of his papers were printed in the reports published yearly by the Seminary. Among his works are *Ueber talmudische Muenzen und Gewichte* (1862), *Das Mathematische im Talmud* (1878), and *Ueber Sabbathjahrcyclus und Jubelperiode* (1857; Eng. tr. by A. Loewy, 1866).

BIBLIOGRAPHY: M. Brann, *Geschichte des juedisch-theologischen Seminars…* (1904), 84–86, 128 (with list of his works); G. Kisch (ed.), *Das Breslauer Seminar* (1963), 323.

[Alexander Tobias / Andreas Brämer (2nd ed.)]

ZUCKERMANN, ELIEZER (1852–1887), pioneer Jewish socialist in Russia. Zuckermann came from a wealthy family of good lineage in Mogilev. When still a youth, he voluntarily taught needy children at the local *talmud torah* and began to contribute to the Hebrew periodicals, **Ha-Meliẓ* and **Ha-Maggid*. Influenced by Pavel *Axelrod, he became a socialist. In 1874 Zuckermann reached Vienna where he worked for a time in the printing press of **Ha-Shaḥar*, which published his stories; he later stayed in a Russian-Jewish youth commune in Berlin. In 1877 he assisted A.S. *Liebermann in publishing **Ha-Emet*. Zuckermann probably drafted the Russian manifesto issued by the Group of Jewish Socialists (Geneva, June 1880), calling upon Jewish Socialists to draw closer the Jewish masses and to propagate socialism in Yiddish. In the fall of 1879 he worked in St. Petersburg for the underground organ of the revolutionary organization *Narodnaya Volya*, but was arrested the following January and imprisoned in the fortress of Petropavlovsk. He was eventually sentenced to eight years' imprisonment and exile. After five years in a Siberian prison, Zuckermann was exiled to a remote village in the Yakutsk region, where he drowned himself.

BIBLIOGRAPHY: E. Zuckermann, *Kitvei* (1940), incl. bibl.; Z. Kroll, *ibid*, 7–54; Deutsch, in: *Zukunft* (1916), 240–5.

[Yehuda Slutsky]

ZUCKERMANN, HUGO (1881–1914), Austrian translator and poet. Zuckermann was born into an assimilated Jewish family in Eger (Cheb), Bohemia. Austrian antisemitism and the emergence of the Zionist movement led him to rediscover his Jewish heritage. Turning to Jewish literature, Zuckermann translated the Song of Songs and works by leading Yiddish writers, notably *Peretz's dramas. After the death of Theodor Herzl, he founded a Jewish student society in his honor and became an active Zionist. Zuckermann also worked to establish a Jewish theater in Vienna. A lieutenant in World War I, Zuckermann regarded his part in the war as revenge for the *Kishinev Pogrom. He was one of the first Austrian casualties on the Eastern front. His *Gedichte*, a slender volume of lyrics, appeared in 1915 (ed. by C. Abeles with a biographical sketch on pp. 7–12). It included the most popular of his war poems, "Das Reiterlied," written in the form of a folksong and expressing readiness to die for the national cause. It has often been reprinted in German anthologies.

BIBLIOGRAPHY: A. Friedmann, *Hugo Zuckermann* (1915).

ZUCKMAYER, CARL (1896–1977), German playwright. Though born of a Jewish mother, Zuckmayer was raised as a Catholic in the Rhineland town of Nackenheim. During World War I he served as an officer on the Western Front and from 1919 worked in the theater and as a freelance writer. In 1924 he joined Bertolt Brecht at Berlin's Deutsches Theater, working for a short time under Max *Reinhardt. Zuckmayer's first success was the prizewinning comedy *Der froehliche Weinberg* (1925), which established the new "matter-of-fact" trend. His reputation was enhanced by the many dramas that followed, notably *Schinderhannes* (1927); *Katharina Knie* (1929); *Der Hauptmann von Koepenick* (1930; *The Captain of Koepenick*, 1932), a powerful satirical attack on Prussian militarism and bureaucracy; and *Der Schelm von Bergen* (1934). Zuckmayer also wrote the screenplay for *Der blaue Engel* ("The Blue Angel", 1930), which was based on Heinrich Mann's novel *Professor Unrat* (1905). Like many other leading anti-Nazi writers, Zuckmayer found his life and career endangered after Hitler came to power and he fled to Switzerland in 1938, emigrating to the U.S. in the following year. From Hollywood he moved to New York, and then spent the war years farming and writing in Vermont. In 1947 he became a cultural adviser to the U.S. Army in Germany and Austria, finally settling in Switzerland in 1958. After World War II he produced an international success with *Des Teufels General* (1946; *The Devil's General*, 1950), the tragic story of an anti-Nazi air force chief. Zuckmayer was much preoccupied with the fate of German Jewry, Jewish characters appearing in several of his dramas, including *Der Hauptmann von Koepenick, Des Teufels General, Der Gesang im Feuerofen* (1950), and *Das kalte Licht* (1955).

His verse collections include *Der Baum* (1926) and *Gedichte* (1960); his novels *Salwàre oder Die Magdalena von Bozen* (1936; *The Moons Ride Over*, 1937) and *Herr ueber Leben und Tod* (1938). Zuckmayer also wrote novellas and short stories, such as *Ein Sommer in Oesterreich* (1937); and two volumes of autobiography, *Second Wind* (1940) and *Als waer's ein Stueck von mir* (1966; *A Part of Myself*, 1970). Four volumes of his collected works appeared in 1960.

BIBLIOGRAPHY: *Fuelle der Zeit. Carl Zuckmayer und sein Werk* (1956), incl. bibl.; I. Engelsing-Malek, *"Amor Fati" in Zuckmayers Dramen* (University of California, Publications in Modern Philology, 61 (1960), incl. bibl.); L.E. Reindl, *Zuckmayer. Eine Bildbiographie* (1962).

[Godfrey Edmond Silverman]

ZUCROW, MAURICE JOSEPH (1899–1975), U.S. aeronautical engineer. Zucrow was born in Kiev and taken to the U.S. in 1914. He became professor of gas turbines and jet propulsion at Purdue University in 1946. Zucrow was a member of several advisory committees on rocket engines and propulsion systems of the National Advisory Committee on Aeronautics, and of the National Aeronautics and Space Administration. He wrote *Principles of Jet Propulsion and Gas Turbines* (1948) and *Aircraft and Missile Propulsion* (2 vols., 1958).

[Samuel Aaron Miller]

ZUELZ (Pol. **Biala**), city in Opole province, S.W. Poland (formerly in Silesia). Although the city appears on the list of places where Jews were martyred during the *Black Death persecutions of 1349, the identification is uncertain. The community itself had a tradition that its beginning was at the end of the 14th century, but the documentary sources date only from the 16th century, when the number of Jewish settlers was very small. In 1564 nine Jewish families lived in a Jewish Quarter (*Judengasse*) in their homes. All Jews were exiled from *Silesia in 1582 with the exception of Zuelz and Gross-Glogau, where many found refuge. In 1591 the local artistocracy sought to persuade the emperor to expel the Jews from Zuelz as well. They found a protector, however, in Hans Christolph von Proskowski, who labored successfully with strenuous Jewish support to secure their position; in 1601 the Jews received verification of their status. Proskowski himself acquired Zuelz in 1606, maintaining a highly liberal attitude toward the Jews in his domain. They succeeded in developing their trading and commercial interests not only within the city but in many surrounding areas as well. In the 17th century Zuelz became a place of refuge for Jews from Poland, Moravia, and Bohemia. By 1647 there were 17 Jewish houses out of 155 in the town. Jews were involved in the silk industry as well as in the production of wool and wax. The community built a small wooden synagogue and school in 1717 that was destroyed by fire in 1769. A new synagogue was built in 1774.

The community had an important talmudic academy that established the reputation of Zuelz as a "learned city" in the 18th and 19th centuries and was the focus of the community's life. Many scholarly rabbis ministered to the community's needs over the years; among them were Joshua Feivel Teomim; Isaac Zelig Caro; Eliezer b. Samuel (d. 1747); Moses Eliezer Lippmann (d. 1810); Meshullam Solomon ha-Kohen (d. 1823); and Aaron b. Baruch (d. 1836). The oldest tombstone found dates from 1640, but the cemetery itself must be somewhat older. In the 18th century there was a growth of the Jewish population; there were 600 in 1724; 1,061 (over half the total population) in 1782; and 1,096 in 1812; thereafter, the Jewish population began to decline: 539 in 1849; 411 in 1858; and 337 in 1866. The community developed a number of philanthropic organizations that were active in the 19th century, the oldest being the *ḥevra kaddisha*. It also possessed a community school founded in 1844, but disbanded in 1870. The community declined further in the 20th century and was officially dissolved in 1914. The sacred objects in its synagogue as well as an invaluable collection of silver ornaments were transferred to Neustadt, which absorbed the small community. By 1929 only nine Jews were left in the city.

BIBLIOGRAPHY: Germ Jud, 2 (1968), 945; I. Rabin, *Die Juden in Zuelz* (1926); M. Grann, *Geschichte der Juden in Schlesien* (1896), passim; idem, *Der Silberschatz der Zuelzer Judengemeinde. Ost und West* (1918), 335–6; B. Brilling, in: *Juedische Familien-Forschung*, 2 (1928–29), 72–76, 177–81; 5 (1938), 952–8.

[Alexander Shapiro]

ZUENZ (Zuelz), ARYEH LEIB BEN MOSES (1773–1883), Polish rabbi and author. Zuenz was a descendant of Leib Zuenz (17th century) who served as rabbi of Holleschau and Pinczow, where Aryeh Leib was born. His great perspicacity was recognized when he was young, and he became known as Leib Ḥarif ("sharp-witted"). He lived in Prague and in Bratislava, and was appointed rabbi of Plotsk. He later went to Praga, a suburb of Warsaw, where he served as rabbi for two years. However, he relinquished this position when he was appointed the head of a yeshivah in the town. A prolific writer, 21 of his books were published and frequently reprinted. After he directed that the inscription on his tombstone should state that he would intercede in Heaven on behalf of anyone who published his books, many Jews came forward to publish them. His works were highly valued in Poland because of their extreme subtlety and pilpulistic method.

Most of his books are on the Talmud and on the Shulḥan Arukh; most important are *Ayyelet Ahavim* (2 pts., 1888–1891) on *Ketubbot*; *Get Mekushar* (Warsaw, 1812) which discusses the ordering of *get* and *ḥaliẓah* and has a commentary, *Tiv Gittin; Simḥat Yom Tov* (1841) on *Beẓah; Gur Aryeh* (1943) on *Ḥullin*; and *Geresh Yeraḥim* (1870) on *Gittin*. He also wrote original interpretations of the Pentateuch, responsa, and sermons.

BIBLIOGRAPHY: A. Walden, *Shem ha-Gedolim he-Ḥadash*, 1 (1864), 429:23; S. Chones, *Toledot ha-Posekim* (1910), 141; J. Shatzky, *Geshikhte fun Yidn in Varshe*, 1 (1947), 169f.

[Itzhak Alfassi]

ZUGOT (Heb. זוּגוֹת; "pairs"; sing. זוּג; *zug*), name given to the pairs of sages responsible for maintaining the chain of the Oral Law from Antigonus of *Sokho, the pupil of Simeon the Just, to Johanan b. *Zakkai. In the sources they are represented as a link between the prophets and the *tannaim* (Pe'ah 2:6; Tosef., Yad. 2:16). Mishnah *Avot* (1:4–12) mentions five *zugot*. The first *zug* was that of *Yose b. Joezer and *Yose b. Johanan of Jerusalem, who flourished at the time of the religious persecutions under Antiochus Epiphanes (174–164 B.C.E.); the second, *Joshua b. Peraḥyah and *Nittai (or, according to some versions, Mattai) the Arbelite; the third, *Judah b. Tabbai and *Simeon b. Shetaḥ, in the days of Alexander *Yannai and *Salome Alexandra; the fourth, *Shemaiah and *Avtalyon, who flourished in the time of Herod; the fifth, *Hillel and *Menahem, after which "Menahem went forth and Shammai entered" (Ḥag. 2:2). According to a mishnaic tradition (*ibid.*), the first in each *zug* was the **nasi* ("elected head of the Sanhedrin"), the second the *av bet din ("elected second to the *nasi*"). R. *Meir upheld this tradition in all cases; but the other rabbis made an exception, holding that "Simeon b. Shetaḥ was *nasi* and Judah b. Tabbai *av bet din*" (Tosef., Ḥag. 2:8). None of the extant sources helps to clarify the exact significance of these titles or of the functions associated with them. Nevertheless, the tradition is not to be rejected, or to be regarded merely as a projection of the organization of the *bet din* at Jabneh and Usha. An allusion to dual appointment in the selection of heads of public institutions at the beginning of the Hasmonean period is to be found in the statement that Johanan the high priest appointed *zugot* to supervise the collection of the tithes (TJ, Ma'as. Sh. 5:9, 56d). These *zugot*, however, according to Geiger (*Urschrift und Uebersetzungen der Bibel* (1857), 116ff., 142, 492), are not to be identified with those under consideration here. Similarly, before the destruction of the Second Temple, there were "two judges of robbery suits" in Jerusalem (Ket. 13:1), and reference is made to 80 *zugot* of pupils of Hillel the Elder (TJ, Ned. 5:7, 39a).

The Mishnah (Sot. 9:9) states that "when Yose b. Joezer of Zeredah and Yose b. Johanan of Jerusalem died, the grape-clusters ceased." The meaning of this expression is not clear, but of all the possible explanations, that of a tradition in the Jerusalem Talmud (TJ, Sot. 9:10, 24a; and see Sot. 47b) is the most plausible, namely, that the difference between this *zug* and the successors was that "the former served in an administrative capacity, while the latter did not serve in an administrative capacity." This apparently means that whereas the leadership of the first *zug*, which flourished before the rule of the Hasmoneans, embraced all spheres, that of the subsequent *zugot* was more restricted, being shared by the Hasmonean kings. In addition to the decrees ascribed to the *zugot* (TJ, Pes. 1:6, 27d and see Shab. 14b), and the ethical maxims and the aphorisms quoted in their names in *Avot* 1, the Mishnah (Ḥag. 2:2) mentions a subject on which all the *zugot* differed between themselves: "Yose b. Joezer says that the laying of hands [on the head of a sacrifice; see **Semikhah*] is not to be performed [on a festival] [for the explanation, see Tosef., Ḥag. 2:10; TJ, Ḥag. 2:3, 78a; Ḥag. 16b], Yose b. Johanan says that it is; Joshua b. Peraḥyah says that it is not to be performed, Nittai the Arbelite says that it is; Judah b. Tabbai says that it is not to be performed, Simeon b. Shetaḥ says that it is; Shemaiah says it is to be performed, Avtalyon says it is not; Shammai says it is not to be done, Hillel says it is."

The question as to why a dispute should have persisted for generations, in particular on the subject of the laying of hands on a sacrifice, with no final decision ever reached on the matter, is one that has puzzled scholars. The various interpretations that have been suggested lack any solid foundation. Nor is there any substance in the different theories that seek to explain this supposed "fundamental controversy" among the *zugot* in terms of trends and schools.

BIBLIOGRAPHY: Graetz, in: MGWJ, 18 (1869), 20–32; Schwarz, *ibid.*, 37 (1893), 164–9; A. Buechler, *Das Synedrion in Jerusalem* (1902), 153ff., 187–93; Zeitlin, in: JQR, 7 (1916/17), 499–517; Frankel, Mishnah, 29–44; Albeck, in: *Zion*, 8 (1942/43), 165–78; Ch. Tchernowitz, *Toledot ha-Halakhah*, 4 (1950), 141–78; Hallewy, in: *Tarbiz*, 28 (1958/59), 154–7; H. Mantel, *Studies in the History of the Sanhedrin* (1961), 1–18; L. Finkelstein, *Pharisees* (1962), index, s.v. individual sages.

ZUKERMAN, JACOB T. (1907–1973), U.S. judge and labor leader. Born in Brooklyn, to immigrant parents from Minsk, Russia, Zukerman accompanied his parents as a child to Arbeiter Ring meetings, Socialist Party affairs, and Jewish gatherings. As early as 1926, he organized the Young Circle League of the Arbeiter Ring, which influenced many future leaders of the parent organization and of related groups. In 1954, he was elected the first American-born president of the Ring. In 1929, Zukerman graduated from New York University's School of Law. From 1932 to 1946 he was administrative assistant to the commissioner of welfare of New York City, and he was for many years director of the National Desertion Bureau (later the Family Location Service) of the Federation of Jewish Charities (1946–65). In 1965, Mayor Robert R. Wagner appointed him a judge of the Family Court for a ten-year term.

Zukerman had a deep and pervasive influence on English-speaking Jews whom he attracted to the Arbeiter Ring.

He was deeply devoted to all aspects of Jewish life and culture, and was known for his humane spirit and his eagerness to serve and advance Jewish causes and the interests of the State of Israel. He was for many years president of the Jewish Labor Committee, a position he held at the time of his death. He was also president of the Forward Association which publishes the Yiddish newspaper the *Jewish Daily Forward*, a member of the Board of the United HIAS Service, a leader in various ORT agencies, and one of the founding directors of the Cooperative Seward Park Housing Corporation.

[Milton Ridvas Konvitz (2nd ed.)]

ZUKERMAN (Zuckerman), PINCHAS (1948–), violinist and conductor; born in Israel. He studied with his father and Ilona Fehér. With the encouragement of Stern, Casals, and the America-Israel and Helena Rubinstein foundations, he continued his studies at New York's Juilliard School with Galamian (1961–67). After he won the coveted Leventritt Award (1967) he achieved world fame as violinist, violist, chamber musician, conductor, and teacher. Zukerman is especially known for his clear articulation, full tone, spontaneity of expressive phrasing, and masterful technique. In chamber music he has appeared with *Barenboim, Jacqueline *du Prè, *Ashkenazy, *Perlman, and the Kalichstein-Laredo-Robinson Trio among others. From 1971 Zukerman turned to conducting orchestras, playing and conducting at the same time. He was appointed artistic director of London's South Bank Summer Music Series (1978–80), and music director of St. Paul Chamber Orchestra, Minnesota (1980–87) and the Baltimore Symphony Orchestra Music Summer Music-Fest (1997–99). He was invited to perform and/or conduct the world's finest orchestras, including the Berlin Philharmonic, Boston Symphony, Chicago Symphony, and the New York Philharmonic. He often played in Israel with the Israel Philharmonic Orchestra and the Israel Chamber Ensemble and in the Israel Festival. A noted exponent of contemporary music, he presented premières of works by Boulez, Lutoslawski, Neikrug, and Takemitsu. His extensive discography includes Classical to Modern violin concertos, as well as the complete Mozart and Beethoven violin sonatas. As a devoted pedagogue, he taught at the Manhattan School of Music, New York (1993), and following his successful appointment as music director of Canada's National Arts Center Orchestra in 1998, he initiated several projects for young musicians. Among his distinctions are an honorary doctorate from Brown University, an Achievement Award from the International Center in New York, and the King Solomon Award by the America-Israel Cultural Foundation. President Reagan awarded him a Medal of Arts and he became the first recipient of the Isaac Stern Award for Artistic Excellence. Zukerman was involved in television specials and documentaries.

BIBLIOGRAPHY: Grove Music Online; *Baker's Biographical Dictionary of Musicians* (1997).

[Uri (Erich) Toeplitz and Yohanan Boehm / Naama Ramot (2nd ed.)]

ZUKERTORT, JOHANNES (1842–1888), chess grandmaster, chiefly in Britain. Zukertort was born in Lublin in 1842. He shrouded his early life in obscurity, but he was probably the son of a Jew who had been converted to Protestantism and acted as a conversionist missionary to the Jews. Zukertort spent some time at a German university, but almost certainly did not take a degree. By the late 1860s he was one of the strongest players in Germany and, in 1872, came to Britain, where he spent the rest of his life, making a living as a chess player and writer. In 1878 he won a big tournament in Paris, and his other performances marked him out as one of the world's leading players. His greatest triumph came in the very big London tournament of 1883 in which the unofficial World Champion Wilhelm *Steinitz and most of the world's best players participated. Zukertort won his first 22 games, one of the greatest feats in chess history. His win against J.H. Blackburne is among the most famous games in chess history. At this point Zukertort suffered a mysterious breakdown, possibly a stroke, and lost three games in a row, although he still easily won first prize. Thereafter his results were mediocre and, in 1886, he lost a match against Steinitz, regarded as the first official match for the World Championship. He died of a stroke at the age of 45. Zukertort was renowned for his phenomenal memory and also for the Munchausen-like accounts he gave of his early life. He stated that he was the son of Baroness Krzyzanovska (sic), that he received a medical degree from Berlin University, that he fought in the Austro-Prussian war of 1866 and was left for dead on the battlefield, and that he was a noted tiger hunter in India. No evidence has been found for any of these claims.

BIBLIOGRAPHY: ODNB online; D. Hooper and K. Whyld, *The Oxford Companion to Chess* (1993), 458–59; H. Golombek (ed.), *Penguin Encyclopedia of Chess* (1981), 522–24; J. Adams, *Johannes Zukertort: Artist of the Chessboard* (1989).

[William D. Rubinstein (2nd ed.)]

ZUKOFSKY, LOUIS (1904–1978), U.S. poet and critic. Zukofsky was born on the Lower East Side of Manhattan to poor immigrants parents, who struggled to provide for his education at Columbia University. He taught English at Brooklyn Polytechnic Institute from 1947 to 1962. His early poems attracted the attention of William Carlos Williams who befriended him. He published various critical articles on Pound's *Cantos* and continued an active but obscure literary life until *All the Collected Short Poems, 1923–1958,* appeared in 1965. A second volume with the same title (poems written in 1956–64) followed in 1966. In 1968 an entire issue of *Poetry* magazine was devoted to him. In 1970 he published a novel *Little* and his poem *A-24* in 1972. His *A*, a poem in 24 sections, was published posthumously by the University of California Press. Zukofsky's other works include *A Test of Poetry* (1948), *Bottom: On Shakespeare* (1963), and *Prepositions* (1967), collected criticism. His *Collected Fiction* was published in 1990, and his *Complete Short Poetry*, in 1991.

The critic Guy Davenport had described him as "one of the three most distinguished living American poets", ranking him with Marianne Moore and Ezra Pound.

In 1976 he received an award from the National Institute of Arts and Letters, and in 1977 he was awarded an honorary doctorate by Bard College.

ADD. BIBLIOGRAPHY: B. Comens, *Apocalypse and After: Modern Strategy and Postmodern Tactics in Pound, Williams, and Zukofsky* (1995); M. Scroggins, *Louis Zukofsky and the Poetry of Knowledge* (1998); idem (ed.), *Upper Limit Music: The Writing of Louis Zukofsky* (1997); S. Stanle, *Louis Zukofsky and the Transformation of a Modern American Poetics* (1994).

ZUKOFSKY, PAUL (1943–), U.S. violinist, conductor, and teacher. Zukofsky was born in Brooklyn. His father was the poet and writer Louis *Zukofsky. He began playing at the age of four. At seven he studied with Galamian, at ten he appeared with the New Haven SO, making his Carnegie Hall debut at 13. Entering the Juilliard School of Music at 16, he earned his B.M. and M.S. in 1964. A virtuoso of great technical skill, he was especially noted for his championship of contemporary works. His repertoire includes works by Ives, Cage, *Glass, and first performances of concertos by Sessions, Wuorinen, Iain Hamilton as well as works by *Babbitt, Carter and *Crumb. Zukofsky's extensive list of recordings includes more than 60 first releases, among them the Bach solo sonatas and partitas and Penderecki's *Capriccio* and an anthology of American violin music written between 1940 and 1970. Zukofsky has edited works for violin by Cage and Steuermann, and written several articles on Cage (1982, 1988, 1993), Brahms (1997), Beethoven (2000), *Schoenberg (1992, 2001), and others as well as a book on 20th-century violin techniques: *All-Interval Scale Book* (1977). Zukosky taught at the Buffalo Center, the New England Conservatory in Boston, and the Berkshire Music Center at Tanglewood. In 1969 he joined the faculty of SUNY, Stony Brook. He held a Guggenheim fellowship (1983–4) and was appointed conductor of the Contemporary Chamber Ensemble at the Juilliard School, where he also taught violin. Zukofsky was director of the Arnold Schoenberg Institute (1989–1995) in Los Angeles and editor of the Institute's journal. He serves as program coordinator of the American Composers Series at the Kennedy Center.

BIBLIOGRAPHY: Grove Music Online; *Baker's Biographical Dictionary of Musicians* (1997).

[Max Loppert / Naama Ramot (2nd ed.)]

ZUKOR, ADOLPH (1873–1976), U.S. motion picture executive. Born in Ricse, Hungary, Zukor went to the U.S. in 1888. He worked in New York and Chicago in the fur business. At first Zukor was interested in motion pictures from the business point of view and opened movie houses. However, he soon foresaw the need for lengthy movies of good quality and turned to production. This idea proved successful when he imported *Queen Elizabeth*, starring Sarah Bernhardt. In 1912 he founded the Famous Players Company, which produced several classics such as *The Prisoner of Zenda* and *The Count of Monte Cristo* (1913). In 1917 he combined with other fledgling production companies to found Paramount Pictures, which became one of the largest movie companies in the world. Zukor was president and chairman of the board. He was also active in Jewish causes.

In 1949 he won an honorary Academy Award whose citation read: "Adolph Zukor, a man who has been called the father of the feature film in America, for his services to the industry over a period of forty years." For Zukor's 100th birthday, Paramount Pictures sold the candles on his birthday cake for $1,000 each, and then donated the proceeds to charity. Zukor lived to be 103. His autobiography, *The Public Is Never Wrong*, was published in 1954.

In 1994 Paramount Pictures Corporation merged with Viacom International, Inc. The merged companies own such corporations as the United Paramount Network (UPN); the Columbia Broadcasting System (CBS) and all its subsidiaries; the Comedy Central network; Blockbuster, Inc; the Spelling Entertainment Corporation and its subsidiaries; Showtime Networks, Inc; the Video Hits 1 (VH1) network; Music Television (MTV) Networks; and the Nickelodeon network.

BIBLIOGRAPHY: W. Irwin, *The House That Shadows Built* (1928).

[Ruth Beloff (2nd ed.)]

ZUKUNFT, DIE ("The Future"), German weekly for "politics, public life, arts and literature," which appeared in Berlin for three decades, every Saturday, from 1892 to 1922 under the editorship of Maximilian *Harden (born Felix Ernst Witkowski, 1861–1927), one of the most controversial figures of the German press. The title seems to have been suggested by Franz Mehring to distinguish the new paper from the journal *Gegenwart* ("The Present"). Harden's political essays, written under the pen name "Keut," and his theater reviews made the periodical an influential platform for intellectual discussion and the mouthpiece of liberal opposition in the German *Kaiserreich*. Due to its topicality, the vigor and erudition of its editor, and the fame of its contributors (among them Stefan *Zweig, Heinrich and Thomas *Mann, Rainer Maria Rilke, Hugo von *Hofmannsthal, Paul *Heyse, and Henrik Ibsen), *Die Zukunft* soon gained numerous readers. Its circulation quickly rose from 6,000 copies per week (40–50 pages each) to 10,000 around 1900, and some 22,000 by 1914. Between 1915 and 1922, however, circulation dropped to less than 1,000 copies per week.

As a result of Harden's deep veneration of Prussian conservatism expressed in the columns of his paper, the aging Otto von Bismarck (1815–1898) made him one of his closest confidants. Yet Harden attacked William II and his entourage with irony and courage. In 1906–07, while Harden was supported by Friedrich von Holstein (1837–1909), a series of articles led to the downfall of Prince Philipp zu Eulenburg (1847–1921), the Kaiser's most influential adviser. In 1897, Harden became a friend of Walther *Rathenau, and published his controversial article "*Hoere Israel!*" in *Die Zukunft*. Georg *Bernhard, however, who had contributed to the paper as "Plutus" from 1901–1903, withdrew upon the advice of August Bebel, after Harden had criticized the Social Democratic Party.

At the outbreak of World War I in August 1914, Harden's *Zukunft* was ardently nationalist and even annexationist, but from November 1915, after the first German military defeat, it became pacifist and supported President Wilson's Fourteen Points of January 1918. Due to Harden's political turn and military censorship, *Die Zukunft* dramatically declined in importance, its readers turning towards papers like Siegfried *Jacobsohn's *Weltbuehne* after 1918. Harden could never come to terms with the new Weimar system, though he advocated a policy of international cooperation and reconciliation. Accordingly, he was blacklisted by the German right wing as "a destructive Jewish intellectual." On July 3, 1922, nine days after the assassination of his friend Walther Rathenau, an attempt was made on Harden's life, from which he never really recovered. On September 30, 1922, the last issue of *Die Zukunft* appeared under the title "After 30 years," and Harden, who realized he could not escape his Jewish origin, emigrated to the Netherlands. Later attempts to revive the paper failed. In 1927, Harden died from pneumonia while taking a cure in Switzerland.

Harden, who had converted to Protestantism in 1881, at times revealed an almost hysterical antisemitism, strongly attacked by Karl *Kraus in his satirical magazine *Die Fackel* (1899–1936). Theodor *Lessing, in his book *Der juedische Selbsthass* (1930), described Harden as a prototype of Jewish self-hatred, which had been particularly stirred up by the *Dreyfus trial. However, it may also be noted that Harden invited Theodor *Herzl in 1897 to state the Zionist case in *Die Zukunft* (an offer which Herzl declined because of Harden's hostile attitude towards William II). From 1917, he maintained friendly relations with the German Zionist Richard *Lichtheim, and the same year stressed the political wisdom of the *Balfour Declaration in his paper.

ADD. BIBLIOGRAPHY: M. Harden (ed.), *Die Zukunft* 1–30 (1892–1922; microfiche reprint 2003); Th. Lessing, *Der juedische Selbsthass* (1930), 167–207; H.F. Young, *Maximilian Harden. Censor Germaniae* (1959); E. Gottgetreu, in: LBIYB, 7 (1962), 215–46; B.U. Weller, *Maximilian Harden und die "Zukunft"* (1970); H.J. Goebel, *Maximilian Harden als politischer Publizist im Ersten Weltkrieg* (1977); H.D. Hellige, in: H.J. Goebel and E. Schulin (eds.), *Walther Rathenau – Maximilian Harden. Briefwechsel 1897–1920* (1983), 15–299; F. Albrecht, in: M. Grunewald (ed.), *Le discours européen dans les revues allemandes, 1871–1914* (1996), 155–76; K. Hecht, "Die Harden-Prozesse" (Ph.D. diss., Munich 1997); S. Armbrecht, *Verkannte Liebe. Maximilian Hardens Haltung zu Deutschtum und Judentum* (1999); M. Sabrow, *Walther Rathenau und Maximilian Harden* (2000); H. Neumann and M. Neumann, *Maximilian Harden* (2003).

[Erich Gottgetreu / Johannes Valentin Schwarz (2nd ed.)]

ZULAY, MENAHEM (1901–1954), Israel researcher of early Ereẓ Israel *piyyut*. Zulay, who was born in Oshcianci, Galicia, settled in Palestine in 1920. In 1925 he was invited to Germany to act as Hebrew tutor to the children of S.Z. Schocken. At the University of Bonn he was awarded a Ph.D. for his study *Zur Liturgie der babylonischen Juden* (1933). He worked at the Schocken Institute for the Study of Hebrew poetry, from its foundation until his death. At the Institute, he studied thousands of photographs of the early Ereẓ Israel *piyyut*, especially those of Yannai, that had been collected from all the libraries of the world in order to identify and classify them.

He published a critical edition of Yannai, *Piyyutei Yannai Melukkatim mi-Tokh Kitvei ha-Genizah u-Mekorot Aherim* (1938); "*Mehkerei Yannai*" in YMHSI, 2 (1936), 213–391; "*Iyyunei Lashon be-Fiyyutei Yannai,*" *ibid.*, 6 (1946), 161–248). He was a member of the Academy of the Hebrew Language. Toward the end of his life he published a series of articles on "The *Piyyut* School of Rav Saadiah Gaon" (*Orlogin*, 6 (1952); 8 (1953); 10 (1954)). His complete work, *Ha-Askolah ha-Paytanit shel Rav Sa'adyah Ga'on* (1969), was published posthumously. The many studies he published constitute only a small part of the abundant material he prepared.

[Yehuda Ratzaby]

ZUNDELEVITCH, AARON (1852–1923), pioneer of the Russian revolutionary movement. Zundelevitch was born in Vilna, studied in various yeshivot and in the Vilna Rabbinical Seminary, and for a time came under the influence of Hebrew secular literature. In 1872 he organized a revolutionary circle among the students of the Vilna Rabbinical Seminary; among its members were Aaron *Liebermann and a number of others who played an important part in the history of the socialist movement. Later on he became a prominent figure in the Russian revolutionary group Narodnaya Volya ("People's Will"). He was a brilliant organizer and was responsible for the dissemination of illegal literature. He played a heroic part in the revolutionary struggle against Czarism and endured many years of misery and torture as a convict in the mines of Siberia.

Zundelevitch advocated the use of terror as a political weapon, but he differed from his colleagues on a number of issues. He did not share their enthusiasm for the Russian peasantry, urged closer cooperation with the German Social-Democrats, who were unpopular among the Russian revolutionaries of the 1870s, and showed great interest in the socialist movement of Western Europe.

Zundelevitch believed that the Jewish religion was a reactionary force, and was equally opposed to Jewish national ideas. He was against a Jewish revolutionary undertaking the assassination of the Czar because "the tendency of the Christian world is to ascribe the sins of one Jew to the entire Jewish people." Zundelevitch benefitted from the amnesty declared after the abortive Russian Revolution of 1905. In 1907 he immigrated to London, where he spent the rest of his life. He opposed the Communist regime in Russia "for their trampling underfoot the ideals of freedom, equality and brotherhood for which generations of revolutionaries made the highest sacrifices."

[Schneiur Zalman Levenberg]

ZUNSER, ELIAKUM (1836–1913), popular Yiddish bard and dramatist, known as **Eliakum Badkhn**. Born in Vilna, Zunser was conscripted in 1856 but was soon released, when Czar Alexander II revoked the oppressive military decrees of his predecessor Nicholas I. In 1856 in the barracks, he composed the song "*Di Poymanes*" ("Child Recruits") lamenting the bitter lot of the child soldiers (see *Cantonists), and after his discharge he wrote "*Di Yeshue*" ("Salvation") celebrating the child draftees' miraculous salvation. In 1857, working in Kovno as a braider of gold lace on uniforms, he came under the influence of the *Musar movement of R. Israel *Salanter, and his songs ("*Der Zeiger*" ("The Watch)" and "*Di Blum*" ("The Flower")) became laden with lyricism and moral sentiment. Singing his songs at festivals and weddings, he soon acquired a reputation as an original bard and decided to make a career as a **badḥan*. He rapidly attained fame as Russia's outstanding wedding bard. Beginning with *Shirim ḥadashim* ("New Songs," 1872), booklet after booklet of his songs was printed and avidly read.

In 1871 Zunser lost seven children during a cholera epidemic and, a year later, his wife. His tragic outlook after these losses was mirrored in poems such as "*Der Potshtover Glekel*" ('The Little Postal Bell') and "*Der Sandek*" ("The Man Holding a Child at Circumcision," 1872), and in his only published drama *Makhaze Mekhires Yoysef* ("The Sale of Joseph," 1874). After his second marriage Zunser lived chiefly in Minsk, serving as the local correspondent for *Kol la-Am*, a Yiddish periodical edited at Koenigsberg by M.L. *Rodkinson. When the pogroms of the early 1880s led to the founding of the pioneering Zionist group *Bilu, Zunser lent his support to the young idealists who were heading for a new life in Palestine. In 1882 he composed the songs "*Shivas Tsien*" ("Return to Zion") and "*Di Sokhe*" ("The Hook Plough") for them, the latter becoming his most popular song both in the Yiddish and Hebrew versions. Its theme was the joy of returning to plow the Jewish earth in the Holy Land. Zunser himself hoped to settle in the Bilu village of Gederah, but in 1889 was compelled to emigrate to New York, where his East Side home and printing shop became a center for Yiddish poets and young Zionists. There he also published poems of the New World (in *Dos Yidishe Tageblat*) about Columbus, Washington, and sweatshops and wrote his autobiography, *Zunsers Biografye Geshribn fun im Aleyn* (ed. by A.H. Fromenson, 1905). A definitive scholarly edition of his complete extant works, *Verk* (including lyrics and melodies) was edited for *YIVO by Mordkhe Schaechter (2 vols., 1964; incl. bibl.).

BIBLIOGRAPHY: S. Liptzin, *Eliakum Zunser, Poet of his People* (1950); M. Schaechter, in: *Eliakum Zunser, Verk*, 2 (1964), 779–88, bibl.; Rejzen, Leksikon, 3 (1929), 259–71; LNYL, 7 (1968), 546–9.

[Sol Liptzin]

ZUNTZ, ALEXANDER (1742–1819), U.S. pioneer merchant. Born in Westphalia, Germany, Zuntz came to America as civilian commissary and adjutant to the Hessian forces employed by England during the American Revolution. Soon after arriving in New York (1779), he became active in Congregation Shearith Israel, and was a leader of the Jewish community during and after the British occupation of the city. In 1784, he was one of the founders of the New York Bank. Though failing in a subsequent business venture, by 1797 he had become prosperous as a broker.

BIBLIOGRAPHY: D. d.S. Pool, *Portraits Etched in Stone* (1952), passim.

[Neil Ovadia (2nd ed.)]

ZUNZ, LEOPOLD (Yom Tov Lippman(n); 1794–1886), philologist, among the founders of the "Science of Judaism" (*Wissenschaft des Judentums). Born in Detmold, Germany, the child of talmud scholar Immanuel Menachem Zunz (1759–1802) and Hendel Behrens (1773–1809), daughter of Dov Beer. In 1795 the family moved to Hamburg where his father and various teachers introduced him to *Hebrew Grammar, the *Talmud, and the *Pentateuch. After the death of his father, Zunz was educated at the **bet-midrash* Samsonsche Freischule at *Wolfenbuettel as of 1803. Samuel Meyer Ehrenberg, an advanced Jewish educator who was appointed director of the school in 1807, recognized Zunz's great talents and helped him in his development; teacher and pupil remained friends until Ehrenberg's death in 1853. Ehrenberg's reforms at the school included the insertion of subjects such as religion, history, geography, French, and German, which Zunz described as a sudden transition from the "middle ages into modern times," and from "Jewish helotism into civic freedom." From 1809 to 1811, Zunz studied at the local high school (Gymnasium), and from 1810 to 1815 was an assistant teacher at the Samsonsche Freischule. In 1811 he read *Ẓemaḥ David* by David *Gans and *Bibliotheca Hebraea* by Johann Christoph *Wolf, which awoke his interest in Jewish history and literature. From 1815 to 1819 he studied at the University of Berlin and acquired a scientific academic grounding; he was particularly influenced by the great classical scholars Friedrich August Wolf (1759–1824) and August Boeckh (1785–1867).

Zunz's scholarly work began in 1817, when he wrote *Etwas ueber die rabbinische Literatur* (1818) and researched *Sefer ha-Ma'alot* by Shem Tov b. Joseph *Falaquera; in 1821 he received his doctorate at the University of Halle for this research. Due to his desire to give Judaism a new definition in keeping with the spirit of the times, he cofounded the *Verein fuer Cultur und Wissenschaft der Juden in 1819, which considered the scientific and historical approach to the "Science of Judaism" as being the best way to achieve society's goals. Zunz edited the *Zeitschrift fuer die Wissenschaft des Judentums* issued by the society (1822) and published three articles in it, including a biography of *Rashi.

Zunz, who then favored the spirit of *religious reform, was invited to deliver sermons in the new synagogue in Berlin starting in May 1820, and in August 1821 he was appointed preacher there, resigning a year later in disappointment with his congregation. A collection of his sermons (*Predigten*) appeared in 1823. He made his living as a member of the editorial board of the Berlin daily newspaper, *Haude und Spenersche*

Zeitung (1824–31) and as director of the primary school of the Jewish community, the Juedische Gemeindeschule (1826–29). His chief interest, however, was his research in Hebrew literature. Zunz used the vast material he had accumulated and the notes he had collected from manuscripts and printed works on his visits to libraries (at Hamburg, the *Oppenheim collection in 1828, and that of H.J. *Michael in 1829) in writing his great work on liturgic addresses which appeared in 1832, *Die gottesdienstlichen Vortraege der Juden historisch entwickelt* (see below).

In 1834–35, Zunz gave 34 public lectures on the Psalms. From September 1835 to July 1836, Zunz served as a preacher to a private religious association in Prague. From 1840 to 1850, he directed a Jewish teachers' seminary (Israelitisches Schullehrerseminar) in Berlin.

His hope that one of the universities would recognize Jewish studies as an academic subject and appoint him as its representative was not fulfilled. In 1848, he sent a letter on this subject to the Prussian minister of culture, but his proposal was turned down. Zunz for his part did not agree to the establishment of separate *rabbinical seminaries for fear of severing the "Science of Judaism" from general intellectual life. He also had little use for the *synods of German progressive rabbis which had begun to convene in 1844, as he could not see any benefit in their reforms; he preferred to carry on his scholarly work alone.

Zunz went on to publish *Toledot R. Azaryah min ha-Adumim* (in Heb. in: *Keren Ḥemed*, 5 (1841); 7 (1843)), 13 articles on Jewish subjects (in the Ersch and Gruber encyclopaedia, 1842), and *Zur Geschichte und Literatur* (1845). In 1850, the community granted him a modest pension. He devoted most of his time to research on the **piyyut*, the **seliḥot*, and various *liturgies, publishing over time *Die synagogale Poesie des Mittelalters* (1855), *Der Ritus des synagogalen Gottesdienstes* (1859), *Literaturgeschichte der synagogalen Poesie* (1865), and additions to the latter (1867). This work required visits to various libraries, including the British Museum, the Bodleian Library, and the library in Paris (1855; where he visited Heinrich *Heine, his friend from the days of the Verein fuer Cultur and Wissenschaft der Juden), and the de *Rossi library at *Parma (1863). Zunz remained barred from the important Vatican library, however, as he was Jewish.

His other literary contributions in the period after 1850 included: the publication of *Moreh Nevukhei ha-Zeman* of Nachman *Krochmal in accordance with the terms of the author's will (1851); articles on Judaism in the *Brockhaus* lexicon (1853); and a biography of his teacher Samuel Meyer Ehrenberg (1854). In honor of his 70th birthday (1864) the Zunz Foundation (Zunzstiftung) was set up in order to support his scholarship and various other undertakings in the "Science of Judaism." In 1874, the death of his wife Adelheid (Bermann (1802–1874)) caused him deep depression. He ceased to work, and only prepared a collection of his articles (*Gesammelte Schriften*), which appeared in three volumes in 1875–76, for publication. The Zunz Foundation issued a jubilee volume in honor of his 90th birthday (1884) entitled *Tiferet Seivah* (Hebrew and German). After an industrious and a passionate life, Zunz died at the age of 91 and was buried at the cemetery of Schoenhauser Allee in Berlin.

Main Research

In *Etwas ueber die rabbinische Literatur* (which appeared in 1818 and was the first attempt to reflect Hebrew literature in all its branches), Zunz outlined the program and aims of the "Science of Judaism" and his own plan of work. According to Zunz, Jewish literature should not be shut within the narrow confines of religious and halakhic tradition, as this literature also embraces the other humanities, as well as natural sciences. A knowledge of Hebrew literature in its broader sense would make possible the recognition of Jewish history as an inseparable part of the history of human culture in general – research into Hebrew literature is part of the humanities in general. He believed that the time was ripe for this research because the rabbinical epoch had come to an end and Hebrew literature had to be evaluated before it and its knowledge would disappear. Further, a scientific report on the Jew's very active past would testify to his talent and readiness to make contributions in the present, which would serve to facilitate obtaining civil rights. After an overview of all subjects to which Jewish culture had contributed in the Disaspora, Zunz returned to his main aim. By treating the rabbinical literature as an integral part of a universal humanistic culture (i. e., philosophy), he hoped to ban all prejudices against Jews and their literature.

Though in his outline for the investigation of Jewish literature, which he later called a "piece of immature work of youth," Zunz had used "only half speech," as he confessed to Ehrenberg, his *Die gottesdienstlichen Vortraege der Juden* was regarded as "no book, but an event; not a literary work but a school" (D. *Kaufmann). After his plan to write a four-volume introduction to the Wissenschaft des Judentums was not realized, he used his collected materials to demonstrate the historical-philological aims of the new "Jewish science." The main text focuses on the *Synagogue and especially its midrashic literature as the pillar of the Jewish nation in the Diaspora. Hundreds of works and thousands of references were combined into a single organic literary structure in which Zunz describes the prophets' teaching, out of which developed the reading of the Torah and of the *Prophets, the *Targum, and the sermons. He focuses on the development of *Oral Law; the activities of the **amoraim* and the **geonim* and their writings; all aspects of **aggadah*; on preaching, its place in intellectual life; and the places of Jewish settlement in which preaching had been customary from ancient times up to the period of the **maskilim* and the religious reformers.

Zunz seldom filled in the historical background of literary works, merely referring to it only to bring out the connection between the periods and the continuity in the tradition of preaching in its various forms. Only details of his research needed correcting. *Sefer Ravyah*, criticisms of Zunz's book by Eliakim Samiler (or *Mehlsack) of Brody, appeared in 1837.

Zunz made use of the latter's corrections and suggestions in preparing a second edition of the *Vortraege*, which appeared in 1892 with N. *Bruell as editor. Despite the scientific and objective character of the book, one can discern in it signs of political controversy and a defense of religious reforms. In the foreword, Zunz links the neglect of Jewish literature with the inferior civil status of the Jewish community; only a knowledge of the spiritual heritage of Jewry would encourage enlightened statesmen to grant the Jew the same rights and civil liberties. The Jew who is familiar with his people's past will know how to reform his religious customs and thereby prepare himself for his new status in society. According to his sympathy for the Reform movement during that time, in the last chapter Zunz approves the various reforms in the synagogues because in this "internal emancipation" he sees a parallel to external political liberation. This scientific book therefore concludes with the hope that the contemporary Jew will yet be a partner in the development of a unified culture for all mankind. (A Hebrew translation by M.A. Zak appeared in Jerusalem in 1947, edited by Ḥanokh Albeck.)

The central idea of *Etwas ueber die rabbinische Literatur* appears again in *Zur Geschichte und Literatur*. In this book he claims it is not right to restrict the scope of Jewish literature and separate it from general culture; the literary productions of the Jews merely supplement general literature, and both exert a mutual influence upon each other. It is true that there were periods of tension and hatred which did not recognize the commands of scholarship, but in the end, the scientific spirit will triumph and Hebrew literature will go forth from its isolation. The chapters deal with the sages of France and Germany in the Middle Ages, collections of manuscripts and printed works, printers and typography, Jewish poets in the south of France, and the history of the Jews of Sicily. The book includes important information from primary sources and accurate records of great historical and literary value. Thoughts on the philosophy of history, announced earlier by the Hegelian thinker and his friend Eduard *Gans, can be found again in the metaphor that Jewish literature is a particular stream that runs into the universal ocean of human culture. While Zunz himself intended to list and arrange his collected materials in order to enlighten the preceived relationship between Jews and the Diaspora societies, the book has been described as impossible to analyze (S. *Schechter) because of its many-sided cultural-historical aspects.

In *Die synagogale Poesie des Mittelalters*, Zunz concentrated on the most characteristic creation of Jewish religious life. At first he decided to limit his research to the *seliḥah* literature that expresses the sorrow of Israel, the suffering of the Exile, faith in the divine covenant, the idea of repentance and beseeching pardon, and the anticipation of the redeemer's coming. Only in the course of the work did he decide to add a discussion on *piyyut* literature, i.e., on the liturgical poetry that later supplemented the prayers. Zunz did not succeed in writing a book that reflected sacred poetry in its entirety, but his work was the first research undertaking of its kind. In the first chapter (The Psalms), a kind of preface to the book, he repeats the idea of the continuity and organic development of Jewish literature. The prophet who announced the word of the Lord to the people and the poet who poured out his soul before God bequeathed their roles to the sages (the authors of the *aggadah* and teachers of the nation) and the *paytanim*. The form of expression underwent change, but the People of Israel both in the biblical era and after the destruction of the Temple was one people. The state fell, but the nation preserved its inner freedom and its creativity. The synagogue became both a political and religious center, a meeting place for the thinker and the poet. In the liturgy are expressed the "history and martyrology of the people, its past and future; the attitude of man's spirit to its origin, the attitude of the individual to mankind and the attitude of man to nature." Historic conditions change, but the covenant between God and Israel stands fast and the synagogue is the witness of this phenomenon.

While in the prefaces to his earlier books Zunz had stressed the organic structure of the history of the human spirit and the universally human framework of Jewish literature, he later abandoned this idea – even if not entirely – and concentrated on the inner life of the Jews. Perhaps the reason for this was his disappointment at the failure of the 1848 Revolution; from then on it was impossible for him to believe in a democratic union of mankind and the revival of its creative powers. Also, he no longer pinned his hopes on religious reforms in modern Judaism. For him, the "Science of Judaism" filled the vacuum which had been created.

Der Ritus des synagogalen Gottesdienstes is a continuation of this work. Zunz traced the change in liturgical customs, according to the places of Jewish dispersion, and described the influence on these customs of various historical phenomena, such as the *Kabbalah, the *Inquisition, the invention of printing, and the contact with Western culture beginning with Moses *Mendelssohn.

With *Literaturgeschichte der synagogalen Poesie*, his pioneering efforts in the field of synagogue poetry came to an end. This work, which is based on research of 500 manuscripts, describes more than 6,000 liturgical pieces and records the history of the *paytanim* and their works up to 1540. Although his intention had been to write an internal history of this literature, he never realized this plan; his talent for producing bibliographies and for performing research proved stronger than his ability to shape historical concepts.

Attitude to Political Life

From his youth, Zunz remained a confirmed democrat and liberal. In his opinion, the state was to be founded on ideals of justice, law, and morality, and must grant basic human freedom and equal rights to all citizens. As a supporter of Enlightenment, he criticized organized religion (the Church) as being opposed to a free state and also demanded total separation of church and state. He regarded the French Revolution and its democratic ideals as the historical point of reference of both the 1830 and 1848 revolutions, and as the basis of a political development which should end with the creation of a European state based upon law and justice (*Rechtsstaat*). Zunz also believed in an amalgamation of Wissenschaft and politics. He claimed that the lack of full civic rights for Jews caused a neglect of their science and vice versa; thus, only through Wissenschaft could full equality be reached. Consequently, he committed himself to participating in numerous public concerns. For example, he was commissioned by the Jewish community of Berlin to write a treatise on Jewish names as a response to a royal decree banning the use of Christian names by Jews (*Namen der Juden* (1837)). In this work, Zunz showed that Jews had always adopted the names found in the Diaspora societies and that the so-called "Christian" names had long been used by Jews. In 1840, he expressed his opinion in a historical-political essay in the *Leipziger Allgemeine Zeitung* against the anti-Jewish imputations of the *Damascus Affair ("Damaskus, ein Wort zur Abwehr"). With his *Kurze Antworten auf Kultusfragen* (1844), he attempted to clarify Jewish religion and culture for the Prussian officials, and he also participated in a revision of the restricted emancipation law of 1812 for the united diet of Prussia in 1847. From 1848 to 1850 he took part in political propaganda, gave background talks to democratic citizens' associations, and was chosen to the electors' council (Wahlmaenner) of the Prussian diet and the German national assembly (Nationalversammlung) in Frankfurt on Main. These activities ceased in the years of reaction (1850–58) and were resumed in 1859 after the death of Frederick William IV. At the beginning of the Bismarckian Era, however, Zunz soon recognized that there was no hope of his democratic and liberal principles being implemented and subsequently withdrew from such activities. A compilation of his political speeches can be found in the collection of his articles (*Gesammelte Schriften*, Volume I).

Contribution to the "Science of Judaism"

Zunz devoted his life to the outline and development of the Wissenschaft des Judentums. According to the modern historical-philological school of F.A. Wolf and A. Boeckh, he intended an exploration of all post-biblical rabbinical or, as he called it, Jewish literature. But instead of modern classical studies (Wissenschaft des Altertums), which treated ancient cultures as completely past, he pursued a substantial interest in the nature of Judaism. In addition to parallels to the modern classics, Zunz participated in the contemporary philosophical discourse about the progress of world history and mankind – most influentially expressed by Johann Gottfried *Herder and Georg Wilhelm Friedrich *Hegel. For him, the historical, cultural and religious achievements of the "Hebrew/Jewish nation" in the Diaspora was revealed in all its written sources. In so doing, Zunz denied several basic values of traditional Judaism, but in their place offered the modern Jew an interest in history. One can discern a definitely negative attitude to the area of the Talmud and the Kabbalah; he considered their spirit as opposed to that of the "Science of Judaism." It is worth noting that among the many subjects in Jewish literature, Zunz chose the most "Jewish": the Midrashim and liturgical poetry. As a researcher he was precise and assiduous, demanding scientific perfection. He did not have disciples, but most of the researchers who followed him learned from him even if they did not accept his ideological premises, and his research served as the foundation and the basis for the "Science of Judaism."

The Zunz Archives

After Zunz's death, his literary estate was presented as a gift to the Zunz Foundation and placed in the *Hochschule fuer die Wissenschaft des Judentums in Berlin. In 1939, the archives were taken to Jerusalem and given to the National and University Library. They include the minute book of the *Verein fuer die Cultur und Wissenschaft der Juden*, documents relating to Zunz's life, among them *Das Buch Zunz* (his diary), drafts of speeches, part of his printed books and articles with comments and additions in his handwriting, and the originals or copies of letters from him and letters received by him or his wife. Microfilm copies of a selection of this material are in the archives of the Leo Baeck Institute in New York. His library, which contained many valuable manuscripts, was bought by the Judith Lady Montefiore College in Ramsgate (1869–1896) and later integrated in the collection of *Jews' College, London.

Legacy

Already during his lifetime Zunz became an, if not *the*, icon of the Wissenschaft des Judentums for scholars like L. *Geiger, G. *Karpeles, M. *Brann and I. *Elbogen, who put much effort into the investigation of his life, work and correspondence (after the Holocaust N.N. *Glatzer was one of those who proceeded with this task). However, at the turn of the 20th century, critical voices increased. Franz *Rosenzweig reported from a conversation with Hermann *Cohen the philosopher's harsh verdict of Zunz: "He could have been a great historian, and was nothing but an antiquarian" (H. Cohen, *Juedische Schriften* (1927)). Shneur Zalman *Shazar blamed Zunz for erecting a wall between Jews and non-Jews out of "the martyrlogium of Jewish history" instead of rejecting such a division, as he had promised (I.S. Rubaschoff, Erstlinge, in: *Der Juedische Wille* (1918)). Finally, Gershom *Scholem accused the Wissenschaft des Judentums and Zunz as its prominent representative (as well as his younger colleague and friend Moritz *Steinschneider) of pursuing a dialectic between constructive and destructive tendencies (G. Sholem, "*Mi-Tokh Hirhurim al Ḥokhmat Yisrael*," in: *Lu'aḥ ha-Areẓ* (1944)). Despite all this criticism, however, fascination for the life and work of Zunz has continued, since he is still to be regarded as one of the most important personalities in the development of the Wissenschaft des Judentums and, arguably, of Jewish studies in general.

BIBLIOGRAPHY: L. Wallach, *Liberty and Letters: The Thoughts of Leopold Zunz* (1959); N.N. Glatzer (ed.), *Leopold and Adelheid Zunz; An Account in Letters, 1815–1885* (1958); idem, in: YLBI, 5 (1960), 122–39; idem (ed.), *Leopold Zunz: Jude – Deutscher – Europaeer* (1964);

S. Baruch (= A.S. Oko), in: *Menorah Journal*, 9 (1923); S. Schechter, *Studies in Judaism*, 3 (1924), 84–142; F. Bamberger, in: PAAJR, 11 (1941), 1–25; L. Geiger, in: ZGJD, 5 (1892), 223–68; S. Maybaum, in: *Zwoelfter Bericht ueber die Lehranstalt fuer die Wissenschaft des Judenthums* (1894); MGWJ, 38 (1894), 481–527; D. Kaufmann, in: ADB, 45 (1900), 490–501; M. Wiener, *Juedische Religion im Zeitalter der Emanzipation* (1933), 177–87; I. Elbogen, in: *Fuenfzigster Bericht der Lehranstalt fuer die Wissenschaft des Judentums* (1936), 14–32; Bernfeld, in: JJGL, 31 (1938), 223–47; A. Altmann, in: YBLI, 6 (1961), 3–59. **ADD. BIBLIOGRAPHY:** A. Altmann, in: *Der Morgen*, 12 (1936), 5–9; I.E. Barzilay, in: JBA, 51 (1993), 173–84; M. Brann, in: MWGJ, 38 (1894), 493–500; idem, in: JJGL, 5 (1902), 159–205, 6 (1903), 120–157; S.S. Cohon, in: HUCA, 31 (1960), 251–76; I. Elbogen, in: MGWJ, 81 (1937), 177–85; idem; in: JJGL, 30 (1937), 131–72 (with bibliography); L. Geiger, in: ZGJD, 5 (1891), 223–68; idem, in: MGWJ, 60 (1916), 245–62, 321–74; idem, in: *Im deutschen Reich*, 5 (1917), 193–201, 6 (1918), 245–50; A. Gottschalk, in: *Judaism*, 29 (1980), 268–94; G. Jacobsohn, in: AZJ, 58 (1894), 385–90; M.-R. Hayoun, in: *Pardès*, 19–20 (1994), 133–43; G. Karpeles, in: AZJ, 58 (1894), 171–73, 199–200, 234–35; D. Kaufmann, in: MWGJ, 38 (1894), 481–93; G. Kisch, in: HUCA, 38 (1967), 237–58; *A. Marx*, PAAJR, 5 (1933–34), 95–153; M.A. Meyer, *The Origins of the Modern Jew. Jewish Identity and European Culture in Germany* (1967); idem, in: YBLI, 16 (1971), 19–41; M.R. Niehoff, in: YBLI, 43 (1998), 3–24; T. Rahe, in: *Judaica*, 42 (1986), 188–99; J. Raphael, in: ZGJ, 7 (1970), 31–36; M. Ritter, in: *Archiv fuer Begriffsgeschichte*, 45 (2003), 121–50; D. Rosin, in: MWGJ, 38 (1894), 504–14; H.I. Schmelzer, in: *Occident and Orient. A Tribute to the Memory of A. Schreiber* (1988), 319–29; I. Schorsch, in: YBLI, 22 (1977), 109–28; idem, in: YBLI, 31 (1986), 281–315; idem, YBLI, 37 (1992), 33–43; M. Simon, in: *Kairos*, 30–31 (1988–1989), 121–32; H. Soussan, *The Science of Judaism. From Leopold Zunz to Leopold Lucas* (1999); H.H. Steinthal, *Ueber Juden und Judentum* (1906), 226–31; J. Theodor, in: MWGJ, 38 (1894), 514–23; C. Trautmann-Waller, *Philologie allemande et tradition juive. Le parcours intellectuel de L. Zunz* (1999); L. Trepp, in: *Emuna*, 7 (1972), 248–54; Veltri, in: JSQ, 7 (2000), 338–51; K.G. Wesseling, in: BBKL, 14 (1998) (with bibliography); L. Wieseltier, in: *History and Theory*, 20 (1981), 135–49.

[Nahum N. Glatzer / Gregor Pelger (2nd ed.)]

ZUR, MENACHEM (1942–), Israeli composer. Born in Tel Aviv, Zur attended the Jerusalem Academy of Music and received a D.M.A in 1976 from Columbia University in New York. He wrote over 100 compositions in all musical genres: orchestral, chamber, vocal, electronic, and one full-scale opera, *Neighbors*. His works are frequently performed in Israel, the U.S., Central America, Europe, and the Far East. Zur served as the chairperson of the Israeli Composer's League in 2001 and was awarded the ACUM (Israeli ASCAP) prize for lifetime achievement and the Prime Minister's prize for composition.

He was constantly engaged, both theoretically and artistically, with the problems of pitch organization in post-tonal music. In his compositions, he uses concepts from set theory and cyclical arrays to create prolongation of motives modeled after *Schenkerian theory of tonal music. He was especially interested in contrapuntal relations among various contrasting bodies of sound, as in the series *Discussions* and in the Concerto for Tuba, Concerto for Piano, Concerto for Violin, Bassoon and Horn.

Although Zur's style is always modern, some works on liturgical texts reveal influences of traditional Jewish music, like *Lamentations* (Alto with Orchestra, 1984), *Combinations* (Children's Chorus with Tape), *The Golem* (Baritone with Orchestra, 1988), *Kedusha Prayer* (Ḥazzan Baritone with Children's Chorus). Some choral works in Hebrew involve a distinct Israeli idiom: *A Tale of Two Sandals* (Children's Chorus, 1985); *Alleluia* (Mixed Chorus); *The Sacrifice of Isaac* (Female Chorus and Piano, 1993). Among his other works are *Keyboard Harmony* (co-author, 1985); Concerto for Orchestra; three symphonies (including no. 2 – *Letters to Schoenberg, Stravinsky and Berg*, 1988–1994); *Centers* (Piano, 1982); *Circles of Time* (Piano, 1993).

BIBLIOGRAPHY: NG²; M. Feingers, "Menachem Zur – A Profile," in: *Israel Music News* (1992).

[Yossi Goldenberg (2nd ed.)]

ẒUR, ẒEVI (1923–), Israeli military commander, the sixth chief of staff of the IDF. Born in Zaslavl, Ukraine, Ẓur went to Palestine in 1925. He joined the *Haganah in 1939, and was battalion commander in the Givati Brigade during the Israeli *War of Independence. After the war he was brigade commander and later chief of staff of the southern command. In 1951 he began to study public administration at Syracuse University, New York, but was recalled to take up an appointment as chief of manpower division at GHQ. In 1956 he became CO of the central command, in 1958, deputy chief of general staff, and then from 1958 to 1961 studied in Paris. In 1961 he was appointed chief of the general staff of the Israeli Defense Forces (1961–63). During his tenure as chief of staff, Israel did not face serious security problems and he devoted himself to upgrading the army's equipment and developing its military doctrine. After he retired from the army, he was director of *Mekorot, the Israeli water company (1964–67). In 1965 he was elected to the *Knesset from the *Rafi party but resigned his seat. In June 1967 he became assistant to the defense minister, Moshe Dayan, a position he held for seven years. From 1974 he served in high managerial positions in the Clal firm. In 2004 he signed a petition supporting Prime Minister Ariel *Sharon's Disengagement Plan.

[Jehuda Wallach]

ZURI (Zuri-Szezak), JACOB SAMUEL (1884–1943), lawyer, authority on Hebrew law, and author. Zuri, who was born in Poland, studied in France and Germany. After immigrating to Palestine after World War I, he lectured for a time at the Jerusalem Law School. In 1927 he moved to Paris and in 1931 to London. Zuri's single scholarly purpose was to introduce into the European study of Greek, Roman, and Islamic law the data of the Jewish legal tradition. He published most of his 31 works in Hebrew, because, as a Zionist, he hoped to lay the foundation for a system of legislation for the coming Jewish state. In his biographical studies and in his analysis of Jewish jurisprudence, Zuri distinguishes between two main currents in rabbinical methodology, the southern, characteristic of Judean scholars, and the northern, of Galilean scholars. These recur in Babylonian Sura and Nehardea-Pumbedita, respectively. Southern methodology seeks for the underlying unity of surface differences. In mishnaic study, a southerner will relate the view of an anonymous Mishnah to the total view held by a tannaitic authority or to an abstract legal principle. Northern methodology concentrates on concrete characteristics of cases and looks for fine individual differences. In mishnaic controversy, the northerner looks for an explanation of difference in the differing circumstances of specific cases. Zuri worked out these principles in, among others, the following works: *Rab, sein Leben und seine Anschauungen* (1918); *Rabbi Akiva* (Heb., 1924); *Rav Ashi* (Heb. 1924); *Tarbut ha-Deromim* (1924); *Toledot Darkhei ha-Limmud* (1914); *Toledot ha-Mishpat ha-Ẓibburi ha-Ivri* (3 vols. 1931–34); and *Tarbut ha-Deromim* (1924). Zuri made a substantial contribution to the study of talmudic history and law. However, his prolixity and occasional inaccuracies, combined with a single-minded adherence to his primary interpretive principle, have limited his impact.

BIBLIOGRAPHY: S. Kanter, in: J. Neusner (ed.), *Formation of the Babylonian Talmud* (1970).

[Jacob Neusner]

ZURICH, capital of the canton of the same name, N. Switzerland. Jews first arrived in Zurich in 1273, settling in a street known as the Judengasse (now the Froschaugasse). They also had a cemetery. Their taxes were paid to Emperor Rudolf I of Hapsburg, but in other respects they were dependent on the town, which undertook to protect them in exchange for a fee of ten marks and authorized them to engage in moneylending. They were also allowed to acquire real property. However they were compelled to remain indoors during Holy Week. Their principal occupation was moneylending, which they practiced on a large scale, dealing with the municipality, the leading aristocratic families, and even lending considerable sums abroad in such towns as Wuerzburg, Venice, and Frankfurt. The reception hall of a Jewish moneylender has been found at Brunngasse 8. The coats of arms of his noble clients bear Hebrew inscriptions.

The rumor that the Jews had caused the plague by poisoning the wells, which spread throughout Switzerland, reached Zurich at the end of 1348. At first the municipal council attempted to protect the Jews, but it was finally forced to cede to the populace. Numbers of Jews were then burnt at the stake on Feb. 22, 1349, and their belongings confiscated by the municipal council. The emperor promptly protested, claiming compensation; once he had received this, he absolved the council from the charge of murder.

The talmudist, Moses of Zurich, author of glosses on the Se-Ma-K (*Sefer Mitzvot Katan*) which are known as *Semak Zurich*, lived in the town during the early 14th century.

In spite of the massacre of 1349, Jews reappeared in the town as early as 1352. Several expulsion orders were issued (1425, 1435, 1436), but the very number of expulsions indicates that the orders were not strictly observed. However when, in 1634, the Jew Eiron (Aaron) of Lengnau, originally of Frankfurt, was executed in Zurich for blasphemy, the Jews were finally and totally expelled.

After the *French Revolution a few Jews attempted to reestablish themselves in Zurich, but it was only after the emancipation of the Jews of Zurich (1862) that a new community, largely formed by migrants from *Endingen and Lengnau and other nearby south German and Alsatian rural communities, was established. The first synagogue was inaugurated in 1883. It was built by disciples of Gottfried Semper. The community grew rapidly until it became the leading one of Switzerland. The secretariat of the Schweizerische Israelitischer Gemeindebund (est. 1904) has its headquarters in the town. In 1895/98 some separatist Orthodox families split away and later East European Jews formed their own community (between 1912 and 1924). The West European Orthodox community erected in 1926 an art-déco synagogue on Freigutstrasse, which was recently renovated. Only in 1961 did the different East European *minyanim* unite in the synagogue on Erikastrasse.

Jews played a prominent role in textile trade and department stores (Julius Brann), not so much in banking, since Protestant families dominated this branch. The private "Bank Julius Bär" (est. 1897) was the biggest Jewish-owned firm. The children of the East European immigrants entered white-collar jobs. The Social Democratic lawyer David Farbstein was their leader between 1898 and 1939. In 1939 the first Jewish community center in Switzerland was opened in Zurich.

In 2005, Zurich had four Jewish congregations – the moderately Orthodox Israelitische Cultusgemeinde (ICZ; 2,596 members), the Orthodox Israelitische Religionsgesellschaft (IRG, 332 families and singles), Agudas Achim (275 families and singles) which follows the East European tradition – and the egalitarian Liberal Jewish congregation Or Chadasch (est. in 1978, 500 members) each possessing its own religious institutions (e.g., four different Jewish cemeteries) and officials. Besides them, there is a sizeable moderate Orthodox *minyan* in the quarter of Wollishofen. Inner-Jewish polarization led to the founding of often rival Orthodox *minyanim* of Chabad, the Belzer Ḥasidim, etc. In the two Jewish old age homes, there exist additional *minyanim*. The only German-language Swiss-Jewish weekly paper, *Tachles,* is edited in Zurich. It succeeded the *Israelitisches Wochenblatt fuer die Schweiz*, which had appeared since 1901. In 2005 *Tachles* bought the American-Jewish *Aufbau* and tried to establish it as a monthly. A full-time Orthodox Jewish school was founded in 1956, which in 1970 had more than 145 pupils from Orthodox families only. A private moderate Orthodox day school was organized by members of the Cultusgemeinde in 1979, which had also about 170 pupils of every type of observance. Religious lessons are provided even after sixth grade, when the day school program ends ("Achinoam"). The youth movements Aguda-youth, Ha-Goshrim, Bnei Akiva, and Ha-Shomer ha-Ẓa'ir (est. in 1933) play an important role in educating the Jewish youth of Zurich.

In 2005 a new constitution of the canton was accepted, including a paragraph on the possible recognition of two democratically organized Jewish communities, the Cultusgemeinde and the Liberal one.

Many Jews moved to the suburbs of Zurich. In the canton of Zurich there were 6,461 Jews (2000), about two-thirds members of the congregations; some Anglo-Saxon families living in central Switzerland (Zug, Lucerne) also belong to them. Since about 1910 Zurich has been the center of Jewish life in Switzerland.

Hebrew Printing

During the 16th and 17th centuries a number of Christian printers in Zurich produced books containing Hebrew type; chief of these was the house of Froschauer (from 1528), which used the type of *Fagius. In 1558 Eliezer b. Naphtali Herz *Treves printed Psalms with a rhymed Yiddish translation by Elijah Baḥur Levita. The same year Hebrew type was used in J. Reuchlin's *Clarorum Verorum Epistolae*. In the 17th and 18th centuries the presses of J.J. Bodmer and of J.H. Heidegger used Hebrew type, the former from 1635 to 1727, the latter from 1673 to 1766. A few Hebrew works were also produced in Zurich in the 19th century.

BIBLIOGRAPHY: Germ Jud, 2 (1968), Germ. Jud., 3/11 (1998) index; Schweizerischer Israelitischer Gemeindebund, *Festschrift zum 50-jaehrigen Bestehen* (1954); A. Weldler-Steinberg, *Geschichte der Juden in der Schweiz* (1966). Hebrew Printing: K.J. Luethi, Hebraeisch in der Schweiz (1926), 32 35; Ḥ.D. Friedberg, *Toledot ha-Defus ha-Ivri be-Eiropah* (1937), 11–12; C. Freimann, *Gazetteer of Hebrew Printing* (1946), 78. **ADD. BIBLIOGRAPHY:** *Festschrift 100 Jahre Israelitische Religionsgesellschaft Zürich* (IRGZ) (1995); *Geschichte der Juden im Kanton Zürich* (2005); ICZ (ed.), *Juden in Zürich* (1981), K. Huser Bugmann, *Schtetl an der Sihl. Einwanderung, Leben und Alltag der Ostjuden in Zürich 1880–1939* (1998), SIG (ed.), *Juedische Lebenswelt Schweiz. 100 Jahre Schweizerischer Israelitischer Gemeindebund* (2004); H. Strauss-Zweig, *David Farbstein (1869–1953). Juedischer Sozialist – sozialistischer Jude* (2002).

[Simon R. Schwarzfuchs / Uri Kaufmann (2nd ed.)]

ẒUR MI-SHELLO (Heb. צוּר מִשֶּׁלּוֹ; lit. "Rock from whose store [we have eaten]"), an anonymous hymn which is generally chanted at the conclusion of the Sabbath meals. This poem functions as an introduction to the *Grace after the Meal, and its four stanzas summarize the contents of that prayer. The first stanza is based on the first paragraph of the Grace which praises God for providing food for all His creatures. The second stanza, relating to the second paragraph of the Grace, expresses Israel's gratitude for the "good land" God has given it. Corresponding to the third paragraph of the Grace, the third stanza asks God to have mercy on Israel and to restore the Temple and the Kingdom of David. The fourth stanza continues the theme of the rebuilding of the Temple and also makes references to the fact that grace is recited over a cup of wine. The refrain of this hymn reads as follows:

> Rock from whose store we have eaten –
> Bless him, my faithful companions.
> Eaten have we and left over –
> This was the word of the Lord (transl. Nina Salaman; see Hertz in bibl.).

Although it makes no references to the Sabbath, *Ẓur mi-Shello* is not recited on weekdays. Nevertheless, Jacob *Emden was of the opinion that one reciting it during the week will be especially blessed (*Siddur Beit Ya'akov*, 156).

BIBLIOGRAPHY: Hertz, Prayer, 413; Idelsohn, Liturgy, 153.

[Aaron Rothkoff]

ẒUR MOSHE (Heb. צוּר מֹשֶׁה), moshav in central Israel, S. of Kefar Yonah, affiliated with Tenu'at ha-Moshavim. Ẓur Moshe was founded in 1937 by settlers from Greece who were joined by others from Turkey and Bulgaria. In the early years they earned their livelihood mainly by working as hired laborers in surrounding villages. Orange groves became the main farming branch, supplemented by poultry and field crops. With the arrival of newcomers from Bulgaria after 1948, the moshav was enlarged, and in 1970 it had 412 inhabitants. In the mid-1990s the population was 543; subsequent large-scale expansion brought it up to 1,410 in 2002. Ẓur Moshe was named after the Greek Zionist leader Moshe Kophinas.

ZUROFF, EFRAIM (1948–), spiritual heir of Simon Wiesenthal, the last of the Nazi hunters; director, *Simon Wiesenthal Center's Israel Office and coordinator of Nazi War Crimes Research for the Simon Wiesenthal Center.

Born in New York City, educated at Brooklyn Talmudical Academy where his father was principal, he completed an undergraduate degree in history (with honors) at Yeshiva University, where his grandfather was dean, and went on *aliyah* in 1970. He obtained a M.A. degree in Holocaust Studies at the Institute of Contemporary Jewry of the Hebrew University, where he also completed his Ph.D., which chronicles the response of Orthodox Jewry in the United States to the Holocaust and focuses on the rescue attempts launched by the Va'ad ha-Hatzalah rescue committee.

In 1978 he was the first director of the Simon Wiesenthal Center in Los Angeles, where he played a leading role in establishing the Center's library and archives and was historical advisor for the Academy award-winning documentary *Genocide*. In 1980 he returned to Israel, where he served as a researcher for the U.S. Justice Department's *Office of Special Investigations. His efforts assisted in the preparation of cases against numerous Nazi war criminals living in the United States.

His work has less of the drama usually associated with the capture of war criminals. Rather it involves a painstaking review of documents with the goal of not only understanding how the deed was done, but by whom, identifying the perpetrator and then engaging foreign leaders and governments with sufficient pressure to have them try Nazi war criminals.

In 1986 his research uncovered the postwar escape of hundreds of Nazi war criminals to Australia, Canada, Great Britain, and other countries, and he rejoined the Wiesenthal Center to coordinate its international efforts to bring Holocaust perpetrators to justice. These efforts have influenced the passage of special laws in Canada (1987), Australia (1989), and Great Britain (1991) which enable the prosecution in those countries of Nazi war criminals.

Since the dismemberment of the Soviet Union and the fall of Communism, Zuroff has played a major role in the efforts to convince Lithuania, Latvia, and Estonia and other post-Communist societies to confront the widespread complicity of their nationals in the crimes of the Holocaust and to prosecute local Nazi collaborators. His public advocacy on these issues has been instrumental in the submission by Lithuania and Latvia of indictments (Lileikis, Gimzauskas) and/or extradition requests (Kalejs, Gecas) against local Holocaust perpetrators. In 1991 he exposed the rehabilitation of Nazi war criminals in Lithuania and led the campaign to stop this process. Zuroff was appointed by the then Israeli Foreign Minister Shimon Peres to serve on the joint Israeli-Lithuanian commission of inquiry established to deal with this issue, which led to the cancelation to date of over 150 rehabilitations granted to individuals who had participated in the murder of Jews during the Holocaust. In 2000 he exposed the rehabilitations granted by the Latvian government to Nazi war criminals; he led the efforts to cancel these pardons, two of which have been rescinded.

In the summer of 2002, together with Aryeh Rubin, founder of the Targum Shlishi Foundation, he launched "Operation: Last Chance," which offers financial rewards for information which will facilitate the conviction and punishment of Nazi war criminals. So far, the project has been initiated in nine countries (Lithuania, Latvia, Estonia, Poland, Romania, Austria, Croatia, Hungary, and Germany) and has yielded the names of over 400 suspects, 85 of which have been submitted to local prosecutors.

At the turn of the 21st century Zuroff directed a research project to identify Nazi war criminals who are receiving special disability pensions from the German government, which passed special legislation to enable their cancelation in 1998. To date, the pensions of 105 individuals who "violated the norms of humanity" have been canceled, several hundred additional cases are currently under active investigation and thousands of other cases are awaiting review by the German Ministry of Social Services.

Zuroff played an important role in the exposure, arrest, extradition, and prosecution of Dinko Sakic, the former commandant of the Croatian concentration camp Jasenovac (nicknamed the "Auschwitz of the Balkans"). In early October 1999, Sakic, who lived for more than 50 years in Argentina, was sentenced in Zagreb to 20 years' imprisonment for his crimes in the first-ever trial of a Nazi war criminal in a post-Communist country.

He has written two books, *Occupation: Nazi-Hunter; The Continuing Search for the Perpetrators of the Holocaust* (1994), which chronicles the belated efforts to prosecute Nazi war criminals in western democracies and explains the rationale for such efforts several decades after the crimes. Also, in 2000 he published a study of the history of the Va'ad ha-Hatzalah, which was awarded an Egit Grant for Holocaust and Jewish Resistance Literature by the Israeli General Federation of Labor (Histadrut) and also received the 1999–2000 Samuel Belkin Literary Award for the best book published by a Yeshiva University alumnus in the field of Jewish studies.

His activities as a Nazi-hunter were the subject of three television documentaries. The first, entitled "The Nazi-Hunter," was produced by ZDF (German Channel 2) in 1999; the second, entitled "The Last Nazi-Hunter," was produced by SWR (German Channel 1 – regional station) in 2004 and the third "The Final Hunt for the Nazis" by France Trois (Channel 3) was broadcast in December 2005.

Zuroff would rather be right than popular. His history of the Va'ad is less a work of the hagiography popular in Orthodox circles today than a serious work of history, which examines not uncritically the work of the Orthodox and demonstrates their unique efforts as well as their dependence on the larger Jewish community for funding and effectiveness. He examines the tendency of Orthodox Judaism to go it alone. He has also been critical of the Israeli government for its lack of interest in pursuing Nazi war criminals.

In 1995 and 1996, Zuroff was invited to Rwanda to assist the local authorities in their efforts to bring to justice the perpetrators of the genocide which took place in that country in spring 1994, and he has served as an official advisor to the Rwandan government. He began his speech in the native language. An activist by temperament as well as by conviction, when he confronts evil, he seeks to undo it rather than understand it.

Since 2001, the Simon Wiesenthal Center's "Annual Status Report on the Worldwide Investigation and Prosecution of Nazi War Criminals," which he writes, is considered the authoritative source on the subject.

[Michael Berenbaum (2nd ed.)]

ẒUR YIGAL (Heb. צור יגאל), community settlement located 5 mi. (8 km.) east of Kefar Sava. The settlement is one of the "star" plan settlements, aimed to expand the Jewish population near the border of the occupied territories. It was founded in 1991 and the first settlers arrived in 1994. In 2002 the population was 6,800. The name Ẓur Yigal comemmorates Yigal Cohen, a member of Knesset who contributed to Israeli settlement.

WEBSITE: www.zur-yigal.muni.il.

[Shaked Gilboa (2nd ed.)]

ZUSYA (Meshulam Zusya) OF HANIPOLI (Annopol; d. 1800), early ḥasidic leader; he was an outstanding disciple of *Dov Baer, the Maggid of Mezhirech, brother of *Elimelech of Lyzhansk, and one of the best known heroes of ḥasidic folktales. Zusya was probably born near Tarnow, Galicia, and at a relatively early age joined the disciples of the Maggid of Mezhirech and interested his brother Elimelech in Ḥasidism. During their youth the two brothers wandered from place to place in the manner of ascetic kabbalists. Many folk legends tell of their wandering and show Zusya as a simple, modest, and benevolent man who despite his meager knowledge of Torah, attained merit because of his innocence and personal righteousness. Zusya's own statements, however, of which few survive in writing, show that he was a scholar. In addition to the close attachment to his brother Elimelech, he formed a friendship with *Shneur Zalman of Lyady. Apparently after the death of the Maggid of Mezhirech, Zusya settled in Hanipoli and Ḥasidim gathered around him. This circle enlarged after Elimelech's death, when some of the latter's Ḥasidim accepted Zusya as their rabbi. His oldest son, MENAHEM ẒEVI HIRSH, succeeded him in Hanipoli. His youngest son, ISRAEL ABRAHAM (1772–1814), served as ḥasidic rabbi and *admor* in Chernyostrov. After Israel Abraham's death, his wife led the Ḥasidim for several years. The few surviving statements of Zusya and his sons were collected in *Menorat Zahav* (ed. by Nathan Neta ha-Kohen, 1902).

BIBLIOGRAPHY: Dubnow, Ḥasidut, index; L.I. Newman, *Ḥasidic Anthology* (1963), index; M. Buber, *Tales of the Ḥasidim* (1968), 238–52; Horodezky, Ḥasidut, index.

[Adin Steinsaltz]

ZUTA (also known as **Yaḥya** and **Abu-Zikri**; 12th century), **nagid* in Egypt. He was also the head of a yeshivah and gave himself the title *Sar Shalom* ("Prince of Peace"), but in reality he acted with great ruthlessness toward the members of his community after he had been appointed *nagid* of Egyptian Jewry in succession to *Samuel b. Hananiah. He secured his position by bribing the caliph al-Fā'iz (1154–1160). As a result of the complaints brought against him by the Jewish community concerning his criminal conduct, he was removed from his position which he had held for 66 days and Samuel was reinstated. After the death of Samuel (shortly after 1159), Zuta made a new effort to secure the position of the *nagid* but failed. During the reign of Saladin (1138–1193), he succeeded in regaining the position in exchange for a yearly payment of 200 dinars, and he held it for about four years from the beginning of the 1160s. As a result of the efforts of Maimonides and R. Isaac b. Sasson, a member of Maimonides' *bet din*, Zuta was excommunicated and ousted from his position, but he succeeded a third time to become the political leader of Egyptian Jewry. However, he served as a *nagid* for 24 years, from 1172 to 1196. Zuta was known to the members of his faction as messiah and *Gaon*. His adherents were accused of being no better than idolaters. To commemorate the ousting of Zuta, in 1196 the poet *Abraham b. Hillel wrote the *Megillat Zuta*, which was published by A. Neubauer, A.E. Harkavy, and D. Kahana. It contains a description of Zuta's activities and his removal.

BIBLIOGRAPHY: Neubauer, in: JQR, 8 (1895/96), 541–51; 9 (1896/97), 721; A.E. Harkavy, *Ḥadashim Gam Yeshanim* (1970), 15–17; Kahana, in: *Ha-Shiloaḥ*, 15 (1905), 175–84; Mann, Egypt, 1 (1920), 234–7; Mann, Texts, 1 (1931), 416–8; Ashtor, Toledot, 1 (1944), 41–42; idem, in: HUCA, 27 (1956), 313–15; Goitein, in: *Tarbiz*, 32 (1962/63), 192. **ADD. BIBLIOGRAPHY:** M. Ben-Sasson, "Maimonides in Egypt: The First Stage," in: *Maimonidean Studies*, 2 (1991), 3–30; M.A. Friedman, "Ha-Rambam, Zuta ve-ha-Muqaddamim – Sippuram shel Sheloshah Haramot," in: *Zion*, 70 (2005), 473–527.

[Abraham David (2nd ed.)]

ZUTA, ḤAYYIM ARYEH (1868–1939), pioneer of Hebrew education in Ereẓ Israel. Born in Kovno, Lithuania, he was one of the first Hebrew teachers in Russia to employ the *Ivrit be-Ivrit* ("Hebrew in Hebrew") system. In 1903 he went to Ereẓ Israel, where he taught in various educational institutions (mainly in Jerusalem) and was a founder of the modern Hebrew school system in the country.

He published articles on Hebrew education and schools and wrote a number of textbooks and stories. His book *Darkhei ha-Limmud shel ha-Tanakh* ("Teaching the Bible," 2 vols., 1935–37) is a major work of Hebrew didactics. *Be-Reshit Darki* ("The Beginning of My Way," 1934) are memoirs of his career as a teacher. His short stories were collected in *Kitvei Ḥayyim Aryeh Zuta*, 3 vols. (1931).

BIBLIOGRAPHY: I. Epstein, in: KS, 12 (1935/36), 290–2; Tidhar, 3 (1949), 1279–80; Rabbi Binyamin, *Keneset Ḥakhamim* (1960), 194–5.

[Gedalyah Elkoshi]

ZUTRA, MAR, the names of three *exilarchs during the fifth and sixth centuries. MAR ZUTRA I (d. c. 414), exilarch from 401 to 409, the successor of Mar Kahana and a contemporary of R. Ashi. It may be that he was the son of Huna b. Nathan, although his father's name does not appear in the sources. Mar Zutra was a student of R. Papa and R. Pappai and he transmitted the teachings of the earlier generations. He associated to a great extent with R. Ashi and Ameimar, and their differing opinions regarding various laws concerning meals are recorded in the Talmud (e.g., Ber. 44b, 50b; Shab. 50b). His piety and character were exemplary, and the title "the pious" was appended to his name (BK 81b; BM 24a). Whenever he had to pronounce a ban on a scholar, he first banned himself and then pronounced it on the culprit. Later, Mar Zutra absolved himself and then absolved the other (MK 17a). He prayed and fasted for the welfare of others but never on his own behalf (TJ, Ma'as. Sh. 5:8, 156d). When Mar Zutra was carried in honor on the shoulders of his audience on the Sabbath before the Pilgrim festivals at a time when he preached on the festival laws, he would repeat the verse (Prov. 27:24): "For riches are not for ever; and doth the crown endure unto all generations?" (Yoma 87a).

MAR ZUTRA II (c. 496–520), exilarch from 512 to 520. He was the son of *Huna, who had previously served as exilarch and was killed during the persecutions instituted by the Persian monarch, Firuz. His mother was the daughter of the head of the academy, Mar Ḥanina. According to tradition, Mar Zutra was born after the entire house of the exilarch had died out, and he was the sole survivor of the House of David, from whom the exilarchs were traditionally descended. During his minority, the exilarchate was administered by his brother-in-law, Mar Paḥra or Paḥda, who bribed the king to retain him in office. When Mar Zutra reached the age of 15, his grandfather induced the king to install him as the legitimate exilarch. The new exilarch took up arms against the Persians, perhaps because of Persian oppression of the Jewish religion. Marching at the head of 400 Jewish warriors, Mar Zutra succeeded in defeating the Persians and setting up an independent Jewish state, with Maḥoza as his residence. The new state survived for seven years, but immorality spread among his followers and they were finally defeated in battle by the Persians. Both Mar Zutra and his grandfather, Ḥanina, were taken prisoner and beheaded, and their bodies were later suspended from crosses on the bridge at Maḥoza.

MAR ZUTRA III (sixth century), the son of Mar Zutra II. According to tradition he was born on the day that his father was executed and was therefore named after him. He later succeeded him as exilarch. He left Babylon to settle in Ereẓ Israel, where he was appointed to an academic position in a college. It is thought that he disseminated knowledge of the Babylonian Talmud in Ereẓ Israel.

In addition to a *tanna* called Zutra who is mentioned in a *baraita* (Ber. 13b), there were also some other *amoraim* of this name: ZUTRA BEN TOBI (third century), a student of Rav and R. Judah who transmitted their teachings (Ber. 7a; Yev. 44a); MAR ZUTRA BEN R. NAḤMAN (b. Jacob; fourth century), who transmitted his father's teachings and who, in his youth, adjudicated a monetary case without previously obtaining the permission of the exilarch and erred in his decision (Sanh. 5a); and MAR ZUTRA BEN MARI (b. Issur; fourth century), the brother of R. Adda the elder (Kid. 65b).

BIBLIOGRAPHY: Hyman, Toledot; Ḥ. Albeck, *Mavo la-Talmudim* (1969), 283–4.

ZVENIGORODKA, city in S. Kiev district, Ukraine. In 1787 the Jewish community of Zvenigorodka numbered 387. In 1897 there were 6,389 Jews (32% of the total population) and in 1926 the number of Jews in Zvenigorodka amounted to 6,584 (36.5% of the total population). Most of the Jews were murdered when the Germans occupied Zvenigorodka in World War II. A 1959 census showed approximately 700 Jews in the town. There was no organized Jewish life. In 1965 private religious services were dispersed by the militia. Most Jews left in the mass exodus of the 1990s,

BIBLIOGRAPHY: I. Erenburg, *Merder fun Felker* (1945), 138–40.

ZVIA (1935–1974), artist. Zvia was born at kibbutz Mishmar ha-Sharon, Ereẓ Israel, and studied art in Tel Aviv before attending the Central School of Art and Crafts, London; she finally settled in England in 1957. Her gifts in traditional techniques were considerable, as draughtsman, painter and portrait-sculptor. But her real talent and interest lay in research, notably into the light properties of acrylics and the use of electric light in sculpture. For these reasons she was employed by both ICI and Osram-GEC, to explore the properties and possibilities of these materials; the elaborate sculptural complexes she produced for these companies were exhibited. As part of her research, she produced a series of charming plastic jewelry. Among her public commissions is a large outdoor sculpture for the University of Sussex, England. She possessed an unusual combination of artistic and scientific accomplishments.

[Charles Samuel Spencer]

ZWEIFEL, ELIEZER (1815–1888), Hebrew author and essayist, one of the first Haskalah writers to view Ḥasidism sympathetically. Zweifel was born in Mogilev. His father belonged to the *Chabad movement, and his traditional education included rabbinic and ḥasidic literature, medieval studies, and Kabbalah. Later, he studied the works of the Haskalah and the Wissenschaft des *Judentums writers in Hebrew and German. After many years of wandering in various Russian towns, earning his living by preaching and teaching, he was appointed lecturer in Mishnah and Talmud in the government rabbinical seminary at Zhitomir in 1853, remaining there until the seminary was closed in 1873. Zweifel was liked by his students, who included A.J. *Paperna and M. *Margolis, and inspired them with a love of Jewish tradition and the Talmud. By nature, he was a moderate; he tried "as far as possible to emphasize the favorable aspect of everything and every person" (preface to his *Shalom al Yisrael*, 3 (1870), 11).

His first book, *Minim ve-Ugav*, appeared in Vilna in 1858. It was a small but variegated collection of scriptural commentaries, homilies, and poems, deprecating the extreme attitudes of the Haskalah toward the devotees of the old religious tradition. The book aroused lively literary controversy, and was criticized with particular severity by *Mendele Mokher Seforim, then a young student, in his pamphlet *Mishpat Shalom* ("Peaceful Judgment," 1860). In *Minim ve-Ugav*, Zweifel employed a unique mixture of biblical, mishnaic, and talmudic language. David *Frischmann exaggerates in calling him "the father of the modern style", but he was undoubtedly one of those who led the change in Hebrew prose from the ornate biblical language to the modern literary style.

Zweifel's most important work was *Shalom al Yisrael* ("Peace to Israel"), which appeared in four parts in Zhitomir and Vilna between 1868 and 1873. The book defended Ḥasidism in terms of modern values and marked a sharp contrast to the general hostility which virtually all *maskilim* had hitherto manifested toward that movement. Ḥasidism, he argued, had a system of ideas of its own, which in many respects resembled the ideas of Philo and Spinoza. His defence of Ḥasidism relates specifically to the early stages of its development, whereas he takes issue with negative aspects which emerged in its later period, especially the cult of the *ẓaddik*. The book includes numerous selections from the writings of Ḥasidim, and of modern Jewish writers who wrote favorably about the movement as well as those who attacked it. Although it contains a wealth of material, the contents are poorly edited and make reading difficult. The book aroused indignation and severe criticism among the *maskilim*, and Jewish censors sympathetic to the Haskalah tried to prevent its publication.

The book sparked a reevaluation of Ḥasidism by scholars and writers, and led to the historical appraisal of the movement by S. *Dubnow and a more romantic one by M.J. *Berdyczewski, S.A. *Horodezky, M. *Buber, and others.

After the closing of the rabbinical seminary in 1873, Zweifel lived in various towns in Russia and Poland, until he finally settled in the house of his daughter at Glukhov. His book *Sanegor* ("Defense Counsel," 1885) is a rebuttal to the accusations leveled against the Talmud by Jewish and gentile critics. Zweifel also wrote hundreds of articles in the Hebrew press, issued several works on ethics in Yiddish, including *Musar Haskel* ("Moral Lesson," 1862) and *Tokhaḥat Ḥayyim* ("Life's Reproof," 1865), and published books by other authors, old and new, whose ideas were akin to his. Zweifel's writings are distinguished by profuse quotations from rabbinic sources and his wide erudition. They lack, however, systematic structure, and today his works are primarily of historical interest.

BIBLIOGRAPHY: Waxman, Literature, 3 (1960^2), 315–9, 341; Lachower, Sifrut, 2 (1929), 251–9, 312–3; Klausner, Sifrut, 6 (1952), 11–80; Rejzen, Leksikon, 2 (1929), 251–9; R. Goldberg, in: *Orlogin*, 12 (1956), 263–6.

[Yehuda Slutsky]

ZWEIG, ARNOLD (1887–1968), German novelist and playwright. Zweig was born in Gross-Glogau, Silesia. In 1915, while a university student, he volunteered for the German army and spent over a year in the trenches. After the war he became a freelance writer, living first in Bavaria and from 1923 in Berlin. There he was for a time editor of the Zionist **Juedische Rundschau*, having, unlike the vast majority of German-Jewish writers, turned to Jewish nationalism. With Lion Feuchtwanger he wrote *Die Aufgabe des Judentums* (1933). When the Nazis came to power, Zweig left Germany for Ereẓ Israel by way of Czechoslovakia, Switzerland, and France. He lived in Haifa where he coedited the short-lived weekly *Orient* (1942–43). In 1948 he settled in East Berlin, remaining there until his death.

Zweig first attracted attention with his *Novellen um Claudia* (1912, *Claudia*, Eng. 1930). The biblical drama *Abigail und Nabal* (1913) and the novella *Aufzeichnungen ueber eine Familie Klopfer* (1911) were followed by a more important drama of Jewish life, the prizewinning *Ritualmord in Ungarn* (1914, revised as *Die Sendung Semaels*, 1918). It was, however, his bestselling novel, *Der Streit um den Sergeanten Grischa* (1927; *The Case of Sergeant Grischa*, 1928), which (translated into nearly 20 languages) spread Zweig's reputation far beyond the German-speaking world. Perhaps the outstanding war novel of the Weimar Republic, this scathing exposure of Prussian justice dealt with the trial and execution of an innocent and inarticulate Russian prisoner of war. Over the years Zweig wrote a series of prose epics on Germany before, during, and after World War I (parts of an eight-volume cycle entitled *Der grosse Krieg der weissen Maenner); Erziehung vor Verdun* (1935; *Education Before Verdun*, 1936); *Einsetzung eines Koenigs* (1937; *Crowning of a King*, 1938); *Junge Frau von 1914* (1931; *Young Woman of 1914*, 1932); and *Die Feuerpause* (1954). The Nazi terror was described in another fine novel, *Das Beil von Wandsbek* (1947; *The Axe of Wandsbeck*, 1947), filmed in 1951; it was published first in Hebrew in 1943.

Zweig's thinking on Jewish problems found expression in the essays *Das ostjuedische Antlitz* (1920); *Caliban* (1927), a study of antisemitism; *Juden auf der deutschen Buehne* (1928); and *Bilanz der deutschen Judenheit 1933* (1934; *Insulted and Exiled*, 1937); his drama *Die Umkehr* (1925), and the novel *De Vriendt kehrt Heim* (1932; *De Vriendt Goes Home*, 1933), based on the tragic career of Jacob Israël de *Haan. During his early Zionist period in Germany, Zweig held that Palestine could change the character of Jewish life everywhere by becoming once again the spiritual center of the Jews and by developing new forms of cooperative living. He nevertheless increasingly held internationalism to be the highest ideal. Zweig never felt at home in Palestine, being unable to adapt himself to a Hebrew-speaking milieu: local publishers were not inclined to translate his books, nor was *Habimah enthusiastic about staging his plays. He favored a binational, Jewish-Arab state and became increasingly critical of Zionist aims. Failing eyesight also increased his aggravations; after the declaration of Israel's independence, Zweig, now more sympathetic to Communism, made a much-publicized return to East Germany, where he succeeded Heinrich Mann as president of the Academy of Arts in 1950. He received many awards, including the International Lenin Peace Prize (1958). His correspondence with *Freud was published in 1968. Toward the end of his life, Zweig evidently reassessed his views on Zionism and courageously refused to sign an East German intellectuals' statement condemning Israel's "aggression" against the Arab states after the Six-Day War of 1967.

BIBLIOGRAPHY: S. Liptzin, *Germany's Stepchildren* (1944), 281–4; *Sinn und Form. Beitraege zur Literatur,* Sonderheft (1952); J. Rudolph, *Der Humanist Arnold Zweig* (1955); H. Kamnitzer, *Erkenntnis und Bekentnis: Arnold Zweig 70 Jahre* (1958); E. Hilscher, *A. Zweig: Brueckenbauer vom Gestern ins Morgen* (1962); *Welt und Wirkung eines Romans; Zu Arnold Zweigs "Der Streit um den Sergeanten Grischa"* (1967), E.L. Freud (ed.), *Letters of Sigmund Freund and Arnold Zweig* (1971).

[Sol Liptzin]

ZWEIG, STEFAN (1881–1942), Austrian playwright, essayist, and biographer. The son of a wealthy Viennese industrialist, Zweig had an early and auspicious start in literature, publishing at the age of 20 his first verse collection, *Silberne Saiten* (1901). When Theodor *Herzl, literary editor of the influential *Neue Freie Presse*, agreed to publish one of his essays, young Zweig was greatly encouraged and he soon became an outstanding member of the "Young Vienna" group. In 1903 he wrote a foreword to a collection of paintings and illustrations by Ephraim Moses *Lilien. Zweig also devoted years of self-effacing work to making the Belgian poet Emile Verhaeren known in German-speaking countries by translating Verhaeren's poetry and other works.

World War I marked a turning point in Zweig's outlook. His fourth play was a powerful pacifist drama, *Jeremias* (1918;

Jeremiah, 1922), first staged in Zurich in 1917 when Zweig was attached to the war archives in Vienna. From 1919 Stefan Zweig lived in Salzburg, where his house became an international literary and cultural center. His friends included the French humanitarian Romain Rolland, whose biography Zweig published (1921) and whose novel *Clérambault* he translated a year later. Zweig's collected verse appeared in 1924.

He became best known for biographies, in which he often grouped three people of similar interests in one volume and attempted to find a common spiritual denominator. *Drei Meister* (1920; *Three Masters*, 1930) contained biographical studies of Balzac, Dickens, and Dostoevski; *Der Kampf mit dem Daemon* (1925) analyzed Hoelderlin, Kleist, and Nietzsche, who fell prey to mental illness or committed suicide; while *Drei Dichter ihres Lebens* (1928; *Adepts at Self-Portraiture*, 1928), discussed Casanova, Stendhal, and Tolstoy. These nine biographies were later incorporated in *Baumeister der Welt* (1935; *Master Builders*, 1939). Other biographies were devoted to Joseph Fouché (1929; Eng., 1930), Napoleon's terrifying minister of police; Marie Antoinette (1932; Eng., 1933); Mary Queen of Scots (1935; Eng., 1935); Magellan (1938; *Conqueror of the Seas*, 1938); and Amerigo Vespucci (1944; *Amerigo: A Comedy of Errors in History*, 1942).

Zweig's only novel, *Ungeduld des Herzens* (1938; *Beware of Pity*, 1939), was a penetrating study of the love of a crippled girl. Like *Marie Antoinette*, and several other works by Zweig, this was later made into a motion picture. *Sternstunden der Menschheit* (1927; *The Tide of Fortune*, 1940) dramatized 12 significant events in the history of the human spirit; *Die Heilung durch den Geist* (1931; *Mental Healers*, 1933), included studies of Mesmer, Mary Baker Eddy, and *Freud, in whose psychoanalysis he was greatly interested; while *Triumph und Tragik des Erasmus von Rotterdam* (1934; *Erasmus of Rotterdam*, 1934) described the man whom Zweig considered his spiritual ancestor and mentor. A gentle, nonpolitical modern humanist, Zweig was deeply concerned about the position of the man of spirit in an increasingly brutalized world. In 1934 he wrote the libretto for Richard Strauss' opera *Die schweigsame Frau*. Its suppression by the Nazis became a cause célèbre. Zweig's correspondence with Strauss (ed. by W. Schuh) was published in 1957. Zweig's brilliant and highly charged style and his psychological penetration are evident from his first collection of stories, *Die Liebe der Erika Ewald* (1904), to his last completed work, *Schachnovelle* (1941; *The Royal Game*, 1944), which foreshadows the triumph of a mechanized civilization over the spirit of man. Three other collections were *Erstes Erlebnis* (1911), sensitive studies of childhood and adolescence; *Amok* (1922; Eng., 1931); and *Verwirrung der Gefuehle* (1927; *Conflicts*, 1927), on adult passions and problems.

Although Zweig took no part in Jewish communal life, some of his short stories deal with Jewish themes. The biblical "*Legende der dritten Taube*"; "*Rahel rechtet mit Gott*"; and "*Buchmendel*," the poignant tale of a Jewish bookseller, are three of those collected in *Kaleidoscope* (1934; Ger., *Kaleidoskop*, 1936). His most ambitious work of this type was *Der begrabene Leuchter* (1937; *The Buried Candelabrum*, 1937). Essays about his fellow writers were included in *Begegnungen mit Menschen, Buechern, Staedten* (1937). In his autobiography, written during World War II, *Die Welt von Gestern* (1942; *The World of Yesterday*, 1943), Zweig sadly observed that "nine-tenths of what the world celebrated as Viennese culture in the 19th century was promoted, nourished, and created by Viennese Jewry."

A prey to increasing pessimism, Stefan Zweig, an inveterate world traveler and a tireless lecturer, settled in England in 1935. He lived first in London and later in Bath, then visited North and South America. Depressed by the fate of Europe, Zweig (together with his second wife, Elisabeth) committed suicide in Petropolis, near Rio de Janeiro. One of the most widely read writers between the world wars, Stefan Zweig is esteemed as a great storyteller, biographer, and humanitarian spirit. The International Stefan Zweig Society was founded in Vienna in 1957.

BIBLIOGRAPHY: J. Romains, *Stefan Zweig, Great European* (1941); S. Liptzin, *Germany's Stepchildren* (1944), 211–25; *Columbia Dictionary of Modern European Literature* (1947); H. Arens, *Stefan Zweig: A Tribute to his Life and Work* (1951); A. Bauer, *Stefan Zweig* (Ger., 1961); F.M. Zweig, *Stefan Zweig. Eine Bildbiographie* (1961); H. Zohn, *Wiener Juden in der deutschen Literatur* (1964), 19–30; W. Schramm, *Stefan Zweig* (Ger., 1961); R.J. Klawiter, *Stefan Zweig; a Bibliography* (1965); R. Dumont, *Stefan Zweig et la France* (1967), includes bibliography; Stern, in: ZGJD, 4 (1967), 247–56; *Haaretz* (Feb. 24, 1967), supplement. **ADD. BIBLIOGRAPHY:** D.A. Prater, *European of Yesterday: A Biography of Stefan Zweig* (2006).

[Harry Zohn]

ZWICKAU, city in *Saxony, Germany. Documentary evidence points to the presence of Jews in the first half of the 14th century. In 1308 Margrave Frederick promised to maintain the privileges of both burghers and Jews. Documents dating from 1330 mention a Jewish street and synagogue. The Jews were expelled from the city in 1430 during the *Hussite wars, although some returned soon after. In 1444 the mint, operated by Jews, was attacked by the burghers, and in 1458 the Jewish quarter was burned down. Jewish settlement dwindled and then disappeared. The modern Jewish community in Zwickau grew from 59 persons in 1875 (only 9 in 1834) to 159 in 1910; 362 in 1925; and 473 in 1932, when 12 charitable and social organizations were functioning. By 1939 only 64 Jews remained in the city; none lived there in 1971. The publisher Salman *Schocken grew up in Zwickau.

There are several memorials dedicated to the destroyed synagogue, the deportations, and the Zwickau Jews who perished during the Nazi era.

BIBLIOGRAPHY: FJW, 329–30; *Germania Judaica*, 2 (1968), 950–1; 3 (1987), 1749–51; PK Germanyah. **ADD. BIBLIOGRAPHY:** A. Diamant, *Zur Chronik der Juden in Zwickau. Dem Gedenken einer kleinen judischen Gemeinde in Sachsen* (1971); K. Fuchs, *Ein Konzern aus Sachsen. Das Kaufhaus Schocken als Spiegelbild deutscher Wirtschaft und Politik 1901 bis 1953* (1990).

ZWOLEN (Pol. **Zwoleń**; Rus. **Zvolen**), town in Kielce province, E. central Poland. In 1578 King Stephen Bathory permitted the Jews to settle and trade in the town. In 1591 King Sigismund III prohibited the Jews of Zwolen from acquiring more than ten houses; they nevertheless owned more houses. In 1815 Zwolen was included in Congress Poland, and henceforth its Jewish population gradually increased, numbering 629 (33% of the total) in 1827; 1,350 (49%) in 1856; 3,242 (56%) in 1897; and 3,787 (51%) in 1921. Apart from petty trade, the Jews of Zwolen engaged in the manufacture of clothes and shoes, in tanning, and foodstuff production.

[Shimshon Leib Kirshenboim]

Holocaust Period

With the beginning of the German occupation in September 1939 the Jews were subjected to economic restrictions, confiscation of property, and forced payments of money. In 1941 people were seized and sent to the Pustkow labor camp. In the summer of 1942 transports of men and women capable of working were sent to the *Skarzysko-Kamienna labor camp. At the end of October 1942 deportations to the extermination camps began. In the process of assembling people about 100 were killed, especially the elderly and sick who could not carry out the Nazi orders. The deportees were sent to *Treblinka. Over 100 Jews who were engaged in putting deportees' property in order for the Germans remained in the city and were later transferred to labor camps.

[Aharon Weiss]

BIBLIOGRAPHY: Halpern, Pinkas, index; B. Wasiutyński, *Ludność żydowska w Polsce w wiekach XIX i XX* (1930), 32; *Słownik geograficzny Królestwa Polskiego*, 14 (1895), 700.

ZYCHLIN (Pol. **Żychlin**), town in Lodz province, near *Kutno, central Poland. A Jewish community existed in Zychlin from the 18th century and in 1765 there were 311 Jews paying the poll tax. In 1780 a synagogue was erected, following a special permit from the archbishop of Gniezno. In 1880 it was replaced by a stone building. There were no restrictions on Jewish settlement in Zychlin. The community numbered 457 (57% of the total population) in 1808; 782 (61%) in 1827; 1,062 (66%) in 1857; 2,268 (47%) in 1897; and 2,701 (40%) in 1921.

[Shimshon Leib Kirshenboim]

Holocaust Period

About 3,500 Jews lived in Zychlin in 1939, forming approximately 50% of the total population. The town fell to the German forces on Sept. 17, 1939, and on the following day all the Jewish men were driven to a village 15 miles away, but after detention in a church for three days were released. In April 1940 the Polish and Jewish intellectuals, especially teachers, were arrested and deported to German concentration camps. The number of Jews was reduced to 2,800 by April 1940. A ghetto was established in July 1940 on a swampy area on the outskirts of the town. The ghetto population increased to 3,500, when a group of Jews deported from a nearby town arrived in Zychlin. The ghetto was not fenced in, so that there was some contact with the outside world. The German police could easily be bribed to facilitate some trade. Members of the *Judenrat and certain other Jews were allowed to leave the ghetto during the day. Labor detachments had to be supplied by the Judenrat almost daily. The American Jewish Joint Distribution Committee supplied relief to the poor and the refugees, but no public kitchen could be organized, and as a result of malnutrition a typhoid epidemic broke out in the ghetto. The regime in the ghetto became more severe in 1942 and those who tried to leave the confines of the ghetto were killed. In February 1942 the German police surrounded and broke into the ghetto, killing hundreds of Jews in the streets, among them most of the Judenrat members and their families. The Jewish police were also liquidated in this *Aktion*. On Purim (March 3) 1942, the Jewish population was assembled in the market place and 3,200 persons were loaded on carts; anyone too weak to climb up on the carts was shot on the spot. The entire Jewish population of Zychlin was thus dispatched to the *Chelmno death camp and murdered.

[Danuta Dombrowska]

BIBLIOGRAPHY: Halpern, Pinkas, index; B. Wasiutyński, *Ludność żydowska w Polsce w wiekach XIX i XX* (1930), 21; Y. Trunk, in: *Bleter far Geshikhte*, 2:1–4 (1949), 64–166; D. Dabrowska, in: BŻIH, 13–14 (1955).

ZYCHLINSKA, RAJZEL (1910–2001). Yiddish poet. Born in Gabin (Gombin), Poland, in the years 1936–38 she lived in Warsaw, before escaping to Russia. After returning to Poland in 1947, she lived in Paris (1948–51), and then settled in New York. Her first poems were published in Warsaw in 1928. The fine economy of her short free lyrics has been much praised; she received the Manger Prize in 1975. Her poems have appeared in major Yiddish anthologies and journals, and have been translated into Hebrew, English, French, and German. In book form she published *Lider* ("Poems," 1936), *Der Regn Zingt* ("The Rain Sings," 1939), *Tsu Loytere Bregn* ("To Clear Shores," 1948), *Shvaygndike Tirn* ("Silent Doors," 1962), *Harbstike Skvern* ("Autumn Squares," 1969), *Di November Zun* ("The November Sun," 1977), and *Naye Lider* ("New Poems," 1993). An English volume of her poetry appeared in 1997: *God Hid His Face: Selected Poems*.

BIBLIOGRAPHY: LNYL, 3 (1960), 712–3.

[Leonard Prager / Carrie Friedman-Cohen (2nd ed.)]

ZYGELBOJM, SAMUEL MORDECAI (pseudonym: **Comrade Arthur**; 1895–1943), Polish Bundist leader. Born in the village Borovica in the province of Lublin, Zygelbojm participated in the convention of the Polish *Bund organizations in December 1917 as the delegate from Chelm. From 1920 to 1936 he lived in Warsaw. In 1924 he became a member of the central committee of the Bund. He was elected member and later secretary of the national council of the Jewish trade unions of Poland and chairman of the leather workers' union (Jewish and non-Jewish). He was also a member of the central commission which headed the country's Socialist trade unions. In the early 1930s he spent a year in the United States to promote Yiddish books. In 1926 he became a member of the municipal council of Warsaw and in 1936 a member of the Lodz municipal council.

When the German forces entered Warsaw (September 1939), the mayor was compelled to hand over 12 public figures as hostages to the Nazis. Zygelbojm volunteered to be one of these hostages. He was put on the Warsaw *Judenrat as the Bund representative. There he opposed the Germans' demand that the Judenrat itself establish the Warsaw ghetto. On the request of his party, he managed to leave the German-occupied territory early in January 1940. At the end of January he attended the meeting of the executive council of the Socialist international in Brussels, where he reported on conditions in German-occupied Poland. In September he reached the U.S. From the spring of 1942 Zygelbojm lived in London, where he was the Bund representative at the national council of the Polish government-in-exile during the peak period of the "Final Solution" (see *Holocaust, General Survey). Zygelbojm received information on the Holocaust and made every attempt to alert Polish, British, and other authorities to take rescue and retaliatory action. He was deeply depressed by the ineffectiveness of official action as exemplified by the Anglo-American Conference on Refugees, held in Bermuda (April 19–30, 1943), and by the brutal repression of the revolt in the Warsaw ghetto. As a protest against the atmosphere of indifference to the tragedy of the Jewish people, Zygelbojm committed suicide on May 12, 1943. This act and the letter he left in explanation stirred public opinion.

BIBLIOGRAPHY: *Stop Them Now* (1942); J. Karski, *Story of a Secret State* (1944); *Ghetto Speaks*, no. 8 (Feb. 1, 1948); LNYL, 3 (1960), 590–4; A.D. Morse, *While Six Million Died* (1968), index; *Zygelbojm-Bukh* (1947); A.S. Stein, *Ḥaver Artur* (Heb. 1953). **ADD. BIBLIOGRAPHY:** G. Pickhan, *Gegen den Strom* (2001).

[Moshe Mishkinsky]

ZYLBERCWEIG, ZALMAN (1894–1972), historian of Yiddish theater. Born in Ozorkow, near Lodz, Poland, to a family descended from the biblical exegete *Malbim, his involvement in the Yiddish theater in Lodz began in 1912, primarily as ensemble manager and translator/adaptor of European repertoire. He also served as a correspondent for the Yiddish press. After living in Palestine and traveling extensively, he settled in New York in 1937, marrying the actress Celia Zuckerberg in 1947. The couple moved to Los Angeles in 1948, where they hosted a Yiddish radio show for 25 years. Zylbercweig wrote, translated, and edited some 30 books. His life's work and signature contribution to Jewish culture was his edition of the six-volume *Leksikon fun Yidishn Teater* ("Encyclopedia of the Yiddish Theater," 1931–69; the first three co-edited with *Jacob Mestel; volume seven, which he also in large part wrote [in press at his death], never appeared). The *New York Times* called it "the most authoritative collection of statistics and biographies of Yiddish stage personalities," and it remains the most important work in the field.

BIBLIOGRAPHY: *Z. Zylbercweig Yoyvel Bukh* (1941), incl. bibl.; Rejzen, Leksikon, 1 (1926), 1078–80; LNYL, 3 (1960), 621–3; M. Ravitch, *Mayn Leksikon*, 2 (1946), 227–9; *New York Times* (Nov. 22, 1964), 121; *New York Times* (July 27, 1972), 34.

[Faith Jones (2nd ed.)]

ZYRARDOW (Pol. **Żyrardów**), city in Warszawa province, E. central Poland. Jews began to settle there in the 1840s. There were 2,310 Jews (23% of the total population) living in Zyrardow in 1897, most of whom were employed as workers and clerks in the local textile factories, while others engaged in small trade, crafts, tailoring, building, carpentry, transport, and mechanics. The Jewish population numbered 2,547 (12% of the total) in 1921, and 2,726 in 1931.

Holocaust Period

At the outbreak of World War II there were about 3,000 Jews in the city. The German army entered the town on Sept. 8, 1939, and immediately began to terrorize the Jewish population, including public executions. During 1940 about 1,000 Jews from other places in Poland were forced to settle there. In February 1941 the entire Jewish population of Zyrardow was made to leave the city. Most of them went to Warsaw and shared the plight of Warsaw Jewry.

The community was not reconstituted after the war.

BIBLIOGRAPHY: B. Wasiutyński, *Ludność żydowska w Polsce w wiekach XIX i XX* (1930), 20; S. Bronsztejn, *Ludność żydowska w Polsce w okresie miedzywojennym* (1963), 278; S. Kalabiński (ed.), *Carat i klasy posiadające w walce z rewolucją 1905–1907 w Królestwie Polskim* (1956), index; T. Brustin-Bernstein, in: *Bleter far Geshikhte*, 4:2 (1951), table 6.

[Stefan Krakowski]

ABBREVIATIONS

GENERAL ABBREVIATIONS

This list contains abbreviations used in the Encyclopaedia (apart from the standard ones, such as geographical abbreviations, points of compass, etc.). For names of organizations, institutions, etc., in abbreviation, see Index. For bibliographical abbreviations of books and authors in Rabbinical literature, see following lists.

*	Cross reference; i.e., an article is to be found under the word(s) immediately following the asterisk (*).
°	Before the title of an entry, indicates a non-Jew (post-biblical times).
‡	Indicates reconstructed forms.
>	The word following this sign is derived from the preceding one.
<	The word preceding this sign is derived from the following one.

ad loc.	*ad locum*, "at the place"; used in quotations of commentaries.
A.H.	*Anno Hegirae*, "in the year of Hegira," i.e., according to the Muslim calendar.
Akk.	Addadian.
A.M.	*anno mundi*, "in the year (from the creation) of the world."
anon.	anonymous.
Ar.	Arabic.
Aram.	Aramaic.
Ass.	Assyrian.
b.	born; *ben, bar.*
Bab.	Babylonian.
B.C.E.	Before Common Era (= B.C.).
bibl.	bibliography.
Bul.	Bulgarian.
c., ca.	Circa.
C.E.	Common Era (= A.D.).
cf.	*confer*, "compare."
ch., chs.	chapter, chapters.
comp.	compiler, compiled by.
Cz.	Czech.
D	according to the documentary theory, the Deuteronomy document.
d.	died.
Dan.	Danish.
diss., dissert,	dissertation, thesis.
Du.	Dutch.
E.	according to the documentary theory, the Elohist document (i.e., using Elohim as the name of God) of the first five (or six) books of the Bible.
ed.	editor, edited, edition.
eds.	editors.
e.g.	*exempli gratia*, "for example."
Eng.	English.
et al.	*et alibi*, "and elsewhere"; or *et alii*, "and others"; "others."
f., ff.	and following page(s).
fig.	figure.
fl.	flourished.
fol., fols	folio(s).
Fr.	French.
Ger.	German.
Gr.	Greek.
Heb.	Hebrew.
Hg., Hung	Hungarian.
ibid	*Ibidem*, "in the same place."
incl. bibl.	includes bibliography.
introd.	introduction.
It.	Italian.
J	according to the documentary theory, the Jahwist document (i.e., using YHWH as the name of God) of the first five (or six) books of the Bible.
Lat.	Latin.
lit.	literally.
Lith.	Lithuanian.
loc. cit.	*loco citato*, "in the [already] cited place."
Ms., Mss.	Manuscript(s).
n.	note.
n.d.	no date (of publication).
no., nos	number(s).
Nov.	Novellae (Heb. *Ḥiddushim*).
n.p.	place of publication unknown.
op. cit.	*opere citato*, "in the previously mentioned work."
P.	according to the documentary theory, the Priestly document of the first five (or six) books of the Bible.
p., pp.	page(s).
Pers.	Persian.
pl., pls.	plate(s).
Pol.	Polish.
Port.	Potuguese.
pt., pts.	part(s).
publ.	published.
R.	Rabbi or Rav (before names); in Midrash (after an abbreviation) – *Rabbah.*
r.	recto, the first side of a manuscript page.
Resp.	Responsa (Latin "answers," Hebrew *She'elot u-Teshuvot* or *Teshuvot),* collections of rabbinic decisions.
rev.	revised.

Rom. Romanian.
Rus(s). Russian.

Slov. Slovak.
Sp. Spanish.
s.v. *sub verbo, sub voce*, "under the (key) word."
Sum Sumerian.
summ. Summary.
suppl. supplement.

Swed. Swedish.

tr., trans(l). translator, translated, translation.
Turk. Turkish.

Ukr. Ukrainian.

v., vv. *verso*. The second side of a manuscript page; also verse(s).

Yid. Yiddish.

ABBREVIATIONS USED IN RABBINICAL LITERATURE

Adderet Eliyahu, Karaite treatise by Elijah b. Moses *Bashyazi.
Admat Kodesh, Resp. by Nissim Ḥayyim Moses b. Joseph |Mizraḥi.
Aguddah, Sefer ha-, Nov. by *Alexander Suslin ha-Kohen.
Ahavat Ḥesed, compilation by *Israel Meir ha-Kohen.
Aliyyot de-Rabbenu Yonah, Nov. by *Jonah b. Avraham Gerondi.
Arukh ha-Shulḥan, codification by Jehiel Michel *Epstein.
Asayin (= positive precepts), subdivision of: (1) *Maimonides, *Sefer ha-Mitzvot;* (2) *Moses b. Jacob of Coucy, *Semag.*
Asefat Dinim, subdivision of *Sedei Ḥemed* by Ḥayyim Hezekiah *Medini, an encyclopaedia of precepts and responsa.
Asheri = *Asher b. Jehiel.
Aeret Ḥakhamim, by Baruch *Frankel-Teomim; pt, 1: Resp. to Sh. Ar.; pt2: Nov. to Talmud.
Ateret Zahav, subdivision of the *Levush*, a codification by Mordecai b. Abraham (Levush) *Jaffe; *Ateret Zahav* parallels Tur. YD.
Ateret Ẓevi, Comm. To Sh. Ar. by Ẓevi Hirsch b. Azriel.
Avir Ya'akov, Resp. by Jacob Avigdor.
Avkat Rokhel, Resp. by Joseph b. Ephraim *Caro.
Avnei Millu'im, Comm. to Sh. Ar., EH, by *Aryeh Loeb b. Joseph ha-Kohen.
Avnei Nezer, Resp. on Sh. Ar. by Abraham b. Ze'ev Nahum Bornstein of *Sochaczew.
Avodat Massa, Compilation of Tax Law by Yoasha Abraham Judah.
Azei ha-Levanon, Resp. by Judah Leib *Zirelson.

Ba'al ha-Tanya – *Shneur Zalman of Lyady.
Ba'ei Ḥayyei, Resp. by Ḥayyim b. Israel *Benveniste.
Ba'er Heitev, Comm. To Sh. Ar. The parts on OḤ and EH are by Judah b. Simeon *Ashkenazi, the parts on YD AND ḤM by *Zechariah Mendel b. Aryeh Leib. Printed in most editions of Sh. Ar.
Baḥ = Joel *Sirkes.
Baḥ, usual abbreviation for *Bayit Ḥadash*, a commentary on Tur by Joel *Sirkes; printed in most editions of Tur.
Bayit Ḥadash, see *Baḥ*.
Berab = Jacob Berab, also called Ri Berav.
Bedek ha-Bayit, by Joseph b. Ephraim *Caro, additions to his *Beit Yosef* (a comm. to Tur). Printed sometimes inside *Beit Yosef*, in smaller type. Appears in most editions of Tur.
Be'er ha-Golah, Commentary to Sh. Ar. By Moses b. Naphtali Hirsch *Rivkes; printed in most editions of Sh. Ar.
Be'er Mayim, Resp. by Raphael b. Abraham Manasseh Jacob.
Be'er Mayim Ḥayyim, Resp. by Samuel b. Ḥayyim *Vital.
Be'er Yizḥak, Resp. by Isaac Elhanan *Spector.
Beit ha-Beḥirah, Comm. to Talmud by Menahem b. Solomon *Meiri.
Beit Me'ir, Nov. on Sh. Ar. by Meir b. Judah Leib Posner.
Beit Shelomo, Resp. by Solomon b. Aaron Ḥason (the younger).
Beit Shemu'el, Comm. to Sh. Ar., EH, by *Samuel b. Uri Shraga Phoebus.
Beit Ya'akov, by Jacob b. Jacob Moses *Lorberbaum; pt.1: Nov. to Ket.; pt.2: Comm. to EH.
Beit Yisrael, collective name for the commentaries *Derishah, Perishah*, and *Be'urim* by Joshua b. Alexander ha-Kohen *Falk. See under the names of the commentaries.
Beit Yizḥak, Resp. by Isaac *Schmelkes.
Beit Yosef: (1) Comm. on Tur by Joseph b. Ephraim *Caro; printed in most editions of Tur; (2) Resp. by the same.
Ben Yehudah, Resp. by Abraham b. Judah Litsch (ליטש) Rosenbaum.
Bertinoro, Standard commentary to Mishnah by Obadiah *Bertinoro. Printed in most editions of the Mishnah.
[Be'urei] Ha-Gra, Comm. to Bible, Talmud, and Sh. Ar. By *Elijah b. Solomon Zalmon (Gaon of Vilna); printed in major editions of the mentioned works.
Be'urim, Glosses to Isserles *Darkhei Moshe* (a comm. on Tur) by Joshua b. Alexander ha-Kohen *Falk; printed in many editions of Tur.
Binyamin Ze'ev, Resp. by *Benjamin Ze'ev b. Mattathias of Arta.
Birkei Yosef, Nov. by Ḥayyim Joseph David *Azulai.
Ha-Buẓ ve-ha-Argaman, subdivision of the *Levush* (a codification by Mordecai b. Abraham (Levush) *Jaffe); *Ha-Buẓ ve-ha-Argaman* parallels Tur, EH.

Comm. = Commentary

Da'at Kohen, Resp. by Abraham Isaac ha-Kohen. *Kook.
Darkhei Moshe, Comm. on Tur Moses b. Israel *Isserles; printed in most editions of Tur.
Darkhei No'am, Resp. by *Mordecai b. Judah ha-Levi.
Darkhei Teshuvah, Nov. by Ẓevi *Shapiro; printed in the major editions of Sh. Ar.
De'ah ve-Haskel, Resp. by Obadiah Hadaya (see *Yaskil Avdi)*.

Derashot Ran, Sermons by *Nissim b. Reuben Gerondi.
Derekh Ḥayyim, Comm. to *Avot* by *Judah Loew (Lob., Liwa) b. Bezalel (Maharal) of Prague.
Derishah, by Joshua b. Alexander ha-Kohen *Falk; additions to his *Perishah* (comm. on Tur); printed in many editions of Tur.
Derushei ha-Ẓelaḥ, Sermons, by Ezekiel b. Judah Halevi *Landau.
Devar Avraham, Resp. by Abraham *Shapira.
Devar Shemu'el, Resp. by Samuel *Aboab.
Devar Yehoshu'a, Resp. by Joshua Menahem b. Isaac Aryeh Ehrenberg.
Dikdukei Soferim, variae lections of the talmudic text by Raphael Nathan*Rabbinowicz.
Divrei Emet, Resp. by Isaac Bekhor David.
Divrei Ge'onim, Digest of responsa by Ḥayyim Aryeh b. Jeḥiel Ẓevi *Kahana.
Divrei Ḥamudot, Comm. on *Piskei ha-Rosh* by Yom Tov Lipmann b. Nathan ha-Levi *Heller; printed in major editions of the Talmud.
Divrei Ḥayyim several works by Ḥayyim *Halberstamm; if quoted alone refers to his Responsa.
Divrei Malkhi'el, Resp. by Malchiel Tenebaum.
Divrei Rivot, Resp. by Isaac b. Samuel *Adarbi.
Divrei Shemu'el, Resp. by Samuel Raphael Arditi.

Edut be-Ya'akov, Resp. by Jacob b. Abraham *Boton.
Edut bi-Yhosef, Resp. by Joseph b. Isaac *Almosnino.
Ein Ya'akov, Digest of talmudic *aggadot* by Jacob (Ibn) *Habib.
Ein Yiẓhak, Resp. by Isaac Elhanan *Spector.
Ephraim of Lentshitz = Solomon *Luntschitz.
Erekh Leḥem, Nov. and glosses to Sh. Ar. by Jacob b. Abraham *Castro.
Eshkol, Sefer ha-, Digest of *halakhot* by *Abraham b. Isaac of Narbonne.
Et Sofer, Treatise on Law Court documents by Abraham b. Mordecai *Ankawa, in the 2nd vol. of his Resp. *Kerem Ḥamar.*
Etan ha-Ezraḥi, Resp. by Abraham b. Israel Jehiel (Shrenzl) *Rapaport.
Even ha-Ezel, Nov. to Maimonides' *Yad Ḥazakah* by Isser Zalman *Meltzer.
Even ha-Ezer, also called *Raban* of *Ẓafenat Pa'ne'aḥ*, rabbinical work with varied contents by *Eliezer b. Nathan of Mainz; not identical with the subdivision of Tur, Shulḥan Arukh, etc.
Ezrat Yehudah, Resp. by *Isaar Judah b. Nechemiah of Brisk.

Gan Eden, Karaite treatise by *Aaron b. Elijah of Nicomedia.
Gersonides = *Levi b. Gershom, also called Leo Hebraecus, or Ralbag.
Ginnat Veradim, Resp. by *Abraham b. Mordecai ha-Levi.

Haggahot, another name for *Rema.*
Haggahot Asheri, glosses to *Piskei ha-Rosh* by *Israel of Krems; printed in most Talmud editions.
Haggahot Maimuniyyot, Comm,. to Maimonides' Yad Ḥazakah by *Meir ha-Kohen; printed in most eds. of Yad.
Haggahot Mordekhai, glosses to *Mordekhai* by Samuel *Schlettstadt; printed in most editions of the Talmud after *Mordekhai.*
Haggahot ha-Rashash on Tosafot, annotations of Samuel *Strashun on the Tosafot (printed in major editions of the Talmud).
Ha-Gra = *Elijah b. Solomon Zalman (Gaon of Vilna).
Ha-Gra, Commentaries on Bible, Talmud, and Sh. Ar. respectively, by *Elijah b. Solomon Zalman (Gaon of Vilna); printed in major editions of the mentioned works.
Hai Gaon, Comm. = his comm. on Mishnah.
Ḥakham Ẓevi, Resp. by Ẓevi Hirsch b. Jacob *Ashkenazi.
Halakhot = Rif, *Halakhot.* Compilation and abstract of the Talmud by Isaac b. Jacob ha-Kohen *Alfasi; printed in most editions of the Talmud.
Halakhot Gedolot, compilation of *halakhot* from the Geonic period, arranged acc. to the Talmud. Here cited acc. to ed. Warsaw (1874). Author probably *Simeon Kayyara of Basra.
Halakhot Pesukot le-Rav Yehudai Ga'on compilation of *halakhot.*
Halakhot Pesukot min ha-Ge'onim, compilation of *halakhot* from the geonic period by different authors.
Ḥananel, Comm. to Talmud by *Hananel b. Ḥushi'el; printed in some editions of the Talmud.
Harei Besamim, Resp. by Aryeh Leib b. Isaac *Horowitz.
Ḥassidim, Sefer, Ethical maxims by *Judah b. Samuel he-Ḥasid.
Hassagot Rabad on Rif, Glosses on Rif, *Halakhot*, by *Abraham b. David of Posquières.
Hassagot Rabad [on Yad], Glosses on Maimonides, *Yad Ḥazakah*, by *Abraham b. David of Posquières.
Hassagot Ramban, Glosses by Naḥmanides on Maimonides' *Sefer ha-Mitzvot;* usually printed together with *Sefer ha-Mitzvot.*
Ḥatam Sofer = Moses *Sofer.
Ḥavvot Ya'ir, Resp. and varia by Jair Ḥayyim *Bacharach
Ḥayyim Or Zaru'a = *Ḥayyim (Eliezer) b. Isaac.
Ḥazon Ish = Abraham Isaiah *Karelitz.
Ḥazon Ish, Nov. by Abraham Isaiah *Karelitz
Ḥedvat Ya'akov, Resp. by Aryeh Judah Jacob b. David Dov Meisels (article under his father's name).
Heikhal Yiẓhak, Resp. by Isaac ha-Levi *Herzog.
Ḥelkat Meḥokek, Comm. to Sh. Ar., by Moses b. Isaac Judah *Lima.
Ḥelkat Ya'akov, Resp. by Mordecai Jacob Breisch.
Ḥemdah Genuzah, , Resp. from the geonic period by different authors.
Ḥemdat Shelomo, Resp. by Solomon Zalman *Lipschitz.
Ḥida = Ḥayyim Joseph David *Azulai.
Ḥiddushei Halakhot ve-Aggadot, Nov. by Samuel Eliezer b. Judah ha-Levi *Edels.
Ḥikekei Lev, Resp. by Ḥayyim *Palaggi.
Ḥikrei Lev, Nov. to Sh. Ar. by Joseph Raphael b. Ḥayyim Joseph Ḥazzan (see article *Ḥazzan Family).
Hil. = Hilkhot ... (e.g. *Hilkhot Shabbat).*
Ḥinnukh, Sefer ha-, List and explanation of precepts attributed (probably erroneously) to Aaron ha-Levi of Barcelona (see article **Ha-Ḥinnukh*).
Ḥok Ya'akov, Comm. to Hil. Pesaḥ in Sh. Ar., OḤ, by Jacob b. Joseph *Reicher.
Ḥokhmat Sehlomo (1), Glosses to Talmud, *Rashi* and Tosafot by Solomon b. Jehiel "Maharshal") *Luria; printed in many editions of the Talmud.
Ḥokhmat Sehlomo (2), Glosses and Nov. to Sh. Ar. by Solomon b. Judah Aaron *Kluger printed in many editions of Sh. Ar.
Ḥur, subdivision of the *Levush*, a codification by Mordecai b. Abraham (Levush) *Jaffe; *Hur* (or *Levush ha-Hur)* parallels Tur, OḤ, 242–697.
Ḥut ha-Meshullash, fourth part of the *Tashbeẓ* (Resp.), by Simeon b. Zemaḥ *Duran.

Ibn Ezra, Comm. to the Bible by Abraham *Ibn Ezra; printed in the major editions of the Bible *("Mikra'ot Gedolot").*
Imrei Yosher, Resp. by Meir b. Aaron Judah *Arik.
Ir Shushan, Subdivision of the *Levush,* a codification by Mordecai b. Abraham (Levush) *Jaffe; *Ir Shushan* parallels Tur, ḤM.
Israel of Bruna = Israel b. Ḥayyim *Bruna.
Ittur. Treatise on precepts by *Isaac b. Abba Mari of Marseilles.

Jacob Be Rab = *Be Rab.
Jacob b. Jacob Moses of Lissa = Jacob b. Jacob Moses *Lorberbaum.
Judah B. Simeon = Judah b. Simeon *Ashkenazi.
Judah Minz = Judah b. Eliezer ha-Levi *Minz.

Kappei Aharon, Resp. by Aaron Azriel.
Kehillat Ya'akov, Talmudic methodology, definitions etc. by Israel Jacob b. Yom Tov *Algazi.
Kelei Ḥemdah, Nov. and *pilpulim* by Meir Dan *Plotzki of Ostrova, arranged acc. to the Torah.
Keli Yakar, Annotations to the Torah by Solomon *Luntschitz.
Keneh Ḥokhmah, Sermons by Judah Loeb *Pochwitzer.
Keneset ha-Gedolah, Digest of *halakhot* by Ḥayyim b. Israel *Benveniste; subdivided into annotations to *Beit Yosef* and annotations to Tur.
Keneset Yisrael, Resp. by Ezekiel b. Abraham Katzenellenbogen (see article *Katzenellenbogen Family).
Kerem Ḥamar, Resp. and varia by Abraham b. Mordecai *Ankawa.
Kerem Shelmo. Resp. by Solomon b. Joseph *Amarillo.
Keritut, [Sefer], Methodology of the Talmud by *Samson b. Isaac of Chinon.
Kesef ha-Kedoshim, Comm. to Sh. Ar., ḤM, by Abraham *Wahrmann; printed in major editions of Sh. Ar.
Kesef Mishneh, Comm. to Maimonides, *Yad Ḥazakah,* by Joseph b. Ephraim *Caro; printed in most editions of *Yad Ḥazakah.*
Keẓot ha-Ḥoshen, Comm. to Sh. Ar., ḤM, by *Aryeh Loeb b. Joseph ha-Kohen; printed in major editions of Sh. Ar.
Kol Bo [Sefer], Anonymous collection of ritual rules; also called *Sefer ha-Likkutim.*
Kol Mevasser, Resp. by Meshullam *Rath.
Korban Aharon, Comm. to *Sifra* by Aaron b. Abraham *Ibn Ḥayyim; pt. 1 is called: *Middot Aharon.*
Korban Edah, Comm. to Jer. Talmud by David *Fraenkel; with additions: *Shiyyurei Korban;* printed in most editions of Jer. Talmud.
Kunteres ha-Kelalim, subdivision of *Sedei Ḥemed,* an encyclopaedia of precepts and responsa by Ḥayyim Hezekiah *Medini.
Kunteres ha-Semikhah, a treatise by *Levi b. Ḥabib; printed at the end of his responsa.
Kunteres Tikkun Olam, part of *Mispat Shalom* (Nov. by Shalom Mordecai b. Moses *Schwadron).

Lavin (negative precepts), subdivision of: (1) *Maimonides, *Sefer ha-Mitzvot;* (2) *Moses b. Jacob of Coucy, *Semag.*
Leḥem Mishneh, Comm. to Maimonides, *Yad Ḥazakah,* by Abraham [Ḥiyya] b. Moses *Boton; printed in most editions of *Yad Ḥazakah.*
Leḥem Rav, Resp. by Abraham [Ḥiyya] b. Moses *Boton.
Leket Yosher, Resp and varia by Israel b. Pethahiah *Isserlein, collected by *Joseph (Joselein) b. Moses.
Leo Hebraeus = *Levi b. Gershom, also called Ralbag or Gersonides.
Levush = Mordecai b. Abraham *Jaffe.
Levush [Malkhut], Codification by Mordecai b. Abraham (Levush) *Jaffe, with subdivisions: *[Levush ha-] Tekhelet* (parallels Tur OḤ 1–241); *[Levush ha-] Ḥur* (parallels Tur OḤ 242–697); *[Levush] Ateret Zahav* (parallels Tur YD); *[Levush ha-Buẓ ve-ha-Argaman* (parallels Tur EH); *[Levush] Ir Shushan* (parallels Tur ḤM); under the name *Levush* the author wrote also other works.
Li-Leshonot ha-Rambam, fifth part (nos. 1374–1700) of Resp. by *David b. Solomon ibn Abi Zimra (Radbaz).
Likkutim, Sefer ha-, another name for *[Sefer] Kol Bo.*

Ma'adanei Yom Tov, Comm. on *Piskei ha-Rosh* by Yom Tov Lipmann b. Nathan ha-Levi *Heller; printed in many editions of the Talmud.
Mabit = Moses b. Joseph *Trani.
Magen Avot, Comm. to *Avot* by Simeon b. Ẓemaḥ *Duran.
Magen Avraham, Comm. to Sh. Ar., OḤ, by Abraham Abele b. Ḥayyim ha-Levi *Gombiner; printed in many editions of Sh. Ar., OḤ.
Maggid Mishneh, Comm. to Maimonides, *Yad Ḥazakah,* by *Vidal Yom Tov of Tolosa; printed in most editions of the *Yad Ḥazakah.*
Maḥaneh Efrayim, Resp. and Nov., arranged acc. to Maimonides' *Yad Ḥazakah* , by Ephraim b. Aaron *Navon.
Maharai = Israel b. Pethahiah *Isserlein.
Maharal of Prague = *Judah Loew (Lob, Liwa), b. Bezalel.
Maharalbaḥ = *Levi b. Ḥabib.
Maharam Alashkar = Moses b. Isaac *Alashkar.
Maharam Alshekh = Moses b. Ḥayyim *Alashekh.
Maharam Mintz = Moses *Mintz.
Maharam of Lublin = *Meir b. Gedaliah of Lublin.
Maharam of Padua = Meir *Katzenellenbogen.
Maharam of Rothenburg = *Meir b. Baruch of Rothenburg.
Maharam Shik = Moses b. Joseph Schick.
Maharash Engel = Samuel b. Ze'ev Wolf Engel.
Maharashdam = Samuel b. Moses *Medina.
Maharḥash = Ḥayyim (ben) Shabbetai.
Mahari Basan = Jehiel b. Ḥayyim Basan.
Mahari b. Lev = Joseph ibn Lev.
Mahari'az = Jekuthiel Asher Zalman Ensil Zusmir.
Maharibal = *Joseph ibn Lev.
Mahariḥ = Jacob (Israel) *Ḥagiz.
Maharik = Joseph b. Solomon *Colon.
Maharikash = Jacob b. Abraham *Castro.
Maharil = Jacob b. Moses *Moellin.
Maharimat = Joseph b. Moses di Trani (not identical with the Maharit).
Maharit = Joseph b. Moses *Trani.
Maharitaẓ = Yom Tov b. Akiva Ẓahalon. (See article *Ẓahalon Family).
Maharsha = Samuel Eliezer b. Judah ha-Levi *Edels.
Maharshag = Simeon b. Judah Gruenfeld.
Maharshak = Samson b. Isaac of Chinon.
Maharshakh = *Solomon b. Abraham.
Maharshal = Solomon b. Jeḥiel *Luria.
Mahasham = Shalom Mordecai b. Moses *Sschwadron.
Maharyu = Jacob b. Judah *Weil.
Maḥazeh Avraham, Resp. by Abraham Nebagen v. Meir ha-Levi Steinberg.
Maḥazik Berakhah, Nov. by Ḥayyim Joseph David *Azulai.

*Maimonides = Moses b. Maimon, or Rambam.
*Malbim = Meir Loeb b. Jehiel Michael.
Malbim = Malbim's comm. to the Bible; printed in the major editions.
Malbushei Yom Tov, Nov. on *Levush,* OḤ, by Yom Tov Lipmann b. Nathan ha-Levi *Heller.
Mappah, another name for *Rema.*
Mareh ha-Panim, Comm. to Jer. Talmud by Moses b. Simeon *Margolies; printed in most editions of Jer. Talmud.
Margaliyyot ha-Yam, Nov. by Reuben *Margoliot.
Masat Binyamin, Resp. by Benjamin Aaron b. Abraham *Slonik
Mashbir, Ha- = *Joseph Samuel b. Isaac Rodi.
Massa Ḥayyim, Tax *halakhot* by Ḥayyim *Palaggi, with the subdivisions *Missim ve-Arnomiyyot* and *Torat ha-Minhagot.*
Massa Melekh, Compilation of Tax Law by Joseph b. Isaac *Ibn Ezra with concluding part *Ne'ilat She'arim.*
Matteh Asher, Resp. by Asher b. Emanuel Shalem.
Matteh Shimon, Digest of Resp. and Nov. to Tur and *Beit Yosef,* ḤM, by Mordecai Simeon b. Solomon.
Matteh Yosef, Resp. by Joseph b. Moses ha-Levi Nazir (see article under his father's name).
Mayim Amukkim, Resp. by Elijah b. Abraham *Mizraḥi.
Mayim Ḥayyim, Resp. by Ḥayyim b. Dov Beresh Rapaport.
Mayim Rabbim, , Resp. by Raphael *Meldola.
Me-Emek ha-Bakha, , Resp. by Simeon b. Jekuthiel Ephrati.
Me'irat Einayim, usual abbreviation: *Sma* (from: *Sefer Me'irat Einayim*); comm. to Sh. Ar. By Joshua b. Alexander ha-Kohen *Falk; printed in most editions of the Sh. Ar.
Melammed le-Ho'il, Resp. by David Ẓevi *Hoffmann.
Meisharim, [*Sefer*], Rabbinical treatise by *Jeroham b. Meshullam.
Meshiv Davar, Resp. by Naphtali Ẓevi Judah *Berlin.
Mi-Gei ha-Haregah, Resp. by Simeon b. Jekuthiel Ephrati.
Mi-Ma'amakim, Resp. by Ephraim Oshry.
Middot Aharon, first part of *Korban Aharon,* a comm. to *Sifra* by Aaron b. Abraham *Ibn Ḥayyim.
Migdal Oz, Comm. to Maimonides, *Yad Ḥazakah,* by *Ibn Gaon Shem Tov b. Abraham; printed in most editions of the *Yad Ḥazakah.*
Mikhtam le-David, Resp. by David Samuel b. Jacob *Pardo.
Mikkaḥ ve-ha-Mimkar, Sefer ha-, Rabbinical treatise by *Hai Gaon.
Milḥamot ha-Shem, Glosses to Rif, *Halakhot,* by *Naḥmanides.
Minḥat Ḥinnukh, Comm. to *Sefer ha-Ḥinnukh,* by Joseph b. Moses *Babad.
Minḥat Yiẓḥak, Resp. by Isaac Jacob b. Joseph Judah Weiss.
Misgeret ha-Shulḥan, Comm. to Sh. Ar., ḤM, by Benjamin Ze'ev Wolf b. Shabbetai; printed in most editions of Sh. Ar.
Mishkenot ha-Ro'im, Halakhot in alphabetical order by Uzziel Alshekh.
Mishnah Berurah, Comm. to Sh. Ar., OḤ, by *Israel Meir ha-Kohen.
Mishneh le-Melekh, Comm. to Maimonides, *Yad Ḥazakah,* by Judah *Rosanes; printed in most editions of *Yad Ḥazakah.*
Mishpat ha-Kohanim, Nov. to Sh. Ar., ḤM, by Jacob Moses *Lorberbaum, part of his *Netivot ha-Mishpat;* printed in major editions of Sh. Ar.
Mishpat Kohen, Resp. by Abraham Isaac ha-Kohen *Kook.
Mishpat Shalom, Nov. by Shalom Mordecai b. Moses *Schwadron; contains: *Kunteres Tikkun Olam.*
Mishpat u-Ẓedakah be-Ya'akov, Resp. by Jacob b. Reuben *Ibn Ẓur.
Mishpat ha-Urim, Comm. to Sh. Ar., ḤM by Jacob b. Jacob Moses *Lorberbaum, part of his *Netivot ha-Mishpat;* printed in major editons of Sh. Ar.
Mishpat Ẓedek, Resp. by *Melammed Meir b. Shem Tov.
Mishpatim Yesharim, Resp. by Raphael b. Mordecai *Berdugo.
Mishpetei Shemu'el, Resp. by Samuel b. Moses *Kalai (Kal'i).
Mishpetei ha-Tanna'im, Kunteres, Nov on *Levush,* OḤ by Yom Tov Lipmann b. Nathan ha-Levi *Heller.
Mishpetei Uzzi'el (Uziel), Resp. by Ben-Zion Meir Hai *Ouziel.
Missim ve-Arnoniyyot, Tax *halakhot* by Ḥayyim *Palaggi, a subdivision of his work *Massa Ḥayyim* on the same subject.
Mitzvot, Sefer ha-, Elucidation of precepts by *Maimonides; subdivided into *Lavin* (negative precepts) and *Asayin* (positive precepts).
Mitzvot Gadol, Sefer, Elucidation of precepts by *Moses b. Jacob of Coucy, subdivided into *Lavin* (negative precepts) and *Asayin* (positive precepts); the usual abbreviation is *Semag.*
Mitzvot Katan, Sefer, Elucidation of precepts by *Isaac b. Joseph of Corbeil; the usual, abbreviation is *Semak.*
Mo'adim u-Zemannim, Rabbinical treatises by Moses Sternbuch.
Modigliano, Joseph Samuel = *Joseph Samuel b. Isaac, Rodi (Ha-Mashbir).
Mordekhai (Mordecai), halakhic compilation by *Mordecai b. Hillel; printed in most editions of the Talmud after the texts.
Moses b. Maimon = *Maimonides, also called Rambam.
Moses b. Naḥman = Naḥmanides, also called Ramban.
Muram = Isaiah Menahem b. Isaac (from: Morenu R. Mendel).

Naḥal Yiẓḥak, Comm. on Sh. Ar., ḤM, by Isaac Elhanan *Spector.
Naḥalah li-Yhoshu'a, Resp. by Joshua Ẓunẓin.
Naḥalat Shivah, collection of legal forms by *Samuel b. David Moses ha-Levi.
*Naḥmanides = Moses b. Naḥman, also called Ramban.
Naẓiv = Naphtali Ẓevi Judah *Berlin.
Ne'eman Shemu'el, Resp. by Samuel Isaac *Modigilano.
Ne'ilat She'arim, concluding part of *Massa Melekh* (a work on Tax Law) by Joseph b. Isaac *Ibn Ezra, containing an exposition of customary law and subdivided into *Minhagei Issur* and *Minhagei Mamon.*
Ner Ma'aravi, Resp. by Jacob b. Malka.
Netivot ha-Mishpat, by Jacob b. Jacob Moses *Lorberbaum; subdivided into *Mishpat ha-Kohanim,* Nov. to Sh. Ar., ḤM, and *Mishpat ha-Urim,* a comm. on the same; printed in major editions of Sh. Ar.
Netivot Olam, Saying of the Sages by *Judah Loew (Lob, Liwa) b. Bezalel.
Nimmukei Menaḥem of Merseburg, Tax *halakhot* by the same, printed at the end of Resp. Maharyu.
Nimmukei Yosef, Comm. to Rif. *Halakhot,* by Joseph *Ḥabib (Ḥabiba); printed in many editions of the Talmud.
Noda bi-Yhudah, Resp. by Ezekiel b. Judah ha-Levi *Landau; there is a first collection *(Mahadura Kamma)* and a second collection *(Mahadura Tinyana).*
Nov. = Novellae, Ḥiddushim.

Ohel Moshe (1), Notes to Talmud, *Midrash Rabbah,* Yad, *Sifrei* and to several Resp., by Eleazar *Horowitz.

Ohel Moshe (2), Resp. by Moses Jonah Zweig.
Oholei Tam. Resp. by *Tam ibn Yaḥya Jacob b. David; printed in the rabbinical collection *Tummat Yesharim.*
Oholei Ya'akov, Resp. by Jacob de *Castro.
Or ha-Me'ir Resp by Judah Meir b. Jacob Samson Shapiro.
Or Same'aḥ, Comm. to Maimonides, *Yad Ḥazakah,* by *Meir Simḥah ha-Kohen of Dvinsk; printed in many editions of the *Yad Ḥazakah.*
Or Zaru'a [the father] = *Isaac b. Moses of Vienna.
Or Zaru'a [the son] = *Ḥayyim (Eliezer) b. Isaac.
Or Zaru'a, Nov. by *Isaac b. Moses of Vienna.
Orah, Sefer ha-, Compilation of ritual precepts by *Rashi.
Oraḥ la-Ẓaddik, Resp. by Abraham Ḥayyim Rodrigues.
Ozar ha-Posekim, Digest of Responsa.

Paḥad Yizḥak, Rabbinical encyclopaedia by Isaac *Lampronti.
Panim Me'irot, Resp. by Meir b. Isaac *Eisenstadt.
Parashat Mordekhai, Resp. by Mordecai b. Abraham Naphtali *Banet.
Pe'at ha-Sadeh la-Dinim and Pe'at ha-Sadeh la-Kelalim, subdivisions of the *Sedei Ḥemed,* an encyclopaedia of precepts and responsa, by Ḥayyim Hezekaih *Medini.
Penei Moshe (1), Resp. by Moses *Benveniste.
Penei Moshe (2), Comm. to Jer. Talmud by Moses b. Simeon *Margolies; printed in most editions of the Jer. Talmud.
Penei Moshe (3), Comm. on the aggadic passages of 18 treatises of the Bab. and Jer. Talmud, by Moses b. Isaiah Katz.
Penei Yehoshu'a, Nov. by Jacob Joshua b. Ẓevi Hirsch *Falk.
Peri Ḥadash, Comm. on Sh. Ar. By Hezekiah da *Silva.
Perishah, Comm. on Tur by Joshua b. Alexander ha-Kohen *Falk; printed in major edition of Tur; forms together with *Derishah* and *Be'urim* (by the same author) the *Beit Yisrael.*
Pesakim u-Khetavim, 2nd part of the *Terumat ha-Deshen* by Israel b. Pethahiah *Isserlein' also called *Piskei Maharai.*
Pilpula Ḥarifta, Comm. to *Piskei ha-Rosh, Seder Nezikin,* by Yom Tov Lipmann b. Nathan ha-Levi *Heller; printed in major editions of the Talmud.
Piskei Maharai, see *Terumat ha-Deshen,* 2nd part; also called *Pesakim u-Khetavim.*
Piskei ha-Rosh, a compilation of *halakhot,* arranged on the Talmud, by *Asher b. Jehiel (Rosh); printed in major Talmud editions.
Pitḥei Teshuvah, Comm. to Sh. Ar. by Abraham Hirsch b. Jacob *Eisenstadt; printed in major editions of the Sh. Ar.

Rabad = *Abraham b. David of Posquières (Rabad III.).
Raban = *Eliezer b. Nathan of Mainz.
Raban, also called *Ẓafenat Pa'ne'aḥ* or *Even ha-Ezer,* see under the last name.
Rabi Abad = *Abraham b. Isaac of Narbonne.
Radad = David Dov. b. Aryeh Judah Jacob *Meisels.
Radam = Dov Berush b. Isaac Meisels.
Radbaz = *David b Solomon ibn Abi Ziumra.
Radbaz, Comm. to Maimonides, *Yad Ḥazakah,* by *David b. Solomon ibn Abi Zimra.
Ralbag = *Levi b. Gershom, also called Gersonides, or Leo Hebraeus.
Ralbag, Bible comm. by *Levi b. Gershon.
Rama [da Fano] = Menaḥem Azariah *Fano.
Ramah = Meir b. Todros [ha-Levi] *Abulafia.
Ramam = *Menaham of Merseburg.
Rambam = *Maimonides; real name: Moses b. Maimon.
Ramban = *Naḥmanides; real name Moses b. Naḥman.
Ramban, Comm. to Torah by *Naḥmanides; printed in major editions. ("Mikra'ot Gedolot").
Ran = *Nissim b. Reuben Gerondi.
Ran of Rif, Comm. on Rif, *Halakhot,* by Nissim b. Reuben Gerondi.
Ranaḥ = *Elijah b. Ḥayyim.
Rash = *Samson b. Abraham of Sens.
Rash, Comm. to Mishnah, by *Samson b. Abraham of Sens; printed in major Talmud editions.
Rashash = Samuel *Strashun.
Rashba = Solomon b. Abraham *Adret.
Rashba, Resp., see also; *Sefer Teshuvot ha-Rashba ha-Meyuḥasot leha-Ramban,* by Solomon b. Abraham *Adret.
Rashbad = Samuel b. David.
Rashbam = *Samuel b. Meir.
Rashbam = Comm. on Bible and Talmud by *Samuel b. Meir; printed in major editions of Bible and most editions of Talmud.
Rashbash = Solomon b. Simeon *Duran.
*Rashi = Solomon b. Isaac of Troyes.
Rashi, Comm. on Bible and Talmud by *Rashi; printed in almost all Bible and Talmud editions.
Raviah = Eliezer b. Joel ha-Levi.
Redak = David *Kimḥi.
Redak, Comm. to Bible by David *Kimḥi.
Redakh = *David b. Ḥayyim ha-Kohen of Corfu.
Re'em = Elijah b. Abraham *Mizraḥi.
Rema = Moses b. Israel *Isserles.
Rema, Glosses to Sh. Ar. by Moses b. Israel *Isserles; printed in almost all editions of the Sh. Ar. inside the text in Rashi type; also called *Mappah* or *Haggahot.*
Remek = Moses Kimḥi.
Remakh = Moses ha-Kohen mi-Lunel.
Reshakh = *Solomon b. Abraham; also called Maharshakh.
Resp. = Responsa, *She'elot u-Teshuvot.*
Ri Berav = *Berab.
Ri Escapa = Joseph b. Saul *Escapa.
Ri Migash = Joseph b. Meir ha-Levi *Ibn Migash.
Riba = Isaac b. Asher ha-Levi; Riba II (Riba ha-Baḥur) = his grandson with the same name.
Ribam = Isaac b. Mordecai (or: Isaac b. Meir).
Ribash = *Isaac b. Sheshet Perfet (or: Barfat).
Rid= *Isaiah b. Mali di Trani the Elder.
Ridbaz = Jacob David b. Ze'ev *Willowski.
Rif = Isaac b. Jacob ha-Kohen *Alfasi.
Rif, *Halakhot*, Compilation and abstract of the Talmud by Isaac b. Jacob ha-Kohen *Alfasi.
Ritba = Yom Tov b. Abraham *Ishbili.
Riẓbam = Isaac b. Mordecai.
Rosh = *Asher b. Jehiel, also called Asheri.
Rosh Mashbir, Resp. by *Joseph Samuel b. Isaac, Rodi.

Sedei Ḥemed, Encyclopaedia of precepts and responsa by Ḥayyim Ḥezekiah *Medini; subdivisions: *Asefat Dinim, Kunteres ha-Kelalim, Pe'at ha-Sadeh la-Dinim, Pe'at ha-Sadeh la-Kelalim.*
Semag, Usual abbreviation of *Sefer Mitzvot Gadol,* elucidation of precepts by *Moses b. Jacob of Coucy; subdivided into *Lavin* (negative precepts) *Asayin* (positive precepts).
Semak, Usual abbreviation of *Sefer Mitzvot Katan,* elucidation of precepts by *Isaac b. Joseph of Corbeil.

Sh. Ar. = *Shulḥan Arukh*, code by Joseph b. Ephraim *Caro.
Sha'ar Mishpat, Comm. to Sh. Ar., ḤM. By Israel Isser b. Ze'ev Wolf.
Sha'arei Shevu'ot, Treatise on the law of oaths by *David b. Saadiah; usually printed together with Rif, *Halakhot;* also called: *She'arim of R. Alfasi.*
Sha'arei Teshuvah, Collection of resp. from Geonic period, by different authors.
Sha'arei Uzzi'el, Rabbinical treatise by Ben-Zion Meir Ha *Ouziel.
Sha'arei Ẓedek, Collection of resp. from Geonic period, by different authors.
Shadal [or Shedal] = Samuel David *Luzzatto.
Shai la-Moreh, Resp. by Shabbetai Jonah.
Shakh, Usual abbreviation of *Siftei Kohen*, a comm. to Sh. Ar., YD and ḤM by *Shabbetai b. Meir ha-Kohen; printed in most editions of Sh. Ar.
Sha'ot-de-Rabbanan, Resp. by *Solomon b. Judah ha-Kohen.
She'arim of R. Alfasi see *Sha'arei Shevu'ot.*
Shedal, see Shadal.
She'elot u-Teshuvot ha-Ge'onim, Collection of resp. by different authors.
She'erit Yisrael, Resp. by Israel Ze'ev Mintzberg.
She'erit Yosef, Resp. by *Joseph b. Mordecai Gershon ha-Kohen.
She'ilat Yavez, Resp. by Jacob *Emden (Yaveẓ).
She'iltot, Compilation arranged acc. to the Torah by *Aḥa (Aḥai) of Shabḥa.
Shem Aryeh, Resp. by Aryeh Leib *Lipschutz.
Shemesh Ẓedakah, Resp. by Samson *Morpurgo.
Shenei ha-Me'orot ha-Gedolim, Resp. by Elijah *Covo.
Shetarot, Sefer ha-, Collection of legal forms by *Judah b. Barzillai al-Bargeloni.
Shevut Ya'akov, Resp. by Jacob b. Joseph Reicher.
Shibbolei ha-Leket Compilation on ritual by Zedekiah b. Avraham *Anav.
Shiltei Gibborim, Comm. to Rif, *Halakhot*, by *Joshua Boaz b. Simeon; printed in major editions of the Talmud.
Shittah Mekubbeẓet, Compilation of talmudical commentaries by Bezalel *Ashkenazi.
Shivat Ẓiyyon, Resp. by Samuel b. Ezekiel *Landau.
Shiyyurei Korban, by David *Fraenkel; additions to his comm. to Jer. Talmud *Korban Edah;* both printed in most editions of Jer. Talmud.
Sho'el u-Meshiv, Resp. by Joseph Saul ha-Levi *Nathanson.
Sh[ulḥan] Ar[ukh] [of Ba'al ha-Tanyal], Code by *Shneur Zalman of Lyady; not identical with the code by Joseph Caro.
Siftei Kohen, Comm. to Sh. Ar., YD and ḤM by *Shabbetai b. Meir ha-Kohen; printed in most editions of Sh. Ar.; usual abbreviation: *Shakh.*
Simḥat Yom Tov, Resp. by Tom Tov b. Jacob *Algazi.
Simlah Ḥadashah, Treatise on *Sheḥitah* by Alexander Sender b. Ephraim Zalman *Schor; see also *Tevu'ot Shor.*
Simeon b. Ẓemaḥ = Simeon b. Ẓemaḥ *Duran.
Sma, Comm. to Sh. Ar. by Joshua b. Alexander ha-Kohen *Falk; the full title is: *Sefer Me'irat Einayim;* printed in most editions of Sh. Ar.
Solomon b. Isaac ha-Levi = Solomon b. Isaac *Levy.
Solomon b. Isaac of Troyes = *Rashi.

Tal Orot, Rabbinical work with various contents, by Joseph ibn Gioia.
Tam, Rabbenu = *Tam Jacob b. Meir.
Tashbaẓ = Samson b. Zadok.
Tashbeẓ = Simeon b. Zemaḥ *Duran, sometimes also abbreviation for Samson b. Zadok, usually known as Tashbaẓ.
Tashbeẓ [*Sefer ha-*], Resp. by Simeon b. Ẓemaḥ *Duran; the fourth part of this work is called: *Ḥut ha-Meshullash.*
Taz, Usual abbreviation of *Turei Zahav*, comm., to Sh. Ar. by *David b. Samnuel ha-Levi; printed in most editions of Sh. Ar.
(Ha)-Tekhelet, subdivision of the *Levush* (a codification by Mordecai b. Abraham (Levush) *Jaffe); *Ha-Tekhelet* parallels Tur, OḤ 1-241.
Terumat ha-Deshen, by Israel b. Pethahiah *Isserlein; subdivided into a part containing responsa, and a second part called *Pesakim u-Khetavim* or *Piskei Maharai.*
Terumot, Sefer ha-, Compilation of *halakhot* by Samuel b. Isaac *Sardi.
Teshuvot Ba'alei ha-Tosafot, Collection of responsa by the Tosafists.
Teshjvot Ge'onei Mizraḥ u-Ma'aav, Collection of responsa.
Teshuvot ha-Geonim, Collection of responsa from Geonic period.
Teshuvot Ḥakhmei Provinẓyah, Collection of responsa by different Provencal authors.
Teshuvot Ḥakhmei Ẓarefat ve-Loter, Collection of responsa by different French authors.
Teshuvot Maimuniyyot, Resp. pertaining to Maimonides' *Yad Ḥazakah;* printed in major editions of this work after the text; authorship uncertain.
Tevu'ot Shor, by Alexander Sender b. Ephraim Zalman *Schor, a comm. to his *Simlah Ḥadashah*, a work on *Sheḥitah.*
Tiferet Ẓevi, Resp. by Ẓevi Hirsch of the "AHW" Communities (Altona, Hamburg, Wandsbeck).
Tiktin, Judah b. Simeon = Judah b. Simeon *Ashkenazi.
Toledot Adam ve-Ḥavvah, Codification by *Jeroham b. Meshullam.
Torat Emet, Resp. by Aaron b. Joseph *Sasson.
Torat Ḥayyim, , Resp. by Ḥayyim (ben) Shabbetai.
Torat ha-Minhagot, subdivision of the *Massa Ḥayyim* (a work on tax law) by Ḥayyim *Palaggi, containing an exposition of customary law.
Tosafot Rid, Explanations to the Talmud and decisions by *Isaiah b. Mali di Trani the Elder.
Tosefot Yom Tov, comm. to Mishnah by Yom Tov Lipmann b. Nathan ha-Levi *Heller; printed in most editions of the Mishnah.
Tummim, subdivision of the comm. to Sh. Ar., ḤM, *Urim ve-Tummim* by Jonathan *Eybeschuetz; printed in the major editions of Sh. Ar.
Tur, usual abbreviation for the *Arba'ah Turim* of *Jacob b. Asher.
Turei Zahav, Comm. to Sh. Ar. by *David b. Samuel ha-Levi; printed in most editions of Sh. Ar.; usual abbreviation: *Taz.*

Urim, subdivision of the following.
Urim ve-Tummim, Comm. to Sh. Ar., ḤM, by Jonathan *Eybeschuetz; printed in the major editions of Sh. Ar.; subdivided in places into *Urim* and *Tummim.*

Vikku'aḥ Mayim Ḥayyim, Polemics against Isserles and Caro by Ḥayyim b. Bezalel.

Yad Malakhi, Methodological treatise by *Malachi b. Jacob ha-Kohen.

Yad Ramah, Nov. by Meir b. Todros [ha-Levi] *Abulafia.
Yakhin u-Vo'az, Resp. by Ẓemaḥ b. Solomon *Duran.
Yam ha-Gadol, Resp. by Jacob Moses *Toledano.
Yam shel Shelomo, Compilation arranged acc. to Talmud by Solomon b. Jehiel (Maharshal) *Luria.
Yashar, Sefer ha-, by *Tam, Jacob b. Meir (Rabbenu Tam); 1st pt.: Resp.; 2nd pt.: Nov.
Yaskil Avdi, Resp. by Obadiah Hadaya (printed together with his Resp. *De'ah ve-Haskel).*
Yaveẓ = Jacob *Emden.
Yehudah Ya'aleh, Resp. by Judah b. Israel *Aszod.
Yekar Tiferet, Comm. to Maimonides' *Yad Ḥazakah*,by David b. Solomon ibn Zimra, printed in most editions of *Yad Ḥazakah.*
Yere'im [ha-Shalem], [Sefer], Treatise on precepts by *Eliezer b. Samuel of Metz.
Yeshu'ot Ya'akov, Resp. by Jacob Meshullam b. Mordecai Ze'ev *Ornstein.
Yiẓhak Rei'aḥ, Resp. by Isaac b. Samuel Abendanan (see article *Abendanam Family).
Ẓafenat Pa'ne'aḥ (1), also called *Raban* or *Even ha-Ezer*, see under the last name.
Ẓafenat Pa'ne'aḥ (2), Resp. by Joseph *Rozin.
Zayit Ra'anan, Resp. by Moses Judah Leib b. Benjamin Auerbach.
Ẓeidah la-Derekh, Codification by *Menahem b. Aaron ibn Zerah.
Ẓedakah u-Mishpat, Resp. by Ẓedakah b. Saadiah Huẓin.
Zekan Aharon, Resp. by Elijah b. Benjamin ha-Levi.
Zekher Ẓaddik, Sermons by Eliezer *Katzenellenbogen.
Ẓemaḥ Ẓedek (1) Resp. by Menaham Mendel Shneersohn (see under *Shneersohn Family).
Zera Avraham, Resp. by Abraham b. David *Yiẓḥaki.
Zera Emet Resp. by *Ishmael b. Abaham Isaac ha-Kohen.
Ẓevi la-Ẓaddik, Resp. by Ẓevi Elimelech b. David Shapira.
Zikhron Yehudah, Resp. by *Judah b. Asher
Zikhron Yosef, Resp. by Joseph b. Menahem *Steinhardt.
Zikhronot, Sefer ha-, Sermons on several precepts by Samuel *Aboab.
Zikkaron la-Rishonim . . ., by Albert (Abraham Elijah) *Harkavy; contains in vol. 1 pt. 4 (1887) a collection of Geonic responsa.
Ẓiẓ Eliezer, Resp. by Eliezer Judah b. Jacob Gedaliah Waldenberg.

BIBLIOGRAPHICAL ABBREVIATIONS

Bibliographies in English and other languages have been extensively updated, with English translations cited where available. In order to help the reader, the language of books or articles is given where not obvious from titles of books or names of periodicals. Titles of books and periodicals in languages with alphabets other than Latin, are given in transliteration, even where there is a title page in English. Titles of articles in periodicals are not given. Names of Hebrew and Yiddish periodicals well known in English-speaking countries or in Israel under their masthead in Latin characters are given in this form, even when contrary to transliteration rules. Names of authors writing in languages with non-Latin alphabets are given in their Latin alphabet form wherever known; otherwise the names are transliterated. Initials are generally not given for authors of articles in periodicals, except to avoid confusion. Non-abbreviated book titles and names of periodicals are printed in *italics*. Abbreviations are given in the list below.

AASOR	*Annual of the American School of Oriental Research* (1919ff.).
AB	*Analecta Biblica* (1952ff.).
Abel, Géog	F.-M. Abel, *Géographie de la Palestine*, 2 vols. (1933–38).
ABR	*Australian Biblical Review* (1951ff.).
Abr.	Philo, *De Abrahamo.*
Abrahams, Companion	I. Abrahams, *Companion to the Authorised Daily Prayer Book* (rev. ed. 1922).
Abramson, Merkazim	S. Abramson, *Ba-Merkazim u-va-Tefuẓot bi-Tekufat ha-Ge'onim* (1965).
Acts	Acts of the Apostles (New Testament).
ACUM	*Who is who in ACUM [Aguddat Kompozitorim u-Meḥabbrim]*.
ADAJ	*Annual of the Department of Antiquities, Jordan* (1951ff.).
Adam	Adam and Eve (Pseudepigrapha).
ADB	*Allgemeine Deutsche Biographie*, 56 vols. (1875–1912).
Add. Esth.	The Addition to Esther (Apocrypha).
Adler, Prat Mus	1. Adler, *La pratique musicale savante dans quelques communautés juives en Europe au XVIIe et XVIIIe siècles*, 2 vols. (1966).
Adler-Davis	H.M. Adler and A. Davis (ed. and tr.), *Service of the Synagogue, a New Edition of the Festival Prayers with an English Translation in Prose and Verse*, 6 vols. (1905–06).
Aet.	Philo, *De Aeternitate Mundi.*
AFO	*Archiv fuer Orientforschung* (first two volumes under the name *Archiv fuer Keilschriftforschung)* (1923ff.).
Ag. Ber	*Aggadat Bereshit* (ed. Buber, 1902).
Agr.	Philo, *De Agricultura.*
Ag. Sam.	*Aggadat Samuel.*
Ag. Song	*Aggadat Shir ha-Shirim* (Schechter ed., 1896).
Aharoni, Ereẓ	Y. Aharoni, *Ereẓ Yisrael bi-Tekufat ha-Mikra: Geografyah Historit* (1962).
Aharoni, Land	Y. Aharoni, *Land of the Bible* (1966).

Ahikar	Ahikar (Pseudepigrapha).
AI	*Archives Israélites de France* (1840–1936).
AJA	*American Jewish Archives* (1948ff.).
AJHSP	*American Jewish Historical Society – Publications* (after vol. 50 = AJHSQ).
AJHSQ	*American Jewish Historical (*Society) *Quarterly* (before vol. 50 =AJHSP).
AJSLL	*American Journal of Semitic Languages and Literature* (1884–95 under the title *Hebraica,* since 1942 JNES).
AJYB	*American Jewish Year Book* (1899ff.).
AKM	Abhandlungen fuer die Kunde des Morgenlandes (series).
Albright, Arch	W.F. Albright, *Archaeology of Palestine* (rev. ed. 1960).
Albright, Arch Bib	W.F. Albright, *Archaeology of Palestine and the Bible* (1935^{3}*).*
Albright, Arch Rel	W.F. Albright, *Archaeology and the Religion of Israel* (1953^{3}*).*
Albright, Stone	W.F. Albright, *From the Stone Age to Christianity* (1957^{2}*).*
Alon, Meḥkarim	G. Alon, *Meḥkarim be-Toledot Yisrael bi-Ymei Bayit Sheni u-vi-Tekufat ha-Mishnah ve-ha Talmud,* 2 vols. (1957–58).
Alon, Toledot	G. Alon, *Toledot ha-Yehudim be-Ereẓ Yisrael bi-Tekufat ha-Mishnah ve-ha-Talmud,* I (1958^{3}), (1961^{2}).
ALOR	Alter Orient (series).
Alt, Kl Schr	A. Alt, *Kleine Schriften zur Geschichte des Volkes Israel,* 3 vols. (1953–59).
Alt, Landnahme	A. Alt, *Landnahme der Israeliten in Palaestina* (1925); also in Alt, Kl Schr, 1 (1953), 89–125.
Ant.	Josephus, *Jewish Antiquities* (Loeb Classics ed.).
AO	*Acta Orientalia* (1922ff.).
AOR	*Analecta Orientalia* (1931ff.).
AOS	American Oriental Series.
Apion	Josephus, *Against Apion* (Loeb Classics ed.).
Aq.	Aquila's Greek translation of the Bible.
Ar.	*Arakhin* (talmudic tractate).
Artist.	Letter of Aristeas (Pseudepigrapha).
ARN^{1}	*Avot de-Rabbi Nathan,* version (1) ed. Schechter, 1887.
ARN^{2}	*Avot de-Rabbi Nathan,* version (2) ed. Schechter, 1945^{2}.
Aronius, Regesten	I. Aronius, *Regesten zur Geschichte der Juden im fraenkischen und deutschen Reiche bis zum Jahre 1273* (1902).
ARW	*Archiv fuer Religionswissenschaft* (1898–1941/42).
AS	*Assyrological Studies* (1931ff.).
Ashtor, Korot	E. Ashtor (Strauss), *Korot ha-Yehudim bi-Sefarad ha-Muslemit,* 1(1966^{2}), 2(1966).
Ashtor, Toledot	E. Ashtor (Strauss), *Toledot ha-Yehudim be-Miẓrayim ve-Suryah Taḥat Shilton ha-Mamlukim,* 3 vols. (1944–70).
Assaf, Ge'onim	S. Assaf, *Tekufat ha-Ge'onim ve-Sifrutah* (1955).
Assaf, Mekorot	S. Assaf, *Mekorot le-Toledot ha-Ḥinnukh be-Yisrael,* 4 vols. (1925–43).
Ass. Mos.	Assumption of Moses (Pseudepigrapha).
ATA	Alttestamentliche Abhandlungen (series).
ATANT	Abhandlungen zur Theologie des Alten und Neuen Testaments (series).
AUJW	*Allgemeine unabhaengige juedische Wochenzeitung* (till 1966 = AWJD).
AV	Authorized Version of the Bible.
Avad.	*Avadim* (post-talmudic tractate).
Avi-Yonah, Geog	M. Avi-Yonah, *Geografyah Historit shel Ereẓ Yisrael* (1962^{3}).
Avi-Yonah, Land	M. Avi-Yonah, *The Holy Land from the Persian to the Arab conquest (536 B.C. to A.D. 640)* (1960).
Avot	*Avot* (talmudic tractate).
Av. Zar.	*Avodah Zarah* (talmudic tractate).
AWJD	*Allgemeine Wochenzeitung der Juden in Deutschland* (since 1967 = AUJW).
AZDJ	*Allgemeine Zeitung des Judentums.*
Azulai	Ḥ.Y.D. Azulai, *Shem ha-Gedolim,* ed. by I.E. Benjacob, 2 pts. (1852) (and other editions).
BA	*Biblical Archaeologist* (1938ff.).
Bacher, Bab Amor	W. Bacher, *Agada der babylonischen Amoraeer* (1913^{2}).
Bacher, Pal Amor	W. Bacher, *Agada der palaestinensischen Amoraeer* (Heb. ed. *Aggadat Amora'ei Ereẓ Yisrael),* 2 vols. (1892–99).
Bacher, Tann	W. Bacher, *Agada der Tannaiten* (Heb. ed. *Aggadot ha-Tanna'im,* vol. 1, pt. 1 and 2 (1903); vol. 2 (1890).
Bacher, Trad	W. Bacher, *Tradition und Tradenten in den Schulen Palaestinas und Babyloniens* (1914).
Baer, Spain	Yitzhak (Fritz) Baer, *History of the Jews in Christian Spain,* 2 vols. (1961–66).
Baer, Studien	Yitzhak (Fritz) Baer, *Studien zur Geschichte der Juden im Koenigreich Aragonien waehrend des 13. und 14. Jahrhunderts* (1913).
Baer, Toledot	Yitzhak (Fritz) Baer, *Toledot ha-Yehudim bi-Sefarad ha-Noẓerit mi-Teḥillatan shel ha-Kehillot ad ha-Gerush,* 2 vols. (1959^{2}).
Baer, Urkunden	Yitzhak (Fritz) Baer, *Die Juden im christlichen Spanien,* 2 vols. (1929–36).
Baer S., Seder	S.I. Baer, *Seder Avodat Yisrael* (1868 and reprints*).*
BAIU	*Bulletin de l'Alliance Israélite Universelle* (1861–1913*).*
Baker, Biog Dict	*Baker's Biographical Dictionary of Musicians,* revised by N. Slonimsky (1958^{5}; with Supplement 1965).
I Bar.	I Baruch (Apocrypha).
II Bar.	II Baruch (Pseudepigrapha).
III Bar.	III Baruch (Pseudepigrapha).
BAR	*Biblical Archaeology Review.*
Baron, Community	S.W. Baron, *The Jewish Community, its History and Structure to the American Revolution,* 3 vols. (1942).

Baron, Social	S.W. Baron, *Social and Religious History of the Jews,* 3 vols. (1937); enlarged, 1-2(1952²), 3-14 (1957–69).
Barthélemy-Milik	D. Barthélemy and J.T. Milik, *Dead Sea Scrolls: Discoveries in the Judean Desert,* vol. 1 *Qumram Cave* I (1955).
BASOR	*Bulletin of the American School of Oriental Research.*
Bauer-Leander	H. Bauer and P. Leander, *Grammatik des Biblisch-Aramaeischen* (1927; repr. 1962).
BB	(1) *Bava Batra* (talmudic tractate). (2) *Biblische Beitraege* (1943ff.).
BBB	Bonner biblische Beitraege (series).
BBLA	*Beitraege zur biblischen Landes- und Altertumskunde* (until 1949–ZDPV).
BBSAJ	*Bulletin,* British School of Archaeology, Jerusalem (1922–25; after 1927 included in PEFQS).
BDASI	*Alon* (since 1948) or *Hadashot Arkhe'ologiyyot* (since 1961), bulletin of the Department of Antiquities of the State of Israel.
Begrich, Chronologie	J. Begrich, *Chronologie der Koenige von Israel und Juda* (1929).
Bek.	*Bekhorot* (talmudic tractate).
Bel	Bel and the Dragon (Apocrypha).
Benjacob, Oẓar	I.E. Benjacob, *Oẓar ha-Sefarim* (1880; repr. 1956).
Ben Sira	see Ecclus.
Ben-Yehuda, Millon	E. Ben-Yedhuda, *Millon ha-Lashon ha-Ivrit,* 16 vols (1908–59; repr. in 8 vols., 1959).
Benzinger, Archaeologie	I. Benzinger, *Hebraeische Archaeologie* (1927³).
Ben Zvi, Eretz Israel	I. Ben-Zvi, *Eretz Israel under Ottoman Rule* (1960; offprint from L. Finkelstein (ed.), *The Jews, their History, Culture and Religion* (vol. 1).
Ben Zvi, Ereẓ Israel	I. Ben-Zvi, *Ereẓ Israel bi-Ymei ha-Shilton ha-Ottomani (*1955*).*
Ber.	*Berakhot* (talmudic tractate).
Beẓah	*Beẓah* (talmudic tractate).
BIES	Bulletin of the Israel Exploration Society, see below BJPES.
Bik.	*Bikkurim* (talmudic tractate).
BJCE	Bibliography of Jewish Communities in Europe, catalog at General Archives for the History of the Jewish People, Jerusalem.
BJPES	Bulletin of the Jewish Palestine Exploration Society – English name of the Hebrew periodical known as: 1. *Yedi'ot ha-Ḥevrah ha-Ivrit la-Ḥakirat Ereẓ Yisrael va-Attikoteha* (1933–1954); 2. *Yedi'ot ha-Ḥevrah la-Ḥakirat Ereẓ Yisrael va-Attikoteha* (1954–1962); 3. *Yedi'ot ba-Ḥakirat Ereẓ Yisrael va-Attikoteha* (1962ff.).
BJRL	*Bulletin of the John Rylands Library* (1914ff.).
BK	*Bava Kamma* (talmudic tractate).
BLBI	*Bulletin of the Leo Baeck Institute* (1957ff.).
BM	(1) *Bava Meẓia* (talmudic tractate). (2) *Beit Mikra* (1955/56ff.). (3) British Museum.
BO	*Bibbia e Oriente* (1959ff.).
Bondy-Dworský	G. Bondy and F. Dworský, *Regesten zur Geschichte der Juden in Boehmen, Maehren und Schlesien von 906 bis 1620,* 2 vols. (1906).
BOR	*Bibliotheca Orientalis* (1943ff.).
Borée, Ortsnamen	W. Borée *Die alten Ortsnamen Palaestinas* (1930).
Bousset, Religion	W. Bousset, *Die Religion des Judentums im neutestamentlichen Zeitalter* (1906²).
Bousset-Gressmann	W. Bousset, *Die Religion des Judentums im spaethellenistischen Zeitalter* (1966³).
BR	*Biblical Review* (1916–25).
BRCI	*Bulletin of the Research Council of Israel* (1951/52–1954/55; then divided).
BRE	*Biblical Research* (1956ff.).
BRF	*Bulletin of the Rabinowitz Fund for the Exploration of Ancient Synagogues* (1949ff.).
Briggs, Psalms	Ch. A. and E.G. Briggs, *Critical and Exegetical Commentary on the Book of Psalms,* 2 vols. (ICC, 1906–07).
Bright, Hist	J. Bright, *A History of Israel* (1959).
Brockelmann, Arab Lit	K. Brockelmann, *Geschichte der arabischen Literatur,* 2 vols. 1898–1902), supplement, 3 vols. (1937–42).
Bruell, Jahrbuecher	*Jahrbuecher fuer juedische Geschichte und Litteratur,* ed. by N. Bruell, Frankfurt (1874–90).
Brugmans-Frank	H. Brugmans and A. Frank (eds.), *Geschiedenis der Joden in Nederland* (1940).
BTS	*Bible et Terre Sainte* (1958ff.).
Bull, Index	S. Bull, *Index to Biographies of Contemporary Composers* (1964).
BW	*Biblical World* (1882–1920).
BWANT	*Beitraege zur Wissenschaft vom Alten und Neuen Testament* (1926ff.).
BZ	*Biblische Zeitschrift* (1903ff.).
BZAW	*Beihefte zur Zeitschrift fuer die alttestamentliche Wissenschaft,* supplement to ZAW (1896ff.).
BŻIH	*Biuletyn Zydowskiego Instytutu Historycznego* (1950ff.).
CAB	*Cahiers d'archéologie biblique* (1953ff.).
CAD	*The* [*Chicago*] *Assyrian Dictionary* (1956ff.).
CAH	*Cambridge Ancient History,* 12 vols. (1923–39)
CAH²	*Cambridge Ancient History,* second edition, 14 vols. (1962–2005).
Calwer, Lexikon	*Calwer, Bibellexikon.*
Cant.	Canticles, usually given as Song (= Song of Songs).

Cantera-Millás, Inscripciones	F. Cantera and J.M. Millás, *Las Inscripciones Hebraicas de España* (1956).
CBQ	*Catholic Biblical Quarterly* (1939ff.).
CCARY	Central Conference of American Rabbis, *Yearbook* (1890/91ff.).
CD	*Damascus Document* from the Cairo *Genizah* (published by S. Schechter, *Fragments of a Zadokite Work*, 1910).
Charles, Apocrypha	R.H. Charles, *Apocrypha and Pseudepigrapha . . .*, 2 vols. (1913; repr. 1963–66).
Cher.	Philo, *De Cherubim*.
I (or II) Chron.	Chronicles, book I and II (Bible).
CIG	*Corpus Inscriptionum Graecarum*.
CIJ	*Corpus Inscriptionum Judaicarum*, 2 vols. (1936–52).
CIL	*Corpus Inscriptionum Latinarum*.
CIS	*Corpus Inscriptionum Semiticarum* (1881ff.).
C.J.	Codex Justinianus.
Clermont-Ganneau, Arch	Ch. Clermont-Ganneau, *Archaeological Researches in Palestine*, 2 vols. (1896–99).
CNFI	*Christian News from Israel* (1949ff.).
Cod. Just.	Codex Justinianus.
Cod. Theod.	Codex Theodosinanus.
Col.	Epistle to the Colosssians (New Testament).
Conder, Survey	Palestine Exploration Fund, *Survey of Eastern Palestine*, vol. 1, pt. I (1889) = C.R. Conder, *Memoirs of the . . . Survey*.
Conder-Kitchener	Palestine Exploration Fund, *Survey of Western Palestine*, vol. 1, pts. 1-3 (1881–83) = C.R. Conder and H.H. Kitchener, *Memoirs*.
Conf.	Philo, *De Confusione Linguarum*.
Conforte, Kore	D. Conforte, *Kore ha-Dorot* (1842^{2}).
Cong.	Philo, *De Congressu Quaerendae Eruditionis Gratia*.
Cont.	Philo, *De Vita Contemplativa*.
I (or II) Cor.	Epistles to the Corinthians (New Testament).
Cowley, Aramic	A. Cowley, *Aramaic Papyri of the Fifth Century B.C.* (1923).
Colwey, Cat	A.E. Cowley, *A Concise Catalogue of the Hebrew Printed Books in the Bodleian Library* (1929).
CRB	*Cahiers de la Revue Biblique* (1964ff.).
Crowfoot-Kenyon	J.W. Crowfoot, K.M. Kenyon and E.L. Sukenik, *Buildings of Samaria* (1942).
C.T.	Codex Theodosianus.
DAB	*Dictionary of American Biography* (1928–58).
Daiches, Jews	S. Daiches, *Jews in Babylonia* (1910).
Dalman, Arbeit	G. Dalman, *Arbeit und Sitte in Palaestina*, 7 vols.in 8 (1928–42 repr. 1964).
Dan	Daniel (Bible).
Davidson, Oẓar	I. Davidson, *Oẓar ha-Shirah ve-ha-Piyyut*, 4 vols. (1924–33); Supplement in: HUCA, 12–13 (1937/38), 715–823.
DB	J. Hastings, *Dictionary of the Bible*, 4 vols. (1963^{2}).
DBI	F.G. Vigoureaux et al. (eds.), *Dictionnaire de la Bible*, 5 vols. in 10 (1912); Supplement, 8 vols. (1928–66)
Decal.	Philo, *De Decalogo*.
Dem.	*Demai* (talmudic tractate).
DER	*Derekh Ereẓ Rabbah* (post-talmudic tractate).
Derenbourg, Hist	J. Derenbourg *Essai sur l'histoire et la géographie de la Palestine* (1867).
Det.	Philo, *Quod deterius potiori insidiari solet*.
Deus	Philo, *Quod Deus immutabilis sit*.
Deut.	Deuteronomy (Bible).
Deut. R.	*Deuteronomy Rabbah*.
DEZ	*Derekh Ereẓ Zuta* (post-talmudic tractate).
DHGE	*Dictionnaire d'histoire et de géographie ecclésiastiques*, ed. by A. Baudrillart et al., 17 vols (1912–68).
Dik. Sof	*Dikdukei Soferim*, variae lections of the talmudic text by Raphael Nathan Rabbinovitz (16 vols., 1867–97).
Dinur, Golah	B. Dinur (Dinaburg), *Yisrael ba-Golah*, 2 vols. in 7 (1959–68) = vols. 5 and 6 of his *Toledot Yisrael*, second series.
Dinur, Haganah	B. Dinur (ed.), *Sefer Toledot ha-Haganah* (1954ff.).
Diringer, Iscr	D. Diringer, *Iscrizioni antico-ebraiche palestinesi* (1934).
Discoveries	*Discoveries in the Judean Desert* (1955ff.).
DNB	*Dictionary of National Biography*, 66 vols. (1921–222) with Supplements.
Dubnow, Divrei	S. Dubnow, *Divrei Yemei Am Olam*, 11 vols (1923–38 and further editions).
Dubnow, Ḥasidut	S. Dubnow, *Toledot ha-Ḥasidut* (1960^{2}).
Dubnow, Hist	S. Dubnow, *History of the Jews* (1967).
Dubnow, Hist Russ	S. Dubnow, *History of the Jews in Russia and Poland*, 3 vols. (1916 20).
Dubnow, Outline	S. Dubnow, *An Outline of Jewish History*, 3 vols. (1925–29).
Dubnow, Weltgesch	S. Dubnow, *Weltgeschichte des juedischen Volkes* 10 vols. (1925–29).
Dukes, Poesie	L. Dukes, *Zur Kenntnis der neuhebraeischen religioesen Poesie* (1842).
Dunlop, Khazars	D. H. Dunlop, *History of the Jewish Khazars* (1954).
EA	El Amarna Letters (edited by J.A. Knudtzon), *Die El-Amarna Tafel*, 2 vols. (1907 14).
EB	*Encyclopaedia Britannica*.
EBI	*Estudios biblicos* (1941ff.).
EBIB	T.K. Cheyne and J.S. Black, *Encyclopaedia Biblica*, 4 vols. (1899–1903).
Ebr.	Philo, *De Ebrietate*.
Eccles.	Ecclesiastes (Bible).
Eccles. R.	*Ecclesiastes Rabbah*.
Ecclus.	Ecclesiasticus or Wisdom of Ben Sira (or Sirach; Apocrypha).
Eduy.	*Eduyyot* (mishanic tractate).

EG	*Enziklopedyah shel Galuyyot* (1953ff.).
EH	*Even ha-Ezer.*
EHA	*Enẓiklopedyah la-Ḥafirot Arkheologiyyot be-Ereẓ Yisrael*, 2 vols. (1970).
EI	*Enzyklopaedie des Islams*, 4 vols. (1905–14). Supplement vol. (1938).
EIS	*Encyclopaedia of Islam*, 4 vols. (1913–36; repr. 1954–68).
EIS^2	*Encyclopaedia of Islam, second edition (1960–2000).*
Eisenstein, Dinim	J.D. Eisenstein, *Oẓar Dinim u-Minhagim* (1917; several reprints).
Eisenstein, Yisrael	J.D. Eisenstein, *Oẓar Yisrael* (10 vols, 1907–13; repr. with several additions 1951).
EIV	*Enẓiklopedyah Ivrit* (1949ff.).
EJ	*Encyclopaedia Judaica* (German, A-L only), 10 vols. (1928–34).
EJC	*Enciclopedia Judaica Castellana*, 10 vols. (1948–51).
Elbogen, Century	I Elbogen, *A Century of Jewish Life* (1960^2).
Elbogen, Gottesdienst	I Elbogen, *Der juedische Gottesdienst ...* (1931^3, repr. 1962).
Elon, Mafte'aḥ	M. Elon (ed.), *Mafte'aḥ ha-She'elot ve-ha-Teshuvot ha-Rosh* (1965).
EM	*Enẓiklopedyah Mikra'it* (1950ff.).
I (or II) En.	I and II Enoch (Pseudepigrapha).
EncRel	*Encyclopedia of Religion*, 15 vols. (1987, 2005^2).
Eph.	Epistle to the Ephesians (New Testament).
Ephros, Cant	G. Ephros, *Cantorial Anthology*, 5 vols. (1929–57).
Ep. Jer.	Epistle of Jeremy (Apocrypha).
Epstein, Amora'im	J N. Epstein, *Mevo'ot le-Sifrut ha-Amora'im* (1962).
Epstein, Marriage	L M. Epstein, *Marriage Laws in the Bible and the Talmud* (1942).
Epstein, Mishnah	J. N. Epstein, *Mavo le-Nusaḥ ha-Mishnah*, 2 vols. (1964^2).
Epstein, Tanna'im	J. N. Epstein, *Mavo le-Sifruth ha-Tanna'im.* (1947).
ER	*Ecumenical Review.*
Er.	*Eruvin* (talmudic tractate).
ERE	*Encyclopaedia of Religion and Ethics*, 13 vols. (1908–26); reprinted.
ErIsr	*Eretz-Israel*, Israel Exploration Society.
I Esd.	I Esdras (Apocrypha) (= III Ezra).
II Esd.	II Esdras (Apocrypha) (= IV Ezra).
ESE	*Ephemeris fuer semitische Epigraphik*, ed. by M. Lidzbarski.
ESN	*Encyclopaedia Sefaradica Neerlandica*, 2 pts. (1949).
ESS	*Encyclopaedia of the Social Sciences*, 15 vols. (1930–35); reprinted in 8 vols. (1948–49).
Esth.	Esther (Bible).
Est. R.	*Esther Rabbah.*
ET	*Enẓiklopedyah Talmudit* (1947ff.).
Eusebius, Onom.	E. Klostermann (ed.), *Das Onomastikon* (1904), Greek with Hieronymus' Latin translation.
Ex.	Exodus (Bible).

Ex. R.	*Exodus Rabbah.*
Exs	Philo, *De Exsecrationibus.*
EẒD	*Enẓiklopeday shel ha-Ẓiyyonut ha-Datit* (1951ff.).
Ezek.	Ezekiel (Bible).
Ezra	Ezra (Bible).
III Ezra	III Ezra (Pseudepigrapha).
IV Ezra	IV Ezra (Pseudepigrapha).
Feliks, Ha-Ẓome'aḥ	*J. Feliks, Ha-Ẓome'aḥ ve-ha-Ḥai ba-Mishnah* (1983).
Finkelstein, Middle Ages	L. Finkelstein, *Jewish Self-Government in the Middle Ages* (1924).
Fischel, Islam	W.J. Fischel, *Jews in the Economic and Political Life of Mediaeval Islam* (1937; reprint with introduction "The Court Jew in the Islamic World," 1969).
FJW	*Fuehrer durch die juedische Gemeindeverwaltung und Wohlfahrtspflege in Deutschland* (1927/28).
Frankel, Mevo	Z. Frankel, *Mevo ha-Yerushalmi* (1870; reprint 1967).
Frankel, Mishnah	Z. Frankel, *Darkhei ha-Mishnah* (1959^2; reprint 1959^2).
Frazer, Folk-Lore	J.G. Frazer, *Folk-Lore in the Old Testament*, 3 vols. (1918–19).
Frey, Corpus	J.-B. Frey, *Corpus Inscriptionum Iudaicarum*, 2 vols. (1936–52).
Friedmann, Lebensbilder	A. Friedmann, *Lebensbilder beruehmter Kantoren*, 3 vols. (1918–27).
FRLT	*Forschungen zur Religion und Literatur des Alten und Neuen Testaments* (series) (1950ff.).
Frumkin-Rivlin	A.L. Frumkin and E. Rivlin, *Toledot Ḥakhmei Yerushalayim*, 3 vols. (1928–30), Supplement vol. (1930).
Fuenn, Keneset	S.J. Fuenn, *Keneset Yisrael*, 4 vols. (1887–90).
Fuerst, Bibliotheca	J. Fuerst, *Bibliotheca Judaica*, 2 vols. (1863; repr. 1960).
Fuerst, Karaeertum	J. Fuerst, *Geschichte des Karaeertums*, 3 vols. (1862–69).
Fug.	Philo, *De Fuga et Inventione.*
Gal.	Epistle to the Galatians (New Testament).
Galling, Reallexikon	K. Galling, *Biblisches Reallexikon* (1937).
Gardiner, Onomastica	A.H. Gardiner, *Ancient Egyptian Onomastica*, 3 vols. (1947).
Geiger, Mikra	A. Geiger, *Ha-Mikra ve-Targumav*, tr. by J.L. Baruch (1949).
Geiger, Urschrift	A. Geiger, *Urschrift und Uebersetzungen der Bibel* 1928^2).
Gen.	Genesis (Bible).
Gen. R.	*Genesis Rabbah.*
Ger.	*Gerim* (post-talmudic tractate).
Germ Jud	M. Brann, I. Elbogen, A. Freimann, and H. Tykocinski (eds.), *Germania Judaica*, vol. 1 (1917; repr. 1934 and 1963); vol. 2, in 2 pts. (1917–68), ed. by Z. Avneri.

GHAT	*Goettinger Handkommentar zum Alten Testament* (1917–22).
Ghirondi-Neppi	M.S. Ghirondi and G.H. Neppi, *Toledot Gedolei Yisrael u-Ge'onei Italyah ... u-Ve'urim al Sefer Zekher Ẓaddikim li-Verakhah . . .*(1853), index in ZHB, 17 (1914), 171–83.
Gig.	Philo, *De Gigantibus.*
Ginzberg, Legends	L. Ginzberg, *Legends of the Jews,* 7 vols. (1909–38; and many reprints).
Git.	*Gittin* (talmudic tractate).
Glueck, Explorations	N. Glueck, *Explorations in Eastern Palestine,* 2 vols. (1951).
Goell, Bibliography	Y. Goell, *Bibliography of Modern Hebrew Literature in English Translation* (1968).
Goodenough, Symbols	E.R. Goodenough, *Jewish Symbols in the Greco-Roman Period,* 13 vols. (1953–68).
Gordon, Textbook	C.H. Gordon, *Ugaritic Textbook* (1965; repr. 1967).
Graetz, Gesch	H. Graetz, *Geschichte der Juden* (last edition 1874–1908).
Graetz, Hist	H. Graetz, *History of the Jews,* 6 vols. (1891–1902).
Graetz, Psalmen	H. Graetz, *Kritischer Commentar zu den Psalmen,* 2 vols. in 1 (1882–83).
Graetz, Rabbinowitz	H. Graetz, *Divrei Yemei Yisrael,* tr. by S.P. Rabbinowitz. (1928 1929^{2}).
Gray, Names	G.B. Gray, *Studies in Hebrew Proper Names* (1896).
Gressmann, Bilder	H. Gressmann, *Altorientalische Bilder zum Alten Testament* (1927^{2}).
Gressmann, Texte	H. Gressmann, *Altorientalische Texte zum Alten Testament* (1926^{2}).
Gross, Gal Jud	H. Gross, *Gallia Judaica* (1897; repr. with add. 1969).
Grove, Dict	*Grove's Dictionary of Music and Musicians,* ed. by E. Blum 9 vols. (1954^{5}) and suppl. (1961^{5}).
Guedemann, Gesch Erz	M. Guedemann, *Geschichte des Erziehungswesens und der Cultur der abendlaendischen Juden,* 3 vols. (1880–88).
Guedemann, Quellenschr	M. Guedemann, *Quellenschriften zur Geschichte des Unterrichts und der Erziehung bei den deutschen Juden* (1873, 1891).
Guide	Maimonides, *Guide of the Perplexed.*
Gulak, Oẓar	A. Gulak, *Oẓar ha-Shetarot ha-Nehugim be-Yisrael* (1926).
Gulak, Yesodei	A. Gulak, *Yesodei ha-Mishpat ha-Ivri, Seder Dinei Mamonot be-Yisrael, al pi Mekorot ha-Talmud ve-ha-Posekim,* 4 vols. (1922; repr. 1967).
Guttmann, Mafte'aḥ	M. Guttmann, *Mafte'aḥ ha-Talmud,* 3 vols. (1906–30).
Guttmann, Philosophies	J. Guttmann, *Philosophies of Judaism* (1964).
Hab.	*Habakkuk* (Bible).
Ḥag.	*Ḥagigah* (talmudic tractate).
Haggai	*Haggai* (Bible).
Ḥal.	*Ḥallah* (talmudic tractate).

Halevy, Dorot	I. Halevy, *Dorot ha-Rishonim,* 6 vols. (1897–1939).
Halpern, Pinkas	I. Halpern (Halperin), *Pinkas Va'ad Arba Araẓot* (1945).
Hananel-Eškenazi	A. Hananel and Eškenazi (eds.), *Fontes Hebraici ad res oeconomicas socialesque terrarum balcanicarum saeculo XVI pertinentes,* 2 vols, (1958–60; in Bulgarian).
HB	*Hebraeische Bibliographie* (1858–82).
Heb.	Epistle to the Hebrews (New Testament).
Heilprin, Dorot	J. Heilprin (Heilperin), *Seder ha-Dorot,* 3 vols. (1882; repr. 1956).
Her.	Philo, *Quis Rerum Divinarum Heres.*
Hertz, Prayer	J.H. Hertz (ed.), *Authorised Daily Prayer Book* (rev. ed. 1948; repr. 1963).
Herzog, Instit	I. Herzog, *The Main Institutions of Jewish Law,* 2 vols. (1936–39; repr. 1967).
Herzog-Hauck	J.J. Herzog and A. Hauch (eds.), *Real-encyklopaedie fuer protestantische Theologie* (1896–1913^{3}).
HḤY	*Ha-Ẓofeh le-Ḥokhmat Yisrael* (first four volumes under the title *Ha-Ẓofeh me-Ereẓ Hagar)* (1910/11–13).
Hirschberg, Afrikah	H.Z. Hirschberg, *Toledot ha-Yehudim be-Afrikah ha-Zofonit,* 2 vols. (1965).
HJ	*Historia Judaica* (1938–61).
HL	*Das Heilige Land* (1857ff.)
ḤM	*Ḥoshen Mishpat.*
Hommel, Ueberliefer.	F. Hommel, *Die altisraelitische Ueberlieferung in inschriftlicher Beleuchtung* (1897).
Hor.	*Horayot* (talmudic tractate).
Horodezky, Ḥasidut	S.A. Horodezky, *Ha-Ḥasidut ve-ha-Ḥasidim,* 4 vols. (1923).
Horowitz, Ereẓ Yis	I.W. Horowitz, *Ereẓ Yisrael u-Shekhenoteha* (1923).
Hos.	Hosea (Bible).
HTR	*Harvard Theological Review* (1908ff.).
HUCA	*Hebrew Union College Annual* (1904; 1924ff.)
Ḥul.	*Ḥullin* (talmudic tractate).
Husik, Philosophy	I. Husik, *History of Medieval Jewish Philosophy* (1932^{2}).
Hyman, Toledot	A. Hyman, *Toledot Tanna'im ve-Amora'im* (1910; repr. 1964).
Ibn Daud, Tradition	Abraham Ibn Daud, *Sefer ha-Qabbalah – The Book of Tradition,* ed. and tr. By G.D. Cohen (1967).
ICC	International Critical Commentary on the Holy Scriptures of the Old and New Testaments (series, 1908ff.).
IDB	*Interpreter's Dictionary of the Bible,* 4 vols. (1962).
Idelsohn, Litugy	A. Z. Idelsohn, *Jewish Liturgy and its Development* (1932; paperback repr. 1967)
Idelsohn, Melodien	A. Z. Idelsohn, *Hebraeisch-orientalischer Melodienschatz,* 10 vols. (1914 32).
Idelsohn, Music	A. Z. Idelsohn, *Jewish Music in its Historical Development* (1929; paperback repr. 1967).

IEJ	*Israel Exploration Journal* (1950ff.).
IESS	*International Encyclopedia of the Social Sciences* (various eds.).
IG	*Inscriptiones Graecae*, ed. by the Prussian Academy.
IGYB	*Israel Government Year Book* (1949/50ff.).
ILR	*Israel Law Review* (1966ff.).
IMIT	*Izraelita Magyar Irodalmi Társulat Évkönyv* (1895 1948).
IMT	International Military Tribunal.
INB	*Israel Numismatic Bulletin* (1962–63).
INJ	*Israel Numismatic Journal* (1963ff.).
Ios	Philo, *De Iosepho.*
Isa.	Isaiah (Bible).
ITHL	Institute for the Translation of Hebrew Literature.
IZBG	*Internationale Zeitschriftenschau fuer Bibelwissenschaft und Grenzgebiete* (1951ff.).
JA	*Journal asiatique* (1822ff.).
James	Epistle of James (New Testament).
JAOS	*Journal of the American Oriental Society* (c. 1850ff.)
Jastrow, Dict	M. Jastrow, *Dictionary of the Targumim, the Talmud Babli and Yerushalmi, and the Midrashic literature,* 2 vols. (1886 1902 and reprints).
JBA	*Jewish Book Annual* (19242ff.).
JBL	*Journal of Biblical Literature* (1881ff.).
JBR	*Journal of Bible and Religion* (1933ff.).
JC	*Jewish Chronicle* (1841ff.).
JCS	*Journal of Cuneiform Studies* (1947ff.).
JE	*Jewish Encyclopedia,* 12 vols. (1901–05 several reprints).
Jer.	Jeremiah (Bible).
Jeremias, Alte Test	A. Jeremias, *Das Alte Testament im Lichte des alten Orients* 1930[4]).
JGGJČ	*Jahrbuch der Gesellschaft fuer Geschichte der Juden in der Čechoslovakischen Republik* (1929–38).
JHSEM	Jewish Historical Society of England, *Miscellanies* (1925ff.).
JHSET	Jewish Historical Society of England, *Transactions* (1893ff.).
JJGL	*Jahrbuch fuer juedische Geschichte und Literatur* (Berlin) (1898–1938).
JJLG	*Jahrbuch der juedische-literarischen Gesellschaft* (Frankfurt) (1903–32).
JJS	*Journal of Jewish Studies* (1948ff.).
JJSO	*Jewish Journal of Sociology* (1959ff.).
JJV	*Jahrbuch fuer juedische Volkskunde* (1898–1924).
JL	*Juedisches Lexikon,* 5 vols. (1927–30).
JMES	*Journal of the Middle East Society* (1947ff.).
JNES	*Journal of Near Eastern Studies* (continuation of AJSLL) (1942ff.).
J.N.U.L.	Jewish National and University Library.
Job	Job (Bible).
Joel	Joel (Bible).
John	Gospel according to John (New Testament).
I, II and III John	Epistles of John (New Testament).
Jos., Ant	Josephus, *Jewish Antiquities* (Loeb Classics ed.).
Jos. Apion	Josephus, *Against Apion* (Loeb Classics ed.).
Jos., index	*Josephus Works,* Loeb Classics ed., index of names.
Jos., Life	Josephus, *Life* (ed. Loeb Classics).
Jos, Wars	Josephus, *The Jewish Wars* (Loeb Classics ed.).
Josh.	Joshua (Bible).
JPESB	Jewish Palestine Exploration Society Bulletin, see BJPES.
JPESJ	Jewish Palestine Exploration Society Journal – Eng. Title of the Hebrew periodical *Kovez ha-Ḥevrah ha-Ivrit la-Ḥakirat Erez Yisrael va-Attikoteha.*
JPOS	*Journal of the Palestine Oriental Society* (1920–48).
JPS	Jewish Publication Society of America, *The Torah* (1962, 1967^2); *The Holy Scriptures* (1917).
JQR	*Jewish Quarterly Review* (1889ff.).
JR	*Journal of Religion* (1921ff.).
JRAS	*Journal of the Royal Asiatic Society* (1838ff.).
JHR	*Journal of Religious History* (1960/61ff.).
JSOS	*Jewish Social Studies* (1939ff.).
JSS	*Journal of Semitic Studies* (1956ff.).
JTS	*Journal of Theological Studies* (1900ff.).
JTSA	Jewish Theological Seminary of America (also abbreviated as JTS).
Jub.	Jubilees (Pseudepigrapha).
Judg.	Judges (Bible).
Judith	Book of Judith (Apocrypha).
Juster, Juifs	J. Juster, *Les Juifs dans l'Empire Romain,* 2 vols. (1914).
JYB	*Jewish Year Book* (1896ff.).
JZWL	*Juedische Zeitschift fuer Wissenschaft und Leben* (1862–75).
Kal.	*Kallah* (post-talmudic tractate).
Kal. R.	*Kallah Rabbati* (post-talmudic tractate).
Katz, England	*The Jews in the History of England, 1485-1850 (1994).*
Kaufmann, Schriften	D. Kaufmann, *Gesammelte Schriften,* 3 vols. (1908 15).
Kaufmann Y., Religion	Y. Kaufmann, *The Religion of Israel* (1960), abridged tr. of his *Toledot.*
Kaufmann Y., Toledot	Y. Kaufmann, *Toledot ha-Emunah ha-Yisre'elit,* 4 vols. (1937 57).
KAWJ	*Korrespondenzblatt des Vereins zur Gruendung und Erhaltung der Akademie fuer die Wissenschaft des Judentums* (1920 30).
Kayserling, Bibl	M. Kayserling, *Biblioteca Española-Portugueza-Judaica* (1880; repr. 1961).
Kelim	*Kelim* (mishnaic tractate).
Ker.	*Keritot* (talmudic tractate).
Ket.	*Ketubbot* (talmudic tractate).

Kid.	*Kiddushim* (talmudic tractate).
Kil.	*Kilayim* (talmudic tractate).
Kin.	*Kinnim* (mishnaic tractate).
Kisch, Germany	G. Kisch, *Jews in Medieval Germany* (1949).
Kittel, Gesch	R. Kittel, *Geschichte des Volkes Israel,* 3 vols. (1922–28).
Klausner, Bayit Sheni	J. Klausner, *Historyah shel ha-Bayit ha-Sheni,* 5 vols. (1950/512).
Klausner, Sifrut	J. Klausner, *Historyah shel haSifrut ha-Ivrit ha-Ḥadashah,* 6 vols. (1952–582).
Klein, corpus	S. Klein (ed.), *Juedisch-palaestinisches Corpus Inscriptionum* (1920).
Koehler-Baumgartner	L. Koehler and W. Baumgartner, *Lexicon in Veteris Testamenti libros* (1953).
Kohut, Arukh	H.J.A. Kohut (ed.), *Sefer he-Arukh ha-Shalem,* by Nathan b. Jehiel of Rome, 8 vols. (1876–92; Supplement by S. Krauss et al., 1936; repr. 1955).
Krauss, Tal Arch	S. Krauss, *Talmudische Archaeologie,* 3 vols. (1910–12; repr. 1966).
Kressel, Leksikon	G. Kressel, *Leksikon ha-Sifrut ha-Ivrit ba-Dorot ha-Aḥaronim,* 2 vols. (1965–67).
KS	*Kirjath Sepher* (1923/4ff.).
Kut.	*Kuttim* (post-talmudic tractate).
LA	Studium Biblicum Franciscanum, *Liber Annuus* (1951ff.).
L.A.	Philo, *Legum allegoriae.*
Lachower, Sifrut	F. Lachower, *Toledot ha-Sifrut ha-Ivrit ha-Ḥadashah,* 4 vols. (1947–48; several reprints).
Lam.	Lamentations (Bible).
Lam. R.	*Lamentations Rabbah.*
Landshuth, Ammudei	L. Landshuth, *Ammudei ha-Avodah* (1857–62; repr. with index, 1965).
Legat.	Philo, *De Legatione ad Caium.*
Lehmann, Nova Bibl	R.P. Lehmann, *Nova Bibliotheca Anglo-Judaica* (1961).
Lev.	Leviticus (Bible).
Lev. R.	*Leviticus Rabbah.*
Levy, Antologia	I. Levy, *Antologia de liturgia judeo-española* (1965ff.).
Levy J., Chald Targ	J. Levy, *Chaldaeisches Woerterbuch ueber die Targumim,* 2 vols. (1967–68; repr. 1959).
Levy J., Nuehebr Tal	J. Levy, *Neuhebraeisches und chaldaeisches Woerterbuch ueber die Talmudim . . .,* 4 vols. (1875–89; repr. 1963).
Lewin, Oẓar	Lewin, *Oẓar ha-Ge'onim,* 12 vols. (1928–43).
Lewysohn, Zool	L. Lewysohn, *Zoologie des Talmuds* (1858).
Lidzbarski, Handbuch	M. Lidzbarski, *Handbuch der nordsemitischen Epigraphik,* 2 vols (1898).
Life	Josephus, *Life* (Loeb Classis ed.).
LNYL	*Leksikon fun der Nayer Yidisher Literatur* (1956ff.).
Loew, Flora	I. Loew, *Die Flora der Juden,* 4 vols. (1924 34; repr. 1967).
LSI	*Laws of the State of Israel* (1948ff.).
Luckenbill, Records	D.D. Luckenbill, *Ancient Records of Assyria and Babylonia,* 2 vols. (1926).
Luke	Gospel according to Luke (New Testament)
LXX	Septuagint (Greek translation of the Bible).
Ma'as.	*Ma'aserot* (talmudic tractate).
Ma'as. Sh.	*Ma'ase Sheni* (talmudic tractate).
I, II, III, and IVMacc.	Maccabees, I, II, III (Apocrypha), IV (Pseudepigrapha).
Maimonides, Guide	Maimonides, *Guide of the Perplexed.*
Maim., Yad	Maimonides, *Mishneh Torah (Yad Ḥazakah).*
Maisler, Untersuchungen	B. Maisler (Mazar), *Untersuchungen zur alten Geschichte und Ethnographie Syriens und Palaestinas,* 1 (1930).
Mak.	*Makkot* (talmudic tractate).
Makhsh.	*Makhshrin* (mishnaic tractate).
Mal.	Malachi (Bible).
Mann, Egypt	J. Mann, *Jews in Egypt in Palestine under the Fatimid Caliphs,* 2 vols. (1920–22).
Mann, Texts	J. Mann, *Texts and Studies,* 2 vols (1931–35).
Mansi	G.D. Mansi, *Sacrorum Conciliorum nova et amplissima collectio,* 53 vols. in 60 (1901–27; repr. 1960).
Margalioth, Gedolei	M. Margalioth, *Enẓiklopedyah le-Toledot Gedolei Yisrael,* 4 vols. (1946–50).
Margalioth, Ḥakhmei	M. Margalioth, *Enẓiklopedyah le-Ḥakhmei ha-Talmud ve-ha-Ge'onim,* 2 vols. (1945).
Margalioth, Cat	G. Margalioth, *Catalogue of the Hebrew and Samaritan Manuscripts in the British Museum,* 4 vols. (1899–1935).
Mark	Gospel according to Mark (New Testament).
Mart. Isa.	Martyrdom of Isaiah (Pseudepigrapha).
Mas.	Masorah.
Matt.	Gospel according to Matthew (New Testament).
Mayer, Art	L.A. Mayer, *Bibliography of Jewish Art* (1967).
MB	*Wochenzeitung* (formerly *Mitteilungsblatt*) *des Irgun Olej Merkas Europa* (1933ff.).
MEAH	*Miscelánea de estudios árabes y hebraicos* (1952ff.).
Meg.	Megillah (talmudic tractate).
Meg. Ta'an.	*Megillat Ta'anit* (in HUCA, 8 9 (1931–32), 318–51).
Me'il	*Me'ilah* (mishnaic tractate).
MEJ	*Middle East Journal* (1947ff.).
Mehk.	*Mekhilta de-R. Ishmael.*
Mekh. SbY	*Mekhilta de-R. Simeon bar Yoḥai.*
Men.	*Menaḥot* (talmudic tractate).
MER	*Middle East Record* (1960ff.).
Meyer, Gesch	E. Meyer, *Geschichte des Alterums,* 5 vols. in 9 (1925–58).
Meyer, Ursp	E. Meyer, *Urspring und Anfaenge des Christentums* (1921).
Mez.	*Mezuzah* (post-talmudic tractate).
MGADJ	*Mitteilungen des Gesamtarchivs der deutschen Juden* (1909–12).
MGG	*Die Musik in Geschichte und Gegenwart,* 14 vols. (1949–68).

MGG²	*Die Musik in Geschichte und Gegenwart, 2nd edition (1994)*
MGH	*Monumenta Germaniae Historica* (1826ff.).
MGJV	*Mitteilungen der Gesellschaft fuer juedische Volkskunde* (1898–1929); title varies, see also JJV.
MGWJ	*Monatsschrift fuer Geschichte und Wissenschaft des Judentums* (1851–1939).
MHJ	*Monumenta Hungariae Judaica,* 11 vols. (1903–67).
Michael, Or	H.Ḥ. Michael, *Or ha-Ḥayyim: Ḥakhmei Yisrael ve-Sifreihem,* ed. by S.Z. Ḥ. Halberstam and N. Ben-Menahem (1965²).
Mid.	*Middot* (mishnaic tractate).
Mid. Ag.	*Midrash Aggadah.*
Mid. Hag.	*Midrash ha-Gadol.*
Mid. Job.	*Midrash Job.*
Mid. Jonah	*Midrash Jonah.*
Mid. Lek. Tov	*Midrash Lekaḥ Tov.*
Mid. Prov.	*Midrash Proverbs.*
Mid. Ps.	*Midrash Tehillim* (Eng tr. *The Midrash on Psalms* (JPS, 1959).
Mid. Sam.	*Midrash Samuel.*
Mid. Song	*Midrash Shir ha-Shirim.*
Mid. Tan.	*Midrash Tanna'im* on Deuteronomy.
Miége, Maroc	J.L. Miège, *Le Maroc et l'Europe,* 3 vols. (1961 62).
Mig.	Philo, *De Migratione Abrahami.*
Mik.	*Mikva'ot* (mishnaic tractate).
Milano, Bibliotheca	A. Milano, *Bibliotheca Historica Italo-Judaica* (1954); supplement for 1954–63 (1964); supplement for 1964–66 in RMI, 32 (1966).
Milano, Italia	A. Milano, *Storia degli Ebrei in Italia* (1963).
MIO	*Mitteilungen des Instituts fuer Orientforschung* 1953ff.).
Mish.	Mishnah.
MJ	*Le Monde Juif* (1946ff.).
MJC	see Neubauer, Chronicles.
MK	*Mo'ed Katan* (talmudic tractate).
MNDPV	*Mitteilungen und Nachrichten des deutschen Palaestinavereins* (1895–1912).
Mortara, Indice	M. Mortara, *Indice Alfabetico dei Rabbini e Scrittori Israeliti ... in Italia ...* (1886).
Mos	Philo, *De Vita Mosis.*
Moscati, Epig	S, Moscati, *Epigrafia ebraica antica* 1935–1950 (1951).
MT	Masoretic Text of the Bible.
Mueller, Musiker	[E.H. Mueller], *Deutisches Musiker-Lexikon* (1929)
Munk, Mélanges	S. Munk, *Mélanges de philosophie juive et arabe* (1859; repr. 1955).
Mut.	Philo, *De Mutatione Nominum.*
MWJ	*Magazin fuer die Wissenshaft des Judentums* (18745 93).
Nah.	Nahum (Bible).
Naz.	*Nazir* (talmudic tractate).
NDB	*Neue Deutsche Biographie* (1953ff.).
Ned.	*Nedarim* (talmudic tractate).
Neg.	*Nega'im* (mishnaic tractate).
Neh.	Nehemiah (Bible).
NG²	*New Grove Dictionary of Music and Musicians* (2001).
Nuebauer, Cat	A. Neubauer, *Catalogue of the Hebrew Manuscripts in the Bodleian Library ...,* 2 vols. (1886–1906).
Neubauer, Chronicles	A. Neubauer, *Mediaeval Jewish Chronicles,* 2 vols. (Heb., 1887–95; repr. 1965), Eng. title of *Seder ha-Ḥakhamim ve-Korot ha-Yamim.*
Neubauer, Géogr	A. Neubauer, *La géographie du Talmud* (1868).
Neuman, Spain	A.A. Neuman, *The Jews in Spain, their Social, Political, and Cultural Life During the Middle Ages,* 2 vols. (1942).
Neusner, Babylonia	J. Neusner, *History of the Jews in Babylonia,* 5 vols. 1965–70), 2nd revised printing 1969ff.).
Nid.	*Niddah* (talmudic tractate).
Noah	Fragment of Book of Noah (Pseudepigrapha).
Noth, Hist Isr	M. Noth, *History of Israel* (1958).
Noth, Personennamen	M. Noth, *Die israelitischen Personennamen.* ... (1928).
Noth, Ueberlief	M. Noth, *Ueberlieferungsgeschichte des Pentateuchs* (1949).
Noth, Welt	M. Noth, *Die Welt des Alten Testaments* (1957³).
Nowack, Lehrbuch	W. Nowack, *Lehrbuch der hebraeischen Archaeologie,* 2 vols (1894).
NT	New Testament.
Num.	Numbers (Bible).
Num R.	*Numbers Rabbah.*
Obad.	Obadiah (Bible).
ODNB online	*Oxford Dictionary of National Biography.*
OḤ	*Oraḥ Ḥayyim.*
Oho.	*Oholot* (mishnaic tractate).
Olmstead	H.T. Olmstead, *History of Palestine and Syria* (1931; repr. 1965).
OLZ	*Orientalistische Literaturzeitung* (1898ff.)
Onom.	Eusebius, *Onomasticon.*
Op.	Philo, *De Opificio Mundi.*
OPD	*Osef Piskei Din shel ha-Rabbanut ha-Rashit le-Ereẓ Yisrael, Bet ha-Din ha-Gadol le-Irurim* (1950).
Or.	*Orlah* (talmudic tractate).
Or. Sibyll.	Sibylline Oracles (Pseudepigrapha).
OS	*L'Orient Syrien* (1956ff.)
OTS	*Oudtestamentische Studien* (1942ff.).
PAAJR	*Proceedings of the American Academy for Jewish Research* (1930ff.)
Pap 4QS^e	A papyrus exemplar of IQS.
Par.	*Parah* (mishnaic tractate).
Pauly-Wissowa	A.F. Pauly, *Realencyklopaedie der klassichen Alertumswissenschaft,* ed. by G. Wissowa et al. (1864ff.)

PD	*Piskei Din shel Bet ha-Mishpat ha-Elyon le-Yisrael* (1948ff.)
PDR	*Piskei Din shel Battei ha-Din ha-Rabbaniyyim be-Yisrael.*
PdRE	*Pirkei de-R. Eliezer* (Eng. tr. 1916. (1965^{2}).
PdRK	*Pesikta de-Rav Kahana.*
Pe'ah	*Pe'ah* (talmudic tractate).
Peake, Commentary	A.J. Peake (ed.), *Commentary on the Bible* (1919; rev. 1962).
Pedersen, Israel	J. Pedersen, *Israel, Its Life and Culture,* 4 vols. in 2 (1926–40).
PEFQS	*Palestine Exploration Fund Quarterly Statement* (1869–1937; since 1938–PEQ).
PEQ	*Palestine Exploration Quarterly* (until 1937 PEFQS; after 1927 includes BBSAJ).
Perles, Beitaege	J. Perles, *Beitraege zur rabbinischen Sprach- und Alterthumskunde* (1893).
Pes.	*Pesaḥim* (talmudic tractate).
Pesh.	Peshitta (Syriac translation of the Bible).
Pesher Hab.	Commentary to Habakkuk from Qumran; see 1Qp Hab.
I and II Pet.	Epistles of Peter (New Testament).
Pfeiffer, Introd	R.H. Pfeiffer, *Introduction to the Old Testament* (1948).
PG	J.P. Migne (ed.), *Patrologia Graeca,* 161 vols. (1866–86).
Phil.	Epistle to the Philippians (New Testament).
Philem.	Epistle to the Philemon (New Testament).
PIASH	*Proceedings of the Israel Academy of Sciences and Humanities* (1963/7ff.).
PJB	*Palaestinajahrbuch des deutschen evangelischen Institutes fuer Altertumswissenschaft,* Jerusalem (1905–1933).
PK	*Pinkas ha-Kehillot,* encyclopedia of Jewish communities, published in over 30 volumes by Yad Vashem from 1970 and arranged by countries, regions and localities. For 3-vol. English edition see Spector, *Jewish Life.*
PL	J.P. Migne (ed.), *Patrologia Latina* 221 vols. (1844–64).
Plant	Philo, *De Plantatione.*
PO	R. Graffin and F. Nau (eds.), *Patrologia Orientalis* (1903ff.)
Pool, Prayer	D. de Sola Pool, *Traditional Prayer Book for Sabbath and Festivals* (1960).
Post	Philo, *De Posteritate Caini.*
PR	*Pesikta Rabbati.*
Praem.	Philo, *De Praemiis et Poenis.*
Prawer, Ẓalbanim	J. Prawer, *Toledot Mamlekhet ha-Ẓalbanim be-Ereẓ Yisrael,* 2 vols. (1963).
Press, Ereẓ	I. Press, *Ereẓ-Yisrael, Enẓiklopedyah Topografit-Historit,* 4 vols. (1951–55).
Pritchard, Pictures	J.B. Pritchard (ed.), *Ancient Near East in Pictures* (1954, 1970).
Pritchard, Texts	J.B. Pritchard (ed.), *Ancient Near East Texts* ... (1970^{3}).
Pr. Man.	Prayer of Manasses (Apocrypha).
Prob.	Philo, *Quod Omnis Probus Liber Sit.*
Prov.	Proverbs (Bible).
PS	*Palestinsky Sbornik* (Russ. (1881 1916, 1954ff).
Ps.	Psalms (Bible).
PSBA	*Proceedings of the Society of Biblical Archaeology* (1878–1918).
Ps. of Sol	Psalms of Solomon (Pseudepigrapha).
IQ Apoc	The *Genesis Apocryphon* from Qumran, cave one, ed. by N. Avigad and Y. Yadin (1956).
6QD	*Damascus Document* or *Sefer Berit Dammesk* from Qumran, cave six, ed. by M. Baillet, in RB, 63 (1956), 513–23 (see also CD).
QDAP	*Quarterly of the Department of Antiquities in Palestine* (1932ff.).
4QDeut. 32	Manuscript of Deuteronomy 32 from Qumran, cave four (ed. by P.W. Skehan, in BASOR, 136 (1954), 12–15).
4QEx^{a}	Exodus manuscript in Jewish script from Qumran, cave four.
4QEx$^{\alpha}$	Exodus manuscript in Paleo-Hebrew script from Qumran, cave four (partially ed. by P.W. Skehan, in JBL, 74 (1955), 182–7).
4QFlor	*Florilegium,* a miscellany from Qumran, cave four (ed. by J.M. Allegro, in JBL, 75 (1956), 176–77 and 77 (1958), 350–54).).
QGJD	*Quellen zur Geschichte der Juden in Deutschland* 1888–98).
IQH	*Thanksgiving Psalms* of *Hodayot* from Qumran, cave one (ed. by E.L. Sukenik and N. Avigad, *Oẓar ha-Megillot ha-Genuzot* (1954).
IQIs^{a}	Scroll of Isaiah from Qumran, cave one (ed. by N. Burrows et al., *Dead Sea Scrolls* ..., 1 (1950).
IQIs^{b}	Scroll of Isaiah from Qumran, cave one (ed. E.L. Sukenik and N. Avigad, *Oẓar ha-Megillot ha-Genuzot* (1954).
IQM	The *War Scroll* or *Serekh ha-Milḥamah* (ed. by E.L. Sukenik and N. Avigad, *Oẓar ha-Megillot ha-Genuzot* (1954).
4QpNah	Commentary on Nahum from Qumran, cave four (partially ed. by J.M. Allegro, in JBL, 75 (1956), 89–95).
IQphyl	Phylacteries *(tefillin)* from Qumran, cave one (ed. by Y. Yadin, in *Eretz Israel,* 9 (1969), 60–85).
4Q Prayer of Nabonidus	A document from Qumran, cave four, belonging to a lost Daniel literature (ed. by J.T. Milik, in RB, 63 (1956), 407–15).
IQS	*Manual of Discipline* or *Serekh ha-Yaḥad* from Qumran, cave one (ed. by M. Burrows et al., *Dead Sea Scrolls* ..., 2, pt. 2 (1951).

IQS^{a}	The *Rule of the Congregation or Serekh ha-Edah* from Qumran, cave one (ed. by Burrows et al., *Dead Sea Scrolls* ..., 1 (1950), under the abbreviation IQ28a).
IQS^{b}	*Blessings* or *Divrei Berakhot* from Qumran, cave one (ed. by Burrows et al., *Dead Sea Scrolls* ..., 1 (1950), under the abbreviation IQ28b).
4QSam^{a}	Manuscript of I and II Samuel from Qumran, cave four (partially ed. by F.M. Cross, in BASOR, 132 (1953), 15–26).
4QSam^{b}	Manuscript of I and II Samuel from Qumran, cave four (partially ed. by F.M. Cross, in JBL, 74 (1955), 147–72).
4QTestimonia	Sheet of Testimony from Qumran, cave four (ed. by J.M. Allegro, in JBL, 75 (1956), 174–87).).
4QT.Levi	*Testament of Levi* from Qumran, cave four (partially ed. by J.T. Milik, in RB, 62 (1955), 398–406).
Rabinovitz, Dik Sof	See Dik Sof.
RB	*Revue biblique* (1892ff.)
RBI	*Recherches bibliques* (1954ff.)
RCB	*Revista de cultura biblica* (São Paulo) (1957ff.)
Régné, Cat	J. Régné, *Catalogue des actes . . . des rois d'Aragon, concernant les Juifs* (1213–1327), in: REJ, vols. 60 70, 73, 75–78 (1910–24).
Reinach, Textes	T. Reinach, *Textes d'auteurs Grecs et Romains relatifs au Judaïsme* (1895; repr. 1963).
REJ	*Revue des études juives* (1880ff.).
Rejzen, Leksikon	Z. Rejzen, *Leksikon fun der Yidisher Literature,* 4 vols. (1927–29).
Renan, Ecrivains	A. Neubauer and E. Renan, *Les écrivains juifs français* ... (1893).
Renan, Rabbins	A. Neubauer and E. Renan, *Les rabbins français* (1877).
RES	*Revue des étude sémitiques et Babyloniaca* (1934–45).
Rev.	Revelation (New Testament).
RGG^{3}	*Die Religion in Geschichte und Gegenwart,* 7 vols. (1957–65^{3}).
RH	*Rosh Ha-Shanah* (talmudic tractate).
RHJE	*Revue de l'histoire juive en Egypte* (1947ff.).
RHMH	*Revue d'histoire de la médecine hébraïque* (1948ff.).
RHPR	*Revue d'histoire et de philosophie religieuses* (1921ff.).
RHR	*Revue d'histoire des religions* (1880ff.).
RI	*Rivista Israelitica* (1904–12).
Riemann-Einstein	*Hugo Riemanns Musiklexikon,* ed. by A. Einstein (1929^{11}).
Riemann-Gurlitt	*Hugo Riemanns Musiklexikon,* ed. by W. Gurlitt (1959–67^{12}), Personenteil.
Rigg-Jenkinson, Exchequer	J.M. Rigg, H. Jenkinson and H.G. Richardson (eds.), *Calendar of the Pleas Rolls of the Exchequer of the Jews,* 4 vols. (1905–1970); cf. in each instance also J.M. Rigg (ed.), *Select Pleas* ... (1902).
RMI	*Rassegna Mensile di Israel* (1925ff.).
Rom.	Epistle to the Romans (New Testament).
Rosanes, Togarmah	S.A. Rosanes, *Divrei Yemei Yisrael be-Togarmah,* 6 vols. (1907–45), and in 3 vols. (1930–38^{2}).
Rosenbloom, Biogr Dict	J.R. Rosenbloom, *Biographical Dictionary of Early American Jews* (1960).
Roth, Art	C. Roth, *Jewish Art* (1961).
Roth, Dark Ages	C. Roth (ed.), *World History of the Jewish People,* second series, vol. 2, *Dark Ages* (1966).
Roth, England	C. Roth, *History of the Jews in England* (1964^{3}).
Roth, Italy	C. Roth, *History of the Jews in Italy* (1946).
Roth, Mag Bibl	C. Roth, *Magna Bibliotheca Anglo-Judaica* (1937).
Roth, Marranos	C. Roth, *History of the Marranos* (2nd rev. ed 1959; reprint 1966).
Rowley, Old Test	H.H. Rowley, *Old Testament and Modern Study* (1951; repr. 1961).
RS	*Revue sémitiques d'épigraphie et d'histoire ancienne* (1893/94ff.).
RSO	*Rivista degli studi orientali* (1907ff.).
RSV	Revised Standard Version of the Bible.
Rubinstein, Australia I	*H.L. Rubinstein, The Jews in Australia, A Thematic History, Vol. I (1991).*
Rubinstein, Australia II	*W.D. Rubinstein, The Jews in Australia, A Thematic History, Vol. II (1991).*
Ruth	Ruth (Bible).
Ruth R.	*Ruth Rabbah.*
RV	Revised Version of the Bible.
Sac.	Philo, *De Sacrificiis Abelis et Caini.*
Salfeld, Martyrol	S. Salfeld, *Martyrologium des Nuernberger Memorbuches* (1898).
I and II Sam.	Samuel, book I and II (Bible).
Sanh.	*Sanhedrin* (talmudic tractate).
SBA	Society of Biblical Archaeology.
SBB	*Studies in Bibliography and Booklore* (1953ff.).
SBE	*Semana Biblica Española.*
SBT	*Studies in Biblical Theology* (1951ff.).
SBU	*Svenkst Bibliskt Uppslogsvesk,* 2 vols. (1962–63^{2}).
Schirmann, Italyah	J.Ḥ. Schirmann, *Ha-Shirah ha-Ivrit be-Italyah* (1934).
Schirmann, Sefarad	J.Ḥ. Schirmann, *Ha-Shirah ha-Ivrit bi-Sefarad u-vi-Provence,* 2 vols. (1954–56).
Scholem, Mysticism	G. Scholem, *Major Trends in Jewish Mysticism* (rev. ed. 1946; paperback ed. with additional bibliography 1961).
Scholem, Shabbetai Ẓevi	G. Scholem, *Shabbetai Ẓevi ve-ha-Tenu'ah ha-Shabbeta'it bi-Ymei Ḥayyav,* 2 vols. (1967).
Schrader, Keilinschr	E. Schrader, *Keilinschriften und das Alte Testament* (1903^{3}).
Schuerer, Gesch	E. Schuerer, *Geschichte des juedischen Volkes im Zeitalter Jesu Christi,* 3 vols. and index-vol. (1901–11^{4}).

Schuerer, Hist	E. Schuerer, *History of the Jewish People in the Time of Jesus*, ed. by N.N. Glatzer, abridged paperback edition (1961).
Set. T.	*Sefer Torah* (post-talmudic tractate).
Sem.	*Semaḥot* (post-talmudic tractate).
Sendrey, Music	A. Sendrey, *Bibliography of Jewish Music* (1951).
SER	*Seder Eliyahu Rabbah.*
SEZ	*Seder Eliyahu Zuta.*
Shab	*Shabbat* (talmudic tractate).
Sh. Ar.	J. Caro Shulḥan Arukh. OḤ – *Oraḥ Ḥayyim* YD – *Yoreh De'ah* EH – *Even ha-Ezer* ḤM – *Ḥoshen Mishpat.*
Shek.	*Shekalim* (talmudic tractate).
Shev.	*Shevi'it* (talmudic tractate).
Shevu.	*Shevu'ot* (talmudic tractate).
Shunami, Bibl	S. Shunami, *Bibliography of Jewish Bibliographies* (1965^{2}).
Sif.	*Sifrei Deuteronomy.*
Sif. Num.	*Sifrei Numbers.*
Sifra	*Sifra* on Leviticus.
Sif. Zut.	*Sifrei Zuta.*
SIHM	Sources inédites de l'histoire du Maroc (series).
Silverman, Prayer	M. Silverman (ed.), *Sabbath and Festival Prayer Book* (1946).
Singer, Prayer	S. Singer *Authorised Daily Prayer Book* (1943^{17}).
Sob.	Philo, *De Sobrietate.*
Sof.	*Soferim* (post-talmudic tractate).
Som.	Philo, *De Somniis.*
Song	Song of Songs (Bible).
Song. Ch.	Song of the Three Children (Apocrypha).
Song R.	*Song of Songs Rabbah.*
SOR	*Seder Olam Rabbah.*
Sot.	*Sotah* (talmudic tractate).
SOZ	*Seder Olam Zuta.*
Spec.	Philo, *De Specialibus Legibus.*
Spector, Jewish Life	*S. Spector (ed.), Encyclopedia of Jewish Life Before and After the Holocaust (2001).*
Steinschneider, Arab lit	M. Steinschneider, *Die arabische Literatur der Juden* (1902).
Steinschneider, Cat Bod	M. Steinschneider, *Catalogus Librorum Hebraeorum in Bibliotheca Bodleiana*, 3 vols. (1852–60; reprints 1931 and 1964).
Steinschneider, Hanbuch	M. Steinschneider, *Bibliographisches Handbuch ueber die . . . Literatur fuer hebraeische Sprachkunde* (1859; repr. with additions 1937).
Steinschneider, Uebersetzungen	M. Steinschneider, *Die hebraeischen Uebersetzungen des Mittelalters* (1893).
Stern, Americans	M.H. Stern, *Americans of Jewish Descent* (1960).
van Straalen, Cat	S. van Straalen, *Catalogue of Hebrew Books in the British Museum Acquired During the Years 1868–1892* (1894).
Suárez Fernández, Docmentos	L. Suárez Fernández, *Documentos acerca de la expulsion de los Judios de España* (1964).
Suk.	*Sukkah* (talmudic tractate).
Sus.	Susanna (Apocrypha).
SY	*Sefer Yeẓirah.*
Sym.	Symmachus' Greek translation of the Bible.
SZNG	*Studien zur neueren Geschichte.*
Ta'an.	*Ta'anit* (talmudic tractate).
Tam.	*Tamid* (mishnaic tractate).
Tanḥ.	*Tanḥuma.*
Tanḥ. B.	*Tanḥuma.* Buber ed (1885).
Targ. Jon	Targum Jonathan (Aramaic version of the Prophets).
Targ. Onk.	Targum Onkelos (Aramaic version of the Pentateuch).
Targ. Yer.	Targum Yerushalmi.
TB	Babylonian Talmud or Talmud Bavli.
Tcherikover, Corpus	V. Tcherikover, A. Fuks, and M. Stern, *Corpus Papyrorum Judaicorum*, 3 vols. (1957–60).
Tef.	*Tefillin* (post-talmudic tractate).
Tem.	*Temurah* (mishnaic tractate).
Ter.	*Terumah* (talmudic tractate).
Test. Patr.	Testament of the Twelve Patriarchs (Pseudepigrapha). Ash. – Asher Ben. – Benjamin Dan – Dan Gad – Gad Iss. – Issachar Joseph – Joseph Judah – Judah Levi – Levi Naph. – Naphtali Reu. – Reuben Sim. – Simeon Zeb. – Zebulun.
I and II	Epistle to the Thessalonians (New Testament).
Thieme-Becker	U. Thieme and F. Becker (eds.), *Allgemeines Lexikon der bildenden Kuenstler von der Antike bis zur Gegenwart*, 37 vols. (1907–50).
Tidhar	D. Tidhar (ed.), *Enẓiklopedyah la-Ḥalutẓei ha-Yishuv u-Vonav* (1947ff.).
I and II Timothy	Epistles to Timothy (New Testament).
Tit.	Epistle to Titus (New Testament).
TJ	Jerusalem Talmud or Talmud Yerushalmi.
Tob.	Tobit (Apocrypha).
Toh.	*Tohorot* (mishnaic tractate).
Torczyner, Bundeslade	H. Torczyner, *Die Bundeslade und die Anfaenge der Religion Israels* (1930^{3}).
Tos.	*Tosafot.*
Tosef.	Tosefta.
Tristram, Nat Hist	H.B. Tristram, *Natural History of the Bible* (1877^{5}).
Tristram, Survey	Palestine Exploration Fund, *Survey of Western Palestine*, vol. 4 (1884) = *Fauna and Flora* by H.B. Tristram.
TS	*Terra Santa* (1943ff.).

TSBA	*Transactions of the Society of Biblical Archaeology* (1872–93).
TY	*Tevul Yom* (mishnaic tractate).
UBSB	United Bible Society, *Bulletin.*
UJE	*Universal Jewish Encyclopedia*, 10 vols. (1939–43).
Uk.	*Ukẓin* (mishnaic tractate).
Urbach, Tosafot	E.E. Urbach, *Ba'alei ha-Tosafot* (1957²).
de Vaux, Anc Isr	R. de Vaux, *Ancient Israel: its Life and Institutions* (1961; paperback 1965).
de Vaux, Instit	R. de Vaux, *Institutions de l'Ancien Testament*, 2 vols. (1958 60).
Virt.	Philo, *De Virtutibus.*
Vogelstein, Chronology	M. Volgelstein, *Biblical Chronology (1944).*
Vogelstein-Rieger	H. Vogelstein and P. Rieger, *Geschichte der Juden in Rom*, 2 vols. (1895–96).
VT	*Vetus Testamentum* (1951ff.).
VTS	*Vetus Testamentum* Supplements (1953ff.).
Vulg.	Vulgate (Latin translation of the Bible).
Wars	Josephus, *The Jewish Wars.*
Watzinger, Denkmaeler	K. Watzinger, *Denkmaeler Palaestinas*, 2 vols. (1933–35).
Waxman, Literature	M. Waxman, *History of Jewish Literature*, 5 vols. (1960²).
Weiss, Dor	I.H. Weiss, *Dor, Dor ve-Doreshav*, 5 vols. (1904⁴).
Wellhausen, Proleg	J. Wellhausen, *Prolegomena zur Geschichte Israels* (1927⁶).
WI	*Die Welt des Islams* (1913ff.).
Winniger, Biog	S. Wininger, *Grosse juedische National-Biographie ...*, 7 vols. (1925–36).
Wisd.	Wisdom of Solomon (Apocrypha)
WLB	*Wiener Library Bulletin* (1958ff.).
Wolf, Bibliotheca	J.C. Wolf, *Bibliotheca Hebraea*, 4 vols. (1715–33).
Wright, Bible	G.E. Wright, *Westminster Historical Atlas to the Bible* (1945).
Wright, Atlas	G.E. Wright, *The Bible and the Ancient Near East* (1961).
WWWJ	*Who's Who in the World Jewry* (New York, 1955, 1965²).
WZJT	*Wissenschaftliche Zeitschrift fuer juedische Theologie* (1835–37).
WZKM	*Wiener Zeitschrift fuer die Kunde des Morgenlandes* (1887ff.).
Yaari, Sheluḥei	A. Yaari, *Sheluḥei Ereẓ Yisrael* (1951).
Yad	Maimonides, *Mishneh Torah (Yad Ḥazakah).*
Yad	*Yadayim* (mishnaic tractate).
Yal.	*Yalkut Shimoni.*
Yal. Mak.	*Yalkut Makhiri.*
Yal. Reub.	*Yalkut Reubeni.*
YD	*Yoreh De'ah.*
YE	*Yevreyskaya Entsiklopediya*, 14 vols. (c. 1910).
Yev.	*Yevamot* (talmudic tractate).
YIVOA	*YIVO Annual of Jewish Social Studies* (1946ff.).
YLBI	*Year Book of the Leo Baeck Institute* (1956ff.).
YMḤEY	See BJPES.
YMḤSI	*Yedi'ot ha-Makhon le-Ḥeker ha-Shirah ha-Ivrit* (1935/36ff.).
YMMY	*Yedi'ot ha-Makhon le-Madda'ei ha-Yahadut* (1924/25ff.).
Yoma	*Yoma* (talmudic tractate).
ZA	*Zeitschrift fuer Assyriologie* (1886/87ff.).
Zav.	*Zavim* (mishnaic tractate).
ZAW	*Zeitschrift fuer die alttestamentliche Wissenschaft und die Kunde des nachbiblishchen Judentums* (1881ff.).
ZAWB	*Beihefte* (supplements) to ZAW.
ZDMG	*Zeitschrift der Deutschen Morgenlaendischen Gesellschaft* (1846ff.).
ZDPV	*Zeitschrift des Deutschen Palaestina-Vereins* (1878–1949; from 1949 = BBLA).
Zech.	Zechariah (Bible).
Zedner, Cat	J. Zedner, *Catalogue of Hebrew Books in the Library of the British Museum* (1867; repr. 1964).
Zeitlin, Bibliotheca	W. Zeitlin, *Bibliotheca Hebraica Post-Mendelssohniana* (1891–95).
Zeph.	Zephaniah (Bible).
Zev.	*Zevaḥim* (talmudic tractate).
ZGGJT	*Zeitschrift der Gesellschaft fuer die Geschichte der Juden in der Tschechoslowakei* (1930–38).
ZGJD	*Zeitschrift fuer die Geschichte der Juden in Deutschland* (1887–92).
ZHB	*Zeitschrift fuer hebraeische Bibliographie* (1896–1920).
Zinberg, Sifrut	I. Zinberg, *Toledot Sifrut Yisrael*, 6 vols. (1955–60).
Ẓiẓ.	*Ẓiẓit* (post-talmudic tractate).
ZNW	*Zeitschrift fuer die neutestamentliche Wissenschaft* (1901ff.).
ZS	*Zeitschrift fuer Semitistik und verwandte Gebiete* (1922ff.).
Zunz, Gesch	L. Zunz, *Zur Geschichte und Literatur* (1845).
Zunz, Gesch	L. Zunz, *Literaturgeschichte der synagogalen Poesie* (1865; Supplement, 1867; repr. 1966).
Zunz, Poesie	L. Zunz, *Synogogale Posie des Mittelalters*, ed. by Freimann (1920²; repr. 1967).
Zunz, Ritus	L. Zunz, *Ritus des synagogalen Gottesdienstes* (1859; repr. 1967).
Zunz, Schr	L. Zunz, *Gesammelte Schriften*, 3 vols. (1875–76).
Zunz, Vortraege	L. Zunz, *Gottesdienstliche vortraege der Juden ...* 1892²; repr. 1966).
Zunz-Albeck, Derashot	L. Zunz, *Ha-Derashot be-Yisrael*, Heb. Tr. of Zunz Vortraege by H. Albeck (1954²).

TRANSLITERATION RULES

HEBREW AND SEMITIC LANGUAGES:

	General	*Scientific*
א	not transliterated[1]	ʾ
בּ	b	b
ב	v	v, b̲
גּ	g	g
ג		ḡ
דּ	d	d
ד		d̲
ה	h	h
ו	v – when not a vowel	w
ז	z	z
ח	ḥ	ḥ
ט	t	ṭ, t
י	y – when vowel and at end of words – i	y
כּ	k	k
כ, ך	kh	kh, k̲
ל	l	l̲
מ, ם	m	m
נ, ן	n	n
ס	s	s
ע	not transliterated[1]	ʿ
פּ	p	p
פ, ף	f	p, f, ph
צ, ץ	ẓ	ṣ, ẓ
ק	k	q, k
ר	r	r
שׁ	sh[2]	š
שׂ	s	ś, s
תּ	t	t
ת		ṯ
ג׳	dzh, J	ǧ
ז׳	zh, J	ž
צ׳	ch	č
◌ָ		å, o, ǒ (short) â, ā (long)
◌ַ	a	a
◌ֲ		a, ᵃ
◌ֵ		e, ẹ, ē
◌ֶ	e	æ, ä, ȩ
◌ֱ		œ, ě, ᵉ
◌ְ	only *sheva na* is transliterated	ə, ĕ, e; only *sheva na* transliterated
◌ִ ◌ִי	i	i
◌ֹ וֹ	o	o, o, o
◌ֻ וּ	u	u, ŭ û, ū
◌ֵי	ei; biblical e	
‡		reconstructed forms of words

1. The letters א and ע are not transliterated.
 An apostrophe (') between vowels indicates that they do not form a diphthong and are to be pronounced separately.
2. *Dagesh ḥazak* (forte) is indicated by doubling of the letter, except for the letter שׁ.
3. Names. Biblical names and biblical place names are rendered according to the Bible translation of the Jewish Publication Society of America. Post-biblical Hebrew names are transliterated; contemporary names are transliterated or rendered as used by the person. Place names are transliterated or rendered by the accepted spelling. Names and some words with an accepted English form are usually not transliterated.

YIDDISH

א	not transliterated
אַ	a
אָ	o
בּ	b
בֿ	v
ג	g
ד	d
ה	h
ו, וּ	u
וו	v
וי	oy
ז	z
זש	zh
ח	kh
ט	t
טש	tsh, ch
י	(consonant) y (vowel) i
יִ	i
יי	ey
ײַ	ay
כּ	k
כ, ך	kh
ל	l
מ, ם	m
נ, ן	n
ס	s
ע	e
פּ	p
פֿ, ף	f
צ, ץ	ts
ק	k
ר	r
ש	sh
שׂ	s
תּ	t
ת	s

1. Yiddish transliteration rendered according to U. Weinreich's Modern *English-Yiddish Yiddish-English* Dictionary.
2. Hebrew words in Yiddish are usually transliterated according to standard Yiddish pronunciation, e.g., חזנות = *khazones*.

LADINO

Ladino and Judeo-Spanish words written in Hebrew characters are transliterated phonetically, following the General Rules of Hebrew transliteration (see above) whenever the accepted spelling in Latin characters could not be ascertained.

ARABIC

ا ء	a[1]	ض	ḍ
ب	b	ط	ṭ
ت	t	ظ	ẓ
ث	th	ع	c
ج	j	غ	gh
ح	ḥ	ف	f
خ	kh	ق	q
د	d	ك	k
ذ	dh	ل	l
ر	r	م	m
ز	z	ن	n
س	s	ه	h
ش	sh	و	w
ص	ṣ	ي	y
ـَ	a	ـَا ى	ā
ـِ	i	ـِي	ī
ـُ	u	ـُو	ū
ـَو	aw	ـِيّ	iyy[2]
ـَي	ay	ـُوّ	uww[2]

1. not indicated when initial
2. see note (f)

a) The EJ follows the *Columbia Lippincott Gazetteer* and the *Times Atlas* in transliteration of Arabic place names. Sites that appear in neither are transliterated according to the table above, and subject to the following notes.

b) The EJ follows the *Columbia Encyclopedia* in transliteration of Arabic names. Personal names that do not therein appear are transliterated according to the table above and subject to the following notes (e.g., Ali rather than ʿAlī, Suleiman rather than Sulayman).

c) The EJ follows the *Webster's Third International Dictionary, Unabridged* in transliteration of Arabic terms that have been integrated into the English language.

d) The term "Abu" will thus appear, usually in disregard of inflection.

e) Nunnation (end vowels, *tanwīn*) are dropped in transliteration.

f) Gemination (*tashdīd*) is indicated by the doubling of the geminated letter, unless an end letter, in which case the gemination is dropped.

g) The definitive article *al-* will always be thus transliterated, unless subject to one of the modifying notes (e.g., El-Arish rather than al-ʿArīsh; modification according to note (a)).

h) The Arabic transliteration disregards the Sun Letters (the antero-palatals (*al-Ḥurūf al-Shamsiyya*).

i) The *tā-marbūṭa* (ο) is omitted in transliteration, unless in construct-stage (e.g., *Khirba* but *Khirbat Mishmish*).

These modifying notes may lead to various inconsistencies in the Arabic transliteration, but this policy has deliberately been adopted to gain smoother reading of Arabic terms and names.

GREEK

Ancient Greek	*Modern Greek*	*Greek Letters*
a	a	*Α; α; ᾳ*
b	v	*Β; β*
g	gh; g	*Γ; γ*
d	dh	*Δ; δ*
e	e	*Ε; ε*
z	z	*Ζ; ζ*
e; e	i	*Η; η; ῃ*
th	th	*Θ; θ*
i	i	*Ι; ι*
k	k; ky	*Κ; κ*
l	l	*Λ; λ*
m	m	*Μ; μ*
n	n	*Ν; ν*
x	x	*Ξ; ξ*
o	o	*Ο; ο*
p	p	*Π; π*
r; rh	r	*Ρ; ρ; ῥ*
s	s	*Σ; σ; ς*
t	t	*Τ; τ*
u; y	i	*Υ; υ*
ph	f	*Φ; φ*
ch	kh	*Χ; χ*
ps	ps	*Ψ; ψ*
o; ō	o	*Ω; ω; ῳ*
ai	e	*αι*
ei	i	*ει*
oi	i	*οι*
ui	i	*υι*
ou	ou	*ου*
eu	ev	*ευ*
eu; ēu	iv	*ηυ*
–	j	*τζ*
nt	d; nd	*ντ*
mp	b; mb	*μπ*
ngk	g	*γκ*
ng	ng	*νγ*
h	–	‘
–	–	’
w	–	*Ϝ*

RUSSIAN

А	A
Б	B
В	V
Г	G
Д	D
Е	E, Ye[1]
Ё	Yo, O[2]
Ж	Zh
З	Z
И	I
Й	Y[3]
К	K
Л	L
М	M
Н	N
О	O
П	P
Р	R
С	S
Т	T
У	U
Ф	F
Х	Kh
Ц	Ts
Ч	Ch
Ш	Sh
Щ	Shch
Ъ	omitted; see note [1]
Ы	Y
Ь	omitted; see note [1]
Э	E
Ю	Yu
Я	Ya

1. Ye at the beginning of a word; after all vowels except ***Ы***; and after **Ъ** and ***Ь***.
2. O after ***Ч***, ***Ш*** and ***Щ***.
3. Omitted after ***Ы***, and in names of people after ***И***.

A. Many first names have an accepted English or quasi-English form which has been preferred to transliteration.
B. Place names have been given according to the *Columbia Lippincott Gazeteer*.
C. Pre-revolutionary spelling has been ignored.
D. Other languages using the Cyrillic alphabet (e.g., Bulgarian, Ukrainian), inasmuch as they appear, have been phonetically transliterated in conformity with the principles of this table.

GLOSSARY

Asterisked terms have separate entries in the Encyclopaedia.

Actions Committee, early name of the Zionist General Council, the supreme institution of the World Zionist Organization in the interim between Congresses. The Zionist Executive's name was then the "Small Actions Committee."

*__Adar__, twelfth month of the Jewish religious year, sixth of the civil, approximating to February–March.

*__Aggadah__, name given to those sections of Talmud and Midrash containing homiletic expositions of the Bible, stories, legends, folklore, anecdotes, or maxims. In contradistinction to **halakhah*.

*__Agunah__, woman unable to remarry according to Jewish law, because of desertion by her husband or inability to accept presumption of death.

*__Aharonim__, later rabbinic authorities. In contradistinction to **rishonim* ("early ones").

Ahavah, liturgical poem inserted in the second benediction of the morning prayer *(*Ahavah Rabbah)* of the festivals and/or special Sabbaths.

Aktion (Ger.), operation involving the mass assembly, deportation, and murder of Jews by the Nazis during the *Holocaust.

*__Aliyah__, (1) being called to Reading of the Law in synagogue; (2) immigration to Ereẓ Israel; (3) one of the waves of immigration to Ereẓ Israel from the early 1880s.

*__Amidah__, main prayer recited at all services; also known as *Shemoneh Esreh* and *Tefillah*.

*__Amora__ (pl. **amoraim**), title given to the Jewish scholars in Ereẓ Israel and Babylonia in the third to sixth centuries who were responsible for the **Gemara*.

Aravah, the *willow; one of the *Four Species used on *Sukkot ("festival of Tabernacles") together with the **etrog, hadas*, and **lulav*.

*__Arvit__, evening prayer.

Asarah be-Tevet, fast on the 10th of Tevet commemorating the commencement of the siege of Jerusalem by Nebuchadnezzar.

Asefat ha-Nivḥarim, representative assembly elected by Jews in Palestine during the period of the British Mandate (1920–48).

*__Ashkenaz__, name applied generally in medieval rabbinical literature to Germany.

*__Ashkenazi__ (pl. **Ashkenazim**), German or West-, Central-, or East-European Jew(s), as contrasted with *Sephardi(m).

*__Av__, fifth month of the Jewish religious year, eleventh of the civil, approximating to July–August.

*__Av bet din__, vice president of the supreme court (*bet din ha-gadol*) in Jerusalem during the Second Temple period; later, title given to communal rabbis as heads of the religious courts (see **bet din*).

*__Badḥan__, jester, particularly at traditional Jewish weddings in Eastern Europe.

*__Bakkashah__ (Heb. "supplication"), type of petitionary prayer, mainly recited in the Sephardi rite on Rosh Ha-Shanah and the Day of Atonement.

Bar, "son of . . . "; frequently appearing in personal names.

*__Baraita__ (pl. **beraitot**), statement of **tanna* not found in *Mishnah.

*__Bar mitzvah__, ceremony marking the initiation of a boy at the age of 13 into the Jewish religious community.

Ben, "son of . . . ", frequently appearing in personal names.

Berakhah (pl. **berakhot**), *benediction, blessing; formula of praise and thanksgiving.

*__Bet din__ (pl. **battei din**), rabbinic court of law.

*__Bet ha-midrash__, school for higher rabbinic learning; often attached to or serving as a synagogue.

*__Bilu__, first modern movement for pioneering and agricultural settlement in Ereẓ Israel, founded in 1882 at Kharkov, Russia.

*__Bund__, Jewish socialist party founded in Vilna in 1897, supporting Jewish national rights; Yiddishist, and anti-Zionist.

Cohen (pl. **Cohanim**), see Kohen.

*__Conservative Judaism__, trend in Judaism developed in the United States in the 20th century which, while opposing extreme changes in traditional observances, permits certain modifications of *halakhah* in response to the changing needs of the Jewish people.

*__Consistory__ (Fr. *consistoire*), governing body of a Jewish communal district in France and certain other countries.

*__Converso(s)__, term applied in Spain and Portugal to converted Jew(s), and sometimes more loosely to their descendants.

*__Crypto-Jew__, term applied to a person who although observing outwardly Christianity (or some other religion) was at heart a Jew and maintained Jewish observances as far as possible (see Converso; Marrano; Neofiti; New Christian; Jadīd al-Islām).

*__Dayyan__, member of rabbinic court.

Decisor, equivalent to the Hebrew *posek* (pl. **posekim*), the rabbi who gives the decision (*halakhah*) in Jewish law or practice.

*__Devekut__, "devotion"; attachment or adhesion to God; communion with God.

*__Diaspora__, Jews living in the "dispersion" outside Ereẓ Israel; area of Jewish settlement outside Ereẓ Israel.

Din, a law (both secular and religious), legal decision, or lawsuit.

Divan, diwan, collection of poems, especially in Hebrew, Arabic, or Persian.

Dunam, unit of land area (1,000 sq. m., c. ¼ acre), used in Israel.

Einsatzgruppen, mobile units of Nazi S.S. and S.D.; in U.S.S.R. and Serbia, mobile killing units.

*__Ein-Sof__, "without end"; "the infinite"; hidden, impersonal aspect of God; also used as a Divine Name.

*__Elul__, sixth month of the Jewish religious calendar, 12th of the civil, precedes the High Holiday season in the fall.

Endloesung, see *Final Solution.

*__Ereẓ Israel__, Land of Israel; Palestine.

*__Eruv__, technical term for rabbinical provision permitting the alleviation of certain restrictions.

*__Etrog__, citron; one of the *Four Species used on *Sukkot together with the **lulav, hadas*, and *aravah*.

Even ha-Ezer, see Shulḥan Arukh.

*__Exilarch__, lay head of Jewish community in Babylonia (see also *resh galuta*), and elsewhere.

*__Final Solution__ (Ger. *Endloesung*), in Nazi terminology, the Nazi-planned mass murder and total annihilation of the Jews.

*__Gabbai__, official of a Jewish congregation; originally a charity collector.

*__Galut__, "exile"; the condition of the Jewish people in dispersion.

***Gaon** (pl. **geonim**), head of academy in post-talmudic period, especially in Babylonia.

Gaonate, office of *gaon.

***Gemara**, traditions, discussions, and rulings of the **amoraim*, commenting on and supplementing the *Mishnah, and forming part of the Babylonian and Palestinian Talmuds (see Talmud).

***Gematria**, interpretation of Hebrew word according to the numerical value of its letters.

General Government, territory in Poland administered by a German civilian governor-general with headquarters in Cracow after the German occupation in World War II.

***Genizah**, depository for sacred books. The best known was discovered in the synagogue of Fostat (old Cairo).

Get, bill of *divorce.

***Ge'ullah**, hymn inserted after the **Shema* into the benediction of the morning prayer of the festivals and special Sabbaths.

***Gilgul**, metempsychosis; transmigration of souls.

***Golem**, automaton, especially in human form, created by magical means and endowed with life.

***Ḥabad**, initials of *ḥokhmah, binah, da'at*: "wisdom, understanding, knowledge"; ḥasidic movement founded in Belorussia by *Shneur Zalman of Lyady.

Hadas, *myrtle; one of the *Four Species used on Sukkot together with the **etrog, *lulav*, and *aravah*.

***Haftarah** (pl. **haftarot**), designation of the portion from the prophetical books of the Bible recited after the synagogue reading from the Pentateuch on Sabbaths and holidays.

***Haganah**, clandestine Jewish organization for armed self-defense in Ereẓ Israel under the British Mandate, which eventually evolved into a people's militia and became the basis for the Israel army.

***Haggadah**, ritual recited in the home on *Passover eve at seder table.

Haham, title of chief rabbi of the Spanish and Portuguese congregations in London, England.

***Hakham**, title of rabbi of *Sephardi congregation.

***Hakham bashi**, title in the 15th century and modern times of the chief rabbi in the Ottoman Empire, residing in Constantinople (Istanbul), also applied to principal rabbis in provincial towns.

Hakhsharah ("preparation"), organized training in the Diaspora of pioneers for agricultural settlement in Ereẓ Israel.

***Halakhah** (pl. **halakhot**), an accepted decision in rabbinic law. Also refers to those parts of the *Talmud concerned with legal matters. In contradistinction to **aggadah*.

Ḥaliẓah, biblically prescribed ceremony (Deut. 25:9–10) performed when a man refuses to marry his brother's childless widow, enabling her to remarry.

***Hallel**, term referring to Psalms 113-18 in liturgical use.

***Ḥalukkah**, system of financing the maintenance of Jewish communities in the holy cities of Ereẓ Israel by collections made abroad, mainly in the pre-Zionist era (see *kolel*).

Ḥalutz (pl. **ḥalutzim**), pioneer, especially in agriculture, in Ereẓ Israel.

Ḥalutziyyut, pioneering.

***Ḥanukkah**, eight-day celebration commemorating the victory of *Judah Maccabee over the Syrian king *Antiochus Epiphanes and the subsequent rededication of the Temple.

Ḥasid, adherent of *Ḥasidism.

***Ḥasidei Ashkenaz**, medieval pietist movement among the Jews of Germany.

***Ḥasidism**, (1) religious revivalist movement of popular mysticism among Jews of Germany in the Middle Ages; (2) religious movement founded by *Israel ben Eliezer Ba'al Shem Tov in the first half of the 18th century.

***Haskalah**, "enlightenment"; movement for spreading modern European culture among Jews c. 1750–1880. See *maskil*.

***Havdalah**, ceremony marking the end of Sabbath or festival.

***Ḥazzan**, precentor who intones the liturgy and leads the prayers in synagogue; in earlier times a synagogue official.

***Ḥeder** (lit. "room"), school for teaching children Jewish religious observance.

Heikhalot, "palaces"; tradition in Jewish mysticism centering on mystical journeys through the heavenly spheres and palaces to the Divine Chariot (see Merkabah).

***Ḥerem**, excommunication, imposed by rabbinical authorities for purposes of religious and/or communal discipline; originally, in biblical times, that which is separated from common use either because it was an abomination or because it was consecrated to God.

Ḥeshvan, see Marḥeshvan.

***Ḥevra kaddisha**, title applied to charitable confraternity (**ḥevrah*), now generally limited to associations for burial of the dead.

***Ḥibbat Zion**, see Ḥovevei Zion.

***Histadrut** (abbr. For Heb. **Ha-Histadrut ha-Kelalit shel ha-Ovedim ha-Ivriyyim be-Ereẓ Israel**). Ereẓ Israel Jewish Labor Federation, founded in 1920; subsequently renamed Histadrut ha-Ovedim be-Ereẓ Israel.

***Holocaust**, the organized mass persecution and annihilation of European Jewry by the Nazis (1933–1945).

***Hoshana Rabba**, the seventh day of *Sukkot on which special observances are held.

Ḥoshen Mishpat, see Shulḥan Arukh.

Ḥovevei Zion, federation of *Ḥibbat Zion, early (pre-*Herzl) Zionist movement in Russia.

Illui, outstanding scholar or genius, especially a young prodigy in talmudic learning.

***Iyyar**, second month of the Jewish religious year, eighth of the civil, approximating to April-May.

I.Ẓ.L. (initials of Heb. ***Irgun Ẓeva'i Le'ummi**; "National Military Organization"), underground Jewish organization in Ereẓ Israel founded in 1931, which engaged from 1937 in retaliatory acts against Arab attacks and later against the British mandatory authorities.

***Jadīd al-Islām** (Ar.), a person practicing the Jewish religion in secret although outwardly observing Islām.

***Jewish Legion**, Jewish units in British army during World War I.

***Jihād** (Ar.), in Muslim religious law, holy war waged against infidels.

***Judenrat** (Ger. "Jewish council"), council set up in Jewish communities and ghettos under the Nazis to execute their instructions.

***Judenrein** (Ger. "clean of Jews"), in Nazi terminology the condition of a locality from which all Jews had been eliminated.

***Kabbalah**, the Jewish mystical tradition:
Kabbala iyyunit, speculative Kabbalah;
Kabbala ma'asit, practical Kabbalah;
Kabbala nevu'it, prophetic Kabbalah.

Kabbalist, student of Kabbalah.

***Kaddish**, liturgical doxology.

Kahal, Jewish congregation; among Ashkenazim, *kehillah*.

*__Kalām__ (Ar.), science of Muslim theology; adherents of the Kalām are called *mutakallimūn.*
*__Karaite__, member of a Jewish sect originating in the eighth century which rejected rabbinic (*Rabbanite) Judaism and claimed to accept only Scripture as authoritative.
*__Kasher__, ritually permissible food.
Kashrut, Jewish *dietary laws.
*__Kavvanah__, "intention"; term denoting the spiritual concentration accompanying prayer and the performance of ritual or of a commandment.
*__Kedushah__, main addition to the third blessing in the reader's repetition of the *Amidah* in which the public responds to the precentor's introduction.
Kefar, village; first part of name of many settlements in Israel.
Kehillah, congregation; see *kahal.*
Kelippah (pl. **kelippot**), "husk(s)"; mystical term denoting force(s) of evil.
*__Keneset Yisrael__, comprehensive communal organization of the Jews in Palestine during the British Mandate.
Keri, variants in the masoretic (*masorah) text of the Bible between the spelling (*ketiv*) and its pronunciation (*keri*).
*__Kerovah__ (collective plural (corrupted) from **kerovez̦**), poem(s) incorporated into the **Amidah.*
Ketiv, see *keri.*
*__Ketubbah__, marriage contract, stipulating husband's obligations to wife.
Kevuz̦ah, small commune of pioneers constituting an agricultural settlement in Erez̦ Israel (evolved later into *kibbutz).
*__Kibbutz__ (pl. **kibbutzim**), larger-size commune constituting a settlement in Erez̦ Israel based mainly on agriculture but engaging also in industry.
*__Kiddush__, prayer of sanctification, recited over wine or bread on eve of Sabbaths and festivals.
*__Kiddush ha-Shem__, term connoting martyrdom or act of strict integrity in support of Judaic principles.
*__Kinah__ (pl. **kinot**), lamentation dirge(s) for the Ninth of Av and other fast days.
*__Kislev__, ninth month of the Jewish religious year, third of the civil, approximating to November-December.
Klaus, name given in Central and Eastern Europe to an institution, usually with synagogue attached, where *Talmud was studied perpetually by adults; applied by Ḥasidim to their synagogue ("*kloyz*").
*__Knesset__, parliament of the State of Israel.
K(c)ohen (pl. **K(c)ohanim**), Jew(s) of priestly (Aaronide) descent.
*__Kolel__, (1) community in Erez̦ Israel of persons from a particular country or locality, often supported by their fellow countrymen in the Diaspora; (2) institution for higher Torah study.
Kosher, see *kasher.*
*__Kristallnacht__ (Ger. "crystal night," meaning "night of broken glass"), organized destruction of synagogues, Jewish houses, and shops, accompanied by mass arrests of Jews, which took place in Germany and Austria under the Nazis on the night of Nov. 9–10, 1938.
*__Lag ba-Omer__, 33rd (Heb. **lag**) day of the **Omer* period falling on the 18th of *Iyyar; a semi-holiday.
Leḥi (abbr. For Heb. *__Loḥamei Ḥerut Israel__, "Fighters for the Freedom of Israel"), radically anti-British armed underground organization in Palestine, founded in 1940 by dissidents from *I.Z.L.
Levir, husband's brother.
*__Levirate marriage__ (Heb. *yibbum*), marriage of childless widow (*yevamah*) by brother (*yavam*) of the deceased husband (in accordance with Deut. 25:5); release from such an obligation is effected through *ḥaliz̦ah.*
LHY, see Leḥi.
*__Lulav__, palm branch; one of the *Four Species used on *Sukkot together with the **etrog, hadas*, and *aravah.*
*__Ma'aravot__, hymns inserted into the evening prayer of the three festivals, Passover, Shavuot, and Sukkot.
Ma'ariv, evening prayer; also called **arvit.*
*__Ma'barah__, transition camp; temporary settlement for newcomers in Israel during the period of mass immigration following 1948.
*__Maftir__, reader of the concluding portion of the Pentateuchal section on Sabbaths and holidays in synagogue; reader of the portion of the prophetical books of the Bible (**haftarah*).
*__Maggid__, popular preacher.
*__Maḥzor__ (pl. **maḥzorim**), festival prayer book.
*__Mamzer__, bastard; according to Jewish law, the offspring of an incestuous relationship.
*__Mandate, Palestine__, responsibility for the administration of Palestine conferred on Britain by the League of Nations in 1922; mandatory government: the British administration of Palestine.
*__Maqāma__ (Ar. pl. **maqamāt**), poetic form (rhymed prose) which, in its classical arrangement, has rigid rules of form and content.
*__Marḥeshvan__, popularly called Ḥeshvan; eighth month of the Jewish religious year, second of the civil, approximating to October–November.
*__Marrano(s)__, descendant(s) of Jew(s) in Spain and Portugal whose ancestors had been converted to Christianity under pressure but who secretly observed Jewish rituals.
Maskil (pl. **maskilim**), adherent of *Haskalah ("Enlightenment") movement.
*__Masorah__, body of traditions regarding the correct spelling, writing, and reading of the Hebrew Bible.
Masorete, scholar of the masoretic tradition.
Masoretic, in accordance with the masorah.
Meliz̦ah, in Middle Ages, elegant style; modern usage, florid style using biblical or talmudic phraseology.
Mellah, *Jewish quarter in North African towns.
*__Menorah__, candelabrum; seven-branched oil lamp used in the Tabernacle and Temple; also eight-branched candelabrum used on *Ḥanukkah.
Me'orah, hymn inserted into the first benediction of the morning prayer (*Yoz̦er ha-Me'orot*).
*__Merkabah__, *merkavah*, "chariot"; mystical discipline associated with Ezekiel's vision of the Divine Throne-Chariot (Ezek. 1).
Meshullaḥ, emissary sent to conduct propaganda or raise funds for rabbinical academies or charitable institutions.
*__Mezuzah__ (pl. **mezuzot**), parchment scroll with selected Torah verses placed in container and affixed to gates and doorposts of houses occupied by Jews.
*__Midrash__, method of interpreting Scripture to elucidate legal points (*Midrash Halakhah*) or to bring out lessons by stories or homiletics (*Midrash Aggadah*). Also the name for a collection of such rabbinic interpretations.
*__Mikveh__, ritual bath.
*__Minhag__ (pl. **minhagim**), ritual custom(s); synagogal rite(s); especially of a specific sector of Jewry.
*__Minḥah__, afternoon prayer; originally meal offering in Temple.

*Minyan, group of ten male adult Jews, the minimum required for communal prayer.

*Mishnah, earliest codification of Jewish Oral Law.

Mishnah (pl. **mishnayot**), subdivision of tractates of the Mishnah.

Mitnagged (pl. ***Mitnaggedim**), originally, opponents of *Ḥasidism in Eastern Europe.

***Mitzvah**, biblical or rabbinic injunction; applied also to good or charitable deeds.

Mohel, official performing circumcisions.

***Moshav**, smallholders' cooperative agricultural settlement in Israel, see moshav ovedim.

Moshavah, earliest type of Jewish village in modern Ereẓ Israel in which farming is conducted on individual farms mostly on privately owned land.

Moshav ovedim ("workers' moshav"), agricultural village in Israel whose inhabitants possess individual homes and holdings but cooperate in the purchase of equipment, sale of produce, mutual aid, etc.

***Moshav shittufi** ("collective moshav"), agricultural village in Israel whose members possess individual homesteads but where the agriculture and economy are conducted as a collective unit.

Mostegab (Ar.), poem with biblical verse at beginning of each stanza.

***Muqaddam** (Ar., pl. **muqaddamūn**), "leader," "head of the community."

***Musaf**, additional service on Sabbath and festivals; originally the additional sacrifice offered in the Temple.

Musar, traditional ethical literature.

***Musar movement**, ethical movement developing in the latter part of the 19th century among Orthodox Jewish groups in Lithuania; founded by R. Israel *Lipkin (Salanter).

***Nagid** (pl. **negidim**), title applied in Muslim (and some Christian) countries in the Middle Ages to a leader recognized by the state as head of the Jewish community.

Nakdan (pl. **nakdanim**), "punctuator"; scholar of the 9th to 14th centuries who provided biblical manuscripts with masoretic apparatus, vowels, and accents.

***Nasi** (pl. **nesi'im**), talmudic term for president of the Sanhedrin, who was also the spiritual head and later, political representative of the Jewish people; from second century a descendant of Hillel recognized by the Roman authorities as patriarch of the Jews. Now applied to the president of the State of Israel.

***Negev**, the southern, mostly arid, area of Israel.

***Ne'ilah**, concluding service on the *Day of Atonement.

Neofiti, term applied in southern Italy to converts to Christianity from Judaism and their descendants who were suspected of maintaining secret allegiance to Judaism.

***Neology; Neolog; Neologism**, trend of *Reform Judaism in Hungary forming separate congregations after 1868.

***Nevelah** (lit. "carcass"), meat forbidden by the *dietary laws on account of the absence of, or defect in, the act of **sheḥitah* (ritual slaughter).

***New Christians**, term applied especially in Spain and Portugal to converts from Judaism (and from Islam) and their descendants; "Half New Christian" designated a person one of whose parents was of full Jewish blood.

***Niddah** ("menstruous woman"), woman during the period of menstruation.

***Nisan**, first month of the Jewish religious year, seventh of the civil, approximating to March-April.

Niẓoẓot, "sparks"; mystical term for sparks of the holy light imprisoned in all matter.

Nosaḥ (**nusaḥ**) "version"; (1) textual variant; (2) term applied to distinguish the various prayer rites, e.g., *nosaḥ Ashkenaz*; (3) the accepted tradition of synagogue melody.

***Notarikon**, method of abbreviating Hebrew works or phrases by acronym.

Novella(e) (Heb. **ḥiddush (im)*), commentary on talmudic and later rabbinic subjects that derives new facts or principles from the implications of the text.

***Nuremberg Laws**, Nazi laws excluding Jews from German citizenship, and imposing other restrictions.

Ofan, hymns inserted into a passage of the morning prayer.

***Omer**, first sheaf cut during the barley harvest, offered in the Temple on the second day of Passover.

Omer, Counting of (Heb. *Sefirat ha-Omer*), 49 days counted from the day on which the *omer* was first offered in the Temple (according to the rabbis the 16th of Nisan, i.e., the second day of Passover) until the festival of Shavuot; now a period of semi-mourning.

Oraḥ Ḥayyim, see Shulḥan Arukh.

***Orthodoxy** (Orthodox Judaism), modern term for the strictly traditional sector of Jewry.

***Pale of Settlement**, 25 provinces of czarist Russia where Jews were permitted permanent residence.

***Palmaḥ** (abbr. for Heb. *peluggot maḥaẓ*; "shock companies"), striking arm of the *Haganah.

***Pardes**, medieval biblical exegesis giving the literal, allegorical, homiletical, and esoteric interpretations.

***Parnas**, chief synagogue functionary, originally vested with both religious and administrative functions; subsequently an elected lay leader.

Partition plan(s), proposals for dividing Ereẓ Israel into autonomous areas.

Paytan, composer of **piyyut* (liturgical poetry).

***Peel Commission**, British Royal Commission appointed by the British government in 1936 to inquire into the Palestine problem and make recommendations for its solution.

Pesaḥ, *Passover.

***Pilpul**, in talmudic and rabbinic literature, a sharp dialectic used particularly by talmudists in Poland from the 16th century.

***Pinkas**, community register or minute-book.

***Piyyut**, (pl. **piyyutim**), Hebrew liturgical poetry.

***Pizmon**, poem with refrain.

Posek (pl. ***posekim**), decisor; codifier or rabbinic scholar who pronounces decisions in disputes and on questions of Jewish law.

***Prosbul**, legal method of overcoming the cancelation of debts with the advent of the *sabbatical year.

***Purim**, festival held on Adar 14 or 15 in commemoration of the delivery of the Jews of Persia in the time of *Esther.

Rabban, honorific title higher than that of rabbi, applied to heads of the *Sanhedrin in mishnaic times.

***Rabbanite**, adherent of rabbinic Judaism. In contradistinction to *Karaite.

Reb, rebbe, Yiddish form for rabbi, applied generally to a teacher or ḥasidic rabbi.

***Reconstructionism**, trend in Jewish thought originating in the United States.

***Reform Judaism**, trend in Judaism advocating modification of *Orthodoxy in conformity with the exigencies of contemporary life and thought.

Resh galuta, lay head of Babylonian Jewry (see exilarch).

Responsum (pl. ***responsa**), written opinion (*teshuvah*) given to question (*she'elah*) on aspects of Jewish law by qualified authorities; pl. collection of such queries and opinions in book form (*she'elot u-teshuvot*).

***Rishonim**, older rabbinical authorities. Distinguished from later authorities (**aḥaronim*).

***Rishon le-Zion**, title given to Sephardi chief rabbi of Ereẓ Israel.

***Rosh Ha-Shanah**, two-day holiday (one day in biblical and early mishnaic times) at the beginning of the month of *Tishri (September–October), traditionally the New Year.

Rosh Hodesh, *New Moon, marking the beginning of the Hebrew month.

Rosh Yeshivah, see *Yeshivah.

***R.S.H.A.** (initials of Ger. *Reichssicherheitshauptamt*: "Reich Security Main Office"), the central security department of the German Reich, formed in 1939, and combining the security police (Gestapo and Kripo) and the S.D.

***Sanhedrin**, the assembly of ordained scholars which functioned both as a supreme court and as a legislature before 70 C.E. In modern times the name was given to the body of representative Jews convoked by Napoleon in 1807.

***Savora** (pl. **savoraim**), name given to the Babylonian scholars of the period between the **amoraim* and the **geonim*, approximately 500–700 C.E.

S.D. (initials of Ger. *Sicherheitsdienst*: "security service"), security service of the *S.S. formed in 1932 as the sole intelligence organization of the Nazi party.

Seder, ceremony observed in the Jewish home on the first night of Passover (outside Ereẓ Israel first two nights), when the *Haggadah is recited.

***Sefer Torah**, manuscript scroll of the Pentateuch for public reading in synagogue.

***Sefirot, the ten**, the ten "Numbers"; mystical term denoting the ten spheres or emanations through which the Divine manifests itself; elements of the world; dimensions, primordial numbers.

Selektion (Ger.), (1) in ghettos and other Jewish settlements, the drawing up by Nazis of lists of deportees; (2) separation of incoming victims to concentration camps into two categories – those destined for immediate killing and those to be sent for forced labor.

Seliḥah (pl. ***seliḥot**), penitential prayer.

***Semikhah**, ordination conferring the title "rabbi" and permission to give decisions in matters of ritual and law.

Sephardi (pl. ***Sephardim**), Jew(s) of Spain and Portugal and their descendants, wherever resident, as contrasted with *Ashkenazi(m).

Shabbatean, adherent of the pseudo-messiah *Shabbetai Ẓevi (17th century).

Shaddai, name of God found frequently in the Bible and commonly translated "Almighty."

***Shaḥarit**, morning service.

Shali'aḥ (pl. **sheliḥim**), in Jewish law, messenger, agent; in modern times, an emissary from Ereẓ Israel to Jewish communities or organizations abroad for the purpose of fund-raising, organizing pioneer immigrants, education, etc.

Shalmonit, poetic meter introduced by the liturgical poet *Solomon ha-Bavli.

***Shammash**, synagogue beadle.

***Shavuot**, Pentecost; Festival of Weeks; second of the three annual pilgrim festivals, commemorating the receiving of the Torah at Mt. Sinai.

***Sheḥitah**, ritual slaughtering of animals.

***Shekhinah**, Divine Presence.

Shelishit, poem with three-line stanzas.

***Sheluḥei Ereẓ Israel** (or **shadarim**), emissaries from Ereẓ Israel.

***Shema** ([Yisrael]; "hear… [O Israel]," Deut. 6:4), Judaism's confession of faith, proclaiming the absolute unity of God.

Shemini Aẓeret, final festal day (in the Diaspora, final two days) at the conclusion of *Sukkot.

Shemittah, *Sabbatical year.

Sheniyyah, poem with two-line stanzas.

***Shephelah**, southern part of the coastal plain of Ereẓ Israel.

***Shevat**, eleventh month of the Jewish religious year, fifth of the civil, approximating to January–February.

***Shi'ur Komah**, Hebrew mystical work (c. eighth century) containing a physical description of God's dimensions; term denoting enormous spacial measurement used in speculations concerning the body of the **Shekhinah*.

Shivah, the "seven days" of *mourning following burial of a relative.

***Shofar**, horn of the ram (or any other ritually clean animal excepting the cow) sounded for the memorial blowing on *Rosh Ha-Shanah, and other occasions.

Shoḥet, person qualified to perform **sheḥitah*.

Shomer, *Ha-Shomer, organization of Jewish workers in Ereẓ Israel founded in 1909 to defend Jewish settlements.

***Shtadlan**, Jewish representative or negotiator with access to dignitaries of state, active at royal courts, etc.

***Shtetl**, Jewish small-town community in Eastern Europe.

***Shulḥan Arukh**, Joseph *Caro's code of Jewish law in four parts:
Oraḥ Ḥayyim, laws relating to prayers, Sabbath, festivals, and fasts;
Yoreh De'ah, dietary laws, etc;
Even ha-Ezer, laws dealing with women, marriage, etc;
Ḥoshen Mishpat, civil, criminal law, court procedure, etc.

Siddur, among Ashkenazim, the volume containing the daily prayers (in distinction to the **maḥzor* containing those for the festivals).

***Simḥat Torah**, holiday marking the completion in the synagogue of the annual cycle of reading the Pentateuch; in Ereẓ Israel observed on Shemini Aẓeret (outside Ereẓ Israel on the following day).

***Sinai Campaign**, brief campaign in October–November 1956 when Israel army reacted to Egyptian terrorist attacks and blockade by occupying the Sinai peninsula.

Sitra aḥra, "the other side" (of God); left side; the demoniac and satanic powers.

***Sivan**, third month of the Jewish religious year, ninth of the civil, approximating to May–June.

***Six-Day War**, rapid war in June 1967 when Israel reacted to Arab threats and blockade by defeating the Egyptian, Jordanian, and Syrian armies.

***S.S.** (initials of Ger. *Schutzstaffel*: "protection detachment"), Nazi formation established in 1925 which later became the "elite" organization of the Nazi Party and carried out central tasks in the "Final Solution."

***Status quo ante** community, community in Hungary retaining the status it had held before the convention of the General Jewish Congress there in 1868 and the resultant split in Hungarian Jewry.

***Sukkah**, booth or tabernacle erected for *Sukkot when, for seven days, religious Jews "dwell" or at least eat in the *sukkah* (Lev. 23:42).

***Sukkot**, festival of Tabernacles; last of the three pilgrim festivals, beginning on the 15th of Tishri.

Sūra (Ar.), chapter of the Koran.

Ta'anit Esther (Fast of *Esther), fast on the 13th of Adar, the day preceding Purim.

Takkanah (pl. ***takkanot**), regulation supplementing the law of the Torah; regulations governing the internal life of communities and congregations.

***Tallit (gadol)**, four-cornered prayer shawl with fringes (*ẓiẓit*) at each corner.

***Tallit katan**, garment with fringes (*ẓiẓit*) appended, worn by observant male Jews under their outer garments.

***Talmud**, "teaching"; compendium of discussion on the Mishnah by generations of scholars and jurists in many academies over a period of several centuries. The Jerusalem (or Palestinian) Talmud mainly contains the discussions of the Palestinian sages. The Babylonian Talmud incorporates the parallel discussion in the Babylonian academies.

Talmud torah, term generally applied to Jewish religious (and ultimately to talmudic) study; also to traditional Jewish religious public schools.

***Tammuz**, fourth month of the Jewish religious year, tenth of the civil, approximating to June-July.

Tanna (pl. ***tannaim**), rabbinic teacher of mishnaic period.

***Targum**, Aramaic translation of the Bible.

***Tefillin**, phylacteries, small leather cases containing passages from Scripture and affixed on the forehead and arm by male Jews during the recital of morning prayers.

Tell (Ar. "mound," "hillock"), ancient mound in the Middle East composed of remains of successive settlements.

***Terefah**, food that is not **kasher*, owing to a defect on the animal.

***Territorialism**, 20th century movement supporting the creation of an autonomous territory for Jewish mass-settlement outside Ereẓ Israel.

***Tevet**, tenth month of the Jewish religious year, fourth of the civil, approximating to December–January.

Tikkun ("restitution," "reintegration"), (1) order of service for certain occasions, mostly recited at night; (2) mystical term denoting restoration of the right order and true unity after the spiritual "catastrophe" which occurred in the cosmos.

Tishah be-Av, Ninth of *Av, fast day commemorating the destruction of the First and Second Temples.

***Tishri**, seventh month of the Jewish religious year, first of the civil, approximating to September–October.

Tokheḥah, reproof sections of the Pentateuch (Lev. 26 and Deut. 28); poem of reproof.

***Torah**, Pentateuch or the Pentateuchal scroll for reading in synagogue; entire body of traditional Jewish teaching and literature.

Tosafist, talmudic glossator, mainly French ($12–14^{th}$ centuries), bringing additions to the commentary by *Rashi.

***Tosafot**, glosses supplied by tosafist.

***Tosefta**, a collection of teachings and traditions of the *tannaim*, closely related to the Mishnah.

Tradent, person who hands down a talmudic statement on the name of his teacher or other earlier authority.

***Tu bi-Shevat**, the 15th day of Shevat, the New Year for Trees; date marking a dividing line for fruit tithing; in modern Israel celebrated as arbor day.

***Uganda Scheme**, plan suggested by the British government in 1903 to establish an autonomous Jewish settlement area in East Africa.

***Va'ad Le'ummi**, national council of the Jewish community in Ereẓ Israel during the period of the British *Mandate.

***Wannsee Conference**, Nazi conference held on Jan. 20, 1942, at which the planned annihilation of European Jewry was endorsed.

Waqf (Ar.), (1) a Muslim charitable pious foundation; (2) state lands and other property passed to the Muslim community for public welfare.

***War of Independence**, war of 1947–49 when the Jews of Israel fought off Arab invading armies and ensured the establishment of the new State.

***White Paper(s)**, report(s) issued by British government, frequently statements of policy, as issued in connection with Palestine during the *Mandate period.

***Wissenschaft des Judentums** (Ger. "Science of Judaism"), movement in Europe beginning in the 19th century for scientific study of Jewish history, religion, and literature.

***Yad Vashem**, Israel official authority for commemorating the *Holocaust in the Nazi era and Jewish resistance and heroism at that time.

Yeshivah (pl. ***yeshivot**), Jewish traditional academy devoted primarily to study of rabbinic literature; *rosh yeshivah*, head of the yeshivah.

YHWH, the letters of the holy name of God, the Tetragrammaton.

Yibbum, see levirate marriage.

Yiḥud, "union"; mystical term for intention which causes the union of God with the **Shekhinah*.

Yishuv, settlement; more specifically, the Jewish community of Ereẓ Israel in the pre-State period. The pre-Zionist community is generally designated the "old yishuv" and the community evolving from 1880, the "new yishuv."

Yom Kippur, Yom ha-Kippurim, *Day of Atonement, solemn fast day observed on the 10th of Tishri.

Yoreh De'ah, see Shulḥan Arukh.

Yoẓer, hymns inserted in the first benediction (*Yoẓer Or*) of the morning **Shema*.

***Ẓaddik**, person outstanding for his faith and piety; especially a ḥasidic rabbi or leader.

Ẓimẓum, "contraction"; mystical term denoting the process whereby God withdraws or contracts within Himself so leaving a primordial vacuum in which creation can take place; primordial exile or self-limitation of God.

***Zionist Commission (1918)**, commission appointed in 1918 by the British government to advise the British military authorities in Palestine on the implementation of the *Balfour Declaration.

Ẓyyonei Zion, the organized opposition to Herzl in connectio with the *Uganda Scheme.

***Ẓiẓit**, fringes attached to the **tallit* and **tallit katan*.

***Zohar**, mystical commentary on the Pentateuch; main textb of *Kabbalah.

Zulat, hymn inserted after the **Shema* in the morning servi ok

e.

ish Congress there in 1868 and the resultant split in Hungarian Jewry.

*__Sukkah__, booth or tabernacle erected for *Sukkot when, for seven days, religious Jews "dwell" or at least eat in the *sukkah* (Lev. 23:42).

*__Sukkot__, festival of Tabernacles; last of the three pilgrim festivals, beginning on the 15th of Tishri.

Sūra (Ar.), chapter of the Koran.

Ta'anit Esther (Fast of *Esther), fast on the 13th of Adar, the day preceding Purim.

Takkanah (pl. ***takkanot**), regulation supplementing the law of the Torah; regulations governing the internal life of communities and congregations.

*__Tallit (gadol)__, four-cornered prayer shawl with fringes (*ẓiẓit*) at each corner.

*__Tallit katan__, garment with fringes (*ẓiẓit*) appended, worn by observant male Jews under their outer garments.

*__Talmud__, "teaching"; compendium of discussion on the Mishnah by generations of scholars and jurists in many academies over a period of several centuries. The Jerusalem (or Palestinian) Talmud mainly contains the discussions of the Palestinian sages. The Babylonian Talmud incorporates the parallel discussion in the Babylonian academies.

Talmud torah, term generally applied to Jewish religious (and ultimately to talmudic) study; also to traditional Jewish religious public schools.

*__Tammuz__, fourth month of the Jewish religious year, tenth of the civil, approximating to June-July.

Tanna (pl. ***tannaim**), rabbinic teacher of mishnaic period.

*__Targum__, Aramaic translation of the Bible.

*__Tefillin__, phylacteries, small leather cases containing passages from Scripture and affixed on the forehead and arm by male Jews during the recital of morning prayers.

Tell (Ar. "mound," "hillock"), ancient mound in the Middle East composed of remains of successive settlements.

*__Terefah__, food that is not **kasher*, owing to a defect on the animal.

*__Territorialism__, 20th century movement supporting the creation of an autonomous territory for Jewish mass-settlement outside Ereẓ Israel.

*__Tevet__, tenth month of the Jewish religious year, fourth of the civil, approximating to December–January.

Tikkun ("restitution," "reintegration"), (1) order of service for certain occasions, mostly recited at night; (2) mystical term denoting restoration of the right order and true unity after the spiritual "catastrophe" which occurred in the cosmos.

Tishah be-Av, Ninth of *Av, fast day commemorating the destruction of the First and Second Temples.

*__Tishri__, seventh month of the Jewish religious year, first of the civil, approximating to September–October.

Tokheḥah, reproof sections of the Pentateuch (Lev. 26 and Deut. 28); poem of reproof.

*__Torah__, Pentateuch or the Pentateuchal scroll for reading in synagogue; entire body of traditional Jewish teaching and literature.

Tosafist, talmudic glossator, mainly French (12–14th centuries), bringing additions to the commentary by *Rashi.

*__Tosafot__, glosses supplied by tosafist.

*__Tosefta__, a collection of teachings and traditions of the *tannaim*, closely related to the Mishnah.

Tradent, person who hands down a talmudic statement on the name of his teacher or other earlier authority.

*__Tu bi-Shevat__, the 15th day of Shevat, the New Year for Trees; date marking a dividing line for fruit tithing; in modern Israel celebrated as arbor day.

*__Uganda Scheme__, plan suggested by the British government in 1903 to establish an autonomous Jewish settlement area in East Africa.

*__Va'ad Le'ummi__, national council of the Jewish community in Ereẓ Israel during the period of the British *Mandate.

*__Wannsee Conference__, Nazi conference held on Jan. 20, 1942, at which the planned annihilation of European Jewry was endorsed.

Waqf (Ar.), (1) a Muslim charitable pious foundation; (2) state lands and other property passed to the Muslim community for public welfare.

*__War of Independence__, war of 1947–49 when the Jews of Israel fought off Arab invading armies and ensured the establishment of the new State.

*__White Paper(s)__, report(s) issued by British government, frequently statements of policy, as issued in connection with Palestine during the *Mandate period.

*__Wissenschaft des Judentums__ (Ger. "Science of Judaism"), movement in Europe beginning in the 19th century for scientific study of Jewish history, religion, and literature.

*__Yad Vashem__, Israel official authority for commemorating the *Holocaust in the Nazi era and Jewish resistance and heroism at that time.

Yeshivah (pl. ***yeshivot**), Jewish traditional academy devoted primarily to study of rabbinic literature; *rosh yeshivah*, head of the yeshivah.

YHWH, the letters of the holy name of God, the Tetragrammaton.

Yibbum, see levirate marriage.

Yiḥud, "union"; mystical term for intention which causes the union of God with the **Shekhinah*.

Yishuv, settlement; more specifically, the Jewish community of Ereẓ Israel in the pre-State period. The pre-Zionist community is generally designated the "old yishuv" and the community evolving from 1880, the "new yishuv."

Yom Kippur, Yom ha-Kippurim, *Day of Atonement, solemn fast day observed on the 10th of Tishri.

Yoreh De'ah, see Shulḥan Arukh.

Yoẓer, hymns inserted in the first benediction (*Yoẓer Or*) of the morning **Shema*.

*__Ẓaddik__, person outstanding for his faith and piety; especially a ḥasidic rabbi or leader.

Ẓimẓum, "contraction"; mystical term denoting the process whereby God withdraws or contracts within Himself so leaving a primordial vacuum in which creation can take place; primordial exile or self-limitation of God.

*__Zionist Commission (1918)__, commission appointed in 1918 by the British government to advise the British military authorities in Palestine on the implementation of the *Balfour Declaration.

Ẓyyonei Zion, the organized opposition to Herzl in connection with the *Uganda Scheme.

*__Ẓiẓit__, fringes attached to the **tallit* and **tallit katan*.

*__Zohar__, mystical commentary on the Pentateuch; main textbook of *Kabbalah.

Zulat, hymn inserted after the **Shema* in the morning service.